Y0-BBX-635

JANUARY — DECEMBER 2006

Published by CQ Press, a division of Congressional Quarterly Inc.
1255 22nd Street, N.W., Suite 400, Washington, DC 20037

Photo credits: *Argus Leader*/Cory Myers (top left); AFP/Getty Images/Thomas Coex (top middle); AFP/Getty Images (top right); Department of Defense/Seaman David P. Coleman, U.S. Navy (bottom left); National Park Service (bottom middle); AP Photo/Chris Polk (bottom right)

ISBN 978-0-87289-544-7
ISSN 1056-2036

CQ Researcher

CQ Researcher is the choice of researchers seeking information on issues in the news. Investigated and written by an experienced journalist, each *CQ Researcher* offers an in-depth, balanced look at a controversial issue. Now in its 80th year, *CQ Researcher* received the prestigious Sigma Delta Chi Award for Journalism Excellence in 1999 for a 10-part series on health care and won the American Bar Association's 2002 Silver Gavel Award for a nine-part series on civil liberties and justice issues.

Each *CQ Researcher* opens with an overview of that issue's topic, followed by a discussion of two to three key questions that drive the debate surrounding the topic. The answers provided are not conclusive, but serve to highlight the range of opinions among the different parties. The overview and issue questions are followed by a background section that places the issue in historical context.

"Current Situation" examines the activities of legislators, citizen groups and others influencing the debate. "Outlook" offers insights by experts on what may happen in the future. In addition to illuminating images, tables and maps, the report illustrates the topic under discussion in the form of statements by representatives of opposing positions. A chronology identifying milestones in the debate and bibliographies of key sources for further research round out the report.

CITING *CQ RESEARCHER*

Sample formats for citing *CQ Researcher* in a bibliography include the ones listed below. Preferred styles and formats vary, so please check with your instructor or professor.

MLA STYLE

Triplett, William. "Teen Driving." CQ Researcher, 7 Jan. 2005: 1–24.

APA STYLE

Triplett, W. (2005, January 7). Teen driving. *CQ Researcher, 15*, 1–24.

CHICAGO STYLE

Triplett, William. "Teen Driving." *CQ Researcher,* January 7, 2005, 1–24.

ACCESSING *CQ RESEARCHER*

CQ Researcher is available in print and online. For access, visit your library or http://library.cqpress.com/cqresearcher.

CQ Researcher

CONTENTS JANUARY — DECEMBER 2006

CQ Researcher

Published by CQ Press, a division of Congressional Quarterly Inc.

thecqresearcher.com

Domestic Violence

Do teenagers need more protection?

On a typical day in the United States, three women are murdered by their spouses or partners, and thousands more are injured. While men are also victims of domestic violence, women are at least five times more likely to suffer at the hands of a loved one. Young people between the ages of 16 and 24 are most at risk. The victims include teens who are abused by their parents as well as young parents who assault each other or their children. Moreover, teen-dating violence touches more than 30 percent of young men and women. The good news is that domestic violence against women has dropped dramatically in recent years. Now Congress has just approved a measure that advocates say will provide much-needed funding to try to stop domestic violence before it starts. Meanwhile, some fathers'-rights and conservative groups say too many domestic-violence programs demonize men, promote a feminist agenda and do not try hard enough to keep families together.

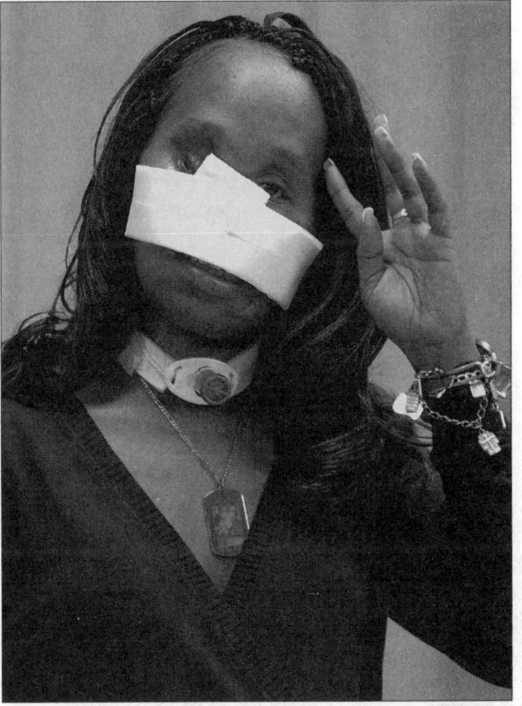

Carolyn Thomas of Waco, Texas, was shot in the face and severely disfigured by her jealous boyfriend. She now speaks to high school groups about domestic violence.

INSIDE

THIS REPORT

The CQ Researcher • Jan. 6, 2006 • www.thecqresearcher.com
Volume 16, Number 1 • Pages 1-24

CQ PRESS

RECIPIENT OF SOCIETY OF PROFESSIONAL JOURNALISTS AWARD FOR EXCELLENCE ◆ AMERICAN BAR ASSOCIATION SILVER GAVEL AWARD

DOMESTIC VIOLENCE

Cover: Carolyn Thomas of Waco, Texas, was shot in the face and severely disfigured by her jealous boyfriend, Terrence Dewaine Kelly, in December 2003. Kelly also shot and killed Thomas' mother and was sentenced to life in prison. (AP Photo/Duane A. Laverty)

CQ Researcher

Jan. 6, 2006
Volume 16, Number 1

MANAGING EDITOR: Thomas J. Colin

ASSISTANT MANAGING EDITOR: Kathy Koch

ASSOCIATE EDITOR: Kenneth Jost

STAFF WRITERS: Marcia Clemmitt, Peter Katel, Pamela M. Prah

CONTRIBUTING WRITERS: Rachel Cox, Sarah Glazer, David Hosansky, Patrick Marshall, Tom Price

DESIGN/PRODUCTION EDITOR: Olu B. Davis

ASSISTANT EDITOR: Melissa J. Hipolit

CQ PRESS

A Division of Congressional Quarterly Inc.

SENIOR VICE PRESIDENT/GENERAL MANAGER: John A. Jenkins

DIRECTOR, LIBRARY PUBLISHING: Kathryn C. Suárez

DIRECTOR, EDITORIAL OPERATIONS: Ann Davies

CONGRESSIONAL QUARTERLY INC.

CHAIRMAN: Paul C. Tash

VICE CHAIRMAN: Andrew P. Corty

PRESIDENT AND PUBLISHER: Robert W. Merry

CQ Researcher (ISSN 1056-2036) is printed on acid-free paper. Published weekly, except March 24, July 7, July 14, Aug. 4, Aug. 11, Nov. 24, Dec. 22 and Dec. 29, by CQ Press, a division of Congressional Quarterly Inc. Annual full-service subscriptions for institutions start at $667. For pricing, call 1-800-834-9020, ext. 1906. To purchase a *CQ Researcher* report in print or electronic format (PDF), visit www.cqpress.com or call 866-427-7737. Single reports start at $10. Bulk purchase discounts and electronic-rights licensing are also available. Periodicals postage paid at Washington, D.C., and additional mailing offices. POSTMASTER: Send address changes to *CQ Researcher*, 1255 22nd St., N.W., Suite 400, Washington, DC 20037.

Domestic Violence

By Pamela M. Prah

The Issues

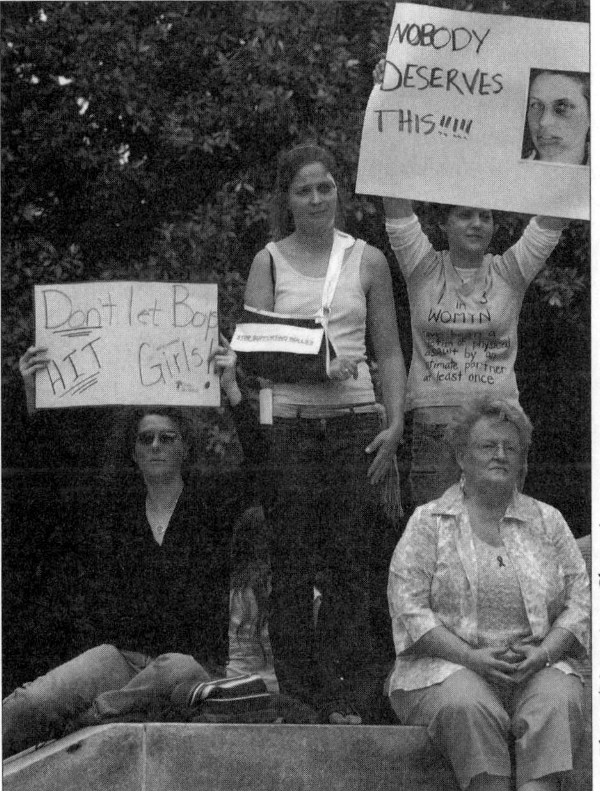

AP Photo/Mary Ann Chastain

Supporters of tougher domestic-violence legislation demonstrate in Columbia, S.C., on April 27, 2005. Congress recently reauthorized the Violence Against Women Act, adding more funding for youth programs and prevention.

Domestic violence doesn't seem to get much attention until a celebrity comes along like O. J. Simpson, the former football star and admitted wife beater who was accused of murdering his ex-wife and her male companion in a fit of jealous rage. Also grabbing headlines was the case of Lorena Bobbitt, the abused Virginia woman who cut off her husband's penis while he slept.*

Yet, on a typical day in the United States, three women are murdered by their spouses, ex-spouses or partners — and thousands more are raped or injured. [1]

They are women like Yvette Cade, 31, from Clinton, Md., who was doused with gasoline and set on fire by her estranged husband. And Jessica Wickiewicz, of Garden City, N.Y., whose boyfriend started punching and kicking her when she was a senior in high school. And Maria, a pregnant 15-year-old from Los Angeles whose boyfriend hit her so hard when she was pregnant that she had to have her baby delivered by cesarean. [2]

Violence against women has been reported since ancient Roman times and has been commonplace in America since Colonial times. But in the last decade, the rate of domestic violence against women has dropped more than 50 percent. [3] And the number of men murdered by their wives, girlfriends and former partners has declined even more dramatically — by some 70 percent since 1976.

Many experts credit the changes to the billons of dollars spent in recent years on shelters, hotlines and legal help for victims and training sessions for police, prosecutors and judges. With more help available, abused women, in particular, recognized they no longer had to resort to violence to get out of a bad relationship.

Despite the positive trends, experts say the true scope of the domestic-violence problem is hard to gauge, because researchers and government agencies use different definitions for the term. Fourteen states, for example, do not include dating violence as a form of domestic violence. Nonetheless, the latest figures from the Department of Justice (DOJ) show more than 588,000 women and more than 100,000 men were physically assaulted, raped or robbed by their "intimate partners" in 2001. [4] And more than 1 million women are stalked. [5]

Researchers are now finding that young people ages 16 to 24 are most at risk. [6] Some teens are exposed to violence at the hands of their parents, while others are young parents themselves and are beating each other and/or their children.

Moreover, teen-dating violence is more prevalent than most parents suspect, since young people usually do not tell their parents about the abuse. Wickiewicz, for example, blamed her high school bruises on cheerleading and hid them under baggy jeans. "It was all a big secret," she said. [7]

While girls and women are much more likely to suffer at the hands of a loved one, men and boys are often victims as well. For 13 years, for example, Karen Gillhespy of Marquette, Mich., brutally abused her husband. Indeed, she broke his ribs, ripped patches of his hair out, beat him with a baseball bat and scratched, bit and kicked him — but he never hit back or filed charges. [8]

In fact, a federal study showed that high school boys are nearly as likely as girls to get hit, slapped or physically hurt by their partners. After surveying youths in Chicago, Dallas, Milwaukee, San Diego and Washington, D.C., the study found that 10 to 17 percent of girls are hit by their boyfriends, and almost the same number of boys — 10 to 15 percent — are abused by their girlfriends. [9]

---

* Simpson was acquitted of the murders of Nicole Brown Simpson and her friend Ronald Goldman, but in a civil trial he was found liable for their deaths and ordered to pay the Goldman family $8.5 million in compensatory damages. A jury in Manassas, Va., acquitted Bobbitt of malicious wounding in January 1994.

Partner Violence Against Women Plummeted

The number of female victims of so-called intimate-partner violence dropped nearly 50 percent — from 1.1 million incidents in 1993 to 588,490 incidents in 2001. Women make up 85 percent of all victims of abuse by either a spouse or ex-partner.

Rates of Non-Fatal Violence by an Intimate Partner*

(per 1,000 persons of each gender; includes rape, sexual assault, robbery and simple or aggravated assault)

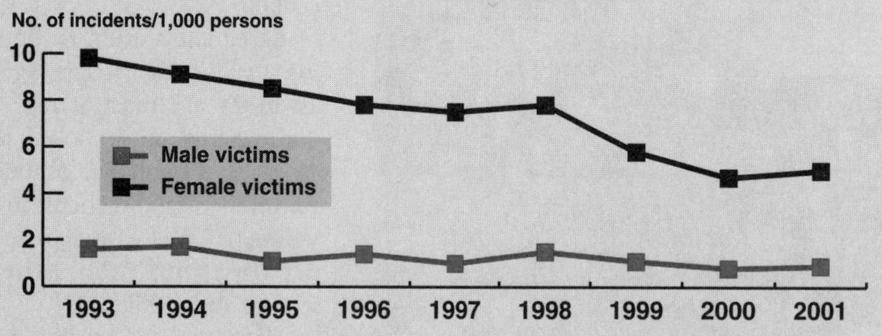

* *Intimate partners include current or former spouses, boyfriends or girlfriends.*

Source: Bureau of Justice Statistics, U.S. Department of Justice, February 2003

The fact that researchers are studying dating violence reflects the recent sea change in how the nation views and deals with domestic violence. Forty years ago, there were no shelters or hotlines for battered women. Police often responded to a domestic-violence call by telling the batterer, typically a man, to walk around the block to cool off. Doctors and health-care providers rarely screened their patients for domestic violence.

But the women's liberation movement of the 1970s shined a spotlight on domestic violence — triggering a wave of state laws dealing with the problem. Much later, the 1994 Violence Against Women Act (VAWA) provided billions of federal dollars to help victims of domestic violence, including funds for legal services and for building local shelters.

The sweeping law — which Congress expanded in December 2005 — also created the National Domestic Violence Hotline and made it a federal crime to cross state lines with the intent of stalking or committing domestic violence. VAWA funding has been used to set up domestic-violence courts as well as specially trained "response teams" to deal with sexual-assault victims.

"Although violent crime has decreased nationwide, it still devastates the lives of many women," says Diane M. Stuart, director of the DOJ's Office on Violence Against Women, who in the 1980s ran a shelter for battered women in Utah. "We have much more work to do."

Today 2,000 shelters provide refuge for victims and information on how to obtain restraining orders against their abusers. Rape-victim advocates offer support in many hospitals, and state courthouses often provide special programs to help guide victims through the legal process.

Businesses also are becoming active on the domestic-violence front, partly because it's the right thing to do and partly because domestic violence costs society, particularly employers. Victims annually lose nearly 8 million days of work, the equivalent of more than 32,000 full-time jobs. [10] In 1995, researchers estimated that domestic violence cost the country more than $5.8 billion — more than $8.3 billion in today's dollars — primarily for medical and mental health care. [11]

In 2005 the DOJ formally kicked off the president's Family Justice Center Initiative, modeled after a San Diego program that brings legal and social services under one roof with victim-support and counseling programs. At the one location, victims can undergo forensic exams, obtain legal advice and even restraining orders against their abusers, speak with a chaplain and meet with a victim's advocate.

"It's a one-stop process. Everything that a person who has been victimized needs is right there," says Stuart.

Advocates and women's groups hope the recent VAWA expansion will usher in a new era that focuses on preventing domestic violence from ever beginning in the first place, rather than treating the victims and punishing the abusers afterwards.

"Many programs today focus on helping adult victims, and prevention has a lesser emphasis, if it is addressed at all," says Esta Soler, president of the Family Violence Prevention Fund, an advocacy group that sponsors campaigns, in partnership with the Advertising Council, to raise awareness about family violence. She says adolescents, young adults and the poor particularly need more attention.

Prevention is key because children who grow up in homes where domestic violence or dating violence occur are more likely to become victims or perpetrators of domestic or dating violence themselves. [12] Abuse also tends to lead to other problems. Young people and adults abused by their spouses or partners are more likely to abuse alcohol or drugs, suffer from eating disorders and engage in risky behavior, such as having unprotected sex. They also are more apt to have mental and physical health problems that make it difficult for them to hold jobs.

Some fathers'-rights and conservative groups, however, say many domestic-violence programs demonize men and promote a feminist and leftist agenda. "The Violence Against Women Act is gender-driven politics being operated through the public purse," says Michael McCormick, executive director of the American Coalition for Fathers and Children. "We're spending nearly $1 billion a year to reinforce in the public's mind that men are indiscriminately attacking women."

As Congress, researchers and advocates debate how best to combat domestic violence, here are some of the questions being asked:

Simple Assault Is Most Common Crime

Nearly three-quarters of the intimate-partner crimes against women and nearly half of those against men were simple assaults.

Types of Violence by Intimate Partners

Violent Crime	No. of female victims	Rate/1,000 females	No. of male victims	Rate/1,000 males
Simple Assault	421,550	3.6	50,310	0.5
Aggravated Assault	81,140	0.7	36,350	0.3
Robbery	44,060	0.4	16,570	0.1
Rape/Sexual Assault	41,740	0.4	---	---
Total	**588,490**		**103,230**	

Source: Bureau of Justice Statistics, U.S. Department of Justice, February 2003

Should the federal government do more to combat domestic violence?

Women's groups say federal programs have contributed to remarkable gains in curtailing domestic violence, sexual assault and stalking. But they say the programs should be expanded to provide more housing options and focus more on prevention. Meanwhile, some fathers'-rights and conservative groups say the programs at the local level that get funds from the federal government demonize men and promote a radical feminist agenda.

In the decade after Congress passed the Violence Against Women Act in 1994, domestic violence dropped more than 50 percent, according to government figures. "VAWA has had a huge impact," says Jill Morris, public policy director of the National Coalition Against Domestic Violence. "It has changed attitudes. It's a great success."

Besides providing billions of dollars to help victims of domestic violence and sexual assault, VAWA forced the issue out into the open. "People are now talking about it in newspapers and in Congress," Morris says.

While lauding VAWA, the coalition and other women's groups say more federal funds should be targeted to help minorities, the disabled, the elderly, victims in rural areas, Native Americans, young people, gays and immigrants who fear being deported. And rape crisis centers should be guaranteed additional federal funds to help counsel victims of sexual assault.

Several states, including Illinois, Massachusetts and Pennsylvania, have waiting lists of sexual assault victims needing counseling, and in many states "rural areas have no services at all," said Mary Lou Leary, executive director of the National Center for Victims of Crime. [13]

Victims also need more housing options, say advocates. "Homelessness does not cause domestic violence, but rather the opposite," according to Lynn Rosenthal, president of the National Network to End Domestic Violence. Half of homeless women and children are fleeing domestic violence, and 38 percent of domestic-violence victims become homeless at some point in their lives, she estimated. [14]

Advocates say victims who live in public housing need protection from their abusers — and sometimes from their landlords. A 39-year-old North Carolina woman, for example, was evicted from her apartment because she was "too loud" after her ex-boyfriend shot her and she jumped from her apartment's second-story balcony to escape his attack. [15] A Michigan woman was evicted because of "criminal activity" in her apartment after her ex-boyfriend returned and attacked her.

Conservative and fathers'-rights groups, however, say VAWA ignores men who are abused. The Safe Homes for Children and Families Coalition and other groups want to rename the law as the Family Violence Prevention Act. They also have pressed for new VAWA language making clear that the law includes programs for men.

"It's a blatant lie to say that new language is not necessary," says David Burroughs, legislative consultant to the coalition. Burroughs says he was denied a VAWA grant because his proposal targeted men and also was rejected for a federal grant to pay for hotel stays for male victims wanting to leave their homes for a cooling-off period. He helped mount a billboard campaign at the Wilmington, Del., Amtrak station to remind Sen. Joseph Biden Jr., D-Del. — lead sponsor of VAWA — that men are abuse victims, too.

VAWA advocates argue, however, that all of the law's provisions are gender neutral. "Nothing in the act denies services, programs, funding or assistance to male victims of violence," says Morris.

Government figures show women overwhelmingly are the victims of domestic violence, with males making up only 15 percent of the victims. [16] But men's groups say more than 100 studies show that men and women are equally likely to initiate domestic violence, adding that 99 percent of the federal funding should not go to programs that help only women.

ALL THE MAKEUP IN THE WORLD CAN'T CHANGE
WHAT HE DOES
1 IN 5 TEENAGERS IS AFFECTED BY TEEN DATING VIOLENCE.*
DON'T HIDE IT.
CALL 1-800-942-6906
STOP Teen Dating Violence
New York State Office for the Prevention of Domestic Violence
George E. Pataki, Governor

Office for the Prevention of Domestic Violence

A high-school student in New York state submitted the winning poster in a statewide contest to increase awareness of teen-dating violence.

Abused men have a hard time finding legal help and shelters — services that get federal funds under VAWA, Burroughs says. About 20 percent of the victims who apply for free legal services are men, but they receive less than 1 percent of the pro bono services, he says, adding that only a handful of domestic-violence shelters nationwide are open to men.

VAWA should be scrapped altogether, says McCormick of the American Coalition for Fathers and Children, although he acknowledges, "the political reality is that it's not going to be withdrawn." The coalition opposes violence against anyone, but McCormick says VAWA funds "a one-sided agenda driven by people who really don't want to see families stay together," namely, feminists and left-wing organizations.

VAWA breaks up families and increases the number of fatherless children, McCormick says, because it funds programs that push couples into divorce instead of trying to get the victim and abuser into counseling.

Lisa Scott, a Bellevue, Wash., attorney specializing in family law, agrees. "VAWA is not about stopping violence," Scott wrote. "It is about greedy special interests slopping at the federal trough, perpetuating gender supremacy for women. If proponents were truly concerned about helping victims, they would demand that all intervention and funding be gender neutral and gender inclusive." [17]

Are judges and police doing enough to protect domestic-violence victims?

Forty years ago, a wife beater would not be arrested unless police actually saw the incident or had a warrant. Police and judges would routinely dismiss the problem as a "family matter."

Things have changed, particularly in the last decade, as police officers, judges and prosecutors have received VAWA-funded training on how to deal with domestic violence. But women's advocates say much still needs to be changed, both in the courtroom and on the police beat.

For instance, Yvette Cade might never have been burned if Judge Richard Palumbo had not dismissed her request for a protective order against her estranged husband. Three weeks later Mrs. Cade's husband walked into the store where she worked, poured gasoline on her and set her on fire. Cade suffered third-degree burns over much of her body. Advocates said Palumbo has a pattern of dismissing temporary protective orders and making flip remarks about domestic violence.* In one instance, he told an abused woman to speak up, even though he had been told her husband had attacked her and crushed her voice box. [18]

"There are judges, for whatever reason, who still don't get it," says Billie Lee Dunford-Jackson, co-director of the Family Violence Project at the National Council on Juvenile and Family Court Judges. But, she quickly adds, "most judges now readily recognize [domestic violence] as a crime and will take steps to protect the victim."

She points to intensive three-day training sessions for judges that the National Judicial Institute on Domestic Violence has sponsored since 1998, largely funded by VAWA. Judges are taught what makes a batterer batter, why victims stay and how to identify and overcome their own biases and blinders when it comes to the problem.

Nationwide, more than 300 judicial systems have established specially designed "domestic-violence courts." [19] Some states have created courts that handle only domestic violence, while others have staff trained who provide

* Palumbo's actions led to his temporary removal from the bench and reassignment to administrative duties on Oct. 26, 2005.

support to victims, Dunford-Jackson explains. New York uses both approaches, with more than 30 domestic-violence courts plus special units that include victims' advocates and staff members who monitor those convicted of domestic violence to ensure they are complying with the terms of their sentence.

Law students also are getting training. As of 2003, most law schools offered educational programming on domestic violence, says Robin R. Runge, director of the American Bar Association's Commission on Domestic Violence.

However, there are still gaps in the system. Most states require volunteers on domestic violence hotlines to complete 40 to 50 hours of training but don't require training for police, judges or lawyers. Even with VAWA, 80 percent of domestic-violence victims are without lawyers to guide them through the process, Runge says. "We've seen the difference having lawyers available" can make, she says. For example, lawyers can help abused women file the legal paperwork more quickly to obtain protection orders, which prohibit their abusers from coming into contact with them.

But, some men's groups say the training given to judges, police and attorneys reinforces the notion that only women are victims. "They are being taught garbage," says Burroughs, of the Safe Homes for Children and Families Coalition.

Some conservatives also argue that women who seek help from domestic-violence legal programs get an edge in their custody or divorce proceedings. VAWA "has little to do with violence and much to do with divorce court," family-law attorney Scott wrote.[20] McCormick of the American Coalition for Fathers and Children says abused women who turn to shelters do not get counseling first but instead are directed to the courthouse to get a restraining order, which helps them in a divorce or child custody case because judges will view the man as abusive and dangerous even if he is not.

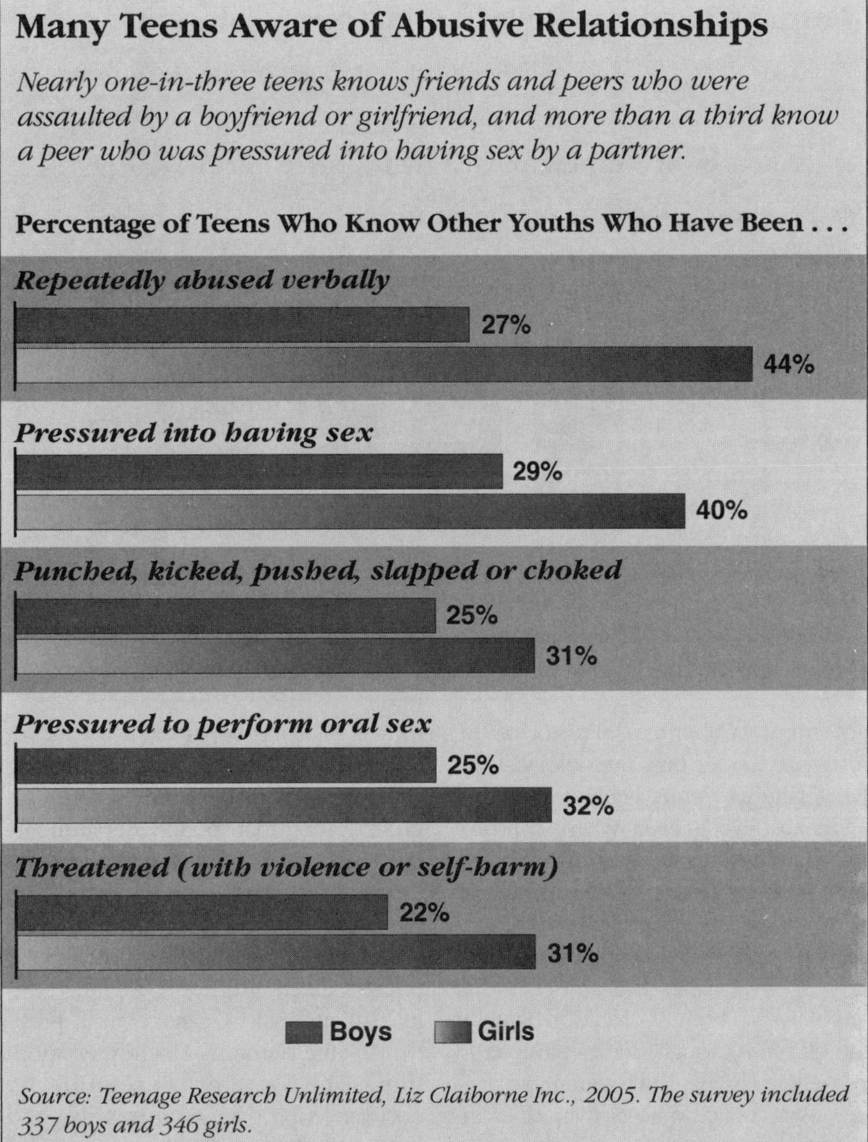
Many Teens Aware of Abusive Relationships
Nearly one-in-three teens knows friends and peers who were assaulted by a boyfriend or girlfriend, and more than a third know a peer who was pressured into having sex by a partner.
Percentage of Teens Who Know Other Youths Who Have Been . . .
Repeatedly abused verbally
27%
44%
Pressured into having sex
29%
40%
Punched, kicked, pushed, slapped or choked
25%
31%
Pressured to perform oral sex
25%
32%
Threatened (with violence or self-harm)
22%
31%
Boys
Girls
Source: Teenage Research Unlimited, Liz Claiborne Inc., 2005. The survey included 337 boys and 346 girls.

Meanwhile, feminists and some domestic-violence experts are backing away from the "mandatory arrest" laws that they pushed states to enact 20 years ago. At least 23 states require police officers to make an arrest when responding to a domestic-violence complaint. But police on the scene often cannot tell the victim from the aggressor, so they arrest both.

States began passing mandatory-arrest laws after a 1984 Minnesota study found that few people arrested under such laws repeated their crimes. But researcher Lawrence Sherman says that states acted too hastily after his first study. His follow-up research showed that mandatory arrests only work in middle-class communities with low unemployment rates, but for some reason, he says, "the new findings got buried."

The new findings showed that unemployed people or those without ties to the community have less to lose by getting arrested and often become angrier. In such cases, mandatory arrest "causes more violence than it prevents,"

Female Teens at Risk for Partner Violence

Females ages 16-24 were the most vulnerable to intimate-partner violence in 1999.

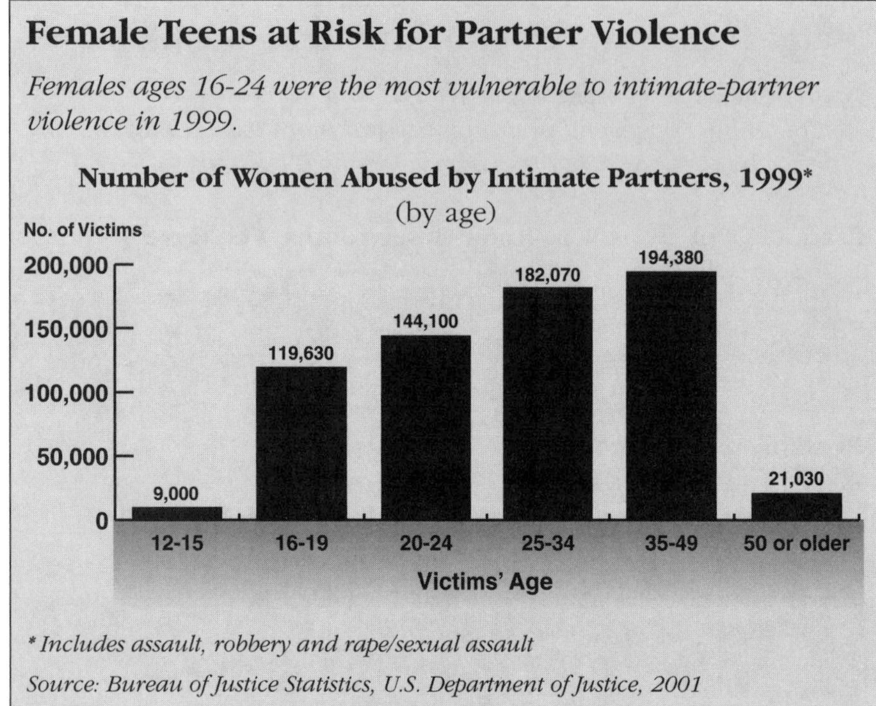

* *Includes assault, robbery and rape/sexual assault*

Source: Bureau of Justice Statistics, U.S. Department of Justice, 2001

according to Sherman, director of the Jerry Lee Center on Criminology at the University of Pennsylvania.

In any event, even when mandatory-arrest laws are in effect, many police officers are reluctant to respond quickly to domestic-violence cases because they are considered so potentially dangerous, with either the abuser or the victim — or both — liable to turn on the officer. Although studies have yet to prove that family disputes are more dangerous to police officers than other incidents, so many officers believe it to be true they often wait for backup before responding to such calls. [21]

However, John Terrill, a spokesman for the National Association of Police Organizations, denies that police treat domestic violence any differently than other cases and supports mandatory-arrest laws.

Some women's groups say a June 2005 U.S. Supreme Court decision undercut efforts to beef up enforcement of mandatory-arrest laws and restraining orders. In *Town of Castle Rock, Colorado v. Gonzales*, the court ruled that a woman did not have the right to sue a police department for failing to enforce a court-ordered restraining order against her husband. [22] Women's groups fear that police departments now will have less incentive to aggressively enforce such orders.

"Mandatory restraining orders aren't worth the paper they're printed on if police officers are not required to enforce them," said Eleanor Smeal, president of the Feminist Majority Foundation. The organization said the decision jeopardizes women's lives and potentially lets police departments off the hook for failing to enforce mandatory orders. [23]

Terrill says police "try to the best of their ability to enforce restraining orders," but sometimes they "get pushed down on the list" of calls police officers must handle. "You can't keep an officer stationed outside the door 24 hours a day."

Should the government do more to protect teens?

The recent expansion of VAWA provides millions of dollars to help teen victims of domestic violence, including dating violence.

Dating violence represents an "epidemic of monumental proportions" among today's youth, says Juley Fulcher, director of public policy at Break the Cycle, a Los Angeles-based group that provides information and legal help to young people experiencing domestic violence. Fulcher points to Justice Department data showing that girls and young women between the ages of 16 and 24 experience the highest rate of non-fatal "intimate-partner" violence, or attacks by a spouse, partner or former spouse or partner — 16 incidents per 1,000 women in this age group compared to six incidents per 1,000 for all women. [24]

"Not enough attention has been paid to finding ways to stop the intimate-partner violence that pervades and sometimes shapes the lives of adolescents and young adults," says Soler, of the Family Violence Prevention Fund.

In 2005, a Gallup survey found that one-in-eight teens ages 13 to 17 knows someone in an abusive relationship with a boyfriend or girlfriend. [25] Another 2005 youth survey, commissioned by Liz Claiborne Inc., the clothing maker, found that one-in-three 13-to-18-year-olds had a friend or peer who had been hit, punched, kicked or slapped by a partner. [26] And up to 18 percent said their partners had threatened to harm themselves if the couple broke up, making the victim feel trapped.

In many cases, teens exposed to violence have fewer options than adults. Many shelters for battered women do not admit their teenage sons. And few shelters accommodate teenage mothers and their children. Teen mothers can be particularly vulnerable to domestic violence. A 2001 study found that a quarter of teen mothers experience violence by their boyfriends or husbands before, during or just after their pregnancies. [27]

Advocates successfully pushed Congress in 2005 to revise the Violence Against Women Act to provide federal money for new programs targeting teens, including programs to educate people working with teens on how to recognize, respond to and provide services to teen victims of domestic and dating violence. Women's groups also wanted middle and high schools to train teachers, coaches and administrators to recognize and address issues related to dating violence and sexual assault.

"Teens must be taught what is healthy and what is not, and services must be offered to help them through this transition," says Fulcher, noting that many teens are dating for the first time and are unsure of the differences between a healthy relationship and an abusive one. A 2003 federal study of schools in Alabama, Idaho, Oklahoma and Utah found that between 11 and 16 percent of female students — and between 4.5 and 7 percent of males — reported being forced to have intercourse. [28]

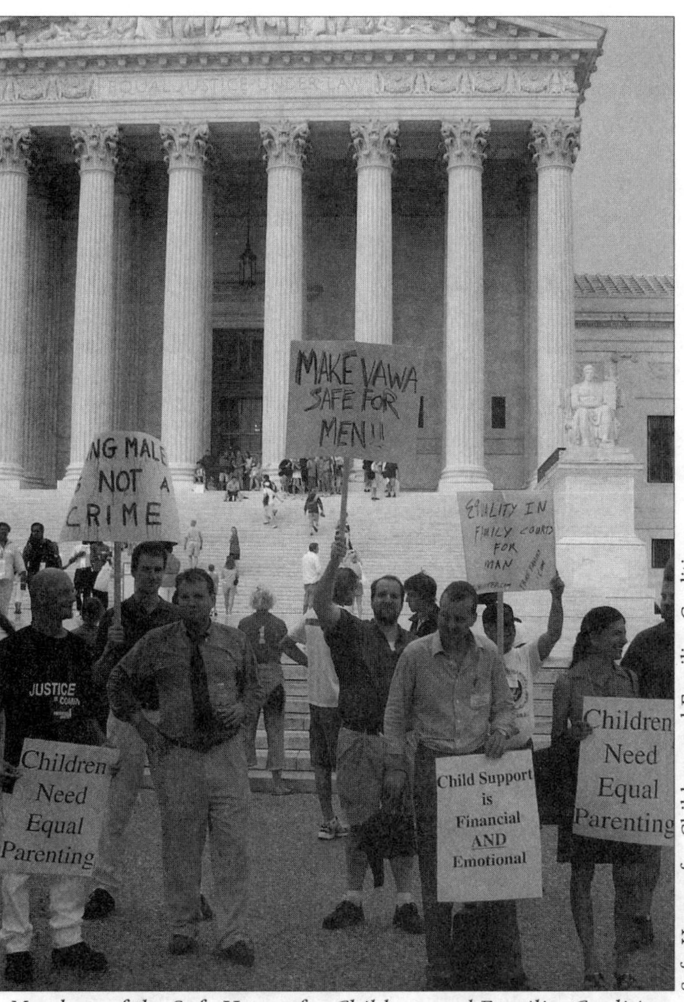

Members of the Safe Homes for Children and Families Coalition call for changes in the Violence Against Women Act during a rally at the U.S. Supreme Court in July 2005. Congress in December 2005 addressed some of their concerns.

Fulcher and other women's groups want the federal government to pay for education programs that involve courts, law-enforcement agencies and youth-based community groups. Only a handful of states — Minnesota, Oklahoma, Utah, Washington and Wyoming — allow minors ages 16 and older to petition for an order of protection without an adult, according to the National Coalition Against Domestic Violence. Moreover, only one county in the United States — Santa Clara, Calif. — has a domestic-violence court just for juveniles.

VAWA already provides grants to reduce sexual assault, rape and other violent crimes on college campuses. "There isn't a university in the country that doesn't have this problem," says Stuart, of the Office on Violence Against Women. Some universities, for example, provide information to all incoming freshmen about sexual assault and other crimes, she says. The programs also "help universities understand that a rape or sexual assault on campus isn't something that can be handled within the university," she says. "It's a crime."

Stuart says she would also like to see secondary schools become more involved, allowing community leaders to come into the schools to share their expertise.

But McCormick, of the American Coalition for Fathers and Children, says the federal government is already too deeply involved in private matters and that talk of domestic violence in the classroom "is not in line with public education." He is particularly concerned that the "education" would in fact be "propaganda" that reinforces feminists groups' one-sided message that men are always the perpetrators.

Burroughs, of the Safe Homes for Children and Families Coalition, says domestic violence is an appropriate topic for schools, even though many school boards may be reluctant to address it because it is a family-related issue and involves sex and sexuality. "We'd be doing young people a favor by teaching them what healthy relationships are," he says, as long as the education doesn't "inject bias" that only women are victims.

BACKGROUND

Women as Property

Well into the 19th century, U.S. laws were influenced by the 1768 English "rule of thumb" law, which allowed a husband to beat his wife as long as the stick was no thicker than his thumb. [29]

Early in America's history, women were viewed as the property of men, much like children or slaves, who could be punished physically for not obeying orders. The Mississippi Supreme Court in 1824 upheld a husband's right to use corporal punishment on his wife, even as women were fighting for equal rights and the right to vote.

Suffrage and temperance movement leaders in the 19th and early 20th centuries saw wife beating as one of society's scourges. The first women's-rights convention was held in Seneca, N.Y., in 1848, and by the 1870s, wife beating was becoming unacceptable, at least legally. In 1871, courts in Alabama and Massachusetts overturned the right of a husband to beat his wife. This change coincided with growing concern over child abuse, which expanded to women's issues.

Maryland became the first state to outlaw wife beating, in 1883, but it took the turbulent 1960s and the women's movement of the 1970s to fundamentally change how Americans viewed domestic violence. [30]

The race riots, violent protests and assassinations of President John F. Kennedy, Sen. Robert F. Kennedy, D-N.Y., and the Rev. Martin Luther King Jr. during the 1960s prompted creation of the President's Commission on the Causes and Prevention of Violence. The panel's national survey gave researchers invaluable — and troubling — data. For instance, about a quarter of all adult men said they could think of circumstances in which it was acceptable for spouses to hit one another. [31]

While abhorring violence in the streets, many Americans still viewed domestic violence as a private matter between family members. For example, after a young woman in New York City named Kitty Genovese was stabbed repeatedly in an alley in 1964 — and her neighbors ignored her screams — many concluded that Americans had become inured to violence. But upon closer examination, the witnesses said they didn't get involved because they thought it was a man beating his wife and felt it wasn't their business to get involved. [32]

Police and judges also were reluctant to intervene in family matters that turned violent. For example, in 1967 the International Association of Police training manual said that "in dealing with family disputes, arrest should be exercised as a last resort."

Getty Images

Former NFL star O. J. Simpson was revealed as a wife beater during his trial for the murders of his ex-wife Nicole Brown Simpson and her friend Ronald Goldman. Simpson was acquitted but in a civil trial was found liable for their deaths and ordered to pay the Goldman family $8.5 million.

Slow Progress

The women's-rights movement of the 1970s helped to change such attitudes about handling domestic violence. It led to establishment of telephone hotlines, support groups and shelters for rape victims — all of which helped battered women admit that they were being beaten at home. The first shelter for battered women opened in 1974 in St. Paul, Minn., and the National Organization for Women created a task force to examine wife beating in 1975.

The judicial and law-enforcement communities also began to step in. In 1977 Oregon became the first state to enact a mandatory-arrest law for domestic-violence incidents. The next year Minnesota became the first state to allow domestic-violence arrests without warrants. By 1980, all but six states had domestic-violence laws. And in 1981, Massachusetts and New Jersey supreme courts ruled that a husband could be criminally liable for raping his wife.

But progress was slow. By the mid-1980s, 22 states still barred police from making arrests without a warrant in domestic-violence cases unless an officer had actually witnessed the battering.

In many cases, police departments beefed up their domestic-violence activities in order to protect against lawsuits. In 1984, a jury awarded a $2.3 million judgment against the Torrington, Conn., police department for failing to protect a woman and her son from her husband's repeated violence. [33] Indeed, while the police were at her house, Tracy Thurman's husband stabbed her 13 times and broke her neck, leaving her partially paralyzed.

Continued on p. 12

Chronology

19th Century

Family violence becomes an issue for charitable organizations. By the 1870s, most states declare wife beating illegal, but there are few services and no shelters to help battered women.

1824
Mississippi Supreme Court says a husband can beat his wife.

1871
Courts in Alabama and Massachusetts overturn the right of a husband to beat his wife.

1960s

Most police and judges view marital violence as a private affair. In most areas, a husband cannot be arrested for wife beating unless police see the incident or have a warrant.

1967
International Association of Chiefs of Police training manual says arrests should be made only as a last resort in family disputes.

1970s

Feminist movement identifies spousal assault and rape as major women's issues, and shelters for battered women are established.

1971
First hotline for battered women is started in St. Paul, Minn.

1977
Oregon becomes first state to require mandatory arrests in domestic-violence incidents.

1978
Minnesota becomes first state to allow arrests without warrants in domestic-violence incidents.

1980s

All states pass domestic-violence legislation, and most mandate or permit the arrest of batterers.

1981
Massachusetts and New Jersey supreme courts say a husband can be charged with raping his wife.

1984
Congress passes Family Violence Prevention and Services Act and the Victims of Crime Act, providing federal funds for domestic-violence programs and shelters.

1985
President Ronald Reagan forces John Fedders, a top Securities and Exchange Commission attorney, to resign after his wife cites 18 years of repeated beatings as grounds for divorce. . . . U.S. surgeon general identifies domestic violence as a major health problem.

1990s

High-profile celebrity cases focus on domestic violence, leading to a new federal law providing money for services to help victims and train officials to deal with domestic violence.

1991
Joint Commission on Accreditation of Hospitals in 1991 requires emergency-room personnel to be trained to identify battered women.

1992
American Medical Association and surgeon general suggest that all women patients be screened for domestic abuse.

1994
Spousal assault gets national attention during the trial of Lorena Bobbitt, a battered woman who cut off her sleeping husband's penis. . . . O. J. Simpson, a sports broadcaster and former football star, is charged with murdering his estranged wife and a male companion. Bobbit and Simpson are both acquitted.

1994
Congress passes Violence Against Women Act (VAWA), establishing community-based programs for domestic violence, training for police and court officials and a national 24-hour hotline for battered women. The law also makes it a federal crime to cross state lines to commit domestic violence.

2000s

Supreme Court limits the types of lawsuits domestic-violence victims can file; Congress targets dating violence and prevention.

2000
Supreme Court says victims of rape and domestic violence cannot sue attackers in federal court. . . . Congress reauthorizes VAWA to include dating violence and stalking.

2005
Supreme Court says a domestic-violence victim cannot sue a police department for failing to enforce a restraining order. . . . Congress updates VAWA to include teen dating and more prevention funds.

Domestic Violence Gets Military's Attention

Master Sgt. William Wright strangled his 32-year-old wife, Jennifer Gail, and buried her in a shallow grave in a North Carolina field. She was among four wives killed in a six-week period in 2002 by their husbands, all soldiers stationed at Fort Bragg, N.C. Three had recently returned from fighting in Afghanistan. [1]

The murders drew considerable media attention and prompted the Pentagon to modify its handling of domestic violence, says Anita Sanchez, spokeswoman for the Miles Foundation, a Connecticut-based advocacy group that deals with domestic violence in the military.

Among other things, the military started requiring troops returning from long deployments to complete a mental health checklist — promptly dubbed the "don't kill your wife survey" by troops. They quickly learned "what to check" to avoid raising red flags, Sanchez says, adding that few services are provided for families on what to expect from their returning soldiers. And with so many troops in Iraq and Afghanistan, many military families are strained and anxious.

Even before the four slayings, concern about domestic violence in the military had prompted lawmakers on Capitol Hill to require the Pentagon to establish a Defense Task Force on Domestic Violence. Established in 1999, it issued several reports and some 200 recommendations before disbanding in 2003.

Maj. Michael Shavers, a Pentagon spokesman, says the Defense Department has made "substantial progress" implementing the task force's recommendations and improving the military's response to domestic violence. For example, the department has funded 22 domestic-violence training conferences over the past two years for commanding officers, judge advocates, law-enforcement personnel, victims' advocates, chaplains, health-care providers and fatality-review team members. The Pentagon also is working with the Family Violence Prevention Fund and the National Domestic Violence Hotline to develop public-awareness campaigns encouraging the military community "to take a stand against domestic violence," Shavers says.

In the last five years, the Miles Foundation reports a dramatic spike in its caseload. In October 2001, the foundation was handling 50 cases a month. Now it has 147 a week, Sanchez says, attributing the increase to greater public awareness of the issue as well as to the confidentiality and privacy the foundation can offer that the military cannot.

Military life, by its very nature, is stressful, making some family members especially vulnerable to domestic violence. Frequent relocations and high unemployment for military spouses, for example, make them more dependent on their service-member partner for income, health care and housing. Moreover, long deployments can cause some soldiers to worry that their spouses are having extramarital affairs. And easy access to weapons also has been shown to be a risk factor in domestic-violence homicides.

Continued from p. 10

That same year, Congress passed the Family Violence Prevention and Services Act and the Victims of Crime Act, which, for the first time, provided money for states to set up shelters for battered women and a national, toll-free hotline for victims of domestic violence. The amount of money provided, however, was "but a trickle," wrote Richard J. Gelles, now dean of the School of Social Work at the University of Pennsylvania and an expert in the field. [34]

By 1987, more than half of the nation's major police departments had adopted "pro-arrest" policies requiring officers to make arrests in domestic-violence cases unless they could document a good reason not to.

Two widely reported cases in the 1980s dispelled the notion that domestic violence affected only the poor or uneducated. In 1985, President Ronald Reagan forced the resignation of John Fedders, a top official at the Securities and Exchange Commission, when Fedders' wife cited 18 years of repeated beatings as grounds for divorce.

Two years later, New York City lawyer Joel Steinberg was convicted of beating his 8-year-old adopted daughter Lisa to death.* During the trial it was also disclosed that Steinberg also routinely beat his companion, Hedda Nussbaum, who hadn't tried to stop the child's abuse. Photos of Nussbaum's badly injured face and vacant stare introduced the nation to "battered women's syndrome," suffered by women living in abusive relationships. Its symptoms include loss of self-esteem, fear, passivity and isolation.

While data suggest that fewer battered women are resorting to violence against their abusers, no one really knows how many women are in prison today for killing or assaulting their abusive partners, says Sue Osthoff, director of the Philadelphia-based National Clearinghouse for the Defense of Battered Women. Recent Justice Department data don't track how many violent crimes committed by women involve spouses or intimates, although a 1991 Justice

* Charlotte Fedders was granted a divorce in 1985. In 1987 John Fedders sought a financial share of his ex-wife's book about her experiences, *Shattered Dreams*, which became a made-for-TV movie; a circuit court judge rejected Fedders' claim. He was never criminally prosecuted and still practices law in Washington. Steinberg was convicted of first-degree manslaughter in 1989 and sentenced to up to 25 years in prison; he was released in 2004. Murder charges against Hedda Nussbaum were dropped after prosecutors concluded she had been too severely battered to protect Lisa. She now works at My Sisters' Place, an organization that helps battered women.

Abuse victims in military families are often reluctant to report incidents of abuse because they know it could jeopardize the spouse's career, along with the family's paycheck, housing and health care.

"Imagine, in the civilian world, that calling a local shelter or confiding in your doctor automatically caused your batterer's employer to find out about his acts of violence and abuse," Judith E. Beals, a member of the Defense Task Force on Domestic Violence, wrote in the group's 2003 report. [2]

Victims' advocates say, however, that in recent years the military has lagged behind the nation in dealing with domestic violence. When the military created its Family Advocacy Programs (FAP) more than 20 years ago, the programs were considered progressive. But over time, experts say, FAP stayed the same while the civilian world changed the way it dealt with domestic violence.

In terms of domestic-violence programs, "the military today is where the country was in the 1980s," Sanchez says. For example, in the 1980s, many civilian hospitals were beginning to make sure they had registered nurses on staff — called SANEs (sexual assault nurse examiners) — trained to examine sexual-assault victims. But Camp Lejeune, a big Marine Corps base in North Carolina, didn't get its first SANE until 2002, Sanchez says. Until recently, sexual-assault victims on some military bases had to be transferred to civilian hospitals to obtain treatment.

Advocates had hoped to persuade Congress in 2005 to add military-specific provisions to the Violence Against Women Act but were told the bill would have to go through the Armed Services and other committees with jurisdiction over military issues, possibly delaying or derailing the entire bill.

Meanwhile, the DOD and the Justice Department's Office on Violence Against Women in 2005 kicked off two domestic-violence demonstration projects that use the "coordinated community response" approach. The projects involve the U.S. Army at Fort Campbell, Ky., and the communities of Hopkinsville, Ky., and Clarksville, Tenn., and the U.S. Navy and the city of Jacksonville, Fla. The projects are expected to provide "lessons learned" and serve as a guide for other military installations.

"There really isn't a set model for coordinating the military and civilian response to domestic-violence incidents, so hopefully we can create one," said Connie Sponsler-Garcia, the Military Projects Coordinator and coordinator of the Jacksonville project. [3]

---

[1] Fox Butterfield, "Wife Killings at Fort Reflect Growing Problem in Military," *The New York Times*, July 29, 2002, p. A9, and "Rash of Wife Killings at Ft. Bragg Leaves the Base Wondering Why," The Associated Press, July 27, 2002.

[2] Judith E. Beals, "The Military Response to Victims of Domestic Violence," 2003. The report comes from the Battered Women's Justice Project, which provides technical advice to the Department of Justice's Office on Violence Against Women.

[3] Kaylee LaRocque, "New Program Will Help Navy Deal with Domestic Violence Cases," *Navy NewsStand*, March 4, 2005.

Department survey of 11,800 female prisoners found that nearly 20 percent were incarcerated for a violent offense committed against an intimate.

Only 125 battered women from 23 states have received clemency since 1978, according to the clearinghouse. Osthoff says many governors and pardon boards are leery of giving battered women a break on their sentences because much of the public opposes early releases for anyone convicted of violent crimes, including battered women. In addition, many believe victims could have avoided violence by turning to today's array of domestic-violence programs.

In the early 1990s the medical community got more involved in domestic violence. The Joint Commission on Accreditation of Hospitals in 1991 required that all emergency room personnel be trained in identifying battered women. The next year the American Medical Association (AMA) and the U.S. surgeon general encouraged the screening of all women patients for domestic abuse.

Few medical organizations, however, supported requiring health-care workers to report patients who were apparent victims of domestic violence to the police or social services, as they are required to do in cases of suspected child abuse.

"Reporting does not ensure that a victim will have access to necessary resources and safeguards, nor does it guarantee prosecution, punishment or rehabilitation of abusers," says Peggy Goodman, director of violence-prevention resources at East Carolina University's Brody School of Medicine in Greenville, N.C. "In fact, [reporting] can further escalate an abusive situation and further endanger the life of the patient," she says. Thus, she says the American College of Emergency Physicians, the AMA and the American College of Obstetrics and Gynecology all oppose mandatory reporting by health-care workers.

The 1990s also ushered in a series of domestic-violence cases that either involved celebrities or made celebrities out of the parties involved because the trials were televised. In 1992, heavyweight boxer Mike Tyson was convicted of raping an 18-year-old beauty-pageant contestant, drawing national attention to date rape. A year later, the issue of spousal assault got national attention when Bobbitt cut off her husband's penis with a knife.

Then, in 1994, O. J. Simpson was arrested and charged with murdering his ex-wife, Nicole Brown Simpson, and her friend, Ronald Goldman. Simpson had pleaded no contest in 1989 to charges that he beat his wife and was fined $700 and sentenced to two years'

Killings of Men Dropped

The number of men killed by so-called intimates dropped by 71 percent between 1976 and 2001. Experts say women now feel they don't have to resort to violence because there are tougher laws to protect them from domestic violence and safer shelters.*

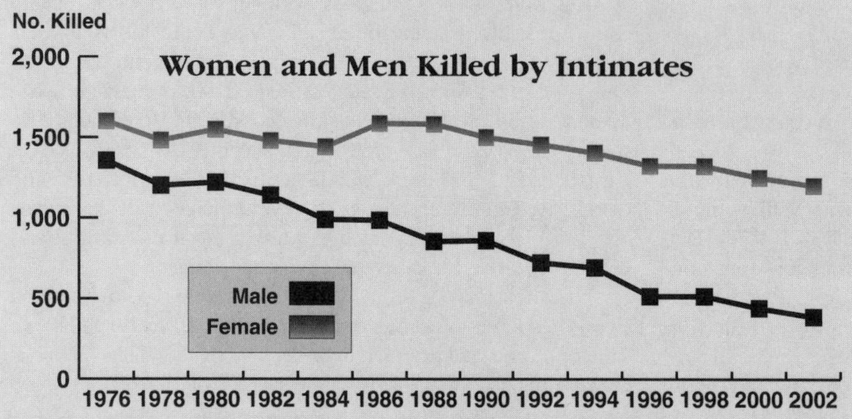

** "Intimates" includes spouses, ex-spouses, boyfriends and girlfriends.*

Source: Bureau of Justice Statistics, U.S. Department of Justice, 2003.

probation. Police records also showed that Mrs. Simpson had frequently made emergency calls to police to report that her husband was beating her.

Congress Acts

Experts say the Simpson case helped prod Congress to approve the Violence Against Women Act in 1994, which proponents call a turning point in the fight against domestic violence. President Bill Clinton, who as a child had witnessed his own mother being beaten by his stepfather, was a strong supporter of VAWA, which was attached to Clinton's crime bill.

The legislation reworked several areas of federal criminal law. It created penalties for stalking or domestic abuse in which an abuser crossed a state line and then physically harmed the victim in the course of a violent crime. VAWA also set new rules of evidence specifying that a victim's past sexual behavior generally was not admissible in federal civil or criminal cases regarding sexual misconduct. The law also allowed rape victims to demand that their alleged assailants be tested for HIV, the virus that causes AIDS.

VAWA encouraged local governments to create "coordinated community responses" bringing together criminal-justice agencies, social-services systems and local shelters and other nonprofits. The strategy is often called the "Duluth model," after the northern Minnesota city where it was developed over a 15-year period. Researchers say the ideal coordinated community response should also involve health-care providers, child-protection services, local businesses, the media, employers and clergy. Health-care providers, in particular, can be important since doctors, nurses and emergency-room workers may see and treat women who don't or can't seek other kinds of assistance.

States in the 1990s also began experimenting with ways to help victims and alternatives to penalizing perpetrators. New Haven, Conn., for example, launched a pilot program that included weekend jail stays combined with counseling. The approach allowed offenders to keep their jobs while remaining behind bars on weekends, when batterers often drink and become abusive. Illinois and Oregon were among the states that put domestic-violence counselors in welfare offices. Washington became the first state to allow battered women to set up confidential addresses their abusers couldn't locate.

Congress updated VAWA in 2000, adding "dating violence" to the definition of domestic violence and urging grant programs to address it. The revised law also created penalties for anyone traveling across state lines with the intent to kill, injure, harass or intimidate a spouse or intimate partner. The revised law also laid out special rules for battered immigrant spouses and their children, allowing them to remain in the United States. Under the old law, battered immigrant women could be deported if they left their abusers, who usually are their sponsors for residency and citizenship in the United States.

Also in 2000, the U.S. Supreme Court invalidated portions of the law permitting victims of rape and domestic violence to sue their attackers in federal court for damages. Ruling in *United States v. Morrison*, the justices said those provisions were unconstitutional under the Commerce and Equal Protection clauses. Victims could still bring damage suits in state courts. In addition, the court said, such violence does not substantially affect interstate commerce and noted that the Equal Protection clause is directed at government actions, not private. The high court's ruling did not affect any VAWA grant programs. [35]

Although the VAWA amendments passed in 2000 with nearly unanimous support, the law had its share of critics. Most of the criticism came from those who complained that violence was a problem of both men and women but that VAWA addressed only the needs of female victims. ■

CURRENT SITUATION

Reworking VAWA

Working until the early-morning hours of Dec. 17, 2005, Congress updated and expanded VAWA, kicking off several new initiatives, including a focus on young people and prevention.

Sen. Biden, the lead sponsor of both the original VAWA and the 2005 updated law, called passage of the new bill "a major victory," saying it "provides cities and towns with the tools they need to combat domestic violence, assist victims and go after abusers when it occurs." [36]

The updated legislation sets aside federal grant money for programs that help teen domestic-violence victims — including those in abusive dating relationships — and focuses more on children exposed to domestic violence at home. It also provides funds to combat domestic violence, sexual assault and dating violence in middle and high schools and expands services for rape victims and rape crisis centers, homeless-youth shelters and homes for runaways.

Targeting federal funds to younger victims "makes sense since we know that the highest rates of intimate-partner violence affect those in the 16-to-24 age group," says Kiersten Stewart, director of public policy at the Family Violence Prevention Fund, which lobbied Congress to enact the original Violence Against Women Act and many of the key revisions in 2005.

Stewart lauded Congress for continuing existing domestic-violence programs and for adding new ones, particularly those that focus on young people. "We're very pleased," she says.

The updated VAWA also includes money for programs to help domestic-abuse victims who are over age 60. It is difficult to say how many older Americans are abused, neglected or exploited, in large part because the problem remains "greatly hidden," says the National Center on Elder Abuse, a Washington, D.C., group that receives funds from the U.S. Administration on Aging. A 1998 federal study estimated that in 1996 some 450,000 Americans 60 and over were victims of physical, emotional or sexual abuse, neglect or financial exploitation. In 90 percent of the cases, a family member was the perpetrator, the study found. [37]

Experts fear that as the U.S. population ages, the number of elder-abuse cases will grow. "It's a hidden epidemic," Daniel Reingold, president and chief executive officer of the Hebrew Home

Is Your Relationship Healthy or Abusive?

Break the Cycle, a nonprofit organization helping young people create lives free of abuse, suggests teens ask themselves the following questions to determine if their relationships are healthy. If teens answer yes to any of these questions, they may be in an abusive or potentially abusive relationship, the organization says.

Does the person I am with:

- Get extremely jealous or possessive?
- Accuse me of flirting or cheating?
- Constantly check up on me or make me check in?
- Tell me how to dress or how much makeup to wear?
- Try to control what I do or whom I see?
- Try to keep me from seeing or talking to my family and friends?
- Have big mood swings — being angry and yelling at me one minute, and the next being sweet and apologetic?
- Make me feel nervous or like I'm "walking on eggshells?"
- Put me down or criticize me and make me feel like I can't do anything right or that no one else would want me?
- Threaten to hurt me?
- Threaten to hurt my friends or family?
- Threaten to commit suicide or hurt himself or herself because of me?
- Threaten to hurt my pets or destroy my things?
- Yell, grab, push, shove, shake, punch, slap, hold me down, throw things or hurt me in any way?
- Break things or throw things when we argue?
- Pressure or force me into having sex or going farther than I want to?

Source: Break the Cycle, www.break-the-cycle.org/

Innovative Programs Fight Domestic Violence

A host of programs around the country are dedicated to fighting and preventing domestic violence. Among those that have been found to work well are:

- **Coaching Boys into Men** — This program from the Family Violence Prevention Fund recognizes the mentoring role coaches have with their athletes and provides training tools to encourage disciplined and respectful behaviors. (www.endabuse.org) A similar effort comes from New York Yankees Manager Joe Torre, who founded the Joe Torre Safe at Home Foundation to prevent others from suffering as he did as a child. Growing up, he stayed away from home, fearful of his own father, who abused his mother. (www.joetorre.org)
- **Cut it Out** — Originally a statewide program created by The Women's Fund of Greater Birmingham and the Alabama Coalition Against Domestic Violence, this program went national in 2003, training hair salon professionals to recognize the signs of domestic abuse and to encourage suspected victims to get help. The project is cosponsored by *Southern Living At Home* magazine, the National Cosmetology Association and Clairol Professional. (www.cutitout)
- **Domestic Violence Prevention Enhancement and Leadership Through Alliances (DELTA)** — These state demonstration projects get funds from the U.S. Centers for Disease Control and Prevention to focus on preventing violence between intimate partners. A program at John Dickenson High School in Wilmington, Del., involves an interactive play for ninth-graders, weekly "healthy relationship" lessons during health class and a weekly after-school club called "Teens Talking About Relationships." Delaware Gov. Ruth Ann Minner (D) awarded the club the 2004 Outstanding Youth Volunteer Service Award. (www.cdc.gov/ncipc/DELTA/default.htm)
- **Family Justice Center, San Diego, Calif.** — Opened in 2002, this program provides "one-stop shopping" for legal, social service and some medical services in downtown San Diego, avoiding the need for abuse victims to go to different locations on different days. It is considered the gold standard for a compact community with good access to mass transit. But researchers have found that such programs are not as efficient for rural areas or spread-out cities that are more auto-dependent. It's a model for President Bush's Family Justice Center program. (www.familyjusticecenter.org)
- **Greenbook Demonstration Initiative** — Named for the report's green cover, this program was launched in 2001 and brings a closer collaboration between child-abuse and domestic-violence services. The project took place in six counties: San Francisco and Santa Clara counties in California; Grafton County, N.H.; St. Louis County, Mo.; El Paso County, Colo.; and Lane County, Ore. Among the key lessons from the Greenbook project: Mothers should not be accused of neglect for being victims of domestic violence, and separating battered mothers and children should be the alternative of last resort. [1] (www.thegreenbook.info/)
- **Judicial Oversight Demonstration Initiative** — This Justice Department program, which began in 1999, establishes closer working relationships between the courts, police departments, district attorneys' offices, probation departments and batterer intervention and victim services. The program was launched in Milwaukee, Wis., Dorchester, Mass., and Ann Arbor, Mich. (www.vaw.umn.edu/documents/1jod/1jod.html)
- **Victim Intervention Program (VIP)** — This program at Parkland Hospital at the University of Texas in Dallas provides staff caseworkers to help determine the health-care and social-service needs of patients who are victims of abuse and provides referrals for other services. Ellen Taliaferro, an emergency physician, founded the program in 1999. (www.parklandhospital.com)

[1] "The Greenbook Demonstration Initiative: Interim Evaluation Report," Caliber Associates, Education Development Center and the National Center for State Courts, Dec. 16, 2004.

for the Aged in Riverdale, N.Y., told *AARP* magazine. [38] That's largely because older victims are ashamed to report the abuse, because they feel they are old enough to know better than to be victimized. Reingold compares the current attention to elder abuse to the domestic-violence and child-abuse movements 25 years ago.

The expanded VAWA also funds programs to educate health-care professionals on how to identify and serve victims of domestic violence. A 2005 report from researchers at Harvard Medical School found that nearly one-third of doctors surveyed fail to document patients' reports of domestic violence, and only 10 percent offer information about domestic abuse to their patients. [39]

The National Network to End Domestic Violence says VAWA's new housing provisions are of particular importance, since 92 percent of homeless women have experienced severe physical or sexual abuse. The new law protects victims of domestic violence or stalking from being evicted from public housing and provides grants for transitional housing for domestic-violence victims.

"The reauthorization of VAWA shows that Congress recognizes domestic violence as a devastating social problem," said network President Rosenthal. [40]

The updated law fails to make the Violence Against Women Act gender neutral, as some men's groups had requested, but contains language

Continued on p. 18

At Issue:

Did Congress improve the Violence Against Women Act?

JILL J. MORRIS
PUBLIC POLICY DIRECTOR, NATIONAL COALITION AGAINST DOMESTIC VIOLENCE

WRITTEN FOR THE *CQ RESEARCHER*, JANUARY 2006

yes

Since Congress passed the bipartisan and groundbreaking Violence Against Women Act (VAWA) in 1994, the criminal-justice and community-based responses to domestic violence, dating violence, sexual assault and stalking have significantly improved. Ten years of successful VAWA programs have helped new generations of families and justice professionals understand that society will not tolerate these crimes.

Congress improved VAWA when it reauthorized it in December 2005. Since 1994, lawmakers have authorized more than $5 billion for states and local programs under VAWA. This relatively small amount has had a huge impact on local communities. For example, the number of women murdered by an intimate partner declined by 22 percent between 1993 and 2001. Also, more women came forward to report being abused in 1998 than in 1993.

VAWA is not only good social policy but also sound fiscal policy. A 2002 university study found that money spent to reduce domestic violence between 1995 and 2000 saved nearly 10 times the potential costs of responding to these crimes. The study estimated that $14.8 billion was saved on medical, legal and other costs that arise from responding to domestic violence. On an individual level, VAWA saved an estimated $159 per victim.

VAWA has fostered community-coordinated responses that for the first time brought together the criminal-justice system, social services and private, nonprofit organizations. With VAWA reauthorized, our local communities can continue to provide life-saving services such as rape prevention and education, victim witness assistance, sexual-assault crisis intervention and legal assistance.

Additionally, VAWA grants help reduce violent crimes on college campuses and provide services for children who witness violence, transitional housing, supervised visitation centers and programs for abused seniors and victims with disabilities.

The updated VAWA will expand programs to fill unmet needs, such as fostering a more community-based response system and addressing housing discrimination, preventing violence, promoting healthy relationships and engaging male allies to encourage positive roles for young men and boys.

The 2005 reauthorization of VAWA was one of the few pieces of legislation that was overwhelmingly supported by members of Congress on both sides of the aisle. Together, Democrats and Republicans agreed that passing VAWA showed that Congress was willing to recommit federal resources to programs that save lives, save money and help future generations of Americans live free from violence.

MICHAEL MCCORMICK
EXECUTIVE DIRECTOR, AMERICAN COALITION FOR FATHERS AND CHILDREN

WRITTEN FOR THE *CQ RESEARCHER*, JANUARY 2006

no

Violence perpetrated against others should be unacceptable regardless of the initiator's sex. But as many lawmakers privately confide, the Violence Against Women Act (VAWA) is not good law. Unfortunately, it has become the third rail of politics: Legislators acknowledge that it is political suicide to oppose passage of the bill. As one chief of staff aptly stated, "You do not want to be one of the few congressmen returning to your district having voted against this legislation, regardless of your reservations."

As a result, VAWA funds a political agenda that addresses domestic violence from a myopic viewpoint. It expands government encroachment into the private sphere of citizens' lives without adequate safeguards to those running afoul of the law and the domestic-violence industry.

Congress had a chance to address the law's shortcomings but failed to do so. For example, therapeutic approaches aimed at preserving the relationship and developing conflict-resolution skills still receive lower priority than law enforcement and relationship-dissolution options. This focus is at odds with stated public-policy objectives of building and maintaining strong, intact families. Congress should have changed this policy and did not.

Congress was correct to include language making clear that VAWA programs cannot discriminate against male victims, but it is still too early to tell whether male victims and their children will indeed get the help they need. Men and their children are not recognized as an underserved population, even though numerous studies indicate men are likely to be victims and suffer injury 15-30 percent of the time.

Even further, Congress made the right move by mandating that the Government Accountability Office study the issue, including the extent to which men are victims of domestic violence. This study will be balanced and give a better idea of how many men are abused and have access to services.

The biggest problem, however, is that VAWA does not recognize the role women play in domestic violence. The updated VAWA reinforces and statutorily codifies the notion that women are victims and men are abusers — a sure-fire way to assure half-baked solutions to a multi-faceted problem. This simplistic view of domestic violence ignores the vast storehouse of data indicating a small minority of both men and women are equally likely to initiate and engage in domestic violence.

Until such fundamental concerns are addressed, VAWA will continue to support a one-sided approach to dealing with domestic violence. Gender politics has no business being funded through the public purse.

Continued from p. 16

specifying that men can't be discriminated against. Rep. James Sensenbrenner Jr., R-Wis., chairman of the House Judiciary Committee and lead VAWA sponsor in the House, said after the bill's passage that the reauthorization "specifies that programs addressing these problems can serve both female and male victims." [41]

Youths from Los Angeles plan programs to publicize and prevent domestic violence against teens at a meeting of Break the Cycle's Youth Voices program.

Break the Cycle

It is widely speculated on Capitol Hill that gay men, who have been excluded from men's groups, could be the biggest beneficiaries of making sure VAWA funds help abused men. While numbers are hard to come by, domestic-violence groups say gays are frequent victims of abuse. "Clearly, it would benefit gay men if the act was gender neutral," Sean Cahill, director of the National Gay and Lesbian Task Force's Policy Institute, told *CQ Weekly*. [42]

McCormick, of the American Coalition for Fathers and Children, is still troubled that the updated law focuses too much on the criminal aspect of domestic violence and not the social problems associated with it. "It still resorts to the nuclear option of blowing up a family," arresting and incarcerating someone who could be falsely accused without even seeing whether counseling could keep the family together, he says.

But McCormick says he's glad the new law authorizes the Government Accountability Office to study the issue, including the extent to which men, women, youths and children are victims of domestic violence, dating violence, sexual assault and stalking. The study will be balanced and provide a better idea of how many men are abused and have access to services, McCormick says.

Finding What Works

While Congress debated reworking VAWA, the Bush administration's Office on Violence Against Women was launching the president's Family Justice Center Initiative. Fifteen centers will get federal funds to provide one-stop help for victims, including legal, medical and social services.

In 2005 family-justice centers opened in Brooklyn, N.Y.; Bexar County, Texas; Alameda County, Calif.; Ouachita Parish, La., and Nampa, Idaho. Additional centers are slated to open in 2006 in St. Louis, Tulsa, Boston and Tampa. The DOJ's Stuart says the centers are examples of approaches that are working. (*See sidebar, p. 16.*)

Meanwhile, 14 states are working with the U.S. Centers for Disease Control and Prevention (CDC) to prevent domestic violence in the so-called DELTA (Domestic Violence Prevention Enhancement and Leadership Through Alliances) program.*

* The 14 states are Alaska, California, Delaware, Florida, Kansas, Michigan, Montana, New York, North Carolina, North Dakota, Ohio, Rhode Island, Virginia and Wisconsin.

Each state project is a little different, since domestic violence and social programs differ from state to state, says Corinne Graffunder, branch chief of the CDC's National Center for Injury Prevention and Control. She says all 14 are innovative because they focus on prevention, not treating the victim or punishing the perpetrator. "That is new," she says.

In Valdez, Alaska, for example, the DELTA program is developing a healthy-relationships curriculum for the local high school. Mayor Bert Cottle proclaimed December 2005 as "White Ribbon Campaign Month" and encouraged all citizens, particularly men, to wear white ribbons in support of preventing domestic violence. And Dane County, Wis., provides programs and discussions for young men about sexual assault and domestic violence. The CDC expects to be able to evaluate the effectiveness of the programs in about three years, Graffunder says.

In New York state, Republican Gov. George Pataki and his wife Libby have spearheaded campaigns targeting teen-dating violence, including a statewide contest in which students were invited to submit posters, songs and music videos to raise awareness of the problem's seriousness. As part of Domestic Violence Awareness month in October 2005, New York kicked off its new "If It Doesn't Feel Right, It Probably Isn't" education campaign and distributed information packets — including copies of the 2005 winning poster — to all high schools in the state. (*See photo, p. 6.*)

"This campaign will serve as a powerful platform to raise awareness about teen dating violence and will let all of New York's teens know that there are resources available to help if they are suffering from abuse," Pataki said. [43]

States also are using welfare offices to help victims of domestic violence, but the efforts have been spotty. Studies have indicated that up to 50 percent of welfare recipients are, or have been, victims of domestic violence and all but three states — Maine, Oklahoma and Ohio — screen welfare recipients for signs of domestic violence. Most states will waive some federal welfare rules pertaining to work, the five-year lifetime limit on cash assistance and child-support requirements for victims of domestic violence. But a recent Government Accountability Office report found that state requirements varied widely and that few welfare recipients received waivers. [44]

The Center for Impact Research, a Chicago anti-poverty research group, found that workers in a local welfare office "overwhelmingly" did not refer welfare recipients to domestic-violence services, says Lise McKean, the center's deputy director. Part of the problem was a cumbersome form that welfare recipients had to fill out and overburdened caseworkers who didn't have the time or interest to pursue the matter.

"The vision of the [welfare] office as the public agency with access to poor women that can identify individuals living with domestic violence and help them gain access to domestic violence services may be unrealistic," the center concluded. [45]

Rather than welfare offices, McKean suggests putting domestic-violence services at employment-service agencies — an approach the center tried in Houston, Chicago and Seattle. [46] Having a domestic-violence counselor on site was key, she says. The case manager did not have to worry whether clients would follow up because the manager could escort them directly to the counselor. Plus, adding domestic violence to a case manger's list of concerns was not a big burden since a specialist was available to handle it.

Experts say domestic violence also should be addressed in marriage and responsible-fatherhood programs. Recent federally funded research found that many of the widely available marriage-education programs were designed and tested with middle-income, college-educated couples and do not address domestic violence. [47]

Some states, such as New York, argue that programs designed to encourage healthy relationships have the positive benefit of reducing the likelihood of both physical and emotional abuse. The Oklahoma Marriage Initiative addresses domestic violence implicitly by focusing on communication and conflict resolution and has recently created a handout telling couples how to identify domestic violence and where to obtain help. [48]

Businesses and nonprofits also are stepping in. Liz Claiborne Inc., Break the Cycle and the Education Development Center, Inc., have created curriculums for ninth- and 10th-graders on dating violence. And 19 schools are participating in the "Love is not abuse" program, which formally began in October 2005.

"Our hope is that this curriculum will help educate teens on how to identify all forms of relationship abuse and understand what types of actions are and are not acceptable in a healthy dating relationship," said Jane Randel, vice president of corporate communications at Liz Claiborne. [49] (*See questionnaire, p. 7.*)

Kraft Foods has sponsored several studies, including the Center for Impact Research's project that looked at how domestic violence affects women's job training and employment. [50] Verizon Wireless has donated more than $8 million to shelters and prevention programs nationwide. Kaiser Permanente has stepped up its efforts to train counselors to perform domestic-violence evaluations and provides resources for patients who need help. The Blue Shield of California Foundation offers free consultations to any employer in California interested in setting up a domestic-violence prevention program in the workplace. [51] ■

OUTLOOK

Focus on Prevention

Most experts say the country has made significant headway in viewing domestic violence as a crime instead of merely a private family matter. But most agree that more focus should be placed on prevention.

"True primary prevention is the next real area on the horizon," says the CDC's Graffunder.

"We're just now beginning to scratch the surface," says Soler, of the Family Violence Prevention Fund. "We can't just intervene after the fact."

"All the recent emphasis has been on the criminal aspect of domestic violence," says Jeffrey L. Edelson, director of the Minnesota Center Against Violence and Abuse at the University of Minnesota. "This is a public health epidemic" that must be tackled in both the courts and public health agencies. "The prevention piece is important."

Until now, prevention has not been a top priority because the immediate concern has been helping victims in crisis and making sure batterers were held accountable and got counseling, says Graffunder. And, she adds, while advocates fighting domestic violence like to envision a day when violence no longer destroys families and lives, "We still have a lot of work to do."

Research and funding still lag behind the needs, advocates say. "We have a pretty good idea what works, but we need documentation by researchers to back it up," says Stuart, of the Justice Department's Office on Violence Against Women. For example, she says, research is particularly lacking on stalking. "Right now, it's hidden. We really don't know how much stalking is out there."

Dunford-Jackson, of the Family Violence Project, also sees a dearth of data. She says judges are always asking for statistics on successful programs and techniques. "We're still in the infancy of domestic-violence research," she says.

Researchers expect to know more from the CDC's DELTA prevention programs once results are in. Advocates are also trying to figure out best practices from several other demonstration projects, such as the "Greenbook" program that provides closer collaboration between child-custody and domestic-violence agencies.

Burroughs of the Safe Homes for Children and Families Coalition is confident that in the coming years male victims of domestic violence will get more attention and federal funds. Soler of the Family Violence Prevention Fund likewise sees a bigger role ahead for men — as major players in prevention.

"Men — as fathers, coaches, teachers and mentors — are in a unique position to influence the attitudes and behaviors of young boys," Soler says. The Family Violence Prevention Fund has two major initiatives aimed at boys, Founding Fathers and Coaching Boys Into Men, which are funded by foundations and private donors.

Fulcher of Break the Cycle says it's critical that more prevention programs target teens. "Now is the time to tell the youth of our nation that we are done pretending, that we will lead them into healthy adulthoods, that we won't tolerate violence and neither should they."

Advocates, however, worry that the budget crunch in Washington caused by Hurricane Katrina and the war in Iraq will mean less money for state and local social and domestic-violence programs, jeopardizing the progress made so far.

"As resources are strained, the decisions that people have to make at the local, community and state levels just get harder and harder," says the CDC's Graffunder. "Prevention doesn't traditionally fare well in those environments." ■

About the Author

Pamela M. Prah is a *CQ Researcher* staff writer with several years previous experience at Stateline.org, *Kiplinger's Washington Letter* and the Bureau of National Affairs. She holds a master's degree in government from Johns Hopkins University and a journalism degree from Ohio University. Her recent reports include "War in Iraq," "Methamphetamines" and "Disaster Preparedness."

Notes

[1] U.S. Department of Justice, Bureau of Justice Statistics, "Intimate Partner Violence, 1993-2001," February 2003.

[2] Prepared testimony of Juley Fulcher and Victoria Sadler before the U.S. Senate Judiciary Committee, July 19, 2005; Allison Klein and Ruben Castaneda, "Md. Burn Victim Told Judge of Fears," *The Washington Post*, Oct. 13, 2005, p. B7 (Cade); Pat Burson, "The Dark Side of Dating," *Los Angeles Times*, June 20, 2005, p. F6 (Wickiewicz).

[3] U.S. Department of Justice, Bureau of Justice Statistics, "Family Violence Statistics," June 12, 2005.

[4] U.S. Department of Justice, *op. cit.*, February 2003.

[5] Testimony of Diane M. Stuart, director, U.S. Department of Justice Office on Violence Against Women before Senate Judiciary Committee, July 19, 2005.

[6] Family Violence Prevention Fund, "Promoting Prevention, Targeting Teens: An Emerging Agenda to Reduce Domestic Violence," 2003.

[7] Burson, *op. cit.*

[8] Becky Beaupre, "Spotlight on female abuser: For 13 years, he never hit her back," *The Detroit News*, April 20, 1997.

[9] Centers for Disease Control and Prevention, "Youth Risk Behavior Surveillance — United States 2003," *Surveillance Summaries*, May 21, 2004.

[10] Centers for Disease Control and Prevention, National Center for Injury Prevention and Control, "Intimate Partner Violence: Fact Sheet," updated October 2005.

[11] Wendy Max, *et al.*, "The economic toll of intimate partner violence against women in the United States," *Violence and Victims 2004*; 19(3), pp. 259-72.

[12] Miriam K. Ehrensaft and Patricia Cohen, "Intergenerational Transmission of Partner Violence: A 20-Year Prospective Study," *Journal of Consulting and Clinical Psychology*, Vol. 71, No. 4, August 2003, pp. 741-753.

[13] Prepared testimony, Senate Judiciary Committee, July 19, 2005.

[14] Prepared testimony of Lynn Rosenthal, president, National Network to End Domestic Violence, Senate Judiciary Committee, July 19, 2005.

[15] *Ibid.*

[16] U.S. Department of Justice, *op. cit.*, February 2003.

[17] Lisa Scott, "Pending federal DV law has little to do with violence and much to do with divorce court, attorney says," *The Liberator*, fall 2005.

[18] Allison Klein and Ruben Castaneda, "Character in a Courtroom Drama," *The Washington Post*, Nov. 17, 2005, p. B1.

[19] Kristin Little, "Specialized Courts and Domestic Violence," National Center for State Courts, May 2003.

[20] Scott, *op. cit.*

[21] Harvey Wallace, *Family Violence: Legal, Medical and Social Perspectives* (2002, 3rd ed.), p. 221.

[22] *Town of Castle Rock v. Gonzales*, 542 U.S. ___ (2005).

[23] "Supreme Court Decision Weakening Restraining Orders Short-Shrifted in the News," *Feminist Daily News Wire*, June 28, 2005.

[24] U.S. Department of Justice, Bureau of Justice Statistics, "Special Report: Intimate Partner Violence and Age of Victim, 1993-1999," 2001.

[25] Gallup Poll, "Adolescents Not Invulnerable to Abusive Relationships," May 24, 2005.

[26] "Liz Claiborne Inc. Omnibuzz Topline Findings: Teen Relationship Abuse Research," February 2005; www.loveisnotabuse.com.

[27] Sally Leidermann and Cair Almo, "Interpersonal Violence and Adolescent Pregnancy: Prevalence and Implications for Practice and Policy," Center for Assessment and Policy Development and National Organization on Adolescent Pregnancy, Parenting and Prevention, 2001.

[28] Centers for Disease Control and Prevention, *op. cit.*, May 21, 2004.

[29] Background drawn from Richard J. Gelles and Claire Pedrick Cornell, *Intimate Violence in Families* (1990) and Harvey Wallace, *Family Violence* (2002).

[30] For background see Sarah Glazer, "Violence Against Women," *CQ Researcher*, Feb. 26, 1993, pp. 169-192.

[31] Gelles and Cornell, *op. cit.*, p. 39.

[32] *Ibid.*

[33] *Thurman v. City of Torrington*, 595 F.Supp. 1521 (Conn. 1984).

[34] Gelles and Cornell, *op. cit.*

[35] *United States v. Morrison*, 529 U.S. 598 (2000).

[36] Statement, Dec. 19, 2005.

[37] "National Elder Abuse Incidence Study, Final Report," Administration for Children and Families and the Administration on Aging, U.S. Department of Health and Human Services, September 1998; www.aoa.gov/eldfam/Elder_Rights/Elder_Abuse/ABuseReport_Full.pdf.

[38] David France, "And Then He Hit Me," *AARP The Magazine*, January/February 2006, p. 81.

[39] Megan Gerber, "How and why community hospital clinicians document a positive screen for intimate partner violence: a cross-sectional study," *BMC Family News*, Vol. 6, p. 48, Nov. 19, 2005.

[40] Statement, Dec. 17, 2005.

[41] *Congressional Record*, Dec. 17, 2005, p. H12122.

[42] Jill Barshay, "Men on the Verge of Domestic Abuse Protection," *CQ Weekly*, Sept. 5, 2005, p. 2276.

[43] Press release, Office of New York Gov. George Pataki, "Governor Promotes Awareness of Teen Dating Violence," Sept. 23, 2005.

[44] Government Accountability Office, "TANF: State Approaches to Screening for Domestic Violence Could Benefit from HHS Guidance," August 2005.

[45] Center for Impact Research, "Less Than Ideal: The Reality of Implementing a Welfare-to-Work Program for Domestic Violence Victims and Survivors in Collaboration with the TANF Department," February 2001.

FOR MORE INFORMATION

American Coalition for Fathers and Children, 1718 M St., N.W., Suite 187, Washington, DC 20036; (800) 978-3237; www.acfc.org. Argues that the Violence Against Women Act destroys families and funds an anti-male, pro-feminist ideological agenda.

Break the Cycle, P.O. Box 64996, Los Angeles, CA 90064; (888) 988-TEEN; www.acfc.org. An advocacy group that educates and empowers youth to build lives and communities free from dating violence and domestic abuse.

Family Violence Prevention Fund, 383 Rhode Island St., Suite 304, San Francisco, CA 94103-5133; (415) 252-8900; www.endabuse.org. Sponsors education campaigns on family violence and was instrumental in lobbying Congress to enact the Violence Against Women Act.

National Coalition Against Domestic Violence, 1633 Q St., N.W., Suite 210, Washington, DC 20009; (202) 745-121; www.ncadv.org. Serves as a national information and referral center for battered women and their children as well as the public, media and allied agencies and organizations.

National Network to End Domestic Violence, 660 Pennsylvania Ave., S.E., Suite 303, Washington, DC 20003; (202) 543-5566; www.nnedv.org. Represents state domestic-violence coalitions and lobbies for stronger domestic-violence measures.

National Resource Center on Domestic Violence, (800) 537-2238; www.nrcdv.org. Provides comprehensive information and resources, policy development and assistance to enhance community response to and prevention of domestic violence.

National Sexual Violence Resource Center, 123 N. Enola Dr., Enola, PA 17025; (877) 739-3895; www.nsvrc.org. Provides information and technical assistance to local and national organizations and the public.

Safe Homes for Children and Families Coalition, 185 Springfield Dr., North East, MD 21901; (410) 392-8244; www.vawa4all.org. Advocates for gender-neutral federal legislation regarding domestic violence.

Stalking Resource Center, 2000 M St., N.W., Suite 480, Washington, DC 20036; (800) 394-2255); www.ncvc.org/src. Part of the National Center for Victims of Crime; serves as an information clearinghouse and peer-to-peer exchange program on stalking.

U.S. Centers for Disease Control and Prevention, National Center for Injury Prevention and Control, Mailstop K65, 4770 Buford Highway, N.E., Atlanta, GA 30341-3724; (770) 488-1506; www.cdc.gov/ncipc/factsheets/ipvoverview.htm. Studies ways to prevent intimate-partner and sexual violence.

U.S. Department of Justice, Office on Violence Against Women, 800 K St., N.W., Suite 920, Washington, DC 20530; (202) 307-6026; www.usdoj.gov. Handles legal and policy issues regarding violence against women and administers Violence Against Women Act grants.

[46] Lise McKean, Center for Impact Research, "Addressing Domestic Violence as a Barrier to Work," October 2004.

[47] Government Accountability Office, *op. cit.*

[48] *Ibid.*

[49] Liz Claiborne Inc., "Love is not abuse" curriculum, Oct. 11, 2005.

[50] McKean, *op. cit.*

[51] Available at www.endabuse.org/workplace/display.php?DocID=33018.

Bibliography

Selected Sources

Books

Gelles, Richard J., *Intimate Violence in Families*, SAGE Publications, 3rd ed., 1997.

Gelles, the then-dean of the University of Pennsylvania's School of Social Work, looks at the myths that hinder understanding of family violence, such as the belief domestic violence is a lower-class phenomenon.

Gosselin, Denise Kindschi, *Heavy Hands, An Introduction to the Crimes of Domestic Violence*, Prentice-Hall, 2000.

A Massachusetts State Police trooper who developed domestic-violence prevention courses for Western New England College examines different kinds of family violence and legal responses, with each chapter providing review questions on domestic violence.

Wallace, Harvey, *Family Violence, Legal, Medical and Social Perspectives*, Third Edition, Allyn and Bacon, 2002.

The director of California State University's Justice Center examines medical and legal responses to domestic violence, particularly among homosexuals and rural victims.

Articles

Beaupre, Becky, "Spotlight on female abuser: For 13 years, he never hit her back," and "No place to run for male victims of domestic abuse," *The Detroit News*, April 20, 1997.

Male victims of domestic violence are sometimes turned away from aid agencies.

Burson, Pat, "The Dark Side of Dating," *Los Angeles Times*, June 20, 2005, p. F6.

The author examines teen-dating violence, giving examples of teens in abusive relationships and how few turn to their parents for help.

Young, Cathy, "Ending Bias in Domestic Assault Law," *The Boston Globe*, July 25, 2005, p. A11.

A libertarian *Reason* magazine editor argues that the Violence Against Women Act helped enshrine a one-sided approach to family violence and that it should be more gender neutral.

Reports and Studies

"Full Report of the Prevalence, Incidence, and Consequences of Violence against Women: Findings from the National Violence Against Women Survey," U.S. Department of Justice, November 2000; www.ncjrs.org/txtfiles1/nij/183781.txt.

The survey quantifies the pervasiveness of domestic violence and its impact on women and society.

"The Greenbook Demonstration Initiative: Interim Evaluation Report," Caliber Associates, Education Development Center and the National Center for State Courts, Dec. 16, 2004.

An innovative pilot program aims to improve coordination between public agencies that deal with domestic violence and child welfare.

"Intimate Partner Violence: Fact Sheet," National Center for Injury Prevention and Control, U.S. Centers for Disease Control and Prevention, updated October 2005.

This backgrounder includes the latest research on domestic violence.

"Intimate Partner Violence, 1993-2001," Bureau of Justice Statistics, U.S. Department of Justice, February 2003.

A federal domestic-violence study looks at abusive relationships involving spouses, boyfriends, girlfriends and ex-spouses and partners.

"Less Than Ideal: The Reality of Implementing a Welfare-to-Work Program for Domestic Violence Victims and Survivors in Collaboration with the TANF Department," February 2001, and "Addressing Domestic Violence as a Barrier to Work," October 2004, Center for Impact Research.

Providing domestic-violence services at welfare agencies does little to help battered women, but putting such services in employment agencies can be beneficial because they help battered women achieve economic independence.

"Liz Claiborne Inc. Omnibuzz Topline Findings: Teen Relationship Abuse Research," February 2005, www.loveisnotabuse.com.

A survey sponsored by the clothing manufacturer shows that more than half of teens surveyed knew friends who had been physically, sexually or verbally abused.

"Promoting Prevention, Targeting Teens: An Emerging Agenda to Reduce Domestic Violence," Family Violence Prevention Fund, 2003.

An advocacy group concludes that the next generation of work in the domestic-violence field must target teens and young parents and emphasize prevention.

Ehrensaft, Miriam, and Patricia Cohen, "Intergenerational Transmission of Partner Violence: A 20-Year Prospective Study," *Journal of Consulting and Clinical Psychology*, Vol. 71, No. 4, August 2003, pp. 741-753.

Children raised in homes where domestic or dating violence occurs are more likely to become victims or perpetrators of such violence.

The Next Step:

Additional Articles from Current Periodicals

Gay Men and Domestic Violence

Mishra, Raja, "A Need for Shelter Havens Elude Many Victims of Gay Domestic Violence," *The Boston Globe*, Dec. 18, 2002, p. A1.
Gay men in cities are as likely to face domestic abuse as heterosexual females, says a new study, but gay victims suffer from a lack of public understanding.

Nichols, Jim, "Court Upholds Domestic Violence Law," *Plain Dealer* (Cleveland), Dec. 22, 2005, p. B5.
An Ohio appeals court ruled that unmarried victims of domestic violence, whether heterosexual or homosexual, have the same legal protections as married ones.

Immigrants and Domestic Violence

The Associated Press, "Battered Immigrants Fear Police as Much as Husbands," *Los Angeles Times*, Oct. 16, 2005, p. A18.
Abused immigrant women often are afraid to go to the police because they are unaware that immigrants who can prove they have been abused by a husband who is a legal U.S. resident can self-petition for a green card.

Somashekhar, Sandhya, "Abuse in the Land of Promise," *The Washington Post*, Oct. 6, 2005, p. T1.
Studies reveal high incidences of domestic violence within the Korean-American community, with abusers taking advantage of their victims' unfamiliarity with American customs.

Zheng, Zen T. C., "Vietnamese Language Legal Guide to Help Victims of Domestic Violence," *The Houston Chronicle*, Dec. 15, 2005, p. 3.
Texas is hoping an information kit in Vietnamese will help victims of domestic violence overcome cultural barriers.

Stalking/Sexual Assault

Ellement, John, and Patricia Wen, "Two Daughters Testify of Rapes and Beatings by Father," *The Boston Globe*, Feb. 12, 2005, p. B3.
Two daughters testified against their father after he was brought to trial on multiple accounts of rape and battery.

Lee, Jeannette J., "Almost Nowhere to Run in Rural Alaska," *The Washington Post*, Nov. 27, 2005, p. A6.
Victims of domestic violence in rural Alaska have little opportunity for help because bad weather and poor roads leave them stranded for days.

Sampson, Hannah, "Abused Wife: Shelter Needed," *The Miami Herald*, April 3, 2002, p. B3.
Because of a lack of local shelters for battered women, Amroutie Ragoobar was forced to take an apartment that her abusive husband was able to easily find and attack her again.

Wilmsen, Steven, "Changing Focus Program Counsels Men Named in Restraining Orders," *The Boston Globe*, April 12, 2002, p. B1.
The Dorchester District Court is providing alleged domestic abusers with advocates to help them navigate the legal system.

Teen-Dating Violence

Abdur-Rahman, Sufiya, "Breaking the Cycle of Teen Dating Violence," *Los Angeles Times*, Feb. 24, 2004, p. 2.
Unlike many organizations helping victims of domestic violence, Los Angeles-based Break the Cycle focuses on teaching youths how to get out of abusive relationships.

Stone Lombardi, Kate, "One Simple Rule for Dating: No Violence," *The New York Times*, April 18, 2004, p. WC4.
A teen-dating violence program was introduced at several all-boys private schools in New York to teach young men that teen-dating violence is a male problem.

Workplace Domestic Violence

Armour, Stephanie, "Domestic Abuse Shows Up At Work," *USA Today*, Oct. 16, 2002, p. B1.
Domestic violence is a growing issue for employers as more women join the work force. More than 70 percent of victims are harassed at work by spouses or significant others.

Belkin, Lisa, "A Haven From Threats That Come From Home," *The New York Times*, Nov. 20, 2005, p. A1.
Domestic violence costs businesses $5 billion annually in lost productivity and health costs.

CITING *THE CQ RESEARCHER*

Sample formats for citing these reports in a bibliography include the ones listed below. Preferred styles and formats vary, so please check with your instructor or professor.

MLA STYLE

Jost, Kenneth. "Rethinking the Death Penalty." The CQ Researcher 16 Nov. 2001: 945-68.

APA STYLE

Jost, K. (2001, November 16). Rethinking the death penalty. *The CQ Researcher, 11*, 945-968.

CHICAGO STYLE

Jost, Kenneth. "Rethinking the Death Penalty." *CQ Researcher*, November 16, 2001, 945-968.

CQ Researcher

Published by CQ Press, a division of Congressional Quarterly Inc.

thecqresearcher.com

Avian Flu Threat

Are we prepared for the next pandemic?

As deaths from bird flu continue to mount in Asia — and now threaten Europe — concern about a worldwide epidemic has prompted calls to action at the highest levels of government. Last month, in response to President Bush's emergency request, Congress approved $3.8 billion to develop new vaccines and stockpile anti-flu medications. Some critics say it's too little too late. If a pandemic hit tomorrow, the nation would have drugs to treat only very few people, no approved vaccine and a public health system that is woefully unprepared for a pandemic. With each new case of human infection, the danger increases that bird flu could easily pass among humans, health authorities warn. But some scientists doubt the virus will mutate into one that is easily transmitted from human to human. So far, most victims had close contact with poultry. But even skeptics agree a flu pandemic is inevitable at some point, and that the nation needs to shore up its response.

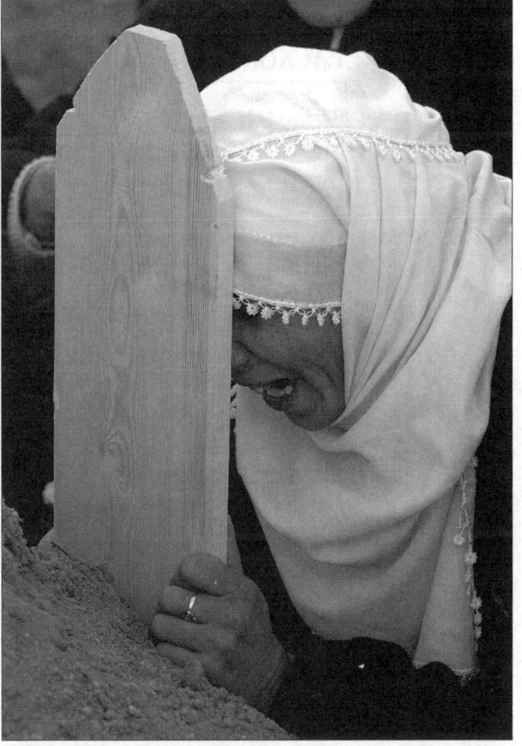

A mother in Turkey mourns at the grave of her 14-year-old son on Jan. 6, 2006. Three of her four children died from avian flu.

INSIDE THIS REPORT

The CQ Researcher • Jan. 13, 2006 • www.thecqresearcher.com
Volume 16, Number 2 • Pages 25-48

CQ PRESS

RECIPIENT OF SOCIETY OF PROFESSIONAL JOURNALISTS AWARD FOR EXCELLENCE ◆ AMERICAN BAR ASSOCIATION SILVER GAVEL AWARD

AVIAN FLU THREAT

Cover: A mother in Turkey mourns at the grave of her 14-year-old son on Jan. 6, 2006. Three of her four children died from avian flu. They were the first human bird-flu fatalities outside East Asia, where at least 75 people have died. (AP Photo/Murad Sezer)

CQ Researcher

Jan. 13, 2006
Volume 16, Number 2

MANAGING EDITOR: Thomas J. Colin

ASSISTANT MANAGING EDITOR: Kathy Koch

ASSOCIATE EDITOR: Kenneth Jost

STAFF WRITERS: Marcia Clemmitt, Peter Katel, Pamela M. Prah

CONTRIBUTING WRITERS: Rachel Cox, Sarah Glazer, David Hosansky, Patrick Marshall, Tom Price

DESIGN/PRODUCTION EDITOR: Olu B. Davis

ASSISTANT EDITOR: Melissa J. Hipolit

CQ PRESS

A Division of Congressional Quarterly Inc.

SENIOR VICE PRESIDENT/PUBLISHER: John A. Jenkins

DIRECTOR, LIBRARY PUBLISHING: Kathryn C. Suárez

DIRECTOR, EDITORIAL OPERATIONS: Ann Davies

CONGRESSIONAL QUARTERLY INC.

CHAIRMAN: Paul C. Tash

VICE CHAIRMAN: Andrew P. Corty

PRESIDENT/EDITOR IN CHIEF: Robert W. Merry

CQ Researcher (ISSN 1056-2036) is printed on acid-free paper. Published weekly, except March 24, July 7, July 14, Aug. 4, Aug. 11, Nov. 24, Dec. 22 and Dec. 29, by CQ Press, a division of Congressional Quarterly Inc. Annual full-service subscriptions for institutions start at $667. For pricing, call 1-800-834-9020, ext. 1906. To purchase a *CQ Researcher* report in print or electronic format (PDF), visit www.cqpress.com or call 866-427-7737. Single reports start at $10. Bulk purchase discounts and electronic-rights licensing are also available. Periodicals postage paid at Washington, D.C., and additional mailing offices. POSTMASTER: Send address changes to *CQ Researcher*, 1255 22nd St., N.W., Suite 400, Washington, DC 20037.

Avian Flu Threat

BY SARAH GLAZER

THE ISSUES

Chickens started dying mysteriously in Srisomboon, in northern Thailand, in August 2004. Like most children in the sleepy village, 11-year-old Sakuntula had daily contact with the birds. When she developed a stomachache and fever, the nurse at a nearby clinic dismissed her symptoms as a bad cold.

Five days later, Sakuntula began coughing up blood and was rushed to the district hospital. Her mother, Pranee Thongchan, was summoned from her job at a garment factory near Bangkok and found her daughter gasping for breath. The child died that night. Two weeks later, Pranee, 26, died, suffering from muscle aches and exhaustion, which were blamed on grief. * Viral pneumonia was listed as the official cause of death, however. [1]

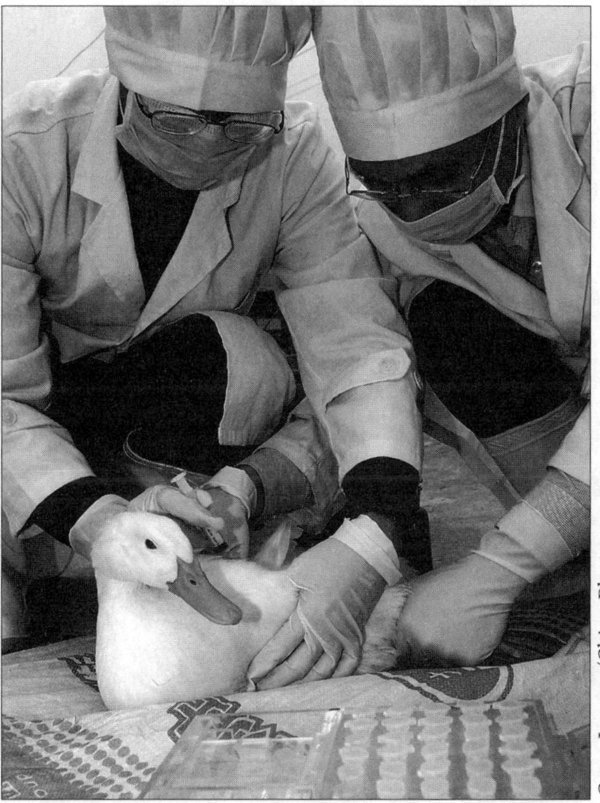

Getty Images/China Photos

Health workers take blood samples from a duck in Sichuan Province, China, on Nov. 11, 2005, to see if it is infected with bird flu. Since 1997, the disease has infected millions of poultry in Asia and Europe. So far, about 75 of the more than 145 people known to be infected by the disease have died.

Then, on Sept. 28, 2004, the World Health Organization (WHO) announced that the mother's death represented the first person-to-person transmission of the avian flu strain known as H5N1.

Researchers received the news with understandable concern. If H5N1 becomes easily transmissible from human to human, a worldwide epidemic — or pandemic — could occur, causing widespread infection and death from a virus to which most humans are believed to have little natural immunity.

The WHO has reassuringly called the Thongchans' daughter-to-mother transmission a "viral dead-end," because the virus does not appear to have mutated into a form that is easily passed from human to human. [2]

Today, the H5N1 virus is "like a key that doesn't quite fit the lock" of human-to-human contagion, explains Michael T. Osterholm, a professor at the University of Minnesota's School of Public Health. "But if you jiggle the key enough times, occasionally it will open the door. The virus is moving closer to the key that would really open the door. That's when you get sustained human-to-human transmission."

And each new human case gives the virus an opportunity to mutate into a fully transmissible strain among people, according to the WHO. International health officials were particularly alarmed by this month's deaths of three children in Turkey, the first victims of the disease reported outside of East Asia. Within a week, more Turks had contracted the disease, apparently after handling infected birds. About 50 others were hospitalized with suspected cases of the bird flu — 20 of them near Ankara, a major metropolitan city that is relatively well off and where humans and animals do not customarily share the same living quarters. By Jan. 9, at least 10 of 81 Turkish provinces reported having found sick birds, compared to only three provinces a few days earlier. [3]

Currently, there is no government-approved vaccine for human avian flu, although there is one for the version that attacks poultry. If a pandemic flu were to hit the United States tomorrow, it could take up to a year after the virus strain was identified to manufacture a targeted vaccine, but domestic-manufacturing capacity would only be able to produce enough doses to cover barely a tenth of the nation's population. *

Currently, the only treatment for the disease is thought to be Tamiflu and Relenza, antiviral medications known to work against seasonal flu. But no one knows for sure how effective they would be against a new pandemic flu strain.

---

* Symptoms of avian flu in humans have ranged from no symptoms to typical flu-like symptoms (fever, cough, sore throat and muscle aches) to eye infections, pneumonia, severe respiratory diseases and other life-threatening complications.

* To create sufficient capacity to cover the entire population, most experts agree the nation needs to convert to new cell-based technology, which has more flexibility to expand the number of doses than current egg-based technology. It would take 2-5 years to get government approval for the new method and to build plants using the new technology.

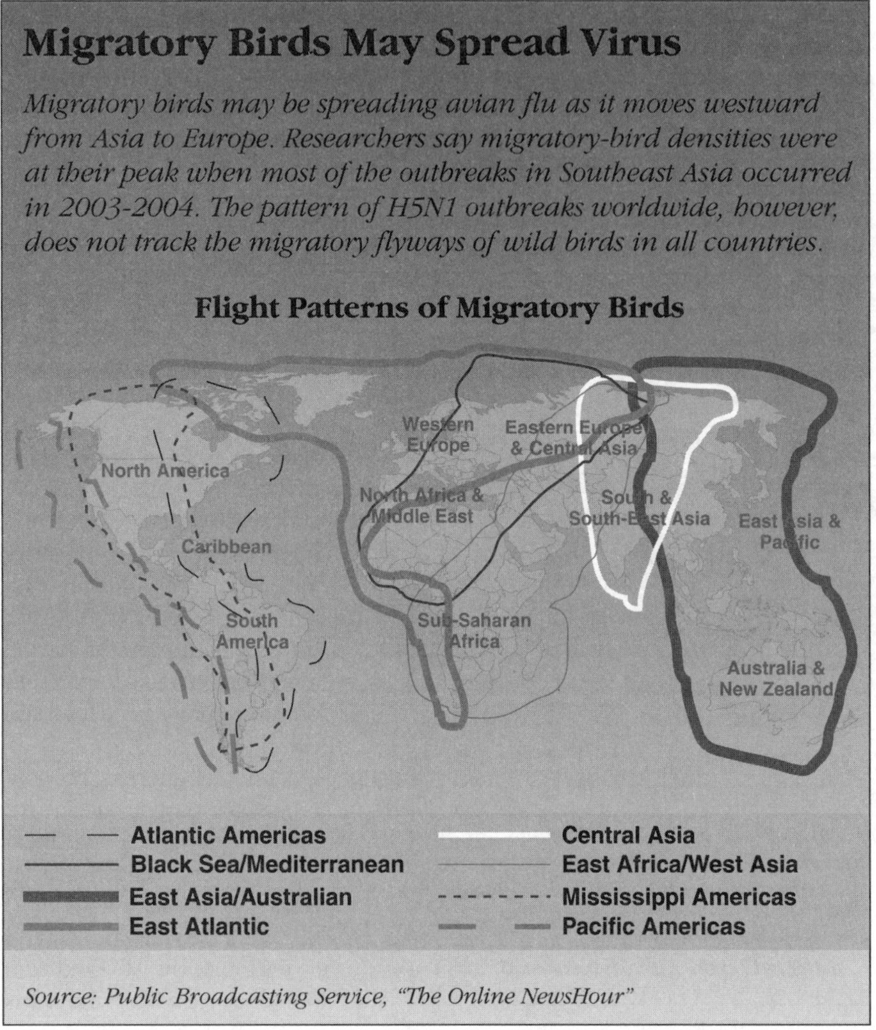

Migratory Birds May Spread Virus

Migratory birds may be spreading avian flu as it moves westward from Asia to Europe. Researchers say migratory-bird densities were at their peak when most of the outbreaks in Southeast Asia occurred in 2003-2004. The pattern of H5N1 outbreaks worldwide, however, does not track the migratory flyways of wild birds in all countries.

Source: Public Broadcasting Service, "The Online NewsHour"

Since 1997, H5N1 outbreaks have infected millions of poultry and more than 140 humans around the world as it has spread from flocks in Southeast Asia to Central Asia and Europe. * More than 75 people have died, about half of those said to be infected. The high 50-percent mortality rate worries experts. However, many think it is probably overstated because milder cases probably are not being reported. And some infected people who may have developed antibodies won't show any symptoms. By contrast, a worldwide flu outbreak in 1918 — the most lethal in recent history — killed only 2.5 percent of its victims, but that amounted to 40 million to 100 million worldwide — including about 675,000 Americans. [4]

But some experts think the avian flu will never mutate into a humanly transmissible virus. Michael Fumento, a senior fellow at the conservative Hudson Institute, maintains that H5N1 was first discovered in Scottish chickens in 1959. "It's therefore been mutating and making contact with humans for 47 years. If it hasn't become transmissible between humans in all that time, it almost certainly won't," he writes. (*See "At Issue," p. 41.*)

Because no one knows whether or when an avian flu pandemic might occur, the U.S. government is in a quandary over how aggressively to act. Some experts believe a global disaster threatens. "The situation right now in Asia is ripe for a perfect storm," says Osterholm. "You've got the virus circulating, you've got it moving closer to human pathogens and you've got a world ill-prepared."

Modern transportation permits a single person to spread disease to several continents within days, as the rapid spread of SARS demonstrated in 2003, when an infected doctor traveling out of China managed to spread the disease to Vietnam, Singapore and Canada within a month. [5] (Although SARS never became the worldwide epidemic that was predicted, before it was effectively contained it had spread to 30 countries, infected 8,000 people and killed 800.)

If a new avian flu pandemic develops, Osterholm paints a bleak picture of nations closing their borders and disrupting global economic trade in self-protection. And since the United States imports 80 percent of the raw materials used to produce crucial pharmaceuticals, he says, medicine would be scarce.

Efforts to contain the disease in Asia — including China's efforts to vaccinate every one of its 14 billion poultry — won't work, some experts say, because some vaccines are likely to be fake or overly diluted. [6] In a phone interview from Hong Kong, virologist Robert Webster of St. Jude Children's Research Hospital in Memphis, Tenn., and one of the world's leading authorities on bird flu, said "crap vaccines" already are being used in China. There are no international standards for agricultural vaccines, he notes.

Administering a weak vaccine causes a "bloody disaster," he explains, because only the symptoms, not the virus itself, tend to disappear. "The chicken doesn't die; instead, if it's infected it goes on pooping out virus for days and days

* Infected birds shed large quantities of the virus in their feces, creating abundant opportunities for exposure. Exposure is considered most likely during slaughter, defeathering, butchering and preparation of poultry for cooking.

and spreads the virus and increases the rate of evolution" of the virus, he says.

H5N1 has also been found in migratory birds, which may explain its spread to Europe, and in ducks, which do not show symptoms but may play an increased role in transmitting H5N1 to both poultry and humans. [7]

The situation looks dire to some advocates. The National Institutes of Health (NIH) is testing an experimental vaccine against a Vietnamese strain of H5N1 that infects humans, and the government has ordered more doses of it to be made. But it will be two to five years before the United States could build enough capacity to vaccinate everyone in the country.

Meanwhile, the government has begun stockpiling Tamiflu, but has only ordered enough to treat 5 percent of the population. (While Relenza is considered as effective as the Tamiflu capsule, it must be inhaled using a special inhaler, making it a less desirable medicine for mass distribution and stockpiling.)

"You can't prevent it if you don't have the vaccine; you can't treat it if you don't have the medication," says Kim Elliott, deputy director of the Trust for America's Health, a public-health advocacy group. [8]

That leaves isolating infected people as the only strategy for preventing spread of the disease. The Centers for Disease Control and Prevention (CDC) has proposed new regulations giving it authority to stop sick travelers from getting off international flights. But, unlike SARS, people with the flu are contagious for about a day before they have symptoms.

"When people push me, I say if society comes apart you have to be prepared to exist for three months with what you have in your house," says Webster. "It won't work, but what else have we got?"

"To have effective quarantine, you have to tell everyone to stay home [because we won't know] who's sick. That's just not possible," says Elliott.

At Least 78 Deaths Reported

The number of humans infected with avian flu doubled between 2004 and 2005, but the outbreak remained in Asia. On Jan. 10, 2006, Turkish health officials reported 15 patients confirmed with the disease and more hospitalized with symptoms suggesting the avian flu — more cases than the World Health Organization's totals (below). Three children in Turkey had died from the infection as of Jan. 10.

Confirmed Avian Flu Cases and Deaths

	2003 cases/ deaths	2004 cases/ deaths	2005 cases/ deaths	2006 cases/ deaths	Total
Cambodia	0/0	0/0	4/4	0/0	4/4
China	0/0	0/0	7/5	1/0	8/5
Indonesia	0/0	0/0	16/11	0/0	16/11
Thailand	0/0	17/12	5/2	0/0	22/14
Turkey	0/0	0/0	0/0	4/2	4/2
Vietnam	3/3	29/20	61/19	0/0	93/42
Total	**3/3**	**46/32**	**93/41**	**5/2**	**147/78**

Source: World Health Organization

In November 2005, President Bush proposed $7.1 billion in emergency funding to prepare for a flu pandemic, mainly to produce and stockpile vaccines and antiviral drugs and to improve reporting of bird flu cases at home and abroad. In December, Congress approved half that amount — $3.8 billion for 2006 — enough to "jump start" the plan this year, according to the Trust for America's Health. [9] The legislation also created sweeping protection from lawsuits for pandemic-vaccine manufacturers, which consumer groups blasted as an "unprecedented giveaway" to drug companies. [10]

But some critics say even the president's full request was too little too late. "That's less than the cost of an aircraft carrier," observes Tara O'Toole, director of the Center for Biosecurity at the University of Pittsburgh Medical School. "If we don't deal with this, we are facing a potential destabilizing and existential threat. You have to have countermeasures. That will require spending real money — money that you measure in [national] defense terms."

Other experts agree with Fumento and doubt this strain of flu will jump from birds to humans. Some believe it could evolve into something no more lethal than typical seasonal flu. "I'm just not persuaded this is a clear-cut case of avian virus waiting to cause the next pandemic," says Peter Palese, a leading microbiologist at Mount Sinai School of Medicine in New York. Like most scientists, Palese expects a flu pandemic of some kind eventually to occur as successive generations lose immunity to older viruses, but he says it could be 20 years from now and bear little relation to H5N1.

Of the 20th century's three flu pandemics, only the 1918 outbreak was extremely lethal. The 1957 and 1968 outbreaks caused about 75,000 and 34,000 U.S. deaths, respectively. Today, a mild pandemic on that scale would cause about 100,000 deaths in the United States — about three times the estimated 36,000 deaths that occur annually from seasonal flu, the Congressional Budget Office (CBO) projects.

Based on the historical frequency of pandemics over the past 300 years, in which mild pandemics have predominated, the chances of a severe pandemic occurring in the future are very small — only 0.3 percent, according to the CBO. [11]

Getty Images/Guang Niu

A pigeon is vaccinated in Beijing in an effort to curb the spread of bird flu. China plans to vaccinate every one of its 14 billion birds. There is no approved vaccine yet for the human version of the disease.

A 1918-scale flu, nonetheless, would infect about 90 million people in the United States and cause 2 million U.S. deaths, according to the CBO.

If a pandemic were to hit tomorrow, most agree our medical system would be woefully unprepared. "If this is anything like 1918, hospitals will be overwhelmed; if hospital workers are home sick with the flu, how you increase capacity becomes almost insoluble," says O'Toole, noting that most hospitals already run at close to 100 percent capacity. "If you ask them to double or triple their capacity, they collapse," she says.

Yet if the president were to start an even more ambitious pandemic-preparedness effort today — such as building new hospitals — the effort would be both costly and possibly unnecessary, as President Gerald Ford discovered with "swine flu." In 1976, the new strain of flu was projected to kill 1 million people, and Ford pushed for a mass-vaccination campaign. But only a few deaths occurred from the swine flu, and the government had to spend millions to compensate hundreds hurt or killed by the vaccine.

President Bush seemed to take note of this inevitable uncertainty when he unveiled his pandemic flu plan on Nov. 1. "While avian flu has not yet acquired the ability to spread easily from human to human, there is still cause for vigilance," he said. "Our country has been given fair warning of this danger to our homeland — and time to prepare. It's my responsibility as president to take measures now to protect the American people from the possibility that human-to-human transmission may occur." [12]

So why is Bush so concerned about preparing for a pandemic? "I have one word for you — [Hurricane] Katrina," says Michael Fumento, a senior fellow at the conservative Hudson Institute, who believes the current bird flu strain will never become a human pandemic.

Yet if a pandemic does arrive soon — whether from this bird flu or another virus — many experts say it could be a disaster, given the nation's beleaguered public health system, inadequate vaccine-production capacity and insufficient stores of antiviral medicine.

Here are some of the questions being debated in Congress, the scientific community and international organizations:

Is the United States prepared for a pandemic?

Top federal health officials have candidly admitted that if a pandemic arrived tomorrow the United States would not be prepared. [13] However, they contend that President Bush's proposal to spend billions on preparation, together with the detailed action plan released by the Department of Health and Human Services (HHS) in November, are steps in the right direction. About 95 percent of the president's proposal would go toward producing and stockpiling vaccines, antiviral drugs and other medical supplies and improving systems for detecting and reporting flu cases here and abroad. [14]

Critics charge that the administration's failure to stockpile antiviral medication earlier or to encourage the development of pre-pandemic vaccines has put the U.S. far behind European countries, which are competing with us for scarce anti-flu medications.

Under the HHS plan, $4.7 billion would be spent to help private companies create production capacity for pandemic influenza vaccine and to build a stockpile. The ultimate goal is to have the capacity to produce enough vaccine for the entire U.S. population — almost 300 million people — within six months of an outbreak.

But current U.S. production capacity falls far short of that goal. The major flu vaccine manufacturer located in the United States is sanofi pasteur, the vaccine-producing arm of the French pharmaceuticals group Sanofi

Aventis, which can produce only about 60 million doses each winter. According to most experts, 600 million doses — two shots for every American — would be needed to protect against a pandemic. "You do the math; it's frightening," says Elliott.

Moreover, there is no federally approved vaccine in the United States to protect against the bird flu strains circulating in Asia. The federal government has tested an experimental H5N1 vaccine in healthy people and is stockpiling the active ingredient needed for the vaccine, known as an antigen, in bulk form. The vaccine requires 12 times as much antigen per dose as seasonal flu vaccine and is expected to require two shots. Based on this formula, some experts say the government will only have enough H5N1 antigen to protect 4 million people by February 2006. [15]

The administration is hoping to stretch that supply with two methods shown in ongoing studies to enhance the immune response — diluting the vaccine with additives known as adjuvants and administering it into the skin rather than the muscle. However, it's unclear how far the supply can be stretched using these methods, according to Bruce Gellin, director of the National Vaccine Program Office, which authored the HHS plan. [16]

It is also unclear whether the H5N1 vaccine being tested by NIH will work against whatever virus appears on our shores. Virologist Webster doubts that it will prevent people from getting sick, though it may prevent deaths. "The viruses that are circulating out here are no longer closely related to the vaccine strain," he said in December, speaking by phone from Hong Kong.

In any case, it will probably be another two to five years before the United States can develop a vaccine and manufacturers can build enough production capacity to vaccinate everyone for a pandemic. (*See sidebar, p. 36.*)

Antiviral medications — such as Tamiflu, which helps people recover from the flu and acts as a preventive — are the second pillar of the administration's pandemic strategy. Under the plan, $1 billion would go toward purchasing enough antiviral drugs for a quarter of the U.S. population — the proportion recommended by the WHO.

However, as of December 2005, the administration had stockpiled only 4.3 million courses of Tamiflu, according to Gellin, far short of the 75 million needed. "There's no question more than 4 million Americans would become sick. We're woefully under-stockpiled there," says Elliott.

In response, Gellin cites computer simulations suggesting a pandemic could be stopped in its tracks by using Tamiflu to treat the small number of people initially infected and by giving it as a preventive to those in the surrounding area. "Three million treatment courses in one model has been shown to be the amount that's needed," he says, adding that the government hopes soon to have enough to treat twice that number of people. However, some experts doubt the government would be able to act fast enough to contain a pandemic this way. (Tamiflu must be taken within 48 hours of becoming ill.)

The United States has ordered 12 million treatment courses of Tamiflu from Roche, the Swiss pharmaceutical giant that developed the drug, but critics say the administration was so slow in placing its order that it is far down on the two-year waiting list behind other countries. And its order would only cover 5 percent of the population. Gellin responds that while the order won't be complete until sometime in 2007, the government will continue to get partial shipments in the intervening months. *

However, as governments were racing to buy Tamiflu, doubts suddenly emerged in late December 2005 about its efficacy, at current doses, after the prestigious *New England Journal of Medicine* reported that half of eight bird flu patients in Vietnam who were treated with Tamiflu had died — including two who developed resistance to the drug. [17]

Under the HHS plan, state and local governments would be largely responsible for distributing vaccines, anti-viral drugs and other medical supplies. But critics say state and local health departments, crippled by years of budget cuts and often sorely understaffed, will be hard-pressed to shoulder the burden. Many said the plan provided too little money for planning and none for implementation. Other critics say many states can't afford the 75 percent share the government is expecting them to kick in to buy 31 million courses of Tamiflu.

"I don't know where the states are going to come up with the money," says Elliott, who calculates the states' share of the cost at $510 million. "Look at Louisiana and Mississippi [post-Katrina]," she says. "They don't have it. It should not matter where you live or what your state's fiscal health is as to whether you get treated during a pandemic."

The administration argues that some $15 billion appropriated since 2001 to counter bioterrorism have helped states build up the same kind of public health capacities that would be needed in a flu pandemic. "Since 9/11 there's been a substantial investment to enhance that infrastructure," says Gellin. "A lot of those investments are helping precisely for the kind of threats we're facing now." Moreover, he says, pandemic planning should be a "shared responsibility" with the states.

But state officials say bioterrorism funds don't make up for cuts in their most crucial resource — people. "The tragedy is the hole was so big that the billions for public health preparedness are not enough when you cut school health programs. When something bad happens, that's where you get your nurses from," says Georges C. Benjamin, executive director of the American Public

---

* Under pressure from the global community, Roche agreed last fall that it would license partner companies to produce Tamiflu.

How Dangerous Is the Virus?

The lethal 1918 "Spanish flu" virus was probably descended from an avian virus and shares some genetic features with today's H5N1 bird flu, but its exact origin remains mysterious, according to molecular pathologist Jeffery K. Taubenberger. He and his research team at the Armed Forces Institute of Pathology recently reconstructed the deadly virus from frozen tissue samples. [1]

Their genetic analysis, published in October 2005, suggested that all eight genes of the 1918 flu came directly from a bird virus and moved into humans after gradually mutating. Federal health officials said at the time that H5N1 flu has already acquired some of the genetic-sequence changes that apparently allowed the 1918 virus to become easily transmissible among humans. [2]

Of the more than 140 people infected with H5N1, most had contact with infected poultry. The potential similarities between the catastrophic 1918 flu and the H5N1 flu — which has caused at least 75 deaths so far — have put the global public health community on edge. [3]

If, as Taubenberger suggests, the 1918 flu was a completely novel virus to which humans had never been exposed — and therefore had developed no immunity — that might help explain why so many people became sick and died. By contrast, the milder pandemics of 1957 and 1968 are believed to have been the combined product of a human flu and an avian virus that exchanged genes after either a human or a pig caught both viruses.

However, this explanation for the greater lethality of the 1918 flu is not universally accepted. It's also possible that the 1918 virus or versions of it had circulated in humans or other animals before it became pandemic, skeptics argue. Because no genetic information exists about any pre-1918 human viruses, no one can know for sure whether the 1918 virus was unique in makeup or whether it may have infected humans at some earlier point.

One of the skeptics, Mount Sinai School of Medicine microbiologist Peter Palese, says, "I don't think we can say [the 1918 flu] was an avian virus that jumped into humans." It's "equally likely" that the 1918 flu was a product of both human and avian viruses, like the 1957 and 1968 pandemics, he says.

Palese is one of several scientists who are not convinced that H5N1 will become a human virus, citing research dating from 1992 indicating that many Chinese already have antibodies to it. "The H5 virus has had ample opportunity to jump from avian populations into humans," he says.

What about mounting reports of humans contracting bird flu since 2003, half of whom have died? Palese thinks the widespread perception from media reports that there has been a jump in cases and a high fatality rate is erroneous. Many bird flu cases probably are not being reported, he says, because they are either mild or asymptomatic (in the case of people with antibodies). So the fatality rate is probably much lower than the apparent 50 percent rate, he says.

Many other scientists also suspect that cases of bird flu are being underreported, especially in China. For example, by the end of 2005, Vietnam had announced more than 90 cases of bird flu, while China — vastly larger than Vietnam — had reported only seven. [4] Some experts, like Palese, suspect that the numbers infected in China are actually in the hundreds. [5]

Nevertheless, the U.S. government is planning for a worst-case scenario with a 2.5 percent death rate, as experienced in

Health Association. "If the resources aren't there, you end up with a big bottle of Tamiflu and no one to manage it."

In a pandemic, up to 5-10 million Americans would need hospitalization — far exceeding the nation's 900,000 staffed hospitals beds. And the flood of patients would overwhelm the need for crucial equipment, such as the nation's 100,000 ventilators, according to the CBO. [18]

The administration's plan contains a long list of recommendations for how hospitals should handle the overflow patients during a pandemic. But "there's no way hospitals could implement even a fraction of what's recommended without federal funds," which are absent from the administration's plan, says the Center for Biosecurity's O'Toole.

Some experts say the administration should put more emphasis on quarantine. "If our states and federal government are only focused on vaccines, and there's no plan for the interim to slow the spread of disease, then it will spread like wildfire," says David Heyman, director of the homeland security program at the Center for Strategic and International Studies and author of a study proposing quarantine guidelines. State officials have been calling him for advice, he said, because they've received so little guidance from the federal government. [19]

But many experts say a quarantine to control pandemic flu won't work. Unlike SARS, people infected with flu can be contagious before they show any symptoms, and some carriers may never show symptoms at all.

However, skeptics like Fumento, at the Hudson Institute, say H5N1 is unlikely to mutate into a human form. And if the next pandemic is not an avian flu, then all the government vaccine efforts aimed at producing an H5N1 vaccine "will be completely useless."

As for the administration's plan in general, "A lot of this is going to be wasted," Fumento says. "It's true of any government crash program. That's how you get $500 toilet seats."

Will liability protection encourage more companies to manufacture vaccines?

"In the past three decades, the

1918. Since influenza viruses also tend to lose lethality over time, some scientists argue that any increase in transmissibility will produce a massive drop in virulence, because killing the host (i.e. humans) impedes a virus' evolution into a more lethal strain. [6]

No one can predict whether the virus will become humanly transmissible, or how virulent it will be, including Robert G. Webster, the scientist at St. Jude Children's Research Hospital in Memphis, Tenn., who has been warning of its potential dangers for years. When asked how serious it might be, all he can do is "hand wave" a guess. "My hand-waving would be if it does go human-to-human, the first wave will be a catastrophe for the world — for two, three, four months," he suggests. "The second wave will be less pathogenic and the third wave will go back to being somewhat benign." This is similar to the pattern observed in ducks, Webster says.

This month, however, Taubenberger and epidemiologist David M. Morens of the National Institutes of Health played down the similarities between the 1918 flu and H5N1. They noted that while the 1918 virus is "avianlike," researchers have been unable to trace the 1918 virus to any particular bird and that there is no historical data indicating that a precursor virus attacked domestic poultry in large numbers, as H5N1 has. No highly pathogenic avian virus has ever been known to cause a human pandemic, they noted. And despite Taubenberger's genetic-sequencing work, the biological basis for converting a virus into a humanly transmissible form — the prerequisite for a human pandemic — remains "unknown," they said. [7]

"The 1918 virus acquired this trait, but we do not know how, and we currently have no way of knowing whether H5N1 viruses are now in a parallel process of acquiring human-to-human transmissibility," they wrote. "Despite an explosion of data on the 1918 virus during the past decade, we are not much closer to understanding pandemic emergence in 2006 than we were in understanding the risk of H1N1 'swine flu' emergence in 1976," which turned out to be a false alarm. [8]

On the reassuring side, if H5N1 were to become a pandemic flu, the availability of modern antibiotics, which did not exist in 1918, would combat secondary bacterial infections, which caused many of the deaths in 1918.

But other unprecedented aspects of the virus worry scientists. The infection now has been found in tigers and domestic cats and in migratory birds, previously considered safe from such viruses. "We have to accept the fact that we're watching the evolution of this virus," says Webster. "Will it ever go human-to-human? Let's hope not. But we'd better be prepared for it."

[1] J. K. Taubenberger, *et al.*, "Characterization of the 1918 influenza virus polymerase genes," *Nature*, Oct. 6, 2005, pp. 889-893.

[2] "Bird Flu and the 1918 Pandemic," editorial, *The New York Times*, Oct. 8, 2005, p. A14.

[3] Congressional Research Service, "Pandemic Influenza: Domestic Preparedness Efforts," Nov. 10, 2005, p. 6.

[4] WHO, "Confirmed number of human cases," Dec. 19, 2005, www.who.int.

[5] See Elisabeth Rosenthal, "Experts Doubt Bird Flu Tallies from China and Elsewhere," *The New York Times*, Dec. 2, 2005, p. A8.

[6] Dennis Normile, "Pandemic Skeptics Warn Against Crying Wolf," *Science*, Nov. 18, 2005, pp. 1112-1113.

[7] Jeffery K. Taubenberger and David M. Morens, "1918 Influenza," *Emerging Infectious Diseases*, January 2006; www.cdc.gov/ncidod/EID/vol12no01/05-0979.htm.

[8] *Ibid.*

number of vaccine manufacturers in America has plummeted, as the industry has been flooded with lawsuits," President Bush declared in his Nov. 1 pandemic speech. The fact that only one major company now manufactures flu vaccine on U.S. soil, Bush said, leaves "our nation vulnerable in the event of a pandemic." [20]

He urged Congress to shield drug makers from lawsuits in order to encourage more of them to manufacture vaccine. A provision providing sweeping protection from liability was approved by Congress in December (*see p. 42*).

The number of manufacturers producing vaccine for the U.S. market has declined precipitously — from 26 companies in 1967 to five today — for all types of vaccines. Only three companies produce flu vaccine for the U.S. market — sanofi pasteur, in Swiftwater, Pa., Chiron, which manufactures its vaccines in England, and MedImmune, based in Gaithersburg, Md.

While thousands of lawsuits claiming vaccine-related injuries to children have flooded the courts in recent years, there have been very few lawsuits — only 10 in the last 20 years — over flu vaccines, according to a recent study in the *Journal of the American Medical Association* (*JAMA*). While two resulted in awards — of $1.9 million and $13.5 million — the rest were settled for much smaller amounts or were dismissed on summary judgment. [21]

Some experts argue that market factors have been more important in discouraging drug makers than liability fears, including the uncertain seasonal demand and the low profitability. Profit margins are much lower for vaccines, which patients receive only once a year, than for drugs for chronic conditions like high blood pressure, which are often taken daily. Indeed, when Wyeth Pharmaceuticals stopped making flu vaccine in 2002, its reasons were "not specifically related to liability," says Wyeth Vice President Peter Paradiso. "We were unable to sell 8-10 million doses out of 20 million in 2002," he says. "It became clear there wasn't a demand for our product."

Nevertheless, insurers' perception of litigation threats has made it difficult for manufacturers to obtain insurance, and a similar perception among manufacturers may have been as important as the reality, the *JAMA* study's authors suggest.

"The economics have not always been favorable, and liability has been a factor in determining the profitability of participating in vaccine manufacturing," says sanofi pasteur spokesman Len Lavenda. "For example, today there are thousands of lawsuits pending against manufacturers of thimerosol" — a mercury additive in childhood vaccines.

But Howard Shlevin, president and CEO of Solvay Pharmaceuticals, in Marietta, Ga., said his company decided in 1998 to build a U.S. flu vaccine plant utilizing the newest cell-based technology, before there was any talk of liability protection. "From Solvay's perspective, if someone wants to give me a free ride, that's nice, but that's not what I'm looking for," he said. The company has, however, applied for a federal grant to help build the new plant, he said.

In any case, most agree that drug companies will need some protection from litigation when it comes to producing a vaccine specifically for a flu pandemic. In a pandemic, there probably won't be enough time to test it extensively for side effects. In addition, notes Lavenda, "When we're talking about a new vaccine combined with a particularly virulent disease and immunizing perhaps 300 million individuals, we have the ingredients for liability exposure far in excess of that normally associated with immunization programs. That's why congressional liability protection is essential for companies supplying pandemic vaccines."

But consumer groups and public health workers' unions maintain that the threat of lawsuits prevents shoddy practices and that the government should not abolish citizens' ability to sue in court unless it also compensates those hurt by the vaccines.

Members of an expert panel convened by the Institute of Medicine (IOM) in 2003 say there are better ways than liability protection to encourage drug companies to produce vaccines. To provide greater supply and price certainty, they recommended the government guarantee an advance purchase of vaccines at a negotiated price. To encourage universal vaccination, they proposed the government require health insurers to cover vaccination and provide government vouchers to people without health insurance. [22]

"Make it worth the manufacturer's while to produce the vaccine. The way other nations do it is by guaranteeing the supply and purchase," says panel member Sara Rosenbaum, chairwoman of the Department of Health Policy at George Washington University. "Until we're ready to do this, I really don't think that an incentive that's speculative at best and meaningless at worst will contribute much to the problem," she said of a sweeping liability approach. The U.S. government already contracts with manufacturers to purchase certain childhood vaccines, which it provides free to children without health insurance under the Vaccines for Children program launched in 1994. [23] Since then, the market for those vaccines has been "robust," according to Rosenbaum. *

Duke University Professor of economics Frank Sloan, who chaired the IOM committee, attributes drug-makers' antipathy to vaccines to low profits, uncertainty about sales and high regulatory costs. "Just taking tort rights away is unjust," he says. "The government regulation of drug companies should be the first guard against contamination" of vaccines like that discovered at Chiron's British plant in 2004. "But suppose it failed? Then you should have tort as a backup." [24]

Should the U.S. government do more to combat avian flu overseas?

Like other wealthy governments, the Bush administration has made its first priority stockpiling enough vaccine to inoculate everyone in the country and enough antiviral medication for those who get the flu. But that approach concentrates most of the world's medical supplies in rich countries. The poorer countries of Asia, like steerage passengers on the doomed *Titanic*, will be left without any lifeboats.

Fewer than 10 countries have domestic vaccine companies working on a pandemic vaccine. Based on present trends, the majority of developing countries would have no access to a vaccine during the first wave of a pandemic and possibly its entire duration, according to the World Health Organization (WHO). Some 23 countries have ordered antiviral drugs for national stockpiles, but the principal manufacturer, Swiss drugmaker Roche, will not be able to fill all orders for at least another year, according to the WHO. [25]

One solution to this bottleneck would be for the government to suspend Roche's Tamiflu patent so other companies could produce it. In October, Sen. Charles E. Schumer, D-N.Y., threatened legislation to this effect unless Roche issued licenses to other companies. [26]

Bowing to international criticism, Roche agreed to license its product to 12 new partners out of 200 interested companies globally to help a number of countries meet their stockpile needs.

For its part, the WHO has recommended that wealthy countries contribute to an international stockpile of antiviral medications and cooperatively develop

Continued on p. 36

* The government also limited the liability of childhood vaccine manufacturers in 1986, when it required families of children injured by routine childhood vaccines to first seek relief through the federal Vaccine Injury Compensation Program before seeking redress in the courts. Seasonal flu vaccines were added to the program in 2004, but vaccines for use in pandemics were not covered.

Chronology

1900s-1970s

"Spanish flu" pandemic kills millions; vaccines and antibiotics become available later.

1918
"Spanish flu" kills up to 100 million, including 675,000 in U.S.

1957
Asian flu kills 75,000 in U.S.

1968
Hong Kong flu kills 700,000 worldwide, 34,000 in U.S.

1976
President Gerald R. Ford orders mass vaccination for "swine flu." Pandemic fizzles, but vaccinations kill 32 and make hundreds sick.

1977
Russian flu, another pandemic that never materializes, infects children and young adults in U.S.

1990s ***H5N1 bird flu is isolated in humans; new antiviral medications enter market.***

1997
H5N1 is first isolated in humans; infects 18 in Hong Kong; six die. Hong Kong slaughters all chickens.

1999
New antiviral drugs, Relenza and Tamiflu, licensed in U.S., Europe.

Early 2000s

Terrorist attacks in U.S. raise concern about possible bioterrorism; bird flu reappears in Asia.

December 2002
President Bush orders smallpox vaccinations for health workers and military; few sign up.

February 2003
Two people contract H5N1 virus in Hong Kong; one dies.

Mid-2003
First wave of H5N1 infection begins with outbreaks in animals in Asia.

December 2003
Bush administration compensates those injured by smallpox vaccine. South Korea reports first avian flu outbreak in chickens.

2004 ***Avian flu spreads through Southeast Asia, killing 32 people in Thailand, Vietnam.***

January 2004
Bird flu appears in poultry in Vietnam, Japan, Thailand; fatalities reported in Vietnam.

Summer 2004
Second wave of H5N1 infection strikes poultry in China, Indonesia, Thailand, Vietnam. Eight more fatalities occur in Thailand, Vietnam.

November 2004
World Health Organization (WHO) warns of possible pandemic.

December 2004
Third wave of infection occurs among poultry in Indonesia, Thailand and Vietnam; new human case reported in Vietnam.

2005 ***Congress approves crash plan to develop and manufacture vaccine and handle a pandemic, as bird flu spreads to more than 20 countries. . . . Cumulative worldwide totals reach more than 140 cases and 75 deaths.***

January 2005
First account of human-to-human transmission of avian flu published by *New England Journal of Medicine.*

March 2005
Bird flu has spread to 20 countries and killed 50 million chickens.

July 2005
Research on dead migratory birds suggests virus is carried along winter migration routes of geese. . . . Russia becomes first European country with virus outbreak in poultry.

October 2005
Virus confirmed in poultry in Turkey, Romania, Croatia.

November 2005
President Bush requests $7.1 billion to boost vaccine capacity, buy drugs.

December 2005
Congress approves $3.8 billion for flu plan, enacts liability protection for vaccine manufacturers. . . . Two cases of resistance to Tamiflu reported in Vietnam.

2006 ***First human victims of H5N1 infection reported outside Asia.***

Jan. 5, 2006
Three children die from H5N1 in Turkey. . . . U.S farmers begin testing chickens for flu. . . . WHO reports 144 infected to date, including 76 fatalities.

New Technique Could Speed Up Vaccine Production

If a flu pandemic were to break out tomorrow, it would take up to a year to develop a vaccine against the virus, by which time it could have circled the globe, creating death and economic havoc worldwide.

Why does it take so long to develop a vaccine? For every dose of flu vaccine, a manufacturer must infect a chicken egg with the particular influenza virus that is causing the new flu epidemic. Using a laborious process that hasn't been updated since the 1950s, a manufacturer aiming to make 20 million doses of a new vaccine must first order 20 million chicken eggs many months before the flu even hits.

"You have to plan in advance for egg deliveries, but there's no assurance you will get them," says Harold Shlevin, CEO of Solvay Pharmaceuticals in Marietta, Ga. "Just the logistics of getting 20 million eggs that you hope will grow properly, isolating and processing them [takes] closer to 9-12 months." Further complicating matters, for a virus that attacks birds as well as humans — such as the H5N1 avian flu now circulating in Asia — the virus could kill the eggs. So manufacturers today face the prospect of "no chickens, no eggs, no vaccine," says Shlevin.

His company has developed a new way to produce flu vaccine that relies on a line of cells harvested from a cocker spaniel's kidney in 1958 and kept alive ever since. President Bush has proposed a $2.8 billion crash program to accelerate development of vaccines using this approach — called cell-based technology — in order to produce enough flu vaccine for every American within six months after a pandemic hits. But it could be another two-to-five years before the United States has such a capacity — the estimated time manufacturers need to obtain government approval and build plants using the new technology.

Under Shlevin's process, rather than ordering millions of eggs, a manufacturer would only need to go to the freezer, pull out a vial of cells, inoculate them with the virus and place them in a large tank, called a bioreactor, to grow.

"If you want to make more simultaneously, you just need another bioreactor," says Shlevin, who likens it to a tank in which beer is brewed. Once the flu strain is isolated, the process could take as little as 90 days, Shlevin estimates.

Solvay is building a plant in Holland to produce a cell-based flu vaccine and has approval to sell it there. Close behind is Chiron, which is conducting clinical trials with cell-based flu vaccine in Europe and expects to apply for approval to sell the vaccine there in 2007.

Normally, it would take another three-to-four years to get the vaccine approved in the U.S. and possibly longer before new plants could be built here, according to Shlevin. However, representatives from both companies say the Food and Drug Administration (FDA) has been discussing expediting their procedure.

The FDA's vaccine advisory committee was asked if it could speed up some of its approval procedures without endangering safety. Panel member David Markovitz, a professor of infectious diseases at the University of Michigan, said he was favorably disposed after Nov. 16 presentations by Chiron and Solvay. Although the meeting was non-binding, Markovitz said, "The fact that the committee was very much in favor would suggest that it's likely to be licensed soon as technology for making flu vaccines."

Markovitz explains that while the vaccine would probably be safe, the residual dog cells could produce cancer in a vaccine recipient, because the cells are "immortalized" — managed so that they "just keep growing," and often some cells are abnormal. But, he adds, "The odds of that in most of these lines seem quite low."

Meanwhile, other vaccine technologies are being tested. The National Institutes of Health (NIH), for instance, is testing a

Continued from p. 34

a "world vaccine." But so far, there's been more talk of coordination than action, according to David Nabarro, the new United Nations official in charge of avian flu. [27]

One computer model suggests that a big flu outbreak in rural Thailand could be contained within a month by giving antiviral medications to the first group of people infected and to uninfected people in the surrounding area. "Several million courses sent to Thailand would be more effective than hoarding [doses] for 300 million people" in the United States, said the model's creator, Emory University Professor of biostatistics Ira Longini. [28]

However, most Asian countries where avian flu has become endemic don't have big stockpiles of the drugs. Cambodia has only 150 doses of Tamiflu, enough for one dose per province, according to CBS' "60 Minutes." [29]

The limited supplies raise a major ethical as well as practical dilemma: Should the United States be prepared to hand over its stockpile of a few million antivirals to a country like Cambodia if the disease emerges there first — if only to protect itself?

A blunt "no," answers Osterholm, because he considers Longini's predictions of stopping the disease "a fairy tale."

For the strategy to work, the first human clusters of virus would have to be rapidly detected, reported and diagnosed. But in far-flung rural villages, local clinic staff usually do not recognize an unusual virus, and lengthy waits are common to get diagnoses from far-off laboratories. "I see no reasonable way to stop the virus in Asia," the University of Minnesota's Osterholm says.

He also doubts it will be possible to keep people from leaving a cordoned-off area. "People are going to flee," he

vaccine against one strain of H5N1 in healthy people and next will test it in the elderly. Like seasonal flu vaccines, it uses a killed, or inactivated, virus. However, during a pandemic an individual influenza strain can undergo changes, a process known as "drift," so a virus stockpiled now might not be effective against a future pandemic strain. For example, the H5N1 strains now circulating in Asia are different from strains that caused the flu in Hong Kong in 1997.

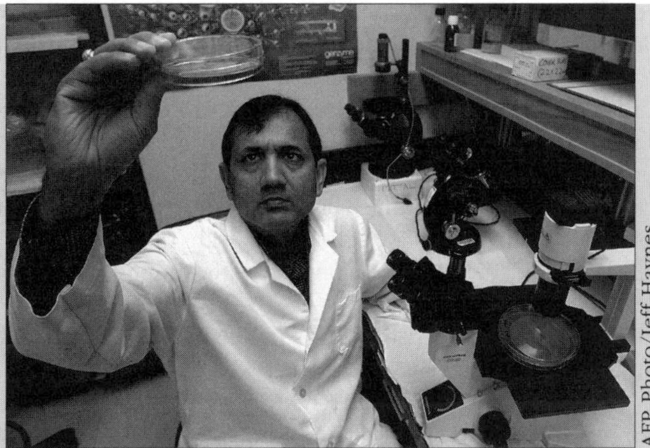

AFP Photo/Jeff Haynes

Purdue University researcher Suresh Metal examines a cell infected with a bird flu gene. U.S. researchers are trying to develop a vaccine in tissue cultures rather than chicken eggs, thus allowing faster production.

A newer-generation vaccine can be made from a live flu virus that has been weakened, or attenuated, so it cannot cause disease. The NIH is developing a live attenuated vaccine for H5N1 with MedImmune Vaccines Inc., which produces FluMist, a nasal spray made from a live attenuated vaccine currently available in the United States.

Live attenuated vaccines appear to create broader protective immunity against strains that have changed over time than vaccines made from killed viruses, according to Ruth Karron, an influenza vaccine expert at the Johns Hopkins Bloomberg School of Public Health. The school will begin testing MedImmune's new, live attenuated vaccine this spring. "We have evidence that this is true for some of the human influenza viruses that circulate each year," she said. For instance, for unknown reasons, FluMist "seems to work better against drifted strains than inactivated influenza vaccine." [1]

Live attenuated vaccine is currently made using egg-based technology but could be made with cell-based techniques once they are available.

Meanwhile, the idea of a single vaccine to protect against all types of flu has always been the "holy grail" for flu vaccine researchers, but no one knows whether it can be achieved. In the event of a pandemic, a universal vaccine would dramatically reduce the turn-around time needed now to develop a vaccine tailored to a specific strain, according to NIH researcher Gary Nabel, who is exploring this possibility. [2]

Finally, researchers are also in the early stages of investigating a DNA-based vaccine, which would inject the DNA from a flu virus into people instead of the killed virus itself, causing a person's cells to make the virus proteins. Theoretically this could speed up production of a vaccine, because the DNA vaccine could be grown in fast-growing bacteria in a matter of weeks. DNA vaccines work well in mice, but "there's no good evidence they induce enough protective immunity in humans," according to Mount Sinai School of Medicine microbiologist Peter Palese. Given the data available now on DNA vaccines, he says, "I would seriously question whether it's really protective against a pandemic strain."

[1] John Hopkins Bloomberg School of Public Health, "Preparing for a Pandemic — Bloomberg School Tests Potential Avian Flu Vaccine," Oct. 19, 2005.

[2] Richard Harris, "Pandemic Flu Spurs Race for New Vaccine Methods," National Public Radio, Dec. 6, 2005, at www.npr.org.

says. Moreover, he asks, what government would be willing to announce that it's the first site of a deadly contagious virus when that news will instantly ostracize them economically?

Conventional wisdom dictates that Tamiflu must be taken within 48 hours of getting sick to be effective, but some recent research suggests that it must be taken within hours of infection, Osterholm says, a near-impossibility in a backward, rural area. And handing out Tamiflu willy-nilly raises the threat that resistance will develop. "Trying to use Tamiflu wisely now is like trying to land a 747 on an aircraft carrier," he maintains.

The WHO acknowledges many of these difficulties in its report recommending shipping Tamiflu from an international stockpile to the first region where the virus takes hold. "While pursuit of this option . . . has no guarantee of success, it nonetheless needs to be undertaken, as it represents one of the few preventive options," the WHO report says. Even if this doesn't stop the virus dead in its tracks, a delay would at least give other countries time to get prepared, it argues. [30]

Once a pandemic hits, nations with vaccine manufacturers are sure to nationalize those industries, preventing any domestically produced vaccine from leaving their borders, warns the Center for Biosecurity's O'Toole, unless some international cooperation forestalls them.

"There's nothing in the president's speech or the [HHS] plan that indicates the United States is going to try to lead a coalition of the world's vaccine manufacturers to maximize the global vaccine supply or has any intention of giving our vaccine away to countries that might be at the center of the storm," she notes. "The blowback from the United States acting as fortress America and having made no attempt to help less developed countries will harm America's standing in the world for a generation."

O'Toole knows it will be hard to persuade government leaders to share scarce vaccine. Her organization recently held a role-playing exercise to find out what would happen if bioterrorists attacked nations with smallpox. Former Secretary of State Madeleine K. Albright played the role of a U.S. president, and former prime ministers played other countries' leaders.

"We saw that national leaders become very ungenerous when their own stocks of vaccine are limited," O'Toole reports. In one scenario, Albright was prepared to share vaccine with Turkey. But when an American city was also attacked, Albright refused to send vaccine, saying, "'We paid for this,'" says O'Toole. "All the other countries did the same thing." ■

BACKGROUND

'Spanish Flu'

Worldwide influenza epidemics — called pandemics — were first documented about 300 years ago, and since then an estimated 10-13 pandemics have occurred. The 20th century saw three flu pandemics: Two were mild, but the 1918-1919 "Spanish flu" epidemic infected an estimated 25-30 percent of the world's population. About 675,000 Americans died from the flu in 1918 — nearly half of all U.S. deaths that year. Worldwide, from 40 million up to 100 million people died. [31]

The 1918 flu was unusual in its high rate of mortality and the large percentage of deaths among young adults between ages 15 and 35, often within hours after the first symptoms appeared. Young people have the strongest immune systems of any age group, and, paradoxically, their immune system response to the foreign virus was so powerful that it killed them, explains author and chronicler of the 1918 epidemic John M. Barry. Many young adults suffered from acute respiratory distress syndrome, in which disease-fighting cells overreact, filling the lungs with fluid and debris, and ultimately suffocating the victim.

In 1997, pathologists noticed something similar in the first six people who died from H5N1 in Hong Kong. Many of the victims' organs were under attack from a "renegade" immune system, Barry writes. Indeed, the deaths reported so far from H5N1 have largely occurred in children and young, healthy adults — a similarity that worries some scientists. [32]

The two milder 20th-century pandemics — in 1957 and 1968 — probably were caused by the exchange of genes between human and avian flu viruses, known as reassortment, which occurred after either a human or a pig caught both viruses.

The second principal mechanism by which flu becomes easily contagious among humans is called adaptive mutation, a more gradual process in which the virus' ability to bind to human cells increases during subsequent infections of humans. Some scientists have suggested that the 1918 flu falls into the latter category.

The 1957 Asian flu outbreak, so-called because it was first identified in Asia, spread to the United States during the summer, killing about 70,000 people. Health officials responded quickly, and limited vaccine supplies were available by August. The 1968 Hong Kong flu killed 33,800 people in the United States, making it the mildest pandemic of the 20th century. A normal seasonal flu outbreak kills about 36,000 Americans each year.

The '57 and '68 pandemics were mild partly because the viruses were less virulent and partly because of advances in medicine. Global detection had improved, allowing public health officials to quickly isolate the viruses, and manufacturers were able to provide vaccines for the two strains. Antibiotics were also widely available to treat secondary bacterial infections, in contrast to 1918, and there were fewer cases of viral pneumonia.

Recent Flu Scares

Several 20th-century flu scares failed to live up to their billing. The 1976 "swine flu" scare began when an 18-year-old soldier at Fort Dix in New Jersey succumbed to a novel virus thought to be related to the Spanish flu virus. After health officials predicted a 1918-scale epidemic, President Ford initiated a program to inoculate every American.

But the pandemic never arrived. Moreover, the vaccination program was stopped after hundreds of people suffered from a rare neurological disorder — Guillain-Barre syndrome — later linked to the vaccine, which killed 32. Congress provided liability protection for the manufacturers and $90 million in compensation for those claiming injuries. [33]

Ever since, the swine flu incident has stood as a cautionary tale to public officials fearful of crying wolf. "In this case, the consequences of being wrong about an epidemic were so devastating in people's minds that it wasn't possible to focus properly on the issue of likelihood," Harvey V. Fineberg, now president of the Institute of Medicine, concluded later. "Nobody could really estimate the likelihood then or now. . . . And at a higher level [The White House] the two — likelihood and consequence — got meshed." [34] In 1977, the so-called Russian flu involved a virus strain that had been in circulation before 1957. The virus primarily sickened children and young adults, who lacked prior immunity to it.

H5N1 Emerges

The current concern about the H5N1 virus dates from 1997, when outbreaks of the highly pathogenic virus occurred in chickens and humans in Hong Kong. Six people died — out of 18 who became sick after handling infected poultry. To prevent further outbreak, Hong Kong's chicken population was slaughtered in three days. Researchers later found that the virus had originated among Chinese geese and found its way into Hong Kong's poultry markets before infecting the first humans. [35]

After several quiet years, the virus reappeared in 2003 — among birds in several Chinese mainland provinces. Alarm bells again sounded that February, when H5N1 infected two people in Hong Kong, killing one. In December, the virus killed two tigers and two leopards in a Thai zoo that had been fed fresh chicken carcasses; it was the first report of influenza causing disease and death in big cats. In January 2004, Vietnam and Thailand reported their first cases of human infection with H5N1. [36]

A second wave of infections began in summer 2004, with reports of infected poultry in China, Indonesia, Thailand and Vietnam. Research showed that H5N1 had become progressively more lethal for mammals and could kill wild waterfowl, long considered a disease-free natural reservoir. More human cases — eight fatal — were reported in Thailand and Vietnam.

In September 2004, researchers found that domestic cats experimentally infected with H5N1 could spread infection to other cats, previously considered resistant to all influenza A viruses — the broad category that includes H5N1. The following month, H5N1 was confirmed in two eagles illegally imported to Brussels, Belgium, from Thailand, and research confirmed that ducks were excreting large quantities of the virus without showing any signs of illness. [37]

How to Avoid Risk

- Poultry and eggs should be fully cooked — no "pink" parts and no runny yolks. Normal temperatures used for cooking poultry (158 degrees F. in all parts of the food) will kill the virus.
- If handling raw poultry in the kitchen, wash hands and disinfect cooking surfaces with hot water and soap. Raw poultry juices should never mix with food eaten raw.
- If you have no contact with birds, the risk is "almost non-existent," according to the World Health Organization.

Source: World Health Organization

The WHO warned in November 2004 that the H5N1 bird flu virus might spark a deadly pandemic. [38] And in 2005 the Institute of Medicine reported H5N1 apparently had accumulated mutations making it both increasingly infectious and deadly in mammals. [39]

Poultry outbreaks in Indonesia, Thailand and Vietnam in December 2004 marked the beginning of a third wave of worldwide infection, according to the WHO. The first — and so far only — human-to-human transmission of avian flu occurred in Thailand in September 2004, according to an early 2005 report in *The New England Journal of Medicine.* [40] Cambodia then reported its first human cases, all fatal, as did Indonesia.

Last April, wild birds began dying at Quinghai Lake in Central China, where hundreds of thousands of migratory birds congregate. More than 6,000 birds died in the ensuing weeks. In July, researchers found transmission of the virus among migratory geese and suggested it may be carried along winter migratory routes. [41] (*See map, p. 28.*)

On July 23, 2005, Russia became the first European country to report an outbreak of the virus — in poultry in Western Siberia — followed by Kazahkstan the next month. By October, the virus was confirmed among poultry in Turkey, Romania and Croatia.

Then in August the British medical journal *Lancet* reported Relenza was at least as effective as Tamiflu, but with fewer side effects and no evidence of resistance. By contrast, it reported resistance levels in up to 18 percent of those taking Tamiflu. The researchers recommended stockpiling both drugs. [42]

Fear of Vaccine

After the attacks on the World Trade Center and the Pentagon on Sept. 11, 2001, U.S. officials increasingly worried that terrorists might attack with a biological weapon, such as anthrax or smallpox. [43] In December 2002, President Bush announced that all frontline health-care workers and military personnel should be vaccinated against smallpox, saying countries like Iraq were harboring secret reserves of smallpox and could use it as a biological weapon. However, many health workers and some hospitals refused to go along with the program, saying the vaccine was not safe. [44]

In response, Congress passed legislation in early 2003 to compensate people injured as a result of receiving the smallpox vaccine. But the compensation program was not launched until the end of that year, which critics said came too late to convince most health-care personnel, and the program fell far short of its goal. [45] Only about 40,000 individuals out of the 500,000 to several million health workers targeted have been vaccinated to date. [46] Labor unions and consumers have cited this failure in arguing that any successful mass-vaccination program for flu must include compensation for injuries. ■

CURRENT SITUATION

Global Efforts

The most dramatic effort to stem the H5N1 virus is taking place in China, where the government is trying to vaccinate an estimated 14 billion domestic chickens and ducks against the virus. In theory, the virus could be stopped this way.

In 2004, when H5N1 was rampant in Asia, Hong Kong did not have a single case in poultry or humans because it "used good vaccines and monitored to see that every chicken imported into Hong Kong was vaccinated with H5N1 vaccine," according to Memphis virologist Webster. But Hong Kong is a small, wealthy city surrounded by water, making it relatively easy to stop every poultry delivery.

By contrast, China is an enormous country, where people — especially in far-flung rural areas — live in close proximity to their poultry and where the prevalence of fake vaccines worries scientists. Government vaccinators have also been seen inoculating birds without wearing gloves and discarding used needles on the ground — raising the potential of further spreading the disease. [47]

When it comes to detecting the virus, the world's early warning system is "weak," the WHO reported last year. Since the countries most affected by avian flu cannot afford to compensate farmers adequately for killing their infected poultry, farmers have little incentive to report outbreaks in the rural areas where most human cases have occurred, WHO concluded. Farmers have suffered more than $10 billion in economic losses already, the organization estimates. [48]

The deadly consequences of failing to report bird flu outbreaks were illustrated in early January 2006, when human cases of bird flu began to multiply in rural eastern Turkey. International health officials said they believed the disease had existed among poultry for months, but because there were no earlier reports of bird flu in the area, humans had no way of knowing they were at risk in handling poultry. [49]

The United States is helping to prevent the spread of H5N1 by funding detection, reporting and education programs. [50] The U.S. Agency for International Development is spending $13.7 million to control and prevent avian flu in Asia, and the Centers for Disease Control and Prevention is spending $6 million on international detection and reporting. But a November 2005 report prepared by the U.N. Food and Agriculture Organization suggested that the amounts committed by member nations so far have been insufficient to control avian flu in animals. [51]

Moreover, the WHO's efforts to get developed countries to cooperate in providing vaccines to developing countries and building an international stockpile of antiviral medications, have had only limited success. [52]

Worldwide, current manufacturers could only produce enough H5N1 bird flu vaccine to inoculate about 1.5 percent of the world's population, which the University of Minnesota's Osterholm says would be "like trying to fill Lake Superior with a garden hose." [53] The scientific journal *Nature* says WHO's fledgling international effort to establish a coalition to fight the spread of the disease is "shaky and far from united or sure in its purpose" and "grossly underfunded." [54]

The discovery in 2004 of the two infected eagles smuggled into Belgium from Thailand in airline carry-on baggage highlighted the severely underpoliced illegal trade in exotic animals — second in size only to the drug trade — as another possible vector for spread of the disease. Robert A. Cook, vice president and chief veterinarian at the Wildlife Conservation Society, calls U.S. laws governing the import of illegal animals "dangerously lax." [55]

Increasingly, new human diseases — such as AIDS and SARS — have originated in wild animals, according to Cook. "You take these animals out of the wild, and they [bring] with them a whole new range of diseases we haven't seen before," he says.

Washington imposed some new import restrictions after monkey pox, which causes fevers and ulcers, infected 71 Midwesterners in 2003. The outbreak was triggered when imported African rodents infected prairie dogs at a pet shop. But it is still legal in the United States to import most exotic species.

Domestic Efforts

On Nov. 1, recalling that the 1918 flu infected one-third of Americans, President Bush unveiled his pandemic plan to the nation. "If history is our guide, there is reason to be concerned," he said. [56]

But in December, when Congress approved only $3.8 billion for pandemic spending — about half the president's $7.1 billion request — lawmakers said the money was enough to get the program started in 2006. [57] Public health advocates hope Congress will appropriate the rest of Bush's request next year.

Of the total, $3 billion is earmarked to prepare for a pandemic, including the purchase of vaccines and antiviral drugs, $350 million for state and local preparedness — more than Bush had requested — and $267 million for overseas detection and reporting of flu cases. The legislation also allows HHS to negotiate contracts with vendors through which states could order antiviral drugs and be reimbursed by the federal government. The legislation would permit the use of federal funds to construct

Continued on p. 42

At Issue:

Is there a serious risk of a human pandemic of avian flu?

MICHAEL T. OSTERHOLM
DIRECTOR, CENTER FOR INFECTIOUS DISEASE RESEARCH AND POLICY, UNIVERSITY OF MINNESOTA

FROM TESTIMONY BEFORE HOUSE COMMITTEE ON INTERNATIONAL RELATIONS, DEC. 7, 2005

yes

We must never forget that influenza pandemics are like earthquakes, hurricanes and tsunamis; they occur. The most recent came in 1957-58 and 1968-69, and although tens of thousands of Americans died in each one, these were considered mild compared to others. According to a recent analysis, [the 1918-19 pandemic] killed 50-100 million people globally. Today, with a population of 6.5 billion — more than three times that of 1918 — even a mild pandemic could kill many millions.

A number of recent events and factors have heightened our concern that a specific near-term pandemic may be imminent. Some important preparatory efforts are under way, but much more needs to be done throughout the world.

Based on our past experiences with outbreaks such as SARS, if an influenza pandemic began today, borders will close, the global economy will shut down, pharmaceutical supplies — including important childhood vaccines — will be in extreme short supply, health-care systems will be overwhelmed and panic will reign. Access to pandemic influenza vaccines and effective antiviral drug treatments will be limited for the entire world for years to come because of our lack of modern vaccines and a grossly inadequate worldwide production capability.

An influenza pandemic will be like a 12-to-18-month global blizzard that will ultimately change the world as we know it today. Foreign trade and travel will be reduced or even ended in an attempt to stop the virus from entering new countries — even though such efforts will probably fail, given the infectiousness of influenza and the volume of illegal crossings that occur at most borders.

One part of pandemic preparedness planning that must receive immediate attention is the implementation of a concept that I have called "critical product continuity" (CPC) — the determination of those products and services that must be available during a pandemic in order to minimize potentially catastrophic collateral health and security consequences — and the subsequent comprehensive actions that must be taken by both governments and the private sector to ensure their availability.

While I have chosen to highlight the issue of critical product continuity and the pharmaceutical industry, there are many other product areas that must be considered as we plan for getting through the next 12-to-18-month pandemic.

MICHAEL FUMENTO
SENIOR FELLOW, HUDSON INSTITUTE

WRITTEN FOR THE *CQ RESEARCHER*, JAN. 4, 2006

no

"It is only a matter of time before an avian flu virus — most likely H5N1 — acquires the ability to be transmitted from human to human, sparking the outbreak of human pandemic influenza." So declared Dr. Lee Jong-wook, director-general of the World Health Organization.

Terrifying statement. False statement.

It is the best-kept secret of the pandemic panic purveyors that H5N1 hasn't just been around since its Hong Kong appearance in 1997 but actually was discovered in Scottish chickens in 1959. It's therefore been mutating and making contact with humans for 47 years. If it hasn't become transmissible between humans in all that time, it almost certainly won't.

Despite what you've been told, H5N1 isn't even slowly mutating in the direction of becoming pandemic. There are no evolutionary pressures upon it to either become more efficiently transmitted from bird to man or man to man. Rather, as one mutation draws the virus closer to human transmissibility, another is as likely to draw it farther away.

Certainly an avian flu pandemic won't let media hysteria dictate its appearance and therefore be upon us before effective vaccines become widely available in a couple of years. If "a matter of time" means several years from now, we'll be quite prepared, thank you.

But aren't we "overdue" for a pandemic, with H5N1 the likeliest cause? Google "avian flu," "pandemic," and "overdue," and you'll get more than 35,000 hits. Anthony Fauci, director of the National Institute of Allergies and Infectious Diseases, insists we're "overdue," explaining that there were three pandemics in the 20th century, the last one 38 years ago.

Yet the time between the second and third pandemics was only 11 years. There's no cycle. As risk-communication expert Peter Sandman of Rutgers University says, the "overdue pandemic" is mere superstition.

None of which should discourage such sensible measures as mass poultry vaccinations, killing infected flocks and teaching Asian farmers to have as little contact with their birds and bird droppings as possible. These steps can reduce or even eliminate the few human cases now occurring and cut the chance of pandemic from nearly zero to zero.

But there is no gain in spreading an epidemic of hysteria. The false fears we sow today we shall reap in the future as public complacency when a monster is truly at the door.

Continued from p. 40

or renovate private facilities for the production of vaccines.

Critics immediately complained that the plan did not specify what localities should do once their hospitals are filled to capacity. European nations are far ahead of the United States in planning so-called surge capacity, according to Elliott, of the Trust for America's Health. "Every single hotel in Great Britain knows whether or not they're going to be a surge hospital," she says.

The plan says health workers should get top priority for vaccinations and allows states to decide who should be in subsequent priority groups. George E. Hardy, Jr., executive director of the Association of State and Territorial Health Officials, says states would like more consistency on who is at the top of the list.

"Whether you live in Alabama or Montana, the priority groups should be the same," he says.

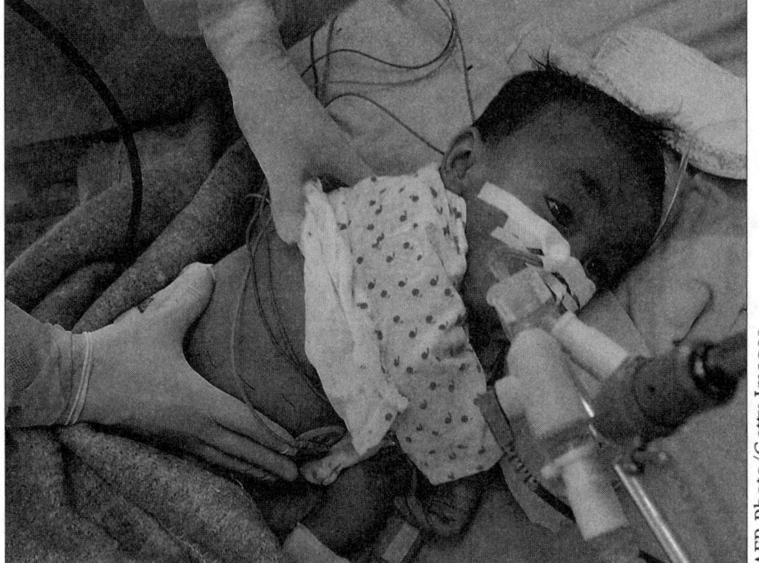

A Vietnamese infant receives avian flu treatment in Hanoi. Health experts say antiviral medications like Tamiflu could lessen the severity of the disease. However, some bird flu patients in Vietnam who took Tamiflu died.

Liability

In December, Congress approved sweeping provisions shielding manufacturers of pandemic vaccines from liability lawsuits. [58] President Bush and GOP lawmakers had argued that the liability protection was necessary to encourage drug makers to get into the vaccine business.

Tacked onto the Defense appropriations bill in the middle of the night, the liability language was immediately attacked as a "backroom deal" by consumer groups complaining that the provision was never subjected to a separate floor vote or discussion.

Senate Majority Leader Bill Frist, R-Tenn., described the measure as "targeted liability protection." Lawsuits could only be brought if the federal government sues on behalf of a patient's wrongful death or serious injury. But the suits can only be brought for "willful misconduct," and negligence or recklessness are not defined as willful misconduct.

"There's no reason to immunize a company against recklessness," says Amy Widman, a lawyer for the Center for Justice and Democracy, arguing that a threat of lawsuits checks corporate irresponsibility.

The center was part of a coalition of five consumer groups that complained to senators that under this narrow definition drug companies would only be held responsible if "the company had actual knowledge the product would kill someone."

The legislation would exempt companies from liability for "countermeasures" — drugs, vaccines or medical devices — designed to protect Americans in public "emergencies," to be defined by the HHS secretary. Consumer advocates said the legislation could cover everything from cholesterol drugs to Tylenol. Widman calls it "a giveaway to drug companies" seeking to incorporate "a lot of things they've been trying to get for many, many years."

"The Republican leadership in Congress cut a backroom deal to give a massive Christmas bonus to the drug companies," Sen. Edward M. Kennedy, D-Mass., said in a statement after the House vote. [59]

But Frist said he was "proud" of the provisions that had been incorporated into the defense appropriations bill. "The bill strikes a reasonable balance where those who are harmed will be fairly compensated and life-saving products will be available in ample supply to protect and treat as many Americans as possible," he said. [60]

The new law directs HHS to sets up a compensation fund to reimburse anyone injured by a vaccine or other medication covered by the legislation. Consumer and labor groups, however, pointed out that no money was appropriated for the fund, which would be inoperable until funded.

Without funding for compensation, said Barbara Coufal, legislative affairs specialist for the American Federation of State, County and Municipal Employees (AFSCME), "We're worried [that] it may never be realized."

Quarantines

In the event of a pandemic, say many public health experts, it may be nearly impossible to isolate the infected from the well, since people infected with the flu are contagious for at least a day before they show symptoms. The more likely scenario would be a wholesale shutdown of public places like schools, workplaces, shopping malls and theatres.

In November, the CDC proposed new quarantine rules that include influenza as one of the illnesses subject to a quarantine ordered by the president. The new rules would also require airlines to keep copies of passenger manifests for 60 days, which could be made available to the CDC within 12 hours if ill passengers arrive on international or domestic flights. [61] But experts say preventing sick or exposed persons from getting off airplanes is unlikely to prevent avian flu from entering the country.

"What if I fly from Thailand to Europe to Canada and drive to Seattle? Are they going to flag me and stop me?" asks the University of Minnesota's Osterholm. "I don't think we're going to stop it."

On Nov. 1, New York City's health department offered free flu vaccines to anyone who showed up at a downtown clinic in an experiment aimed at simulating what might happen during a major outbreak. Many people waited more than three hours, prompting some to wonder whether the city could handle a real emergency. [62]

"Most state and local public health agencies lack the people, money and political clout to manage an epidemic," according to the Center for Biosecurity at the University of Pittsburgh. [63]

Governors have put most of their health dollars into mandatory programs like Medicaid, according to Elliott rather than public health departments where spending is discretionary. "We have an aging work force and not a lot of new blood coming in because it's not a lucrative profession," she says. There are not enough workers now to handle regular vaccinations and health needs, she points out.

On the other hand, since 9/11, every state has developed a federally funded plan for responding to a bioterrorist attack. "We're much better prepared than we were a year ago," says Hardy of the Association of State and Territorial Health Officials. However, federal funds for state and local bioterrorism preparedness programs were cut 14 percent in the fiscal 2006 appropriations bill, which the Trust for America called "ill-advised" in view of their pandemic responsibilities.

"The first thing we learned in Hurricane Katrina is you put public health leaders in charge of a health crisis, not first responders" like police, says Elliott, of the Trust for America's Health. "Otherwise we have situations like triaging folks in an airport and putting masses of people in a convention center with no water or sanitary facilities. Public health officials would never have done that."

Late-Breaking News

Multiplying human cases of bird flu appeared in early January 2006 in Turkey, putting health officials in Europe on "high alert." An unusual cluster of human cases (15 confirmed as of Jan. 10), including some 50 other people hospitalized for possible H5N1, raised the possibility that the virus might have mutated to become more contagious to humans. But as of Jan. 11, WHO scientists had detected no changes in the H5N1 virus samples from Turkey that might make it more transmissible to humans. [64]

American chicken farmers apparently are taking the disease more seriously, given the announcement that nearly all flocks would be tested for avian flu starting Jan. 16. [65] With the fall bird migration ended, some experts declared that North America had dodged the bird flu — at least for the 2005-2006 winter flu season. But international health officials warned that Europe might still be vulnerable from the spring 2006 migration. [66] ■

OUTLOOK

Economic Disaster?

Many experts hope a pandemic doesn't arrive for another five years or so, which would give the United States time to increase manufacturing capacity for vaccines. The administration is pinning its hopes on the new cell-based vaccines that would take less lead time than today's old-fashioned technology.

Meanwhile, NIH researchers are working on developing a universal vaccine that would prevent all flu strains — considered the holy grail of vaccine researchers.

Many agree that new, more effective antiviral medications need to be developed, especially if resistance develops in whatever flu strain hits our shores. But others say it's most important to rebuild the U.S. public health system, so there will be enough workers to vaccinate and treat the sick.

The gloomiest forecast is painted by the University of Minnesota's Osterholm, who foresees a collapse in our increasingly global economy if a pandemic forces nations to shut down their borders. For instance, most masks, gloves and syringes are manufactured offshore, as are the raw materials for antibiotics. As a result, modern medicine's advantages won't really be available, he predicts.

"When a pandemic flu hits, we'll go back to 1918 medicine; we're going to care for people in large gyms and stadiums; we will have a major shortage of intravenous equipment; we'll have a shortage of antibiotics and health-care workers, and no masks are being stockpiled. So you tell me how that's different from 1918. If you don't call that a perfect storm, I don't know what is."

But some economists say the U.S. economy is so resilient that even a severe pandemic — like that in 1918 — would not produce an economic disaster. A mild pandemic like that in 1968 would "probably not cause a recession and might not be distinguishable from the normal variation in economic activity," according to a recent CBO report. [67]

There are so many gaps in the scientific knowledge about viruses that "there is no scientific basis to predict anything," according to Masato Tashiro, director of the WHO's Collaborative Center for Influenza Surveillance and Research at Japan's National Institute of Infectious Diseases in Tokyo. [68]

Although some scientists are skeptical that H5N1 bird flu will cause the next pandemic, and others believe it will be mild, virtually everyone agrees there will be another flu pandemic eventually, and that the country should start preparing now. ■

Notes

[1] This description is from Mike Davis, *The Monster at Our Door* (2005), pp. 4-8.

[2] *Ibid.*, p. 7.

[3] Elisabeth Rosenthal, "Bird Flu Reports Multiply in Turkey, Faster Than Expected," *The New York Times*, Jan. 9, 2006, p. A4.

[4] Institute of Medicine, *The Threat of Pandemic Influenza: Are We Ready? A Workshop Summary* (2005), p. 8.

[5] For background, see Mary H. Cooper, "Fighting SARS," *CQ Researcher*, June 20, 2003, pp. 569-592.

[6] That is the number needed in order to kill all poultry in China over a year's time.

[7] Institute of Medicine, *op. cit.*, p. 19.

[8] http://healthyamericans.org.

[9] Trust for America's Health, press release, "TFAH commends U.S. House of Representatives for Passing Down Payment," Dec. 19, 2005.

[10] "Don't Support a Defense Spending Bill that Has Backroom Special Interest Protections," Dec. 20, 2005, letter to senators from U.S. PIRG and other interest groups at www.uspirg.org.

[11] Congressional Budget Office (CBO), "A Potential Influenza Pandemic: Possible Macroeconomic Effects and Policy Issues," Dec. 8, 2005, p. 6.

[12] White House, "President Outlines Pandemic Influenza Preparations and Response," Nov. 1, 2005, at www.whitehouse.gov/news/releases/2005/11/20051101-1.html.

[13] See for example, comments by Anthony Fauci on CBS' "60 Minutes:" "Right now . . . if we had an explosion of H5N1 we would not be prepared for that;" "Chasing the Flu," Dec.4, 2005, at www.cbsnews.com/stories/2005/12/02/60minutes/main1094515.shtml.

[14] The president's proposal and HHS plan can be found at www.pandemicflu.gov.

[15] Congressional Budget Office, *op. cit.*, p. 22.

[16] Sanofi pasteur announced Dec. 15 study results showing it could produce an H5N1 vaccine requiring only four times as much antigen using adjuvants. See "Sanofi says H5N1 vaccine with adjuvant may go further," Dec. 15, 2005, at www.cidrap.umn.edu.

[17] Andrew Jack, "Deaths cast doubt over use of Tamiflu," *Financial Times*, Dec. 22, 2005, p. 6.

[18] CBO, *op. cit.*, p. 29.

[19] David Heyman, "Model Operational Guidelines for Disease Exposure Control," Nov. 2, 2005, at www.csis.org/index.php?option=com_csis_pubs&task=view&id=2504.

[20] White House press release, "President Outlines Pandemic Influenza Preparations and Response," Nov. 1, 2005.

[21] Michelle M. Mello and Troyen A. Brennan, "Legal Concerns and the Influenza Vaccine Shortage," *JAMA*, Oct. 12, 2005, pp. 1817-1820.

[22] Institute of Medicine, *Financing Vaccines in the 21st Century: Assuring Access and Availability* (2003), at www.nap.edu.

[23] www.cdc.gov/nip/vfc/Parent/parent_home.htm#1.

[24] In October 2004, British government regulators withdrew the license from Liverpool, England, flu vaccine manufacturer Chiron after 4 million doses were found to be contaminated. On Oct. 5, 2004, Chiron announced that it could not provide its expected production of 46-48 million doses of flu vaccine — about half the expected U.S. influenza vaccine supply — setting off a major shortage of flu vaccine in the winter flu season of 2004.

[25] World Health Organization (WHO), *Responding to the Avian Influenza Pandemic Threat: Recommended Strategic Actions* (2005), p. 2. Also see Ira M. Longini, Jr., *et al.*, "Containing Pandemic Influenza at the Source," *Science*, Aug. 12, 2005, pp. 1083-1087.

[26] See press releases from Sen. Schumer "As Avian Flu Closes in on U.S. Schumer Calls for Immediate Action: Demands Suspension of Tamiflu Patent So Vaccine Can be Mass-Produced," Oct. 16, 2005, and "Schumer Praises Roche Agreements with 2 Major U.S. Generic Drug Companies," Dec. 8, 2005.

[27] See Council on Foreign Relations, Conference on the Global Threat of Pandemic Influenza, Session 2: Containment and Control, Nov. 16, 2005 at www.cfr.org/publication/9244/council_on_foreign_relations_conference_on_the_global_threat_of_pandemic_influenza_session_2.html. David Nabarro is U.N. System Coordinator for Avian and Human Influenza.

[28] Quoted in Michael Fumento, "Fuss and Feathers: Pandemic Panic Over the Avian Flu," *The Weekly Standard*, Nov. 21, 2005.

[29] "60 Minutes," *op. cit.*

[30] WHO, *op. cit.*, p. 12.

[31] CBO, *op. cit.*, p. 6. It is unclear why the outbreak was called the "Spanish flu," since it did not originate in Spain or hit that country particularly hard. Some theorize that the term arose because of heavy coverage by Spanish newspapers.

[32] John M. Barry, *The Great Influenza* (2004), p. 250.

[33] Laurie Garrett, "The Next Pandemic?" *Foreign Affairs*, July/August 2005, pp. 3-23.

[34] Quoted in *ibid.*, p. 10.

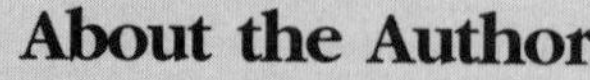

About the Author

Sarah Glazer, a New York freelancer, is a regular contributor to the *CQ Researcher*. Her articles on health, education and social-policy issues have appeared in *The New York Times*, *The Washington Post*, *The Public Interest* and *Gender and Work*, a book of essays. Her recent *CQ Researcher* reports include "Increase in Autism" and "Gender and Learning." She graduated from the University of Chicago with a B.A. in American history.

[35] *Ibid.*; also see Institute of Medicine (2005), p. 13.
[36] WHO, "H5N1 Avian Influenza: Timeline," Oct. 28, 2005.
[37] *Ibid.*
[38] "Avian Flu Timeline," *Nature* Web site at www.nature.com/nature/focus/avianflu/timeline.html.
[39] Institute of Medicine (2005), p. 12.
[40] K. Ungchusak, *et al.*, "Probable Person-to-person Transmission of Avian Influenza A (H5N1)," *The New England Journal of Medicine*, Jan. 27, 2005, pp. 333-40.
[41] WHO, *ibid.*
[42] *Nature* Web site, *op. cit.*
[43] For background, see David Masci, "Smallpox Threat," *CQ Researcher*, Feb. 7, 2003, pp. 105-128.
[44] Jeffrey Gettleman, "Threats and Responses: Biological Defenses," *The New York Times*, Dec. 19, 2002, p. A19.
[45] The program hoped to vaccinate 500,000 people, but by October 2003 only 37,901 had been vaccinated. A hundred people suffered injuries. See *CIDRAP News*, "Study shows few serious problems among smallpox vaccinees," Dec. 14, 2005, at www.cidrap.umn.edu.
[46] CBO, *op. cit.*, p. 27.
[47] Howard W. French, "Bird by Bird China Tackles Vast Flu Task," *The New York Times*, Dec. 2, 2005, p. A1.
[48] WHO, "Responding to the Avian Influenza Pandemic Threat," *op. cit.*
[49] Elisabeth Rosenthal, "Bird Flu Reports Multiply in Turkey, Faster Than Expected," *New York Times*, Jan. 9, 2006, p. A4.
[50] In September, Bush announced an International Partnership on Avian and Pandemic Influenza, a global network that requires participating countries that face an outbreak to provide samples to the WHO. As of Nov. 1, 88 countries had joined the effort.
[51] *Ibid.*
[52] Congressional Research Service, *Pandemic Influenza: Domestic Preparedness Efforts*, Nov. 10, 2005, p. 17.
[53] Based on current doses of H5N1 vaccine, Osterholm calculates that capacity exists for about 100 million of the world's population of about 6.5 billion.
[54] "On a Wing and a Prayer," *Nature*, May 26, 2005, pp. 385-386, www.nature.com/nature.
[55] William B. Karesh and Robert Cook, "The Human-Animal Link," *Foreign Affairs*, July/August 2005, pp. 38-50.
[56] White House, "President Outlines Pandemic Influenza Preparations and Response," Nov. 1, 2005.
[57] "House Approves Pandemic Funding Far Below Bush Request," *CIDRAP News* at www.cidrap.umn.edu/cidrap/content/influenza/panflu/news/dec1905funding.html.
[58] Sheryl Gay Stolberg, "Legal Shield for Vaccine Makers is Inserted into Military Bill," *The New York Times*, Dec. 20, 2005, p. A26.
[59] *Ibid.*
[60] Sen. Bill Frist press release, "Frist Hails Passage of FY06 Defense Appropriations Conference Report," Dec. 21, 2005.
[61] Lawrence K. Altman, "C.D.C. Proposes New Rules in Effort to Prevent Disease Outbreak," *The New York Times*, Nov. 23, 2005, p. A22.
[62] Shadi Rahimi, "Just a Drill, But Flu Shots were Real, And Popular," *The New York Times*, Nov. 2, 2005, p. A1.
[63] Center for Biosecurity, "National Strategy for Pandemic Influenza," Nov. 7, 2005.
[64] See Rosenthal, *op. cit.*, Jan. 9, 2006; Reuters, "Turkey Struggles with Bird Flu as Children Fall Ill," *The New York Times*, Jan. 7, 2006, and Elisabeth Rosenthal, "New Bird Flu Cases in Turkey Put Europe on 'High Alert,' " *The New York Times*, Jan. 7, 2006, p. A3.
[65] Donald G. McNeil Jr., "U.S. Farmers to Begin Testing Chickens for Flu," *The New York Times*, Jan. 6, 2006, p. A19.
[66] See "If the Avian Flu Hasn't Hit, Here's Why. Maybe," *The New York Times*, Jan. 1, 2006, "News of the Week in Review," p. 10, and U.N. Food and Agriculture Organization, "Wild Birds and Avian Influenza," at www.fao.org/ag/againfo/subjects/en/health/diseases-cards/avian_HPAIrisk.html.
[67] CBO, *op. cit.*, pp. 1-2.
[68] Dennis Normile, "Pandemic Skeptics Warn Against Crying Wolf," *Science*, Nov. 18, 2005, p. 1113.

FOR MORE INFORMATION

American Public Health Association, 800 I St., N.W., Washington, DC 20001-3710; (202) 777-APHA; www.apha.org. Represents public health professionals worldwide.

Association of State and Territorial Health Officials, 1275 K St., N.W., Suite 800, Washington, DC 20005-4006; (202) 371-9090; www.astho.org. Represents chief health officials.

Center for Biosecurity, University of Pittsburgh Medical Center, The Pier IV Building, 621 E. Pratt St., Suite 210, Baltimore, MD 21202; (443) 573-3304; www.upmc-biosecurity.org. An independent organization concerned with epidemics caused by natural and terrorist agents.

Center for Infectious Disease Research & Policy, University of Minnesota, Academic Health Center, 420 Delaware St., S.E., MMC 263, Minneapolis, MN 55455; (612) 626-6770; www.cidrap.umn.edu. Carries daily breaking news on avian flu on its Web site.

Center for Justice and Democracy, 80 Broad St., Suite 1600, New York, NY 10004; (212) 267-2801; http://centerjd.org. A consumer group active on liability issues involving vaccine manufacturers.

pandemicflu.gov. The official U.S. government Web site on pandemic flu and avian flu is managed by the Department of Health and Human Services, with links to the White House and other federal agencies.

Pharmaceutical Research and Manufacturers Association of America, 1100 15th St., N.W., Washington, DC 20005; (202) 835-3400. www.phrma.org. Represents the country's leading pharmaceutical research and biotechnology companies.

Trust for America's Health, 1707 H St., N.W., 7th Floor, Washington, DC 20006; (202) 223-9870; http://healthyamericans.org. A nonprofit public health advocacy group.

U.S. Centers for Disease Control and Prevention, 1600 Clifton Rd., Atlanta, GA 30333; (404) 639-3534; www.cdc.gov. The chief federal health agency dealing with avian flu.

Bibliography

Selected Sources

Books

Barry, John M., *The Great Influenza: The Epic Story of the Deadliest Plague in History*, Penguin Books, 2004.
This history of the deadly 1918 influenza pandemic cites similarities with the H5N1 bird flu now in Asia. Barry is distinguished visiting scholar at the Center for Bioenvironmental Research of Tulane and Xavier universities.

Davis, Mike, *The Monster at Our Door: The Global Threat of Avian Flu*, The New Press, 2005.
Science writer Davis expresses outrage at poor countries' lack of access to vaccines and antiviral medicines and recommends governments take over their manufacture if the free market can't distribute them cheaply.

Garrett, Laurie, *The Coming Plague: Newly Emerging Diseases in a World Out of Balance*, Penguin Books, 1994.
In a wide-ranging look at modern diseases that some have compared to Rachel Carson's celebrated *Silent Spring*, a Pulitzer Prize-winning journalist warns that infectious microbes pose increasing danger as humans disrupt the Earth's ecology.

Articles

Fumento, Michael, "Fuss and Feathers: Pandemic Panic over the Avian Flu," *The Weekly Standard*, Nov. 21, 2005; www.weeklystandard.com.
A senior fellow at the conservative Hudson Institute downplays the risk of bird flu and charges that politicians, public health officials and the press are crossing the line between informing the public and starting a panic.

Garrett, Laurie, "The Next Pandemic?" *Foreign Affairs*, July/August 2005, pp. 3-23.
Journalist Garrett, now a senior fellow at the Council on Foreign Relations, describes the recent history of H5N1 and why it might create the next pandemic.

Karesh, William B., and Robert A. Cook, "The Human-Animal Link," *Foreign Affairs*, July/August 2005, pp. 38-50.
Two veterinarians explain why diseases like bird flu that originate in animals are a growing threat to humans.

Normile, Dennis, "Pandemic Skeptics Warn Against Crying Wolf," *Science*, Nov. 18, 2005, pp. 1112-1113.
Some scientists doubt that H5N1 bird flu will become the next human pandemic and worry the "current hype" could undermine efforts to prepare for the next genuine pandemic.

Osterholm, Michael T., "Preparing for the Next Pandemic," *Foreign Affairs*, July/August 2004, pp. 24-37.
A professor of public health at the University of Minnesota discusses why the world is unprepared for a pandemic and what steps should be taken.

Orent, Wendy, "Chicken Little," *The New Republic*, Sept. 12, 2005; www.tnr.com.
Those warning of a new H5N1 epidemic are being alarmists, the author says.

Taubenberger, Jeffery K., and David M. Morens, "1918 Influenza: The Mother of All Pandemics," *Emerging Infectious Diseases*, January 2006; www.cdc.gov/ncidod/EID/vol12no01/05-0979.htm.
Taubenberger, the scientist who sequenced the genes of the 1918 flu, and epidemiologist Morens downplay earlier reported similarities between the 1918 virus and H5N1 virus.

Reports and Studies

Congressional Budget Office, *A Potential Influenza Pandemic: Possible Macroeconomic Effects and Policy Issues*, Dec. 8, 2005; www.cbo.gov.
A severe flu pandemic would cause a recession, the CBO concludes in this up-to-date summary of policy debates over avian flu.

Congressional Research Service, *Pandemic Influenza: Domestic Preparedness Effort*, Nov. 10, 2005; www.fas.org/sgp/crs/homesec/RL33145.pdf.
The CRS provides a good overview of efforts by domestic and international agencies to prepare for a pandemic as well as proposed legislative approaches.

Institute of Medicine, *Financing Vaccines in the 21st Century: Assuring Access and Availability*, 2003; www.nap.edu.
A panel of experts recommended that the government mandate health-insurance coverage of vaccination in order to encourage drug companies to get into the vaccine market.

Institute of Medicine, *The Threat of Pandemic Influenza: Are We Ready?*, 2005; www.nap.edu.
This report, which grew out of a 2004 workshop at the Institute of Medicine, contains papers by contributors as well as recommendations on how to prepare for a pandemic.

World Health Organization, *Responding to the Avian Influenza Pandemic Threat: Recommended Strategic Actions*, 2005; www.who.int/csr/resources/publications/influenza/WHO_CDS_CSR_GIP_05_8-EN.pdf.
After assessing the global threat of H5N1 flu virus, this report recommends that nations contribute to a worldwide stockpile of antiviral medications, among other steps.

The Next Step:

Additional Articles from Current Periodicals

Flu Vaccines

Alonso-Zaldivar, Ricardo, "GOP's Flu Plan Would Shield Makers," *Los Angeles Times*, Nov. 17, 2005, p. A21.
Republicans supported a bill creating liability protection for avian flu vaccine manufacturers.

Chang, Alicia, "Flu Patients Die Despite Drug," *The Miami Herald*, Dec. 22, 2005, p. A4.
Two Vietnamese bird flu patients died after receiving early and aggressive treatment with Tamiflu, suggesting the dosage doctors consider ideal might not be enough.

Seno, Alexandra A., "The Business of the Flu," *Newsweek*, Nov. 14, 2005, p. 34.
The threat of an avian flu pandemic is revolutionizing the beleaguered vaccine industry.

Sipress, Alan, "Bird Flu Experts Warn Against Bad Vaccines," *The Washington Post*, Nov. 22, 2005, p. A24.
Health officials worry that improper vaccination of chickens and ducks in East Asia may be spreading bird flu.

Skoloff, Brian, "Counterfeit Bird Flu Drug Confiscated," *The Houston Chronicle*, Dec. 19, 2005, p. A3.
U.S. customs agents confiscated more than 50 fake shipments of Tamiflu, saying Asian suppliers sent them to individuals who ordered the drug on the Internet.

Migratory Birds

Bridges, Andrew, "Migrating Birds Not Linked to Flu," *The Miami Herald*, Dec. 29, 2005, p. A6.
Scientists have not linked the spread of the bird flu to the migratory patterns of wild birds.

Schofield, Matthew, "Spring's Bird-Flu Threat Gets European Scientists Hustling," *The Philadelphia Inquirer*, Dec. 24, 2005, p. A10.
Europe is busy preparing for the arrival of migrating birds this spring, which many believe will carry the bird flu after mixing with migratory birds from Southeast Asia in Africa.

Pandemic Fears

Blue, Laura, "Steps Ahead of Bird Flu," *Time International*, Nov. 28, 2005, p. 40.
Canada was the first country to develop a comprehensive influenza-preparedness plan.

Gorman, Christine, "How Scared Should We Be?" *Time*, Oct. 17, 2005, p. 30.
Gorman provides a primer on the risks of a major flu epidemic and how the government is preparing to counter an outbreak.

Piller, Charles, "A Virus Stalks the Henhouse," *Los Angeles Times*, Dec. 13, 2005, p. A1.
California poultry and egg farms are stepping up security measures to prevent a bird flu outbreak.

Wehrfritz, George, and Rod Nordland, "A Costly Disease," *Newsweek*, Oct. 24, 2005, p. 34.
Experts say an avian flu epidemic could cost the United States six times its conventional flu costs and shave 5 percent off Asia's GDP.

Turkey

Altman, Lawrence K., "Official Says Bird Flu Virus in Turkey is No Mutation," *The New York Times*, Jan. 11, 2006, p. A10.
World health officials said they have not found evidence suggesting new mutations in the avian flu virus responsible for recent outbreaks in Turkey.

Rosenthal, Elisabeth, "A Scientific Puzzle: Some Turks Have Bird Flu Virus But Aren't Sick," *The New York Times*, Jan. 11, 2006, p. A10.
Five more bird flu cases were detected in Turkey's capitol this week, but several victims show no disease symptoms, and none has died.

Williams, Daniel, and Alan Sipress, "Fifteenth Turk Found to Have Bird Flu," *The Washington Post*, Jan. 11, 2006, p. A15.
Authorities confirmed the 15th case of bird flu in Turkey and more infected birds in areas thought to be virus free, causing experts to say the flu has spread more quickly and broadly in Turkey than originally believed.

CITING *THE CQ RESEARCHER*

Sample formats for citing these reports in a bibliography include the ones listed below. Preferred styles and formats vary, so please check with your instructor or professor.

MLA STYLE

Jost, Kenneth. "Rethinking the Death Penalty." The CQ Researcher 16 Nov. 2001: 945-68.

APA STYLE

Jost, K. (2001, November 16). Rethinking the death penalty. *The CQ Researcher, 11*, 945-968.

CHICAGO STYLE

Jost, Kenneth. "Rethinking the Death Penalty." *CQ Researcher,* November 16, 2001, 945-968.

CQ Researcher

Published by CQ Press, a division of Congressional Quarterly Inc.

thecqresearcher.com

Future of Newspapers

Will print papers survive in an online world?

The nation's $59 billion newspaper industry is facing an uncertain future even while its biggest companies are enjoying enviable profits averaging around 20 percent. Newspaper circulation has been declining for many years, especially among young adults. Now, newspapers are losing readers and some advertising to the Internet. In fact, only 52 percent of adults read the paper on a typical weekday. Many newspapers are working on redesigns aimed at making their print editions more readable. Most also have created Web sites to deliver news and information, including special features and interactive options not included in the print product. But newspaper executives are struggling to incorporate their online editions into viable business plans. Meanwhile, slipping profit margins are resulting in layoffs at several of the major newspaper companies and opening up the country's second-largest — Knight Ridder — to a possible takeover.

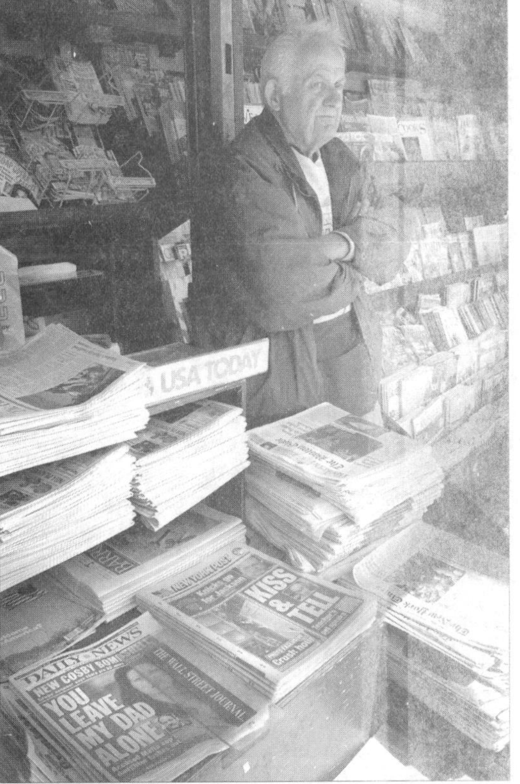

The days may be numbered for vendor Joe Carney, in Cambridge, Mass. Newspapers are losing readers to new print, online and broadcast competitors.

INSIDE THIS REPORT

The CQ Researcher • Jan. 20, 2006 • www.thecqresearcher.com
Volume 16, Number 3 • Pages 49-72

CQ PRESS

RECIPIENT OF SOCIETY OF PROFESSIONAL JOURNALISTS AWARD FOR EXCELLENCE ◆ AMERICAN BAR ASSOCIATION SILVER GAVEL AWARD

Cover: Joe Carney sells newspapers at Harvard Square in Cambridge, Mass. Newspapers are losing readers and ad revenues — partly due to free, online competition — and are being squeezed by rising production and delivery costs. (Getty Images/Melanie Stetson Freeman)

CQ Researcher

Jan. 20, 2006
Volume 16, Number 3

MANAGING EDITOR: Thomas J. Colin

ASSISTANT MANAGING EDITOR: Kathy Koch

ASSOCIATE EDITOR: Kenneth Jost

STAFF WRITERS: Marcia Clemmitt, Peter Katel, Pamela M. Prah

CONTRIBUTING WRITERS: Rachel Cox, Sarah Glazer, David Hosansky, Patrick Marshall, Tom Price

DESIGN/PRODUCTION EDITOR: Olu B. Davis

ASSISTANT EDITOR: Melissa J. Hipolit

CQ PRESS

A Division of Congressional Quarterly Inc.

SENIOR VICE PRESIDENT/PUBLISHER: John A. Jenkins

DIRECTOR, LIBRARY PUBLISHING: Kathryn C. Suárez

DIRECTOR, EDITORIAL OPERATIONS: Ann Davies

CONGRESSIONAL QUARTERLY INC.

CHAIRMAN: Paul C. Tash

VICE CHAIRMAN: Andrew P. Corty

PRESIDENT/EDITOR IN CHIEF: Robert W. Merry

CQ Researcher (ISSN 1056-2036) is printed on acid-free paper. Published weekly, except March 24, July 7, July 14, Aug. 4, Aug. 11, Nov. 24, Dec. 22 and Dec. 29, by CQ Press, a division of Congressional Quarterly Inc. Annual full-service subscriptions for institutions start at $667. For pricing, call 1-800-834-9020, ext. 1906. To purchase a *CQ Researcher* report in print or electronic format (PDF), visit www.cqpress.com or call 866-427-7737. Single reports start at $10. Bulk purchase discounts and electronic-rights licensing are also available. Periodicals postage paid at Washington, D.C., and additional mailing offices. POSTMASTER: Send address changes to *CQ Researcher*, 1255 22nd St., N.W., Suite 400, Washington, DC 20037.

Future of Newspapers

BY KENNETH JOST

THE ISSUES

Money manager Bruce Sherman didn't waste words in his Nov. 1, 2005, letter to the board of directors of Knight Ridder Inc. — the country's second-largest newspaper chain.

Sherman reminded the board that his Florida-based investment company, Private Capital Management, holds 19 percent of the company's stock and that he had alerted board members in July to his firm's "concerns" with Knight Ridder's" stock performance.

Then Sherman dropped his bombshell: He told the board he wanted Knight Ridder put on the auction block, since it was continuing to have "difficulties . . . in realizing the fair value of the company for its shareholders."

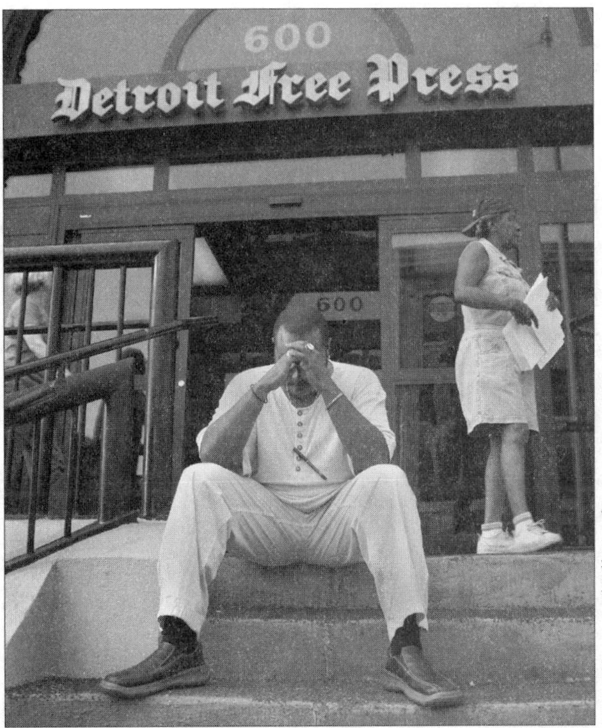

Getty Images/Bill Pugliano

James Hill, an assistant managing editor at the Detroit Free Press, *reacts to the news on Aug. 3, 2005, that Knight Ridder Inc. was selling the paper to the giant Gannett chain, which publishes 99 daily newspapers. Despite healthy profits, Knight Ridder is under pressure from big institutional investors to put itself on the auction block.*

Sherman's demand might have led casual readers of the financial pages to surmise that Knight Ridder was bleeding money and losing customers. In fact, its 32 daily newspapers in such cities as Miami, Philadelphia and San Jose, Calif., had a total circulation of 3.4 million — second only to industry giant Gannett. (*See graph, p. 56.*) And the company's 19.4 percent profit margin — up from 14.4 percent in 1994 — would be considered extraordinary in most industries, where the average profit is only about half that high. [1]

But that's not healthy enough for today's Wall Street. The stock price of Knight Ridder, one of the nation's most respected media organizations, peaked near $80 per share in early 2004 but slumped into the low $50s in 2005. And the institutional investors who hold ever-larger stakes in publicly traded newspaper companies care more about stock prices and shareholder returns than about Pulitzer prizes, foreign news coverage or community service.

"There is pressure from Wall Street," says John Morton, a longtime newspaper-industry analyst in Silver Spring, Md., and columnist for *American Journalism Review*. "And Wall Street has become notoriously very short-term oriented."

"There is more pressure on companies to increase profit margins every year, to increase shareholder return every year," says Richard Rodriguez, executive editor of the *Sacramento Bee* and president of the American Society of Newspaper Editors (ASNE). "That, in turn, has placed pressure on newsrooms either to hold down or cut spending. It's a trend that over a period of time is going to cut into the quality of journalism."

The Knight Ridder board is meeting Sherman's demand — as required by corporate law — by agreeing to look at offers from prospective purchasers. So far, according to news reports, possible bidders include McClatchy Newspapers, which publishes the *Bee*, and several consortia of private equity firms. But some analysts are predicting no sale will materialize. And Knight Ridder itself could deflect the shareholder revolt by buying back a chunk of its stock. (*See sidebar, p. 60.*)

Whatever the outcome for Knight Ridder, the story dramatizes the seemingly paradoxical state of the U.S. newspaper industry in the early 21st century. Newspaper companies are bigger than ever, newspapers fatter and their bottom lines written in double-digit black ink. Morton says the average profit margin of publicly traded newspaper companies is 20.5 percent.

Newspapers may be making extraordinary profits, but they are competing with a plethora of new print, online and broadcast competitors. The competition includes all-news, business-news and sports-news cable networks, several prime-time TV news magazines, thousands of newsletters, weeklies and alternative newspapers and hundreds of online news sources.

And newspapers are losing readers. Circulation has been declining in recent years following decades of subpar growth, including plummeting readership among young people. Currently, only 52 percent of adults read a newspaper on a typical weekday. Lagging circulation has combined with stagnant advertising growth in the past year to trigger layoffs and cutbacks at some of the company's biggest newspapers, including *The New York Times*.

Number of Newspapers Declined

The number of U.S. daily newspapers declined more than 17 percent in the past 50 years, reflecting the demise of afternoon papers.

Source: Newspaper Association of America, from Editor & Publisher *data*

Other experts are less sanguine. Philip Meyer, a former reporter and Knight Ridder executive who now holds the Knight professorship in journalism at the University of North Carolina in Chapel Hill, says Wall Street is pushing newspapers too hard for short-term profits while newspaper executives themselves are too timid in meeting the challenges of a new media environment.

"Newspapers had it so good for so long that they developed a risk-averse mentality," Meyer says. "To figure out new ways of delivering the news is going to require some risk-taking."

As the newspaper industry copes with a myriad of editorial and financial challenges, here are some of the questions being debated:

More ominously, newspapers are under pressure from Internet rivals that offer news, information and even classified advertising for free. To young Internet enthusiasts, print newspapers are relics of an earlier age — uncompetitive in so many ways with online media and bad for trees besides.

Newspaper executives and industry officials insist the pessimistic picture is wrong in some respects and overdrawn in others. They say newspaper companies are strong today and will continue to be strong well into the foreseeable future.

"The industry is in very strong shape financially," says John Sturm, president and chief executive officer of the Newspaper Association of America (NAA), the industry's principal trade association. "Operating margins continue to be very healthy compared to other industry sectors. The industry has good access to capital, there's good internal cash flow and there are substantial investments being made in the online world and other products."

"The general financial picture is quite good," agrees Rodriguez. "That's why it's a little surprising to hear all this talk about the death of the newspaper industry. Right now, there's a bit of piling on."

As for the emergence of online media, industry officials say newspapers have been rushing to develop online editions ever since the mid-1990s. They say newspapers are better situated than Internet rivals like Google, Yahoo and AOL to fully exploit the potential uses of the new technology — and make money while doing it.

"We were among the first to get involved online," says John Kimball, the Newspaper Association's senior vice president and chief marketing officer. "Newspapers are in almost any market the best-known brand and the most visited Web site in that market."

Some experts similarly discount dire warnings for the industry. "Newspapers have been the real news utility for the community," says former *New York Times* reporter Alex Jones, director of the Joan Shorenstein Center for the Press, Politics and Public Policy at Harvard University. "That's never been challenged. Newspapers have a lot more information in them than a one-hour or two-hour TV newscast. If they can parlay that news information on the Web, then they can sustain a business."

Is the newspaper industry in financial jeopardy?

Donald Graham, chairman and chief executive officer of the Washington Post Co., was far from upbeat when he reported to investors and analysts in December on the state of the company's flagship newspaper. Circulation at the *Post* was down, advertising revenues were up only modestly, newsprint was more expensive and profits were diminishing. And just outside the gates, ambitious Web competitors such as Google were creating "clever products . . . designed to make our life harder." [2]

Many of the newspaper executives who spoke at back-to-back media conferences sponsored by financial firms UBS and Credit Suisse First Boston tried to be more positive. In recapping the conferences, however, Goldman Sachs' respected analyst Peter Appert discounted the executives' optimistic predictions on ad revenue and earnings and warned of likely staff cuts in 2006. And to top the week off, Prudential Equity Research Group downgraded its recommendation on New York Times Co. stock to a far-from-enthusiastic "neutral." [3]

The newspaper industry's trade association discounts the gloom-and-doom talk, however — and so do many veteran industry-watchers. "The fundamentals of the business are extremely strong," says Conrad Fink, a professor at the University of Georgia's Grady College of Journalism and Mass Communication in Athens and author of a leading textbook on newspaper management.

As two markers of that strength, Fink notes that newspapers are "almost without exception" the dominant source of news and advertising in their communities and are among the "strongest brand names" in any business. Above all, he emphasizes, newspapers are extremely profitable — with a 20 percent operating margin, almost double the average profits of companies in the benchmark S&P 500.

So why the gloom and doom? Some experts say Wall Street is primarily to blame. "Wall Street wants them to have more," says Morton. "Wall Street is not interested in what you've done in the past. They want to know what you're going to do in the future." [4]

Some experts, however, see more troubling signs for the industry now and in the near future. The economic picture "is changing — obviously," says Tom Rosensteil, a former *Los Angeles Times* reporter who now heads the Project for Excellence in Journalism in Washington. "It's worse in some places than in others."

Rosensteil says the long-term decline in print circulation has accelerated in some places in recent years. "That's really raised questions about whether we're beginning to see the structural shift away from people not reading newspapers in print at all to reading newspapers online or not at all," he says.

In time, shifting to online may be financially advantageous because of the reduced costs of production and distribution, Rosensteil explains — but not yet. "Right now, newspapers can make a lot more from their print editions than from their online editions," he says. "What you can get from the advertiser in an online edition doesn't compare to what you can get for the print edition. And right now the online edition is given away."

Readership Declined Among All Age Groups

Newspaper readership in America has been declining among all age groups since 1970. The greatest declines were among readers 18-34. The smallest decline was among readers over 55.

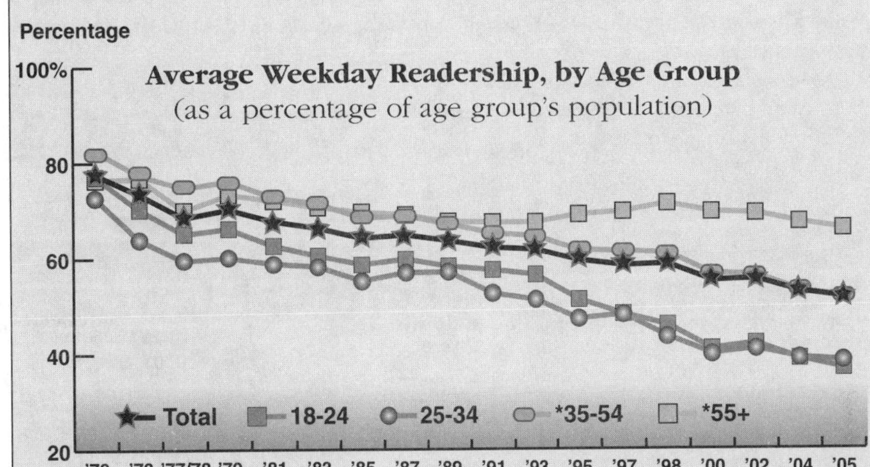

** For 1973, "35-54" actually represents "35-49" and "55+" actually represents "50+."*

*** Beginning in 1998, readership data are based on only the top 50 markets, so figures are not comparable to previous years.*

Source: Newspaper Association of America

For its part, the Newspaper Guild-Communications Workers of America — the major union representing the industry — says newspapers' future should be bright, but only if managements invest in the research and planning needed to adapt. "You should be thriving when you can deliver content to more people than ever imagined and in a more targeted way than ever before," says Guild President Linda Foley. "It's the fault of these companies in not investing in research and development and not investing in the tools they need."

"For years, they didn't have to worry about that," Foley concludes. "If you were a newspaper, you made money."

Meyer says Wall Street's pressure for exceptionally high earnings clouds the industry's long-term prospects. "Wall Street can't see past its nose," says Meyer. "It is goading companies that don't have some cushion between them and Wall Street into harvesting their assets and running the companies into the ground. It's pushing newspaper companies into sacrificing their long-term interests for short-term gains."

Media-industry consultant Merrill Brown counters that blaming Wall Street is neither justified nor useful. "Public ownership is part of the challenge of management in a difficult media environment," says Brown, a longtime newspaper and magazine journalist before helping found CourtTV and later MSNBC.com. "The public marketplace will reward managements that see the future in clear terms, but the ones that don't will be justifiably punished."

Seeking Ways to Lure Young Readers

When it comes to luring more young readers back to daily newspaper reading, the Readership Institute of Northwestern University in Chicago has good news and bad news.

First, the good news: Newspapers can be reinvented to make them more attractive to people under age 30.

Now, the bad news: It won't be easy.

Institute researchers based their conclusions on six years of investigation into newspaper readers' habits and motivations. In the Front Page Study — completed in May 2005, researchers teamed up with editors and reporters at the *Star Tribune* in Minneapolis to develop two different versions of the front page and an inside page for a typical news day, then tested the reactions of the target audience — self-supporting, childless under-30s with a range of occupations.

The results strongly indicated that the most effective way to reach those readers was through a reader-centered approach to newspaper editing and design, which the Institute calls "editing for experience." The approach begins with "choosing the effects you want to create in your audience, then picking and crafting content to get those results." [1]

Attention: Gay Brits
The Royal Navy is recruiting more gay sailors. Is America next?
Say it ain't so
Find out why the Jayhawks call it quits
Tuesday
February 22, 2005
StarTribune
Metro Edition
License, registration and saliva, please ...
Cops want DNA from all of those arrested for felonies.
Data collectors duped into giving criminals information on Minnesotans.
Missing: 2,000 IDs and piece of mind
SHOULD POKER BE A CRIME?
One year ago, armed agents raided a St. Cloud poker game with guns blazing. This weekend a state legislator called for legalizing Texas Hold 'em.

Courtesy Minneapolis *Star Tribune*

Readers liked the lively "Experience" version of the Star Tribune *front page.*

Editors were guided by three experiential goals identified by the Readership Institute as feelings, emotions and motivations that cause people to read daily newspapers more: "gives me something to talk about," "looks out for my interests" and "turned on by surprise and humor."

The 140 targeted readers looked at three page versions: the Original Paper that was actually published; the Improved Paper, which included the same stories recrafted to change emphasis, play and approach to enhance the three chosen experiences; and the Experience Paper, in which the three experiences drove both story choice and presentation.

For example, the Experience Paper jettisoned a lead story about a woman who planned to walk every street of Minneapolis as holding little interest for young readers. The replacement, a centerpiece about legalizing Texas Hold 'Em poker, was cast in an engaging pro-con debate format and included information about how to play and where to practice online.

A story about legislation requiring police to collect DNA from any Minnesotan arrested on a felony was reshaped to speak directly to the reader. The original headline, "Broader DNA Collection Law Proposed," became "License, Registration and Saliva please. . . ." The original third-person, institutional account was edited to offer many entry points, to break out useful information in marginalia and boxes

But Jones cautions that both Wall Street and newspaper management may need to lower their expectations for the industry. "With an economic model that is increasingly fragmenting the advertising business and the growth of alternatives in terms of classified-advertising business, newspapers are probably going to have to adjust their expectations as to what is an acceptable level of profit, especially as the transition is made from print to online," he says.

Will newspapers succeed online?

As head of the newspaper editors' trade association, *Sacramento Bee* editor Rodriguez naturally worries about the declining circulation of print newspapers. But he worries a bit less about the industry's overall prospects because of what he sees when stopping at a coffee house on a typical Sunday morning.

"Everybody there was looking for information — whether it was the people who were buying the *Bee* or the people reading their computers," Rodriguez says. "There wasn't anyone in that coffeehouse who wasn't looking for information."

A decade after the first surge of online editions, virtually everyone in or around newspapers realizes that computers are a big part of the industry's future — and serving computer users may be key to its long-term survival. But getting to the online *there* from the print *here* is proving to be no easy task.

"They are doing better than the doomsday scenario, but worse than they should be doing," says Pablo Boczkowski, an associate professor at

and to point readers to a debate in the next day's paper. A new lead, or opening paragraph, addressed readers' interests directly: "If you're ever arrested for a felony in Minnesota, you may soon be asked to open wide and give a sample of saliva along with your fingerprint."

Respondents preferred the Experience Paper over the other two by a ratio of roughly 3-to-1, scoring it much higher on such criteria as: more likely to catch your attention, more visually appealing, more likely to get you to read, more memorable, easier to get information, would cause you to mention when talking with friends, story selection, looks out for your interests and makes the news more interesting.

Emotions Attract Most Readers

Among three versions of a Star Tribune *front page, an "experience version" proved the most popular.*

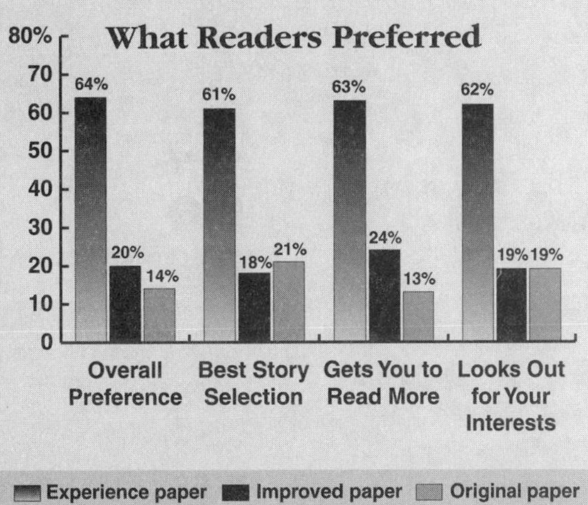

Source: Readership Institute, 2005

"Experiences are a way of converting traditional news judgment from editors' definitions (what's most interesting, what's most important, what you just can't believe happened) to readers' definitions of how they react (what makes readers feel informed, what gives them something to talk about, what tells them the paper is looking out for their interests)," said *Star Tribune* Editor Anders Gyllenhaal.

The young readers' clear preference for the Experience Paper over the Improved Paper supported researchers' contention that reversing the decline in daily newspaper readership will require an editorial revolution within the dailies' hard-news core, not just stylistic changes around the edges.

"What we heard from these young adult Minnesotans is typical of what we hear from young Americans everywhere," the study overview reported. "Newspapers are OK, but they don't compel and engage."

But making them more compelling, while doable, will require altering long-entrenched editorial practices. "Newspapers tend to talk about topics, keeping a distance between themselves, the topic and the reader," noted team leader Nancy Barnes, assistant managing editor at the *Star Tribune*. "In this experiment we actively sought to talk to readers directly, and engage them every step along the way. That makes the newspaper seem more personal. It goes against our natural instinct, however."

The overall lesson was "Yes, you can do that," said Mary Nesbitt, managing director of the Readership Institute. But, she continued, "The degree of change you need to make is substantial. It's not just a matter of redesigning the look of the front page. It is that, but it is a lot more than that. You have to consider, given your target audience, how are you defining news in the first place. Where are you going to look for news? What approach or angle do you take with the story? And then how do you present it effectively?"

— Rachel S. Cox

[1] "Reinventing the Newspaper for Young Adults," Readership Institute, April 2005, p. 1. Available at www.readership.org/experience/startrib_overview.pdf.

Northwestern University in Evanston, Ill., and author of the recent book *Digitizing the News*. "They are still, to a certain extent, tied to a world that is no longer viable."

"The approach of most newspaper organizations is to put their print product onto the Web," says Mary Nesbitt, managing director of the Readership Institute at Northwestern's Media Management Center. "The platform has changed, the look of it certainly, but it's basically transferring one to the other."

The critique may be generally true, but there were exceptions even in the early days of online newspapers in the late '90s. In his book, Boczkowski notes as one example the "Virtual Voyager" features on HoustonChronicle.com, which used online technologies to take readers along almost in real time on such experiences as a month-long trip on old Route 66. [5]

Today, more and more online newspapers are offering distinctive features that are not — and could not be — published in print editions. Newspaper Web sites commonly combine related editorial or advertising content into extensive packages that would take up way too much space in a print edition.

Newspaper sites also typically include interactive features that allow readers to comment on issues from the serious to the mundane and — unlike letters to the editor — to participate in ongoing dialogues with other readers, and perhaps reporters and editors as well. In early January 2006, for example, visitors to nytimes.com

Gannett Is Nation's Largest Newspaper Group

Gannett Co. is the nation's largest newspaper chain in number of daily papers and circulation. Its 99 daily papers include the nation's largest-selling newspaper, USA Today, *with 2.3 million circulation. Knight Ridder and Tribune Co. trail in second and third places in overall circulation. Knight Ridder is currently looking at offers from prospective purchasers, including the ninth-ranked McClatchy Co., but some experts believe no sale will materialize.*

Combined Circulation of the Largest Newspaper Groups
(in thousands)

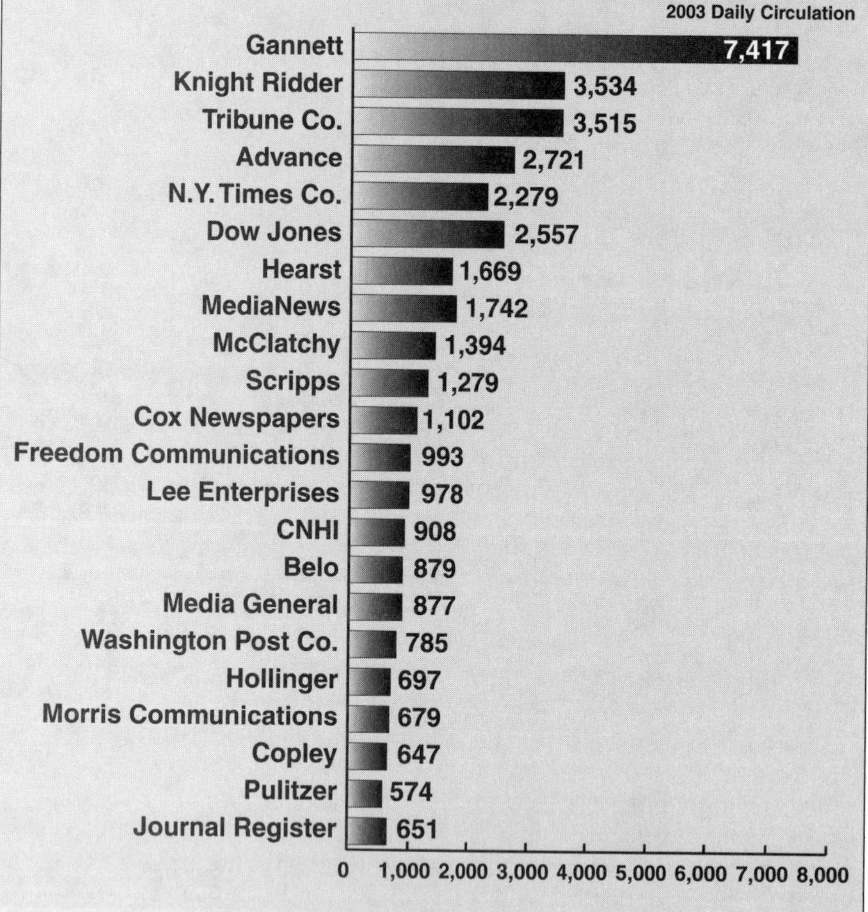

Sources: Journalism.org, Editor and Publisher Yearbook; PEJ *Research*

could discuss Israel's pullout from Gaza, the University of Texas' victory in the Rose Bowl, comedian Jon Stewart's selection to host the Oscars or the future of plastic surgery.

Web competitors, however, are busy doing similar things. Google News offers users headlines and news stories from around the world, continuously updated throughout the day (http://news.google.com). Google Groups allows users to create or join a mailing list or discussion forum on topics of individual interest (http://groups.google.com). Users can also track their favorite topics simply by clicking on a star next to the particular subject.

Industry officials insist that newspapers can meet the challenges posed by Internet competitors and note that rivals are in fact pulling much of their content from print sources. "Everybody says the Internet is eating our lunch," says the Newspaper Association's Kimball. "The reality is that newspapers are providing the lunch."

Kimball and Rodriguez both concede, however, that newspapers have their work cut out for them to make online editions successful. Economically, newspaper companies need to get more revenue from online editions by raising rates and convincing advertisers that the money is well spent. L. Gordon Crovitz, president of Dow Jones' electronic publishing division, alluded to the issue in remarks to the UBS media conference in December. "The challenge for all of us," Crovitz said, "is to do the hard work that's necessary to keep informing advertisers of the value of online advertising." [6]

"We've got a long way to go," Rodriguez says. "We understand as an industry the imperative of getting more technologically savvy. We're still struggling with the structure of how to make that happen."

Industry observers agree on the challenges but offer somewhat different prescriptions. Rosenstiel says the future lies online. "In time, you're going to have to let go of that print focus," he says. "To really build a better journalism you have to think of the Internet as the better platform."

But Northwestern's Boczkowski cautions newspapers not to overlook the print product. "The future of newspapers lies in the intersection of print and non-print options," he says. "There is a lot that is wonderful about the print newspaper. It's not that newspaper companies should abandon the print business, but they should reinvent it for our time."

Can newspapers attract more younger readers?

The demographics of newspaper readership are more than discouraging for the industry. Young people, simply put, are not reading the newspaper as much as their parents or grandparents did — and the numbers keep declining with each new generation. One study found that in 1972 a majority of the people in every age group above the age of 30 read a newspaper every day; three decades later, in 2002, daily newspaper readers were in the majority only among people in their late 50s or older. [7]

"Cohorts of high newspaper readers are being replaced by cohorts who read at lower levels," says Nesbitt of the Readership Institute. "Newspapers still reach a high proportion of the adult population, but it's no longer as entrenched a daily habit as it once was."

Experts offer a variety of explanations for the declining readership. The University of Georgia's Fink suggests that the trend toward waiting to get married is one factor. "Traditionally we waited until they got married, had a household and took on responsibilities, and then they became newspaper readers," and that all once happened at an early age, Fink says. "Now they wait to do all that. And if you haven't read a newspaper by the time you're 30, you're not going to start then."

For his part, David Mindich, a former CNN editor who now chairs the journalism department at St. Michael's College in Colchester, Vt., sees a declining interest among young people in serious news from any media — print, broadcast or online. He blames many institutions besides newspapers. "We no longer use the news in our discussions at the dinner table or in the classrooms as we once did," Mindich says. "We need a total change in our society to change educational expectations, workplace expectations, the expectations of the Federal Communications Commission."

Newspaper Circulation Declined

The number of papers sold daily in the United States dropped by nearly 10 percent, or more than 5 million papers, from 1960-2004. During the same period, the U.S. population increased 115 million.

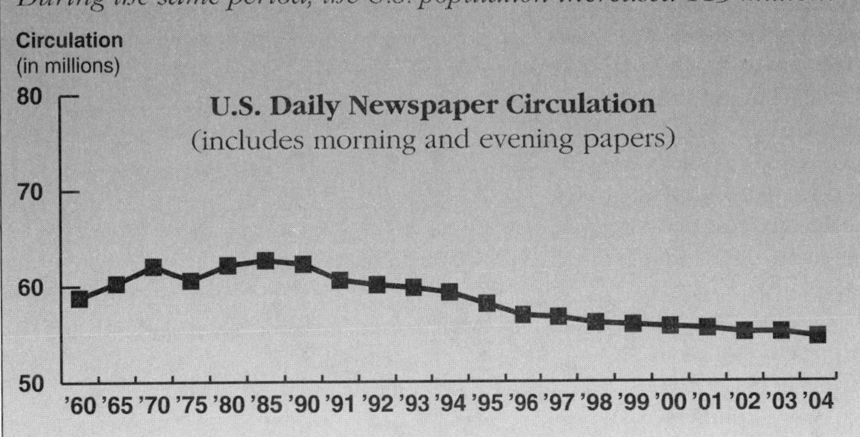

Source: National Newspaper Association, based on Editor & Publisher *data*

The advent of the Internet further weakens the appeal of the print newspaper. "Our school systems have been training people to get information by computer keyboard and screen," says industry analyst Morton. *Bee* editor Rodriguez says young people especially like the control they can exercise in using online media. "They want it where they want it, when they want it, how they want it," he says. "And they don't want to pay for it."

Newspaper Association officials acknowledge the change in reading habits among young people but point to evidence that young people continue to find newspapers valuable — whether in print or online. "They don't read the newspaper the way their parents or grandparents did," says Kimball. "They don't sit down before or after work and go through the newspaper cover to cover. But if you ask them if they used the newspaper during the course of the day, you get a different picture. Over half of the people ages 12-17 are saying they are using the newspaper on a regular basis."

The Project for Excellence in Journalism's Rosensteil also believes the declining readership among young people has been somewhat exaggerated and, in any event, says the Internet can help counter the trend. "With the advent of the Internet, there is more reason to believe that young people will be news consumers," he says. "The notion that people under a certain age don't read at all was overstated. They do read, and they now have a medium that they prefer where they can read what they want when they want it."

Other experts, however, fear that over time online newspapers will differ markedly from print editions — and not for the better. Stories online will be shorter, Boczkowski says, because people read them at work or on the run. And online editions will devote less space to substantive news about politics or government and more to entertainment and culture. "There will be far less of the hard news and far more of the soft news — and softer treatment of the hard news," he says.

But Mindich and the Readership Institute's Nesbitt both say newspapers can — and must — find ways to com-

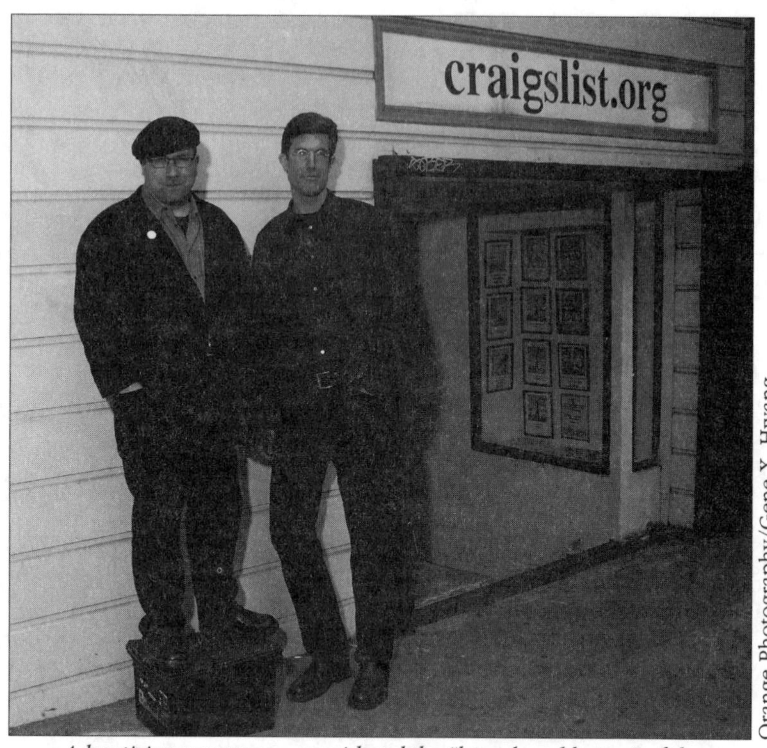

Orange Photography/Gene X. Hwang

Advertising revenue — considered the "bread and butter" of the newspaper business — has been down in recent years, growing less than 3 percent a year compared to about 5 percent historically. Many blame the disappearing ads in newspapers on the emergence of Craigslist.org, a San Francisco-based nonprofit community Web site that offers free, local classified ads on the Internet. Now in many cities, the site was founded by Craig Newmark, left, with CEO Jim Buckmaster.

municate important information to young readers in ways that they will find appealing. "Anecdotally, I've seen that there are many young kids who are following the news closely online," Mindich says. He says editors who substitute soft for hard news are selling young people short.

Nesbitt agrees. She says the key is to present stories in ways that better convey their importance and their interest to readers — both young and old. "Younger adult readers are not stupid," she says. "They react very badly to being talked down to. But they also don't want to be bored to tears by stories that are not well told, stories that are of no interest to them in the first place." ■

BACKGROUND

Growing the Press

Newspapers grew in number, circulation and economic and political importance as the United States itself grew through the 19th and 20th centuries in size, in population and in two other preconditions for a mass medium: industrialization and urbanization. Organizationally, newspapers changed from an "entrepreneurial" model — owned and operated by individuals or families in the community served — to a model of corporate ownership, increasingly in the late 20th century as parts of large newspaper chains. The transformation helped make newspapers a big — and profitable — business, but the effects of corporate ownership on the quality of journalism are sharply debated. [8]

Boston was home of the American Colonies' first newspapers. *Publick Occurrences Both Foreign and Domestick*, a three-page newspaper (with one page deliberately left blank), appeared once in 1690 only to be shut down by authorities; eight years later, the homesick printer returned to London. *The News-Letter* debuted in 1704 and remained as the first continuously published newspaper in the Colonies — one of five in Boston by the time of the Revolutionary War. Most of the early newspapers — more than 2,100 founded between 1690 and 1820 — folded after two years or less, victims of insufficient advertising and unaffordable subscription prices. Still, as historian Frank Luther Mott notes, newspapers played a vital role in spreading news about the war for independence and emerged after the Revolution "with a newly found prestige" that would make them "a power of the first importance." [9]

The number of newspapers increased rapidly in the early years of the Republic — from 37 at the end of the Revolutionary War to 1,258 in 1835 — but most depended on outside financing, for example from political parties. The introduction of the steam-driven press in 1825, along with advances in the manufacture of paper and ink, laid the foundation for mass production. Circulation lagged, however, until the advent of the "penny press," beginning with the *New York Sun* in 1833. *The Sun* and dozens of imitators over the next decade emphasized local crime and court news in newspapers priced to reach a mass audience large enough to attract advertisers. "The penny papers," notes David Demers, an associate professor of communications at Washington State University, "were specifically created to make a profit." [10]

More explosive growth followed in the late 19th century: From 1870 to 1900 the number of general-circulation daily newspapers quadrupled from 574 to 2,226, while circulation increased

Continued on p. 60

Chronology

1900-1960 *Number of newspapers begins long-term decline; circulation begins to lag behind population growth after end of World War II.*

1903
Charles L. Knight becomes part owner of *Akron Beacon Journal* in Ohio; buys out partner four years later; brings his sons John S. and James L. into the business as they reach adulthood; leaves paper to them upon his death in 1933.

1906
Herman Ridder gains complete ownership of German-language daily *Staats Zeitung* in New York; his sons later acquire *Journal of Commerce* (1926) and then begin expanding company with medium-sized papers in Midwest, California, elsewhere.

1950s
Knight Newspapers has well-regarded daily newspapers in several major cities; Ridder Publications has a dozen dailies in mid-sized cities.

1960s-1970s *Major newspaper companies "go public" — raising capital by selling stock on public markets; some create two classes of stock to preserve family control; industry becomes more concentrated.*

1966
Gannett Co. goes public, with single class of stock.

1967
New York Times Co. goes public, with control vested in second class of stock held by Ochs-Sulzberger family trust.

1969
Knight Newspapers and Ridder Publications both go public, each with single class of stock; Knight and Ridder families have sufficient stock holdings for effective control.

1974
Knight Newspapers and Ridder Publications merge to form country's second-largest newspaper chain.

1980s *Newspapers fail with first ventures into electronic products; newsrooms computerized; circulation begins to fall.*

1980
Columbus (Ohio) *Dispatch* debuts "electronic edition" with phone access to contents of *Dispatch* and three other newspapers; folds experiment two years later.

1982
Gannett launches *USA Today*, national newspaper relying on colorful graphics and ultra-short stories.

1983
Knight Ridder begins market trial of Viewtron videotext service; folds three years later.

1987
Nationwide daily newspaper circulation peaks at 62.8 million.

1990s *Newspapers aggressively develop online editions as World Wide Web emerges.*

1993
New York Times goes online with "@Times" on AOL; three years later, develops its own site: *New York Times* on the Web.

1995
P. Anthony "Tony" Ridder advances to chairman and chief executive officer of Knight Ridder; raises company's operating margin over next decade to 19 percent.

1998
Publicly traded newspaper companies account for nearly half of daily circulation nationwide.

1999
All but two of 100 biggest newspapers have online editions.

2000-Present *Newspapers face increasing competition from online rivals; readership declines, especially among young people.*

2000
Swedish Metro International launches first youth-oriented commuter tabloid in United States with *Metro Boston*; U.S. companies follow suit: Tribune Co.'s *RedEye* in Chicago (2002), Washington Post Co.'s *Express* (2003).

2004
Nationwide daily newspaper circulation falls to 54.6 million, 13 percent below 1987 peak.

2005
Wave of layoffs in industry cuts 2,200 jobs through attrition, buyouts. . . All but two of 20 biggest U.S. newspapers report decline in circulation for period ending Sept. 30 . . . . Knight Ridder's biggest institutional investor writes letter on Nov. 1 demanding that board pursue "competitive sale" of company; company mulling bids as of January 2006.

Knight Ridder's Uncertain Future

Two-and-a-half months after Knight Ridder's biggest investor forced the nation's second-largest newspaper chain to put itself up for sale, its future remains uncertain.

California-based McClatchy Co. and three teams of private equity investors appear to be among the most serious potential bidders. [1] Industry giant Gannett Co. and William Dean Singleton's rapidly growing Denver-based MediaNews Group, may also be interested.

Formal bids for the $4.2 billion company are due after all potential bidders receive financial presentations in January from Knight Ridder (KR). Its board of directors could accept a bid or reject them all and decide not to sell.

In the meantime, KR's news operations, including 32 daily newspapers and a popular Internet news site, continue functioning. But there is speculation that a cost-conscious purchaser might try to cut labor expenses by 5 percent or more. [2]

Florida money manager Bruce Sherman, whose Private Capital Management (PCM) owns 19 percent of KR stock, touched off the corporate turmoil in November 2005, demanding that the KR board "aggressively pursue the competitive sale of the company."

After initial doubt about a sale, speculation is shifting in the direction of an eventual deal. Several other possible scenarios remain, however, including a "buyback" of PCM shares by KR. And any proposed sale might draw opposition from unions or federal antitrust agencies. For example, McClatchy could have problems acquiring KR's *St. Paul Pioneer Press* since it already owns its Twin Cities competitor, the *Star Tribune*.

Depending on the buyer, a sale could extinguish the names of two journalistic families, each with a century of owning newspapers. [3] Charles L. Knight bought the *Akron* (Ohio) *Beacon Journal* in 1903, guided his sons John S. and James L. into the business, and left it to them upon his death in 1933. With Jack focused on editorial and Jim on business, Knight Newspapers acquired and upgraded papers in bigger cities: the *Miami Herald* (1937), *Detroit News* (1940) and *Chicago Daily News* (1944). The company was profitable, the newspapers respected. *The Herald* picked up its first Pulitzer in 1950 for a series on organized crime, the *Detroit News* in 1967 for coverage of local race riots.

Herman Ridder, a second-generation German-American, bought the German-language daily *Staats Zeitung* in 1906. His sons kept the paper alive despite anti-German sentiment during World War I, purchased the New York-based *Journal of Commerce* in 1926 and later picked up small- and medium-sized newspapers in monopoly markets. By the mid-1950s, the company had a dozen daily papers, and — in contrast to Knight Newspapers — no overarching philosophy of journalistic excellence.

The merger of the two chains in 1974 stemmed from ordinary corporate considerations. [4] Bernard H. Ridder Jr., president of Ridder Publications, saw no obvious successor among his brothers and cousins. Knight Newspapers, ably guided by Business manager Alvah Chapman, wanted to grow. Chapman called Ridder in March and proposed a merger, and by November it was complete. Headquartered in Miami, the new company had 35 papers with daily circulation of 3.8 million.

Both companies had gone public in 1969, but family members held the biggest blocks: John Knight's two surviving sons held 46 percent of Knight Newspapers; family members owned 50 percent of Ridder Publications. For financial reasons, both companies had gone public with a single class of stock instead of guarding family control with a second, super-voting class of stock. When the companies merged, tax considerations again dictated a single class of stock. The result — unforeseen but foreseeable — was to leave Knight Ridder vulnerable to a shareholder revolt.

At the time of the merger, P. Anthony "Tony" Ridder, one of eight fourth-generation cousins in the business, was business manager of the *San Jose Mercury News*. Two decades later, he had advanced to become KR's chairman and chief executive officer. In the meantime, KR newspapers had earned widespread respect — none more than the *Philadelphia Inquirer*, which collected 17 Pulitzer prizes under an aggressive editor, Eugene Roberts. But in the late 1980s, Ridder had clamped down on Roberts' budget. Frustrated, Roberts unexpectedly resigned in 1990.

Continued from p. 58

more than fivefold to 15 million. With rapid industrialization and urbanization, manufacturers relied on newspapers to reach buyers, and newspapers reaped the profits. Meanwhile, newspapers' editorial content was also being transformed, first with the birth of "new journalism" in the 1870s — emphasizing better writing, attractive makeup and editorial independence — followed by the mixture of reformism and sensationalism derogatorily labeled "yellow journalism." [11]

Three famous newspaper publishers brought these contrasting approaches to New York City in the 1880s and '90s after buying up struggling papers. Joseph Pulitzer used yellow journalism to turn the *World* into a moneymaker, only to be bested by William Randolph Hearst's yellow journalism at the rival *Journal*. Meanwhile, Adolph Ochs aimed at a higher class of readers at the *Times* with dignified coverage of "All the News That's Fit to Print" — a slogan that still appears every day in the left "ear" of the front page of the paper's print editions.

The newspaper industry continued to mature through the 20th century editorially and financially and — despite some apprehension — continued to prosper even as radio and television emerged as competing news media. Editorially, the 20th century saw the rise of specialized reporters, foreign correspondents and political columnists. Financially, circulation nearly doubled, and advertising revenue more than tripled between 1910 and the last pre-Depression benchmark of 1930. But the number of daily

As head of the company since 1995, Ridder has continued to focus on the company's bottom line — with some success. [5] The company's profit margin has increased to 19.4 percent from 14.4 percent, the stock price from $26 in 1995 to a peak near $80 in May 2004. But the company's price has sagged since then. And three of the papers are pulling down the company's profitability: the *Inquirer*, straining under high labor costs; the *Mercury News*, lagging in advertising revenue because of the dotcom bust; and the competitively pressured *Pioneer Press*. The dip caused concern for Sherman and PCM. Two other big institutional investors are backing Sherman's tactic: Southeastern Asset Management, Inc., and Harris Associates LP. Together, they hold 36 percent of KR stock.

Knight Ridder Inc.

Knight Ridder Chairman P. Anthony "Tony" Ridder.

The other potential bidders identified in published accounts are Blackstone Group LP of New York and Providence Equity Partners, in partnership with the New York buyout firm Kohlberg Kravis Roberts; and Thomas H. Lee Partners LP of Boston in a joint bid with Texas Pacific Group of Dallas and other investment firms. Either of those bids is thought most likely to envision restructuring KR and then selling it — in whole or piece by piece — for a profit.

Despite the inevitable angst among KR employees, industry and labor officials caution against pessimism. "When you look at Knight Ridder, maybe it's not performing as well as it has," says Richard Rodriguez, executive editor of the *Sacramento Bee* and president of the American Society of Newspaper Editors. "But it's still a pretty healthy company."

"You're not going to wind up with those newspapers going out of business," says Linda Foley, president of the Newspaper Guild, a unit of the Communications Workers of America.

Although the bidding process has been guarded, McClatchy has figured prominently in speculation both because of its recent interest in acquisitions and its positive journalistic reputation. The company began expanding in 1979 beyond its three *Bee* newspapers in California (Sacramento, Modesto, Fresno) to buy papers in Alaska, Washington state, South Carolina and North Carolina. *The Star Tribune* was purchased in 1998.

At first, Gannett was described as uninterested. Then it was reported to have submitted a bid only to withdraw it. A Gannett spokeswoman called that story "ridiculous" but declined to comment further.

Privately owned MediaNews Group, whose more than 40 daily newspapers have a circulation of nearly 2 million, is reportedly planning a bid with two venture capital firms. Since the mid-1980s, Singleton has been buying papers nationwide and gaining a reputation for journalistic quality.

[1] See Joseph DiStefano, "Potential Buyers of Knight Ridder Still Emerging," *The Philadelphia Inquirer*, Jan. 12, 2006, p. C2; Pete Carey, "Knight Ridder Meets With First Potential Buyer," *San Jose Mercury News*, Jan. 14, 2006, p. 1.

[2] See "Morgan Stanley Pinpoints Knight Ridder's 'Underperforming Papers,' " editorandpublisher.com, Dec. 1, 2005.

[3] See Davis Merritt, *Knightfall: Knight Ridder and How the Erosion of Newspaper Journalism Is Putting Democracy at Risk* (2005), pp. 29-45.

[4] *Ibid.*, pp. 46-59.

[5] Background in part from Joseph Menn, "Moment of Truth for Media Chief," *Los Angeles Times*, Dec. 25, 2005, p. C1; Devin Leonard, "Tony Ridder Just Can't Win," *Fortune*, Dec. 24, 2001, p. 99.

newspapers stood at 2,202 in 1910 and declined slowly and steadily for the rest of the century. [12]

Despite the growth of group ownership, by 1960 only three newspaper chains had achieved national scope: Hearst, Scripps-Howard and Newhouse. More typical of the more than 100 newspaper groups at the time was Gannett, now the nation's largest but then comprising only 16 dailies in medium-sized cities in New York and New Jersey. [13] Among other chains, John S. Knight had expanded beyond his father's *Akron Beacon Journal* to acquire, among others, newspapers in Miami, Detroit, Chicago and Charlotte, N.C. (Knight sold the *Chicago Daily News* in 1956 for a then-record $24 million.) Meanwhile, Ridder Publications had grown from the family's original property — the New York-based German-language daily *Staats Zeitung* — into a chain with 13 dailies and seven Sundays in such mid-sized cities as St. Paul, Minn.; Wichita, Kan.; and San Jose, Calif. [14]

Going Public

The consolidation of the newspaper industry proceeded apace in the late 20th century with a continuing decline in the number of dailies and an even sharper decline in the number of independently owned papers. The increasing size of the largest newspaper chains, along with rising fixed costs of newspaper production, drove many of the best-known companies to "go public" — that is, to raise

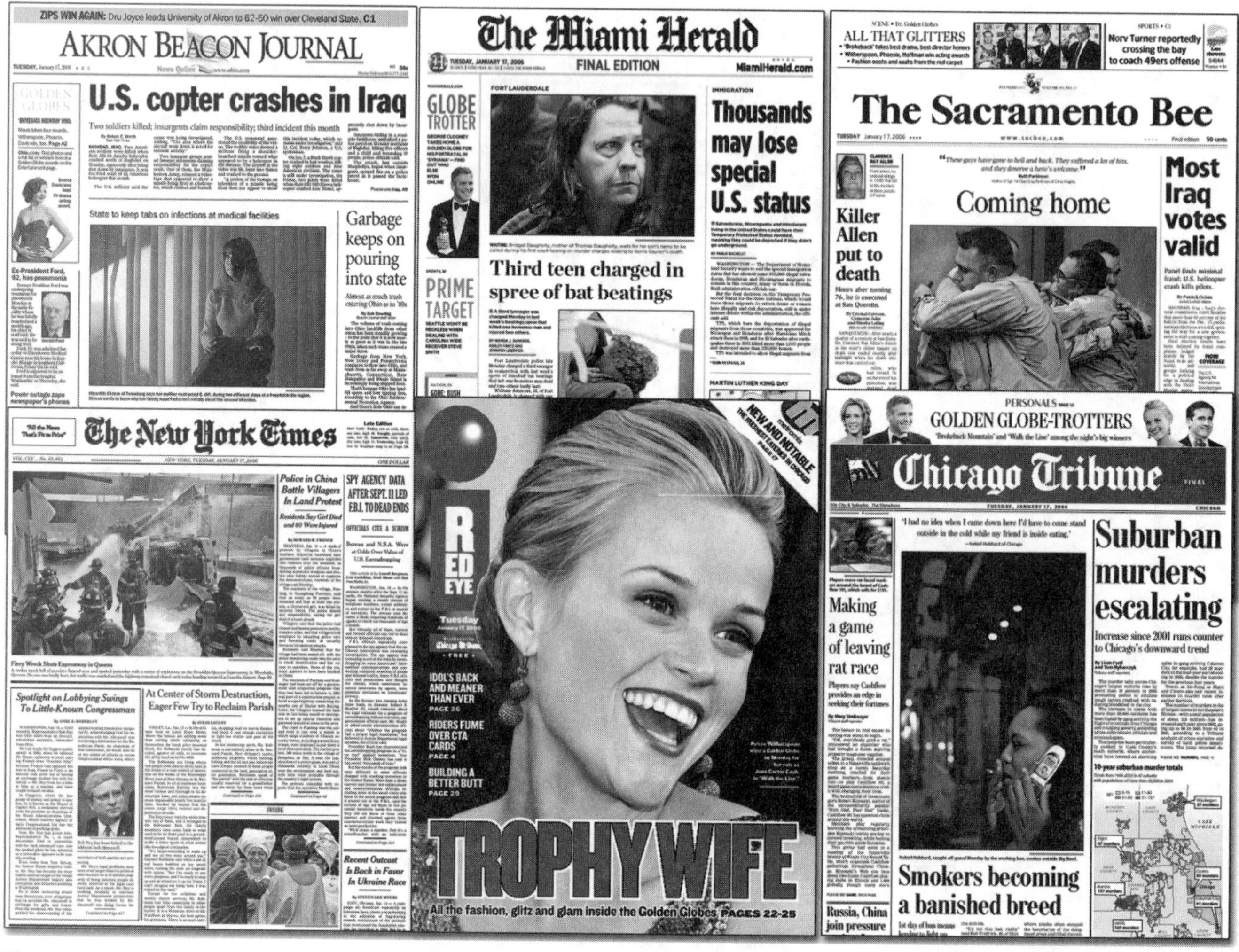
ZIPS WIN AGAIN: Dru Joyce leads University of Akron to 62-50 win over Cleveland State, C1

AKRON BEACON JOURNAL

U.S. copter crashes in Iraq

Two soldiers killed; insurgents claim responsibility; third incident this month

State to keep tabs on infections at medical facilities

Garbage keeps on pouring into state

Ex-President Ford, 92, has pneumonia

Power outage zaps newspaper's phones

The Miami Herald

FINAL EDITION

MiamiHerald.com

GLOBE TROTTER

PRIME TARGET

Third teen charged in spree of bat beatings

IMMIGRATION

Thousands may lose special U.S. status

MARTIN LUTHER KING DAY

ALL THAT GLITTERS

Norv Turner reportedly crossing the bay to coach 49ers offense

The Sacramento Bee

Coming home

Killer Allen put to death

Most Iraq votes valid

The New York Times

Police in China Battle Villagers In Land Protest

SPY AGENCY DATA AFTER SEPT. 11 LED F.B.I. TO DEAD ENDS

Fiery Wreck Shuts Expressway in Queens

Spotlight on Lobbying Swings To Little-Known Congressman

At Center of Storm Destruction, Eager Few Try to Reclaim Parish

Recent Outcast Is Back in Favor In Ukraine Race

NEW AND NOTABLE

RED EYE

IDOL'S BACK AND MEANER THAN EVER

RIDERS FUME OVER CTA CARDS

BUILDING A BETTER BUTT

TROPHY WIFE

All the fashion, glitz and glam inside the Golden Globes PAGES 22-25

PERSONALS

GOLDEN GLOBE-TROTTERS

Chicago Tribune

Making a game of leaving rat race

Suburban murders escalating

Increase since 2001 runs counter to Chicago's downward trend

Smokers becoming a banished breed

Russia, China join pressure

Newspapers are using more and larger photographs and bolder graphics on their front pages in an effort to hold on to readers, especially younger Americans. Some papers are also distributing free tabloids, such as the Tribune Co.'s RedEye *in Chicago (bottom, center).*

capital by selling stock on publicly traded markets. The increase in public ownership resulted in increased pressure to push profits higher and higher, even at companies still controlled by newspaper-publishing families. [15]

The changes in the industry's economic structure took place against a backdrop of continuing concern about circulation and readership. Circulation had been growing slower than population since the 1960s and began falling in absolute terms for daily papers by the mid-1980s and for Sunday papers by the 1990s, according to industry figures. By 2004, circulation for daily papers had fallen to 54.6 million — 13 percent below the 1987 peak of 62.8 million. Sunday circulation of 57.8 million was 8 percent below the 1993 peak. [16]

Readership figures were even bleaker. The percentage of adults who read a newspaper on an average weekday declined from 78 percent in 1970 to 64 percent in 1989; the figure continued falling through the 1990s and the first years of the 21st century except for a post-9/11 uptick in 2002. By 2005, a bare majority of adults — 51.6 percent — read a newspaper on a typical weekday. The decline was especially sharp among young adults. From 1972 to 1998, the percentage of adults ages 30-39 who read a newspaper on a typical weekday plummeted from 73 percent to 30 percent. [17] (*See graph, p. 53.*)

Lagging circulation was both cause and effect of the simultaneous decrease in the number of daily newspapers. The number of afternoon papers dropped by nearly half from 1950 to 1998 as people turned to television instead of newspapers for news at the end of the workday. (*See graph, p. 52.*) On the other hand, the number of morning and Sunday papers both increased — driven largely by the birth of new newspapers in suburbia. Meanwhile, annual newspaper revenue continued to increase by 5 percent or so since the 1960s, even though the industry lost overall advertising revenue with increased competition from radio and television. [18]

The movement toward public ownership began in the 1960s for reasons only partly related to the industry's concerns about circulation and readership. Ben Bagdikian, a former reporter turned industry critic, says tax laws encouraged the trend by giving favorable treatment to companies that used retained profits to acquire other companies. [19] But Jones of Harvard's Shorenstein Center says the 19th-century tradition of family-owned newspapers simply could not be preserved in a 20th-century economy where newspapers were both bigger and more profitable.

"In the 19th century, newspapers went from one family to another," says Jones, who covered the press for the *Times* in the 1980s. "But when newspapers became a way of making money, there came a point where a newspaper could only be acquired by another newspaper because no family could afford it."

The *Times* was, in fact, among the earliest newspaper companies to go public, in 1967. [20] Gannett, still a regional newspaper chain, had gone public a year earlier. Knight and Ridder each went public in 1969 — five years before they merged. Among other major present-day companies, the Washington Post Co. went public in 1971, the Tribune Co. in 1983, McClatchy in 1988 and Scripps-Howard in 1998. By then, the 17 publicly traded newspaper companies owned a total of 313 dailies and 244 Sunday papers, with a combined daily circulation of 24.7 million — or almost 44 percent of total newspaper circulation (and more than half of the total Sunday circulation).

Many of the companies — including the Times, the Post and McClatchy — structured stock ownership to preserve family control by creating two classes of stock and vesting effective power in stock owned by family members or (in the Times' case) a family-controlled trust. Knight and Ridder, however, both went public in 1969 with a single class of stock. Alvah H. Chapman, a Knight executive who went on to be chairman and CEO of the merged Knight Ridder, later said that the idea of creating two classes of stock was never seriously considered because Jack Knight was expected to hold most of the stock and thus maintain control of the company. When the two companies merged, they again issued only one class of stock. [21]

Simultaneously with the trend toward public ownership, newspapers were moving toward more "soft" news — celebrities, scandals, gossip and human interest stories — and less coverage of government and international news. From 1977 to 1997, the amount of "soft news" in U.S. news media increased to 43 percent from 15 percent, according to a survey by the Project for Excellence in Journalism. [22] Emblematic of the trend was Gannett's nationwide newspaper *USA Today*, founded in 1982, which relied heavily on colorful graphics and ultra-short stories and de-emphasized government reporting.

Jones says going public helped many of the companies, including the Times. "Going public saved the company," he says. "It made it possible for the Times to acquire other companies that allow the business to survive."

But others are more critical. In their study, journalism professors Gilbert Cranberg, Randall Bezanson and John Soloski conclude that investors in publicly traded companies are "concerned with . . . continuously improved profitability" and "indifferent to news or, more disturbingly, its quality." And because publicly traded companies control a large segment of the industry, their practices "are becoming the standards to which all newspapers must subscribe in order to survive." [23]

Going Online

Newspaper companies began experimenting with non-print technologies in the 1980s, but the ventures were financially unsuccessful. With the advent of the World Wide Web in the 1990s, newspapers intensified their efforts to develop new, non-print products, using several strategies to try to attract readers/users and advertisers. These ventures incurred even bigger losses than the experiments in the '80s. But companies decided to stay with the ventures — viewing the costs as necessary investments for a shift into online distribution essential for the industry's long-term survival. [24]

The various electronic experiments depended first on the computerization of the newsroom: the shift from typewritten copy later set into type by composing room typographers to word-processed copy prepared by newsroom staff on computer screens. By the 1990s, computer terminals were ubiquitous. The technological change reduced labor costs and neutralized composing-room unions; in time, the change also would be seen as giving editorial staff more flexibility and control over the final product.

With content no longer bound to paper, the newspaper industry buzzed with excitement in the 1980s over ways to deliver the news electronically. [25] As Northwestern University's Boczkowski notes, the option that drew the most interest was videotext: transmittal of information stored in a computer database over telephone lines to a dedicated terminal, specially adapted television set or personal computer. The technology — developed by the British Post Office in the 1970s — got its first commercial application in the United States when the *Columbus* (Ohio) *Dispatch* began publishing an "electronic edition" in 1980 that provided access (at $5 per hour) to the

Dispatch and three other papers: *The New York Times, The Washington Post* and the *Los Angeles Times*. The two-year test was a bust. Boczkowski posits several reasons, including lack of original content and no critical mass of personal computer users. Whatever the reasons, the industry took the failed experiment as proof that electronic delivery posed no threat to established newspapers.

In 1979 Knight Ridder had started its own videotext experiment by creating a separate subsidiary in a joint venture with AT&T. The "Viewtron" service debuted in a field test in 1980, and a market trial began in 1983. By the end of the first year, the service — available through phone lines, not personal computers — had only 2,800 subscribers. Knight Ridder belatedly began offering it to the rapidly growing personal computer market, but not soon enough to salvage the experiment. It folded in 1986 after estimated losses of $50 million.

Other technical alternatives to print newspapers also failed in the 1980s. Teletext transmitted text and rudimentary graphics over television broadcast signals; viewers could then use special decoder equipment to view the content on their TV screens. Several newspapers tried but failed to make it into a profitable business. The *Chicago Sun Times* closed its three-year experiment in 1984 after concluding that cable TV subscribers would not pay extra for the service. Newspapers also experimented with simpler technologies: audiotext, which allowed phone users automated access to newspaper content, and fax delivery of specially customized "papers." But those experiments also proved commercially unsuccessful.

Despite the setbacks, the newspaper industry continued to be interested in electronic delivery and moved quickly to exploit opportunities with the exploding growth of the World Wide Web in the mid-1990s. [26] By 1999 all but two of the 100 largest U.S. dailies had online services. The online papers had their own staffs: 100 people at *The Washington Post's* Digital Ink as of 1997, 90 at *The Wall Street Journal's* Interactive Edition and 84 at USA Today Online. The online papers also had readers. The editor of *The New York Times* on the Web estimated 250,000 daily visitors to the site as of 1999, compared to the print newspaper's daily circulation of somewhat more than 1 million. One survey indicated that overall the proportion of people who read a newspaper online at least once a week increased from 4 percent in 1995 to 15-26 percent in 1998.

Online papers consisted primarily of "repurposed" content from the print editions — derisively called "shovelware." But newspapers quickly saw that they could do more on the Web than in print — and that they needed to do more to fully exploit the online editions' potential, editorially and financially. One strategy, Northwestern's Boczkowski says, was to "recombine" content — for example, putting together content on a specific subject, sometimes combined with e-mail reminders and updates. Newspaper morgues represented a mother lode of recombinable content, and newspapers quickly recognized that they could sell archived stories once the material was digitized.

A second strategy was (in Boczkowski's phrasing) to "re-create" content — that is, to develop content primarily or exclusively for online sites. He notes as one distinctive example the Web version of the *Philadelphia Inquirer's* "Blackhawk Down," which expanded the *Inquirer's* 30-part series on the 1993 battle between U.S. soldiers and Somalian rebels into a 30-part hypermedia package on Phillynews.com.

Despite the bustle and buzz, by the end of the 1990s the online ventures had failed to prove themselves as commercially viable. Several of the biggest newspaper chains reported eight-figure losses at an annual media conference in 1998: $35 million for Tribune Corporation, $23 million for Knight Ridder, $20 million for Times Mirror and $10 million to $15 million for the New York Times Co. At the next year's event, Alan Spoon, then president of the Washington Post Co., said the company expected to spend $100 million on online ventures despite previous losses. "This isn't the time for neatness in Internet models," he said. [27] ■

CURRENT SITUATION

Shrinking the Newsroom

The cartoon shows a roaring figure labeled "Accountants" in a King Kong-like pose holding a fistful of money as he appears to topple Chicago's landmark Tribune Tower, corporate headquarters of a newspaper chain now with 11 dailies.

The barbed image by Nick Anderson of Louisville's *Courier-Journal* is one of 100 satirical depictions posted on the Association of American Editorial Cartoonists' Web site in early December 2005 to protest the elimination of staff cartoonist positions at two of the Tribune Co.'s biggest newspapers, the *Los Angeles Times* and *Baltimore Sun*.

The cartoonists' "Black Ink Monday" did nothing to reverse the Tribune Co.'s cost-cutting moves, but the silent protest helped focus attention on two examples of an industrywide wave of cutbacks that eliminated an estimated 2,000 positions at newspapers around the country in 2005. [28]

In the year's biggest cut, the New York Times Co. announced on Sept. 20

Continued on p. 66

At Issue:

Is corporate ownership of newspapers hurting journalism?

yes

ROBERT W. MCCHESNEY
PRESIDENT, FREE PRESS
***CO-AUTHOR,* TRAGEDY & FARCE: HOW THE AMERICAN MEDIA SELL WARS, SPIN ELECTIONS, AND DESTROY DEMOCRACY**

WRITTEN FOR THE *CQ RESEARCHER*, JANUARY 2006

It is true that from the very beginning of our Republic, the press system has been commercial, in the hands of profit-seeking owners. But the Founders had no illusions that profit-driven journalism would produce the caliber of journalism necessary for the American constitutional experiment to succeed. Behind the leadership of Madison and Jefferson, the government instituted a series of massive public subsidies, in the form of printing contracts and reduced postal rates, to spawn a much more vibrant print culture than would have existed otherwise.

The great strength of private, profit-motivated control over the press has been its structural independence from the government. Its weakness has been a willingness to put commercial gain over public service. The system worked best in competitive markets, when it was relatively easy for people to start a viable, new newspaper if they were dissatisfied with the existing options.

This model collapsed by the end of the 19th century. Newspaper markets increasingly became monopolistic, virtually closing down the option of an individual, even a supremely wealthy individual, of successfully launching a new newspaper in an existing market. U.S. journalism increasingly was awash in profit-obsessed sensationalism and corruption, along with partisan, right-wing politics.

This crisis threatened the legitimacy of the industry and led to the emergence of professional journalism as the solution. Professional journalism has its strengths; it bans explicit corruption and demands factual accuracy while giving journalists some autonomy from the dictates of owners and advertisers. Its main weakness is the uncritical dependence upon "official sources" as the basis of political news.

The strengths of professional journalism have been undermined over the past generation as profit-driven corporate media giants have slashed resources for international, investigative and serious, local journalism. Instead, we have seen more coverage of trivial and salacious stories masquerading as news. Owners have little commercial incentive to challenge the politicians who control the lucrative subsidies and policies upon which they depend.

Regrettably, the Internet will not solve the attack on journalism. It requires more competitive markets with more diverse and local ownership; a commitment to a well-funded and heterogeneous nonprofit and non-commercial media sector; and thoughtful political solutions to the most fundamental of political problems.

no

DAVID DEMERS
ASSOCIATE PROFESSOR OF COMMUNICATION, EDWARD R. MURROW SCHOOL OF COMMUNICATION, WASHINGTON STATE UNIVERSITY

WRITTEN FOR THE *CQ RESEARCHER*, JANUARY 2006

Few journalists and scholars would dispute the notion that corporate newspapers wield a great deal of power and, like other bureaucratic institutions, sometimes misuse that power. However, the notion that the transition from the entrepreneurial to the corporate form of organization is destroying good journalism and democratic principles has several major flaws.

To begin with, most of the scholarly research simply fails to support it. Scores of studies have examined the impact of chain ownership or corporate structure on decision-making, editorial content, newsroom behaviors, allocation of resources and organizational values. These studies show that corporate newspapers are more profitable, primarily because they benefit from economies of scale.

But the empirical evidence strongly shows that corporate newspapers place less emphasis on profits as an organizational goal and more on product quality. Chain and corporate newspapers are more vigorous editorially. They produce content that is more critical of traditional or established political and economic power groups and elites.

My own national probability surveys support these findings and also show that editors and reporters at corporate newspapers have more autonomy from owners and supervisors.

So how could the critics be so wrong? They base their arguments on personal experiences or anecdotes, rather than probability surveys, comparative case studies, or historical/longitudinal research. Personal experience can be a valid method for understanding the world. But it can also mislead.

The critical perspective also fails to account for the role newspapers and other news media have played historically as facilitators of change. The critics assume that as a newspaper becomes more "corporatized," the more it promotes the interests of its owners and other corporate and business elites.

All media provide broad-based support for dominant institutions and values, to be sure. But the anti-change position is inconsistent with a large body of historical and empirical research.

During the last century, corporate news media have played a key (if sometimes late) role in promoting the goals of many social movements, including those seeking expansion of rights for women, minorities, the working class, environmentalists, homosexuals and the poor. Such changes certainly have not eliminated discrimination or injustice, but they have altered the power structure and that, in turn, helps explain why our country has a relatively high degree of political stability.

Continued from p. 64

that it was reducing its overall work force by 4 percent, or 500 jobs, including 45 positions in the *Times'* newsroom and another 35 editorial jobs at the *Times*-owned *Boston Globe*. On the same day, Knight Ridder's Philadelphia newspapers announced cutbacks that would trim the *Inquirer's* newsroom by 15 percent — or 75 positions — and the *Daily News'* by nearly 20 percent, or 25 positions.

Two days later, Knight Ridder's *San Jose Mercury News* followed suit with a 15 percent reduction in its newsroom work force from 330 to 280. The *Sun* and the Tribune-owned *Newsday*, the Long Island-based tabloid, had announced job cuts earlier in the year. Tribune Co. had cut some 600 publishing jobs in 2004, most outside the newsrooms. Among others, the *Los Angeles Times*, *Wall Street Journal* and *Washington Post* also had trimmed newsroom staffs in the previous few years.

The job cuts — envisioned coming from buyouts and attrition instead of layoffs — were blamed primarily on lagging advertising revenue. *The Times*, for example, said its ad revenue in August 2005 was 0.8 percent below the figure for August 2004. Analyst Morton says industrywide advertising revenue has been growing less than 3 percent per year compared to an historic annual growth rate around 5 percent.

The Internet is one big reason for the slump. Some classified advertising is being lost to free online services such as Craigslist.org. Commercial advertisers are also re-evaluating their newspaper ad budgets as consumers do more of their shopping online.

Courtesy WashingtonPost.com

Online newspapers like WashingtonPost.com typically include interactive features that allow readers to participate in ongoing dialogues with other readers, and perhaps reporters and editors as well.

Lagging circulation is also to blame. Among the 20 highest-circulation newspapers in the country, only *The New York Times* and the *Star-Ledger* of Newark, N.J., reported increases in the six months ending Sept. 30 compared to the same period the previous year. The *Inquirer's* circulation, for example, was down by 3 percent from the previous year, while the *Globe's* fell 8 percent.

Executives and industry officials generally minimize the importance of the job losses. In an Oct. 14 conference call to investors and analysts, Knight Ridder chairman and CEO Tony Ridder said both Philadelphia papers had been "overstaffed." "We're just bringing them into line," Ridder said. The local newspaper guild president disagreed. "We don't think the staff is too large," said Harry Holcomb, an *Inquirer* business reporter. [29]

"That's a cyclical matter that every industry has gone through in the past," says the NAA's Kimball. "Nobody writes a headline when people add jobs, it's only when they eliminate them."

"It's still in editors' hands what they're going to do," says ASNE President Rodriguez. "Editors don't have their hands tied. They have to make hard decisions and prioritize."

Morton says the cuts reflect Wall Street's emphasis on keeping earnings up, but he is not overly alarmed. "These are not horrible cuts," he said following the *Times'* and Philadelphia announcements. [30] Other industry watchers, however, are more concerned.

"What you've got is a gigantic negative-feedback circle here," says Esther Thorson, a journalism professor at the University of Missouri in Columbia. "You take resources out of the newsroom. As a result, quality goes down, and [then] circulation goes down, and you leave an opportunity for competitors to come into the market, leading to taking more resources out of the newsroom." [31]

Looking for Readers

Washington, D.C., commuters have a choice of any number of newspapers to read on their morning bus or subway ride. In addition to the long-dominant *Washington Post* and its conservative rival *The Washington Times*, commuters have easy access to the Washington edition of *The New York Times* or *The Wall Street Journal* — all available by home delivery or from newsboxes at most of the busiest bus stops and subway stations.

Nowadays, however, they can also read *Express*, a free tabloid published by the Post, edited with a 15-minute commute in mind and aggressively hawked at bus stops and subway stations since its debut in August 2003.

Free papers are one of the newspaper industry's desperate efforts to try to reverse or at least stem the decline in circulation now in its second decade. "It's a way of getting people into the newspaper habit," says Nesbitt of Northwestern's Readership Institute. But a study by a market research firm released in November 2005 raises questions whether giveaway papers are helping established newspapers with their main target: young people between age 18 and 34, most of whom are not daily print newspaper readers.

Free newspapers are not a new idea: many big cities have free, entertainment-oriented weekly newspapers that make their money from movie and music advertising and classifieds. The recently launched commuter and youth papers are different, however, in trying to provide a daily, general-subject-matter alternative to established, paid-circulation newspapers.

A Swedish firm, Metro International, pioneered the quick-read paper for commuters in several European cities before bringing the idea to Boston in January 2000 and Philadelphia a year later. The *Post* is one of several mainstream newspapers that responded by launching free tabloids themselves, both to protect their home turfs and to try to grow their own readership. [32]

Express is a tabloid-sized paper, usually around 24 pages, with wire-service copy and some staff-written articles but no stories written by regular *Post* reporters. Publisher Christopher Ma, a Post Co. vice president, said at its launch that *Express* was intended to complement, not compete with, the *Post*. "It's a way for the Post Co. to reach an audience that by virtue of lifestyle and time limitations finds it difficult to read newspapers frequently," Ma said. [33]

Chicago, Cincinnati, Dallas and New York are among the other cities with free tabloids from the same companies that publish paid-circulation dailies. In some cities, there are even rival free papers. In New York, the Tribune Co.'s *amNew York* competes with the Swedish firm's *Metro*. The Tribune's *RedEye* in Chicago prompted the *Sun Times* to launch the *Red Streak*, but it folded in December 2005.

Some newspapers are also giving away classified ads to try to hold readers. The *San Diego Union-Tribune* began in August 2005 to offer free, three-line classified ads for seven days to anyone offering to sell an automobile or merchandise for $5,000 or less. "In this day and age when newspapers are struggling for readership, offering free classifieds can be an enticement to read the paper," says industry analyst Morton. [34]

The Newspaper Association's Sturm says free papers are one of several ways for newspapers to hold and actually grow their audience despite declining circulation. "Readership has been fairly stable," says Sturm. "More people read newspapers than buy one. And newspapers have been adding audience by niche publications, ethnic publications, free publications and, in particular, online with newspaper Web sites."

A study by Scarborough Research, a market research firm, however, may dampen newspaper companies' hopes that the free tabloids are enticing non-readers into the newspaper habit. [35] The study, presented Oct. 26, 2005, at a symposium in Prague, Czech Republic, dispelled some publishers' concerns that the free tabloids are siphoning readers away from mainstream papers. But it suggested that most of the people reading the giveaway papers are already reading mainstream newspapers. In New York, for example, 78 percent of *amNew York* readers and 71 percent of *Metro* readers said they had also read one or more other newspapers on the previous day.

"Most free daily readers are strong newspapers readers — both free and paid," James Collins, senior vice president of information systems and custom analytics at Scarborough, said in a statement. "Rather than competing with their paid counterparts, free dailies are being used in a complementary fashion by most of their readers." ■

OUTLOOK

Going Private?

If going public is the problem for newspapers, perhaps going private is the solution. That at least is the suggestion of Douglas McCollam, a legal affairs journalist and contributing editor to *Columbia Journalism Review* (*CJR*).

Writing in *CJR's* January/February 2006 issue, McCollam suggests publicly traded newspaper companies should turn to private investors to avoid the adverse effects that he says result from Wall Street's focus on stock prices and short-term profits. [36] In corporate-finance jargon, a "leveraged buyout" would allow a company to borrow money from private investors in order to buy back all its stock from shareholders, he says.

In comparison to public shareholders, McCollam contends, private equity investors would be less focused on "the quarterly earnings treadmill." And even if some proved to be "every bit as rapacious as the most aggressive fund manager," they would still be better than "the lineup of bloodless managers and mandarins currently squeezing the life out of journalism."

Experienced industry analysts discount the likelihood of any widespread use of the tactic. "The reality of daily newspapers is what it is," says media consultant Brown. "They're not all going to be taken private any time soon." Indeed, McCollam acknowledges that newspaper executives such as New York Times Co. Chairman Arthur O. Sulzberger Jr. and the Washington Post Co.'s Graham say public ownership has benefited their companies.

In their study, professors Cranberg, Bezanson and Soloski proposed a series of corporate and legal reforms to encourage newspaper companies to put more emphasis on journalistic quality than on short-term profit. [37] They would, for example, require that journalistic quality be given a larger role in determining pay incentives for corporate managers and publishers and that it be the only factor in any incentives for editors. They would also require more detailed financial reporting by newspaper companies and reorient government policy to actively foster competition instead of simply protecting existing companies from competition.

Nearly five years after their book's publication, none of their proposals has been widely adopted.

Within the industry, the main question today is not corporate structure or governance but market strategy: how to reposition the print-producing newspaper companies of the 20th century in the increasingly online media environment of the 21st. *Sacramento Bee* Editor Rodriguez believes newspaper companies are up to the challenge.

"Five years from now, you'll see the newspaper industry is very much alive, very strong," he predicts. "You'll see that we've integrated online with print, that we are hiring different kinds of people with multimedia skills and that we're on television more promoting our product as well as doing more direct chats online.

"You'll see a real emphasis on watchdog journalism in which the main emphasis will be newspapers or the newspaper company looking out for readers," he says. "You'll see more participatory events, interactive events with readers, readers' opinions more prominently displaced on Web sites, newspapers acting as a guide to the Web site and more back and forth."

"You'll still see us in a state of confusion about the future of the newspaper industry," Rodriguez concedes in conclusion. "It won't shake out in five years. It's an evolution that will take place over a couple of generations."

No one denies that online is bound to become a more influential medium in the future and that the influence of mainstream newspaper companies is likely to diminish as a result. "They still have a lot going for them," says Northwestern University's Boczkowski. "But their relative importance has decreased dramatically, and I don't think there's any reasonable chance it will go back up in the foreseeable future."

"The big guy is still print. Online is the baby," Boczkowski concludes. "But in 10 to 15 years, it may be the reverse."

Newspaper Guild President Foley echoes management's insistence that newspapers remain the dominant news source, even online. "Where do people go for the news?" she asks rhetorically. "They don't go to Yahoo. They don't go to Google. They go to the newspaper sites."

But Foley also emphasizes that newspapers have to do better at getting revenue from their online products. "They are attracting the eyeballs," she says. "They just need to figure out how to make money out of having those eyeballs."

Former journalists Jones and Meyer are among those who say newspaper companies — and their shareholders — need to adjust their financial expectations downward. "If they can find a way to be satisfied with lower margins, newspapers can survive long enough to make the transition," Meyer says. Nothing in the stock market's recent behavior, however, suggests that investors are following the advice. As newspaper companies' bottom lines have sagged, stock prices have taken a licking.

Still, industry officials and experienced industry-watchers believe newspapers — the print products as well as the companies that produce them — are not about to go extinct. "The newspaper will be one of the instruments you will use to deliver news and information to your readers," says the University of Georgia's Fink. "A lot of Americans will have newsprint ink on their hands for a long time yet — not as many, but a lot."

"I am extremely confident that whatever the content is, it will be coming to the marketplace through the newspapers' brand," says the Newspaper Association's Kimball. "It may be distribution vehicles that we haven't even heard from, but they will be owned by the newspaper." ■

About the Author

Associate Editor **Kenneth Jost** graduated from Harvard College and Georgetown University Law Center. He is the author of the *Supreme Court Yearbook* and editor of *The Supreme Court from A to Z* (both *CQ Press*). He was a member of the *CQ Researcher* team that won the 2002 ABA Silver Gavel Award. His recent reports include "Death Penalty," "Right to Die" and "Supreme Court's Future."

Notes

1 Some background drawn from Joseph Menn, "Moment of Truth for Media Chief," *Los Angeles Times*, Dec. 25, 2005, p. C1; Joseph Menn

and James Rainey, "As Knight Ridder Goes, So May News Industry," *Los Angeles Times*, Nov. 8, 2005, p. C1. Sherman's letter was posted on *The Wall Street Journal's* Web site: www.wsj.com.

[2] Graham's prepared remarks to the Credit Suisse First Boston media conference on Dec. 6, 2005, are posted on the Washington Post Co.'s Web site (www.washpost.com). The quoted remark is from Jay DeFoore, "Print vs. Online Battle at 'Wash Post' with Froomkin in Middle," editorandpublisher.com, Dec. 12, 2005.

[3] See Julie Bosman, "Newspapers Offer a Case for Keeping Them Around," *The New York Times*, Dec. 8, 2005, p. C4; Jennifer Saba, "Goldman Sachs Thinks More Job Cuts on the Way," editorandpublisher.com, Dec. 13, 2005; Jennifer Saba, "Prudential Downgrades The New York Times Co.," editorandpublisher.com, Dec. 7, 2005.

[4] The Diane Rehm Show, "The Future of Newspapers," WAMU-FM, Jan. 3, 2005.

[5] Pablo J. Boczkowski, *Digitizing the News: Innovation in Online Newspapers* (2004), pp. 105-139.

[6] Quoted in Bosman, *op. cit.*

[7] Data from the study by Wolfram Peiser are cited in David T.Z. Mindich, *Tuned Out: Why Americans Under 40 Don't Follow the News* (2005), p. 28.

[8] For a concise history, see David Pearce Demers, *The Menace of the Corporate Newspaper: Fact or Fiction?* (1996), pp. 31-57. See also Michael Emery, Edwin Emery and Nancy L. Roberts, *The Press and America: An Interpretive History of the Mass Media* (9th ed.), 1999; Frank Luther Mott, *American Journalism: A History, 1690-1960* (3d. ed.), 1962.

[9] *Ibid.*, p. 108.

[10] Demers, *op. cit.*, p. 39.

[11] Emery & Emery, *op. cit.*, pp. 162-163 (new journalism), p. 192 (yellow journalism).

[12] See Demers, *op. cit.*, p. 47.

[13] See Mott, *op. cit.*, pp. 814-817.

[14] See Davis Merritt, *Knightfall: Knight Ridder and How the Erosion of Journalism Is Putting Democracy at Risk* (2004), pp. 28-45.

[15] Some background drawn from Gilbert Cranberg, Randall Bezanson and John Soloski, *Taking Stock: Journalism and the Publicly Traded Company* (2001). See also Demers, *op. cit.*, pp. 49-53. For additional background, see David Hatch, "Journalism Under Fire," *CQ Researcher*, Oct. 10, 2003, pp. 845-868.

[16] "The Source: Newspapers by the Numbers," Newspaper Association of America, 2005, p. 17. Mott notes that circulation did not keep pace with overall population growth in the 1940s and 1950s, but attributes the lag in part to the high birth rates of the Baby Boom decades. Circulation did slightly exceed the increase in adult population for those two decades, he says. See Mott, *op. cit.*, pp. 804-805.

[17] See Patrick G. Marshall, "Hard Times at the Nation's Newspapers," *Editorial Research Reports*, Aug. 24, 1990, p. 481; "The Source," *op. cit.*, p. 7; Merrill Brown, "Abandoning the News," *Carnegie Reporter*, spring 2005.

[18] Cranberg *et al.*, *op. cit.*, pp. 24-25. Cranberg is a professor emeritus, University of Iowa; Bezanson is a professor at the University of Iowa College of Law and Soloski, formerly at the University of Iowa, is now dean of the University of Georgia's Grady College of Journalism and Mass Communication.

[19] Cited in Demers, *op. cit.*, p. 50.

[20] For details, see Cranberg *et al.*, *op. cit.*, Appendix A (pp. 155-196).

[21] Quoted in Merritt, *op. cit.*, p. 56.

[22] Neil Hickey, "Money Lust: How Pressure for Profit is Perverting Journalism," *Columbia Journalism Review*, July/August 1998. For background, see Kathy Koch, "Journalism Under Fire," *CQ Researcher*, Dec. 25, 1998, pp. 1121-1144.

[23] Cranberg *et al.*, *op. cit.*, pp. 8, 10-11.

[24] Background drawn largely from Boczkowski, *op. cit.*

[25] *Ibid.*, pp. 20-32.

[26] *Ibid.*, pp. 51-55.

[27] Lucia Moses, "Newspapers, present and future: Good in 1999! Better in 2000?" *Editor & Publisher*, Dec. 11, 1999, p. 30, quoted in Boczkowski, *op. cit.*, p. 67.

[28] See Mark Fitzgerald, "The Shrinking Staff," *Editor & Publisher*, Dec. 1, 2005. For other overviews, see Katharine Q. Seelye, "Jobs Are Cut as Ads and Readers Move Online," *The New York Times*, Oct. 10, 2005, p. C1; Frank Ahrens, "N.Y. Times, Philadelphia Papers Plan Job Cuts," *The Washington Post*, Sept. 21, 2005, p. D1.

[29] Ridder was quoted in Jennifer Saba, "Philly in Hot Seat on KR Conference Call," editorandpublisher.com, Oct. 14, 2005; Holcomb was quoted in Jennifer Saba, "The Philadelphia Story: 'A Big Disruption,'" *Editor & Publisher*, Dec. 1, 2005.

[30] Quoted in Ahrens, *op. cit.*

[31] Quoted in Fitzgerald, *op. cit.*

[32] Some background drawn from Lucia Moses, "They're Young and Daily Growin'," *Editor & Publisher*, Nov. 3, 2003, p. 4.

[33] Quoted in Frank Ahrens, "Post Co. to Launch Free Tabloid," *The Washington Post*, July 11, 2003, p. E1.

[34] Morton's quote, originally given to the Union-Tribune, was repeated in "San Diego Union-Tribune to Offer Free Classifieds," editorandpublisher.com, Aug. 29, 2005.

[35] Jennifer Saba, "Study Suggests Free Papers Complement Paid Papers," editorandpublisher.com, Oct. 26, 2005.

[36] Douglas McCollam, "A Way Out? How Newspapers Might Escape Wall Street and Redeem Their Future," *Columbia Journalism Review*, January/February 2006, pp. 18-21.

[37] Cranberg, *et al.*, *op. cit.*, pp. 141-153.

FOR MORE INFORMATION

American Society of Newspaper Editors, 11690B Sunrise Valley Dr., Reston, VA 20191-1409; (703) 453-1122; www.asne.org. Membership organization for newspaper editors.

Newspaper Association of America, 1921 Gallows Road, Suite 600, Vienna, VA 22182-3900; (703) 902-1600; www.naa.org. The newspaper industry's principal trade association.

The Newspaper Guild, Communications Workers of America, 501 Third St., N.W., Suite 250, Washington, DC 20001; (202) 434-7177; www.newsguild.org. A labor union representing journalists and other media workers.

Project for Excellence in Journalism, 1850 K St., N.W., Suite 850, Washington, DC 20006; (202) 293-7394; www.journalism.org. A Columbia University Graduate School of Journalism initiative aimed at raising journalism standards.

Readership Institute, 301 Fisk Hall, Northwestern University, 1845 Sheridan Road, Evanston, IL 60208-2110; (847) 491-9900; www.readership.org. Conducts research for the newspaper industry on readership-building best practices.

Bibliography

Selected Sources

Books

Boczkowski, Pablo J., *Digitizing the News: Innovation in Online Newspapers*, The MIT Press, 2004.

Boczkowski, an associate professor at Northwestern University, recounts the newspaper industry's growing use of online media from the early and largely unsuccessful experiments in the 1980s through the proliferation of newspaper Web sites beginning in the mid-1990s. Includes notes, 27-page bibliography.

Cranberg, Gilbert, Randall Bezanson, and John Soloski, *Taking Stock: Journalism and the Publicly Traded Newspaper Company*, Iowa State University Press, 2001.

Three well-known professors provide, from a critical perspective, detailed information about ownership, control and "organizational behavior and dynamics" of publicly traded newspaper companies. Cranberg is professor emeritus of journalism, University of Iowa; Bezanson is a professor at the University of Iowa College of Law; and Soloski, formerly at the University of Iowa, is dean of the University of Georgia's Grady College of Journalism and Mass Communication.

Demers, David Pearce, *The Menace of the Corporate Newspaper: Fact or Fiction?* Iowa State University Press, 1996.

Demers, a professor at Washington State University's School of Communication, argues that the growth of corporate ownership of newspapers has been misunderstood and presents research indicating that corporate ownership has not reduced journalistic professionalism or independence. Includes detailed notes, 22-page bibliography.

Emery, Michael, Edwin Emery and Nancy L. Roberts, *The Press and America: An Interpretive History of the Mass Media* (9th ed.), Allyn and Bacon, 1999.

The most comprehensive single-volume history of journalism in the United States emphasizes editorial more than financial aspects in recounting the growth and development of newspapers from Colonial times to the present as well as the 20th-century development of radio and television. Includes detailed notes and a 73-page, chapter-by-chapter bibliography. Roberts, a professor of journalism and mass communication at the University of Minnesota, completed the most recent edition following the deaths of Michael Emery and his father Edwin, who were, respectively, professors at California State University, Northridge, and Minnesota.

Merritt, Davis, *Knightfall: Knight Ridder and How the Erosion of Newspaper Journalism Is Putting Democracy at Risk*, Amacom, 2005.

The longtime Knight Ridder journalist traces the history of the pre-merger Knight and Ridder newspaper chains and critically recounts what he views as an increasing emphasis on corporate profits at the expense of journalistic quality. Merritt had been a reporter or editor with Knight or Knight Ridder for more than 40 years, including 23 years as editor of the *Wichita Eagle*, before he was effectively eased out of that position in the early 1990s. Includes brief chapter notes; Knight Ridder Chief Executive Tony Ridder did not agree to an interview or provide other materials.

Meyer, Philip, *The Vanishing Newspaper: Saving Journalism in the Information Age*, University of Missouri Press, 2004.

Meyer, a longtime Knight Ridder journalist and now a professor of journalism at the University of North Carolina-Chapel Hill, describes the book as "an attempt to isolate and describe the factors that made journalism work as a business in the past and that might also make it work with the changing technologies of the present and future." Includes page notes.

Mindich, David T.Z., *Tuned Out: Why Americans Under 40 Don't Follow the News*, Oxford University Press, 2005.

Mindich, a former CNN editor and now chair of the journalism department at St. Michael's College, Colchester, Vt., argues that young people have "largely abandoned traditional news" but says they are "ready to interact with the news if [news media] just provide the right conditions for them to do so." Includes notes, nine-page bibliography.

Mott, Frank Luther, *American Journalism: A History: 1690-1960* (3d ed.), Macmillan, 1962.

Mott, a longtime professor at the University of Missouri before his death, published the first edition of his comprehensive history of American newspapers in 1940 and updated the work through the 1950s in the last edition. Includes page notes and section-by-section bibliographical notes.

Article

Menn, Joseph, "Moment of Truth for Media Chief," *Los Angeles Times*, Dec. 25, 2005, p. C1.

Menn gives a good overview of the tenure of Knight Ridder chairman and CEO Tony Ridder and the pending demand by the company's biggest institutional investor to put itself up for sale.

Reports and Studies

Brown, Merrill, "Abandoning the News," *Carnegie Reporter*, Vol. 3, No. 2 (spring 2005) (www.carnegie.org/reporter).

The veteran journalist and media-business consultant argues that to survive, news organizations need to work with bloggers and other independent citizens and journalists to develop new products that will be more engaging to readers, particularly young people.

The Next Step:

Additional Articles from Current Periodicals

Circulation

Ahrens, Frank, "NY Times, Philadelphia Papers Plan Job Cuts," *The Washington Post*, Sept. 21, 2005, p. D1.
The *New York Times* will cut 4 percent of its work force, and the *Philadelphia Inquirer* will reduce its staff by 15 percent in an attempt to offset decreased ad revenue and circulation.

Dotinga, Randy, "Amid Newsroom Layoffs, Hard Questions Arise About Future of Print Journalism," *The Christian Science Monitor*, Nov. 9, 2005, p. 2.
Journalism experts say improving the quality of articles is not the answer to the newspaper industry's recent problems.

Seelye, Katharine Q., "Newspaper Daily Circulation Down 2.6%," *The New York Times*, Nov. 8, 2005, p. C8.
Newspaper circulation fell 2.6 percent in the six-month period that ended in September — the largest decrease since 1991.

Smith, Adam, "The Rise of the Free Press," *Time International*, May 23, 2005, p. 44.
Free newspapers are flourishing throughout the world, becoming some of the most widely circulated newspapers.

"Study: Traditional News Media See No Growth in Audience," *The Houston Chronicle*, March 17, 2004, p. 10.
Online journalism and ethnic or alternative sources of news, such as Spanish newspapers, are the only forms of news media seeing audience growth.

Economics

Ahrens, Frank, "Wall Street Journal to Narrow Its Pages," *The Washington Post*, Oct. 12, 2005, p. D1.
High newsprint costs are forcing Dow Jones & Co., publisher of *The Wall Street Journal*, to reduce the size of the paper.

Fabrikant, Geraldine, "In a Big Bet on Newspapers, A Shy Investor Makes News," *The New York Times*, Dec. 8, 2005, p. C1.
Money manager Bruce S. Sherman is betting that the newspaper industry will survive the Internet onslaught and is pushing for the sale of Knight Ridder in order to boost his client's investments.

Mulligan, Thomas S., "Timing of Possible Sale May Work Against Knight Ridder," *Los Angeles Times*, Nov. 21, 2005, p. C1.
Chronic circulation and advertising declines facing major newspaper chains might hinder the sale of Knight Ridder Inc.

Online Newspapers

O'Brien, Timothy L., "The Newspaper of the Future," *The New York Times*, June 26, 2005, p. A1.
The Lawrence Journal-World, the newspaper of Lawrence, Kan., showcases important guidelines for the future of newspapers by offering a variety of services in its online version.

Seelye, Katharine Q., "Jobs Are Cut as Ads and Readers Move Online," *The New York Times*, Oct. 10, 2005, p. C1.
Pessimism about the newspaper industry's ability to overcome economic woes and the rapid expansion of the Internet continue to drive down the price of newspaper stocks.

Tedeschi, Bob, "Newspaper Ad Circulars Find Their Way Online," *The New York Times*, Oct. 31, 2005, p. C1.
Gannett, the nation's largest newspaper publisher, will displays banner ads on its newspaper Web sites that readers can expand into a virtual version of the weekly, local advertising circulars found in print newspapers.

Readership

Kirk, Jim, and H. Gregory Meyer, "RedEye, Red Streak Go Nose-to-Nose," *Chicago Tribune*, Oct. 31, 2002, p. 1.
As readership continues to decline, two Chicago newspapers are introducing tabloid editions aimed at younger readers.

Rainey, James, "Black and White and Read by Fewer," *Los Angeles Times*, Oct. 10, 2005, p. C1.
Many journalists are dispirited by the recent editorial-job cuts at major newspaper companies.

Samuelson, Robert J., "Demographics and the Marketplace," *The San Diego Union-Tribune*, April 18, 2002, p. B14.
The Wall Street Journal is being redesigned in order to connect with younger customers and women.

CITING *THE CQ RESEARCHER*

Sample formats for citing these reports in a bibliography include the ones listed below. Preferred styles and formats vary, so please check with your instructor or professor.

MLA STYLE

Jost, Kenneth. "Rethinking the Death Penalty." The CQ Researcher 16 Nov. 2001: 945-68.

APA STYLE

Jost, K. (2001, November 16). Rethinking the death penalty. *The CQ Researcher, 11*, 945-968.

CHICAGO STYLE

Jost, Kenneth. "Rethinking the Death Penalty." *CQ Researcher*, November 16, 2001, 945-968.

In-depth Reports on Issues in the News

Are you writing a paper?

Need backup for a debate?

Want to become an expert on an issue?

For 80 years, students have turned to the *CQ Researcher* for in-depth reporting on issues in the news. Reports on a full range of political and social issues are now available. Following is a selection of recent reports:

Civil Liberties
Right to Die, 5/05
Immigration Reform, 4/05
Gays on Campus, 10/04

Crime/Law
Death Penalty Controversies, 9/05
Domestic Violence, 1/06
Methaphetamines, 7/05
Identity Theft, 6/05
Marijuana Laws, 2/05
Supreme Court's Future, 1/05

Education
Academic Freedom, 10/05
No Child Left Behind, 5/05
Gender and Learning, 5/05

Energy/Transportation
SUV Debate, 5/03

Environment
Saving the Oceans, 11/05
Endangered Species Act, 6/05
Alternative Energy, 2/05

Health/Safety
Avian Flu Threat, 1/06
Birth-Control Debate, 6/05
Disaster Preparedness, 11/05
Domestic Violence, 1/06
Drug Safety, 3/05
Marijuana Laws, 2/05

International Affairs
Future of European Union, 10/05
War in Iraq, 10/05
Exporting Democracy, 4/05

Social Trends
Cosmetic Surgery, 4/05
Celebrity Culture, 3/05
Media Bias, 10/04

Terrorism/Defense
Re-examining 9/11, 6/04

Youth
Bullying, 2/05
Teen Driving, 1/05
Athletes and Drugs, 7/04

Upcoming Reports

Global Warming, 1/27/06
Rebuilding New Orleans, 2/3/06
Eating Disorders, 2/10/06
Pension Crisis, 2/17/06
Energy Conservation, 2/24/06
Presidential Power, 3/3/06

ACCESS

The CQ Researcher is available in print and online. For access, visit your library or www.thecqresearcher.com.

STAY CURRENT

To receive notice of upcoming *CQ Researcher* reports, or learn more about *CQ Researcher* products, subscribe to the free e-mail newsletters, *CQ Researcher Alert!* and *CQ Researcher News*: www.cqpress.com/newsletters.

PURCHASE

To purchase a *CQ Researcher* report in print or electronic format (PDF), visit www.cqpress.com or call 866-427-7737. Single reports start at $10. Bulk purchase discounts and electronic rights licensing are also available.

SUBSCRIBE

A full-service *CQ Researcher* print subscription—including 44 reports a year, monthly index updates, and a bound volume—is $688 for academic and public libraries, $667 for high school libraries, and $827 for media libraries. Add $25 for domestic postage.

The *CQ Researcher Online* offers a backfile from 1991 and a number of tools to simplify research. For pricing information, call 800-834-9020, ext. 1906, or e-mail librarysales@cqpress.com.

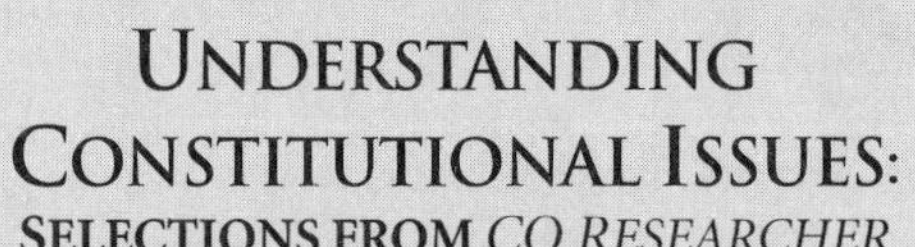

Understanding Constitutional Issues focuses on four key themes — governmental powers and structure, security, liberty, and equality — to help students develop a deeper understanding of the relation between current events and constitutional issues and principles. Integrating eighteen *CQ Researcher* reports, *Understanding Constitutional Issues* makes important connections clear, such as those between civil liberties and security; and privacy and liberty.

June 2004 • 8 1/2 x 11 • Approx. 432 pages • Paperback • ISBN 1-56802-885-7 • $39.95

To Order: Call Toll-Free: 866.4CQ.PRESS (427.7737)
Fax: 800.380.3810 • Web: www.cqpress.com
E-mail: customerservice@cqpress.com

CQ Press, 1255 22nd Street, NW, Suite 400 • Washington, DC 20037

CQ Researcher

Published by CQ Press, a division of Congressional Quarterly Inc.

thecqresearcher.com

Climate Change

Is tougher action needed to slow rising temperatures?

Scientists generally agree that the globe has warmed over the past 40 years, due largely to human activities that raise carbon-dioxide levels in the atmosphere. The Kyoto Protocol mandating limits on carbon emissions took effect in 2005, eight years after it was written. But the United States — the world's biggest carbon emitter — has not ratified the treaty. Debate over global warming has shifted from whether human activities are causing climate change to whether the possible changes will be severe enough to justify the hefty expense of developing cleaner-energy technologies. Economists and even some energy companies have recently proposed taxing carbon as an incentive to consumers and industry to shift to low-carbon fuels. Some multi-state coalitions also hope to issue tradable emissions permits to industry. Congress has begun to show some interest, but the Bush administration still argues strongly against any mandates to cut carbon-fuel use.

Dramatic evidence of global warming can be seen at Montana's Glacier National Park, where fewer than 30 of the original 150 glaciers remain, all greatly reduced in size.

INSIDE THIS REPORT

The CQ Researcher • Jan. 27, 2006 • www.thecqresearcher.com
Volume 16, Number 4 • Pages 73-96

CQ PRESS

RECIPIENT OF SOCIETY OF PROFESSIONAL JOURNALISTS AWARD FOR EXCELLENCE ◆ AMERICAN BAR ASSOCIATION SILVER GAVEL AWARD

CLIMATE CHANGE

THE ISSUES

BACKGROUND

CURRENT SITUATION

OUTLOOK

SIDEBARS AND GRAPHICS

FOR FURTHER RESEARCH

Cover: Dramatic evidence of global warming can be seen at Montana's Glacier National Park, where fewer than 30 of the original 150 glaciers remain, all greatly reduced in size. (National Park Service)

CQ Researcher

Jan. 27, 2006
Volume 16, Number 4

MANAGING EDITOR: Thomas J. Colin

ASSISTANT MANAGING EDITOR: Kathy Koch

ASSOCIATE EDITOR: Kenneth Jost

STAFF WRITERS: Marcia Clemmitt, Peter Katel, Pamela M. Prah

CONTRIBUTING WRITERS: Rachel Cox, Sarah Glazer, David Hosansky, Patrick Marshall, Tom Price

DESIGN/PRODUCTION EDITOR: Olu B. Davis

ASSISTANT EDITOR: Melissa J. Hipolit

CQ PRESS

A Division of Congressional Quarterly Inc.

SENIOR VICE PRESIDENT/PUBLISHER: John A. Jenkins

DIRECTOR, LIBRARY PUBLISHING: Kathryn C. Suárez

DIRECTOR, EDITORIAL OPERATIONS: Ann Davies

CONGRESSIONAL QUARTERLY INC.

CHAIRMAN: Paul C. Tash

VICE CHAIRMAN: Andrew P. Corty

PRESIDENT/EDITOR IN CHIEF: Robert W. Merry

CQ Researcher (ISSN 1056-2036) is printed on acid-free paper. Published weekly, except March 24, July 7, July 14, Aug. 4, Aug. 11, Nov. 24, Dec. 22 and Dec. 29, by CQ Press, a division of Congressional Quarterly Inc. Annual full-service subscriptions for institutions start at $667. For pricing, call 1-800-834-9020, ext. 1906. To purchase a *CQ Researcher* report in print or electronic format (PDF), visit www.cqpress.com or call 866-427-7737. Single reports start at $10. Bulk purchase discounts and electronic-rights licensing are also available. Periodicals postage paid at Washington, D.C., and additional mailing offices. POSTMASTER: Send address changes to *CQ Researcher*, 1255 22nd St., N.W., Suite 400, Washington, DC 20037.

Climate Change

By Marcia Clemmitt

The Issues

"I'm sitting up in Alaska where I can see that we are experiencing climate change," Sen. Lisa Murkowski, R-Alaska, told a Senate hearing last July. [1]

Indeed, said whale hunter Percy Nusunginya, ocean ice "used to be 20 to 30 feet thick, but now it is more like 10 feet." Like many of Murkowski's constituents, Nusunginya believes climate changes caused by global warming could be dangerous to his way of life. He fishes through pack-ice air holes 300 miles inside the Arctic Circle. "We are definitely warming up; the polar pack ice has all but gone." [2]

"Alaska is melting," agrees Richard A. Muller, a physics professor at the University of California at Berkeley, noting, "Even a small rise in average temperature is a looming catastrophe." [3] He recalls seeing "drunken trees" along the roadside — their shallow roots loosened in the softening soil — crazily leaning houses and meadows sunken three feet lower than the surrounding forest because the permafrost had melted. [4]

Getty Images/Anne-Christine Poujoulat

A heat wave throughout Europe last summer sends French bathers to the beach at Fos-sur-Mer, near Marseilles. Climate experts blame human-caused global warming for lethal summer temperatures in 2003 that killed 25,000 Europeans, including 15,000 in France.

Across the globe, evidence of global warming is piling up:

- The number of glaciers in Montana's Glacier National Park has dropped from 150 — when the park was created in 1910 — to fewer than 30 today, all greatly shrunken.
- The legendary snows of Tanzania's Mount Kilimanjaro have melted about 80 percent since 1912 and could be gone by 2020. [5]
- Rising sea levels are killing Bermuda's coastal mangrove forests.
- World ocean temperatures have risen by a net 0.11 degrees Fahrenheit over the past four decades.

The evidence shows that human-caused warming is causing rapid, hard-to-predict and potentially dangerous change, James Hurrell, director of the Climate and Global Dynamics Division at the National Center for Atmospheric Research, told the Senate Energy and Natural Resources Committee in July. Global temperatures today are more than 1 degree Fahrenheit warmer than at the beginning of the 20th century, he said, and the rates of increase were greatest in recent decades: Nine of the last 10 years are among the warmest since 1860. As ocean temperatures warmed, global sea levels rose about 4-6 inches during the 20th century, he added.

"The climate is changing, and the rate of change as projected exceeds anything seen in nature in the past 10,000 years," Hurrell said. And while specific changes in some regions "might be benign . . . global warming will be disruptive in many, many ways," potentially causing "drought, heat waves, wildland fires and flooding" in some local areas. [6]

Now, a year after the first international treaty on climate change — the Kyoto Protocol — took effect, the ground is shifting in the debate over global warming. Today, only a few skeptics say warming is not occurring — mostly due to increased atmospheric concentration of so-called greenhouse gases * (GHGs) like carbon dioxide, which is emitted during the burning of fossil fuels, and methane gas, from animals and other sources. [7]

"Greenhouse gas concentrations in the atmosphere are now higher than at any time in the last 750,000 years," Hurrell said.

But the climate change debate is far from over. Arguments now center not on whether human-induced global warming is occurring but whether it is enough of a threat to warrant spending money to stop it. The Bush administration and most Republican

* The concentration in the atmosphere of some gases, such as CO_2, water vapor and ozone, increases the atmosphere's tendency to trap heat, much like the glass in a greenhouse.

Impact of Climate Change Around the World

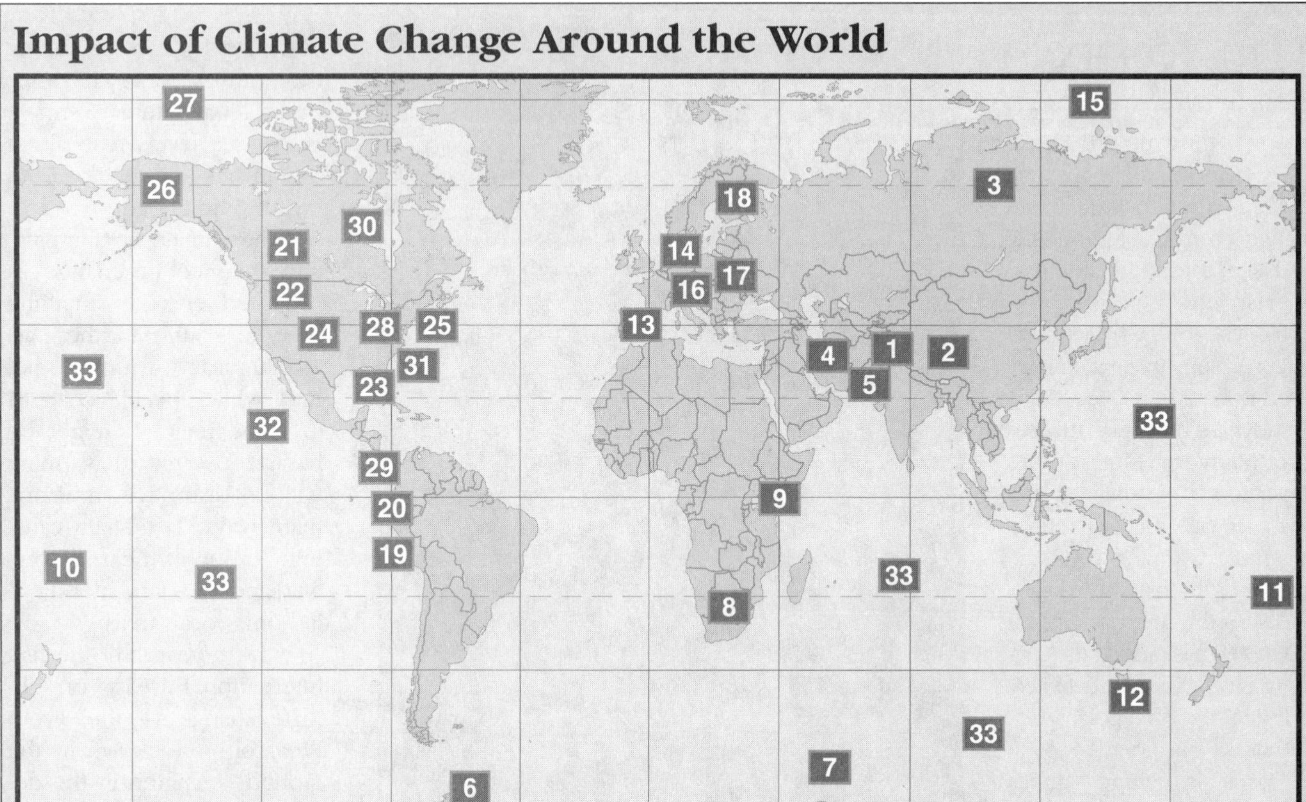

1. **Garhwal Himalayas, India:** Glaciers are retreating at record pace; scientists predict all central and eastern Himalayan glaciers will be lost by 2035.
2. **Tibet:** Ice-core records indicate the last decade has been the warmest in 1,000 years, with annual temperatures increasing 0.4 degrees F. per decade.
3. **Siberia:** Large amounts of tundra permafrost are melting, as much as eight inches per year in some regions.
4. **Iran:** Two years of extreme drought dried up 90 percent of the wetlands in 2001.
5. **Pakistan:** The longest drought on record — from 1999-2001 — affected 2.2 million people and 16 million livestock.
6. **Antarctic Peninsula:** Adelie penguin population dropped 33 percent over the past three decades as their winter ice habitat disappeared.
7. **Southern Ocean:** Waters around Antarctica rose 0.3 degrees F. between 1950-1980.

Source: Union of Concerned Scientists; www.climatehotmap.org

members of Congress say no. Even lawmakers like Murkowski say action isn't warranted unless scientists can prove beyond doubt that dangerous levels of warming — caused by human activity — will occur.

Meanwhile, like Alaska, many states eye global warming as potentially devastating. New Hampshire officials warn that climate change threatens the twin foundations of the state's lucrative tourist industry. A ski season shortened by 20 percent, for instance, could cost $84 million a year in lost tourism revenue. [8] And warmer temperatures also could decimate the maple-dominated forests that attract admirers of colorful fall foliage to the Northeast. [9]

Outside the United States there is widespread support for action, probably because the consequences of human-induced climate change seem more apparent. In Europe, for example, an extreme heat wave in 2003 killed more than 25,000 people — nearly 15,000 of them in France. In May 2002, southeastern India suffered that country's highest-ever one-week death toll from heat; temperatures rose to 120 degrees Fahrenheit, and more than 1,200 people died.

"We are . . . conducting a vast experiment in the composition of the Earth's atmosphere" by allowing emissions to rise, said British environmentalist George Marshall of the activist group Rising Tide. "We have no right . . . to

8. **Southern Africa:** The warmest and driest decade was recorded in 1985-1995.
9. **Mount Kilimanjaro, Tanzania:** Eighty-two percent of the ice has disappeared since 1912; scientists predict all will be gone by 2020.
10. **Fiji:** The average shoreline has been receding half a foot per year for the past 90 years.
11. **American and Western Samoa:** Both are experiencing land loss as ocean waters rise, with Western Samoa's shoreline receding 1.5 feet per year for the past 90 years.
12. **Heard Island (Australia):** Air temperature has risen while the glaciers have decreased in size.
13. **Spain:** Half of all glaciers present in 1980 are gone.
14. **Denmark and Germany:** October 2001 was the warmest October on record, with temperatures in Germany up to 7 degrees F. above average.
15. **Arctic Ocean:** Ice volume decreased by 40 percent compared to 20-40 years ago.
16. **Europe:** Many butterfly species shifted their ranges northward by 22-150 miles.
17. **Europe:** Spring events, such as flowering, have advanced by six days, and autumn events, such as leaf coloring, have been delayed by about five days.
18. **Turku, Finland:** The growing season has lengthened by 10 days over the last century.
19. **Andes Mountains, Peru:** The Qori Kalis glacier's retreat rate accelerated sevenfold between 1963-1995.
20. **Chiclayo, Peru:** Average minimum temperatures increased substantially throughout the country.
21. **Edmonton, Alberta, Canada:** Warmest summer on record occurred in 1998.
22. **Glasgow, Montana:** For the first time, temperatures remained above 0 degrees F in December (1997).
23. **Florida:** During a June heat wave in 1998, temperatures remained above 95 degrees F for 24 days in Melbourne.
24. **USA:** An autumn heat wave from mid-November to early December in 1998 broke or tied more than 700 daily-high temperature records.
25. **Chesapeake Bay:** Marsh and island losses are occurring as the sea level is rising at three times the historical rate.
26. **Interior Alaska:** Permafrost thawing is causing the ground to subside 16-33 feet in places.
27. **Arctic Ocean:** The area covered by sea ice decreased by 6 percent from 1978-1995.
28. **Washington, D.C.:** Cherry trees are blossoming earlier.
29. **Monteverde Cloud Forest, Costa Rica:** Warmer Pacific Ocean temperatures have caused a reduction in dry-season mists, causing the disappearances of 20 species of frogs and toads.
30. **Western Hudson Bay, Canada:** The early spring breakup of sea ice has disrupted polar bear hunting patterns, causing decreased weight among adults and a decline in birthrate since the early 1980s.
31. **Bermuda:** Rising sea level is causing salt water to inundate and kill coastal mangrove forests.
32. **Pacific Ocean, Mexico:** Coral reefs are under severe stress due to higher temperatures and other factors.
33. **World Oceans:** Temperatures have risen by a net 0.11 degrees F. over the past four decades.

argue to future generations . . . that we were waiting to achieve a full scientific understanding" before acting. [10]

But Stephen Milloy, an adjunct scholar at the libertarian Cato Institute in Washington, warns that the precautionary principle leading Europeans to try to avert climate change now could result in "regulation based on irrational fears." [11]

Such regulation could seriously damage the economy, say many GOP congressional leaders, arguing that the known risks do not justify the potential costs of requiring businesses to limit energy use.

"The United States Senate is standing on firmer ground than ever against mandatory reduction of carbon dioxide, which could effectively throw our nation into an economic depression," said Sen. James Inhofe, R-Okla., chairman of the Senate Environment and Public Works Committee. [12]

But as more scientists and citizens express concern about dangerous environmental changes, some Republican lawmakers have begun to waver. "I have come to accept that something is happening with the Earth's climate," Senate Energy Committee Chairman Pete Domenici, R-N.M., said last July. And while he wasn't sure yet what should be done, he promised to hold more hearings. [13]

Climate Change May Affect Public Health

The environment has long been known to play a big role in human health — from waterborne diseases like cholera to allergies caused by ragweed pollen. Now some researchers are blaming human-induced climate warming for killer European heat waves and even for increased incidence of malaria.

In response, many experts argue that public-health systems must prepare for new challenges. Planetary warming may stress already overburdened public-health systems, especially in developing countries. (*See graph, p. 79.*)

In some cities, air quality is particularly susceptible to warming, as evidenced by that fact that summer ozone pollution and stagnant air masses make it harder for people with asthma or cardiovascular disease to breathe, according to Harvard Medical School's Center for Health and the Global Environment. [1] The more severe drought and flood conditions predicted by some climate scientists could also mean widespread death and injury from worsened malnutrition, floods and landslides.

The range and severity of infectious diseases also may shift as climate alters.

The Harvard researchers say the range of malaria, one of the most disabling and widespread infectious diseases, already may be shifting and expanding due to climate change. Before the 1970s, for example, malaria did not afflict Africa's highlands. With warming, however, mountain glaciers have melted, and malaria-carrying mosquitoes have expanded their range into the mountains.

Conservative analysts, however, dispute the idea that malaria has only recently spread to non-tropical regions. Global-warming enthusiasts "made this up," says Myron Ebell, director of global warming and international environmental policy at the big-business-funded Competitive Enterprise Institute. "Even in the Little Ice Age, we had malaria and dengue fever [another mosquito-borne disease] in Washington, D.C., and Oslo [Norway]."

But that criticism misses the point, according to Jonathan Patz, an associate professor of environmental studies and population health at the University of Wisconsin-Madison. The malaria parasite does show up in temperate regions, Patz says, but it's not a problem because the disease's ability to spread is restricted in moderate climates.

Patz says the danger comes if malaria spreads into a region that has become warmer, which some scientists say may be already happening in Africa. In warm climates, malarial parasites can thrive, and the disease spreads easily, becoming difficult for medicine to halt.

"You can't just do one thing and make it go away," Patz says, so the spread into additional, warming regions would be a serious health threat.

"The lesson for the future is that we need to take a multipronged approach to the health effects of climate change," he continues. "Number one, we need a strong public-health infrastructure. There also must be an awareness that these longtime environmental pressures can make disease prevention even harder."

For example, if extreme weather events occur more often, as most climate-change models predict, floods that may have contaminated public water systems every 20 or 30 years in the past may become much more frequent. Then "there's a need to build that into public-health planning," says Patz. "This is where environmental policy becomes the same as public-health policy."

Putting environmental considerations back into the forefront of public health is in some ways a return to the past, Patz says. Before antibiotics and pesticides, "we used to be very environmentally oriented"" in medicine, concerned with sanitation and the spread of disease. "Medical schools used to have strong departments of vector ecology" — the study of organisms like mosquitoes that don't cause disease but carry disease-causing pathogens — "but these were dismantled."

That focus needs to come back, Patz says.

[1] "Climate Change Futures: Health, Ecological and Economic Dimensions," Center for Health and Global Environment, Harvard Medical School, www.climatechangefutures.org/pdf/CCF_Report_Final_10.27.pdf.

Even among those who urge action, however, there's little agreement on how best to reduce GHGs. Some economists recommend imposing "carbon taxes" to discourage excessive use of carbon-based fuels. Last May, New Zealand became the first country to impose such a tax, which is expected to add about 6 percent to household energy costs and 9 percent to business energy costs. [14] Also last spring Paul Anderson — CEO of Duke Energy, a Charlotte, N.C., power company — surprised many by vowing to lobby Congress for a similar tax.

Unlike some other incentives, a tax could reach all energy-consuming sectors, including motorists, Anderson said. It also would encourage everyone to conserve fuel, to make "low-carbon fuel choices" and encourage development of low-carbon technology, he said. [15]

However, conservatives and many business leaders adamantly oppose a carbon tax. It "makes people poorer and gives government too much revenue," says Marlo Lewis, a senior fellow at the pro-market Competitive Enterprise Institute (CEI).

Congress has not yet contemplated a carbon tax, but some lawmakers from both parties support capping GHGs. Since 2003, Sens. John McCain, R-Ariz., and Joseph I. Lieberman, D-Conn., have sought an emissions cap as well as establishment of a permit system allowing low emitters to sell their permits to high emitters. Last year, Sen. Jeff Bingaman, D-N.M., proposed another cap-and-trade plan that would limit the cost of extra permits, potentially making it less objectionable to business. Similar proposals in the House have not advanced.

In the absence of federal legislation, seven Mid-Atlantic and Northeastern states tentatively agreed to launch a regional cap-and-trade system for greenhouse gas emissions in 2009.

Meanwhile, by 2012, under the Kyoto Protocol, worldwide GHG emissions would be lowered to 5 percent below 1990 levels. The European Union (EU) implemented a regional cap-and-trade system to make it easier for high-emitting EU countries to comply.

But critics point out that even if all participating nations meet their initial Kyoto targets, global emissions will drop only minimally, not nearly enough to affect planetary temperature. The first round of cuts "doesn't even begin to address the problem," says Berkeley's Muller.

"Only a couple of nations" will meet their targets, says Patrick Michaels, a senior fellow at the Cato Institute.

Furthermore, the three nations considered key to substantial long-term reduction — China, India and the United States — are not part of Kyoto's first round. The United States, which emits an estimated 20 percent of all GHGs, has not ratified the protocol. Cutting U.S. emissions below 1990 levels on the required timetable would have been impossible, says Raymond Kopp, a senior fellow at Resources for the Future, a nonpartisan environmental research group. [16]

The U.S. economy and energy use have skyrocketed since 1990, so to reach the 1990 baseline the United States would have had to cut emissions 30 percent, Kopp says, adding, "There is no possible way the U.S. could agree to that target."

In summer 2005, the Bush administration — which acknowledges that human-caused global warming is occurring but opposes taxes and mandatory emissions limits — launched its own initiative, the Asia-Pacific Partnership on Clean Development and Climate. The group, which includes the United States, China, India, Japan,

Ethiopia Is Most 'Vulnerable' Nation

Ethiopia is considered as the country most vulnerable to the effects of global climate change. Vulnerable nations tend to be the least developed and characterized by weak governance systems, high poverty, poor access to water and sanitation and recent armed conflict. Ironically, such nations contribute least to climate change.

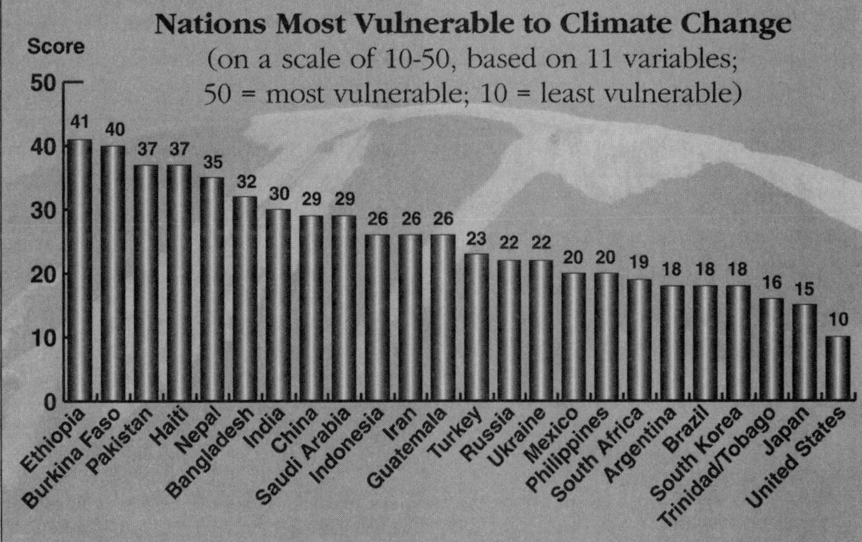

Source: Pew Center on Global Climate Change, "Climate Data: Insights and Observations," December 2004; Kilimanjaro photo by Jennifer Prophet

South Korea and Australia, will promote private-sector development and the distribution of clean-energy technologies. [17]

Meanwhile, rapidly developing nations like China and India specifically were exempted from the first round of Kyoto cuts. Yet the two huge countries are expected to add most to global emissions over the next century, as cars and electricity come to more of their 2-billion-plus populations. [18]

Despite deficiencies in Kyoto and the current cap-and-trade systems, they represent important first steps, Kyoto supporters say. Everybody understands that the emissions reductions that will be achieved under Kyoto's first round "are but a fraction of what we need," says Elliot Diringer, director of international strategies at the Pew Center on Global Climate Change. Nevertheless, the treaty establishes a legal framework for more significant future reductions, he says, and for "the countries that have accepted targets, it's driving them down the road" toward emissions cutbacks.

As economists, scientists and lawmakers weigh the risk of serious climate change against the cost of strategies that might avert it, here are some questions that are being debated:

Is the world at risk for dangerous climate change?

Climate-change skeptics once argued that the globe was not warming and that, even if it were, there was no proof that human activity had triggered the change. Now few hold such views. Instead, debate centers on whether the changes are likely to be dangerous to humans and the planet.

"The global mean temperature has been going up at a moderate pace from the 1970s, and we know that human

Top Greenhouse Gas Emitters

The United States, China and the 25-member European Union emit half of the world's CO_2 and other greenhouse gases (GHGs). Wealthier countries tend to have higher rates of consumption and more energy-intensive lifestyles, thus generating more emissions. Australia, the United States and Canada have some of the highest per-capita emissions. By contrast, the four largest developing countries — China, India, Indonesia and Brazil — account for 44 percent of Earth's population but only 24 percent of global emissions.

Country	Percent of world GHGs	Tons of carbon emissions per capita
United States	20.6%	6.6
China	14.8	1.1
European Union	14.0	2.8
Russia	5.7	3.6
India	5.5	0.5
Japan	4.0	2.9
Germany	2.9	3.2
Brazil	2.5	1.3
Canada	2.1	6.3
United Kingdom	2.0	3.1
Italy	1.6	2.5
South Korea	1.6	3.1
Ukraine	1.6	2.9
Mexico	1.5	1.4
France	1.5	2.3
Indonesia	1.5	0.7
Australia	1.4	6.8
Iran	1.3	1.9
South Africa	1.2	2.6
Spain	1.1	2.6

Source: Pew Center on Global Climate Change, "Climate Data: Insights and Observations," December 2004

activity is likely to contribute," says Myron Ebell, director of the climate change and international environment program at the Competitive Enterprise Institute. The pro-business group once argued strenuously that human activity was not causing warming.

Indeed, the planet's biodiversity has already been affected by the human-induced warming that has occurred to date, some scientists argue, pointing out that some stressed species have had to migrate closer to Earth's poles or further up mountains where it is cooler. Large-scale extinctions of such species are likely in the modern world where human development limits the ability of animals and plants to migrate.

Over the long term, failing to limit human contributions to global warming risks potentially catastrophic consequences for most countries, scientists told the Senate Energy and Natural Resources Committee last July. While modest warming will have "both positive and negative impacts," said Mario Molina, a professor of earth, atmosphere and planetary sciences at the Massachusetts Institute of Technology (MIT), above a certain threshold "the impacts turn strongly negative for most nations, people and biological systems."

Molina warned of "devastating impacts" on ecosystems and biodiversity, severe flooding in urban centers and island nations, "significantly more destructive and frequent" droughts and floods, seriously affected agricultural productivity, exacerbated disease and dislocated populations. [19]

But Lewis, at CEI, says, "There is really no scientific cause for alarm. Yes, there will be change, and, yes, it will have costs and benefits, but to describe it as a catastrophe in the making? No."

Computer climate models only predict extreme changes when they're fed "unrealistic data," Ebell says. For example, modelers often exaggerate how much GHG emissions will rise because they overestimate the future wealth and energy usage of developing nations, he says. "If you put totally implausible numbers into models, you get these scary results."

Richard Lindzen, a professor of meteorology at MIT, agrees that climate models that produce scary scenarios are clearly inaccurate. Currently, planetary temperatures have risen by only "one-third to one-sixth" as high as the models project, he writes, "So either the models are greatly overestimating the sensitivity of the climate to manmade GHG or the models are correct but some unknown process is canceling the warming." Thus, in arguing for climate alarmism, "we are choosing the second possibility" and assuming that whatever is canceling the warming "will soon cease." [20]

But Stephen Schneider, co-director of Stanford University's Center for Environmental Science and Policy, says Lindzen's argument confuses the planet's temperature in its early stages of responding to GHG-induced warming with the final temperature it will register once a new equilibrium is reached. For example, he says, if a small steel ball at 50 degrees Fahrenheit is dropped into a large bucket of 70-degree water, the ball and water eventually will reach an equilibrium temperature near 70 degrees. But if you measure the ball's temperature after only an hour, it might have warmed up to only 55 degrees. Expecting to observe the full warming effect of past emissions today "would be like expecting the ball to hit 70 degrees in the first second," Schneider argues.

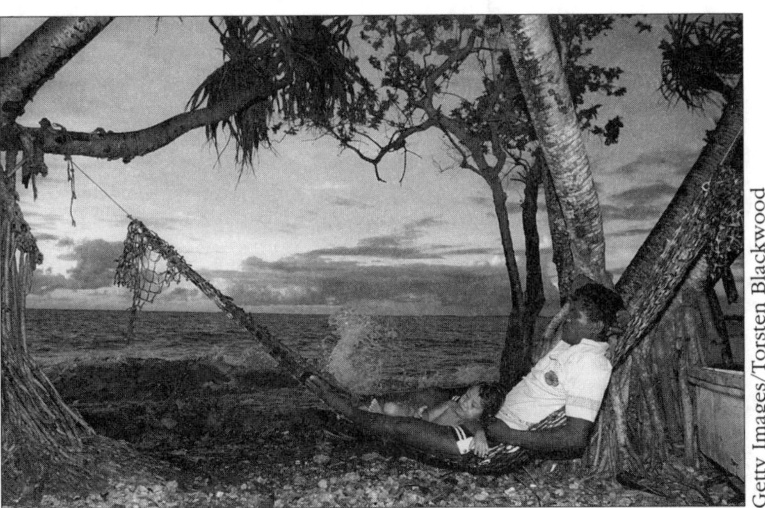

Getty Images/Torsten Blackwood

High tides breach a seawall on Tuvalu, in the South Pacific, in 2004. Islands and developing nations generally are most vulnerable to the effects of global climate change.

Evidence suggesting that dangerous warming is a real possibility — though not a certainty — has piled up in recent years as computer models have improved and satellite data have become available, Schneider says. "I got into this in 1970, and there were 10 papers worth reading. Now there are 1,000," he says.

His conclusion: Climate-change effects "may be either negligible or catastrophic," he says. But, he cautions, those who dispute that climate change could reach dangerous levels "totally rule out catastrophic" as a possibility, even though that's not justified by scientific findings.

Should the United States cap greenhouse gas (GHG) emissions?

Supporters of mandatory limits say slowing GHG emissions is like buying life insurance: It's a reasonable precaution that's worth the cost if a dire possibility turns out to be real.

Among academic economists, for example, "there is a 95 percent consensus" that, given the magnitude of the threat and the risk, "there should be action," says Professor Robert Stavins, of Harvard's John F. Kennedy School of Government.

But opponents argue that government regulation is an expensive burden that would cripple business' ability to develop new technology. "I don't see any plausible justification for turning the global economy upside down," says CEI's Lewis. "Kyoto-like policies are simply all cost for no benefit." Even if Kyoto countries meet their initial commitments, he says, the amount of warming that will occur by 2050 will be only slightly lower than it would have been otherwise.

Capping U.S. energy use in line with protocol requirements would cost between $67 billion and $400 billion, he says. "Is it worth spending that" to accomplish a "reduction that is probably too small for anybody to reliably detect?" he asks. Environmentalists "say that you shouldn't gamble with the only environment you have. But we shouldn't gamble with the only economy we have, either."

Many advocates of emissions limits say that the warming slowdown projected by 2050 under the Kyoto cuts is an important first step in a long-term process. And the costs over several years only amount to 0.5 to 3.5 percent of the nation's annual gross domestic product (GDP).[21]

Worldwide, the total cost of stabilizing atmospheric concentrations of carbon dioxide could run as high as $18 trillion, according to Schneider and environmental economist Christian Azar, of Sweden's Chalmers University of Technology. But that is only 3 to 5 percent of annual global GDP, they argue, which the global economy can absorb fairly easily. Since global income is likely to grow by 2 to 3 percent annually, they say, the total cost of stemming climate change "would be overtaken after a few years of income growth."[22]

Moreover, limiting emissions to avert warming is just like taking precautions to mitigate other potential problems, which most people do in their everyday lives, says Peter Wilcoxen, an economist who directs the Center for Environmental Policy and Administration at Syracuse University's Maxwell School. "I compare it to driving on a slippery, icy road," he says. "We don't know if we'll have a bad accident, a minor fender-bender or get down the road with no problem." But, usually, "if we don't have to drive, we don't. And if we do have to drive, we slow down. By analogy, that means we should reduce emissions" where it's relatively painless, such as using more insulation.

Fear that government will impose costly anti-pollution regulations and later discover that the threat was non-existent are overblown, says economist Frank Ackerman, director of research and policy programs at Tufts University's Global Development and Environment Institute. Europe has operated on the better-safe-than-sorry principle to impose environmental restrictions for decades, he says, and the United States did the same in the 1970s and '80s, with the Clean Air and Clean Water acts.

Since then, there has been almost no evidence that the regulation slowed growth or harmed businesses, says Ackerman, while most of the once-suspected threats — such as asbestos and lead — have turned out to be even more damaging than originally thought.

"Where are the big, expensive, false positives?" he asks. "Where did we spend ourselves into poverty mitigating a problem?"

Harvard's Stavins points out that the United States has significant experience with cap-and-trade policies, starting with local air-pollution permits in the '70s. Emissions limits had their biggest success in the 1980s, he says, when industry successfully removed lead from gasoline using tradable permits among refineries.

In fact, Stavins says, the cap-and-trade program used for lead is a good model for a GHG cap. That's because, as with lead, he explains, it's relatively easy to enforce CO_2 limits at the plants where fuel is produced, but next to impossible to monitor emissions from the millions of individual cars, businesses and homes that burn fossil fuels.

Should Congress enact a carbon tax?

Ask an economist, and you're likely to hear that a carbon tax is an ideal way to slow GHG emissions because it would discourage the use of carbon-intensive fuels. Taxes are simple, effective and multifunctional, they say. Conservative analysts and many business people, however, argue that a tax would only drain private-sector dollars from projects that could help humanity cope with global warming.

A carbon tax would encourage a shift from carbon-intensive fuels like coal while spreading its effects across several industries, says economist Gilbert Metcalf, of Tufts University, raising prices no more than about 4 percent. Meanwhile, he adds, it could produce "really significant revenue" at a time when the federal treasury is experiencing rising deficits. Metcalf estimates a carbon tax of about 10 cents extra on a gallon of gasoline could raise $40 billion a year in revenues.

No one knows exactly how much cutting GHG emissions would cost industry. In such a case, says Harvard's Stavins, economists usually prefer a tax to tradable permits because a company's costs are more predictable.

"With cap and trade, you can be surprised in a bad way," says Metcalf, noting that a limit imposed by lawmakers could turn out to be extremely expensive for industry.

Nevertheless, says Stavins, "politically, a tax is worse." Spurred by the tax, businesses would spend money to cut emissions but also pay taxes on what they failed to cut — a double whammy. Many economists argue that a carbon tax would encourage businesses to develop less carbon-intense technologies, but conservatives generally reject that argument.

"There's no evidence that by making energy more costly you can midwife the technological leap," says the CEI's Lewis. In Europe, where gasoline prices run as high as $7 a gallon — of which taxes make up an average 60 percent — "where is the great leap forward into the new future?" Europeans drive smaller cars and more diesels, but have not developed low-carbon technology, he says.

Instead, "if you want a technology revolution, you really need prosperity, capital," while a carbon tax would drain capital from the private sector, he says.

Kopp of Resources for the Future counters that, in fact, raising fuel prices has spurred market demand in Europe for hybrid cars, which run on a combination of gasoline and electric battery power. "As gas prices go up, the demand for hybrids is quite high," he says.

But Lewis says recent U.S. history hasn't backed up that idea. The gasoline price hikes of late 2005, haven't caused Americans to drive less, for example, he says.

In fact, retort advocates of emission controls, many Americans *are* buying hybrids.

Syracuse's Wilcoxen says people change their behaviors only if they believe a price change will last. For example, technological change did happen during the oil-price hikes of the 1970s, he points out. "U.S. energy consumption leveled off. We stabilized fossil-fuel consumption," he says. "People thought the price change was going to be permanent, so they started buying smaller cars and insulating their homes."

With both taxes and limits on GHG emissions having their drawbacks and detractors, a growing number of economists propose a "hybrid," or "safety-valve," system that incorporates elements from both.

To effectively control emissions, any "policy will have to be in effect longer than any other policy in the history of the world," says Wilcoxen. That's nearly impossible with either a pure tax or a pure cap-and-trade system, he says. "A huge constituency" would lobby to abolish the cap-and-trade policy every year because of its unpredictable costs, and political opposition to taxes is a given.

A hybrid plan would allow the government to impose caps, and then issue free permits to each company for the level of emissions it was allowed. But if cutting emissions to that level became too difficult, a company could buy a one-year permit from the government at a set, relatively low price, says Wilcoxen. Knowing the price of the extra permit in advance would make the system of caps as predictable as a tax and also bring in some revenue for the government, he says. ■

Continued on p. 84

Chronology

1800s-1910s

In the first stage of the Industrial Revolution, coal burning increases greenhouse gases (GHGs) like carbon dioxide in the atmosphere. Some scientists theorize GHGs are warming the planet.

1827
French scientist Jean-Baptiste Fourier hypothesizes that the atmosphere acts like a "greenhouse," keeping Earth warmer than it would be otherwise.

1896
Swedish scientist Svante Arrhenius speculates that carbon-dioxide buildup may warm the atmosphere.

1920s-1950s

The opening of oil fields in Texas and the Middle East in the 1920s accelerates fossil-fuel use. Scientists first report that the globe has been warming.

1931
Severe drought begins turning the Plains States into a Dust Bowl that lasts nearly a decade. Some scientists blame the greenhouse effect.

1957
U.S. scientist David Keeling begins continuous monitoring of atmospheric carbon-dioxide levels and finds them rising year after year.

1960s-1980s

Scientific conferences and Department of Energy researchers focus attention in the 1960s on climate change. Improved computer modeling and satellite data collection speed climate-science development.

1979
First World Climate Conference calls on governments to prevent potential human-caused changes to climate.

1985
Scientific conference in Villach, Austria, predicts that GHGs will cause the largest planetary temperature rise in human history during the first half of the 21st century, possibly raising sea levels by a meter.

1988
United Nations sets up Intergovernmental Panel on Climate Change to analyze new scientific findings.

1990s

The hottest years in recorded climate history occur; many nations push for international agreements to slow climate change.

1992
U.N. Framework Convention on Climate Change is signed in Rio de Janeiro, pledging nations to voluntarily reduce GHG emissions.

1994
Fearful of flooding, the Alliance of Small Island States asks for a 20 percent cut in global GHG emissions by 2005.

1996
At a meeting of Framework Convention members, U.S. delegates agree to press for legally binding emissions cuts.

1997
The resulting Kyoto Protocol calls for legally binding emissions cuts in industrialized countries, averaging 5.4 percent by 2010. U.S. Senate declares the United States will not ratify a treaty that doesn't require "meaningful" emissions cuts by developing nations.

2000s

Kyoto Protocol is ratified, committing countries to binding cuts in GHG emissions. . . . Industrialization accelerates in India and China, with the potential to push global GHG emissions higher.

2001
Reneging on a campaign pledge, President George W. Bush withdraws the United States from Kyoto Protocol talks.

August 2003
Severe heat wave kills thousands in Europe.

2004
One of the world's largest insurance companies, Swiss Re, estimates that within a few years climate-change damage will cost $150 billion annually. . . . Australian scientists develop a vaccine to reduce methane — a GHG — emitted by animals.

2005
Kyoto Protocol takes effect, following ratification by Russia in 2004. . . . New Zealand becomes first country to enact a carbon tax. . . . Seven Northeastern states form the Regional Greenhouse Gas Initiative to limit GHG emissions.

Jan. 11, 2006
First meeting of President Bush's Asia-Pacific Partnership on Clean Development and Climate is held.

Setting a Value on the Future

As concern about climate change grows, policymakers increasingly find themselves at odds over how to balance current priorities against future threats.

Frank Ackerman, an environmental economist at Tufts University, in Boston, says traditional economic analysis is the wrong approach. A traditional economic analysis might conclude that initiatives to limit future climate changes impose unacceptable costs and sacrifices on the current generation, says Ackerman. For example, cutting carbon emissions means people must drive their cars less now.

Traditionally, however, dollars spent to purchase future benefits are discounted by economists by a few percentage points for each year the benefit will be deferred, reducing their "present-value" worth, Ackerman explains. Such "discounting" makes sense when we're figuring out how much money we can afford each month, for example, on a mortgage. "But is the fate of the Earth something that should be treated the same way?" Ackerman asks.

He argues that instead of looking to economists for answers, legislators should come to grips with the fact that setting environmental policy "will be a political process, even though we don't want to admit it."

Making political value judgments about the future requires a brand of ethical analysis that differs from what most people are used to, says Stephen Gardiner, an assistant professor of philosophy at the University of Washington.

In ethical terms, the traditional economic method of "discounting" future benefits amounts to "taking advantage" of our position in time, says Gardiner. In other words, we enjoy the pleasures of our energy-intense technology, even though it may impose substantial costs — even "catastrophic costs" — on people who have the misfortune to live after us.

Crafting policy to protect future generations "is not completely new," says Gardiner. But for climate change, "the issue is on a bigger scale, and the lag time is very pronounced," so the actions we take today may not be evident for hundreds of years. That being the case, Gardiner doubts lawmakers will be willing to act aggressively.

Until that happens, he says, they will naturally find it "politically convenient not to deal with" climate change.

Conservative analysts have a different view of our responsibility toward the future, however. Taking government action today is likely to only cripple the future and rob private citizens of money they could use to adapt to climate change, says Myron Ebell, director of global warming and international environmental policy at the industry-funded Competitive Enterprise Institute.

Instead of draining off money to pay taxes or meet government-imposed energy regulations, lawmakers should take a hands-off approach that will allow wealth to develop. Wealth and technological knowledge and sophistication help people deal with environmental challenges, he says. "A wealthy Bangladesh could deal with a typhoon."

Meanwhile, support for more attention to climate change as an ethical and moral problem has been building in an unusual constituency. Some evangelical Christians, traditionally identified with conservative, anti-environmentalist views, are developing a policy on global warming that may call for curbing greenhouse gas (GHG) emissions. [1]

The Evangelical Environmental Network (EEN) says that "nearly 500 Christian leaders" have signed its Evangelical Declaration on the Care of Creation.

"Urgency is required" to address warming because "we're making long-term decisions now" that will affect GHG emissions for decades, the group says. [2] "Addressing global warming is a new way to love our neighbors. Poor children will be hurt the most, and it is their stories we must remember when thinking and praying about global warming."

The EEN urges leaders to be "good stewards of natural resources" and support "government policies to do the same." It applauds a non-binding Senate resolution passed in June 2005 that dubs the Bush administration's approach on climate change as "insufficient." [3]

---

[1] Mark Bixler, "Leaders Direct Clout at Global Warming," *Atlanta Journal-Constitution*, Dec. 27, 2005.

[2] Evangelical Environmental Network, "Global Warming Briefing for Evangelical Leaders," www.creationcare.org/responses/faq.php.

[3] *Ibid.*

Continued from p. 82

BACKGROUND

An Uncertain World

Making climate-change policy would be much easier if scientists could predict the timing — and precise causes — of Earth's future temperature changes. But the climate system is exquisitely complicated, and the most science can provide is a broad consensus on a range of possibilities.

As early as the 1890s scientists — including Svante Arrhenius of Sweden and P.C. Chamberlain of the United States — theorized that CO_2 buildup in the atmosphere might cause climate change. But climate science, which depends on complex computer models and hard-to-gather present and past data on temperature variation, is a developing science.

Among scientists, there is a general — though not a unanimous — consensus that global warming is real, says Berkeley's Muller. "The evidence that the Earth has been warming over the past 100 years is pretty solid."

But consensus on that last point has changed in recent years. A decade ago, most scientists believed global warming began around the early 1900s and was caused by a jump in carbon dioxide emissions due to human activities like cutting forests and burning fuels. Today, most scientists believe that human activity has only caused the warming that has occurred since 1960, Muller says.

For the European Union, that consensus has been enough for governments to justify imposing limits. In the United States, however, many lawmakers in Congress fear that government regulation will harm free markets. That fear — combined with growing worry that climate change also could damage the economy — spurs politicians to demand quantifiable answers from scientists before imposing mandates on businesses.

"We're looking for a little more certainty" before committing to a climate-change policy, Alaska's Sen. Murkowski said at the Senate Energy hearing in July.

For many lawmakers, government action is not justifiable unless the risks of harm definitively outweigh economic losses that might result from emissions limits, which, one way or another, would force Americans to consume less fossil energy. Only data definitively quantifying the impact of human-induced climate change could establish that. But climate models can't provide that certainty.

Top Models

A scientific model in climatology is a set of ideas — expressed as mathematical equations — about how climate responds to changing conditions, such as varying amounts of energy from the sun and changing proportions of atmospheric gases. Fed with data about past and current conditions and projected future events, such as changing levels of CO_2 emissions, a computer model predicts future climate scenarios.

Scientists cannot state such scenarios as definitive, however, because of what Stanford's Schneider describes as "a cascade of uncertainties" in developing both models and data.

Climate models are based on ideas about how the atmosphere works, derived in part from historical data about the way the climate has shifted through the ages. But, "there are problems aplenty," even in figuring out today's temperatures around the world, let alone comparing them to the past or attributing change to specific causes, Muller wrote. "An accurate thermometer didn't exist until the 1900s."

To determine temperatures in earlier times, scientists examine the widths of tree rings, the ratio of oxygen isotopes in glacial ice, variations in species of microscopic animals found in sediment and historical records of occurrences, such as harbor closures. But, such proxy measurements are also affected by elements of the weather, Muller adds, such as rainfall, cloud cover and storm patterns. "Most proxies are sensitive to local conditions, and extrapolating to global climate can be hazardous." [23]

Like the data, the models being used are also works in progress, Muller says. Climate science is developing "fairly rapidly," he says, but not as rapidly as the science of storm prediction, for example, which now gives meteorologists much more certainty about the projected paths of hurricanes. In climatology, "we're still groping for the simple principles that we can use to predict things," he says.

Gauging the probability of future scenarios requires accurate descriptions of physical processes, such as how clouds reflect heat, as well as other factors, like future population growth, economic development and energy technologies. The multitude of factors and the degree of uncertainty means that different climate analyses "will arrive at very different estimates of the probability of dangerous climate change in 2100," explains Schneider. [24]

"How should you look at emerging data? Well, you don't get all excited about a block of ice melting off Antarctica and think that we will all drown," says Schneider. But, he adds, neither should one dismiss the corroborating evidence that is emerging, mostly in the form of "fingerprints" — specific examples of climate change that one would expect if the planet were warming substantially and if human activity was driving the change.

For example, over the past several decades the stratosphere — between nine and 31 miles above Earth's surface — has cooled, while surface temperatures have warmed. This suggests that GHG emissions and not increased sunshine are responsible for the trend, says Schneider. But could it be an accident, or from some other cause? he asks. "No single, new study will prove or disprove warming," he says.

For more certainty, scientists have sought many such "fingerprints," and observations from many fields now tend to confirm human-caused warming, which might rise high enough to be dangerous, says Schneider.

For example, scientists have tallied how many bird species return north from the tropics earlier each spring and how many plants sprout earlier each growing season. Recent data show about 80 percent of bird and plant cycles are occurring earlier.

Taken individually, no study allows a clear conclusion about climate change. "But when you get a lot of data like this, it tells you that, in fact, the dice are loaded in favor of warming," says Schneider.

Still, much remains a mystery. Controversy rages, for example, over the role of South America's huge Amazon rainforest in climate change. In the past, the Amazon was able to soak up large amounts of carbon dioxide from the atmosphere, providing a brake on atmospheric GHG buildup. Today, however, some scientists argue that widespread deforestation has actually made the Amazon rainforest a net contributor to GHG emissions, as trees are burned and debris rots.

Modeling and assembling data "take a long time" and don't yield clear-cut answers, Schneider acknowledges. "I know that's very frustrating for politicians and the media."

According to Muller, those frustrations are hindering development of climatology by substituting political battles for unbiased, unhurried study. Currently, climatology is "so primitive in its achievement, yet so important, that the combination is disastrous," he says.

Traditionally, science has advanced when rigorous, self-critical thinkers follow facts where they lead. But, because of its potential environmental and economic impact, climate science has attracted some honorable but agenda-driven scientists — on both sides of the issue, Muller says. "I see many well-meaning scientists dropping their scientific training because they're trying to be helpful" by producing the definitive answers policymakers crave, he says.

In the long run, climate science will be better served if researchers "present results with caution, and insist on equivocating," according to Muller. "Leave it to the president and his advisers to make decisions based on uncertain conclusions." [25]

But some climate-change critics are more cynical about their scientific opponents' motives. Cato's Michaels, for example, contends some scientists tout scary climate dangers just to keep federal research funds flowing. "They perceive they aren't going to get any attention if they don't overstate the case," he says. They're afraid if they express uncertainties, "the $2.5 billion gravy train will grind to a halt."

The Odds

Many climate researchers find a strong probability that increasing GHG emissions will push average global temperatures up 3.6 to 5.4 degrees Fahrenheit * in the 21st century — and possibly even 9 degrees Fahrenheit or more.

For example, according to Thomas Wigley, a senior scientist at the U.S. National Center for Atmospheric Research, and Sarah Raper, of the United Kingdom's University of East Anglia, there's a 90 percent probability that Earth's surface temperature will rise between 3 and 8.8 degrees Fahrenheit by 2100. [26]

Similarly, researchers at the University of North Carolina and Massachusetts Institute of Technology say current models predict a 50 percent chance of mean surface temperatures rising by more than 4.3 degrees Fahrenheit by 2100, and a 97.5 percent chance that the increase will be less than 8.8 degrees. [27]

Temperature changes in those ranges would "very likely" cause more hot days and more heat waves on all continents, leading to increased heat-related deaths and serious illness among the elderly and the urban poor, according to a majority of the U.N.'s International Panel on Climate Change (IPCC).

Increased heat also could have a devastating impact on tourism in poor, tropical countries, making them too hot to visit. There is also a 90-percent-plus probability that many regions would see more intense precipitation, increasing floods, mudslides and avalanches. [28]

Worsening regional drought conditions are only slightly less likely, with a 67-90 percent probability that many continents will have drier summers. That could reduce crop yields — potentially triggering famine — and shrink drinking-water resources, Schneider notes. [29]

Many scientists agree on the IPCC's probability assessments. But even if the whole world agreed, policy decisions would still not be easy, observed a National Academy of Sciences panel in 2000. "The word 'safe' . . . depends on both viewpoint and value judgment" and "changes dramatically" if you live in a country "with sufficient resources for adaptation" or in a poor country or small island nation whose residents have few relocation options. [30]

Further complicating things, climate change is a more all-encompassing issue — both in space and time — than any that humanity has dealt with before. For one thing, GHG emissions anywhere affect climate-related events everywhere. "When you think of air pollution — that's many times simpler," says Kopp of Resources for the Future. Greenhouse gas emissions come from so many sources "that it's off the charts. It may look like problems that we've had in the past, but it's exquisitely [more] complicated."

Moreover, in addition to long lag times between changes in emissions levels and climate alteration, a turn from carbon-intensive to low-carbon technologies can't be done on a dime. "You have automobile fleets all over the world, and they have about a 10-to-15-year lifespan," Kopp says.

Voluntary vs. Mandatory

The 1992 U.N. Framework Convention on Climate Change (UNFCCC) was launched to stabilize GHG emissions at 1990 levels by 2000, mainly through voluntary GHG reductions by industrialized countries.

By March 1994, 50 nations had ratified the treaty, bringing it into full effect. The United States, which had ratified it in 1992, was among 189 countries that signed the agreement. Soon after the UNFCCC took effect, however, several countries began to doubt that emissions reductions could be accomplished voluntarily. In response, UNFCCC participants in December 1997 negotiated an amendment to the treaty, the Kyoto Protocol, calling for legally binding emissions cuts.

Kyoto was not the quick sell the UNFCCC had been. It did not go into effect until February 2005 — after enough countries (those producing at

* Or 2 to 3 degrees Celsius. Most scientific studies use Celsius.

least 55 percent of total emissions) ratified the agreement.

Although the United States was heavily involved in the long negotiation that produced the Kyoto accord in 1997, it has not ratified — and probably won't ratify — the agreement.

Meanwhile, many Kyoto signatories recognize a host of as-yet-unsolved problems with the treaty. These include continuing questions about how to get the private sector to alter the way it uses energy, how to involve developing nations without crippling their growing economies and whether affordable technologies can be developed to replace carbon-based fuels.

Europeans initially proposed a tax on GHG emissions — in order to persuade the private sector to change its ways. But U.S. businesses and many lawmakers adamantly opposed new taxes, and Europeans settled on a system that U.S. negotiators preferred — setting up a timetable for meeting national emissions targets. In recent years, however, U.S. lawmakers and the Bush administration have remained hostile to that approach as well.

In 1997, in response to the Clinton administration's participation in the Kyoto talks, the U.S. Senate rejected mandatory cuts when it approved, 95-0, the so-called Byrd-Hagel resolution. The non-binding resolution called on the United States to refuse mandatory cuts unless developing countries also were required to limit emissions, and backers demonstrated the limits would not harm the U.S. economy. [31]

Today, most Kyoto backers and critics agree the protocol is flawed, but supporters nonetheless praise it as an essential first step. "A sound international agreement" is vital on climate change because the issue has a serious "free-rider problem," says Harvard's Stavins. That is, if some countries cut emissions severely to avert warming — and incur the costs of doing so — other countries can benefit just as much, even if they keep emitting. Such problems require treaties and other legal means to push countries to participate against what may seem to be their own self-interest.

But Kyoto is "not a good structure, even if the U.S. were on board," Stavins argues. The treaty imposes targets that are "too little, too fast," mandating quite large cuts over the next five years but setting no long-term goals for the ensuing years. That's left too many countries worried that they won't meet initial targets, which has set off a new scramble to establish a long-term structure.

©worldviewofglobalwarming.org/Gary Braasch

Decreasing ice habitat on the Antarctic Peninsula over the past 30 years has caused the Adelie penguin population to drop by one-third.

Despite problems, the protocol is an important milestone, given the transborder nature of warming and other environmental matters, says Ackerman of Tufts. "Warts and all, it's the beginning of a process where the world tries to negotiate its way toward something."

New Technology

In the 18th and 19th centuries, the Industrial Revolution opened the way to human-triggered climate change. Mushrooming industries in Europe and North America burnt coal and, later, oil and gasoline, emitting GHGs into the atmosphere. Meanwhile, logging worldwide felled forests that had once soaked up carbon dioxide from the air. [32]

And if technology got us into the global-warming dilemma, technology will have to get us out, many climate experts say. "We are not going to solve the problem without new technologies," many of which already exist but aren't being used, says Pew's Diringer. Heavy use of fossil fuels, especially coal, is the problem, he says. Potential solutions include fossil-fuel alternatives, cleaner ways to burn fossil fuels and more efficient machines. [33]

But no technology will be adequate on its own, and all have costs and drawbacks, says Alan Nogee, director of the clean energy program at the Union of Concerned Scientists, which advocates strong steps to avert global warming. "There's no silver bullet."

A top priority is to develop cleaner ways to burn coal. Despite its high carbon content, many developed nations — including the United States and Australia — depend heavily on domestic coal deposits for electricity, as do China and many other developing nations. [34] The Energy Information Administration (EIA) estimates that by 2025 energy demand by developing nations — primarily China and India — will be more than twice the level in 2002. In fact, by 2025 demand for

Did 'Warming' Cause Recent Hurricanes?

The ferocity of Hurricane Katrina and the record-high number of hurricanes spawned in the North Atlantic in the last two hurricane seasons have dramatically focused public attention on the question of whether global warming — and the resulting warmer ocean temperatures — might be causing more and stronger hurricanes.

The debate stems from the belief that warmer ocean temperatures "fuel" hurricanes — both in frequency and intensity. However, as with all controversies related to climate change, bitter debate rages, even as the science slowly develops.

"Katrina has nothing to do with global warming. Nothing," financial analyst and American Enterprise Institute fellow James K. Glassman confidently declared online in *Capitalism Magazine*. "Giant hurricanes are rare, but they are not new." [1]

Hurricane analysts who "have been around a long time . . . don't think this is human-induced global warming," meteorologist and hurricane-science pioneer William Gray of Colorado State University's Tropical Meteorology Project told Glassman. "The people that say that it is are usually those that know very little about hurricanes." [2]

But hurricane scientists like Gray "don't know a lot about global climate," shot back Judith Curry, chair of Georgia Institute of Technology's School of Earth and Atmospheric Science. "Their conclusions are based on their investigation of North Atlantic hurricanes" only — which represent only about 10 percent of hurricanes, worldwide — and "the North Atlantic does not have anything to do with what goes on globally." [3]

However, scientists aren't sure whether ocean temperatures actually cause hurricanes to intensify or even whether there is a correlation between warmer ocean temperatures and hurricane strength. Many other factors, such as the El Niño global weather phenomenon, can cause more frequent hurricanes, say weather and climate scientists.

Scientists agree on a few points, however, including the fact that global warming isn't needed to account for recent storms. Before Katrina, three other storms of similar magnitude occurred before the 1970s — two in 1935 and one in 1969 — the period of most of the human-induced global warming that has occurred so far. [4]

Moreover, more than one known climate cycle affects the number and severity of hurricanes in the region, causing hurricane-heavy periods to alternate with periods of fewer severe storms. One heavy-storm cycle, driven by so-called El Niño Oscillations, began in 1995, and "every year since . . . has seen above-average hurricane activity, with one exception." [5]

But as scientists seek telltale "fingerprints" of climate change in weather cycles, some are turning up evidence of a correlation between recent storms and the slow planetary warming that's occurred over the past33 years, says the Pew Center on Global CLimate Change.

For example, as surface temperatures of tropical seas have risen in hurricane basins around the world since 1970, the frequency of very intense hurricanes has almost doubled, according to Curry and a colleague. [6]

Sea-surface temperatures are rising globally at the same time that atmospheric water vapor is increasing. That means that "the environment in which . . . hurricanes form is changing . . . in ways that provide more fuel for them," said Kevin Trenberth, head of climate analysis at the National Center for Atmospheric Research. A March 2004 hurricane in the South Atlantic off Brazil "was the first of its kind, and it's clear evidence that things are changing," Trenberth said. [7]

Are these correlations real? Do they indicate a long-term trend associated with global warming? No one knows for certain quite yet. However, "evidence . . . is starting to emerge of a human fingerprint in hurricane trends," concluded a recent cover story in the British magazine *New Scientist*. "It is not yet proof, but neither can it be ignored." [8]

---

[1] James K. Glassman, "Hurricane Katrina and Global Warming," *Capitalism Magazine*, Sept. 3, 2005, http://capmag.com.

[2] Quoted in James K. Glassman, "Hurricanes and Global Warming: Interview with Meteorologist Dr. William Gray," *Capitalism Magazine*, Sept. 12, 2005, http://capmag.com.

[3] Quoted in "The Evidence Linking Hurricanes and Climate Change: An Interview With Judith Curry," *Environmental Science & Technology Online News*, American Chemical Society, Oct. 20, 2005, http://pubs.acs.org.

[4] "Was Katrina's Power a Product of Global Warming?" Pew Center on Global Climate Change, www.pewclimate.org/.

[5] *Ibid.*

[6] Peter Webster *et al.*, "Changes in Tropical Cyclone Number, Duration, and Intensity in a Warming Environment," *Science*, Sept. 16, 2005, pp. 1844-1846.

[7] Quoted in "Hurricanes and Global Warming News Conference," Center for Health and Global Environment, Harvard Medical School, Oct. 21, 2004.

[8] Fred Pearce, "The Gathering Storm," *New Scientist*, Dec. 3, 2005, p. 36.

energy in the developing world will be 9 percent higher than in existing industrialized countries, and climbing, according to the EIA.

Two technologies that show promise are coal gasification — which breaks coal down into its component parts and separates out the carbon — and coal sequestration — which stores the separated carbon long-term in the ground or underwater. But much more research and investment are needed before either technology is adaptable and affordable. Other alternative energy sources, from windmills to nuclear plants, also have roles to play, but they are controversial: Conservative analysts and industry tout nuclear power while environmentalists want a larger role for renewables. [35]

"Clearly, renewables are not going to be an immediate solution," says University of Michigan Professor of political science Barry Rabe. "Solar costs are still pretty high." But there has been considerable progress in-

Continued on p. 90

At Issue:

Should the U.S. join an international treaty on climate change?

yes

SEN. JAMES JEFFORDS, I-VT.
RANKING MINORITY MEMBER, SENATE COMMITTEE ON ENVIRONMENT AND PUBLIC WORKS

FROM STATEMENT POSTED ON SEN. JEFFORDS' WEB SITE, DECEMBER 2005

One of the most important issues facing mankind is the problem of human-induced climate change. The broad consensus within the scientific community is that global warming has begun, is largely the result of human activity and is accelerating.

Global warming will result in more extreme weather, increased flooding and drought, disruption of agricultural and water systems, threats to human health and loss of sensitive species and ecosystems. We must take action now to minimize these effects, for our children, our grandchildren and future generations.

[In December 2005], 189 countries met in Montreal to discuss global climate change. . . . Members of my staff traveled to Montreal and met with representatives and negotiators from other countries. They witnessed firsthand how the Bush administration worked very hard to dissuade other countries from agreeing to even discuss further commitments. This is not the position that our nation should be taking. We should be leading the way on climate change, not burying our head in the sand. . . .

The overwhelming majority of Americans support taking some form of action on climate change. A recent poll found 73 percent of Americans believe the U.S. should participate in the Kyoto Treaty. . . . The study found that 83 percent of Americans favor "legislation requiring large companies to reduce greenhouse-gas emissions to 2000 levels by 2010 and to 1990 levels by 2020." The current administration is completely out of step with the American public on this issue.

I am both discouraged and heartened by the outcome of the talks in Montreal. Those of us who care about stopping climate change did everything we could to help aid these talks, and despite the Bush administration resistance, the international dialogue on climate change will continue.

But dialogue is not nearly enough, and the consequences of additional delay are dire. The U.S. has been and remains the largest emitter of greenhouse gases. It has a responsibility to its own people and to the people of the world to be a leader on this issue. Thus far, it has been anything but a leader, and these talks highlighted that fact.

I look forward to the day when I can once again be proud of the United States' role in these talks, when we can enter these negotiations having done our part. I believe that is what we agreed to in 1992, when the Senate ratified the climate treaty, and it is high time we live up to our obligation.

no

SEN. JAMES INHOFE, R-OKLA.
CHAIRMAN, SENATE COMMITTEE ON ENVIRONMENT AND PUBLIC WORKS

FROM STATEMENT DELIVERED IN SENATE, JAN. 4, 2005

As I said on the Senate floor on July 28, 2003, "much of the debate over global warming is predicated on fear, rather than science." I called the threat of catastrophic global warming the "greatest hoax ever perpetrated on the American people," a statement that, to put it mildly, was not viewed kindly by environmental extremists and their elitist organizations. I also pointed out, in a lengthy committee report, that those same environmental extremists exploit the issue for fundraising purposes, raking in millions of dollars.

Since my detailed climate change speech in 2003, the so-called skeptics continued to speak out. What they are saying, and what they are showing, is devastating to the alarmists. They have amassed additional scientific evidence convincingly refuting the alarmists' most cherished assumptions.

Let's ask some simple questions. Is global warming causing more extreme weather events of greater intensity, and is it causing sea levels to rise? The answer to both is an emphatic "No." The number of such disasters in Asia, and the deaths attributed to them, [have been] declining fairly sharply over the last 30 years.

Or let's take hurricanes. A team led by the National Oceanic and Atmospheric Administration's Dr. Christopher Landsea concluded that the relationship of global temperatures to the number of intense land-falling hurricanes is either non-existent or very weak.

What about sea-level rise? In a study published in *Global and Planetary Change*, Dr. Nils-Axel Morner of Sweden found "there is no fear of massive future flooding as claimed in most global warming scenarios."

What I have outlined today won't appear in *The New York Times*. Instead you'll read much about "consensus" and Kyoto and hand wringing by its editorial writers that unrestricted carbon-dioxide emissions from the United States are harming the planet. You'll read nothing, of course, about how Kyoto-like policies harm Americans, especially the poor and minorities, causing higher energy prices, reduced economic growth and fewer jobs.

After all, that is the real purpose behind Kyoto, as Margot Wallstrom, the European Union's environmental minister, said in a revealing moment of candor. To her, Kyoto is about "leveling the playing field" for businesses worldwide. In other words, we can't compete, so let's use a feel-good treaty, based on shoddy science, fear and alarmism — and which will have no perceptible impact on the environment — to restrict America's economic growth and prosperity. Unfortunately for Ms. Wallstrom and Kyoto's staunchest advocates, America was wise to her scheme, and it has rejected Kyoto and similar policies convincingly.

Continued from p. 88

corporating variable power sources like wind — which are produced in small, non-centralized facilities — into electric-transmission grids, Rabe says.

Conservatives in the United States, however, counter that renewables like wind have little future. "The wealthy, connected, liberal people of Nantucket will say, 'You're not putting a windmill in the middle of my [ocean] view,' " says Cato's Michaels.

But Rabe says states like Nebraska and Texas that have abundant, cheap land are already generating wind power.

Europe, Japan and even China and India are also embracing renewables, says Nogee. "We invented the technologies in their modern form," he says. "But the failure of the U.S. government to provide consistent support means most of the markets have shifted abroad, including the manufacturing capability and the jobs."

Europe has a high target for renewable energy in its electric supply — 21 percent by 2010. However, as of May 2005, the European Environment Agency notes that Europeans have made only slow progress toward that goal and in fact went backwards in one recent year — 2002. The EU will need "significant further growth" to meet the ambitious goal. Most EU countries still depend on hydropower to meet the renewables quota, and there is little further capacity for dam building. Denmark and Finland, which have strong government policies to promote renewable development, are ahead of the pack. [36]

Despite Europe's difficulties, however, most analysts still say that the EU is well ahead of the United States on renewable energy.

China also enacted "ambitious" renewable-energy requirements for power generation that went into effect in January 2006, according to the environmental group Worldwatch Institute. And India now has the world's fourth-largest wind power industry.

Nevertheless, renewable sources can't meet all of the world's energy needs, and nuclear power "obviously" must also be considered, despite worries over terrorism, Alexander Downer, Australia's minister of foreign affairs, told the six-nation Asia-Pacific Partnership on Clean Development and Climate on Jan. 11. Australia, which does not use nuclear, hopes to export nuclear fuel to China. [37] U.S. Energy Secretary Samuel Bodman warned that nuclear materials exports were vulnerable to theft by terrorists and called on China to agree to anti-terror safeguards so the plan could proceed. [38]

Some industry leaders in the United States would like to see more nuclear plants, says Rabe, but they make many states nervous. Even in Illinois, where nuclear already generates more than 40 percent of electrical power, "ask them which Chicago suburb wants" the next nuclear plant, Rabe quips.

Increasing energy efficiency is also expected to play a role in reducing greenhouse gases, but the private sector will undoubtedly need a push — such as tougher efficiency standards — says Duke Energy's Anderson.

"The only way to reduce emissions is to consume less fuel," said Anderson. "Yet U.S. government fuel-efficiency standards for cars haven't changed since 1990. And the average fuel efficiency for new cars and trucks fell from 22.1 miles per gallon in 1988 to 20.4 miles per gallon in 2001. We're heading in the wrong direction." [39] ■

CURRENT SITUATION

Kyoto Crash?

Following a December global warming summit in Montreal, countries participating in the Kyoto Protocol are assessing how to reach targets for reducing GHGs without cooperation from three of the world's biggest current and potential emitters: China, India and the United States.

After acknowledging that most countries won't be able to meet their initial Kyoto targets, "signatories started talking about post-2012 commitments," says Resources for the Future's Kopp. But he says ratifying nations feel pressured to commit themselves to completely unrealistic cuts in order to maintain the appearance of movement toward Kyoto's goals without cutbacks by the United States, the world's biggest CO_2 emitter.

The EU is talking about "draconian" cuts that would compensate — on paper anyway — for non-participation by the United States, he says. "But when it came to talking about what they really want to do, it didn't happen."

The meeting had been called to assess progress and plot future action. As in the negotiations leading to Kyoto, especially tense discussions centered on how the United States and China will participate in future agreements.

The U.S. delegation initially avoided participating in substantive conversations, says Kopp, but in the closing hours, "China signaled a willingness to get involved." That put pressure on the United States to offer at least minimal future involvement, but it promised only to participate in informal talks.

Nevertheless, says Kopp, "If the [EU] can move China, it may be able to move the U.S." However, China is an easier sell right now, he says, because it is investing in energy resources for rapid, anticipated growth.

Syracuse's Wilcoxen says the news that most signatories probably won't meet their initial Kyoto targets was not a big surprise. "A lot of countries signed and ratified [the treaty] knowing that it was lies," he says. "Japan had known for five years they couldn't meet the targets."

Committing to the Kyoto targets-and-timetables approach was "a well-intentioned mistake," Wilcoxen adds. He says other mechanisms — such as carbon taxes and fixed-price annual emissions permits for high emitters — would work better than the emissions caps set out by the treaty. He calls the Kyoto process "a horrible waste of time" that "set the whole process back 10 or 12 years because there's been all this arguing over what is fundamentally flawed anyway."

Meanwhile, Europe's emissions-trading mechanism for Kyoto may be damaging European trade while failing to hold down emissions, Kopp says. The EU has not found a way to cap transportation emissions, which "are out of control," he says. That puts most of the burden on industries important to international trade, such as the power and manufacturing sectors. EU politicians say they would be willing to accept that outcome, if they were protected from losing out on trade to non-participating countries like China and the United States.

"You can imagine the difficult position this puts the EU in," says Kopp.

Washington Wavers

Although the federal government is still largely on the climate-change sidelines, the Bush administration proposed an initiative in 2005, and interest is growing in the Senate. The House remains aloof, however.

"Congress is currently shifting," says the Pew Center's Diringer. Senators have twice rejected the McCain-Lieberman cap-and-trade proposal to slow GHG emissions. But in June 2005, a Senate majority expressed interest in considering — if not acting on — the problem. Fifty-three senators voted for the Senate Climate Change Resolution — a non-binding resolution "finding" that there is a scientific consensus that human-caused climate change is occurring, and that "mandatory steps will be required to slow" GHG emissions.

The vote was "a bellwether that would have been hard to conceive of a year earlier," Diringer says.

The Senate also has a new climate-change proposal to consider, alongside McCain-Lieberman. New Mexico Sen. Bingaman's proposal to cap GHG emissions for U.S. industries would ease the cost of additional emissions permits for companies that couldn't initially meet their mandatory cuts.

While some climate-change proposals have seen debates, votes and some hearings in the Senate over the past few years, similar proposals introduced in the House have languished, and House leaders with jurisdiction over energy and environment issues have expressed extreme skepticism about global warming. Last year, for example, Chairman Joe Barton, R-Texas, of the House Committee on Energy and Commerce, caused an outcry among scientists when he launched an inquiry into the work of several climate scientists whose data has been cited by the IPCC, suggesting that the international panel was unjustly biased toward belief in global warming.

For his part, President Bush's new Asia-Pacific Partnership will share ideas and promote private-sector development of clean energy technologies. [40]

It's not clear what initiatives the partnership will pursue because "there's no budget for it yet," says the CEI's Lewis. But, like other conservative analysts, Lewis says the organization has promise and will give the world "a place to go after Kyoto, which contains the seeds of its own destruction."

For the new group, says Lewis, the administration wanted to start with a handful of countries that are large emitters, because "when you are dealing with a small number of people, you can do something serious."

But skeptics like Diringer note that, unlike Kyoto, the partnership "doesn't commit anybody to anything," so legislators won't feel an obligation to fund the initiative. "They will only be given the funding level that you can squeeze out of Congress in a given year."

Four partnership members — China, India, Japan and South Korea — have ratified Kyoto, although only Japan is required to make significant emissions cuts under that treaty. Partners Australia and the United States are not Kyoto members.

Action in States

While Congress may be moving at glacial speed to mitigate global warming, states are moving "at the speed of light," says the University of Michigan's Rabe.

In 1999, when he first began speaking on state climate-change initiatives, an environmental economist told Rabe that, "No state acting rationally would ever do this," he recalls. "Now, I can't keep up with what is happening."

Worries about energy availability and the rising cost of natural gas are spurring states to conserve energy and utilize alternative fuel sources — moves that will also cut GHG emissions. For example, 21 states now have mandated "renewable portfolio standards" (RPS) — requiring a portion of electrical power to be generated from renewable sources. "A year ago it was 17," says Rabe.

States with renewable standards represent over half the U.S. population, and standards have been enacted on a bipartisan basis, Rabe says. In fact, 16 of the 21 governors who have approved renewable standards have been Republicans.

Some states perceive threats in climate change, while others see opportunities. Sparsely populated New Mexico and Nebraska, for example, see economic opportunities in developing wind and solar power on their vast, open spaces.

Even states with strong oil and coal industries, such as Pennsylvania and Illinois, are on the renewables bandwagon, says Rabe. And in oil-rich Texas, Republican Gov. Rick Perry in summer 2005 raised the state's renewable standard — first enacted under then-Gov. George W. Bush — to require that about 5 percent of power be generated from renewables by 2009 — and double that by 2025.

Several states are also establishing multi-state partnerships to cap and trade GHG emissions. In December 2005, seven Mid-Atlantic and Northeastern states tentatively agreed to launch the Regional Greenhouse Gas Initiative, allowing emitters in the region to buy and sell emissions permits after caps are put into effect in 2009. ■

OUTLOOK

Momentum Gathers

Both supporters and critics of the Kyoto Protocol are searching for better ways to cut emissions and involve developing countries. And, as debate shifts from whether human activity is causing climate change to how likely it is to be dangerous, the United States may be edging closer to action.

The Senate is still far from endorsing government action to stem climate change, and the Bush administration and the House remain adamantly opposed. "We're a long way from passing anything in Congress," says Ebell of the Competitive Enterprise Institute.

But some analysts see movement in the Senate. Sen. Bingaman's proposal to cap emissions while limiting the cost to industry "could have a vote in the Senate" in a year or two, says Kopp, of Resources for the Future. "And it could pass there, though it won't in the House."

For actual federal enactment of a global-warming plan, "we probably need a change of administration," says Kopp.

And Congress is highly unlikely to ratify Kyoto or any other international agreement on climate change anytime soon, says economist Wilcoxen of Syracuse University. "But it is within the realm of political possibility in the next five years," he says.

On the international scene, "a lot will happen in the next 24 months," Kopp says, particularly since China signaled interest at the Montreal meeting in getting involved.

Pew's Diringer hopes to see multiple, overlapping new protocols and organizations develop involving both Kyoto signatories and non-Kyoto countries working together to stem emissions, he says. For example, "you could have Kyoto and non-Kyoto countries" working together to disperse new technology, he suggests.

At present, though, the administration's Asia-Pacific Partnership remains a threat to new post-Kyoto international agreements, "because the administration's aim in part is to take the conversation outside the [U.N. framework]," Diringer says.

Unless more binding agreements happen, however, current Kyoto members will hesitate to commit to longer-term goals, Diringer warns.

"From a competitive [economic] standpoint, nobody can get involved [in Kyoto] without losing out," especially if others, such as the United States and China, don't go in, he says. Given the EU's current struggles, "it's very hard to imagine there'll be the political will to go further."

For that reason, says Kopp, future international climate talks will be a much bigger deal, with nations sending trade, transportation, energy and finance officials as well as environment ministers. Countries now realize "that you've got to have the other ministers in it too, because the environment ministers don't think of all the consequences."

Such a change might actually open up new possibilities, Kopp suggests. "That kind of multi-sector talk also gives you more policies to put on the table, so it might make it easier to make deals." ■

About the Author

Staff writer **Marcia Clemmitt** is a veteran social-policy reporter who previously served as editor in chief of *Medicine and Health*, a Washington industry newsletter, and staff writer for *The Scientist*. She has also been a high school math and physics teacher. She holds a liberal arts and sciences degree from St. John's College, Annapolis, and a master's degree in English from Georgetown University. Her recent reports include "Birth Control," "Academic Freedom" and "Saving the Oceans."

Notes

[1] Quoted in "Senate Energy and Natural Resources Committee Holds Hearing on Climate Change," transcript, Congressional Quarterly, July 21, 2005, www.cq.com.

[2] Quoted in Kate Bissell, "Alaskan People Tell of Climate Change," Aug. 8, 2005, www.newsvote,bbc,co.uk.

[3] Richard A. Muller, "Alaska is Melting: Can Kyoto Save It?" *Technology Review On Line*, April 16, 2004.

[4] *Ibid.*

[5] "Fast Facts on Global Warming," National Geographic," http://news.nationalgeographic.com.

[6] Quoted in Senate Energy and Natural Resources Committee, *op. cit.*

[7] For background, see Mary H. Cooper, "Global Warming Treaty," *CQ Researcher*, Jan. 26, 2001, pp. 41-64.

[8] "Potential Climate Change Impacts in New Hampshire," Office of Planning, City of Keene, www.ci.keene.nh.us.

[9] Climate Change and New Hampshire, Office of Policy, Planning and Evaluation, U.S. Environmental Protection Agency.

[10] Quote in "Truth Will Out; Global Warming Is Caused By Human Activity," British Broadcasting Corporation, www.open2.net.

[11] Stephen Milloy, "U.S. Should Not Import European Laws," *Junk Science*, Nov. 12, 2005, www.foxnews.com.

[12] Quoted in David Mildenberg, "Duke CEO Not Finding Favor on His Call for a Carbon Tax," *Charlotte* [North Carolina] *Business Journal*, May 9, 2005.

[13] Quoted in Senate Energy and Natural Resources Committee, *ibid.*

[14] John Vidal, "New Zealand First To Levy Carbon Tax," *The Guardian*, May 5, 2005.

[15] Quoted in "Paul Anderson, CEO of Duke Energy," *Sunday Sunrise Transcript*, March 13, 2005, http://seven.com.au/sundaysunrise/transcripts/19440.

[16] For background on China, see Peter Katel, "Emerging China," *CQ Researcher*, Nov. 11, 2005, pp. 957-980.

[17] Fact Sheet: President Bush and the Asia-Pacific Partnership on Clean Development, The White House, July 27, 2005, www.state.gov/g/oes/rls/fs/50314.htm.

[18] For background, see Peter Katel, "Emerging China," *CQ Researcher*, Nov. 11, 2005, pp. 957-980, and David Masci, "Emerging Inda," *CQ Researcher*, April 19, 2002, pp. 329-360.

[19] Quoted in Senate Energy and Natural Resources Committee, *op. cit.*

[20] Richard Lindzen, "Is There a Basis for Global Warming Alarm?" presentation at the Yale Center for the Study of Globalization, Oct. 21, 2005.

[21] *World Factbook*, "U.S. Central Intelligence Agency," www.cia.gov/cia/publications/factbook/geos/us.hrml.

[22] Christian Azar and Stephen Schneider, "Are the Economic Costs of Stabilizing the Atmosphere Prohibitive?" *Ecological Economics*, February 2002.

[23] Richard A. Muller, "Medieval Global Warming: The Peril of Letting Politics Shape the Scientific Debate," *Technology Review*, Dec. 17, 2003.

[24] Stephen Schneider, *Climate Change*, http://stephenschneider.stanford.edu/Climate/ClimateFrameset.html.

[25] Muller, *op. cit.*

[26] Quoted in "Communicating Uncertainty in the Science of Climate Change," International Center for Technology Assessment, www.icta.org/doc/Uncertainty%20in%20science-9-04.pdf.

[27] *Ibid.*

[28] Schneider, *op. cit.* For the original source, see "Climate Change 2001: Impacts, Adaptation, and Vulnerability," Intergovernmental Panel on Climate Change, 2001, www.grida.no/climate/ipcc_tar/wg2/009.htm#tabspm1.

[29] *Ibid.*

[30] *Climate Change Science: An Analysis of Some Key Questions*, National Academy of Sciences, 2000, p. 18.

[31] www.nationalcenter.org/KyotoSenate.html.

[32] For background, see Spencer Weart, *The Discovery of Global Warming*, June 2005, www.aip.org/history/climate/; and Mary H. Cooper, "Global Warming," *CQ Researcher*, Nov. 1, 1996, pp. 961-984.

[33] For background, see Mary H. Cooper, "Alternative Fuels," *CQ Researcher*, Feb. 25, 2005, pp. 173-196.

[34] Katel, *op. cit.*

[35] For background, see Jennifer Weeks, "Domestic Energy Development," *CQ Researcher*, Sept. 30, 2005, pp. 809-832.

[36] "Renewable Energy Consumption: May 2005 Assessment," European Environment Agency, themes.eea.eu.int/IMS/ISpecs/ISpecification20041007132201/IAssessment111650 4213343/view_content.

[37] Stephanie Peating, "Nuclear Question Looms Large at Climate Change Talks," *Sydney* [Australia] *Morning Herald*, Jan. 12, 2006.

[38] *Ibid.*

[39] Paul Anderson, "Taking Responsibility," address delivered at a *Charlotte Business Journal* industry breakfast, April 7, 2005.

[40] Fact sheet, "President Bush and the Asia-Pacific Partnership on Clean Development," The White House, July 27, 2005, www.state.gov/g/oes/rls/fs/50314.htm.

FOR MORE INFORMATION

Center for Health and the Global Environment, Harvard Medical School. 401 Park Dr., Boston, MA 02215; (617) 384-8530; http://chge.med.harvard.edu/. Researches the health implications of climate change.

Climate Change, http://stephenschneider.stanford.edu/. The Web site of Stanford climatologist Stephen Schneider, a believer in human-induced warming.

The Discovery of Global Warming, www.aip.org/history/climate/. A detailed history of climate-change science.

Energy Information Administration, 1000 Independence Ave., S.W., Washington, DC 20585; (202) 586-8800; www.eia.doe.gov/. Official government source for statistics on energy use.

Intergovernmental Panel on Climate Change, www.ipcc.ch/about/about.htm. Organization formed by the United Nations and the World Meteorological Organization.

National Climatic Data Center, 151 Patton Ave., Asheville, NC 28801-5001; (828) 271-4800; www.ncdc.noaa.gov/oa/about/ncdccontacts.html. Government agency that collects historical and current climate data.

Pew Center on Climate Change, 2101 Wilson Blvd., Suite 550, Arlington, VA 22201; (703) 516-4146; www.pewclimate.org. Nonprofit organization that issues information and promotes discussion by policymakers on the science, economics and policy of climate change.

RealClimate.org. www.realclimate.org. Climate scientists provide responses to emerging data and opinion regarding global warming.

Resources for the Future, 1616 P St., N.W., Washington, DC 20036; (202) 328-5000; www.rff.org. A nonpartisan think tank that conducts research on global warming and other environmental issues.

Still Waiting for Greenhouse, www.john-daly.com/. Web site founded by the late Australian global-warming skeptic John Daly.

World Climate Report, www.worldclimatereport.org. Analysis of new data and opinion on climate change, from the point of view of global-warming skeptics.

Bibliography

Selected Sources

Books

Cox, John D., *Climate Crash: Abrupt Climate Change and What it Means for Our Future*, Joseph Henry Press, 2005.

A science journalist explains how scientists discovered that very abrupt and extreme climate changes have occurred throughout Earth's history. He describes the uncertainties that surround the fundamental question: Could human greenhouse gas emissions help trigger an abrupt, catastrophic climate event?

Houghton, John, *Global Warming: The Complete Briefing*, Cambridge University Press, 2004.

A co-chair of the Scientific Assessment Working Group of the U.N.'s Intergovernmental Panel on Climate Change gives a full account of the scientific and ethical dimensions of global warming. The book provides references to the original scientific sources and pays special attention to how energy use relates to climate change.

Maslin, Mark, *Global Warming: A Very Short Introduction*, Oxford University Press, 2005.

One of a series of general introductions to current topics, the book summarizes the current debate over warming, focusing mainly on findings of the Intergovernmental Panel on Climate Change. Maslin is an associate professor at the University of London's Environmental Change Research Center.

Michaels, Patrick J., *Meltdown: The Predictable Distortion of Global Warming by Scientists, Politicians, and the Media*, Cato Institute, 2004.

A climatologist at the University of Virginia and senior fellow at the libertarian Cato Institute argues that global warming has been hyped by scientists, advocates and journalists with vested interests in overstating research findings and the need for policy responses.

Tennesen, Michael, *Complete Idiot's Guide to Global Warming*, Alpha Books, 2004.

A science journalist provides a primer on the basic scientific and policy concepts in the climate-change debate.

Victor, David G., *Climate Change: Debating America's Policy Options*, Council on Foreign Relations Press, 2004.

An associate professor of political science at Stanford University lays out arguments for three possible U.S. policy options on climate change — relying on wealthy nations' ability to adapt to change; reinvigorating the Kyoto Protocol; and establishing a worldwide market for low-carbon technologies.

Weart, Spencer, *The Discovery of Global Warming*, Harvard University Press, 2004.

A historian of science recounts the long process through which scientists discovered and explored human-induced climate change, beginning in the late 19th century. Written for the general reader, the book describes the enabling technologies, blind alleys, uncertainties and disagreements found along the way. Weart updates and augments the book with much more detail on his Web site: www.aip.org/history/climate/.

Articles

Gardiner, Stephen M., "The Global Warming Tragedy and the Dangerous Illusion of the Kyoto Protocol," *Ethics and International Affairs*, 2004.

An assistant professor of philosophy at the University of Washington outlines ethics issues involved in setting policy on global warming.

Pearce, Fred, "The Gathering Storm," *New Scientist*, Dec. 3, 2005, p. 36.

A science journalist explains and updates the scientific controversy over global warming and hurricanes.

Reports and Studies

The Center for Health and the Global Environment, "Climate Change Futures: Health, Ecological and Economic Dimensions," Harvard Medical School, November 2005.

Public-health analysts who believe that climate change may be dangerous describe its potential health-related consequences.

International Climate Change Taskforce, "Meeting the Climate Challenge," January 2005; www.tai.org.au/Publications_Files/Papers&Sub_Files/Meeting%20the%20Climate%20Challenge%20FV.pdf.

Policy experts assembled by think tanks in the United States, United Kingdom and Australia make recommendations for government actions to reduce human-caused greenhouse gas emissions.

National Research Council Ocean Studies Board, "Abrupt Climate Change: Inevitable Surprises," *National Academies Press*, June 2002.

An expert panel of scientists describes the growing evidence for episodes of very abrupt climate changes throughout Earth's history. The report discusses the possibility that such abrupt change will occur in the future, triggered by human-induced global warming or possibly by other factors.

The Next Step:

Additional Articles from Current Periodicals

Climate Change

"Lessons of the Past," *The Houston Chronicle*, Jan. 2, 2006, p. B6.
Civic and business leaders in Galveston, Texas, must come to terms with the effects of climate change by limiting coastal development and curbing emissions.

McFarling, Usha Lee, "Core Evidence That Humans Affect Climate Change," *Los Angeles Times*, Nov. 25, 2005, p. A24.
An ice core extracted from Antarctica shows that the levels of carbon dioxide and methane are higher than they have been in the past 650,000 years.

McFarling, Usha Lee, "Warming Trend Detected in Pacific," *Los Angeles Times*, Jan. 7, 2006, p. A9.
Scientists are blaming the human production of greenhouse gases for the warming of Southern California's coastal waters to their highest temperature level in 1,400 years.

Nelson, Bryn, "Link Found Between Frogs' Extinction, Global Warming," *Los Angeles Times*, Jan. 12, 2006, p. A15.
Two-thirds of Central and South America's harlequin frog species has vanished because of a killer fungus strengthened by global warming, says a new study.

Emissions Trading

Bennett, Drake, "Emission Control," *The Boston Globe*, Dec. 18, 2005, p. K1.
Economists support the decision by Gov. Mitt Romney, R-Mass., to pull out of a Northeastern plan to limit greenhouse gas emissions (GHGs) because it lacked a price cap on emissions permits.

Dilanian, Ken, "The Pollution Trade," *The Philadelphia Inquirer*, Oct. 19, 2005, p. C1.
Europe's plan to reduce emissions of gases that cause global warming features the system of carbon-emissions trading that the U.S. negotiated into the Kyoto treaty.

Kramer, Andrew E., "In Russia, Pollution is Good For Business," *The New York Times*, Dec. 28, 2005, p. C1.
Russia is selling its right to release carbon dioxide into the air to other countries that produce more carbon dioxide than is permitted by the Kyoto treaty.

Penson, Stuart, "EU Launching Emissions-Trading Plan," *The Houston Chronicle*, Jan. 1, 2005, p. 9.
The European Union will launch the world's first international carbon dioxide emissions trading scheme today, forcing energy-intensive businesses to monitor and lower their carbon emissions or face a penalty.

Energy Efficiency

Bernasek, Anna, "Real Energy Savers Don't Wear Cardigans. Or Do They?" *The New York Times*, Nov. 13, 2005, p. 5.
The U.S. must work with market forces to create an effective energy policy to reduce the cost of energy-efficient technology and force consumers to cut back on energy use.

Salant, Katherine, "Energy-Efficient Homes Can Help Curb Global Warming," *The Washington Post*, Dec. 31, 2005, p. F6.
Buildings account for 85 percent of greenhouse gases in the U.S., causing the Department of Energy to initiate a new program to reduce energy needs in new houses by 50 percent.

Kyoto Protocol

Spaeth, Anthony, and Maryann Bird, "A Real Fix or Just Hot Air?" *Time International*, Aug. 8, 2005, p. 22.
Australia and the United States unveiled the Asia-Pacific Partnership on Clean Development and Climate last week.

Spotts, Peter N., "Downside of Cleaner Air: More Warming," *The Christian Science Monitor*, Dec. 27, 2005, p. 3.
Scientists warn that reducing emissions of aerosols, which include pollutants but also have a cooling effect on the atmosphere, could cause global temperatures to rise quickly.

Spotts, Peter N., "U.S. Stand Poses Hurdle at Environmental Talks," *The Christian Science Monitor*, Dec. 2, 2005, p. 4.
Participating nations are trying to convince developing nations to join the Kyoto Protocol.

Citing The *CQ Researcher*

Sample formats for citing these reports in a bibliography include the ones listed below. Preferred styles and formats vary, so please check with your instructor or professor.

MLA Style

Jost, Kenneth. "Rethinking the Death Penalty." The CQ Researcher 16 Nov. 2001: 945-68.

APA Style

Jost, K. (2001, November 16). Rethinking the death penalty. *The CQ Researcher, 11*, 945-968.

Chicago Style

Jost, Kenneth. "Rethinking the Death Penalty." *CQ Researcher*, November 16, 2001, 945-968.

CQ Researcher

Published by CQ Press, a division of Congressional Quarterly Inc.

thecqresearcher.com

Rebuilding New Orleans

Should flood-prone areas be redeveloped?

Five months after Hurricane Katrina flooded most of New Orleans, some 80 percent of the "Crescent City" remains unrepaired. Damage is estimated at $35 billion. Most schools and businesses are still closed, and two-thirds of the 460,000 residents have moved out. How many will return remains troublingly uncertain. Municipal leaders only this month began setting up a process to decide which of the city's 73 neighborhoods can be resettled and which would be left uninhabited to soak up future floodwaters. Questions about who will help the city's poorer residents — many of them African-American — hang over the city, along with concern about how much of New Orleans' storied popular culture will survive. Meanwhile, as a new hurricane season approaches, efforts to repair and strengthen the protective system of levees, canals and pumps lag behind schedule.

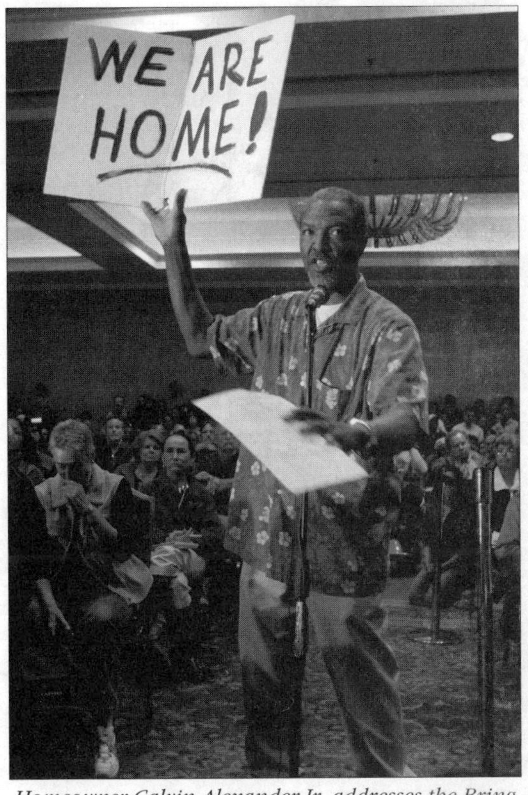

Homeowner Calvin Alexander Jr. addresses the Bring New Orleans Back Commission on Jan. 11, 2006. Many African-American residents fear their devastated neighborhoods won't be rebuilt.

INSIDE THIS REPORT

The CQ Researcher • Feb. 3, 2006 • www.thecqresearcher.com
Volume 16, Number 5 • Pages 97-120

CQ PRESS

RECIPIENT OF SOCIETY OF PROFESSIONAL JOURNALISTS AWARD FOR EXCELLENCE ◆ AMERICAN BAR ASSOCIATION SILVER GAVEL AWARD

Cover: Homeowner Calvin Alexander Jr. addresses the Bring New Orleans Back Commission on Jan. 11, 2006. Many African-American residents fear their devastated neighborhoods won't be rebuilt. (Getty Images/Chris Graythen)

CQ Researcher

Feb. 3, 2006
Volume 16, Number 5

MANAGING EDITOR: Thomas J. Colin

ASSISTANT MANAGING EDITOR: Kathy Koch

ASSOCIATE EDITOR: Kenneth Jost

STAFF WRITERS: Marcia Clemmitt, Peter Katel, Pamela M. Prah

CONTRIBUTING WRITERS: Rachel Cox, Sarah Glazer, David Hosansky, Patrick Marshall, Tom Price

DESIGN/PRODUCTION EDITOR: Olu B. Davis

ASSISTANT EDITOR: Melissa J. Hipolit

CQ PRESS

A Division of
Congressional Quarterly Inc.

SENIOR VICE PRESIDENT/PUBLISHER:
John A. Jenkins

DIRECTOR, LIBRARY PUBLISHING: Kathryn C. Suárez

DIRECTOR, EDITORIAL OPERATIONS:
Ann Davies

CONGRESSIONAL QUARTERLY INC.

CHAIRMAN: Paul C. Tash

VICE CHAIRMAN: Andrew P. Corty

PRESIDENT/EDITOR IN CHIEF: Robert W. Merry

CQ Researcher (ISSN 1056-2036) is printed on acid-free paper. Published weekly, except March 24, July 7, July 14, Aug. 4, Aug. 11, Nov. 24, Dec. 22 and Dec. 29, by CQ Press, a division of Congressional Quarterly Inc. Annual full-service subscriptions for institutions start at $667. For pricing, call 1-800-834-9020, ext. 1906. To purchase a *CQ Researcher* report in print or electronic format (PDF), visit www.cqpress.com or call 866-427-7737. Single reports start at $10. Bulk purchase discounts and electronic-rights licensing are also available. Periodicals postage paid at Washington, D.C., and additional mailing offices. POSTMASTER: Send address changes to *CQ Researcher*, 1255 22nd St., N.W., Suite 400, Washington, DC 20037.

Rebuilding New Orleans

BY PETER KATEL

THE ISSUES

Hurricane Katrina's floodwaters surged through tens of thousands of houses in New Orleans, including Dennis and Linda Scott's tidy, two-story brick home on Farwood Drive. The first floor has since been gutted, the ruined furnishings and appliances discarded.

Five months after floodwaters breached the city's levees and drainage canals, every other house for miles around is in the same deplorable shape. [1]

Like the Scotts, most of the residents who evacuated the sprawling New Orleans East area cannot decide whether to return, uncertain if their solidly middle class, mostly African-American neighborhoods will ever come back to life.

The disaster that began when Katrina's Category 3 winds hit New Orleans on Aug. 29, 2005, grinds on. [2] Yet the Scotts and their neighbors feel lucky to be alive.

"I'm one of the fortunate ones," says Scott, 47, who fled to Houston with his wife before the storm hit.

Linda's teaching job was swept away when the floods closed down the schools, so she's staying in Texas while Dennis works on the house and goes to his job as a communications specialist at Louis Armstrong International Airport. Their next-door neighbors, an elderly couple who stayed home, were drowned. Some three-quarters of Louisiana's 1,070 Katrina deaths occurred in New Orleans, where about 70 percent of the victims were age 60 and older. [3]

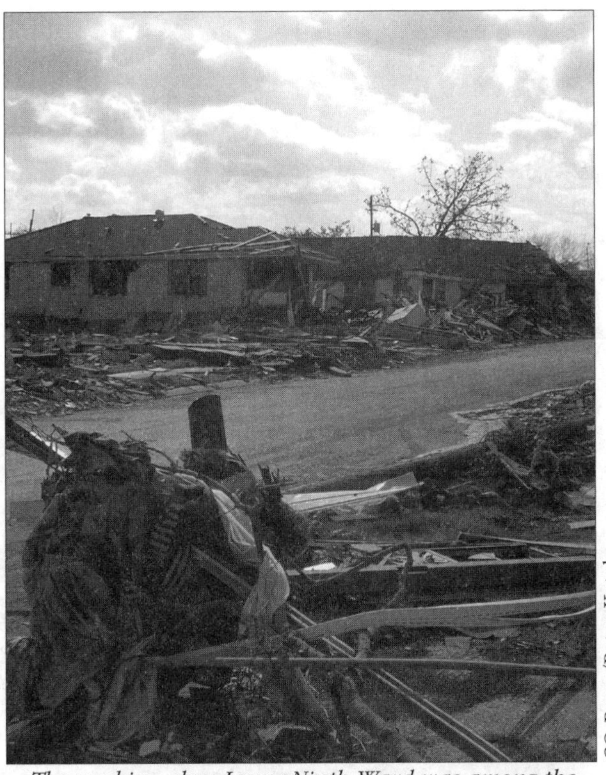

CQ Press/Peter Katel

The working-class Lower Ninth Ward was among the hardest-hit New Orleans neighborhoods. A rebuilding plan proposed by the Bring New Orleans Back Commission in early January would give residents a role in deciding whether heavily flooded neighborhoods would be resettled. An earlier plan by the Urban Land Institute sparked controversy among African-Americans when it proposed abandoning unsafe areas, including parts of the Lower Ninth.

But "the east" is not alone. Similar devastation also afflicts some older neighborhoods, where lush gardens and sprawling villas reflect the city's French and Spanish heritage. [4]

The continuing devastation mocks President Bush's stirring promise two weeks after the storm to mount "one of the largest reconstruction efforts the world has ever seen." [5]

Indeed, when the Senate Homeland Security and Governmental Affairs Committee toured the city four months later, members were "stunned" to see that "so much hasn't been done," said Chairwoman Susan Collins, R-Maine. [6]

Floodwaters up to 20 feet deep covered about 80 percent of the city and didn't recede until late September. [7] Fully half the city's homes — 108,731 dwellings — suffered flooding at least four feet deep, according to the Bring New Orleans Back Commission (BNOBC) formed by Mayor Ray Nagin. In some neighborhoods, Hurricane Rita, which struck later in September, brought additional flooding. [8]

Losses in destroyed and damaged property, added to losses resulting from the shrinkage of the city's economy, amount roughly to $35 billion, estimates Stan Fulcher, research director of the Louisiana Recovery Authority in Baton Rouge.

Most residents are still gone, largely because most jobs — except those that involve either tearing down houses or fixing them up — have disappeared. Plans are only starting to be made to rebuild the city, and no one knows how much reconstruction money will be available.

Does Scott have a future in New Orleans? "I'm on hold," he replies.

That response comes up a lot among the city's residents and evacuees, often accompanied by a sense that the rest of the country has moved on — or views the French-founded, majority-African-American city as somehow foreign or not worth rebuilding.

"This is America you're talking about," lawyer Walter I. Willard says in frustration.

So American, in fact, that jazz was born there — amid a culture formed by the peculiarities of the city's slavery and segregation traditions. [9] "The West Africans [slaves] were allowed to play their music in Congo Square on Sundays. That happened nowhere else in the United States," famed New Orleans-born trumpeter Wynton Marsalis says. [10]

Flooding Affected Most of Greater New Orleans

Flood water up to 20 feet deep covered more than three-quarters of New Orleans when storm surges pushed by Hurricane Katrina breached levees in 34 places. The Lower Ninth Ward and the New Orleans East district were among the hardest-hit areas.

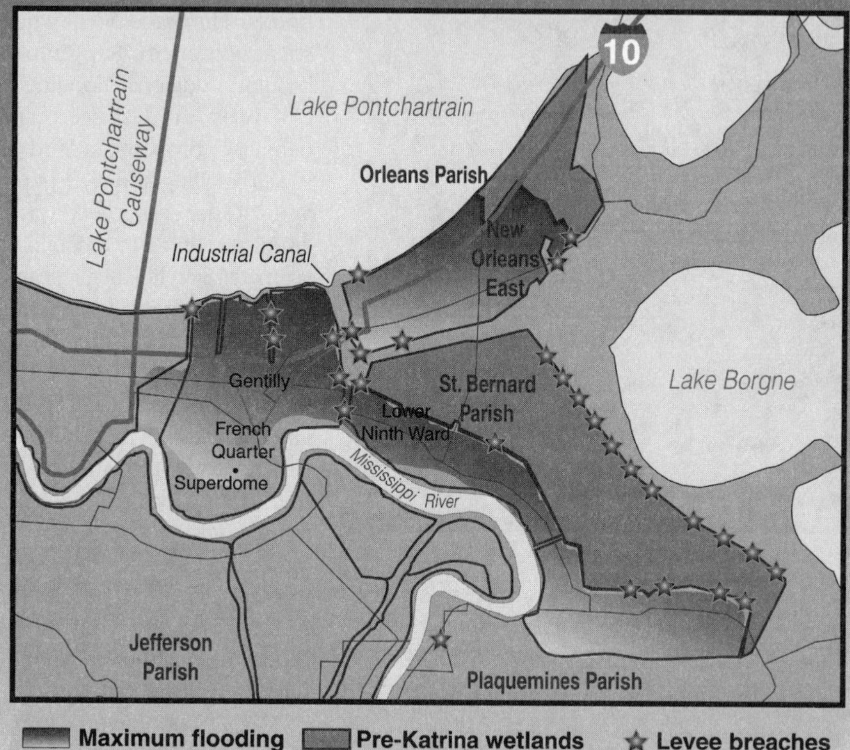

Source: Federal Emergency Management Agency

Slavery's legacy of racial and class divide has been part of the Katrina story from the beginning. New Orleans is two-thirds African-American, and the thousands of impoverished residents who were without cars to flee the approaching hurricane were overwhelmingly black. [11] "As all of us saw on television," President Bush acknowledged, "there's . . . some deep, persistent poverty in this region. That poverty has roots in a history of racial discrimination, which cut off generations from the opportunity of America." [12]

Bush also conceded that the federal response to Katrina amounted to less than what its victims were entitled to — a point reinforced in early 2006, when Sen. Collins' committee released a strikingly accurate prediction of Katrina's likely effects, prepared for the White House two days *before* Katrina hit. [13]

But in a sense, New Orleans was crumbling from within even before the floods washed over the city. "The city had a lot of economic and social problems before — economics, race, poverty, crime, drugs," says musician and Xavier University Prof. Michael White. "Our failure to deal with harsh realities has sometimes been the problem."

In 2004, for example, the city's homicide rate hit 59 per 100,000 — the nation's highest. [14]

In that post-Katrina climate — fed by bitter memories of institutional racism — the African-American community is concerned that developers are planning to reduce the black portion of the city's population. U.S. Housing and Urban Development Secretary Alphonso Jackson, who is African-American, intensified those fears when he said, "New Orleans is not going to be as black as it was for a long time, if ever again." [15]

The concern remained an issue into early 2006, when Mayor Nagin, also African-American, declared on Jan. 16 that the city "should be a chocolate New Orleans . . . a majority-African-American city. It's the way God wants it to be." [16] The following day, after furious reactions from both the white and black communities, Nagin apologized. [17]

Nagin's provocative language aside, fears of a demographic shift seem well-founded. In late January, sociologist John R. Logan of Brown University said he had conducted a study that showed about 80 percent of New Orleans' black residents were unlikely to come back, in part because their neighborhoods wouldn't be rebuilt. [18]

The BNOBC sparked the most recent chapter of the race and redevelopment debate. The commission's rebuilding plan, unveiled in early January, would give residents of the most heavily flooded neighborhoods four months to help figure out if their districts could be resettled. Homeowners in neighborhoods that can't be revived could sell their houses to a government-financed corporation for 100 percent of the pre-Katrina values, minus insurance payouts and mortgage obligations. The overall plan would cost more than $18 billion. [19] Federal, state and city approval is needed. [20]

Nowhere did the commission say that the poorest and most heavily damaged African-American neighborhoods should be abandoned. But the Washington-based Urban Land Institute (ULI), flatly recommended against extensive rebuilding in the most flood-prone areas, by implication including much of the

More Than 400,000 Residents Left Home States

Six times more Louisiana residents are still displaced from their homes than Mississippians. Of the more than 750,000 residents from both states displaced by Katrina, more than half are still living outside their home states.

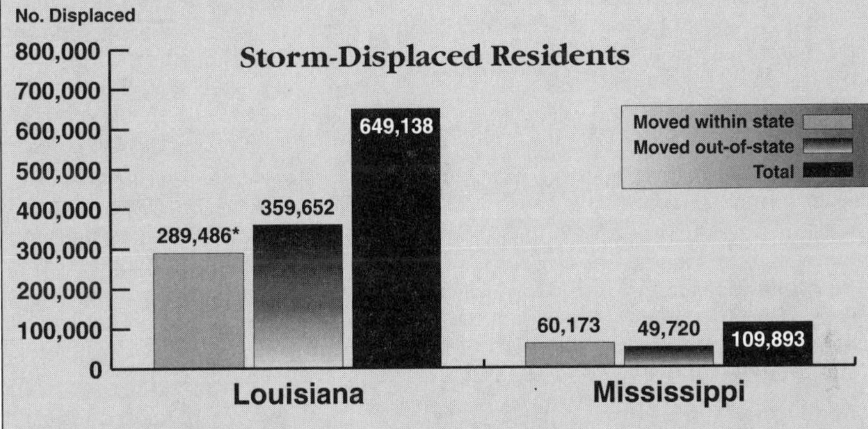

** Based on the number of FEMA aid applicants who have not returned to their pre-Katrina addresses.*

Source: Louisiana Recovery Authority

working-class, largely African-American Lower Ninth Ward. [21]

Under the Jim Crow segregation system that lasted into the 1960s, residents point out, the Lower Ninth was the only place where African-Americans could buy property. "These people struggled to buy a little bit of land they could call home," says contractor Algy Irvin, 60, standing in the wrecked living room of his mother's house on Egania Street.

Irvin recalls earning $35 a week mopping hospital floors and paying $18 a week for his own $1,200 lot on nearby Tupelo Street — now also a ruin. "You can see why people don't want a fat-cat developer coming in, making millions," he says, giving voice to a common suspicion that declaring the neighborhood unsafe is merely a cheap means of clearing out its present inhabitants to make way for lucrative development. But Irvin adds, "If people are compensated, that's another story."

Post-Katrina television coverage also gave the impression that New Orleans' African-American population was uniformly poor. In fact, the city had a substantial black middle class. "I had no clue that people couldn't get out of here," says Anne LaBranche, an African-American from New Orleans East, who returned to the city in January after staying with friends in Birmingham, Ala. "I do not know a person who doesn't own a car."

The LaBranches are moving into a house owned by her father-in-law. Her physician husband Emile, whose family practice was destroyed by Katrina along with all the patients' records, has been looking for work. But other medical offices say they aren't hiring until they know how many people are coming back.

Across town, Cory Matthews, 30, a medical-technology salesman, also wonders whether he still has a place in the city. He is rebuilding the flood-damaged Uptown house he shares with his girlfriend, but as he puts up new Sheetrock and rewires, he worries that his physician customer base has shrunk. "I'm hoping we're making the right move," he says.

Certainly, nobody is expecting redevelopment to bring speedy population growth. An estimated 135,000 people remain in New Orleans — less than a third of the 462,000 pre-Katrina population. Nagin's commission projects 247,000 residents by September 2008, while a more optimistic consultant projects 252,000 by early 2007. [22] The totals, however, don't specify whether the residents will be laboring at construction sites or behind desks.

Jay LaPeyre, president of the Business Council of New Orleans and the River Region, says laborers are desperately needed "for every type of manual labor — from skilled electricians and plumbers to low-skilled apprentices and trainees to service jobs at Burger King."

That kind of talk makes white-collar New Orleanians nervous. Tulane University, one of the city's major high-end employers, laid off 230 of its 2,500 professors. [23] Nearly all 7,500 public school employees were laid off as well, though some were rehired by the handful of charter schools that have sprung up. [24]

"It's become a blue-collar market," says Daniel Perez, who lost his night-manager job at the swanky Royal Sonesta Hotel after business dropped off. Perez applied in vain for dozens of professional or managerial jobs. He had almost decided to leave New Orleans before finally landing a position as a sales manager for *USA Today.*

For now, at least, even the service-industry job market is thinning, though the profusion of help-wanted signs in the functioning parts of the city convey a different impression. A planned Feb. 17 reopening of Harrah's Casino, for example, will take place with only half the pre-Katrina payroll of 2,500, says Carla Major, vice president for human resources.

Continued on p. 103

Can New Orleans' Musical Culture Be Saved?

Sunpie and the Louisiana Sunspots have the crowd at the House of Blues rocking as the group pounds out "Iko-Iko," a New Orleans standard with Creole lyrics and an irresistible beat.

The first night of Carnival is under way in the French Quarter, and the club is filling up for a long evening of music, with three more acts to follow. In the less touristy Marigny neighborhood, jazz pianist Ellis Marsalis is starting a slightly more sedate set at popular Snug Harbor.

Four months after Katrina hit, New Orleans is making music again. "So far, it's gone better than I would have thought, given the total lack of tourism," says Barry Smith, proprietor of the Louisiana Music Factory, where CDs and vinyl records of New Orleans artists account for some three-quarters of the stock of jazz, blues and gospel artists — both world-renowned and known only to locals. "I've definitely experienced a big increase in the number of local customers coming to the store, and a lot of the people who came here to work — from construction workers to Red Cross volunteers."

Few if any places in the United States come even close to New Orleans as an incubator of musical style and talent. As far back as 1819, a visitor wrote about the African music being played at Congo Square. And by the early 20th century, a musical tradition had formed in which Louis Armstrong — arguably the century's most influential musician — came of age. [1]

Courtesy www.ellismarsalis.com

Legendary jazz pianist Ellis Marsalis is a popular performer in Old New Orleans, which was largely spared by the flooding.

"All American music in the 20th century was profoundly shaped and influenced by New Orleans music," Tom Piazza writes in *Why New Orleans Matters*. [2]

The career of famed musician/producer Allen Toussaint illustrates the city's musical power. Toussaint wrote such 1960s hits as "Mother in Law" and produced and arranged the 1973 hit "Right Place, Wrong Time" for fellow New Orleans resident "Dr. John," as well as the disco standard "Lady Marmelade."

"He helped invent things we take as everyday in music — certain beats, certain arrangements," his partner in a record label said recently. [3]

Toussaint fled New Orleans after Katrina and has spoken optimistically of the city's future prospects. [4] But away from the club scene and music stores, the future looks less bright.

That's because the city's music springs from the very streets that Katrina emptied — the fabled "social aid and pleasure clubs," fraternal organizations that sponsor the Mardi Gras "Indian tribes," as well as the brass-band funeral processions that nourished jazz. All these influential institutions are maintained by people who mostly live paycheck to paycheck, says Michael White, a clarinetist and music scholar who holds an endowed chair in arts and humanities at New Orleans' Xavier University. [5]

The New Orleans establishment recognizes the problem. "Financial losses for social aid and pleasure clubs, Mardi Gras Indian tribes and [brass band] second-line companies are conservatively estimated at over $3 million," the Bring New Orleans Back Commission reports. [6]

"These were poor people, but people who spent a lot of money on these events," says White, a New Orleans native who comes from a long line of musicians. "The thing of money is serious. If people don't have jobs, they're not going to be able to participate."

White himself suffered another kind of loss — his vast collection of vintage instruments and memorabilia that included a trumpet mouthpiece from jazz saint Sidney Bechet; 4,000 rare CDs and even rarer vinyl recordings; photographs of New Orleans musical legends and notes and tapes of interviews with musicians who have since died. All were stored at his house — and it's all gone.

Is resurrecting an entire popular culture any more possible than restoring White's collection? "It's not like there's a central entity that can be rebuilt," says Piazza. "What steps can be taken to repatriate as many members of the African-American community and other communities — people who don't have the same kinds of resources as others to come back and rebuild, or who lived in areas where logistical challenges to rebuilding are all but insurmountable? That is the most difficult question about cultural renewal."

---

[1] For background, see Geoffrey C. Ward and Ken Burns, *Jazz: A History of America's Music* (2000), pp. 7-16; 40-46.

[2] Tom Piazza, *Why New Orleans Matters* (2005), p. 37.

[3] Quoted in Deborah Sontag, "Heat, and Piano, Back in New Orleans," *The New York Times*, Sept. 20, 2005, p. E1; for additional background see, "Inductees: Allen Toussaint," Rock+Roll Hall of Fame and Museum, undated, http://rockhall.com/hof/inductee.asp?id=200.

[4] *Ibid.*

[5] Ward and Burns, *op. cit.*, pp. 7-16.

[6] "Report of the Cultural Committee, Mayor's Bring New Orleans Back Commission," Jan. 17, 2006, pp. 8-9, www.bringneworleansback.org.

Continued from p. 101

On his Jan. 11 visit, President Bush touted New Orleans as still "a great place to visit." But his motorcade had skirted most of the devastation, going nowhere near, for instance, the Scotts' deserted neighborhood. [25]

"We can't move forward until we have positive information on what's happening," Scott says. "There are no banks, no schools, no electricity. We just want to be home."

As officials plan the city's future, here are some of the questions being debated:

Katrina Costs Dwarf Previous Disasters

Hurricane Katrina cost the Federal Emergency Management Agency $25 billion in the Gulf Coast — nearly three times more than the 2001 terrorist attacks on the World Trade Center and eight times more than Hurricane Rita, which followed on the heels of Katrina. The money pays for such services as temporary housing, unemployment assistance, crisis counseling and legal aid.

Disaster	FEMA Cost Estimate* ($ in billions)
Hurricane Katrina (2005)	$24.6
World Trade Center (2001)	$8.8
Hurricane Rita (2005)	$3.4
Hurricane Ivan (2004)	$2.6
Hurricane Wilma (2005)	$2.5
Hurricane Georges (1998)	$2.3
Hurricane Andrew (1992)	$1.8
Hurricane Hugo (1989)	$1.3
Loma Prieta Earthquake (1989)	$0.87
Hurricane Alberto (2000)	$0.6

** Flood-insurance reimbursements not included*

Source: FEMA, December 2005

Should some neighborhoods not be rebuilt?

The buzzword summing up the single toughest question about New Orleans' future is "footprint." That's urban-planner jargon for a city's shape and the amount of space it occupies. In New Orleans, the term has become code for the idea that flood-prone districts are best turned back into open-space "sponges" to absorb nature's future onslaughts.

But would that help? New Orleans and the entire Gulf Coast are sinking. New Orleans was built on sandy soil to begin with, but oil and gas extraction and upriver levee construction — which reduces the delta area's natural landfill process, called silting — have exacerbated the problem. And sea levels are rising due to global warming. [26] As a result, writes Virginia R. Burkett of the U.S. Geological Survey's National Wetlands Research Center in Louisiana, by 2100 parts of New Orleans "could lie [about 23 feet] below water level during a Category 3 hurricane." [27]

Even so, the extensive levee system was designed to defend the entire metropolitan area from floods. So the Katrina disaster didn't grow out of the development of flood-prone lands that never should have been urbanized, say opponents of shrinking the footprint. Instead, they argue, the catastrophe grew out of human failure in engineering, construction or maintenance — or in all three.

"If we can build levees in Iraq, we can build levees on the Gulf Coast," says Sen. Mary Landrieu, D-La. "And if we can build hospitals in Baghdad and Fallujah, we can most certainly rebuild our hospitals in this metropolitan area." [28]

But congressional power brokers aren't in the mood to redevelop flood-prone areas. "We are committed to helping the people of Louisiana rebuild," said House Appropriations Committee member Rep. Ray LaHood, R-Ill. But, "we are not going to rebuild homes that are going to be destroyed in two years by another flood. We are not just going to throw money at it." [29]

Some who call the flood a man-made failure don't oppose redesigning the city in a more environmentally sensible way — even if it means abandoning their own neighborhoods. "It's not what I want, but I could live with it," says LaBranche, who with her husband owns a home, an office building and rental properties in New Orleans East. "I don't want to go through this again."

But who should decide? "The idea that everybody gets to have what they want" is not practical, says business leader LaPeyre. He wants the government to use its power of eminent domain — the right to condemn private property and compensate the owner — to prevent redevelopment of areas unsuitable for residential and business use. [30]

Private companies, such as utility and insurance companies — will also influence decisions about where development will occur. "The market will do better than most people claim," he says. "If you're not going to have good services, most people will say, 'I don't want to live there.' "

Others argue that a neighborhood's residents should have a big voice. The Bring New Orleans Back Commission proposed letting residents of heavily

Katrina Saved Worst for New Orleans

Nearly 90 percent of Katrina's flood and storm damage occurred in Louisiana — more than half of it in New Orleans. The other three states affected by Katrina suffered only 12 percent of the damages.

Property Damage from Hurricane Katrina's Flood and Storm Surge*
($ in billions)

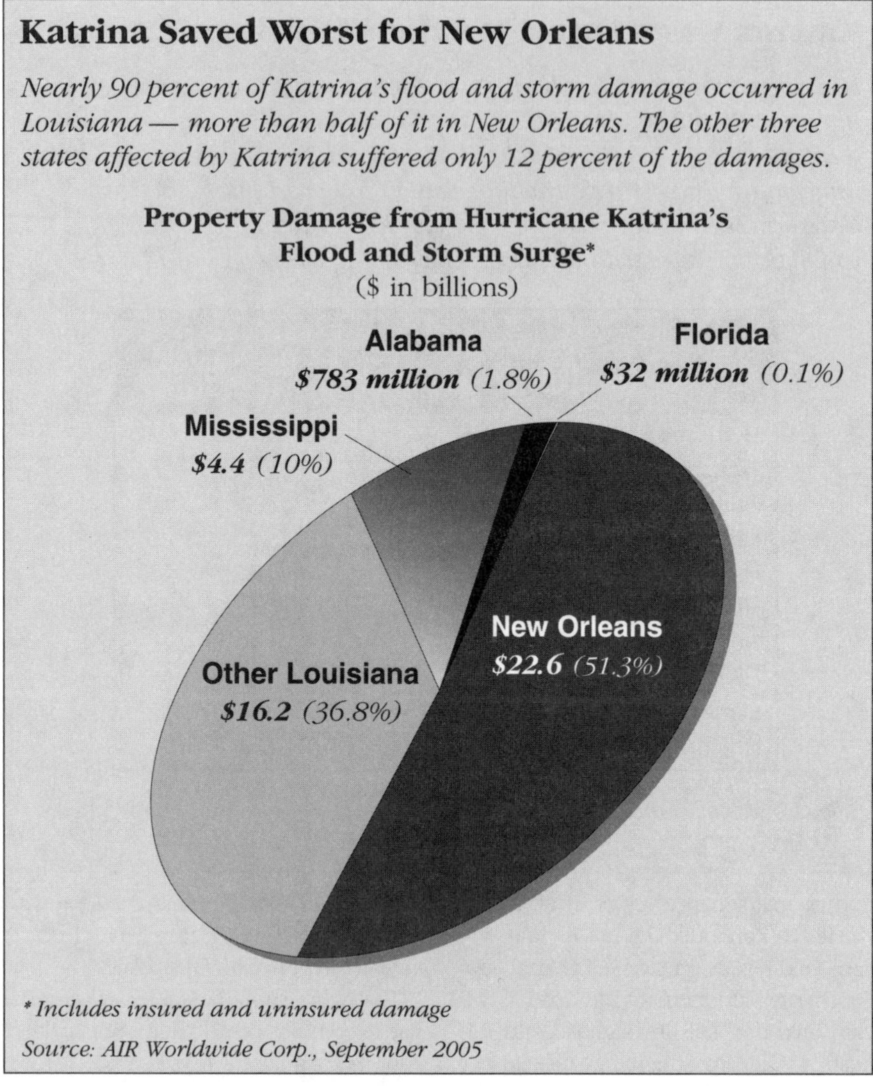

* *Includes insured and uninsured damage*

Source: AIR Worldwide Corp., September 2005

damaged neighborhoods work with urban and financial planners to determine if their districts could be revived. The "neighborhood planning teams" would have until May to decide. The procedure grew out of opposition to the Urban Land Institute's recommendation against rebuilding in flood-prone areas.

"In an arbitrary and capricious manner to say that these areas — which were populated by black people because they were directed there — should now be turned into green space deepens the wound," says Councilwoman Cynthia Willard-Lewis, who represents several of the city's eastern neighborhoods. Many of the houses can be repaired and the communities brought back, she says, adding that she suspects the plan "was not based on what was safe but on whom they wanted to return."

William Hudnut, a former mayor of Indianapolis who holds the Urban Land Institute's public policy chair, says city leaders do not have the courage to tell residents what they don't want to hear. "The footprint has to be smaller and development more compact," he says. "An honest, tough-minded approach to rebuilding is part of what leadership is all about. It may be that some people would lose their political base or lose their jobs. But if a thing is worth doing, it's worth doing well and worth standing up for."

Ari Kelman, an environmental historian at the University of California at Davis, concedes that some neighborhoods should be abandoned. At the same time, he says, low-income African-American residents have well-founded fears that any planning and decision system will be stacked against them.

"People who don't have money also don't have power," says Kelman, author of a 2003 book on the interplay between human design and nature in New Orleans. "When politics get cooking in New Orleans, it's likely that the poor are going to get screwed."

Should the levee system be upgraded to guard against a Category 5 storm?

The levee system surrounding New Orleans was designed to withstand a Category 3 hurricane. Katrina had weakened to Category 3 by the time it made landfall, but the wall of water it sent ashore — the hurricane's "surge" — was born when the storm was still offshore and raging at Category 4 and 5 strength. [31]

So far, official attention has focused on possible errors in design, construction or maintenance of the levees. But many are also asking whether the system should be upgraded to protect against a Category 5 hurricane — the most powerful. Among Louisianans in general and New Orleanians in particular, support for a Category 5 system seems nearly universal.

"I would like to see the levees brought to Category 5 for my safety and that of my family and properties," says LaBranche, the displaced New Orleans homeowner.

But some government experts say a Category 5 levee system is a pipe dream. They point out Category 5 is open-ended, taking in all hurricanes whose winds exceed 155 mph and create storm surges greater than 18 feet. "What's the top end for a Cat 5 hurricane?" asked Dan Hitchings, director of Hurricane Katrina recovery for the Corps of Engineers. "There isn't one." [32]

That argument carries little weight in Louisiana. Some Louisiana lawmakers say that if the below-sea-level Netherlands can protect itself from floods, New Orleans shouldn't settle for less. "They built once-in-1,000-years flood protection," Sen. Landrieu told a rally of some 75 displaced New Orleanians outside the White House last December. "We don't even have once-in-100-years [protection]."

No hurricanes strike in the North Sea, which surrounds the Netherlands. But the tiny country, some of which lies more than 20 feet below sea level, is vulnerable to powerful storms with winds that can reach 60 mph. Following a 1953 storm that killed more than 1,800 people, the country redesigned its protective system in ways that many New Orleanians say should serve as a model. [33]

The Netherlands system was designed to withstand a once-in-10,000-years storm. New Orleans' levees were designed for a once-in-200-300-years storm, says the Corps of Engineers. [34]

In addition, say Louisiana officials, a Category 5 system would probably cost about $32 billion. [35]

"It will probably be a pretty staggering price tag," acknowledges Craig E. Colten, a geography professor at Louisiana State University in Baton Rouge and author of a recent book on New Orleans' flood-protection history. But the long-term value of property protection would make an upgraded system a wise investment, he added, citing the prosperous Netherlands, an international shipping center.

Getty Images/Robyn Beck

Skip LaGrange takes a break from cleaning out his flooded home in the Mid-City section of New Orleans, on Oct. 5, 2005. An estimated 135,000 people are now living in New Orleans — less than a third of the 462,000 pre-Katrina population.

But Rep. Richard Baker, R-La., cautions that debating a Category 5 upgrade now could distract from the immediate and urgent tasks facing New Orleans. "Construction toward a Category 5 standard would be a decade-long project," he says. "The statistical probabilities of a Category 5 hitting New Orleans are fairly small, especially since we just got hit. I think we have time."

No one denies the need for fixing the existing flood-protection system. The Bush administration has proposed $1.6 billion to restore the system to a Category 3 level of protection, and another $1.5 billion for further improvements. [36] Thus far, however, it has stayed out of the Category 5 argument. At a White House briefing on the new flood-protection plan, Donald E. Powell, the administration's coordinator of post-hurricane recovery projects, would only say that after the proposed improvements, "The levee system will be better, much better, and stronger than it ever has been in the history of New Orleans." [37]

The White House plan also includes a study, backed by Mayor Nagin, of whether a substantial upgrade to the system is needed. A preliminary report is due in May.

However, city officials argue that a system capable of protecting against a Category 5 storm is well within the range of engineering possibilities and would be good for both the city's and the country's economy. "We need to build toward Category 5 to provide . . . assurance to [potential] investors," says Gary P. LaGrange, director of the Port of New Orleans, and to protect the port, an essential part of the nation's trade system.

Should the nation pay for New Orleans to be rebuilt?

So far, Congress has committed $98.9 billion for post-hurricane recovery and rebuilding programs throughout the Gulf Coast, the Senate Budget Committee calculated. The funding came in two emergency appropriations in September totaling $62.3 billion, followed by several smaller spending authorizations. In December, expanding on a request by Bush, Congress redirected $23.4 billion in funds previously appropriated. [38]

It's uncertain, however, how much will go to New Orleans.

In any event, money appropriated so far includes $6.2 billion in Community Development Block Grants intended for Louisiana, and $22 billion for reimbursements to Gulf Coast homeowners from the federal flood-insurance program. But even with the emergency injections of cash, the flood-insurance program is "bankrupt," Senate Banking Committee Chairman Richard Shelby, R-Ala., said on Jan. 25. The acting director of the Federal Emergency Management

Agency (FEMA) insurance division said the agency has paid out $13.5 billion in claims arising from the 2005 hurricane season — nearly as much as the agency has paid out in its 37-year existence. And 30 percent of the 239,000 claims have yet to be resolved. [39]

Federal hurricane-recovery coordinator Powell has been advocating directing much of the block grant money to the estimated 20,000 New Orleans homeowners who didn't have flood insurance because their neighborhoods weren't designated as flood plains. [40]

Given the huge costs involved and all the unknowns, lawmakers from other parts of the country are not exactly champing at the bit to pay for rebuilding New Orleans. The city's tenuous hydrological situation and the likelihood that it will be flooded again by other hurricanes lead some Americans to question whether the rest of the country should have to pay to rebuild the city in such a precarious location.

"There is a lot of — I suppose you can call it 'Katrina fatigue' — that people are dealing with out in the heartland," Rep. Henry Bonilla, R-Texas, told Louisiana Gov. Kathleen Babineaux Blanco, a Democrat, at a House Select Katrina Response Investigation Committee hearing last Dec. 14.

The situation has rekindled a long-simmering debate about whether Americans in the heartland should pay to constantly bail out people — usually those living on the coasts — who choose to live in areas prone to floods, hurricanes, landslides and earthquakes. "Is it fair to make people living in Pennsylvania or Ohio pay billions for massive engineering projects so that some of the people of New Orleans can go back to the way things were and avoid the hard choices that nature presents them?" asks economist Adrian Moore of the libertarian Reason Foundation of Los Angeles. [41]

Some lawmakers agree, although only a few have spoken out. "It looks like a lot of that place could be bulldozed," House Speaker Dennis Hastert, R-Ill. said shortly after the hurricane, raising hackles. He later explained he only meant that danger zones shouldn't be resettled. [42]

New Orleanians respond that other disaster-prone areas, including hurricane-exposed Florida coastal cities, get rebuilt with few questions asked about viability. "People build on mountainsides in California that fall in the ocean," notes Perez, the newspaper sales manager. "We're not the only vulnerable area in the country."

In addition, points out Republican Louisiana Sen. David Vitter, 25 percent of the nation's energy and most of the Midwest's grain exports are shipped through the port of New Orleans. "If people don't think there's a national stake in rebuilding New Orleans, that's fine. But they should get used to much higher gasoline prices," he said. "And people can forget about getting crops to foreign markets. You need a major city as the hub of all that activity."

But if federal funds are forthcoming to rebuild the city, they should have some serious accountability strings attached, given the city's long history of corruption and dysfunction, some argue. "A lot of . . . our constituents now are telling us that they [don't] want us to support funding for the Gulf region at this point without strong plans of accountability," Bonilla said.

Recognizing those sentiments — as well as the reality that the country is at war and its debt and deficits are rising — Louisiana politicians have proposed two major plans that they say would lower the federal spending burden for rebuilding New Orleans and the rest of the state.

But the White House has already refused to back one of these plans. Its author, Rep. Baker, proposed establishing a public corporation to buy or finance repairs on storm-damaged property. Homeowners who sold their houses to the corporation would get 60 percent of the pre-Katrina value of their holdings. The corporation would then resell the homes, if possible, and turn the proceeds back to the Treasury. Nagin's BNOBC adopted the idea, which some of its members called crucial to reviving the city.

"We were concerned about creating additional federal bureaucracies, which might make it harder to get money to the people," Bush said, explaining his rejection of Baker's idea. [43]

On Feb. 1, according to Baker's office, three former Republican governors of Louisiana — Murphy J. "Mike" Foster, Charles E. "Buddy" Roemer III, and David Treen — urged Bush to change his mind concerning Baker's bill, which they called the only practical method of disposing of thousands of ruined residential and business properties.

The congressman has been vowing to press ahead with his proposal, sponsored in the Senate by Sen. Landrieu. Bush's negative response would "constrict the opportunities for rapid redevelopment, and that's tough," said Reed Kroloff, architecture dean at Tulane University and a BNOBC member. [44]

But developer Joseph Canizaro, who helped put together the commission's plan, said block grant money and other unspecified funds could be found for a property buyback. [45]

The other plan to lower direct federal spending is a longstanding proposal to boost the state's share of money that the federal government earns from petroleum leases on the Outer Continental Shelf in the Gulf of Mexico off Louisiana's coast. One-quarter of U.S. crude oil production comes from Louisiana's offshore waters. [46]

The cost of repairing the state's hurricane-protection system "can be paid for simply by giving Louisiana our fair share of oil and gas revenues from the Outer Continental Shelf," Gov. Blanco told Bonilla at the House Select Committee hearing.

Coastal states like Louisiana receive 27 percent of the revenues from oil and gas leases from waters within their

Continued on p. 108

Chronology

1700s-1800s

From the time of its founding, New Orleans' vulnerability to nature is seen as the price of its incomparably strategic location.

1718
New Orleans is founded on a natural levee along a bend in the Mississippi River.

1892
Adolph Plessy of New Orleans is arrested after testing segregation laws by riding in a "white" train car. U.S. Supreme Court later upholds his conviction in landmark *Plessy v. Ferguson* decision.

1900-1947

A catastrophic flood reminds the city of its dangerous location.

1927
Massive Mississippi floods see many African-Americans forced into levee-reinforcement work; two rural parishes are deliberately flooded to save New Orleans.

1929
The U.S. Army Corps of Engineers begins building a spillway on the Mississippi to channel floodwater away from New Orleans.

1930s

Expansion of city drainage systems allows urban expansion, but new neighborhoods are strictly segregated.

Sept. 17-19, 1947
A Category 4 hurricane overwhelms levees, causing flooding over nine square miles of the city.

1950s-1970s

The city expands into drained wetlands, increasing its vulnerability to floods.

1950
Land drained for suburban expansion reaches 49,000 acres.

Sept. 7, 1965
Hurricane Betsy slams the city with Category 3 winds, pushing a 10-foot storm surge through some levees.

Oct. 27, 1965
President Lyndon B. Johnson signs the Flood Control Act, which includes funding for a hurricane-protection system in New Orleans.

Aug. 17, 1969
Category 5 Hurricane Camille devastates Mississippi and Alabama, but reinforced protective systems keep most of New Orleans safe.

May 3, 1978
Heavy rainstorm flooding damages more than 70,000 homes.

1980s-1990s

Attempts by the city to guard against rainstorm floods prove inadequate, as fears of vulnerability to hurricanes begin to grow.

April 1982
Rainstorm-caused floods damage 1,400 homes and other buildings.

1983
City expands pumping and drainage systems.

May 8-10, 1995
Flooding damages thousands of homes, causes six deaths.

2000-Present

Fears of hurricane vulnerability grow, as journalists and government officials warn about the weakness of the city's defenses.

June 23-June 26, 2002
Times-Picayune warns of New Orleans' hurricane vulnerability.

Sept. 26, 2002
Hurricane Isidore hits Louisiana after weakening to a tropical storm, but still causes major flooding.

July 2004
FEMA officials conduct a drill featuring Category 3 "Hurricane Pam" hitting New Orleans and predict serious flooding, massive evacuation.

Aug. 29, 2005
Hurricane Katrina makes landfall east of New Orleans.

Sept. 15, 2005
President Bush visits New Orleans and pledges a massive disaster-recovery effort.

Jan. 11, 2006
Bring New Orleans Back Commission releases an "Action Plan" for re-creating the city.

Jan 17, 2006
Senators of both parties visit New Orleans and criticize slow progress on recovery.

Jan. 26, 2006
President Bush explains why he refused to support the creation of a public corporation to buy flood-damaged homes.

June 1
Hurricane season begins; repairs and improvements to levee system due for completion.

Experts Blame Levees, Not Storm

The newspaper headlines blamed "Killer Storm Katrina" for devastating New Orleans. But engineers largely blame the levees designed and built by the U.S. Army Corps of Engineers.

A team of experts who examined the protective system found no fewer than 34 storm-induced levee breaches, indicating that the engineering failures were far wider than initial reports indicated. [1]

"The performance of many of the levees and floodwalls could have been significantly improved, and some of the failures likely prevented, with relatively inexpensive modification," the team concluded. The simple addition of concrete "splash slabs," for instance, might have prevented soil levee tops from eroding.

In fact, even a task force assembled by the Corps of Engineers itself concluded "integral parts of the . . . hurricane-protection system failed." [2]

With the June 1 start of the 2006 hurricane season approaching, the Corps is trying to patch the immediate problems. Engineers and lawmakers, meanwhile, are evaluating the system's performance. So far, a lethal combination of design, construction and maintenance errors appears to underlie the disaster.

Blame extends from state-appointed "levee boards" responsible for inspection and maintenance to the Corps of Engineers, Sen. George Voinovich, R-Ohio, told the Senate Homeland Security and Governmental Affairs Committee on Dec. 14. And Congress deserved blame too, he said: "We have been penny-wise and pound-foolish" on funding upkeep and completion of the New Orleans levee system.

The Lake Pontchartrain and Vicinity Hurricane Protection Project includes 125 miles of levees, floodwalls and other structures. The system was supposed to bar storm surges from Lake Pontchartrain and channel any flooding out of the city via a series of canals. [3]

Though Congress approved the project in 1965, it was unfinished when Katrina struck. In the city itself, construction was 90 percent complete, but the lack of completion has not been blamed for the system's failure. [4] Rather, the devastation was intensified by the environmental changes in southern Louisiana since the system was first designed, the *Times-Picayune* reported as early as 2002. [5]

As the oil and gas industry expanded, the Corps of Engineers built or approved the necessary navigation channels in southern Louisiana and the Gulf of Mexico. And the industry expansion swallowed one-third to one-half of the wetlands — which have been disappearing at a rate of at least 25 square miles a year. Experts now know wetlands play a critical role during hurricanes, slowing storms as they make landfall. [6]

Continued from p. 106

three-mile jurisdictions (federal waters extend another 197 miles). By contrast, states with oil and gas production on public lands receive 50 percent of the federal revenues, leading coastal states to feel they are entitled to a larger share of offshore revenues. [47]

Sen. Landrieu last year pushed a bill to grant coastal states 50 percent of the take from oil and gas leases in the areas off their shores. The bill died at year's end, but she is planning to revive it this year (*see p. 112*).

Rather than creating a new revenue source, however, the proposal would merely divert money to the state before the funds reach federal coffers, which bothered Bonilla. "It is wise when states and local governments come before us to show what they are doing to help themselves in terms of raising whatever revenue dollars you can," Bonilla told Blanco. "People would want to know . . . what is Louisiana doing in terms of everything you possibly can do to help yourself and not just look at the federal government and say, 'We need you to help us pay for these things.' "

But, he added, Americans would not "turn their back on those who want to help themselves." ■

BACKGROUND

Island City

New Orleans has been battling with nature ever since explorer Jean-Baptiste Le Moyne de Bienville founded the city in 1718. Its original name, in fact, reflected the city's relationship to the four bodies of water surrounding it — the Mississippi River, Lake Pontchartrain, Lake Borgne and the Gulf of Mexico. He called it *L'Isle de la Nouvelle Orléans* — the Island of New Orleans. [48]

"His enthusiasm for the river's commercial benefits blinded him to many of the challenges of building a city in the delta," environmental historian Kelman writes. These included: epidemics; "terrible to nonexistent" drainage; dampness; and "the threat of catastrophic flooding."

Still, Bienville's insight into the river's economic importance was on the money. The Mississippi was unrivalled as a highway deep into the North American continent, and remains so today. Some 500 million tons of goods — including about 60 percent of U.S. grain exports — are shipped downriver to the southern Louisiana port complex, which includes New Orleans. [49]

So when Katrina made landfall across the region's depleted wetlands, the poorly designed and built levees and floodwalls couldn't withstand the full force of the storm surge.

A section of floodwall along the London Avenue Canal was so weakened that it likely would have been breached by the floodwaters — if the barrier on the opposite side of the canal hadn't failed first, an engineer told the Senate Environment and Public Works Committee on Nov. 17. "Multiple, concurrent failure mechanisms" were present, said Larry Roth, deputy executive director of the American Society of Civil Engineers. "The wall was badly out of alignment and tilting landward; as a result of the tilt, there were gaps between the wall and the supporting soil."

Additional pressure on the flood barriers came from the Mississippi River Gulf Outlet (MRGO), a 76-mile long canal built to give ships a shortcut from the Gulf to the Port of New Orleans. Instead, it gave Katrina a straight shot into the city — a "hurricane alley" — said Sen. David Vitter, R-La., who has called, along with others, for the canal's closure. The Corps says it will not conduct its annual dredging of the waterway, and hurricane experts say it may become less dangerous as it becomes shallower. [7]

Meanwhile, engineers have suggested that some residential areas be abandoned — to provide a flood-absorbing floodplain — and building codes amended to require that houses be elevated.

But the levee system also must be dealt with, Roth said. "If we are to rebuild the city," he said, "we must also rebuild its protections." [8]

---

[1] The team was assembled by the National Science Foundation (NSF), the American Society of Civil Engineers (ASCE) and the University of California at Berkeley. See R. B. Seed, *et al.*, "Preliminary Report on the Performance of the New Orleans Levee Systems in Hurricane Katrina on Aug. 29, 2005," Nov. 2, 2005, Figure 1.4, p. 1-10, www.ce.berkeley.edu/~inkabi/KRTF/CCRM/levee-rpt.pdf.

[2] "Performance Evaluation Plan and Interim Status, Report 1 of a Series: Performance Evaluation of the New Orleans and Southeast Louisiana Hurricane Protection System," Interagency Performance Evaluation Task Force, Jan. 10, 2006, Appendix A, p. 2, https://ipet.wes.army.mil.

[3] *Ibid*, pp. 1.2-1.3; Seed, *et al.*, *op. cit.*, p. A-2.

[4] "Performance Evaluation Plan," *op. cit.*, Appendix A, p. 2.

[5] John McQuaid and Mark Schleifstein, "Evolving Danger; experts know we face a greater threat from hurricanes than previously suspected," *The Times-Picayune* (New Orleans), June 23, 2002, p. A1.

[6] John McQuaid and Mark Schleifstein, "Shifting Tides," *The Times-Picayune* (New Orleans), June 26, 2002, p. A1.

[7] John Schwartz, "New Orleans Wonders What to Do With Open Wounds, Its Canals," *The New York Times*, Dec. 231, 2005, p. A26; Seed, *et al.*, *op. cit.*, p. 3.1; Matthew Brown, "Corps suspends plans to dredge MRGO," *The Times-Picayune* (New Orleans), Breaking News Weblog, Nov. 21, 2005, www.nola.com/t-p/.

[8] For background, see Larry Roth statement to Senate Committee on Environment and Public Works, Nov. 17, 2005, http://epw.senate.gov/hearing_statements.cfm?id=249000.

The first of New Orleans' protective barriers — called levees from the French verb "to lift" — were natural. In fact, New Orleans exists in the first place because the Mississippi's waters helped create a high section of riverbank along the section of the river that forms a crescent embracing old New Orleans — known today as the French Quarter. The sloping, natural levee was only 12 feet above sea level.

Settlers soon began adding to nature's work. Throughout the 18th and early 19th centuries — during the first period of French rule, the Spanish colonial period that followed in 1768-1801 and the French restoration in 1801-1803 — levees were built far upstream, and raised continually after flooding.

The levee work continued after the United States bought the city and vast swaths of the new nation's interior in 1803 for $15 million, or about 3 cents an acre. Nine years after the so-called Louisiana Purchase, Louisiana became a state.

From the beginning, many people realized that building ever-higher levees up and down the river prevented its energy from being dissipated naturally in periodic floods. By the time the Mississippi reached New Orleans, it would be dangerously high and flowing at maximum force.

"We are every year confining this immense river closer and closer to its own bed — forgetting that it is fed by over 1,500 streams — and regardless of a danger becoming every year more and more impending," State Engineer P. O. Herbert warned in 1846. He argued for flood outlets along the river, but landowners resisted, not wanting their plantations flooded. [50]

In 1849, the river broke through several upstream levees, one of them 17 miles above New Orleans. The resultant flooding in the lowest section of New Orleans forced 12,000 mostly poor residents to abandon their dwellings or try to coexist with the water.

Afterward, the city raised the levees higher still. But A. D. Wooldridge, the state engineer who succeeded Herbert, declared in 1850 that reliance on levees "will be destructive to those who come after us." By then, some rose 15 feet.

Dynamiting the Levee

The engineers' warnings came to pass in early 1927. A series of rainstorms, coupled with unusually heavy spring runoff, swelled the huge river and overwhelmed the levees. Floodwater inundated 28,545 square miles of the Mississippi Valley as far north as Illinois, killing 423 people. By mid-April, more than 50,000 people had fled their homes. [51]

In New Orleans, powerful pumps kept floodwaters at bay — until a bolt of lightning disabled the power plant that kept the pumps humming.

A group of city leaders, who had formed the Citizens Flood Relief Committee, began campaigning to stop the flooding of the city by blowing a hole in the levee some 12 miles downstream.

Residents of the two thinly populated wetland parishes downstream, St. Bernard and Plaquemines, largely made their living fishing and trapping muskrats for their fur. The New Orleans political class persuaded Louisiana Gov. Oramel Simpson that those rural activities were worth sacrificing to protect New Orleans. Simpson gave the "river parish" residents three days to clear out. Muskrat trapping took years to recover.

Getty Images/Robyn Beck

Engineers inspect a Katrina-damaged section of the London Avenue Canal on Sept. 21, 2005, three days before Hurricane Rita hit and reopened some levees that had been partially repaired. The city's flood-control system may not be completely repaired by June 1, the start of the 2006 hurricane season.

For the poor African-Americans living along the river's southern reaches, the 1927 flood left bitter memories of racial oppression and death. Especially in Mississippi, thousands of black men were conscripted into labor gangs that shored up the levee, often working at gunpoint. Some drowned as they worked, and a community leader who refused a summons because he'd been working all night was shot on the spot.

The race-hatred exacerbated by the flood triggered a vast expansion of the "great migration" of African-Americans from South to North. [52] For the black community, 1927 established a connection between natural disaster, racism and black exodus — a chain of events that many would later see repeating itself with Katrina.

New Expansion

The 1927 disaster led to improved federal flood-control systems and also launched a continuing debate over whether all Americans should have to pay to protect people living in disaster-prone places. [53]

In New Orleans, the 1927 flood also undermined the total dependence on levees for protection. Two years later, the Corps of Engineers began building a spillway at Bonnet Carré that could release river water into Lake Pontchartrain if the Mississippi rose to 20 feet in New Orleans. The spillway was completed in 1936.

By then, New Orleans residents had other reasons to feel safer. Electric and gasoline-powered motors had relieved major drainage problems. In a city sitting below sea level in a swampy area, difficulties in disposing of human and other waste had long endangered health and lowered the quality of life. Mosquito-borne yellow fever alone killed about 41,000 people between 1817 and 1905.

Draining surrounding swampland also allowed the opening up of new lands for settlement. From the 1930s to the post-World War II years, acreage to the north, east and west of the original city were transformed from wetlands into tract-housing territory. The suburbanization expanded into Jefferson Parish, just outside of the city.

Within New Orleans itself, the amount of land that had been drained for settlement expanded from 12,349 acres in 1895 to more than 90,000 by 1983.

On a dry day, the newly drained territory appeared suitable for housing. But after Katrina, the local paper, the *Times-Picayune*, published an 1878 map showing that nearly every part of the city that flooded in 2005 had been uninhabited in the years before the land was drained. Early residents understood exactly where not to live, the paper concluded. [54]

Hurricanes and Floods

Since the city's founding, the protective levee system had aimed mainly at holding back Mississippi flooding. But beginning in the mid-20th century, a series of powerful hurricanes changed the perception of where danger lay.

In 1947, a 112-mile-an-hour hurricane (they didn't have names yet) brought two-foot floods in a nine-square-mile area. Hurricanes Flossy (1956) and Hilda (1964) caused some damage but were dwarfed by the 160-mile-an-hour winds of Hurricane Betsy in 1965. Floodwaters reached eight feet in parts of the city; 75 people died, and 7,000 homes suffered damage.

In response, Congress passed the Flood Control Act of 1965, which funded expansion of the levee and canal system in and around New Orleans to protect against what today would be classified as a Category 3 hurricane. [55]

In 1969, just as construction of the expanded system began, Hurricane Camille slammed the Gulf Coast. Mississippi was hit hardest, but a section of the New Orleans levee complex also failed, flooding part of the city.

In succeeding years, even rainstorms became problematic. Nine inches of rain during a 1978 storm caused flooding of up to 3.5 feet in low-lying sections, damaging 71,500 homes. A series of heavy rainstorms between 1979 and 1995 also caused widespread damage, and in 1998, Hurricane Georges, a Category 2 storm that barely touched New Orleans, brought a water surge to within a foot of topping the levees. [56]

Waiting for the Big One

The steady growth in the number and intensity of hurricanes during the 1990s fed unease in New Orleans and prompted the *Times-Picayune* to publish — at the beginning of the 2002 hurricane season — a series of articles unflinchingly examining the risks New Orleans faced. "Officials at the local, state and national level are convinced the risk is genuine and are devising plans for alleviating the aftermath of a disaster that could leave the city uninhabitable for six months or more," the authors presciently wrote. [57]

In January 2005, Ivor van Heerden, deputy director of the Louisiana State University (LSU) Hurricane Center, told a conference on "coastal challenges" that a Category 3 or above storm striking New Orleans or any other coastal Louisiana city would be a "disaster of cataclysmic proportion." [58]

By then, the city's new-and-improved flood-protection system consisted of about 125 miles of levees, floodwalls and flood-proofed bridges and other barriers. In Orleans Parish, the renovation work was 90 percent complete. [59]

On Aug. 28, as Hurricane Katrina was rolling through the Gulf and heading for New Orleans, the National Weather Service called it "a most powerful hurricane with unprecedented strength." After landfall, "Most of the area will be uninhabitable for weeks, perhaps longer." [60]

Mayor Nagin, a newcomer to politics, had ordered the city evacuated. But buses for the tens of thousands of elderly and poor residents who didn't own cars were never dispatched.

Even before Katrina touched down near New Orleans on the morning of Aug. 29, a storm surge breached the levees along the Inner Harbor Navigation Canal (the "Industrial Canal"). At about the same time, an 18-foot surge from Lake Borgne pushed through a wall along the Mississippi River Gulf Outlet east of St. Bernard Parish and the Lower Ninth Ward. The resulting flooding soon reached the Lower Ninth. [61]

Over the next few hours, additional surges over the Industrial Canal sent even more floodwater into the Lower Ninth. Then, with Katrina moving westward near Lake Pontchartrain, another section of levee along the Industrial Canal gave way, followed by a breach of the 17th Street Canal floodwall, flooding the western end of the parish. [62]

In the days following the storm, New Orleans became an international symbol of government dysfunction. Tens of thousands of residents unable to evacuate clung to rooftops or flocked to the New Orleans Superdome, which was unequipped to receive them. By Sept. 12, FEMA Director Michael Brown had resigned under pressure — only days after being congratulated by President Bush. Belatedly, federal officials organized bus convoys and flights out of the city. [63]

Then, on Sept. 24, Hurricane Rita, a Category 3 storm, hit the Gulf Coast. New Orleans didn't lie directly in the storm's path, but the hurricane reopened some partly repaired levee breaches. As a result, the Lower Ninth Ward and the Gentilly neighborhood flooded again. Elsewhere in Louisiana and East Texas, the damage was far worse, with tens of thousands left homeless. [64]

By early December, only 10 percent of the city's businesses were up and running, and 135,000 residents, at most, had stayed or returned. They had a name for the only fully functioning part of the city — a strip of high ground that includes the French Quarter and other sections of old New Orleans: Like explorer Bienville, they called it "the island." [65] ■

CURRENT SITUATION

Redevelopment Plans

On Jan. 11, the Bring New Orleans Back Commission released its "Action Plan" for rebuilding the city, but action doesn't seem to be on the near horizon.

The plan recommended the formation of 13 neighborhood-planning committees, with work on recommendations to start on Feb. 20, finish by May 20 and be submitted to the city for approval by June 20. Reconstruction would begin by Aug. 20. [66]

Within days of the plan's release, however, a FEMA official said updated floodplain maps of the city wouldn't be available until the summer, depriving crucial information to homeowners considering rebuilding.

"If I were putting my lifetime savings in the single, biggest investment I'll ever make, I'd want to make sure I had minimized every possible risk," said Tulane's Kroloff, chairman of the commission's urban-design subcommittee. [67]

The delay in obtaining the updated flood-zone information would slow the reconstruction timetable, Kroloff said, but wouldn't prevent the neighborhood committees from canvassing past and present residents. "There are some people who are going to return no matter what, and some who aren't," he said. [68]

Other obstacles could further slow the plan's execution. Congress may not approve Rep. Baker's proposal to create a public corporation to buy and sell distressed properties, although BNOB Commissioner Canizaro hopes funds can be rounded up from FEMA and elsewhere. [69] The Louisiana legislature would have to create the nonprofit entity, provisionally entitled the Crescent City Recovery Corp., and New Orleans voters would have to OK changes to the city charter to authorize it. [70]

That vote could come as soon as April. But it remains to be seen how receptive voters will be to measures recommended by Nagin and the commission, especially in light of the criticism that greeted the plan when it was unveiled. Some property owners attacked the proposal as a land grab.

"If you come to take our property, you'd better come ready," homeowner Rodney Craft of the Lower Ninth Ward told the commissioners. [71]

"I hear the politicians talk, and nothing is being said — nothing," says Gail Miller, a retired New Orleans police officer who has returned to her home in New Orleans East, living upstairs but cooking in a motor home she and her husband park in the driveway. "The political situation worries me — the levees don't worry me a bit."

Another widespread worry is education. Since the state took over 102 of the city's 117 schools by designating them as a "recovery district," only about 8,000 of 60,000 pre-Katrina students are attending the handful of public and parochial schools that are operating. [72]

"One of the barriers to families returning is that the state took over the schools and is not opening them," says Councilwoman Willard-Lewis.

Many residents say, however, that reopening the schools as they were wouldn't be much help. The Urban Land Institute reported that before Katrina the public school system had an "educational quotient" ranking of 1 out of 100 — the nation's lowest. [73]

"Everybody knew that public education was broken before the storm," says Heather Thompson, a New Orleans native and Harvard Business School student. A graduate of the public schools' only secondary-level crown jewel, Benjamin Franklin High School, Thompson helped organize a consulting project by four dozen of her fellow business students to recommend recovery ideas for schools and other elements of civic life. [74]

Meanwhile, the shortage of school space seems likely to continue. "I want to get the very best leaders and the very best teachers for every child in Orleans Parish," said State Education Superintendent Cecil Picard, adding that he expects 15,000 public-school students when classes reopen in August. [75]

Port Bounces Back

Giant cranes are swinging containers off and on ships, warehouses are filled with bundles of rubber and coils of steel, and trucks headed inland are filling up with coffee beans. The Port of New Orleans is back up and running, though only months ago a quick comeback seemed improbable.

"On Aug. 30, somebody told me it would be six months before we got the first ship back," port Director LaGrange says. "I said our goal was to be at 70 percent of pre-Katrina activity by March 1 — the six-month anniversary [of Katrina]. We're pushing 65 percent now."

Immediately after Katrina struck, while Americans watched thousands of human tragedies unfolding in real time on television, shippers and merchants focused on the southern Louisiana port complex — the country's fourth-largest. [76] "The longer the ports remained closed, the greater the risk that we'd all be paying higher prices for coffee, cocoa, lumber, steel, zinc, aluminum and any number of other things," said Mark M. Zandi, chief executive of the Economy.com research firm. [77]

In a seeming paradox, Katrina largely spared the riverfront port area. Like the old French Quarter, most of the port sits atop the natural levee on which Bienville founded the city. However, a major container terminal and a new cold-storage warehouse in eastern New Orleans were both destroyed.

Louisiana politicians frequently cite the port's importance to the economy as an argument for rebuilding New Orleans to its pre-Katrina scale. When she heard that the port might be able to function at full strength with a city somewhat smaller than pre-Katrina New Orleans, Sen. Landrieu, responded: "Where are the workers going to come from? You can't have a port without New Orleans."

LaGrange takes a more nuanced view. "You've got to have the work force here," he says, and they will need "the support services that a city provides — transit, schools, places to worship, grocery stores, gasoline stations. But if the city, for some reason, is smaller, I don't think that would be a tremendous effect on the output of the port."

Continued on p. 114

At Issue:

Should New Orleans be completely rebuilt on its old footprint?

yes

SEN. MARY LANDRIEU, D-LA.
MEMBER, SENATE APPROPRIATIONS COMMITTEE

WRITTEN FOR THE *CQ RESEARCHER*, JANUARY 2006

More than five months ago, Hurricane Katrina and the subsequent breaks in numerous flood-control levees decimated one of our nation's greatest cities, my hometown, New Orleans.

Some have since questioned whether or not we should rebuild New Orleans, saying that we should abandon a city that has contributed so much to our great nation.

New Orleans is the capitol of our nation's energy coast. It was put there for a reason. We did not go there to sunbathe. We went there to set up the Mississippi River, to tame that river, to create channels for this country to grow and prosper. New Orleans was established so the cities and communities along the Mississippi River would have a port to trade with the world.

The indispensible Higgins boats that saved us during World War II were built in New Orleans. Forty-three thousand people built those boats and headed them out to Normandy. We're going to rebuild our shipping industry. We're going to rebuild our maritime industry, we will maintain our great port and we will continue to provide the energy that keeps our lights on across the nation.

Just because parts of New Orleans are below sea level is no reason to allow this great city to die. The Netherlands is a nation that is 21 feet below sea level at its economic heart, yet they still operate Europe's largest port — just as we operate America's largest port system.

The Dutch have proved that you can live below sea level and still keep your feet dry. They believe in an integrated system of water management. After a flood destroyed their nation in 1953, the Dutch said "Never again," and today they have created the world's most advanced storm-protection and flood-control system. If a nation half the size of Louisiana can do it, then surely the United States of America can.

We can and should rebuild every neighborhood — but maybe not exactly the way we did it the first time. This time we can build better, smarter, stronger neighborhoods.

One fact is certain: Every, single American citizen who calls New Orleans home has a right to come back and rebuild their neighborhoods, and the federal government should generously support that right.

New Orleans helped build America, and now America must help rebuild New Orleans, because America needs that great city — right where it is.

no

WILLIAM HUDNUT
JOSEPH C. CANIZARO CHAIR IN PUBLIC POLICY, URBAN LAND INSTITUTE

WRITTEN FOR THE *CQ RESEARCHER*, JANUARY 2006

There are those who understandably feel that New Orleans should be rebuilt in its entirety, and that blocks and neighborhoods throughout the pre-Katrina city should be rebuilt house by house as resources permit.

The emotional tug of going back to one's "roots" is strong. One cannot blame the City Council and others for demanding that all areas of the city, especially East New Orleans and the Lower Ninth, as well as Lakeview and Gentilly, be rebuilt simultaneously. But we need to ask: Is such a plan realistic? Does it make sense?

The city will not have the resources to take care of a widely dispersed population, and not all the evacuees will be returning. Critics of a smaller city dismiss such plans and ideas as "arrogant," "elitist" and "racist," because the low-lying areas are where mostly black and low-income residents lived before Katrina. But the questions persist.

I can think of two compelling reasons to envision a smaller New Orleans in the future. It will have a smaller population, and it will be safer.

As is often said, "Demography is destiny." If New Orleans once had 465,000 people, that was once and no more. The city was losing population before Katrina and has shrunk to a little over 100,000 today, with prospects of that number climbing to perhaps 250,000 by the time Katrina's third anniversary rolls around.

Is it prudent to think that this smaller number of people should occupy all the territory that almost twice that number did before August 2005, especially when the city will not have the financial resources, police, fire and EMS services and the like to care for such a scattered population? Two keys to a successful, vibrant city are diversity and density, which a sprawled-out land base does not provide.

Katrina has given New Orleans a chance to reinvent itself as a more compact, connected city on a smaller footprint. The city's recovering economy built on restored building blocks — culture, food, music, art, entertainment, tourism, bioscience and medical research, the port, energy production — will attract people back into mixed-use, mixed-income, racially balanced, pedestrian-friendly neighborhoods carefully planned by citizens, with parks, open space, new wetlands and light-rail transit added to the mix. All of that can be accomplished on less space than the city occupied heretofore.

Who was it that said, "Small is beautiful?"

Continued from p. 112

Politics and Legislation

New Orleans' future lies in many hands, but federal lawmakers may be the most important, because they control the biggest money source.

"We are at your mercy," Gov. Blanco told Senate Homeland Security Committee members as they toured the disaster zone on Jan. 17. "We are begging you to stay with us." [78]

Landrieu plans to revive her proposal to channel 50 percent of offshore petroleum-lease revenues to the state. The money would be earmarked for post-Katrina reconstruction, says her spokesman, Adam Sharp.

Besides the Landrieu and Baker proposals, Louisiana politicians will continue to push for $2.1 billion in supplemental Medicaid funds to help pay for health care for Katrina victims — many suddenly homeless and unemployed — who had to enter the federally subsidized medical insurance program for low-income people. Congress adjourned at year's end without passing the Medicaid bill, but Landrieu says she'll also continue to push for that.

The fact that none of these proposals passed while Katrina's devastation was fresh would seem to show that the state's politicians "have some work to do" to get Congress' attention, said one of Baker's aides. Blanco, meanwhile, is preparing to call a special 12-day legislative session, beginning on Feb. 6. She wants state lawmakers to make the "levee boards" that supervise maintenance more accountable. The boards were widely criticized — even ridiculed — for laxity, following Katrina. [79]

Getting the schools going again remains a priority, and Blanco must hammer together by May a plan to reorganize the city's school system, now largely under state control. The state Board of Elementary and Secondary Education would have to rule on the plan. The BNOBC in January proposed a leaner administrative office — one superintendent and four or five assistants — and expanded authority for principals, who would be able to hire and fire their own staffs. Differences between "have" and "have-not" schools would be eliminated under the plan, and early-education programs would be initiated. [80]

Meanwhile, the often-criticized Blanco tangled with the City Council over what she called its resistance to installing FEMA-supplied trailers for needy families. The council was responding, in part, to complaints from some residents who objected to trailer villages in their neighborhoods.

"Disagreements over housing must end — and must end now," she told the council on Jan. 5. Council members denied that they had obstructed trailer installation. After a subsequent meeting between the governor and council members, sites for a total of 40,000 trailers were identified. [81]

Even the demolition of unsafe houses stirred controversy. When it appeared the city was about to bulldoze some Lower Ninth Ward houses deemed unsafe, residents and some council members sought a court order to stop it. U.S. District Judge Martin L. C. Feldman then OK'd a deal between the Nagin administration and Lower Ninth Ward residents requiring at least seven-days' notice before demolition. [82]

The court-approved settlement apparently resolved the demolition issues, but political conflicts between Nagin and the council remain. The beleaguered mayor is among the candidates up for re-election on April 22. ■

OUTLOOK

Pessimism and Paralysis

Optimism is in short supply in New Orleans, notwithstanding the brave talk of Louisiana politicians. The failure of the flood-protection system, the tragedy and chaos of the early days of the disaster and the devastated conditions that remain in much of the city five months after Katrina have not provided grounds for much hope.

President Bush, in his State of the Union address on Jan. 31, devoted 162 of the speech's 5,432 words to New Orleans, proposing no specific, new remedies. "As we meet . . . immediate needs, we must also address deeper challenges that existed before the storm arrived," Bush said, citing a need for better schools and economic opportunity. Among Louisiana politicians, even the president's fellow Republicans felt left out. "I was very disappointed at how small a part those national challenges — and I think are national challenges — were given in the speech," Sen. Vitter told the *Times-Picayune.*

"There's no sense of urgency from the city government, the state government or the federal government," says Dennis Scott, looking out on his devastated New Orleans East neighborhood.

Indeed, as of late January, the U.S. Army Corps of Engineers had completed only 16 percent of the levee repairs scheduled for completion by June 1, when the 2006 hurricane season begins. [83]

An outsider draws essentially the same conclusion as Scott. "The lack of unity in the political establishment is the paralyzing factor," says the Urban Land Institute's Hudnut. "There's almost a political stand-off between the governor's office, the mayor's office, the City Council and the Bring New Orleans Back Commission; but this is also partially a Washington issue. I don't see a lot of leadership coming from the White House team."

Republican Hudnut is one of many politicians and ordinary citizens to question the high cost of the war in Iraq with the needs of New Orleans. The war's direct cash cost alone through November 2005 was calculated at

$251 billion, according to a study released in January by two former Clinton administration officials. [84] Thompson, the Harvard Business School student working on redevelopment plans, observes that the government ought to be able to "make money appear" for New Orleans in the same way as deficit financing is arranged for the war.

If talking openly about race relations holds promise for making them better, the New Orleans disaster might have served some purpose. Some black New Orleanians wonder aloud, though, if the color of the majority of the city's residents hasn't also slowed down the pace of recovery. Anne LaBranche, the doctor's wife from New Orleans East, can't think of any other reason.

"This was a man-made problem," she says, referring to the failure of the flood-protection system. And yet, previous hurricane damage in Florida and other Gulf Coast states has been paid for without debate on whether people should be living in such potentially risky areas, she says. "President Bush says he resents it when people say 'racism,' so tell me what it is," she says quietly. "Why the different treatment?"

If New Orleans has one advantage concerning race, it may be that the city's geography tends to throw people of different colors together more than in other locales. Another point in the city's favor is New Orleanians' loyalty to their city. It remains to be seen whether that's enough to overcome the economic, political and environmental obstacles.

Piano technician David Doremus has lived in New Orleans most of the past 30 years. He and his wife live in the unflooded Algiers neighborhood on the Mississippi's west bank, and they are committed to remaining in town with their daughters.

While he's unsure about how much piano tuning and rebuilding work he'll have in the near future, he can't imagine anywhere else that offers the pace of life, the social graces and the fishing that he enjoys in New Orleans — as well as the musical variety. "I work for a recording studio, and one of the first sessions I worked on after the storm was with Allen Toussaint and Elvis Costello," he says.

So Doremus is ready to commute 40 miles to work at a friend's piano business in Covington, La., for a year, if he has to, or even work at Home Depot. "My family back in Virginia thinks I'm nuts," he adds. "And my wife's family in Pittsburgh thinks she's nuts."

If the Doremuses are crazy, New Orleans needs all the nuts it can muster. ■

Notes

[1] Gary Rivlin, "Anger Meets New Orleans Renewal Plan," *The New York Times*, Jan. 12, 2006, p. A18.

[2] When Hurricane Katrina made landfall at Buras, La., 35 miles east of New Orleans at about 6 a.m., it was originally rated at Category 4, the classification for storms with wind speeds of 131-155 mph. The National Hurricane Center later revised that classification down to Category 3, with winds of 111-130 mph. Some 24 hours before reaching Louisiana, Katrina varied between categories 4 and 5. For further detail, see Peter Whoriskey and Joby Warrick, "Report Revises Katrina's Force," *The Washington Post*, Dec. 22, 2005, p. A3; Richard D. Knabb, *et al.*, "Tropical Cyclone Report: Hurricane Katrina, 22-30 August, 2005," National Hurricane Center, Dec. 20, 2005, p. 3, www.nhc.noaa.gov/pdf/TCR-AL122005_Katrina.pdf; and National Aeronautics and Space Administration, "Hurricane Season 2005: Katrina," www.nasa.gov/vision/earth/lookingatearth/h2005_katrina.html.

[3] Nicholas Riccardi, "Most of Louisiana's Identified Storm Victims Over 60," *Los Angeles Times*, Nov. 5, 2005, p. A11; Nicholas Riccardi, Doug Smith and David Zucchino, "Katrina Killed Along Class Lines," *Los Angeles Times*, Dec. 18, 2005, p. A1.

[4] While Katrina had weakened to Category 3 upon reaching Louisiana, the surges it created began when the storm was at categories 4 and 5 strength. For further detail, see "Tropical Cyclone Report," *op. cit.*, p. 9.

[5] "President Discusses Hurricane Relief in Address to the Nation," White House, Sept. 15, 2005, www.whitehouse.gov/news/releases/2005/09/print/20050915-8.html.

[6] Bill Walsh, "Senators say recovery moving at snail's pace," *The Times-Picayune* (New Orleans), Jan. 18, 2006, p. A1.

[7] Ralph Vartabedian, "New Orleans Should be Dry by End of Week," *Los Angeles Times*, Sept. 19, 2005, p. A8; "Performance Evaluation Plan and Interim Status, Report 1 of a Series: Performance Evaluation of the New Orleans and Southeast Louisiana Hurricane Protection System," Interagency Performance Evaluation Task Force, Jan. 10, 2006, p. 1, https://ipet.wes.army.mil.

[8] "Action Plan for New Orleans: The New American City," Bring New Orleans Back Commission, Urban Planning Committee, Jan. 11, 2006, Introduction, www.bringneworleansback.org.

[9] "It was not unusual for slaves to gather on street corners at night, for example, where they challenged whites to attempt to pass. . . ," historian Joseph G. Tregle is quoted in Eugene D. Genovese, *Roll, Jordan, Roll: The World the Slaves Made* (1972), pp. 412-413.

[10] Quoted in Reed Johnson, "New Orleans: Before and After," *Los Angeles Times*, Sept. 5, 2005, p. E1. For more background on Congo Square, see Craig E. Colten, *An Unnatural Metropolis: Wresting New Orleans From Nature* (2005), p. 72; and Gerald Early, "Slavery," on Web site for "Jazz," PBS documentary, www.pbs.org/jazz/time/time_slavery.htm.

[11] "A Strategy for Rebuilding New Orleans, Louisiana," Urban Land Institute, Nov. 12-18, 2005, p. 17, www.uli.org/Content/NavigationMenu/ProgramsServices/AdvisoryServices/KatrinaPanel/ULI_Draft_New_Orleans%20Report.pdf.

[12] "President Discusses Hurricane Relief," *op. cit.*

[13] Joby Warrick, "White House Got Early Warning on Katrina," *The Washington Post*, Jan. 24, 2005, p. A2.

[14] Steve Ritea and Tara Young, "Cycle of Death: Violence Thrives on Lack of Jobs, Wealth of Drugs," *The Times-Picayune* (New Orleans), p. A1; Adam Nossiter, "New Orleans Crime Swept Away, With Most of the People," *The New York Times*, Nov. 10, 2005, p. A1. Dan Baum, "Deluged, When Katrina hit, where were the police?" *The New Yorker*, Jan. 9, 2006, p. 59.

[15] Quoted in, Joel Havemann, "New Orleans' Racial Future Hotly Argued," *Los Angeles Times*, Oct. 1, 2005, p. A14.

[16] Brett Martel, The Associated Press, "Storms Payback From God, Nagin Says," *The Washington Post*, Jan. 17, 2006, p. A4.

[17] Manuel Rog-Franzia, "New Orleans Mayor Apologizes for Remarks About God's Wrath," *The Washington Post*, Jan. 18, 2006, p. A2.

[18] James Dao, "Study Says 80% of New Orleans Blacks May Not Return," *The New York Times*, Jan. 27, 2006, p. A16.

[19] *Ibid.*; see also "Action Plan," (pages unnumbered); Frank Donze and Gordon Russell, "Rebuilding proposal gets mixed reception," *The Times-Picayune* (New Orleans), Jan. 12, 2006, p. A1.

[20] Donze and Russell, *ibid.*; Rivlin, *op. cit.*

[21] "A Strategy for Rebuilding," *op. cit.*; Frank Donze, "Don't write us off, residents warn," *The Times-Picayune* (New Orleans), Nov. 29, 2005, p. A1.

[22] "Action Plan," Introduction, *op. cit.*; Gordon Russell, "Comeback in Progress," *The Times-Picayune* (New Orleans), Jan. 1, 2006, p. A1.

[23] "Battered by Katrina, Tulane University forced into layoffs, cutbacks," The Associated Press, Dec. 9, 2005.

[24] Susan Saulny, "Students Return to Big Changes in New Orleans," *The New York Times*, Jan. 4, 2006, p. 13; Steven Ritea, "School board considers limited role," *The Times-Picayune* (New Orleans), Dec. 7, 2005, p. A1.

[25] Elizabeth Bumiller, "In New Orleans, Bush Speaks With Optimism But Sees Little of Ruin," *The New York Times*, Jan. 13, 2006, p. A12.

[26] For background, see Marcia Clemmitt, "Climate Change," *CQ Researcher*, Jan. 27, 2006, pp. 73-96.

[27] Virginia R. Burkett, "Potential Impacts of Climate Change and Variability on Transportation in the Gulf Coast/Mississippi Delta Region," Center for Climate Change and Environmental Forecasting, Oct. 1-2, 2002, p. 7, http://climate.volpe.dot.gov/workshop1002/burkett.pdf. Burkett is chief of the Forest Ecology Branch of the U.S. Geological Survey's National Wetlands Research Center, in Lafayette, La.

[28] In 2006, the Bush administration does not plan to seek new funds for reconstruction in Iraq. See, Ellen Knickmeyer, "U.S. Has End in Sight on Iraq Rebuilding," *The Washington Post*, Jan. 2, 2006, p. A1.

[29] Michael Oneal, "GOP Cools to Katrina Aid," *Chicago Tribune*, Nov. 12, 2005, p. A7.

[30] For background, see Kenneth Jost, "Property Rights," *CQ Researcher*, March 4, 2005, pp. 197-220.

[31] R. B. Seed, *et al.*, "Preliminary Report on the Performance of the New Orleans Levee Systems on August. 29, 2005," University of California at Berkeley, American Society of Civil Engineers, Nov. 2, 2005, pp. 1.2-1.4.

[32] Schwartz, *op. cit.*

[33] For details, see John McQuaid, "The Dutch Swore It Would Never Happen Again," "Dutch Defense, Dutch Masters," "Bigger, Better, Bolder," *The Times-Picayune* (New Orleans), Nov. 13-14, 2005, p. A1.

[34] "Performance Evaluation Plan," *op. cit.*, appendix A-2. John Schwartz, "Category 5: Levees are Piece of $32 Billion Pie," *The New York Times*, Nov. 29, 2005, p. A1.

[35] *Ibid.*

[36] Richard W. Stevenson and James Dao, "White House to Double Spending on New Orleans Flood Protection," *The New York Times*, Dec. 16, 2005, p. A1.

[37] *Ibid.*

[38] President Bush said on Jan. 26 the congressional appropriations amounted to $85 billion. For background and detail, see Joseph J. Schatz, "End-of-Session Gift for the Gulf Coast," *CQ Weekly*, Dec. 26, 2005, p. 3401; "Cost of Katrina Nearing $100 Billion, Senate Budget Says," *CQ Budget Tracker News*, Jan. 18, 2006; "Senate Budget Committee Releases Current Tally of Hurricane-Related Spending," Budget Committee, Jan. 18, 2006, http://budget.senate.gov/republican. "Press Conference of the President," [transcript] Jan. 26, 2006, www.whitehouse.gov/news/releases/2006/01/ 20060126.htm..

[39] Quoted in Jacob Freedman, "Additional Flood Funds Needed to Cover Extensive Gulf Coast Damage," *CQ Today*, Jan. 25, 2006; Statement of David I. Maurstad, Acting Director/Federal Insurance Administrator, Mitigation Division, Federal Emergency Management Agency, Committee on Senate Banking Housing and Urban Affairs, Jan. 25, 2006, http://banking.senate.gov/_files/ACF43B7.pdf.

[40] Frank Donze, Gordon Russell and Lauri Maggi, "Buyouts torpedoed, not sunk," *The Times-Picayune* (New Orleans), Jan. 26, 2006, p. A1.

[41] Adrian Moore, "Rebuild New Orleans Smarter, Not Harder," Reason Foundation, Jan. 11, 2006, /www.reason.org/commentaries/moore_20060111.shtml.

[42] David Greising, *et al.*, "How Do They Rebuild a City?" *Chicago Tribune*, Sept. 4, 2005, p. A1.

[43] "Press Conference of the President," *op. cit.*

[44] Donze, Russell and Maggi, *op. cit.*

[45] *Ibid.*

[46] Robert L. Bamberger and Lawrence Kumins, "Oil and Gas: Supply Issues After Katrina," Congressional Research Service, updated Sept. 6, 2005, p. 1, www.fas.org/sgp/crs/misc/RS22233.pdf. For background on offshore leases, see Jennifer Weeks, "Domestic Energy Development," *CQ Researcher*, Sept. 30, 2005, pp. 809-832.

[47] Marc Humphries, "Outer Continental Shelf: Debate Over Oil and Gas Leasing and Revenue Sharing," Congressional Research Service, Uupdated Oct. 27, 2005, pp. 1-4. http://fpc.state.gov/documents/organization/56096.pdf.

[48] Unless otherwise indicated, all material in this section comes from Colten, *op. cit.*; and Ari Kelman, *A River and Its City: The Nature of Landscape in New Orleans* (2003).

[49] Caroline E. Mayer and Amy Joyce, "Troubles Travel Upstream," *The Washington Post*, Sept. 5, 2005, p. A23.

[50] Colten, *op. cit.*, pp. 25-26.

[51] For background, see C. Perkins, "Mississippi River Flood Relief and Control," *Editorial Research Reports*, 1927, Vol. 2; and M. Packman, "Disaster Insurance," *Editorial Research Reports 1956*, Vol. I.

[52] John M. Barry, *Rising Tide: The Great Mississippi Flood of 1927 and How it Changed America* (1998), pp. 311-317; p. 332

[53] For background, see "Economic Effects of the Mississippi Flood," *Editorial Research Reports, 1928*, Vol. I.

About the Author

Peter Katel is a *CQ Researcher* staff writer who previously reported on Haiti and Latin America for *Time* and *Newsweek* and covered the Southwest for newspapers in New Mexico. He has received several journalism awards, including the Bartolomé Mitre Award for drug coverage from the Inter-American Press Association. He holds an A.B. in university studies from the University of New Mexico. His recent reports include "Lobbying Boom," "Immigration Reform" and "Emerging China."

[54] Gordon Russell, "An 1878 Map Reveals that Maybe Our Ancestors Were Right to Build on Higher Ground," *The Times-Picayune* (New Orleans), Nov. 3, 2005, p. A1.
[55] "Performance Evaluation Plan," *op. cit.*, Appendix A, p. 1; Willie Drye, " 'Category Five': How a Hurricane Yardstick Came To Be," *National Geographic News*, Dec. 20, 2005, http://news.nationalgeographic.com/news/2005/12/1220_051220_saffirsimpson.html.
[56] John McQuaid and Mark Schleifstein, "The Big One," *The Times-Picayune* (New Orleans), June 24, 2002, p. A1.
[57] *Ibid.*
[58] Ivor van Heerden, "Using Technology to Illustrate the Realities of Hurricane Vulnerability," Jan. 25, 2005, www.laseagrant.org/forum/01-25-2005.htm.
[59] "Performance Evaluation Plan," *op. cit.*, Appendix A, pp. 2-3.
[60] "Urgent Warning Proved Prescient," *The New York Times*, Sept. 7, 2005, p. A21.
[61] "How New Orleans Flooded," in "The Storm That Drowned a City," NOVA, WGBH-TV, October 2005, www.pbs.org/wgbh/nova/orleans/how-nf.html.
[62] *Ibid.*
[63] See Pamela Prah, "Disaster Preparedness," *CQ Researcher*, Nov. 18, 2005, pp. 981-1004.
[64] "Rita's Aftermath," *Los Angeles Times*, Sept. 28, 2005, p. A1; Shaila Dewan and Jere Longman, "Hurricane Slams Into Gulf Coast; Flooding Spreads," *The New York Times*, Sept. 25, 2005, p. A1.
[65] Anne Rochell Konigsmark, "Amid ruins, 'island' of normalcy in the Big Easy," *USA Today*, Dec. 19, 2005, p. A1; Gordon Russell, "Comeback in Progress," *The Times-Picayune* (New Orleans), Jan. 1, 2006, p. A1.
[66] "Action Plan," *op. cit.*, Sec. 4, (pages unnumbered).
[67] Gordon Russell and James Varney, "New flood maps will likely steer rebuilding," *The Times-Picayune* (New Orleans), Jan. 15, 2006, p. A1.
[68] *Ibid.*
[69] *Ibid.*
[70] *Ibid.*
[71] Russell and Donze, *op. cit.*, Jan. 12, 2006.
[72] Ritea and Saulny, *op. cit.*
[73] "A Strategy for Rebuilding New Orleans," *op. cit.*, p. 19.
[74] For background, see, George Anders, "How a Principal in New Orleans Saved Her School," *The Wall Street Journal*, Jan. 13, 2006, p. A1.

FOR MORE INFORMATION

Bring New Orleans Back Commission, www.bringneworleansback.org. The commission has been issuing detailed redevelopment plans.

The Brookings Institution, Katrina Issues and the Aftermath Project, Metropolitan Policy Program, 1775 Massachusetts Ave., N.W., Washington, DC 20036; (202) 797-6139; www.brookings.edu/metro/katrina.htm. The think tank provides policy proposals, commentary and statistics.

Center for the Study of Public Health Impacts of Hurricanes, CEBA Building, Suite 3221, Louisiana State University, Baton Rouge, LA 70803; (225) 578-4813; www.publichealth.hurricane.lsu.edu. A research center focusing on disaster prevention and mitigation.

Federal Emergency Management Agency, 500 C St., S.W., Washington, DC 20472; (202) 566-1600; www.fema.gov. The lead federal agency on disaster recovery; provides information on relief program requirements and application deadlines.

Greater New Orleans Community Data Center, www.gnocdc.org. A virtual organization that provides links to the city's most recent social, economic and demographic statistics.

Louisiana Recovery Authority, 525 Florida St., 2nd Floor, Baton Rouge, LA 70801; (225) 382-5502; http://lra.louisiana.gov. The state government's post-disaster reconstruction agency; provides information on the aid flowing to New Orleans.

New Orleans Area Habitat for Humanity, P.O. Box 15052, New Orleans, LA 70175; (504) 861-2077, www.habitat-nola.org. A self-help housing organization building new homes in the city and nearby suburbs.

Savenolamusic, www.savenolamusic.com/index.php. An exhaustive listing of performance bookings and other resources (including medical assistance) for New Orleans musicians, including those forced out of the city.

Urban Land Institute, 1025 Thomas Jefferson St., N.W., Suite 500 West, Washington, DC 20007; (202) 624-7000; www.uli.org. The nonprofit organization for land-use and development professionals is the New Orleans city government's disaster-recovery consultant.

[75] Steve Ritea, "La. won't run N.O. schools by itself," *The Times-Picayune* (New Orleans), Jan. 3, 2006, p. B1.
[76] Vanessa Cieslak, "Ports in Louisiana: New Orleans, South Louisiana, and Baton Rouge," Congressional Research Service, Oct. 14, 2005, p. 1, http://fpc.state.gov/documents/organization/57872.pdf.
[77] Keith L. Alexander and Neil Irwin, "Port Comes Back Early, Surprisingly," *The Washington Post*, Sept. 14, 2005, p. D1.
[78] Bill Walsh, "Senators say recovery moving at a snail's pace," *The Times-Picayune* (New Orleans), Jan. 18, 2006, p. A1.
[79] Ed Anderson, "Special session set to begin Feb. 6," *The Times-Picayune* (New Orleans), Jan. 12, 2006, p. A2.
[80] Steve Ritea, "Nagin's schools panel issues reforms," *The Times-Picayune* (New Orleans), Jan. 18, 2006, p. A1; "Rebuilding and Transforming: A Plan for World-Class Public Education in New Orleans," Bring New Orleans Back Commission, Jan. 17, 2006, pp. 10, 48.
[81] Ed Anderson, "N.O. needs 7,000 more trailer sites, Blanco says," *The Times-Picayune* (New Orleans), Jan. 9, p. A1.
[82] Adam Nossiter, "New Orleans Agrees to Give Notice on Home Demolitions," *The New York Times*, Jan. 18, 2006, p. A10.
[83] Spencer S. Hsu, "Bush's Post-Katrina Pledges," *The Washington Post*, Jan. 28, 2006, p. A12.
[84] Linda Bilmes and Joseph Stiglitz, "The Economic Costs of the Iraq War: An Appraisal Three Years After the Beginning of the Conflict," http://ksghome.harvard.edu/~lbilmes/paper/iraqnew.pdf. Former Deputy Assistant Commerce Secretary Bilmes is now at the Kennedy School of Government at Harvard; Stiglitz, a Nobel laureate economist, teaches at Columbia University.

Bibliography

Selected Sources

Books

Colten, Craig E., *An Unnatural Metropolis: Wresting New Orleans from Nature*, Louisiana State University Press, 2005.
A Louisiana State University, Baton Rouge, geographer chronicles the city's ongoing efforts to tame its watery environment.

Dyson, Michael Eric, *Come Hell or High Water: Hurricane Katrina and the Color of Disaster*, Basic Civitas Books, 2006.
A professor of humanities at the University of Pennsylvania — and a prolific author and commentator on issues of race and culture — dissects what he views as structural racism, government incompetence and class warfare against the poor in the Katrina disaster.

Kelman, Ari, *A River and its City: The Nature of Landscape in New Orleans*, University of California Press, 2003.
Using New Orleans' long and complicated relationship with the Mississippi River as a framework, an environmental historian at the University of California, Davis, examines why New Orleans developed as it did.

Piazza, Tom, *Why New Orleans Matters*, HarperCollins, 2005.
A jazz historian, novelist and New Orleans resident who evacuated the city during Katrina argues that American culture will be poorer if the working people who keep the city's traditions alive are permanently uprooted from the city.

Ward, Geoffrey C., and Ken Burns, *Jazz: A History of America's Music*, Alfred A. Knopf, 2000.
An author of popular history (Ward) and a renowned documentary filmmaker provide — with contributions by jazz scholars — a one-volume history of America's major cultural creation, with much attention to New Orleans' role.

Articles

Baum, Dan, "Deluged: When Katrina hit, where were the police?" *The New Yorker*, Jan. 9, 2006, p. 50.
A writer recounts how police and city government coped — or failed to — in the post-hurricane disaster.

Cooper, Christopher, "Old-Line Families Escape Worst of Flood and Plot the Future," *The Wall Street Journal*, Sept. 8. 2005, p. A1.
A profile of one of New Orleans' aristocrats brings the city's social inequalities to light in dispassionate fashion.

McQuaid, John, and Mark Schleifstein, "In Harm's Way," "Evolving Danger," "Left Behind," "The Big One," "Exposure's Cost," "Building Better," "Model Solutions," "Tempting Fate," "Shifting Tides," [series] *The Times-Picayune*, June 23-June 26, 2002.
Three years before Katrina, two reporters spell out the city's growing vulnerability to a massive hurricane, virtually telling the Katrina story.

Sontag, Deborah, "Delrey Street," *The New York Times*, Oct. 12, 2005, p. A1; Oct. 24, 2005, p. A1; Nov. 12, 2005, p. A9; Nov. 14, 2005 p. A1; Dec. 2, 2005, p. A20; Jan. 9, 2006, p. A1.
In a series of detailed profiles, a *New York Times* reporter examines how the lives of families from New Orleans' Lower Ninth Ward have been upended by Katrina.

Tizon, Alex Tomas, and Doug Smith, "Evacuees of Hurricane Katrina Resettle Along a Racial Divide," *Los Angeles Times*, Dec. 12, 2005, p. A1.
Two reporters analyzed change-of-address data to draw early conclusions on the racial effects of the disaster.

Reports and studies

"Action Plan for New Orleans: The New American City," Bring New Orleans Back Commission, Urban Planning Committee, Jan. 11, 2006, www.bringneworleansback.org.
Civic leaders and officials provided the first detailed plan for redevelopment of New Orleans.

"An Unnatural Disaster: The Aftermath of Hurricane Katrina," Scholars for Progressive Reform, Sept. 2005, www.progressivereform.org/Unnatural_Disaster_512.pdf.
A liberal organization analyzes the disaster as a failure of unrestrained energy development and inadequate government regulation.

Katz, Bruce, *et al.*, "Katrina Index: Tracking Variables of Post-Katrina Reconstruction," updated Dec. 6, 2005, The Brookings Institution, www.brookings.edu/metro/pubs/200512_katrinaindex.htm.
To be updated periodically, this report compiles and organizes statistics in order to show economic and social trends as New Orleans recovers.

Seed, R. B., *et al.*, "Preliminary Report on the Performance of the New Orleans Levee Systems in Hurricane Katrina on August 29, 2005," University of California at Berkeley, American Society of Civil Engineers, National Science Foundation, Nov. 2, 2005, www.berkeley.edu/news/media/releases/2005/11/leveereport_prelim.pdf.
Engineering experts provide an early look at the failures of the levee system that led to disaster.

The Next Step:

Additional Articles from Current Periodicals

Deciding Whether to Return

Eisenberg, Daniel, "The Displaced: Which Way is Home?" *Time*, Nov. 28, 2005, p. 40.
Journalists follow five groups of Katrina survivors from Louisiana and Mississippi as some return to the Gulf Coast and others vow never to return.

Pomfret, John, "Evacuees Begin to Put Down Roots," *The Washington Post*, Oct. 22, 2005, p. A8.
New Orleans evacuees living in Austin, Texas, find it difficult to return to the city because of new jobs and new schools.

Thomas-Lester, Avis, "Tough Decisions About Studying in New Orleans," *The Washington Post*, Jan. 19, 2006, p. T15.
Students displaced from colleges affected by Katrina must decide whether to stay at their temporary schools.

Turner, Allan, "Some New Orleans Evacuees Homesick, Some Sick of Home," *The Houston Chronicle*, Dec. 9, 2005, p. A1.
New Orleanians displaced by Katrina discuss whether they want to return home or stay in their new locations.

Emotional Trauma

Connolly, Ceci, "Katrina's Emotional Damage Lingers," *The Washington Post*, Dec. 7, 2005, p. A3.
The emotional scars lingering after Katrina are far beyond what mental-health experts in the United States have ever confronted.

Levy, Clifford J., "Wrestling With Memories Amid Mounds of Trash," *The New York Times*, Dec. 28, 2005, p. A12.
New Orleans residents grapple with throwing away destroyed possessions that invoke memories.

Mehren, Elizabeth, "Study is Tracing Hardships of Katrina Survivors," *Los Angeles Times*, Jan. 6, 2006, p. A24.
Gulf Coast residents affected by Katrina are exhibiting signs of weariness, anxiety and pessimism.

Olsen, Lise, "Fleeing the Storms Was Just the Start of Troubles for the Elderly, As Many Are Isolated From Their Families and Have No Home Left," *The Houston Chronicle*, Nov. 28, 2005, p. A1.
Thousands of elderly residents displaced by Katrina and Rita are left scarred from the stress of being moved, losing everything and remaining isolated from families.

Radcliffe, Jennifer, "HISD Schools Suffering 'Compassion Fatigue,' " *The Houston Chronicle*, Dec. 25, 2005, p. B6.
Fights, arrests and suspensions characterize the greater Houston area's school systems four months after they absorbed 20,000 students displaced from New Orleans.

Flood Control in the Netherlands

Martin, Susan Taylor, "To Live Below Sea Level, Ask Dutch," *St. Petersburg Times* (Florida), Nov. 6, 2005, p. A1.
Americans are visiting the Netherlands to see whether lessons learned there on how to protect an area below sea level can be applied to New Orleans.

Nickerson, Colin, "Holland Goes Beyond Holding Back the Tide," *The Boston Globe*, Dec. 5, 2005, p. A1.
The Netherlands is endeavoring to make itself "climate-proof" by inventing techniques beyond dikes and dams to cope with the accelerated rise of rivers and sea levels.

Sterling, Toby, "Katrina's Force Stuck Holland, Too," *The Philadelphia Inquirer*, Nov. 18, 2005, p. A2.
Dutch flood defenses are some of the best in the world, but after seeing Katrina's level of destruction, the government is reassessing its system of dams, seawalls and surge barriers.

Repairing Levees

Axtman, Kris, "Search for Weak Link in Big Easy's Levees," *The Christian Science Monitor*, Dec. 30, 2005, p. 3.
Engineers in New Orleans know that the levees failed because of improper design but wonder if the entire system can be upgraded and refortified or if it needs a complete overhaul.

Crenson, Matt, "Will Levee Repairs Be Ready in Time?" *The Miami Herald*, Jan. 15, 2006, p. A11.
The U.S. Corps of Engineers expects to have all the levees in New Orleans restored to pre-Katrina condition by June 1, the start of hurricane season, but critics say new projects need to be implemented to make the city safe.

CITING THE *CQ RESEARCHER*

Sample formats for citing these reports in a bibliography include the ones listed below. Preferred styles and formats vary, so please check with your instructor or professor.

MLA STYLE

Jost, Kenneth. "Rethinking the Death Penalty." The CQ Researcher 16 Nov. 2001: 945-68.

APA STYLE

Jost, K. (2001, November 16). Rethinking the death penalty. *The CQ Researcher, 11*, 945-968.

CHICAGO STYLE

Jost, Kenneth. "Rethinking the Death Penalty." *CQ Researcher*, November 16, 2001, 945-968.

CQ Researcher

Published by CQ Press, a division of Congressional Quarterly Inc.

thecqresearcher.com

Eating Disorders

Is societal pressure to be thin to blame?

Tabloids and TV entertainment shows are full of gossipy reports about young, pencil-thin Hollywood actresses who might be anorexic or bulimic. Eating disorders, however, are far from glamorous. Anorexia has the highest mortality rate of any mental illness. Up to 35 million Americans have an eating disorder. Moreover, contrary to the old stereotype, overachieving white girls from affluent families are not the only victims. Also afflicted are men, middle-aged women, African-Americans and children as young as 8. Many Americans blame the nation's obsession with appearances for causing eating disorders, but genetics and brain chemistry also play roles. Public-health experts say Web sites that give tips on hiding eating disorders should be closed down, while patients' advocates are pushing Congress to require insurers to cover more of the costs of treatment and to make eating disorders a national priority — just like obesity.

Actress Lindsay Lohan reportedly said recently she had an eating disorder, but she later claimed Vanity Fair *magazine misquoted her.*

INSIDE THIS REPORT

The CQ Researcher • Feb. 10, 2006 • www.thecqresearcher.com
Volume 16, Number 6 • Pages 121-144

Recipient of Society of Professional Journalists Award for Excellence ◆ American Bar Association Silver Gavel Award

THE ISSUES

BACKGROUND

CURRENT SITUATION

OUTLOOK

SIDEBARS AND GRAPHICS

FOR FURTHER RESEARCH

Cover: Actress Lindsay Lohan was quoted recently as saying she had an eating disorder, but she later claimed *Vanity Fair* magazine misquoted her. Lohan and other super-thin celebrities are often pictured as "thin-spirations" on eating-disorder Web sites. (AP Photo/Chris Polk)

CQ Researcher

Feb. 10, 2006
Volume 16, Number 6

MANAGING EDITOR: Thomas J. Colin

ASSISTANT MANAGING EDITOR: Kathy Koch

ASSOCIATE EDITOR: Kenneth Jost

STAFF WRITERS: Marcia Clemmitt, Peter Katel, Pamela M. Prah

CONTRIBUTING WRITERS: Rachel Cox, Sarah Glazer, David Hosansky, Patrick Marshall, Tom Price

DESIGN/PRODUCTION EDITOR: Olu B. Davis

ASSISTANT EDITOR: Melissa J. Hipolit

CQ PRESS

A Division of Congressional Quarterly Inc.

SENIOR VICE PRESIDENT/PUBLISHER: John A. Jenkins

DIRECTOR, LIBRARY PUBLISHING: Kathryn C. Suárez

DIRECTOR, EDITORIAL OPERATIONS: Ann Davies

CONGRESSIONAL QUARTERLY INC.

CHAIRMAN: Paul C. Tash

VICE CHAIRMAN: Andrew P. Corty

PRESIDENT/EDITOR IN CHIEF: Robert W. Merry

CQ Researcher (ISSN 1056-2036) is printed on acid-free paper. Published weekly, except March 24, July 7, July 14, Aug. 4, Aug. 11, Nov. 24, Dec. 22 and Dec. 29, by CQ Press, a division of Congressional Quarterly Inc. Annual full-service subscriptions for institutions start at $667. For pricing, call 1-800-834-9020, ext. 1906. To purchase a *CQ Researcher* report in print or electronic format (PDF), visit www.cqpress.com or call 866-427-7737. Single reports start at $10. Bulk purchase discounts and electronic-rights licensing are also available. Periodicals postage paid at Washington, D.C., and additional mailing offices. POSTMASTER: Send address changes to *CQ Researcher*, 1255 22nd St., N.W., Suite 400, Washington, DC 20037.

Eating Disorders

BY PAMELA M. PRAH

THE ISSUES

Anna Westin, of Chaska, Minn., and Shelby Starner, of Stroudsburg, Pa., both had eating disorders they tried to hide.

Anna wore baggy clothes to conceal her shrinking, starving body. Shelby, who had a multi-album recording contract by age 14, perfected vomiting into Snapple bottles — up to 14 times a day — to avoid clogging the sinks and alerting her parents. [1]

The disorders eventually killed them both. Anna committed suicide at age 21 after battling anorexia for five years. Shelby died of bulimia at 19.

"Anna knew she had an eating disorder," says her mother. "She hated it and wanted to be free of it. That drove her to suicide."

Anorexia, bulimia and compulsive eating affect an estimated 35 million Americans, according to the National Eating Disorders Association (NEDA).

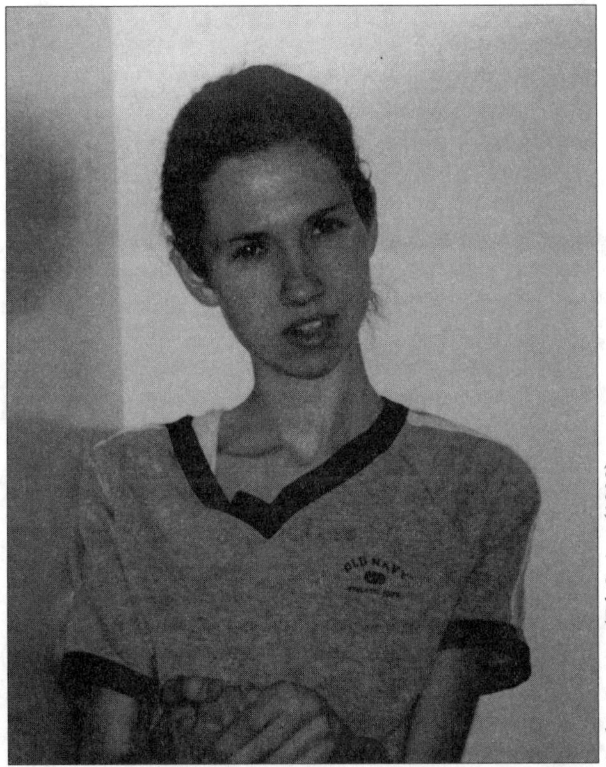

Corbis Images/Ed Quinn (1999)

Jennifer Shortis has suffered from an eating disorder since age 15, when she began dieting with friends in Baldwinville, Mass. Within months, she had developed anorexia. Now 24, she weighs 76 pounds and is still struggling to regain a normal weight. Anorexia has the highest mortality rate of any mental illness, with death often caused by suicide. As many as 35 million Americans may have an eating disorder.

Victims of eating disorders are obsessed with food and the fear of getting fat. Anorexics either refuse to eat enough to maintain a normal weight or eat only enough to survive, typically seeing themselves as fat even though they often are dangerously thin.

Bulimics generally follow a so-called binge-and-purge cycle — compulsively eating large amounts of food and then offsetting weight gain by vomiting, fasting, exercising excessively or misusing laxatives, diuretics or enemas.

Eating disorders are considered serious mental illnesses; anorexia has the highest mortality rate of any mental illness, with death often caused by suicide. [2]

While anorexia and bulimia are distinct diagnostic categories of eating disorders, binge, or compulsive, eating is not an official category of mental illness, nor is obesity. [3] Binge eaters differ from bulimics in that they don't try to purge their food.

Anorexia and bulimia are commonly — and mistakenly — thought to primarily afflict overachieving white girls from affluent families. "Eating disorders are truly an equal-opportunity disease," says Ellen Rome, a pediatrician in Cleveland and spokeswoman for the Academy for Eating Disorders in Chicago. "We are seeing it in all walks of life," including among men, middle-aged women, blacks, Hispanics, rich and poor.

"One of the myths is that it's 'other' people who have these disorders," says psychologist Douglas Bunnell, past president of the Seattle-based NEDA. "They are everybody's sister, daughter, wife, friend. You know someone with an eating disorder. You may not be able to spot it necessarily, but people with these disorders are living among us."

And physicians say eating disorders are appearing in younger and younger patients. "It's not uncommon to find 8- and 12-year-olds with these disorders," says Rome.

But there are no reliable statistics on whether eating disorders are on the rise or just being diagnosed more often, because they aren't tracked by the federal government. "It's a national disgrace that we still don't have published data on how many people have an eating disorder," says Ruth Striegel-Moore, who heads the psychology department at Wesleyan University in Middletown, Conn., and specializes in eating disorders.

However, NEDA estimates that up to 10 million females and 1 million males struggle with anorexia or bulimia, or both. Among U.S. women, about 1 percent are anorexic and up to 5 percent are bulimic, says Bunnell, director of the Renfrew Center of Southern Connecticut, a respected eating-disorder clinic in Wilton. Another 25 million are estimated to suffer from binge eating. (*See chart, p. 127.*)

The death of 32-year-old pop singer Karen Carpenter in 1983 from an eating disorder helped raise awareness of the problem, but today the diseases are everyday fodder for the tabloids and entertainment shows. "We do sort of make anorexia glamorous," says Bunnell, who

Most Americans Aware of Eating Disorders

Ninety percent of American adults know about at least one eating disorder. Women are more likely than men to blame the media for causing eating disorders, while men tend to blame lack of willpower.

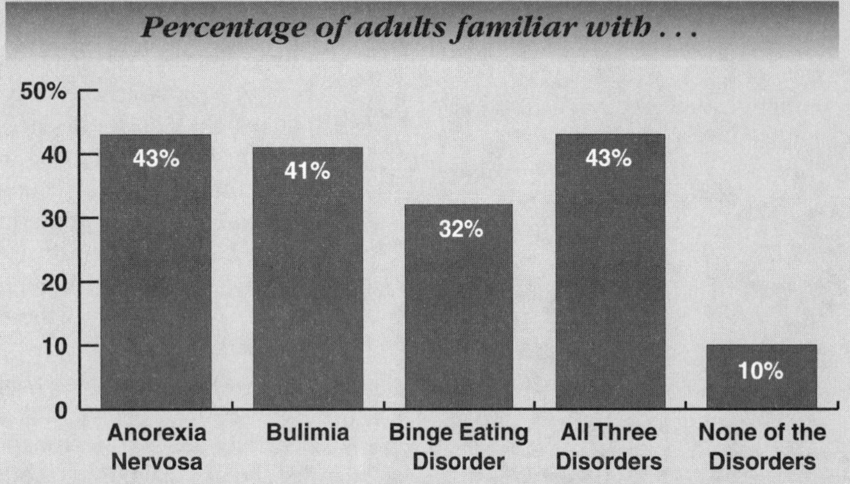

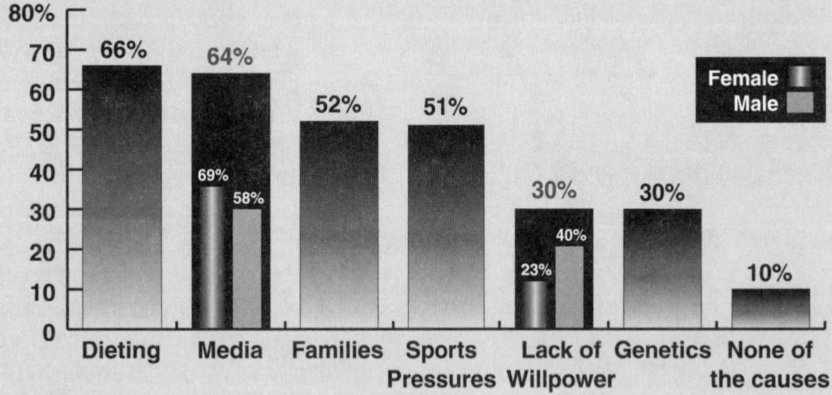

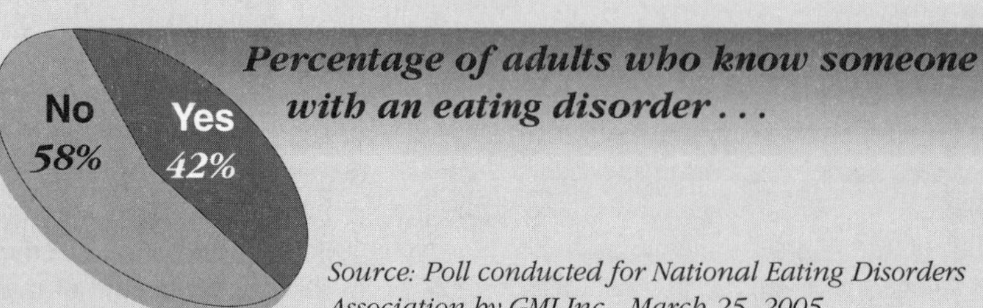

Source: Poll conducted for National Eating Disorders Association by GMI Inc., March 25, 2005

fears the celebrity focus and attention "almost marginalize the illness."

But experts say eating disorders are caused by a complex mix of biological, psychological and social factors, such as brain chemistry, metabolism, coping skills and personality — along with a culture that promotes thinness. Activities that require a lean appearance — such as acting, dancing, modeling, gymnastics or distance running — also increase the risk of developing an eating disorder. (*See sidebar, p. 132.*)

Sarah Putnam, 21, a senior at North Carolina's Elon University, changed her major from musical theater to corporate communications because the pressure to be thin in theater "was obviously killing me." Putnam had initially enrolled at Wagner College, in Staten Island, N.Y., where she says theater students shared ideas for staying thin, such as taking laxatives and exercising excessively. Her 25-pound weight loss — to just 100 pounds — won her praise from faculty and friends. At one point, she says, she was throwing up six times a day. She says she got help when her eating disorder "had completely taken over my life."

Recent research now suggests that genetics may play a bigger role than previously thought. While an "anorexia gene" has yet to be discovered, research indicates that people may be born with a predisposition to developing an eating disorder.

"Genes load the gun, environment pulls the trigger," the Illinois-based National Association of Anorexia Nervosa and Associated Disorders (ANAD) explains on its Web site. [4]

Victims of eating disorders typically try to hide their problem and balk at getting help. Some, like Shelby, instead turn to Web sites that promote anorexia and bulimia as choices and lifestyles rather than as diseases — sites that many experts say should be shut down. The sites offer tips on how to avoid detection, such as throwing up while showering to conceal the sounds of vomiting and wearing hidden ankle weights to fool doctors during weigh-ins. Particularly startling are the sites' "thinspirations" — galleries of photos of unusually thin people, typically actresses, such as Lindsay Lohan, Nicole Ritchie, Mary-Kate Olsen and Calista Flockhart.

Sufferers who do seek help are in for a long haul. Anorexia treatment typically takes five to seven years. Inpatient care for an eating disorder can cost up to $30,000 a month and more than $100,000 for outpatient therapy and medical monitoring, according to ANAD.

Treatment is costly because both mental and physical problems are involved. Irregular heartbeats and electrolyte imbalances are common in both anorexic and bulimic patients, as are psychiatric disorders like anxiety, depression and obsessive-compulsive disorder. Many victims also have alcohol and drug problems.

Insurance rarely covers more than a small portion of the costs. Kitty Westin says her insurance company's refusal to cover Anna's treatment and the financial burden her daughter knew she was putting on the family contributed to her suicide. For years, mental health advocates have lobbied Congress, with little success, to require more insurance coverage for eating disorders and other mental illnesses.

Mary Ellen Clausen, an eating-disorders activist in Syracuse, N.Y., says treatments for her two daughters have cost more than $1 million over eight years. Insurance has paid for some, but the family has largely footed the bill. "Our 401(k)s are a thing of the past," she says. "We have re-mortgaged our house, taken out loans and maxed out all our credit cards."

Since treatment is successful only about half of the time for anorexia and bulimia, researchers are seeking new approaches. For bulimics, cognitive therapy, medication and nutritional counseling appear promising. Medication — typically an anti-depressant — appears less effective for anorexics until after they gain weight.

Many Teens Worry About Weight Gain

Nearly one-fifth of female teens and nearly 10 percent of the boys have starved themselves for 24 hours or more to lose weight or avoid gaining weight.

Percentage of Students Nationwide Who . . .

Went without eating for 24 hours or more

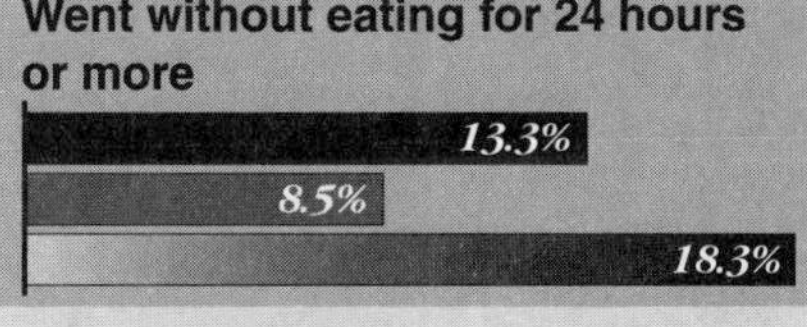

Took diet pills, powders, or liquids

9.2%
7.1%
13.0%

Vomited or took laxatives

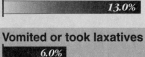

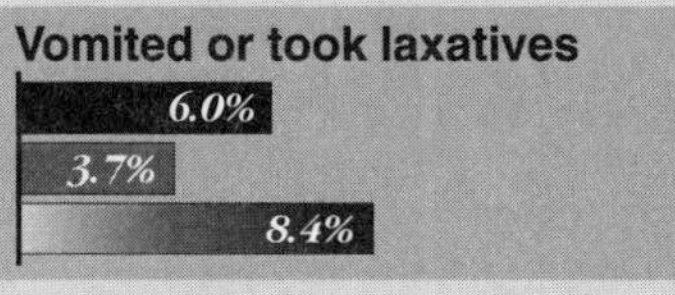

Total Male Female

Source: National Center for Chronic Disease Prevention and Health Promotion, Youth Risk Behavior Surveillance System, May 2004

Ironically, while 11 million Americans with eating disorders are virtually starving themselves, the United States is facing an obesity epidemic affecting some 60 million people. Obesity and binge eating aren't recognized as eating disorders, but some experts think they should be. Meanwhile, they warn, many people with obesity may have real eating disorders but are not getting help.

As eating-disorder experts and family members lobby Congress for more research funds and insurance coverage, here are some of the questions people are asking:

Should binge eating and obesity be categorized as eating disorders?

Experts disagree about whether binge eating and obesity — which affect some 85 million adult Americans — should be considered distinct eating disorders like anorexia and bulimia.

The authoritative *Diagnostic and Statistical Manual of Mental Disorders* (*DSM*), published by the American Psychiatric Association (APA), recognized anorexia and bulimia as mental disorders in 1980. Currently the *DSM* lists binge eating in a catch-all "eating-disorders category otherwise not specified." Obesity is not included at all.

The distinction is important because mental health professionals use the manual to diagnose and treat patients with eating problems, and insurance companies use it to figure out whether to pay for treatment, explains Pauline Powers, president of the National Eating Disorders Association, professor of psychiatry at the University of South Florida and member of an APA working group on eating disorders. The catch-all category offers less guidance to mental health professionals, and some insurance companies are more restrictive in their coverage for this category, treating the condition as less serious than anorexia and bulimia. [5]

"The more definitive a disease is, the more likely insurance will cover it," says Annie Hayashi, a spokeswoman for the National Association of Anorexia Nervosa and Associated Disorders. "It's much more difficult to get coverage" for patients diagnosed with binge eating, since it's included in the broader category, she says.

Hayashi notes that the association's history reflects the evolving study of eating disorders — it was founded in 1976, three years before the term bulimia nervosa was even coined.

Many experts, including Powers, predict binge eating will be listed as a third, distinct type of eating disorder the next

Continued on p. 127

Does Hollywood 'Cause' Eating Disorders?

The 1983 death of anorexic pop singer Karen Carpenter first alerted the American public to the deadly danger of eating disorders. But today celebrities and their eating disorders are frequent topics for Hollywood gossip sheets, TV shows and online blogs.

"The media reflect and exacerbate the problems," argues Ellen Rome, a pediatrician in Cleveland and spokeswoman for the Chicago-based Academy for Eating Disorders. "These teen girls watch and read and observe and emulate."

Psychologist Douglas Bunnell, a past president of the National Eating Disorders Association (NEDA), agrees. However, he cautions, by portraying the most extreme cases, the media can end up "marginalizing the illness." He says his patients will look at scrawny celebrity photos and conclude, " 'See, I'm not anorexic. I am not like that.' "

On the other hand, Bunnell adds, "When they put Mary-Kate Olsen, Lindsay Lohan or whoever the star of the moment is who has an eating disorder out there, they are showing how shocking it is, and how people shouldn't develop these disorders."

New York psychotherapist Steven Levenkron, who treated Carpenter before her death, wrote in a 2001 book that in some cases the media attention balloons "into circus sideshows," becoming "a spectator sport for the non-afflicted public." [1]

Getty Images/Nick Elgar

Kate Dillon became a plus-size model after battling anorexia as a super-thin model.

The tribulations of Rachel and Clare Wallmeyer, 34-year-old Australian twins who have been fighting anorexia for 20 years, have been chronicled on TV in their homeland for years and became a story for U.S. entertainment shows in 2005. [2] At one point, the twins lived on watermelon, Diet Coke and at least 20 laxatives a day, and their combined weight was 105 pounds. Since 2003, the U.S. show "Entertainment Tonight" has been following the treatment of former TV reporter Melissa Dehart, who at one point dropped to 56 pounds.

But media coverage of eating disorders is not new. Talk-show host Oprah Winfrey covered the story of Rudine, a woman who died in 1995 weighing only 38 pounds, while Maury Povich hosted the anorexic twins Michaela and Samantha Kendall. Michaela died in 1994 and Samantha died three years later. [3]

Model Kate Dillon said she got the idea to purge from a TV movie. At five feet 11 inches tall and a size 4, she was anorexic when she appeared in *Vogue* and *Elle.* She quit modeling in the mid-1990s when she was ordered to lose 20 pounds from her 125-pound frame. "I wanted freedom from this ideal, from these cultural ideals. I wanted freedom to be who I was," she said during PBS's "Dying To Be Thin" broadcast in 2000. [4] Now she is a plus-size supermodel. "Plus size is no different than skinny, it's just another way of being beautiful," she said.

Dillon is not alone in speaking publicly about her problem. The roster of celebrities sharing their stories include actress and 1980s fitness guru Jane Fonda; Jamie-Lynn DiScala, from HBO's "Sopranos," who contemplated suicide while suffering for years with anorexia and bulimia; and singer-dancer Paula Abdul, the "American Idol" judge who in 2005 won an award from NEDA for discussing her own struggles with eating disorders.

Eating-disorder support and research organizations often take issue with advertisements they think promote or trivialize eating disorders. The National Association of Anorexia Nervosas and Associated Disorders successfully lobbied several companies, including Chanel, Hershey Foods and Revlon, to get them to change or pull ads touting slogans like, "You can never be too rich or too thin." And NEDA is currently targeting Spencer Gifts for its T-shirts that flippantly read, "I beat Anorexia."

The group "About Face" takes a more sarcastic approach when criticizing the culture of thinness. In 1995, it plastered hundreds of copies of a poster around San Francisco that spoofs a Kate Moss ad for perfume with "Emaciation Stinks: Stop Starvation Imagery." The group also has a poster with a circus theme showing caged models that says, "Please Don't Feed the Models."

But experts are clear that the media and Hollywood, by themselves, can't prompt someone to become anorexic or bulimic. "It's almost normative now for 16-year-old girls to loathe their bodies. That's certainly a byproduct of the culture," says Bunnell, adding, "I don't think the culture causes eating disorders, but it absolutely contributes to it."

---

1 Steven Levenkron, *Anatomy of Anorexia* (2001).

2 "Can These Anorexic Twins Be Saved?" *The Insider,* Nov. 3, 2005, http://insider.tv.yahoo.com/celeb/3278/.

3 Cynthia R. Kalodner, *Too Fat or Too Thin?* (2003), p. 4.

4 Transcript, "Dying to Be Thin," PBS, Dec. 12, 2000. www.pbs.org/wgbh/nova/transcripts/2715thin.html.

Continued from p. 125

time the association updates its manual — probably in 2011. Meanwhile, the APA is planning in the next few months to update its treatment guidelines for all eating disorders, greatly expanding the section on binge eating.

Binge eaters rapidly consume excessive amounts of food and feel as though they can't stop. But unlike bulimics, they usually don't try to get rid of the food by vomiting, fasting, using laxatives or other unsafe ways.

Binge eating can lead to serious health complications, such as diabetes, hypertension, cardiovascular disease and obesity, but little is known about it or its prevalence. "Presumably, more people are affected by binge eating, but we just don't know," says Bunnell. NEDA estimates that 25 million Americans struggle with binge eating. "Some binge eaters may be on their way to a formal eating disorder or on the way out of it. We don't know."

The medical and research communities generally recognize binge eating as an eating disorder but disagree over whether it should be considered a distinct disorder — separate from bulimia — or simply a non-purging form of bulimia, says Wesleyan University's Striegel-Moore.

She says the popularity of today's "super-size" meals — some of which would qualify as a binge — is helping to drive the disorder. "We live in a society where overeating has become normative . . . and is promoted."

Meanwhile, combating obesity is a top public health priority. In 2001, then-U.S. Surgeon General David Satcher issued a "call to action" to prevent and reduce obesity, a problem he feared "could reverse many of the health gains achieved in the U.S. in recent decades." [6]

But there's disagreement over whether obesity is linked to eating disorders.

ANAD's Hayashi says her association considers obesity an eating disorder, but "not everyone agrees."

Eating Disorders Affect Up to 35 Million

More than one-in-four adults — about 58 million Americans — suffer from a mental disorder in any given year, according to the National Institute of Mental Health. Up to 35 million may have an eating disorder. Here are some of the most common mental disorders:

Eating disorders — Anorexia and bulimia affect nearly 10 million females and 1 million males. Binge eating (not considered a distinct eating disorder) affects an estimated 25 million men and women, according to the National Eating Disorders Association. (There are no comprehensive federal statistics on eating disorders for males and females.)

Mood disorders — Affect some 21 million American adults, or about 9.5 percent of the U.S. population 18 and older. Common mood disorders and the number of adults affected are:

• Bipolar disorder, or manic depression	5.7 million
• Dysthymic disorder, or chronic, mild depression	3.3 million
• Major depression	14.8 million

Anxiety disorders — Affect some 40 million adult Americans. Common anxiety disorders and the number of adults affected include:

• Generalized anxiety disorder	6.8 million
• Obsessive-compulsive disorder	2.2 million
• Panic disorder	6 million
• Post-traumatic stress disorder	7.7 million

Other mental disorders include —

• Agoraphobia, or the intense fear and anxiety of any place or situation where escape might be difficult	1.8 million
• Alzheimer's disease	4.5 million
• Attention-deficit hyperactivity disorder	4.6 million 18-44-year-olds
• Schizophrenia	about 2.4 million

Sources: National Institute of Mental Health; National Eating Disorders Association

Advocates of making obesity an eating disorder say that including it in the *DSM* will help medical professionals find the proper treatment for obese people. Opponents, however, argue that not all obese people have eating disorders and that including them all would neither be accurate nor helpful to everyone.

"I think obesity is an eating disorder, but I'm in the minority," says Powers.

However, NEDA's Bunnell cautions that "being obese doesn't necessarily mean that a person has an eating disorder," noting that an eating disorder is a psychiatric diagnosis associated with a variety of emotional and physical factors. "Obesity doesn't tell you that about a person."

Striegel-Moore agrees that some binge eaters are obese, but says adamantly:

Understanding Anorexia and Bulimia

There are two types of anorexics: those who eat very little and those who eat very little and compensate for eating with intense exercise, laxatives, enemas, diuretics or vomiting. Some alternate between the two types. There are also two types of bulimics: those who binge and then purge, and those who rely on fasting or excessive exercise.

Anorexic and bulimic binges are similar, but there are differences. Anorexics may consider eating a handful of grapes a binge and force themselves to throw up. Bulimics binge on thousands of calories. Anorexics are invariably too thin, but bulimics can be slightly underweight, normal weight, overweight or even obese.

Anorexia is diagnosed when a person:

- Weighs at least 15 percent less than is normal for their height;
- Fears gaining weight or becoming fat and sees himself or herself as overweight but is actually dangerously thin. Anorexics tend to be perfectionists who are extremely critical of themselves and their bodies.
- Has stopped having menstrual periods.

Bulimia is diagnosed when a person:

- Binges (compulsively eats large amounts of food in a short time);
- Purges at least twice a week for three months by vomiting, misusing laxatives, diuretics, enemas, fasting or excessive exercise.
- Has a distorted self-image.

Source: American Psychiatric Association

"Obesity is not an eating disorder." By definition, she says, a psychiatric disorder must be associated with "clinically significant impairment," and not all individuals who are obese experience such impairment. "To be an eating disorder, there has to be disturbance in body image and eating behavior. Not all individuals evidence such symptoms. So, unless there are behavioral or body-image symptoms, obesity does not represent an eating disorder."

Many observers doubt the APA will include obesity as a distinct disorder when it updates its manual. Powers predicts certain syndromes related to obesity, such as "night-eating syndrome," will be listed as eating disorders, but not obesity. Night-eating syndrome is characterized by eating 25 percent of a person's daily calorie count after dinner.

Does insurance adequately cover eating disorders?

Kitty Westin doesn't exactly say that Blue Cross-Blue Shield of Minnesota killed her daughter in 2000 — only that the insurer's refusal to pay for Anna's treatment for anorexia helped push her to suicide.

Like many families, the Westins were shocked to discover the family's "Cadillac" health-insurance plan covered only a small portion of the cost of treatment, which extended several years and cost tens of thousands of dollars. Westin says the insurer refused to pay even after the hospital said Anna could die without it.

"It blew us away," she says, adding that Anna felt she was a burden on her family and that the insurer's refusal to pay "contributed to her despair."

The Westins and the state of Minnesota sued the insurer and won an out-of-court settlement in June 2001 that required Blue Cross-Blue Shield to set up an independent, three-member panel to review all denials of insurance coverage. (The state, county and insurer each select a member.) Two other Minnesota health-insurance carriers voluntarily agreed to the provisions of the settlement. "It made a huge difference in Minnesota," Westin says.

Larry Akey, a spokesman for America's Health Insurance Plans (AHIP), says 47 states require mental health coverage, and 95 percent of his group's 1,300 members provide some sort of mental-health benefit, which may include eating disorders. [7] But eating-disorder experts say many states allow insurers to charge higher co-pays for mental health services or to limit services, and only 22 states require insurers to cover treatment for eating disorders that is equal to coverage for physical disorders.

By severely limiting coverage or not covering treatment at all, victims' families and health professionals contend that insurers threaten the recovery of eating-disorder sufferers. Many insurers limit the number of days they will pay for hospitalization for eating disorders, and it's usually not enough to properly treat the patient, says ANAD's Hayashi, especially for anorexics, where the first priority is getting them to gain weight.

However, anorexics are expensive to the health-care system, costing about as much as treating patients with schizophrenia — a chronic, debilitating mental disorder, says Wesleyan's Striegel-Moore. Anorexics can develop abnormal blood clotting, osteoporosis, dehydration and kidney problems, while bulimics may suffer from bowel problems, abdominal pain and erosions in the teeth, stomach and esophagus.

However, while insurers may cover treatment for these physical complications, they often balk at covering psychological counseling for what caused the complications in the first place, creating what Striegel-Moore calls "perverse situations." If an anorexic is so depressed she jumps out the window and breaks her leg, an insurer will pay for treating the leg but not the eating disorder that prompted her to jump, she says. "It's a real problem."

In the end, Striegel-Moore says, the policy is penny-wise and pound-foolish, because victims often end up in the emergency room — one of the most expensive places to receive care — for treatment of related ailments. "People with eating disorders are high consumers of health services [for their physical ailments], because they are not getting the [mental health] services that would treat their eating disorders," she says.

Activist Clausen of upstate New York discovered the peculiarities of the health-insurance system when both her daughters developed eating disorders. After her oldest daughter tried to commit suicide, the insurance company paid for her intensive care but refused to fully cover the treatment for the eating disorder that made her suicidal, says Clausen. She says the insurance battles left her emotionally and financially drained and threatened her daughter's recovery. The insurer would cover only 14 days of treatment, so she was discharged just as she was getting better, and the cycle started all over again.

Insurers argue that they are simply offering the benefits employers request and can afford. "Many purchasers opt for some limits to medical care to keep premiums affordable and to keep the array of benefits they offer as broad as possible," says AHIP's Akey.

Claire Sheahan, a spokeswoman for the Blue Cross-Blue Shield Association, says people often blame the insurance company for not offering certain benefits, "but it's not the insurer's choice. Every benefit is negotiated with the employer."

According to a 2005 poll of 1,500 adults commissioned by NEDA, 76 percent of respondents said eating disorders should be covered by insurance companies "just like any other illness." The results show that "the public agrees not only that eating disorders are serious illnesses but also that they deserve — and demand — treatment and adequate insurance coverage," said NEDA. [8]

However, say medical experts, insurers often use the APA's formal criteria for diagnosing eating disorders as excuses "to exclude coverage." For example, says Powers, one of the four criteria for determining if a female is anorexic is the loss of menstrual periods. Some insurers will refuse to cover female anorexic patients who don't lose their periods but are otherwise clearly anorexic.

Another criterion for anorexia is that the person weighs at least 15 percent less than the normal weight for their height. "Let's say someone has lost 13 percent," says Bunnell of NEDA. "That doesn't mean they aren't anorexic." Similarly, one of the criteria for bulimia is bingeing or purging twice a week. "Suppose you binge or purge 1.5 times a week?"

Should Web sites promoting anorexia and bulimia be shut down?

Shelby Starner's mother, Kathy Benn, says her talented daughter got tips for hiding her bulimia from Internet sites that promote anorexia and bulimia as lifestyles rather than diseases. "These Web sites make it seem

Are Your Eating Habits Healthy?

If you answer yes to more than five of the following questions, you may be thinking too much about food and weight, according to the National Association of Anorexia Nervosa and Associated Disorders (ANAD). The quiz is not intended, however, to diagnose an eating disorder. People with questions or concerns about their eating habits can obtain a list of professionals and support groups in their area by contacting ANAD at (847) 831-3438 or anad20@aol.com.

1. Are you constantly thinking about your weight and food?
2. Are you dieting strictly and/or have you lost a lot of weight?
3. Are you more than 10 percent below your healthy weight?
4. Are people concerned about your weight?
5. Is your energy level down?
6. Do you constantly feel cold?
7. Are your periods abnormal or have they stopped?
8. Are you overeating and feeling out of control?
9. Are you vomiting, using laxatives or water pills, herbal agents, or trying to fast as a way to control your weight?
10. Are you over-exercising or do others consider your exercise excessive?
11. Does your weight fluctuate drastically?
12. Do any of the above interfere with your enjoyment of life, relationships or everyday functioning?

Source: National Association of Anorexia Nervosa and Associated Disorders, 2006

like eating disorders are a trend and a cool thing to do," she told the *Pittsburgh Tribune-Review* not long after Shelby's death at age 19. [9] "These girls don't realize that people die from this. It's terrifying."

Shelby's bulimia caused an imbalance of her body's electrolytes, which caused her brain to swell and led to a fatal seizure.

Experts say there are probably thousands of Web sites and blogs that promote anorexia (dubbed pro-"ana" sites) or bulimia (pro-"mia" sites). Although many have been around since the late 1990s, the pro-ana sites became more widely known in 2001 after exposés by *Time* and other publications as well as TV shows like "Oprah" and "Dr. Phil."

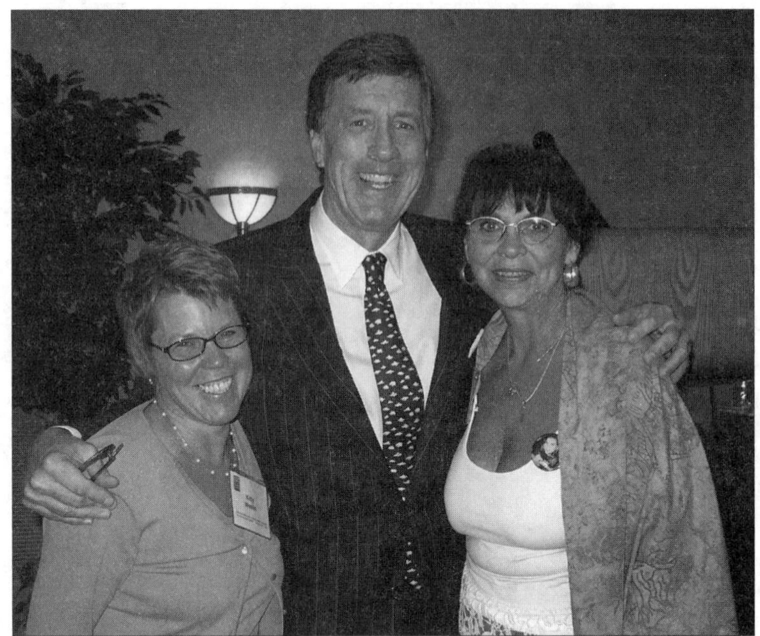
EDC Photo/Mark Lerro

Kitty Westin, left, and Sharon Haugen became eating-disorder activists after their daughters died from the illness. Rep. Jim Ramstad, R-Minn., supports equal insurance coverage for eating disorders, or mental-health parity.

Many experts say the sites are dangerous and should be shut down. But others say they provide support to sufferers and give researchers new insights.

"These sites are just awful," says Rome of the Academy for Eating Disorders. In addition to the photos of ultra-thin people, some contain "reverse triggers," or photos of extremely overweight people. Many are interactive with blogs and discussion boards.

Benn isn't alone in blaming the sites for giving young people ideas. According to a 2005 study, 66 percent of teens who had visited a pro-ana or pro-mia site said they had tried some of the weight-loss techniques suggested. [10]

"Ana's Underground Grotto" is one of many sites clearly promoting an eating disorder. "This is a pro-ana Web site," it declares. "That means this is a place where anorexia is regarded as a lifestyle and a choice, not an illness or disorder. There are no victims here."

Most of the pro-ana sites also provide warnings. For example, "Thin Files" advises, "If you are currently in recovery from an eating disorder or if you are offended or otherwise disturbed by the existence of pro-ana, I suggest you go no further." And "Blue Dragon" says its tips "are to give you fresh ideas on how to stay on track so that you don't fall into a depression and kill yourself — not to teach you how to 'not eat.' "

Blogs like www.miafriends.org are full of suggestions, such as always carry a plastic Ziploc bag or a large cup with a lid to vomit into. Visitors to the sites, mostly teenage and college-age women, post before-and-after photos of themselves; images of waiflike models, actresses and even tiny Tinkerbell from "Peter Pan" adorn the sites. In an essay on "40 reasons not to eat," one threatens, "If you eat, you'll look like those disgusting, fat, ghetto and trailer-trash hookers on 'Jerry Springer.' "

The National Eating Disorders Association says the sites could "encourage a 'cult'-type destructive support system." The Academy for Eating Disorders says there is always a "creative tension" between respecting free speech and protecting vulnerable individuals, particularly children. "It's important to note that the peak age of onset of eating disorders is during adolescence, and thus these sites target largely an audience of children," says the academy's Web site. [11]

Several years ago, eating-disorder researchers and support groups began prodding major Internet servers to take down the sites or delete them from search engines. Yahoo! encourages groups like ANAD to alert the company of online content that may be illegal or harm children, says spokeswoman Mary Osako. ANAD's Hayashi estimates that hundreds of such sites have been taken down, but more pop up to replace them.

Some pro-ana sites are clearly frustrated by efforts to silence them. "Ana's Underground Grotto" notes that several sites that had linked to its site had been changed to "anti-pro-ana sites" or have gone dead or offline. The notice adds that it will no longer list sites hosted by Geocities, Tripod, Angelfire, Homestead or myweb.ecomplanet because those links "continually get deleted."

Lori Rosenthal, a professor of psychology at Boston's Emerson College, says the sites provide support for sufferers and useful information for researchers. "These sites offer social support and friendship," she says, and

Continued on p. 132

Chronology

Early History

The first medical account of ailments now known as eating disorders appears in the 17th century.

First Century
The ancient Romans abhorred being fat and set aside so-called vomitoriums where people who stuffed themselves with enormous amounts of food could throw up.

Middle Ages
Devout Christians refuse food as a way to get closer to God, but by the late Middle Ages women who fast excessively are thought to possess evil spirits.

1689
Richard Morton, the king of England's physician, describes cases of "nervous consumption" in his medical textbook, *Phthisiologia: or, A Treatise of Consumptions.*

1873
Sir William Gull, an English physician, coins the term "anorexia nervosa" and describes it as "a perversion of the ego."

1903
French neurologist Pierre M.F. Janet describes a woman's compulsive eating in his book *Les Obsessions et la Psychasthenie.*

1960s-1980s

Researchers suggest that anorexics act out their frustrations and feelings of inadequacy by restricting their eating. . . . Eating disorders are generally attributed to dysfunctional families.

1967
The media's ideal for beauty shifts from full-figured women to waif-like Twiggy, the 92-pound British teen fashion model.

1976
Vivian Meehan, a nurse in Highland Park, Ill., creates National Association of Anorexia Nervosa and Associated Disorders.

1979
University of London researcher Gerald Russell coins the term bulimia nervosa.

1980
American Psychiatric Association (APA) recognizes anorexia and bulimia as separate mental disorders.

1983
Pop singer Karen Carpenter, 32, dies of a heart attack after a two-year battle with anorexia.

1989
Congress creates National Eating Disorders Awareness Week.

1990s

Researchers determine that genetics and brain chemistry may play a bigger role than societal pressures in determining whether someone develops an eating disorder.

1991-92
National Collegiate Athletic Association finds that eating disorders exist in most men's and women's college sports.

1996
Mental Health Parity Act requires lifetime and annual dollar limits on mental health care to equal the benefits for treatment of physical ailments.

1998-99
Doctors in London find that increased levels of the brain chemical serotonin, which affects mood and appetite, may be linked to anorexic behavior; University of Pittsburgh researchers find that decreased serotonin activity may cause bulimic behavior.

2000s

Experts debate whether binge eating should be a distinct and separate type of eating disorder.

January 2000
"Healthy People 2010," the federal government's health priorities for the next decade, seeks to reduce the number of people who relapse after getting help for eating disorders.

2001
Web sites promoting eating disorders as a lifestyle, not a disorder, become popular.

2005
State lawmakers in Iowa, Oregon and Washington require insurers to provide coverage for mental disorders equal to that for physical illnesses; the measures bring to 22 the number of states that cover treatment for eating disorders.

2006
APA plans to update its treatment guidelines for eating disorders, including a larger section on binge eating. By 2011, the APA is expected to list binge eating as a separate eating disorder, alongside anorexia and bulimia.

Athletic Culture Can Encourage Eating Disorders

After failing to make the all-around competition at the 1992 Olympics, gymnast Kerri Strug began training with a new coach and eating less. If she were a little leaner or lighter, the 14-year-old thought, maybe she would perform better. Besides, her new coach frequently weighed his gymnasts, adding to the pressure. [1]

Eventually, the 4-foot-9-inch gymnast weighed 78 pounds when her team won the first U.S. Olympic gold medal for gymnastics in 1996.

"I did lose a lot of weight in 1993, and my parents were very concerned," Strug says today. But she says it wasn't an eating disorder. "I did not stop eating but was eating very little for someone exercising eight hours a day. All was taken care of within a matter of weeks. My parents ordered me my favorite cake, and I was back to eating what I wanted in moderation versus just fruit, veggies and protein."

Most athletes with eating disorders can be found in sports where athletes are judged partly on physical appearance or where a really thin body is necessary for good competition, says Virgina Overdorf, a professor of movement science at William Patterson College in Wayne, N.J. For instance, while only about 3 percent of the general population develops eating disorders, up to 60 percent of athletes who compete in "aesthetic sports" — like gymnastics, diving and figure skating — develop disorders, says Teri McCambridge, an assistant professor of pediatrics at the Johns Hopkins University School of Medicine.

Similarly, long-distance runners, jockeys and cross-country skiers have a higher incidence of eating disorders than athletes in other sports. The belief "that the thinner athlete is the better athlete" pervades some sports cultures and encourages athletes to lose weight, says Ron Thompson, a psychologist in Indiana and a fellow at the Academy for Eating Disorders in Chicago.

Even a sport like wrestling, which may not require leanness per se, breeds athletes "who think they can improve performance by losing weight," says Leigh Cohn, publisher of Gurze Books, which specializes in eating disorders and education, and co-author of the 2000 book, *Making Weight: Healing Men's Conflicts with Food, Weight, and Shape.*

Thompson and his associate Roberta Sherman identified a phenomenon they called "sport body stereotypes," which dictate how athletes in different sports are expected to look. Distance runners are supposed to be thin, for instance, while football players are supposed to be larger. Athletes trying to maintain the body stereotypes associated with aesthetic and lean sports are more at risk of developing an eating disorder, says Thompson.

Aesthetic and lean sports tend to be individual sports rather than team sports, and their athletes often share a personality type — the "perfectionist personality," says McCambridge. Characterized by a competitive drive for excellence, the perfectionistic personality is often found in both athletes and eating-disorder patients and can cause athletes to have more difficulty than the general population in maintaining a healthy diet.

Thompson explains that athletes, like those suffering from anorexia nervosa, exhibit a mental toughness, are never satisfied with their performance and make decisions based on what they think will please those around them. These traits allow athletes "to keep going when they are out of juice," says Cohn, "in the same way anorexics can stop themselves from eating even though they're hungry."

Some experts say coaches can unwittingly encourage eating disorders by suggesting an athlete lose weight without encouraging healthy weight-loss practices, according to McCambridge. Moreover, she says, a coach might attach punishment to weight gain, telling athletes they can't play unless they make a certain weight.

But Overdorf doesn't believe coaches cause eating disorders. While they may make careless comments about weight,

Continued from p. 130

often in a more effective and reader-friendly manner than more formal eating-disorder treatment sites.

Rosenthal acknowledges the sites are potentially dangerous, but she doesn't think they should be shut down. Aside from free-speech concerns, she says, the sites have much to teach. For example, by reading the sites and their discussion boards, she says, researchers can glean new insights into how anorexics and bulimics feel and why some refuse to get treatment. Preliminary results of her current study show that two-thirds of those who join the pro-ana discussion boards are looking for someone to talk to, and one-third are looking for tips on how to starve themselves.

Walter H. Kaye, professor of psychology at the University of Pittsburgh School of Medicine's Western Psychiatric Institute and Clinic, agrees. "If you weigh 60 pounds and you think you're fat, even though that's a very real feeling to you, other people might look at you and be mystified," Kaye said. "But these Web sites probably make these girls feel like there is someone that understands them and won't judge them." [12] ■

BACKGROUND

Saints and Witches

In the Middle Ages, women who starved themselves were first considered saints — then they were denounced as witches and finally they were seen as just plain unhealthy.

In the 14th century, St. Catherine of Siena, for example, died of starvation at the age of 33 after eating only

those comments only affect athletes already predisposed to an eating disorder, she says.

Thompson blames the athletic culture that views some eating-disorder symptoms as normal — even desirable. For example, up to 67 percent of female athletes experience amenorrhea, the loss of menstruation, which is a common symptom of an eating disorder, explains Thompson. Even though amenorrhea can be harmful to women, many coaches don't see it as a problem. For instance, Thompson found that less than half of 3,000 National Collegiate Athletic Association coaches that he surveyed thought amenorrhea was abnormal and needed intervention. Many even thought it was advantageous, as it prevented menstruation from impairing performance.

Getty Images/Tony Duffy (1996)

Olympic gold medalist Kerri Strug and other athletes in "aesthetic" events are at risk for developing eating disorders.

Other research suggests that athletic participation can protect against eating disorders by building self-esteem, Thompson says, but mainly at non-elite levels in non-lean sports. And Mark F. Reinking, an assistant professor of physical therapy at St. Louis University, co-authored a study comparing disordered-eating symptoms of female collegiate athletes and non-athletes. The female athletes did not show more disordered-eating symptoms than the non-athletes. In fact, "athletes had a more normalized body satisfaction than the non-athletes," says Reinking. [2]

However, female athletes participating in lean sports were more at risk for developing disordered-eating behavior, suggesting that sports that don't emphasize leanness, like basketball and field hockey, might protect athletes from developing eating disorders.

Antonia Baum, a psychiatrist at George Washington University Medical Center, speculates that some athletes might join a sport because it provides an environment that could facilitate an eating disorder. Nancy Clark, director of nutrition services at Sports Medicine Associates, in Brookline, Mass., and author of *Sports Nutrition Guidebook*, agrees. "Many women get into sports, and they're disguised as athletes," she writes, such as "the teenage girl who gets into running, where really the goal is to burn off calories." [3]

— Melissa J. Hipolit

[1] Eli Saslow, "Strug's Golden Years Come After Olympics," *The Washington Post*, Aug. 10, 2004, p. D3.

[2] Mark F. Reinking and Laura E. Alexander, "Prevalence of Disordered-Eating Behaviors in Undergraduate Female Collegiate Athletes and Nonathletes," *Journal of Athletic Training*, March 2005, pp. 47-51.

[3] Barbara Maston, "Sports Women; Anorexia: It's Not Going Away," *The Boston Globe*, April 9, 2003, p. E12.

bread, raw herbs and water since age 25. In his 1985 book *Holy Anorexia*, Rudolph M. Bell, a professor of Italian history at Rutgers State University, documents 261 cases of women starving for religious reasons between 1206 and 1934. [13] Many were elevated to sainthood and praised for helping the sick at their own health's expense.

But toward the end of the Middle Ages, women who fasted were thought to possess evil spirits and were accused of being witches bent upon destroying the Catholic Church.

By the 17th and 18th centuries, however, women who wasted away were considered neither witches nor saints but simply victims of poor health. In fact, many women who supposedly died from consumption, known today as tuberculosis, are now thought to have suffered from anorexia.

Richard Morton, the physician to the king of England, is credited with the first reference to anorexia in medical literature in 1689 when he described cases of "nervous consumption" in *Phthisiologia: or, A Treatise of Consumptions.* Morton defined the disorder as separate from "consumption." [14]

Ironically, one of Morton's first cases involved a man. Today anorexia is widely seen as a "woman's disease," and men often refrain from getting help because of the stigma.

In the 1870s, medical accounts of anorexia came from E. C. Lasegue, a French professor of medicine, and W. W. Gull, a London surgeon. In 1873 Gull coined the term "anorexia nervosa" (from the Greek word for "lack of appetite"). Gull defined anorexia as an independent disease while Lasegue thought it was a "peripheral," or a disorder of the nervous system. Both agreed, however, that anorexia was a psychological disease.

In 1888, the British medical journal *Lancet* published 11 articles over a two-month period regarding anorexia, greatly boosting awareness of the disorder.[15] By the 1940s, the medical community generally accepted anorexia as a psychological disorder.[16]

Early researchers gave various reasons for eating disorders. French neurologist Pierre M. F. Janet, a pioneer in psychiatry, linked anorexia and the loss of appetite in young girls to emerging adolescent sexuality. So did Sigmund Freud, the founder of psychoanalysis. Both concluded that anorexic girls feared adult womanhood and sex and wanted to stay thin and childlike.

In the 1960s and '70s, Hilde Bruch, a professor of psychiatry at Baylor College of Medicine in Houston, suggested that anorexics had an "inadequate sense of self" and restricted their eating to act out their frustration and feelings of inadequacy. Her treatments focused on helping anorexics "find a voice."[17] Bruch's 1979 book about anorexia nervosa, *The Golden Cage*, is widely considered a classic.

Arthur Crisp, chairman of psychiatry at St. George's Hospital Medical School in London, also was influential, arguing that anorexia was a way to cope and avoid adolescence; Gerald Russell of the University of London researched anorexics' intense fear of fatness.

Russell coined the term "bulimia nervosa" in 1979 and helped develop the disorder's diagnostic criteria. Bulimia, Greek for "bull's appetite," has a sparser record in the medical books, but not in history. The first modern bulimia case was described in 1903 by Janet in *Les Obsessions et la Psychasthenie.*

But reports of people bingeing and purging have been around for centuries. Ancient Romans, for example, visited so-called vomitoriums during feasts so they could regurgitate and eat some more. Emperors Claudius and Vitellius may be the first documented cases of individuals who binged and purged.[18]

EDC Photo/Mark Lerro

"Anorexia and bulimia were certainly foreign to me until I woke up three years ago and realized they were eating me alive," actor Tommy Schrider of New York told a congressional briefing in December 2003. "Never in my wildest dreams could I ever have conceived of the debilitating despair, the soul-crushing hopelessness that my eating disorder wreaked upon me."

Social Pressure

Cultural shifts and fashion fads have profoundly affected how women want to look and how much they think they should weigh. In the United States, plumpness once signaled that a woman was well fed and affluent. By the early 1900s, however, women wanted to look like the "Gibson Girl" created by illustrator Charles Dana Gibson and popularized by magazines such as *Scribner's* and *Harpers*. With her incredibly tiny waist, the Gibson girl gave women a nearly impossible ideal to achieve.

The 1920s ushered in the "flappers," pencil-thin women who wore loose-fitting dresses that exposed arms and legs. In the 1940s and '50s, the full figure again was the ideal, popularized by movie stars like Ava Gardner, Jane Russell and Marilyn Monroe. But that changed in the 1960s when a 97-pound British model known as Twiggy (Leslie Hornby Armstrong) hit the fashion runway, and many women tried to look like her. Before Twiggy, the average fashion model weighed just 8 percent less than the average American woman, but today fashion models are thinner than 98 percent of American women.[19]

Many experts say the first Barbie doll, launched in 1959 by Mattel, epitomizes the unrealistic expectations that American pop culture puts on girls and women. The average American girl has at least one Barbie by the time she is 3 years old. But if Barbie were a real person, she would stand 5'9" and weigh a mere 110 pounds, with the unrealistic body measurements of 39-18-33.

"Barbie, Tinkerbell, and countless others . . . reinforce the societal message about the value of thinness," writes psychologist Cynthia R. Kalodner in her 2003 book *Too Fat or Too Thin?*[20]

In the 1970s, few people talked about eating disorders, and little was known about them. When Vivian Meehan, a nurse at a hospital in Highland Park, Ill., discovered that her daughter had anorexia nervosa, she found little information about it and no support systems. After she put an ad in the local newspaper asking if anyone was interested in discussing the ailment, she was bombarded with calls. In 1976, she formed the National Association of Anorexia Nervosa and Associated Disorders, one of the country's first organizations devoted to eating disorders.

Four years later, the American Psychiatric Association recognized anorexia and bulimia as separate mental disorders.

In the late 1970s, Argentinian psychiatrist Salvador Minuchin, who practiced in Philadelphia, theorized that family behavior shapes the anorexic's eating habits and recommended that treatment involve the entire family. In the early 1980s, New York psychotherapist Steven Levenkron described anorexics as seeing themselves as either being in charge of everything — including food intake and weight — or being completely powerless. His novel *The Best Little Girl in the World* was made into a TV movie in 1981, giving many Americans their first glimpse of eating disorders.

People with eating disorders also tend to have certain personality traits that may play a role in their illness. For example, anorexia sufferers often have low self-esteem, are perfectionistic and need to be liked or in control. Researchers speculate that focusing on weight loss and food allows anorexics to ignore — possibly unconsciously — problems that are too painful or seem too difficult to solve.

Eating disorders often occur in early adolescence, either just as a person enters puberty, or just before or in early adulthood. Researchers speculate that as a girl's body begins to develop, she starts worrying about getting "fat" in places where she wasn't before. Girls also may feel powerless as their bodies change, so they react by taking total control of what they eat.

Eating disorders are often triggered by seemingly trivial incidents like a brother teasing his sister about her weight or a coach's off-hand remark. Significant life events also can act as a trigger, such as being sexually or physically abused as a child, starting high school or college, beginning a new job or getting married or divorced.

Complex Treatment

The complexity of eating disorders calls for treatment focusing on both the body and mind. Anorexics first must gain weight and receive medical treatment to correct the likely damage to their hearts and other organs caused by starving themselves. For bulimics, the goal is to stop the purging, so the focus is on learning new patterns of regular, non-binge meals and healthy, but not excessive, exercise.

Experts say that all eating-disorder patients benefit from some form of psychotherapy to deal with their underlying emotional issues. This can include cognitive-behavior therapy in which the therapist and patient work together to identify illogical thinking patterns about food, body image, weight and perfection, or interpersonal therapy, in which patients look at their interactions with others that may exacerbate, but not actually cause, the eating disorder. In many cases, treatment also must tackle serious accompanying psychiatric disorders, such as depression, anxiety, panic, obsessive-compulsive disorder and alcohol and drug problems.

Just as the 1990s were ending, researchers in the United States and Britain were finding that brain chemistry and genetics play a bigger role in the onset of eating disorders than originally thought. Doctors at London's Maudsley Hospital found in late 1998 that increased levels of the brain chemical serotonin, which affects mood and appetite, may be linked to anorexic behavior, while University of Pittsburgh researchers found that decreased serotonin activity may cause bulimic behavior. [21]

These studies suggest that people with eating disorders have variations in their genes for serotonin receptors. Low levels of serotonin are found in people who are depressed, while high levels are found in anxious or overwhelmed people who are perfectionists. According to one theory, bingeing helps people with low serotonin levels increase those levels, making them feel better. Conversely, withholding food can make people with high serotonin levels feel calmer.

In essence, goes the thinking, eating too much or too little actually makes the person feel better. ■

CURRENT SITUATION

New Research

Eating disorders are more widespread than originally thought and probably run in families, but researchers are still trying to figure out why.

Recent studies by Striegel-Moore of Wesleyan University dispel the notion that eating disorders are maladies of young, white girls. Her research indicates that young, black women also suffer from eating disorders. But few studies have included or targeted minorities, so there are little reliable data.

Most experts think rates for men are much higher than studies suggest. "You probably hear the ratio that 1-in-10 patients will be male, but it's probably more like 1-in-6," says Bunnell, of the National Eating Disorders Association. Males are even more reluctant to seek treatment because eating disorders are seen as a "women's disease."

Indeed, they feel the same cultural pressure to be svelte that women feel, says Bunnell, citing billboards "with perfect male bodies that none of us could ever have." Men now "get to feel what women have felt for 40 years," he adds.

Treatment centers also are seeing older women — in their 30s, 40s, 50s and even 60s — seeking help. The big question is whether they have newly developed the disease or have had the disorder since they were younger but were never properly diagnosed.

Medical experts have always suspected that people with eating disorders "cycle" from being anorexic then to bulimic and then back again, and now they are more clearly seeing that. "About one-third, if not more, of patients who have anorexia nervosa will transition into bulimia within two years of their illness. That is the general trend," says Bunnell.

But the disease and its causes are widely misunderstood by the general public, according to a 2005 poll. Most American women blamed dieting and media coverage as the primary reasons people developed eating disorders, while men said it was caused by lack of willpower. (*See graph, p. 124.*)

Research debunks another widely held myth about eating disorders: that they are the result of bad parenting. "It's clear that 'bad parenting' is not, per se, a risk factor" for developing an eating disorder, says Striegel-Moore.

However, many families are still faulted and shut out from treatment, says Clausen, who founded Ophelia's Place, a resource center in upstate New York for those with eating disorders. Clausen says she felt blamed for her two daughters having eating disorders, and that she "had to fight to get into therapy" with her daughters. "We need to involve the families," she says.

In fact, one of the most promising new treatments for young anorexics involves the entire family. The so-called Maudsley Method, developed at London's Maudsley Hospital, neither blames the family for "causing" the disease nor the anorexic for "getting" it. Instead, everyone helps the anorexic manage and treat the disorder. Parents are told that food functions as medicine for the anorexic, just as insulin is medicine for a diabetic. So the parents must ensure the anorexic gets his or her medicine. The treatment appears less effective for older adolescents, adults or those who binge and purge.

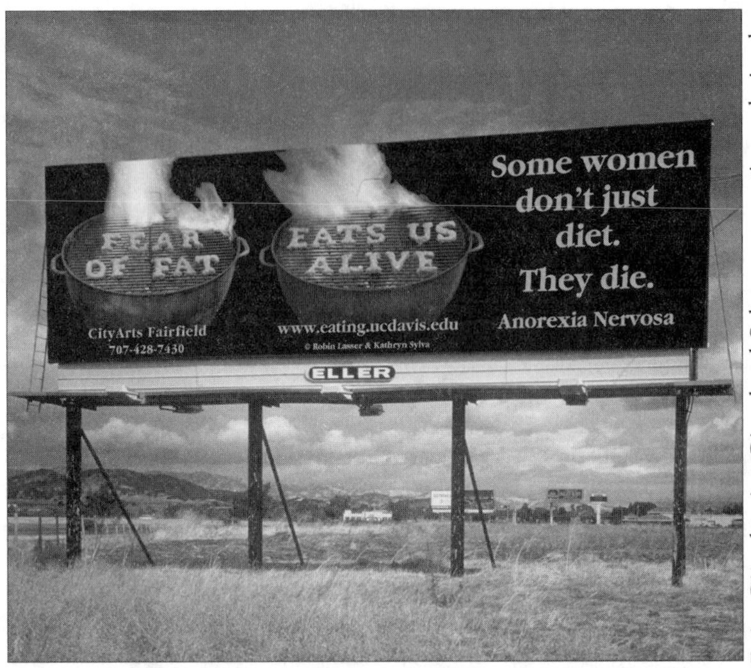

Eating Disorders in a Disordered Culture, www.eating.ucdavis.edu

A nationwide public-art campaign to raise awareness of eating disorders was launched in the late 1990s by artists Robin Lasser, of San Jose State University, and Kathryn Sylva of the University of California, Davis. Above, one of their billboards in Fairfield, Calif.

Families may also play another, even larger role: Research increasingly shows that eating disorders tend to run in families. The National Alliance on Mental Illness estimates, for example, that a girl has a 10 to 20 times higher risk of developing anorexia nervosa if she has a sibling with the disease.

Differences in brain wiring also play a role. Researchers at the University of Pittsburgh found in 2005 that a chemical deep inside the brain, called dopamine, could make an anorexic unable to accept that they are too thin or the seriousness of their condition. [22]

Researchers also are finding that psychotropic medications — which affect emotions — can help treat eating disorders. Antidepressants have helped bulimics but seem to work for anorexics only after they reach a normal weight.

Professionals increasingly agree that the first step in treating anorexia is to help the person gain weight, then dive into therapy or medication. "It's very hard to do psychotherapy with a starving brain," says Bunnell.

Striegel-Moore acknowledges "the picture is totally bleak" for anorexics because no treatment has proven to be clearly superior to others — at least not until they've begun to gain weight. "It's really an emergency."

Cognitive therapy appears to work in about 50 percent of bulimia cases, says Striegel-Moore.

Continued on p. 138

At Issue:

Does insurance adequately cover eating disorders?

KAREN IGNAGNI
PRESIDENT AND CEO, AMERICA'S HEALTH INSURANCE PLANS

WRITTEN FOR THE *CQ RESEARCHER*, FEBRUARY 2006

yes

Eating disorders such as bulimia and anorexia are serious conditions that can have devastating consequences for individuals and their loved ones. Accordingly, more than 95 percent of all employer-sponsored health insurance plans provide some benefits for treatment of these and other mental health disorders. More than nine-out-of-10 people buying insurance on their own choose policies that have mental health coverage.

The issue with which policymakers and health-care stakeholders must grapple is how to ensure that coverage for services related to eating disorders is accessible to all those who need it.

In the past, many legislators gravitated to coverage mandates. Today, however, lawmakers are increasingly recognizing that coverage mandates often have unintended consequences. Many states have put the brakes on new mandates because they have been found to raise costs and thus inhibit access to coverage, as well as usurp employer and consumer purchasers' decision-making authority.

The discussion about coverage for eating disorders underscores the need for more data about which courses of treatment best help patients. Indeed, our entire health-care system suffers from a dearth of information about which therapies, technologies and providers are the safest and most effective.

Rather than taking a disease-by-disease approach to making health care more affordable and accessible, policymakers should focus on three priorities:

- Evaluating how health costs can be brought under control to ensure that consumers and purchasers can get the coverage they want.
- Determining the consequences of having legislators construct benefit packages that employers and individuals must purchase.
- Finding the tipping point for employers and individuals to determine when mandates, however well intentioned, prevent the purchase of insurance.

Those afflicted with eating disorders deserve access to health-care services based on the best available medical evidence. Legislators need to encourage more research to determine what works rather than imposing coverage on purchasers. Collaboration among all stakeholders will do far more to improve treatment options and quality of care for eating disorders than mandating coverage requirements.

JEANINE C. COGAN, PH.D.
POLICY DIRECTOR, EATING DISORDERS COALITION FOR RESEARCH, POLICY & ACTION

WRITTEN FOR THE *CQ RESEARCHER*, FEBRUARY 2006

no

Treatment for mental disorders in general and eating disorders in particular is not adequately covered by most health-insurance plans. For this reason, Congress passed legislation in 1996 requiring insurance companies to end their practice of capping the dollars spent on treatment for mental illness and reimburse for these conditions on par with the treatment of physical illness.

The intent of the law was to stop discrimination based on mental illness and provide parity for mental health treatment. Unfortunately, the insurance industry evaded the spirit of the law by replacing the caps on dollars spent for mental health treatment with caps on the number of visits to be reimbursed.

This practice has notable consequences for people suffering from eating disorders. The death rate for women with anorexia is 12 times greater than the general death rate for women in the same age group. Moreover, research indicates that as the length of treatment decreases for people with eating disorders, the risk for relapse and death increases.

According to a congressional briefing at the Renfrew Center, a residential treatment facility, prior to the proliferation of reimbursement caps eating-disorder patients stayed an average of 50 days. In 2001 the average stay had dropped to only 15 days, and the rate of returning patients rose to 33 percent compared to 10 percent when more days were reimbursed.

Other research corroborates this trend. Examining the changing patterns of hospitalization in eating-disorder patients, Wiseman and her colleagues found that readmissions of eating-disorder patients increased 27 percent between 1985 and 1998 as lengths of stays were briefer, and weight at discharge was lower.

And Baran and his colleagues found that the majority of patients discharged while still at a low weight are eventually readmitted. This suggests that the economic rationale for shortening eating-disorder treatment is canceled out by the higher costs associated with relapse and readmissions.

This documented trend of the revolving door results in sicker patients and higher death rates. As the duration of eating-disorder symptoms is prolonged, the prognosis for recovery decreases and the mortality rate increases.

Clearly, for people with severe eating disorders, adequate health-insurance reimbursement is not simply good public policy, it is a lifesaver. As such, the Eating Disorders Coalition is working with Congress toward the passage of mental health parity legislation that would continue to eliminate obstacles for life-saving treatment.

Continued from p. 136

Stalled in Congress

Eating-disorder experts haven't had much luck convincing Congress to make it easier for victims of eating disorders — and other mental disorders — to get insurers to pay for treatment. However, they hope the federal government's campaign to combat obesity will translate into more attention, research and federal dollars devoted to eating disorders.

The only federal law related to eating disorders was a 1989 congressional resolution establishing a National Eating Disorders Awareness Week. "That just goes to show how little has happened legislatively" regarding eating disorders, says Jeanine C. Cogan, policy director of the Eating Disorders Coalition for Research, Policy & Action, which is lobbying Congress to make eating disorders "a public-health priority."

High on the coalition's wish list is "mental health parity," which would require insurers to cover mental illness at the same level as physical illnesses. Although Congress passed a federal mental health parity law in 1996, it didn't prohibit insurers that offer mental health benefits from charging higher co-pays for those benefits than they charge for physical illnesses or from imposing stricter limits on treatment for mental illness. Mental health advocates have been lobbying for a broader version even before the 1996 bill passed.

Cogan says anorexics who are forced to be discharged from hospitals before they've gained enough weight usually end up being readmitted later, thus costing the health-care system more over the long term. In the 1980s, for example, before the widespread use of managed-care contracts, anorexic patients used to stay 50 days in a hospital getting treatment, and only 10 percent returned for further treatment. Now, she says, the average stay is only 15 days, but 33 percent of the patients return.

Cogan admits that mental health parity "seems stalled" and unlikely to pass as long as the House Republican leadership, particularly House Speaker J. Dennis Hastert R-Ill., opposes the measure. Many House Republicans, employers and insurance companies oppose parity, arguing that it would increase costs for employers at a time when many businesses are already struggling to pay for health care.

Meanwhile, most states require some level of coverage for mental illnesses, including eating disorders, but the requirements vary widely. While 47 states have a law or regulation affecting mental health coverage, many allow insurers to charge higher co-pays for mental health services or to limit service, says Lee Dixon, director of the Health Policy Tracking Service, in Falls Church, Va.

Only 26 states have what Dixon calls true "parity." But four of those (Hawaii, Montana, Oklahoma and South Dakota) specifically exclude eating disorders from coverage. The remaining 22 states treat eating disorders as mental disorders and are covered.

When the movement to get mental health parity began at the state level nearly a decade ago, attention focused on biologically based mental illnesses like schizophrenia and bipolar disorder, Dixon says. Since then, research has shown that there is a biological basis for most, if not all, mental illnesses — including eating disorders.

In the meantime, eating-disorder experts are optimistic the nation's preoccupation with obesity will focus more attention on eating disorders. "A lot of funding is being directed to obesity now," says Rome, of the Academy for Eating Disorders. "We would love to have some funding for eating-disorder work as well."

NEDA
What's going on in her mind is even scarier.

National Eating Disorders Association

People with eating disorders have a mental illness that distorts their body image, as dramatized in a poster from the National Eating Disorders Association. Men and women who starve themselves to stay thin can die from the resulting organ damage.

NEDA estimates that the National Institutes of Health in 2005 spent $647 million on Alzheimer's research — a disease that affects 4.5 million people — but only $12 million on anorexia, which affects an estimated 11 million.

Some experts worry, however, that encouraging obese Americans to lose weight may trigger eating disorders. "The more we intensify our efforts to eliminate obesity, if we don't do it in a meaningful way it could lead to eating disorders," Cogan says. She notes that research has shown that for some people, their eating disorder developed after going on a diet. "We have to be careful."

The coalition also hopes Congress will direct the Centers for Disease Control and Prevention to do a better job tracking the number of people who die of eating disorders. As it stands, anorexia and bulimia are rarely put on a death certificate. Instead, the death is usually attributed to the physical ailment that killed the person, such as heart failure or low electrolytes. ■

OUTLOOK

New Medications

Many eating-disorder experts believe researchers eventually will find better ways to help sufferers and prevent others from developing the disorder in the first place.

"We've come quite a way in understanding how to treat a substantial number of people with bulimia and anorexia nervosa — that's the good news," says NEDA's Bunnell. "The bad news is that we are talking about only about 50 percent of the patients responding to those therapies. We are left with what do we do with the other 50 percent."

Several new medications hold promise. A schizophrenia medication called olanzapine has shown some benefit for anorexics, says the APA's Powers. And topiramate, a drug used to control seizures, may reduce frequency of bulimics' bingeing and purging. Another treatment, called "vagus nerve stimulation" — currently used to treat epilepsy and depression — also may help bulimics. The vagus nerve starts in the brain, goes down the neck where it affects the vocal cords, the acid content of the stomach and other organs. Some researchers think the treatment might help bulimics stop vomiting.

"There is a lot of exciting work being done," Powers says.

Experts also hope research on the genetic link will eventually help professionals predict who is most likely to develop anorexia, possibly intervening earlier to prevent the onset of the disorder.

Meanwhile, efforts continue to help the general public better understand that eating disorders are serious illnesses and not just diets gone bad. "Clearly, these aren't choices, they are illnesses," says Powers.

"We are near a tipping point with public awareness about eating disorders," says Bunnell. "My hope would be that in five years it would be common for mothers to talk to their daughters about their risks," particularly if the family has a history of eating disorders.

"We have to talk about it," agrees New York activist Clausen, whose two daughters continue to battle eating disorders. "There's still a stigma, a denial" associated with eating disorders.

Westin agrees. She says her family in Minnesota was swamped with calls and letters from families "thanking us for being honest" by stating in Anna's death notice that she died of anorexia, something that was "unheard of" before then, she says.

Both mothers launched eating-disorder centers in their areas because no facilities were available nearby. While more information is available now, advocates worry that the media "glorifies and trivializes" the illnesses, says Cogan of the eating-disorders coalition. She hopes that in the next five to 10 years people will acknowledge eating disorders as serious illnesses that are an important public-health issue.

The more people know about eating disorders, the more they may seek help. "Eating disorders are very serious illnesses," Westin says, "but they should never be fatal." ■

High on the Eating Disorder Coalition's wish list is "mental health parity," which would require insurers to cover mental illnesses at the same level as physical illnesses.

Notes

[1] More information about both young women can be found at www.annawestinfoundation.org/annastory.htm and "Living With Bulimia:

Kathy Benn," Aug. 11, 2005, www.webmd.com/content/article/109/109397.htm.

2 National Eating Disorders Association, "Statistics: Eating Disorders and Their Precursors," 2005.

3 For background, see Alan Greenblatt, "Obesity Epidemic," *CQ Researcher*, Jan. 31, 2003, pp. 73-104.

4 National Association of Anorexia Nervosa and Associated Disorders, "Facts About Eating Disorders," 2005; www.anad.org/site/anadweb/content.php?type=1&id=6982.

5 Cynthia R. Kalodner, *Too Fat or Too Thin?* (2003), p. 33.

6 U.S. Department of Health and Human Services, "The Surgeon General's Call to Action to Prevent and Decrease Overweight and Obesity," December 2001; www.surgeongeneral.gov/topics/obesity/.

7 For background, see Jane Tanner, "Mental Health Insurance," *CQ Researcher*, March 29, 2002, pp. 265-288.

8 "American Public Opinion on Eating Disorders," poll conducted for National Eating Disorders Association by GMI Inc., March 25, 2005.

9 Jill King Greenwood, "Online Anorexia," *Pittsburgh Tribune-Review*, Dec. 4, 2005.

10 Lucile Packard Children's Hospital at Stanford, press release, "Web Sites Promoting Eating Disorders Are Widely Used by Adolescents with the Condition, Say Researchers at Stanford and Lucile Packard Children's Hospital," May 16, 2005.

11 Academy for Eating Disorders, "Position Statement on Pro-Anorexia Web Sites," www.aedweb.org/policy/pro-anorexia_sites.cfm.

12 Greenwood, *op. cit.*

13 Rudolph M. Bell, *Holy Anorexia* (1985).

14 Background drawn from LeeAnn Alexander-Mott and D. Barry Lumsden, *Understanding Eating Disorders* (1994).

15 Kalodner, *op. cit.*, p. 52.

16 For background, see Richard L. Worsnop, "Eating Disorders," *CQ Researcher*, Dec. 18, 1992.

17 James Lock and Daniel le Grange, *Help Your Teenager Beat An Eating Disorder* (2005).

18 Kalodner, *op. cit.*

19 National Eating Disorders Association, "The Facts & Statistics," www.nationaleatingdisorders.org.

20 Kalodner, *op. cit.*

21 "Genetic clues to eating disorders," *BBC News*, Jan. 21, 1999.

22 University of Pittsburgh press release, "Specific regions of brain implicated in anorexia nervosa, finds Univ. of Pittsburgh study," July 7, 2005.

FOR MORE INFORMATION

Academy for Eating Disorders, 60 Revere Dr., Suite 500, Northbrook, IL 60062-1577; (847) 498-4274; www.aedweb.org. An international organization for professionals in the field.

Alliance for Eating Disorders Awareness, P.O. Box 13155, North Palm Beach, FL 33408-3155; (866) 662-1235; www.eatingdisorderinfo.org. Disseminates information to parents and caregivers about warning signs, dangers and consequences of eating disorders.

American Psychiatric Association, 1000 Wilson Blvd., Suite 1825, Arlington, VA 22209; (703) 907-7300; www.psych.org. Represents physicians who specialize in mental illnesses, including eating disorders.

Anorexia Nervosa and Related Eating Disorders, www.anred.com. Nonprofit organization provides information about eating disorders, including self-help tips and a survey.

Eating Disorder Referral and Information Center, 2923 Sandy Pointe, Suite 6, Del Mar, CA 92014-2052; (858) 792-7463; www.edreferral.com. Provides referrals to eating-disorder practitioners, treatment facilities and support groups nationwide.

Eating Disorders Coalition for Research, Policy & Action, 611 Pennsylvania Ave. S.E., #423, Washington, DC 20003-4303; (202) 543-9570; www.eatingdisorderscoalition.org. Lobbies Congress for more federal attention to eating disorders.

National Alliance on Mental Illness, Colonial Place Three, 2107 Wilson Blvd., Suite 300, Arlington, VA 22201-3042; (703) 524-7600; www.nami.org. Provides information on eating disorders and advocates on behalf of victims of those and other mental conditions.

National Association of Anorexia Nervosa and Associated Disorders, Box 7, Highland Park, IL 60035; (847) 831-3438; www.anad.org. Provides hotline counseling, a national network of free support groups and referrals.

National Eating Disorders Association, 603 Stewart St., Suite 803, Seattle WA 98101; (800) 931-2237; www.nationaleatingdisorders.org. The largest U.S. organization in the field was formed in 2001 with the merger of Eating Disorders Awareness and Prevention and the American Anorexia Bulimia Association.

National Institute of Mental Health, 6001 Executive Blvd., Bethesda, MD 20892; (301) 443-4513; www.nimh.gov. Federal agency that studies eating disorders.

"Something Fishy," www.somethingfishy.org; This Web site on eating disorders calls itself a "pro-recovery" site, as opposed to sites that promote eating disorders as lifestyles, rather than diseases. Provides information in easy-to-understand terms.

About the Author

Pamela M. Prah is a *CQ Researcher* staff writer with several years previous reporting experience at Stateline.org, *Kiplinger's Washington Letter* and the Bureau of National Affairs. She holds a master's degree in government from Johns Hopkins University and a journalism degree from Ohio University. Her recent reports include "War in Iraq," "Disaster Preparedness" and "Domestic Violence."

Bibliography

Selected Sources

Books

Kalodner, Cynthia R., *Too Fat Or Too Thin?* Greenwood Press, 2003.
The director of the counseling psychology program at Maryland's Towson State University provides a practical guide to eating disorders, including lists of books, movies and Web sites for students and parents interested in learning more.

Levenkron, Steven, *Anatomy of Anorexia*, W.W. Norton & Co., 2001.
A New York psychotherapist stresses the importance of detecting early symptoms of anorexia and outlines various treatment options.

Lock, James, and Daniel le Grange, *Help Your Teenager Beat An Eating Disorder*, The Guilford Press, 2005.
Two professors of psychiatry provide a roadmap for parents whose children have eating disorders, explaining the latest research in easy-to-understand language. Lock is director of the Eating Disorders Program for Children and Adolescents at Stanford University; le Grange is director of the eating-disorders program at the University of Chicago Hospitals.

Articles

"Body Image in Hollywood: Sending Wrong Messages?" CNN, Nov. 25, 2005.
A report on Hollywood's obsession with being super-thin includes interviews with Jane Fonda, Paula Abdul and Jamie-Lynn DiScala about their eating disorders.

"Dying To Be Thin," PBS, Dec. 12, 2000; www.pbs.org/wgbh/nova/thin/.
NOVA talks to medical experts about eating disorders and provides tips for teachers interested in discussing the topic in class.

Matson, Barbara, "Sports Women; Anorexia: It's Not Going Away," *The Boston Globe*, April 9, 2003, p. E12.
Female athletes in sports that value a lean appearance — like gymnastics, figure skating and distance running — are at high risk for developing an eating disorder.

Reaves, Jessica, "Anorexia Goes High Tech," *Time*, July 31, 2001.
Reaves' report was one of the first national articles to examine the wave of pro-anorexia Web sites that started to flood the Internet in the late 1990s.

Silverman, Lauryn, "Hunger's Diary," Youth Radio, also aired on National Public Radio's "Morning Edition," May 16, 2005; www.youthradio.org/health/npr050516_anorexia.shtml.
This first-person account of her struggle with anorexia by a high-school junior from Berkeley, Calif., won the 2005 Gracie Allen Award from the American Women in Radio and Television.

Tyre, Peg, "No One To Blame," *Newsweek*, Dec. 5, 2005, pp. 51-60.
A review of the latest advances and treatment for anorexia, including new findings related to genetics.

Reports and Studies

"American Public Opinion on Eating Disorders: A Poll Conducted on Behalf of the National Eating Disorders Association," GMI Inc., March 2005.
Most American women blame dieting and media coverage as the primary causes of eating disorders, while men blame a lack of willpower. Neither is accurate.

American Psychiatric Association Work Group on Eating Disorders, "Practice Guidelines for the Treatment of Patients with Eating Disorders," *American Journal of Psychiatry*, January 2000, pp. 1-39.
The latest guidance from the APA on eating disorders, slated to be updated in 2011.

Centers for Disease Control and Prevention, Department of Health and Human Services, *National Youth Risk Behavior Surveillance, 2003*, May 2004; www.cdc.gov/mmwr/PDF/SS/SS5302.pdf.
Eighteen percent of high-school girls admit fasting for 24 hours or longer to trim down, while 11 percent tried diet pills or powders and 8 percent took laxatives or threw up, according to the latest government report.

National Association of Anorexia Nervosa and Associated Disorders, "A Brief Review of Therapies Used in the Treatment of Eating Disorders," 2005; www.anad.org/site/anadweb/content.php?type=1&id=6901.
Patricia Santucci, a physician, explains the major methods used to treat eating disorders, including one of the newest therapies, the Maudsley approach.

National Institute of Mental Health, "Eating Disorders: Facts About Eating Disorders and the Search for Solutions," 2001; www.nimh.nih.gov/Publicat/eatingdisorders.cfm.
A government booklet describes the symptoms, causes and treatments for eating disorders, with information on getting help.

The Next Step:

Additional Articles from Current Periodicals

Adult Women

Morris, Bonnie Rothman, "Older Women, Too, Struggle With a Dangerous Secret," *The New York Times*, July 6, 2004, p. F5.

Doctors who are seeing a growing number of adult women with eating disorders suspect they have struggled with weight and body image throughout their lives.

White, Tanika, "A New Midlife Crisis: Fear of Food," *Los Angeles Times*, Dec. 4, 2005, p. A22.

As adult women develop eating disorders in higher numbers, experts blame media images that suggest older women should look like 20-year-olds as well as older women's feelings of loss of control over their lives.

African-Americans

Brodey, Denise, "Blacks Join Whites in Threatening-Disorder Mainstream," *Intelligencer Journal* (Lancaster, Pa.), Sept. 20, 2005, p. B5.

More African-American girls are seeking help for severe eating disorders than ever before, and experts are wondering if they receive proper treatment.

Tharp-Taylor, Shannah, "Anorexia in Blacks Gets New Scrutiny," *Chicago Tribune*, Aug. 25, 2003, p. 1.

Eating-disorder experts are researching whether African-American anorexics are more common than previously thought.

Athletes

Case, Christa, "First Steps to Curb Eating Disorders Among Top Athletes," *The Christian Science Monitor*, Aug. 26, 2004, p. 11.

Many experts believe the attributes that produce athletic success, like perfectionism and strict discipline, can lead to eating disorders.

Hersh, Philip, "Are Ski Jumpers Too Thin?" *Chicago Tribune*, Jan. 16, 2002, p. 7.

Ski-jumping techniques favor lighter athletes, pushing jumpers to develop eating disorders.

Josephs, Ira, "Ounce of Prevention," *The Philadelphia Inquirer*, March 6, 2005, p. D1.

Wrestling has gone through a steady period of reform, helping to eliminate fasting and purging, after three NCAA wrestlers died in 1997.

Liddane, Lisa, "Athletic Females at Risk for Disorder," *Chicago Tribune*, Aug. 21, 2002, p. 7.

Female athletes are at risk for developing a health-threatening disorder termed the 'female athlete triad,' which is the lost of menstruation due to disordered eating that causes bones to become porous and brittle.

Norwood, Robyn, "Fed Up With the Hunger," *Los Angeles Times*, July 21, 2004, p. A1.

Jockeys are beginning to push for an increase in the minimum weights horses carry after years of pressure from owners and trainers to be as light as rules permit triggered numerous eating disorders.

Binge Eating

The Associated Press, "Some Can Blame Genes for Binge Eating, Researchers Suggest," *The Houston Chronicle*, March 20, 2003, p. A12.

A study focused on a gene that helps the brain regulate appetite suggests mutations in the gene can make the body feel too much hunger and can lead to binge eating.

Squires, Sally, "Secret Lives of Bingers and Nighttime Noshers," *Los Angeles Times*, Jan. 23, 2006, p. F4.

Clinical experience and a few studies suggest binge-eating disorder and night-eating syndrome are two distinct disorders that affect about 2 percent of the general population.

Celebrities

Hagen, Mindy B., "Actress Recounts Exercise-Bulimia Struggle," *The Herald-Sun* (Durham, N.C.), Feb. 22, 2005, p. C1.

"Sopranos" star Jamie-Lynn DiScala was almost recast after losing 40 pounds due to an eating disorder — exercise bulimia.

Leibrock, Rachel, "The Skinny on the Stars Lindsay Lohan and Nicole Richie: What's Putting Young Hollywood in the Thick of Ultra-Thin?" *Sacramento Bee*, June 7, 2005, p. E1.

Young celebrities like Lindsay Lohan, Mary-Kate Olsen and Nicole Richie undergo extreme weight loss after becoming famous.

Susman, Carolyn, "Lohan Battles Bulimia and Denial," *Palm Beach Post* (Florida), Feb. 1, 2006, p. E1.

Actress Lindsay Lohan admitted to *Vanity Fair* that she suffers from bulimia but later claimed she was misquoted, leading psychologists to speculate she is in denial about her problem.

Witlin, Dawn, "Rail-Thin Celebs Motivate Many With Eating Disorders," *The Boston Herald*, Nov. 21, 2005, p. 3.

Images of emaciated celebrities, like Nicole Richie, reinforce extreme dieting and provide many young Americans with "thin-spiration."

Genetics

Roan, Shari, "Seeking a Genetic Link to Anorexia Nervosa," *Los Angeles Times*, April 7, 2003, p. 3.
Scientists suspect a number of genes — not just one — cause personality traits common to people who develop anorexia, prompting the U.S. government to fund research to search for the genes.

Shell, Ellen Ruppel, "The Ancestry of Anorexia Blame Biology, Not Parenting, New Theory Suggests," *The Boston Globe*, Dec. 30, 2003, p. D1.
Psychologist Shan Guisinger theorizes that anorexics have a biological adaptation in their genes that causes their bodies to shut off hunger signals.

Insurance Coverage

Barnard, Anne, "Wasting Away Women Suffering From Eating Disorders Finally Get the Medical and Psychological Attention They Need," *The Boston Globe*, July 1, 2003, p. C4.
Doctors and the families of eating-disorder patients are finding private dollars to support new treatment centers for the disorders after insurance companies refuse to pay for treatment after a patient leaves the hospital.

Galloway, Angela, " 'Great Leap' On Mental Health Law Mandates Equal Insurance Coverage," *The Seattle Post-Intelligencer*, March 10, 2005, p. B1.
Lawmakers in Washington passed a mental health parity bill requiring insurance companies to cover psychiatric care on the same terms as medical or surgical care.

Waterhous, Therese S., "Treating Anorexia: The Question of Insurance," *The Seattle Times*, Nov. 10, 2004, p. F2.
All major insurance companies consider eating disorders to be behavioral-health issues that qualify for mental health benefit provisions — which often offer less coverage — and not medical coverage.

Obesity

The Associated Press, "Teenage Girls' Radical Dieting Can Cause Obesity, Study Says," *The Houston Chronicle*, April 21, 2005, p. B2.
Researchers found that adolescent girls who use harsh weight-control measures, including skipping meals, vomiting and using laxatives, are more likely to become obese than those who eat high-fat foods or sometimes gorge themselves.

Roan, Shari, "A Reluctance to Broach the Topic of Weight," *Los Angeles Times*, May 9, 2005, p. F4.
Parents of obese children are reluctant to talk to their children about their weight, fearing it might trigger an eating disorder, but doctors and eating-disorder experts say that with obesity on the rise in the United States, parents must intervene.

Treatment

Gollob, Beth, "When Food Becomes the Enemy," *The Daily Oklahoman*, Dec. 27, 2005, p. A13.
Tulsa's Laureate Clinic and Psychiatric Hospital helps patients with eating disorders by using art therapy, separate programs for children and adults and teaching healthy eating and exercise habits.

Roan, Shari, "Just One Rule: Eat," *Los Angeles Times*, Oct. 3, 2005, p. F1.
A controversial new family-centered approach to treating eating disorders engages a patient's entire family in therapy, teaching parents and siblings how to outmaneuver attempts to avoid food.

Uhlman, Marian, "A Way Station to Cure Eating Disorders," *The Philadelphia Inquirer*, Aug. 5, 2002, p. E1.
Philadelphia's Renfrew Center exclusively treats eating disorders, utilizing many forms of therapy, from individual counseling and group sessions to monitored eating and gentle exercise.

Vuong, Mary, "A Desire to Be Perfect Can Make Treating the Eating Disorder Difficult," *The Houston Chronicle*, July 7, 2004, p. 1.
A gold standard for treating anorexia nervosa has not been developed because of resistant patients, their development of other disorders — like depression — and the stigma that the problem is self-inflicted.

Citing The *CQ Researcher*

Sample formats for citing these reports in a bibliography include the ones listed below. Preferred styles and formats vary, so please check with your instructor or professor.

MLA Style

Jost, Kenneth. "Rethinking the Death Penalty." The CQ Researcher 16 Nov. 2001: 945-68.

APA Style

Jost, K. (2001, November 16). Rethinking the death penalty. *The CQ Researcher, 11*, 945-968.

Chicago Style

Jost, Kenneth. "Rethinking the Death Penalty." *CQ Researcher,* November 16, 2001, 945-968.

In-depth Reports on Issues in the News

Are you writing a paper?

Need backup for a debate?

Want to become an expert on an issue?

For 80 years, students have turned to the *CQ Researcher* for in-depth reporting on issues in the news. Reports on a full range of political and social issues are now available. Following is a selection of recent reports:

Civil Liberties
Right to Die, 5/05
Immigration Reform, 4/05
Gays on Campus, 10/04

Crime/Law
Death Penalty Controversies, 9/05
Domestic Violence, 1/06
Methaphetamines, 7/05
Identity Theft, 6/05
Marijuana Laws, 2/05
Supreme Court's Future, 1/05

Education
Academic Freedom, 10/05
Intelligent Design, 7/05
No Child Left Behind, 5/05
Gender and Learning, 5/05

Environment
Climate Change, 1/06
Saving the Oceans, 11/05
Endangered Species Act, 6/05
Alternative Energy, 2/05

Health/Safety
Avian Flu Threat, 1/06
Birth-Control Debate, 6/05
Disaster Preparedness, 11/05
Domestic Violence, 1/06
Drug Safety, 3/05
Marijuana Laws, 2/05

International Affairs
Future of European Union, 10/05
War in Iraq, 10/05
Exporting Democracy, 4/05

Social Trends
Future of Newspapers, 1/06
Cosmetic Surgery, 4/05
Celebrity Culture, 3/05

Terrorism/Defense
Re-examining 9/11, 6/04

Youth
Bullying, 2/05
Teen Driving, 1/05
Athletes and Drugs, 7/04

Upcoming Reports

Pension Crisis, 2/17/06
Presidential Power, 2/24/06
Elite High School Programs, 3/3/06
Whistleblowers, 3/10/06
Mining Safety, 3/17/06

ACCESS

The CQ Researcher is available in print and online. For access, visit your library or www.thecqresearcher.com.

STAY CURRENT

To receive notice of upcoming *CQ Researcher* reports, or learn more about *CQ Researcher* products, subscribe to the free e-mail newsletters, *CQ Researcher Alert!* and *CQ Researcher News*: www.cqpress.com/newsletters.

PURCHASE

To purchase a *CQ Researcher* report in print or electronic format (PDF), visit www.cqpress.com or call 866-427-7737. Single reports start at $10. Bulk purchase discounts and electronic rights licensing are also available.

SUBSCRIBE

A full-service *CQ Researcher* print subscription—including 44 reports a year, monthly index updates, and a bound volume—is $688 for academic and public libraries, $667 for high school libraries, and $827 for media libraries. Add $25 for domestic postage.

The *CQ Researcher Online* offers a backfile from 1991 and a number of tools to simplify research. For pricing information, call 800-834-9020, ext. 1906, or e-mail librarysales@cqpress.com.

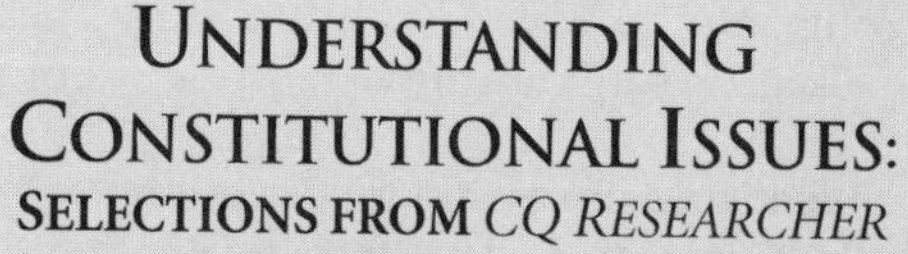

Understanding Constitutional Issues focuses on four key themes — governmental powers and structure, security, liberty, and equality — to help students develop a deeper understanding of the relation between current events and constitutional issues and principles. Integrating eighteen *CQ Researcher* reports, *Understanding Constitutional Issues* makes important connections clear, such as those between civil liberties and security; and privacy and liberty.

June 2004 • 8 1/2 x 11 • Approx. 432 pages • Paperback • ISBN 1-56802-885-7 • $39.95

To Order: Call Toll-Free: 866.4CQ.PRESS (427.7737)
Fax: 800.380.3810 • Web: www.cqpress.com
E-mail: customerservice@cqpress.com

CQ Press, 1255 22nd Street, NW, Suite 400 • Washington, DC 20037

CQ Researcher

Published by CQ Press, a division of Congressional Quarterly Inc.

thecqresearcher.com

Pension Crisis

Are traditional pensions becoming obsolete?

Many private pension plans won't be able to pay the benefits they have promised; they are underfunded by an estimated $450 billion. Even the federal agency that insures them is in the red $23 billion — and its shortfall could hit $142 billion in 20 years. The biggest pension failures have involved companies in struggling industries such as auto, steel and airlines — but even healthy corporations such as IBM, Verizon and Hewlett-Packard have recently frozen their pension plans. Congress is crafting legislation to make the nation's private pension system more stable, but many observers worry that tightening funding rules could lead more companies to drop their pension programs. It seems certain that more of the responsibility of saving for retirement will fall to individuals — and Americans are notoriously bad savers. As the first wave of baby boomers turns 60 this year, many experts warn that they and coming generations won't be able to retire as comfortably as their parents.

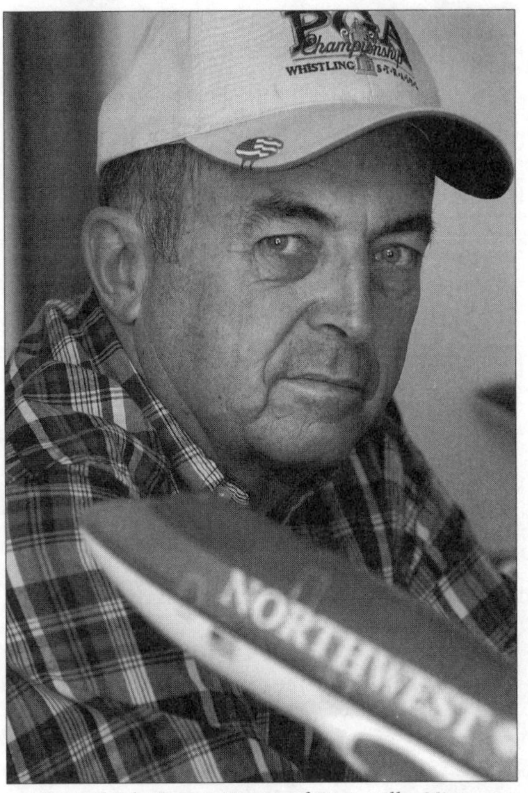

Retired pilot Les McNamee of Burnsville, Minn., may not get his full pension because Northwest Airlines filed for bankruptcy protection.

INSIDE THIS REPORT

The CQ Researcher • Feb. 17, 2006 • www.thecqresearcher.com
Volume 16, Number 7 • Pages 145-168

CQ PRESS

RECIPIENT OF SOCIETY OF PROFESSIONAL JOURNALISTS AWARD FOR EXCELLENCE ◆ AMERICAN BAR ASSOCIATION SILVER GAVEL AWARD

THE ISSUES

BACKGROUND

CURRENT SITUATION

OUTLOOK

SIDEBARS AND GRAPHICS

FOR FURTHER RESEARCH

Cover: Retired pilot Les McNamee of Burnsville, Minn., is among thousands of current and former Northwest Airlines workers who may not get their full pension benefits because the company has filed for bankruptcy protection. (AP Photo/Craig Lassig)

CQ Researcher

Feb. 17, 2006
Volume 16, Number 7

CQ PRESS
A Division of
Congressional Quarterly Inc.

CQ Researcher (ISSN 1056-2036) is printed on acid-free paper. Published weekly, except March 24, July 7, July 14, Aug. 4, Aug. 11, Nov. 24, Dec. 22 and Dec. 29, by CQ Press, a division of Congressional Quarterly Inc. Annual full-service subscriptions for institutions start at $667. For pricing, call 1-800-834-9020, ext. 1906. To purchase a *CQ Researcher* report in print or electronic format (PDF), visit www.cqpress.com or call 866-427-7737. Single reports start at $10. Bulk purchase discounts and electronic-rights licensing are also available. Periodicals postage paid at Washington, D.C., and additional mailing offices. POSTMASTER: Send address changes to *CQ Researcher*, 1255 22nd St., N.W., Suite 400, Washington, DC 20037.

Pension Crisis

BY ALAN GREENBLATT

THE ISSUES

Joe Necastro had no trouble finding work when he came home to Warren, Ohio, after serving on an aircraft carrier in Vietnam. Within a week, he landed a job in the test lab at Ajax Magnethermic Corp., a heavy-equipment maker.

Necastro had a good run with Ajax — 35 years. But as he neared retirement, the company struggled, was sold and began eliminating benefits — first severance pay, then health insurance.

Finally, the company shut down. But ownership had been dispersed among so many shell companies that none could be held legally responsible for the shortfall in the company's pension fund.

"Not sold, not bankrupt? How do I get pension?" Necastro wrote in a note to himself. [1]

Ajax's pension money had been set aside, but the value of its stock market holdings had declined, leaving only about half as much left as was needed to fulfill the company's pension promises. Luckily for Necastro and other older workers, the federal Pension Benefit Guaranty Corporation (PBGC) stepped in. Set up by Congress in 1974, PBGC promised to make good their pensions — but at a rate much reduced for some workers. *

However, the outcome could have been worse. At least Necastro and his buddies will receive a share of the pensions they were promised. Only 30,000 U.S. companies even offer guaranteed pensions today, down from a high of 112,000 companies in 1985. And the outlook for millions of workers, like Necastro, who counted on their employer-sponsored pensions, has become much cloudier.

In recent months, major companies such as United Airlines and auto-parts giant Delphi have turned to PBGC to relieve them of pension promises they can no longer keep. Verizon, IBM and Hewlett-Packard have all decided either to deny traditional pension plans to new hires or to suspend their existing pension programs altogether.

Meanwhile, company pension plans are underfunded by some $450 billion, while the PBGC is itself running a deficit of $22.8 billion.

Getty Images/Barry Williams

General Motors is closing nine plants in North America by 2008, including its facility in Doraville, Ga. Older companies like struggling GM must support multiple generations of retirees but have fewer active workers contributing to their pension funds. Hard times in the steel, airline and auto industries have caused huge deficits in corporate pension funds and the federal fund that guarantees private pensions.

But that deficit could quadruple over the next decade, according to a study released in September 2005 by the Congressional Budget Office. It estimated that PBGC shortfalls could reach nearly $87 billion over the next decade — and possibly $142 billion in 20 years.

"Based on this report, the choice is either for pensioners to lose over $100 billion in promised retirement benefits or for taxpayers to get slapped with a $100-billion bill for failed private pension plans. Neither is acceptable," said House Budget Committee Chairman Jim Nussle, R-Iowa. [2]

Three decades ago, pensions in both the government and private sectors were fixtures of the American workplace. Employers proudly touted retirement plans that provided set payments for life in order to recruit workers, and employees saw their pensions as an assurance that they would be provided for in their old age.

But today, huge funding deficits have put traditional pension plans under a severe strain. Newer companies refuse to offer them, while more established employers are doing everything they can to limit their pension liabilities.

As part of an emerging, historic change, many companies are shifting the responsibility of paying and planning for retirement onto individual workers. Other companies, meanwhile, have maintained pension programs they can't sustain — and are shifting their cost to the already underfunded PBGC, which is funded with pension-plan contributions from employers.

In recent years, the PBGC's finances have been severely strained by

* The maximum annual payout is currently $47,659.08 per person. So retirees with pensions above that amount get penalized.

Ten Firms Had $11 Billion in Pension Shortfalls

The 10 largest pension defaults of the past 30 years were in the steel, aluminum or airline industries. Their $11 billion in pension debts represented about half of the claims turned over to the Pension Benefit Guaranty Corporation (PBGC) during that period.

Top 10 Firms Presenting Pension Claims to the PBGC (1975-2004)

Firms	Claims (in $ billions)	No. of Participants	Average Annual Claim*
1. Bethlehem Steel	$3.754	97,015	$37,668
2. LTV Steel	$1.962	80,376	$24,418
3. National Steel	$1.146	35,404	$32,382
4. Pan American Air	$0.841	37,485	$22,438
5. US Airways Pilots	$0.726	7,168	$101,294
6. Weirton Steel	$0.688	9,196	$74,890
7. Trans World Airlines	$0.668	34,171	$19,560
8. Kaiser Aluminum	$0.565	17,591	$32,175
9. Eastern Air Lines	$0.552	51,187	$10,798
10. Wheeling-Pitt Steel	$0.495	22,144	$22,364
Top 10 total	**$11.397**	**391,737**	**$28,862**
All other total	**$9.303**	**1,009,097**	**$9,264**
TOTAL	**$20.700**	**1,400,834**	**$14,761**

** The maximum annual PBGC payout is $47,659 per person.*

Source: Pension Benefit Guaranty Corporation (PBGC), "Pension Insurance Data Book, 2004"

high-profile business failures, such as the LTV and Bethlehem steel companies. Several U.S. airlines, under intense pressure from new, low-cost airlines that do not offer traditional pension programs, have been particularly pinched by their burgeoning old-style pension obligations. Last year, United Airlines defaulted on its four pension plans, handing over $9.8 billion in pension shortfalls to PBGC. US Airways also reached a deal with PBGC last year, resolving $2.7 billion in pension obligations. Other bankrupt airlines, Delta and Northwest, are next in line and may add as much as $12 billion to PBGC's deficit.

But the airline industry isn't alone. In October the PBGC said it might have to assume responsibility for $4.1 billion of the $10.8 billion pension deficit faced by Delphi, which was spun off from General Motors. GM's own pension plan, meanwhile, is in serious jeopardy. [3]

Worried that taxpayers may be forced to make up the PBGC's shortfall, both the House and the Senate late last year passed bills designed to tighten up pension-funding rules. Lawmakers are expected to reconcile their competing proposals in the coming weeks (*see p. 159*).

"Not long ago, workers used to be pretty sure of a good pension plan. That's not the case anymore," said Charles E. Grassley, R-Iowa, chairman of the Senate Finance Committee, citing factors both within and outside lawmakers' purview. "We need to fix the problems within our control." [4]

Indeed, some experts lay the blame for underfunded pensions at Congress' doorstep, saying that federal pension rules make it too easy for corporations to wiggle out of their commitments — and then leave it to the PBGC to clean up their pension messes.

"Congress repeatedly has passed legislation that enables corporations to underfund their pensions, overstate their profits and postpone to another day any action that would lead them to keep their promises to employees," writes Martha Paskoff Welsh, an adviser on pension reform to the president of the liberal-leaning Century Foundation. [5]

When Congress passed the law governing private pensions 30 years ago, lawmakers never envisioned that entire industries — not just a few companies — would go bankrupt and struggle to meet their pension obligations. But that is exactly what has happened in many of the industrial sectors — including steel, auto and the airlines — that have traditionally provided the most generous retirement benefits. Now companies in these fields say they can't afford to expend their remaining assets on workers who are no longer active.

Others say pension funds should have been managed and funded separately from each company's main operations, with accounts that should be sacrosanct and dedicated to meeting old pension promises, even in companies that are far from robust. Regardless, all companies — and governments — are struggling with demographic changes as well.

For one thing, pensions have become much more expensive than originally envisioned, primarily because life expectancy has grown. In 1950, the average life expectancy in the United States was 68.2 years. In 2002, it was up to 77.3 years. [6] The oldest baby boomers — the enormous generation born in the years following World War II — turn 60 this year, and it's been estimated that two-thirds of all the world's people who have ever reached age 65 are alive today.

The demographic changes mean relatively fewer people are working full time today — and paying into Social Security and other pension funds — compared to the number who are retired. "Back in the '30s, when Social Security started, there were 35 workers for every retiree," says David Wyss, chief economist for Standard & Poor's. Today, that ratio is fast approaching 2-to-1.

Similarly, older companies like struggling General Motors, which have fewer active workers contributing to their pension funds, must continue supporting multiple generations of retirees. Indeed, GM has been called "a pension budget fund and health-insurance business that happens to make cars." [7]

"The system really was designed in an era when everybody thought that the work force would continually grow," says Carol A. Weiser, a benefits lawyer at Sutherland, Asbill & Brennan in Washington.

While American companies like GM and Ford struggle to pay their pension and health "legacy costs," rivals such as Toyota don't have nearly the same level of benefits eating into their bottom lines.

Over the last decade, virtually no company has created a traditional pension plan that offers workers "defined benefits" — guaranteed monthly payments after retirement. Instead, newer companies, such as Southwest Airlines and Microsoft, offer "defined-contribution" plans, such as tax-deferred 401(k) accounts. In defined-contribution plans, workers contribute a certain percentage of their salaries to their own retirement accounts, which their employer may fully or partly match. But the employer is not obliged to pay out any additional funds once the worker retires.

Defined-contribution plans actually slightly surpassed defined-benefit plans in total assets in 1997; both currently hold roughly $2 trillion in reserves.

Number of Traditional Pension Plans Fell

American companies have been terminating their company-sponsored defined-benefit pension plans for years. Today, fewer than 30,000 companies offer employer-sponsored plans, down from an all-time high of 112,208 in 1985. Firms increasingly are sponsoring defined-contribution programs, such as 401(k) plans.

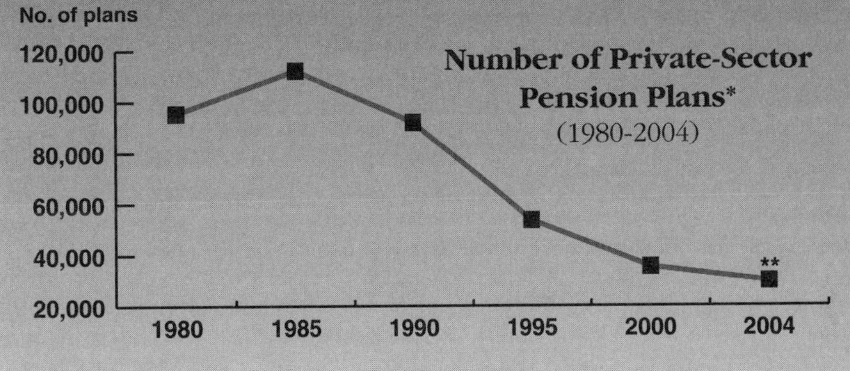

** Sponsored by single employers*

*** Estimated*

Source: "Pension Insurance Data Book 2004," Pension Benefit Guaranty Corp.

Due to sluggish bond and stock markets in recent years, companies still offering traditional pensions — which rely on investment income — have not been able to accumulate assets fast enough to match their growing liabilities. To make up the difference, companies have had to contribute more cash out of their general operating budgets, causing further problems for companies that were struggling anyway. Some are even turning to investments in risky hedge funds (*see p. 163*).

But even healthy companies have been cutting back on their pension benefits. According to Watson Wyatt, a global consulting firm, 11 percent of the *Fortune* 1000 companies with defined-benefit plans froze or terminated them in 2004 — up from 7 percent the year before.

Some argue that such moves are necessary to compete in today's global marketplace. "The Cold War actually protected American workers, because there weren't that many places where you could get cheap labor," says John J. McFadden, a compensation expert at The American College in Bryn Mawr, Pa. But for today's employers, he says, "Any long-term obligation looks bad to them."

Companies that still run pension plans complain that they are highly regulated, answering to three separate federal agencies (the PBGC, the Internal Revenue Service and the Labor Department). Having to meet more stringent funding requirements, as Congress and the Bush administration want, could drive still more companies to drop their traditional pension plans, some argue.

"Some of the proposals are so draconian that they're going to be counterproductive and will drive some companies out of business or out of defined-benefit plans," says Alan Reuther, legislative director for the United Auto Workers (UAW). "The result will be more of the risk of retirement being shifted onto the backs of workers."

Reuther questions "the post-modern notion that blue-collar workers should

San Diego's 'Bad Habit'

Numerous state and local governments face billion-dollar pension deficits, but San Diego's problem is particularly intense. Possibly because of what has been called a "corrupt conspiracy," the mayor recently resigned and several other officials were indicted. [1]

The trouble began a decade ago, when the city was tapped to host the 1996 Republican National Convention. To pay for refurbishing the convention center, officials dipped into the city's pension fund rather than raising taxes or issuing bonds. It was the beginning of a bad habit.

As the economy began slowing, local officials continued using pension dollars for other purposes. "The key, Nobel Prize-winning breakthrough in economics was the discovery that the unfunded pension liability was a big hole where you could hide your debt," says City Attorney Michael Aguirre. In 2002, for example, unable to give raises to its employees, the city instead offered 25 percent pension increases — despite having just lowered the city's cash contributions into the fund.

"Under the corrupt scheme," editorialized *The San Diego Union-Tribune* last October, "the City Council agreed to increase pension benefits significantly if the retirement board, controlled by the labor unions and other city employees, approved a plan allowing the city to underfund the pension system." [2] Under the agreement, union officials were allowed to jack up their personal pensions in violation of tax rules.

The underfunding plan was approved despite the warnings of Diann Shipione, a pension board trustee, that over the long run it could bankrupt the city. [3] A private attorney for the board also warned it was probably illegal. [4]

Running for re-election in 2004, Mayor Dick Murphy denied that the city was in serious financial difficulty, even as its pension deficit was nearing the billion-dollar mark. He narrowly won but resigned a few months later, after *Time* named him one of the nation's three worst mayors. [5]

In December 2005, Aguirre reported that the city had already run up $10 million in legal bills. [6] The city was also spending heavily to try to make up its pension deficit, by then estimated at $1.4 billion. Last year it increased its annual contributions to the pension fund from about $80 million to $160 million and, according to Councilman Scott Peters, will soon raise them to more than $200 million — serious money in a city with a $2.5 billion budget.

On Jan. 6, 2006, the former pension system's director, staff attorney and five former trustees were indicted for conspiracy and fraud.

Although San Diego's problems are extreme, and the alleged conspiracy unusual, such financing decisions have become commonplace. Many governments that saw tax revenues start to dry up while their pension systems were still making money in the financial markets found it less painful to defer pension payments than to close police stations and libraries.

"Every single decision made in San Diego over the last 20 years was made in other cities as well," says former California Finance Director Steve Peace, also a former state senator from San Diego.

But San Diego's massive system failure has served as a warning to other governments. Just as emergency managers across the country are re-examining their plans in the wake of Hurricane Katrina, says Mark Funkhouser, city auditor in Kansas City, Mo., "most of us ran quick and looked at our pension systems to see if there was anything obviously out of line."

In San Diego, said newly elected Mayor Jerry Sanders, "one thing has become clear to me: San Diego's government systems are badly in need of repair." [7]

---

1 "Corrupt Conspiracy; Internal memo details crooked pension scheme," *The San Diego Union-Tribune*, Oct. 6, 2005, p. B10.

2 *Ibid.*

3 Philip J. LaVelle, "Whistle-blower Was Right, But Feels No Vindication," *The San Diego Union-Tribune*, Jan. 7, 2006, p. A16.

4 "City Attorney to Sue San Diego Union Leaders, Pension Panel Members," Copley News Service, Oct. 4, 2005.

5 Terry McCarthy, "The Worst Mayors in America," *Time*, April 25, 2005, p. 22.

6 Craig Gustafson, "S.D.'s Tab for Lawyers: $10 million," *The San Diego Union-Tribune*, Dec. 22, 2005, p. B1.

7 "San Diego Mayor Wants Resignation Letters from City's Managers," The Associated Press, Jan. 3, 2006.

---

be responsible for their own retirements because giant corporations can't handle it." [8] Many pension experts say companies that were able to offer pension benefits on the cheap when their funds' pension investments were profiting in the markets shouldn't complain now that those investments aren't earning as much — meaning the companies must contribute more.

"If the funding rules worked in insuring that companies had contributed sufficient assets to protect the liabilities, then we wouldn't be having this conversation," says Bradley D. Belt, executive director of the PBGC.

Whether the fault lies with increasing global competition, poor investment payoffs or complex accounting rules, the fact is that more and more companies are closing their traditional pension plans. Although these are often replaced with 401(k) or other individual retirement accounts (IRAs), defined-benefit plans provide the greatest security to retirees — a federally insured guarantee of payment until death.

It's becoming clear that individual Americans will have to finance more of their own retirements. And because Americans are poor savers, it's likely that many will struggle.

"The golden age of retirement as our fathers knew it won't be what it used to be," says James Morris, senior vice president for retirement at SEI Investments, in Oaks, Pa.

As the pension debate continues in Congress and elsewhere, here are some of the questions people are asking:

Are traditional pension plans becoming obsolete?

Private pension plans historically have offered "defined" benefits promising fixed monthly payments from retirement until death. The benefits were based on a formula — say, 1.5 percent of the worker's salary times the number of months at the firm.

But because Americans are living longer, companies must pay benefits much longer for each person than they had projected. As a result, troubled companies, such as United Airlines, have divested themselves of their defined-benefit pension plans, turning over their assets and liabilities to the Pension Benefit Guaranty Corporation (PBGC).

Meanwhile, newer companies like Microsoft and Southwest Airlines never offered employees the old-fashioned plans. Financial-services companies say it's been years since they've seen the launch of any new defined-benefit plans. At the same time, many healthy companies, such as Hewlett-Packard and Verizon, decided in 2005 that they wouldn't enroll new hires into their existing defined-benefit plans.

All of this leaves many observers wondering whether traditional pension plans are quickly becoming outmoded. "It's probably fair to say that a traditional defined-benefit plan has less relevance in today's world," says the PBGC's Belt.

Clearly, traditional pension plans don't have the cachet they once did. But most *Fortune* 1000 companies still offer them, and no one thinks they will disappear anytime soon. Dallas Salisbury, president of the Employee Benefit Research Institute, says traditional pensions will remain in demand in industries where workers tend to stay put for a long period of time, such as government and utilities.

Corporate Pensions Are $450 Billion Short

Total underfunding of defined-benefit pension plans rose from $50 billion in 1990 to nearly a half-trillion dollars in 2004.

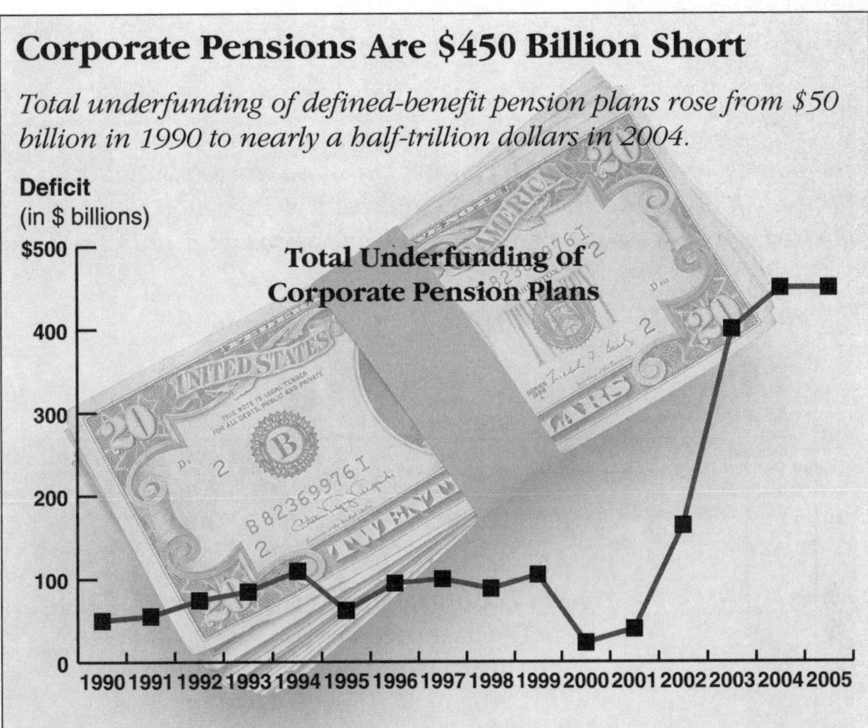

Source: Pension Benefit Guaranty Corporation

Traditional private pensions cover 21.6 million workers and continue to offer many advantages: They help to pool risk and cost less per person to administer than individual retirement accounts. [9] And the vast majority of them, despite the headline failures, are well-funded. "Many of these plans, even those that have been frozen and closed to new participants, will be around for up to 100 years," Salisbury predicts.

And these plans continue to serve the same purpose they always have — helping attract and retain skilled workers. "They are an important work-force management tool," says Bob Shepler, director of corporate finance and tax at the National Association of Manufacturers. "Employers want to reward their employees for staying with the company throughout their career."

At times, pension plans have also offered an even more tangible benefit to employers. During the 1990s, many companies were able to provide generous retirement benefits at no cost to themselves because their pension-plan investments were performing well in the booming stock market. Some did so well that companies were able to draw out funds and count them as pure profit.

"Nobody said anything about pension plans bankrupting companies during the 1990s, because the investment earnings of pension plans were fattening the bottom lines of all these companies," says McFadden, at The American College. "Ten percent of IBM's earnings in the '90s were due to pension funds. Now that's turned around, and companies are claiming pensions are pulling them down."

Shepler warns that the long-term viability of traditional pensions depends to a large extent on the final shape of legislation currently being negotiated in Congress. The bills being considered would shore up the PBGC, which is funded by premiums from companies offering traditional pension plans. But talk of tightening up pension-funding rules over a short timeframe frightens many companies.

Pension Fund Has $23 Billion Deficit

The federal Pension Benefit Guaranty Corporation (PBGC) has a $23 billion deficit because of the growing number of failed companies and underfunded pension plans. But the Congressional Budget Office warns the shortfall could reach $142 billion in the next 20 years unless steps are taken to tighten pension-funding rules.

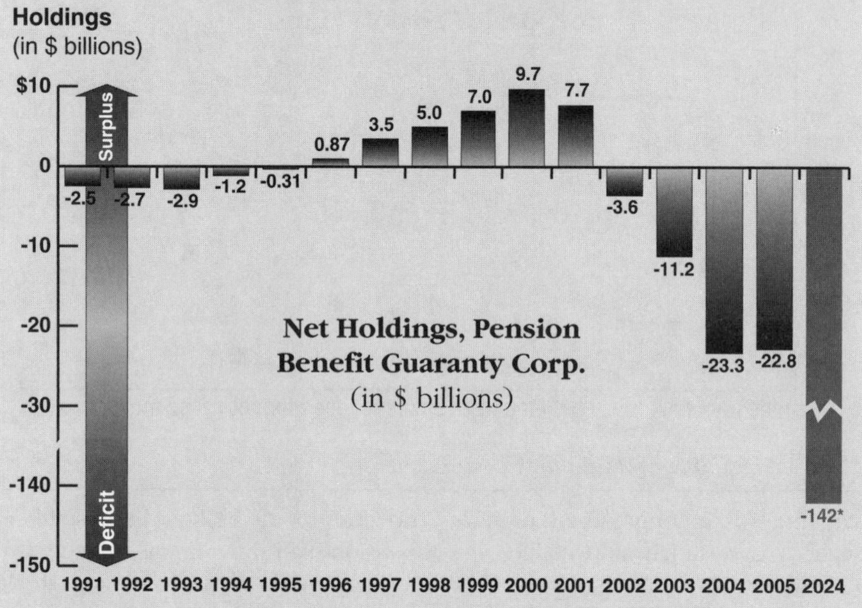

* *Projected*

Source: PBGC Annual Reports (1980-2004), "Pension Insurance Data Book 2004," Pension Benefit Guaranty Corporation; Congressional Budget Office

"You want to breathe as much life into the defined-benefit plans that are left as you can without making demands that cannot be met," says North Carolina state Treasurer Richard H. Moore.

Olivia S. Mitchell, who directs the Pension Research Council at the University of Pennsylvania's Wharton School, doubts that Congress will be able to strike the right balance. She warns that lawmakers may shore up troubled plans at the expense of companies that have managed their pension liabilities well.

"If you raise premiums to clear up past mistakes [by other companies], you may drive out those companies that remain [in the PBGC system]," she says. "To try to charge higher premiums on companies still running defined-benefit plans, it seems to me, might cause a death spiral."

Others warn that no matter what Congress does, many companies will try to unload their pension plans as soon as they can. (Companies are penalized if they end pension plans with future liabilities that aren't 100 percent covered by current assets.) Many executives say it's simply too expensive to offer generous benefits into an unpredictable future when competitors aren't offering the same sort of packages.

"You're going to see less and less of the overall pension dollar go to defined-benefit plans every year," says Stephen W. Skonieczny, a New York-based partner in the employee-benefits group of Dechert LLP, an international law firm. "I don't know whether it will be 10 years or 15 years down the road, but the day will come when there aren't going to be any more defined-benefit plans."

Should employers fund their workers' retirements?

U.S. employers are under no obligation to offer their workers any sort of retirement income. Big firms began offering pensions over a century ago in hopes of retaining skilled workers. Pensions became commonplace following World War II, a staple of employment in heavy-manufacturing industries.

Even A. J. "Jim" Norby, who lobbies for pensioners as president of the National Retiree Legislative Network, says that pensions, like salaries and other benefits, "are a pure labor-relations issue." He adds: "There's no reason to pay an employee a pension, unless the employer decided that the employee was valuable enough to offer him one."

Moreover, even at their peak, traditional U.S. pension plans were hardly universal. At best, according to the Pension Research Council's Mitchell, less than half the American work force received retirement benefits. Now, as more and more companies are moving away from the old-fashioned fixed-income pension model, and fewer employees are spending their entire careers with one employer, companies are taking a fresh look at how much they are obligated to help pay for employees' retirement.

Not surprisingly, labor unions strongly favor pensions. "We think society has an obligation to ensure that people have adequate retirement income," says the UAW's Reuther. "The employer-based system has been a major element of providing that protection."

Many employers still want to offer retirement benefits, in hopes of attracting and retaining talented people. As fewer employers offer traditional defined-benefit pension plans, thousands of employers have set up 401(k) and other retirement accounts into which they may pour a certain percentage of workers' current salaries.

"Most companies feel an obligation to help their employees accumulate wealth for retirement," says Lynn D. Dudley, vice president of retirement policy at the American Benefits Council, which lobbies for big employers that sponsor pension plans. "The surveys I've seen on that point are very strong."'

Shepler of the National Association of Manufacturers agrees but emphasizes that pensions are a voluntary management tool. "Employers cannot provide pensions at the expense of the business," he says. "There's a need to strike a balance."

Getty Images/Tim Boyle

Newer companies like Southwest Airlines offer "defined-contribution" pension plans, such as tax-deferred 401(k) accounts, rather than traditional plans that offer workers "defined benefits," or guaranteed monthly payments after retirement. Under the newer plans, workers contribute a certain percentage of their salaries to their own retirement accounts, which their employer may match or partly match.

Although offering a pension is voluntary, once a company promises to pay pensions it is legally obligated to pay out the full amount. Companies can alter their pension policies at any time, but once an individual retires, it's nearly impossible for the former employer to alter a worker's benefits package. "To renege on what they promised is virtually stealing from you, because you've already earned it," says C. William Jones, president of the Association of BellTel Retirees.

For that reason, many companies worried about being stuck with future liabilities are reducing current workers' benefits. "Employers don't like to use their compensation money for people who don't work there any more," says McFadden, at The American College.

Still, retirement packages are generally considered a good idea. Federal tax policy gives breaks to companies and workers to encourage employer-based pensions. "The combination of the employer system and Social Security is really what made a good retirement for Americans," says Anna Rappaport, a benefits consultant in Chicago and former president of the Society of Actuaries.

Rappaport says there's nothing "magic" about employer-sponsored pensions, but notes that many people, and perhaps society as a whole, have come to rely on them. Moreover, the plans — which involve automatic contributions usually withheld from the employee's paycheck — tend to encourage better savings rates than individual retirement accounts. "People who have employer-sponsored plans are much more likely to save than those who don't," she says.

In fact, Americans are up to 20 times more likely to save if they're automatically enrolled in an employer-sponsored plan compared with those who are not enrolled, says Brian H. Graff, executive director of the American Society of Pension Professionals and Actuaries.

That creates a tension, he says. Some people believe the current system "is too paternalistic," Graff explains. "Our employer-based system forces savings upon people, and some might prefer to take the money and spend it. But as a practical matter, if we don't have this paternalism, people won't save."

The Bush administration, which puts a premium on individual responsibility, has recommended expanded tax breaks and incentives to get more individuals to save for retirement on their own.

But many people disagree, says Graff. "Lots of folks believe that, given the fact that Social Security isn't going to get any bigger, the only way we're going to get the vast majority of Americans to a comfortable retirement is through these employer-sponsored plans," he says, "So we should do everything we can to encourage them."

Morris, of SEI Investments, hopes policymakers address the question of legal liability for companies that want to help their employees better manage their retirement savings. Many companies are shy about offering detailed advice, he says, because they're afraid they'll be held responsible if investments don't pay off.

That kind of advice will be increasingly helpful as time goes on, suggests employee-benefits attorney Diane M. Morgenthaler, a partner at McDermott Will & Emery in Chicago. "We've begun a trend [in which] employees will have to take more and more responsibility for their own retirements," she says. "While there will be employer benefits, we'll see more and more individuals funding their own retirements."

Will today's working Americans be able to retire comfortably?

With many major employers backing away from their historic commitment to pension plans, some economists and other observers are concerned that Americans who are today in their 50s — or younger — won't be able to retire as comfortably as earlier generations.

"Unlike their parents and grandparents, they're unlikely to find an employer at the end of their working life who will replace a good deal of their income," says Graff. "Younger workers need to assume more responsibility for their future than ever before because of this trend of shifting expenses away from employer to employee."

Other trends are foreboding, as well. Social Security benefits may decline in the future. And Medicare, the federal health insurance program for seniors, is running a long-term deficit, leading some to worry that retirees will have to spend most of their limited income on health care. "Imagine accumulating your 401(k) money, and all of it has to be spent just to cover your health-insurance premiums," says Laurence J. Kotlikoff, an economist at Boston University.

But not everyone is pessimistic. Some experts point out that traditional pension plans are usually being replaced with 401(k) and other defined-contribution plans. While there's a danger that individuals can outlive their savings under such plans, they also offer the opportunity to save adequately for retirement.

Salisbury, the president of the Employee Benefit Research Institute, says many people in the newer pension plans have saved enough to create as much retirement income as workers who left the investment decision-making to their company under an old-fashioned plan. The average monthly retirement check from a defined-benefit plan is about $775 — about as much as one could earn from a modest 5 percent return on a $186,000 individual retirement account. And the average 401(k) balance, it turns out, for those between 60 and 65 years of age with 30 years of service is now $190,000, he says.

Other statistics also indicate that many older workers have managed to save that much in their retirement accounts. But younger workers are saving much less than they'll need for retirement, often in the belief that they will catch up later, say many economists.

Salisbury says with today's highly mobile work force many more Americans could fare better under newer plans like the 401(k) than with traditional pension plans. The federal government also has allowed other tax-free or deferred-tax plans designed to encourage retirement savings, such as Roth IRAs. The Bush administration has pushed expansion of such plans. The current pension bills under debate in Congress may make 401(k) enrollment automatic for many employees — giving many workers no choice but to save for retirement.

It would also help, Kotlikoff says, if the financial-services marketplace would do more to create and promote annuity plans, which would allow individuals to invest their retirement savings in a way that would pay out a set monthly amount. In too many cases, retirees withdraw their retirement money in a lump sum, leaving them vulnerable if they spend it down too quickly. "Employees need longevity protection," he says.

However, Kotlikoff and other economists are not sure that, as the retirement burden falls more and more on workers rather than companies, individuals will take adequate advantage of various savings plans. "Anybody who is age 40 — if you're not contributing at least 10 percent of your income, you should worry," says Larry Zimpleman, executive vice president of Prudential Financial Group, in Des Moines, Iowa.

The Wharton School's Mitchell hopes people will change their saving habits. "Just because there's some degree of financial illiteracy doesn't mean people can't learn and won't learn," she says. "That's good, because they're going to have to learn."

That is, such changes will have to occur if Americans are going to continue to enjoy the same levels of comfort in retirement as their immediate forebears. "People will live longer and work longer — and will have to invest more wisely, because I don't think that safety net is going to be there," says Morris, of SEI Investments. "The notion of retiring and playing golf every day, that's kind of an antiquated idea." ■

BACKGROUND

Railroad Ties

Veterans' pensions date back to the Revolutionary War, but private companies didn't provide pensions until after the Civil War. Older Americans were cared for by their families or, more often, continued working. In the 19th century, roughly 75 percent of all males over age 65 were still working. [10]

The antebellum economy had consisted largely of farms and small-scale handicraft-production firms. But during the latter half of the 19th century, the Industrial Revolution took hold, leading to a vast expansion in manufacturing. Between 1870 and 1910, the manufacturing work force

Continued on p. 156

Chronology

1940s-1960s

Pension plans become common in heavy industry during the postwar economic boom.

1949
Ford Motor Co. capitulates to union demands for pensions, setting off a stampede of employer-funded plans. . . . Supreme Court supports National Labor Relation Board's contention that pensions are a proper issue for collective bargaining.

1960
Forty percent of private-sector workers are covered by employer-sponsored pension plans.

1963
Automaker Studebaker collapses, reneging on generous pension increases offered in recent years.

1970s-1990s

Pensions become more regulated and begin to lose favor among employers, who migrate toward newer retirement accounts.

1974
Congress passes Employee Retirement Income Security Act (ERISA), setting standards for private-sector retirement accounts and creating the Pension Benefit Guaranty Corporation (PBGC).

1978
Congress allows creation of 401(k) accounts, enabling workers to defer tax liabilities on a percentage of their income until retirement.

1986
Tax Reform Act requires broader pension coverage of rank-and-file workers and faster vesting schedules, prompting some employers to drop their traditional pension plans.

1990
Congress updates ERISA, imposing an excise tax on money removed from pension funds by cash-strapped companies.

1991
Congress sets PBGC premiums at $19 a year per plan participant.

1997
Defined-contribution plans such as 401(k) accounts surpass traditional pensions in total cash reserves; Congress creates the Roth IRA, a retirement account funded with non-deductible contributions that are not taxed when used after retirement.

1999
IBM converts its traditional defined-benefit pension plan into a cash-balance plan, triggering an age-discrimination lawsuit. A 2003 ruling held the plan was discriminatory.

2000s

Pensions lose favor with employers; many plans fail in a bad investment climate.

2001
President Bush's Commission to Strengthen Social Security recommends ways to overhaul the program that would introduce personal investment accounts; a tax bill increases contribution limits for 401(k) accounts and IRAs.

2002
PBGC posts losses of $11 billion; House passes Pension Security Act, limiting the amount of employee 401(k) contributions that can be invested in company stock and promoting worker education concerning retirement; bill dies in Senate.

May 10, 2005
United Airlines receives court permission to terminate its four employee pension plans — the largest pension default since passage of ERISA.

July 15, 2005
San Diego Mayor Dick Murphy resigns in disgrace over the city's $1.4 billion pension deficit; a new election is held in November.

Nov. 10, 2005
Federal Accounting Standards Board requires corporations to make pension liabilities more clear in their earnings statements and to count their liabilities against profits.

Nov. 15, 2005
PBGC reports a $22.8 billion deficit — a slight improvement on its $23.3 billion deficit in 2004.

Nov. 16, 2005
Senate votes 97-2 in favor of a measure to create more stringent pension-funding rules; House passes its version, 294-132, on Dec. 15.

Dec. 20, 2005
New York City transit workers worried about pensions and other benefits shut down the city's public transportation network for three days during the holidays.

Jan. 6, 2006
IBM freezes traditional defined-benefits pension plan and switches to a 401(k) plan, saying the move will save billions.

Feb. 1, 2006
Congress increases PBGC premiums from $19 to $30 per participant per year.

Pension Failures Take Human Toll

Ellen Saracini's husband, Vincent, had been the pilot of United Flight 175, one of the planes that terrorists crashed into the World Trade Center on Sept. 11, 2001.

But when the bankrupt United last year turned its underfunded pension fund over to the federal Pension Benefit Guaranty Corporation (PBGC), Saracini's widow's pension was cut in half — to $47,000 a year, the maximum payout allowed by the beleaguered agency, which is already running a $23 billion deficit.

"I can't help but ask myself at what point are companies allowed to take away so much from the lives of dedicated employees and their families," Saracini wrote in an "online hearing" organized by Rep. George Miller of California, ranking Democrat on the House Education and the Workforce Committee. "The PBGC's decision to allow United Airlines to end their pensions is just wrong." [1] More than 2,000 other unhappy United workers also responded.

Another United pilot, Gerald Innella, saw his pension of roughly $126,000 a year cut by nearly $80,000, forcing him and his wife to sell their retirement home and move in with younger relatives. [2]

As more and more companies suspend or end their traditional pension plans, many workers and their dependents are feeling similarly shortchanged. The prospect of workers reaching the end of their careers, only to find themselves financially strapped through no fault of their own, has been an important factor in the political debate on regulating pensions.

In California, Republican Gov. Arnold Schwarzenegger was forced to back down from his proposal last year to end the traditional defined-benefit pension for state and school employees after it became clear that the benefits of widows and orphans left behind by firefighters and police officers would have been cut.

"If someone were to get disabled on the job or lose their life, their families are not going to have the guaranteed security that this pension program provides for them right now," complained Heather McCormack, the widow of a fire captain who died on the job. [3]

Companies that offer defined-benefit plans cannot legally change the benefits of retirees, short of a failure such as United's. But it's perfectly legal to suspend, cancel or change plans for current workers. Many companies are refusing to enroll new workers into their pension plans. Others have suspended the benefits offered to current employees, meaning they will only receive the level of benefits they have already earned but will rack up nothing more in their retirement accounts.

Employers, after all, are under no obligation to provide retirement benefits; in fact, most don't. So a smaller check from PBGC is still more than most retired workers get.

But in industries where pensions have been a fact of life at least since World War II, the sudden threat to their well-being is causing anxiety. Personal bankruptcies have increased more than sixfold since 1980. Some economists blame the erosion of programs such as pensions and retiree health benefits for making the financial road so much bumpier for millions of Americans.

Continued from p. 154

quadrupled (from 3.5 million to 14.2 million workers). Family ties grew weaker as people sought factory work in large cities, away from their extended families.

Large corporations, led by the railroads, began offering pensions to help maintain a stable work force. Pensions kept workers attached to a company for long careers and also encouraged older, more expensive workers to leave the payroll. Simply putting older workers out on the street would have dispirited younger workers, who might grow concerned over their own fates.

"To keep worn-out, incapacitated workers on the payroll is an economic waste," writes law Professor James A. Wooten, of the State University of New York at Buffalo, summarizing the thinking of the day. "To turn such [people] adrift is not humane and exercises a depressing influence upon workers still in the prime of life." [11]

Industrial pensions first arose in the 1860s in Prussia, the heart of German industry. Workers who reached age 65 retired in exchange for limited pension payments for the rest of their lives. In 1875, American Express Co., then a transcontinental freight hauler, set up the first U.S. employer-sponsored pension plan, followed in 1880 by the Baltimore and Ohio Railroad. [12]

Railroads depended on pensions to develop experienced, permanent administrative staff to run their giant bureaucracies. Railroads sponsored most of the pension plans developed over the next several decades, but by the early 20th century several banks and utilities also provided pensions.

At first, pensions were discretionary — gratuities from a grateful employer for long and faithful service. But some began to frame pensions as a moral obligation to superannuated workers. In a 1912 book on old age, Lee Wielling Squier wrote, "From the standpoint of the whole system of social economy, no employer has a right to engage men in any occupation that exhausts the individuals' industrial life in 10, 20 or 40 years, and then leave the remnant floating on society at large as a derelict at sea." [13]

Congress, though, remained mostly sympathetic to the so-called personnel theory of private pensions, sharing the corporate view that they were

"Business and government used to see it as their duty to provide safety nets against the worst economic threats we face," said Yale University political scientist Jacob S. Hacker, author of the book *The Great Risk Shift*. "But more and more, they're yanking them away." [4]

Five United Airlines flight attendants, ages 55-64, created a provocative calendar to publicize concern about the airline's pension plan.

Because the United Auto Workers union agreed in November to allow General Motors (GM) to cut its retiree health-care liability by $15 billion, Gerald Roy, a retired GM employee, now pays monthly premiums and other medical expenses for the first time. Although that pinches, he worries more about his son, Jerry, who works for Delphi — the auto-parts maker spun off from GM in 1999. Delphi is operating under bankruptcy and threatening, like United, to hand its pension obligations over to the PBGC.

"What worries me most, or bothers me the most," said the senior Roy, "is him working for 28 years for GM, and he might lose his retirement." [5]

The younger Roy sounds more sanguine, telling *The New York Times*, "People survive somehow." Indeed, many workers are trying to find ways to change their financial positions, given the state of their employers and their pension funds. Hundreds of pilots have lobbied Congress to raise their mandatory retirement age from 60 to 65, giving them more time to recover money lost to pension cuts. [6]

Some flight attendants have tried measures that are both more creative and, perhaps, more desperate. At the top of the list are the five United flight attendants, ages 55 to 64, who posed provocatively in scanty costumes for a 2006 calendar called "Stewardesses Stripped (of Their Pension)." [7]

---

[1] Her testimony is available at http://edworkforce.house.gov/democrats/unitedsaracinitestimony.html.

[2] Dale Russakoff, "Human Toll of a Pension Default," *The Washington Post*, June 13, 2005, p. A1.

[3] Chuck Carroll and Rodney Foo, "Governor's Pension Proposal Denounced," *San Jose Mercury News*, March 26, 2005, p. 1B.

[4] Quoted in Peter S. Gosselin, "If America Is Richer, Why Are Its Families So Much Less Secure," *Los Angeles Times*, Oct. 10, 2004, p. A1.

[5] Danny Hakim, "For a G.M. Family, the American Dream Vanishes," *The New York Times*, Nov. 19, 2005, p. A1.

[6] Bloomberg News, "Pilots Ask Congress to Raise Retirement Age," *Los Angeles Times*, May 26, 2005, p. C3.

[7] Tim Gray, "Pension Roulette," *AARP Bulletin*, July-August 2005.

primarily a means for managing workforce needs. The 1921 Revenue Act exempted income from pension and profit-sharing trusts — becoming the first tax incentive for employers to establish retirement-income benefits for workers.

But employees remained at risk. They received nothing if their employers went bankrupt, and only about 50 percent lived long enough — generally, to age 65 — to enjoy full benefits. Reformers viewed pensions as deferred wages and wanted companies to guarantee that more workers would actually receive pension payments. But corporations shunned the idea of creating special accounts that could be viewed as representing individual employees' assets.

Instead, pension plans became profit centers for companies during the roaring 1920s. Meanwhile, because of the way pension plans were set up, companies "demanded a sacrifice of liberty and mobility, what [Supreme Court Justice] Louis Brandeis called the 'new peonage,' in exchange for this shadowy benefit," writes historian Steven Sass. [14]

By 1935, when establishment of the Social Security System created a federal retirement plan for most Americans, only 3 to 4 million workers — less than 15 percent of the work force — were covered by private plans, mostly sponsored by a few older businesses that imposed strict age and years-of-service requirements. [15] That number would soon shrink. During the Great Depression, nearly 10 percent of companies that had provided pensions discontinued or suspended parts of their plans. Another 10 percent reduced benefits.

"Private pensions would henceforth be tied tightly to the need to reward key employees, and plan benefits would flow more swiftly to the higher-compensated employees," according to Sass. [16]

Social Security and other New Deal programs pushed federal income taxes higher — up to 70 percent on top earners. Pension plans became attractive shelters for highly paid workers because the benefits were taxed more lightly than straight income. After years of fighting between Congress and Treasury officials over lost revenue, lawmakers passed the 1942 Revenue Act requiring broad employee participation in the plans, so top management couldn't create sheltering plans just for themselves.

Postwar Boom

As income taxes applied to more people during World War II, the tax relief afforded by pension plans became valuable to the general work force. Wartime wage-and-price controls also sparked a big increase in the number of companies offering pensions because companies were encouraged to offer non-inflationary compensation. Between September 1942 and December 1944, the IRS approved more than 4,000 plans. By 1945, 6.5 million employees were covered by private pensions — triple the number in 1938. [17]

Meanwhile, unions — which could not negotiate for wage increases because of wage controls — revised their long-held view of pensions as merely management tools and began to see them as desirable. After the war, the United Mine Workers began administering a multi-employer pension plan, to which several mining companies contributed. And Walter Reuther, head of the UAW, made pensions a priority.

In 1947, Ford tentatively agreed to create the first pension plan in the automobile industry but backed out after passage of the Taft-Hartley Act. By limiting union activity, the law in effect gave the company greater concessions than it had been able to extract from the UAW during negotiations about pensions and other contract issues. (In 1949, the Supreme Court supported the National Labor Relation Board's contention that pensions were a proper issue for collective bargaining.)

The old "human-depreciation" idea, which held that companies had a responsibility to care for personnel in old age, just as they would pay to replace worn-out machinery, took root in 1949 with the report of a fact-finding board appointed by President Harry S Truman to rule on a labor dispute.

"The human machines, like the inanimate machines, have a definite rate of depreciation," the board concluded. "We think that all industry, in the absence of adequate government programs, owes an obligation to workers to provide for maintenance of the human body . . . and full depreciation in the form of old-age retirement." [18]

U.S. Steel balked at the obligation at first, but the report influenced the Ford-UAW negotiations (autoworkers tended to be younger than steel workers). Ford began offering pensions in 1949, followed by General Motors the next year, triggering a pension gold rush; by 1960, 40 percent of private-sector workers were covered. [19]

The rise of collectively bargained pension rights — especially in sectors with union-administered, multi-employer plans such as construction, building trades and trucking — bred a sense of worker connection to their unions that began to replace the old model under which pensions were a tool to engender loyalty to a specific employer. There were investigations into allegations that some unions abused their pension funds, notably the mob-influenced Teamsters under James R. Hoffa, who used the money in part to reward his allies.

Getty Images/Chip Somodevilla

Reps. George Miller, D-Calif., at left, and Jan Schakowsky, D-Ill., join members of the Association of Flight Attendants and the Machinists' union on May 10, 2005, to urge a Chicago bankruptcy court to reject a proposed pension agreement between United Airlines and the Pension Benefit Guaranty Corporation.

UAW chief Reuther wanted workers' pensions to be more secure and seized on the collapse of Studebaker as a public relations opportunity to press his point. When Studebaker closed its South Bend, Ind., auto plant in 1963, its pension fund was $15 million short. After negotiations with the union local, some retirees received their full pensions, but vested employees under age 60 received only about 15 percent of the value of their pensions. Those who weren't vested, including employees under 40, got nothing. [20]

Four months later, a presidential commission said basic fairness and the substantial federal tax subsidy enjoyed by private pensions obligated pension funds to deliver promised benefits. The UAW pushed its case that pensions should be insured, but businesses scoffed. Sen. Jacob K. Javits, R-N.Y., who was sympathetic toward the idea of greater worker security, held hearings and helped plant human-interest stories that helped shift media coverage of the issue.

"Each year, thousands of Americans who think they are 'covered' fail to get the retirement benefits they've been counting on," reported *Reader's Digest* in 1971. "In the end, Congress will have to act if the pension rights of millions of Americans are to be protected." [21]

The effort moved some state legislatures to take up bills, leading business groups to lobby Congress for preemptive federal legislation. The landmark Employee Retirement Income Security Act of 1974 (ERISA) created "a far more complex institution, with the government joining employers and unions as an active and assertive participant," writes Sass. [22] In addition to creating the PBGC, it said companies offering pensions would have to adhere to federal funding and vesting rules. It also authorized the use of IRAs, setting the stage for later steps to encourage workers to save more for retirement. [23]

After ERISA

But passage of ERISA, in retrospect, marked the high-water mark for traditional, defined-benefit pension plans. Four years after its passage, Congress created a new retirement vehicle, known as a 401(k) after its location in the Revenue Act. As with many traditional pension plans, these accounts were initially created to give corporate executives the chance to shelter parts of their income (the top individual tax rate was then 70 percent). But within a few years, companies made them available more broadly to workers, and by 1985 assets in 401(k) accounts totaled $91 billion. [24] By 1997, defined-contribution plans such as 401(k)s held bigger reserves than traditional pensions, which currently cover just about 20 percent of all U.S. workers.

Employers argued that 401(k) accounts were better for workers than traditional pensions because they were fully portable — vested workers lost nothing if they changed jobs. But 401(k)s were also cheaper for employers, who put a set amount — say, 3 percent of the worker's salary — into the accounts and then their obligation was finished. Unlike traditional plans, they had no obligation after the worker retired.

In any event, traditional pension funds much bigger than Studebaker have failed in recent years. Some blame generous benefits, such as the "30 and out" early-retirement plans negotiated in the early 1970s by the UAW, which allowed retirement after 30 years of service. Others say even if companies struggle, their pension funds should still be healthy at the time of bankruptcy if they were being managed properly. Pension accounting, based on fluctuating rates of return on investments and largely maintained in secrecy, adds to the confusion.

"Depending on whom you talk to," writes Roger Lowenstein in *The New York Times*, "General Motors' mammoth pension fund is either fully funded or, as the PBGC maintains, it is $31 billion in the hole." [25]

Recent history is full of examples of companies whose pensions were supposedly healthy but turned out to be billions short after the dust of bankruptcy settled. Pension plans in general have been struggling recently due to a confluence of factors. Aside from people living longer and forcing companies to pay out more benefits than they had anticipated, stock market performance has been sluggish since 2000, forcing pension sponsors to compensate for poor returns by putting more cash into their funds.

"Each year, thousands of Americans who think they are 'covered' fail to get the retirement benefits they've been counting on."

— Reader's Digest, 1971

Congress' Pension Plan Considered Generous

As members of Congress consider strengthening the private pension system, they do so in the knowledge that their own pension plan is more generous than most.

Just how much money lawmakers receive upon retirement depends on their length of service and other factors. They generally get between $40,000 and $55,000 a year. Members can receive their full pension by age 60 if they have served for 10 years or more. In some cases they can begin collecting at an even younger age. [1] In addition, lawmakers' pensions include automatic cost-of-living increases that most private-sector workers don't get.

Congressional pensions have been the source of a good deal of populist anger, much of it vented on the Internet. David Keating, senior counselor for the National Taxpayers Union, once said they were "yet another example of Congress run amok. The end results of this system are huge costs for taxpayers and incentives for members to stay longer and longer." [2]

Congressional pensions are not only generous but also more secure than private-sector plans. It would take an act of Congress to change them, after all. And even felons such as former Rep. Randy "Duke" Cunningham, R-Calif. — who pleaded guilty to taking $2 million in bribes — can continue to collect their payments while in prison. (Two Democratic senators recently introduced a bill to cancel pensions in such instances.) [3]

But it's not true, as many Web sites claim, that congressmen pay no Social Security taxes. Between Social Security and their pension plan, members of Congress contribute about 8 percent of their salaries to their own retirement coverage — a higher percentage than most federal employees.

---

[1] Patrick J. Purcell, "Retirement Benefits for Members of Congress," Congressional Research Service, Jan. 21, 2005.

[2] Jennifer S. Thomas, "Congress Taking Look at Its Pensions," *The St. Petersburg Times*, Jan. 28, 1995, p. A1.

[3] George E. Condon Jr., "Cunningham Has Become a Symbol of Corruption," Copley News Service, Feb. 9, 2006.

Many companies that went bankrupt or had underfunded pension plans have dumped their pension obligations onto the PBGC in recent years, including Kaiser Aluminum and Kemper Insurance. But the biggest pension problems have been in older, struggling industries — the airlines, auto manufacturing and steel. PBGC Executive Director Belt told the Senate Finance Committee in June that "United, US Airways, Bethlehem Steel, LTV and National Steel would not have presented claims in excess of $1 billion each, and with funded ratios of less than 50 percent — if the [funding] rules worked."

The biggest pension failure in U.S. history occurred last spring, when United Airlines declared bankruptcy and turned its pension obligations, including a $10 billion deficit, over to the PBGC. Like many other companies, United failed to change its habits when the boom years of the 1990s came to a close. Between 2000 and 2002 the company did not put any contributions into its four pension plans. Yet in 2002, even as the struggling company was lobbying for federal bailouts in the wake of the Sept. 11, 2001, terrorist attacks, it granted a 40 percent pension increase to its ground employees. [26]

If Belt blames the funding rules, the Wharton School's Mitchell blames ERISA itself. "ERISA [depended on] risk pooling. That concept doesn't work when entire industries go under, and that's what we're seeing. They never really had thought that entire industries would go down the tubes." ■

CURRENT SITUATION

Congress Acts

From a purely economic perspective, "the last few years have not been kind to assets accumulating within pension systems," says Zimpleman, of the Prudential Financial Group. The worst-case scenario for traditional pensions, he says, is "low interest rates and poor equity markets — just what has been the scenario for the past five or six years."

But current pension problems appear to stem from more than just a cyclical downturn. Corporate America has experienced an unprecedented rash of failures, with too many companies making pension promises they couldn't keep. Their failures, in turn, have put pressure on healthier companies, which have had to both take up the slack in funding the federal pension-guarantee system and compete against businesses that have sloughed part of their labor costs onto the government.

The Bush administration has grown concerned that the string of billion-dollar bankruptcies could lead to a taxpayer bailout of the private pension system. PBGC is funded by contributions from corporate pension sponsors, who currently pay $30 a year per plan participant. But the fund now owes $22.8 billion more than it has in reserves.

Continued on p. 162

At Issue:

Should Congress give airlines more time to pay down their pension debt?

yes

DUANE WOERTH
PRESIDENT, AIR LINE PILOTS ASSOCIATION INTERNATIONAL (ALPA)

FROM TESTIMONY BEFORE HOUSE SUBCOMMITTEE ON AVIATION, JUNE 22, 2005

Our industry has lost over $30 billion in the last four years and is projected to lose at least $5 billion this year. . . . When we add to this grim financial condition the factors of historically low interest rates and poor stock-market returns, we have a "perfect storm" for the pension woes we currently face. As a result of this witches' brew, we are on guard for even more pension-plan terminations. . . .

But ALPA believes these drastic results can be avoided with creativity and foresight — and appropriate legislative reforms.

Logically, since a pension plan is a long-term proposition, it should be funded over the long term. This would require reasonably predictable, level, periodic contributions, similar to the way homeowners pay their mortgage.

But when a deficit-reduction contribution is required . . . extraordinarily large contributions [are] required over very brief periods of time. This is like asking homeowners to pay off their 30-year house mortgage as if it were a car loan — over only three to five years — far too short a time to meet far too large an obligation.

But the devastating consequences of more pension-plan terminations in the airline industry can be avoided if appropriate legislation is enacted now. We believe the current pension-funding crisis is only temporary.

Given sufficient time, we believe that interest rates will rise, stock-market performance will improve and airline profitability will return. Sound retirement policy should not allow an employer to break its pension promise to employees just because of negative economic and financial conditions expected to last only a few short years. This is especially so when such negative conditions are viewed in the context of a pension plan, the duration of which is measured in decades.

Under current law, the only way an airline can avoid burdensome pension costs is by entering bankruptcy and terminating the plans. But if more and more airlines choose to shed their pension liabilities in bankruptcy, it sets up the potential for the "domino effect," in which all the other legacy carriers are incentivized, or even forced, to file bankruptcy in order to achieve the same cost savings and "level the playing field."

We believe that providing relief from the deficit-reduction contribution rules will go a long way toward removing the pension-plan termination incentive to enter bankruptcy, and will, as a result, help prevent further bankruptcies in the U.S. airline industry.

no

BRADLEY D. BELT
EXECUTIVE DIRECTOR, PENSION BENEFIT GUARANTY CORPORATION

FROM TESTIMONY BEFORE HOUSE SUBCOMMITTEE ON AVIATION, JUNE 22, 2005

Congress and the administration have been sympathetic to the plight of the airline industry. After Sept. 11, [2001] Congress created the Air Transportation Stabilization Board to administer up to $10 billion in loan guarantees to help [the] struggling industry.

Today, nearly four years later and with passenger traffic at record levels, the plea from certain carriers is for a different form of loan guarantee. That is what pension-funding rule changes represent — a loan from the pension plan to the company, co-signed by the PBGC [Pension Benefit Guaranty Corporation] and underwritten primarily by financially healthy companies whose premiums finance the insurance program.

Pension underfunding is neither an accident nor the result of forces beyond a company's control. On the contrary, it is a largely predictable and controllable byproduct of decisions made by corporate management. In the case of the airlines, a series of decisions allowed pensions to become significantly underfunded. Companies did not contribute as much cash as they could when times were good, and in certain cases contributed no cash at all when it was needed most. In some cases, they granted generous benefit increases that are proving difficult to afford.

These issues are not unique to the airline industry. We saw the same weaknesses lead to the same bad outcomes with the steel industry a few years ago. . . . Because the PBGC receives no federal tax dollars, and its obligations are not backed by the full faith and credit of the United States, losses suffered by the insurance fund must, under current law, be covered by higher premiums.

Not only will healthy companies be subsidizing weak companies with underfunded plans, they may also face the prospect of having to compete against a rival firm that has shifted a significant portion of its ongoing labor costs onto the government — clearly at issue in the airline industry.

Companies that sponsor pension plans have a responsibility to live up to the promises they have made to their workers and retirees. Yet under current law, financially troubled companies have shortchanged their pension promises by nearly $100 billion, putting workers, responsible companies and taxpayers at risk.

It is difficult to imagine that healthy companies would want to continue in a retirement system . . . in which the sponsor-financed insurance fund is running a substantial deficit. By eliminating unfair exemptions from risk-based premiums and restoring the PBGC to financial health, the administration's proposal will revitalize the defined-benefit system.

Continued from p. 160

The administration has supported tightening funding requirements and wants to see pension accounting become both clearer and more transparent to workers and auditors. It also wants to restrict companies from making unrealistic pension promises.

"The maze that has been created by the current funding rules is virtually incomprehensible," Labor Secretary Elaine Chao said in a recent speech outlining the administration's proposals. "If the government is going to ensure that companies can prudently plan for their workers' retirement, employers shouldn't need a rocket scientist to do so." [27]

Members of Congress have had to walk a tightrope as they work to turn the administration's ideas into legislation. Most agree pensions should be better funded, but there's little desire to ask taxpayers to assume responsibility for bailing out troubled funds — especially when most taxpayers don't have traditional pensions themselves. There's also concern that if funding rules become too stringent, more and more companies will get out of defined-benefit pensions.

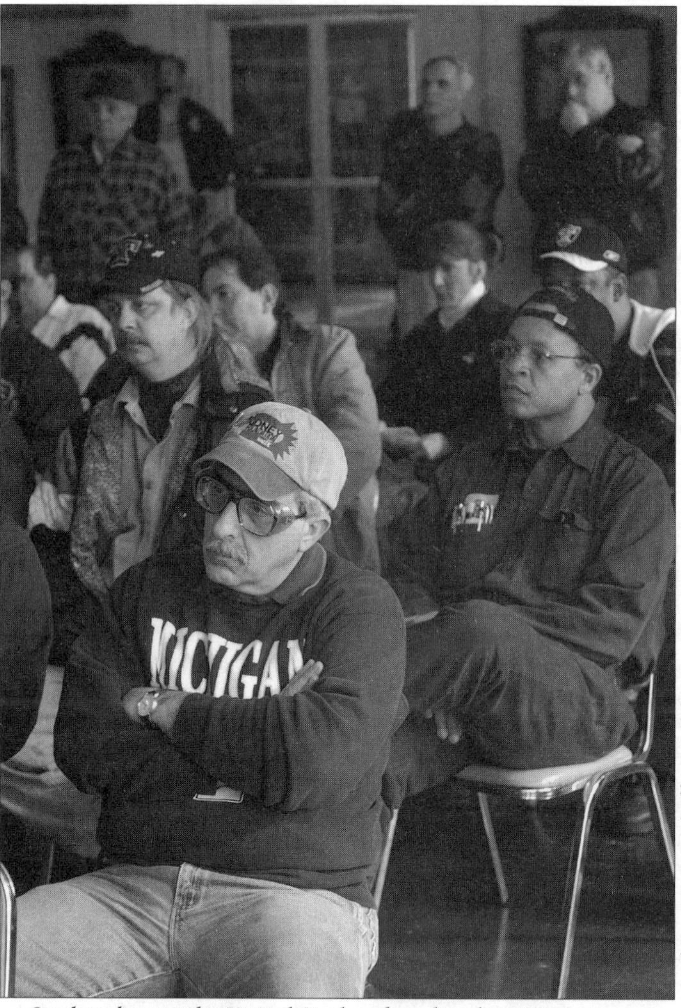

AFP/Getty Images/Jeff Kowalsky

Steelworkers at the United Steelworkers local in River Rouge, Mich., listen to a discussion of their battered industry in March 2002. Steel firms that have filed for bankruptcy in recent years have presented unfunded pension claims in excess of $1 billion each to the Pension Benefit Guaranty Corporation.

"The key to all this is trying to strike a balance between improving the financial condition of both the PBGC and employer plans, yet recognize that this is a voluntary system," says Larry Sher director of retirement policy at Buck Consultants, in New York. "The last thing you want to do is push more and more companies out of the system and end up with very few defined-benefit plans left — and those that are left poorly funded."

Congress recently raised annual PBGC premiums from $19 to $30 per participant per year. Because such a move raises revenue, it was included in the fiscal 2006 budget package, which cleared Congress on Feb. 1. "No one is doing cartwheels about that," says Aliya Wong, director of pension policy for the U.S. Chamber of Commerce, but she thinks employers can live with it.

The rest of the pension-reform package still must be hashed out in a Senate-House conference.

The bill passed by the Senate on Nov. 16 would require companies to fund 100 percent of their pension obligations, giving underfunded companies seven years to make up the difference. If their plans are less than 80 percent funded at the end of seven years, companies would be barred from promising any additional benefit increases. [28] The bill also would require regulatory agencies to consider a company's credit rating, assuming that those with "junk-bond" status would be more likely to default. Fearing the measure will hurt automakers, Michigan's two Democratic senators cast the only votes against it.

Many companies complain that they are penalized, through excise taxes, if they contribute extra to their plans in good years. "Right now, there are rules that prevent companies from putting in extra money during market upticks, or when the business cycle is in their favor," says Shepler, of the National Association of Manufacturers. On the premise that such contributions are helpful in the long run, the House bill, passed Dec. 15, would allow employers to make additional deductible contributions to plans funded up to 150 percent of their current liability. (The Senate bill would allow contributions up to 180 percent.)

As with the Senate bill, the House measure also freezes benefits when plans are less than 80 percent funded. But the Senate measure gives airlines 20 years to make up any underfunding

— a provision not included in the House bill. And the Bush administration has threatened to veto any bill that gives preference to a single industry. Supporters of the amendment, however, oppose burdening struggling airlines with more pension contributions than they can afford.

Cash-Balance Plans

Business leaders also are watching the regulation of so-called hybrid, or cash-balance plans, which combine features of traditional pensions and defined-contribution plans. Under a cash-balance plan, an employer sets up an account for each employee and funds it much like a traditional pension plan, with the employer paying the whole cost. Once the employee retires, the employer pays out the balance but is not responsible for making additional payments. The plans can be portable, so the employees can carry balances along to their next job.

"Cash-balance plans are the future," says Graff, of the American Society of Pension Professionals and Actuaries. "There's a whole world of companies that don't have defined-benefit plans at all, and a lot are thinking about the cash-balance design."

Cash-balance plans are widely used in Japan and have been fairly popular in the United States. Their growth was hampered, though, when a judge ruled in 2003 that IBM's cash-balance plan discriminated against older workers, who stood to lose money during the conversion from their traditional pension plan. Other courts have looked favorably on the plans, but businesses say Congress needs to clarify that the plans pass legal muster. Both of the pending pension-reform measures attempt to do that.

"Clearly, there needs to be greater legal certainty attached to being able to offer cash-balance plans," says the PBGC's Belt.

Regardless of the final state of the legislation, tougher accounting rules are inevitable. In November, the Financial Accounting Standards Board (FASB) announced that by the end of 2006 it would put forward new rules that "would take the effect of pension obligations out of the footnotes and [put them] directly onto corporate balance sheets," according to the Center on Federal Financial Institutions. [29] Moreover, by 2009, FASB will recommend comprehensive changes to all aspects of pension accounting.

Although the coming new standards promise greater clarity and less underfunding, they could have the unintended effect of pushing more companies out of traditional pensions. More companies are expected to be tempted to move their pension investments away from stocks and into bonds, which pay a fixed rate of return. That would reduce the volatility of their plan's assets but would cost companies more up front because they would have to put more into the plan initially.

Boston University economist Kotlikoff favors more investments in the safer but generally lower-performing bond market. "There's no reason that a firm that makes a commitment to pay somebody a pension, which is really a bond-like liability, should then be allowed to take money and gamble in the stock market, and if it does poorly make taxpayers pay for it," he says. Most pension managers today split their investments, putting about 60 percent in stocks and 40 percent in bonds.

Some pension managers, however, have steeply increased their investments in risky hedge funds: Pension investments in hedge funds are expected to reach $300 billion by 2008, up from $5 billion a decade ago. [30]

Despite the risk, pension managers have been lining up to invest. "We are trying to meet our 8 percent [rate of return], so our board decided to look at other investment options," said Roselyn Spencer, executive director of the City of Baltimore Employees' Retirement System, which has put about $55 million, or 5 percent of its assets, in hedge funds. [31]

If rule changes force pension managers to invest more conservatively, effectively forcing businesses to increase their cash contributions, more companies probably would freeze their defined-benefit plans, refuse to cover new workers or even terminate their pensions altogether.

"If they get too tough and demand too much reality, it will throw everybody out of this business," says North Carolina Treasurer Moore, who oversees one of the few traditional state pension plans that is 100 percent funded as well as the nation's largest public 401(k) plan.

Public Pensions

Pension plans for government workers don't have to be fully funded, and most aren't. They operate under a different set of rules than private companies. Governments only need to keep enough cash on hand to pay out that year's benefits. But many are struggling to do even that.

According to Wilshire Associates Inc., Illinois ranks worst among the 50 states in its per capita unfunded pension liability, averaging $3,406 for each state resident, or a 2004 funding level of just 42.6 percent (meaning there were assets to cover less than half the amount the state would expect to pay out). Chicago's Civic Federation reports that Illinois has not funded its full pension bill in 35 years, and its five major funds are $35 billion in the red — more than 80 percent of the state's annual budget of $43 billion. At least 16 other states are in worse shape: Their pension deficits exceed their total annual budgets. [32]

The situation is the same in many localities. "It was always easy to pay off the retirees by promising money in the future, but knowing that appropriating the money was the next council's job, the next governor's job," says Wyss of Standard & Poor's.

Many legislatures and localities will have to invest large sums in their pension systems this year or make them less generous. That may be tough politically, as Gov. Schwarzenegger found last year when he attempted to shift state employees into a 401(k)-style retirement plan. Firefighters and public-safety officers balked, and the fallout damaged Schwarzenegger's entire "reform" agenda. Alaska, however, succeeded in shifting its employees to a defined-contribution system last year, and Michigan has closed its defined-benefit pension plan to some new employees. Other legislatures — including Colorado, New Jersey and New Mexico — are looking at less drastic changes, such as having employees contribute more to their pensions or paying out benefits at a later age.

Several states have started defined-contribution plans and are offering their employees the choice between enrolling in them or a traditional pension plan. "This compromise does not really change much," writes Lowenstein, the financial writer. "Most employees who are given the choice opt, quite naturally, to keep their pensions." [33] ■

OUTLOOK

Continuing Pressure

Despite the current challenges, it's too early to write off traditional defined-benefit plans, most of which are well-funded. Many observers believe Congress can breathe new life into the pension system by straightening out the rules on cash-balance plans, which are generous to employees but eliminate employers' fear of unknown liabilities. Clarifying funding rules for traditional pension plans in ways that are acceptable to the business community will also relieve a lot of pressure.

"With appropriate changes in law, I think we will be able to meet the challenges down the road," says Belt of the Pension Benefit Guaranty Corporation.

Salisbury, of the Employee Benefit Research Institute (EBRI), is more skeptical. To make plans more secure, he says, companies will have to put more money in them, which will prove a bitter pill.

"At this point, the Senate bill, the House bill and the administration proposal all are likely to hasten the decline of defined-benefit plans and in the long term harm the PBGC, even though in the short term they will strengthen PBGC's cash flow," Salisbury adds. If such provisions pass, "A very large number of plan sponsors say it will cause them to consider freezing or terminating plans."

If most individuals determine that traditional, defined-benefit pension plans offer more security, but fewer employers believe they can afford to provide them, what is the likely outcome as the baby boomers reach retirement age? Most observers believe individual workers will face increased responsibility for their own retirements — and that many of them will fall short financially.

"There has to be some sort of replacement for the assets that defined-benefit plans pay people — there are over $2 trillion in defined-benefit plans," says Shepler, of the National Association of Manufacturers. "I'm not saying defined-contribution plans are bad, but the trends show that people are just not amassing the large amounts of wealth that people figured they would when they put these plans in."

States such as Texas are stepping up their financial-education efforts and, as word gets out that individuals will have to take more responsibility for their own retirements, more Americans may do a better job saving. EBRI has found that about two-thirds of Americans say they are behind on their personal savings, but almost all of them believe they can catch up. They may get some help from Congress, which is considering making employee enrollment in 401(k) plans automatic in most cases. Investment broker Merrill Lynch has run magazine advertisements recently comparing the retirement portfolios of older parents and their middle-aged children, suggesting that younger people face "more potential pitfalls."

Veteran pension consultant Rappaport warns that the fashionable, current idea — of making people work longer so they can save more for retirement and put fewer years of strain on their pension plans — may fall short. "It's great for people to plan to work later," she says, "but one of the things we've been finding in our research is that almost four out of 10 people retire earlier than they had planned to, due to health or losing a job."

About the Author

Alan Greenblatt is a staff writer at *Governing* magazine. He previously covered elections, agriculture and military spending for *CQ Weekly*, where he won the National Press Club's Sandy Hume Award for political journalism. He graduated from San Francisco State University in 1986 and received a master's degree in English literature from the University of Virginia in 1988. His recent reports include "Upward Mobility," "The Partisan Divide" and "Media Bias."

Thus, today's workers will not only have to change their savings habits but will also have to worry about future cuts to Social Security and government retiree health coverage, which appear to be unsustainable at current levels.

"It all adds up to a probable declining standard of living for retirees, compared with what we have expected to see," says The American College's McFadden. ■

FOR MORE INFORMATION

American Society of Pension Professionals & Actuaries, 4245 North Fairfax Dr., Suite 750, Arlington, VA 22203l; (703) 516-9300; www.asppa.org. A national organization for career retirement-plan professionals.

Center on Federal Financial Institutions, 734 15th St., N.W., Suite 502, Washington, DC 20005; (202) 357-5770; www.coffi.org. A nonprofit organization focused on the federal government's lending and insurance programs.

Center for Retirement Research, Boston College, 550 Fulton Hall, Chestnut Hill, MA 02467; (617) 552-1762; www.bc.edu/centers/crr/index.shtml. A center devoted to research of retirement issues that fosters communication between academics and policymakers.

Employee Benefit Research Institute; 2121 K St., N.W., Suite 600, Washington, DC 20037; (202) 659-0670; www.ebri.org. A research organization that studies employee-benefit programs and public policy affecting them.

Employee Benefits Security Administration, U.S. Department of Labor, 200 Constitution Ave., N.W., Washington, DC 20210; (866) 444-3272; www.dol.gov/ebsa. Federal agency responsible for the regulation of pension and welfare benefit plans.

Pension Benefit Guaranty Corporation, 1200 K St., N.W., Washington, DC 20005; (202) 326-4000; www.pbgc.gov. A federal corporation that insures private pension plans.

Pension Research Council, Wharton School of the University of Pennsylvania, 3620 Locust Walk, Philadelphia, PA 19104; (215) 898-7620; prc.wharton.upenn.edu/prc/prc.html. An academic center that sponsors research on private pensions, Social Security and related benefit plans.

Pension Rights Center, 1350 Connecticut Ave., N.W., Suite 206, Washington, DC 20036; (202) 296-3776; www.pensionrights.org. An advocacy group dedicated to protecting pension recipients.

U.S. Chamber of Commerce, 1615 H St., N.W., Washington, DC 20062; (202) 659-6000; www.uschamber.com. A federation representing 3 million businesses as well as trade associations and state and local chambers.

Notes

[1] Adam Geller, "When a Pension's Not There," *The Philadelphia Inquirer*, Dec. 31, 2005, p. D1.

[2] The Associated Press, "Pension Deficit Is Expected to Surge," *Los Angeles Times*, Sept. 16, 2005, p. C3.

[3] Eduardo Porter and Mary Williams Walsh, "Benefits Go the Way of Pensions," *The New York Times*, Feb. 9, 2006, p. C1.

[4] Quoted in Adriel Bettelheim, "Moving to Close the Pension Gap," *CQ Weekly*, Oct. 1, 2005, p. 2624; for background, see Mary H. Cooper, "Employee Benefits," *CQ Researcher*, Feb. 4, 2000, pp. 65-88.

[5] Martha Paskoff Welsh, "The Role of Congress in Pension Defaults," The Century Foundation, June 15, 2005; www.tcf.org/list.asp?type=NC&pubid=1034.

[6] National Center for Health Statistics, "National Vital Statistics Reports," Sept. 18, 2003; www.cdc.gov/nchs.

[7] "Now for the Reckoning", *The Economist*, Oct. 15, 2005, Special Report (2).

[8] Roger Lowenstein, "The End of Pensions?" *The New York Times Magazine*, Oct. 30, 2005.

[9] "Employee Benefits in Private Industry," National Compensation Survey, Bureau of Labor Statistics, March 2005.

[10] Steven A. Sass, *The Promise of Private Pensions* (1997), p. 4.

[11] James A. Wooten, *The Employee Retirement Security Act of 1974* (2004), p. 20.

[12] For background, see Mary H. Cooper, "Retirement Security," *CQ Researcher*, May 31, 2002, pp. 481-504.

[13] Quoted in Dan M. McGill, *Fundamentals of Private Pensions* (4th ed.), 1979, p. 17.

[14] Sass, *op. cit.*, p. 61.

[15] James H. Schulz, *The Economics of Aging* (6th ed.), 1995, p. 227.

[16] Sass, *op. cit.*, p. 101.

[17] *Ibid.*, p. 118.

[18] McGill, *op. cit.*, p. 18.

[19] Lowenstein, *op. cit.*, p. 56.

[20] Wooten, *op. cit.*, p. 76.

[21] Quoted in *ibid.*, p. 169.

[22] Sass, *op. cit.*, p. 225.

[23] For background, *Congress and the Nation, Vol. IV: 1973-1976* (1977), p. 690.

[24] Donald L. Bartlett and James B. Steele, "The Broken Promise," *Time*, Oct. 31, 2005, p. 47.

[25] Lowenstein, *op. cit.*, p. 56.

[26] *Ibid.*

[27] Quoted in "Elaine Chao Delivers Remarks at the National Press Club on Retirement Security," CQ Transcriptions, Jan. 10, 2005.

[28] See Michael R. Crittenden, "Senate Solidly Backs Pension Rewrite," *CQ Weekly*, Nov. 18, 2005, p. 3138.

[29] Douglas J. Elliott, "PBGC: Effects of Proposed Accounting Changes," Center on Federal Financial Institutions, Nov. 14, 2005.

[30] Riva D. Atlas and Mary Williams Walsh, "Pension Officers Putting Billions Into Hedge Funds," *The New York Times*, Nov. 27, 2005, p. A1.

[31] Ben White, "As Hedge Funds Go Mainstream, Risk Is Magnified," *The Washington Post*, Aug. 11, 2005, p. D1.

[32] Peter Harkness, "Shortfalls in the Long Haul," *CQ Weekly*, Oct. 28, 2005, p. 2898.

[33] Lowenstein, *op. cit.*, p. 56.

Bibliography

Selected Sources

Books

Sass, Steven A., *The Promise of Private Pensions: The First 100 Years*, Harvard University Press, 1997.
The associate director of the Center for Retirement Research at Boston College concludes that traditional pensions have faltered in recent years because of the decline of labor unions and the old-line corporations that supported them.

Wooten, James. A., *The Employee Retirement Security Act of 1974: A Political History*, University of California Press, 2004.
A law professor at the State University of New York at Buffalo shows how Congress overcame strong opposition from business to make pension funding a policy matter of national importance.

Articles

Atlas, Riva D., and Mary Williams Walsh, "Pension Officers Putting Billions Into Hedge Funds," *The New York Times*, Nov. 27, 2005, p. A1.
Pension plans and other large institutions are expected to put $300 billion into lightly regulated hedge-fund investments.

Bartlett, Donald L., and James B. Steele, "The Broken Promise," *Time*, Oct. 31, 2005, p. 32.
Veteran reporters conclude that congressional rules have made it easy for unscrupulous corporations to mismanage their pension funds and rip off retirees.

Bettelheim, Adriel, "Moving to Close the Pension Gap," *CQ Weekly*, Oct. 1, 2005, p. 2624.
The writer puts the current congressional debate over pension policy into historical context.

"Corrupt Conspiracy; Internal Memo Details Crooked Pension Scheme," *The San Diego Union-Tribune*, Oct. 6, 2005, p. B10.
A newspaper editorial outlines how alleged collusion between San Diego officials and the pension board led to the city underfunding its pension plan by $1.4 billion.

Greenhouse, Steven, "Transit Strike Reflects Nationwide Pension Woes," *The New York Times*, Dec. 24, 2005, p. A1.
A holiday transit strike in New York City over pensions and other benefits was emblematic of public-finance problems across the country.

Hakin, Danny, "For a G.M. Family, the American Dream Vanishes," *The New York Times*, Nov. 19, 2005, p. A1.
Four generations of the Roy family have relied on General Motors for employment, but they sense its good jobs and retirement plans have drawn to an end.

Harkness, Peter, "Shortfalls in the Long Haul," *CQ Weekly*, Oct. 28, 2005, p. 2898.
The publisher of *Governing* magazine examines the reasons why pensions have become a major thorn irritating the skins of state and local government officials.

Hinden, Stan, "Ready, Set . . . Retire?" *The Washington Post*, Dec. 25, 2005, p. B1.
A former retirement columnist warns that problems with private pensions, Social Security and health-insurance programs will cause a troubled old age for baby boomers.

Lowenstein, Roger, "The End of Pensions?" *The New York Times Magazine*, Oct. 30, 2005, p. 56.
A business writer suggests that government rules allowing corporations to underfund their pension systems caused the current woes. He argues that defined-contribution plans, such as 401(k) accounts, should be more carefully regulated because so many more people now depend on them.

Peterson, Jonathan, "Airline Execs Seek Revised Pension Rules," *Los Angeles Times*, June 8, 2005, p. C1.
The chief executives of Delta and Northwest airlines told the Senate they would need more time to properly fund their pension plans or they would be forced into bankruptcy. (Both airlines went bankrupt in September.)

Russakoff, Dale, "Human Toll of a Pension Default," *The Washington Post*, June 13, 2005, p. A1.
The failure of United Airlines' pension plan has put a strain on thousands of workers.

Walsh, Mary Williams, "Pensions: Big Holes in the Net," *The New York Times*, April 12, 2005, p. G1.
Despite regulations, it's almost impossible for plan participants to determine the financial health or underlying rules governing their pensions.

Reports and Studies

"Information on Cash Balance Plans," Government Accountability Office, October 2005.
Most workers receive bigger benefits under defined-benefit plans, but many companies provide additional money during transitions to cash-balance plans.

Passantino, George, and Adam B. Summers, "The Gathering Pension Storm," Reason Foundation, 2005.
The authors conclude that governments have been slower than the private sector in shifting from traditional pension plans and now promise "extravagant" retirement benefits to workers that are hurting taxpayers.

The Next Step:

Additional Articles from Current Periodicals

Congressional Action

Abrams, Jim, "House Passes Bill Seeking to Fix Pensions," *The Philadelphia Inquirer*, Dec. 16, 2005, p. C2.
The House passed legislation that would require companies to meet their pension obligations to employees.

Newton-Small, Jay, "Firms Seek Protection in Cash-Balance Plans," *The Philadelphia Inquirer*, Jan. 29, 2006, p. E3.
Several companies are battling the American Association for Retired Persons (AARP) to influence congressional negotiators overhauling the U.S. pension system.

Walsh, Mary Williams, "Veto Threat As Senators Approve Pension Bill," *The New York Times*, Nov. 17, 2005, p. C1.
The Senate passed a bill that would require companies to close pension-fund shortfalls within seven years but would allow major airlines 20 years to do so.

Pension Benefit Guaranty Corporation (PBGC)

Gordon, Marcy, "Future of Pension Insurer Shaky," *The Houston Chronicle*, Nov. 16, 2005, p. 2.
The PBGC, which insures the private pensions of 44 million workers, has a $22.8 billion deficit and may run out of money.

Vrana, Debora, "PBGC to Assume United's Pensions," *Los Angeles Times*, March 12, 2005, p. C1.
The PBGC agreed to take over the underfunded pensions of more than 36,000 ground workers at United Airlines.

Public-Sector Pensions

Abate, Tom, "Public Pensions on the Table," *The San Francisco Chronicle*, Jan. 16, 2005, p. E1.
California Gov. Arnold Schwarzenegger (R) proposed that guaranteed payments to public retirees be phased out.

Broder, John M., "Five Officials in San Diego Are Indicted Over Pensions," *The New York Times*, Jan. 7, 2006, p. A8.
A federal grand jury indicted current and former city pension officials, accusing them of conspiring to enact a pension plan that would enrich themselves.

Dolan, Jack, and Michael Vasquez, "Higher City Tax Revenue Offset by Pension Bills," *The Miami Herald*, Sept. 22, 2005, p. A1.
Miami is expected to spend $80 billion on the city's generous pension funds, causing officials to fear a taxpayer backlash.

Lewis, Raphael, "Treasurer Mulls Idea of Opening Up State Pension Fund," *The Boston Globe*, April 8, 2005, p. B3.
Massachusetts Treasurer Timothy P. Cahill is considering allowing state residents to invest in the state's pension plan.

Struggling Industries

Fernandez, Bob, "A Reversal of Fortune," *The Philadelphia Inquirer*, April 10, 2005, p. E1.
U.S. Bankruptcy Court judges allowed five steel companies to cut severance benefits and move $6.4 billion in long-term pension obligations to the PBGC.

Hensel Jr., Bill, "Pension Proposal Irks Continental," *The Houston Chronicle*, Sept. 29, 2005, p. 1.
Continental Airlines opposes a new congressional proposal that may give competitors an edge by allowing them to delay payments of their underfunded pension plans for several years.

Trumball, Mark, "GM Cutbacks Portend Tougher Road Ahead," *The Christian Science Monitor*, Nov. 22, 2005, p. 2.
General Motors will have to cut 30,000 workers and close several factories because of competition from Asian carmakers and past promises to thousands of now-retired workers to fund their pensions and health care.

Traditional Pensions

Crenshaw, Albert B., "Make 'em Provide Pensions," *The Washington Post*, Jan. 29, 2006, p. F1.
Crenshaw argues that Congress should require companies to provide pensions to workers, even as it seems the system is becoming outmoded, in order to avoid a large number of retirees turning to the government for help in 20 years.

Walsh, Mary Williams, "More Companies Ending Promises For Retirement," *The New York Times*, Jan. 9, 2006, p. A1.
Many thriving American companies are freezing their traditional pension plans and emphasizing 401(k) plans.

Citing The *CQ Researcher*

Sample formats for citing these reports in a bibliography include the ones listed below. Preferred styles and formats vary, so please check with your instructor or professor.

MLA STYLE

Jost, Kenneth. "Rethinking the Death Penalty." The CQ Researcher 16 Nov. 2001: 945-68.

APA STYLE

Jost, K. (2001, November 16). Rethinking the death penalty. *The CQ Researcher, 11*, 945-968.

CHICAGO STYLE

Jost, Kenneth. "Rethinking the Death Penalty." *CQ Researcher*, November 16, 2001, 945-968.

CQ Researcher

Published by CQ Press, a division of Congressional Quarterly Inc.

thecqresearcher.com

Presidential Power

Is Bush overstepping his executive authority?

President Bush has been busy defending the administration's electronic-surveillance program against critics who say it unconstitutionally violates citizens' civil liberties. Bush says the surveillance is vital to the nation's anti-terrorism efforts, but critics say the president has overstepped his powers and infringed on Congress' constitutional authority, inviting opposition at home and criticism abroad. Other questions about the president's possible abuse of presidential power involve the administration's use of military tribunals and its alleged use of torture, as well as its refusal to support a congressional inquiry into the response to Hurricane Katrina. What's needed, critics say, is Supreme Court action limiting the administration's exercise of executive power. But administration supporters reject claims that Bush has gone further than previous wartime presidents and stress that as commander in chief he has the power to do everything he deems necessary to protect the country.

President Bush speaks to the press at the National Security Agency in early January after discussing his controversial electronic-surveillance program with personnel at the top-secret agency.

INSIDE

This Report

The CQ Researcher • Feb. 24, 2006 • www.thecqresearcher.com
Volume 16, Number 8 • Pages 169-192

Recipient of Society of Professional Journalists Award for Excellence ◆ American Bar Association Silver Gavel Award

THE ISSUES

BACKGROUND

CURRENT SITUATION

OUTLOOK

SIDEBARS AND GRAPHICS

FOR FURTHER RESEARCH

Cover: President Bush speaks to the press at the National Security Agency, in Fort Meade, Md., in early January after discussing his controversial electronic-surveillance-program with personnel at the top-secret agency. (Getty Images/Paul J. Richards)

CQ Researcher

Feb. 24, 2006
Volume 16, Number 8

MANAGING EDITOR: Thomas J. Colin

ASSISTANT MANAGING EDITOR: Kathy Koch

ASSOCIATE EDITOR: Kenneth Jost

STAFF WRITERS: Marcia Clemmitt, Peter Katel, Pamela M. Prah

CONTRIBUTING WRITERS: Rachel Cox, Sarah Glazer, David Hosansky, Patrick Marshall, Tom Price

DESIGN/PRODUCTION EDITOR: Olu B. Davis

ASSISTANT EDITOR: Melissa J. Hipolit

CQ PRESS

A Division of
Congressional Quarterly Inc.

SENIOR VICE PRESIDENT/PUBLISHER: John A. Jenkins

DIRECTOR, LIBRARY PUBLISHING: Kathryn C. Suárez

DIRECTOR, EDITORIAL OPERATIONS: Ann Davies

CONGRESSIONAL QUARTERLY INC.

CHAIRMAN: Paul C. Tash

VICE CHAIRMAN: Andrew P. Corty

PRESIDENT/EDITOR IN CHIEF: Robert W. Merry

CQ Researcher (ISSN 1056-2036) is printed on acid-free paper. Published weekly, except March 24, July 7, July 14, Aug. 4, Aug. 11, Nov. 24, Dec. 22 and Dec. 29, by CQ Press, a division of Congressional Quarterly Inc. Annual full-service subscriptions for institutions start at $667. For pricing, call 1-800-834-9020, ext. 1906. To purchase a *CQ Researcher* report in print or electronic format (PDF), visit www.cqpress.com or call 866-427-7737. Single reports start at $10. Bulk purchase discounts and electronic-rights licensing are also available. Periodicals postage paid at Washington, D.C., and additional mailing offices. POSTMASTER: Send address changes to *CQ Researcher*, 1255 22nd St., N.W., Suite 400, Washington, DC 20037.

Presidential Power

BY KENNETH JOST

THE ISSUES

The impressive resume of Rep. Heather Wilson of New Mexico notes her service as an Air Force officer and National Security Council aide, not to mention the doctorate she holds in international relations. Those credentials propelled her into a lead role in shaping House Republicans' messages after the Sept. 11, 2001, terrorist attacks and during the Iraq war. President Bush repaid Wilson for supporting the administration's policies with a campaign visit in October 2002 to boost her hard-fought bid for re-election to a third term.

Wilson found herself questioning the president's policies, however, after *The New York Times* reported in December 2005 that Bush had secretly authorized a program for intercepting telephone calls and e-mail traffic between suspected members of the al Qaeda terrorist network overseas and people within the United States. *The Times'* story said the surveillance program — carried out by the super-secret National Security Agency (NSA) — appeared to violate the 1978 Foreign Intelligence Surveillance Act (FISA), which requires judicial approval for any domestic wiretapping. *

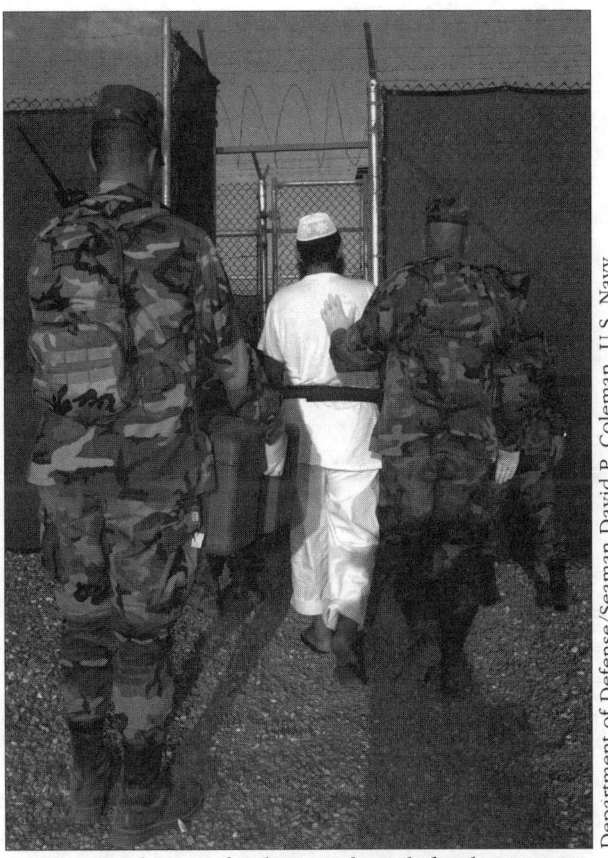

Department of Defense/Seaman David P. Coleman, U.S. Navy

Critics say the use of military tribunals for detainees at the U.S. Naval Station at Guantánamo Bay, Cuba, reflects President Bush's alleged abuse of presidential power, as do the administration's alleged torture of prisoners and its electronic-surveillance program.

Wilson was reportedly concerned enough to share her doubts with Rep. Jane Harman, a California Democrat who serves with her on the House Intelligence Committee. With the administration continuing to defend the program, Wilson went public with her doubts on Feb. 7, telling *The Times* she had "serious concerns" about the program and calling for the Intelligence Committee to conduct a "painstaking" review. [1]

Wilson's break exemplified growing GOP skepticism over Bush's claim that he has the power to institute the surveillance program with or without congressional authorization. "You think you're right," Senate Judiciary Committee Chairman Arlen Specter, R-Pa., told Attorney General Alberto Gonzales during a daylong hearing on Feb. 6, "but a lot of people think you're wrong."

The rumblings of discontent finally got the administration to move away from what critics called its high-handed dealings with Congress over the program. Bush and other officials had been insisting the administration had adequately consulted Congress by holding briefings on the program for the so-called Gang of Eight — the bipartisan leaders of Congress and the chairmen and ranking Democrats on the House and Senate Intelligence committees. Broader disclosure would have risked leaks, Vice President Dick Cheney said on Feb. 7. [2]

After Wilson's statements, however, the administration agreed to give detailed briefings to all Intelligence committee members.

The surveillance controversy epitomizes what many observers say has been Bush's extraordinarily expansive view of presidential power. "Bush has been more assertive of presidential prerogatives than any president in American history," says Michael A. Genovese, a professor of political science at Loyola Marymount University in Los Angeles and author of an historical overview of presidents from Washington through Clinton. "It's the imperial presidency on steroids." [3]

Democrats have pounced on the surveillance program to buttress criticism of Bush for bypassing Congress on anti-terrorism policies and a range of other issues. Sen. Patrick J. Leahy, D-Vt., ranking Democrat on the Judiciary Committee, calls Bush "a president prone to unilateralism." Bush is drawing criticism from a variety of interest groups as well.

---

* The surveillance program is widely described as "domestic spying." Administration officials say the phrase is misleading because the program targets communications between someone outside the United States who is suspected of being a member or agent of al Qaeda or an affiliated terrorist organization and someone in the United States. They prefer to call it the "terrorist surveillance program."

Americans Split Over Warrantless Wiretapping

Polls indicate Americans are closely divided on the wisdom and the legality of the program of warrantless electronic surveillance that President Bush authorized after the 9/11 terrorist attacks. The most recent poll — taken after Attorney General Alberto Gonzales' Feb. 6 appearance before the Senate Judiciary Committee — found a bare majority of those responding opposed to the program. An earlier poll by the same news organizations showed a bare majority in favor.

Do you think the Bush administration was right or wrong in wiretapping these conversations without obtaining a court order?

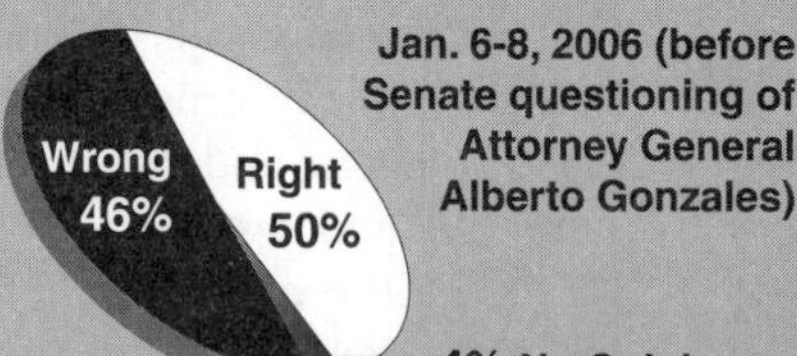

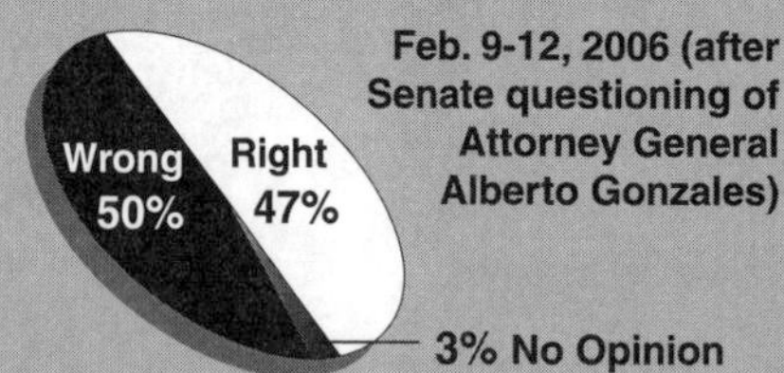

Do you think George W. Bush — definitely broke the law, probably broke the law, probably did not break the law or definitely did not break the law when he authorized wiretapping of American citizens' communications?

*Source: CNN/*USA Today*/Gallup Polls; results are based on telephone interviews with 1,000 U.S. adults, ages 18 and older.*

"The president has advanced sweeping powers as commander in chief that I find totally unconvincing and troublesome," says Timothy Lynch, director of the criminal-justice project at the libertarian Cato Institute. "I do believe that he has overstepped the bounds of his office in a number of instances."

"The current surveillance of Americans is a chilling assertion of presidential power that has not been seen since the days of Richard Nixon," says Anthony Romero, executive director of the American Civil Liberties Union (ACLU). President Nixon's claim of authority to conduct warrantless domestic wiretapping was soundly rejected by the U.S. Supreme Court in a landmark 1972 decision, Romero noted at a Jan. 17 news conference. [4] Romero spoke as he announced the ACLU had filed suit in federal court in Michigan challenging the legality of Bush's surveillance program.

Administration critics cite other evidence of Bush's expansive post-9/11 view of presidential power. They note that he invoked the president's authority as commander in chief — established in Article II of the Constitution — to designate foreigners and U.S. citizens as "enemy combatants" and detain them for years without charging them with a crime and with only limited opportunities to challenge their confinements. The Supreme Court dealt the administration a temporary setback in June 2004, later negated by Congress, by requiring hearings or some form of judicial review for the detainees.

Bush also came under sharp criticism for a memo written by a Justice Department lawyer in August 2002 that argued the president could authorize torture in interrogating suspected terrorists. The White House disavowed the memo after it was disclosed in June 2004. Despite evidence of abuse of Iraqi prisoners and others, Bush and other officials contend that U.S. policy prohibits torture or any other cruel, degrading or inhumane treatment of detainees. [5]

Administration supporters reject claims that Bush has gone further than previous wartime presidents. "Earlier presidents asserted much more sweeping authority in the name of the president's power as commander in chief," says Kris Kobach, a professor at the University of Missouri School of Law in Kansas City and former counselor to Bush's first attorney general, John Ashcroft. Kobach cites Franklin D. Roosevelt's wiretapping during World War II and Harry S Truman's seizure of the nation's steel mills during the Korean War — a move struck down by the Supreme Court as beyond the president's powers. "President Bush's actions appear minor by comparison," Kobach says. (*See sidebar, p. 184.*)

But presidential scholar Richard Pious, chairman of the Department of Political Science at Barnard College in New York City, says that even if Bush has followed other presidents in claiming broad powers during wartime, he has been "one of the most overbearing" of presidents in his relations with Congress, critics and subordinates. "There's a deft way [of using power], and then there's the Bush way," Pious says. "He's been a bull in a china shop."

Bush entered the White House in 2001 convinced that the presidency had been weakened since Nixon was forced to resign in August 1974, following the Watergate scandal. That view is held at least as strongly by Cheney, who was chief of staff to Nixon's successor, Gerald R. Ford. [6]

With the controversy over electronic surveillance at a peak in mid-December, Cheney stoutly defended the administration's record in trying to restore presidential power. "I believe in a strong, robust executive authority, and I think that the world we live in demands it," Cheney told reporters traveling with him on Air Force Two on Dec. 20. In wartime, he added, the president "needs to have his constitutional authority unimpaired." [7]

Bush voiced similar views on Feb. 10. "Sept. 11 changed the way I think," Bush told GOP House lawmakers during a retreat in Cambridge, Md. "I told the people exactly what I felt at the time, and I still feel it, and that is we must do everything in our power to protect the country." [8]

Critics, however, say Bush's broad view of presidential powers is inviting opposition at home and criticism abroad. "When you disembody the president from the rule of law, you change the very structure of government," says Genovese. "You want to empower the Congress and the president to fight terror, but you don't want to give them the store."

As the debate over presidential power in the post-9/11 world continues, here are some of the questions being considered:

Has President Bush overstepped his authority in the war against terrorism?

When reports surfaced in late April 2004 that U.S. servicemembers had mistreated Iraqi captives in Baghdad, President Bush quickly denounced the abuse. [9] But his comments were clouded by disclosures in June of memoranda by government lawyers suggesting the president could authorize torture even in the face of a congressional statute and international treaties prohibiting such practices.

"Congress may no more regulate the president's ability to detain and interrogate enemy combatants than it may regulate his ability to direct troop movements on the battlefield," a ranking Justice Department official wrote. [10]

Over the next 18 months, an indignant Sen. John McCain, R-Ariz., who was tortured as a prisoner of war during the Vietnam conflict, led an ultimately successful effort in Congress to write into law a specific prohibition of torture or any "cruel, inhuman or degrading" treatment of prisoners at the hands of U.S. servicemembers. Although Bush signed the measure on Dec. 30, 2005, he included a "signing statement" that suggested he was not bound by it. "The executive branch shall construe [the law] in a manner consistent with the constitutional authority of the president to supervise the unitary executive branch and as commander in chief," the statement read. [11] *

Throughout the controversy, administration officials have depicted the dispute as largely theoretical, saying that Bush has restated official U.S. policy against the use of torture. And one administration supporter suggests that Bush's signing statement carries little weight. "Signing statements have only the effect that the courts choose to give them — which is minimal in almost all cases," says the University of Missouri's Kobach.

Still, Bush's decision to risk further public and congressional criticism on the detainee-treatment issue continues his policy of claiming broad presidential powers and resisting efforts to limit the scope of his authority. Bush adopted a similar posture in defending the electronic-surveillance program after it was disclosed in December. In a radio address the next day, Bush said he instituted the program under his authority as commander in chief and intended to continue it despite criticism.

"The American people expect me to do everything in my power under our laws and Constitution to protect them and their civil liberties," Bush said. "And that is exactly what I will continue to do, so long as I'm the president of the United States." [12]

Critics contend that Bush has gone beyond his lawful powers and violated both congressional laws and the Constitution not only with his electronic-surveillance program but also with other policies as well. The accusations of presidential lawbreaking received high-profile attention in January from the man who lost the presidency to Bush in 2000: former Vice President Al Gore. Gore charged Bush with "breaking the law repeatedly and insistently," citing the electronic-surveillance program as the latest example.

"If the president has the inherent authority to eavesdrop, imprison citizens on his own declaration, kidnap foreign citizens off the streets of other countries and torture, then what can't he do?" Gore asked in a major speech in Washington on Jan. 16 cosponsored by the liberal American Constitution Society and the conservative-libertarian Liberty Coalition. He added: "A president who breaks the law is a threat to the very structure of our government."

* The unitary executive theory holds that under the Constitution Congress cannot limit the president's authority to control executive branch officials. Some proponents of the theory say it also gives the president powers unspecified in Article II. The Supreme Court has rejected the theory.

A Republican Party spokeswoman denigrated Gore's speech as politically motivated. "Gore's incessant need to insert himself in the headline of the day is almost as glaring as his lack of understanding of the threats facing America," Republican National Committee spokeswoman Tracey Schmitt said in a statement. "While the president works to protect Americans from terrorists, Democrats deliver no solutions of their own, only diatribes laden with inaccuracies and anger."

With the electronic-surveillance debate continuing, administration officials are defending the practice on statutory grounds and as within the president's inherent powers as commander in chief. In legal memoranda and in Gonzales' testimony before the Senate Judiciary Committee, the Justice Department claims that the Sept. 14, 2001, congressional resolution authorizing the use of military force against al Qaeda or other terrorist organizations gives the president power to conduct warrantless electronic surveillance against the enemy both outside and within the United States.

Administration supporters echo that argument while continuing to defend the surveillance program as a natural part of the president's war-making powers. "It would be remarkable if our president was not attempting to use all the forces available to him to intercept the enemy's communications," says Todd Gaziano, director of legal and judicial studies at the conservative Heritage Foundation in Washington. "When we're at war, all of our enemy communications should be intercepted if at all possible."

Critics say the administration is wrong on both points. The argument that the 2001 use-of-force resolution supersedes the specific prohibition against domestic warrantless wiretapping is "laughable," says Geoffrey Stone, a law professor at the University of Chicago and author of a book on civil liberties in wartime. In a similar vein, Stone says intelligence gathering is "not sufficiently connected" to the use of force to be encompassed within the president's commander-in-chief powers.

Office of Rep. Heather Wilson

Rep. Heather Wilson, R-N.M., has questioned the president's program for intercepting telephone calls and e-mail traffic between suspected terrorists overseas and people within the United States.

Polls show the public closely divided on the issues. The *Los Angeles Times* and Bloomberg News in late January found a narrow plurality of respondents — 49 percent to 45 percent — supporting the program. A later poll by CNN-*USA Today*-Gallup — taken in February after Gonzales' appearance — found a bare majority opposed to the program: 50 percent to 47 percent. In a second question, 49 percent of those responding thought Bush may have violated the law in authorizing the program while 47 percent believed he had not. [13]

Has President Bush infringed on Congress' constitutional powers?

After 14 coal miners died in two separate accidents in West Virginia in January, the Senate Labor Appropriations Subcommittee called in the head of the Mine Safety and Health Administration (MSHA) to ask what the agency was doing to prevent future tragedies. Acting Administrator David Dye spent an hour on the witness stand on Jan. 23 telling the senators that there was more safety enforcement than ever before.

Once the questions were over, Dye started to leave, saying that he could not stay to answer follow-ups after testimony from other witnesses. "There's 15,000 mines in the United States, and we've got some really pressing matters," Dye said.

With dripping sarcasm, subcommittee Chairman Specter told Dye that the senators also had "other pressing matters" — pointing to the planned hearings on the NSA surveillance program as one example. "So we don't think we're imposing too much to keep you here for another hour," Specter said. Undeterred, Dye departed, leaving aides behind to field any other questions.

As slights go, it was a small one — but nonetheless indicative of what many observers see as the Bush administration's disdain for Congress as a supposedly coequal branch of government. "Bush has been more successful than any president I've seen in asserting presidential powers and in giving Congress the back of his hand," says Norman Ornstein, a resident scholar at the American Enterprise Institute and a Congress-watcher for more than 40 years.

Among other examples, the White House in January refused a request by a Senate committee investigating the government's response to Hurricane Katrina for presidential aides' e-mail correspondence on the subject. Earlier, the administration had turned aside efforts by Senate Democrats during confirmation hearings for Supreme Court nominees John G. Roberts Jr. and Samuel A. Alito Jr. to obtain documents from their time as Justice Department lawyers in the 1980s.

The debate over the electronic-surveillance program pitted the president against Congress in a higher-stakes confrontation. From *The Times'* initial disclosure on Dec. 16, lawmakers in both parties faulted the administration for giving Congress too little information about the program. Five members of the Senate Intelligence Committee — including Republicans Chuck Hagel of Nebraska and Olympia Snowe of Maine — signed a letter on Dec. 20 calling for the panel to conduct "an immediate inquiry" into the program.

Democrats were especially critical of the administration's failure to brief the full membership of the two Intelligence committees about the program. They gained support for their critique in January from the Congressional Research Service (CRS), which said the limited briefings to House and Senate leaders violated a broad disclosure requirement contained in a 1991 law.

The law, an amendment to the National Security Act passed as part of the 1991 intelligence authorization measure, required that the two congressional Intelligence committees be kept "fully and currently informed" of U.S. "intelligence activities." Limited disclosures to the so-called Gang of Eight were allowed only for "covert operations." [14]

The administration's belated decision in February to provide more detailed briefings to both Intelligence committees may have mooted the disclosure issue. Earlier, however, CRS lawyers also voiced strong doubts about the program's legal basis. In a 44-page memorandum, attorneys Elizabeth Bazan and Jennifer Elsea concluded that courts had previously upheld Congress' power to regulate intelligence gathering and were "unlikely" to find that Congress had expressly or implicitly authorized the program.

Nevertheless, during his Judiciary Committee appearance Attorney General Gonzales rejected suggestions by senators in both parties for steps to strengthen the legal basis for the program. Specter suggested the administration present the program to the Foreign Intelligence Surveillance Court — the special court created to consider applications for warrants under FISA. Several other senators seemed almost to plead with Gonzales to join in supporting legislation to authorize the program. Gonzales said the administration would listen to ideas from Congress, but made no promises.

The stirrings of resistance from within GOP ranks to Bush's position represent a departure from the mostly unified and nearly unquestioning support that Hill Republicans gave to the White House during Bush's first term. "Clearly, the executive branch is doing whatever it can to maximize its influence. That's as natural as it can be," says Marc Hetherington, an associate professor of political science at Vanderbilt University in Nashville. "What strikes me as interesting is how little Congress has done to stop it."

Ornstein agrees. The reason, he says, is that from the start of his administration, congressional Republicans have seen their fate as "inextricably linked" to Bush's. "They saw themselves as field soldiers much more than they saw themselves as an independent, distinct branch of government," Ornstein explains. "They saw oversight as something that could embarrass the president — and therefore did little to nothing."

The rumblings of independence within GOP ranks, however, may remind Bush of the risks of being too high-handed with Congress. "Maybe it's short-sighted to be so blunt with the legislative branch," says John Marini, an associate professor of political science at the University of Nevada-Reno and a critic of what he called "the imperial Congress" that was under Democratic control during the Reagan presidency in the 1980s.

"The legislative branch has more power than any of the other branches," Marini says. "Congress has the power to slap the president down at any time. The bulk of the power is in the legislature if it's willing to use it."

Should the courts limit the Bush administration's claims of executive power?

Just after launching the war in Afghanistan, President Bush issued an executive order on Nov. 13, 2001, allowing establishment of so-called "military commissions" to try suspected terrorists captured there or elsewhere. Critics questioned the legal basis for the order, but Bush pointed to Congress' Sept. 14 use-of-force resolution as giving him the authority needed to set up the tribunals.

After several years of legal skirmishes, the Supreme Court agreed in November 2005 to hear a challenge to Bush's order brought by Salim Ahmed Hamdan, a one-time driver for al Qaeda leader Osama bin Laden and a detainee at Guantánamo since 2002. But now the Bush administration wants the court to dismiss Hamdan's case, saying that Congress in December eliminated the federal courts' power to hear challenges by Guantánamo detainees except after final decisions in their cases by the military tribunals.

How Bush Defends 'Roving Wiretaps'

In April 2004, during the presidential campaign, President Bush was drumming up support for the USA Patriot Act before a law-enforcement group in Buffalo, N.Y.

Bush acknowledged controversy over the anti-terrorism law's controversial "roving wiretaps," which allow government investigators to listen in on conversations as targets move from one cell phone to another.

But Bush promised the law did not affect constitutional safeguards: "Now, by the way, any time you hear the United States government talking about wiretap, it requires — a wiretap requires a court order. Nothing has changed, by the way. When we're talking about chasing down terrorists, we're talking about getting a court order before we do so." [1]

Bush failed to mention, however, that in 2001, just as Congress was shaping the Patriot Act, he had secretly authorized a program of warrantless eavesdropping on telephone calls and e-mail traffic between people in the United States and members or supporters of the terrorist group al Qaeda overseas. Bush had approved the surveillance by the super-secret National Security Agency after receiving assurances from Justice Department lawyers that the program was legal despite provisions in the Foreign Intelligence Surveillance Act (FISA) requiring a warrant for any domestic wiretaps.

Information about the surveillance program emerged only in December 2005, after *The New York Times* blazoned it across the front page. The revelation provoked a debate on Capitol Hill and around the country not only about the program but also about the president's legality in authorizing it. *The Times* said it had withheld the story for nearly a year at the administration's request, for national security reasons. [2]

The White House quickly moved to defend the program. Bush refused to confirm the existence of the program in a previously scheduled interview on Dec. 16 on PBS' "NewsHour with Jim Lehrer." The next day, however, Bush acknowledged the program, insisting it was "consistent with U.S. law and the Constitution." [3]

While continuing to shield most details of the program, Bush and other administration officials — notably, Vice President Dick Cheney and Attorney General Alberto Gonzales — are unswervingly defending it. The legal defense — detailed in a 42-page Justice Department memorandum — rests on both the president's inherent constitutional powers as commander in chief and on the Authorization to Use Military Force approved by Congress three days after the 9/11 terrorist attacks. [4]

Intelligence gathering directed against an enemy is one of the "traditional and accepted incidents of force," the memo argues. On that basis, the president as commander in chief has inherent power to use any intelligence methods — including wiretaps, which Presidents Woodrow Wilson and Franklin D. Roosevelt both authorized during the 20th century's two world wars. The use-of-force resolution "confirms and supplements" that power, the memo contends.

As for FISA, the Justice Department memo notes the act prohibits warrantless wiretaps unless authorized by a separate statute. It goes on to contend that the use-of-force resolution provides that separate authorization. Even without that argument, the memo says, FISA should be interpreted narrowly to avoid a constitutional clash with the president's powers as commander in chief.

Most of the legal scholars and experts weighing in on the issue — representing a range of ideological viewpoints — reject the administration's ultimate conclusion, as does the nonpartisan Congressional Research Service. [5] Two main points seem to command wide agreement among the critics:

- That the 1978 FISA law validly limits whatever inherent power the president may have exercised in the past to gather intelligence on the enemy;
- That Congress' broadly phrased authorization to use "all necessary and appropriate force" against those responsible for the 9/11 attacks cannot be read to permit warrantless wiretapping within the United States in violation of FISA.

In defending the administration's position, Gonzales ran into a buzz saw of criticism from Democrats and some Republicans in a daylong appearance before the Senate Judiciary Committee on Feb. 6. The committee is now planning a second daylong hearing with supporters and opponents of the program.

Meanwhile, the administration is sending signals that it might agree to legislation on the issue, which — if passed — could eliminate some, though not all, of the legal arguments against the program.

---

[1] For the full text of Bush's remarks, see *Weekly Compilation of Presidential Documents*, April 26, 2004, pp. 638-645 (www.gpoaccess.gov/wcomp/). For coverage, see Steve Orr, "Bush Makes Case for Anti-Terror Act," *Rochester Democrat and Chronicle*, April 21, 2004, p. A1; Dan Herbeck, "Freedom vs. Security at Issue," *Buffalo News*, April 21, 2004, p. A1.

[2] See James Risen and Eric Lichtblau, "Bush Lets U.S. Spy on Callers Without Courts," *The New York Times*, Dec. 16, 2005, p. A1. See also James Risen, *State of War: The Secret History of the CIA and the Bush Administration* (2006), pp. 39-60.

[3] For the text of the Dec. 17 address, see *Weekly Compilation of Presidential Documents*, Dec. 26, 2005, pp. 1880-1882. Bush was also questioned at length about the program in a news conference on Dec. 19. *Ibid.*, pp. 1885-1896.

[4] U.S. Deparment of Justice, "Legal Authorities Supporting the Activities of the National Security Agency Described by the President," Jan. 19, 2006 (www.usdoj.gov/opa/whitepaperonnsalegalauthorities.pdf).

[5] See Congressional Research Service, "Presidential Authority to Conduct Warrantless Electronic Surveillance to Gather Foreign Intelligence Information," Jan. 5, 2006; critical commentary can be found in op-ed articles in many newspapers, on the Web site www.findlaw.com, and on various interest group Web sites, including the American Civil Liberties Union's (www.aclu.org/nsaspying).

McCain's anti-torture legislation that cleared Congress in December included a provision — the so-called Graham-Levin amendment — barring Guantánamo detainees from challenging their detentions in federal court. Instead, it provided for limited review of the tribunals' final decisions by the D.C. Circuit.

"Congress made clear that the federal courts no longer have jurisdiction over actions filed on behalf of Guantánamo detainees," the government argues in a motion filed with the high court in Hamdan's case on Jan. 12. The government filed a similar motion urging the U.S. Court of Appeals for the District of Columbia to throw out two pending cases brought on behalf of about 60 other Guantánamo detainees. [15]

Hamdan's lawyer, Georgetown University Law Center Professor Neal Katyal, argues that Bush's order creating the tribunals established "a new form of military jurisdiction" without congressional authority and in violation of the Geneva Conventions. Dismissing the case, he writes in response to the government motion, would mean that most broad challenges to the tribunals "could never be brought at all."

Administration supporters, in fact, want to limit any review of the detainees' cases. "The idea that the military ought to be spending its time going through case by case presenting detailed evidence is ridiculous," says Richard Samp, senior attorney at the conservative Washington Legal Foundation, who has filed briefs supporting the government in the Supreme Court and D.C. Circuit cases.

Lawyers for the detainees counter that many of them are in fact innocent of any terrorism charge and that, in any event, they deserve a fair hearing. "The idea of justice is not to let people go. It is to let these people have a hearing," says Bill Goodman, legal director for the New York-based Center for Constitutional Rights, which brought the major detainee cases.

The cases have given Bush's critics their best opportunity so far to test the president's powers in court. The Supreme Court in June 2004 rejected the administration's broad efforts to deny or severely limit suspected terrorists' ability to challenge their detentions in court. In one decision, *Hamdi v. Rumsfeld*, the court upheld the president's authority to detain U.S. citizens as enemy combatants but required that they be given "a meaningful opportunity to contest the factual basis for the detention before a neutral decisionmaker." In a second ruling, *Rasul v. Bush*, the court held that federal courts have jurisdiction over habeas corpus challenges filed by aliens held at Guantánamo. [16]

The administration moved to minimize the impact of the rulings. In the citizen enemy-combatant case, the government released Yaser Hamdi in October 2004 on the condition that he renounce his U.S. citizenship and relocate to Saudi Arabia, where he held dual citizenship. Later, the government transferred a second U.S. citizen held as an enemy combatant, Jose Padilla, from a naval brig to a federal jail in January 2006 after obtaining an indictment against him for aiding terrorist activity abroad. Padilla is now awaiting trial in Miami while asking the high court to rule his previous three-year detention without charges unlawful. [17]

Meanwhile, the Defense Department is devising rules for Combatant Status Review Tribunals to be held for detainees at Guantánamo, but the rules in some ways limit detainees' procedural rights. At the same time, the government wants the federal courts in Washington — where the Guantánamo cases all have been consolidated — either to postpone action or to rule in favor of the legality of the tribunals and their procedures.

The D.C. Circuit handed the administration a major victory on July 15, 2005, by upholding the president's power under the use-of-force resolution to create the tribunals and rejecting other challenges to their procedures. Congress appeared to buttress the administration's stance with the Graham-Levin amendment. However, the amendment sponsors differ on whether it applies to the pending cases. Republican Lindsey Graham of South Carolina says it does, while Democrat Carl Levin of Michigan says it does not. The issue turns partly on a close reading of a somewhat complex statute. But Hamdan's lawyers argue that applying the law retroactively would amount to "the extraordinary step of stripping the federal courts — and [the Supreme Court] in particular — of jurisdiction over seminal pending cases."

Congress intended that exact result, Samp says. "Now that Congress has told the courts that they shouldn't get involved, I hope the courts will finally take the hint," he says. In response, Goodman contends that the law amounts to an unconstitutional suspension of habeas corpus and — even if valid — applies only to future cases, not those already pending. ■

BACKGROUND

'The Executive Power'

The framers of the Constitution provided in Article II that "the executive power" of the new national government "shall be vested in a President of the United States of America." Some of the president's powers were specified, but the list was not as long or as inclusive as the "enumerated" powers of Congress in Article I.

The meaning of the text and the intention of the framers have been debated through history up to the present day. Over time, the presidency has gained power. But each president has had to establish his own power anew in the face of opposition or resistance from other power centers: Congress, the courts, the federal bureaucracy and public opinion. [18]

The Constitutional Convention met in 1787 with a consensus that the new government needed a stronger executive than was provided in the

Articles of Confederation. Nevertheless, Article II is the "poorest drafted" part of the Constitution, according to historian Forrest McDonald, an emeritus professor at the University of Alabama. Delegates turned to laying out the president's powers only after devising the Electoral College system for the election of the president and rejecting the strong minority viewpoint for a "plural" chief executive. With time running out, the framers left the president's powers "ambiguous and undecided," McDonald says. For example, the article divides the power of appointment between the Senate and the president but says nothing about removing an officer. (Alexander Hamilton, who supported a strong chief executive, nonetheless believed the Senate had to consent.) Still, two provisions in particular point toward a strong executive: the designation of the president as commander in chief and the broad duty to "take care that the laws be faithfully executed."

Despite its ambiguities, Article II gave the president opportunities to act if he took them. George Washington (1789-1797) did. He established the precedents of firing Cabinet officers, vetoing legislation on constitutional grounds and controlling foreign policy. Among pre-Civil War presidents, several others stretched the office's powers beyond Article II's stated terms. Despite doubts about his own authority, Thomas Jefferson (1801-1809) completed the Louisiana Purchase unilaterally, choosing speed over constitutional niceties.

More boldly, Andrew Jackson (1829-1837) declared the president — not Congress — to be "the direct representative" of the American people. He successively defied the Supreme Court (by refusing to help enforce a controversial decision), Congress (by vetoing renewal of the national bank) and the Southern states (by rejecting their power to nullify acts of Congress). James K. Polk (1845-1849) followed his mentor Jackson's example by stretching the president's power — most notably, by provoking the war with Mexico that expanded the country's borders to the Pacific.

In his effort to save the Union, Abraham Lincoln (1861-1865) construed the president's power more broadly than anyone before or perhaps since, according to political scientist Genovese. Newly inaugurated and with Congress not in session, Lincoln responded to the Southern states' secession and the firing on Fort Sumter by commencing military action, calling for new troops, declaring a blockade of Southern ports and suspending habeas corpus. He acted unilaterally again in issuing the Emancipation Proclamation. But McDonald says Lincoln also allowed Congress to help direct military operations and sought after-the-fact legislative support for his decision to free the slaves. And despite Chief Justice Roger Taney's ruling to the contrary, Lincoln always believed he had followed the law in suspending habeas corpus.

The strong presidents had their critics. Jackson's opponents labeled him "King Andrew," Lincoln's called him a "dictator."

Through the 19th century, however, Congress was far and away more powerful than the president. Presidents only sparingly proposed legislation. They tangled with Congress over spending and with the Senate over appointments. Among post-Civil War presidents, only Grover Cleveland (1885-1889, 1893-1897) stood up to Congress — and he only with the negative power of the veto. As the young scholar Woodrow Wilson wrote in 1885, Congress was "unquestionably the predominant and controlling force" in national affairs. [19]

Imperial Presidency?

The president's power increased in the 20th century as the national government itself grew more powerful, playing a larger role in domestic social and economic policies and acting more assertively in world affairs. Presidents assumed a major role in initiating legislation for Congress to consider and became figures of international importance as the United States emerged as the world's strongest nation, both economically and militarily. Yet even successful presidents stumbled by considering their powers more sweeping than they actually were. And the growth of presidential power halted with the backlash in the late 1960s and early '70s against what historian Arthur Schlesinger Jr. lastingly labeled "the imperial presidency." [20]

The modern presidency began taking shape under William McKinley (1897-1901), who used his experience as a former senator to gather legislative power into the White House and led the United States into its first overseas conflict: the Spanish-American War. After McKinley's assassination, Theodore Roosevelt (1901-1909) moved more boldly at home and abroad, presenting an ambitious domestic legislative agenda and a determination — in political scientist Genovese's phrasing — to "dominate" the world stage. Most significantly, Roosevelt personalized the presidency as never before. He viewed himself as "the steward of the people" and his office as a "bully pulpit" from which he could shape public opinion.

Wilson (1913-1921) likewise became — in McDonald's words — the nation's "chief legislator" at home and a commanding figure abroad. But his presidency ended with the Senate's rejection of the Versailles Treaty, due in part to Wilson's refusal to compromise with opponents.

Franklin D. Roosevelt (1933-1945) combined all these strands, according to McDonald: chief legislator, national symbol, world leader — and man on a white horse. Elected with a mandate to lift the nation out of the Great

Continued on p. 180

Chronology

Before 1900

Congress is generally the dominant branch of the government.

20th Century

Presidents become more powerful with advent of modern communications and U.S. emergence as world power.

1933-1945
Franklin D. Roosevelt takes office with mandate to lift U.S. out of Great Depression; Congress passes his "New Deal" economic-recovery program but rebuffs his 1937 effort to "pack" Supreme Court.

1951
States ratify 22nd Amendment, limiting future presidents to two terms.

1952
Supreme Court says President Harry S Truman exceeded his authority in seizing steel mills during Korean War.

1963
After assassination of President John F. Kennedy, Lyndon B. Johnson wins passage of ambitious agenda.

1972
Supreme Court says President Richard M. Nixon cannot order warrantless wiretapping in domestic-security cases.

1973
War Powers Act requires Congress' approval before U.S. forces are sent into combat.

1974
Congressional Budget and Impoundment Control Act limits president's authority to withhold spending approved by Congress. . . . Supreme Court orders Nixon to turn over tapes of Watergate-related conversations; evidence of Nixon's role in cover-up forces him to resign.

1978
Foreign Intelligence Surveillance Act (FISA) requires judicial warrant from special court for foreign-intelligence gathering inside U.S. . . . Congress requires appointment of independent counsel to investigate alleged wrongdoing by president.

1980s ***Ronald Reagan becomes first two-term president since Eisenhower.***

1986-1987
Iran-contra scandal weakens Reagan.

1990s ***Bill Clinton is first Democratic president to serve two full terms since FDR.***

1990
Congress approves President George H. W. Bush's request that U.S. lead U.N. coalition in Persian Gulf War against Iraq.

1997
Supreme Court rules a president can be sued for unofficial actions.

1998
Clinton's sexual liaison with White House intern is revealed; House in December impeaches Clinton for perjury and obstruction; after Senate trial, Clinton is acquitted in February 1999.

1999
Congress allows independent-counsel act to expire.

2000-Present

President Bush moves to strengthen executive powers.

2001
President George W. Bush quickly moves to reassert executive prerogatives; after 9/11 terrorist attacks Congress passes Authorization to Use Military Force resolution aimed at al Qaeda, the group blamed for attacks, and USA Patriot Act. . . . Bush creates military tribunals to try enemy combatants captured in Afghanistan.

2002
At Bush's request, Congress authorizes U.S. invasion of Iraq. . . . Justice Department memo claims president has power to authorize torture of detainees; memo is disavowed when disclosed in 2004.

2004
Supreme Court backs president's authority to hold "enemy combatant" but says U.S. citizens must be given hearing, and aliens can use habeas corpus to challenge detention. . . . Bush re-elected.

2005
Bush is said to have authorized secret electronic surveillance of phone calls, e-mails between suspected terrorists overseas and persons in the U.S.; Bush, others defend program, despite criticism that it is illegal. . . . Detainee Treatment Act bars torture or abusive treatment of detainees, limits legal challenges to confinement.

2006
White House signals open mind on possible legislation to authorize warrantless surveillance program. . . . Supreme Court due to hear challenge to military tribunals.

New Anti-Torture Law Questioned

Reports that the CIA secretly imprisons foreigners in countries that might condone torture have raised questions about whether President Bush has overstepped his authority and violated international laws in his war against terrorism.

If the U.S. president can "kidnap foreign citizens off the streets of other countries and torture, then what can't he do?" asked former Vice President Al Gore in a Jan. 16 speech outlining concerns about the expansion of executive power during the Bush presidency. [1]

And experts doubt that anti-torture measures passed by Congress in December — authored by former Navy pilot and Vietnam prisoner of war Sen. John McCain, R-Ariz. — will halt the practice.

President Bush neither confirms nor denies the existence of secret CIA prisons or that the United States transfers foreign citizens to other countries to be interrogated. However, he told reporters in November that the United States is at war with an enemy "that lurks and plots and plans and wants to hurt America again. And so, you bet, we'll aggressively pursue them, but we'll do so under the law." But he quickly added, "We do not torture." [2]

According to the press reports, after the 9/11 terrorist attacks the CIA initiated a covert anti-terrorism program involving so-called extraordinary rendition, in which the agency helps capture suspected terrorists abroad and transfers them to third countries where they are subjected to interrogation techniques that some lawyers say violate anti-torture treaties. Rep. Edward Markey, D-Mass., condemned the practice as "an extrajudicial, secret process in which the CIA or some other U.S. government entity acts as prosecutor, judge and jury and without any due process may send a detainee to any country in the world, including some of the planet's most notorious human-rights abusers." [3]

Then in November *The Washington Post* disclosed that the CIA has been hiding and interrogating terrorist captives in secret prisons around the world, including in Eastern European democracies. [4] After the revelations touched off an uproar both at home and in Europe, the detainees allegedly were moved to similar CIA facilities elsewhere, referred to as "black sites" in classified documents. [5]

The European Union and human-rights organizations say the practice may violate international and domestic laws, including the U.N. Convention against Torture and the European Convention on Human Rights. Forcibly detaining a person and then refusing to acknowledge the detention or allow the person legal protection is called a "forced disappearance," says Human Rights Watch. "The U.S. has long condemned other countries that engage in forced disappearances" and helped draft U.N. condemnations of such activities — with no exceptions for national security, the group says. [6]

The allegations about the renditions and secret prisons further damaged America's reputation abroad, already severely tarnished by the 2004 exposé of detainee abuse in U.S. military prisons in Iraq and Afghanistan. [7]

Secretary of State Condoleeza Rice tried to assure European officials last December that the U.N. convention applies to U.S. personnel "wherever they are, whether they are in the United States or outside of the United States." [8]

Despite the assurances, both the European Union's Parliament and the Council of Europe — the continent's main human-rights organization — launched separate investigations into whether the CIA may have illegally transferred prisoners through European airports. Now questions are being raised as to whether European governments may have cooperated secretly with the United States. On Feb. 20, 2006, German prosecutors announced they were investigating whether Germany acted as a silent partner in the abduction of Khaled el-Masri, a German citizen of Arab descent who was mistaken for a terrorism suspect. El-Masri says he was abducted while on vacation in Macedonia in 2003 and flown to an American prison in Afghanistan, where he was held and tortured for five months. [9]

In December, amid new outrage over allegations that the administration had approved surveillance of U.S. citizens' telephone and e-mail communications, Congress began to push back against Bush's controversial wartime tactics. Both chambers inserted language drafted by McCain into the 2006 Defense appropriations and authorization bills prohibiting Americans from engaging in "cruel, inhuman and degrading" treatment of prisoners anywhere in the world and restricting the U.S. military to interrogation techniques listed in the U.S. Army *Field Manual*.

"It's an important first step, but it definitely hasn't solved the problem," says Joanne Mariner, director of the counterterrorism program at Human Rights Watch. Questions still remain, according to her and others, as to how it will be enforced, exactly what the Army *Field Manual* — which is being revised — will say, and who will define torture or cruel, inhuman and degrading treatment for CIA personnel.

In addition, says Mariner, it addresses only the behavior of U.S. personnel, so it will not specifically prevent the CIA from "outsourcing torture" to interrogators in other countries.

Continued from p. 178

Depression, he wrote the most ambitious legislative agenda in U.S. history — known as the New Deal — and got it enacted within 100 days. His radio "fireside chats" established the model of personal communication between the president and the people. He led the nation and the world in defeating German Nazism in Europe and Japanese aggression in the Pacific.

But FDR also stumbled — most notably when Congress rejected his 1937 plan to "pack" the Supreme Court. And his legacy was clouded by the two-term constitutional amendment ratified six years after his death and the

Enforcement of the McCain amendment was complicated by the inclusion of another provision — written by Sens. Lindsey Graham, a South Carolina Republican, and Democrat Carl Levin of Michigan — prohibiting the 500-plus detainees at Guantánamo Bay, Cuba, from challenging their detention or treatment in a U.S. court.

"If the McCain law demonstrates to the world that the United States really opposes torture, the Graham-Levin amendment risks telling the world the opposite," said Tom Malinowski, Washington advocacy director at Human Rights Watch. The treatment of Guantánamo Bay detainees will remain "shrouded in secrecy, placing detainees at risk for future abuse." [10]

Robert K. Goldman, an American University law professor and former president of the Inter-American Commission on Human Rights, agrees the McCain amendment has great symbolic value overseas. "It helps to clean up our image, which has been so battered around the world," he said. But Scott L. Silliman, executive director of Duke Law School's Center on Law, Ethics and National Security, says the measure allows CIA and Justice Department lawyers to determine which interrogation techniques CIA and civilian interrogators can use. [11]

And effective policing by those departments is unlikely, said Eugene Fidell, president of the National Institute of Military Justice. "You could have a wonderful McCain amendment, but if there's no enforcement mechanism, it's worthless or worse than worthless because it would be an empty promise." [12]

Many experts agree enforcement appears doubtful. After having unsuccessfully tried to get Congress to exempt CIA operatives from McCain's abuse ban, President Bush signed the two laws reluctantly, saying on both occasions that he would enforce the provisions "in a manner consistent with the constitutional authority of the president to supervise the unitary executive branch and as commander in chief." Many read his statement as signaling his intention to disregard the law. [13]

But McCain and Sen. John W. Warner, R-Va., chairman of the Senate Armed Services Committee, said in a statement on Jan. 4, 2006, that they expect the president to abide by the law. "We believe the president understands Congress's intent in passing by very large majorities legislation governing the treatment of detainees," they said, and that Congress had specifically declined "to include a presidential waiver of the restrictions included in our legislation." Further, they said, their committee "intends through strict oversight to monitor the administration's implementation of the new law."

Meanwhile, the European Parliament was scheduled to begin hearings into the secret prison allegations on Feb. 23. "The fact that Europe is investigating this and not the U.S. Congress is disappointing," says Human Rights Watch's Mariner.

— *Kathy Koch*

Getty Images/Paul J. Richards

German citizen Khaled el-Masri, shown on TV, says he was illegally abducted, detained and tortured last year in a secret overseas prison.

[1] The speech is available at www.acslaw.org.

[2] Michael A. Fletcher, "Bush Defends CIA's Clandestine Prisons; 'We Do Not Torture,' President Says," *The Washington Post*, Nov. 8, 2005, p. A15.

[3] Randy Hall, " 'Outsourcing Torture' Condemned by Dems, Activists," CNSNews.com, March 11, 2005.

[4] Dana Priest, "CIA Holds Terror Suspects in Secret Prisons; Debate Is Growing Within Agency About Legality and Morality of Overseas System Set Up After 9/11," *The Washington Post*, Nov. 2, 2005, p. A1.

[5] Dana Priest, "Covert CIA Program Withstands New Furor; Anti-Terror Effort Continues to Grow," *The Washington Post*, Dec. 30, 2005, p. A1.

[6] "Questions and Answers: U.S. Detainees Disappeared into Secret Prisons: Illegal under Domestic and International Law," Human Rights Watch Backgrounder, Dec. 9, 2005, http://hrw.org/backgrounder/usa/us1205/index.htm.

[7] For background, see Mary H. Cooper, "Privatizing the Military," *CQ Researcher*, June 25, 2004, pp. 565-588.

[8] Glenn Kessler and Josh White, "Rice Seeks To Clarify Policy on Prisoners; Cruel, Inhuman Tactics By U.S. Personnel Barred Overseas and at Home," *The Washington Post*, Dec. 8, 2005, p. A1.

[9] Don Van Natta Jr., "Germany Weighs if It Played Role in Seizure by U.S.," *The New York Times*, Feb. 21, 2006, p. A1.

[10] Quoted at http://hrw.org/english/docs/2005/12/16/usdom12311.htm.

[11] Quoted in Seth Stern, "McCain's Detainee Language May Give Non-Military Interrogators Leeway, Experts Say," *CQ Today*, Dec. 18, 2005.

[12] *Ibid.*

[13] Quoted in John M. Donnelly, "Bush Signs Defense Authorization Bill, Repeats Reservations," *CQ Today*, Jan. 9, 2006.

repudiation decades later of his wartime internment of Japanese-Americans.

The Cold War's ever-present threat of nuclear war focused attention and power all the more on the president. Meanwhile, the advent of television magnified the president's ability to speak directly to the people. Yet each of the first three Cold War presidents — Harry S Truman (1945-1953), Dwight D. Eisenhower (1953-1961) and John F. Kennedy (1961-1963) — was politically weakened by congressional opposition. In addition, domestic- and national-security apparatuses were growing within the executive branch, largely out of public view and, to some extent, beyond the president's control.

After Kennedy's assassination, Lyndon B. Johnson (1963-1969) took up his predecessor's mantle and used his unequaled mastery of legislative skills to push through Congress a "Great Society" program that rivaled if not surpassed Roosevelt's New Deal. After a landslide election in 1964, however, his presidency crashed and burned in Vietnam. Johnson claimed congressional support for the war on the dubious authority of the controversial Gulf of Tonkin resolution. Despite his doubts about a possible victory, he staved off defeat in Vietnam to avoid being tagged "soft on communism" by the military or congressional Republicans. But by 1968 the war was so unpopular he had to step aside rather than seek re-election.

Richard M. Nixon (1969-1974) expanded presidential powers past the breaking point. Campaigning, he claimed he had a "secret plan" to end the war; in office, he continued the conflict and secretly expanded it into neighboring Cambodia with no congressional sanction. Domestically, he achieved many successes working with a Democratic-controlled Congress, but he angered lawmakers by claiming the authority to "impound" congressionally approved spending.

By the time the Watergate scandal forced Nixon to resign, the office was being weakened. Congress passed the War Powers Act of 1973 to control the president's military powers; a year later, the Congressional Budget and Impoundment Control Act rejected the president's authority to withhold spending. And the Supreme Court's decision in *United States v. Nixon* (1974) requiring him to turn over the Watergate tapes to a special prosecutor put judicial teeth behind the truism that — whatever his powers — the president was not above the law. [21]

'Beleaguered' Presidents

Presidents of the late 20th century governed with the burdens created by two national traumas. The Vietnam War made the public wary of military conflicts abroad, while the Watergate scandal left them cynical about government and fearful of official abuses. Three of the five presidents had tenures cut short by the voters, while the two who served the constitutional maximum of two terms were beset by scandals exploited by Congresses controlled by the opposite party. The neoconservative scholar Aaron Wildavsky saw the presidency as "beleaguered," while political scientist Genovese says each successive president left the office weaker than before. [22]

The first two post-Watergate presidents, Gerald R. Ford (1974-1977) and Jimmy Carter (1977-1981), used low-key styles to try to regain public trust. But Ford never recovered from his 1974 decision to pardon Nixon for his Watergate crimes, saving him from a possible trial. With Ford in the White House, the Senate in 1976 responded to a damning report on the CIA as both incompetent and unaccountable by creating a new Select Committee on Intelligence to strengthen congressional oversight of the agency. The House created a counterpart committee the next year.

Carter famously promised in his 1976 campaign that he would never lie to the American people, but his moralistic persona proved ill-suited to national leadership and to managing a Congress controlled by elders of his own party. He also signed the 1978 law providing for appointment of independent counsels to investigate the president or high-ranking executive officials — a statute that would come to bedevil presidents of both parties.

Ronald Reagan (1981-1989) and Bill Clinton (1993-2001) both came to the White House with well-honed communications skills and well-developed policy views. Both had significant legislative successes in their first terms. Both were willing to commit U.S. troops to overseas missions in less than clear-cut threats to national security. And both won re-election to second terms only to struggle to hold power in the face of political scandals.

Reagan faced a challenge to his credibility and character with the disclosure in November 1986 that the United States had traded arms to Iran in exchange for American hostages and used the illegal profits to funnel aid to the U.S-backed contras seeking to topple the leftist regime in Nicaragua. Reagan's initial denial — "We did not trade weapons or anything else for hostages" — gave way in March 1987 to an admission that "the facts and the evidence" said otherwise. The scandal resulted in an investigation by a special House-Senate committee and a subsequent critical report as well as the appointment of an independent counsel with ensuing criminal prosecutions. Reagan remained personally and politically popular, but his power in his final two years was at an ebb.

Clinton faced questions about his character throughout his presidency, but they came to a head with the disclosure in January 1998 that he had had sexual encounters with an intern, Monica Lewinsky, inside the White House. Clinton initially denied that he had had "sexual relations with that woman" and repeated that denial in a sworn deposition only to admit an "improper physical relationship" in a grand-jury appearance in August. After receiving a harshly critical report from independent counsel Kenneth Starr, the House voted in November to impeach Clinton for perjury (two counts), obstruction of justice and abuse of office. The trial in the Republican-controlled Senate ended in February 1999 with Clinton's acquittal, but he was left severely weakened for his last two years in office. Clinton's legal troubles also produced a Supreme Court decision, *Clinton v. Jones* (1997), holding that a president could be sued while in office for actions unrelated to his official duties. [23]

By the turn of the century, Reagan and Clinton could be credited with revitalizing the president's role as Legislator in Chief — but with mixed results in the face of opposition-controlled Congresses for much of their time in office. Along with George H. W. Bush (1989-1993), they also renewed the commander in chief's power to send troops abroad without a congressional say-so: Reagan to Grenada, Bush to Panama and Clinton in different contexts to Haiti, Somalia and Kosovo. And Bush asked for and got authorization from Congress in 1990 for the U.S. role in the United Nations-mandated Gulf War.

More broadly, however, the presidency suffered from what Genovese calls the "highly personalized, excessively partisan and deeply hurtful" political climate. As a result, he says, "the presidency became a smaller, less dignified office." [24]

Post-9/11 President

George W. Bush came to office in January 2001 determined to restore what both he and his vice president, Cheney, viewed as the lost powers of the presidency. The terrorist attacks of Sept. 11, 2001, forged these views into a hard-and-fast policy of asserting maximum presidential authority to fight a war against terrorism at home and abroad.

The Bush-Cheney doctrine got its first test in a domestic policy setting. As head of an energy task force created by Bush in his first month in office, Cheney invoked the president's need for candid advice in refusing to divulge details about its proceedings before release of the group's final report in May 2001 and during a legal battle extending through May 2005. The administration rebuffed requests for information about the task force from Congress and later successfully fought a suit by two interest groups to use federal access laws to learn of the group's contacts with industry executives.

The White House responded to the 9/11 attacks by simultaneously defending Bush's power as commander in chief to take military action on his own and working with Congress on a resolution to authorize the use of force. Initially, the administration wanted authority to "deter and pre-empt" future acts of terrorism or aggression. But lawmakers insisted on a narrower resolution directed only against those responsible for the Sept. 11 attacks. It cleared Congress on Sept. 14 — three days after the attacks — with one dissenting vote in the House and none in the Senate.

The administration also had to settle for somewhat less than it wanted in the USA Patriot Act, the broad counterterrorism measure passed by Congress on Oct. 25, 2001. The law increased penalties for terrorism and expanded federal law-enforcement powers in terrorism-related investigations. But Congress balked at the administration's request to indefinitely detain immigrants suspected of terrorism. It also inserted a "sunset" clause to terminate some of the act's provisions after four years. And, significantly for later developments, it included no authority to use foreign-intelligence-gathering wiretaps within the United States.

Bush also drew criticism on Capitol Hill when he issued an executive order on Nov. 13 authorizing military tribunals to try non-citizens suspected of terrorism. "I need to have that extraordinary option at my fingertips," Bush said a few days later. Democrats and some libertarian-minded Republicans complained, but Bush refused to back off — foreshadowing the stout legal defense of the program that administration lawyers have waged ever since.

With the war in Afghanistan ended in December 2001, the administration in early 2002 began focusing on Iraq. By June, Bush was explicitly warning of a possible pre-emptive strike — prompting lawmakers to warn against initiating military action without congressional approval. A White House-drafted resolution served as the basis for a measure finally approved in October that authorized Bush to use "necessary and appropriate" force against "the continuing threat posed by Iraq" and to enforce "all relevant" U.N. Security Council resolutions against Iraq. The House approved the measure, 296-133; the Senate, 77-23. Under pressure from Congress and from the United States' main ally — Britain — Bush continued seeking United Nations approval for the action almost up until the day the United States invaded Baghdad on March 19, 2003.

Despite quick success in removing Saddam Hussein from power and subduing the Iraqi army, the United States remains bogged down in a deadly fight with a stubborn insurgency in Iraq. With no final resolution, Bush has been faced with a steady stream of complaints about faulty intelligence — particularly on the issue of Iraq's suspected weapons of mass destruction — and poor planning and execution of postwar reconstruction.

Meanwhile, the administration was coming under increasing criticism in Congress and elsewhere for abuse and torture of suspected terrorists captured in Afghanistan and elsewhere and held at Guantánamo Bay. Rejecting the administration's arguments for a free hand, the Supreme Court in June 2004 ruled that detainees could go to federal courts to challenge their confinement.

By late 2005, Bush was being politically weakened by other issues — notably, the administration's flawed response to Hurricane Katrina in August. [25] Polls showed Bush's public approval sagging. Despite resistance by the White House, both the Senate and House included anti-torture provisions in military-funding measures. On Dec. 15, Bush met with McCain

Youngstown Decision Offers Test for President's Powers

Can President Bush authorize the National Security Agency to monitor telephone calls between a U.S. citizen and a suspected terrorist overseas without a judicial warrant? Can he order a foreign terror suspect to be tried before a military tribunal without access to federal courts?

Many experts think the answers are contained in a landmark Supreme Court decision overturning President Harry S Truman's seizure of the nation's steel mills in 1952 to avert a strike during the Korean War. In a concurring opinion in the decision, *Youngstown Sheet & Tube Co. v. Sawyer*, Justice Robert H. Jackson set out a three-tiered structure for judging the scope of the president's power — now recognized as the starting point for any constitutional decision in the area.

Supreme Court Justice Robert H. Jackson.

Jackson — who had served as attorney general under one of the nation's most powerful presidents, Franklin D. Roosevelt, and was chief U.S. prosecutor at the Nuremberg war-crimes trial in Germany in 1945 and 1946 — reasoned that the chief executive's power depends in part on what, if anything, Congress has said about a particular subject. The president's authority "is at its maximum," wrote Jackson, when he acts "pursuant to an express or implied authorization of Congress." In such instances, the president's power includes "all that he possesses in his own right plus all that Congress can delegate."

By contrast, the president's power "is at its lowest ebb" when he "takes measures incompatible with the expressed or implied will of Congress," Jackson said. Under those circumstances, the president "can rely only upon his own constitutional powers minus any constitutional powers of Congress over the matter."

In the middle are cases where the president has acted "in absence of either a congressional grant or denial of authority," Jackson said. He called this area "a zone of twilight" in which the president and Congress may share authority or the distribution of power between the two branches may be uncertain.

In those instances, Jackson continued, congressional "inertia, indifference or quiescence" may either enable or at least invite the president to act on his own. And the legality of the president's actions, he concluded, would depend "on the imperatives of events and contemporary imponderables rather than on abstract theories of law."

Bush and his supporters argue that the electronic surveillance and military tribunals fit squarely into Jackson's first category. They say Congress gave Bush the needed powers on Sept. 14, 2001, when it passed the Authorization to Use Military Force against the perpetrators of the 9/11 terrorist attacks. And even if the use-of-force resolution is not read that broadly, administration officials and supporters argue, the president has inherent authority to gather intelligence against a foreign enemy and provide for trials of captured enemy combatants.

Opponents of Bush's policies say the electronic surveillance falls squarely in Jackson's "lowest ebb" category — where Congress has prohibited the president's actions. They say the Foreign Intelligence Surveillance Act specifically requires a court warrant for any foreign-intelligence gathering within the United States. As for military tribunals, the administration's critics contend that despite the president's powers as commander in chief to capture and hold enemy combatants, he cannot bypass provisions of the Uniform Code of Military Justice or the Geneva Conventions that govern hearings for detainees.

In the steel-seizure case, Jackson had no difficulty in concluding that Truman had no congressional authorization for his action. In fact, he argued, it ran afoul of the procedure Congress set out in the Taft-Hartley Act for putting an industry back to work after a strike. He then rejected the Truman administration's arguments that the president had the power to put the steel mills back to work in the face of contrary congressional legislation.

"No doctrine that the Court could promulgate would seem to me more sinister and alarming than that a President whose conduct of foreign affairs is so largely uncontrolled, and often even is unknown, can vastly enlarge his mastery over the internal affairs of the country by his own commitment of the Nation's armed forces to some foreign venture," Jackson wrote.

"With all its defects, delays and inconveniences, men have discovered no technique for long preserving free government except that the Executive be under the law, and that the law be made by parliamentary deliberations," Jackson concluded. "Such institutions may be destined to pass away. But it is the duty of the Court to be last, not first, to give them up."

at the White House and agreed to accept the restriction.

Trying to put the best face on the reversal, Bush told reporters, "We've been happy to work with [Sen. McCain] to achieve a common objective, and that is to make clear that this government does not torture." [26] ■

Continued on p. 186

At Issue:

Is the administration's electronic-surveillance program legal?

yes

ROBERT F. TURNER
CO-FOUNDER, CENTER FOR NATIONAL SECURITY LAW, UNIVERSITY OF VIRGINIA LAW SCHOOL

WRITTEN FOR THE *CQ RESEARCHER*, FEBRUARY 2006

Critics who call President Bush a "lawbreaker" for authorizing National Security Agency surveillance of international communications between suspected al Qaeda operatives abroad and people inside our country are focusing on the wrong "law." In reality, this is a constitutional issue pitting privacy interests protected by the Fourth Amendment against the president's independent "executive" and "commander-in-chief" powers. The 1978 Foreign Intelligence Surveillance Act (FISA) could no more usurp authority vested by the Constitution in the president's discretion than Congress could narrow the Fourth Amendment's protections by mere statute.

John Jay explained in *Federalist No. 64* that the new Constitution left the president free "to manage the business of intelligence as prudence might suggest"; and Washington, Jefferson, Madison, Hamilton and Chief Justice Marshall each noted that the grant of "executive power" to the president included control over foreign relations. In *Marbury v. Madison*, Marshall noted that the Constitution gave the president important political powers about which "the decision of the executive is conclusive."

In 1818, Rep. Henry Clay reasoned it would be improper for Congress to inquire into foreign-intelligence activities authorized by the president. And in the landmark 1936 *Curtiss-Wright* case, the Supreme Court found Congress "powerless to invade" the president's "plenary and exclusive power" over international diplomacy.

The Fourth Amendment binds in peace and war, but in neither is it absolute. It prohibits only "unreasonable" searches and seizures — a standard obviously affected when Congress authorizes war — and the idea that warrantless surveillance of our nation's enemies during wartime is "unreasonable" finds no support in historic practice or judicial opinions. The test involves balancing the privacy interest against the governmental interest, and the Supreme Court has repeatedly observed: "no governmental interest is more compelling than the security of the Nation."

The courts are clearly with the president. When the Supreme Court held in the 1972 *United States v. United States District Court* case that warrants would be required for national security wiretaps of purely domestic targets (like the Black Panthers), it carefully distinguished its holding from a case involving foreign agents. In 2002, the FISA Court of Review observed that every federal appeals court to consider the issue has held the president has independent constitutional power to authorize warrantless foreign-intelligence wiretaps, and noted "FISA could not encroach upon the president's constitutional power."

no

KATE MARTIN
DIRECTOR, CENTER FOR NATIONAL SECURITY STUDIES

WRITTEN FOR THE *CQ RESEARCHER*, FEBRUARY 2006

When Congress authorized secret wiretaps of Americans in the 1978 Foreign Intelligence Surveillance Act (FISA), it required special orders from the FISA court. It did so in order to implement the Fourth Amendment's command that searches be authorized by judicial warrant to safeguard individual privacy against arbitrary government invasion.

Congress explicitly prohibited any future president from conducting warrantless eavesdropping and made FISA and the criminal wiretap laws "the exclusive means" for carrying out electronic surveillance in the Untied States. Congress refused to enact any exception for "inherent presidential power" and made it a crime for government officials to wiretap without a warrant.

The president now claims the power to act in violation of FISA as well as the Fourth Amendment's warrant requirement, citing his commander-in-chief authority. But the president's authorization of such wiretapping — done in secret and deliberately withheld from the public and the Congress — is unprecedented. Nothing in the Constitution authorizes the president to violate the law or to decide on his own to secretly wiretap Americans — even during wartime.

The Justice Department pays lip service to the principle that the president is bound by the law when it argues that Congress gave the president this power in the authorization to use force against al Qaeda, and that such warrantless surveillance is "reasonable." The authorization argument is too frivolous to respond to in this limited space. The president's real claim is that he has exclusive power to conduct such wiretaps, that Congress may not limit that power, and judges may not review it.

The Supreme Court has never upheld such a claim of monarchical power. To the contrary, it reiterated in the *Hamdi* case: "Whatever power the . . . Constitution envisions for the Executive in its exchanges with other nations or with enemy organizations in times of conflict, it most assuredly envisions a role for all three branches when individual liberties are at stake."

The president can make no claim of necessity for exercising exclusive power. Following the law and obtaining a warrant would not make it impossible to conduct surveillance necessary to prevent future attacks. Courts would issue warrants for surveillance of communications with al Qaeda, which is manifestly reasonable. The Congress would amend FISA if the president demonstrates the necessity, as it has already done since the 9/11 terrorist attacks. The secret program of warrantless surveillance is illegal and unconstitutional.

Continued from p. 184

CURRENT SITUATION

Detainee Cases

Four years after President Bush ordered the use of military tribunals for suspected terrorists captured in Afghanistan, the administration is now hoping a new law passed by Congress will prevent hundreds of detainees from challenging his action in federal court. Lawyers for the detainees, however, say the government's interpretation of the law is either wrong or unconstitutional.

In December 2005, when Congress passed McCain's anti-torture measure, known officially as the Detainee Treatment Act, it was responding to the Supreme Court's June 2004 decision to allow federal courts to hear habeas corpus petitions filed by detainees held at the U.S. Naval Station at Guantánamo Bay. The act — signed by Bush as part of the Defense Department annual funding measure — provides instead that "no court, justice or judge shall have jurisdiction" to consider a habeas corpus petition filed by any Guantánamo detainee.

Justice Department lawyers now cite the act in asking the Supreme Court to dismiss the Hamdan case, which the justices had agreed to consider in November. The act "plainly divests the courts of jurisdiction" to hear Hamdan's pretrial challenge to the military tribunal, the government wrote in the motion filed with the Supreme Court on Jan. 12. The government is similarly asking the federal appeals court for the D.C. Circuit to dismiss consolidated cases brought on behalf of about 60 other Guantánamo detainees.

In all of the cases, the government is contending that the new law requires detainees to wait until their cases are decided by the so-called combatant status-review tribunals before coming to federal court. The law also provides that any appeals go to the D.C. Circuit, which would exercise only limited review over the tribunals' decisions.

Detainees' lawyers say the law does not apply to any of the pending cases. The two principal sponsors of the provision — Sens. Graham and Levin — disagree over whether it applies retroactively. If the law is held to apply to Hamdan's case, his lawyer, Georgetown Professor Katyal, argues that Congress cannot suspend habeas corpus except by a more explicit provision and, in any event, has acted improperly by barring the use of habeas corpus only by Guantánamo detainees.

The high court had already scheduled arguments in the Hamdan case for March 28 before the government's motion to dismiss in January. Katyal urged the justices either to reject the motion altogether or, alternatively, to consider the issue along with the merits of the case in the March arguments.

In their action in November, the justices agreed to consider two issues Hamdan raised after the D.C. Circuit had rejected his claims. The first is whether Bush had the power to establish the military tribunals either under his inherent authority or under the use-of-force resolution Congress passed in September 2001. The second issue is whether federal courts can enforce a provision of the Geneva Conventions that, according to lawyers for the detainees, requires a formal court-martial to first determine whether detainees are entitled to prisoner-of-war status with additional procedural safeguards.

Two lawyers on opposing sides of the case speculate that the court may be reluctant to dismiss Hamdan's appeal altogether. "The government is going to have a tough row to hoe on the jurisdictional issue," says Samp of the Washington Legal Foundation.

Pamela Karlan, a Stanford University law professor who filed an amicus brief in support of Hamdan, notes that under the late Chief Justice William H. Rehnquist, the high court "did not shy away from asserting its jurisdiction over a wide range of issues." While the court's direction under Chief Justice John G. Roberts Jr. is not yet clear, Karlan stresses that the government wants to block any ruling on Hamdan's legal argument until after the military tribunal has decided his case. "The government is saying not only that the Supreme Court can't hear the case but that none of the courts below can hear it," she explains.

Roberts will not be participating in the case because he was one of the judges in the D.C. Circuit's ruling. By recusing himself, Roberts raises the possibility of a 4-4 split, which would leave the appeals court's ruling for the government standing. If the justices hear the case on March 28, a decision would be expected in late June.

Surveillance Program

Congress may be backing away from a detailed inquiry into the operations of the NSA electronic-surveillance program as the administration moves toward accepting legislative proposals to provide specific legal authorization for it.

Legislation could complicate court challenges to the surveillance, which in any event face daunting obstacles and are unlikely to be ruled on any time soon.

The Senate Intelligence Committee gave the administration a significant victory Feb. 16 by refusing to take up a motion by the panel's Democratic vice chairman, West Virginia's John D. Rockefeller IV, to open an inquiry on the surveillance program. Republicans have an 8-7 majority on the committee, but two GOP senators — Snowe and Hagel — had called for an inquiry in December. [27]

Committee Chairman Pat Roberts of Kansas strongly opposes any inquiry as "unwarranted" and potentially "detrimental to this highly classified program." In the days before the committee's meeting, the White House helped Roberts resist the inquiry by signaling that the administration would provide more details on the program to the Intelligence Committee and that it might accept legislation to authorize the program with more congressional oversight.

Following the closed-door meeting, Roberts told reporters the committee had adjourned without voting on Rockefeller's motion. Rockefeller criticized the delay, saying the committee had "once again abdicated its responsibility" to oversee intelligence activities. For her part, Snowe said in a statement that it was "imperative" for the administration to provide more information about the program before the committee's next scheduled meeting on March 7.

Meanwhile, leaders of the House Intelligence Committee reportedly agreed to open an inquiry into the program, but the scope of the planned review was unclear. New Mexico's Rep. Wilson, who chairs the panel's Subcommittee on Technical Intelligence, told *The New York Times* that the review would have "multiple avenues." But *The Times* quoted a spokesman for committee Chairman Peter Hoekstra, R-Mich., as saying the review would not be "an inquiry into the program" but an examination of ways to "modernize" the FISA statute. [28]

Two GOP senators are promoting separate proposals for legislation on the issue. Judiciary Committee Chairman Specter is drafting a measure to require the attorney general to seek permission from the FISA court to eavesdrop on U.S. communications, to identify who was being monitored and why and to apply for reauthorization every 45 days. The proposal also would authorize the court to rule on whether the program was constitutional.

Sen. Mike DeWine, R-Ohio, a member of both the Judiciary and Intelligence committees, is instead proposing that Congress simply exempt eavesdropping on al Qaeda or other terrorist groups from FISA's warrant requirement. His proposal also would require the NSA to provide newly created Intelligence subcommittees with more details on the surveillance.

The White House continues to say that no legislation is needed to authorize the program, but press secretary Scott McClellan said on Feb. 16 the administration is willing to "work with Congress on legislation that would not undermine the president's ability to protect Americans." Between the two senators' proposals, DeWine's appears to sit better with the White House. DeWine said White House counsel Harriet Miers called him on Feb. 15 to discuss his proposal and suggested only minor changes.

Opponents of the program, meanwhile, are pressing ahead with legal challenges. [29] The ACLU and the Center for Constitutional Rights (CCR) filed separate suits in federal courts in Detroit and New York, respectively, challenging the program as a violation of the First and Fourth Amendments and separation-of-powers principles. The ACLU says criminal-defense lawyers, journalists, scholars and nonprofit organizations are among those who fear their communications with people in predominantly Muslim countries are being monitored without just cause. The CCR filed suits in its own behalf.

Separately, two Washington-based groups — the Electronic Privacy Information Center and People for the American Way — are suing the Justice Department and the NSA, respectively, under the federal Freedom of Information Act (FOIA) to try to force disclosure of legal opinions and operational details of the program. In a preliminary ruling on Feb. 16, U.S. District Judge Harry Kennedy directed the Justice Department to turn over documents within 20 days or provide a list of documents being withheld.

In addition, the Electronic Frontier Foundation, a San Francisco-based, free-speech advocacy group, is suing major telephone companies, claiming their cooperation with the NSA surveillance program violates customers' privacy rights. The suit is pending in federal court in San Francisco.

The suits face a variety of legal hurdles, including questions about the legal standing of the plaintiffs in the ACLU and CCR suits and broad exemptions for intelligence activities in the FOIA actions.

And even if courts allow the cases to proceed, they are unlikely to issue substantive rulings in the near future. "All these cases take a long period of time," says Caroline Frederickson, the ACLU's Washington legislative director. ■

OUTLOOK

Presidential Weakness?

The political scientist Richard Neustadt focused his landmark 1960 study *Presidential Power* not on the strength of the office but on its weakness — with formal powers effectively limited by the other branches of government, private interest groups, the press and public opinion. In a revised edition 30 years later, Neustadt repeated the same theme. The office is inherently weak, he wrote, "in the sense of the great gap between what is expected [of the president] and assured capacity to carry through." [30]

George W. Bush entered the White House in 2001 believing the office had been weakened even further. But he seemed to defy its weaknesses with a strategy of boldness. Working with Republican majorities in both houses of Congress, he won major legislative victories in his first months and then gained enough support after the 9/11 terrorist attacks to wage a quick war in Afghanistan and to get congressional approval a year later for a second war in Iraq.

Today, Bush seems to be paying a price for flexing his political power. With the conflict in Iraq continuing and his domestic agenda stalled, Bush's boldness is now seen on Capitol Hill as highhandedness and among much of the public as manipulativeness or outright deception. His approval ratings hover in the low 40 percent range, and some polls indicate a voter shift toward Democrats and away from Republicans. [31]

Bush's slippage may not be simply a backlash to his style of governing, historian McDonald says. "It's a very, very divided country," McDonald says. "The backlash would have come whether he'd been bold or not."

Whatever the reason, the co-equal branches of government are pushing back, if tentatively. The Supreme Court in 2004 rejected Bush's boldest claims in the enemy-combatant cases for his actions to be completely free of judicial review even if they upheld some presidential power to detain them. The cases "were not a tremendous victory for the president," says John McGinnis, a conservative constitutional law expert at Northwestern University in Evanston, Ill.

On Capitol Hill, the Republican-controlled Congress showed virtually no interest in the Social Security privatization proposal that Bush showcased in his 2005 State of the Union address. The laundry list of domestic proposals in his 2006 address on Jan. 31 seems to have been forgotten within a matter of days.

Instead, the major news from Capitol Hill in February has been the tough grilling administered to Attorney General Gonzales on the electronic-surveillance program and the tongue-lashing delivered to Homeland Security Secretary Michael Chertoff from a special House committee for the bungled response to Hurricane Katrina.

American Enterprise Institute scholar Ornstein thinks resistance, even from GOP lawmakers, was inevitable. "At some point, they will have had enough," he says. "They will realize they are a majority." Still, Ornstein does not expect a direct confrontation between the White House and Congress soon. "It's going to be a while," he says.

For its part, the White House may be coming around to giving Congress a greater role on the two issues — electronic surveillance and detainees — that the administration had previously chosen to handle on its own. Bush ultimately agreed to Sen. McCain's anti-torture proposal. And the White House is signaling that it will accept some legislative fix on the electronic-surveillance program.

Bradford Berenson, a Washington lawyer who served as associate White House counsel in Bush's first term, says the administration should work with Congress on the issues. "Congress should become involved," Berenson remarked at a Feb. 16 forum at Georgetown University Law Center in Washington. "It is the right policymaker to engage with the administration."

Appearing on the same panel, Sen. Specter said both the president and the Congress need to do a better job of the separate roles that each has in the constitutional order. "He's got to tell us more in a democracy," Specter said, "and the Congress has to be a lot more assertive than it has been." ■

About the Author

Associate Editor **Kenneth Jost** graduated from Harvard College and Georgetown University Law Center. He is the author of the *Supreme Court Yearbook* and editor of *The Supreme Court from A to Z* (both *CQ Press*). He was a member of the *CQ Researcher* team that won the 2002 ABA Silver Gavel Award. His recent reports include "Supreme Court's Future" and "Future of Newspapers."

Notes

[1] For *The Times'* original story, see James Risen and Eric Lichtblau, "Bush Lets U.S. Spy on Callers Without Courts," Dec. 16, 2005, p. A1. For Wilson's comments and later reaction, see Eric Lichtblau, "Republican Who Oversees N.S.A. Calls for Wiretap Inquiry," *The New York Times*, Feb. 8, 2006, p. A1, and Sheryl Gay Stolberg, "Republican Speaks Up, Leading Others to Challenge," *The New York Times*, Feb. 11, 2006, p. A1. Some background on Wilson drawn from CQ's *Politics in America* (13th ed., 2005).

[2] Cheney was interviewed on "The NewsHour with Jim Lehrer," Public Broadcasting Service, Feb. 7, 2006.

[3] See Michael A. Genovese, *The Power of the American Presidency 1789-2000* (2001).

[4] *United States v. U.S. District Court*, 407 U.S. 297 (1972). The decision is commonly called the *Keith* case after the federal district court judge whose ruling was upheld by the Supreme Court.

[5] For background, see David Masci, "Torture," *CQ Researcher*, April 18, 2003, pp. 345-368.

[6] For previous background, see Adriel Bettelheim, "Presidential Power," *CQ Researcher*, Nov. 15, 2002, pp. 945-968.

[7] Quoted in Peter Baker and Jim VandeHei, "Clash Is Latest Chapter in Effort to Widen Executive Power," *The Washington Post*, Dec. 21, 2005, p. A1.

[8] Quoted in Stolberg, *op. cit.* Bush apparently was unaware that his microphone was on and his remarks audible to reporters.

[9] For background, see Mary H. Cooper, "Privatizing the Military," *CQ Researcher*, June 25, 2004, pp. 565-588.

[10] The Aug. 1, 2002, memo signed by Jay S. Bybee, then director of the Office of Legal Counsel, can be found on FindLaw.com (http://news.findlaw.com/hdocs/docs/doj/bybee80102ltr.html. For coverage of Bybee's memo, see Dana Priest and R. Jeffrey Smith, "Memo Offered Justification for Use of Torture," *The Washington Post*, June 8, 2004, p. A1. For

coverage of similar memoranda, see Neil A. Lewis and Eric Schmitt, "Lawyers Decided Ban on Torture Didn't Bind Bush," *The New York Times*, June 23, 2004, p. A1.

[11] For Bush's signing statement, see *Weekly Compilation of Presidential Documents*, Jan. 2, 2006, pp. 1918-1919. For coverage, see two articles by Charlie Savage in *The Boston Globe*: "Bush Could Bypass New Torture Ban," Jan. 4, 2006, p. A1; "3 GOP Senators Blast Bush Bid to Bypass Torture Ban," Jan. 5, 2006, A3.

[12] See Peter Baker, "President Says He Ordered Domestic NSA Spying," *The Washington Post*, Dec. 18, 2005, p. A1. For background, see Kenneth Jost, "Civil Liberties Debates," *CQ Researcher*, Oct. 24, 2003, pp. 871-894; and David Masci, "Civil Liberties in Wartime," *CQ Researcher*, Dec. 12, 2001, pp. 1017-1040.

[13] See Ronald Brownstein, "Bush's Ratings Sink, but Trust Remains," *Los Angeles Times*, Jan. 27, 2006, p. A1; CNN/*USA Today*/Gallup Poll, www.usatoday.com (posted Feb. 14, 2005).

[14] Congressional Research Service, "Statutory Procedures Under Which Congress Is To Be Informed of U.S. Intelligence Activities, Including Covert Actions," Jan. 18, 2006.

[15] The Supreme Court case is *Hamdan v. Rumsfeld*, 05-184. For court decisions, briefs and selected articles, see www.hamdanvrumsfeld.com. The D.C. Circuit cases are *Al Odah v. United States*, 05-5064, and *Boumediene v. Bush*, 05-5062.

[16] The citations are *Hamdi v. Rumsfeld*, 542 U.S. 507, and *Rasul v. Bush*, 542 U.S. 466, both June 28, 2004.

[17] The case is *Padilla v. Hanft*, 05-533. The Supreme Court had dismissed Padilla's habeas corpus petition on a procedural issue, *Rumsfeld v. Padilla*, 542 U.S. 426 (June 28, 2004), but he filed a new petition to "cure" the defect.

[18] Historical background drawn in part from Genovese, *op. cit.*, and Forrest McDonald, *The American Presidency: An Intellectual History* (1994).

[19] Woodrow Wilson, *Congressional Government* (1885), p. 31, cited in Genovese, *op. cit.*, p. 104.

[20] Arthur M. Schlesinger Jr., *The Imperial Presidency* (1973).

[21] The citation is *United States v. Nixon*, 418 U.S. 683 (1974). For background, see Kenneth Jost, "Independent Counsels Re-Examined," *CQ Researcher*, May 7, 1999, pp. 377-400.

[22] Aaron Wildavsky, *The Beleaguered Presidency* (1991); Genovese, *op. cit.* Wildavsky died in 1993.

[23] The citation is *Clinton v. Jones*, 520 U.S. 681 (1997).

[24] *Ibid.*, p. 189. See also Adriel Bettelheim, "State of the Presidency: What Bush Inherits," *CQ Weekly*, Jan. 20, 2001, p. 162.

[25] For background, see Pamela Prah, "Disaster Preparedness," *CQ Researcher*, Nov.18, 2005, pp. 981-1004.

[26] See John M. Donnelly and Anne Plummer, "After Long Fight, McCain Wins Bush's Support on Treatment of Detainees," *CQ Today*, Dec. 15, 2005.

[27] See Mary Speck, "Revamp of Spy Program Gets Boost," *CQ Today*, Feb. 16, 2006; and these Feb. 17 stories: Charles Babington and Carol D. Leonnig, "Senate Rejects Wiretapping Probe," *The Washington Post*; and Greg Miller and Maura Reynolds, "Spying Inquiry Blocked by GOP," *Los Angeles Times*.

[28] See Eric Lichtblau and Sheryl Gay Stolberg, "Accord in House to Hold Inquiry on Surveillance," *The New York Times*, Feb. 17, 2006.

[29] Cases discussed and Web sites for more information include *American Civil Liberties Union v. National Security Agency* (www.aclu.org/nsaspying); *Center for Constitutional Rights v. Bush* (www.ccr-ny.org/v2/legal/govt_misconduct/docs/NSAcomplaintFINAL11706.pdf); *Electronic Privacy Information Center v. Department of Justice* (www.epic.org); *People for the American Way Foundation v. National Security Agency* (http://media.pfaw.org/pdf/civil_liberties/PFAWFvsNSAComplaint.pdf); and *Hepting v. AT&T Corp.* (www.eff.org).

[30] Richard E. Neustadt, *Presidential Power and the Modern Presidents: The Politics of Leadership from Roosevelt to Reagan* (1990), p. ix. Neustadt died in 2003.

[31] See Dan Balz, "Bush's Midterm Challenge: Rebuilding Public Support May Bolster GOP Candidates," *The Washington Post*, Jan. 29, 2006, p. A1.

FOR MORE INFORMATION

American Civil Liberties Union, 125 Broad St., 18th floor; New York, NY 10004; (212) 549-2500; 122 Maryland Ave., N.E., Washington, DC 20002; (202) 544-1681; www.aclu.org. The ACLU filed a broad legal challenge to the warrantless electronic-surveillance program established by President Bush after the 9/11 terrorist attacks.

American Constitution Society for Law and Policy, 1333 H St., N.W., 11th Floor, Washington, DC 20005; (202) 393-6181; www.acslaw.org. A liberal educational organization focusing on preserving individual rights and liberties; co-sponsored former Vice President Al Gore's Jan. 16 speech on presidential power.

The Cato Institute, 1000 Massachusetts Ave., N.W., Washington, DC 20001; (202) 842-0200; www.cato.org. Public-policy organization that advocates limited government.

Center for Constitutional Rights, 666 Broadway, 7th floor, New York, NY 10012; (212) 614-6464; www.ccr-ny.org. Founded in 1966; has been coordinating legal representation of detainees held at the U.S. Naval Station, Guantanamo Bay, Cuba.

Center for National Security Studies, 1120 19th St., N.W., 8th floor, Washington, DC 20036; (202) 721-5650; www.cnss.org. A research and advocacy organization, founded in 1974 and now affiliated with George Washington University, that seeks to prevent claims of national security from eroding civil liberties and constitutional protections.

Center for the Study of the Presidency, 1020 19th St., N.W., Suite 250, Washington, DC 20036; (202) 872-9800; www.thepresidency.org. A nonpartisan center founded in 1979 to further the understanding and functioning of the U.S. presidency.

Federalist Society, 1015 18th St., N.W., Suite 425, Washington, DC 20036; (202) 822-8138; www.fed-soc.org. Founded in 1982 to promote conservative and libertarian views in opposition to what it saw as a dominant liberal ideology at U.S. law schools.

Heritage Foundation, 214 Massachusetts Ave., N.E., Washington DC 20002; (202) 546-4400; www.heritage.org. Founded in 1973; seeks to formulate and promote conservative public policies.

Bibliography

Selected Sources

Books

Genovese, Michael A., *The Power of the American Presidency 1789-2000*, Oxford University Press, 2001.
A professor of political science at Loyola Marymount University provides an historical overview of the growth — and limits — of presidential power with individual portraits of each chief executive from George Washington through Bill Clinton. Includes appendices, notes and an 11-page bibliography. Genovese is also co-editor with Robert J. Spitzer of *The Presidency and The Constitution: Cases and Controversies* (Palgrave Macmillan, 2005), a compilation of excerpts of major Supreme Court decisions affecting presidential powers.

McDonald, Forrest, *The American Presidency: An Intellectual History*, University Press of Kansas, 1994.
A professor emeritus at the University of Alabama describes his book as "a history of the idea of the presidency — how it was born, how it was initially implemented, how it has evolved, and what it has become through practice."

Neustadt, Richard E., *Presidential Power and the Modern Presidents: The Politics of Leadership from Roosevelt to Reagan*, Free Press, 1990.
The late professor of political science at Harvard University emphasized the personal rather than the formal aspects of presidential power in an updated version of his classic study, originally written in 1960. Includes detailed notes.

Wildavsky, Aaron, *The Beleaguered Presidency*, Transaction Publishers, 1991.
A longtime professor of political science at the University of California-Berkeley until his death in 1993 argued that Lyndon B. Johnson's presidency ushered in a period of significantly increased criticism that left him and subsequent presidents "beleaguered" — under perpetual assault. Includes brief chapter notes.

Yoo, John, *The Powers of War and Peace: The Constitution and Foreign Affairs After 9/11*, University of Chicago Press, 2005.
A law professor at the University of California-Berkeley and formerly a high-ranking Justice Department lawyer under President George W. Bush, argues that the Constitution vests "the bulk" of powers over foreign and military affairs to the president. Includes detailed notes.

On the Web

The White House's Web site is at www.whitehouse.gov. *The Weekly Compilation of Presidential Documents* can be found at www.gpoaccess.gov/wcomp/index.html. The Presidency Research Group, a section of the American Political Science Association, provides articles, bibliographies, course syllabi and other information on line at http://cstl-cla.semo.edu/Renka/prg/; the moderator is Russell Renka, a professor of political science at Southeast Missouri State University, Cape Girardeau.

Books on the Presidency From CQ Press

CQ Press publishes a number of reference works and college texts about the U.S. presidency.

Michael Nelson's comprehensive two-volume ***Guide to the Presidency*** (8th ed., 2006) provides an array of factual information about the institution and the presidents, along with analytical chapters that explain the structure and operations of the office and the president's relationship to Congress and to the Supreme Court. ***The Presidency A to Z*** (3rd ed., 2003) is a one-volume encyclopedia with more than 300 alphabetical, easy-to-read entries.

Nelson, a professor of political science at Rhodes College, is also editor of ***The Presidency and the Political System*** (8th ed., 2006), a collection of 21 essays examining presidential powers and perceptions, and co-editor with Richard Ellis of ***Debating the Presidency: Conflicting Perspectives on the Executive*** (2006), pro-con essays written as debate resolutions on a series of pivotal issues facing the modern presidency.

The Politics of the Presidency (Joseph A. Pika and John Anthony Maltese, rev. 6th ed., 2006) provides an in-depth assessment of the institution, the individuals who have served, the presidents' interactions with the public and their impact on public policy. For a substantive look at the current administration, ***The George W. Bush Presidency: Appraisals and Prospects*** (edited by Colin Campbell and Bert A. Rockman, 2004) is a collection of essays that provides measured and nuanced assessments of Bush's accomplishments, failures and frustrations at a particularly eventful time in U.S. history. For an innovative theoretical study, ***Going Public*** (Samuel Kernell, 3rd ed., 1997) examines the increasingly frequent presidential practice of appealing for support directly to the public.

The Presidents, First Ladies, and Vice Presidents: White House Biographies, 1789-2005 (Daniel C. Diller and Stephen L. Robertson, 2005) highlights the public and private lives of chief executives, their wives and their seconds-in-command. Other reference titles include ***Presidential Elections 1789-2004*** (2005), a comprehensive guide to the history and evolution of U.S. presidential elections, and ***Presidential Winners and Losers: Words of Victory and Concession*** (John Vile, 2002), a collection of more than 500 speeches and other documents from George Washington to George W. Bush relating to the outcome of elections.

The Next Step:

Additional Articles from Current Periodicals

Courts

Goldstein, Amy, and Jo Becker, "Alito Hearings Conclude," *The Washington Post*, Jan. 14, 2006, p. A3.
Confirmation hearings for Supreme Court nominee Samuel A. Alito Jr. explored his support for the "unitary executive theory," which Bush embraced to justify controversial anti-terrorism policies.

Lewis, Neil A., "Court Gives Bush Right to Detain U.S. Combatant," *The New York Times*, Sept. 10, 2005, p. A1.
A federal appeals court panel ruled that President Bush had the authority to detain American citizens as enemy combatants if they fought U.S. forces on foreign soil.

Richey, Warren, "Military Tribunals to Get a Test in Supreme Court," *The Christian Science Monitor*, Nov. 8, 2005, p. 1.
The Supreme Court will examine whether the president can try al Qaeda suspects before military commissions.

Weinstein, Henry, "Debating the Power of the Presidency," *Los Angeles Times*, Aug. 14, 2005, p. A20.
Supreme Court nominee John G. Roberts Jr. may have a big impact on executive power, probably sympathizing with presidential claims of authority.

Electronic Surveillance

"Surveillance Static," *The Houston Chronicle*, Feb. 8, 2006, p. B10.
Sen. Lindsey Graham, R-S.C., and other Republicans expressed fears about Bush's secret surveillance program.

Balz, Dan, and Claudia Deane, "Differing Views on Terrorism," *The Washington Post*, Jan. 11, 2006, p. A4.
Americans are divided sharply along partisan lines over the legitimacy of Bush's domestic eavesdropping program.

Barr, Bob, "Presidential Snooping Damages the Nation," *Time*, Jan. 9, 2006, p. 34.
Former Rep. Bob Barr, R-Ga., rejects the Bush administration's defense of its secret electronic-surveillance program.

Ebrahim, Margaret, "Warrantless Surveillance Debated During Ford Term," *The Philadelphia Inquirer*, Feb. 5, 2006, p. A10.
Debate over warrantless domestic wiretaps in terrorism investigations also erupted during the Ford administration.

Yen, Hope, "Bush Broke Law in Spying Request, Specter Says," *The Houston Chronicle*, Feb. 6, 2006, p. A6.
Sen. Arlen Specter, R-Pa., said Bush violated the Foreign Intelligence Surveillance Act when he failed to seek court approval for secret domestic surveillance.

Executive Power

Feldman, Noah, "Who Can Check the President?" *The New York Times Magazine*, Jan. 8, 2006, p. 52.
Feldman profiles the history of the presidency, the Bush administration's push to extend presidential power and the role of the Supreme Court and Congress in checking the president's power.

Stevenson, Richard W., "For This President, Power is There for the Taking," *The New York Times*, May 15, 2005, p. 3.
Stevenson says Bush has not fundamentally altered the presidency in ways that will outlast his tenure, arguing that what the president has done is a product of a particular time and place.

Wartime

Russell, Gail, "Senate Target: Bush's War Powers," *The Christian Science Monitor*, Feb. 1, 2006, p. 1.
The Republican-controlled Congress has gone along with the Bush administration's moves to aggressively expand presidential power in wartime, but that deference may be coming to an end.

Savage, David G., "The Power of the President," *Los Angeles Times*, Feb. 6, 2006, p. A10.
Bush argues the president has an "inherent authority" to act without first seeking congressional approval in wartime.

Silva, Mark, "In the Midst of Conflict, George W. Bush is Not the First to Stretch the Powers of the Executive," *Chicago Tribune*, Jan. 12, 2006, p. C1.
Bush belongs to a long line of presidents who asserted extraordinary powers in wartime, but some legal scholars and critics say he is claiming war powers like few before him.

Citing The *CQ Researcher*

Sample formats for citing these reports in a bibliography include the ones listed below. Preferred styles and formats vary, so please check with your instructor or professor.

MLA Style

Jost, Kenneth. "Rethinking the Death Penalty." The CQ Researcher 16 Nov. 2001: 945-68.

APA Style

Jost, K. (2001, November 16). Rethinking the death penalty. *The CQ Researcher, 11*, 945-968.

Chicago Style

Jost, Kenneth. "Rethinking the Death Penalty." *CQ Researcher*, November 16, 2001, 945-968.

CQ Researcher

Published by CQ Press, a division of Congressional Quarterly Inc.

thecqresearcher.com

AP and IB Programs

Can they raise U.S. high-school achievement?

The lighter side of the challenging Advanced Placement program at California's El Cajon Valley High School brightens a student.

More than 25 percent of first-year college students need remedial courses. Concern about the ability of American high-school graduates to handle college-level work has led some schools to offer Advanced Placement (AP) and International Baccalaureate (IB) programs. Engaging students in more challenging coursework appears to boost learning and achievement, although there is little research on the effects of AP and IB programs. Higher-income students are much more likely to be offered AP and IB classes or other challenging learning experiences than students from disadvantaged educational or socioeconomic backgrounds. Over the past decade, most school reform has focused on the elementary grades, but a growing number of states are now concentrating on improving the college readiness of their high-school students. But critics say the effort is wasted if younger students aren't given adequate preparation for high school.

INSIDE THIS REPORT

The CQ Researcher • March 3, 2006 • www.thecqresearcher.com
Volume 16, Number 9 • Pages 193-216

CQ PRESS

RECIPIENT OF SOCIETY OF PROFESSIONAL JOURNALISTS AWARD FOR EXCELLENCE ◆ AMERICAN BAR ASSOCIATION SILVER GAVEL AWARD

THE ISSUES

BACKGROUND

CURRENT SITUATION

OUTLOOK

SIDEBARS AND GRAPHICS

FOR FURTHER RESEARCH

Cover: The lighter side of the challenging Advanced Placement program at California's El Cajon Valley High School brightens a student. (AVID Center)

CQ Researcher

March 3, 2006
Volume 16, Number 9

MANAGING EDITOR: Thomas J. Colin

ASSISTANT MANAGING EDITOR: Kathy Koch

ASSOCIATE EDITOR: Kenneth Jost

STAFF WRITERS: Marcia Clemmitt, Peter Katel, Pamela M. Prah

CONTRIBUTING WRITERS: Rachel Cox, Sarah Glazer, David Hosansky, Patrick Marshall, Tom Price

DESIGN/PRODUCTION EDITOR: Olu B. Davis

ASSISTANT EDITOR: Melissa J. Hipolit

CQ PRESS

A Division of Congressional Quarterly Inc.

SENIOR VICE PRESIDENT/PUBLISHER: John A. Jenkins

DIRECTOR, LIBRARY PUBLISHING: Kathryn C. Suárez

DIRECTOR, EDITORIAL OPERATIONS: Ann Davies

CONGRESSIONAL QUARTERLY INC.

CHAIRMAN: Paul C. Tash

VICE CHAIRMAN: Andrew P. Corty

PRESIDENT/EDITOR IN CHIEF: Robert W. Merry

CQ Researcher (ISSN 1056-2036) is printed on acid-free paper. Published weekly, except March 24, July 7, July 14, Aug. 4, Aug. 11, Nov. 24, Dec. 22 and Dec. 29, by CQ Press, a division of Congressional Quarterly Inc. Annual full-service subscriptions for institutions start at $667. For pricing, call 1-800-834-9020, ext. 1906. To purchase a *CQ Researcher* report in print or electronic format (PDF), visit www.cqpress.com or call 866-427-7737. Single reports start at $10. Bulk purchase discounts and electronic-rights licensing are also available. Periodicals postage paid at Washington, D.C., and additional mailing offices. POSTMASTER: Send address changes to *CQ Researcher*, 1255 22nd St., N.W., Suite 400, Washington, DC 20037.

AP and IB Programs

BY MARCIA CLEMMITT

THE ISSUES

In Pflugerville, Texas, outside Austin, high-school senior Joshua Garza gets a $5 gift card every time he attends an after-class review session for his Advanced Placement (AP) calculus class. If he passes the standardized exam in May, he'll receive $100, and possible college credit. * And his calculus teacher will get an extra $100 for each student who passes. [1]

Garza has taken five AP classes in high school, but so far he has tried only one exam, which he didn't pass. But he's not in it for the money or even the college credit; he wanted the challenge. "AP classes prepare me for more rigorous classes in college," he said. They teach "discipline and time management, which are skills I need." [2]

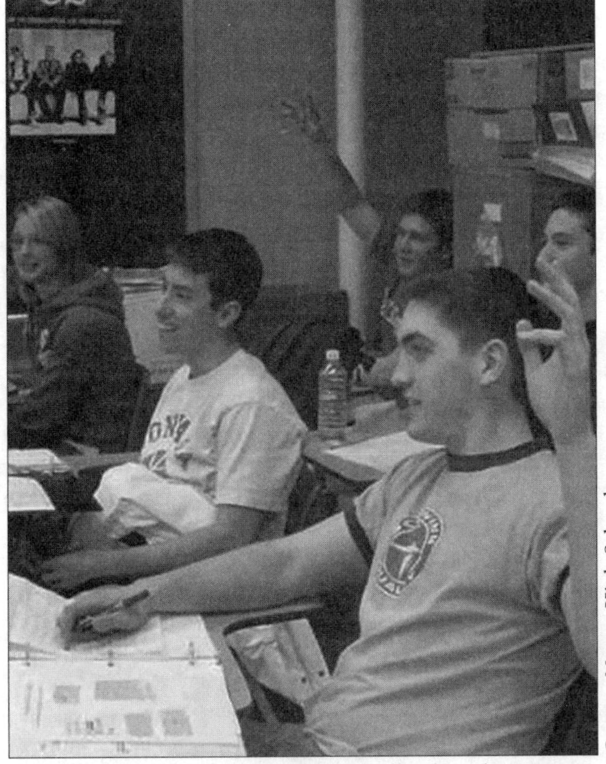

George Mason High School

George Mason High School, in Falls Church, Va., is among more than 450 U.S. schools that offer International Baccalaureate diplomas. Research shows that challenging coursework improves student achievement, but little data specifically shows the effects of IB and AP programs. Rigorous academic programs are far more likely to be offered to affluent rather than disadvantaged students, though increasing numbers of minority students are taking AP courses.

An anonymous donor provided a $1 million grant for Pflugerville's AP incentives, but many other communities get help as well in drumming up interest in advanced high-school programs like AP and the International Baccalaureate (IB), which is typically offered to 11th and 12th graders. **

In fact, encouraging greater enrollment in such programs is one of the hottest new trends in secondary education. Over the past four summers, for example, a group of businesses in Greensboro, N.C., helped the Guilford County School District award four cars, 20 laptop computers and nearly two-dozen $1,500 scholarships to AP students. Last year's winner of a new car — Laura St. Cyr, a freshman at North Carolina's Elon University — was eligible because she passed five or more AP tests. [3]

Arkansas, Florida, South Carolina and Florida are among the states that have recently begun paying students to take AP exams. [4] A 2004 Arkansas law requires all high schools to offer either the IB diploma or AP courses in four major subject areas by 2008. A 2005 Minnesota law authorizes full or partial state payment of exam fees for all public and private students, and a 2005 Texas law requires universities and colleges to offer credit for IB and AP.

The efforts appear to be paying off: In the last five years the number of students taking AP exams swelled from about 400,000 to more than 600,000. And while only 479 U.S. schools offer IB diplomas, that figure is up from less than 400 three years ago — a 20 percent increase. (A total of 610 American schools offer some part of the IB program, which includes a K-10 curriculum.) [5]

But fundamental questions remain: Will getting students to take AP and IB classes rescue public schools from mediocrity, as many educators and public officials hope? Or will bright kids from affluent families be the main beneficiaries?

Since 1992, the federal Advanced Placement Incentive Program has provided federal grants for AP programs, particularly to encourage lower-income students to participate. In his recently released annual budget proposal, President Bush calls for training 70,000 new teachers of AP and IB math and science courses.

Such efforts are needed, say AP and IB enthusiasts, because high schools are a weak link in the U.S. education system. For example, on the 2003 Trends in International Mathematics and Science Survey (TIMSS), U.S. fourth-graders did better on the math test than fourth-graders in countries ranging from Australia and Norway to the Slovak Republic

---

* Grading is on a 1-5 scale, with 1 equivalent to an F, 3 equal to a C and 5 equal to an A. Many universities give college credit for high-school AP courses if the student scores at least a 3 on an AP final exam.

** Internationally accepted IB diplomas are awarded to students who pass written and oral exams and submit a lengthy research paper after completing an intense, two-year, comprehensive curriculum.

High-School Graduation Requirements Lag

Only 10 states had high-school graduation requirements that matched the course requirements for admission to public universities in their states. Twenty-eight states had no alignment.

Alignment Between Requirements for High-School Graduation and College Admission*

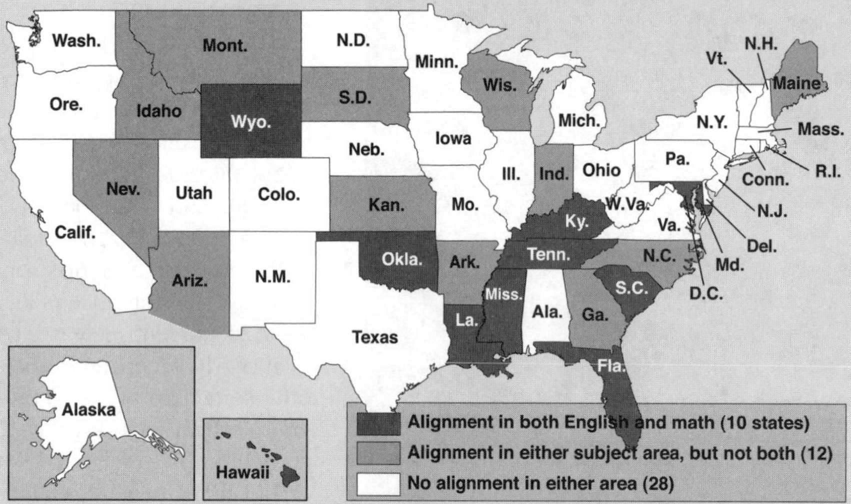

* *Based on the number of courses required by high schools and state colleges/universities*

Source: American Association of State Colleges and Universities, February 2005

and Sweden. But by age 15 the tables had turned, with students in those countries outscoring U.S. students on the math portion of the 2003 Program for International Student Assessment (PISA). [6]

American high schools have fallen behind in preparing students for college and work, according to a survey of 1,487 recent, public high-school graduates, 400 employers and 300 college faculty members. Among the graduates, 39 percent of those in college and 39 percent of those in the work force said there were significant gaps in their high-school preparation. And 46 percent of the workers said they lacked preparation for jobs they hoped to get in the future. [7]

Among the employers, 41 percent were dissatisfied with the ability of graduates to understand complicated materials. Overall, only 18 percent of the professors thought most of their students were "extremely" or "very well" prepared for college, but the percentage dropped to 7 percent at two-year colleges. Overall, professors said half of the high-school graduates aren't prepared to do college-level math or college-level writing. [8]

Advocates argue that AP and IB programs can improve learning for low-achieving as well as above-average students. "Many communities have found that adding AP really turns a school around," according to education reporter Jay Mathews, originator of the Challenge Index. Published by *Newsweek*, it ranks school quality based on the proportion of students who take AP and IB tests. [9] Moreover, he adds, AP and IB courses "give average students a chance to experience the trauma of heavy college reading lists and difficult college examinations." [10]

Even students who only scored a 2 on their AP exam "come back from college and tell me they did really well in freshman English because they'd been so well prepared," said Michael Watkins, guidance director at W. T. White High School in Dallas. [11]

Preliminary research at DePaul University shows that IB programs may prepare disadvantaged students well for college, says Brian Spittle, the school's assistant vice president for enrollment management. After tracking the progress of 44 Chicago IB graduates enrolled at DePaul, the university found that 97 percent went on to enroll as sophomores after completing the freshman year, compared to 85 percent of freshmen overall. The IB students also had a slightly higher college GPA — 3.1 compared to 3.0 for all freshmen — and took a heavier courseload: 15 hours per quarter, on average, compared to the 13-hour average.

Those results are especially striking given the socioeconomic background of the IB students, says Spittle. Of the IB group, 79 percent are eligible for federal Pell grants for low-income students, compared to 24 percent of DePaul freshmen. Twenty-seven percent of the IB students — but only 7 percent of DePaul freshmen overall — are African-American, and 39 percent are Hispanic, compared to 13 percent overall. Sixty-six percent of the IB students are first-generation collegians, compared to 33 percent of all DePaul freshmen. [12]

But many researchers warn against viewing AP and IB as a panacea for what ails U.S. education. "I don't know what you're smoking" if you see AP "as a massive solution," says Michael Kirst, an education professor at Stanford University. AP was intended to provide college-level classes for advanced students likely to attend selective colleges, he points out. Rather than more AP courses, he says, most students need more college-preparatory work to ready them for the expectations of the two-year community colleges and four-year regional universities that most high-school graduates attend, he says.

Meanwhile, unchallenging courses and lack of college readiness remain a big problem, says Kirst, who heads Stanford's Bridge Project to improve the transition from high school to college. "We have not increased significantly our graduation rate" from four-year colleges, and "tons" of new college students end up in remedial courses rather than credit-bearing classes, he says.

But simply injecting more challenging coursework in the upper grades will leave far too many high-school students behind, says Samuel Stringfield, co-director of the Nystrand Center of Excellence in Education at the University of Louisville. Particularly hard-hit will be low-income and minority students, who need more — and earlier — help to succeed, Stringfield says.

Furthermore, many educators point out, the most devastating high-school achievement gaps involve dropouts and students who barely achieve literacy — often from the most disadvantaged neighborhoods. Offering more challenging courses to high-school students may increase college attendance rates for "borderline kids," says Stringfield, but it won't affect the dropout rate "for kids in trouble."

What clearly makes the most difference in raising high-school achievement is attending a rigorous middle school, Stringfield argues. "So, is AP the answer?" he asks. "No, it's better middle-school programs," coupled with external supports like tutoring. "If you want to see [AP] fail and become last year's fad, try it by itself."

As educators and lawmakers struggle to create high schools for the 21st century, here are some of the questions they are considering:

Number of AP Exam Takers Rose

Twenty-three percent of the U.S. high-school students who graduated in 2005 took an AP exam at some point in high school, compared with 16 percent in 2000. The percentage that received a score of 3 or better (equal to a "C" on a scale of 1-5) rose from 10.2 percent of all high-school graduates in 2000 to 14.3 percent in 2005.

Participation in AP by Schools in U.S.

Public schools	11,498
Non-public schools	3,075
Avg. no. of AP courses offered:	8

Total high-school graduates who took an AP exam during high school

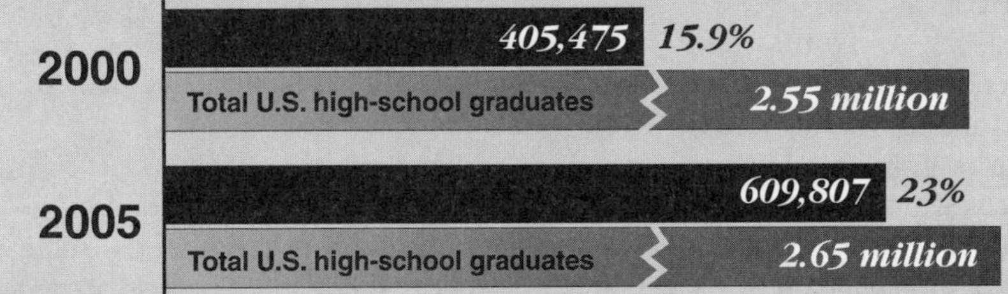

Total high-school graduates who earned a 3 or higher on an AP exam

Source: The College Board, "Advanced Placement: Report to the Nation 2006"

Are AP and IB programs effective?

When judged on whether they achieve the goals for which they were designed, both AP and IB programs generally get good marks. AP courses provide college-level curricula, and graduates who score high enough on the final exam usually receive college credit for their AP work. Likewise, IB graduates end up with a diploma that satisfies pre-college requirements at selective universities around the world.

Some educators question, however, whether IB, and particularly AP, courses succeed in improving high schools across the board, which is the reason many high schools are now using them. For example, AP's presumably college-level work has become a standard substitute for other college-preparatory courses in many schools. But critics worry that the switch may shortchange rank-and-file students on the college preparation they really need. IB programs get less criticism on these grounds because they are designed as college-prep — not college-level — courses, although some colleges offer credit for completing the IB diploma.

Getty Images/Paul J. Richards

President Bush greets AP students at the School of Science and Engineering at Yvonne A. Ewell Townview Magnet Center in Dallas. Bush's new budget proposal calls for training 70,000 AP and IB math and science teachers.

AP courses, however, are presumably advanced enough to gain credit at selective colleges. Yet most high-school college-prep courses lag far behind the skill levels needed to succeed at even the local community college, says Stanford's Kirst. Before schools replace their college-prep courses with AP, they should figure out what level of college prep is needed for regional universities and local community colleges and then design their college-prep courses to meet those needs, Kirst says. (*See map, p. 196.*)

Robert Sternberg, a Tufts University psychologist who studies learning, agrees. Adopting AP just because it's there — before figuring out what schools want to accomplish — is a cart-before-the-horse approach, he says.

But Aaron Pallas, a professor of the sociology of education at Columbia University Teachers' College, praises AP and IB courses for being tied to curricula developed by subject-matter experts rather than by individual teachers. Thus, the programs are more likely to serve broad, significant educational goals, he says, and the standards and syllabi are public so educators can see if the courses "reflect the competencies we want students to master."

Moreover, standard AP and IB exams, which are devised and graded by people outside of a student's school, change the dynamic in classrooms for the better, says John Bishop, an associate professor of human resource studies at Cornell University. [13] In other classes, students typically tell the teacher, " 'Hey, let's have an enjoyable class. We can't really do all this work you're assigning,' " says Bishop. And in many cases "teachers cave in."

However, when demanding external tests loom on the horizon, suddenly, teachers, parents and students are "all on one team, trying to prove that they can live up to the standard," he says. The shift is especially pronounced in low-income neighborhoods, he says, where schools want to show that their ability to achieve should not be underestimated.

Such external assessments are also usually better than individual teachers' exams, says Bishop, noting that high-school exams devised by teachers are "pretty awful," mainly testing memorization and seldom calling on students to integrate information and ideas. But a National Research Council report had the same complaint about AP and IB math and science courses, pointing out many AP and IB syllabi push teachers to cover so many topics that shallow memorization too often replaces deep understanding. [14]

In addition, said Lawrence Weschler, director of the New York Institute of the Humanities, judging from his daughter's AP experience in European history and English, some AP courses may encourage too much cramming for the test. "The kids got very involved in the causes of World War I and wanted to talk about it, but the teacher said they couldn't because they had to move on and cover all the material for the test." And in AP English, he complained, her poetry unit assignment was to do little more than devise two multiple-choice questions about a poem that might be used on the test. [15]

But the IB program, insists Carol Solomon, who heads both the AP and IB programs at Richard Montgomery High School, in Rockville, Md., encourages students to take a full range of pre-college courses. It's "an integrated program that does not just say to students, 'Take advanced college work,' " she says.

Also on the positive side, the National Research Council said the AP and IB programs challenge students and represent the higher expectations that high schools should promote. In particular, the IB curriculum's required two-year Theory of Knowledge seminar fosters "metacognition" — the practice of monitoring one's own learning, the panel pointed out. Research shows that strong metacognitive skills "are characteristics of experts in any field, as well as of school-age learners," the report said. [16]

The Theory of Knowledge course "helps students become critical thinkers and readers, which should prepare them for anything college throws at them," says Robert Snee, principal of George Mason High School in Falls Church, Va., which has had an IB program since the early 1980s. "We like to think of it as a total package that prepares students better for college than anything else," he says.

AP may be another matter, however, say some researchers. "I'm increasingly convinced that AP is doing a great job at its original role" — allowing a few advanced kids who are already bored with high-school-level work to earn college credit — says Kristin Klopfenstein, an assistant professor of economics at Texas Christian University, in Fort Worth. But AP courses are now widely viewed as standard college-prep courses. "And I am not at all convinced that AP is doing a good job of preparing kids for the rigors of college.

"It's important that we remember that AP courses are college level," she continues. They "throw you in the deep end" rather than preparing you to swim there.

Louisville's Stringfield says that while anything that increases the opportunity to learn is "at least vaguely going in the right direction," some schools adopt AP to make them look good, without actually changing what and how they teach or figuring out what best suits students' needs. "Some schools just put a fancier name on the same old, same old," he says.

U.S. High-School Graduation Rate Lags

At least 90 percent of the high-school students in six nations graduated in 2005 compared with only 73 percent in the United States.

Country	Graduation Rate
1. Germany	97%
2. Greece	96
3. Norway	92
4. Ireland	91
5. Japan	91
6. Switzerland	90
7. Czech Republic	88
8. Hungary	87
9. Denmark	86
10. Poland	86
11. Finland	84
12. France	81
12. Italy	81
14. Iceland	79
15. Sweden	76
16. United States	73
17. Luxembourg	71
18. Spain	67
19. Slovak Republic	56
20. Turkey	41

Source: Organization for Economic Cooperation and Development, 2005

Should AP and IB be more broadly available?

Most educators say all students who want to earn early college credit should have the chance to do so. But critics are concerned that broadening AP access both dilutes the program and encourages schools to neglect their responsibility to make the rest of the curriculum as challenging as possible for all students.

But AP is not necessarily out of reach for most college-bound students, says Cornell's Bishop. "People have the impression that it's beyond the pale" to propose an AP standard for college-bound students generally, he says. But AP exam requirements are similar to regular graduation requirements in most industrialized countries, including France, Canada and the Netherlands, he says, proving that AP-level courses should not be viewed as "only achievable by the most intelligent students."

AP may seem out of reach to many Americans in part because U.S. middle and high schools lag so far behind world standards, says Bishop. "We lose a lot of ground in the period between the end of eighth grade and the end of high school." But in a globally competitive world, "if you want to have a population of young Americans who compare with Europe and East Asia, then you need as many students as possible" taking courses like AP, Bishop says.

Critics complain, however, that schools around the country seem to be focusing more on getting the maximum number of students into AP courses than on improving teaching overall — a trend that hurts AP as well as non-AP students. "In my four sections of AP English, about 40 percent of the 96 students do not have the motivation and/or the ability to do the work and are making it difficult for me to push the other half to their limits," said Patrick Welsh, a veteran English teacher at T. C. Williams High School in Alexandria, Va., and occasional newspaper columnist on education. "If we had a traditional college-prep course for those who are having difficulty, they would learn much more than they are learning now sitting in my AP course." [17]

"The basic mission of schools" is "to take their students and stretch them as far as possible," he said. "The number of kids taking AP tests is but one tiny measure of whether a school fulfills that mission." [18]

Today, many students try to take as many AP courses as possible, starting as early as possible. The trend has been driven by college admissions policies that favor students with AP courses on their transcripts and high schools that weight AP courses much more heavily when they compute grade-point averages. (*See sidebar, p. 208.*)

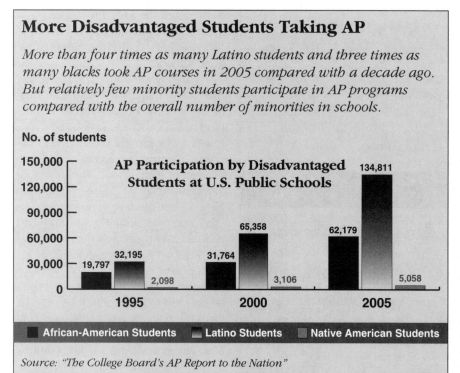

More Disadvantaged Students Taking AP

More than four times as many Latino students and three times as many blacks took AP courses in 2005 compared with a decade ago. But relatively few minority students participate in AP programs compared with the overall number of minorities in schools.

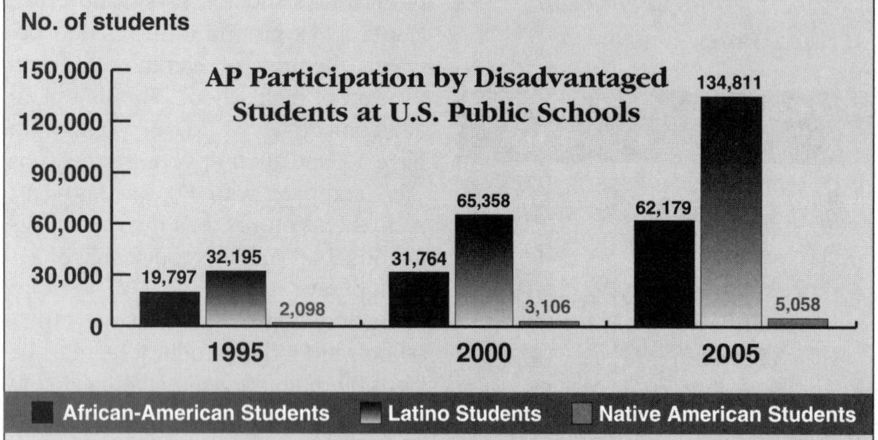

AP Participation by Disadvantaged Students at U.S. Public Schools

No. of students

Year	African-American Students	Latino Students	Native American Students
1995	19,797	32,195	2,098
2000	31,764	65,358	3,106
2005	62,179	134,811	5,058

Source: "The College Board's AP Report to the Nation"

Philosophy Professor William Casement, founder of the Great Books program at Minnesota's University of St. Thomas, fears the trend undermines the original mission of AP programs — offering college-level work to advanced students. "Originally, AP was for high-school seniors," wrote Casement. "Today 11th-, 10th- and ninth-graders comprise between 40 and 50 percent of AP students."

As a result, he notes, many students skip non-AP courses and go straight to AP. "Readiness for college study requires intellectual growth and a maturation process," Casement contends. "How many 15- and 16-year-olds are truly ready?"

Some researchers argue that even "gifted" students often don't mesh well with AP and IB courses. A study led by Professor Carolyn Callahan of the University of Virginia's Curry School of Education found that many AP and IB classes use a one-size-fits-all teaching strategy best suited for memorization whizzes who learn well in lecture classes.

Based on surveys and site visits to 15 schools in four states, Callahan and her colleagues concluded that most IB and AP classes are "dominated by lectures, rapid-fire discussions and heavy reliance on motivated students taking initiative." Students who take the classes "accept and expect 'one-size-fits-all' learning," and "appear to believe these instructional approaches are the most efficient methods for covering a large amount of content in a short period of time," said Callahan's group. [19]

After an expanded survey of 22 high schools in nine states, Callahan again concluded that current AP and IB courses do not accommodate the varied learning styles even of many gifted students. "The rigidity of the programs" discourages teachers from accommodating a broad ranger of learners, the researchers said. "Unique students meet with resistance and cognitive dissonance" from teachers and fellow students.

To accommodate a broader range of AP and IB learners, they said teachers must "recognize that 'modifying' does not equal 'dumbing down.' " But such problems are solvable, say other educators, and opening the highest level of education to a broad swath of high-schoolers is worth the extra effort. [20]

In Washington state's Bellevue School District, pushing AP enrollment has driven up academic achievement schoolwide, says Superintendent Michael Riley. "The mission of the Bellevue School District is to give every student the kind of education traditionally reserved for America's elite class, [which] will allow the student to graduate from college, not just be admitted to college," Riley wrote. "Nationwide only about 25 percent of our high-school students receive this kind of education." An elite, college-prep curriculum would include four years of English, four years of math, three years of lab science, three years of social studies, at least two years of a world language and one or more AP or IB courses. [21]

Research shows that a challenging high-school curriculum is the best predictor of whether a student will graduate from college, says Riley. But, unlike Europe, the United States does not make AP or IB programs available universally but doles them out to the kids who "qualify," or to those "savvy enough to request it," he adds. "In our district, we believe all students can be AP or IB students" if they receive good teaching, strong elementary- and middle-school preparation and adequate supports like tutoring. [22]

Riley says Bellevue's results speak for themselves: In last year's 1,000-member senior class, 84 percent completed at least one AP or IB course, and 44 percent completed four or more. Even more impressive, 68 percent of seniors from low-income neighborhoods and 82 percent of those taking English as a second language took at least one AP or IB course. [23]

Can advanced high-school courses close the achievement gap?

Proponents of expanding AP and IB accessibility say it will raise achievement for all students, reducing the achievement gap between advantaged and disadvantaged students. But others say the worst gaps begin in elementary and middle school, and that adding advanced-level high-school courses won't answer those students' needs.

American middle-school and high-school students overall show mediocre achievement in international comparisons, but "huge gaps . . . continue to leave the children of low-income, African-American and Latino families" far behind even their lagging American peers, said Kati Haycock, director of the nonprofit Education Trust. Citing statistics that she calls "potentially devastating" for both the students and the country, Haycock noted that while one-fifth to one-quarter of white and Asian students leave high school without learning "basic" math skills, one-half to two-thirds of Latino and African-Americans "suffer the same fate." [24]

Large dropout rates among African-American and Hispanic students continue to plague the U.S. education system. Each year 1.3 million students drop out before graduation — producing a U.S. graduation rate far lower than in Europe. In addition, studies show that dropouts earn less, on average, than those with high-school diplomas, and their job prospects are significantly curtailed, says Bob Wise, a former West Virginia governor who heads the nonprofit Alliance for Excellent Education.

Cornell's Bishop says pulling up a school's achievement by increasing enrollment in advanced classes works better than trying to push from below using minimum-competency tests, which penalizes high failure rates.

Minimum competency seeks to set a minimum standard, achieve it and keep raising the bar, Bishop explains. But the method backfires if the initial standard is too high, he says, risking increased dropouts among those who fail the tests.

"Some schools try to set up [minimum competency] tests so that you get huge failure rates," hoping that teachers and students will rise to the stiff challenge, Bishop says. But then teachers end up "teaching to the test," which does not lead to excellence because test questions aim at the low end of what students should achieve.

On the other hand, encouraging more students to try AP and IB tests pulls the whole school's achievement up gradually, Bishop argues, as teachers aim their instruction at the higher standard, and a growing number of students learn that they can achieve more.

Richard Montgomery's Solomon agrees. Her school's muscular AP and IB programs have made the school "a place where committed teachers come and stay," she says. IB students are selected competitively — about 800 apply each year for 100 slots — but since IB teachers must also teach non-IB courses, she points out, instructional "best practices" promulgated by the International Baccalaureate Organization reach all students. "Once you start building that critical mass," the belief "that school is a place for learning . . . affects almost every child."

"You won't find a school that's had IB for three years or more that will say the program didn't affect the whole school," echoes Snee of George Mason, where IB teachers also teach non-IB. The program "raises the bar for students generally." Only about 10 percent of George Mason's students come from disadvantaged households, but Snee says he "absolutely" would initiate IB if he headed a school in a low-income area.

In the past decade, South Side High School, in Rockville Centre, Long Island, has attacked the achievement gap by pushing students into ever-more challenging classes, with a focus on IB, says Principal Carol Burris.

"Higher achievement follows from a more rigorous curriculum," writes Burris. And since African-American and Hispanic students are consistently over-represented in lower-track classes, "a highly proficient student from a low socioeconomic background has only a 50-50 chance" of being placed in a higher track with more challenging classes, she writes. [25]

"We are very careful" to maintain a [balanced] student mix in each course section, Burris points out. As a result, all students' performance on the New York state Regents' exams has improved, and there has been a "dramatic" narrowing of the achievement gap, according to Burris. [26]

Many Students Need Remedial Courses

More than a quarter of the first-year college students in two-year and four-year institutions need remediation in reading, writing or mathematics.

First-Year College Students Requiring Remedial Courses

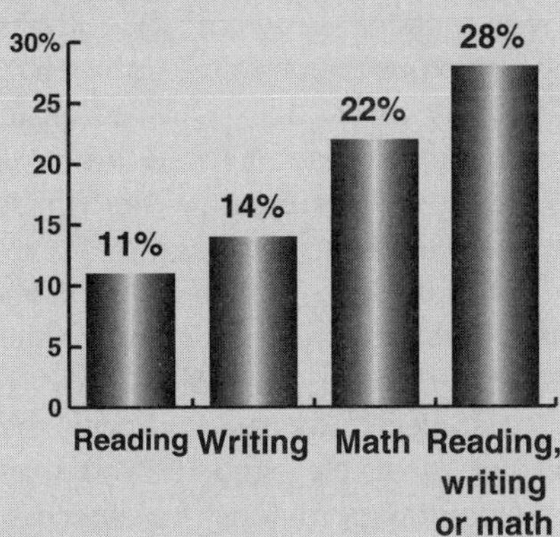

Source: "The Expectations Gap: A 50-State Review of High School Graduation Requirements," Achieve, Inc., 2004.

In 2000, 88 percent of the school's white and Asian students but only 32 percent of the African-American and Hispanic graduates earned Regents diplomas, which are awarded for passing at least eight end-of-course exams covering major subject areas. By 2003, 82 percent of African-American and Hispanic seniors and 97 percent of whites and Asians earned diplomas. [27]

When South Side began detracking, it also dropped AP classes in favor of IB, which Burriss calls the "new frontier" for raising schoolwide achievement. More and more students began choosing IB, and Burris now envisions a future when the upper grades are IB-only. About half the students aim for the full IB diploma, and as enrollments have risen IB scores have not declined.

But even at a suburban, middle-class school like South Side, with about one-fifth African-American and Hispanic students and 13 percent of students from disadvantaged homes, considerable extra effort is needed to help students manage challenging work. [28] Teachers give extra-help periods daily, and "every other day we have support classes," Burris says.

But, she contends, if the school wanted to switch to IB-only in the upper grades, teachers will have to work harder at differentiating instruction to suit different learners. "We talk about cooperative learning, multiple intelligences, tiering assignments with readings at different reading levels on the same topic," she explains. "That's hard stuff. It's going to take us some years to really get that right."

To succeed, teachers must have an "instinctual understanding that the playing field is not level for all children," says Burris. Luckily, she says, her faculty tend to be "reformers at heart."

Other supports are also needed, such as tutoring and giving students information about college standards and life. That's the philosophy of AVID — Advancement Via Individual Achievement — a California-based nonprofit that establishes school-based programs around the country. "Rigor without support is a recipe for failure," says AVID Communications Director Adam Behar.

The group helps establish advanced courses in schools where most students come from non-college-going families, and achievement expectations are low. "We start with the position that all students — with very few exceptions — are capable of taking a rigorous courseload," says Behar. "One way to do that" is to enroll in challenging courses like IB and AP, "but they need support — and that's often the missing piece."

But AVID doesn't claim its programs can directly raise achievement for the lowest-performing or most disadvantaged students. We succeed with the "average, invisible" student who may have low expectations for success. "We're really good at turning 1.8-to-2.5 GPAs into 3-to-3.5 GPAs," says Behar. Nevertheless, he notes, AVID schools experience "a kind of ripple effect" when going to college suddenly becomes "kind of cool."

However, other researchers say that with education money tight, it is short-sighted to focus too much on AP and IB if it siphons resources from earlier interventions or lower-achieving students. Pushing AP and IB too hard puts the cart before the horse because many students lack the necessary preparation, says Eric Hanushek, a senior fellow at the Hoover Institution, a conservative think tank based at Stanford University. The most important first step may be to improve the quality of instruction, particularly in the early grades.

"AP is expensive to institute," agrees Texas Christian University's Klopfenstein. "You take teachers away and give them a small class. I would much rather see the money spent on early intervention."

Even though the biggest achievement gap exists among minority and low-income students, resources for those students remain scarcest in many states, according to a new report by the Education Trust. In 27 of 49 states, the highest-poverty school districts spent $907 less per student in 2005 than the richest districts. [29] Nationwide, districts that enrolled the most students of color spent $614 less per student than districts with the least minority students. "The result is that children who have less in their personal lives end up with less in . . . their lives spent as students preparing to be educated citizens," says the Trust. The spending gaps have been "effectively unchanged over the six years" the group has tracked education funding.

Fewer resources mean fewer academically challenging courses for low-income and minority students, according to a new report by Clifford Adelman, a senior research analyst at the U.S. Department of Education who in 1999 discovered a strong link between challenging high-school curricula and college graduation rates. The "academic intensity" of a student's high-school curriculum still counts more than anything else "in providing momentum toward completing a bachelor's degree," he writes in an updated version of his original analysis, "Answers in the Toolbox." But low-income and minority students have much less chance to encounter high-level academic courses, he writes. [30] ■

BACKGROUND

It's Not Academic

Low interest in challenging academics has long been a feature of

Continued on p. 204

Chronology

1950s-1970s

Public high schools increasingly offer a cafeteria-style curriculum, with many non-academic options and less college-prep emphasis. States establish "minimum-competency" tests for high-school students. The Advanced Placement (AP) program is launched for gifted students, while the International Baccalaureate (IB) program is developed to provide an international university-entrance diploma.

1951
United Nations Educational, Scientific and Cultural Organization founds the International Schools' Association (ISA) to develop curricula and teaching methods to advance international understanding.

1956
The first AP tests are given.

1963
ISA receives a grant to develop a common curriculum and exam program that would meet the admissions requirements of any university in the world.

1970
The first IB diploma exams are given. Twenty schools worldwide have IB programs.

1980s-1990s

U.S. middle-school and high-school students fall behind international students. As efforts to establish national curricular standards lag, states begin establishing new graduation requirements and standards. AP and IB enrollments increase.

1983
"A Nation at Risk" report calls for a more challenging high-school curriculum.

1992
Congress establishes Advanced Placement Fee Payment Program to subsidize exam fees for low-income students.

1995
The first Trends in International Mathematics and Science Study (TIMSS) is released. Successive TIMSS reports through 2003 show that U.S. students score well as fourth-graders, fall to average by middle school and are among the lowest performers by the end of high school. . . . States nationwide begin drafting statewide academic standards.

1998
Congress renames AP fee-subsidy program the Advanced Placement Incentive Program, adding grants for states to train teachers to offer AP in low-income schools. . . . *Newsweek* publishes first "Challenge Index" listing the 100 U.S. high schools with the highest number of AP and IB tests taken compared to the number of seniors in the school.

1999
"Answers in the Toolbox" study by Education Department analyst Clifford Adelman shows that taking difficult high-school courses, such as trigonometry or calculus, is the surest indicator that a student will graduate from college. . . . American Civil Liberties Union files a class-action lawsuit charging that California provides unequal access to AP courses for minority students.

2000s

No Child Left Behind (NCLB) law expands federal influence on education, but high schools still are exempt from most requirements. Federal government and states strengthen incentives to broaden access to AP and IB. States look to align high-school graduation standards with college admission requirements.

2002
President Bush signs NCLB law requiring high schools to employ only "highly qualified" teachers and to administer state achievement tests to all students at least once during grades 10 to 12.

2005
Congress rejects Bush's bid to extend nationally required annual testing through high school. . . . Minnesota requires state colleges to give college credit to high-scoring AP and IB students; Colorado adds AP and IB measures to high-school accreditation standards; Tennessee urges governor to fund statewide AP expansion; 13 states form the American Diploma Project Network and pledge to align high-school standards with skills and knowledge needed for college.

2006
Congress raises hackles in some states when it passes budget bill allowing the secretary of Education to certify certain high-school curricula "rigorous" enough for their low-income graduates to be eligible for new Academic Competitiveness Grants. Bill authors explain that they are not authorizing the federal government to set high-school curriculum standards. . . . College Board launches audit program to ensure that AP courses meet quality standards.

'Bored' Students Sparked AP Program

Advanced Placement (AP) courses were launched in the early 1950s by educators worried that bright but bored students might drop out of high school, depleting the nation's pool of academic talent.

The Ford Foundation-sponsored pilot program featured 12 secondary schools and 12 colleges offering college credit based on high-school students' test scores in any of 11 academic areas. [1]

The exams were "open to any able high-school student, wherever he may be and whether he achieved his knowledge through his own efforts, through tutorial assistance, or by taking special courses." In the 1955-56 school year, the nonprofit College Board took over management of AP testing. In 1956, 1,229 students from 110 high schools took 2,199 exams; the group attended 138 different colleges that September, although nearly half enrolled at five elite schools — Harvard, Yale, Princeton, Cornell and the Massachusetts Institute of Technology. [2]

In the 1960s, The College Board began offering summer training workshops to AP teachers at universities. By 2005 students could take AP tests in 34 subject areas.

The number of students taking AP exams has risen quickly in recent years. In the graduating class of 2005, around 610,000 of the nation's 2.7 million high-school seniors — or 23 percent — had taken at least one AP exam. That's up from 15.9 percent — 405,000 — of seniors in the class of 2000. Altogether, 2005 graduates took more than 1.5 million individual AP exams. [3] The most popular exams in 2005 were U.S. history (207,817 test takers), English literature and composition (203,697), English language and composition (162,357), AB calculus — the easier of two calculus options ((141,732), U.S. government and politics (103,224) and biology (88,223), according to The College Board.

Individual colleges determine how much, if any, credit is offered, based on a range of possible scores from 1 to 5. A score of 3 generally is considered equivalent to a C in an introductory college-level course. Scores of 3, 4, or 5 typically earn credit, although only less selective colleges offer credit for 3s.

In recent years, a few highly selective colleges have severely limited the credit they offer for AP courses. Harvard, for example, generally requires a 5 for credit and doesn't offer any credit for some tests, such as the U.S. government and politics exam.

In 2005, 14.3 percent of graduates scored 3 or higher on at least one exam, compared with 10.2 percent in 2000. [4]

In response to concerns that AP's growing popularity has led schools to simply relabel courses with the AP name, The College Board in early 2006 launched an audit system. Beginning with the 2007-08 school year, AP designations will be officially granted only to courses that have passed the audit, which includes an evaluation of the course syllabi, method of instruction and other factors.

Rise of the International Baccalaureate Program

The International Baccalaureate program has its roots in the "international education" movement that began in the early 1950s. That's when the United Nations Educational, Scientific and Cultural Organization (UNESCO) established the International Schools' Association (ISA) to find practical curricula and teaching methods that would "enhance international understanding." [5]

In 1963, ISA received a grant to develop a common curriculum and exam program that could meet admission requirements for any university in the world, mainly to serve students such as diplomats' children who lived abroad with their families. [6]

While AP courses were created to help individual students meet their educational goals, true to its UNESCO roots, the IB program has broader aims.

Three main principles underlie IB education, according to the International Baccalaureate Organization (IBO), in Geneva, Switzerland:

- providing a broad general education that includes the basic knowledge and thinking skills secondary students will need to pursue university studies;
- giving students a "balanced," well-rounded curriculum while allowing some individual choice in what to study; and

Continued from p. 202

American high schools, according to some historians. [31] "Since at least the 1930s, the function of high schools for many, many students has been primarily custodial," says Jeffrey Mirel, a professor of educational studies and history at the University of Michigan.

High-school enrollment has risen dramatically over the past century or so, swelling from 6 percent of the nation's 14- to 17-year-olds in 1890 to 92.2 percent by 1970. During much of the 20th century, economic conditions made it desirable to keep as many teens as possible in school and out of the job market, which Mirel says helped to lower academic standards. [32]

Since the late 19th century, the nation has "been fighting about whether our high schools should be college prep for the masses or . . . a 'cafeteria-style curriculum' " in which time-in-seat is the primary criterion for a diploma, even if the time is mostly spent in nonacademic classes like home economics and physical education, Mirel writes.

The country came close to creating a national curriculum in 1893, when a committee of college presidents and other luminaries headed by Harvard University President Charles Eliot issued the "Report of the Committee of Ten on Secondary School Studies." [33]

• developing international understanding and citizenship as a means to "a more peaceful, productive future." [7]

Because IB navigates the divide between many national education systems, "it was developed as a deliberate compromise between the specialization required in some national systems and the breadth preferred in others," says the IBO. [8]

IB courses such as math and literature may be taken individually, and students who take the courses may also take IB assessment tests. Graded on a 1 to 7 scale, IB exams are taken at the end of each two-year course and include both oral and written portions. As with AP, some colleges offer credit for the exams; scores of 5, 6, or 7 usually are required for college credit. Students who take the entire IB diploma curriculum and pass the associated exams earn an IB diploma accepted at universities worldwide and also earn college credit at some colleges.

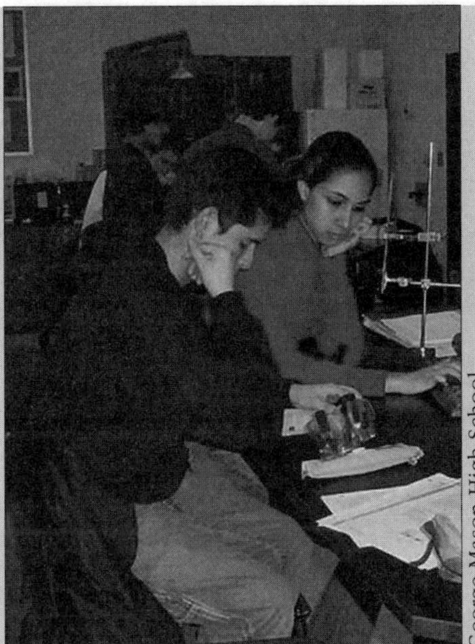

George Mason High School

IB students ponder a lab experiment at George Mason High School, in Falls Church, Va.

The full IB diploma program includes two-year courses in a student's native literature and language; a second language, either modern like Spanish or classical like Latin or Greek; social studies such as history or economics, with a global focus; math and computer science; the arts and a laboratory-science course that includes opportunities for students to develop and pursue their own research questions.

In IB lingo, those courses form a "hexagon" that is centered on three other key pieces of the IB curriculum. In a two-year required Theory of Knowledge (TOK) course, students examine philosophical questions related to knowledge and learning. TOK exams consist of 1,200-to-1,600-word essays marked by an international team of exam assessors, as in other IB courses. In recent exams, students could choose from lists of questions like these: Can a machine know? Can we know something that has not yet been proven true? "All ethical statements are relative"; by examining the justifications for — and implications of — making this claim, decide whether or not you agree with it.

Rounding out the curriculum is an "extended essay," an "independent, self-directed piece of research, culminating in a 4,000-word paper," plus a requirement for a specified number of hours spent in outside activities, including sports, arts groups and social-service projects. [9]

Like the AP program, IB also offers teacher-training seminars and suggests syllabi.

Currently, 1,740 schools in 122 countries offer IB, which includes a K-10 curriculum as well as the diploma course; 620 of those schools are in the United States. The diploma program is offered by 1,355 schools in 121 countries, including 479 in the United States. [10]

---

[1] *They Went to College Early*, The Fund for the Advancement of Education, 1957.

[2] *Ibid.*

[3] *Advanced Placement: Report to the Nation 2006*, The College Board, p. 79, apcentral.collegeboard.com.

[4] *Ibid.*

[5] G. Renaud, of UNESCO, 1974, quoted in G. Harold Poelzer and John F. Feldhusen, "The International Baccalaureate: A Program for Gifted Secondary Students," *Roeper Review*, March 1997, p. 168.

[6] *Ibid.*

[7] "A Basis for Practice: The Diploma Program," International Baccalaureate Organization, www.ibo.org.

[8] *Ibid.*

[9] *Ibid.*

[10] IB World School Statistics, www.ibo.org.

This influential document recommended a traditional array of studies in Greek and Latin, math, chemistry, natural history, government and economics. It argued that studying Greek and Latin "trains the mind" and that geography "enhances the powers of observation and reasoning."

The classics approach of the Committee of Ten was largely superseded by a 1918 report, "The Cardinal Principles of Secondary Education," prepared not by university chiefs but by education specialists, public officials and high-school principals. Greatly influenced by the progressive, utilitarian philosophy of educator John Dewey, it emphasized "health, command of fundamental processes, worthy home membership, vocation, citizenship, worthy use of leisure and ethical character."

The same emphasis on psychology and real-world applications was also apparent in *The Curriculum*, a groundbreaking book also published in 1918 by University of Chicago education Professor Franklin Bobbitt. It argued that human life "consists in the performance of specific activities. Education that prepares for life is one that prepares definitely and adequately for these specific activities."

It was this philosophy, as interpreted variously by local school districts — many of them dealing with newly diverse populations brought about by

History and English Are Most Popular

U.S. history and English literature and language were the most-popular AP exams among students in the class of 2005. Many educators worry about the relatively low interest in advanced math and science tests. The least-popular AP exam was in French literature (793 students).

The 10 Most-Popular AP Exams Among the Class of 2005

	(Exam)	(No. of students)
1.	U.S. History	(207,817)
2.	English Literature and Composition	(203,697)
3.	English Language and Composition	(162,357)
4.	Calculus AB (the less-challenging level)	(141,732)
5.	U.S. Government and Politics	(103,224)
6.	Biology	(88,223)
7.	Spanish Language	(71,517)
8.	Psychology	(68,847)
9.	Statistics	(61,018)
10.	European History	(58,474)

Source: "The College Board's AP Report to the Nation 2006"

immigration — that would hold sway in the United States for much of the 20th century.

By 1920 the advocates of a cafeteria-style high school had won, with most schools offering curricula with low-academic rigor, according to Mirel. They also had begun tracking students.

By 1920, most big-city high schools were offering four high-school tracks: college prep, commercial (primarily preparation for secretarial work), vocational (industrial arts and home economics) and general, which merely offered a high-school diploma without specific preparation for educational or vocational endeavors. Most students still enrolled in academic classes like foreign languages and science, but that changed as the 20th century wore on.

Two factors led ever-growing proportions of students into low-challenge curricula. First, waves of new immigration and industrialization resulted in burgeoning enrollments, and some education leaders believed that the new high-school students were less intelligent than previous generations. Secondly, a series of economic crises — starting with the Great Depression and ending with the return to the work force of World War II veterans — made it good economic sense to keep students out of the labor market ias long as possible.

To keep students from dropping out, schools allowed them to take easier classes. For example, from 1928 to 1943, health and physical education (PE) courses increased from 4.9 to 11.5 percent of total course-taking nationwide. "These courses were entertaining, relevant to young people's lives outside of school, required little or no homework, and . . . were amenable to high student/teacher ratios," writes Mirel. Over the next half-century, health and PE were the fastest-growing courses: By 1973 they were second only to English classes in the percentage of students taking the courses nationwide. [34]

As a result, high school became a "hothouse for youth culture," from the raw energy of the hot-rod cruising 1950s to the rock 'n' roll counterculture of the 1960s, explains Mirel. Teachers increasingly resorted to an unspoken bargain with students that led to further abandonment of rigorous academics: "I'm not going to demand too much of you if you don't give me a hard time." [35]

Starting Small

While academically undemanding high schools were popular with many Americans, as early as the 1950s some policymakers began to worry about a gap between public high-school preparation and college requirements, and about a potential talent drain as some bright students grew bored with school.

The concern led to the establishment in 1951 of a Ford Foundation pilot program — the School and College Study of Admission with Advanced Standing — which eventually became today's Advanced Placement program. (*See sidebar, p. 204.*)

"Many able students, marking time in an unchallenging high-school environment, lose interest in education and do not go on to college," said a 1957 history of the program from the foundation's Fund for the Advancement of Education. [36]

By the 1955-56 school year, the program had grown from a pilot involving a few schools and colleges to a full-fledged national program. In 1956, 1,229 students from 110 high schools took 2,199 exams and attended 138 different colleges that September. Nearly half enrolled at five elite schools — Harvard, Yale, Princeton, Cornell and the Massachusetts Institute of Technology. [37]

Over the decades, the proportion of high schools participating in AP grew to about 60 percent. About 10 times as many students participate in AP today as in 1980, and the number of subjects for which there are AP exams has grown from 11 to 34. [38]

In the 1960s, international educators — led by the International Schools Association established by the U.N. Educational, Scientific and Cultural Organization (UNESCO) — sought to solve another education dilemma: how to create a common curriculum and diploma that universities around the world would recognize, mostly to serve students living abroad, such as the children of diplomats and international businessmen. (*See sidebar, p. 204.*) [39]

To earn an IB diploma, students must complete a two-year comprehensive curriculum that includes science, math, the student's native language and a second language, history and the arts as well as the Theory of Knowledge course. They must also complete a 4,000-word essay based on self-directed research and participate in creative and service projects in the community.

After opening at a handful of international schools around the world in 1970, IB diploma programs today exist at 1,348 schools in 121 countries, including 479 schools in the United States.

Many Graduates Are Deficient in Reading

Only 51 percent of U.S. high-school graduates are ready for college-level reading, according to the 2005 ACT test. White students, females and graduates from affluent families are the most prepared; African-Americans and Latinos are among the least prepared.

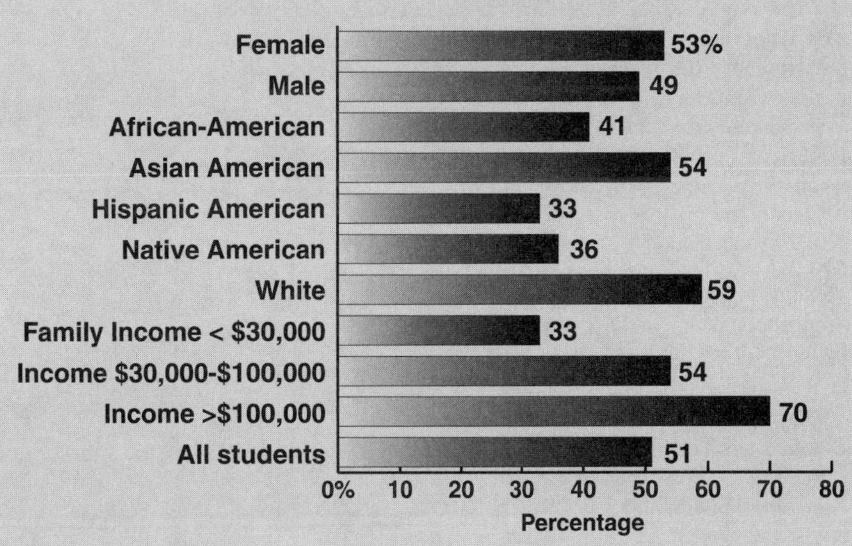

Source: "Reading Between the Lines: What the ACT Reveals About College Readiness in Reading," ACT, Inc., March 2006. Findings are based on 1.2 million high-school students who took the ACT; 27% were from the East, 40% from the Midwest, 14% from the Southwest and 19% from the West.

Reform Movement

During the 1980s and '90s, as standardized test scores declined — particularly on international comparative tests — and businessmen complained that American graduates were unprepared for the work force, U.S. presidents from both parties called for a common core curriculum nationwide and mandatory testing to ensure that students were learning the material.

But resistance both from the right and the left led Congress repeatedly to reject mandatory nationwide standards or testing. Conservatives generally objected to the idea of the federal government interfering in curriculum development, which has historically been done by the nation's 15,000 local school districts. And liberals feared that without a massive injection of additional funding, imposing mandatory testing and achievement standards on disadvantaged inner-city schools would ensure their failure.

In the end, each of the 50 states drafted its own statewide academic standards — a situation many called untenable, since they varied widely in rigor and content. [40]

By the late 1990s, states were trying to strengthen their statewide standards, and many even adopted mandatory testing — called high-stakes tests — as a prerequisite for graduation. But often the tests were not properly aligned with the new, statewide curricula, causing high failure rates. Low test scores in some states triggered heated parental rebellion against the mandatory testing. [41]

Then in 2001, newly elected President George W. Bush jumped into the fray, proposing his No Child Left Behind law (NCLB). Adopted on Jan. 8, 2002 — a year after his inauguration — it authorized around $135 billion in extra federal funding for education over five years in exchange for mandatory math and reading testing in grades 3 through 8. The tests were to be developed by the states and aligned with statewide academic standards. [42]

States Back AP, IB

In passing NCLB, Congress and President Bush gave the federal

Continued on p. 210

Does AP Predict College Success?

Taking challenging classes — not necessarily Advanced Placement courses — is the best predictor of a student's eventual success in college, according to several recent studies. They take issue with the greater emphasis some high schools and colleges place on AP courses than on other tough classes.

"The original goal of AP was to have upper-middle-class kids who were bored take courses at the college level," and the program does a "great job" for those students, says Kristin Klopfenstein, an assistant professor of economics at Texas Christian University, in Fort Worth. "Now, however, AP has taken on a second job" — acting as the marker by which college admissions officers pinpoint the most highly qualified applicants.

Courtesy of Texas Christian University

College admissions officers use the AP program to pinpoint the most highly qualified students, says Assistant Professor Kristin Klopfenstein, of Texas Christian University.

In addition, many high schools "weight AP courses much, much heavier" when computing student grade-point averages (GPAs), says Klopfenstein. That practice gives AP students an additional leg up on college admissions, especially in states like Florida, Texas and California, where high GPAs earn public high-school students automatic admission to some universities.

But those practices don't jibe with what research is finding, says Klopfenstein. In a study of 28,000 Texas high-school graduates who attended four-year public universities, "AP doesn't provide additional predictive power" to pinpoint the students who will succeed in college, she says. In fact, she says, students who take challenging courses in general, like trigonometry or precalculus, are most likely to succeed on campus. AP is "not a necessary component" of such a curriculum, Klopfenstein says. Earlier research that suggested taking AP courses specifically predicted college success "didn't control for the rest of the curriculum experience," she says.

While research on the question is scant, some studies seem to buttress Klopfenstein's argument. For example, a 2004 study by education researchers from the University of California-Berkeley found that while scoring high on AP exams "is strongly related to college performance," the "number of AP and honors courses taken in high school bears little or no relationship to students' later performance in college," after controlling for other academic and socioeconomic factors. [1]

Based on a sample of 81,445 University of California freshmen between 1998 and 2001, Berkeley education researchers concluded that "many students who take AP courses do not complete the associated AP exams, and merely taking AP or other honors-level courses in high school is not a valid indicator of the likelihood that students will perform well in college. . . . AP coursework, by itself, contributes almost nothing to the prediction of college performance," However, "AP examination scores are among the very best predictors," according to the UC data. [2]

Meanwhile, substantial research backs up the idea that the most successful college students are those who took the highest number of solid academic courses, in all curriculum areas, throughout high school.

"No matter how one divides the universe of students, the curriculum measure" predicts "a higher percent of those earning bachelor's degrees" than any other factor in students' pre-college background, such as standardized test scores or GPAs, says U.S. Department of Education senior analyst Clifford Adelman. "The academic intensity and quality of one's high-school curriculum" is a "dominant determinant" of whether a student earns a college degree, according to his study, which followed a national sample of students from high school to age 30, he says. [3]

Furthermore, the impact of a high-quality high-school curriculum is a "much greater" predictor of college success for African-American and Latino students than for white students, Adelman says. [4]

Adelman's study included AP courses as one factor among several in his measure of challenging curricula, so it does not address the AP question directly. However, he does identify one curriculum area as "a key marker in precollegiate momentum." The "tipping point" for math courses that point to college success is "now firmly above Algebra II," Adelman says. [5]

---

[1] Saul Geiser and Veronica Santelices, "The Role of Advanced Placement and Honors Courses in College Admissions," Research and Occasional Paper Series, Center for Studies in Higher Education, University of California, Berkeley, 2004.

[2] *Ibid.*

[3] Clifford Adelman, "Answers in the Toolbox: Academic Intensity, Attendance Patterns, an d Bachelor's Degree Attainment," U.S. Department of Education, 1999.

[4] *Ibid.*

[5] Clifford Adelman, *The Toolbox Revisited*, U.S. Department of Education, 2006.

At Issue:

Should schools encourage most high-school students to take AP and IB courses?

yes

JOHN BISHOP
ASSOCIATE PROFESSOR OF HUMAN RESOURCE STUDIES, CORNELL UNIVERSITY

WRITTEN FOR THE *CQ RESEARCHER*, MARCH 2006

I encourage students to take rigorous, externally examined courses like Advanced Placement (AP) and the International Baccalaureate (IB) because they will learn more and benefit more from what they learn. Let's look at the evidence. Students from countries that require everyone to take AP-style exams — such as Australia, Denmark and France — score more than a grade-level equivalent ahead of students from equally advanced nations that don't require such exams.

Similarly, students from Canadian and German provinces with AP-style exams outperform students from provinces that lack such exams. Finally, Americans taking externally examined AP/IB classes learn considerably more during the year than equally able students taking other classes.

Why? First, the teachers are better prepared. Nations and provinces with external exam systems expect even middle-school teachers to have majored in the subjects they teach. Outside of AP/IB, however, most history, chemistry and physics classes in America are taught by teachers who did not major or minor in the subject during college. Second, externally set and graded exams protect AP teachers from pressures to reduce the difficulty and amount of work they assign and instead push them to demand more of their students and themselves. The teacher becomes the coach of a team where every member's effort and success is valued.

Most important, AP students have willingly taken on the challenge of higher standards. They are not competing against each other, so they no longer feel they must hide their interest for fear of being considered a "suck up." Class discussions are more animated because everyone has read and thought about last night's assignment. Learning is more fun.

There are, of course, exceptions to these generalizations. But please do not avoid AP because it's "too hard" or "only for the gifted." Lots of students with 500 SATs take AP and get college credit. In Europe and Asia, calculus starts in high school. Why should we be different?

Ignore the adults who tell you AP is unnecessary because they succeeded without AP. You face a much more competitive world. Real wage rates of young adults without a bachelor's degree are significantly below their level in 1970. Even maintaining the standard of living of your parents will require you to develop skills that substantially exceed those your parents brought to the labor market a generation ago.

Don't wait for college. Seek out challenges now, and you will develop habits of mind that will serve you for the rest of your life.

no

KIRK A. JOHNSON
SENIOR POLICY ANALYST, THE HERITAGE FOUNDATION

FROM "EXPANDING OPPORTUNITY FOR LOW-INCOME HIGH-SCHOOL STUDENTS: PELL GRANTS VS. ADVANCED PLACEMENT CLASSES," MARCH 2004

There are two basic ways that bright high-school students can perform college-level work. First, they may enroll in Advanced Placement (AP) or International Baccalaureate (IB) classes. The second way is simply to take one or more classes at a community college or state university. Virtually all states have a program that allows high-school students to take such classes.

Federal programs have clearly favored the establishment of AP courses. The No Child Left Behind legislation authorized Advanced Placement Incentive Program Grants, which provided roughly $24 million annually to state and local education agencies to fund AP and pre-AP programs in low-income communities.

But high-school-based AP classes may not be the most efficient and cost-effective means to expand access to higher education for low-income students. Generally speaking, AP classes are far more expensive to operate than regular high-school classes. Taking into account differences in the average class size and teacher's pay, the cost of the typical AP class is more than twice that of the average, non-AP high-school class.

Another drawback is that these courses may duplicate classes that are currently being offered in institutions of higher education. Classes similar to those in AP programs can be found at virtually all of the nearly 2,100 community colleges and state universities across America.

For the most part, these institutions already have the infrastructure to offer these types of classes, and they exist in close proximity to high-school students — especially those in low-income urban areas. In short, expanding AP programs would tend to duplicate the kinds of classes that are already available at a broad range of colleges and universities.

As an alternative to the AP system, Pell grants could be offered to bright, low-income high-school students as a fiscally responsible way to expand their access to college-level classes. Using the $24 million the federal government currently spends on the Advanced Placement Incentive Program every year, more than 18,500 low-income students could be given $1,200 Pell grants, enabling them to take a class in both the fall and spring semesters.

Such a program would have the ancillary benefit of allowing students to choose from a wider variety of classes than might be offered in a limited, school-based AP program. Under a Pell grant program, for example, low-income students who might be particularly gifted in computers could take computer science courses at a local junior college — an option they would not enjoy in most AP programs.

Continued from p. 207

government an unprecedented, dominant role in education policy for the nation. But it kept one tradition intact: The new federal requirements mostly applied to elementary schools, leaving most policy-setting for high schools to states and localities.

However, NCLB does "basically outlaw" a common high-school practice that interferes with offering challenging coursework: assigning teachers to subjects in which they don't have a college major or minor, says Richard Ingersoll, a professor at the University of Pennsylvania's Graduate School of Education. Beginning this school year, NCLB requires high schools to have "highly qualified" teachers in each class. School principals frequently run afoul of that requirement as they try to juggle faculty to cover a complex schedule, he says.

But, Ingersoll points out, it is usually lower-track classes — which disproportionately enroll low-income and minority students — that are most likely to have misassigned teachers. "The equity people go bonkers at that," he says, but it is unclear whether and how NCLB can enforce the ban on misassignment.

In addition, over the past several years, federal policymakers have continued to encourage high schools to strengthen their academic course content, mostly because U.S. students lag behind on international comparative tests. As a result, federal grants have helped many states develop incentive programs to increase AP and IB participation and have partially paid AP and IB fees for low-income students.

Many state legislators have concluded that all local school districts should increase participation in AP and, to a lesser extent, IB courses. But offering students equitable access to educational opportunity has been a long-term struggle for states, since public schools are financed mainly through local property taxes. Because of that approach, poor areas get less money per student than rich areas — something that no other industrialized country does. [43]

Perhaps nowhere has the struggle for educational equity been more apparent than in efforts to make AP courses accessible to students from all economic backgrounds. In 1999, for example, the American Civil Liberties Union (ACLU) filed a class-action suit against the state of California on behalf of a group of minority students, who the ACLU said had no access to AP courses. In response, some California legislators have proposed requiring every high school in the state to offer six AP courses, and the ACLU has worked with educators to devise a solution. To date, the case has no judicial resolution. ■

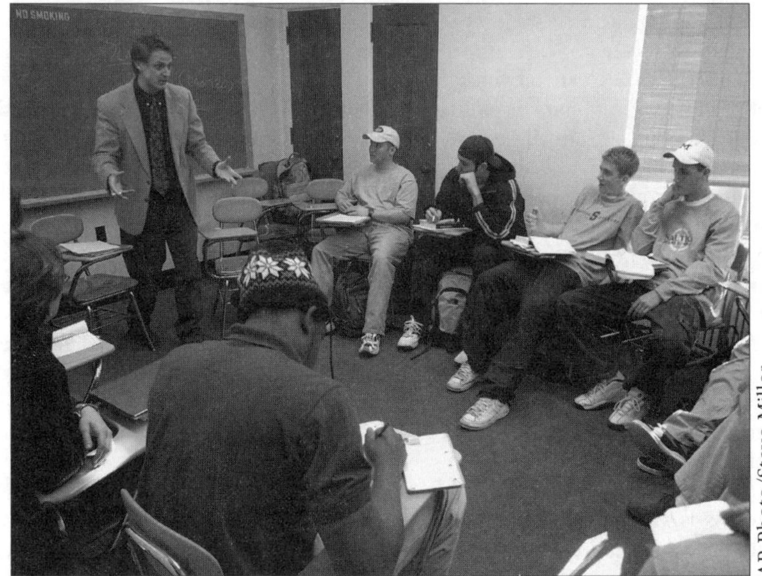

AP Photo/Steve Miller

A course in basic writing at the University of Connecticut, in Storrs, helps students polish sub-par skills. More than 25 percent of first-year college students need remedial courses in writing, reading or math.

CURRENT SITUATION

States Resist

In 2006, the struggle to make U.S. high schools more academically challenging continues, even as state representatives fight off federal attempts to standardize high-school learning.

For the past few years, President Bush's budget proposals for education have raised the hackles both of members of Congress and state lawmakers. First, Bush's budgets for implementing NCLB were below authorization by about $7 billion in fiscal 2003 and $9 billion below in fiscal 2004, for example. [44] This year's presidential budget for fiscal 2007, released in January, also curtails NCLB funding.

In addition, last year Bush proposed extending NCLB's mandatory yearly reading and math testing to grades nine through 11.

By 2005, however, states were complaining bitterly that the federal 2006 budget severely underfunded existing NCLB requirements, and they were in no mood to accept more. "The well has been poisoned," said California Rep. George Miller, the top-ranking Democrat on the House Education and the Workforce Committee. "Given the history of this administration in not funding [NCLB], no member of Congress is going to put their chips on this plan." [45]

Even moderate Republican Rep. Michael Castle of Delaware, chairman of the House Education Subcommittee, who supports Bush's testing proposal, declared it "dead on arrival" because so many conservative Republicans opposed it.

States would welcome help from the federal government to increase high-school rigor, but it must be the right kind of help, says former West Virginia Gov. Wise, now president of the nonprofit Alliance for Excellent Education coalition. "Rigor demands resources. Dollars are important," he says. "You have to be willing to get good teachers and supply extra help."

Also on Wise's wish list are federal incentives for states to form "P-16" or "P-20" councils to begin coordinating state instructional programs from preschool through graduate school.

Meanwhile, in another budget bill enacted last month, Congress ran afoul of both state-control advocates and some college leaders when it authorized new Academic Competitiveness Grants. Based on a Bush proposal, the grants would assist low-income students to study math, science, engineering and high-demand foreign languages. [46]

Critics decry the law's stipulation that students can only receive the money if they've completed a high-school curriculum deemed "rigorous" by the secretary of Education. That gives the Education Department too much say over high-school policy-making, critics say.

But the measure's authors quickly shot off a letter to Education Secretary Margaret Spellings insisting that prior federal education law "prohibits the secretary from establishing any curriculum in any school, public or private." [47]

While states have cautioned federal lawmakers to lie low, state governments have launched their own initiatives to increase the rigor of high-school curricula, both through AP and IB and other means, such as centering diploma requirements on skills and knowledge that state colleges and universities say students require to succeed on campus.

In 2005 legislative action, for example, Illinois created a public-awareness program to inform parents of the importance of AP courses; Minnesota required its state colleges and universities to award college credit to students scoring a 3 or higher on an AP exam or a 4 or higher on IB exams; and Colorado revised its high-school accreditation standards to include the percentage of students enrolled in AP and IB courses. [48]

In addition, 13 governors and the nonprofit group Achieve formed the American Diploma Project (ADP) Network, which has pledged to work with employers and colleges to align their high-school graduation requirements with students' post-graduation needs. Currently 22 states are ADP members. ■

OUTLOOK

Challenge for All?

Many educators believe that after years of talk without action, a change is sure to come to U.S. high schools. But much more research and more and better data from schools is needed before educators will know exactly what works for high schools, say education analysts. Otherwise, says the University of Louisville's Stringfield, too many education proposals become "politicized" rather than based on knowledge.

Finding out what works will take more meaningful data, agrees David Conley, director of the Center for Education Policy Research at the University of Oregon. For example, to find out which curricula work best, "what goes on in classes — not just course titles — needs to be studied."

Meanwhile, efforts to bridge the high-school-college gap are in their infancy and will increase, researchers say. "The whole high-school-college connection is just getting going," says Conley. Unfortunately, the high-school standards movement of the 1990s "was misguided" and will need to be thoroughly overhauled, he says, because states established graduation standards without first figuring out what students need to succeed in postsecondary education and training.

Conley sees high schools and colleges working together much more closely in the future. For example, "Can you imagine submitting a paper" in a high-school class "and having them say, 'You're ready for college in sentence construction and punctuation but not in organization?' " Such helpful assessments eventually will become the norm, he predicts.

AP and IB programs are good models because they base student assessment on meaningful curricula and train teachers, says Kirst of Stanford. However, "we need to take these models and adapt them" to the academic standards set for most U.S. high-schoolers, as Colorado, Illinois and Maine are doing. "We're groping at it, and I think we'll see more in five or 10 years."

When it comes to expanding top students' access to the most challenging courses, like AP, online education is the wave of the future, says Hanushek of the Hoover Institution. "If you have a high school of 50 kids, you can't offer German IV very easily," he says. "But distance education is starting to work." Especially in the West, "some states are beginning to use it effectively."

Many researchers say the United States is on the brink of undertaking major high-school reform, after discussing it without action for more than

20 years. "The country is currently at the will-building stage," says former Gov. Wise. Economic changes will galvanize that will eventually, he says. "The folks laid off at Ford plants will realize that, though they got their good jobs with a high-school degree, when Ford retools and starts hiring again, their sons and daughters won't get a job the same way."

AP and IB will play a large role in that process, says Cornell's Bishop. "Essentially, we're in a slow transition from a low-standard system to one that's much more like the European system," he says.

When it comes to AP and IB, "everybody can't do them right now. But we're moving in the direction that more and more can take them and succeed," he continues. "It's a slow movement." But as pressure builds for students to take challenging courses, schools will be forced to hire better teachers and increase other learning supports. "It'll take us 10, 15 or 20 years."

The problems of low achievement and dropouts "are solvable," says Michigan's Mirel. And while better-trained teachers are part of a solution, it will take more than just ensuring that teachers study more subject-matter courses. Ensuring that all math teachers have at least college math minors, for example, won't do the trick, he says. Many people who know subject matter have trouble communicating it effectively to others, let alone to students of widely varying abilities and learning styles, he notes. To do the job right, schools of education must "give teachers better ways to teach."

The bottom line, says Mirel, is that to sustain the U.S. economy and maintain democracy by producing an informed public, the education system must tackle "the great challenge of the 21st century:" learning how to teach challenging courses to kids of all levels of ability. ■

Notes

[1] Whitney L. Becker, "AP Classes Gaining in Popularity, But Passing Rates Lag," *Austin American-Statesman*, Feb. 1, 2006.

[2] *Ibid.*

[3] Tamar Lewin, "The Two Faces of AP," *New York Times Education Life Supplement*, Jan. 8, 2006.

[4] "Tons of Test Takers," *Inside Higher Ed*, Feb. 8, 2006, www.insidehighered.com.

[5] IB Statistics, www.ibo.org/school/statistics/. The International Baccalaureate Organization expanded its programs to include middle school in 1994 and elementary school in 1997. As with IB for 11th- and 12th-graders, schools must be certified by IBO to offer the comprehensive curricula, which focus on interdisciplinary learning, development of thinking and learning skills, communication and research skills and global and environmental understanding.

[6] "Comparing NAEP, TIMSS, and PISA in Mathematics and Science," National Center for Education Statistics, U.S. Department of Education, http://nces.ed.gov/timss/pdf/naep_pisa_comp.pdf.

[7] "Rising to the Challenge: Are High School Graduates Prepared for College and Work?" survey by Peter D. Hart Research Associates/Public Opinion Strategies, February 2005, conducted for Achieve, a group of governors and business leaders pushing for more rigorous high-school curricula.

[8] *Ibid.*

[9] Jay Mathews, "The 100 Best High Schools In America," *Newsweek*, June 2, 2003, p. 48.

[10] Jay Mathews, "Inside the Challenge Index: Rating High Schools," *Washingtonpost.com*, May 27, 2003. For additional recent coverage, see Jay Mathews, "As AP Expands, Studies Disagree on Its Value," *The Washington Post*, Feb. 28, 2006, p. A8.

[11] Lewin, *op. cit.*

[12] For background, see Ann R. Martin, "International Baccalaureate Programs Making Impact on City Schools," *Chicago Tribune Special Section: Education Today*, Jan. 15, 2006.

[13] For background, see "Testing in Schools," Kenneth Jost, *CQ Researcher*, April 20, 2001, pp. 321-344.

[14] *Ibid.*

[15] *Ibid.*

[16] *Learning and Understanding: Improving Advanced Study of Mathematics and Science in U.S. High Schools* (2002), National Research Council Committee on Programs for Advanced Study. The Theory of Knowledge philosophy seminar examines complex questions about the nature of knowledge and its relationship to truth, belief and perception.

[17] *Ibid.*

[18] Quoted in Jay Mathews, "Is AP Good for Everybody? It's Debatable," *The Washington Post*, April 10, 2005, p. B3.

[19] Carolyn M. Callahan, Ellen P. Hench, Catherine M. Brighton, "Advanced Placement and International Baccalaureate Programs," presentation to the National Association for Gifted Children, November 2002.

[20] *Ibid.*

[21] Michael N. Riley, "A District Where Everyone's on the Advanced Track," School Administrator, American Association of School Administrators, Jan. 1, 2005.

[22] *Ibid.*

About the Author

Staff writer **Marcia Clemmitt** is a veteran social-policy reporter who previously served as editor in chief of *Medicine and Health*, a Washington industry newsletter, and staff writer for *The Scientist*. She has also been a high school math and physics teacher. She holds a liberal arts and sciences degree from St. John's College, Annapolis, and a master's degree in English from Georgetown University. Her recent reports include "Birth Control," "Academic Freedom," "Saving the Oceans," and "Climate Change."

[23] *Ibid.*

[24] Kati Haycock, "Still at Risk," *Thinking K-15, Education Trust*, Summer 2002.

[25] Carol Corbett Burris and Kevin G. Welner, "Closing the Achievement Gap by Detracking," *Phi Delta Kappan*, April 2005, p. 594.

[26] *Ibid.*, p. 596.

[27] *Ibid.*, p. 597.

[28] *Ibid.*, p. 596.

[29] *The Funding Gap 2005*, The Education Trust, 2006.

[30] Clifford Adelman, *The Toolbox Revisited: Paths to Degree Completion From High School Through College*, U.S. Department of Education, February 2006.

[31] For background, see Jeffrey Mirel and David Angus, *The Failed Promise of the American High School, 1890-1995* (1999).

[32] Unless otherwise noted, this historical background is taken from Jeffrey Mirel, "The Traditional High School," *Education Next*, Hoover Institution, Winter 2006, www.educationnext.org.

[33] Unless otherwise noted, information below is from Charles S. Clark, "Education Standards," *CQ Researcher*, March 11, 1994, pp. 217-240.

[34] *Ibid.*

[35] *Ibid.*

[36] "They Went to College Early, Evaluation Report Number 2," The Fund for the Advancement of Education, 1957.

[37] *Ibid.*

[38] www.apcentral.collegeboard.com.

[39] For background, see G. Harold Poelzer and John F. Feldhusen, "The International Baccalaureate: A Program for Gifted Secondary Students," *Roeper Review*, March 1997, p. 168.

[40] For background, see Clark, *op. cit.*, and Kathy Koch, "National Education Standards," *CQ Researcher*, May 14, 1999, pp. 401-424.

[41] For background, see Jost, *op. cit.*

[42] For background, see Barbara Mantel, "No Child Left Behind," *CQ Researcher*, May 27, 2005, pp. 469-492.

[43] For background, see Kathy Koch, "Reforming School Funding," *CQ Researcher*, Dec. 10, 1999, pp. 1041-1064.

[44] Vincent L. Ferrandino and Gerald N. Tirozzi, "Getting Ahead of No Child Left Behind," *Education Week*, Nov. 20, 2002 (fiscal 2003); Howard Dean, "No Child Left Behind Should Be More Than a Slogan," *Seattle Times*, Jan. 8, 2004 (fiscal 2004).

FOR MORE INFORMATION

Achieve, Inc., 1775 Eye St., N.W., Suite 410, Washington, DC 20006; (202) 419-1540; www.achieve.org. An independent, bipartisan group formed by state governors and business leaders to promote higher academic standards.

Alliance for Excellent Education, 1201 Connecticut Ave., N.W., Suite 901, Washington, DC 20036; (202) 828-0828; www.all4ed.org. A nonprofit research and advocacy group that pushes for development of national and state policies to help at-risk high-school students attain college and workplace readiness.

AVID, AVID Center, 5120 Shoreham Place, Suite 120, San Diego, CA 92122; (858) 623-2843; www.avidcenter.org. A nonprofit group that establishes in-school support programs to help low-achieving students tackle a college-prep curriculum.

The Bridge Project, Stanford Institute for Higher Education Research, Stanford University School of Education, 485 Lasuen Mall, Stanford, CA 94305-3096; (650) 725-1235; www.stanford.edu/group/bridgeproject/. A research group that studies efforts to link colleges with public-school systems to improve students' college readiness.

The College Board, 45 Columbus Ave., New York, NY 10023; (212) 713-8000; http://apcentral.collegeboard.com/. A nonprofit membership organization of colleges and universities that produces and manages the Advanced Placement program.

Education Next, Hoover Institution, Stanford University; www.educationnext.org/. The online quarterly journal on education reform is published by the conservative think tank.

The Education Trust, 1250 H St., N.W., Suite 700, Washington, DC 20005; (202) 293-1217; www2.edtrust.org/edtrust. An independent nonprofit research and advocacy group that focuses on closing the achievement gap in learning and college preparation for low-income and minority students.

International Baccalaureate Organization, Route des Morillons 15, Grand-Saconnex, Geneva CH-1218, Switzerland; www.ibo.org. The nonprofit education foundation that supports international education and develops, manages and conducts student assessments for the IB program and its participating schools.

National Center for Accelerated Schools PLUS, University of Connecticut, Neag School of Education, 2131 Hillside Road Unit 3224, Storrs, CT 06269-3224; (860) 486-6330; www.acceleratedschools.net. A national collaborative of universities and schools that brings curricula and learning strategies developed for gifted and talented students to all students in 1,500 affiliated schools, mostly in low-income communities.

National Center for Education Statistics, 1990 K St., N.W., Washington, DC 20006; (202) 502-7300; http://nces.ed.gov/. The U.S. Department of Education office that provides data on student attendance and achievement and international comparisons.

[45] Gil Klein, "Bush's High School Reform Plan Bombs," Media General News Service, Jan. 17, 2005.

[46] "The Gift Colleges Don't Want," *Inside Higher Ed*, Jan. 24, 2006, www.insidehighered.com.

[47] Rep. John Boehner and Rep. Michael Enzi, letter to U.S. Education Secretary Margaret Spellings, Feb. 1, 2006, http://edworkforce.house.gov.

[48] *Recent State Policies/Activities: High School — Advanced Placement*, Education Commission of the States, www.ecs.org.

Bibliography

Selected Sources

Books

Angus, David L., and Jeffrey E. Mirel, *The Failed Promise of the American High School, 1890-1995*, Teachers College Press, 1999.

Two University of Michigan professors of education history put the long battle over curriculum choices into historical context and discuss the ramifications of giving students a range of curriculum choices.

Conant, James Bryant, *The American High School Today: A First Report to Interested Citizens*, McGraw Hill, 1959.

A former Harvard University president offers his much-discussed recommendations for improving high schools.

Kirst, Michael W., and Andrea Venezia, (eds.), *From High School to College; Improving Opportunities for Success in Postsecondary Education*, Jossey Bass Publishers, 2004.

The directors of Stanford University's Bridge Project present case studies of efforts to align high-school standards and graduation requirements with the skills and knowledge required by postsecondary institutions.

Mathews, Jay, and Ian Hill, *Supertest: How the International Baccalaureate Can Strengthen Our Schools*, Open Court, 2005.

An education reporter (Mathews) and the director general of the IB program recount both the international history of IB and its use at a U.S. high school.

Articles

Lewin, Tamar, "The Two Faces of AP," *The New York Times Education Life Supplement*, Jan. 8, 2006.

Lewin describes current debates over the value of AP courses and exams for college preparation, based on interviews with students, high-school teachers and college admission officers with wide-ranging views on AP's importance.

Mathews, Jay, "Inside the Challenge Index — Rating High Schools," *The Washington Post*, May 27, 2003.

Mathews, a *Washington Post* reporter who devised the Challenge-Index high-school quality ranking system explains why he believes that the number of students in a high school who take Advanced Placement and International Baccalaureate exams is a good measure of school quality.

Mollison, Andrew, "Surviving a Midlife Crisis," *Education Next*, The Hoover Institution, Winter 2006, www.educationnext.org.

A veteran education writer recounts the history of the AP program and outlines the current research controversies over AP's relationship to success in college.

Reports and Studies

"Advanced Placement Report to the Nation, 2006," The College Board, February 2006.

The organization that operates the AP program reports on 2005 test results and participation rates.

"Measuring Up 2004: The National Report Card on Higher Education," National Center on Public Policy and Higher Education, September 2004.

The nonprofit think tank examines state-by-state trends in college preparation as well as college graduation rates and the affordability of secondary education. It finds college preparation has been improving in many states.

"A Nation at Risk," The National Commission on Excellence in Education, April 1983, www.ed.gov/pubs/NatAtRisk/index.html.

A panel of education experts convened by President Ronald Reagan issues a harsh assessment of what American high-school students learn and calls for tougher graduation requirements in academic subjects.

"On Course for Success: A Close Look at Selected High School Courses that Prepare Students for College and Work," ACT, Inc., and The Education Trust, 2005.

Analysts describe in detail curricula, course syllabi and teaching practices from high schools whose graduates have a record of college success.

"Ready or Not: Creating a High School Diploma That Counts," The American Diploma Project, 2004.

Education think tanks describe specific high-school curricula and class syllabi that employers as well as college and university instructors say would better prepare high-school students.

Adelman, Clifford, "The Toolbox Revisited," U.S. Department of Education, February 2006.

A senior government education analyst finds that a challenging high-school courseload is the strongest predictor of whether a student will graduate from college.

Venezia, Andrea, Michael W. Kirst and Anthony L. Antonio, "Betraying the College Dream: How Disconnected K-12 and Postsecondary Education Systems Undermine Student Aspirations," Stanford University Bridge Project, 2003.

Stanford University professors of education argue that public school systems are too disconnected from local colleges and universities and that the disconnect allows school curricula to lag behind college requirements.

The Next Step:

Additional Articles from Current Periodicals

Achievement Gap

Freedman, Samuel G., "The Achievement Gap in Elite Schools," *The New York Times*, Sept. 28, 2005, p. B7.
Public schools in affluent communities are trying to develop techniques to address persistent achievement gaps between white, super-achieving students and minority, low-income stragglers.

Martin, Ann R., "International Baccalaureate Programs Making Impact on City Schools," *Chicago Tribune*, Jan. 15, 2006, p. C1.
Many low-income, minority students are participating in International Baccalaureate programs in Chicago public schools.

Mathews, Jay, "Schools See IB Degree As Way to Boost Minority Achievement," *The Washington Post*, Aug. 17, 2005, p. B1.
The IB program at Mount Vernon High School in Alexandria, Va., is improving minority achievement.

Pinzur, Matthew I., "Hispanic Teens Excel on Exams," *The Miami Herald*, Feb. 8, 2006, p. B1.
Florida's Miami-Dade County leads the world in Hispanic students' performance on Advanced Placement examinations.

Advanced Placement (AP)

Helderman, Rosalind S., "Virginia Colleges To Accept AP Credit," *The Washington Post*, Sept. 16, 2004, p. B1.
Virginia high-school students could accumulate as many as 13 college credits by taking AP, IB or community-college classes, saving an average of $5,000 in tuition.

Ohlemacher, Stephen, "More Seniors Took Advanced Placement Tests in '05, Passed," *The Boston Globe*, Feb. 8, 2006, p. A4.
More public high-school seniors took and passed AP tests nationwide in 2005 than ever before, but racial gaps persisted.

Spencer, Jason, "As School Districts Race to Expand AP Offerings, Disparities in Scores Have Some Asking If All Programs Are Up to Standard," *The Houston Chronicle*, Nov. 13, 2005, p. B1.
Houston schools with mostly minority and low-income students are enrolling more students in AP classes but are not graduating more students with college credits.

College Remedial Courses

"Colorado Grads Not Prepared for College," *The Denver Post*, Dec. 19, 2005, p. B7.
Nearly one-third of the Colorado high-school graduates attending a state college need remedial work.

Cloud, John, "Who's Ready for College?" *Time*, Oct. 14, 2002, p. 60.
Conservatives view remedial college courses as fiscal frills for the lazy, but others say they are necessary.

Schevitz, Tanya, "CSU Falls Short of Its Proficiency Goals For Freshman," *The San Francisco Chronicle*, March 16, 2005, p. B2.
Nearly half of all freshmen in California's state-university system in 2004 were not ready for college-level English.

Thompson, Lynn, " 'Math Gap' Equals Trouble For Students Heading For College," *The Seattle Times*, Feb. 1, 2006, p. H14.
Almost half the students in Washington going directly from high school to community college in 2004 needed remedial math.

International Baccalaureate

Erikson, Helen, "Bill Offers a Fast Track to College," *The Houston Chronicle*, June 15, 2005, p. B2.
A proposed law would give students who earn an IB diploma at least a year of credit at any Texas college.

Graham, Kristen A., "Think Globally, Teach Locally," *The Philadelphia Inquirer*, May 19, 2005, p. A1.
Public and private highs schools in and around Philadelphia are beginning to offer the IB program.

Mendez, Teresa, "An Elite Curriculum Meets An Amalgam of Students," *The Christian Science Monitor*, July 26, 2005, p. 12.
New York City's Baccalaureate School for Global Education, with an even mix of black, Latino, Asian and white students, is seeing if IB can work for all students.

CITING THE *CQ RESEARCHER*

Sample formats for citing these reports in a bibliography include the ones listed below. Preferred styles and formats vary, so please check with your instructor or professor.

MLA STYLE

Jost, Kenneth. "Rethinking the Death Penalty." CQ Researcher 16 Nov. 2001: 945-68.

APA STYLE

Jost, K. (2001, November 16). Rethinking the death penalty. *CQ Researcher, 11*, 945-968.

CHICAGO STYLE

Jost, Kenneth. "Rethinking the Death Penalty." *CQ Researcher*, November 16, 2001, 945-968.

CQ Researcher

Published by CQ Press, a division of Congressional Quarterly Inc.

thecqresearcher.com

Nuclear Energy

Should the U.S. build more nuclear power plants?

President Bush has recommended building more nuclear energy plants in response to high oil and natural gas costs and continuing concern about global warming. Advocates say nuclear power is the only large-scale energy source that does not contribute to global climate change. The Energy Department is working with industry to find sites for new, safer reactors, and Congress has approved subsidies for companies that build the first plants. Opponents fear that accidents or terrorist strikes on reactors could contaminate large areas, and that nuclear fuel could be stolen and used for weapons. They also argue the United States does not have an acceptable, long-term policy for managing nuclear waste and that renewable energy is safer, cleaner and more affordable. Meanwhile, critics say a nuclear pact recently proposed by Bush between India and the United States undercuts nuclear non-proliferation efforts.

More than 25 years ago, fears sparked by an accident at the Three Mile Island nuclear plant in Pennsylvania stalled U.S. development of nuclear power. Now energy companies are again considering building new nuclear plants.

INSIDE THIS REPORT

The CQ Researcher • March 10, 2006 • www.thecqresearcher.com
Volume 16, Number 10 • Pages 217-240

CQ PRESS

RECIPIENT OF SOCIETY OF PROFESSIONAL JOURNALISTS AWARD FOR EXCELLENCE ◆ AMERICAN BAR ASSOCIATION SILVER GAVEL AWARD

NUCLEAR ENERGY

Cover: More than 25 years ago, fears sparked by an accident at the Three Mile Island nuclear plant in Pennsylvania stalled U.S. development of nuclear power. Now energy companies are again considering building new nuclear plants. (Lonna M. Malmsheimer)

CQ Researcher

March 10, 2006
Volume 16, Number 10

MANAGING EDITOR: Thomas J. Colin

ASSISTANT MANAGING EDITOR: Kathy Koch

ASSOCIATE EDITOR: Kenneth Jost

STAFF WRITERS: Marcia Clemmitt, Peter Katel, Pamela M. Prah

CONTRIBUTING WRITERS: Rachel Cox, Sarah Glazer, David Hosansky, Patrick Marshall, Tom Price

DESIGN/PRODUCTION EDITOR: Olu B. Davis

ASSISTANT EDITOR: Melissa J. Hipolit

CQ PRESS

A Division of Congressional Quarterly Inc.

SENIOR VICE PRESIDENT/PUBLISHER: John A. Jenkins

DIRECTOR, LIBRARY PUBLISHING: Kathryn C. Suárez

DIRECTOR, EDITORIAL OPERATIONS: Ann Davies

CONGRESSIONAL QUARTERLY INC.

CHAIRMAN: Paul C. Tash

VICE CHAIRMAN: Andrew P. Corty

PRESIDENT/EDITOR IN CHIEF: Robert W. Merry

CQ Researcher (ISSN 1056-2036) is printed on acid-free paper. Published weekly, except March 24, July 7, July 14, Aug. 4, Aug. 11, Nov. 24, Dec. 22 and Dec. 29, by CQ Press, a division of Congressional Quarterly Inc. Annual full-service subscriptions for institutions start at $667. For pricing, call 1-800-834-9020, ext. 1906. To purchase a *CQ Researcher* report in print or electronic format (PDF), visit www.cqpress.com or call 866-427-7737. Single reports start at $10. Bulk purchase discounts and electronic-rights licensing are also available. Periodicals postage paid at Washington, D.C., and additional mailing offices. POSTMASTER: Send address changes to *CQ Researcher*, 1255 22nd St., N.W., Suite 400, Washington, DC 20037.

Nuclear Energy

By Jennifer Weeks

The Issues

Critics scoffed when plans were announced in 2002 to spend $1.8 billion upgrading the Browns Ferry nuclear power plant in northern Alabama, which had been sitting idle since a 1985 fire and a series of operating problems.

"For the same amount of money, they could build a brand-new reactor that's safer and has a longer life," said David Lochbaum, director of the Union of Concerned Scientists' (UCS) Nuclear Safety Project and a former Browns Ferry engineer. "It's like trying to dust off an eight-track tape player rather than buying a DVD system." [1]

But after extensive modifications, the 25-year-old plant is scheduled to restart in May 2007, and with a higher power output. "This investment will pay dividends for the families, businesses and industry of the [Tennessee] Valley in the forms of low-cost power, cleaner air and economic growth," said Bill Baxter, director of the Tennessee Valley Authority (TVA). [2]

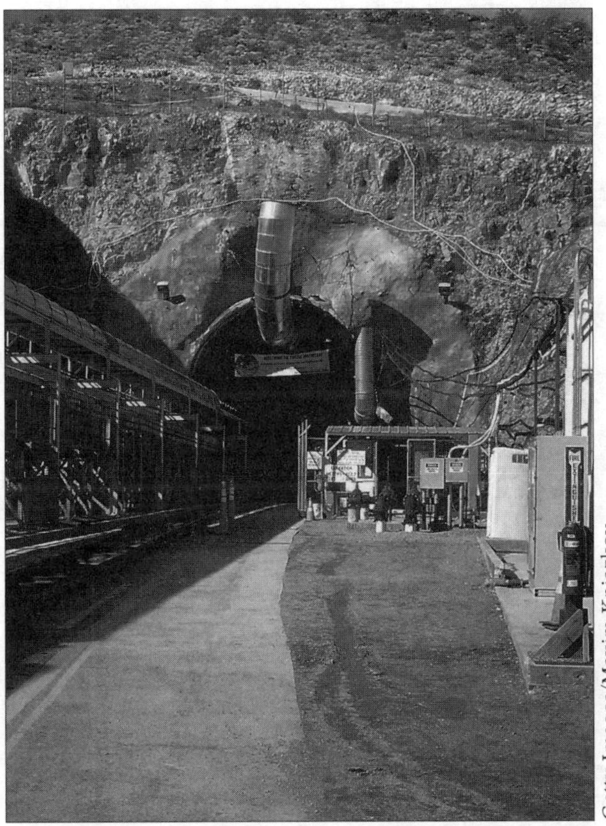

Getty Images/Maxim Kniazkov

Construction of the Department of Energy's nuclear-waste repository inside Nevada's Yucca Mountain is far behind schedule. If licenses are granted and the facility is completed, it will store sealed casks containing 70,000 tons of high-level radioactive waste from commercial power plants as well as atomic fuel from nuclear ships.

Nuclear advocates see the resurrection of Browns Ferry as a sign that nuclear power, which has produced about 20 percent of U.S. electricity annually since 1990, is poised for new growth. They say it offers the best option for addressing the nation's converging challenges of rising energy demand, high fossil-fuel prices, unreliable foreign energy suppliers and concerns about air pollution and climate change.

In his 2006 State of the Union address, President Bush complained that America is "addicted" to oil and proposed increasing research on energy sources, including nuclear power, to reduce U.S. reliance on imported oil. "By applying the talent and technology of America, this country can dramatically improve our environment, move beyond a petroleum-based economy and make our dependence on Middle East oil a thing of the past," said Bush.

"The United States needs more electricity production capacity starting after 2010," says Marvin Fertel, senior vice president of the Nuclear Energy Institute (NEI). Congress is considering new restrictions on the amount of pollutants — including sulfur dioxide, nitrogen oxide, mercury and carbon dioxide — power plants can emit after that date. That would severely limit energy companies' ability to use coal, even as dwindling supplies have driven up natural gas prices. What the nation needs is other options, he adds. "Nuclear plants are performing well, and the industry has consolidated and become more efficient, so they offer operating certainty and price stability."

But before nuclear power can become a more important source of non-polluting energy, the industry and policymakers must first figure out how to lower the cost of building and operating modern nuclear plants, reduce the risk of nuclear accidents, manage radioactive waste and prevent nuclear proliferation. [3]

"We can't assume that society will continue to accept nuclear energy unless we can sufficiently reduce its proliferation, waste, safety and terrorism liabilities — and it's an open question as to whether we can manage those risks," says John Holdren, a professor of environmental policy at Harvard University and co-chair of the National Commission on Energy Policy.

But the rewards of successfully expanding nuclear energy would be far-reaching, according to Holdren, helping to address both global climate change and the growing competition for natural gas. [4] "It can't be the whole solution, but it would help," he says.

The threat of nuclear-weapons development by Iran and North Korea and the recent controversy over U.S. nuclear assistance to India underscore the concern about proliferation. (*See sidebar, p. 228.*)

On March 2, Bush proposed helping India meet its growing civilian energy needs while allowing it to

Nuclear Plants Operate in 31 States

The 103 commercial nuclear power plants operating in 31 states produce about 20 percent of the nation's electricity. The newest plant is Tennessee's 1996 Watts Bar 1; the oldest plant is Nine Mile 1 in New York state, built in 1969.

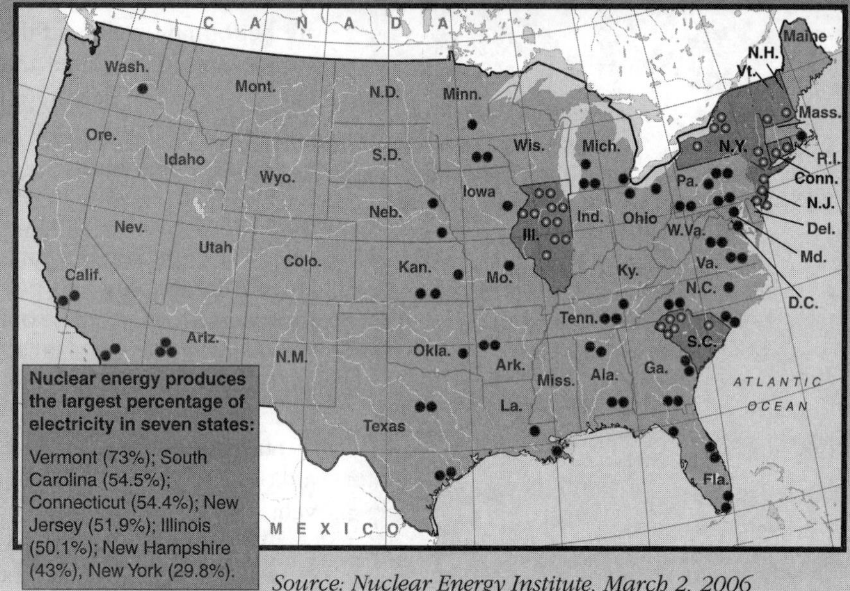

Source: Nuclear Energy Institute, March 2, 2006

continue developing nuclear weapons. Supporters said the pact was essential to maintaining nuclear stability in the region, but critics said it undermined nuclear non-proliferation efforts.

"I'm trying to think differently," Bush said in New Delhi. "Not to stay stuck in the past, and recognize that by thinking differently, particularly on nuclear power, we can achieve some important objectives: one of which is less reliance on fossil fuels, second, to work with our partners to help both our economies grow and thirdly is to be strong in dealing with nonproliferation issues." [5]

In 2004, the nation's 103 existing nuclear plants — down from 111 in 1990 — were producing power at a record 90.5 percent of total licensed capacity, up from 66 percent in 1990. [6] With power consumption projected to rise sharply in the next several decades, nuclear advocates say it's time for expansion.

"In the 21st century, our nation will need more electricity, more safe, clean, reliable electricity," said Bush while visiting Maryland's Calvert Cliffs nuclear plant in June 2005. "It is time for this country to start building nuclear power plants again." [7]

No new nuclear plants have been ordered in the United States since 1979, when an accident at the Three Mile Island plant near Middletown, Pa., triggered a partial meltdown. There were no injuries, but the resulting opposition to new plants continues today. "Nuclear energy is too expensive, it's unsafe and we don't have a good solution for handling high-level waste," says Anna Aurilio, legislative director of the U.S. Public Interest Research Group (US PIRG). Moreover, she says, the industry's optimistic cost estimates for new plants "are not borne out by the facts."

Nuclear-energy critics say the Nuclear Regulatory Commission (NRC) is not aggressive enough at regulating the industry, citing the 2002 discovery that corrosion at Ohio's Davis-Besse nuclear plant had nearly eaten through the steel around the reactor's radioactive core. The General Accounting Office (now the Government Accountability Office) called the incident the most serious at a U.S. commercial reactor since Three Mile Island. The NRC failed to detect the corrosion because its oversight "did not produce accurate information on plant conditions," said the GAO. [8]

For its part, the NRC levied a record $5.45 million fine against the plant's owners in 2005. In early 2006 the owners agreed to pay a $28 million fine to escape criminal prosecution for providing false information to the NRC about the reactor; three former plant employees eventually were indicted by a federal grand jury. [9]

Lochbaum says plant owners should be required to fix known safety problems more quickly and the NRC should have more sophisticated ways to monitor reactors as they age. "Surprises keep coming up," he says. "We haven't done a good job of picking the most vulnerable areas to monitor for aging, and sometimes inspections look at the right areas but don't catch problems." *(See "At Issue," p. 233.)*

While the NRC describes itself as "a pain in the neck" regulator forbidden by law from promoting nuclear power, Lochbaum also says the NRC is under pressure to do just that. "Congress and the administration have been hammering the NRC to get out of the industry's way and not be a regulatory burden, and the commission has heard the message," he says. For example, he says, before the problems at Davis-Besse were uncovered, the NRC had diverted personnel from inspections there to work on extending reactor licenses, a contention the NRC denies.

Overall safety at U.S. nuclear plants has improved dramatically since the 1980s. "There's no such thing as perfect safety, but the probability of an accident is far smaller today than it was 10 or 20 years ago," says Robert Budnitz, head of the Nuclear and Risk Science Group at Lawrence Livermore National Laboratory and former NRC research director. "Significant events," such as reactor shutdowns and problems with important safety equipment, fell from an average of 0.9 per year per plant in 1989 to 0.02 in 2003, and unplanned automatic shutdowns declined nearly tenfold from 1980 through 2004. [10]

"The industry is proud of this improvement, and it has a right to be proud," says Budnitz. "Nuclear operators have analyzed the causes of failures at reactors and reduced accidents and safety events significantly. Better training has made the work-force culture at nuclear plants more professional and respectful of rules, and the industry has become much more responsible about policing itself."

But an even more ominous cloud has descended over nuclear safety since the terrorist attacks of Sept. 11, 2001. Many Americans now worry that terrorists might target nuclear reactors, especially since the 9/11 hijackers reportedly discussed crashing jet planes into a nuclear facility near New York City. [11]

Although the NRC has tightened security requirements, ordered more frequent and realistic attack training and insists there are multiple, redundant layers of safety and security to protect against even a large commercial aircraft, critics say plants still are vulnerable. Officials in communities surrounding nuclear plants now worry that residents cannot be evacuated quickly in emergencies, especially if populations have increased since the plants were built. (While the NRC evaluates evacuation plans, primary off-site evacuation responsibility lies with local authorities.)

As lawmakers and communities debate the need for more nuclear power plants, here are some issues they will consider:

Industry Safety Has Improved

The decreasing number of so-called significant events at U.S. nuclear plants each year is one of many indicators of the industry's improving safety record, according to the Nuclear Regulatory Commission.

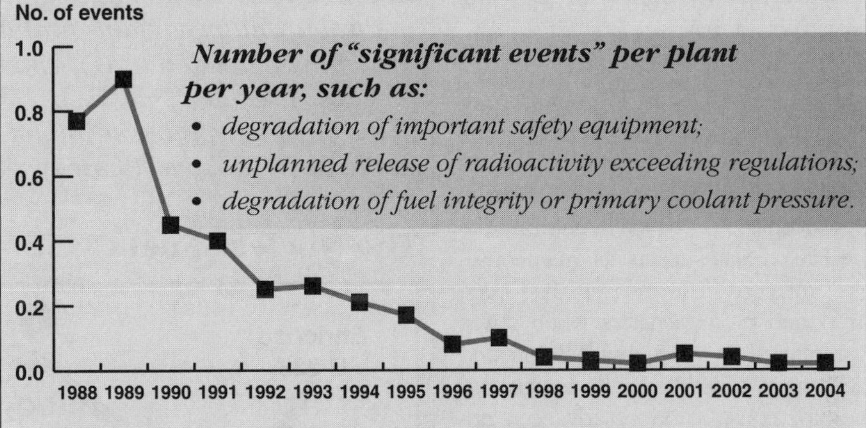

Source: Nuclear Regulatory Commission, "NRC Information Digest," December 2005

Can nuclear power "solve" the global-warming problem?

Now that scientific consensus affirms that greenhouse-gas emissions from human activities are warming Earth's climate, the nuclear industry contends that nuclear power is the best option for meeting rising energy demand without exacerbating climate problems. Nuclear reactors generate electricity without emitting carbon dioxide and other pollutants — called greenhouse gases — that hold heat in the atmosphere. Power plants burning coal, oil and natural gas produced 39 percent of U.S. carbon dioxide emissions in 2003. [12]

But nuclear-power capacity would have to expand dramatically to eliminate enough greenhouse emissions to make a difference. Nuclear plants generated 789 terawatt-hours * of electricity in 2004 — or about 22 percent of the nation's electrical power. By 2030 the U.S. Energy Information Administration (EIA) predicts that nuclear plants will generate only about 871 terawatt-hours — and that's if six new 1,000-megawatt reactors are built and 2,000 megawatts of uprates (capacity increases) are made at existing plants. But demand will have risen so sharply by then, says the EIA, that nuclear power will end up providing only about 16 percent of total U.S. power generation — a smaller share than it provides today. [13]

To significantly reduce climate change, according to a 2003 Massachusetts Institute of Technology (MIT) study, world nuclear capacity would have to roughly triple by 2050, with the United States adding 200 or more new reactors. [14] Industry representatives admit that growth on anything approaching this scale would be a serious challenge.

Even so, some prominent environmentalists have called recently for rethinking the issue of nuclear power in view of the potential threat from climate change. "Renewable energies, such as wind, geothermal and hydro are part of the solution," wrote Greenpeace co-founder Patrick Moore in early 2005. "Nuclear energy is the only non-greenhouse-gas-emitting power source that can effectively replace fossil fuels and satisfy global demand." [15]

* A terawatt is equivalent to 1 trillion watts.

However, most environmental organizations remain strongly opposed to nuclear energy because of unresolved concerns about safety and radioactive waste. Bishop Hugh Montefiore, former chairman of the British group Friends of the Earth, was forced to leave the board in late 2004 because of his support for nuclear power.[16]

In June 2005, Sens. John McCain, R-Ariz., and Joseph I. Lieberman, D-Conn., put the issue to a test when they offered a revised version of their Climate Stewardship Act, which would require the United States to cut its greenhouse-gas emissions. The measure had been supported by 43 senators when it was first offered in 2003, but McCain and Lieberman added federal loan guarantees for construction of advanced nuclear reactors and other zero-greenhouse-gas energy plants to the 2005 version. "The idea that a zero-emission technology such as nuclear has little or no place in our energy mix is just as antiquated, out-of-step and counterproductive as our continued dependence on fossil fuels," said McCain.[17]

However, the measure was defeated by a wider margin than in 2003 after nearly all major environmental groups opposed the inclusion of nuclear power. "Adding expensive and unnecessary subsidies to a global-warming bill doesn't increase support for doing something about the issue," argues US PIRG's Aurilio.

Producing Electricity From Nuclear Fuel

Processing uranium to produce fuel to generate electricity is known as the "nuclear fuel cycle." It involves converting the mined uranium into a gas, which is then "enriched" through a physical-separation process into nuclear fuel. Since only 1 percent of natural uranium contains uranium-235 (U-235), with atoms that are easily split and thus is useful for producing energy, the processing requires that the U-235 be extracted from the 99 percent of the ore that contains uranium-238 (U-238) — which is not useful for producing electricity.

The Nuclear Fuel Cycle

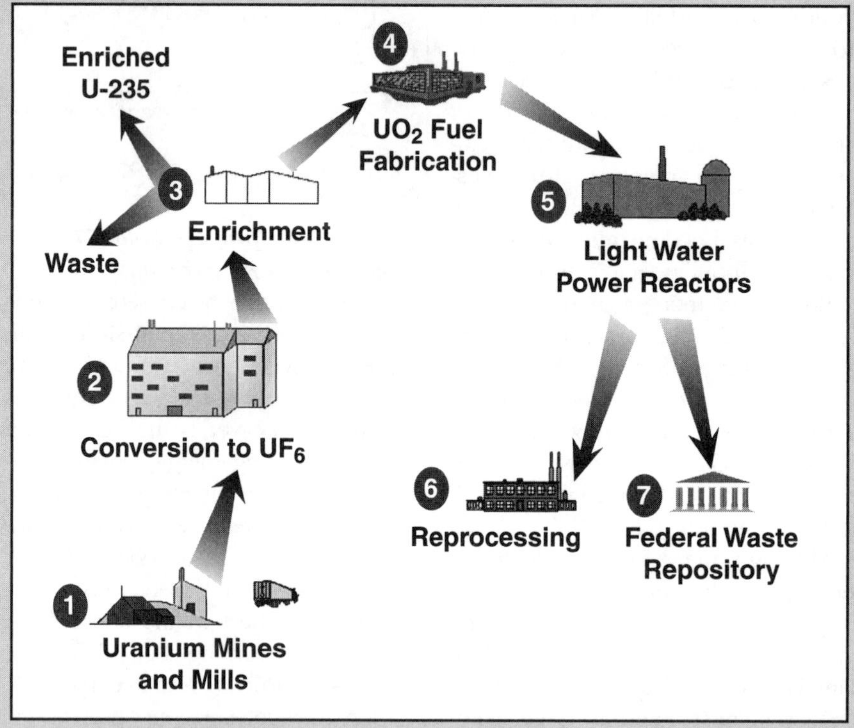

Source: U.S. Nuclear Regulatory Commission

The United States has limited options for meeting rising electricity demand without increasing greenhouse emissions. Environmentalists want investments in energy conservation and renewable fuels such as wind and solar energy. Renewable sources other than hydropower generated about 2 percent of U.S. electricity supplies in 2004, and the EIA says this share will increase only slightly by 2030. But policy choices could substantially increase renewable energy's market share, according to the bipartisan National Commission on Energy Policy, which estimated that with more funds for research and development and binding limits on greenhouse-gas emissions, non-hydro renewable-energy sources could generate up to 10 percent of U.S. electricity supplies by 2020.[18]

But even though oil and gas prices have risen sharply since 2000, fossil fuels today are still cheaper than many renewables. Coal is generally still the cheapest fuel for electricity generation, "especially since carbon dioxide emissions are not subject to any kind of nationwide cap," says Karen Palmer, an economist at the environmental group Resources for the Future.

National limits on emissions — like those proposed by McCain and Lieberman — would make renewable fuels and nuclear power more competitive with coal and natural gas, because fossil-fuel-burning plants would have to buy allowances for emissions that exceed their limits, increasing the cost of their electricity. "Even a small carbon tax

Steps in the Nuclear Fuel Cycle

1. Uranium Mining and Milling: Uranium is mined using either surface or underground techniques, depending on the depth of the ore. A mill then grinds the ore and separates out concentrated uranium oxide, called "yellowcake." (It takes about 200 tons of yellowcake to produce the fuel needed to run a large 1,000-megawatt reactor for a year.)

2. Conversion: The yellowcake is converted into a gas, uranium hexafluoride (UF_6).

3. Enrichment: The UF_6 gas is enriched through a physical process, typically diffusion through a membrane or separation in a centrifuge, to raise the amount of "fissile," or splittable, uranium-235 (U-235) in the gas from its natural level of 0.7 percent to about 3.5 percent or more. The enriched gas then moves to the next stage of the fuel cycle, fuel fabrication. The waste material — known as depleted uranium, tails or tailings — contains less than 0.25 percent U-235 and cannot be used for energy. Nearly twice as dense as lead, depleted uranium has other commercial uses.

4. UO_2 Fuel Fabrication: The enriched uranium gas is converted into uranium dioxide (UO_2) powder and pressed into fuel pellets, which are inserted into thin tubes to form fuel rods. The sealed rods are assembled into clusters to form fuel assemblies that are used in the core of the nuclear reactor.

5. Light Water Power Reactors: Hundreds of fuel assemblies make up the core of a nuclear reactor, where the U-235 isotope splits in a chain reaction that produces heat used to produce steam for driving an electric generator. In U.S. reactors, the core is cooled by normal, or "light," water. Some foreign reactors use "heavy" water, which has more deuterium and tritium, to both cool the core and help support the chain reaction. After the fuel is consumed, or "spent," it is removed from the reactor and stored in on-site ponds or air-cooled facilities for several years while its radioactivity and heat subside.

6. Reprocessing: About 1 percent of the spent fuel is fissionable U-235 and about 1 percent is plutonium that was produced in the reactor. Reprocessing separates the uranium and plutonium from waste products. The recovered uranium can be returned to the conversion plant to be reconverted to UF_6. The plutonium can be blended with enriched uranium to produce a mixed oxide fuel in a fuel-fabrication plant. The remaining high-level radioactive wastes can be stored in liquid form and subsequently solidified. Currently, reprocessing occurs in Europe and Russia, but not in the United States.

7. Federal Waste Repository: Unreprocessed spent fuel eventually will be encapsulated in sturdy, stainless steel canisters and buried in stable rock structures deep underground. Several countries are working on creating federal waste repositories, but a final disposal of spent fuel has not yet occurred. The Department of Energy is attempting to license a permanent disposal site at Yucca Mountain, in Nevada.

would benefit nuclear, although it probably won't be enough by itself to be a deciding factor in building new nuclear plants," says Palmer. But the Bush administration strongly opposes mandatory limits on greenhouse-gas emissions, which it says would increase energy prices and harm the economy.

Similarly, building more nuclear power plants will do little to reduce current U.S. dependence on imported oil in the short term because petroleum products are used mainly in the transportation sector (oil only produces about 3 percent of the nation's electricity supply). However, over the long term nuclear power could help facilitate a shift to a hydrogen-based economy, particularly in transportation. In 2003 the Bush administration launched a Hydrogen Initiative aimed at reducing U.S. oil consumption and pollution from motor vehicles by commercializing hydrogen fuel-cell vehicles and other hydrogen applications. [19]

Using hydrogen as fuel does not produce greenhouse gases if the hydrogen is made using a carbon-free electricity source. If hydrogen is made by chemically separating it from natural gas or coal, carbon dioxide is produced as a byproduct that can either be captured and stored or released into the atmosphere.

Hydrogen can also be extracted from water, using electricity; if the electricity comes from a plant powered by fossil fuel, the process still produces greenhouse-gas emissions. Nuclear reactors can provide the electricity needed for hydrogen extraction without emitting carbon dioxide, although the process is more expensive than separating hydrogen from fossil fuels. But advanced "Generation IV" reactors being developed for deployment after 2030 could produce hydrogen from water more efficiently. [20]

In any case, hydrogen production is not a factor in near-term decisions on nuclear power because other major elements of a hydrogen economy, such as distribution systems and cheaper fuel cells, have yet to be developed. "It's not going to happen tomorrow, but if we're going to go to large-scale hydrogen, then we should produce it with non-emitting technologies, and if nuclear plants can do it efficiently and economically, we should look at that," says NEI's Fertel.

Does the U.S. have a viable program for managing nuclear waste?

For more than 30 years, U.S. policy for managing high-level nuclear waste has centered on a "once-through" fuel cycle in which fuel is irradiated once in a reactor, then disposed of permanently in an underground repository. Today, frustration with the slow progress of the government's efforts to build a repository for the nuclear waste is undermining some policymakers' support for this approach. [21]

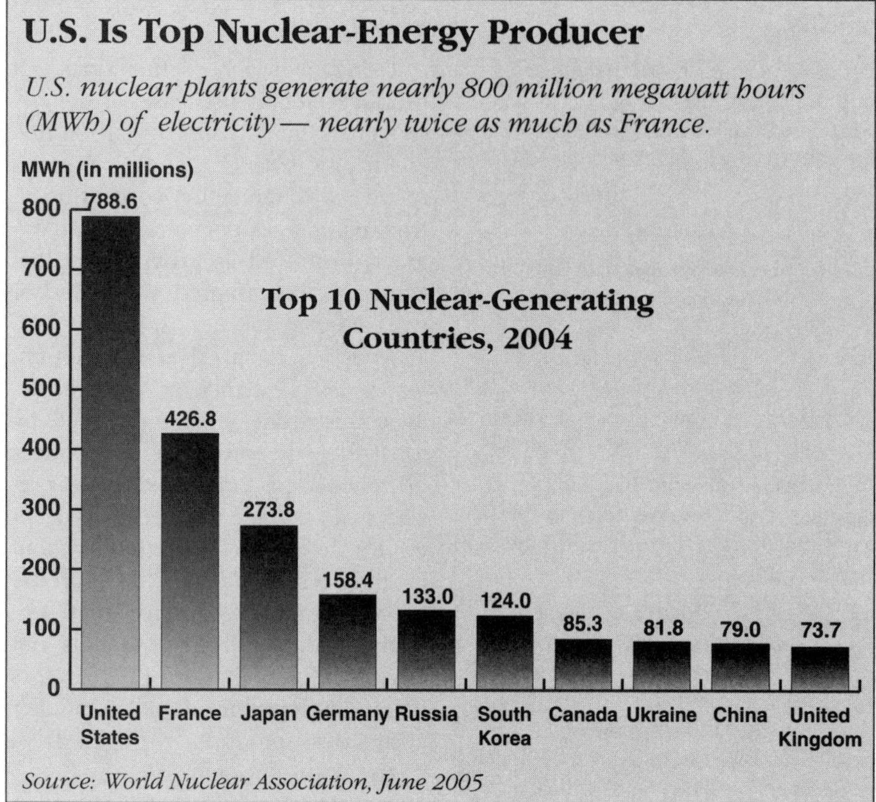

The Nuclear Waste Policy Act of 1987 directed the Department of Energy (DOE) to build a repository deep inside Nevada's Yucca Mountain to store 70,000 tons of high-level nuclear waste, mainly from commercial nuclear power reactors. DOE was to devise a repository capable of containing spent fuel for tens of thousands of years while its radioactive emissions decay to natural background levels.

After more than 20 years and $4 billion of scientific analysis, Energy Secretary Spencer Abraham in February 2002 formally recommended Yucca Mountain as a suitable site for the repository, and both Congress and President Bush approved the recommendation.

"A repository at Yucca Mountain will bring together the location, natural barriers and design elements necessary to protect the health and safety of the public, including those Americans living in the immediate vicinity, now and long into the future," Abraham said in a letter to Bush. [22]

Since then, however, the project has hit several new roadblocks. Until recently, DOE estimated that the site would be ready to start accepting waste by 2010 (well past its original target date of 1998), but now the department has stopped forecasting an official opening date. [23]

Environmental groups and Nevada officials say the waste could leach from the repository during the thousands of years it would be stored, exposing people nearby to dangerous radiation. In July 2004, the U.S. Circuit Court of Appeals rejected the Environmental Protection Agency's (EPA) proposed standard for radiation exposure in the area surrounding Yucca Mountain. [24] The EPA had proposed an overall dose of no more than 15 millirem per year (about equal to three chest X-rays) for 10,000 years after the repository closes. But Congress had directed EPA to conform its standard to the National Academy of Sciences' estimated time of peak exposure risk, which was hundreds of thousands of years into the future. [25]

EPA then proposed adding a limit of 350 millirem per year for the period lasting from 10,000 years after the repository is closed up to 1 million years. Lawrence Livermore's Budnitz says DOE was prepared to meet EPA's original standard for protecting the public from radiation for 10,000 years, but that the revised standard will require further study.

"We have a very strong understanding of doses for the first 10,000 years, and we should be able to meet those criteria," he says. "But until EPA's new analysis of doses over 1 million years is done and evaluated, it's premature to say whether we have that understanding. Whatever the final standard is, the NRC will have to approve the license, and it will carry out a stringent review of the repository so the public can have confidence in the decision."

However some experts question the EPA's revised standard. "It's a cop-out," says Allison Macfarlane, a senior research associate and nuclear waste expert at MIT. "The waste canisters will fail after about 100,000 years, so the radiation doses increase significantly after that point, but you can't estimate doses a million years out."

Nevada is challenging the EPA standards in court, along with the DOE's plan to designate federal lands in Nevada for a rail line to ship waste to the site. Some nuclear critics argue that moving spent fuel cross-country could lead to accidental releases of radiation, but a 2006 study by the National Academy of Sciences found "no fundamental technical barriers to the safe transport of spent nuclear fuel and high-level radioactive waste in the United States." [26] Nuclear-waste shipments would cross some 43 states.

Robert Loux, director of the Nevada nuclear projects office, says the DOE is redoing its Yucca Mountain hydrology model — showing how water moves through the site — because of data-quality questions and is launching a broader re-evaluation of the entire program that may last for several years.

"The program at DOE is in chaos, and the regulatory foundation will probably be uncertain for a very long time because EPA's standards have been repeatedly thrown out of court," says Loux. "Our view is that the project is dead, and that sooner or later the industry will recommend that Congress pull the plug. Congress could legislate standards, but that doesn't improve the site or DOE's competence to develop a repository."

But the DOE insists that Yucca Mountain will be licensed and constructed. "This project will fulfill a government obligation to the commercial nuclear power industry, and it will remove what has been a major impediment to new nuclear construction in this country. And we are committed to completing this important project," Energy Secretary Samuel Bodman said in May 2005. [27]

However, Congress has underfunded administration requests for research and development for the Yucca Mountain project. Work on a nuclear-waste repository is funded partly by a user fee of 0.1 cents per kilowatt-hour on nuclear electricity, paid into a Nuclear Waste Fund that can only be used for work on a repository. Since the fund was created in 1982, electricity customers have paid more than $24 billion into the fund, and the balance is growing at more than $1 billion annually, plus interest.

But Congress frequently appropriates less for the fund than DOE requests, because under current budget procedures payments into the fund are treated as general revenues that go into the federal treasury, not as collections to offset spending on a repository. Thus Congress has little incentive to spend all of the money on the repository.

Since the fund currently stands at just over $16 billion, nuclear industry and state energy officials argue that Congress has been using the money to offset federal budget deficits in other areas and have demanded assurances the funds are spent only on the repository. DOE has also called on Congress to revise its budgeting practices so that enough funds will be appropriated to carry out work on Yucca Mountain. [28]

"The nation's electric ratepayers have been paying for a nuclear-waste repository for over 20 years," Robert Garvin, chairman of the Wisconsin Public Service Commission, told the House Energy and Commerce Committee in March 2005. "It is past time for ratepayers to get what they have paid for." [29]

The DOE is required to report to Congress between January 2007 and 2010 on whether the nation needs a second repository to handle high-level waste. Yucca Mountain is legally limited to storing 70,000 metric tons of spent fuel, but DOE has estimated that up to 105,000 tons of commercial spent fuel and other radioactive waste may require disposal by 2035. [30]

"Yucca Mountain is basically full today because of the substantial quantities of spent waste that [already] exist around our country" and are waiting to be transferred to Yucca, Bodman said recently. [31]

Congress has several options for addressing this dilemma, including increasing the limit on Yucca Mountain storage (which DOE has said is technically possible), or directing DOE to begin looking for a second repository site. The Bush administration, however, supports a third, more controversial and costly option: reprocessing spent fuel to reduce the volume that must be stored. (*See sidebar, p. 228.*)

Should the United States subsidize new nuclear reactors?

According to a study published in 2000, the nuclear power industry received $145 billion worth of federal subsidies from 1943 to 1999, including both direct benefits, such as research-and-development funding, and indirect benefits such as liability limits that reduce plant owners' insurance premiums. [32] But critics question whether new nuclear plants should receive further federal subsidies, given the scope of past government support and the fact that the industry is now developing its fourth generation of reactors.

In the Energy Policy Act of 2005, Congress approved several additional incentives for building advanced nuclear plants, including $2 billion in risk insurance to compensate for construction delays at up to six new reactors; a tax credit of 1.8 cents per kilowatt-hour for electricity generated by the first new reactors; and loan guarantees for innovative technologies that reduce air pollution and greenhouse-gas emissions, including advanced, new nuclear plants. It also extended the federal cap on nuclear plant liability through 2025.

"With the practical steps in this bill, America is moving closer to a vital national goal," said President Bush in signing the bill on Aug. 8, 2005. "We will start building nuclear plants again by the end of this decade."

Nuclear advocates point out that reactor owners pay all or part of many costs that other energy sources are not required to cover, such as waste disposal and decommissioning closed plants. And incentives for the first, few nuclear power plants are justified, they argue, because of the enormous amounts of capital involved and the history of long regulatory delays in the 1970s and '80s.

A "systematic, disciplined program to build nuclear power plants" is justified, the NEI's Fertel told Congress in April 2005, because nuclear power is "a strategic national asset." Thus, a comprehensive program is needed to address the business concerns — including licensing and regulatory issues, development of new plant designs and financing — that could block new plant construction, he said. [33]

Many energy experts agree that some support for new nuclear plants is justified. Both the 2003 MIT nuclear power study and the 2004 report of the National Commission on Energy Policy recommended that the government share costs with industry for designing and licensing a few, new advanced-design reactors. "Government subsidies for first movers in a new generation of reactor construction are the entry fee that will give us a chance to show whether we can build cheaper and safer reactors," says energy commission co-chair Holdren.

Fiscal conservatives argue that the nuclear industry itself should bear the financial risks of building new plants. When the Senate was debating the 2005 Energy Policy Act, Sen. John E. Sununu, R-N.H., unsuccessfully tried to strike loan guarantees for new reactor construction, which he said would set "a terrible precedent, putting the taxpayers on the hook for billion-dollar loans to successful, private, profitable corporations." Although he supports nuclear power, Sununu said, the measure would leave the federal government liable for the full value of the loans if the projects failed.

The Nuclear Energy Institute points out in a recent report that government-industry partnerships frequently have been used to strengthen the nation's infrastructure: "This approach has worked to bolster the country's transportation, rural electrification, telecommunications, land and water projects," the institute said, noting that similar approaches were used to promote merchant marine modernization and to help the airlines survive the economic downturn that ensued after the 9/11 terrorist attacks. [34]

That may be true, say opponents, but nuclear power has already received enough support. "These measures are simply corporate welfare," says Jill Lancelot, president of Taxpayers for Common Sense. "This is a mature industry — it's over 50 years old, and it's had cradle-to-grave subsidies that distort price signals and undermine the natural market forces of the energy industry. It's time for the industry to stand on its own feet — innovation should be a cost of doing business for nuclear power."

Other energy industries, including oil, gas, coal and renewable energy, receive various forms of government support ranging from research and development funds to tax credits and "portfolio standards" that require electricity suppliers to generate a specific fraction of their energy from specified fuels. The effectiveness of any of these measures depends in large part on how they are designed. [35]

In any case, nuclear plant owners want federal and state regulations to treat nuclear energy the same as other non-polluting energy sources. Under so-called "cap-and-trade" regulations, traditional energy producers receive credits that allow them to produce specific levels of emissions each year. Sources that produce less pollution than they are allowed can sell their extra credits to other plants that emit more than their allowances.

Nuclear advocates say nuclear plants that do not produce emissions should be rewarded with allowances that they can sell, which would reduce their cost of producing power and make them more competitive with polluting plants.

In 2003, New Hampshire revised its regulations controlling emissions of nitrogen oxides (NOx), a primary ingredient of smog, so that the Seabrook nuclear plant could receive NOx emission credits if it is allowed to increase its power output because nuclear plants generate power without emitting NOx. Other states have been reluctant to let nuclear plants receive this kind of credit for "avoided" emissions, but the industry argues that any plant that produces emission-free energy — whether it uses wind, solar energy or nuclear power — should be credited. [36]

Most environmentalists support awarding credits for emission-free electricity generation to renewable-energy sources but argue that nuclear power is a well-established industry that does not need this type of support to gain market share, and that nuclear energy has negative environmental impacts that should not be rewarded with subsidies.

In a 2004 report, the National Association of State PIRGs predicted that the Seabrook nuclear plant might receive up to one-third of the allowances that New Hampshire had set aside under its NOx-control program to encourage cleaner power sources. "The risk of catastrophic radiation release due to accident or sabotage, the dangers posed by routine emissions of radiation and the as-yet unresolved problems surrounding the long-term storage of nuclear waste mean that nuclear power cannot be considered an environmentally acceptable solution to the problem of climate change," the association argued. [37] ■

BACKGROUND

A New Industry

Civilian nuclear power emerged after World War II as a spin-off from the top-secret atomic bomb program. In 1946 Congress placed nuclear-research facilities under civilian control and created the Atomic Energy Commission (AEC) to manage the new industry. [38]

But while politicians saw nuclear energy as an important symbol of American scientific and technical leadership, private firms had little interest in what they viewed as a risky, new field. Early U.S. nuclear-energy research was driven mainly by scientists and the armed forces: *Business Week* reported in 1950 that "AEC people have had to beat on desks in order to find a company willing to take on projects." [39]

To increase business interest, Congress in 1954 allowed private companies to own nuclear-power reactors, and in 1957 the Price-Anderson Act capped private liability for reactor accidents at $560 million, allaying utilities' fears that they would be unable to obtain insurance for the potentially

Continued on p. 228

Chronology

1970s ***Nuclear power expands following oil shocks.***

October 1973
Arab members of the Organization of Petroleum Exporting Countries (OPEC) embargo oil shipments to the United States. . . . U.S. utilities order 41 new nuclear reactors.

1974
India detonates a "peaceful" nuclear weapon, raising global concern over nuclear proliferation.

1977
President Jimmy Carter declares a national energy crisis, introduces measures to reduce U.S. dependence on oil imports and bans reprocessing of spent nuclear fuel to avoid stockpiling weapons-grade plutonium.

1979
A partial meltdown at the Three Mile Island nuclear plant near Middletown, Pa., triggers cancellations of plans for new plants and tighter regulations on reactors.

1980s ***An explosion at a nuclear plant in Chernobyl, Ukraine, increases concern about nuclear power safety.***

Jan. 7, 1983
Nuclear Waste Policy Act directs Department of Energy (DOE) to take charge of spent nuclear fuel by Jan. 31, 1998.

April 26, 1986
An explosion at the Chernobyl nuclear power plant kills 50 emergency workers and causes thousands of cases of radiation illness in Ukraine and surrounding countries.

1987
Congress directs DOE to research underground storage of nuclear waste at Nevada's Yucca Mountain.

1990s ***Nuclear reactor performance improves as regulators take steps to support new plant construction.***

1991
Inspections after the first Persian Gulf War reveal a massive, secret, nuclear-weapons program in Iraq, prompting the International Atomic Energy Agency (IAEA) to seek stronger powers to inspect nuclear facilities worldwide.

1992
Energy Policy Act revises U.S. reactor-licensing rules to reduce construction delays by awarding single licenses to construct and operate nuclear reactors.

1995
Nuclear Non-Proliferation Treaty of 1968, now with 177 member countries, is extended and made permanent.

1997
The U.S. and more than 150 other nations sign the Kyoto Protocol, which sets targets and timetables for cutting industrialized countries' greenhouse-gas emissions to slow global climate change.

1998
Baltimore Gas and Electric applies for 20-year license extension at its Calvert Cliffs plant. . . . DOE misses its deadline for beginning to store commercial nuclear fuel wastes. . . . India and Pakistan test nuclear weapons from materials obtained for peaceful purposes.

2000s ***Energy companies become more positive about building new nuclear plants.***

2001
President Bush's energy policy calls for expanding nuclear power.

2002
Opposition group reveals that Iran is building a uranium-enrichment plant that could be used for civilian or military purposes. IAEA reveals Iran has carried out secret nuclear research for 18 years.

2003
New Hampshire awards economic credits to the Seabrook nuclear power plant as a non-polluting energy source. . . . North Korea withdraws from Nuclear Non-Proliferation Treaty.

2004
Nine U.S. nuclear energy companies form the NuStart consortium to seek licenses for advanced nuclear reactors at two sites by 2011.

2005
Energy Policy Act of 2005 provides loan guarantees and tax credits for new, advanced nuclear reactors and extends liability protection for the nuclear industry. . . . DOE delays the opening date for the nuclear waste repository at Yucca Mountain.

2006
In his State of the Union address, President Bush calls for more reliance on nuclear power to break America's "addiction" to oil. . . . On March 2 Bush agrees to a controversial plan to end a decades-long moratorium on sales of nuclear fuel and reactor components to India, allowing it to expand its nuclear power while continuing to develop nuclear weapons.

India and the Challenge of Non-Proliferation

The recent announcement of what President Bush called a "historic" nuclear pact between the United States and India has generated concern about continuing nuclear weapons proliferation and the threat of nuclear terrorism.

"This deal not only lets India amass as many nuclear weapons as it wants, it looks like we made no effort to try to curtail them," said George Perkovich, vice president for studies at the Carnegie Endowment for International Peace." [1]

Under the agreement, announced on March 2, the United States would end its longstanding ban on the sale of civilian nuclear fuel and reactor components to India — which has refused to sign the Nuclear Non-Proliferation Treaty (NPT) — while allowing it to continue developing nuclear weapons. [2]

Supporters said the deal would help India fulfill its civilian energy needs while creating a strategic partner for the United States in a volatile region. Critics say it sets a dangerous precedent that may undermine efforts to prevent other nations, such as Iran and North Korea, from developing nuclear weapons in defiance of international treaties.

The proposed deal is "an absolute torpedo aimed at the midship of the whole nuclear non-proliferation regime," says Jonathan Schell, author of *The Unconquerable World: Power, Nonviolence, and the Will of the People.* It paves the way for the "new nuclear world order" of unlimited and unconstrained proliferation heralded by Indian Prime Minister Manmohan Singh, he said. [3]

But supporters of the deal say Bush is merely being a realist, acknowledging that India has had nuclear weapons for 30 years. "This deal brings a country that's been developing nuclear programs . . . into the non-proliferation mainstream," said Richard Boucher, the new assistant secretary of State for South and Central Asian Affairs. "As they develop nuclear power, it's better for us to be cooperating with them than not." The deal would increase the percentage of India's nuclear capacity that is under international safeguards from the current 19 percent to 65 percent, he said, and "over time . . . up to 90 percent." [4]

Besides being a realist, Bush is being a pragmatist, said Ashton Carter, co-director of the Preventive Defense Project at Harvard's Kennedy School of Government and a former assistant secretary of Defense. Bush wants a "strategic partnership" in a region where two of India's neighbors, China and Pakistan, have nuclear weapons. India can serve as "a counterweight to China if one is required sometime in the future," Carter said. And "if something goes wrong in Pakistan, we want to have neighbors who help us." [5]

Nevertheless, he said, "avoiding nuclear terrorism and nuclear proliferation is the most important security objective of the United States." Terrorists are most likely to seek nuclear weapons, but they also can use nuclear materials produced in nuclear power programs.

Since the Soviet Union's breakup in 1991, the three non-Russian republics where nuclear weapons had been stored — Ukraine, Belarus and Kazakhstan — have returned those weapons to Russia and joined the NPT as non-nuclear states. Now, the United States and other countries are helping to upgrade security for Russia's thousands of nuclear weapons and radioactive materials — reportedly about 180 tons of separated plutonium and 1,100 tons of highly enriched uranium (HEU), which is used for nuclear weapons. But security has only been upgraded at half of Russia's nuclear-materials storage sites. [6]

In December 2005, the federal commission appointed to analyze the Sept. 11, 2001, terrorist attacks gave the U.S. government a "D" grade on its efforts to secure weapons of

Continued from p. 226

severe damage that a major nuclear accident might cause. [40]

These and other federal incentives gradually stimulated private investments in nuclear power. By 1960, only three commercial nuclear plants had been licensed, but applications increased through the decade, spurred by sharply rising demand for electricity. By 1970, 20 reactors were operating, and dozens more were under construction. However, opponents blocked several projects they claimed were unsafe, including two plants in California and Oregon that were located on earthquake faults. Meanwhile, some facilities experienced serious accidents — including partial meltdowns at a prototype mobile reactor at Idaho Falls in 1961 and an experimental breeder reactor — for plutonium production — near Detroit in 1966.

However, these events received little media coverage, and public views of nuclear energy remained positive. [41]

Limiting Nuclear Weapons

Scientists and U.S. leaders recognized from the outset that civilian nuclear reactors and facilities for processing uranium and spent nuclear fuel could be used to produce highly enriched uranium or plutonium, both of which could be used to make nuclear weapons. To prevent this, the U.S. proposed in the 1946 Baruch Plan that an international organization be established to control nuclear weapons and nuclear power activities — from mining uranium to operating nuclear reactors. The Soviet Union, which wanted to develop nuclear weapons, rejected the plan. [42]

In 1953 President Dwight D. Eisenhower again called for peaceful cooperation on nuclear energy. In his "Atoms for Peace" speech, Eisenhower proposed creating an agency at the United Nations to promote civilian applications of nuclear technology worldwide. Eisenhower's initiative led to the establishment in 1957 of the International Atomic Energy Agency (IAEA), which was charged with ensuring that nuclear plants were not producing nuclear weapons. [43]

mass destruction, noting, "Countering the greatest threat to America's security is still not the top national-security priority of the president and the Congress." [7] In fact, in his 2005 budget, Bush requested cuts in funds to safeguard nuclear weapons in Russia. [8]

Under the NPT, non-nuclear weapons states that sign the pact have an "inalienable right" to develop peaceful nuclear energy. Honoring this commitment while limiting the spread of nuclear weapons has been a longstanding U.S. challenge. [9]

Since 1978, the United States has required non-nuclear weapons countries to open their entire nuclear programs to "full-scope" International Atomic Energy Agency (IAEA) monitoring before they can receive nuclear exports from the United States. But by the time those conditions were imposed, several countries had developed or researched nuclear weapons using materials and technologies imported from abroad — often after pledging to use the equipment for peaceful purposes. Three such countries — India, Israel and Pakistan — refused to sign the NPT and thus remain outside of the pact.

Today, with Iran and North Korea suspected of carrying out nuclear weapons research at civilian facilities, persuading their leaders to give up their nuclear programs is widely considered the world's foremost non-proliferation challenge.

Because many countries have cheated on non-proliferation commitments, experts say access to the nuclear fuel cycle should be restricted. In 2004, President Bush urged major nuclear-supplier countries to stop selling enrichment and reprocessing technology to countries that did not already have them. [10] And IAEA Director General Mohamed ElBaradei, upon accepting the 2005 Nobel Peace Prize, recommended establishing an international fuel bank and a multinational system for producing, supplying and disposing of nuclear fuel so countries would not have to develop enrichment and reprocessing facilities on their own. [11]

ElBaradei also stressed the need to strengthen international safeguards and verification systems. The United States, however, spent less than $5 million on technical-safeguards research and development in 2005. [12] "The IAEA has inspectors deployed throughout the world at nuclear facilities, and some relatively modest investments in better technologies would make them much more effective," says Steve Fetter, dean of the University of Maryland's School of Public Policy.

1 Quoted in Steven R. Weisman, "Dissenting on Atomic Deal," *The New York Times*, March 3, 2006, p. A10.

2 Elisabeth Bumiller and Somini Sengupta, "Bush and India Reach Pact That Allows Nuclear Sales," *The New York Times*, March 3, 2006, p. A1.

3 Quoted from WBUR's OnPoint Show, "Nuclear Ambitions," March 7, 2006. Also see David Von Drehle, "The Multipolar Unilateralist," *The Washington Post*, March 5, 2006, p. B2.

4 WBUR, *ibid.*

5 *Ibid.*

6 "The Security of WMD Related Material in Russia," Annual Report for the NATO Parliamentary Assembly, December 2005, www.nato-pa.int/Default.asp?SHORTCUT=695.

7 9/11 Public Discourse Project, "Final Report on 9/11 Commission Recommendations," Dec. 5, 2005, p. 4.

8 Miles A. Pomper, "Bush Stresses Importance of Nunn-Lugar Programs but Cuts Funds in 2005 Budget Request," Arms Control Association, March 2004.

9 For background, see Mary H. Cooper, "Nuclear Proliferation and Terrorism," *CQ Researcher*, April 2, 2004, pp. 297-320.

10 "President Announces New Measures to Counter the Threat of WMD," Feb. 11, 2004, www.whitehouse.gov.

11 "Nobel Lecture by IAEA Director General and Nobel Peace Prize Laureate 2005 Dr. Mohamed ElBaradei," www.iaea.org.

12 American Physical Society, *op. cit.*, pp. 6-13.

By this time, though, the nuclear club was already growing. Britain exploded its first atomic bomb in 1952, followed by France in 1960. In 1963 President John F. Kennedy predicted that within a decade the U.S might face "a world in which 15 or 20 or 25 nations may [have] these weapons. I regard that as the greatest possible danger and hazard." [44] China tested its first weapon the following year.

These steps lent urgency to talks that had been in process since 1958 on a treaty to limit the spread of nuclear weapons. [45] Under the Nuclear Non-Proliferation Treaty, signed by 98 countries in 1968, all members other than the five declared nuclear-weapons states pledged never to develop nuclear weapons. In return, the treaty guaranteed signatories access to peaceful nuclear materials and technologies. [46]

Momentum Stalls

A series of upheavals in the 1970s sharply undercut public support for nuclear power and halted new reactor orders by 1980. [47]

When Arab oil-producing states embargoed oil exports to the United States in 1973 to protest American support for Israel, the resulting spike in energy prices made nuclear power more competitive with fossil fuels — at least in the short term. But households and businesses responded by conserving energy, reducing demand for electric power. State regulators became less willing to approve rate hikes or let companies pass costs through to customers. As a result, many utilities ran short of cash and had to borrow money at high interest rates, increasing the already steep costs of building new reactors.

The emergence of an environmental movement helped to blunt nuclear power's growth. New laws such as the National Environmental Policy Act of 1970 subjected reactors to environmental reviews, further prolonging the licensing process and driving up construction costs. [48]

Activists also began to question the safety of nuclear power. For example, the Union of Concerned Scientists asserted in 1971, citing information from government researchers, that the Atomic Energy Commission was not looking closely enough at possible flaws in reactors' emergency core-cooling systems and called for a halt to licensing new nuclear plants. [49]

Nuclear waste also became an issue in the 1970s. U.S. policy called for reprocessing spent fuel, recycling plutonium in reactors and putting remaining wastes in an underground repository. But in 1972 work on a Kansas repository was canceled after the site proved geologically unsuitable. Instead, the commission proposed building a surface interim-storage facility, but it was unclear whether or when it would be ready. With public concern growing, several states barred construction of new reactors until a permanent solution was found for managing nuclear waste. [50]

As questions mounted, critics charged that the AEC was paying more attention to expanding nuclear power than to safety and waste-management issues. In 1974 President Gerald R. Ford abolished the AEC and replaced it with two agencies: the Energy Research and Development Agency (which later became the Energy Department) to promote nuclear power, and the Nuclear Regulatory Commission (NRC) to regulate it. Three years later Congress abolished its Joint Committee on Atomic Energy, which was viewed as highly secretive and too supportive of the nuclear industry. Many other committees began holding open hearings that further publicized nuclear controversies.

Concerns increased during this period that nuclear-power programs abroad were furthering the spread of nuclear weapons. In 1974 India tested what it called a "peaceful" atomic weapon that was fueled with plutonium made in a civilian reactor, and a 1975 CIA report described Taiwan, South Korea, Pakistan, Argentina, Brazil, Libya, South Africa, Iran, Egypt and Spain as "threshold states" that could produce nuclear weapons by 1985. [51]

In 1977, President Jimmy Carter indefinitely deferred reprocessing and commercial development of breeder reactors — used to create plutonium — in an effort to discourage other countries from developing plutonium stockpiles. This meant the United States would only follow a "once-through" fuel cycle, sending spent fuel directly to a repository after using it once in a reactor.

On March 28, 1979, a reactor at the Three Mile Island plant near Middletown, Pa., suffered a partial core meltdown after a stuck valve drained too much cooling water from the reactor. [52] Although the accident was ultimately found to have released only small amounts of radiation, it sharply increased public fear of nuclear power. Many standing reactor orders were canceled, and new orders ceased completely. New safety requirements led to expensive modifications at operating reactors and plants under construction.

For the next decade, the nuclear industry struggled to regain momentum. President Ronald Reagan lifted the ban on commercial reprocessing, but private industry did not pursue the technology because of its high cost. The Nuclear Waste Policy Act of 1982 set timetables for developing two underground waste repositories, but the Energy Department was unable to find communities willing to host them. [53]

In 1987 Congress designated Yucca Mountain as the only site to be studied, drawing protests from Nevada that it had been chosen because of its small population, not because it was technically suitable. [54]

Against this backdrop the number of U.S. reactors grew from 71 in 1980 to 111 in 1990 as projects were completed, but many were finished far behind schedule and over budget. After an explosion at Ukraine's Chernobyl reactor in May 1986 killed dozens and sent a radioactive cloud across Western Europe, concerns about safety increased, although utilities stressed that the Chernobyl reactor had a different and riskier design than U.S. nuclear plants.

One of the most controversial projects, the Shoreham reactor on Long Island, was shut down in 1988 without ever going online after New York Gov. Mario M. Cuomo refused to certify that the region could be safely evacuated in an emergency. The $5.3 billion loss was absorbed by utility investors and electricity customers on Long Island.

A New Era?

In the 1990s, nuclear advocates began laying the groundwork for a new generation of reactors. The Energy Policy Act of 1992 streamlined licensing procedures by creating a combined license to build and operate nuclear plants. [55] Formerly, utilities had to obtain construction licenses and then apply for operating licenses, giving opponents two chances to block new plants and often leading to design changes during construction. The new approach also allowed the NRC to pre-approve reactor sites and standardize plant designs.

The 1992 law also spurred a major restructuring of the electric-power industry, leading many states to begin deregulating their retail power markets, opening them up to competition. [56] Although many observers predicted that nuclear plants would close because reactors' high capital costs made them unable to compete with cheaper fuels, nuclear power survived deregulation handily. Many utilities that owned only one or two reactors sold them to larger power companies that could run them more efficiently. Power output at U.S. reactors rose from 66 percent of total licensed capacity in 1980 to 88.1 percent in 2000 as operators reduced shutdowns for maintenance and unplanned safety problems. [57]

Deregulation gave nuclear power operators "an incentive to improve their performance," says economist Palmer of Resources for the Future. "It's one of the success stories of competition."

As nuclear plants' performance improved, NRC approvals of applications for power uprates rose from 13 in the 1980s to 33 in the 1990s. [58] These increases in licensed reactor output allowed nuclear plants to maintain their share of the electric-power market even though several older reactors closed in the 1990s. In 1998, reactor owners began applying to extend their 40-year operating licenses for another 20 years. The NRC approved each of these requests after conducting thorough plant-safety reviews. To date, over 100 power uprates have been granted, often in the form of multiple, incremental increases at a single site. The NRC is required to grant the increase if a plant meets safety and environmental requirements. The same holds true for the 39 license extensions granted so far.

In his 2001 energy plan, President Bush strongly endorsed expanding nuclear power, but the 9/11 terrorist attacks raised questions about whether nuclear reactors might be similarly targeted. [59] NRC Chairman Richard Meserve stated in September 2002 that it would be prudent "to presume that al Qaeda may consider nuclear facilities as potential targets." [60] The commission tightened security requirements at nuclear plants and increased the size of a likely attacking force in contingency plans.

In 2004, the National Academy of Sciences (NAS) warned Congress that if terrorist attacks partially or totally drained pools at reactor sites, where highly radioactive spent fuel rods are stored underwater, the fuel's zirconium cladding could catch fire and release large amounts of radiation. The report recommended steps to make spent fuel pools less vulnerable, such as rearranging the fuel to distribute heat loads evenly and adding water-spray systems to cool the fuel if pools were damaged. [61]

Over the next several years, fossil fuel prices rose sharply as oil and gas supplies tightened, improving the competitive position of nuclear plants. Additionally, because world uranium supplies were plentiful and distributed among many supplier countries, advocates contended that increased use of nuclear power would help insulate the U.S. economy against unstable fuel prices.

But as work on the Yucca Mountain repository lagged farther behind schedule, the problem of managing nuclear waste remained the industry's Achilles' heel. The DOE missed its 1998 deadline for starting to accept spent fuel from nuclear plant owners, forcing a growing number of energy companies to store spent fuel at their reactor sites in dry casks, once the fuel had cooled enough to be removed from cooling pools.

By the end of 2004, a total of 49 reactors were storing spent fuel onsite in casks, and another 45 facilities were building or planning to build onsite storage. [62] Three courts had found DOE in breach of its contractual responsibility to accept spent fuel, creating major potential liabilities for taxpayers. ■

Current Situation

Licensed to Build

Encouraged by NRC's streamlining of the licensing process and nuclear power's improving economics, energy companies are edging closer to building new reactors, although none have made firm commitments yet.

Exelon, Entergy and Dominion Resources have applied for early permits to build new reactors at existing nuclear plant sites in Illinois, Mississippi and Virginia, respectively, and Southern Company plans to apply for an early site permit at its Vogtle, Ga., nuclear plant this year. [63] If the applications are approved, the companies can bank the licenses while they decide whether to build new units.

As many as seven other companies and groups of companies are preparing to apply for licenses to build "Generation III" advanced nuclear plants at other existing reactor sites, mainly in the South. [64] The new plants would be simpler, more rugged and have more safety features than 1970s- and '80s-era Generation II reactors now operating in the United States and most other nuclear countries. [65] The NRC has certified four Generation III designs and is reviewing others. Certification, which is valid for 15 years, means the NRC has approved the reactor designs as safe for general use, so their safety features cannot be challenged during licensing of specific projects.

While no application to the NRC is expected until well into 2007, the companies have indicated plans to build as many as 17 new reactors.

The Department of Energy's Nuclear Power 2010 program, which aims to reduce barriers to construction of new nuclear plants, is paying half of the cost of first-time demonstrations of NRC's new combined construction/operating license process at two sites, a project expected to cost about $1.1 billion. [66]

"Showing the new plants can be built on schedule and on budget, including licensing, is one of the nuclear industry's biggest challenges, given some of the cost overruns that occurred in the 1980s," says NEI's Fertel. "The 1992 reforms to the licensing process do a lot to address past risks and should provide investors with a high degree of certainty at the time when they will be required to commit capital."

Reprocessing Used Nuclear Fuel

There are two ways to handle nuclear waste — store it or reprocess it. Neither alternative comes without risks and costs, and the Bush administration proposes reprocessing — the more controversial approach.

Commercial nuclear-reactor fuel consists of enriched-uranium pellets, which are sealed in long metal rods. The fuel rods are packaged in assemblies (bundles) that can weigh more than 1,000 pounds. Used or "spent" fuel assemblies are removed from reactors when they have absorbed so many neutrons that they can no longer sustain a chain reaction, although they still contain substantial amounts of uranium and plutonium. They are highly radioactive and must be cooled underwater in pools for at least several years before they can be processed.

Countries that practice a "once-through" fuel cycle, like the United States, Canada and Sweden, send spent fuel to a final disposition site or store it until a site is ready. Others, including France, Russia and Japan, reprocess it. Reprocessing involves breaking down used fuel and using various chemical methods to separate its components, after which the uranium and plutonium can be re-fabricated into new fuel. The remaining waste includes actinides (long-lived radioactive substances such as americium and neptunium) and fission products (shorter-lived, highly radioactive substances such as iodine, cesium and strontium). Countries that reprocess need disposal sites for these high-level radioactive wastes.

Today, commercial reprocessing is done using the PUREX process, which was developed during World War II to separate plutonium for use in nuclear weapons. PUREX involves dissolving spent fuel in nitric acid and then adding a solvent to recover uranium and plutonium from the solution. Because it produces separated plutonium that can be used for nuclear weapons, PUREX is viewed as a proliferation risk and is done under strict safeguards to prevent plutonium from being stolen or diverted. According to the Department of Energy, nuclear weapons can be made using as little as 4 kilograms (about 10 pounds) of plutonium, a mass roughly the size of a soft drink can. [1] Commercial reprocessing plants typically process several tons of plutonium each year.

DOE is researching two new approaches to reprocessing that advocates believe are more "proliferation-proof" than PUREX because they produce plutonium that is mixed with highly radioactive elements and therefore is less usable for weapons. [2] The UREX+ method is similar to PUREX but leaves the plutonium mixed with neptunium and other elements. Another technique, pyroprocessing, uses molten salt instead of acid to dissolve the fuel and passes an electric current through the solution to separate out plutonium, other actinides and some fission products.

In countries using PUREX, reprocessing has consistently cost more than a once-through fuel cycle because reprocessing spent fuel and fabricating plutonium into reactor fuel are more expensive than making new fuel from fresh uranium. [3] Reprocessing U.S. spent fuel and recycling the long-lived transuranic elements in reactors would cost between \$50 billion and \$100 billion more than disposal in underground repositories. [4]

The Bush administration's proposed Global Nuclear Energy Partnership (GNEP) program would use UREX+ or pyroprocessing to reprocess spent fuel, then recycle the actinides in reactors that use fast-moving neutrons to break these products down to shorter-lived substances. The cost of this approach remains highly uncertain: In a February budget briefing, Deputy Energy Secretary Clay Sell said, "[W]e are seeking to develop these technologies; we are seeking to lessen the amount of uncertainty as to what it would cost to build these facilities on a commercial scale, and ultimately we hope to be in a position to make a judgment about the commercial viability of this approach in the coming years." Sell acknowledged, however, that the administration's \$250 million funding request for fiscal 2007 "is expected to increase dramatically in the coming years." [5]

[1] U.S. Department of Energy, "Restricted Data Declassification Decisions, 1946 to the Present (RDD-7)," Jan. 1, 2001, online at www.fas.org/sgp/ othergov/doe/rdd-7.html#I23, item II-L-33.

[2] U.S. Department of Energy, Global Nuclear Energy Partnership, "Why Do We Need Advanced Fuel Separation Techniques?", www.gnep.energy.gov/ pdfs/factSheetPrimerAdvSseperation.pdf.

[3] Steve Fetter and Frank von Hippel, "Is U.S. Reprocessing Worth the Risk?" *Arms Control Today*, September 2005.

[4] National Academy of Sciences, *Nuclear Wastes: Technologies for Separation and Transmutation* (1996), p. 7.

[5] DOE press briefing on the Global Nuclear Energy Partnership, Feb. 6, 2006, www.energy.gov/print/3171.htm.

Reprocessing Ban

While momentum may be building for construction of new nuclear plants, the slow progress at the Yucca Mountain repository has prompted calls to revisit the U.S. ban on reprocessing commercial spent fuel. Reprocessing could buy extra time for work on the repository and might mean that more nuclear waste could be stored there over the long term, but this step is controversial because past U.S. reprocessing activities at civilian and military facilities have run over budget and generated large quantities of highly radioactive waste.

DOE's Advanced Fuel Cycle Initiative (AFCI), part of its nuclear energy research program, is studying ways to treat spent fuel and recycle plutonium. This research "could provide an alternative to building multiple Yucca Mountains while still supporting an expanding role for nuclear power in this country," William Magwood, director of DOE's Office of Nuclear Energy, told Congress in March 2005. Reprocessing could not only extend the useful life of the Yucca repository, Magwood says, but also reduce the radiotoxicity of the wastes stored there, cutting to less than 1,000 years the time needed for the wastes to decay to the relatively harmless toxicity of natural

Continued on p. 234

At Issue:

Do aging nuclear reactors pose higher safety risks?

DAVID LOCHBAUM
DIRECTOR, NUCLEAR SAFETY PROJECT, UNION OF CONCERNED SCIENTISTS

WRITTEN FOR THE *CQ RESEARCHER*, MARCH 2006

yes

A product's chance of failure over its lifetime is represented by what is called the "bathtub curve." Failure is most likely early in life, the break-in phase, and late in life, the wear-out phase. The break-in portion of nuclear power's bathtub curve is labeled with names like Sodium Reactor Experiment, SL-1, Fermi Unit 1, Three Mile Island and Chernobyl — serious reactor accidents in the first months of operation. The wear-out portion of nuclear power's bathtub curve has no labels — yet.

The average age of the nuclear power reactors operating in the United States is more than 26 years. Over half have had their 40-year operating licenses extended for another 20 years, and most of the rest are in line for extensions. All U.S. nuclear power reactors are heading toward — if not already in — the wear-out phase of their lifetimes.

While nuclear reactors are operating with an increasing risk of failure, policies have diminished the chances for early detection and correction of aging problems. Reactor owners, citing low failure rates occurring during the flat portion of the bathtub curve, have successfully petitioned the Nuclear Regulatory Commission (NRC) for significant reductions in the scope and frequency of safety tests and inspections. Checks that had been performed on a monthly basis are now being performed quarterly. Other checks that had been conducted annually are now being done biannually, or even less frequently. Thus, U.S. nuclear reactors are moving closer to the wear-out phase of the bathtub curve with a strobe light, rather than a spotlight, on their safety levels.

This disturbing trend is exacerbated by another recent development. The NRC has approved increases of up to 20 percent in the maximum power levels at which nuclear reactors can operate. The higher temperatures and flows occurring at increased power levels cause equipment to wear out faster. For example, flow vibrations at the Quad Cities nuclear plant in Illinois caused a large metal component above the reactor core to shake itself apart — twice.

Operating aging nuclear reactors at increased power levels with fewer safety checks is a recipe for disaster. To avoid balancing the nuclear bathtub curve with reactor names on the wear-out phase, prompt steps must be taken to ensure there is a powerful spotlight on safety, not a weak strobe light.

Sadly, last year's energy bill contained ample provisions for more nuclear plants but nothing to remedy the NRC's flickering focus on safe reactor operation.

SCOTT PETERSON
VICE PRESIDENT, COMMUNICATIONS, NUCLEAR ENERGY INSTITUTE

WRITTEN FOR THE *CQ RESEARCHER* MARCH 2006

no

An industry commitment to safety and training, combined with a system of close monitoring and strict regulation, has placed nuclear power plants among the nation's safest industrial facilities.

The Nuclear Regulatory Commission (NRC) regulates commercial and institutional uses of nuclear energy. As part of this oversight, the NRC assigns at least two full-time resident inspectors to each nuclear plant site. They conduct daily inspections, providing close surveillance of the plant, its equipment and operations. In addition, the typical nuclear plant site undergoes about 2,500 hours of inspections per reactor each year.

The NRC developed a new reactor-oversight process that was implemented industrywide in April 2000. This process is more sharply focused on areas of plant operation that are most important to safety and provides the public, the government and the industry timely, understandable and meaningful assessments of plant performance.

The NRC also reviews applications for nuclear plant license renewals. This is a stringent process that takes into account numerous factors regarding a reactor's ability to continue operation, including the effectiveness and safety of existing equipment.

The industry's overarching commitment to safety extends beyond meeting federal regulations. This desire to maintain the highest level of safety and efficient operation of nuclear plants motivates the industry's investment in sound systems and properly functioning equipment.

Companies operating nuclear power plants have an integrated plan for managing the condition of plant systems, structures and components. That includes monitoring the integrity of primary system materials and maintaining the condition of plant equipment. With more than 40 years of experience, companies have learned how equipment wears, and they can refurbish or replace the vast majority of equipment before it fails. When the operation of an important component degrades or fails, companies make detailed root-cause analyses and take corrective actions.

It is for these reasons that the so-called bathtub curve does not appropriately apply to America's existing nuclear power plants. Clearly, these plants already have safely surpassed the first phase, or break-in period. Given that the speculative back end of the bathtub curve would be due to fatigue or depletion of materials, the ongoing preventative and corrective maintenance performed at nuclear plants addresses these issues.

Continued from p. 232

uranium ore. [67] This would allow more waste to be stored at Yucca Mountain, advocates argue, because the heat of the waste determines how far apart canisters need to be spaced in the repository. To accelerate this process, Congress added $50 million to the fiscal 2006 energy appropriations bill for DOE to develop a plan to reprocess all U.S. commercial spent nuclear fuel and recycle its plutonium content, with instructions to start finding sites for the facilities by mid-2006. "It is essential to continue development of the Yucca Mountain repository," said the bill's sponsor, Rep. David Hobson, R-Ohio, "but it is also essential to pursue alternative approaches to spent nuclear fuel so that we do not have to develop eight more Yucca Mountains by the end of this century." [68]

The Bush administration has requested $250 million in its fiscal 2007 budget to launch a Global Nuclear Energy Partnership (GNEP), under which the U.S. would lease fresh nuclear fuel to other countries and take back spent fuel for disposition (which the U.S. already does with fuel it supplies to scientific-research reactors around the world to prevent the spent fuel from being used for weapons).

Using technologies currently under development, the United States would reprocess both the foreign and domestic spent fuel, using the resulting plutonium and other actinides (long-lived radioactive elements) as fuel for advanced "burner" reactors that would break them down into shorter-lived materials. [69]

The partnership would enable expansion of nuclear power in the United States and around the world, promote non-proliferation and help resolve nuclear waste disposal issues, Energy Secretary Bodman told the Senate Energy Committee on Feb. 9. "[T]he United States will work with key international partners to develop and demonstrate new proliferation-resistant technologies to recycle spent nuclear fuel to reduce waste," he said. And new technologies developed through the project would reduce the volume and radiotoxicity of nuclear waste, greatly reducing the amount of waste needing permanent storage at Yucca Mountain and delaying the need for an additional repository indefinitely, he said.

The Energy Department has not released long-term cost estimates for GNEP, but developing new reprocessing plants and fast reactors to break down transuranic wastes could cost $40 billion or more over the next several decades. [70] "These advanced reprocessing techniques and fast reactors have not been commercially deployed, so we don't know whether they are technically feasible or how much they'll cost, although they are almost certain to cost more than conventional reprocessing," says physicist Steve Fetter, dean of the University of Maryland's School of Public Policy.

The Bush administration wants private companies and foreign governments to contribute, but early reactions from U.S. nuclear plant owners were lukewarm because executives reportedly did not see GNEP as helping to build support for new power plants. "We'll all cheer DOE from the sidelines," said one utility official in early February. [71]

The trade newsletter *Electricity Daily* called a resumption of reprocessing "an entirely bad idea" and predicted that it would be "wildly uneconomic," noting that DOE has been working to clean up a civilian reprocessing site at West Valley, N.Y., since 1980 and does not expect to be finished until 2008. [72]

Many energy experts argue that because spent nuclear fuel can be stored in dry casks at reactors for at least 50 years, there is no need to make a near-term commitment to an expensive reprocessing program. They further argue that since plutonium separated during reprocessing can be stolen or diverted for use in nuclear weapons, the United States should not resume reprocessing any earlier than necessary because it could spur proliferation threats around the globe.

The Bush administration argues that reprocessing techniques envisioned for GNEP will produce plutonium unsuitable for nuclear weapons because it would be mixed with other actinides. But some scientists doubt the new techniques would be proliferation-proof. "Almost all of these elements are usable for nuclear weapons, although they may complicate the design issues," says Fetter. "And other countries might alter the technologies to produce materials that could be used in nuclear weapons. GNEP raises more questions than it answers."

A May 2005 report by the American Physical Society on resolving nuclear power's proliferation problem concluded that it was not "urgent" for the United States to initiate reprocessing or develop additional repositories. The panel recommended refocusing the Advanced Fuel Cycle Initiative — away from reprocessing and onto proliferation-resistant fuel cycle options.

"We should not be stampeded into anything," says Ernest Moniz, a professor of physics at MIT and former Energy under secretary. "The right course is long-term surface or sub-surface storage of spent fuel." The nuclear industry continues to press for licensing of the Yucca Mountain repository and to criticize Congress for appropriating less money out of the Nuclear Waste Fund than consumers have paid into it. NEI's Fertel says nuclear owners view reprocessing as a long-term strategy, not as an alternative to geologic disposition.

"If we're going to build a large number of nuclear plants in the coming decades," says Fertel, "then it makes sense to look at whether we're going to close the fuel cycle, and to do research and development on some key questions: What technology is the safest, most efficient and most proliferation-resistant, what kind of fuel would be used, and what kind of reactor would we use? But our timeline is 30 to 50 years, and whether you close the fuel cycle and move to reprocessing or not, you still need a repository." ■

OUTLOOK

Doubts About Expansion

While conditions for building new nuclear plants appear to be improving, experts outside the nuclear industry remain skeptical that a major nuclear expansion is on the horizon.

Based on the subsidies included in the 2005 Energy Policy Act, the Energy Information Administration predicts that 9,000 megawatts of new nuclear capacity will be added through 2030, including 3,000 megawatts of uprates at existing plants and 6,000 megawatts of new plants (about six large reactors). [73] Energy analysts agree that even though streamlined licensing regulations have lowered the barriers to building new plants, lingering issues — especially waste management — could still undercut support for new reactors.

Incentives in the new law should resolve the financial risk issues, says MIT's Moniz, but until there is a "near-term prospect" of disposing of spent fuel at Yucca Mountain, it could be very complicated to get a new plant licensed.

Reprocessing advocates appear ready to press for a change in U.S fuel-cycle policy, if only to move spent fuel somewhere soon. "Yucca Mountain started out as something everybody thought could stay on time, stay within budget and get done," said Sen. Pete Domenici, R-N.M., a leading congressional reprocessing advocate. "It turns out none of that is true — it's not on time, we still haven't cleared some of the worst hurdles. So we have to stick with it, [but] what role it will inevitably play is still undetermined, in my opinion." [74]

Most environmentalists maintain that conservation and renewable energy are the safest and cheapest ways to keep the lights on and the air clean. They view reprocessing as expensive and a proliferation threat, and oppose the Bush administration's Global Nuclear Energy Partnership proposals. "It's the height of hypocrisy to support activities that will make energy and environmental problems worse at a time when funds are being cut for energy programs that help people, like weatherization and efficiency," says US PIRG's Aurilio.

Plant security could also fuel new concerns about expanding nuclear power, especially if any incidents take place at operating plants or it becomes clear that terrorists are targeting reactors. Details of the new design-basis threat (DBT) — the minimum size of an attacking force that commercial reactor owners must be ready to fight off — implemented by the NRC in 2004 are classified, but the standard reportedly directs nuclear plant owners to maintain enough security to defend against a force less than the size of the 9/11 attackers. The commission is currently reviewing the DBT and putting the new standards into regulations after taking public comments, says NRC public affairs Director Brenner. [75]

"Every nuclear power plant in the United States meets the requirements for providing assurance that their activities . . . do not constitute an unreasonable risk to the public health and safety," said NRC Chairman Nils Diaz on Dec. 2, 2004. "However, the NRC continues to be vigilant, cognizant of the threat and of the need to ensure that every one of our licensees is performing at the levels needed for . . . the protection of the public." [76]

Critics argue that the NRC is overly focused on how much security the industry can afford, citing examples such as a June 2005 agency staff paper, which stated the revised design-basis threat "is not based on worst-case scenarios but rather on actual adversary characteristics demonstrated worldwide and a determination as to those characteristics against which a private security force could reasonably be expected to provide protection." [77]

"That's backwards," says Danielle Brian, director of the Project on Government Oversight. "What we really need is an assessment of the threat and what it takes to handle it. If this is the best that industry can do on security, then we should rethink whether industry should be in charge of security."

The privately owned plants are guarded by well-trained private security forces, often staffed with ex-military personnel, and all have arrangements with local law-enforcement agencies for supplemental assistance, Brenner says. An attacking force larger than the DBT is considered by NRC regulation to be "an enemy of the United States" that would call into play additional federal assets.

Meanwhile, reactors are continuing to win approvals for uprates and license extensions. Most local communities seem willing to live with existing reactors, but winning public approval and millions of dollars in federal support to build the first next-generation reactors will be a much higher hurdle. "That's where the rubber will meet the road," says Aurilio. "Will Congress spend hundreds of millions of dollars more on this industry when budgets are tight?"

Furthermore, even if new plants can be built safely in the United States, a nuclear disaster abroad — like Chernobyl in 1986 — would quickly sour domestic opinion on nuclear energy again. The fate of nuclear power in the United States thus is tightly linked to the adoption of stronger safety requirements and barriers against proliferation worldwide.

"Many nuclear energy proponents don't recognize that one accident or proliferation incident anywhere will shut down an expansion of nuclear power worldwide," says Harvard's Holdren. "If we're going to do this, it's important to do it right." ■

Notes

[1] Quoted in David Firestone, "Utility Board Votes to Restart a Nuclear Reactor in Alabama That Has Been Idle Since 1985," *The New York Times*, May 17, 2002, p. A12.

[2] Tennessee Valley Authority, "TVA Board Approves Browns Ferry Unit 1 Recovery, Extended Operations," May 16, 2002.

[3] *The Future of Nuclear Power*, Massachusetts Institute of Technology (2003); and National Commission on Energy Policy, "Ending the Energy Stalemate: A Bipartisan Strategy to Meet America's Energy Challenges," December 2004.

[4] For background, see Marcia Clemmitt, "Climate Change," *CQ Researcher*, Jan. 27, 2006, pp. 73-96.

[5] President Bush was quoted on "Nuclear Ambitions," WBUR Radio, "OnPoint," March 7, 2006. See Jim VandeHei and Dafna Linzer, "U.S., India Reach Deal On Nuclear Cooperation," *The Washington Post*, March 3, 2006, p. A1.

[6] Nuclear Energy Institute, "U.S. Nuclear Industry Capacity Factors (1980-2004)," www.nei.org.

[7] "President Discusses Energy Policy, Economic Security," June 22, 2005, www.whitehouse.gov.

[8] Government Accountability Office, "Nuclear Regulatory Commission: Challenges Facing NRC in Effectively Carrying Out Its Mission," May 26, 2005, p. 11.

[9] Tom Henry, "FirstEnergy To Pay $28 Million Fine for Lying," *Toledo Blade*, Jan. 21, 2006, p. 1.

[10] Nuclear Energy Institute, "Significant Events at U.S. Nuclear Plants: Annual Industry Average (1998-2003)," and "Unplanned Automatic Scrams per 7,000 Critical Hours," www.nei.org.

[11] *Final Report of the National Commission on Terrorist Attacks Upon the United States* (2004), p. 245.

[12] Environmental Protection Agency, "Inventory of U.S. Greenhouse Gas Emissions and Sinks: 1990-2003," April 2005, p. 60.

[13] Energy Information Administration, "Annual Energy Outlook 2006 Overview," December 2005, p. 15.

[14] *The Future of Nuclear Power*, *op. cit*, p. 3.

[15] Patrick Moore, "Environmental Movement Has Lost Its Way," *The Miami Herald*, Jan. 28, 2005.

[16] " 'Nuclear' Bishop Quits Campaign," BBC News, Oct. 22, 2004.

[17] *Congressional Record*, June 22, 2005, p. S7023.

[18] National Commission on Energy Policy, *op. cit.*, p. 62.

[19] For background, see Mary H. Cooper, "Alternative Energy," *CQ Researcher*, Feb. 25, 2005, pp. 173-196.

[20] National Research Council, *The Hydrogen Economy: Opportunities, Costs, Barriers, and R&D Needs* (2001), pp. 94-97.

[21] For background, see Brian Hansen, "Nuclear Waste," *CQ Researcher*, June 8, 2001, pp. 489-504.

[22] Letter from Energy Secretary Spencer Abraham to President George W. Bush, Feb. 14, 2002, www.ocrwm.doe.gov/ymp/sr/salp.pdf.

[23] Daniel Whitten, "Meeting Shows Industry Frustration Over Repository Project's Difficulties," *Inside Energy With Federal Lands*, Jan. 16, 2006, p. 12.

[24] The case is *Nuclear Energy Institute, Inc., v. Environmental Protection Agency*, July 9, 2004.

[25] National Academy of Sciences, *Technical Bases for Yucca Mountain Standards* (1995).

[26] National Academy of Sciences, Committee on Transportation of Radioactive Waste, *Going the Distance? The Safe Transport of Spent Nuclear Fuel and High-Level Radioactive Waste in the United States*, pre-publication draft, National Academies Press (2006), p. SR.1.

[27] Remarks of Secretary of Energy Samuel W. Bodman, Nuclear Energy Assembly, May 17, 2005, www.energy.gov.

[28] Testimony of Theodore Garrish, deputy director, Office of Civilian Radioactive Waste Management, before the House Energy and Commerce Subcommittee on Energy and Air Quality, March 10, 2005.

[29] Testimony of Robert Garvin before House Energy and Commerce Subcommittee on Energy and Air Quality, March 10, 2005.

[30] Mark Holt, "Civilian Nuclear Waste Disposal," *Congressional Research Service Issue Brief IB92059*, Aug. 2, 2005, p. CRS-6.

[31] Press briefing by Energy Secretary Samuel W. Bodman, Feb. 6, 2006, www.energy.gov/news/3169.htm.

[32] Marshall Goldberg, "Federal Energy Subsidies: Not All Technologies Are Created Equal," Renewable Energy Policy Project, July 2000.

[33] Testimony of Marvin Fertel before House Government Reform Subcommittee on Energy and Resources, April 28, 2005.

[34] Nuclear Energy Institute, "Nuclear Energy: Powering America's Future," February 2005, p. 5.

[35] For background, see Energy Information Administration, "Federal Financial Interventions and Subsidies in Energy Markets 1999: Primary Energy," September 1999, www.eia.doe.gov/oiaf/servicerpt/subsidy/pdf/sroiaf(99)03.pdf.

[36] Nuclear Energy Institute, "Powering the Future With Environmentally Sound Nuclear Energy," 2003, p. 5.

[37] National Association of State PIRGs, "Stopping Global Warming Begins at Home," September 2004, p. 12, www.newenergyfuture.com/newenergy.asp?id2=14276.

[38] For background, see F. P. Huddle, "Control of Atomic Energy," *Editorial Research Reports 1946* (Vol. I); and B. W. Patch, "International Control of Atomic Energy," *Editorial Research Reports 1948* (Vol. I), both available from *CQ Researcher Plus Archive*, CQ Electronic Library, http://library.cqpress.com.

[39] Quoted in Brian Balogh, *Chain Reaction: Expert Debate and Public Participation in American Commercial Nuclear Power, 1945-1975* (1991), p. 97.

[40] For background, see W. T. Stone, "Atomic Information," *Editorial Research Reports 1953* (Vol. II); and M. Packman, "Atomic Energy for Industry," *Editorial Research Reports 1955*, *CQ Researcher Plus Archive*, CQ Electronic Library, http://library.cqpress.com.

[41] Balogh, *op. cit.*, pp. 234-37.

[42] See "New Approaches to Atomic Control," *Editorial Research Reports 1954* (Vol. I); and W. Sweet, "Strategic Arms Debate," *Editorial Research Reports 1979* (Vol. I), *CQ Researcher Plus Archive*, CQ Electronic Library, http://library.cqpress.com.

[43] See Packman, *op. cit.*, and W. Korns, "Atomic Power Race," *Editorial Research Reports 1957* (Vol. I), *CQ Researcher Plus Archive*, CQ Electronic Library, http://library.cqpress.com.

[44] President John F. Kennedy, News Conference No. 52, March 21, 1963.

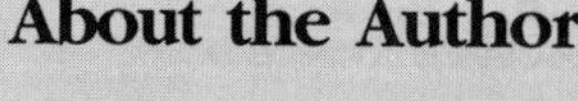

About the Author

Jennifer Weeks is a freelance writer in Watertown, Mass., who specializes in energy and environmental issues. She has written for *The Washington Post*, *The Boston Globe Magazine* and other publications, and has 15 years' experience as a public-policy analyst, lobbyist and congressional staffer. She has an A.B. degree from Williams College and master's degrees from the University of North Carolina and Harvard

[45] For background, see Mary H. Cooper, "Non-Proliferation Treaty at 25," *CQ Researcher*, Jan. 27, 1995, pp. 73-96.
[46] For background, see J. Kuebler, "Atomic Proliferation," *Editorial Research Reports 1965* (Vol. I), *CQ Researcher Plus Archive*, CQ Electronic Library, http://library.cqpress.com.
[47] For background, see R. C. Deans, "Nuclear Power Options," *Editorial Research Reports 1971* (Vol. II); S. Stencel, "Nuclear Safeguards," *Editorial Research Reports 1974* (Vol. II); available at *CQ Researcher Plus Archive*, CQ Electronic Library, http://library.cqpress.com.
[48] For background, see J. Hamer, "Environmental Policy," *Editorial Research Reports 1974* (Vol. II), available at *CQ Researcher Plus Archive*, CQ Electronic Library, http://library.cqpress.com.
[49] For background, see Ian A. Forbes, *et al.*, "Cooling Water," *Environment*, January/February 1972, pp. 40-47.
[50] For background, see S. Stencel, "Nuclear Waste Disposal," *Editorial Research Reports 1976* (Vol. II); available at *CQ Researcher Plus Archive*, CQ Electronic Library, http://library.cqpress.com.
[51] Central Intelligence Agency, "Managing Nuclear Proliferation: The Politics of Limited Choice," December 1975, declassified Aug. 21, 2001, and published by the National Security Archive, www.gwu.edu/~nsarchiv/NSAEBB/NSAEBB155/prolif-15.pdf.
[52] For details, see U.S. Nuclear Regulatory Commission, "The Accident at Three Mile Island," www.nrc.gov/reading-rm/doc-collections/fact-sheets/3mile-isle.html; and W. Sweet, "Determining Radiation Dangers," *Editorial Research Reports 1979* (Vol. II), available at *CQ Researcher Plus Archive*, CQ Electronic Library, http://library.cqpress.com.
[53] For background, see M. Leepson, "Nuclear Power's Future," *Editorial Research Reports 1983* (Vol. II), at *CQ Researcher Plus Archive*, CQ Electronic Library, http://library.cqpress.com.
[54] For background, see Brian Hansen, "Nuclear Waste," *CQ Researcher*, June 8, 2001, pp. 489-504.
[55] For background, see Rodman D. Griffin, "Alternative Energy," *CQ Researcher*, July 10, 1992, pp. 573-596.
[56] For background, see Adriel Bettelheim, "Utility Deregulation," *CQ Researcher*, Jan. 14, 2000, pp. 1-16.
[57] Nuclear Energy Institute, "U.S. Nuclear Industry Capacity Factors (1998-2004)," www.nei.org.

FOR MORE INFORMATION

National Association of Regulatory Utility Commissioners, 1101 Vermont Ave., N.W., Suite 200, Washington, DC 20005; (202) 898-2200; www.naruc.org. Represents agencies that regulate telecommunications, energy and water utilities.

National Commission on Energy Policy, 1616 H St., N.W., 6th Floor, Washington, DC 20006; (202) 637-0400; www.energycommission.org. A bipartisan group of energy experts developing a long-term energy strategy.

Nuclear Energy Institute, 1776 I St., N.W., Suite 400, Washington, DC 20006; (202) 739-8000; www.nei.org. The nuclear power industry's advocacy organization promotes beneficial uses of nuclear energy and technologies.

U.S. Nuclear Regulatory Commission, 1 White Flint North, 11555 Rockville Pike, Rockville, MD 20852-2738; (301) 415-8200; www.nrc.gov. Regulates nuclear reactors and the transport, storage and disposal of nuclear materials.

Project for Government Oversight, 666 11th St., N.W., Suite 500, Washington, DC 20001-4542; (202) 347-1122; www.pogo.org. A nonprofit group that investigates misconduct in federal agencies.

Union of Concerned Scientists, 2 Brattle Square, Cambridge, MA 02238-9105; (617) 547-5552; www.ucsusa.org. An alliance dedicated to "rigorous scientific analysis with innovative thinking and committed citizen advocacy."

U.S. Public Interest Research Group (PIRG), 218 D St., S.E., Washington, DC 20003; (202) 546-9707; www.uspirg.org. A nonprofit watchdog group.

[58] Nuclear Regulatory Commission, "Power Uprates for Nuclear Plants," July 2004.
[59] For background, see Mary H. Cooper, "Energy Security," *CQ Researcher*, Feb. 1, 2002, pp. 73-96.
[60] "One Year After — Reflections on Nuclear Security," speech by Dr. Richard A. Meserve, Sept. 11, 2002, NRC press release No. S-02-024.
[61] National Academy of Sciences, "Safety and Security of Commercial Spent Nuclear Fuel Storage: Public Report," 2005, pp. 5-8. See also Shankar Vedantum, "Storage of Nuclear Spent Fuel Criticized," *The Washington Post*, March 28, 2005, p. A1.
[62] Nuclear Energy Institute, "Status of Used Nuclear Fuel Storage at U.S. Commercial Nuclear Plants," October 2005, www.nei.org.
[63] See www.nrc.gov/reactors/new-licensing/esp.html and "Southern Nuclear Mulls Nuclear Generation Units at Vogtle," *Atlanta Business Chronicle*, Aug. 19, 2005.
[64] Nuclear Energy Institute, "New Nuclear Power Plants," www.nei.org.
[65] World Nuclear Association, "Advanced Nuclear Power Reactors," December 2005, www.world-nuclear.org/info/inf08.htm.
[66] Testimony of Deputy Energy Secretary Clay Sell before Senate Committee on Energy and Natural Resources, April 26, 2005.
[67] Testimony of William D. Magwood IV before House Appropriations Subcommittee on Energy and Water Development, March 15, 2005.
[68] *Congressional Record*, Nov. 9, 2005, p. H10058.
[69] Department of Energy, "The Global Nuclear Energy Partnership," www.gnep.energy.gov.
[70] Daniel Horner and Elaine Hiruo, "DOE Releases Details On Nuclear Initiative, Spurring Little Excitement In Industry," *Nuclear Fuel*, Feb. 13, 2006, p. 1.
[71] *Ibid.*
[72] Kennedy Maize, " 'Reprocessing Dead End," *Electricity Daily*, Feb. 6, 2006.
[73] Energy Information Administration, *op. cit.*, p. 7.
[74] Quoted in "U.S. Drafting Plan for Nuke Energy Use," National Public Radio, "All Things Considered," Dec. 29, 2005.
[75] See Mark Thompson, "Are These Towers Safe?" *Time*, June 20, 2005, p. 43.
[76] "Protecting Our Nation," speech by NRC Chair Nils Diaz, Dec. 2, 2004, www.nrc.gov/reading-rm/doc-collections/commission/speeches/2004/s-04-020.html.
[77] Nuclear Regulatory Commission, "Proposed Rulemaking to Revise 10 CFR 73.1, design basis threat (DBT) Requirements," SECY-05-0106, www.nrc.gov/reading-rm/doc-collections/commission/secys/2005/secy2005-0106/2005-0106scy.pdf.

Bibliography

Selected Sources

Books

Allison, Graham T., *Nuclear Terrorism: The Ultimate Preventable Catastrophe*, Times Books, 2004.

The director of Harvard's Belfer Center for Science and International Affairs argues the United States needs to prevent terrorists from stealing a bomb or the nuclear materials needed to build one.

Duffy, Robert J., *Nuclear Politics in America: A History and Theory of Government Regulation*, University Press of Kansas, 1997.

A professor of political science at Colorado State University explains how supporters and opponents of nuclear energy have shaped policy toward the nuclear industry.

Garwin, Richard L., and Georges Charpak, *Megawatts and Megatons: A Turning Point in the Nuclear Age?* Knopf, 2001.

U.S. nuclear weapons designer Garwin and French physicist Charpak explain how nuclear reactors operate, how nuclear bombs explode and options for managing radioactive materials.

Macfarlane, Allison M., and Rodney C. Ewing, eds., *Uncertainty Underground: Yucca Mountain and the Nation's High-Level Nuclear Waste*, MIT Press, 2006.

Experts from science, industry and government discuss the unresolved scientific and technical issues surrounding using Yucca Mountain to store high-level nuclear waste.

Articles

"The Shape of Things To Come?" *The Economist*, July 9, 2005.

The picture remains mixed for nuclear energy, but concerns about climate change are improving prospects for new reactor construction.

Alvarez, Lisette, "Finland Rekindles Interest in Nuclear Power," *The New York Times*, Dec. 12, 2005, p. A10.

Finland is building a new nuclear power plant after years of public debate, spurred by rising energy prices and concerns about global climate change.

Thompson, Mark, "Are These Towers Safe?" *Time*, June 20, 2005, pp. 34-48.

An investigation into nuclear power plant security in the post-9/11 era questions whether the U.S. nuclear industry has done enough to protect reactors from terrorist attacks.

Wald, Matthew L., "A New Vision for Nuclear Waste," *Technology Review*, December 2004, pp. 34-48.

A *New York Times* technology writer argues that Yucca Mountain is a flawed site for a nuclear waste repository and that the U.S. should study other options for managing spent nuclear fuel.

Wolfsthal, Jon B., "The Nuclear Third Rail: Can Fuel Cycle Capabilities Be Limited?" *Arms Control Today*, December 2004.

Under the Nuclear Non-Proliferation Treaty, countries can reprocess plutonium or enrich uranium as long as they do not use them for weapons, but this policy may change in response to Iran's clandestine nuclear program. The challenge is persuading non-nuclear weapons states to give up fuel-cycle technology.

Reports and Studies

"The Future of Nuclear Power: An Interdisciplinary MIT Study," Massachusetts Institute of Technology, 2003.

Engineering experts assert that nuclear power could be an important tool for responding to global climate change, but that the industry faces major waste, safety, proliferation and cost issues that must be overcome first.

"Vision 2020: Nuclear Energy and the Nation's Future Prosperity," Nuclear Energy Institute, 2002.

The nuclear industry's trade organization details its case for building 50,000 megawatts of new nuclear power capacity by 2020.

Lochbaum, David, "U.S. Nuclear Plants in the 21st Century: The Risk of a Lifetime," Union of Concerned Scientists, May 2004.

A nuclear engineer with 20 years of experience at U.S. commercial reactors describes the risks of nuclear power at various points in reactors' operating lives and argues for better enforcement of safety regulations, especially at older reactors.

National Research Council, *Disposition of High-Level Waste and Spent Nuclear Fuel: The Continuing Societal and Technical Challenges*, 2001.

Managing nuclear waste is an urgent problem worldwide and poses both social and technical challenges. Countries that have addressed the issue through open, democratic and flexible processes have made the most progress.

Nivola, Pietro S., "The Political Economy of Nuclear Energy in the United States," *Policy Brief #138*, Brookings Institution, 2004.

U.S. nuclear power capacity has not been growing because the nation has had other, cheaper options, not because of excessive government regulation.

The Next Step:

Additional Articles from Current Periodicals

Energy Security

Bennett, Drake, "Nuclear Options Talk of Nuclear Energy As A Viable Alternative to Fossil Fuels Is Back In Fashion, Even Among Some Environmentalists," *The Boston Globe*, June 5, 2005, p. D1.

The United States and Europe are demonstrating new interest in nuclear energy as an alternative to fossil fuels.

Gugliotta, Guy, "Nuclear Energy Initiative Holds Uncertainties," *The Washington Post*, Feb. 19, 2006, p. A9.

Bush says his new nuclear energy plan could cure America's dependence on foreign oil, but supporters and opponents of the plan say it relies on unproven technologies.

Haynes, Tim, "Can Nuclear Power By Safe?" *The Boston Globe*, July 8, 2003, p. C1.

Nuclear energy proponents argue that pebble-bed modular reactors (PBMR) are safer, cheaper and easier to operate than traditional nuclear plants.

Hutchenson, Ron, "Pushing a Nuclear Revival," *The Philadelphia Inquirer*, June 23, 2005, p. C1.

President Bush visited the Calvert Cliffs Nuclear Power Plant in Maryland to push for Senate approval of an energy bill that would help the domestic nuclear industry.

Wilkie, Dana, "Nuclear Power Poised For Comeback," *The San Diego Union-Tribune*, July 31, 2005, p. A1.

Congress' new energy plan includes billions of dollars to build new nuclear plants.

Managing Spent Fuel

The Associated Press and *The Washington Post*, "N-Waste Storage on Reservation OK'd," *The Seattle Times*, Sept. 10, 2005, p. A6.

The Nuclear Regulatory Commission (NRC) approved plans for a nuclear waste storage site on the Skull Valley Goshute Indian Reservation in Utah, but several state officials oppose the facility.

Davidson, Keay, "Yucca Mountain Studies Must Be Redone," *The San Francisco Chronicle*, Feb. 18, 2006, p. B2.

Department of Energy officials said studies into the safety of turning a Nevada mountain into a nuclear waste site will have to be redone following charges that data in the original studies were fabricated.

Vartabedian, Ralph, "Nuclear Waste Outpaces Solutions," *Los Angeles Times*, June 12, 2005, p. A1.

Growing U.S. stockpiles of nuclear waste are forcing nuclear plants to use outdoor storage casks while waiting for the government to find a permanent storage solution.

Wald, Matthew L., "Scientists Try to Resolve Nuclear Problem With an Old Technology Made New Again," *The New York Times*, Dec. 27, 2005, p. F3.

Congress voted to give $50 million to the Energy Department to explore a new method of reprocessing spent nuclear fuel that would reuse a much larger fraction of the waste.

Weir, Fred, and Howard LaFranchi, "Russia and U.S. As Global Nuclear Waste Collectors?" *The Christian Science Monitor*, Feb. 7, 2006, p. 1.

Russia and the United States proposed a plan to provide energy-starved countries with fuel to generate nuclear power and then take back the dangerous, spent fuel.

National Security and Nuclear Power

Bender, Bryan, "Official At Nuclear Power Station Alleges Retaliation," *The Boston Globe*, March 1, 2006, p. A3.

A senior official at Connecticut's Millstone Nuclear Power Station was removed from his job after he complained that the plant's electronic security system was seriously flawed.

Davidson, Keay, "Nuclear Safety Study Denied Data," *The San Francisco Chronicle*, Feb. 10, 2006, p. A14.

The Nuclear Regulatory Commission refused to share classified information with investigators looking into the risk of terrorist attacks on shipments of spent nuclear fuel.

Morgan, Curtis, "FPL Says Turkey Point Nuclear Power Plant Is Secure," *The Miami Herald*, Dec. 18, 2005, p. A16.

Executives at Florida Power and Light have turned the Turkey Point nuclear plant into a heavily guarded encampment.

CITING THE *CQ RESEARCHER*

Sample formats for citing these reports in a bibliography include the ones listed below. Preferred styles and formats vary, so please check with your instructor or professor.

MLA STYLE

Jost, Kenneth. "Rethinking the Death Penalty." CQ Researcher 16 Nov. 2001: 945-68.

APA STYLE

Jost, K. (2001, November 16). Rethinking the death penalty. *CQ Researcher, 11,* 945-968.

CHICAGO STYLE

Jost, Kenneth. "Rethinking the Death Penalty." *CQ Researcher,* November 16, 2001, 945-968.

CQ Researcher

Published by CQ Press, a division of Congressional Quarterly Inc.

cqresearcher.com

Coal Mining Safety

Are underground miners adequately protected?

The year has started off tragically for the coal industry, which provides the fuel to generate half the nation's electricity. The deaths of 12 men in an explosion at the Sago mine in West Virginia — and nine more mining fatalities soon afterwards — have raised questions about whether the nation's 75,000 coal miners are adequately protected. Critics say the Bush administration rarely penalizes mine operators who violate safety rules. But the Mine Safety and Health Administration (MSHA) says its strict enforcement has led to the lowest number of fatalities in history — just 22 deaths in 2005 compared to 66 in 1990. West Virginia already has passed tougher state rules, and its congressional delegation advocates similar protections nationwide. Meanwhile, MSHA has issued new rules requiring coal operators to report accidents within 15 minutes and to stock more breathing devices underground. The agency also is testing the reliability of wireless communications and tracking technologies used in Australia but rarely in the U.S.

A makeshift memorial honors David Lewis, one of 12 West Virginia coal miners killed following an explosion in the Sago mine in early January.

INSIDE THIS REPORT

CQ Researcher • March 17, 2006 • www.cqresearcher.com
Volume 16, Number 11 • Pages 241-264

CQ PRESS

RECIPIENT OF SOCIETY OF PROFESSIONAL JOURNALISTS AWARD FOR EXCELLENCE ◆ AMERICAN BAR ASSOCIATION SILVER GAVEL AWARD

COAL MINING SAFETY

THE ISSUES

BACKGROUND

CURRENT SITUATION

OUTLOOK

SIDEBARS AND GRAPHICS

FOR FURTHER RESEARCH

Cover: A makeshift memorial at the Barbour County courthouse honors David Lewis, one of 12 West Virginia coal miners killed following an explosion in the Sago mine in early January. (Getty Images/Mark Wilson)

CQ Researcher

March 17, 2006
Volume 16, Number 11

MANAGING EDITOR: Thomas J. Colin
ASSISTANT MANAGING EDITOR: Kathy Koch
ASSOCIATE EDITOR: Kenneth Jost
STAFF WRITERS: Marcia Clemmitt, Peter Katel, Pamela M. Prah
CONTRIBUTING WRITERS: Rachel Cox, Sarah Glazer, David Hosansky, Patrick Marshall, Tom Price
DESIGN/PRODUCTION EDITOR: Olu B. Davis
ASSISTANT EDITOR: Melissa J. Hipolit

CQ PRESS
A Division of Congressional Quarterly Inc.

SENIOR VICE PRESIDENT/PUBLISHER: John A. Jenkins
DIRECTOR, LIBRARY PUBLISHING: Kathryn C. Suárez
DIRECTOR, EDITORIAL OPERATIONS: Ann Davies

CONGRESSIONAL QUARTERLY INC.
CHAIRMAN: Paul C. Tash
VICE CHAIRMAN: Andrew P. Corty
PRESIDENT/EDITOR IN CHIEF: Robert W. Merry

CQ Researcher (ISSN 1056-2036) is printed on acid-free paper. Published weekly, except March 24, July 7, July 14, Aug. 4, Aug. 11, Nov. 24, Dec. 22 and Dec. 29, by CQ Press, a division of Congressional Quarterly Inc. Annual full-service subscriptions for institutions start at $667. For pricing, call 1-800-834-9020, ext. 1906. To purchase a *CQ Researcher* report in print or electronic format (PDF), visit www.cqpress.com or call 866-427-7737. Single reports start at $10. Bulk purchase discounts and electronic-rights licensing are also available. Periodicals postage paid at Washington, D.C., and additional mailing offices. POSTMASTER: Send address changes to *CQ Researcher*, 1255 22nd St., N.W., Suite 400, Washington, DC 20037.

Coal Mining Safety

By Pamela M. Prah

The Issues

"Hi Deb and Sara. I'm still OK at 2:40 p.m.," trapped West Virginia miner George Hamner Jr. wrote in a Jan. 2 note to his family. "The section is full of smoke & fumes so we can't escape. We are all still alive at this time." [1]

Eight hours earlier, an explosion had trapped Hamner and 12 other men 260 feet underground in the Sago mine, near Tallmansville. With just an hour's worth of emergency oxygen each, they waited in the dark, unaware that noxious gases were keeping rescuers at bay.

Rescue attempts played out on national television as the country hoped for a miracle to rival the dramatic rescue of nine miners from a flooded section of the Quecreek Mine in western Pennsylvania in 2002. But the miracle never came.

Getty Images/Jeff Swensen

Grieving mourners leave a funeral service last Jan. 10 for Fred Ware Jr., one of 12 miners who died after an explosion at the Sago mine in West Virginia. Critics say lax mine safety is lightly punished, but the Mine Safety and Health Administration says its strict enforcement has lowered the fatality rate to just 22 coal mining deaths in 2005.

Adding to the tragedy, family members initially were told that all but one of the miners had survived, only to be informed hours later the reverse was true. It took nearly two days for rescuers to recover the bodies of 12 Sago miners, including the 55-year-old Hamner.

His family and many others say the miners might be alive today if the coal company had been required to equip the mine with a wireless communications system. Rescuers could have used it to tell the miners their best chance of survival was to try to get out rather than barricade themselves inside.

"It breaks my heart to know that there's modern technology that could have prevented my husband's death, and the Sago mine wasn't equipped with it," Deborah Hamner told a congressional forum on mine safety on Feb. 13. [2]

Hamner's anguished complaint must have seemed eerily familiar to the families of 13 miners who died following explosions at the Jim Walter Resources mine in Brookwood, Ala., on Sept. 23, 2001. As in the Sago disaster, many miners' families blamed poor communications, inadequate oxygen and the federal government's seeming indifference. However, because the deaths occurred shortly after the Sept. 11, 2001, terrorist attacks killed nearly 3,000 people, they were largely ignored by the press.

Then came the Sago disaster and a string of other coal mining accidents that killed nine other miners in West Virginia, Kentucky and Utah in early 2006. This time a bright national spotlight zeroed in on the coal mining industry and the federal agency responsible for enforcing mine safety standards, the Mine Safety and Health Administration (MSHA, pronounced Em-Sha).

"For so long, the public thought these types of accidents were a thing of the past," says former coal miner Paul Rakes, a professor of history at West Virginia University's Institute of Technology. "Today, when people are aware, minute by minute, of men being trapped underground, they can sympathize with that slow death."

MSHA says the high-tech devices that critics say could have prevented Sago are unreliable or untested, or don't provide two-way communication. "There are a lot of misconceptions," says Robert M. Friend, acting deputy assistant secretary of Labor for mine safety and health.

Nevertheless, since Sago, the agency says it is aggressively seeking the latest communication technology that will work inside mines. The effort includes dispatching engineers to Australia to look at the electronic "Tracker Tagging system," which allows rescuers to identify a miner's general location underground. The agency also is visiting the few U.S. mines that have technology that lets rescuers above ground send text messages to trapped miners. But neither system offers two-way communication between miners and rescuers, says Friend, a 28-year MSHA veteran.

The recent fatalities occur as coal is making a comeback. With oil prices skyrocketing, the government and industry are again eying the country's

Western Coal Coveted for Low Sulfur Content

Some 1,400 coal mines operate in the United States; Wyoming is the biggest source. Surface mines in the Powder River Basin, spanning the Wyoming-Montana border, produce nearly 40 percent of the U.S. supply. The low sulfur content of subbituminous Powder River coal generates less heat — but less pollution — when burned. The rest of the nation's coal comes mostly from the Appalachian Mountains and the Midwest, largely from underground mines that yield high-sulfur bituminous coal.

Coal-Bearing Areas of the United States

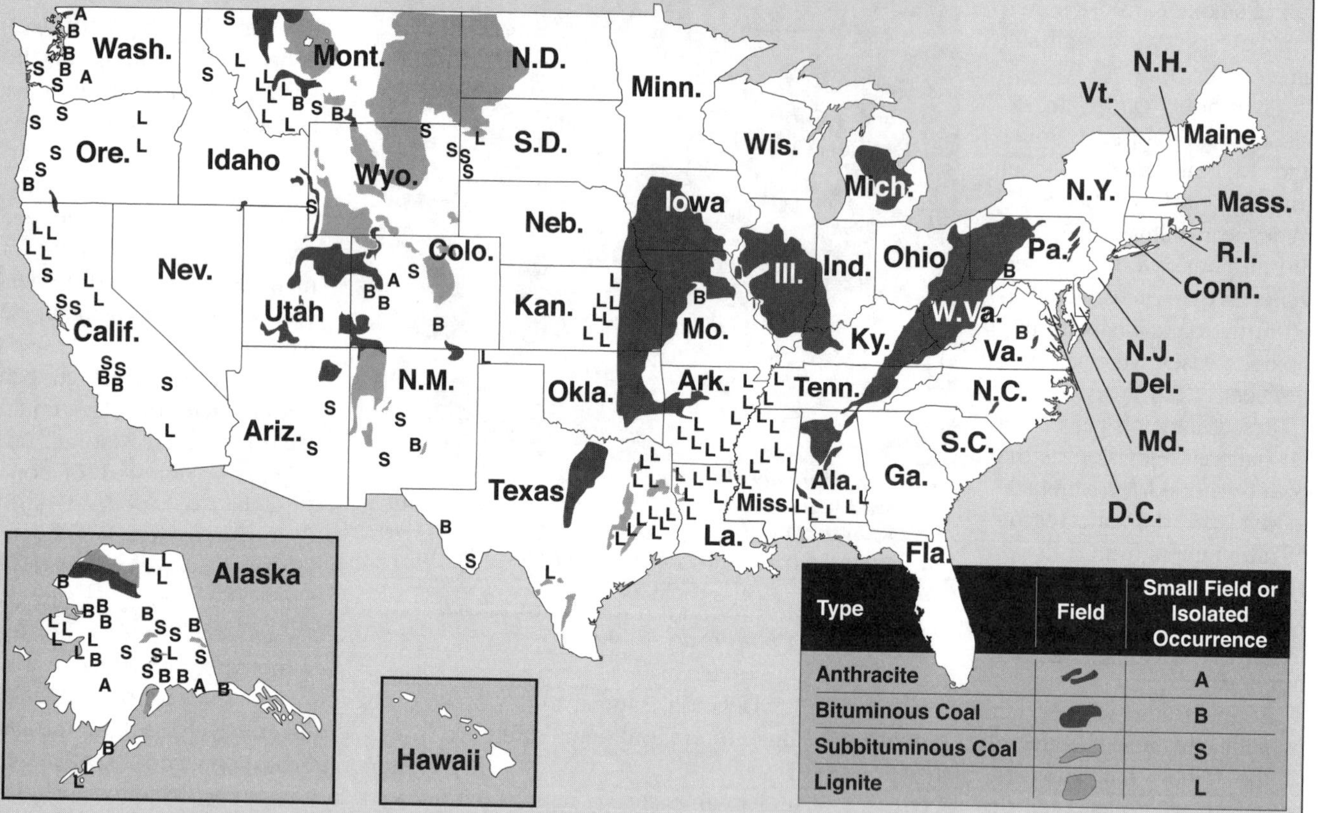

Type	Field	Small Field or Isolated Occurrence
Anthracite		A
Bituminous Coal		B
Subbituminous Coal		S
Lignite		L

Sources: U.S. Geological Survey; Texas Bureau of Economic Geology; Louisiana Geological Survey; Colorado Geological Survey

vast coal resources and new technologies to make burning coal more environmentally friendly. The United States has enough coal to last 250 years and currently mines more than 1 billion tons a year. But with production picking up, the National Mining Association estimates 50,000 new miners will be needed over the next five to seven years as demand rises and aging workers retire. (*See sidebar, p. 256.*)

Miners' families, labor unions and other critics say the Sago disaster and others might have been prevented if the Bush administration hadn't treated coal companies too leniently and shelved more than a dozen important safety standards initiated by the Clinton administration. MSHA fined Sago's owner, the International Coal Group, for 208 safety violations before the Jan. 2 accident, most of them for less than $250, according to Sen. John D. Rockefeller IV, D-W.Va. "If fines are going to be that predictable and that small, it's much easier for the company to pay the fine than fix the problem," Rockefeller said during a March 2 Senate hearing.

However, the Bush administration and the coal industry cite last year's record-low fatality rate — 22 deaths — as evidence that MSHA is enforcing federal safety rules. In the early 20th century, 2,000 to 3,000 miners died every year, the agency points out. [3]

"MSHA inspectors vigorously enforce the law," MSHA Acting Administrator David Dye told the Senate panel. "We don't take our enforcement responsibilities lightly."

West Virginia lawmakers quickly passed tougher safety rules after the

Sago accident, and the state's congressional delegation wants similar protections nationwide. The West Virginia law requires underground miners to have electronic tracking equipment and extra oxygen supplies. It also calls for the creation of a "rapid response" system for mine accidents. Pennsylvania and New Mexico are also poised to toughen their state mining safety rules. Other states considering beefing up mine safety protection include Illinois, Kentucky, Missouri, Ohio, Utah and Virginia (*see p. 254*).

"It's unfortunate that every coal mine health and safety law on the books is written with the blood of coal miners," said Rep. Nick Rahall, D-W.Va., whose congressional district includes several coal mining communities. [4] Most of the federal mine safety laws written during the 20th century followed West Virginia mining accidents. For example, the 1907 Monongah explosion that killed 362 men and boys led to the creation of the Federal Bureau of Mines, which studied mine safety but lacked enforcement powers. And the 1968 explosion that killed 78 at a mine in Farmington prodded Congress a year later to pass the Mine Safety and Health Act, which empowered the federal government to inspect and close down unsafe mines.

MSHA wants Congress to allow the agency to raise the existing $60,000 cap on fines to $220,000 — for flagrant violators. But otherwise the administration says current federal mine safety law works fine.

Meanwhile, the agency has issued "emergency" standards — including requiring operators to stock extra breathing devices underground, an idea MSHA dropped when President Bush took office. "They're fixing something that they screwed up the first time. Better late than never," said Tony Oppegard, a Kentucky mine safety attorney and former senior MSHA official during the Clinton administration. [5]

Production Up, Fatalities Down

U.S. coal production has increased by 83 percent since 1970, while mine fatalities have dropped by 92 percent. Modern technology and new mine safety laws are responsible for the changes, experts say.

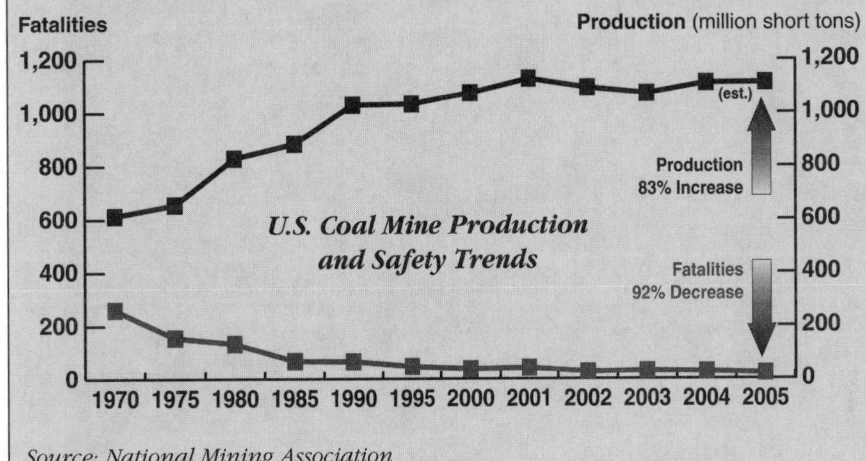

Source: National Mining Association

MSHA also is soliciting input from the industry, unions and others on several ideas, such as requiring mine operators to build underground "safe rooms," or rescue chambers. In late January, just such a safeguard kept 72 Canadians alive during a fire in a potash mine.

For its part, the coal industry is hoping Congress doesn't act too hastily. "What occurred in West Virginia is tragic, but I don't think it points to any systemic failures, either in the administration of the mine act or the administration of mine safety programs or a systemic failure in anything the industry is doing," says Bruce Watzman, vice president for safety and health at the National Mining Association, which represents the nation's 325 mining companies.

It would be a "big mistake" for Congress and MSHA to rush in and make sweeping changes until the Sago investigation is completed, agrees Robert Ferriter, manager of the mine safety program at the Colorado School of Mines in Golden. "Right now, quite frankly, a lot of it is political grandstanding."

As Congress scrutinizes whether enough is being done to keep miners safe, here are some questions people are asking:

Is the Bush administration adequately enforcing federal mine safety rules?

MSHA insists it has beefed up enforcement during the Bush administration, but critics say it relies too heavily on voluntary compliance and rarely penalizes coal companies for safety violations.

Since President Bush took office, say labor unions and advocacy groups, the administration has gutted worker protections and coddled corporate interests. [6] "What we've seen is a change of culture at MSHA, from an agency that enforces the law to what is more an 'enforcement counseling' agency," says Phil Smith, a spokesman for the United Mine Workers of America (UMW). He says MSHA essentially tells coal operators, "Let's all sit down and see if there is a problem." And if there is, Smith says, "the agency responds, 'You guys really should fix this. We're going to let it slide until you do.' "

AP Photo/Charles Rex Arbogast

United Mine Workers of America

Deep Underground

Second-generation miner Ron Bryant Jr. (top) uses a waist-level remote-control panel to operate a 40-ton continuous mining machine 450 feet below the surface in Galatia, Ill. During a safety drill in February at the Loveridge mine in West Virginia (bottom), miners erect a ventilation curtain to direct fresh air to the miners' location so that methane gas won't build up to explosive levels.

Rep. George Miller, D-Calif., ranking Democrat on the House Education and Workforce Committee, echoes the union charges. "This administration has not only failed to make the safety and health of mine workers a priority, it has also undermined the mine safety program through regulatory rollbacks, budget cuts and unqualified leadership," he said during a March 1 committee hearing.

MSHA is a "paper tiger," said J. Davitt McAteer, who headed the mine safety agency during the Clinton administration. "The numbers indicate that they haven't done much in the area of enforcement." [7]

The Bush administration, however, says MSHA issued 18 percent more citations at coal mines in 2005 than it did during Clinton's last year in office and that the number of "significant and substantial" citations has gone up 11 percent. [8] "MSHA is neither soft on enforcement nor soft on assessments," MSHA Acting Administrator Dye told the Senate Committee on Health Education, Labor and Pensions on March 2.

But Ferriter says the number of citations that MSHA writes "doesn't tell you whether the citations were eventually dropped or led to improvements in safety. For instance, many of the 208 citations MSHA levied against Sago appeared to be repeat violations, he says. All of those citations resulted in $132,000 in fines.

The New York Times reported recently that none of the individual fines against Sago since 2004 has exceeded $460, less than one-thousandth of 1 percent of the $110 million net profit reported last year by the mine's owner, International Coal Group. [9]

"The companies don't see these fines as a compliance requirement," says the UMW's Smith. "They see them as just another cost of doing business."

The Bush administration agrees the fines are too low and has asked Congress to more than triple the $60,000 maximum penalty for flagrant violators — to $220,000. Neal Merrifield, head of MSHA's Office of Assessment, points out that MSHA uses a complex, six-step process for determining penalties — a system laid out by Congress that MSHA cannot change. "Our hands are really tied," he says.

Not only are MSHA fines low, say critics, but they also are usually reduced and rarely collected. In January, Knight Ridder Newspapers reported that fewer than half the fines levied by MSHA between 2001 and 2003 — about $3 million — were ever paid. [10]

But Merrifield, an ex-miner who grew up not far from the Sago mine, disputes Knight Ridder's figures and says that in the past decade MSHA has collected 80 percent of its penalties. Year-to-year penalty-collection comparisons like Knight Ridder's are misleading, he says, because coal operators typically contest the fines and litigation can take years to resolve. And even when an operator is fined, judges sometimes reduce the penalty, he says. For example, after the 13 deaths in Brookwood, Ala., in 2001, MSHA levied a $435,000 fine that was slashed to $3,000 by an administrative law judge. MSHA is appealing the reduction to the Federal Mine Safety and Health Commission.

"Who knows how long that will take?" Merrifield asks.

Twice in February, the agency sued Kentucky mine operators who chronically failed to pay MSHA penalties, including the Simpson Mining Co., which owed $1 million in fines. [11] The UMW's Smith calls such aggressive actions "really, really rare" and a "public relations reaction" to the recent accidents.

MSHA's Dye says computer problems have prevented the agency from sending delinquent fines to the Treasury Department for collection ever since 2003. "Can't you walk them across the street?" Sen. Hillary Clinton, D-N.Y., asked during the March 2 hearing of the Senate Committee on Health Education, Labor and Pensions. "What kind of message does that send?"

But Dye told the panel that shutting down parts of a mine is a more powerful tool than levying fines. MSHA closed down parts of the Sago mine 18 times until all the 208 violations were corrected, he said. "If you close down a production area until the hazard is abated, that can cost a company in lost revenues anywhere from $50,000 to $150,000 for a single shift," Dye told the senators. But MSHA does not have authority to preemptively close entire mines or shut down production because of unpaid fines.

MSHA admits criminal cases and convictions are down, with guilty pleas dropping 54 percent since 2001. In the first four years of the Bush administration, the federal government averaged 3.5 convictions a year, compared to an average of 7.75 in the four years before that, according to Knight Ridder. "That's correct," Merrifield responds, but accidents and fatalities also were down during that same period.

"Mining is one of the heaviest regulated and inspected industries in this country," he says, adding, "There will always be a need for stiff and strong enforcement, [but] we can't inspect every inch of every single mine, every single day."

The coal industry agrees with MSHA that talk of lax enforcement is inaccurate. Luke Popovich, a spokesman for the National Mining Association, says such criticism is inflammatory and partisan and ignores steady improvement in safety over the last 20 years. "The only way to indict an administration or an industry for neglecting mine safety," he says, "is by overlooking the fact that the figures give a different story."

Democrats say MSHA enforcement has been curtailed by Bush budget cuts. Between 2001 and 2005, the enforcement staff was cut by 190 full-time inspectors, according to a report by Democrats on the House Education and the Workforce Committee. [12] And a 2003 report from congressional auditors found that MSHA inspectors failed to make timely follow-ups on 48 percent of citations. [13]

But Friend says MSHA has enough inspectors and has completed 99 percent of its mandated inspections — four a year for every underground coal mine and two yearly for surface mines

Mining Fines Among the Lowest

Many industries pay fines of more than $1 million for violations of federal regulations, but mining industry fines are limited to $60,000 for each violation of a health and safety standard.

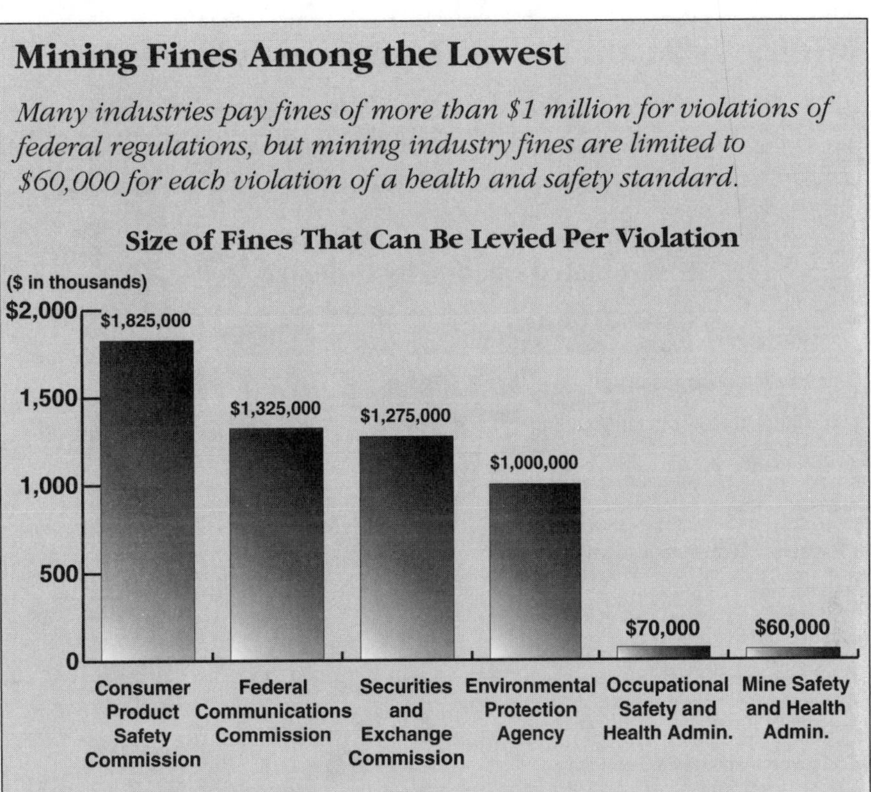

Source: USA Today, *Feb. 10, 2006*

Mining Is Second-Most-Dangerous Job

With 28 deaths per 100,000 employees, mining has the nation's second-highest rate of work-related deaths (right graph). A total of 152 miners of all types died in 2004 (left graph).

Number of Deaths and Rate of Work-Related Deaths, by Industry, 2004*

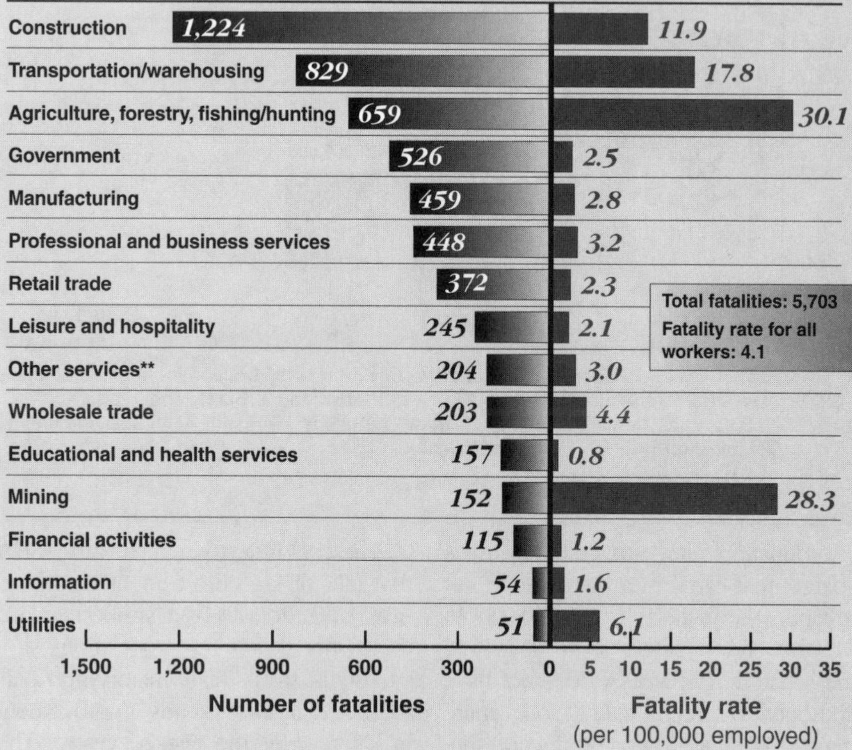

* *Industry figures do not include data for government employees, which are provided separately. Employment data based on the 2004* Current Population Survey *and Department of Defense figures.*

** *Excluding public administration*

Sources: Bureau of Labor Statistics, Current Population Survey, *"Census of Fatal Occupational Injuries"; Department of Defense, 2004*

— plus unannounced spot checks and other inspections.

The industry confirms that MSHA is making the inspections but questions whether the process is the most efficient use of the agency's time and resources. "Some mines in our country are so expansive that for an inspector to complete an inspection he begins at the first day of the quarter and closes that inspection out at the last day of the quarter. And then he immediately rolls into the next one," the NMA's Watzman says, which means, essentially, that an MSHA inspector is on hand nearly every day. "That doesn't seem to us to be a very efficient way to conduct business."

Does the mining industry have too much influence over MSHA?

Critics say the Bush administration has filled key MSHA positions with officials more interested in profits than in worker safety. As a result, say unions and Democrats, MSHA in the past five years has revoked or delayed at least 18 new rules that could make mining safer.

The administration and the coal industry dispute those charges and also say MSHA's top officials have many years of mining experience that uniquely qualify them to run the agency.

President Bush picked David Lauriski, an executive at Energy West Mining, to head MSHA until he left in November 2004. The agency's previous deputy assistant secretaries under Bush also came from mining: John Caylor had held management positions at Cyprus Minerals Co., Amax Mining Co. and Magma Copper Co. and John Correll held management jobs at Amax Mining and Peabody Coal Co.

"From the outset, the Bush administration filled top-level positions at the Mine Safety and Health Administration with officials from the industry it is charged with regulating," said a report issued in January by Democrats on the House Education and the Workforce Committee. [14]

The coal industry sees it differently. "I take comfort, quite honestly, knowing that the people who are running the agency, who are making the most important decisions, have mining experience," says Watzman of the National Mining Association. He says Lauriski's appointees, combined, had more than 100 years in mining.

During a Jan. 23 hearing, Sen. Robert Byrd, D-W.Va., asked MSHA officials point blank whether the agency is too cozy with the coal industry. "There's no cronyism between me and anyone in the industry," said MSHA Acting Administrator Dye. [15]

However, since Bush came into office, his mining officials have withdrawn or delayed 18 safety proposals because the rules would have forced coal companies to spend more time and money changing their practices, say the UMW and other critics. The proposals ranged from requiring miners to get more training and standardizing accident investigations to cutting miners' exposure to coal dust.

Rep. Miller said MSHA "didn't drop the regulations because they had better ideas. The 'better idea' was that the regs shouldn't exist." [16]

But Watzman says many of the proposals had such low priorities that they had lain dormant for many years, including during the Clinton era. For example, he says, one of the withdrawn proposals — to make conveyor belts more flame-resistant — came from former President George H. W. Bush — the president's father. However, the new, more flame-resistant conveyor belt that would have been developed to meet the new standard would have given off toxic gases if it did catch fire. "So they were introducing one hazard to replace another potential hazard," Watzman says.

Getty Images/Gene J. Puskar

The last of nine miners trapped for three days in the flooded Quecreek mine in Somerset, Pa., is brought to the surface in July 2002.

Democrats, however, say at least two of the 18 pulled safety proposals might have helped speed the rescue and increase the survival chances for the 14 miners killed in recent accidents in West Virginia. One proposal would have encouraged every mine operator to establish two fully trained and equipped rescue teams, and another would have ensured that "self-rescue" breathing devices were properly inspected and provided more than an hour of oxygen.

During a Jan. 23 hearing on the Sago accident, Sen. Tom Harkin, D-Iowa, whose father had been a miner, asked MSHA's Dye why the Bush administration dropped a proposal to update technology, such as using underground text-messaging devices. Dye cited several problems, including "reliability issues." [17]

In another hearing, Sen. Edward M. Kennedy, D-Mass., the ranking Democrat on the Senate Health, Education, Labor and Pensions Committee, wanted assurances from Richard M. Stickler, President Bush's pick to fill the top MSHA spot, that the agency would work to guarantee that every mine has a rescue team.

"No, senator, I cannot commit to that at this time," Stickler said during his Jan. 31 Senate confirmation hearing. [18] Some mines are very small, he said, making it unfeasible to station rescuers at each mine.

Kennedy expressed concerns that Stickler may be too close to the mining industry to effectively run MSHA. Stickler spent 30 years with BethEnergy Mines, working his way up from rank-and-file miner to corporate executive before leaving to head the Pennsylvania Bureau of Deep Mine Safety from 1997 to 2003. He was at the bureau when the nine Quecreek miners were rescued.

"Mr. Stickler's history is long on coal production experience but short on ensuring worker safety," Kennedy said during Stickler's confirmation hearing. [19]

The UMW opposes Stickler's nomination. "We want someone who hasn't spent his entire career figuring out how to circumvent safety laws so that they can increase production," Smith says.

Stickler, who followed his father and grandfather into the mines, told the Senate panel that he is the right man for the job. "I want this job because I have 'been there,' and I believe that I can contribute something positive to this agency," he said. [20] A Senate panel voted on March 8 to confirm Stickler, sending the nomination to the full Senate.

Are tougher mine-safety laws needed?

The Bush administration says sweeping, new mine-safety laws are premature, particularly since MSHA is improving mining safety with new rules. Several key members of Congress, however, say MSHA has been too complacent for too long and that only new laws will force the agency to beef up enforcement and require the latest safety technologies.

Lawmakers representing West Virginia introduced legislation in Congress on Feb. 1 requiring heftier penalties against coal companies that repeatedly violate safety standards. "It's obvious that something is very, very wrong at MSHA," said Sen. Byrd, the bill's lead Senate sponsor. [21] "The rescue procedures for miners are woefully inadequate."

In Byrd's measure, coal operators would have to station rescue teams at each mine, store additional breathing devices underground and have emergency communication and tracking devices that allow miners to contact rescuers. Rep. Rahall, the bill's lead House sponsor, complained that as technology enables companies to mine more coal in less time with fewer workers, "advances that could improve the conditions for workers . . . were tragically shoved aside." [22]

A day before the legislation was unveiled, Stickler told a Senate panel that, "in general, the [current] laws are adequate." If confirmed, he promised to "do everything possible" to get new mine technology approved and used in the mines, including communication devices for contacting rescuers. [23]

Labor unions endorse the legislation, arguing that coal companies won't voluntarily make the changes until MSHA forces them to — and the agency so far has refused to do that. UMW President Cecil Roberts told a Senate panel in January that when he was in the mines 30 years ago the miners' connection to the outside world was a telephone line. Despite technological advances since then, he said, the typical mine today still has "one telephone line from the surface to the working sections of the mine." [24]

But unions are leery about a wholesale overhaul of the Mine Safety and Health Act. "We don't want to reopen the Mine Safety and Health Act," says the, UMW's Smith. "It's not necessary. It's a good act."

The coal industry has neither endorsed nor opposed the West Virginia measure but cautions Congress against "quick fixes" that might not work. For example, certain electronic equipment may not work properly in all mines. "Unless proven effective in underground conditions, some devices might impart a false sense of security and lead miners to take unnecessary risks," wrote Kraig R. Naasz, president and CEO of the National Mining Association. [25]

But labor unions, some Democrats and former MSHA Administrator McAteer question the industry's claims that the technology is unreliable and shouldn't be mandated. About a dozen U.S. mines already use "personal emergency devices" (PEDs), worn on the belt, that allow miners to be tracked by aboveground monitors and alerted in case of danger. Eight years ago, 45 miners wearing the devices escaped a fire at the Willow Creek Mine in Helper, Utah. The technology has been available, McAteer told a Senate panel in January, and "can be put in the all the mines in this country." [26] He estimated that the device costs about $20 per miner, but both MSHA and the manufacturer say PEDs cost about $200.

Whatever the price, the device only allows one-way communication, so there is no way to know if the miners received the information. "We want uninterruptible, ground-penetrating, wireless two-way communication," NMA's Watzman says. The technology, he says, is "not yet where we ultimately want it to be."

The mining industry also says the proposed bill could threaten 100 working coal mines, primarily in the West, by nullifying a 2004 Bush administration reversal of a longstanding policy that required coal operators to build two separate tunnels — one to take the coal out of the mine and another to blow in fresh air. NMA's Watzman says 100 mines use ventilation systems that essentially use the same tunnel for both taking out coal and blowing in air. Critics say that creates a greater hazard because the air could feed a fire, making escape more difficult.

"Those mines are in very serious trouble" if the measure is enacted, Watzman says. The West Virginia delegation says the fire at the Alma No. 1 mine in West Virginia that killed two miners in January might have been prevented had MSHA kept the rule on the books.

In the meantime, MSHA in February announced "emergency" mine evacuation standards that address some, but not all, of lawmakers' concerns raised by the Sago accident. [27] The standards, published in the *Federal Register* on March 9, will require mine operators to inform the agency within 15 minutes of an accident. Some two hours passed before MSHA was notified of the Jan. 2 Sago accident. The new rules also require operators to provide miners with emergency air devices containing extra oxygen — to be stored in the mines — and to install "lifelines," such as ropes with reflective tape, along primary and alternate escape routes.

The UMW's Smith calls the emergency standards "good steps in the right direction" but says the more sweeping changes outlined in the West Virginians' legislation are still needed. The NMA said it "fully supports" the emergency rule and that the "regulations standardize practices that are voluntarily employed at many of the nation's coal mines." [28] ■

BACKGROUND

Canaries and Rats

During the 19th century, coal fueled the nation's industrial revolution, heated homes and powered an expanding network of locomotives and steamboats. Homeowners dubbed the coal they used for heating as "dusty diamonds,"

Miners used picks and shovels, often for 10 hours a day; boys as young as 8, known as breakers, picked up the smaller pieces. Today, coal is largely mined by sophisticated, computerized machines, but hazards remain.

Continued on p. 252

Chronology

1800s *Coal becomes the principal fuel for locomotives and increasingly is used to heat homes and fuel steamboats.*

1890
United Mine Workers of America (UMW) is founded.

Sept. 10, 1897
Police fire on striking coal miners in Lattimer, Pa., killing 19 and wounding 40. The incident helps spur unionism in the mines.

1900-1940s

Mining disasters kill 2,000-3,000 miners each year.

1907
In the worst coal mining disaster in U.S. history, an explosion and resulting fires in Monongah, W. Va., kill 362 men and boys.

1910
Congress creates the Bureau of Mines, but it lacks enforcement authority.

1920
Labor leader John L. Lewis, a former miner, becomes president of the UMW and one of the most effective advocates for miners.

1922
Twenty-two people are killed near Herrin, Ill., when striking coal miners attack workers hired to replace them.

1933
National Industrial Recovery Act grants workers the right to form unions, sparking UMW growth from 100,000 members to 600,000.

1950-1990s

Congress gradually toughens federal mining requirements.

1952
After 220 miners are killed in explosions in Centralia and West Frankfort, Ill., in the 1940s, Congress passes the Mine Safety Act, which requires annual inspections and safeguards and sets penalties for violators; mines employing fewer than 15 miners are exempt.

1966
Mine Safety Act is revised to cover small mines.

1968
A coal mine explosion in Farmington, W. Va., kills 78 miners and spurs passage the following year of the Federal Coal Mine Health and Safety Act, empowering the government to close unsafe mines.

1973
Mine Enforcement and Safety Administration (MESA) is spun off from the Bureau of Mines as the first federal agency with the sole purpose of protecting miners.

1977
Mine Safety and Health Act renames MESA as Mine Safety and Health Administration (MSHA) and moves it to Department of Labor from the Interior Department.

1991
MSHA proposes $7 million in fines against mine operators for falsifying coal-dust samples. Owners plead guilty, pay reduced fines.

1995
A Republican proposal to disband MSHA and fold its responsibilities into the Occupational Safety and Health Administration fails to pass.

2000-Present

Democrats and unions blame mining accidents on lax enforcement of safety standards.

Sept. 23, 2001
Explosions kill 13 miners at the Jim Walter Resources No. 5 mine in Brookwood, Ala.

July 24, 2002
Nine miners are dramatically rescued after three days in a flooded section of the Quecreek mine in Somerset, Pa.

Jan. 2, 2006
Twelve miners die after an explosion at West Virginia's Sago mine.

Jan. 19, 2006
Two more West Virginia miners die in a fire at the Aracoma Alma mine. . . . In response, state lawmakers require electronic tracking equipment in mines and extra supplies of oxygen. . . . The state's congressional delegation proposes similar federal legislation.

March 1-2, 2006
Congressional panels grill MSHA officials about mine safey and enforcement and the use of electronic tracking and communications equipment.

March 9, 2006
New mine evacuation regulations require coal operators to report accidents within 15 minutes and store more emergency oxygen devices underground.

April 20-22, 2006
State-of-the-art mining technologies will be the focus of an international symposium at Wheeling Jesuit University in Wheeling, W. Va., sponsored by federal and state mining officials.

Different Mining, Different Hazards

The accident at West Virginia's Sago mine has focused attention on underground coal mining, but surface, or strip, mining is actually far more common.

Most U.S. coal is mined using surface mining, which involves bulldozing and removing several layers of rock and dirt to get to the coal. Surface mines are less dangerous than underground mines because they lack explosive methane gas, the risk of falling roofs and other hazards associated with underground mines.

It generally costs less to strip mine coal and requires fewer workers than underground mining to produce the same quantity of coal. Underground mining made up only 33 percent of production in 2005, but it accounted for 14 of the 22 fatalities that year — 64 percent. [1]

However, surface mines have their own hazards, both physical and environmental.

In surface mining, workers often blast the area with explosives first, then use huge earthmoving equipment such as power shovels or draglines to scoop off the layers of soil and rock. Once the coal is exposed, smaller shovels are used to load it into trucks. In some cases, operators remove the tops of mountains to get to the coal, known as mountaintop removal. This involves using a dragline to remove the rock and earth to create a flat area that can be mined.

Most fatalities in surface mines involve the large trucks, conveyors and front-end loaders. "The trucks are so huge that the wheels are bigger than a pickup," says Phil Roberts, professor of history at the University of Wyoming in Laramie. Drivers of those massive trucks could run over a passenger car "like running over a cardboard box."

Two surface miners in Kentucky were killed when an unattended coal truck rolled into the area where they were eating lunch. And last August another miner died when the bulldozer he was operating on a surface mine overturned. [2]

While accident and fatality rates may be lower in surface mining, the environmental concerns are significant. Coal operators are required by the 1977 Surface Mining Control and Reclamation Act to "reclaim" the land after they remove the coal, but some unscrupulous operators simply abandon the mines instead of restoring the land. Water that runs off surface mines often erodes the soil to the point that it is unusable and pollutes rivers and lakes with sulfuric acid. In his book *Lost Mountain*, Kentucky native Erik Reece, whose father worked in the mines, estimates that 47 percent of Kentucky's rivers and streams are too polluted for drinking, fishing or swimming because of surface mining. [3]

One of the biggest changes in the U.S. coal industry has been the development in the 1970s of surface mines in the Rocky Mountains' Powder River Basin, which spans the Wyoming-Montana border. Coal from the basin, coveted for its low sulfur content, now makes up nearly 40 percent of all U.S. coal. [4]

Wyoming became the country's top coal producer in 1990 after surpassing West Virginia and Kentucky. [5] Wyoming's coal now comes almost exclusively from surface mines, a marked difference from the 1880s, when underground mining was so prevalent that mining safety measures were put into the state's constitution, says Roberts. "Families here are very grateful that we have a different kind of mining operation," he says.

The coal in the Powder River Basin wasn't always prized. In the early years of mining, Powder River coal was considered lower grade because of its low sulfur content. Sulfur levels determine the amount of heat — and air pollution — the coal generates. Powder River coal, technically called subbituminous, generates less heat than other types of coal, but its low sulfur means that electric companies that burn it don't have to install expensive "scrubbers" to get rid of its airborne emissions. [6] Coal from other parts of the country, primarily bituminous, produces more heat but also more pollution.

Surface mining in the West picked up just as organized labor's clout was on the wane. As a result, many surface mines are not unionized. The United Mine Workers of America (UMW) represents up to 45,000 of the nation's 75,000 coal miners, primarily in states east of the Mississippi, but there is no union in the Powder River Basin.

Now, according to UMW spokesman Phil Smith, the union has launched a nationwide organizing campaign at Peabody Energy, the world's largest coal company, which operates mines from Appalachia to the Power River Basin.

[1] Figures from the National Mining Association and MSHA, "End of Year," 2005, www.msha.gov/stats/charts/coal2005yearend.asp.

[2] For descriptions of fatal coal accidents, see MSHA's "Fatalgrams" at http://www.msha.gov/fatals/fab.htm.

[3] Erik Reece, *Lost Mountain*, (2006).

[4] "Coal Production and Number of Mines by State and Coal Rank, 2004" U.S. Energy Information Administration, www.eia.doe.gov/cneaf/coal/page/acr/table6.html.

[5] Duane Lockard, *Coal: A Memoir and Critique* (1998), p. 17.

[6] *Ibid.*

Continued from p. 250

Underground mines build up explosive, lethal gases, chiefly methane and carbon monoxide. Miners also face the risk of cave-ins, fires, suffocation from lack of proper ventilation and even drowning. The Quecreek miners were trapped when they accidentally broke into an adjacent abandoned mine, unleashing millions of gallons of water. It took rescuers three days to drill 240 feet to reach the miners and pull them to safety.

In the 1800s, canaries were the miners' early-warning "technology." If the birds stopped chirping and died, miners knew the level of noxious gases was too high and ran for their lives. Miners also befriended mine rats, thought to be able to detect subtle vibrations that signaled danger. If the rats suddenly scurried away, the miners followed, wrote author Barbara Freese in *Coal: A Human History.* [29]

New laws and technologies have replaced the canaries and rats, but safety progress usually has come only after deadly disasters forced lawmakers to act.

From the late 1800s to the early 1900s, coal companies' influence over miners extended well beyond their jobs, making it hard for them to complain about unsafe working conditions. In the mining towns that proliferated in Pennsylvania, West Virginia and Wyoming — known as coal "patches" or camps — miners often lived in company-owned homes and shopped in company stores. Companies even had their own form of money, called "scrip," which could only be spent at company stores and facilities.

Some coal operators gave out scrip in advance for wages not-yet earned, keeping many miners in debt to the company, which often set high prices at its stores. Singer Tennessee Ernie Ford captured the miner's plight in his 1955 hit "Sixteen Tons:"

You load sixteen tons, what do you get?
Another day older and deeper in debt.
Saint Peter don't you call me 'cause I can't go.
I owe my soul to the company store.

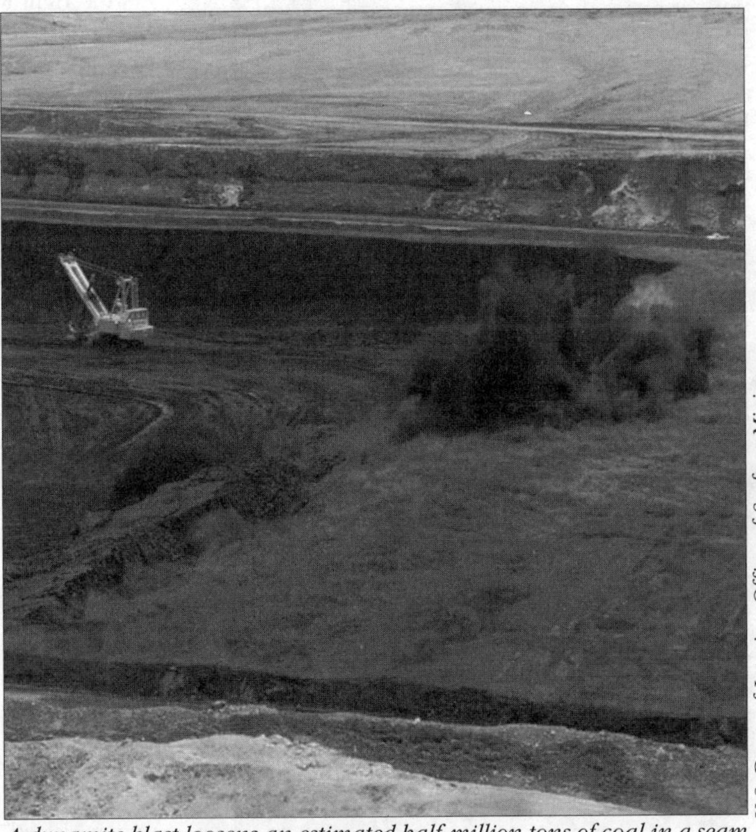

U.S. Dept. of Interior, Office of Surface Mining

A dynamite blast loosens an estimated half-million tons of coal in a seam 80 feet thick at a Kerr-McGee Coal Corp. surface mine in Gillette, Wyo.

Unwilling to complain to a company with so much control over their lives, the workers eventually — and perhaps inevitably — turned to labor unions. The United Mine Workers was formed in 1890, but it was during John L. Lewis' 40-year tenure as president (1920-1960) that the union became one of the most powerful and militant in the country.

Accidents and Unions

Improvements in working conditions typically occurred after fatal accidents caught the public's attention. The worst coal mining disaster in American history occurred in 1907 at Monongah, W. Va. The official death toll was 362 miners, but Duane Lockard, a professor emeritus of politics at Princeton University and author of *Coal: A Memoir and Critique*, contends at least 550 people died, including children and immigrants whose families in Europe didn't know their loved ones were missing. Lockard's grandfather helped bring out the remains of victims. [30]

Within days of the Monongah tragedy, two coal mine explosions in Pennsylvania and one in Alabama killed 329 other miners, followed the next year by three explosions that killed 280 miners in Wyoming, Pennsylvania and West Virginia. [31] And the toll kept rising. In the nation's third-deadliest mining accident, a fire in Cherry, Ill., killed 259 miners in 1909.

The spate of deadly accidents prompted Congress to create the Bureau of Mines in 1910, but many miners felt it didn't go far enough. Indeed, the bureau lacked authority to inspect mines or enforce safety procedures. For the next 20 years, accidents took the lives of about 2,000 miners each year. [32]

After three decades of lobbying, miners and unions convinced Congress to empower the bureau to inspect mines and publicize its findings. But it could only make recommendations, not enforce them.

Miners and their union often clashed with operators, sometimes violently, in demanding better working conditions and wages. Shortly after Lewis became UMW president, 10 miners, union officials and townspeople were killed in a gunfight during the "Matewan Massacre" in West Virginia, as the union was trying to organize miners throughout the

Library of Congress

United Mine Workers of America

Mining in the Past

Coal miners ride into a mine in Maidsville, W. Va., in 1938 (top). New laws in the 1930s helped workers unionize and won them better working conditions. Led by the dynamic John L. Lewis (bottom), the United Mine Workers of America grew from 100,000 members in the early 1930s to 600,000 by 1940.

state. The town's mayor died in the infamous incident, which was memorialized in John Sayles' critically acclaimed 1987 film "Matewan."

The 1930s and '40s was a seminal period for organized labor. With the dynamic Lewis at the helm, the UMW capitalized on new laws that helped workers unionize and won them better working conditions. The 1933 National Industrial Recovery Act and the 1935 National Labor Relations Act guaranteed most private-sector workers the right to form unions. The new laws helped the UMW bolster its membership from 100,000 in the early 1930s to 600,000 by 1940. [33] The Fair Labor Standards Act in 1938 guaranteed a minimum wage and workweek and limited child labor.

During World War II, miners were pressured to produce more quickly because coal was vital to the production of steel and chemicals used in military equipment. About one-third of the nation's mines had been mechanized, which speeded production but introduced new hazards, says Rakes of West Virginia University. The new machinery was loud, created much more dust and used electrical systems that increased the possibility of sparking gas explosions. Coal was so important to the war effort that the federal government twice took over the mines during strikes. [34]

Leading strikes during the war made Lewis one of the most hated public figures in America, but the coal miners loved him. Indeed, by 1949 they were among the nation's highest-paid industrial workers, with health and pension plans enjoyed by few others. [35] By the 1950s, however, demand for coal was declining as power plants, businesses and homes turned to oil and gas, and thousands of miners lost their jobs. [36]

Safety Laws

Coal miners, however, were still dying on the job. An explosion in Centralia, Ill., that killed 111 men in 1947 raised public awareness and spurred Congress to act, if somewhat belatedly. [37] Five years later, lawmakers passed the Federal Mine Safety Act, which required annual inspections, safeguards and penalties for violators.

A 1968 explosion in Farmington, W. Va., that killed 78 miners was the first coal mining disaster viewed nationally via television, says Rakes. Rescuers could not locate all the victims, and 19 remain entombed in the mine. This time, lawmakers responded quickly, passing the Federal Coal Mine Health and Safety Act of 1969. The law sought to prevent explosions and accidents through tougher enforcement and, for the first time, took action to eliminate "black lung disease" — a respiratory ailment caused by prolonged exposure to coal dust — and compensate miners suffering from the disease.

The new law also allowed the federal government, again for the first time, to issue mandatory fines for violating mine safety standards and criminal penalties for willful violations. In addition, inspectors were empowered to close unsafe mines, and miners were given the right to request federal inspections.

A fire at a silver mine in Kellogg, Idaho, in 1972, killed 91 miners and prompted the federal government to create the Mine Enforcement and Safety Administration (MESA) from the Bureau of Mines. It became the first federal agency charged solely with assuring a safe, healthful working environment for all miners.

Congress, however, was concerned with Bureau of Mines enforcement. A General Accounting Office (now the Government Accountability Office) report found that during inspections the previous year inspectors made less than one-third of the required safety inspections. [38] Meanwhile, mining accidents continued; at the Scotia mine in Letcher County, Ky., in 1976 two explosions killed 26 men, including three MESA inspectors.

In 1977 President Jimmy Carter transferred MESA from the Interior Department to the Labor Department and renamed it the Mine Safety and Health Administration. The new law required at least four complete inspections of all underground mines annually and two of all surface mines.

Carter was a big proponent of coal. Following the 1973 OPEC oil embargo, he sought to nearly double coal production and consumption by 1985 and reduce American dependence on oil and gas. [39]

Rakes, who had been a miner for 20 years in West Virginia, saw a "remarkable change" once MSHA began inspecting mines. "The chances that we used to take we wouldn't think of doing because of MSHA," he says. Once "MSHA forced the issue," he says, the company implemented numerous safety practices, such as making sure each section of the mine had its own air supply, that workers wore reflective clothing and that methane monitors would automatically shut down machines if gas build-ups reached a certain level.

Nonetheless, the 1980s saw more miners' deaths and again more congressional scrutiny, including charges by some lawmakers that MSHA was not enforcing safety laws any better than MESA. Critics also worried that Republican President Ronald Reagan's budget cuts threatened enforcement. In the first 20 days of 1982, 14 coal miners died in explosions. [40]

The spotlight returned to the coal industry in April 1991 — this time for fraud. Under President George H. W. Bush, Labor Secretary Lynn Martin charged 850 coal operators with tampering with coal dust samples to show that the air in their mines was safe. The department proposed some $7 million in fines, but dozens of coal companies pleaded guilty and paid lesser fines. [41]

When Bill Clinton was elected president, he appointed McAteer, a frequent critic of MSHA, to head the agency. McAteer, an attorney, had headed the Occupational Safety and Health Law Center, a workplace advocacy group. During McAteer's stint, MSHA initiated more worker training, noise restrictions and limits on

Coal Generates Most U. S. Power

Coal generated 50 percent of the nation's electricity in 2004, and experts believe it will supply almost 60 percent by 2030 because of the nation's rising power needs.

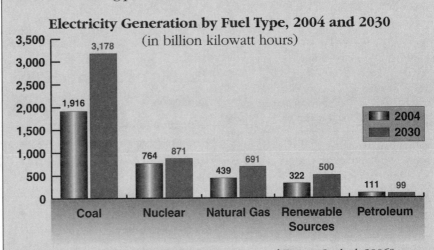

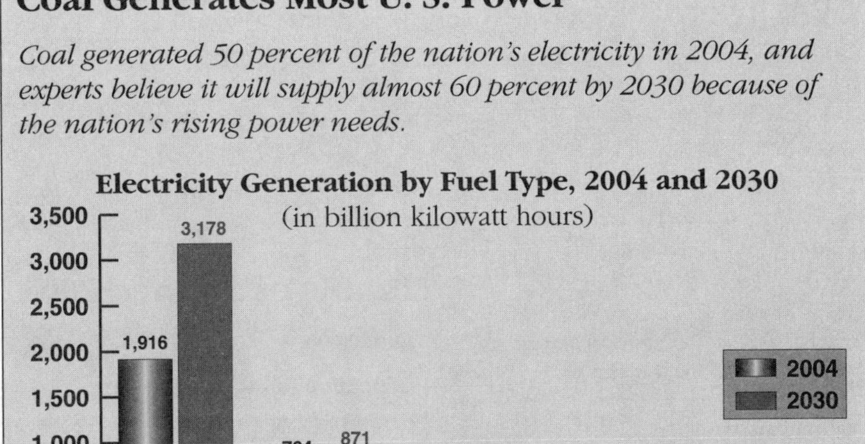

Source: Energy Information Administration, "Annual Energy Outlook 2006"

Wanted: Next Generation of Miners

Just one day after 13 miners were trapped in West Virginia's Sago mine, 22-year-old Ryan Boyd began coal-mining classes at West Virginia University's Academy of Mine Training and Energy. "Mining is the job that pays the most here," Boyd said. "It puts food on the table and roofs over heads." [1]

In 1923 the coal industry employed 863,000 miners. Today it employs 75,000. Yet in less than a decade, the industry will need 50,000 new recruits to replace retiring miners and meet the growing demand for coal. "We are going to lose an entire generation of miners in the next five to seven years, and we need to replace them," says Bruce Watzman, vice president for safety and health at the National Mining Association.

The looming miner shortage is an outgrowth of the OPEC oil embargo of 1973, which prompted the United States to rely more on its coal resources. Through the 1980s and '90s, however, few new miners were hired, thanks in part to new technology that increased production with fewer workers. Now, just as production is picking up, many miners hired in the '70s are preparing to retire.

Some coal experts say the Sago disaster and other safety issues will have little impact on recruiting the next generation of miners, in large part because the pay is excellent. The starting salary for an underground or surface miner is between $55,000 and $60,000, says Phil Smith, a spokesman for the United Mine Workers of America (UMW), which represents about 45,000 miners. With overtime, some miners can earn more than $100,000 a year. "That's pretty good pay no matter where you live," Smith says.

But the coal industry must fight the misperception that miners are low-skilled, uneducated, rural worker who can't find work elsewhere. "That is just not true," says Smith.

Smith explains that miners must complete between six months to a year of training before taking a state test to become certified. Each state has its own test, but all states require certification, he says.

No longer a pick-and-shovel job, most coal today is mined using sophisticated equipment and technology. "You're talking about people operating pieces of machinery that can be worth $30 million that are all computer driven," Watzman says.

Not only is the pay excellent, but, for some, working close to nature and in a rural area is part of the appeal. "I want to stay in West Virginia," said Boyd, an avid hunter and fisherman. "I was born and raised here. I love West Virginia." And while mining has its risks, Boyd isn't too worried: "You're just as likely to get killed on the highway." [2]

Paul Rakes, a former coal miner and now a professor of history at West Virginia University's Institute of Technology in Montgomery, W. Va., can relate. "The coal mine is an exciting place," he says. "It's fun."

Profile of a Miner, 2004

Average age:	50
Education (all U.S. miners):	
Less than high school	*14.9%*
High school diploma	*62.1*
Some college	*10.3*
Associate degree	*6.9*
Bachelor's degree	*3.4*
Master's degree	*2.3*
Earnings:	
Average hourly	*$21.57*
Average weekly	*$1,029.59*
Average annual	*$50,000*

Totals do not add to 100 due to rounding.

Sources: National Mining Association, Bureau of Labor Statistics

[1] Tom Vanden Brook, "Recruits hungry for good jobs head off to coal mines," *USA Today*, Feb. 15, 2006, p. B1.
[2] *Ibid.*

the amount of diesel fumes from underground coal-mining equipment.

When Republicans took over the House in the mid-1990s, as part of their efforts to streamline federal agencies they tried to fold MSHA into the larger Occupational Safety and Health Administration (OSHA), which enforces safety rules for other industries. The legislation — "a giant step in the wrong direction" for miner safety, said McAteer — never passed. [42] In 1995, however, Congress succeeded in closing the Bureau of Mines and transferring its duties to other agencies. ■

CURRENT SITUATION

States Act

Coal mining safety is being scrutinized at a level unseen for decades, with probes under way by Congress, the states, MSHA and the industry itself.

State and federal investigators are still investigating the Sago accident, but West Virginia already has implemented sweeping changes to its state mining safety rules. Meanwhile, Pennsylvania and New Mexico are working on similar measures, and several reforms have been proposed by congressional lawmakers.

"Sometimes you see states waiting for the federal government to act," says Kate Burke, an energy policy specialist at the National Conference of State Legislatures (NCSL) in Denver. "But not in this case."

Continued on p. 258

At Issue:

Is the administration adequately enforcing mine safety rules?

yes

DAVID G. DYE
ACTING ASSISTANT SECRETARY OF LABOR FOR MINE SAFETY AND HEALTH

FROM TESTIMONY BEFORE THE SENATE COMMITTEE ON HEALTH, EDUCATION, LABOR AND PENSIONS, MARCH 2, 2006

MSHA [Mine Safety and Health Administration] inspectors vigorously enforce the law — with the support of the entire agency, top to bottom. Last year, MSHA issued the highest number of citations and orders since 1994. In recent years, MSHA increased its use of "withdrawal orders" to gain compliance with the standards. This is a powerful enforcement tool, [which] requires miners to be removed from the area affected by the violation, often resulting in disruptions to production. The number of withdrawal orders increased 20 percent over the last five years. MSHA issued more withdrawal orders in both 2004 and 2005 than in any year since 1994. . . . Any MSHA violation must be abated within a specified time frame before the penalty is assessed. In the case of withdrawal orders, the hazard must be abated before miners are allowed to work in the area or activity affected by the hazard.

The statistics show our strong enforcement record very clearly. From FY2000 to FY2005:

- Total citations and orders issued by MSHA at all mines increased by 5 percent (119,183 to 125,161);
- Total citations and orders issued at coal mines increased by 19 percent (56,870 to 67,756);
- Total "significant and substantial" citations and orders issued at coal mines increased by 13 percent (23,586 to 26,717);
- MSHA enforcement personnel have significantly increased the issuance of withdrawal orders to coal mine operators who exhibit an unwarrantable failure to comply with the regulations. Unwarrantable failure orders are one of the most severe enforcement actions inspectors can take, and in each of the last two years MSHA inspectors issued more such orders than in any year in the last 10 years.

I want to make something clear: MSHA's inspectors diligently and vigorously enforce the law. However, the Mine Act does not give MSHA authority to preemptively close entire mines because of the number or frequency of violations. Nor does the Mine Act include the authority to close or seize a mine because of unpaid fines or penalties.

While we are proud of our enforcement and compliance record, we know there is more to do. We are currently engaged in a thorough investigation of the recent tragic accidents at the Sago and Alma mines. We are determined to learn from these accidents.

no

CECIL E. ROBERTS
PRESIDENT, UNITED MINE WORKERS OF AMERICA

WRITTEN FOR *CQ RESEARCHER*, MARCH 2006

Recent tragic events in America's coalfields demonstrate all too well that the government has failed miserably to protect those who toil in the nation's mines.

The primary mine safety law was enacted nearly 40 years ago in recognition that mine operators cannot be trusted to police themselves and to put safety before the bottom line. Developing improved health and safety standards is one of the primary purposes of the Mine Act, along with ensuring operator compliance and encouraging research to help prevent illness and accidents.

Regrettably, the Mine Safety and Health Administration (MSHA) hasn't met these priorities. Instead of focusing exclusively on improving miners' health and safety, the agency has focused on helping operators produce more coal while methodically stripping away miners' protections, despite the specific mandate from Congress.

The United Mine Workers of America appreciates the work of MSHA's inspectors and other personnel, but the agency's top policymakers have not done their job. As the tragedies at the Sago and Alma mines in West Virginia demonstrate, there is a serious void in the regulatory framework for underground miners confronting an emergency. In fact, MSHA has been going backwards in providing miners with needed protections. The agency scrapped 18 proposed rules — among them protections that might have saved the miners who perished at Sago and Alma.

To its credit, MSHA has recently initiated a rulemaking that might help trapped miners survive an accident. It would require companies to immediately notify MSHA of emergencies, store additional oxygen supplies underground and install "lifelines" — special cables along escape routes for miners to hold onto that indicate the way out.

We support these efforts, but we must ask: Why did MSHA wait so long? Why wasn't it looking for these solutions 10 and 20 years ago? Besides, rulemaking is pointless if the rules aren't enforced.

The bottom line is that MSHA spends too much effort at "compliance assistance" and too little on enforcement. The agency must bolster its expertise and prepare for transition as many of its inspectors approach retirement. Finally, MSHA needs to do a better job seeking and enforcing meaningful fines and penalties for Mine Act violations.

The status quo is inadequate. When the government failed the Sago and Alma miners, it failed all miners. Coal mining is still dangerous, but we can do a lot more than we are doing today to make it safer.

Continued from p. 256

In fact, it took West Virginia lawmakers just one day to revise the state mining law. Passage of the bill on Jan. 23 "was truly historic and set the tone for a series of reforms on both the state and federal level that will have a real and lasting impact on miners and their families for many years to come," said Democratic Gov. Joe Manchin, whose uncle was killed in the deadly 1968 Farmington explosion. [43] The governor also wants legislation requiring every mine in the state to have at least one rescue chamber stocked with enough air, food and water to keep survivors alive for at least 24 hours.

Illinois, Kentucky, Missouri, Ohio, Utah and Virginia also are considering beefing up mine safety protection, says Burke. Alabama is considering a 24-hour mine accident operations center linked to its Department of Homeland Security, while an Arizona measure would have the state mine inspector report directly to the governor.

West Virginia also initiated a "stand down for safety," which called for the state's 550 coal mines to cease production during each shift to allow for safety checks by supervisors and workers. The Bush administration liked the idea so much that MSHA expanded the idea nationwide, persuading operators to take a one-hour safety timeout on Feb. 6. [44]

Congress Debates

Congressional Democrats wasted little time painting the Bush administration as soft on the coal industry at workers' expense. Within weeks of the Sago accident, Democrats on the House Education and the Workforce Committee issued a report lambasting MSHA's enforcement record under the current administration. [45] In February, they brought in the families of miners killed this year to speak out while chastising their GOP counterparts for failing to hold hearings.

"This forum, hopefully, will lead to official hearings so we can pass legislation such as the West Virginia delegation has introduced," said Robert C. Scott, D-Va. [46] Many House Democrats are pushing for a vote on the delegation's bill, which calls for tougher MSHA penalties and updated safety standards, including required use of communications and tracking devices.

The Senate acted more quickly. Four weeks after the Sago accident, Republican Sen. Arlen Specter of coal-rich Pennsylvania put MSHA on the hot seat. As chairman of the Appropriations subcommittee with jurisdiction over mining safety, Specter questioned whether budget cuts had affected MSHA and vowed to press for "adequate funding" for job safety. Acting Administrator Dye assured Specter the agency has managed its resources and personnel well, but he left the hearing before it was over, even though a clearly annoyed Specter had asked him to stay.

> **"Why did miners have to die before MSHA took these steps?"**
>
> ***— Sen. Robert C. Byrd, D-W. Va.***

Specter has introduced legislation similar to the West Virginia proposal, but his bill also would impose $100 "user fees" for each serious violation of the mining law. The additional money from fines collected would be spent on research and training, and the Federal Mine Safety and Health Commission could no longer reduce fines for flagrant and habitual violators. Specter's bill would impose higher civil penalties than the West Virginia proposal — up to $500,000 for flagrant violations.

A March 1 hearing held by the House Education and the Workforce's Subcommittee on Workforce Protections erupted into a shouting match between Chairman Charlie Norwood, R-Ga., and Rep. Miller, the ranking Democrat, who complained that the panel's first mine safety hearing in five years was too short and MSHA's answers inadequate. "No wonder nothing gets done," Miller said.

The Sago disaster clearly has moved many members of Congress. Sen. Johnny Isakson, R-Ga., now carries the photograph of one of the dead miners given to him during a two-hour visit with the miners' families. Wyoming Republican Sen. Michael B. Enzi, who chairs the Senate Health, Education, Labor and Pensions Committee, promised the families his panel would approve legislation "that will move mine safety into the 21st century." Wyoming is the country's top coal producer, although most of its coal is mined on the surface.

Technology has emerged as a key issue in Congress. "We talked with astronauts on the moon; why in the dickens can't we talk to those men underground?" Rep. Norwood asked during his panel's March 1 hearing.

Rep. Tom Price, R-Ga., was equally incredulous. "It seems inconceivable to me that we can't tell where miners are located underground. I can't believe that technology isn't out there." Isakson, chairman of the Senate Subcommittee on Employment and Workplace Safety, argues better technology could have prevented the Sago disaster and spearheaded a Feb. 15 Senate roundtable discussion on mine-safety technologies. [47]

Friend, the acting deputy assistant Labor secretary for mine safety and health, says MSHA already has visited four U.S. mines that use personal emergency devices (PEDs), which were developed and are more widely used in Australia. He also stresses that the "tracker" locator system used in a few underground mines in Australia and China is not foolproof. Essentially, a miner wears a transmitter that sends out a unique, pulsed signal to receivers positioned underground. Rescuers could identify a miner's zone but not his precise location. MSHA estimates the cost of installing the system in a typical mine at $100,000. While in Australia, MSHA plans to examine rescue chambers there.

Getty Images/Spencer Platt

Mike Kasavich ends his 10-hour shift at the Mathies coal mine in western Pennsylvania. The mine closed not long after this photo was taken in August 2001, and the veteran miner says he misses mining. "I enjoyed it," says Kasavich, now 51. "It was fascinating work."

"Is there anything that works 100 percent?" Friend asks. "We haven't found it. We want the very best and the very latest to protect miners, but we also want to make sure it works before we mandate it."

Some experts expect robotics to play a bigger role in rescue operations, but the technology has not been approved by MSHA. "I know of no other single technology that holds as much promise to transform the capacity for mine response and rescue," said William "Red" Whittaker, a robotics professor at Carnegie Mellon University in Pittsburgh. [48] He predicts that robots will be as common in the mining industry as they are today in automobile assembly and space exploration.

MSHA Reacts

Some members of Congress are clearly angry at what they see as MSHA inaction. During a March 2 hearing, Sen. Byrd pressed MSHA for a time frame for publishing and implementing the "emergency standard" announced by the agency in February, which requires more oxygen, lifelines and quicker notification. "When are you going to get off your duff?" Byrd demanded. Dye said MSHA was working as fast as it could. The standards were published in the *Federal Register* on March 9.

Other lawmakers were skeptical of the agency's flurry of activity since Sago. "This is a real busy agency since the disaster," Rep. Miller said during the March 1 hearing. "What were we doing before Sago?"

In addition to the emergency standard, MSHA in January published a wide-ranging proposal seeking comments on a host of safety measures, including whether rescue chambers should be required in coal mines, the role of robotics in mine rescue operations and whether underground mining operations should use thermal and infrared imagers — which provide video pictures of heat emitted by objects underground. [49]

MSHA also held a public hearing on March 13 to get comments on the latest communication technologies available. And MSHA, the National Institute for Occupational Safety and Health (NIOSH) and West Virginia mining officials are holding an international symposium in Wheeling on April 20-22 to bring together technology developers, equipment manufacturers and other experts to discuss state-of-the-art safety technologies.

"Why did miners have to die before MSHA took these steps?" Byrd asked.

The UMW supports MSHA's reviews and public hearings on new technology, but Dennis O'Dell, the union's occupational health and safety administrator, asked during a March 1 House hearing, "Why didn't the agency do this decades ago?"

For its part, the mining industry hopes Congress will not act until after July 1, when the commission created by the industry in January to study new mining safety advances presents its findings.

NIOSH agrees with MSHA that the PEDs advocated by some congressional Democrats work well in some, but not all, mines. Jeffery Kohler, associate director for mining and construction at NIOSH's Pittsburgh office, says PEDs should be "promptly deployed" to all mines where they work to see how they can be more widely used.

He stresses, however, that improving communication systems is "only one piece of the puzzle." For example, MSHA also should consider updating existing basic safety requirements to make mines "more survivable" in an explosion, he says, such as those dealing with mine seals and ventilation controls. At Sago, for example, the mine seal blew out, and the explosion spread into the mine.

"Hardening" existing systems to withstand a mine explosion should be a high priority, Kohler says, adding that the technology to do that already exists but hasn't been tested in mines. "It's doable," he insists.

The heightened scrutiny of underground mine safety has produced a small blizzard of new safety products. Since Sago, MSHA has received more than 70 proposals from manufacturers and distributors of emergency communication and tracking systems, and more arrive on a daily basis, says Friend. All equipment used in underground coal mines must be approved by MSHA.

To promote improved mining technology, the Senate in February included in its budget measure a proposal from West Virginia's Sen. Rockefeller that would provide tax incentives to help pay for underground safety devices. The House budget proposal does not include the incentives, so it's up to congressional negotiators to determine whether to include them in the final tax bill. ■

OUTLOOK

Changes Predicted

Industry and government mining officials and labor unions expect the Sago accident to bring new technology and new safety practices into many of the country's mines. The question remains, however, whether Congress or MSHA will mandate such changes or if the industry will implement new practices on its own.

"History has shown that industry does learn from these events and does make changes," says Kohler of NIOSH.

Watzman of the National Mining Association also sees changes ahead. "Technology will continue to evolve; it's going to have to," he says. "We will have to continue to advance the productivity gains that we've made."

Ferriter of the Colorado School of Mines also agrees, noting that the mining industry works hard to make mines safe because it's the right thing to do and good for the bottom line. "A safe mine is a more productive mine and a more profitable mine," he says.

Many labor and industry officials, academics and safety experts predict, however, that Congress will only "fine tune" federal mine safety law, not overhaul it. "The 1969 and 1977 acts were powerful vehicles for the improvement of mine health and safety," says Kohler. We don't need anything that sweeping."

Politicians, however, appear eager to show they are doing something to prevent future Sagos. "You can't overlook the political season we're in," says NMA spokesman Popovich. "This is an election year. That's part of it." Several coal states were considered key swing states in the last presidential election.

The Sago accident also resonated with the public, which will keep the pressure on regulators and Congress, says Rakes of West Virginia University, whose own father once was trapped for three hours in a coal mine. "No one wants another one of these accidents to occur on their watch."

But Freda Sorah, whose husband Joe died in the Jim Walter Resources explosion in Alabama in 2001, doubts that any improvements will be made. After watching the Sago coal tragedy unfold on TV, she said, "The more I watched, the madder I got, rehearing the same promises that I had heard approximately four years earlier — broken promises from the Mine Safety and Health Administration . . . and many other politicians." ■

About the Author

Pamela M. Prah is a *CQ Researcher* staff writer with several years previous reporting experience at Stateline.org, *Kiplinger's Washington Letter* and the Bureau of National Affairs. She holds a master's degree in government from Johns Hopkins University and a journalism degree from Ohio University. Her recent reports include "War in Iraq," "Disaster Preparedness" and "Domestic Violence."

Notes

[1] Text of letter from George Hamner released at a Feb. 13 congressional forum.

[2] From transcript of mine safety forum held by House Education and the Workforce Committee Democrats, Feb. 13, 2006.

[3] www.msha.gov/MSHAINFO/FactSheets/MSHAFCT2.htm.

[4] The Associated Press, "Bodies of Two Coal Miners Found in W. Va.," Jan. 22, 2006.

[5] As quoted in "Reversal: Mine-safety devices to be required," *The Herald Leader* [Lexington, Ky.], Feb. 8, 2006, p. A1.

[6] For background, see David Hatch, "Worker Safety," *CQ Researcher*, May 21, 2004, p. 445-468.

[7] Seth Borenstein and Linda J. Johnson, "Under Bush, mine-safety enforcement eased," Knight Ridder, *The Philadelphia Inquirer*, Jan. 8, 2006.

[8] Mine Safety and Health Administration press release, Jan. 23, 2006.

[9] Ian Urbina and Andrew W. Lehren, "U.S. Is Reducing Safety Penalties for Mine Flaws," *The New York Times*, March 2, 2006, p. A1.

[10] Borenstein and Johnson, *op. cit.*

[11] MSHA press releases, Feb. 6, 2006, and Feb. 24, 2006.

[12] House Committee on Education and the Workforce, Democratic staff, "Review of Federal Mine Safety and Health Administration's

Performance from 2001 to 2005 Reveals Consistent Abdication of Regulatory and Enforcement Responsibilities," Jan. 31, 2006, p. 6.

[13] Government Accountability Office, "Mine Safety: MSHA Devotes Substantial Effort to Ensuring Safety and Health of Coal Miners, But Its Programs Could Be Strengthened," September 2003, p. 20.

[14] House Democratic staff report, *op. cit.*

[15] Transcript, hearing of the Senate Appropriations Subcommittee on Labor, Health and Human Services, and Education, Jan. 23, 2006.

[16] Joby Warrick, "Federal Mine Agency Considers New Rules to Improve Safety," *The Washington Post*, Jan. 31, 2006, p. A3.

[17] Senate Appropriations Subcommittee, *op. cit.*

[18] Alex Wayne, "Mine Safety Nominee Says Current Laws Suffice But New Technology is Needed," *CQ Today*, Jan. 31, 2006.

[19] Ian Urbina, "Mine Safety Nominee Fields Tough Questions from Senators," *The New York Times*, Feb. 1, 2006, p. A1.

[20] Prepared testimony, Richard Stickler, nominee for assistant secretary of Labor for mine safety and health, Jan. 31, 2006.

[21] Press release, Sen. Robert Byrd (D-W.Va.), Jan. 25, 2006.

[22] Press release, Rep. Nick Rahall (D-W.Va.) Feb. 1, 2006.

[23] Wayne, *op. cit.*

[24] Senate Appropriations hearing, *op. cit.*

[25] Kraig R. Naasz, "Solutions, not quick fixes," *USA Today*, Feb. 2, 2006.

[26] Senate Appropriations hearing, *op. cit.*

[27] MSHA press release, Feb 7, 2006; www.msha.gov/MEDIA/PRESS/2006/NR060207.asp.

[28] Press release, National Mining Association, Feb. 8, 2006.

[29] Barbara Freese, *Coal: A Human History* (2003).

[30] Duane Lockard, *Coal: A Memoir and Critique* (1998), p. 64.

[31] *Ibid.*, p. 66.

[32] U.S. Department of Labor, Mine Safety and Health Administration, "Coal Fatalities for 1900 Through 2005;" www.msha.gov/stats/centurystats/coalstats.htm.

[33] For background, see K. P. Maize, "America's coal economy," *Editorial Research Reports 1978* (Vol. I), at *CQ Researcher Plus Archive*, CQ Electronic Library, http://library.cqpress.com.

[34] Paul H. Rakes, "Casualties on the Homefront: Scotts Run Mining Disasters During World War II," *West Virginia History Journal, Vol. 53* (1994), pp. 95-118.

FOR MORE INFORMATION

American Coal Foundation, 101 Constitution Ave., N.W., Suite 525 East, Washington, DC 20001-2133; (202) 463-9785; www.teachcoal.org. An industry-backed group that provides lesson plans about coal mining for teachers to use in classrooms.

Appalachian Citizens Law Center, 207 W. Court St., Suite 202, Prestonsburg, KY 41653-7725; (606) 886-1442; www.appalachianlawcenter.org. A nonprofit law firm that provides free legal services to miners seeking federal black-lung benefits and those who say they were mistreated after complaining about unsafe conditions.

Energy Information Administration, 1000 Independence Ave., S.W., Washington, DC 20585; (202) 586-8800; http://eia.doe.gov. The federal agency that provides official energy statistics, including projections for coal production and use.

Mine Safety and Health Administration, 1100 Wilson Blvd., Arlington, VA 22209-3939; (202) 693-9400; www.msha.gov. The federal agency responsible for enforcing mine safety laws; provides historical data on fatalities and other information on its Web site.

National Institute for Occupational Safety and Health, Mining and Construction Division, P.O. Box 18070, 626 Cochrans Mill Road, Pittsburgh, PA 15236; (412) 386-5301; www.cdc.gov/niosh. The federal research agency that focuses on reducing workplace injuries and fatalities; Web site includes ongoing research and latest findings.

National Mining Association, 101 Constitution Ave., N.W., Suite 500 East, Washington, DC 20001; (202) 463-2600; www.nma.org. The trade group that represents mining interests.

United Mine Workers of America, 8315 Lee Highway, Fairfax, VA 22031; (703) 208-7200; www.umwa.org. The labor union that represents 45,000 of the nation's coal miners.

U.S. Coal Resource Databases, U.S. Geological Survey; http://energy.er.usgs.gov/products/databases/CoalQual/index.htm. An online government database that provides the location, quantity and physical and chemical characteristics of U.S. coal resources.

[35] Freese, *op. cit.*, p. 159.

[36] For background, see M. Packman, "Coal in trouble," *Editorial Research Reports 1954* (Vol. II), at *CQ Researcher Plus Archive*, CQ Electronic Library, http://library.cqpress.com.

[37] For background, see L. Wheildon, "Mine safety," *Editorial Research Reports 1947* (Vol. II) at *CQ Researcher Plus Archive*, CQ Electronic Library, http://library.cqpress.com.

[38] Lockard, *op. cit.*, p. 82.

[39] For background, see Maize, *op. cit.*

[40] Ben A. Franklin, "Coal Mine Safety Comes Under Fire," *The New York Times*, Jan. 22, 1982, p. A14.

[41] Frank Swoboda, "Coal Firms to Plead Guilty; Falsification of Mine Dust Samples Alleged," *The Washington Post*, Oct. 22, 1991, p. A1.

[42] MSHA press release, June 19, 1995.

[43] West Virginia Gov. Joe Manchin statement, Jan. 27, 2006.

[44] U.S. Department of Labor press release, "MSHA to Expand West Virginia, 'Stand Down for Safety' Nationwide on Feb. 6," Feb. 1, 2006.

[45] House Committee on Education and the Workforce, Democratic staff, *op. cit.*

[46] *Ibid.*

[47] Nancy Zuckerbrod, The Associated Press, "Lawmakers check out mine safety upgrades," *Pittsburgh Post-Gazette*, Feb. 16, 2006.

[48] John Roach, "Robots, Virtual Reality Touted as Mine-Safety Solutions," *National Geographic News*, Jan. 27, 2006.

[49] U.S. Department of Labor, MSHA, proposed rule, *Federal Register*, Jan. 25, 2006, pp. 4223-4226.

Bibliography

Selected Sources

Books

Freese, Barbara, *Coal: A Human History*, Perseus Publishing, 2003.

An assistant attorney general of Minnesota who helped enforce her state's air-pollution laws looks at the human and environmental impacts of mining and burning coal.

Lockard, Duane, *Coal: A Memoir and Critique*, University Press of Virginia, 1998.

A professor emeritus of politics at Princeton University who followed his grandfather and father into the mines chronicles his family's coal mining experience and sketches key developments affecting the industry.

Articles

Borenstein, Seth, and Linda J. Johnson, "Under Bush, Mine-Safety Enforcement Eased," *The Philadelphia Inquirer*, Jan. 8, 2006, p. A1.

Fewer than half the fines levied by the Mine Safety and Health Administration (MSHA) between 2001 and 2003 — about $3 million — have been paid. MSHA disputes the figures.

Frank, Thomas, "Mining Fines Among Smallest" and "Fines May Not Bring Compliance," *USA Today*, Feb. 10, 2006, pp. A1, A3.

Two articles exploring MSHA penalties contend that the federal government levied a larger fine — $550,000 — for the 2004 Super Bowl showing of Janet Jackson's breast than it did for the 2001 deaths of 13 Alabama miners.

Jackson, David, "Disaster at No. 5 Mine," *Chicago Tribune*, Sept. 22, 2002, p. C1.

The first of a three-part special series called "The Human Cost of Coal Mining," that ran Sept. 22-24, 2002. The first article describes the confusion at the Jim Walter Resources No. 5 Mine in Alabama after a Sept. 23, 2001, explosion trapped 13 miners. The second article looks at the botched rescue and the third examines the low penalties coal companies face for violations.

Rakes, Paul H., "Casualties on the Homefront: Scotts Run Mining Disasters During World War II," *West Virginia History Journal*, Vol. 53 (1994), pp. 95-118.

A former coal miner who is now a history professor at West Virginia University's Institute of Technology looks at the new hazards that mechanization and war brought to mining in the 1940s.

Roberts, Phil, "Frontier Wyoming's Most Dangerous Occupation: The Quest for Mining Safety in Wyoming's Coal Industry," University of Wyoming, updated 2002.

A professor of history at the University of Wyoming explains how coal mining has changed in Wyoming, the country's top coal producer. The article is part of the university-published series "Buffalo Bones: Stories from Wyoming's Past."

Tollefson, Jeff, "Mine Safety Regulations In a New Spotlight," *CQ Weekly*, Jan. 30, 2006, pp. 270-271.

In the wake of West Virginia's Sago mine disaster, state and national lawmakers are scrutinizing the roles of government and coal companies in improving safety.

Urbina, Ian, and Andrew W. Lehren, "U.S. Is Reducing Safety Penalties for Mine Flaws," *The New York Times*, March 2, 2006, p. A1.

The Bush administration has decreased major fines for mining companies; none of the fines at the Sago mine since 2004 exceeded $460, a tiny fraction of the $110 million net profit reported by the International Coal Group.

Reports and Studies

"Focus on Coal Mining: Safety Hazards, Health Hazards and Mine Rescue," National Institute for Occupational Safety and Health, updated 2006; www.cdc.gov/niosh/topics/minerescue/.

This informative series on key mine safety issues — such as methane, mine ventilation and miner training — is available online from the federal agency responsible for preventing workplace injuries.

"Mine Safety: MSHA's Programs for Ensuring the Safety and Health of Coal Miners Could be Strengthened," U.S. Government Accountability Office, Jan. 23, 2006.

Testimony from the investigative arm of Congress highlights findings of a 2003 GAO report that concluded MSHA failed to make follow-up inspections after ordering mine operators to make safety changes regarding ventilation and roof support.

"Questions and Answers on the Sago Mine Accident," Mine Safety and Health Administration, January 2006.

This is one of several online MSHA publications following the Sago mine accident. Others include explanations of MSHA penalties and rescue efforts at Sago. All are available online at www.msha.gov.

"Review of Federal Mine Safety and Health Administration's Performance from 2001 to 2005 Reveals Consistent Abdication of Regulatory and Enforcement Responsibilities," U.S. House Committee on Education and the Workforce, Democratic staff, Jan. 31, 2006.

The committee's minority staff contends the Bush administration has undermined MSHA through regulatory rollbacks, budget cuts and appointments of officials who are too close to the coal industry.

The Next Step:

Additional Articles from Current Periodicals

Bush Administration

Klein, Rick, "Democrats Asking Congress to Review Safety, Enforcement," *The Boston Globe*, Jan. 5, 2006, p. A18.

After the recent West Virginia mine tragedy, Democrats requested congressional hearings into mine safety and the Bush administration's enforcement of mine regulations.

Schorr, Daniel, "Deregulation and the Sago Mine," *The Christian Science Monitor*, Jan. 13, 2006, p. 9.

Members of the Bush administration, especially former House Majority Leader Tom DeLay, fostered a deregulatory attitude in the government toward the mining industry.

Urbina, Ian, and Andrew W. Lehren, "U.S. Is Reducing Safety Penalties For Mine Flaws," *The New York Times*, March 2, 2006, p. A1.

The Bush administration decreased major fines for safety violations by mining companies since 2001 and failed to collect the fines in almost half of the cases, according to *The New York Times*.

Emergency Technologies

Brook, Tom Vanden, "CEO: Mine Passageway Unblocked," *USA Today*, Jan. 10, 2006, p. A3.

International Coal Group CEO Ben Hatfield said wireless communication systems, which the coal industry has been slow to adopt, might have saved some of the Sago mine disaster victims.

Clayton, Mark, "Ahead, High-Tech Help For Mine Rescues," *The Christian Science Monitor*, Jan. 11, 2006, p. 3.

New, advanced safety technologies like mine-rescue robots, illuminated rescue lifelines, laser pointers and fuel-cell technology are awaiting approval for use in coal mines.

Messina, Lawrence, "West Virginia Lawmakers OK Mine Safety Measure," *Chicago Tribune*, Jan. 24, 2006, p. C10.

West Virginia lawmakers passed a bill that requires coal operators to issue emergency communicators and electronic tracking devices to all miners underground.

Safety Laws and Regulations

Frank, Thomas, "Mines Given a Month to Store More Oxygen," *USA Today*, March 8, 2006, p. A3.

MSHA has ordered mine operators to adopt new emergency safety rules by April, including storing more underground oxygen tanks and extra training in lifesaving.

Harris, Gardiner, "Endemic Problem of Safety in Coal Mining," *The New York Times*, Jan. 10, 2006, p. A13.

An examination of the mine industry reveals that certain problems are endemic, such as the use of old safety equipment, lax enforcement of regulations and a culture that discourages safety complaints.

Rubinkam, Michael, "Emotions Become Heated With Coal in Short Supply," *The Houston Chronicle*, Feb. 27, 2005, p. 2.

Coal companies in Schuylkill County, Pa., are rationing coal to customers because federal inspectors are increasingly citing anthracite mines for safety violations.

Urbina, Ian, "Mine Safety Nominee Fields Tough Questions From Senators," *The New York Times*, Feb. 1, 2006, p. A21.

Richard M. Stickler, the GOP's nominee to be the nation's top mine safety regulator, responded to questions at his Senate confirmation hearing from Democrats who believe he is too cozy with the mine industry to enforce stricter safety regulations.

Safety Violations

Frank, Thomas, "Senators Urge Bigger Fines For Mines," *USA Today*, March 3, 2006, p. A3.

Democratic senators told David Dye, acting head of MSHA, that fines against coal mines — typically a few hundred dollars — are too small to make coal companies abide by safety regulations.

Grimm, Fred, "Tunnel Vision Turns Coal Mines Into Death Pits," *The Miami Herald*, Jan. 12, 2006, p. B1.

MSHA inspection records reveal that poor safety conditions at the Sago mine might have contributed to the recent disaster; the mine was cited last year with 205 safety violations.

Citing The *CQ Researcher*

Sample formats for citing these reports in a bibliography include the ones listed below. Preferred styles and formats vary, so please check with your instructor or professor.

MLA STYLE

Jost, Kenneth. "Rethinking the Death Penalty." CQ Researcher 16 Nov. 2001: 945-68.

APA STYLE

Jost, K. (2001, November 16). Rethinking the death penalty. *CQ Researcher, 11,* 945-968.

CHICAGO STYLE

Jost, Kenneth. "Rethinking the Death Penalty." *CQ Researcher,* November 16, 2001, 945-968.

CQ Researcher

Published by CQ Press, a division of Congressional Quarterly Inc.

cqresearcher.com

Protecting Whistleblowers

Do employees who speak out need better protection?

From prisoner abuse at Abu Ghraib prison to fraud at Enron, some of the most dramatic revelations of corporate and government wrongdoing have come from insiders. The Whistleblower Protection Act and other laws are designed to shield employees who reveal wrongdoing from retaliation by vengeful bosses. But federal employees who claim they were harassed after blowing the whistle lose their cases far more often than they win. They lose so often, in fact, that some whistleblower advocates urge potential whistleblowers to become anonymous sources for reporters instead. National-security employees are in an especially delicate position, because what they want to disclose may involve secret information. Several bills now before Congress aim to strengthen protections for whistleblowers, including those in intelligence agencies.

Bunnatine H. Greenhouse, a U.S. Army Corps of Engineers contracts supervisor, was demoted in 2005 after challenging Iraq war contracts awarded to a subsidiary of the Halliburton Co.

INSIDE THIS REPORT

CQ Researcher • March 31, 2006 • www.cqresearcher.com
Volume 16, Number 12 • Pages 265-288

RECIPIENT OF SOCIETY OF PROFESSIONAL JOURNALISTS AWARD FOR EXCELLENCE ◆ AMERICAN BAR ASSOCIATION SILVER GAVEL AWARD

THE ISSUES

BACKGROUND

CURRENT SITUATION

OUTLOOK

SIDEBARS AND GRAPHICS

FOR FURTHER RESEARCH

Cover: Bunnatine H. Greenhouse, a U.S. Army Corps of Engineers contracts supervisor, was demoted in 2005 after challenging Iraq war contracts awarded to a subsidiary of the Halliburton Co. She is contesting her demotion. (Getty Images/Chip Somodevilla)

CQ Researcher

March 31, 2006
Volume 16, Number 12

CQ PRESS

A Division of Congressional Quarterly Inc.

CQ Researcher (ISSN 1056-2036) is printed on acid-free paper. Published weekly, except March 24, July 7, July 14, Aug. 4, Aug. 11, Nov. 24, Dec. 22 and Dec. 29, by CQ Press, a division of Congressional Quarterly Inc. Annual full-service subscriptions for institutions start at $667. For pricing, call 1-800-834-9020, ext. 1906. To purchase a *CQ Researcher* report in print or electronic format (PDF), visit www.cqpress.com or call 866-427-7737. Single reports start at $10. Bulk purchase discounts and electronic-rights licensing are also available. Periodicals postage paid at Washington, D.C., and additional mailing offices. POSTMASTER: Send address changes to *CQ Researcher*, 1255 22nd St., N.W., Suite 400, Washington, DC 20037.

Protecting Whistleblowers

BY PETER KATEL

THE ISSUES

When Sgt. Samuel Provance learned U.S. forces at Abu Ghraib prison near Baghdad were abusing Iraqi prisoners, he knew he had to do something. But there was pressure to remain silent, he testified before the House National Security Subcommittee on Feb. 14, sitting ramrod straight at a gleaming, wooden witness table.

"I was told that the honor of my unit and the Army depended on either withholding the truth or outright lies," he said. [1]

Nonetheless, Provance informed his superiors, and then reporters, that Military Intelligence officers had directed the abuses — contrary to official claims that rogue troops were responsible. In response, the Army revoked his security clearance and demoted him.

Getty Images/Linda Spillers

Former FBI translator Sibel Edmonds, at her home in Alexandria, Va., was dismissed by the FBI after exposing alleged wrongdoing and incompetence. The U.S. Supreme Court refused to hear her case after government lawyers said they couldn't argue against her lawsuit without revealing state secrets.

The Defense Department presented no witness to contradict Provance's account. Nor were other witnesses' allegations of reprisals disputed. They told of being harassed, fired or forced to resign for revealing a number of national security foul-ups, including the alleged cover-up of early discoveries concerning the Sept. 11, 2001, terrorists; a botched FBI terrorism investigation; foreign infiltration of the top-secret National Security Agency (NSA) and poor security at U.S. nuclear power plants.

"We need national-security whistleblowers to tell us when things go wrong," said Subcommittee Chairman Christopher Shays, R-Conn. "But those with whom we trust the nation's secrets are too often treated like second-class citizens when it comes to asserting their rights to speak truth to power."

In recent years, whistleblowers have exposed wrongdoing or incompetence hidden behind walls of corporate or government secrecy, from the financial fraud that led to the Enron collapse to the tobacco industry's lies about the cancer-causing nature of cigarettes.

In the process, whistleblowers often become media heroes. In 2002, FBI agent Colleen Rowley was named one of *Time* magazine's "Persons of the Year" for revealing FBI incompetence before the Sept. 11, 2001, terrorist attacks. Also named were two corporate whistleblowers — former Enron Vice President Sherron Watkins and WorldCom auditor Cynthia Cooper. [2]

Today, with the war in Iraq beginning its fourth year and debate intensifying over the government's counterterrorism tactics, national-security whistleblowers increasingly have come in conflict with government efforts to control information affecting the country's safety.

"When they go out and talk to the public about a highly classified program, they harm the national security of this country," Attorney General Alberto R. Gonzales told the Senate Judiciary Committee on Feb. 6.

But whistleblowers and their defenders contend that government officials often use secrecy rules to stifle politically embarrassing truths. "New whistleblower protections should immediately be established for members of the executive branch who report evidence of wrongdoing — especially where it involves . . . the sensitive areas of national security," former Vice President Al Gore said in a January speech. [3]

Sen. Frank Lautenberg, D-N.J., has introduced a bill to prevent government officials from claiming secrecy when whistleblowers try to denounce wrongdoing or prove retaliation. And Rep. Todd R. Platts, R-Pa., and Sen. Daniel Akaka, D-Hawaii, introduced whistleblower-protection bills last year. The Senate Homeland Security and Governmental Affairs Committee approved the Akaka bill, and the House Government Reform Committee OK'd Platts' proposal, but neither bill has moved to the full Congress.

The bills were introduced against the backdrop of high-stakes court battles between whistleblowers and the executive branch. Last November the

Whistleblower Suits Recovered $9.6 Billion

More than 5,100 "qui tam" (whistleblower) suits have been filed against companies allegedly cheating the federal government since the False Claims Act was updated in 1986 to offer more protection and financial incentives to whistleblowers. During the same period, more than $9.6 billion was recovered.

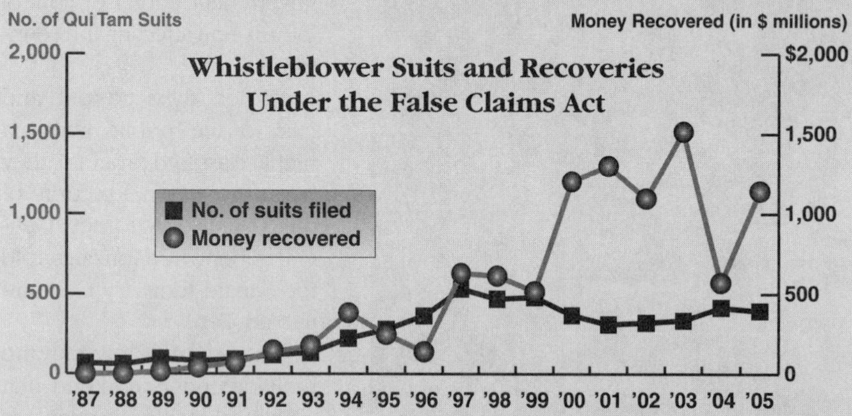

What Is a Qui Tam *Suit?*

The False Claims Act allows citizens and organizations with evidence of fraud against the government to sue the wrongdoer on behalf of the government. Such actions are known as qui tam, or "whistleblower" lawsuits. Qui tam *is part of a longer Latin phrase* (qui tam pro domino rege quam pro se ipso in hac parte sequitur) *that means "he who brings an action for the king as well as for himself." The person filing a successful suit receives 15-30 percent of the money recovered.*

Sources: Taxpayers Against Fraud; Project on Government Oversight

U.S. Supreme Court refused to hear an appeal by former FBI translator Sibel Edmonds, who claims she was fired for exposing alleged wrongdoing and incompetence. However, the justices refused to hear Edmonds' appeal after government lawyers said they couldn't argue against her lawsuit without revealing state secrets — an argument lower court judges had accepted. [4]

But the justices have agreed to decide whether government employees have a constitutionally protected free-speech right to report wrongdoing. The case involves a Los Angeles deputy district attorney who contends his rights were violated when he was demoted for denouncing a search warrant that contained inaccurate information. Justice Department lawyers have filed a brief in the case, arguing that the First Amendment doesn't cover public employees who speak out in the course of their jobs. [5]

Stephen Kohn, a Washington lawyer specializing in representing whistleblowers, calls the government's position "outrageous" and potentially disastrous for employees who try to report wrongdoing.

Even if the court determines the First Amendment doesn't always protect public employees from reprisals, they still are shielded by the federal whistle-blower-protection system established by Congress about 30 years ago.

The system for intelligence-community whistleblowers largely revolves around the inspectors general offices attached to — but independent of — the various federal agencies. But inspectors' powers are limited. For example, a report by the Justice Department's inspector general concluded that Edmonds did have legitimate grounds for voicing suspicions about a colleague's possible ties to a foreign intelligence service. "Edmonds had her case reviewed by the FBI, which did not, and still has not, adequately investigated these allegations," said the January 2005 report, noting the bureau also failed to prove that Edmonds' firing was justified. [6] In response, the FBI launched a new investigation of her allegations. [7]

A separate law, the Intelligence Community Whistleblower Protection Act of 1998, allows intelligence-service employees to report wrongdoing of "urgent concern" to Congress. [8] "Exercising one's rights under this act is an appropriate and responsible way to bring questionable practices to the attention of those in Congress charged with oversight of the intelligence agencies," CIA Director Porter Goss wrote just before Shays held his hearing. "And it works." As House Intelligence Committee chairman in 1998, Goss was one of the law's authors.

But intelligence analyst Russell Tice, who was fired by the NSA last year after warning that a colleague might be a foreign spy, told Shays' subcommittee the agency had barred him from reporting his concerns to Congress on the grounds that House and Senate Intelligence Committee members didn't have the security clearances required to hear about certain NSA and Defense Intelligence Agency operations. But a Jan. 9 letter from the agency did tell Tice that no members or staff of the Intelligence committees were "cleared to receive the information" concerning "Special Access Programs" that Tice wanted to disclose. The letter added that Tice had to inform the Defense Department and NSA of what he wanted to say, and be directed by them how to deal with the congressional committees.

No one disputes that national-security whistleblowing raises legitimate worries about the country's safety. Even former CIA and Defense Department analyst Richard M. Barlow, whose career was shattered after he spoke up, says he was troubled by *The New York Times'* disclosure of the NSA's warrantless electronic spying on U.S. citizens. [9] (*See sidebar, p. 276.*)

"I can understand how White House people are concerned that this stuff ended up in *The Times*," says Barlow, an expert on Pakistan's nuclear-arms program. "This is not good."

Barlow conjectures that if NSA employees had had a reliable channel to pass information about wrongdoing to Congress — and if lawmakers had been more receptive to whistleblowers — the revelations might never have wound up in the headlines. Critics like Barlow point to Abu Ghraib whistleblower Provance as proof that those who step forward become sitting ducks for payback by their superiors.

Still, a Defense official suggested that Provance hadn't taken full advantage of the whistleblower-protection system. Under questioning by Shays, Jane Deese, director of military-reprisal investigations for the Pentagon's inspector general, called Provance's account "disturbing" but added that he had never filed a complaint.

After the hearing, one of Provance's lawyers, Deborah Pearlstein of Human Rights First, said Provance had likely concluded on the basis of what he'd already suffered that he would worsen his situation by filing a retaliation complaint.

Asked by Rep. Henry Waxman, D-Calif., how his superiors had reacted to his accounts of detainee abuse, Provance said their responses made clear that "anything that I had to say was just going to be avoided or ignored."

Before You Blow the Whistle . . .

Employees should consider the following checklist before becoming whistleblowers, according to three whistleblower advocacy groups.

1. Consult your loved ones — *This is a family decision, and you want to have your spouse, family and/or close friends on your side.*

2. Check for skeletons in your closet — *Is there a peccadillo or something in your past that could be used against you?*

3. Document, document, document — *Keep records of important documents; your access to agency documents might be denied after whistling.*

4. Do not use government resources — *Do not use agency resources, such as phones and fax machines, when engaging in whistleblowing.*

5. Check to see who will support your account — *If you can't count on co-workers or others to defend your case, consider waiting.*

6. Consult an attorney early — *Seek legal advice before you intervene.*

7. Choose your battles — *Don't fight personnel issues, because the advantage is with the employer, not the employee.*

8. Identify allies — *Share your knowledge with others at the agency that might have interest in your evidence.*

9. Have a plan — *Create a step-by-step action plan, including how the agency will respond and how you will counter its response.*

10. Get career counseling — *Consider where your actions will leave you in a year, two years, five years.*

Sources: "The Art of Anonymous Activism: Serving the Public While Surviving Public Service"; Project on Government Oversight, Government Accountability Project, Public Employees for Environmental Responsibility

Trained as an intelligence and computer expert, Provance says that since being demoted from sergeant to specialist he has been relegated to "picking up trash and guard duty and things of that nature."

As the fight over whistleblower protection heats up again, here are some of the leading issues in debate:

Are federal whistleblowers adequately protected?

Whistleblower expert Kohn says some 40 laws protect federal whistleblowers — at least in theory. They include a little-known 2002 statute that makes job retaliation a crime when directed at someone who provided truthful information about the "commission or possible commission" of a federal crime. [10]

"That is an extremely powerful tool," says Kohn, who has written five books on whistleblowing. "It prohibits the gagging of federal employees, even those involved in highly sensitive national-security issues. They can go to federal law enforcement under this law." Kohn says the law has not been used much, but he expects lawyers to begin invoking it in whistleblower cases.

Dozens of states have enacted laws providing varying degrees of protection to government whistleblowers. In the federal system, the extent of protection varies by agency. For instance, employees who work in fields affecting public health and safety, such as nuclear power, aviation, trucking and environmental protection, can take complaints of retaliation directly to the Labor Department and, depending on the response, directly to federal District Court.

Those employees and most other federal employees — except national-security workers — fall under the Office of Special Counsel (OSC) and the Merit Systems Protection Board (MSPB). Whistleblowers can take cases of alleged serious retaliation — such as firing or suspension — to the board. Complaints of transfers, blocked promotions and the like can be reported to the OSC if the alleged reason was retaliation or another prohibited practice. If the OSC doesn't act within 120 days, employees can bring their cases to the MSPB. The OSC can also conduct preliminary disclosures of serious misconduct in agencies and require full-scale investigations by the agencies themselves if the allegations seem to be well-founded.

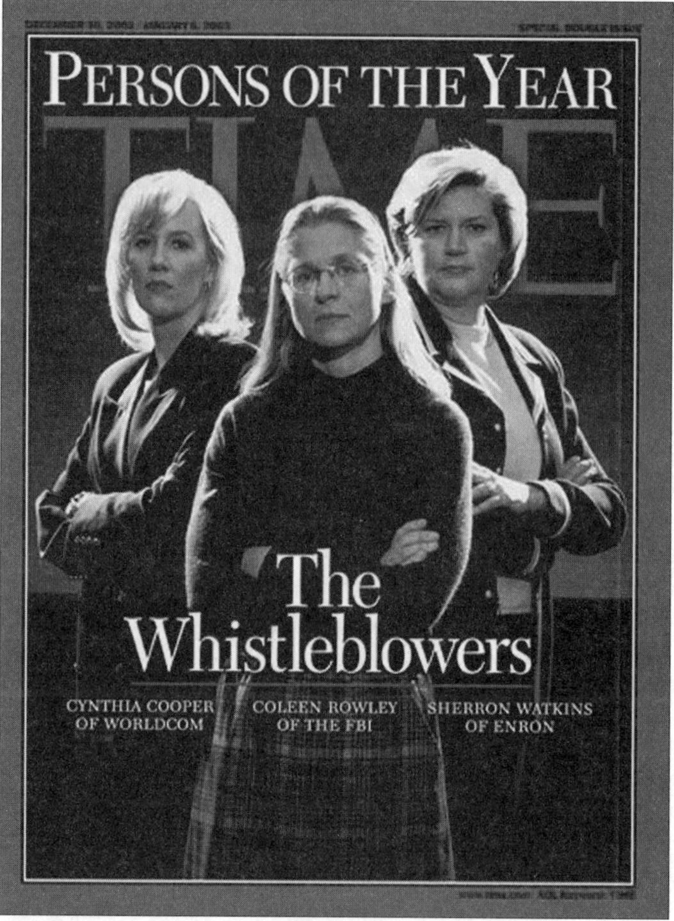

Time, Inc.

Time *tapped three whistleblowers as its "Persons of the Year" in 2002: auditor Cynthia Cooper, who revealed phony accounting practices at WorldCom; FBI agent Colleen Rowley, who documented bureau failure to follow-up leads before the 9/11 terrorist attacks; and Enron Vice President Sherron Watkins, who warned about massive financial irregularities at the now bankrupt firm.*

If the OSC concludes an employee has been improperly treated, it can ask the MSPB to postpone the personnel action about to be taken against the worker. But if the MSPB rejects that request, the OSC cannot appeal that decision. [11] The Court of Appeals for the Federal Circuit, created in 1982, has exclusive jurisdiction over appeals of board decisions.

But Kohn and other experts advise whistleblowers to sue in federal District Court — alleging violations of their First Amendment free-speech rights, for example — rather than going to the MSPB and the OSC. "If you enter that box, you will get a ruling from somebody that says you are not a real whistleblower, which undermines your ability to go to Congress and the press and get your issues addressed," he says.

For instance, of the 120 Federal Circuit rulings on the merits of whistleblower appeals between 1994 and 2005, only one went in favor of the employee, according to Thomas Devine, legal director of the Government Accountability Project. And of the 52 whistleblowers that took their cases to the MSPB from 1999 to March 13, 2006, only two prevailed, Devine says. [12]

Board General Counsel Martha Schneider does not dispute the figures. But she says the board works within limits set by the Federal Circuit and the 1987 Whistleblower Protection Act (WPA). The court set a key precedent in 1999 when it ruled that in order for whistleblowers to sustain their cases, a "disinterested observer" would have to agree that misconduct had occurred. "The WPA is not a weapon in arguments over policy or a shield for insubordinate conduct," the court said. [13] Since that ruling, a single witness on behalf of a government agency has been enough to knock down employees' cases.

And, Schneider says, the WPA statute itself is "fairly narrow" in its definition of the kinds of activities that whistleblowers get protected for reporting — a violation of law, regulation or gross mismanagement; gross waste of funds; abuse of authority; or a "substantial and specific danger" to public health or safety. Given those limits, Schneider says, it is "harder for whistleblowers to prevail."

In reality, some whistleblower advocates say, the board has long been hostile to employees who appear before it. In 1994, the House Committee on Post Office and Civil Service reported that it had heard "extensive testimony at hearings that the MSPB and the Federal Circuit have lost credibility with the practicing bar for civil service cases." [14]

Devine says members of the three-member board are traditionally "minor-league political appointees who know they won't rise up the political food chain by helping people who challenge abuses of power by the president or his political appointees." Board Chairman Neil A. G. McPhie, a former Virginia senior assistant state attorney general, did not respond to a request for comment.

Whistleblower advocates direct even harsher criticism at the Office of Special Counsel, headed by Bush appointee Scott J. Bloch. Bloch draws criticism for both his handling of whistleblowers and personnel issues in his own agency. A complaint filed against Bloch by whistleblower advocacy groups and others charges he issued an illegal gag order, transferred employees he considered disloyal and disposed of cases often without interviewing the employees who filed the complaints. (*See sidebar, p. 278.*)

Backlog of Whistleblower Cases Reduced

In an effort to clear out its large backlog of whistleblower cases, the Office of Special Counsel (OSC) closed nearly three times as many cases in 2004 as it did in 2003. Only eight of the 18 cases alleging government fraud, mismanagement or abuse were substantiated in 2004. In 2005, however, despite a caseload half as large, twice as many cases were substantiated.

OSC Disposition of Whistleblower Disclosures

	FY2003	FY2004	FY2005
Total cases pending	1,091	1,262	583
Referred to agency for investigation	11	18	19
Substantiated by agency	13	8	16
Processed and closed	401	1,154	473

Source: Office of Special Counsel, fiscal 2007 Congressional Budget Justification and Performance Budget Goals

Is the Bush administration hostile to whistleblowers?

No contemporary president has generated much enthusiasm among whistleblower advocates.

"Every administration's Justice Department has objected to every whistleblower bill since the [1978] Civil Service Reform Act," a Democratic congressional aide says, asking not to be named. "They have an institutional bias, because they would always be defending an agency against a whistleblower. So any bill that helps a whistleblower means they might lose cases."

Indeed, in an April 12, 2005, letter to Congress on Akaka's proposed bill, Assistant Attorney General William E. Moschella cited strong opposition by the Clinton administration in 1998 to a proposal to extend whistleblower protection to employees whose reports of alleged wrongdoing included classified information.

Even so, President Bush stands out for his insistence on controlling government information, say whistleblower advocates. "The Bush administration is much more aggressive in regard to whistleblowers [in its] secrecy policies, which creates more possibilities for retaliation and creates a chilling effect," says Beth Daley, an investigator with the Washington-based Project on Government Oversight. [15]

The administration has created a new category of "sensitive but unclassified" information that agencies are prohibited from disclosing — though a definition of the category has yet to be hammered out. So far, prohibited data include information on shipments of hazardous materials, injury rates among workers at the Portland, Ore., airport and plans for a liquefied natural gas power plant on Long Island Sound.

Bush has ordered National Security Director John D. Negroponte to come up with a governmentwide definition of "sensitive but unclassified" information in order to enhance information sharing "amongst those entities responsible for protecting our communities from future attack," said Negroponte spokesman Carl Kropf. [16] Negroponte's office declined to discuss the effect of the classification on national-security whistleblowers.

Taken alone, a new category of classified information might not sound alarming in post-9/11 America. But the policy worries the whistleblower-protection network, particularly in view of other recent efforts by the federal government to either withhold information from the public or retaliate against those who reveal irregularities.

For instance, the government has secretly reclassified more than 55,000 intelligence and diplomatic documents in the National Archives that had been publicly available for years, some dating back to the Korean War. The reclassification began under President Clinton in 1999, when the CIA and other agencies objected to the unsealing of what they considered secret information following a 1995 presidential declassification order. The reclassification intensified under Bush. [17]

After disclosure of the program prompted outrage from historians, Allen Weinstein, director of the National Archives, announced a halt, pending talks with the spy and military agencies. He also asked the agencies to do their best to restore to public access as many of the newly reclassified files as possible. [18]

Only Three Whistleblowers Won Their Cases

Only three out of 172 employees in recent years won their cases after claiming employers retaliated against them for revealing problems. Under the 1999 Whistleblower Protection Act, retaliation claims can be filed with either the Merit Systems Protection Board or the Court of Appeals for the Federal Circuit.

Status of Whistleblowers' Retaliation Claims

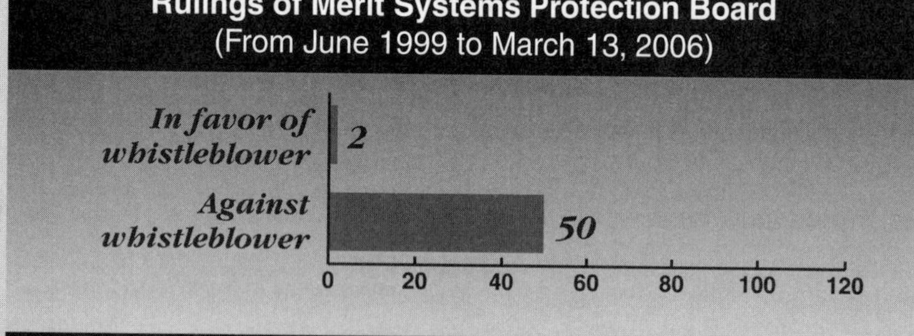

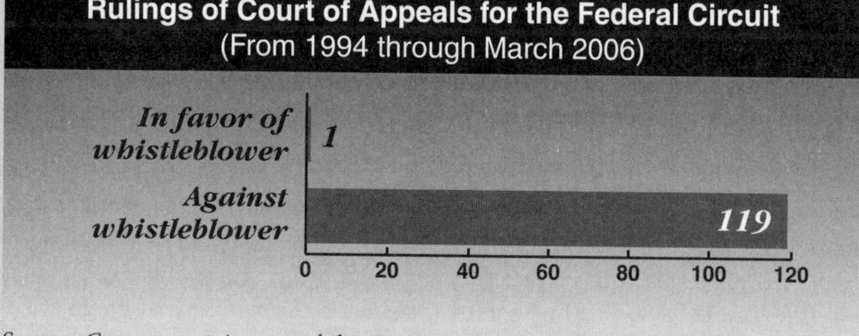

Source: Government Accountability Project , March 2006

In 2005 the U.S. Army Corps of Engineers demoted Bunnatine H. Greenhouse, a contracts supervisor who challenged Corps contract awards to Kellogg Brown & Root — a subsidiary of Halliburton (formerly headed by Vice President Dick Cheney), which received more than $10 billion in contracts for work in Iraq. The Corps said it was not retaliating against Greenhouse, but her lawyer argued that was the only explanation, given her stellar track record before the Halliburton issues arose. [19] Greenhouse's challenge of her demotion is pending.

Medicare actuary Richard Foster was threatened with dismissal in 2003 if he told Congress that a prescription-drug reimbursement plan (since enacted) would cost $100 billion more than administration officials had claimed. The inspector general of the Health and Human Services Department (HHS) later concluded that Foster's boss did not act illegally because Foster had no independent right to inform Congress. [20]

HHS' position reflected a May 21, 2004, memo to the department from then-Assistant Attorney General Jack L. Goldsmith, who concluded that government officials' powers include control of what information Congress gets to see. "Executive privilege," he wrote, referring to the doctrine of presidential secrecy, "applies governmentwide, and is not limited to presidential decision making. . . . Presidents George [H.W.] Bush, Bill Clinton and George W. Bush each asserted executive privilege against congressional committees to protect intra-agency deliberative materials prepared for senior officers in executive departments." [21]

Goldsmith was disputing a Congressional Research Service (CRS) memo declaring that Congress' right to information trumps any gag orders on employees. "Congress has a clear right and recognized prerogative . . . to receive from officers and employees of the agencies and departments of the United States accurate and truthful information regarding the federal programs and policies," wrote Jack Maskell, a CRS legislative attorney. [22]

In 2004 U.S. Park Police Chief Teresa Chambers was fired after telling reporters that her officers were unable to patrol Washington-area parks because of a new policy that they maintain a bigger presence at national monuments. A Merit Systems Protection Board judge upheld the dismissal, saying she had broken the chain of command by going public. [23]

Jeff Ruch, executive director of Public Employees for Environmental Responsibility, said the Chambers case cast an especially big shadow because the police chief didn't see herself as a whistleblower but as the agency's spokesperson. "Now the line between whistleblowing and simply telling the truth is increasingly blurred," Ruch says. "A lot of times, the people we work with don't realize they're whistleblowing by being inconveniently candid."

Consciously or not, however, the employees are colliding with the Bush administration doctrine that high-ranking officials — not their subordinates — decide what information to release. A "fundamental principle" of presidential authority, Goldsmith wrote in his memo on the Medicare matter, is that "his subordinates must be free from certain types of interference from the coordinate branches of government." [24]

Whistleblower advocates argue that with both the executive branch and Congress controlled by Republicans, the normal checks and balances — specifically congressional oversight — do not exist. "The Republicans are not going to do any oversight of themselves," says Kris J. Kolesnik, who helped draft the 1989 Whistleblower Protection Act (WPA) as an aide to Sen. Charles Grassley, R-Iowa. Kolesnik, also a Republican, is now executive director of the National Whistleblower Center.

Administration officials say they support whistleblower-shield systems. Last April, as the administration prepared to establish a new personnel system for civilians at the Pentagon — the National Security Personnel System (NSPS) — then-Navy Secretary Gordon England (now deputy secretary of Defense) told the Senate Armed Services Committee that the new system "will not remove whistleblowing protections."

But an official of the American Federation of Government Employees, which opposes the system, says the NSPS would wreck whatever protections exist. Mark Roth, the union's general counsel, points to an appeal system in which the Merit Systems Protection Board would be able to overturn a boss' personnel action only if it were found "totally unwarranted," which would mean that any infraction by an employee would be enough to sustain a demotion or disciplinary move.

On Feb. 27, U. S. District Judge Emmet G. Sullivan accepted the union's arguments in barring the Pentagon from putting most of the NSPS into operation. "The appeals system is the antithesis of fairness," the judge wrote. [25] England said he expected his department to appeal the ruling. [26]

Getty Images/Adam Rountree

Tobacco industry whistleblower Jeffrey Wigand, right, who revealed that Brown & Williamson officials knew cigarettes caused cancer, joins New York City Mayor Michael Bloomberg as he announces his Smoke-Free Air Act on Oct. 9, 2002.

Should civil servants anonymously leak information to reporters instead of becoming whistleblowers?

The firings and demotions experienced by some government whistleblowers discourage others from going through official channels to reveal wrongdoing. Instead, some insiders protect their jobs by leaking information anonymously to the press.

The consequences of whistleblowing can be even more serious for workers at intelligence agencies, where both law and workplace culture demand observance of secrecy rules. At the least, their security clearances can be revoked — effectively ending their careers. In some cases, they can be prosecuted for revealing state secrets. Thus, it was not surprising that the recent press reports about warrantless NSA domestic spying were based on anonymous sources.

"All reporters know that the very best stories — the most important, the most sensitive — rely on them," wrote reporter James Risen, who broke the domestic-spying story in the *Times* and authored a new book about the intelligence community and the war in Iraq. Without information from "current and former officials from the Bush administration, the intelligence community and other parts of the government," the book couldn't have been written. [27]

But CIA Director Goss has little tolerance for leakers. "Those who choose to bypass the law and go straight to the press are not noble, honorable or patriotic," Goss wrote. "Nor are they whistleblowers. Instead, they are committing a criminal act that potentially places American lives at risk." [28]

Goss told a Senate Intelligence Committee hearing in February that reporters writing stories based on NSA leaks should be hauled before a grand jury and "asked to reveal who is leaking this information." [29] In fact, the Bush administration has instigated a criminal investigation that could end in just that. [30]

Rather than leak to the press, FBI whistleblower Rowley worked within the system, sending a 13-page letter to FBI Director Robert S. Mueller III and copies to two members of the Joint Intelligence Committee.

Nevertheless, Rowley acknowledges that exceptional circumstances justify extraordinary measures, citing the notorious 1968 massacre of Vietnamese civilians at My Lai by U.S. troops and FBI Assistant Director Mark Felt's leaks — as "Deep Throat" — to *The Washington Post* during the Watergate scandal. "When your bosses are destroying evidence and outright lying — then, yes, you actually have to go outside the chain of command." (Rowley retired from the FBI and is running as a Democrat for a U.S. House seat in Minnesota.)

Still, given the potential risks of whistleblowing, some whistleblower advocates encourage employees to leak information about misdeeds. "We talk people out of blowing the whistle, says Ruch of Public Employees for Environmental Responsibility (PEER). If you think about it, if an agency is forced to confront the issue directly and can't blame it on a disgruntled employee, that's very good terrain to be on."

"The Art of Anonymous Activism," published by the Project on Government Oversight (POGO), the Government Accountability Project and PEER, advises employees on how to leak information. "Throwing away your entire career, particularly if there are other ways to ventilate the problem, is imprudent and counterproductive," the booklet argues.

But lawyer Kohn argues that even anonymous leakers can endanger their careers. For one thing, he says, while bosses and co-workers usually can figure out an anonymous source's identity, a leaker who suffers retaliation might not be able to prove that his boss has identified him.

But Rep. Shays responds that when whistleblowers follow the official chain of command it often leads to a dead end: "Leaks happen because whistleblowers are not getting heard."

Administration officials show little sympathy for that argument — or for leakers. Attorney General Gonzales told the Senate Judiciary Committee on Feb. 6 the Intelligence Community Whistleblower Protection Act protects employees wanting to report misconduct. "The danger or problem of going to the media as an initial matter is that you have some people . . . whose motivation . . . can be questioned in terms of why are they doing that," Gonzales said. ■

BACKGROUND

Civil War Abuses

When Civil War contractors were discovered selling the Union Army gunpowder cut with sawdust and other shoddy supplies, Congress authorized civil servants and citizens to sue cheaters on the government's behalf and share any money recovered with the government. [31]

Although the 1863 False Claims Act was groundbreaking legislation, it only dealt with whistleblowers reporting abuses by private contractors. It did not address insider accounts about public servants. President Theodore Roosevelt set the stage for such legislation when he barred employees in 1902 from contacting Congress on their own. [32]

The dispute over lawmakers' access to direct information from the executive branch agencies simmered through 1912, when Congress passed the Lloyd-Lafollette Act, which prohibited the firing of employees who contacted Congress. [33]

The early laws provided the only legal backing to civil servants reporting improper conduct until Congress took a comprehensive look at whistleblowing in 1978.

In 1972, journalist-historian Taylor Branch defined whistleblowers as political descendants of the turn-of-the-century journalistic crusaders known as muckrakers, who specialized in exposing corporate and government corruption. [34]

Muckraking's heyday had faded by the time insiders began blowing the whistle on government and corporate misdeeds during the government-reform movement of the 1960s. Ralph Nader, an advocate of corporate accountability and government transparency, immediately saw whistleblowers' value in arousing the public as well as politicians.

On Jan. 30, 1971, Nader organized a Conference on Professional Responsibility, which kicked off a campaign for legislation encouraging employees to tell Congress about government misdeeds while protecting them from retaliation. "The willingness and ability of insiders to blow the whistle is the last line of defense ordinary citizens have against the denial of their rights and the destruction of their interests by secretive and powerful institutions," Nader wrote. [35]

Nader and his allies had been inspired by four young staffers for Sen. Thomas J. Dodd, D-Conn., the father of today's Sen. Christopher J. Dodd, D-Conn. In 1965, they gave investigative reporter Jack Anderson copies of documents from Dodd's files that indicated he was pocketing campaign contributions. Anderson's articles led to Dodd's 1967 censure by the Senate for misusing political funds. [36]

Dodd's downfall notwithstanding, most government whistleblowing has been centered on the executive branch. In 1968, shortly after the Dodd exposé, a civilian Air Force financial analyst, A. Ernest Fitzgerald, told a congressional subcommittee that the cost of developing the C-5A transport plane was $2 billion over budget. Fitzgerald was forced out of his job but challenged his ouster in court and was reinstated in 1982.

In 1987, Fitzgerald made news again when he forced the Reagan administration to back down from requiring employees to take a secrecy pledge aimed at keeping government information out of the hands of Congress and the press. [37]

Fitzgerald's stand against wasteful military spending became a national news story, but he remained an inside-the-Beltway Washington figure. Defense analyst Daniel Ellsberg,

Continued on p. 276

Chronology

1960s-1970s

Whistleblowers reveal government misdeeds during Vietnam War and Watergate scandal.

1968
Pentagon fires A. Ernest Fitzgerald for revealing cost overruns in developing the C-5A transport plane. He was reinstated in 1982.

1971
Consumer advocate Ralph Nader launches drive for whistleblower-protection laws.

1973
Prosecutors drop charges against former Pentagon analyst Daniel Ellsberg for leaking the "Pentagon Papers" to *The New York Times.*

1978
Congress passes first, comprehensive whistleblower legislation, the Civil Service Reform Act.

1980s ***Congress strengthens the new statute.***

1984
Merit Systems Protection Board finds most employees are still fearful of reporting wrongdoing.

1987
Congress passes Whistleblower Protection Act (WPA), but Republican President Ronald Reagan vetoes it the next year, claiming it would be a vehicle for the merely disgruntled.

1989
President George H.W. Bush signs a toned-down version of the WPA.

1990s ***New generation of whistleblowers makes sensational disclosures of corporate and government wrongdoing.***

1992
Congress halts mental health exams for military whistleblowers and restores cash awards to whistleblowers who save the government money.

1993
Democratic Vice President Al Gore encourages whistleblowers as part of the Clinton administration's "Reinventing Government" effort.

1994
Congress strengthens WPA, allowing whistleblowers to challenge agency decisions to alter their working conditions or order them to undergo psychiatric testing.

1995
Former tobacco-industry scientist Jeffrey Wigand reveals the cover-up of smoking hazards by Brown & Williamson Tobacco Co.

1996
Aircraft maker McDonnell-Douglas pays fines for accounting fraud revealed by whistleblowers.

1997
Internal Revenue Service auditor Jennifer Long tells Congress the IRS targets lower-income taxpayers seen as easy targets. . . . On Oct. 24, a federal District judge in Houston rules the False Claims Act is unconstitutional; Supreme Court later overturns the decision.

1998
FBI agrees to pay large settlement to former crime laboratory official Frederic Whitehurst, who revealed manipulation of FBI lab results.

2000s ***National-security whistleblowers face retaliation.***

2002
FBI agent Colleen Rowley reveals FBI's pre-9/11 incompetence.

2003
Medicare actuary Richard Foster is threatened with dismissal after threatening to tell Congress the Bush administration is low-balling cost estimates for its prescription-drug reimbursement plan.

2004
Army Sgt. Samuel A. Provance is reduced in rank after revealing abuses at Abu Ghraib prison in Iraq.

March 2005
Bills introduced by Sen. Daniel Akaka, D-Hawaii, and Rep. Todd R. Platts, R-Pa., would close loopholes in the whistleblower law.

Aug. 28, 2005
Army Corps of Engineers demotes contract specialist Bunnatine H. Greenhouse after she complains of irregularities in Iraq war contracts.

Nov. 28. 2005
U.S. Supreme Court refuses to hear appeal by FBI whistleblower Sibel Edmonds.

Feb. 14, 2006
Sen. Frank R. Lautenberg, D-N.J., introduces bill aimed at shielding national-security whistleblowers. . . . House National Security Subcommittee holds hearings on whistleblowers.

Feb. 17, 2006
Supreme Court calls for reargument in case of Los Angeles prosecutor Richard Ceballos, who was demoted after revealing that a warrant contained false information.

The Downfall of Richard M. Barlow

Praise for his skills, friends in high places and four years of high-level national-security work — Richard M. Barlow can claim it all. What he lacks is a career.

Barlow was forced out of his job at the Defense Department in 1989. He's been trying to get it back ever since — along with his pension — with help from powerful supporters.

"As a message to whistleblowers, Rich's case is chilling," says former Assistant Secretary of State Robert Gallucci, dean of Georgetown University's School of Foreign Service, who is trying to persuade Congress to restore Barlow's retirement pay.

Barlow's adversaries tended to criticize him for being too rigid — and not a team player. His supporters said he was honest — and accurate — to a fault. Indeed, Victor Rostow, a former director of negotiations policy at the Pentagon, said Barlow's views "may have been absolutely right, but in the atmosphere of the creation of policy, being absolutely right is sometimes a hindrance. . . . There's a point at which you have to back off." [1]

Barlow's downfall began in 1987 at a closed-door briefing for the House Subcommittee on South Asian Affairs on Pakistan's nuclear weapons program. Barlow, then a brash, young CIA specialist, had the temerity to contradict testimony by Gen. David Einsel, a top National Intelligence Council official.

At the time, the Reagan administration wanted to keep aid flowing to Pakistan, which had been helping the United States oppose the Soviet Union's takeover in Afghanistan. But after the outlines of Pakistan's nuclear program surfaced, Congress had imposed two conditions on aid: The president was forced to certify that Pakistan wasn't building a nuclear weapon. And no aid could go to any country that was illegally obtaining U.S. materials of any kind to build a nuke. [2]

Years later, after Barlow sued to get his job back, a Court of Claims judge conceded, "We can safely assume that General Einsel's testimony was materially incorrect." [3]

Yet, abrasiveness aside, Barlow had delivered his testimony under orders from his bosses at the CIA, which months later awarded him a "certificate for exceptional accomplishment." Nonetheless, the episode effectively ended Barlow's agency career, and he quit and joined the Defense Department as a proliferation specialist in 1989.

Again, he clashed with a superior over Pakistan, this time after learning the CIA was still misinforming Congress about Pakistan's nuclear weapons in order not to jeopardize the $1.4 billion sale of F-16 fighters by the U.S. to Pakistan. Barlow had reported to his bosses that the planes were being modified to carry nuclear weapons. Told he'd be fired, Barlow quit. [4]

Over the years, as more details surfaced about Pakistan's weapons program — including black-market sales of nuclear technology by A. Q. Khan, then the director of Pakistan's nuclear weapons program, — Barlow's accuracy was confirmed. [5] But the Defense Department refused to rescind its actions against him, even when a General Accounting Office (now the Government Accountability Office) report called the Pentagon's case against Barlow legally unsupported. The 1997 report noted that even the Pentagon did not accept an account by Barlow's boss, Gerald Brubaker, that Barlow had threatened to contact Congress over the matter on his own. [6]

By 1998, it was clear that even Barlow's influential lawyer, former Assistant Defense Secretary Paul C. Warnke, had failed. Although Warnke had persuaded congressional leaders from both sides of the aisle to pressure the Pentagon to rescind its personnel actions, it wouldn't budge. [7] Then, Sen. Jeff Bingaman, D-N.M., introduced a "private relief bill" to obtain for Barlow the equivalent of the $1.1 million retirement pay he had forfeited when he was forced out of government. [8]

The bill never got out of committee. Instead, the Senate in 1998 sent Barlow's case to the U.S. Court of Claims, which designates a judge to act as a hearing officer for Congress. [9] Four years later, Senior Judge Eric G. Bruggink concluded that Defense had acted within the law. In doing so, he accepted an account that Barlow had threatened to contact Congress about Pakistan's nuclear weapons on his own — a conclusion previously rejected by the Defense Department itself. "Mr. Barlow was a probationary employee who was terminated because of performance deficiencies and personality conflicts," Bruggink wrote. [10]

Continued from p. 274

on the other hand, achieved international fame in 1971 for leaking the secret Defense Department history of the Vietnam War known as the "Pentagon Papers." Ellsberg was arrested weeks after *The New York Times* began publishing the long account, but charges that he had violated the Espionage Act were dropped after government agents illegally tapped his phone. [38]

Legal Shields

The men who monitored Ellsberg's calls — and also broke into his psychiatrist's office in search of damaging information — became infamous when they were caught breaking into the Democratic National Committee's offices at the Watergate Hotel. [39] The resulting cover-up and Watergate scandal led to President Richard M. Nixon's resignation. [40]

After Watergate, lawmakers and the public viewed administration officials bent on secrecy as villains and whistleblowers as heroes. In 1978, Congress responded to the popular mood by including whistleblower-protection measures in the Civil Service Reform Act. "These conscientious civil servants deserve statutory protection rather than bureaucratic harassment and intimidation," said a Senate report on the legislation. The law cre-

Bruggink's decision ignited a delayed behind-the-scenes dispute centering on the decision to bow to the government's wishes on excluding evidence. Aides to Sens. Susan Collins, R-Maine, chairwoman of the Senate Homeland Security and Governmental Affairs Committee, and Joseph I. Lieberman of Connecticut, the committee's ranking Democrat, told Barlow that Bruggink's report was the last word. But the staffers agreed to meet with Gallucci, Joseph Ostoyich, who took over the case from Warnke, and Louis Fisher, then a senior specialist in separation of powers at the Congressional Research Service. [11]

Richard Barlow

Former Defense Department nuclear-proliferation expert Richard Barlow.

Fisher argued that Bruggink had not been obliged simply to accept the secrecy claim but could have reviewed documents and admitted some of them or sent the case back to the Senate because full evidence was unavailable. As it was, Fisher wrote, the court allowed the government to introduce the evidence it wanted, while denying Barlow the same right. [12] "My pitch was that the court didn't do what it was supposed to do to get at the facts," Fisher says. "The record is pretty clear that the court failed in its duty."

Barlow, for his part, faults congressional lawmakers. "You can hardly blame the executive branch for pushing its power and authority as far as Congress lets them push it," he says. "We're dealing with a Congress that's not been engaging in any checks and balances or oversight — giving the signal that the executive can do whatever it wants."

As for the misinformation about Pakistan's nuclear weapons that Congress received, "There is something to the idea that Congress sort of half-wanted to be misled in the '80s," Gallucci says. "People like Rich were going to force them to look at it in the eye. He really did get screwed."

[1] Rostow testified at a 2002 hearing before a Court of Claims judge.

[2] For background on Pakistan's nuclear arms program, see Douglas Frantz, "From Patriot to Proliferator," *Los Angeles Times*, Sept. 23, 2005; Richard Weintraub, "Pakistan Faces Woes From Within, Without; Nuclear Question Threatens Ties to the U.S.," *The Washington Post*, July 28, 1987, p. A10, and Richard Weintraub "Pakistan Denies Connection to any Nuclear-Export Plot," *The Washington Post*, July 22, 1987, p. A1.

[3] See 53 Fed. Cl. 667, 2002 Court of Claims, pp. 4-5; a fuller account of the episode and of its consequences can be found in Seymour Hersh, "On the Nuclear Edge," *The New Yorker*, March 29, 1993, www.newyorker.com/printables/archive/040119fr_archive02.

[4] General Accounting Office [now, Government Accountability Office], "Inspectors General: Joint Investigation of Personnel Actions Regarding a Former Defense Employee," July 10, 1997, pp. 2-3.

[5] For background, see Mary H. Cooper, "Nuclear Proliferation and Terrorism," *CQ Researcher*, April 2, 2004, pp. 297-320.

[6] General Accounting Office, *op. cit.*

[7] Warnke, who died in 2001, was also a former director of the Arms Control and Disarmament Agency. Barlow provided to *CQ Researcher* a file of correspondence between Senate Armed Services Committee Chairman Strom Thurmond, R-S.C., other lawmakers, and Defense officials.

[8] 105th Congress, 2d Session, S. 2274, "For the relief of Richard M. Barlow of Santa Fe, N.M.," July 8, 1998; press release, "Bingaman Seeks Compensation for Pentagon Whistleblower," Office of Sen. Bingaman, July 8, 1998. Barlow spent most of the 1990s working under a consulting contract with Sandia National Laboratories in New Mexico.

[9] Louis Fisher, "National Security Whistleblowers," Congressional Research Service, Dec. 30, 2005, pp. 35-38, www.pogo.org/m/gp/gp-crs-nsw-12302005.pdf.

[10] Federal Court of Claims, *op. cit.*

[11] Fisher joined the staff of the Library of Congress' law library on March 6, 2006, after 35 years at CRS. See, Yochi J. Dreazen, "Expert on Congress's Power Claims He Was Muzzled for Faulting Bush," *The Wall Street Journal*, Feb. 9, 2006, p. A6.

[12] Louis Fisher, "Congressional Research Service memorandum to: Jennifer Hemingway, Senate Committee on Homeland Security and Governmental Affairs, Nov. 25, 2005."

ated the Merit Systems Protection Board (MSPB) and the Office of Special Counsel (OSC) to prosecute prohibited personnel practices, such as reprisals against whistleblowers.

But the protection process was complicated and fraught with limitations, and few employees used it. Fear of reprisals grew stronger during the early years of the Reagan administration. Indeed, the percentage of employees keeping quiet about official misconduct doubled between 1980 and 1983, according to an MSPB study. [41]

Acknowledging that reality, Congress passed the Whistleblower Protection Act of 1987, which would have authorized the OSC to appeal MSPB decisions in federal court and made it easier for whistleblowers to claim they were victims of retaliation. But President Reagan pocket-vetoed the bill in 1988, calling it a way for undeserving employees to avoid firing, demotion or other action.

The following year, Congress passed and President George H.W. Bush signed a toned-down version of the bill — with the OSC's appeal power removed.

But even the new legal protections proved less than solid. A 1994 MSPB survey found retaliation on the upswing, with 37 percent of respondents saying they had suffered retaliation for exercising their rights — including re-

Critics Question Agency's Commitment

Whistleblower advocates say the chief federal official charged with protecting whistleblowers who are federal employees is out to sabotage employee rights.

A formal complaint filed by employees and whistleblower-advocacy organizations charges that Scott J. Bloch, who heads the Office of Special Counsel (OSC), issued an illegal gag order and transferred employees he considered disloyal.

"Complainants' allegations against Special Counsel Bloch . . . go to the heart of OSC's credibility and effectiveness as a watchdog of the [federal] merit system," said the Government Accountability Project, the Project on Government Oversight, Public Employees for Environmental Responsibility and Human Rights Campaign. Their initial complaint was filed on March 3, 2005. [1]

Whistleblower advocates say Bloch's personnel practices reflect the OSC's performance in handling whistleblower cases. "This OSC is even worse than the others," says Washington lawyer Stephen M. Kohn, who often represents whistleblowers. While OSCs in previous years filed a couple of cases, he says, "this one does straight-out nothing."

For its part, the OSC reports it referred 19 whistleblower allegations to federal agencies for investigation last year, and that 16 were substantiated.

The complaint against Bloch charges that his methods of trimming the office's case backlog included closing cases "at breakneck speed" — often without even interviewing complainants alleging retaliation. [2]

Bloch, who took office in January 2004, has dismissed the allegations as false — the product of disgruntled employees and administration opponents. "They don't like the success Bush officials are having in dealing with the bureaucracy," he said. [3]

Rep. Tom Davis, R-Va., chairman of the House Government Reform Committee, congratulated Bloch last May for reducing the agency's historically massive backlog of whistleblower and other cases, which had been cited in a critical report by the General Accounting Office. "We appreciate the professional seriousness with which you . . . reduced the existing backlogs," Davis said, in a letter cosigned by Rep. Jon G. Porter, R-Nev., chairman of the House Federal Workforce Subcommittee. "Unfortunately, this activity, while beneficial to whistleblowers, was regarded with suspicion by activists who claim to work on behalf of whistleblowers." [4]

The whistleblower advocates cited leaked OSC reports, a practice Bloch excoriated. "It's unfortunate that we have a leaker or leakers in our office who went to the press rather than coming to me," Bloch said. [5] He later ordered that any "official comment on or discussion of confidential or sensitive internal agency matters with anyone outside OSC" had to be approved by him or his immediate staff, according to the complaint. That directive violated both the First Amendment and a federal law authorizing federal workers to disclose information to Congress, the complaint argues. [6]

Bloch himself told Federal News Radio he is pro-whistleblower. "Any time we can give more protection to whistleblowers and make sure that they understand that they're protected, it's a good thing. . . . They do have an agency that does go to bat for them. It is true that some don't get as much justice as they wish or as quickly as they ought to. We are making significant progress in that." [7]

The interview didn't touch on the charges against Bloch's management of the agency. Loren Smith, the OSC's congressional and public affairs director, says Bloch doesn't want to discuss the complaint until investigators have examined the allegations.

The complaint that received the most attention said Bloch flouted federal law by refusing to pursue cases involving employees who report discrimination based on sexual orientation. Bloch ignited the controversy shortly after taking office by removing references to sexual-orientation discrimination from his agency's Web site. He later said that while discriminating against

porting fraud, waste or abuse — up from 24 percent in 1983. And fewer than 20 percent of employees who filed complaints with the MSBP were successful in their cases. [42]

The OSC's record was even more dismal. A 1994 report by the House Post Office and Civil Service Committee found that the agency had not litigated a single case to restore a whistleblower's job — even though 400 to 500 employees had filed cases with the OSC since its 1979 creation. [43]

Employees also fared badly in the U.S. Court of Appeals for the Federal Circuit, the only court authorized to hear appeals of MSPB decisions. In one case, the House Post Office panel said a judge violated congressional intent in upholding the firing of a Department of the Army employee who claimed her dismissal was retaliation for whistleblowing. The department had not even been required to prove that the whistleblowing played no part in her firing.

That case helped persuade Congress in 1994 to amend the law, allowing employees to challenge an agency decision to change their working conditions or order them to get psychiatric testing. The new law also authorized the MSPB to reinstate employees at the same job level they would be occupying if the prohibited personnel practice hadn't occurred and reimburse the employees for attorney's fees and back pay.

Famous Whistleblowers

Despite weaknesses in the protection laws, corporate and gov-an employee's sexual "conduct" would be illegal, discriminating against an employee's sexual "orientation" might not be. [8]

Following a storm of criticism from gay-rights advocates and administration critics, White House spokesman Trent Duffy said, "The president believes that no federal employee should be subject to unlawful discrimination. That's longstanding federal policy that prevents discrimination based on sexual orientation." [9]

In response, Bloch seemed to adjust his view, announcing he'd concluded after a legal review that his office could investigate claims of discrimination based on sexual orientation when the discrimination was rooted in an assumption about an employee's private conduct. [10] But a month later, he told the Senate Homeland Security and Government Affairs Subcommittee that he didn't have legal authority to defend workers who suffer discrimination simply because they are gay.

U.S. Office of Special Counsel

Scott J. Bloch, special counsel, federal Office of Special Counsel.

Senators of both parties responded by lecturing Bloch on how to treat employees. Rep. George Voinovich, R-Ohio, said he had learned that 10 of the 12 Washington staffers ordered transferred by Bloch had left the agency rather than transfer to offices in Dallas and Detroit. Bloch said he'd had no intention of harming any employees. "Your actions don't comport with your words," Sen. Frank R. Lautenberg, D-N.J., told the counsel. [11]

Beth Daley, senior investigator for the Project on Government Oversight, says she has little hope that the agency assigned to investigate the allegations against the OSC — the Office of Personnel Management (OPM) — will pursue the case energetically. "We're not holding our breath," she says.

"Depending on the complexity, it could take three or four months," says Norbert Vint, the OPM's assistant inspector general for investigations. As to the complainants' low confidence, Vint says, "I can't comment on their opinion. Our opinion is that we will do a thorough investigation."

---

[1] Detailed allegations are contained in "Statement in Support of Complaint of Prohibited Personnel Practices Against U.S. Special Counsel Scott J. Bloch," March 3, 2005; "Amended Complaint," March 31, 2005, both available at, http://pogo.org/p/government/OSCcompendium.html.

[2] *Ibid.*, p. 22.

[3] Tim Kauffman, "Spotlight; New counsel reviews whistleblower, bias laws," *Federal Times*, March 22, 2004, p. 22.

[4] For background, see, "U.S. Office of Special Counsel: Strategy for Reducing Persistent Backlog of Cases Should be Provided to Congress," General Accounting Office [now, Government Accountability Office], GAO 04-36, March 2004, www.gao.gov/new.items/d0436.pdf.

[5] Kauffman, *op. cit.*

[6] "Statement in Support of Complaint," *op. cit.*, pp. 26-28.

[7] "Are whistleblowers protected?" Jan. 1, 2006, available at www.osc.gov/library.htm.

[8] Tim Kauffman, "OSC to study whether bias laws covers gays," *Federal Times*, March 15, 2004, p. 4.

[9] Jerry Seper, "Bush backs policy against bias; Challenges counsel's decision on sexual orientation," *The Washington Times*, April 2, 2004, p. A6.

[10] Office of Special Counsel," Results of Legal Review of Discrimination Statute," press release, April 4, 2004, www.osc.gov.

[11] Stephen Barr, "Senators Criticize Special Counsel's Treatment of Employees," *The Washington Post*, May 25, 2005, p. B2, and Christopher Lee, "Official Says Law Doesn't Cover Gays," *The Washington Post*, May 25, 2005, p. A25.

ernment insiders continued speaking out in the mid-1990s. In 1996, whistleblowers at the McDonnell Douglas Corp. revealed more than $1 billion in overruns on development of the Air Force's C-17 cargo jet, triggering a Pentagon investigation, dramatic congressional hearings and the forced retirement of three generals. The company paid a $500,000 fine to the Securities and Exchange Commission to settle charges it misled stockholders about the C-17 project. In settling, the company neither admitted nor denied wrongdoing. [44]

The year before, in an even more sensational case, Jeffrey Wigand, a former research director for Brown & Williamson Tobacco Corp., testified the company had opposed developing safer cigarettes in order to escape liability for the negative health effects of cigarettes. [45]

Although Brown & Williamson had already fired Wigand, it sued him for breaking a confidentiality agreement. But the firm dropped the suit as a prelude to a massive 1998 settlement between the tobacco industry and a group of state attorneys general and private lawyers in which major tobacco firms agreed to pay $206 billion over 25 years to end states' anti-tobacco lawsuits. [46]

Another tobacco whistleblower leaked documents showing that Brown & Williamson executives knew that cigarettes caused cancer. [47] Merrell Williams, a paralegal for a Louisville law firm, secretly photocopied the documents and gave them to a prominent plaintiffs' lawyer, who turned them over to Rep. Waxman, then chairman of the House Health and Environment Subcommittee.

The documents were crucial to the tobacco settlement, and Williams — when his name surfaced — became a hero to anti-tobacco advocates.

In a more public display of whistleblowing, Jennifer Long, an IRS auditor in Houston, and six colleagues — hidden behind screens, their voices disguised — told the Senate Finance Committee that some auditors targeted low-income taxpayers seen as defenseless but didn't cite wealthier citizens for violations because they could afford lawyers to challenge IRS examiners. [48]

Long's bosses took steps to fire her, but they backtracked after Finance Committee Chairman William V. Roth, R-Del., complained to the IRS commissioner and described the attempted firing as "contempt of Congress." [49]

Even as the IRS and tobacco dramas were playing out, complex whistleblower allegations were surfacing from the worlds of law enforcement and national security.

At the FBI, Frederic Whitehurst, a chemist in the explosives library, began telling superiors in the early 1990s that laboratory reports were scientifically flawed and typically slanted against defendants. [50] By 1994, his complaints had prompted an internal investigation. The conclusion: Whitehurst was "an idealist and perfectionist who sees everything as black or white." [51]

Whitehurst demanded an independent investigation, and a Justice Department inspector general concluded he had been largely correct. [52] In 1998, in return for Whitehead's resignation, the FBI agreed to pay the 50-year-old chemist the salary and pension he would have received if he had retired at 57 — a deal worth about $1.1 million. The FBI also paid $258,580 of Whitehurst's legal costs. Then, to settle a Whitehurst lawsuit against Justice, the department paid him $300,000. Typical settlements in such lawsuits were $5,000, said Whitehurst's lawyer. [53]

Whistleblowing by Richard Nuccio, a State Department official involved in peace talks between the Guatemalan government and left-wing guerrillas, didn't end so happily. In 1995, he reported possible CIA human-rights abuses to Rep. Robert Torricelli, D-N.J., who passed the information to *The New York Times*. After Nuccio was identified as the source, the CIA revoked his security clearance for releasing the information without authorization. [54]

The Senate Intelligence Committee then proposed a new provision in the Intelligence Authorization Act allowing executive-branch employees to disclose classified information to congressional committees or to their own representatives if doing so revealed improprieties or threats to the public. [55] But President Clinton vowed to veto any intelligence bill that contained the provision, and House-Senate conferees removed the whistleblower shield. [56] Without his security clearance, Nuccio lost his job. [57]

He wasn't the only national-security whistleblower involved in sensitive matters. In the late 1980s, former Defense Department and CIA specialist on nuclear proliferation Barlow lost his Defense job after running afoul of U.S. policy toward Pakistan and its nuclear ambitions. [58]

Post-9/11 Whistleblowing

After the terrorist attacks, whistleblowers focused an often-searing spotlight on the competence of government intelligence officials.

First came FBI agent Rowley, who in 2002 accused top FBI officials of blocking efforts to probe more deeply into Zacarias Moussaoui, whom agents had arrested shortly before 9/11 in Minneapolis, where he'd been taking flying lessons. She also criticized the failure to follow up a Phoenix agent's inquiries about Arab men studying aviation. [59]

Testifying before the Senate Judiciary Committee made Rowley a media superstar. Her prominence may have insulated her from retaliation, but Judiciary Committee members also got Mueller to pledge there would be no reprisals against her. Soon afterward, Rowley and two other whistleblowers became *Time's* "Persons of the Year." [60]

Accompanying her on the magazine's cover were corporate whistleblowers Sherron Watkins, the Enron vice president who had warned Chairman Ken Lay the firm faced financial collapse; and WorldCom auditor Cynthia Cooper, whose accounts of phony accounting practices helped push the telecom giant into bankruptcy. [61]

In the years that followed, however, national-security whistleblowers eclipsed their private-sector counterparts, including Richard A. Clarke, counterterrorism director at the National Security Council under presidents Clinton and Bush. Clarke asked to be reassigned after his pre-9/11 warnings about the al Qaeda terrorist network went — as he saw it — unheeded. [62]

After leaving government in 2003, Clarke described his failed whistleblowing in a 2004 book, *Against All Enemies: Inside America's War on Terror*. When then-National Security Director Condoleezza Rice and other officials challenged his account, Clarke repeated his charges before the bipartisan commission investigating pre-9/11 security breaches. [63]

The Iraq war became a new field for whistleblowers. Corps of Engineers contract supervisor Greenhouse raised questions about contracting irregularities in a series of billion-dollar contracts awarded to the Halliburton subsidiary Kellogg Brown & Root. [64] In 2005, Greenhouse was demoted for allegedly poor job performance, but the Corps' commander said retaliation had not been the motive. [65] She is contesting her demotion. ■

Continued on p. 282

At Issue:

Should Congress expand whistleblower rights?

THOMAS DEVINE
LEGAL DIRECTOR, GOVERNMENT ACCOUNTABILITY PROJECT

FROM A LETTER TO THE U.S. SENATE, MARCH 13, 2006

yes

Twelve years of hostile court rulings against whistleblowers by the federal Circuit Court of Appeals have effectively rewritten the Whistleblower Protection Act (WPA) — against congressional intent. Since the 1994 vote to strengthen the WPA, whistleblowers have suffered a 1-119 track record there for decisions on the merits.

The federal Circuit Court translated explicit statutory language to provide legal protection for "any" lawful disclosure of wrongdoing to mean "almost never." This was done through rulings that disqualify whistleblower protection for the most common disclosures of wrongdoing, such as those made to a supervisor or during the course of one's job duties.

The impact of these and other rulings [has] made the Whistleblower Protection Act the most powerful reason for government workers who witness fraud, waste or abuse to remain silent. We cannot expect public servants to defend our families and our tax dollars if they cannot defend themselves.

A status quo that is bad for whistleblowers is also bad for the taxpayers. Secrecy breeds corruption. In an era of record government spending, we need whistleblowers . . . to guard against waste, fraud and abuse and so that we know the true cost of programs. We need them for homeland security — to allow Congress to act against vulnerability to terrorists caused by bureaucratic negligence at our nuclear weapons facilities, at our airports and elsewhere. We need them to protect the health of America's families — whether to warn about government-approved painkillers that have killed tens of thousands or government-inspected meat and poultry that have hospitalized hundreds of thousands more.

Genuine rights are long overdue for those who champion accountability within the federal bureaucracy. After the Enron and MCI scandals, Congress gave state-of-the-art whistleblower rights to corporate workers [that are] far stronger than what are available for federal employees. Those defending America's families need protection against retaliation as much as those defending America's stock values.

Just before Christmas, United Nations Under Secretary General Christopher Bernham unveiled a whistleblower policy for U.N. employees that is far stronger than the WPA. The new policy is based largely on the best practices of other nations, whose whistleblower protections also have surpassed those in the United States. Mr. Bernham . . . effectively insisted on and won some of the precise protections for U.N. employees that are not available for federal workers in the United States.

WILLIAM E. MOSCHELLA
ASSISTANT ATTORNEY GENERAL
DIRECTOR, OFFICE OF LEGISLATIVE AFFAIRS, U.S. DEPARTMENT OF JUSTICE

FROM A LETTER TO THE U. S. SENATE, APRIL 12, 2005

no

The WPA [Whistleblower Protection Act] already provides adequate protection for legitimate whistleblowers. The federal Circuit appropriately has recognized that the purposes of the WPA must be taken into account in determining whether a disclosure is one protected by the WPA. These limitations are reasonable and serve to further the purpose of the WPA to protect legitimate whistleblowers.

The proposed expansive definition [of whistleblower complaints] has the potential to convert any disagreement or contrary interpretation of a law, no matter how trivial or frivolous, into a whistleblower disclosure. Such an increase in the number of frivolous claims would impose an unwarranted burden upon federal managers. Given the expanded definition of disclosure, it would be exceedingly easy for employees to use whistleblowing as a defense to every adverse personnel action.

Nearly every federal employee will, sometime during the course of his or her career, disagree with a statement or interpretation made by a supervisor, or during the course of performing his or her everyday responsibilities report an error that may demonstrate a violation of a law, rule or regulation. Without the ability to take the context — the time, the place, the motive — of the alleged disclosure into account, even trivial matters would become elevated to the status of protected disclosures.

Conceivably, any time a supervisor suspected wrongdoing by an employee and determined to look into the matter, the "investigation" could be subject to challenge. Employees would be able to delay or thwart any investigation into their own or others' wrongdoing.

The Constitution not only generally establishes the president as the head of the executive branch but also makes him commander in chief of all military forces, the sole organ of America's foreign affairs and the officer in the government with the express duty (and corresponding authority) to take care that the laws are faithfully executed.

The executive branch remains committed to accommodating Congress' legitimate oversight needs in ways that are consistent with the executive branch's constitutional responsibilities. However, a process exists by which this has been and may be done.

The process of dynamic compromise between the branches, whereby each branch seeks an optimal accommodation by evaluating the needs of the other, cannot function where every covered employee of the executive branch is vested with the right to decide for himself or herself — without any official authorization — [what] disclosures are appropriate.

Continued from p. 280

CURRENT SITUATION

Legislative Potential

Sen. Lautenberg is proposing the most far-reaching measures to strengthen whistleblower protections. His Whistleblower Empowerment, Security, and Taxpayer Protection Act of 2006 would bring spy-agency workers under the Whistleblower Protection Act. That would guarantee whistleblowers alleging retaliation access to federal District Court, authorize them to ask for special prosecutors to investigate the retaliation and subject bosses to fines for retaliating against whistleblowers.

"Right now, managers who retaliate against whistleblowers get off basically scot-free, even though whistleblower retaliation is against the law," Lautenberg said in a statement.

But many question whether Congress is in the mood for such a sweeping change. "It would take a miracle for it to pass on its own," says Devine of the Government Accountability Project. For instance, the bill would have to pass through the Senate Intelligence and Judiciary committees, where objections would be likely. The National Security Whistleblowers Coalition, organized by dismissed FBI translator Edmonds, helped draft the bill, which she says answers a need for sweeping legislation.

Devine and some other whistleblower advocates are pinning their hopes on the measures introduced last year by Sen. Akaka and Rep. Platts. The bills would close loopholes in existing whistleblower law by:

- Ensuring that federal employees could get whistleblower protection even if discovering the wrongdoing they are reporting is part of their job;
- Allowing employees to use classified information to report wrongdoing to Congress;
- Allowing whistleblowers to appeal MSPB decisions to federal Circuit courts for a period of five years, helping to end the Federal Circuit's monopoly over jurisdiction; and
- Providing a review mechanism for employees whose security clearance is revoked.

Although the administration opposes both measures, they passed their respective committees last year, and the Senate legislation had been approved in committee in two previous years. After an administration official testified the Senate bill could make managing federal employees more difficult, the Senate Homeland Security and Governmental Affairs Committee said in its 2005 report on the bill, "We can take other steps to deter and weed out frivolous whistleblower claims, but we cannot begin to calculate the potential damage to the nation should good-faith whistleblowing become chilled by a hostile process."

Nevertheless, the bill never reached the floor. Advocates of stronger whistleblower legislation say only public pressure can force congressional leaders to allow legislation to reach the full House and Senate, but more optimistic advocates say the political climate may be changing.

"We are hearing more about people disclosing issues of national concern and getting in trouble for it," says a Democratic Senate aide. "I think the American people aren't going to stand for it."

But Sen. Akaka says his bill's immobility after committee approval last year has led him to consider tacking it onto other legislation in the form of amendments. Whatever the Bush administration's attitudes toward whistleblowers may be, Akaka says, lawmakers aren't leaping to defend them. "The reactions and responses indicate they would rather not touch the issue," he says. Whistleblowers can affect "a lot of special interests that members have."

Free Speech at Work

A Supreme Court ruling this summer may limit public employees' whistleblower rights.

The high court last year heard arguments in the landmark case — involving a Los Angeles search warrant containing false information — but revisited it on March 21 after Justice Samuel A. Alito Jr. joined the court. [66]

The case essentially revolves around the following questions: Does the constitutional right to free speech apply to public employees who speak or write as part of their jobs? Can such employees speak or write about corruption or improprieties they witness at their jobs?

The Bush administration argues that the First Amendment doesn't apply in such cases. "Constitutional rights are personal, and when a public employee speaks in carrying out his job duties, he has no personal interest in the speech," U.S. Solicitor General Paul D. Clement argues in his brief. [67]

Victory in that argument would be a giant step back for employees, says whistleblower lawyer Kohn. "It would permit you to fire many whistleblowers," he says. "It's such a gigantic issue because 98 percent of all whistleblowers go to management first. And the majority would deny to your face that they were whistleblowers; the majority say they were just doing their job. The moment you stop that type of conduct from being protected, you undermine almost all whistleblower cases."

Furthermore, Kohn contends, existing Supreme Court precedents give public employees on-the-job First Amendment rights on issues of public concern, even if they deal with those issues as part of their jobs.

The high-stakes legal dispute evolved after a deputy Los Angeles prosecutor investigated a defense lawyer's motion to throw out a search warrant that had authorized a search that led to drug and firearms charges. [68] Prosecutor Richard Ceballos concluded that the warrant contained false information and that the deputy sheriff who obtained it may have lied. Ceballos argued to his boss that the criminal charges should be thrown out, and he said as much in court. But after the hearing, he was demoted and transferred to a distant office.

Ceballos sued District Attorney Gil Garcetti and Los Angeles County, claiming the punitive actions taken against him violated his First Amendment right to free speech. A U.S. District Court and the U.S. 9th Circuit Court of Appeals agreed. Garcetti (now out of office) and the county appealed to the Supreme Court, arguing they acted legally against Ceballos because he had no free speech on matters involving his job.

But his lawyers argue that stifling whistleblowing is a bad idea: "It is not in any government agency's best interest 'to fly blind' because its employees are afraid to report corruption or abuse." [69]

While Solicitor General Clement argues that public employees would be protected if they spoke out as citizens instead of as civil servants, his brief warns that any employee whose job duties include reporting wrongdoing is generally "prohibited from speaking to the press about an ongoing investigation without the permission of his employer, [who] may well discipline him for violating the prohibition."

Ceballos' chief lawyer, Bonnie Robin-Vergeer of the nonprofit Public Citizens Litigation Group of Washington, calls the government position "startling and extreme." And as a practical matter, no employee who calls the press as a citizen to report wrongdoing would escape discipline. "It's just what it looks like," she says of the government position. "It means the public employee really can't speak on matters of public concern." ■

OUTLOOK

Open Floodgates?

Nothing generates protection for whistleblowers better than scandal, says whistleblowers' lawyer Kohn. After Enron and WorldCom imploded, Congress passed the Sarbanes-Oxley Act of 2002, which gave corporate insiders the right to file federal lawsuits if they suffered retaliation after reporting wrongdoing. [70]

Now, he contends, the Bush administration's policy of controlling information is breeding new cadres of insiders. Inevitably, information about misconduct will surface, he says, generating pressure for more laws.

"Whistleblowers can save our government a lot of grief, a lot of money and correct some of the inequities and problems our government has," Sen. Akaka says. "The whistleblowers who have come forward to disclose security lapses and, in particular, threats to public health and safety since 9/11, have brought renewed attention to those who alert the public to government wrongdoing."

The public has no trouble grasping whistleblowers' role, Kohn says. "If you look at most other areas of employment discrimination, there hasn't been that much movement, but in the whistleblower field they keep passing laws." The public is saying to companies and agencies, he adds, " 'the more you don't get the message that things have changed, the laws are going to get tougher and tougher.' "

However, whistleblower protection can mean almost anything, depending on who's talking. "It's become a motherhood issue," says Ruch of Public Employees for Environmental Responsibility. "It's like the environment; no one's anti-environment. So officials will say, we're in favor of whistleblower protection, but we're also in favor of flexibility — increasing management prerogatives to hire and fire." Flexibility, he says, can become a euphemism for facilitating retaliation against whistleblowers.

Furthermore, as efforts to combat terrorism continue indefinitely, expanded presidential wartime powers pose a danger for whistleblowers, especially given any administration's built-in aversion to whistleblowers. But, says Rep. Shays, "This war against Islamist terror is going to last a long time, so you need to be even more alert that powers aren't abused. With more power there has to be more congressional oversight." And for oversight to be effective, "You need to empower people to speak out when they see wrongdoing — and they need to be protected."

Right now, the level of protection for national-security whistleblowers is "pathetic," he acknowledges. Even Congress provides no whistleblower protection for its own employees, he points out.

Shays insists whistleblowers can help a president stay on top of an issue. "They share things that need to be disclosed, and the sooner they're disclosed, the better."

For her part, FBI whistleblower Rowley is sure that if she were speaking out now, rather than soon after 9/11, she would have paid a price in retaliation. "I think they view me as a big mistake," she says. "I ended up having a certain amount of power. I even criticized [Attorney General John] Ashcroft. I don't think it would happen again. Now they would say, 'Next time, we'll fire whistleblowers from the start.' "

Rowley, however, accepts the validity of the executive branch's "floodgates" argument — that a wave of trivial whistleblower complaints could overwhelm the federal personnel system and Congress. But that should not doom whistleblower protection, says Rowley. "Someone has to be a gatekeeper," she says.

Barlow, the former Defense nuclear-proliferation expert, rejects the "floodgates" argument entirely. "Federal employees do not go marching down to

Congress unless it's something serious," he says. "Whistleblowers are always going to get screwed by their colleagues. It's human nature; you're never going to make that go away." Criminalizing retaliation would help control that behavior, he adds.

Kohn agrees. "The thing that has hurt whistleblowers the most is having former friends and colleagues turn their backs on them," he says, especially since the difference between winning and losing a case "is obtaining evidence and getting witnesses."

Whistleblower advocate and former Senate aide Kolesnik says the solution is to negotiate a good settlement — one that allows a whistleblower to walk away from a job without having doomed his future prospects. Whatever shape protection may take, he says, whistleblowers still must rely on their common sense: "You have to know the law and know what you're doing." ■

Notes

[1] For background on Provance's disclosures to the press, see Douglas Jehl and Kate Zernike, "The Struggle for Iraq: Abu Ghraib," *The New York Times*, May 28, 2004, p. A11.

[2] For background see James Kelley, "Year of the Whistleblowers," *Time*, Dec. 30, 2002.

[3] A transcript of Gore's Jan.16, 2006, speech is available at www.washingtonpost.com/wp-dyn/content/article/2006/01/16/AR2006011600779.html.

[4] Linda Greenhouse, "Justices Reject F.B.I. Translator's Appeal on Termination," *The New York Times*, Nov. 29, 2005, p. A22.

[5] For background see Nat Garrett, "Tomorrow's Argument: *Garcetti v. Ceballos*, Oct. 11, 2005, Scotusblog, www.scotusblog.com/movabletype/archives/2005/10/tomorrows_argum_11.html; and "Brief for the United States as Amicus Curiae Supporting Petitioners," *Gil Garcetti, et al., v. Richard Ceballos*, Case No. 04-473, www.usdoj.gov/osg/briefs/2004/3mer/1ami/2004-0473.mer.ami.pdf.

[6] "A Review of the FBI's Actions in Connection With Allegations Raised by Contract Linguist Sibel Edmonds, Unclassified Summary," U.S. Department of Justice, Office of the Inspector General, January 2005, www.usdoj.gov/oig/special/0501/index.htm.

[7] "Statement by the FBI Regarding the Office of Inspector General's Report," press release, Jan. 14, 2006, www.fbi.gov/pressrel/pressrel05/011405.htm.

[8] Louis Fisher, "National Security Whistleblowers," Congressional Research Service, Dec. 30, 2005, pp. 33-35, www.pogo.org/m/gp/gp-crs-nsw-12302005.pdf.

[9] James Risen and Eric Lichtblau, "Bush Lets U.S. Spy on Callers without Courts," *The New York Times*, Dec. 16, 2005, p. A1.

[10] Federal statute 18 USC 1513(e), "Retaliating against a witness, victim, or an informant."

[11] L. Paige Whitaker and Michael Schmerling, "Whistleblower Protections for Federal Employees," Congressional Research Service, updated May 18, 1998, pp. 2-10, http://whistle20.tripod.com/crswhistle.pdf.

[12] For background, see earlier Devine testimony, "Statement of Tom Devine," Senate Governmental Affairs Committee, Nov. 12, 2003, http://hsgac.senate.gov/_files/111203devine.pdf.

[13] *LaChance v. White, Court of Appeals for the Federal Circuit*, 98-3249, http://caselaw.lp.findlaw.com/cgi-bin/getcase.pl?court=fed&navby=case&no=983249.

[14] House Report 103-769, 103d Cong., 2nd Session, 12 (1994), quoted in Fisher, *op. cit.*, p. 31.

[15] For background on executive branch authority, see Kenneth Jost, "Presidential Power," *CQ Researcher*, Feb. 24, 2006, pp. 169-192.

[16] Lancy Gay, "Government withholds 'sensitive-but-unclassified' information," Scripps-Howard News Service, Feb. 2, 2006, www.shns.com/shns/g_index2.cfm?action=detail&pk=UNCLASSIFIED-02-02-06.

[17] Scott Shane, "U.S. Reclassifies Many Documents in Secret Review," *The New York Times*, Feb. 20, 2006, p. A1.

[18] Scott Shane, "Archivist Urges U.S. to Reopen Classified Files," *The New York Times*, March 3, 2006, p. A1.

[19] Erik Eckholm, "Army Contract Official Critical of Halliburton Pact is Demoted," *The New York Times*, Aug. 29, 2005, p. A9.

[20] Tony Pugh, "Medicare Drug Costs Ordered Withheld," *The Miami Herald*, March 12, 2004, p. A1, and Tony Pugh, "Concealing Drug Bill Cost Called Legal," *The Miami Herald*, July 7, 2004, p. C1.

[21] Department of Justice, "Authority of Agency Officials to Prohibit Employees From Providing Information to Congress, Letter Opinion for the General Counsel, Health and Human Services," May 21, 2004, www.usdoj.gov/olc/crsmemoresponsese.htm.

[22] Congressional Research Service memorandum To: Hon. Charles Rangel; From: Jack Maskell, April 26, 2004, www.pogo.org/m/gp/wbr2005/AppendixD.pdf.

[23] Marty Niland, "National Park Service Fires Chambers," The Associated Press, July 9, 2004; Derrill Holly, "Judge Upholds Park Police Chief's Firing," The Associated Press, Oct. 8, 2004.

[24] Department of Justice, *op. cit.*

[25] *American Federation of Government Employees AFL-CIO et al. v. Donald H. Rumsfeld*, Civ. No. 05-2183 (EGS), Memorandum Opinion; see also, Christopher Lee, "Court Blocks DOD's New Rules for Workers," *The Washington Post*, Feb. 28, 2006, p. A1.

[26] Tim Kauffman and Mollie Ziegler, "DoD will proceed with NSPS plan, despite adverse court ruling," *FederalTimes.com*, Feb. 28, 2006, http://federaltimes.com/index.php?S=1565465.

[27] James Risen, *State of War: The Secret History of the CIA and the Bush Administration* (2006).

[28] Porter Goss, "Loose Lips Sink Spies," *The New York Times*, Feb. 10, 2005, p. A25.

[29] David Johnston, "Inquiry Into Wiretapping Article Widens," *The New York Times*, Feb. 12, 2006, p. A26.

[30] *Ibid.*

[31] For background see Charles S. Clark, "Whistleblowers," *CQ Researcher*, Dec. 5, 1997,

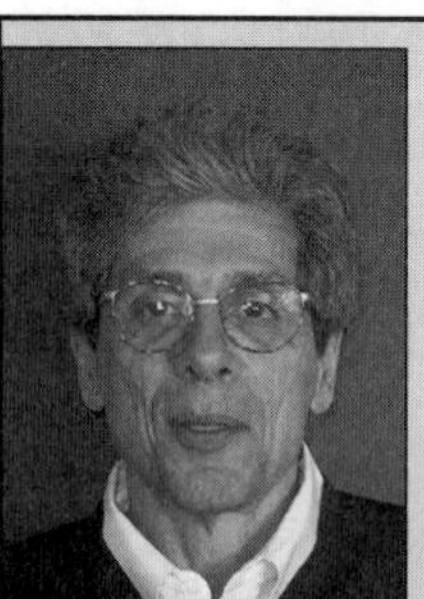

About the Author

Peter Katel is a *CQ Researcher* staff writer who previously reported on Haiti and Latin America for *Time* and *Newsweek* and covered the Southwest for newspapers in New Mexico. He has received several journalism awards, including the Bartolomé Mitre Award for drug coverage from the Inter-American Press Association. He holds an A.B. in university studies from the University of New Mexico. His recent reports include "Immigration Reform" and "Rebuilding New Orleans."

pp. 1059-1078.
[32] Fisher, *op. cit.*, pp. 3-4.
[33] *Ibid.*
[34] Taylor Branch in Charles Peters and Taylor Branch, *Blowing the Whistle: Dissent in the Public Interest* (1972), pp. 3-31.
[35] Ralph Nader, Peter J. Petkas and Kate Blackwell, *Whistle Blowing: The Report of the Conference on Professional Responsibility* (1972), p. 7.
[36] E.W. Kenworthy, "Censure of Dodd is asked in Ethics Panel's Report for 'Dishonor' of Senate," *The New York Times*, April 28, 1967, p. A1; *Congress and the Nation*, Congressional Quarterly, Vol. II, 1965-68, pp. 900-902.
[37] Nader *et al.*, *op. cit.*, pp. 40-41; Molly Moore, "A. Ernest Fitzgerald: Analyst Who Knows the Price of Exposing Cost Overruns," *The Washington Post*, Feb. 23, 1987; Richard Halloran, "U.S. Drops Threat on Disputed Pledge of Secrecy," *The New York Times*, Aug. 22, 1987, p. A8.
[38] Stuart Taylor Jr., "Disclosing Secrets to the Press: U.S. Calls it Espionage," *The New York Times*, Oct. 8, 1984, p. A13.
[39] Information in this section is drawn from Whitaker and Schmerling, *op. cit.*, except where indicated.
[40] *Congress and the Nation*, *op. cit.*, pp. 989-990; *Congress and the Nation*, Vol. IV, 1973-1976, pp. 948-949.
[41] Cited in, Whitaker and Schmerling, *op. cit.*, pp. 2-3.
[42] U.S. Merit Systems Protection Board, "Working for America: An Update," July 1994, pp. vii, 20-21, www.mspb.gov/studies/work2.pdf.
[43] *Congress and the Nation*, Vol. IX, 1993-1996, pp. 820-821.
[44] Ralph Vartabedian, "McDonnell Douglas to Pay $500,000 to Settle Charges on C-17 Program," *Los Angeles Times*, June 25, 1996, p. D1.
[45] Henry Weinstein, "At White House, Red Carpet for Tobacco Whistle-Blowers," *Los Angeles Times*, July 19, 1997, p. D1; Barry Meier, "The Spoils of Tobacco Wars," *The New York Times*, Dec. 22, 1998, p. C1.
[46] *Ibid.* For background, see Kenneth Jost, "High-Impact Litigation," *CQ Researcher*, Feb. 11, 2000, pp. 89-112. Lawyers for anti-tobacco plaintiffs and the industry originally settled on a figure of $246 billion, but Congress refused to authorize that amount.
[47] Richard Leiby, "Smoking Gun," *The Washington Post*, June 23, 1996, p. F1.
[48] Albert B. Crenshaw and Stephen Barr, "IRS Official Reports Double Standard," *The Washington Post*, April 28, 1998, p. A4.
[49] David Johnston, "On Tax Day, IRS Prepared to Fire Star Whistle-Blower," *The New York Times*, April 17, 1999, p. A1.
[50] Richard A. Serrano, "1994 Internal FBI Probe Revealed Only Minor Flaws With Crime Lab," *Los Angeles Times*, March 7, 1997, p. A20.
[51] *Ibid.*
[52] David Johnston, "Report Criticizes Scientific Testing at F.B.I. Crime Lab," *The New York Times*, April 16, 1997, p. A1.
[53] "Justice Dept. to Pay Settlement to FBI Whistle-Blower Whitehurst," The Associated Press, March 12, 1998.
[54] Thomas Newcomb, "In From the Cold: The Intelligence Community Whistleblower Protection Act of 1998," *Administrative Law Review*, fall 2001.
[55] *Ibid.*
[56] *Ibid.*
[57] Frank del Olmo, "Perspective on the CIA; Blow the Whistle, Get Blown Away," *Los Angeles Times*, Dec. 5, 1996, p. B9.
[58] For background see Seymour M. Hersh, "A Reporter At Large: On the Nuclear Edge," *The New Yorker*, March 29, 1993, www.newyorker.com/printables/archive/040119fr_archive02.
[59] James Risen and David Johnston, "Traces of Terror: The Intelligence Reports; Agent Complaints Lead F.B.I. Director to Ask For Inquiry," *The New York Times*, May 24, 2002, p. A1.
[60] Eric Lichtblau, "Bureaucracy is Hobbling the FBI, Rowley Testifies," *The New York Times*, June 7, 2002, p. A1; "3 Whistle-Blowers Get Time Magazine Honors," The Associated Press, Dec. 23, 2002, in *The New York Times*, p. A14.
[61] *Ibid.*, The Associated Press.
[62] National Commission on Terrorist Attacks Upon the United States, *The 9/11 Commission Report* (2004), pp. 201-205.
[63] Judith Miller, "Former Terrorism Official Faults White House on 9/11," *The New York Times*, March 22, 2004, p. A18; Dan Eggen and Walter Pincus, "Ex-Aide Recounts Terror Warnings," *The Washington Post*, March 25, 2004, p. A1.
[64] T. Christian Miller, "Halliburton Contracts Bypassed Objections," *Los Angeles Times*, Oct. 29, 2004, p. A1.
[65] Eckholm, *op. cit.*, p. A9.
[66] "Supreme Court to Rehear Whistleblower Case," The Associated Press, Feb. 17, 2006.
[67] "Brief for the United States as Amicus Curiae Supporting Petitioner," Department of Justice, p. 9.
[68] Background on the case is drawn from briefs for respondent (Ceballos), petitioner (Garcetti) and *amicus curiae* (the United States), all available at www.scotusblog.com/movabletype/archives/2005/10/tomorrows_argum_11.html.
[69] *Ibid.*, p. 44.
[70] For background on Sarbanes-Oxley, see *CQ Almanac Plus*, 2002, 107th Congress, 2nd Session, Vol. LV111," pp. 11-3, 11-4.

FOR MORE INFORMATION

Government Accountability Project, 1612 K St., N.W., Suite 1100, Washington, DC 20006; (202) 408-0034; www.whistleblower.org. Founded 28 years ago to represent whistleblowers, among other watchdog duties.

Merit Systems Protection Board, 1615 M St., N.W., Washington, DC 20419; (202) 653-7200; www.mspb.gov. Quasi-judicial agency hears cases of alleged retaliation against whistleblowers.

National Security Whistleblowers Coalition, PO Box 20210, Alexandria, VA 22320; www.nswbc.org. Aids intelligence and military whistleblowers.

National Whistleblower Center, PO Box 3768, Washington, DC 20007; (202) 342-1902; www.whistleblowers.org. Runs an attorney-referral service, mounts test-case litigation and provides other services.

Office of Special Counsel, 1730 M St., N.W., Washington, DC 20036; (202) 254-3600; www.osc.gov. A federal agency that investigates whistleblower reports and other employee allegations.

Project on Government Oversight, 666 11th St., N.W., Suite 500, Washington DC 20001; (202) 347-1122; www.pogo.org. Investigates alleged government misconduct, works with whistleblowers and advocates on their behalf.

U.S. Court of Appeals for the Federal Circuit, 717 Madison Place, N.W., Washington DC 20439; (202) 633-6550; www.fedcir.gov. Hears federal government whistleblower cases; Web site contains texts of relevant decisions.

Bibliography

Selected Sources

Books

Ellsberg, Daniel, *Secrets: A Memoir of Vietnam and the Pentagon Papers*, Penguin, 2003.
The most famous — or notorious, depending on one's point of view — whistleblower of the Vietnam War-era tells the story of how and why he made the Pentagon Papers public.

Kohn, Stephen M., *Concepts and Procedures in Whistleblower Law*, Quorum, 2000.
A Washington lawyer who specializes in whistleblower litigation lays out the legal and bureaucratic fundamentals of the federal system designed to protect whistleblowers.

Swartz, Mimi, with Sherron Watkins, *Power Failure: The Inside Story of the Collapse of Enron*, Currency, 2004.
Watkins, the corporate whistleblower who sounded the alarm about the imminent collapse of the Houston-based company, was a major source, but not the only one, for Swartz, an editor at muckraking *Texas Monthly*.

Articles

Alonso-Zaldivar, Ricardo, "Bag Scanning System Called Easily Foiled," *Los Angeles Times*, Feb. 28, 2002, p. A11.
The account of major airport security lapses by whistleblower Bogdan Dzakovic of the Federal Aviation Administration was one of the most shocking revelations to emerge from post-9/11 investigations.

Hersh, Seymour, "On the Nuclear Edge," *The New Yorker*, March 29, 1993.
A leading investigative reporter's account of near-nuclear war between India and Pakistan includes the first coverage of the case of CIA and Pentagon whistleblower Richard M. Barlow.

Leiby, Richard, "Smoking Gun: Merrell Williams, ex-actor, is the most important leaker of documents since Daniel Ellsberg," *The Washington Post*, June 23, 1996, p. F1.
A reporter digs into motivations of a law firm paralegal who photocopied and distributed thousands of pages of tobacco industry documents.

Miller, T. Christian, "Halliburton Contracts Bypassed Objections," *Los Angeles Times*, Oct. 29, 2004, p. A1.
A reporter dissects the case of Bunnatine H. Greenhouse, the Army Corps of Engineers contract analyst whose objections to a series of Iraq contracts for a subsidiary of a politically well-connected company led to her demotion.

Pugh, Tony, "Medicare Drug Costs Ordered Withheld," *The Miami Herald*, March 12, 2004, p. A1.
The silencing of a government expert who argued that the Bush administration was low-balling Medicare drug-plan cost estimates was first reported by a Washington reporter for Knight Ridder newspapers.

Rose, David, "An Inconvenient Patriot," *Vanity Fair*, September 2005, p. 264.
FBI translator Sibel Edmonds, who took her whistleblowing against the bureau all the way to the Supreme Court, is profiled at length.

Reports and Studies

"Homeland and National Security Whistleblower Protections: The Unfinished Agenda," Project on Government Oversight, April 2005.
A Washington-based watchdog and advocacy organization argues its case for strengthening career protection for whistleblowers at law-enforcement and intelligence agencies.

"A Review of the FBI's Actions in Connection With Allegations Raised by Contract Linguist Sibel Edmonds," U.S. Department of Justice, Office of the Inspector General, Office of Oversight and Review, Unclassified Summary, January 2005.
The only publicly accessible part of the report of an investigation of whistleblower Edmonds' charges shows how the inspector-general system functioned in this recent, high-profile case.

"U.S. Office of Special Counsel: Strategy for Reducing Persistent Backlog of Cases That Should be Reported to Congress," General Accounting Office (now the Government Accountability Office), March 2004.
Congress' investigative arm opens a window into the workings of one of the agencies empowered to protect whistleblowers. The Office of Special Counsel's reported backlog has since been reduced, but the report was a key factor in the continuing debate over how whistleblowers fare at the agency.

Fisher, Louis, "National Security Whistleblowers," Congressional Research Service, Dec. 30, 2005.
The former senior specialist in separation of powers analyzes in detail, but in layman's language, the law and legislative history concerning whistleblowers from the spy establishment. Fisher is now at the Library of Congress' Law Library.

Whitaker, L. Paige, and Michael Schmerling, "Whistleblower Protections for Federal Employees," Congressional Research Service, May 18, 1998.
Two analysts examine the system set up to protect federal whistleblowers.

The Next Step:

Additional Articles from Current Periodicals

Federal Government and Whistleblowers

Kaufman, Marc, "Attempt to Discredit Whistle-Blower Alleged," *The Washington Post*, Nov. 24, 2004, p. A19.

Food and Drug Administration officials allegedly tried to anonymously smear an agency safety officer who challenged the FDA's drug safety policies.

Pear, Robert, "Congress Moves to Protect Federal Whistle-blowers," *The New York Times*, Oct. 3, 2004, p. 29.

Both parties want to protect federal employees who expose government wrongdoing, but the administration says it interferes with the president's authority.

Iraq/Counterterrorism

Eckholm, Erik, "Army Demotes Halliburton Contract Critic," *Chicago Tribune*, Aug. 29, 2005, p. 4.

A top Army contracting official, Bunnatine Greenhouse, was demoted after criticizing a large, non-competitive contract with Halliburton Co. for work in Iraq.

Hastings, Deborah, "Suit Accuses Contractor of Bilking Millions in Iraq," *The Houston Chronicle*, May 1, 2005, p. A25.

Two former employees of Custer Battles, a private security firm that has won millions of dollars in contracts for work in Iraq, allege the company defrauded the government.

Lichtblau, Eric, "Justice Review Backs FBI Whistle-Blower's Claims on Terror Case," *The Houston Chronicle*, Dec. 4, 2005, p. A14.

Undercover operative Mike German accused the FBI of retaliating against him after he revealed how bureau officials mishandled a Florida terror investigation.

Meyer, Josh, "CIA Official Challenges Agency on Terrorism," *Los Angeles Times*, Nov. 9, 2004, p. A16.

Senior CIA counterterrorism official Michael Scheuer refuses to stop publicly criticizing the agency's response to the al Qaeda terrorist network, arguing that uncorrected management problems since Sept. 11 continue to put the U.S. at risk.

White, Josh, and Scott Higham, "Soldier: Military Intelligence Behind Abuse," *The Miami Herald*, May 20, 2004, p. A25.

Sgt. Samuel Provance, the first military-intelligence service-member to speak openly about abuses at Abu Ghraib prison, says military-intelligence officials directed the interrogation techniques in question.

National Security

Fisher, William, "Corruption-U.S.: With the Feds, No Good Deed Goes Unpunished," IPS-Inter Press Service, Feb. 20, 2006.

Five former employees of the FBI, National Security Agency, Defense Department and Energy Department told a House committee how national-security whistleblowers have little legal protection against retaliation.

Hentoff, Nat, "The FBI Retroactively Classified Information About Edmonds' Claims Provided to Congressional Staff," *Chicago Sun-Times*, July 29, 2004, p. 43.

Sens. Patrick Leahy, D-Vt., and Charles Grassley, R-Iowa, are investigating documents that the government reclassified after FBI translator Sibel Edmonds blew the whistle on translation problems within the agency before Sept. 11.

Marks, Alexandra, "National Security vs. Whistle-Blowing," *The Christian Science Monitor*, Jan. 24, 2006, p. 2.

Government employees who uncover potentially illegal actions at work are having problems blowing the whistle and proving their case because the Bush administration has increased the amount of government material that is classified.

Shane, Scott, "Bipartisan Support Emerges For Federal Whistle-Blowers," *The New York Times*, Feb. 17, 2006, p. A17.

Some congressional Republicans are joining Democrats in supporting government employees who say they were punished for disclosing sensitive information on reported abuses.

Chaddock, Gail Russell, "A Surge in Whistle-Blowing . . . and Reprisals," *The Christian Science Monitor*, Feb. 16, 2006, p. 1.

Since Sept. 11, the number of government insiders alleging wrongdoing in government has surged and so has government retaliation against the whistleblowers.

CITING THE *CQ RESEARCHER*

Sample formats for citing these reports in a bibliography include the ones listed below. Preferred styles and formats vary, so please check with your instructor or professor.

MLA STYLE

Jost, Kenneth. "Rethinking the Death Penalty." CQ Researcher 16 Nov. 2001: 945-68.

APA STYLE

Jost, K. (2001, November 16). Rethinking the death penalty. *CQ Researcher, 11*, 945-968.

CHICAGO STYLE

Jost, Kenneth. "Rethinking the Death Penalty." *CQ Researcher*, November 16, 2001, 945-968.

CQ Researcher

Published by CQ Press, a division of Congressional Quarterly Inc.

thecqresearcher.com

Rising Health Costs

Can costs be cut without hurting care quality?

Medical costs have more than doubled over the last decade, and health insurance premiums have risen nearly five times faster than wages. Americans are spending far more on health care than residents of any other industrialized country while receiving lower-quality care overall. Meanwhile, big U.S. businesses that provide health coverage to workers complain that the high costs are crippling their ability to compete with companies abroad whose workers get government-subsidized care. The Bush administration is encouraging consumers to switch to consumer-directed health plans, whose high copayments would force them to shop for more cost-effective care. But critics argue that individuals can do little to control costs. Instead, they argue, the plans would primarily benefit the wealthy and that society must make hard choices about which care should be paid for by public and private dollars.

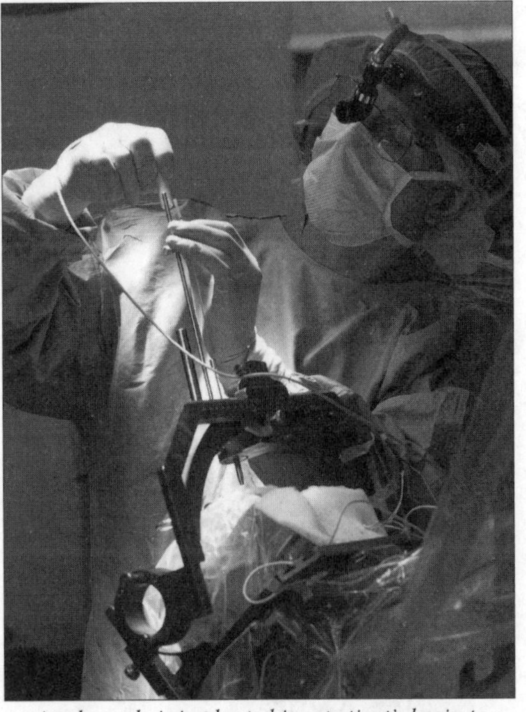

An electrode is implanted in a patient's brain to reduce the symptoms of Parkinson's disease. The development of such high-tech procedures contributes to rising health costs.

INSIDE THIS REPORT

CQ Researcher • April 7, 2006 • www.cqresearcher.com
Volume 16, Number 13 • Pages 289-312

CQ PRESS

RECIPIENT OF SOCIETY OF PROFESSIONAL JOURNALISTS AWARD FOR EXCELLENCE ◆ AMERICAN BAR ASSOCIATION SILVER GAVEL AWARD

THE ISSUES

BACKGROUND

CURRENT SITUATION

OUTLOOK

SIDEBARS AND GRAPHICS

FOR FURTHER RESEARCH

Cover: To reduce the symptoms of Parkinson's disease, an electrode is implanted in the brain of a patient at the Robert Wood Johnson University Hospital, in New Brunswick, N.J. Such high-tech procedures contribute to rising health costs along with better care. (AP Photo/Brian Branch-Price)

CQ Researcher

April 7, 2006
Volume 16, Number 13

MANAGING EDITOR: Thomas J. Colin

ASSISTANT MANAGING EDITOR: Kathy Koch

ASSOCIATE EDITOR: Kenneth Jost

STAFF WRITERS: Marcia Clemmitt, Peter Katel, Pamela M. Prah

CONTRIBUTING WRITERS: Rachel Cox, Sarah Glazer, David Hosansky, Patrick Marshall, Tom Price

DESIGN/PRODUCTION EDITOR: Olu B. Davis

ASSISTANT EDITOR: Melissa J. Hipolit

CQ PRESS

A Division of Congressional Quarterly Inc.

SENIOR VICE PRESIDENT/PUBLISHER: John A. Jenkins

DIRECTOR, LIBRARY PUBLISHING: Kathryn C. Suárez

DIRECTOR, EDITORIAL OPERATIONS: Ann Davies

CONGRESSIONAL QUARTERLY INC.

CHAIRMAN: Paul C. Tash

VICE CHAIRMAN: Andrew P. Corty

PRESIDENT/EDITOR IN CHIEF: Robert W. Merry

CQ Researcher (ISSN 1056-2036) is printed on acid-free paper. Published weekly, except March 24, July 7, July 14, Aug. 4, Aug. 11, Nov. 24, Dec. 22 and Dec. 29, by CQ Press, a division of Congressional Quarterly Inc. Annual full-service subscriptions for institutions start at $667. For pricing, call 1-800-834-9020, ext. 1906. To purchase a *CQ Researcher* report in print or electronic format (PDF), visit www.cqpress.com or call 866-427-7737. Single reports start at $10. Bulk purchase discounts and electronic-rights licensing are also available. Periodicals postage paid at Washington, D.C., and additional mailing offices. POSTMASTER: Send address changes to *CQ Researcher*, 1255 22nd St., N.W., Suite 400, Washington, DC 20037.

Rising Health Costs

By Marcia Clemmitt

The Issues

Zoila Garcia, who works the 10 p.m. to 6 a.m. shift as a janitor at the University of Miami, recently developed a blood clot in her calf that needs surgery. But her job doesn't offer health insurance, and she can't afford the $4,000 procedure.

"Where do you get that money?" making only $6.70 an hour, she asks. [1]

Other Americans are in similar predicaments. Jeannie Brewer's job as a contract physician at the Alta Bates-Summit Medical Center in Oakland, Calif., doesn't provide health insurance either. So Brewer — who has suffered from depression, multiple sclerosis and back problems and has two diabetic daughters — has been paying $15,000 to $20,000 a year in medical bills out of her own pocket in recent years. Finally, in June 2005, she filed for personal bankruptcy, "after having liquidated every single asset I ever had." [2]

Economists estimate more than $2 trillion will be spent in the United States on medical care this year — about $6,830 per person — which amounts to 16 percent of the nation's gross domestic product (GDP). [3] That's far more than any other industrialized country: In 2002, the most recent year for which international comparisons are available, Americans spent an average of $5,267 per person on health care, compared to $3,446 in Switzerland and $3,093 in Norway, the next biggest per-capita spenders. [4]

Furthermore, U.S. government actuaries predict that U.S. health spending will double by 2015 — to more than $12,300 per person — and account for 20 percent of the nation's GDP. [5]

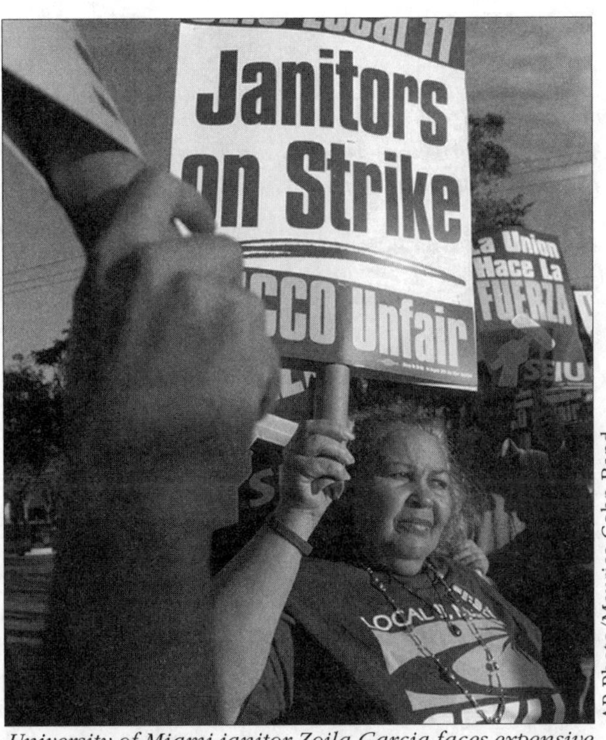

AP Photo/Maurice Cohn Band

University of Miami janitor Zoila Garcia faces expensive surgery for a blood clot in her leg but has no insurance and can't afford the $4,000 operation. Rising costs have made health care too expensive for tens of millions of Americans, including many with health coverage. In the last five years, insurance premiums jumped 73 percent, but wages rose only 15 percent.

Relentlessly rising U.S. health-care costs have made health insurance too expensive for many employers to offer and health care itself too costly for tens of millions of Americans, from the 46 million who are uninsured to low- and middle-income workers with insurance. In the last five years, insurance premiums jumped 73 percent, but wages rose only 15 percent, according to Drew Altman, president of the nonprofit Kaiser Family Foundation, which tracks health-care issues. During the same period, workers' annual payroll deductions for health insurance went up $1,100, on average. [6] Health coverage alone "is eating up about a quarter of the increase in workers' earnings," Altman said. [7] Moreover, says Katherine Baicker, an associate professor of public policy at the University of California, Los Angeles, and a member of President Bush's Council of Economic Advisors, much of the apparent stagnation in wage growth can be attributed to the fact that a greater percentage of workers' compensation is now provided through health-care benefits instead of higher wages.

"Most employees don't realize how much their employer is actually spending to provide them with health care," says Baicker. A family health-insurance policy now costs nearly $11,000 a year — more than a full-time, minimum-wage worker earns. [8]

With such high costs, it's not surprising that fewer employers — especially small companies — are offering health insurance, said Altman. In the last five years, 266,000 companies have stopped offering it. As a result, only 60 percent of Americans receive health insurance through their employers today, down from 69 percent in 2000. And the trend "is mostly affecting lower-wage workers, who are the folks who really take it on the chin," said Altman.

Public-sector employers are under even more pressure, often caught between the "rock" of expensive health insurance and the "hard place" of budget cutbacks. Health-insurance costs have risen to a level where they are "seriously impacting school resources," Paul Burrow, an Iowa public school teacher who chairs the State Employees Benefits Association Board, told the Senate Health Appropriations Subcommittee. For example, teachers in Oskaloosa last year effectively took no increase in salary to enable the district to pay for a 19-percent increase in premiums, he added, and in at least two Iowa districts the cost of family coverage "already equals the salary of a beginning teacher." [9]

Health Costs to Top $4 Trillion

Health spending is expected to rise to more than $4 trillion by 2015 (top graph), or one-fifth of the nation's projected $20 trillion gross domestic product (middle). At the same time, health expenditures are projected to rise to more than $12,000 per person (bottom).

U.S. Health Expenditures
(1993-2015)

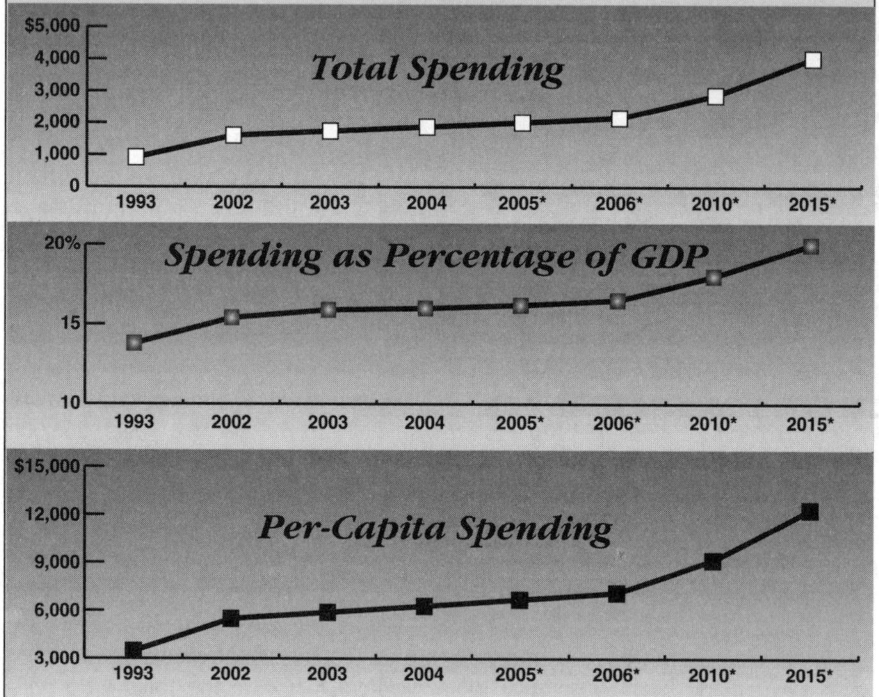

* *Projected*

Source: Christine Borger, et al., *"Health Spending Projections Through 2015: Changes On The Horizon,"* Health Affairs, *published online Feb. 22, 2006.*

The number of Americans without health insurance — mostly lower-wage workers — has steadily risen over the past 30 years, according to a study by two professors at the University of California, San Diego. [10] They attribute the phenomenon almost entirely to the fact that per-capita health-care spending has increased far more rapidly than income. At the current rate of growth, they predict, the number of uninsured Americans will reach 56 million by 2013, or 27.8 percent of the working-age population. [11] High health-care costs discourage the uninsured from getting needed treatment. A 2003 national survey found that 82 percent of insured people suffering from one of 15 serious symptoms had talked to a health professional about their symptoms, but only 37 percent of the uninsured with similar symptoms consulted a health professional. [12]

Rising costs also affect public hospitals, community-health and mental-health clinics and Medicaid — which covers poor children, their mothers and the disabled. As a result such tax-supported health programs gobble up ever-bigger bites from state budgets, says former Oregon Gov. John Kitzhaber, an emergency physician and organizer of the Archimedes Project, a campaign to encourage states to undertake large-scale health reform.

"Since 2003, Medicaid has exceeded the cost of primary and secondary education as the largest item in many state budgets," says Kitzhaber. Out-of-control health costs are "undermining our ability to invest in our public school system, which offers the best opportunity of success" for American children.

Worse, the nation's highest-in-the-world health spending isn't necessarily buying the highest-quality health care. (*See chart, p. 293.*) While new drugs and medical technology have improved longevity and quality of life for many Americans, the United States is ranked 37th by the World Health Organization (WHO) in providing overall quality care, based on adult and infant mortality rates, says economist Len Nichols, director of the health-policy program at the progressive New America Foundation think tank. The United States also ranks 24th among industrialized nations in life expectancy.

Other recent studies have also shown that high spending does not necessarily ensure high-quality care. For instance, in states where the spending is highest for Medicare — the federally subsidized health insurance program for the elderly and disabled — the quality of care is lower than in states that spend less, according to a study at Dartmouth College. [13] (*See graph, p. 302.*)

Many economists say America spends more than any other country on health care because, unlike all other industrialized countries, it does not provide universal health-care insurance. Countries that ensure all citizens a basic level of health care end up spending less because they have a strong motivation to hold costs down by limiting which treatments are subsidized and/or aggressively negotiating lower prices.

In Switzerland, for example, every resident is required to buy private health insurance, with the government picking up part of the tab for lower-income residents. But because of the substantial subsidies and the commitment to insure everyone, Swiss cantons — similar to U.S. states — strictly control insurers' price negotiations. [14] The Swiss end up spending about two-thirds as much as Americans on health, while covering the entire population. [15]

Besides spending more overall, Americans pay the highest health-care prices, according to Gerard Anderson, a professor of health policy and management at Johns Hopkins University. For example, in 2002 the average cost for a day in a U.S. hospital was $2,434, compared to $870 in Canada. [16]

Efforts to control costs have had limited, temporary success. In the mid-1990s, for example, managed-care insurance plans successfully pressured doctors and hospitals to lower prices and limit some services, but after a public backlash spending began to rise again.

The Bush administration has suggested controlling health costs by encouraging the establishment of so-called consumer-directed health plans (CDHPs) — insurance coverage that requires individuals to pay larger-than-normal portions of their health-care costs out of pocket.

Spending more of their own money on health care — rather than relying on comprehensive insurance coverage — will motivate patients "to find out more about what health care costs and what they're getting for their money," said Gail Wilensky, a senior fellow at the nonprofit research organization Project HOPE. [17]

But economists say eventually the United States will have to take much tougher action. "The situation has become genuinely nasty," according to Henry Aaron, an economist at the liberal/centrist Brookings Institution. "Costs are rising fast, just as budgets, public and private, are tightening." [18] One option is to follow other industrialized nations in limiting what kind of care is provided, such as paying only for

U.S. Spends More, Gets Less Health Coverage

The United States spends far more for health care than 29 other countries but has fewer doctors per 1,000 population than most of them. The U.S. ranks last in the percentage of its population that is eligible for government-mandated hospitalization insurance.

Spending on Health Care by the U.S. and Other Industrialized Countries, 2002

Country	Per-capita ($U.S.*)	Percent of GDP	Doctors per 1,000 population	% of Population eligible for mandated hospitalization insurance#
Australia**	$2,504	9.1%	2.5	100.0%
Austria	2,220	7.7	3.3	99.0
Belgium	2,515	9.1	3.9	99.0
Canada	2,931	9.6	2.1	100.0
Czech Republic	1,118	7.4	3.5	100.0
Denmark	2,583	8.8	3.3	100.0
Finland	1,943	7.3	3.1	100.0
France	2,736	9.7	3.3	99.5
Germany	2,817	10.9	3.3	92.2
Greece	1,814	9.5	4.5**	100.0
Hungary	1,079	7.8	3.2	99.0
Iceland	2,807	9.9	3.6	100.0
Ireland	2,367	7.3	2.4	100.0
Italy	2,166	8.5	4.4	100.0
Japan**	2,077	7.8	2.0	100.0
South Korea	996	5.1	1.5	100.0
Luxembourg	3,065	6.2	2.6	100.0
Mexico	553	6.1	1.5	68.5
Netherlands	2,643	9.1	3.1	74.1
New Zealand	1,857	8.5	2.1	100.0
Norway	3,083	9.6	3.0**	100.0
Poland	654	6.1	2.3	na
Portugal	1,702	9.3	3.2**	100.0
Slovak Republic	698	5.7	3.6	na
Spain	1,646	7.6	2.9	99.3
Sweden	2,517	9.2	3.0	100.0
Switzerland	3,446	11.2	3.6	99.5
Turkey	446+	6.6+	1.3	55.1++
United Kingdom	2,160	7.7	2.1	100.0
United States	**5,267**	**14.6**	**2.4****	**46.0**

** Represents purchasing power parity.*
*** 2001*
+ 2000
++ 1990
 # Based on data available as of 1997
Source: Organization for Economic Cooperation and Development, 2004

Slicing the Big Pie

Taxes fund nearly half of all U.S. health spending (left graph). Hospitals get the biggest share of health-care dollars while drugs get only 12 percent (right graph).

Projected 2006 Health-Care Spending

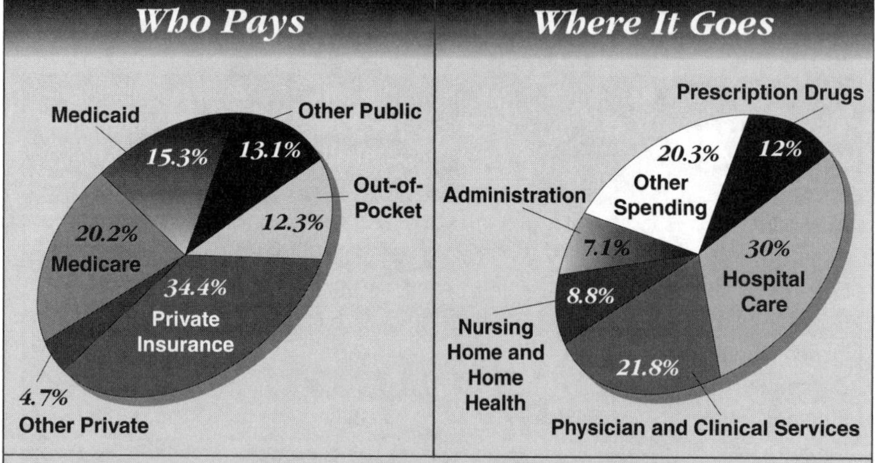

Source: Centers for Medicare and Medicaid Services

cost-effective treatments, he says, acknowledging that "rationing" would be unpopular and hard to introduce to the decentralized U.S. system.

"If we do not ration, we are going to be spending a very great deal of money on health-care services, an increasing, absolute amount of which is not going to be worth what it costs society to provide," Aaron says.

As economists, lawmakers and consumers wrestle with rising costs, here are some of the major questions being debated:

Will cutting costs harm Americans' health?

Much of the higher health spending in the past few decades has gone toward new drugs, surgical techniques and high-tech diagnostic devices, many of which have helped people live longer, healthier lives. And emphasizing cost control could jeopardize progress in the search for new cures, say some economists. But others argue that European nations — and many lower-spending U.S. states — score as high or higher than high-spending U.S. regions on many health measures, indicating that health can be improved while cutting spending.

Opponents of cost controls, like Duke University economist Henry Grabowski, note that American pharmaceutical companies now lead the world in introducing important new drugs, thanks largely to high drug prices. Between 1993 and 2003, he points out, U.S. companies introduced 48 percent of the world's innovative drugs, 52 percent of all biotech drugs and 55 percent of all "orphan" drugs that treat rare diseases.

That success depends on continued strong financing, says Grabowski, who conducted a study partially funded by drugmaker AstraZeneca. For example, development of new drugs would drop off if Congress imposed price controls on Medicare's new prescription-drug benefit, he says.

Likewise, medical-technology discoveries have been a major driver of higher costs, but imposing cost controls on technology could impede medical innovation, according to a landmark 2001 study by Harvard economist David Cutler and physician Mark McClellan, a former Stanford economist who now heads the Medicare and Medicaid programs. They analyzed spending growth between the 1950s and 1999 and improvements in longevity and quality of life for five medical conditions and found that higher spending had bought health improvements that far exceeded the cost for heart attacks, low-birth weight babies, depression and cataracts. For breast cancer, however, the benefits were roughly equivalent to the higher costs. They concluded that the quality-adjusted price of medical care is actually falling — not rising. [19]

Meanwhile, cost controls have made health care less accessible for Europeans and Canadians, according to George Halvorson, CEO of Kaiser Permanente, a nationwide health-care delivery organization, and George Isham, medical director of HealthPartners, a Minnesota-based health maintenance organization (HMO). "In most countries with government-run health systems, a great many specialized services are in very short supply . . . because the government doesn't have the money for more," they argued. [20]

For example, the average British patient had to wait more than 29 weeks to get elective surgery in 2000, according to Halvorson and Isham. "This 'rationing' keeps British costs at about half of U.S. costs," they concluded, but the British system "isn't anywhere near as responsive to patient needs."

However, some physicians say, Americans often pay for services that are not health- or life-enhancing. "My mother is 88 and very frail," said physician and former Gov. Kitzhaber. After a physical exam showed signs of a possible tumor, the normal procedure would have involved an endoscopy, a colonoscopy and "a whole lot of things that she had no desire to have done," he said. The

Continued on p. 296

Elderly Won't Cause Health-Cost Tsunami

In coming decades, the elderly in the United States and other industrialized nations not only will be older than today's seniors, but there will be more of them. While that certainly will mean higher health spending, many economists say the biggest growth in health-care costs will be caused by new technologies, not the growing elderly population.

In fact, the United States won't experience the same huge senior demographic wave as many other countries for nearly 20 years, said Johns Hopkins University economist Gerard Anderson. For example, in 2000, the over-65 crowd comprised only 12.5 percent of the U.S. population, compared to 17.1 percent in Japan and 15.2 percent in Germany. The American over-65 population is not projected to hit 16.6 percent until 2020. [1]

After analyzing two decades of national spending data, Brandeis University economists concluded that 72 percent of future health-spending growth will be caused by expensive new technology and higher prices. Only 18 percent of the higher spending will be due to population growth and only 10 percent to an aging population. [2]

Getty Images/Joe Raedle

The aging of the nation's population will account for only 10 percent of future health-care spending increases, according to Brandeis economists.

As Princeton University economist Uwe Reinhardt described it, the economic impact of the additional elderly on health-care costs "isn't a tsunami, but a little ripple." Evidence for that conclusion comes from countries like Germany and France, whose demographics already mirror what the United States will look like in two decades, Reinhardt said. [3]

Aging has had less impact than many expected because health-care costs, while highest in the last year of life, aren't the same for every patient, said Harvard University economist David Cutler. As lifespans lengthen and death rates decline, a smaller share of the elderly will be in their expensive last year at any given time, he explained. In addition, more people will die in their 80s or 90s, rather than earlier, and studies show that end-of-life costs generally decline for very old people, in part because their families and doctors make different choices about their care. [4]

Cost pressures due to aging are expected to ease over time for two reasons, according to economists at the Organization for Economic Cooperation and Development (OECD), a group of 30 industrialized democracies, including the United States. First, increases in longevity "are assumed to translate into additional years of good health," which should help hold down medical cost increases. Second, because medical costs are highest in the last months of life, increased longevity will cut costs for every age cohort of the elderly. As people live longer, more and more individuals will " 'exit' an age group by moving into an older group" rather than " 'exit' by dying," thus lowering the group's average costs. [5]

Medicare data demonstrate the lower cost of end-of-life care for much older people, according to the late Norman Levinsky, a professor of medicine at Boston University Medical School. In a study of 1996 Medicare spending for patients in their last year of life, Levinsky and his colleagues calculated per-patient costs averaged $35,300 in Massachusetts and $27,800 in California for patients 65 to 74. But costs dropped to $22,000 in Massachusetts and $21,600 in California for dying patients 85 or older. [6]

However, future generations could throw a monkey wrench into this benign scenario if they turn out to be less healthy than anticipated, according to Dana Goldman, director of health economics at the RAND Corporation, a Santa Monica, Calif., research organization. "The past few decades have witnessed alarming increases in obesity and diabetes among the young," and "disability rates for the young have risen within all demographic and economic groups," Goldman said. That could mean future cohorts of the elderly would be more costly to treat. [7]

But while the aging population may not substantially drive up health costs overall in the United States, it could still alter the health-care payment landscape dramatically, moving more and more private-sector spending into the public Medicare and Medicaid programs, according to Cutler.

Meanwhile, under current laws, the general tax revenues that help fund Medicare will grow to only 3.8 percent of GDP by 2050. Thus, to meet costs, Medicare spending would have to be cut by more than half from its projected level. "No one has a way to do that," Cutler said. [8]

---

[1] Gerard F. Anderson and Peter Scott Hussey, "Population Aging: A Comparison Among Industrialized Countries," *Health Affairs*, May/June 2000.

[2] Quoted in "Hospital Forum Airs Predictions on Health-Care Future," *Medicine & Health Perspectives*, May 5, 2003.

[3] Quoted in *ibid.*

[4] David M. Cutler, "The Potential for Cost Savings in Medicare's Future," *Health Affairs* Web site, Sept. 26, 2005; www.healthaffairs.org.

[5] "Projecting OECD Health and Long-Term Care Expenditures: What Are the Main Drivers?" Organization for Economic Cooperation and Development, Economics Department Working Paper No. 477, www.oecd.org/eco, February 2006.

[6] Norman G. Levinsky, *et al.*, "Influence of Age on Medicare Expenditures and Medical Care in the Last Year of Life," *Journal of the American Medical Association*, Sept. 19, 2001, p. 1349.

[7] Dana P. Goldman *et al.*, "Consequences of Health Trends and Medical Innovation for the Future Elderly," *Health Affairs* Web site, Sept. 25, 2005; www.healthaffairs.org.

[8] Cutler, *op. cit.*

Health Insurance Premiums Fluctuated

Annual growth in the cost of health-insurance premiums fluctuated dramatically over the last two decades, dipping precipitously in the early 1990s after Congress began discussing universal health insurance. At the same time, inflation and earnings remained relatively flat. In the mid-1990s, a backlash against managed-care restrictions designed to cut costs caused premium growth rates to rise again. Although the rate of premium growth turned downward in 2003, experts doubt it will drop to 1996 levels.

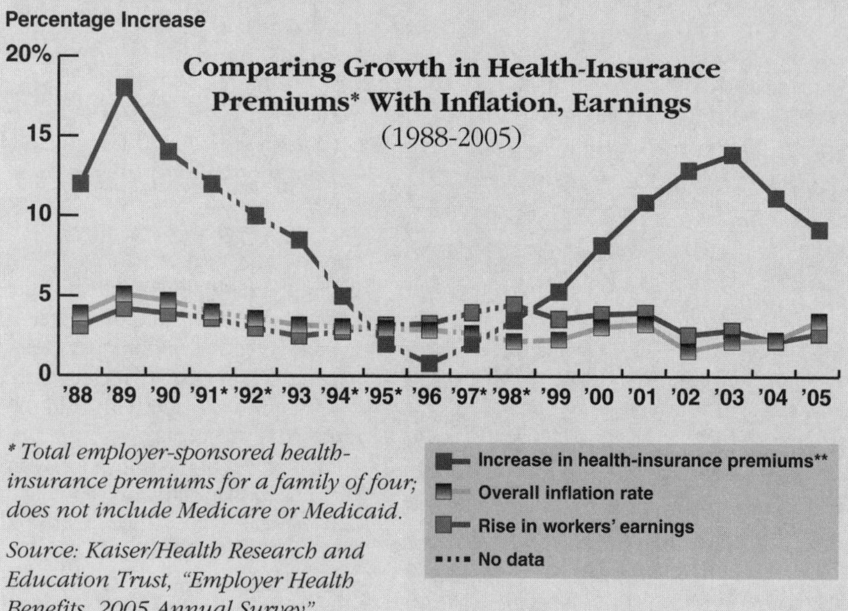

** Total employer-sponsored health-insurance premiums for a family of four; does not include Medicare or Medicaid.*

Source: Kaiser/Health Research and Education Trust, "Employer Health Benefits, 2005 Annual Survey"

Continued from p. 294

doctor recommended re-checking her blood work in a few weeks to see how she was doing, but Kitzhaber asked him, "Why continue to check the blood work on an 88-year-old woman who has decided she doesn't want a bunch of treatment? You're not going to change the outcome." [21]

Evidence clearly shows that much of today's higher health-care spending does not improve health and may even harm it, according to Dartmouth Medical School Professor of Medicine Elliott Fisher. Medicare spending varies widely across the United States, and an extensive analysis shows that "higher spending is associated with lower quality, worse access to care and no gain in satisfaction," he said. In fact, higher spending "is associated with a small increase in the risk of death." [22]

According to a Medicare study at Dartmouth, patients in high-spending states showed no significant difference on nine out of 26 quality measures and, in fact, did worse on 15. Those in higher-spending states, for instance, were less likely to obtain mammograms at recommended intervals, annual eye exams for diabetics and beta-blocking drugs after heart attacks. The researchers hypothesize that in lower-spending areas a patient is more likely to depend on a single general practitioner who ensures that cost-effective, preventive procedures are prescribed. In high-spending areas, on the other hand, patients visit specialists more than twice as often as in lower-spending areas, but specialists are more expensive and don't usually coordinate overall care.

According to some economists, using cost controls to reverse the American trend of favoring specialty care over primary care — provided by internists, general practitioners and pediatricians — could reap huge cost savings while promoting better health. The U.S. physician mix consists of about one-third generalists and two-thirds specialists, unlike countries such as Australia and Canada, where generalists make up about half of all doctors. [23]

An American is three times more likely to see a specialist than a British patient. [24] And U.S. specialists earn more than generalists. The median annual income for anesthesiologists, for example, was $321,686 in 2004, compared to $156,010 for family-practice doctors. [25] U.S. specialists also earn more than their counterparts abroad.

However, studies show that having more specialists in a region does not improve care. Adding one additional primary-care physician per 10,000 population produces a 6 percent drop in mortality from all causes and a 3 percent drop in infant mortality, according to Barbara Starfield, a professor of health policy at the Johns Hopkins Bloomberg School of Public Health. But having an above-average number of neonatologists — infant specialists — does not decrease the infant death rate in a region, she says, nor does having more specialists increase the number of people whose cancer is diagnosed at earlier, more treatable stages. [26]

Deciding what care to pay for based on evidence of what works could substantially cut costs without harming health, argues Karen Davis, president of the Commonwealth Fund, which supports international research on health care and insurance. [27] Many studies now demonstrate techniques that preserve care quality while lowering costs, she said, such as having advanced-practice nurses visit frail, elderly patients. They could detect serious conditions early, cutting those patients' annual health costs by 36 percent. In another study a hospital decreased average maternity costs from $1,622 to $1,480 per person by encouraging obstetricians not to induce labor until at least the 39th week of pregnancy. [28]

Davis challenged the "typical assumption" that other countries are "rationing effective care" and "have long waiting lists." While U.S. patients do wait shorter times for surgery, she pointed out, sick Americans wait longer to see a doctor than patients in other countries, and more Americans rely on emergency rooms for primary care.

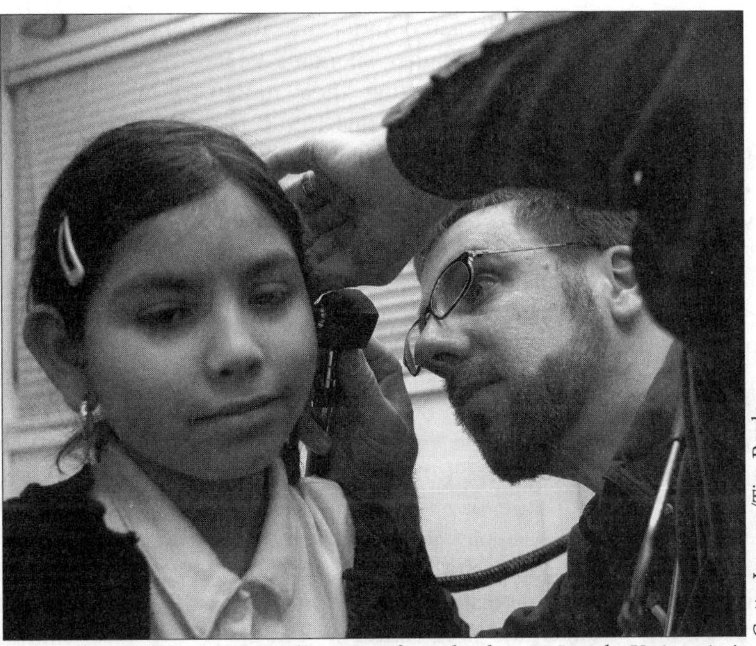

Getty Images/Tim Boyle

A fourth-grader in Cicero, Ill., gets a free checkup at Loyola University's Pediatric Mobile Health Unit, which serves needy children in the Midwest. Some economists say using fewer specialists and more primary-care doctors — such as internists and pediatricians — could save money while promoting better health.

Would health care be cheaper if everyone were insured?

As the cost of health care becomes further and further out of reach for uninsured Americans, U.S. lawmakers face policy and ethical dilemmas. [29] On one hand, it would cost a whopping $48 billion a year, according to one estimate, to extend health-insurance coverage to the nation's 46 million uninsured. [30] But some economists argue that much of those costs would be offset by other economic gains and that covering only a small number of the uninsured — such as more mothers with young children — could cost even more than universal coverage.

If all uninsured Americans had health coverage, the average annual cost of the care they receive now would rise by 39 percent — from $2,034 per person to $2,836 — or $802 per person, according to Jack Hadley and John Holahan, economists at the liberal-leaning Urban Institute. [31]

"From a purely selfish economic perspective . . . leaving the uninsured in their current predicament turns out to be cheaper than stepping up to underwrite with added taxes a move to universal coverage," said Princeton University Professor of economics Uwe Reinhardt.

While Congress wants to take small steps to help at least some people get more coverage — such as enabling small businesses to pool administrative costs to save money on insurance — Senate Majority Leader Bill Frist, R-Tenn., a cardiologist, said it would be "impossible to get to 100 percent" coverage. His own home state of Tennessee has been "going bankrupt" trying to achieve universal coverage, he said. [32]

Furthermore, offering everyone the same level of comprehensive health insurance enjoyed by most Americans would increase demand for services — and thus overall spending — because insurance itself drives up costs, says Brookings' Aaron. "By shielding patients from all or most of the cost of care, insurance encourages patients to demand all care, however small the benefit and however high the cost of producing it." [33]

Nevertheless, Hadley and Holahan argue, covering everyone could be cheaper than covering only a few, small additional groups, because if everyone were covered, programs that specifically fund uninsured care could be dismantled and tens of billions of dollars redirected to subsidizing universal coverage. [34]

Currently, uninsured patients receive about $125 billion worth of care annually and pay only about 26 percent of the cost. Public and private programs that serve the uninsured — such as community health centers and special payments to hospitals serving large numbers of the uninsured — pick up some of the tab while hospitals provide the rest, passing some of the costs on to other patients. [35]

Moreover, an expert government panel has estimated that covering the uninsured would create $65 billion to $130 billion worth of improved health and productivity annually, more than enough to make the cost of coverage worthwhile. [36]

The uninsured often foster ineffective, excessive spending because they wait until their health condition reaches a critical stage and end up in the emergency room — instead of getting more cost-effective preventive care in a physician's office, said Kitzhaber. He related the penny-wise-but-pound-foolish case of Douglas Schmidt, an Oregon man who suffered from a seizure disorder. In February 2003, to balance the budget in a recession, the Oregon legislature discontinued prescription-drug coverage for the medically needy, he said. Without his anti-seizure medication, Schmidt went into a sustained grand mal seizure, suffered serious brain damage and ended up on a ventilator in intensive care for months. Schmidt died in November 2003 after life support was withdrawn.

Schmidt's anti-seizure medication would have cost $14 a day, Kitzhaber said, while his intensive care cost $7,500 a day — more than $1.1 million — "all of which was simply billed back to the state." [37]

Every country with universal coverage spends less on health care than the United States because their governments have an incentive to hold down costs, say some economists. They do that by paying only for treatments shown to be effective and negotiating price cuts from suppliers and health providers.

"Countries with national health systems . . . often [have] historically low levels of spending," said Julian Le Grand, a professor of social policy at the London School of Economics. The United Kingdom, for instance, spends about half as much of its GDP on health care as the United States. (*See chart, p. 293.*) [38]

Does the U.S. health-care industry charge too much?

Some economists say U.S. health spending is the highest in the world because the American health-care industry charges higher prices for the same services and enjoys larger profits than its counterparts in other countries. Moreover, those higher prices and profits do not necessarily buy more or better-quality health care, they argue.

Opponents of that view contend that higher U.S. profits often underwrite necessary but underfunded services — such as uninsured care and research and development — and that income disparity between U.S. jobs in general is much wider than in other countries.

Johns Hopkins' Anderson says that despite their higher spending Americans are not getting their money's worth. Studies show that U.S. patients get less health care than residents of many other industrialized countries, he said, citing statistics showing that in 2000 the United States had fewer physicians per 1,000 people; fewer doctor visits per capita and fewer hospital admissions per 1,000 people than the median for industrialized countries belonging to the 30-member Organization for Economic Cooperation and Development (OECD).

In an earlier study Americans were found to pay 40 percent more per capita than the Germans for four diseases — diabetes, gall stones, breast cancer and lung cancer — but got 15 percent fewer services. Many OECD countries also have more high-tech imaging devices — such as MRIs (magnetic resonance imaging) and CT (computerized tomography) scanners — per capita than the United States. Less care but higher overall costs means U.S. prices are significantly higher, Anderson explains. [39]

For example, U.S. physicians' incomes are much higher, according to an analysis by Princeton's Reinhardt. In 1996 — the last year for which international comparisons are available — the average American physician's income was $199,000, compared to the OECD median of $70,324. [40]

And U.S. providers are determined to keep their incomes high, even when Medicare and private insurers strive to keep prices down, said the Commonwealth Fund's Davis. "[P]hysicians respond to reduced fees by working longer hours, seeing more patients, having patients come back more frequently and performing more billable procedures," she told the Senate Health Appropriations Subcommittee. [41]

For example, she said, when Congress enacted Medicare cuts in 1997, average physician incomes dropped over the next few years; in response, doctors began performing more services. Between 2000 and 2001, the number of doctor visits by Medicare beneficiaries increased by 4.3 percent, while use of some lab tests grew 22 percent and brain MRIs increased 15 percent.

"It is hard to believe that Medicare beneficiaries suddenly demanded 15 percent more brain MRIs," said Davis. More plausibly, she said, doctors simply took it upon themselves to schedule more patients for the non-invasive, high-paying, diagnostic procedures — at least partly in order to boost revenues.

Reinhardt points out that there is a wider disparity between American doctors' incomes and other U.S. workers' salaries than there is in other OECD countries. In 1996, for instance, U.S. doctors' average income was about 5.5 times the average U.S. worker's salary. By comparison, German doctors earned 3.4 times the average worker's income, Australians, 2.2 times and Swedes, 1.5 times. [42]

But economists say it is not surprising that U.S. providers are high earners, given other features of the U.S. economy. The income disparity for all U.S. occupations is far wider than in other OECD countries, Reinhardt said, so the disparity between American doctors' incomes and the average worker is well in line with salary differences between other top U.S. professionals and other workers. The incomes of skilled health workers "are determined partly with reference to the incomes that equally able and skilled professionals can earn elsewhere in the economy," he said.

Moreover, the higher American physicians' incomes may be justifiable because medical education leaves U.S. doctors with substantial debt, unlike in OECD countries where governments often subsidize medical students, according to Reinhardt. In 2004, more than 80 percent of U.S med-school graduates were in debt. [43]

Continued on p. 300

Chronology

1920s-1950s

Health costs increase, and U.S. reformers press for social insurance covering all citizens. Large industries begin offering health coverage to workers.

1932
Committee on the Cost of Medical Care details the growing difficulties families face in paying for care.

1948
President Harry S Truman's National Health Insurance initiative fails after the American Medical Association criticizes it, and some congressional Republicans compare it to communism.

1960s-1970s

Medical science advances, costs rise and the U.S. government provides health coverage for poor mothers with young children, the disabled and the elderly. President Richard M. Nixon and Congress offer grants to develop health maintenance organizations (HMOs) to control costs.

1960
U.S. health spending totals $28 billion, or 5.2 percent of gross domestic product (GDP).

1965
President Lyndon B. Johnson signs Medicare and Medicaid programs into law.

1971
President Nixon imposes wage-and-price controls on medical services.

1980s

New rules reduce Medicare spending, but as payments fall hospitals charge private insurers more.

1980
Health spending tops $255 billion, or 9.1 percent of GDP.

1983
Medicare begins reimbursing hospitals for overall treatment of illnesses rather than for individual services.

1990s

Health-spending growth slows as employers embrace managed care, and President Bill Clinton promises health-system reforms. By mid-decade, Clinton's plan is stalled, consumers lash back against managed care and spending rises again.

1993
First lady Hillary Rodham Clinton leads an effort to reform the health-care system by compromising between government price controls and competition among private health plans.

1997
A presidential commission urges Congress to protect patients from potentially harmful managed-care cost controls. . . . Congress cuts Medicare and Medicaid.

1999
An Institute of Medicine panel casts doubt on the quality of U.S. health care, finding that tens of thousands of patients die and hundreds of thousands are injured each year from medical errors. . . . Backlash from medical providers leads Congress to undo the 1997 Medicare payment cuts.

2000s

Congress enacts tax breaks for consumer-directed health plans (CDHPs) and health safety accounts (HSAs). States and the federal government begin studying the cost-effectiveness of medical treatments.

2000
Health spending totals $1.4 trillion, or 13.8 percent of GDP.

2001
Oregon uses research on drug effectiveness to determine how much Medicaid will pay for them.

2003
Congress enacts tax breaks for HSAs and a research program to compare treatment costs and effectiveness.

2004
Dartmouth University analysts find that Medicare patients get worse care in states where spending is higher.

2005
Health insurer Aetna discloses what it pays physicians in Cincinnati.

2006
Health spending totals $2.2 trillion — 16.5 percent of GDP. . . . President Bush proposes greatly expanded tax breaks for HSAs. . . . White House asks insurers and employers to pressure providers to reveal their prices and quality ratings.

2011
First baby boomers are eligible for Medicare, increasing the proportion of subsidized health spending.

2015
Health spending projected to rise to more than $4 trillion — 20 percent of GDP.

Should the Rich Pay More for Health Care?

As an emergency physician and public official, John Kitzhaber viewed health-care delivery two ways. As a doctor, he was trained to "use every resource on the person in front of me, regardless" of how few resources that may leave for others, he says. But as Oregon's governor (1995 to 2003), he realized, "you can't practice medicine one person at a time. You can't make a healthy system that way."

Unfortunately, "We've created a system where we lavish unlimited resources on one person at a time, but we give little thought to the big-picture consequences of those person-by-person decisions," says Kitzhaber, who founded and runs The Archimedes Movement, a campaign to encourage states to undertake large-scale health reform.

Some economists now say rising costs are creating a health-care dilemma that may force Americans to debate fundamental principles about rights to care. A growing number of workers cannot afford health insurance and end up paying much higher prices than insured people for the same care.

"Our health-care system is in real trouble, but we are not even discussing the fundamental cause" — a "mismatch between demand and the available supply," said Humphrey Taylor, chairman of the Harris Poll. The key question is "whether health care is, or should be, more a common good (i.e., an entitlement) or more a private economic good, where you get what you are willing and able to pay for. We should debate that." [1]

To some, providing basic health-care resources to everyone is a self-evident ethical principle. "There are 10,000 technical issues involved with health-system reform, but one fundamentally moral question: Who shall be allowed to sit at our health-care table of plenty?" asks economist Len Nichols, who directs the health-policy program at the progressive New America Foundation think tank. "Many scriptural traditions and much humanistic philosophy admonish full communities to feed the hungry. . . . For us to deny [health care] because of cost is tantamount to denying food to the starving poor." [2]

But David Kelley argues that entitling all citizens to receive health care unfairly imposes government control on taxpayers and on physicians and other care providers. "If health care is a right, then government is responsible for seeing that everyone has access to it, just as the right to property means that government must protect us against theft," says Kelley, founder and senior fellow of the Objectivist Center, a think tank that espouses limited government and laissez-faire capitalism. "A political system that tries to implement a right to health care will necessarily involve forced transfers of wealth to pay for programs, loss of freedom for health-care providers, higher prices and more restricted access by all consumers." [3]

The range of opinion is so broad that the country probably can't come to a single conclusion about how to allocate health resources, said Gail Wilensky, a senior fellow at Project HOPE, a nonprofit research organization, and a former head of the Medicare and Medicaid programs. "Should ethical issues be a part of national health policy?" Wilensky asks. She does not believe they will be, because the United States has a heterogeneous population that is very different ethnically, religiously and racially. "It would be very difficult for us to have a single, uniform policy with regard to rationing of health care." [4]

With regard to a sense of responsibility, she continues, "we are clearer for some populations. Most people would agree that the poor . . . will need some or a lot of help [to finance] their own health care." Even within that basic consensus, however, there is disagreement over who is considered poor, she added.

The Bush administration is promoting expansion of consumer-directed health plans (CDHPs), which require consumers to pay more for health care than in traditional insurance coverage and are designed to encourage consumers to shop for the most cost-effective treatments. Encouraging more cost-conscious buying is basically sound, says Uwe Reinhardt, professor of economics at Princeton University, but current proposals put disproportionate demands on lower-income people, he says.

CDHPs generally require owners to spend $4,000-$6,000 a year out of pocket. "To a waitress and a husband with $40,000 or less family income, $4,000 is a huge hit," says Reinhardt. But for a two-lawyer household with an annual

Continued from p. 298

Physicians also earn high incomes because they face long, irregular working hours; more than one-third of full-time physicians and surgeons worked 60 hours or more a week in 2004, according to the U.S. Bureau of Labor Statistics. [44]

And while many segments of the U.S. health system are overpaid, others are woefully underfunded. The behavioral and psychiatric units of the Children's Hospital and Research Center in Oakland, Calif., suffered deficits "in excess of $2 million" over the past two years, according to that hospital's May 2005 Web posting. "Most insurance providers now pay us only half or less of what it actually costs to provide these services." [45]

"Many inner-city hospitals caring for large numbers of uninsured patients continue to struggle financially," said the Center for Studying Health System Change. For example, in northern New Jersey, suburban hospitals have expanded into new buildings while "hospitals in declining urban areas . . . have struggled" just to keep existing facilities upgraded. And in Miami, the county hospital system "is facing significant deficits stemming in part from charity-care needs growing faster than . . . funding from a dedicated half-penny sales tax." [46] ■

income in the $200,000 range, a $4,000 deductible "is nothing. It's a skiing trip."

A more ethical and effective approach would be to increase CDHP deductibles on a sliding scale, based on income, Reinhardt suggests, with a family earning $200,000 obligated for $20,000-$30,000 — five times the deductible paid by a family that earns one-fifth their income. "This should be the debate," he says.

Similarly, tax breaks proposed by the Bush administration for consumers who use CDHPs also favor the well-off, who get proportionally higher tax deductions than the poor, says Stuart Butler, vice president of domestic and economic policy studies at the conservative Heritage Foundation, "It's very badly targeted. I would have liked to see the administration moving more in the direction of a tax-credit approach" that would target lower-income people only.

Former Gov. John Kitzhaber, D-Ore., an emergency physician, urges states to undertake large-scale health reform.

Under the existing system, the poor end up paying more for all health services than the rich. Low-income people and individuals without insurance face so-called discriminatory pricing when they purchase health services. That's because pharmacies, hospitals and other health providers offer volume discounts to insurers and large government-subsidized programs like Medicare and Medicaid. But the uninsured or self-insured don't get those discounts and often are billed at highly inflated list prices. Conservative advocates worry that CDHP-insured people may face similar price discrimination for services they pay for out of pocket.

"Typically, a hospital will charge uninsured patients three, four, five or even 10 times as much as what an insured patient pays for the same procedures or services," according to K. B. Forbes, head of Consejo de Latinos Unidos, an advocacy group based in East Los Angeles. [5] In Fort Myers, Fla., for example, an uninsured man who broke his leg paid $15,100 for a procedure that would have cost an insurer around $5,500, Forbes says, and an uninsured woman was charged $7,271 for a cesarean section that would have cost an insurer around $3,600.

The Consejo group focuses its efforts on the Hispanic community, in part because Hispanics are least likely to have health insurance. In 2004, 34.3 percent of non-elderly Hispanics were uninsured, compared to 29.1 percent of American Indians/Alaska Natives, 21.2 percent of non-Hispanic blacks and 13.2 percent of non-Hispanic whites. [6]

High charges for uninsured people are "economic discrimination that impacts minorities," Forbes said. "We have a responsibility to protect their rights and livelihood." [7]

---

1 Humphrey J. F. Taylor, "The Health Care Debate We Are Not having Now," EyeNet, American Academy of Ophthalmology, March 2003.

2 Len M. Nichols, "Outline of the New America Vision for a 21st-Century Health-Care System," *Issue Brief #1*, New America Foundation Health Policy Program, January 2006.

3 David Kelley, "Is There a Right to Health Care?" www.objectivistcenter.org.

4 Gail Wilensky, interview, "Healthcare Crisis: Who's at Risk" www.pbs.org.

5 K. B. Forbes, "Unconscionable," http://hospitalpricing.com, Oct. 27, 2003.

6 *The Uninsured: A Primer*, Kaiser Commission on Medicaid and the Uninsured, January 2006.

7 Quoted in "Latino Advocacy Group Calls on Hospitals to Invoke Six-Month National Moratorium on Lawsuits Against Uninsured Patients," *Hispanic Business*, www.hispanicbusiness.com.

BACKGROUND

High Tech, High Cost

In the early 20th century, medicine began to morph from a hands-on, low-tech profession — with matching low pay — to the high-tech, expensive health system we know today. [47]

But University of Pennsylvania medical historian Rosemary Stevens warns that it's easy to be beguiled by tales of kindly 19th-century physicians who made house calls and accepted chickens for payment from farmers. "We over-romanticize the past," she told the Public Broadcasting Service. "Doctors went to bedsides to give cheer because they often couldn't do anything else." [48]

Over the last half-century, however, medicine has had "a very, very different potential," dominated by drugs and technology with the potential to prevent and cure disease. "Antibiotics only came into general use in the 1940s," Stevens pointed out.

But the higher cost of the new and more effective drugs and technologies posed a public-policy conundrum and ethical dilemma: Who, if anyone, should be ensured access to care, and

Medicare Spending Varies Widely

Federal health-care spending for the elderly varies widely, largely because patients in some cities see more doctors and specialists than in other cities. In Miami, for instance, Medicare spends more than twice as much on the average beneficiary as in Rapid City. Numerous studies show, however, that patients are healthier in cities where expenditures are lower, in part because seeing a lot of specialists does not result in coordinated, preventive care.

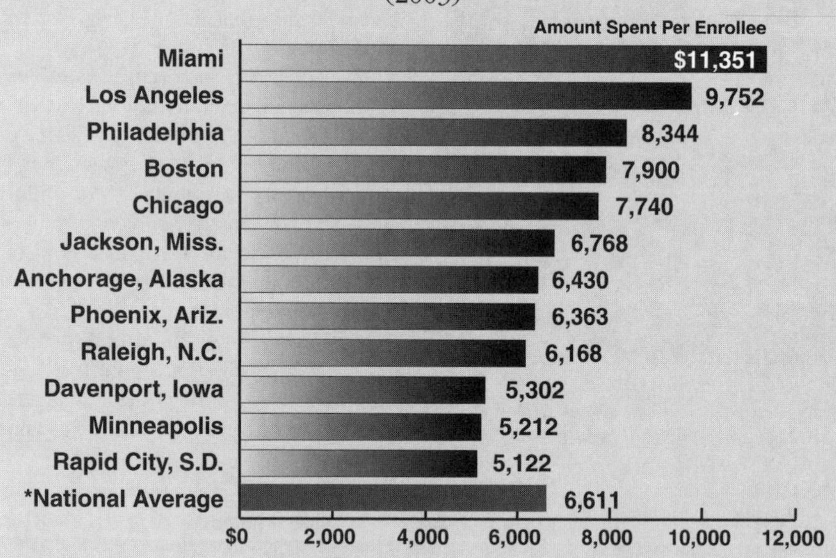

Source: Dartmouth Atlas of Health Care database, http://cecsweb.dartmouth.edu/release1/datatools/bench_s1.php

at whose expense? By the end of the 1990s, all of the OECD countries except Mexico, Turkey and the United States had answered that question by instituting some version of universal or near-universal coverage. [49]

Over the past 40 years, health spending worldwide has consistently risen faster than national incomes. Finland, Ireland, New Zealand and the United Kingdom have been the most successful — and the United States the least successful — at keeping health spending from greatly outpacing national income growth. [50] By 1960, U.S. annual spending on health care was already 50 percent higher per capita than in any other OECD country, and it continued to rise, growing an average of 2.4 percentage points faster than gross domestic product between 1960 and 2000. [51]

During the 1990s, spending growth slowed because employers had turned to cost-conscious managed-care insurers for employees' coverage, and health providers reined in cost increases in hope of warding off the large-scale health-system reform sought by President Bill Clinton. By 1996, however, Clinton's reform effort — led by first lady Hillary Rodham Clinton — had spectacularly failed, doctors and patients were lashing back against managed-care restrictions, and spending began rising again.

Sticker Shock

When it comes to predicting how high a nation's health-care spending will rise, John Poisal, an actuary for the federal Centers for Medicare and Medicaid Services, says that, in essence, "income drives the bus." As personal and national incomes rise, he explains, people worldwide spend increasing amounts on health care.

As medicine develops new treatments and technologies and serves ever more consumers, spending is pushed higher, not always for good clinical reasons, according to Kenneth Thorpe, chairman of the Department of Health Policy and Management at Emory University's Rollins School of Public Health in Atlanta. [52] Health spending, he explains, rises for three main reasons:

- Some diseases, such as diabetes, are more common;
- Doctors have begun treating some chronic conditions like high blood pressure, high cholesterol and depression at earlier stages; and
- Many new drugs and technologies have been invented.

Medical innovation is a major cost driver, Thorpe said. For example, spending per newborn infant increased fivefold between 1987 and 2002, due almost entirely to new technology.

Meanwhile, the U.S. health system has its own unique cost generators, which helps explain why U.S. spending is the highest in the world. To begin with, the non-centralized American system has steep administrative costs. Between 1970 and 1998, for example, the number of people holding administrative jobs — such as claims processors, billing clerks and business managers — in U.S. health care swelled 24-fold, according to David Himmelstein and Steffie Woolhandler, associate professors of medicine at Harvard Medical School, who advocate a single-payer health system in which the federal government would provide insurance to everyone. During the same period, the number of doctors and other clinical workers grew only two-and-a-half-fold.[53] By 1999, the administrative costs of insurers, employers and health providers amounted to about 24 percent of total health spending, Himmelstein and Woolhandler estimate, compared with Canada, for example, which spends only about half as many of its health dollars on administrative paperwork.[54]

Meanwhile, U.S. prices for goods and services also have risen higher than elsewhere, largely because hundreds of individual insurers, employers and government programs each buy care on their own, enabling doctors, hospitals and drug companies to charge higher prices than those in countries with single-payer government systems or government oversight of insurers' prices.[55]

Technology also enters the U.S. system more easily and disperses more quickly than in other industrialized countries. In Germany, for example, only about 20 percent of new technologies are approved for payment after careful costs/benefit analysis by health providers and government officials, said Anne Haas, senior officer for health policy at AOK Bundesverband, the largest government-approved and regulated company among those managing Germany's cradle-to-grave social-insurance system.[56]

In the United States, on the other hand, not only do doctors and hospitals increase usage of new technologies unchecked, but only a handful of poorly funded U.S. organizations analyze clinical technology before insurers pay for it, said Robert Laszewski, North American chairman of the Global Medical Forum, a nonprofit group that studies cost issues. The U.S. health system "may be the biggest supply-side economy in the universe" with "an unfettered ability to simultaneously create both supply and cost," Laszewski said.[57]

Getty Images/Jim Watson

President George W. Bush calls for the use of consumer-directed health plans (CDHPs) in a policy address in February at the headquarters of Wendys International, in Dublin, Ohio. Bush says CDHPs will encourage consumers to "shop around until you get the best treatment for the best price."

John Wennberg, director of Dartmouth Medical Schools' Center for Clinical Evaluative Services and a pioneer in studying how medical costs vary regionally, says that "ignorance and silence" surround the question: How much care is the right amount?

"For example, how frequently should a doctor schedule office visits with a patient chronically ill with diabetes? Every three months? Every six months? The fact is, nobody knows or has supported research to find out," he says.

Cost-Control Battles

In the mid-20th century — as health-care spending began its steep upward climb — U.S. policymakers started looking for ways to keep care affordable.

"The puzzle over what to do about the high costs of health care — who pays for it and are we getting what we pay for — has confounded every administration since Truman's 60 years ago," said Risa Lavizzo-Mourey, president of the Robert Wood Johnson Foundation, a major source of funding for health-policy research. "Richard Nixon is the first president I can remember who warned us of a 'crisis' in [health] costs." Nixon called for a new system "that makes high-quality health care available to every American in a dignified manner and at a price he can afford."[58]

In 1971, Nixon ordered wage-and-price controls for health care, along with other parts of the economy, in hope of reining in inflation and stemming the crisis in health-care affordability. "I was brought into the White house in 1971 and was told by . . . the president that if [health spending] reached 8 percent of GDP . . . the American way would deteriorate," said Stuart Altman, former deputy director of Nixon's Cost-of-Living Council and now a professor of health policy at Brandeis University.[59]

While the controls held costs down somewhat, they sparked passionate resistance by businesses and health providers. The administration ended the program in 1974.

Over the years, some insurers have tried "bundling" medical charges — paying for the entire treatment of an injury or illness rather than allowing providers to charge easily inflatable prices for individual goods and services like the notorious $10 aspirin appearing on many a hospital bill.

In an effort to encourage a market-based program combining bundling with preventive health care, Nixon pushed Congress to provide funds to encourage development of enough health-maintenance organizations (HMOs) to enroll about 40 million people by 1976. [60]

By 1973, Congress had handed out some $7 million in HMO planning grants. But the initiative drew fire from the American Medical Association (AMA), the nation's largest physicians' organization, which resisted having doctors abandon their individual practices to work as employees on HMO staffs.

Many liberal commentators also denounced Nixon's plan, arguing that the country needed universal national health coverage rather than limited, market-based expansion of HMOs. Ultimately, the Watergate scandal forced Nixon's resignation from office in 1974, ending his ambitious — though mostly ill-fated — efforts to control health costs.

Through the 1970s and '80s, health spending continued to soar. Medicare costs, for example, grew an average of 19 percent annually from 1979 to 1982. [61] In response, Medicare began to develop charge-bundling programs for various health sectors — an effort that continues today. In 1983, Medicare introduced its first such "prospective payment system" (PPS) — the Diagnosis-Related-Group (DRG) system — in which hospitals are paid a set amount for a patient's entire stay, based on the diagnosis.

The DRG-PPS system helped hold down Medicare hospital costs and was eventually copied by many private insurers and overseas governments. But in the late 1980s, with providers earning less from Medicare, they got tougher in price negotiations with private insurers, causing workers' insurance premiums and overall spending to soar again.

In response, employers turned again to Nixon's HMO idea. In the late 1980s and early '90s, more and more companies adopted managed-care coverage for their workers and scored some cost-control victories as their HMOs bargained aggressively with providers. In addition, Clinton entered office in 1992 promising large-scale health reform, and the prospect of a government-regulated system scared some health organizations into voluntarily slowing cost increases.

By 1996, however, Congress had blocked the Clinton plan, and doctors had made common cause with patients to oppose HMO restrictions. With Congress threatening to enact a Patients' Bill of Rights that would ban managed care from imposing certain cost-control measures — such as limiting which doctors a patient could see — insurers and employers backed off aggressive cost controls, and spending rose anew. [62]

Although the PPS approach had worked in the Medicare program, providers began using other methods to obtain higher payments — many that probably didn't improve patient care. For example, when Medicare began paying more for catheterization — the insertion of a thin tube into the artery to take measurements such as blood pressure inside the heart — in heart-attack victims, "you can imagine what happened to catheterization rates," says White House adviser Baicker. ■

CURRENT SITUATION

Savvier Shopping

In 2006, health spending continues to climb with no slowdown in sight. The Medicare PPS still functions, and some managed-care cost-containment practices remain in place, such as emphasizing preventive care and carefully managing drug utilization by high-cost patients. But the 21st century has seen only one new idea for keeping costs down: President Bush's consumer-directed health plans.

CDHPs are insurance plans in which individuals pay larger-than-usual health costs out of their own pockets, often aided by health savings accounts (HSAs), to which employers may contribute. In 2003 at the president's urging, Congress made HSA contributions by employers and individuals tax deductible, much like today's flexible-spending accounts. However, unlike flexible-spending accounts, unspent balances in HSAs roll over from year to year, and workers can take their HSAs with them when they change jobs.

This year, in hope of expanding CDHPs' reach, the administration has proposed major additional tax breaks, particularly aimed at the self-employed and those who do not buy health coverage through their jobs. Under the plan, HSA owners would get a tax credit — in addition to the existing tax deductibility — and an additional deduction for premiums paid for HSA-related health coverage. Higher-income taxpayers would get bigger tax breaks in absolute dollars, since their higher tax brackets give them bigger deductions.

The hope is that CDHPs would encourage workers to "shop around until

Continued on p. 306

At Issue:

Should the government do more to lower Medicare drug costs?

yes

DEAN BAKER
CO-DIRECTOR, CENTER FOR ECONOMIC AND POLICY RESEARCH

FROM "THE EXCESS COST OF THE MEDICARE DRUG BENEFIT," INSTITUTE FOR AMERICA'S FUTURE, FEBRUARY 2006

The waste and inefficiency built into the 2003 Medicare Modernization Act (MMA) will add more than $800 billion to the cost of prescription drugs to the government and beneficiaries over its first decade, compared to a drug bill designed to maximize efficiency.

Congress deliberately structured the bill to ensure that multiple private insurance companies would provide the benefit rather than Medicare. This design substantially increased the cost of the program for seniors and the disabled, leaving many with large drug expenses. The structure designed by Congress also made the program more costly for the federal government and state governments.

The waste built into the MMA is easy to show. . . . The Congressional Budget Office (CBO) projected that the marketing and the profits of the insurance industry would add $38 billion to the cost of the MMA over the first eight years, due to the fact that Medicare is not allowed to use its bargaining power to gain discounts from the industry.

Virtually every other country in the industrialized world imposes some constraint on drug prices, either through formal price controls or negotiated prices. Consumers in these countries pay, on average, between 35 and 55 percent less than consumers in the United States. The [negotiated] discounts obtained by the Veterans Administration were even larger.

If Medicare was allowed to use its bargaining power to negotiate prices . . . it could almost certainly obtain discounts that are at least as large as the highest discounts obtained in other countries, since it would be by far the biggest drug buyer in the world. If Medicare could negotiate the same schedule of prices as Australia (the lowest-cost country), the savings over the first eight years of the drug benefit would be almost $560 billion.

The combined savings from having Medicare negotiate prices directly with the industry and from having Medicare directly offer the benefit instead of private insurers would be more than $600 billion . . . from 2006 to 2013. These savings are so large it would be possible to fully pay for all drugs for Medicare beneficiaries, with no premiums, deductibles or copayments. Alternatively, it would be possible to have a modest schedule of copayments, comparable to those in most private health-insurance plans, and save federal and state governments more than $100 billion compared to the spending projected in the MMA.

no

CENTER FOR HEALTH POLICY STUDIES

FROM THE HERITAGE FOUNDATION WEB SITE, WWW.HERITAGE.ORG, NOV. 5, 2005

While price controls guaranteeing cheap prescription drugs for everyone may sound appealing, the consequences of imposing price controls would harm seniors and all Americans.

Commerce Department researchers recently examined the prescription-drug markets in member countries of the Organization for Economic Cooperation and Development (OECD) and determined that these "governments have relied heavily on government fiat rather than competition to set prices, lowering drug spending through price controls applied to new and old drugs alike." The study found that price controls in OECD countries caused a $6 billion to $8 billion annual reduction in funding for drug research and development worldwide.

The impact of price controls would vary with the degree to which the controls were set below market prices. According to a recent study published by the National Bureau of Economic Research, a 40-45-percent cut in pharmaceutical prices "would have a significant impact on the incentives for private firms to invest in research and development." The study estimated that under such price controls, the number of compounds moving from the laboratory into human trials would decrease by 50-60 percent.

Because of the uncertainties involved, fewer compounds moving into clinical trials directly translates into fewer new products — the effects of which wouldn't be fully felt for several decades because of the long development cycle. Moreover, because of the spillover effects of [research and development], less activity today reduces the possibilities for new opportunities in the future.

Not only would price controls add to the delay in the development of drugs and eliminate new drugs, they would also delay the introduction of new drugs into the market. The Boston Consulting Group found that the more interference in the market in a given country, the longer it took approved drugs to reach the marketplace.

With the passage of the Medicare Modernization Act in 2003, the government dramatically increased its activity in the prescription-drug market. Not surprisingly, as cost estimates for benefits soar, some in Congress are looking toward price regulation as a way to hold expenses down. . . . [L]egislation has been proposed that would allow the federal government to "negotiate" the prices of drugs covered by the benefit. "Negotiate," however, is misleading. What the term really means is price controls.

No politician, over the course of 4,000 years of experience, has yet devised a humane system of price controls that spares consumers from the risks of shortages and declines in quality.

Continued from p. 304

you get the best treatment for the best price," said President Bush in a February speech at the Dublin, Ohio, headquarters of the Wendy's restaurant chain. HSAs provide tax-favored savings from which workers may pay for health care, Bush explained. "When you inject this type of thinking in the system, price starts to matter. You begin to say, well, maybe there's a better way to do this, and a more cost-effective way." [63]

So far, no one knows how many people have set up HSAs. However, the insurance-industry group America's Health Insurance Plans estimates that as of January 2006, 3.2 million people were enrolled in the high-deductible CDHP insurance that HSA owners must purchase to qualify for tax breaks. That's up from 438,000 enrollees in September 2004. [64]

If new tax incentives are enacted that attract more people into CDHPs, there's a good chance patients could exercise their purchasing clout to get more value for their health dollars, says Baicker.

However, critics argue that even widespread adoption of HSAs won't do much to slow spending, since the highest-spending patients are very sick and incur their expenses far beyond the level of CDHP deductibles. But Baicker says that — counting both the deductible and patient copayments for things like doctors'-office visits and prescriptions — about 50 percent of all health spending is "in the cost-sensitive range," or enough to make a real difference if patients start demanding value for their dollars.

But Baicker agrees with administration critics who say CDHP enrollees can't really make cost-sensitive purchases today because, she says, "they don't have the information needed" to compare the cost and quality of health providers.

Price Transparency

Bush has recently been meeting privately with large employers and insurers, urging them to undertake voluntary initiatives to publish cost and quality information, says Roy Ramthum, a senior adviser at the Treasury Department. To "get people more used to caring about price," the White House also will ask Medicare, the Federal Employee Health Benefit Plan and the Department of Defense's TriCare insurance to begin telling enrollees the prices of treatments, even though most of their members don't face high out-of-pocket expenses, Ramthum says.

Aetna insurance already has launched a transparency program, making available online the prices it has negotiated with Cincinnati-area doctors for various medical procedures, says Ramthum. [65] Similar efforts are in the development pipeline at other large insurers and employers, and four bills were introduced last year in Congress to require disclosure. But no committee or floor debates have been scheduled so far on these measures.

It's no wonder hearings have not been scheduled, given the continuing opposition by health providers like hospitals and doctors to disclosing price and quality information. Meanwhile, Bush is pressing forward. But publicly accessible price and quality transparency "has been promised for 20 years," says Princeton's Reinhardt. Yet, so far, almost no comparative information is available to the public, he says. "I can just see the [American Hospital Association] going nuts over the very idea of forcing that much competition. Providers don't like this. They are powerful, and they will fight you every step of the way." [66]

For evidence of congressional reluctance to even produce cost-benefit information — let alone publish it — one need look no further than the Effective Health Care program authorized by Congress in 2003 as part of Medicare prescription-drug legislation. It authorized $50 million a year for research on what treatments give the best value for the dollar, but Congress — at the suggestion of the White House — only provided $15 million for each of the program's first two fiscal years, and there is no indication the funding will rise. [67] That is less than one-thousandth of 1 percent of total spending in the $2-trillion U.S. health-care system.

Even this modest program has aroused opposition among health providers. For example, drug and medical-device companies also have complained recently that they want more input into whatever research is funded. [68]

Even if more consumer information were available, accelerated expansion of CDHPs is unlikely for the present, because Congress probably will not act on Bush's proposal this year, say congressional health leaders. No suitable tax legislation is scheduled to come out of the Senate that could include Bush's proposals, said Senate Finance Committee Chairman Charles Grassley, R-Iowa, on March 7. "Without that, I don't see how you move things like this." Furthermore, said Grassley, "before we add more tax subsidies, we first should look to see if we can make the incentives we have today work better." [69]

Employers and states also have a role in helping trim costs, most analysts agree. However, large health-care purchasers are not exactly "sitting there with lots of big weapons they haven't deployed yet to attack this problem," said the Kaiser foundation's Altman. They are already managing chronic diseases like diabetes, switching patients to generic drugs and similar actions.

For example, in Pennsylvania a new state program has begun sending "unsales" representatives to doctors' offices to convince them to prescribe drugs based on clinical evidence rather than sales pitches from brand-name pharmaceutical companies and to use cheaper generic drugs where appropriate. The Pennsylvania Department of Aging hopes the project can help bring down spending while improving care. "We're trying to go directly to the physicians . . . and have a dialogue . . . about prescribing practices that we think should be corrected," said Thomas Snedden, who heads the drug-assistance program. [70]

On April 4, Massachusetts enacted an ambitious, bipartisan plan to require — and heavily subsidize — all state residents to buy health coverage. With insurance reforms to cut costs, the law aims to cover 95 percent of uninsured people in the state in three years. [71]

Over the years, however, funding shortfalls, health-provider opposition and disagreement about program goals have characterized many such programs. In Indianapolis, for instance, four different employer coalitions have tried since 1996 to spur local health providers to adopt quality and transparency programs, according to analysts at the Center for Studying Health System Change. But none "has had a sustained impact" — in part because the employers haven't been able to agree about what type of data should be released. [72] ■

OUTLOOK

Higher and Higher

Many economists and lawmakers confess they are fresh out of new ideas for slowing health spending. Nevertheless, in the next few decades, the United States must slam the brakes on rising health costs or begin slashing spending in other areas in order to afford health care.

Until now, rising health costs have seemed relatively affordable — at least for middle- and upper-income people — because prices have been rising from a relatively low base in the 1960s, says Michael Chernew, a professor of health management and policy at the University of Michigan. Today, however, with health spending already consuming more than 16 percent of GDP, rapid growth in health costs quickly translates into something the country almost certainly cannot afford, he says.

Even if the growth of health spending could be slowed through the year 2075 to a rate just one percentage point faster than GDP — about half as fast as it's grown historically — the United States still would spend a little more than half of its cumulative annual income increases on health. That's steep, but not completely unaffordable, since nearly half of each year's income growth would still be left over to spend on other priorities. [73]

But if health spending continues to grow two percentage points faster than GDP each year — the historical average — big trouble looms quickly, Chernew explains. Under the 2 percentage-point scenario, 44.9 percent of the increase in per-capita income between 1999 and 2010 goes to health care. Then, from 2010-2050, health care eats up 87.8 percent of income growth. "You get to use only a little over 10 percent of your new raise for anything" else, Chernew says. Then from 2050-2075, things would get even worse: 165.6 percent of the increase in GDP would go to health care. "In other words, spending on everything but health care would actually drop" year to year, even though incomes kept going up, he explains.

If that happened, the United States would have to resort to some kind of health-care rationing, even though the U.S. health-care system currently has no idea how to use clinical evidence to parcel out health care rationally, says Aaron of the Brookings Institution. "We need to acquire a great deal of knowledge," he continues. The nation will face choices that "will strain the democratic fabric" of society, because of the "emotional content and economic stakes involved."

On the bright side, says Chernew, the question is how to cut future growth in health spending, not how to give up current spending levels. "The prospect isn't as scary as some may think," he says. "Things will still get better, just less better than they otherwise might."

Despite arguments that physicians and insurance companies make too much money, "this isn't a villain situation," says Jack Meyer, president of the nonpartisan Economic and Social Research Institute. "Is it a problem that a neurosurgeon earns $500,000 a year?" he asks, pointing out that Yankee third-baseman Alex Rodriguez earns $25 million a year — "50 times what the neurosurgeon is making."

Rather than searching for a villain, Meyer says, we must acknowledge, "we have met the enemy and he is us." Americans expect unlimited health care with little financial pain, he says. Generous insurance benefits enjoyed by well-insured people drive up premium costs for everyone, and many workers expect to retire early, even though Medicare would be easier to sustain if the eligibility age were nudged up by a few years.

For the hard answers, "we have to look in the mirror," says Meyer. "Americans don't like being told to wait, let alone being told, 'No.' " ■

Notes

[1] Quoted in Ana Menendez, "While Shalala Lives in Luxury, Janitors Struggle," *The Miami Herald*, March 1, 2006.

[2] "Coping Without Health Insurance," transcript, "Newshour With Jim Lehrer," www.pbs.org, Nov. 28, 2005.

[3] Stephen Heffler, *et al.*, "U.S. Health Spending Projections for 2004-2014," *Health Affairs* Web site, Feb. 23, 2005. Gross national product is roughly equivalent to the nation's total spending.

[4] Gerard F. Anderson, *et al.*, "Health Spending in the United States and the Rest of the Industrialized World," *Health Affairs*, July/August 2005.

[5] Christine Borger, *et al.*, "Health Spending Projections Through 2015: Changes on the Horizon," *Health Affairs* Web site, Feb. 22, 2006.

[6] Employer Benefits Survey, 2005, The Kaiser Family Foundation and Health Research and Educational Trust, September 2005, p. 7.

[7] "2005 Annual Employer Health Benefits Survey, transcript," www.kaisernetwork.org, Sept. 14, 2005.
[8] Employer Benefits Survey, 2005, *op. cit.*
[9] Paul Burrow, testimony before Senate Appropriations Subcommittee on Labor, Health and Education, May 14, 2003.
[10] Richard Kronick and Todd Gilmer, "Explaining the Decline in Health Insurance Coverage, 1979-1995," *Health Affairs*, March/April 1999.
[11] Todd Gilmer and Richard Kronick, "It's the Premiums, Stupid: Projections of the Uninsured Through 2013," *Health Affairs* Web site, April 5, 2005.
[12] Jack Hadley and Peter J. Cunningham, "Perception, Reality, and Health Insurance," *Issue Brief No. 100*, Center for Studying Health System Change, October 2005.
[13] Katherine Baicker and Amitabh Chandra, "Medicare Spending, the Physician Workforce, and Beneficiaries' Quality of Care," *Health Affairs* Web site, April 7, 2004.
[14] For background, see Jim Landers, "Swiss Health-Care System Might Serve as Model for U.S.," *Dallas Morning News*, Feb. 20, 2006.
[15] *Ibid.*
[16] Anderson, *et al.*, *op. cit.* Data are for 2002, the latest year for which international comparisons are available.
[17] Quoted in "President Participates in Panel Discussion on Health-Care Initiatives," transcript, www.whitehouse.gov, Feb. 16, 2006.
[18] Henry G. Aaron, "The Unsurprising Surprise of Renewed Health-Care Cost Inflation," *Health Affairs* Web site, Jan. 23, 2002. For background, see "Setting Limits on Medical Care," *Editorial Research Reports*, Nov. 23, 1990, available at *CQ Researcher Plus Archive*, CQ Electronic Library, http://library.cqpress.com.
[19] David M. Cutler and Mark McClellan, "Is Technological Change in Medicine Worth It?" *Health Affairs*, September/October 2001.
[20] George C. Halvorson and George J. Isham, *Epidemic of Care* (2003), p. 48.
[21] John Kitzhaber, transcript, Citizens' Health-Care Working Group, Public Meeting, Portland, Ore., Sept. 23, 2005.
[22] "Supply, Prices — Not Quality — Push Spending Upward," *Perspectives, Medicine & Health*, June 23, 2003.
[23] Medicare Payment Advisory Commission, "Report to the Congress: Medicare Payment Policy," March 2006, p. 15. For background, see Bob Adams, "Primary Care," *CQ Researcher*, March 17, 1995, pp. 217-240.
[24] Barbara Starfield, *et al.*, "The Effects of Specialist Supply on Populations; Health: Assessing the Evidence," *Health Affairs* Web site, March 15, 2005.
[25] "Physician Compensation and Production Report, 2005," Medical Group Management Association.
[26] Starfield, *op. cit.*
[27] Karen Davis, "Taking a Walk on the Supply Side: 10 Steps to Control Health-Care Costs," The Commonwealth Fund, April 2005, www.cmwf.org.
[28] *Ibid.*
[29] Keith Epstein, "Covering the Uninsured," *CQ Researcher*, June 14, 2002, pp. 521-544.
[30] Jack Hadley and John Holahan, "The Cost of Care for the Uninsured: What Do We Spend, Who Pays, and What Would Full Coverage Add to Medical Spending?" *Issue Update*, Kaiser Commission on Medicaid and the Uninsured, May 2004.
[31] *Ibid.*
[32] "Frist: 100 Percent Coverage Impossible. 93 Percent Not Working So Well Either," *Medicine & Health*, Feb. 9, 2004.
[33] Henry J. Aaron, William B. Schwartz and Melissa Cox, *Can We Say No: The Challenge of Rationing Health Care* (2005), p. 2.
[34] Hadley and Holahan, *op. cit.*
[35] *Ibid.*
[36] Institute of Medicine Committee on the Consequences of Uninsurance, *Hidden Costs, Value Lost*, National Academies Press, 2003.
[37] Kitzhaber, transcript, *op. cit.*
[38] Julian Le Grand, "Methods of Cost Containment: Some Lessons from Europe," paper delivered at the International Health Economics Association, San Francisco, June 2003.
[39] Gerard F. Anderson, *et al.*, "It's the Prices, Stupid: Why the United States is so Different From Other Countries," *Health Affairs*, May/June 2003.
[40] Uwe E. Reinhardt, Peter S. Hussey and Gerard F. Anderson, "U.S. Health-Care Spending in an International Context," *Health Affairs*, May/June 2004.
[41] Karen Davis, "American Health Care: Why So Costly?" testimony before Senate Appropriations Subcommittee on Labor, Health, and Education, June 11, 2003.
[42] Reinhardt, Hussey and Anderson, *op. cit.*
[43] "Physicians and Surgeons," *Occupational Outlook Handbook, 2006-07 Edition*, U.S. Department of Labor, Bureau of Labor Statistics.
[44] *Ibid.*
[45] For background, see Adriel Bettelheim, "Hospitals' Financial Woes," *CQ Researcher*, Aug. 13, 1999, pp. 689-704.
[46] Insurance Update: May 4, 2005, Children's Hospitals and Research Center, Oakland, www.childrenshospitaloakland.org.
[47] For background, see Aaron, Schwartz and Cox, *op. cit.*
[48] Rosemary A. Stevens, interview, PBS, "Healthcare Crisis," www.pbs.org, 2000.
[49] Gerard F. Anderson and Jean-Pierre Poullier, "Health Spending, Access, and Outcomes: Trends in Industrialized Countries," *Health Affairs*, May/June 1999.
[50] Anderson and Poullier, *op. cit.*
[51] *Ibid.*, Reinhardt, Hussey and Anderson, *op. cit.*
[52] Kenneth E. Thorpe, "The Rise in Health-Care Spending and What to Do About It," *Health Affairs*, November/December 2005.
[53] David Himmelstein and Steffie Woolhandler, *Bleeding the Patient: The Consequences of Corporate Healthcare* (2001).
[54] Steffie Woolhandler, Terry Campbell and David Himmelstein, "Costs of Health-Care Administration in the United States and Canada," *New England Journal of Medicine*, Aug. 21, 2003, p. 768.
[55] Reinhardt, Hussey and Anderson, *op. cit.*
[56] Quoted in "Analysts Want to Buy Value, but Public May Not Be Ready," *Medicine &*

About the Author

Staff writer **Marcia Clemmitt** is a veteran social-policy reporter who previously served as editor in chief of *Medicine and Health*, a Washington industry newsletter, and staff writer for *The Scientist*. She has also been a high school math and physics teacher. She holds a liberal arts and sciences degree from St. John's College, Annapolis, and a master's degree in English from Georgetown University. Her recent reports include "Saving the Oceans," "Climate Change" and "AP and IB Programs."

Health Perspectives, Dec. 13, 2004.

[57] *Ibid.*

[58] Risa Lavizzo-Mourey, "The State of the Union's Health Care," www.rwjf.org, January 2006.

[59] Quoted in "The 12th Princeton Conference — How Will the States Pay for Health Care?" transcript, May 20, 2005, www.kaisernetwork.org.

[60] For background, see Sarah Glazer, "Managed Care," *CQ Researcher*, April 12, 1996, pp. 313-336; and Adriel Bettelheim, "Managing Managed Care," *CQ Researcher*, April 16, 1999, pp. 305-328.

[61] Judith Mistichelli, "Diagnosis Related Groups (DRGs) and the Prospective Payment System: Forecasting Social Implications," *Cope Note 4*, National Reference Center for Bioethics Literature, http://bioethics.georgetown.edu.

[62] For background, see Kenneth Jost, "Patients' Rights," *CQ Researcher*, Feb. 5, 1998, pp. 97-120.

[63] George W. Bush, "President Discusses Health Care," address delivered Feb. 15, 2006, www.whitehouse.gov.

[64] John Reichard, "Ignagni: 'Young Immortals' Aren't Dominating HSA Enrollment," *CQ Healthbeat*, March 9, 2005.

[65] For background, see Vanessa Fuhrmans, "Insurer Reveals What Doctors Really Charge," *The Wall Street Journal*, Aug. 18, 2005.

[66] Uwe E. Reinhardt, "A Primer for Journalists on Reforming American Healthcare: Proposals in the Presidential Campaign," unpublished paper, September 2004.

[67] John Reichard, "First Finding of Landmark Program to Get Better Value for Medicare: Drugs as Good as Surgery for GERD," *CQ Healthbeat*, Dec. 14, 2005.

[68] John Reichard, "Big Lobbies Angling to Reshape Landmark Research Program," *CQ Healthbeat*, Jan. 11, 2006.

[69] John Reichard, "No HSA Markup This Year," *CQ Healthbeat*, March 8, 2006.

[70] Scott Hensley, "Harvard Professor Helps Team in Pennsylvania Publicize Alternatives to Pricey Pills," *The Wall Street Journal*, March 13, 2006, p. A1.

[71] William C. Symonds, "In Massachusetts, Health Care for All?" *Business Week Online*, April 4, 2006.

[72] "What's Driving Spending? More Stuff, No Brakes," *Perspectives, Medicine & Health*, Sept. 22, 2003.

[73] Michael E. Chernew, Richard A. Hirth and David M. Cutler, "Increased Spending on Health Care: How Much Can the United States Afford?" *Health Affairs*, July/August 2003.

FOR MORE INFORMATION

Alliance for Health Reform, 1444 I St., N.W., Suite 910, Washington, DC 20005; (202) 789-2300; www.allhealth.org. A nonpartisan, nonprofit group that disseminates information about ways to improve access to affordable health care.

California Healthcare Foundation, 476 Ninth St., Oakland, CA 94607; (510) 238-1040; www.chcf.org. An independent philanthropy that commissions and disseminates research on the way health care is delivered and financed in California.

Center for Studying Health System Change; 600 Maryland Ave., S.W. #550, Washington, DC 20024; (202) 484-5261; www.hschange.com. A nonpartisan policy-research group that chronicles long-term trends in American health care through a multi-year, in-depth survey of 12 cities.

Citizens' Health Care Working Group; www.citizenshealthcare.gov. Established by Congress in 2003, the 14-member panel is holding nationwide public hearings on health-care reform and will recommend to Congress how to extend affordable care to all.

Commonwealth Fund, One East 75th St., New York, NY 10021; (212) 606-3800; www.cmwf.org. A private foundation that funds independent research on health-care cost, access and quality in the United States and abroad.

Consejo de Latinos Unidos, 820 South Indiana St., East Los Angeles, CA 90023; (800) 474-7576; www.consejohelp.org. A nonprofit advocacy group that informs and assists uninsured Latinos and others on how to fight high hospital charges.

Council for Affordable Health Insurance, 127 S. Peyton St., Suite 210, Alexandria, VA 22314; (703) 836-6200; www.cahi.org. This advocacy organization made up of insurers that sell individual, small-group and consumer-directed health plans disseminates market-oriented proposals for improving access to affordable care.

Heritage Foundation, 214 Massachusetts Ave., N.E., Washington DC 20002-4999; (202) 546-4400; www.heritage.org. A conservative think tank that analyzes health-care-policy proposals from a free-market perspective.

Kaiser Family Foundation, 1330 G St., N.W., Washington, DC 20005; (202) 347-5270; www.kff.org. A nonprofit private foundation that conducts and disseminates research on national health-care issues including access, quality and cost.

National Business Group on Health, 50 F St., N.W., Suite 600, Washington, DC 20001; (202) 628-9320; www.wbgh.org. A national organization of more than 200 large employers and companies that provides information on health-care cost and quality issues.

National Coalition on Health Care, 1200 G St., N.W., Suite 750, Washington, DC 20005; (202) 638-7151; www.nchc.org. A nonprofit, nonpartisan group that advocates for improved access to affordable coverage and improved health-care quality. Its 100 members include associations of insurers, labor organizations, businesses, consumer groups and health providers.

New America Foundation, 1630 Connecticut Ave., N.W., 7th Floor, Washington, DC 20009; (202) 986-2700; www.newamerica.net. A nonpartisan, nonprofit research and information group seeking public-policy options to ensure affordable, portable health coverage and high-quality care for all.

Bibliography

Selected Sources

Books

Aaron, Henry J., William B. Schwartz and Melissa Cox, *Can We Say No: The Challenge of Rationing Health Care*, Brookings Institutions Press, 2005.
Brookings economists argue that rising health-care costs will force the U.S. to follow Great Britain in imposing top-down decisions about who can have what health care.

Cutler, David M., *Your Money or Your Life: Strong Medicine for America's Health Care System*, Oxford University Press, 2004.
A Harvard University economics professor finds that while expensive medical advances of the past half-century have improved health overall, substantial amounts of low-value care also have been provided.

Gingrich, Newt, *Saving Lives and Saving Money*, The Alexis de Tocqueville Institution, 2003.
A former Republican speaker of the House outlines a plan for cutting health costs and improving quality by promoting preventive care and investing in information systems to help consumers become better health-care buyers.

Halvorson, George C., and George J. Isham, *Epidemic of Care*, Jossey-Bass, 2003.
The CEO and the medical director of two leading managed-care organizations examine policy alternatives and new medical practices that might reduce rising health costs.

Articles

Appleby, Julie, and Sharon Silke-Carty, "Ailing GM Looks to Scale Back Generous Health Benefits," *USA Today*, June 23, 2005.
Rising health-care costs are a significant contributor to the financial woes of the large U.S. automaker.

Mullan, Fitzhugh, "Wrestling with Variations: An Interview with Jack Wennberg," *Health Affairs* Web exclusive, Oct. 7, 2004, www.healthaffairs.org.
A former chief of the federal Bureau of Health Professions discusses medical-cost and practice variations with the Dartmouth Medical School professor who pioneered the study of regional variations in health spending.

Reports and Studies

"2005 Employer Benefits Survey," Kaiser Family Foundation and Health Research and Education Trust, 2005.
This annual national survey of employers details current trends in health-care coverage and spending.

"Health Status, Health Insurance, Health Services Utilization: 2001," Household Economic Studies, U.S. Census Bureau, February 2006.
The latest Census Bureau survey describes the health status and health-service-usage patterns of different economic and demographic groups.

"Hidden Costs, Value Lost: Uninsurance in America," Institute of Medicine Committee on the Consequences of Uninsurance, National Academy Press, 2003.
An expert panel analyzes recent research on the financial, health and productivity burdens of having substantial numbers of people uninsured.

Doty, Michelle M., Jennifer N. Edwards and Alyssa L. Holmgren, "Seeing Red: Americans Driven Into Debt by Medical Bills," The Commonwealth Fund, August 2005.
Analysts estimate that about two-in-five American adults have trouble paying medical bills, based on a biennial insurance survey conducted by the nonprofit fund.

Hadley, Jack, and Peter J. Cunningham, "Perception, Reality, and Health Insurance," Center for Studying Health System Change, October 2005.
Economists describe how health status and patterns of seeking health care vary between the insured and the uninsured, based on a multiyear, national survey.

Hadley, Jack, and John Holahan, "The Cost of Care for the Uninsured: What Do We Spend, Who Pays, and What Would Full Coverage Add to Medical Spending?" The Kaiser Commission on Medicaid and the Uninsured, May 2004.
Economists from the liberal-leaning Urban Institute explain how the uninsured population affects American health-care financing overall.

Lesser, Cara S., Paul B. Ginsburg and Laurie E. Felland, "Initial Findings From HSC's 2005 Site Visits: Stage Set for Growing Health-Care Cost and Access Problems," Center for Studying Health System Change, August 2005.
Economists who have tracked the health-care systems in 12 U.S. cities for a decade report that many hospitals and physician-owned clinics are increasing their capacity, a trend expected to push costs higher.

Tu, Ha T., "Rising Health Costs, Medical Debt and Chronic Conditions," Center for Studying Health System Change, September 2004.
About 57 million working-age Americans have chronic illnesses, and more than one-in-five has trouble paying medical bills, according to a national survey.

The Next Step:

Additional Articles from Current Periodicals

Consumer-Directed Health Plans

Colliver, Victoria, "Workers Like Old Health Plans," *The San Francisco Chronicle*, Dec. 10, 2005, p. C1.
Employees enrolled in consumer-directed health plans (CDHPs) are less satisfied than those participating in more traditional health plans, according to the Employee Benefit Research Institute and the Commonwealth Fund.

Costello, Daniel, "Hospital Bills — But With Interest," *Los Angeles Times*, Dec. 12, 2005, p. F1.
CDHPs are fueling the growth of medical credit cards that give participants more time to pay off high deductibles and expenses.

Gearon, Christopher J., "High Deductible, High Risk," *The Washington Post*, Oct. 18, 2005, p. F1.
High-deductible health plans feature low-premiums but can cause large out-of-pocket expenses if the participant's health falters.

Goldstein, Josh, "Coming Soon, But Slowly," *The Philadelphia Inquirer*, Jan. 27, 2006, p. D1.
Philadelphia employers are showing interest in CDHPs, and the region's major insurers offer an array of such plans, but there are few subscribers.

Hundley, Kris, "Hey, Doc, Can You Give Me A Deal?" *St. Petersburg* [Florida] *Times*, March 13, 2005, p. D1.
Health-care experts wonder how successful individuals will be in negotiating lower prices for medical services when using CDHPs.

Neikirk, William, and Judith Graham, "The Health-Care Guessing Game," *Chicago Tribune*, Feb. 12, 2006, p. C3.
Many employees are unhappy with the CDHPs being pushed by President Bush, and critics say the plans favor the healthy and the rich at the expense of the sick and poor.

Vrana, Debora, "Insurer Group to Open Bank," *Los Angeles Times*, Dec. 5, 2005, p. C1.
Blue Cross-Blue Shield plans to open a bank to enable consumers who use health savings accounts to keep cash available for out-of-pocket expenses.

Employers and Health Costs

Christoffersen, John, "On Strike For Health Care," *The Philadelphia Inquirer*, March 2, 2006, p. C2.
Medical benefits are the central issue in labor disputes across the country, as companies with aging work forces and increasing costs reduce medical coverage for employees.

Granito, Alison, "Wal-Mart Chief: Health-Care Fix Will Require Cooperation," *The Seattle Times*, Feb. 27, 2006, p. B2.
CEO Lee Scott told U.S. governors that Wal-Mart's expansion of employees' health benefits will not reduce soaring health-care costs.

Lamb, Gregory M., "Small Companies Ask, 'How About a Raise Instead of a Medical Plan?' " *The Christian Science Monitor*, Aug. 29, 2005, p. 13.
Small businesses are trying to save money by offering extra goodies to workers — such as cash payments or extra donations to their retirement or health savings accounts — if they don't sign up for company medical plans.

Rising Costs

Francis, David R., "Why the Healthcare Crises Won't Go Away," *The Christian Science Monitor*, July 18, 2005, p. 17.
Many conservative business and health-policy experts support a market solution to controlling rising health-care costs, but critics say the plan will fail because medical care is not really a "market" in the traditional economic sense.

Halper, Evan, "Benefits Tab Seen as Major Fiscal Drag," *Los Angeles Times*, Feb. 18, 2006, p. B1.
California has guaranteed health benefits for current and future retirees that could cost more than $70 billion.

Lauerman, John, "Drugs Now Win Approval More Quickly, Cutting Costs," *The Philadelphia Inquirer*, March 8, 2006, p. C2.
Drugmakers are cutting the time it takes to test and win approval for new medicines, suggesting that higher prices are not linked to rising research and development costs.

Citing the *CQ Researcher*

Sample formats for citing these reports in a bibliography include the ones listed below. Preferred styles and formats vary, so please check with your instructor or professor.

MLA STYLE

Jost, Kenneth. "Rethinking the Death Penalty." CQ Researcher 16 Nov. 2001: 945-68.

APA STYLE

Jost, K. (2001, November 16). Rethinking the death penalty. *CQ Researcher, 11*, 945-968.

CHICAGO STYLE

Jost, Kenneth. "Rethinking the Death Penalty." *CQ Researcher*, November 16, 2001, 945-968.

CQ Researcher

Published by CQ Press, a division of Congressional Quarterly Inc.

cqresearcher.com

Future of Feminism

Are women returning to a 1950s mind-set?

The founders of the feminist movement some 40 years ago envisioned a glorious new era of equality for working women. But today more than half of employed parents can't take time off to care for sick children, and day care costs more than tuition at a state university. To be sure, women have made tremendous strides: Most mothers are in the work force today, and women account for half the managerial jobs and half the law-school graduates. But women still lag behind male counterparts in many ways, including wages. Many U.S. jobs are not "mother friendly," leading some women to opt off of the career treadmill and forcing out blue-collar workers. Some sociologists are asking whether feminism has failed, particularly in its inability to transform domestic life, where women still do the bulk of household chores. Indeed, some disparage women for returning to a 1950s mind-set — when "a woman's place was in the home." But some young feminists assert that child rearing should be respected work.

Philadelphia author Miriam Peskowitz, 41, says most employers don't enable women to combine work and parenting.

INSIDE THIS REPORT

CQ Researcher • April 14, 2006 • www.cqresearcher.com
Volume 16, Number 14 • Pages 313-336

CQ PRESS

RECIPIENT OF SOCIETY OF PROFESSIONAL JOURNALISTS AWARD FOR EXCELLENCE ◆ AMERICAN BAR ASSOCIATION SILVER GAVEL AWARD

THE ISSUES

BACKGROUND

CURRENT SITUATION

OUTLOOK

SIDEBARS AND GRAPHICS

FOR FURTHER RESEARCH

Cover: Philadelphia author Miriam Peskowitz, 41, says most employers don't enable women to combine work and parenting. She runs a Web site for feminist mothers, www.playgroundrevolution.com. (Miriam Peskowitz)

CQ Researcher

April 14, 2006
Volume 16, Number 14

MANAGING EDITOR: Thomas J. Colin

ASSISTANT MANAGING EDITOR: Kathy Koch

ASSOCIATE EDITOR: Kenneth Jost

STAFF WRITERS: Marcia Clemmitt, Peter Katel, Pamela M. Prah

CONTRIBUTING WRITERS: Rachel S. Cox, Sarah Glazer, David Hosansky, Patrick Marshall, Tom Price

DESIGN/PRODUCTION EDITOR: Olu B. Davis

ASSISTANT EDITOR: Melissa J. Hipolit

CQ PRESS

A Division of
Congressional Quarterly Inc.

SENIOR VICE PRESIDENT/PUBLISHER:
John A. Jenkins

DIRECTOR, LIBRARY PUBLISHING: Kathryn C. Suárez

DIRECTOR, EDITORIAL OPERATIONS:
Ann Davies

CONGRESSIONAL QUARTERLY INC.

CHAIRMAN: Paul C. Tash

VICE CHAIRMAN: Andrew P. Corty

PRESIDENT/EDITOR IN CHIEF: Robert W. Merry

CQ Researcher (ISSN 1056-2036) is printed on acid-free paper. Published weekly, except March 24, July 7, July 14, Aug. 4, Aug. 11, Nov. 24, Dec. 22 and Dec. 29, by CQ Press, a division of Congressional Quarterly Inc. Annual full-service subscriptions for institutions start at $667. For pricing, call 1-800-834-9020, ext. 1906. To purchase a *CQ Researcher* report in print or electronic format (PDF), visit www.cqpress.com or call 866-427-7737. Single reports start at $10. Bulk purchase discounts and electronic-rights licensing are also available. Periodicals postage paid at Washington, D.C., and additional mailing offices. POSTMASTER: Send address changes to *CQ Researcher*, 1255 22nd St., N.W., Suite 400, Washington, DC 20037.

Future of Feminism

By Sarah Glazer

The Issues

A bus driver is fired for arriving three minutes late to work because her son had an asthma attack. A divorced mother loses her janitor's job for missing a day of work after her retarded son's babysitter didn't show up. A telephone-company clerk is ordered to attend a two-week training course out of town on the first day of her return from maternity leave — or be fired. [1]

It wasn't supposed to be this way. In the 1970s, founders of the feminist movement envisioned a glorious, new era of equality: Women doing the same job as men would get the same pay. The glass ceiling keeping women out of the executive suite would be shattered. And child care woes would be banished by a network of reliable, inexpensive day-care centers.

Xerox Corp.

Xerox CEO Anne Mulcahy is a rarity among female executives. While women account for half the nation's managerial jobs, fewer than 2 percent are CEO's for Fortune *500 companies. Many young women today see the new feminist frontier as reshaping the workplace so parents — including fathers — have more flexibility to take care of children without economic penalties or loss of job status.*

To the dismay of the early feminists, however, more than half of employed parents today can't take time off to care for sick children; day care costs more than tuition at a state university. [2] The United States remains one of only five countries — out of 168 — that does not mandate paid maternity leave. [3] And many employers, to remain globally competitive, require blue-collar employees to work overtime and white-collar employees to put in 70-hour weeks. [4]

On the other hand, feminists back then would have been astounded to see that most mothers are in the work force today and that women account for half the managerial jobs and half the law-school graduates.

Nonetheless, many wonder why women haven't risen further. Women may be managers, but fewer than 2 percent are CEOs for *Fortune* 500 companies; women make up half the new hires at law firms but only 17 percent of the partners in 2005. [5] And, women still earn less than men — only 77 cents to a man's dollar, on average — a gap that widens as women get older and have children. [6] (*See graph, p. 316.*)

In the march toward equality, women's growing participation in the labor force has been hailed as a major indicator that men and women have attained equality. But that march stalled in 2000 at 77 percent for women ages 25-44. [7] About 60 percent of all women age 16 and over are in the labor force, compared to nearly 75 percent of men. [8]

In a controversial 2003 article, *The New York Times* declared that an "opt-out revolution" was under way among professional women who had left their jobs to stay home with children. The article raised questions about whether women were returning to the values of 1950s domesticity, when middle-class women viewed wifedom and motherhood as a lifetime occupation. [9] Several economists have since disputed that there was a real decline beyond the job losses suffered by both men and women during the dot-com bust. (*See sidebar, p. 327.*)

Some experts also point out that professional women with advanced degrees represent only a small portion of all working women, many of whom do not have the luxury of quitting a job, and that career women often leave their jobs reluctantly. [10] However, the tug between home and workplace is not an entirely upper-class phenomenon.

"For social workers, nurses or teachers, the salaries are so low that once they add in babysitting costs the numbers don't work out. So they end up quitting," says Philadelphia author Miriam Peskowitz, who interviewed 70 families for her 2005 book *The Truth Beyond the Mommy Wars: Who Decides What Makes a Good Mother?*

Working mothers get three-and-a-half hours less sleep per week than non-working mothers in order to spend more quality time with their children, according to new research by University of Maryland sociologist Suzanne Bianchi. "There may be a point of exhaustion where the quality of life is so low that women cut back and say, 'This isn't working. Something's got to give,'" says Bianchi. What "gives" is usually their job, she adds.

Women Still Earn Less Than Men

Women's wages continued their steady climb relative to men's in the 1990s — but more slowly. By 2004, women earned 77 percent as much as men doing similar work on an annual basis and an all-time high of 80 percent on a weekly basis. In 2004, median annual earnings were nearly $10,000 more for men than for women (inset).*

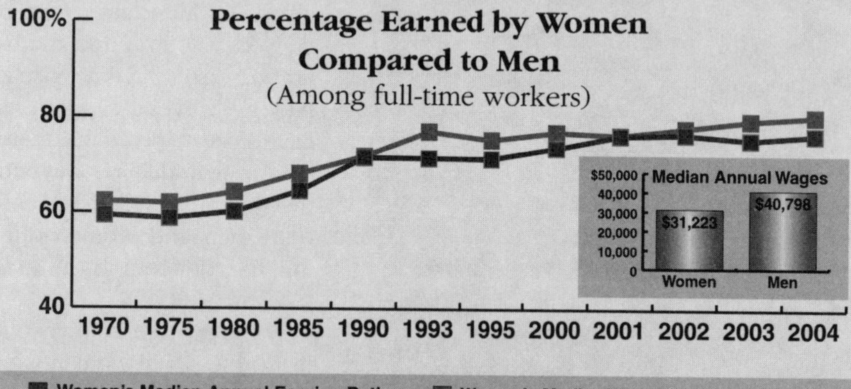

** Annual earnings ratio data include self-employed workers. Weekly data are for wage and salary workers and are not restricted to full-year workers.*

Source: "The Gender Gap Ratio," Institute for Women's Policy Research

When employers today demand long hours or mandatory overtime, they assume that most workers can behave as if they have spouses at home to take care of the kids. [11] Joan Williams, a professor at the University of California's Hastings College of Law, has documented more than 600 suits by employees who claim employers discriminated against them because they are parents. "Case law shows that women aren't opting out — they're being pushed out by bias," Williams says.

Women in their 20s and 30s see the new feminist frontier as reshaping the workplace so parents (including men) have more time and flexibility to take care of children without economic penalties. Mothers' groups are coalescing around a legislative agenda that includes the right to paid sick and parental leave and part-time work with benefits.

"This is a set of issues that's very important to swing voters — namely women," says Karen Kornbluh, policy director for Sen. Barack Obama, D-Ill. While business interests oppose measures that could increase the cost of hiring, some major corporations argue that flexible work schedules actually improve productivity by reducing burnout and turnover (*see p. 328*).

Yet the biggest, most established women's organizations have failed to make workplace flexibility a top priority and are losing fresh blood as a result, say some critics within the movement. Less than a quarter of young women identify themselves as feminists, according to a 2001 Gallup Poll. [12]

"Where the woman's movement has stalled is in work-family issues," says Leslie Calman, vice president for external relations at the International Center for Research on Women (ICRW) and a longtime feminist activist. "There's an ambivalence" at the major women's organizations, she says, about the choice to stay home with children. Yet, "Scratch any woman in her 20s and 30s, and the issue is flex-time, child care, male-female sharing of work at home. Women's organizations have taken themselves out of the middle-class picture by focusing exclusively on reproductive rights."

In just the past year, for example, major women's groups like the National Organization for Women (NOW) have campaigned — unsuccessfully — against the nominations of two Supreme Court justices with conservative abortion records and a new abortion ban in South Dakota. Polls show the majority of Americans support legal abortion, but with restrictions, and some critics say the women's movement's refusal to acknowledge that ambivalence is costing it potential supporters.

"If pro-choice people were more willing to adopt the position of those in the middle — that abortion should be legal but every effort made to reduce its incidence — a lot more people would join our movement," says Frances Kissling, president of Catholics for a Free Choice. "A lot of young feminists are very appreciative of someone saying this and feel that feminists since the '70s shut them down when they express feelings about the issue."

Nancy Keenan, president of NARAL Pro-Choice America, says "the right to choose is not a single issue; it's tied to fundamental rights of freedom and privacy for women. It's linked to other policies the women's movement has fought for, including women's independence to make economic decisions." Recent threats to women's rights, including South Dakota's ban and the refusal of some pharmacists to dispense birth control, have led many young women who were not otherwise politically active to contact her organization, she says.

As for the charge that the movement has neglected family issues, "The people who are saying that don't know what the feminist movement is doing," protests Eleanor Smeal, president of the Feminist Majority Foundation and a former president of NOW. "The women's-rights movement has been [fighting for] publicly funded child care as long as I've known. Who testified on behalf of family leave before Congress? * I did in the mid-1980s on the part of all women's groups!"

Yet a host of new Web sites, blogs and organizations sprouting online reveal a fresh approach to reaching women in their 20s and 30s. Alison Stein, 25, says she deliberately avoided the word feminist when recruiting members in this age group for a new women's organization. But concerns about balancing work and family proved a powerful draw. "It's the issue people should be using to get younger women involved," says Stein, founder and director of the Younger Women's Task Force of the National Council of Women's Organizations, an umbrella group representing 20 million women.

Meanwhile, *New York Times* columnist Maureen Dowd worries that young women's distaste for feminism goes deeper than disliking the label. "Narcissism trumps feminism" is how she describes young women's seeming obsession with looking sexy to attract a man — which she calls a "cultural rejection of what the early feminists fought so hard for." Citing the growing taste for cosmetic surgery, Barbie-doll dimensions and "The Bachelor" reality TV show — in which women claw one another's eyes out to get a man — she quips, "If you had sat [*Ms.* magazine founder] Gloria Steinem in a chair in 1968 and shown her the future, would she even have bothered?"

Here are some of the questions being raised in the workplace, the political arena and online:

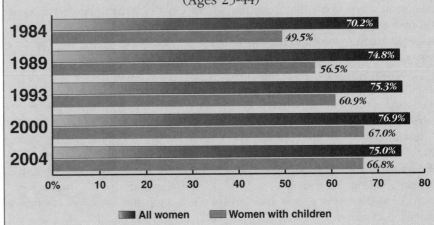

Mothers Are Not 'Opting Out'

The percentage of women in the work force increased from 1984 until 2000, when it began to drop. The decline was roughly the same for women with children and all women, undercutting anecdotal theories that more mothers today are "opting out" of the work force to stay home with their children.

Percentage of Women Working
(Ages 25-44)

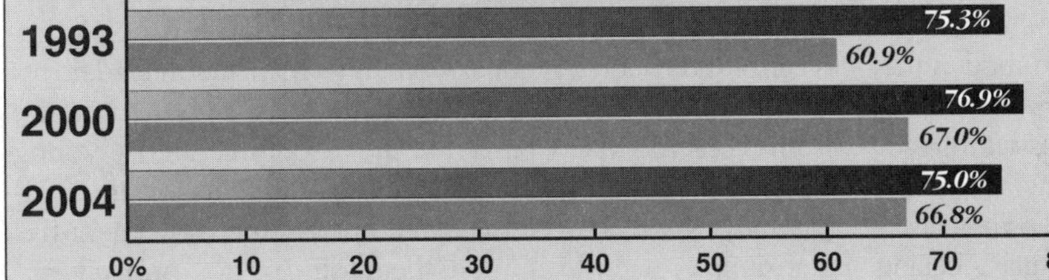

Source: "Are Women Opting Out? Debunking the Myth," Center for Economic and Policy Research, December 2005

Has feminism failed?

Since the 1970s, women have made huge strides. Yet for every advance, questions arise as to why women are not doing better.

Most of the women's movement's early efforts focused on direct discrimination in hiring, promotion and pay. But some experts now believe women's failure to earn as much as men or to climb to the top of the corporate ladder is due to "indirect" discrimination, which penalizes women for being society's child bearers.

"Why are women's earnings still different from men's if we've had all this equality? It's indirect discrimination," says Martha Farnsworth Riche, former director of the U.S. Census Bureau and a demographer at Cornell University's Center for the Study of Economy and Society. Motherhood changes women's work-life decisions, she points out, which results in economic penalties. After having children, a professional woman may decide to become a teacher so she can have summers off — and her pay declines — or she won't take a promotion because it's too time-consuming, Riche observes.

The tendency to interrupt work for a few years, scale back hours or take advantage of parental-leave policies keeps women from advancing, according to many economists. When women initially enter the work force, they earn almost as much as men: 87 cents to a man's dollar between ages 25 and 29. But when they start having children, women fall behind. By the time they reach their early 40s, women earn only 71 cents to a man's dollar. [13]

Interruptions in women's careers account for up to a third of the gender pay gap, according to one study. [14]

* The Family and Medical Leave Act, which provides 12 weeks of unpaid family leave, was signed by President Bill Clinton in 1993.

Cornell University economist Francine D. Blau has also found that about 40 percent of the wage gap remains "unexplained" after taking into account such factors as women's tendency to enter lower-paid professions. That suggests direct discrimination still plays a role, she says. (*See sidebar, p. 319.*)

The pay gap might also increase with age because women hit the infamous "glass ceiling" at the top of their professions, says Blau, explaining that the gap becomes most pronounced among women in the top 10 percent of salaries. All these factors help explain why women occupy only 16 percent of corporate officers' chairs even though they fill half of the nation's managerial jobs. [15]

Law Professor Williams contends that many women hit the "maternal wall" of discrimination before they ever reach the glass ceiling. For example, a civil engineer in Pennsylvania was awarded $3 million in a lawsuit because she was passed over for promotion after the birth of her son. She testified that the president of the company asked her, "Do you want to have babies or do you want a career here?" [16]

Yet such work-life issues have been a low priority for feminist organizations like NOW, argues the ICRW's Calman. That's partly because feminist leaders "want to be CEOs, to be empowered in male ways and run things," she says. "They know if a woman stays home it's less likely she will be a CEO." Calman recalls a meeting where a mother with an advanced business degree said she was staying home with her child. "What a waste!" was the muttered reaction from a leader of a feminist organization.

But it seems like the right decision to younger women who want to care for their children at home but keep their hand in a career. "Many of us are saying you can be a stay-at-home mom and a feminist," says Philadelphia author Peskowitz, 41, who runs a Web site (www.playgroundrevolution.com) for feminist mothers. But she says most employers don't enable women to effectively combine work and parenting, pointing to her own fall in status and pay when she decided to teach part time.

"For previous generations it was about access [to the workplace]; for this generation it's parenting," says Amy Richards, 36, co-founder of Third Wave Foundation, a feminist foundation based in New York City that aims to combat inequality for women ages 15-30. She is writing a book titled *Opting In: The Case for Motherhood and Feminism.*

To criticism that the movement has overly focused on abortion rights, national women's-organization leaders respond that abortion rights form the basis for the economic rights young women are seeking. Some young feminists agree but say the movement has turned them off by not publicly acknowledging that abortion is often a difficult and sad decision. "Coming out about these things and having open conversations does point to political solutions," says Jennifer Baumgardner, a New York author and maker of "I Had an Abortion," a documentary film.

Others say the movement needs to think about ways to restructure the workplace to make part-time work more of an option and less economically precarious. "Most studies show most women would like to be in the work force at least part time; that's a bit of a reality check on the idea that women are returning to values of the 50s," says Judith Stadtman Tucker, founder of the Web site Mothers Movement Online.

But some movement leaders warn that the focus of new mothers' groups on part-time work is largely the province of middle-class and upper-class mothers. "For a lot of women part-time work is not viable because they don't have the income that allows them to go part-time," says Deven McGraw, chief operating officer of the National Partnership for Women and Families.

Policies to support working mothers — like paid leave and subsidized child care — have trouble succeeding because they're expensive and involve big government, notes Katha Pollitt, a feminist columnist for *The Nation* magazine. Day care's expense is one reason more women's groups aren't working on it, according to Smeal of the Feminist Majority Foundation. "Funding is very difficult in this area," she says. "You've got centers costing $10,000-$20,000 per child annually."

But many young mothers want more time with their children at home, not institutional day care. Baumgardner, who has a toddler, says "some of the things imagined 30 years ago aren't solutions I'd imagine now. When I think of government-run day care, I think of the post office in my neighborhood. It's disgusting and has bullet-proof windows."

Conservative critic Kate O'Beirne, author of the new book *Women Who Make the World Worse and How Their Radical Feminist Assault Is Ruining Our Schools, Families, Military, and Sports*, writes, "The feminist movement has long been on a collision course with what we know to be true about the natural bond between mother and child." [17] Feminist demands for equality have denied the biological differences between men and women by insisting — erroneously — that women are every bit as committed to their careers as men are, she argues. The disparity in wages between women with children and men is "not sex discrimination but rather the result of choices mothers freely make in their desire to balance work and family responsibilities." [18]

But many women say their decision to drop out of the workplace was not a "free choice." Hunter College sociologist Pamela Stone studied professional women who dropped out of their careers when they had children and found most wanted to continue

Gender Pay Gap Hits Mothers Hardest

The "59 cents" pin was a fashion favorite among feminists in the 1970s to protest the lower income women earned, on average, for every dollar made by men. But the pin became obsolete by 1989, when women earned almost 69 cents on the dollar, narrowing the wage gap. [1]

Women's wages have continued to climb — but more slowly. By 2004, women earned 77 percent as much as men on an annual basis and an all-time high of 80 percent on a weekly basis.

But the good news hides even bigger disparities in earnings, economists say, by ignoring the fact that most women either work part time or drop out of the labor force to care for their families. When those differences are taken into account, women earn about 60 percent less than men over a 15-year period — a cumulative loss of more than $270,000 each — according to the Institute for Women's Policy Research. [2]

The good news also ignores the fact that women earn almost the same as men until they reach the age of childbearing and more important, child-rearing. From ages 25 to 29, they earn 87 cents to a man's dollar. By the time they reach the 40-44 age group, their earnings plunge to 71 cents to a man's dollar. [3]

One study found that before childbearing, the wages of highly skilled mothers and non-mothers were not significantly different. But highly skilled women experience an 8 percent reduction in their wages during the first five years after they have a child compared to childless women. After 10 years, the penalty rises to more than 20 percent — even after taking into account any reduction in mothers' working hours. [4]

Economists describe this as a "motherhood penalty." Some economists say the penalty stems from the extended leaves mothers often take from their jobs, but others say that work interruptions account for only about one-third of the gender earnings gap.

"There's all kinds of evidence to suggest mothers are discriminated against," says Cornell University sociologist Shelley Correll. She recently asked students to evaluate the résumés of hypothetical job applicants with comparable work experience. She found that women with children were given poorer evaluations than men or women without children and were held to higher standards of punctuality. [5]

"A large component of the gender wage gap is really that mothers' wages are depressed," says Correll. "If women don't have children, they tend to do pretty well at work."

Some people say women can't expect to have it all — if they want to do as well as men they could choose not to have children. But says Correll: "As a society, this can't be a solution; you'd be saying no women should have children."

"If women don't have children, they tend to do pretty well at work."

— Cornell University sociologist Shelley Correll

Several studies have shown that the more housework women do the lower their wages are — even after adjusting for the possibility that lower-earning women do more housework because they can't afford to hire a cleaning lady. [6] And the motherhood penalty is worse for women with a high-school diploma than for those with a college degree, perhaps because they work in more rigid jobs. "If I have to leave at 4:30 for a child-related emergency, it's more likely to be noticed" at such a workplace, suggests Correll.

Cornell economist Francine Blau finds that after she adjusts for obvious factors, like the fact that women often enter lower-paid occupations than men, about 41 percent of the wage gap is unexplained. The biggest wage gap — for older women at the highest salary levels — suggests they're bumping up against the proverbial glass ceiling. "We've made so much progress that what is left are more subtle, unconscious barriers," she says. "The remaining barriers may be hard to correct."

[1] Francine D. Blau and Lawrence M. Kahn, "The U.S. Gender Pay Gap in the 1990s: Slowing Convergence," National Bureau of Economic Research, October 2004; www.nber.org. Women earned 59.7 percent of men's earnings in 1979.

[2] "Still a Man's Labor Market: The Long Term Earnings Gap," Institute for Women's Policy Research, June 4, 2004; www.iwpr.org.

[3] Sylvia Ann Hewlett and Carolyn Buck Luce, "Off-Ramps and On-Ramps," *Harvard Business Review*, March 2005, pp. 1-10, 4.

[4] Carrie Conaway, "Paying the Price," *Regional Review*, Federal Reserve Bank of Boston, First Quarter 2005, pp. 27-29.

[5] Shelley J. Correll and Stephen Benard, "Getting a Job: Is There a Motherhood Penalty?" June 13, 2005 (unpublished paper).

[6] Conaway, *op. cit.*, pp. 27-29.

working at least part time, but their employers were too inflexible. "These women have been seen as the poster girls for the failure of feminism," she says. "They're not. It's the failure of major institutions of society."

Poor, single working moms and those on welfare often face this dilemma far more cruelly, as they can often afford only inferior child care, and each hour of child care purchased reduces their disposable income. In 1973, the late Sen. Daniel Patrick Moynihan, D-N.Y., wrote, "If American society recognized home-making and child rearing as productive work . . . the receipt of welfare might not imply dependency. But we don't. It may be hoped that the

Working Moms Do Most 'Home' Work

Fathers do more housework and child care now than they did in 1965, but working mothers today spend twice as many hours as dads at both tasks.

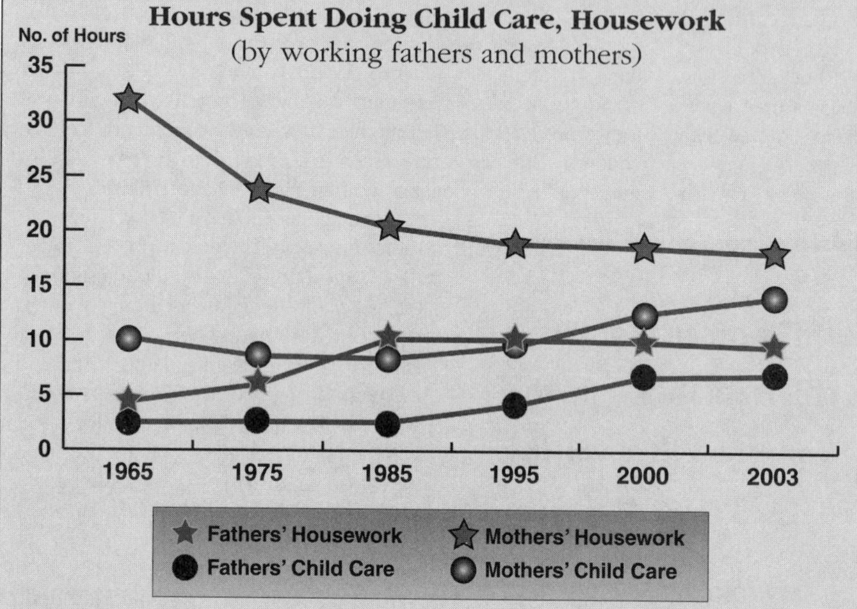

Source: Suzanne Bianchi, et al., *"Maternal Employment and Family Caregiving," Department of Sociology and Maryland Population Research Center (MPRC), University of Maryland, Dec. 9, 2005*

women's movement of the present time will change this."

Although some feminists argued that a mother's child rearing should be treated like paid work, the movement did not succeed in applying this philosophy to mothers on welfare during Moynihan's lifetime. But in recent years some states — notably Minnesota and Montana — have created programs to pay welfare mothers to stay home to care for their own children instead of telling them to find work and farm their children out to child care. [19]

Is there a glass ceiling at home?

"Think about it. Who routinely unloads the dishwasher, puts away the laundry and picks up the socks in your house? Who earns the largest share of the money? Who calls the shots?" author Judith Warner asked recently in a *New York Times* op-ed. The answers for many families are the same as they were 50 years ago, she pointed out, even though the outside world for women has changed enormously since then. The feminist revolution remains incomplete because of its failure to reshape domestic life, she argued. [20]

Research shows that mothers still do twice as much housework as their husbands and are usually expected to be responsible for child care. [21] Could this "second shift" at home be keeping them from advancing in the workplace?

Yes, argues Linda Hirshman, a retired professor of philosophy and women's studies at Brandeis University, in a widely debated piece in the liberal *American Prospect* magazine. The number of women in elite jobs doesn't come close to men's, she argues, because "the real glass ceiling is at home." In describing housework as repetitive tasks that interfere with women's flourishing, she harks back to pioneering feminist Betty Friedan's original radical critique in *The Feminine Mystique:* "Vacuuming the living room floor — with or without make-up — is not work that takes enough thought or energy to challenge any woman's full capacity." [22]

The issue of the unfair division of labor in the home is "what the workplace was [for feminists in] 1964 and the vote in 1920," Hirshman argues. Her solution for women: Train for high-paying jobs and marry down, so your job doesn't get sacrificed for his.

Since 1965, fathers have actually more than doubled the number of hours they spend on housework — to 9.6 hours week — and nearly tripled the number of hours they spend on child care — to about 7 hours a week. But women still spend nearly twice as much time as men on both housework (18 hours) and child care (14 hours), according to University of Maryland sociologist Bianchi. [23] *(See graph at left.)*

It may be a noble ideal to get men to do half the housework and child care, but they won't do it as long as the workplace penalizes them for it, cautions Hastings law Professor Williams. "We've got a workplace designed to marginalize anyone not available to the employer all the time," she says. "Men earn 70 percent of the family income, and masculinity is defined as the provider role. They can't do half at home and live up to expectations placed on them as men. The key pressure point is the workplace."

Several recent studies of employees in high-powered professions find that only those who spend more time on child rearing than their colleagues suffer career or earnings penalties. A study of financial-services professionals found that both women and men who took advantage of a firm's family-sick-leave policy earned less than their peers. "In other words, so long as you don't spend too much time on your family, then it need not affect your career to have one," concludes Joyce P. Jacobsen, chairwoman of the Wesleyan University economics department, in a recent review of the studies. [24]

Conservatives bristled at Hirshman's contention that women who stay home handling diapers and garbage have "voluntarily become untouchables." "The domestic sphere may not offer the sort of brutalizing, dominating power Hirshman admires, but it is the realm of unmatched influence," responded *New York Times* columnist David Brooks. "If there is one thing we have learned over the past generation, it is that a child's IQ, mental habits and destiny are largely shaped in the first few years of life, before school or the outside world has much influence." [25]

Getty Images/Alex Wong

New York Times *columnist Maureen Dowd, author of the 2005 book* Are Men Necessary?, *sees young women's seeming obsession with their appearance as a "cultural rejection of what the early feminists fought so hard" to achieve.*

Likewise, argues feminist economist Nancy Folbre of the University of Massachusetts-Amherst, "the notion that feminism equals participation in paid employment seems simplistic and formulaic and outdated to me." Women lose something when they focus entirely on paid work, she says, because "the true rewards of life come from relationships that are not driven by pecuniary gain or career ambition."

Folbre has long argued that a mother caring for a child is a valuable economic activity that the family would otherwise have to purchase. "It's a set of services that men have taken for granted; literally it's a grant — it's a gift," she says. But it's hard to get men to share the load, she acknowledges.

"But what if you have a choice between getting your partner to take on more responsibility for care work or just ending the relationship? Which hurts your family more?" she asks. "A lot of women are facing this choice." If those women decide to continue doing the extra work themselves, "I don't think that indicates a loss of commitment to feminist ideals," she says. "It's just a practical decision that taking care of family and relationships is for them more important."

Most conservatives argue that women freely choose to stay at home because they prefer domestic tasks. "I'm not sure the average mother would be happy if half of the child rearing was done by men," says University of Virginia sociologist W. Bradford Wilcox. He recently found that traditionally minded women who do most of the housework are more content with their marriages than feminist women. [26] "The question is whether men will ever engage in family life on a 50-50 basis," Wilcox says. "No society in the world has come to that point." Even in egalitarian Sweden, women do most of the child rearing and dominate such traditionally female occupations as social services and health care, according to Wilcox.

Economist Jacobsen suggests that when the wife earns more money, the man will stay home with the kids because it makes economic sense. For example, since her husband retired, he's been in charge of the children's schedules, while she pursued a hard-charging career.

Richards of the Third Wave Foundation is her family's main breadwinner. When she's expected to take care of her two children after a stressful day, she finds herself having a typical male reaction: "Listen, my work brings in the money; yours doesn't."

But she doesn't see that macho reaction as the solution. "To me, the ultimate goal of feminism was not to have women and men switching those roles but not to have them based on economics in the first place."

Are women returning to a 1950s mind-set?

New York investment banker Shannon O'Hara, 38, the mother of two, has been surprised at how lonely her career path has been. * Only

---

* Her name has been changed to protect her privacy.

one other female business-school classmate is still working, and hardly any other mothers from her daughter's private school are working. Even more surprising, she says, most of them look askance at her as if to ask, "Your husband doesn't make enough money to support you?"

O'Hara thinks most of her female business-school classmates threw in the towel because of a combination of male chauvinism at work and strains on their families. Her typical workday is 7 a.m. to 7 p.m. and involves frequent overnight travel. "It hits you every time you miss something," like a child's school play, she says. But one reason she keeps working is to send a positive message to her daughter. "It's a crime if after all this education, you can do whatever you want but the message is — go marry some rich guy."

Marrying some rich guy seems to be frequently on the minds of young women, according to some observers of today's dating scene. Among women in their 20s and early 30s, "There's this incredible, intense anxiety about commitment and a feeling that marriage is men's to bestow," says Kamy Wicoff, 33, a New York writer whose book on marriage in her generation, *I Do But I Don't*, is scheduled to be published in June. "You look at your 20s as not 'real life' but as a fun, single phase." Eventually, marriage becomes necessary, she says, "because a career doesn't sustain you."

In interviews with 80 college-educated young women, Wicoff was surprised by how much they were spending on clothes and beauty products — $30,000 was one woman's estimate of her yearly expenditures. These young women are, in essence, a "product on the marriage market," she says, "so they have to spend a lot on their appearance."

The statistics about certain groups of elite women back up Wicoff and O'Hara's anecdotes. A survey of three Harvard Business School graduating classes found that only 38 percent of women end up in full-time careers; a broader study showed that a third of white women with MBAs are not working full time. [27]

To learn what happens to women with advanced degrees, Brandeis University's Hirshman interviewed about 80 percent of the 41 women who announced their weddings in *The New York Times* social pages over three Sundays in 1996. She found that — at about age 40 — nearly all of the college graduates with careers were home with their children. Half the married women with children were not working at all, and among those working part time, several were a long way from their original career paths. [28]

While this trajectory sounds a lot like the 1950s, when women ended their careers after they married, does it represent a broader trend? *Nation* columnist Pollitt pooh-poohs the idea. The women who announce their weddings in the *Times* are "a very small class of elite women who come from wealthy families and plan to marry wealthy men," she says. "Those women never had a commitment to the work force." Moreover, it makes economic sense to quit, she adds, "if you marry some guy and he's a bond trader making $1 million, and you have a choice working as a lawyer for $200,000."

While about 20 percent of women say they want to stay home with children as their life's work, the rising number of women in the labor force tells another story. According to the most recent figures from the Bureau of Labor Statistics, female participation in the labor force rose steadily from 43 percent of all women in 1970 to 60 percent by 2000 and only receded slightly — to 59 percent in 2004, the most recent year for which the bureau has statistics. [29] Even if women's work force participation has reached a plateau, there's no hint that it's moving backwards in any significant way.

Indeed, recent research suggests that rather than dropping out permanently from the work force, professional women are taking temporary "off-ramps," averaging about two years, before returning to work, according to a recent survey by economist Sylvia Ann Hewlett in the *Harvard Business Review*. Even in this group, most women cannot afford to quit their careers entirely, the survey found. Less than a third of the women said they had quit because their spouse's income was sufficient for the family to live on. [30]

In addition to the pull of family, there were "push" factors that made women head out the office door, such as unstimulating assignments once they became mothers and a lack of advancement opportunity. [31] Indeed, work-related reasons were more important in pushing professional women with children to leave their jobs than a desire to return to traditional family roles, Hunter College sociologist Stone found. In interviews with more than 50 professional women in seven metropolitan areas, only 20 percent said they'd found their permanent calling in caring for children.

Most were ambivalent about quitting their jobs, and many said the decision was "protracted and agonizing," according to Stone. Before dropping out, these women had averaged 13 years in the world of 60-hour workweeks in male-dominated fields like law, business and the sciences. [32]

Among the most common reasons for leaving was workplace inflexibility — either an inability to negotiate a part-time schedule or a conviction that the employer would never even consider it. "Women who get into Harvard Law School believe in the system — jobs have to be 60-plus hours a week," says Stone.

The women Stone interviewed "wanted to create a sense of family and have a presence in their children's lives," she says. Many were married to men in hard-driving jobs who were rarely home. The women "were not willing to have

Continued on p. 325

Chronology

1920s *Women's-rights advocates shift their focus from the domestic sphere to legal equality and voting rights.*

1920
The 19th Amendment gives women the right to vote.

1960s *Women win landmark victories in the fight for workplace equal rights.*

1963
Equal Pay Act guarantees "equal pay for equal work."

1964
Author Betty Friedan condemns housewifery in *The Feminine Mystique*. . . . Civil Rights Act bans sex discrimination against women.

1965
Head Start is established.

1966
Friedan founds National Organization for Women (NOW).

1968
Newspaper want ads that seek "men only" are ruled illegal.

1970s *Feminists win the* Roe v. Wade *abortion decision but lose on child care legislation and the Equal Rights Amendment (ERA).*

1971
President Richard M. Nixon vetoes Comprehensive Child Development Act, which would have established child care programs.

1972
Title IX of the Education Act forbids federally funded educational programs, including sports, from discriminating on the basis of sex. . . . Congress passes the ERA.

1973
Supreme Court legalizes abortion nationwide in *Roe v. Wade*.

1977
Indiana becomes the 35th and last state to ratify the ERA, three states shy of the 38 needed.

1978
Pregnancy Disability Act classifies pregnancy as a medical disability and bans discrimination on the grounds of pregnancy or childbirth.

1980s *More mothers enter the labor force, prompting feminists to argue for more focus on family issues.*

1981
Friedan argues in *The Second Stage* that the women's movement should help improve family conditions through flexible work policies.

1987
Half of women with infants are employed at least part time.

1990s *Women in labor force peak at 60 percent.*

1992
Third Wave Foundation founded for young feminists.

1993
President Bill Clinton signs Family and Medical Act requiring large employers to offer workers 12 weeks of unpaid leave to care for a child or relative.

2000s *Mothers' groups agitate for more government and workplace support; pro-choice movement loses major abortion battles.*

2000
The percentage of working mothers with infants drops for the first time since measurements began in 1976.

2001
Ann Crittenden's *The Price of Motherhood* argues mothers should get more flexible policies in the workplace.

2002
California becomes first state to require paid parental leave.

April 27, 2005
Sen. Edward M. Kennedy, D-Mass, introduces bill to provide seven days of paid sick leave for a parent or a sick child.

Sept. 29, 2005
Senate confirms Judge John G. Roberts Jr. to Supreme Court over opposition of pro-choice groups.

November 2005
Flexible work policies are supported by 53 corporations.

Jan. 31, 2006
Senate confirms Judge Samuel A. Alito to Supreme Court, over opposition of pro-choice groups.

March 6, 2006
South Dakota becomes first state to ban abortions since *Roe v. Wade*.

Is Raunch the New Feminism?

Many '70s-era feminists are horrified by the raunchy behavior among today's young women — breast-baring "Girls Gone Wild" videos, the mainstreaming of pornography, stripper chic (stripping and pole-dancing classes at health clubs) and exhibitionistic, promiscuous dressing. Sex-oriented "Cake" parties for women are only one form of "raunch" reported by *New Yorker* writer Ariel Levy in her recent book *Female Chauvinist Pigs.*

Some observers of today's young, female social scene — notably *New York Times* columnist Maureen Dowd in her 2005 book *Are Men Necessary?* — worry that today's young women are elevating a concern with sexual allure over the struggle for equality in the workplace and the political arena.

According to Levy, embracing pornography and raunch is a way for women to thumb their noses at the moralizing of the Second Wave feminists of the '70s, some of whom fought to outlaw pornography as degrading. As even Dowd acknowledges, "If you talked about heels or babies or cute guys, it was considered frivolous."

But Levy says raunch is also a "garbled attempt at continuing the work of the women's movement" — the strand that sought to liberate women's enjoyment of their sexuality. In today's incarnation, however, she says young women are embracing just one kind of sexuality, in which they're desired as sex objects but don't get to enjoy sex themselves. [1]

Getty Images/Frazer Harrison

Lessons in stripping and pole dancing are popular at Sheila Kelley's S Factor Studio in Los Angeles.

Younger feminists retort that much of this concern is misplaced. Being proud of one's female body *is* being a feminist, they say, and wearing a tight shirt isn't being slutty but is the modern equivalent of giving up bras. "There is power in being sexual," insists Jennifer Baumgardner, 35, a New York author and filmmaker. "Younger people have been informed by the feminists of 30 years ago, who thought it was important to have sexual expression, whether that takes the form of bondage or stripping."

Has the feminist movement failed to convey to today's young women the message that females should not be treated as sex objects? "I don't buy it for a second," Baumgardner answers. "My philosophy of feminism is more about the freedom to do things — not protecting girls from pop culture."

But the celebration of sexuality has taken some disturbing forms in a culture where prostitution, porn stars and stripping are increasingly popularized in fashion, movies and on the Internet.

"Girls are latching onto that notion and acting it out. One way is being paid to give boys blowjobs in the bathroom at school," says Mandy Van Deven, 26, director of community organizing at Girls for Gender Equity, which works with middle-school girls in low-income Brooklyn neighborhoods. The answer she gets from the girls? "Sure, it's a bit like prostitution, but because you're the one in control of your sexuality, you're deciding what you do. It's better than the girl doing it and not getting paid for it."

There's no clinical data comparing the percentage of girls vs. boys that perform oral sex or statistical evidence that there's more oral sex among teens than in years past. But in interviews with 50 boys and girls ages 12-18, Levy found plenty of anecdotes. "What all of these adolescent incidents have in common are, of course, exhibitionism and oral sex — oral sex for the boys, that is," she reports. [2]

With a lot more casual sex going on, and the pressure to "do it" starting as early as age 11 or 12, some young women express concern that the balance of power has tipped too far toward men, who now expect sexual intercourse on the first or second date. "I grew up with boys who felt entitled by the idea they could have sex with girls in a way that they didn't have a generation before," says 33-year-old Kamy Wicoff, a New York writer whose book on marriage in her generation, *I Do But I Don't,* will be published this June. "There was no code of behavior that protected women."

While some women have responded by adopting the same ho-hum attitude toward sex as men — as portrayed in the popular TV series "Sex and the City" — others decry their mothers' liberated generation, which they see as having created higher divorce rates and latchkey children. They look back to an idealized era when family roles were more clearly defined.

Women in their early 30s "have seen this total wreckage" from the baby boomer generation's social upheaval, says Wicoff. "A lot of women want to skip their mothers' generation as role models and go back to their grandmothers.' "

---

[1] Ariel Levy, *Female Chauvinist Pigs* (2005), pp. 74-75.

[2] *Ibid.*, p. 144.

Continued from p. 322

their children taken care of entirely by caregivers," she says. And women who shifted to part-time or job-share positions often found themselves "mommy tracked" — given demotions that played a role in their decision to quit. Many of these women "tried to hold onto their job," says Stone. "They left as a last resort." ■

BACKGROUND

Suffrage Movement

The American women's movement initially had two goals: equality in the public sphere and improvement in the domestic sphere. Equality in public life won out as the primary goal of both the 19th-century suffrage movement and the 1970s women's movement, argues retired Brandeis University sociologist Janet Zollinger Giele in *Two Paths to Women's Equality.* [33]

The suffragists emphasized the sameness of men and women when arguing that women had an equal right to the vote, education and the professions. Another camp — dubbed "maternal feminists" by historians — emphasized women's roles in caring for children and fought for legislation protecting them with shorter workweeks and less dangerous work.

Today, concerns about women's differences are resurfacing, as young women raised to expect workplace equality find their status impeded once they become mothers. "Many equal-rights advocates seemed to think of women as men and so skipped the problem of the family," Giele writes of the 1970s feminist movement. "But . . . one of the main reasons women lack equal education, employment and pay is that they have unequal (and greater) responsibilities for family and children."

In her first public address before the New York Senate, Elizabeth Cady Stanton — one of the founders of the women's-rights movement — demanded that married women be able to earn money, share marital property and custody of children and obtain a divorce. Partly in response, the legislature in 1848 passed the Married Women's Property Act, allowing wives to hold property in their own name. In 1857 and 1860 the state's lawmakers amended the act to allow women to collect their own earnings, share joint custody of their children and inherit equally with their children when widowed. Other states soon enacted similar laws. [34]

But husbands were left with full control of all property created during the marriage. During the Industrial Revolution of the mid-19th century, men began working outside the home as manufacturing jobs replaced farming. But wives' household labor remained intense — typically including gardening, canning, sewing, raising animals, making soap and caring for children. Nevertheless, the courts viewed women's home labor as voluntary. It was no longer considered labor; it was "love." [35]

After the Civil War, the suffragists' agenda shifted to legal equality — specifically the right to vote — and in 1920 the 19th Amendment to the Constitution gave women the right to vote, after having been pending in Congress for 45 years. [36] Since then, suffragists' descendants have focused on gender equality rather than differences between the sexes. For example, after the National Woman's Party proposed the Equal Rights Amendment in 1923, it opposed any form of protective legislation for working women, including shorter hours. [37]

During World War II, women were aggressively recruited into the workplace to aid the war effort. [38] Nevertheless, in the mid-1940s, 43 states still limited the daily and weekly hours a woman could work outside the home, and 15 states prohibited night work for women.

Yet partly because of women's enormous wartime contributions, the Equal Rights Amendment — which had been introduced in every Congress since 1923 — was briefly resurrected in 1946. Although backed by President Harry S Truman and both major parties, a divided Congress failed to pass the measure. [39]

Modern Movement

During the 1960s, women around the country organized local consciousness-raising groups that pushed for a more egalitarian workplace role for women. Friedan's enormously influential 1963 book *The Feminine Mystique* attacked the traditional division of labor between men and women, describing the home as a "concentration camp" for full-time housewives. [40] She founded the National Organization for Women in 1966.

Another major feminist organization, the National Association for the Repeal of Abortion Laws (NARAL) was formed in 1969, later becoming NARAL Pro-Choice America.

The 1960s and '70s saw the passage of tough, new civil-rights laws. In 1963 the Equal Pay for Equal Work Act made it illegal to pay a man more than a woman for the same job. In 1964, the Civil Rights Act forbade gender discrimination in hiring and promotion. In 1968, the Equal Employment Opportunity Commission ruled that help-wanted ads specifying "men only" were illegal. And in 1972, Title IX of the Education Act mandated that all educational programs receiving federal funding, including sports, could not discriminate on the basis of sex. [41]

By the late 1970s, women's expectations about working had been transformed. [42] In 1966, nearly 75 percent

Library of Congress

Suffragists picket at the Republican Party convention in Chicago in 1920. The American women's movement initially sought both equality in the public sphere and improvement in the domestic sphere, but equality in public life became the primary goal.

of women graduating from four-year colleges had majored in female-dominated subjects like education. But by the early 1970s, female undergraduates were moving into career-oriented concentrations that often required advanced degrees. As more women majored in subjects like business, they also entered the work force in larger numbers. While only about half of the women born in the 1930s worked, about 80 percent of those born in 1950 worked. The 1970s saw the largest increase in women's labor-force participation in history. [43]

Harvard economist Claudia Goldin cites the advent of the birth-control pill in the late 1960s as a major influence on these changes. By lowering the risk that pregnancy could derail a career, the "pill" lowered the costs to young, unmarried women of pursuing careers that required substantial, early investments of time. The Supreme Court's 1973 *Roe v. Wade* decision legalizing abortion also contributed to the sense that women's fates were no longer tied to childbearing. [44]

In 1972 Congress passed the Equal Rights Amendment, declaring, "Equality of rights under the law shall not be denied or abridged by the United States or any state on account of sex." Five years later, Indiana became the last state to ratify the ERA. But the amendment was not ratified — missing that goal by three states — considered a major defeat for the women's-rights movement.

In 1978, the Pregnancy Disability Act gave workplace recognition to women's biological differences. Treating pregnancy as no different from a medical disability that would require a man to take time off, it was America's first national policy on employment and motherhood and the first step toward parental leave.

Child Care, Parental Leave

In the 1960s, the United States began to develop a fragmentary child care system. The establishment of Head Start centers in 1965 coincided with a dramatic rise in mothers entering the work force. Responding to reports of scandalous conditions in unlicensed facilities, a coalition of child-development experts, feminists and minority groups lobbied for the Comprehensive Child Development Act, which would have established early-childhood-education programs designed to break the cycle of poverty. Although passed by Congress in 1971, President Richard M. Nixon vetoed it.

Efforts to revive the act in 1975 and 1979 failed, according to Giele, because feminists' major efforts then were focused on the Equal Rights Amendment and reproductive rights. As a result, she says, their support for the idea that universal child care should be available to help liberate women was "mainly rhetorical." [45]

By 1987, half the mothers of infants under age 1 were employed at least part time. Working mothers in the 1980s became increasingly aware that little provision had been made for their other job — caring for children. Many began to propose parental leave as the best way to handle the conflicting demands of work and family. At the same time, radical feminist writers like Kate Millet were declaring that women would never be free until the family was obliterated.

Friedan lashed out against this viewpoint, arguing that feminism was ready to move to *The Second Stage*, as she titled her 1981 book. By focusing on "individualistic" women's rights like abortion, she argued, the women's movement had developed a blind spot about the family, abandoning the subject to conservatives. She urged the movement to move beyond prizing work above family and to focus on expanding parental leave and getting more flexible workplace policies and better child care centers.

In 1993, after an eight-year battle and two vetoes by President George H. W. Bush, a coalition of women's groups and conservatives overcame business opposition to pass the Family and Medical Leave Act. Signed into

Are Mothers Opting Out of Work?

A *New York Times Magazine* cover story, "The Opt-Out Revolution," asked in 2003: "Why don't more women get to the top?" and answered "They choose not to." [1] After decades of climbing, the percentage of career women with infants working or seeking employment began to decline slightly in 2000, a trend the *Times* interpreted as evidence that professional mothers were deserting the work force.

Starting at 31 percent in 1976, the percentage of mothers with infants who were working rose almost every year until hitting a high of 58.7 percent in 1998 and then began to drop, from 55 percent in 2000 to 53 percent in 2004. [2]

More recently, the *Times* reported last September that undergraduate women at Yale were planning to quit their jobs when they enter their 30s to have children, setting off a storm of controversy in the blogosphere about whether they represent a larger trend. [3] The *Times* survey was not based on a scientific sample, according to Cornell University sociologist Shelley Correll.

Economist Heather Boushey at the Center for Economic and Policy Research points out that a recession following the dot-com bust in the early 2000s led to sustained job losses for both men and women — both mothers and non-mothers. [4] Others say the increasing proportion in the female population of young Hispanic women — who are culturally less inclined to work outside of the home — might also have brought the rates down. [5] Taken together, many economists agree that the trend since 2000 has been one of leveling out rather than a decline. Nevertheless, "we haven't explained why it's leveled out," says Katharine Bradbury, a senior economist at the Federal Reserve Bank of Boston.

"We don't know for sure if it's a pause or consolidation or a kind of longer-run plateau," says Cornell economist Francine Blau. She speculates that the cause of the leveling off may be that women are simply running out of time. "The division of labor within the family is still relatively unequally divided between men and women. That's at least a possible limit this is bumping up against."

Nancy Folbre, a professor of economics at the University of Massachusetts-Amherst, says women have cut back on the easy household chores, like cooking and cleaning. "All along the way, women have done their best to protect quality time with their kids," she observes. She suggests mothers may quit rather than sacrifice this time with children.

Based on women's past patterns, opting out seems unlikely as a permanent aspect of women's lives, argues Harvard University economist Claudia Goldin. A Mellon Foundation study of 10,000 women who graduated from college by 1981 found that on average the women in the survey spent only 1.6 years out of the labor force. [6]

It's too early to tell if women who finished school 10 years ago and are now in their early 30s will follow a similar pattern. But other patterns, such as women having babies at later ages and fairly constant employment and marriage rates, "don't spell big opt-out to me," Goldin concludes. [7]

And compared to the 1980s, women are opting in: Women are half as likely to opt out of employment today because of children than they were in 1984, according to Boushey. [8]

Today more than 70 percent of women with children are either working full time, part time or looking for work. But University of Maryland sociologist Suzanne Bianchi says this statistic hides another reality: Only about a third work full time year-'round; many are working part time or only part of the year.

"There's room to go in terms of full-time, year-'round" employment for women, Bianchi says. Her studies show that the average working parent works 65 hours a week if both paid work and child care and housework are included. "Women cut back their labor-force participation when they have really high child care demands," says Bianchi. "That's one way they find time."

The fact that young mothers take time off from work once they have children may also reflect a younger generation's confidence that they can return to their careers at the same wage and rank that they left.

"Our grad students have babies while they're in graduate school," Bianchi observes. "It doesn't signal that they're not committed to finishing their degree or getting a job the way it did 30 years ago."

Although statistics show that mothers are penalized in terms of wages and promotions if they step out of the work force, young people are "making a bet they won't suffer those wage penalties," observes Bianchi. "Some of us are skeptical."

---

[1] Lisa Belkin, "The Opt-Out Revolution," *The New York Times Magazine*, Oct. 26, 2003, p. 42.

[2] Linda Hirshman, "Homeward Bound," *American Prospect*, Dec. 20, 2005.

[3] Louise Story, "Many Women at Elite Colleges Set Career Path to Motherhood," *The New York Times*, Sept. 20, 2005.

[4] Heather Boushey, "Are Women Opting Out? Debunking the Myth," Center for Economic Policy Research, December 2005, www.cepr.net.

[5] "More About Women in the Labor Force, March 12, 2006, Demo Memo at http://demomemo.blogspot.com/2006/03/more-about-women-in-labor-force.html.

[6] Claudia Goldin, "Working it Out," *The New York Times*, March 15, 2006, p. A27.

[7] *Ibid.*

[8] Heather Boushey, "Are Mothers Really Leaving the Workplace?" Council on Contemporary Families, March 28, 2006. at http://www.contemporary-families.org/subtemplate.php?t=briefingPapers&ext=pr306.

law by President Bill Clinton, it permits workers to take 12 weeks of unpaid leave to care for a sick family member, bond with a new baby or recover from their own illness without losing their jobs or health insurance. More than 50 million Americans have taken job-protected leave since the law's enactment, according to the National Partnership for Women and Families, the leading advocacy group for the legislation.

The 1970s feminists are often referred to as Second Wave feminists to emphasize their lineage from the 19th-century suffragists. In January 1992, Rebecca Walker, daughter of the African-American writer Alice Walker, declared in *Ms.* magazine "I am the Third Wave" and later that year founded the Third Wave Foundation aimed at women 18-35. Richards, co-founder of the foundation, says the movement was reacting against the Second Wave's "very narrow definition of feminism" that many young women found overly puritanical.

"Could I be a feminist and acknowledge I liked Barbie when I was a kid? For anyone to acknowledge you liked Barbie was to concede you'd been duped by the patriarchy," says Richards. "What Third Wave said was, 'If something appeals to you, it doesn't preclude feminism.' " ■

CURRENT SITUATION

Avoiding Labels

Young women rarely identify themselves as feminists today. Only 25 percent of women considered themselves feminists in 2001, according to a Gallup Poll, down a percentage point from a similar poll in 1999. [46] But the data also show that basic feminist issues have more popular support than the label itself. [47]

Many young women associate the word feminist with the stereotype of a '60s-era bra-burning, hairy-legged activist. Others disavow the label because they believe most feminist activists are middle-aged, says Stein, of the Younger Women's Task Force.

"I went to a meeting of a national women's group and was the youngest in the room by 20 years," says Stein, who founded the task force a year ago to reach women in their 20s and 30s. [48] Her group solicited members in places where activists aren't usually sought — like churches and health clubs — to discuss the most pressing issues in their lives as young women. The task force now has more than 3,000 members in 11 chapters. Their solicitations deliberately avoid using the word feminist, especially when it comes to semi-rural areas like Pennsylvania's Poconos. "Trust me," Stein says, "if they used that word, they would have few people at their meeting."

Some chapters lobby on traditional feminist issues like abortion rights, but work-life-balance issues are most likely to get younger women involved, Stein says. "Every woman knows how hard it is to balance this stuff, and every woman wants to talk about it."

That's the focus of the Mothers Movement Online Web site, whose founder, Judith Stadtman Tucker — a former full-time graphic designer — says she became a feminist after becoming a mother. Until recently, Web sites like Tucker's and mothers' groups have lacked the backing of big grass-roots organizations.

But Tucker senses "a reinvigorated interest" at NOW, one of the largest old-line feminist organizations. At its national conference last year, NOW resolved to start an initiative around mothers' and caregivers' economic rights. Tucker belongs to a committee that has formed to advocate for paid parental leave and expansion of the existing Family Medical Leave Act to include employees at firms with fewer than 50 employees, among other family-friendly initiatives.

Those issues are also part of the platform of Momsrising.org, a new organization being formed by moveon.org co-founder Joan Blades and Kristin Rowe-Finkbeiner, author of the 2004 book *The F-Word: Feminism in Jeopardy*. Rowe-Finkbeiner's own poll of college women found that most were turned off by the word "feminist." "Many young women haven't seen the penalties of being a woman until they have children," she says.

According to Rowe-Finkbeiner, the gender wage gap in the United States is higher than in other industrialized countries because "we don't have paid family leave, subsidized child care or health care" — all programs momsrising.org will seek. Rowe-Finkbeiner and Blades have co-authored a new book, *The Motherhood Manifesto*, which argues that the federal government needs to revamp its policies along European lines to support working mothers and children.

"In countries with paid leave, women don't take the same wage hit when they come back to work, and society is more supportive," Rowe-Finkbeiner says.

Family and Sick Leave

Nearly half the nation's private-sector employees are not covered by the Family and Medical Leave Act (FMLA) because they work part time or for businesses with fewer than 50 employees. Family-leave-advocacy groups want the bill expanded to cover more employees and other family needs like attending parent-teacher conferences.

But expansion is unlikely because of opposition from business groups, which want to crack down on what they see as abuses under the existing law — changes family advocates say would weaken the law. Michael Eastman, director of labor law policy at the U.S. Chamber of Commerce, says personnel managers commonly complain that employees use the law to duck out of work for minor conditions like a cold or a broken toe.

Continued on p. 330

At Issue:

Are women giving up by opting out?

yes

LINDA HIRSHMAN
AUTHOR, GET TO WORK: A MANIFESTO FOR WOMEN OF THE WORLD, TO BE PUBLISHED IN JUNE 2006.

WRITTEN FOR *CQ RESEARCHER*, APRIL 2006

It's now around 20 percent harder for a girl to get into college than a guy. Since more women want to go to college than men, colleges have responded by discriminating against them in order to preserve something like a 50-50 ratio.

The colleges justify this sexist, punitive behavior on the grounds that the more women outnumber men on any given campus, the less men want to go there. And we must have men in our colleges, even dumb ones, or we will lose the status race for sure. Because girls don't confer status.

Women are a lot less likely to confer status because they will opt out of the workplace — get tenure and quit, if their employer won't run a day-care center for them. As Princeton President Shirley Tilghman once said, Princeton aims to train the future leaders of society. And ex-tenured, retired academics won't become leaders and they won't become the kind of alumnae who give big bucks to their alma mater.

Why do you think colleges give preference to the children of their alums, maintain the sexist and drunken fraternity culture, pay their football coaches more than their physicists? Out of love for humanity, as Adam Smith famously asked, or for their dumber but harder-working male alums' donations? And it's all perfectly legal.

Recently, the Web site of the American Conservative Union carried an essay advising employers to stay away from employees who demand day-care centers or risk bankruptcy. Even the fabled 100 Best Companies for Working Mothers (*Working Mother* magazine) produced only a feeble 30 percent rate for company child care programs. Imagine what the other hundred-thousand companies are like.

Although employers can't refuse to hire women, they turn them into failures in a thousand unseen ways. The chipper new book *This Is How We Do It*, from *Working Mother* CEO Carol Evans, extols the virtues of Flex Track, sequencing, job sharing and all the other heart-warming ways that women find to limit the demands of the workplace. What Evans does not tell her readers is that, cozy anecdotes aside, those strategies bring with them almost certain career suicide. The law profession: 40 percent female; law partnerships: 17 percent female.

Are these part-time lawyers letting down the team? Well, put yourself into the mind-set of a partner with limited mentoring time. Anticipating that she is twice as likely to demand part-time work sometime in the prime career years, what does a new, young, female law associate look like? Unless she's extraordinary, she looks like a losing proposition, that's what.

no

MIRIAM PESKOWITZ
AUTHOR, THE TRUTH BEHIND THE MOMMY WARS: WHO DECIDES WHAT MAKES A GOOD MOTHER

SHE RUNS THE WEB SITE WWW.PLAYGROUNDREVOLUTION.COM.

Once upon a time, I had a low-paying, high-prestige job. I was a professor at a major public university. I taught religious and women studies. I won teaching awards and research grants, I published well and received tenure at a relatively young age. My job was a good one, at least for someone without children.

Unfortunately, this good job didn't come with the basic elements that workers who are also parents need. It didn't offer paid maternity leave or paternity leave, at least not at my job level. It didn't offer high-quality, subsidized, on-site child care. Nor did it offer backup child care. There didn't seem to be any of the other supports that working parents might need, such as part-time work with fair wages and prorated benefits.

Not wanting to totally ditch my career when my first child was born, I left my position for the uncertainties of part-time work at another university. A shame, really, for the university that had just tenured me. It had invested tens of thousands of dollars over and above salary into my research and scholarship. What odd, shortsighted vision: I'm offered a job for life but not sustained through the relatively short period in which parents of young children need the most help.

Did I opt out? Absolutely not. When workplaces don't provide the basic supports mothers and fathers need, that's no opting out. Training women to take professional jobs but not supporting us as working mothers is a squeeze-out, a force-out.

Some feminists call us disappointments. I disagree. The new feminist movement now organizing around motherhood does not offer solutions that blame individual women and label them failures. It sees the core problem: The workplace hasn't changed to support family life, nor have schools, nor our health-care system, nor our public policies. Our society favors productivity over caretaking and hasn't yet risen to the humane challenge of rebalancing both. For now, mothers are caught in the middle.

It's not a politically retrograde choice to leave a workplace that squeezes you too tight; to refuse to work all day for pay and work all evening at home; to refuse the exhaustion of our mothers, amplified by the huge rise in the hours we are expected to work.

No, this is called a boycott. It's called resistance, and it needs a voice and it needs a path. Some very articulate moms, from both the low-income and high-income points on the economic spectrum are providing just this voice and path. This is the new, mother-supporting and family-friendly feminism.

Continued from p. 328

"Their condition flares up every Friday at 4 p.m. or after the weekend," he says. "Employers need more tools to help them combat chronic absenteeism; I'm talking about fraudulent use of the FMLA."

California is the only state that provides paid leave, funded by monthly employee contributions. Since 2002, workers have been able to take up to six weeks — at partial pay — to care for a new baby or sick relative.

Sen. Edward Kennedy, D-Mass., introduced a bill in April 2005 — the Healthy Families Act — that would give workers the right to seven days of paid leave if they or a child falls sick. It has strong support from family-advocacy groups and the National Partnership for Women and Families, which points out that nearly half the nation's workers have no paid sick leave. [49]

"When both parents are working, you don't have a structure anymore where you have someone staying home with a sick child," says McGraw. "A lot of our low-wage families can't afford to be docked a day of pay; it can be the difference in being able to pay the rent that month."

The Chamber of Commerce opposes the bill, contending it could become another major headache like the FMLA. As for the argument that workers shouldn't have to lose their jobs for carrying out parental duties, Eastman says market forces rather than congressional mandates should solve that problem. "Word gets around if you're a bad employer," he says. "People start to look elsewhere."

Workplace Flexibility

Some prominent corporations have taken a different tack, arguing that workplace flexibility can help retain experienced workers while improving performance and the bottom line. A coalition of 53 companies, including such giants as Philip Morris and Time Warner, released a report last November supporting flex-time, part time, job-sharing and telecommuting as good business practices. [50]

"Flexibility drives financial performance and is a key management tool," says Donna Klein, president of the nonprofit group that released the report, Corporate Voices for Working Families. Companies using flexible approaches have less absenteeism, less turnover, less burnout and increased ability to recruit and retain good workers, according to Klein.

In an effort to stem the loss of experienced women attorneys, several leading law firms have recently begun to offer the option of working part time while staying on track to make partner. It costs a firm $200,000-$300,000 to replace a third-year associate, according to Cynthia Calvert, co-director of the Project for Attorney Retention, and some firms have vowed to "stop the bleeding," in the words of a leading partner of one such firm.

When Calvert's Project surveyed firms in Washington, D.C., in 1999-2000, it could not find a single firm where a part-time lawyer had made partner. By 2004, almost every one of the 60 firms surveyed said they no longer disqualified part-time attorneys from the partnership track, and 40 percent had conferred partnership status on attorneys who had worked part time, according to Calvert.

The political polarization over such issues stems from the initial portrayal of flexibility as an accommodation to women, Klein suggests. "In reality, men are as anxious to have flexibility as women," she says. Indeed, for younger Gen X and Gen Y workers, "flexibility is at the top of the list of what they want from a corporation, and they are asking for it in campus recruitment data."

Taking their cue from Europe, some mothers' groups want to go further, citing a British law that allows employees to request part-time work unless the employer can show it is economically harmful. [51]

Kornbluh, of Sen. Obama's office, has proposed following the British model "because women are the ones who pay the price for the lack of flexibility." Bill Clinton ran on his support for the family leave bill and won married women's votes in 1992 and 1996, Kornbluh observes, and work flexibility could be a similar draw for this group of voters.

But the Chamber's Eastman cautions that such legislation might increase the cost of doing business and make it more difficult to create jobs. For example, if a company has to hire another half-time worker to do the rest of the job, it could mean providing a second benefits package, which can be costly, he observes. Pointing to the current unrest in France over employment laws, Eastman notes unemployment among French youth exceeds 20 percent but that employers are discouraged from making new hires because the required benefits package is so expensive.

The group Workplace Flexibility 2010 is trying to build nationwide consensus on improving flexible working conditions. The organization grew out of a decade of research that concluded, "there is a mismatch between the structure of work and the structure of family," says Katie Corrigan, co-director of the group at the Georgetown University Law Center.

"A lot of different constituencies have a stake in the game beyond families with children," she says, such as semi-retired elderly, baby boomers caring for aging parents and Gen X-ers who want time to go bungee jumping. [52]

Some states also are showing interest. Thirteen states have created rules requiring state agencies to allow part-time work, and 12 states provide benefits to part-time employees. [53]

At the same time, however, global competition and communications technology are pushing employers to either outsource jobs to countries that don't require benefits or switch to non-fulltime employees who don't qualify for expensive benefits. Nearly a quarter of the work force is employed in non-standard positions such as part time, temporary, freelance, on call or self-employed, and many companies are cutting back health and pension packages. [54]

Reproductive Rights

When it comes to abortion rights, many feminist groups feel they've been under constant assault in recent years. They not only lost two battles against pro-life Supreme Court justices (Chief Justice John Roberts and Associate Justice Samuel Alito) but also watched as South Dakota banned abortions, the Food and Drug Administration refused to allow over-the-counter sales of emergency contraception and some pharmacists have refused to dispense birth control. [55]

Most polls show that a majority of Americans support legal abortion, with restrictions. [56] In the words of President Clinton, abortion should be "safe, legal and rare." The National Abortion Rights Action League's name change — to NARAL Pro-Choice America — seems to reflect a squeamishness about using the word abortion, although the group's leaders deny that was the reason for the change.

Within the next two to three years, if the increasingly conservative Supreme Court overturns *Roe v. Wade*, abortion's legality would again be determined by state law as it was before the landmark 1973 decision. "We will have to take the case to the states and convince people on the basis of its merits, not constitutional rights," says Kissling of Catholics for a Free Choice, "and it will depend on our ability to convince them that we take it seriously."

In a widely debated article published in winter 2004-2005, Kissling argued, "The pro-choice movement will be far more trusted if it openly acknowledges that the abortion decision involves weighing multiple values and that one of those values is fetal life." [57] While longtime feminists came down hard on her, Kissling says, "For younger feminists, the question of abortion as a complex issue or a sad issue seems less troublesome."

Documentary filmmaker Baumgardner agrees. "There's a lot more interest in listening to what women and men having abortion experiences say. You can know it's the right thing and know it's a sacrifice of some kind, too."

Leaders in the abortion-rights movement insist they *do* acknowledge this reality and have pushed for greater access to contraception in order to make abortions rarer. "For each woman, it is a morally complex issue," says NARAL Pro-Choice America President Keenan.

As for the current political situation, Keenan said her organization has seen an increase in membership in the last three to four years, with inter-generational responses rising since the South Dakota ban. "The sleeping majority here has watched these politicians overstep several times," she says. Now, "people are very upset that pharmacists can deny them prescriptions for contraception."

For her part, columnist Pollitt says, "We'd all love to move on from this issue, but I don't see how that is possible; the other side doesn't want compromise." There's a certain complacency among middle-class pro-choicers, she suggests, while low-income women — those who have to sleep in their cars overnight to get service in states with only one abortion clinic — are rarely heard from. "The people most affected by restrictions placed on abortions so far are those women who are not politically active," says Pollitt.

Pro-choice leaders predict that the majority of Americans will become more politicized as they realize that extremists want to outlaw not only abortion but also birth control. For example, when South Dakota's legislature outlawed some forms of contraception, says Keenan, the governor refused to sign the law because right-wing groups didn't think they could prevail in the Supreme Court.

"They're starting to show their hand," says Smeal, of the Moral Majority. And Keenan interprets Bush's lukewarm response to the South Dakota ban as "code for 'Put the brakes on.' " ■

OUTLOOK

Personal Politics

Judging from all the Web sites run by young feminists and mothers, a vibrant new women's movement appears to be sprouting. But as Calman at the International Center for Research on Women points out, "A Web site is not a movement."

Mother's Movement Online founder Tucker agrees that for the kinds of family-work issues she supports the movement is "very much at the consciousness-raising stage." A major problem, she says, is the fact that issues most affecting women today don't fit neatly into past categories: "Is it feminist? Is it labor?"

Today, young women are most likely to experience gender discrimination in isolation, such as when trying to negotiate a part-time job that keeps them on the career track but leaves time for child raising. But some young feminists say they don't measure a movement's success in the number of women that join an organization like NOW or respond to urgent e-mail blasts. "Going into that office with as much information as you can get is exactly the way movements are built," maintains Baumgardner, co-author of *Grass Roots: A Field Guide for Feminist Activism*. "That *is* grass roots; it's every individual root in the grass; it's the work of individuals; it's not relating to a big parent organization."

Amy Nassisi, a San Mateo, Calif., mother, recently formed a group to do just that. Her Flexibility Alliance will disseminate profiles of women who managed to negotiate flexible work arrangements — something she herself didn't manage to do when her daughter was born. "I could have made a much more successful proposal to my boss had I had these profiles to show him," she says, "and that would have made him feel more comfortable."

But other activists say women will have to get more involved in politics at a higher level if they want to reshape society's attitude toward women's role. Women currently compose less than 15 percent of Congress. Sixty-five percent of women between ages 18 and 24 did not even vote in the 2000 presidential election, compared to 65 percent of women over 44 who did, according to Momsrising.org co-founder Rowe-Finkbeiner.

The 1970s feminists started their movement around kitchen tables with the slogan "the personal is political." Third Wave's Richards believes "the opposite has to happen with this generation; we have to look at politics to see how it affects our lives." The new slogan should be, "The political is personal." ■

Notes

1 These are union arbitration cases reported in Joan Williams, "One Sick Child Away from Being Fired: When 'Opting Out' Is Not an Option," Center for WorkLife Law, University of California, Hastings College of Law, March 14, 2006, pp. 3, 32; www.worklifelaw.org. The three mothers took their grievances to union arbitration.

2 Karen Kornbluh, *et al.*, "Workplace Flexibility: A Policy Problem," *Work and Family Program Issue Brief #1*, New America Foundation, May 2004, and Williams, *ibid.*, p. 18.

3 Peter Svensson, "Compared to Rest of World, U.S. Mothers Get Short Shrift," *The Houston Chronicle*, Aug. 1, 2005, p. 1.

4 Dual-earner couples work 91 hours a week, up 10 hours from 1977. Kornbluh, *et al.*, *op. cit.*

5 Two percent statistic: "Women at the Top in the 1970s and 2002," *Regional Review*, Federal Reserve Bank of Boston, First Quarter 2005, p. 2. This special issue presented papers from a March 3, 2004, conference, "Reaching the Top: Challenges and Opportunities for Women Leaders." Seventeen percent statistic: Project on Attorney Retention; www.PARDC.org.

6 Institute for Women's Policy Research, "The Gender Wage Ratio: Women's and Men's Earnings," August 2005; www.iwpr.org.

7 Heather Boushey, "Are Women Opting Out? Debunking the Myth," Center for Economic Policy Research, December 2005, p. 5; www.cepr.net.

8 www.bls.gov/opub/working/page3b.htm.

9 Lisa Belkin, "The Opt-Out Revolution," *New York Times Magazine*, Oct. 26, 2003, pp. 42-47, 58, 85-86.

10 Research finding that professional women are highly conflicted about interrupting careers is reported in Pamela Stone and Meg Lovejoy, "Fast-Track Women and the 'Choice' to Stay Home," *Annals of American Academy of Political and Social Sciences*, November 2002, pp. 62-83.

11 The Fair Labor Standards Act of 1938 provides workers the right to time-and-a-half pay for hours worked over a 40-hour week. But workers have no protections if they turn down overtime. See Karen Kornbluh, "Win-Win Flexibility," New America Foundation, June 2005; www.newamerica.net. Kornbluh is former director of the New America Foundation Work & Family Program.

12 Ariel Levy, *Female Chauvinist Pigs* (2005), p. 86.

13 Sylvia Ann Hewlett and Carolyn Buck Luce, "Off-Ramps and On-Ramps," *Harvard Business Review*, March 2005, pp. 1-11, p. 4.

14 Cited in Stone and Lovejoy, *op. cit.*, p. 64.

15 Cathy E. Minehan, "An Introduction," *Regional Review*, Federal Reserve Bank of Boston, First Quarter 2005, p. 2.

16 Joan C. Williams and Nancy Segal, "Beyond the Maternal Wall: Relief for Family Caregivers Who are Discriminated Against on the Job," *Harvard Women's Law Journal*, Vol. 26, 2003, p. 130.

17 Kate O'Beirne, *Women who Make the World Worse and How their Radical Feminist Assault is Ruining Our Schools, Families, Military, and Sports* (2006), p. 23.

18 *Ibid.*, p. 48.

19 For further information see Sarah Glazer, "Helping Welfare Mothers to Stay Home," p. 314, in "Mothers' Movement," *CQ Researcher*, April 4, 2003, pp. 297-320.

20 Judith Warner, "The Parent Trap," *The New York Times*, Feb. 8, 2006, p. A21.

21 Suzanne Bianchi, *et al.*, "Maternal Employment and Family Caregiving," Dec. 9, 2005, Figure 1 (unpublished paper).

22 Linda Hirshman, "Homeward Bound," *American Prospect*, Dec. 20, 2005.

23 Bianchi, *et al.*, *op. cit.*

24 Joyce P. Jacobsen, "Choices & Changes," *Regional Review*, Federal Reserve Bank of Boston, First Quarter 2005, pp. 17-21.

25 David Brooks, "The Year of Domesticity," *The New York Times*, Jan. 1, 2006, p. WK8.

26 See Meghan O'Rourke, "Desperate Feminist Wives: Why Wanting Equality Makes Women Unhappy," *Slate*, March 7, 2006.

27 Hewlett and Luce, *op. cit.*, p. 1.

28 Hirshman, *op. cit.*

29 For women age 16 and over, the labor-force participation rate was 59 percent in 2004. See "Women in the Labor Force: A Data Book," Bureau of Labor Statistics, 2005 at www.bls.gov/cps/wlf-databook2005.htm.

30 *Ibid.*

31 Hewlett and Luce, *op. cit.*, p. 4.

32 Stone and Lovejoy, *op. cit.*, pp. 62-83.

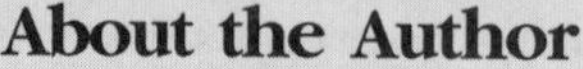

About the Author

Sarah Glazer, a New York freelancer, is a regular contributor to the *CQ Researcher*. Her articles on health, education and social-policy issues have appeared in *The New York Times*, *The Washington Post*, *The Public Interest* and *Gender and Work*, a book of essays. Her recent *CQ Researcher* reports include "Increase in Autism" and "Gender and Learning." She graduated from the University of Chicago with a B.A. in American history.

[33] Unless otherwise noted, information in this section is from Janet Zollinger Giele, *Two Paths to Women's Equality: Temperance, Suffrage and the Origins of Modern Feminism* (1985), pp. 179, 183.
[34] Ann Crittenden, *The Price of Motherhood* (2001), p. 86.
[35] *Ibid.*, p. 47.
[36] For background, see "Equal Rights Amendment," *Editorial Research Reports*, April 4, 1946, available at *CQ Researcher Plus Archive*, CQ Electronic Library, http://library.cqpress.com.
[37] For background, see "Sex Equality and Protective Laws," *Editorial Research Reports*, July 13, 1926, available at *CQ Researcher Plus Archive*, CQ Electronic Library, http://library.cqpress.com.
[38] For background, see "Women in War Work," *Editorial Research Reports*, Jan. 26, 1942, and "Women Workers After the War," *Editorial Research Reports*, April 22, 1944, both available at *CQ Researcher Plus Archive*, CQ Electronic Library, http://library.cqpress.com.
[39] For background, see "Equal Rights Fight," *Editorial Research Reports*, Dec. 15, 1978, available at *CQ Researcher Plus Archive*, CQ Electronic Library, http://library.cqpress.com.
[40] Betty Friedan, *The Feminine Mystique* (1963), p. 282.
[41] For background, see "Women in Sports," *Editorial Research Reports*, May 6, 1977; and "Women in Sports," *CQ Researcher*, May 11, 2001, pp. 401-424; and "Racism in America," *Editorial Research Reports*, May 13, 1964, available at *CQ Researcher Plus Archive*, CQ Electronic Library, http://library.cqpress.com.
[42] Claudia Goldin, "From the Valley to the Summit," *Regional Review*, Federal Reserve Bank of Boston, First Quarter 2005, pp. 5-12.
[43] *Ibid.*
[44] *Ibid.*
[45] Giele, *op. cit.*, p. 194.
[46] Levy, *op. cit.*, p. 86.
[47] "Feminism: What's in a Name?" Sept. 3, 2002, at www.gallup.com.
[48] NOW and the Feminist Majority say they do not keep membership statistics by age.
[49] See www.nationalpartnership.org.
[50] "Business Impacts of Flexibility: An Imperative for Expansion," Corporate Voices for Working Families, November 2005; www.cvworkingfamilies.org. For background see Kathy Koch, "Flexible Work Arrangements," *CQ Researcher*, Aug. 14, 1998, pp. 697-720.
[51] Kornbluh, *op. cit.*, June 2005.

FOR MORE INFORMATION

Bureau of Labor Statistics, Postal Square Bldg., 2 Massachusetts Ave., N.E., Washington, DC 20212-0001; (202) 691-5200; www.bls.gov. A federal agency that posts statistics on women's participation in the labor force on its Web site.

Center for WorkLife Law, 200 McAllister St., San Francisco, CA 94102; (415) 565-4640; www.worklifelaw.org. Based at the University of California's Hastings College of Law; focuses on parental discrimination.

Corporate Voices for Working Families, 1899 L St., N.W., Suite 250, Washington, DC 20035; (202) 429-0259; www.cvworkingfamilies.org. A coalition of 53 companies that support flexible work policies.

Families and Work Institute, 267 Fifth Ave., 2nd Floor, New York, NY 10016; (212) 465-2044; www.familiesandwork.org. Provides research data on the changing family, changing work force and changing community.

Feminist Majority Foundation, 1600 Wilson Blvd., Suite 801, Arlington, VA 22209; (703) 522-2214; www.feminist.org. Works to advance women's equality.

Institute for Women's Policy Research, 1707 L St., N.W., Suite 750, Washington, DC 20036; (202) 785-5100; www.iwpr.org. Conducts research on women.

Mothers Movement Online, www.mothersmovement.org. Web site features information and opinions about the well-being of mothers.

NARAL Pro-Choice America, 1156 15th St., N.W., Suite 700, Washington, DC 20005; (202) 973-3000; www.prochoiceamerica.org. Formerly the National Abortion Rights Action League.

National Organization for Women (NOW), 1100 H St., N.W., 3rd Floor, Washington, DC 20005; (202) 628-8669; www.now.org. The oldest grass-roots organization of the women's movement, founded in 1966.

National Partnership for Women and Families, 1875 Connecticut Ave., N.W., Suite 650, Washington, DC 20009; (202) 986-2600; www.nationalpartnership.org. Advocates for family leave and other family-friendly policies.

Third Wave Foundation, 511 W. 25th St., Suite 301, New York, NY 10001; (212) 675-0700; www.thirdwavefoundation.org. Feminist organization aimed at ages 15-30.

Younger Women's Task Force, 1050 17th St., N.W., Suite 250, Washington, DC 20036; (202) 293-4505; www.ywtf.org. A project of the National Council of Women's Organizations aimed at attracting younger women.

[52] www.law.georgetown.edu/workplaceflexibility2010/index.cfm.
[53] "Opportunities for Policy Leadership on Part-Time Work," Issue 4, *Policy Leadership Series*, Sloan Work and Family Research Network, 2006, www.bc.edu/wfnetwork.
[54] See Kornbluh, *et al.*, "Workplace Flexibility: A Policy Problem," *op. cit.* For background see Marcia Clemmitt, "Rising Health Costs," *CQ Researcher*, April 7, 2006, pp. 289-312, and Alan Greenblatt, "Pension Crisis," *CQ Researcher*, Feb. 17, 2006, pp. 145-168.
[55] For background, see Marcia Clemmitt, "Birth-Control Debate," *CQ Researcher*, June 23, 2005, pp. 565-588.
[56] See www.pollingreport.com/abortion.htm.
[57] Frances Kissling, "Is there Life After Roe? How to Think about the Fetus," *Conscience*, Winter 2004/5, pp. 11-18.

Bibliography

Selected Sources

Books

Dowd, Maureen, *Are Men Necessary? When Sexes Collide*, G.P. Putnam's Sons, 2005.
The New York Times columnist views the contemporary scene and concludes "Materialism has defeated feminism."

Crittenden, Ann, *The Price of Motherhood: Why the Most Important Job in the World is Still the Least Valued*, Metropolitan Books, 2001.
The former *Times* reporter galvanized mothers with her argument that they are exploited by U.S. society.

Friedan, Betty, *The Feminine Mystique*, W.W. Norton, 2001.
Originally published in 1963, Friedan's analysis of suburban wives' dissatisfaction triggered the feminist movement.

Giele, Janet Zollinger, *Two Paths to Women's Equality: Temperance, Suffrage, and the Origins of Modern Feminism*, Twayne Publishers, 1995.
A sociologist argues that feminists who fought to protect women's roles as caregivers lost the fight.

Levy, Ariel, *Female Chauvinist Pigs: Women and the Rise of Raunch Culture*, Free Press, 2005.
A magazine writer asks if young women's supposedly liberated sexuality is simply a distasteful imitation of male voyeurism.

O'Beirne, Kate, *Women Who Make the World Worse: and How Their Radical Feminist Assault Is Ruining Our Families, Military, Schools and Sports*, Sentinel, 2006.
A conservative commentator argues that feminists are denying biological gender differences when they disdain women who want to stay home with children.

Articles

Baumgardner, Jennifer, "Feminism is a Failure, and Other Myths," *AlterNet*, Posted Nov. 17, 2005, at www.alternet.org.
Taking a critical look at Levy's book (above), Baumgardner says women need better examples of "powerful sexuality."

Brooks, David, "The Year of Domesticity," *The New York Times*, Jan. 1, 2006, pp. WK 8.
A conservative columnist argues that women make a rational choice when they leave the workplace to care for their children.

Goldin, Claudia, "Working it Out," *The New York Times*, March 15, 2006, p. A27.
A Harvard economist argues that college-educated women aren't opting out of the work force for good.

Hewlett, Sylvia Ann, and Carolyn Buck Luce, "Off-Ramps and On-Ramps: Keeping Talented Women on the Road to Success," *Harvard Business Review*, March 2005, pp. 1-10.
In a widely cited article, the authors argue business and law are suffering a brain drain of career women because of inflexible workplaces.

Hirshman, Linda, "Homeward Bound," Dec. 20, 2005, *American Prospect* at www.prospect.org.
A retired professor of philosophy at Brandeis University ignited controversy with her recipe for breaking the "glass ceiling" at home so that women are free to achieve feminist goals.

Kissling, Frances, "Is There Life after Roe?" *Conscience*, winter 2004-5, pp. 11-18.
The president of Catholics for a Free Choice argues that the pro-choice movement must acknowledge that abortion is "a profoundly moral question."

Porter, Eduardo, "Stretched to the Limit, Women Stall March to Work," *The New York Times*, March 2, 2006, p. A1.
The *Times'* latest contribution to the opt-out debate was spurred by continuing declines in women's labor-force participation.

Saletan, William, "Is Abortion Bad? From: William Saletan To: Katha Pollitt," *Slate*, Feb. 1, 2006, at www.slate.com.
Slate columnist Saletan argues that pro-choice advocates should acknowledge moral quandaries, and columnist Katha Pollitt of *The Nation* disagrees; part of a week-long debate.

Traister, Rebecca, "The F Word," *Salon*, July 5, 2005, at www.salon.com.
Traister discusses why the word "feminism" turns off so many younger women.

Warner, Judith, "The Parent Trap," *The New York Times*, Feb. 8, 2006, p. A21.
The feminist revolution is incomplete because no national policies make work and family life compatible, she says.

Reports and Studies

Boushey, Heather, "Are Women Opting Out? Debunking the Myth," Center for Economic and Policy Research, December 2005.
Boushey argues that the percentage of women in the labor force hasn't declined.

Center for Worklife Law, "One Sick Child Away from Being Fired: When Opting Out Isn't an Option," March 14, 2006, at www.workLifelaw.org.
The Hastings College of Law center reports on 90 union arbitration cases in which workers argued they had been disciplined for carrying out parental responsibilities.

The Next Step:

Additional Articles from Current Periodicals

Child Care

Clausen, Lisa, "Putting a Price on Our Children," *Time International*, March 13, 2006, p. 40.
Australian parents complain that child care is harder to find and afford and are asking the government to help.

Langan, Fred, "Want Cheap Day Care? Consider Canada," *The Christian Science Monitor*, April 6, 2006, p. 6.
Canada's Parliament will debate whether to create a nationwide subsidized child care system.

Family Leave

An, Caroline, "State Family-Leave Money Often Not Enough, Study Says," *San Bernardino Sun*, Dec. 11, 2005.
Most Californians say the state's paid family-leave plan only provides for them to be paid up to 55 percent of their salaries.

Greenhouse, Steven, "As Demands on Workers Grow, Groups Push For Paid Family and Sick Leave," *The New York Times*, March 6, 2005, p. 23.
Take Back Your Time is a Seattle-based coalition seeking legislation in 21 states to give workers paid sick days.

Joyce, Amy, "Can You Spare Some Time?" *The Washington Post*, May 8, 2005, p. F6.
Most states are not providing more parental leave than the 12 weeks of unpaid leave required by federal law.

Svensson, Peter, "Compared to Rest of World, U.S. Mothers Get Short Shrift," *The Houston Chronicle*, Aug. 1, 2005, p. 1.
Out of 168 nations, only five — including the United States — do not provide some form of paid maternity leave.

Feminism Today

Bower, Amanda, "The Mommy Brain," *Time*, May 2, 2005, p. W13.
A Pulitzer Prize-winning reporter argues motherhood makes moms smarter.

Cavendish, Lucy, "Housewife No Longer A Dirty Word," *The Seattle Post-Intelligencer*, Nov. 20, 2005, p. D6.
Cavendish argues that being a housewife has made her happier than when she was a working mom.

Cohen, Patricia, "Today, Some Feminists Hate the Word 'Choice' " *The New York Times*, Jan. 15, 2006, p. 3.
Lawyer and scholar Linda R. Hirshman coined and then denounced the term "choice feminism."

Feldmann, Linda, "Face of Feminism in 2004," *The Christian Science Monitor*, April 23, 2004, p. 1.
Today's young women laugh at the old notions of feminism but care a lot about reproductive rights.

Ganahl, Jane, "Soon We'll Be Ordered to Wear Dresses," *The San Francisco Chronicle*, Nov. 20, 2005, p. D2.
Ganahl contends that feminism is alive and well after 23 young girls from Pennsylvania organized a national boycott against sexist t-shirts made by Abercrombie and Fitch.

Ryan, Maureen, "Mommy Wars Rage On, and So Do the Inequalities," *Chicago Tribune*, April 14, 2004, p. C6.
Ryan believes women should work together to reduce the inequalities still facing women.

Varner, Lynne K., "Moms On the Front Lines of America's Culture Wars," *The Seattle Times*, Nov. 9, 2004, p. B6.
Varner is uncomfortable with the recent political mood of women who desire a return to traditional values.

Minority Moms

Buckner Farmer, Lori, "A Living Reference," *The Houston Chronicle*, Dec. 25, 2005, p. 13.
Lonnae O'Neal Parker discusses what it is like to be a married, professional, black, middle-class mother in her new book *I'm Every Woman: Remixed Stories of Marriage, Motherhood and Work*.

Clemetson, Lynette, "Work vs. Family, Complicated By Race," *The New York Times*, Feb. 9, 2006, p. G1.
Well-educated black women in a Washington suburb discuss how the "opt-out" debate does not resonate with them.

CITING THE *CQ RESEARCHER*

Sample formats for citing these reports in a bibliography include the ones listed below. Preferred styles and formats vary, so please check with your instructor or professor.

MLA STYLE

Jost, Kenneth. "Rethinking the Death Penalty." CQ Researcher 16 Nov. 2001: 945-68.

APA STYLE

Jost, K. (2001, November 16). Rethinking the death penalty. *CQ Researcher, 11*, 945-968.

CHICAGO STYLE

Jost, Kenneth. "Rethinking the Death Penalty." *CQ Researcher*, November 16, 2001, 945-968.

CQ Researcher

Published by CQ Press, a division of Congressional Quarterly Inc.

cqresearcher.com

Port Security

Are new anti-terrorism measures adequate?

The controversy over an Arab company's plan to operate terminals at six U.S. seaports put port security at the top of lawmakers' agenda. But some security experts say the firestorm over the ill-fated Dubai Ports World deal masks a bigger problem: the failure of the United States to invest enough on security — including infrastructure upgrades, advanced radiation-detection equipment and manpower — to prevent terrorists from smuggling radioactive bombs or other dangerous materials into one of the more than 360 U.S. seaports. Only 5 percent of the 11.3 million shipping containers arriving at U.S. seaports last year were examined, leading some members of Congress to call for inspections of all U.S.-bound containers. The Bush administration defends its port security strategy and vows to install more radiation-detection devices at U.S. and overseas ports and to expand programs that ask U.S. businesses and foreign governments to voluntarily heighten security overseas.

A Customs officer uses a hand-held radiation-detection device to inspect a cargo container arriving at a U.S. port.

INSIDE THIS REPORT

CQ Researcher • April 21, 2006 • www.cqresearcher.com
Volume 16, Number 15 • Pages 337-360

CQ PRESS

RECIPIENT OF SOCIETY OF PROFESSIONAL JOURNALISTS AWARD FOR EXCELLENCE ◆ AMERICAN BAR ASSOCIATION SILVER GAVEL AWARD

THE ISSUES

BACKGROUND

CURRENT SITUATION

OUTLOOK

SIDEBARS AND GRAPHICS

FOR FURTHER RESEARCH

Cover: A Customs officer uses a hand-held radiation-detection device to check a container truck entering a U.S. seaport. (Government Accountability Office)

CQ Researcher

April 21, 2006
Volume 16, Number 15

MANAGING EDITOR: Thomas J. Colin

ASSISTANT MANAGING EDITOR: Kathy Koch

ASSOCIATE EDITOR: Kenneth Jost

STAFF WRITERS: Marcia Clemmitt, Peter Katel, Pamela M. Prah

CONTRIBUTING WRITERS: Rachel S. Cox, Sarah Glazer, David Hosansky, Patrick Marshall, Tom Price

DESIGN/PRODUCTION EDITOR: Olu B. Davis

ASSISTANT EDITOR: Melissa J. Hipolit

CQ PRESS

A Division of Congressional Quarterly Inc.

SENIOR VICE PRESIDENT/PUBLISHER: John A. Jenkins

DIRECTOR, LIBRARY PUBLISHING: Kathryn C. Suárez

DIRECTOR, EDITORIAL OPERATIONS: Ann Davies

CONGRESSIONAL QUARTERLY INC.

CHAIRMAN: Paul C. Tash

VICE CHAIRMAN: Andrew P. Corty

PRESIDENT/EDITOR IN CHIEF: Robert W. Merry

CQ Researcher (ISSN 1056-2036) is printed on acid-free paper. Published weekly, except March 24, July 7, July 14, Aug. 4, Aug. 11, Nov. 24, Dec. 22 and Dec. 29, by CQ Press, a division of Congressional Quarterly Inc. Annual full-service subscriptions for institutions start at $667. For pricing, call 1-800-834-9020, ext. 1906. To purchase a *CQ Researcher* report in print or electronic format (PDF), visit www.cqpress.com or call 866-427-7737. Single reports start at $10. Bulk purchase discounts and electronic-rights licensing are also available. Periodicals postage paid at Washington, D.C., and additional mailing offices. POSTMASTER: Send address changes to *CQ Researcher*, 1255 22nd St., N.W., Suite 400, Washington, DC 20037.

Port Security

BY PAMELA M. PRAH

THE ISSUES

A truck driver in Indonesia picks up a shipment of designer sneakers made for a big U.S. firm. But before delivering the load to a port in Jakarta, he stops to let al Qaeda members stash a radioactive bomb inside the sealed container. The "dirty bomb" is encased in lead to avoid radiation-detection equipment used at many ports.

U.S. Customs officers based in Jakarta, however, neither open the container nor screen it for radioactivity because the Indonesian shipper and the big-name U.S. sneaker firm are on the government's list of "trusted" companies. When the container arrives at its destination — a warehouse in Chicago — terrorists detonate the bomb. The radioactive blast causes several deaths, devastating environmental damage and potentially long-term health risks.

Getty Images/David McNew

The Port of Los Angeles is the busiest of the nation's 361 seaports. Many security experts say the government and private industry aren't doing enough to prevent terrorists from smuggling a "dirty bomb" or other weapon of mass destruction into the United States in a container.

Retired Coast Guard Cmdr. Stephen Flynn recently described that chilling, hypothetical scenario to congressional committees in calling for tighter port security. A former security specialist for presidents George H.W. Bush and Bill Clinton, Flynn, now a senior fellow at the Council on Foreign Relations, says the story is not all that far-fetched.

Indeed, the Department of Homeland Security (DHS) found numerous security breaches at foreign and U.S. ports that could easily allow terrorists to smuggle weapons of mass destruction (WMD) into the United States, according to The Associated Press. The three-year study, yet to be released, reportedly found that sealed shipping containers could be opened en route to the United States without detection. [1]

More than 11 million containers entered the 361 U.S. ports in 2005 from more than 100 countries, and container traffic is expected to grow by some 10 percent each year in the future.

In addition to health and environmental havoc, a dirty bomb exploding at a U.S. port would cause "staggering economic damage," said Sen. Susan Collins, R-Maine, chairwoman of the Senate Homeland Security and Governmental Affairs Committee. As a security precaution, officials likely would immediately shut down all U.S. ports, she said, and imports would come to a grinding halt for several days, creating a container-ship backup that would take months to untangle.

Supplies of imported food, medicine, raw materials and consumer goods from bananas to computers to toys would quickly run out, costing the economy an estimated $58 billion, according to the consulting firm Booz Allen Hamilton. [2] A Congressional Budget Office report likened the economic impact to the aftermath of the Sept. 11, 2001, terrorist attacks or Hurricane Katrina. [3]

The Bush administration insists its efforts to beef up port security are on track. [4] "I'd be the first person to tell you we have more work to do, but . . . a lot of work has been done," Homeland Security Secretary Michael Chertoff told the Heritage Foundation on March 20. [5]

But others are skeptical. "The ports are not secure," warned former Gov. Thomas Kean, R-N.J., co-leader of the bipartisan investigation of the Sept. 11 terrorist attacks known as the 9/11 Commission. [6] "You and I can walk today into the port of New York . . . and get into areas where people shouldn't get." The commission last December graded the administration on port security and gave it a "D" for failing to screen more cargo. [7]

New government studies show U.S. port security programs are highly vulnerable to terrorists. Only 5 percent of the estimated 11.3 million containers arriving at American ports last year were either physically inspected by Customs agents or screened with X-ray-like imaging machines capable of detecting unusually dense objects,

U.S. Port Security Spans the Globe

U.S. Customs inspects suspicious containers in 44 foreign seaports as part of its Container Security Initiative (CSI). By the end of 2007, the program is slated to operate in 58 ports and cover 85 percent of U.S.-bound maritime cargo. In addition, the Department of Energy's Megaports program to combat nuclear smuggling operates radiation-detection equipment at five major foreign seaports, with another seven slated to be added. Other U.S. programs in 36 countries — primarily in the former Soviet Union and Eastern Europe — guard against smuggling of nuclear materials.

U.S. Port Security Operations Overseas

Sources: U.S. Customs; Government Accountability Office, 2006

such as a dirty bomb encased in lead that would elude radiation detectors. Ports overseas are even more vulnerable: Only 2.8 percent of containers destined for the United States were screened for radiation in 2005, and only about one-third of 1 percent were X-rayed. [8]

"This is a massive blind spot," said Sen. Norm Coleman, R-Minn., chairman of the Senate Homeland Security Committee's Permanent Subcommittee on Investigations, noting that more than 60 percent of U.S. ports lack basic radiation detectors. In addition to lax seaport security, federal investigators in late 2005 passed through Canadian and Mexican border checkpoints into Texas and Washington carrying enough radioactive material to make two dirty bombs. [9]

Moreover, if terrorists did attack a U.S. port today, the response likely would be poorly coordinated, according to a recent Department of Justice report. Lack of preparedness and interagency squabbling between the Coast Guard and FBI could result in a "potentially disastrous" delay, it said. "[N]one of the FBI's intelligence reports [has] assessed the threat and risk of terrorists smuggling a WMD in a shipping container aboard a cargo ship," the 117-page report said. And while both the Coast Guard and the FBI now have specialized anti-terror SWAT teams, during a mock terrorist strike on a ferry in Connecticut last year the FBI "repeatedly blocked the Coast Guard's efforts, saying the FBI was the lead federal agency," the report said. [10]

Policing sea shipments entering the country is a massive, multi-agency job. The Coast Guard and U.S. Customs and Borders Protection (CBP), formerly Customs, oversee anti-terrorism efforts at ports, while state and local governments administer 126 "port authorities" that either handle day-to-day port operations themselves or hire private operating companies. Local governments also provide law enforcement. The Port Authority of New York and New Jersey's 1,600-member police department, for instance, is one of the nation's largest police organizations.

Some critics say the federal government has radically overhauled airport security since 9/11 but paid scant attention to seaports. The administration, however, says the system of "layered security" it has developed since 9/11 focuses on identifying threats overseas before they reach the United States. "Our nation's ports in the global supply chain are far safer today than they were before the terrorist attacks of Sept. 11," Jayson Ahern, assistant commissioner for CBP field operations, told lawmakers in March. Nearly 200 Customs agents are stationed in 44 foreign ports looking for suspicious U.S.-bound cargo, he noted. [11]

Nevertheless, national outrage erupted when reports surfaced in February that an Arab-owned company, Dubai Ports World, planned to take over terminal operations at six U.S. ports, "When you read in the paper that a foreign company may run a terminal at a port near the 9/11 attack, people get afraid," said Republican Sen. Lindsey Graham of South Carolina. [12]

Not long after a poll showed that an overwhelming majority — 66 percent — of Americans opposed the deal, Dubai Ports World agreed to have U.S. firms run the disputed U.S. terminals. [13] Only 9 percent of respondents thought port security is "a lot better" since Sept. 11, while 34 percent felt airports were safer.

Largest U.S. Ports Have Foreign Partners

The Port of Los Angeles, busiest of the nation's 361 ports, has corporate partners from five nations. Terminals at four of the nation's five biggest ports are operated by foreign-owned firms.

Foreign Operating Partners at the Five Biggest U.S. Ports 2005

Port Location	Foreign Partners	Total TEUs*
Los Angeles	Japan, Denmark, Singapore, China, Taiwan	4.9 million
Long Beach	Hong Kong, China, Japan, South Korea	4.4 million
New York	Denmark, Hong Kong, United Kingdom	3.4 million
Charleston	Denmark, Japan	1.5 million
Savannah	None; operated by Georgia Ports Authority	1.5 million

** The standard unit of measure for container capacity is the TEU (for "twenty-foot equivalent unit"). U.S. shippers typically use 40-foot containers, which are counted as two TEUs of cargo.*

Sources: U.S. Transportation Maritime Administration and American Association of Port Authorities, 2006

But security experts say concern about an Arab-owned company running major U.S. ports missed the more important security threat. "The maximum danger to the United States is where cargo is loaded on its way to our shores, not where the cargo is offloaded. By then it will be too late," says Daniel Goure, former director of the Pentagon's Office of Strategic Competitiveness and now vice president of the conservative Lexington Institute think tank.

DHS Secretary Chertoff claims federal authorities screen "100 percent" of containers entering the United States, but critics point out that often simply means inspectors have looked at the paperwork — a ship's manifest that lists its cargo — which security experts say is unreliable.

Flynn wants the United States to replicate a security program being tested in Hong Kong that requires every container entering the port to undergo scanning and radiation detection. (*See sidebar, p. 349.*) "This is not a pie-in-the-sky idea," he says, claiming such a system would cost only $10 to $25 per container. The Bush administration says the concept is good but that the technology is unproven and the program untested.

Critics also say the Coast Guard and Customs are overburdened and underfunded. Since 9/11, for example, the number of hours the Coast Guard patrols U.S. waters each week has increased by 1,220 percent, but its funding has not dramatically increased. [14] (*See graph, p. 354.*) Others complain that the administration is overdue on drafting new rules requiring background checks and proper identification for those with access to U.S. ports.

Meanwhile on Capitol Hill, proposals are pending to toughen rules for screening U.S.-bound containers and to increase funding for port security. As Congress debates beefing up port security, here are some questions people are asking:

Are U.S ports secure?

The Bush administration says it has implemented numerous port-security measures since 9/11, but critics say neither port personnel nor the thousands of cargo containers that arrive daily are properly screened.

AFP/Getty Images/Lo Sai Hung

A truck passes through a portal radiation-detection system that scans cargo for nuclear materials at a port in Hong Kong, one of two that is testing enhanced security operations.

For instance, three times in 2005 a 24-year-old man from Stockton, Calif., snuck into Oakland's port and stowed away on ships traveling to Los Angeles, Long Beach and Taiwan. "Isn't that a suggestion that, at least at Oakland, we have a real problem?" asked Rep. Dan Lungren, R-Calif., chairman of the House Homeland Security Subcommittee on Economic Security, Infrastructure Protection and Cybersecurity. [15]

Subcommittee member Jane Harman, D-Calif., added that twice last year illegal Chinese immigrants were found inside shipping containers at the port of Los Angeles, but it "could have been terrorists or the components for a radiological bomb" instead. [16]

Others point out that the administration still hasn't instituted the Transportation Worker Identification Credential, known as TWIC, mandated by the Maritime Transportation Security Act of 2002. The law required anyone with port access to be identified using biometric information such as fingerprints or iris scans, following extensive background checks.

"We still don't know whether it's an American or a foreign operator who is on our docks," said Noel Cunningham, a security consultant and former director of operations and emergency management for the Port of Los Angeles. The current system of relying on drivers' licenses and employee IDs is "just not acceptable," he said. [17]

The Government Accountability Office (GAO) last year blamed bureaucratic obstacles for some of the TWIC delays. The Transportation Security Administration (TSA), created after the 9/11 attacks, initially envisioned TWIC-style IDs at all airports, seaports and railroad terminals beginning in August 2004. But implementation was delayed when the agency was moved in 2003 from the Department of Transportation to the newly created Department of Homeland Security, the GAO said. [18]

In the meantime, port operators have spent "hundreds of millions of dollars" on new security measures — such as fencing, lighting and video surveillance — says Kurt Nagle, president and chief executive officer of the American Association of Port Authorities. But the operators have been reluctant to develop new ID programs, he says, because of the impending TWIC program.

Homeland Security Secretary Chertoff admitted on March 20 that TWIC "has languished for too long" and promised to start it within months. [19]

The International Longshore and Warehouse Union (ILWU), among others, wants all workers with port access — including non-union truckers — covered by TWIC so union members won't be held to higher standards than other workers. The unions also fear that TWIC background checks may cost union members their jobs because of past criminal convictions unrelated to terrorism. "We want a fair process," says ILWU Legislative Director Lindsay McLaughlin.

The ILWU and other transportation unions say some aspects of port security have deteriorated since 9/11. "Real security measures have yet to be implemented and our ports remain extremely vulnerable," the AFL-CIO's Transportation Trades Department said in a March 23 statement asking the government to step up enforcement and provide more funding for security.

For example, some terminal operators replaced guards with cameras to make sure container seals have not been broken, but the image resolution is often too low to tell, McLaughlin says. In addition, not all terminal operators are ensuring that containers marked "empty" are actually empty, he says, and regulations requiring hazardous cargo to be properly documented and separated from other cargo are often ignored.

"Our port security is full of holes that need to be fixed," McLaughlin says.

Others say the United States should be inspecting more than just 5 percent of the incoming cargo. "Five percent . . . is unacceptable given the threats we face," Sen. Frank Lautenberg, D-N.J., told the Senate Permanent Subcommittee on Investigations on March 28. He called for inspections or scans of all arriving containers.

Customs spokesman John Mohan acknowledges the 5 percent figure may sound low but says those inspections follow a 100 percent screening before all goods leave foreign ports. Carriers must provide manifest information electronically at least 24 hours before containers are loaded onto a vessel, Mohan explains. Customs then checks the information against databases and watch lists maintained by the DHS's National Targeting Center to determine if the cargo poses a threat.

In addition to the 24-hour Customs rule, the Coast Guard requires that all international vessels file "notices of arrival" 96 hours before arriving in a U.S. port.

The Lexington Institute's Goure is not concerned that less than 10 percent of the cargo entering the United States is actually inspected. "You don't want to have to inspect more than just a small fraction," he says, lauding the administration's strategy of "pushing the borders out" to track and inspect more cargo while it's still overseas.

But critics say federal authorities have no way of knowing if the information on the shipping inventories is accurate. The 24-hour rule is a good start, says Christopher Koch, president and chief executive officer of the World Shipping Council, but authorities should also demand more details — better cargo descriptions, names of the sellers and buyers of the goods, point of origin, name of the broker and name and address of the business that "stuffed," or loaded, the container.

The Bush administration also touts its 180 new "radiation portal monitors" that now screen incoming cargo for nuclear and radiological materials. Before 9/11, no such monitors were used, Customs' Ahern told a Senate Homeland security panel on March 28. Currently, radiation monitors scan 37 percent of arriving international cargo, but the goal is 98 percent by December 2007, said DHS Assistant Secretary Stewart Baker.[20]

France Lags in Container Inspections

France inspected less than half the high-risk containers flagged by U.S. Customs inspectors. By comparison, the United Kingdom inspected more containers than it was asked to look at, and Japan inspected more than three-quarters.

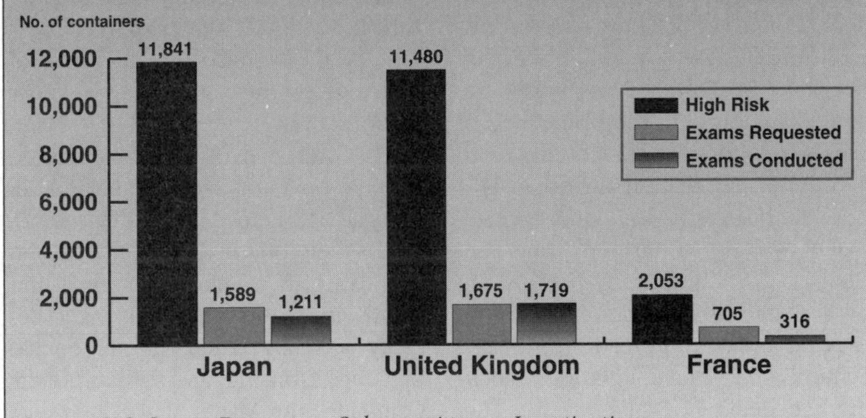

Source: U.S. Senate Permanent Subcommittee on Investigations

Customs also has deployed 12,400 handheld radiation-detection devices.

The radiation-screening equipment is promising technology, Koch says, but the devices often set of false alarms. Bananas, brocolli and kitty litter, for example, set off the equipment because they contain potassium.

"The technology is conceptually attractive," Koch says, "but a real-world evaluation of the technology . . . is clearly needed."

But cargo screening is not the only security problem. Ports are attractive terrorist targets for several reasons, according to John F. Frittelli, a transportation specialist at the Congressional Research Service and author of the 2003 book, *Port and Maritime Security, Background and Issues.*[21] The thousands of trucks serving U.S. ports every day provide opportunities for terrorists to sneak themselves or dangerous materials inside. And the hundreds of cargo ships are easy targets for fast-moving boats. In addition, many ports allow fishing and recreational boats to dock nearby, giving terrorists access to the bigger ships.

Security experts also fear that terrorists could:

- Seize a large cargo ship and crash into a bridge or waterfront refinery;
- Sink a cargo ship in a major shipping channel, blocking traffic;
- Blow up a large ship carrying volatile fuel;
- Attack an oil tanker, disrupting world oil markets and causing serious environmental damage; or
- Seize a cruise ship and threaten to kill the passengers if demands are not met.

Should foreign firms be barred from operating cargo terminals in U.S. ports?

The proposed lease of six U.S. port facilities to Dubai Ports World, a company based in the United Arab Emirates (UAE), was blocked after it triggered a furor in the United States. Critics said foreign-owned firms — particularly those with ties to terrorists — should be barred from controlling such crucial infrastructure as ports, which provide access to the rest of the country. The 9/11 Commission's

Kean said the Dubai deal "doesn't make any sense," noting that two of the 9/11 hijackers came from the UAE and that terrorists' money has been laundered through Dubai. [22]

Some of the deal's staunchest opponents were lawmakers from New York, which suffered grievously on Sept. 11 and whose port — the country's third largest — would have been operated by Dubai Ports under the deal. "Outsourcing the operations of our largest ports to a country with a dubious record on terrorism is a homeland security and commerce accident waiting to happen," said Sen. Charles E. Schumer, D-N.Y. Along with Sen. Hillary Rodham Clinton, D-N.Y., and Rep. Peter King, R-N.Y., Schumer introduced legislation blocking the deal. [23]

The Bush administration and others, however, point out that foreign companies already run many U.S. port facilities without compromising security. In fact, a British company — the Peninsular and Oriental Steam Navigation Co. — had already been operating the six terminals in question. Dubai Ports World had planned to take over the operations at the six terminals (in New York, Miami, Newark, Philadelphia, New Orleans and Baltimore) once it bought Peninsular.

In response to the public outcry, however, Dubai Ports World promised that once its purchase of Peninsular and Oriental was finalized, as it was in March, the company would lease the six U.S. terminals to an American company. It is still seeking bids from U.S. firms for those terminals.

A terminal operator leases terminal space from a state or local port authority only to load and unload cargo. The port authorities own, manage and maintain the physical infrastructure of a port, such as the docks and piers. Customs agents check cargo, and the Coast Guard oversees security. The arrangement is similar to those at U.S. airports, where foreign airlines may lease a terminal, but security is still the TSA's responsibility.

About 80 percent of U.S. ports lease some or all of their terminals to third-party operators, including foreign firms. For instance, companies from China, Denmark, Japan, Singapore and Taiwan operate more than 80 percent of the terminals at the Port of Los Angeles, the nation's largest. (*See chart, p. 341.*)

The presence of so many foreign terminal operators, said Homeland Security adviser Frances Fragos Townsend, means there is little difference between a British firm running a terminal and a UAE firm. [24] Assistant Homeland Security Secretary Baker told the Senate Banking, Housing and Urban Affairs Committee in March that a terminal operator — whether foreign or domestic — does not have "a unique insight into the breadth and depth of [Department of Homeland Security] security measures" nor can a terminal operator with ill intent get access "to inside information to avoid or evade DHS scrutiny." [25]

But critics weren't convinced. "For a port manager to run the ports, they have to interface with our security forces," Rep. King said. "They have to work with the Coast Guard, they have to work with all the local authorities, which means they are within our defense perimeter. They know exactly what is being done as far as security, so they can easily infiltrate, they can easily take advantage of that." [26]

But James Jay Carafano, a senior fellow for national security at the Heritage Foundation, told the House Armed Services panel that terrorists "don't need to buy a $7 billion company to penetrate maritime." Instead, they can just take cues from smugglers, he said. "The Mafia doesn't buy FedEx to smuggle. The Mafia makes low-level penetrations." [27]

Flynn and other security experts insist that foreign operation of port terminals doesn't make those ports more vulnerable. "We need to know what's in the box more than we need to know who is moving them around a container yard," Flynn said. [28]

At one point, President Bush implied that those questioning the Dubai deal were racist and only concerned because the firm is Arab. "It sends a terrible signal to friends around the world that it's OK for a company from one country to manage the port, but not a country that plays by the rules," he said. [29]

Arsalan T. Iftikhar, national legal director of the Council on American-Islamic Relations in Washington, was more direct. The outcry over the Dubai Ports World deal, he said, "was nothing more than knee-jerk, xenophobic and political 'cherry-picking' by certain political leaders seeking to bolster their national security platform in a midterm election year." (*See "At Issue," p. 353.*)

But some of the president's staunchest supporters rejected the racism accusations, insisting their concerns were based on the UAE's past involvement in supporting international terrorists. "I don't believe you can treat the United Arab Emirates the same as you treat Great Britain," King, chairman of the House Homeland Security Committee, told NBC's "Meet the Press." [30]

The UAE was one of three countries that openly supported the Taliban in the 1990s, opponents of the deal noted. "Their track record is terrifying," said Rep. Duncan Hunter, R-Calif., chairman of the House Armed Services Committee. [31] Other critics pointed out that when the Pakistani nuclear scientist A. Q. Khan wanted to sell black-market nuclear-weapons materials to Iran and North Korea, he used UAE middlemen and smuggled the contraband in shipping containers through Dubai. [32]

Opponents also stressed that Dubai Ports World is not simply a company located in the UAE but is owned by the government itself.

Getty Images/David McNew

Cargo containers are stacked high on the deck of a vessel at the Port of Los Angeles. Critics of port security say only 5 percent of the 11 million containers that arrived in the United States in 2005 were inspected.

However, the Bush administration and others say the UAE is now a trustworthy and important U.S. ally. It allows the United States and its allies to dock 131 warships and 590 military command ships in its ports, said Sen. Ted Stevens, R-Alaska, chairman of the Senate Commerce, Science and Transportation Committee. Sen. John McCain, R-Ariz., agreed, noting that the UAE hosts the U.S. Air Force at Al Dhafra, the UAE air-warfare and fighter-training center, and that the UAE government has worked to stop terrorist money-laundering. "We are dealing with a friend and an ally on this issue." [33]

Goure of the Lexington Institute called Schumer, Clinton and King "the axis of idiocy," charging that they had "totally misconstrued the issue for pure political gain."

The rising xenophobia and anti-Arab sentiment, he said, echoes concerns raised by some Americans when the Japanese bought Lincoln Center in New York City and other U.S. properties in the 1990s. "It's this weird notion that if they buy [U.S. facilities] that it means they're stronger and we're weaker. None of this makes a rat's ass difference," he says. The biggest danger "is at the port of embarkation, where cargo is loaded on its way to our shores, not where the cargo is offloaded."

Is the administration doing enough to improve port security abroad?

Homeland-security experts and the Bush administration agree that oversight of foreign ports is key to ensuring that U.S. ports are safe, but some experts say the administration's post-9/11 efforts to improve overseas port security fall short.

Customs launched two programs in 2002 aimed at preventing terrorists from smuggling dangerous materials into the United States from foreign ports: The Container Security Initiative (CSI) and the Customs-Trade Partnership Against Terrorism (C-TPAT). The CSI posts U.S. Customs agents at foreign ports, where they can target and screen U.S.-bound shipments deemed "high risk" by the United States. Participating ports must install radiation-detecting equipment. The 44 foreign ports currently participating in CSI handle about 75 percent of the containers entering the United States. By the end of the year, the administration expects 50 ports to be participating, covering 82 percent of the U.S.-bound cargo, Customs' Ahern said.

However, GAO investigators found that only 17.5 percent of containers that U.S. officials tagged as "high-risk" were given follow-up inspections by U.S. officials overseas. [34] Some of the foreign host countries have either been "unwilling or unable to share their intelligence" with U.S. officials, and the radiation-detection equipment varies widely from country to country, the Senate Permanent Subcommittee on Investigations reported in March. Moreover, investigators said, Customs agents cannot force suspicious containers to be opened. Ports in France, for example, refused to inspect about 60 percent of the cargo deemed high-risk by U.S. agents. (*See graph, p. 343.*)

Equally troubling, says Sen. Carl Levin D-Mich., ranking Democrat on the Senate Homeland Security investigations panel, Customs relies on cargo manifests — which security experts say are undependable — to identify "high-risk containers." The system has never been tested or validated, Levin adds.

The U.S. government uses a computerized model known as the Automated Targeting System to determine which containers might be "high risk." But as Flynn's nightmare scenario involving Indonesian-made sneakers shows, the CSI program doesn't take into account the many stops foreign-made products — even those from "trusted" shippers — can make between the factory and the ship. "All a terrorist organization need do is find a single weak link within a trusted shipper's complex supply chain, such as a poorly paid truck driver taking a container from a remote factory to a loading port," Flynn said in March.

Nearly 10,000 businesses have applied to take part in C-TPAT, the other major Customs initiative. It promises companies fewer inspections if they agree to voluntarily beef up their security measures. Thus far, Customs has reviewed the security plans of 5,800 firms but has validated only 1,545 of the plans. Ahern told the House Homeland Security Committee in March he is "not happy" with the agency's progress in checking the plans but hopes to have 65 percent of the applications reviewed by year's end. [35]

GAO concluded last year, however, that C-TPAT does not necessarily improve security because U.S. officials do not check to see if companies are doing what they promised in their security plans. [36]

However, C-TPAT can be a good investment for businesses. After toymaker Hasbro spent $200,000 to join the program in 2002 and get its plan validated, its inspections dropped from 7.6 percent of all containers in 2001 to 0.66 percent in 2003. That saved the company more than a half a million dollars in inspection costs, says Rep. Lungren, who has proposed legislation to expand the program.

Henry H. Willis, an analyst at the RAND Corporation, says the government has no way to ensure that CSI and C-TPAT work. The World Shipping Council's Koch agrees, noting that because both programs are voluntary, "It's hard to measure their effectiveness." Nevertheless, he insists, they are "absolutely valuable" and should be expanded.

Critics also worry that Customs won't have enough time or manpower to follow up and make sure that companies involved in C-TPAT continue to use top-of-the-line security procedures. Today Customs has 88 specialists on staff to review and monitor companies' security plans. Another 40 are to join the agency by late spring, Ahern told Coleman's panel.

Some experts say the two programs give a false sense of security because terrorists can figure out which shipments inspectors routinely designate as low risk. "Because name-brand companies like Wal-Mart and General Motors are widely known to be considered low-risk, terrorists need only to stake out their shipment routes and exploit the weakest points to introduce a weapon of mass destruction," wrote Flynn and Lawrence M. Wein, a faculty member at Stanford University's Center for International Security and Cooperation. [37]

"A terrorist cell posing as a legal shipping company for more than two years or a terrorist truck driver hauling goods from a well-known shipper can also be confident of being perceived as low risk," Wein and Flynn wrote. The entire program, Flynn testified, relies on the honor system.

The Bush administration in 2003 also launched Megaports, a Department of Energy program designed to prevent nuclear materials from entering the United States. Under the program, the United States has installed radiation-detection systems in ports in Greece, the Bahamas, Sri Lanka, the Netherlands and Spain and is working on installation arrangements with Belgium, China, the U.A.E., Honduras, Israel, Oman, the Philippines, Singapore and Thailand. The administration hopes to work out deals with 21 other countries, David G. Huizenga, deputy assistant secretary of the agency, testified during a March 28 hearing by the Senate Homeland Security and Governmental Affairs Subcommittee on Investigations.

But GAO investigators warned that corruption is a "pervasive problem" in some countries that received radiation-detection equipment. Border-security authorities in those countries turned off the devices or ignored alarms, GAO's director of Natural Resources and Environment, Gene Aloise, said during the same March 28 Senate hearing.

Lawmakers also worry that there are too many federal agencies with jurisdiction over port security, creating problems of coordination and overlapping responsibilities. The agencies include Customs, the Coast Guard, the Transportation Security Administration and the Domestic Nuclear Detection Office — all within the DHS — plus the departments of State, Transportation and Defense.

However, insists Vayl Oxford, director of the Nuclear Detection Office, the groups now have a "daily dialogue" that didn't exist before 9/11. "It's a great step forward," he told Coleman. ■

BACKGROUND

Taxes and Smugglers

For decades, port security meant preventing thieves — including organized crime — from stealing cargo. For the government, it meant collecting taxes, or duties, on imported goods and looking for smuggled goods or drugs.

Customs and the Coast Guard were established — primarily to collect taxes — shortly after the United States became a country. The Tariff Act of July 4, 1789, allowed the government to collect duties on imported goods to raise money and pay off debts. Four weeks later, on July 31, 1789, Congress created the Customs Service to collect those taxes at ports of entry. [38]

Customs collections funded the country's expansion — including purchases of Louisiana, Oregon, Florida and Alaska — and for building the nation's lighthouses, the military and naval academies and Washington, D.C.

The Coast Guard's history is more complicated because it involves several independent but overlapping federal agencies. [39] The Revenue Cutter Service, created in 1790, officially became the Coast Guard in 1915. It primarily ensures that tariffs are paid, ships are protected from pirates and that neither products nor humans are smuggled into the country. Intercept-

Continued on p. 348

Chronology

1700s-1950s

The two federal agencies responsible for port security — Customs and the Coast Guard — are created early in the nation's history, primarily to collect taxes.

1789
The Customs Service is created and a year later the Revenue Cutter Service, which is renamed the Coast Guard in 1915.

1917
German saboteurs attack an ammunition depot near New York Harbor prompting passage of the Espionage Act giving the Coast Guard authority over U.S. waters.

Dec. 7, 1941
The U.S. naval base at Pearl Harbor, Hawaii, is attacked by the Japanese, forcing the United States into World War II. During the war, airplanes and blimps patrol U.S. ports and coastlines for German and Japanese submarines.

1950
Congress amends the Espionage Act, expanding the Coast Guard's authority to harbors, ports and waterfront facilities.

1960s-1990s

Coast Guard's focus shifts to enforcing environmental and safety standards, intercepting illegal drugs and helping Cuban refugees.

1980
Coast Guard launches the so-called Mariel boatlift to assist the 125,000 Cubans — including many prisoners and mental patients — who had suddenly been released by Cuban President Fidel Castro and were trying to reach U.S. shores in 1,700 overcrowded boats.

2000s

Following the Sept. 11, 2001, terrorist attacks, the Coast Guard launches the largest port-security operation since World War II, and Customs tightens scrutiny overseas of U.S.-bound cargo.

January 2002
Container Security Initiative allows U.S. Custom agents at foreign ports to screen high-risk containers bound for the United States. . . . Customs-Trade Partnership Against Terrorism promises fewer Customs inspections for companies that voluntarily beef up security.

October 2002
The consulting firm Booz Allen Hamilton estimates that the detonation of a radioactive, or "dirty bomb," at a U.S. port could force all American ports to be shut down for 12 days, at a cost of $58 billion.

Nov. 25, 2002
President George W. Bush signs the Maritime Transportation Security Act requiring the nation's 361 commercial seaports to develop anti-terrorism plans and an ID system for port workers.

Nov. 20, 2003
Congress creates the Department of Homeland Security, which absorbs Customs, Border Patrol and the Coast Guard.

July 1, 2004
A security regime for international shipping approved in 2002 by the International Maritime Organization, a branch of the United Nations, goes into effect. The requirements parallel the United States' Maritime Transportation Security Act of 2002 by requiring ports and shipping companies to review their operations to prevent terrorists from infiltrating the maritime sector.

May 2005
Congressional investigators find that only 17.5 percent of the cargo identified by U.S. officials overseas as high risk is being properly inspected and examined.

September 2005
President Bush issues the National Strategy for Maritime Security.

Dec. 5, 2005
The 9/11 Commission issues a "report card" faulting U.S. efforts to improve cargo screening and security at critical infrastructure.

February 2006
Arab-owned Dubai Ports World announces controversial plans to run terminals at six U.S. ports, prompting hearings and proposals to block foreigners from operating U.S. ports and to improve port security.

March 2006
Senate investigators find that port inspectors overseas screen less than 3 percent of U.S.-bound containers for radiation. The Bush administration promises to install 620 radiation devices at the top U.S. ports by December 2007.

April 2006
Department of Homeland Security Secretary Michael Chertoff inspects Hong Kong's pilot program for screening all containers with radiation and scanning detectors.

Continued from p. 346

ing "contraband" — whether it be slaves, narcotics or, during Prohibition, liquor — has been the Coast Guard's most challenging responsibility.

AFP/Getty Images/Lo Sai Hung

Homeland Security Secretary Michael Chertoff (front right) tours a port in Hong Kong that is operating a pilot program to show cargo can be screened with both radiation-detection and X-ray-type machines without disrupting trade.

The Sept. 11 terrorist attacks were not the first foreign attacks on the United States that resulted in new laws to protect U.S. waterways. In 1916, during World War I, German agents in 1916 blew up ammunition stored on an island near New York Harbor that was bound for the Allied powers in Europe. [40] The next year, after the United States entered the war, Congress passed the Espionage Act of 1917, giving the Coast Guard authority over U.S. waters. [41]

During World War I, uniformed Customs intelligence officers were responsible for security and operations support for port and federal/military activities and formed a special intelligence bureau at the Port of New York. In World War II, the Coast Guard was not only involved in every major invasion abroad but also rescued more than 1,500 survivors of torpedo attacks in areas adjacent to the United States.

In the early 1960s, the Coast Guard's focus shifted to helping refugees fleeing Cuba after communist Fidel Castro took power in 1959. The assistance ended in 1965, when the United States imposed new restrictions on Cuban immigration, but it restarted with the 1980 "Mariel boatlift." The effort to help 125,000 Cubans trying to reach U.S. shores in 1,700 overcrowded boats was the largest Coast Guard operation ever undertaken in peacetime. [42] In the 1970s the Coast Guard and Customs launched drug-interdiction efforts in the "war on drugs" that continue today.

War on Terror

Experts say the "war on terrorism" is fundamentally different from the "war on drugs." Drug smugglers seek secret routes that can be used repeatedly, which allows federal agencies to look for patterns of behavior by the smugglers. Terrorists, on the other hand, prize methods that have never been used and likely will be used only once, explained transportation specialist Frittelli. [43]

One of the earliest maritime terrorist attacks occurred in 1985, but not in the United States, Frittelli points out. Palestinian terrorists seized the *Achille Lauro* cruise ship in the Mediterranean and demanded that Israel release 50 Arab prisoners. To demonstrate their resolve, the attackers shot and killed a wheelchair-bound Jewish-American passenger, Leon Klinghoffer, and threw his body overboard. And in 2000, suicide bombers rammed a small boat filled with explosives into the destroyer *USS Cole* during a refueling stop in Aden, Yemen, killing 17 U.S. sailors. [44]

After the 9/11 attackers brought terrorism to U.S. shores, however, the Coast Guard created the largest port-security operation since World War II, according to Frittelli. The Coast Guard now maintains "security zones" around waterside facilities, Navy vessels and cruise and cargo ships entering or leaving ports. Coast Guard cutters and aircraft have been diverted from other assignments to patrol the new security zones as well as coastal waters.

In addition to CSI and C-TPAT — the two anti-terrorism port programs launched by Customs after 9/11 — Congress created the new Transportation Security Administration with a mandate to develop an ID and background-check program for all transportation workers, including dock workers.

But the Maritime Transportation Security Act signed by President Bush in November 2002 was the first legislation devoted to port security, requiring U.S. ports to develop "security and incident-response plans." Since then the Coast Guard has reviewed and approved security plans

Does Hong Kong Have the Answer?

Some security experts think a pilot port security program in Hong Kong may represent the "Holy Grail" of modern port security technology.

Since March 2005, all containers entering two Hong Kong ports have been scanned for both radiation and large, dense objects that — according to the shipper's cargo manifest — don't seem to belong in the shipment. Digital images of the containers' contents are then stored in a database.

The Hong Kong initiative is "a true model of where we might be able to go" with port security, says Stephen E. Flynn, a senior fellow at the Council on Foreign Relations and former Coast Guard commander. The density scanning is particularly important, he explains, because radiation sensors would not detect a radioactive "dirty bomb" wrapped in lead. But gamma-ray (similar to X-rays) machines single out unusually dense objects.

The program is funded by the Container Terminal Operators Association of Hong Kong and Hutchison Port Holdings, one of the world's largest port operators, and receives no government funding. Shipping companies and terminal operators say they support the program because it might prevent a terrorist event that could shut down port operations for days or weeks, costing billions of dollars, said Hutchison Senior Vice President Gary Gilbert. [1] If the program were mandated worldwide, Gilbert said, it would not only deter terrorism but also provide a way for investigators to track shipments to their port of origin if there is an incident, possibly avoiding an entire maritime shutdown.

Shippers and the Bush administration call the Hong Kong initiative a good start but not a panacea. "The technology is not totally proven," Michael Jackson, deputy secretary of the Department of Homeland Security (DHS), told the House Homeland Security Committee on April 4. "We need to do more testing."

Christopher Koch, president and CEO of the World Shipping Council, concurs, noting that today's radiation devices cannot distinguish between deadly radiation and low-level, natural radiation emitted by such products as kitty litter and bananas. The result would be countless "nuisance alarms," he says.

Moreover, said Jayson Ahern, assistant commissioner for field operations at U.S. Customs and Border Protection, the Hong Kong screening operation has been "completely oversold. It is not doing 100 percent of the containers." [2]

Jackson also complains that so far no one is reviewing the images of the container contents being collected. The images are "basically going onto a disk and being stored," he said.

But shippers point out that it's only a pilot program, designed to show that the technology exists to scan for both radiation and density. There were never plans to analyze the data, says Alison Williams, a spokeswoman at SAIC, the San Diego-based company that provides the screening machines. Instead, the objective was designed to show that accurate screening information could be collected without impeding the flow of commerce, she says.

The program is still working on its other objective: to show the U.S. government that if the system were deployed in foreign terminals the database could be useful, Williams says. "There have been a number of U.S. delegations to see the system in operation in Hong Kong, but there still is not a definitive statement from DHS" regarding the program, she says. Nevertheless, the operators have agreed to continue running it while DHS studies the system.

DHS Secretary Michael Chertoff visited the project on April 1 and calls it "very innovative," says DHS spokesman Russ Knocke. "He wanted to see the pilot firsthand to see if there are any elements that could be applicable here," he says, adding that not analyzing the data is a concern.

Several lawmakers have advocated that all U.S.-bound containers be screened or inspected, but many do not spell out whether they mean screening for radiation, density or both.

For the program to work worldwide, Flynn says Customs would need 400 agents reviewing the images. Currently, Customs has 80 agents stationed abroad, designated to look for suspicious cargo bound for the United States as part of a voluntary program called the Customs-Trade Partnership Against Terrorism, but the agency says another 40 agents are to be posted to that program by May. [3]

Meanwhile, the question of who would pay for such a global screening system remains unanswered. At an April 3 Senate forum, Hutchison's Gilbert suggested that taxpayers pay for the personnel to examine the data and shippers pay for the technology. Clark Kent Ervin, former DHS inspector general and now a homeland security expert at the Aspen Institute, endorsed an even split for the cost of new radiation monitors. [4]

But Knocke warns that "technology alone for supply-chain security is not the only solution. What's needed, he says, is "a combination of personnel, technology, private-sector participation, business practices and the layered security defense that we have throughout the container supply chain."

[1] Pamela Hess, "Pilot port security program data unused," United Press International, April 4, 2006.

[2] Transcript of House Homeland Security Subcommittee on Economic Security, Infrastructure Protection and Cybersecurity Hearing on Port Security, March 16, 2006.

[3] House Homeland Security Subcommittee, *op. cit.*

[4] Tim Starks "Experts Recommend Increased Port Security," *CQ Today*, April 3, 2006.

for 3,200 maritime facilities in the nation's ports. [45]

The Coast Guard also has completed security checks at all 55 U.S. ports the federal government deems "strategic" due to their economic or military importance. For example, during Operation Desert Storm in 1991 about 90 percent of military equipment and supplies was shipped through "strategic" ports. [46] If those ports were attacked, "not only could massive

The Revolutionary, Versatile Shipping Container

Gone are the days when burly longshoremen wielding lethal-looking metal hooks unloaded cargo from ships — bundle by bundle and crate by crate — storing it in warehouses to await loading onto trucks.

Today, more than 90 percent of the world's cargo moves in standard-sized containers stacked like children's blocks on ships as long as football fields. When the ships dock, the containers are loaded directly onto freight cars or trucks by giant gantry cranes, which inspired the robotic creatures in George Lucas' film, "The Empire Strikes Back."

More than 11 million containers arrived in U.S. ports in 2005, with 12 million expected this year, says Christopher Koch, president of the World Shipping Council. A typical container today is 20-, 40- or 45-feet long and can be equipped with special technologies such as refrigeration units or hanger systems for clothing. A 40-foot container can hold 4,403 VCRs, 267,000 video games or 10,000 pairs of shoes, according to the American Association of Port Authorities.

The ease with which containers can be moved around helped foster the rapid globalization of international trade by reducing both labor costs and transport time. [1] Today a standard container with 32 tons of cargo can be shipped from China to the United States for as little as $2,000. [2]

"The world has become dependent upon the box — and the box, in return, has changed the world," German filmmaker Thomas Greh said in a Web site posting about his 2004 documentary film, "The Container Story."

The re-release of Greh's documentary coincides with the 50th anniversary of the first container shipped — in 1956, from Newark, N.J., bound for Houston. [3] Containers were invented by a North Carolina farmer's son, Malcolm McLean, who had started his own trucking company during the Great Depression. Frustrated by the inefficiency of the dockside loading and unloading process, McLean asked himself, "Wouldn't it be great if my [tractor] trailer could simply be lifted up and placed on the ship?" [4]

McLean eventually died a very rich man, having sold his Sea-Land shipping business for $160 million in 1969. But, while he and the world's consumers benefited from containers, others did not. As the first container ship left Newark harbor, International Longshoremen's Association official Freddy Fields was asked how he liked the new ship. "I'd like to sink that sonofabitch," Fields replied. [5]

Unsuccessful longshoremen's strikes followed the introduction of containers. As shipping costs plummeted, so did dockworkers' jobs. Containers and other new technologies slashed the number of West Coast longshoremen's jobs from more than 100,000 in the 1970s to 10,500 today. [6]

Intermodal shipping containers — as they're technically called — are nearly indestructible and typically last for decades. McLean probably never imagined his invention would one day be recycled as temporary offices, living quarters, schools and medical facilities in remote locations.

"Construction companies often own their own containers and ship supplies, tools and equipment to job sites in a container. Then they use the empty container as an office while the project is ongoing," says construction supervisor Tom Koch, who has worked in container "offices" on projects in Guam and Tajikistan. "When the project is finished, they load all the equipment back into the container and ship it home."

Some companies donate their old containers. In the 1990s Coca-Cola donated a container to Soweto's Nanto primary school in South Africa, which leased it out to a convenience

civilian casualties be sustained, but the Defense Department could also lose precious cargo and time and be forced to rely heavily on its overburdened airlift capabilities," according to a 2002 GAO report. [47]

The 2002 law also required vessels to install special tracking devices that transmit a unique identifying signal to a receiver located at the port and to other ships in the area. The system relies on global positioning systems, digital communication equipment and other technology to provide port officials and other vessels nearby with a vessel's identity, position, speed and course. Such a system aims to provide an "early warning" if a vessel is in a location where it shouldn't be. The system is operational in 12 major U.S. ports, but all ports nationwide are scheduled to have it eventually.

Last September President Bush issued a blueprint for improving port security, called the National Strategy for Maritime Security. [48] The 30-page plan calls for beefing up existing programs but does not propose any new initiatives. It dovetails with eight "supporting" plans, such as the International Outreach and Coordination Strategy and the Maritime Infrastructure Recovery Plan.

U.S. Coast Guard Commandant Admiral Thomas Collins said the strategy builds on the nation's "layered defense as the government and private-sector improve their coordination during maritime incidents." [49]

But Flynn of the Council on Foreign Relations says all of the plans and activity "should not be confused with real capability." He told a Senate Homeland Security panel on March 28 that the administration's approach on port security has been piecemeal, "with each agency pursuing its signature program or programs with little regard for other initiatives." ■

store operator. Thousands of donated containers have been converted into schools, community centers, homes, even restaurants and beauty salons in Africa. [7] Seattle architects Robert Humble and Joel Egan have turned old shipping containers into modular homes, designed a mobile medical unit for Doctors Without Borders and a base camp in rural Siberia for Earth Corps, which is helping to develop ecotourism at Lake Baikal. [8]

The windowless containers have also reportedly been used for more nefarious purposes — such as places to secretly torture prisoners in Afghanistan or Iraq. [9] "Around Iraq, in the back of a Humvee or in a shipping container, there's no camera," an Army interrogator told a documentary filmmaker. "And there's no one looking over your shoulder, so you can do anything you want." [10]

Since containers are large enough for people to live in, they are sometimes used to smuggle large groups of illegal immigrants with enough food and water for a long sea journey. In April, 22 illegal Chinese immigrants were found inside a sealed cargo container at Seattle's Harbor Island. [11]

And while sealed shipping containers have dramatically reduced the amount of pilferage that once occurred during shipments, security experts worry that terrorists could sneak a radioactive "dirty bomb" into a locked shipping container bound for the United States. Pakistani nuclear scientist A. Q. Khan, for example, confessed in 2004 that he smuggled nuclear-weapons materials to Libya, Iran and North Korea in containers. [12]

U.S. Customs and Border Protection

Food, water and makeshift toilets are among the debris left behind after 22 Chinese immigrants arrived in Seattle after 15 days in a 40-foot container.

[1] Marc Levinson, *The Box: How the Shipping Container Made the World Smaller and The World Economy Bigger* (2006).

[2] Christian Caryl, "The Box Is King," *Newsweek International*, April 10, 2006.

[3] www.containerstory.com.

[4] Quoted from "Who Made America?" PBS, www.pbs.org/wgbh/theymadeamerica/whomade/mclean_hi.html.

[5] *Ibid.*

[6] From David Bacon and Freda Coodin, "Bush Threatens West Coast Dockers' Right to Strike," *Labor Notes*, September 2002.

[7] Michael Wines, "Africans find a refuge in cast-off 'big boxes,' " *The New York Times*, Aug. 8, 2004.

[8] See www.cargotecture.com/contact.html.

[9] See Michael Ignatieff, "Lesser Evils," *The New York Times Magazine*, May 2, 2004, p. 46.

[10] Alessandra Stanley, "The Slow Rise of Abuse That Shocked the Nation," *The New York Times*, Oct. 18, 2005, p. E5.

[11] Lornet Turnbull, "Stowaways say each paid $10,000," *The Seattle Times*, April 12, 2006.

[12] For background, see Mary H. Cooper, "Nuclear Proliferation and Terrorism," *CQ Researcher*, April 2, 2004, pp. 297-320.

CURRENT SITUATION

The Fast Track

In the wake of the controversial Dubai Ports World deal, the administration is fast-tracking several port-security initiatives that had been languishing for years, including installing more radiation-detection devices in U.S. ports and issuing the first-ever identification cards for port workers. And lawmakers on Capitol Hill finally are getting traction on a flurry of port-security proposals.

"The controversy focused much-needed attention on the issue of port security," said Sen. Collins on March 21, when she was named "Port Person of the Year" by the American Association of Port Authorities. [50]

Democrats, however, quickly seized on the Ports World controversy as a potential election-year issue and began pushing for more money for port security. "If the Republicans are now deciding to get on board, then we welcome them, because for so long they have been on a sinking ship, basically saying that our ports are secure," said Rep. Bennie Thompson of Mississippi, ranking Democrat on the House Homeland Security Committee. [51]

In March Congress received three separate GAO reports showing weaknesses in the country's port defenses. Among the findings:

- U.S. port operators are delaying deployment of radiation portal monitors, fearing they will slow shipping. [52]
- DHS plans to buy "advanced" radiation portal monitors that will cost between $330,000 and

Getty Images/Stephen Chernin

Getty Images/David McNew

Inspection Technology at Work

U.S. Customs inspectors cut off a padlock in order to examine a shipping container in Jersey City (top). Inspectors also use X-ray-type devices and radiation detectors when inspecting containers. A Department of Homeland Security inspector inside a mobile scanning unit at the Port of Los Angeles examines X-ray images of a shipping container (bottom).

Continued from p. 350

$460,000 apiece without really knowing if they work better than the existing devices costing $49,000 to $60,000. [53]

- Customs officers are not required to verify that shippers of radiological material actually obtained required licenses, and Customs lacks access to Nuclear Regulatory Commission (NRC) data that could authenticate a license. [54]

Ahern told Sen. Coleman's March 28 Homeland Security hearing that Customs is working hard to improve its programs. In addition to being able to screen 98 percent of inbound containers for radiation by December 2007, the agency plans to deploy 60 mobile radiation portal monitors in seaports by the end of 2006, he says. GAO investigators caution, however, that the schedule is ambitious.

Ahern also promised to establish new procedures so Customs officials do not get fooled by fake documents, as they did during GAO's recent undercover sting operation at Mexican and Canadian border crossings. Investigators were allowed to bring radioactive material into the United States after producing fake documents showing they had an NRC license. The GAO had downloaded examples of the documents they needed on the Internet and used off-the-shelf computer software to create copies.

DHS Deputy Secretary Jackson says ID cards for port workers are a "very high priority" and that the department plans to issue them in "months, not years." Both the TSA and the Coast Guard are working on regulations, he explained, and in late March the administration published a notice seeking firms with the technological background to run certain parts of the program.

But some on Capitol Hill complain that the administration is not acting quickly enough. A House Homeland

Continued on p. 354

At Issue:

Is it racist to ban Arab companies from operating U.S. ports?

ARSALAN T. IFTIKHAR
NATIONAL LEGAL DIRECTOR, COUNCIL ON AMERICAN-ISLAMIC RELATIONS

WRITTEN FOR *CQ RESEARCHER*, APRIL 2006

yes

Unfortunately, the whole Dubai Ports World fiasco was nothing more than knee-jerk, xenophobic and political "cherry-picking" by political leaders seeking to bolster their national-security platform in a midterm election year.

Although these leaders have now become the self-anointed vanguards of our port security, their disingenuous arguments that port "security" being outsourced to an Arab company would somehow put that security at risk is based on nothing more than anti-Muslim, anti-Arab sentiment that is, unfortunately, becoming pervasive within the Washington Beltway.

Note that none of these elected officials gave a bloody hoot while Dubai Ports World was being fully vetted and blessed by the Committee on Foreign Investment in the United States (CFIUS), which includes representatives from the departments of Treasury, Defense and Homeland Security.

The *Wall Street Journal* editorial board took the naysayers to task by questioning why these politicians "believe Dubai Ports World has been insufficiently vetted for the task at hand. So far, none of the critics provided any evidence that the administration hasn't done its due diligence."

Another insincere argument advanced by these politicians is that we as Americans cannot outsource port "security" to an Arab Muslim nation. The editorial board at the *Los Angeles Times* found this argument to be equally as vapid. "The notion that the Bush administration is farming out port 'security' to hostile Arab nations is alarmist nonsense. Dubai Ports World would be managing the commercial activities of these U.S. ports, not securing them," wrote the *Times*.

Nonetheless, these "superhawks" still do not believe that an Arab and Muslim company has the moral equilibrium to merely hire longshoremen, many of whom are red-blooded Americans and card-carrying members of the AFL-CIO.

This is where xenophobia takes over. Baltimore Mayor Martin O'Malley asked: "Do we want to turn over the port of Baltimore, home of the 'Star-Spangled Banner,' to the United Arab Emirates? Not so long as I'm mayor."

The knee-jerk rhetoric was so eloquently epitomized by Sen. Charles Schumer, D-N.Y., who said: "Let's say skinheads had bought a company to take over our port. . . . I think the outcry would have been the same."

When jingoistic references to our national anthem and silly comparisons of Arabs to skinheads become political talking points, you know racism and xenophobia cannot be far behind.

U.S. REP. DUNCAN HUNTER, R-CALIF.
CHAIRMAN, HOUSE ARMED SERVICES COMMITTEE

WRITTEN FOR *CQ RESEARCHER*, APRIL 2006

no

We're in an age that unites terrorism and technology. So we must critically examine America's vulnerabilities, especially those in our infrastructure — such as in our ports and power plants — where disasters would paralyze commerce or imperil populations.

Unfortunately, there's no perfect protection against attack. Therefore, vigilance is paramount — especially regarding who controls our nation's critical infrastructure. That is why I introduced legislation to ensure that critical national-security assets remain in the hands of reliable, American-controlled companies.

The proposed legislation would require the secretary of Defense to maintain a list of assets so vital that their destruction would cripple our ability to maintain national security, economic security or public safety. Further, American citizens must control sensitive or classified aspects of the national-defense critical infrastructure. Appropriate U.S. authorities must also search 100 percent of inbound cargo.

Ensuring American control of key U.S. assets isn't new. For example, businesses that perform classified defense work must have an American CEO and outside directors who are U.S. citizens who cannot be removed except with Department of Defense permission. In domestic airlines, U.S. citizens must comprise top management. Indeed, many foreign investments in the United States leave U.S. management intact. Despite what critics say about the economic impact of such measures, America has long been foreign investment's favorite destination — perhaps because we ensure a safe, stable society.

National security, not simple economic opportunity, comes first. The Committee on Foreign Investment in the United States (CFIUS) apparently forgot this when it OK'd the deal to shift major port terminal operations to government-controlled Dubai Ports World, overlooking facts like these: In 2003, over U.S. protests, customs officials in the United Arab Emirates allowed Dubai to transship 66 high-speed electrical switches, which can be used to detonate nuclear weapons. Dubai also rejected U.S. requests to inspect containers holding the switches.

Yet, Dubai's track record somehow passed muster at CFIUS, which let the president down. Accordingly, my legislation mandates the administration be notified of mergers, acquisitions or takeovers being reviewed by CFIUS.

The drive to globalization shouldn't dupe us into letting down our guard regarding critical American assets and infrastructure. If that makes me a protectionist, as critics say, I'll say it again: America is worth protecting.

Port Security Funding Has Increased

Federal funding for port security has increased by more than 600 percent since the terrorist attacks on Sept. 11, 2001, to about $1.6 billion in 2005 says the Bush administration (top). But U.S. port authorities complain that in the past three years they received only 19 percent of the $3.8 billion in federal grants they requested to upgrade security infrastructure, such as lighting, fencing and security cameras (bottom).

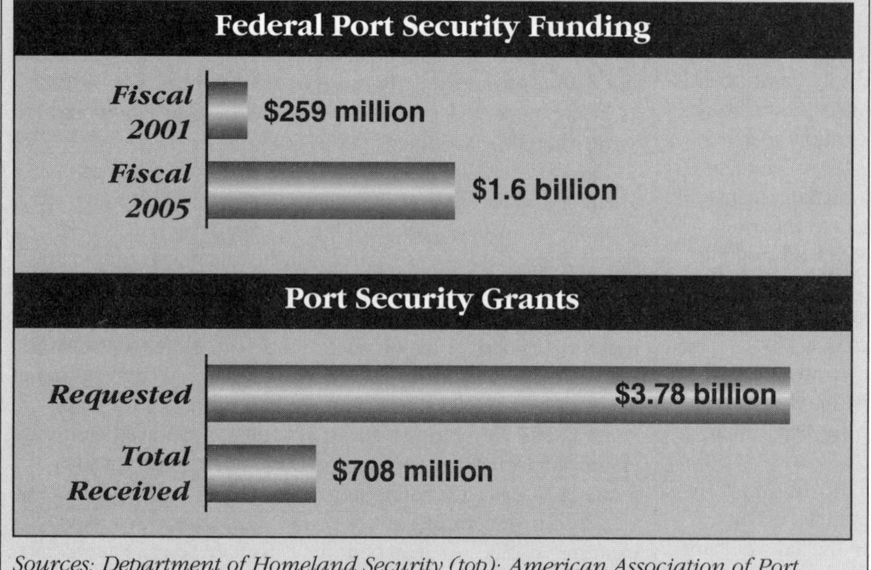

Sources: Department of Homeland Security (top); American Association of Port Authorities

Continued from p. 352

Security panel on March 30 approved the first piece of port-security legislation since the Dubai Ports World dustup. The bipartisan SAFE Port Act, proposed by California Reps. Lungren and Harman, would require the DHS to develop timelines for installing radiation equipment in ports and launching the TWIC program. It would also establish procedures for restoring port operations in the event of an attack and improving the CSI and C-TPAT programs.

On March 30, Lungren's Subcommittee on Economic Security, Infrastructure Protection and Cybersecurity approved the measure, increasing to $821 million the amount of federal funds set aside each year for port security — including a $20 million increase earmarked for speeding up the TWIC identification cards. [55]

Democrats were defeated in efforts to include amendments requiring full inspection of every cargo container and increasing the number of port inspectors by 1,600 over four years. The full House is expected to vote on the measure in May.

A similar bill in the Senate, introduced by Collins and Sen. Patty Murray, D-Wash., would provide quicker processing, or "green lanes," to shippers who meet strict security requirements along with $400 million in security grants. Collins' committee has held a hearing on the measure and expects to vote on it in April.

Lungren stresses that neither his bill nor Collins' is "an afterthought" to the recent Dubai Ports World controversy and that their efforts began months before the deal made headlines.

Homeland Security Deputy Secretary Jackson declined on April 5 to endorse the Collins and Lungren measures but said nonetheless that he looked forward to the "passage of bipartisan legislation that will strengthen our work in the maritime domain." It was the first time DHS has supported any of the pending legislation to beef up port security.

Meanwhile, a larger transportation bill approved by the Senate Commerce, Science and Transportation Committee in late February would authorize random inspections of cargo entering the United States and provide $729 million annually for port security. In April, the House Transportation and Infrastructure Committee approved a bill that would require greater oversight of transfers of ownership or operation of port facilities and limit a port terminal's top security post to U.S. citizens. (*See "At Issue," p. 353.*)

Money Matters

Port facilities may soon see more federal dollars. A Senate panel in April earmarked an additional $648 million for port security in an emergency fiscal 2006 budget package to help finance the war in Iraq. The additional funding includes $227 million for port-security grants, $211 million for Customs to purchase 60 additional cargo-container inspection systems, $23 million for 50 additional Customs port inspectors, $23 million for the Coast Guard to triple the number of port-security plan specialists, $32 million for Customs to hire 85 container-security specialists and $132 million to deploy more than 300 additional radiation portal monitors at U.S. seaports. [56]

The full Senate is scheduled to take up the emergency bill after the Easter recess. The House in March narrowly rejected, 208-210, an amendment that would have added $825 million for port security to the emergency measure.

As for fiscal 2007, many proposed measures increase money for port security. In recent years Democrats had tried repeatedly to increase spending on port security, but Republicans had blocked them. This year, however, key Republicans in both chambers have called for more funding.

Getty Images/Brendan Smialowski

Security expert and former Coast Guard commander Stephen Flynn of the Council on Foreign Relations tells a congressional committee that the United States has not done enough since the terrorist attacks of Sept. 11, 2001, to beef up port security.

"Regrettably, the administration's budget shortchanges port security," said Collins, who wants a separate stream of federal funds for port security rather than the administration's approach, which folds in money for ports with all other transportation projects. [57]

The administration points out that funding for port security has increased more than 600 percent since 9/11. The Department of Homeland Security spent $1.6 billion on port security in fiscal 2005, compared to $259 million before 2001. Overall, the federal government will spend $2.8 billion this year on port security, including the Department of Energy's Megaports program, says Jackson. [58]

But critics say that amount falls short. The Coast Guard has estimated the cost of installing adequate port-security measures at $5.4 billion. [59] "While billions of homeland-security dollars have been allocated to airports, first responders and research and development, only a modest amount has been made available for port security," says Nagle of the Association of Port Authorities.

Rep. Harman estimates that $9 of every $10 spent on transportation security since 9/11 has gone to airports. "We have severely underfunded ports," she said on April 4.

Unions also insist that more federal funds are needed, among other things, to teach workers how to recognize a security breach and how to evacuate during an emergency. Unions also want access to the security plans that port operators are required to write but are not required to share with unions, says McLaughlin of the International Longshore and Warehouse Union.

Meanwhile, proposed immigration reform — if it passes — might also result in additional Customs agents, money and equipment. The Senate left for its Easter break without wrapping up work on how to deal with the highly charged issue of illegal immigration. Tucked into comprehensive immigration legislation proposed by Senate Majority Leader Bill Frist, R-Tenn. — already included in a House-passed version — is language that would add more maritime border security and technology. But prospects are mixed on whether Congress will pass a bill this year.

Finally, none of the pending measures to bar foreign, government-owned companies from controlling U.S. ports has passed. Several measures also would overhaul the process by which mergers and acquisitions of American companies by foreigners are reviewed by the Committee on Foreign Investment in the United States (CFIUS), the interagency panel that approved Dubai Ports World's lease proposal.

A Senate panel in April approved a measure that would retain Treasury as the lead agency of CFIUS but make the process more transparent. Another measure, proposed by Collins, would create a new panel headed by DHS to review transactions with national-security concerns. ■

OUTLOOK

'Time Is of the Essence'

Security experts hope intensified port-security concerns will force Congress and the Bush administration to give ports the same protection that airports received after 9/11.

"The hullabaloo surrounding the Dubai Ports World deal injected a sense of urgency into the need for important port-security reform," says Rep. Lungren.

Rep. Harman calls the House Homeland Security panel's quick approval of the SAFE Port Act "nothing short of a miracle." It shows that "Congress is appropriately focused" after years of giving short shrift to port security. "Time is of the essence."

Sen. Murray of Washington state likewise says immediate action by Congress is needed. "Let's make the changes now, on our terms, before there's a deadly incident."

Meanwhile, there is wide agreement that it will take more time and money to completely secure the ports. "We have a long way to go to make this a reality," says Collins.

Regardless of what Congress does, the administration plans to continue relying on voluntary compliance by private companies via the C-TPAT program and by foreign governments under the CSI and Megaports programs. It also plans to continue looking for new and better screening technologies. "I am convinced that we can make great progress in the near term," says DHS Deputy Secretary Jackson.

DHS Secretary Chertoff expects that by year's end two-thirds of the containers entering the United States will be screened for radiation either overseas or in this country. But he also stresses that his department won't be consumed by port mania: "My job is not to go from protecting the ports to protecting the railroads to protecting this and protecting that, following along as the media focuses in fits and starts on the particular news of the day." [60]

Experts like Flynn of the Council on Foreign Relations, however, worry that the current attention on ports will fade and little will change. "Should terrorists strike in a major U.S. seaport today, Americans, I believe, will experience a post-Katrina sense of dismay and frustration at how little the federal government has been investing to effectively safeguard this critical national-security and economic-security asset," he says.

Sen. Coleman agrees: "If we think that the terrorists are going to ignore our vulnerabilities and not find the kinks in our supply chain, we are mistaken."

Some lawmakers fear it will take more than good intentions to get the government to act. Rep. Gene Taylor of Mississippi, a former member of the Coast Guard Reserve and ranking Democrat on the House Armed Services Committee, said in March, "It's going to take a 9/11-type maritime-industry-based disaster for our country to do what we should be doing." [61] ■

About the Author

Pamela M. Prah is a *CQ Researcher* staff writer with several years previous reporting experience at Stateline.org, *Kiplinger's Washington Letter* and the Bureau of National Affairs. She holds a master's degree in government from Johns Hopkins University and a journalism degree from Ohio University. Her recent reports include "Disaster Preparedness," "Eating Disorders" and "Coal Mining Safety."

Notes

[1] Ted Bridis, "Port Security Lapses Raise Fears of Attacks," The Associated Press, March 12, 2006.

[2] Booz Allen Hamilton, "Port Security War Game, Implications for U.S. Supply Chains," 2002.

[3] Congressional Budget Office, "The Economic Costs of Disruptions in Container Shipments," March 29, 2006.

[4] For background, see Martin Kady II, "Homeland Security," *CQ Researcher*, Sept. 12, 2003, pp. 749-772; and Patrick Marshall, "Policing the Borders," *CQ Researcher*, Feb. 22, 2002, pp. 145-168.

[5] Remarks of Homeland Security Secretary Michael Chertoff at the Heritage Foundation, March 20, 2006.

[6] Transcript, MSNBC, "Hardball with Chris Matthews," Feb. 27, 2006; www.msnbc.msn.com/id/11605058/.

[7] "Final Report on 9/11 Commission Recommendations," Dec. 5, 2005, www.9-11pdp.org/press/2005-12-05_report.pdf.

[8] Senate Permanent Subcommittee on Investigations, Committee on Homeland Security and Governmental Affairs, "An Assessment of U.S. Efforts to Secure the Global Supply Chain," March 30, 2006.

[9] Government Accountability Office, "Border Security: Investigators Successfully Transported Radioactive Sources Across Our Nation's Borders at Selected Locations," March 2006.

[10] Department of Justice, Office of the Inspector General Audit Division, "The Federal Bureau of Investigation's Efforts to Protect the Nation's Seaports," March 2006; www.usdoj.gov/oig/reports/FBI/a0626/final.pdf.

[11] Transcript, House Homeland Security Subcommittee on Economic Security, Infrastructure Protection and Cybersecurity Hearing on Port Security, March 16, 2006.

[12] Transcript, CBS News, "Face the Nation," Feb. 26, 2006.

[13] According to a March *USA Today*/CNN/Gallup Poll, www.usatoday.com/news/polls/2006-03-02-poll.htm#ports.

[14] Government Accountability Office, "Maritime Security, Enhancements Made, But Implementation and Sustainability Remain Key Challenges," May 17, 2005, p. 12.

[15] Transcript of March 16, 2006, hearing, *op. cit.*

[16] *Ibid.*

[17] *Ibid.*

[18] Government Accountability Office, May 17, 2005, *op. cit.*, p. 20-21.

[19] Chertoff remarks, Heritage Foundation, *op. cit.*

[20] Prepared testimony of Homeland Security Assistant Secretary Stewart Baker before the House Coast Guard and Maritime Transportation Subcommittee, March 9, 2006.

[21] John F. Frittelli, *Port and Maritime Security, Background and Issues*, Novinka Books, 2003.

[22] Transcript, Fox News, "Hannity & Co.," March 1, 2006.

[23] Press releases, Sen. Charles E. Schumer, Feb. 16 and 26, 2006.

[24] Transcript, White House press briefing of Assistant to the President for Homeland Security and Counterterrorism Frances Fragos Townsend, Feb. 23, 2006; www.whitehouse.gov/news/releases/2006/02/20060223-5.html.

[25] Transcript, Senate Banking, Housing and Urban Affairs Committee hearing, March 2, 2005.

[26] "Meet the Press," Feb. 26, 2006.

[27] Transcript, House Armed Service Committee Hearing on Dubai Purchase of U.S. Port Facilities, March 2, 2006.

[28] *Ibid.*

[29] White House transcript, "President Discusses Port Security," Feb. 21, 2006; www.whitehouse.gov/news/releases/2006/02/20060221-2.html.

[30] "Meet the Press," *op. cit.*

[31] Press release, Rep. Duncan Hunter, March 2, 2006.

[32] For background, see Mary H. Cooper, "Nuclear Proliferation and Terrorism," *CQ Researcher*, April 2, 2004, p. 297-320.

[33] Transcript, Senate Commerce, Science and Transportation Committee Hearing on U.S Port Security, Feb. 28, 2005.

[34] Government Accountability Office, "Container Security, A Flexible Staffing Model and Minimum Equipment Requirements Would Improve Overseas Targeting and Inspection Efforts," April 2005.

[35] March 16, 2006 transcript, *op. cit.*

[36] Government Accountability Office, "Cargo Security, Partnership Program Grants, Importers Reduced Scrutiny with Limited Assurance of Improved Security," March 2005.

[37] Lawrence M. Wein and Stephen E. Flynn, "Think Inside the Box," *The New York Times*, Nov. 29, 2005, p. A27.

[38] Background on Customs from "U.S. Customs Service, Over 200 Years of History," www.cbp.gov/xp/cgov/toolbox/about/history/history.xml.

[39] U.S. Coast Guard History, www.uscg.mil/hq/gcp/history/h_USCGhistory.html.

[40] The site of the 1916 incident, known as the "Black Tom Island explosion," is today a portion of Liberty State Park.

[41] Carmela Karnoutsos, "Jersey City, Past and Present Web Site Project," New Jersey City University, 2004; www.njcu.edu/programs/jchistory/About.htm.

[42] For background, see "Refugee Policy," *Editorial Research Reports*, May 30, 1980, available at CQ Electronic Library, *CQ Researcher Plus Archive*, http://library.cqpress.com.

[43] John F. Frittelli, *Port and Maritime Security, Background and Issues* (2003).

[44] For background, see David Masci, "War on Terrorism," *CQ Researcher*, Oct. 12, 2001, pp. 817-848.

[45] Baker testimony, March 9, 2006, *op. cit.*

[46] Frittelli, *op. cit.*, p. 50.

FOR MORE INFORMATION

American Association of Port Authorities, 1010 Duke St., Alexandria, VA 22314; (703) 684-5700; www.aapa-ports.org. Represents more than 150 port authorities in the United States, Canada, the Caribbean and Latin America.

Council on Foreign Relations, 58 East 68th St., New York, NY 10021; (212) 434-9400; www.cfr.org. A nonpartisan think tank that has long been concerned about port security.

International Longshore and Warehouse Union, AFL-CIO, 1188 Franklin St., 4th Floor, San Francisco, CA 94109; (415) 775-0533; www.ilwu.org. Represents 42,000 workers, primarily on the West Coast.

U.S. Coast Guard, 2100 Second St., S.W., Washington, DC 20593; (202) 267-1587; www.uscg.mil. A Department of Homeland Security (DHS) agency that plays a lead role in patrolling waters in and around U.S. ports.

U.S. Customs and Border Protection, 1300 Pennsylvania Ave., N.W., Washington, DC 20229; (202) 354-1000; www.cbp.gov. A DHS agency that screens cargo and cargo manifests at home and in foreign ports for dangerous materials.

U.S. Department of Homeland Security, Washington, DC 20528; (202) 282-8000; www.dhs.gov. The Cabinet-level department with overall responsibility for protecting U.S. ports.

World Shipping Council, 1015 15th St., N.W., Suite 450, Washington, DC 20005; (202) 589-1230; www.worldshipping.org. A trade group representing more than 40 shipping companies, including the largest container lines.

[47] General Accounting Office (now the Government Accountability Office), "Combating Terrorism, Actions Needed to Improve Force Protection for DOD Deployments Through Domestic Seaports," October 2002.

[48] www.whitehouse.gov/homeland/maritime-security.html#intro.

[49] Press release, Department of Homeland Security, "National Strategy for Maritime Security Supporting Plans Announced," Oct. 26, 2005.

[50] Press release, American Association of Port Authorities, March 22, 2006.

[51] "Ports Deal News Tracker," *The Wall Street Journal*, March 16, 2006.

[52] Government Accountability Office, "Combating Nuclear Smuggling: Corruption, Maintenance and Coordination Problems Challenge U.S. Efforts to Provide Radiation Detection Equipment to Other Countries," March 2006.

[53] Government Accountability Office, "Combating Nuclear Smuggling: DHS Has Made Progress Deploying Radiation Detection Equipment at U.S. Ports of Entry, But Concerns Remain," March 2006.

[54] Government Accountability Office, "Border Security," March 2006, *op. cit.*

[55] Tim Starks, "House Panel OKs $821 Million for Beefed Up Port Security," *CQ Weekly Report*, April 3, 2006, p. 924.

[56] Press release, Senate Appropriations Committee, "Appropriations Committee Reports Supplemental Bill," April 4, 2006.

[57] John M. Donnelly and Tim Starks, "A Plethora of Port Security Bills," *CQ Weekly*, March 6, 2006, p. 604.

[58] From testimony before the House Homeland Security Committee on April 4, 2006.

[59] Memo of House Subcommittee on Coast Guard and Maritime Transportation Hearing on Foreign Operations of U.S. Port Facilities, March 9, 2006.

[60] Chertoff speech before Heritage Foundation, *op. cit.*

[61] House Armed Services Committee hearing, March 2, 2006, *op. cit.*

Bibliography

Selected Sources

Books

Flynn, Stephen, *America the Vulnerable, How Our Government Is Failing to Protect Us From Terrorism*, HarperCollins, in cooperation with the Council on Foreign Relations, 2004.
A former Coast Guard commander concludes that while the Bush administration has waged an aggressive war against terrorists abroad it has neglected to protect critical U.S. infrastructure, including ports.

Frittelli, John F., *et al.*, *Port and Maritime Security, Background and Issues*, Novinka Books, 2003.
Experts on security at the Library of Congress' Congressional Research Service give a concise history of maritime security and lay out the key issues facing Congress, including funding levels.

Articles

Bridis, Ted, "Port Security Lapses Raise Fears of Attacks," The Associated Press, March 12, 2006.
A Department of Homeland Security study slated for release this fall finds that cargo containers can be opened secretly and that there are serious security lapses at foreign and American ports, aboard ships and on trucks and trains.

Carafano, James Jay, "The Administration Misses an Opportunity," The Heritage Foundation, March 2, 2006.
A former director of Military Studies at the Army's Center of Military History says the Bush administration should have used the Dubai deal to explain how ports can be made more secure, which includes providing more funds to the Coast Guard and Customs.

Cohen, William S., and James M. Loy, "Fact, Not Fear," *The Wall Street Journal*, Feb. 28, 2006.
The former Defense secretary and the former administrator of the Transportation Security Administration say Congress should not let the "inflamed rhetoric" over the Dubai port deal distract them from the more important task of identifying "the substantial gaps that exist in our current port security system."

Goure, Daniel, "Right Issue — Wrong Port," Lexington Institute, Feb. 28, 2006.
A military expert says Americans should be most concerned about the ports where cargo is loaded, not where it arrives and is unloaded.

Plummer, Anne, "Hill Scrutiny of Ports Deal Intensifies," and Donnelly, John, and Tim Starks, "A Plethora of Port Security Bills," *CQ Weekly*, March 6, 2006, pp. 603-604.
Two analyses of the dispute over the proposed Dubai Ports World deal outline the various proposed port security bills.

Wein, Lawrence, and Stephen E. Flynn, "Think Inside the Box," *The New York Times*, Nov. 29, 2005, p. A27.
A management professor and faculty member of Stanford's Center for International Security and Cooperation (Wein) and a senior fellow at the Council on Foreign Relations argue that President Bush's border security reform and immigration proposals won't protect the country from what the authors say is the gravest risk: the possibility that a ship, truck or train will import a 40-foot cargo container in which terrorists have hidden a "dirty bomb."

Reports and Studies

"An Assessment of U.S. Efforts to Secure the Global Supply Chain," Senate Permanent Subcommittee on Investigations, Committee on Homeland Security and Governmental Affairs, March 30, 2006.
Senate investigators find that only 2.8 percent of containers destined for the United States in 2005 were screened overseas with radiation detectors, while less than 1 percent (0.38 percent) were screened with X-ray-type imaging technology.

"Combating Nuclear Smuggling: Corruption, Maintenance and Coordination Problems Challenge U.S. Efforts to Provide Radiation Detection Equipment to Other Countries," and "Combating Nuclear Smuggling: DHS Has Made Progress Deploying Radiation Detection Equipment at U.S. Ports of Entry, But Concerns Remain," both Government Accountability Office, March 2006.
A series of reports by the congressional watchdog agency finds U.S. seaport operators have delayed deployment of radiation-detection equipment, fearing that corrupt border security officials overseas could compromise the effectiveness of the devices given to foreign ports by the United States.

"The Economic Costs of Disruptions in Container Shipments," Congressional Budget Office, March 29, 2006.
Congressional investigators estimate that an unexpected shutdown of the ports of Los Angles and Long Beach could cost up to $150 million a day.

"Port Security War Game, Implications for U.S Supply Chains," Booz Allen Hamilton Inc., 2002.
The consulting firm concludes after a two-day "war game" involving government and private industry that a dirty bomb delivered at a U.S. seaport could force the government to shut down all U.S. ports for up to 12 days at a cost of $58 billion.

Willis, Henry H., and David S. Ortiz, "Evaluating the Security of the Global Containerized Supply Chain," RAND, 2004.
The authors lay out the challenges of trying to keep cargo secure while en route to U.S. ports.

The Next Step:

Additional Articles from Current Periodicals

Foreign Ports

Bridis, Ted, and John Solomon, "Hong Kong Firm to Check U.S.-Bound Cargo," *The Philadelphia Inquirer*, March 26, 2006, p. A6.

A Hong Kong company will soon operate a radiation-detection device in the Bahamas to check cargo bound for the United States without American Customs agents present, worrying some in Congress.

Caryl, Christian, "The Box is King," *Newsweek International*, April 10, 2006.

The shipping container that revolutionized global commerce is now causing security concerns worldwide.

Fattah, Hassan M., and Eric Lipton, "Gaps in Security Stretch All Along the Way From Model Port in Dubai to U.S.," *The New York Times*, Feb. 26, 2006, p. 26.

Security experts say port security concerns should shift from U.S. to foreign ports, where cargo is first placed on U.S.-bound ships.

Lee, Christopher, "Progress 'Limited' On Seaport Security," *The Washington Post*, May 4, 2005, p. A17.

U.S. efforts to provide foreign customs officials with advanced cargo-screening equipment are faltering because some countries have been reluctant to cooperate.

Lipton, Eric, "Loopholes Seen in U.S. Efforts to Secure Overseas Ports," *The New York Times*, May 25, 2005, p. A6.

The Department of Homeland Security's importer and port programs, which are intended to block threats overseas before they reach American shores, are proving flawed.

Port Security Technology

Hall, Mimi, "Most of the Containers Moving Through U.S. Ports Unchecked," *USA Today*, March 15, 2006, p. A3.

Equipment for monitoring cargo entering America's ports, including gamma-ray machines, is too expensive for wide use.

Shukovsky, Paul, "Nation's Ports Soon to Tighten Cargo Checks, But Some Say Radiation Monitors For Containers Aren't Enough," *The Seattle-Post Intelligencer*, Jan. 11, 2005, p. A1.

Detectors used to uncover atomic or "dirty bombs" being smuggled into the country will soon be installed at ports around the United States.

White, Ronald D., "Plan Unveiled to Speed Cargo Processing," *Los Angeles Times*, Feb. 2, 2005, p. C2.

U.S. Customs and Border Protection revealed a new plan to hide wireless sensors inside cargo containers at ports worldwide to monitor tampering.

U.S. Ports

Alonso-Zaldivar, Ricardo, "Customs Chief to Resign," *Los Angeles Times*, Sept. 28, 2005, p. A11.

Customs Commissioner Robert C. Bonner acknowledged that he will leave his post after helping create the Container Security Initiative and the Customs-Trade Partnership Against Terrorism.

Borenstein, Seth, "Other Security Issues Lost in Ports-Deal Fuss," *The Philadelphia Inquirer*, Feb. 23, 2006, p. A17.

Officials say the Bush administration's controversial approval of an Arab firm to run operations at six U.S. ports is deflecting attention from other port security issues.

Eckert, Toby, "U.S. Has Big Gaps in Cargo Container Security, Senate Study Finds," *The San Diego Union-Tribune*, March 30, 2006, p. A3.

Only a small number of containers are examined abroad, and the system used to identify potentially troublesome cargo is unreliable, according to a new study.

Hensel, Bill Jr., "Port of Houston Seeks More Customs Officers," *The Houston Chronicle*, March 10, 2006, p. 1.

Port representatives say Houston needs 125 to 150 additional Customs officers to properly inspect cargo shipments.

Turnbull, Lornet, "15 Days in a Metal Box, Only to be Locked Up," *The Seattle Times*, April 6, 2006, p. A1.

Port security guards in Seattle discovered 22 Chinese stowaways in a cargo container from Shanghai.

CITING THE *CQ RESEARCHER*

Sample formats for citing these reports in a bibliography include the ones listed below. Preferred styles and formats vary, so please check with your instructor or professor.

MLA STYLE

Jost, Kenneth. "Rethinking the Death Penalty." CQ Researcher 16 Nov. 2001: 945-68.

APA STYLE

Jost, K. (2001, November 16). Rethinking the death penalty. *CQ Researcher, 11*, 945-968.

CHICAGO STYLE

Jost, Kenneth. "Rethinking the Death Penalty." *CQ Researcher*, November 16, 2001, 945-968.

In-depth Reports on Issues in the News

Are you writing a paper?
Need backup for a debate?
Want to become an expert on an issue?

For 80 years, students have turned to the *CQ Researcher* for in-depth reporting on issues in the news. Reports on a full range of political and social issues are now available. Following is a selection of recent reports:

Civil Liberties
Right to Die, 5/05
Immigration Reform, 4/05
Gays on Campus, 10/04

Crime/Law
Domestic Violence, 1/06
Death Penalty Controversies, 9/05
Methamphetamines, 7/05
Identity Theft, 6/05
Marijuana Laws, 2/05
Supreme Court's Future, 1/05

Education
Academic Freedom, 10/05
Intelligent Design, 7/05
No Child Left Behind, 5/05
Gender and Learning, 5/05

Environment
Nuclear Energy, 3/06
Climate Change, 1/06
Saving the Oceans, 11/05
Endangered Species Act, 6/05
Alternative Energy, 2/05

Health/Safety
Rising Health Costs, 4/06
Pension Crisis, 2/06
Avian Flu Threat, 1/06
Domestic Violence, 1/06
Disaster Preparedness, 11/05
Birth-Control Debate, 6/05
Marijuana Laws, 2/05

International Affairs
Future of European Union, 10/05
War in Iraq, 10/05

Social Trends
Future of Feminism, 4/06
Future of Newspapers, 1/06
Cosmetic Surgery, 4/05

Terrorism/Defense
Presidential Power, 2/06

Youth
Bullying, 2/05
Teen Driving, 1/05
Athletes and Drugs, 7/04

Upcoming Reports

Native Americans' Plight, 4/28/06
Transgender Issues, 5/5/06
Controlling the Internet, 5/12/06
Energy Conservation, 5/19/06
Teen Spending, 5/26/06
War on Drugs, 6/2/06

ACCESS

The *CQ Researcher* is available in print and online. For access, visit your library or www.cqresearcher.com.

STAY CURRENT

To receive notice of upcoming *CQ Researcher* reports, or learn more about *CQ Researcher* products, subscribe to the free e-mail newsletters, *CQ Researcher Alert!* and *CQ Researcher News*: www.cqpress.com/newsletters.

PURCHASE

To purchase a *CQ Researcher* report in print or electronic format (PDF), visit www.cqpress.com or call 866-427-7737. Single reports start at $10. Bulk purchase discounts and electronic rights licensing are also available.

SUBSCRIBE

A full-service *CQ Researcher* print subscription—including 44 reports a year, monthly index updates, and a bound volume—is $688 for academic and public libraries, $667 for high school libraries, and $827 for media libraries. Add $25 for domestic postage.

The *CQ Researcher Online* offers a backfile from 1991 and a number of tools to simplify research. For pricing information, call 800-834-9020, ext. 1906, or e-mail librarysales@cqpress.com.

CQ Researcher

Published by CQ Press, a division of Congressional Quarterly Inc.

cqresearcher.com

American Indians

Are they making meaningful progress at last?

Winds of change are blowing through Indian Country, improving prospects for many of the nation's 4.4 million Native Americans. The number of tribes managing their own affairs has increased dramatically, and an urban Indian middle class is quietly taking root. The booming revenues of many Indian-owned casinos seem the ultimate proof that Indians are overcoming a history of mistreatment, poverty and exclusion. Yet most of the gambling houses don't rake in stratospheric revenues. And despite statistical upticks in socioeconomic indicators, American Indians are still poorer, more illness-prone and less likely to be employed than their fellow citizens. Meanwhile, tribal governments remain largely dependent on direct federal funding of basic services — funding that Indian leaders and congressional supporters decry as inadequate. But government officials say they are still providing essential services despite budget cuts.

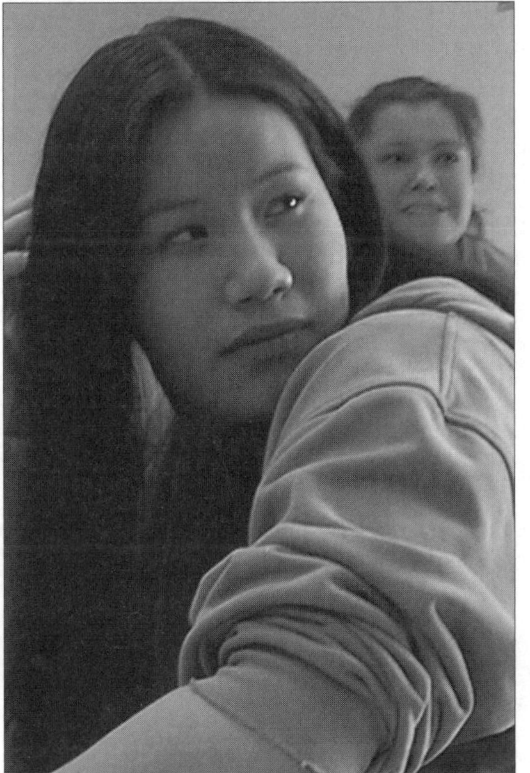

Nicole Boswell, an American Indian high-school student in White Earth, Minn., dreams of being a psychologist on her tribe's reservation.

INSIDE THIS REPORT

CQ Researcher • April 28, 2006 • www.cqresearcher.com
Volume 16, Number 16 • Pages 361-384

RECIPIENT OF SOCIETY OF PROFESSIONAL JOURNALISTS AWARD FOR EXCELLENCE ◆ AMERICAN BAR ASSOCIATION SILVER GAVEL AWARD

Cover: Nicole Boswell, an Indian high-school student in White Earth, Minn., dreams of being a psychologist on her tribe's reservation. (AP Photo/Minnesota Public Radio, Dan Gunderson)

CQ Researcher

April 28, 2006
Volume 16, Number 16

MANAGING EDITOR: Thomas J. Colin

ASSISTANT MANAGING EDITOR: Kathy Koch

ASSOCIATE EDITOR: Kenneth Jost

STAFF WRITERS: Marcia Clemmitt, Peter Katel, Pamela M. Prah

CONTRIBUTING WRITERS: Rachel S. Cox, Sarah Glazer, David Hosansky, Patrick Marshall, Tom Price

DESIGN/PRODUCTION EDITOR: Olu B. Davis

ASSISTANT EDITOR: Melissa J. Hipolit

CQ PRESS

A Division of
Congressional Quarterly Inc.

SENIOR VICE PRESIDENT/PUBLISHER: John A. Jenkins

DIRECTOR, LIBRARY PUBLISHING: Kathryn C. Suárez

DIRECTOR, EDITORIAL OPERATIONS: Ann Davies

CONGRESSIONAL QUARTERLY INC.

CHAIRMAN: Paul C. Tash

VICE CHAIRMAN: Andrew P. Corty

PRESIDENT/EDITOR IN CHIEF: Robert W. Merry

CQ Researcher (ISSN 1056-2036) is printed on acid-free paper. Published weekly, except March 24, July 7, July 14, Aug. 4, Aug. 11, Nov. 24, Dec. 22 and Dec. 29, by CQ Press, a division of Congressional Quarterly Inc. Annual full-service subscriptions for institutions start at $667. For pricing, call 1-800-834-9020, ext. 1906. To purchase a *CQ Researcher* report in print or electronic format (PDF), visit www.cqpress.com or call 866-427-7737. Single reports start at $10. Bulk purchase discounts and electronic-rights licensing are also available. Periodicals postage paid at Washington, D.C., and additional mailing offices. POSTMASTER: Send address changes to *CQ Researcher*, 1255 22nd St., N.W., Suite 400, Washington, DC 20037.

American Indians

By Peter Katel

The Issues

It's not a fancy gambling palace, like some Indian casinos, but the modest operation run by the Winnebago Tribe of Nebraska may just help the 2,300-member tribe hit the economic jackpot.

Using seed money from the casino, it has launched 12 businesses, including a construction company and an Internet news service. Projected 2006 revenues: $150 million.

"It would be absolutely dumb for us to think that gaming is the future," says tribe member Lance Morgan, the 37-year-old Harvard Law School graduate who runs the holding company for the dozen businesses. "Gaming is just a means to an end — and it's done wonders for our tribal economy."

Indian casinos have revived a myth dating back to the early-20th-century Oklahoma oil boom — that Indians are rolling in dough. [1] While some of the 55 tribes that operate big casinos indeed are raking in big profits, the 331 federally recognized tribes in the lower 48 states, on the whole, endure soul-quenching poverty and despair.

Getty Images/Mario Tama

Jerolyn Fink lives in grand style in the housing center built by Connecticut's Mohegan Tribe using profits from its successful Mohegan Sun casino. Thanks in part to booming casinos, many tribes are making progress, but American Indians still face daunting health and economic problems, and tribal leaders say federal aid remains inadequate.

Arizona's 1.8-million-acre San Carlos Apache Reservation is among the poorest. The rural, isolated community of about 13,000 people not only faces devastating unemployment but also a deadly methemphetamine epidemic, tribal Chairwoman Kathleen W. Kitcheyan, told the Senate Indian Affairs Committee in April.

"We suffer from a poverty level of 69 percent, which must be unimaginable to many people in this country, who would equate a situation such as this to one found only in Third World countries," she said. Then, speaking of the drug-related death of one of her own grandsons, she had to choke back sobs.

"Our statistics are horrific," says Lionel R. Bordeaux, president of Sinte Gleska University, on the Rosebud Sioux Reservation in South Dakota. "We're at the bottom rung of the ladder in all areas, whether it's education levels, economic achievement or political status." [2]

National statistics aren't much better:

- Indian unemployment on reservations nationwide is 49 percent — 10 times the national rate. [3]
- The on-reservation family poverty rate in 2000 was 37 percent — four times the national figure of 9 percent. [4]
- Nearly one in five Indians age 25 or older in tribes without gambling operations had less than a ninth-grade education. But even members of tribes with gambling had a college graduation rate of only 16 percent, about half the national percentage. [5]
- Death rates from alcoholism and tuberculosis among Native Americans are at least 650 percent higher than overall U.S. rates. [6]
- Indian youths commit suicide at nearly triple the rate of young people in general. [7]
- Indians on reservations, especially in the resource-poor Upper Plains and West, are the nation's third-largest group of methemphetamine users. [8]

The immediate prognosis for the nation's 4.4 million Native Americans is bleak, according to the Harvard Project on American Indian Economic Development. "If U.S. and on-reservation Indian per-capita income were to continue to grow at their 1990s' rates," it said, "it would take half a century for the tribes to catch up." [9]

Nonetheless, there has been forward movement in Indian Country, though it is measured in modest steps. Among the marks of recent progress:

Conditions on Reservations Improved

Socioeconomic conditions improved more on reservations with gambling than on those without gaming during the 1990s, although non-gaming reservations also improved substantially, especially compared to the U.S. population. Some experts attribute the progress among non-gaming tribes to an increase in self-governance on many reservations.

Socioeconomic Changes on Reservations, 1990-2000*
(shown as a percentage or percentage points)

	Non-Gaming	Gaming	U.S.
Real per-capita income	+21.0%	+36.0%	+11.0%
Median household income	+14.0%	+35.0%	+4.0%
Family poverty	-6.9	-11.8	-0.8
Child poverty	-8.1	-11.6	-1.7
Deep poverty	-1.4	-3.4	-0.4
Public assistance	+0.7	-1.6	+0.3
Unemployment	-1.8	-4.8	-0.5
Labor force participation	-1.6	+1.6	-1.3
Overcrowded homes	-1.3	-0.1	+1.1
Homes lacking complete plumbing	-4.6	-3.3	-0.1
Homes lacking complete kitchen	+1.3	-0.6	+0.2
College graduates	+1.7	+2.6	+4.2
High school or equivalency only	-0.3	+1.8	-1.4
Less than 9th-grade education	-5.5	-6.3	-2.8

** The reservation population of the Navajo Nation, which did not have gambling in the 1990s, was not included because it is so large (175,000 in 2000) that it tends to pull down Indian averages when it is included.*

Source: Jonathan B. Taylor and Joseph P. Kalt, "Cabazon, The Indian Gaming Regulatory Act, and the Socioeconomic Consequences of American Indian Governmental Gaming: A Ten-Year Review, American Indians on Reservations: A Databook of Socioeconomic Change Between the 1990 and 2000 Censuses," Harvard Project on American Indian Economic Development, January 2005

- Per-capita income rose 20 percent on reservations, to $7,942, (and 36 percent in tribes with casinos, to $9,771), in contrast to an 11 percent overall U.S. growth rate. [10]
- Unemployment has dropped by up to 5 percent on reservations and in other predominantly Indian areas. [11]
- Child poverty in non-gaming tribes dropped from 55 percent of the child population to 44 percent (but the Indian rate is still more than double the 17 percent average nationwide). [12]

More than two centuries of court decisions, treaties and laws have created a complicated system of coexistence between tribes and the rest of the country. On one level, tribes are sovereign entities that enjoy a government-to-government relationship with Washington. But the sovereignty is qualified. In the words of an 1831 Supreme Court decision that is a bedrock of Indian law, tribes are "domestic dependent nations." [13]

The blend of autonomy and dependence grows out of the Indians' reliance on Washington for sheer survival, says Robert A. Williams Jr., a law professor at the University of Arizona and a member of North Carolina's Lumbee Tribe. "Indians insisted in their treaties that the Great White Father protect us from these racial maniacs in the states — where racial discrimination was most developed — and guarantee us a right to education, a right to water, a territorial base, a homeland," he says. "Tribes sold an awful lot of land in return for a trust relationship to keep the tribes going."

Today, the practical meaning of the relationship with Washington is that American Indians on reservations, and to some extent those elsewhere, depend entirely or partly on federal funding for health, education and other needs. Tribes with casinos and other businesses lessen their reliance on federal dollars.

Unlike other local governments, tribes don't have a tax base whose revenues they share with state governments. Federal spending on Indian programs of all kinds nationwide currently amounts to about $11 billion, James Cason, associate deputy secretary of the Interior, told the Senate Indian Affairs Committee in February.

But the abysmal conditions under which many American Indians live make it all too clear that isn't enough, Indians say. "This is always a discussion at our tribal leaders' meetings," says Cecilia Fire Thunder, president of the Oglala Sioux Tribe in Pine Ridge, S.D. "The biggest job that tribal leaders have is to see that the government lives up to its responsibilities to our people. It's a battle that never ends."

Indeed, a decades-old class-action suit alleges systematic mismanagement of billions of dollars in Indian-owned assets by the Interior Department —

a case that has prompted withering criticism of the department by the judge (*see p. 375*).

Government officials insist that, despite orders to cut spending, they've been able to keep providing essential services. Charles Grim, director of the Indian Health Service, told the Indian Affairs Committee, "In a deficit-reduction year, it's a very strong budget and one that does keep pace with inflationary and population-growth increases."

In any event, from the tribes' point of view, they lack the political muscle to force major increases. "The big problem is the Indians are about 1 percent of the national population," says Joseph Kalt, co-director of the Harvard Project. "The voice is so tiny."

Faced with that grim political reality, Indians are trying to make better use of scarce federal dollars through a federally sponsored "self-governance" movement. Leaders of the movement say tribes can deliver higher-quality services more efficiently when they control their own budgets. Traditionally, federal agencies operate programs on reservations, such as law enforcement or medical services.

But since the 1990s, dozens of tribes have stepped up control of their own affairs both by building their own businesses and by signing self-governance "compacts" with the federal government. Compacts provide tribes with large chunks of money, or block grants, rather than individual grants for each service. Then, with minimal federal oversight, the tribes develop their own budgets and run all or most services.

The self-governance trend gathered steam during the same time that Indian-owned casinos began booming. For many tribes, the gambling business provided a revenue stream that didn't flow from Washington.

According to economist Alan Meister, 228 tribes in 30 states operated 367 high-stakes bingo halls or casinos in 2004, earning an estimated $19.6 billion. [14]

Revenues From Casinos Almost Doubled

Revenue from Indian gaming operations nearly doubled to $19.4 billion from 2000-2004. The number of Indian casinos increased from 311 to 367 during the period.

Indian Gaming Revenues
(2000-2004)

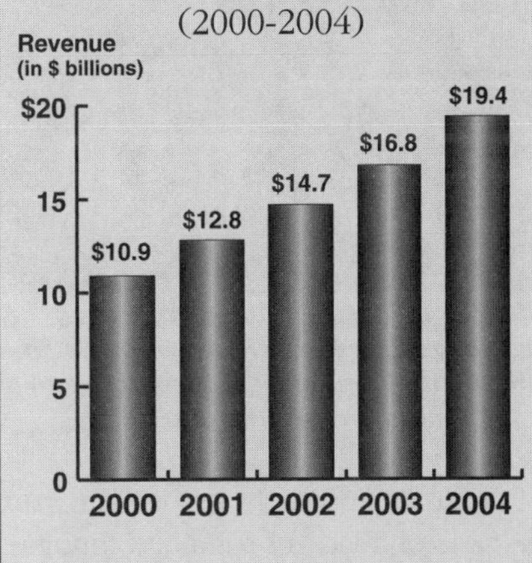

Source: Indian Gaming Commission

The gambling houses operate under the 1988 Indian Gaming Regulatory Act (IGRA), which was made possible by a U.S. Supreme Court ruling upholding tribes' rights to govern their own activities. [15] A handful of tribes are doing so well that $80 million from six tribes in 2000-2003 helped fuel the scandal surrounding one-time Washington super-lobbyist Jack Abramoff, whose clients were among the most successful casino tribes. [16]

If the Abramoff scandal contributed to the notion of widespread Indian wealth, one reason may be the misimpression that tribes don't pay taxes on their gambling earnings. In fact, under the IGRA, federal, state and local governments took in $6.3 billion in gambling-generated tax revenues in 2004, with 67 percent going to the federal government. In addition, tribes paid out some $889 million in 2004 to state and local governments in order to get gambling operations approved. [17]

The spread of casinos has prompted some cities and counties, along with citizens' groups and even some casino-operating tribes, to resist casino-expansion plans.

The opposition to expansion is another reason tribal entrepreneur Morgan doesn't think gaming is a good long-range bet for Indians' future. His vision involves full tribal control of the Indians' main asset — their land. He argues for ending the "trust status" under which tribes can't buy or sell reservation property — a relic of 19th-century protection against rapacious state governments.

Indian Country needs a better business climate, Morgan says, and the availability of land as collateral for investments would be a big step in that direction. "America has a wonderful economic system, probably the best in the world, but the reservation tends to be an economic black hole."

As Indians seek to improve their lives, here are some of the issues being debated:

Is the federal government neglecting Native Americans?

There is wide agreement that the federal government bears overwhelming responsibility for Indians' welfare, but U.S. and tribal officials disagree over the adequacy of the aid Indians receive. Sen. John McCain, R-Ariz., chairman of the Senate Indian Affairs Committee, and Vice Chairman Byron L. Dorgan, D-N.D., have been leading the fight for more aid to Indians. "We have a full-blown crisis . . . particularly dealing with children and elderly, with respect to housing, education and health care," Dorgan told the committee on Feb. 14. He characterized administration proposals as nothing more than "nibbling around the edges on these issues . . . making a few adjustments here or there.' "

Administration officials respond that given the severe federal deficit, they are focusing on protecting vital programs. "As we went through and prioritized our budget, we basically looked at all of the programs that were secondary and tertiary programs, and they were the first ones on the block to give tradeoffs for our core programs in maintaining the integrity of those," Interior's Cason told the committee.

For Indians on isolated reservations, says Bordeaux of the Rosebud Sioux, there's little alternative to federal money. He compares tribes' present circumstances to those after the buffalo had been killed off, and an Army general told the Indians to eat beef, which made them sick. "The general told them, 'Either that, or you eat the grass on which you stand.'"

But David B. Vickers, president of Upstate Citizens for Equality, in Union Springs, N.Y., which opposes Indian land claims and casino applications, argues that accusations of federal neglect are inaccurate and skirt the real problem. The central issue is that the constitutional system is based on individual rights, not tribal rights, he says. "Indians are major recipients of welfare now. They're eligible. They don't need a tribe or leader; all they have to do is apply like anybody else."

Pat Ragsdale, director of the Bureau of Indian Affairs (BIA), acknowledges that Dorgan's and McCain's criticisms echo a 2003 U.S. Commission on Civil Rights report, which also called underfunding of Indian aid a crisis. "The government is failing to live up to its trust responsibility to Native peoples," the commission concluded. "Efforts to bring Native Americans up to the standards of other Americans have failed in part because of a lack of sustained funding. The failure manifests itself in massive and escalating unmet needs." [18]

AP Photo/William Lauer

Controversial Whiteclay, Neb., sells millions of cans of beer annually to residents of the nearby Pine Ridge Reservation in South Dakota. Alcohol abuse and unemployment continue to plague the American Indian community.

"Nobody in this government disputes the report, in general," says Ragsdale, a Cherokee. "Some of our tribal communities are in real critical shape, and others are prospering."

The commission found, for example, that in 2003 the Indian Health Service appropriation amounted to $2,533 per capita — below even the $3,803 per capita appropriated for federal prisoners.

Concern over funding for Indian programs in 2007 centers largely on health and education. Although 90 percent of Indian students attend state-operated public schools, their schools get federal aid because tribes don't pay property taxes, which typically fund public schools. The remaining 10 percent of Indian students attend schools operated by the BIA or by tribes themselves under BIA contracts.

"There is not a congressman or senator who would send his own children or grandchildren to our schools," said Ryan Wilson, president of the National Indian Education Association, citing "crumbling buildings and outdated structures with lead in the pipes and mold on the walls." [19]

Cason told the Indian Affairs Committee the administration is proposing a $49 million cut, from $157.4 million to $108.1 million, in school construction and repair in 2007. He also said that only 10 of 37 dilapidated schools funded for replacement by 2006 have been completed, with another 19 scheduled to finish in 2007. Likewise, he said the department is also behind on 45 school improvement projects.

McCain questioned whether BIA schools and public schools with large Indian enrollments would be able to meet the requirements set by the national No Child Left Behind Law. [20] Yes, replied Darla Marburger, deputy assistant secretary of Education for policy. "For the first time, we'll be providing money to . . . take a look at how students are achieving in ways that they can tailor their programs to better meet the needs of students." Overall, the Department of Education would spend about $1 billion on Indian education under the administration's proposed budget for 2007, or $6 million less than in 2006.

McCain and Dorgan are also among those concerned about administration plans to eliminate the Indian Health Service's $32.7 million urban program, which this year made medical and counseling services available to some 430,000 off-reservation Indians at 41 medical facilities in cities around the nation. (*See Sidebar, p. 372.*) The administration argues that the services were available through other programs, but McCain and Dorgan noted that "no evaluation or evidence has been provided to support this contention." [21]

Indian Health Service spokesman Thomas Sweeney, a member of the Citizen Potawatomi Nation of Oklahoma, says only 72,703 Indians used urban health centers in 2004 and that expansion of another federal program would pick up the slack. [22]

In Seattle, elimination of the urban program would cut $4 million from the city's Indian Health Board budget, says Executive Director Ralph Forquera. "Why pick on a $33 million appropriation?" he asks. In his skeptical view, the proposal reflects another "unspoken" termination program. You take a sub-population — urban Indians — and eliminate funding, then [you target] tribes under 1,000 members, and there are a lot of them. Little by little, you pick apart the system."

The IHS's Grim told the Senate committee on Feb. 14 the cuts were designed to protect funding that "can be used most effectively to improve the health status of American Indian and Alaskan Native people."

Have casinos benefited Indians?

Over the past two decades, Indian casinos have become powerful economic engines for many tribal economies. But the enthusiasm for casinos is not unanimous.

"If you're looking at casinos in terms of how they've actually raised the status of Indian people, they've been an abysmal failure," says Ted Jojola, a professor of planning at the University of New Mexico and a member of Isleta Pueblo, near Albuquerque. "But in terms of augmenting the original federal trust-responsibility areas — education, health, tribal government — they've been a spectacular success. Successful gaming tribes have ploughed the money either into diversifying their economies or they've augmented funds that would have come to them anyway."

Tribes with casinos near big population centers are flourishing. The Coushatta Tribe's casino near Lake Charles, La., generates $300 million a year, enough to provide about $40,000 to every member. [23] And the fabled Foxwoods Resort Casino south of Norwich, Conn., operated by the Mashantucket Pequot Tribe, together with Connecticut's other big casino, the Mohegan Tribe's Mohegan Sun, grossed $2.2 billion just from gambling in 2004. [24]

There are only about 830 Coushattas, so their benefits also include free health care, education and favorable terms on home purchases. [25] The once poverty-stricken Mashantuckets have created Connecticut's most extensive welfare-to-work program, open to both tribe members and non-members. In 1997-2000, the program helped 150 welfare recipients find jobs. [26]

Most tribes don't enjoy success on that scale. Among the nation's 367 Indian gambling operations, only 15 grossed $250 million or more in 2004 (another 40 earned $100 million to $250 million); 94 earned less than $3 million and 57 earned $3 million to $10 million. [27]

"We have a small casino that provides close to $3 million to the tribal nation as a whole," says Bordeaux, on the Rosebud Sioux Reservation. The revenue has been channeled into the tribe's Head Start program, an emergency home-repair fund and other projects. W. Ron Allen, chairman of the Jamestown S'Klallam Tribe in Sequim, Wash., says his tribe's small casino has raised living standards so much that some two-dozen students a year go to college, instead of one or two.

Efforts to open additional casinos are creating conflicts between tribes that operate competing casinos, as well as with some of their non-Indian neighbors. Convicted lobbyist Abramoff, for example, was paid millions of dollars by tribes seeking to block other tribal casinos. [28]

Some non-Indian communities also oppose casino expansion. "We firmly believe a large, generally unregulated casino will fundamentally change the character of our community forever," said Liz Thomas, a member of Tax Payers of Michigan Against Casinos, which opposes a casino planned by the Pokagon Band of Potawotami Indians Tribe in the Lake Michigan town of New Buffalo, where Taylor and her husband operate a small resort.

"People are OK with Donald Trump making millions of dollars individually," says Joseph Podlasek, executive director of the American Indian Center of Chicago, "but if a race of people is trying to become self-sufficient, now that's not respectable."

Nevertheless, some American Indians have mixed feelings about the casino route to economic development. "I don't think anyone would have picked casinos" for that purpose, says the University of Arizona's Williams. "Am I ambivalent about it? Absolutely. But I'm not ambivalent about a new fire station, or Kevlar vests for tribal police fighting meth gangs."

"There's no question that some of the money has been used for worthwhile purposes," concedes Guy Clark, a Corrales, N.M., dentist who chairs the National Coalition Against Legalized Gambling. But, he adds, "If you do a cost-benefit analysis, the cost is much greater than the benefit." Restaurants and other businesses, for example, lose customers who often gamble away their extra money.

Even some Indian leaders whose tribes profit from casinos raise caution flags, especially about per-capita payments. For Nebraska's Winnebagos, payments amount to just a few hundred dollars, says CEO Morgan. What bothers him are dividends "that are just big enough that you don't have to work or get educated — say, $20,000 to $40,000."

But there's no denying the impact casinos can have. At a January public hearing on the Oneida Indian Nation's attempt to put 17,000 acres of upstate New York land into tax-free "trust" status, hundreds of the 4,500 employees of the tribe's Turning Stone Resort and Casino, near Utica, showed up in support. "When I was a kid, people worked for General Motors, General Electric, Carrier and Oneida Ltd.," said casino Human Resources Director Mark Mancini. "Today, people work for the Oneida Indian Nation and their enterprises." [29]

For tribes that can't build independent economies any other way, casinos are appealing. The 225,000-member Navajo Nation, the biggest U.S. tribe, twice rejected gaming before finally approving it in 2004. [30] "We need that infusion of jobs and revenue, and people realize that," said Duane Yazzie, president of the Navajos' Shiprock, N.M., chapter. [31]

But the Navajos face stiff competition from dozens of casinos already in operation near the vast Navajo reservation, which spreads across parts of Arizona, New Mexico and Utah and is larger than the state of West Virginia.

Would money alone solve American Indians' problems?

No one in Indian Country (or on Capitol Hill) denies the importance of federal funding to American Indians' future, but some Indians say it isn't the only answer.

"We are largely on our own because of limited financial assistance from the federal government," said Joseph A. Garcia, president of the National Congress of American Indians, in his recent "State of Indian Nations" speech. [32]

Fifty-two tribal officials and Indian program directors expressed similar sentiments in March before the House Appropriations Subcommittee on the Interior. Pleading their case before lawmakers who routinely consider billion-dollar weapons systems and other big projects, the tribal leaders sounded like small-town county commissioners as they urged lawmakers to increase or restore small but vital grants for basic health, education and welfare services.

"In our ICWA [Indian Child Welfare Act] program, currently we have a budget of $79,000 a year," said Harold Frazier, chairman of the Cheyenne River Sioux, in South Dakota. "We receive over 1,300 requests for assistance annually from 11 states and eight counties in South Dakota. We cannot give the type of attention to these requests that they deserve. Therefore, we are requesting $558,000."

To university President Bordeaux, federal funding is vital because his desolate reservation has few other options for economic survival. "What's missing is money," he says.

Money is crucial to improving Indians' health, says Dr. Joycelyn Dorscher, director of the Center of American Indian and Minority Health at the University of Minnesota-Duluth. Especially costly are programs to combat diabetes and other chronic diseases, says Dorscher, a Chippewa. While health programs have to be carefully designed to fit Indian cultural patterns, she says, "Everything comes down to time or money in the grand scheme of things."

But with funding from Washington never certain from year to year, says the Harvard Project's Kalt, "The key to economic development has not been federal funding" but rather "tribes' ability to run their own affairs."

For tribes without self-government compacts, growing demands for services and shrinking funding from Washington make keeping the dollars flowing the highest priority. "We're always afraid of more cutbacks," says Oglala Sioux President Fire Thunder.

But an Indian education leader with decades of federal budgetary negotiations acknowledges that problems go beyond funding shortfalls. "If you ask students why they dropped out, they say, 'I don't see a future for myself,' " says David Beaulieu, director of Arizona State University's Center for Indian Education. "Educators need to tie the purposes of schooling to the broad-based purposes of society. We're more successful when we tie education to the meaning of life."

The University of Arizona's Williams says a tribe's success and failure may be tied more to the way its government is organized than to how much funding it gets.

Williams says the first priority of tribes still using old-style constitutions should be reorganization, because they feature a weak executive elected by a tribal council. "That's what the BIA was used to," he explains. "It could play off factions and families, and the economic system would be based on patronage and taking care of your own family." Under such a system, he adds, "there's not going to be any long-term strategic planning going on." [33]

Yet other needs exist as well, says the American Indian Center's Podlasek. "It's so difficult for us to find a place to do a traditional ceremony," he says. "We had a traditional healer in town last month, and he wanted to build a sweat lodge. We actually had to go to Indiana. Doing it in the city wasn't even an option." ■

BACKGROUND

Conquered Homelands

Relations between Indian and non-Indian civilizations in the Americas began with the Spanish Conquistadors' explorations of the 1500s, followed by the French and British. By turns the three powers alternated policies of enslavement, peaceful coexistence and all-out warfare against the Indians. [34]

By 1830, with the Europeans largely gone, white settlers moved westward into Georgia, Mississippi and Alabama.

Unwilling to share the rich frontier land, they pushed the Indians out. President Andrew Jackson backed the strategy, and Congress enacted it into the Indian Removal Act of 1830, which called for moving the region's five big tribes into the Oklahoma Territory.

If the law didn't make clear where Indians stood with the government, the treatment of Mississippi's Choctaws provided chilling evidence. Under a separate treaty, Choctaws who refused to head for Oklahoma could remain at home, become citizens and receive land. In practice, none of that was allowed, and Indians who stayed in Mississippi lived marginal existences.

Georgia simplified the claiming of Cherokee lands by effectively ending Cherokee self-rule. The so-called "Georgia Guard" reinforced the point by beating and jailing Indians. Jackson encouraged Georgia's actions, and when Indians protested, he said he couldn't interfere. The lawsuit filed by the Cherokees eventually reached the Supreme Court.

Chief Justice John Marshall's 1831 majority opinion, *Cherokee Nation v. Georgia*, would cast a long shadow over Indians' rights, along with two other decisions, issued in 1823 and 1832. "Almost all Indian policy is the progeny of the conflicting views of Jackson and Marshall," wrote W. Dale Mason, a political scientist at the University of New Mexico. [35]

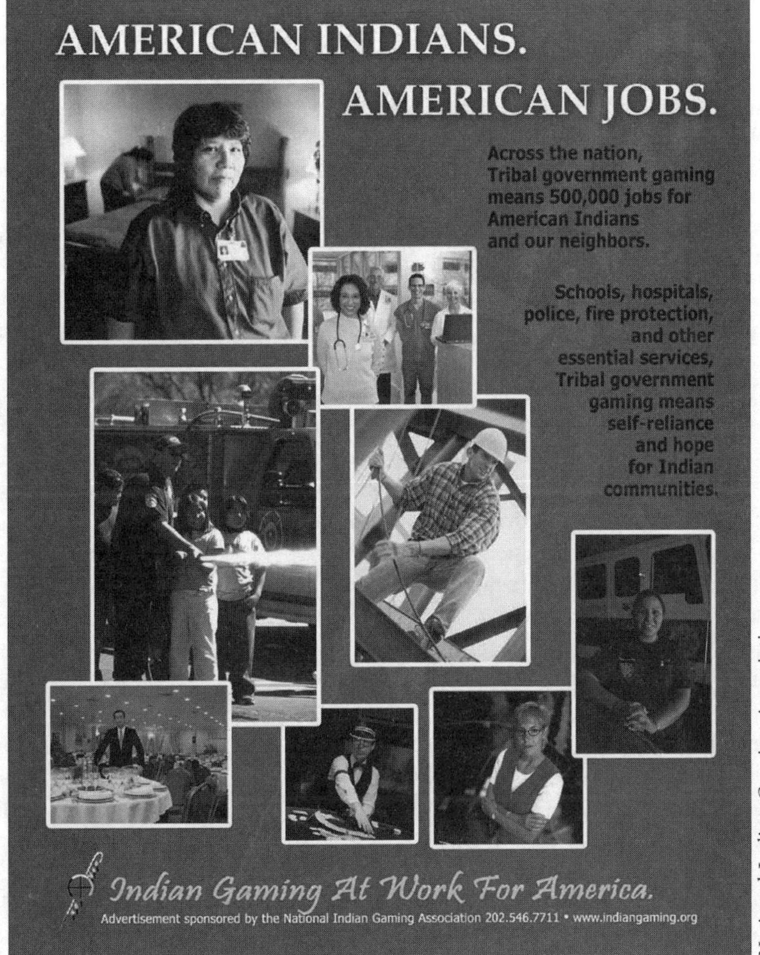

AMERICAN INDIANS.
AMERICAN JOBS.
Across the nation, Tribal government gaming means 500,000 jobs for American Indians and our neighbors.
Schools, hospitals, police, fire protection, and other essential services, Tribal government gaming means self-reliance and hope for Indian communities.
Indian Gaming At Work For America.
Advertisement sponsored by the National Indian Gaming Association 202.546.7711 • www.indiangaming.org

National Indian Gaming Association

A National Indian Gaming Association advertisement touts the benefits of tribal gaming operations to American Indian communities. Some 228 tribes in 30 states operated 367 high-stakes bingo halls or casinos in 2004.

In concluding that the court couldn't stop Georgia's actions, Marshall defined the relationship between Indians and the U.S. government. While Marshall wrote that Indians didn't constitute a foreign state, he noted that they owned the land they occupied until they made a "voluntary cession." Marshall concluded the various tribes were "domestic dependent nations." In practical terms, "Their relations to the United States resembles that of a ward to his guardian." [36]

Having rejected the Cherokees' argument, the University of Arizona's Williams writes, the court "provided no effective judicial remedy for Indian tribes to protect their basic human rights to property, self-government, and cultural survival under U.S. law." [37]

Along with the *Cherokee* case, the other two opinions that make up the so-called Marshall Trilogy are *Johnson v. M'Intosh* (also known as *Johnson v. McIntosh*), and *Worcester v. State of Georgia*. [38]

In *Johnson*, Marshall wrote that the European empires that "discovered" America became its owners and had "an exclusive right to extinguish the Indian title of occupancy, either by purchase or by conquest. The tribes of Indians inhabiting this country were fierce savages. . . . To leave them in possession of their country was to leave the country a wilderness." [39]

However, Marshall used the 1832 *Worcester* opinion to define the limits of state authority over Indian tribes, holding that the newcomers couldn't simply eject Indians.

"The Cherokee nation . . . is a distinct community occupying its own territory . . . in which the laws of Georgia can have no force," Marshall wrote. Georgia's conviction and sentencing of a missionary for not swearing allegiance to the state "interferes forcibly with the relations established between the United States and the Cherokee nation." [40] That is, the federal government — not states — held the reins of power over tribes.

According to legend, Jackson remarked: "John Marshall has made his decision — now let him enforce it." Between Jackson's disregard of the Supreme Court and white settlers' later manipulation of the legal system to vacate Indian lands, the end result was the dispossession of Indian lands.

Forced Assimilation

The expulsions of the Native Americans continued in the Western territories — especially after the Civil War. "I instructed Captain Barry, if possible to exterminate the whole village," Lt. Col. George Green wrote of his participation in an 1869 campaign against the White Mountain Apaches in Arizona and New Mexico. "There seems to be no settled policy, but a general policy to kill them wherever found." [41]

Some military men and civilians didn't go along. But whether by brute force or by persuasion, Indians were pushed off lands that non-Indians wanted. One strategy was to settle the Indians on reservations guarded by military posts. The strategy grew into a general policy for segregating Indians on these remote tracts.

Even after the Indians were herded onto lands that no one else wanted, the government didn't respect reservation boundaries. They were reconfigured as soon as non-Indians saw something valuable, such as mineral wealth.

The strategy of elastic reservation boundaries led to the belief — or rationalization — that reservations served no useful purposes for Indians themselves. That doctrine led to a policy enshrined in an 1887 law to convert reservations to individual landholdings. Well-meaning advocates of the plan saw it as a way to inculcate notions of private property and Euro-American culture in general.

All tribal land was to be divided into 160-acre allotments, one for each Indian household. The parcels wouldn't become individual property, though, for 25 years.

Indian consent wasn't required. In some cases, government agents tried persuading Indians to join in; in others, the divvying-up proceeded even with many Indians opposed. In Arizona, however, the government backed off from breaking up the lands of the long-settled Hopis, who resisted attempts to break up their territory. The vast Navajo Nation in Arizona, Utah and New Mexico was also left intact.

While widely reviled, the "forced assimilation" policy left a benign legacy for the affected Indians: the grant of citizenship. Beyond that, the era's Indians were restricted to unproductive lands, and with little means of support many fell prey to alcoholism and disease.

The bleak period ended with President Franklin D. Roosevelt. In his first term he appointed a defender of Indian culture, John Collier, as commissioner of Indian affairs. Collier pushed for the Indian Reorganization Act of 1934, which ended the allotment program, financed purchases of new Indian lands and authorized the organization of tribal governments that enjoyed control over revenues.

Termination

After World War II, a new, anti-Indian mood swept Washington, partly in response to pressure from states where non-Indians eyed Indian land.

Collier resigned in 1945 after years of conflict over what critics called his antagonism to missionaries proselytizing among the Indians and his sympathies toward the tribes. The 1950 appointment of Dillon S. Myer — fresh from supervising the wartime internment of Japanese-Americans — clearly reflected the new attitude. Myer showed little interest in what Indians themselves thought of the new policy of shrinking tribal land holdings. "I realize that it will not be possible always to obtain Indian cooperation. . . . We must proceed, even though [this] may be lacking." [42]

Congress hadn't authorized a sweeping repeal of earlier policy. But the introduction of dozens of bills in the late 1940s to sell Indian land or liquidate some reservation holdings entirely showed which way the winds were blowing. And in 1953, a House Concurrent Resolution declared Congress' policy to be ending Indians' "status as wards of the United States, and to grant them all of the rights and privileges pertaining to American citizenship." A separate law granted state jurisdiction over Indian reservations in five Midwestern and Western states and extended the same authority to other states that wanted to claim it. [43]

The following year, Congress "terminated" formal recognition and territorial sovereignty of six tribes. Four years later, after public opposition began building (spurred in part by religious organizations), Congress abandoned termination. In the meantime, however, Indians had lost 1.6 million acres.

At the same time, though, the federal government maintained an associated policy — relocation. The BIA persuaded Indians to move to cities — Chicago, Denver and Los Angeles were the main destinations — and opened job-placement and housing-aid programs. The BIA placed Indians far from their reservations to keep them from returning. By 1970, the BIA estimated that 40 percent of all Indians lived in cities, of which one-third had been relocated by the bureau; the rest moved on their own. [44]

Activism

Starting in the late 1960s, the winds of change blowing through American society were felt as deeply in Indian Country as anywhere. Two books played a crucial role. In 1969, Vine Deloria Jr., member of a renowned family of Indian intellectuals from Oklahoma, published his landmark history, *Custer Died For Your Sins*, which portrayed American history from the Indians' viewpoint. The following year, Dee Brown's *Bury My Heart at Wounded Knee* described the settling of the West also from an Indian point of view. The books astonished many non-Indians. Among young Indians,

Continued on p. 373

Chronology

1800s United States expands westward, pushing Indians off most of their original lands, sometimes creating new reservations for them.

1830
President Andrew Jackson signs the Indian Removal Act, forcing the Cherokees to move from Georgia to Oklahoma.

1832
Supreme Court issues the last of three decisions defining Indians' legal status as wards of the government.

1871
Congress makes its treaties with tribes easier to alter, enabling non-Indians to take Indian lands when natural resources are discovered.

Dec. 29, 1890
U.S. soldiers massacre at least 150 Plains Indians, mostly women and children, at Wounded Knee, S.D.

1900-1950s Congress and the executive branch undertake major shifts in Indian policy, first strengthening tribal governments then trying to force cultural assimilation.

1924
Indians are granted U.S. citizenship.

1934
Indian Reorganization Act authorizes expansion of reservations and strengthening of tribal governments.

1953
Congress endorses full assimilation of Indians into American society, including "relocation" from reservations to cities.

1960s-1980s In the radical spirit of the era, Native Americans demand respect for their traditions and an end to discrimination; federal government concedes more power to tribal governments, allows gambling on tribal lands.

1969
American Indian Movement (AIM) seizes Alcatraz Island in San Francisco Bay to dramatize claims of injustice.

July 7, 1970
President Richard M. Nixon vows support for Indian self-government.

Feb. 27, 1973
AIM members occupy the town of Wounded Knee on the Pine Ridge, S.D., Sioux Reservation, for two months; two Indians die and an FBI agent is wounded.

1988
Indian Gaming Regulatory Act allows tribes to operate casinos under agreements with states.

1990s Indian-owned casinos boom; tribal governments push to expand self-rule and reduce Bureau of Indian Affairs (BIA) supervision.

1994
President Bill Clinton signs law making experimental self-governance compacts permanent.

March 27, 1996
U.S. Supreme Court rules states can't be forced to negotiate casino compacts, thus encouraging tribes to make revenue-sharing deals with states as the price of approval.

June 10, 1996
Elouise Cobell, a member of the Blackfeet Tribe in Montana, charges Interior Department mismanagement of Indian trust funds cheated Indians out of billions of dollars. The case is still pending.

Nov. 3, 1998
California voters uphold tribes' rights to run casinos; state Supreme Court later invalidates the provision, but it is revived by a 1999 compact between the tribes and the state.

2000s Indian advocates decry low funding levels, and sovereignty battles continue; lobbying scandal spotlights Indian gambling profits.

2000
Tribal Self-Governance Demonstration Project becomes permanent.

2003
U.S. Commission on Civil Rights calls underfunding for Indians a crisis, saying federal government spends less for Indian health care than for any other group, including prison inmates.

Feb. 22, 2004
Washington Post reports on Washington lobbyist Jack Abramoff's deals with casino tribes.

March 29, 2005
U.S. Supreme Court blocks tax exemptions for Oneida Nation of New York on newly purchased land simply because it once owned the property.

April 5, 2006
Tribal and BIA officials testify in Congress that methamphetamine addiction is ravaging reservations.

Budget Cuts Target Health Clinics

When Lita Pepion, a health consultant and a member of the Blackfeet Nation, learned that her 22-year-old-niece had been struggling with heroin abuse, she urged her to seek treatment at the local Urban Indian Clinic in Billings, Mont.

But the young woman had so much trouble getting an appointment that she gave up. Only recently, says Pepion, did she overcome her addiction on her own.

The clinic is one of 34 federally funded, Indian-controlled clinics that contract with the Indian Health Service (IHS) to serve urban Indians. But President Bush's 2007 budget would kill the $33-million program, eliminating most of the clinics' funding.

Indians in cities will still be able to get health care through several providers, including the federal Health Centers program, says Office of Management and Budget spokesman Richard Walker. The proposed budget would increase funding for the centers by nearly $2 billion, IHS Director Charles W. Grim told the Senate Indian Affairs Committee on Feb. 14, 2006. [1]

AP Photo/Salt Lake Tribune

Native Americans in downtown Salt Lake City, Utah, demonstrate on April 21, 2006, against the elimination of funding for Urban Indian Health Clinics.

But Joycelyn Dorscher, president of the Association of American Indian Physicians, says the IHS clinics do a great job and that, "It's very important that people from diverse backgrounds have physicians like themselves."

Others, however, including Pepion, say the clinics are poorly managed and lack direction. Ralph Forquera, director of the Seattle-based Urban Indian Health Institute, says that while the clinics "have made great strides medically, a lack of resources has resulted in services from unqualified professionals." In addition, he says, "we have not been as successful in dealing with lifestyle changes and mental health problems."

Many Indian health experts oppose the cuts because Indians in both urban areas and on reservations have more health problems than the general population, including 126 percent more chronic liver disease and cirrhosis, 54 percent more diabetes and 178 percent more alcohol-related deaths. [2]

Indian health specialists blame the Indians' higher disease rates on history, lifestyle and genetics — not just on poverty. "You don't see exactly the same things happening to other poor minority groups," says Dorscher, a North Dakota Chippewa, so "there's something different" going on among Indians.

In the view of Donna Keeler, executive director of the South Dakota Urban Indian Health program and an Eastern Shoshone, historical trauma affects the physical wellness of patients in her state's three urban Indian clinics.

Susette Schwartz, CEO of the Hunter Urban Indian Clinic in Wichita, Kan., agrees. She attributes Indians' high rates of mental health and alcohol/substance abuse to their long history of government maltreatment. Many Indian children in the 19th and early 20th centuries, she points out, were taken from their parents and sent to government boarding schools where speaking native languages was prohibited. "Taking away the culture and language years ago," says Schwartz, as well as the government's role in "taking their children and sterilizing their women" in the 1970s, all contributed to Indians' behavioral health issues.

Keeler also believes Indians' low incomes cause their unhealthy lifestyles. Many eat high-fat, high-starch foods because they are cheaper, Pepion says. Growing up on a reservation, she recalls, "We didn't eat a lot of vegetables because we couldn't afford them."

Opponents of the funding cuts for urban Indian health centers also cite a recent letter to President Bush from Daniel R. Hawkins Jr., vice president for federal, state and local government for the National Association of Community Health Centers. He said the urban Indian clinics and community health centers are complementary, not duplicative.

While Pepion does not believe funding should be cut entirely, she concedes that alternative health-care services are often "better equipped than the urban Indian clinics." And if American Indians want to assimilate into the larger society, they can't have everything culturally separate, she adds. "The only way that I was able to assimilate into an urban society was to make myself do those things that were uncomfortable for me," she says.

But Schwartz believes a great benefit of the urban clinics are their Indian employees, "who are culturally competent and sensitive and incorporate Native American-specific cultural ideas." Because of their history of cultural abuse, it takes a long time for Native Americans to trust non-Indian health providers, says Schwartz. "They're not just going to go to a health center down the road."

Dorscher and Schwartz also say the budget cuts could lead to more urban Indians ending up in costly emergency rooms because of their reluctance to trust the community health centers. "Ultimately, it would become more expensive to cut the prevention and primary care programs than it would be to maintain them," Dorscher says.

— Melissa J. Hipolit

---

[1] Prepared testimony of Director of Indian Health Service Dr. Charles W. Grim before the Senate Committee on Indian Affairs, Feb. 14, 2006.

[2] Urban Indian Health Institute, "The Health Status of Urban American Indians and Alaska Natives," March 16, 2004, p. v.

Continued from p. 370

the volumes reflected and spurred on a growing political activism.

It was in this climate that the newly formed American Indian Movement (AIM) took over Alcatraz Island, the former federal prison site in San Francisco Bay (where rebellious Indians had been held during the Indian Wars), to publicize demands to honor treaties and respect Native Americans' dignity. The takeover lasted from Nov. 20, 1969, to June 11, 1971, when U.S. marshals removed the occupiers. [45]

A second AIM-government confrontation took the form of a one-week takeover of BIA headquarters in Washington in November 1972 by some 500 AIM members protesting what they called broken treaty obligations. Protesters charged that government services to Indians were inadequate in general, with urban Indians neglected virtually completely.

Another protest occurred on Feb. 27, 1973, when 200 AIM members occupied the village of Wounded Knee on the Oglala Sioux's Pine Ridge Reservation in South Dakota. U.S. soldiers had massacred at least 150 Indians at Wounded Knee in 1890. AIM was protesting what it called the corrupt tribal government. And a weak, involuntary manslaughter charge against a non-Indian who had allegedly killed an Indian near the reservation had renewed Indian anger at discriminatory treatment by police and judges.

The occupation soon turned into a full-blown siege, with the reservation surrounded by troops and federal law-enforcement officers. During several firefights two AIM members were killed, and an FBI agent was wounded. The occupation ended on May 8, 1973.

Disease Toll Higher Among Indians

American Indians served by the Indian Health Service (IHS) — mainly low-income or uninsured — die at substantially higher rates than the general population from liver disease, diabetes, tuberculosis, pneumonia and influenza as well as from homicide, suicide and injuries. However, Indians' death rates from Alzheimer's disease or breast cancer are lower.

Health Status of American Indians * Compared to General Population
(deaths per 100,000 population)

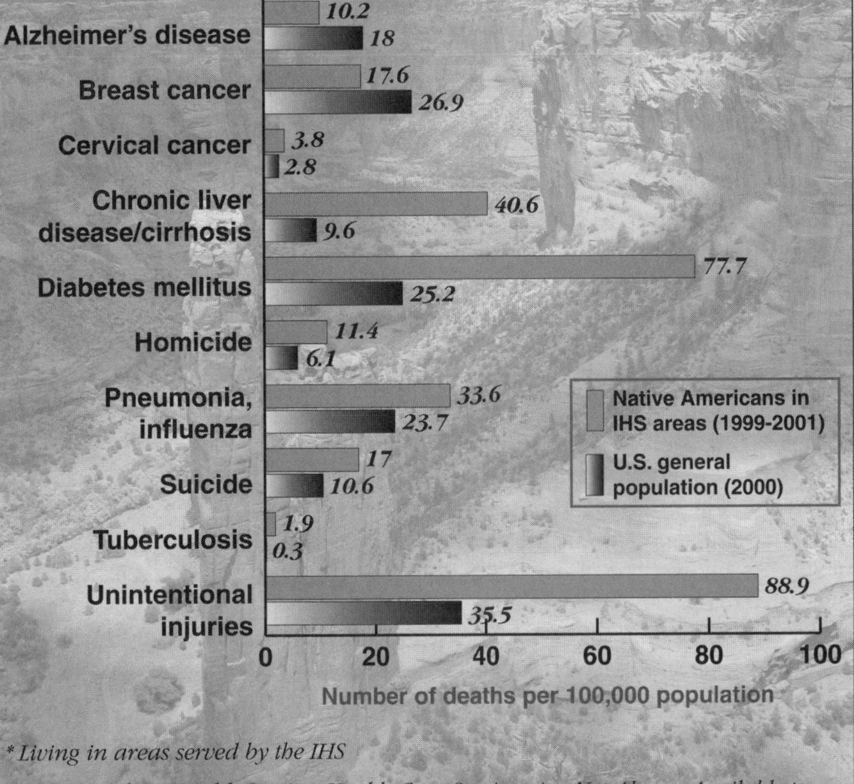

** Living in areas served by the IHS*

Source: "Indian Health Service: Health Care Services Are Not Always Available to Native Americans," Government Accountability Office, August 2005

Background image: Canyon de Chelly, Navajo Nation, Arizona (Navajo Tourism)

Self-Determination

Amid the surging Indian activism, the federal government was trying to make up for the past by encouraging tribal self-determination. [46]

In 1975, Congress passed the Indian Self-Determination and Education Assistance Act, which channeled federal contracts and grants directly to tribes, reducing the BIA role and effectively putting Indian communities in direct charge of schools, health, housing and other programs.

And to assure Indians that the era of sudden reversals in federal policy had ended, the House in 1988 passed a resolution reaffirming the "constitutionally recognized government-to-government relationship with Indian tribes." Separate legislation set up a "self-governance demonstration project" in which eligible tribes would sign "compacts" to run their own governments with block grants from the federal government. [47]

By 1993, 28 tribes had negotiated compacts with the Interior Department. And in 1994, President Bill Clinton signed legislation that made self-governance a permanent option.

For the general public, the meaning of newly strengthened Indian sovereignty could be summed up with one word: casinos. In 1988, Congress enacted legislation regulating tribal gaming operations. That move followed a Supreme Court ruling (*California v. Cabazon*) that authorized tribes to run gambling operations. But tribes could not offer a form of gambling specifically barred by the state.

American Indian Center/Warren Perlstein

Native American children and adults in the Chicago area keep in touch with their cultural roots at the American Indian Center. About two-thirds of the nation's Indians live in urban areas.

The law set up three categories of gambling operations: Class I, traditional Indian games, controlled exclusively by tribes; Class II, including bingo, lotto, pull tabs and some card games, which are allowed on tribal lands in states that allow the games elsewhere; and Class III, which takes in casino games such as slot machines, roulette and blackjack, which can be offered only under agreements with state governments that set out the size and types of the proposed casinos.

Limits that the Indian Gaming Regulatory Act put on Indian sovereignty were tightened further by a 1996 Supreme Court decision that the Seminole Tribe couldn't sue Florida to force negotiation of a casino compact. The decision essentially forced tribes nationwide to make revenue-sharing deals with states in return for approval of casinos. [48]

Meanwhile, particularily on reservations from Minnesota to the Pacific Northwest, a plague of methamphetamine addiction and manufacturing is leaving a trail of death and shattered lives. By 2002, Darrell Hillaire, chairman of the Lummi Nation, near Bellingham, Wash., said that members convicted of dealing meth would be expelled from the tribe. [49]

But the Lummis couldn't stop the spread of the scourge on other reservations. National Congress of American Indians President Garcia said early in 2006: "Methamphetamine is a poison taking Indian lives, destroying Indian families, and razing entire communities." [50] ■

CURRENT SITUATION

Self-Government

Some Indian leaders are advocating more power for tribal governments as the best way to improve the quality of life on reservations.

Under the Tribal Self-Governance Demonstration Project, made permanent in 1994, tribes can replace program-by-program grants by entering into "compacts" with the federal government, under which they receive a single grant for a variety of services. Some 231 tribes and Alaskan Native villages have compacts to administer a total of about $341 million in programs. Of the Indian communities now living under compacts, 72 are in the lower 48 states. [51]

Under a set of separate compacts, the Indian Health Service has turned over clinics, hospitals and health programs to some 300 tribes and Alaskan villages, 70 of them non-Alaskan tribes.

The self-governance model has proved especially appropriate in Alaska, where the majority of the native population of 120,000 is concentrated in 229 villages, many of them remote, and compact in size, hence well-suited to managing their own affairs, experts say.

Another advantage of Alaska villages is the experience they acquired through the 1971 Alaska Native Claims Settlement Act, which granted a total of $962 million to Alaska natives born on or before Dec. 18, 1971, in exchange for giving up their claims to millions of acres of land. Villages formed regional corporations to manage the assets. In addition, all Alaska residents receive an annual dividend ($946 in 2005) from natural-resource royalty income. [52]

"The emergence of tribal authority is unprecedented in Indian Country's history," says Allen, of the Jamestown S'Klallam Tribe, one of the originators of the self-governance model. "Why not take the resources you have available and use them as efficiently as you can — more efficiently than currently being administered?" [53]

But the poorer and more populous tribes of the Great Plains and the Southwest have turned down the self-governance model. "They can't afford to do it," says Michael LaPointe, chief of staff to President Rodney Bordeaux of the Rosebud Sioux Tribe. "When you have a lot of poverty and not a lot of economic activity to generate tribal resources to supplement the unfunded mandates, it becomes impossible."

In contrast with the Jameston S'Klallam's tiny membership of 585 people, there are some 24,000 people on the Rosebud Siouxs' million-acre reservation. The tribe does operate law enforcement, ambulances and other services under contracts with the government. But it can't afford to do any more, LaPointe says.

A combined effect of the gambling boom and the growing adoption of the self-governance model is that much of the tension has gone out of the traditionally strained relationship between the BIA and tribes. "BIA people are getting pushed out as decision-makers," Kalt says. Some strains remain, to be sure. Allen says he senses a growing reluctance by the BIA to let go of tribes. "They use the argument that that the BIA doesn't have the money [for block grants]," he says.

BIA Director Ragsdale acknowledges that tougher financial-accounting requirements sparked by a lawsuit over Interior Department handling of Indian trust funds are slowing the compact-approval process. (*See "Trust Settlement" below.*) But, he adds, "We're not trying to hinder self-governance."

Limits on Gambling

Several legislative efforts to limit Indian gaming are pending. Separate bills by Sen. McCain and House Resources Committee Chairman Richard Pombo, R-Calif., would restrict tribes' ability to acquire new land for casinos in more favorable locations.

More proposals are in the pipeline. Jemez Pueblo of New Mexico wants to build a casino near the town of Anthony, though the pueblo is 300 miles away. [54]

In eastern Oregon, the Warm Springs Tribe is proposing an off-reservation casino at the Columbia River Gorge. And in Washington state, the Cowlitz and Mohegan tribes are planning an off-reservation casino near Portland. [55] The process has been dubbed "reservation shopping."

Under the Indian Gaming Regulatory Act of 1988, a tribe can acquire off-reservation land for casinos when it is:

- granted as part of a land claim settlement;
- granted to a newly recognized tribe as its reservation;
- restored to a tribe whose tribal recognition is also restored; or
- granted to a recognized tribe that had no reservation when the act took effect.

The most hotly debated exemption allows the secretary of the Interior to grant an off-reservation acquisition that benefits the tribe without harming the community near the proposed casino location. Both Pombo and McCain would repeal the loophole created by this so-called "two-part test." Under Pombo's bill, tribes acquiring land under the other exemptions would have to have solid historic and recent ties to the property. Communities, state governors and state legislatures would have to approve the establishment of new casinos, and tribes would reimburse communities for the effects of casinos on transportation, law enforcement and other public services.

McCain's bill would impose fewer restrictions than Pombo's. But McCain would give the National Indian Gaming Commission final say over all contracts with outside suppliers of goods and services.

The bill would also ensure the commission's control over big-time gambling — a concern that arose from a 2005 decision by the U.S. Court of Appeals for the District of Columbia that limited the agency's jurisdiction over a Colorado tribe. The commission has been worrying that applying that decision nationwide would eliminate federal supervision of casinos.

McCain told a March 8 Senate Indian Affairs Committee hearing that the two-part test "is fostering opposition to all Indian gaming." [56]

If the senator had been aiming to soften tribal opposition to his bill, he didn't make much headway. "We believe that it grows out of anecdotal, anti-Indian press reports on Indian gaming, the overblown issue of off-reservation gaming, and a 'pin-the-blame-on-the-victim' reaction to the Abramoff scandal," Ron His Horse Is Thunder, chairman of the Standing Rock Sioux Tribe of North Dakota and South Dakota, told the committee. He argued that the bill would amount to unconstitutional meddling with Indian sovereignty.

But the idea of restricting "reservation-shopping" appeals to tribes facing competition from other tribes. Cheryle A. Kennedy, chairwoman of the Confederated Tribes of the Grand Ronde Community of Oregon, said her tribe's Spirit Mountain Casino could be hurt by the Warm Springs Tribes' proposed project or by the Cowlitz and Mohegan project. [57]

Pombo's bill would require the approval of new casinos by tribes that already have gambling houses up and running within 75 miles of a proposed new one.

The House Resources Committee heard another view from Indian Country at an April 5 hearing. Jacquie Davis-Van Huss, tribal secretary of the North Fork Rancheria of the Mono Indians of California, said Pombo's approval clause would doom her tribe's plans. "This provision is anti-competitive," she testified. "It effectively provides the power to veto another tribe's gaming project simply to protect market share."

Urban Indians: Invisible and Unheard

Two-thirds of the nation's 4.4 million American Indians live in towns and cities, but they're hard to find. [1] "Indians who move into metropolitan areas are scattered; they're not in a centralized geographical area," says New Mexico Secretary of Labor Conroy Chino. "You don't have that cohesive community where there's a sense of culture and language, as in Chinatown or Koreatown in Los Angeles."

Chino's interest is professional as well as personal. In his former career as a television journalist in Albuquerque, Chino, a member of the Acoma Pueblo, wrote an independent documentary about urban Indians. His subjects range from a city-loving San Franciscan who vacations in Hawaii to city-dwellers who return to their reservations every vacation they get. Their lives diverge sharply from what University of Arizona anthropologist Susan Lobo calls a "presumption that everything Indian is rural and long, long ago." [2]

Indian society began urbanizing in 1951, when the Bureau of Indian Affairs (BIA) started urging reservation dwellers to move to cities where — it was hoped — they would blend into the American "melting pot" and find more economic opportunity and a better standard of living. [3]

But many found the urban environment oppressive and the government assistance less generous than promised. About 100,000 Indians were relocated between 1951 and 1973, when the program wound down; unable to fit in, many fell into alcoholism and despair. [4]

Still, a small, urban Indian middle class has developed over time, partly because the BIA began systematically hiring Indians in its offices. Indians keep such a low profile, however, that the Census Bureau has a hard time finding them. Lobo, who consulted for the bureau in 1990, recalls that the agency's policy at the time was to register any household where no one answered the door as being in the same ethnic group as the neighbors. That strategy worked with urban ethnic groups who tended to cluster together, Lobo says, but not with Native Americans because theirs was a "dispersed population."

By the 2000 census that problem was resolved, but another one cropped up. "American Indians are ingenious at keeping expenses down — by couch-surfing, for instance," Lobo says. "There's a floating population that doesn't get counted because they weren't living in a standard residence."

But other urban Indians live conventional, middle-class lives, sometimes even while technically living on Indian land. "I am highly educated, a professor in the university, and my gainful employment is in the city of Albuquerque," says Ted Jojola, a professor of planning at the University of New Mexico (and a member of the Census Bureau's advisory committee on Indian population). "My community [Isleta Pueblo] is seven minutes south of Albuquerque. The reservation has become an urban amenity to me."

Some might see a home on Indian land near the city as a refuge from discrimination. "There have been years where you couldn't reveal you were native if you wanted to get a job," says Joseph Podlasek, executive director of the American Indian Center of Chicago.

Joycelyn Dorscher, president of the Association of American Indian Physicians, recalls a painful experience several years ago when she rushed her 6-year-old daughter to a hospital emergency room in Minneapolis-St. Paul, suspecting appendicitis. The young intern assigned to the case saw an Indian single mother with a sick child and apparently assumed that the daughter was suffering from neglect. "She told me if I didn't sit down and shut up, my daughter would go into the [child-protective] system," recalls Dorscher, who at the time was a third-year medical student.

Even Chino, whose mainstream credentials include an M.A. from Princeton, feels alienated at times from non-Indian city dwellers. He notes that Albuquerque officials ignored Indians' objections to a statue honoring Juan de Oñate, the 16th-century conqueror who established Spanish rule in what is now New Mexico. "Though native people protested and tried to show why this is not a good idea," Chino says, "the city went ahead and funded it." [5]

In the long run, Chino hopes a growing presence of Indian professionals — "we're not all silversmiths, or weavers" — will create more acceptance of urban Indians and more aid to combat high Indian dropout rates and other problems. "While people like having Indians in New Mexico and like visitors to get a feel for the last bastion of native culture," he says, "they're not doing that much for the urban Indian community, though we're paying taxes, too."

[1] Urban Indians were 64 percent of the population in 2000, according to the U.S. Census Bureau. For background, see, "We the People: American Indians and Alaska Natives in the United States," U.S. Census Bureau, 2000, p. 14, www.census.gov/prod/2006pubs/censr-28.pdf.

[2] "Looking Toward Home," *Native American Public Telecommunications*, 2003, www.visionmaker.org.

[3] Donald L. Fixico, *The Urban Indian Experience in America* (2000), pp. 9-11.

[4] *Ibid.*, pp. 22-25.

[5] Oñate is especially disliked at Acoma, Chino's birthplace, where the conqueror had the feet of some two-dozen Acoma men cut off in 1599 after Spanish soldiers were killed there. For background, see Wren Propp, "A Giant of Ambivalence," *Albuquerque Journal*, Jan. 25, 2004, p. A1; Brenda Norrell, "Pueblos Decry War Criminal," *Indian Country Today*, June 25, 2004.

Trust Settlement

McCain's committee is also grappling with efforts to settle a decade-old lawsuit that has exposed longstanding federal mismanagement of trust funds. In 1999, U.S. District Judge Royce Lamberth said evidence showed "fiscal and governmental irresponsibility in its purest form." [58]

The alternative to settlement, McCain and Dorgan told the Budget Committee,

Continued on p. 378

At Issue:

Should tribes open casinos on newly acquired land?

ERNEST L. STEVENS, JR.
CHAIRMAN, NATIONAL INDIAN GAMING ASSOCIATION

FROM STATEMENT BEFORE U.S. HOUSE COMMITTEE ON RESOURCES, NOV. 9, 2005

yes

Indian gaming is the Native American success story. Where there were no jobs, now there are 553,000 jobs. Where our people had only an eighth-grade education on average, tribal governments are building schools and funding college scholarships. Where the United States and boarding schools sought to suppress our languages, tribal schools are now teaching their native language. Where our people suffer epidemic diabetes, heart disease and premature death, our tribes are building hospitals, health clinics and wellness centers.

Historically, the United States signed treaties guaranteeing Indian lands as permanent homes, and then a few years later, went to war to take our lands. This left our people to live in poverty, often on desolate lands, while others mined for gold or pumped oil from the lands that were taken from us.

Indian gaming is an exercise of our inherent right to self-government. Today, for over 60 percent of Indian tribes in the lower 48 states, Indian gaming offers new hope and a chance for a better life for our children.

Too many lands were taken from Indian tribes, leaving some tribes landless or with no useful lands. To take account of historical mistreatment, the Indian Gaming Regulatory Act (IGRA), provided several exceptions to the rule that Indian tribes should conduct Indian gaming on lands held on Oct. 17, 1988.

Accordingly, land is restored to an Indian tribe in trust status when the tribe is restored to federal recognition. For federally recognized tribes that did not have reservation land on the date IGRA was enacted, land is put into trust. Or, a tribe may apply to the secretary of the Interior. The secretary consults with state and local officials and nearby Indian tribes to determine whether an acquisition of land in trust for gaming would be in the tribe's "best interest" and "not detrimental to the surrounding community."

Now, legislation would require "newly recognized, restored, or landless tribes" to apply to have land taken in trust through a five-part process. Subjecting tribes to this new and cumbersome process discounts the fact that the United States mistreated these tribes by ignoring and neglecting them, taking all of their lands or allowing their lands to be stolen by others.

We believe that Congress should restore these tribes to a portion of their historical lands and that these lands should be held on the same basis as other Indian lands.

STATE REP. FULTON SHEEN, R-PLAINWELL
MICHIGAN HOUSE OF REPRESENTATIVES

FROM STATEMENT TO U.S. HOUSE COMMITTEE ON RESOURCES, APRIL 5, 2006

no

The rampant proliferation of tribal gaming is running roughshod over states' rights and local control and is jeopardizing everything from my own neighborhood to — as the Jack Abramoff scandal has demonstrated — the very integrity of our federal political system.

In 1988, Congress passed the Indian Gaming Regulatory Act (IGRA) in an effort to control the development of Native American casinos and, in particular, to make sure that the states had a meaningful role in the development of any casinos within their borders. At that time, Native American gambling accounted for less than 1 percent of the nation's gambling industry, grossing approximately $100 million in revenue.

Since that time, the Native American casino business has exploded into an $18.5 billion industry that controls 25 percent of gaming industry revenue. Despite this unbridled growth, IGRA and the land-in-trust process remain basically unchanged.

When Congress originally enacted IGRA, the general rule was that casino gambling would not take place on newly acquired trust land. I believe Congress passed this general rule to prevent precisely what we see happening: a mad and largely unregulated land rush pushed by casino developers eager to cash in on a profitable revenue stream that is not burdened by the same tax rates or regulations that other businesses have to incur. "Reservation shopping" is an activity that must be stopped. And that is just one component of the full legislative overhaul that is needed.

IGRA and its associated land-in-trust process is broken, open to manipulation by special interests and in desperate need of immediate reform. It has unfairly and inappropriately fostered an industry that creates enormous wealth for a few select individuals and Las Vegas interests at the expense of taxpaying families, small businesses, manufacturing jobs and local governments.

Our research shows that while local and state governments receive some revenue-sharing percentages from tribal gaming, the dollars pale in comparison to the overall new costs to government and social-service agencies from increased infrastructure demands, traffic, bankruptcies, crime, divorce and general gambling-related ills.

I do not think this is what Congress had in mind. Somewhere along the way, the good intentions of Congress have been hijacked, and it is time for this body to reassert control over this process. It is imperative that Congress take swift and decisive steps today to get its arms around this issue before more jobs are lost and more families are put at risk.

Continued from p. 376

is for the case to drag on through the courts. Congressional resolution of the conflict could also spare the Interior Department further grief from Lamberth. In a February ruling, he said Interior's refusal to make payments owed to Indians was "an obscenity that harkens back to the darkest days of United States-Indian relations." [59]

Five months later, Lamberth suggested that Congress, not the courts, may be the proper setting for the conflict. "Interior's unremitting neglect and mismanagement of the Indian trust has left it in such a shambles that recovery may prove impossible." [60]

The court case has its roots in the 1887 policy of allotting land to Indians in an effort to break up reservations. Since then, the Interior Department has been responsible for managing payments made to landholders, which later included tribes, for mining and other natural-resource extraction on Indian-owned land.

But for decades, Indians weren't receiving what they were owed. On June 10, 1996, Elouise Cobell, an organizer of the Blackfeet National Bank, the first Indian-owned national bank on a reservation, sued the Interior Department charging that she and all other trust fee recipients had been cheated for decades out of money that Interior was responsible for managing. "Lands and resources — in many cases the only source of income for some of our nation's poorest and most vulnerable citizens — have been grossly mismanaged," Cobell told the Indian Affairs Committee on March 1.

The mismanagement is beyond dispute, said John Bickerman, who was appointed to broker a settlement. Essentially, Bickerman told the Senate Indian Affairs Committee on March 28, "Money was not collected; money was not properly deposited; and money was not properly disbursed."

As of 2005, Interior is responsible for trust payments involving 126,079 tracts of land owned by 223,245 individuals — or, 2.3 million "ownership interests" on some 12 million acres, Cason and Ross Swimmer, a special trustee, told the committee.

Bickerman said a settlement amount of $27.5 billion proposed by the Indian plaintiffs was "without foundation." But the Interior Department proposed a settlement of $500 million based on "arbitrary and false assumptions," he added. Both sides agree that some $13 billion should have been paid to individual Indians over the life of the trust, but they disagree over how much was actually paid.

Supreme Court Ruling

Powerful repercussions are expected from the Supreme Court's latest decision in a centuries-long string of rulings involving competing claims to land by Indians and non-Indians.

In 2005, the high court said the Oneida Indian Nation of New York could not quit paying taxes on 10 parcels of land it owns north of Utica. [61]

After buying the parcels in 1997 and 1998, the tribe refused to pay property taxes, arguing that the land was former tribal property now restored to tribal ownership, and thereby tax-exempt. [62]

The court, in an opinion written by Ruth Bader Ginsburg, concluded that though the tribe used to own the land, the property right was too old to revive. "Rekindling the embers of sovereignty that long ago grew cold" is out of the question, Ginsburg wrote. She invoked the legal doctrine of "laches," in which a party who waits too long to assert his rights loses them. [63]

Lawyers on both sides of Indian law cases expect the case to affect lower-court rulings throughout the country. "The court has opened the cookie jar," Williams of the University of Arizona argues. "Does laches only apply to claims of sovereignty over reacquired land? If a decision favoring Indians is going to inconvenience too many white people, then laches applies — I swear that's what it says." Tribes litigating fishing rights, water rights and other assets are likely to suffer in court as a result, he argues.

In fact, only three months after the high court decision, the 2nd U.S. Circuit Court of Appeals in New York invoked laches in rejecting a claim by the Cayuga Tribe. Vickers of Upstate Citizens for Equality says that if the 2nd Circuit "thinks that laches forbids the Cayugas from making a claim because the Supreme Court said so, you're going to find other courts saying so."

In Washington, Alexandra Page, an attorney with the Indian Law Resource Center, agrees. "There are tribes in the West who have boundary disputes on their reservations; there are water-law cases where you've got people looking back at what happened years ago, so the Supreme Court decision could have significant practical impact. The danger is that those with an interest in limiting Indian rights will do everything they can to expand the decision and use it in other circumstances." ■

OUTLOOK

Who Is an Indian?

If advocates of Indian self-governance are correct, the number of tribes running their own affairs with minimal federal supervision will keep on growing. "The requests for workshops are coming in steadily," says Cyndi Holmes, self-governance coordinator of the Jamestown S'Klallam Tribe.

Others say that growth, now at a rate of about three tribes a year, may be nearing its upper limit. "When you look at the options for tribes to do self-governance, economics really drives whether they can," says LaPointe of the Rosebud

Sioux, whose tribal government doesn't expect to adopt the model in the foreseeable future.

But the longstanding problems of rural and isolated reservations are not the only dimension of Indian life. People stereotypically viewed as tied to the land have become increasingly urban over the past several decades, and the view from Indian Country is that the trend will continue.

That doesn't mean reservations will empty out or lose their cultural importance. "Urban Indian is not a lifelong label," says Susan Lobo, an anthropologist at the University of Arizona. "Indian people, like everyone else, can move around. They're still American Indians."

Ho-Chunk, Inc.

Harvard Law School graduate Lance Morgan, a member of Nebraska's Winnebago Tribe, used seed money from his tribe's small casino to create several thriving businesses. He urges other tribes to use their casino profits to diversify. "Gaming is just a means to an end," he says.

For Indians, as for all other peoples, moving around leads to intermarriage. Matthew Snipp, a Stanford University sociologist who is half Cherokee and half Oklahoma Choctaw, notes that Indians have long married within and outside Indian society. But the consequences of intermarriage are different for Indians than for, say, Jews or Italians.

The Indian place in American society grows out of the government-to-government relationship between Washington and tribes. And most tribes define their members by what's known as the "blood quantum" — their degree of tribal ancestry.

"I look at it as you're kind of USDA-approved," says Podlasek of the American Indian Center. "Why is no other race measured that way?"

Podlasek is especially sensitive to the issue. His father was Polish-American, and his mother was Ojibway. His own wife is Indian, but from another tribe. "My kids can be on the tribal rolls, but their kids won't be able to enroll, unless they went back to my tribe or to their mother's tribe to marry — depending on what their partners' blood quantum is. In generations, you could say that, by government standards, there are no more native people."

Snipp traces the blood-quantum policy to a 1932 decision by the Indian Affairs Commission, which voted to make one-quarter descent the minimum standard. The commissioners were concerned, Snipp says, reading from the commission's report, that thousands of people "more white than Indian" were receiving "shares in tribal estates and other benefits." Tribes are no longer bound by that decision, but the requirement — originally inserted at BIA insistence — remains in many tribal constitutions.

On the Indian side, concern over collective survival is historically well-founded. Historian Elizabeth Shoemaker of the University of Connecticut at Storrs calculated that the Indian population of what is now the continental United States plummeted from a top estimate of 5.5 million in 1492 to a mere 237,000 in 1900. Indian life expectancy didn't begin to rise significantly until after 1940. [64]

Now, Indians are worrying about the survival of Indian civilization at a time when Indians' physical survival has never been more assured.

Even as these existential worries trouble some Indian leaders, the living conditions that most Indians endure also pose long-term concerns.

Conroy Chino, New Mexico's Labor secretary and a member of Acoma Pueblo, says continuation of the educational disaster in Indian Country is dooming young people to live on the margins. "I'm out there attracting companies to come to New Mexico, and these kids aren't going to qualify for those good jobs."

Nevertheless, below most non-Indians' radar screen, the Indian professional class is growing. "When I got my Ph.D. in 1973, I think I was the 15th in the country," says Beaulieu of Arizona State University's Center for Indian Education. "Now we have all kinds of Ph.D.s, teachers with certification, lawyers." And Beaulieu says he has seen the difference that Indian professionals make in his home state of Minnesota. "You're beginning to see an educated middle class in the reservation community, and realizing that they're volunteering to perform lots of services."

In Albuquerque, the University of New Mexico's Jojola commutes to campus from Isleta Pueblo. Chairman of an advisory committee on Indians to the U.S. Census Bureau, Jojola shares concerns about use of "blood quantum" as the sole determinant of Indian identity. "A lot of people are saying that language, culture and residence should also be considered," he says.

That standard would implicitly recognize what many Indians call the single biggest reason that American Indians have outlasted the efforts of those who wanted to exterminate or to assimilate them. "In our spirituality we remain strong," says Bordeaux of the Rosebud Sioux. "That's our godsend and our lifeline." ■

Notes

[1] For background, see "The Administration of Indian Affairs," *Editorial Research Reports 1929* (Vol. II), at *CQ Researcher Plus Archive*, CQ Electronic Library, http://library.cqpress.com.

[2] For background see Phil Two Eagle, "Rosebud Sioux Tribe, Demographics," March 25, 2003, www.rosebudsiouxtribe-nsn.gov/demographics.

[3] "American Indian Population and Labor Force Report 2003," p. ii, Bureau of Indian Affairs, cited in John McCain, chairman, Senate Indian Affairs Committee, Byron L. Dorgan, vice chairman, letter to Senate Budget Committee, March 2, 2006, http://indian.senate.gov/public/_files/Budget5.pdf.

[4] Jonathan B. Taylor and Joseph P. Kalt, "American Indians on Reservations: A Databook of Socioeconomic Change Between the 1990 and 2000 Censuses," Harvard Project on American Indian Economic Development, January 2005, pp. 8-13; www.ksg.harvard.edu/hpaied/pubs/pub_151.htm. These data exclude the Navajo Tribe, whose on-reservation population of about 175,000 is 12 times that of the next-largest tribe, thus distorting comparisons, Taylor and Kalt write.

[5] *Ibid.*, p. 41.

[6] McCain and Dorgan, *op. cit.*

[7] "Injury Mortality Among American Indian and Alaska Native Youth, United States, 1989-1998," *Morbidity and Mortality Weekly Report*, Centers for Disease Control and Prevention, Aug. 1, 2003, www.cdc.gov/mmwr/preview/mmwrhtml/mm5230a2.htm#top.

[8] Robert McSwain, deputy director, Indian Health Service, testimony before Senate Indian Affairs Committee, April 5, 2006.

[9] *Ibid.*, p. xii.

[10] Taylor and Kalt, *op. cit.*

[11] *Ibid.*, pp. 28-30.

[12] *Ibid.*, pp. 22-24.

[13] The decision is *Cherokee Nation v. Georgia*, 30 U.S. 1 (1831), http://supreme.justia.com/us/30/1/case.html.

[14] Alan Meister, "Indian Gaming industry Report," Analysis Group, 2006, p. 2. Publicly available data can be obtained at, "Indian Gaming Facts," www.indiangaming.org/library/indian-gaming-facts; "Gaming Revenues, 2000-2004," National Indian Gaming Commission, www.nigc.gov/TribalData/GamingRevenues2004 2000/tabid/549/Default.aspx.

[15] The ruling is *California v. Cabazon Band of Mission Indians*, 480 U.S. 202 (1987), http://supreme.justia.com/us/480/202/case.html.

[16] For background, see Susan Schmidt and James V. Grimaldi, "The Rise and Steep Fall of Jack Abramoff," *The Washington Post*, Dec. 29, 2005, p. A1. On March 29, Abramoff was sentenced in Miami to 70 months in prison after pleading to fraud, tax evasion and conspiracy to bribe public officials in charges growing out of a Florida business deal. He is cooperating with the Justice Department in its Washington-based political-corruption investigation. For background see Peter Katel, "Lobbying Boom," *CQ Researcher*, July 22, 2005, pp. 613-636.

[17] Meister, *op. cit.*, pp. 27-28. For additional background, see John Cochran, "A Piece of the Action," *CQ Weekly*, May 9, 2005, p. 1208.

[18] For background, see, "A Quiet Crisis: Federal Funding and Unmet Needs in Indian Country," U.S. Commission on Civil Rights, July, 2003, pp. 32, 113. www.usccr.gov/pubs/na0703/na0731.pdf.

[19] Ryan Wilson, "State of Indian Education Address," Feb. 13, 2006, www.niea.org/history/SOIEAddress06.pdf.

[20] For background see, Barbara Mantel, "No Child Left Behind," *CQ Researcher*, May 27, 2005, pp. 469-492.

[21] McCain and Dorgan, *op. cit.*, pp. 14-15.

[22] According to the Health and Human Services Department's budget proposal, recommended funding of $2 billion for the health centers would allow them to serve 150,000 Indian patients, among a total of 8.8 million patients. For background, see "Budget in Brief, Fiscal Year 2007," Department of Health and Human Services, p. 26, www.hhs.gov/budget/07budget/2007BudgetInBrief.pdf.

[23] Peter Whoriskey, "A Tribe Takes a Grim Satisfaction in Abramoff's Fall," *The Washington Post*, Jan. 7, 2006, p. A1.

[24] Meister, *op. cit.*, p. 15.

[25] Whoriskey, *op. cit.*

[26] For background see Fred Carstensen, *et al.*, "The Economic Impact of the Mashantucket Pequot Tribal National Operations on Connecticut," Connecticut Center for Economic Analysis, University of Connecticut, Nov. 28, 2000, pp. 1-3.

[27] "Gambling Revenues 2004-2000," National Indian Gaming Commission, www.nigc.gov/TribalData/GamingRevenues20042000/tabid/549/Default.aspx.

[28] Schmidt and Grimaldi, *op. cit.*

[29] Alaina Potrikus, "2nd Land Hearing Packed," *The Post-Standard* (Syracuse, N.Y.), Jan. 12, 2006, p. B1.

[30] For background see "Profile of the Navajo Nation," Navajo Nation Council, www.navajonationcouncil.org/profile.

[31] Leslie Linthicum, "Navajos Cautious About Opening Casinos," *Albuquerque Journal*, Dec. 12, 2004, p. B1.

[32] For background, see "Fourth Annual State of Indian Nations," Feb. 2, 2006, www.ncai.org/News_Archive.18.0.

[33] For background see Theodore H. Haas, *The Indian and the Law* (1949), p. 2;

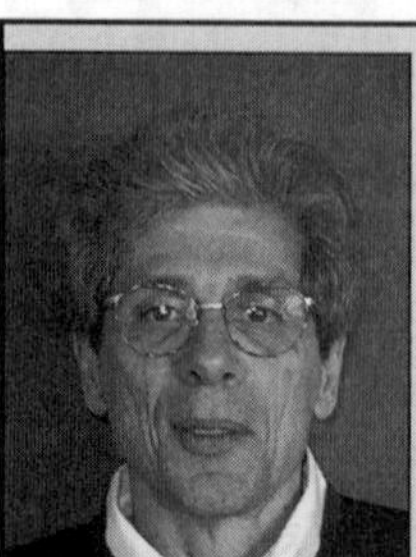

About the Author

Peter Katel is a *CQ Researcher* staff writer who previously reported on Haiti and Latin America for *Time* and *Newsweek* and covered the Southwest for newspapers in New Mexico. He has received several journalism awards, including the Bartolomé Mitre Award for drug coverage from the Inter-American Press Association. He holds an A.B. in university studies from the University of New Mexico. His recent reports include "Immigration Reform" and "Rebuilding New Orleans."

thorpe.ou.edu/cohen/tribalgovtpam2pt1&2.htm#Tribal%20Power%20Today.

[34] Except where otherwise noted, material in this section is drawn from Angie Debo, *A History of the Indians of the United States* (1970); see also, Mary H. Cooper, "Native Americans' Future," *CQ Researcher*, July 12, 1996, pp. 603-621.

[35] W. Dale Mason, "Indian Gaming: Tribal Sovereignty and American Politics," 2000, p. 13.

[36] *Cherokee Nation v. Georgia, op. cit.*, 30 U.S.1, http://supct.law.cornell.edu/supct/html/historics/USSC_CR_0030_0001_ZO.html.

[37] Robert A. Williams Jr., *Like a Loaded Weapon: the Rehnquist Court, Indians Rights, and the Legal History of Racism in America* (2005), p. 63.

[38] *Johnson v. M'Intosh*, 21 U.S. 543 (1823), www.Justia.us/us21543/case.html; *Worcester v. State of Ga.*, 31 U.S. 515 (1832), www.justia.us/us/31/515/case.html.

[39] *Johnson v. M'Intosh, op. cit.*

[40] *Worcester v. State of Ga., op. cit.*

[41] Quoted in Debo, *op. cit.*, pp. 219-220.

[42] Quoted in *ibid.*, p. 303.

[43] The specified states were Wisconsin, Minnesota (except Red Lake), Nebraska, California and Oregon (except the land of several tribes at Warm Springs). For background, see Debo, *op. cit.*, pp. 304-311.

[44] Cited in Debo, *op. cit.*, p. 344.

[45] For background see Troy R. Johnson, *The Occupation of Alcatraz Island: Indian Self-Determination and the Rise of Indian Activism* (1996).

[46] For background, see Mary H. Cooper, "Native Americans' Future," *CQ Researcher*, July 12, 1996, pp. 603-621.

[47] For background see "History of the Tribal Self-Governance Initiative," Self-Governance Tribal Consortium, www.tribalselfgov.org/Red%20Book/SG_New_Partnership.asp.

[48] Cochran, *op. cit.*

[49] For background see Paul Shukovsky, "Lummi Leader's Had It With Drugs, Sick of Substance Abuse Ravaging the Tribe," *Seattle Post-Intelligencer*, March 16, 2002, p. A1.

[50] "Fourth Annual State of Indian Nations," *op. cit.*

[51] Many Alaskan villages have joined collective compacts, so the total number of these agreements is 91.

[52] For background see Alexandra J. McClanahan, "Alaska Native Claims Settlement Act (ANCSA)," Cook Inlet Region Inc., http://litsite.alaska.edu/aktraditions/ancsa.html; "The Permanent Fund Dividend," Alaska Permanent Fund Corporation, 2005, www.apfc.org/alaska/dividendprgrm. cfm?s=4.

[53] For background see Eric Henson and Jonathan B. Taylor, "Native America at the New Millennium," Harvard Project on American Indian Development, Native Nations Institute, First Nations Development Institute, 2002, pp. 14-16, www.ksg.harvard.edu/hpaied/pubs/pub_004.htm.

[54] Michael Coleman, "Jemez Casino Proposal At Risk," *Albuquerque Journal*, March 10, 2006, p. A1; Jeff Jones, "AG Warns Against Off-Reservation Casino," *Albuquerque Journal*, June 18, 2005, p. A1.

[55] For background see testimony, "Off-Reservation Indian Gaming," House Resources Committee, Nov. 9, 2005, http://resourcescommittee.house.gov/archives/109/full/110905.htm.

[56] Jerry Reynolds, "Gaming regulatory act to lose its 'two-part test,' " *Indian Country Today*, March 8, 2006.

[57] Testimony before House Resources Committee, Nov. 9, 2005.

[58] Matt Kelley, "Government asks for secrecy on its lawyers' role in concealing document shredding," The Associated Press, Nov. 2, 2000.

[59] "Memorandum and Order," Civil Action No. 96-1285 (RCL), Feb. 7, 2005, www.indiantrust.com/index.cfm?FuseAction=PDFTypes.Home&PDFType_id=1&IsRecent=1.

[60] "Memorandum Opinion," Civil Action 96-1285 (RCL), July 12, 2005, www.indiantrust.com/index.cfm?FuseAction=PDFTypes.Home&PDFType_id=1&IsRecent=1.

[61] Glenn Coin, "Supreme Court: Oneidas Too Late; Sherrill Declares Victory, Wants Taxes," *The Post-Standard* (Syracuse), March 30, 2005, p. A1.

[62] *Ibid.*

[63] *City of Sherrill, New York, v. Oneida Indian Nation of New York*, Supreme Court of the United States, 544 U.S._(2005), pp. 1-2, 6, 14, 21.

[64] Elizabeth Shoemaker, *American Indian Population Recovery in the Twentieth Century* (1999), pp. 1-13.

FOR MORE INFORMATION

Committee on Indian Affairs, U.S. Senate, 838 Hart Office Building, Washington, DC 20510; (202) 224-2251; http://indian.senate.gov/public. A valuable source of information on developments affecting Indian Country.

Harvard Project on American Indian Economic Development, John F. Kennedy School of Government, 79 John F. Kennedy St., Cambridge, MA 02138; (617) 495-1480; www.ksg.harvard.edu/hpaied. Explores strategies for Indian advancement.

Indian Health Service, The Reyes Building, 801 Thompson Ave., Suite 400, Rockville, MD 20852; (301) 443-1083; www.ihs.gov. One of the most important federal agencies in Indian Country; provides a wide variety of medical and administrative information.

National Coalition Against Legalized Gambling, 100 Maryland Ave., N.E., Room 311, Washington, DC 20002; (800) 664-2680; www.ncalg.org. Provides anti-gambling material that touches on tribe-owned operations.

National Indian Education Association, 110 Maryland Ave., N.E., Suite 104, Washington, DC 20002; (202) 544-7290; www.niea.org/welcome. Primary organization and lobbying voice for Indian educators.

National Indian Gaming Association, 224 Second St., S.E., Washington, DC 20003; (202) 546-7711; www.indiangaming.org. Trade association and lobbying arm of the tribal casino industry.

Self-Governance Communication and Education Tribal Consortium, 1768 Iowa Business Center, Bellingham, WA 98229; (360) 752-2270; www.tribalselfgov.org. Organizational hub of Indian self-governance movement; provides a wide variety of news and data.

Upstate Citizens for Equality, P.O. Box 24, Union Springs, NY 13160; http://upstatecitizens.org. Opposes tribal land-claim litigation.

Bibliography

Selected Sources

Books

Alexie, Sherman, *The Toughest Indian in the World*, Grove Press, 2000.

In a short-story collection, an author and screenwriter draws on his own background as a Spokane/Coeur d'Alene Indian to describe reservation and urban Indian life in loving but unsentimental detail.

Debo, Angie, *A History of the Indians of the United States*, University of Oklahoma Press, 1970.

A pioneering historian and champion of Indian rights provides one of the leading narrative histories of the first five centuries of Indian and non-Indian coexistence and conflict.

Deloria, Vine Jr., *Custer Died For Your Sins: An Indian Manifesto*, University of Oklahoma Press, 1988.

First published in 1969, this angry book gave many non-Indians a look at how the United States appeared through Indians' eyes and spurred many young Native Americans into political activism.

Mason, W. Dale, *Indian Gaming: Tribal Sovereignty and American Politics*, University of Oklahoma Press, 2000.

A University of New Mexico political scientist provides the essential background on the birth and early explosive growth of Indian-owned gambling operations.

Williams, Robert A., *Like a Loaded Weapon: The Rehnquist Court, Indians Rights, and the Legal History of Racism in America*, University of Minnesota Press, 2005.

A professor of law and American Indian Studies at the University of Arizona and tribal appeals court judge delivers a detailed and angry analysis of the history of U.S. court decisions affecting Indians.

Articles

Bartlett, Donald L., and James B. Steele, "Playing the Political Slots; How Indian Casino Interests Have Learned the Art of Buying Influence in Washington," *Time*, Dec. 23, 2002, p. 52.

In a prescient article that preceded the Jack Abramoff lobbying scandal, veteran investigative journalists examine the political effects of some tribes' newfound wealth.

Harden, Blaine, "Walking the Land with Pride Again; A Revolution in Indian Country Spawns Wealth and Optimism," *The Washington Post*, Sept. 19, 2004, p. A1.

Improved conditions in many sectors of Indian America have spawned a change in outlook, despite remaining hardships.

Morgan, Lance, "Ending the Curse of Trust Land," *Indian Country Today*, March 18, 2005, www.indiancountry.com/content.cfm?id=1096410559.

A lawyer and pioneering tribal entrepreneur lays out his vision of a revamped legal-political system in which Indians would own their tribal land outright, with federal supervision ended.

Robbins, Ted, "Tribal cultures, nutrition clash on fry bread," "All Things Considered," National Public Radio, Oct. 26, 2005, transcript available at www.npr.org/templates/story/story.php?storyId=4975889.

Indian health educators have tried to lower Native Americans' consumption of a beloved but medically disastrous treat.

Thompson, Ginger, "As a Sculpture Takes Shape in New Mexico, Opposition Takes Shape in the U.S.," *The New York Times*, Jan. 17, 2002, p. A12.

Indian outrage has clashed with Latino pride over a statue celebrating the ruthless Spanish conqueror of present-day New Mexico.

Wagner, Dennis, "Tribes Across Country Confront Horrors of Meth," *The Arizona Republic*, March 31, 2006, p. A1.

Methamphetamine use and manufacturing have become the scourge of Indian Country.

Reports and Studies

"Indian Health Service: Health Care Services Are Not Always Available to Native Americans," Government Accountability Office, August 2005.

Congress' investigative arm concludes that financial shortfalls combined with dismal reservation conditions, including scarce transportation, are stunting medical care for many American Indians.

"Strengthening the Circle: Interior Indian Affairs Highlights, 2001-2004," Department of the Interior (undated).

The Bush administration sums up its first term's accomplishments in Indian Country.

Cornell, Stephen, *et al.*, "Seizing the Future: Why Some Native Nations Do and Others Don't," Native Nations Institute, Udall Center for Studies in Public Policy, University of Arizona, Harvard Project on American Indian Economic Development, John F. Kennedy School of Government, Harvard University, 2005.

The authors argue that the key to development lies in a tribe's redefinition of itself from object of government attention to independent power.

The Next Step:

Additional Articles from Current Periodicals

Drug Smuggling on Reservations

Kershaw, Sarah, "Through Indian Lands, Drugs' Shadowy Trail," *The New York Times*, Feb. 19, 2006, p. 1.
Law-enforcement officials say Indian reservations have become a critical link in the drug trade, as criminal organizations have found havens in the wide-open and isolated Indian lands.

Riley, Michael, "Porous Border Stokes a Crucible of Pain and Smuggling on Tribal Land," *The Denver Post*, June 6, 2004, p. A1.
The Tohono O'odham Nation reservation, west of Tucson, has become a major corridor for smuggling drugs from Mexico, providing easy, fast money to residents who have nothing.

Indian Education

Dell'Angela, Tracy, "Dakota Indians Say Kids Trapped in 'School-to-Prison' Pipeline," *Chicago Tribune*, Nov. 29, 2005, p. C1.
Indian students in South Dakota's Winner School District are punished at disproportionate rates and are leaving the district in large numbers, causing many civil-rights activists to declare the district is racist in disciplining tribal children.

Mapes, Lynda V., "Indian Elders Help Write Lessons That Reflect Culture, Spur Reading," *Chicago Tribune*, Jan. 6, 2005, p. 10.
Administrators and teachers at Chinook Elementary School in Auburn, Wash., have used a supplemental curriculum based on content recommended by Indian elders to improve children's reading scores.

Silverman, Julia, "Indian Teachers Sought," *The Philadelphia Inquirer*, April 2, 2003, p. A8.
Universities across the West are starting to recruit and train American Indian teachers and place them at schools with large native populations, hoping to lower the high dropout rates and raise test scores.

Walker, Cheryl, "Charter School Helps Indian Students Succeed," *The San Diego Union-Tribune*, July 23, 2005, p. NI6.
Michelle Parada and Mary Ann Donohue founded the All Tribe American Indian Charter School to foster an environment for Indians to gain self-confidence and graduate from high school.

Methamphetamine

McKosato, Harlan, "Reservations Are Targets of Meth, More," *The Santa Fe New Mexican*, Feb. 19, 2006, p. F1.
The former host of the nationwide radio show, "Native America Calling," compares methamphetamine use on reservations to crack cocaine use in the inner city.

Murr, Andrew, "A New Menace on the Rez," *Newsweek*, Sept. 27, 2004, p. 30.
Meth is becoming the drug of choice on Indian reservations because drug networks believe there are fewer police.

Riley, Michael, "A Mexican Drug Gang Infiltrates an Alcoholism-Riddled Wyoming Indian Reservation to Sell a New Addiction," *The Denver Post*, Nov. 6, 2005, p. A1.
The Sinaloan Cowboys came to the Wind River Reservation in Wyoming four years ago and have shifted many tribal members' alcohol addiction to meth.

Tribal Sovereignty

Greenhouse, Linda, "Court Upholds Tribal Power It Once Denied," *The New York Times*, April 20, 2004, p. A12.
The Supreme Court ruled that tribes now have the authority to prosecute members of other tribes for crimes committed on their reservations.

Hecox, Walter, and Rebecca Schild, "Western Tribes Recapturing Control Over Their Lives," *The Denver Post*, June 19, 2005, p. E1.
Indian individuals and tribes are increasingly exercising their sovereign authority in areas of culture and language, social and political conditions and the environment, according to the Colorado College State of the Rockies Project.

The Associated Press, "Gregoire, 2 Tribes Reach Agreement on Tax Collection," *The Seattle Times*, Jan. 27, 2006, p. B5.
Gov. Christine Gregoire, D-Wash., and two tribes agreed that the state will continue to collect gas taxes on the tribes' reservations despite a recent District Court ruling that it would infringe on their tribal sovereignty.

CITING THE *CQ RESEARCHER*

Sample formats for citing these reports in a bibliography include the ones listed below. Preferred styles and formats vary, so please check with your instructor or professor.

MLA STYLE

Jost, Kenneth. "Rethinking the Death Penalty." CQ Researcher 16 Nov. 2001: 945-68.

APA STYLE

Jost, K. (2001, November 16). Rethinking the death penalty. *CQ Researcher, 11*, 945-968.

CHICAGO STYLE

Jost, Kenneth. "Rethinking the Death Penalty." *CQ Researcher*, November 16, 2001, 945-968.

CQ Researcher

Published by CQ Press, a division of Congressional Quarterly Inc.

cqresearcher.com

Transgender Issues

Should gender-identity discrimination be illegal?

People who do not identify with their biological sex are a small proportion of the population, but the issues they pose for law, medicine and society are significant. Trans people say they experience widespread discrimination in employment, housing and other areas. Eight states and more than 80 local governments have passed laws prohibiting discrimination based on gender identity, and transgender advocacy groups want Congress to follow suit. Many government and private employers already have "trans-inclusive" non-discrimination policies and help transgender workers fit in comfortably with colleagues and customers. Meanwhile, transgender advocates are urging health-insurance companies to cover the cost of sex-change procedures and calling on psychiatrists to delete or change the designation of "gender identity disorder" as a mental illness. But social conservatives oppose laws to bar gender discrimination and say transgender people are mentally ill and need therapy to help them accept their biological sex.

Diane Schroer — formerly Army Special Forces Lt. Col. Dave Schroer — is suing the Library of Congress for sex discrimination.

INSIDE THIS REPORT

CQ Researcher • May 5, 2006 • www.cqresearcher.com
Volume 16, Number 17 • Pages 385-408

CQ PRESS

RECIPIENT OF SOCIETY OF PROFESSIONAL JOURNALISTS AWARD FOR EXCELLENCE ◆ AMERICAN BAR ASSOCIATION SILVER GAVEL AWARD

THE ISSUES

BACKGROUND

CURRENT SITUATION

OUTLOOK

SIDEBARS AND GRAPHICS

FOR FURTHER RESEARCH

Cover: Diane Schroer — formerly Army Special Forces Lt. Col. Dave Schroer — is suing the Library of Congress for sex discrimination. (Diane Schroer)

CQ Researcher

May 5, 2006
Volume 16, Number 17

MANAGING EDITOR: Thomas J. Colin

ASSISTANT MANAGING EDITOR: Kathy Koch

ASSOCIATE EDITOR: Kenneth Jost

STAFF WRITERS: Marcia Clemmitt, Peter Katel, Pamela M. Prah

CONTRIBUTING WRITERS: Rachel S. Cox, Sarah Glazer, David Hosansky, Patrick Marshall, Tom Price

DESIGN/PRODUCTION EDITOR: Olu B. Davis

ASSISTANT EDITOR: Melissa J. Hipolit

CQ PRESS

A Division of Congressional Quarterly Inc.

SENIOR VICE PRESIDENT/PUBLISHER: John A. Jenkins

DIRECTOR, LIBRARY PUBLISHING: Kathryn C. Suárez

DIRECTOR, EDITORIAL OPERATIONS: Ann Davies

CONGRESSIONAL QUARTERLY INC.

CHAIRMAN: Paul C. Tash

VICE CHAIRMAN: Andrew P. Corty

PRESIDENT/EDITOR IN CHIEF: Robert W. Merry

CQ Researcher (ISSN 1056-2036) is printed on acid-free paper. Published weekly, except March 24, July 7, July 14, Aug. 4, Aug. 11, Nov. 24, Dec. 22 and Dec. 29, by CQ Press, a division of Congressional Quarterly Inc. Annual full-service subscriptions for institutions start at $667. For pricing, call 1-800-834-9020, ext. 1906. To purchase a *CQ Researcher* report in print or electronic format (PDF), visit www.cqpress.com or call 866-427-7737. Single reports start at $10. Bulk purchase discounts and electronic-rights licensing are also available. Periodicals postage paid at Washington, D.C., and additional mailing offices. POSTMASTER: Send address changes to *CQ Researcher*, 1255 22nd St., N.W., Suite 400, Washington, DC 20037.

Transgender Issues

BY KENNETH JOST

THE ISSUES

The Library of Congress appeared to have found an ideal candidate in fall 2004 for a position as terrorism research analyst with the Congressional Research Service (CRS).

Dave Schroer, a recently retired Army Special Forces officer, had experience in anti-terrorism work and had seen combat in Panama, Haiti and Rwanda. Schroer also held master's degrees in history and international relations and had helped brief top officials in Washington, including Vice President Dick Cheney.

After a salary offer had been extended and accepted, Schroer invited CRS Assistant Director Charlotte Preece to lunch. Then, over Chinese food at a Capitol Hill restaurant, Schroer dropped a bombshell. After gently asking Preece how much she knew about transsexuals, Schroer drew a deep breath: "I want to start work as Diane," she said. (*See glossary, p. 389.*)

Lt. Col. Dave Schroer, here on duty in Haiti in 1994, is now Diane Schroer (see cover photo) after undergoing hormone treatments and some sex-change procedures. She is suing the Library of Congress for sex discrimination, contending it withdrew a job offer after learning she was planning to report to work as a female. Transgender people say they experience widespread discrimination in the workplace and elsewhere.

For Diane Schroer, the coming-out represented the culmination of a lifelong struggle with feeling to be a woman, not a man. It also came amid a four-year transition that included a difficult divorce and equally difficult and expensive medical procedures.

For CRS, Schroer's transition also proved difficult — in fact, disqualifying. According to Schroer, Preece called the next day to rescind the job offer. For its part, the library denies that a final job offer was made and claims that Schroer "failed to satisfy the position's national-security requirements." Preece declines to comment.

Stunned, disappointed and ultimately angry, Schroer contested the decision through the library's internal procedures. When that failed, she turned to the American Civil Liberties Union (ACLU), which contended in a federal suit that refusing to hire her was illegal sex discrimination under Title VII of the Civil Rights Act of 1964. [1]

Schroer's lawyers face an uphill challenge. Title VII traditionally has protected against discrimination based on a person's biological sex, but not on the basis of gender identity. The Library of Congress relies on that view in claiming that it acted "appropriately" in Schroer's case. But times may be changing.

A slowly growing number of states and municipalities have enacted laws that protect transgender people from discrimination based on gender identity or expression. (*See map, p. 388.*) Some courts are also rethinking the issue. In fact, U.S. District Judge J. Willard Robertson gave Schroer a preliminary victory on March 31, 2006, by rejecting the government's effort to dismiss the suit.

"We're in an early stage of what I hope will be the ultimate legal recognition that discrimination against transgender people is sex discrimination under federal law," says Sharon McGowan, an attorney with the ACLU's Lesbian, Gay, Bisexual and Transgender (LGBT) Rights Project.

Equally, if not more important, transsexuals are increasingly visible in day-to-day life. Transmen and transwomen — people who have "transitioned" from female to male (FTM) or male to female (MTF) — are "coming out" in increasing numbers to their families, friends, neighbors and co-workers. Accounts and depictions in news stories and in popular culture, such as the widely acclaimed 2005 film "Transamerica," are beginning to overcome ignorance — and the visceral discomfort many people feel — about transsexuals.

The number of transsexuals in the United States is uncertain and subject to dispute. The American Psychiatric Association (APA) estimates that 1-in-30,000 men and 1-in-100,000 women undergo sex-change surgery at some

Transgender Discrimination Banned in 89 Places

Minneapolis passed the first transgender anti-discrimination law in 1975. Today 89 states, cities and counties have similar laws banning gender-identity discrimination in employment, housing or the use of public accommodations. The laws cover 31 percent of the nation's population, or 86 million people.

Jurisdictions Banning Gender-Identity Discrimination

States / Counties / Selected cities

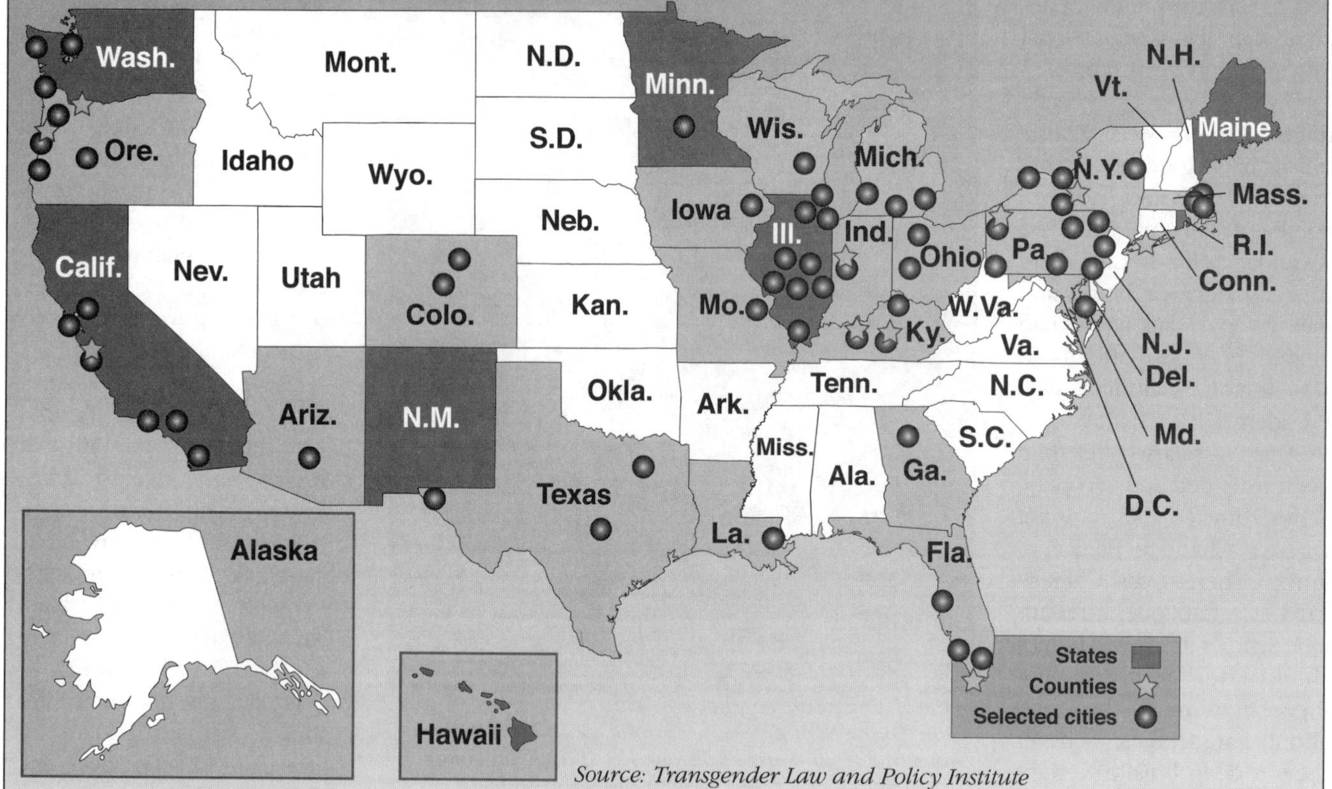

Source: Transgender Law and Policy Institute

point in their lives, but transgender advocates regard the decades-old estimate as conservative.

Using more recent data on the number of surgeries in the United States, Lynn Conway, a transgender professor emerita of electrical engineering and computer science at the University of Michigan in Ann Arbor, calculates the number of post-operative MTF transsexuals at 40,000 and hypothesizes three to five times that number of pre-op MTFs. The number of FTM transsexuals is widely thought to be lower, but no one really knows. [2]

Whatever their exact number, transsexuals do not produce the same degree of public astonishment that ex-G.I. George Jorgensen did when he returned to the United States in 1953 as Christine, after a sex-change operation in Denmark. "It's just not as shocking to people any more," says Mara Keisling, executive director of the National Center for Transgender Equality in Washington, D.C. "As more and more people are coming out, people are understanding that we are worthy of having jobs. And as more and more diversity-trained children are growing up, they're understanding that everybody is just people."

Still, Keisling and other transgender advocates, including broad gay-rights organizations such as Human Rights Campaign and the National Gay and Lesbian Task Force, emphasize that life still can be pretty tough for transgender people. Without an anti-discrimination law, transgender people may have no recourse when — as often happens — they are rejected for a job, refused an apartment or denied service because of their gender identity.

Transgender people may face disapproval — or even arrest — for using a public restroom that corresponds to their gender identity but not their biological sex. (*See sidebar, p. 392.*) And — even more than gay men or lesbians — transgender people appear to be disproportionately the victims of hate crimes. [3]

Sex and Gender: A Primer

Sex and **gender** are often used interchangeably, but the terms have different meanings. Biological or genetic sex is determined at birth, typically by the physical appearance of the genitalia.

Gender refers to an individual's outward appearance and behavior and, more importantly, self-identification as male or female. For most people, sex and gender correspond.

Transgender is the umbrella term coined in the 1970s to refer to people who do not identify with the sex designated at birth. The term encompasses transsexuals, cross-dressers and (in some usages) intersexed persons.

A **transsexual** — an older term — is someone who changes his or her original sex through medical procedures. A **transwoman**, or MTF, changes from male to female; a **transman**, or FTM, from female to male.

Hormone-replacement therapy is the use of testosterone or other male hormone for FTMs or estrogen for MTFs to produce some of the secondary sex characteristics of the gender the person is transitioning into, such as facial hair for FTMs or breast enlargement for MTFs. Some secondary sex characteristics — notably, voice modulation for MTFs — are changed only through instruction and practice.

Sex-reassignment surgery entails a mastectomy (removal of the breasts) for FTMs ("top surgery") and may entail genital reconstruction for either MTFs or FTMs ("bottom surgery"). For MTFs, complete reassignment surgery includes removal of the testes (castration) and penis (penectomy) and creation of a vagina and labia (vaginoplasty). For FTMs, the surgery includes creation of a penis by using the clitoris and its surrounding tissue (metoidioplasty) or tissue from other parts of the body (phalloplasty). Many, perhaps most, transsexuals do not undergo genital surgery; in particular, the results of a phalloplasty are not completely satisfactory, although surgical techniques are said to be improving.

Sexual orientation refers to an individual's physical or affectional attraction to individuals of the same sex, opposite sex or both. Transgender people have varying sexual orientations: Some are attracted to persons of the opposite gender ("straight"), some to persons of the same gender ("gay" or "lesbian"), and some to both ("bisexual").

A **cross-dresser** likes to wear clothes associated with the opposite gender but does not want to change his or her physical sex. (The older term "transvestite" is now widely viewed as pejorative.) Most male cross-dressers prefer female sex partners.

Intersex refers to someone born with ambiguous genitalia, an abnormally small penis or abnormally large clitoris or other atypical reproductive or sexual anatomy. Experts estimate that 1 percent of the population is born with this condition. (The older term, "hermaphrodite," is now viewed as pejorative.) Chromosome testing may be needed to designate their sex (XX chromosome for females, XY for males). Genital surgery may be used to attempt to create genitalia corresponding to the designated sex. The common practice of performing this surgery with the parents' consent soon after birth or in infancy is now viewed with disfavor by some intersexed persons.

In one high-profile case, Gwen Araujo, a "trans" California teenager, was beaten and strangled in 2002 after a sexual encounter with two men. Evidence at trial showed the men had become angry after learning Araujo's biological sex, but jurors rejected prosecutors' efforts to punish the offense as a hate crime motivated by Araujo's gender identity. (*See sidebar, p. 396.*)

Conservative advocacy groups voice strong disapproval of transgenderism. "A man with a man's DNA, Adam's apple, male physique and male brain construction who believes with all his heart he's a woman is someone who's seriously confused, not someone who's trapped in the wrong body," says Robert Knight, director of the Culture and Family Institute, an affiliate of the conservative Concerned Women for America. "It's misplaced compassion to aid and abet someone's abnormal fantasy and to perpetuate their misery."

Many psychiatrists agree. "We psychiatrists should work to discourage those adults who seek surgical sex reassignment," writes Paul McHugh, a professor emeritus at Johns Hopkins University School of Medicine in Baltimore, who made the controversial decision to close the school's gender identity clinic in 1979 after 13 years in operation. "We have wasted scientific and technical resources and damaged our professional credibility by collaborating with madness rather than trying to study, cure and ultimately prevent it." [4]

"Our view is that generally a person's sex is fixed at birth. It should not be changed," says Peter Sprigg, vice president for policy of the Family Research Council (FRC). The self-identified Christian pro-family group opposes laws to prohibit discrimination based on sexual orientation. Sprigg says he similarly opposes "any sort of protections from discrimination based on self-proclaimed gender identity."

Transgender protections are, in fact, a somewhat recent add-on to the push for gay rights laws. [5] The gay and lesbian rights organizations that emerged in the 1970s had, at best, ambivalent views toward transgender people. Cross-dressers and drag queens hindered efforts to win social acceptance, while people who underwent full-scale sex reassignment — like the professional tennis player Renee Richards — engendered more curiosity and discomfort than understanding or approval.

As the push for gay rights laws gained steam in the 1980s and '90s, conventional wisdom had it that transgender protections would complicate and possibly derail the campaigns. Today, however, established gay rights organizations say transgender protections must be included in non-discrimination legislation. "We as a GLBT [gay, lesbian, bisexual and transgender] community have decided that we want the entire community protected," says Christopher Labonte, legislative director of Human Rights Campaign.

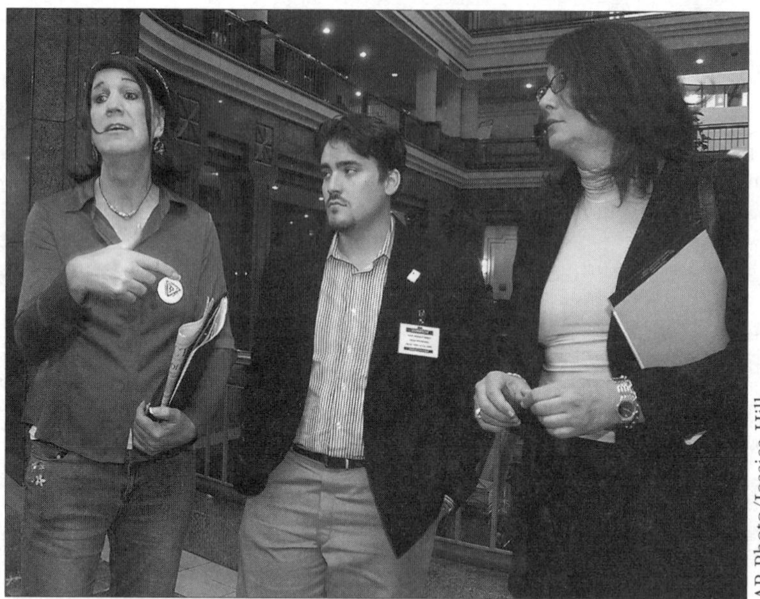
AP Photo/Jessica Hill

Transsexuals (from left) Jerimarie Liesegang, Adam Nichols and Rachel Goldberg wait to testify on March 24 in Hartford, Conn., in favor of a bill prohibiting discrimination against transgendered people. Eight states and 81 municipalities have banned discrimination against transsexuals in employment, housing or public accommodations.

Apart from the legal issues somewhat common to their gay, lesbian and bisexual allies, transsexuals face two health-related issues distinctive to them. Gender identity disorder (GID) is officially listed as a mental illness in the DSM. Transgender advocates say the diagnosis stigmatizes transgender people and generally favor deleting or significantly revising it. (*See "At Issue," p. 401.*)

At the same time, the vast majority of health-insurance plans do not cover the substantial costs of sex-reassignment procedures, which include ongoing hormone replacement therapy (testosterone for transmen, estrogen for transwomen) and genital surgery, which is performed in some but not all cases. Transgender advocates dispute the argument sometimes offered that sex-change procedures amount to "elective" cosmetic surgery.

As transgender advocates press their case, here are some of the major arguments being made:

Should "gender identity disorder" continue to be classified as a mental illness?

Back in the 1970s, psychiatrist Paul Fink played an influential role in getting the American Psychiatric Association to remove homosexuality from the *DSM.* The decision followed a two-decade campaign by homosexual groups, who argued that classifying homosexuality as a mental illness was clinically inaccurate and unfairly stigmatizing to gay men and lesbians.

Some transgender activists are making similar arguments today in an effort to remove "gender identity disorder" (GID) from the upcoming *DSM-V,* the revision due out in 2011. But Fink, a professor at Temple University's School of Medicine in Philadelphia who says he has treated more than 40 transsexuals in his practice, disagrees.

"Transsexualism is a diagnosis," Fink says, and psychiatrists have a vital role to play in acting as "ombudsman" during a patient's transition. As for the stigma, "I do not believe that the diagnosis stigmatizes anyone worse than the stigma that the transsexuals receive every single day."

The current *DSM-IV* calls for a diagnosis of GID only with evidence of "a strong or persistent cross-gender identification" and "persistent discomfort about one's assigned sex or a sense of inappropriateness in the gender role of that sex." Adults with GID are described as "preoccupied with their wish to live as a member of the other sex." Among children, boys with GID are described as preoccupied with "traditionally feminine activities," while girls are said to display "intense negative reactions" toward feminine attire or appearance.

The manual lists a separate diagnosis for "transvestic fetishism," defined as cross-dressing among heterosexual or bisexual men typically "for the purpose of sexual excitement." [6]

As with the previous classification of homosexuality as mental illness, transgender advocates say listing GID in the *DSM* gives a misleading picture of transgender people and their lives. After transitioning, transgender people can lead normal, productive, healthy lives, the advocates argue.

Many transgender people do have mental health problems, such as depression or substance abuse, Keisling acknowledges. But, she adds, "Most of those are related to gender identity only because of how we're treated, not because of gender identity itself."

In any event, Keisling says the GID diagnosis is misleading because it suggests the possibility of a "cure" through psychotherapy, medication or both. "Nobody has found a way to do talk therapy or use a drug to talk someone out of that," she says.

Dan Karasic, a clinical professor of psychiatry at the University of California in San Francisco and current president of the Association of Gay and Lesbian Psychiatrists, agrees. "There isn't really evidence of effective psychotherapy that in any demonstrable way makes people who have a transgender identity happy not expressing that," he says.

Some transgender advocates, however, call for revising the depiction of GID in the *DSM* rather than simply deleting it. They agree that the current diagnosis is stigmatizing but argue that, as a practical matter, a clinical definition is needed to access the medical procedures for sex reassignment.

"Difference is not disease," activist and author Kelley Winters writes on her Web site, www.gidreform.org. "It is time for culturally competent psychiatric policies that recognize the legitimacy of cross-gender identity and yet distinguish gender dysphoria [distress] as a serious condition, treatable with medical procedures." [7]

The head of an American Psychological Association task force on transgender issues acknowledges mixed feelings on the issue. "There's a very practical reason for it staying there, but there are many reasons for wanting it removed," says Margaret Schneider, who heads a program in psychological counseling at the University of Toronto. The task force, due to complete a report by September 2006, will not deal directly with the diagnosis issue, she notes.

For their part, anti-gay organizations view transgenderism undeniably as mental illness and oppose hormonal therapy or surgery to enable gender switching. "I would certainly consider it a psychiatric disorder," says the Family Research Council's Sprigg. Assisting patients to change from one gender to another "basically amounts to collaborating in a mental illness rather than treating it," he says.

"The good news is that no one is born homosexual or transsexual," the pro-family Traditional Values Coalition says on its Web site. "These are mental conditions that can be treated through religious-based or psychological therapies." [8]

While defending the current GID diagnosis, psychiatrists Fink and Spitzer both appear to stop short of claiming any ability to "cure" patients of the desire to change genders. "When they begin to act, dress and appear like their chosen sex, they are much more at home, much more comfortable, much more convincing of that gender," Fink says. As for sex-reassignment surgery, "I'm not against it," Spitzer says. "If it helps — and apparently it does help — that's fine, let them do it."

With the long lead-time in revising the *DSM*, any resolution of the debate is several years away. Many APA members will resist any change. "Conceptually, it's a mental disorder," says Robert Spitzer, a professor at the New York State Psychiatric Institute in New York City. Prejudice against transgender persons "is a separate issue," he says.

But Keisling and other transgender advocates insist some reform is needed. "The way it is in there doesn't make any sense," she says. "It doesn't make any sense clinically, theoretically or morally."

Should gender-identity discrimination be illegal?

Krystal Etsitty was born a male but was already transitioning to female when the Utah Transit Authority hired her as a bus driver in 2001. She had legally changed her name, was taking estrogen and was trying to save up the money for sex reassignment surgery.

Shortly after she was hired, Etsitty told her supervisor that she was a transsexual. The supervisor was supportive, but other managers were not. Etsitty claims in a federal sex-discrimination suit that the transit authority fired her in February 2002 after the operations manager and a human resources official raised concerns about potential liability from Etsitty's using women's restrooms at public facilities along her bus routes.

Etsitty sees no problems with using the restroom that corresponds to her gender identity. "Who goes inside a stall but just yourself?" Etsitty is quoted as saying. But U.S. District Court Judge David Sam rejected her suit, saying the company had legitimate reasons for firing her. "Concerns about privacy, safety and propriety are the reason that gender-specific restrooms are universally accepted in our society," Sam wrote in the June 2005 ruling. [9]

Restroom use is emblematic of the barriers transgender people must overcome to gain acceptance among employers, co-workers or customers in the workplace. An unscientific survey by the San Francisco-based Transgender Law Center in February and March 2006 found that more than half of the transgender people responding — 57 percent — claimed to have experienced discrimination in the workplace. Only 25 percent of respondents were employed full time. [10]

"We get calls virtually every day from somebody who has been fired from his or her job," Keisling says. "And generally when transgender people get fired, they don't just lose their jobs. They lose their careers."

Transgender advocates say prohibiting discrimination against transsexuals should be no more controversial than protecting other minorities. "It is a basic American value that we should be judged on the basis of the work we do and not on our personal characteristics," says Lisa Mottet, a transgender-rights lawyer with the Task Force (formerly, the National Lesbian and Gay Task Force).

Social conservatives disagree. "The decision to present yourself as something other than your biological sex is a choice," says Sprigg. "It's something where an employer should be free to make a decision whether that's appropriate or not."

Which Restrooms Should Transgenders Use?

Helena Stone says it's "wonderful" to use the women's restroom where she works. But the 71-year-old transgender telephone repair worker had to go to court to earn that right after being arrested by a New York City subway policeman who insisted she use the men's room.

Stone's run-in with the Metropolitan Transportation Authority (MTA) illustrates, in unusually dramatic fashion, the problems encountered by transgender people over the mundane but unavoidable need to use restrooms at work or school or in a public facility.

Transgender people feel most comfortable and secure using restrooms that correspond to their transitioned gender. "If we're going to have gender-segregated bathrooms, it should be based on the gender that a person is expressing," says Christopher Daley, director of the Transgender Law Center in San Francisco. [1]

Transitioning women face a specific danger of harassment or worse if forced to use a men's restroom, Daley adds. "It's not only insulting to her but would put her at great risk," he says.

Still, the non-trans world sometimes reacts with surprise or discomfort when a masculine-appearing transwoman goes into the ladies' room or, less frequently, when a feminine-appearing transman goes into the men's room. As a solution to the problem, transgender advocates are calling for gender-neutral, single-user restrooms in public facilities. [2]

While bathroom stalls can provide privacy, locker rooms at schools, workplaces or health clubs pose a more difficult issue. But transgender advocates note that locker rooms can be equipped with curtained showers and dressing areas for privacy.

Stone, a longtime Verizon employee who transitioned a decade ago, caught the attention of an MTA police officer after she was assigned to do repair work at Grand Central Terminal in 2005. According to Stone and her lawyer, Michael Silverman of the Transgender Legal Defense and Education Fund, the officer arrested her in September on disorderly conduct charges for no apparent reason and then a few months later.

On the second occasion, the officer came to Stone's office, used derogatory terms and threatened to arrest her if he ever saw her coming out of the women's restroom. The officer followed through with the threat on Jan. 12, taking her to jail in handcuffs and charging her with two counts of disorderly conduct.

The MTA ultimately agreed to dismiss all the charges against Stone and adopted a policy confirming the right to use a restroom corresponding to one's gender. "Anyone can use any bathroom they want if they view themselves as that particular sex," says MTA spokesman Tim O'Brien. Police have been instructed on the policy, he adds.

Silverman acknowledges that non-transgender people have "real concerns" about the restroom issue. "I don't think they're making up their discomfort," he says. "None of these are the simplest issues."

For her part, Stone is happy that she can go to the restroom of her choice. "It feels wonderful," she says. "That's who I am. That's where I belong."

[1] For a detailed backgrounder from an advocacy viewpoint, see Transgender Law Center, "Peeing in Peace: A Resource Guide for Transgender Activists and Allies," 2005. Daley is not transgender.

[2] See Patricia Leigh Brown, "A Quest for a Restroom That's Neither Men's Room Nor Women's Room," *The New York Times*, March 4, 2005, p. A14.

"These laws are aimed at criminalizing opposition to gender confusion," says Knight. "Civil rights laws are enforced against someone. In this case they would be enforced against anyone who thought it odd that a man came to work one day in a dress."

Despite those arguments, a slowly growing number of employers are voluntarily adopting policies to prohibit discrimination on the basis of gender identity or expression, including 82 companies among the *Fortune* 500, according to a tally by Human Rights Campaign. [11] Ann Reesman, general counsel of the Equal Employment Advisory Council, a Washington-based employers association, says most companies today would not refuse to hire a qualified transsexual applicant "unless there's a job-related reason for it."

Citing the Utah case, however, Reesman says co-worker discomfort over the restroom issue is a legitimate concern for employers. "Unless the bathroom problem is solved, there's a big problem," she says. But she acknowledges that single-user unisex bathrooms — an alternative suggested by transgender advocates — can resolve the issue.

For her part, Keisling contends that employers are wrong in practical terms to be reluctant to hire a transgender applicant. "The traits that allow a person to succeed in transition are also the traits that you want in an employee: courage, focus and integrity," she says.

Life for transgender people is often "fragile" not only in the workplace but also in other areas, Keisling says. Landlords may refuse to rent to transsexuals or evict after learning a tenant is transgender. In child-custody disputes, transgender parents may not simply be limited on visitation but may be barred altogether from seeing their children.

Transgender advocates are pushing bills to prohibit discrimination against transsexuals at the same time that lawyers are arguing — as in Schroer's case — that discrimination is already illegal under federal civil rights law. "When someone is transgender, that discrimination is motivated by the person's sex or by stereotypes," says Christopher Daley, director of the

Transgender Law Center. "Either way, we should find that people should be protected."

Meanwhile, transgender advocates say they are advancing on the legislative front. With laws on the books in eight states and 81 local governments, nearly one-third of the nation's population — about 86 million people — live in jurisdictions where discrimination against transsexuals is illegal, according to a tally by the Transgender Law and Policy Institute.

"It's still a relatively new kind of legislation," says Paisley Currah, a founder of the institute and an associate professor of political science at Brooklyn College, City University of New York. "A lot of progress has been made."

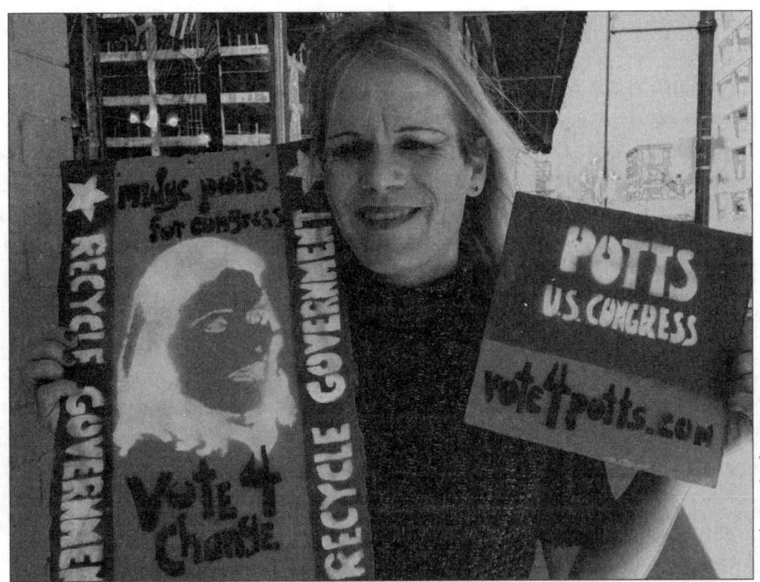

AP Photo/John S. Stewart

Transgender political candidate Midge Potts is running to unseat Rep. Roy Blunt, R-Mo. Potts calls herself a fiscally conservative Republican.

Should health insurance or taxpayers cover the cost of sex-change procedures?

Late in 2001 — almost eight years after his 1994 transition — Marcus Arana developed an abscess at the site of his testosterone injections. Arana, a discrimination investigator with the San Francisco Human Rights Commission, was hospitalized for 13 days and out of work for six months. His medical bills totaled nearly $100,000.

The vast majority of transgender people have to pay medical bills like those on their own — not only for the immediate costs of sex-change procedures but also for hormone therapy and other ongoing treatments. But Arana was fortunate — the city of San Francisco had decided in early 2001 to include transgender health benefits in its employee health plans.

Some critics on the city's Board of Supervisors questioned providing coverage for what they depicted as cosmetic surgery. But transgender advocates and their allies called the policy change a simple question of fairness. "This is very much a civil rights issue," said board member Mark Leno, the principal supporter of the move. "This is about equal benefits for equal work." [12]

The main stumbling block to the change, however, was the practical concern about the potential cost, according to Arana, who was instrumental in adoption of the policy and continues to be involved in its implementation. He recalls that city officials and the administrators of the city's self-insured health plan feared that the cost would swell as transgender people from across the country sought out employment with the city to take advantage of the new benefit. To control costs, benefits were capped at $50,000, and coverage was provided only after a year's employment.

Sex-change procedures, in fact, are costly. Male-to-female surgery can cost as much as $50,000; female-to-male surgery can cost $75,000 or more. Testosterone therapy for transmen can cost around $500 a year, estrogen therapy for transwomen somewhat more.

With limited actuarial information, San Francisco health plan administrators projected that 35 people would access the benefit during the first year at an average cost of $50,000 — for a total cost of more than $1.75 million. To cover the expected cost, the plan increased the required employee contributions by $1.70 per month, about $20 per year.

The estimates have proved wildly exaggerated, Arana says. Over the next three years, the health plan collected $4.6 million to cover the benefit and paid out only $156,000 on seven claims for surgery. Based on that experience, the $50,000 cap on benefits has been raised to $75,000 and the one-year exclusion eliminated. In addition, the three health-maintenance organizations (HMOs) that offer coverage to city employees are also now offering similar benefits.

Nationally, transgender health benefits should be provided as a matter of equity, Keisling of the National Center for Transgender Equality believes. "It's indisputably a medical condition," she says. But coverage would have only limited effect, she says, because most transgender people lack health insurance altogether. "It would really, really help people who have insurance, but most transgender people don't."

Coverage for transgender health costs under Medicaid — the federal-state program for indigent health care — could help more people, but the use of public funds for sex-change operations or hormone therapy invites political attack. A few states cover sex-change procedures, but transgender advocates do not call attention to the issue. When Washington state's auditor criticized the state Medicaid agency's decision to pay for a sex-change operation two years earlier, the legislature tried but failed to bar use of public funds for the procedure. The Medicaid agency, however, is now changing its policy and refusing to pay for such procedures on the grounds that the surgery is "experimental." [13]

Anti-gay organizations see no reason to provide transgender health benefits. "I certainly don't think any health insurance that's provided by the government or covered by taxpayers should cover it," says the Family Research Council's Sprigg. "And health-insurance companies should not be required to cover it."

The University of California has followed San Francisco in providing transgender health benefits, and so have a handful of private employers, according to Arana. Some other municipalities have inquired about the policy but not adopted it.

A few companies cover the costs in their health plans, Arana says. But health-insurance experts have little information about the subject. "We have no data on that topic," says Suzanne Zagata-Meraz, a spokeswoman for Chicago-based Hewitt and Associates, which surveys health-insurance practices annually. "It's a subject that we've been thinking about asking about in our surveys but we haven't."

Keisling says the lack of insurance coverage stems from social disapproval of transgenderism. "The insurance companies can get away with not covering it because it's a stigma," she says.

For his part, Arana says San Francisco's experience shows that cost should not be an obstacle to providing the benefit. "The worst fears aren't being realized," he says. But the benefit is still important, he says, even if only a few people use it.

"Only a small number of people are going to have open-heart surgery every year, but that doesn't mean we shouldn't offer [coverage]," he says. "A small number of people are going to need the benefit, and for them we ought to provide it." ■

BACKGROUND

Gender Variations

The biological differentiation between male and female is a basic fact of life recognized in the biblical account of creation.

But, as science writer Deborah Rudacille notes in her 2005 book *The Riddle of Gender*, gender variations also have an ancient lineage — from the sex-changing gods of Greek and Roman mythology to cross-dressing men and women in many cultures. Scientific discoveries beginning in the 19th century better explained the biological basis for sex differences and laid the groundwork for the first medical sex-change procedures for humans in the 20th century. [14] *

The modern science of sexology owes its development to work by the German physiologist Arnold Berthold (1801-1863), who in 1848 and 1849 explained the role of the testes in the development of male sex characteristics by experimentally castrating young male chickens. The castrated cockerels did not develop typical male sexual behavior or characteristics, but reimplantation of the testes brought about normal development. By 1912, the Austrian physician and researcher Eugen Steinach (1861-1944) had advanced Berthold's insights by transplanting female sex glands into male guinea pigs and vice versa. The genetic males developed female sex characteristics after the transplants, while the females came to display male behavior.

Steinach was mentor to the two physicians credited with exploiting the discoveries from animal research for purposes of sex reassignments in humans: the German Magnus Hirschfeld (1868-1935) and the German-born American Harry Benjamin (1885-1986). Hirschfeld, a homosexual and cross-dresser himself, founded the Institute for Sexual Science in Berlin. He reported in 1918 on the first incomplete female-to-male reassignments (removal of the sexual organs without creating new genitalia) performed in 1912 and later referred the patient whose 1931 surgery marked the first complete FTM reassignment (removal of the male sex organs and creation of a vagina and labia.) A longtime advocate for homosexual rights, he fled Germany as the Nazis were coming to power and died two years later in France.

In contrast to Hirschfeld's motivation, Benjamin was drawn to the physiology of sex through his practice in geriatrics. He embraced Steinach's belief that vasectomies could rejuvenate elderly male patients and sought to popularize the procedure both in Europe and the United States. His interest in hormonal research also led him to arrange funding for American researchers who in the 1930s first isolated male sex hormones (androgens). The medical writer Paul de Kruif brought the discoveries to wide public attention with his 1945 book *The Male Hormone*. Meanwhile, researchers in the United States and Germany were moving in the 1920s and '30s toward isolating female sex hormones (estrogens). By 1941, both natural and synthetic estrogens were available in the United States.

A small number of male-to-female and female-to-male reassignments were performed in Europe in the 1930s and '40s, but sex-change procedures were little known outside a limited number of physicians and researchers until the transformation of George to Christine Jorgensen in 1951 and 1952. Jorgensen, a 26-year-old photographer in the Bronx, N.Y., had struggled with gender-identity issues from his youth. After enrolling in medical-assistants' school to learn about sex hormones in 1948, he proceeded

Continued on p. 397

* According to embryologists, as the human fetus develops in the womb, it initially has both types of sex organs, but one sex normally becomes predominant by the time of birth.

Chronology

Before 1950

Biology of sex differences explored.

1930, 1931
First reported complete female-to-male (FTM) surgery in 1930; first reported complete male-to-female (MTF) surgery in 1931.

Mid- and late 1930s
Male sex hormones isolated; natural and synthetic female sex hormone becomes available.

1950s-1960s

Sex change hits the headlines.

1953
Christine Jorgensen returns to U.S. after sex-change surgery in Denmark.

1966
Johns Hopkins medical school opens gender identity clinic, begins performing sex-change surgeries. . . . Drag queens in San Francisco resist police manhandling. . . . Harry Benjamin publishes *The Transsexual Phenomenon*, the first book on the subject.

1969
Transvestites are among the New Yorkers pelting police during raid at Stonewall Inn, landmark event in gay rights movement; transgender people are ignored or shunned during movement's early years.

1970s-1980s

Transgender advocates win first legislative victories.

1975
Minneapolis revises definition of sexual orientation in non-discrimination law to include gender identity; Los Angeles and Champaign and Urbana, Ill., are only other cities to pass such laws in decade.

1979
Janice Raymond publishes *The Transsexual Empire*, criticizing transsexuals from feminist perspective. . . . Johns Hopkins School of Medicine closes gender identity clinic; other universities follow suit.

1980
Standards of care published by Harry Benjamin International Gender Dysphoria Association call for transsexuals to have approval from two psychiatrists and live in opposite gender for full year before undergoing sex-reassignment surgery.

1983, 1986
Harrisburg, Pa., and Seattle prohibit gender discrimination.

1990s ***Transgender movement begins to form.***

1993
Minnesota becomes first state with a law banning discrimination because of gender identity; similar laws passed in more than 20 localities during decade. . . . Brandon Teena, a preoperative teenage FTM, is killed in Nebraska on New Year's Eve.

1999
All-volunteer National Transgender Advocacy Coalition forms as first nationwide trans advocacy group. . . . "Boys Don't Cry," a movie about Brandon Teena's killing, is widely acclaimed, with Oscar for Hillary Swank in lead role.

2000-Present

Transgender people come out in increasing numbers.

2001
San Francisco provides health benefits to city employees for sex-change procedures. . . . Rhode Island passes trans-inclusive non-discrimination law.

2002
Kansas Supreme Court bars MTF transsexual from inheriting estate of late husband, saying marriage was invalid. . . . Trans teenager Gwen Araujo brutally killed in Calif.; assailants convicted of murder in 2005.

2003
American Psychiatric Association debates "gender identity diagnosis" at annual meeting in prelude to revision of *Diagnostic and Statistical Manual of Mental Disorders* (*DSM*). . . . National gay rights organizations agree on including gender identity in proposed Employment Nondiscrimination Act in Congress; no hearings held on bill.

2004
Florida appeal court bars custody rights for transsexual Michael Kantaras on ground his marriage to woman was void.

2005
Diane Schroer, transgender Army veteran, sues Library of Congress for sex discrimination. . . . "Transamerica," sympathetic story of pre-operative transsexual woman, gains wide audience; popular films "Rent" and "Breakfast on Pluto" have cross-dressers in featured roles.

2006
Local New Jersey school board puts transgender teacher Lily McBeth back on eligibility list after absence for sex-change procedures.

The Murder of Gwen Araujo

Eddie Araujo Jr. wanted to be a girl from an early age and by age 17 began dressing and living as a female named Gwen. [1] On the evening of Oct. 3, 2002, she left her home near San Francisco to hang out with a wild crowd of 20-somethings. She did not return.

As shown in testimony in two murder trials, Gwen previously had had sexual encounters with several of the men in the group. At the gathering, according to some accounts, they became enraged upon learning — and confirming by forced inspection — that Gwen had male genitalia. Three assailants beat and bludgeoned her inside the house and then took her to the garage and strangled her with a rope. Along with a fourth man, the assailants then drove to the foothills of the Sierra Nevadas and buried Gwen. (The cable television network Lifetime is scheduled to air a docudrama, "The Gwen Araujo Story," in June 2006.)

Araujo's death and the convictions of the four men for murder or manslaughter represent for the transgender community the same kind of hate crime that the 1998 murder of the homosexual Wyoming college student Matthew Shepard represents for the gay community. But Araujo's death drew far less attention. Shepard's death, for example, was reported on the front page of *The New York Times* (Oct. 13, 1998); Araujo's killing appears to have gone unmentioned in the newspaper until it carried a brief wire service account of the mistrial in the defendants' first trial on June 23, 2004.

Police and prosecutors in many jurisdictions also tend to give less attention to crimes against transgender people than to other offenses, say transgender advocates. "Very often, the crimes are not taken seriously," says Mara Keisling, executive director of the National Center for Transgender Equality. "Victims are often treated as suspects, or victims are told, 'What did you expect?' because of the way they're dressed."

Statistics on crimes against transgender people in the United States are imprecise. Keisling cites a common estimate of one killing per month in recent years. Gwen Smith, 39, a married, transgender Web designer in Antioch, Calif., maintains a Web site (www.rememberingourdead.org) listing about 350 transgender murder victims in the United States and other countries dating from the 1970s.

Transgender people are particularly vulnerable to assaults, robberies or other personal crimes because many live in marginal neighborhoods. As in Araujo's case, many of the crimes are especially violent. "We call it overkill," Keisling says. [2]

The attention given to Araujo's case represented a positive sign, Keisling says, because media coverage was "respectful," in part because Araujo's family was "so supportive and so articulate." Alameda County prosecutors charged the offense as first-degree murder and asked for an enhanced sentence under California's hate crime law — one of eight state hate crime statutes that cover offenses motivated by gender identity or expression. [3]

Horizons Foundation

Gwen Araujo, 17, was killed after it was discovered she was a transsexual.

The initial trial in the case ended with a hung jury. The second trial ended on Sept. 13, 2005, with the second-degree murder convictions of two defendants — Michael W. Magidson and Jose A. Merel — but acquittal on the hate crime charge. One juror explained afterward that jurors believed the crime was motivated by anger, not by Gwen's gender. The jury deadlocked on a third defendant, Jason Cazares, but on Dec. 16 he pleaded no contest to voluntary manslaughter. The fourth defendant, Jason Nabors, earlier had pleaded guilty to voluntary manslaughter and testified against the other three in the trials.

Magidson and Merel each were sentenced to 15 years to life in prison. Cazares received a six-year term. Nabors is expected to be sentenced to 11 years' imprisonment.

On the eve of the Magidson and Merel sentencing, Gwen's mother, Sylvia Guererro, wrote about the mix of emotions she felt: anger at the killing and the defendants' efforts to blame Gwen; gratitude for the support from family, friends and strangers — and sadness. "I'm sad," Guererro wrote, because "other transgender women have been killed since Gwen's murder, and we don't have a realistic end in sight to that violence." [4]

---

[1] Reconstruction drawn from Wikipedia (visited April 2006) and corroborated in news accounts. For coverage of the verdicts against two of the defendants, see Henry K. Lee, "2 Guilty in 2nd Degree in Araujo Slaying," *The San Francisco Chronicle*, Sept. 13, 2005, p. A1. See also Bob Moser, "The Murder of a Boy Named Gwen," *Rolling Stone*, Feb. 10, 2005.

[2] For an overview, see Bob Moser, " 'Disposable People'," Southern Poverty Law Center, winter 2003 (www.splc.org).

[3] The other states are Connecticut, Hawaii, Minnesota, Missouri, New Mexico, Pennsylvania and Vermont. See Transgender Law and Policy Institute (www.transgenderlaw.org).

[4] Sylvia Guererro, "Life after Gwen," SFGate.com, Jan. 25, 2006 (posted at Araujo Trial Update, www.transgenderlaw.org).

Continued from p. 394

to self-administer estrogens and was pleased with the resulting physical and emotional changes. Soon afterward, Jorgensen traveled to Denmark, where — with government approval — she underwent castration in 1951 and a penectomy (surgical removal of the penis) a little over a year later.

Word of the operation leaked out from a family friend, and the news spread worldwide. Jorgensen initially wanted to avoid publicity, but in a letter to Benjamin in 1953 said she had decided to seek it out with the hope that "when the next 'Christine' comes along the sensationalism will be decreased." [15] She later became an actress and entertainer.

Benjamin came to be a link to the next critical development for transsexualism: the establishment of the Gender Identity Clinic at Johns Hopkins University School of Medicine in Baltimore in 1966. The clinic was founded by a Johns Hopkins psychologist, John Money, whose interest stemmed from his study in the 1950s of intersex persons — people born with ambiguous genitalia or sex characteristics. As Rudacille recounts, Money coauthored a seminal paper in 1955 that endorsed "corrective plastic surgery" not only for intersex persons — who make up 1 percent of the population — but also for adolescents or adults whose biological sex "flagrantly contradicted . . . their gender role and orientation." [16]

Encouraged by Benjamin, Money pushed hard — in the face of resistance from his Johns Hopkins colleagues — to win approval for the opening of a clinic that would perform sex-reassignment surgeries. The clinic had been operating for several months when the news hit the front page of *The New York Times*. [17] The story noted that Johns Hopkins was the first U.S. hospital to officially support the procedure. A few other universities followed suit. But resistance continued at Hopkins, which finally closed the clinic 13 years later.

Uncommon Cause

Transgender people were present at the creation of the gay liberation movement in the 1960s. But they were largely ignored or even shunned well into the 1990s. Many in the gay rights movement viewed transgenderism as incompatible with the prevailing conformist politics of gay men and feminist ideology of lesbians. Efforts to ban discrimination based on gender identity advanced only slowly: As late as 2001, only 5 percent of the nation's population lived in jurisdictions with such laws.

The contemporary gay liberation movement is typically traced to the riot that resulted from a police raid on the Stonewall Inn, a gay bar in New York City's Greenwich Village, in June 1969. As unearthed by the transgender San Francisco historian Susan Stryker, however, a similar though smaller confrontation with police had occurred three years earlier at Compton's Cafeteria, a seedy diner frequented by drag entertainers.

Police came to the cafeteria one evening in August 1966 — the exact date is uncertain — after the manager called to report a disturbance. Stryker's film "Screaming Queens" depicts the spontaneous brawl after an officer manhandled one of the queens during what became the first instance of collective resistance to police harassment of transgender people. The episode also ushered in some changes, including social services for transsexuals and repeal of the city's ordinance banning cross-dressing. [18]

Drag queens may have been the first to feel the brunt of police harassment when police raided the Stonewall Inn three summers later — and possibly also the first to fight back. While accounts of the sequence of events on the night of June 23 differ, there is agreement that young transvestites were among those who heckled and pelted the police as many of the bar's gay male patrons were being shoved into waiting paddy wagons.

Despite their common cause that night, gay men and lesbians later parted company from transgender people. "They rather explicitly excluded transgender people from the movement," Keisling says today. The predominantly white, middle-class gay men who founded the Queer Activist Alliance saw the multiethnic drag queens of the street as invitations for public derision and contempt. Lesbians viewed them as anti-feminist — "men who impersonate women for entertainment and profit," as they were described at the city's gay pride parade in 1973. [19]

Transsexuals suffered a more concrete setback at the end of the decade, when Johns Hopkins closed its Gender Identity Clinic and stopped performing sex-change surgery. McHugh, a confirmed opponent of the procedure, had become head of psychiatry in 1975. McHugh commissioned a post-surgical study of the clinic's patients by fellow psychiatrist Jon Meyer. Meyer found that the patients voiced no regrets about having undergone the procedures but they continued to have many of the same psychological problems they had had before their surgeries. Meyer's conclusions were — and continue to be — sharply disputed, but McHugh relied on them in his decision in October 1979 to close the clinic. Other universities followed suit. [20]

Transsexuals also were making little progress on the legal front. Minneapolis became the first city to pass an anti-discrimination law protecting transgendered people in 1975, when it amended its definition of "affectional preference" in an ordinance passed the year before to include the phrase "having or projecting a self-image not associated with one's biological maleness or one's biological femaleness." As transgender lawyers Currah and Shannon Minter note, however, the "historic moment" drew little notice: The amendment was passed in a flurry of progressive legislation enacted just before a newly elected, more conservative mayor was about to take office. [21]

The push for statewide legislation in Minnesota revealed a split over whether to include protection for transsexuals in gay rights legislation — a debate that was to be played out repeatedly elsewhere in coming years. Some of the leading activists called for covering transsexuals, but the lead sponsor — state Sen. Allan Spear, a Democrat and the country's first openly gay male politician — argued pragmatically that a trans-inclusive provision would kill any bill. As it happened, the state legislature in 1975 rejected a trans-inclusive amendment but proceeded to defeat Spear's measure anyway.

By the late '70s, gay rights measures were facing stiffened resistance following a campaign by singer Anita Bryant, which led to Miami's repeal of its anti-discrimination ordinance in 1978. In the difficult political climate that prevailed through the 1980s, transgender activists managed to get trans-inclusive provisions included in anti-discrimination ordinances in only seven cities — most notably, Los Angeles and Seattle. Minnesota became the first state to pass a trans-inclusive statute in 1993. Another two-dozen localities followed suit during the remainder of the '90s, but only in 2001 did Rhode Island become the second state to prohibit discrimination based on gender identity.

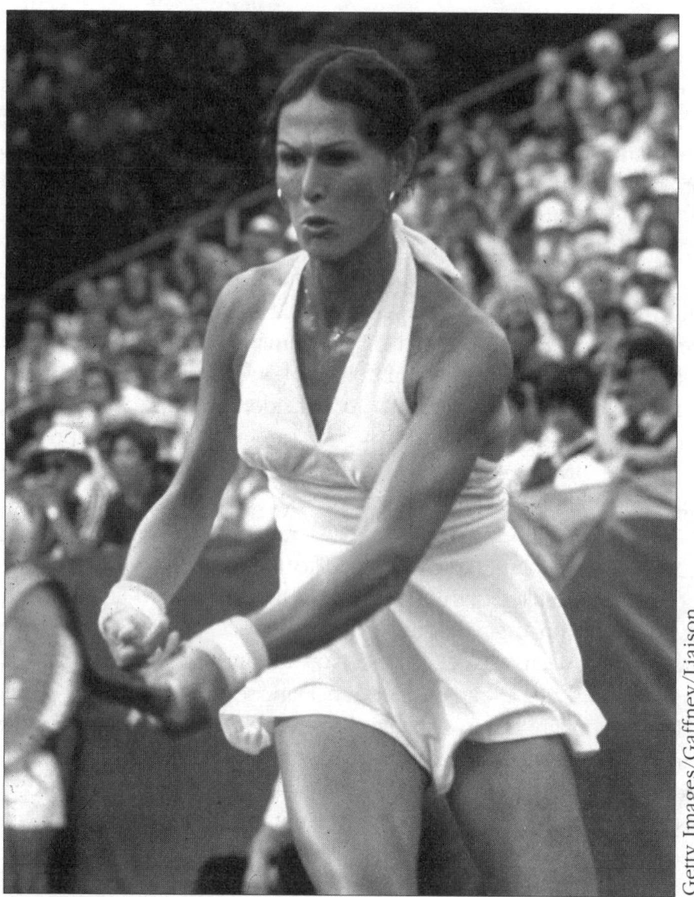

Getty Images/Gaffney/Liaison

Renee Richards plays professional tennis in the 1970s after winning a court fight allowing her to compete as a woman. Before undergoing sex-reassignment surgery, she was Richard Raskind, an amateur tennis champion and married eye surgeon. She later expressed misgivings about her decision.

Trans Action

Transgender people were becoming more visible and transgender advocates more vocal by the late 1990s, and their efforts began producing more results in the new century. The number of jurisdictions with trans-inclusive anti-discrimination legislation grew, the APA opened debate on the diagnosis of GID, and hate crimes against transsexuals drew increasing attention. Progress for trans activists was slow and uneven, however, and their increased visibility caused social conservatives to broaden their anti-gay messages to include opposition to transgender rights as well.

An instance of the increased visibility for transgender people came with the 1999 film "Boys Don't Cry," the story of Brandon Teena, an FTM teenager in Nebraska killed in 1993 by two friends enraged by what they saw as his deception. Besides focusing on the issue of hate crimes, the movie also gave unaccustomed attention to an FTM transsexual. The film won an Oscar in March 2000 for Hillary Swank, who cheered trans activists in her acceptance speech by referring to Brandon with the masculine pronoun. Three years later, the cable channel HBO gave a happier account of transsexualism with a TV drama, "Normal," which sympathetically portrayed a married man's decision to transition to female.

Trans activists were also focusing on transgender issues through conventional political and public education activities. The all-volunteer National Transgender Advocacy Coalition formed in 1999 as the first nationwide group specifically focused on trans issues. Operating with a Washington, D.C., mailing address, the group's executive director, Vanessa Edwards Foster, used press releases and news-media interviews over the course of several years to focus on issues ranging from unfavorable court rulings to jokes about transsexuals on late-night talk shows. (The group is largely inactive today; Foster is executive director of the Texas Gender and Information Network.) Keisling helped found NCTE in 2003 as the first professionally staffed national trans-advocacy group. Equally if not more important, transgender-related projects were also started at the older and better financed gay rights organizations as well as the ACLU.

Some successes followed. The San Francisco Human Rights Commission got its first transgender member in 2001, just as the city was moving to approve transgender health benefits for employees.

'Reluctant Activist' Sues Library of Congress

Dave Schroer had a "boringly normal" childhood growing up in a Chicago suburb in the 1960s and early '70s. From early on, however, "I knew something was amiss. Something wasn't right." Only now does Diane Schroer understand what was wrong — what she calls "the itch that refuses to be scratched."

Schroer's transition from male to female over the last four years came at the end of a childless 18-year marriage and a 26-year career in the military. But the struggle goes back much further — back to Dave's teenage years when he sometimes tried on his mother's clothes when no one else was at home.

The occasional cross-dressing continued after marriage, always in secret. True cross-dressers enjoy the practice, but for Dave it was "unsatisfying." Only in his mid-40s — and only after "considerable research" — did he realize that "it was more than that."

Schroer's research led to the online transgender community — "God love the Internet!" she exclaims. Then in October 2003, as a woman, Schroer went to the Southern Comfort Conference in Atlanta, an annual event described as the world's largest gathering of transgender people.

The conference gave Schroer new friends and a new resolve. "I needed time to re-rack my life," she says now. Back home, Dave told his wife. "She didn't want to deal with it," Schroer recalls today. At the time, he had "no idea of transitioning," Schroer continues. "I didn't see these things as absolutely, mutually exclusive."

The divorce, which became final in November 2005, was "brutal and hugely expensive." The coming-out, however, proved to be less difficult than Schroer had been forewarned. Her best friend, an Army buddy, was surprised but immediately supportive. Diane's two brothers and their families have also embraced her. "I can almost count on one hand the number of friends I've lost," she says today.

The sex-change procedures, on the other hand, have been difficult: more than 12 hours of plastic surgery to feminize her face, 150 hours of hair-removing electrolysis and repeated hair transplants on the scalp; genital surgery may come this fall. She's satisfied with the results. So far, at 5-foot-10 and 175 pounds, Schroer still has man-size dimensions, but with wig, makeup and nice clothes, "I don't look like a truck driver in a dress," she says.

Schroer admits that she procrastinated in coming out to Congressional Research Service (CRS) officials at the Library of Congress when she applied for a job as a terrorism research analyst in late 2004. "I wasn't too thrilled about having to tell my future employer this," she says. When she did, the CRS assistant director slept on the new information overnight and then withdrew what Schroer had understood to be a job offer extended and accepted.

Defending the federal sex-discrimination suit filed in June 2005 on Schroer's behalf by the American Civil Liberties Union, lawyers for the library say there was no final job offer. ACLU lawyer Sharon McGowan says the distinction is unimportant. Schroer was told she was the most qualified of three finalists for the job, the attorney says, so refusing to hire her amounted to "an adverse employment action" based on gender.

With the lawsuit pending, Schroer is working for a consulting company that has contracts with the Department of Homeland Security. She bought a house in Alexandria and hopes, eventually, to unpack and settle in. She has made friends in the neighborhood, but they know her only as Diane. "Which is just fine," she adds.

Conditioned in the military to avoid the media, Schroer has become what she calls "a reluctant activist," having done several print interviews and appeared on the ABC newsmagazine "20/20."

What does she want from the lawsuit? "I would hope that the government would say in very unequivocal terms that what they did was wrong, that that kind of hiring practice is unacceptable," she says.

"It would be nice if they gave me the job just as they had before," she adds. McGowan thinks that is unrealistic, but Schroer says: "I honestly don't know. I think that's fair. I think that's right."

And what if she loses? "I guess I'll go on about my business — living my life, doing my best to get by just like everyone else."

By 2003, the vast majority of states had laws or regulations permitting transsexuals to change the sex designated on their birth certificate. New Mexico and California added gender identity to state anti-discrimination laws in 2003; Maine and Illinois followed suit in 2004. In a significant strategic change the same year, Human Rights Campaign and other gay rights organizations announced that they would insist on including gender identity with sexual orientation in the proposed federal Employment Nondiscrimination Act (ENDA).

Along with the successes came at least as many defeats or disappointments. Trans activists were especially angry that as New York neared passage of a gay rights measure in 2002, the major lobbying group, the Empire State Pride Agenda, rebuffed their strenuous efforts to add gender identity to the measure. "This is one of the most divisive things I've seen in my 30 years in the movement," activist Allen Roskoff remarked. [22]

Courts also rejected rights for transsexuals in two closely watched marriage-related cases, nullifying the unions in both instances on the grounds that an individual's sex is fixed at birth. In 2002, the Kansas Supreme Court barred J'Noel Gardiner, an MTF transsexual, from receiving half of the $2.5 million estate of her late husband on the grounds that their purported marriage was invalid under Kansas law. [23]

Michael Kantaras, a transsexual man, initially fared better in a custody dispute when a Florida judge in 2003 favored him over the mother of their two children in their divorce case. (Kantaras had legally adopted the older child; the younger child was artificially conceived during the marriage.) But a state appeal court reversed the decision in July 2004, rejecting any custody rights for Kantaras on the grounds that he was legally a woman and the marriage was void. [24]

Despite the lobbying and litigation, transgender issues remained below most Americans' radar screens. When the APA debated the GID issue at its annual meeting in San Francisco in May 2003, the event went unreported except in the association's own newsletter. [25] When anti-gay forces mounted an ultimately unsuccessful effort to try to repeal Maine's trans-inclusive anti-discrimination law in 2005, the heated campaign was fought primarily over traditional gay rights questions with very little attention to transgender issues. And the murder trial in the Araujo case drew only a fraction of the news-media coverage that had been given a few years earlier to the killing of the gay Wyoming college freshman Matthew Shepard and the trial of his assailants.

Nevertheless, transgender visibility measurably advanced in late 2005 thanks to the coincidental release of three commercial films that featured trans characters. Trans activists especially praised the film "Transamerica" for a realistic depiction of the experience of a pre-operative MTF transsexual coming out to her biological son. The film was widely acclaimed, and Felicity Huffman garnered an Oscar nomination for best actress for her performance in the role. Two other well-received films — "Rent" and "Breakfast in Pluto" — had cross-dressers in featured roles. ■

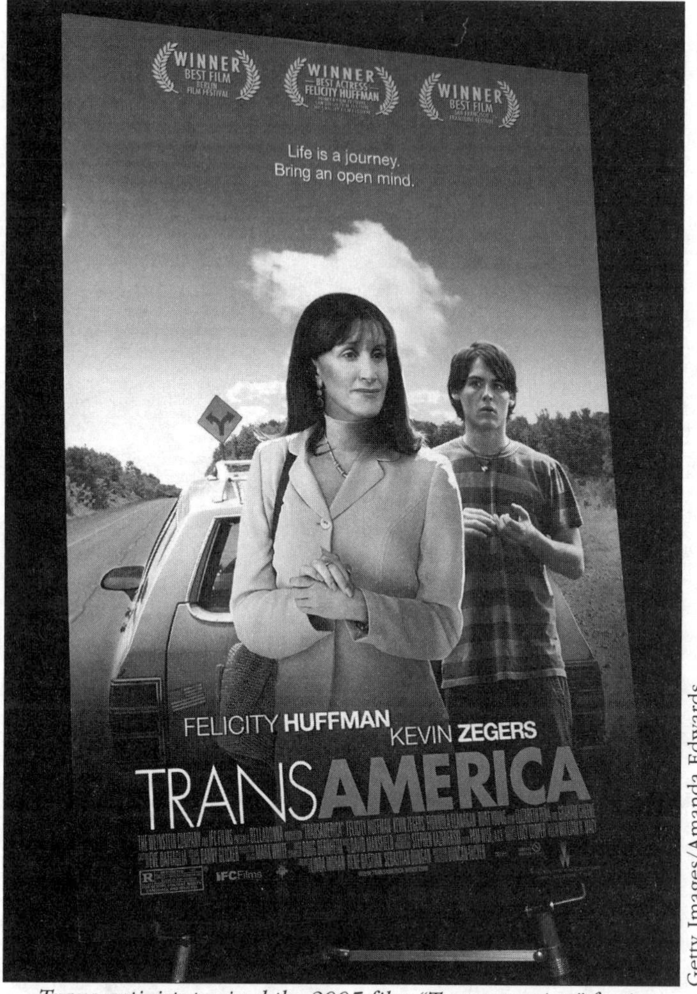

Getty Images/Amanda Edwards

Trans activists praised the 2005 film "Transamerica" for its realistic depiction of a pre-operative male-to-female transsexual coming out to her biological son. Felicity Huffman received an Oscar nomination for best actress.

CURRENT SITUATION

Fighting Over the Law

Transgender advocates are celebrating passage of a trans-inclusive non-discrimination law in Washington state, but opponents hoping to repeal the measure in a November referendum are calling the broadened coverage an invitation to confusion and litigation.

The enactment of the law in January 2006 came 29 years after the introduction of the first bill in the state to ban discrimination on the basis of sexual orientation and some three years after the prime sponsor agreed to broaden the bill to include "gender expression or identity." [26]

Despite the conventional wisdom that a trans-inclusive provision complicates gay rights legislation, transgender issues apparently did not play a prominent role in the final rounds of lobbying and debate over the measure. But opponents are emphasizing the act's protections for transgender people as they try to gather the 112,440 signatures needed to put the measure before Washington voters in November.

"Under this law, 'sexual orientation' includes how you look, how you act, how you feel about yourself and how you express yourself," says Tim Eyman, a veteran initiative organizer who calls his current drive Let the Voters Decide. "It's a Pandora's box of a law. That's going to be an aspect of the campaign that's going to give the voters pause." Eyman says that only 8,718 signatures had been gathered as of April 27.

Transgender advocates appear to be trying to soften opposition by minimizing somewhat its potential impact, especially in the workplace. Marcia Botzer, a trans activist and lobbyist on the measure, says for example that the law would allow an employer to require a

Continued on p. 402

At Issue:

Should gender identity disorder be considered a mental illness?

ROBERT L. SPITZER, M.D.
PROFESSOR OF PSYCHIATRY, NEW YORK STATE PSYCHIATRIC INSTITUTE

WRITTEN FOR *CQ RESEARCHER*, MAY 2006

yes

Dr. Karasic argues for eliminating gender identity disorder (GID) from *DSM-V* as it applies to children. He states: "The diagnostic criteria do not require the child to identify as the other sex — only that the child exhibit behaviors more typical of the other sex."

That is not true. Criterion A states: A strong and persistent cross-gender identification. The B criterion states: Persistent discomfort with his or her sex or sense of inappropriateness in the gender role of that sex. The diagnosis is not given merely because the child exhibits behaviors more typical of the other sex.

Consider this true case (supplied by Dr. Kenneth Zucker): "A 2-year-and-10-month-old boy was referred for assessment. When asked his name, he says he is 'Snow White.' Since age 2 he has insisted that he wants to be a girl. He wants to grow up to be a mommy. When told by his parents that he will grow up to be a daddy, he bursts into tears and is inconsolable. He likes to wear dresses in nursery school and only plays with girls. He sits to urinate."

Does such a child have a mental disorder? Apparently Dr. Karasic would say no because he did not actually insist that he was a girl. This is absurd.

Dr. Karasic says: "GID in children is used as a surrogate diagnosis for children suspected to be pre-homosexual by therapists trying to prevent homosexuality."

Not true. GID in children first appeared in *DSM-III* in 1980, largely formulated by Dr. Richard Green, a staunch advocate of regarding homosexuality as a normal variant (see Ronald Bayer's *American Psychiatry and Homosexuality*). It is not true that all therapists treating GID (there aren't that many) have as their goal the preventing of the later development of homosexuality.

Regarding GID in adults, Dr. Karasic says the *DSM* diagnosis should not "pathologize transgendered people who have adjusted well by modifying their bodies and/or presentation of gender." Granted that hormone therapy or surgery may now be the only treatment that we can now offer the adult with GID.

But surely something remains profoundly wrong psychologically with individuals who are uncomfortable with their biological sex and insist that their biological sex is of the opposite sex. The only diagnosis that is appropriate for such cases is GID.

DAN KARASIC, M.D.
PROFESSOR OF PSYCHIATRY, UNIVERSITY OF CALIFORNIA; PRESIDENT, ASSOCIATION OF GAY AND LESBIAN PSYCHIATRISTS

WRITTEN FOR *CQ RESEARCHER*, MAY 2006

no

The American Psychiatric Association (APA) periodically revises its official list of diagnostic criteria, the *Diagnostic and Statistical Manual* (*DSM*). For the next edition, *DSM-V*, the APA will re-examine all diagnoses, including gender identity disorder (GID). The last edition states, "it must be admitted that no definition adequately specifies precise boundaries for the concept of 'mental disorder,' " but "neither deviant behavior (e.g., political, religious, or sexual) nor conflicts that are primarily between the individual and society are mental disorders unless the deviance or conflict is a symptom of a dysfunction." Given the imprecision in separating variance from pathology, the current diagnosis of GID warrants careful re-assessment.

There are two sets of criteria for GID in the *DSM*, for children and for adolescents and adults. The diagnostic criteria for children and adults differ, and the diagnoses apply to different groups of people — not the same people at different ages. Most boys with GID do not grow up to be transgender adults, but rather, gay and bisexual men. The diagnostic criteria do not require the child to identify as the other sex — only to exhibit behaviors more typical of the other sex. Gender behavior outside of traditional gender roles is not mental illness. Programs for gender-variant children emphasize supporting the child and his/her family, rather than trying to force conformity to stereotypical gender roles.

GID in children is used as a surrogate diagnosis for children suspected to be pre-homosexual by therapists trying to prevent homosexuality. Since homosexuality is not a *DSM* disorder, and "reparative therapy" for homosexuality has been condemned by the APA, a surrogate for pre-homosexuality should not be a *DSM* disorder.

The diagnosis of GID in adults also needs reassessing. The diagnosis does not distinguish between the distress of gender dysphoria and the healthy adaptations transgendered people make to relieve gender dysphoria. The criterion of stress or social/occupational dysfunction may be caused by societal discrimination, rather than individual dysfunction. The diagnosis should not include those who change their appearance and social role and are no longer impaired by gender dysphoria, but instead are hampered by societal prejudice.

Patients would be better served by a narrower diagnosis that describes psychological distress about one's gender but does not pathologize transgendered people who have adjusted well by modifying their bodies and/or presentation of gender.

Continued from p. 400

transgender person to take time off while transitioning or to reassign the employee afterward. There are processes in place to negotiate about transitions in workplaces," she says.

Nationally, major gay rights groups insist that including protection for transgender persons helps efforts to pass anti-discrimination measures. "The community is strongest when we stand together," says HRC Legislative Director Labonte. "Since 2003, every bill that has passed has included the whole community. We have not seen any erosion of support when the entire community was included."

On Capitol Hill, however, Rep. Barney Frank, D-Mass., an openly gay lawmaker and major ally of gay rights organizations, disagrees with the strategy. Frank helped win House passage in September of a bill to define as hate crimes offenses motivated by the victim's sexual orientation or gender identity, but he now says the trans-inclusive provision caused the measure to stall in the Senate. [27]

For that reason, Frank says he continues to oppose including gender identity in the gay rights groups' major legislative goal: the Employment Nondiscrimination Act (ENDA), which would ban workplace discrimination on the basis of sexual orientation. "My strategy was to get people used to voting on transgender issues," Frank says. "It had more of a negative effect [on the hate-crime bill] than I'd thought it would."

Conservative groups continue to oppose any bills that include sexual orientation or gender identity in employment discrimination or hate-crime laws. "We feel every citizen should be given equal protection against violence rather than specifying certain categories for a heightened form of protection," says the Family Research Council's Sprigg. As for anti-discrimination measures, Sprigg says protections should be given only for characteristics "inborn, immutable, involuntary, innocuous and/or in the Constitution."

AP Photo/Mary Godleski

Lily McBeth, 71, is happy to be back as a substitute elementary school teacher in Eagleswood, N.J., after undergoing a sex change and experiencing some parental opposition to returning to the classroom.

Transgender advocates continue making slow progress in gaining anti-discrimination protections. In April, Bloomington, Ind., became the second city in the state and the 81st locality in the country to prohibit discrimination based on gender identity or expression. The ordinance provides for voluntary mediation of complaints.

Currah of the Transgender Law and Policy Institute says municipal ordinances are "symbolically important" but acknowledges they have limited impact because local human-rights agencies are usually underfunded. Statewide laws have greater potential impact, he says, but are also harder to pass. So far, eight have been enacted.

As for federal legislation, all LGBT groups concede that the Republican-controlled Congress will not act on any broad anti-discrimination measure whether or not it covers transgender persons. But Mottet of the National Lesbian and Gay Task Force says legislators at state and local levels are supportive "when they're educated about who transgender people are and the discrimination that they face at work and in other parts of their lives."

Looking for Acceptance

After a year's absence, Lily McBeth is glad to be getting back in the classroom as a substitute elementary school teacher in tiny Eagleswood, N.J. "Oh, what a joy!" the 71-year-old transgender retired sales executive says in an e-mail to friends.

McBeth took herself off the school board's list of substitute teachers in January 2005 as she transitioned from male to female. When she applied to go back on the rolls, some parents in the working-class community protested. The school board voted 4-1 in March to list McBeth as available for assignment, but she went nearly two months without a call, even though before her transition she had had frequent work. [28]

McBeth's struggles for self-acceptance after a lifetime of gender conflict and for acceptance by others amid community conflict typify the lives of many transgender people. "I was in this conflicted state, and as a result so was everybody around me," transgender author Jamison Green recalls of his own transition beginning in the late 1980s. Initially frightened, he was relieved when he finally started transitioning. "I realized it was the right thing for me because I stopped having a conflict," he says.

In a contrary view, however, Renee Richards, who made headlines as a transgender professional tennis player in the 1970s, now advises against sex-change procedures in midlife or later. "I don't want anyone to hold me out as an example to follow," Richards, who is now a physician, remarked in a 1999 interview. "I get a lot of letters from people who are considering having this operation," she explained, "and I discourage them all." [29]

Mental-health professionals say transgender people vary in their ability to resolve their personal conflicts. "Some are coping well," says University of Toronto psychologist Schneider. "Some are not coping well."

"There are those with clinically significant dysphoria [distress] about the difference between their gender identity and their bodies," says psychiatrist Karasic. "But there are also quite many transgender people who are living their lives quite successfully."

Both Karasic and Schneider say the difficulties transgender people face from society compound the adjustment problems. "I see this as not only a psychological issue but also a social-justice issue," Schneider says. "It's a social-justice issue because it's an issue of discrimination."

The workplace presents the most serious problem, say transgender advocates. While overall statistics are unavailable, transgender groups firmly believe that transgender people are underemployed and unemployed at disproportionate rates to the population as a whole. The unscientific March 2006 survey of transgender San Franciscans by the Transgender Law Center supports that view. About 35 percent of the 194 respondents were unemployed, compared to 4.7 percent of the city's population as a whole. And those who were employed also had relatively low incomes, with only a small fraction — between 4 percent and 8 percent — making more than the city's median household income of $60,000. [30]

Workplace conditions are improving, however, according to transgender advocates. "We've seen a tremendous, exponential growth in the number of companies that recognize transgender employees as part and parcel of the success of their company," says Daryl Herrschaft, director of HRC's workplace project. HRC offers to help companies with newly transitioning workers to prepare other employees for the changes and resolve restroom and other issues.

Housing also can present difficult issues for transgender people. The San Francisco survey found only 5 percent of those responding owned their own homes, 10 percent said they were homeless and another 31 percent lived in "unstable situations." More than one-fourth — 27 percent — claimed to have suffered housing discrimination. [31]

Transgender people can encounter difficulties in dealing with any number of other social or governmental institutions. "A lot of social services are sex-segregated, such as drug treatment, homeless shelter or foster care," says Currah at the Transgender Law and Policy Institute. Working with other transgender groups, the institute negotiated an agreement with the New York City Department of Homeless Services in February 2006 to assign clients to shelters based on their gender identity.

Prisons present a more serious problem. Transgender inmates face "a high risk of sexual violence in jails and prisons," according to Daley, including rape and unnecessary strip searches. Prison administrators often resort to administrative segregation to protect transgender inmates instead of taking affirmative steps to ensure their safety, Daley says.

McBeth got more than a taste of the public disapproval in the nationally publicized dispute over relisting her as a substitute teacher in the first months of 2006. But the difficulties receded when she returned to hugs and congratulations from the other teachers at the elementary school in late April.

"They knew who I was, they knew who I was as a person," McBeth told a reporter that evening. "It was recognition that I was a person of worth, and that's what this is all about." ■

OUTLOOK

Trans Formations

Emboldened by the sexual revolution and a succession of liberation movements — for women, blacks, gays — transgender people are coming out in greater numbers in the United States, demanding legal rights and social acceptance. [32] And with each day the number of Americans who have encountered or will encounter a transgender person in their daily lives grows.

Transgender advocates believe those day-to-day interactions are key to gaining legal protections against what they see as widespread discrimination in the workplace and elsewhere.

"More and more transgender people are out," says Keisling, of the National Center for Transgender Equality. "They're educating their families, their schools, their churches. They're willing to say this is wrong and this has to get fixed."

"People initially are so prejudiced about it because they think it's a sexual perversion," says author Green. "Once people hear about it, they feel much more positive about it."

Even social conservative opponents recognize the transformation. "Christine Jorgensen looked like a singular phenomenon," the Culture and Family Institute's Knight recalls. "Now it looks like a movement. You have a transgender movement complete with Web site, organizations, funding and official support from the homosexual, activist movement. That's what's changed."

From one perspective, the transgender movement's progress can be viewed as limited and slow. No federal legislation explicitly prohibits discrimination on the basis of gender, and the inclusion of the gender identity provision in a hate-crime bill has apparently stalled it in the Senate following House passage. Only eight states have "trans-inclusive" non-discrimination measures, all but one adopted since 2000.

Transgender people are diagnosed by psychiatrists as mentally disordered, yet the medical costs of treating the condition — hormone replacement, cosmetic surgery, genital reconstruction — are not covered by health insurance (except for San Francisco city employees). After complaints from conservative groups, the Internal Revenue Service recently refused to allow tax deductions for sex-change medical expenses — contradicting previous rulings on the issue. [33]

Transgender advocates, however, see the glass as filling up. "We've progressed much faster than I expected," says author Green.

Keisling also professes optimism about winning protections against gender discrimination. "We're getting there," she says. "Eventually, the whole country will get covered."

Courts may provide a quicker path to anti-discrimination protections. Diane Schroer's case against the Library of Congress is being watched closely for further developments, as is the appeal in the case of the fired Salt Lake City bus driver Krystal Etsitty. Before Etsitty's case, some federal and state courts had been receptive to arguments that an adverse employment action based on gender identity does amount to sex discrimination under established civil rights laws.

Transgender advocates are less optimistic about eliminating or reforming the GID diagnosis in the *DSM*. APA committee leaders working on the issue "are not amenable to listening to the concerns," says GID reform advocate Winters.

Opponents say the transgender movement will encounter more resistance with increased visibility. "They run the risk of alienating people who were sort of benignly accepting of the homosexual movement and then wake up and say, 'My goodness, things have gone too far,'" says Knight.

Knight worries, however, that the APA may drop the designation of GID. "A saner psychiatric profession that isn't dominated by the politically correct homosexual lobby would have no problem diagnosing this and advocating help for people afflicted with it," he says.

For her part, Schroer views herself not as afflicted, but as lucky. "I wouldn't trade my life for anything, and I don't regret a second of it," she says. Yes, she might have transitioned earlier if she had "understood all the pieces in the puzzle." But she "loved" the Army, the people she met and the things she accomplished.

"My constant dedication to my work and hard-driving attitude was clearly an outgrowth of the frustration over being transgender," Schroer concludes. "But it forced me to be a better officer and achieve things that are not possible for most. It's difficult to curse something that does that for you in life." ■

About the Author

Associate Editor **Kenneth Jost** graduated from Harvard College and Georgetown University Law Center. He is the author of the *Supreme Court Yearbook* and editor of *The Supreme Court from A to Z* (both *CQ Press*). He was a member of the *CQ Researcher* team that won the 2002 ABA Silver Gavel Award. His reports include "Gays on Campus" and "Gay Marriage."

Notes

1 The case is *Schroer v. Billington*, 05-1090 (U.S. District Court for the District of Columbia). Legal papers from both sides can be found on the ACLU's Web site: www.aclu.org/lgbt/transgender/12255res20050602.html. For coverage, see Petula Dvorak, "The Right Person for the Job: Library of Congress Accused of Transgender Bias," *The Washington Post*, June 2, 2005, p. B1; "Special Forces Commander Transitions from Man to Woman," ABC News, "20/20," Oct. 21, 2005 (abcnews.go.com/2020).

2 Lynn Conway, "How Frequently Does Transsexualism Occur?" http://ai.eecs.umich.edu/people/conway/TS/TSprevalence.html.

3 For background see Kenneth Jost, "Hate Crimes," *CQ Researcher*, Jan. 8, 1993, pp. 1-24.

4 Paul McHugh, "Surgical Sex," *First Things*, November 2004, pp. 34-38 (www.firstthings.com).

5 For background see Kenneth Jost, "Gay-Rights Update," *CQ Researcher*, April 14, 2000, pp. 305-328.

6 American Psychiatric Association, *Diagnostic and Statistical Manual of Mental Disorders* (*DSM-IV-TR*), 4th ed. (2000), pp. 576-582 (gender identity), and pp. 574-575 (transvestic fetishism).

7 Winters previously wrote under the pen name Katherine Wilson.

8 See Traditional Values Coalition, www.traditionalvalues.org. The Web site lists 18 organizations that provide "ministry and counseling resources for those struggling with same-sex attractions and other gender identity disorders.

9 The case, pending before the 10th U.S. Circuit Court of Appeals, is *Etsitty v. Utah Transit Authority*, 05-4193. Some details from coverage by Pamela Manson in *The Salt Lake Tribune*: "UTA Stereotyping Suit Dismissed," June 28, 2005, p. C1; "Sex Change Leads to Lawsuit Against UTA," July 3, 2004, p. B2. For opposing legal briefs, see these Web sites: Transgender Law Center (www.transgenderlawcenter.org); Equal Employment Advisory Council (www.eeac.org).

10 Transgender Law Center, "Good Jobs Now! A Snapshot of the Economic Health of San Francisco's Transgender Communities," March 2006.

[11] Human Rights Campaign, "Workplace Discrimination: Gender Identity or Expression," www.hrc.org/Template.cfm?Section=Transgender_Issues&Template=/TaggedPage/TaggedPageDisplay.cfm&TPLID=26&ContentID= 31022 (visited April 2006).

[12] Quoted in Rachel Gordon, "S.F. Set to Add Sex Change Benefits," *The San Francisco Chronicle*, Feb. 16, 2001, p. A1. For other coverage, see John M. Glionna, "San Francisco Benefits May Cover Sex Changes," *Los Angeles Times*, Feb. 23, 2001, p. A3.

[13] See Ralph Thomas, "Tax Dollars and a Sex Change: A Story of One Patient," *The Seattle Times*, April 11, 2006, p. A1, and related story, "Few Private Policies Cover Sex Changes," p. A11.

[14] Background drawn largely from Deborah Rudacille, *The Riddle of Gender: Science, Activism and Transgender Rights* (2005).

[15] Quoted in *ibid.*, p. 90.

[16] Quoted in *ibid.*, p. 107.

[17] Thomas Buckley, "A Changing of Sex by Surgery Begun at Johns Hopkins," *The New York Times*, Nov. 21, 1966, p. 1.

[18] See Susan Stryker, "Roots of the Transgender Movement: The 1966 Riots at Compton's Cafeteria," *Critical Moment*, Issue 13 (November/December 2005), www.criticalmoment.org. The film "Screaming Queens" by Victor Silverman and Susan Stryker was broadcast on KQED-TV, San Francisco, in July 2005.

[19] Quoted in Rudacille, *op. cit.*, p. 158.

[20] For coverage, see Jane E. Brody, "Benefits of Transsexual Surgery Disputed as Leading Hospital Halts the Procedure," *The New York Times*, Oct. 2, 1979, p. C1.

[21] Paisley Currah and Shannon Minter, "Transgender Equality: A Handbook for Activists and Policymakers," National Center for Lesbian Rights/Policy Institute of the National Gay and Lesbian Task Force, 2000, p. 19. Subsequent events in Minnesota also taken from their account.

[22] Quoted in Shaila K. Dewan, "On Eve of Gay Rights Vote, Bill Is Besieged From Within," *The New York Times*, Dec. 16, 2002, p. B3.

[23] See Anne Lamoy and Stacy Downs, "Transsexual Loses Battle for Estate," *The Kansas City Star*, March 16, 2002, p. A1.

[24] See coverage by William R. Levesque in the *St. Petersburg Times*: "What Is a Man? Court Has an Answer," July 24, 2004, p. 1A; "Transsexual Man Wins Custody of Two Children," Feb. 22, 2003, p. 1B. Kantaras and his ex-wife later agreed to share custody after airing their dispute on the "Dr. Phil" television program.

FOR MORE INFORMATION

American Psychiatric Association, 1000 Wilson Blvd., Suite 1825, Arlington, VA 22209-3901; (703) 907-7300; www.psych.org. Promotes the availability of high-quality psychiatric care.

American Psychological Association, 750 1st St., N.E., Washington, DC 20002-4242; (202) 336-5500; www.apa.org. Works toward improving the qualifications, training programs and competence of psychologists.

Concerned Women for America, 1015 Fifteenth St., N.W., Suite 1100, Washington, DC 20005; (202) 488-7000; www.cwfa.org. A conservative organization that voices strong disapproval of transgenderism.

Harry Benjamin International Gender Dysphoria Association, 1300 South Second St., Suite 180, Minneapolis, MN 55454; (612) 624-9397; www.hbigda.org. A professional organization devoted to the understanding and treatment of gender identity disorders. The association will change its name in fall 2006 to World Professional Association for Transgender Health (WPATH).

Human Rights Campaign, 1640 Rhode Island Ave., N.W., Washington, DC 20036-3278; (202) 628-4160; www.hrc.org. A political and lobbying organization working for lesbian and gay equal rights.

National Center for Lesbian Rights, 870 Market St., Suite 370, San Francisco, CA 94102; (415) 392-6257; www.nclrights.org. The legal center handles various lesbian-rights issues, with special emphasis on child custody and same-sex adoption issues.

National Center for Transgender Equality, 1325 Massachusetts Ave., N.W., #700, Washington, DC 20005; (202) 903-0112; www.nctequality.org. A social-justice organization devoted to ending discrimination and violence against transgender people.

Traditional Values Coalition, 139 C St., S.E., Washington, DC 20003; (202) 547-8570; www.traditionalvalues.org. The non-denominational, grassroots church lobby says it focuses on issues involving religious liberties, marriage, the right to life and the homosexual agenda.

Transgender Law Center, 870 Market St., Room 823, San Francisco, CA 94102; (415) 865-0176; www.transgenderlawcenter.org. A civil rights organization advocating for transgender communities.

[25] See Ken Hausman, "Controversy Continues to Grow Over DSM's GID Diagnosis," *Psychiatry News*, July 18, 2003, p. 25.

[26] Text of the bill, HB 2661, can be found on the Washington legislature's Web site: www.leg.wa.gov/pub/billinfo/2005-06/Pdf/Bills/Session%20Law%202006/2661-S.SL.pdf. The definition of "gender expression or identity" is found in sec. 4, paragraph 15. Gov. Christine Gregoire signed the bill into law on Jan. 31, 2006. Her remarks can be found on the governor's Web site: www.governor.wa.gov. For coverage of the pivotal legislative vote, see Chris McGann, "A Long-Awaited Win for Gay Rights: Senate OKs State Anti-Bias Bill," *Seattle Post-Intelligencer*, Jan. 28, 2006, p. A1.

[27] See Elizabeth Weill-Greenberg, "Frank says trans issue stalled Senate hate crimes measure," The washingtonblade.com, Dec. 21, 2005.

[28] For background, see Kristen A. Graham, "At Last, a Substitute Finds Her True Self," *The Philadelphia Inquirer*, March 21, 2006, p. B1.

[29] Dr. Renee Richards, "The Liaison Legacy," *Tennis Magazine*, March 1999, p. 31.

[30] Transgender Law Center, *op. cit.*, pp. 2-3.

[31] *Ibid.*, p. 3.

[32] For background, see Sandra Stencel, "Homosexual Legal Rights," *Editorial Research Reports 1974* (Vol. I); and W. B. Dickinson Jr., "Negro Voting," *Editorial Research Reports 1964* (Vol. II); Richard L. Worsnop, "Sexual Revolution: Myth or Reality," *Editorial Research Reports 1970* (Vol. I), all available from *CQ Electronic Library Plus Archive*, http://library.cqpress.com.

[33] Internal Revenue Service, "Request for Chief Counsel Advice: Medical Expense Deduction," No. 200603025, released Jan. 20, 2006, cited at Transgender Law and Policy Institute, Jan. 25, 2006 (www.transgenderlaw.org).

Bibliography

Selected Sources

Books

Bloom, Amy, *Normal: Transsexual CEOs, Crossdressing Cops, and Hermaphrodites with Attitude*, Random House, 2002.

The book comprises separate magazine-length profile-essays of transsexuals, cross-dressers and hermaphrodites. Bloom is an author and practicing psychotherapist. Includes four-page bibliography.

Califia, Patrick, *Sex Changes: The Politics of Transgenderism* (2d ed.), Cleis Press, 2003.

Califia, a transgender author, therapist and activist, provides a well-researched contemporary history of transsexuality along with a strongly argued thesis that diversity in gender identity is "a rich and valuable part of human physicality and society." Includes chapter notes, 11-page list of cited works.

Currah, Paisley, Richard M. Juang and Shannon Price Minter (eds.), *Transgender Rights*, University of Minnesota Press, 2006 [forthcoming September 2006].

The 15 essays comprehensively cover the transgender civil rights movement, including legal protections for transgender people, the history of transgender communities and the politics of transgender advocacy. Includes detailed chapter notes and the text of the proposed International Bill of Gender Rights. Currah is associate professor of political science at Brooklyn College, City University of New York, and Minter is legal director of the National Center for Lesbian Rights; they are both founding members of the Transgender Law and Policy Institute. Juang is an assistant professor of English at Susquehanna College.

Green, Jamison, *Becoming a Visible Man*, Vanderbilt University Press, 2004.

The transgender author and public speaker provides an informative account of female-to-male transitions, including his own, along with insightful commentary on gender identity and expression and public attitudes toward the issues. Includes seven-page bibliography.

Karasic, Dan, and Jack Drescher (eds.), *Sexual and Gender Diagnoses of the Diagnostic and Statistical Manual (DSM): A Reevaluation*, Haworth Press, 2006.

The book provides a thorough and balanced review of the debate over the sexual and gender diagnoses in the American Psychiatric Association's *Diagnostic and Statistical Manual of Mental Disorders* (*DSM-IV*) and proposals to revise those diagnoses in the new edition due out in 2011. Drescher is training and supervising analyst at the William Alanson White Institute in New York City; Karasic is a clinical professor of psychiatry at the University of California in San Francisco.

Rudacille, Deborah, *The Riddle of Gender: Science, Activism, and Transgender Rights*, Pantheon, 2005.

Rudacille, a science writer at Johns Hopkins University, provides a thorough and lucid account of transgenderism from early history through the 19th- and 20th-century discoveries of the biological basis of sex differences and the late-20th-century debates over diagnosis, treatment and legal status of transgender people. Includes notes, five-page bibliography.

Articles

McHugh, Paul, "Surgical Sex," *First Things*, Jan. 26, 2005.

McHugh, who closed the gender identity clinic at Johns Hopkins University School of Medicine when he headed the department of psychiatry in the 1970s, argues strongly against assisting patients with sex-change therapies or surgeries. *First Things* is published by the conservative Institute on Religion and Public Life.

Reports and Studies

Currah, Paisley, and Shannon Minter, *Transgender Equality: A Handbook for Activists and Policymakers*, National Center for Lesbian Rights/Policy Institute of the National Gay and Lesbian Task Force, 2000.

The 100-page report, available at www.transgenderlaw.org, covers the history and then-current status of the transgender movement. Includes endnotes, organization list and other reference materials.

Human Rights Campaign, *Transgender Americans: A Handbook for Understanding*, November 2005.

The 50-page pamphlet, available at www.hrc.org, provides an overview of transgender history and advocacy along with brief "stories" and photographs of transsexual individuals. Includes endnotes.

Traditional Values Coalition, "A Gender Identity Disorder Goes Mainstream," April 2005.

The four-page "special report" by the socially conservative Christian lobbying organization, available at www.traditionalvalues.org, argues that transgender individuals "need professional help, not societal approval or affirmation." Ongoing criticism of transgender advocacy through press releases and other statements can be found on the coalition's Web site as well as the Web site of the Culture and Family Institute, an affiliate of the conservative Concerned Women for America (www.cwfa.org).

The Next Step:

Additional Articles from Current Periodicals

Courts

Mitchell, Kirk, "Inmate Sues State Prison to Get Sex-Change Operation," *Chicago Tribune*, March 29, 2006, p. 6.

Christopher "Kitty" Grey, an inmate at Colorado's Limon Correctional Facility, has asked the state's Supreme Court to grant him a sex-change operation, saying he is a woman in a man's prison.

Renaud, Jean-Paul, "Transgender People Are Finding It's Tougher to Change a Name," *Los Angeles Times*, Aug. 28, 2004, p. B6.

Increasing concerns about identity theft are making it difficult for transgender people to change their name to match their preferred gender; the California Supreme Court only grants such changes with proof of surgery and a $300 fee.

Simmons, Ann M., "Couple Sue Over Marriage Rule," *Los Angeles Times*, Dec. 6, 2004, p. B3.

A Los Angeles couple is suing U.S. immigration services for denying residency to the husband, a non-U.S. citizen, because the wife underwent a sex change to become a woman.

Stetson, Erik, "Couple Navigating Murky Legal Ground," *Chicago Tribune*, Feb. 2, 2005, p. A3.

Since Michael Howden underwent a sex change to become a woman, the status of his marriage is in question: Is it a heterosexual or a same-sex marriage?

Gender Identity Disorder

Reeves, Hope, "Youth Permitted to Dress As Female," *The New York Times*, Jan. 10, 2003, p. B7.

New York's Supreme Court ruled that a 17-year-old male living in a foster-care home may dress as a woman after a psychiatrist diagnosed him with gender identity disorder.

Scott, Megan, "The Price and Pain on the Road to Transformation," *St. Petersburg Times* (Florida), Feb. 25, 2005, p. E3.

Twenty percent of the 3,000 people diagnosed with gender identity disorder in the United States have gender-altering surgery.

Thomas, Ralph, "Tax Dollars and a Sex Change: A Story of One Patient," *The Seattle Times*, April 11, 2006, p. A1.

Washington Medicaid officials acknowledge gender identity disorder is a real and serious medical condition but also say sex-change surgery is risky and unproven, furthering the debate over whether taxpayers should pay for sex-change operations.

Legislation

Budoff, Carrie, "Rendell Broadens Protection Against Gender-Identity Bias," *The Philadelphia Inquirer*, July 29, 2003, p. B1.

Democratic Gov. Edward Rendell of Pennsylvania issued an executive order to protect the 80,000 employees in his Cabinet agencies from discrimination based on "gender identity or expression."

Workplace Issues

Dwyer, Kelly Pate, "An Employee, Hired as a Man, Becomes a Woman. Now What?" *The New York Times*, July 31, 2005, p. 1.

Employers are struggling with what to do when employees announce they are switching genders.

Geranios, Nicholas K., "Discrimination Trial Wraps Up," *The Seattle Times*, May 18, 2005, p. B4.

A federal judge will decide if a U.S. Customs and Border Protection employee, Tracy Nichole Sturchio, who underwent a sex change, suffered discrimination from co-workers.

Lewis, Diane E., "Firm Offers Transgender Protections," *The Boston Globe*, July 29, 2005, p. C1.

Raytheon Co. became the first of the nation's six big defense firms to expand its equal-opportunity employment policy to include transgender and transsexual workers.

Loviglio, Joann, "Officer Navigating Sex Change," *The Philadelphia Inquirer*, March 1, 2004, p. B10.

Heladio Gonzalez, a 36-year member of the Philadelphia police force, is preparing for gender-reassignment surgery, making her the first transgender officer in department history.

CITING *CQ RESEARCHER*

Sample formats for citing these reports in a bibliography include the ones listed below. Preferred styles and formats vary, so please check with your instructor or professor.

MLA STYLE

Jost, Kenneth. "Rethinking the Death Penalty." CQ Researcher 16 Nov. 2001: 945-68.

APA STYLE

Jost, K. (2001, November 16). Rethinking the death penalty. *CQ Researcher, 11*, 945-968.

CHICAGO STYLE

Jost, Kenneth. "Rethinking the Death Penalty." *CQ Researcher*, November 16, 2001, 945-968.

CQ Researcher

Published by CQ Press, a division of Congressional Quarterly Inc.

cqresearcher.com

Controlling the Internet

Can it survive as an uncensored global network?

Governments and corporations are increasingly concerned about political and economic threats posed by a freewheeling, global Internet. Many experts warn the "Net" may fragment into "walled gardens" that block users' freedom to communicate and innovate. In the U.S., telephone and cable companies already have won the right to block competing Internet service providers like Earthlink from using their high-speed broadband lines. Now advocates for an open Internet worry that broadband providers will use their market power to slow or block access to controversial Web sites or competing businesses like Internet telephone. The activists want Congress to require the companies to treat all Internet content the same. Abroad, more nations are expanding broadband access for economic reasons, even as they crack down on citizens who access controversial material or express dissenting opinions via the Net. In the face of such turmoil, civic groups worldwide are seeking new forms of governance to keep the Internet secure and uncensored.

A sunny day lures a laptop user to San Francisco's Union Square, one of 801 public sites in the city with wireless Internet access.

INSIDE

THIS REPORT

CQ Researcher • May 12, 2006 • www.cqresearcher.com
Volume 16, Number 18 • Pages 409-432

CQ PRESS

RECIPIENT OF SOCIETY OF PROFESSIONAL JOURNALISTS AWARD FOR EXCELLENCE ◆ AMERICAN BAR ASSOCIATION SILVER GAVEL AWARD

CONTROLLING THE INTERNET

Cover: A sunny day lures a laptop user to Union Square, one of 801 public sites in San Francisco with wireless Internet access, 368 of them free. (Getty Images/Justin Sullivan)

CQ Researcher

May 12, 2006
Volume 16, Number 18

MANAGING EDITOR: Thomas J. Colin

ASSISTANT MANAGING EDITOR: Kathy Koch

ASSOCIATE EDITOR: Kenneth Jost

STAFF WRITERS: Marcia Clemmitt, Peter Katel, Pamela M. Prah

CONTRIBUTING WRITERS: Rachel S. Cox, Sarah Glazer, David Hosansky, Patrick Marshall, Tom Price

DESIGN/PRODUCTION EDITOR: Olu B. Davis

ASSISTANT EDITOR: Melissa J. Hipolit

CQ PRESS

A Division of Congressional Quarterly Inc.

SENIOR VICE PRESIDENT/PUBLISHER: John A. Jenkins

DIRECTOR, LIBRARY PUBLISHING: Kathryn C. Suárez

DIRECTOR, EDITORIAL OPERATIONS: Ann Davies

CONGRESSIONAL QUARTERLY INC.

CHAIRMAN: Paul C. Tash

VICE CHAIRMAN: Andrew P. Corty

PRESIDENT/EDITOR IN CHIEF: Robert W. Merry

CQ Researcher (ISSN 1056-2036) is printed on acid-free paper. Published weekly, except March 24, July 7, July 14, Aug. 4, Aug. 11, Nov. 24, Dec. 22 and Dec. 29, by CQ Press, a division of Congressional Quarterly Inc. Annual full-service subscriptions for institutions start at $667. For pricing, call 1-800-834-9020, ext. 1906. To purchase a *CQ Researcher* report in print or electronic format (PDF), visit www.cqpress.com or call 866-427-7737. Single reports start at $10. Bulk purchase discounts and electronic-rights licensing are also available. Periodicals postage paid at Washington, D.C., and additional mailing offices. POSTMASTER: Send address changes to *CQ Researcher*, 1255 22nd St., N.W., Suite 400, Washington, DC 20037.

Controlling the Internet

By Marcia Clemmitt

The Issues

Critics of a proposed, new America Online (AOL) policy discovered in April that AOL apparently was blocking e-mails mentioning DearAOL.com — a Web site set up by 600 organizations opposed to the policy.

"I tried to e-mail my brother-in-law about DearAOL.com, and AOL sent me a response as if he had disappeared," said Wes Boyd, co-founder of MoveOn.org, a liberal political group. "When I sent him an e-mail without the DearAOL.com link, it went right through." [1]

AOL blamed the blockage on a brief technical glitch. "A glitch is a glitch is a glitch," said AOL Communication Director Nicholas Graham. "As many as 65 other domains . . . were impacted," even though they had no connection to DearAOL. [2]

AFP/Getty Images/Genya Savilov

Waving "Orange Revolution" flags, Ukrainians gather in Kiev's Independence Square on Aug. 24, 2005, the 14th anniversary of Ukraine's break from the Soviet Union. During the Orange Revolution, which pressured the government to overturn 2004 election results as fraudulent, community Web sites posted information about where protesters needed assistance.

But many DearAOL activists note the timing of the blockage suspiciously coincided with their latest petition drive opposing AOL's plan to allow mass mailers to pay a fee to bypass AOL's spam filters.

Activists fear that under AOL's proposed rule change, messages from "poorer" users — such as nonprofit charities and political groups — would be blocked while commercial ads would sail through. They also worry that major portions of the Internet would be off-limits to citizens of certain countries.

The DearAOL activists note that it's not the first time a big Internet service provider (ISP) has blocked access to content it opposed, nor does the collateral blocking of unaffiliated sites necessarily prove it was an accident, given that last year Telus, a Canadian phone company and ISP, blocked access to a Web site run by its striking employees' union. In the process, access to more than 700 unrelated Web sites was blocked. [3]

In the United States, the battle for Internet control is playing out over revision of the landmark 1996 Telecommunications Act, which deregulated the telecommunications industry to increase competition. [4] Much of the debate centers on so-called Net neutrality — or requiring ISPs to treat all Internet content equally.

Neutrality advocates say the policy has enabled the Internet to foster rapid innovation. With no gatekeeper regulating traffic, tiny start-up companies and college students have created a plethora of innovative products and services — from instant messaging and podcasting to e-Bay, search engines and Amazon.com. "The key to the Net's extraordinary innovation is that it doesn't allow a term like 'allow,' " wrote Lawrence Lessig, a professor of cyberlaw at Stanford University. [5]

But telephone and cable companies, which own the wires over which most Internet traffic travels, want to replace the Net's traditional "open-pipe" structure with a system of priority channels that "sniff" data to determine content and shift some traffic to high-priority lanes. Such a system is needed, the companies say, to ensure higher quality of service for customers downloading bandwidth-gobbling video, for example, and to raise funds to pay for extending fiber-optic cable and other infrastructure to carry today's much faster broadband Internet.

But media advocates say telephone and cable companies mostly want to protect their key businesses — video and voice transmissions — from new competitors offering the same services via broadband.

The big ISPs hope to remake the Internet in the "entertainment model," where big-money players control distribution channels, determining which content makes it onto the movie or television screen, says Jeffrey Chester, executive director of the Center for Digital Democracy. "Phone and cable companies know that if there's an open wire, their business is over," now that broadband connections are fast enough to carry video and voice telephony. "They have to make sure that their own content can receive premium treatment."

Such a model, Chester argues, is dangerous for democracy because the Internet is not just an entertainment

Internet Access Limited by 20 States

Twenty states have laws restricting municipally operated broadband lines and/or laws limiting consumers' right to attach equipment to their Internet lines. Five of the anti-municipal broadband laws were passed in 2005.

Local and State Laws Controlling Internet Access

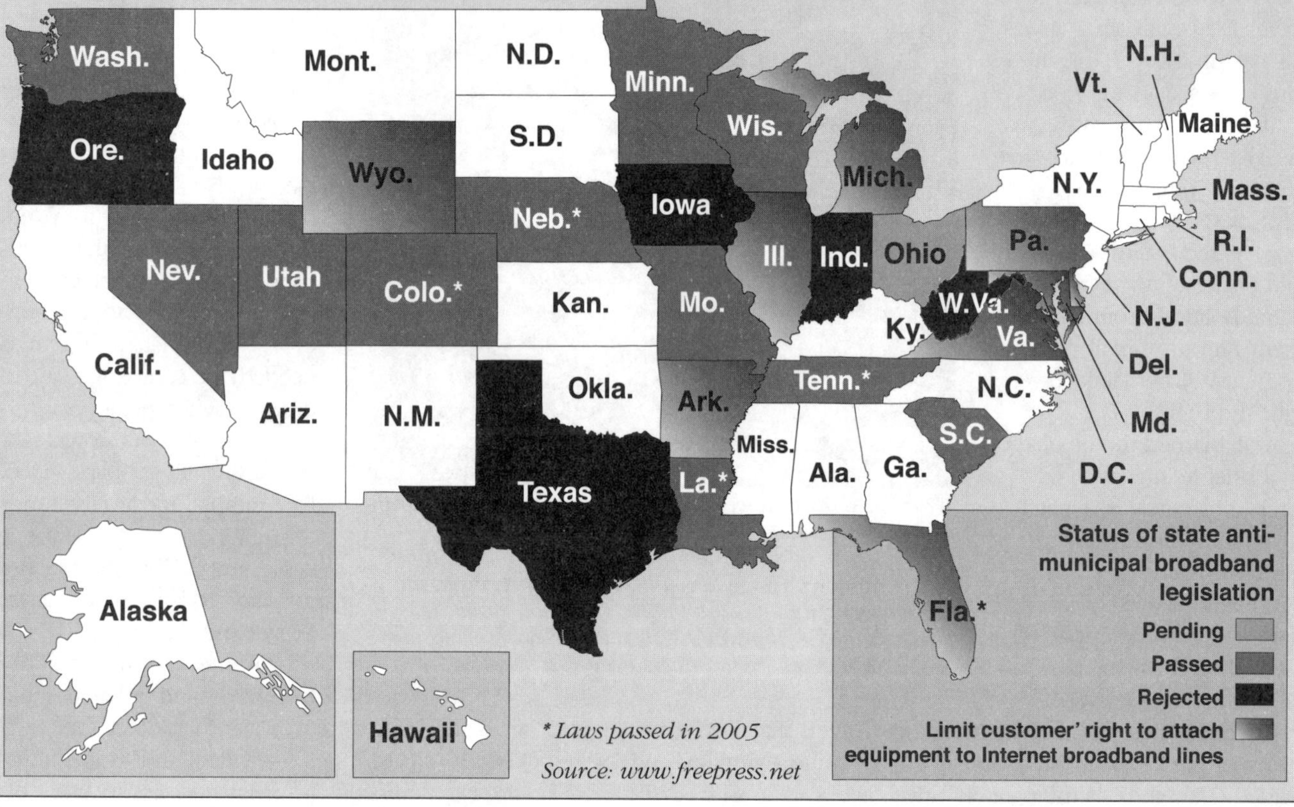

Status of state anti-municipal broadband legislation

Pending

Passed

Rejected

Limit customer' right to attach equipment to Internet broadband lines

** Laws passed in 2005*

Source: www.freepress.net

medium but also a forum for discussion of public issues. And if some information moves faster, then other information necessarily moves more slowly, he notes. The slower information may never be seen, he adds, which spells death to Web sites where visibility is key. If ISPs can shunt some information to slower lanes while reserving the fast lanes for selected content, what happens to "content necessary for civic participation?" he asks.

David Isenberg, a fellow at Harvard Law School's Berkman Center for the Internet and Society, agrees on the link between Internet freedom and democracy. Freedom of Internet communication is "fundamental to freedom of speech," and "violating it should be anathema to democracy," he says.

Some members of Congress, mostly Democrats, are pushing so-called Net-neutrality legislation that would prohibit ISPs from prioritizing service by content. But after heavy lobbying by the cable and telephone industries, the House Energy and Commerce Committee on April 26 defeated a Net-neutrality amendment while finalizing its version of the telecom law overhaul. Chairman Joe L. Barton, R-Texas, said that while he supports the Federal Communications Commission (FCC) watching for potentially anti-competitive or censorial ISP treatment of Internet content, he doesn't believe "all the Draconian things" people predict will happen without a Net-neutrality amendment. [6]

A new group — the "Save the Internet" coalition — says it is rapidly gaining individual and institutional supporters. By early May, the group claimed more than a half-million signatures on a petition demanding a Net-neutrality law. Backers range from the liberal MoveOn.org to conservative bloggers like "Instapundit" Glenn Reynolds and "Right Wing News." [7]

"Whenever you see people from the far left and the far right joining together about something that Congress is getting ready to do . . . what Congress is getting ready to do is basically un-American," said Craig Fields, director of Internet operations for Gun Owners of America. [8]

While some worry that powerful corporations want to stifle Internet freedom, others warn that various authoritarian governments in recent years have walled their citizens off from much of the Internet, even as they have promoted broadband use as an economy booster.

Indeed, repressive governments have much to fear from an unfettered Internet. Modern telecommunications played a major role in Ukraine's "Orange Revolution," which "pressured the government to overturn its 2004 election results as fraudulent." [9] Demonstrators used cell phone messaging technology to gather "smart mobs" of protesters, while community Web sites posted information about where protesters needed assistance. [10]

China has promoted Internet use as a tool for economic growth while squelching certain content. With some 111 million Internet users, China is second only to the United States in total users but has strictly limited their access. China blocks Web sites, censors citizens' Web searches and tracks down people who publish critical opinions or information on blogs. The Chinese government — with the acquiescence of Google, Yahoo! and other search engines — not only censors Web sites that question government actions but also those dealing with teen pregnancy, homosexuality, dating, beer and even jokes. [11] (*See sidebar, p. 424.*)

Free-Internet advocates also complain that broadband rollout in the United States has stalled — particularly in rural areas. "This country needs a national goal . . . to have universal, affordable access for broadband technology by the year 2007," said President George W. Bush in March 2004. [12] But critics say that because of phone and cable company foot-dragging and the lack of a national broadband strategy, Bush's goal can't possibly be reached and, in fact,

Off-Limits Web Sites

Sites that help Internet users in non-democratic countries avoid detection and those offering gambling are the most censored — after pornography and political dissent — among nations monitored by the OpenNet Initiative.

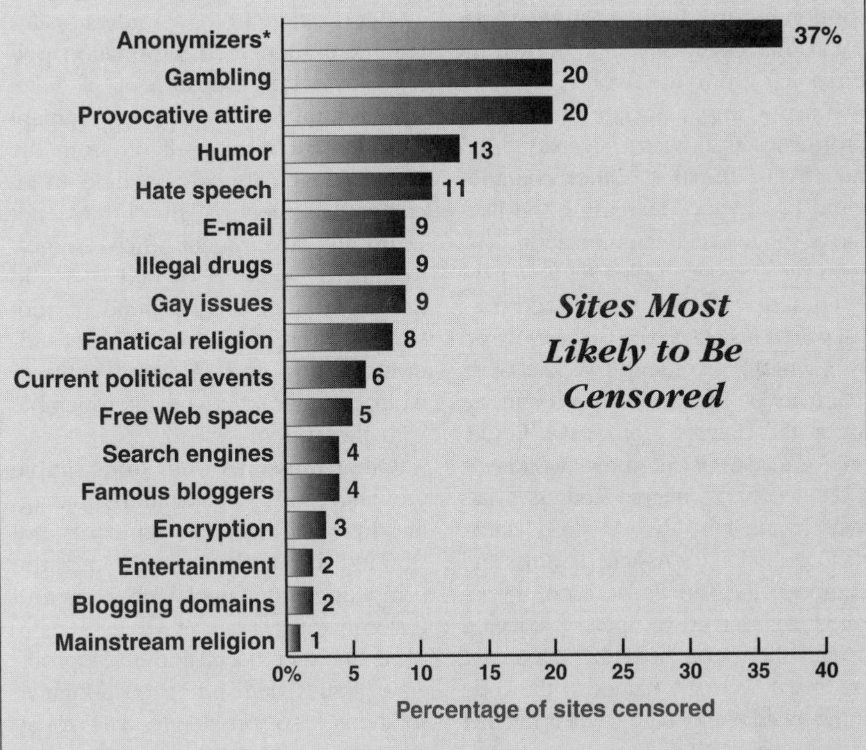

* *Sites that help online users remain untraceable*

Sources: Wired, *OpenNet Initiative, Reporters Without Borders*

the United States has fallen behind other industrialized countries in access to broadband. (*See graph, p. 422.*)

Installing fiber to carry broadband Internet to rural America is extremely expensive, says David Farber, distinguished career professor of computer science and public policy at Carnegie Mellon University. "I could run fiber to every ranch in Montana, but nobody would pay for it," he says. Nevertheless, private phone and cable companies are trying to block rural governments' efforts to offer residents broadband service on their own if the private market doesn't offer it or the service costs too much.

But low population density is not the obstacle to full broadband penetration so much as the lack of a national strategy to achieve that goal, says the advocacy group Free Press. It notes other low-density countries, such as Iceland and Canada, have more broadband coverage than the United States. [13]

As government, the telecom industry and Internet users debate control of the Net, here are some of the questions being discussed:

Is the global Internet in danger of being dismantled?

Enthusiasts say the Internet embodies the dream of a global medium allowing people on opposite sides of the planet to communicate as easily as if they were in the same room. Today, however, some say the global Internet is in danger of being fragmented into separate, unconnected networks.

For instance, authoritarian governments are building firewalls to block citizens' access to certain parts of the Net, especially the Web sites of opposition groups. In the past few years, China "has essentially shut its own Internet off from the world Internet," says Jean Camp, associate professor of informatics at Indiana University. "And they're just the first. Other countries could do it," too, increasing the likelihood of Internet fragmentation.

In late February, China set up a master list of new Chinese Internet addresses that will be maintained on Chinese-owned "root servers," according to Michael Geist, chairman of Internet and e-commerce law at the University of Ottawa in Ontario, Canada. [14] Until now, worldwide coordination of Internet addresses has been handled by the U.S.-based Internet Corporation for Assigned Names and Numbers (ICANN). In addition, 13 so-called root-server computers scattered around the globe hold the master list that maps Web site names to the code numbers corresponding to their Internet addresses, or URLs.

China's action "doesn't mark the end of a global, interoperative Internet," but it demonstrates that countries may not always cooperate to keep the global Internet interoperable, said Geist. The global system would "break" if a parallel system duplicated existing addresses and diverted them to different computers, for example, or adopted different technical operating procedures.

The results of such an alternative Internet could be "creepy," says Lauren Weinstein, co-founder of People for Internet Responsibility. Different sites would pop up for the same Web address typed into computers in different countries. International e-mails might not get through, and variable or incompatible standards would stymie those trying to develop new business and communications applications, says Weinstein.

"The Internet . . . exists only if there is agreement about core functionality," he says. "For it to work, there has to be an awful lot of cooperation," and if enough countries become disgruntled with the current system, a split could develop.

But David Gross, coordinator for communications and information policy at the U.S. Department of State, says it's unlikely that a government would risk cutting itself off from the global community by launching an incompatible root system. "I have not heard any government official suggest that there would be benefits . . . in the creation of an independent root system" using existing Internet addresses. Gross said. "Any new network would . . . want to be interoperable with the current system."

Other pressures stem from simple growing pains. Organizations managing Internet technical standards are strained by rapid growth and the competing agendas of Web users and governments. [15]

As Internet users and uses proliferate, issues demanding collaborative solutions also proliferate, but today there is no specific structure to resolve them, says Weinstein. Despite its mind-boggling sophistication, the Internet is, in fact, in its "infancy," he says.

To keep the system interoperable, a new governance structure must develop that is embraced by an unusually diverse group of players, including governments, domestic and international businesses and individual users, says John Mathiason, an adjunct professor for international education and distance learning at Syracuse University. Today the world is just beginning to develop such a system, he says.

Dealing with copyright violations — such as the illegal downloading of music — is only one of many complications that must be worked out, he says. Currently, music copyright laws can be circumvented using servers located in countries that are not party to international copyright treaties, Mathiason says. If the Internet allows circumvention of national boundaries, he says, "You need to work out how conflicting schemes of copyright, commercial transactions and money are going to work."

Such protections don't yet exist, and more unresolved issues keep popping up, Mathiason says. "In a technical sense, the Internet is very robust," he says. "But, from a political point of view, it's very fragile. There is a great motivation by many people to keep it global and open. But when you have a conflict, then the issue is up in the air."

Today, ICANN is the closest thing to an Internet governing organization, although ostensibly it only manages certain technical parameters — mainly involving Internet addresses — and bases its decisions on input from businesses, governments and users around the world.

"The U.S. has been a very light-handed steward from the beginning," says Susan Crawford, an assistant professor of law at Cardozo Law School in New York City and ICANN board member. "ICANN becomes the issue of contention because the domain name system" — the Internet's system of coordinated address names and their corresponding code numbers — "is one of the very few choke points where you could censor content."

But even ICANN's "light-handed" approach to regulating the Internet has come under fire, in part because, while independent, it operates under the auspices of the U.S. Department of Commerce. For example, last summer, after long deliberation, ICANN announced that it would create a new "dot xxx" Internet domain where pornography Web sites could voluntarily register. The move was controversial worldwide but became more so when, shortly thereafter, ICANN reversed the decision at the behest of the Commerce Department, after heavy lobbying by conservative groups.

Commerce's intervention raised hackles and was seen as "very inappropriate," since it imposed a U.S. policy position on the Internet without consultation, says Crawford. In fact, Commerce's surprise intervention probably got more people worldwide to come down in favor of the xxx domain than would ever have done so otherwise, says Mathiason.

In another controversial move, ICANN in 2005 at the behest of the U.S. government, transferred ownership of the Internet domain for Kazakhstan — "dot kz" — from a group of Kazakhstan Internet users to an organization owned by the Kazakh government "without requiring consent from the existing owners," said Kieren McCarthy, a British technology writer. It also turned Iraq's domain over to a government-run group.[16]

"Previously, ICANN would take no action . . . unless both sides were in complete agreement," he said. "Now, ICANN had set itself up as the de facto world authority on who should run different parts of the Internet."[17]

Tension between the United States and other governments over non-Internet issues such as the Iraq war are exacerbating disgruntlement with ICANN, say some Internet scholars. "People just don't have the same good faith now that Washington will stay benevolent and not do anything to abuse its authority," said Lee McKnight, an associate professor of information economics and technology policy at Syracuse University's School of Information Studies.[18]

ICANN — and other organizations being considered to take over Internet management, such as the United Nations — are too likely to become enmeshed with the aims of big business and wealthy governments to make good long-term stewards, say many public-policy analysts. The only way to stave off a fragmented Net lies in civic groups stepping up to develop worldwide consensus on Internet issues, they argue.

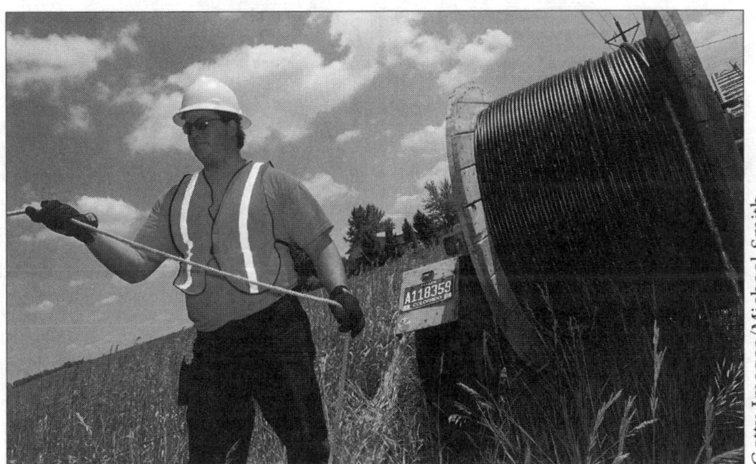

Getty Images/Michael Smith

A worker helps install fiber-optic cable onto telephone lines in Louisville, Colo. President George W. Bush has called for "universal, affordable access for broadband technology by the year 2007," but critics say the goal can't be reached because of phone and cable company foot-dragging and the lack of a national broadband strategy.

"The world is on the path to more globalized governance" though the road is long, says Milton Mueller, a professor of the political economy of communications at Syracuse University and co-founder of ICANN's Noncommercial Users Constituency.

Should telephone and cable companies be allowed to control the Internet?

As significantly faster broadband connections become the norm, telephone and cable companies that own the so-called last-mile wires connecting homes and businesses to the Internet say they need more control over how data travels and what kind of data users send in order to improve security, transmission quality and broadband access.

However, Internet-freedom advocates say the Internet only works when it's an "open pipe," with all data treated the same, and when users are free to place whatever software or hardware they want at the "pipe ends" without asking permission — just as electricity customers can plug in either a computer network or a toaster. Without these key qualities, the Internet cannot continue to foster business innovation and the open discussion crucial to democracy, say open-Net advocates.

Cable and telephone companies want permission to alter the open-pipe structure so they can "prioritize" and speed transmission of some data. Allowing companies to speed transmission of some content, such as video, would increase competition by allowing ISPs to specialize, says Chistopher Yoo, a professor of technology and entertainment law at Vanderbilt University Law School.

But others say allowing network owners to slow or speed data will mean that only wealthy individuals and companies would get higher-speed service, leaving poorer, non-commercial users and start-up businesses in slower-moving cyber obscurity. Such a system would also stifle innovation and allow cable and telephone companies to block, slow or charge exorbitant fees to companies like Vonage, which offers Voice Over Internet Protocol (VOIP), or telephone service via the Internet.

"Because the network is neutral, the creators of new Internet content and services need not seek permission . . . or pay special fees to be seen online," said Vinton Cerf, a key Internet software developer and Chief Internet Evangelist for Google. "As a result, we have seen an array of unpredictable new offerings" — from blogging to VOIP — "that might never have evolved had central control of the network been required."[19]

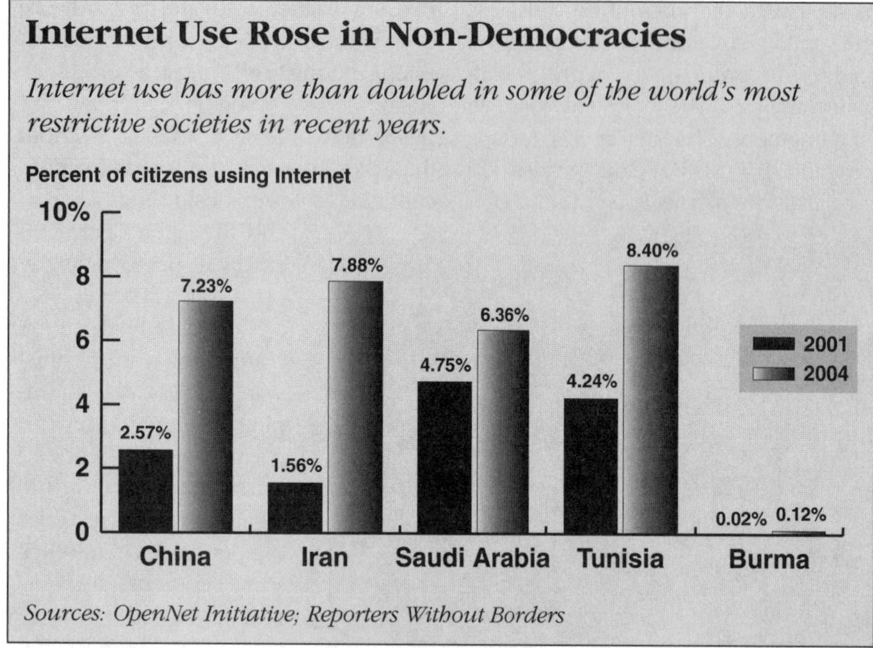

A neutral net is "critical" to America's competitiveness, he adds. "In places like Japan, Korea, Singapore and the United Kingdom, higher bandwidth and neutral broadband platforms are unleashing waves of innovation that threaten to leave the U.S. further and further behind," says Cerf.

In defending their proposal to charge customers more for priority transmission, some phone companies insist that some companies have already asked to be able to pay more for faster service.

"It's probably true that companies are . . . willing to pay for better treatment, but I think they're doing it out of fear," said Jeff Pulver, an Internet analyst. "It's legalized extortion." [20]

As for blocking telephone company competitors like Vonage, Ed Whitacre, CEO of SBC Communications, said he's not worried that his business will be eclipsed by online competitors, because he controls their transmission lines. "How do you think they're going to get to customers?" Whitacre asked. "Through a broadband pipe. Now what [Vonage and other Internet businesses] would like to do is use my pipes free, but I ain't going to let them do that. . . . The Internet can't be free in that sense, because we and the cable companies have made an investment and for a Google or Yahoo or Vonage . . . to expect to use these pipes free is nuts!" [21]

But some technology scholars say Whitacre's plan could amount to double-charging. "This is a pretty dumb thing . . . to say," wrote Edward Felten, professor of computer science and public affairs at Princeton University. "If I were an SBC broadband customer, I'd be dying to ask Mr. Whitacre exactly what my monthly payment is buying if it isn't buying access to Google, Yahoo, Vonage and any other $%&^ Internet service I want to use." Many SBC customers sign up for the company's broadband services only to get access to Vonage or Google, so "why should Google pay SBC for this? Why shouldn't SBC pay Google instead?" [22]

Yoo acknowledges that there might be a "limited incentive" for cable Internet providers to discriminate against competing ISPs or for a telephone company to discriminate against VOIP providers. But "since different people want different things from the Internet," he says, encouraging "network diversity" would create a more vibrant marketplace where network providers can "compete on a basis other than price."

Moreover, allowing telecom companies to charge companies extra for priority online treatment would not put innovators at a disadvantage, as many fear, says James Gattuso, a senior fellow at the conservative Heritage Foundation. Instead, start-ups might be first in line to pay for priority transmission, because "if I were starting up a computing application, I would want to be able to say my new service is faster," he says. And start-ups "can get capital to pay for prioritized treatment," Gattuso says. "Money is easier to get than visibility." (*See "At Issue," p. 425.*)

Verizon's chief technology officer, Mark Wegleitner, says contrary to neutrality-advocates' fears, network owners have a strong incentive to help customers reach as many Web sites as possible. "We think the richest, broadest choice . . . makes for a happier consumer," he said. [23]

But others argue that if companies can "sniff" data packets and speed some information along faster than the rest it will hamper democratic discourse online. Web sites with controversial views might be relegated to the slow lanes, says the Center for Digital Democracy's Chester. And since nonprofits with "dot org" Internet addresses — where much of the civic discourse takes place online — often have little cash, their Internet communications will be shunted to the equivalent of a cyber "dirt road," he says. "This is being framed as a business story, but it's also a battle for the soul of our communications system."

In addition, start-up content providers could be strangled by red tape, he warns. "Today, anyone can open up a Web site and compete" for Internet users' attention. "Tomorrow, you'll have to show up at the office of the phone and cable companies" to get permission to attach your new application to the network, he says.

Advocates of a neutral Internet law say history indicates that phone and

A World of Online Communities

Because the Internet developed free of corporate control, it's been a source of innovation, giving rise to new technologies and forums, including some that threaten traditional businesses and values. That's in stark contrast to the "entertainment model" phone and cable companies want to impose on the Internet, which critics say would limit such innovation.

A relative newcomer is **Meetup — www.meetup.com** — which helps people establish interest groups in their local communities. Founded in 2002, it claims 2 million members, including French-, Italian-, Japanese- and Spanish-speakers' groups, stay-at-home-moms' groups and book clubs.

Social-networking sites, where users post profiles and garner "friend" lists, are booming. **MySpace — www.myspace.com** — used by young people and celebrities alike, boasts 50 million members, and **Friendster — www.friendster.com** — 24 million. In South Korea, 15 million people — one-third of the population — belong to CyWorld. [1]

Partisan political networking and blogging sites have flourished over the past few years, but a recent entry, **Essembly — www.essembly.com** — hopes to exploit the social-networking phenomenon on a non-partisan basis. Essembly members post profiles, blog and list friends, as on MySpace, but they also participate in site-wide political dialogue.

Since Hurricane Katrina hit the Gulf Coast in 2005, a volunteer Internet service, the **Katrina People Finder Project — www.katrinalist.net** — has helped people locate missing loved ones. Along with a team of other computer experts, David Geilhufe developed a new computer tool, People Finder Information Formats, to aggregate data from various sources into one searchable, convenient source. [2]

New kinds of people-to-people links — often for the purpose of bypassing banks and other traditional institutions — pop up continually on the Internet. Several new sites feature people-to-people banking. **Kiva — www.kiva.org** — enables individuals in the United States to offer micro-financing help to entrepreneurs in developing countries by partnering with local organizations. Lenders can chip in capital in amounts as small as $25 to help people start bakeries, print shops and hair salons. Kiva reports 100 percent of its loans have been repaid or are being repaid.

Prosper — www.prosper.com — links up people who want to borrow money or are willing to lend it, for a return. Would-be borrowers seek cash to attend school, renovate a house, start a business or buy a big present for a 40th anniversary, and Prosper lenders name their own interest rates.

In keeping with the Internet principle that the more people a network links the more value it has, Internet entrepreneurs and activists have long developed applications aimed at bringing more people online, sometimes for free.

For example, **FON software — http://en.fon.com/** — helps Wi-Fi (Wireless Fidelity) users worldwide get access to wireless Internet wherever they go, in return for registering to share their own wireless access with other FON members who pass by.

Internet services to help users get around government censorship also are under continual development by activists around the world.

Psiphon — developed by researchers at the University of Toronto — and the **Free Network Project**, or **Freenet**, developed by Scottish network technologist Ian Clarke, use computer networks in non-censoring countries to help people in information-censoring regimes communicate anonymously and freely.

To many Internet enthusiasts, the Net is first and foremost a publishing medium, and as faster broadband connections become the norm, the range of what's published continually expands. At photo-sharing site **Flickr — www.flickr.com** — members file, store and share their photos. And, true to the Internet's community-building tradition, Flickr members engage in plenty of two-way conversation about what they see. For example, in several popular ongoing games, Flickr members snap and post mystery photos in a favorite city, like New York, Chicago or London, and fellow urban-enthusiasts try to guess where the photo was taken.

Among the newest wrinkles are sites where users can upload and share videos. The hot, new video site **YouTube — www.YouTube.com** — started up last year in the garage of two young techies looking to share home videos. Among the current offerings on the site created by Chad Hurley and Steve Chen — a sample guitar lesson posted by a group of music teachers advertising their pay services; a video art installation of a chair that disassembles then reassembles itself to music; performance clips of aspiring comics; and home and travel videos from around the world, from street dancing in Japan to scary driving behavior in India.

And of course, big advertisers also show up on YouTube, counting on the passing traffic — 30 million videos are viewed daily — to drum up interest in everything from new Nike sneakers to upcoming movies like "Superman Returns." [3]

---

[1] Micah L. Sifty, "Essembly.com: Finally, a Friendster for Politics," *Personal Democracy Forum*, March 13, 2006, www.personaldemocracy.com.

[2] Tin Zak, transcript, "Interview with Ethan Zuckerman," *Globeshakers*, Oct. 3, 2005, www.pghaccelerator.org.

[3] "YouTube: Way Beyond Home Videos," *Business Week online*, April 10, 2006, www.businessweek.com.

cable companies will not respect the Net's open nature on their own. According to Public Knowledge, a non-profit that advocates for a free and open Internet, ISPs have tried to manipulate how broadband subscribers use the Net and have forbidden subscribers from using their broadband connections to provide content to the public — flying in the face of the Internet's tradition of offering publishing power to ordinary people. [24]

Other broadband contracts forbid home users from logging onto virtual private networks (VPNs), needed by telecommuters to access their workplace networks from home. And, until the FCC intervened last year, Madison River Telephone Co., which serves rural counties in Illinois and several Southern states, blocked subscribers from using Vonage's VOIP service. [25] The wireless company Clearwire, in Kirkland, Wash., blocks broadband services — such as streaming video or VOIP — that use a lot of bandwidth, and broadband providers have successfully lobbied for laws in nine states limiting how broadband consumers can use their own computers. [26]

Content blocking for ideological reasons also has occurred, according to Public Knowledge. Last year the Canadian ISP Telus blocked a Web site set up by a labor union representing Telus employees, who were in a dispute with the company. [27]

Should local governments be allowed to provide broadband Internet service?

Far fewer Americans have access to affordable broadband than citizens in other developed countries, and too few Americans have a choice of broadband Internet service providers — especially in rural areas. At the end of 2005, only 24 percent of rural households were using high-speed Internet at home, compared to 39 percent of urban and suburban households. [28]

Running TV cables or upgrading phone lines to isolated homes in rural areas costs more and returns less profit than stringing cable or phone lines in high-density urban or suburban areas, so rural areas are usually the last to get new telecom services.

To overcome the problem, many local governments have begun installing or are considering installing their own networks, either on their own or in partnership with private companies. Local groups argue that such government-initiated efforts can spur more competitive broadband markets and widen access. But the cable and phone companies offering Internet services say government-provided broadband services siphon off subscription money that the companies could use to extend their broadband infrastructure.

In Sanborn, Iowa — population 1,300 — "we have lost nearly 50 percent of our subscribers" over the past four years to a municipal broadband service, not because of high prices or poor services but due to unfair competition, said Douglas Boone, CEO of the Premier Communications phone company, told the Senate Commerce Committee on Feb. 14. [29] Private ISPs cannot compete with local governments' broadband offerings, he said, because localities don't pay taxes, which eat up "more than 40 percent of our profits. It is difficult to compete when the local municipality starts . . . with a 40 percent discount." [30]

Furthermore, since most municipal broadband is in rural areas, the projects pose the biggest threat to the smallest ISPs, which generally serve rural areas neglected by the bigger cable and phone companies, according to Brett Glass, owner of a tiny wireless — Lariat.Net — in Laramie, Wyo. Subsidized local broadband networks also crowd out small wireless start-ups, which could mean less competition in the long run because wireless ISPs are potentially the biggest competitive threat to cable and telephone ISPs, he said. [31]

Opponents also argue that locally subsidized broadband is probably an unfair and inefficient use of public dollars. "It is unlikely that more than a small number of residents would benefit," wrote Joseph Bast, president of the Chicago-based free-market think tank Heartland Institute, making it hard to "justify the steep cost" that would be borne by all local taxpayers. The cost also can't be justified in the name of overall community improvement, he argued, because "it is fanciful to imagine that municipal broadband is a cost-effective way to promote economic development." [32]

But advocates of municipal broadband point out that many of the projects are not competing against private business. "The overwhelming majority of current projects are the result of a public-private partnership," wrote city officials from four small Texas towns in a Feb. 13 letter to Sen. Kay Bailey Hutchison, R-Texas. They called the claim that the public-sector broadband threatens the private sector "a red herring." [33]

Supporters of municipal broadband also argue that the usual ban against the public sector competing with the private sector does not apply to broadband infrastructure because broadband is a public, not a private, good.

If high-speed Internet services "were a purely private good . . . like, say, golf clubs, I could buy an argument against government provision," said Thomas Rowley, a fellow at the University of Missouri-based Rural Policy Research Institute. But "its benefits go far beyond the individual user to improve an entire community's economy, schools, health care and public safety. As with all these services, if the private sector cannot or will not . . . provide it to all at affordable prices, the public sector must." [34] ■

BACKGROUND

Born in the USA

In the early 1960s, a nuclear clash between the Cold War superpowers, the United States and the Soviet Union, seemed imminent. U.S. researchers wondered: Could they build a communications network that could survive nuclear combat? [35] Their efforts spurred creation of the Internet, whose technological and social ramifications we are

Continued on p. 420

Chronology

1960s-1970s

Computer researchers develop non-centralized, user-controlled computer networks.

1965
MIT researcher Lawrence Roberts creates first long-distance computer network, linking machines in Massachusetts and California.

1969
University of California at Los Angeles becomes the first node of ARPANET, the Internet's Pentagon-funded precursor.

1971
Michael Hart starts Project Gutenberg to put copyright-free works online.

1972
E-mail is invented and dubbed the first Internet "killer app."

1973
England and Norway become the Net's first international connections.

1974
AT&T declines invitation to run the Internet.

1975
First ARPANET mailing lists link people with shared interests.

1980s-1990s

Businesses join research institutions online. Internet viruses and spam invented.

1982
Sending messages gets easier as a University of Wisconsin server automatically links computer numbers to names, in the prototype of the Domain Name System (DNS).

1984
Internet-wide DNS introduced. The Net has over 1,000 directly connected computers — called "hosts," or Internet service providers (ISPs).

1988
Cornell graduate student Robert Morris, son of a network-security expert, sends the first self-replicating virus.

1989
Internet has over 100,000 hosts.

1990
"The World" (world.std.com) is the first commercial ISP. The first remotely operable machine — the Internet Toaster — goes online.

1992
Internet has more than 1 million hosts.

1993
White House, U.N. go online.

1994
U.S. immigration lawyers Martha Siegel and Lawrence Cantor send out first spam, advertising their firm.

1996
Phone companies ask Congress to ban Internet telephones. Congress passes Telecommunications Act but doesn't ban the phones . . . . China requires Net users and ISPs to register with the police . . . . Saudi Arabia confines access to universities and hospitals.

1998
Private, nonprofit Internet Corporation for Assigned Numbers (ICANN) takes over DNS under a U.S. government contract.

1999
Somalia gets an ISP; Bangladesh and Palestinian Territories register domains.

2000s

Battles over Internet control heat up. Broadband allows voice and video to travel over the Internet. U.S. phone and cable industries consolidate and offer broadband.

2000
Yahoo! bans auctions of Nazi memorabilia when it is unable to block French users from the product listings, as ordered by a French court.

2001
Internet2 — an ultra-fast broadband network for U.S. research institutions — carries a live musical, "The Technophobe and the Madman."

2002
FCC rules that cable broadband operators don't need to give competing ISPs access to their lines.

2003
First World Summit on the Information Society discusses global governance and access for developing nations.

2005
FCC rules phone companies don't need to give competing ISPs free access to broadband connections. India's domain, "dot in," swells from 7,000 sites in 2004 to more than 100,000 in 2005. . . . China jails dissident based on Net writings handed over by Yahoo!

2006
Google launches controversial Chinese search engine that censors information. . . . Congress considers "Net neutrality" legislation. . . . ICANN contract expires in September, and governments and citizens' groups mull global governance for the Internet.

Rights Group Names 15 Internet 'Enemies'

Reporters Without Borders, an international organization working to restore the press' right to inform citizens, recently listed the following 15 countries as "enemies of the Internet" because of their restrictive Internet policies:

Belarus: President Alexander Lukashenko often blocks access to opposition parties' Web sites, especially at election time. In August 2005, he harassed youths posting satirical cartoons online.

Burma: Home Internet connections are prohibited; access to opposition sites is systematically blocked, and Internet café computers record what customers are searching every five minutes for government-spying purposes.

China: Censorship technology and spying block all government criticism on the Internet. Intimidation, including the world's largest prison for cyber-dissidents, forces self-censorship by users. Some blogs and discussion groups post real-time news about events in China, but censors remove the postings later. China is exporting its cyber-surveillance expertise to other repressive countries, including Zimbabwe, Cuba and Belarus.

Cuba: Citizens may not buy computers or access the Internet without Communist Party authorization. Some Cubans get connected illegally but can only access a highly censored, government-controlled version of the Internet.

Iran: Ministry of Information blocks access to hundreds of thousands of Web sites, especially those dealing with sex and providing independent news. Several bloggers were imprisoned recently, including Mojtaba Saminejad, who got a two-year sentence for insulting Ayatollah Ali Khamenei.

Libya: There is no independent media, and the government controls the Internet, blocking access to dissident exile sites and targeting cyber-dissidents.

Maldives: Several opposition Web sites are filtered by President Maumoon Abdul Gayoom's regime. One of four people arrested in 2002 is still in prison for helping to produce an e-mailed newsletter criticizing government policies.

Nepal: King Gyanendra Bir Bikram Shah Dev's regime controls Internet access of citizens. Most online opposition publications, especially those seen as close to Maoist rebels, have been blocked inside the country. Bloggers discussing politics or human rights are under constant pressure from the authorities.

North Korea: The government only recently allowed a few thousand privileged citizens access to a highly censored version of the Internet, including about 30 pro-regime sites.

Saudi Arabia: The government blocks access to 400,000 sites to protect citizens from content — mainly sex, politics or religion — that violates Islamic principles and social standards.

Syria: The government restricts Internet access to a small number of privileged people, filters the Web and closely monitors online activity.

Tunisia: President Zine el-Abidine Ben Ali blocks opposition publications and other news sites, discourages e-mail because it is difficult to monitor and jails cyber-dissidents.

Turkmenistan: Internet use is essentially prohibited; there are no Internet cafés, and a censored version of the Web is only accessible through certain companies and international organizations.

Continued from p. 418

only today beginning to understand.

Traditional networks — like the phone system and Post Office — route messages through central switching points and are vulnerable to complete breakdown if vital nodes are knocked out. Paul Baran, an electrical engineer at the RAND Corporation, a think tank focusing on military issues, proposed a network with many nodes, each able to route data on to another network point until the data reached its destination. He also proposed chopping messages into smaller "packets" of digitized information. Each packet is separately addressed and travels on its own to the designated addressee computer.

The network plan — which several other researchers envisioned at the same time — seemed inefficient, but was in truth "extremely rugged," designed with doomsday in mind, explained technology and science fiction writer Bruce Sterling. Each digital packet "would be tossed like a hot potato from node to node to node, more or less in the direction of its destination, until it ended up in the proper place. If big pieces of the network had been blown away, that simply wouldn't matter; the packets would still stay airborne, lateralled wildly across the field by whatever nodes happened to survive." [36]

In 1969, the concept was made operational for the first time, when seven large computers at U.S. research institutions were linked into a non-centralized packet-switching communications network. Funded by the Defense Department's Advanced Research Projects Agency (DARPA), ARPANET allowed researchers to transmit data — and even program each other's computers — via dedicated high-speed lines.

Scientists were enthusiastic about ARPANET, which gave them access to hard-to-come-by user time on remote fast computers. By 1972, the network had 37 nodes. Through the 1970s, other computer networks in the United States and abroad were linked to the so-called ARPANET, and the Internet — the network of networks — was born.

From its earliest days the Internet's radically decentralized structure gave it an unprecedented ability to develop in ways that its inventors never anticipated, a characteristic at the heart of today's battles over the Net.

ARPANET was built to facilitate high-tech computing and government com-

Controlling Net Traffic

Here are the five most common ways that governments, primarily non-democratic states, control access to the Internet.

Filter Web content at national level
Arrest and prosecute cyber-dissidents
Monitor cyber-cafés
Require registration of Web sites
Use Web-filtering software

Sources: OpenNet Initiative; Reporters Without Borders

Uzbekistan: The state security service often asks Internet service providers (ISPs) to temporarily block access to opposition sites. Some Internet cafés warn users will be fined for viewing pornographic or banned political sites.

Vietnam: Filters "subversive" Internet content, spies on cyber-café users and jails cyber-dissidents.

Countries to Watch

Bahrain: Has begun to regulate the Internet; requires all online publications, including forums and blogs, to be officially registered.

Egypt: Censorship is minor, but the government has taken steps since 2001 to control online material; some criticism of the government is unwelcome.

European Union (EU): Holds ISPs responsible for content of Web sites they host, requiring them to block any page considered illegal; EU is studying a proposal to oblige ISPs to retain records of customers' online activity.

Kazakhstan: Online publications are under scrutiny because many government scandals have been revealed on Web sites. President Nursultan Nazarbayev's regime blocked two opposition party sites in October 2005.

Malaysia: Government intimidation of online journalists and bloggers has increased, notably at the country's only independent Internet daily, whose journalists have been threatened and its premises searched.

Singapore: The government intimidates Internet users, bloggers and Web site editors.

South Korea: Filters the Internet, blocking pornographic sites and publications that "disturb public order," including pro-North Korea sites; users who go too far in expressing anti-government opinions are punished.

Thailand: Filters the Internet to fight pornography, but has extended censorship well beyond this.

United States: Laws to prevent intercepting online traffic do not guarantee enough privacy; U.S. Internet firms, including Google, Yahoo!, Cisco Systems and Microsoft, are working with China to censor their material in China.

Zimbabwe: The government reportedly is getting Chinese equipment to monitor citizens' Internet usage; state telecom monopoly TelOne asked ISPs in June 2004 to sign contracts allowing it to monitor e-mail traffic and requiring them to block material the government deems illegal.

Source: Reporters Without Borders, 2005.

munications. But, to the surprise of many, high-tech users quickly adapted the system to a down-to-earth pursuit — sending mail electronically for free. By 1973 e-mail made up 75 percent of network traffic.

By 1975, users had developed another new application — mailing lists to broadcast individual messages to large numbers of subscribers. These discussion lists gave birth to the first Internet communities — groups around the world connected by networked computers and common interests. While some lists were work-related, many were not. The most popular of the early unofficial lists was SF-Lovers, a list for discussing science fiction.

As the Internet quietly fostered new ways of communicating, the traditional communications industry remained aloof. Internet users paid for the use of phone lines to transmit their data, but otherwise phone companies paid little attention to the Net. "We were fortunate in that there was absolutely no commercial Internet industry out there," said Robert Kahn, a former DARPA network developer who later founded the nonprofit Corporation for National Research Initiatives to promote information-infrastructure development. "There were no . . . Internet service providers; there was no commercial anything. So nobody . . . saw the original Internet initiative as a threat to their business." In fact, AT&T made a conscious decision to stay out of computer networking, he pointed out. "They thought they could make more money by selling . . . the underlying circuits." [37]

AT&T — at the time a telephone monopoly — was kept informed of ARPANET's progress but wasn't impressed. AT&T executive Jack Osterman said of one DARPA proposal, "First, it can't possibly work, and if it did, damned if we are going to allow the creation of a competitor to ourselves." [38]

In 1974, AT&T turned down an offer to run ARPANET. [39]

Battle of the Band

During the 1980s the decentralized Internet mushroomed from less than 1,000 host computers, mostly in the United States, to millions worldwide, but the telephone and cable companies largely continued to ignore it. The Internet expanded from the research sector to

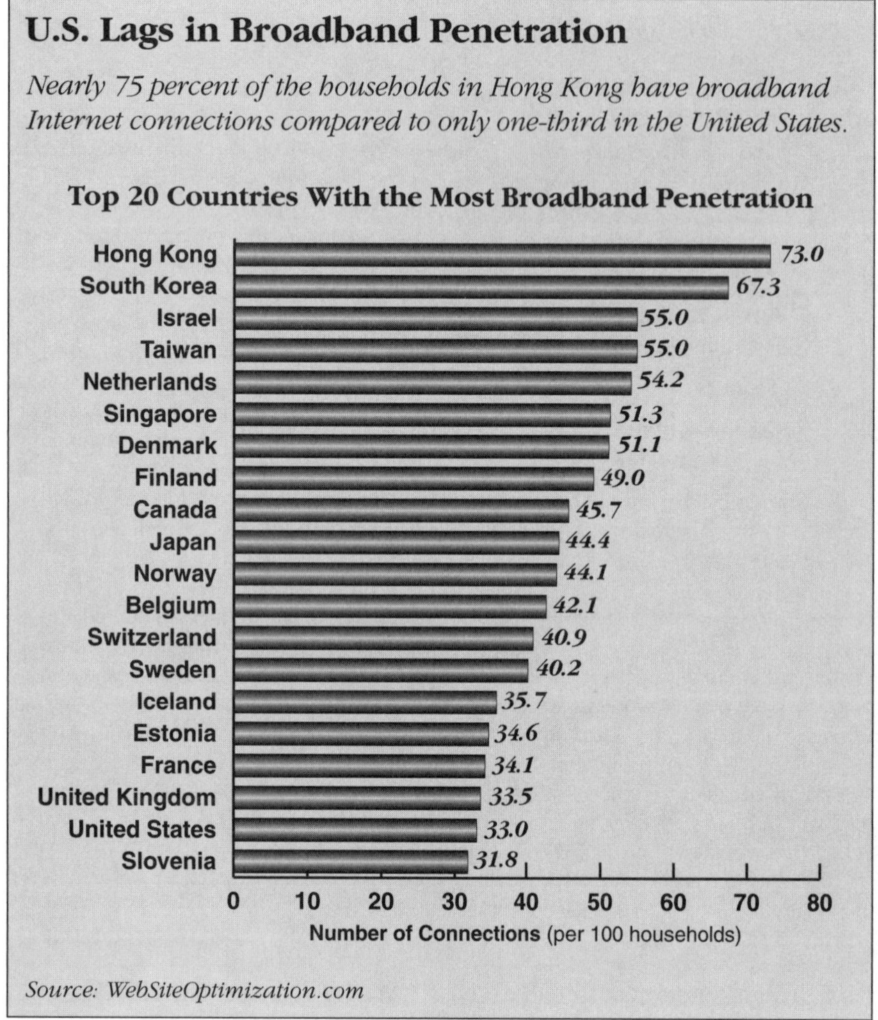

the commercial sector in the mid- to late-'90s and began spawning e-commerce businesses and new ways to communicate, like the now ubiquitous Web sites. Nervous about potential competition, phone companies asked Congress in the mid-1990s to ban Internet telephony, but legislators refused.

A new world emerged in the late 1990s when broadband technology, using cable and optical fiber to transmit data at high speeds, allowed Internet users to send not just text but video and voice messages. While top speeds get faster all the time, the International Telecommunications Union defines broadband as transmissions of 256 kilobytes per second (Kbps) or faster — for both uploading and downloading — while the U.S. FCC deems broadband as transmissions of 200 Kbps or faster.

As communications digitized and speeded up, the telecommunications landscape changed for its dominant industries — telephone and cable-TV companies.

First, cable operators began offering Internet connections over their lines. Phone companies responded by adding so-called digital subscriber lines (DSL), which are broadband-capable wires with a range of speeds at around 128 Mbps — much slower than cable broadband.

Furthermore, the freewheeling, innovative Internet could now provide the telecommunication industries' two big-money products — video and voice communications.

In 1996, when Congress overhauled federal telecom law for the first time in several years, legislators believed they had created a framework for a competitive telecom marketplace that would last well into the future. [40] However, few foresaw that within a few years Internet companies like Google Video or Vonage would offer video and telephone service that would directly compete with the cable and phone companies — who own the transmission lines over which those competing products would travel.

The 1996 act was "oblivious to the power of the Internet and technology to revolutionize everything," said Michael Powell, who was appointed by President George W. Bush and chaired the FCC from 2001 to 2005. [41]

In the past few years, with Congress not yet willing to wade into telecom law again, the FCC, courts and state legislatures have been left to sort out increasingly bitter battles over broadband.

Phone companies have long been regulated as "common carriers' — open channels required to accept all traffic without discrimination, in return for being free of legal liability for communications they carry. Cable companies were not deemed common carriers; however, prior to 2002, the FCC required them to lease their broadband-Internet lines to competing ISPs on reasonable terms.

But the key principle of the 1996 act — and a guiding principle for the Bush administration — was that the telecom industry would do best if it were freed from government regulation. And, beginning in 2000, cable companies insisted they were unable to expand broadband access because regulation was crippling them. Cable operators' top complaint — the "open access" requirement to lease lines to competing ISPs.

In 2002 the FCC granted their request, saying that when consumers purchase cable-modem service, they are buying only an "information" service, not a traditional two-way communications service like telephone service. The decision exempted cable-modem providers from opening their lines to competing ISPs and from other rules.

Not all FCC commissioners were happy. Commissioner Michael Copps wrote that without open access "the Internet — which grew up on openness — may become the province of dominant carriers, able to limit access . . . to all but their own ISPs," a consequence he called "ironic." [42]

AFP/Getty Images/Romeo Gacad

A university student in Manila logs onto the new Yahoo! Philippines site. Atypically, more than half the country's Internet users are women. Internet use is growing rapidly in Southeast Asia and the rest of the world, including societies that closely monitor, and censor, citizens' access.

Independent ISPs continued to insist that the Internet is a two-way communications system and fought in court for access to cable lines. But in June 2005, in *National Cable and Telecommunications Association v. Brand X Internet Services*, the Supreme Court sided with cable, overturning a lower court's ruling. [43]

The *Brand X* ruling opened the door for telephone companies to make the same argument — that broadband Internet services carried on phone lines shouldn't be subject to the century-old common-carrier rules. In August 2005, the FCC agreed. Beginning in August 2006, phone companies will no longer have to offer competing ISPs, such as AOL, free access to DSL connections. Phone companies will be able to sell or lease access to their DSL lines for whatever they deem fair value, although they will still be required to offer competitors free access to their slower dial-up connections.

As a result, most non-cable and non-telephone company ISPs "will disappear," says Crawford of Cardozo Law School. "The phone companies will just swallow them up, and there'll be much less choice of Internet providers." Phone and cable companies themselves will begin selling "bundles of services" — such as local and long-distance phone service along with DSL Internet service — that consumers will have no choice but to purchase.

Nevertheless, the FCC's decision will encourage "greater investment in . . . broadband networks," argued James C. Smith, senior vice president of SBC Communications, in defending their decision. [44]

But Internet advocates and some regulators are skeptical. Having one big phone company and one big cable company as the sole broadband providers in an area doesn't foster innovation and low price, says Copps. "I thought the '96 act was pretty clear in saying, 'Let's have competing providers, then deregulate.' But we kind of got it in reverse, deregulating before the competition had materialized."

Indeed, although the '96 law was intended to promote competition, the opposite has happened: The telephone and cable industries have been consolidating ever since — a worrisome fact because the Internet is a key communications channel for democracy, says Copps. In 2005, for example, the FCC approved a merger between SBC Communications and AT&T but bound the company to an enforceable Net-neutrality provision — barring the broadband giant from discriminating among Internet content — for two years. "This allows time for Congress to address the issue and for the American people to become involved," Copps says.

As in many other countries, U.S. phone companies pledged in the 1990s to upgrade infrastructure for high-speed access. In the United States, Congress and the FCC loosened some regulations on the telephone industry, in part because companies argued they would use the extra profits to modernize transmission lines.

Many other governments, such as Japan and South Korea, aggressively monitored infrastructure improvements in their countries to be sure they were made. In many countries, phone companies remained heavily regulated monopolies, which could be compelled to build infrastructure. But the U.S. government relied on what it believed would be market incentives for the private sector to wire the country for broadband, without establishing a clear policy for getting it done or fully debating the economics of doing so.

Meanwhile, in the United States, rural regions, especially, have been fighting back against the big telecom companies' reluctance to extend broadband. With little or no broadband available in some markets or prices too high for lower-income families, local governments have set up their

Googling in China Has Its Limits

As governments around the world bring more of their citizens online, they also are censoring information and opinion on the Internet and using networking technology to track down and punish political dissidents, according to Reporters Without Borders, a free-media advocacy group based in France.

Google has drawn press and congressional criticism recently for setting up a Chinese version of its Google.com search engine — Google.cn — which censors search results in line with government information-suppression guidelines. For example, a search for Tiananmen Square on Google.com turns up many images of tanks confronting unarmed demonstrators in 1989. But the same search on Google.cn produces smiling tourists posing for snapshots but few demonstrators.

"In countries such as China, where the mainstream media is subject to censorship, the Internet seemed to be the only way for dissidents to freely express their opinions," Reporters Without Borders Washington representative Lucie Morillon told the House Committee on International Relations on Feb. 15. "But, thanks to some U.S. corporations, Chinese authorities have managed to gradually shut down this 'open window' to the world." [1]

For example, both Google's and Yahoo's China sites have blocked some access to the U.S. government's Voice of America Web site and Radio Free Asia, as well as various other media sites around the world, Morillon said.

Meanwhile, Internet companies take varying approaches to dealing with Chinese-government repression, said Rebecca MacKinnon, a former Beijing bureau chief for CNN and now a fellow at Harvard Law School's Berkman Center for Internet and Society.

The anti-virus capability of Cisco Systems' "router" computers is, in effect, a built-in censorship device, said MacKinnon. By selling routers to China, the company is helping the Chinese government keep its citizens under surveillance and crack down on their political activity, she said, although it's not clear whether Cisco provides Chinese authorities with much training on the machines' capabilities. [2]

Microsoft provides instant messaging and Hotmail e-mail service to China but operates the programs on servers located outside of China to avoid having to hand over data to Chinese authorities. However, Microsoft also runs a Chinese version of its blog site, MSN Spaces, and censors the site according to Chinese requirements. It was widely criticized late last year when it deleted the work of blogger Zhao Jing, not just for Chinese viewers but worldwide. The company has since refined its processes so that global viewers can still read blogs blocked to Chinese Internet users, according to MacKinnon.

Unlike Microsoft and Google, Yahoo! runs its Chinese-language products on servers inside China and thus must comply with Chinese police requests to hand over information, noted MacKinnon. That compliance has led to the jailing of at least three dissidents, MacKinnon writes. "If I were one of those people or their loved ones, I would never forgive Yahoo!," she said. Recently, Reporters Without Borders reported that Yahoo cooperation also led Chinese officials to a fourth cyber-dissident, Wang Xiaoning, who received a 10-year prison sentence in 2003. [3]

To avoid such dilemmas, Google won't offer some products, such as Gmail or Blogger, on Google.cn "until we're comfortable that we can do so in a manner that respects our users' interest in the privacy of their personal communications," Andrew McLaughlin, Google's senior policy counsel, wrote on the company's blog [4]

"Filtering our search results" on Google.cn in accord with China's censorship requirements "clearly compromises our mission," but "failing to offer Google search at all to a fifth of the world's population . . . does so far more severely," McLaughlin argued.

Google's argument is that Google.cn users actually will get more information if Google itself does the filtering, because Google's filtering tools are more finely developed than the "very broad sweeps" of government censors, says Lauren Weinstein, co-founder of People for Internet Responsibility. While the claim is "not inaccurate technically," Weinstein says, it opens the company up "to a damaging side effect" — charges of hypocrisy. The perception has been created that the company may not be as committed to principles of privacy as it has always claimed, he says.

"And perceptions alone can do a lot of damage," he adds. For example, Google recently fought a U.S. Department of Justice request to turn over millions of search results in the name of protecting users' privacy. But, in the future, skeptics will remember that, in China, "you caved," and they'll ask, in light of that, " 'What happens next time?' " Weinstein says.

[1] Testimony before House Committee on International Relations, Feb. 15, 2006, www.rsf.org.

[2] Rebecca MacKinnon, "America's Online Censors," *The Nation*, Feb. 24, 2006.

[3] "Still No Reaction from Yahoo! After Fourth Case of Collaboration With Chinese Police Uncovered," Reporters Without Borders, April 28, 2006, www.rsf.org.

[4] Andrew McLaughlin, "Google in China," Official Google Blog, Jan. 2, 2006, http://googleblog.blogspot.com/2006/01/google-in-china.html.

own fiber or wireless "pipes."

The governments often use fiber line already laid by a municipally owned power company or cooperate with private companies. The ISP Earthlink, for instance, is deploying wireless transmitters on light poles in Philadelphia to offer a lower-cost connection, which the city will subsidize for some low-income residents.

But cable and phone companies have been fighting such efforts, lobbying state legislators to stave off what they see as publicly subsidized competition. Fourteen states now have laws restricting localities' ability to offer communications services to residents. ■

Continued on p. 426

At Issue:

Should Congress require Internet service providers to treat all content the same?

REP. EDWARD J. MARKEY, D-MASS.
RANKING MEMBER, HOUSE SUBCOMMITTEE ON TELECOMMUNICATIONS AND THE INTERNET

WRITTEN FOR *CQ RESEARCHER*, MAY 2006

yes

Ever since the Internet was first opened to commercial use in the early 1990s, it has been defined by its open exchange of ideas — an exchange that has fostered tremendous innovation and economic growth.

The Internet's traditional open architecture was protected by rules enforced by the Federal Communications Commission (FCC) that prohibited telecommunications carriers from engaging in discriminatory practices. However, those legal protections, which embodied the notion of "network neutrality," were removed by the FCC in August 2005. The telecommunications legislation now moving through Congress places the very nature of the Internet under attack by failing to provide strong, effective network-neutrality rules.

In essence, network neutrality means that broadband network owners such as AT&T or Verizon cannot discriminate against unaffiliated content providers on the Net but rather have to stay neutral with regard to the content flowing through their networks. Moreover, the phone companies cannot charge access fees to certain companies in exchange for faster content distribution to high-bandwidth customers, or to provide enhanced quality-of-service assurances.

Finally, the principle of network neutrality also protects consumers' freedom to use their choice of gadgets with their broadband connection, from computer modems and VOIP [voice over Internet protocol] phones, to Wi-Fi routers and other whiz-bang gizmos just over the horizon.

Without these protections, the open, free-market nature of the Internet — perhaps the purest example of a level playing field that we have ever seen — would be hijacked by large broadband-network owners and discarded in favor of a tiered superhighway of bandwidth haves and have-nots.

The current debate over network neutrality presents us with a choice: Should we favor the vision for the Internet's future as warped by a small handful of very large companies or should we safeguard the dreams of thousands of inventors, entrepreneurs, small businesses and other independent voices?

Already, we have begun to see the grass roots rise up in opposition to Rep. Joe Barton's telecom bill, with over 250,000 backers of an open and unrestricted Internet signing a petition to Congress. Lawmakers should listen to these voices and ensure that broadband network owners treat all forms of content the same so that we do not lose the open architecture that has allowed the Internet to become such a success.

JAMES L. GATTUSO
SENIOR FELLOW IN REGULATORY POLICY, HERITAGE FOUNDATION

WRITTEN FOR *CQ RESEARCHER*, MAY 2006

no

Should Internet network owners, such as telephone and cable TV companies, be required to treat all Internet content equally? The idea — known as network neutrality — seems at first glance unobjectionable. What could be wrong with requiring neutrality? A lot, actually.

The key issue is whether network owners should be allowed to offer priority service, for a fee, to content providers who want it. Under a "network-neutral" system, all data is treated the same, with bits being transported to their destinations on a first-come, first-served, basis.

But what if a content provider wants higher-quality service? A firm providing Internet phone calls, for instance, may want to ensure that voice conversations have no delay. Why should it be banned from paying more to the network owner for priority transmission? Such differentiation is hardly a new concept. In the non-Internet world, priority service is offered for everything from package delivery to passenger trains.

Differentiation could also help provide much-needed Internet investment. A content provider, for instance, might contract with a network owner to provide capital for capacity expansion. But the incentive to do so is eliminated if it is required to allocate that new capacity on a first-come, first-served basis.

Regulation proponents argue, nevertheless, that network owners could abuse their power — perhaps blocking specific Web sites to further their own interests. But this is extremely unlikely. No major U.S. network operator has ever blocked a Web site, and if one does, consumers would switch to another operator in a nanosecond.

Rhetoric to the contrary, today's broadband market is a competitive one, with cable and telephone companies fighting each other for customers, and other technologies — such as wireless and satellite — also on offer. Moreover, if a network owner somehow does abuse its power, existing competition law is more than sufficient to address the problem.

Imposing new rules on the Internet would also invite endless litigation. Regulators would be drawn into years-long, lobbyist-driven policy quagmires as to whether this or that action is allowed or banned, and even what prices could be charged. This would be a bonanza for lobbyists and lawyers but would hurt innovation, investment and Internet users.

Proponents of neutrality regulation say the future of the Internet is at stake. They are right. These harmful and unnecessary new rules should be rejected.

U.S. Lags in Internet Speed

Downloading a typical DVD movie in the United States takes 18 times longer than in Japan.

Country	Internet Connection	Time
Japan	(26Mbit/s)	20 minutes
S. Korea	(20Mbit/s)	26 minutes
Belgium	(3Mbit/s)	44 minutes
Denmark	(2Mbit/s)	4.5 hours
USA	Cable Modem (1.5Mbit/s)	6 hours

Note: 1 megabit per second (Mbit/s) = 1 million bits per second

Source: International Telecommunication Union, Sept. 26, 2003

Continued from p. 424

CURRENT SITUATION

Fighting for the Net

Congress is overhauling the 1996 telecom law just 10 years after it was enacted. This time, a top priority will be extending the nation's broadband capabilities — barely a blip on the radar screen a decade ago. "Net neutrality" will also be a major new buzzword in the debate.

Over the past year, a growing chorus of advocacy and consumer groups and Internet companies have argued that Congress should require Internet carriers to treat Net content neutrally, rather than shunting chosen data to high-priority — and presumably more expensive — lines. But cable and telephone companies say that preventing them from developing such higher-priced traffic amounts to excessive regulation and that offering priority services is the only way they can afford to roll out broadband to the entire country.

On April 27, the cable and telephone industries won round one of the battle when the House Energy and Commerce Committee approved its telecom bill, after rejecting, 22-34, a Net-neutrality provision sponsored by Rep. Edward J. Markey, D-Mass.

"There is a fundamental choice," said Markey. "It's the choice between the bottleneck designs of a . . . small handful of very large companies and the dreams and innovations of thousands of online companies and innovators." [45]

The final measure, drafted by Texas Republican Barton, instead authorized the FCC to investigate allegations that carriers are treating Internet content unfairly and to fine companies up to $500,000 for blocking or degrading access to Web sites.

The Senate also is expected to debate telecom overhaul legislation this year, although no schedule has been announced. Sen. Ron Wyden, D-Ore., has introduced a bill mandating that ISPs treat all Internet content equally, and Sens. Olympia Snowe, R-Maine, and Byron Dorgan, D-N.D., have drafted a similar bipartisan measure.

Senate Commerce Committee Chairman Ted Stevens, R-Alaska, said he supports neutrality in principle but isn't sure yet what will be in the bill. "We're going to have an enormous number of items that people want to put in," he said. [46]

Not surprisingly in a congressional election year, lobbying has intensified, as have political donations — just as they did in 1996, also an election year.

On April 26, the big computer-chip maker Intel joined a long list of computer and Internet companies — including Microsoft, Google, eBay and Amazon — and advocacy groups from across the political spectrum to push for a neutrality law. The retirees group AARP, the liberal political group MoveOn.org, the American Library Association and the libertarian Gun Owners of America all favor neutrality.

Meanwhile, critics of the telecom industry say phone and cable companies may be paying their way into the hearts of cash-strapped legislators running for re-election. As of March 31, for example, cable giant Comcast was Barton's top 2006 campaign contributor and AT&T was his fourth-biggest donor, according to the political funding Web site OpenSecrets.org. In Barton's 2003-2004 campaign, Comcast was his third-biggest donor and SBC was in second place.

Some Democrats who opposed Markey's Net-neutrality amendment also have financial ties to telecom. Rep. Bobby Rush, D-Ill., cosponsored Barton's telecom bill and is the founder of the Rebirth of Englewood Community Development Corp., a group in his home district that recently received a $1 million grant from the SBC Foundation. [47]

As Congress discusses telecom overhaul, other broadband-related bills are also up for consideration. In the House, Texas GOP Rep. Pete Sessions has introduced legislation to prevent municipalities from setting up broadband networks in localities where private broadband service is available. In the Senate, John McCain, R-Ariz., and Frank R. Lautenberg, D-N.J., are sponsoring a bill to allow local governments to offer broadband service.

However, few expect a comprehensive bill to pass in 2006. The '96 telecom law was several years in the making, and "I don't see why this would be any easier," said Carol Mattey, a former deputy chief of the FCC now with Deloitte & Touche's regulatory consulting practice. [48]

Whither ICANN?

This year also marks a significant milestone in the quest for global Internet governance. ICANN's current contract with the U.S. government to run the Internet's domain-name addressing system expires in September, and international groups have been discussing a possible new governance structure for several years.

Until the late 1990s, individual U.S. researchers and some small organizations ran the Internet's technical functions on behalf of the U.S. government. That structure was in keeping with the Net's history as a U.S.-developed technology. But as the 21st century neared, the Internet's swelling size and increasing global importance led President Bill Clinton to turn over control of Internet addresses to ICANN, a private, nonprofit group that manages technical aspects of the Net with input from private and public groups worldwide.

The U.S. government's intention, expressed in a series of contracts between ICANN and the Commerce Department, has been to eventually move toward more global control. Last year, however, the Bush administration announced that the international search for an alternate governing body had focused too much on government controls and that the United States would not turn over Net functions to international government bureaucrats — such as the United Nations — who might stifle innovation or be too strongly influenced by repressive governments. [49]

The U.S. government is currently considering all options for the close of the current ICANN contract in September, says a spokesman for the Commerce Department's National Telecommunications and Information Administration, which oversees the agreement. At an international summit in November, participants agreed to create an Internet Governance Forum consisting of government, business and civil-society groups to discuss global Internet governance.

The goal is to create a forum with multiple stakeholders that will meet sometime in mid-2006 in Athens. The group will try to come to global consensus on the top issues involving the Internet, such as spam, cyber-crime, the intersection of national law and Internet principles on censorship. ■

Getty Images/Peter Parks

Google CEO Eric Schmidt unveils the firm's Chinese name in Beijing on April 12, 2006. With 111 million Internet users, China is second only to the United States in total number of users. The Chinese government — assisted by Google, Yahoo! and other computer companies — censors Web sites that question government actions or deal with teen pregnancy, homosexuality, dating, beer and even jokes.

OUTLOOK

Wireless Is 'Happening'

If the Internet survives as an open medium, it may be because users — from software engineers to teenagers with pages on MySpace.com — demand security mechanisms that allow innovation while preventing domestic and international threats to Internet freedom, say technology experts.

Today, "the fact that tens of millions of machines in consumer hands are hooked up to networks that can convey reprogramming in a matter of seconds means that those computers stand exposed to near-instantaneous change" by malicious viruses and crippling loads of network-drowning spam, according to Jonathan Zittrain, professor of Internet governance at Oxford University.

The very real threat of Internet meltdown in a world of non-techie users will inevitably lead to a Net "locked down" by governments and ISPs in ways that eliminate user choice and innovation, Zittrain said, unless open-Internet supporters demand or develop improved network security and reliability while retaining users' ability to be creative. [50]

For example, personal computers could be sold with keyboard switches. In "red" mode, a PC would run whatever software it encountered, like PCs today; in "green" mode, it would run only software certified by its ISP. Users would pay more for an Internet connection that allowed them to run "red." [51]

"Corporate mass-market software" that dominates today's Net was developed with little thought to security, says Peter

Neumann, principal scientist at the SRI Computer Science Laboratory in Menlo Park, Calif., and co-founder of People for Internet Responsibility. In a universally online world that could lead to a disastrous shutdown of vital Net-based systems, such as power, air-traffic control or electronic voting, he notes.

"The government has typically said the market will solve" security problems, but Microsoft and others "are making scads of money while all but ignoring security," he continues. Meanwhile, the industry has its "head in the sand" and won't change unless "we have enough people who understand the big picture" and take responsibility for it, Neumann says.

For U.S. consumers to make market choices on Internet service, a real market must develop, with three or more competing services available everywhere, not just the phone and cable companies that dominate today, said former FCC Chairman Powell. "We believe magical things happen at three," he said. [52]

Currently, wireless ISPs remain the best hope, although whether wireless technology is up to the job remains an open question. Some say wireless is poised to emerge strong in urban and rural areas. Nine years ago, "it was a technological curiosity," but today "it's happening," says Steve Stroh, a writer and an analyst for the broadband wireless Internet industry. He cites Trump Tower in Manhattan, which recently installed a wireless network for the entire building, and hundreds of rural wireless ISPs — called WISPs — that increasingly can extend broadband connections over long distances. An operator in eastern Washington state, for example, can reach customers 30-to-40 miles from its transmission point via large antennas, Stroh says.

To flourish, wireless needs access to dedicated bands on the electromagnetic spectrum, says Stroh, which could be a special problem in the United States, where — unlike in some other countries — much prime spectrum is already allocated to users like the Department of Defense. The spectrum issue is on Congress' agenda, with some legislators proposing to dedicate empty spaces in local broadcast TV spectra to wireless ISPs, for example.

The Internet's continued ability to allow unfettered communication and innovation rides on the outcome of all these debates, say longtime Net users like Karl Auerbach, a San-Francisco-based computer-network developer and former ICANN board member.

"These Internet governance debates are the visible aspects of the most significant change in the conception of nation-states, national sovereignty and the relationship of the individual to his/her government since at least the end of the Napoleonic wars," he says. ■

About the Author

Staff writer **Marcia Clemmitt** is a veteran social-policy reporter who previously served as editor in chief of *Medicine and Health*, a Washington industry newsletter, and staff writer for *The Scientist*. She has also been a high school math and physics teacher. She holds a liberal arts and sciences degree from St. John's College, Annapolis, and a master's degree in English from Georgetown University. Her recent reports include "Saving the Oceans," "Climate Change" and "AP and IB Programs."

Notes

1 Quoted in "AOL Censors E-Mail Tax Opponents," Electronic Frontier Foundation media release, April 13, 2006.

2 John Byrne, "Update: AOL Says Emails Protesting Its Own Service Blocked By Accident," *The Raw Story* blog, April 14, 2006.

3 Tom Barrett, "To Censor Pro-Union Web Site, Telus Blocked 766 Others," *The Tyee*, Aug. 4, 2005, http://thetyee.ca.

4 For background, see David Masci, "The Future of Telecommunications," *CQ Researcher*, April 23, 1999, pp. 329-352.

5 Lawrence Lessig, "Architecting Innovation," *The Industry Standard*, Sept. 8, 2001.

6 Quoted in Declan McCullagh, "Democrats Lose House Vote on Net Neutrality," ZDNet.com, http://news.zdnet.com.

7 *Save The Internet* blog, www.savetheinternet.com.

8 Quoted in *ibid.*

9 For background, see Kenneth Jost, "Russia and the Former Soviet Republics," *CQ Researcher*, June 17, 2005, pp. 541-564.

10 Daniel Henninger, "Here's One Use of U.S. Power Jacques Can't Stop," *The Wall Street Journal*, Dec. 17. 2004.

11 Declan McCullagh, "No Booze or Jokes for Googlers in China," CnetNews.com, http://news.com, Jan. 27, 2006.

12 "Promoting Innovation and Competitiveness," President Bush's Technology Agenda, March 26, 2004, www.whitehouse.gov.

13 S. Derek Turner, "Why Does the U.S. Lag Behind?" *Free Press*, February 2006.

14 Michael Geist, "The Credible Threat," Circle ID, Feb. 28, 2006, www.circleid.com.

15 Quoted in Declan McCullagh, "Internet Showdown in Tunis," CNET News.com, Nov. 11, 2005; http://news.com.com. For background, see Charles S. Clark, "Regulating the Internet," *CQ Researcher*, June 30, 1995, pp. 561-584.

16 Kieren McCarthy, "2005: The Year the U.S. Government Undermined the Internet," *The Register*, Dec. 29, 2005, www.theregister.co.uk.

17 *Ibid.*

18 Amol Sharma, "World Seeks a Wider Web Role," *CQ Weekly*, Nov. 14, 2005, p. 3042.

19 Testimony before Senate Committee on Commerce, Science and Transportation, Feb. 7, 2006.

20 Quoted in Marguerite Reardon, 'Qwest CEO Supports Tiered Internet," ZDNet.com, http://news.zdnet.com.

21 Quoted in "At SBC, All's Well About Scale and Scope," *Business Week Online*, Nov. 7, 2005.

22 Edward Felten, "Net Neutrality and Competition," *Freedom to Tinker* blog, www.freedom-to-tinker.com.

23 Quoted in Marguerite Reardon, "Verizon Says Net Neutrality Overhyped," CNET News.com,

March 31, 2006, http://news.com.com.

[24] John Windhausen, Jr., "Good Fences Make Bad Broadband," *A Public Knowledge White Paper*, Public Knowledge, Feb. 6, 2006.

[25] *Ibid.*

[26] *Ibid.* The nine states are Arkansas, Delaware, Florida, Illinois, Maryland, Michigan, Pennsylvania, Virginia and Wyoming.

[27] *Ibid.*

[28] John Horrigan, "Rural Broadband Internet Use," Pew Internet and American Life Project, February 2006.

[29] Quoted in "Senate Commerce, Science, and Transportation Committee Holds Hearing on Communications Issues," Congressional Transcripts, Feb. 14, 2006, www.cq.com.

[30] *Ibid.*

[31] Quoted in Dana Blankenhorn, "You Get Muni Broadband by Demanding It," ZDNet blog, April 5, 2006.

[32] Joseph L. Bast, "Municipally Owned Broadband Networks: A Critical Evaluation (Revised Edition)," www.heartland.org, October 2004.

[33] ww.baller.com/pdfs/Texas_2-14-06.pdf.

[34] Thomas D. Rowley, "Where No Broadband Has Gone Before," Rural Policy Research Institute, Aug. 19, 2005.

[35] For background, see *The Internet's Coming of Age, Committee on the Internet in the Evolving Information Infrastructure* (2001); and Barry M. Leiner, *et al.*, "A Brief History of the Internet," Internet Society, www.isoc.org.

[36] Bruce Sterling, "A Short History of the Internet," *The Magazine of Fantasy and Science Fiction*, February 1993.

[37] "Putting It All Together With Robert Kahn," *Ubiquity: An ACM IT Magazine and Forum*, www.acm.org.

[38] Quoted in Lawrence Lessig, "It's the Architecture, Mr. Chairman," http://cyber.law.harvard.edu/works/lessig/cable/Cable.html.

[39] Scott Bradner, "Blocking the Power of the Internet," *Networkworld*, Jan. 6, 2006, www.networkworld.com.

[40] For background, see Masci, *op. cit.*; and Kathy Koch, "The Digital Divide," *CQ Researcher*, Jan. 28, 2000, p. 41-64.

[41] Quoted in Elizabeth Wasserman, "The New Telecom Wars: Looking to Update a Landmark Law," *CQ Weekly*, Nov. 14, 2005, p. 3049.

[42] Michael Copps, Dissenting Statement, GN. No. 00-185, www.fcc.gov.

[43] *National Cable and Telecommunications Association v. Brand X Internet Services*, 543 U.S., 2005.

[44] Quoted in "FCC Reclassifies DSL as Data Service," Analyst Views, IT Analyst Information on Demand, Northern Light, Sept. 20, 2005, www.centerformarketintelligence.com.

[45] Quoted in Declan McCullagh, "Republicans Defeat Net Neutrality Proposal," CNet News.com, April 6, 2006, http://news.com.com.

[46] Quoted in Declan McCullagh, "Senator: Net Neutrality May Not Happen," ZDNet News, March 22, 2006, http://news.zdnet.com.

[47] "Donation Explanation Has Phony Ring," *Chicago Sun-Times*, April 26, 2006.

[48] Quoted in Kelly M. Teal, "1996 Telecom Act Turns 10," *New Telephony*, Feb. 8, 2006, www.newtelephony.com.

[49] Tim Receveur, "United States Says No UN Body Should Control Internet," *Washington File*, USInfo, U.S. State Department, Oct. 24, 2005, http://usinfostate.gov.

[50] Jonathan Zittrain, "The Generative Internet," 2005; www.oiprc.ox.ac.uk/EJWP0306.pdf.

[51] *Ibid.*

[52] Quoted in "Michael Powell: We Need That Third Pipe," *IP Democracy*, April 3, 2006, www.ipdemocracy.com.

FOR MORE INFORMATION

Berkman Center for Internet and Society, Harvard Law School, Baker House, 1587 Massachusetts Ave., Cambridge, MA 02138; (617) 495-7547; http://cyber.law.harvard.edu. A research program investigating legal, technical and social developments in cyberspace, in the United States and worldwide.

Center for Democracy and Technology, 1634 I St., N.W., #100, Washington, DC 20006; (202) 637-9800; www.cdt.org. Advocates preservation of constitutional freedoms and democratic values in the developing digital world.

Center for the Digital Future at the University of Southern California Annenberg School, 300 South Grand Ave., Suite 3950, Los Angeles, CA 90071; (213) 437-4433; www.digitalcenter.org. A research program investigating the Internet's effects on individuals and societies.

Electronic Frontier Foundation, 454 Shotwell St., San Francisco, CA 94110; (415) 436-9333; www.eff.org. A nonprofit organization that advocates for and litigates on technological issues involving privacy, free speech, freedom to innovate and consumer rights.

Free Press, 100 Main St., PO Box 28, Northampton, MA 01061; (877) 888-1533; www.freepress.net. A national, nonpartisan organization that promotes public participation in debate on media policy and development of more competitive and public-interest-oriented media.

ICANN Watch, www.icannwatch.org. Membership organization of technology experts who study and write about management and policy issues affecting the Internet's domain-name address system.

Internet Governance Project, School of Information Studies, Syracuse University, Syracuse, NY 13244; (315) 443-5616; www.internetgovernance.org. An interdisciplinary group of academic researchers analyzing issues of global governance for the Internet.

National Cable and Telecommunications Association, 1724 Massachusetts Ave., N.W., Washington, DC 20036; (202) 775-3550; www.ncta.com. Represents the cable industry, the largest single provider of broadband Internet services in the United States.

Pew Internet and American Life Project, 1615 L St., N.W., Suite 700, Washington, DC 20036; (202) 419-4500; www.pewinternet.org. Provides data and analysis on Internet usage and its effects on American society.

Progress and Freedom Foundation, 1444 I St., N.W., Suite 500, Washington, DC 20005; (202) 289-8928; www.pff.org. A free-market-oriented think tank that studies public policy related to the Internet.

Bibliography

Selected Sources

Books

Borgman, Christine, *From Gutenberg to the Global Information Infrastructure: Access to Information in the Networked World*, MIT Press, 2003.
A professor of information studies at the University of California, Los Angeles, describes the technical and policy tradeoffs that libraries, universities, readers and researchers face as they shift from a culture of books to a world of online information.

Goldsmith, Jack, and Timothy Wu, *Who Controls the Internet? Illusions of a Borderless World*, Oxford University Press, 2006.
Professors specializing in cyberlaw at Harvard and Columbia, respectively, describe threats the global Internet has posed to national regimes. They argue national government have and are exercising power to control the Internet.

Thierer, Adam, and Wayne Crews, eds., *Who Rules the Net?: A New Guide to Navigating the Proposed Rules of the Road for Cyberspace*, Cato Institute, 2003.
Two libertarian analysts assembled essays that discuss the challenges of regulating cyberspace, including how international cyber-disputes should be settled and whether a multinational treaty should govern the Internet.

Yassini, Rouzbeh, *et al.*, *Planet Broadband*, Cisco Press, 2003.
An electrical engineer and advocate of cable broadband explains how broadband works and describes how high-speed Internet connections may change how consumers, businesses and researchers use the Net.

Articles

Chester, Jeffrey, "The End of the Internet?" *The Nation online*, www.thenation.com, Feb. 1, 2006.
An advocate of an open-access Internet describes the conflict between traditional Internet values and the economic and policy agendas of the phone and cable industries.

Cukier, Kenneth Neil, "No Joke," *Foreign Affairs*, foreignaffairs.org, Dec. 28, 2005.
A journalist describes U.S. and international views of Internet control and how changes in the way the Internet works are altering those views.

Goldsmith, Jack, and Timothy Wu, *Digital Borders*, *Legal Affairs*, January/February 2006, www.legalaffairs.org.
Law professors at Harvard and Columbia, respectively, describe incidents in which national laws collide with traditional Internet principles like freedom of expression.

Hu, Jim, and Marguerite Reardon, "Cities Brace for Broadband War," CNET News.com, May 2, 2005, http:/news.com.com.
Battles are heating up between cities and towns that want to develop government-sponsored broadband networks and regional phone and cable companies that accuse local governments of engaging in unfair competition.

MacKinnon, Rebecca, "America's Online Censors," *The Nation online*, www.thenation.com, Feb. 24, 2006.
A fellow at Harvard Law School's Berkman Center for Internet and Society explores the economics and ethics of U.S. computer companies' cooperation with Chinese-government Internet censorship.

Manjoo, Farhad, "One Cable Company to Rule Them All," *Salon*, Salon.com, March 17, 2004.
A journalist discusses potential threats to Internet access posed by consolidation of media ownership.

Reardon, Margaret, "Broadband for the Masses?" CNET News.com, www.com,com, April 14, 2004.
Jim Baller — a lawyer for local governments — describes court challenges to their attempts to build broadband networks and defends such initiatives.

"Seven Questions: Battling for Control of the Internet," *Foreign Policy*, www.foreignpolicy.com, November 8. 2005.
Stanford University law professor and Internet expert Lawrence Lessig discusses conflicts between the United States and European Union over who should control the granting of Internet domain names.

Zittrain, Jonathan, "Without a Net," *Legal Affairs*, January/February 2006, www.legalaffairs.org.
An Oxford University professor of Internet governance describes why burgeoning Internet-security threats like computer viruses mean that Internet law and technology require overhaul.

Studies and Reports

***The Internet's Coming of Age*, Committee on the Internet in the Evolving Information Infrastructure, National Research Council, 2001.**
An expert panel recommends policies to accommodate more widespread Internet usage and new technologies.

***Signposts in Cyberspace: The Domain Name System and Internet Navigation*, *Computer Science and Telecommunications Board*, National Research Council, 2005.**
An expert panel explains the Internet's address system and recommends policy to stabilize its future governance.

The Next Step:

Additional Articles from Current Periodicals

China and Internet

Grossman, Lev, and Hannah Beech, "Google Under the Gun," *Time*, Feb. 13, 2006, p. 53.
The authors consider the ethics of Google's compliance with Communist Party censorship regulations in China.

MacDonald, G. Jeffrey, "Congress's Dilemma: When Yahoo in China's Not Yahoo," *The Christian Science Monitor*, Feb. 14, 2006, p. 1.
Giving up a majority stake of its China service to a Chinese company in October 2005 may protect Yahoo from a congressional investigation of Yahoo's alleged censorship.

Pan, Philip P., "Chinese Media Assail Google," *The Washington Post*, Feb. 22, 2006, p. A9.
Several Chinese newspapers criticized Google, suggesting that the Chinese government is unhappy with the company's efforts to block "harmful information" from its search results.

Yardley, Jim, "Google Chief Rejects Putting Pressure on China," *The New York Times*, April 13, 2006, p. C7.
Google CEO Eric E. Schmidt announced the company would not lobby China to change its censorship laws.

Digital Divide

Althaus, Dudley, and Joan Grillo, "Getting the Working Class Wired Up," *The Houston Chronicle*, Oct. 14, 2005, p. A6.
A new low-income subdivision on the edge of Mexico City offers Internet access with every home.

Heim, Kristi, "Global Digital Divide Grows Wider, UW Research Finds," *The Seattle Times*, March 21, 2006, p. C1.
The world's supply of computers, Internet hosts and secure servers is narrowly distributed among a small group of countries, according to University of Washington researchers.

Piedra, Jennifer Mooney, "Bills' Aim: Discounted PCs For Kids," *The Miami Herald*, April 11, 2006, p. A1.
Florida legislators are proposing legislation to sell discounted computers and Internet service to the disadvantaged.

Internet2

Bray, Hiawatha, "Music Suites Hit Use of Fast Network," *The Boston Globe*, April 13, 2005, p. A1.
The music and movie industries will launch lawsuits today against college students who have been sharing movies and music over a fast experimental network called Internet2.

Kessler, Michelle, "Internet2 is Higher-Tech Version of Regular Internet," *USA Today*, April 14, 2005, p. B3.
Kessler explains Internet2 — who uses it, who pays for it, how one uses it and why it is needed.

Walker, Leslie, "Internet's Speed Increases As It Turns 35 Years Old," *The Washington Post*, Sept. 5, 2004, p. F6.
Scientists are rapidly improving quasi-private versions of the Internet, including the super-high-speed Internet2 network.

Municipal Broadband

Carpenter, Dave, "Chicago Wants to Make the Entire City Wireless," *St. Louis Post-Dispatch*, Feb. 19, 2006, p. A8.
Chicago wants to offer wireless broadband, joining the Wi-Fi bandwagon that includes Philadelphia and San Francisco.

Lazaroff, Leon, "Debate Sizzles on the Wiring of U.S. Towns," *Chicago Tribune*, May 27, 2005, p. C8.
Telecom giants SBC and Verizon, along with cable providers such as Comcast and Mediacom, are trying to prohibit small towns from creating their own municipal networks.

Van, Jon, "Iowa Towns in Internet's Fast Lane," *Los Angeles Times*, Aug. 28, 2005, p. A1.
Iowa's Cedar Falls Utility offered affordable high-speed data connections years before the local cable TV operator.

Wirzbicki, Alan, "Getting Wired: Rural Towns Offer Own High-Speed Connection," *The Boston Globe*, Sept. 18, 2005, p. A17.
Several rural New England towns are offering their own broadband Internet and cable TV services.

CITING *CQ* RESEARCHER

Sample formats for citing these reports in a bibliography include the ones listed below. Preferred styles and formats vary, so please check with your instructor or professor.

MLA STYLE

Jost, Kenneth. "Rethinking the Death Penalty." CQ Researcher 16 Nov. 2001: 945-68.

APA STYLE

Jost, K. (2001, November 16). Rethinking the death penalty. *CQ Researcher, 11*, 945-968.

CHICAGO STYLE

Jost, Kenneth. "Rethinking the Death Penalty." *CQ Researcher*, November 16, 2001, 945-968.

CQ Researcher

Published by CQ Press, a division of Congressional Quarterly Inc.

cqresearcher.com

Energy Efficiency

Is enough being done to save energy?

President Bush recently responded to escalating energy prices by suspending government purchases for the Strategic Petroleum Reserve, relaxing environmental rules for gasoline formulation and launching investigations into possible price manipulation. Soon after, Congress began debating a flurry of energy proposals, including allowing exploration in the Arctic National Wildlife Refuge, streamlining refinery regulations, expanding tax credits for hybrid vehicles and reforming fuel-economy standards for cars. With Congress polarized, the outcomes are unclear, but voter unrest over high gasoline prices might prompt the passage of some bipartisan legislation. Environmental groups are hoping for proposals focusing on promoting energy efficiency. Since the Arab oil embargo of 1973, fuel-economy standards and other energy-efficiency measures have produced energy savings throughout the economy. But market barriers prevent the adoption of many measures, and there is disagreement about how far government should go to promote them.

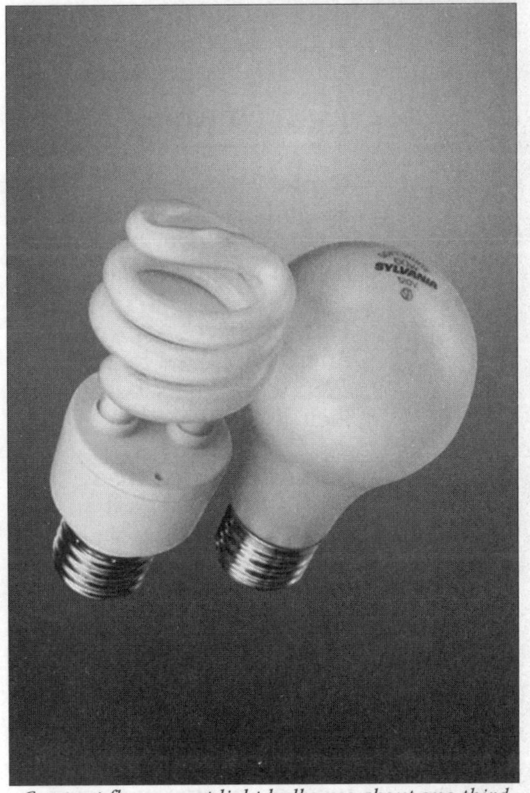

Compact fluorescent light bulbs use about one-third the energy of comparable incandescent bulbs and last up to 10 times longer.

Inside This Report

CQ Researcher • May 19, 2006 • www.cqresearcher.com
Volume 16, Number 19 • Pages 433-456

Recipient of Society of Professional Journalists Award for Excellence ◆ American Bar Association Silver Gavel Award

Cover: Compact fluorescent light bulbs use about one-third the energy of comparable incandescent bulbs and last up to 10 times longer, according to the Alliance to Save Energy.

CQ Researcher

May 19, 2006
Volume 16, Number 19

MANAGING EDITOR: Thomas J. Colin

ASSISTANT MANAGING EDITOR: Kathy Koch

ASSOCIATE EDITOR: Kenneth Jost

STAFF WRITERS: Marcia Clemmitt, Peter Katel, Pamela M. Prah

CONTRIBUTING WRITERS: Rachel S. Cox, Sarah Glazer, David Hosansky, Patrick Marshall, Tom Price

DESIGN/PRODUCTION EDITOR: Olu B. Davis

ASSISTANT EDITOR: Melissa J. Hipolit

CQ PRESS

A Division of Congressional Quarterly Inc.

SENIOR VICE PRESIDENT/PUBLISHER: John A. Jenkins

DIRECTOR, LIBRARY PUBLISHING: Kathryn C. Suárez

DIRECTOR, EDITORIAL OPERATIONS: Ann Davies

CONGRESSIONAL QUARTERLY INC.

CHAIRMAN: Paul C. Tash

VICE CHAIRMAN: Andrew P. Corty

PRESIDENT/EDITOR IN CHIEF: Robert W. Merry

CQ Researcher (ISSN 1056-2036) is printed on acid-free paper. Published weekly, except March 24, July 7, July 14, Aug. 4, Aug. 11, Nov. 24, Dec. 22 and Dec. 29, by CQ Press, a division of Congressional Quarterly Inc. Annual full-service subscriptions for institutions start at $667. For pricing, call 1-800-834-9020, ext. 1906. To purchase a *CQ Researcher* report in print or electronic format (PDF), visit www.cqpress.com or call 866-427-7737. Single reports start at $10. Bulk purchase discounts and electronic-rights licensing are also available. Periodicals postage paid at Washington, D.C., and additional mailing offices. POSTMASTER: Send address changes to *CQ Researcher*, 1255 22nd St., N.W., Suite 400, Washington, DC 20037.

Energy Efficiency

BY BARBARA MANTEL

THE ISSUES

When members of Congress went home for spring break, angry constituents gave them an earful about gas prices that had risen to near or more than $3 per gallon. So when lawmakers returned to Washington in late April, they were determined to show voters their concern.

Republicans and Democrats alike threw out a flurry of energy proposals, including investigating possible price-gouging, opening the Arctic National Wildlife Refuge to oil drilling, easing environmental regulations on refineries and reforming fuel-economy standards.

But in a polarized Congress in an election year, getting agreement on any of these will be difficult, to say the least. And besides, some analysts say there's not enough emphasis on reducing demand. "With energy-supply markets tied in a straitjacket, moderating demand is our only real choice for the near term," said Steven Nadel, executive director of the American Council for an Energy-Efficient Economy, an independent policy group. The way to reduce demand, said Nadel, is to improve energy efficiency.

Increasing energy efficiency involves building buildings and developing appliances, industrial processes and vehicles that use less energy but deliver the same or better service. It doesn't mean turning down the thermostat and shivering; it means installing an energy-efficient furnace and keeping the thermostat setting the same.

Since government efficiency programs were created soon after the 1973 Arab oil embargo, America's "energy intensity" — the amount of energy the economy uses to produce a dollar of gross domestic product — has been reduced by more than 40 percent. [1]

"If the U.S. were operating today at the same energy intensity as in 1973, we'd be consuming about 186 quadrillion Btus * each year, instead of the 100 quadrillion that we actually do," says Joe Loper, vice president of research and analysis at the Alliance to Save Energy, a coalition of business, government, environmental and consumer groups.

Gas sells for over $3 a gallon in San Francisco in early May. Faced with unhappy motorists, lawmakers have proposed solutions ranging from investigating possible price-gouging to drilling for oil in the Arctic National Wildlife Refuge. But some experts say the best way to reduce prices is by reducing demand through improved energy efficiency.

The nation's improved energy intensity is not due entirely to better energy efficiency. An estimated 25 to 50 percent of the reduction is due to structural changes in the economy, such as the shift away from manufacturing. Still, energy efficiency has played a significant role, and examples abound in all sectors of the economy:

- The average fuel economy of new cars and light trucks increased from 15 miles per gallon (mpg) in 1975 to 26 mpg by 1987, although that has dropped recently to 24 mpg.
- The average electricity used by new refrigerators has been cut by more than half since 1972.
- The energy used to produce a ton of paper has fallen 27 percent over 20 years. [2]

Despite the improved efficiency of appliances, vehicles and manufacturing, overall U.S. energy consumption has continued to increase — though at a slower rate — primarily because of population growth and economic expansion. American energy consumption has risen from about 75 quadrillion Btus in 1973 to about 100 quadrillion Btus in 2004, according to the Department of Energy, and will jump another 30 percent by 2025. [3]

But it doesn't have to be that way, some experts say. "Americans can still cost-effectively save half the electricity they use . . . and at least that much of the oil and gas," estimates the Rocky Mountain Institute, a research and consulting nonprofit. "Achieving these technical potentials . . . would take several decades, but pursuing them is clearly worthwhile." [4]

Meanwhile, energy costs have been climbing. The inflation-adjusted

---

* A Btu, or British thermal unit, is a measure of energy equal to the amount of heat required to raise the temperature of one pound of water by 1 degree Fahrenheit.

Oil Is Largest U.S. Energy Source

More than 90 percent of the energy used in the United States in 2004 came from non-renewable sources, including 40 percent from oil. Renewable sources, such as wind and water power, produced 6 percent (left graph). Of the four main users of energy, industry accounted for one-third of total energy use (right graph).

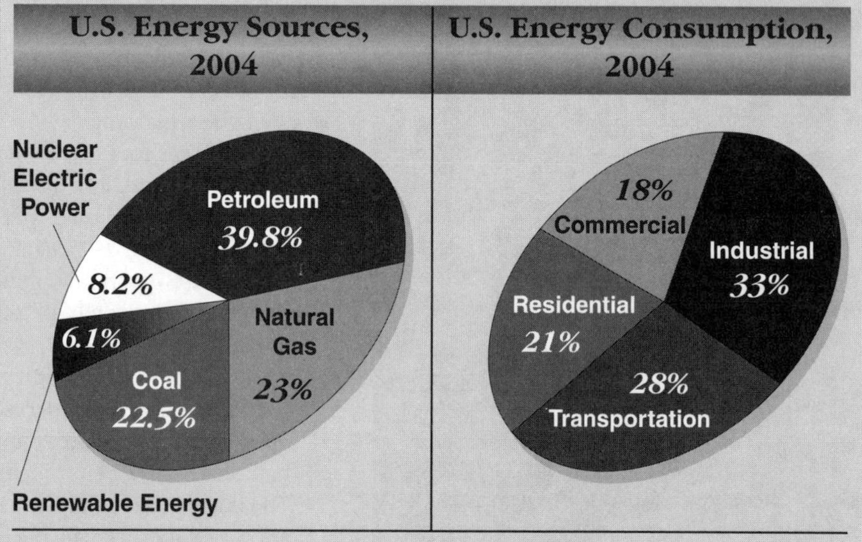

Note: Percentages may not add to 100 due to rounding

Source: U.S. Energy Information Administration

price of residential natural gas rose 29 percent this winter compared to last winter, and residential heating oil jumped 22 percent. [5] The inflation-adjusted price of gasoline in late April increased 27 percent over last year. [6]

But it's not just rising costs that are lending urgency to the call for reduced energy consumption. "The past decade was the hottest of the past 150 years and perhaps the past millennium," according to the nonpartisan Pew Center on Global Climate Change. [7] The Earth is warming, and a growing scientific consensus says it is partly due to the release of carbon dioxide and other greenhouse gases that result from burning fossil fuels. Rising sea levels and changes in precipitation are likely and, coupled with warming, could threaten ecosystems, biological diversity and even human health, according to the center.

In fact, a growing number of scientists believe the Earth may be approaching a "tipping point" — beyond which corrective action to reduce greenhouse gas emissions will be useless to prevent catastrophic disruptions. These concerns were heightened after release of a British report in January warning that a rise of 3 degrees C from current temperatures could lead to the irreversible destabilization of Arctic ice sheets or reversal of the Earth's ability to absorb carbon dioxide. This temperature level is well within most climate-change projections. [8]

Concern about air pollution, overloading the electrical grid and disruptions in oil supplies and subsequent price shocks are also cited as reasons to shrink energy demand.

Price shocks are a real threat, says Ann Korin, co-director of the Institute for the Analysis of Global Security. "Our most critical supply chain, our energy lifeline, is open to terrorism," she says. For instance, a quarter of the world's oil reserves is controlled by Saudi Arabia, whose reserves are concentrated in just eight oil fields. Most of its processing is concentrated in a single enormous facility.

While the utility, residential and commercial sectors of the U.S. economy have reduced their oil use dramatically since the 1970s, the transportation sector burns up 40 percent more than it did then and now accounts for more than two-thirds of total U.S. oil consumption. [9] Oil use "has become even more concentrated in the sector that . . . has historically demonstrated the least ability to respond to price shocks by switching to alternative fuels," noted a report by the Department of Energy's Oak Ridge National Laboratory. [10] "America is addicted to oil," said President Bush in his State of the Union address in February.

The United States must do a better job of developing alternative fuels and increase car and truck efficiency, the Oak Ridge report concluded.

But federal funding for energy-efficiency research, development and demonstration projects has dropped 12 percent since 2002, and President Bush's proposed fiscal 2007 budget would slash such programs even more. [11] Facing a growing federal deficit, the president has proposed cutting funding by 9 percent for the voluntary ENERGY STAR program, which identifies and promotes energy-efficient products. He also would reduce by 30 percent funding for programs that help energy-intensive industries improve efficiency and that help local groups weatherize low-income homes. [12]

The proposal quickly came under attack from a coalition of companies, trade associations, environmental and energy-efficiency organizations, state and local government agencies and consumer advocates. "Now is the time to invest more, not less, in technologies

Energy-Saving Tips for Homeowners

Heating and Cooling: These use the most household energy. Clean filters, radiators, warm-air registers and baseboard heaters. Select ENERGY STAR furnaces when replacing equipment.

Insulation: Inspect insulation and then visit the Department of Energy's ZIP Code Insulation Program (www.ornl.gov/~roofs/Zip/ZipHome.html) to determine the recommended level for a locality. Add more if needed.

Ducts: Many duct systems are poorly insulated. Ducts that leak heated air into unheated spaces can add hundreds of dollars a year to bills. Seal leaky ducts with heat-approved tape and then insulate them. For new construction, run ducts through conditioned spaces rather than a crawl space or attic.

Appliances and Lighting: These account for the second-largest energy consumption. Compact fluorescent bulbs can reduce lighting energy use by as much as 75 percent and bulbs last 4-10 times longer than incandescent bulbs. Consider purchasing ENERGY STAR appliances when replacing equipment.

Laundry: Ninety percent of the energy used for laundry is for heating the water. Wash clothes in cold water, and only wash full loads. ENERGY STAR washing machines use 50 percent less energy than standard washers.

Water Heating: This is the third-largest home energy expense. Turn down the thermostat on the water heater. Install low-flow faucets. Insulate the water heater, being careful not to cover thermostat or the top, bottom and burner compartment of a gas heater. Insulate the first six feet of water pipes connected to heater. Drain a quart of water from tank every three months to remove sediment that impedes heat transfer. Consider buying an energy-efficient water heater.

Windows: Windows can account for 10-25 percent of the heating bill, and during the summer, sunny windows make the air conditioner work two-to-three times harder. Install storm windows to reduce heat loss in winter, and weatherize current ones. Keep South windows clean in winter and South-facing curtains closed in summer. Consider installing high-performance windows if renovating, although it will take many years to recoup the investment.

Home Office and Electronics: In general, ENERGY STAR office equipment — personal computers, monitors, printers, copiers and fax machines — use half the electricity of standard equipment. Laptops use much less energy than desktop computers. Three-quarters of the electricity used to power home electronics like televisions, stereos and computers is consumed while the products are turned off. Unplug equipment when not in use or switch off power strips.

and practices that promise the quickest, cleanest and cheapest means of addressing tight energy supplies and extraordinarily high prices," the group said in a statement to Congress. [13]

Critics are also concerned about staffing changes at the Department of Energy. Dan Reicher, former assistant secretary of Energy for energy efficiency and renewable energy under President Bill Clinton, calls the administration's decision to close all six regional energy-efficiency offices "one of the saddest examples of the administration's indifference to energy efficiency." The Energy Department contends the closings will reduce administrative overhead. But Reicher says the staff in those offices needs to be in the field to properly help homeowners, businesses and industry adapt energy-efficiency measures to local conditions.

While the federal government is cutting back its funding for efficiency programs, some states, like California, New York and Texas, are aggressively expanding their energy-efficiency requirements for appliances and equipment and are setting energy-saving targets for utilities. While some of these programs depend on state funding, others depend on federal money.

As the nation grapples with budget cuts, rising energy prices and national security and climate concerns, here are some of the questions being asked:

Are homeowners and businesses doing enough to improve energy efficiency using existing technology?

Melanie and Mike Jones just couldn't get their house in Swansea, Ill., warm last winter. Despite a thermostat set at 74 degrees, she slept in socks, long pants and a sweatshirt. But when her toddler asked to sleep in a sweater too, Jones and her husband decided to take action, putting plastic on windows, caulking outside faucets, insulating light switches and having the furnace checked.

When the 1,940-square-foot ranch house did not get warmer, the Joneses called in a professional energy auditor. Not only did the heating ducts leak, but one section was split open. "Hot air was going into the crawl space," says Melanie Jones. "That's not where you want it to go!"

The Department of Energy recommends a host of ways to make residential and commercial buildings — which account for 39 percent of U.S. energy consumption — more energy efficient. [14] They range from quick fixes like cleaning furnace filters and switching to compact fluorescent bulbs to long-term investments like sealing leaky ducts and adding insulation. (*See box above.*)

Despite major improvements in the energy efficiency of buildings since the 1970s, experts say much more can be done. The Alliance to Save Energy estimates buildings could be up to 30 percent more efficient within the next decade relying only on technologies "already in the market and known to be feasible and cost-effective." [15]

Heating Uses Most Energy at Home

Americans use as much energy to heat their homes as they use for their appliances and lighting. Hot water, air conditioning and refrigerators consume about a third of total home energy.

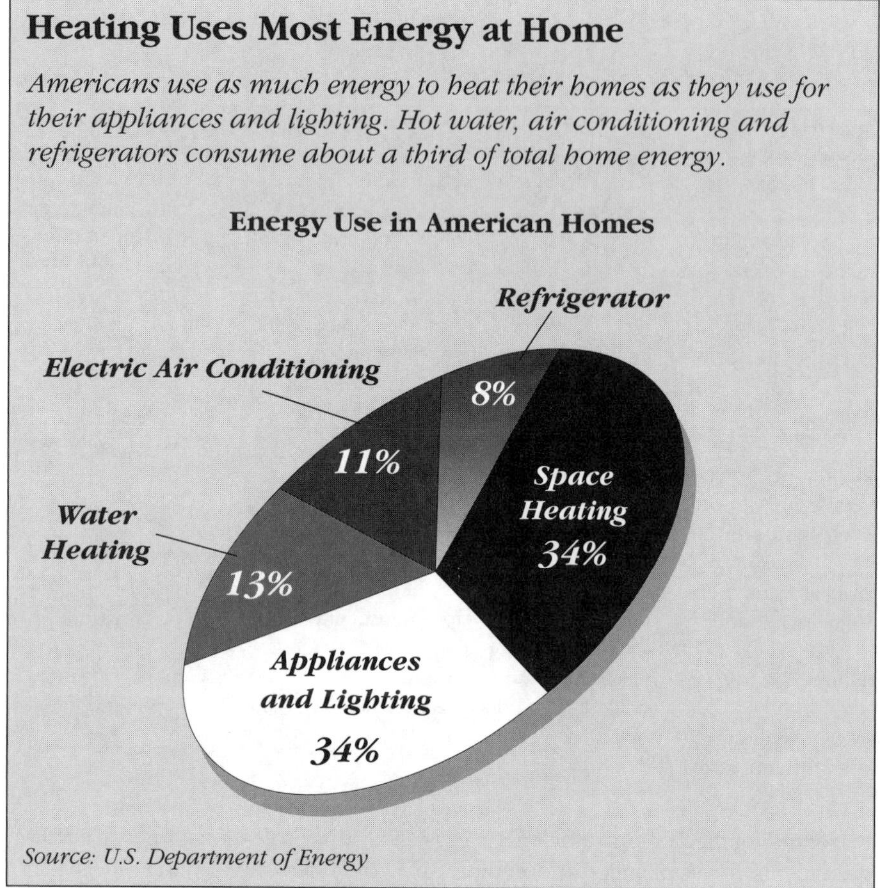

Source: U.S. Department of Energy

"There's tremendous potential," says Marilyn Brown, interim director of the engineering, science and technology division at the Oak Ridge laboratory. For example, commercial buildings could install reflective roofs to block heat in summer, she says. Although reflective roofs provide a quick return on investment, they are being installed on only "a small fraction" of commercial roofs today, according to Brown. Moreover, only 40 percent of residences and less than 30 percent of commercial buildings are well insulated, and less than a third of new windows purchased today are highly efficient, she says.

Obstacles — mainly upfront costs — must be overcome if energy-efficient products and construction techniques are to further penetrate the building sector, experts say. While options like switching to fluorescent light bulbs are relatively cheap, others are expensive. The Joneses spent $2,000 to repair their ductwork, and — depending on natural gas prices — won't recoup the costs for three years. They also spent considerable time on government Web sites learning about home energy use and energy audits. Many consumers and small-business owners don't have that kind of time or find the process daunting.

There is also the "split-incentive" problem: When a builder spends the extra money to make homes more energy efficient, it is the buyer who reaps the energy savings.

Many government programs are designed specifically to overcome these kinds of market barriers. They include the ENERGY STAR program, minimum energy-efficiency standards for appliances and programs to help industry improve efficiency. A National Academy of Sciences review of such programs concluded their net economic benefits exceeded their costs by more than 300 percent. [16]

The story is much the same in the industrial sector, which accounts for 33 percent of U.S. energy consumption. [17] Great strides have been made, but much more can be done, say efficiency experts. A Department of Energy report estimates that energy use in the industrial sector could be cut by 6 percent using currently available technology and improved equipment maintenance. [18] Even more energy could be saved with products and processes that require more research and development.

The Oak Ridge laboratory conducts energy audits of industrial plants, sending experts to review energy use and recommend ways to improve efficiency. "We have identified hundreds of millions of dollars in potential energy savings in just a couple of dozen plants," says Brown, "and these investments would have less than a two-year payback period — and some would be almost immediate." The measures range from replacing old motors with variable-speed models to sealing leaks in compressed air and steam systems.

As in the building sector, however, there are barriers. Many companies are large and complex, with no one accountable for energy-efficiency improvements. Even when someone is designated for the job, says Christopher Russell, director of the industrial team at the Alliance to Save Energy, that person often lacks clout. "I know people who were given the position of energy manager but didn't have the authority," he says, "and they quit."

Manufacturers also are reluctant to interrupt production to fix something they may not consider broken, especially if their energy costs are less than 5 percent of expenses.

" 'I've got only so many hours in the day,' " Russell hears from plant managers, " 'and do I want to use those hours to make widgets or to tune up my machinery?' "

Industrial plants adopt only 30-40 percent of the recommendations made during an energy audit, Russell says. "If fuel prices go up high enough, maybe you'll hear a different song," he says.

They certainly have had an impact at Pinehall Brick in Winston-Salem, N.C. Earlier this year, the company slightly increased the size of the holes in its bricks to reduce their weight in the kiln. "If you fire the same number of bricks, but they weigh less, you'll use less energy," said company President Fletcher Steele. The change has cut his energy use by 2.5 percent, he estimates. [19]

Alliance to Save Energy

Insulating the attic, along with sealing leaks to the outside with caulking and weather stripping, can reduce home heating and cooling bills up to 20 percent, according to the Alliance to Save Energy.

Should the federal government raise CAFE standards for cars?

After the Arab oil embargo of 1973, Congress passed the Energy Policy Conservation Act, requiring automakers to meet corporate average fuel economy (CAFE) standards set by the National Highway Traffic Safety Administration (NHTSA) and Congress. The near-term goal was to double the fuel economy of new cars by 1985 to 27.5 miles per gallon.

But there hasn't been much movement since. The CAFE standard for passenger cars has remained at 27.5 mpg for the past 16 years, and environmental groups say that's long enough. "We cannot simply drill our way out of our current gasoline-supply woes," says the Union of Concerned Scientists. [20] The group wants fuel-economy standards raised to more than 40 mpg by 2015, and 55 mpg by 2025.

While the idea of raising standards has gained some traction in Congress recently, the auto industry remains extremely skeptical, and technology — its feasibility, its cost and its desirability to consumers — is at the center of the debate.

In 2001, the National Academy of Sciences studied the efficacy of the CAFE program for Congress. It concluded that as the standards rose between 1975 and 1984, automakers used advances in the efficiency of engines, drive trains and aerodynamics to improve fuel economy. Fuel economy gained "62 percent without any loss of performance." But after 1985, as the government held CAFE standards steady, the industry concentrated technological advances "principally on performance and other vehicle attributes." Fuel economy remained essentially unchanged, while vehicles became 20 percent heavier and acceleration 25 percent faster. [21]

It wouldn't take hydrogen fuel cells, plug-in hybrids or space-age materials to raise fuel economy again, experts say. It could be done with current technology, and power and performance would not have to suffer, they say.

"Honda, Toyota and BMW are leading the pack," using such innovations as multi-valve engines, variable valve timing and lift, six-speed transmissions and low-rolling-resistance tires, says Alan Crane, a researcher who worked on the National Academy of Sciences report. "You would see a lot more implementation of these new technologies if the CAFE standards were raised."

According to the Union of Concerned Scientists, integrating these technologies into an SUV the same size and acceleration as the Ford Explorer could raise its fuel economy from 21 mpg to 36 mpg. But the improvements would add more than $2,000 to the cost of the vehicle and take up to five years to recoup through gasoline savings. [22]

"The technology is available, but will consumers pay for it?" asks Eron Shosteck, a spokesperson for the Alliance of Automobile Manufacturers. "What we have found is that some will and some won't, and some get very resentful [about buying] technology that they don't want to spend the money on."

Since CAFE standards are weighted to sales, it's not enough for carmakers to produce more fuel-efficient vehicles, says Shosteck. Consumers must buy them if carmakers are to meet government targets.

Safety is another concern. "The downweighting and downsizing that occurred in the late 1970s and early 1980s, some of which was due to CAFE standards, probably resulted in an additional 1,300 to 2,600 traffic fatalities in 1993," the National Academy of Sciences reported. [23] Critics of CAFE standards have seized on that conclusion to argue against raising them.

But two members of the panel that wrote the report sharply challenged that conclusion. David Greene, a corporate fellow at the Oak Ridge laboratory, called the evidence of a link between fuel economy, weight reduction and traffic fatalities or injuries

Energy Efficiency Reduces U.S. Consumption

Since 1973, the United States has saved more energy through efficiency and conservation efforts than the amount of energy it consumed from petroleum.

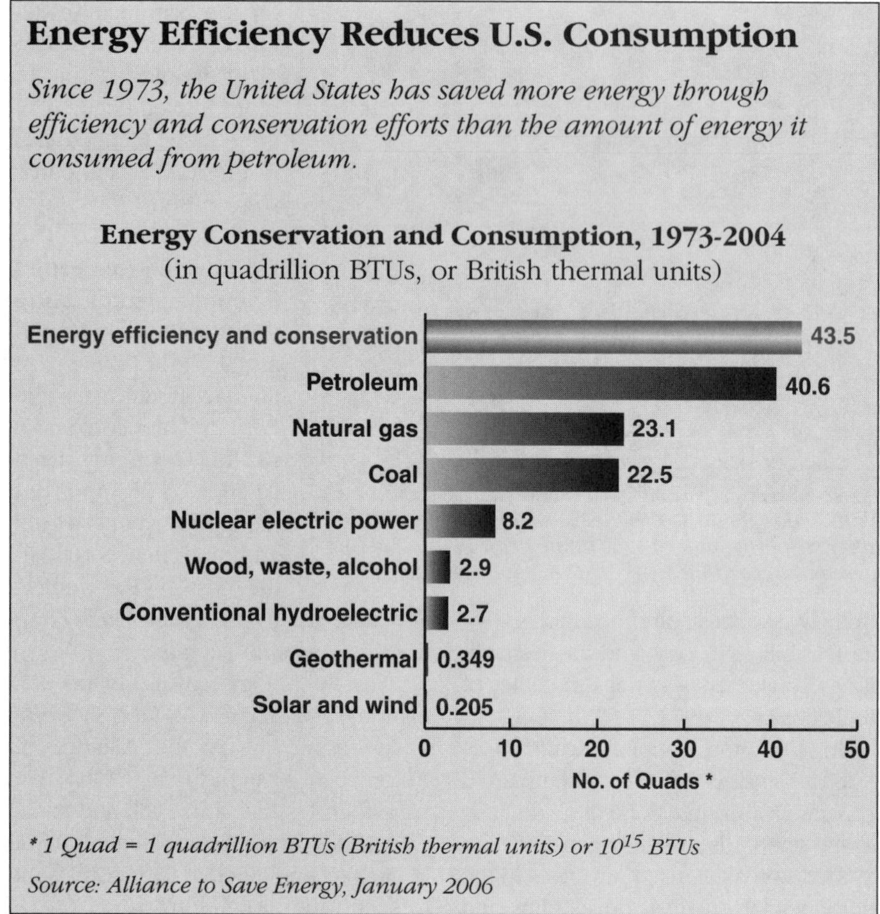

** 1 Quad = 1 quadrillion BTUs (British thermal units) or 10^{15} BTUs*

Source: Alliance to Save Energy, January 2006

"highly dubious." Moreover, he said, weight reduction is just one way automakers can respond to higher CAFE standards. They can also adopt innovations in engine technology, transmission design and aerodynamics. [24]

Some of the greatest potential to reduce fuel consumption is in light trucks, which include SUVs, minivans and pickup trucks. Their CAFE standard, 21.6 mpg for this model year, is lower than for cars. But that is going to change for some of the smaller models. On March 29, NHTSA strengthened the light truck CAFE standard and overhauled the way the standards are set.

"The new standards represent the most ambitious fuel-economy goals for light trucks ever developed in the program's 27-year history," said Secretary of Transportation Norman Y. Mineta. "And more importantly, they close loopholes that have long plagued the current system." [25]

Under the plan, the heaviest SUVs — those weighing between 8,500 and 10,000 pounds, such as Hummers — for the first time will be subject to fuel-economy regulation. However, the heaviest pickup trucks, which make up 80 percent of the 8,500-10,000 pound weight class, will still be exempt.

In addition, instead of applying an average standard for light trucks as it has done in the past, NHTSA assigned a standard to each vehicle based on its size, or "footprint." The smaller the footprint, the more stringent the fuel-economy standard a vehicle would have to meet. Thus, the CAFE standard for the large Hummer 2 model will increase to 22 mpg in model year 2011, while the fuel-economy standard for the smaller Jeep Wrangler will rise to 28.6 mpg. The goal is to discourage automakers from designing smaller vehicles as light trucks instead of passenger cars just to take advantage of the truck category's historically lower CAFE standard.

While many environmental groups have long sought to close the light-truck loophole, the new regulations create their own problem: They may encourage carmakers to produce more of the largest SUVS and pickups because they have the lowest CAFE standards.

Environmentalists also attacked the administration's proposal on other fronts. The continued exemption of heavier pickup trucks is shortsighted, they said, and the fuel-economy standards are too low and the fuel savings too small. "You're talking about saving 11 billion gallons of gasoline over about 20 years," says David Friedman, research director of the Clean Vehicles Program at the Union of Concerned Scientists. "That's less than a month's worth of gasoline."

On May 2, 2006, California, Massachusetts and eight other states sued to force the Bush administration to toughen the standards for light trucks, alleging that it had failed to consider the standards' impact on air quality and greenhouse gas emissions. "The Bush administration is pushing for fuel-economy standards that appear to be authored by the oil and auto industries," said Massachusetts Attorney General Thomas F. Reilly. [26]

But the Alliance of Automobile Manufacturers called the new fuel-economy standards "a challenge." [27] It pointed out they are expected to cost the industry $6.7 billion during model years 2008-2011. As for raising fuel-economy standards for passenger cars, Transportation Secretary Mineta said the administration would oppose any increase without reforms to the program, such as tailoring fuel-economy standards to car size as it did for light trucks.

As an alternative to raising fuel-economy standards, economists often propose raising the excise tax on gasoline. Making gasoline more expensive

Energy Policy Act Gets Mixed Reviews

In August 2005, President Bush signed the Energy Policy Act into law — the first major piece of federal energy legislation in 13 years.

It took Congress five years to draft the law after considering and then dropping several controversial provisions, including allowing oil drilling in the Arctic National Wildlife Refuge and raising fuel-economy targets for cars.

The law has its share of critics, from conservatives who say the government should not meddle in energy markets to consumers who say it did nothing to lower energy prices. But those who advocate energy efficiency as one of the most effective ways to reduce the nation's dependence on oil and cut greenhouse gas emissions gave the bill a cautious thumbs up.

"It's a modest down payment," says Steven Nadel, executive director of the American Council for an Energy-Efficient Economy. "But it doesn't do nearly enough and much more is needed." Nadel's organization estimates that the energy-efficiency sections of the law will reduce U.S. energy use by about 2 percent in 2020.

While the bill gives $2.6 billion in tax incentives to the oil and gas industry to promote energy development and distribution, it also contains several provisions designed to promote energy efficiency. For instance, it adopts energy-efficiency standards on 16 products, many of which were already subject to standards in some states, including dehumidifiers and traffic signals. The energy council estimates the standards will account for 40 percent of the anticipated energy savings in 2020.

The law also authorizes a variety of tax incentives. Consumers who buy hybrid vehicles between 2006 and 2010, for example, can receive up to $3,400 in tax credits, depending on the vehicle's fuel economy and weight. But the credit will be phased out once a manufacturer has sold 60,000 eligible vehicles. While some manufacturers probably won't reach that sales threshold for years, Toyota estimates it will have sold 60,000 hybrids by the second quarter of this year.

Bradley Berman, editor of hybridcars.com, doubts the tax credits will increase hybrid sales much. "It creates a general climate of acceptance of hybrids," says Berman, "but I don't believe it is increasing the number of hybrids on the road." The biggest problem for hybrids is lack of availability, he says, because demand for many models exceeds supply.

Homeowners, too, can receive tax credits for adding insulation, metal roofs, energy-efficient windows, furnaces, hot-water heaters and central air conditioners. The total credit cannot exceed $500, and the improvements must be made by the end of 2007.

"We're already seeing the manufacturers of these products advertising to contractors and pushing these incentives," says Nadel.

The law also encourages efficient construction of new homes and buildings. Builders whose new homes use 50 percent less energy for space heating and cooling than is required by current energy codes can receive a $2,000 tax credit. But the homes must be built by the end of 2007. Unfortunately, says Nadel, builders need much more time to learn how to construct such energy-efficient homes because very few exist today.

"If the credit expires in 2007," says Nadel, "it will nip this project in the bud." The same problem exists for the tax deduction offered to commercial builders, most of whom won't be able to design and build a qualifying project in such a short period.

Several other programs depend on federal funding, but Bush's proposed fiscal 2007 budget often doesn't supply it. For instance, the Energy Policy Act authorized $90 million for a major public-awareness campaign on how to save energy. "But it was not funded — not one cent," says Kara Saul Rinaldi, policy director at the Alliance to Save Energy.

Efficiency experts say such a campaign would be more than just good public relations. A similar $30 million campaign in California during that state's 2001 energy crisis contributed significantly to a 7 percent drop in energy use, according to the American Council for an Energy-Efficient Economy. [1] The law also authorized increased funding to help states develop and enforce energy-efficient building codes, but the president's budget zeroes out the entire program.

"That's terrible," says Rinaldi, because "every building built today may last 100 years."

House Energy and Commerce Committee Chairman Joe Barton, R-Texas, also criticized the president's budget. The administration "dropped the ball on everything in the Energy Policy Act," said Barton. ""I don't think there's a member of the committee on either side of the aisle who is happy with the budget." [2]

Testifying before Barton's committee in March, Energy Secretary Samuel Bodman said that cuts needed to be made to accommodate the president's increases in science-program funding and the initiative to increase nuclear power. [3]

[1] National Public Radio, "Talk of the Nation/Science Friday," Sept. 30, 2005.

[2] Quoted in Mary O'Driscoll, "Energy Policy: DOE 'dropped the ball' on EP Act Funding, Barton says," *Environment and Energy Daily*, March 10, 2006.

[3] *Ibid.*

---

would cause consumers to demand more fuel-efficient cars, they argue. But in the current environment of $3 gas, politicians are calling for lowering gasoline taxes, not raising them. (*See "At Issue," p. 449.*)

Can states do more to encourage energy efficiency?

States have long been the laboratories for energy-efficiency policies, often serving as the inspiration for federal programs. For instance, when the federal government declined to set minimum efficiency standards for appliances like refrigerators and room air conditioners in the early 1980s, several states set their own. The federal government eventually followed suit, after manufacturers said national standards were better than a patchwork of state rules.

States use various tools to encourage energy efficiency, ranging from appliance standards and energy codes for buildings to tax incentives and public education. But experts say states could be doing much more. Only half of the states have energy-efficiency programs, and many of them need to be strengthened, according to experts.

"We clearly are finding much more efficiency potential out there than any state is realizing," says Neal Elliot, industrial program director at the American Council for an Energy-Efficient Economy.

In response to rising energy prices, strains on electricity grids, environmental concerns and advances in technology, several states have begun to do more. Many have turned once again to appliance standards. Since 2004, 10 states have established new energy-efficiency standards for products.[28] And Congress, again taking its cue from the states, incorporated 16 of the state standards into the Energy Policy Act of 2005.

California, for example, set new standards for external-power supplies, swimming-pool pumps, home electronics, commercial refrigerators and lighting, while Massachusetts set new standards for residential furnaces, lighting and electronic equipment. The Northeast Energy Efficiency Partnerships, which works with states to promote efficiency, estimates that if all states in its region adopted new or updated energy-efficiency standards, by 2020 they could reduce projected growth in annual electricity consumption by 24 percent, cut projected growth in peak demand by as much as 55 percent and reduce annual carbon emissions by more than 6 million metric tons.[29]

Building energy codes — like efficiency standards — have been around for decades. California created the first state energy code in 1978. Florida soon followed, as did New York, Minnesota, Oregon, Washington and others.

Energy codes, which are included in state residential and commercial building codes, typically set standards for the thermal properties of windows, doors and skylights, for the amount of insulation in ceilings, walls and basements, and for proper size of heating and cooling equipment. But only 20 states have adopted the most up-to-date version of the model energy code endorsed by the Department of Energy, and enforcement remains a big problem.

While the code is set by the state, local officials conduct the building inspections. "Our best-guess estimate for the Northeast is that we have maybe 50-percent compliance with the energy component of the building code," says Jim O'Reilly, policy director of the Northeast partnerships. "A local building inspector is typically more concerned with making sure fire-retardant materials are used and making sure smoke detectors meet code."

California is an exception. Its building energy code is considered the nation's most stringent and best enforced, and the state says it is responsible for 25 percent of its electricity savings over the past 30 years.[30]

To improve local enforcement of energy codes, regional organizations like the partnerships train local officials, architects and builders, using Energy Department funds. But this funding would be eliminated by President Bush's budget request for 2007.

"That's potentially a big problem," says O'Reilly.

While appliance standards and building codes are mandates, states also try to transform the marketplace in other ways. They offer rebates to consumers who buy ENERGY STAR products and to businesses that buy high-efficiency motors; they pay to weatherize low-income homes and they mount education campaigns to promote efficiency and conservation.

States often pay for these programs by having local utilities assess customers a small surcharge, usually a fraction of a cent per kilowatt-hour, and then pool the money into "a public benefit fund." Sometimes the state administers the efficiency programs, sometimes the utility does; sometimes it's a quasi-state agency or nonprofit.

Twenty-five states have such funds, but they're all "running out of money," says Elliot of the American Council for an Energy-Efficient Economy. Once consumers and businesses learn about the rebates or the weatherization programs, Elliot says, they rush to demand them and the programs "max out." In early 2005, heating and air-conditioning rebate programs in California ran short of cash, and later that year the state authorized utilities to increase the surcharge on customer bills.

In some states, legislatures have raided the funds. O'Reilly says the Connecticut legislature began to siphon off $1 million a month from its public benefit fund in 2003 to help pay the state's own energy bills. "Once they did that and there wasn't a great hue and cry, they went and grabbed the whole thing," he says. Some of the money was eventually returned, but the program was cut in half.

"Even if you had public programs that weren't threatened by funding diversion," says O'Reilly, "even if you had building energy codes that were more effectively enforced and even if you had a list of product and appliance standards being set in all states, we as a region are still capturing only a fraction of what is technically achievable in terms of energy efficiency."

Energy-efficiency advocates would like to see states follow the lead of Texas, California and Connecticut, which have adopted energy-efficiency "portfolio standards" that set firm targets for energy savings by electric utilities. Texas, for instance, requires utilities to use energy-efficiency measures to meet 10 percent of the growth in

Continued on p. 444

Chronology

1970s *Energy crises spark interest in conservation.*

1970
Domestic oil production begins to decline.

Oct. 20, 1973
Arab members of the Organization of Petroleum Exporting Countries (OPEC) embargo oil exports to the U.S., triggering energy crisis.

1975
Congress adopts CAFE (corporate average fuel economy) standards.

1977
President Jimmy Carter creates Energy Department and boosts funds for energy efficiency and renewable-energy research.

1978
CAFE standards take effect. . . . Congress passes National Energy Act of 1978, a comprehensive energy measure that includes energy-efficiency tax credits.

1979
Iranian revolution triggers second oil crisis, doubling crude oil prices.

1980s *As oil prices fall, interest in energy efficiency cools.*

January 1981
Crude peaks at $34 a barrel. . . . Inflation leads to global recession.

1986
Crude prices plummet to $12 a barrel. . . . National Highway Traffic Safety Administration (NHTSA) relaxes CAFE standard for model years 1986-1989 as demand for small cars falls.

1987
President Ronald Reagan vetoes, then signs, National Appliance Energy Conservation Act. . . . CAFE standards are raised to 27.5 mpg for cars and 20.7 mpg for light trucks, including SUVs.

1990s *Clinton administration strengthens efficiency programs while GOP-controlled Congress reduces funds for them. . . . Falling oil prices spur demand for SUVs.*

1991
Persian Gulf War refocuses national attention on energy issues. . . . Environmental Protection Agency (EPA) launches Green Lights, the nation's first voluntary energy-efficiency effort and the precursor to the current ENERGY STAR program.

1992
President George H. W. Bush signs comprehensive Energy Policy Act.

1994
U.S. oil imports exceed domestic production for the first time.

1996
National energy-efficiency standard requires manufacturers to increase the energy efficiency of new refrigerators by 30 percent.

December 1998
Crude prices fall to $10 a barrel, boosting consumer demand for SUVs and other gas guzzlers.

1999
President Bill Clinton orders federal government to reduce its energy use 35 percent from 1985 levels by 2010. . . . Honda releases the Insight, first hybrid car in U.S.

2000s *A Republican White House and sympathetic Congress reduce spending on government energy-efficiency programs while pressing for increased domestic production of fossil fuels.*

2000
Toyota releases the Prius, the first hybrid, four-door sedan in the U.S.

May 2001
President George W. Bush directs Vice President Dick Cheney to develop a national energy policy. Developed in secret, it calls for intensified domestic-energy production, including drilling in the Arctic National Wildlife Refuge. Courts later rule Cheney does not have to reveal the industry representatives he met with.

August 2005
Bush signs Energy Policy Act, which includes incentives for improvements in energy efficiency and purchases of hybrid cars but does not increase vehicle fuel economy.

February 2006
President Bush's fiscal 2007 budget proposes further reductions in funding for energy-efficiency programs.

March 2006
Federal government raises fuel-economy standards for light trucks.

April-May 2006
Gas prices climb above $3 a gallon. Bush temporarily halts purchases for the Strategic Petroleum Reserve, orders investigation into alleged price manipulation, asks Congress to repeal certain oil-industry tax incentives and suggests reforming CAFE standards for cars. Members of Congress introduce energy-conservation bills aimed at lowering energy prices.

More Builders Going 'Green'

When the Alta Ski Resort in Utah's Wasatch Mountains was planning a new mid-mountain ski shelter, it decided to "go green."

"We're on public land," says Tom Whipple, Alta's facilities supervisor. "So I think we've always been good stewards, and this is the next step."

The three-level Watson Shelter opened this season. To reduce the impact on the environment, the deck is made of recycled materials, and water is sterilized with ultraviolet light instead of chemicals. The restrooms use waterless urinals, automatic faucets and low-flow toilets. To save on energy, the building makes maximum use of daylight, uses fluorescent bulbs with occupancy sensors and contains energy-efficient windows, high-efficiency boilers and a computer-controlled heating and ventilation system.

Building "green" is catching on, but for a while no one knew exactly what the term meant. Then in 1993, a group of architects and building professionals founded the U.S. Green Building Council to define and standardize the process. Seven years later, the organization, now a coalition of architects, building professionals, environmentalists, utilities and government officials, introduced a rating system for sustainable building that has quickly become a sought-after imprimatur.

The system is called LEED — Leadership in Energy and Environmental Design — and buildings are rated in five categories:

- site sustainability
- water efficiency
- materials and resources
- indoor environmental quality, and
- energy efficiency.

A commercial building receives points in each category, and the total determines its rating, ranging from certified, silver and gold to platinum — the highest.

"Energy efficiency plays the largest role in terms of points," says Tom Hicks, the council's LEED vice president. "This reflects not only the impact to the bottom line but also the broader impacts to the environment."

To receive a LEED rating, the owners of a planned building must first register it. The number of registrations has climbed dramatically since LEED was introduced — from 400 in 2003 to 1,000 last year, bringing the total number of registered buildings to more than 4,000. Once a building is complete, it can be rated. About 400 buildings currently have LEED ratings.

Several are in New York City. In March, 7 World Trade Center — the last building to fall in the 2001 terrorist attacks and the first to be rebuilt — received a gold LEED certification. Its developer, Larry A. Silverstein, said certification won't stop there.

"Everything we do at 7 World Trade Center we will do at the Freedom Tower . . . and at all subsequent World Trade Center buildings," said Silverstein. [1] The 7 World Trade building has a public park, state-of-the-art clear glass, a high-efficiency air-filtration system, high-efficiency steam-to-electricity turbine generators and a system to harvest rainwater for cooling the building and irrigating the park.

Just a few blocks away, a 292-unit luxury apartment building that opened in 2003, the Solaire, is also certified gold, and the neighborhood expects seven other LEED-certified apartment buildings to be completed in the next few years. Solaire leasing manager Lydia Haran said green features were the primary selling point. "We learned from the leasing process that . . . other factors were secondary; that there was a pent-up demand for green luxury high rises." [2]

It's not just private developers who are registering for LEED certification. More than two-dozen U.S. cities now require municipal buildings to meet LEED standards, and nearly a dozen states have done the same for state-owned buildings. [3]

Still, LEED-registered buildings represent just 5 percent of the commercial building market, and most of those buildings are large, averaging 100,000 square feet. The average commercial building in the United States is 15,000 square feet.

"Smaller builders may not have the same financial abilities as the larger builders," says Hicks. But he adds, the costs are surprisingly low. "People think that these buildings must cost 20 percent more to build, but it's actually less than 2 percent more." The time it takes to recoup these added costs depends on several factors, including the amount of water and energy saved and their costs.

Currently, LEED ratings are available only for commercial and institutional buildings, but the U.S. Green Building Council is developing LEED ratings for homes as well.

Meanwhile, the National Association of Home Builders has issued a set of guidelines for builders interested in constructing green homes. According to an association survey, interest is climbing: In 2005, green building represented $7.4 billion worth of the residential market, or 2 percent of housing starts. In 2010, green building will represent $19-$38 billion worth of the residential market, or 5-10 percent of housing starts. [4]

[1] U.S. Green Building Council, 7 World Trade Center Earns LEED Certification, March 27, 2006. www.usgbc.org/News/USGBCNewsDetails.aspx?ID=2225.

[2] Gracella Hapgood, "Green Gets Green," *Continental.com/magazine*, December 2005, p. 72.

[3] U.S. Green Building Council, "LEED Initiatives in Governments and Schools," March 21, 2006.

[4] National Association of Home Builders, "Key Points from the Green Building Survey," www.nahb.org/fileUpload_details.aspx?contentID=56262.

Continued from p. 442

energy demand each year. The rule became effective in 2004. New Jersey is developing an efficiency portfolio standard, and Rhode Island and Maine are considering them as well. Energy-efficiency portfolio standards are similar to the renewable portfolio standards that already exist in 21 states and which require utilities to meet a certain percentage of energy demand through renewable sources. ■

BACKGROUND

Rapid Change

Wood fuel was America's primary source of energy for 200 years, but after a rapid period of industrialization in the late 1800s, coal came to dominate and by the end of World War I accounted for 75 percent of the nation's energy use. [31]

Petroleum and natural gas grew in importance after discovery of the vast Spindletop oil reserve in Texas in 1901 and the advent of mass-produced automobiles. Americans turned to automobiles as their chief form of transportation, spurring suburban development and the construction of a vast network of roads and highways. [32] Trucks took business away from railroads, and railroads themselves began switching from coal to diesel. Homeowners began to use cleaner-burning natural gas in their furnaces and ranges. By 1947, annual consumption of petroleum and natural gas exceeded that of coal and then quadrupled in a single generation.

"Neither before nor since has any source of energy become so dominant so quickly," according to the Department of Energy. [33]

For much of this time, the country produced almost all the energy it consumed. But by the late 1950s, it began to rely more heavily on imported oil. Economic growth, rising personal income and a growing number of automobiles on the road stimulated the demand for oil, just as domestic production began to decline. Between 1970 and 1973, imports of crude oil and petroleum products doubled.

That rising dependence on imports proved critical when on Oct. 20, 1973, the Arab members of the Organization of Petroleum Exporting Countries (OPEC) cut off all shipments to the United States for five months in retaliation for its support of Israel in the Yom Kippur War. [34] By November, oil supplies were critically low, prompting panic buying and long lines at the pump. Energy shortages threatened almost every sector of the economy.

U.S. Fish and Wildlife Service/Getty Images

President Bush asked lawmakers in April to approve energy exploration in the Arctic National Wildlife Refuge as part of his plan to ease rising prices. He also asked Congress to repeal $2 billion in tax breaks for energy companies and expand tax breaks to buyers of hybrid cars.

The public looked to government for solutions, and two years later Congress passed the Energy Policy Conservation Act of 1975, which created the Strategic Petroleum Reserve to soften the economic impact of future disruptions in oil supplies. To encourage domestic production, the law began a phased deregulation of U.S. oil prices, which had risen much less than world prices during the embargo, largely due to price controls imposed by President Richard M. Nixon.

The law also promoted energy efficiency, and automobiles were a natural target. The oil embargo and the resulting energy shortages had brought into sharp focus the fuel inefficiency of U.S. cars. The average fuel economy of new cars had fallen from 14.8 mpg in model year 1967 to 12.8 mpg in 1974. [35] The law established corporate average fuel economy (CAFE) standards for new cars.

In early 1977, newly elected Democratic President Jimmy Carter devised a National Energy Plan and called the challenge of reducing America's dependence on foreign oil the "moral equivalent of war." At the president's request, Congress created the Department of Energy to coordinate energy policy and, after much negotiation, passed the National Energy Act of 1978, which significantly increased funding for energy efficiency and renewable-energy research and development.

Carter could have used a period of energy stability to organize his new department and implement its programs, but in January 1979 the Iranian revolution triggered a second oil crisis, greatly disrupting the flow of oil to world markets and sending world oil prices soaring. In response, Carter called for increased production, conservation and development of alternative fuels as well as the continued decontrol of U.S. oil prices.

This second energy crisis combined with Carter's inability to free American hostages from the U.S. Embassy in Tehran contributed to Carter's loss to Republican Ronald Reagan in the 1980 presidential election. [36]

Falling Prices

Reagan reversed Carter's emphasis on energy efficiency and alternative fuels and even advocated abolishing the Department of Energy, which he said had not "produced a quart of oil or a lump of coal or anything else in the line of energy." [37]

Funds for efficiency and conservation programs at the Department of Energy were slashed by more than 50 percent — from $730 million in 1981 to $333 million in 1989 — and funding for alternative-energy research plummeted from $1 billion to $116 million. [38] Reflecting his GOP administration's free-market philosophy, Reagan accelerated the schedule for energy price decontrol.

The public's interest in energy efficiency flagged along with the president's. After OPEC increased production in 1986, oil prices plunged from $30 a barrel to $12. Consumers began to turn away from smaller, more fuel-efficient cars and began their love affair with minivans and SUVs.

Paradoxically, just as energy prices were falling President Reagan did support one of the country's most far-reaching energy-efficiency programs. In 1987, he signed the National Appliance Energy Conservation Act, which set federal energy-efficiency standards for commonly used appliances.

Reagan's successor, Republican George H. W. Bush, continued the emphasis on deregulating oil and gas, but he also renewed funding for research and development of energy efficiency and alternative fuels. The Bush administration also ushered in a non-regulatory approach. In 1992, the Environmental Protection Agency (EPA) launched ENERGY STAR, a voluntary labeling program designed to identify and promote energy-efficient products to reduce greenhouse gas emissions. Computers and monitors were labeled first, eventually followed by office equipment, major appliances, lighting and home electronics.

That same year, Bush signed the Energy Policy Act. It encouraged oil and gas exploration in coastal U.S. waters while improving building energy codes, equipment standards and the management of energy use by the federal government — the nation's biggest energy consumer.

AP Photo/Frank Franklin II

Installing a high-efficiency natural gas furnace can help lower home heating bills. Heating accounts for the biggest chunk of the energy used in a typical home.

When Democrat Bill Clinton took over the White House in 1993, his energy policy reflected the growing concern about the dangers of global warming and the part played by the burning of fossil fuels in creating greenhouse gas emissions. In his first Earth Day address on April 21, Clinton announced that the United States would stabilize greenhouse gas emissions at 1990 levels by the year 2000. In October, the administration unveiled its Climate Change Action Plan. Energy efficiency and conservation measures counted for about 70 percent of the plan's anticipated emissions reductions. [39]

Sustained Price Rise

In the late 1990s, energy prices began to rise again. In March 1999, OPEC production cuts sent the price of world crude oil from less than $11 a barrel to $24.50 a barrel by December. [40] Disruptions in the flow of oil from Venezuela and Nigeria further restricted production. Meanwhile, world demand for oil increased, propelled in part by rapid economic growth in China and India, which were becoming major energy consumers.

Natural gas prices in the United States also were rising. The bitterly cold winter of 2000-2001 caused a surge in demand for gas for home heating and electrical generation, and by the beginning of the decade, demand exceeded domestic supplies.

In May 2001, against this backdrop of shortage and rising prices, newly elected President George W. Bush presented his national energy policy emphasizing increasing domestic production of oil, gas, coal and nuclear power. The president called for opening the Arctic National Wildlife Refuge to oil and gas exploration, reducing barriers to drilling on other public lands and easing regulations for the licensing of power plants and gas refineries. Bush's plan also called for an expansion of the ENERGY STAR program and efficiency standards for appliances. [41]

"Energy production and environmental protection are not competing priorities," said the president. [42]

Environmental groups and congressional Democrats immediately attacked the plan. "Who would benefit?" asked David Hawkins, director of the Climate Center at the Natural Resources Defense Council, an environmental group. "The oil, coal and auto industries, which shoveled millions of dollars into Bush campaign coffers. Who loses? Anyone who likes to breathe." [43]

Not until the summer of 2005, with oil reaching almost $60 a barrel and gasoline just under $2.50 a gallon, did Congress approve the Energy Policy Act of 2005. "After years of debate and division, Congress passed a good bill," President Bush said as he signed it on Aug. 8. "I'm confident that one day Americans will look back on this bill as a vital step toward a more secure and more prosperous nation that is less dependent on foreign sources of energy."

The law provides $2.6 billion in tax credits for oil and gas production and refining, streamlines approval procedures for drilling on public lands, expedites federal judicial review for permitting natural gas pipelines and liquefied natural gas terminals and promotes the development of clean coal. Consumer advocates and environmental groups promptly attacked the plan as doing little to lower gasoline prices, while conservatives attacked it for doing too much. "With oil flirting with $60 a barrel, you don't need to provide new incentives for development, new incentives for production and exploration," said Jerry Taylor, a senior fellow at the libertarian Cato Institute. [44]

With regard to energy efficiency, the law gives manufacturers and consumers tax incentives to speed the adoption of energy-efficient technologies and sets minimum energy-efficiency standards for 16 products.

By the spring of 2006, energy prices had reached new historic highs. Crude oil breached the $70 per barrel mark, and gasoline climbed above $3 a gallon in some regions. In April, Bush announced a plan that he said would ease rising prices. He directed the Justice Department to investigate possible price gouging and temporarily halted government purchases of oil to fill the Strategic Petroleum Reserve. He also asked Congress to repeal $2 billion in tax breaks for energy companies, expand tax breaks to buyers of hybrid cars and approve energy exploration in the Arctic National Wildlife Refuge. ■

CURRENT SITUATION

Efficiency Lawsuit

Environmentalists, 15 states and two consumer groups are suing the Energy Department for failing to toughen minimum energy-efficiency standards for 22 household and commercial products. The department is between six and 13 years behind schedule updating federally mandated standards for products like dishwashers, central air conditioners and furnaces. For instance, a new, stronger energy-efficiency standard for home furnaces is 12 years overdue.

The department blames its own internal rulemaking process for the delays. Congressional Democrats blame the delays on mismanagement, and efficiency advocates cite budget cuts. Almost everyone agrees the delays will cost consumers money.

According to the American Council for an Energy-Efficient Economy, existing standards will save nearly 400 billion kilowatt-hours per year by 2020 or about $34 billion at current electricity and natural gas prices. "Updating all the standards now pending at the Department of Energy could save another 180 billion kilowatt-hours per year by 2030 . . . worth about $15 billion per year at current prices." [45]

While the delays straddle three different administrations, past administrations at least caught up on some. The Clinton administration issued 10 efficiency standards, says Katherine Kennedy, a senior attorney at the Natural Resources Defense Council, one of the parties in the lawsuit. "Bush senior's administration issued five standards," she continued. "But the current administration has not issued any strengthened energy standards at all."

On Jan. 31, 2006, the Energy Department released a schedule for bringing the standards up to date. "This aggressive schedule shows our commitment to greater efficiency by issuing new standards for all products in the backlog by June of 2011, just five years from now," said Acting Assistant Secretary for Energy Efficiency and Renewable Energy Douglas L. Faulkner. [46]

But the groups suing the department were far from mollified. "It leaves aside until after 2011 any action on two of

Gas Tax Hasn't Changed in a Decade

The federal excise tax on gasoline has remained virtually unchanged — at about 18 cents per gallon — since 1994. Today, many economists want Congress to raise the tax in hopes it will force consumers to demand more fuel-efficient cars. But with gas currently selling for more than $3 a gallon, politicians want the tax lowered, not raised.

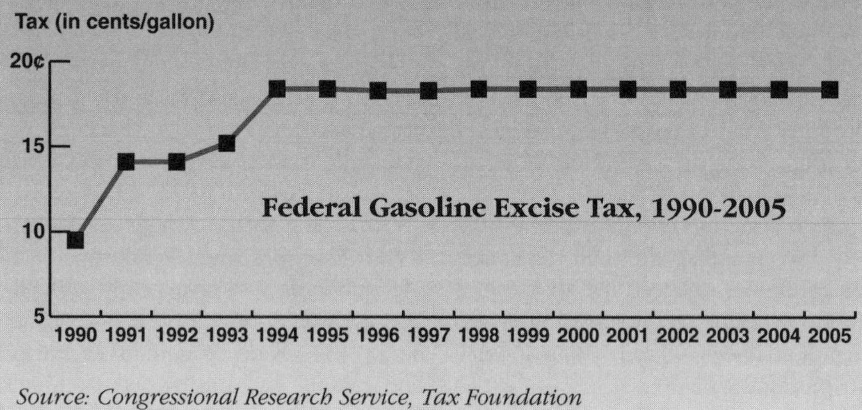

Source: Congressional Research Service, Tax Foundation

the standards that have the potential for the biggest energy savings — residential refrigerators and residential furnace fans," says Andrew deLaski, executive director of the nonprofit Appliance Standards Awareness Project.

In addition, the schedule is voluntary. "There is no reason to believe that [the Department of Energy] will meet the deadlines in this plan," says Kennedy, "when they have missed so many deadlines in past plans."

The plaintiffs in the lawsuit have proposed their own schedule with earlier deadlines and are asking the court to make those deadlines binding.

Automakers Sue California

While California is one of the states suing the federal government over appliance standards, automakers are suing California over its anti-climate-change law.

In July 2002, former Democratic California Gov. Gray Davis signed the nation's first law to control the amount of greenhouse gases emitted in auto exhaust. Two years later, the California Air Resources Board issued regulations to implement the law, which gives automakers until 2009 to develop an auto fleet emitting 22 percent fewer greenhouse gases by 2012 and 30 percent fewer by 20016.

Automakers immediately protested, and in December 2004 the Alliance of Automobile Manufacturers, the Association of International Automobile Manufacturers and California auto dealers challenged the law in federal court. "This regulation is inconsistent with federal law, as well as fundamental principles for sound regulation of motor vehicles," said Fred Webber, president and CEO of the manufacturers' alliance. [47]

California and the automakers disagree on almost every point: the legality of the law, its cost to consumers and its impact on vehicle choice.

Virtually all vehicle greenhouse gas emissions are carbon dioxide, and the only way to reduce those is to improve fuel economy, say automakers. But only the federal government can set fuel-economy standards, the manufacturers' alliance says and calls the California law a backdoor attempt by a state to set fuel-economy standards. [48]

California lawmakers counter that the state is setting emissions, not fuel-economy standards, and that it has authority to do so under the federal Clean Air Act. California regulators say the technology to reduce vehicles' greenhouse emissions is readily available and would add less than $400 to the cost of a car or small SUV in 2012 and just over a $1,000 in 2016. Moreover, they estimate that car buyers would more than recoup these costs over the lifetime of the vehicle with savings at the gas pump.

The Alliance of Automobile Manufacturers, however, puts the cost at triple those amounts and says drivers would never completely recoup them. It also says Californians would see fewer models on sales lots and full-size pickup trucks might disappear altogether.

Nine states, including New York, have pledged to adopt the California standards. And after Canada threatened to copy the California law, automakers and the Canadian government reached a voluntary agreement in March 2005 to reduce greenhouse gas emissions from cars sold there. Automakers already have a voluntary agreement with the European Union.

Environmental groups say the Canadian pact weakens the carmakers' lawsuit. "When they go into court and say, 'Your honor, we can't do this,' we can point out that they have agreed to do this just north of us in Canada," said Daniel Becker, director of the Sierra Club's global warming program. [49]

But automakers say the Canadian pact has no bearing on the U.S. lawsuit. Canada has the authority to reach a voluntary agreement with carmakers, but states, automakers argue, don't have the authority to set fuel-economy standards. "So it is apples and oranges,"

Continued on p. 450

At Issue:

Should gas taxes be raised to encourage energy conservation?

ROBERT H. FRANK
PROFESSOR OF ECONOMICS, JOHNSON GRADUATE SCHOOL OF MANAGEMENT, CORNELL UNIVERSITY

WRITTEN FOR *CQ RESEARCHER*, MAY 2006.

yes

Suppose a politician proposed a policy that would, if adopted, produce hundreds of billions of dollars in savings for American consumers, significant reductions in traffic congestion, major improvements in air quality, large reductions in greenhouse gases and substantially reduced dependence on Middle East oil. This policy would also require no net cash outlays from American families, no additional regulations and no expansion of the bureaucracy.

Although it sounds too good to be true, such a policy could be enacted by Congress tomorrow — namely, a $2-a-gallon tax on gasoline whose proceeds were refunded to American families in reduced payroll taxes.

On average, a family of four currently consumes almost 2,000 gallons of gasoline annually. If all families continued to consume gasoline at the same rate after the imposition of a $2-a-gallon tax, the average family would pay $4,000 in additional gasoline taxes annually. A family with two earners would then receive an annual payroll tax refund of $4,000.

But that is not how things would play out. Suppose, for example, that the family was about to replace its aging Ford Explorer, which gets 15 mpg. It would have a strong incentive to consider Ford's new Focus wagon, which can haul almost as much cargo and gets more than 30 miles per gallon.

Experience from the 1970s confirms that consumers respond to higher gasoline prices not just by buying more efficient cars but also by taking fewer trips, forming carpools and moving closer to work. If families overall bought half as much gasoline as before, the rebate would be only $2,000 for the representative two-earner family. In that case, this family could not buy just as much gasoline as before unless it spent $2,000 less on everything else.

One barrier to the adoption of higher gasoline taxes has been the endless insistence by proponents of smaller government that all taxes are bad. But as even the most enthusiastic free-market economists concede, current gasoline prices are far too low, because they fail to reflect the environmental and foreign policy costs associated with gasoline consumption. Government would actually be smaller, and we would all be more prosperous, if not for the problems caused by what President Bush has called our addiction to oil.

In the warmer weather they will have inherited from us a century from now, perspiring historians will struggle to explain why this proposal was once considered politically unthinkable.

BEN LIEBERMAN
SENIOR POLICY ANALYST, HERITAGE FOUNDATION

WRITTEN FOR *CQ RESEARCHER*, MAY 2006.

no

Raising the excise tax on gasoline is clearly not the solution to the energy challenges Americans face. The last thing drivers struggling with $2.90-a-gallon gas need is the government deliberately raising the price even higher.

There is no doubt that a large enough tax increase on motor fuels would reduce consumption by forcing the public — low-income persons disproportionately — to drive less, and pricing some at the margins off the roads entirely. Indeed, the gas tax may well be the most regressive tax in existence, especially for those who drive to low-wage jobs. But the goal of our nation's energy policy should not be reductions in use per se, especially if achieved by punishing the American consumer. The aim should be to help people, not hurt them, and for that we want energy that is more affordable, not less.

Some argue that a higher gasoline tax would encourage people to drive more fuel-efficient cars. It would, but those cars are already available for those who want them. Coercing people through economic necessity to choose smaller and less safe vehicles can hardly be considered a favor to them.

Others believe that a heftier gas tax is needed to encourage alternative fuels and vehicles. But are we better off with alternatives that are so expensive that they can't compete with oil even at today's high prices? Granted, petroleum use has its costs — geopolitical as well as economic — but that does not mean that alternatives are necessarily better.

An economically viable alternative would be a very good thing, but there is no reason to believe that high gasoline taxes will spur any rapid technological advances toward that end. Consider the fact that Europe has for years accepted the "wisdom" of higher fuel taxes — in many nations there the taxes alone exceed $3 per gallon. Yet despite years of such high prices, European automotive engineers — including the vaunted Germans — have failed to come up with a gasoline or diesel alternative that can grab significant market share. Similarly, high taxes on gasoline here are unlikely to lead to miracle breakthroughs, just a bigger cost burden for motorists.

Rather than raising taxes, Congress should be taking steps to ensure that energy is as affordable as market forces will allow. These steps include removing the stiff restrictions on new, domestic oil production in the Arctic National Wildlife Refuge and offshore, and streamlining regulations that hamper needed refinery expansions and make gasoline more expensive to produce. Affordable energy should be seen as the solution, not the problem.

Department of Energy Efficiency Programs

Building Technologies Program: Conducts research and development of emerging building technologies and promotes integration of new technologies. Helps states to implement and enforce building energy codes and sets energy-efficiency standards for appliances and equipment.

ENERGY STAR: Identifies and promotes energy-efficient products, buildings and practices through a voluntary labeling program. ENERGY STAR labels exist for more than 35 products, including office equipment, residential heating and cooling equipment, lighting, home electronics and major appliances.

Industrial Technologies Program: Partners with energy-intensive industries to reduce energy consumption. Conducts research and development of technologies common to many industries, like sensors and combustion, to increase efficiency. Works with industry to implement energy-management practices in plants.

Distributed Energy and Electric Reliability Program: Develops advanced technologies to strengthen the nation's electric-energy infrastructure. Conducts research, development, demonstration, technology transfer and educational activities in partnership with utilities, state agencies, universities and national laboratories.

Weatherization Assistance Program: Enables low-income families to permanently reduce their energy bills by making their homes more energy efficient.

State Energy Program: Provides funding to states to design and carry out their own energy-efficiency and renewable-energy programs.

FreedomCAR and Fuel Partnership: Focuses on the research needed to develop technologies, such as fuel cells and advanced hybrid propulsion systems, needed to produce vehicles using little or no gasoline and producing few emissions.

Continued from p. 448

said Gloria Bergquist, a spokeswoman for the Alliance of Automobile Manufactures. [50]

Hybrid Potential

The California law comes at a particularly difficult time for U.S. automakers. General Motors and Ford plan to cut 60,000 jobs and close or idle more than two-dozen facilities in the next several years. These restructuring plans are designed to reverse billions of dollars of losses suffered as health-care costs have climbed and sales of SUVs and pickups have slumped in the face of rising gasoline prices.

Analysts say rising gasoline prices pose a serious threat to domestic automakers. "If the automakers do not change the fuel economy from where it is today, they will lose a lot of money," says Walter S. McManus, director of the Automotive Analysis Division at the University of Michigan Transportation Research Institute. McManus expects high or rising oil prices to be the norm for the next two decades.

The institute modeled the potential effects of average gasoline prices at $3.37 a gallon compared to a baseline of $1.96 a gallon. The report predicted that sales of cars and light trucks in North America would decline 14 percent in model year 2009 and profits would shrink by $17.6 billion, with U.S. automakers absorbing the brunt of the reductions "because of their dependence on SUV and pickup sales." [51]

McManus and other auto analysts say the technology is there to improve fuel economy, although retooling plants could cost billions of dollars. Among the available technologies are things like six-speed automatic transmissions, automated manual transmissions, variable valve lift, dual cam phasers, turbocharging and hybrids. Of them all, hybrids may offer the most fuel savings.

Hybrid vehicles run off a rechargeable battery and gasoline. Their engines are smaller, and when the vehicle is stopped, the gasoline motor shuts off and the electric motor and battery take over. Hybrids often recover braking energy and use it to charge the battery.

But hybrid vehicles are currently less than 1.5 percent of the U.S. market, and Toyota dominates. The sales of its Prius alone are more than all other hybrids combined. Next is Honda and then Ford. Trailing far behind are General Motors and DaimlerChrysler. "What I'm afraid of is that some of these companies are setting themselves up for a repeat of the 1970s," says Friedman, of the Clean Vehicles Program at the Union of Concerned Scientists, "when there was an oil embargo, gas lines and gas-price spikes and the Big Three automakers didn't have the products that consumers needed."

All the automakers plan to introduce more hybrids. "We expect roughly half of our lineup to be available as a hybrid option," says Mike Moore, a Ford spokesman. General Motors is adding three hybrid models in model year 2007, and DaimlerChrysler plans to unveil a hybrid Dodge Durango. The forecasting firm JD Powers expects hybrids to account for 3.5 percent of U.S. sales by 2012. [52]

Bradley Berman, the editor of hybridcars.com, an informational Web site, calls that estimate conservative. "It's not based on market potential," says Berman.

But predicting market potential is difficult. Hybrid technology can add several thousands of dollars to the price of a vehicle, and the length of time needed to recoup that cost depends on how much one drives, the price of gasoline and the vehicle's fuel economy. *Consumer Reports*, a product-rating publication, tested hybrids in city and highway driving and found that most fell far short of the estimates published on their fuel-economy labels. [53]

Toyota Motor Co.

The Toyota Prius outsells all other hybrids combined. Hybrid vehicles now account for less than 1.5 percent of the U.S. market, but that's expected to rise to 3.5 percent by 2012.

If hybrids are to go mainstream, automakers say they must get the price of the vehicles down. "We've said we want to sell 1 million hybrids a year by about 2012," explained Dave Hermance, executive engineer for advanced-technology vehicles at Toyota. "To do that, we need to reduce costs and thus reduce the manufacturer's suggested retail price premium by about $1,000." [54]

But many environmental groups are concerned that some automakers are reducing that price premium by weakening the hybrid technology and barely improving gas mileage. "There are good hybrids and bad hybrids in the marketplace," says Friedman of the Union of Concerned Scientists.

For instance, says Friedman, the hybrid Chevrolet Silverado pickup truck doesn't deserve the name hybrid. The engine does idle-off at stops, but it doesn't accelerate from stops using the electric motor, it doesn't have regenerative braking and it can't run on just the electric motor and the battery, as the most advanced hybrids do. "And the Silverado only gets a 10 percent increase in fuel economy over the conventional version, whereas the Honda Civic and the Toyota Prius do much better than that," says Friedman.

"This is the part where the market hasn't quite adjusted. They think hybrids should get 50 miles per gallon," said Steve Poulos, a General Motors hybrid engineer. "The reality is you have to look by class of vehicle." The Silverado is a full-size pickup, and owners tend to drive a lot of miles, said Poulos. [55] Thus, even a 10 percent improvement in fuel economy would save them a lot of money. ■

OUTLOOK

Will Congress Act?

Since late April, lawmakers in Congress have been responding to voters' complaints about rising gasoline prices by scrambling to put together an energy bill. Fearing how gasoline prices will play in the November elections, Republicans and Democrats have been floating a variety of ideas and sharp words.

In early May, House Republicans called a Senate Republican proposal to mail American households a $100 rebate "silly" and "insulting." The Senate leadership promptly shelved it.

The remaining proposals being seriously debated would not have an immediate impact on gasoline prices. In fact, their impact could take years to be felt. They include giving the Federal Trade Commission greater authority to crack down on price gouging, withdrawing $2 billion in oil-industry tax breaks, streamlining refining regulations, drilling in the Arctic National Wildlife Refuge (ANWR), expanding tax credits for hybrid vehicles and raising the fuel-economy standards for passenger cars.

However, it is uncertain which proposals will make it out of Congress. "The House has the capacity to pass bills that very strongly favor the producer-based solutions, but you can't get enough votes in the Senate to pass those," says Bruce Oppenheimer, a professor of political science at Vanderbilt University. "And the House is unwilling to adopt solutions that the Senate would tolerate that are more heavily weighted toward conservation and alternative-fuels-based solutions."

"It's really a question of whether the frustration of the public with energy prices will be enough to bring forth a bipartisan legislative initiative," says Kara Saul Rinaldi, director of policy at the Alliance to Save Energy. "And something that would pass this Congress could not have a lot of the most contentious issues in there."

Those contentious issues include drilling for oil in ANWR and raising the fuel-economy standards for passenger cars. Although several Republicans who formerly opposed raising standards have now said they would consider it, past proposals have failed by wide margins.

Moreover, Transportation Secretary Mineta said the administration opposes any hikes in fuel-economy standards until Congress gives the department the authority to reform the program. Mineta would like to replace the average fleetwide standard of the current system with different standards for each size car, as it did for light trucks in March. But several prominent Democrats, including Rep. John Dingell, D-Mich., have expressed reluctance to give Congress such authority, and the Alliance of Automobile Manufacturers said it may be premature to adopt a new system for cars with "the ink barely dry on the recent light-truck rule." [56]

This is not the first time the current Congress has responded to rising energy prices with a flurry of proposals. After Hurricane Katrina interrupted the flow of energy supplies last September, more than 40 energy bills were introduced. Several were aimed at increasing efficiency.

The Health Care for Hybrids Act, introduced by Sen. Barack Obama, D-Ill., would help automakers meet rising health-care costs if at least half of the savings were reinvested in hybrids and alternative-fuel vehicles or in retooling manufacturing plants. Two broader bills would set specific oil-saving targets and would increase incentives for the purchase of efficient vehicles, provide incentives for fuel stations to install alternative-fuel pumps and provide incentives to speed the commercialization of technologies that could reduce gasoline use.

Congress will continue to hold hearings on energy policy, and the fate of any of these proposals depends, partly, on the course of energy prices this summer.

"The rug gets pulled back out of everything if energy prices go down again," says Oppenheimer. ■

Notes

1 Energy Information Administration, "Monthly Energy Review March 2006." Gross domestic product is the annual output of goods and services in the United States.

2 American Council for an Energy-Efficient Economy, "Energy Efficiency Progress and Potential;" www.aceee.org/energy/effact.htm.

3 Energy Information Administration, "Annual Energy Outlook 2006."

4 Rocky Mountain Institute, "Meeting Our Needs With Efficiency," www.rmi.org/sitepages/pid318.php.

5 Energy Information Administration, March 2006, *op. cit.*

6 American Petroleum Institute, "U.S. Pump Price Update — April 26, 2006," http://apiec.api.org/filelibrary/PumpPriceUpdate.pdf.

7 Pew Center on Global Climate Change, "Basic Science;" www.pewclimate.org/globalwarming-basics/basic_science/.

8 Department for Environment, Food and Rural Affairs, United Kingdom, "Avoiding Dangerous Climate Change," *Executive Summary*, Jan. 30, 2006, pp. 2-3. See also Juliet Eilperin, "Debate on Climate Shifts to Issue of Irreparable Change; Some Experts on Global Warming Foresee 'Tipping Point' When It Is Too Late to Act," *The Washington Post*, Jan. 29, 2006, p. A1.

9 Energy Information Administration, "Annual Energy Review 2004."

10 David L. Greene and Nataliya I. Tishchishyna, "Costs of Oil Dependence: A 2000 Update," Oak Ridge National Laboratory, p. 3.

11 "Federal Energy-Efficiency Programs Deserve Significant Increases in FY 2007 Funding," Alliance to Save Energy; www.ase.org/files/2903_file_Budget_Statement.pdf.

12 Alliance to Save Energy, Legislative Alert, "President's FY2007 Budget Would Cut Energy-Efficiency Funding," pp. 2-3.

13 *Ibid.*

14 Alliance to Save Energy, "Building on Success: Policies to Reduce Energy Waste in Buildings," July 2005, p. 6.

15 *Ibid.*, p. 8.

16 National Academy of Sciences, "Energy Research at DOE: Was it Worth It?" 2001, p. 6.

17 National Association of Manufacturers, "Efficiency and Innovation in U.S. Manufacturing Energy Use," 2005, p. 3.

18 Department of Energy, "Energy Use, Loss and Opportunities Analysis: U.S. Manufacturing & Mining," 2004, pp. 1, 72.

19 Timothy Aeppel and Melanie Trottman, "As Energy Costs Soar, Companies Retool Operations," *The Wall Street Journal*, April 22, 2006, p. A1.

20 Union of Concerned Scientists, "Clean Vehicles," www.ucsusa.org/clean_vehicles/fuel_economy/.

21 National Academy of Sciences, "Effectiveness and Impact of Corporate Average Fuel Economy (CAFE) Standards," 2002, p. 3.

22 Union of Concerned Scientists, "Building a Better SUV," September 2003, p. 3.

23 National Academy of Sciences, 2002, *op. cit.*

24 David L. Greene, "Improving the Nation's Energy Security: Can Cars and Trucks Be Made More Fuel Efficient?" testimony before House Science Committee, Feb. 9, 2005, p. 7.

25 U.S. Department of Transportation, www.dot.gov/affairs/cafe032906.htm.

26 Danny Hakim, "10 States, in Challenge to U.S., Plan Suit to Force Better Mileage Rules for S.U.V.'s," *The New York Times*, May 2, 2006. The article came out the day before the formal filing of the suit.

27 "Statement of the Alliance of Automobile Manufacturers before House Committee on Energy and Commerce," May 3, 2006, p. 7.

28 Appliance Standards Awareness Project, press release, March 15, 2006; www.standardsasap.org/press21.htm.

29 Northeast Energy Efficiency Partnerships, "Energy Efficiency Standards: A Low-Cost, High Leverage Policy for Northeast States," pp. i-ii.

30 American Council for an Energy-Efficient

About the Author

Barbara Mantel is a freelance writer in New York City whose work has appeared in *The New York Times*, the *Journal of Child and Adolescent Psychopharmacology* and *Mamm Magazine*. She is a former correspondent and senior producer for National Public Radio and has won several journalism awards, including the National Press Club's Best Consumer Journalism Award and Lincoln University's Unity Award. She holds a B.A. in history and economics from the University of Virginia and an M.A. in economics from Northwestern University.

Economy, "Energy Efficiency's Next Generation: Innovation at the State Level," November 2003, p. 9.

[31] Energy Information Administration, "History of Energy Use in the United States," www.eia.doe.gov/emeu/aer/eh/frame.html.

[32] For background, see Mary H. Cooper, "Alternative Energy," *CQ Researcher*, Feb. 25, 2005, p. 182. For background, see "Ten Years of Federal Aid in Road Building," *Editorial Research Reports 1927* (Vol. III), available in *CQ Researcher Plus Archive*, http://library.cqpress.com.

[33] Energy Information Administration, "History of Energy Use in the United States;" www.eia.doe.gov/emeu/aer/eh/frame.html.

[34] Daniel Yergin, *The Prize* (1991), p. 608. For background, see Sandra Stencel, "Middle East Reappraisal," *Editorial Research Reports*, Dec. 12, 1973, available in *CQ Researcher Plus Archive*, http://library.cqpress.com.

[35] Congressional Research Service, *CRS Issue Brief*, "Automobile and Light Truck Fuel Economy: The CAFE Standards," June 19, 2003, p. 2.

[36] Yergin, *op. cit.*, pp 699-702.

[37] Department of Energy, Energy History Series, "Department of Energy 1977-1994," November 1994, p. 31.

[38] White House, "Budget of the United States Government, Fiscal Year 2007."

[39] Department of Energy, November 1994, *op. cit.*, p. 85.

[40] Congressional Research Service, "Energy Policy: Conceptual Framework and Continuing Issues," Jan. 18, 2006, p. 1.

[41] For background, see Mary H. Cooper, "Energy Policy," *CQ Researcher*, May 25, 2001, pp. 441-464; and Cooper, "Alternative Energy," *op. cit.*

[42] The White House, "Remarks by the President to Capital City Partnership," May 17, 2001; www.whitehouse.gov/news/releases/2001/05/20010517-2.html.

[43] Natural Resources Defense Council, press release, "NRDC Offers Responsible Alternative to Bush Energy Plan," May 17, 2001.

[44] CNBC, "Morning Call," Aug. 1, 2005.

[45] American Council for an Energy-Efficient Economy, press release, "Coalition Praises DOE for First Step Toward Setting New Energy-Saving Appliance Standards," Feb. 1, 2006.

[46] Department of Energy, press release, "Department Sets Aggressive Schedule for New Appliance Standards," Feb. 1, 2006.

[47] Alliance of Automobile Manufactures, "Automakers and Dealers Cite Federal Law, Marketplace Principles in Challenging Carbon Dioxide Law," Dec. 7, 2004.

FOR MORE INFORMATION

Alliance to Save Energy, 1200 18th St., N.W., Suite 900, Washington, DC 20036; (202) 857-0666; www.ase.org. A nonprofit organization that promotes energy efficiency worldwide to achieve a healthier economy, a cleaner environment and greater energy security.

Alliance of Automobile Manufacturers, 1401 I St., N.W., Suite 900, Washington, DC 20005; (202) 326-5500; www.autoalliance.org. A trade association of nine car and light truck manufacturers including BMW group, DaimlerChrysler, Ford, General Motors, Mazda, Mitsubishi Motors, Porsche, Toyota and Volkswagen.

American Council for an Energy-Efficient Economy, 1001 Connecticut Ave., N.W., Suite 801, Washington, DC 20036; (202) 429-8873; www.aceee.org. A nonprofit organization dedicated to advancing energy efficiency.

American Petroleum Institute, 1220 L St., N.W., Washington, DC 20005; (202) 682-8000; www.api.org. The primary trade association of the oil and natural gas industry.

Environmental Protection Agency, ENERGY STAR Web site, www.energystar.gov. Provides information about the government's voluntary labeling program that promotes energy-efficient products and buildings.

Edison Electric Institute, 701 Pennsylvania Ave., N.W., Washington, DC 20004; (202) 508-5000; www.eei.org. An association of U.S. shareholder-owned electric companies, international affiliates and industry associates worldwide.

Hybridcars.com, www.hybridcars.com. A Web site providing information about hybrid vehicles and the hybrid-vehicle marketplace.

Rocky Mountain Institute, 1739 Snowmass Creek Road, Snowmass, CO 81654-9199; (970) 927-3851; www.rmi.org. A nonprofit that works with businesses, individuals, governments and communities to promote the efficient use of resources.

The Tax Incentive Assistance Project, www.energytaxincentives.org. A Web site that provides information to consumers and businesses about federal income-tax incentives for energy-efficient products and technologies.

Union of Concerned Scientists, 2 Brattle Square, Cambridge, MA 02238; (617) 547-5552; www.ucsusa.org. A nonprofit partnership of scientists and citizens combining scientific analysis, policy development and citizen advocacy to achieve practical environmental solutions.

U.S. Department of Energy, Energy Efficiency Web site, www.energy.gov/energyefficiency/index.htm. Describes energy-efficiency programs and provides an extensive list of homeowner tips for saving energy.

U.S. Green Building Council, 1015 18th St., N.W., Suite 508, Washington, DC 20036; (202) 828-7422; www.usgbc.org. A coalition of building-industry leaders working to promote buildings that are environmentally responsible, profitable and healthy.

[48] *Ibid.*

[49] Miguel Bustillo, "Canada OKs Auto Emissions Pact," *Los Angeles Times*, March 24, 2005.

[50] *Ibid.*

[51] University of Michigan Transportation Research Institute, "How Oil Prices Threaten Automakers' Profits and Jobs," July 2005, p. iv.

[52] J. D. Power and Associates, "44 Hybrid and 26 Diesel Models Anticipated in U.S. Market by 2012," June 28, 2005.

[53] ConsumerReports.org, "High Cost of Hybrid Vehicles, Sizing Up the Savings & Costs," April 2006.

[54] *Ibid.*

[55] hybridCARS.com; www.hybridcars.com/silverado-sierra.html.

[56] "White House Plan On CAFE Reform Legislation Faces Stiff Opposition," *Energy Washington Week*, May 10, 2006.

Bibliography

Selected Sources

Books

Kemp, William H., *Smart Power: An Urban Guide to Renewable Energy and Efficiency*, New Society, 2006.
Kemp, a developer of control systems for low-environmental-impact hydroelectric utilities worldwide, has written an accessible guide for homeowners interested in using less energy or adopting renewable-energy technologies.

Wulfinghoff, Donald R., *Energy Efficiency Manual*, Energy Institute Press, 2000.
Wulfinghoff, an engineer and publisher of Energy Institute Press, has written a technical how-to guide for anyone interested in improving energy efficiency in a home, commercial building or industrial plant.

Yergin, Daniel, *The Prize: The Epic Quest for Oil, Money & Power*, Free Press, 1991.
Yergin, the co-founder and chairman of Cambridge Energy Research Associates, won a Pulitzer Prize for his account of the struggle for wealth and power that surrounds the quest for oil in the 20th century.

Articles

Aeppel, Timothy, and Melanie Trottman, "As Energy Costs Soar, Companies Retool Operations," *The Wall Street Journal*, April 22, 2006, p. A1.
Industrial companies are examining energy use and finding ways to improve energy efficiency in order to cut costs as energy prices continue to rise.

Freeman, Sholnn, "Light Trucks' Mileage Rules Toughen," *The Washington Post*, March 30, 2006, p. D1.
The federal government raised the fuel-economy standards for light trucks and reformed the process for setting those standards, but environmentalists say the rules are too lax and the fuel savings too low.

"Gentlemen, Start Your Engines," *The Economist*, Jan 21, 2006, p. 77.
Hybrid vehicles may not be all they are cracked up to be, but U.S. drivers are interested in more fuel-efficient cars.

Hulse, Carl, "Plan for $100 Gas Rebate Appears to Be All but Dead," *The New York Times*, May 3, 2006, p. A16.
To deal with rising gas prices, congressional Republicans proposed giving taxpayers a $100 rebate, but the plan met with scorn.

Simon, Richard, "Congress Ready to Approve Energy, Highway Measurers," *Los Angeles Times*, July 29, 2005, p. A18.
After years of negotiations and many compromises, Congress approves the Energy Policy Act of 2005.

Reports and Studies

Alliance to Save Energy, *Building on Success: Policies to Reduce Energy Waste in Buildings*, July 2005.
The alliance discusses and recommends more than 40 government policies that it says would help cut energy use in buildings.

American Council for an Energy-Efficient Economy, *Energy Efficiency's Next Generation: Innovation at the State Level*, November 2003.
The council presents innovative policies and programs at the state level that it says can make a substantial difference in improving energy efficiency.

Congressional Research Service, *Energy Policy: Conceptual Framework and Continuing Issues*, Jan. 18, 2006.
This report examines the many issues that shaped U.S. energy policy from the 1973 Arab oil embargo to the present, and includes a discussion of unresolved energy issues such as drilling in the Arctic National Wildlife Refuge.

National Academy of Sciences, *Effectiveness and Impact of the Corporate Average Fuel Economy (CAFE) Standards*, 2001.
Researchers determined that CAFE standards helped to raise fuel economy while also contributing to an increase in fatalities in the late 1970s and 1980s as carmakers reduced the size and weight of cars.

National Association of Manufacturers, *Efficiency and Innovation in U.S. Manufacturing Energy Use*, 2005.
The association describes opportunities for manufacturers to become more energy efficient and presents case studies of best practices.

Northeast Energy Efficiency Partnerships, *Energy Efficiency Standards: A Low-Cost, High-Leverage Policy for Northeast States.*
The authors say that energy-efficiency standards for appliances and equipment are among the lowest-cost, highest-benefit energy policies that states have ever adopted and recommend that states adopt standards for 10 additional products.

University of Michigan Transportation Research Institute, *In the Tank: How Oil Prices Threaten Automakers' Profits and Jobs*, July 2005.
The authors discuss how high gasoline prices and the resulting slump in SUV sales are cutting into profits and jobs at domestic automakers, who need to make fuel efficiency their top priority.

The Next Step:

Additional Articles from Current Periodicals

Energy Prices

Eilperin, Juliet, "Resistant Lawmakers Now Back Higher Gas Mileage Standards," *The Washington Post*, May 4, 2006, p. A5.
Several lawmakers now indicate they may consider raising fuel-economy standards for passenger cars for the first time in more than 30 years.

Foss, Brad, "Oil Drops Below $70," *The Houston Chronicle*, May 5, 2006, p. 1.
Gasoline supplies grew last week, reversing two months of declines that led to high gas prices and prompted the House Energy Committee to ask major oil companies for detailed information about their investment priorities.

Molloy, Tim, "Bigger Tax Break Goes to Buyers of Gas Guzzlers," *The Philadelphia Inquirer*, Feb. 26, 2006, p. A18.
Federal tax rules that took effect last month allow a tax credit of up to $3,150 for anyone buying a hybrid car, while small-business owners who purchase SUVs weighing more than three tons get deductions up to $25,000.

Valcourt, Josee, "A Resentful Swipe at Big Oil," *The Houston Chronicle*, April 11, 2006, p. 3.
Chrysler's chief spokesman accused major oil companies of greed and indifference to the environment, furthering tensions between the oil and auto industries because of higher gas prices.

Wald, Matthew L., "Plan to Reshape Mileage Standards Could Buoy Detroit," *The New York Times*, May 7, 2006, p. 34.
Raising fuel-economy standards for cars might help Detroit automakers by showing them that investment in new tooling and technology to produce high-mileage vehicles will pay back for years to come.

Federal Funding of Energy Efficiency

Athavaley, Anjali, "Grants to Help Clear the Air," *The Houston Chronicle*, July 29, 2004, p. 10.
Texas businesses are receiving $80 million in grants from the state to help clean the air, with many companies using the money to install more fuel-efficient engines in cars, boats, trains and trucks.

Lewis, Raphael, "As Energy Costs Soar, Legislative Plan Pairs Incentives, Relief," *The Boston Globe*, Sept. 23, 2005, p. A1.
Massachusetts legislators unveiled an $80 million package of tax credits and deductions to encourage energy efficiency, which is likely to be passed.

Neikirk, William, "Budget Cuts May Dim President's Energy Plan," *Chicago Tribune*, Feb. 22, 2006, p. C1.
Bush is proposing cutbacks in programs to increase the energy efficiency of buildings, appliances and vehicles.

Romero, Simon, "Much Talk, Mostly Low Key, About Energy Independence," *The New York Times*, Feb. 2, 2006, p. C1.
Federal funding for research in energy efficiency has declined 14 percent since 2002, and the Bush administration has not pressured Detroit to produce more energy-efficient cars.

Tompor, Susan, "Rules Limit Tax Breaks For Energy Upgrades," *The Houston Chronicle*, April 3, 2006, p. 1.
Homeowners hoping to save money on taxes by making energy-efficient home improvements should read the rules.

Lawsuits

Baker, David R., "SUV Mileage Knocked," *The San Francisco Chronicle*, May 3, 2006, p. C1.
Ten states sued the federal government over SUV gas-mileage standards they consider too lax.

Clayton, Mark, "A 'Green' Spurt For U.S. Businesses?" *The Christian Science Monitor*, Oct. 28, 2005, p. 2.
Despite numerous environmental suits, Wal-Mart wants to get all its energy from renewable sources.

Gormley, Michael, "15 States, NYC Sue U.S. Agency," *The Philadelphia Inquirer*, Sept. 8, 2005, p. C3.
Fifteen states and New York City sued the U.S. Department of Energy for failing to set tougher energy standards required by Congress.

CITING *CQ RESEARCHER*

Sample formats for citing these reports in a bibliography include the ones listed below. Preferred styles and formats vary, so please check with your instructor or professor.

MLA STYLE

Jost, Kenneth. "Rethinking the Death Penalty." CQ Researcher 16 Nov. 2001: 945-68.

APA STYLE

Jost, K. (2001, November 16). Rethinking the death penalty. *CQ Researcher, 11*, 945-968.

CHICAGO STYLE

Jost, Kenneth. "Rethinking the Death Penalty." *CQ Researcher*, November 16, 2001, 945-968.

In-depth Reports on Issues in the News

Are you writing a paper?

Need backup for a debate?

Want to become an expert on an issue?

For 80 years, students have turned to *CQ Researcher* for in-depth reporting on issues in the news. Reports on a full range of political and social issues are now available. Following is a selection of recent reports:

Civil Liberties
Right to Die, 5/05
Immigration Reform, 4/05
Gays on Campus, 10/04

Crime/Law
Domestic Violence, 1/06
Death Penalty Controversies, 9/05
Methamphetamines, 7/05
Identity Theft, 6/05
Marijuana Laws, 2/05
Supreme Court's Future, 1/05

Education
Academic Freedom, 10/05
Intelligent Design, 7/05
No Child Left Behind, 5/05
Gender and Learning, 5/05

Environment
Nuclear Energy, 3/06
Climate Change, 1/06
Saving the Oceans, 11/05
Endangered Species Act, 6/05
Alternative Energy, 2/05

Health/Safety
Rising Health Costs, 4/06
Pension Crisis, 2/06
Avian Flu Threat, 1/06
Domestic Violence, 1/06
Disaster Preparedness, 11/05
Birth-Control Debate, 6/05
Marijuana Laws, 2/05

International Affairs
Future of European Union, 10/05
War in Iraq, 10/05

Social Trends
Controlling the Internet, 5/06
American Indians, 4/06
Future of Feminism, 4/06

Terrorism/Defense
Port Security, 4/06
Presidential Power, 2/06

Youth
Bullying, 2/05
Teen Driving, 1/05

Upcoming Reports

Teen Spending, 5/26/06
War on Drugs, 6/2/06
Impact of Blogs, 6/9/06
Pork-Barrel Politics, 6/16/06
Reviving Downtowns, 6/23/06
Drinking on Campus, 6/30/06

ACCESS

CQ Researcher is available in print and online. For access, visit your library or www.cqresearcher.com.

STAY CURRENT

To receive notice of upcoming *CQ Researcher* reports, or learn more about *CQ Researcher* products, subscribe to the free e-mail newsletters, *CQ Researcher Alert!* and *CQ Researcher News*: www.cqpress.com/newsletters.

PURCHASE

To purchase a *CQ Researcher* report in print or electronic format (PDF), visit www.cqpress.com or call 866-427-7737. Single reports start at $10. Bulk purchase discounts and electronic rights licensing are also available.

SUBSCRIBE

A full-service *CQ Researcher* print subscription—including 44 reports a year, monthly index updates, and a bound volume—is $688 for academic and public libraries, $667 for high school libraries, and $827 for media libraries. Add $25 for domestic postage.

CQ Researcher Online offers a backfile from 1991 and a number of tools to simplify research. For pricing information, call 800-834-9020, ext. 1906, or e-mail librarysales@cqpress.com.

CQ Researcher

Published by CQ Press, a division of Congressional Quarterly Inc.

cqresearcher.com

Teen Spending

Are teenagers learning to manage money wisely?

Teenage American consumers spent a mind-boggling $159 billion last year on everything from movies and French fries to clothes and iPods. Experts say teens are spending more than ever before because they have more to spend. About 10 percent of teens have credit cards, nearly twice that number have debit cards and about 20 percent get money simply by asking their parents for it. Consumer advocates — as well as rappers and professional football players — say kids aren't learning how to use "plastic" wisely. In fact, parents themselves are setting poor examples. Credit card loan delinquencies are at record levels, while Americans' saving rate is at an all-time low. Critics say the credit card industry is too aggressive in marketing to younger and younger kids. The Bush administration and some members of Congress are pushing for more financial-literacy courses earlier in schools. Meanwhile, only a few states require schools to teach personal finance.

"How do these look?" asks a young shopper in Daly City, Calif. Teenage U.S. consumers spent $159 billion in 2005.

INSIDE THIS REPORT

CQ Researcher • May 26, 2006 • www.cqresearcher.com
Volume 16, Number 20 • Pages 457-480

CQ Press

Recipient of Society of Professional Journalists Award for Excellence ◆ American Bar Association Silver Gavel Award

Cover: "How do these look?" asks a young shopper in Daly City, Calif. Teenage U.S. consumers spent $159 billion in 2005. (Getty Images/Justin Sullivan)

CQ Researcher

May 26, 2006
Volume 16, Number 20

CQ Researcher (ISSN 1056-2036) is printed on acid-free paper. Published weekly, except March 24, July 7, July 14, Aug. 4, Aug. 11, Nov. 24, Dec. 22 and Dec. 29, by CQ Press, a division of Congressional Quarterly Inc. Annual full-service subscriptions for institutions start at $667. For pricing, call 1-800-834-9020, ext. 1906. To purchase a *CQ Researcher* report in print or electronic format (PDF), visit www.cqpress.com or call 866-427-7737. Single reports start at $10. Bulk purchase discounts and electronic-rights licensing are also available. Periodicals postage paid at Washington, D.C., and additional mailing offices. POSTMASTER: Send address changes to *CQ Researcher*, 1255 22nd St., N.W., Suite 400, Washington, DC 20037.

Teen Spending

By Pamela M. Prah

The Issues

Eric Simmons' parents figured that giving him a debit card with a set limit was a good way for him to learn about managing money. So every month, the high school senior in Annandale, Va., gets $300 added to his debit card.

But Eric recently exceeded the limit on his debit card and then racked up hundreds of additional dollars on a credit card his mother got for him and his older sister for gas, school supplies and emergencies. And although Nancy Simmons discourages her son from buying online, he has spent hundreds of dollars on the Internet for shoes, clothes and accessories for his motorized scooter and remote-control car.

Simmons admits she "enables" her son's excessive spending by paying his bills and that she should have set stricter limits with him earlier. "I need to sit down and talk with him," she says.

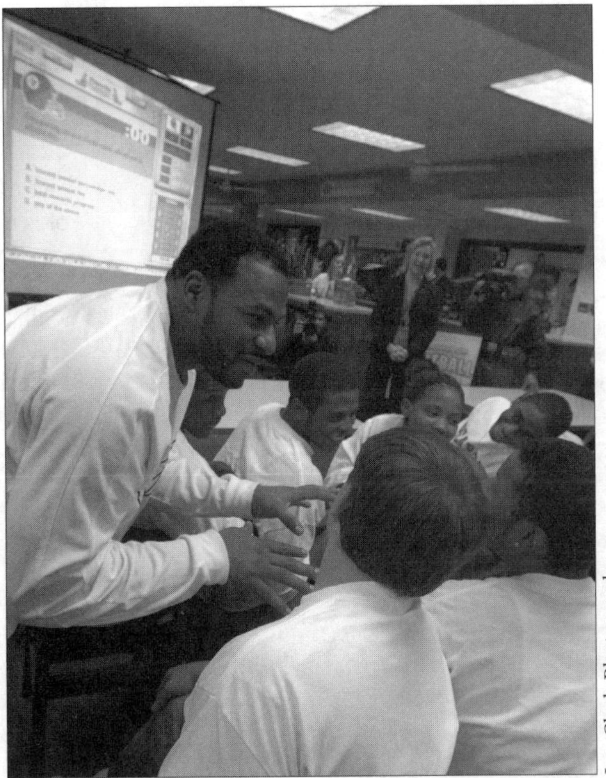

Joe Clark Photography

Running back Jerome Bettis of the Pittsburgh Steelers coaches a team of students in a game of "Financial Football" at Pittsburgh's Peabody High School. The animated money-management computer game incorporates lessons from Visa's Practical Money Skills for Life. *Experts say teens are spending more than ever before but aren't learning how to use credit wisely.*

Eric is part of the so-called Echo Baby Boomer Generation — the more than 75 million Americans, including at least 25 million teens, born between 1977 and 1994. Not since their baby boomer parents were teenagers themselves has a group of teens been so large and so coveted by product-pitching marketers. And they have an unprecedented amount of money to spend on whatever they want, from clothes to iPods to custom ring tones for their cell phones.

Many teens, like Eric, have access to debit and credit cards, a notion that just 20 years ago — when "plastic" was widely restricted to adults — was unimaginable. But critics say the industry has gone too far marketing to younger and younger kids, citing the Hello Kitty debit cards that Legend Credit Inc. launched in 2004 trying to attract the preteen set, often called the "tweens." (*See story, p. 468.*) "Don't think for a second the companies marketing these cards have our children's best interests in mind," wrote *Washington Post* financial columnist Michelle Singletary in a recent column condemning the use of credit cards among young people. "They have one goal — to hook a customer as early in life as possible." [1]

Unfortunately, say consumer advocates, parents aren't teaching their kids how to use credit or debit cards or manage money. The average teen owes about $230, and about one-in-four youths ages 16-18 already is more than $1,000 in the red, says an April 2006 study from the Charles Schwab Foundation, a private, nonprofit organization created by the financial-services company. [2]

Many experts also worry about the long-term ramifications of young people not learning to save and going into debt at an early age. When today's young generation retires, the experts say, many employers will no longer be offering workers pensions, which provide a set amount of money each month. And with Social Security coffers quickly depleting, they say it is crucial for people today to begin saving for their own retirement. [3]

Estimates of how much American teenagers spend vary. Teenage Research Unlimited (TRU), a Chicago-based teen-marketing company, estimates that teens spent $159 billion last year, which is about $20 billion more than the entire 2006-07 Texas state budget. [4] The figure is up from $122 billion in 1997, the first year the company did the survey, says TRU Vice President Michael Wood, but down 6 percent from 2004. Wood attributes the dip to parents being skittish about the economy, making them more tightfisted, and rising gas prices. "Teens who drive are watching an unprecedented amount of their budget flowing directly into their gas tanks," he says. But teens are optimistic about 2006, with nearly half of the teens surveyed (47 percent) saying they think they'll spend more in 2006 than they did last year.

Many Teens Clueless About Money Matters

Two-thirds of teenagers consider themselves knowledgeable about shopping for a good deal, but less than half say they know about money matters ranging from credit cards to balancing a checkbook.

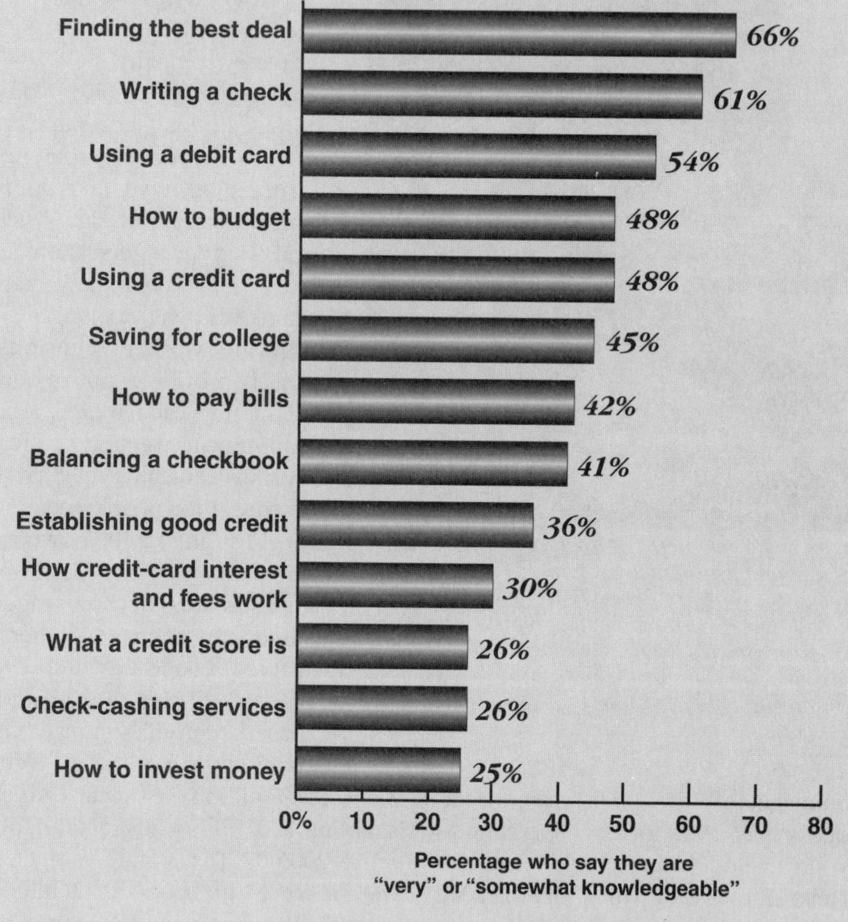

Source: "Teens and Money," Charles Schwab Foundation, April 19, 2006

Today's teens are spending more because they have more money at their disposal, says Diane Crispell, executive editor of GfK Roper Consulting in New York, which has provided snapshots of U.S. teen spending habits since 1990 in the *Roper Youth Report.*

Traditionally, teens have received money for doing household chores (37 percent) or from their allowance (29 percent), says Crispell. Katy and Jenny Burgess, 14-year-old twins from Indianapolis, Ind., get most of their spending money from chores. "If we want something, we have to work for it," says eighth-grader Katy, whose family operates a farm.

But in recent years a growing number of teens — about one-in-five today, and mainly girls — have been getting spending money simply by asking for it, Crispell says.

"If I need something, I ask for it," says Brittany Guenther, a ninth-grader at Bishop Ireton High School in Alexandria, Va. She typically garners about $50 per shopping spree.

Her friend Liz Guttman, on the other hand, negotiates. "I try to strike a deal; whatever they're willing to give, I take," she says. Both 15-year-olds recently were shopping for clothes — the most common item on a teen girl's shopping list — at Pentagon City Mall, outside Washington.

For boys, food and video games rank high, while CDs and personal-care products are popular among both boys and girls, the Roper survey shows. TRU's Wood says the technology category "has exploded" of late, with more teens buying video games and consoles, cell phones, wireless products and iPods.

Another new wrinkle on the teen-buying scene: Teenagers often don't have to wait until they have the money or their parents take them to the mall — They buy online with credit cards. Today's teen generation is the first to grow up shopping via the Internet.

"Everything has to be instantaneous," says Don Montuori, publisher of *Packaged Facts,* published by MarketResearch.com, a market research firm in New York City.

About 10 percent of teens have credit cards, and nearly twice that number have debit cards, says Wood. Visa USA, which has dubbed this younger set Generation Plastic or Gen P, estimated last year that payments via plastic — including online commerce — now account for about 53 percent of spending among 18-24-year-olds. [5]

While teens under 18 must have a parent co-sign for a credit card, there is no minimum age for debit or prepaid cards, explains Rhonda Bentz, vice president, Visa USA. Visa is among the companies that have developed cards especially for young people that parents can load with cash. Another is Payjr, which this summer plans to launch its version of a prepaid spending card exclusively for

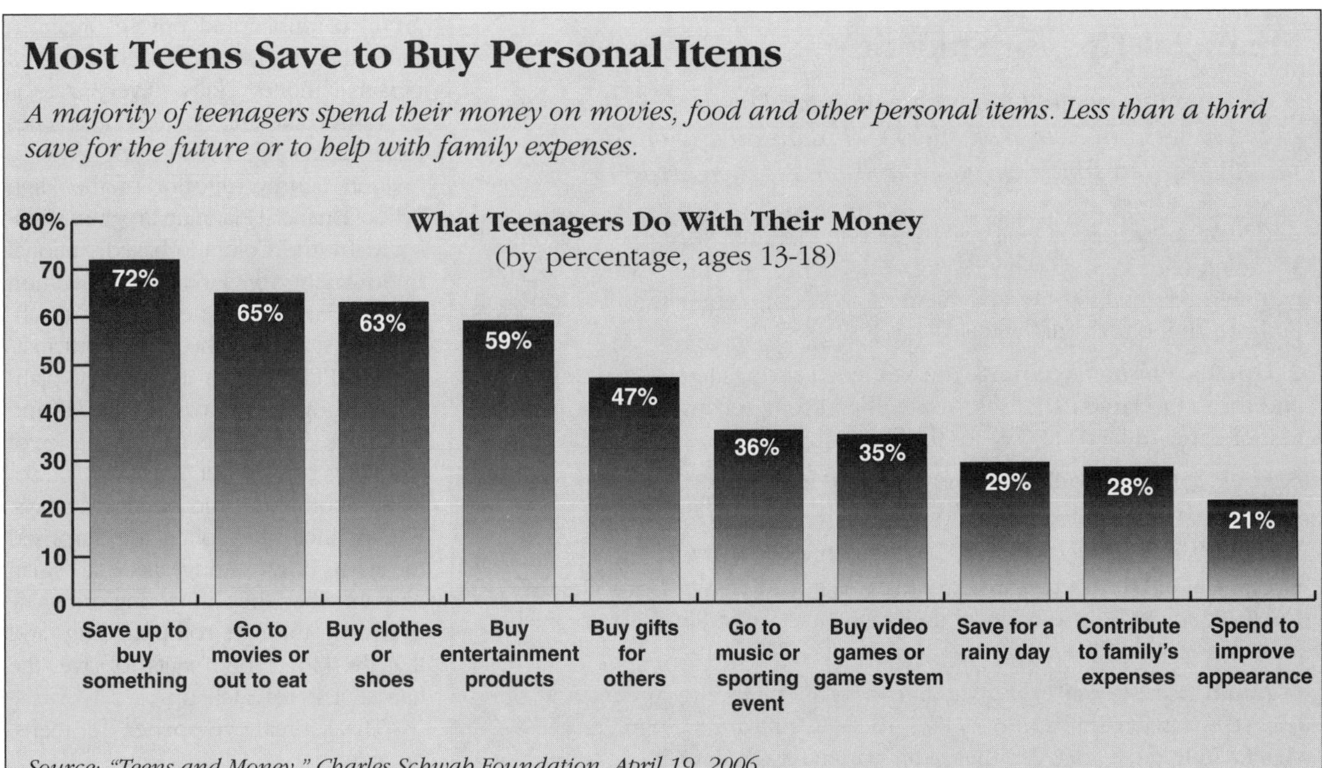

teens. Payjr President and Chief Executive Officer David Jones says the company is considering calling the card "scrilla," the rap term for money, in order to attract teens.

Many teens get their first credit card just as they arrive at college or during their freshman year, and many run up credit card debt on top of their student loans. Some put their tuition on plastic, with the intention of paying it off, and spend their student loans and other financial aid on books, pizzas and daily living expenses. Today's typical undergraduate has four credit cards and owes more than $2,000, according to the Nellie Mae Corp., an education lender in Braintree, Mass. [6]

In fact, parents themselves are setting a poor example. The nation's credit car loan delinquencies have reached a record high, the savings rate is among the lowest in the industrialized world and the average family has $9,000 in credit card debt. [7]

"I don't think a lot of adults should have credit cards, let alone teens," says Dallas Salisbury, chairman of the American Savings Education Council, which sponsors the national "Choose to Save" campaign. Credit cards "lead people to overspend and run up debt."

Unless young people start to save more, "the end result will continue to be inadequate savings, overuse of credit and high rates of personal bankruptcies," says Salisbury who also is president and CEO of the Employee Benefit Research Institute.

About a dozen states now require schools to teach personal finance, but the Bush administration and some members of Congress are pushing for more financial literacy earlier in schools.

As policymakers, educators and parents debate the issues, here are some questions people are asking:

Are teens being taught to manage their money?

Many states today require students to take money-management courses. Seven states — Alabama, Georgia, Idaho, Illinois, Kentucky, New York and Utah — require students to take a personal-finance course before graduating from high school, up from two states in 2002, according to the National Council on Economic Education (NCEE). Nine states require that students be tested on personal finance. [8]

It is unclear, however, whether the courses change spending behavior, says NCEE President and CEO Robert F. Duvall. "We've only just begun to address that," he says.

In addition, the curriculum quality and difficulty of the financial-education requirements varies from state to state. Many of the state mandates are "relatively weak," says Stephen Brobeck, executive director of the Consumer Federation of America. For instance, some of the requirements can be met simply by attending three of four class sessions. Other states lack financial-education classes but cover some of the concepts in math, economics and social-studies classes, says Laura Levine, executive director of the Jump$tart Coalition for Personal Financial Literacy, a

Financial Tips for Students

A money-management program co-founded by the U.S. Bankruptcy Court in Western New York offers 10 tips on staying out of debt, managing your finances and establishing a good credit rating.

1. Create a Budget: A realistic budget will identify exactly how you are spending your money — including your "needs" vs. your "wants" — and will help you budget the repayment of any debt you incur and how much you can spend on your "wants."

2. Open a Savings Account: You will need savings for both emergencies and for future large expenses. You will go broke relying on high-interest-rate credit-card loans to pay for these.

3. Look for Ways to Save Money: Buying at shopping clubs and with coupons, looking for the cheapest gas price, going to discount movie theaters and utilizing student discounts will help you save money.

4. Use Cash, Debit Card or Checking Account Instead of a Credit Card: People who use cash for their purchases spend less, so use cash if a purchase is under $20 or if you can eat it or drink it.

5. Avoid Credit Card Debt: Credit cards have high interest fees and often lead to late payments and over-limit fees. This means you will pay significantly more for everything you purchase. Remember, if you don't have any extra money in your budget to repay it within a reasonable amount of time with interest, you can't afford the purchase.

6. Pay Your Bills on Time: Paying your bills late, including credit card, rent, telephone, utility and cell-phone bills, hurts your credit rating.

7. Always Pay Debts Off as Quickly as Possible: Research the best credit card for rates and fees, and don't charge anything on it that you can't pay for at the end of the month. If you can't pay your credit card balance off in full, pay at least 10 percent of the balance. Never make just the minimum payment, and stop charging until you have paid off your balance.

8. Minimize Your Student-Loan Debt: Keep it to a minimum. Before choosing a college, ask yourself if the job you are likely to get after college justifies the loan debt you will incur at that institution.

9. Other Things to Avoid: Impulse shopping on the Internet, expensive behaviors like gambling and drugs, opening multiple store charge accounts, more than three-year car loans and pawn shops, rent-to-own and payday loan establishments. Also, don't open credit card accounts to get "free stuff." Those accounts will hurt your credit rating, even if you don't use them.

10. Remember the Consequences of Consumer Debt: Credit card and other consumer debt could hurt your future chances for a job, student loan, admission to graduate school, apartment or car loan. Today, everyone is pulling credit checks and using them to make decisions about your future.

Source: Credit Abuse Resistance Education (CARE), www.careprogram.us

group of public and private organizations that promotes development of personal money skills. "Every state is so vastly different" in how it teaches teens to manage money, she says.

John Parfrey, director of the High School Financial Planning Program sponsored by the Colorado-based National Endowment for Financial Education (NEFE), speaks frequently with teachers and students who have participated in NEFE courses in financial planning, budgeting, savings, credit and insurance. Today's teens "have a lot of spending power but not a lot of sophistication about the basics," he says. For instance, they often are surprised to learn how setting aside a small amount when they are young can grow over time through compounding, and that the longer one waits to save, the harder it is to catch up.

"That's a real eye-opener" for teens, he says.

Parfrey says students who have participated in the NEFE financial-planning course appear to have changed the way they save and spend money. For example, three months after completing the course, about 60 percent said they were more focused on buying only things that they really need and trying to save more. [9]

Judge John C. Ninfro II, chief judge of the U.S. Bankruptcy Court for the Western District of New York, has been visiting local schools since 1997, when he realized that many of the people in financial trouble who end up in his courtroom had never received financial-literacy education. "That is still true today," says Ninfro, who in 2002 formed the Credit Abuse Resistance Education (CARE) program (www.careprogram.us), which arranges visits by bankruptcy experts to high schools and colleges in 31 states to help students avoid credit problems.

"Our nation's high-school students are financially illiterate in too many ways, especially about credit cards," Ninfro says. For instance, kids are always shocked to discover that an $80 pair of running shoes can end up costing $120 if they are bought on credit and not quickly paid off in full, he says.

Boston Bar Association

Students from South High School in Worcester, Mass., went to bankruptcy court to hear bankruptcy lawyer M. Ellen Carpenter, above, and Judge Joel B. Rosenthal discuss what happens when people spend beyond their means. The courtroom visit capped a financial-literacy program sponsored by the U.S. Bankruptcy Court for Massachusetts and the Boston Bar Association.

Recent surveys suggest that Scott Murray, a 16-year-old junior at Fairmount Heights High School in Prince George's County, Md., and his friends are typical teenagers when it comes to money matters. Although his mother talks to him about finances, he says he's not sure whether he has a credit or debit card. His friend Chris Grant, also 16 and a student at nearby Largo High School, says he thinks he has a savings account but is not sure. Neither of them is trying to save money.

"Most people I know don't save," says Murray.

Most teens say they recognize the importance of good money habits, including how to shop for deals and write a check, but less than half know how to budget money, use a credit card or save for college, according to the Charles Schwab Foundation's April survey. [10] And while one-third of teens owe money, only half say they are concerned about paying it back, the foundation found.

In the latest Jump$tart Coalition survey, the average high-school senior scored only 52 percent on a test of their knowledge of credit cards, saving and retirement. [11] The results were actually slightly worse than in 1997, when seniors scored 57 — an all-time high. "Our survey is fairly consistent in depicting the insufficient knowledge that young people have about money matters," says Levine.

A 2005 NCEE study gave high-school students an "F" on their understanding of basic financial concepts, such as annual percentage rates, inflation and interest. [12] Most didn't know, for example, that keeping cash in a piggy bank or under the mattress held a greater risk of losing value than investing the money in the stock market or mutual funds.

Many teens enter college without understanding the basics or the long-term consequences of poor money management. Researchers from Ohio State University found, for example, that 45 percent of college freshmen incorrectly thought their parents would be responsible for their credit card debts until age 21, and few were aware that late credit card payments could mean higher interest rates on car loans and mortgages. [13] The Government Accountability Office (GAO) found in 2005 that less than 20 percent of youths ages 18-24 knew their credit history could affect employment. [14]

Linda Sherry, who tracks credit and debit card issues for Consumer Action, a San Francisco-based consumer advocacy group, says many adults — not to mention teens — don't realize that a single late payment can allow a credit card company to impose much higher interest rates on the account. Even worse, some card companies routinely use credit reports to track customers' credit behavior on other credit cards. Here too, a single late payment on another credit card can lead a company to double or triple interest rates on their own card, even if the customer's payments on their card have been paid on time, she says. "People are always shocked" when they learn that, she says, and "most teens don't know about it."

Nancy Simmons says her son Eric thought his debit card simply would not work if his account ran out of money. He didn't realize he was racking up a slew of overdrawn penalties. She says the bank waved all but one $35 late fee after she and her son went in and talked with bank officials, but they made clear the bank wouldn't be as understanding the next time.

Should teens have credit cards?

Do credit cards teach teens about managing money or create the next generation of overspenders? Laura Fisher, a spokeswoman for the American Bankers Association (ABA), says teens can learn important lessons about budgeting and managing their money by using credit cards. They not only help teens establish credit but also give parents a sense of security from knowing their child has enough money during emergencies, she says.

"A secure card with set, low limits is a good way to get started," she says, suggesting a card with a $300 limit, the lowest that many credit card companies and banks offer.

But most card companies don't publicize their lowest-limit cards. When Nan Mead, a spokeswoman for the National Endowment for Financial Education, was shopping for a credit card for her son, she had to specifically ask for a

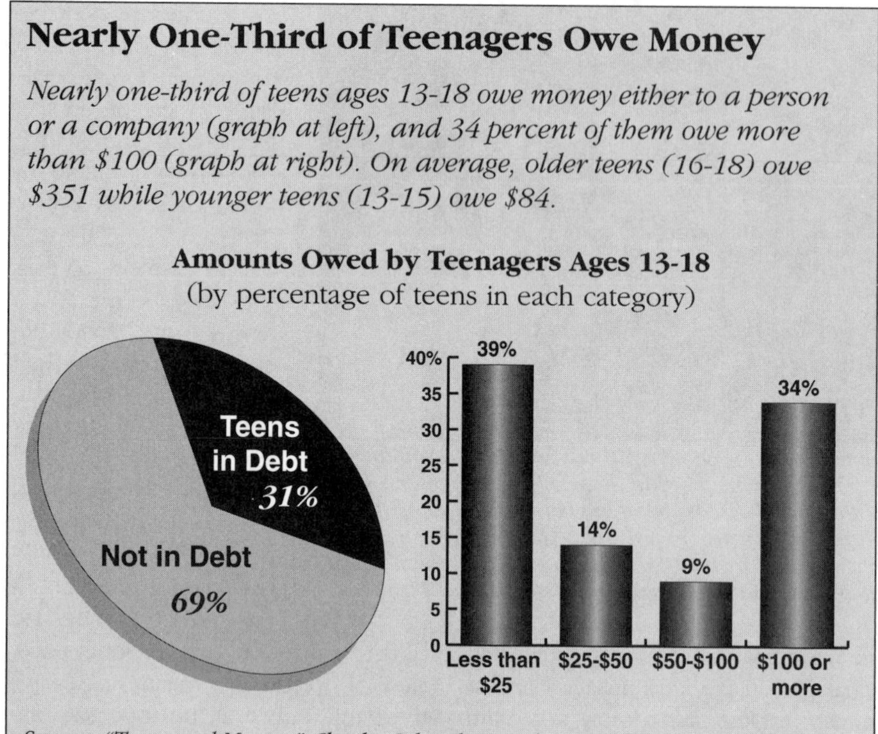

Nearly One-Third of Teenagers Owe Money

Nearly one-third of teens ages 13-18 owe money either to a person or a company (graph at left), and 34 percent of them owe more than $100 (graph at right). On average, older teens (16-18) owe $351 while younger teens (13-15) owe $84.

Source: "Teens and Money," Charles Schwab Foundation, April 19, 2006

lower limit on the card. "The credit card companies don't advertise that. Parents have to be proactive."

And giving a credit card to a teen is a double-edged sword, she says. A credit card can help develop a teen's credit, but if a parent doesn't provide the proper "context" youths often don't learn the dangers of running up high bills and paying only the minimum amount, she says.

Fisher agrees. "Education is key," she says. "Kids have to understand credit isn't magic money. They have to pay it back."

Banks and credit card companies have kicked off a credit education program that included, for example, 39,000 presentations by ABA members to 1.5 million teens in the past four years as part of the association's "Get Smart About Credit" program, Fisher says.

Pamela Erwin, senior vice president of the Wells Fargo Foundation, says credit cards are a good idea for teens but only if teens receive direction. Otherwise it is akin to handing over the car keys to a teen without any driving lessons. Cards are a way of life, she says, but "whether you are a teen or an adult, you still need a roadmap."

No federal agency tracks how many teens have credit cards, and estimates from lenders and others vary widely, but as teens get older, clearly more get plastic. Only 5 percent of 13-14-year-olds have their own credit cards; by age 17, the percentage climbs to 9.8 percent and then doubles to 19.6 percent for teens 18 and older, according to an April poll by Junior Achievement, a Colorado organization that teaches young people about business. [15]

The poll found that more than 15 percent of teens with credit cards make only the minimum payment, which some teens don't realize means taking months or years longer to pay off the debt. The report notes it would take a teen making minimum payments more than nine years and almost $2,000 in interest fees to pay off a credit card with a $1,000 balance and 18 percent interest rate.

Teens who want and get their own credit card should also then have to pay the balance, says Mead. "Otherwise, they see no consequence of overspending, and that can lead to significant problems down the line."

"We do not encourage parents to give their children credit cards," says Brobeck of the Consumer Federation of America. The argument that they can help teens learn to handle money doesn't hold water, he says, because "most parents bail out their children, and the children don't learn the responsibility" of having and using credit cards.

Levine of the Jump$tart Coalition says there is no magic age for giving a teen a credit card; it depends on a teen's level of maturity. "There are a lot of young adults not mature enough to handle a credit card," she says.

Some consumer advocates argue that the credit card industry is more interested in roping in new customers at an early age than in teaching good financial skills.

Many teens get their first credit card as they head off to college. The latest Nellie Mae survey found that of the 76 percent of undergraduates in 2004 who had their own credit cards, 43 percent got it during their freshman year, and less than a quarter had the card before entering college. [16]

Marie O'Malley, vice president of marketing for Nellie Mae, said undergraduates are becoming more responsible in their use of credit. Five years ago, typical undergraduates owed nearly $3,000 on their credit cards; today it's just over $2,000, according to Nellie Mae. "The message of using credit responsibly is getting out," says O'Malley. Only 4 percent of students with credit cards said their parents paid their card bills, the survey found. [17]

But data from the federal government suggest many more parents are bailing out their kids' card debts. Jacqueline King, director of the American Council on Education's Center for Policy Analysis, says Department of Education data show that 56 percent of undergraduates

Continued on p. 466

Rappers, Contests Tout Wise Spending

In an effort to grab teenagers' attention, financial-literacy advocates are using online games, contests and celebrities to promote wise spending habits.

Visa USA, for instance, has recruited National Football League players — including the Denver Broncos' Jake Plummer, Atlanta Falcons' Warrick Dunn and Jerome Bettis of the Super Bowl champion Pittsburgh Steelers — to help get teenagers' attention. They visited classrooms in 17 cities last season to play an animated computer game called "Financial Football" with students that combines the structure and rules of the NFL with financial-education questions. [1]

Visa also offers two online games — "Smart Money Quiz Show" and "Road Trip to Savings" — geared to young, cyber-savvy teens (www.practicalmoneyskills.com).

Outside the classroom, rappers like LL Cool J, Alicia Keyes and Nas plug financial literacy through the Hip-Hop Summit Action Network (HSAN), created by hip-hop pioneer Russell Simmons and veteran civil rights activist Benjamin Chavis Muhammad. The network in March kicked off the Hip-Hop Summit on Financial Empowerment's "Get Your Money Right" nationwide tour in Detroit, followed by shows in New York in April. The tour planned to open in Miami Gardens, Fla., in May where rappers Remy Ma, MC Lyte, Pitbull and Doug E. Fresh were scheduled to join experts from Chrysler Financial in urging fans to be financially responsible. Other hip-hop artists will be on hand this fall when the tour moves to Atlanta, Los Angeles and Dallas.

Getty Images/Paul Hawthorne

Rapper Doug E. Fresh urges youths to be financially responsible.

"The biggest misconception probably comes from the hip-hop community itself . . . that the money lasts forever," LL Cool J said at the New York summit. "You have to do the right thing with it." [2] HSAN offers a "Get Your Money Right" workbook on its Web site (http://hsan.org/).

A team of seniors from Blackman High School in Murfreesboro, Tenn., won a free trip to Washington, D.C., by turning a hypothetical $100,000 into $150,263 over 10 weeks as part of the "Capitol Hill Stock Market Game Challenge." Students nationwide played The Stock Market Game (www.stockmarketgame.org) developed by the Foundation for Investor Education. Teachers have used the game in classrooms since 1977 to teach young people about saving and investing and how the capital markets work.

Other financial companies and nonprofits offer various games and materials online, but the information is often difficult to find unless teens and parents know where to look. Here are links to some online resources:

- **Merrill Lynch —** Since launching its free "Investing Pays Off" program in 2001, the big financial-services company estimates it has provided its curriculum, which is broken down into courses for various age groups, to at least 1 million students, including many who are home-schooled. The company also has teamed up with "Sesame Street's" Elmo to teach younger children about the basics of saving, spending and planning. (www.ml.com/philanthropy/ipo/volunteer/curriculumletter.html).
- **National Endowment for Financial Education —** The nonprofit's online games and puzzles can be found at www.nefe.org/hsfppportal/index.html.
- **Wells Fargo —** The bank's "Hands on Banking" Web site (www.handsonbanking.org) has received 16 million visitors since it was launched in January 2004; at least 10 percent of the visitors clicked on the Spanish version. The company also has distributed more than 400,000 CDs and trained more than 5,000 Wells Fargo volunteers to assist in money-skill instruction for age groups ranging from fourth grade to adulthood.
- **U.S. Treasury Department —** The federal agency says it will soon add a youth link to its www.mymoney.gov Web site, which provides personal-finance information, including how to choose and use credit cards, get out of debt, protect credit records, start a savings-and-investment plan and understand Social Security benefits. In 2001 the government developed the Money Smart financial education program (www.fdic.gov/consumers/consumer/moneysmart/index.html), endorsed last year by the National School Boards Association and available in six languages.

[1] Visa/NFL press release, Dec. 6, 2005; www.practicalmoneyskills.com./english/presscenter/releases/120605.php.

[2] "Rappers urge financial responsibility," The Associated Press, April 23, 2006, and statement from Hip-Hop Summit Action Network at http://hsan.org/.

Continued from p. 464

had a credit card during the 2003-2004 school year, and 25 percent said parents helped pay the bill. The students polled included those at four-year universities as well as community and trade schools.

Salisbury of the American Savings Education Council says teens and credit cards are not a good mix. "A credit card doesn't teach you about money. It doesn't develop a sense of living within your means," he says. When he was in college, he says, he had $15 for food each week, "and when that cash was gone, it was gone." With credit cards, however, while there is a point in which card companies will stop approving purchases, that limit is typically thousands of dollars.

Janet Bodnar, a columnist for *Kiplinger's Personal Finance* magazine and author of *Raising Money Smart Kids*, advocates teaching money management a step at a time, first with cash, then with a checking account linked to a debit card and finally a credit card.

"Giving kids credit cards too early does more harm than good," she warned recently. [18]

Should teens be given prepaid credit cards?

Teens who don't have their own credit cards and can't use their parents' can still make purchases using prepaid cards, which some financial experts say teach teens how to manage their money. But critics say that many of these products come with high hidden fees.

Prepaid cards differ from regular credit or debit cards because they contain a set amount. Special prepaid cards for teens enable parents to determine how much money is on the card, track the teen's spending at anytime and "reload" the card with additional funds online or through an 800 number.

Bentz of Visa USA says parents love the prepaid cards because they teach their teens how to manage money, and teens love them because they give teens freedom, make them feel like adults and are easy to use for online purchases. Visa launched the program after parents asked for an alternative to other cards and because the company recognized that "the teen market is significant," says Bentz.

Visa estimates that "hundreds of thousands" of teens use the "Visa Buxx Cash Card," a prepaid card designed specifically for teens, says Bentz, who tracks teen issues for Visa.

But Sherry of Consumer Action prefers debit cards linked to a teen's checking account, because many prepaid products come with unusually high transaction fees or hidden charges. "I don't like them at all," she says.

Bentz says the terms of using a Buxx Cash Card vary among the five banks that issue the cards. "We encourage parents to do the research," she says. Based on the banks' online disclosure notices, National City Visa Buxx cards have a $15 annual fee, a $1 fee for each ATM withdrawal and a $2.50 charge for loading the card if the money comes from a bank other than National City. Sandy Spring Bank's Visa Buxx card has a monthly service fee of $2, a $1 "inactivity fee" if the card is not used and a $15 penalty for overdrafts. Wachovia has a $12 one-time account-setup fee and a $1.50 charge if the teen withdraws cash from an ATM more than twice a month.

In July, Payjr plans to launch its version of a prepaid spending card that the company thinks may boost teen online shopping. "Until now, most teen spending was always done at the mall," says CEO Jones. Unlike other prepaid cards, he says, Payjr won't have excessive penalties if a teen spends more money than is in the account. "That is not teaching kids how to manage money, but taking advantage of them. We won't have abusive fees."

The company is still working on the details for its cards but says it envisions teaming up with MTV, Nickelodeon, Yahoo, Abercrombie & Fitch and other companies that Jones says are popular among teens. They're even considering allowing teens to upload their own photos and design their own cards. Payjr already offers a free online program that allows parents to manage their children's chores and allowances online, using instant messaging, e-mail and text messaging, for example, to notify teens when money has been deposited.

NEFE's Mead says prepaid cards can be a great way for parents to teach teens about fiscal responsibility, particularly if it is their first experience with "plastic." Teens can learn how to pace themselves and make sure they don't run out of money. And if the teen is responsible, she argues, buying online with a debit card is not much different from buying in a store. But if the parent is simply "pouring money into the debit account" without the teen tracking expenses or paying for it, then the lesson is lost.

Some critics, however, say allowing teens to buy online with plastic encourages overspending.

Clearly, teens today are not reluctant to purchase online, whether it's with their own credit card, their parents' card or a prepaid card. The April Junior Achievement survey found that nearly 60 percent of teens who have their own credit cards had bought items online with their cards. [19] Teenage Research Unlimited found that 42 percent of teens have made an online purchase, most commonly using their parents' credit cards. And 46 percent used other payment methods, such as prepaid cards and PayPal, an affiliate of eBay that lets anyone with an e-mail address send and receive online payments using a credit card or bank account.

Sherry says parents need to discuss the pros and cons of shopping at the mall vs. on the Internet and to make sure teens are aware of the penalties if they overspend. Levine of Jump$tart agrees. "It's not shopping online that is a problem, it's when it's unsupervised," she says. A debit card is a great tool for shopping online, "but with any tool, parental supervision and involvement are key." ■

Continued on p. 468

Chronology

1940s-90s

Teenagers in the 1950s become the first generation to show economic and cultural clout. Over the decades, music, clothes and snacks top the list of "must-haves" for teens.

1941
The word "teenager" is first cited in an article in *Popular Science* magazine to describe an age group that would soon became of keen interest to marketers.

1949
The Diners' Club card — the first universal credit card — is introduced, aimed at middle-class American adults.

1965
A survey by *Seventeen* indicates teenage girls spend $450 million a year for cosmetics and toiletries.

1980
Teenage shoppers pump $39 billion into the U.S. economy.

1990s

Credit companies begin to drop the requirement that anyone under 21 must have an adult co-signer to get a credit card. Teens begin getting their own cards.

March 10, 1994
Aggressive marketing to college students by credit card companies prompts a House Banking, Finance and Urban Affairs panel to hold hearings on "kiddie" credit cards.

May 1997
The newly formed Jump$tart Coalition for Personal Finance Literacy tests high-school seniors, who correctly answer only 57 percent of financial questions. The coalition finds no improvement in students' scores over the next nine years.

June 1999
A controversial study by the Consumer Federation of America linking college students' debt with suicides draws widespread attention.

2000s

Rising levels of personal bankruptcies and concerns about easy access to credit cards prompt new education campaigns.

2001
Treasury Department develops money-based math curriculum for use by schools to teach young people about personal finance.

May 2002
Nearly a third of youths ages 12-17 admit to feeling pressure to buy clothes and other products because their friends have them.

April 2003
Congress declares April as Financial Literacy Month.

December 2003
President George W. Bush signs the Fair and Accurate Credit Transactions Act into law, mandating creation of a Web site, toll-free hotline and national financial-literacy strategy.

October 2004
Treasury Department's Financial Literacy and Education Commission launches www.mymoney.gov and 1-888-mymoney to provide the public with information on personal-finance matters. . . . Hello Kitty debit cards are unveiled in a bid to attract preteens.

April 2005
President Bush signs Bankruptcy Abuse Prevention and Consumer Protection Act into law, which requires anyone filing for bankruptcy to get credit counseling. It also urges states to develop financial-literacy programs for elementary and secondary schools . . . . National Council on Economic Education (NCEE) gives high-school students an "F" grade for their poor understanding of basic financial concepts.

January 2006
For the first time since the Great Depression, Americans' personal-savings rate dips below zero into negative territory.

April 2006
Bush administration unveils National Strategy for Financial Literacy, a blueprint for improving Americans' understanding of issues such as credit management, retirement savings and home ownership.

May 2006
U.S. Senate Banking Committee holds hearing on financial literacy. Some senators express concern that the Bush administration's blueprint for financial literacy fails to provide a coherent strategy for getting more Americans financially savvy. Federal Reserve Chairman Ben Bernanke calls financial literacy vital for consumers and U.S. financial markets. He also promises to encourage banks that offer credit cards to include on consumers' monthly statements how many months or years it would take to pay off the full balance if a consumer only makes the minimum payment, a common practice for young people . . . . Securities and Exchange Commission launches podcasts to teach young people about investing and stocks on its Web site (www.sec.gov/investor).

How Marketers Woo Tweenagers

Audrey Sorensen celebrated her birthday with her "tween" friends, getting the Tutti-Frutti Manicure Delight at the CapeCodder Resort's spa in Hyannis, Mass. Meanwhile, in Washington, D.C., two 11-year-olds received prepaid credit cards for their birthdays. [1]

Some 29 million 8-12-year-olds — the so-called tweens — have emerged as a potentially lucrative consumer group that marketers are aggressively wooing. But critics worry the trend is encouraging young children to grow up too fast.

The tween market is far from being monolithic, says Don Montuori, publisher of *Packaged Facts*, published by Market Research.com, a market research firm in New York City. "There are nuanced differences," he says. He estimates that today's tween market includes 16.4 million 8-to-11-year-olds and nearly 13 million 12-to-14-year-olds and that their buying power totals $39 billion. But regardless of their chronological age, "everyone is trying to 'age up,' " he says. "The 12-year-olds want to be 14, and the 16-year-olds want to be 21."

Tweens generally have less money ($10 a week) than their older teenage siblings ($30), according to the 2005 *Roper Youth Market* report, published by GfK Roper Consulting. The 8-to-12-year-old set is more likely to plan for their "teen-type" purchases, such as video games for boys and clothing for girls, while buying snack foods is still the most popular way tweens spend their money on impulse, according to the report. [2]

According to Montuori's *Market Research* report, tweens say they get to choose "some or most" of the movies they see, the toys and dolls they buy, the brands of jeans and sneakers they wear and the fast-food restaurants they frequent. [3] "And when it comes to providing leeway to their kids as consumers, parents generally trust girls more than they do boys," Monturori says.

Tweens also spend more time playing video games and wanting the various accessories that go with them, such as lights, magnifiers, vibrating buttons, speakers, headphones and carrying cases. Kids in the 8-to-10-year-old age group spend about an hour and 25 minutes every day playing a video or computer game, while the slightly older 11-to-14-year-olds spend only an hour and nine minutes, according to a March 2005 Kaiser Family Foundation study. [4] Older teens ages 15-18 spend less than an hour playing video games.

Michele Stockwell, director of social and family policy for the Progressive Policy Institute, a liberal think tank, says marketers most often exploit tweens' strong desire to be older. Tween girls can now buy padded push-up bras, midriff-baring tops and high-heeled shoes in their sizes, she writes in a 2005 paper, "Childhood for Sale: Consumer Culture's Bid for Our Kids." [5]

By the time they're 12, both boys and girls are big consumers of hair-styling products, moisturizers and cologne to help them look and feel older. Most girls 12-14 are already using lipstick and lip-gloss (86 percent), nail polish (82 percent), eyebrow pencils (66 percent), eye shadow (80 percent) and mascara (53 percent), according to Marketresearch.com. In Hyannis, CapeCodder owner Deb Catania said she started offering manicure and spa treatments for tweens and teens because there was a demand. [6]

Tweens also are paying big bucks to redecorate their bedrooms, fueled in part, experts say, by the popularity of home-makeover TV shows. The average parent spent $76 over a three-month period on room decor and accessories for their tweenaged child, according to the New York market research firm NPD Group. [7] Jumping on the tween room-makeover bandwagon, movie stars Mary-Kate and Ashley Olsen — who have been acting since they were infants — now offer their own line of furniture and rugs.

Tweens also have clear brand preferences. "Today's tweens are the most brand-conscious generation in history," writes Juliet B. Schor, a sociology professor at Boston College, in her 2004

Continued from p. 466

BACKGROUND

Teen Market Emerges

While references to "teens" have been around for centuries, the word "teenager" was first cited in a 1941 article in *Popular Science* magazine to describe an age group that quickly became of keen interest to marketers. [20]

Until the Great Depression, many young Americans worked instead of attending high school. The Depression forced young Americans into schools so farm and factory jobs could go to adults. This shift created the first "teenage" generation.

"Teenagers occupy a special place in American life," journalist Thomas Hine writes in *The Rise & Fall of the American Teenager*. "They are envied and sold to, studied and deplored. . . . Some see these young people as barbarians at the gates, and others look forward greedily to large numbers of new consumers." [21]

Teen power began to grow in the 1950s — both culturally and economically — when marketers feared that adult demand for big-ticket items like cars, washing machines and other goods, which had been pent up during World War II, had been met and was coming to an end. But clean-cut '50s-era teenage girls clad in bobbysocks and poodle skirts were eager to buy, kicking off a teen spending spree.

Journalist Landon Y. Jones contends that youths born during the postwar baby boom were the "first generation of children to be isolated by Madison

book *Born to Buy: The Commercialized Child and the New Consumer Culture.* [8] When 8-to-14-year-olds ask for something, more than 90 percent of their requests include a particular brand, according to Schor.

Marketers have discovered they must go where the kids are in order to tap into the tween market. Television outlets such as Viacom's Nickelodeon and Time Warner's Cartoon Network are trying to reach tweens with ads at theme parks, on Web sites and in magazines such as *CosmoGirl* and *Teen People.* "If we are really going to be a part of kids' lives, we've got to be with them wherever they go," a Nickelodeon executive told *Advertising Age* last year. [9]

Marketers say they must expand into non-traditional media because 60 percent of 12-to-14-year-olds say they fast-forward or skip commercials whenever possible. This indifference to traditional media requires new tactics, says Montuori, such as e-mail marketing, cell phone text-messaging, mall tours and Web-based sweepstakes. Data also suggest movie theaters are an effective way to reach this market: More than 40 percent of young teens say they notice ads when they are in the theater, according to Marketresearch.com.

Stockwell warns of the "unwelcome and unhealthy consequences for the children and families on the receiving end of all that marketing and consumerism." [10] Youths as young as 11 no longer consider themselves "children," according to Media Awareness Network, a Canadian nonprofit that says the Toy Manufacturers of America have changed their target market of birth to 14, to birth to 10 years of age. [11] Twenty years ago, the publisher of *Seventeen* magazine said its target audience was 16 years old, but now it caters to 11- and 12-year-olds. [12]

Schor says that too much consumerism at a young age can lead to major problems, including depression, anxiety and low self-esteem. "Day by day, marketers are growing bolder," she says, and year by year, "the harmful effects" mount.

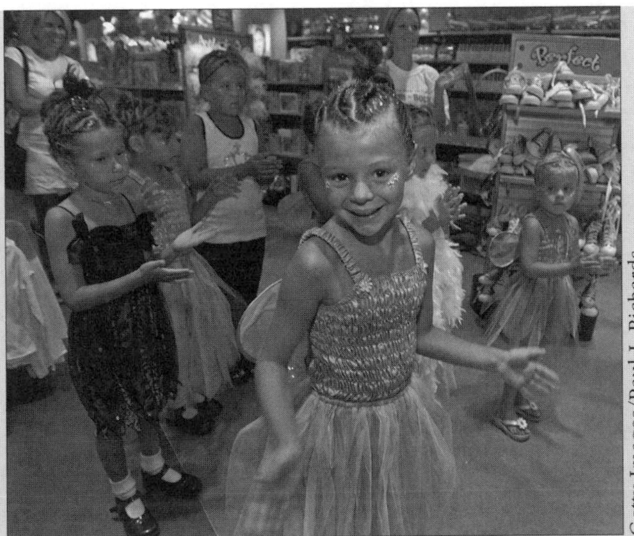
Getty Images/Paul J. Richards

Youngsters take a dance lesson at Club Libby Lu at the Tysons Corner Mall in McLean, Va.

[1] Marie Ewald, "Facials for 13-year-olds? Spas target teens," *The Christian Science Monitor,* May 14, 2004; and Michelle Singletary, "Credit Cards for Kids? Not in My House," *The Washington Post,* April 2, 2006, p. F1.

[2] "Roper Youth Report," GfK Roper Consulting, September 2005.

[3] "The U.S. Tween Market," *Packaged Facts,* MarketResearch.com, May 2005.

[4] "Generation M: Media in the Lives of 8-18-Year-Olds," Kaiser Family Foundation, 2005; www.kff.org/entmedia/7251.cfm

[5] Michelle Stockwell, "Childhood for Sale: Consumer Culture's Bid for Our Kids," Progressive Policy Institute, August 2005.

[6] Ewald, *op. cit.*

[7] Erin Clark, "What a Tween Wants . . . Now," *Children's Business,* April 1, 2004.

[8] Juliet B. Schor, *Born to Buy: The Commercialized Child and the New Consumer Culture* (2004), p. 25.

[9] *Packaged Facts, op. cit.*

[10] Stockwell, *op. cit.*

[11] www.media-awareness.ca/english/parents/marketing/issues_teens_marketing.cfm.

[12] Robin Rauzi, "The Teen Factor: Today's Media-Savvy Youths Influence What Others are Saying and Hearing," *Los Angeles Times,* June 9, 1998, p. F1.

Avenue as an identifiable market. . . . From the cradle, the baby boomers [were] surrounded by products created especially for them." [22]

It didn't take long for advertisers to notice. Ever since, they have been trying to woo the 13-19 set, the vast group that has determined what is popular in music, movies, snack food and clothing — from the "flower children" of the 1960s to the disco and punk cultures of the '70s and '80s to rap of the '90s. [23]

Ad companies have tried various tactics to lure teens to spend, including using sex. But in the 1980s they began to pitch their appeal to younger markets, including the controversial Calvin Klein jean ads in 1980 featuring 15-year-old actress and model Brooke Shields, asking: "What comes between me and my Calvins? Nothing." [24]

That year teenage shoppers pumped an estimated $39 billion into the U.S. economy, according to a Rand Youth Poll, which also found that nearly 70 percent of young people surveyed said they spent money on things they later realized they did not want. [25] Calvin Klein, meanwhile, continued to push the envelope with controversial, sex-oriented ads.

Banking Deregulation

Deregulation of the banking industry in the 1980s and the prosperity of the '90s ushered in new ways for teens to spend money. [26] At the same time, credit card companies in the early 1990s dropped the requirement that youths under 21 needed a co-signer to get a credit card, explains Robert Manning, a finance professor at the Rochester

Institute of Technology, in his 2000 book *Credit Card Nation*. [27]

When they were introduced in the 1950s, credit cards were typically geared for the middle class and — until the late 1970s — state usury laws prevented banks from charging excessive interest on the accounts. A 1978 U.S Supreme Court decision and banking deregulation in the 1980s, however, changed all that, allowing the banks to charge high interest rates. [28] The high court followed up in 1996 with another decision lifting restrictions on the amount of late fees a card company could charge. [29]

Manning and other critics say the rulings encouraged card companies to specifically seek out high-risk, low-income customers, such as college students. Some companies charged interest rates as high as 30 percent to cover the risk of giving cards to young customers with little income or credit history. The campaigns often included offers of free gifts for college students and showed up unsolicited in their campus mailboxes.

The aggressive marketing to college students prompted Rep. Joseph P. Kennedy II, D-Mass., in 1994 to ask the House Subcommittee on Consumer Credit to hold hearings on "kiddie" credit cards. Officials from MasterCard and Visa defended their practices and detailed various programs they had instituted to educate young consumers.

"College students are adults and are treated as such by the bankcard industry," said Visa Senior Vice President and General Counsel Paul Allen, noting the average student used a credit card responsibly. [30]

Some of those students, however, were running up staggering debts with heartbreaking consequences. A 1999 study conducted by Manning and the Consumer Federation of America linked college students' suicides with their anxiety over high credit card debt, drawing widespread attention from the media and policymakers. [31] Among the students was Mitzi Pool, an 18-year-old University of Oklahoma freshman who hanged herself after calling her mother and expressing remorse about losing her part-time job and maxing out three credit cards. [32]

In 2001, Iowa Attorney General Tom Miller lamented that "more and more students are slipping into high credit card debt with very serious long-term consequences" and quoted an administrator at Indiana University who said, "We lose more students to credit card debt than to academic failure." [33]

Between 1999 and 2001, at least 24 states considered — but only Arkansas and Louisiana approved — legislation to either study the effects of credit cards on college students or to limit credit card solicitation at institutions of higher education. [34]

The American Council on Education's King says that in the 1990s many parents were surprised their college-age students could get credit cards without their signatures and didn't know their kids were running up debt. Now, she says, some colleges ban credit card solicitation on campus, while others include financial-literacy information during orientation with freshmen and their parents.

Financial Literacy

Although Congress held several hearings in the 1990s on marketing credit cards to college students, it enacted no new laws. Sen. Christopher Dodd, D-Conn., a member of the Senate Banking Committee and a frequent critic of the credit card industry, has blamed the "very, very powerful" industry for blocking changes, including his proposal requiring anyone under 21 to prove they have the financial capacity to pay or have a parent co-sign when applying for a credit card.

"We've lost that every time I've offered it," Dodd said in a 2004 Public Broadcasting Service report, "Secret History of the Credit Card." [35]

In the early 2000s, however, growing concern prompted many banks and credit card companies to launch their own public-education campaigns to improve financial literacy. Many now offer free financial-literacy curricula for schools and online games (*see p. 465*).

The dot-com crash and the Sept. 11, 2001, terrorist attacks quickly ended the good times of the 1990s. But despite a recession, consumers — including teens — continued to buy, and often it was on credit. Rising levels of bankruptcies, including a troubling number of people under 25, and identity theft through credit cards prompted Congress in the 2000s to pass legislation calling for new efforts to teach young people about managing money.

The Fair and Accurate Credit Transaction Act of 2003 (FACTA), which primarily aimed to help consumers fight identity theft, also mandated creation of a Web site and a toll-free hotline directing consumers to personal-finance resources and a national financial-literacy strategy.

Congress also passed a resolution that year marking April as Financial Literacy Month, a move spearheaded by Reps. Rubén Hinojosa, D-Texas, and Judy Biggert R-Ill., and Sen. Daniel Akaka, D-Hawaii.

Two years later, the Bankruptcy Abuse Prevention and Consumer Protection Act of 2005 required that anyone filing for bankruptcy receive credit counseling and urged states to develop financial-literacy programs for elementary and secondary schools.

Akaka also added a provision to the Bush administration's landmark No Child Left Behind law setting aside $1.5 million to promote economic and financial literacy. [36] The National Council on Economic Education, which won the grants during the program's first two years, has provided subgrants to hundreds of local groups to bolster financial-literacy education. ■

CURRENT SITUATION

Wooing Youngsters

Politicians, business leaders, consumer groups and even pro football players and rappers are ramping up efforts to encourage teens to save and to spend their money wisely. But they are competing against a barrage of ads targeting teens as well as their parents, who are racking up billions in debt themselves.

"We have a long way to go," says Rep. Hinojosa, who frequently talks to parents and young people on money matters as co-founder and current co-chair of the House Financial and Economic Literacy Caucus.

Today's teens spend so much because they have been bombarded with ads to buy nearly since birth, say experts. The advertising industry spent $100 million pitching products to teens and kids in 1983, primarily through TV ads. But today, 150 times as much — $15 billion — is spent wooing young customers, according to a 2006 report from the Center for a New American Dream, a coalition of nonprofits that "helps Americans consume responsibly to protect the environment, enhance quality of life and promote social justice." [37]

Marketers today not only use TV and radio but also the Internet and the classroom to pitch their products — ranging from soft drinks and junk food to computers — to teens. [38] The Channel One television network, for example, provides video equipment to schools if classes watch daily news broadcasts liberally punctuated by promotional materials and commercials. [39]

"Contemporary American tweens and teens have emerged as the most brand-oriented, consumer-involved and materialistic generation in history," writes Juliet B. Schor, a sociology professor at Boston College, in her 2004 book *Born to Buy: The Commercialized Child and the New Consumer Culture.* [40] (*See sidebar, p. 468.*)

Personal-Finance Courses Required

Seven states require personal-finance courses before high-school graduation.

Require Personal-Finance Course Before Graduation

Alabama • Georgia
Idaho • Illinois
Kentucky • New York
Utah

Require Testing on Personal Finance

Connecticut • Georgia
Idaho • Illinois
Indiana • Kentucky
Michigan • Oregon
Virginia

Source: National Council on Economic Education, March 2005

The perpetual advertising adds to teens' pressure to buy more things, says the Center for a New American Dream, which along with the World Wildlife Fund launched the "Be, Live, Buy Different" campaign calling on kids to be socially aware consumers. According to a 2002 poll conducted by the center, nearly a third of teens between ages 12 and 17 admitted to feeling pressure to buy things like clothes, shoes and CDs just because their friends had them, and more than half said they bought certain products to make them feel better about themselves. [41]

The center also found that kids asked for things, on average, nine times before they parents finally gave in. "As a result of unprecedented levels of advertising and marketing aimed at kids, our children feel intense pressure to try to bolster their sense of self-esteem at the mall, and they will go to incredible lengths to get their parents to give in," said Executive Director Betsy Taylor. [42]

Apparently, however, parents often give in to their kids' demands because they enjoy the products as much as their children, according a recent poll. This is a shift from generations past when parents and teens clashed over clothes and culture, said Yankelovich Inc., a marketing research firm, in its latest *Youth Monitor.* [43] Nearly 3-in-4 parents said they and their child had a lot in common when it comes to things they like to do and buy, ranging from the latest camera phones and iPods to blockbuster hits such as "Shrek 2."

"We have to remember that today's parents are, to a significant degree, the MTV, original "Star Wars," "Star Search" generation," Yankelovich said. "So in some respects, the ruling pop culture of their youth is frequently echoed in today's pop culture." [44]

National Strategy

While admitting that times have changed, Rep. Hinojosa wishes more parents emulated his own father when it comes to teaching money skills. As a 10-year-old growing up after World War II, Hinojosa was required to sock away a portion of his allowance and earnings into his piggy bank. When he earned $200, his father took him to the bank and opened a savings account. Hinojosa's own children got savings accounts when they were 12 and began investing in the stock market at 14.

"Young people can be trained to save early, and that continues through adulthood," he says.

But not enough teens and their parents are getting the message. "Most of our children haven't yet grasped

College Students Favor Debit Cards

Debit card use among college students surpassed credit cards and ATM cards in 2003. Today nearly three-quarters of college students use debit cards while less than half use credit cards.

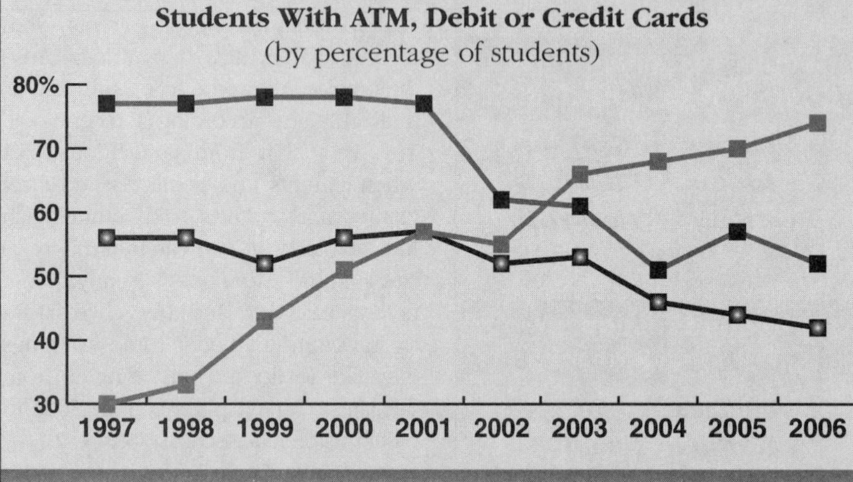

Source: Student Monitor LLC, 2006

the most basic financial and economic concepts that will enable them to prepare for their future," said Rep. Biggert, the other caucus co-chair, after the House approved a resolution for the third-straight year marking April as Financial Literacy Month. [45] As the leading congressional advocates for financial education, Biggert, Hinojosa and Akaka hosted a financial-literacy fair on Capitol Hill on April 25.

The Bush administration is also promoting financial literacy and trying to determine what works in the classroom, says Dan Iannicola, Jr., deputy assistant Treasury secretary for financial education, who participated in the department's recent 15-city tour touting Financial Literacy Month. Iannicola is surprised that so few young people seem to understand the consequences of using plastic, such as finance charges, compounding interest and fees. They also seem unaware that someone is watching how they use credit cards, and that their history shows up on a credit report. "I liken [credit reports] to a grade point average," a concept that students understand, he says.

He recently returned from Chicago with U.S. Treasurer Anna Escobedo Cabral, who was publicizing the National Strategy for Financial Literacy, a blueprint for improving Americans' understanding of credit management, retirement savings and home ownership. [46] The strategy describes programs the administration hopes communities will institute, including a money-based math curriculum developed by the Treasury Department in 2001 (www.publicdebt.treas.gov/mar/marmonetymath.htm) and a report on how schools can integrate financial education into their curricula (www.treasury.gov/financialeducation). The strategy also highlights programs that teach financial education to college freshmen, high-school dropouts seeking their GEDs and male juveniles in correctional facilities.

The 159-page strategy was developed by the Financial Literacy and Education Commission, made up of 20 federal agencies and headed by the Treasury Department, which was mandated by the Fair and Accurate Credit Transaction Act of 2003. By the end of this year, Iannicola expects to begin airing public-service announcements on credit literacy, another requirement of the law, which also mandated creation of a Web site (www.mymoney.gov) and toll-free hotline (1-888-mymoney).

Hinojosa and Biggert say the commission's report is a good start but doesn't go far enough. Biggert wants the commission expanded to include private-sector representatives; Hinojosa wants a hearing on the national strategy.

During a hearing on financial literacy held by the Senate Banking Committee on May 23, several senators expressed concern that the commission's report merely showcased some "best practices" but failed to provide a strategy to make more Americans financially literate. "The report is useful . . . but we need to do more," agreed Federal Reserve Chairman Ben S. Bernanke, who also is a member of the Financial Literacy and Education Commission. The Fed kicked off its "There's a Lot to Learn About Money" campaign in 2003 and provides information on personal finance, including resources for teachers, on its Web site (www.federalreserveeducation.org).

Sen. Richard Shelby, R-Ala., the committee's chairman, saying he was worried that young people were getting mired in credit card debt because they only pay the minimum amount listed on their statement, wondered if legislation was needed. Bernanke said the Fed was working on "guidance" to persuade banks that offer credit cards to include on each bill how many months or years it would take to pay off the full balance if a consumer only made the minimum payment.

The U.S. Securities and Exchange Commission, which regulates the stock markets, is trying podcasts to get the word out to young people about investing, SEC Chairman Christopher Cox told the Senate panel. The podcasts "Welcome

Continued on p. 474

At Issue:

Do credit card companies market too aggressively to youths?

TRAVIS B. PLUNKETT
LEGISLATIVE DIRECTOR, CONSUMER FEDERATION OF AMERICA

WRITTEN FOR *CQ RESEARCHER*, MAY 2006

yes

Many credit card issuers have targeted the least sophisticated and riskiest consumers in recent years, including young people, and encouraged them to run up high, often unsustainable levels of debt. This practice has proven to be very profitable for many credit card issuers, but it can have devastating consequences for consumers.

Starting in the early 1990s, card issuers targeted massive marketing efforts at college campuses across the country, resulting in a sharp growth in credit card debt among college-age and younger Americans. As a result, Americans under age 35 continue to show more signs of trouble managing credit card debt than any other age group.

Between the mid-1990s and 2004, the amount of credit card debt held by students graduating from college more than doubled, to $3,262. Americans under 35 are less likely to pay off their card balances every month than average Americans. They are paying more for debt obligations than in the past and are increasingly likely to pay more than 40 percent of their incomes on credit card debt.

Not surprisingly, more young Americans are declaring bankruptcy than in the past. Moreover, there is increasing evidence that credit card companies are now targeting high-school students with card offers. They are also marketing branded debit cards to adolescents, in part to encourage these young consumers to use similarly branded credit cards when they are older.

Young people are also financially vulnerable to the questionable pricing and business practices adopted by issuers to increase the profitability of lending to riskier customers. These abusive practices include "universal default," in which a consumer must suddenly pay a sharply higher interest rate on their outstanding balance with one credit card company because of a minor problem with another creditor.

Many creditors have also significantly increased their penalty fees, even for small transgressions like a payment that is made only a few hours late. Until recently, issuers also decreased the size of minimum payments that consumers had to pay, encouraging them to carry more debt for longer periods.

Several pieces of legislation have been introduced in Congress in recent years that would prevent credit card companies from targeting young people with unsustainable offers of credit and prohibit abusive fee and interest-rate practices. Unless credit card issuers adopt considerably more restraint in marketing and extending credit to less-sophisticated borrowers, the Consumer Federation of America will continue to urge Congress to adopt such restrictions.

LOUIS J. FREEH
VICE CHAIRMAN AND GENERAL COUNSEL, MBNA CORP.

FROM TESTIMONY BEFORE U.S. SENATE BANKING COMMITTEE, MAY 17, 2005

no

In discussing student marketing, it is important to note that we make every effort to ensure that credit card offers are not sent to people under the age of 18.

MBNA does promote its products to college-aged customers by partnering with more than 700 colleges and universities, primarily through the college alumni associations. By working closely with school administrators, we have earned the confidence and trust of most of America's premier educational institutions. . . .

Before granting credit to a college student, analysts familiar with the needs and abilities of college students review each application and decline more than half. . . . Most college student applicants report a separate income, and many already have an established credit history.

When evaluating an application, we consider the college students' projected performance as an alumnus, and when we grant credit, we typically assign a line of between $500 and $1,000. If a college student attempts to use his or her card beyond the credit line, we typically refuse the charge. And we do not re-price these accounts based on behavior.

Once a college student becomes a cardholder, MBNA delivers its "Good Credit, Great Future" brochure in a Welcome Package. The brochure highlights sound money-management habits, including guidance on how to handle a credit card responsibly. We also maintain a Web site aimed at college-aged consumers, highlighting many of the same tips. MBNA also conducts on-campus credit-education seminars, and we provide articles concerning responsible credit use for student and parent publications.

The performance of our college-student portfolio mirrors closely that of the national experience, as reported in [Government Accountability Office] reports and several independent studies. However, our accounts have much smaller credit limits and much smaller balances than the norm, our college student customers utilize their cards less often than the norm and these accounts are less likely to incur fees. Our experience has also been that college students are no more likely to mishandle their accounts than any other group of customers.

When we grant a card to a college student, we think of it as the beginning of what we hope will be a long relationship. . . . Given this, we have absolutely no interest in encouraging poor credit habits. In fact, everyone's interest is best served when college students make responsible use of credit. That is our goal in every situation, and certainly when dealing with college-aged customers.

Continued from p. 472

to Your Money" and "Hot Stock Tips" are available on the SEC's Web site (www.sec.gov/investor).

Meanwhile, Sen. Akaka is pushing legislation that would create a pilot program requiring college students to get credit counseling and a financial-literacy program that gives grants to organizations that ban or discourage credit card marketing on campus.

Iannicola says states and schools should have the flexibility to figure out how best to integrate financial-literacy courses and that federal or state mandates may not be the best answer. But that is precisely the direction some states are taking. Seven states passed legislation in 2005 requiring financial education in schools, and New York and Illinois this year introduced measures to beef up their existing financial-education standards, according to a report from Citigroup. [47]

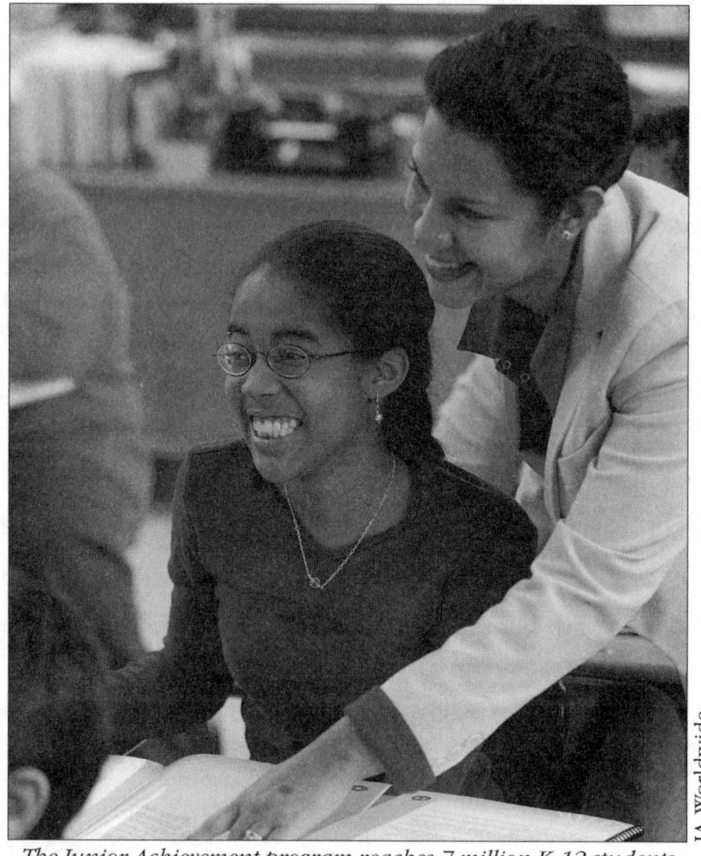

JA Worldwide

The Junior Achievement program reaches 7 million K-12 students around the globe, including this youth at the A.H. Middle School in Richmond, Va. In-school and after-school programs cover financial literacy, career development, economics and related areas.

Shock Therapy

Some bankruptcy judges have turned to shock therapy to teach teens about the consequences of excessive debt. In March about 90 high-school juniors from Worcester, Mass., got a taste of the real world when they watched a mock consumer bankruptcy case in U.S. Bankruptcy Court in Boston.

"If many of the 25,000 debtors who filed for bankruptcy in Massachusetts last year better understood the risks of credit, they might have been able to avoid bankruptcy," said Chief Bankruptcy Judge Joan Feeney, who in 2004 created a task force with the Boston Bar Association to devise a financial-literacy curriculum. [48]

In Western New York state, Bankruptcy Court Judge Ninfro visits about 20 high schools and colleges each year, describing to students some of the cases he sees in his bankruptcy courtroom, such as the man who owed $20,000 on credit cards and lost his $60,000 job.

"Mounting credit card debt is a ticket to bankruptcy," he says. U.S. bankruptcy filings in the federal courts skyrocketed a record 30 percent in 2005, according to the Administrative Office of the U.S. Courts. More than 2 million individuals and businesses filed for bankruptcy in 2005, up from the 1.6 million the previous year and more than in any 12-month period in the history of the federal courts. Many people filed before the Bankruptcy Abuse Prevention and Consumer Protection Act of 2005 went into effect in October 2005. The act made it harder for people to file for bankruptcy. [49]

Many financial institutions today are trying to boost financial education. Citigroup, for example, has committed $200 million over 10 years to address financial literacy around the world. [50]

Meanwhile, the National Endowment for Financial Education (NEFE) plans to focus more attention on credit card fraud, Internet transactions and parental involvement. "The new materials will emphasize parents," NEFE's Parfrey says. "There's a real disconnect between parents and kids."

Experts agree that while it's important that teens learn about money in school, it's even more important for the lessons to begin at home. "By far, the largest influence on kids and how they behave financially is watching their parents," says Salisbury of the American Savings Education Council.

Parents are doing some things right, Salisbury says, just not enough. Most parents encourage their children to save, and eight out of 10 say they teach their kids to compare prices, he says, citing a 2001 council survey. [51] But only half the parents said they taught their kids how to track expenses and make a budget, and even fewer have taught them about different kinds of investments.

Even though the council's study is somewhat dated, Salisbury says the results are consistent with other reports showing that many parents carry large balances on their credit cards and don't have family budgets.

An overwhelming number of teens — 94 percent — say they are likely to go to their parents with money questions, but many are reluctant to sit down and talk with their kids about finances, especially those who feel their own habits are not exemplary, says Mead of the National Endowment for Financial Education. She urges parents to set aside a monthly "family money night" to discuss financial matters, such as the importance of saving, how to make a budget and what groceries and other necessities cost per week.

Levine of Jump$tart says that whether parents feel prepared or qualified to talk is beside the point, because it's not just what they say but what they do. "If you spend and charge too much, it's hard to expect that your teenage son or daughter won't," she says. "Parents have to set a good example." ■

OUTLOOK

Train Wreck?

Most financial experts are only cautiously optimistic that today's teens will be smarter than their parents about money, but others are downright bleak in their assessments.

"It's a train wreck waiting to happen," says Parfrey of the National Endowment for Financial Education.

The problem is that many of today's teens won't have pensions to fall back on when they retire, as their parents do. "Young people need to increase their financial IQ now if they are to survive in a world where there will be no Social Security, the costs of health care and college tuition for their kids will skyrocket, gas will be $5 to $6 a gallon and job security will totally be a thing of the past," says New York state Bankruptcy Judge Ninfro.

NEFE's Mead agrees. "Kids today are facing financial issues that their parents didn't," she says. "They will have to be much more financially savvy." Much depends on whether more schools teach financial literacy and whether the lesson is reinforced at home, she says; it may take "several generations."

Levine of the Jump$tart Coalition for Personal Financial Literacy predicts more states will require financial literacy in schools and hopes parents will reinforce the message at home. "It's so important that financial literacy become part of a child's formal education — in school, after school and at home.

"You wouldn't hand a kid a musical instrument and see if they can learn how to play it," she says. "Why would money be any different?"

But with young people being bombarded with ads that promote living rich and on credit, "We have a big challenge," says Duvall of the National Council on Economic Education.

Deputy Assistant Secretary of the Treasury Iannicola says the financial-literacy movement for both teens and adults is in its adolescence. "It's not new anymore, but it's not in full maturity," he cautions. And like any other social movement, it will take time before most Americans start changing their spending and saving habits, he says, citing the years of urging before Americans began using their seat belts and designating a non-drinking driver.

Ninfro likens today's spendthrift ways to the popularity of smoking in the 1950s, before the dangers were widely known. He predicts that just as millions of Americans have stopped smoking because of the cancer risk, they will, over time, stop running up thousands of dollars of debt once they realize the financial consequences.

Young adults who racked up debt and bad credit histories as teenagers are losing out on jobs, student loans, apartments, admission to graduate school and more because of their abuse of credit, he says. "We need to get young people the message," he says. "Education is really the only way." ■

Notes

[1] Michelle Singletary, "Credit Cards for Kids? Not in My House," *The Washington Post*, April 2, 2006, p. F1.

[2] "Teens & Money 2006 Survey," Charles Schwab Foundation, April 2006.

[3] For background see Alan Greenblatt, "Pension Crisis," *CQ Researcher*, Feb. 17, 2006, pp. 145-168.

[4] Ann Holdsworth, "Teens Cash In," *Fiscal Notes*, Texas Comptroller, August 2005.

[5] "Generation Fact Sheet," Visa USA Research, 2005.

[6] "Undergraduate Students and Credit Cards in 2004," Nellie Mae Corp., May 2005.

[7] Consumer Federation of America, 2005.

[8] The nine states are Connecticut, Georgia, Idaho, Illinois, Indiana, Kentucky, Michigan, Oregon and Virginia, as reported in "Survey of the States," National Council on Economic Education, March 2005.

[9] "Evaluation of the NEFE High School Financial Planning Program, 2003-2004," University of Minnesota.

[10] "Teens & Money 2006 Survey," *op. cit.*

[11] 2006 Jump$tart Questionnaire; www.jumpstart.org.

[12] "What American Teens & Adults Know About Economics," National Council on Economic Education, April 2005.

[13] Creola Johnson, "Maxed Out College Students: A Call to Limit Credit Card Solicitation on College Campuses," *Journal of Legislation and Public Policy*, New York University Law School, Vol. 8, No. 2, p. 195, June 2005.

[14] Government Accountability Office, "Credit Reporting Literacy: Consumers Understood the Basics but Could Benefit from Targeted Educational Efforts," March 2005.

[15] Junior Achievement, "2006 Interprise Poll on Teens and Personal Finance," April 18, 2006.

[16] Nellie Mae, *op. cit.*

[17] *Ibid.*

[18] Janet Bodnar, "Just Say 'No' to Plastic," *Kiplinger.com*, Aug. 11, 2005.

[19] Junior Achievement, *op. cit.*

[20] Thomas Hine, *The Rise & Fall of the American Teenager* (1999).

[21] *Ibid.*

[22] For background, see William V. Thomas, "Trends in Advertising," *Editorial Research Reports, 1981* (Vol. II) at *CQ Press Researcher Plus Archive*, CQ Electronic Library, http://library.cqpress.com.

[23] For background, see Helen B. Shaffer, "Youth Market," *Editorial Research Reports 1965* (Vol. II) at *CQ Researcher Plus Archive*, CQ Electronic Library; http://library.cqpress.com.

[24] Thomas, *op. cit.*

[25] *Ibid.*

[26] For background, see Richard L. Worsnop, "Consumer Debt," *CQ Researcher*, Nov. 15, 1996, pp. 1009-1032.

[27] Robert D. Manning, *Credit Card Nation* (2000).

[28] The Supreme Court case is *Marquette National Bank of Minneapolis v. First Omaha Serve Corp.* (439 U.S. 299).

[29] The Supreme Court case is *Smiley v. Citibank (South Dakota), N.A.* (517 U.S. 735).

[30] Transcript of House Banking, Finance and Urban Affairs Subcommittee on Consumer Credit and Insurance, March 10, 1994.

[31] Robert D. Manning, "Credit Cards on Campus: The Social Consequences of Student Debt," Consumer Federation of America, June 8, 1999.

[32] *Ibid.*

[33] www.iowaattorneygeneral.org/consumer/press_releases/2001/campus_cc_debt.html.

[34] General Accounting Office, "Consumer Finance: College Students and Credit Cards," June 2001, pp. 53-66. The office has since been renamed the Government Accountability Office.

[35] www.pbs.org/wgbh/pages/frontline/shows/credit/.

[36] For background, see Barbara Mantel, "No Child Left Behind," *CQ Researcher*, May 27, 2005, pp. 469-492.

[37] "Tips for parenting in a commercial culture," *New American Dream*, April 2006.

[38] For more background, see David Masci, "The Consumer Culture," *CQ Researcher*, Nov. 19, 1999, pp. 1001-1016.

[39] For background, see Patrick Marshall, "Advertising Overload," *CQ Researcher*, Jan. 23, 2004, pp. 49-72.

[40] Juliet B. Schor, *Born to Buy: The Commercialized Child and the New Consumer Culture* (2004), p. 21.

[41] Center for a New American Dream, press release, 2002.

[42] *Ibid.*

[43] *Yankelovich Youth Monitor*, press release, June 2005.

[44] *Ibid.*

[45] Rep. Judy Biggert, press release, April 7, 2006.

[46] www.mymoney.gov/ownership.pdf.

[47] "The Drive for Financial Literacy," Citigroup, 2006. The seven states are Missouri, South Carolina, Texas, Virginia, Washington, West Virginia and Wyoming.

FOR MORE INFORMATION

American Savings Education Council, 2121 K St., Suite 600, N.W., Washington, DC 20037-1896; (202) 659-0670; www.choosetosave.org. A coalition of government and industry institutions to educate people on all aspects of personal finance.

Consumer Credit Counseling Service, 9009 West Loop South, Suite 700, Houston, TX 77096; (800) 873-2227; www.cccsintl.org. Helps people nationwide solve debt problems by providing counseling on personal finances.

Consumer Federation of America, 1620 I St., N.W., Suite 200, Washington, DC 20006; (202) 387-6121; www.consumerfed.org. A leading critic of credit card marketing to young people.

Credit Abuse Resistance Education (CARE), 1400 U.S. Courthouse, 100 State St., Rochester, NY 14814; (585) 613-4200; www.careprogram.us. A national program founded by Judge John C. Ninfro of the U.S. Bankruptcy Court in Western New York that provides resources, speakers and information to schools and colleges.

FederalReserveEducation.org. The Federal Reserve's online resource includes materials specifically geared toward teachers and high school and college students.

Jump$tart Coalition for Personal Financial Literacy, 919 18th St., N.W., Suite 300, Washington, DC 20006; (202) 466-8604; www.jumpstart.org. Regularly surveys high-school students' knowledge of basic money matters.

Junior Achievement, One Education Way, Colorado Springs, CO 80906; (719) 540-8000; www.ja.org. A nonprofit dedicated to educating young people about business and entrepreneurship.

National Council on Economic Education, 1140 Avenue of the Americas, New York, NY 10036; (212) 730-7007; www.ncee.net. A network of state and university centers that promote financial literacy in the classroom and track state developments.

National Endowment for Financial Education, 5299 DTC Blvd., Suite 1300, Greenwood Village, CO 80111; (303) 741-6333; www.nefe.org. Provides curriculum and materials for classrooms and researches financial-education issues.

Securities and Exchange Commission, 100 F St. N.E., Washington, DC 20549; 1-800-SEC-0330; www.sec.gov/investor.shtml. The federal agency charged with protecting investors provides information about saving and investing.

U.S. Financial Literacy and Education Commission (1-888-mymoney); www.mymoney.gov. Provides educational materials on financial issues.

About the Author

Pamela M. Prah is a *CQ Researcher* staff writer with several years previous reporting experience at Stateline.org, *Kiplinger's Washington Letter* and the Bureau of National Affairs. She holds a master's degree in government from Johns Hopkins University and a journalism degree from Ohio University. Her recent reports include "Disaster Preparedness," "Eating Disorders" and "Coal Mining Safety."

[48] Boston Bar Association, press release, March 27, 2006.

[49] www.uscourts.gov/Press_Releases/bankruptcyfilings032406.html.

[50] Citigroup, *op. cit.*

[51] "Parents, Youth & Money Survey," American Education Savings Council and Employee Benefit Research Institute, April 2001.

Bibliography

Selected Sources

Books

Hine, Thomas, *The Rise & Fall of the American Teenager*, Avon Books, 1999.

A journalist traces the culture of youth in America, including what he calls the media-blitzed consumerism of today's teens.

Manning, Robert D., *Credit Card Nation*, Basic Books, 2000.

A finance professor at Rochester Institute of Technology examines how credit card companies targeted the college student market in the late 1980s and early 1990s and finds student credit card debt much higher than is commonly reported.

Schor, Juliet B., *Born to Buy: The Commercialized Child and the New Consumer Culture*, Scribner, 2004.

A sociology professor at Boston College says today's teens are the most brand-oriented, consumer-involved and materialistic generation in history and concludes that the onslaught of advertising aimed at children hurts kids' emotional and social well-being.

Articles

Bodnar, Janet, "Just Say 'No' to Plastic," *Kiplinger.com*, Aug. 11, 2005.

This column on teaching teens personal finance by the author of *Raising Money-Smart Kids* advocates teaching money management a step at a time, first with cash, then with a checking account linked to a debit card and finally a credit card.

Singletary, Michelle, "Credit Cards for Kids? Not in My House," *The Washington Post*, April 2, 2006, p. F1.

A *Washington Post* business columnist lambastes the credit card industry for marketing to young people.

Reports and Studies

"Credit Reporting Literacy: Consumers Understood the Basics but Could Benefit from Targeted Educational Efforts," U.S. Government Accountability Office, March 2005.

The congressional watchdog agency finds that less than 20 percent of 18-24-year-olds know their credit history can affect employment.

"Parents, Youth & Money Survey," American Education Savings Council and Employee Benefit Research Institute, April 2001.

The two sponsors of the national "Choose to Save" campaign find that only half of parents say they taught their kids how to track expenses and how to make a budget, and even fewer have taught their kids about different kinds of investments.

"Personal Finance 2006," Junior Achievement, April 2006.

An organization that educates young people about business and entrepreneurship finds that about 16 percent of teenage credit card holders make only the minimum payment.

"2006 Jump$start Questionnaire," Jump$start Coalition for Personal Financial Literacy, April 2006.

The group's annual survey of high-school seniors finds that students earned an average score of only 52 percent on a test of their knowledge of credit cards, saving and retirement.

"Undergraduate Students and Credit Cards in 2004," Nellie Mae Corp., May 2005.

The student-loan lender finds that of the 76 percent of undergraduates in 2004 who had their own credit cards, nearly a quarter had the card before entering college, while 43 percent got it during their freshman year.

"What American Teens & Adults Know About Economics," April 2005; and "Survey of the States," National Council on Economic Education, March 2005.

The first report from a network of state and university centers promoting the teaching of economics gives high-school students an "F" on their understanding of basic financial concepts; the second describes how each state deals with personal finance in the classroom.

"Youth Report," GfK Roper Consulting, September 2005.

A consulting firm finds that while the number of teens who get money from household chores and allowance has remained about the same in recent years, a growing number of teens get money simply by asking for it.

Johnson, Creola, "Maxed Out College Students: A Call to Limit Credit Card Solicitation on College Campuses," *Journal of Legislation and Public Policy*, New York University Law School, Vol. 8, No. 2, June 2005.

An Ohio State University researcher finds that few college students are aware that late credit card payments could mean higher interest rates on car loans and mortgages.

Manning, Robert D., "Credit Cards on Campus: The Social Consequences of Student Debt," Consumer Federation of America, June 8, 1999.

A controversial 1999 study links college students' debt with suicides, drawing considerable attention from the media and state and federal policymakers.

The Next Step:

Additional Articles from Current Periodicals

College Students

Barker, Tim, "College Students' Futures Clouded by Plastic," *Los Angeles Times*, March 19, 2006, p. A12.

A national debate has erupted over whether credit card companies should be allowed to recruit new users on college campuses.

Hoover, Eric, "Students Carry Lower Credit-Card Balances," *The Chronicle of Higher Education*, June 3, 2005, p. 28.

A majority of college students frequently use credit cards when making purchases, but they are carrying slightly lower credit card balances than they did four years ago, according to a new study by Nellie Mae.

McLaughlin, Mary-Beth, "Area College Students Warn Against Credit Card Debt," *The Toledo Blade*, May 16, 2006.

The amount of credit card debt college students face after graduating is a growing cause for concern, especially because more students are using the cards to finance their education.

Financial Literacy

"Teaching Kids About Money Certainly Makes Lots of Cents," *The Miami Herald*, April 23, 2006, p. 40.

Al Duarte, vice president of education at the InCharge Education Foundation in Orlando, Fla., presents six steps parents should take when teaching their kids about finances.

Aversa, Jeannine, "Teens Come Up Short When Asked How Money Works, Survey Says," *St. Louis Post-Dispatch*, April 6, 2006, p. B6.

Teenagers answered correctly only 52.4 percent of questions about personal finance and economics on a nationwide survey released by the Federal Reserve.

Dinnen, Steve, " 'Kids, I'd Like You to Meet Your Money. . .,' " *The Christian Science Monitor*, Sept. 26, 2005, p. 13.

Parents owe it to their children to teach them how to save, budget and invest their money at an early age.

Glod, Maria, "Schools Bank On Teaching Kids How to Save," *The Washington Post*, May 22, 2006, p. A1.

Educators and policymakers are beginning to insist that the basics of money management, including the importance of saving, become part of school offerings.

Hannah-Jones, Nikole, "Visa Counsels Durham Students on Finance," *The* [Charlotte, N.C.] *News and Observer*, May 23, 2006.

Visa wants to teach young adults how to responsibly use their credit cards, so the company is teaching students nationwide an online personal-finance program.

Kristof, Kathy M., "Teaching How to Save, Invest at a Tender Age," *Los Angeles Times*, May 14, 2006, p. C3.

A.G. Edwards, a St. Louis-based investment company, recently contributed $450,000 to fund a program it's calling Nest Egg Knowledge for Kids, aimed at teaching the underage set how to handle finances.

Lykins, Lorrie, "Teens Find Bringing Bling Isn't So Cheap," *St. Petersburg Times*, April 24, 2006, p. 1.

Pinellas County libraries are presenting a free financial-literacy program designed to educate Florida high-school students on budgeting, financial planning, establishing credit, managing credit cards and avoiding debt.

Radcliffe, Jennifer, "A 'Necessary' Lesson in Personal Finance," *The Houston Chronicle*, Nov. 15, 2005, p. A4.

A new Texas law requires personal-finance literacy to be added to the state's economics curriculum in the 2006-2007 school year and to be included in a class required for high-school graduation by 2008-2009.

Marketing to Teens

Deam, Jenny, "Targeting Kid Consumers, Children and Parents Find Ads' Influence Tough to Shut Out," *The Denver Post*, July 23, 2002, p. F1.

Advertisements aimed at children and teens are more sophisticated and intense than ever, with marketers zeroing in on specific age groups and personality types.

Tedeschi, Bob, "Teenagers Are Among Online Retailers' Most Sought-After Customers," *The New York Times*, Feb. 28, 2005, p. C3.

Online retailers are tailoring their Web sites for difficult-to-reach teenage customers, designing them to answer the question "what's in it for me?" and offering advice on cool, new trends.

Timberlake, Cotton, and Lisa Kassenaar, "Meet the Newest Lovers of Luxury Goods: Teens With Parents Who Don't Bat an Eye at Buying a $900 Purse," *The Seattle Times*, Nov. 27, 2005, p. L1.

Teenagers are luxury stores' new customers along Madison and Fifth avenues in New York City, paying for expensive items with mom's and dad's credit cards.

Teens and Credit Cards

Alsever, Jennifer, "Teenagers and Their Plastic, the Rites of Passage," *The New York Times*, June 25, 2005, p. C5.

Teenagers are showing a lack of enthusiasm for credit cards, with just 15 percent of teenagers surveyed this spring saying they were interested in obtaining a credit card in their own name, down from 34 percent in 2000.

Bunkley, Nick, "Teens Skip the Malls, Shop Online," *Chicago Tribune*, Feb. 19, 2006, p. Q5.
A growing number of teens are discovering online shopping as a way to avoid the crowds, browse a broad selection of merchandise and save money.

Clark, Kim, "The Perils of Plastic," *U.S. News & World Report*, Dec. 12, 2005, p. 63.
The writer offers tips to teens with credit cards on how to avoid debt.

Houtz, Jolayne, "Look Who's Whipping Out the Credit Card: High Schoolers," *The Seattle Times*, April 23, 2006, p. A1.
Consumer advocates say high-school students are being aggressively targeted by the credit card industry.

Johnson, Patt, "Teens Approve of Debit," *Des Moines Register*, Oct. 20, 2005, p. A1.
Parents and financial experts agree that debit cards can act as financial training wheels for teens before they get a credit card.

Sandomir, Richard, "In His First Endorsement, Young Selects A Debit Card," *The New York Times*, April 22, 2006, p. D6.
Vince Young, the former University of Texas quarterback, has chosen to endorse NetSpend's prepaid debit cards because he says "it keeps college kids from going in debt."

Shanley, Will, "U.S. Teens Steady on Credit; Poll Shows 10 Percent Have Cards, A Slight Drop From 2005," *The Denver Post*, April 18, 2006, p. C4.
The percentage of teenagers nationwide who own credit cards has not increased in recent years because credit card companies have become hesitant to issue plastic to teens, and parents are eschewing credit cards for prepaid spending cards.

Tween Market

D'Innocenzio, Anne, "Toy Manufacturers Set Out After A New Market: 'Tween Girls," *The Philadelphia Inquirer*, Sept. 21, 2000, p. F5.
Toy manufacturers are beginning to target new electronic toys to tween girls after finding they are interested in girl-friendly high-tech toys.

Frey, Christine, "The Buying Power of Tweens — 'It's All About Them,' " *The Seattle Post-Intelligencer*, July 31, 2004, p. E1.
Because "tweens" (children ages 8-12) account for $260 billion in U.S. spending annually, companies have targeted them for the past 10 years.

Henerson, Evan, "Latest Troll Dolls Sport 'Spell Phones' and 'Tpods,' " *Chicago Tribune*, Jan. 30, 2005, p. Q6.
DIC Entertainment is tweaking the Troll doll brand name in an effort to appeal to the coveted tween audience.

Jones, Terril Yue, "The Preteen Tech Consultants," *Los Angeles Times*, Nov. 25, 2005, p. C1.
Technology and consumer electronics companies increasingly are crafting advertisements aimed at tweens, realizing that they have a large say in how their parents spend money.

Noguchi, Yuki, "Cellphone Companies Seek Untouched 'Tween' Market," *The Miami Herald*, July 8, 2005, p. C3.
Having already captured nearly 70 percent of the U.S. population in service contracts, wireless companies are reaching out for tween customers.

Rose, Marla Matzer, "Tween Power," *The Seattle Post-Intelligencer*, June 24, 2003, p. E1.
The tween demographic group is using its sizable buying power to turn its favorite celebrities into multimedia sensations, purchasing their albums, movies, cosmetics and clothing lines.

Sheets, David, "Kiddie Calls Are on the Horizon For the Growing 'Tween Market," *St. Louis Post-Dispatch*, Feb. 12, 2005, p. 3.
The world's No. 2 toymaker, Hasbro Inc., is going after the growing 'tween market with ChatNow, a walkie-talkie-like device that is similar to a mobile phone with an effective range of two miles.

Yerak, Becky, "Mother May I Get A Facial? Yes, You May," *Chicago Tribune*, Oct. 1, 2005, p. C1.
Marshall Field's department store will open a new salon and spa for toddlers to preteens, and consumer experts say others will follow based on the strength of the tween market.

CITING *CQ RESEARCHER*

Sample formats for citing these reports in a bibliography include the ones listed below. Preferred styles and formats vary, so please check with your instructor or professor.

MLA STYLE

Jost, Kenneth. "Rethinking the Death Penalty." CQ Researcher 16 Nov. 2001: 945-68.

APA STYLE

Jost, K. (2001, November 16). Rethinking the death penalty. *CQ Researcher, 11*, 945-968.

CHICAGO STYLE

Jost, Kenneth. "Rethinking the Death Penalty." *CQ Researcher*, November 16, 2001, 945-968.

In-depth Reports on Issues in the News

Are you writing a paper?

Need backup for a debate?

Want to become an expert on an issue?

For 80 years, students have turned to *CQ Researcher* for in-depth reporting on issues in the news. Reports on a full range of political and social issues are now available. Following is a selection of recent reports:

Civil Liberties
Right to Die, 5/05
Immigration Reform, 4/05
Gays on Campus, 10/04

Crime/Law
Domestic Violence, 1/06
Death Penalty Controversies, 9/05
Methamphetamines, 7/05
Identity Theft, 6/05
Marijuana Laws, 2/05
Supreme Court's Future, 1/05

Education
Academic Freedom, 10/05
Intelligent Design, 7/05
No Child Left Behind, 5/05
Gender and Learning, 5/05

Environment
Nuclear Energy, 3/06
Climate Change, 1/06
Saving the Oceans, 11/05
Endangered Species Act, 6/05
Alternative Energy, 2/05

Health/Safety
Rising Health Costs, 4/06
Pension Crisis, 2/06
Avian Flu Threat, 1/06
Domestic Violence, 1/06
Disaster Preparedness, 11/05
Birth-Control Debate, 6/05
Marijuana Laws, 2/05

International Affairs
Future of European Union, 10/05
War in Iraq, 10/05

Social Trends
Controlling the Internet, 5/06
American Indians, 4/06
Future of Feminism, 4/06

Terrorism/Defense
Port Security, 4/06
Presidential Power, 2/06

Youth
Bullying, 2/05
Teen Driving, 1/05

Upcoming Reports

War on Drugs, 6/2/06
Impact of Blogs, 6/9/06
Pork-Barrel Politics, 6/16/06
Reviving Downtowns, 6/23/06
Drinking on Campus, 6/30/06
Latin America, 7/21/06

ACCESS

CQ Researcher is available in print and online. For access, visit your library or www.cqresearcher.com.

STAY CURRENT

To receive notice of upcoming *CQ Researcher* reports, or learn more about *CQ Researcher* products, subscribe to the free e-mail newsletters, *CQ Researcher Alert!* and *CQ Researcher News*: www.cqpress.com/newsletters.

PURCHASE

To purchase a *CQ Researcher* report in print or electronic format (PDF), visit www.cqpress.com or call 866-427-7737. Single reports start at $10. Bulk purchase discounts and electronic rights licensing are also available.

SUBSCRIBE

A full-service *CQ Researcher* print subscription—including 44 reports a year, monthly index updates, and a bound volume—is $688 for academic and public libraries, $667 for high school libraries, and $827 for media libraries. Add $25 for domestic postage.

CQ Researcher Online offers a backfile from 1991 and a number of tools to simplify research. For pricing information, call 800-834-9020, ext. 1906, or e-mail librarysales@cqpress.com.

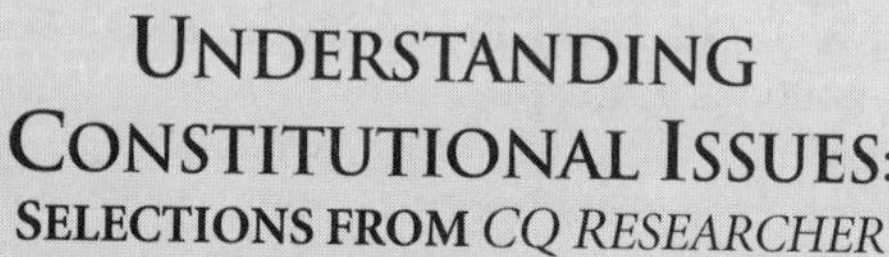

Understanding Constitutional Issues focuses on four key themes — governmental powers and structure, security, liberty, and equality — to help students develop a deeper understanding of the relation between current events and constitutional issues and principles. Integrating eighteen *CQ Researcher* reports, *Understanding Constitutional Issues* makes important connections clear, such as those between civil liberties and security; and privacy and liberty.

June 2004 • 8 1/2 x 11 • Approx. 432 pages • Paperback • ISBN 1-56802-885-7 • $39.95

To Order: Call Toll-Free: 866.4CQ.PRESS (427.7737)
Fax: 800.380.3810 • Web: www.cqpress.com
E-mail: customerservice@cqpress.com

CQ Press, 1255 22nd Street, NW, Suite 400 • Washington, DC 20037

CQ Researcher

Published by CQ Press, a division of Congressional Quarterly Inc.

cqresearcher.com

War on Drugs

Should nonviolent drug users be subject to arrest?

President Bush's anti-drug campaign has increasingly focused on a law-enforcement model that attacks the "supply side" of the illegal drug industry — traffickers, smugglers and users — rather than on helping users through prevention and treatment, the so-called demand side. He also would like more middle and high schools to conduct random drug tests, although few have signed on. And although the Food and Drug Administration in April declared that smoked marijuana lacks any known medicinal properties, 12 states now bar state prosecution of those who use marijuana for medical purposes. The number of people arrested annually on marijuana-related charges has skyrocketed — from 400,000 in the 1980s to about 700,000 — partly because low-level drug offenders now can be diverted to one of more than 1,750 new "drug courts," where their cases are dismissed if they stay straight. The Bush administration says it has struck the right balance between treatment and law enforcement.

A Coast Guardsman watches over 11.5 tons of cocaine seized in the war on drugs. Since 2001, the United States has increased by 64 percent the amount spent on interdiction, while drug treatment and prevention funds have increased by 2 percent.

INSIDE THIS REPORT

CQ Researcher • June 2, 2006 • www.cqresearcher.com
Volume 16, Number 21 • Pages 481-504

CQ PRESS

RECIPIENT OF SOCIETY OF PROFESSIONAL JOURNALISTS AWARD FOR EXCELLENCE ◆ AMERICAN BAR ASSOCIATION SILVER GAVEL AWARD

WAR ON DRUGS

Cover: A Coast Guardsman watches over 11.5 tons of cocaine seized in the war on drugs. Since 2001, the United States has increased by 64 percent the amount spent to halt illegal drug shipments, destroy foreign coca fields and arrest dealers and users, as treatment and prevention funds increased by 2 percent. (USCG photo/Petty Officer Brian N. Leshak)

CQ Researcher

June 2, 2006
Volume 16, Number 21

MANAGING EDITOR: Thomas J. Colin
ASSISTANT MANAGING EDITOR: Kathy Koch
ASSOCIATE EDITOR: Kenneth Jost
STAFF WRITERS: Marcia Clemmitt, Peter Katel, Pamela M. Prah
CONTRIBUTING WRITERS: Rachel S. Cox, Sarah Glazer, David Hosansky, Patrick Marshall, Tom Price
DESIGN/PRODUCTION EDITOR: Olu B. Davis
ASSISTANT EDITOR: Melissa J. Hipolit

CQ PRESS
A Division of
Congressional Quarterly Inc.

SENIOR VICE PRESIDENT/PUBLISHER: John A. Jenkins
DIRECTOR, LIBRARY PUBLISHING: Kathryn C. Suárez
DIRECTOR, EDITORIAL OPERATIONS: Ann Davies

CONGRESSIONAL QUARTERLY INC.
CHAIRMAN: Paul C. Tash
VICE CHAIRMAN: Andrew P. Corty
PRESIDENT/EDITOR IN CHIEF: Robert W. Merry

CQ Researcher (ISSN 1056-2036) is printed on acid-free paper. Published weekly, except March 24, July 7, July 14, Aug. 4, Aug. 11, Nov. 24, Dec. 22 and Dec. 29, by CQ Press, a division of Congressional Quarterly Inc. Annual full-service subscriptions for institutions start at $667. For pricing, call 1-800-834-9020, ext. 1906. To purchase a *CQ Researcher* report in print or electronic format (PDF), visit www.cqpress.com or call 866-427-7737. Single reports start at $10. Bulk purchase discounts and electronic-rights licensing are also available. Periodicals postage paid at Washington, D.C., and additional mailing offices. POSTMASTER: Send address changes to *CQ Researcher*, 1255 22nd St., N.W., Suite 400, Washington, DC 20037.

War on Drugs

BY PETER KATEL

THE ISSUES

Pablo Rayo Montaño and Rita Faye Myers are about as different as two people could be. But America's 33-year-old war on drugs targeted them both with equal tenacity.

Montaño smuggled more than 15 tons of cocaine a month from Colombia to the United States and Europe, according to the U.S. Drug Enforcement Administration (DEA). His enterprise was so vast, the DEA says, he had his own "navy," including a small submarine. [1]

Myers, by contrast, was anything but an international drug lord. A longtime drug addict, she is serving 21 years in an Alabama prison for forging a prescription for the synthetic opiate Dilaudid.

Since President Richard M. Nixon declared "war" on drugs in 1973, federal spending on the anti-drug campaign — stopping big-time drug smugglers and arresting users and sellers — has increased 30-fold — from $420 million in 1973 to $12.7 billion this fiscal year. [2]

And while drug use has shrunk since the peak years of the late 1970s and early '80s, half of the nation's 2005 high-school graduates reported having used an illegal drug at some point; the number of new heroin users has increased to more than 100,000 a year; and local officials across the country say methamphetamine production and use are devastating their communities and over-burdening their resources. [3]

But federal drug policy continues to focus on marijuana use because it is seen as a "gateway" to harder drugs, even as some drug experts call the gateway theory a myth. As a result of a shift in federal drug policy, drug arrests have nearly tripled since 1980. About 1.7 million people were arrested on drug charges in 2004, about 700,000 of them for marijuana. [4] "The drug war met its goal of arrest and incarceration and seizures," says Kevin Zeese of Takoma Park, Md., president of Common Sense for Drug Policy and a longtime writer and activist on drug law, "yet the problem has gotten worse."

Drug-war advocates call such assertions absurd. The vast majority of Americans don't use illegal drugs, and "drug use by teens is going down," notes the Web site of the St. Petersburg, Fla.-based Drug Free America Foundation. "That's a failure?" As for marijuana, the country's most widely abused drug, the foundation cites 2004 testimony by National Institute on Drug Abuse (NIDA) Director Nora Volkow, who said "early exposure to marijuana increased the likelihood of a life filled with drug and addiction problems." [5]

AP Photo/*Daily Post-Athenian*/Ben Benton

Workers from the McMinn County Sheriff's Department clean up the toxic remains of a suspected methamphetamine lab in Niota, Tenn. Local officials across the country say the federal government's continued focus on marijuana users is giving short shrift to the growing problem of meth abuse.

Such personal and social costs are reason enough to maintain the drug war, say enforcement advocates. "How are we doing in the war on cancer? Or crime? Or poverty?" asks Robert L. DuPont, former drug czar under presidents Gerald R. Ford and Jimmy Carter, when asked if the war on drugs is working. "Drugs are the only [societal] problem where [some critics say] the correct answer is supposed to be zero."

In fact, he says, drug prohibition has been far more effective in reducing drug use than the use of persuasion — without arrests — has been in reducing cigarette and alcohol use, which also impose serious personal and social costs.

However, critics of the government's approach to the drug war argue that officials should emphasize reducing demand by funding drug treatment programs rather than spending billions of dollars attacking the supply of drugs by trying to eradicate Latin American coca fields, halt illegal drug shipments and lock up users like Myers.

But the Bush administration insists that it has struck the right balance and is reaping success on both fronts. "We put as much emphasis on driving down demand as on attacking supply," says David Murray, assistant to White House Office of National Drug-Control Policy (ONDCP) Director John P. Walters. The administration vowed to reduce drug use among young people by 25 percent over five years, Murray explains. "We're four years out, and we're at a

Enforcement Shifts Focus

Although cocaine use remained steady and marijuana use has risen only slightly since 1991, marijuana arrests have increased steadily while cocaine arrests have dramatically declined. Critics say the shift is the result of federal law-enforcement policies that focus on marijuana because it is the most commonly used drug and some say it is a "gateway" to harder drug use.

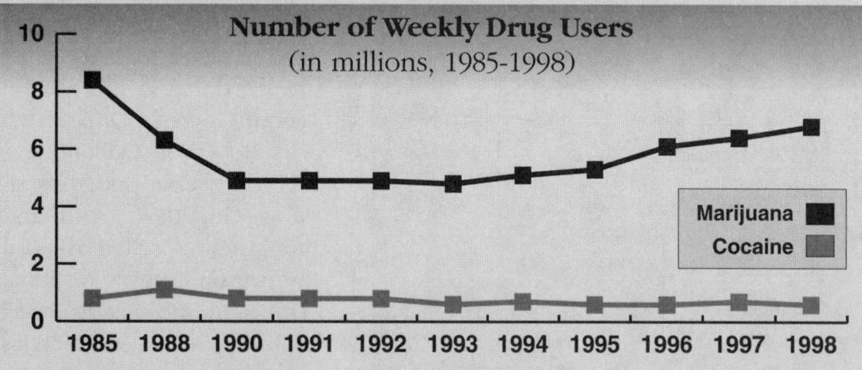

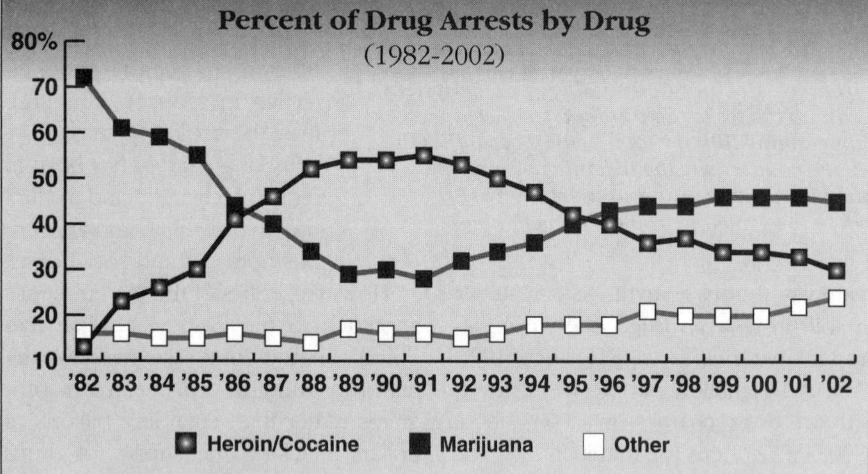

Source: "Substance Abuse: The Nation's Number One Health Problem," U.S. Department of Health and Human Services; "The War on Marijuana," The Sentencing Project

19 percent reduction. In Colombia . . . cultivation [of drug crops] is down and their productivity is dropping."

But Sen. Charles E. Grassley, R-Iowa, chairman of the Senate International Narcotics Control Caucus, dismisses the ONDCP's drug-eradication statistics as "mumbo-jumbo" (*see p. 496*).

Meanwhile, at home, drug-war strategy has evolved into a mixture of arrest, court-supervised drug treatment and — often in the case of repeat offenders like Myers — incarceration. Even some advocates of imprisonment concede that punishments for users can far outweigh the crimes, but they say the judicial system is frustrated by repeat offenders.

"This is a little, old woman who has a sixth-grade education — a pleasant, nice person who was an addict," says District Judge Orson L. "Pete" Johnson, after Myers appeared before him in February charged with smoking crack cocaine. That arrest violated her parole on the Dilaudid charge.

Circuit Judge Julian King of Talladega, Ala. — who had handed down Myers' 21-year sentence — acknowledges that Myers "has a sickness" but cites her record of past convictions, failed treatment, missed court dates and flouted probation rules. "I send people to drug rehab constantly," he explains, but "it's hard to treat someone unless the person is willing to seek help. She had been afforded help in the past, and it hadn't been very successful."

In drug-war jargon, Myers has not responded to "demand reduction" — drug prevention and treatment. Law-enforcement activities, especially those that target drug shipments and traffickers, are defined as "supply reduction." For 2007, President Bush is proposing boosting supply-side funding from about 62 percent in 2006 to about 65 percent of the anti-drug budget, while demand-reduction programs would drop from 38 percent to about 36 percent. [6]

John Carnevale, an economist who served in the ONDCP during the Clinton administration, says that during Bush's six years in office, there has been "a real shift in resources" from demand reduction to supply reduction. Compared to 2001, when the last Clinton-era budget was in effect, he says, Bush's latest budget proposal would step up demand-side funding by about 2 percent, while supply-side funding will have jumped 64 percent. Meanwhile, Carnevale says, "I don't see much of an effect in terms of reducing consumption." (*See graph, p. 485.*)

But Murray says looking at federal dollars alone is misleading, because federal agencies are better suited to supply-side work, while states and localities are better at treatment. "The federal government can't neglect the border," Murray says. "And the city of

San Francisco doesn't send troops to Colombia to help eradicate coca."

Crop eradication aside, the DEA and other federal agencies are engaged in a constant battle with foreign and domestic traffickers. Along with Montaño's capture, results this year include the April arrests of 16 people in the United States and eight in Colombia in connection with an alleged money-laundering and drug-smuggling operation that funneled $7 million a week in drug profits back to South America. And the year began with discovery of a lighted, ventilated, 2,400-foot-long tunnel — along with two tons of marijuana — being used for smuggling drugs into the country under the border with Mexico. [7]

However, the Bush administration *is* proposing a major increase — from about $10 million to $69 million — in federal funds for "drug courts," which cropped up across the country in the 1990s. The courts were set up to keep drug offenders out of jail by providing a period of court-supervised treatment, during which defendants submit to periodic drug tests and often are required to get and keep a full-time job. Generally, their charges are dropped if they pass the drug tests, while defendants who fail the tests are jailed for short periods of time or face standard court proceedings where they might get longer jail terms. [8]

Since the first drug court opened in Miami in 1989, more than 1,750 have been established nationwide handling at least 70,000 defendants a year. A 2005 Government Accountability Office (GAO) study found that recidivism by drug-court defendants can run 35 percent less than in conventional courts, although not all drug courts are that successful. The study noted that defendants run the gamut from nonviolent first-time arrestees to people with "extensive criminal histories" and records of failed drug treatment. [9]

Even though drug courts generally have been successful at reducing recidivism, some analysts say they are part of the reason arrest rates have risen so steeply. More people are being arrested for minor drug charges, such as marijuana possession, today than in the past because the police know the non-jail drug court option exists, says Marc Mauer, assistant director of The Sentencing Project, a nonprofit that advocates eliminating sentencing disparities. "That's either good news or bad news, depending how you look at it."

Of the 500,000 inmates serving time on federal, state and local drug charges of all kinds, most weren't jailed just for possession. [10] The Sentencing Project found that 54 percent of prisoners doing time on state drug charges were sentenced for trafficking, while 43 percent were charged with either possession or possession with intent to distribute. [11]

As for the most popular illegal drug, "Marijuana defendants are less likely to end up in prison," says Mauer. "[So] the system does filter out high cases and low cases to a certain extent." Still, some 30,000 state and federal prisoners are doing time for marijuana, he says, slightly fewer than half of whom are high-level players who'd been involved in smuggling, money-laundering or trafficking. More than 7,000 marijuana prisoners are nonviolent first offenders who weren't trafficking. [12]

In any case, marijuana-prohibition advocates have already lost the war of ideas, contends Ethan Nadelmann, executive director of the New York-based Drug Policy Alliance. "We have a rising cultural acceptance of marijuana," he says, pointing out that 96 million Americans — about 40 percent of the population 12 years old and up — have tried pot at least once, according to government statistics. [13]

Nevertheless, drug czar Walters made a point of announcing this year's drug-war strategy — with a continued focus on stopping marijuana use — in Denver, Colo., where citizens voted 54-46 percent last November to decriminalize possession of one ounce or less of marijuana. "Marijuana is the single biggest cause of [drug] treatment in this country by far," said Walters. [14]

Interdiction, Arrests Get Bigger Budget Bite

During the Bush administration, a growing proportion of the drug-control budget has been earmarked for eradicating Latin American coca fields, interdicting illegal drug shipments and arresting drug dealers and users. Since 2001, the amount spent on such "supply-reduction" activities jumped 64 percent — from $5 billion to $8.2 billion — while the amount spent on drug treatment and prevention, called demand reduction, increased only 2 percent, from $4.4 billion to only $4.5 billion.

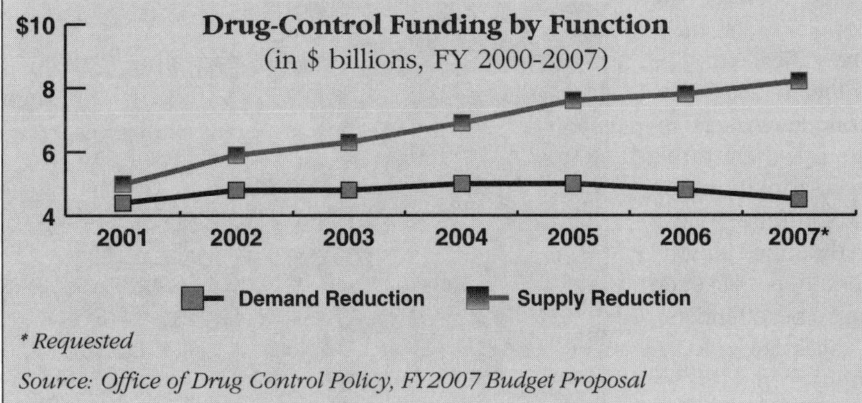

* Requested

Source: Office of Drug Control Policy, FY2007 Budget Proposal

But Walters' continued emphasis on going after marijuana use is leading even some drug-war advocates to complain that the federal government is giving short shrift to the growing problem of methamphetamine abuse. "The ONDCP has done nothing but repeat its intention to provide a methamphetamine strategy," the House Government Reform Committee said in a March analysis of federal drug policy. [15]

Meanwhile, the popularity of hard-line strategies may be fading. In 2004, New York lawmakers reduced the state's notoriously harsh "Rockefeller" laws mandating lengthy sentences of even first-time offenders.

Still, law-enforcement officials acknowledge that street arrests, which account for the bulk of drug detentions, fall most heavily on poor neighborhoods, where many drug deals take place in the open. "What we do well is arrest and prosecute," says David Soares, elected as district attorney of New York's Albany County in 2004 as an opponent of the state's Rockefeller laws. "What we don't do well is stabilize these communities [which] are suffering from . . . a lot of poverty."

As the drug war grinds on, it provokes some of these intensely debated questions:

Should drug use be treated as a law-enforcement issue or a public-health matter?

Those who advocate decriminalizing drugs argue that the urge to take mind-altering substances lies deep in the human psyche. Attempts to eradicate drug use are doomed and represent an impractical impulse to try to control natural behavior, say supporters of legalization.

"Law enforcement should be involved at the fringes — enforcing Driving Under the Influence, for instance," says Zeese of Common Sense for Drug Policy. "As far as personal consumption goes, the more important concern is making sure that people have access to health care if they get in trouble. But the vast majority don't end up needing treatment."

AP Photo/Steve Ruark

Drug-free for 11 years, James Craig inspects a space his flourishing demolition company recently cleared out. After 31 years as a heroin and cocaine addict, Craig says a Maryland drug court helped him finally kick the habit — something 22 methadone programs and more than a dozen drug treatment programs failed to do. The nation's 1,750 drug courts keep 70,000 non-violent drug offenders out of jail by providing them with court-supervised treatment.

One veteran drug warrior doesn't mind conceding that point, even as he upholds the law-enforcement approach. "Not everybody who's smoked marijuana needs treatment," says DuPont, the former drug-policy director who runs two consulting companies on drugs in schools and the workplace. What they need, he says, is a solid reason to quit, and getting arrested is enough to scare many people straight.

They should quit, he says, because society shouldn't have to bear the enormous costs of drug abuse. A 2002 ONDCP report estimates that drug abuse costs the nation $180.9 billion a year in lost productivity and spending on law enforcement, prisons and health care. [16]

Prohibition is what makes those costs so high, say decriminalization advocates.

"Our approach now is that we make it as dangerous as possible to use drugs," says Allan Clear, executive director of the New York-based Harm Reduction Coalition. "That's why so many people are living with HIV and Hepatitis C related to injection-drug use." Drug laws prohibit people from buying syringes over the counter, he said, so people have to share needles, adding to both infection rates.

The coalition provides training and advice to needle-exchange programs in New York and Oakland, Calif., which provide clean injecting tools to heroin, cocaine or methamphetamine addicts in return for used syringes. "Harm-reduction" doctrine accepts that some people will continue using drugs, notwithstanding the illegality. Hence, Clear says, "You must be able to help them protect themselves and their families from total destruction," while arresting those who commit crimes to finance their addictions.

Law-enforcement advocates — and some recovering addicts as well — argue that criminal penalties prevent drug trafficking from expanding and force drug abusers to get treatment — in effect, saving their lives. "After experiencing this environment for 60 or 90 days, they have these epiphanies," says a recovering addict at Regional Addiction Prevention Inc. (RAP), a 36-year-old treatment program based in Washington, D.C. "But someone [first] said, 'Your option is this, or I'm going to revoke your probation or parole.' "

Hubert Williams, president of the non-profit Police Foundation, favors police pressure but argues that it's not being aimed at the right target. "If we want to use the standard of the number of people we arrest — about 1.7 million people get busted every year — but these numbers deal with quantity not quality. We're busting people for use — not trafficking. We need a new strategy that doesn't focus on the ghetto and the inner city, . . . [one] that brings together intelligence and analyses on the big gangs — [like] the Bloods, the Crips, the Jamaican posses, Russian Mafia. Bust them and bring them down."

Nadelmann, of the Drug Policy Alliance, says drug use should be decriminalized, with police action reserved for those who harm other people. And even drug treatment shouldn't always be mandatory. "It's not even clear that drug use should be an issue of public health if it doesn't present public health problems," he says.

When drug use is defined as a crime, Nadelmann says, poor people inevitably bear the brunt of drug enforcement because better-off people with drug problems get sent to psychotherapists. Poor people get stuck with court-supervised programs in which success is measured by testing "clean" for drug use.

However, Albany County District Attorney Soares fears the effects of simply decriminalizing drugs. While he advocates sentencing reform and expanding treatment opportunities, he says, "I am not for legalization. I have seen the devastation alcohol has wreaked in communities. I don't believe in making more of these substances available."

RAP's staff trainer and clinical supervisor Rahman Abdullah — a recovered heroin addict — also opposes decriminalization. But he says policymakers don't seem to understand that the drug war has been accompanied by a steady climb in violence and desperation in poor communities, as each crop of street drug dealers is replaced by an even more violent generation. "All the young people born right now, they're going to start thinking that this is the norm, and they're going to take it a little further."

Should the federal government focus its drug-enforcement strategy on interdiction?

Tension has persisted for four decades between promoters of a "supply-side" approach to drug-control policy and those recommending a "demand-side" approach. Supply-siders say the government should focus on eradicating drug crops abroad and seizing drugs either being smuggled into the United States or domestically grown or manufactured. Demand-siders advocate reducing U.S. demand for illegal drugs by spending more money on addiction treatment and programs to persuade users to quit taking drugs and youngsters to refrain from taking them in the first place.

The federal government argues that cutting off the supply of drugs and shrinking the number of users are both essential. "These things have to be in balance," says Murray, drug czar Walters' assistant. "If [traffickers] don't have money, they can't buy protection. How do you attack the market? You can go after it one way or the other, but you'd better do both simultaneously; they augment each other."

But some drug-war veterans say that supply-side spending has gotten far more attention from the Bush administration. As former Clinton ONDCP official Carnevale points out, interdiction funding increased dramatically — by $3.2 billion — between 2001 and Bush's proposed 2007 budget, while demand-reduction funding increased by only $49 million.

"You can see a real shift in resources. The shift is so dramatic, and in my mind irrational," says Carnevale, who, in fact, supports the war against drugs. "[But] I don't see much of an effort in terms of reducing consumption."

Moderate critics like Carnevale stop short of condemning supply-side efforts. "If we wanted to impact the amount of people using drugs," says Police Foundation president Williams, "then we've got to suppress the amount of drugs available for abuse."

Opponents of interdiction, on the other hand, are more blunt. "Interdiction and eradication have consistently made the drug problem worse," says Zeese, of Common Sense for Drug Policy. For example, he explains, after the Reagan administration shut down seaborne and airborne marijuana smuggling from Colombia in the early 1980s, "The Colombians switched to cocaine, which is more profitable and easier to smuggle. So we had a giant cocaine glut, which led to crack."

Because there was an excess of cocaine on the market, drug sellers aggressively began pushing crack cocaine — the cheaper, more addictive, smokable form of cocaine — which devastated America's inner cities in the late 1980s, triggering a crime wave characterized by drive-by shootings, teenagers killing each other in drug turf wars and unprecedented rates of drug addiction.

That record of violence raises the pressure on federal officials to stop the drug problem at the source of most illicit drugs — farmers' fields and clandestine laboratories in Latin America and Asia. But critics of the interdiction strategy say it can't possibly overcome socioeconomic imbalances between nations. "I don't blame any foreign country, especially a poor country, that exports drugs to a rich country that demands it," says Clear of the Harm Reduction Coalition.

And, though crop-eradication programs typically include programs to provide farmers with alternative crops, these are never as profitable, Clear says. "You have to offer farmers a viable alternative."

Even supply-reduction advocates like the Police Foundation's Williams concede that deeper issues are also at play. Demand-reduction proponents like Zeese insist that supply isn't the overriding issue. "At some point we have to begin to ask the question: What is

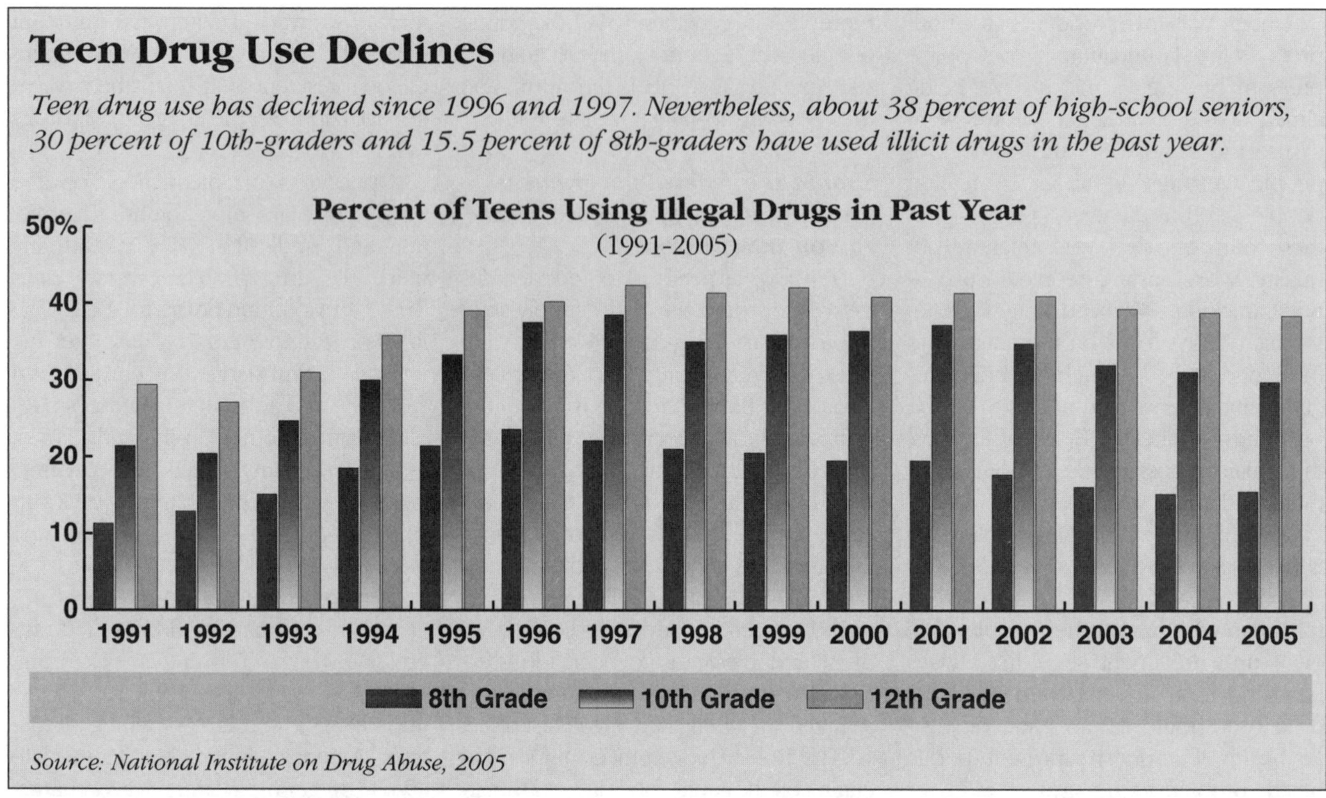

Teen Drug Use Declines

Teen drug use has declined since 1996 and 1997. Nevertheless, about 38 percent of high-school seniors, 30 percent of 10th-graders and 15.5 percent of 8th-graders have used illicit drugs in the past year.

Source: National Institute on Drug Abuse, 2005

it that makes Americans, particularly our youth, so much in need of escaping from the psychological environments in which they are situated?" he says.

But the moderates say advocates of both interdiction and demand reduction should acknowledge that drug use will always exist. Acting against supply "simply drives up the street price, and therefore increases the crime and all the other things that go along with it," says David Keene, chairman of the American Conservative Union (ACU), who quickly adds that doing nothing about supply also bothers him. "Given . . . human nature, you will never eradicate the problem; you want something that keeps it under control."

Like its predecessors, the Bush administration seems to share Keene's conclusion. The White House ONDCP's 2006 drug control strategy document speaks about "reducing" drug use, not eliminating it, and the agency says "healing drug users" is a priority. [17]

Some fervent drug warriors voice skepticism. In a lengthy analysis of administration strategy, the House Committee on Government Reform, whose Criminal Justice, Drug Policy and Human Resources Subcommittee oversees drug-war efforts, concluded that the administration's rhetoric about balancing supply-side and demand-side programs was empty.

"Since prevention comprises only 11.7 percent of the entire FY 2007 drug-control budget and represents a 19.3 percent decrease in prevention funding from that enacted in FY 2006, the committee questions the administration's claim that it has 'set a bold agenda' in its prevention efforts," the committee reported. [18]

Should middle and high schools randomly test students for drug use?

For the Bush administration, screening middle- and high-school students at random for evidence of drug use occupies a top spot in the drug-war priority list. "The aim here is not to punish children but to send them this message: We love you, and we don't want to lose you," Bush said in his 2004 State of the Union address. [19]

Despite the administration's promotion of testing, the number of schools actually testing students remains small. So far random testing — in public schools at least — is limited to students involved in extracurricular programs, in part because it's the only testing that has withstood a court challenge. In 2002 the U.S. Supreme Court ruled 5-4 that random drug tests of students participating in extracurricular activities was constitutional because they travel and room together in out-of-town competitions and meetings, and thus have a reduced expectation of privacy. [20]

Random testing of all public school students — even if a student does not show any outward signs of using drugs — has not become a widespread practice, in part because administrators fear being sued on Fourth Amendment grounds for searching a student without just cause.

Despite the Supreme Court's blessing, however, most public schools also

Will Nevada Legalize Pot?

As America's premiere adult playground, Nevada has always pushed the envelope on cultural mores. Modern legalized casino gambling was born there, and a 1971 law legalized brothels in most Nevada counties. [1] Now Nevada could become the first state to treat marijuana like alcohol — making it legal, but regulated and taxed.

In November state voters will decide whether adults in Nevada can legally possess up to one ounce of pot for their own pleasure. Only those over 21 would be allowed to buy pot, and the penalty for killing or injuring someone while driving under the influence of either alcohol or marijuana would be doubled to 40 years. [2]

The Marijuana Policy Project (MPP) wrote the proposed law and organized the campaign to sell it to voters in a referendum. The nonprofit has been campaigning for 11 years to abolish criminal penalties for marijuana use — experience that led them to name the Nevada organization the Committee to Regulate and Control Marijuana. Drug-war critics have always been turned off by the word "legalization," says Ethan Nadelmann, executive director of Drug Policy Alliance, which is not involved in the Nevada campaign.

In most states, the modern marijuana decriminalization movement has involved only exempting "medical marijuana" users from prosecution, as Nevada did in 2000. * (*See p. 495.*) In addition, first and second offenses for possessing non-medical marijuana are only misdemeanors in Nevada and do not carry any jail time (although treatment may be required). Third offenses are also classified as misdemeanors but can bring a sentence of up to one year; any further offenses are felonies. [3]

But Nevada's present arrangement still results in thousands of arrests each year, says Neal Levine, campaign manager for the legalization drive. "We had 86,000 people sign the petition to put this on the ballot," he says. "We're saying, why not pull marijuana out of the criminal market . . . put it into a tightly regulated market where we can have sensible safeguards and have some control."

Surveys show the measure faces an uphill fight. A poll commissioned by the *Las Vegas Review-Journal* showed opinion running 56-34 against, with only 10 percent of those surveyed undecided. In 2004, the MPP failed to get a similar measure on the ballot, when 2,000 petition signatures from newly registered voters were disqualified. Two years before that, marijuana legalization was on the ballot — but lost by a 61-39 margin. Campaigners blame the defeat largely on the fact that the measure would have allowed up to three ounces of pot — which voters apparently felt was too much. [4]

Levine says his organization's polling shows opinion "roughly even." But Nadelmann says it is "highly unusual" for an initiative to emerge victorious with less than 50 percent going in. He calls the Nevada campaign "premature."

Stan Olsen, executive director for intergovernmental affairs of the Las Vegas Metropolitan Police Department, says, "People know what the drug culture has created in this country, and it's not a good thing. They know that the people pushing this are for one thing — getting loaded." A former lieutenant, Olsen says the medical marijuana law has worked well, but he dismisses the argument that ending marijuana prohibition would free police to pursue violent criminals. "You can say, 'Let's legalize burglary — it's nonviolent and happens when people aren't home.' "

But Levine says most Nevadans feel that arresting people just for smoking or possessing small quantities of marijuana makes no sense. And Nevada "is a very pragmatic state."

* During the late 1970s six states — Alaska, California, Colorado, Maine, Ohio and Oregon — decriminalized marijuana, but the laws were later repealed.

[1] Roger Dunstan, "History of Gambling in the United States," chapter II in *Gambling in California*, January 1997, California State Library [online, book-length study], www.library.ca.gov/CRB/97/03/Chapt2.html; and "The ultimate sin tax: Nevada considers taxing hookers," The Associated Press, 2/26/03, www.cnn.com/2003/US/West/02/26/brothel.tax.ap.

[2] "Regulation of Marijuana Initiative," www.regulatemarijuana.org/home/06init.

[3] "State-by-State Laws," National Organization for the Reform of Marijuana Laws, updated 9/22/05, www.norml.org/index.cfm?wtm_view=&Group_ID=4550.

[4] Ed Vogel, "Marijuana measure opposed," *Las Vegas Review-Journal*, April 11, 2006, p. B1; Ed Vogel, "Marijuana hearing rejected," *Las Vegas Review-Journal*, Sept. 29, 2004, p. B4.

don't randomly test kids involved in extracurricular activities. In fiscal 2005, only 55 of the nation's 14,000 school districts received U.S. Department of Education grants — which range from $65,000 to $300,000 — to finance drug-test programs, a department spokesman says. Those 55 districts oversee only 152 of the nation's 23,000 public high schools. [21]

However, the actual number of schools requiring drug tests is unknown, because some schools test without seeking federal grants. Based on press reports, the ONDCP estimates that up to 650 schools and school districts — how many of each is unknown — may be randomly testing students.

The National School Boards Association has no estimates of the number of schools conducting drug tests. "We don't care one way or the other," says association attorney Lisa E. Soronen. "We want them to have the option. This is a political issue that the Bush administration is interested in. We like to focus on things like student achievement."

As for the absence of official data on how many schools test, Soronen says, "It's been suggested to me that the government doesn't really want to know because not that many schools are doing it."

However, Drug czar Walters is leading the charge to expand the number of schools that randomly drug-test students. "I would say it is a keystone of our domestic policy," says Walters' assistant Murray. "It is fully accepted that addiction and dependency is a disease. Between the ages of 12 and 18, kids acquire a pattern of behavior. If they don't start during that time of great vulnerability, the likelihood of becoming dependent is remote."

But the University of Michigan's Institute for Social Research — whose annual "Monitoring the Future" survey is the leading source on national student drug consumption trends — says drug testing does not deter drug use. The institute's survey of 722 schools found that those that test for drugs and those that don't have virtually identical drug-use rates. [22]

But testing advocates immediately complained that schools that may have conducted a single drug test were lumped in with those that tested regularly. [23]

The criticism is valid, acknowledges Lloyd R. Johnston, a social psychologist who has directed the "Monitoring the Future" survey since it began in 1975. But, he ran a follow-up study, he says, that added data from 209 additional schools and distinguished between types of testing programs. The second survey also showed drug testing does not reduce drug consumption. In fact, it seemed to have the opposite effect: Schools with random drug testing showed 20.8 percent of students using illicit drugs — while schools with no testing showed a 16.7 percent rate. [24]

However, Johnston points out, "You can't conclude [based on those findings] that no form of drug testing would be effective," noting that the number of schools conducting random tests — only 0.8 percent of the sample — may be too small to draw definitive conclusions.

Drug-test boosters acknowledge that they lack comprehensive data showing that testing lowers drug use. But the absence doesn't temper their enthusiasm. "It has a certain logical, common-sense aspect to it — if people know that a test is possible and if they know there are some consequences to testing positive, they should be less likely to use," says Herbert Kleber, a psychiatrist who directs the substance abuse division of the Columbia University Medical School in New York and was deputy drug czar of demand reduction under President George H. W. Bush.

But Carnevale, another ONDCP veteran, says the drug-policy community's consensus on testing is that it's "silly," given the absence of treatment programs for kids who test positive. Otherwise, "What do you do with the information? Do you throw the students off the cheerleader team, call their parents?"

What should happen, drug-testing advocates say, is a temporary response. "There's no law-enforcement involvement, no expulsion," says Elizabeth Edwards, a school drug-test promoter with the Arizona High-Intensity Drug Trafficking Areas. [25] "[Usually,] it is a short-term suspension from extracurricular activity. Once a student is clean, he goes back to the activity."

In reality, a student who tests positive a second time "may get thrown off the team or expelled," says Nadelmann, of the Drug Policy Alliance. "The argument that this is not about punishment is a lie. If you push the proponents on that issue, they'll say, 'Well, there's got to be sanctions.' "

Still hovering in the background is the question of whether public schools should test *all* students. Logically speaking, "If you want to test, why wouldn't you want to test all students?" says Bill Bond of Paducah, Ky., a retired school principal who is an expert on testing matters for the National Association of Secondary School Principals, which takes no position on the issue.

Private schools are free to test all students, lawyers say, but a public school would likely be challenged on the grounds it was violating the constitutional prohibition against unreasonable searches and seizures by government entities. "It would certainly provoke litigation," says Graham Boyd, director of the American Civil Liberties Union's Drug Policy Reform Project, based in Santa Cruz, Calif.

Boyd represented a 13-year-old student and his father who sued the only public school known to have tried the approach. The challengers won, when U.S. District Judge Sam Cummings of Lubbock, Texas, ruled in 2001 that the Lockney Independent School District's universal student testing program exacted "a great price to citizens' constitutionally guaranteed rights to be secure in their 'persons, houses, papers, and effects.' "

The district didn't appeal the decision. [26] ■

BACKGROUND

The Pragmatic President

When President Nixon took office in 1969, America's consumption of illegal drugs was shifting from a hidden, marginal activity to a symbol of youth revolt and the basis of a new, underground economy. [27]

Until then, drugs had been slowly climbing the scale of government priorities.

Criminal-justice system jurisdiction over narcotics hadn't existed until 1912, when the United States joined the 1912 Hague Opium Convention, the first international accord to clamp down on opiates and cocaine. In 1930, Congress created the Bureau of Narcotics and in 1937 passed the Marijuana Tax Act, designed to prohibit marijuana use.

By the time Nixon began his first term, though, most college campuses seemed to be enveloped in a haze of marijuana

Continued on p. 492

Chronology

1900s-1950s

The federal government bans marijuana and addictive drugs, but illicit drug use gradually spreads, particularly among entertainers and artists.

1912
United States signs the Hague Opium Convention, which limits opium, heroin and cocaine to medical and other legitimate uses.

1937
The Marijuana Tax Act effectively bans growing, sale and consumption of marijuana.

1953
William S. Burroughs, a founding member of the "beat" movement of writers and poets, publishes the autobiographical *Junky* (later *Junkie*), the first modern account of heroin addiction.

1960s-1970s

The modern era of drug consumption begins, as "recreational" use spreads onto college campuses and into middle-class society.

1967
Thousands gather in San Francisco for the "Human Be-In," marked by open consumption of pot and the hallucinogen LSD.

1970s-1980s

Government's anti-drug policy undergoes major shifts under successive presidents, while drug-use patterns also change.

June 17, 1971
President Richard M. Nixon launches an "all-out offensive" on drugs, establishing the first White House anti-drug office.

1973
New York's Republican Gov. Nelson A. Rockefeller signs mandatory sentencing laws aimed at drug kingpins that snare many low-level dealers as well.

1979
Drug use peaks, as 25 million Americans — 14.1 percent of the population — regularly consume illegal substances.

1986
At President Ronald W. Reagan's behest, anti-drug budget for 1987 doubles to $3.9 billion, with most funds earmarked for law enforcement.

1988
Responding to new crack cocaine epidemic, Congress enacts mandatory-minimum sentences for crack possession.

1990s

Drug-policy debate intensifies, driven in part by beefed up anti-drug operations abroad and state "medical marijuana" initiatives.

1995
Lee Brown, President Clinton's first drug czar, resigns after Congress and the administration reject his emphasis on drug treatment.

1996
California voters pass an initiative shielding medical-marijuana users from state prosecution; 11 other states eventually follow suit.

2000s

U.S. Supreme Court rules on school drug tests and medical marijuana, while states pass medical-marijuana protection laws and arrests keep the pressure on drug users.

2000
The Clinton administration and the Colombian government launch "Plan Colombia," which aims to greatly reduce coca planting and cocaine production.

2002
In *Pottawatomie v. Earls*, the U.S. Supreme Court rules that students involved in competitive extracurricular activities may be tested for drug use even if they're not suspected of taking drugs.

2003
The University of Michigan's Institute for Social Research finds no evidence that school drug testing prevents drug use.

2004
Police arrest 1.7 million people nationwide for drug-law violations — 22 percent more than in 1995.

2005
Supreme Court rules, in *Gonzales* (originally, *Ashcroft*) *v. Raich*, that state medical marijuana laws can't overturn the federal prohibition on the drug.

March 9, 2006
House Committee on Government Reform criticizes administration's emphasis on law enforcement over treatment and the absence of a comprehensive strategy against methamphetamines.

Edgy Montana TV Ads Target Methamphetamines

A baby-faced boy sits on a ratty couch in a drug den and swears, "I'm trying it just this once." A group of emaciated, stringy-haired methamphetamine burnouts around him suddenly bursts out laughing, as if they've never heard anything so naive.

The edgiest, most intensive, anti-drug advertising campaign in the United States is under way in a seemingly unlikely setting: Montana — Big Sky Country. Edited, lit and scripted for fast pace, stark visuals and real teen-speak, the 30-second spots hammer home one point — don't take that first hit of meth. Most feature teenagers about to try the super-stimulant suddenly facing gaunt versions of themselves covered in sores, surrounded by filth and groveling for their next hit.

A growing methamphetamine plague accounts for 73 percent of all drug crime in Montana, compared to 17 percent nationwide. [1] Now, Montanans are getting the anti-meth message virtually everywhere they turn — on TV, radio, billboards and the Internet. [2]

"Our theory: if we can change attitudes, we can change behavior," says Thomas Siebel, creator and financier of the Montana Meth Project.

The 53-year-old software entrepreneur — who in 2005 sold his Siebel Systems company to Oracle Corp. for $5.5 billion — has long divided his time between California and Montana, where he owns ranches. [3] In recent years, he started hearing from a friend who is a sheriff that a methamphetamine epidemic was ruining lives, overwhelming social services and filling the jails and prisons in Montana.

Yet most Montanans were in denial, says Michael McGrath, the state's attorney general. "Not in our town," was what he heard as recently as five years ago.

Wondering what he could do, Siebel reasoned, "Law enforcement is important, treatment is important, but the area that was least resourced and least understood — and intuitively struck me as offering a lot of potential — was prevention."

So in 2005, he sank $5.5 million of his own money into a campaign designed to take anti-product advertising to places it's never been, because the traditional approach left him underwhelmed. "Most of the other ads that I see are talking down to kids, or rolling out some authority figure."

Instead, Siebel hired Tony Kaye — director of the 1998 film "American History X" about working-class American neo-Nazis — whose in-your-face style generated a lot of buzz. In addition to TV ads, the campaign broadcasts radio spots featuring real teenagers recounting their lives as meth addicts (the TV ads use actors).

"I came to the point where I was selling myself for meth," says a 15-year-old named Cindy from Browning, Mont., on one of the radio ads.

The ads have gotten the state's 928,000 residents talking. That's not surprising, because Siebel blanketed the state with the ads. During the first phase of the campaign, which ran from September to February, Siebel ran 60,000 minutes of radio and TV ads and 150 newspaper ad pages. "I can hardly go anywhere where this doesn't come up," says Attorney General McGrath.

But the ads aim to foster more than conversation. The project commissioned a comprehensive baseline survey in August 2005 of how teens perceive risk from methamphetamine use, and then conducted the first of a series of follow-ups in March. The March survey found that the percentage of teens believing that even trying methamphetamines once poses an increased risk of brain damage jumped from 70 percent to 80 percent. Those who perceived a greater risk of tooth decay from using meth rose from 48 percent to 59 percent and those who saw a greater risk of neglecting hygiene rose from 56 percent to 71 percent — all issues raised by the commercials. According to the survey report, increasing perception of risk is critical in convincing teens to avoid meth. [4]

Siebel, a Republican, tries to shy away from criticizing other approaches to fighting drug abuse. But he has his doubts. "Our rate of incarceration is greater than that of any population on planet Earth and doesn't seem to be having much of an effect. I suspect you could double the prison population in the state of Montana and it wouldn't have any effect on meth use. [It] seems to me we are dealing with . . . a mental disease as [if it were] a criminal problem."

[1] "Courts and Crime," in "Meth-Free Montana," Montana Department of Justice, 2006, http://methfreemt.org/courts.

[2] All the ads can be viewed and listened to at www.montanameth.org.

[3] Mike Musgrove, "Oracle to Buy Siebel for $5.53 Billion," *The Washington Post*, Sept. 13, 2005, p. D5.

[4] "Montana Meth Use & Attitudes Survey," Montana Meth Project, April 19, 2006, p. 9, www.montanameth.org/documents/MMP_Survey_April_2006.pdf.

Continued from p. 490

smoke. New psychedelic drugs such as LSD and long-established substances such as heroin and amphetamines were equally plentiful.

Unable or unwilling to ignore the issue, Nixon was the first president to attempt to create a policy aimed at curbing drug-taking. When he began his second term, the drug-control spending package for 1973 that he pushed through Congress amounted to $420 million — more than eight times the amount appropriated before his presidency.

Though Nixon resigned under pressure in 1974 for covering up the series of political scandals known collectively as "Watergate," some experts call his drug policy more sensible and better-managed than those of his successors. His policy included providing heroin addicts with methadone, which satisfies the drug craving without producing a high; establishing treatment programs for hard-core drug users rather than locking them up; and focusing efforts on drug addicts in poor neighborhoods rather than on middle-class youthful experimenters.

All in all, Nixon combined pragmatic actions with his hard-line "law and order" rhetoric, coining the "war" metaphor for the anti-drug campaign in 1973.

Nixon's strategy influenced the drug policies of his successors Ford and Carter, whose administrations spanned a period marked by widespread acceptance of drug use. In fact, President Carter in 1977 called for decriminalization of marijuana possession, and six states — Alaska, California, Colorado, Maine, Ohio and Oregon — passed laws decriminalizing marijuana during the late '70s, laws that were later repealed. Even former drug czar DuPont declared his support for decriminalization.

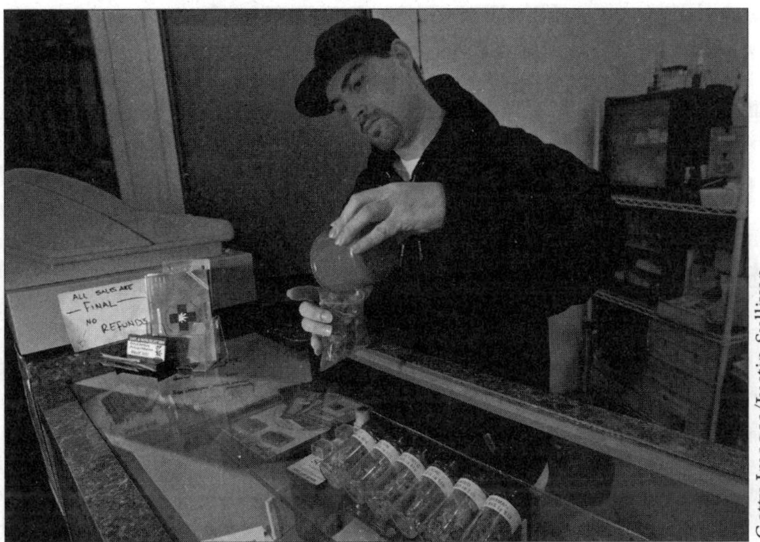

Getty Images/Justin Sullivan

Alternative Herbal Health Services worker Jason Beck packages medical marijuana in San Francisco. California is one of a dozen states that legalized pot use for medical purposes. The Food and Drug Administration in April declared that there is no scientific evidence supporting use of the drug for medical treatment.

By 1978-79, however — as drug use among youths was reaching an all-time high — an anti-drug backlash led by an Atlanta-based "parents movement" had developed. The movement eventually morphed into National Families in Action, an anti-drug lobbying group that became influential in the development of federal drug policy — particularly the government's tough stance against marijuana use among youths. [28]

Having risen to political prominence as governor of California during the 1964 Free Speech Movement revolt at the University of California at Berkeley, President Ronald W. Reagan took office in 1981 knowing the political value of taking a hard line on "culture war" issues. Before his administration was over, he had more than doubled the drug-enforcement budget from $800 million to $1.7 billion in 1987, with 90 percent of the money going to law enforcement rather than treatment. The following year, the anti-drug budget more than doubled again, to $3.9 billion. With that increase, the government did step up funding for drug-use prevention and education, including for first lady Nancy Reagan's "Just Say No" anti-drug campaign. But about three-quarters of the anti-drug budget was still being used to cut off supplies.

By 1987, fewer than 4 percent of the 6.5 million drug users who needed treatment had access to subsidized treatment.

Crack Boom

If Reagan had been president in the '70s, he would have been swimming against the tide. But a sudden change in the social climate surrounding drug use favored his hard-line approach.

Halfway through his administration, a new version of an old drug soared to terrifying popularity. Crack cocaine, as it was called, came to national attention in 1985 and seemingly overnight became the dominant drug in U.S. cities, including New York, Miami, Los Angeles, Detroit and in the shadow of the U.S. Congress in the slums of Washington, D.C. [29]

Crack was a new, cheap, smokable form of cocaine. Unlike cocaine's expensive powder form — which had enjoyed glamour status among musicians, celebrities, models and their hangers-on, as it had in the early 20th century — crack was cooked up in apartment ovens by drug traffickers who combined powder cocaine with baking soda. The resultant "rocks" made a popping sound as they were smoked, hence the name "crack." They also offered an immediate and powerful but short-lasting high. As crack addiction spread and more and more people sought to keep their high going, they created a booming consumer market. Dealers congregated in poor black and Latino neighborhoods. There, the sudden rush to buy crack coincided with a loss of job possibilities for uneducated young people, triggering a crime wave of historic proportions.

The crack market became the economic bedrock of entire communities and the source of livelihood for thousands of individuals. For them, nothing was as important as protecting their corner of the market. Nearly a decade of skyrocketing drug-related crimes ensued, often characterized by gunfights between rival gangs of dealers, which peaked in most cities in 1996. [30]

But one of its results is still being felt: the breakup of families, as crack-addicted parents — often single mothers — neglected or abandoned their children, who were left to relatives or in the care of foster parents. In New York alone, child abuse and neglect cases skyrocketed from 36,305 in 1985 to 59,353 in 1989.

Interdiction Campaign

Demand for crack fueled a cocaine processing and smuggling business based in Colombia, where traffickers soared to prosperity virtually overnight. They were swimming in wealth that went far beyond what marijuana profits had offered. The *narcotraficantes* built palatial homes and gunned down anyone who got in their way, up to and including judges, public officials and even a presidential candidate, Luís Carlos Galán, murdered in 1989 by a hit-man for drug kingpin Pablo Escobar. [31]

Smugglers were brazenly shipping the cocaine into the United States by the planeload, often offloading their cargoes in remote areas of the South and Southwest. The volume of cocaine being smuggled into the United States from Colombia became so enormous that traffickers set up shop in the United States, typically in Miami, bringing with them their lavish lifestyles and ruthless business practices. By the late 1980s, killings by "cocaine cowboys" outraged Floridians and set alarm bells ringing in Washington.

The Reagan administration set up a South Florida Task Force under the National Narcotic Border Interdiction System, an inter-agency group made up of members of the DEA and the U.S. Customs Service and headed by then-Vice President George H. W. Bush. By the time Bush became president in 1988, the stage was set for even more dramatic action.

Crack was generating so much violence and misery that 35 percent of the public, according to one survey, considered drugs the nation's top priority. In Washington, D.C., alone, the number of murders rose by 64 percent in 1988. "Take my word for it," Bush vowed in his inaugural address. "This scourge will stop!" [32]

In 1989 Bush ordered the U.S. invasion of Panama and the toppling of its strongman, Gen. Manuel Noriega, partly on the grounds that Noriega was wanted on U.S. drug-trafficking charges. In 1992, Noriega was convicted of eight out of 10 charges and sentenced to 40 years in prison. Bush hailed the conviction as a "major victory against the drug lords." [33]

Meanwhile, Congress, too, was eager to show leadership and to prove that it was tough on crime. At the end of 1988, lawmakers created a new Office of National Drug Control Policy — to be based in the White House — whose Cabinet-rank director would coordinate the 30-odd federal agencies involved in the drug war. [34]

The first director was William J. Bennett, an aggressive, conservative ideologue who made up in combativeness what he lacked in background on the drug issue. His thundering that drug-taking and drug-decriminalization advocacy grew from moral decay set him against even some of his staff who favored expanding drug treatment opportunities. Bennett argued arrest would force people into treatment. [35]

However, the biggest success of Bush's targeting of foreign drug kingpins occurred after the new Clinton administration had taken over. In 1993, Colombian police, aided by U.S. Army "Delta Force" operatives, tracked down and killed Escobar, the most notorious of the Colombian cocaine tycoons. [36]

War on Pot

President Bill Clinton took office as the first president to have admitted ingesting an illegal drug. His insistence that he "didn't inhale" when trying marijuana as a Rhodes Scholar in England in the late '60s was roundly ridiculed. [37]

Drug use came to touch Clinton's life in another way as well. As governor of Arkansas, he'd been notified that his half-brother, Roger, who had become hooked on cocaine, was under investigation for dealing the drug. Roger eventually was arrested, pleaded guilty to trafficking and served a year in prison. While campaigning, Bill Clinton cited the episode in rejecting calls to decriminalize drugs. "If drugs were legal, I don't think he'd be alive today," he said of his brother. [38]

However, Roger Clinton had also benefited from drug treatment, and Clinton favored expanding treatment. After taking office he proposed increasing spending on treatment and cutting back on interdiction.

But in 1993, when a new drug-use survey showed that the number of high-school kids smoking marijuana was going up again, Clinton's past left him vulnerable to predictable attacks for being soft on drugs. So his 1994 budget proposed putting more police on the streets and locking up three-time felons. [39]

In this climate, Clinton's first drug czar, former New York police commissioner Lee Brown, resigned in 1995 after both Congress and the administration rebuffed his calls for emphasizing treatment over incarceration. Clinton replaced Brown with retired Gen. Barry McCaffrey, a combat veteran of Vietnam and the Gulf War whom no one could accuse of being soft on any threat to the nation.

McCaffrey, who also had headed the Army's Southern Command that oversaw drug-eradication efforts in Bolivia and Peru, favored stepping up interdiction along the U.S.-Mexico border. But he also came to favor drug treatment. And he frequently made a show of rejecting the "war" metaphor for anti-drug efforts. Instead, he called drugs a "cancer."

The late 1990s saw the beginnings of a potential new drug epidemic. Use of methamphetamine, an addictive super-stimulant, spread east and south from California and Hawaii. Rural communities in the West and South proved especially receptive to the drug, which proved particularly devastating to families, because meth-addicted parents are notoriously neglectful of their children. [40]

By 2005 the National Association of Counties called methamphetamine the No. 1 drug problem for local governments. Though experts disagree on whether the meth boom was morphing into a full-blown national epidemic, there is no dispute about the damage the drug causes to individuals and families, including — in some reported cases — irreversible brain damage. ■

CURRENT SITUATION

Politics vs. Science

Meanwhile, the controversy surrounding the medical potential of marijuana remains the soft spot in the government's continuing war on drugs. Since 1996 a dozen states have exempted anyone smoking pot for medical reasons from state criminal penalties, despite federal officials' admonitions about the danger of loosening prohibitions on marijuana. As recently as January, 2006, Rhode Island lawmakers enacted a two-year medical marijuana law that makes state residents eligible for cards granting them the right under state law to smoke marijuana if a physician certifies that they would benefit medically. [41] The success of the medical-marijuana proposals has shown the political power of linking marijuana-law reform to legalization of medical marijuana.

This April, the FDA declared that smoked marijuana lacks any known medicinal properties, prompting denunciations from drug-war critics and some scientists. But the statement has quieted the congressional critic who prompted the FDA statement in the first place. Rep. Mark Souder, R-Ind., chairman of the Criminal Justice, Drug Policy and Human Resources Subcommittee, did not respond to the FDA statement, which he had been demanding for three years. Nor did a Souder spokesman respond to two requests for comment.

The FDA announcement was seen by many scientists as a political repudiation of the 1999 book-length report by the Institute of Medicine (IOM) — an advisory body to the National Academies of Science, Engineering and Medicine — which concluded that some of marijuana's chemical components showed promise in treating pain, nausea associated with chemotherapy and HIV/AIDS-related "wasting syndrome." [42]

"There was pretty good agreement among the panel that THC [tetrahydracannibinol] has good benefit, and it's in marijuana," said Billy R. Martin, a professor of pharmacology and toxicology at Virginia Commonwealth University, who was one of the principal investigators for the IOM study. [43] THC is the euphoria-producing ingredient in marijuana.

The FDA announcement came on the heels of two strongly worded letters Souder sent to FDA Acting Commissioner Andrew C. Eschenbach during the first three months of this year, protesting the agency's failure to rebut those who advocate marijuana as medication. In Souder's second letter, on March 15, he questioned whether the FDA took seriously "the threat posed by marijuana, our nation's most abused drug." Souder also noted that he'd gotten no answer to his Jan. 18 letter, in which he had written: "I am exasperated at the FDA's failure to act against the fraudulent claims about 'medical' marijuana." [44]

On April 20, the FDA posted a statement on its Web site saying "there is currently sound evidence that smoked marijuana is harmful." The statement went on to note that the growing number of state medical marijuana laws were "inconsistent with efforts to ensure that medications undergo the rigorous scientific scrutiny of the FDA approval process and are proven safe and effective." [45]

Souder had been pressing the FDA for a medical-marijuana statement since September, 2003. Since then Maryland, Montana, Vermont and Rhode Island enacted laws that shield from state prosecution anyone who smokes marijuana for medical purposes *

The FDA statement also followed years of insistence by drug-enforcement advocates that the entire medical-marijuana movement really aims at lifting the ban on marijuana entirely. "Medical-marijuana is a Trojan Horse issue, backed by a larger marijuana legalization effort," Michael Dermody, a spokesman for the Drug Free America Foundation, said when the Supreme Court was preparing to hear arguments on the issue. [46]

With voters and legislators so receptive to arguments for medical marijuana, advocates have continued to push for adoption of similar provisions, despite the U.S. Supreme Court's 2005 rejection of the argument that states can regulate marijuana use within their borders. The 6-3 ruling stopped short, however, of declaring state medical-marijuana laws null and void. [47]

However, the DEA said it wouldn't use the decision to target medical-marijuana users. "We don't target sick and dying people," DEA Administrator Karen Tandy said. [48]

* Maryland's law doesn't eliminate prosecution but limits punishment to a $100 fine.

Still, by ruling on the narrow issue of federal precedence in marijuana laws, the Supreme Court left a legal question mark lingering between medical-marijuana states and the federal government, say some lawyers. California Attorney General Bill Lockyer told the state's Health Services Department that carrying out the state's medical-marijuana law — issuing ID cards to certified users and related steps — would not break federal law. While federal agents are free to enforce the federal marijuana prohibition as they see fit, he wrote, "Under the Constitutional principles of dual sovereignty, the federal government cannot force state officials to enforce federal laws," he wrote. Meanwhile, the ACLU saw enough room in the Supreme Court decision to file a lawsuit seeking a federal judge's approval of a medical-marijuana program in the city of Santa Cruz, Calif. "The federal government cannot force California or the city of Santa Cruz to make medical marijuana use a crime," Allen Hopper, an ACLU lawyer said. [49]

For now, the federal government appears be at a bit of legal standoff with the states. The DEA is not arresting medical marijuana users, but it has raided medical marijuana providers in California when it concluded they were distributing the drug for non-medical uses.

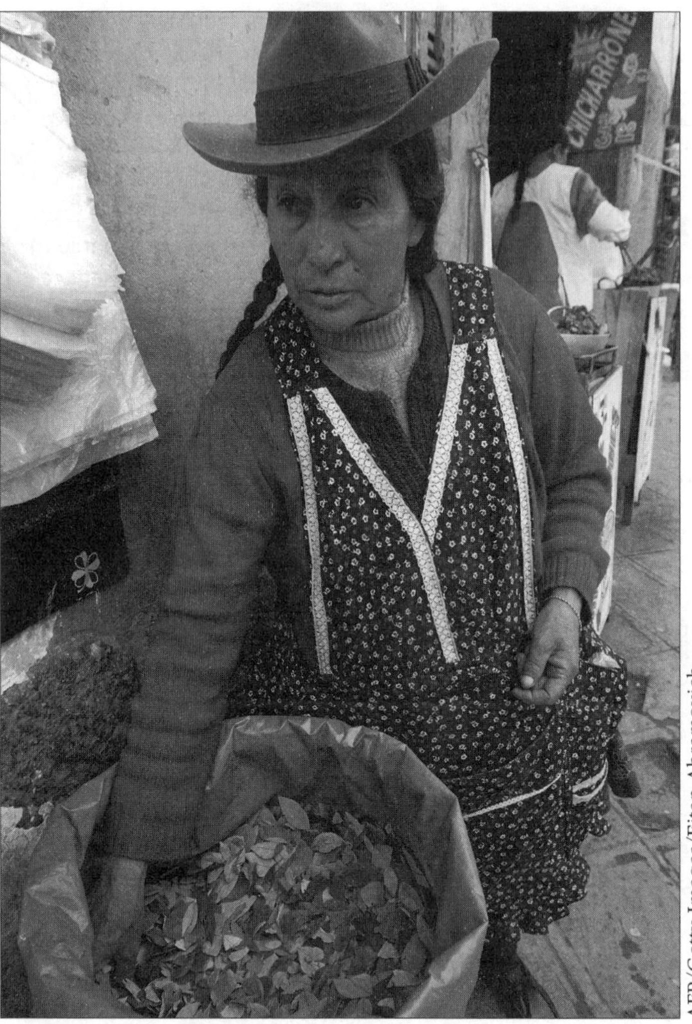

AFP/Getty Images/Eitan Abramovich

A peasant woman sells coca leaves in Peru, where the leaves traditionally are used for tea and chewing. They are also the raw material for cocaine, about 190 tons of which leave Peru each year, making it the world's second biggest cocaine producer. Critics of the U.S. drug war say interdiction can't overcome socioeconomic imbalances between nations unless poor farmers are offered profitable alternative crops.

Supplies Fluctuate

The top Senate Republican overseer of U.S. anti-drug efforts abroad says he doesn't believe the administration's reports of success eradicating coca and opium crops in Colombia. In fact, Sen. Grassley calls ONDCP's efforts to defend its conclusions "a bunch of mumbo-jumbo."

Since Grassley is co-chairman of the Senate Caucus on International Narcotics Control, the congressional panel most directly concerned with foreign drug supply, his face-off with UNDCP, which began with an April 26 letter to drug czar Walters, packed an explosive punch. [50] It questions the credibility of ONDCP reports that cocaine and heroin supplies are dwindling in U.S. cities, based on rising price and diminishing purity.

"[T]hese assumptions may be premature and perhaps even unfounded," Grassley wrote in a detailed, four-page letter. He said ONDCP had cherry-picked price and purity data from a single six-month period. The System to Retrieve Information from Drug Evidence (STRIDE), where the numbers come from, shows constant up-and-down movement of price and purity, Grassley contends. [51]

The United States has focused its coca eradication efforts on Colombia — the center of the world's cocaine trade — since the late 1980s. The Clinton administration expanded the campaign in 2000, when it joined the Colombian government in launching "Plan Colombia," which aims to crush the FARC — the Spanish initials for Revolutionary Armed Forces of Colombia — a left-wing guerrilla army with deep roots in cocaine and heroin production and trafficking — by aerial spraying of its coca and poppy crops. (Right-wing paramilitary forces, who also are heavily involved in the cocaine business, have partially demobilized). [52]

The Bush administration is also working to lessen poppy cultivation in

Continued on p. 498

At Issue:

Should schools randomly test students for drug use?

BERTHA K. MADRAS, PH.D.
DEPUTY DIRECTOR OF DEMAND REDUCTION, OFFICE OF NATIONAL DRUG CONTROL POLICY

WRITTEN FOR *CQ RESEARCHER*, MAY 2006

yes

Drug abuse is a serious public health threat. Among the number of adverse consequences attributed to drugs, evidence is mounting for a link between marijuana use and mental health problems.

When he entered office, President Bush pledged to the American people that he would reduce youth drug use by 25 percent in five years. We are on the right track. Teen drug use is down almost 20 percent over the last four years; however, drugs are prevalent and persist in our communities and schools. For example, 50 percent of high-school seniors have tried an illegal drug in their lifetime. Surveys also indicate students with an average grade of "D" or below were four times more likely to have used marijuana in the past year than "A" students.

For years, schools have tested for tuberculosis and other communicable diseases because of the public health threat. Random student drug testing extends this strategy to protect against the disease of substance abuse. Drug testing is effective not only as a prevention measure but also in helping students who have initiated drug use. Accumulating evidence indicates that drug testing serves as a powerful deterrent. After implementing a testing program, Polk County schools in Florida saw a 24-percent decline in marijuana use among athletes, combined with increased participation in extracurricular activities.

Student drug testing should support, but not supplant, other important prevention efforts in homes and communities. Parents are the most powerful influence on their children's attitudes toward drugs. However, teens in school often face peer pressure to try drugs. Student drug testing helps young people resist peer pressure by giving them a credible reason to say "no."

The U.S. Supreme Court ruled that random student drug testing is not a violation of privacy. After carefully weighing the question of privacy, the court ruled that a school's interest in protecting children from the influence of drugs outweighs their expectation of privacy. The court protected privacy issues by mandating that results be kept confidential, shared only with the parents of the student, and by referring the student to the appropriate level of counseling or treatment; not punishment.

Drug testing has proven remarkably effective at reducing drug use in American schools, businesses and the military and medical professions. For example, drug testing of airline pilots and school bus drivers has made our skies and roads safer. As a deterrent, few methods deliver clearer results. Our children deserve the same protective strategies.

ETHAN NADELMANN AND JENNIFER KERN
EXECUTIVE DIRECTOR, RESEARCH ASSOCIATE, DRUG POLICY ALLIANCE

WRITTEN FOR *CQ RESEARCHER*, MAY 2006

no

The nation's drug czar is so obsessed with marijuana and student drug testing that leading Republicans in Congress have called for his resignation for ignoring serious methamphetamine problems around the country. His obsession ill serves America's teenagers. Random drug testing of students is costly, ineffective, counterproductive and disrespectful of basic American principles.

Schools pay roughly $42 per screen; that's $21,000 for a high school testing 500 students. One school, in Dublin, Ohio, spent $35,000 to detect 11 students who tested positive; it then junked the program and hired two full-time substance-abuse counselors to implement prevention programs for the entire student body and help those most in need.

The largest study ever conducted on the topic compared 94,000 students in schools with and without a drug-testing program and found no differences in illegal drug use. Drug testing provides a false sense of assurance and only limited information about student behaviors. The standard test has a short window of detection for most drugs other than marijuana, and most tests reveal nothing about alcohol, tobacco, MDMA (Ecstasy), OxyContin or inhalants.

Drug testing deters some students from participating in extracurricular activities and then punishes those who test positive by suspending them from these activities. It thus removes students from the very thing keeping them engaged and supervised after school. Random testing also creates bizarre incentives. Binge drinking starts to make more sense because it's less detectable than pot. Ditto for more dangerous, illegal drugs. And some students try to cheat the tests by drinking bleach or iodine.

Some programs give parents no choice whether their children will be tested or not. Students' privacy rights are shunted aside. False accusations and violations of medical privacy and confidentiality are legitimate concerns. Treating young people with instinctive and institutional suspicion undermines relations of trust. And young Americans are taught that they live in a society in which privacy and sovereignty over one's mind and body are diminished while intrusive surveillance is routine.

Concerned parents, students and school administrators should look instead to alternatives that focus on keeping kids safe. The California PTA has partnered with the Drug Policy Alliance to promote both honest drug education and restorative justice principles for dealing with teens who get into trouble. (See www.safety1st.org.) We think that makes better sense than drug testing our children without cause.

Continued from p. 496

Afghanistan, the world's No. 1 source of heroin's essential ingredient. In 2005, according to the U.N. Office on Drugs and Crime, poppy cultivation decreased 21 percent, but favorable weather raised per-field yields by 39 percent. And Afghan drug traffickers' 2005 revenues of $2.7 billion amount to 52 percent of the country's gross domestic product. "The chain of narco-dollars goes from the districts to the highest levels of government," a member of the Afghan parliament told *Newsweek* magazine. [53]

However, the heroin from Afghan poppies primarily ends up in Europe, so Colombian drug production is a bigger problem in relation to U.S. drug supplies than Afghan heroin, even though taming Afghanistan's drug trade is a key U.S. foreign policy objective. Colombia supplies 50 percent of the heroin and 90 percent of the cocaine in the United States, according to DEA operations chief Michael Braun. [54]

The drug czar's office concedes that the latest data from Colombia indicate "mixed results."

Indeed, the State Department's 2006 International Narcotics Control Strategy Report states that in 2005 144,000 hectares (355,830 acres) of Colombian territory was planted in coca — 39,000 more (96,370 acres) than was reported in 2004. [55]

Nevertheless, says Murray, assistant to ONDCP Director Walters, "In areas where we sprayed, we have territory that's more stable, hundreds of tons of drugs removed from the world market, and the weakening of subversive and terrorist structures."

Asked about Grassley's critique, Murray says he sent a detailed explanation of the calculation methods used to produce the ONDCP's analyses of eradication progress. Although he would not release the response, he says, "What we're doing is working. We know it is producing an effect on available coca in Colombia."

Conservative Disaffection

Drug-war politics are shifting as conservative support for hard-line drug laws erodes. In the process, some longtime alliances are being strained and new ties are being formed.

Conservative disaffection with drug prohibition isn't new in itself. *National Review* founder William F. Buckley and conservative economic guru and Nobel laureate Milton Friedman have been drug-war critics for decades. [56] But today more conservatives are warming to that point of view.

"There's been a movement of people saying there must be a better way than the war on drugs," says Keene of the American Conservative Union, a lifelong veteran of Republican politics. "There has been a continuing discussion about two things — one, we spend all this money on the war on drugs, which doesn't seem to do much; and, two, we send all these people to prison whose bunk space might better be taken by others."

Disaffection hasn't reached "cataclysmic" proportions, Keene says. But he says it's likely younger conservatives are increasingly dismissive of government drug policy, especially when it comes to marijuana. Keene himself, a professional lobbyist whose political résumé includes service on the staff of Vice President Spiro T. Agnew, during the Nixon administration, isn't part of the young set. But he signs on to some of its criticism of federal marijuana policy.

"I certainly have no objections to medical marijuana," says Keene. "I think that's a state issue, and a lot of conservatives share that view."

He acknowledges that pushing for easing of marijuana prohibitions would be irresponsible if the government's "gateway" assertion that marijuana leads to more dangerous drugs is correct. But, he says, "I'm not convinced" by the gateway thesis.

To be sure, disenchantment with the drug war hasn't entirely swept right-wing circles. This year, conservative hard-liners on drugs were incensed by the fact that two big guns in the anti-drug-war movement — the Drug Policy Alliance and the Marijuana Policy Project — cosponsored the annual Conservative Political Action Conference (CPAC), which the ACU helps organize and draws right-wing Republicans from around the country.

"What on earth were the CPAC organizers thinking?" Rep. Souder asked, in comments read into the *Congressional Record* on Feb. 8. Noting that George Soros — a billionaire financier of many liberal causes, including opposition to President Bush's 2004 reelection — funds the Drug Policy Alliance, Souder asked: "Why would the American Conservative Union allow extremist liberals like George Soros . . . to access a meeting of conservatives?" [57]

Cliff Kincaid — a pioneer in right-wing analysis of mainstream media and editor of the *Accuracy in Media* report, a conservative journalism watchdog publication — wrote: "Having put most of the left-wing political movement and many liberal Democrats on his payroll, it is apparent that Soros is now working to manipulate the conservative movement. It is surprising that CPAC is facilitating his scheme." [58]

Indeed, drug-war critics are seeking alliances in previously unfriendly quarters. Bill Piper, the Drug Policy Alliance's national policy director, calls the receptive attitude among some conservatives one of the most important recent developments in drug policy, prompted by a growing social and political consensus toward drug use, drug problems and the high cost of interdiction, he says. "Everyone knows treatment is much cheaper" than police action, Piper says.

In one CPAC event that especially angered Souder, Kincaid and others debated the Drug Policy Alliance's Nadelmann and Rob Kampia, executive director of the Marijuana Policy Project.

"We take issues on which there are significant differences of opinion," Keene says, responding to the criticism. "Whenever you do that on drugs or gambling, or a number of issues, there are people who say, 'What the hell did you do that for? We're all agreed.' "

However, Keene says, "No, we're not."

OUTLOOK

Opinion Sharply Divided

Indeed, opinions on the future of drug policy vary just as sharply.

Ex-drug czar DuPont says the combined effects of law-enforcement action and workplace and school drug testing are making drug-taking less fashionable, hence less attractive to young people. "Take Ecstasy," he says. "Ecstasy has been stigmatized. It happened with cocaine as well."

If drug-testing is expanded to cover all drivers involved in traffic accidents, as DuPont advocates, social acceptance of drug use would drop off even more sharply, he says. "Drugged driving is as big a problem as drunk driving," he says. "If we made use of modern [drug-testing] technology on the highway, that would have as great an effect on drug use as anything."

But the Drug Policy Alliance's Piper contends that a national social consensus is developing that takes a more tolerant view of drug use and how to treat addiction. "The demographic trends are on our side," he says, arguing that younger people take a more liberal view of drug use than older generations.

"Medical marijuana will almost certainly be legal nationwide" within the next decade, he predicts, "and several states will have legalized marijuana in a way similar to alcohol." He also expects states to stop incarcerating low-level drug offenders.

However, what to do about harder drugs such as heroin remains an open question, concedes the Drug Policy Alliance's Nadelmann. "We're all divided on that," he says. "It's not an easy issue."

Advocates of the drug war depict legalization as an all-or-nothing proposition — one with terrible consequences. "If we legalized heroin," DuPont says, "a lot of people wouldn't use heroin, but the people who would use it would be the most vulnerable — young people, poor people, people with various handicaps. The consequences would be so visible so quickly that you would get a reimposition of prohibition."

But even if drug policy becomes less harsh toward drug users, District Attorney Soares of Albany County, N.Y., cautions that changing drug laws take far longer than some people imagine. He doesn't foresee a sudden repudiation of tough state anti-drug statutes, such as his state's Rockefeller laws — roundly criticized by drug-law critics because they, in effect, require street drug dealers to be sentenced as drug lords — even though he himself was elected as an opponent of the laws. "The laws have been on the books for more than 30 years, so I don't expect wholesale changes to be made in a year," he says. "Change is going to be gradual."

However, no one doubts that support for treatment will increase in coming years. Former ONDCP official Carnevale says privacy protection for treatment records will be a key issue as medical record-keeping becomes increasingly digitized. Standard-setting organizations are developing privacy guidelines so that sensitive information in drug treatment records "is protected as it moves through the system," he says.

Seventy-year-old Ronald Clark, founder and CEO of Washington's RAP residential treatment program, anticipates a comeback for long-term programs that treat addiction and its related social ills and causes. "I have to believe that things are going to turn around in the next 10 years," he says.

But an opposing trend is running strong, he acknowledges. "There's a great emphasis on trying to find a pill — another methadone," he says, referring to the heroin substitute that prevents addiction withdrawal without providing a high. "It's very scary that people would rather spend money on that."

Clark also worries that declining drug-use rates could be overturned when combat veterans from Iraq and Afghanistan return to the United States and follow the pattern of previous wars and treat their post-combat stress with drugs. There were spikes in illicit drug use after the Korean and Vietnam wars, and some soldiers came home with addictions.

"We don't know what's going to happen when these guys come back."

Notes

[1] "Three islands, $70 million in Assets Seized in DEA Drug Bust," Drug Enforcement Administration, press release, May 17, 2006, www.dea.gov/pubs/pressrel/pr051706p.html.

[2] "Crime in the United States, 2004, Uniform Crime Reports," Federal Bureau of Investigation, pp. 278-280, www.fbi.gov/ucr/cius_04; Michael Massing, *The Fix* (2000), p. 116; "Drug Control Funding Tables," Office of National Drug Control Policy, 2006, http://ondcp.gov/publications/policy/07budget/partii_funding_tables.pdf.

[3] Lloyd D. Johnston, *et al.*, "Monitoring the Future: National Results on Adolescent Drug Use, Overview of Key Findings, 2005," National Institute on Drug Abuse, p. 10, www.monitoringthefuture.org/pubs/monographs/overview2005.pdf. The number of new users in 2004 was 118,000, "Results from the 2002 National Survey on Drug Use and Health," Substance Abuse and Mental Health Services Administration, September, 2003,

http://oas.samhsa.gov/nhsda/2k2nsduh/results/2k2Results.htm#chap6; and update, www.drugabusestatistics.samhsa.gov/nsduh/2k4nsduh/2k4Results/2k4Results.htm#5.4.

[4] "Crime in the United States, 2004," *op. cit.*; Ryan S. King and Marc Mauer, "Distorted Priorities: Drug Offenders in State Prisons," The Sentencing Project, September, 2002, p. 1, wwwsentencingproject.org.

[5] "What's right with the fight? Facts versus fiction," Drug Free America Foundation Inc. [undated], www.dfaf.org/whatsright/fact.php; "Statement for the Record, Nora D. Volkow, M.D.," April 1, 2004, www.nida.nih.gov/Testimony/4-1-04aTestimony.html.

[6] "Drug Control Funding Tables," *op. cit.*

[7] For background, see Joshua Goodman, "Colombia, U.S. Authorities Arrest 24 in Money Laundering Bust," The Associated Press, April 27, 2006; Onell R. Soto, Leslie Berestein, "2,400-foot Smuggling Tunnel 'Beats Them All,' " *The San Diego Union-Tribune*, Jan. 26, 2006, p. A1.

[8] "National Drug Control Budget, Executive Summary," February, 2006, www.whitehousedrugpolicy.gov/publications/policy/07budget/parti_exec_summ.pdf.

[9] "Adult Drug Courts," Government Accountability Office, February, 2005, pp. 46-47, www.gao.gov/new.items/d05219.pdf; C. West Huddleston III, *et al.*, "Painting the Current Picture: A National Report Card on Drug Courts and Other Problem Solving Court Programs in the United States," National Drug Court Institute, May 2005, p. 7, www.ndci.org/publications/10697_PaintPict_fnl4.pdf; "National Drug Control Strategy," The White House, February, 2006, p. 14, www.whitehousedrugpolicy.gov/publications/policy/ndcs06, pp. 5-6.

[10] "Crime in the United States, 2004," *op. cit.*

[11] King and Mauer, *op. cit.*, pp. 11-12.

[12] For background, see, Ryan S. King, Marc Mauer, "The War on Marijuana: The Transformation of the War on Drugs in the 1990s," The Sentencing Project, May, 2005, www.thesentencingproject.org.

[13] Cited in, "Marijuana, Overview," Office of National Drug Control Policy, updated Feb. 27, 2006, www.whitehousedrugpolicy.gov/drugfact/marijuana/index.html.

[14] Valerie Richardson, "Drug Control Strategy Launched," *Washington Times*, Feb. 9, 2006; Christopher N. Osher, "Denver Legalizes Possession," *Denver Post*, Nov. 3, 2005, p. B1; Christopher N. Osher, "Pro-pot group seeks state vote," *Denver Post*, Dec. 28, 2005, p. B1.

[15] "2006 Congressional Drug Control Budget and Policy Assessment: A Review of the 2007 National Drug Control Budget and 2006 National Drug Control Strategy," House Committee on Government Reform, March, 2006, p. 10, www.souder.house.gov/UploadedFiles/2006DrugControlBudget&PolicyAssessment.pdf.

[16] "The Economic Costs of Drug Abuse in the United States, 1992-2002," Office of National Drug Control Policy, December, 2004, pp. vi-xiii, www.whitehousedrugpolicy.gov/publications/economic_costs/economic_costs.pdf.

[17] "National Drug Control Strategy," *op. cit.*

[18] 2006 Congressional Drug Control Budget and Policy Assessment, *op. cit.*, p. 16.

[19] Quoted in National Drug Control Strategy, *op. cit.*, p. 9.

[20] *Board of Ed. of Independent School Dist. No. 92 of Pottawatomie Cty. v. Earls*, 536 U.S. 822 (2002), http://caselaw.lp.findlaw.com/scripts/getcase.pl?court=US&vol=000&invol=01-332.

[21] "U.S. Department of Education Office for Safe and Drug-Free Schools, School-based Student Drug-Testing Programs," www.ed.gov/programs/drugtesting/05awards-drgtst.pdf; and "Digest of Education Statistics, 2004, Table 93, http://nces.ed.gov/programs/digest/d04/tables/dt04_093.asp.

[22] Ryoko Yamaguchi, Lloyd D. Johnston, Patrick M. O'Malley, "Relationship Between Student Illicit Drug Use and School Drug-Testing Policies," *Journal of School Health*, April, 2003, p. 159, www.monitoringthefuture.org/pubs/text/ryldjpom03.pdf.

[23] Robert L. DuPont, "Commentary," Institute for Behavior and Health, June 5, 2003, www.studentdrugtesting.org.

[24] Ryoko Yamaguchi, Lloyd D. Johnston, Patrick M. O'Malley, "Drug Testing in Schools: Policies, Practices and Association with Student Drug Use," Institute for Social Research, The University of Michigan, 2003, www.rwjf.org/files/research/YESOccPaper2.pdf.

[25] High-Intensity Drug Trafficking Area (HIDTA) programs are ONDCP-funded task forces of federal, state and local law-enforcement agencies in regions with high volumes of drug activity. Nationwide, 28 HIDTA programs are operating. For background, see, "High-Intensity Drug Trafficking Areas," Office of National Drug Control Policy, [undated], www.whitehousedrugpolicy.gov/hidta/index.html.

[26] Quoted in, "District drops drug-test policy," The Associated Press, April 29, 2001.

[27] For further background, see Mary H. Cooper, "Drug-Policy Debate," *CQ Researcher*, July 28, 2000, pp. 595-620; information in this section is also drawn, unless otherwise indicated, from Massing, *op. cit.*, pp. 37-50, 166-178.

[28] For background, see Patrick Marshall, "Marijuana Laws," *CQ Researcher*, Feb. 11, 2005, pp. 125-148.

[29] For example, see Linda Diebel, "A mother is killed in front of her children. Schoolkids are armed. Life in Washington, D.C. has become so terrifying the American capital is SCARED TO DEATH," *Toronto Star*, Oct. 20, 1991, p. H1.

[30] "Crack's Decline: Some Surprises Across U.S. Cities," National Institute of Justice, July, 1997, www.ncjrs.gov/txtfiles/165707.txt.

[31] For background, see Guy Gugliotta, Jeff Leen, *The Kings of Cocaine: Inside the Medellín Cartel* (1989).

[32] Quoted in Massing, *op. cit.*, p. 190.

[33] Sam Vincent Meddis, Deborah Sharp, "Bush calls Noriega conviction 'victory against drug lords,'" *USA Today*, April 10, 1992, p. A1; Larry Rohter, "After 7 Months and a Final Skirmish, the Noriega Case Goes to the Jury," *The New York Times*, April 4, 1992, p. A29; Sam Vincent Meddis, "Noriega goes on the offensive," *USA Today*, July 13, 1992, p. A8.

[34] Massing, *op. cit.*, p. 191.

About the Author

Peter Katel is a *CQ Researcher* staff writer who previously reported on Haiti and Latin America for *Time* and *Newsweek* and covered the Southwest for newspapers in New Mexico. He has received several journalism awards, including the Bartolomé Mitre Award for drug coverage from the Inter-American Press Association. He holds an A.B. in university studies from the University of New Mexico. His recent reports include "Immigration Reform" and "Rebuilding New Orleans."

[35] *Ibid.*, pp. 191-205.
[36] Mark Bowden, *Killing Pablo: The Hunt for the World's Greatest Outlaw* (2001).
[37] David Maraniss, Clinton's Life Shaped by Early Turmoil, *The Washington Post*, Jan. 26, 2002, p. A1.
[38] *Ibid.*
[39] For background, see Patrick Marshall, "Three-Strikes Laws," *CQ Researcher*, May 10, 2002, pp. 417-432.
[40] For background, see Pamela Prah, "Methamphetamine," *CQ Researcher*, July 15, 2005, pp. 591-607.
[41] "Medical Marijuana," Drug Policy Alliance, April 10, 2006, www.drugpolicy.org; "Active State Medical Marijuana Programs," National Organization for the Reform of Marijuana Laws, Dec. 1, 2004, www.norml.org/index.cfm?Group_ID=3391; M. L. Johnson, "Rhode Island Launches Medical Marijuana Program," The Associated Press, March 31, 2006.
[42] "Marijuana as Medicine? The Science Beyond the Controversy," 2000, p. 6, http://darwin.nap.edu/books/0309065313/html/6.html; see also Kathy Koch, "Medical Marijuana," *CQ Researcher*, Aug. 20, 1999, pp. 705-728.
[43] Quoted in Mary Beckman, "One drug, two takes," *Los Angeles Times*, May 1, 2006, p. F1.
[44] See Souder's letters of Jan. 18 and March 15, 2006, http://reform.house.gov/CJDPHR/News/DocumentSingle.aspx?DocumentID=40988; and http://reform.house.gov/CJDPHR/News/DocumentSingle.aspx?DocumentID=38555.
[45] "Inter-Agency Advisory Regarding Claims That Smoked Marijuana is a Medicine," U.S. Food and Drug Administration, April 20, 2006, www.fda.gov/bbs/topics/NEWS/2006/NEW01362.html.
[46] Quoted in, Nina Totenberg, "Supreme Court to Rule on Medical Marijuana," "Morning Edition," National Public Radio, Nov. 29, 2004, www.npr.org/templates/story/story.php?storyId=4190119.
[47] *Gonzales v. Raich*, 545 U.S._(2005), http://wid.ap.org/scotus/pdf/03-1454P.ZO.pdf; Linda Greenhouse, "Justices Say the U.S. May Prohibit the Use of Medical Marijuana," *The New York Times*, June 7, 2005, p. A1.
[48] David G. Savage, "Justices Rule U.S. Can Ban Medical Pot," *Los Angeles Times*, June 7, 2005, p. A1.
[49] Lockyer letter, July 15, 2005, at, www.aclu.org/FilesPDFs/ca%20ag%20post-raich%20opinion%20to%20cdhs.pdf; Hopper quoted in, "Round Two Begins in Legal Fight to Force Feds to Honor State Medical Marijuana Laws," ACLU press release, Jan. 31, 2006, www.aclu.org/drugpolicy/medmarijuana/24002prs20060131.html.
[50] "Grassley Concerned About ONDCP Assessment of Effectiveness of Plan Colombia," Center for International Policy, press release, April 26, 2006, [includes text of letter, confirmed by ONDCP and Grassley staff], http://ciponline.org/colombia/060426gras.htm.
[51] *Ibid.*
[52] "War and Drugs in Colombia," International Crisis Group, Jan. 27, 2005, www.crisisgroup.org/library/documents/latin_america/11_war_and_drugs_in_colombia.pdf.
[53] Quoted in, Ron Moreau, Sami Yousafzai, "A Harvest of Treachery," *Newsweek*, Jan. 9, 2006, p. 32; for background, see also, "Afghanistan Opium Survey 2005," U.N. Office on Drugs and Crime, pp. 3-20, www.unodc.org/pdf/afg/afg_survey_2005.pdf.
[54] Testimony, House Subcommittee on the Western Hemisphere, March 30, 2006.
[55] "International Narcotics Control Strategy Report, 2006," Bureau of International Narcotics and Law Enforcement Affairs, State Department, pp. 7-11, www.state.gov/p/inl/rls/nrcrpt/2006/vol1/html/.62106.htm; "2005 Coca Estimates For Colombia," Office of National Drug-Control Policy, April 14, 2006, www.whitehousedrugpolicy.gov/news/press06/0411406.html.
[56] "The War on Drugs is Lost," Symposium, *National Review*, July 1, 1996, www.nationalreview.com/12feb96/drug.html.
[57] Hon. Mark E. Souder, "George Soros' Infiltration of CPAC," *Congressional Record*, Feb. 8, 2006, pp. E94-E95, http://frwebgate1.access.gpo.gov/cgi-bin/waisgate.cgi?WAISdocID=871505338684+2+0+0&WAISaction=retrieve.
[58] *Ibid.*

FOR MORE INFORMATION

ACLU Drug Law Reform Project, 1101 Pacific Ave., Suite 333, Santa Cruz, CA 95060; (831) 471-9000; www.aclu.org/drugpolicy. Civil liberties group involved in key lawsuits on school drug testing and other flashpoints of controversy in the drug war.

Drug Policy Alliance, 70 W. 36th St., 16th floor, New York, NY 10018; (212) 613-8020; www.drugpolicy.org. National organization funded by billionaire financier George Soros; opposes existing drug policy.

Harm Reduction Coalition, 22 West 27th Street, 5th Floor, New York, NY 10001; (212) 213-6376; www.harmreduction.org. Promotes needle-exchange programs that give injection-drug users tools to avoid spreading HIV and other diseases.

National Families in Action, 2957 Clairmont Road, N.E., Suite 150, Atlanta, GA 30329; (404) 248-9676; www.nationalfamilies.org. Pushes for harder government line against drugs; information clearinghouse on family-related drug issues.

Montana Meth Project, P.O. Box 8944, Missoula, MT 59807; (406) 721-2538; www.montanameth.org. Promotes innovative ad campaign aimed at persuading young people to avoid methamphetamines.

National Institute on Drug Abuse, 6001 Executive Blvd., Room 5213, Bethesda, MD 20892; (301) 443-1124; www.drugabuse.gov/NIDAHome.html. Part of the National Institutes of Health; presents the scientific case on why drugs are harmful.

Office of National Drug-Control Policy, P.O. Box 6000, Rockville, MD 20849; (800) 666-3332; http://ondcp.gov. Known as office of the White House "drug czar;" coordinates federal policy and serves as administration's lead voice on drug matters.

United Nations Office on Drugs and Crime, Vienna International Centre, P.O. Box 500, A-1400 Vienna, Austria; (011-431) 260-600; www.unodc.org/unodc/index.html. A key player in international anti-drug efforts and a valuable information source on drug eradication efforts.

Bibliography

Selected Sources

Books

Baum, Dan, *Smoke and Mirrors: The War on Drugs and the Politics of Failure*, Back Bay Books, 1997.
A prolific journalist, now a writer for *The New Yorker*, dissects the drug war, concluding that its results have been disastrous.

MacCoun, Robert J., and Peter Reuter, *Drug War Heresies: Learning from Other Vices, Times and Places*, Cambridge University Press, 2001.
A University of California, Berkeley, law professor (MacCoun) and a public policy professor at the University of Maryland (Reuter) conduct a rigorous and nonpartisan analysis of drug policy and how to reduce the harmful effects of both drugs and anti-drug laws.

Mares, David R., *Drug Wars and Coffeehouses: The Political Economy of the International Drug Trade*, CQ Press, 2006.
In a rigorous and non-polemical study, a political science professor at the University of California, San Diego, analyzes the workings of the drug industry and the ways in which various countries' laws affect it.

Massing, Michael, *The Fix*, University of California Press, 2000.
Examining drug-policy shifts since the Nixon administration, a widely published freelance journalist concludes that Nixon's strategies were more rational and effective than those since then.

Articles

Boyum, David, and Mark A. R. Kleiman, "Breaking the Drug-Crime Link," *The Public Interest*, Summer 2003, pp. 19-38.
A policy consultant and a public-policy professor at UCLA conclude that testing parolees and probationers for drug use and locking them up if they test positive would offer fast and dramatic results in breaking the link between drugs and crime.

Lakshmanan, Indira A. R., "$4 Billion Later, Drugs Still Flow in Colombia," *The Boston Globe*, May 21, 2006.
A *Boston Globe* reporter provides a balanced, comprehensive look at drug eradication in Colombia, where the campaign to uproot the cocaine industry has a long way to go.

Morarjee, Rachel, "An Afghan province where heroin rules and police look the other way," *Financial Times* (London), April 13, 2006.
A correspondent for one of Europe's leading newspapers provides a ground-level view of the anti-drug campaign in Afghanistan, where many police are in the narcotics trade themselves.

Satterfield, Jamie, "One by One, Ex-cops Face Judge's Justice," *Knoxville* (Tenn.) *News-Sentinel*, July 14, 2005.
Five members of the Campbell County Sheriff's Office beat and tortured a paroled drug dealer whom they suspected of returning to his old ways — the entire session surreptitiously captured on a tape recorder by the victim's wife.

Zernike, Kate, "Potent Mexican Meth Floods In As States Curb Domestic Variety," *The New York Times*, Jan. 23, 2006, p. A1.
The reporter describes in-depth a trend state and county officials have been warning about for some time — methamphetamines from Mexico that are replacing the home-grown variety.

Reports and Studies

"Adult Drug Courts: Evidence Indicates Recidivism Reductions and Mixed Results for Other Outcomes," Government Accountability Office, February 2005.
Congress' watchdog office examines a vast amount of data generated by the country's 1,700-plus drug courts, concluding that results are uneven but that they can keep people from getting back into trouble.

"Marijuana Abuse," National Institute on Drug Abuse, July 2005.
The government's research agency on drugs presents the science on why marijuana is more dangerous than drug-decriminalization advocates acknowledge.

"Who's Really in Prison for Marijuana?" Office of National Drug Control Policy, May 18, 2005.
The White House drug czar presents data to back up its statement that most of those imprisoned on marijuana convictions are traffickers, growers and smugglers.

"FY '07 Drug Budget: Demand Reduction Being De-Emphasized," Carnevale Associates LLC, February 2006.
A former ONDCP official concludes that the Bush administration is raising law-enforcement spending at the expense of "demand reduction."

Longshore, Douglas, *et al.*, "Evaluation of the Substance Abuse and Crime Prevention Act: Cost Analysis," University of California, Los Angeles, Integrated Substance Abuse Programs, April 5, 2006.
A new California program requiring all non-violent drug offenders to be offered treatment and probation instead of incarceration saves substantial amounts of money.

The Next Step:

Additional Articles from Current Periodicals

Drug Courts

Lay, Donald P., "Rehab Justice," *The New York Times*, Nov. 18, 2004, p. A31.
Judge Lay argues that Congress needs to follow the lead of the states and modify its sentencing policies to incorporate elements of the drug court model.

Osher, Christopher N., "Task Force Rules in Favor of Drug Court," *The Denver Post*, April 20, 2006, p. B1.
Denver's Crime Prevention and Control Commission endorsed a proposal to help unclog the city's jails by creating a drug court that emphasizes treatment for drug users.

Zielinksi, Danielle, "Drug Court Program is Tough But Effective," *St. Louis Post-Dispatch* (Missouri), April 23, 2006, p. D9.
Buchanan County's drug court program has been very successful, with a recidivism rate significantly lower than individuals who go though other programs, like incarceration.

Harm Reduction

Costello, Daniel, "Addicts Learn to Save Others From Death," *Los Angeles Times*, Oct. 31, 2005, p. B1.
Training addicts to save their brethren from drug overdoses has helped reduce the number of accidental overdoses in San Francisco.

Fulbright, Leslie, "Needles Available Without Prescription," *The San Francisco Chronicle*, Dec. 15, 2004, p. B5.
Contra Costa supervisors approved legislation allowing pharmacists to sell hypodermic needles without requiring a prescription, hoping to curb the spread of HIV, hepatitis C and other blood-borne diseases.

Lewis, Mike, "Canada's Radical Plan For Social Costs of Heroin Use," *The Seattle Post-Intelligencer*, Feb. 7, 2005, p. A1.
Canada's North American Opiate Medications Initiative will distribute daily doses of heroin to a small, screened group of longtime addicts for free, hoping to stem drug-related crimes and the spread of blood-borne diseases.

Rosenberg, Steven, "Addicted to Saving Lives," *The Boston Globe*, Jan. 8, 2006, p. 1.
Former heroin addict Harry Leno now distributes clean syringes to heroin addicts in Massachusetts.

Staples, Brent, "How Needle Exchange Programs Fight the AIDS Epidemic," *The New York Times*, Oct. 25, 2004, p. A20.
New York City's AIDS prevention program called CitiWide Harm Reduction is one of nine city syringe exchange programs that has reduced the HIV infection rate of drug addicts from 50 percent to a little more than 15 percent.

Interdiction

Chu, Henry, "Plan Colombia Fails to Stem Cocaine Supply," *Los Angeles Times*, Sept. 18, 2005, p. A10.
President Bush wants to extend Plan Colombia, a five-year, $3 billion strategy to combat narco-trafficking between Colombia and the United States, but authorities say it appears to have had little effect on overall supply.

Rich, Eric, "Drug Search a Sore Subject," *The Washington Post*, May 13, 2004, p. B5.
Students at Kent County High School in Maryland were forced to endure a drug search by the Sheriff's office and two girls were forced to remove clothing.

Marijuana Decriminalization

Harris, Gardiner, "FDA Declares Marijuana Has No Medical Value," *Chicago Tribune*, April 21, 2006, p. C3.
The Food and Drug Administration announced that "no sound scientific studies" support the medical use of smoked marijuana, contradicting a 1999 review by top government scientists.

Lewis, Mike, "Two Years Later, Little Fallout From Seattle's Pot Initiative," *The Seattle Post-Intelligencer*, Nov. 23, 2005, p. A1.
Since Seattle voted to make low-level marijuana busts a low police priority, law enforcement officials have not claimed that the law sent a pro-drug message, nor has there been increased support to legalize pot.

Simon, Stephanie, "Denver is First City to Legalize Small Amount of Pot," *Los Angeles Times*, Nov. 3, 2005, p. A10.
Denver became the first city in the nation to eliminate all penalties for adults possessing less than an ounce of marijuana.

CITING *CQ RESEARCHER*

Sample formats for citing these reports in a bibliography include the ones listed below. Preferred styles and formats vary, so please check with your instructor or professor.

MLA STYLE

Jost, Kenneth. "Rethinking the Death Penalty." CQ Researcher 16 Nov. 2001: 945-68.

APA STYLE

Jost, K. (2001, November 16). Rethinking the death penalty. *CQ Researcher, 11*, 945-968.

CHICAGO STYLE

Jost, Kenneth. "Rethinking the Death Penalty." *CQ Researcher*, November 16, 2001, 945-968.

In-depth Reports on Issues in the News

Are you writing a paper?
Need backup for a debate?
Want to become an expert on an issue?

For 80 years, students have turned to *CQ Researcher* for in-depth reporting on issues in the news. Reports on a full range of political and social issues are now available. Following is a selection of recent reports:

Civil Liberties
Right to Die, 5/05
Immigration Reform, 4/05
Gays on Campus, 10/04

Crime/Law
Domestic Violence, 1/06
Death Penalty Controversies, 9/05
Methamphetamines, 7/05
Identity Theft, 6/05
Marijuana Laws, 2/05
Supreme Court's Future, 1/05

Education
Academic Freedom, 10/05
Intelligent Design, 7/05
No Child Left Behind, 5/05
Gender and Learning, 5/05

Environment
Nuclear Energy, 3/06
Climate Change, 1/06
Saving the Oceans, 11/05
Endangered Species Act, 6/05
Alternative Energy, 2/05

Health/Safety
Rising Health Costs, 4/06
Pension Crisis, 2/06
Avian Flu Threat, 1/06
Domestic Violence, 1/06
Disaster Preparedness, 11/05
Birth-Control Debate, 6/05
Marijuana Laws, 2/05

International Affairs
Future of European Union, 10/05
War in Iraq, 10/05

Social Trends
Controlling the Internet, 5/06
American Indians, 4/06
Future of Feminism, 4/06

Terrorism/Defense
Port Security, 4/06
Presidential Power, 2/06

Youth
Bullying, 2/05
Teen Driving, 1/05

Upcoming Reports

Impact of Blogs, 6/9/06
Pork-Barrel Politics, 6/16/06
Reviving Downtowns, 6/23/06
Drinking on Campus, 6/30/06
Turmoil in Latin America, 7/21/06
Social (Cyber) Networking, 7/28/06

ACCESS

CQ Researcher is available in print and online. For access, visit your library or www.cqresearcher.com.

STAY CURRENT

To receive notice of upcoming *CQ Researcher* reports, or learn more about *CQ Researcher* products, subscribe to the free e-mail newsletters, *CQ Researcher Alert!* and *CQ Researcher News*: www.cqpress.com/newsletters.

PURCHASE

To purchase a *CQ Researcher* report in print or electronic format (PDF), visit www.cqpress.com or call 866-427-7737. Single reports start at $10. Bulk purchase discounts and electronic rights licensing are also available.

SUBSCRIBE

A full-service *CQ Researcher* print subscription—including 44 reports a year, monthly index updates, and a bound volume—is $688 for academic and public libraries, $667 for high school libraries, and $827 for media libraries. Add $25 for domestic postage.

CQ Researcher Online offers a backfile from 1991 and a number of tools to simplify research. For pricing information, call 800-834-9020, ext. 1906, or e-mail librarysales@cqpress.com.

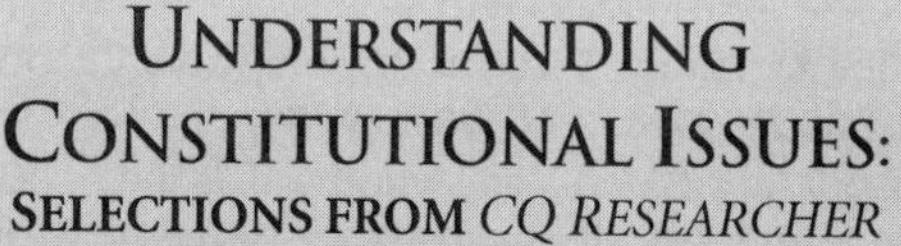

Understanding Constitutional Issues focuses on four key themes — governmental powers and structure, security, liberty, and equality — to help students develop a deeper understanding of the relation between current events and constitutional issues and principles. Integrating eighteen *CQ Researcher* reports, *Understanding Constitutional Issues* makes important connections clear, such as those between civil liberties and security; and privacy and liberty.

June 2004 • 8 1/2 x 11 • Approx. 432 pages • Paperback • ISBN 1-56802-885-7 • $39.95

To Order: Call Toll-Free: 866.4CQ.PRESS (427.7737)
Fax: 800.380.3810 • Web: www.cqpress.com
E-mail: customerservice@cqpress.com

CQ Press, 1255 22nd Street, NW, Suite 400 • Washington, DC 20037

CQ Researcher

Published by CQ Press, a division of Congressional Quarterly Inc.

cqresearcher.com

Blog Explosion

Are blogs a passing fad or a lasting revolution?

The term "blog" was coined only in 1997, but less than 10 years later the blogging phenomenon is sweeping across the United States and around the world. Millions of bloggers are filling the blogosphere with everything from personal journals and family photographs to political advocacy and journalistic commentary. Blogophiles say the blogging revolution is changing politics, business and popular culture for the better by reducing the influence of elites and institutions and allowing for wider public participation and greater interactivity. Some skeptics, however, question whether blogging is anything more than an Internet fad. And some critics say public-policy blogs spew too much unchecked information and over-hyped rhetoric into the political process. But with easy-to-use software and growing interest among individuals as well as businesses and government, the blogging phenomenon appears unlikely to peak any time soon.

Garrett M. Graff became the first blogger credentialed to cover the White House in March 2005.

INSIDE THIS REPORT

CQ Researcher • June 9, 2006 • www.cqresearcher.com
Volume 16, Number 22 • Pages 505-528

CQ PRESS

RECIPIENT OF SOCIETY OF PROFESSIONAL JOURNALISTS AWARD FOR EXCELLENCE ◆ AMERICAN BAR ASSOCIATION SILVER GAVEL AWARD

Blog Explosion

Cover: Garrett M. Graff, a 23-year-old writer, became the first blogger credentialed to cover the White House on March 11, 2005, when he was writing the Fishbowl DC blog. (AP Photo/Ron Edmonds)

CQ Researcher

June 9, 2006
Volume 16, Number 22

CQ Press

A Division of Congressional Quarterly Inc.

CQ Researcher (ISSN 1056-2036) is printed on acid-free paper. Published weekly, except March 24, July 7, July 14, Aug. 4, Aug. 11, Nov. 24, Dec. 22 and Dec. 29, by CQ Press, a division of Congressional Quarterly Inc. Annual full-service subscriptions for institutions start at $667. For pricing, call 1-800-834-9020, ext. 1906. To purchase a *CQ Researcher* report in print or electronic format (PDF), visit www.cqpress.com or call 866-427-7737. Single reports start at $10. Bulk purchase discounts and electronic-rights licensing are also available. Periodicals postage paid at Washington, D.C., and additional mailing offices. POSTMASTER: Send address changes to *CQ Researcher*, 1255 22nd St., N.W., Suite 400, Washington, DC 20037.

Blog Explosion

BY KENNETH JOST AND MELISSA J. HIPOLIT

THE ISSUES

Time magazine's special issue promised to reveal "the lives and ideas of the world's most influential people," and many of the faces on the May 8 cover were instantly recognizable: President Bush, Al Gore and Hillary Rodham Clinton from the world of politics. Computer billionaire Bill Gates. Entertainment queen Oprah Winfrey. Rock star turned global activist Bono.

Down toward the bottom, however, *Time* anointed two media stars less familiar to most Americans but well known to the increasing number of news junkies who turn to cyberspace for information and opinion about the day's events.

Matt Drudge appeared in his trademark fedora, looking much the same as the taboo-defying conservative did in 1998 when his online Drudge Report broke the story of President Bill Clinton's liaison with White House intern Monica Lewinski.

Off to Drudge's left, Arianna Huffington presented an image of pensive glamour evoking her dual life as celebrity socialite and proprietress of HuffingtonPost.com, a new but widely read liberal compendium of political news and opinion.

Getty Images/Andrew H. Walker

Former conservative socialite Arianna Huffington created HuffingtonPost.com, a year-old liberal political blog that has risen to the top rank of blogs, with an estimated 1.3 million visitors in April 2006. Huffington says blogging has "leveled the playing field" between the traditional media and the new, independent media who have only a laptop and an Internet connection.

Time's selection of Drudge and Huffington from among many better-known media heavyweights represented the kind of event the weekly news magazine might have noted on its "Milestones" page:

"**ARRIVED**. *The Age of the Blog, the interactive, globally connected medium of communication with revolutionary potential to make politics more democratic, business more productive and knowledge and culture more diffuse."* [1]

The word "blog" — short for "Web log" — may nevertheless still seem like somewhat obscure jargon to many Americans. A countercultural computer geek coined the word less than 10 years ago to describe the process of logging on a personal site items he found interesting while surfing the World Wide Web. Nearly three-fourths of the country's Internet users had never read a blog as of November 2004, according to a survey by the Pew Internet and American Life Project. [2]

Today, however, the so-called blogosphere has exploded, with more than 42 million sites and counting, according to the blog-finding service Technorati. Admittedly, many of them are little more than personal diaries, such as the growing number of intimacy-revealing blogs published by high-school and college students. (*See sidebar, p. 518.*) But businesses, politicians and even government agencies are now starting blogs to provide information to — and invite feedback from — customers and constituents. (*See sidebar, p. 516.*)

In addition, a growing number of political blogs provide breaking news not found in mainstream media along with corrections or complaints about news coverage and sharp, often vituperative commentary about national and world events. "Blogs have become the new information ecosystem, part of the conversation about policy," says Rebecca MacKinnon, a research fellow at the Berkman Center for Internet and Society at Harvard Law School in Cambridge, Mass. (*See chart, p. 512.*)

Blogging has also become a global phenomenon and a valuable tool for human-rights and pro-democracy activists in challenging repressive regimes. Bloggers and other Web activists face risks, however. The Egyptian government jailed at least six bloggers among other dissidents in May 2006. China has jailed several Web activists and — with the assistance of U.S.-based Internet service providers — blocked some anti-government sites. And Iran jailed some 20 online journalists and bloggers in January 2005. Some were released after international

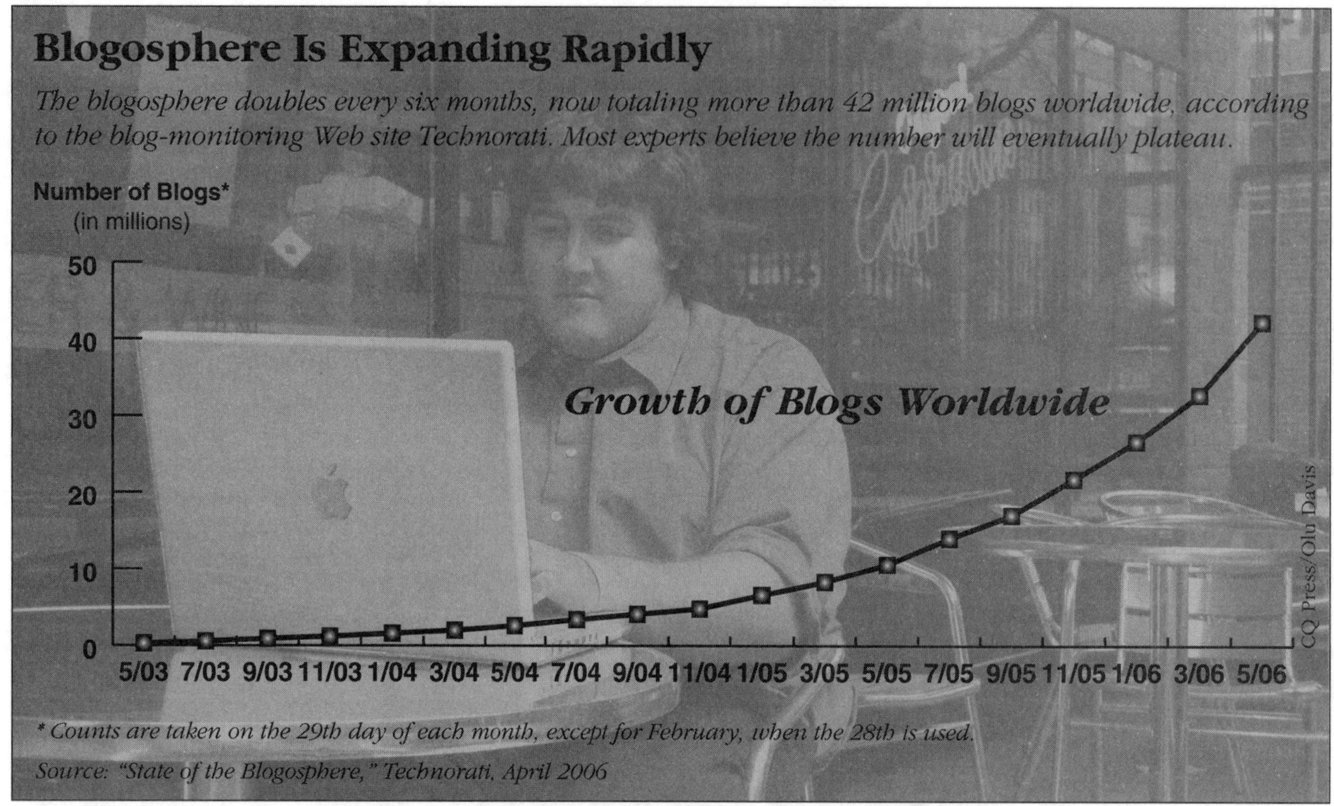

Blogosphere Is Expanding Rapidly

The blogosphere doubles every six months, now totaling more than 42 million blogs worldwide, according to the blog-monitoring Web site Technorati. Most experts believe the number will eventually plateau.

* *Counts are taken on the 29th day of each month, except for February, when the 28th is used.*

Source: "State of the Blogosphere," Technorati, April 2006

criticism, but human-rights groups say the government continues to persecute bloggers critical of the regime. [3]

Blogs offer two comparative advantages over other media. Bloggers face few barriers to entry: Anyone with a computer and the nominal costs of easy-to-use software and a Web hosting service can start a blog. The ease of start-up is beguiling, however. The vast majority of blogs go idle after a short period of time. For readers, blogs offer the opportunity to provide instantaneous feedback and to engage in freewheeling dialogue with other blog readers unlimited by space or time.

"Blogs give people the ability to talk to each other, and they're finding that they have more trust in people like themselves, at least in some key areas, than they have in traditional sources of information," says David Kline, a business journalist, consultant and co-author of the book *blog! how the newest media revolution is changing politics, business and culture.*

Drudge himself reportedly dislikes the word "blog," and the Drudge Report invites e-mail and tips but, unlike true blogs, no interactive feedback. Huffington sees her recognition from *Time*, however, as "a tribute to the influence of the blogosphere," which she says "has leveled the playing field between the media haves and the media have-only-a-laptop-and-an-Internet-connection crowd."

In fact, both Drudge and Huffington have clearly arrived in terms of their visibility in political and media circles. Drudge's site drew around 2.7 million "unique" visitors in April 2006, according to the media-tracking service Nielsen/Net.* "Anybody who's dealing with the political world or the political media world, they're checking Drudge's site every day," says Robert Cox, managing editor of TheNationalDebate.com and president of the newly founded Media Bloggers Association.

* A "unique visitor" is anyone who goes to a site at least once during the time period.

Huffington's site, which debuted on May 9, 2005, rose within a year to the top rank of blogs. Nielsen/Net estimated 1.3 million visitors in April 2006. "It creates a place for liberals to gather and takes some of the oxygen from conservative sites like the Drudge Report," says the liberal political satirist Al Franken. [4] In the *Time* issue, he claims tongue-in-cheek credit for converting the onetime Newt Gingrich acolyte to her self-described views today as "a compassionate and progressive populist."

The mainstream print and broadcast media continue to draw far more readers and viewers than blogs, however — even in head-to-head competition online. NewYorkTimes.com, for example, was reporting 29 million unique visitors per month in March 2006. [5] "We haven't gotten to the point that blogs swamp in readership the aggregate of all newspapers and magazines," says Eugene Volokh, a UCLA law professor and author of a widely read legal-affairs blog, The Volokh Conspiracy.

In contrast to traditional media, bloggers have no established career path, no prescribed course of dues-paying jobs before reaching prime time or the front page. Drudge used a job in the gift shop at CBS Studios in Los Angeles in the early 1990s to gather Hollywood-type gossip for a report that started as an e-mail newsletter and then broadened into political gossip as it moved onto the World Wide Web in 1996. Before starting her blog, Huffington was a columnist and critic in London in the 1970s and an author and socialite after moving to the United States in the 1980s.

Easy access makes the blogosphere "extremely competitive," according to media historian Paul Starr, a professor of sociology and public affairs at Princeton University in New Jersey. But it is unclear "how deeply entrenched the early leaders will be, how long they will be able to maintain the edge that they now enjoy," says Starr, author of the Pulitzer Prize-winning *The Creation of the Media*.

The biggest blogs, however, not only appear to have staying power but also — thanks to advertising — are making their creators rich. Drudge's site has been estimated to be worth as much as $120 million; Huffington has made lucrative deals with Internet giants AOL and Yahoo. *Time* itself hosts one of the older blogs: Andrew Sullivan's Daily Dish, while Mickey Kaus's Kausfiles is featured on the online magazine *Slate.com*.

Still, media watchers emphasize that blogs depend on mainstream media for much of their raw material. "They don't go out and do investigative reporting," says Kline. "But as a complement to traditional media, blogs have been very helpful, adding a real slice of life to reporting, uncovering a lot of mistakes in the mainstream media and allowing more diverse voices to be heard."

As the number of blogs and blog readers continues to grow, here are some of the questions being debated:

Most Blog Readers Are Young and Democrats

Internet users between ages 18-29 read blogs more than other age groups, and 28 percent of them read blogs frequently or occasionally. Democrats read blogs more often than Republicans or Independents.

Percent of Internet Users Who Read Blogs
(By Age)

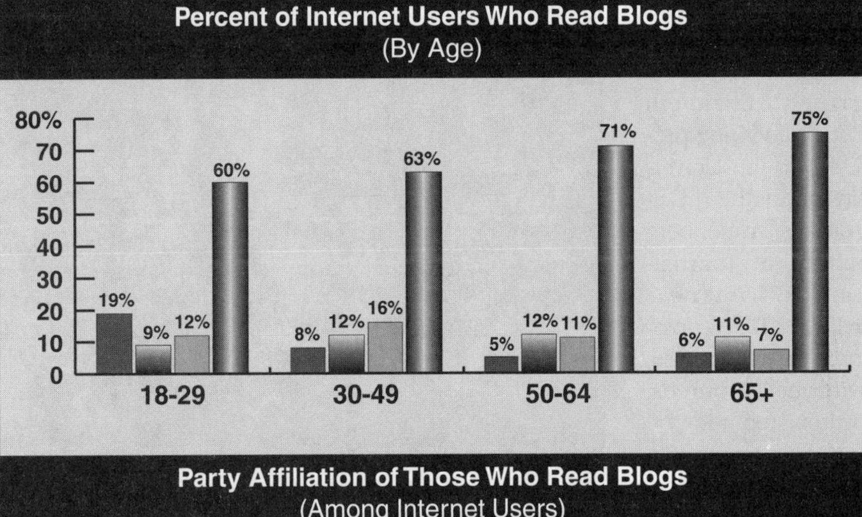

Party Affiliation of Those Who Read Blogs
(Among Internet Users)

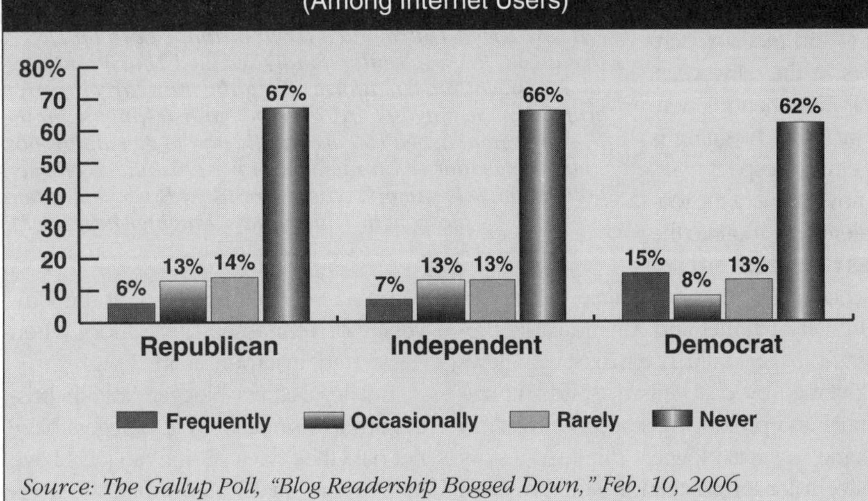

Source: The Gallup Poll, "Blog Readership Bogged Down," Feb. 10, 2006

Should policymakers be influenced by political blogs?

One month away from becoming Senate majority leader, Sen. Trent Lott, R-Miss., put his foot in his mouth at Sen. Strom Thurmond's 100th birthday bash on Dec. 5, 2002, by fondly recalling the presidential campaign the South Carolinian waged in 1948 on a segregationist platform. Noting that his home state of Mississippi had voted for Thurmond, Lott remarked, "If the rest of the country had followed our lead, we wouldn't have had all these problems over all these years."

Initially, Lott's gaffe went unreported except for a brief mention on ABCNews.com. But the story erupted in the blogosphere, pushed initially by the liberal Joshua Micah Marshall (talkingpointsmemo.com) and the conservative Glenn Reynolds (Instapundit.com). Eventually, the mainstream media took up the missed story, and an abashed Lott had to give up the GOP leadership.

Even as bloggers were demonstrating their impact, however, a noted journalism professor was dismissing their abilities and their role. "Bloggers are navel gazers," Elizabeth Osder, a visiting professor at the University of Southern California's Annenberg School of Journalism, told *Wired News* in 2002. "This is opinion without expertise, without resources, without reporting." [6]

Osder reflected a common view of blogging among journalists and media-watchers in the early years of the phenomenon. But now, blogging is getting respect. "It's moving out of the toddler stage and into the early elementary school age," says Lee Rainie, director of the Pew Internet and American Life Project. Bloggers influence mainstream news coverage by checking facts, adding material and prolonging stories, he says. "In some respects bloggers can keep a story alive a lot longer than it would've been alive in the pre-Internet era."

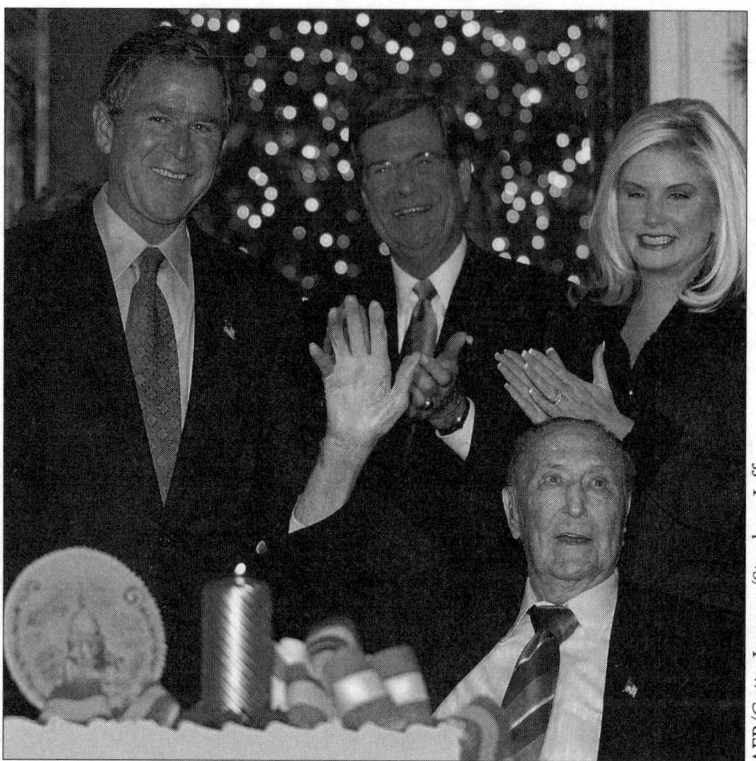
AFP/Getty Images/Stephen Jaffe

At Sen. Strom Thurmond's 100th birthday bash on Dec. 5, 2002, Sen. Trent Lott, R-Miss., center, fondly recalled Thurmond's 1948 campaign on a segregationist platform. The gaffe went largely unreported until it erupted in the blogosphere, and the mainstream media then took up the story. An abashed Lott eventually had to give up his post as Senate majority leader — an incident many attribute to bloggers' newfound political muscle. Among others, President Bush, left, attended the party, along with Thurmond's daughter Julie, right.

With literally millions of bloggers, generalizations are necessarily treacherous. But among the highest-profile political bloggers, several of them started — like Huffington and Drudge — without the kind of background or experience ordinarily associated with admission into the top echelons of the commentariat. Marshall, for example, had been in journalism for only two years when he started Talking Points Memo in 2000 at the age of 31. Reynolds was a 41-year-old professor at the University of Tennessee Law School when he started Instapundit in 2001.

But legal-affairs blogger Volokh bristles at the insinuation that bloggers have not paid their dues. "Some bloggers have many more qualifications than the average journalist writing on a particular field," he says. Others may have no special expertise but "end up producing good stuff because they're smart people."

Author Kline acknowledges the uneven quality of some blog content. "A great deal of it is uninformed — maybe 95 percent," he says. "But much of what I read in the newspapers is garbage. And most academic writing is terrible."

As with the Lott story, however, Huffington says bloggers have played an important role by running ahead on controversies that mainstream media were either missing or downplaying, such as the re-examination of the "60 Minutes II" story on President Bush's Air National Guard service and the reassessment of the prewar coverage of Iraq's supposed weapons of mass destruction. "These stories would not have gotten the traction they did without the blogosphere," she says.

But Tom Rosensteil, director of the Washington-based Project on Excellence in Journalism, says bloggers depend on mainstream media to have an impact on events. "If you track the cases where blogs have been influential, it's because they've influenced other political leaders or the media," the former *Los Angeles Times* media critic says.

Whether direct or indirect, bloggers' influence appears to have become a recognized fact of political life. "They have a considerable readership," says Princeton's Starr, who is co-editor of the liberal monthly *The American Prospect*. "I don't see how anybody can ignore them."

Geneva Overholser, a longtime journalist and now a professor at the University of Missouri School of Journalism in Columbia, agrees, but says readers need better information to evaluate individual blogs. She also worries about a seeming lack of diversity in the blogosphere. "We're not seeing the diversity of voices across the old lines of sex, race, socioeconomic level," she says. "Could we really say it's just as easy to find a poor Latina writing a blog that will be heard as it is to find some 35-year-old white guy writing for us?"

Daily Blog Postings Approach 1.5 Million

By the end of March, blog postings had surpassed 1.4 million per day— or nearly 60,000 per hour. Postings depend on the news. For instance, postings spiked after the 2004 presidential election, Hurricane Katrina, the death of Terry Schiavo, the subway bombings in London and the youth protests in France and the Duke University lacrosse team scandal.

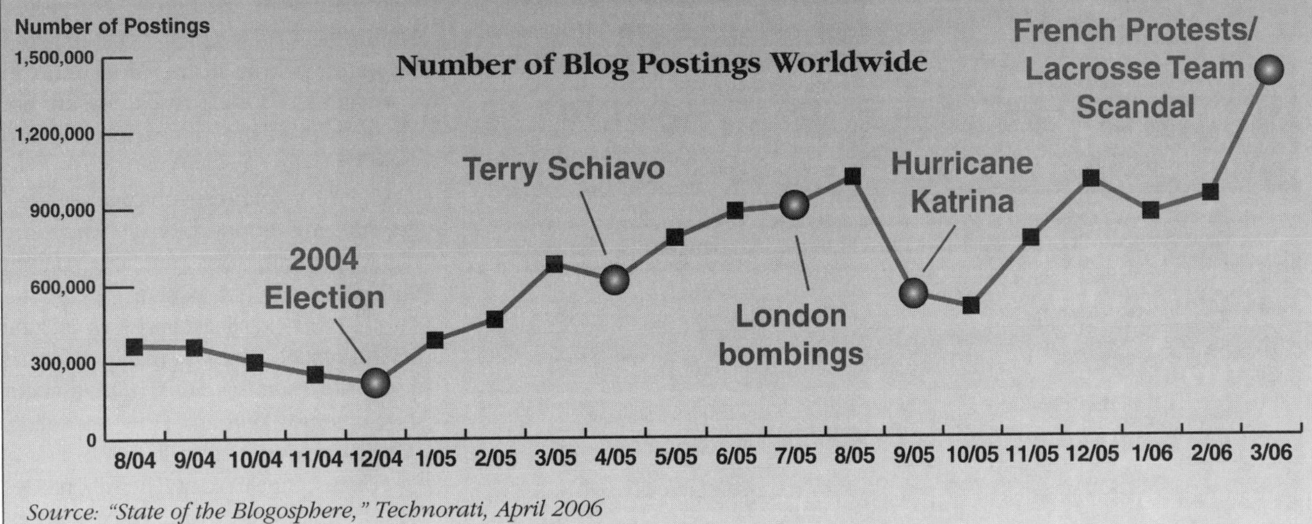

Source: "State of the Blogosphere," Technorati, April 2006

Meanwhile, Osder sounds different on the subject today from four years ago. Blogging is "absolutely a wonderful new way to hear the voices of people you might not have heard before," she says. "I think of it more as a way for people in public office to have a new and legitimate ear on their community."

Should blogs tone down their political rhetoric?

Barely an hour after the American Bar Association (ABA) announced it had rated as "unqualified" President Bush's judicial nominee Michael Wallace, one of the bloggers on the pro-Bush site ConfirmThem.org vented his reaction.

"This is complete and utter b.s.," wrote Stephen Dillard ("feddie") in his May 10 posting. "Mike Wallace is clearly qualified to serve as a federal appellate judge, and the hacks that issued this rating ought to be ashamed of themselves. Lord, how I loathe the ABA."

A few days later, the liberal blogger Jerry Tenuto ("Lone Star Iconoclast") weighed in from the opposite perspective on another Bush nominee, Brett Kavanaugh.

"Brett Kavanaugh is just another shiftless Republican sycophant, ready to do the bidding of the King . . . er, Herr Oberst Karl Rove, that is," Tenuto wrote in the posting on OpEdNews.com. "They've really got this Fuhrer prinzip concept working overtime."

Although such caustic blogosphere rhetoric cheers partisans, some fear it risks aggravating political divisions and coarsening political dialogue. Media historian Starr, however, says blogs cannot be blamed for the political divisions in the country.

"You have, in general, a more polarized and more partisan politics, and at the same time you have the development of the blogs," says Starr. "The two feed off each other."

Bloggers themselves defend the sharp language as part of an American tradition and an essential element of their appeal. "There is a long, proud tradition of incendiary, controversial political rhetoric in America that goes back to the days before the Declaration of Independence," says Cox, of the Media Bloggers Association.

At the same time, blog expert Kline is one of many media watchers who expect the tone to change over time. "I don't think the degree of snarkiness is going to last," Kline says. "This phenomenon is going to evolve. The political conversations now, people just talk at each other. Over time, they'll become more reasoned."

Starr notes that blog technology invites intemperate postings. "There is less of a filter with the blogs because somebody's keystrokes go up immediately," says Starr. "Even if that writer has second thoughts, it's too late."

But Rosensteil of the Project on Excellence in Journalism says some bloggers do claim to filter out inflammatory rhetoric. "They try to be more provocative, but the most obstructionist and divisive stuff is kept out," he says.

For some bloggers, sharp rhetoric is part of their appeal. "I'm preaching to the choir for a reason," says Markos

Liberal Political Blogs Are Most Popular

Although conservative blogs dominated immediately after the 9/11 terrorist attacks, most of the top 12 political blogs today are liberal. A blog's popularity is measured by how many other sites link to it, considered a vote of confidence for that blog. The rankings refer to how the Web site ranks among the 100 most popular blogs of all types.

Top 12 Political Blogs

Overall Rank Among All Blogs	Blog/Blogger	Site	No. of Web Sites Linking to This Blog
6	**Daily Kos** Liberal political analysis written by conservative-turned-liberal author Markos Moulitsas Zuniga.	**www.dailykos.com**	**11,798**
10	**Huffington Post** Liberal commentary by conservative-turned-liberal Arianna Huffington.	**www.huffingtonpost.com**	**8,960**
16	**Michelle Malkin** Written by conservative journalist and author Michelle Malkin; focuses on immigration issues.	**www.michellemalkin.com**	**7,165**
17	**Instapundit** Libertarian/conservative; written by University of Tennessee law Professor Glenn Reynolds.	**www.instapundit.com**	**6,460**
19	**Crooks & Liars** Liberal virtual magazine by former Duran Duran musician John Amato; features audio and video clips.	**www.crooksandliars.com**	**6,406**
5	**Think Progress** Liberal; edited by Judd Legum, research director at the Center for American Progress and former Clinton-era assistant to White House Chief of Staff John Podesta.	**www.thinkprogress.org**	**5,586**
35	**Wonkette** Gossipy, satirical blog on Washington, D.C., politics created by journalist Ana Marie Cox.	**www.wonkette.com**	**4,177**
39	**Talking Points Memo** Liberal political commentary, reporting from Joshua Micah Marshall, a columnist for the Capitol Hill newspaper, *The Hill*.	**www.talkingpointsmemo.com**	**3,879**
55	**AMERICAblog** Liberal blog with focus on the Bush administration, the radical right and gay civil rights; edited by writer and political consultant John Aravosis.	**www.americablog.blogspot.com**	**3,402**
56	**Little Green Footballs** Neoconservative war blog by software engineer and guitarist Charles Johnson.	**www.littlegreenfootballs.com**	**3,401**
59	**Power Line** Conservative blog dealing with policy issues such as income inequality and campaign finance reform written by lawyers John H. Hinderaker and Scott W. Johnson.	**www.powerlineblog.com**	**3,346**
71	**Eschaton** News and politics from liberal points of view; edited by Duncan Black, a senior fellow at Media Matters for America.	**www.atrios.blogspot.com**	**3,147**

Source: Technorati.com, as of June 1, 2006

Moulitsas Zuniga, whose liberal blog DailyKos reportedly draws 500,000 visitors monthly. "It's because we're trying to organize, we're trying to fundraise, we're trying to win elections." [7]

Huffington, however, says she aims at a wider audience. "I don't think we just preach to the choir," she says. Huffington says her blog is bookmarked by many people in the media and in government. "Obviously, these are not all people of the same political persuasion," she says.

UCLA's Volokh cautions against overgeneralizing about blogs. "Some are highly partisan, some are less partisan and some are not partisan at all," he says. In fact, legal affairs blogs include several widely read primarily informational sites, such as SCOTUSBlog about the Supreme Court and How Appealing, which covers appellate litigation.

For his part, Cox of TheNationalDebate.com says the marketplace will operate over time as a check on the kind of rhetoric seen in the blogosphere now. "Bloggers, like anyone else advocating a political point of view, must compete in the marketplace of ideas," he says. "This marketplace is self-correcting. Those that employ language in a way that offends the sensibilities of their readers will find themselves with a dwindling audience and decreased influence."

Journalism Professor Overholser agrees. "There are all kinds of blogs," says Overholser. "Some will seek to be balanced, though most are indeed opinionated. Among the opinionated, some will be shrill, others more thoughtful and fair-minded. We consumers will choose among them, and the ones we choose will flourish."

Should bloggers have the same rights and privileges as reporters?

Sen. Richard J. Lugar, R-Ind., cheered journalism groups in May when he and a group of four bipartisan cosponsors introduced a bill to establish a federal shield law giving reporters a qualified privilege to protect confidential sources of information. "This is important legislation that all Americans should support," David Carlson, president of the Society of Professional Journalists, said in a May 18 press release. [8]

Bloggers had less reason to cheer, however. Lugar's bill would limit the protection to established print, broadcast and cable media — and exclude bloggers. "This bill is more like an 'affirmative action' program for corporate media," says Cox. "It grants special privileges to entities or persons based solely on their relationship to a corporate media organization."

Lugar says the issue is still open for discussion. "As to who is a reporter, this will be a subject of debate as this bill goes farther along," Lugar said in an online reply to a question after introducing the bill. [9] And journalists and media watchers are themselves uncertain about how far into the blogosphere to extend special privileges established for journalists.

"There's so much variety," says Steve Outing, a columnist for *Editor and Publisher Online* who covers interactive media. "Anything from a high-school student who has a personal blog all the way up to a *New York Times* reporter who might be blogging for *The New York Times* or maybe they have a personal blog."

As free-speech expert Volokh notes, the First Amendment itself guarantees certain rights to anyone — whether or not in the news media. The government cannot censor blogs, for example. But journalist shield laws passed by some states are the only protection for guarding confidential sources after the Supreme Court in 1974 refused to recognize a journalists' privilege under the First Amendment.

In addition, governmental and private organizations routinely must decide who qualifies as a member of the media in order to grant them special seating or access to news events. Bloggers marked an important milestone in 2004 when both the Republican and Democratic parties credentialed online journalists — including some bloggers — to cover their national conventions. [10]

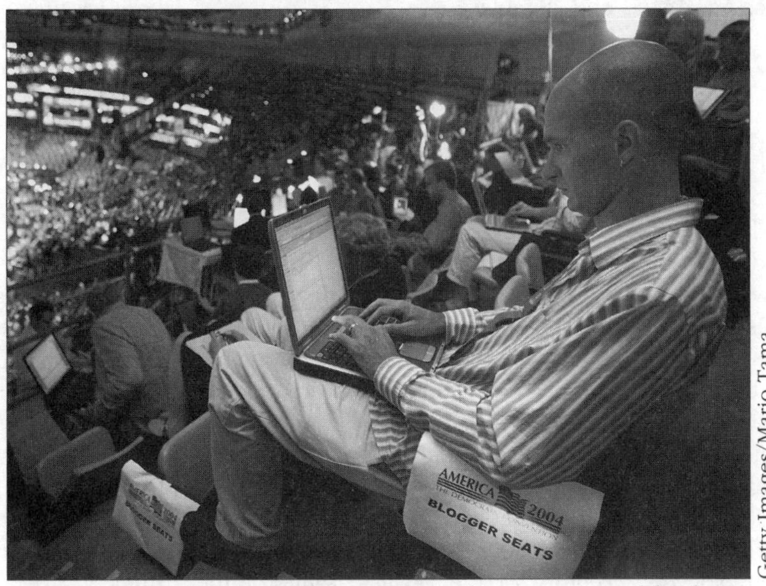

Getty Images/Mario Tama

Bloggers post on their Web logs in a special section reserved for them during the Democratic National Convention in July 26, 2004, in Boston, Mass. Bloggers marked an important milestone when both the Republican and Democratic parties credentialed some bloggers to cover their 2004 national conventions.

For his part, Cox says the rule for bloggers is simple: "When bloggers are acting in a journalistic capacity, they should have the full protections afforded to anybody else who's operating as a journalist. If a blogger is reporting on a story — interviewing people, gathering information, reporting facts and putting together a story — they are a journalist. How they publish is irrelevant. The fact that bloggers are self-published doesn't speak to the issue of what they're doing to produce their content."

Carlson, director of the Interactive Media Lab at the University of Florida in Gainesville, agrees on protections for journalist bloggers but says it is necessary to draw a line between bloggers who are journalists and those who are not. One way to draw the line, Carlson says, is between bloggers who are doing "original reporting" and those who are only "stating opinion" or "regurgitating what others have written."

"You can't necessarily say someone who only does opinion is not a journalist, but often they are not," Carlson continues. "And you can't necessarily say anyone who's doing original reporting is a journalist. But most often they are."

However, Duncan Black, a senior fellow at Media Matters for America and a blogger, says original reporting should not be a prerequisite for a blogger to be treated like other journalists. "What bloggers do fits well within the news media if we broaden [the definition of media] to include the kind of talk shows we find on cable news, public-affairs programs that include news analysis, AM talk radio," he says. "The news media is much broader than people like to think sometimes."

Corporate affiliation should be irrelevant, Black adds. "A press ID from *The New York Times* shouldn't give you special privileges," he says. Rosensteil agrees. "From a journalistic point of view, the technology exists now that you don't need an organization to practice journalism," he says.

Moreover, Cox notes, the mainstream media now are moving rapidly into the blogosphere themselves. "It's not an us [bloggers] versus them [mainstream media] issue," says Cox. "It very much used to be, but now it's gone. When the *New York Times*, *Washington Post*, *National Journal*, CBS News all have bloggers, there's no longer a dichotomy." ■

BACKGROUND

Before Blogs

Modern-day bloggers trace their antecedents back to Ice Age cave painters and to the political pamphleteers of the early centuries of the print revolution. In U.S. history, their ancestry can be seen in the openly partisan press of the 19th and early 20th centuries, the muckraking journalists of the progressive era and the rambunctious hosts of mid- and late 20th-century talk radio. Now with an inexpensive platform that was available to none of those ancestors, bloggers have a unique ability to disseminate their messages — chatty or substantive, informational or opinionated — in real time, 24/7, to an audience as large and far-flung as a global computer network will allow. [11]

The connection between bloggers and cave painters came to blog expert Dan Burstein on a visit to southwestern France. [12] Burstein writes of learning for the first time that the pictorial decorations went on in some instances for generations or longer. With no written language, the painters and storytellers of prehistory used visual images to describe and comment on their ideas and beliefs on the topics of their day — hunting, initiation rites, sickness, mortality, the afterlife. The automotive blog Inside Line sees the same connection. "People blog because cave paintings are obsolete," a Jan. 10, 2006, post reads.

Cave painting was indeed a limiting medium. Reaching a wider audience awaited the development of written languages and a writing "platform." The Egyptians came up with papyrus around 3000 B.C. Europeans used sheepskin parchment. The Chinese initially used bamboo and silk, but around 200 B.C. developed a technique of using wood pulp to make what came to be called "paper" when it reached Europe more than 1,000 years later. Despite modern-day derision of "dead tree" media, paper was truly a breathtaking breakthrough: it used an abundant natural resource to produce a communications medium both portable and durable.

Publishing was a labor-intensive process dependent on monks and Talmudic scholars, however, until the development of movable type and the printing press. The Chinese pioneered movable type beginning in the 11th century. Clay type was used first, then wood and finally metal.

In the mid-15th century German goldsmith Johann Gutenberg combined metal type with a mechanical printing press. The invention spread quickly, and books — once a luxury — became by contemporary standards cheap and plentiful, as did pamphlets, like the anticlerical writings of the English Puritan John Milton in the mid-17th century or the political satire of the Anglo-Irish author Jonathan Swift in the early 18th. In America, Thomas Paine's pro-independence pamphlet "Common Sense" (1776) sold half a million copies and is widely credited with helping swing popular sentiment toward revolution. [13]

The Industrial Revolution made printing even cheaper in the 19th century, as the United States was developing what was then the world's most efficient and reliable postal system. News was cheap: It was the era of the "penny newspaper." And with the invention of the telegraph, news could travel even faster.

Throughout this period, U.S. newspapers were highly partisan. "There's nothing that we see on any blog that compares to the scurrilous kind of attacks newspapers would print about politicians in those days," says author Kline. At the turn of the century, journalist-authors like Ida Tarbell, Lincoln Steffens and Upton Sinclair created the model of investigative reporting. President Theodore Roosevelt labeled them "muckrakers," even as he congratulated them for attacking the "grave evils" of the day.

The advent of radio and television made news even cheaper and quicker. Advertising-supported over-the-air broadcasting gradually became a big business — "the biggest of Big Media," as journalist-turned-blogger Dan Gillmor puts it. [14] Broadcasting became too profitable to risk being too controversial. Simultaneously, newspapers generally were moving away from outright partisanship toward an ethos of objectivity and professionalism. In the process, today's bloggers suggest, print and broadcast media alike became more centralized and homogenized — and less interesting.

The era gave rise, however, to a few mavericks who can be viewed as forerunners of today's bloggers, with the best example being I. F. Stone (1907-1989), says media historian Starr. After two decades as a journalist and author, Stone in 1953 started his own publication, *I. F. Stone's Weekly*, and filled it for 18 years with hard-hitting articles often based on close examination of government documents left unread by mainstream reporters.

Talk-radio hosts can also be seen as antecedents for bloggers. Call-in shows date from 1945, but the format exploded in the late 1980s when the Federal Communications Commission's repeal of the Fairness Doctrine eliminated stations' need to ensure balanced viewpoints. Over the next decade the rise of conservative hosts like Rush Limbaugh — and the eventual emergence of a few, less successful liberal counterparts — stemmed from a shared

Continued on p. 516

Chronology

1970s-1980s

Early days of computer networking; electronic bulletin boards emerge, Internet is born.

1990s

World Wide Web launched; first weblogs follow.

1991
First World Wide Web site brought online by British computer scientist Sir Tim Berners-Lee.

1993
Mosaic Web browser simplifies creating Web pages.

1994
Swarthmore College student Justin Hall starts Web-based diary "Justin's Links from the Underground," seen as forerunner of personal blogging.

1996
Matt Drudge migrates gossipy Hollywood-based Drudge Report from e-mail distribution to Web.

1997
Jorn Barger begins publishing "RobotWisdom," coins the word "weblog" to describe process of logging the Web as he surfed.

1998
Drudge Report breaks story of President Clinton's liaison with White House intern Monica Lewinsky.

1999
Pyra Labs creates "Blogger," easy-to-use software for creating blogs. . . . Fewer than 100 blogs known to be in existence.

2000-Present

Blogs number in the millions, but are unread by most Americans.

2001
Terrorist attacks of 9/11 bring outpouring of conservative, pro-war sentiments on "war blogs."

2002
New York Times word maven William Safire devotes July 28 column to origins, usage of "blog" . . . Bloggers Glenn Reynolds (Instapundit) and Joshua Micah Marshall (TalkingPointsMemo) publicize Senate GOP Leader Trent Lott's praise for Strom Thurmond's segregationist presidential campaign in 1948; controversy picked up by mainstream media, forces Lott to relinquish post.

2003
Teen blog site MySpace.com is founded; acquired by Rupert Murdoch's NewsCorp in 2005 for $580 million. . . . Howard Dean uses Internet, blogs to raise funds, mobilize support for 2004 presidential campaign; folds campaign in February 2004 after faring badly in Iowa, New Hampshire.

May 2004
Senate staffer Jessica Cutler fired for writing sexy "Washingtonienne" blog from office computer but gets six-figure book deal from episode.

July 2004
Bloggers credentialed for political party conventions.

September-Novemer 2004
Conservative blogs sharply attack CBS report questioning President Bush's service in Texas Air National Guard; controversy hastens Dan Rather's retirement as news anchor, forces network to acknowledge flaws in report. . . . Bush and Democratic challenger John Kerry both use blogs in presidential campaigns. . . . Media Bloggers Association formed.

January 2005
Iran jails 20 online journalists and bloggers.

February 2005
Gallup Poll shows a third of Internet users read blogs at least occasionally, but nearly two-thirds never do.

May 2005
Business Week cover story tells businesses to use blogs for market research, consumer feedback. . . . Ariana Huffington debuts liberal blog HuffingtonPost.com.

March 2006
Federal Election Commission says political blogs not subject to federal campaign finance laws.

April 2006
Los Angeles Times columnist's blog on California politics is suspended after he was found to have posted comments on site and elsewhere under an assumed name.

May 2006
Matt Drudge, Ariana Huffington named by *Time* magazine as among world's 100 most influential people. . . . California state appeals court says bloggers entitled to same protection for confidential sources as other journalists. . . . Bloggers tracked by Technorati surpass 42 million. . . . Egypt jails at least six bloggers among other dissidents.

Businesses Ignore Blogosphere at Their Peril

The Kryptonite lock company's slogan — "Tough Locks for a Tough World" — refers to the protection its locks offer against "real world" thieves. But the Canton, Mass., manufacturer of high-end bicycle locks learned that cyberspace is a tough world, too, especially for businesses that ignore the blogosphere.

Kryptonite still feels the impact of the September 2004 blogosphere eruption that occurred when someone using the name "unaesthetic" posted on a discussion site the fact that the company's ubiquitous U-shaped lock could be picked with the plastic casing of a ballpoint pen. Within two days, a number of blogs, including the consumer electronics site engadget, had posted a video demonstrating how to perform the trick. Hundreds of thousands of people read about the lock's flaw, and cyclists in chatrooms and blogs expressed their alarm.

Two days later the company promised a tougher line of locks, but bloggers stayed on the case. The blog-monitoring Web site Technorati estimated that 1.8 million Internet users read about the lock's flaws. Finally, 10 days after word initially broke, the company said it would exchange any lock for free. [1] The incident cost the company's parent company Ingersoll-Rand an estimated $10 million. [2]

Donna Tocci, the company's media chief, now checks 30-40 blogs a day for discussions about its products. [3]

"This wouldn't happen today," says Steve Rubel, a senior vice president and author of the blog "Micro Persuasion" at the Edelman public relations firm. "Kryptonite didn't respond fast enough, and it spun out of control."

Love it or hate it, businesses are coming to grips with the blogosphere and learning that when managed well it can help the bottom line — or at least public relations. For instance, when a Manhattan blogger complained that he could not find Degree Sport deodorant in his neighborhood, manufacturer Unilever not only e-mailed him to tell him where he could find it but also sent him a free case of the antiperspirant, Rubel says.

In another example of how blogs can improve customer relations, Microsoft employee Robert Scoble's blog (http://scobleizer.wordpress.com/) was credited with helping reduce external criticism of the company's launch of MSN Space in 2004. Scoble then co-authored *Naked Conversations*, describing how blogs are changing communications between business and customers. Microsoft Chairman Bill Gates wrote admiringly on the book jacket that Scoble was "building a connection" to customers, adding, "Maybe they'll tell us how we can better improve our products."

Everyone who follows business blogs has a favorite story about how they have helped or hurt any given firm, says David Kline, co-author of *blog! how the newest media revolution is changing politics, business, and culture.*

Nevertheless, only a fraction of America's biggest companies have embraced the blog's power so far. As of April 18 of this year, 29 — or only 5.8 percent — of *Fortune* 500 companies were blogging, according to a "wiki" launched by Chris Anderson of *Wired* magazine and Ross Mayfield of Socialtext, a maker of enterprise social software for collaboration. [4] *

But companies ignore the blogosphere at their peril, as Dell computer manufacturer found out. Writer, publisher and interactive journalism expert Jeff Jarvis complained on his blog (Buzzma-

* A wiki — the Hawaiian word for quick — is a Web page that readers can edit.

Continued from p. 514

distrust between host and listeners of "the media" and the listeners' ability to voice their opinions on the air.

Meanwhile, a new communications technology was emerging. Rudimentary elements of computer networking dated from the 1960s. The electronic bulletin boards of the 1980s allowed computer users to dial up individual sites for information. Then in the early 1990s came the World Wide Web: a global information space accessible to any Internet-connected computer with the use of click-and-point technology. A new chapter in media history was about to begin.

Birth of Blogs

The first bloggers began blogging in the mid-'90s before the word "blog" had been coined or the technology for widespread use had been developed. The pioneers were computer experts who were and remain little known outside the information-technology community. The advent of easy-to-use software at the end of the decade allowed non-geeks to begin blogging. Then, in the first years of the new century, the Sept. 11, 2001, terrorist attacks showed that the new technology could facilitate national conversation about cataclysmic events while the toppling of Senate Republican leader Lott demonstrated that bloggers could have real impact on politics and government. [15]

The British computer scientist Sir Tim Berners-Lee brought the first World Wide Web site online on Aug. 6, 1991. He had developed the concept of hypertext in the 1980s as a means of facilitating the sharing and updating of computer-stored information among researchers. In 1989 he saw the potential to join his hypertext markup language (HTML) software with the Internet to allow information-sharing globally. And, as blogger Gillmor notes,

chine) that his Dell laptop kept crashing and recounted his fruitless efforts to get Dell customer support to help. His subsequent blog post announcing that he planned to buy an Apple laptop became one of the most trafficked posts for weeks.

"If something is happening on the Internet and you're not aware of it, whether you're a company or a major brand or a government agency, there's a price to pay," says Sue MacDonald, marketing manager at Nielsen Buzzmetrics, which helps companies navigate "consumer-generated media," including blogs. Many firms now check what people are saying about them online, but they do so only on an ad hoc basis.

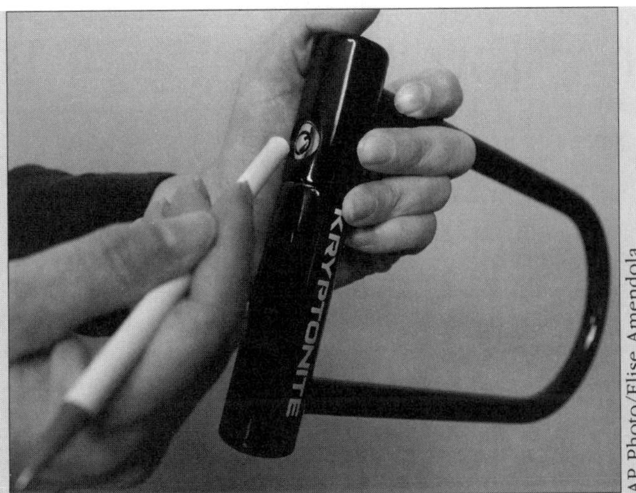

AP Photo/Elise Amendola

Word spread through cyberspace like wildfire in 2004 after a blogger mentioned that the famous U-shaped Kryptonite-brand lock could be easily opened with the plastic casing of a ballpoint pen.

Yet Kline says when people shop online, it is the customer comments rather than advertising or newspapers that have the most important impact on purchasing decisions. He cites *Edelman Annual Trust Barometer*, a survey of 2,000 opinion leaders in 11 countries conducted by the world's biggest public relations firm. Its most recent survey found that participants believe what "a person like me" says about a company or its products more than what anyone else says. Among U.S. participants this tendency leapt from just 20 percent in 2003 to 68 percent in 2005. [5]

Jason Goldman, product manager for Google's blogging service called Blogger, says that at conferences and other gatherings in the last 18 months, there has been a "groundswell" of people getting specifically involved in helping businesses start their own blogs. "The fact that it has already penetrated close to 6 percent among the last bastion of traditional businesses is rather surprising," he says. The percentage of smaller companies blogging, particularly Internet start-ups, was far higher, he adds.

Kline says blogging will dramatically change the way companies advertise. "Now people can go on their blogs and say, I had a lousy experience with a Dell computer, and it has an evident, noticeable impact. In the future, the database miners will be less important than those who can derive relevant meaning from even a small sample of consumers in their own words," he says. "Customers are going to become co-creators in terms of marketing strategy."

— Elaine Monaghan

[1] See David Kirkpatrick, *et al.*, "Why There's No Escaping the Blog," *Fortune*, Jan. 10, 2005.

[2] Ben Delaney, "Kryptonite on level ground six months after U-lock publicity crisis," *Bicycle Retailer*, April 1, 2005.

[3] See "The Blog in the Corporate Machine — Corporate Reputations," *The Economist*, Feb. 11, 2006.

[4] www.socialtext.net/bizblogs/index.cgi.

[5] www.edelman.com/news/ShowOne.asp?ID=102.

Berners-Lee also envisioned two-way communication: the ability to read from *and* to write to documents found on the Web. [16]

Programmers at the National Center for Supercomputing Applications in Champaign, Ill., made the next breakthrough: the development of Mosaic, the first Web browser to provide a multimedia, graphical user interface to the Internet. The leader of the team, Marc L. Andreessen, went on to found the company that later became Netscape. With Mosaic, Web pages were relatively easy to create, and some early forms of what Gillmor calls "personal journalism" emerged. He counts Justin's Links from the Underground by Swarthmore College student Justin Hall as "perhaps the first serious weblog."

"It was journalism," Hall explained later, "but it was mostly about me." [17]

Credit for naming the practice goes to Jorn Barger, a computer geek from the age of 11 and an active participant in the early 1990s in Usenet, the pre-Web computer communications network. On Dec. 17, 1997, Barger began posting short comments and links on his Robot Wisdom Web site. He coined the term "weblog," which he defined in a September 1999 posting as "a webpage where a weblogger . . . 'logs' all the other webpages she finds interesting." By then, Barger was reporting getting 1,500-2,000 hits a day, the term was being shortened to "blog," and the new phenomenon was being heralded — in the words of tech journalist Jon Katz — as "the freshest example of how people use the Net to make their own, radically different new media." [18]

Pyra Labs, a start-up company in San Francisco founded in 1999 by Evan Williams and Meg Hourihan, provided the last of the initial building blocks: an easy-to-use software dubbed "Blogger." The service was made available, for free, in August 1999 — at a time

Teens and 'Gen-Y' Love to Blog

Alongside her photograph and personal information on her MySpace weblog, 19-year-old Jenna from Cross Plains, Tenn., praises her "wonderful" boyfriend Jeremy, adding, "even though he can be a dork sometimes."

A 22-year-old from Salt Lake City wrote on his blog that when he revealed that he was homosexual, his father had kicked him in the groin. "The only people I can really count on in this difficult time is you all," he wrote.

Teens and Internet users who belong to Generation Y — the 18-to-28 age group — are in the vanguard of the blogging revolution, revealing their true loves, rating their teachers, coming out, finding dates, sharing passions and even mourning deaths in public.

"The younger generations have no problem expressing their whole life on their blog," says Mark Jen, a product manager at Plaxo, a company that maintains contact information for more than 10 million Internet users. In fact, 38 percent of Internet users ages 12 to 17 read blogs, while 19 percent say they have created one. Forty-one percent of Generation Y Internet users read blogs and one in five have created one of their own, according to a survey released in December 2005 by the Pew Internet and American Life Project. Blog creation trails off significantly in older age groups, dropping to 9 percent for the 29-40 and 51-59 age groups, 3 percent for the 41-50- and 60-69-year-olds and 4 percent for those 70-plus. [1]

But for young people, blogging has opened the door to a new sense of community, says Jen, 23. For instance, Sara, a 23-year-old from San Francisco, reported finding 42 new "friends" in her first day of MySpace membership.

The enormously popular teen blogging site attracted 48 million visitors in April and was the eighth most trafficked site. Founded in 2003, the site was bought for $580 million in July 2005 by Rupert Murdoch's News Corp.

Teens also use blogs — and flex their blog muscle — in innovative ways. Eight million students around the world use RateMyProfessors.com, which allows college and university students to give frank, anonymous assessments of their teachers. More than 3 million school kids in the United States, Canada, the United Kingdom and Ireland have posted 9.2 million ratings on a sister site, RateMyTeachers.com.

The most rated college is Grand Valley State University in Allendale, Mich., where teachers get marks of good, average or poor — and a red chili pepper if they are "hot." Here, a teacher can learn a student was so bored he counted 137 tiles on the ceiling during a lecture.

Similarly, Facebook.com, a two-year-old online social directory, claims 7.5 million members from more than 2,200 colleges, 22,000 high schools and 2,000 companies and is the seventh-most trafficked site. Two-thirds of the membership visits the site daily, spending an average of 20 minutes viewing photos and profiles of peers or updating their own information.

Bearing in mind recent examples of online predators taking advantage of teens on the Internet, Rep. Michael Fitzpatrick (R-Pa.) has introduced a bill that would restrict minors from accessing commercial social networking Web sites and chat rooms at schools and public libraries. [2] Mobilizing America's Youth, a group that works to increase political participation by the young, opposes the bill, although it agrees with the intent: to protect Internet users. Spokesman Damien Power

when blogs may have numbered fewer than 100. As software developer Matthew McKinnon wrote two years later, Blogger allowed anyone with a Web site to set up a blog "in about two minutes" and to update the site any time from anywhere. [19] As word of the free service spread, the number of blogs grew. The software was rewritten in 2002 so that it could be licensed, and the advertising-supported blogspot began to emerge as the dominant software. By then, the number of blogs was estimated at 40,000. [20]

At that point, blogging was also generating its first intramural spat: complaints from early bloggers about the rise of so-called "war bloggers" in the aftermath of the Sept. 11 terrorist attacks. As the U.S.-led invasion of Afghanistan got under way, several hawkish blogs emerged — notably, Glenn Reynolds' Instapundit — to vent indignation and to chronicle and support the military actions. In contrast to the techies' "inward-looking" sites, Reynolds said his and other sites were "outward-looking" — focused on a larger audience. [21] Old-line bloggers flinched at the newcomers' political slant and at the spike in attention, but the visibility was paying off in eyeballs. Reynolds was counting nearly 20,000 visitors a day by mid-2002.

By the end of the year, the broader-focused blogs were being depicted as a new power center, based on their role in forcing Lott to step down as Senate Republican leader. Mainstream media missed the story of Lott's Dec. 5 remarks at first, but the story gained legs thanks to venting from hundreds of bloggers ranging across the political spectrum. "The Internet's First Scalp," the *New York Post* declared in a headline. [22]

Reynolds and liberal counterpart Joshua Micah Marshall demurred. "I think you can exaggerate the role of the blogs in this," Reynolds said, while Marshall took exception to what he called "blog triumphalism." [23]

Whether exaggerated or not, the episode sent a clear warning to journalists and politicians alike: Ignore the bloggers at your peril.

said Facebook.com allows users to block other users and to report unsolicited messages to site administrators. [3]

However, the ease with which teenagers and young adults "let it all hang out" on their blogs — particularly descriptions of illegal activities like drug or alcohol use — could come back to haunt them. Police regularly trawl MySpace for evidence of crimes both big and small.

Rayann VonSchoech, a community-services officer with the Sacramento Police Department's gang-suppression unit, has bookmarked about 30 MySpace blogs to check for faces matching gang street names or other signs of a looming crime. [4] "I already have a bank full of gangsters," she said. Her colleague Detective Sam Blackmon estimated that the Internet helps provide clues to about 10 percent of the city's gang arrests. [5]

And in Riverton, Kan., five students were arrested in April on suspicion of plotting a school shooting attack after posting a threatening message on MySpace.com. [6]

AP Photo/W.A. Harewood

Georgia State University student Pamela Elder accesses her Facebook.com blog, where she has reconnected with old friends. The two-year-old online social directory claims 7.5 million members from more than 2,200 colleges, 22,000 high schools and 2,000 companies.

Marketers have begun to view the popularity of such sites among the youthful market sector as a vast untapped advertising opportunity. But the younger generation is suspicious of advertisers, so companies are cautious.

"We don't tell clients to market *to* teens," says Steve Rubel, a prominent blogger and senior vice president at the global public relations firm Edelman. "We say you should market *with* teens."

He adds, "You need to figure out what their motivations are and help them succeed, and at the same time . . . integrate your brand into that experience."

— Elaine Monaghan

[1] The Pew survey can be found at www.pewinternet.org/PPF/r/144/report_display.asp.

[2] See Timothy Taylor and Stephanie Woodrow, "Youths to Congress: Don't Block MySpace," *Roll Call*, May 22, 2006.

[3] *Ibid.*

[4] Carrie Peyton Dahlberg, "Many eyes on teens' space; Law enforcement combs popular Web site where youths let it all hang out," *The Sacramento Bee*, May 30, 2006.

[5] *Ibid.*

[6] Marcus Kabel, "Five Students Arrested in Foiled Southeast Kansas School Shooting," *Belleville News-Democrat*, April 20, 2006.

Power of Blogs

With blogging still in its first decade, the number of blogs has skyrocketed along with readership. Bloggers continued to demonstrate their power by helping force the resignations of two media heavyweights in 2005: CBS News anchor Dan Rather and CNN President Eason Jordan. Political candidates also began to use blogs as fund-raising and mobilizing tools — most notably, former Vermont Gov. Howard Dean in his unsuccessful bid for the Democratic presidential nomination in 2004. But the intermingling of journalistic and political roles by some bloggers raised a variety of legal and ethical issues.

The blogosphere's growth has been nothing short of phenomenal. From fewer than 1 million blogs at the start of 2003, the number doubled every six months through early 2006. News coverage of blogs also increased. *The New York Times* used the word in 28 articles in 2002 and 553 articles in 2005. Blog readership also grew rapidly, as the number of adults who have read blogs increased more than fourfold — from 13.2 million in May 2003 to 57 million by January 2006, according to the Pew Internet center. Significantly, more than one out of 10 Internet users have also posted material or comments on other people's blogs. [24]

In 2004 Dean's Internet-driven presidential campaign created a surge of interest in blogs and other online tools among politicians, voters and political journalists. Dean went from a blip on the political radar screen in early 2003 to the presumed Democratic front-runner by the end of the year primarily on the strength of using the Internet to raise more than $40 million from 300,000 donors. At one point his campaign weblog drew 100,000 visitors a day. The excitement about Web-based politics deflated when Dean's Web support failed to materialize at the polls: he ended his campaign on Feb. 18 after losing badly in the Iowa caucuses in January and the New Hampshire primary in early February 2004. [25]

Both President Bush and the eventual Democratic nominee John Kerry did pick up Dean's idea of using blogs as a tool to communicate with supporters and volunteers — but in different formats. An Associated Press Internet reporter described Bush's campaign blog as "flashier," Kerry's more substantive, and noted that Kerry's blog allowed visitors to post comments, while Bush's did not. [26] Bush "didn't get in trouble" for not having an interactive blog, Professor Davis remarks today. "His supporters didn't punish him for it, and he won."

Bloggers did play an important part, however, in helping the president's campaign combat questions that resurfaced late in the campaign about Bush's service in the Texas Air National Guard in the 1960s. The CBS program "60 Minutes II" aired a story on Sept. 8, 2004, claiming that newly discovered documents provided by an anonymous source showed that then-Lt. Bush had received favorable treatment in the Guard and failed to fulfill some service requirements. Rather, a correspondent on the program and then in his 24th year as "CBS Evening News" anchor, reported the story.

An array of conservative bloggers — led by FreeRepublic.com — immediately questioned the authenticity of the documents and accused Rather and CBS of political bias. "You can almost say that conservative bloggers acted as a fire brigade" on the story, says David Perlmutter, a professor of journalism at the University of Kansas who is writing a book on political blogs. Under heavy attack, Rather announced in November that he would step down as anchor in March 2005. Then, after an independent investigation, CBS News conceded in January 2005 that it could not authenticate the documents, fired the story's producer and demoted three other executives connected with the program.

In another episode, CNN President Jordan was forced to resign in February 2005 after comments he made two weeks earlier blaming the U.S. military for the deaths of 12 journalists in Iraq. As with the so-called Rathergate story, conservative blogs publicized the comments as evidence of liberal bias by CNN and eventually dragged mainstream media into covering the story. Jordan's resignation under pressure cheered conservatives but left one leading blogger ambivalent. "I wish our goal were not taking off heads but digging up truth," Jeff Jarvis of buzzmachine.com told *The New York Times.* [27]

Different ethical issues were raised by the role of two political bloggers in South Dakota's hotly contested 2004 Senate race. Senate Democratic Leader Tom Daschle was running neck and neck with Rep. Jim Thune, a Republican strongly supported by national GOP leaders. It turned out that two bloggers, Jon Lauck and Jason Van Beek, who sharply attacked Daschle on their sites, were paid $27,000 and $8,000, respectively, by the Thune campaign, though the campaign did not disclose the payments until after the election. Thune won by about 4,700 votes, and Van Beek now has a full-time job in Thune's Senate office. The campaign insisted at the time that the bloggers were paid for research, not for blogging. [28] ■

CURRENT SITUATION

Gaining Respect

Bloggers and other Internet sites are savoring two important legal victories that recognize confidential-source protections for online journalists and exempt all unpaid Internet political activity from federal campaign-finance regulation.

In a closely watched trade-secrets case, a state appeals court in California ruled on May 26 that online journalists are entitled to the same protection as other news organizations against being forced to divulge confidential sources. The ruling blocks Apple Computer from learning the identities of individuals who leaked inside information to two bloggers in 2004 about a then unreleased digital-music device the company was developing. [29]

Meanwhile, the Federal Election Commission (FEC) decided on March 27 to extend to bloggers and other online publications the same exemption enjoyed by traditional news media: Bloggers will not be required to disclose their costs of covering federal election campaigns. Under the commission's decision, even overtly partisan blogs organized to support a particular candidate or party need not disclose their expenditures unless actually controlled by the candidate or party. [30]

Blogging advocates praised both decisions. "Bloggers should be treated the same as the media under campaign finance law," says Adam Bonin, a Philadelphia lawyer who represented three liberal bloggers before the FEC.

Media Bloggers Association President Cox calls the California decision "another step up in the ladder of building the case law around blogging."

The Apple case stemmed from the pre-release publication of details of the company's new "Asteroid" device in November 2004 on two Web sites devoted to Apple products: Power Page, published by Pennsylvania blogger Jason O'Grady, and Apple Insider, published by the pseudonymous "Kasper Jade." Apple filed suit in state court claiming the two sites had appropriated valuable trade secrets and then tried to use pretrial discovery to find out who leaked the information.

O'Grady and "Jade" both invoked California's journalist shield law in refusing, but the trial judge said the privilege did not apply because the theft

Continued on p. 522

At Issue:

Is blogging increasing public participation in politics?

ROBERT COX
PRESIDENT, MEDIA BLOGGERS ASSOCIATION

WRITTEN FOR *CQ RESEARCHER*, JUNE 2006

yes

Since blogs first "arrived" on the political scene during the 2004 election, blogging has increased popular participation in politics. Blog readership and blog creation have been growing at a phenomenal rate, with political blogging the most active part of the blogosphere.

The question is not whether blogging has increased political participation but rather will that continue as political professionals strive to co-opt blogging for their own ends. Professor Richard Davis (at right) has rightly warned that those in the past who have heralded a new technology as transforming American democracy have been disappointed. Television was to allow more Americans to engage in the great issues of the day, but in the years since the watershed Kennedy-Nixon debates the long-term trend has been a decline in voter turnout.

It is certainly reasonable to fear that political power brokers will seek to control spin on the blogs, just as they do in the rest of the media. Meanwhile, with Rupert Murdoch's purchase of MySpace and the acquisition of About.com by *The New York Times*, large media institutions are already staking out their online claims.

Blogs are fundamentally different from previous mass-communications technologies like newspapers, radio and television. Because they reside on the Internet and are inexpensive to own and operate, anyone with online access can utilize an infinitely scalable, near-free distribution system to reach a global audience. They not only are interactive but also permit information to flow in multiple directions and to be distributed on multiple levels. More important, as Davis notes, blog reading is "purposive," requiring "affirmative steps" that make it ideal for attracting and organizing citizens willing to actively engage in a political campaign. The "netroots" efforts on behalf of Howard Dean's campaign in 2004 demonstrated the power of blogs as a fundraising tool.

The question is not whether blogs increase political participation — they do — but how that participation will manifest itself in the political process. Politicians now realize that blogs have the potential to be a disruptive force in the political power structure. Professor Davis is right to worry that politicians are taking steps to avoid being disintermediated out of the political process, but squelching bloggers is about as effective as squeezing mercury. Traditional gatekeepers in the political process are fighting a rearguard action as blogging redefines the political landscape, levels the information playing field and gives millions of Americans a voice they never had in our national political dialogue.

RICHARD DAVIS
PROFESSOR OF POLITICAL SCIENCE, BRIGHAM YOUNG UNIVERSITY

WRITTEN FOR *CQ RESEARCHER*, JUNE 2006

no

Blogs provide another vehicle for political expression. In that sense, they increase political participation. But if political participation is defined more broadly, blogs potentially fall short.

For example, if we mean increased involvement by bloggers in political activities such as voting, donating, communicating with public officials, community service, and so forth, then there is no evidence blogs have performed that function.

And if we mean involving more people who have not previously been involved in politics, then that seems unlikely as well. That's because the political-blog audience consists of the already highly political. According to a recent survey by Harris Interactive, 52 percent of daily, political-blog readers also listen to talk radio at least several times a week and 86 percent watch network or cable news broadcasts. Among the general public, only 37 percent listen to talk radio, and 71 percent watch network news.

But some might say that will change as blog use grows. That argument is based on a premise that fails to consider human behavior. The mere existence of a technology does not change people's interests, attitudes and political behavior. For example, when people go online, they do much the same thing they used to do through other means: write to family and friends, trade stocks, follow sports scores or pay attention to politics. They are not more likely to engage in activities in which they have little interest.

Political blogs are even less likely than the Internet generally to reach citizens who are not politically interested or active. They are a niche of the blogosphere and of the Internet that the less politically interested must search out and find. Why would they do so? Perhaps if they were angry about some governmental decision, they would. But the stimulus would be their anger, not blogs.

The digital divide between rich and poor feared in the 1990s actually became a divide between the politically interested and active — who found e-mail, Web sites, and online discussion a new mechanism for gathering political information and expressing themselves — and the politically less interested, who used the Internet for other things.

Political blogs are part of that digital divide as well. The politically interested will gravitate to them while the majority who see politics primarily as a civic duty, if even that, will go elsewhere.

Continued from p. 520

of trade secrets amounted to a crime. On appeal, Apple pressed its argument that the bloggers could not claim protection of the law at all, but the San Jose-based appeals court disagreed. "The shield law is intended to protect the gathering and dissemination of news, and that is what petitioners did here," Justice Conrad Rushing wrote in the 69-page opinion.

"Bloggers who practice journalism are journalists . . . and therefore are entitled to the same protection afforded to any other journalist. Period," says Cox.

The FEC's decision largely reaffirmed the agency's initial stance to leave Internet political activity essentially unregulated. A federal judge in Washington in 2004 ordered the agency to reconsider the issue in a suit brought by the House sponsors of the Bipartisan Campaign Reform Act (BCRA), the 2002 measure commonly known by the names of its Senate sponsors: Sens. John McCain, R-Ariz., and Russ Feingold, D-Wis.

In its new regulation, the FEC decided federal candidates must disclose expenditures for paid political advertising on the Internet but left all other Internet political communications unregulated. The rules "totally exempt individuals who engage in political activity on the Internet from the restrictions of the campaign-finance laws," FEC Chairman Michael Toner said before the March 27 vote.

For bloggers, the FEC action adds Web sites and any other Internet or electronic publications to the definition of news media in a longstanding exemption from having to report the costs of news coverage, editorials or commentaries. "Bloggers and others who communicate on the Internet are entitled to the press exemption in the same way as traditional media entities," the commission wrote in explaining the rule.

The commission had taken the same stance in an advisory ruling in November 2005, telling the pro-Democratic blog Fire Up that it did not need to disclose its spending as campaign contributions. A coalition of public-interest groups favoring campaign finance regulation had opposed the exemption. "This looked much more like a partisan political organization," explains Paul Ryan, FEC program director for the Campaign Legal Center.

Prominent bloggers on the left and right both praised the FEC's rule. "This is a tremendous win for speech," said Mike Krempasky of the conservative blog RedState.org. Liberal blogger Duncan Black, writing under the pseudonym Artios, said: "This could have been an utter disaster, but it appears to have all worked out in the end." [31]

For their part, the campaign-finance groups say they are satisfied with the FEC's overall position, but Ryan still voices concern about the broad media exemption. "Whenever the FEC opens an exemption, the window for abuse opens," he says.

Blogging at Work

A police union in suburban Washington, D.C., is watching its online message board more carefully these days after some officers were discovered to have posted racist, sexist and anti-immigrant comments on the site.

A *Los Angeles Times* columnist is no longer writing a political blog for the newspaper because he posted comments on the newspaper's Web site and elsewhere on the Web under pseudonyms.

A marine zoologist is out of a job after the Academy of Natural Sciences in Philadelphia fired her for posting comments about her job on her site and on MySpace.com.

Along with all the marvels of blogging come at least a fair share of new problems. Blogging culture invites the posting of information that in the pre-Internet world might have been kept private and messages that might have been left unwritten — or at least undelivered.

Employers and employees are among those working out rules for blogging — mostly by trial and error. The vast majority of companies appear to have no written policies on the subject. But a blogger activist who says he lost out on a job because of one of his postings counts more than 60 other bloggers who have been fired or disciplined for blog-related reasons.

The most famous workplace victim is Jessica Cutler, a twenty-something former staffer for Sen. Mike DeWine, R-Ohio, who was fired in May 2004 for writing up her active sex life under the cyberhandle "Washingtonienne." Cutler thought the anonymous blog would amuse her girlfriends, only to discover that others were not amused after the blog was publicized through another blog: Wonkette, a widely read Washington gossip and politics site.

Cutler landed on her feet, however. She received a six-figure advance to write a thinly fictionalized account of her experiences under the title *The Washingtonienne: A Novel.* [32]

Curt Hopkins, a journalist-blogger (MorphemeTales) and founder of the now-defunct Committee to Protect Bloggers, began counting blog-related job actions in December 2004 shortly after a public-radio network cited one of his postings in rejecting him for a staff position. By May 2006, Hopkins' list included 61 individuals who had been fired, four who had been disciplined and two, including himself, who were "not hired." Hopkins shut down the blog-protection committee in May for lack of funding.

While no one was fired in the police blog episode, the Montgomery County (Md.) Fraternal Order of Police suffered a black eye in March 2006 when *The Washington Post* disclosed that some officers had anonymously posted offensive comments on the union's password-protected message board. One referred to immigrants as "beaners," and another called a black policewoman a "ghetto" officer. The department responded by restricting access to the site from county computers, while the union promised to monitor the site and remove offensive messages. [33]

The *Los Angeles Times* suspended columnist Michael Hiltzik's Golden State blog in April after he acknowledged posting comments on his own blog and other sites under two assumed names. (The pseudonymous postings were disclosed by another blogger.) The *Times* said it was suspending the blog because Hiltzik had violated ethics guidelines requiring editors and reporters to identify themselves when dealing with the public. Hiltzik continues to write a political column with the same name, however, for the newspaper's print editions. [34]

Meanwhile, the blogosphere is treating marine zoologist Jessa Jeffries as a martyr of sorts after the Academy of Natural Sciences in Philadelphia fired her because her blog (Jessaisms) contained identifiable references to the museum along with racy details about sex and drinking. "Blogger Fired for Actually Having a Life," the widely read Thought Mechanics blog declared in a May 18 posting. Jeffries was unapologetic in her blog post about the firing, but she later told *The New York Times:* "I probably shouldn't have been blogging about work." [35]

Workplace policies on blogging, however, are murky at best. In a survey by the Society for Human Resources Management, only 8 percent of the HR professionals responding said their companies had written policies on the subject. But Jonathan Segal, a Philadelphia employment-law attorney, says it may be too early to try to write detailed policies on employee blogging. "It's so gray, every time you try to write a rule you can come up with a hundred ways that the rules won't work," he says.

For its part, the Electronic Frontier Foundation, a San Francisco-based advocacy group, cautions that more and more bloggers are getting in trouble over the issue and that legal protections for work-related blogging are limited.

"None of this should stop you from blogging," the group says. "Freedom of speech is the foundation of a functioning democracy, and Internet bullies shouldn't use the law to stifle legitimate free expression." [36] ■

OUTLOOK

'Starting Discussions'

Blogging enthusiasts see the phenomenon as far more than an entertaining hobby or short-lived fad. They see blogs as the dawning of a new media age that will replace top-down journalism and government- and corporate-controlled information with ever more interactive communication and ever more democratic political and economic life.

"Traditional media send messages," the French software executive Loïc le Meur proclaims on his blog. "Blogs start discussions."

Clearly, blogging has yet to reach its potential — in politics, business or culture. Blogs are continuing to increase in number and applications: podcasting and videoblogs are now emerging. "There's lots more innovation and development to be done," says the Pew center's Rainie. "It's very much an unfolding, evolving form."

But a Gallup Poll in February suggests that popular interest in blogging may be leveling off — and at a somewhat low level. Under the headline "Blog Readership Bogged Down," Gallup reports that only 9 percent of Internet users say they frequently read blogs and another 11 percent occasionally. The figures are essentially unchanged from a year earlier. [37]

The number of blogs may itself be misleading, since most are inactive after a couple of weeks. "Most blogs are like diets," says Rosensteil at the Project for Excellence in Journalism. "They're started and then abandoned."

Blogging's influence may also be blunted by its very successes, as the institutions that bloggers are self-consciously challenging adapt the tool for their own uses. Businesses, political candidates and government agencies are learning how to use blogs to promote their products, campaigns or services. It remains to be seen whether they will be transformed by the bottom-up communication that results or whether they will simply learn how to use blogs to manipulate consumer taste and voter behavior.

News organizations are also rapidly adding blogs to their Web sites. "The blogosphere and the mainstream media world are getting blended now and will probably blend more in the future," says Rainie. "The notion that they are separate realms and competing realms will fade."

Blogging has certainly increased the number of voices in the news media and the amount of information and opinion available for news junkies. Independent blogs are making "big media" somewhat more accountable through the fact-checking and agenda-setting functions Rainie cites. At the same time, Rosensteil says readers take the independent blogs with a grain of salt.

"People who read blogs don't necessarily think of them as accurate," he says. "They view them as interesting opinion, but they don't think of them as The Associated Press. They have a feel for what they're getting."

In addition, some in the "old media" fret that minute-by-minute postings in short bursts have little, if any, lasting value, informational or literary. "Blogging is the closest literary culture has come to instant obsolescence," Washington writer Trevor

Butterworth concludes in a lengthy critique in the London-based *Financial Times*. "No Modern Library edition of the great polemicists of the blogosphere to yellow on the shelf; nothing but a virtual tomb for a billion posts. . . ." [38]

Bloggers are also worried about a potential threat to their most valuable resource: unhampered access to the Internet. Some major telephone and cable companies want to charge extra for delivering some high-bandwidth services through their wires faster than others. They say they need the revenue to pay for network infrastructure improvements. But bloggers are part of a coalition that wants Congress to block the idea by requiring non-discriminatory access to the Internet — so-called net neutrality. They argue that the proposed charges would make it harder for "everyday people" to have their voices heard on the Web. [39]

Despite all those reservations and caveats, blogging advocates remain convinced that blogs are an important and lasting tool for self-expression and self-empowerment. "The fact that anybody, anywhere, can create their own media, publish their own opinions and information on the Web — that is not going away," says MacKinnon at Harvard's Berkman Center. "In fact, that is going to become more pervasive."

"Blogging will last," says UCLA's Volokh, "because it taps into one of the most fundamental desires of many humans, which is to express their views — and to get the pleasures both selfish and selfless of knowing that others are listening and — one hopes — being enlightened and helped by the spreading of those views."

Author Kline agrees. "The idea of ordinary people talking to each other about what's important in the world, the ability to reach vast audiences and to maneuver around the official sources of power — that's going to survive," he says. "There's no way this is going to fade, and people are just going to go back and be passive recipients of politics, business, information, products and services. That genie is definitely out of the bottle." ■

Notes

[1] See "The People Who Shape Our World," *Time*, May 8, 2006, (www.time.com). For individual entries, see Ana Marie Cox, "Matt Drudge: Redefining What's News," p. 171; Al Franken, "Arianna Huffington: The Woman Who Made a Sharp Left," p. 172. Some background on Drudge and Huffington drawn from Wikipedia (visited May 2006).

[2] Pew Internet and American Life Project, "The state of blogging," January 2005; www.pewinternet.org/PPF/r/144/report_display.asp.

[3] See Daniel Williams, "New Vehicle for Dissent Is a Fast Track to Prison; Bloggers Held Under Egypt's Emergency Laws," *The Washington Post*, May 31, 2006, p. A10; Tom Zeller Jr., "Internet Firms Facing Questions About Censoring Online Searches in China," *The New York Times*, Feb. 15, 2006, p. C3; Megan K. Stack, "Iran Attempts to Pull the Plug on Web Dissidents," *Los Angeles Times*, Jan. 24, 2005, p. A3.

[4] Quoted in Eric Deggans, "Huffington Beats Odds as Blogger," *St. Petersburg* (Fla.) *Times*, May 10, 2006, p. 1A.

[5] *Ibid.*

[6] Noah Schachtman, "Blogs Make the Headlines," *Wired News*, Dec. 23, 2002.

[7] Quoted in David Kline and Dan Burstein, *blog! how the newest media revolution is changing politics, business, and culture* (2005), p. 17.

[8] For background, see Kenneth Jost, "Free-Press Disputes," *CQ Researcher*, April 8, 2002, pp. 293-316.

[9] www.nationalreview.com.

[10] See Anick Jesdanun, "Democrats Credential Bloggers; Republicans Say They Will, Too," The Associated Press, July 9, 2004.

[11] For background, see Kline and Burstein, *op. cit.*; Dan Gillmor, *We the Media: Grassroots Journalism by the People, for the People* (2004).

[12] Dan Burstein, "From Cave Painting to Wonkette: A Short History of Blogging," in Kline & Burstein, *op. cit.*, pp. xii-xiii.

[13] See Emily Eakin, "The Ancient Art of Haranguing Has Moved To the Internet, Belligerent as Ever," *The New York Times*, Aug. 10, 2002, p. B9.

[14] Gillmor, *op. cit.*, p. 4.

[15] Some background drawn from Wikipedia entries on individuals and computer technologies. For an overview, see Steven Levy, *et al.*, "Living in the Blog-osphere," *Newsweek*, Aug. 26, 2002, p. 42.

[16] Gillmor, *op. cit.*, pp. 11-12. For a first-person account, see Tim Berners-Lee and Mark Fischetti, *Weaving the Web: Origins and Fu-*

About the Authors

Associate Editor **Kenneth Jost** graduated from Harvard College and Georgetown University Law Center. He is the author of the *Supreme Court Yearbook* and editor of *The Supreme Court from A to Z* (both *CQ Press*). He was a member of the *CQ Researcher* team that won the 2002 ABA Silver Gavel Award. His recent reports include "The Future of Newspapers" and "Free-Press Disputes."

Melissa J. Hipolit is the assistant editor of *CQ Researcher*. She graduated *magna cum laude* from Hobart and William Smith Colleges with a bachelor's degree in history. She has contributed to recent reports, including "American Indians," "Death Penalty Controversies," "Eating Disorders" and "Emerging China."

ture of the World Wide Web (1999). Berners-Lee, who was knighted in 2004, is now director of the World Wide Web Consortium.

[17] Gillmor, *op. cit.*, p. 12.

[18] Jon Katz, "Here Come the Weblogs," Slashdot.com, May 24, 1999, reprinted in Editors of Perseus Publications, *We've Got Blog: How Weblogs Are Changing Our Culture* (2002). As reprinted, the article carries the date May 24, 2001, an apparent mistake.

[19] Matthew McKinnon, "King of the Blogs," *Shift*, summer 2001, linked from "Pyra Labs," *Wikipedia* (visited May 2006).

[20] Steven Levy, "Will the Blogs Kill Old Media?" *Newsweek*, May 20, 2002, p. 52.

[21] Quoted in David F. Gallagher, "A Rift Among Bloggers," *The New York Times*, June 10, 2002, p. C4.

[22] John Podhoretz, "The Internet's First Scalp," *The New York Post*, Dec. 13, 2002, p. 41.

[23] Quoted in Mark Jurkowitz, "The Descent of Trent Lott Brings the Rise of Bloggers," *The Boston Globe*, Dec. 26, 2002, p. D1.

[24] Total readership from Pew Internet and American Life Project, forthcoming report, July 2006; blog posting data from previous report, January 2005.

[25] Some background from Liz Halloran, "The Blogger's Life: Online Deaniacs Vow to Stay Involved," *Hartford Courant*, Feb. 20, 2004, p. D1; Michael Cudahay and Jock Gill, "The Political Is Personal — Not Web-Based," *Pittsburgh Post-Gazette*, Feb. 1, 2004, p. E1.

[26] Anick Jesdanun, "Product Review: Bush, Kerry sites lackluster after bar raised in Democratic primaries," The Associated Press, July 15, 2004.

[27] Quoted in Katharine Q. Seelye, "Bloggers as News Media Trophy Hunter," *The New York Times*, Feb. 14, 2005, p. C1.

[28] See Eric Black, "In New Era of Reporting, Blogs Take a Seat at the Media Table," *The* (Minneapolis) *Star Tribune*, March 9, 2005.

[29] The case is *O'Grady v. Superior Court, Calif. Court of Appeal, Sixth District* (May 26, 2006). For coverage, see Howard Mintz, "Apple Loses Case Against Bloggers," *San Jose Mercury News*, May 27, 2006, p. A1.

[30] See Federal Election Commission, "Internet Communications," Notice 2006-8, published in *Federal Register*, Vol. 71, No. 70 (April 12, 2006), p. 18589. For coverage, see Adam Nagourney, "Agency Exempts Most of Internet From Campaign Spending Laws," *The New York Times*, March 28, 2006, p. A15; Eric Pfeiffer, "FEC to Leave Alone Web Political Speech," *The Washington Times*, March 28, 2006, p. A6.

[31] Both quoted in Thomas B. Edsall, "FEC Rules Exempt Blogs From Internet Political Limits," *The Washington Post*, March 28, 2006, p. A3.

[32] See April Witt, "Blog Interrupted," *Washington Post Magazine*, Aug. 15, 2004, p. W12; Jonathan Yardley, "Capitol Hill Siren's Tell-All Fiction," May 24, 2005, p. C1.

[33] See Ernesto Londono, "Union's Online Controls Greeted Warily," *The Washington Post*, April 1, 2006, and earlier stories by same writer March 28 and March 31.

[34] See Katie Hafner, "At Los Angeles Times, a Columnist Who Used a False Web Name Loses His Blog," *The New York Times*, April 24, 2006, p. C1.

[35] Anna Bahney, "Interns? No Bloggers Need Apply," *The New York Times*, May 25, 2006, p. G1.

[36] See Electronic Frontier Foundation, "Legal Guide for Bloggers," April 20, 2006.

[37] "Blog Readership Bogged Down: Audience Skews Slightly Young," Gallup News Service, Feb. 10, 2006. The results were based on a telephone survey of 1,013 randomly selected adults Dec. 5-8, 2005; the margin of error is plus or minus 3 percentage points. See also "Bloggy, We Hardly Knew Ye," *Chicago Tribune* (editorial), Feb. 22, 2006, p. C16; for a reply, see Eric Zorn, "Post This: Blogs' Demise Highly Exaggerated," *Chicago Tribune*, Feb. 23, 2006, p. C5.

[38] Trevor Butterworth, "Time for the Last Post," *Financial Times*, Feb. 18, 2006, *Weekend Magazine*, p. 18.

[39] For opposing views, see *Hands Off the Internet*, www.handsoff.com, and www.SavetheInternet.com. For background, see Marcia Clemmitt, "Controlling the Internet," *CQ Researcher*, May 12, 2006, pp. 409-432.

FOR MORE INFORMATION

Berkman Center for Internet and Society, Harvard Law School, Baker House, 1587 Massachusetts Ave., Cambridge, MA 02138; (617) 495-7547; http://cyber.law.harvard.edu. A research program investigating legal, technical and social developments in cyberspace.

Electronic Frontier Foundation, 454 Shotwell St., San Francisco, CA 94110-1914; (415) 436-9333; www.eff.org. A nonprofit working to protect digital rights; represented two of the Web sites involved in the Apple case.

Media Bloggers Association; (928) 223-5711; http://mediabloggers.org. A nonpartisan organization dedicated to promoting blogging as a distinct form of media and helping to extend the power of the press, with all the rights and responsibilities that entails, to every citizen.

Pew Internet and American Life Project, 1615 L St., N.W., Suite 700, Washington, DC 20036; (202) 419-4500; www.pewinternet.org. Explores the impact of the Internet on families, communities, work and home, daily life, education, health care and civic and political life.

Project for Excellence in Journalism, 1850 K St., N.W., Suite 850, Washington, DC 20006; (202) 293-7394; www.journalism.org. A Columbia University Graduate School of Journalism initiative aimed at raising journalism standards.

Reporters Committee for Freedom of the Press, 1101 Wilson Blvd., Suite 1100, Arlington, VA 22209; (703) 807-2100; www.rcfp.org. A nonprofit providing free legal assistance to help journalists defend their First Amendment rights.

Society of Professional Journalists, 3909 N. Meridian St., Indianapolis, IN 46208; (317) 927-8000; www.spj.org. Dedicated to the perpetuation of a free press as the cornerstone of democracy.

Bibliography

Selected Sources

Books

Armstrong, Jerome, and Markos Moulitsas Zuniga, *Crashing the Gates: Netroots, Grassroots, and the Rise of People-Powered Politics*, Chelsea Green, 2006.
Liberal bloggers Armstrong (MyDD) and Moulitsas (DailyKos) present strategies for revitalizing progressive politics and "revolutionizing" the Democratic Party.

Davis, Richard, *Politics Online: Blogs, Chatrooms and Discussion Groups in American Democracy*, Routledge, 2005.
A professor of political science at Brigham Young University calls online political discussion "a new force in American politics," examines the kind of people who participate and evaluates its potential as a tool for democratic governance.

Editors of Perseus Publishing, *We've Got Blog: How Weblogs Are Changing Our Culture*, Perseus Publishing, 2002.
This collection of 34 first-person accounts and essays from bloggers includes an eight-page glossary and two-page list of "helpful" sites in building your own blog and understanding weblog culture.

Gillmor, Dan, *We the Media: Grassroots Journalism by the People, for the People*, O'Reilly Books, 2004.
A former business columnist for the *San Jose* (Calif.) *Mercury News* and now president of the Center for Citizen Media writes with conviction about "journalism's transformation from a 20th-century mass-media structure to something profoundly more grassroots and democratic."

Kline, David, and Dan Burstein, *blog! how the newest media revolution is changing politics, business, and culture*, CDS Books, 2005.
The authors provide overviews and more than 30 interviews with or commentaries by major bloggers covering the impact of blogs on politics and policy, business and economics, and media and culture. Appendices list most popular blogs as of May 2005 and the authors' recommended blogs by subject matter. Kline, a journalist, and Burstein, a journalist and venture capitalist, are also co-authors of *Road Warriors: Dreams and Nightmares Along the Information Highway* (Dutton, 1995).

Reynolds, Glenn, *An Army of Davids: How Markets and Technology Empower Ordinary People to Beat Big Media, Big Government, and Other Goliaths*, Nelson Current, 2006.
Conservative blogger Reynolds (Instapundit) argues that technology is evening out the balance of power between the individual and the organization.

Scoble, Robert, and Shel Israel, *Naked Conversations: How Blogs Are Changing the Way Businesses Talk With Customers*, John Wiley, 2006.
Business blogger Scoble and former public relations executive Israel use 50 case histories to argue that blogging is an efficient and credible method of business communication. Includes overview of blogging culture internationally and suggestions for how to blog successfully in a crisis.

Articles

Bai, Matt, "Can Bloggers Get Real?" *The New York Times Magazine*, May 28, 2006, p. 13.
The writer questions whether blogs and other online political tools will fundamentally change the nature of U.S. politics.

Baker, Stephen, and Heather Green, "Blogs Will Change Your Business," *Business Week*, May 2, 2005, p. 56.
The cover story — written in the form of blog postings over a five-day period — advises businesses to consider blogs as an invaluable tool for market research and consumer feedback.

Butterworth, Trevor, "Time for the Last Post," *Financial Times*, Feb. 18, 2006, *Weekend Magazine*, p. 16.
The writer debunks blogging's "evangelists," insisting most blogs are "overblown, boring and don't make a penny."

Perlmutter, David D., "Political Blogs: the New Iowa?" *The Chronicle of Higher Education*, May 26, 2006, p. 38.
The article raises questions about the role of blogs in the next presidential election. Perlmutter, who recently joined the faculty of the University of Kansas School of Journalism and Mass Communications, also publishes a political-analysis blog: www.policybyblog.squarespace.com.

Rosen, Jeffrey, "Your Blog or Mine?" *The New York Times Magazine*, Dec. 19, 2004, p. 19.
Blogs are transforming "the boundaries between public and private," according to Rosen, a journalist and law professor at George Washington University.

Reports and Studies

Pew Internet and American Life Project, "The state of blogging," January 2005 (www.pewinternet.org/PPF/r/144/report_display.asp).
The four-page data memo shows blog readership increasing despite most Americans' unfamiliarity with the practice. An updated report is to be published in July 2006.

The Next Step:

Additional Articles from Current Periodicals

Bloggers and Journalists

Bernton, Hal, "War Blog Rings True For Many," *The Seattle Times*, Nov. 10, 2005, p. D1.

Michael Yon and his blog (michaelyon.blogspot.com) belong to a broader network of war bloggers whose blogs about the Iraq war offer an alternative source from the mainstream media for readers wanting to learn about the war.

Gillin, Beth, "A 'Blogswarm' Stings Old Media Into Action," *The Philadelphia Inquirer*, Aug. 18, 2005, p. E1.

When bloggers join together and disparage the mainstream media for not paying attention to stories they deem worthy, they can sometimes push them to cover stories they wouldn't have otherwise.

Kurtz, Howard, "Washington Post Blogger Resigns Amid Allegations," *The Seattle Times*, March 25, 2006, p. A6.

Ben Domenech, a conservative blogger hired by *The Washington Post's* Web site, resigned after allegations of plagiarism.

Last, Jonathan, "One Last Thing," *The Philadelphia Inquirer*, April 23, 2006, p. D5.

Last argues that while bloggers play a useful role, they discount news-gathering in favor of news analysis, which is only a tiny part of real journalism,.

Parker, Kathleen, "All About Bloggers," *Chicago Tribune*, Dec. 29, 2005, p. C27.

The writer values the role of the new "citizen journalists" but worries about the power blogs are garnering — untempered by restraint or accountability.

Young, Cathy, "When Blog Hysteria Does Real Harm," *The Boston Globe*, Oct. 24, 2005, p. A15.

After a 21-year-old student at the University of Oklahoma blew himself up outside the school's football stadium, bloggers and the mainstream media brought out the worst in each other by perpetuating rumors.

Blogs in Politics

Chaddock, Gail Russell, "Their Clout Rising, Blogs Are Courted By Washington's Elite," *The Christian Science Monitor*, Oct. 27, 2005, p. 1.

Washington politicians are eager to engage bloggers because of their power to shape debate.

Johnson, Steve, "Blah, Blah, Blogs," *Chicago Tribune*, May 5, 2006, p. C1.

Officeholders' blogs are trendy, but they tend to read like press releases or repackaged campaign material rather than the casual, interactive communication that defines other blogs.

Mannies, Jo, "Bloggers' Scrutiny Keeps Missouri Politicians Jumping," *St. Louis Post-Dispatch*, Oct. 9, 2005, p. C6.

Missouri's political blogs are fast becoming a major influence in regional politics.

VandeHei, Jim, "Blogs Attack From Left As Democrats Reach For Center," *The Washington Post*, Jan. 28, 2006, p. A6.

Fiery liberals raising their voices on political blogs are butting heads with elected Democrats who are trying to appeal to a much broader audience.

Wangsness, Lisa, "In Blogosphere, Democrats Provide A First," *The Boston Globe*, May 22, 2006, p. B1.

Political bloggers in Massachusetts got statewide candidates together to answer their questions for the first time ever.

Blogs in the Workplace

Griffin, Greg, "Treading With Caution Into the Blogosphere, Web Logs Can Be Useful Tools," *The Denver Post*, May 1, 2005, p. K1.

Legal experts say companies should make sure blogs are covered in workplace policies.

Joyce, Amy, "Blogged Out of a Job," *The Washington Post*, Feb. 19, 2006, p. F6.

The number of workplace policies explaining the company's rules on blogging is small, but several employers have disciplined workers for personal blogs.

Osterman, Rachel, "Blog Complaints Can Get Disgruntled Workers Fired," *The Seattle Post-Intelligencer*, May 30, 2005, p. F3.

Employees are airing workplace complaints through their personal blogs, and some are getting fired for it.

Citing *CQ Researcher*

Sample formats for citing these reports in a bibliography include the ones listed below. Preferred styles and formats vary, so please check with your instructor or professor.

MLA Style

Jost, Kenneth. "Rethinking the Death Penalty." CQ Researcher 16 Nov. 2001: 945-68.

APA Style

Jost, K. (2001, November 16). Rethinking the death penalty. *CQ Researcher, 11*, 945-968.

Chicago Style

Jost, Kenneth. "Rethinking the Death Penalty." *CQ Researcher*, November 16, 2001, 945-968.

In-depth Reports on Issues in the News

Are you writing a paper?

Need backup for a debate?

Want to become an expert on an issue?

For 80 years, students have turned to *CQ Researcher* for in-depth reporting on issues in the news. Reports on a full range of political and social issues are now available. Following is a selection of recent reports:

Civil Liberties
Right to Die, 5/05
Immigration Reform, 4/05
Gays on Campus, 10/04

Crime/Law
War on Drugs, 6/06
Domestic Violence, 1/06
Death Penalty Controversies, 9/05
Methamphetamines, 7/05
Identity Theft, 6/05
Marijuana Laws, 2/05

Education
Academic Freedom, 10/05
Intelligent Design, 7/05
No Child Left Behind, 5/05
Gender and Learning, 5/05

Environment
Nuclear Energy, 3/06
Climate Change, 1/06
Saving the Oceans, 11/05
Endangered Species Act, 6/05
Alternative Energy, 2/05

Health/Safety
Rising Health Costs, 4/06
Pension Crisis, 2/06
Avian Flu Threat, 1/06
Domestic Violence, 1/06
Disaster Preparedness, 11/05
Birth-Control Debate, 6/05
Marijuana Laws, 2/05

International Affairs
Future of European Union, 10/05
War in Iraq, 10/05

Social Trends
Controlling the Internet, 5/06
American Indians, 4/06

Terrorism/Defense
Port Security, 4/06
Presidential Power, 2/06

Youth
Teen Spending, 5/06
Bullying, 2/05
Teen Driving, 1/05

Upcoming Reports

Pork-Barrel Politics, 6/16/06
Reviving Downtowns, 6/23/06
Drinking on Campus, 6/30/06
Turmoil in Latin America, 7/21/06
Social Networking, 7/28/06
Treatment of Detainees, 8/18/06

ACCESS

CQ Researcher is available in print and online. For access, visit your library or www.cqresearcher.com.

STAY CURRENT

To receive notice of upcoming *CQ Researcher* reports, or learn more about *CQ Researcher* products, subscribe to the free e-mail newsletters, *CQ Researcher Alert!* and *CQ Researcher News*: www.cqpress.com/newsletters.

PURCHASE

To purchase a *CQ Researcher* report in print or electronic format (PDF), visit www.cqpress.com or call 866-427-7737. Single reports start at $10. Bulk purchase discounts and electronic rights licensing are also available.

SUBSCRIBE

A full-service *CQ Researcher* print subscription—including 44 reports a year, monthly index updates, and a bound volume—is $688 for academic and public libraries, $667 for high school libraries, and $827 for media libraries. Add $25 for domestic postage.

CQ Researcher Online offers a backfile from 1991 and a number of tools to simplify research. For pricing information, call 800-834-9020, ext. 1906, or e-mail librarysales@cqpress.com.

CQ Researcher

Published by CQ Press, a division of Congressional Quarterly Inc.

cqresearcher.com

Pork Barrel Politics

Do earmarks lead to waste and corruption?

Ever since the country was founded, congressional lawmakers have curried favor with hometown voters by providing funds — known as earmarks — for local projects and favored firms. Recently, however, the number of earmarks has skyrocketed from 2,000 projects worth $10.6 billion in 1998 to 15,584 items totaling $32.7 billion in 2004. Defenders of such spending argue it aids valuable local projects like parks and after-school programs that might otherwise go unfunded. But critics warn that such pork barrel politics also fuels corruption. Former Rep. Randy "Duke" Cunningham, R-Calif., recently pleaded guilty to accepting $2.4 million in bribes to direct earmarked funds to defense contractors. Opponents of uncontrolled earmarking also complain that local "pork" projects take funds away from national needs. A current defense spending bill, for example, would divert money from troop support and other Pentagon priorities to local defense contractors for lower-priority projects.

Former Rep. Randy "Duke" Cunningham, R-Calif., apologizes on Nov. 28, 2005, after pleading guilty to taking $2.4 million in bribes to sponsor earmarks.

INSIDE THIS REPORT

CQ Researcher • June 16, 2006 • www.cqresearcher.com
Volume 16, Number 23 • Pages 529-552

RECIPIENT OF SOCIETY OF PROFESSIONAL JOURNALISTS AWARD FOR EXCELLENCE ◆ AMERICAN BAR ASSOCIATION SILVER GAVEL AWARD

THE ISSUES

BACKGROUND

CURRENT SITUATION

OUTLOOK

SIDEBARS AND GRAPHICS

FOR FURTHER RESEARCH

Cover: Former Rep. Randy "Duke" Cunningham, R-Calif., apologizes on Nov. 28, 2005, after pleading guilty to taking $2.4 million in bribes to sponsor defense-related earmarks. He was sentenced to more than eight years in federal prison. (AP Photo/Lenny Ignelzi)

CQ Researcher

June 16, 2006
Volume 16, Number 23

MANAGING EDITOR: Thomas J. Colin

ASSISTANT MANAGING EDITOR: Kathy Koch

ASSOCIATE EDITOR: Kenneth Jost

STAFF WRITERS: Marcia Clemmitt, Peter Katel

CONTRIBUTING WRITERS: Rachel S. Cox, Sarah Glazer, David Hosansky, Patrick Marshall, Tom Price

DESIGN/PRODUCTION EDITOR: Olu B. Davis

ASSISTANT EDITOR: Melissa J. Hipolit

EDITORIAL INTERN: Nicholas Sohr

CQ PRESS

A Division of Congressional Quarterly Inc.

SENIOR VICE PRESIDENT/PUBLISHER: John A. Jenkins

DIRECTOR, LIBRARY PUBLISHING: Kathryn C. Suárez

DIRECTOR, EDITORIAL OPERATIONS: Ann Davies

CONGRESSIONAL QUARTERLY INC.

CHAIRMAN: Paul C. Tash

VICE CHAIRMAN: Andrew P. Corty

PRESIDENT/EDITOR IN CHIEF: Robert W. Merry

CQ Researcher (ISSN 1056-2036) is printed on acid-free paper. Published weekly, except March 24, July 7, July 14, Aug. 4, Aug. 11, Nov. 24, Dec. 22 and Dec. 29, by CQ Press, a division of Congressional Quarterly Inc. Annual full-service subscriptions for institutions start at $667. For pricing, call 1-800-834-9020, ext. 1906. To purchase a *CQ Researcher* report in print or electronic format (PDF), visit www.cqpress.com or call 866-427-7737. Single reports start at $10. Bulk purchase discounts and electronic-rights licensing are also available. Periodicals postage paid at Washington, D.C., and additional mailing offices. POSTMASTER: Send address changes to *CQ Researcher*, 1255 22nd St., N.W., Suite 400, Washington, DC 20037.

Pork Barrel Politics

BY MARCIA CLEMMITT

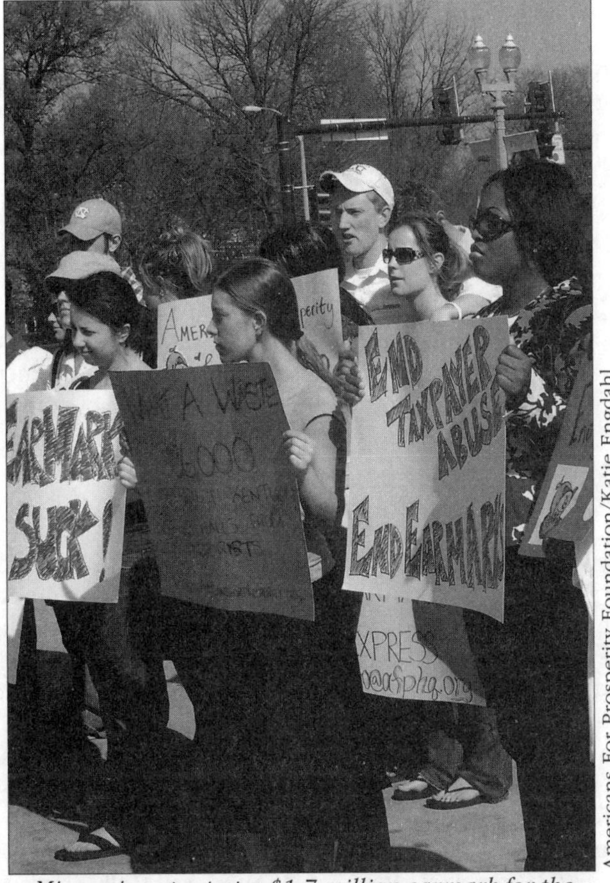

Americans For Prosperity Foundation/Katie Engdahl

Missourians protest a $1.7 million earmark for the Missouri Historical Society and Museum in St. Louis, on April 12, 2006. The museum will house the papers of former House Majority Leader Richard A. Gephardt, D-Mo. Critics say the skyrocketing number of earmarks is diverting funds from critical national needs, including the war in Iraq.

THE ISSUES

Rep. Ken Calvert, R-Calif., bought a weedy, trash-strewn four-acre lot in his home district for $550,000 a year ago and sold it recently for nearly $1 million.

In the past, the transaction might have been viewed as just another smart business deal. But in the wake of the bribery conviction of former Rep. Randy "Duke" Cunningham, also a California Republican, and the brewing scandal involving Rep. William J. Jefferson, D-La. — eyebrows and questions have been raised over Calvert's deal.

During the time Calvert and a partner owned the property, he also requested and received $9.5 million in federal funds to upgrade a nearby freeway interchange and support new commercial development. "Even for a speculator like Calvert," the near doubling of the land's price in a year was "an unusually good deal," made possible in part by transportation improvements in the region, said a front-page *Los Angeles Times* article. [1]

Calvert has not been charged with any wrongdoing. And he firmly says he sought the funds — known as earmarks — only to benefit residents of his district. "All my life in public service, I've never done anything to enrich myself using the position I hold," he said. [2]

But with Cunningham already in prison for accepting bribes in exchange for earmarks for defense contractors and the Justice Department investigating up to 2,000 cases of alleged public corruption — according to Heritage Foundation researcher Ronald Utt — public suspicion is unusually high that legislators routinely trade the promise of earmarked funds for money.

Earmarks are monies members of Congress secure for their hometowns or businesses they favor. Although they have a long history, in the past decade Republican congressional leaders have greatly increased the number of earmarks granted by Appropriations committees — a change some analysts say is leading to more corruption on Capitol Hill and irresponsible spending that shortchanges needy projects and wastes taxpayers' money.

It's especially disturbing if earmarks are granted corruptly in defense bills, said Norm Ornstein, a longtime congressional analyst with the free-market American Enterprise Institute (AEI) think tank. "This is nauseating on so many levels," said Ornstein. The earmarks that Cunningham — a decorated Vietnam War veteran — sponsored in exchange for bribes were "worse than just taking money. It is taking money and undermining everything he presumably stood for." [3]

Normally, lawmakers sponsor local earmarks — or political "pork" — to help their home districts and improve their own re-election chances. Thousands of local projects were aided, such as the Cowgirl Hall of Fame in Fort Worth, Texas, and the teapot museum in Sparta, N.C. There were also tax breaks for favored companies and orders for military aircraft that the Pentagon never requested but whose production would protect jobs in lawmakers' hometowns. (*See sidebar, p. 537.*) In a recent and "depressing development," however, says Utt, evidence seems to be piling up that there is a growing "connection between personal profit and earmarks, and I think we're just seeing the tip of the iceberg."

"The members are turning the appropriations process into an ATM machine," lamented Rep. David R. Obey, D-Wis., the top-ranking Democrat on the House Appropriations Committee. [4]

In the past, earmarks were generally awarded based on the seniority of the member seeking the appropriation. But after Republicans became the majority party in Congress in 1995, they began using earmarks to help GOP lawmakers with shaky electoral margins win over voters in their districts and to reward legislators who voted for bills

Number of Earmarks Has Skyrocketed

Between 1995 and 2005, the number of pork barrel projects, or earmarks, increased by 940 percent after Republicans took control of Congress. The number dropped in 2005 amid emerging corruption scandals and growing concerns over the deficit.

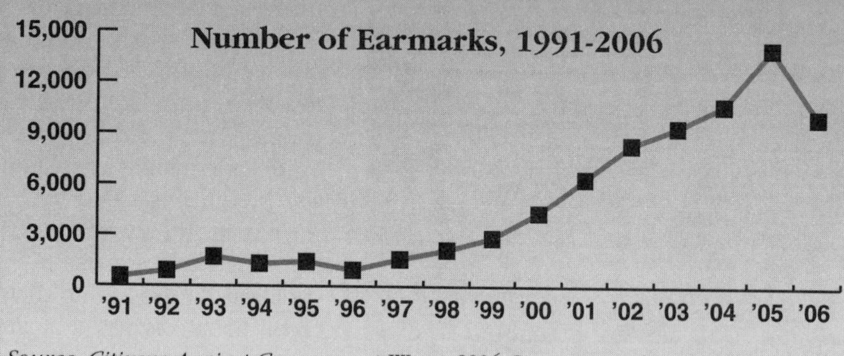

Source: Citizens Against Government Waste, 2006 Congressional Pig Book

the leadership favored. As a result, earmark requests have mushroomed to the point that they compromise the ability of Congress and federal agencies to do their jobs by diverting money from vital needs, say some analysts.

For example, the 2006 defense spending bill contained 2,837 earmarks costing $11.2 billion, up from 587 earmarks worth $4.2 billion in fiscal 1994. While the number of earmarks has skyrocketed, the cost of the average earmark has plummeted. In 1970, there were only 12 defense earmarks costing an average of $466 million; the average earmark sought for fiscal 2006 cost just $3.9 million. [5]

The marked shift from a limited number of high-dollar earmarks to thousands of low-cost items demonstrates a major change in the way lawmakers view earmarks, according to Steve Ellis, vice president for programs at the budget-watchdog group Taxpayers for Common Sense.

"You could argue that those dozen 1970 earmarks worth nearly a half-billion dollars each may have represented legitimate policy disagreements between the executive and legislative branches. But it's clear that the $3.9-million average earmark in 2006 represented members of Congress eager to steer federal . . . defense dollars back home for pork barrel needs and political favors," Ellis told the Senate Homeland Security and Government Affairs Committee in March. [6]

That raises serious questions about lawmakers' priorities, he said. "One area you would think we could all agree on is that adequately providing for our men and women in uniform is of the utmost importance," he said. "Evidently, some members of Congress think some other items are of utmost importance, like the Outdoor Odyssey adventure camp in Boswell, Pa., and paying for Montana's Lewis and Clark Bicentennial." [7]

Such projects divert funds from more important needs, such as providing fully armored Humvees and adequate body armor for troops in Iraq, say Ellis and others.

Moreover, sorting through tens of thousands of earmark requests that flood congressional appropriators annually is now a bigger-than-full-time job that distracts lawmakers and their aides from monitoring how executive-branch agencies are using taxpayers' money, says former Democratic House Appropriations staffer Scott Lilly, a senior fellow at the Center for American Progress, a liberal think tank. "I was glad to leave [Congress,] because I got tired of people sticking pieces of paper [containing earmark requests] in my pockets" on the House floor, Lilly says.

The roughly 15,000 earmark requests that appropriators receive during a congressional session produce "a stack of paper 10 feet high," says Lilly. "The subcommittees have had to detail people from the [federal] agencies [under their jurisdiction] to come down and log them in."

For instance, a recent highway bill had 6,350 earmarks, or 15 per House district, he continues. "If you were going to do a conscientious job of finding the 15 most pressing traffic problems in your district, you'd probably have to look in detail at 50 to 60 problem areas to find that 15," he says. It's ludicrous to imagine congressional staffs could or should do that. "That's why we have state highway departments."

However, many lawmakers defend the granting of numerous small earmarks. Because they must come in under budget caps just like any other spending, said Rep. Mike Simpson, R-Idaho, earmarks divert funds away from bigger federal programs, thereby helping to balance the federal budget. Earmarks generally "go to projects that are short-term in nature and small in scope," he said, limiting the growth of the federal government, where large programs tend to operate in perpetuity. [8]

With the Cunningham scandal as a backdrop, Congress this year is considering reforms, not to limit the numbers of earmarks but to make lobbying for them more transparent.

Transparency will prevent federal funds from being used for corrupt or ill-advised purposes, said earmark critic Sen. Tom Coburn, R-Okla. "A recent Congressional Research Service [CRS] report shows that 96 percent of the 12,852 appropriations earmarks [granted in fiscal 2006] were hidden within report language" attached at the back of bills, Coburn told the Homeland Security Committee. (The CRS is Congress' nonpartisan research arm.)

In other words, the language was "slipped in behind closed doors at the last minute in the middle of the night," Coburn said. "Everyone knows that conference reports become public almost immediately before they have to be voted on, which makes it almost impossible for members to know what they're voting for." [9]

Both the Senate and House have passed bills this year to require more transparency in lobbying and earmarking, but congressional watchdog groups say the bills contain far too many loopholes. In any case, the measures appear to be stalled.

Meanwhile, challengers in a handful of congressional races around the country are confronting incumbent legislators on earmarks. But because lawmakers — and hometown constituents — usually benefit from earmarks, many observers think the criticism of earmarks may not resonate much with voters, giving lawmakers little incentive to clean up the practice.

The public tends to be ambivalent and confused about the issue, says William Hartung, director of the World Policy Institute's Arms Trade Research Center at the New School university in New York. "When people see things like education getting cut, and then they see other things like local earmarks being funded, it feeds into the cynicism that all members of Congress are in it for the money," he says.

Nonetheless, it's not certain that being an avid earmarker — even one suspected of corruptly doling out earmarks — will lose a legislator votes, he says. "Voters are happy about their own local performing-arts center," even if it was funded by an earmark, says Hartung.

As Congress ponders whether to limit pork barrel spending, here are some of the questions lawmakers, voters and political analysts are considering:

Military Bills Get Most 'Pork'

More than a third of appropriations earmarks end up being tacked onto defense and military bills. Critics say military measures are popular vehicles for earmarks because a president would never veto a defense spending bill, especially in wartime. But earmarks often divert money from more crucial, national needs, say critics, such as supplying adequate body armor for troops in Iraq.

Earmarks Appropriated in 2006, by Function

(By percentage of total earmarks)

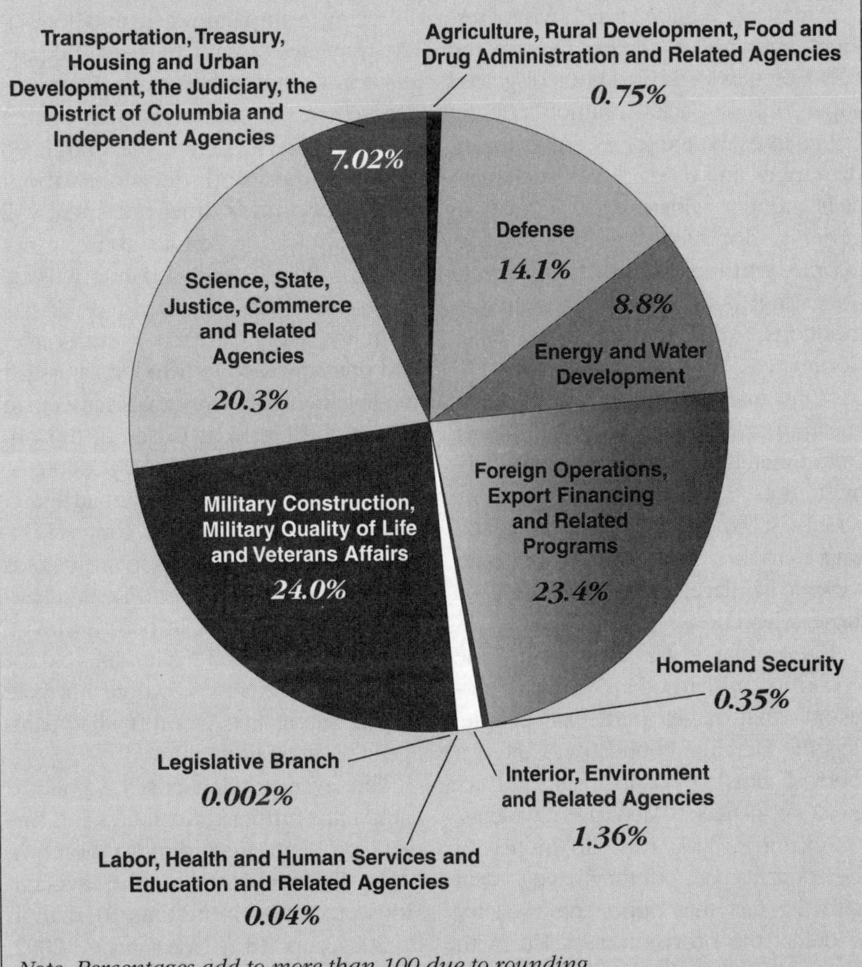

Note: Percentages add to more than 100 due to rounding.

Source: Congressional Research Service, "Earmarks in FY2006 Appropriations Acts," March 6, 2006

Does earmarking lead to bribery and congressional corruption?

Lawmakers' ability to provide billions of dollars to constituents and donors invites bribery, say some analysts. But others counter that personal character flaws — not earmarks — foster corruption.

"I have an opportunity to help the state. I do it with earmarks," said longtime Sen. Richard J. Durbin, D-Ill. "They're very open. There's nothing secret or sinister about them." [10]

Abuse of legislative power, not earmarks, leads to corruption says former Rep. David E. Skaggs, D-Colo., executive director of the Center for Democracy and Citizenship Program at the Council for Excellence in Government. "When you're a member of Congress, you have influence over many policy and spending decisions, and, sadly, members can use those powers unwisely and be corrupted. Ultimately, it's about the kind of people involved."

American League of Lobbyists President Paul Miller agrees. Despite the flood of news stories about disgraced super-lobbyist Jack Abramoff offering bribes in exchange for earmarks for Indian tribes and other clients, such practices are not widespread, he said. In general, "lobbyists are not 'bribing' people, and members of Congress are not being 'bought' for campaign contributions," Miller told the House Rules Committee. [11]

"One man broke the law by lying, cheating and stealing from his clients. Unfortunately, he called himself a lobbyist. But . . . Jack Abramoff was not a lobbyist. By definition, Jack Abramoff was a crook. . . . No matter what rules we put in place, there will always be those who choose to break them." [12]

But earmarks are more susceptible to corruption than other legislative provisions that target particular people, says the Heritage Foundation's Utt. If a lobbyist aims to obtain a targeted tax break or increased Medicare payments, for example, "you can slip money to the congressman, but they have to deal with the fact that opponents" will try to defeat the provision, says Utt. With earmarks, however, "there's nobody on the other side," making the payment seem an assured path to results.

Conservative activist Grover Norquist, president of the anti-tax group Americans for Tax Reform, agrees. "You don't pay people for a 'maybe,' " he says. "But when I can just scribble it into" a bill — as generally happens with earmarks — "that's what makes the temptation greater."

Currently, there are too many earmarks granted with too little public transparency, said AEI's Ornstein. "The out-of-control earmarking phenomenon has led to a culture of corruption," he said. "The ethical compass on Capitol Hill is out of whack," creating a "legislative process that has lost the transparency, accountability and deliberation that are the core of the American system." [13]

"Diverting taxpayer money to pet projects is a positive-feedback loop of lobbying, campaign cash and legislative paybacks," said Ellis, of Taxpayers for Common Sense. [14] Earmarks "are corrosive to the political system generally because the decentralized and unsupervised decisions about how public funds should be spent will ultimately lead to serious abuse, if not outright fraud," said a January issue paper from Ellis' group. [15]

In the past, earmarks were scarcer and primarily used to help legislators get funding for high-priority goals, rather than leaving the president to set all the priorities, said Rep. Obey. By contrast, today's large number of earmarks corrupts the process because congressional leaders award earmarks to sway votes on other bills, he added. "When a chairman uses an earmark in order to [twist] a member's arm and make him vote for a bill that he otherwise would not vote for on substantive grounds, that damages this institution." [16]

The ever-growing cost of political campaigns further exacerbates the earmark problem. According to the Campaign Finance Institute, the average House race cost more than $1 million in 2004, up 18 percent from 2002. Senate races in 2004 each cost an average of $6.5 million, up 57 percent from 1998, the last time the 2004 seats were contested. [17]

"The escalating cost of campaigns has put intense pressure on members of Congress, even those with safe seats, and lobbyists to raise and contribute substantial sums of money," Thomas Mann, a senior fellow at the Brookings Institution, told the House Rules Committee. [18]

"At the same time, more opportunities exist for members of Congress and their leaders to deliver benefits to lobbyists and their clients," he continued. "These include earmarks in appropriations and authorization bills . . . added late in the legislative process under the veil of secrecy. . . . These conditions foster practices that risk conflicts of interest and unethical or illegal behavior." [19]

Does earmarking hamper the government's ability to do its work?

Critics maintain that the growing use of earmarks displaces funding for other federal projects and diverts Congress' attention from more important matters. Supporters, however, argue that legislators often know better than federal bureaucrats what local districts need and that the power to grant or withhold earmarks helps congressional leaders pass key legislation.

Virtually everyone agrees that reducing earmarks would not dent the rising federal budget deficit. As a potential budget-buster, congressional pork is "way way way way way down the list," representing only a tiny percentage — usually estimated at no more than 1-2 percent — of federal dollars, explains James Horney, a senior fellow at the liberal-leaning Center on Budget and Policy Priorities (CBPP).

Nevertheless, earmark critics note, as the budget grows tighter, pork can shave dollars from other important federal programs. Over the past two years, for instance, supplemental spending bills for the wars in Iraq and Afghanistan have been larded with pork projects that divert dollars from vital military-support services, according to Winslow Wheeler, a former Senate staffer who is a visiting fellow at the nonpartisan Center for Defense Information. In 2004, Congress "pushed the pork in the defense budget to an all-time high . . . $8.9 billion," said Wheeler, while funding "wartime operations at only a fraction of what nearly all analysts agree" was needed. [20]

"The Armed Services Committee raided . . . combat-readiness" funds, he continued, partly in order to free dollars for both defense-related and non-defense-related pork, such as aid for Alaskan fisheries. The committee cut Army depot weapons maintenance by $100 million in that part of the bill, he added, just when the repair backlog from the two wars had grown to unmanageable proportions, and cut $1.5 billion for transportation and consumables such as helicopter rotor blades, tank tracks, spare parts, fuel, food and much more. [21]

Earmarking in the 2004 defense bill was typical of current bills that clearly add "unnecessary spending" that can delay or impair other work, says Hartung of the New School university. With members out to get projects in their districts funded, "it sets up a kind of corrupt process," he says, in which big-picture thinking about defense priorities runs a distant second to pushing through projects in key members' districts.

A pending defense spending bill, for example, includes more than $200 million to start production on several new C-17 cargo planes, even though the Pentagon wants only the C-17s already in production. But shutting off production of the C-17 in 2008 would eliminate more than 6,000 jobs at the Long Beach, Calif., Boeing plant where the planes are made, so Sen. Dianne Feinstein, D-Calif., successfully pressed other lawmakers to begin advance-funding more planes. When completed, the newly ordered planes will cost at least an additional $1.6 billion. [22]

In the end, some important military items "don't get funded because they're not in the districts of key members" who promise each other, " 'I'll do your program if you'll do mine,' " Hartung says. One item that perennially loses out to weapons and aircraft produced at legislators' local plants, he says, is the military's day-to-day operations and management budget, which tends to lack "big, sexy items."

Funds are being cut to make room for earmarks at other federal agencies as well, says the Heritage Foundation's Utt, because Congress first sets an overall budget cap before any separate agency appropriations are considered. "So the more and more earmarks you have, you are pulling dollars out" from other items, says Utt, citing the "defunding" of an office that maintained a valuable national transportation database in order to pay for earmarks.

Not only does pork "cripple the federal agencies," says Thomas Schatz, president of the nonpartisan Citizens Against Government Waste (CAGW), but it creates inequities because it "distributes funding disproportionately" among the states. In this year's supplemental spending bill, for example, lawmakers shaved dollars from the main measure — which focuses on war needs and hurricane relief — to make room for local drought-relief funds, says Schatz. But at the moment, "drought relief is just not as critical as hurricane relief . . . and the fact that they view these projects as coequal with everything else we spend money on is troubling."

The 15,000 earmarks that flow into appropriators' "in" boxes each session divert lawmakers' attention from larger policy questions and "consume the rest of the legislative process," says former Democratic congressional aide Lilly. The extra paperwork prevents committees from being good stewards of the federal coffers, such as overseeing how well the Centers for Disease Control and Prevention has prepared for avian flu, he adds.

Lilly told senators in March that the mushrooming of earmarks amounts to "an implicit deal" between the executive branch and Congress: "We will allow you to make a fool of yourself on the 2 percent of the federal budget that you earmark if you will give us free rein over the other 98 percent of . . . spending.' " [23] But it's a bad bargain, Lilly said, because it means "Congress is not performing its constitutional responsibility to hold the federal bureaucracy accountable." [24]

Nevertheless, local pork is a time-honored, successful means to speed "passage of legislation of national importance" by "trading projects for members' votes for broad public policy," according to Diana Evans, a professor of political science at Trinity College in Hartford, Conn., and a leading expert on earmarks. Congress perpetually faces the dilemma of how to pass laws that benefit the nation when members are unavoidably preoccupied with pleasing local constituents to ensure re-election, she writes. [25]

Moreover, writes Washington attorney Wesley Bizzell, federal agencies would shortchange many significant projects if lawmakers didn't direct funds to them. "While many in the media deride these earmarks as 'pork' or 'government waste,' " he said, earmarks "help worthy projects that may not otherwise receive the attention they deserve by the federal government," such as technology improvements for local police departments. [26]

In addition, local projects do serve the national interest, argue many lawmakers and their constituents. For example, California's Sen. Feinstein wrote that the C-17 funding she is pushing "would allow the production line to remain open beyond 2008," ensuring that if more C-17s are needed at that time "there will be no disruption in . . . production." [27]

Likewise, the *Meridian* [Mississippi] *Star* editorialized earlier this year that while pork barrel politics "is a huge problem in this country," the entire nation would benefit from a controversial $700-million Gulf Coast railroad relocation earmark that Mississippi's senators tried to include in this year's supplemental spending bill for the Iraq and Afghanistan wars and hurricane relief. Even though $300 million in federal funds helped rebuild the railroad last year after

Local Projects Get Federal Pork

Critics, such as Citizens Against Government Waste, say earmarks usually direct too much money to too few Americans, seldom relate to the purpose of the department from which the money is being diverted and support items local taxpayers or private companies should be funding themselves.

Examples of Earmarks in Fiscal 2006 Appropriations Bills

Agriculture

$1.4 million — Curriculum development, Mississippi Valley State University
$248,000 — Iowa Vitality Center

Defense

$3.4 million — Research on ways to capture energy from the Northern Lights
$1 million — Gaming-technology software initiative
$8.3 million — Breath-alcohol testing equipment
$4 million — For a Toledo, Ohio, shipyard that is closing

Foreign Operations

$13.5 million — For a private group building a cafe and a YMCA in Ireland

Homeland Security

$78.6 million — For Island Class Patrol Boats, now considered ineffective at drug interdiction
$10 million — For private bus companies, including one that takes vacationers to the Hamptons on Long Island

Interior

$400,000 — Library, Missoula, Mont.
$100,000 — Community center, Ocean Springs, Miss.
$350,000 — Decorative landscaping, Chicago

Commerce, Justice, and Science

$2.5 million — Laser dry-cleaning, Goddard Space Flight Center
$250,000 — Girls Inc., an Alabama nonprofit promoting girls' self-esteem
$315,000 — YMCA, Jackson, Miss.
$2 million — Virginia community colleges to develop a Web portal
$100,000 — Belle Grove Plantation, Va.

Transportation, Treasury and Housing and Urban Development

$550,000 — Museum of Glass, Tacoma, Wash.
$50,000 — Capitol Hill Baseball and Softball League, Washington, D.C.
$325,000 — Seattle Aquarium
$250,000 — Historical Globe Theater, Odessa, Texas
$750,000 — Youth/recreation center, Canton, Ohio
$950,000 — Parking lot, Joslyn Art Museum, Omaha, Neb.
$100,000 — Community swimming complex, California Lutheran University

Source: Citizens Against Government Waste, 2006 Congressional Pig Book

Hurricane Katrina, the paper said, all Americans would benefit from paying again this year to yank up the line and relocate it farther from the coast to allow construction of a beachfront highway. [28]

The new highway would force stores and restaurants to relocate farther from the beach, where they would be exposed to "less damage during a storm," the paper reasoned. "And the fewer . . . buildings damaged or destroyed, the lighter the federal government's recovery tab after a storm." [29]

Should earmarks be banned?

Recent reports about lawmakers trading earmarks for cash from lobbyists have spurred some calls for a ban. In the 2006 George Washington University Battleground Poll in February, for example, 59 percent of voters said they favored ending earmarks. [30] But many legislative analysts argue that all legislative powers, not just earmarks, can be misused by unethical lawmakers.

As Congress ponders bills to limit corruption, syndicated columnist Dick Morris, a former political consultant who managed President Bill Clinton's 1996 campaign, said "serious reform" should include a "ban [on] earmarking in Appropriations bills. [31]

"Voters have long since understood it is a fiction that a legislator is fighting for a specific earmark to help the district," wrote Morris. "They know he is really doing it to get campaign contributions." Presidents have perennially argued that if they had the power to veto single items in bills, they could keep a lid on the more egregious pork spending, he noted. However, the Supreme Court in 1998 declared the "line-item" presidential veto unconstitutional. [32] After that happened, said Morris, "the natural next step" is to ban earmarking. "It deserves to be ended."

Heritage Foundation Senior Fellow Brian Riedl would like to see Congress impose a one-year moratorium on pork spending while it enacts a permanent ban on legislation that specifically names businesses, organizations or locations to receive federal grants. "Lobbying reform is . . . helpful, but as long as lawmakers continue to distribute government grants, organizations will find a way to lobby and financially influence them," he said. [33]

Continued on p. 538

Funds for Cowgirls, Teapots and Rain Forests

Christmas came early to tiny Sparta, N.C. Tucked into the vast $142.5 billion 2006 discretionary spending bill recently passed by Congress was $500,000 to build the Sparta Teapot Museum, which supporters say will attract tourists.

"Congress should take a look in the mirror and ask itself: Does funding an indoor rain forest in Iowa, a Cowgirl Hall of Fame in Texas, a teapot museum in North Carolina, a zoo exhibit in Illinois or maple research in Vermont benefit the national interest?" said Rep. Jeff Flake, R-Ariz., at a March 16 House hearing. [1]

In recent years, Congress has approved thousands of earmarks for special interests without attempting to determine which, if any, are actually worthy of federal funds, say budget watchdog groups. As a result, they argue, earmarking directs too much money to some areas and not enough to others and funds projects that local taxpayers should pay for, as well as some they don't even want.

In the $23 billion highway bill Congress passed in 2005, for example, Alaska got earmarks worth more than $1 billion, even though Alaska's 660,000 population is only slightly bigger than the population of a single congressional district according to Scott Lilly, a senior fellow at the progressive think tank Center for American Progress. [2]

Funding that's out of proportion to the population benefiting from it is common in the world of earmarks, according to Citizens Against Government Waste (CAGW), whose annual *Congressional Pig Book* chronicles federal spending on earmarks.

Last year, for example, the Police Department in Wasilla, Alaska (population 7,700) snagged $150,000 for technology upgrades, while Baltimore — population 600,000-plus — only received $100,000, CAGW says. [3]

An even bigger winner in the police-upgrade derby: Tiny Harpers Ferry, W.Va., got $100,000 for its three-man police force. "This is the same size force as the fictional town of Mayberry on the 'Andy Griffith Show,' " CAGW says.

Targeted funding for special interests frequently turns up in bills where you'd least expect it, says Lilly, such as a special tax break to manufacturers of fishing-tackle boxes tucked into a 2005 energy bill. [4]

In 2004, the Foreign Operations Appropriations bill contained $100,000 for goat-meat research in Texas. [5] In another case of an earmark funded in an odd place, $2 million was provided under the Justice Department's Community-Oriented Policing Services (COPS) program last year to the First Tee initiative, which provides "learning facilities and educational programs that promote character development and life-enhancing value through the game of golf."

COPS "began under President Clinton with the goal of adding 100,000 more police to the streets," says CAGW President Thomas Schatz. But "it is safe to say that First Tee would not put one cop on the street." [6]

Equally disturbing, says Schatz, is that First Tee is one of many earmark earners that could afford to pay its own way. Among its supporters are the Professional Golf Association, Nike and the World Golf Foundation, which is supported by Shell, IBM and Nextel. "Clearly," First Tee could operate "without relying on handouts from taxpayers," says Schatz. [7]

Similarly, the Grammy Foundation, supported by the lucrative pop music industry, got $150,000 in 2004. [8]

Some earmarks seem to be directed to places that don't even want them.

In 2002, for example, Rep. Sam Graves, R-Mo., got $273,000 for the Blue Springs Youth Outreach Unit to combat Goth culture, which a Graves spokesperson said was spurring 35 local kids to take drugs, self-mutilate, sacrifice animals and engage in violence "that possibly could lead up to what happened at Columbine in 1999." But "then a funny thing happened," said Schatz. Outreach "finally admitted that many of the claims they made in their grant proposal were unfounded" and ended up returning $132,000 to the federal government. [9]

And then there was the $50-million grant to build the "world's largest enclosed rain forest" as a tourist attraction in Coralville, Iowa. Congress enacted the funding in January 2004, but no local government stepped up to help finance the $200 million project. In November 2005, earmark sponsor Sen. Charles E. Grassley, R-Iowa, froze the funds until $50 million in matching funds can be raised. [10]

A $1.5-million roads project in Alaska was intended to provide easy access between timber cutting in the Tongass National Forest and a private timber mill. About the time the earmark was approved, however, the Forest Service halted the timber cutting, so the roads will "provide access to a timber sale that no longer exists," says the watchdog group Taxpayers for Common Sense. "They are, quite literally, roads to nowhere." [11]

Many lucky neighborhoods also are holding winning tickets in the earmarks lottery. Last year, among thousands of other similar spending items, Congress anted up $550,000 for a Museum of Glass in Washington state; $100,000 for ice-skating rinks in Toledo, Ohio; $75,000 to Lancaster, Ohio, for a glass-blowing museum and $350,000 for Columbia County, New York, to renovate an old stone Shaker barn.

---

[1] Quoted in "Eliminating 'Earmarks,' " Congressional Quarterly Committee Testimony, March 16, 2006.

[2] Quoted in *ibid.*

[3] *2006 Congressional Pig Book*, Citizens Against Government Waste, www.cagw.org.

[4] Quoted in "Eliminating 'Earmarks,' " *op. cit.*

[5] *Congressional Pig Book*, *op. cit.*

[6] Quoted in *ibid.*

[7] *Ibid.*

[8] Ken Silverstein, "The Great American Pork Barrel," *Harper's* online, July 2005, www.harpers.org.

[9] Quoted in "Eliminating 'Earmarks,' " *op. cit.*

[10] Quoted in *ibid.*

[11] "Earmark to Nowhere," *The Wastebasket: A Weekly Bulletin on Government Waste*, Taxpayers for Common Sense, Nov. 29, 2004.

Continued from p. 536

CAGW's Schatz argues that the federal government has no business funding local projects. "Some members of Congress claim it is better that local officials, rather than Washington bureaucrats, make the decisions on where funding should occur," Schatz told senators earlier this year. "We agree, but we think that doesn't mean members of Congress get to decide. Instead, most of those programs should be paid for out of local taxes, or even private dollars." After all, he added, "It is highly unlikely I will ever use a bike path in Montana." [34]

But many lawmakers disagree. "We each understand the unique needs, challenges and opportunities of our districts better than other members, and we should be able to present the case for our requests on their merits," said Rep. Melissa Bean, D-Ill., at a House Rules Committee hearing in March. While she doesn't favor an outright ban, she does see the need for more transparency, pointing out that, "Every year, questionable projects are found . . . inserted in the dead of night." And that misuse of earmarks calls into question Congress' dedication "to spending tax dollars wisely." [35]

Rep. Adam Putnam, R-Fla., says ending earmarks would create "a caste system in the House of the haves [lawmakers who sit on Appropriations committees] and the have-nots." Without earmarks, lawmakers who do not sit on Appropriations committees would have no way "to help their community college, their school district, [or] their particular road needs." [36]

House Appropriations Committee member Obey says earmarks themselves are not the problem; their excessively high number is the problem because it forces lawmakers to focus all their attention on local earmarks rather than big-picture items. For a recent spending bill for Labor, Education and Health and Human Services, Obey said, "I got only two calls from members asking me . . . what happened to this education program or that education program," he said. "Every other call I got from both sides of the aisle was, 'How are my earmarks?' The tail [wags] the dog." [37]

"The Constitution gives Congress the unfettered power to spend," says Lilly, of the Center for American Progress. "Just because Congress uses the power foolishly sometimes doesn't mean it isn't important for them to have it."

Some earmarks are in the national interest and could have been initiated only by Congress, Lilly says, citing funds used to build an interpretive visitors' center for the U.S. military cemetery in Normandy, France, site of the World War II D-Day invasion. Although thousands of veterans visit Normandy every year, Lilly says, before the money for a new center was earmarked the cemetery had only a "tiny, little visitors' center" that was inadequate to educate travelers about the memorial's historical significance.

"Congress uses earmarks to set funding priorities and direct executive-branch activities," said Douglas Holtz-Eakin, chairman of international economics at the Council on Foreign Relations and former head of the Congressional Budget Office and the Office of Management and Budget under President George W. Bush. "New procedures to constrain that practice could weaken lawmakers' ability to set priorities . . . thereby strengthening the power of the executive branch over the use of . . . funds." [38]

"To say there shouldn't be any [earmarks] means we defer to political appointees and [federal] civil servants on all funding matters," says former Rep. Skaggs, D-Colo. "But we shouldn't assume that all good discretion and prioritization happens in the executive branch." ■

BACKGROUND

Bringing Home the Bacon

Pork barrel politics has long been a staple of the American political diet. (The term grew out of the pre-Civil War custom of handing out salt pork from barrels to underfed slaves, who rushed to grab it.)

But in the past decade, the practice of doling out political pork has exploded to the point that earmarks now directly fund individual universities, local parks and performing-arts centers, as well as specific companies, such as weapons manufacturers. Not surprisingly, earmarks have drawn increased attention from critics of government spending. And last year former California Rep. Cunningham was imprisoned for taking millions of dollars in bribes in exchange for garnering earmarks for military contractors. The scandal involving lobbyist Abramoff, who showered members of Congress with favors, also has led the media and some lawmakers to turn up the heat on congressional pork. [39]

Pork barrel spending traditionally appeared in appropriations bills that Congress passes annually to fund federal agency operations, measures that — unlike other legislation — must be passed annually to avoid a government shutdown. But unlike traditional pork barrel projects, says Citizens Against Government Waste, earmarks generally represent questionable uses of federal tax dollars, are often sought by only one chamber of Congress, are not awarded through competitive bids, have not been requested by the president, are not part of a larger federal program authorized by Congress, have not been publicly debated in congressional hearings and serve narrow rather than national interests.

Continued on p. 540

Chronology

1790s-1970s

Despite criticism that pork barrel funding is unconstitutional, it gradually becomes accepted practice for road and water projects.

1790
Treasury Secretary Alexander Hamilton wins lawmakers' votes to establish a navy by offering shipbuilding and port jobs to 10 different states.

1817
South Carolina Sen. John C. Calhoun introduces bill to build highways connecting the Eastern United States to the West, but President James Madison vetoes it, arguing that Congress cannot legally fund projects that don't promote the general welfare.

1909
England's *Westminster Gazette* publishes the first print usage of "pork barrel" to describe politically motivated funding.

1970
Annual defense spending bill contains 12 earmarks.

1976
Former Senate aide Gerald Cassidy becomes a lobbyist and quickly obtains $32 million in earmarks to launch a nutrition research center at Boston's Tufts University.

1977
President Jimmy Carter loses the support of the Democrat-led Congress when he threatens to veto water-project earmarks he says are environmentally unsound.

1980s

Universities seek earmarked research funds. Congressional Republicans, the minority party, criticize earmarks as wasteful.

1980
Defense appropriations bill has 62 earmarks.

1983
Columbia University and The Catholic University of America use their political connections to get congressional appropriations. Columbia becomes the first university to use earmarked funds to construct a building — a chemistry building. Catholic's money is used for traditional research. American Association of Universities declares a moratorium on seeking earmarks, but some schools ignore it.

1984
Businessman J. Peter Grace and investigative reporter Jack Anderson found Citizens Against Government Waste (CAGW) to trim public spending.

1987
President Ronald Reagan vetoes a spending bill because it has 121 earmarks. A highway authorization bill contains 152 earmarks, up from only 10 in 1982.

1990s

Earmarks increase as more universities and companies lobby for them, and Republicans gain control of Congress.

1991
CAGW publishes its first *Congressional Pig Book* and lists 541 pork barrel projects.

1995
Congress' new Republican majority awards earmarks to lawmakers who vote for leadership-approved bills.

2000s

Lobbying for earmarks increases, and some lawmakers are accused of earmark-related corruption.

2003
Rep. Ralph Regula, R-Ohio, a candidate to chair the House Appropriations Committee, removes Democrat-sponsored earmarks from his subcommittee bill to prove he'll distribute pork in line with GOP leadership goals. . . . An omnibus spending bill's $23 billion in earmarks includes $224,000 to repair a public swimming pool in Sparks, Nev. Rep. Jim Gibbons, R-Nev., asked for the money because he felt guilty for clogging the pool with tadpoles as a boy.

2005
Annual defense appropriations bill has 2,671 earmarks. CAGW's *Pig Book* counts 13,997 earmarks in annual spending bills overall, for a cost of $27.3 billion — nearly $100 for each person in the United States.

2006
Rep. Randy "Duke" Cunningham, R-Calif., is sentenced to eight years in prison for taking $2.4 million in bribes to procure defense-related earmarks. . . . Rep. Alan B. Mollohan, D-W.Va., resigns from the House Ethics Committee, accused of directing earmarks to nonprofit groups he founded. . . . House and Senate pass earmark and lobbying reform legislation. . . . Inquiry continues into recent earmarks possibly connected to jailed super-lobbyist Jack Abramoff.

Universities Haul in Research Earmarks

Since the 1930s, the federal government has funded scientific research at universities. For decades, grants were awarded competitively, based on expert peer reviews. [1]

Beginning in the late 1970s, however, some universities and lawmakers decided the peer-review process favored elite Eastern schools; some figured they might do better if they sought earmarked funding. They were right.

Over the past two decades, earmarked research funds have skyrocketed, and lawmakers responsible for the change believe they're helping level the playing field in what they call the rigged game of peer review.

"Can you see the University of Idaho and Boise State University getting grants in competition with the Massachusetts Institute of Technology (MIT) and other big-name Eastern universities if some bureaucrat in Washington was making the decision?" asked Sen. Larry Craig, R-Idaho, who directs funding to his local universities. [2]

Ironically, it was big-name schools that first sought and got earmarked funding. In 1977, Boston's Tufts University received the first research earmark. In 1983, New York's Ivy League Columbia University and the Washington, D.C.-based Catholic University of America began using their connections to lawmakers to seek and win direct appropriations. Columbia procured a first-of-its-kind research-related earmark to fund university facilities.

But earmarking created immediate controversy in the research community.

"No issue divided the membership [of the American Association of Universities] so strongly" during the 1980s, wrote the group's public affairs officer, Ann Leigh Speicher. [3] In 1983, the group approved a resolution against seeking earmarks, but through the 1980s and '90s, more and more universities began hiring lobbyists to get them into the earmark game.

Some academics argued that earmarked funds tarnished the image of science as an objective pursuit. Earmarking research funding is "the same phenomenon that used to result in sewers and bridges," said Robert Park, a University of Maryland physics professor. "Academic science has now replaced the sewers as the place where the money goes." [4]

But recipients of earmarked funds at research universities say they have the same rights as other institutions to seek tax-supported funding. "People talk about sordid — they'd better read the Constitution," said John Silber, former president of Boston University. "I've got a right to appeal to the Congress. Every citizen does. If that's dirty, the whole country's dirty." [5]

In the new century, while debates over academic earmarking continue, the number of research earmarks has risen dramatically along with earmarks for other purposes. For example, fiscal 2006 spending bills contained $2.4 billion for earmarked scientific research, up 63 percent since 2003, according to the American Association for the Advancement of Science. [6] Academic earmarks grew fourfold between 1996 and 2003, according to *The Chronicle of Higher Education*. [7]

Universities' lobbying expenditures have grown alongside the growth in earmarks — from $23 million in 1998 to $62 million in 2003. [8] The lobbying has paid off, according to management professors John M. de Figueiredo of MIT and the University of Toronto's Brian S. Silverman. In fiscal 2003, they report, congressional appropriators funded 1,964 academic earmarks, totaling around $2 billion, or just over 10 percent of all federal funding for academic research. Between 1980 and 2003, earmarked research funding grew 59-fold, compared to only a 2.4-fold increase in overall federal research funding, they say. [9]

Lobbying appears to have aided that growth, according to their analysis, with each $1 increase in lobbying expenditures

Continued from p. 538

In addition, earmarks are not limited to appropriations bills. Lawmakers can benefit their towns or a favored company through all kinds of bills, further complicating any proposal to eliminate or overhaul the earmarking process. For example, a defense authorization bill can direct the Pentagon to purchase a specific company's weapon or product by simply describing the product in intricate detail without naming the manufacturer. Alaska's notorious "bridges to nowhere" — which first received, then lost, earmarked funds during last year's debate over the budget deficit — were first earmarked in a transportation authorization bill, not an appropriations bill. [40]

Similarly, says Horney of the Center on Budget and Policy Priorities, a lawmaker can craft a tax break that targets a handful of companies or even a single company, again without ever mentioning the specific firm. Virtually any legislation can be engineered to serve specific interests through an earmark-like provision, says Scott Adler, an associate professor of political science at the University of Colorado. That's why legislators seek certain committee assignments, not just seats on the spending committees, he says. Whether it's an agriculture, civil service or science panel, "you look across the committees, and it's very clear that members select onto it to serve their constituents' interest," such as by promoting a local NASA installation or crafting a farm-subsidy program, he says.

Constitutional Powers

Federal dollars have always flowed to legislators' favored regions and organizations, but even in the nation's earliest days Congress repeatedly debated the propriety of such spending.

For example, an early Congress refused to lend money to a glass manufacturer on the grounds that the Constitution directed Congress to act only

associated with a $1.56 increase in earmarks for a university with no local senator or congressman on an appropriations committee and a $4.50 boost in earmarks for institutions with a local member on one of the panels. [10]

Earmarked or not, scientific research funding often finds its way onto lists of silly-sounding federal spending projects. To spotlight such projects, the late Sen. William Proxmire, D-Wis., began handing out "Golden Fleece Awards " in 1975 to federal programs he considered not just wasteful but silly or outrageous. His first award went to the National Science Foundation, for an $84,000 study about why people fall in love. [11]

In fact, over the years, "there were more Proxmire Golden Fleece Awards for peer-reviewed science than there were for congressional earmarks," said former Sen. J. Bennett Johnston, D-La. [12]

But as earmarks proliferate, scientific pork has come in for increased criticism from government-spending critics. In its *2006 Congressional Pig Book*, for example, the watchdog organization Citizens Against Government Waste (CAGW) says many science projects don't seem to have clear national goals yet continue to attract funding year after year.

For example, last year, a $3.4-million earmark went to the University of Alaska's High Frequency Active Auroral Research Program (HAARP), "which was initially designed to capture energy from the aurora borealis but is now being configured to heat up the ionosphere to improve military communications. CAGW has identified $105.9 million appropriated for HAARP since 1995." [13]

The relative productivity of earmarked vs. competitively awarded federal science funding remains an open question. However, research by University of Toronto economics Professor A. Abigail Payne suggests that peer review may beat out earmarked funding in promoting scientific excellence.

Payne finds that earmark-funded research results in more scientific papers being published, but other scientists cite those papers less often. The number of citations an academic paper receives is often held to be a measure of its quality. An additional $1 million in earmarked funding to a university boosts the number of scientific articles it publishes by between 21 and 42 articles. But the quality of the articles — measured by the number of citations per article — declines by between 9 and 57 percent, Payne concluded. [14]

[1] For background, see James D. Savage, *Funding Science in America: Congress, Universities, and the Politics of the Academic Pork Barrel* (2000).

[2] Quoted in Tom Finnigan, "All About Pork," Citizens Against Government Waste, May 2006.

[3] Ann Leigh Speicher, "The Association of American Universities: A Century of Service to Higher Education," undated, http://aau.edu.

[4] Quoted in Tim Weiner, "Lobbying for Research Money, Colleges Bypass Review Process," *The New York Times*, Aug. 24, 1999, p. A1.

[5] Quoted in *Ibid.*

[6] "R&D Earmarks Hit New Record of $2.4 billion," American Association for the Advancement of Science, Jan. 4, 2006.

[7] "Congressional Earmarks for Higher Education, 1990-2003," *The Chronicle of Higher Education*, Sept. 26, 2003, http://chronicle.com/stats.pork/.

[8] Alan B. Krueger, "The Farm-Subsidy Model of Financing Academia," *The New York Times*, May 26, 2005, p. C2.

[9] John M. de Figueiredo and Brian S. Silverman, "How Does the Government (Want to) Fund Science? Politics, Lobbying and Academic Earmarks," March 16, 2004.

[10] *Ibid.*

[11] "The Golden Fleece Award," Taxpayers for Common Sense, undated, www.taxpayer.net/awards/goldenfleece/about.htm.

[12] Quoted in "Earmarking of Science: Definitions, Interpretations, and Implications," a workshop by the American Association for the Advancement of Science, Oct. 3, 2001.

[13] *2006 Congressional Pig Book*, Citizens Against Government Waste, p. 10.

[14] A. Abigail Payne, "Do Congressional Earmarks Increase Research Output at Universities?" Nov. 10, 2002, http://ideas.repec.org/p/wpa/wuwppe/0111002.html.

to promote the "general welfare," not local interests. Another bill that proposed paying a bounty to New England cod fishermen was deemed unconstitutional because it would "gratify one part of the Union by oppressing the other." [41]

Federal funding should support "great national works only, since if it were unlimited it would be liable to abuse and might be productive of evil," wrote President James Monroe in 1822. [42]

As the 19th century progressed and the nation needed public infrastructure to support commerce and expand into the Western frontier, Congress gradually became more amenable to handing out funds for local lighthouses, dams, harbors, canals and roads. Soon, earmarks became a key way for lawmakers to please local voters and aid their re-election hopes, according to Evans of Trinity College. "The purpose of such projects was described in 1888 by [British historian] James Bryce, who wrote that 'grants from the federal treasury for local purposes' were routinely employed by members of Congress seeking to secure their renominations." [43]

Securing federal funds for local projects gives incumbents a big electoral boost, according to scholars. For example, an additional $100 per person, or a total of $50 million, in federal funding procured for the home district translates into a 2 percent increase in votes for an incumbent House member, according to University of Chicago economics Professor Steven Levitt and Massachusetts Institute of Technology political science Professor James Snyder. [44]

And the majority party historically uses earmarked dollars to hold onto that status. For example, although states with both Democratic and Republican senators pull in earmarks, states whose senators represent the majority party get more pork dollars, according to Michael Crespin, an American Political Science Association fellow, and Charles Finocchiaro, an assistant professor of political science at the State University of New York at Buffalo. In the past decade, "states with a majority

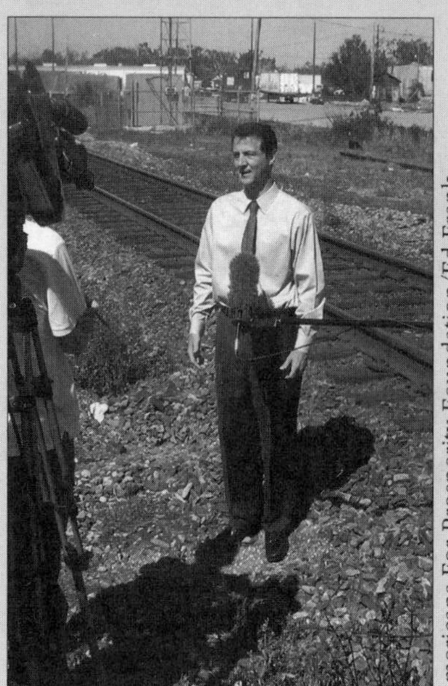

Earmarks Help Local Projects

A mentor helps a camper with her reading at the Outdoor Odyssey camp in Boswell, Pa., (upper left), which received $500,000 in earmarks in a defense spending bill, while Montana's Lewis and Clark Bicentennial celebration (lower right) received $1.6 million. The Museum of Glass (upper right) in Tacoma, Wash., received $550,000 in earmarks in 2006, and the CSX Railroad in Gulfport, Miss., was slated to receive $700 million to relocate the railroad — rebuilt with federal funds after Hurricane Katrina last year. The CSX funds were cancelled following protests by watchdog groups like Americans For Prosperity; organization President Tim Phillips is pictured (lower left).

delegation received 21 percentage points more pork [annually, on average] than states with a minority-party delegation," they wrote. [45]

Presidents, on the other hand, have long been hostile to legislative earmarks. In 1977, during his first months in office, President Jimmy Carter announced he would end funding for more than 300 water projects that he deemed wasteful and environmentally suspect. In the late 1980s, President Ronald Reagan vetoed more than 100 earmarked projects. Neither action came without a price, however. After his threat, Carter faced growing difficulty getting the Democratic Congress to vote his way, and top Republican lawmakers banded together to override Reagan's veto.

Congress resists executive-branch efforts to control pork, say analysts, because presidential budgets usually include their own pork proposals, also tied to bids for political advantage. Presidents use earmarks "to reward political supporters, campaign contributors and sometimes members of Congress" who voted in favor of a White House proposal, said Barry Anderson, a longtime staff member at the White House Office of Management and Budget (OMB). [46]

After Congress appropriates funds for federal agencies, the executive branch sets the agenda, with presidential appointees and civil servants disbursing funds as they see fit, says Keith Ashdown, vice president for policy at Taxpayers for Common Sense. Lobbyists for special interests "can go to the agencies as easily as to Congress," Ashdown says. But presidential pork is far more difficult to track than legislative earmarks, he points out.

While congressional earmarks are written into publicly accessible bills — albeit frequently without the exact name of the recipient or congressional sponsor attached — no one, not even OMB, keeps track of presidential pork, said Anderson. "Of course, we had every reason not to," he said.

"Unlike with appropriations bills, where there's a document," there's no way of knowing whether a presidential earmark has been directed to "some key district or state" for political gain, says CAGW's Schatz.

Alaska Received Most 'Pork' Per Citizen

Alaskans received nearly $500 per person in earmarks in 2006, more than the residents of any other state. Georgians, in comparison, received the least — $12 apiece. Overall, Hawaii took in the most in earmarks, with projects totaling nearly a half-billion dollars.

Top 25 States in Value of Earmarks Per Capita

(National average: $30.55)

2006 Rank	State	Total 2006 Earmarks (in millions)	Earmarks/ Capita
1	Alaska	$325.1	$489.87
2	Hawaii	$482.4	$378.29
3	D.C.	$100.2	$182.07
4	West Virginia	$239.1	$131.58
5	Mississippi	$372.9	$127.68
6	North Dakota	$78.5	$123.35
7	Montana	$99.6	$106.41
8	Nevada	$167	$69.15
9	New Mexico	$129	$66.90
10	South Dakota	$49.5	$63.74
11	New Hampshire	$81.7	$62.36
12	Vermont	$32.1	$51.52
13	Idaho	$70.3	$49.17
14	Rhode Island	$52.2	$48.46
15	Alabama	$203	$44.55
16	Kentucky	$185.4	$44.43
17	Washington	$253.1	$40.25
18	Utah	$97.6	$39.51
19	Louisiana	$177.7	$39.29
20	Delaware	$32.8	$38.90
21	Arizona	$228.1	$38.40
22	Colorado	$177.3	$38.00
23	Maryland	$210.9	$37.65
24	Wyoming	$18.6	$36.47
25	Missouri	$188.1	$32.43

Source: Citizens Against Government Waste, 2006 Congressional Pig Book

Pork Rises

Congressional earmarking held at relatively steady levels between 1955 and 1995, when Democrats made up the majority in Congress, and GOP lawmakers slammed earmarking as wasteful and corrupting. When Republicans captured the Capitol Hill majority a decade ago, however, Republican leaders eager to consolidate electoral gains and enact an ambitious agenda discovered the uses of pork, and earmarking grew to unprecedented levels.

"Ten years ago, the majority of members had never had an earmark," says former House Appropriations aide Lilly. "There weren't nearly as many, and they were mostly large and went to very senior members of leadership and members of the Appropriations committees."

Several of the annual spending bills — such as the one that funds the departments of Labor, Education and Health and Human Services — never had any earmarks. And members seeking earmarks had to "argue why it was a good idea" to Appropriations subcommittee staff and members, Lilly says.

In those days Republican lawmakers repeatedly attacked pork barrel politics. Democrats' proclivity for pork "is not only a personal affront to me but reflects the arrogance of the Democrat-controlled leadership in Congress," Rep. Daniel Manzullo, R-Ill., said in 1993. "While we fund frivolous projects, veterans' spending is given secondary priority," he complained. [47]

After 1995, however, the new Republican majority quickly changed its tune and the method by which earmarks are handed out. While Democrats were in control of the House, seats on Appropriations panels had been awarded largely on the basis of seniority. But then-House Majority Leader Tom DeLay, R-Texas, took a new approach, often assigning new members elected by narrow margins to the prestigious committees. The strategy helped members with slim re-election chances impress constituents and opened the door for those members to access campaign funds from special interests seeking earmarks. [48]

The plan worked. For example, Rep. Anne Northrup, R-Ky., was first elected to Congress in 1996 by a margin of just 1,200 votes in Louisville, a traditionally Democratic district. Placed immediately onto the Appropriations Committee, Northrup quickly increased earmarks for Louisville to levels exceeding those of some small states, such as Delaware and Nebraska. In the process, she raised $1.9 million for her 1998 campaign, which she won with

51.5 percent of the vote, and $3.3 million for the 2004 election, in which she captured 60 percent of the vote. [49]

In response to such successes, Republican leaders began increasing the number of earmarks — while generally decreasing their individual dollar size — to spread the bounty. The CRS found recently that between fiscal 1994 and fiscal 2006 defense earmarks grew from 1.76 percent to 2.36 percent of the Pentagon's discretionary budget, while the number of defense earmarks grew from 587 to 2,847. [50] During the same period, agriculture earmarks grew from 313 provisions accounting for 1.5 percent of the Department of Agriculture's budget to 704 projects and 3.0 percent of the budget. In energy and water development, earmarks grew from 1,574 to 2,436, with the percentage of the budget devoted to earmarks fluctuating between about 20 and 30 percent. Department of Transportation earmarks grew from 140 earmarks — 2.4 percent of the budget — to 2,820 — 3.4 percent. [51]

The schedule for adding earmarks to bills also has changed. From 1995 to 1999, most pork was added when the House and Senate passed their initial bills, according to Crespin and Finocchiaro. Beginning in 2000, however, more earmarks were added during the House-Senate conferences that reconcile the two chambers' versions of legislation before final passage. "This may be an indication of different members being bought off in order to secure passage of the bills," they write. [52]

Earmarks have exploded because "the Republican leadership is sympathetic to them and willing to do them," says the University of Colorado's Adler. When a lawmaker helps someone in his district, it attracts votes even from people who don't directly benefit, because "people remember reading it in the paper," he says.

The fact that Republican lawmakers have piled on the pork they previously shunned surprises many. But conservative activist Norquist says it's not really unexpected. In Congress "there's always a temptation to spend more unless there's political pushback," he says, and while virtually all Republican constituencies "wish you'd spend less money, it's not a vote-moving issue" and "they're not demanding it."

CAGW's Schatz agrees. Whether a conservative or a liberal, he says, "it's rare that someone loses an election for spending too much money."

For Republican leaders, passing priority GOP legislation has become more important than fiscal conservatism, said Ellis of Taxpayers for Common Sense.

"Pork has become a tool to enforce discipline," said Ellis. "Denying prime committee assignments or chairmanships are too blunt. But cutting someone's earmarks can be modulated and provides an annual opportunity to remind someone of the consequences of failing to toe the line." [53]

Loads of Lobbyists

As the number of available earmarks has grown, so has the number of universities, cities and companies lining up to claim them. They often hire Washington lobbyists to do the job, as evidenced by today's booming lobbying industry. [54]

Since 2000, the number of individuals registered to lobby in Washington has doubled to around 35,000. [55] And between 1988 and 2005, the number of firms that sought lobbyist representation on spending issues swelled from 1,447 to well over 4,000. [56]

"The lion's share of that is earmarks," says Ashdown of Taxpayers for Common Sense, pointing out that today many lobbyists are dedicated to gaining earmarks rather than lobbying for policy changes.

"In less than a decade, an entire industry of Gucci-clad lobbyists has sprung up," the group says. "In this new reality, there are two types of communities: those that have a lawmaker on the Appropriations Committee" — and thus are able to get earmarks for themselves — "and those that are shaken down by some lobbyist promising to get federal cash for your local day care, park or community center." [57]

Earmark seekers tout their lobbyists' success. The resort town of Orange Beach, Ala., for example has paid $60,000 a year since 2003 to lobbyist Stewart Van Scoyoc and credits his firm with securing $3.4 million in federal earmarks. [58]

The combination of more earmarks, more lobbyists and increasingly expensive political campaigns has spurred questionable deals and full-fledged scandals that have made news around the country. In March, for example, former California Republican Rep. Cunningham was sentenced to eight years and four months in prison for accepting $2.4 million in bribes from contractors and lobbyists in exchange for earmarking defense contracts. [59] Reps. Katherine Harris, R-Fla., and Virgil Goode, R-Va., recently came under fire for accepting funds from defense contractor Mitchell Wade, then seeking earmarks for his company. [60] Both deny any impropriety.

Rep. Alan B. Mollohan, D-W.Va., was forced to resign his senior spot on the House Ethics Committee following allegations that he directed $250 million in earmarks to five nonprofit organizations he established. Citizens Against Government Waste named him the "porker of the month" in April. [61]

The government is also investigating whether House Appropriations Chairman Jerry Lewis, R-Calif., engaged in sweetheart deals directing earmarks to clients of former congressman-turned-lobbyist Bill Lowery. Fueling suspicion is the fact that top Lewis aide Jeff Shockey has worked for Lowery and garnered $600,000 in severance from the lobbying firm before rejoining Lewis' committee staff last year. [62]

The recent scandals have put earmarks on the public's radar, says Utt

Continued on p. 546

At Issue:

Is Congress doing enough to end corrupt earmarking?

REP. DAVID DREIER, R-CALIF.
CHAIRMAN, HOUSE RULES COMMITTEE

FROM REMARKS ON THE HOUSE FLOOR, MAY 3, 2006

yes

The Lobbying Accountability and Transparency Act of 2006 (HR 4975) seeks to uphold the highest standards of integrity when it comes to Congress' interaction with outside groups.

This legislation does increase transparency and accountability through toughening up disclosure and tightening the rules. This legislation will fulfill the public's right to know who is seeking to influence their Congress.

This legislation will provide brighter lines of right and wrong and more rigorous ethics training so that everyone can understand what is right and what is wrong here. I was taught that as a kid, but obviously there has been some confusion, and in the past there have been gray areas. This legislation creates that clear definition and provides an opportunity for greater training for members and staff so they can have an understanding of it.

This legislation will significantly reform the earmark process to foster more responsible and accountable government spending.

The speaker, the majority leader, I, the whip, and others made a very strong commitment, working with the Appropriations Committee, [to language] the Senate has passed [that] we think is very good. The language says that when we look at the issue of earmark reform so we can have greater accountability when it comes to spending, that it should not simply focus on the appropriations process. It should be universal and go across the board to the other committees as well.

This legislation will considerably increase fines and penalties for violating the transparency and accountability provisions. This legislation will give new authority to the House inspector general to perform random audits of lobbyist-disclosure forms and refer violations to the Department of Justice. It will not permit business as usual. It will not perpetuate the status quo.

These is no question whatsoever that this bill, regardless of what anyone says about it, represents progress, a move in the right direction. There is no question at all that it is a vast improvement over the status quo.

After we pass this bill, let me tell you what is next on our agenda: more reform — the Republican part of reform. The drive for reform never stops. We have demonstrated that consistently in the past, and we will continue to do so in the future. It is a continuous, ongoing process that takes both perseverance and commitment.

REP. RUSH HOLT, D-N.J.

FROM REMARKS ON THE HOUSE FLOOR, MAY 3, 2006

no

Having been entrusted by our constituents with the responsibility to serve their interest in this body, we hold a sacred trust to represent them openly, honestly and selflessly. Serving as a public official necessarily and rightly subjects an individual to heightened scrutiny of behavior. It is tragic that scurrilous actions perpetrated by members of this body have further eroded the trust that Americans place in their electoral and representative system. Congress must act expeditiously and strongly to restore this trust.

Unfortunately, HR 4975 [the Lobbying Accountability and Transparency Act of 2006] is nothing more than a sham. It is a feeble attempt to fool the public — a package of half-hearted cosmetic changes that merely nibble at the edges of a fundamentally flawed governing ethos.

Sunshine, as they say, is the best disinfectant, and HR 4975 does not do nearly enough to allow the public to know the interaction between elected officials and lobbyists. HR 4975 contains no meaningful disclosure requirements [for] lobbyist campaign-finance activities on behalf of members of Congress. We must let the public know about fundraisers, events "honoring" members or outright contributions that special-interest lobbyists are lavishing upon elected officials. The bill has been stripped of any such requirements.

It is clear that the practice of earmarking is not the ideal way to fund the needs of the nation. Basing funding decisions not on merit but on the influence and seniority of a member of Congress inherently does a disservice to the nation. Earmarking needs to be severely restricted. At a minimum, each member should be willing to fully disclose the requesting organization or person and explain the purpose of the project publicly. Unfortunately, HR 4975 fails to achieve this goal. Its disclosure requirements apply only to appropriations bills — not to authorization or tax bills. It's a half-measure, at best, that would do nothing to stop wasteful and unnecessary projects like [Alaska's] "Bridge to Nowhere."

The Washington Post calls this bill "a watered-down sham." *USA Today* calls it an "outrageous substitute for needed reform." Third-party interest groups like Common Cause condemned this weak and inadequate effort to kick the can down the road. We have an historic opportunity to reform the way business is conducted in Washington, D.C., and we are poised to miss that opportunity.

Continued from p. 544

of the Heritage Foundation. While "it has yet to draw much interest on talk radio or television news, today most newspapers now have a team of reporters on the earmark issue."

"What seems to have fueled the current outrage over pork is the link with lobbyists," says Evans of Trinity College. "What smells bad to people is that you get a lobbyist coming in, and they're getting a contingency fee . . . and the company or lobbyist is giving money to the member's campaign."

In the past, the rule for legislators dealing with lobbyists was: "If you can't take their money at breakfast and screw them in the afternoon, you don't belong in this business," wrote Richard Lowry, editor of the conservative *National Review*. [63]

But GOP leaders have forged much closer relationships with lobbyists, even bringing them into the so-called whip operations to help pressure legislators for votes. "The institutionalization of the lobbyists into the whip operation was a mistake," said an anonymous source quoted by Lowry. "It's too cozy. And I'm a lobbyist." [64] ■

CURRENT SITUATION

Pork Chopped

With lawmakers clearly benefiting from earmarks, Congress remains ambivalent about changing the system, despite some public displeasure. Nevertheless, in the current scandal-ridden climate lawmakers are seeking fewer earmarks this year but have defeated attempts to strip out some earmarks from pending bills. And while both the House and the Senate have approved bills aimed at cleaning up lobbying and earmarking, passage of a final bill is uncertain.

Last year, with the Cunningham and Abramoff scandals simmering, Congress' ardor for earmarks cooled somewhat. For example, between fiscal 1994 and 2005, earmarks for the Labor, Education and Health and Human Services departments had swelled from five to 3,014. The fiscal 2006 bill, however, was trimmed back to eight earmarks. [65]

This year, earmark requests from individual lawmakers are down again. For example, total requests to seven of the 10 House Appropriations subcommittees dropped 42.6 percent between 2005 and 2006 — from 26,954 last year to 15,470. [66]

But the drop-off in requests doesn't necessarily mean anything, says Donald Wolfensberger, a former aide to House Rules Committee Republicans, who directs the Congress Project at the Woodrow Wilson International Center for Scholars. "It's hard to say where this is all going to come out," he says. "There is currently some self-restraint on the number of requests. But the more important number is how many they are going to grant."

Lawmakers like Sen. Coburn and Rep. Jeff Flake, R-Ariz., who try to shoot down earmarks have met with little success. In April, Coburn managed to strip a $15 million seafood-promotion earmark from the supplemental war and hurricane-cleanup spending bill, but several large earmarks remained in the bill — such as the $700 million to relocate the CSX Railroad in Mississippi (later removed by conferees). [67] On the House side, Flake's efforts to strip certain earmarks have been defeated by large margins. [68]

And neither the White House nor congressional conservatives have embraced the cause of ending earmarks, says the Heritage Foundation's Utt. "The president himself has let it be known that it's only [whether] the total [spending falls under a White House-set cap] that matters to him. They don't care what's in it," says Utt, referring to the current defense supplemental spending bill. "That's a remarkable thing to say."

Bills Stalled

Most congressional watchdog groups say House and Senate measures passed this spring designed to curb lobbying and earmark abuses are more cosmetic than substantive. And, as summer approaches — not to mention the fall congressional election — lawmakers may have lost whatever enthusiasm they had for the measures.

The Senate passed its bill March 29, on a 90-8 vote. The House measure passed by a slim 217-213 margin on May 3. The two bills vary considerably, however, and while the Senate has appointed members to a conference committee to hash out the differences, House leaders have yet to name conferees.

Both bills would require lobbyists to disclose more details about their activities. The Senate bill would ban senators and staff from accepting gifts from registered lobbyists, while the House would require lobbyists to report any gifts over $10. The House legislation would label earmarks in appropriations bills with the name of the lawmaker who requested them. The Senate bill has a more expansive provision, requiring sponsors of earmarks in all bills — not just appropriations — to be named.

But watchdog groups say the bills are riddled with loopholes that make them ineffective, even if Congress manages to iron out differences and pass legislation.

The Senate passed "unacceptable" legislation, while the House "passed a completely fraudulent bill," said Common Cause, the League of Women Voters, Public Citizen and several other groups on May 31. "The entire House bill . . . virtually left intact the corrupting way of life on Capitol Hill and the financial perks from influence seekers," the groups said. [69]

Among other issues, the groups said, the House Rules Committee watered down some provisions before taking that chamber's bill to the floor. For example, the original bill asked the Government Accountability Office, Congress' audit and research arm, to study the extent to which lobbyists receive contingency fees for securing clients' earmarks. Although contingency fees for lobbying are illegal, many Congress-watchers say they are common practice.

"Judging by the amount I've heard about it, it's a pretty regular occurrence," illegal or not, says Ashdown of Taxpayers for Common Sense. "They structure it legally in a way that it appears to be a retainer" — a straight fee for time and services, not based on whether an earmark was procured — "but it's really a contingency fee," he says. Despite these suspicions, the current bill does not mention contingency fees.

As for the Senate bill, "everything they did, there's a simple way around it," Ashdown said. For example, he said, a ban on adding earmarks in the last few hours of Senate deliberations could be easily circumvented by adding them even later — during the House-Senate conference committee. "Based on what the Senate passed . . . Duke Cunningham could come back to Congress today and rip off the government for tens of millions more, and we wouldn't know it," he said. [70]

The Senate bill also defined earmarks as targeted funding that goes straight to an external entity like a defense contractor or local government office, exempting funds that first pass through a federal agency. That's "a massive loophole," says Ashdown. In some areas, such as defense, many earmarks already take this form and would thereby be excused from the transparency provisions, he says. "You could basically start writing any of these [earmark provisions] so they got redefined as going to the Department of Labor, Defense, whatever."

A major issue stalling the bills is a Senate-proposed requirement that staffers wait a year after leaving their jobs on Capitol Hill before lobbying Congress. The House bill doesn't have such a ban. Congressional aides who see high-paid lobbying careers in their futures are apparently lobbying their bosses today to nix the provision.

"There's a lot of under-the-radar pushback" on the waiting period, said Sen. Susan Collins, R-Maine, who chairs the Senate Homeland Security and Governmental Affairs Committee. [71]

Despite transparency requirements in both pending measures, appropriations bills have been emerging this year without sponsors' names attached to earmarks, raising the hackles of those who want a crackdown. "We ought to follow what we passed out of the House" and name earmark sponsors, said Flake. [72]

With plenty else on lawmakers' plates, the chances of Congress passing earmark and lobbying reforms this year look doubtful to many. "Getting between a lawmaker and an earmark is like trying to take a ribeye away from a dog," said Ashdown. [73]

"I'm skeptical" that a law will emerge this year, says Evans of Trinity College. "We're so deep in the election cycle now, and there are so many other issues on the table. The only way it could is if this election gets nationalized around the issue."

But Wolfensberger of the Congress Project thinks Congress is slowly moving toward a compromise bill, with House leaders having indicated that they'd be willing to adopt some of the Senate's slightly tougher provisions. "I think they will pass a bill," he says. ■

OUTLOOK

Nonstop 'Gravy Train'?

Few analysts envision a major crackdown on earmarks — either corrupt or simply excessive — because legislators value them too much.

Conservative anti-tax activist Norquist, however, says current corruption scandals could make earmarks a winning issue for some congressional challengers this fall.

"Some people will lose elections," he says, while acknowledging that spending is not an issue that has cost elections before. "But the corruption angle may change that." When it comes to outrage over government spending, "I think the public understands a $10 million earmark better than a $100 billion entitlement program."

After the November elections, Republicans could very likely return to their anti-earmarking roots, says former Democratic House aide Lilly. If Democrats regain control of Congress, Republicans would again become stout earmark opponents, he says.

If Democrats gain the congressional majority, it's not clear whether earmark levels would stay high or return to earlier levels. "Democrats have less of a philosophical problem with using federal money to address local problems," says Evans.

And if federal budget problems worsen, interest in limiting earmarks could increase. "There are still towns, cities and colleges that haven't caught on to the earmark" gravy train, says Lilly, so it's likely that "more people will come in to ask for them. After a few years we will get to a point where there is no more money, but there will still be more people asking and therefore more people Congress will have to say 'no' to." That could lead to a painful reconsideration, he says.

Congress will seriously question earmarking only when it "starts to get serious about the deficit," says the Congress Project's Wolfensberger. That may require emergence of another political figure like 1992 presidential candidate Ross Perot, who "impresses upon people how serious it is." [74]

A "reform-minded president could threaten vetoes," says the New School's Hartung. "The president could very well win on that, if the public mood was right," but victory would come at a price. "They'd then need to figure out how to relate to the Hill on other matters," because legislators would push back.

It's corrupt earmarks, given in exchange for money and favors, that are most alarming, says the Heritage Foundation's Utt. To weed those out, democracy's traditional means of checks and balances — the press and the courts — will eventually suffice, though it will take time, he says. "Eventually, a free press and an independent judiciary work," he says. Currently, "the publicity is starting to bring things out."

But no one predicts that Congress will ever swear off pork barrel politics. "Members think it helps them get re-elected. Leaders think it helps them get bills passed," says Evans. "So where is the incentive to stop?" ■

Notes

[1] Tom Hamburger, Lance Pugmire and Richard Simon, "Rep. Calvert's Land of Plenty," *Los Angeles Times*, May 15, 2006, p. A1.

[2] Quoted in *ibid.*

[3] Quoted in George E. Condon, Jr., "Congressman's Betrayal of Troops Called Greatest Sin," Copley News Service, Dec. 1, 2005, http://signonsandiego.printthis.clickability.com.

[4] Tom Coburn, statement delivered to hearing of Senate Committee on Homeland Security and Government Affairs, March 16, 2006, http://hsgac.senate.gov/_files/031606CoburnOpen.pdf.

[5] Steve Ellis, "Earmark Reform: Understanding the Obligation of Funds Transparency Act," testimony before Senate Homeland Security and Government Affairs Committee, March 16, 2006.

[6] *Ibid.*

[7] *Ibid.*

[8] Quoted in David Bauman, "Legislator Takes Stand in Support of Earmarks," *Government Executive* online, www.Govexec.com, March 24, 2006.

[9] Quoted in "Eliminating 'Earmarks,' " Congressional Quarterly committee testimony, March 16, 2006, www.cq.com.

[10] Quoted in Dori Meinert, "'Earmarks Bring In Millions In Federal Funds," Copley News Service, April 26, 2006.

[11] Quoted in "Lobbying Revision," Congressional Quarterly Committee Testimony, March 2, 2006, www.cq.com.

[12] *Ibid.*

[13] *Ibid.*

[14] Quoted in "Eliminating 'Earmarks,' " *op. cit.*

[15] "The Corrupting Power of Earmarks," Taxpayers for Common Sense, Jan. 20, 2006, www.taxpayer.net.

[16] Quoted in "House Rules Committee Holds Hearing on Lobbying Reform," *op. cit.*

[17] "House Winners Average $1 Million for the First Term; Senate Winners Up 47 Percent," press release, Campaign Finance Institute, Nov. 5, 2004, www.cfinst.org.

[18] Quoted in "Lobbying Revision," *op. cit.*

[19] *Ibid.*

[20] Winslow Wheeler, "Don't Mind If I Do," *The Washington Post*, Aug. 22, 2004, p. B1.

[21] *Ibid.*

[22] "Bill Shorts Gear for Troops," The Associated Press, April 21, 2006.

[23] Quoted in "Eliminating 'Earmarks,' " *op. cit.*

[24] *Ibid.*

[25] Diana Evans, *Greasing the Wheels* (2004), p. 14.

[26] Wesley Bizzell, "Congressional Earmarks Are More Than Just Pork," *Corrections Today*, American Correctional Association, October 2004, www.winston.com/pdfs/Judicial_web10-2004.pdf.

[27] "Senate Supplemental Appropriations Bill Adds $227.5 Million for Advance Procurement of C-17s," *California Chronicle*, April 4, 2006, www.californiachronicle.com.

[28] "Porkbusters Pick on Wrong Project," *The Meridian Star*, www.meridianstar.com.

[29] *Ibid.*

[30] "GW Battleground 2006 Poll Reveals Environment Is Negative Towards All, Partisan Politics Is Creating Distrust," press release, George Washington University News Center, March 2, 2006, www.gwu.edu.

[31] Dick Morris, "Abramoff Scandal Should Lead to Appropriation Earmarking Reform," Cagle Syndicate, Jan. 21, 2006.

[32] For background, see Kenneth Jost, "Line-Item Veto," *CQ Researcher*, June 20, 1997, pp. 529-552.

[33] Brian Riedl, "How Pork Corrupts," *The Washington Times*, Jan. 29, 2006, www.hhrf.org.

[34] Quoted in "Eliminating 'Earmarks,' " *op. cit.*

[35] Quoted in "Lobbying Revision," *op. cit.*

[36] Quoted in "House Rules Committee Holds Hearing on Lobbying Reform," *op. cit.*

[37] *Ibid.*

[38] Testimony before Senate Committee on Rules and Administration, July 9, 2003, www.cbo.gov.

[39] Unless otherwise noted, information in this section comes from Diana Evans, *op. cit.*; Tom Finnigan, "All About Pork," Citizens Against Government Waste, May 2006; and Ronald Utt, "A Primer on Lobbyists, Earmarks, and Congressional Reform," *Heritage Foundation Backgrounder*, April 2006.

[40] For coverage, see Todd Wilkinson, "Alaska's 'bridges to nowhere,' " *The Christian Science Monitor*, June 15, 2004, p. 2.

[41] Finnigan, *op. cit.*

[42] Thomas Schatz, testimony before House Budget Committee, May 25, 2006.

[43] Evans, *op. cit.*, p. 4.

[44] Steven D. Levitt and James M, Snyder, "The Impact of Federal Spending on House Election Outcomes," *The Journal of Political Economy*, February 1997, pp. 30-53, www.jstor.org.

[45] Michael H. Crespin and Charles J. Finocchiaro, "Parties and the Politics of Pork in

About the Author

Staff writer **Marcia Clemmitt** is a veteran social-policy reporter who previously served as editor in chief of *Medicine and Health*, a Washington industry newsletter, and staff writer for *The Scientist*. She has also been a high school math and physics teacher. She holds a liberal arts and sciences degree from St. John's College, Annapolis, and a master's degree in English from Georgetown University. Her recent reports include "Saving the Oceans," "Climate Change" and "AP and IB Programs."

the U.S. Senate," paper delivered at Duke University conference, "Party Effects in the U.S. Senate," April 7-8, 2006.

[46] Unless otherwise noted, information in this section is drawn from Jackie Calmes, "In Search of Presidential Earmarks," *The Wall Street Journal*, Feb. 21, 2006, p. A6.

[47] Quoted in "Grand Old Porkers," Minority Staff of the House Appropriations Committee, 2003, www.house.gov/appropriations_democrats/.

[48] Ken Silverstein, "The Great American Pork Barrel," *Harper's* online, July 2005, www.harpers.org.

[49] *Ibid.*

[50] "Earmarks in Appropriations Acts," CRS Appropriations Team, Congressional Research Service, Oct. 13, 2005; "Earmarks in FY2006 Appropriations Acts," CRS Appropriations Team, Congressional Research Service, March 6, 2006.

[51] *Ibid.*

[52] Crespin and Finocchiaro, *op. cit.*

[53] Steve Ellis, "Speech Regarding the Explosion of Earmarks on Capitol Hill," undated, Taxpayers for Common Sense, www.taxpayer.net/budget/katrinaspending/catospeech.htm.

[54] For background, see Peter Katel, "Lobbying Boom," *CQ Researcher*, July 22, 2005, pp. 613-636.

[55] Richard Lowry, "Say It Ain't So: How the GOP Majority Lost Its Way," *National Review*, Feb. 13, 2006, p. 32.

[56] "Pulled Pork," *The Wastebasket: A Weekly Bulletin on Government Waste*, Taxpayers for Common Sense, March 15, 2006, www.taxpayer.net.

[57] *Ibid.*

[58] "The Bankrollers: Lobbyists' Payments to the Lawmakers They Court, 1998-2006," Congress Watch, May 2006.

[59] Peter Pae and Dan Morain, "Cozying Up To Power," *Los Angeles Times*, May 8, 2006, p. C1.

[60] Michael Kranish, "Congress Bribery Probe Could Deepen," *The Boston Globe*, May 19, 2006, p. A1.

[61] "CAGW Names Rep. Mollohan Porker of the Month," Citizens Against Government Waste, April 24, 2006, www.cagw.org.

[62] Peter Pae, "Lewis Surfaces in Probe of Cunningham," *Los Angeles Times*, May 11, 2006.

[63] Lowry, *op. cit.*

[64] *Ibid.*

[65] "Earmarks in Appropriations Acts," *op. cit.*; "Earmarks in FY2006 Appropriations Acts," *op. cit.*

FOR MORE INFORMATION

American Association for the Advancement of Science, 1200 New York Ave., N.W., Washington, DC 20005; (202) 326-6400; www.aaas.org. The world's largest scientific membership organization tracks research-related earmarks in legislation.

American League of Lobbyists, P.O. Box 30005, Alexandria, VA 22310; (703) 960-3011; www.alldc.org. Advocates for the rights of lobbyists and sets standards for the lobbying industry.

Americans for Prosperity Foundation, 1726 I St., N.W., 10th Floor, Washington, DC 20036; (202) 349-5880; http://americansforprosperity.org. Promotes fiscal conservatism, low taxes and low government spending at the federal and state levels; sponsored a national "Earmarks Express" tour to highlight wasteful spending.

Association of American Universities, 1200 New York Ave., N.W., Suite 550, Washington, DC 20005; (202) 408-7500; www.aau.edu. An organization of research universities that develops policy positions for academia on appropriations issues.

Citizens Against Government Waste, 1301 Connecticut Ave., N.W., Suite 400, Washington, DC 20036; (202) 467-5300; www.cagw.org. Works to eliminate waste and inefficiency in the federal government; its annual *Congressional Pig Book* lists pork barrel projects in appropriations bills.

Citizens for Ethics and Responsibility in Washington, 1400 I St., N.W., Suite 450, Washington, DC 20005; (202) 588-5565; http://jackinthehouse.org. A watchdog group that provides information about and brings lawsuits against public officials suspected of involvement in bribery or other corrupt dealings with special interests.

Porkbusters: Blogging the Waste Out of Government; http://truthlaidbear.com/porkbusters/index.php. A group of conservative bloggers dedicated to bringing attention to pork barrel spending.

Porkopolis: Rants on Pork Barrel Spending and Libertarian Commentary; http://porkopolis.blogspot.com/. Libertarian blogger Mario Delgado provides links to news reports about pork barrel spending.

Taxpayers for Common Sense, 651 Pennsylvania Ave., S.E., Washington, DC 20003; 1(800)-taxpayer; www.taxpayer.net. A nonpartisan watchdog group that provides information about wasteful government spending; sponsors the "Golden Fleece Awards" to call attention to spending items it considers frivolous.

[66] Peter Cohn, "Panel's Overhaul of Earmark Practices Appears to Have an Effect," *Government Executive*, March 23, 2006, www.govexec.com.

[67] Anne Plummer, "Coburn Has Mixed Success Cutting Spending in War Bill," *CQ Today*, April 27, 2006.

[68] Steven T. Dennis and Liriel Higa, "Even With Earmark Battles, House on Pace to Finish Spending Bills by July 4," *CQ Today*, May 26, 2006.

[69] "Statement of Reform Groups on House-Senate Conference on So-Called Lobbying and Ethics 'Reform' Bill," Campaign Legal Center, May 31, 2006, www.campaignlegalcenter.org.

[70] Quoted in Gail Russell Chaddock, "Senate Lobby Reform: Strong Enough?" *The Christian Science Monitor*, March 31, 2006, p. 3.

[71] Quoted in Martin Kady II, "Lobbying Overhaul Drive Runs Out of Gas," *CQ Today*, May 16, 2006.

[72] Quoted in *ibid.*

[73] Quoted in Silverstein, *op. cit.*

[74] For background, see Marcia Clemmitt, "Budget Deficit," *CQ Researcher*, Dec. 9, 2005, pp. 1029-1051.

Bibliography

Selected Sources

Books

Evans, Diana, *Greasing the Wheels: Using Pork Barrel Projects to Build Majority Coalitions in Congress*, Cambridge University Press, 2004.

A political science professor at Connecticut's Trinity College says congressional leaders and presidents often trade local pork for votes to pass legislation they believe is in the national interest.

Savage, James D., *Funding Science in America: Congress, Universities, and the Politics of the Academic Pork Barrel*, Cambridge University Press, 2000.

A University of Virginia professor of politics traces the growth of earmarks for academic research, which began to boom in the 1980s after some universities complained that the traditional process of awarding federal grants on the basis of competitive peer review put lesser-known universities at a disadvantage.

Articles

Allison, Wes, "Projects Touchy for Lawmakers," *St. Petersburg Times*, March 11, 2006, p. A1.

When the newspaper asked members of Congress representing Florida to disclose what earmarks they asked for and which they received, few lawmakers responded in detail.

Bauman, David, "Here to Stay," *Government Executive*, www.GovExec.com, Feb. 13, 2006.

A new lobbying community has emerged in the last decade, dedicated to procuring earmarks for clients ranging from the Florida Public Transportation Association to the Country Music Hall of Fame.

Budoff, Carrie, "From Staff to Lobbyist: The Ties That Bind," *The Philadelphia Inquirer*, April 17, 2006, www.centredaily.com.

Former congressional staffers set up lucrative lobbying shops, using connections to their old Capitol Hill bosses to gain earmarked funds for clients.

Calmes, Jackie, "In Search of Presidential Earmarks," *The Wall Street Journal*, Feb. 21, 2006, p. A6.

The White House earmarks funds for political reasons just as Congress does, but they're harder to detect.

Cochran, John, "Budget Villian, Local Hero," *CQ Weekly*, June 12, 2006, p. 1606.

The number of congressional earmarks have mushroomed. Critics say they waste money and foster corruption. But local beneficiaries praise lawmakers who procure federal largesse, so the practice is expected to continue.

Epstein, Keith, "A World of Secrets," *The Tampa Tribune*, March 24, 2006, http://news.tbo.com.

The congressional bribery case involving former Rep. Randy "Duke" Cunningham, R-Calif., offers glimpses into a secret world of back-room deals over congressional earmarks.

Kirkpatrick, David D., "Rise of Lobbyist Shines a Light on House Ties," *The New York Times*, June 3, 2006.

A former aide to House Appropriations Committee Chairman Rep. Jerry Lewis, R-Calif., now a lobbyist specializing in obtaining earmark funds, draws legal scrutiny over her Capitol Hill connections.

Lowry, Richard, "Say It Ain't So: How the GOP Majority Lost Its Way," *National Review*, Feb. 13, 2006, p. 32.

After decades of decrying the evils of pork barrel spending as the minority party, Congress' GOP majority embraces pork as a tool for accomplishing legislative goals.

Ochoa, Julia, "Money a Motivator in I-75 Earmark?" *Naples [Florida] News*, April 16, 2006, www.naplesnews.com.

House appropriator Rep. Don Young, R-Alaska, may have helped a Florida county get federal road funding in exchange for campaign contributions in the state.

Silverstein, Ken, "The Great American Pork Barrel: Washington Streamlines the Means of Corruption," *Harper's*, July 2005, posted online Feb. 9, 2006, www.harpers.org.

As congressional leaders turn more often to earmarks as a way to gain lawmakers' votes, a new lobbying industry grows in Washington, with many complex ties to members of Congress.

Wheeler, Winslow, "Defense Pork: Putting Lipstick on the Pig," *Mother Jones*, March 21, 2006, www.mojones.com.

Proposed earmarking and lobbying reforms might not slow the growth of defense-related earmarking.

Reports and Studies

"Earmarks in Appropriation Acts: FY1994, FY1996, FY1998, FY2000, FY2002, FY2004, FY2005," Congressional Research Service Appropriations Team, Oct. 13, 2005.

Congress' nonpartisan research arm describes recent trends in earmarking for each federal department.

Utt, Ronald D., "A Primer on Lobbyists, Earmarks, and Congressional Reform," *Heritage Foundation Backgrounder*, April 27, 2006.

An analyst at the conservative think tank describes the different legislative provisions that qualify as earmarks, chronicles historical trends in earmarking and lobbying for earmarks and makes recommendations for reform.

The Next Step:

Additional Articles from Current Periodicals

Bribes and Congress

Broder, John M., "Congressman Pleads Guilty to Bribery, Then Resigns," *The Houston Chronicle*, Nov. 29, 2005, p. A1.

Rep. Randy "Duke" Cunningham, R-Calif., resigned from Congress after pleading guilty to taking at least $2.4 million in bribes to help friends and campaign contributors win defense contracts.

Coile, Zachary, "Corruption and the Politics of Pay-to-Play," *The San Francisco Chronicle*, Dec. 4, 2005, p. A1.

Republicans recaptured the House in 1994 by portraying Democrats as too corrupt to lead after a series of scandals. Now the GOP is under fire for ethical problems including bribes.

Powers, Ashley, and Richard Simon, "San Bernardino County Records Are Subpoenaed," *Los Angeles Times*, June 3, 2006, p. B3.

A federal grand jury is examining the relationship between Rep. Jerry Lewis, R-Calif., and Washington lobbyist Bill Lowery that may have led to favorable treatment for the lobbyist's clients.

Earmark Reform

Chaddock, Gail Russell, "Bold Bid to Cut 'Pork' in Congress," *The Christian Science Monitor*, May 2, 2006, p. 1.

Republicans — aware that a recent poll showed Americans saying ending earmarks should be a top priority for Congress — are growing anxious about this fall's elections.

Hulse, Carl, "A First Small Step Against Pet Projects," *The New York Times*, April 29, 2006, p. A9.

The Senate voted to eliminate $15 million for a seafood marketing campaign from an emergency spending bill, showing how sentiment is shifting away from earmarks.

Milligan, Susan, "Loophole Weakens Lobbying Reform Bill," *The Boston Globe*, April 2, 2006, p. A1.

A loophole in a new bill meant to reduce the number of earmarks approved by Congress will allow almost half of proposed pork-barrel projects to slip through.

Murray, Shailagh, "Capital's New Four-Letter Word," *The Washington Post*, Jan. 27, 2006, p. A21.

A budget crisis and scandals involving legislative favors are spurring a government watchdog movement that is turning "pork" into a bad word.

Lobbying Scandals

Goldstein, Steve, "Specter Begins Inquiry Into Staff, Lobbyist Ties," *The Philadelphia Inquirer*, Feb. 18, 2006, p. A4.

Sen. Arlen Specter, R-Pa., is investigating whether his senior staffer Vicki Siegel Herson secured funds for clients of her lobbyist husband Michael Herson.

Kirkpatrick, David D., "Lobbyist Says Client Paid Half of Town House's Cost," *The New York Times*, June 7, 2006, p. A20.

Letitia Hoadley White, a former top House defense appropriations aide admitted a military contractor paid half the cost of her million-dollar town house.

Marsh, Bill, "Capital Alert: The Unfolding Story of Brent Wilkes," *The New York Times*, May 21, 2006, p. 16.

Congress is investigating California defense contractor Brent R. Wilkes, identified as a co-conspirator in the case of Rep. Randy "Duke" Cunningham and accused of giving bribes.

Mississippi Railroad Project

Simon, Richard, and Maura Reynolds, "GOP Senators Spurn Bush's Order to Cut Bill," *Los Angeles Times*, April 27, 2006, p. A4.

Republican Senators acquired enough votes to defy a veto threat from President Bush on an emergency spending bill that includes pet projects.

Whoriskey, Peter, "Priorities of Earmarks Are Disputed," *The Washington Post*, May 24, 2006, p. A3.

A Senate bill to address emergency spending for the wars in Iraq and Afghanistan and Hurricane Katrina relief included a $700 million earmark to reroute a Mississippi train line damaged by Katrina that was already rebuilt at a cost of at least $250 million.

CITING *CQ RESEARCHER*

Sample formats for citing these reports in a bibliography include the ones listed below. Preferred styles and formats vary, so please check with your instructor or professor.

MLA STYLE

Jost, Kenneth. "Rethinking the Death Penalty." CQ Researcher 16 Nov. 2001: 945-68.

APA STYLE

Jost, K. (2001, November 16). Rethinking the death penalty. *CQ Researcher, 11*, 945-968.

CHICAGO STYLE

Jost, Kenneth. "Rethinking the Death Penalty." *CQ Researcher*, November 16, 2001, 945-968.

CQ Researcher

Published by CQ Press, a division of Congressional Quarterly Inc.

cqresearcher.com

Downtown Renaissance

Are center cities finally returning to health?

After World War II, suburban job and population growth in the United States far outstripped that of cities, leading many to worry that downtowns were doomed. In recent years, however, many cities have revived their fortunes by fashioning downtowns that are attractive and — for the first time in decades — drawing in new residents. Once-forlorn urban centers from San Diego to Philadelphia are now busy construction zones that are filling up with trendy shops and restaurants. But despite the good news, downtowns are still grabbing only a tiny fraction of metropolitan growth. Some skeptics worry that the downtown renaissance is fragile, largely built on upscale shopping and entertainment — relatively new trends that could easily change. But others believe downtowns, having once again become the most vital parts of many cities, will provide a model for future development — even in the suburbs.

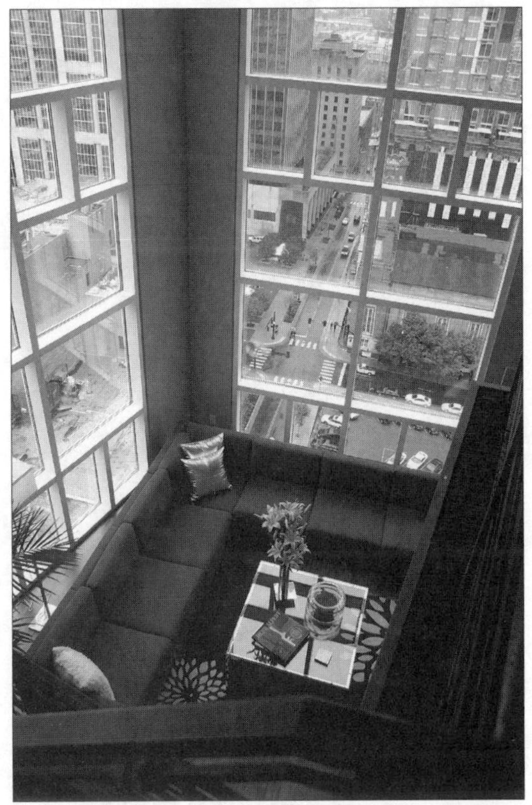

A renovated penthouse condominium overlooks Nashville's vibrant downtown. The $1.2 million, 23rd-floor duplex was featured in the city's 2006 downtown home tour.

INSIDE THIS REPORT

CQ Researcher • June 23, 2006 • www.cqresearcher.com
Volume 16, Number 24 • Pages 553-576

CQ Press

Recipient of Society of Professional Journalists Award for Excellence ◆ American Bar Association Silver Gavel Award

Cover: A renovated penthouse condominium overlooks Nashville's vibrant downtown. The $1.2 million, 23rd-floor duplex was featured in the city's 2006 downtown home tour. (Nashville Downtown Partnership)

CQ Researcher

June 23, 2006
Volume 16, Number 24

MANAGING EDITOR: Thomas J. Colin

ASSISTANT MANAGING EDITOR: Kathy Koch

ASSOCIATE EDITOR: Kenneth Jost

STAFF WRITERS: Marcia Clemmitt, Peter Katel

CONTRIBUTING WRITERS: Rachel S. Cox, Sarah Glazer, Alan Greenblatt, Patrick Marshall, Tom Price

DESIGN/PRODUCTION EDITOR: Olu B. Davis

ASSISTANT EDITOR: Melissa J. Hipolit

EDITORIAL INTERN: Nicholas Sohr

CQ PRESS

A Division of Congressional Quarterly Inc.

SENIOR VICE PRESIDENT/PUBLISHER: John A. Jenkins

DIRECTOR, LIBRARY PUBLISHING: Kathryn C. Suárez

DIRECTOR, EDITORIAL OPERATIONS: Ann Davies

CONGRESSIONAL QUARTERLY INC.

CHAIRMAN: Paul C. Tash

VICE CHAIRMAN: Andrew P. Corty

PRESIDENT/EDITOR IN CHIEF: Robert W. Merry

CQ Researcher (ISSN 1056-2036) is printed on acid-free paper. Published weekly, except March 24, July 7, July 14, Aug. 4, Aug. 11, Nov. 24, Dec. 22 and Dec. 29, by CQ Press, a division of Congressional Quarterly Inc. Annual full-service subscriptions for institutions start at $667. For pricing, call 1-800-834-9020, ext. 1906. To purchase a *CQ Researcher* report in print or electronic format (PDF), visit www.cqpress.com or call 866-427-7737. Single reports start at $10. Bulk purchase discounts and electronic-rights licensing are also available. Periodicals postage paid at Washington, D.C., and additional mailing offices. POSTMASTER: Send address changes to *CQ Researcher*, 1255 22nd St., N.W., Suite 400, Washington, DC 20037.

Downtown Renaissance

BY ALAN GREENBLATT

THE ISSUES

One fine May afternoon, Sam Kleckley was sitting in downtown Greenville, S.C., enjoying watching people meandering across the new pedestrian bridge overlooking the waterfalls cascading down the Reedy River. Nodding toward a wedding party posing for pictures, he said, "It's amazing the number of people who came here for prom pictures, too."

The chance for photo ops is new in downtown Greenville. A few years ago, a large vehicular bridge blocked the view of the falls. Today it's gone, and the 18-month-old pedestrian bridge and the park surrounding it are the city's leading tourist attraction.

But they're not the only draw in a downtown that suddenly finds itself crowded with shoppers and folks hunting for places to eat. Main Street, which had only four restaurants 20 years ago, now boasts more than 75. There's a busy performing-arts center, and the new minor league ballpark just up the street has largely silenced local complaints about the home team's quirky name, The Drive. And the number of downtown residential units has jumped 50 percent in the last five years.

"It is phenomenal," says Kleckley, owner of a restaurant with an impressive river view. "Ten years ago, this area was like a slum."

Greenville's revitalization *is* phenomenal, but it's far from unique. After decades of decline, America's downtowns are making a comeback. From Phoenix to Philadelphia, from Memphis to Minneapolis, once derelict areas have become clean, chic and expensive.

"If you look at the numbers, there's no question that downtowns are coming back and are healthy in ways that we never expected," says David Feehan, president of the International Downtown Association.

Greenville suffered many of the same woes that befell other American cities after World War II, when an explosion of cars and road building lured city dwellers to the suburbs. Even today, Greenville accounts for only 56,000 residents in a sprawling county of 400,000.

Noel St. John

Lunchtime crowds pack Atlanta's Fairlie-Poplar Historic District for weekly concerts. Across the country, once moribund downtown areas have become clean, chic and expensive, thanks in part to new convention centers, stadiums and performing-arts complexes. But some critics say downtowns' newfound popularity will fade as affluent city dwellers start families and move to the suburbs. Meanwhile, they say, low-income residents are being forced out of gentrifying neighborhoods.

But central business districts were never meant as places to live. They were where people went to work and shop. And they were famous for their huge department stores, women's-wear shops and, improbable as it may seem, car dealers. But the retail outlets and car dealerships soon followed their customers to the suburbs, where giant malls began rising in the 1940s. By 2000, downtown retail sales accounted for less than 5 percent of the nation's total, says Feehan.

Office workers still came downtown to shop, since many jobs remained in the cities, even through the worst of times. But casual visitors stayed away: Parking was scarce and expensive, many retail outlets had closed and crime became a major concern, particularly after a crack epidemic left drug addicts, homelessness and panhandlers in its wake. Cities in the 1970s and '80s were "places of crime and danger," says Paul Levy, president of the Philadelphia Center City District.

Downtowns had become the empty center of the metropolitan donut. But while suburban population and job growth continue to outpace downtowns, central cities are experiencing an undeniable, if perhaps fragile, renaissance. A strong economy and better policing techniques, as pioneered in New York City, have helped bring crime way down. Violent crimes dropped by 32 percent between 1995 and 2004, according to the FBI. [1]

Moreover, says Feehan, between 1995 and 2005 major crimes declined 58 percent in U.S. cities. Business-improvement districts (BIDs) such as Levy's, invested heavily in sprucing up

Suburbs Outpacing Central Cities

Suburbs throughout the United States are growing rapidly, especially in the South and West. In contrast, central cities are growing more slowly. In the Midwest, however, they are declining.

Population Change in Central Cities and Suburbs of Large Metropolitan Areas, 2000-2004
(By percent change)

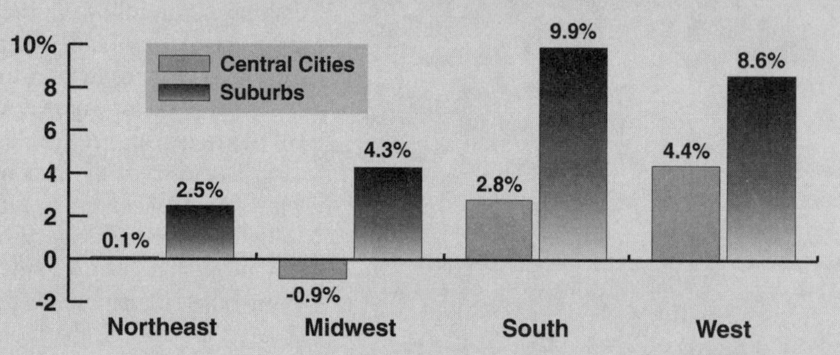

Source: The Brookings Institution, "Living Cities Census Series," September 2005

appearances, which helped downtowns look cleaner and safer. Many BIDs imposed levies or even helped pass tax increases that paid for new convention centers, stadiums and performing-arts complexes.

Movies and television shows like "Ally McBeal" and "Sex and the City" began depicting urban living as the lifestyle choice of hip, single, young adults. "The cultural change reflected demographic change," says Levy, "and these things are reinforcing each other."

Today, many young people aspire to live in cities because that's where the action is. For a generation that grew up knowing only the vast, anonymous spaces of shopping malls and suburban sprawl, downtowns feel richer in history and a sense of place. "People are looking for denser social experiences, a greater sense of civic life," says Alison Isenberg, a Rutgers University historian and author of the 2004 book *Downtown America*. "That's something that's very hard to find in suburbs."

Fifteen or 20 years ago, feasibility studies suggested no one would want to live downtown. But after a few developers took a risk and began converting abandoned old buildings into condos, the "loft" spaces became an important new trend.

"In the studies, no one could get it in their minds what it was like to live downtown," says Richard T. Reinhard, managing director of urban development and public infrastructure at the Urban Land Institute. "Yet when the product was put on the market, people discovered it was something that they really liked."

The lofts, coffee shops and hookah bars that now are common in many contemporary downtowns are catnip to young people. Older folks whose children are grown — so-called empty nesters — also find themselves drawn back to city living. Many baby boomers, it seems, find they no longer need 5,000-square-foot homes in suburban cul-de-sacs and instead prefer to walk to work or to downtown attractions.

Some worry that the influx of middle- and upper-income residents is driving out long-term, low-income residents. But others say that busier downtowns, which were never primarily residential areas, are a boon. Downtowns that once were barren after 6 o'clock are now bustling at night with tourists or residents with more disposable income than children. In Greenville, ballgames, outdoor concerts and other events draw people downtown and encourage them to loiter at restaurants and cafes. "There's something going on every night from Wednesday on," says Kleckley, the restaurant owner.

Many cities now rely on a similar formula of attractions and leisure spending, leading some critics to warn that downtowns are becoming Disneyfied versions of themselves — all with the same chain restaurants and not enough sustainable business activity of substance, such as legal and professional services. Downtowns certainly don't command the same dominant share of either jobs or retail sales they once did. Indeed, the Census Bureau stopped tracking downtown retail sales in 1977 because the number had become such a small percentage of overall metropolitan sales — just 4 percent compared with 50 percent in 1920. Thus, rather than being revitalized, downtowns are being reinvented, Isenberg suggests.

Despite the naysaying, there's no question that dozens of American downtowns are livelier places than they were just a few years ago. "If we're filling up the buildings and we're attracting middle- and upper-income people and we're having lively streets and restaurants, where's the problem?" wonders Feehan. "I don't see it."

As people contemplate the changing nature of downtowns and their future, here are some of the questions they're debating:

Are downtowns making a sustainable comeback?

Greenville has drawn people back downtown using several methods that have become popular with city governments: It helped build a large hotel for business meetings, a pair of large performing-arts venues and the new ballpark. Those attractions provided anchors for downtown development along Main Street, encouraging both people and retailers to return to the area.

Although many downtowns today clearly are healthier than they were a few years ago, many experts fear their success is not built on solid foundations. Because many reviving downtowns rely heavily on entertainment, skeptics wonder how long such "urban theme parks" will remain popular. And downtown growth — in terms of business, retail and residential — still represents only a fraction of the continued oceanic swelling of American suburbs.

"The numbers are pretty overwhelming that what is happening in downtowns is real but very, very small compared to suburbs," says Joel Kotkin, a senior fellow at the New America Foundation and author of several books and studies about cities. "Perhaps most troubling, there is not a huge amount of job growth in most of the traditional downtowns, even though we have a strong [nationwide] expansion. My sense is that many cities are becoming more residential, in part, because the office demands are not there."

Downtowns might be able to survive as "Disneylands for adults," as Kotkin calls them, but some analysts worry they'll lose their shine over time. New downtown residents are overwhelmingly young professionals who may very well move back to the suburbs soon after starting families because, while public schools in many large cities have shown measurable improvement of late, they remain poor performers compared to suburban schools.

"Clearly, cities can maintain a certain amount of vitality with empty nesters and young professionals, but to sustain their health there has to be more infrastructure," says Lorlene Hoyt, a professor of urban studies and planning at MIT. "That's the big litmus test even

Downtown Revival Lagging in Some Cities

Only five downtown areas are fully developed in the United States, including Boston and Chicago, according to a Brookings Institution study. Another five are on the verge of taking off, and a baker's dozen are emerging. However, St. Louis and Detroit are among a dozen cities experiencing population declines.

Status of Downtowns in Major Cities

Fully Developed — *Large, densely settled, sustained positive household growth in past three decades; highly educated, relatively affluent populace has highest rates of homeownership.*

Boston, **Chicago**, **Lower Manhattan**, **Midtown Manhattan**, **Philadelphia**

Emerging — *Located primarily in the South and West, smaller and far less dense than fully developed downtowns; only experienced growth in the 1990s and are much less affluent; show promise of becoming fully developed if high household growth rates continue.*

Atlanta, **Baltimore**, **Charlotte**, **Cleveland**, **Denver**, **Los Angeles**, **Memphis**, **New Orleans**, **Norfolk**, **Portland, Ore.**, **San Diego**, **San Francisco**, **Seattle**

About to Take Off — *Larger than emerging downtowns but slightly less dense; experienced greater losses in households between 1970-1990 than emerging downtowns but made a comeback in the '90s with higher rates of homeownership and educational attainment; relatively more affluent than emerging downtowns.*

Chattanooga, **Dallas**, **Miami**, **Milwaukee**, **Washington, D.C.**

Slow-Growing — *Majority are in the South and West; the smallest and least dense of all the downtown categories. Experienced growth in the 1990s after significant losses in the previous two decades; generally lower average education attainment rates and less affluence than cities above.*

Albuquerque, **Austin**, **Boise**, **Colorado Springs**, **Columbus, Ohio**, **Indianapolis**, **Lafayette**, **Phoenix**, **Pittsburgh**, **Salt Lake City**

Declining — *Primarily in the Midwest and South, these downtowns are smaller and have less density; all lost households in each of the last three decades and by 2000 had just 65 percent of the households they had in 1970; small percentage of downtown residents have bachelor's degrees.*

Cincinnati, **Columbus, Ga.**, **Des Moines**, **Detroit**, **Jackson, Miss.**, **Lexington, Ky.**, **Mesa, Ariz.**, **Minneapolis**, **Orlando**, **San Antonio**, **Shreveport**, **St. Louis**

Source: The Brookings Institution, "Living Cities Census Series," September 2005

City Shoppers Find Plenty of Merlot, But No Diapers

The Park Slope section of Brooklyn is now stroller infested, a prime place for parents wanting to raise their children in a leafy, upscale neighborhood. It is still adjusting, however, to its new demographics, with well-publicized disputes between parents and the childless as more and more places become child-friendly — even taverns. [1]

But the neighborhood hasn't fully given itself over to the prerogatives of parents. For one thing, there aren't enough disposable diapers. Eager shoppers are known to form long lines at the few places that carry the products whenever a delivery is expected.

Even in cities that have thriving downtown office and entertainment districts filled with crowded restaurants and condo and loft dwellers, retail has been slow to follow. Downtowns and their big department stores dominated retail during the first half of the 20th century, but only a paltry amount of goods are sold downtown today. "Even the office worker" — once the most loyal group of downtown shoppers — "has to be competed for against the suburban mall," says Alison Isenberg, author of *Downtown America*.

Shopping in urban areas is a lot different than in the suburbs, where well-stocked big-box and warehouse stores come equipped with lifetime supplies of groceries, household goods and other sundry items that are either hard to find in the inner city or are sold after a high markup in small convenience stores.

But that may be changing, at least in some places. Wal-Mart, the world's largest retailer, announced in April that it would open 50 stores in blighted urban areas over the next couple of years. [2] Its rival, Target, has already opened stores in several urban malls, including a two-story location in its hometown of Minneapolis. Even supermarkets, which have been fleeing urban settings since the 1970s, are returning. [3]

People may not want to drive very far to buy the goods and services that they need on a daily basis, such as groceries and dry cleaning. But, as with live entertainment or sports, suburbanites have become willing to come downtown for "destination shopping" — unique boutiques that have items that can't be found anywhere else, or stores that make shopping into an event.

"You don't go to Williams-Sonoma just to buy a frying pan," says David Feehan, president of the International Downtown Association. "It's all about the experience. They can teach you how to prepare French meals."

But author Joel Kotkin, a skeptic about the extent of downtown revivals, is dubious that downtown retail is going to make a dent in suburban sales. "It's very difficult in American cities now to find a unique anything," he says. "Why go to a Gap in Harvard Square when there's a Gap in every shopping mall?"

Although downtowns have found it tough to attract retail outlets, that is only natural, says Christopher B. Leinberger, a visiting fellow at the Brookings Institution. Retailers are followers of real estate, he says, reluctant to enter downtown markets until there is enough population in place to support them.

"The housing must be in place before a grocery can build a store," he says. "As a downtown redevelops, there are not enough households initially to justify the conventional grocery store."

Limitations on land present special challenges for big stores, especially for parking. But there are enough people moving into some downtowns to more than justify the headaches. In Manhattan, for example, more than 40 cash registers at the 59,000-square-foot Whole Foods store at Columbus Circle, on the Upper West Side, barely keep up with the crowds at lunch time and during the evening rush hour. [4]

"Grocery stores in particular are finding urban locations exceedingly profitable due to less shelf space devoted to low-profit paper goods, like diapers, and more space for more profitable take-out food for busy professional households," Leinberger concluded in a Brookings research brief. [5]

---

[1] Chris Erikson, "Lowering the Bar," *The New York Post*, Dec. 20, 2005, p. 42.

[2] Abigail Goldman, "Wal-Mart Plans Stores in Ailing Urban Areas," *Los Angeles Times*, April 5, 2006, p. C3.

[3] Alan Ehrenhalt, "The Grocery Gap," *Governing*, April 2006, p. 9.

[4] Teri Karush Rogers, "Turning Supermarkets Into Restaurants, Too," *The New York Times*, Aug. 28, 2005, p. 3:24.

[5] Christopher B. Leinberger, "Turning Around Downtown: Twelve Steps to Revitalization," Brookings Institution, March 2005, p. 19.

---

for people who are big city lovers — the quality of the public schools, outdoor space, the ability to pick up the things you need without having to take a large chunk out of your day."

Indeed, says Meg Boyco, a loft dweller in downtown St. Louis, having to drive miles to buy groceries or rent videos gets old fast. "It seems nice, but are people going to grow old here?" she asked. "Is it going to be people moving in and out for three years at a time, while they get established and then bump into the suburbs?" [2]

However, downtown boosters note that even in their heyday, downtowns weren't home to very many people. And they don't think downtowns will ever return as singularly important economic centers. But that doesn't mean urban centers can't become healthier.

"Some people are saying that downtown revitalization is a myth because the numbers aren't growing like in the suburbs," says Feehan, of the International Downtown Association. "Of course not — it's a built area."

And even if they only appeal to a limited subset of people — young professionals and empty nesters — that's still a sizable, growing market as baby boomers retire and the 25-to-35-year-old cohort expands. After all, points out Christopher B. Leinberger, a visiting fellow at the Brookings Institution's Metropolitan Policy Program, three-quarters of U.S. households do not have school-age children.

"Clearly, downtowns play a central role in the identity of a region," says Lee Munnich, director of the state and local policy program at the University of Minnesota's Hubert H. Humphrey Institute of Public Affairs. "They're still major employment centers, and they're increasingly a place where people are choosing to live and spend their leisure time."

Cities long sought magic bullets — such as sports arenas or free parking — to solve their downtown woes. "The history of downtowns contains a lot of false optimism," says Otis White, an Atlanta-based consultant to cities. "There was always a search for an easy solution to fixing downtowns, but they were in the grip of bigger forces than beautification can deal with."

Since then, says Rutgers historian Isenberg, cities have realized that no one thing — whether retail, residential or entertainment — is going to restore downtowns. Rather, the mix of attractions will need regular updating and maintenance, just as shopping centers and industrial parks do, and downtowns will have to be adaptable. And unlike the urban-renewal movement of the 1950s and '60s — when entire neighborhoods were destroyed, hundreds of acres at a time, to make way for new developments — planners today "envision more incremental progress," she argues.

"There is no, one, stable set of ideas, no one stable set of needs that can be met downtown," Isenberg says. "What we see as aesthetically pleasing today, or what we want to see downtown, will be different in 30 years."

Does gentrification hurt longtime residents?

Much of the recent downtown revitalization has been fostered by tax breaks. Cities often agree to forego a percentage of property taxes to get more attractive properties built. In Houston's rapidly gentrifying Third Ward,

Pittsburgh Cultural Trust (both)

Transformation in Pittsburgh

In the 1980s, the Harris Theater was one of many X-rated attractions in downtown Pittsburgh. Today the dramatically revitalized central city features a dozen theaters and performance spaces and numerous art galleries.

Top Cities Are Fun, Hip and Affordable

The cities that Americans most want to live in feature good values in home prices, reasonable costs of living, high quality of life, access to quality health care and a strong economy, according to a survey by Kiplinger's Personal Finance. *Here are the top 10 cities on the magazine's list of the 50 most desirable cities:*

1. Nashville, Tenn. — *Affordable homes, mild climate, lively entertainment scene.*

2. Minneapolis-St. Paul, Minn. — *Hip and progressive atmosphere with a Midwestern sensibility, multiple cultural outlets, professional teams in all four major sports, a dozen universities and colleges and a diverse economy.*

3. Albuquerque, N.M. — *Resort-town ambience, boomtown economy but reasonable prices.*

4. Atlanta, Ga. — *Vibrant city with a rich history, good health care, hip cultural scene and genteel neighborhoods shaded by magnificent dogwood and magnolia trees.*

5. Austin, Texas — *State capital features a medley of culture, history and politics, including the University of Texas, the Zachary Scott Theater and the Umlauf Sculpture Garden and Museum.*

6. Kansas City — *Straddling the Kansas and Missouri state line, offers stately houses, downtown suburbs, world-class museums and barbecue.*

7. Asheville, N.C. — *A virtually franchise-free downtown with fine cuisine, unique crafts, live-music venues, fine arts and beautiful mountain views.*

8. Ithaca, N.Y. — *In the scenic Finger Lakes region, liberal home of Cornell University; farms provide rich assortment of organic products.*

9. Pittsburgh, Pa. — *Undergoing an ongoing renaissance; distinctive neighborhoods, tree-lined streets, glittering skyscrapers, upscale shops and a diversified economy.*

10. Iowa City, Iowa — *Oasis on the prairie bursting with creative and intellectual energy, including an annual jazz festival, a Shakespeare festival and the home of the University of Iowa.*

Source: "50 Smart Places to Live," Kiplinger's Personal Finance, *June 2006*

however, Texas state Rep. Garnet Coleman is using the same tax-financing arrangements to put limits on growth.

A board he partially controls has been buying up land in order to keep it away from developers who want to tear down low-cost housing and replace it with high-priced condominiums. He's also trying to impose restrictive deeds and covenants on existing properties to ensure that they are used only for rental housing in perpetuity.

"We can give tax abatements out the wazoo for lofts and condominiums," Coleman told *Governing* magazine. "The question is . . . whether we are willing to spend the same money on people who need a nice, affordable, clean place to live." [3]

While Coleman's tactics are unusual, his motivation is not. As middle- and upper-income people move into downtowns, there has been widespread concern that lower-income residents will be priced out of their longtime neighborhoods.

In May the Los Angeles City Council approved a one-year moratorium on conversions of 14,000 single-room occupancy (SRO) hotel rooms, which generally serve the poor, into high-end condos. It is also considering a broader slowdown on residential redevelopment.

"Landlords were evicting tenants so they could flip those properties," says Eva Kandarpa, an aide to Councilwoman Jan Perry, who sponsored the ordinance. "We wanted to stop that until we could come up with a comprehensive plan for more affordable housing."

Columbia University urban-planning professor Lance Freeman lauds the goal of trying to get more affordable housing built but says trying to halt gentrification won't achieve that aim. In a 2005 study, Freeman concluded that residents of gentrifying neighborhoods were no more likely to move than residents of non-gentrifying neighborhoods. Older neighborhoods tend to have a high turnover in any event, he found, but improvements in gentrifying areas — such as increased jobs and falling crime rates — were likely to be a boon to long-term residents, who then are more inclined to stay. [4]

Freeman concedes, however, that lower-income residents may feel the wealthier newcomers change the fabric of the community, and renters may be forced out if the affordable housing stock is limited. Even so, cities that do not gentrify will be no better off, he says.

"It's hard to argue that cities are better off if housing is affordable because no one wants to live there," he says.

Similarly, Duke University economist Jacob Vigdor, who has studied gentrification in Boston, says gentrification is a symptom, not the cause of housing-affordability problems. In other words, residents are often displaced because land values throughout a regional market are going up — not just in their neighborhood — which encourages new development that in turn attracts new people.

No one is going to go to the expense of renovating an old warehouse, Vigdor says, until property values have already climbed enough to justify the investment. "People assume that the arrival of yuppies [young urban professionals] causes price escalation," he says. "But when the prices start to go up, that's what gets developers' juices flowing."

In addition, since unused, old warehouses — along with schools, jails, office buildings and even grain elevators — often are converted into urban housing, that means no one is being displaced, say some downtown boosters. If no one was living there previously, how can they be forced out?

"A lot of downtowns historically have not had much in the way of housing," Freeman says. "If you add housing to the downtown, and no one was living there previously or it was predominantly manufacturing, then you wouldn't expect much displacement."

But such analyses don't sit well with longtime residents of New York's Harlem or San Francisco's Mission District, who feel their neighborhoods are being overrun by latte-sippers who are driving up property costs and forcing them out. To prevent that, many cities require developers of high-end projects to create a certain number of affordable-housing units.

"Lower-class housing and work-force housing are diminishing," says Donald J. Borut, executive director of the National League of Cities. "Where cops and teachers can afford to live — it's not a small issue."

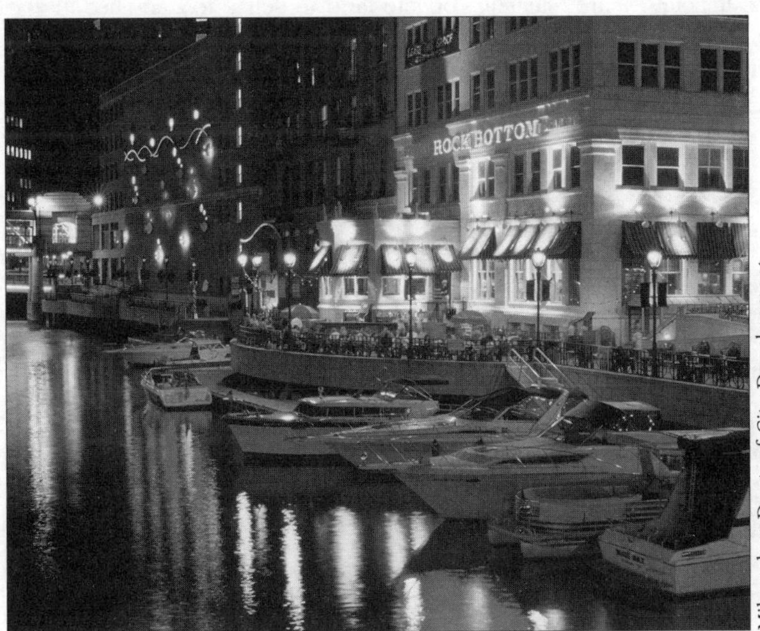

Milwaukee Dept. of City Development

Milwaukee's popular River Walk blossomed from the city's once-undeveloped waterfront in the late 1990s. It now features condominiums, restaurants and entertainment.

"Atlanta is gentrifying at a very substantial rate," says Larry Keating, a professor of city and regional planning at Georgia Institute of Technology, who recently chaired a gentrification task force for the City Council. "The displacement [of low-income renters] is substantial."

While urban improvements enhance a city's overall tax base, he says, they reduce the amount of affordable housing, forcing poor residents to the city's fringes or the suburbs, tearing apart their social networks.

"Absolutely, people are being displaced," says Brookings' Leinberger. He recommends policies to help transfer some of cities' growing wealth into programs to subsidize affordable housing.

He mordantly recalls a multi-panel cartoon that illustrates some of the negative social dynamics associated with gentrification. The first panel shows a white couple moving out to the suburbs during the 1950s and extolling their good fortune. The second shows an African-American couple moving to the suburbs during the 1990s and feeling equally lucky to be leaving the city. The last panel shows the white couple returning happily to the city, saying, "It worked."

Should greater restrictions be placed on government use of eminent domain to acquire land?

Some recent downtown development, especially major projects covering many acres, has been fostered by cities using their power of eminent domain — the process of condemning private land for public use.

The Constitution forbids governments from "seizing" private property without compensating its owners, but cities have long used eminent domain — or condemnation — to force owners to sell when it is determined that the land is needed for the public's benefit. Although governments usually buy property through normal real estate transactions, they sometimes use eminent domain to take control of large parcels of land rather than having to deal with scattered holdouts reluctant to sell.

In the past, local governments used eminent domain to acquire land for public infrastructure, such as roads, bridges, railroads or schools. But during the urban-renewal movement that flourished from the 1940s to the 1960s, they began using eminent domain for economic purposes, taking over blighted sections of towns — often occupied primarily by African-Americans or poor residents — that were ripe for redevelopment.

Recently, cash-strapped cities have begun using their powers of eminent domain again to promote economic development by condemning commercially viable properties or middle-income homes to make way for pricier hotels, retail shops or condominiums. The higher-end use of the land will bring in greater tax revenues, the cities argue, thus benefiting the common good. For example, Greenville employed eminent domain to acquire rundown riverfront warehouses for a large hotel, office, condo and artists' studio complex.

CBS' "60 Minutes" highlighted a city that went so far as to redefine "blighted" to include park-side homes with only a single-car garage so middle-class homes could be condemned to make way for upscale condos with a park view. In Minnesota, a car dealership was forced to sell out five years ago to make way for Best Buy's $160 million corporate headquarters in suburban Richfield.

"We cannot understand how giving our property to a multibillion-dollar company like Best Buy serves a 'public purpose' as the law mandates," said Barbara Jerich, general counsel for Walser Automotive Group. [5]

Cities and developers, however, point out that a big electronics headquarters, for example, generates more income and jobs than a car dealer and a few dozen homes, benefiting the entire community. Losing such a moneymaker due to the intransigence of a single property owner would have been a big blow to the area, said the project's supporters.

Nevertheless, the practice has stirred up stiff resistance among affected landowners, who claim cities are "stealing" private land to sell it to rich developers at reduced rates. When a city condemns land, it normally only pays the appraised value for the land — usually lower than the price developers would have to pay on the open market. If a redevelopment project is such a wise investment, argue affected landowners, developers should just buy the land on the open market.

Getty Images/Mark Wilson

A critic of the Supreme Court's controversial Kelo v. New London *decision makes his position clear at a Senate Judiciary Committee hearing last year. The court ruled that New London, Conn., could force homeowners to sell their land to make way for a $350 million pharmaceutical factory.*

The simmering controversy burst into the open in 2005, when the U.S. Supreme Court ruled in *Kelo v. New London* that New London, Conn., could legally force landowners in the "distressed municipality" to sell their land to make way for a $350 million pharmaceutical factory. Fifteen homeowners didn't want to sell, but in a 5 to 4 decision the Supreme Court ruled that the increased potential economic activity generated by the plant justified the city's taking of the land. Swelling the tax base amounted to a "public purpose," the court ruled. [6]

"Promoting economic development is a traditional and long accepted function of government," Justice John Paul Stevens wrote. "Clearly, there is no basis for exempting economic development from our traditionally broad understanding of public purpose." [7]

But in her dissenting opinion Justice Sandra Day O'Connor wrote: "Under the banner of economic development, all private property is now vulnerable to being taken and transferred to another private owner, so long as it might be upgraded. The specter of condemnation hangs over all property. Nothing is to prevent the state from replacing any Motel 6 with a Ritz-Carlton, any home with a shopping mall or any farm with a factory."

If eminent domain was not a sexy topic before, *Kelo* turned it into one, stirring up a hornet's nest of opposition in cities across the country. "I was down about the decision for about 20 minutes," recalls Scott Bullock, a senior attorney with the libertarian Institute for

Continued on p. 564

Chronology

1940s-1960s

Downtowns lose business and cities lose population to suburbs.

1948
Downtown's share of retail trade — nearly one-third before the Great Depression — falls to 11 percent.

1949
Housing Act provides federal funds to help cities acquire and clear slum and blighted property for private redevelopment.

1961
Jane Jacobs publishes *The Death and Life of Great American Cities*, arguing that small, dense mixed-use neighborhoods are more vital and safer than huge developments.

1965
Congress creates Department of Housing and Urban Development (HUD), the first Cabinet-level agency devoted to urban problems.

1968
Assassination of civil rights leader the Rev. Martin Luther King Jr. sparks rioting in 125 cities, killing 39 and damaging 2,600 buildings.

1970s-1980s

Federal government scales back its commitment to urban programs; cities begin attracting specialty shops and new customers.

1973
President Richard M. Nixon freezes most HUD programs to control costs and address allegations of mishandled funds.

1974
Congress approves Community Development block grants for city infrastructure improvements.

1975
President Gerald R. Ford refuses federal aid to financially ailing New York City, prompting *Daily News* headline, "Ford to City: Drop Dead."

1976
Developer James Rouse opens Faneuil Hall Marketplace in historic Boston building, beginning string of urban "festival" markets.

1977
Community Development Reinvestment Act requires lenders to invest in their areas of service.

1984
Newsweek declares "The Year of the Yuppie" in response to the growing number of affluent white-collar workers in some cities.

1987
President Ronald Reagan abolishes revenue sharing, which distributed federal funds to states and cities.

1990s-2000s

The nation's improving economy helps revive cities that provide professional or technological services; cities succeed in developing a mix of attractions that lure some downtown inhabitants.

1991
Driven partly by the crack cocaine epidemic of the late 1980s, the U.S. homicide rate peaks at 9.8 per 100,000 population, largely affecting urban areas.

1992
U.S. Conference of Mayors leads thousands in March on Washington, proposes "Marshall Plan for the Cities" to be paid for with $35 billion in new federal funds. . . . Baltimore opens Camden Yards stadium, a much-imitated home for baseball's Orioles that is integrated with its downtown, its bustling harbor and the city's mass-transit system.

1993
Congress rejects President Bill Clinton's $16 billion economic-stimulus package for cities.

1995
Clinton creates urban-empowerment and enterprise zones in cities receiving federal funds and tax incentives for development and social services.

2000
Eight of the 15 cities that had been among the nation's 15 largest in 1950 have lost population for the fifth census in a row.

2004
Chicago opens its downtown Millennium Park, a $475 million, 24-acre sculpture garden.

2005
President George W. Bush's budget would slash Community Development Block Grants. . . . U.S. Supreme Court upholds cities' ability to take control of private property through eminent domain in *Kelo v. New London* case. . . . Hurricane Katrina devastates New Orleans.

2006
During the first five months of the year, 23 state legislatures pass bills to restrict cities' use of eminent domain. . . . Federal housing officials announce that more than 5,000 public housing units in New Orleans will be razed in favor of mixed-income developments.

'Walkable Urbanity' Livens Up the 'Burbs

The population of Sugar Hill, Ga., about 40 miles north of Atlanta, has tripled over the last decade, leading local officials to try to think of new ways to improve things. When they polled townspeople about the changes they would most like to see, the answer was overwhelming: They wanted a lively, pedestrian-friendly downtown.

Sugar Hill is now building itself a downtown — from scratch — along a road that will be lined with 15-foot-wide sidewalks. Developers are eager to start filling in the area with stores and restaurants.

"They wanted that hometown, downtown walking area, and that's what the mayor and council have said they'll have," says City Manager Bob Hail. "We are not renovating. We are doing the 'build it and they will come.' "

Sugar Hill is not the first place in the area to try to create instant urbanism. Many communities within the sprawling 17-county metro Atlanta region have decided they need town centers, both to provide a distinct identity for their communities and to afford residents the pleasures of a walkable downtown shopping and entertainment district without having to drive into the big city.

"Deprived by the difficulty of driving to social and cultural activities, people are bringing those activities to the suburbs," says Michael M. Sizemore, whose firm designed a downtown for Smyrna, 35 miles west of Sugar Hill. "When they do, it starts to provide the anchor or catalyst for revitalizing their downtowns."

The suburbs are associated with strip malls and other signs of sprawl, but some observers predict they will increasingly become convenient, urban-style gathering places. "There is so much pent-up demand for walkable urbanity that it cannot all be satisfied in the traditional downtown," says Christopher B. Leinberger, an urban strategist and developer.

Even more common than the creation of new downtowns is the phenomenon of older suburbs attempting to revitalize central business and shopping districts — often located near mass-transit lines — that had long been neglected. In Decatur, which sits along Atlanta's eastern border, the shopping district is undergoing extensive renovation, and the first new downtown residential units are being built since the Great Depression, all within easy walking distance of a stop on Atlanta's citywide rail system.

"The 1950s and 60s suburban ideal was you don't want to live anywhere near a storefront, you want to get as far away as possible from commercial development," said Brian J. Nickerson, director of the Michaelian Institute for Public Policy and Management at Pace University in New York City. "Now, you want to live above the storefront." [1]

In many suburbs, old-fashioned shopping malls are giving way to "town centers" or "lifestyle centers" — shopping complexes that mimic some of the qualities of the walkable downtowns. In some cases, this amounts to a direct swap. In Centennial, Colo., the 1974-vintage Southglenn Mall will be replaced with a development called The Streets at Southglenn that will feature — in addition to about 100 stores — sidewalk cafes, shaded walkways and little nooks for relaxing.

More than 60 lifestyle centers will open around the country this year and next, compared with just one traditional covered mall, according to the International Council of Shopping Centers. [2] "In both suburban downtowns and new town developments, you've got civic leaders and developers trying to replicate the success of urban downtowns," says Brad Segal, president of Progressive Urban Management Associates, a development-consulting firm in Denver.

Segal questions the staying power of the new shopping developments, warning they offer too many of the same chain stores and have a homogeneous, cookie-cutter feel as a result. Urban "downtowns have a competitive advantage in terms of organic qualities that have evolved over time — they have 100 or 200 years of history, and you can see it," he says. "These new lifestyle centers are really a product of 2006."

For now, though, it is clear that many suburbs covet sophisticated little shopping areas of their own. Perhaps the new downtown designers in Sugar Hill will be able to pull a page from Smyrna's successful urban playbook. Retail sales and property values there have increased so much that the city has been able to lower its property tax rates every year since construction of the downtown began in the late 1980s.

"For about a half-mile all around it, there are all kinds of development," Sizemore says. "If you create a place that's great for everybody, starting with the kids, everybody wants to be there, and they're willing to pay for it."

[1] Debra West, "Adding More Urban to Suburbia," *The New York Times*, May 14, 2006, Section 14WC, p. 1.

[2] Thaddeus Herrick, "Fake Towns Rise, Offering Urban Life Without the Grit," *The Wall Street Journal*, May 31, 2006, p. A1.

Continued from p. 562

Justice in Arlington, Va., who argued New London landowner Susette Kelo's case before the court. Then he saw O'-Connor's passionate dissent and realized she had handed him a gift. "I read the dissenting opinions and realized that there's a real opportunity here to take what was a terrible decision and turn it into something that was very positive for property owners."

Indeed, both conservatives and liberals opposed the decision. Conservatives disliked the apparent expansion of governmental power over private property. Liberals — recalling the massive displacement of poor communities during the urban-renewal movement — feared the practice could be used to once again force low-income citizens from their homes to make way for the wealthy.

Before the decision, nine state supreme courts had already forbidden the use of eminent domain to build revenues or employment. [8] In fact, Justice Stevens explicitly pointed out that states have the power to curb the use of eminent domain — and many have quickly done so. In the past year, two-dozen states have passed new restrictions on the use of eminent domain, and bills to restrict the practice have been introduced in Congress and nearly every state legislature. Initiatives are on the ballot in four states, and petitions are circulating in California and eight other states to put it before voters in November, according to the American Planning Association.

"What I don't like is where somebody has a higher and better use in their minds, and they give the land to a private developer," says Indiana state Rep. David Wolkins, who sponsored a bill that would discourage the practice by narrowing the state's definition of blight and forcing redevelopment agencies to pay ousted owners 150 percent of the appraised value of a property.

Similar arguments were made in Iowa, where the legislature this year voted to restrict the use of eminent domain to areas that are 75 percent blighted. But developers and local officials say that's a bad idea, because areas targeted for redevelopment will have to decline further before a city can step in to improve them. They cite the example of downtown Des Moines, which was legally declared a slum 30 years ago — dominated by dilapidated buildings, abandoned stores and seedy hotels. The city has since helped foster an impressive renaissance, using eminent domain to make way for several office and retail complexes and other projects that have increased the taxable value of the area by more than $1 billion.

"We would not have the development activity we have within the downtown core right now if we didn't have eminent domain," says Councilwoman Christine Hensley, who represents the area. The legislature went overboard in reaction to anti-*Kelo* emotions, she says. Sounding emotional herself, she adds, "It pisses me off." Perhaps responding to such reasoning — if not the emotion — Gov. Tom Vilsack vetoed the eminent-domain bill.

Indianapolis Mayor Bart Peterson says eminent domain should be left intact because it is self-regulating — taking private property is usually so controversial public officials don't do it unless it's absolutely necessary. "Elected officials rightly know they cannot go around taking property at will," he says.

If they didn't know it before, they've certainly gotten the message since *Kelo*. Ironically, the decision didn't expand local governments' powers; it merely affirmed them. But in so doing, the court set the stage for a political backlash that has left many cities with more limited tools for promoting economic development.

In that regard, says the National League of Cities' Borut, "It was like winning the Super Bowl and then not having a team." ■

San Diego Convention and Visitors Bureau

San Diego's PETCO Park, a new open-air stadium built in the East Village area near the historic Gaslamp Quarter, is part of a comprehensive plan to revitalize the city's aging downtown.

BACKGROUND

Industrial Age

America's cities grew rapidly as the country industrialized in the late 19th century, and millions left their

Milwaukee Dept. of City Development

Phoenix Convention Center

Harlem Community Dev. Corp./Francisco Guzman

Blossoming Cities

(Top): Architect Santiago Calatrava designed a recent addition to the Milwaukee Art Museum, right. New condos are rising nearby. (Middle): Several big projects in Phoenix, including expansion of the Convention Center, are pumping new life into the city. (Bottom): New York's Harlem has undergone a dramatic revival that has seen the arrival of new businesses and residents and restoration of the world-famous Apollo Theater.

farms or their home countries and poured into American downtowns. Between 1790 and 1890, the total U.S. population grew 16-fold — but the nation's urban population grew to 139 times its 1790 size. [9]

Downtowns were often referred to as the cities' heart, with streetcars bringing workers in each morning and carrying them home each night. Not every town had a skyscraper or an opera house, but they all had commercial Main Streets, points out author Isenberg in *Downtown America.* [10] Downtowns also served as a melting pot for the cities — the one area where people from all over came and felt welcome.

"The central business district was the one bit of turf common to all," writes historian Jon C. Teaford. "Along the downtown thoroughfares, wealthy financiers passed by grubby beggars, rubbed shoulders with horny-handed porters and draymen and jostled for space with clerks and stenographers." [11]

Downtowns were also home to railroad and ferry terminals, department stores and often the cities' sole business and financial districts. As late as 1890, downtowns were often the only part of town with electricity. [12] They were compact, crowded places for industry and shopping, often occupying less than a square mile but generating more trade than the rest of the city combined. And they generated a huge percentage of urban property-tax valuations — more than 20 percent in St. Louis, for example, and almost half in Cincinnati. [13]

Downtowns in the early 20th century also became great manufacturing centers, and it was convenient to have lawyers, accountants and other professional services nearby. Convenience also drew women shoppers downtown, where they could find everything they wanted in one of the mammoth department stores that dominated retail sales. Novelist William Kennedy recalls "booming, bustling" downtown

Albany, where "crowds were six abreast on the sidewalks at high noon and all day Saturday, when all the trolley cars were crowded, and you had to stand in line to get into the movies." [14]

By 1925, the 18 cities with populations of more than 400,000 had grown by an average of 71 percent since the dawn of the century. Los Angeles had ballooned by 609 percent; Detroit had more than tripled. [15] As cities grew more crowded, many families became willing to ride an hour to distant neighborhoods or out to the country to avoid living under or over another family. As a result, cities desperately needed rapid transit, especially as automobile traffic began to clog downtown streets.

Many cities talked of building subways to deliver every resident to within a half-mile of his job, but few invested the large sums required. By the late 1920s, New York and Boston boasted more than 90 percent of the nation's subway traffic. [16]

Moving on Out

Faced with congestion and high downtown land values, industry began to move out of the central cities by the late 1920s, first to peripheral neighborhoods and then to suburbs. In suburban Dearborn, Mich., Ford's River Rouge facility — the largest factory in the world when it opened in 1928 — was more than double the size of downtown Detroit. Secondary business districts also began to spring up, with some professional firms moving their administrative offices out and banks beginning to set up branch offices.

Retailers soon followed suit. Because a central-city location no longer guaranteed proximity to shoppers, a proliferation of chain stores moved into the suburbs. Joseph Appel, president of Wanamaker's department store, wrote in 1928 that it was time for the store to go to its customers rather than try "to force them to come to us." [17]

The Great Depression of the 1930s, which hit inner cities disproportionately hard, accelerated the trend outward. Hotels and other downtown properties fell widely into receivership, and more office buildings were being torn down during the decade than were going up. Desperate owners tore down tall buildings, replacing them with one- or two-story parking lots, in order to decrease their tax burdens and generate some income. Chicago's land value dropped by as much as 78.5 percent from 1930 to 1935, while New York City's assessed values by 1939 had dropped below 1889 levels. [18] *Business Week* declared in 1940: "Every American city of 6,000,000 or 6,000 population shows symptoms of identical dry rot at its core." [19]

City of Greenville

Newly revitalized Greenville, S.C., turned the Reedy River and its scenic falls into the city's most popular attraction. Main Street, which had only four restaurants 20 years ago, now boasts more than 75. There's also a performing-arts center and a new minor league ballpark just up the street.

By the end of World War II, central-business-district organizations had sprung up in most cities to lobby for tax and zoning policies that would promote downtowns as places worth visiting. They studied how to improve transportation and even the idea of banning downtown traffic, but the forces favoring the decentralization of commerce were ultimately much stronger.

After the war, even though the nation's economy boomed, downtowns stagnated. The newly built parking lots didn't generate jobs, and new freeways meant that more and more downtown land was devoted to traffic and parking and less to trade. Congestion remained a problem, prompting many big businesses to follow heavy industry to the suburbs. [20] Several insurance companies moved from New York to leafy Westchester County, just north of Manhattan, as did General Foods, Standard Oil and other large corporations. Cargill, the country's largest grain trader, left Minneapolis for Lake Minnetonka. [21] In 1948, 80 percent of the new manufacturing, retail and wholesale jobs were being created in the suburbs. [22]

That year, in fact, downtowns' share of the nation's retail trade, which had been nearly one-third in 1929, plummeted to just 11 percent. [23] (The first regional shopping center had been built in Los Angeles a year earlier.) Over the next six years, retail sales downtown climbed by just 1.6 percent while increasing 32.3 percent in suburbs. [24]

As the president of the TG&Y variety store chain declared, "We do not think the housewives (who are our main customers) will drive miles and miles to get downtown when they can obtain the same merchandise in better facilities in the suburbs." [25]

Urban 'Jungles'

During the early 1950s, 84 percent of the nation's population growth occurred in the 168 metropolitan areas, but less than 2 percent was in central cities.

"The upper and middle classes were moving to the periphery and the suburbs," writes MIT urban historian Robert M. Fogelson in his 2001 book *Downtown*. "But the lower class, many of whose members belonged to one or another of the nation's ethnic and racial minorities, were staying put — some because they did not want to move, others because they could not afford to." [26]

As downtown retailers lost their best customers, private interests sought to raze the slums in the inner city to make way for large-scale development. Local governments hoping for increased property assessments were eager to help them. A 1955 *Life* magazine article, headlined "An Encroaching Menace," captured the tone of their plea: "The slums of Chicago each year have pushed closer to the heart of the city. Some of the worst came only six blocks from the glittering skyscrapers. There a newly aroused and desperate city stopped them." [27]

States such as New York and New Jersey gave private companies the power of eminent domain, authorizing them to acquire land for redevelopment. Congress got involved, passing the Housing Act of 1949, which further spurred urban clearance and redevelopment. In theory, private initiatives were supposed to improve and rebuild low-income housing, but that rarely happened. By 1961, 126,000 residential units had been demolished but only 28,000 built to replace them. [28] A study that year found that in 60 cities that had undertaken urban-renewal projects, 60 percent of the dispossessed simply relocated to other substandard housing. [29]

During the 1960s, Presidents John F. Kennedy and Lyndon B. Johnson dramatically expanded the scope of federal urban policy. In 1965, Johnson created the Department of Housing and Urban Development (HUD), the first Cabinet-level position to address the problems of urban America. Its first major initiative — Model Cities — sought to include community wishes in comprehensive rebuilding plans.

But inner cities continued to become islands of ethnicity due to "white flight" to the suburbs. Between 1960 and 1970, the white population of the 20 largest Northeastern and Midwestern cities fell by more than 2.5 million, or 13 percent. The decline was even more precipitous in the 1970s, dropping by another 4 million, or 24.3 percent. [30] Meanwhile, the black share of central city populations shot up 725 percent from 1960 to 1968. [31]

The urban riots of the late 1960s and early '70s made matters worse. Anecdotal and newspaper accounts suggested that rioters in Los Angeles, Harlem, Washington and elsewhere targeted white merchants they felt had long cheated them economically. Whatever the rationale, riots certainly did not help urban America's fortunes.

As Rutgers University's Isenberg writes, "certainly people were less likely to make shopping excursions with riot threats hanging in the air." [32] Suburbanites began to think of downtown as a dangerous no-man's land. In 1969, a *Newsweek* cover report looked at "The Sick, Sick Cities."

With the central cities continuing to lose jobs, many local leaders despaired. St. Louis Mayor A. J. Cervantes declared in 1968: "We just can't make it anymore."

New Orleans Mayor Moon Landrieu echoed the sentiment: "The cities are going down the pipe."

HUD Secretary George Romney said in 1972, "The whole social web that makes living possible [in the cities] is breaking down into a veritable jungle." [33]

A year later, President Richard M. Nixon froze most HUD programs following allegations the funds were being mishandled. He folded Model Cities and other urban-renewal programs into Community Development Block Grants, which gave localities wide discretion over the types of programs that could be funded. Cities foundered financially, as exemplified by New York City's $726 million budget deficit in 1975. President Gerald R. Ford's refusal to aid the city led to the memorable New York *Daily News* headline, "Ford to City: Drop Dead," which Ford believed cost him the 1976 election.

Hitting Bottom

Ford's opponent, Jimmy Carter, created new grant programs to send money directly to neighborhoods, rather than passing it through lower levels of government. During his first year in office, Congress approved the Community Development Reinvestment Act, which required banks to invest funds in the communities they served.

Many of Carter's programs for cities, though, were dismantled by his successor, Ronald Reagan. In fact, Reagan was following a Carter administration advisory panel that recommended helping city residents move to the suburbs. The federal government's role should be "to assist communities to adjust to redistributional trends, rather than attempt to reverse them," the commission concluded." [34]

Reagan eliminated Carter's Office of Neighborhoods and cut programs for cities by nearly a quarter during his first two years in office. He ended federal revenue sharing, by which Washington

Continued on p. 570

At Issue:

Are downtowns undergoing a real renaissance?

DAVID FEEHAN
PRESIDENT, INTERNATIONAL DOWNTOWN ASSOCIATION

WRITTEN FOR *CQ RESEARCHER*, JUNE 2006

yes

The evidence is irrefutable: Downtowns in the United States have made a remarkable, perhaps historic, comeback. After decades of decline, disinvestment and near abandonment, American downtowns are experiencing what can only be called a renaissance.

This remarkable phenomenon is not without its critics and cynics. The most prominent of these, however, blithely ignore the overwhelming body of evidence and instead engage in sensationalistic arguments based on highly selective data and flawed reasoning. Often they compare downtown growth with suburban growth, which is a bit like comparing a minivan and a sports car — they both are gasoline-powered vehicles with four wheels, but with decidedly different purposes and ancestries.

Let's look at the facts: In the early 1990s, an economist studying downtown's economic importance found that it contributed more than $19 in tax revenues to various taxing bodies for every dollar in services it consumed. City managers, finance directors and other city officials have confirmed that these numbers are reasonably representative of most downtowns and central cities in the United States. Clearly, downtown is the economic engine that pulls the city's train. Strong downtowns make stronger core cities possible, which in turn helps to support regional economic health.

The downtown office market is showing strength and resiliency. Occupancy rates nationally since 1990 have favored downtowns over suburbs. The downtown housing market is strong and has grown explosively in many cities, including cities of every size and region — from New York, Philadelphia and Washington to Miami, Los Angeles and Seattle; and from Memphis to Des Moines to Fort Worth to Albuquerque. People want to live downtown and will pay a premium to do so.

Dining, entertainment, sports, meetings and conventions and tourist attractions have all expanded in downtowns. Crime is at historic lows. Downtown public spaces not only look better but also are managed better than ever through a plethora of public-private partnerships and business-improvement districts.

Downtowns are stronger than at any time in the past 50 years, and as downtowns continue to improve they provide the resources cities need to improve neighborhoods, schools and services. The downtown renaissance is little more than a decade old, and it may take another decade or two for urban neighborhoods to catch up. But now, with revitalized downtowns, they may have the resources and opportunity to do so. Few would argue that this is a very important goal.

JOEL KOTKIN
IRVINE SENIOR FELLOW, NEW AMERICA FOUNDATION

WRITTEN FOR *CQ RESEARCHER*, JUNE 2006

no

Even amidst a strong economic expansion, the most recent census data reveal a renewed migration out of our urban centers. This gives considerable lie to the notion, popularized over a decade — particularly among the media — that cities are enjoying a historic rebound.

In 1999 *The Economist* suggested "Americans [are] abandoning their love affair with far-flung suburbs and shopping malls." The recovery in some downtowns, suggested Jonathan Fanton, president of the MacArthur Foundation, heralded a new "urban renaissance."

But this may be more wishful thinking than reality. Since 1950 more than 90 percent of all growth in U.S. metropolitan areas has been in the suburbs. Nor is this trend showing any sign of turning around. Census data show that since 2000 even healthy urban centers like New York, Boston, Portland, Ore., and San Francisco have experienced slowing or declining population growth. Meanwhile, suburbs in those regions and elsewhere have been capturing an ever-expanding percentage of both people and jobs.

The simple fact is that most Americans — including 86 percent of all Californians, according to a recent survey — express a great preference for single-family homes, which for most means choosing suburbia. Unless there is some radical and unexpected change, most new population growth and expansion of the built environment (which is estimated to grow 50 percent by 2030) will occur in the suburbs, particularly in the South and West — places dominated by low-density, automobile-dependent growth.

The tapering housing bubble has created a false notion of an urban renaissance driven by, among other things, empty nesters returning to the city. In many urban cores, from New York to San Diego, large numbers of condo units — in some cases upwards of a third — have been bought not by new urbanites but by speculators. So we have the odd phenomenon of more housing units, at higher costs, but fewer full-time residents.

Instead of luring the "hip and cool" with high-end amenities, cities should address issues that concern businesses as well as middle-class families. These include such basic needs as public safety, maintenance of parks, improving public schools and cutting taxes — in other words, all those unsexy things that contribute to maintaining a job base and upward mobility.

Cities can't thrive merely as amusement parks for the rich, the nomadic young and tourists. To remain both vital and economically relevant, they must remain anchored by a large middle class, and by families and businesses that feel safe and committed to the urban place.

Continued from p. 568

sent funds to other levels of government to spend as they saw fit.

Without the federal government to help them out, city and business leaders decided they were responsible for improving the lot of the cities. Many businesses were willing to pay additional assessments in order to clean up downtowns and make them safer. The first business-improvement district (BID) was created in New Orleans in 1975, and BIDs became widespread in the 1980s.

Cities also welcomed their first good retail news in decades with the creation of "festival marketplaces" — shopping areas built in historic districts or among the ruins of old industrial sites, including Ghirardelli Square in San Francisco, the Inner Harbor in Baltimore and Faneuil Hall in Boston. Although often criticized as Potemkin villages — pockets of prosperity that did little for the wider city surrounding them — they were successful and widely imitated. They appealed to the nostalgia many people felt for the downtowns of yore — before crime, congestion and despair overran the cities. The American city, as Isenberg points out, had become a commodity to be marketed rather than a place in decline to be ignored.

At the same time, the National Trust for Historic Preservation's Main Street program began encouraging downtown business owners in small communities to properly restore their storefronts as a way to use the charm of a community's historic ambience to revive struggling local economies. Scores of communities across the country have benefited from the downtown face-lifts under Trust guidance, helping them battle the often overpowering competition from regional malls and discounters. [35]

Some cities, such as New York, Denver and Houston, even enjoyed job growth during the 1980s with the rise of the service sector, but older industrial cities such as Detroit, Philadelphia and Baltimore were left behind. Jobs continued their exodus to the suburbs. During a three-year period, Atlanta's suburbs gained twice as many jobs as the city; the suburbs of St. Louis, Chicago and San Francisco gained five times as many jobs as those cities, and Detroit's suburbs outstripped the city by nearly 700 percent. [36]

The cities, meanwhile, continued to struggle, having fallen into a downward spiral. Whites who fled the cities during the 1960s grew increasingly reluctant to come to downtowns that had become scenes of poverty, crime and drug abuse — particularly given the crack epidemic of the 1980s.

Likewise, homelessness became a headline issue, as the share of the nation's poor who lived in central cities had increased by a third since 1960. [37] In 1992, *Business Week* declared, "The breeding ground for economic misery is the American city." [38]

The sense of urban uncertainty continued into the booming 1990s despite falling crime rates, a growing economy and a set of exceptionally gifted mayors, including Rudolph Giuliani of New York, Ed Rendell of Philadelphia and Richard M. Daley of Chicago.

Even Rendell, after a highly praised tenure during which he pulled Philadelphia back from the brink of bankruptcy, said as he left office in 1998, "Forget all the good things I've done. Philadelphia is dying." [39] ■

CURRENT SITUATION

Success Stories

Rendell's pessimism aside, his city has thrived in recent years. Or, at least its center city has. The downtown is now home to a thriving arts district anchored by the massive Kimmel Center. Condos around Rittenhouse Square are in great demand, and a city that once had no outdoor cafes now has 167. The prosperity that surrounds the downtown area is starting, slowly, to spread to blighted areas around it.

Levy, of the Philadelphia Center City District, argues that rather than being caught in a vicious downward cycle, as they were for decades, cities are starting to recover.

Levy and some other urban observers say that cities, ironically, have the federal government to thank, because when the government turned its back on the cities, local officials realized they could only depend on themselves. "The withdrawal of federal agencies has done more for the cities than all previous federal activities combined," says MIT's Hoyt. "Now you have business-improvement districts, universities and hospitals partnering with cities and raising resources in creative ways."

The federal government today is only minimally interested in helping cities. For the past two years the Bush administration has tried to slash funding for Community Development Block Grants — the last major source of federal grants for local governments — and to merge it with other economic-development programs within the Commerce Department. Although the program still exists, city and county lobbyists aren't optimistic that it will remain robust. The administration also wants to eliminate the Section 8 rental-assistance program and Hope VI grants to cities to rebuild housing.

"The federal doctor doesn't make house calls anymore," says Levy. Cities have relatively few champions in GOP-dominated Washington. Urbanites historically do not vote for Republicans.

"It's hard to think of urban constituencies to whom the Republicans owe anything," says Michael S. Greve, director of the American Enterprise Institute's Federalism Project.

So cities are pulling up their bootstraps and doing for themselves. Using BIDs, downtown employers collect taxes to pay for the services they once sought from government. "They allowed people to tax themselves extra to get signage, plantings, additional police services," says urban consultant White. "The rise in property values has more than covered whatever people have paid in taxes."

In the 1990s, cities tried various schemes to draw people back downtown, spending billions on new sports stadiums and convention centers. With his 1997 book, *The Rise of the Creative Class*, Richard Florida convinced many civic leaders that the path to prosperity lies not in granting tax breaks to businesses but in presenting the right blend of social and cultural amenities to attract well-educated workers.

However, none of the ideas proved to be a magic bullet. [40] Sports stadium promoters' promises of thousands of new jobs and millions in additional city revenues rarely panned out, but the improvement ideas did begin to rouse central cities from their long slumber and pessimism. [41]

Cities entered into partnerships with the private sector to construct multimillion-dollar projects. Government used its eminent-domain power to amass land, secured tax-exempt financing and provided fast-track approvals. Private partners determined what the market wanted, and together they built convention centers, performing-arts facilities, hotels and other ambitious projects that began to attract people back downtown, albeit in fits and starts.

Cities eventually learned how to attract people with money. Consider the sprawling desert city of Phoenix. Having grown from 100,000 people in 1950 to more than 1 million today, it is a classic Sun Belt town, better known for ranch-resort tourism than for downtown vitality. It has no distinguishing topography and little historical cachet.

Getty Images/David McNew

Suburban houses rise next to a dairy farm east of Los Angeles. Despite odors, flies and pollution from hundreds of dairy farms in the surrounding Chino Basin, the quest for affordable, new homes draws a steady stream of immigrants from the city.

"Phoenix had sprawled out to the suburbs and pretty much abandoned the central city," says City Councilman Claude Mattox. Left behind were "the homeless, vagrants and prostitutes."

But today, with new baseball, basketball and hockey facilities, two major new museums and two concert halls, an upscale retail complex and a $600 million expansion of the convention center, Phoenix draws tens of thousands of people downtown every night. Convinced that sports and tourism weren't enough to make downtown healthy, city leaders have also promoted residential construction and gave the planned site of a new football stadium to a big biomedical campus.

"Over the last two or three years, the residential part is starting to kick in, creating quite a vibrant area," says Maricopa County Administrator David R. Smith.

In March, city voters approved an $878 million bond package to help fund a wide variety of projects, most aimed at revitalizing downtown. Eventually, a chunk of Arizona State University will move into the city from suburban Tempe, drawing 15,000 students, faculty and administrators downtown.

Phoenix's success story has been replicated in many other cities. Although the specific details may differ, downtowns have become chic places for young professionals and empty nesters to buy low-maintenance lofts and condos, surrounded by a mix of outdoor cafes, entertainment options and plenty of people-watching. For instance, Washington, D.C.'s Seventh Street corridor — next door to Chinatown — had historically been an important shopping district. But a decade ago it was rundown and lined with vacant buildings. In 1997, a new basketball arena was opened up nearby, followed by a popular museum and dozens of restaurants — including one with an $18 million interior.

On a recent Friday night, patrons browsed in a bookstore before curtain time at the neighboring Shakespeare Theater. Teenagers watched a "bucket drummer" banging on seven upside-down plastic tubs. Small kids won tee shirts and balloon hats from a radio station's street festival. Inside a new retail alley designed to look like old cast-iron storefronts, a line snaked round and doubled back on itself at a cineplex showing thrillers, cartoons, hip-hop comedies and independent films.

Buffalo's BID sponsors a downtown concert series that now draws 8,000 to 12,000 people a week. Detroit has had more housing starts than any other jurisdiction in Michigan in the last two years. A developer in Nashville is building a 65-story, luxury condo tower. [42]

Cities and their private partners have learned to integrate stadiums and ballparks into neighborhoods in ways that encourage people to walk around and see other things. As a result, downtowns are animated after the 9 to 5 workday, and retailers have added five or six hours to their business day.

However, downtowns are still relatively small potatoes in the broader economic scheme of things. Few central cities have attracted more than a few thousand new residents, while suburbs — including new towns sprouting up on the far metropolitan fringe — continue to draw millions. Attracting just 2 percent of the city's population to live downtown remains an elusive goal almost everywhere.

But downtowns have always been primarily places for commerce, and the fact that so many people with high disposable incomes are either living downtown or visiting regularly represents an impressive turnaround.

Cities still have a long way to go in some fundamental areas, such as lowering the disparities in wealth between loft-dwellers and the poor and providing higher-quality education. But Levy argues that rather than being caught in a vicious downward cycle, as they were for decades, cities are starting to build on their increasing strengths and attractiveness.

"I don't think we're going to have downtowns dominating regions like they did in 1900," he says, "but we're long past the point where downtowns are embarrassments to their regions." ■

OUTLOOK

Multicentered Regions

Levy of the Philadelphia Center City District and many others speak of "multicentered regions," in which commerce is spread among many business districts. Brookings fellow Leinberger says while sprawling cities like Los Angeles and Atlanta were once the model of urban development, Washington now represents the future.

Washington's Metro system, he says, has fostered a series of thriving downtown commercial districts scattered along the subway lines — not just around the downtown Seventh Street area but in suburbs such as Bethesda and Silver Spring in Maryland and Arlington and Alexandria in Virginia. Most building permits now being issued in the region, Leinberger says, are for attached properties rather than the stand-alone projects that define sprawl.

Kotkin, the New America Foundation fellow who is perhaps the leading debunker of downtown cheerleading, argues that America's future lies in the suburbs, just as it has for decades. Downtowns may be attracting a few more people, but they represent a paltry share of the nation's population growth, he says.

"I'm not saying it's not real, but it's not significant," Kotkin says. "Most real-estate bankers and analysts — not, of course, developers and their PR people — will tell you the condo market is overbuilt."

Even downtown boosters are concerned that center cities won't attract a stable, long-term population until the public schools improve. Test scores are up even in some tough districts, such as Chicago, Boston and Philadelphia, but inner-city schools as a rule cannot compete with private or suburban schools. Until they can, only small numbers of affluent parents will raise their families in or around downtowns.

"The quality of school systems is actually an economic-development tool," says Steve Moore, president of the Washington DC Economic Partnership. "You want people to stay for years and raise their kids here."

Moore points out, however, that cities have become "cool for a particular kind of person," if not for parents of school-age children. Brad Segal, a development consultant in Denver, thinks downtowns will benefit from demographic trends that will lead to increased numbers of those particular kinds of persons — both young workers without children and older adults with grown children — who have been repopulating center cities.

About the Author

Alan Greenblatt is a staff writer at *Governing* magazine. He previously covered elections, agriculture and military spending for *CQ Weekly*, where he won the National Press Club's Sandy Hume Award for political journalism. He graduated from San Francisco State University in 1986 and received a master's degree in English literature from the University of Virginia in 1988. His recent reports include "Upward Mobility," "The Partisan Divide" and "Media Bias."

Segal also believes that more people will be drawn to downtowns and inner suburbs because of the same factors that kicked off the gentrification trend of the 1970s — they're fed up with long commutes, congestion and the rising cost of gasoline. "Urban living is a far more resource-efficient way of life," Segal says. "The ability to recapture time is a huge factor that will move people more toward urban living. The long-term economics of resource depletion are going to push us back into cities whether we like it or not."

Despite recent spikes, however, gas prices eat up a smaller portion of personal spending than they did back in 1981. And most cities, despite their glitzy, new downtown neighborhoods, are still losing population, or at least population share, to the suburbs.

"When they talk about 5,000 units in downtown L.A., does anyone understand what that means in a region of 15 million people?" asks Kotkin. "Some of these downtowns are going to have a lot of nomadic people." ■

FOR MORE INFORMATION

International Downtown Association, 1250 H St., N.W., 10th Floor, Washington, DC 20005; (202) 393-6801; www.ida-downtown.org. The association provides information and support to business-improvement districts.

Metropolitan Policy Program, Brookings Institution, 1775 Massachusetts Ave., N.W., Washington, DC 20036; (202) 797-6139; www.brookings.edu/metro. The think tank's urban program issues studies and supports scholars whose work can help communities grow in sustainable ways.

National League of Cities, 1301 Pennsylvania Ave., N.W., Suite 550, Washington, DC 20004; (202) 626-3000; www.nlc.org. The nation's oldest and largest association representing municipal governments.

National Trust for Historic Preservation, 1785 Massachusetts Ave., N.W., Washington, DC 20036; (202) 588-6000; www.mainstreet.org. Sponsors educational activity and advocates for neighborhood conservation, preservation law and downtown Main Street initiatives.

Urban Land Institute, 1025 Thomas Jefferson St., N.W., Suite 500 West; Washington, DC 20007; (202) 624-7000; www.uli.org. Initiates research into trends in land use and property development.

Notes

[1] Terry Frieden, "FBI: Violent crime rate drops again," CNN.com, Oct. 17, 2005, www.cnn.com/2005/LAW/10/17/crime.rate/. For recent coverage, see Rick Lyman, "Surge in Population in the Exurbs Continues," *The New York Times*, June 21, 2006, p. A10.

[2] Quoted in Matt Sepic, "St. Louis Escapes Its Rust-Belt Past," National Public Radio, May 17, 2006.

[3] John Buntin, "Land Rush," *Governing*, March 2006, p. 26.

[4] Lance Freeman, "Displacement or Succession?: Residential Mobility in Gentrifying Neighborhoods," *Urban Affairs Review*, 2005, p. 463.

[5] Scott Carlson, "Richfield Wins Court Battle to Condemn Car Dealership Site," *St. Paul Pioneer Press*, Jan. 20, 2001, p. 1C.

[6] For background see Kenneth Jost, "Property Rights," *CQ Researcher*, March 4, 2005, pp. 197-220.

[7] Linda Greenhouse, "Justices Uphold Taking Private Property for Development," *The New York Times*, June 24, 2005, p. A1.

[8] Avi Salzman and Laura Masnerus, "For Homeowners, Anger and Frustration at Court Ruling," *The New York Times*, June 24, 2005, p. A20.

[9] Arthur M. Schlesinger Jr., "The City in American Civilization," in *American Urban History* (1969), p. 35.

[10] Alison Isenberg, *Downtown America: A History of the Place and the People Who Made It* (2004), p. 7.

[11] Jon C. Teaford, *The Twentieth Century American City*, 2nd ed. (1993), p. 17.

[12] Robert M. Fogelson, *Downtown: Its Rise and Fall, 1880-1950* (2001), p. 13.

[13] *Ibid.*, p. 193.

[14] William Kennedy, *O Albany!* (1983), p. 8.

[15] Robert A. Beauregard, *Visions of Decline: The Postwar Fate of U.S. Cities* (1993), p. 75.

[16] Fogelson, *op. cit.*, p. 109.

[17] *Ibid.*, p. 199.

[18] Isenberg, *op. cit.*, p. 129.

[19] *Ibid.*, p. 142.

[20] For background, see "Business Migrates to the Suburbs," *CQ Researcher*, Nov. 14, 1986.

[21] Fogelson, *op. cit.*, p. 387.

[22] Michael A. Burayidi, ed., *Downtowns: Revitalizing the Centers of Small Urban Communities* (2001), p. 1.

[23] Fogelson, *op. cit.*, p. 223.

[24] Isenberg, *op. cit.*, p. 174.

[25] *Ibid.*, p. 178.

[26] Fogelson, *op. cit.*, p. 318.

[27] Isenberg, *op. cit.*, p. 188.

[28] Herbert J. Gans, "The Failure of Urban Renewal," in *American Urban History*, *op. cit.*, p. 568.

[29] *Ibid.*, p. 569.

[30] W. Dennis Keating *et al.*, eds., *Revitalizing Urban Neighborhoods* (1996), p. 207.

[31] Beauregard, *op. cit.*, p. 171.

[32] Isenberg, *op. cit.*, p. 239.

[33] Beauregard, *op. cit.*, p. 201.

[34] For background, see Charles S. Clark, "Revitalizing the Cities," *CQ Researcher*, Oct. 13, 1995, pp. 897-920.

[35] For background see Richard L. Worsnop, "Historic Preservation," *CQ Researcher*, Oct. 7, 1994, pp. 865-888.

[36] Beauregard, *op. cit.*, p. 231.

[37] *Ibid.*, p. 259.

[38] Christopher Farrell and Michael Mandel, "The Economic Crisis of Urban America," *Business Week*, May 18, 1992, p. 38.

[39] Quoted in William H. Hudnut, *Cities on the Rebound* (1998), p. 1.

[40] William Fulton, "The Panacea Patrol," *Governing*, October 2004, p. 62.

[41] Alan Ehrenhalt, "Ballpark Dreaming," *Governing*, November 2004, p. 6.

[42] Lisa Chamberlain, "Creating Demand for City Living in Nashville," *The New York Times*, June 21, 2006, p. C10.

Bibliography

Selected Sources

Books

Fogelson, Robert M., *Downtown: Its Rise and Fall, 1880-1950*, Yale University Press, 2001.
An MIT professor of urban studies and history examines how downtowns lost their retail dominance.

Isenberg, Alison, *Downtown America: A History of the Place and the People Who Made It*, University of Chicago Press, 2004.
A Rutgers University historian examines downtowns during the 20th century, with particular attention to how retail trends reflected broader racial and economic issues.

Articles

Boddy, Trevor, "Vancouverism vs. Lower Manhattanism," Archnewsnow.com, Sept. 20, 2005.
The architecture critic for the *Vancouver Sun* explains how the downtown population of the British Columbia city doubled over the past 15 years, making it the highest residential density urban area in North America.

Buntin, John, "Land Rush," *Governing*, March 2006, p. 26.
Residential development is taking off around downtown Houston and other cities, but some feel that the government should intervene to preserve old neighborhoods.

Chan, Sewell, "Standard & Poor's Upgrades City's Credit Rating to Best Ever," *The New York Times*, May 23, 2006, p. B1.
A major bond-rating agency upgraded New York City's debt rating, citing surging tax revenues, new money for school construction and a new retiree health-insurance trust fund.

DiMassa, Cara Mia, and Roger Vincent, "Retailers Not Sold on Grand Avenue," *Los Angeles Times*, April 25, 2006, p. A1.
A leading architect and influential civic boosters are promoting new office and condo towers along Grand Avenue in Los Angeles but failing to lure high-end retailers back.

Hampson, Rick, "Studies: Gentrification a Boost for Everyone," *USA Today*, April 19, 2005, p. 1A.
Studies suggest gentrification drives comparatively few low-income residents from their homes, but anecdotal testimony indicates the poor are being priced out of their homes.

Leroux, Charles, and Ron Grossman, "Putting the 'Chic' Back in Chicago," *Chicago Tribune Magazine*, Feb. 5, 2006, p. 10.
Areas such as North Kenwood/Oakland, which had long struggled, have suddenly become fashionable.

MacGilless, Alec, "Region's Job Growth a Centrifugal Force," *The Washington Post*, June 18, 2006, p. A1.
Job and population growth in the National Capital Area continue to be much stronger in suburbs far from Washington, to the dismay of planners who wished for more density and better integration with transit.

Maler, Kevin, "Suburbs Want Downtowns of Their Own," *The New York Times*, April 30, 2006, Sec. 11, p. 10.
An increasing number of suburbs around Minneapolis-St. Paul are building their own downtowns.

Mehren, Elizabeth, "States Acting to Protect Private Property," *Los Angeles Times*, April 16, 2006, p. A1.
In response to a Supreme Court decision allowing cities to take control of properties for private development, all but three states have considered legislation to curb the practice.

Montgomery, Lori, "Education Becoming Top Issue for D.C.," *The Washington Post*, May 24, 2006, p. A1.
Business leaders with a stake in Washington's economic revival argue that healthy public schools are vital.

Mui, Ylan Q., "Wal-Mart to Enter Urban Markets," *The Washington Post*, April 5, 2006, p. D1.
The leading retailer announces it will build stores in more than 50 blighted urban areas.

Reports and Studies

Birch, Eugenie L., "Who Lives Downtown," Living Cities Census Series, Brookings Institution, November 2005.
An analysis of 44 cities finds that downtown populations are growing after decades of decline.

Freeman, Lance, "Displacement or Succession?: Residential Mobility in Gentrifying Neighborhoods," *Urban Affairs Review*, 2005, p. 463.
A Columbia University urban-planning professor finds that gentrification plays a minor role, if any, in displacing poor city dwellers.

Kotkin, Joel, "The New Suburbanism: A Realist's Guide to the American Future," The Planning Center, November 2005.
Despite urban planners' love for central cities, suburbs will continue as the stage for America's future growth.

Leinberger, Christopher B., "Turning Around Downtown: Twelve Steps to Revitalization," The Brookings Institution, March 2005.
A consultant lays out the template for revitalizing downtowns, from initial planning through housing strategy to attracting retail.

The Next Step:

Additional Articles from Current Periodicals

Downtown Revival

Chamberlain, Lisa, "Creating Demand for City Living in Nashville," ***The New York Times*****, June 21, 2006, p. C10.**
A pioneering developer has created a market for residential housing in the central business district.

Huffstutter, P.J., "A Still-Struggling Detroit Puts On Its Game Face," ***Los Angeles Times*****, Feb. 3, 2006, p. A10.**
Officials hope to show off downtown Detroit's revival during the Super Bowl, but critics say the reality is grim.

Johnson, Patt, "Hungry For Visitors At Locust Street Mall Food Court," ***The Des Moines Register*****, May 19, 2006.**
While residential and office developments are blossoming in downtown Des Moines, Iowa, restaurants and retail outlets are struggling.

Nelson, Tim, "Jail Slated to Become Condos on the Minnesota Riverfront," ***Chicago Tribune*****, Jan. 7, 2006, p. W14.**
A vacant jail and an abandoned office building in St. Paul will be turned into 300 new condos as the city tries to bring new residents downtown.

Eminent Domain

Richey, Warren, "Battle Over Property Rights Goes On, Despite Ruling," ***The Christian Science Monitor*****, Jan. 4, 2006, p. 2.**
Residents of the Fort Trumbull neighborhood in New London, Conn., are still living in their homes six months after the Supreme Court ruled the city could seize them.

Yednak, Crystal, "Eminent Domain Now Big Business," ***Chicago Tribune*****, Jan. 3, 2006, p. 1.**
Property owners in Chicago are upset the city is using eminent domain to provide cheap land to private companies.

Gentrification

Adler, Linda, "Affordable Housing Reaches Quandary," ***The Houston Chronicle*****, March 8, 2006, p. 2.**
Apartments are rapidly being demolished, and rents are rising, causing consumers to struggle with home affordability.

Dewan, Shaila, "Gentrification Changing Face of New Atlanta," ***The New York Times*****, March 11, 2006, p. A1.**
Gentrification has expanded Atlanta's tax base and eradicated blight, but it has also reduced the black share of the city's population — long a symbol of African-American success.

Morales, Laura, "Developer Pledges $6 Million to Community," ***The Miami Herald*****, Feb. 16, 2006, p. 3.**
Council members in Coconut Grove, Fla., have asked condo developers to ensure that low-income residents can stay in the neighborhood, soon to be taken over by new condos.

Schwartzman, Paul, "Whose H Street Is It, Anyway?" ***The Washington Post*****, April 4, 2006, p. B1.**
Old and new residents of gentrifying Northeast Washington argue over zoning laws, with new residents wanting fast-food restaurants removed from the neighborhood and longtime residents seeing it as a war on black Washington.

Suburban Growth

Herrick, Thaddeus, "Fake Towns Rise, Offering Urban Life Without the Grit," ***The Wall Street Journal*****, May 31, 2006, p. A1.**
Faux downtowns are popping up in suburban areas across the country, offering urban benefits without city realities.

Nicholson, Heather L., "Experts Predict Longer Commutes As Suburbs Grow," ***The Houston Chronicle*****, June 1, 2006, p. 1.**
Transportation and development experts predict major suburban expansion west of the city by 2035, causing much longer commutes.

Rodkin, Dennis, "Sprawl Blossoms," ***Chicago Tribune*****, Jan. 8, 2006, p. C1.**
Bob Bruegmann, a professor at the University of Illinois at Chicago, argues in his new book, *Sprawl: A Compact History*, that suburban growth is good, providing a pleasant lifestyle for people at all economic levels.

CITING *CQ RESEARCHER*

Sample formats for citing these reports in a bibliography include the ones listed below. Preferred styles and formats vary, so please check with your instructor or professor.

MLA STYLE

Jost, Kenneth. "Rethinking the Death Penalty." CQ Researcher 16 Nov. 2001: 945-68.

APA STYLE

Jost, K. (2001, November 16). Rethinking the death penalty. *CQ Researcher, 11*, 945-968.

CHICAGO STYLE

Jost, Kenneth. "Rethinking the Death Penalty." *CQ Researcher*, November 16, 2001, 945-968.

CQ Researcher

Published by CQ Press, a division of Congressional Quarterly Inc.

cqresearcher.com

National Service

Should community service be required?

More than 65 million Americans now volunteer for charitable and service organizations, and President Bush wants to push the total to 75 million by 2010. But the president appears to have lost some of his enthusiasm for volunteerism. In his 2002 State of the Union address, Bush called on more Americans to volunteer to help their neighbors. But now the administration wants drastic cuts in AmeriCorps, the domestic Peace Corps-type program created by President Bill Clinton in 1993. Experts say the issue could move into the spotlight in coming years if Bush's support wanes, and candidates for public office pick up the banner of national service. Supporters argue that requiring national service will foster national unity and inspire more volunteerism from Americans young and old. Critics counter, however, that making service compulsory negates the whole purpose of volunteering — giving one's time willingly to help others.

The Experience Corps pairs retirees with inner-city children in 14 cities for tutoring and mentoring.

INSIDE THIS REPORT

CQ Researcher • June 30, 2006 • www.cqresearcher.com
Volume 16, Number 25 • Pages 577-600

RECIPIENT OF SOCIETY OF PROFESSIONAL JOURNALISTS AWARD FOR EXCELLENCE ◆ AMERICAN BAR ASSOCIATION SILVER GAVEL AWARD

THE ISSUES

BACKGROUND

CURRENT SITUATION

OUTLOOK

SIDEBARS AND GRAPHICS

FOR FURTHER RESEARCH

Cover photograph: Alex Harris

CQ Researcher

June 30, 2006
Volume 16, Number 25

MANAGING EDITOR: Thomas J. Colin
ASSISTANT MANAGING EDITOR: Kathy Koch
ASSOCIATE EDITOR: Kenneth Jost
STAFF WRITERS: Marcia Clemmitt, Peter Katel
CONTRIBUTING WRITERS: Rachel S. Cox, Sarah Glazer, Alan Greenblatt, Patrick Marshall, Tom Price
DESIGN/PRODUCTION EDITOR: Olu B. Davis
ASSISTANT EDITOR: Melissa J. Hipolit
EDITORIAL INTERN: Nicholas Sohr

CQ PRESS

A Division of Congressional Quarterly Inc.

SENIOR VICE PRESIDENT/PUBLISHER: John A. Jenkins
DIRECTOR, LIBRARY PUBLISHING: Kathryn C. Suárez
DIRECTOR, EDITORIAL OPERATIONS: Ann Davies

CONGRESSIONAL QUARTERLY INC.
CHAIRMAN: Paul C. Tash
VICE CHAIRMAN: Andrew P. Corty
PRESIDENT/EDITOR IN CHIEF: Robert W. Merry

CQ Researcher (ISSN 1056-2036) is printed on acid-free paper. Published weekly, except March 24, July 7, July 14, Aug. 4, Aug. 11, Nov. 24, Dec. 22 and Dec. 29, by CQ Press, a division of Congressional Quarterly Inc. Annual full-service subscriptions for institutions start at $667. For pricing, call 1-800-834-9020, ext. 1906. To purchase a *CQ Researcher* report in print or electronic format (PDF), visit www.cqpress.com or call 866-427-7737. Single reports start at $10. Bulk purchase discounts and electronic-rights licensing are also available. Periodicals postage paid at Washington, D.C., and additional mailing offices. POSTMASTER: Send address changes to *CQ Researcher*, 1255 22nd St., N.W., Suite 400, Washington, DC 20037.

National Service

BY JOHN GREENYA

THE ISSUES

Stefanie Huber didn't know quite what to expect when she applied to work with seriously ill children as a member of the National Civilian Community Corps (NCCC). But the 25-year-old Monroe, Wis., native says the camp in New York state was magical, and she wants to return this summer.

"It's an amazing place," she says. "The kids are there to have fun. You kind of forget they even have illnesses — so do they, I think, as much as they possibly can. I'm applying to go back." [1]

But another stint is unlikely. President George W. Bush's fiscal 2007 budget calls for eliminating funding for the NCCC. The NCCC puts 1,100 Americans ages 18-24 to work for 10 months on service projects like the camp, but primarily involving disaster relief. NCCC volunteers are housed in dorms on five campuses around the country, and hundreds were deployed to the Gulf Coast region to support relief efforts after Hurricane Katrina.

The NCCC is part of AmeriCorps, which was created by President Bill Clinton in 1993 as a kind of domestic Peace Corps. In addition to the NCCC AmeriCorps includes two other programs in which members work for small stipends: VISTA (Volunteers in Service to America) supplies 6,000 full-time workers to help nonprofit, faith-based and community organizations in impoverished areas. [2] AmeriCorps State and National provides federal grants and volunteers to public and nonprofit groups. Bush's budget also calls for cutbacks in overall AmeriCorps funding.

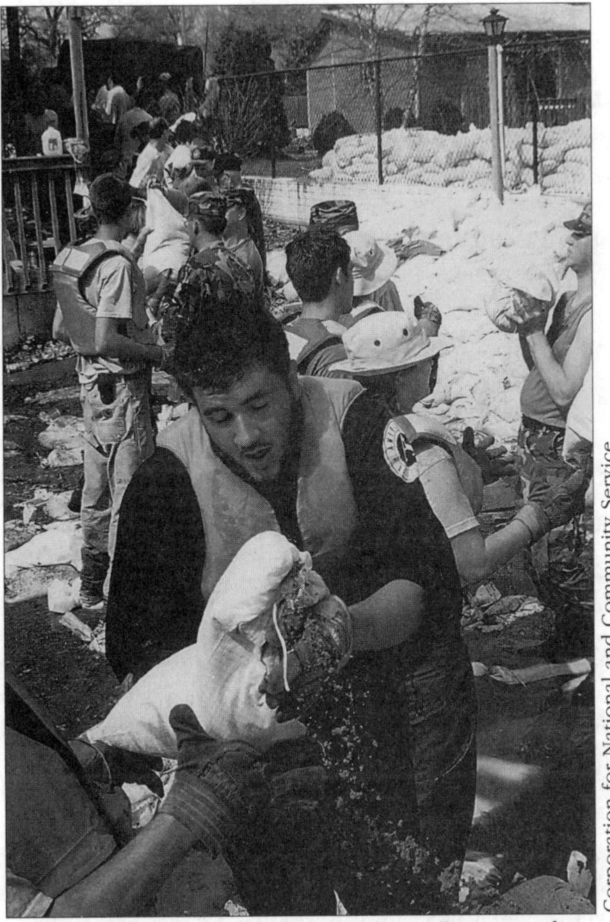

Corporation for National and Community Service

An AmeriCorps member helps with sandbagging after recent flooding. To help pay for the Iraq war and damage from Hurricane Katrina, President Bush proposes abolishing the National Civilian Community Corps, whose 1,100 members focus on disaster-relief work. The corps is one of three AmeriCorps programs created by President Clinton in 1993 as a kind of domestic Peace Corps.

"I couldn't believe it," says Katie Crumley, 26, a former VISTA volunteer, when she heard Bush wanted to abolish the NCCC. "It didn't make sense that he would be cutting this program after it had just been shown how crucial disaster relief was to this country!"

While researching spring-break volunteer opportunities in the Gulf Coast region, Crumley, a graduate student at the University of Minnesota, came across dozens of youth groups looking for help rebuilding New Orleans. "Like the young people who volunteered following the Sept. 11, 2001, terrorist attacks, they are motivated by the horrific media images to help out in whatever way they can," she wrote in a letter to *The Minnesota Daily*. "Why is the president denying them the opportunity? Our young people are ready; you just need to tell them where to go."

In his 1961 inaugural address, Democratic President John F. Kennedy famously urged Americans, "Ask not what your country can do for you; ask what you can do for your country."

Four decades later, President Bush surprised his fellow Republicans with a similar challenge in his 2002 State of the Union address: "My call tonight is for every American to commit at least two years — 4,000 hours over the rest of your lifetime — to the service of your neighbors and your nation."

Bush established his own domestic national-service program, the U.S.A. Freedom Corps. But in supporting not just volunteerism but government-financed national service, the president had gone against his party's leaders.

"Congressional Republicans are still upset because they weren't able to kill off Clinton's AmeriCorps," wrote *Time* columnist Margaret Carlson, "and now it's coming back at them stronger than ever, as the linchpin of Freedom Corps."

Indeed, Carlson noted, then-House Majority Leader Dick Armey, R-Texas, once called AmeriCorps a "welfare program for aspiring yuppies," and Sen. Rick Santorum, R-Pa., has described it as a sweet deal for those "picking up trash in a park and singing Kumbaya." [3]

High-School Volunteerism Has Risen

Volunteerism among high-school seniors rose from about two-thirds of students in the early 1990s to three-quarters by 2003. Volunteerism among 10th-graders rose slightly during that period and remained steady among 8th-graders.

Students Who Have Volunteered in the Past Year (2003)
(by percentage)

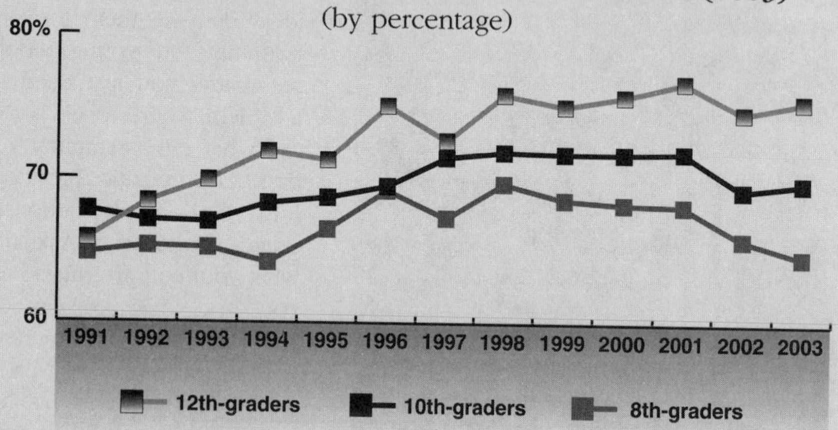

Source: "Volunteering Among Young People," Center for Information & Research on Civil Learning & Engagement, February 2004, using "Monitoring the Future" surveys.

The critics are especially critical of the NCCC program, which they say is far more costly than other government-sponsored service programs.

But there is resistance to the Bush administration's efforts to downsize AmeriCorps and abolish the NCCC — and it has support from a variety of quarters. There's the spirit of youths like Crumley, who asked, "Where is that strong call for national service that followed Sept. 11?" [4] And the Rev. William J. Byron, a Jesuit priest and professor at Loyola College in Baltimore, says there is a deep reservoir of goodwill about volunteerism following Katrina.

Rep. Charles Rangel, D-N.Y., reiterated the call for "shared sacrifice" in 2003 when he introduced a bill to reinstitute the military draft. [5] The measure called for mandatory military service for everyone between the ages of 18 and 26 but would allow citizens to work for AmeriCorps-type service programs as a substitute for military service. The legislation received little support.

Advocates for national service say it could become a major debate topic in congressional elections this fall and even in the presidential election in 2008. Former President Clinton recently announced that his new book will be about public service and citizen activism. [6] And former President George H. W. Bush — who initiated his own "thousand points of light" call to volunteerism in 1989 — and his wife Barbara sounded the drum for service as co-speakers at The George Washington University graduation ceremonies in May. "You'll get a lot more satisfaction by tucking a child into bed, seeing a victim of Hurricane Katrina moving back into their home," said Mrs. Bush. "It's best to invest in the lives of people." [7]

Many of the new graduates already had firsthand experience with public service because they had attended high schools that required community service for graduation. For instance, schools in Fort Lauderdale (Broward County), Fla., and Bellevue, Wash., require 40 hours of community service to graduate, while Maybeck High School in Berkeley, Calif., requires 60 hours and Incarnate Word High School in San Antonio and Woodrow Wilson High School in Washington, D.C., both require 100 hours.

Students overseas are even more familiar with the idea of national service, which is required by many other nations, some of which allow civilian service instead of mandatory military service. (*See sidebar, p. 589.*)

Now that President Bush has backed away from his support for national service, the debate over it may become heated. According to *New York* magazine columnist Michael Tomasky, "it has always been an article of faith [among Republicans] that government action, even in wartime, frustrates the growth of civil society, which must come from below." [8]

Alex Totman, valedictorian of the 2006 graduating class at Brunswick High School in Maine, found his mandatory service inspiring, and a key element of his education. He spent his 20 hours of required community service working in a hunger-prevention program unloading boxes, sorting food items and serving hot meals — none of which shows up in his grade point average. 'It was a pretty powerful experience, the realization that there is hunger and poverty everywhere," he said. [9]

Like civilian national service, the idea of bringing back the draft has been debated for decades, but with one big difference: When talking about national service, no one asks what would be the effect of "another 9/11."

In January 2002, the debate went national when Rep. Rangel made his first draft proposal. It required all citizens (or permanent residents) between ages 18 and 26 to complete two years of compulsory service, either in the military or in a civilian capacity. Rangel conceded from the start that he knew the bill had little chance of passing; his point in introducing it, he said, was to highlight what he perceived as the unfairness of the current all-volunteer military system, which fills most of its ranks with young men and women from the nation's lower socioeconomic stratum. "I believe in . . . shared sacrifice," Rangel said at the time. [10]

Former Common Cause President David Cohen argues that requiring all citizens to perform national service — either military or civilian — would have a "bonding" effect on all the nation's citizens. "It's important to create universals," he says, "because they are a way of showing we are in this together."

As Congress considers President Bush's proposal to cut national service programs, here are some of the questions being debated:

Most High-School Students Volunteer

More than 80 percent of incoming college freshmen performed community service work in high school in 2003 — up from two-thirds of freshmen in 1989. Some researchers say the increased activity reflects occasional volunteering by college-bound seniors seeking to pad their resumes, rather than regular service.

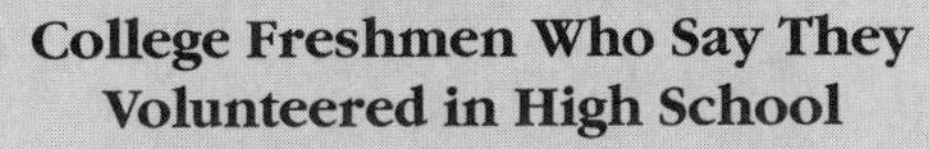

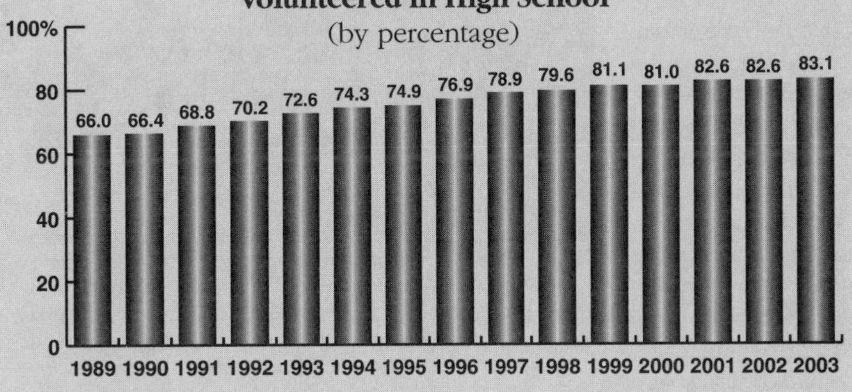

Source: Higher Education Research Institute

Should national service be mandatory?

Some Americans say national service should be required of everyone; others believe service should never be coerced.

This fundamental split is not new. Americans have always been divided on the question of whether some form of national service should be mandatory. In part, the dichotomy stems from two seemingly contradictory strains in the American character: a deep belief in helping others — especially the less fortunate — and an equally strong sense of self-reliance.

The conflict is further complicated by politics, religion and economics. Liberals tend to favor compulsory national service, while conservatives oppose it. Religious conservatives firmly believe that good works should be done because people want to do them, not because it's required by the government; many non-religious Americans feel the same way.

"Enrollment in a government-funded self-improvement project or acceptance of a government job [cannot] be called true service," wrote Bruce Chapman, founder and co-director of the conservative Discovery Institute. "Indeed, when coercion or inducements are provided, as in the various national service schemes, the spirit of service is to that degree corrupted." [11] *(See "At Issue," p. 593.)*

Others, including some government officials, oppose mandatory service because they say the cost of setting up and operating a nationwide national service program would be prohibitive. When the White House announced it was eliminating the NCCC's funding, Tom Schatz, president of Citizens Against Government Waste, told Fox News, "We thought AmeriCorps was always expensive. I give the administration credit for evaluating a program and proposing its elimination."

Likewise, James Bovard, president and founder of the Competitive Enterprise Institute, said, "It's always been a boondoggle, and it will always be a boondoggle when you are rounding up people and paying them for doing good deeds. Bush's cuts are a nice gesture, [but] only if it's a step toward abolishing the whole program." [12]

Younger commentators are also divided, but perhaps even more passionate. "Opponents [of a mandatory-service requirement] assert that the government has no right to claim a year of its young citizens' lives," writes Vanderbilt University sophomore Sean Harris, who says he'd be happy to give a year or two to national service. "But in my opinion the government does have that right and should exercise it. As citizens of the U.S., we enjoy the protection of American law and the shelter of the American government. In return for this protection, all citizens owe this country any service it requests, so long as that service is meaningful." [13]

Ann Maura Connolly, vice president of Voices for National Service, said,

"Now is not the time to be cutting [the NCCC] after there has been this huge surge in people wanting to serve, especially among young people, particularly after 9/11 and Katrina." [14]

Ben Schiffrin, writing in *The Harvard Journal of Legislation*, argued that while mandatory national service seeks a just end, it goes about it the wrong way. "A return to the draft is not the way to redress either the problems faced by minorities that force them into military service or the reluctance of other young Americans to represent their country," he wrote. "At the same time, military and civilian national service should be made more attractive so that more young Americans choose to serve voluntarily. Increased pay and benefits, better service conditions and greater candor from politicians considering military action may induce more young elites to represent their county." [15]

Lance Bell

World War II veterans gather with students at Allegany High School in Cumberland, Md., following the completion of their oral-history book and film project. The school's oral-history program has been recognized by the state's Department of Education as a premiere example of service learning.

Gary L. Yates, president and CEO of the California Wellness Foundation, argued that "mandatory national service would provide a way for the youth of this nation to give something back for the freedoms they enjoy and to work side-by-side with other young Americans for a common national purpose." [16]

"The result would be a better understanding of the strength of our diversity and increased participation in the voting booth," he continued. "For some, the military may be an option, as it was for me; for others, the ability to work in a nursing home, recreation facility or day-care center may be a life-altering experience. The benefits will surely be safer, healthier and more civicly engaged youth and adults."

Rep. Rangel's bill would have allowed Americans to work in either a national service or military capacity to fulfill a mandatory two-year service obligation. When he introduced the measure, Rangel, a decorated Korean War veteran, said he mainly wanted to use the proposal to illustrate the fact that the war in Iraq was being fought, almost exclusively, by the poor and minorities.

Accusing Rangel of attacking the president unfairly, the Republican House leadership rushed his bill to a vote without hearings or debate. They reportedly were worried about a growing buzz on the Internet that the administration was considering reinstituting the draft if Bush won re-election in 2004. [17] The measure was defeated overwhelmingly, with only two Democrats — Reps. John Murtha of Pennsylvania and Pete Stark of California — voting for it.

Conservative commentator Stanley Kunitz complained Rangel's bill "would create a giant, make-work government program for the millions of drafted Americans who would not serve in the military (not to mention the cost of feeding, housing and managing a huge section of the population)." The benefits from inculcating an "ethic of service" among the nation's youth would be outweighed by the cost factor, he continued. The same goal can be achieved by setting up junior Reserve Officer Training Corps (ROTC) programs in high schools and reviving ROTC programs at the nation's most prestigious college campuses, he said, while avoiding "the drawbacks of a compulsory national service program." [18]

Actually, Congress in 2002, with very little debate, approved a program (dubbed the National Call to Service program) to allow U.S. troops to fulfill part of their military obligation by serving in AmeriCorps. A later effort to establish a pilot program in which recruits could spend at least part of their service time in the Peace Corps was roundly defeated in February 2006, after complaints that it would compromise the Peace Corp's neutral image as a non-military organization. [19]

Should AmeriCorps be saved?

Of AmeriCorps' three programs — AmeriCorps State and National, VISTA and the National Civilian Community Corps — only the NCCC is on the chopping block.

The president's fiscal 2007 budget would cut $22 million from the program, leaving only $5 million for shutting down the five NCCC camps. [20]

In a letter calling for restoration of the NCCC cuts, Sen. Barbara Mikulski, D-Md., called the corps "a reputable program with a proven track record." She noted that NCCC volunteers have built and renovated approximately 5,500 houses, tutored more than 300,000 students, constructed 7,800 miles of hiking trails, cleared damaged trees from thousands of acres ravaged by wildfires and supported 4.6 million people in disaster areas. They have also brought their training in CPR, first aid, disaster response and firefighting to every national disaster since the program was established, most recently after Katrina. All told, Mikulski said they have provided more than 250,000 service hours, valued at $3.8 million, to more than 50 different projects.

Negative reaction to the proposed Bush cuts in NCCC has been coming from both sides of the political aisle. In the House, several dozen mostly Democratic lawmakers followed the lead of Republicans Chris Shays of Connecticut and Tom Osbourne of Nebraska and Democrats David Price of North Carolina and Tennessee's Harold Ford, Jr. The four sponsored a letter signed by 53 other members urging the House leadership to restore the NCCC funds.

"The NCCC is a trained force that can immediately be deployed," they wrote. "The service NCCC members provided to [Katrina] evacuees was invaluable, and so is the NCCC. . . . If additional steps must be taken to enhance and reform the NCCC, we look forward to working with the [administration] to make the necessary changes." [21]

Rep. Shays is a longtime supporter of national service. In February 2006, the 115-member Voices for National Service coalition gave him a lifetime achievement award for his support. [22]

Meanwhile, some analysts praise the work done by the NCCC but say it costs too much money. The Office of Management and Budget (OMB) report accompanying the White House announcement of the cuts put the annual cost per worker at $27,859. In the other non-residential AmeriCorps programs, there is a per-participant cost of $16,000. Some opponents also don't like the fact that the members are paid, which, they say, violates the "spirit of service."

Bush-appointee David Eisner — CEO of the Corporation for National and Community Service, which oversees AmeriCorps — was in the unenviable position of having to defend the cuts. Eisner, who gets good marks from most national service proponents for his commitment to the program, said that while the president is committed to national service, "he is also committed to controlling spending and reducing the deficit. That entails some hard choices for discretionary spending." Nonetheless, Eisner's disappointment was apparent: "This is a difficult decision," he wrote, "given the popularity of the program with our participants and partners, particularly in disaster response." [23]

Some national service opponents were blunt in their reaction to the cuts. Libertarian author Bovard, a longtime critic of the program (and more recently also of President Bush) wrote, "Bush was far more interested in exploiting it to show his own benevolence so he sharply expanded its membership rolls and volunteers." [24]

OMB said the NCCC "has not demonstrated efficiencies in controlling costs per participant" and that compared to other federally funded residential programs "is far more expensive. For example, the average per-day program cost for an NCCC participant

AmeriCorps Members 'Make a Difference'

Nearly all participants in the AmeriCorps State and National and NCCC programs felt they made a difference in the life of at least one person, and a large majority felt the experience helped them gain a new perspective on their beliefs and attitudes.

AmeriCorps Members' Perceptions of Accomplishments
(By percentage)

	State and National (Strongly agree/ Agree)	NCCC (Strongly agree/ Agree)
You felt you made a difference in the life of at least one person	97%	91%
You felt you made a contribution to the community	94	91
You were exposed to new ideas and ways of seeing the world	87	89
You re-examined your beliefs and attitudes about yourself	84	85
You felt like part of the community	90	76
You changed some of your beliefs and attitudes	79	77
You did things you never thought you could do	77	78
You learned more about the "real world"	77	65

Source: Corporation for National and Community Service, "Serving Country and Community: A Longitudinal Study of Service in AmeriCorps," December 2004

Majority of Youths Oppose Mandated Service

More than half of the young people polled in 2002 opposed requiring high-school students to perform community service in order to graduate. But more than 80 percent favored opportunities for paid community service to earn money for college.

Attitudes Toward Community Service Requirements
(Among 15-to-25-year-olds)

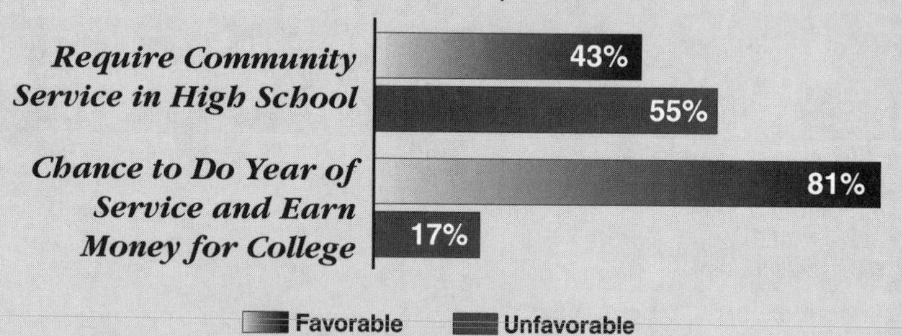

Source: Center for Information & Research on Civic Learning & Engagement/ Council for Excellence in Government Youth Survey, 2002

with an average 10-month length of stay is estimated at $72, compared to $27 for the National Youth Challenge program." [25]

Should community service be required for high-school graduation?

Performing a certain number of hours of community service in conjunction with academic courses — known as service learning — is a statewide requirement for high-school graduation in Maryland, the District of Columbia and various schools and school districts (and some colleges) elsewhere. Officials in several cities and states are considering implementing such requirements, including those in New Jersey, Michigan and Chicago.

Proponents of required service learning say volunteerism builds students' self-esteem, reinforces classroom learning and performs a valuable community service. Opponents say when the service is required the meaning of service is diminished. They also argue that it's not fair for schools to require an activity that is not academic.

Opposition to mandatory service is not surprising. While Americans have always been generally supportive of volunteerism, they have resisted compulsory civilian and military service, except in times of national emergency. More than half of youths ages 15-25 polled recently opposed unpaid community-service graduation requirements, but 81 percent favored it if they were paid and able to earn money for college. (*See graph above.*)

Aric Herndon was a 14-year-old Eagle Scout in Chapel Hill, N.C., when he and his parents, and the parents of another student, went to court in 1995 to oppose the school district's requirement that students perform 50 hours of community service during high school. They argued that the service requirement "violates parents' right to direct and control the upbringing and education of their children" under the 14th Amendment to the Constitution. The students and parents also argued that requiring them to perform community service violates the constitutional right to freedom from involuntary servitude, personal liberty and privacy.

The Fourth U.S. Circuit Court of Appeals affirmed a lower court ruling rejecting the parents' suit, saying the service requirement did not violate the students' constitutional rights. The court held that the service requirement was "in no way comparable to the horrible injustice of human slavery," as the plaintiffs had alleged.

Chapman, of the Discovery Institute, opposes compulsory service in general but finds required service learning in schools less offensive. "We definitely need to encourage voluntary service by all ages, including especially the young," he wrote. "But compulsory service isn't really service in the same moral sense, any more than there is some virtue in meeting the obligation of paying one's taxes. What is required by law cannot be offered as a gift. It is far better to instill an expectation of genuine lifetime service and charity and to incorporate into all careers the opportunity for service in hours outside work and as an extra effort during work." [26]

School-connected programs, however, "plainly are not as objectionable as government-mandated and financed programs performed in lieu of a regular job," he says. "Most high-school 'volunteers' are only expected to put in, say, 60 hours of service, with no pay, at a charity of their choice. This is performed more as an extracurricular activity than as a job substitute, so the impact and cost are much less. Some students plainly do game the system, while many apparently benefit and do some good for the charities that take them on."

Still, Chapman writes: "Does a child who must perform service to graduate from high school develop a high sense of what it means to help others?"

In the view of Alice Joyce, service-learning coordinator at Chapel Hill High School, the answer is an enthusiastic yes. Students at the 1,800-student school participate in a range of activities, from Meals on Wheels, to helping in the Community Kitchen and at men's and women's shelters. They work with families in the waiting room at a local hospital, helping them make phone calls. They partner with lonely elderly people at nursing homes. "It's a wonderful program," Joyce says.

The essays that students are required to write in their senior year, reflecting on their service experience, are often "extremely moving," says Joyce. "They feel community service has helped shape their idea of what they want to do in the future. And it often boosts their self-esteem. They feel better about themselves and better understand their place in the world."

Peace Corps

A Peace Corps urban youth development volunteer in Nicaragua leads the boys' soccer team he organized on a hike. He also teaches English to high-school students. More than 180,00 volunteers have served in the Peace Corps since its start in 1961.

Joyce notes that the program's requirements have been tightened in recent years to bar participation in activities that benefit private groups, such as country clubs, neighborhood pools and church congregations, rather than the community at large. "Some parents and students think it's not fair — that it's a value judgment to exclude certain activities," she says.

Michael Lind, Whitehead senior fellow at the New America Foundation, a liberal think tank, supports requiring service learning in school but objects to compulsory programs for adults. "There's nothing wrong with requiring students to do something for their community," he says. "That's different from requiring adults. When you are in public school, you are a ward of the state until graduation and the state can make your graduation contingent on whatever requirements it sees fit.

"Bringing groceries to poor people, restoring the environment, tutoring younger kids — such activities are all part of the legitimate educational mission of school," he continues. "Education is not simply memorizing and regurgitating data but training students to be good citizens, helping them acquire the habit of good citizenship early."

Nonetheless, Lind says, "I'm sure you'll find some scrooge to attack" service learning.

Lind argues, however, that people will be more active as adults if they are not compelled to serve. "Once you graduate and are a legal adult, it's a huge deprivation of liberty to conscript people for any service unless there's an overwhelming public necessity."

Sara Helms, a doctoral candidate at the University of Maryland, College Park, studied Maryland's service-learning requirement for her dissertation. [27] Each Maryland school district is permitted to come up with its own state-approved program, but generally students can fulfill the 75-hour requirement throughout their public-school tenure, although most do it from sixth to 10th grade.

With more and more schools contemplating service requirements, Helms thinks more research is needed into the long-term effects of such programs. She found that while students report completing more service activity as eighth-graders, this result is not found in 12th grade.

The lingering question, she says, is whether their volunteering will pick up again after they leave school, or whether it will simply fade away. "Maybe they will come back to volunteering later," she says. "But we need more information on whether these programs are doing what [school officials] think they are doing." ■

BACKGROUND

Wartime Service

In the nation's early days, mutual-aid activities were typically informal and non-governmental, ranging from "the shared harvests of the early colonists to the shared burdens of the early slaves, from the barn-raisings and quilting bees of the westward migration to the city settlement houses of the great northward immigration . . . to the committed participation of the civil rights movement," said a report by the Commission on National and Community Service. [28]

While those activities were voluntary, they were also private. Whenever the government has suggested requiring citizens to help one another or the government itself, the response has not always been enthusiastic. In his 1988 book *A Call to Civic Service.* Northwestern University sociology Professor Charles Moskos wrote, "At certain times, national service is held out as a civic ideal against which all other public activities can be measured; at other times, it is a marginal factor, dismissed as irrelevant or utopian." [29]

One of the first examples of national service was, of course, the Colonial militias, in which all the soldiers were volunteers. According to Moskos, they were "reinvigorated" by the Revolutionary War, only to wax and wane in the two centuries since.

In the late 19th century, "muscular Christianity" was in vogue, leading to the formation of such organizations as the YMCA and YWCA and the Boy and Girl Scouts. [30] In 1906, the celebrated American philosopher and pacifist William James (brother of novelist Henry James) called on young Americans to channel their war-like energies into the pursuit of peace. His 1910 essay, "The Moral Equivalent of War," was described by conservative icon William F. Buckley decades later as "a kind of charter instrument of national service." [31]

In the past, wartime governments have debated and sometimes enacted national service and labor-conscripting measures that would be considered fairly Draconian by today's standards. For instance, the Selective Service System (the military draft) enacted during World War I included so-called "Work or Fight" regulations designed to induce able-bodied men to transfer from non-essential to essential occupations.

In 1917 to 1918, as the wartime labor market grew increasingly tight, states passed "compulsory work laws." Largely an expression of "anti-slacker" sentiment, they were designed to move male workers (usually between ages 18 and 50) from occupations seen as unnecessary to more productive industries. For instance, when New York's compulsory work law went into effect on June 1, 1918, Police Commissioner Richard E. Enright said: "No human parasite is going to escape, and every man investigated will have to prove that he is in a useful occupation." The law would be enforced, police said, against "fortune tellers, gamblers, wire and rope dancers, touts, lounge lizards, loafers on golf courses, barkers for sightseeing cars, Chinatown guides, dope fiends, chair warmers in hotels and public places, hangers-on in pool rooms, and various other groups." [32]

Compulsory national service has been proposed and debated — and sometimes adopted — during non-wartime. Perhaps best-known is the Civilian Conservation Corps (CCC) created by President Franklin D. Roosevelt during the Great Depression. During its nine years of existence, 1933-1942, the CCC sent 2.5 million unemployed young people to rural areas to do conservation work. At its peak in 1935, the corps had 500,000 on its rolls.

During World War II, as millions of young men were being drafted, President Roosevelt called for passage of a national service law that would last at least as long as the war. Calling national service "the most democratic way to wage war," Roosevelt claimed it would "prevent strikes, and with certain appropriate exceptions . . . make available for war production or for any other essential services every able-bodied adult in this nation." [33]

Although Roosevelt's proposal was supported by the War Production Board, the War Manpower Commission, the Selective Service System, the War Food Administration and various farm organizations, opposition from labor and management organizations convinced Congress to block adoption of the plan in 1944. The next year Roosevelt again proposed national service legislation, and bills were passed by both houses in February and March. But before the conference report resolving differences in the two bills could be adopted the war in Europe had ended. [34]

Peace Corps

The next major national service program was JFK's Peace Corps, which beginning in 1961 sent volunteers to work for two-year periods on development projects in Third World countries. The Peace Corps' busiest year was 1966, when 15,556 Americans were working in nations around the globe. At that same time, several people associated with the Peace Corps pushed the idea of universal voluntary service by all young Americans, but the proposed program became another casualty of the mounting costs of the war in Vietnam.

The 1970s saw the creation of the federal Youth Conservation Corps (YCC) and Young Adult Conservation Corps (YACC), but they were always much smaller than the Peace Corps.

Continued on p. 588

Chronology

1933-1964 *Early efforts to encourage volunteerism find fruition in President Johnson's Great Society programs.*

1933
To help the unemployed during the Great Depression, President Franklin D. Roosevelt establishes the Civilian Conservation Corps.

1940
Congress passes first peacetime draft in American history. Except for a short period after World War II, the draft remains in force until 1973.

1948
Selective Service Act requires 18-year-old men to register.

March 1, 1961
President John F. Kennedy establishes the Peace Corps.

1964
President Lyndon B. Johnson establishes VISTA (Volunteers in Service to America).

1970s-1990s

Presidents of both parties push initiatives to increase national service by young Americans.

July 1971
President Richard M. Nixon creates ACTION as the umbrella agency for the Peace Corps and VISTA.

1976
Habitat for Humanity International is founded by Millard and Linda Fuller in Georgia to build housing for low-income families.

Aug. 18, 1988
Republican presidential candidate George H.W. Bush calls for Americans to become "A Thousand Points of Light" through volunteer work.

1990
President Bush signs National and Community Service Act authorizing programs to engage citizens in service. . . . Points of Light Foundation is founded.

September 1993
Maryland legislature approves statewide compulsory community-service requirement for high-school graduation. . . . . President Bill Clinton signs National and Community Service Trust Act providing education funds for individuals performing national service.

September 1994
AmeriCorps sends out its first group of volunteers — 20,000 young men and women.

2000-Present

Terrorist attacks spark a surge of patriotism and volunteerism.

Sept. 11, 2001
Terrorists fly hijacked planes into World Trade Center, Pentagon.

November 2001
Sens. Evan Bayh, D-Ind., and John McCain, R-Ariz., introduce Call to Service Act to greatly expand the scope of national service.

January 2002
In his State of the Union message, President George W. Bush calls on all American citizens to give 4,000 hours to community service over their lifetimes. He also proposes to expand AmeriCorps by 50 percent to give more Americans a chance to serve.

December 2002
Congress passes defense authorization bill that includes a provision, based on the Bayh-McCain bill, that would allow some military volunteers the option of serving for 18 months in the military and then serving two years in the Peace Corps, one year in AmeriCorps or six years in the inactive reserves.

January 2003
Rep. Charles Rangel, D-N.Y., proposes legislation to reinstate the draft. It is overwhelmingly defeated.

Fall 2003
Democratic presidential candidates Gen. Wesley Clark and Sens. John Kerry, D-Mass., and John Edwards, D-N.C., call for expanding national service, making it a major issue in the Democratic primary debate.

January 2004
Congress gives AmeriCorps a record funding increase to expand to 75,000 members.

2005
Republican Study Committee, a caucus of conservative House members, proposes eliminating Corporation for National and Community Service as part of its $500 billion "Operation Offset" plan to cut spending in order to pay for federal aid following Hurricane Katrina. . . . Rep. Rangel submits new draft bill.

2006
Bush administration proposes eliminating the National Civilian Community Corps (NCCC) and cutting the corporation's budget by $22 million in 2007. A proposal to restore the NCCC cuts is under consideration, but the bill has not yet been debated, and the outcome is unclear. . . . Rep. Rangel again submits a draft bill.

'I Felt Like I Was Entering a War Zone'

Community-service volunteers today range from teenagers to retirees, and the projects they work on are just as varied — from assisting in disaster relief and tutoring schoolchildren to manning food banks and visiting nursing-home residents.

Carrie Ann Smith, 25, a graduate of Buffalo State College, worked as a forest ranger before joining AmeriCorps in upstate New York, where she worked with at-risk youths. After Hurricane Katrina, she volunteered to go to Slidell, La., to assist in the cleanup.

"I can still feel that nervousness, those butterflies of excitement and anxiety, buzzing around in the pit of my stomach the night before we left," she later wrote. "Thirty days of my life was the least I could give, and I would again." [1]

Smith found a landscape of total devastation. "Homes were nothing but standing wreckage. Clothes, drapes and blankets hung randomly in the trees, weighed down by muck and mud. I felt like I was entering a war zone. I felt the pain and frustration that still loomed in the air, but most of all I felt the need to help, to serve and to make a difference."

Naomi Baskin

Retiree Naomi Baskin found her "passion" in tutoring youngsters.

Like many volunteers who left comfortable existences to help disaster victims, Smith came away enriched by the experience and confident that working for AmeriCorps is the right career path. "Being in Louisiana transformed me," she says. "I became a more compassionate and understanding person, and that has benefited me not only in my career but in my personal life as well."

Retiree Naomi Baskin of San Francisco has experienced the same joy of helping others in need.

During her career selling real estate, Baskin envisioned many alluring post-retirement activities, but tutoring underprivileged youths was not one of them. Six years ago, however, she began working with Experience Corps, a nonprofit volunteer program for older Americans.

"I just love it," she says. "I found my passion late in life, and I get far more reward than I give."

Baskin tutors Latino and African-American youngsters from second to eighth grade. "My goal, which is an uphill battle for many of the kids, is to get them to discover the joy of reading," she says. "Those who come from underprivileged homes and whose very struggle is just to survive are the biggest challenge. I want so much to instill in them that the only way to 'break out' is to get an education. My biggest reward is when I get that 'aha' moment. A letter I received from a 10-year-old boy I tutored best illustrates this point. He wrote: 'Ms. Naomi, you make my brain accelerate.' "

Like Baskin, Wash Gjebre, a newspaper reporter, worried about the prospect of having too much free time on his hands after retirement. At a friend's suggestion, he reluctantly joined the local Salvation Army board, only to find that it sparked what he called a "life-altering change."

"Clearly, it's been a transition with a purpose," he said. "I learned later that volunteerism offered a personal fulfillment that would take the ennui out of the empty hours in retirement." [2]

---

[1] www.americorps.gov/for_individuals/current/stories.

[2] Wash Gjebre, "First Person: Doing Unto Others," *The Pittsburgh Post-Gazette*, Nov. 12, 2005.

Continued from p. 586

Various national leaders had hoped to see a much-expanded Peace Corps. Peace Corps co-founder and former U.S. Sen. Harris Wofford, D-Pa., recalls, "In one of his last interviews, Robert Kennedy said he thought the Peace Corps idea should become part of the whole of life, not just a passing episode for a relative handful of people. But no such escalation of the idea has yet been tried." [35]

Wofford and others were elated when Defense Secretary Robert S. McNamara — a leader of what pacifist James would have considered "the war party" — took up the idea of national service. In a 1966 speech, McNamara suggested that the inequity of having only "a minority of eligible young men" drafted into the military could begin to be rectified by "asking every young person in the United States to give two years of service to his country — whether in one of the military services, in the Peace Corps or in some other volunteer developmental work at home or abroad."

But the White House quickly threw cold water on the suggestion and eventually, in Wofford's words, "made it clear that because of the mounting costs of the conflict in Vietnam there would be no money for any such large, new venture." [36]

In the 1980s, many scholars viewed national service as vital to America. Northwestern University sociologist Moskos in 1981 proposed linking federal aid for higher education to a voluntary national service system that would include military-reserve duty or civilian work. "The ideal of citizenship obligation ought to become part of growing up in America," he wrote. University of Chicago sociologist Morris Janowitz argued in a 1984 book that citizen service is necessary to restore the balance between citizenship's rights and obligations, and to rebuild patriotism in modern form. [37]

Others saw national service as a way to instill a sense of civic duty in all Americans. "Military veterans, Peace Corps alumni and, ironically, immigrants, are now virtually the only Americans who experience a sense of citizenship earned rather than simply received," said a 1986 Ford Foundation study conducted by former Carter administration officials Richard Danzig and Peter Szanton. "As a result, they often value themselves and their country more highly. Forms of national service that require sacrifice, intensive effort or some risk might offer that sense to all." [38]

1,000 Points of Light

The next major federal effort toward national service came during the administration of President George H. W. Bush, with passage of a 1990 law creating the 21-member Commission on National and Community Service, an independent, nonpartisan body charged by Congress with supporting and encouraging voluntary national service. According to Professor Paul C. Light of New York University, the first President Bush "launched his 'Points of Light' volunteering initiative in 1989 to call all

Many Nations Offer Service Alternatives

Unlike the United States, many nations require all youths to serve in the military or perform community service. Here is a sampling of some of the programs around the world:

Cyprus — *Military service of 25 months is mandatory for all men ages 18-50. Conscientious objectors can either choose 33 months of unarmed service in the army or 38 months of community work.*

Denmark — *Four months of military service is mandatory for all men 18-27. Conscientious objectors can serve six months dealing with domestic disasters or perform foreign-aid work in a Third World country.*

Finland — *Military service is mandatory for all men for at least six months. Non-military service of 13 months is available for conscientious objectors.*

Germany — *Nine months of military service is mandatory for men 18-23. Conscientious objectors may petition for permission to become foreign-development aides for at least 18 months.*

Jamaica — *The National Youth Service Corps was established in 1973 and re-established in 1995 amid major concerns about the high level of youth unemployment and academic underachievement. The program combines training in career skills, re-socialization and work experience.*

Kenya — *The 42-year-old National Youth Service program has 18 camps across the country where unemployed, unmarried men and women between 18 and 22 serve for two to three years. They receive formal job training aimed at preparing them to join the work force.*

Malaysia — *The National Service Program was created in 2003 to strengthen cultural identity and build national identity among Malaysian youth. More than 80,000 conscripts participate.*

Mexico — *Men 18 years of age must register for military service, lasting one year, with selection made through a lottery system. Those interested in community service can participate in literacy campaigns as teachers, or as physical-education instructors.*

Nigeria — *One-year's participation in a national service program is mandatory for all high school and university graduates.*

Norway — *Military service is mandatory for men 18-44 and lasts 18 months. Pacifists can apply for 13 months of non-military service.*

Papua New Guinea — *After performing civilian service, participants in the National Youth Service may use their service awards to launch micro-enterprise businesses.*

Switzerland — *Military service is obligatory for all men and includes 17 weeks of basic training as well as annual three-week refresher courses. Conscientious objectors can choose 390 days of community service instead of military service.*

Taiwan (Republic of China) — *Military service is mandatory for all men, lasting 16 months. Draftees may also request alternative service, usually in community-service areas, which requires a longer service period.*

Sources: Center for Social Development, George Warren Brown School of Social Work, Washington University; Answers.com

Corporation for National and Community Service (all)

AmeriCorps in Action

In exchange for a year of full-time work or sustained part-time community service, AmeriCorps members receive education awards of up to $4,725 for higher education, job training or to repay student loans. The program is open to Americans 17 and older. ***Top:*** *Members assist at a Habitat for Humanity home site in New Orleans being readied for victims of Hurricane Katrina.* ***Middle:*** *AmeriCorps team members helped this family in Florida while aiding Federal Emergency Management Agency recovery efforts following the hurricanes that hit Florida in 2004.* ***Bottom:*** *Members perform stream clearing and a variety of other environmental tasks.*

Americans, including corporations, schools and places of worship, to claim society's problems as their own and to help solve them." [39]

In 1992, during his successful campaign for president, then Gov. Clinton, D-Ark., enthusiastically endorsed the idea, calling for what he termed a season of service: "Just think of it: millions of energetic young men and women serving their country by teaching children, policing the streets, caring for the sick, working with the elderly or people with disabilities, building homes for the homeless, helping children to stay off drugs and out of gangs — giving us all a real sense of home and limitless possibilities." [40]

Clinton's new program called for paying the young volunteers to help them afford college or job training, but Congress approved only half of what the president had sought.

President George W. Bush followed with his own largely unexpected endorsement of national service in 2002. As journalist Richard Just later wrote, "In a political masterstroke, Bush surprised his critics, and many supporters, by proposing an even wider-ranging plan to support and expand national service. . . . Freedom Corps was one of the most well received policies put forth in Bush's address." [41]

Bush's plan sought to increase the ranks of service groups like AmeriCorps by 200,000 young men and women. He also called on all Americans to serve. "My call tonight is for every American to commit at least two years — 4,000 hours over the rest of your lifetime — to the service of your neighbors and your nation."

It was an effort, as Bush put it, "to sustain and extend the best that has emerged in America." Bush created the U.S.A. Freedom Corps to act as a clearinghouse to match up thousands of expected new volunteers with the thousands of new volunteer opportunities Bush promised to create by expanding AmeriCorps, the Peace Corps and the Senior Corps. [42]

When Bush made his own call for national service, there already existed a solid network of federal and community-based programs providing volunteer services and opportunities. Several of the programs, such as the Peace Corps, ACTION, VISTA and the Job Corps, were remnants of President Lyndon B. Johnson's Great Society programs of the 1960s. But under President Bush, the Corporation for National and Community Service has greatly expanded its faith-based programs.

The corporation "is committed to President Bush's initiative to strengthen the work of faith-based and small community organizations, which provide compassionate care to millions of Americans," it reported in 2004. "These organizations effectively tackle some of our nation's most intractable problems. In doing so, they turn around individuals' lives and give hope to countless communities in need." [43] ■

Tutoring Is Most Popular AmeriCorps Job

Nearly 90 percent of AmeriCorps members from State and National programs and the National Civilian Community Corps (NCCC) tutored or mentored, reflecting the program's commitment to children. NCCC members generally do more physical activities, such as cleaning trails and construction work.

Tasks Performed by AmeriCorps Members
(By percentage participating)

Task	State and National (%)	NCCC (%)
Tutor, mentor or take care of children, teens or adults	82.3%	88.4%
Clean trails or do other environmental work	62.4	97.3
Organize or do administrative work for programs that help needy individuals	59.1	55.1
Help renovate, construct or clean offices or buildings for needy people	49.4	86.8
Help care for sick, elderly or homeless people	42.6	66.8
Work involving disaster relief	---	29.5

Source: Corporation for National and Community Service, "Serving Country and Community: A Longitudinal Study of Service in AmeriCorps," December 2004

CURRENT SITUATION

Expanding AmeriCorps

Whenever he flies into any American city, President Bush has a ritual: As soon as he descends from Air Force One, he greets and publicly recognizes a local volunteer. He's met more than 465 volunteers since March 2002, reinforcing one of the few beliefs that he shares with former President Clinton: the importance of national service. [44]

Bush has expanded AmeriCorps, the mainstay of the Clinton-created Corporation for National and Community Service, by half — to 75,000 new volunteers each year. Under Bush, the corporation has a goal of increasing the number of Americans who volunteer to 75 million by 2010, from about 65.4 million today. [45]

In 2002 Bush created a new White House office, the U.S.A. Freedom Corps, to encourage Americans to volunteer. And he signed a law in 2003 — the National Call to Service Initiative — that allowed military recruits to enlist for 18 months, rather than the typical four years, followed by a period of service in AmeriCorps. Some 4,300 recruits had taken advantage of the shorter enlistments through the end of fiscal 2005, according to the Department of Defense. A spokeswoman, Lt. Col. Ellen Krenke, says the Pentagon is aiming to enlist 4,000 more recruits through the program and that the department has been pleased with the results, despite at first resisting the idea.

"The department considers this program a valuable tool in the mix of enlistment options," she said.

Congress sidestepped a minor flap over the military recruitment program last February, when it blocked efforts to expand the call-to-service option to allow recruits to finish their commitments in the Peace Corps rather than AmeriCorps. Peace Corps officials had worried that their agency would be perceived as being connected to the military. [46]

Yet the idea of federal government investments in community service remains controversial. "There's a hard core of Republicans who have always looked askance at the idea," says Will Marshall, president of the Progressive Policy Institute, who helped Clinton develop his national service agenda in the early 1990s.

Budget Cuts

This year, the debate over federal volunteer programs has become entwined with the ongoing recovery from Hurricane Katrina.

Last September, the Republican Study Committee, a caucus of conservative House members, proposed eliminating the Corporation for National and Community Service as part of its $500 billion "Operation Offset" plan to cut spending in order to pay for federal aid to Katrina victims. Cutting the corporation would have saved $3 billion over five years and $6.5 billion over 10 years. [47]

In May, the Senate rejected an attempt by Sen. John Thune, R-S.D., to divert $20 million from the corporation's NCCC program in order to boost spending on veterans' health programs. NCCC advocates said the money was needed to pay volunteers assisting with Katrina recovery efforts in New Orleans. [48]

Despite his verbal support for national service programs, President Bush — constrained by the expenses of both the war in the Middle East and Hurricane Katrina — had not only proposed eliminating the NCCC in his fiscal 2007 budget but also proposed cutting the corporation's budget by $22 million in 2007.

CEO Eisner said the agency was "disappointed" but that the bill is "one step in a long process." [49] House appropriators chose to preserve the NCCC however, cutting other service programs instead. [50]

And despite the looming budget cuts, overall spending on federal service programs such as AmeriCorps has grown about 17 percent since Bush took office.

In June, the House Appropriations Committee cut funding for the Corporation for National and Community Service even deeper than Bush proposed: 9 percent, to $822.9 million.

Service Learning and the Draft

Compulsory service for high-school students, known as service learning, has not gained traction in Congress, though it has gained popularity in schools across the country. Service learning is a teaching method that engages young people in solving problems within their schools and communities as part of their academic studies or other type of intentional learning activity. One state (Maryland), the District of Columbia and school districts around the nation (as well as many colleges and universities) now require students to perform from 20 to 100 hours as a volunteer during their school career in order to graduate.

"There is a growing momentum to require service learning — not just service alone — across the nation," says Sarah Pearson, a senior program associate at the American Youth Policy Forum.

But Pearson worries that the No Child Left Behind (NCLB) law has discouraged many schools from pursuing service learning. "The NCLB juggernaut has literally scared schools into improving student academic performance by placing a clear emphasis on raising literacy and math skills and de-emphasizing service learning and subjects like art, history and civics," she says. "Schools could creatively use service learning to improve students' interest in reading and math, but I don't know if schools have recovered from the stresses of NCLB yet to take a more creative approach to learning."

American Red Cross/Daniel Cima

An American Red Cross volunteer hands out drinks to emergency workers in New York City after the Sept. 11, 2001, terrorist attacks. More than 1 million Americans volunteer for the Red Cross.

Given the nation's general attitudes about service, compulsory national service most likely would take the form of a military draft. During the 2004 presidential campaign, rumors that the government would revive the military draft if Bush were re-elected spread through the Internet, based largely on Rep. Rangel's controversial 2003 legislation to revive the draft. The rumors became so widespread the White House was forced to officially deny them, and the House eventually called Rangel's measure up for a vote, just so the rumor could be laid to rest. The measure was defeated 402 to 2 on Oct. 5, 2004. Reps. Pete Stark, D-Calif., and John P. Murtha, D-Pa., were the only members in favor. Even Rangel voted against his own bill, calling the GOP's tactic "a prostitution of the legislative process." [51]

Continued on p. 594

At Issue:

Should military or civilian service be required?

ROBERT E. LITAN
DIRECTOR, ECONOMIC STUDIES PROGRAM, BROOKINGS INSTITUTION

FROM "THE OBLIGATIONS OF SEPT. 11, 2001" *

yes

Though one good reason for adopting universal service now is to respond to the military and homeland threat, universal service makes sense in other ways in this time of national peril.

First, universal service could provide some much-needed "social glue" in an embattled American society that is growing increasingly diverse — by race, national origin and religious preference — and where many young Americans from well-to-do families grow up and go to school in hermetically sealed social environments.

A service program in which young people from different backgrounds work and live together would do far more than college ever could to immerse young Americans in the diversity of our country. It would also help sensitize more fortunate young men and women to the concerns and experiences of others from different backgrounds and give them an enduring appreciation of what life is like "on the other side of the tracks."

Second, universal service could promote civic engagement, which Harvard social scientist Robert Putnam has persuasively argued in *Bowling Alone*, has been declining — or at least was before Sept. 11. Some who perform service for the required period may believe their civic responsibilities will thereby be discharged, but many others are likely to develop an appreciation for helping others that could change the way they lead the rest of their lives.

Third, young people serving in a civilian capacity in particular would help satisfy unmet social needs beyond those associated with homeland security: improving the reading skills of tens of millions of Americans who cannot now read English at a high-school level; cleaning up blighted neighborhoods and helping provide social, medical and other services to the elderly and low-income individuals and families.

Finally, universal service would establish firmly the notion that rights for ourselves come with responsibilities to others. Of course, the Constitution guarantees all citizens certain rights — free speech, due process of law, freedom from discrimination, voting — without asking anything of them in return. But why shouldn't citizens be required to give something to their country in exchange for the full range of rights to which citizenship entitles them?

BRUCE CHAPMAN
PRESIDENT AND CEO, THE DISCOVERY INSTITUTE

FROM "A BAD IDEA WHOSE TIME HAS PASSED" *

no

Universal service never was a good idea, and it grows worse with time. It fails militarily, morally, financially and politically.

For almost a century, universal service has brought forth new advocates, each desiring to enlist all youth in something. Only the justifications keep changing. Today's justification is "homeland security." But is it realistic to suggest that youth who help guard a public or private facility (let alone those who stuff envelopes at some charity's office) are "shouldering the burden of war" in the same way as a solider in Afghanistan?

Except in times of mass conflict, such as the Civil War and the two world wars, there has never been much of a reason for universal service.

We eliminated the draft three decades ago in part because the armed services found that they needed relatively fewer recruits to serve longer than conscription provided. As the numbers that were needed shrank, the unfairness of the draft became ever more apparent — and offensive. Youth, ever ingenious, found ways to get deferments, decamp to Canada. Many of the young people who objected to military service availed themselves of alternative service, but no one seriously believed that most conscientious objectors were shouldering the burden of war in a way comparable to those fighting in the field.

Trying to justify universal service on moral grounds is also a mistake, and a serious one. Morally, service isn't service to the extent it is compelled. Advocates such as Litan are on especially shaky ground when charging that citizens should be "required to give something to their country in exchange for the full range of rights to which citizenship entitles them." This cuts against the grain of U.S. history and traditions. To require such service before the rights of citizenship are extended is simply contrary to the purposes for which the country was founded and has endured.

The way to get a nation of volunteers is to showcase voluntary service, praise it, reward it and revere it. The way to sabotage voluntary service is to coerce it, bureaucratize it, nationalize it, cloak it in political correctness and pay for it to the point where the "volunteer" makes out better than the poor soul of the same age who works for a living. Universal service would be a civic virtue perverted into a civic vice.

* Both excerpts adapted from E.J. Dionne Jr., Kayla Meltzer Drogosz and Robert E. Litan, eds., *United We Serve: National Service and the Future of Citizenship* (2003); reprinted with permission of the Brookings Institution Press.

Continued from p. 592

The draft rumors prompted House Majority Leader Tom DeLay, R-Texas, to charge, "This campaign is a baseless and malevolent concoction of the Democrat Party, and everyone in this chamber knows it. It has one purpose — to spread fear. To spread fear among an unsuspecting public, to undermine the War on Terror, to undermine our troops, to undermine our cause, and most of all, to undermine our commander in chief in an election year." [52]

Administration officials including President Bush and Defense Secretary Donald H. Rumsfeld said they have absolutely no plans to restore the draft and believe that the all-volunteer military is the proper way to field troops." [53]

"We will not have a draft so long as I'm the president of the United States," Bush told a cheering crowd in Iowa. "We do not need a draft," Rumsfeld said during a radio interview with Sean Hannity. "We've got, you know, 295 million people in this country and we have an active force of about 1.4 million and we are having no trouble at all attracting and retaining the people that we need to serve in the Armed Forces." [54]

Jean-Christian Bourcart

A Teach for America volunteer works on a project with sixth-grade science students in New York City.

The country's lack of support for a draft, though, raises questions by some researchers about the public's true commitment to service. "Americans are always for national service — except when we are not," Brookings Institution scholars wrote in a 2003 paper on national service. Citing debate over the draft, they asked, "How firm is our belief in service?" [55]

In May 2005 Rangel introduced a bill that would require all Americans between ages 18-26 to perform 15 months of service in the military or in a national-defense-related civilian position. But Stark is his only co-sponsor, and the measure has been given no attention by the Republican-controlled House Armed Services Committee, where it now awaits action. [56]

In 2006 Rangel introduced a new version of his universal service bill, which would require two years of service, not 15 months. [57] "Our military is more like a mercenary force than a citizen militia," he said as he introduced the measure. "It is dominated by men and women who need an economic leg-up. I don't expect my bill to pass; my purpose in introducing this legislation is for it to serve as a constant reminder that we have lost 2,200 of the best, brightest and bravest Americans, have had thousands more maimed and countless Iraqi citizens killed. As the president speaks of a national response involving the military option, military service should be a shared sacrifice.

"Right now, the only people being asked to sacrifice in any way are those men and women who with limited options chose military service and now find themselves in harm's way in Iraq. A draft would ensure that every economic group would have to do their share, and not allow some to stay behind while other people's children do the fighting.

"I dare anyone to try to convince me that this war is not being fought predominantly by tough, loyal and patriotic young men and women from the barren hills and towns of rural and underprivileged neighborhoods in urban America where unemployment is high and opportunities are few." [58] ■

OUTLOOK

If the Democrats Win

Advocates of national service say it would get a boost if the Democrats regain control of the House or the Senate (or both) this November — or if they win back the White House in 2008.

Traditionally, Democrats have supported national service and Republicans have opposed it. But there have been exceptions. Republican Rep. Shays is among Congress' strongest advocates of national service, and President Bush has been very supportive, though less noticeably in recent years.

As the first CEO of the Corporation for National and Community Service, Peace Corps co-founder Wofford takes a long view of national service. "There are lots of effort currently to get the [national service] rocket going up again," he says. As for the fate of funding for the NCCC, Wofford says, "all signs are good in the Senate," but, he adds, "a good fight is better than no fight at all."

Wofford likes to remind people that the idea for the NCCC was left over from the administration of the first President Bush and that Clinton pushed it after he was elected.

"It was the first piece of Clinton-proposed legislation to pass," Wofford says, adding that he thinks there are more Republicans in favor of national service than is generally believed to be the case.

John Gomperts, CEO of the Experience Corps, agrees. He was Wofford's top aide at the Corporation for National and Community Service. "President George W. Bush has actually been quite supportive, and he actually helped national service grow some, but it was never at the center of what he is all about. For the idea to really take wing, it has to be closer to the heart of what the country's leader really thinks and cares about."

"I think the nation likes the idea," of AmeriCorps, says Wofford, adding that Gallup polls consistently show support for it. But most Americans don't know enough about what it does. When he held a focus group with young Americans several years ago, they were surprised to learn that far more young people had served in AmeriCorps than in the Peace Corps over its long history. *

"They almost got angry about it and wanted to know why we didn't tell them that!" says Wofford, adding that AmeriCorps is "doing better and better with college students."

As CEO of Youth Service America, a national resource center for community service, Steven A. Culbertson plays a key role in helping to expand the impact of the youth service movement. In a letter to Corporation for National and Community Service Chairman Eisner, Culbertson noted, "We have worked to make service to others the common expectation and common experience of all young Americans. We know that most of the adults who volunteer in the United States . . . had their first experience when they were children." [59]

* To date, about 400,000 men and women have served in AmeriCorps and about 182,000 in the Peace Corps.

Indeed, Culbertson said on Global Youth Service Day last April, "Young people are powerful change makers around the world. They possess the energy and ingenuity to help tackle the world's most complex problems, which make them assets and resources for our communities." [60] ■

Notes

[1] Quoted in Mike Leverton, "AmeriCorps Experience Exhilarating," *The Monroe* (Wis.) *Times*, Feb. 16, 2006, p. 1.

[2] For background see Sarah Glazer, "Faith-Based Initiatives," *CQ Researcher*, May 4, 2001, pp. 377-400.

[3] Margaret Carlson, "All Together Now — Think national service just means singing Kumbaya? Bush knows better," *Time*, Feb. 11, 2002, p. 33.

[4] Katie Crumley, "Whatever Happened to Bush's Call for Service," *The Minnesota Daily*, March 1, 2006.

[5] "Rangle Calls for Mandatory Military Draft," CNN.com, Dec. 30, 2002.

[6] Motoko Rich, "Clinton Plans to Write a Book about Activism and Service," *The New York Times*, May 18, 2006, p. A24.

[7] David Nakamura, "Bushes Banter for GWU Grads," *The Washington Post*, May 22, 2006, p. B3.

[8] Michael Tomasky, "Party in Search of a Notion," *The American Prospect*, May 2006, p. 20.

[9] Jim McCarthy, "BHS Student Takes Lead in Revamping Community Service Policy," *Brunswick Times-Record*, May 16, 2006.

[10] "House Opposes Military Draft Bill," Fox News, Oct. 6, 2004.

[11] Quoted in Melissa Bass, "National Service in America: Policy (Dis)Connections Over Time," *CIRCLE Working Paper 11*, October 2003, www.civicyouth.org.

[12] Kelly Beaucar Vlahos, "AmeriCorps on the Chopping Block," Fox News, March 20, 2006.

[13] Sean M. Harris, "Serving Up a Different System," *Current*, Dec. 5, 2005.

[14] Vlahos, *op. cit.*

[15] Ben Schiffrin, "Recent Developments, Universal National Service Act," *Harvard Journal of Legislation*, winter 2004, p. 337.

[16] Gary L. Yates, President and CEO, *California Wellness Foundation News*, Feb. 1, 2002.

[17] "Antiwar Democrat pushes again for military draft," The Associated Press, May 27, 2005.

[18] Stanley Kunitz, "Think ROTC," *The National Review Online*, Jan. 9, 2003.

[19] Alan Cooperman, "Congress Moves to Underline the 'Peace' in Peace Corps," *The Washington Post*, Feb. 17, 2006, p. A17.

[20] The NCCC bases are in Perry Point, Md.; Sacramento, Calif.; Washington, D.C.; Charleston, S.C.; and Denver.

[21] Letter, March 16, 2006.

[22] "U.S. Representative Christopher Shays Honored by Voices for National Service in Recognition of His Leadership of National Service," www.house.gov/shays/news/2006/february.

[23] "Message on Fiscal year 2007 from David Eisner, CEO, Corporation for National and Community Service," Feb. 6, 2006.

[24] Vlahos, *op. cit.*

[25] AmeriCorps National Civilian Community Corps Assessment, ExpectMore.gov, March 2006.

[26] Bruce Chapman, "A Bad Idea Whose Time Has Passed: The Case against Universal Service," in *United We Serve: National Service and the Future of Citizenship* (2003), p. 111.

[27] Sara Helms, "Involuntary Volunteering: The Impact of Mandated Service in Public Schools," unpublished dissertation, University of Maryland, College Park, June 2006.

[28] Quoted in "What You Can Do For Your Country," a report by the Commission on National and Community Service, Jan. 19, 1993, p. 48. For background, see Marc Leepson, "National Service," *CQ Researcher*, June 25, 1993, pp. 553-576.

[29] Charles Moskos, *A Call to Civic Service: National Service for Country and Community* (1988).

[30] *Ibid.*

[31] Quoted in *Gratitude: Reflections on What We Owe to Our Country* (1990).

[32] See B. W. Patch, "Compulsory Labor Service," *Editorial Research Reports*, Feb. 17, 1942, available at *CQ Researcher Plus Archive*, CQ Electronic Library, http://library.cqpress.com.

[33] For background, see F. P. Huddle, "Universal Military Service," *Editorial Research Reports*, April 15, 1944, available at *CQ Researcher Plus Archive*, CQ Electronic Library, http://library.cqpress.com.

[34] *Ibid.*

[35] Harris Wofford, *Of Kennedys and Kings* (1993), pp. 456-457.

[36] *Ibid.*

[37] Quoted in R. K. Landers, "Blueprints for National Service," in *Editorial Research Reports, 1986* (Vol. II), available in *CQ Researcher Plus Archives*, CQ Electronic Library.

[38] Richard Danzig and Peter Szanton, *National Service: What Would It Mean?* (1986), p. 277.

Danzig was principal deputy assistant Defense secretary for manpower and logistics during the Carter administration; Szanton was an associate director of the Office of Management and Budget.

[39] Paul C. Light, "The Volunteering Decision: What Prompts It? What Sustains It?" *The Brookings Review*, fall 2002, p. 46.

[40] William J. Clinton, Acceptance Speech to the Democratic National Convention, New York, N.Y., July 16, 1992; www.americanpresidents.org/presidents/president.asp?PresidentNumber=41.

[41] Richard Just, "Whatever Happened to National Service?" *The Washington Monthly*, March 2003.

[42] Quoted in *Ibid.*

[43] "Faith-based and Community Initiatives," *Issue Brief*, Corporation for National and Community Service, June 2004.

[44] USA Freedom Corps, "About USA Freedom Corps," www.usafreedomcorpos.gov/about_usafc/call/index.asp.

[45] Corporation for National and Community Service, "Volunteering in America: State Trends and Rankings, 2002-2005," June 2006.

[46] Cooperman, *op. cit.*

[47] Republican Study Committee, "Operation Offset: RSC Budget Options 2005," Sept. 22, 2005.

[48] Liriel Higa and Anne Plummer, "Senate Supplemental Fattened Up," *CQ Weekly*, May 8, 2006, p. 1236.

[49] Corporation for National and Community Service, "CEO Message on House Subcommittee Action on Fiscal Year 2007 National Service Budget;" nationalservice.gov/about/newsroom/statements_detail.asp?tbl_pr_id=394.

[50] Michael Teitelbaum, "Hits for Service Programs, One Targeted for Elimination," *CQ Today*, Feb. 6, 2006.

[51] John M. Donnelly, "House Bill to Bring Back the Draft Inspires Nothing but Political Crossfire," *CQ Today*, Oct. 5, 2004.

[52] Quoted on FoxNews.com, "House Opposes Military Draft Bill" Oct. 2, 2004.

[53] Carl Hulse, "Bill to Restore the Draft Is Defeated in the House," *The New York Times*, Oct. 5, 2004, p. A16.

[54] *Ibid.*

[55] E.J. Dionne, Jr. and Kayla Meltzer Drogosz, "The Promise of National Service: A (Very) Brief History of an Idea," *The Brookings Institution Policy Brief No. 120*, June 2003.

[56] "Universal National Service Act of 2005," introduced May 26, 2005.

[57] HR 4752, "Universal National Service Act of 2006," introduced Feb. 14, 2006.

FOR MORE INFORMATION

American Red Cross, 2025 E St., N.W., Washington, DC 20006; (202) 303-4498; www.redcross.org. Volunteers provide disaster relief and medical services to victims around the world.

AmeriCorps, 1201 New York Ave., N.W., Washington, DC 20525; (202) 606-5000; www.americorps.org. Funnels volunteers to more than 3,000 nonprofits, public agencies and faith-based and community organizations across the country.

Experience Corps, 2120 L St., N.W., Washington, DC 20037; (202) 478-6190; www.experiencecorps.org. Volunteer organization for Americans over age 55 who tutor children in inner-city schools.

National Service-Learning Partnership, 1825 Connecticut Ave., N.W., Suite 800, Washington, DC 20009-5721; (202) 884-8356; www.service-learningpartnership.org. Based at the Academy for Educational Development, the partnership is dedicated to advancing service learning as a core part of every young person's education.

Peace Corps, 1111 20th St., N.W., Washington, DC 20526; 1 (800) 424-8580; www.peacecorps.gov. Volunteers work on education, youth outreach and community development, the environment and information technology in 71 countries.

Salvation Army, 615 Slaters Lane, P.O. Box 269, Alexandria, VA 22313; www.salvationarmyusa.org. Provides assistance including disaster-relief services, day-care centers, summer camps, holiday assistance, services for the aging, AIDS education and substance-abuse rehabilitation.

United Peace Relief, P.O. Box 933, Ukiah, CA 95482; (707) 462-2439; www.unitedpeacerelief.org. Responds to disasters with conventional and alternative medical and humanitarian relief.

U.S.A. Freedom Corps, 1600 Pennsylvania Ave., N.W., Washington, DC 20500; 1 (877) 872-2677; www.usafreedomcorps.gov. Partners with national service programs to place interested individuals in service projects across the country.

Youth Service America, 1101 15th St., Suite 200, Washington, DC 20005; (202) 296-2992; www.ysa.org. Partners with other organizations to involve youths in service projects.

About the Author

John Greenya is a freelance writer in Washington, D.C., who has written for *The Washington Post, New Republic, New York Times* and other publications. He has taught writing at The George Washington University and is the author of several books, including *Silent Justice: The Clarence Thomas Story* and *P.S. A Memoir*, written with the late Pierre Salinger. He holds a B.A. in English and history from Marquette University and an M.A. in English from The Catholic University.

[58] From a statement issued Feb. 14 when he re-introduced his national service bill.

[59] Letter from Steven A. Culbertson, president & CEO, Youth Service America, to David Eisner, Chief Executive Officer, Corporation for National and Community Service, Oct. 12, 2004.

[60] Quoted in "Young People Around the World Stand Up and Take Action for the 7th Annual Global Youth Service Day, April 21-23, 2006, press release, www.ysa.org.

Bibliography

Selected Sources

Books

Buckley, William F., *Gratitude: Reflections on What We Owe to Our Country*, Random House, 1990.
Buckley contends that young people should be encouraged through various rewards and sanctions to give a year of service out of gratitude for the civil liberties they have inherited.

Byron, William J., *Quadrangle Considerations*, Loyola University Press, 1989.
A former president of Catholic University presents the pros and cons of national service and discusses its future.

Chapman, Bruce, *Wrong Man in Uniform: Our Unfair and Obsolete Draft and How We Can Replace It*, Trident Press, 1967.
The co-founder and director of the Discovery Institute opposes both the draft and national service.

Coles, Robert, *The Call of Service: A Witness to Idealism*, Houghton Mifflin, 1993.
A Harvard psychiatrist and advocate for civil and children's rights examines volunteerism in literature while recounting the experiences of a lifetime given to volunteering.

Dionne, E.J., Jr., Kayla Meltzer Drogosz, and Robert E. Litan, eds., *United We Serve: National Service and the Future of Citizenship*, Brookings Institution Press, 2003.
Essays from a wide range of scholars, public officials and educators explore the pros and cons of national service.

Danzig, Richard, and Peter Szanton, *National Service: What Would It Mean?* Lexington, 1986.
Former Carter administration officials contend that national service could instill a sense of civic duty in all Americans.

Moskos, Charles C., *A Call to Civic Service*, Free Press, 1988.
A military sociologist at Northwestern University argues the nation needs more individual service instead of a government-led national service program.

Olasky, Marvin, *The Tragedy of American Compassion*, Regnery, 1993.
A professor of history and journalism at the University of Texas argues that care for the poor should be the responsibility of private individuals and organizations.

Wofford, Harris, *Of Kennedys and Kings*, University of Pittsburgh Press, 1992.
The co-founder of the Peace Corps and the first CEO of the Corporation for National and Community Service describes the basis of modern thinking on national service.

Articles

Bandow, Doug, "National Service: The Enduring Panacea," *Cato Policy Analysis No. 130*, March 22, 1990.
A long-time opponent of national service argues that we need "service," not "national service."

Broder, David, "Hard-Line Hostility for a Volunteer Initiative," *The Washington Post*, Sept. 4, 2002, p. A21.
The veteran *Washington Post* political reporter explains "why it is so stunning that the Citizen Service Act, which would reform and expand the main volunteer-community programs, is being blocked by the House Republican leadership, apparently to spare a minority of hard-core conservatives from having to vote on the measure before Election Day."

Bumiller, Elizabeth, "Bush Urges Graduates to Volunteer in Community Service," *The New York Times*, May 22, 2005, p. 15.
Reports of the protests at Calvin College during a commencement address by President George W. Bush underscored the small but growing voice of the Christian left.

Bush, George W., "Heal The World, Be A Volunteer," *Parade Magazine*, April 21, 2002, p. 14.
The president explains why he values volunteer national service and repeats his call to take part.

Just, Richard, "Whatever Happened to National Service? How a Bush Policy Pledge Quietly Disappeared," *The Washington Monthly*, March 2003.
Just tries to explain why an issue "championed by a popular wartime president, favored by the vast majority of Americans and supported by both parties has floundered so badly."

Lawrence, Stratton, "Americut?" *Charleston City Paper*, March 29, 2006, p. 1.
The author explores what could happen to volunteerism if the Bush administration's cuts in the AmeriCorps budget are not restored, suggesting they "could not come at a worse time."

Reports and Studies

Department of Labor, Bureau of Labor Statistics, "Volunteering the United States," Dec. 9, 2005; www.bls.gov/cps/.
Contains data on U.S. volunteering — defined as "persons who did unpaid work (except for expenses) through or for an organization." About 65.4 million people volunteered through or for an organization at least once between September 2004 and September 2005; the proportion of the population that volunteered was 28.8 percent, the same as in each of the prior two years.

The Next Step:

Additional Articles from Current Periodicals

AmeriCorps

Brodeur, Nicole, "Troubled Teens Find Purpose," *The Seattle Times*, May 17, 2005, p. B1.

City Year, part of the AmeriCorps national-service network, pairs troubled middle-schoolers with Corps members, who help the children with academics, anger management and conflict resolution.

Lee, Christopher, "AmeriCorps Civilian Program Faces $22 Million Budget Cut," *The Washington Post*, Feb. 28, 2006, p. A13.

President Bush says AmeriCorps' National Civilian Community Corps is "ineffective" and wants to shut it down.

Steele, Jeffrey, "Piling Up Good Will, Not Debts," *Chicago Tribune*, Sept. 18, 2005, p. 7.

Many graduate students look to AmeriCorps as a way to help finance their education.

Experience Corps

Rosen, Ruth, "Share Your Experience," *The San Francisco Chronicle*, May 24, 2004, p. B7.

The majority of Experience Corps volunteers who help struggling children to read are African-Americans who feel connected to their neighborhoods and want to help the next generation succeed.

"Grandparents Helping in the Classroom," *The Christian Science Monitor*, March 9, 2006, p. 8.

Students from six Baltimore schools tutored by Experience Corps volunteers had higher reading scores than their peers who did not receive the assistance and fewer misbehavior referrals, according to a study by the Johns Hopkins Center on Aging and Health.

Vitez, Michael, "Pioneered in Philadelphia, A Reading Program May Help Redefine How America Views Aging," *The Philadelphia Inquirer*, May 11, 2006, p. R1.

Experience Corps was pioneered in Philadelphia and now helps thousands of children in 14 cities, including children in 40 Philadelphia schools.

Mandatory Service

Asimov, Nanette, "Governor Taps Predecessor's Idea," *The San Francisco Chronicle*, July 31, 2004, p. A12.

Republican Gov. Arnold Schwarzenegger and his California Performance Review team want to institute mandatory community service for public college students.

Eisner, Jane, "To Make Us Stronger," *The Philadelphia Inquirer*, May 30, 2004, p. C1.

Eisner contends that requiring youths to perform two years of national service would help with national defense at home and bring Americans together.

Loth, Renee, "Patriotism Redefined," *The Boston Globe*, Aug. 10, 2004, p. A19.

Loth argues that Americans should enact universal national service, which appeals to both conservatives and liberals.

Post-Katrina Efforts

Gillum, Jack, "College Grads Going to 'Work' For New Orleans," *USA Today*, June 19, 2006, p. D6.

Many recent college graduates are forgoing jobs to volunteer in New Orleans.

Leiser, Ken, "AmeriCorps Steps Up, Digs In," *St. Louis Post-Dispatch*, Jan. 23, 2006, p. A1.

Members of the St. Louis-based AmeriCorps emergency response team are helping residents in Pass Christian, Miss., clean up after Katrina destroyed three-quarters of the town's homes and businesses.

Nolan, Bruce, "Student Aid Takes on New Meaning in New Orleans," *The Houston Chronicle*, March 25, 2006, p. 1.

College students from around the country are volunteering to help residents in New Orleans recover from Hurricane Katrina.

Rosen, David S., "Fort Bend Volunteers Build Habitat House," *The Houston Chronicle*, Nov. 10, 2005, p. 1.

More than 100 employees of Houston-based Tyco affiliates are building a new house in the city for Habitat for Humanity after being inspired by recent disasters like Hurricane Katrina.

Simmons, Amy M., "Hurricane Alters Tulane Graduates' Paths," *Los Angeles Times*, May 12, 2006, p. A5.

Tulane University students displaced by Hurricane Katrina have been inspired to volunteer since returning, helping with the cleanup of Katrina debris, tutoring local high-school students and making plans to join Teach for America or AmeriCorps.

Schools and Services

"Louisiana's Governor Calls For a Student 'Summer of Service,' " *The Houston Chronicle*, Jan. 28, 2006, p. B8.

Gov. Kathleen Blanco, D-La., pledged to join forces with faith groups, Habitat for Humanity and other volunteer organizations to encourage college students nationwide to come and help with reconstruction efforts in the state.

Bombardieri, Marcella, "At Tufts, Civic Engagement Stretches Across the Globe," *The Boston Globe*, March 14, 2004, p. C1.

Tufts University's College of Citizenship and Public Service is one of the most ambitious attempts by a research university to make public service part of its core academic mission.

Labbe, Theola S., "Volunteers Sign Up For Youth Service Day," ***The Washington Post*****, March 17, 2005, p. T3.**
Thousands of Washington, D.C., students from elementary school to college will plant trees, visit nursing homes and read to children during National Youth Service Day.

Loller, Travis, "TSU Project Combines Service Projects, Learning," Tennessean.com, June 15, 2006.
Tennessee State University's new Center for Service Learning and Civic Engagement is leading the way in a growing trend to integrate community service and academics in the state.

Soler, Eileen, "Teens Earn Points By Caring For Homeless Animals," ***The Miami Herald*****, May 20, 2004, p. 1.**
Students in Broward County can satisfy their mandatory community service requirement through a new program at the Humane Society that lets them help homeless animals at the society or on outside, self-directed projects.

Teach for America

Lewin, Tamar, "Options Open, Top Graduates Line Up to Teach to the Poor," ***The New York Times*****, Oct. 2, 2005, p. 1.**
Ivy league graduates are applying in droves to Teach for America, a program that places recent grads into poor schools to teach for two years; 12 percent of Yale's graduates and 8 percent of Harvard's and Princeton's applied in 2005.

Pope, Justin, "Teaching Program is Luring in More College Graduates," ***The Houston Chronicle*****, June 18, 2006, p. A6.**
Nearly 19,000 college seniors applied to Teach for America this year, and more than four in five were rejected.

Woodall, Martha, "A 5-Week Boot Camp For Aspiring Teachers," ***The Philadelphia Inquirer*****, Aug. 1, 2005, p. B1.**
Hundreds of recent college grads recently completed Teach for America's intensive summer training institute at Temple University, learning methods, techniques and educational theories to prepare for teaching special-education students.

Volunteerism

Gergen, David, "Teaching For A Better America," ***The Boston Globe*****, Oct. 22, 2005, p. A15.**
Experience is showing that the most valuable contribution Teach for America volunteers make comes after they finish their service: Sixty percent of alums still work fulltime in education, and half work with low-income communities.

MacDonald, G. Jeffrey, "On A Mission — A Short-Term Mission," ***USA Today*****, June 19, 2006, p. D6.**
Critics say short-term mission trips can be counterproductive, with untrained missionaries offending indigenous populations and undermining hard-earned relationships.

Nigel, Duara, "Vilsack Congratulates Iowa's Volunteers," ***Des Moines Register*****, June 13, 2006, p. B5.**
Four states in the Midwest topped a Corporation for National and Community Service study ranking state's on their populations' volunteer participation; Utah came in first with 48 percent of residents volunteering.

Portillo, Ely, and Sadia Latifi, "U.S. Volunteerism is Flat, Survey Says," ***The Miami Herald*****, June 13, 2006, p. A6.**
The rate at which Americans volunteer has remained flat at 28.8 percent since 2002, or an average of 50 hours per year, according to a new study by the Corporation for National and Community Service.

Tighe, Theresa, "As Volunteers Age, Charities Are Finding Fewer and Fewer Young Replacements," ***St. Louis Post-Dispatch*****, Dec. 2, 2005, p. D9.**
Several charities in St. Louis are struggling to find younger volunteers to replace aging help.

Woodall, Martha, "City's Schools to Get Extra Summer Help," ***The Philadelphia Inquirer*****, Jan. 13, 2005, p. B3.**
Teach for America will move its Northeast summer training camp from New York City to Philadelphia, bringing 750 prospective teachers to the area.

Citing *CQ Researcher*

Sample formats for citing these reports in a bibliography include the ones listed below. Preferred styles and formats vary, so please check with your instructor or professor.

MLA Style

Jost, Kenneth. "Rethinking the Death Penalty." CQ Researcher 16 Nov. 2001: 945-68.

APA Style

Jost, K. (2001, November 16). Rethinking the death penalty. *CQ Researcher, 11*, 945-968.

Chicago Style

Jost, Kenneth. "Rethinking the Death Penalty." *CQ Researcher*, November 16, 2001, 945-968.

CQ Researcher

Published by CQ Press, a division of Congressional Quarterly Inc.

cqresearcher.com

Change in Latin America

Are anti-U.S. sentiments on the rise?

Winds of discontent are again blowing through Latin America, threatening U.S. influence in the region. Washington promoted political and economic transformations that swept the continent in the 1990s, but the resulting leap from dictatorship to democracy has left many political and governmental institutions weak. And despite promises of expanded opportunities, some 70 percent of the region's 500 million people live on $300 a month or less. Income inequality between rich and poor is stark, and growing. Stoking the inevitable bitterness is Venezuela's combative president, Hugo Chávez, who has made himself the Bush administration's rival for regional leadership. Skyrocketing oil revenues are turning his petroleum-rich country into a financial powerhouse. Meanwhile, critics of U.S. support for free trade say unrestricted commerce will weaken Latin American countries at the expense of North American business interests.

A supporter of Venezuelan President Hugo Chávez demonstrates last year in Caracas against President George W. Bush and U.S. "imperialism."

INSIDE THIS REPORT

CQ Researcher • July 21, 2006 • www.cqresearcher.com
Volume 16, Number 26 • Pages 601-624

CQ PRESS

RECIPIENT OF SOCIETY OF PROFESSIONAL JOURNALISTS AWARD FOR EXCELLENCE ◆ AMERICAN BAR ASSOCIATION SILVER GAVEL AWARD

CHANGE IN LATIN AMERICA

Cover: A supporter of Venezuelan President Hugo Chávez demonstrates last year in Caracas against President George W. Bush and U.S. "imperialism." (AFP/Getty Images/Andrew Alvarez)

CQ Researcher

July 21, 2006
Volume 16, Number 26

MANAGING EDITOR: Thomas J. Colin

ASSISTANT MANAGING EDITOR: Kathy Koch

ASSOCIATE EDITOR: Kenneth Jost

STAFF WRITERS: Marcia Clemmitt, Peter Katel

CONTRIBUTING WRITERS: Rachel S. Cox, Sarah Glazer, Alan Greenblatt, Patrick Marshall, Tom Price

DESIGN/PRODUCTION EDITOR: Olu B. Davis

ASSISTANT EDITOR: Melissa J. Hipolit

EDITORIAL INTERN: Nicholas Sohr

CQ PRESS

A Division of Congressional Quarterly Inc.

SENIOR VICE PRESIDENT/PUBLISHER: John A. Jenkins

DIRECTOR, LIBRARY PUBLISHING: Kathryn C. Suárez

DIRECTOR, EDITORIAL OPERATIONS: Ann Davies

CONGRESSIONAL QUARTERLY INC.

CHAIRMAN: Paul C. Tash

VICE CHAIRMAN: Andrew P. Corty

PRESIDENT/EDITOR IN CHIEF: Robert W. Merry

CQ Researcher (ISSN 1056-2036) is printed on acid-free paper. Published weekly, except March 24, July 7, July 14, Aug. 4, Aug. 11, Nov. 24, Dec. 22 and Dec. 29, by CQ Press, a division of Congressional Quarterly Inc. Annual full-service subscriptions for institutions start at $667. For pricing, call 1-800-834-9020, ext. 1906. To purchase a *CQ Researcher* report in print or electronic format (PDF), visit www.cqpress.com or call 866-427-7737. Single reports start at $10. Bulk purchase discounts and electronic-rights licensing are also available. Periodicals postage paid at Washington, D.C., and additional mailing offices. POSTMASTER: Send address changes to *CQ Researcher*, 1255 22nd St., N.W., Suite 400, Washington, DC 20037.

Change in Latin America

By Peter Katel

The Issues

Presidents don't talk this way — at least not in front of a microphone — and not about other global leaders. But Hugo Chávez of Venezuela plays by his own protocol rules. Last March, on his weekly TV call-in show, Chávez called President George W. Bush "Mr. Danger," declaring: "You are a donkey, Mr. Danger. . . . You are a coward, a genocidal murderer . . . an alcoholic. In other words, you are a drunk. You are immoral. You are scum, Mr. Danger." [1]

Chávez launched the outburst in response to a White House national security paper describing him as a "demagogue." [2] The episode was the latest showing how relations between the Bush administration and Latin America's self-styled defender against percieved U.S. imperialism have been deteriorating in recent years.

AFP/Getty Images

President Hugo Chávez of Venezuela, left, welcomes Cuban President Fidel Castro to Caracas in June 2005. The virulently anti-U.S. Chávez claims that only massive government spending can help poverty-stricken Latin America, not trade pacts promoted by Washington.

"The kind of rhetoric we hear coming out of Caracas is disturbing," says Assistant Secretary of State for Western Hemisphere Affairs Thomas A. Shannon. "It's all about not seeing the region as the Americas but as South America against everybody else. It's a rhetoric of confrontation. It's a negative message."

Chávez's attitude toward the Bush White House hardened after the administration greeted news of a short-lived 2002 coup by saying Chávez had resigned and blaming him for riling opponents. [3] This year, as Latin America's election season rolls on, Chávez has stepped up the tirades — which often accompany his cheerleading for political allies in neighboring countries.

Voters across the region have their pick of competing solutions to the poverty and inequality plaguing Latin America. U.S.-backed free-market economic policies that swept through in the 1990s were supposed to have improved living conditions by now. But some 360 million people — 70 percent of the area's population (including the Caribbean) — live on less than $10 a day. [4]

The poverty prompts "repeated calls for change in Latin America," warned Luis Alberto Moreno, president of the Inter-American Development Bank (IDB), in June. Without immediate progress, he continued, "the very legitimacy of the development effort will be called into question." [5]

Moreno is promoting a free-market development model that relies on expanded trade and entrepreneurship — a strategy known as "neoliberalism" or the "Washington consensus." Chávez leads those who claim neoliberalism has failed and that massive government spending alone can deliver the level of economic progress the region needs. [6]

The most recent face-off between the two doctrines occurred in Mexico's presidential election on July 5, when free-market conservative Felipe Calderón apparently edged out left-of-center Andrés Manuel López Obrador, who demanded a recount. [7]

As recently as 1988, when computer trickery robbed a left-wing candidate of victory, Mexico — then a one-party state masquerading as a democracy — had no vote-result challenge mechanism. And 20 years earlier, a demand for genuine democracy led thousands of students and others into the streets in Mexico City — where troops acting on presidential orders gunned down hundreds. [8]

The massacre joined a long list of Latin American death-squad killings, military coups and civil wars — many U.S.-supported — that claimed tens of thousands of leftists, supposed leftists, politicians of various stripes and ordinary civilians from the 1960s until the early '90s. With democratic elections now established regionwide, state terror and guerrilla attacks are largely in the past, except in Colombia, where a 42-year-old guerrilla conflict still smolders. [9]

Yet Latin America's cavernous socioeconomic gap has deepened under neoliberal policies. "In the past, there was a much wider state social safety net," says Eduardo Gamarra, director of Florida International University's Latin American and Caribbean Center in Miami, because people had jobs with benefits — often in state-owned industries. "That was dismantled, and the informal economy grew enormously."

Poverty and Income Inequality Plague Region

Sprawling Latin America — usually defined as the 31 predominantly Spanish-, Portuguese- and French-speaking countries of South America, Central America, Mexico and the Caribbean — has a population of some 500 million and an average per capita income of $3,260 (not including Cuba). Although the economy is improving overall, disparities between rich and poor have long defied solution.

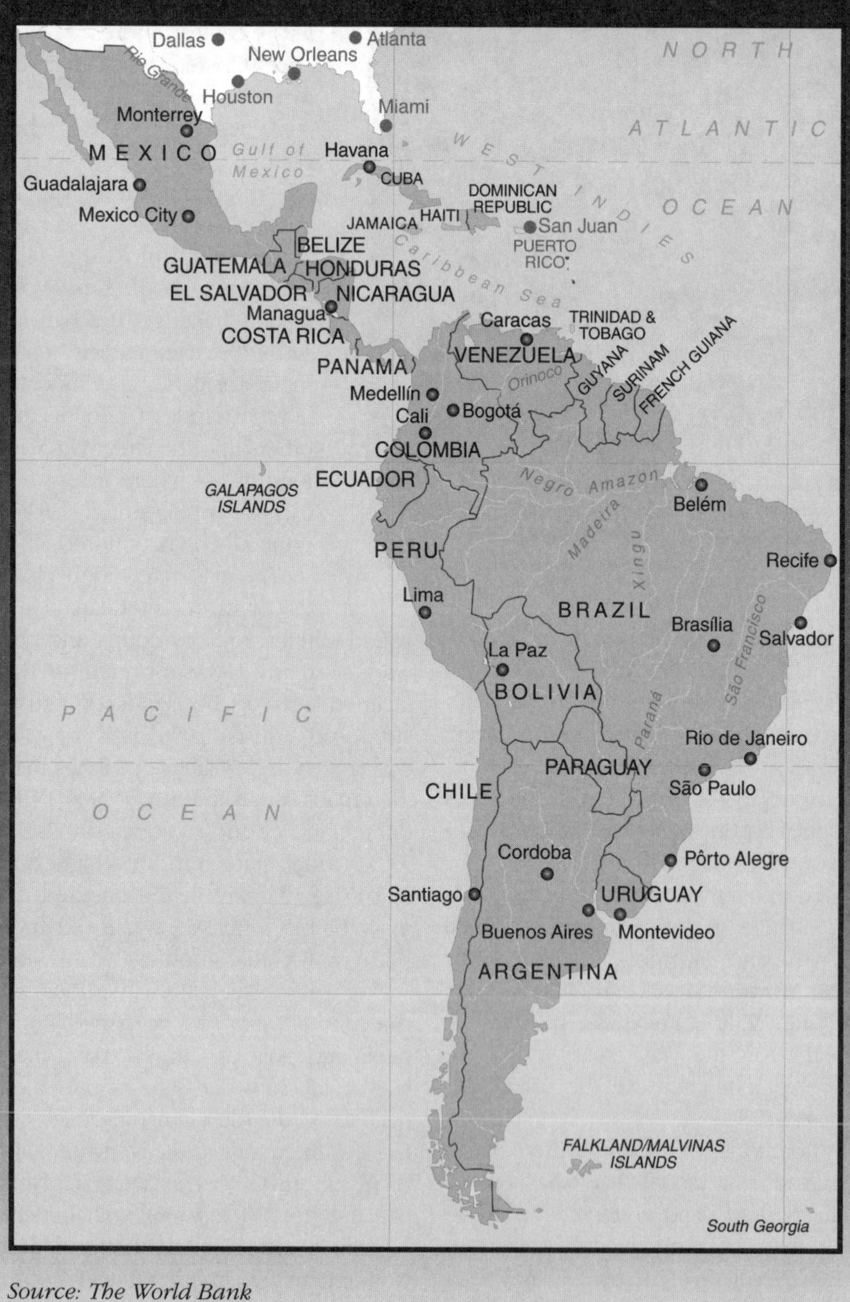

Source: The World Bank

Gamarra and others don't blame neoliberal measures for all of Latin America's problems. Economic growth has been slower than population growth, effectively preventing widespread improvement in living conditions.

But voters appear to be disillusioned with the free-market recipe and with local business elites seen as profiting from inside deals. Since the decade began, Latin America's giant, Brazil, as well as its big-league oil power, Venezuela, have elected left-wing presidents. So have Bolivia, Uruguay and Ecuador. And Argentina and Peru elected presidents from populist-nationalist parties. Even in Mexico, López Obrador's near-victory underscores the political punch he packs with his promise of socioeconomic reform. Another four presidential elections in Latin America are scheduled in 2006. [10] In one of those races, in Nicaragua, Chávez is backing a former Sandinista leader, Daniel Ortega.

Nevertheless, political differences from country to country stand out as much as the similarities. The hostile reception Chávez sometimes receives is telling. In Peru, Alan García, himself a left-of-center populist, won the presidency in June after Chávez denounced him as corrupt. "The country has . . . defeated Mr. Hugo Chávez's efforts to incorporate us in his expansionist strategy," García told cheering supporters. [11] Last November, Chávez called Mexico's outgoing conservative President Vicente Fox a "puppy of the American empire," prompting outrage across the Mexican political spectrum.

"We don't want any head of state to insult the president of Mexico," a left-wing congressman said. [12]

Chávez also has run into trouble in Brazil. Latin America's biggest country is led by a longtime hero of the left — Luiz Inácio Lula da Silva — a factory worker who rose to head his country's left-labor party before winning the presidency in 2002. [13]

But any notion that left-wing politics transcends national interests collapsed

The United States gave an estimated $1.8 billion in financial assistance to Latin America and the Caribbean last year. More than half went to Venezuela and other Andean countries.

U.S. Assistance to Latin America, Fiscal 2005
(in $ millions)

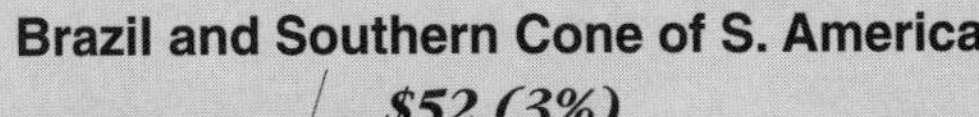

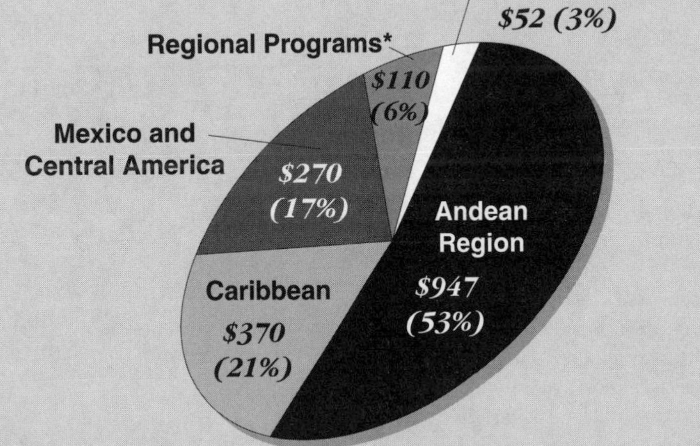

** Includes trade-capacity building and migration and refugee assistance*

Source: Congressional Research Service, "U.S. Foreign Assistance to Latin America and Caribbean," March 30, 2005

on May 1, 2006, when Bolivia's newly elected president, Evo Morales — a Chávez protégé — nationalized Bolivia's natural gas industry. Under the new arrangement, big operators — including, ironically, a state-owned Brazilian company — would be allowed to stay only if they agreed to turn over up to 82 percent of the gas they produce to Bolivia's state-owned firm.

Chávez hailed the move. But in Brazil, where major industries run on Bolivian gas, political opponents lashed out at da Silva for having been duped by his nominal left-wing comrades. In response, Brazil's foreign minister said da Silva had upbraided Chávez by phone. Another da Silva ally accused Chávez of meddling in other countries' business. [14]

Da Silva has followed pro-business economic policies while investing in social programs, but he has eschewed Chávez-style denunciations of the United States. The overall approach wins bipartisan praise from Washington and international bankers. At the recent IDB conference, former President Bill Clinton praised Brazil's "Bolsa Escola," a scholarship program that pays poor families if they send their children to school. (Mexico and Colombia have similar programs). [15]

Clinton acknowledged that the free-trade message he'd preached to Latin America in the early 1990s had been incomplete. "We bought the logic of trade that had been true since the end of World War II, that it would lift all boats," Clinton said, "and it doesn't lift all boats without the proper kind of internal economic and social policies." [16]

The IDB wants those policies to include grass-roots projects that bring immediate social benefits, such as giving the poor access to bank credit so they can start or expand businesses. The bank is now promoting such "micro" level activities serving "real people," as opposed to its traditional, big-project approach.

Chávez, who has been using Venezuela's prolific oil revenues to finance projects across the hemisphere, often casts his approach in military terms. "The [U.S.] imperialist forces are starting to strike against the people of Latin America and the world," the former paratrooper boomed to a stadium full of anti-globalization activists in Brazil last year. "And it's up to our soldiers to defend the people and not submit themselves to the interests of the empire." [17]

Despite Chávez's hostile rhetoric, Venezuela maintains an active trade relationship with the United States, supplying about 11 percent of U.S. oil imports. In fact, the United States buys 57 percent of Venezuela's oil exports, making it Venezuela's biggest oil customer. [18]

"Chávez is not going to cut off his nose to spite his face," says Fadel Gheit, chief petroleum analyst at Oppenheimer & Co., a New York investment firm. The United States lies only days away from Venezuelan ports, but distant oil-consumers, such as China, would have to be charged less in order to compensate for higher shipping costs, Gheit says. "Chávez is not going to deny his people $2 million to $4 million a day of additional revenue just to stick it to the U.S."

As newly democratic Latin America strives to improve economic conditions for its impoverished masses, here are some of the key questions being debated:

Is Chávez a visionary leader or a destructive demagogue?

Ever since he led a failed coup 16 years ago, Chávez has been a hero to Venezuela's masses. The attempted overthrow of the president was aimed ultimately at overhauling a corrupt, two-party system that was sharing little of Venezuela's oil wealth with the poor. [19]

Continued on p. 607

Playing Coca Politics Bolivian-Style

Evo Morales burst onto the South American scene in the early 1990s as leader of a Bolivian peasant farmers' organization opposed to government policies based on the U.S.-sponsored war on drugs.

The farmers wanted to keep growing coca plants — the raw material for cocaine but also used for millennia as a traditional herbal remedy for the rigors of high-altitude life. [1] The government — at U.S. insistence — wanted to eradicate the coca crop. The political boost Morales got from his venture into coca politics helped elect him president.

But drug-war politics differ from country to country. "In Colombia, being the leader of the coca-growers would never be your path to power," says Adam Isacson, director of the Latin America demilitarization program at the liberal Center for International Policy. Colombian President Alvaro Uribe — who celebrates his closeness to President Bush and expanded coca eradication and military action against widely despised drug-trafficking guerrillas — was re-elected in May by a landslide 62 percent of the vote. [2]

Getty Images/Gerard Cerles

Bolivian President Evo Morales

Bolivia, on the other hand, has a history of suspicion of U.S. policies. And the indigenous tradition of coca-leaf consumption runs stronger in Bolivia than in Colombia. Indeed, Bolivians who grow coca — cocaleros — enjoy a degree of legal protection, as do the leaves, which offer roughly the same stimulant buzz as a cup of coffee. [3]

Even Pope John Paul II conferred what amounted to a papal blessing on coca in 1988, when he drank coca-leaf tea before his plane landed in La Paz, the 13,000-foot-high capital. [4]

Also in 1988, Bolivia's congress responded to American pressure on coca cultivation. With U.S. cocaine use booming and Bolivia the center of the illegal cocaine trade, President George H. W. Bush wanted to eradicate the Bolivian crop. [5] But eradication was out of the question, so lawmakers decreed that 30,000 acres could be dedicated to coca cultivation; additional coca acreage was marked for destruction. [6]

By 1995, however, U.S. officials acknowledged that coca cultivation was trending upward. So Washington told Bolivia to destroy 4,320 acres or forfeit at least $87 million in aid. [7]

Popular discontent with Washington's interference in Bolivian affairs lifted Morales to the forefront of political life and, eventually, to a congressional seat. "We are not going to stop growing coca," he said in 2001. "We will defend ourselves from this government, which has decided to blindly obey the orders of Washington with no thought given to its own citizens." [8]

For years, pro-U.S. politicians such as President Gonzalo Sánchez de Lozada insisted that Morales and his allies — by suggesting that coca farmers were merely following ancestral traditions — were distorting reality. In fact, many coca cultivators were working hand-in-glove with cocaine processors, the politicians said.

"These aren't just poor innocent farmers," Sánchez de Lozada said in 1995. [9]

When Morales was running in the 2002 presidential election, U.S. Ambassador Manuel Rocha threatened that U.S. aid might be cut off if Bolivians chose Morales. "The Bolivian electorate must consider the consequences of choosing leaders somehow connected with drug trafficking and terrorism," Rocha said.

Morales' support shot from 4 percent to about 21 percent, and he came in second — paving the way for his victory three years later. [10]

In the early months of his administration, there was little warming between Morales and the Bush administration. "The new . . . Morales administration in Bolivia has displayed a lackluster commitment to coca reduction," Anne W. Patterson, assistant secretary of State for international narcotics and law enforcement, told the House Western Hemisphere Subcommittee in March.

Morales says he can protect cocaleros while cracking down on cocaine traffickers, and critics of the drug war agree. "The international community should give the Bolivian government the breathing room it needs . . . to implement the new approach," wrote two drug-war critics in June. [11]

---

[1] For background, see "Coca-growers' leaders released, march on La Paz to continue," BBC Summary of World Broadcasts, Sept. 9, 1994; "Seven dead in Bolivian clashes with coca growers," Agence France Presse, April 19, 1997.

[2] For re-election details, see Chris Kraul, "Uribe's Second Term is a First," *Los Angeles Times*, May 29, 2006, p. A16.

[3] For a summary of the cultural significance of coca, see Becky Branford, "Coca quandary for hard-up Bolivia," BBC, April 14, 2006, http://new.bbc.co.uk/1/hi/world/americas/4902192.stm.

[4] For an account of the Pope's trip, see, William R. Long, "Rich Countries Obligated to Aid Poor, Pope Says," *Los Angeles Times*, May 11, 1988, p. A8.

[5] Bradley Graham, "Bolivia Runs Risks in Drug Drive," *The Washington Post*, July 17, 1986, p. A1.

[6] Branford, *op. cit.*

[7] William R. Long, " 'Coca Power' Winning Bolivian Drug War," *Los Angeles Times*, Sept. 24, 1995, p. A1.

[8] Anthony Faiola, "In Bolivia's Drug War, Success Has Price," *The Washington Post*, March 4, 2001, p. A1.

[9] Long, *op. cit.*

[10] Hector Tobar and Andrew Enever, "U.S. Envoy Criticized in Messy Aftermath of Bolivian Vote," *Los Angeles Times*, July 6, 2002, p. A3; Jeffrey D. Rosner and Mark Feierstein, "Hindering Reform in Latin America," [Op-Ed] *The Washington Post*, Aug. 6, 2002, p. A15.

[11] Kathryn Lebedur and Colletta A. Youngers, "Crisis or Opportunity: Bolivian Drug Control Policy and the U.S. Response," Andean Information Network, Washington Office on Latin America, June 2006, p. 10; www.wola.org/publications/AIN-WOLA%20Drug%20Policy%20Memo%20FINAL%20brief.pdf.

Continued from p. 605

In 1998 Chávez was elected president by an overwhelming vote and is expected to win again when presidential elections are held this December. With his political opposition disorganized, Chávez's Fifth Republic Movement party also controls Congress. And, according to his opponents, Chávez supporters run the country's highest court. Cementing his image as the hope of the poor, Chávez has brought thousands of Cuban doctors to serve in clinics in Venezuelan slums, established subsidized markets and improved water delivery and other services. [20]

Meanwhile, thanks to oil revenues, Venezuela reportedly has committed $25.6 billion to programs throughout the region, including: $10 billion for a Latin America-wide anti-poverty program; $4.3 billion for Brazilian energy projects; $30 million for Bolivian social welfare projects and an estimated $2 billion for nearly 100,000 barrels of low-cost oil daily for energy-strapped Cuba. [21]

Even the U.S. poor aren't being neglected. The Venezuelan state oil company's U.S. subsidiary, Citgo, reportedly distributed 44.5 million gallons of heating oil at discounts of up to 40 percent to low-income consumers in New England last winter. [22]

As further outreach to the region, Chávez helped President Eduardo Kirchner pay off Argentina's remaining $9.8 billion debt to the International Monetary Fund (IMF), thus eliminating the IMF's supervisory role in Argentina's economy. Chávez also announced plans to build a 5,000-mile oil pipeline to Argentina. [23]

"We want to find a solution — for real, for real — to the tragedy of inequality," Chávez said. "Let's change the model; let's leave capitalism behind. From Venezuela, we say, let's go forward to a new kind of socialism, a 21st-century socialism; a model for equality and for justice." [24]

But socialism is a big tent. One of Chávez's opponents on Dec. 3 will be another socialist, Teodoro Petkoff, who was a Castro-inspired guerrilla leader in the 1960s. Now editor of the opposition newspaper *TalCual*, Petkoff aligns himself with such left-of-center reformers as da Silva of Brazil, Michelle Bachelet of Chile and Tabaré Vásquez of Uruguay — none of whom has insulted Bush or attacked trade with the United States. Petkoff argues that Chávez is less interested in social equality than with building his own power. He says Chávez's administration is "essentially personality-dominated, with strong traits of militarism, messianism and authoritarianism." [25]

For instance, Chavez has committed $3.7 billion toward the biggest arms purchase in recent Latin American history, including: 24 Sukhoi fighter jets, 15 helicopters and 100,000 assault rifles from Russia and eight patrol vessels and light warships from Spain. And he has begun forming a citizens' militia to repel what he says is a coming U.S. attack. [26] "Two Sukhois just passed in front of my window at low altitude," said Ibsen Martínez, a Venezuelan writer and columnist, during Venezuela's July 5th independence day celebrations, questioning why Venezuela needs advanced warplanes.

Jorge G. Castañeda, a professor of politics and Latin American studies at New York University who was Mexican President Fox's foreign minister in 2001-2003, says Chavez "is attempting, with some success, to split the hemisphere into two camps: one pro-Chávez, one pro-American. . . . He also frequently picks fights with Fox and Bush and is buying arms from Spain and Russia. This is about as close to traditional Latin American populism as one can get — and as far from a modern and socially minded left as one can be." [27]

But a leading left-wing Colombian congressman says critics like Petkoff and Castañeda prefer house-broken leftists. "They're trying to foster the idea of a well-behaved left that will serve the oligarchies of Latin America by administering their countries," says Gustavo Petro of Bogotá, a former guerrilla leader who now belongs to the leftist Independent Democratic Center party.

Petro says Chavez's domestic policies can't be exported like oil, but he adds that trying to separate him from more moderate left-wing leaders ignores the reality on the ground. "You can identify a common agenda," says Alexander Main, an American who is an adviser to Venezuela's foreign ministry. "There is a growing consensus that countries

Millions Lack Sanitation, Water, Electricity

Nearly 30 percent of people in Latin America don't have basic sanitation, 20 percent have no piped water and 8 percent lack electricity.

Availability of Basic Services in Latin America and the Caribbean*
(2003-2004)

Service	Percentage of Population	Number Without Access (in millions)
Electricity	7.8%	41
Sanitation	28.8	153
Piped Water	19.7	105

** Excludes Argentina, the Bahamas, Haiti, Nicaragua and Bolivia*

Source: World Bank, "Inequality in Latin America and the Caribbean: Breaking With History," 2004

Millions Earn Less Than $2 a Day

More than half of the people in five Latin American nations earn less than $2 a day. Chileans and Uruguayans earn the most.

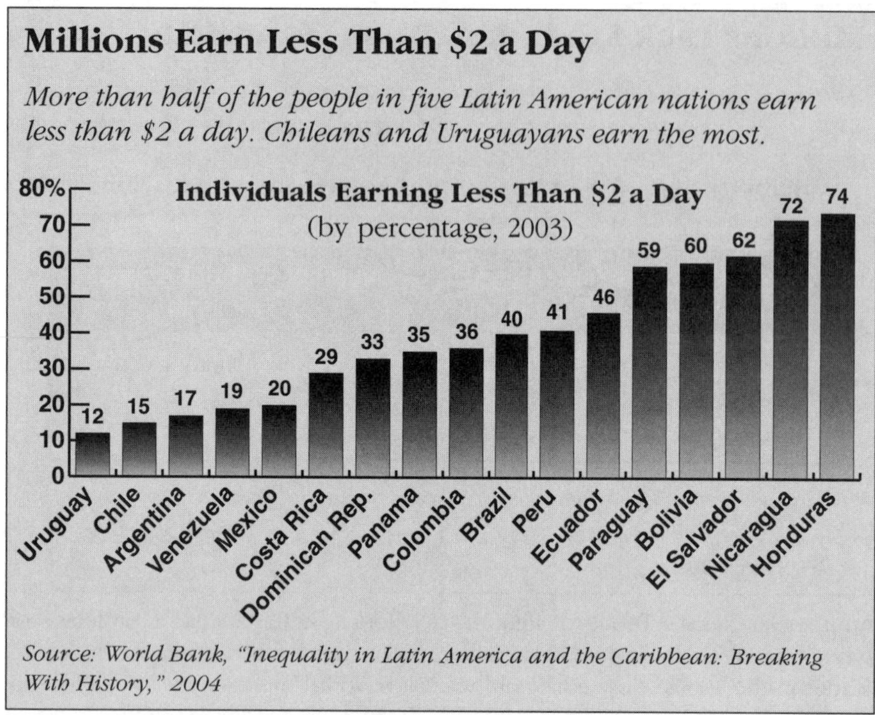

Source: World Bank, "Inequality in Latin America and the Caribbean: Breaking With History," 2004

should take back control of their economies; the emphasis on the role of the state is coming back. It's a return to the developmental policies that Latin America had before the 1980s, before the Washington consensus became standard policy. So Chávez's message carries weight."

But it's a message whose strength may be fading, says Michael Shifter, vice president for policy at Inter-American Dialogue, a Washington think tank. "We're seeing the risks of overreaching," he says, noting the defeat of the Chávez-endorsed presidential candidate in Peru. "He just wants to control everything; the Latin Americans don't want anyone to control them, whether it's George Bush or Hugo Chávez."

Mark Weisbrot, co-director of the liberal Center for Economic and Policy Research, argues that Chávez critics are mischaracterizing the Peruvian results. Candidate Ollanta Humala, Chávez's favorite, got 47.5 percent of the vote in his first bid for office. "The media are portraying it as a big defeat for Chávez, but the region is still moving in the direction of increased national economic policies and a reduced influence of the United States."

Are Latin Americans growing more anti-American?

Anti-U.S. feeling is part of the political landscape in Latin America, where the region's 800-pound gorilla has been asserting dominance for nearly two centuries. However, American visitors typically are greeted warmly, and 61 percent of Latin Americans report positive feelings about the United States as a country — which hasn't changed since 1995, according to Latinobarómetro, a respected survey covering 18 countries.

"If we had asked about President Bush, we would have gotten a far different result," says Cristóbal Hunneus, research director of Mori Chile, the polling firm that conducts the survey.

"There's a special dislike and distrust for the policies of the Bush administration," says Shifter. "People really don't like what's going on in the rest of the world." Moreover, "Unilateral military action is an especially sensitive issue in this region," he says, alluding to past U.S. interventions in Latin America.

But Latin America is so vast there is plenty of room for regional variants. In Colombia, views of the United States are dominated by the four-decade war against the government by the FARC (Fuerzas Armadas Revolucionarias de Colombia — the Revolutionary Armed Forces of Colombia). The guerrillas' kidnappings, cocaine trafficking and other crimes have brought widespread public loathing — and a deadly paramilitary response.

"Anti-Americanism doesn't have much resonance in Colombia," says Adolfo Meisel, director of the Colombian central bank's Center for Regional Economic Studies in Cartagena. "The United States is seen as an ally in the fight against the FARC, and against drug trafficking."

Colombian congressman Petro agrees the FARC has alienated most Colombians, but he blames Bush for a "deeply aggressive and irrational foreign policy" that transcends Iraq. The former guerrilla leader points to U.S. efforts in Colombia to eradicate coca and opium-poppy crops and provide military counterinsurgency training and assistance, costing more than $630 million. "Practically speaking, the country is living under occupation," Petro says. [28]

But most Colombians apparently either disagree, or don't mind: Petro's party was overwhelmed in the May 28 presidential election by conservative incumbent Alvaro Uribe, a stalwart U.S. ally who received nearly triple the left-wing candidate's 22 percent of the vote. [29]

In Bolivia, argues Gamarra of Florida International University, Bush isn't an especially big factor in the country's anti-Americanism, which predates Bush. "It's rather simplistic," he says. "Nationalisms are always very simplistic." He acknowledges, however, that Bush has deepened antagonism by turning conflicts with Chávez and Bolivia's Morales into ideological battles. "It's in their interest to play it up and in our interest to play it down. When we make it ideological, we're going to lose every time."

But even American officials acknowledge that the Iraq war has complicated things. "This is just something we have to live with," says U.S. diplomat Shannon. "We're a global power, we have security concerns that are related to our larger global interests and a necessity to protect ourselves. We're going to have to make decisions that we think are right and responsible, irrespective of how people are going to respond."

Chávez advocates portray the Venezuelan government as anti-Bush, not anti-American. "Chávez and others in government are always careful to differentiate between the American people and problems they have with the Bush administration," says foreign policy adviser Main. "The long-term goal is to keep strong relations with the U.S., with the hope that another administration will have more reasonable policies toward Venezuela and the rest of the world."

Nevertheless, Chávez's attacks on Washington feature typical Marxist rhetoric about imperialism vs. socialism, reflecting a view that blames the United States for the region's woes, with little discussion of the role of native ruling classes.

"I don't blame the United States for acting like an empire," says Juan Claudio Lechín, a prominent Bolivian economist-turned-novelist whose father was a legendary left-wing union leader and politician. "But our elites have devoted themselves simply to making money, shrugging off their responsibilities for what the people are demanding."

Is a regionwide free-trade pact possible?

After the North American Free Trade Agreement (NAFTA) with Mexico and Canada was launched in 1994, the Clinton administration proposed an even bigger trade deal — the Free Trade Area of the Americas (FTAA) — to eliminate obstacles to commerce throughout Latin America. [30]

Negotiations were to be completed by the end of 2005, but U.S. enthusiasm for the pact didn't catch on, and the FTAA talks have disappeared into limbo. For one thing, NAFTA didn't live up to its promise to create well-paid jobs in Mexico. Instead, millions of Mexican workers — legal and otherwise — sought opportunities in the expanding U.S. economy. [31]

In addition, the failure of the World Trade Organization (WTO) to cut farm subsidies in wealthy countries across the globe, including the United States, undercut the FTAA. A pending WTO agreement on subsidy cuts would have been incorporated in the FTAA, but on July 1 WTO talks in Geneva collapsed. [32]

With a global trade accord uncertain at best, U.S. trade policy in Latin America has shifted to smaller-scale trade pacts, which Shannon says demonstrate that the FTAA remains alive as a principle. "We keep a large hemispheric agreement as our objective but then begin to build, through bilateral and sub-regional free-trade agreements, a free-trade linkage throughout the hemisphere, which would create a structure that eventually could be linked to create an FTAA," he says.

Accordingly, the United States has negotiated several free-trade agreements recently in the region, including a bilateral deal with Chile that took effect in 2004; last year's Central America Free Trade Agreement (CAFTA-DR), which includes seven Central American countries and the Dominican Republic; a tentative agreement with Colombia completed in February; and an agreement with Peru, approved by Peru's congress in June. [33]

But trade complications remain. Colombia, for example, is arguing with the United States over how many U.S. chicken leg quarters to allow in, given Colombian poultry producers' worries that unrestrained, cheaper U.S. exports will drive them out of business. [34]

Meanwhile, the Bush administration froze trade talks with Ecuador after the government there handled a dispute with Los Angeles-based Occidental Petroleum Corp. by unilaterally canceling the company's operating contract. Occidental had invested a reported $900 million in Ecuador to produce 100,000 barrels of oil a day. In Costa Rica, Nobel Peace Prize laureate Oscar Arias squeaked through a presidential election with a 41-40 percent victory last February, largely because he supported the CAFTA-DR, which the country's congress has yet to approve. [35]

For Venezuelan government adviser Main, these disputes indicate that FTAA probably will never be approved. "At least in its current terms, it doesn't favor a lot of Latin American countries" since it would allow the United States to retain its agricultural subsidies, he says.

But others say the picture isn't entirely bleak for bilateral trade. Stephen Johnson, an analyst at the conservative Heritage Foundation, notes that growing unhappiness in Uruguay over the so-called Mercosur trade agreement with Argentina, Brazil and Paraguay has sparked interest in trade deals with the United States. [36] If other Mercosur members follow Uruguay's example, Johnson says, "Perhaps the U.S. would be able to jump-start the FTAA process and do a detour around the issue of agricultural subsidies that is still being decided in the WTO."

But even Arias, who put his presidential hopes on the line by supporting free trade with the United States, sees little hope for FTAA — and he blames the United States. "The U.S. government spends roughly $20 billion per year to subsidize agribusiness, artificially depressing global crop prices and depriving the poorest farmers in the world of money they need to survive," Arias wrote in March. As long as subsidies remain at that level, he agued, "There is little chance [the FTAA] will be adopted." [37]

In Central America, though, with CAFTA-DR already negotiated and largely ratified, Costa Rica would be foolish to back out, Arias has said. "Costa Rica has no choice but to insert itself more and more in the global economy," he said. "We need to tell Costa Ricans. . . . 'There is no other way.' "[38]

But Chávez insists there is another approach. "God save us from these so-called free-trade agreements, which are nothing but a way to impose the FTAA," Chávez declared in April on his weekly TV-radio program. "We are proposing to Latin America's peoples and governments treaties of liberation and trade with justice. . . . When Venezuela, for example, sends fertilizer to some farm cooperatives in Nicaragua, we provide it on credit, at low cost . . . while the United States government proposes free-trade agreements, which without any doubt harm these peoples and increase their dependence on the empire."[39]

For all of Chávez's rhetoric, numbers paint a picture that no Latin American government looking to expand trade can afford to ignore, says Gamarra of Florida International University. "Chávez might be able to hand out $20 billion here or $30 billion there, but the Venezuelan economy still generates the same economic activity as Minneapolis."[40] ■

BACKGROUND

'Good Neighbor'?

After Latin America freed itself from Spanish and Portuguese rule in the 19th century, the United States became the region's main political and economic force, swallowing up about half of Mexico after the War of 1846; helping to oust Spain from Cuba and Puerto Rico in 1898 and dominating the early oil industry in Mexico and Venezuela.[41]

In 1938, relations between the United States and Latin American nations — typically dominated by strongmen ("caudillos") — took a dramatic turn. President Lázaro Cárdenas nationalized Mexico's oil industry following a dispute between Mexican workers and the American and British companies that controlled petroleum production. Although the companies were compensated, they mounted a worldwide boycott of Mexican oil and persuaded equipment sellers not to do business with Mexico. The industry's retaliation hamstrung the expansion of Mexico's oil industry for the next 30 years even though the Franklin D. Roosevelt administration — which had a policy of non-intervention in the region — did not retaliate against Mexico.[42]

To this day, Mexico commemorates the nationalization in a patriotic holiday, and Cárdenas' act still resounds throughout the hemisphere — most recently in Bolivia.

In his first inaugural address in 1933, Roosevelt had described his administration as a "good neighbor" to Latin America who "respects the rights of others." But in the Cold War tension that emerged after World War II, U.S. presidents feared the Soviet Union would make inroads in Latin America unless Washington stepped in.

Guatemala provided the first test. Left-winger Jacobo Arbenz Guzmán was elected president in 1950 and began a land-reform program that alarmed big landowners as well the U.S.-based United Fruit Co., which ran banana plantations. United Fruit lobbied the Eisenhower administration to intervene.[43] In 1954, the Central Intelligence Agency (CIA) mounted a coup in Guatemala, installing a right-wing colonel in power and launching a period of more than 30 years in which the Guatemalan military effectively — and ruthlessly — ruled the country.[44]

The overthrow of Arbenz deepened anti-Americanism in the country and prompted the departure of a young, communist-leaning Argentine doctor — Ernesto Guevara, later known worldwide as Che — who had moved to Guatemala to take part in the reforms.[45]

Alliance for Progress

Guevara went to Mexico City and fell in with a group of Cuban exiles led by a young Havana lawyer named Fidel Castro. After forming a small guerrilla army, Castro and his followers clandestinely returned to Cuba in 1956 and launched a war against the government of dictator Fulgencio Batista, who had become unpopular with the middle class.[46]

On New Year's Day 1959, Castro's forces decisively defeated the military, and Batista fled into exile. Over the next two years, Castro became (or, some historians say, revealed himself to be) thoroughly anti-American and pro-Soviet. In 1961, the United States organized a small group of Cuban exiles to topple Castro, but they were defeated at the Bay of Pigs after expected U.S. air support never appeared.

The following year, the discovery of Soviet nuclear missiles in Cuba led to the brink of atomic war, but the measured response by President John F. Kennedy (JFK) allowed Soviet leader Nikita Khrushchev to withdraw the missiles without losing face.

To the United States, Castro embodied the long-feared communist menace to the Americas. But many Latin Americans reveled in his defiance of the United States. In any event, the repressive policies that would come to characterize Castro's rule showed up early.[47]

"Revolutionary justice is based not on legal precepts but on moral conviction," Castro announced in March 1959 after personally throwing out the acquittals of 44 members of the Batista-era air force who had been accused of war crimes. After Castro replaced the court's judges and named the defense minister as prosecutor, the men were convicted and sentenced to up to 30 years in prison. Guevara, meanwhile, was conducting trials and executions of accused war criminals from the Batista regime. Cubans who

Continued on p. 612

Chronology

1930s-1950s

United States changes from benevolent neighbor to Cold War warrior.

March 18, 1938
President Lázaro Cárdenas nationalizes Mexico's oil industry.

1954
CIA-backed coup topples Guatemala's democratically elected left-wing president, Jacobo Arbenz Guzmán.

Jan. 1, 1959
Fidel Castro seizes power in Cuba from U.S.-backed dictator Fulgencio Batista.

1960s-1970s

Cuba becomes a Soviet ally; U.S. praises democratic reform while backing repressive regimes.

March 19, 1961
President John F. Kennedy launches Alliance for Progress aid program.

April 15, 1961
U.S.-backed anti-Castro guerrillas are defeated by Cuban troops at the Bay of Pigs.

Oct. 9, 1967
Communist revolutionary Ernesto "Che" Guevara is executed during a failed guerrilla mission to Bolivia.

Sept. 11, 1973
Chilean military overthrows elected left-wing President Salvador Allende and establishes a dictatorship.

March 24, 1976
Argentina's military takes over the government and steps up its "dirty war" against the left.

1979
Sandinista National Liberation Front overthrows Nicaragua's Anastasio Somoza regime.

1980s

South American military regimes begin collapsing as the United States deepens its involvement in Central American.

March 24, 1980
Right-wing gunmen assassinate human-rights activist Archbishop Oscar Romero of El Salvador.

December 1981
U.S.-trained Salvadoran soldiers massacre 800 women and children and elderly people in guerrilla stronghold. . . . Elected civilian president takes office in Argentina, following military junta's collapse.

Dec. 20, 1989
President George H. W. Bush sends troops to Panama to arrest strongman Manuel Noriega for drug trafficking.

1990s

U.S. pushes free markets in Latin America as democracy spreads.

Jan. 16, 1992
Salvadoran guerrillas sign peace accord with the government.

1993
Congress ratifies North American Free Trade Agreement (NAFTA) among the U.S., Canada and Mexico.

1994
Ernesto Zedillo becomes president of Mexico.

1998
Hugo Chávez wins Venezuelan presidency, sweeping past candidates from traditional political parties.

2000s

Unsuccessful neoliberal policies of the '90s lead to populists' growing power.

2001
Corruption sends Argentine economy into a tailspin.

2002
Venezuelan business leaders topple Chávez, but the coup quickly collapses.

2004
Illegal Mexican emigration to the U.S. reportedly peaks at more than a half-million people a year.

2005
Evo Morales, former leader of Bolivia's coca farmers, elected president.

May 28, 2006
Alvaro Uribe, Colombia's law-and-order president, wins re-election.

June 2, 2006
George W. Bush administration opposes U.N. Security Council seat for Venezuela.

June 5, 2006
Peru's Alan García says his presidential election victory is a defeat for Venezuela's Chávez, who campaigned for García's opponent.

July 6, 2006
Conservative Felipe Calderón narrowly wins Mexico's presidential election, defeating former Mexico City Mayor Andrés Manuel López Obrador, who vows to challenge the results.

Latino Workers in U.S. Send Billions Home

The single biggest infusion of cash into the Latin American economy owes nothing to trade pacts, corporate investments or development projects. Instead, Latin Americans working in the United States have built a vast financing system based on money sent home, or "remittances," in economists' jargon. All told, they will pump some $60 billion into the Americas in 2006.

On average, each worker sends home about $1,100 to $3,000 a year. At least 15 percent of that is over and above what households need for food and other immediate needs, says Donald Terry, director of the Inter-American Development Bank's (IDB) Multilateral Investment Fund. "That is $9 billion-plus," Terry says. "That's about as much as the IDB and the World Bank are likely to lend this year to Latin America and the Caribbean. And the [remittance] money goes where you want it to go. It's not filtered through the 'lords of development' like me." [1]

This year's $60 billion in projected remittances represents a near-doubling in only four years from $32 billion in 2002. Further increases are projected for the near future, though economic improvements in home countries could eventually lessen both migration and remittances. [2]

Remittances are virtually as old as labor migration, but governments and the development establishment have zeroed in on them only in the past five years. For some officials, the magnitude of the flow opens the possibility of channeling the funds into projects of the kind that typically depend on foreign aid. [3]

Terry and others argue, however, that remittances can't replace development assistance. "Foreign aid, hopefully, goes principally to build what are called public goods," such as schools. "Remittances are private flows that don't build public goods."

Exceptions do exist. The Mexican state of Zacatecas, which has been sending people to work in the United States for decades, is credited with starting a tradition in which migrants abroad form clubs that finance roads, sewage systems and other public works back home. [4]

But the generosity of some migrants doesn't change the bottom line about remittances. "These family transfers represent the ultimate in family values: hard work, thrift, sacrifice and hope for a better future," Terry argues in a paper published by the United Nations. "Underlying all of them is one basic fact: It's their money." [5]

The IDB encourages people on both ends of the remittance connection to use banks to send and deposit funds and to persuade banks to seek customers among remittance recipients. [6]

Typically, banks and low-income people in Latin America have little to do with each other. "There is an assumption among some banks that because most money recipients are low-income individuals who predominantly use the money for consumption, they are not potential bank customers," wrote Manuel Orozco, a leading expert on remittances. A political scientist born in Nicaragua, Orozco is executive director of the Remittances and Rural Development Project at Inter-American Dialogue, a Washington think tank. [7]

Linking remittance recipients and banks would enable recipients to use deposits as collateral for loans to build or expand businesses and homes, generating more economic activity.

"My mantra is to give people more options to use their money," Terry says. "If you give [people] the option of a savings account or a loan, we can help their communities and not make it so necessary to leave home" to find good jobs.

---

1 For details on average annual amounts, see "All in the Family: Latin America's Most Important Financial Flow," Inter-American Dialogue, January 2004, p. 7; www.thedialogue.org/publications/country_studies/remittances/all_family.pdf.

2 *Ibid.*, p. 4; for the future of remittances, see Pedro de Vasconcelos, *et al.*, "Improving the Development Impact of Remittances," United Nations Expert Group Meeting on International Migration and Development, July 6-8, 2005, p. 9; www.un.org/esa/population/publications/ittmigdev2005/P10_DeVasconcelos.pdf.

3 Geri Smith, "Channeling the Remittance Flood," *Business Week Online*, Dec. 28, 2005; www.businessweek.com/bwdaily/dnflash/dec2005/nf20051228_4272.htm.

4 See Chris Kraul, "Tapping Generosity of Emigrants," *Los Angeles Times*, July 8, 2000, p. A1.

5 Quoted in Vasconcelos, *op. cit.*, p. 9.

6 Manuel Orozco, "Enabling Environments? Facing a Spontaneous or Incubating Stage," Inter-American Dialogue, Jan. 28, 2002, p. 14; www.thedialogue.org/publications/country_studies/remittances/Enabling%20environments.pdf.

7 *Ibid.*, p. 9.

Continued from p. 610

resisted the communist transformation of Cuba fled or were imprisoned. [48]

After the "Cuban Missile Crisis," Castro and his Soviet backers organized and encouraged guerrilla movements throughout the hemisphere. These efforts suffered a setback in 1967 when Guevara was executed without trial by U.S.-aided Bolivian forces during a failed mission to launch a Latin American communist revolution. [49]

After the Bay of Pigs disaster, JFK threw his administration behind the Alliance for Progress, an aid program for Latin America. The administration aimed to align the United States with anti-communist democrats in the region who would offer alternatives to Soviet-style revolution, such as land reform, new schools and expanded health care. [50]

"We call for social change by free men — change in the spirit of Washington and Jefferson, of Bolivar and San Martin and Martí," Kennedy declared. "Our motto is what it has always been — progress yes, tyranny no — *Progreso si, tiranía no!*" [51]

In practice, however, genuine democrats were scarce among the region's leaders, and the United States found its closest friends among military and business leaders, who viewed liberal reforms as a threat. In Argentina, Guatemala, Brazil, Chile and elsewhere local rulers — often supported by U.S. officials and CIA agents — met calls for reform with roundups, imprisonment and worse. "During the Kennedy years alone, military men overthrew six popularly elected Latin American presidents," wrote Stephen G. Rabe, a University of Texas historian. "The military men who seized power . . . during the 1960s had trained under U.S. direction." [52]

'Dirty Wars'

In Brazil, the military overthrew an elected president in 1964. In 1968, Mexican troops acting under presidential orders massacred some 300 students and supporters conducting a peaceful, pro-democracy protest. [53] In 1973, the military overthrew Chile's elected, leftist president, Salvador Allende. A junta led by Gen. Augusto Pinochet subsequently killed or "disappeared" some 4,000 people identified as leftist enemies of the regime. Another 28,459 were imprisoned and tortured. [54]

In 1976, Argentina's military overthrew the weak civilian government that had been under attack by guerrillas. In the so-called dirty war that intensified after the coup, left-wingers and anyone suspected of left-wing ties were killed — 22,000 victims in 1976-78 alone. [55]

For decades, critics of U.S. policy maintained that Washington had strong ties to the region's repressive governments. Some of the charges were confirmed as early as 1975, when the Senate Intelligence Committee reported that CIA funding for right-wing political activities in Chile — including plotting the 1973 overthrow of Allende — ran to $8 million between 1963 and 1973. Documents declassified in 2000 showed the head of Pinochet's secret police had been a CIA informant. [56]

The documents also reflect American disenchantment with Pinochet and support for the opposition movement that eventually ended military rule in 1988, when Chilean voters removed Pinochet. [57]

Events in Argentina followed a similar course. During the Ford administration in 1976 Secretary of State Henry A. Kissinger gave what some have interpreted as a green light to the Argentine military to repress dissidents. "If there are things that have to be done, you should do them quickly," Kissinger told the foreign minister, an admiral. [58]

However, President Jimmy Carter's State Department pressured Argentina's generals to respect human rights, though some historians argue the Defense Department conveyed support for the dirty war. Military rule collapsed in 1983 after Great Britain routed Argentine forces, which had tried to reclaim the British Falkand Islands. [59]

In the late 1970s long-simmering political and social conflicts erupted in Central America — mainly in Nicaragua, Guatemala and El Salvador.

In 1979, for instance, the left-wing Sandinista guerrilla army — named after legendary anti-U.S. fighter César Sandino — ousted Nicaraguan dictator Anastasio Somoza, who had virtually inherited the country from his father and grandfather. [60] Washington had long backed Somoza, but he lost U.S. support as he increased repression. Meanwhile, the Sandinistas who dominated the new government had received extensive help from Cuba. But opposition parties remained legal, as did private business — policies that Castro himself had recommended, apparently in an effort to keep the new government from becoming isolated. [61]

But anti-communist ex-Sandinistas joined with Somoza supporters to form a guerrilla army that was quickly dubbed the "contras" (the "antis"). Despite a 1984 congressional prohibition on funding for military or paramilitary operations in Nicaragua, the contras secretly received extensive backing from the Reagan administration, which had taken office in 1981. To evade the law, Reagan aides devised a scheme to sell weapons to Iran, with profits to go to the contras. They did get funds, but disclosure of the operation triggered a scandal that tarnished the Reagan presidency. [62]

In El Salvador, Archbishop Oscar Romero was assassinated in 1980 while celebrating mass in San Salvador, the capital. Romero had advocated human rights, defying the right-wing military and rich agribusiness families that dominated the country. The U.N.-organized Commission on the Truth for El Salvador concluded in 1993 that leading right-wing politician Roberto d'Aubuisson — a former army major — had ordered the killing. The commission also found "substantial evidence" that a top military commander had a part in ordering the murders of three American nuns and a lay churchwoman, all of them critics of the U.S. role in El Salvador, in 1980. [63]

Romero's assassination spurred fighting that continued through the 1980s, with left-wing guerrillas who controlled part of the countryside battling with the U.S.-backed regular army forces. In the cities, security forces regularly assassinated people considered "subversive." The right-wing death squads, along with U.S.-backed security forces, committed 85 percent of the 22,000 atrocities investigated by the truth commission; left-wing guerrillas committed the remainder. [64]

By the end of the 1980s, Central America's wars were winding down. The Sandinistas were voted out of power in 1989. U.N.-sponsored peace talks helped achieve peace in El Salvador and Guatemala, where some 200,000 people had been killed during a 36-year civil war. [65]

As Central Americans were moving toward peace, Mexicans were becoming more and more dissatisfied with the Revolutionary Institutional Party (PRI), which had held power continuously since 1929. [66]

Opposition parties were tolerated, or even subsidized, but only if they didn't threaten the PRI's grip on power. By 1988, citizen discontent had reached the point that Carlos Salinas de Gortari won the presidency only through rigged election results.

Salinas signed the North American Free Trade Agreement with the United States and Canada and pressed for its ratification by the U.S. Congress in 1993. The treaty was a milestone in the rise of what Latin Americans call "neoliberalism" — unrestricted access to their markets and industries.

Following NAFTA's Jan. 1, 1994, start date, foreign investment in Mexico soared to $12 billion a year, and Mexican exports tripled to more than $160 billion. But well-paying jobs that would keep Mexicans from migrating to the United States — a key NAFTA promise — didn't materialize, especially after the economic boom in China began attracting Western investment. [67] Instead, illegal Mexican migration to the United States increased from about 332,000 in 1993 to 530,000 in 2000, continuing at lower numbers thereafter before rising again in 2004. [68]

Salinas' presidency ended amid corruption scandals. His successor, Ernesto Zedillo, strengthened Mexico's election system for the 2000 presidential race. In that election, Vicente Fox, a farmer and business executive from central Mexico representing the traditional center-right National Action Party (PAN) also appealed to the influential center-left. With its support, he won the election and opened what was widely hailed as a new political era in Mexico.

Turbulent Times

The 1990s began an era of South American turbulence marked by the rise and fall of a new generation of powerful politicians who — unlike the caudillos of the past — were elected to office.

Peruvians, responding to economic chaos and guerrilla violence, in 1990 elected political outsider Alberto Fujimori, who crushed the ultra-violent Maoist Shining Path insurgency and dominated the political scene for a decade. He fled to Japan after videotapes surfaced showing his intelligence czar handing out bribes to members of congress. [69]

In Argentina, President Carlos Saúl Menem's crash was equally spectacular. He too took office amid economic crisis, in 1989, and responded by privatizing state-owned companies and opening the country to trade and investment. The overhaul made Menem a favorite of the United States and the multinational banking community. [70] But in 1999, as his second term was ending, Menem and his top officials were ensnared in scandals, many involving payoffs in privatization deals. By 2001, the economy teetered near collapse despite an emergency IMF loan of nearly $40 billion and the forced resignation of Menem's successor. The crisis was blamed on cheap Brazilian imported goods, loss of consumer confidence and the high level of foreign debt necessitated by the mountains of public funds siphoned off by corruption. [71]

Colombia, meanwhile, faced its own unique problems. The vastly expanded illegal drug industry intensified the fighting between the government and FARC guerrillas. In the 1980s, far-right paramilitaries entered the conflict and, like their FARC opponents, made money from drugs. [72]

In 2000, the Clinton administration and the Colombian government agreed to combine anti-drug and anti-guerrilla strategies under the so-called Plan Colombia. It included herbicide spraying of coca and heroin poppy crops, aid to farmers who switched to non-drug crops and military assistance. The Bush administration embraced the plan, and it is still in force.

In Venezuela, decades of mismanagement and corruption by the two established political parties led army Lt. Col. Hugo Chávez to attempt a coup in 1992. Although the attempt failed, he emerged as a champion of the masses and in 1998 was elected president. He quickly forged a bond with Castro and engineered passage of a new Venezuelan constitution that conferred broader powers on the presidency. In addition to bringing in thousands of Cuban doctors to work in Venezuelan slums, he began establishing himself as the alternative to neoliberalism, becoming a hero to many American and European leftists. [73]

Chávez's relationship with Washington deteriorated after he was briefly ousted by a coup in 2002 and the Bush administration, instead of condemning the overthrow of a democratically elected president, said the country's chaotic political climate had forced him to resign. Other Latin governments, however, condemned the coup, which collapsed after two days. [74]

Chávez's popularity and aggressive international presence grew as rising oil prices filled Venezuela's coffers, igniting a stream of commentary and debate over Latin America's turn to the left. [75] ■

CURRENT SITUATION

Mexican Election

Andrés Manuel López Obrador, the fiery politician who — apparently — barely lost the Mexican presidential election on July 2, wants his followers to take to the streets until all ballots are recounted. The former Mexico City mayor, who ran on the Democratic Revolutionary Party ticket, didn't say what he would do if Mexico's Electoral Tribunal rejected his appeal. But his spokesman, Gerardo Fernandez Noroña, said cryptically, "The other road is insurrection." [76]

Meanwhile, president-elect Felipe Calderón of the conservative National Action Party accepted congratulations from President Bush and other world leaders and tried to convey the image of a dynamic leader. "This is a plural country," he said, "and everyone's first responsibility, especially mine, is reconciliation." [77]

On July 5 Mexico's independent Federal Electoral Institute announced that Calderón had outpolled López Obrador by 244,000 votes — roughly 0.6 percent of the 41 million votes cast. [78]

As expected, Calderón swept northern and central Mexico, where industry and agribusiness are centered and Calderón's free-market ideology has long been popular. Support for government programs to counter poverty and inequality runs strong in Mexico's poorer southern states, where López Obrador dominated.

Outside experts say the close results mean Calderón will have to bend to the left. "He is going to have to put poverty reduction at the top of his list," said former U.S. ambassador to Mexico James R. Jones, a consultant on Latin American business.

The country's socioeconomic profile would seem to have created the ideal conditions for victory for a crowd-pleasing politician who vowed to better the lot of the hungry masses. [79] About half of Mexico's 100 million people live in poverty, though the $6,770 average per capita income is Latin America's highest. [80] To boost the economy, López Obrador vowed to revise NAFTA. Many on both sides of the border say Mexican business and agriculture can't compete with cheap U.S. imports that have flooded Mexico since NAFTA went into effect in 1994. [81]

But Jorge G. Castañeda, a former foreign minister under Fox, says voters defied stereotyping by not flocking to López Obrador. "Let's suppose López Obrador was a charismatic, change-inspiring candidate who was the candidate of the poor in a country where the poor are the overwhelming majority," Castañeda says. "Then explain to me why he didn't win by 20 points."

AFP Photo/Getty Images/Antonio Scorza

Houses perch precariously on a hillside in the Rocinha shantytown of Rio de Janeiro, Brazil, reflecting the overcrowding and poverty afflicting Latin America.

Distrust is a factor, even within López Obrador's own party, say Castañeda and others, pointing out that Cuauhtémoc Cárdenas — the son of Mexico's most revered 20th-century president and the 1988 challenger who tried to end the Institutional Revolutionary Party's monopoly on power — never endorsed López Obrador.

Reaching Out

The Inter-American Development Bank knows it has a problem. The IDB is a major source of low-cost financing for projects designed to reduce poverty and inequality in Latin America, but socioeconomic inequality remains widespread.

"It is clear that we need to reach the majority of people in the region," says Donald Terry, manager of the bank's Multilateral Investment Fund. "We want to make it more relevant."

Only a handful of countries in Africa and the former Soviet Union exceed Latin America's pattern of concentrated wealth. The World Bank concluded that the richest 10 percent of Latin Americans receive 40 to 47 percent of the region's income. By contrast, the wealthiest 10 percent in the United States receive 31 percent of the nation's income. [82]

To close the gap, the bank launched an initiative in June to generate projects that would make an immediate difference to ordinary Latin Americans' lives. Over the next five years, the bank plans to double spending on basic infrastructure programs, such as water and sewer service, to $1 billion; create a new $1 billion loan program for small and medium-sized businesses; and triple — to $15 million — the amounts available from private lenders for small-scale "micro-credit" loans. The bank is also studying ways to help millions of marginalized citizens obtain birth certificates or other proof of citizenship so they can gain access to social services and schools. Some 8.5 million of the region's children lack birth certificates.

The bank's initiative is designed to stimulate business development, rather than fund government-owned enterprises, so private firms will employ more people, said IDB President Moreno. Such a market orientation has become the dominant approach among Latino businesspeople and many politicians since the 1990s.

An influential advocate of the market approach, economist Hernando de Soto of Peru, helped shape the bank's initiative. After studying poor people's assets in the region, he concluded that homes, land and businesses that lie outside the formal economy — and thus are untitled — represent $1 trillion in market value. But since the owners don't have deeds to prove ownership, they can't get mortgages to borrow against their assets to expand businesses, improve homes or pay for schooling. What they have, says de Soto, is "dead capital." [83]

Even with all those assets lying fallow, the region's economy has reached a level of stability that makes the IDB initiative possible, Moreno says. Since 2002, the region has experienced steady economic expansion, with GDP growth of 4.1 percent projected for 2006.

If that projection holds, regional growth in 2003-2006 will have reached 4.1 percent — compared with 2.6 percent in 1990-2002. [84] But that is still below projected growth levels of developed nations, which are projected to attain GDP growth of 5.7 percent during the same period (4.8 percent if China is left out). [85]

However, warns economist Liliana Rojas Suárez, a senior fellow at the Center for Global Development, "Growth has been very volatile over the last decade. There's no assurance or confidence it could continue at the current pace."

Economic uncertainty aside, the bank must convince Latin Americans that the initiative represents a real break from past programs. "I don't see a lot of difference," says Alejandro Gaviria, dean of economics at the University of the Andes in Bogotá. "The bank has been involved with micro-credit for quite some time. Now they're to focus even more on that. Apart from that, I don't see anything really different."

At the June IDB conference, when Latin American reporters largely echoed Gaviria's skepticism, Moreno responded: "This is an initiative that's pragmatic, that's socially oriented, that's dynamic and that's aimed at achieving concrete results. Typically, institutions of this size don't focus on this kind of work. That's what's new."

U.N. Fight

U.S. opposition to Venezuela's efforts to obtain a temporary seat on the United Nations Security Council has also exacerbated tensions between the Bush administration and Venezuela. Both Venezuela and Guatemala are competing for the seat, and U.S. officials have made clear that they're backing Guatemala.

As a Security Council member, Venezuela could block U.S. initiatives on such matters as dealing with Iran's development of nuclear technology. [86] "Venezuela in international institutions, in multilateral organizations, has an agenda which is peculiar, which is not necessarily related to the organizations themselves, and which always has a confrontational and conflicted edge," Assistant Secretary of State Shannon said on June 2. [87]

Shannon's tone didn't begin to match the intensity of remarks by his Venezuelan counterpart, Mari Pili Hernandez, vice minister of foreign affairs for North American Affairs. "It is illegitimate, disrespectful, shameful and immoral that the United States is trying to pressure friendly, sister nations to vote against Venezuela," she said in a written statement in June. [88]

The Security Council seat is one of 10 that rotate among U.N. members that do not have permanent places on the council. *

"Guatemala was one of the founding members of the U.N. but has never served on the Security Council," Deputy Secretary of State Robert B. Zoellick said. "So, not surprisingly, when you face issues like we'll be facing, such as Iran, it's good to have a country that has been at the heart of the U.N. system and who appreciates the role that it can play." [89]

Some five weeks later, Frank C. Urbancic, the State Department's principal deputy coordinator for counterterrorism, testified in Congress that Venezuelan diplomats were obstructing U.S. efforts to strengthen anti-terrorism efforts in the region. At one inter-governmental meeting in March, "The Venezuelan delegation . . . asserted that the United States is the biggest security threat in the region," Urbancic told the House Subcommittee on International Terrorism and Nonproliferation. He also cited growing ties between Venezuela and Iran, and Colombian guerrilla activity on Venezuelan territory. "In the international community's fight against terrorism, Venezuela is a liability," Urbancic said. [90]

U.S. officials can only hope they fare better in the Security Council race than they did in a contest last year for secretary-general of the Organization of American States (OAS). "The Bush administration's mishandling of a situation that called for diplomacy and strategic thinking has had huge costs for U.S. credibility and influence in the region," said Inter-American Dialogue's Shifter. [91]

Traditionally, the U.S.-supported candidate always got the OAS job. But hemispheric dynamics have shifted. With Venezuela lobbying actively for rejection of whomever the United States backed, the Bush administration first

* Permanent Security Council members are the United States, France, Britain, the Russian Federation and China.

Continued on p. 618

At Issue:

Is the U.S. winning the drug war in Latin America?

ANNE W. PATTERSON
ASSISTANT SECRETARY OF STATE FOR INTERNATIONAL NARCOTICS AND LAW ENFORCEMENT

FROM TESTIMONY BEFORE THE HOUSE WESTERN HEMISPHERE SUBCOMMITTEE, MARCH 30, 2006

yes

The eradication and interdiction efforts of our partner nations have, with U.S. support, kept hundreds of tons of cocaine, heroin and marijuana out of our country. Today, U.S. cocaine consumption has leveled off and casual use is down substantially, while drug abuse is growing throughout the hemisphere. The inter-American dialogue on drugs has changed accordingly. The United States plays an important leadership role but is no longer alone in pressing for effective action.

Countries are seizing more drugs, extraditing more fugitives, participating in more cross-border operations and rooting out and punishing corruption. All around the Americas, countries are opting for creative ways to work with their neighbors. Mexico and Colombia are staunch allies. El Salvador stepped forward to host the new International Law Enforcement Academy for the Americas.

Andean countries, Central American states and Mexico reported seizing 365 metric tons of cocaine worth tens of billions of dollars on the street. Mexican authorities . . . uncovered over $40 million in currency hidden in cargo bound for Colombia. U.S. and international support assisted Colombia in aerially eradicating [343,500 acres] and manually eradicating another [76,600 acres] of illegal coca. Peru manually eradicated [nearly 29,700 acres] of coca and seized 11 tons of drugs. Mexico eradicated [more than 49,400 acres] of opium poppy and [74,000 acres] of marijuana and seized 30 tons of cocaine, 1,700 tons of marijuana and nearly a ton of methamphetamine.

[White House Office of National Drug Control Policy] figures show that the use of illegal drugs by teenagers in the United States has dropped by nearly 20 percent since 2001. From 2003 to 2004, the purity of heroin in the U.S. decreased by 22 percent while the price rose by 30 percent. Since February 2005, a similar, albeit preliminary, pattern has been seen with cocaine, although these drugs are still readily available. However, we believe overall demand has begun to stabilize.

I firmly believe if the United States were not supporting counter-narcotics programs in the Americas the situation here would be dramatically worse. Without a concerted effort to eliminate drugs at their source, we would have rising addiction rates because more drugs would be available at lower prices.

We have a huge amount of work to do. It is both a "war" to be fought and won and an ongoing effort to protect our country from foreign criminal threats.

JOY OLSON
EXECUTIVE DIRECTOR, WASHINGTON OFFICE ON LATIN AMERICA

FROM TESTIMONY BEFORE THE HOUSE WESTERN HEMISPHERE SUBCOMMITTEE, MARCH 30, 2006

no

U.S. drug policy in Latin America has been ineffective at achieving its own goals and has generated much collateral damage. We have lost sight of the fundamental need — to reduce drug consumption and the associated damage to society.

The supply-control strategies into which we have poured so many billions of dollars have patently failed to shrink drug availability. The . . . main illicit drugs targeted by U.S. efforts in Latin America — cocaine and heroin — remain readily available at near-record low prices.

The area under coca cultivation in the Andes for 2005 . . . will be roughly . . . 442,000 acres — only 3 percent lower than the estimate for the year 2000.

In 1989, the U.S. Congress made the U.S. military the "single lead agency" in the detection and monitoring of drugs coming into the United States. While the military initially resisted this role, they did what any democratic military does when assigned a job by the civilians: They embraced the role. They also turned to their partners in the region — Latin American militaries — for help.

Use of the military does provide short-term results, but lasting impact requires dismantling trafficking networks. Only police and judicial institutions can do this. By investing in military approaches we are not investing in long-term solutions.

U.S. drug policy in the region is plagued by short-term thinking that leads to tactical victories that often make the problem worse and create collateral damage. Every time we are "successful" in eradicating drug production through forced eradication, we displace people who move elsewhere, often moving production and environmental damage with them. When we are "successful" through interdiction in limiting trafficking in one area, it moves somewhere else, bringing corruption and violence to a new country or region.

In the past three years I have had countless conversations about U.S. drug policy in the region with U.S. policymakers from both side of the aisle. The overwhelming sentiment is that . . . current policy does not work but that . . . it is political suicide to challenge the policy or think outside the box.

I have also traveled extensively throughout the [United States] over the past year giving public presentations. Not one person stood up and said, "Why are you questioning this successful policy?"

Continued from p. 616

threw its support behind a candidate from El Salvador, in part to reward it for having sent troops to Iraq. But the Salvadoran candidate got so little support he withdrew. The administration then backed Mexican Foreign Minister Luis Ernesto Derbez. [92]

But with some nations reluctant to go along with the United States, the Chilean candidate — then-Interior Minister José Miguel Insulza — won the most votes and became secretary-general. [93]

Now, the United States is pressuring Chile not to support Venezuela's Security Council bid. [94] "The Chileans aren't going to go along," predicts a U.N. staffer, who asked to remain anonymous. "They don't want to be seen as puppets of the United States." ■

OUTLOOK

Spring Forward?

Free and fair elections have arrived in Latin America to stay, say most observers. Moreover, the emergence of forceful, new leaders such as Venezuela's Chávez, Bolivia's Morales, Colombia's Uribe and Argentina's Kirchner — shows that honest elections can coexist with the much older tradition of the caudillo — the strongman.

"Caudillos are not going to go away," says Shifter of Inter-American Dialogue. "The new model of leaders do have legitimacy; they are elected, but they certainly are operating in a weak institutional context."

By all accounts, justice systems in which all citizens are treated the same are the weak points in Latin American political culture. But little hope exists that strong courts and other institutions will be established in most countries over the next 10 to 15 years.

"I don't see it happening" in the poorest countries, says the Heritage Foundation's Johnson. "If you have judges that don't even have courtrooms, who sit in offices and write opinions that most people don't see, they're susceptible to bribes, and a small-business man sued by a large corporation may never get a fair break."

Bolivian novelist Lechín agrees that development of institutions that lessen the ruling classes' political and economic power is essential. "With these elites, Latin America isn't going to get anywhere," he says.

With Fidel Castro's departure from the scene perhaps imminent — he turns 80 in August — Cuba is virtually certain to undergo major changes during the next decade. The Bush administration's Commission on Assistance to a Free Cuba is preparing a second set of recommendations to President Bush (the first was made in 2004), reportedly designed to step up pressure on the Castro regime to democratize. [95]

Oswaldo José Payá Sardiñas, a leading Cuban dissident who has led the drafting of a grass-roots transition plan, said that under its terms, "There will be no lynchings, no revenge, no exclusions. Those now in power will have the same rights as all citizens. There will be no uncontrolled privatizations, but there will be a guarantee for the right of all Cubans to a free economy, the right to have private enterprise and to trade freely." [96]

Changes in Cuba will be accompanied by dramatic demographic upheavals regionwide. In the next two decades, the population of Latin America and the Caribbean is projected to grow by 44 percent, from 559 million in 2005 to 702 million in 2025. [97] Population pressure on poor Andean and Central American countries, in particular, is likely to foster more populist measures, and perhaps more immigration to the United States, Johnson says.

But what some analysts call populist, others call pro-growth. Weisbrot of the Center for Economic and Policy Research says the left-wing surge in Latin America will see a growing reliance on government spending to spur economic development — a repeat of what authoritarian governments did to foster growth in the 1940s-1960s. "I'm very optimistic. I think most of the region is going to return to the status of normal, developing countries that actually grow."

At the same time, he says, global economic developments are likely to lessen Latin America's dependence on the U.S. market. "Almost all economists recognize that the U.S. trade deficit is not sustainable, and adjustments to lessen it will cause the U.S. market for imports to shrink over the next decade," Weisbrot says. "That is going to have a huge impact on countries that export a lot to the United States. They're going to be forced to diversify their markets."

Petro, the left-wing Colombian congressman from Bogotá, also sees a bright future. The key, he says, is that Latin Americans seeking socioeconomic change need no longer fear for their lives. "Thirty years ago, we had the beginnings of a Latin American spring, when people on the left in various countries tried to undertake peaceful change," Petro says. Instead, tens of thousands were hunted down and killed.

"I don't believe that that experience will be repeated," Petro says. "Societies will be able to take up the issue of social inequality, and to deepen democracy," he says. "Another spring is here." ■

Notes

[1] "Chávez Calls Bush Coward Over Iraq War," BBC Monitoring Latin America — Political, March 20, 2006.

[2] Pablo Bachelet, "White House labels 3 Latin American countries as 'challenges,' " *The Miami Herald*, March 16, 2006.

[3] Karen DeYoung, "U.S. Seen as Weak Patron of Latin Democracy," *The Washington Post*, April 16, 2002, p. A15; Alexandra Olson,

"Dramatic Two Days in Venezuela," The Associated Press, April 16, 2002.

[4] "Building Opportunity for the Majority," Inter-American Development Bank, June 2006; www.iadb.org/bop/about.cfm?language=En&parid=2; for additional information, see "Improving on the Latin rate of growth," *The Economist*, May 20-26, 2006, pp. 40-41. For a detailed study of inequality and its roots, see Guillermo Perry, *et al.*, "Inequality in Latin America and the Caribbean: Breaking With History?" The World Bank, 2003, summary, pp. 2-4; http://lnweb18.worldbank.org/LAC/LAC.nsf/ECADocByUnid/4112F1114F594B4B85256DB3005DB262?Opendocument.

[5] Luis Alberto Moreno, "Building Opportunity for the Majority," June 12, 2006; www.iadb.org/NEWS/articledetail.cfm?Language=En&parid=5&artType=SP&artid=3124.

[6] *The Economist, op. cit.*

[7] James C. McKinley Jr. and Ginger Thompson, "Conservative Wins in Mexico In Final Tally," *The New York Times*, July 7, 2006, p. A1. See also Hector Tobar and Richard Boudreaux, "Now the Leftist Has the Lead in Mexico," *Los Angeles Times*, July 6, 2006, p. A1.

[8] For accounts of the 1968 and 1988 events, see Julia Preston and Samuel Dillon, *Opening Mexico: The Making of a Democracy* (2004), pp. 70-81, 379-382 (1968); pp. 158-180 (1988).

[9] For an account of the coup-and-guerrilla era and its fading, see Jorge G. Castañeda, *Utopia Unarmed: The Latin American Left After the Cold War* (1992).

[10] Elections have already been held in Bolivia, Colombia, Costa Rica, Chile, Honduras, Peru and Mexico. Countries with elections scheduled in 2006 are Brazil, Ecuador, Nicaragua and Venezuela. For dates and candidates in each race, see *CIA World Factbook*, www.cia.gov/cia/publications/factbook/.

[11] Quoted in Juan Forero, "Failure in '90, Ex-President Wins in Peru in a Comeback," *The New York Times*, June 5, 2006, p. A13. See also Agence France-Presse, "Peru's Garcia insists on respect in relations with Venezuela," June 6, 2006.

[12] Congressman Juán José García Ochoa quoted in Hector Tobar, "Feuding Fox, Chavez Recall Envoys," *Los Angeles Times*, Nov. 15, 2005, p. A3.

[13] For background, see David Masci, "Trouble in South America," *CQ Researcher*, March 14, 2003, pp. 225-248.

[14] Juan Forero, "Seeking United Latin America, Venezuela's Chavez is Divider," *The New York Times*, May 20, 2006, p. A1.

[15] For praise of the Brazilian model from World Bank officials, see David De Ferranti and Vinod Thomas, "Why eyes are on Brazil; a new model of growth," *International Herald Tribune*, Dec. 24, 2003, p. A6; for Brazilian business-community views, see Larry Rohter, "Brazil's Opposition Shelters President From Scandal, For Now," *The New York Times*, Aug. 14, 2005, p. A3. For background on "Bolsa Escola," see Jon Jeter, "Brazil Pays its Poor to Send Kids to School," *The Washington Post*, July 1, 2003, p. A7.

[16] "Building Opportunity for the Majority: Luis Alberto Moreno and President William Clinton," dialogue transcript, June 15, 2006; http://idbdocs.iadb.org/wsdocs/getdocument.aspx?docnum=758538.

[17] Quoted in Joseph Contreras and Phil Gunson, "Venezuela: Balance of Power," *Newsweek*, Atlantic edition, Feb. 14, 2005, p. 36.

[18] "Energy Security: Issues Related to Potential Reductions in Venezuelan Oil Production," U.S. Government Accountability Office, June 2006; www.gao.gov/new.items/ d06668.pdf. For U.S. oil import figures, see, "U.S. imports by country of origin," Energy Information Administration [updated regularly], http://tonto.eia.doe.gov/dnav/pet/pet_move_impcus_a2_nus_ep00_im0_mbbl_m.htm.

[19] Tim Padgett, "Crackdown in Caracas," *Time*, March 3, 2003, p. 33; Tim Padgett, "Tracking Hurricane Hugo," *Time*, July 11, 2005, p. 40.

[20] Peter Beaumont, "Review: The New Kid in the Barrio," *The Observer* [London], May 7, 2006, p. 6; Brian Ellsworth, "Dispatches From Chavez' Venezuela," *Slate*, Aug. 12, 2004; www.slate.com/id/2105063/entry/2105064.

[21] José Suárez-Náñez, "A $25,8 millardos asciende solidaridad económica de Venezuela en la región," *El Nacional* [Caracas], Feb. 4, 2006. The sources cited were statements by Chávez, central bank announcements and documentation of appropriations. A veteran Venezuelan public-sector economist says the absence of hard documentation makes the numbers impossible to confirm.

[22] Juan Forero, "Chavez Uses Aid to Win Support in the Americas," *The New York Times*, April 4, 2006, p. A1; Andres Oppenheimer, "Chávez making friends while Bush earning enmity," *The Miami Herald*, Feb. 9, 2006, p. A12; Tim Padgett, "Venezuela's Oil Giveaway," Time.com, Feb. 7, 2006; "Citgo's Low Cost Heating Oil Program, undated press release; www.citgo.com/CommunityInvolvement/HeatingOil.jsp.

[23] Larry Rohter, "As Argentina's Debt Dwindles, President's Power Steadily Grows," *The New York Times*, Jan. 3, 2006, p. A1; "Kirchner defendió en Madrid la inversión estatal," [In Madrid, Kirchner defended state investment], *La Nación* [Buenos Aires], June 23, 2006.

[24] Hugo Rafael Chávez Frías, "Inauguración del Diálogo Ministerial Sobre la Carta Social de las Américas," Venezuelan Ministry of Foreign Affairs, Aug. 28, 2005, www.mre.gov.ve/Noticias/Presidente-Chavez/A2005/Discurso-240.htm.

[25] Teodoro Petkoff, "Las dos izquierdas," *Revista Digital Consenso*, No. 4, October 2005; www.consenso.org/05/articulos/06_01.shtml.

[26] Guy Dinmore, "Chavez jet deal seen as 'waste of money,' " *Financial Times* [London], June 16, 2006, p. 5; Juan Forero, "Venezuela's Rag-Tag Reserves Are Marching As to War," *The New York Times*, June 11, 2006, p. A3.

[27] Jorge G. Castañeda, "Latin America's Left Turn," *Foreign Affairs*, May-June, 2006; www.foreignaffairs.org/20060501faessay85302/jorge-g-castaneda/latin-america-s-left-turn.html.

[28] "U.S. Aid to Colombia Since 1997: Summary Tables," Center for International Policy, updated June 13, 2006, http://ciponline.org/colombia/aidtable.htm.

[29] Chris Kraul, "Uribe's Second Term is a First," *Los Angeles Times*, May 29, 2006, p. A16.

[30] For background see Mary H. Cooper, "Rethinking NAFTA," *CQ Researcher*, June 7, 1996, pp. 481-504; and David Masci, "U.S.-Mexico Relations," *CQ Researcher*, Nov. 9, 2001, pp. 921-944.

[31] Jeffrey S. Passel and Roberto Suro, "Rise, Peak, and Decline: Trends in U.S. Immigration 1992-2004," Pew Hispanic Center, Sept. 27, 2005, pp.10-12.

[32] Paul Blustein, "Trade Ministers Give Up on Compromise," *The Washington Post*, July 2, 2006, p. A18; Jeffrey L. Schott, "Does FTAA Have a Future?" Institute for International Economics, November 2005, pp. 1, 10.

[33] Rachel van Dongen, "Expiration of Fast Track a Blow to Bush Strategy," *CQ Weekly*, June 5, 2006, p. 1535.

[34] Andres Oppenheimer, "Colombian tycoons wage a battle against free trade," *The Miami Herald*, March 2, 2006, p. A10.

[35] Hal Weitzman, "Ecuador erupts in protests over US oil group," *Financial Times* [London], May 10, 2006, p. A6; Richard Lapper and Hal Weitzman, "US deplores Ecuador decision to revoke Occidental contract," *Financial Times* [London], May 17, 2006, p. A8; Elisabeth Malkin, "Central American Trade Deal is Being Delayed by Partners," *The New York Times*, March 2, 2006, p. C3.

[36] Benedict Mander, "Uruguayans lose faith in Mercosur trade pact," *Financial Times* [London], March 21, 2006, p. 9.
[37] Oscar Arias, "Latin America's Shift to the Center," *The Washington Post*, March 15, 2006, p. A19.
[38] Stephen Kinzer, "The Trouble with Costa Rica," *The New York Review of Books*, June 8, 2006, p. 56.
[39] Hugo Chávez, "Aló Presidente," April 2, 2006, www.alopresidente.gob.ve/docs/Alocuciones/Alo_Presidente_251.pdf.
[40] The Minneapolis area's gross metropolitan product in 2004, the latest figure available, was about $145 billion; Venezuela's present GDP is about $153 billion. See "The Role of Metro Areas in the U.S. Economy," *Global Insight*, U.S. Conference of Mayors, Jan. 13, 2006, p. 12, www.mayors.org/74thWinterMeeting/metroeconreport_January2006.pdf; "Venezuela," *CIA World Factbook*, updated July 11, 2006, www.odci.gov/cia/publications/factbook/print/ve.html.
[41] Unless otherwise indicated, information in this section is drawn from Williamson, *op. cit.*
[42] For background, see Thomas E. Skidmore and Peter H. Smith, *Modern Latin America* (1989), pp. 232-233.
[43] Stephen Schlesinger and Stephen Kinzer, *Bitter Fruit: The Untold Story of the American Coup in Guatemala* (1983); also see Kate Doyle and Peter Kornbluh, "CIA and Assassinations: The Guatemala 1954 Documents," *National Security Archive Electronic Briefing Book No. 4*, [undated], www.gwu.edu/~nsarchiv/NSAEBB/NSAEBB4.
[44] *Ibid.*
[45] Jon Lee Anderson, *Che: A Revolutionary Life* (1997), pp. 128-159.
[46] Material in this section drawn from Hugh Thomas, *Cuba: The Pursuit of Freedom* (1971).
[47] See Human Rights Watch reports and position papers, including, "Cuba: Human Rights Concerns for the 61st Session of the U.N. Commission on Human Rights," March 10, 2005; http://hrw.org/english/docs/2005/03/10/cuba10306.htm.
[48] Castro quoted in Thomas, *op. cit.*, p. 1202; for purges, see pp. 1244-1256; for Guevara and executions, see Anderson, *op. cit.*, pp. 375-425.
[49] Anderson, *op. cit.*, pp. 393-395, 418-421, 435, 677-678, 707.
[50] Information in this section drawn from Stephen G. Rabe, *The Most Dangerous Area in the World: John F. Kennedy Confronts Communist Revolution in Latin America* (1999).
[51] "Modern History Sourcebook: John F. Kennedy on the Alliance for Progress," Fordham University, March 13, 1961, www.fordham.edu/halsall/mod/1961kennedy-afp1.html.
[52] *Ibid.*, pp. 141-142.
[53] Julia Preston and Samuel Dillon, *Opening Mexico: The Making of a Democracy* (2004), pp. 70-81, 379-382.
[54] For a recent estimate of the number killed and disappeared, see Larry Rohter, "Colonel's Death Gives Clues to Pinochet Arms Deals," *The New York Times*, June 19, 2006, p. A6; the number of torture victims was determined in 2005 by Chile's Presidential Commission on Political Imprisonment and Torture; see "La Comisión Sobre Prisión Política y Tortura," May 2005, www.comisiontortura.cl/inicio/index.php.
[55] "On 30th Anniversary of Argentine Coup," National Security Archive, March 23, 2006; www.gwu.edu/~nsarchiv/NSAEBB/NSAEBB185/index.htm.
[56] Christopher Marquis and Diana Jean Schemo, "Documents Shed Light on Assassination of Chilean in U.S.," *The New York Times*, Nov. 14, 2000, p. A14.

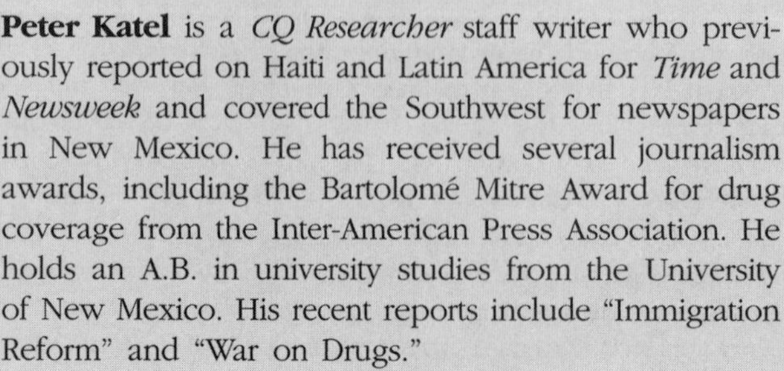

About the Author

Peter Katel is a *CQ Researcher* staff writer who previously reported on Haiti and Latin America for *Time* and *Newsweek* and covered the Southwest for newspapers in New Mexico. He has received several journalism awards, including the Bartolomé Mitre Award for drug coverage from the Inter-American Press Association. He holds an A.B. in university studies from the University of New Mexico. His recent reports include "Immigration Reform" and "War on Drugs."

[57] *Ibid.*
[58] Diana Jean Schemo, "Papers Show No Protest by Kissinger on Argentina," *The New York Times*, Aug. 27, 2004, p. A3; see also, "Kissinger to Argentines on Dirty War: 'The Quicker You Succeed the Better,' " National Security Archive, Dec. 4, 2003; www.gwu.edu/~nsarchiv/NSAEBB/NSAEBB104.
[59] "The Pentagon and the CIA Sent a Mixed Message to the Argentine Military," National Security Archive, March 28, 2003; www.gwu.edu/~nsarchiv/NSAEBB/NSAEBB8; Williamson, *op. cit.*, pp. 477-483.
[60] For Sandino background, see Williamson, *op. cit.*, p. 324.
[61] Skidmore and Smith, *op. cit.*, pp. 318-322.
[62] Johanna Neuman, "Ronald Wilson Reagan, 1911-2004," *Los Angeles Times*, June 6, 2004, p. A1.
[63] "From Madness to Hope: The 12-Year War in El Salvador," *The Commission on the Truth for El Salvador*, Part 4, Chapter 4, 1993, www.usip.org/library/tc/doc/reports/el_salvador/tc_es_03151993_casesD1_2.html#D1; Tim Golden, "U.N. Report Urges Sweeping Changes in Salvador Army," *The New York Times*, March 16, 1993, p. A1.
[64] *Ibid.* See also Guy Gugliotta and Douglas Farah, "12 Years of Tortured Truth on El Salvador," *The Washington Post*, March 21, 1993, p. A1, and Tracy Wilkinson, "Officials, Death Squads Get Most Salvador Blame," *Los Angeles Times*, March 16, 1993, p. A1.
[65] Larry Rohter, "Guatemalans Formally End 36-Year Civil War, Central America's Longest and Deadliest," *The New York Times*, Dec. 29, 1996, p. A8; Mireya Navarro, "Guatemalan Army Waged 'Genocide,' New Report Finds," *The New York Times*, Feb. 25, 1999, p. A1; an English-language version of the commission report is available from American Association for the Advancement of Science, http://shr.aaas.org/guatemala/ceh/report/english/toc.html.
[66] Information in this section drawn from Preston and Dillon, *op. cit.*
[67] For background see Peter Katel, "Emerging China," *CQ Researcher*, Nov. 11, 2005, pp. 957-980.
[68] Geri Smith and Cristina Lindblad, "Was NAFTA Worth It?" *Business Week*, Dec. 22, 2003, p. 34; Passel and Suro, *op. cit.*
[69] Sebastian Rotella and Natalia Tarnawiecki, "Fujimori Has Peru Waiting, Wondering," *Los Angeles Times*, Sept. 18, 2000, p. A1.
[70] Sebastian Rotella, "Special Report: Latin America; 3 Degrees of Hardships," *Los Angeles Times*, Jan. 10, 1999, p. C1.

FOR MORE INFORMATION

Center for Economic and Policy Research, 1611 Connecticut Ave., N.W., Suite 400, Washington, DC 20009; (202) 293-5380; www.cepr.net. The liberal think tank's reports on Latin America focus on economic and political issues.

Center for International Policy, 1717 Massachusetts Ave., N.W., Suite 801, Washington, DC 20036; (202) 232-3317; http://ciponline.org. The liberal think tank provides data and analysis on Colombia, Cuba and Central America.

The Heritage Foundation, 214 Massachusetts Ave., N.E., Washington, DC 20002; (202) 546-4400; www.heritage.org. The conservative think tank actively studies Latin America.

Human Rights Watch, 350 Fifth Ave., 34th floor, New York, NY 10118; (212) 290-4700; http://hrw.org. The nonpartisan human rights advocacy organization prepares investigative reports on the region.

Inter-American Development Bank, 1300 New York Ave., N.W., Washington, DC 20577; (202) 623-1000; www.iadb.org. The bank funds projects to promote socioeconomic improvement.

Inter-American Dialogue, 1211 Connecticut Ave., N.W., Suite 510, Washington, DC 20036; (202) 822-9002. The nonpartisan think tank produces research focusing on trade, remittances and government accountability.

Latin American and Caribbean Center, Florida International University, University Park, DM 353, Miami, FL 33199; (305) 348-2894; http://lacc.fiu.edu/index. The center studies remittances, anti-crime policies and the Colombian diaspora.

Washington Office on Latin America, 1630 Connecticut Ave., N.W., Suite 200, Washington, DC 20009; (202) 797-2171; http://wola.org. The longtime left-liberal group focuses on human rights and public safety.

[71] Sebastian Rotella and Chris Kraul, "IMF Announces $49.7-Billion Rescue Package for Argentina," *Los Angeles Times*, Dec. 19, 2000, p. A1; Clifford Krauss, "With No Hope For Economy, Many Argentines Are Leaving," *The New York Times*, Nov. 24, 2000, p. A3; Hector Tobar, "Rioting Forces President Out in Argentina," *Los Angeles Times*, Dec. 21, 2001, p. A1; Larry Rohter, "Blows Keep Coming for Argentina in Long Crisis," *The New York Times*, June 26, 2002, p. W1.

[72] For the history of the drug boom, see Guy Gugliotta and Jeff Leen, *Kings of Cocaine: Inside the Medellín Cartel, an Astonishing True Story of Murder, Money and International Corruption* (1989); for a narrative of political violence in the 1980s and '90s, see Steven Dudley, *Walking Ghosts: Murder and Guerrilla Politics in Colombia* (2006). The Center for International Policy maintains a vast Web site of documents and statistics.

[73] Beaumount, *op. cit.*; Ellsworth, *op. cit.*

[74] DeYoung, *op. cit.*; Olson, *op. cit.*

[75] For a sampling of representative views, see, Castañeda, "Latin America's Left Turn," *op. cit.*; Mark Weisbrot, "Latin American 'Populism' Doing Well," Center for Economic and Policy Research, March 19, 2006; www.cepr.net/columns/weisbrot/2006_03_19.htm.

[76] Quoted in Richard Boudreaux and Carlos Martínez, "Lopez Obrador Files Challenges," *Los Angeles Times*, July 10, 2006, p. A4; López Obrador paraphrased in James C. McKinley Jr. and Ginger Thompson, "Leftist Predicts Unrest Without Complete Recount of Mexican Election," *The New York Times*, p. A1, July 9, 2006.

[77] McKinley and Thompson, *ibid.*

[78] Manuel Roig-Franzia, "Mexico Vote Tally Gives Free-Trader a Narrow Victory," *The Washington Post*, July 7, 2006, p. A1.

[79] Marla Dickerson, "Placing Blame For Mexico's Ills," *Los Angeles Times*, July 1, 2006, p. C1, and Ginger Thompson, "Mexican Election to Hinge on a Conflicted Middle Class," *The New York Times*, July 2, 2006, p. A8.

[80] "Mexico Country Brief," The World Bank, updated April 2006; http://web.worldbank.org/WBSITE/EXTERNAL/COUNTRIES/LACEXT/MEXICOEXTN/0,,menuPK:338407~pagePK:141132~piPK:141107~theSitePK:338397,00.html.

[81] *Ibid.*

[82] Guillermo Perry, *et al.*, "Inequality in Latin America and the Caribbean: Breaking With History?" The World Bank, 2003, summary, pp. 2-4; http://lnweb18.worldbank.org/LAC/LAC.nsf/ECADocByUnid/4112F1114F594B4B85256DB3005DB262?Opendocument.

[83] "Mapping Dead Capital," June 2006, Inter-American Development Bank; www.iadb.org/bop/mapping_capital.cfm?language=En&parid=4.

[84] "Preliminary Overview of the Economics of Latin America and the Caribbean, 2005," Economic Commission for Latin America and the Caribbean, December 2005, pp. 13-17; www.eclac.cl/publicaciones/DesarrolloEconomico/2/LCG2292PI/LCG2292_i_Chapter_1.pdf.

[85] *Ibid.*, p. 14.

[86] Paul Richter and Maggie Farley, "U.S. is Aiming to Block Venezuela's Bid for U.N. Role," *Los Angeles Times*, June 19, 2006, p. A1.

[87] "On-the-record briefing," June 2, 2006, U.S. State Department; www.usemb.gov.do/OAS_GA/on-the-record_briefing.htm.

[88] "Vice-ministra: es 'inmoral' presión de EEUU contra Venezuela," The Associated Press, June 21, 2006.

[89] "Press Availability at the General Assembly of the Organization of American States," U.S. State Department, June 5, 2006; www.state.gov/s/d/rem/2006/67591.htm.

[90] "Venezuela: Terrorism Hub of South America?," Frank C. Urbancic, principal deputy coordinator, counterterrorism, U.S. State Department, July 13, 2006, http://www.state.gov/s/ct/rls/rm/2006/68968.htm.

[91] Hector Tobar and Paul Richter, "Leftist-backed Chilean Likely to Head OAS," *Los Angeles Times*, April 30, 2005, p. A7.

[92] *Ibid.*

[93] *Ibid.*

[94] "Daily Press Briefing," U.S. State Department, June 20, 2006; www.state.gov/r/pa/prs/dpb/2006/68134.htm.

[95] Pablo Bachelet, "Report urges funding Castro foes," *The Miami Herald*, June 30, p. A1. A State Department spokesman refuses to comment on the draft.

[96] Oswaldo José Payá Sardiñas, "The Unstoppable Cuban Spring," *The Washington Post*, July 1, 2006, p. A25.

[97] "2005 World Population Data Sheet," Population Reference Bureau, 2005, p. 8; www.prb.org/pdf05/05WorldDataSheet_Eng.pdf.

Bibliography

Selected Sources

Books

Anderson, Jon Lee, *Che: A Revolutionary Life*, Grove Press, 1997.
The New Yorker foreign correspondent moved to Cuba to research this detailed but exciting portrait of Che Guevara and his era.

Blustein, Paul, *And the Money Kept Rolling In (and Out): Wall Street, the IMF and the Bankrupting of Argentina*, Public Affairs, 2006.
The economics correspondent for *The Washington Post* spares neither foreign bankers nor Argentina's political class in examining Latin America's most recent financial meltdown.

Castañeda, Jorge G., *Utopia Unarmed: The Latin American Left After the Cold War*, Vintage Books, 1994.
A former Mexican foreign minister, now a professor of politics and Latin American and Caribbean Studies at New York University, surveys the effects of global politics on Latin American reformers and revolutionaries during the past 40 years.

Dudley, Steven, *Walking Ghosts: Murder and Guerrilla Politics in Colombia*, Routledge, 2006.
The Miami Herald's correspondent in Colombia explores the intersection of politics and homicide in one of Latin America's deadliest countries.

Wilkinson, Daniel, *Silence on the Mountain: Stories of Terror, Forgetting and Betrayal in Guatemala*, Duke University Press, 2004.
The cruel politics and history of Guatemala are examined at ground level in this personal but rigorous account by the deputy director of the Americas division of Human Rights Watch.

Williamson, Edwin, *The Penguin History of Latin America*, Penguin Books, 1992.
A professor of Hispanic studies at the University of Edinburgh has written an invaluable overall history of the vast and varied region.

Articles

"Improving on the Latin Rate of Growth," *The Economist*, May 20, 2006, p. 40.
Improving the region's economic performance is essential but by no means simple.

Grandin, Greg, "Latin America's New Consensus," *The Nation*, May 1, 2006, www.thenation.com/doc/20060501/grandin.
Latin America is turning away from made-in-U.S.A. policies, a development that left-leaning academics find heartening.

Naím, Moisés, "The Good Neighbor Strategy," *Time*, July 9, 2006, p. 34.
Repairing U.S. relations with Latin America is within President Bush's grasp, if he chooses to take the opportunity.

Oppenheimer, Andres, "In Latin America, it's the left versus the left," *The Miami Herald*, May 7, 2006, p. A16.
Politics in the region is more complicated than it seems on the surface — or than some may wish.

Pearlstein, Steven, "World Puts the Brakes on the Rush to Globalization," *The Washington Post*, July 5, 2006, p. D1.
Latin America's disillusionment with neoliberalism is part of the growing skepticism toward unrestrained trade and investment.

Rohter, Larry, "Visit to U.S. Isn't a First for Chile's First Female President," *The New York Times*, June 8, 2006, p. A1.
Chile's new president spent some childhood years in Washington and is now uncomfortable with too much praise from the Bush administration.

Reports and Studies

"Erasing the Lines: Trends in U.S. military programs with Latin America," Center for International Policy, Latin America Working Group Education Fund, Washington Office on Latin America, December 2005.
The United States is devoting what may be disproportionate attention to training and aiding Latin American military and security forces.

"Lost in Transition: Bold Ambitions, Limited Results for Human Rights Under Fox," Human Rights Watch, 2006.
High hopes for major improvements in human rights under Mexico's new democracy were only partly realized.

Johnson, Stephen, "Venezuela's New Chokehold on Civil Society," Heritage Foundation, July 7, 2006.
The Venezuelan government is stepping up control of nongovernmental organizations in an effort, critics say, to stifle dissent.

Perry, Guillermo, *et al.*, "Inequality in Latin America and the Caribbean: Breaking With History?," World Bank, 2003.
Deeply rooted and pervasive inequality constitutes an enormous — and so far intractable — obstacle to social and economic progress.

The Next Step:

Additional Articles from Current Periodicals

Chávez and U.S.

"Chavez Warns Rice: Don't 'Mess' With Me," *Chicago Tribune*, Feb. 20, 2006, p. 24.

Venezuelan President Hugo Chávez warned U.S. Secretary of State Condoleezza Rice that her diplomatic efforts to turn Latin American nations against Venezuela would fail.

The Associated Press, "U.S. Alarmed by Chavez's Plan to Build a Gun Factory," *The Houston Chronicle*, June 19, 2006, p. A11.

Chávez's plan to build the first Russian assault weapon factory in South America is increasing fears that Venezuela could start arming leftist allies in the region.

Kraul, Chris, "U.S. Eyes Venezuela-Iran Commercial Alliance," *Los Angeles Times*, June 24, 2006, p. A15.

The United States is trying to prevent Venezuela from securing the rotating Latin American seat on the United Nations Security Council because of Chávez' growing relationship with Iran.

Sullivan, Kevin, "Chavez Casts Himself as the Anti-Bush," *The Washington Post*, March 15, 2005, p. A1.

Chávez has been traveling the globe looking for new markets for his country's oil.

Mexico's Election

Chardy, Alfonso, "Mexico's New Prosperity Belies Its Old Poverty and Migration," *The Philadelphia Inquirer*, June 25, 2006, p. A19.

Mexico's recent economic expansion has been less than the country needs, and the current presidential election reflects the remaining gap between the rich and the poor.

Harman, Danna, "Obrador Lures Mexico's 50 Million Poor," *The Christian Science Monitor*, June 26, 2006, p. 6.

Mexico's leftist presidential candidate, Andrés Manuel López Obrador, has centered his campaign on the impoverished half of the country's 100 million people.

McKinley, James C., and Ginger Thompson, "Conservative Wins in Mexico in Final Tally," *The New York Times*, July 7, 2006, www.nytimes.com.

Election officials declared Thursday that conservative candidate Felipe Calderón had won Mexico's presidential race.

Tobar, Hector, and Paul Richter, "Mexican Election Sure to Affect Ties With U.S.," *The Seattle Times*, June 19, 2006, p. A7.

U.S. officials are watching Mexico's presidential election closely because one candidate rejects the U.S. model and the other could strengthen Mexico-U.S. ties.

Socioeconomic Equality

Bussey, Jane, "A Struggle For Hearts and Minds," *The Miami Herald*, June 26, 2006, p. G6.

The Inter-American Development Bank is working on a new initiative to help Latin America, emphasizing entrepreneurs and private initiatives — not trade agreements.

Chauvin, Lucien, "Peru Gives Its Poor More Money, But There's a Catch," *The Christian Science Monitor*, Oct. 14, 2005, p. 1.

The government will give $30 a month to Peru's poorest families if they enroll their children in school and provide basic health care.

Dellios, Hugh, "Incentives Enlisted in War on Poverty," *Chicago Tribune*, June 12, 2005, p. 3.

Latin American officials are visiting Mexico to learn about a $3-billion-a-year poverty program that aids needy families if they comply with health and education requirements.

McDonnell, Patrick J., "Bolivia Leader Nationalizes Natural Gas, Oil Industries," *Chicago Tribune*, May 2, 2006, p. 1.

Bolivian President Evo Morales nationalized the country's natural gas and oil industry, saying that foreign companies plundered Bolivia's resources for decades.

Sanchez, Marcela, "A New Path on Latin Poverty?" *The Washington Post*, Feb. 18, 2006, p. A33.

The World Bank recently acknowledged that Latin America needs to cut poverty to boost growth after years of arguing that economic growth through market reform politics and the deregulation of private industry would end poverty.

CITING *CQ RESEARCHER*

Sample formats for citing these reports in a bibliography include the ones listed below. Preferred styles and formats vary, so please check with your instructor or professor.

MLA STYLE

Jost, Kenneth. "Rethinking the Death Penalty." CQ Researcher 16 Nov. 2001: 945-68.

APA STYLE

Jost, K. (2001, November 16). Rethinking the death penalty. *CQ Researcher, 11*, 945-968.

CHICAGO STYLE

Jost, Kenneth. "Rethinking the Death Penalty." *CQ Researcher*, November 16, 2001, 945-968.

CQ Researcher

Published by CQ Press, a division of Congressional Quarterly Inc.

cqresearcher.com

Cyber Socializing

Are Internet sites like MySpace potentially dangerous?

Internet socializing has become hugely popular, and Web sites that help people meet potential dates, find new friends and keep track of old ones are big business. Hundreds of sites attract tens of millions of users, and more sites come online daily. Born along with the Internet in the early 1970s, online socializing has helped people worldwide link to others with common interests for conversation and support. Nevertheless, new social-networking sites like Facebook and MySpace raise more troubling privacy issues than traditional Internet chat rooms. Visitors to such sites can access not only individuals' posted profiles but also profiles of their friends. Parents and law-enforcement agencies worry that predators can use the information to contact vulnerable teens. Some states are considering requiring tighter security and confidentiality, and a bill introduced in the House of Representatives would require schools and libraries to block teenagers from the sites.

Paul Schnetlage and Cait Lynch married in March 2006 after meeting through the online dating service Match.com. Both are 24 and live in Reston, Va.

INSIDE THIS REPORT

CQ Researcher • July 28, 2006 • www.cqresearcher.com
Volume 16, Number 27 • Pages 625-648

CQ PRESS

RECIPIENT OF SOCIETY OF PROFESSIONAL JOURNALISTS AWARD FOR EXCELLENCE ◆ AMERICAN BAR ASSOCIATION SILVER GAVEL AWARD

Cover photograph: Jessica Lynch

CQ Researcher

July 28, 2006
Volume 16, Number 27

CQ PRESS

A Division of
Congressional Quarterly Inc.

CQ Researcher (ISSN 1056-2036) is printed on acid-free paper. Published weekly, except March 24, July 7, July 14, Aug. 4, Aug. 11, Nov. 24, Dec. 22 and Dec. 29, by CQ Press, a division of Congressional Quarterly Inc. Annual full-service subscriptions for institutions start at $667. For pricing, call 1-800-834-9020, ext. 1906. To purchase a *CQ Researcher* report in print or electronic format (PDF), visit www.cqpress.com or call 866-427-7737. Single reports start at $15. Bulk purchase discounts and electronic-rights licensing are also available. Periodicals postage paid at Washington, D.C., and additional mailing offices. POSTMASTER: Send address changes to *CQ Researcher*, 1255 22nd St., N.W., Suite 400, Washington, DC 20037.

Cyber Socializing

BY MARCIA CLEMMITT

THE ISSUES

Last year, Eddie Kenney and Matt Coenen were kicked off the Loyola University swim team after officials at the Chicago school found they belonged to a group that posted disparaging remarks about their coaches on the Internet social-networking site Facebook. [1]

Like many people who post profiles and photos and exchange messages on cyber-networking sites like Facebook, MySpace, Xanga and Bebo, the students were shocked to find that university officials, not just their friends, were checking out the site. But Facebook, whose 8 million members are high-school or college students, alumni or faculty and staff members, is considered slightly less risky than sites with open membership rolls.

Nevertheless, said Kenney, who has since transferred to Purdue, "Facebook is dangerous right now. I've learned my lesson. You're supposed to have fun with this Facebook thing, but you need to be careful." [2]

But others see greater dangers than a lack of privacy lurking on social-networking Web sites. Last month, a 14-year-old Texas girl and her mother filed a $30 million lawsuit against MySpace, claiming the girl had been sexually assaulted by a 19-year-old man she met on the site. The man allegedly contacted the girl through her MySpace site in April, posing as a high-school senior. After a series of e-mails and phone calls, they arranged a date, when the alleged assault occurred. [3]

MySpace shares blame for the incident, the lawsuit argues, because users aren't required to verify their age, and security measures intended to prevent contacts with children under age 16 are "utterly ineffective." [4]

Getty Images/Bill Pugliano

Katherine Lester, 17, and her father leave the courthouse in Caro, Mich., on June 29, 2006, after prosecutors decided not to treat her as a runaway for flying to the Middle East to meet a man she had met on the Internet. As cyber socializing grows, so do fears that the Internet exposes the vulnerable — especially the young — to sexual predators.

Though computer networking was developed in the late 1960s to allow scientists to access remote computers for research, its users — initially just academic researchers — quickly saw its possibilities as a socializing tool. As early as 1973, for example, 75 percent of electronic traffic was e-mail, much of it purely social in nature.

Over the past 15 years, a slew of new Internet applications — from chat rooms to instant messaging and, most recently, social-networking Web sites — have made online socializing easier than ever. By the end of 2004, for example, about 70 million adults logged onto the Internet every day in the United States alone — up from 52 million four years earlier — and 63 percent of American adults were Internet users. Teens were logging on at even higher rates — 87 percent of those ages 12 to 17. [5]

Today, a great deal of online activity remains social in nature. For example, in a survey by the nonprofit Pew Internet and American Life Project, 34 percent of the people who said the Internet played an important role in a major decision they'd made said they had received advice and support from other people online. [6] And 84 percent of Internet users belong to a group or organization with an online presence; more than half joined only after they got Internet access. Members of online groups also say the Internet brings them into more contact with people outside their social class or their racial or age group. [7]

But as Internet socializing grows, so do fears that the practice exposes the vulnerable — especially young people — to sexual predators. [8] Some also worry that networking sites create added peer pressure for teens to engage in risky behavior, such as posting risqué pictures of themselves.

In the cyber social world, there has always been the possibility that the friendly stranger chatting about mountain biking or a favorite rock band is not who he says he is. Older socializing technologies, such as Internet discussion boards and chat rooms, allow users to converse about favorite topics, from quilting to astrophysics. Participants generally use screen names — pseudonyms — and conversation

Teens Feel Safe on MySpace

More than 80 percent of teens believe the cyber-networking site MySpace is safe. Teens spend an average of two hours a day, five days a week on the site. However, 83 percent of parents of MySpace users worry about online sexual predators.

What Teens Say About MySpace	What Parents of MySpace Users Say
• Typically visit 2 hours a day, 5 days a week • 7-9% have been approached for a sexual liaison • 20% feel MySpace negatively affects school, job, family and friends • 83% believe MySpace is safe • 70% would be comfortable showing their parents their MySpace page • 35% are concerned about sexual predators on MySpace • 15% are concerned that MySpace fosters social isolation • 36% are concerned about meeting online friends in person • 46% believe there are "some, but not too many," sexual predators on MySpace	• 38% have not seen their teen's MySpace page • 43% don't know how often their teens are on MySpace • 50% allow their teen to have a computer in the bedroom • 62% have never talked to their teen about MySpace • 83% worry about sexual predators on MySpace • 75% worry MySpace fosters social isolation • 81% worry about their teen meeting online friends in person • 63% believe there are "quite a few" sexual predators on MySpace

Source: Larry D. Rosen, "Adolescents in MySpace: Identity Formation, Friendship and Sexual Predators," California State University, Dominguez Hills, June 2006

centers on the forum topic, often with a minimum of personal information exchanged.

But social-networking sites have greatly increased Internet users' ability to discover other users' full personal information. For instance, newer social-networking sites utilize a personal profile — usually with photos and detailed descriptions of the person's likes and dislikes — as well as the names of friends with whom the person e-mails or instant messages. The page owner also can post comments and message on friends' pages.

Thus, while most Internet social networkers use pseudonyms, the wealth of information on their pages — plus information gleaned by reading their friends' pages — allows strangers to learn far more about a user than they could about someone posting a comment in a traditional cyber chat room. [9]

Moreover, today most cyber social-network users are between 12 and 25 years old. The largest networking site, MySpace, had more than 51 million unique U.S. visitors in May and boasts about 86 million members. [10] Traffic on the site jumped 367 percent between April 2005 and April 2006 while overall traffic on the top 10 social-networking sites grew by 47 percent. [11] Similarly, adult-oriented online dating sites are also attracting tens of millions of users. (*See sidebar, p. 636.*)

By now, most people — including teens — know it's risky to post personal information such as last name and phone number on the Internet, says Michelle Collins, director of the exploited child unit at the National Center for Missing and Exploited Children (NCMEC). But on today's social-networking sites, "You're only as safe as your friends are," says Collins. For example, a teenage girl may think she's playing it safe by not naming her school on MySpace, "but if she has four friends who all reveal the name of their school, then anyone who reads their pages can surmise" that she also goes there and could potentially track her down.

Last spring, concern about child predators spurred the Suburban Caucus — a new group in the House of Representatives — to introduce the Deleting Online Predators Act (DOPA). Building on the 2000 Children's Internet Protection Act (CIPA), DOPA would require schools and libraries to block young people's access to Internet sites through which strangers can contact them. [12]

The bill's purpose is to shield children from being approached by strangers when using the Internet away from home, an aim that's important to suburban families, according to sponsor Rep. Michael Fitzpatrick, R-Pa. "One-in-five children has been approached sexually on the Internet," he told a House subcommittee on June 10. "Child predation on the Internet is a growing problem." [13]

But many wonder if DOPA addresses the right problem. For one thing, the "one-in-five" figure is "more complicated than is being implied," given today's cultural norms, says Tim Lordan, executive director of the nonprofit Internet Education Foundation. As one teenage girl admitted, " 'Dad, if I wasn't getting sexually solicited by my peers, I would be doing something wrong,' " says Lordan.

"The media coverage of predators on MySpace implies that 1) all youth are at risk of being stalked and molested because of MySpace; and 2) prohibiting youth from participating in MySpace will stop predators from attacking kids," said Danah Boyd, a University of California, Berkeley, doctoral student who studies how teens use online technology. "Both are misleading; neither is true. . . . Statistically speaking, kids are more at risk at a church picnic or a Boy Scout outing than . . . when they go to MySpace." [14]

In fact, the NCMEC report from which the one-in-five figure originates shows that 76 percent of online sexual solicitations "came from fellow children," and 96 percent of the adult solicitations came from adults 18 to 25, said Boyd. "Wanted and unwanted solicitations are both included. In other words, if an 18-year-old asks out a 17-year-old and both consent, this would still be seen as a sexual solicitation." [15]

Cyberspace presents no more danger than the real world, says Michigan State University Professor of Psychology Linda Jackson. "But there are dangers," she says, "such as the ease with which you can give away your information."

Unwary users giving out private information — perhaps permanently, since so much Internet content is archived — is the chief new danger posed by social networking, say many analysts.

Most teenagers who post MySpace pages "seem to have the sense that nobody is watching" except their closest friends, says Tamyra Pierce, an assistant professor of mass communication at California State University, Fresno, who is studying social-networking use among high-school students. For example, "a boy who posted about banging a mailbox last night" apparently was unaware that the posting exposed him to vandalism charges, she says.

"Teenage girls would be petrified if you read their diary, yet they are now posting online stuff that is much more personal," said Jeffrey Cole, director of the University of Southern California's Center for the Digital Future. "Clearly kids need guidance." [16]

Given the popularity of online socializing, it would be impossible to ban it, says Kaveri Subrahmanyam, an associate professor of psychology at California State University, Los Angeles. "The Internet is here to stay. If you ban it, they'll find a way to get around the ban. It will become a cat-and-mouse game," she says. "We need to teach kids how to keep safe."

Young Adults Are Most Likely to Date Online

About one-in-10 Internet users — or 16 million people — visited an online dating site in 2005. Those ages 18-29 were most likely to have used an online dating site.

Online Daters
(% of Internet users who have visited a dating site)

All Internet Users	**11%**
Sex	
Men	12%
Women	9
Race/Ethnicity	
White	10%
Black	13
Hispanic	14
Location	
Urban	13%
Suburban	10
Rural	9
Age	
18-29	18%
30-49	11
50-64	6
65+	3
Education Level	
Less Than High School	14%
High School Grad	10
Some College	11
College+	10

Source: Pew Internet and American Life Project, March 5, 2006

Unfortunately, the new dangers posed by sites like MySpace "have not been integrated into the society's knowledge base," said Kevin Farnham, author of a book of safety tips for social-networking. "Common-sense teaching is [not] automatically passed from parents to child." [17]

But predators are not the only ones reading social-networking sites. Some employers routinely scan pages posted by job candidates, with potentially disastrous results, says Matthew Smith, a professor of communications at Ohio's Wittenberg University. "You may put up a birthday-party picture of yourself in your underwear, thinking you are showing how carefree you are," says Smith. "But a future employer may see it and decide you're irresponsible."

And the federal government may be next. The National Security Agency (NSA) is funding "research into the mass harvesting of the information that people post about themselves on social networks," according to Britain's *New Scientist* magazine. [18]

"You should always assume anything you write online is stapled to your résumé," said Jon Callas, chief security officer at PGP, a maker of encryption software. [19]

As lawmakers, parents and Internet companies confront new Internet security issues, here are some of the questions being discussed.

Is cyberspace more dangerous than real space?

Some legislators and worried parents warn that the online world increases opportunities for sexual predators to reach victims. Likewise, some women won't use online dating services because they fear they might meet unsavory characters. But defenders of online socializing argue that real-life encounters pose just as much risk of unwanted sexual advances or of being bullied or defrauded.

"There's a child-abuse epidemic that we don't even know about on

Survival Tips for Online Socializing

In the long run, the Internet is good for teens, bolstering their social development, creativity and even writing skills. Dangers do exist, however, mainly caused by teenagers not understanding how easily strangers can access posted information.

There's clear evidence that writing and creating art, music and videos on the social Internet is building literacy and creative skills in today's teens, says Northwestern University Professor of Communications Studies Justine Cassell.

In the early 1990s, educators were concerned about seriously declining interest in writing by American students. But today, "we have striking evidence that kids are willing to write, when they weren't before," a change that many analysts attribute to the popularity of e-mail, instant messaging and blogging, says Cassell. Today's teens even show sophisticated understanding of literary niceties such as tailoring one's writing style to suit the audience. "They don't use emoticons [symbols] with parents," for example, because they "understand that's a dialect," she says.

Benefits aside, however, dangers and misunderstandings also exist, exacerbated by the fact that kids have raced ahead of many adults in their use of Internet socializing tools, says John Carosella, vice president for content at the Internet security company Blue Coat. "We are the first generation of Internet parents, and we need to learn how our job has changed," Carosella says.

Here are experts' tips for handling the online social world:

- Parents must learn how to use the technology, says Cassell. "At the very least, IM (instant message) your kids." Parents who IM "report much less fear about the technology and more happiness because their kids keep in touch," she says.
- Parents should play with Internet search engines "to learn how easily they turn up information and then share that knowledge as they talk with their children about Internet privacy," she says.
- Privacy rules between parents and kids can't remain the same in an Internet world, says Kaveri Subrahmanyam, an associate professor of psychology at California State University, Los Angeles. "If it's a kid's diary, you don't look at it." But diaries are different from MySpace pages, "because nobody else is looking at them," Subrahmanyam says.

  When it comes to publicly posted information that strangers can access, "You do need to know what they do," she says. "You can say to your child, 'I don't need to know the content of the IM, but I do need to know whom you're sending it to.' "
- Age matters when it comes to teens understanding Internet privacy issues, according to Zheng Yan, an education professor at the State University of New York at Albany. Only children ages 12 to 13 or older can grasp the Internet's "social complexity," such as the large number of strangers who can access information posted on Web sites.[1]
- Web sites vary widely in how much public and private access they allow to posted material, and it's important to think about this when posting, says Alex Welch, founder and CEO of the photo-sharing Web site Photobucket. On Photobucket, the photo albums of people under age 18 are automatically kept private.

  However, even if they weren't, posting photos on Photobucket would be less risky than posting the same pictures on a social-networking site like MySpace, says Welch. That's because on MySpace photos are linked to additional personal information that may pique strangers' interest and provide clues to help them contact posters.
- It's also important to consider the future, including how employers or college admissions officers might view your online postings, says Henry Jenkins, director of the comparative media studies program at the Massachusetts Institute of Technology. Much of what appears on the Internet today ends up archived somewhere and can be retrieved tomorrow, he says. "Kids don't recognize the permanence of what they put up there."
- Adults will probably learn a lot about the Internet from their children, and they should be open to that, says Jenkins. Parents "need to recognize that some unfamiliar experiences look scarier from the outside than they are. Take time to understand what you're seeing."

  Talking about teens' MySpace pages can open the door to family discussions of important, sometimes touchy issues, like contemporary fashion, media images and ideals, Jenkins says. "Ask your kid how they choose to represent themselves" on their MySpace pages "and why."
- Teens — and adults — who socialize on the Web should remember that, "when it comes to the rules for getting to know people," the Internet "parallels our world perfectly," says Patricia Handschiegel, founder and CEO of StyleDiary.net, a social-networking site focused on fashion.

  Often, young people have "a false sense that you can't be tracked" by people they correspond with online, Handschiegel says. "If you want to correspond, fine, but take your time getting to know people. Watch for cues" to ulterior motives, "such as somebody pushing too fast to know you."

[1] Bruce Bower, "Growing Up Online," *Science News*, June 17, 2006, p. 376, www.sciencenews.org/articles/20060617/bob9.asp.

the Internet, which is how it stays so invisible, when a 45-year-old man engages in sexually explicit dialogue with a 12-year-old girl," says John Carosella, vice president for content control at Blue Coat Systems, a maker of security software and other tools for online communication.

"When it happens in real life you know it's happening," but on the Internet, even the girl herself may not know it's happening initially, he says. "This is why it can go on with such facility, and it's so easy to escalate because nobody can overhear it."

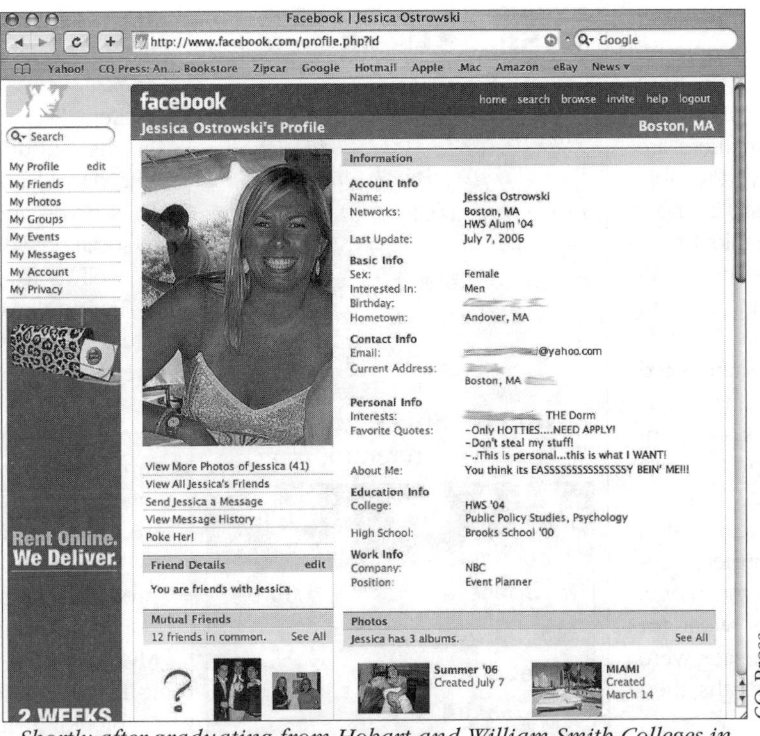

CQ Press

Shortly after graduating from Hobart and William Smith Colleges in 2004, Jessica Ostrowski joined the popular college social-networking site Facebook. She lives in Boston but stays connected to friends nationwide through the site, which has 8 million members.

Internet communication is riskier than real-life meetings, according to Carosella, because many of the cues humans use to size up other people — such as gestures and tone of voice — are missing. "Most of our evolutionary clues [to risk] are stripped out" of online encounters, he says.

In addition, online acquaintances can do harm — especially to young people — even without offline meetings, he says. The Internet "is the most powerful tool yet invented" capable of bringing "every aspect of human behavior from the most sublime to the most debauched and depraved" right into our own homes, he says. And it's burgeoned so fast that "we've had no time to figure out how to deal with it."

Carosella also suggests that — while there is not enough research yet to prove it — easy access to online porn may prime some people to become aggressive or engage in sexual predation. "Lots of data suggest that pornography is a very significant factor in the emergence of criminal, aggressive behavior," he says. "You're whipping around the most powerful urge that people have. And the Internet has made pornography more accessible, more private, more extreme."

Moreover, peer pressure among teens may encourage risky sexual expression on cyber-networking sites, says Pierce of California State University. "The more stuff they have that is graphic and shocking, like links to porn and photos in risqué poses, the more friends they have on their lists," she says of recent studies of MySpace and Xanga and their use by more than 300 local high-school students. "Most who have upward of 500 friends have links to porn sites and graphic stuff."

Looking at social-networking sites can sometimes expose teenagers to porn, even when they don't seek it out, says Pierce. For example, in a group of 50 to 60 sites she recently examined, 10 contained automatic links that unexpectedly shift the viewer to a pornography site.

It "concerns me that our youth may be exposed to pornography" at the inadvertent click of a mouse, she says. "I don't know if individuals in the porn industry are creating 'fake' MySpace sites and then autolinking them or if the young persons themselves are getting involved. I just know that what appeared to be an innocent, young person's site automatically turned into porn" when the site user's photo was clicked.

Collins of the National Center for Missing and Exploited Children says the Internet provides a "target-rich environment" for pedophiles. "Twenty years ago, people had to go to a park or a soccer game" to meet children and teens, she says. And the Internet allows predators to learn more about a potential victim, which may help him build a relationship.

There's little disagreement that dangers can lurk on the Internet. However, many analysts note that, even as Internet socializing has burgeoned, sex crimes have been decreasing, and data do not indicate an increase in sexual predation due to teens going online. "There is no evidence that the online world is more dangerous," says Justine Cassell, a professor of communications studies at Northwestern University.

In fact, predatory crimes against girls have declined during the past decade, even as the Internet was bringing more young people online, she says. All national data sets show that from 1994 to 2004, single-offender crimes, including assaults, by men against 12-to-19-year-old girls decreased, demonstrating that the online world has not put young people in more danger, says Cassell.

The number of sexual-abuse cases substantiated by child-protection agencies "dropped a remarkable 40 percent between 1992 and 2000," and evidence shows it was a "true decline," not a change in reporting methodology, wrote sociology Professor David Finkelhor and Assistant Professor of Psychology Lisa M. Jones, of the University of New Hampshire's Crimes Against Children Research Center. [20]

Meanwhile, says Collins, tips about online enticement of young people reported to the NCECM have risen from 50 reports a week in 1998 to about 230 a week. But does that mean there are more online incidents today? Probably not, says Collins. "More people know where to report it today," thanks to the center's education campaigns and social-networking companies' putting links to NCECM's tipline on their sites. In addition, "more people, more kids, are wired today than ever before," Collins notes.

Even teenagers' fascination with online porn may be something of a passing fancy, not a long-term, negative behavior change, says Michigan State's Jackson, who recently completed research that tracked teens' Internet usage. "We went everywhere they went for 16 months," she says. "Porn sites were popular for the first three months, then it really died down."

As for the dangers of online dating, Eric Straus, CEO of Cupid.com, a popular dating site, rates the dangers of online and offline dating as about equal. Meeting potential romantic partners online is "a numbers game," and the Web lets you search for geographic proximity or mutual interests across a wide variety of potential dates. But "you shouldn't be fooled into feeling safe" from deception in either environment, he says. "If you talk to 100 people online, some are going to be unsavory. If you meet them in a bar, and they say they're not married, you shouldn't believe that either, and if you give them your phone number, that's dangerous."

New technology always spurs panic, says Paul DiMaggio, a sociology professor at Princeton. "MySpace is generating the same fear reaction that films and vaudeville got," says DiMaggio. "And all new technology and media generate more hysteria than threat."

"A lot of the behavior on sites like MySpace has been going on in teen hangouts for generations," wrote Anne Collier, editor of *NetFamilyNews*. [21] Dangerous behavior existed, "but parents weren't privy to it."

"One child being molested by an online predator is too many and has to be addressed," says Lordan, of the Internet Education Foundation. "Nevertheless, statistically, most molestations are family and acquaintance molestations, and the chance of your child being dragged through the computer screen by a predator is low."

Furthermore, "a lot of the stories that you hear" about teens running off with adults they met on MySpace, for example, "appear to be kids who would get in trouble in some other way if it weren't for the Internet," he says. "Once you start digging down, these don't appear to be typical families."

All youngsters are not at equal risk of being victimized, says Collins. "Some kids are using the Internet to fill a void, and these kids are going to be more susceptible," she says.

MySpace Users Are Most Loyal

Two-thirds of the visitors to MySpace return each month — more than any other social-networking site. MSN Groups caters to those with special interests, such as computers, cars, music, movies or sports.

Top Five Socializing Sites
(based on retention rate)

Site	Retention Rate (%)*
MySpace	67.0
MSN Groups	57.6
Facebook	51.7
Xanga.com	48.9
MSN Spaces	47.3

** Based on the number of March 2006 visitors who returned to the site in April*

Source: Nielsen/NetRatings

Should schools and public libraries block access to social-networking sites?

Rep. Fitzpatrick and other members of the Suburban Caucus have introduced legislation that would require public schools and libraries to bar access to social-networking sites and chat rooms as well as to pornography sites.

For adults, online social-networking sites "are fairly benign," but "for children they open the door to many dangers," including online bullying and exposure to child predators that have turned the Internet into a virtual hunting ground for children," Fitzpatrick said on the House floor May 9. [22]

"There are thousands of online predators who are trying to contact our kids using powerful engines like MySpace.com," said Rep. Mark Kirk, R-Ill. [23]

Blocking Internet social tools, at least temporarily, is a valid response, says Carosella of Blue Coat Systems. While educational responses are vital in the long run, "we haven't invented [that education] yet."

Furthermore, "while we are developing our educational response, predators are building and improving their game plans. It's an arms race," says Carosella. Blocking access in schools and libraries "is absolutely an answer," because supervision currently "is completely inadequate."

But critics of such proposals say blocking access is nearly impossible without inadvertently blocking valuable portions of the Internet. "It's brain-dead to say you should stop people from using some technology," says John Palfrey, clinical professor of law and executive director of Harvard Law School's Berkman Center for Internet and Society, pointing out that the technology isn't going away.

Boyd, of the University of California, pointed out that because technology plays a major role in the business world, it is unwise to deprive students of it in schools and libraries. "The law is so broadly defined that it would limit access to any commercial site that allows users to create a profile and communicate with strangers." While it ostensibly targets MySpace, as written it would block many other sites, she said, including blogging tools, mailing lists, video and pod-cast sites, photo-sharing sites and educational sites like NeoPets, where kids create virtual pets and participate in educational games. [24]

Moreover, she continued, many technology companies now are using social software, such as features that help users find information, get recommendations and share ideas. "This would all be restricted," she wrote. [25]

Lynn Bradley, director of the American Library Association's government relations office, agrees. Fitzpatrick's proposal "is like using a water hose to brush your teeth." The legislation could also affect distance-learning programs, which use many technologies that the legislators want blocked. "Rural schools have increasingly started to rely on distance learning to supplement their curricula," said Bradley. "It would appear to us on reading this bill that [such programs] would be swept up in the blockage." [26]

Henry Jenkins, director of comparative media studies at the Massachusetts Institute of Technology (MIT), says it would be unwise to keep teachers and librarians away from social-networking technology because "they are the best people to teach people how to use it constructively and safely." And, while Fitzpatrick's bill contains loopholes for educational uses, history suggests that fear and uncertainty would likely stop many schools from using those loopholes, he adds.

Blocking access at public schools and libraries would also worsen the already troubling "digital divide," says Jenkins. [27] Children in wealthier families could still access school-blocked Internet sites from home, but students without Internet at home "will be shut out," he says.

Policymakers who propose blocking as a "silver bullet" don't know how

Freshmen Share Many Personal Details

Most University of North Carolina freshmen reveal their birthday and hometown on social-networking sites. But only 16 percent give out more detailed personal information, like cell phone numbers.

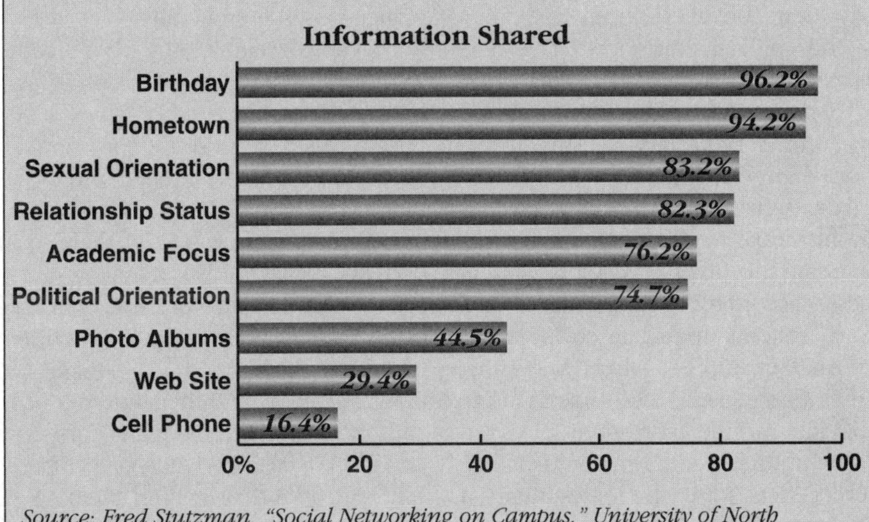

Source: Fred Stutzman, "Social Networking on Campus," University of North Carolina, Chapel Hill, 2006

important online socializing is to teenagers, says the Internet Education Foundation's Lordan. "Kids feel quite attached to their own space," whether on MySpace or another site, and are "incredibly worried" about it being taken away, he says. If sites are blocked, "they'll go underground."

The bill should be called the "Send Social Networking Sites Off Shore Act," says Lordan, because there are social-networking sites all over the world and "stories of kids creating these sites themselves." If that happens, "we can't even help them."

Moreover, there are serious technical barriers, such as age verification, he says. Many blocking proposals would depend on age verification of site users, either to block out older users who might prey on kids or to keep younger kids from using the sites. But "age verification is a problem even in the real world," where kids use fake ID cards to buy alcohol and cigarettes, says Loran, and the problem is "worse in the online world."

Does Internet social networking foster good relationships?

For nearly as long as the Internet has existed, people have used it to stay in touch with old friends and meet new ones. [28] For just as long, skeptics have argued that online relationships are less rich, real and reliable than real-world interactions and that Internet socializing actually isolates people. Over the years, studies have found evidence bolstering both sides of the question.

No online community can support human bonding the way real-world communities do, said Clifford Stoll in his 1996 best-seller *Silicon Snake Oil: Second Thoughts on the Information Superhighway.* "What's missing from this ersatz neighborhood? A feeling of permanence, a sense of location, a warmth from the local history. Gone is the very essence of a neighborhood: friendly relations and a sense of being in it together." [29]

Some studies have found that Internet usage pulls people away from their real-world friends and family and isolates the user. Research by Stanford University's Institute for the Quantitative Study of Society (SIQSS), for example, finds that Internet use directly relates to social isolation. Based on survey findings, the Stanford researchers say that for every hour a person spends online, their face-to-face time with family and friends decreases by 23.5 minutes. [30]

Furthermore, "face-to-face interaction with close [friends and family] qualitatively differs from interactions in the virtual world online and is more important to one's psychological wellness," according to Lu Zheng, a Stanford doctoral student in sociology. [31]

Another SIQSS analysis found that "the more time people spend using the Internet the more they lose contact with their social environment." Internet users, for example, spend much less time talking on the phone to friends and family, according to the study. [32]

"E-mail is a way to stay in touch, but you can't share a coffee or a beer with somebody on e-mail or give them a hug," said SIQSS Director Norman Nie. "The Internet could be the ultimate isolating technology that further reduces our participation in communities." [33]

But other analysts insist that Internet socializing strengthens online and offline relationships. What looks to some like a "fading away" of social life as Internet usage increases is actually just a shift to new communication modes that strengthen many people's social ties, says a recent report from the Pew Internet and American Life Project and the University of Toronto. [34]

"The traditional human orientation to neighborhood- and village-based groups is moving toward communities . . . oriented around geographically dispersed social networks," the Pew report said. "The Internet and e-mail play an important role in maintaining these . . . networks" and "fit seamlessly" into people's social lives. As a result, the study concluded, Americans today "are probably more in contact with members of their communities and social networks than before."

For example, the analysts found that those who e-mail 80-100 percent of their closest friends and family weekly also speak regularly by phone with 25 percent more of their closest associates than those who e-mail less. For so-called second-tier (or "significant") social ties, the effects were even more pronounced: Those who weekly e-mail 80-100 percent of their second-tier contacts also regularly telephone twice as many of those contacts as do people who do not e-mail their friends. [35] Furthermore, 31 percent of those surveyed said their Internet use had increased their number of second-tier contacts — while only 2 percent said it had decreased them. [36]

A Canadian study of a housing development found similar results. University of Toronto researchers found that residents with high-speed connections had more informal, friendly contact with neighbors than residents who were not on the Internet. [37] Residents with broadband service knew the names of 25 neighbors, on average, compared to non-wired residents, who knew eight. Wired residents made 50 percent more visits to neighbors' homes than non-wired people, and their visits were more widely scattered around the housing development, according to the paper. [38]

And in a new and interesting wrinkle, the Internet may be helping to keep the lines of communication open between people on both sides of the recent Middle East violence. Since the cross-border shelling between Israel and Lebanon erupted earlier this month, Internet message boards, discussion forums and blogs have exploded with posts from Israeli and Lebanese nationals commenting on the fighting. "The fact that the citizens of two warring countries are maintaining a dialogue while a war is going on cannot be ignored," said Lisa Goldman, a Canadian-born freelance journalist who blogs from Tel Aviv and who points out that Internet discussions and socializing between Israelis and Lebanese predated the current conflict. [39]

Another significant new phenomenon among adolescents equipped with cell phones, instant messaging and social-networking pages is "tele-cocooning," says MIT's Jenkins. Coined by Mimi Ito, a research scientist at the University of Southern California's Annenberg Center for Communication, tele-cocooning refers to "carrying your friends around with you, using technology to be literally in contact with them all the time."

Online socializing also helps kids who would otherwise have a hard time finding friendships, says Jenkins. "Kids who may be outcasts, or pariahs, or have interests that nobody in their school shares now can go online and meet kids all around the country who like the same comic books, music and sports," Jenkins says. "I watched my son go through that."

In addition, while online socializing creates opportunities for deception or misunderstanding, meeting people online first can sometimes help avoid superficial judgments. The Internet allows disadvantaged or physically different people to socialize without suffering the instantaneous negative judgment that may happen in person.

"If people consider you unattractive, for example — you have moles, a big nose — . . . you can get negative reactions in public," says Wittenberg's Smith. "Online, I can talk about my love of pets or my work with my church. I can put down what is lovable about me and bypass whatever I think is keeping me from getting fulfilled relationships" offline.

Internet dating also saves time, says Mark Brooks, editor of *Online Personals Watch*. "The great thing about Internet dating is being able to

Continued on p. 636

Chronology

1960s-1980s

As the Internet develops, its academic and technical users begin socializing online.

1967
The term "six degrees of separation" enters the lexicon after Yale University psychologist Stanley Milgram claims to experimentally validate the theory that any two people on Earth are connected by an average of six intermediate contacts.

1972
E-mail is invented and quickly becomes the most widely used tool on the first wide-scale computer network, ARPANET.

1975
First ARPANET mailing lists link people with shared interests.

1979
First Usenet newsgroups are established.

1982
Carnegie Mellon University computer-science Professor Scott Fahlman invents the first emoticon, the smiley :-)

1988
Internet Relay Chat is invented, allowing computer users to exchange real-time messages with a group.

1990s

People flock to the Internet, mostly drawn by socializing tools like e-mail and chat rooms. Worries grow about sexual predators contacting teens through online socializing, but sex crimes against teenagers decrease overall.

1990
John Guare's play "Six Degrees of Separation" captures the public imagination with its portrayal of the power of social networks.

1994
Netscape's Mosaic Web browser is offered free on the company's Web site, helping draw millions of non-technical users online.

1996
AOL introduces the Buddy List, which alerts users when friends are online and ready to IM (instant message) each other.

1997
Sixdegrees.com becomes one of the first Internet social sites to link users to friends of friends, through three "degrees of separation." . . . AOL introduces AIM, allowing users for the first time to IM non-AOL users.

1998
eHarmony.com, the first online dating site to require users to complete a personality-matching test, is founded by evangelical Christian Neil Clark Warren.

2000s

Social-networking sites become teenagers' socializing tool of choice, while rock bands and other performers begin using the sites to build and strengthen their fan bases. Lawmakers become concerned that cyber social networking makes it easier for sexual predators to find teens.

2000
President Bill Clinton signs the Children's Internet Protection Act (CIPA), requiring federally subsidized public and school libraries to use filtering software to block children's access to pornography.

2001
Columbia University Professor Duncan Watts uses forwarded e-mails to confirm Milgram's six-degrees-of-separation finding.

2003
MySpace is founded. . . . The U.S. Supreme Court upholds CIPA's requirement for public libraries to block Internet sites. . . . Vermont Gov. Howard Dean becomes a leading contender for the 2004 Democratic presidential nomination by using the social-networking site Meetup to spur grass-roots organization.

2005
News Corp., a global company headed by Australian media mogul Rupert Murdoch, buys MySpace for $580 million. . . . Several state legislatures consider bills requiring online dating sites to conduct background checks of users.

2006
NBC's television newsmagazine "Dateline" films sting operations around the country in which adults pose as teens in Internet chat rooms and arrange to meet sexual predators. . . . The Deleting Online Predators Act is introduced in Congress to require federally subsidized schools and libraries to block children's access to social-networking sites, chat rooms and other socializing technology. . . . Social software continues to spread with Internet companies including AOL, Netscape, Google and Yahoo jumping on board. . . . Americans spend $521 million on online dating, making it one of the biggest income generators on the World Wide Web.

Do You Take This Online Stranger . . . ?

Soon after moving to Washington, D.C., from upstate New York to attend community college, Cait Lynch signed up with the popular Internet dating site Match.com. "I'd just moved to the area and I didn't really know anyone. I was interested in meeting new people," she says. Moreover, her mother had met her husband of eight years online. "I figured if it went well for her, I should give it a shot."

After a few months, Lynch came across a promising profile. Paul Schnetlage was getting his master's degree at Johns Hopkins University, and they shared an interest in cafes, movies, reading and art. Moreover, they were the same age — 22 — and both were in school full time while working.

After e-mailing for a month, they met for coffee, and Paul admitted he had "met several really strange girls" before meeting her. For her part, Lynch says she "didn't take anything seriously at all" on the site. Nonetheless, their relationship slowly blossomed, and last March, nearly two years after meeting, they married. Without Match.com, "I don't think I ever would have met someone like Paul," says Lynch, who works for a real estate developer. Her husband is a software designer.

Launched in 1995 as the first online dating service, Match.com now has some 15 million paid members. It claims that more than 300 marriages or engagements occur between members or former members each month and that 400,000 people find the person they are seeking each year. The "vast majority aren't marriages," says spokesperson Kristin Kelly, "but a lot of people are telling us they found a great relationship."

Today, Internet sites devoted to matchmaking constitute one of the top online income generators, with the U.S. market valued at $521 million. [1] Nearly one-third of American adults know someone who has used a dating Web site, according to the Pew Internet and American Life Project. [2]

But after steady increases in membership, the 25 most-visited online dating sites showed a 4 percent decline in American visitors in the past year compared to a 4 percent increase in the total U.S. Internet audience. [3]

"There is a natural limit to the number of people who want to participate in this industry, and they are getting to that number," explained Jupiter Research analyst Nate Elliot." [4]

And Mary Madden, a Pew senior research specialist, points out the Internet is still very low on the list of ways people meet their significant others. "We asked all Internet users who are married or in a committed relationship if they met their partner online or offline, and only 3 percent said they met them online," she says.

There are clearly cases where online dating does foster meaningful relationships, says Barbara Dafoe Whitehead, co-director of Rutgers University's National Marriage Project. "But to what degree it's a very reliable source of finding a partner is the open question," she says.

Stan Woll, a psychology professor at California State University, Fullerton, says Internet dating sites are good at introducing people to large numbers of potential mates they might not otherwise meet. However, he finds that the number of possibilities tends to make members overlook people they would ordinarily enjoy. "There is an array of other people, and you keep wanting to go on and find somebody better or closer," argues Woll.

Andrea Baker, a sociology professor at Ohio University and author of the 2005 book *Double Click: Romance and Commitment of Online Couples*, argues that online dating sites are better than chance meetings at helping members find partners with common interests.

But online dating has its drawbacks. Whitehead says she often hears criticism about untruthful member profiles. Lynch says members she met online often embellished their résumés to enhance

Continued from p. 634

find the right people," something that is harder in the real world, where there's no search function, he says. By meeting someone online first, "I don't need to go out with somebody who smokes or who has kids. You can ask the difficult questions up front."

Social-networking sites also draw criticism for their emphasis on having a lengthy list of friends, as sites like MySpace tend to do. Encouraging the how-many-friends-do-my-friends-have game sets up bad behaviors, according to technology entrepreneur Christopher Allen. "It is not the number of connections but the quality" that counts, a fact obscured by concentration on long friend lists, he said. [40]

Social networking is based on a faulty view of friendship — the "premise that . . . if A is a friend of B, and B is a friend of C, then A can be a friend of C, too," said the University of California's Boyd. "Just because you're friends with somebody doesn't mean their friends are similar" to the friends you would choose. [41]

A social-networking site can also be used as "an electronic bathroom wall," potentially increasing the reach of school bullying, says NCMEC's Collins. "There's capacity for large-scale humiliation," Collins says, citing an incident in which a girl created a page laden with pornography and put an ex-friend's name on it.

But Boyd isn't so sure. "Bullying, sexual teasing and other peer-to-peer harassment are rampant among teenagers" because they are "tools through which youth learn to make meaning of popularity, social status and cultural norms," she said. It is unclear whether online embarrassment is any more damaging than offline humiliation, she added, conceding the Internet "may help spread rumors faster." [42] ■

their appeal, such as the man who said he liked chess but didn't know the rules when they sat down to play. And the Pew project found that 66 percent of Internet users think cyber dating is dangerous because its puts personal information online. [5]

Online-dating experts have found that people are turning to the Internet to find love for a number of different social and cultural reasons. For instance, busy work schedules make it harder for people to find compatible partners in the offline world, Baker says.

The Internet also allows busy singles to meet people who live across town whom they would not normally bump into, contends Kelly. It can "cut across boundaries that used to limit people's opportunities to meet people, like geography," adds Whitehead.

Compared to a generation ago, people are much more likely to live in a city where they did not grow up, Kelly points out. Because people's lives are no longer dictated by geography, traditional "friendship networks are down," says Bernardo Carducci, a professor of psychology at Indiana University Southeast. He argues that people are lonely and don't have a local friendship network that can produce dates.

Yahoo Drew Most Visitors

Each month Internet dating sites entice millions of hopeful visitors searching for the perfect mate.

Top 10 Dating Sites

Site	Unique Visitors (in thousands)
Yahoo! Personals	6,052
Match.com Sites	3,893
MarketRange Inc.	2,676
Spark Networks	2,638
Mate1.com	2,354
True.com	2,093
eHarmony.com	1,796
Love@AOL	1,516
Zencon Technologies Dating Sites	1,091
Lovehappens.com	976

Source: comScore Media Metrix, a division of comScore Networks, Inc., January 2006

And Whitehead and Kelly agree that singles are also turning to the Internet to find a mate because they are not finding them in the old places, such as college or high school.

While online-dating sites do provide more conveniences, Madden says the majority of people she surveyed did not find online dating more efficient than offline dating. Users "still have the complex challenges of negotiating relationships [including] norms and social skills that are different from face-to-face communication."

Some, like Carducci, describe online dating as just one more tool in the dating arsenal. Others, including Whitehead, think it is a big tool that is going to have a lasting force in society.

Kelly predicts that "some of the stigma about online dating is a generation gap" that will disappear over time.

— Melissa J. Hipolit

[1] Ginanne Brownell, "The Five-Year Itch," *Newsweek*, Feb. 27, 2006.

[2] Pew Internet and American Life Project, "Online Dating," March 5, 2006.

[3] comScore Media Metrix, January 2006.

[4] Brownell, *op. cit.*

[5] Pew Internet and American Life Project, *op. cit.*

BACKGROUND

Wired Love

Virtually all communications technology, no matter why it was developed, has quickly become a socializing tool, with teenagers usually leading the way. And — from the telegraph to MySpace — parents have always worried what kind of trouble teens may get into with the new technology.

Northwestern's Cassell recounts a newspaper story entitled "Wired Love," which describes how a father followed his 16-year-old daughter to a tryst she'd arranged with a man she had met online and was arrested after threatening to kill the man and the girl. The father had bought his daughter the new technology — a telegraph — according to the 1886 story in the magazine *Electrical World*.

"At first people thought the telegraph would be good for girls," who might land jobs as telegraph operators, says Cassell. "But in the 1880s, an attempt was made to legislate who could be a telegraph operator because people worried that girls would contact men through the device," she says.

In the early 1900s, similar worries and proposals for legislation arose about the telephone, she says. The anti-telephone "rhetoric was identical to anti-MySpace rhetoric today," stressing "fears that girls were at risk," she says.

Yet socializing has always been a top human need, as the history of communications technology has shown, says Wittenberg's Smith. When new technologies change how people communicate, people always use them for social interactions — rather

What's Next for the Social Net?

The mega social-networking site MySpace boasts more than 30 million visitors a day. But with the bulk of its users teenagers, Internet industry observers say the MySpace phenomenon may have peaked and that teens are ready to move on to the next big thing.

But social-networking technology — from people searches to video sharing — is here to stay. And Internet entrepreneurs are scrambling to develop new ways to give social-networking sites more staying power and attract a broader — and older — audience.

"Could it be that MySpace peaked" this past April?" mused Scott Karp, a technology and publishing analyst. "When a fad becomes overhyped, teens will eventually retreat," and MySpace daily traffic began falling off somewhat in late spring, Karp said. [1]

Some observers seconded Karp's observation. "MySpace is hot now, but teen audiences are the most fickle market ever invented," wrote Mathew Ingram, an online business writer for the Toronto *Globe and Mail.* "MySpace has gone (or is becoming) mainstream, and mainstream is the kiss of death." [2]

Media mogul Rupert Murdoch, whose News Corp. bought MySpace last year for $580 million, has been reticent about how he plans to make money on the free site. But the man who once described newspapers' paid classified advertising as "rivers of gold," confounded the industry recently when he announced that he will offer free classified advertising on MySpace. [3]

Social-networking sites are really about communicating with people you know or specifically want to know, not publication to strangers, according to Dalton Caldwell, founder and CEO of the social-networking site imeem.com. "You don't want to see strangers' home movies," Caldwell says.

Some people in the social-networking business think of the sites as "destinations," cool places to hang out and spend time, says Caldwell. But that's a recipe for a site whose popularity wanes fairly quickly, Caldwell believes. "The site'll be like a night club. It'll be cool for a while, but then it'll fade."

But a site envisioned as a collection of popular, useful, top-of-the-line communication tools won't likely suffer that fate, because "you're plugging into something that people always do." IM — instant messaging — for example, "is not a fad. It hasn't changed since its inception" because it's "a cool tool that people continue to want to use," Caldwell says.

A big draw of social networking will always be connection, especially for the older-than-teenage crowd that entrepreneurs hope to lure in bigger numbers, says Mark Brooks, editor of *Online Personals Watch.* Facebook — a site that caters to college students — has an advantage for the long run in that regard, says Brooks. Providing a connecting point for school pals that will help them avoid losing touch with old friends, Facebook "hits people at their point of pain," Brooks says.

The fact that the site provides a venue to keep in touch with old school mates will eventually "drive Facebook beyond MySpace," Brooks predicts.

To draw older, hopefully more permanent users than MySpace's teens, some entrepreneurs are developing sites where people can join groups discussing topics of interest rather than hanging out and posting personal profiles. Such sites are similar to traditional Internet social venues like Yahoo Groups, whose thousands of discussion groups are focused on individual topics like hobbies or alternative sexual lifestyles.

than just for business or educational use, he says.

The telephone, for example, was first marketed as a tool to speed up workplace transactions, says Smith. When the fledgling phone industry found that people were getting on and talking for a long time, they "were horrified," he says. For example, for efficiency's sake a single party line was usually assigned to several families to share. "But people wanted to get on and yak," clogging up the lines for their neighbors, he says.

Internet socializing, which began almost as soon as computer networks were established in the late 1960s, also took network developers by surprise. By 1973, e-mail — much of it purely social in nature — made up 75 percent of traffic on ARPANET, the computer network designed by the Department of Defense to allow researchers to exchange data and access remote computing capability. [43]

By 1975, ARPANET users had developed the first Internet communities, mailing lists through which people could send messages on topics of interest to a whole list of others who shared their passions. Some lists were work-related, but lists linking science-fiction fans and wine-tasting enthusiasts were among the most popular.

In 1978, computer scientists developed Usenet, a network intended to allow Internet users to exchange technical information about the Unix computer operating system. Again, to the surprise of its developers, Usenet almost immediately became a tool for long-distance socializing. Usenet's "originators underestimated the hunger of people for meaningful communication," wrote Internet historians Michael and Ronda Hauben, pointing out that the possibility of "grass-roots connection of people" around the globe is what attracted users. [44]

Although other online groups joined Usenet, until the early 1990s most users were technical people and academics. In the early 1990s, however, America Online and Netscape began making it easy for non-technical users to move online. AOL, in particular, popularized

Unlike traditional discussion groups, however, the new "social media" groups capitalize on social networking's ability to connect an individual not only to friends but also to friends of friends, says Tom Gerace, founder and CEO of Gather.com, a social-networking site aimed at adults.

Gather's approach is to encourage its users — envisioned as the sort of folks who are regular listeners to National Public Radio, for example — to post thoughts on subjects ranging from politics to recipes. Those postings constitute a new "social media," movie reviews and political rants composed not by professional journalists but by any interested Internet user. Sites like Gather then use social networking's "friends of friends" structure to help people link up to the posting they'll be most interested in, because they interest others in their circle of contacts, says Gerace.

Gather users will also provide "social filtering" of the media they create, providing links and reviews that will bring the best socially created content to the top of the heap, Gerace says. The site currently pays members a modest fee if content they create gets high marks from fellow users. And "eventually some writers will earn a living" by creating top-ranked Gather content, Gerace says.

Content is also king at Buzznet, a social-networking site on which users share writings, photo, music and video celebrating popular culture, especially music. "A classic social network is all about your profile, but on Buzznet our emphasis is 100 percent focused on what you're producing," says co-founder Anthony Batt.

Buzznet "is the upside-down version of MySpace," says Batt. It's a catalog of people. We're about . . . what people are interested in. You connect with an interest, then you meet the people." Buzznet founders plan to build on its success to found other communities linked by different interests, potentially attracting different age groups, says Batt.

But Buzznet is not the replacement for MySpace that its founders expected it to be, says Batt. "People tend to have three stops. They hang out on MySpace, write a bit at LiveJournal" — a blogging and social-networking site — "and then spend time with us."

Online dating services will ultimately succumb to the social-networking boom, predicts Markus Frind, creator and owner of the Canada-based dating site Plentyoffish.com. Unlike most other dating sites, Plentyoffish is free to users. Frind's operation is "half social networking," because, unlike most other dating sites, Plentyoffish doesn't attempt proactive matchmaking. Instead, like MySpace, Plentyoffish simply allows members to post profiles, converse and arrange outside meetings — one-on-one dates or multi-member parties — on their own.

Contrary to what MySpace and Facebook members claim, the social-networking sites "are all about sex," says Frind. "People go there to hook up," and they're succeeding at it, he says. Eventually, that success will pull most people away from online dating services — which charge — to social-networking sites, which are free. "The hot girls are only on the social-networking sites now, not on dating sites. It's socially unacceptable for hot girls to say they're looking for dates," Frind says. "Eventually, all the guys will follow them there."

[1] Scott Karp, "Has the MySpace Downturn Begun?" *Publishing 2.0*, May 25, 2006, http://publishing2.com.

[2] Quoted in *ibid.*

[3] Murdoch was interviewed on "The Charlie Rose Show," on July 20, 2006. Also see "Murdoch predicts demise of classified ads," *Financial Times*, Nov. 24, 2005.

chat rooms, where people can exchange messages in real time. The live nature of chat room discussions raised new fears among parents because users were generally anonymous. Some chat rooms were eventually found to be heavily trafficked by pedophiles. By 1997, AOL had 14,000 chat rooms, which accounted for about a third of the time AOL members spent online. [45]

Later, AOL introduced instant messaging (IM) — real-time e-mail discussions with one person — and buddy lists, which alert users when friends are online and available to receive IMs.

"Community is the Velcro that keeps people there," said AOL President Theodore Leonsis. [46]

Six Degrees

In the 1960s, Yale University psychologist Stanley Milgram tested and apparently verified the theory that any two people on Earth are connected to each other by an average of six intermediate contacts. [47]

Scientific doubt remains about the validity of Milgram's so-called "six-degrees-of-separation" theory, but the idea has intrigued the popular imagination. In the late 1990s, Internet developers recognized that the Internet provides tools to seek and contact others in the farther circles of connection. For example, those who post personal Web pages invite friends to link their personal pages to theirs, then their friends link to their friends, creating a chain of social linkages.

In 1997, the pioneering Web site Sixdegrees.com allowed users to send and post messages viewable by their first, second and third-degree contacts. [48] Founder Andrew Weinreich, a lawyer-turned-entrepreneur, explained social networking's usefulness in business and social terms.

"Say you're coming out of college and you want to be a lawyer in Dallas. You ask, 'Who knows an environmental lawyer in Dallas?' You want advice. We give you a shot at that." Less serious queries also pay off, said Weinreich. "You can get a movie review from Siskel and Ebert, but wouldn't you rather hear it from friends you trust?" [49]

The first really big-name social-networking site, Friendster, was launched in 2002, and the block-buster site, MySpace, quickly followed, in 2003. While other sites also attract visitors in the millions, MySpace struck gold with a concept that, for the first time, brought teen Internet users together at a single spot.

"Curiosity about other people" drove social networking's initial fast growth, says Brooks, of *Online Personals Watch*. "But to make a site grow you need to hit something more powerful than curiosity," something that attracts key people or "connectors" — the "socialites . . . or loudmouths . . . those who run into hundreds of other people all the time," Brooks says.

MySpace seized upon music as a tool to reach the young "connectors." The site contacted music promoters and got band members to engage with the popular people on the site, said Berkeley's Boyd. The bands then created their own pages on MySpace, giving musicians an opportunity to link to multiple kids' pages. "Eventually, other young people followed the young people that followed the music," she says. [50]

And follow they have. With more than 80 million members, MySpace was growing by about 250,000 members a day in early 2006. [51] Exact rankings among the world's top Web sites shift daily, but MySpace averages the sixth-highest number of daily visitors, alongside English-language sites Yahoo, Microsoft Network, Google and eBay, and several Chinese-language sites. That translates to more than 30 million users visiting MySpace daily. [52]

Following right behind have been advertisers, with everybody who wants to contact young people putting up a MySpace page. Even the Marine Corps began collecting "friends" in early 2006. Some 12,000 people now link their pages to the Corps' page, and at last count 430 people had contacted recruiters through the site. [53]

AP Photo/*The Patriot Ledger*/Greg Derr

Flight instructor Harold Spector, 67, is arrested last April in Marshfield, Mass., where he'd flown in his private plane to meet what he thought was a 15-year-old girl he'd been "talking" to in an Internet chat room. Spector was charged with attempted statutory rape and attempting to entice a minor under age 16 for sex after the "girl" turned out to be two police officers.

Techno Kids

What has really brought MySpace to public attention, however, is not its sheer numbers, but its demographics.

Teens and young adults make up the overwhelming majority of users, triggering fear among parents, law-enforcement agencies and some legislators that the site may offer sexual predators easier access to young victims or encourage adolescents to engage in unhealthy behavior, such as posting sexually suggestive photos of themselves.

"The dangers our children are exposed to by these sites are clear and compelling," said Rep. Fitzpatrick. [54]

These worries aren't new and didn't start with social networking, says MIT's Jenkins. "Children and young people have always been early adopters of technology," he says, noting that the Boy Scouts were early users of radio, and in the 19th century children used toy printing presses to create magazines and newspapers.

But the speed with which new technologies appear on the scene today, combined with teens' propensity to quickly embrace new technologies, makes it especially difficult for parents, lawmakers and technology companies to figure out how to respond, says Blue Coat's Carosella. "The social behaviors that involve the Internet are not going to go away." In fact, "the kids . . . are inventing these behaviors."

"Kids are always one or two steps ahead" of older generations, says California State University's Subrahmanyam. "Chat, IM, social networking have all developed as teen-heavy technology," she says. "That makes sense, because figuring out sex and their own place in the social order . . . makes talking with peers very important."

But while teens have long discussed sex and relationships via instant messaging, adolescent interchanges on sites like MySpace "can now be seen by others," she adds.

Background Checks

While most of the uproar over potential dangers in online socializing concerns teenagers and children, some fear that online dating sites may also make it easier for sexual predators to reach adult victims.

Continued on p. 642

At Issue:

Should Congress require schools and public libraries to block social-networking Web sites?

REP. MICHAEL FITZPATRICK, R-PA.
SPONSOR, DELETING ONLINE PREDATORS ACT

FROM REMARKS ON HOUSE FLOOR, MAY 9, 2006

yes

My most important job is my role as a father of six children. In a world that moves and changes at a dizzying pace, being a father gets harder all the time. Technology is one of the key concerns I have as a parent, specifically the Internet and the sites my kids visit, register with and use on a daily basis.

One of the most interesting and worrying developments of late has been the growth in what are called "social-networking sites." Sites like MySpace, Friendster and Facebook have literally exploded in popularity in just a few short years.

For adults, these sites are fairly benign. For children, they open the door to many dangers, including online bullying and exposure to child predators that have turned the Internet into a virtual hunting ground for children. The dangers our children are exposed to by these sites are clear and compelling. MySpace, which is self-regulated, has removed an estimated 200,000 objectionable profiles since it started in 2003.

This is why I introduced the Deleting Online Predators Act as part of the Suburban Caucus agenda. Parents have the ability to screen their children's Internet access at home, but this protection ends when their child leaves for school or the library. The Deleting Online Predators Act requires schools and libraries to implement technology to protect children from accessing commercial networking sites like MySpace.com, and chat rooms, which allow children to be preyed upon by individuals seeking to do harm to our children.

Additionally, the legislation would require the Federal Trade Commission [FTC] to design and publish a unique Web site to serve as a clearinghouse and resource for parents, teachers and children for information on the dangers of surfing the Internet. The Web site would include detailed information about commercial networking sites like MySpace. The FTC would also be responsible for issuing consumer alerts to parents, teachers, school officials and others regarding the potential dangers of Internet child predators and others and their ability to contact children through MySpace.com and other social-networking sites.

In addition, the bill would require the Federal Communication Commission to establish an advisory board to review and report commercial social-networking sites like MySpace.com and chat rooms that have been shown to allow sexual predators easy access to personal information of, and contact with, our nation's children.

HENRY JENKINS
DIRECTOR, COMPARATIVE MEDIA STUDIES PROGRAM, MASSACHUSETTS INSTITUTE OF TECHNOLOGY

FROM INTERVIEW POSTED ONLINE BY THE MIT NEWS OFFICE, ACCESSED JULY 2006

no

As a society, we are at a moment of transition when the most important social relationships may no longer be restricted to those we conduct face-to-face with people in our own immediate surroundings. We are learning how to interact across multiple communities and negotiate with diverse norms. These networking skills are increasingly important to all aspects of our lives.

Just as youth in a hunting society play with bows and arrows, youth in an information society play with information and social networks. Rather than shutting kids off from social-network tools, we should be teaching them how to exploit their potential and mitigate their risks.

Much of the current policy debate around MySpace assumes that the activities there are at best frivolous and at worst dangerous to the teens who participate. Yet a growing number of teachers around the country are discovering that these technologies have real pedagogical value.

Teachers are beginning to use blogs for knowledge-sharing in schools; they use mailing lists to communicate expectations about homework with students and parents. They are discovering that students take their assignments more seriously and write better if they are producing work that will reach a larger public rather than simply sit on the teacher's desk. Teachers are linking together classrooms around the country and around the world, getting kids from different cultural backgrounds to share aspects of their everyday experience.

Many of these activities would be threatened by the proposed federal legislation, which would restrict access to these sites via public schools or library terminals. In theory, the bill would allow schools to disable these filters for use in educationally specified contexts, yet, in practice, teachers who wanted to exploit the educational benefits of these tools would face increased scrutiny and pressure to discontinue these practices.

Teens who lack access to the Internet at home would be cut off from their extended sphere of social contacts.

Wouldn't we be better off having teens engage with MySpace in the context of supervision from knowledgeable and informed adults? Historically, we taught children what to do when a stranger telephoned them when their parents are away; surely, we should be helping to teach them how to manage the presentation of their selves in digital spaces.

Many Americans Know Online Daters

Nearly one-third of American adults know at least one person who has used an online dating Web site.

Percent (of U.S. adults)	No. of People	Who Know Someone Who Has . . .
31%	63 million	used a dating Web site
26	53 million	dated a person they met on a dating site
15	30 million	been in a long-term relationship or married someone they met online

Source: Pew Internet and American Life Project, "Online Dating," March 5, 2006

Continued from p. 640

In the past year and a half, legislators in several states, including California, Florida, Illinois, Michigan, Ohio, Texas and Virginia, proposed requiring online dating sites to conduct criminal background checks of all prospective members or prominently inform users that they do not conduct such checks. [55]

The bills were suggested by Herb Vest, founder and CEO of the True.com dating service, which checks the criminal and marital backgrounds of its members. "The primary motivation is to protect people from criminal predation online," said Vest. "I can't imagine anyone with a hatful of brains being against that." [56]

Many online daters think dating sites already take such precautions, said Republican Florida state Rep. Kevin Ambler, who sponsored a similar bill in Florida last year after hearing that 20 percent of survey respondents thought background checks were already required on dating sites. "Many online daters have a false sense of security," he said. [57]

But some Internet companies and dating sites say the bills aren't needed or would create a false sense of security. "It would be just as easy to argue that True.com should be required to post labels on each page, saying, 'Warning. True.com's background searches will not identify criminals using fake names,' " said Kristin Kelly, a spokeswoman for the Match.com dating site. [58]

True.com has contracted with Rapsheets.com, a private firm trying to build a national database of criminal convictions, according to the Internet Alliance, an advocacy group whose members include the dating sites Match.com and eHarmony.com, as well as other Internet companies such as eBay, AOL and Yahoo. But mechanisms for tracking criminal convictions are state-based, the group points out, and some states decline to participate in national databases. So it is impossible for Rapsheets to have complete information, they said. [59]

Internet Alliance also argues that new laws aren't needed because unregulated dating services — such as newspaper ads and singles hotlines — have run "smoothly for years without legislative interference," while "providing even less information [than] a typical online profile."

So far, the bills have gone nowhere. The Michigan House passed a bill, but it later died in the state Senate. In Florida, bills were approved in committee last year but did not advance. A California bill that would have fined online dating services $250 for each day they don't conduct background checks was introduced but later pulled from consideration. ■

CURRENT SITUATION

Big Brother

Nowadays, teenagers aren't the only ones hanging out on MySpace.com. Law-enforcement officials now are increasingly staking out the site, looking to head off crimes. Some high-profile arrests in MySpace-related cases have raised concerns about social networking similar to worries that arose in the 1990s about chat rooms.

For example, a 39-year-old Pennsylvania man faces federal charges that he molested a 14-year-old Connecticut girl he met through her MySpace page. The girl had listed her age as 18. In another Connecticut case, a 22-year-old man traveled from New Jersey to visit an 11-year-old girl, whom he molested in her home while her parents slept. [60]

Besides monitoring for sexual predation, law-enforcement officials worry that teenagers may use MySpace to plot violence or vandalism. For example, a 15-year-old New Jersey girl was charged with harassment when school officials found an apparent "hit list" on her MySpace page. In Denver, a 16-year-old boy was arrested after allegedly posting photos of himself holding handguns on MySpace. [61] And in Riverton, Kan., five high-school boys were arrested in April after school officials found a message on one boy's MySpace page apparently threatening a Columbine-style shooting. Law-enforcement officers later found weapons and documents related to a plot in a student's bedroom and in school lockers. [62]

Meanwhile, the NBC program "Dateline" recently highlighted potential online dangers to children from adults. In a series of programs, "Dateline" photographed men who had arranged to meet what they thought were young teenagers but were actually adult members of an activist group. While the encounters took place in chat rooms, not on social-networking sites, the shows raised further alarms.

In response, Rep. Fitzpatrick introduced his Deleting Online Predators Act. It would expand the anti-pornography Children's Internet Protection Act (CIPA) by requiring schools and libraries to prohibit access to any commercial social-networking site or chat room through which minors could access sexual material or be subject to sexual advances.

"This is a new and evolving problem" that requires amendments to CIPA, since social networking didn't exist when that law was written, said Michael Conalle, Fitzpatrick's chief of staff. [63]

But the American Library Association said the bill is so broadly written that it would block not only education that would teach kids to go online safely but also "a wide array of other important applications and technologies." [64]

Lordan of the Internet Education Foundation said evidence suggests that more teens are abused in their own homes and neighborhoods than online. "We could end up diverting resources" to attack online predation "when the main need is really elsewhere," he says.

Although the House Energy and Commerce Committee has held subcommittee hearings on Fitzpatrick's bill, and it has been discussed on the House floor, discussions so far have focused heavily on child pornography on the Internet. No action on the legislation has yet been scheduled, and no bills have been introduced in the Senate.

Safety First

State attorneys general, parents, entrepreneurs and social-networking companies recently have launched safety initiatives for online socializing.

Connecticut Attorney General Richard Blumenthal, for example, has asked social-networking companies to implement tougher measures to block teenagers' access to pornography and rid the sites of sexual predators. Voluntary efforts, once the state and businesses agree on what steps should be taken, would "avoid the costs and time required for any sort of legal action," he said. [65]

In April, MySpace hired Hemanshu Migam — Microsoft's former director of consumer security and child safety and a former federal prosecutor of online child-exploitation cases — to manage its safety, privacy and customer-education programs. The company also partnered with the National Center for Missing and Exploited Children and the Advertising Council to post public-service announcements about online safety on TV, MySpace and other Internet sites. [66]

While acknowledging the company's first steps, Blumenthal said he had urged MySpace to adopt other, "more significant, specific measures," such as tougher age-verification efforts and free software for parents to block MySpace from home computers. [67]

Alarms about social networking also are drawing interest from parents' groups and some entrepreneurs. In Utah, for example, the state parent-teacher association is creating materials to teach parents how to make their children safe online. It will also recommend filtering and blocking software to parents in collaboration with Blue Coat, the Internet security company. [68]

Other Internet-technology developers also are offering help. Sales have tripled in the last three years for programs like eBlaster, Content Protect, IM Einstein and Safe Eyes, which allow parents to monitor their kids' e-mails, instant messages and online chats in real time from a separate computer — such as while the parent is at work. [69] Software developer Alex Strand, for instance, has established MySpace-watch.com, where users can sign up to monitor changes — such as new photos, additional listed friends — on a MySpace Web page for free.

"I started it as . . . a way for parents to check out what their kids are doing," said Strand. [70] ■

OUTLOOK

Here to Stay

In the future, online communications and social networking will become even more deeply rooted in our lives, say most analysts.

That makes it imperative to learn as much as possible about how online activities affect people, says Carosella, of Blue Coat Systems. "There's a critical role for mental health and social scientists," he says. "We should be doing studies on why there are so many sexual predators out there. Where did they all come from? Is there a vicious cycle between easy access to pornography online and the emergence of online predators?"

Future generations will make even more use of social networking, predicts Diane Danielson, who created www.DWCFaces.com, a social-networking site for businesswomen. "We will see Generation Y bringing their social networks into the workspace," she says, referring to the 20-25-year-old age group. "They will also remain connected to more people from their high schools and colleges" thanks to the persistent presence on social-networking sites of links to Web sites like Classmates.com. "In a transient society, a social network Web page might be your most consistent address."

Social networking may also transform some political campaigns into more grass-roots affairs, says Zephyr Teachout, a professor of constitutional law at Vermont Law School, who directed Internet organizing for

Howard Dean's 2004 presidential campaign. Dean encouraged people around the country to communicate on their own via social-network software, allowing local and individual momentum to drive many activities. "We discovered that the human need to be political is important" and, if tapped, increases participation, she says. "But to do it you need a candidate willing to devolve power."

When media mogul Rupert Murdoch's News Corp. bought MySpace last year for $580 million, some speculated that the conservative Murdoch might use the site to influence the politics of the site's young users, perhaps by pushing Republican-slanted commentary on the site during the 2008 presidential election cycle. Many analysts doubt whether such an effort could succeed, though, since social-networking users have notoriously fled sites when owners have tried to exercise regulatory clout.

But Murdoch says he spent $1.5 billion in the past year to buy MySpace and other online companies to empower people to create their own content. "Technology is shifting power away from the editors, the publishers, the establishment, the media elite. Now it's the people who are taking control," he said. [71]

As Internet technology draws more people to publish their personal information in cyberspace, a new set of ethics is needed for presenting oneself, says Bill Holsinger-Robinson, chief operating officer of Spout.com, a social-networking site focused on film. "I see it as harking back to earlier, simpler times — a town square where people can gather."

When town squares were common, he says, "there was a certain sense of responsibility on how we presented ourselves. We've lost that. Now we have to reinvent it for a new generation." ■

Notes

[1] Erik Brady and Daniel Libit, "Alarms Sound Over Athlete's Facebook Time," *USA Today*, March 8, 2006.

[2] Quoted in *ibid.*

[3] Clair Osborn, "Teen, Mom Sue MySpace.com for $30 Million," *Austin American-Statesman*, June 20, 2006.

[4] Quoted in *ibid.*

[5] "Internet: The Mainstreaming of Online Life," Pew Internet and American Life Project, www.pewinternet.org.

[6] John Horrigan and Lee Rainie, "The Internet's Growing Role in Life's Major Moments," Pew Internet and American Life Project, April 19, 2006.

[7] "Internet: The Mainstreaming of Online Life," *op. cit.*

[8] For background, see Brian Hansen, "Cyber-predators," *CQ Researcher*, March 1, 2002, p. 169-192.

[9] For background, see David Masci, "Internet Privacy," *CQ Researcher*, Nov. 6, 2998, pp. 953-976.

[10] "Social Networking Sites Continue to Attract Record Numbers as MySpace.com Surpasses 50 Million U.S. Visitors in May," PRNewswire, comScore Networks, Inc., June 15, 2006.

[11] Marshall Kirkpatrick, "Top 10 Social Networking Sites See 47 Percent Growth," the socialsoftwareweblog, May 17, 2006, http://socialsofware.weblogsinc.com.

[12] For background, see Kenneth Jost, "Libraries and the Internet," *CQ Researcher*, June 1, 2001, pp. 465-488.

[13] Michael Fitzpatrick, testimony before House Energy and Commerce Subcommittee on Oversight and Investigations, June 10, 2006.

[14] Henry Jenkins and Danah Boyd, "Discussion: MySpace and Deleting Online Predators Act," interview published online by Massachusetts Institute of Technology News Office, May 24, 2006, www.danah.org/papers/MySpaceDOPA.html.

[15] *Ibid.*

[16] Quoted in Anne Chappel Belden, "Kids' Tech Toys: High-Tech Communication Tools," Parenthood.com, http://parenthood.com.

[17] Kevin Farnham, reply to "Friendster Lost Steam. Is MySpace Just a Fad?" Corante blog, March 21, 2006, http://man.corante.com.

[18] Paul Marks, "Pentagon Sets Its Sights on Social Networking in Washington," *NewScientist.com*, June 9, 2006, www.newscientist.com.

[19] Quoted in *ibid.*

[20] David Finkelhor and Lisa M. Jones, "Explanations for the Decline in Sexual Abuse Cases," *Juvenile Justice Bulletin*, U.S. Department of Justice, Office of Juvenile Justice and Delinquency Prevention, January 2004, www.ojp.usdoj/gov/ojjdp.

[21] Quoted in Larry Magid, "Plug In, or Pull the Plug," Staysafe.org for Parents, www.staysafeonline.com.

[22] *Congressional Record*, House, May 9, 2006, p. H2311.

[23] *Ibid*, p. H2315.

[24] Jenkins and Boyd, *op. cit.*

[25] *Ibid.*

[26] Quoted in Robert Brumfield, "Bill Calls for MySpace Age Limit," *eSchoolNews online*, May 16, 2006, www.eschoolnews.com.

[27] For background, see Kathy Koch, "The Digital Divide," *CQ Researcher*, Jan. 28, 2000, pp. 41-64.

[28] For background, see Marcia Clemmitt, "Controlling the Internet," *CQ Researcher*, May 12, 2006, pp. 409-432.

[29] Clifford Stoll, *Silicon Snake Oil: Second Thoughts on the Information Highway* (1996), p. 43.

[30] Killeen Hanson, "Study Links Internet, Social Contact," *The Stanford Daily Online Edition*, Feb. 28, 2005.

[31] Quoted in *ibid.*

[32] Norman H. Nie and Lutz Erbring, "Internet and Society: A Preliminary Report," Stanford Institute for the Quantitative Study of Society, Feb. 17, 2000.

[33] Quoted in *ibid.*

About the Author

Staff writer **Marcia Clemmitt** is a veteran social-policy reporter who previously served as editor in chief of *Medicine and Health*, a Washington industry newsletter, and staff writer for *The Scientist*. She has also been a high-school math and physics teacher. She holds a liberal arts and sciences degree from St. John's College, Annapolis, and a master's degree in English from Georgetown University. Her recent reports include "Climate Change," "Controlling the Internet" and "Pork Barrel Politics."

[34] Jeffrey Boase, John B. Horrigan, Barry Wellman and Lee Rainie, "The Strength of Internet Ties," Pew Internet and American Life Project, Jan. 25, 2006.

[35] *Ibid.*

[36] *Ibid.*

[37] Barry Wellman, Jeffrey Boase and Wenhong Chen, "The Networked Nature of Community: Online and Offline," *IT & Society*, summer 2002, pp. 151-165, www.itandsociety.org.

[38] *Ibid.*

[39] Sheera Claire Frenkel, "Israelis and Lebanese Are Still Talking — on the Net," *The Jerusalem Post*, July 21, 2006.

[40] Christopher Allen, "My Advice to Social Networking Services," Life With Alacrity blog, Feb. 3, 2004, www.lifewithalacrity.com.

[41] Quoted in Michael Erard, "Decoding the New Cues in Online Society," *The New York Times*, Nov. 27, 2003.

[42] Quoted in Jenkins and Boyd, *op. cit.*

[43] For background, see *The Internet's Coming of Age* (2000).

[44] Michael Hauben and Ronda Hauben, "The Social Forces Behind the Development of Usenet," First Monday, www.firstmonday.org.

[45] "Internet Communities," *Business Week Archives*, May 5, 1997, www.businessweek.com.

[46] Quoted in *ibid.*

[47] For background, see Judith Donath and Danah Boyd, "Public Displays of Connection," *BT Technology Journal*, October 2004, p. 71.

[48] Doug Bedell, "Meeting Your New Best Friends," *The Dallas Morning News*, Oct. 27, 1998.

[49] Quoted in *ibid.*

[50] Danah Boyd, "Friendster Lost Steam. Is MySpace Just a Fad?" March 21, 2006, www.danah.org.

[51] Dawn Kawamoto and Greg Sandoval, "MySpace Growth Continues Amid Criticism," ZDNet News, March 31, 2006, http://news.zdnet.com.

[52] MySpace traffic details from www.alexa.com.

[53] Audrey McAvoy, "Marines Trolling MySpace.com for Recruits," *Chicago Sun-Times*, July 25, 2006.

[54] *Congressional Record*, *op. cit.*, p. H2310.

[55] For background, see Javad Heydary, "Regulation of Online Dating Services Sparks Controversy," *E-Commerce Times*, March 3, 2005, www.ecommercetimes.com.

[56] Quoted in "Online Dating Background Checks?" CNNMoney.com, April 25, 2006, http://cnnmoney.com.

[57] Quoted in *ibid.*

[58] Quoted in Declan McCullagh, "True Love With a Criminal Background Check," C/Net News.com, Feb. 28, 2005, http://news.com.com.

FOR MORE INFORMATION

Apophenia: Making Connections Where None Previously Existed, www.zephoria.org/thoughts/. News, data and commentary on the social Internet by social-media researcher Danah Boyd.

Berkman Center for Internet and Society, Harvard Law School, Baker House, 1587 Massachusetts Ave., Cambridge, MA 02138; (617) 495-7547; http://cyber.law.harvard.edu. A research program investigating legal, technical and social developments in cyberspace.

Center for the Digital Future, University of Southern California Annenberg School, 300 South Grand Ave., Suite 3950, Los Angeles, CA 90071; (213) 437-4433; www.digitalcenter.org. A research program investigating the Internet's effects on individuals and society.

Crimes Against Children Research Center, University of New Hampshire, 20 College Rd., #126 Horton Social Science Center, Durham, NH 03824; (603) 862-1888; www.unh.edu/ccrc/. Studies criminal victimization of young people and how to prevent it, including online.

Internet Education Foundation, 1634 I St., N.W., Suite 1107, Washington, DC 20006; (202) 638-4370; www.neted.org. Educates the public and lawmakers about the Internet as a tool of democracy and communications; the industry-supported GetNetWise project (www.getnetwise.org) disseminates information on safety and security.

Many2Many, http://many.corante.com/. Academics and technical experts provide information and commentary on social networking in this blog.

National Center for Missing and Exploited Children, 699 Prince St., Alexandria, VA 22314-3175; (703) 274-3900; www.missingkids.com. Provides education and services on child exploitation to families and professionals; maintains a CyberTipline and other resources for reporting and combating exploitation via the Internet.

Online Personals Watch, http://onlinepersonalswtach.typepad.com. A blogger and industry veteran provides news and commentary on social networking and online dating.

Pew Internet and American Life Project, 1615 L St., N.W., Suite 700, Washington, DC 20036; (202) 419-4500; www.pewinternet.org. Provides data and analysis on Internet usage and its effects on American society.

Progress and Freedom Foundation, 1444 I St., N.W., Suite 500, Washington, DC 20005; (202) 289-8928; www.pff.org. A free-market-oriented think tank that examines public policy related to the Internet.

[59] "Online Dating," white paper from Internet Alliance, www.internetalliance.org.

[60] "Twenty Youths Suspended in MySpace Case," The Associated Press, March 3, 2006.

[61] "MySpace in the News," *Bergen* [New Jersey] *Daily Record*, May 14, 2006, www.dailyrecord.com.

[62] "Charges Mulled in Alleged School Shooting Plot," The Associated Press, April 23, 2006. For background, see Kathy Koch, "School Violence," *CQ Researcher*, Oct. 9, 1998, pp. 881-904.

[63] Quoted in Declan McCullagh, "Congress Targets Social Network Sites," C/Net News.com, May 11, 2006, http://news.com.com.

[64] Michael Gorman, "ALA Opposes 'Deleting Online Predators Act,' " May 15, 2006, statement, American Library Association.

[65] Quoted in "Making MySpace Safe for Kids," Newsmaker Q&A, *Business Week online*, March 6, 2006, www.businessweek.com.

[66] Maria Newman, "MySpace.com Hires Official to Oversee Users' Safety," *The New York Times*, April 12, 2006.

[67] Quoted in *ibid.*

[68] "Utah PTA and Blue Coat Systems Join Forces to Drive Greater Internet Safety, Community Action," Blue Coat Systems press release, June 20, 2006, www.bluecoat.com.

[69] See Ned Potter, "Watching Your Kids Online," ABCNews.com, July 24, 2006.

[70] Quoted in Stefanie Olsen, "Keeping an Eye on MySpace," C/Net News.com, June 29, 2006, http://news.com.com.

[71] Spencer Reiss, "His Space," *Wired*, July 14, 2006, www.wired.com.

Bibliography

Selected Sources

Books

Farnham, Kevin M., and Dale G. Farnham, *MySpace Safety: 51 Tips for Teens and Parents*, How To Primers, 2006.
Parents of a veteran teenage MySpace user explain what their experiences have taught them about how social networking works and what safety rules families should follow.

Rheingold, Howard, *The Virtual Community: Homesteading on the Electronic Frontier*, The MIT Press, 2000.
A technology analyst and longtime participant in Internet communities recounts the history of the social Internet and his two decades of personal experience with it.

Articles

Armental, Maria, "Site Started by New Jersey Teens Is Growing Fast," *Asbury Park Press*, May 16, 2006, www.app.com.
MyYearbook.com, a social-networking site created by two New Jersey high-school students in 2005, has membership rolls that are growing by about 40 percent a month. The brother and sister team who created it became millionaires before high-school graduation earlier this year when an investor paid $1.5 million for a 10-percent stake in the operation.

Bower, Bruce, "Growing Up Online," *Science News Online*, June 17, 2006, www.sciencenews.org.
Research psychologists dissect the appeal of Internet social-networking software to teenagers and describe the findings in several recent studies of how teenagers behave online.

Brumfield, Robert, "Bill Calls for MySpace Age Limit," *eSchoolNews online*, May 16, 2006.
Educators discuss the possible effects on schools and students of a congressional proposal to require schools and public libraries to block social software.

Hof, Robert D., "Internet Communities," *Business Week*, May 5, 1997, *Business Week Archives*, www.businessweek.com.
As women, teenagers and non-technical users flock online, Internet use turns away from pre-created content toward socializing and Internet communities sharing common interests.

Koppelman, Alex, "MySpace or OurSpace?" *Salon.com*, June 8, 2006, www.salon.com.
A growing number of school administrators and law-enforcement officials regularly monitor MySpace and other social-networking sites in search of evidence of rule-breaking and criminal activity. The practice is raising awareness among teens that spaces they believed were private are not and also is raising questions about how far schools can go in policing students' out-of-school activities.

Leonard, Andrew, "You Are Who You Know," *Salon.com*, June 15, 2004.
Social-networking entrepreneurs and Internet analysts explain why Internet technology led to development of social software and why they believe social networks matter, online and off.

Marks, Paul, "Pentagon Sets Its Sights on Social Networking Websites," *New Scientist*, June 9, 2006, NewScientist.com.
The National Security Agency is researching the possibility of mining social-networking sites for data to assemble extensive personal profiles of individuals and their social circles to help sniff out terrorist plots.

Reiss, Spencer, "His Space," *Wired*, July 14, 2006, www.wired.com.
Since media mogul Rupert Murdoch paid $580 million to buy MySpace in 2005, technology and business analysts have argued about whether Murdoch can make the investment pay by selling advertising and/or using the site as a distribution channel for music and video content.

Studies and Reports

Boase, Jeffrey, John B. Horrigan, Barry Wellman and Lee Rainie, *The Strength of Internet Ties*, Pew Internet and American Life Project, January 2006.
Statistics show that the Internet and e-mail aid users in maintaining social networks and providing pathways to support and advice in difficult times, according to University of Toronto and Pew researchers.

Finkelhor, David, Kimberly J. Mitchell and Janis Wolak, *Online Victimization: A Report on the Nation's Youth*, Crimes Against Children Research Center, University of New Hampshire, June 2000.
In cooperation with the National Center for Missing and Exploited Children and the U.S. Department of Justice Office of Juvenile Justice and Delinquency Prevention, University of New Hampshire researchers detail national statistics on online crimes against children and teens, online sexual solicitation of young Internet users and responses to Internet sexual solicitations by young people, their families and law enforcement.

Lenhart, Amanda, and Mary Madden, *Teen Content Creators and Consumers*, Pew Internet and American Life Project, November 2005.
Creating and sharing content through blogs, videos and other sites is an integral part of online social life for today's teens.

The Next Step:

Additional Articles from Current Periodicals

Internet Dating

English, Bella, "Pet Lovers Find Animal Attraction Hard to Resist," *The Houston Chronicle*, Feb. 19, 2006, p. 4.
Dan Cohen's animalattraction.com is a dating site that pairs people up based on their love of animals.

Kloer, Phil, "Site Offers Truth About Personal Ads on Net," *Chicago Tribune*, Aug. 7, 2005, p. B3.
Truedater.com allows online daters to post reviews of anyone they have dated from a variety of sites, depicting what that person is really like as opposed to his or her personal ad.

Noveck, Jocelyn, "Internet Dating Comes of Age — Middle Age," *The Miami Herald*, March 25, 2006, p. E4.
People over 50 are increasingly turning to Internet dating sites to find romance.

Internet Safety

Briscoe, Daren, " 'Netbangers,' Beware," *Newsweek*, March 13, 2006, p. 31.
Street gangs are setting up Web pages to communicate with one another and pick online fights with rival gangs.

Helderman, Rosalind S., "Law Directs Schools to Teach About Cyber-Safety," *The Washington Post*, March 30, 2006, p. T1.
A new Virginia law will require the state's public schools to teach students about Internet safety.

Sharos, David, "Internet Safety Fears Spark Education Efforts," *Chicago Tribune*, May 8, 2006, p. 8.
Law-enforcement officials, school administrators and software companies have begun to address social-networking issues, including pedophiles trolling for youngsters on the Web and the sharing of too much personal information by minors in chat rooms.

Wyss, Jim, "Chaperoning On The Net," *The Miami Herald*, Feb. 8, 2006, p. C1.
A background screening company will police a new gaming-meets-dating site that uses fantasy and role-playing.

MySpace.com

Gaither, Chris, and Dawn C. Chmielewski, "MySpace Takes Measures to Make Hip Youth Web Site Predator-Free," *The Houston Chronicle*, April 12, 2006, p. 8.
The social-networking site MySpace.com has hired a former federal prosecutor to patrol the service and launched ads warning kids about Internet predators.

Gunderson, Matt, "Police Delete Minor Users From Website," *The Boston Globe*, Feb. 23, 2006, p. 1.
Police in Pepperell, Mass., have launched a campaign to erase profiles of local children who are underage or misrepresenting their ages on MySpace.

Jesdanun, Anick, "Popularity of MySpace Soars, Sphere of Influence Expands," *Chicago Tribune*, Feb. 13, 2006, p. 1.
MySpace, created just over two years ago, quickly eclipsed Friendster as the top social-networking site and now has more than twice the traffic of Google.

Mitchell, Dan, "MySpace No Longer Their Space?" *The New York Times*, June 3, 2006, p. C5.
Internet experts contend that MySpace might lose popularity among teens because of increasing reports that the site is dangerous, cluttered and beset by technical problems.

Teens Online

Lenhart, Jennifer, "Teens' Online Boasting Leads to Arson Arrests," *The Washington Post*, May 13, 2006, p. B2.
Two Maryland teenagers who set fires around their neighborhood for several months were caught after boasting about their exploits on MySpace.

McDonald, Soraya Nadia, " 'Facebooking' The Rage on College Campuses," *The Seattle Times*, July 4, 2005, p. C4.
Facebook.com, an online directory created to connect the higher-education world through social networks, is an Internet sensation on college campuses.

Prichard, Oliver, "Web Network 'Friends' Who Can Be Anything But," *The Philadelphia Inquirer*, Dec. 11, 2005, p. A23.
Teens are increasingly congregating on social-networking sites for interaction, self-expression, mischief-making and risk-taking.

Citing *CQ Researcher*

Sample formats for citing these reports in a bibliography include the ones listed below. Preferred styles and formats vary, so please check with your instructor or professor.

MLA Style

Jost, Kenneth. "Rethinking the Death Penalty." CQ Researcher 16 Nov. 2001: 945-68.

APA Style

Jost, K. (2001, November 16). Rethinking the death penalty. *CQ Researcher, 11*, 945-968.

Chicago Style

Jost, Kenneth. "Rethinking the Death Penalty." *CQ Researcher*, November 16, 2001, 945-968.

CQ Researcher

Published by CQ Press, a division of Congressional Quarterly Inc.

cqresearcher.com

Drinking on Campus

Have efforts to reduce alcohol abuse failed?

Tremendous media attention has been focused on heavy college drinking during the past decade, but drinking habits have changed little. Alcohol is still the drug of choice among young people, especially on college campuses. Each year, some 1,700 students die due to drunken driving or other alcohol-related incidents. This year, the Duke University lacrosse team made the news when an exotic dancer accused three of its members of raping her at an alcohol-fueled party. Studies have found that rates of binge drinking and its often-devastating outcomes have remained remarkably stable over time, despite various attempts to reduce alcohol consumption on campus. According to the National Institute of Alcohol Abuse and Alcoholism, too many college alcohol programs are not supported by research. As a result, there is considerable debate about what colleges and surrounding communities can do to reduce excessive drinking among students.

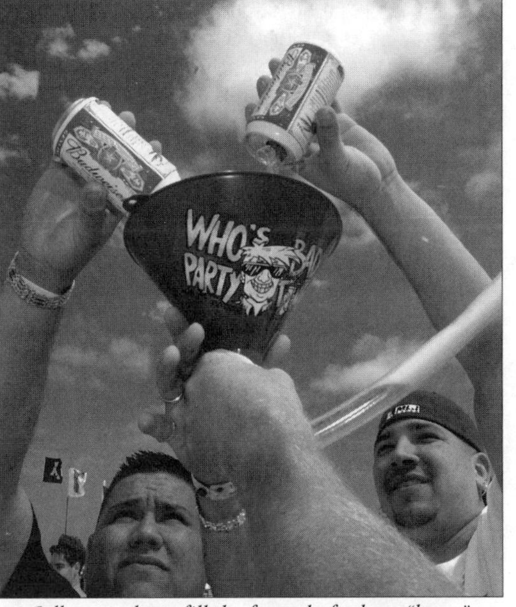

College students fill the funnel of a beer "bong" during spring break at South Padre Island, Texas. Bongs are commonplace on U.S. campuses.

INSIDE THIS REPORT

CQ Researcher • Aug. 18, 2006 • www.cqresearcher.com
Volume 16, Number 28 • Pages 649-672

DRINKING ON CAMPUS

Cover photograph:Newsmakers/Joe Raedle

CQ Researcher

Aug. 18, 2006
Volume 16, Number 28

MANAGING EDITOR: Thomas J. Colin

ASSISTANT MANAGING EDITOR: Kathy Koch

ASSOCIATE EDITOR: Kenneth Jost

STAFF WRITERS: Marcia Clemmitt, Peter Katel

CONTRIBUTING WRITERS: Rachel S. Cox, Sarah Glazer, Alan Greenblatt, Patrick Marshall, Tom Price

DESIGN/PRODUCTION EDITOR: Olu B. Davis

ASSISTANT EDITOR: Melissa J. Hipolit

EDITORIAL INTERN: Nicholas Sohr

CQ PRESS

A Division of Congressional Quarterly Inc.

SENIOR VICE PRESIDENT/PUBLISHER: John A. Jenkins

DIRECTOR, LIBRARY PUBLISHING: Kathryn C. Suárez

DIRECTOR, EDITORIAL OPERATIONS: Ann Davies

CONGRESSIONAL QUARTERLY INC.

CHAIRMAN: Paul C. Tash

VICE CHAIRMAN: Andrew P. Corty

PRESIDENT/EDITOR IN CHIEF: Robert W. Merry

CQ Researcher (ISSN 1056-2036) is printed on acid-free paper. Published weekly, except March 24, July 7, July 14, Aug. 4, Aug. 11, Nov. 24, Dec. 22 and Dec. 29, by CQ Press, a division of Congressional Quarterly Inc. Annual full-service subscriptions for institutions start at $667. For pricing, call 1-800-834-9020, ext. 1906. To purchase a *CQ Researcher* report in print or electronic format (PDF), visit www.cqpress.com or call 866-427-7737. Single reports start at $15. Bulk purchase discounts and electronic-rights licensing are also available. Periodicals postage paid at Washington, D.C., and additional mailing offices. POSTMASTER: Send address changes to *CQ Researcher*, 1255 22nd St., N.W., Suite 400, Washington, DC 20037.

Drinking on Campus

BY BARBARA MANTEL

THE ISSUES

High-school softball player Laura Smith hoped to play on a varsity team in college, and like thousands of other athletes, she visited various schools during her senior year. But during a visit last March to California State University at Chico, the 17-year-old's college career almost ended before it started.

While attending a party hosted by team members, Smith (not her real name) became unresponsive after heavy drinking. Luckily, someone called 911. At 1 a.m., paramedics rushed her to a hospital to be treated for alcohol poisoning.* Smith was released five hours later.

AP Photo/Phoummarath family

Phanta "Jack" Phoummarath, right, was 18 when he died from alcohol poisoning at a University of Texas fraternity party last December. His parents, left, sued the fraternity, Lambda Phi Epsilon, alleging Jack had been forced to drink heavily during a hazing ritual. "We don't want any family to go through what we have had to go through," said his sister. More than 1,700 college students die annually in alcohol-related incidents.

Following Smith's close call, Chico State Athletic Director Anita Barker promptly canceled the remainder of the softball season and kicked the players who attended the party off the team, several of whom were underage. "This is not the kind of behavior we expect," Barker said. "The magnitude and gravity of the situation warrants swift and decisive action that sends a message this behavior is unacceptable." [1]

In fact, several alcohol-related deaths have occurred at Chico State. Last year, a 21-year-old fraternity pledge died during a hazing ritual. In 2001, a 19-year-old was hit by a train after passing out drunk on the tracks. And the year before, an 18-year-old student died after drinking a bottle of brandy at a fraternity party. [2]

While the deaths at Chico and other campuses capture media and public attention, they only hint at the extent of heavy drinking among college students and the harm that results. In the early 1990s, Harvard University's School of Public Health showed that 44 percent of students questioned in a nationwide survey reported binge drinking — consuming five or more drinks in a row for men and four or more for women — during the two weeks prior to the survey. Other studies have shown similar results. [3]

Since then, both houses of Congress have passed resolutions asking college presidents to address the problem, and colleges have instituted various initiatives to reduce college drinking. The National Institute on Alcohol Abuse and Alcoholism formed a special task force in 1998, and the surgeon general in 2000 set a goal of reducing college binge drinking by 50 percent within 10 years.

Surveys show that goal will be difficult, if not impossible, to meet: Heavy, episodic drinking continues to be a stubborn problem on campuses across the United States.

"Drinking is a very big part of the American college experience," says Emma Ross, a rising senior at the University of Chicago. "Rarely does someone participate in an evening activity (aside from going to the movies) that doesn't involve drinking, and when they do drink it is not uncommon for someone to get incredibly drunk. Also, large college parties are generally not very fun if one isn't drunk. They are loud and impersonal, so no one would want to be at a party and not be drinking."

Depending on the study, the number of college students who binge drink is holding steady or falling only slightly.

For instance, Harvard's "College Alcohol Study" showed that "remarkably similar proportions of students were classified as binge drinkers in 2001, as in previous survey years (44.4%)." [4] The University of Michigan's "Monitoring the Future" survey finds a similar percentage: 41.7 percent in 2004, roughly the same as in the early 1990s but down slightly from 1980, when the survey began. (*See graph, p. 662.*)

"I would definitely say that there is a binge-drinking culture at the University of Southern California," says Sean Fish, a senior at the Los Angeles campus. "Many students, many of my friends and myself, are guilty of binge drinking." But Fish considers it a problem only when it happens two or more times a week.

While studies show that frequent binge drinking is becoming more common, paradoxically the percentage of

---

* Consuming large amounts of alcohol can lead to unconsciousness and then death because vital organs, such as the heart and lungs, can be slowed to the point of stopping.

Consequences of Excessive Drinking

Every year, some 1,700 students die from alcohol-related injuries, nearly 100,000 are victims of alcohol-related sexual abuse and more than 2 million are cited for drunken driving.

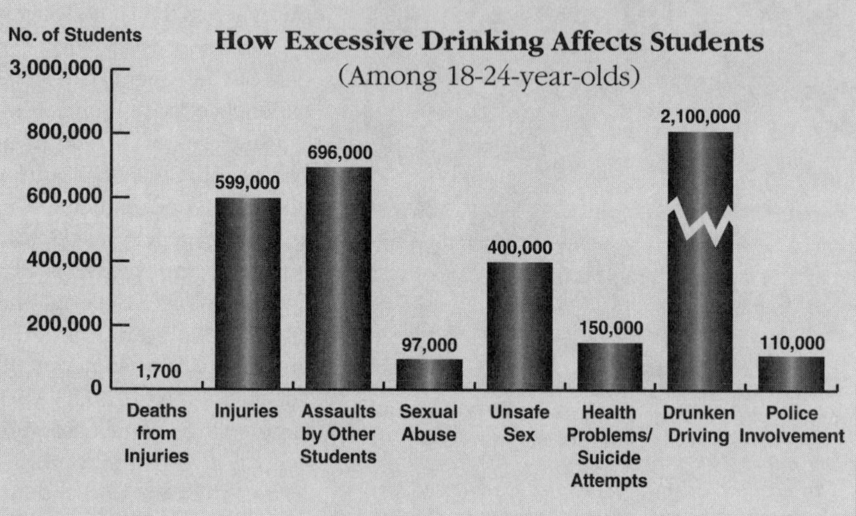

Source: National Institute on Alcohol Abuse and Alcoholism

students abstaining from alcohol is also increasing, indicating that student drinking habits are becoming more polarized between those who don't partake and those who do — heavily.

How alarming are these trends? That depends on whether one focuses on the sizable minority who binge drink or the majority who don't.

"Alcohol use on college campuses is certainly a problem, but hardly the epidemic it is made out to be," writes Aaron White, an assistant professor of psychiatry and an alcohol researcher at Duke University Medical Center. "Not all college drinkers get out of hand, drink to get drunk or require treatment for alcohol poisoning." [5]

It may not be an epidemic, but it is a chronic problem, says Ralph Hingson, a professor of public health at Boston University and an investigator at its Youth Alcohol Prevention Center. "If over 40 percent of college students are consuming five or more drinks on any one occasion, I consider that a very substantial minority," says Hingson. "And remember, drinkers don't just harm themselves."

Excessive drinking causes a variety of negative consequences, including blackouts, injury, unintended and unprotected sex, impaired driving, poor grades, property damage, fights, arrests and sexual violence. (*See graph above.*) In the 2001 "College Alcohol Study," about 30 percent of students who drank in the past 30 days reported missing a class because of alcohol, 21 percent had unplanned sex because of alcohol and about 13 percent reported getting injured — all somewhat higher than in 1993. [6]

There are also secondhand effects, as Hingson points out. About 48 percent of students had to care for a drunken student, 60 percent had their sleep or study interrupted and about 20 percent experienced an unwanted sexual advance. [7]

The fatal consequences of heavy drinking are also on the rise. The number of alcohol-related deaths among college students has increased faster than the college population. In 2001, an estimated 1,717 college students ages 18 to 24 died from alcohol-related accidental injuries, including motor vehicle crashes; that's an increase of 6 percent (adjusted for college population growth) over the 1,575 deaths in 1998. [8]

"How can this be if the percentage of students that binge drink has remained relatively stable?" Duke University's White asks rhetorically. He explains that categorizing students as either binge or non-binge drinkers does not reveal *how much* they actually drink. For instance, a female student would be considered a binge drinker if she had four drinks or 40 drinks, but the danger from consuming 40 drinks would be quite different.

"It is entirely possible that peak levels of consumption beyond the binge threshold have been skyrocketing for years, and we have simply missed this fact," says White. [9]

He recently reported that roughly half of all males categorized as binge drinkers actually consumed 10 or more drinks, twice the binge threshold, at least once in the two weeks before being questioned. [10] However, the study — using data from a single, online college survey — did not measure whether the amount consumed by bingers has changed over time.

Whether they drink five or 20 drinks in a single sitting, bingers are not a representative slice of the college population. "I see problem drinking more among freshmen," says Caroline Stevens, who graduated last spring from Beloit College in Wisconsin. "By the time you graduate, drinking is not such a big deal, and it's much less common to get drunk."

Stevens' impressions are statistically correct. According to several studies, the students who drink the most are males, whites, fraternity members, athletes and first-year students. Students who drink the least are those who attend two-year institutions, religious schools, historically black colleges and universities and commuter schools. [11]

Even though many colleges and universities have tailored and directed their alcohol messages to those most at risk, the rate of heavy, episodic college drinking shows little or no improvement.

"For the most part, schools have not based their prevention efforts on strategies identified and tested for effectiveness by research," according to a report from the National Institute on Alcohol Abuse and Alcoholism. [12]

In today's environment of heightened awareness but unimpressive results, here are some of the questions being debated:

National Social Norms Resource Center

Posters displayed at the University of Arizona use social norms marketing to change students' misperception about their peers' drinking habits. An increasing number of schools are using social norms marketing to reduce social pressure to binge drink.

Do social norming and online tools convince students to drink more responsibly?

"I honestly am not sure what a college can do about drinking. I think a lot of students just view it as part of the college experience."

— Julie Price, senior, The College of William and Mary, Williamsburg, Va.

For decades schools have tried to educate students about the risks of excessive drinking. But simply providing them with information doesn't seem to work. Now an increasing number of schools are changing their approach by turning to a controversial method known as social norms marketing.

The technique is based on a simple premise. Studies show that students consistently overestimate how much their peers drink and underestimate how many abstain. By giving students accurate information, such as that less than a majority — 44 percent — of students nationwide binge drink, social norms marketing campaigns hope to reduce the social pressure to drink to excess.

Like many students, William and Mary's Price overestimates her peers' drinking habits. "I would say that binge drinking probably occurs among a majority of students on a regular basis," she says.

Social norms marketing campaigns usually involve a series of ads in various campus venues. At Florida State University (FSU), for example, the campaign features ads on campus shuttle buses, billboards and radio and TV spots, says Mary B. Coburn, vice president for student affairs. "A typical ad has been a picture of actual students debunking the myth that everybody is doing it," she says.

FSU's campaign, begun in 2000, is funded by the Anheuser-Busch Foundation. The alcoholic-beverage industry often funds social norms campaigns, as do federal and state agencies. Proponents say social norming celebrates what students are doing right rather than denouncing what they are doing wrong, and that it works.

"We have case studies at different universities showing that when a norm campaign corrects misperceptions of drinking . . . we get parallel reductions in actual heavy drinking behavior and in negative consequences," says Michael Haines, director of the National Social Norms Resource Center, at Northern Illinois University in Dekalb.

But Henry Wechsler, director of Harvard's "College Alcohol Study," calls the case studies "very rudimentary." For instance, they used no control group for comparison, says Wechsler, and they did not take into account other alcohol programs on campus that may influence drinking behavior. FSU, for instance, also has limited students' access to alcohol and has implemented programs to educate students about the risks of drinking.

Wechsler's own study — comparing the results of the "College Alcohol Study" at schools that say they use social norms marketing with schools that don't — concluded that there is no difference in student drinking behavior between the two. "If you really believe that the industry is going to back a method that is going to cut down on sales of alcohol, then you're an idealist," says Wechsler. "Their job is to sell alcohol."

But proponents of social norms marketing attacked Wechsler's study. "Given the prestigious academic platform of a Harvard project, the public would logically assume that the study has merit," wrote researchers at the Higher Education Center for Alcohol and Other Drug Abuse and Violence Prevention, a nonprofit funded by the U.S. Department of Education. "But it does not." [13]

Wechsler's study, the researchers said, failed to distinguish between schools doing legitimate social norms marketing and those that said they were doing the marketing but in fact were not making a serious effort. Putting up a few posters, these researchers said, does not constitute a social norms marketing campaign.

Experimental studies are needed, but so far only a limited one has been conducted. Researchers at San Diego State University introduced a social norms marketing campaign into one residence hall at a large university and used another residence hall as a control for comparison. "The campaign successfully corrected students' misperceptions of drinking norms but had no effects, or counterintuitive effects, on drinking behaviors," the study concluded. [14] However, the campaign was short, just six weeks, and the study took place at only one school.

The results of the first national experimental study of social norms marketing will be published in the *Journal of Studies on Alcohol* in a few months. Project Director Laura Gomberg Towvim, of the Higher Education Center, says a social norms marketing campaign implemented for three years at nine schools produced "a protective effect against increases in alcohol consumption" compared to nine control schools. In other words, drinking did not decline at the schools where the campaign was implemented, but neither did it increase, as it did at schools without a campaign.

Given that only a protective effect was observed, experts expect the debate about the efficacy of social norms marketing to continue.

Meanwhile, colleges increasingly are using online tools to encourage students to reduce excessive drinking. Nearly 2,400 college campuses are using an interactive course called "Alcohol 101 Plus," created by the Century Council, a nonprofit funded by American distillers that promotes responsible drinking. And more than 500 colleges and universities, up from 23 three years ago, now require students to take "AlcoholEdu," developed by Outside the Classroom, a private company that receives no alcohol-industry money.

"We have two simple goals: to promote abstention and reduce risk for drinkers," says Brandon Busteed, Outside the Classroom's founder and CEO. "But nowhere in the course do we tell a student not to drink." Instead, it explains the risks of behaviors like drinking and driving, chugging and playing drinking games.

Students begin by answering confidential, pre-survey questions about their drinking behaviors. They then take the course, which uses audio-visual presentations and is customized depending on the survey answers.

Students enter their height, weight, sex and typical drinking pattern and are told how soon they will reach levels of impairment. They also are shown videos of drinking situations and asked to make decisions about when to drink and how much. There are short quizzes, a final exam and a short post-course survey. The entire process takes about three hours. Students are given a follow-up survey two months later.

According to a recent study, a group of fraternity and sorority members who took the online course had modest reductions in heavy drinking and its negative consequences compared to a control group that did not take the course. But, overall, research about such online programs is scant, and even the author of the study says he's surprised by AlcoholEdu's rapid adoption, given the lack of hard evidence that it works. [15]

"There is still plenty to prove, and we are aware of that," says Busteed.

Ralph Blackman, president and CEO of the Century Council, agrees. "But that doesn't mean you don't do it," he says. "Education is the key to helping students make responsible decisions about alcohol."

Focusing on the individual decision-maker, however, appears not to be enough.

"By just focusing on the individual, we ignore the broader environment that encourages heavy alcohol use by students," says Traci Toomey, director of the alcohol epidemiology program at the University of Minnesota.

Should colleges ban or restrict alcohol on campus?

Studies indicate that the college environment promotes excessive drinking. College-bound high-school students drink less than their non-college-bound peers, but the trend reverses itself once they reach college, where they end up drinking more. [16]

In an effort to change the physical, social, economic and legal environment in which college students make decisions about drinking, many schools are adopting a strategy called environmental management.

A majority of schools, for instance, now offer alcohol-free or substance-free housing (*see Sidebar, p. 664*).

Others sponsor alcohol-free social events. For instance, the West Virginia University Up All Night program offers free food and activities every Thursday, Friday and Saturday night.

"They have cool things like arts and crafts, laser tag, pool and bowling," says Jared Russell, a sophomore. "When I'm hungry late at night, I go for the free food. I've gone a lot, actually, and I think a lot of people use it as an alternative to going to bars and drinking."

But when schools move beyond offering alcohol-free options to limiting access to alcohol, the response is often quite different, as Robert Carothers discovered. When Carothers first arrived at the University of Rhode Island 15 years ago as the new president, he was given the task of improving academics.

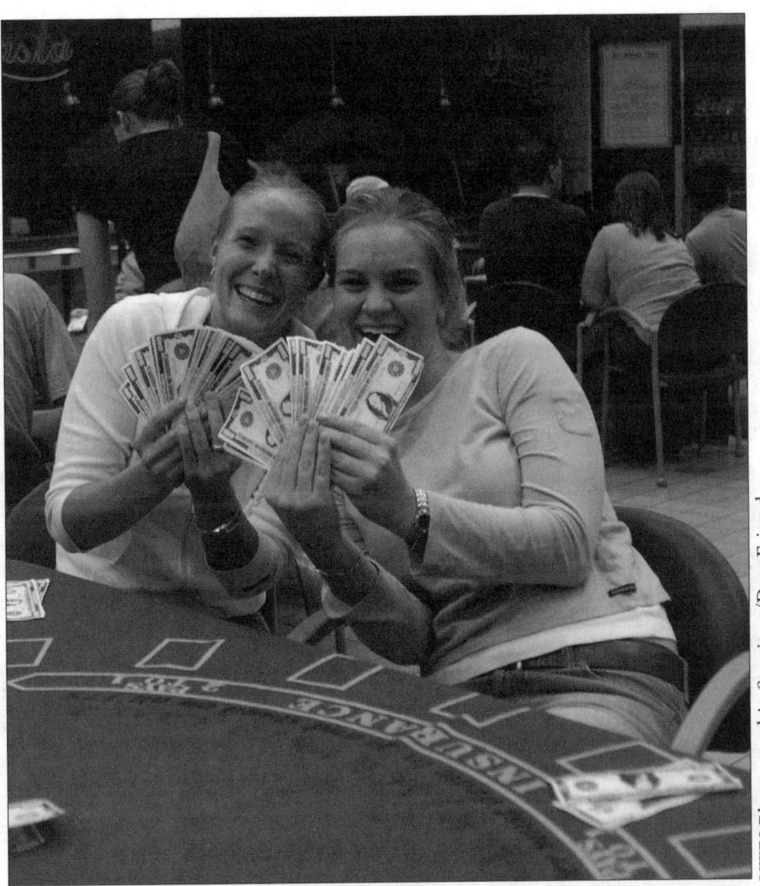

UWV Photographic Services/Dan Friend

West Virginia University students gamble at one of the school's Up All Night events. The popular program offers alcohol-free weekend entertainment alternatives to the heavy-drinking college party scene.

"I found I wasn't going to achieve that with a significant portion of the community hung over from Thursday to Monday," he says. "So that had to be taken on."

Ten years ago, Carothers convinced the university to adopt a policy of no alcohol at campus events, including faculty dinners, university fundraisers, parties at fraternity and sorority houses, parties in dormitories, sporting events and even during homecoming weekend. This was a dramatic change for a school once known as URHigh.

"It was very, very difficult to stay the course in the face of criticisms," recalls Carothers. Some alumni refused to attend homecoming, and "we had a terrible time when we went through this with the fraternities. I closed 10 fraternities because they just didn't get it." Many donors, several of whom had been fraternity members, weren't pleased.

But binge drinking has dropped significantly at the university since then, according to Carothers, and donations are up, as are SAT scores of applicants. The school, he says, is no longer attracting the hard-partying crowd.

According to a recent study, one in three schools now bans alcohol on campus for all students, regardless of age. And more than 40 percent restrict alcohol use at athletic contests, homecoming, tailgate parties, dances, concerts and other events. [17]

But critics say these policies just drive student drinking off campus or underground. When the University of Southern California banned alcohol sales at sporting events a few years ago, it didn't stop the drinking, says senior Sean Fish. "A lot of people have made the decision to get more intoxicated before the game since they can't drink at the game, and that leads to rowdiness at the gates."

"Data suggest that the crackdowns as they're practiced now change the location of drinking without changing the behavior, making it more dangerous," says Haines, of the National Social Norms Resource Center. "The heavy drinking is taking place off campus in a non-monitored environment."

But that argument assumes that drinking on campus — at sporting events, tailgate parties, fraternity parties or in campus bars — is properly monitored and inherently safer. Many researchers say that is not the case and that underage and intoxicated students often have no trouble being served alcohol anywhere.

Still, no one wants to see drinking just change locations. Toomey of the University of Minnesota says colleges need to work with their communities to crack down in town as well. "We need to put controls in as many places as possible. There is not one thing that is going to fix it all," says Toomey.

Proponents of environmental management recommend that colleges:

Signs of Alcohol Poisoning

Alcohol is a depressant and slows down many of the body's vital functions. Consuming large amounts of alcohol can lead to unconsciousness and then death because the heart and lungs can be slowed to the point of stopping.

Alcohol poisoning may have occurred if there are signs of:

- Mental confusion, stupor, coma or inability to be roused
- Vomiting
- Seizures
- Slow breathing (fewer than eight breaths per minute)
- Irregular breathing (10 seconds or more between breaths)
- Hypothermia (low body temperature), bluish skin color, paleness

If alcohol poisoning is suspected:

- Call 911. Do not try to gauge drunkenness. Do not wait for all symptoms to be present.
- Try to wake the person.
- Turn the person on her/his side so that if vomiting occurs, the airway will not be blocked. Stay with the person so they don't roll over onto their back.
- Check skin color and temperature and monitor the breathing. If the skin is pale, bluish and clammy then the person is not getting enough oxygen.
- Be aware that a person who has passed out may die.

If alcohol poisoning goes untreated:

- Hypothermia (low body temperature) can occur.
- Hypoglycemia (too little blood sugar) can lead to seizures.
- Severe dehydration from vomiting can cause seizures, permanent brain damage or death.

Source: National Institute on Alcohol Abuse and Alcoholism

- Work with restaurants, bars and taverns to train servers to check age identification, to recognize the signs of intoxication and to have the confidence to refuse an alcohol sale;
- Ask police to conduct regular compliance checks of alcohol-serving establishments;
- Work with town leaders to reduce the number of bars near campus;
- Help the town develop ordinances and a program to crack down on rowdy off-campus parties.

"When you have a private house that's used for loud and noisy parties, the police put a big, red circle right on it," says Carothers of the University of Rhode Island, which pays for some of the extra town police needed for the job. Two or three red circles can lead to fines for the landlord, who then usually voids the students' leases.

"Hey, this is New England," says Carothers. "We use the big, red scarlet letter here."

The number of colleges trying comprehensive environmental management has not been tallied. But there are many barriers to its adoption, including the cost of extra policing, the challenge of community organizing, the need for strong leadership and the common belief that such an approach punishes the majority for the transgressions of a few.

Bob Saltz, a senior research scientist at the Prevention Research Center of the Pacific Institute for Research and Evaluation, in Berkeley, Calif., refutes the notion that banning alcohol unfairly punishes moderate drinkers. Using data from a student survey, he says, "We added up all the problems by the type of drinker, and there were so many more light and moderate drinkers than extreme drinkers, that — even though their risk of problems is lower for individuals — as a group, they were responsible for the bulk of the problems."

But the research on environmental management is far from extensive. Saltz is conducting an experiment at 14 universities in California, and Harvard's Wechsler studied 10 schools that implemented similar strategies in a program called "A Matter of Degree."

Overall, Wechsler found no statistically significant change in drinking or in negative consequences due to drinking. But at the five colleges with the most comprehensive environmental-management programs, he found statistically significant declines in alcohol consumption, alcohol-related harms and secondhand effects compared to control schools.

Should colleges restrict alcohol advertising and marketing to students?

Advocates of environmental management also recommend reducing the advertising and marketing of alcohol to college students. Distillers voluntarily no longer advertise in college newspapers, and brewers do so only with school permission. But the biggest controversy is over alcohol advertising at or during college sporting events.

"The time has come to sever the tie between college sports and drinking — completely, absolutely and forever," said University of Miami President Donna Shalala. [18] Three years ago, the school phased out stadium signs from Bacardi, Budweiser, Coors and Miller and replaced them with the logos of banks and soft drinks.

The University of Florida went further and banned alcohol commercials during local broadcasts of its games. In fact, 246 colleges — about a quarter of the members of the National Collegiate Athletic Association (NCAA) — have banned such ads. [19] Between 2001 and 2003, alcohol ads on college sports broadcasts dropped from 5,737 to 4,747. [20]

These colleges have signed "The College Commitment," created by the Center for Science in the Public Interest (CSPI), a consumer-advocacy group. They agree not only to ban alcohol advertisements on local sports broadcasts but also pledge to pressure their athletic conferences to ban alcohol ads from conference broadcasts. So far the Big South and Ivy League conferences have climbed on board.

And in June, the Big Ten Conference signed an agreement with Fox Cable Networks to create the Big Ten Channel, a national network that will not accept alcohol advertising. "This is the first time that a major conference has told the telecaster there will be no alcohol ads principally because the ads are incompatible with conference values," says George Hacker, director of the CSPI's alcohol policies project.

But beer companies, which lead the alcohol industry in college advertising, are not thrilled. "They're certainly welcome to do what they want, although we'd rather they didn't do that," says Jeff Becker, president of The Beer Institute, a trade group for brewers. "A lot of our consumers are sports-minded people."

Banning alcohol ads on college sports broadcasts is not the way to attack underage drinking, says Becker. Most viewers of college sports, he points out, are adults. According to Nielsen Media Research, 89 percent of college football viewers and 86 percent of college basketball fans are 21 or older. [21] "The advertising targets adults, period," says Becker. "We don't think youth drinking has anything to do with advertising."

But research seems to show a link. The latest study, a survey of individuals 15 to 26 years of age, concluded that youths who saw more alcohol advertisements drank more, on average. [22] "These studies are all finding statistically significant correlations" between advertising and youth drinking, says David Jernigan, executive director of the Center on Alcohol Marketing and Youth at Georgetown University. They also contradict the industry argument that alcohol advertising only causes brand switching.

Others say that local marketing by bars and liquor stores may have more of an impact on college drinking than televised beer ads. "There are a lot of bar specials here," says Russell, the West Virginia University sophomore. "I've memorized them all." For instance, if a bar is offering free Jack Daniels and Coke until 11 p.m., Russell says, his friends will usually go there and get drunk. "Then if they have money, they'll spend it buying more drinks after 11 p.m."

Recent research shows that the greater the number of drink specials and price discounts at local bars and liquor stores, the more binge drinking there is at nearby colleges. However, such studies show only a correlation, not causation. Heavy drinking by students could be inducing bars and restaurants to compete for their patronage by lowering prices, instead of the other way around. But researchers point out that under the laws of economics, high demand usually causes prices to rise, not fall. [23]

Getty Images/Sara D. Davis

Duke University lacrosse player David Evans proclaims his innocence after being indicted with two other team members for allegedly sexually assaulting an exotic dancer at a team party in May. The team has a reputation for wild parties, and in the past three years 15 team members have faced alcohol-related charges, including underage alcohol possession and public urination.

In any case, a growing number of colleges are cutting back on the amount of alcohol marketing allowed on campus. FSU, for instance, outlawed flyers from bars and liquor stores after such handbills "littered the campus uncontrollably," said Michael Smith, director of the school's Florida Center for Prevention Research. [24]

Other schools are working with town leaders, local bars and liquor stores to eliminate alcohol specials and promotions. In Lincoln, Neb., for instance, business owners, City Council members, prevention specialists, law enforcement officials and alcohol distributors formed a coalition in the 1980s to reduce the irresponsible sale and serving of alcohol in town. Recently, the University of Nebraska joined in. The school works with the town to enforce state laws restricting happy hours, free drinks and one-price drink specials. Most bars comply, say college officials, but there are always some that try to skirt the law.

"A bar can have a policy that says the first drink is $3 and the second is 1 cent," says Linda Major, director of student involvement at Nebraska. "They aren't technically violating the law because the second drink isn't free." Other times, bar managers allow servers to make up their own specials on the spot. "They'll flip a coin with a customer and the drink is half price," says Major.

The university — working with the City Council, other bar owners, law-enforcement officials and the business-improvement association — will then pressure the bar owner to eliminate alcohol specials that violate the spirit of the law. "The chief of police is the co-chair of our coalition," says Major's colleague Tom Workman. "In order to do any of this, you have to have a whole community ready."

But when there are no laws restricting happy hours and drink specials, the situation can get complicated. For instance, in 2004, when Madison, Wis., was considering requiring bars to close earlier and to pay for extra law enforcement in order to cut down on rowdy drinking by University of Wisconsin students, bars owners volunteered instead to eliminate all happy hours and drink specials on weekends.

But eight months later, three university students sued 24 bars and the local Tavern League — and eventually the university and the town council — for price fixing. The students won, and the case is now on appeal in federal district court. So far, legal fees for the bar owners exceed half a million dollars. ■

BACKGROUND

Temperance and Prohibition

Alcohol has long been a part of American life, but Americans can't seem to make up their minds about its proper role. From Colonial times to the temperance era, and from Prohibition to the present, attitudes toward alcohol have undergone major shifts.

For early settlers, a stiff drink "kept off chills and fevers," and a few glasses "aided digestion," according to the social history *Drinking in America.* Beer and cider were the preferred beverages, and even children were served alcohol at meals. "Simply stated, most settlers drank often and abundantly." [25]

But drunkenness was a crime throughout the Colonies, and the penalties could be severe, including fines, imprisonment, whipping and serving time in the stocks, which a historian has called "the Colonial era's equivalent of the alcoholism-treatment facility." [26]

By the early 19th century, Americans were drinking nearly three times as much as they do today, and most continued to believe that alcohol imparted health, eased fevers, cured colds and even relieved snakebite. But as consumption rose to unprecedented levels, "an awareness of the dangers of drink began to emerge, and the first American temperance movement took hold," wrote historian David Musto. [27]

In 1826, one of the most dynamic speakers of the time, the Rev. Lyman Beecher, called for a crusade against alcohol. By 1855, about a third of the nation's 40 states and territories had banished the sale of alcohol. "Alcohol consumption fell to less than a third of its pretemperance level," wrote Musto, "and never again reached the heights of the early republic." [28]

But abstinence fell out of favor during the Civil War, and some states repealed their alcohol prohibitions in the 1860s. In other states, the laws fell into disuse or the courts found them unconstitutional.

By the turn of the century, the abstinence movement was again gaining momentum, culminating in ratification of the 18th Amendment to the U.S. Constitution in 1919 barring the "manufacture, sale or transportation of intoxicating liquors" within the United States as well as all imports and exports of alcoholic beverages. The Prohibition amendment became effective in January 1920 and remained in effect nearly 14 years.

On the positive side, medical evidence suggests that Prohibition reduced mortality from alcoholism and cirrhosis of the liver. But that doesn't mean that Americans stopped drinking. Many stockpiled alcohol before Prohibition took effect. There were rural and urban stills, "medicinal liquor," industrial alcohol, underground breweries and imports smuggled from Canada, Britain and the Caribbean. Prohibition fostered the growth of entrenched criminal organizations and "secret" drinking establishments known as speakeasies.

Continued on p. 661

Chronology

1970s ***As 18-year-olds are being drafted for the Vietnam War, states lower the minimum drinking age.***

1971
Federal government creates National Institute of Alcohol Abuse and Alcoholism to combat alcohol abuse. . . . On July 5, Congress gives 18-year-olds the right to vote, prompting many states to lower the drinking age.

1980s ***Anti-alcohol-abuse movement gains momentum; minimum drinking age is raised.***

1983
College organizations create the Inter-Association Task Force on Alcohol and Other Substance Issues, which sponsors National Collegiate Alcohol Awareness Week.

July 17, 1984
Minimum Uniform Drinking Age Act requires states to set their minimum drinking age to 21 or risk losing federal highway funds.

Oct. 27, 1986
Drug-Free Schools and Communities Act establishes and expands drug abuse and prevention programs in schools.

Nov. 18, 1988
President Ronald Reagan signs omnibus anti-drug bill requiring drug-free workplace policies and health labels on alcoholic beverages.

December 1988
By now, all 50 states have raised the minimum drinking age to 21. Legal challenges to the laws fail.

1990s ***Federal government steps up its campaign against underage drinking and drunken driving.***

Sept. 15, 1990
National Commission on Drug-Free Schools calls alcohol and tobacco the most misused drugs and criticizes the alcohol and tobacco industries for targeting youth.

Jan. 27, 1992
White House releases anti-drug strategy that for the first time addresses underage drinking.

Dec. 7, 1994
Harvard University's "College Alcohol Study" finds that 44 percent of surveyed students binge drink.

1995
Federal Zero Tolerance Law mandates that by Oct. 1, 1998, states must pass "zero-tolerance" laws — prohibiting anyone under 21 from driving with any measurable blood alcohol content (BAC) — or risk losing highway safety funds.

March 1997
Two national fraternities — Phi Delta Theta and Sigma Nu — announce they will ban alcohol from chapter houses beginning July 1, 2000. Within five years, both grade-point averages and membership levels at Phi Delta rise, while insurance premiums drop.

August-November 1997
After alcohol-related deaths of students at several colleges, including MIT, the nation becomes more aware of the scope of the campus binge-drinking problem.

1998
By now, zero-tolerance legislation has passed in all 50 states.

2000-Present ***States toughen drunken-driving laws as more colleges try to reduce student alcohol use.***

Oct. 23, 2000
Congress passes and President Bill Clinton signs law redefining drunken driving by lowering the legal BAC level from 0.10 percent to 0.08. By year's end, 21 states lower their limits to the new threshold.

2001
An estimated 1,717 college students between ages 18-24 die from alcohol-related unintentional injuries, including motor vehicle crashes; by comparison there were 1,575 such deaths in 1998.

March 2002
Study shows that 44 percent of surveyed students say they are binge drinkers — unchanged from eight years earlier — while the percentage of students abstaining from alcohol has risen.

April 2002
National Institute on Alcohol Abuse and Alcoholism releases "A Call to Action," advocating adoption of research-based programs to reduce alcohol use on campus and for increased research into the problem.

July 2004
By now, all 50 states and the District of Columbia have set 0.08 BAC as the threshold for drunken driving.

June 21, 2006
The Big Ten Conference and Fox Cable Networks announce that their new Big Ten Channel, devoted to Big Ten athletic and academic programs, will not broadcast alcohol ads.

Do European Students Really Drink Less?

Julie Price, a senior sociology major at the College of William and Mary in Williamsburg, Va., has often heard the argument: American kids binge drink because alcohol is a forbidden fruit until age 21, and kids rebel against the restriction by drinking to excess. European youths, on the other hand, learn to drink alcohol in moderation because they have wine at the dinner table with their parents from an early age. The minimum drinking age across most of Europe is 18 — 16 in Spain — so alcohol is not a forbidden substance there.

As a result, the theory goes, European youths do not abuse alcohol as a way to challenge authority. Thus, if the minimum drinking age in the United States were lowered from 21 to 18, there would be less sneaking around and less binging among American college students, say those who follow this reasoning.

"But given what I saw in Scotland," says Price, who spent her spring semester studying there, "I'm not so sure." Her Scottish classmates — who can drink legally at age 18 — were drunk more often and "much earlier in the day" than her fellow students are at William and Mary, she says.

Although there is sparse data comparing the drinking patterns of U.S. and European college students, detailed surveys comparing the drinking patterns of 10th-graders tend to disprove the theory. The surveys show that in comparison to American 16-year-olds, more European 16-year-olds drink — and drink heavily. [1]

For instance, 35 percent of the U.S. 10th-graders surveyed reported drinking in the past 30 days. In many European countries — including Austria, Germany, Denmark, Ireland and the United Kingdom — more than 70 percent of the surveyed students reported drinking in the past 30 days. Only Turkey, a Muslim country, had a lower rate of 20 percent.

As for binge drinking, 22 percent of those surveyed in the United States reported recently drinking five or more drinks in one sitting, compared to 40 percent reporting heavy drinking among respondents in many European countries. [2]

Moreover, while 18 percent of the American 16-year-olds reported being drunk in the past 30 days, only six European countries — Turkey, France, Romania, Portugal, Greece and Cyprus — had lower percentages. Italy's percentage was nearly identical to America's. Most countries had more than a quarter of their 16-year-olds reporting intoxication, with the highest numbers in Northern Europe: 61 percent in Denmark; 53 percent in Ireland; 48 percent in Austria and 46 percent in the United Kingdom. [3]

"This idea that all we have to do is lower the drinking age to solve our problem is not supported by this data," says Joel Grube, director of the Prevention Research Center at the Pacific Institute for Research and Evaluation. "It's a much broader and complex cultural issue."

European Teens Drink More

Youths in Europe drink nearly twice as heavily as teens in the United States.

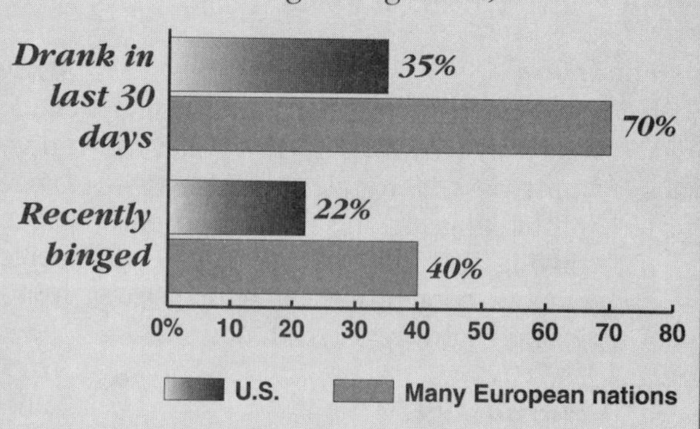

Source: U.S. Department of Justice, May 2005

The European researchers who studied the survey data did not offer explanations for the differences in drinking patterns between Northern and Southern European countries. But Grube says it is interesting that the countries with the lowest intoxication rates are Mediterranean countries.

"To some extent, I think people who argue that there is a different culture in those countries — that alcohol is more integrated into the meals — are absolutely correct."

But that culture is changing, Grube says. In Spain, for instance, there is anecdotal evidence that teenagers are beginning to drink like Northern Europeans. They are switching from wine to beer, and their intoxication levels are rising. "It's hard to know why," he says.

Northern European drinking patterns also are changing, Grube says. "Ireland, contrary to people's perception, was a low-alcohol-consuming country for youth about 20 years ago, and now it's among the highest," he says, adding that the reason for the change is unclear. One theory posits that a vastly improving economy has put more discretionary income into the hands of youths. In addition, it has become more socially acceptable for young women in Ireland to drink.

"And they are definitely drinking more," says Grube.

1 "Youth Drinking Rates and Problems: A Comparison of European Countries and the United States," Office of Juvenile Justice and Delinquency Prevention, U.S. Department of Justice, May 2005, p. 2.

2 *Ibid.*, p. 3.

3 *Ibid.*, p. 4.

Continued from p. 658

Nevertheless, Prohibition did significantly reduce alcohol consumption among adults and youth. "College students remained fairly temperate, at least through the mid-1920s — the wild sprees depicted in the novels of F. Scott Fitzgerald notwithstanding." [29] It was visiting alumni who did most of the excessive drinking. Contemporary surveys showed considerable support for Prohibition among college students at the time.

But the success of Prohibition in cutting alcohol consumption contained the seeds of its eventual defeat. As problem drinking waned, so did the public's concern. Failures of enforcement, growing violence and the Great Depression all caused the nation to overwhelmingly reject Prohibition in 1933 and return to the states the broad power to regulate alcohol.

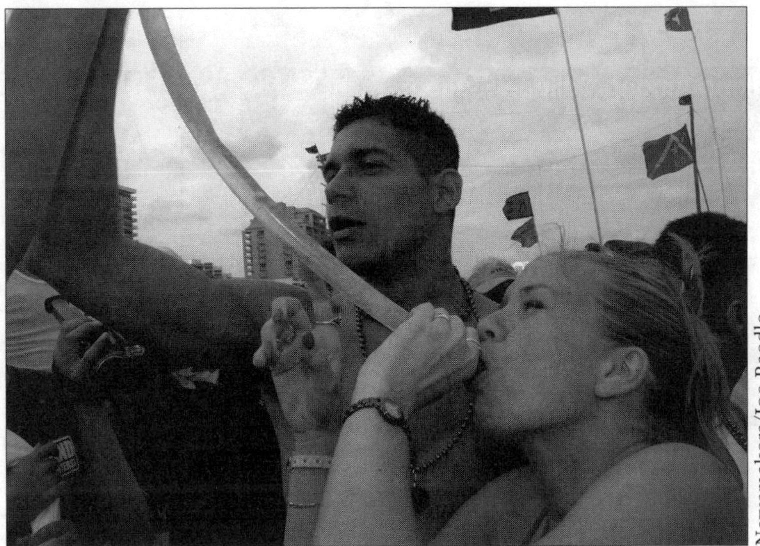

Newsmakers/Joe Raedle

A college student in Texas chugs beer through a bong during spring break. The rate for female binge drinkers has risen slightly in recent years.

Minimum Drinking Age

After Prohibition was repealed, most states established 21 as the minimum legal drinking age, but as adult consumption of alcohol rose, so did concerns about college drinking. In response, researchers Robert Straus and Selden D. Bacon undertook one of the first comprehensive surveys of college drinking in the early 1950s.

"Stereotypes of college drinking include the belief that most students drink, that they do so heavily and frequently, and that dangerous and disgraceful behavior often ensues," they wrote. However, based on their research, the authors observed that adult perceptions of college drinking were "very far from the reality." [30]

In fact, they reported, only 21 percent of college men and 10 percent of the women reported drinking more than once a week. When they did drink, the amounts were usually modest. Only 9 percent of men and 1 percent of women reported drinking large amounts of beer, and only 4 percent of men and less than half a percent of women reported drinking large amounts of wine. Liquor, however, was more popular: 29 percent of men and 7 percent of women reported drinking large amounts of spirits. [31]

But as the decades passed, drinking among college students became more common. Then in 1971, as young men were being drafted during the Vietnam War, enactment of the 26th Amendment to the U.S. Constitution lowered the voting age from 21 to 18. Many states then lowered their minimum legal drinking ages to 18 or 19, based on the argument that if young people were responsible enough to vote and to go to war, they were responsible enough to drink.

In the 1970s and '80s, however, studies began to show that alcohol-related traffic crashes were increasing significantly among young people ages 18 to 20 in states with lower drinking ages. The public — led by the powerful grassroots group Mothers Against Drunk Driving (MADD) — began to demand that the drinking age be raised again to 21.

"It now appears that a third era of temperance is under way in the U.S.," Musto wrote in 1996. [32]

MADD was established in 1980 by a mother whose 13-year-old daughter had been killed by a drunken driver. By the end of 1982 it boasted 100 chapters. Pushing for tougher laws at the state and federal level, MADD marshaled support for the more than 100 new state anti-drunken driving laws passed by the end of 1983.

Largely as a result of MADD's lobbying, Congress in 1984 enacted the Minimum Uniform Drinking Age Act, which required that a portion of federal highway funds be withheld from states that do not raise the minimum drinking age to 21. Four years later, every state had complied.

"Raising the age to 21 led to an immediate decline of roughly 15 percent or so in teen drinking," says Alexander Wagenaar, professor of epidemiology and health policy research at the University of Florida. "And this is despite weak enforcement." The National Highway Traffic Safety Administration (NHTSA) estimates that the laws save nearly 1,000 lives a year.

But assessing the impact on college students alone is difficult. There are few high-quality studies focusing so narrowly, but of those that do, none have been able to link higher-minimum drinking age laws to lower alcohol consumption

Frequent Bingeing Increased

Binge drinking among college students remained virtually unchanged between 1993 and 2001, but frequent bingeing (more than once a week) increased among both men and women. Meanwhile, the gap increased between those who don't drink and those who binge frequently (top). While occasional bingeing rose among blacks and Asians, it decreased among Hispanics and Native Americans (bottom).

	1993	2001
Prevalence of Drinking Among College Students (by percentage)		
Binge drinkers, total	43.9%	44.4%
Abstainers, total	16.4	19.3
Frequent bingers, total	19.7	22.8
Female bingers	17.1	20.9
Male bingers	22.4	25.2
Binge Drinkers Among College Students (by percentage)		
Whites	49.5%	50.2%
African Americans	16.7	21.7
Hispanics	39.7	34.4
Native Americans	39.3	33.6
Asians	23.1	26.2

Source: Henry Wechsler, et al., *"Trends in College Binge Drinking During a Period of Increased Prevention Efforts,"* Journal of American College Health, *March 2002*

among college students. "If one assumes that the minimum legal drinking age is less effective on college campuses," researchers wrote, "perhaps it is due to lax enforcement and particularly easy access to alcohol by underage youth in such settings." [33]

Others argue that the higher drinking age has increased the allure of alcohol on college campuses by making it a "forbidden fruit" and has caused students to "pre-game:" load up on alcohol before going out.

"Before the age was increased, we had a very different environment," said Ronald Liebowitz, president of Vermont's Middlebury College. "You had kids drinking beer and getting sick on beer, but you didn't have gross alcohol poisoning and binge drinking." [34]

Liebowitz is among many college administrators who advocate a lower minimum drinking age. In a 2000 survey of 330 directors of student affairs, 39 percent preferred a drinking age below 21. [35] No state, however, is seriously considering such a proposal.

Instead, states have adopted a range of additional policies to attack underage and excessive drinking. Many states have toughened penalties on the use of false identification or withdrawn driving privileges of minors guilty of any alcohol violation. All states have adopted laws that set blood-alcohol concentration (BAC) levels at almost zero for drivers under 21.

In another MADD-promoted campaign, states also lowered the BAC limit for all drivers, after President Bill Clinton in 2000 signed a law requiring states to reduce the legal BAC from 0.10 to .08 or risk losing federal highway funds. Despite heavy lobbying against the measure by the alcohol industry, all states had complied by July 2004. [36]

'Responsible Drinking'

As the "third era of temperance" took hold in the 1980s, the alcohol industry developed its own programs to encourage "responsible drinking." They generally involved distributing brochures for parents and training material for alcohol servers, providing funds for campus programs and launching national advertising campaigns.

Anheuser-Busch, for instance, says it has spent more than $500 million since 1982 on such programs. Its latest advertising campaign, "Responsibility Matters," extols "the good practices of adults who exercise personal responsibility by designating a driver, calling a cab when they or a friend is too drunk to drive and talking to their children about underage drinking. [37]

"No company benefits when its products are misused, something acknowledged by the company's thousands of employees who are raising children, living and working in this society and driving on the same highways as everyone else," says Anheuser-Busch's Web site. [38]

But some critics — such as the Marin Institute, an industry watchdog in San Raphael, Calif. — call industry-sponsored responsibility advertising a "public relations ploy." The industry is trying to "avoid responsibility for the consequences of its products and shift blame to individual consumers," the institute said. [39]

Research shows that youths ages 16-22 are not impressed by responsibility advertising from beer companies. In one study, participants rated brewer-sponsored ads as "less informative, believable, on-target, and effective" than conventional public-service announcements sponsored by the government or advocacy groups.

And when asked why brewers sponsor responsibility advertisements, respondents ranked the "improvement of the company's image and selling its beer" higher on the companies' agendas than preventing drunken driving. [40] ■

Delta Sigma Phi, University of Virginia (both)

Party Time

University of Virginia students play popular drinking games, including flip cup and beer pong, at the Delta Sigma Phi fraternity house (top). UVa students get ready to party (bottom). Students at many schools "pre-game," or drink in their rooms before going out.

CURRENT SITUATION

Greek Scene

When it comes to drinking, fraternity and sorority members are way ahead of the rest of the college pack. Three-quarters of fraternity or sorority house residents reported binge drinking in a 2001 survey of 119 colleges — far higher than other student groups. [41]

"Alcohol consumption is the fraternity's social lubricant," writes Harvard alcohol researcher Wechsler, lead author of the study. "Most students who join fraternities expect alcohol to be central to their experience, even though they are likely to be legally underage."

As a fraternity member told Wechsler:

"I am not an advocate for responsible college drinking; in fact, I am quite the opposite. I party hard and I party a lot, but what the 1980s labeled as a 'party animal' has now taken on the label of 'binge drinker.' So what if I bong three beers at a time and often play drinking games that drain a case of beer between four people in less than 75 minutes? I drink often and a lot, but I know my limits and I don't wake up each morning needing a drink. If you look hard and ask students, you'll see that alcohol has become an institution at parties. A party is not a party without it. . . . By the way, I am only 20 years old and my parents know full well how much I drink. In fact, more than 90 percent of the parents of the men in our fraternity know how much their kids are drinking, and they aren't worried about it." [42]

Fraternity members are paying a price for heavy drinking. Nearly twice as many fraternity residents as non-fraternity residents fall behind in schoolwork, argue with friends, damage property, have unprotected sex or suffer injuries. They also are more likely to drink and drive or ride with a drunken driver. [43]

Continued on p. 666

Substance-free Dorms Offer Peace and Quiet

During her freshman year at Vassar College in Poughkeepsie, N.Y., Kathryn Thomas chose to live in a "wellness" corridor in her dorm. "I wanted a quiet place for studying," she said. In fact, her floor eventually became a refuge for other students "who come and stay until they know the party on their floor has died down." [1]

Her corridor is part of a growing trend. Colleges and universities across the country have been offering students the option of living in so-called substance-free housing, where no alcohol, tobacco and other drugs are used. Institutions ranging from small, liberal arts colleges like Franklin & Marshall to large public universities like the State University of New York have reserved halls and suites for students — most often freshmen — who sign up. Upperclassmen, who usually choose their own roommates, have less of a need for the school to set the rules.

Parents like having the option. "Sometimes we get students who complain that their parents filled out the housing form," says Katherine Steele, dean of students for residential life at the University of the South in Sewanee, Tenn., a liberal arts college where 6 percent of the 1,400 students choose substance-free housing.

But Steele believes that most students choose substance-free housing on their own. Otherwise, she thinks she would see more violations of the policy. This year the school had only one or two violations, she says.

"Students understand that it is a commitment, and it's a commitment to each other," says Steele. Like most schools, the University of the South relies on head residents and student proctors to enforce residence hall policies and report violations.

In a survey at the University of Michigan, students said they chose substance-free housing in order to:

- Avoid roommate problems associated with alcohol or drug use (78 percent),
- Live in an atmosphere conducive to studying (59 percent),
- Satisfy parents (26 percent),
- Abide by religious preferences (22 percent).

Another 6 percent said they made the choice because of a family member with a substance-abuse problem. [2]

Some parents may wonder why colleges need substance-free housing — especially for younger students — when, by law, all residences with younger students should be alcohol free.

"We have an alcohol policy that says if you're under 21, you have to adhere to state and federal laws," says Rob Wild, an assistant director of residential life at Washington University in St. Louis, Mo., where 20 percent of first-year students request the special housing. "But we know that students make choices about alcohol; we try to limit the really dangerous and disruptive behaviors."

For instance, Wild says, a head resident is not going to cite a 19-year-old for drinking a beer in her dorm room on a Friday night, unless she lives on a substance-free hall.

Students who choose to live in substance-free housing do not promise to abstain completely, only in the residence. Nevertheless, a Harvard study shows that students living in substance-free dorms were three-fifths less likely than students living in unrestricted residences to engage in heavy, episodic drinking and were also less likely to fall behind in schoolwork, ride with a drunken driver, get in trouble with police or damage property. [3]

> **"You're less likely to have the occasional broken window, or a student shooting off a fire extinguisher or vomiting"**
>
> ***— Katherine Steele,***
> ***Dean of Students for Residential Life, Univ. of the South, Sewanee, Tenn.***

"You're less likely to have the occasional broken window, or a student shooting off a fire extinguisher or vomiting," says Steele. "It's really frustrating how living spaces can get treated sometimes."

Does substance-free housing have an impact on overall campus culture? "That's a good question," says Wild, and he doesn't have an answer. Even the Harvard researchers found it difficult to distinguish cause and effect.

"While the difference in heavy, episodic drinking rates may be due to self-selection of determined non-drinkers into these residences, the lower rates [of heavy drinking] may also be due to the influence that such an environment has on students," said the researchers. [4]

Nevertheless, Wild and a growing number of college administrators believe that offering substance-free housing is an important option for students who want to avoid the noise, mess and disruptions associated with heavy drinking.

---

[1] Tamar Lewin, "Clean Living on Campus," *The New York Times*, Nov. 6, 2005.

[2] "Preventing Alcohol-Related Problems on Campus: Substance-Free Residence Halls," Higher Education Center for Alcohol and Other Drug Prevention, 1997, p. 4.

[3] Henry Wechsler, *et al.*, "Drinking Levels, Alcohol Problems, and Second-hand Effects in Substance-Free College Residences," *Journal of Studies on Alcohol*, January 2001, press release.

[4] *Ibid.*

At Issue:

Should federal and state excise taxes on alcohol be raised to curtail underage drinking?

DAVID L. ROSENBLOOM
DIRECTOR, YOUTH ALCOHOL PREVENTION CENTER, BOSTON UNIVERSITY SCHOOL OF PUBLIC HEALTH

WRITTEN FOR *CQ RESEARCHER*, JULY 2006

yes

Higher taxes on alcohol will yield important public health and safety benefits. Since taxes on beer range from 2 cents a gallon in Wyoming to $1.07 a gallon in Alaska, it is possible to know the real-world consequences of these taxes. For example, the five states with the lowest beer taxes have teen binge-drinking rates that are twice as high as the five states with the highest beer taxes. Higher alcohol tax states have lower alcohol-related teen driving deaths. Research has also shown that increasing the total price of alcohol decreases drinking and driving among all age groups. Today, there are about 600,000 alcohol-related violent incidents a year on American college campuses. Researchers estimate that a 10 percent increase in the price of alcohol would reduce problem drinking enough to avoid about 200,000 of these incidents every year.

Increasing alcohol taxes will not have much effect on most people. About a third do not drink any alcohol. Many adults drink and enjoy alcoholic beverages in moderation without harm to their health and safety. However, drinking teenagers and alcoholics consume so much that even a modest increase in the price of each drink will reduce their total consumption — and that is a good thing. Recent research has shown that alcohol has damaging long-term effects on adolescent brain development. Increasing the price through taxes is the quickest and most effective way to avoid some of this damage. Similarly, making it more expensive for alcoholics to continue their self-destructive, compulsive drinking may encourage some of them to seek the effective treatment that is now available — and increased alcohol taxes might pay for it.

In most of the country, alcohol taxes no longer provide any of these benefits because their impact has been eaten away by inflation. Many states have not raised their taxes in decades. In Massachusetts, the beer tax was set at 11 cents a gallon in 1975 — about 3 cents a gallon in current terms. State and federal governments need to raise alcohol taxes to a meaningful level and then index them to inflation to make sure they continue to save lives in the future.

A significant majority of all voters — including those who drink — consistently favor increasing alcohol taxes. The only opposition is from the alcohol industry and politicians who have taken the pledge against taxes — but not rum.

ROGER BRINNER
CHIEF ECONOMIST, THE PARTHENON GROUP, BOSTON

WRITTEN FOR *CQ RESEARCHER*, JULY 2006

no

Would higher alcohol taxes work as well as other alternatives to reduce underage or abusive drinking? The clear answer from the most careful economic research is "No."

The best study — a meticulous econometric analysis by Thomas Dee of the U.S. government's "Monitoring the Future" student data from 1977-1992 — found beer taxes were not statistically related to either "moderate" or "binge" drinking rates.

Research appearing to find substantial deterrence effects of alcohol taxes is badly flawed. It erroneously attributes declining alcohol consumption trends (across states or across time) to price increases without accounting for the correct explanations of legal penalties and enforcement, server training, parental involvement, counseling and peer norms programs.

Quite simply, higher taxes are relatively impotent policy tools. Abusive drinkers either ignore taxes or seek cheaper alcohol options. Potential teen drinkers know they risk parental punishment, significant fines, community service, lost privileges in school activities and driver's license suspension. A tax mainly encourages responsible, moderate adult drinkers to reduce their purchases, trade down to lower-priced brands or swap lower alcohol-concentration products for those with higher alcohol content — like beer for distilled spirits. Moderate-drinking adults — clearly not the policy target — pay the vast majority of alcohol taxes, rather than problem drinkers.

Moreover, the collateral damage from excise taxes is great. As moderate-drinking adults reduce their purchases, good-paying jobs are lost at the producer, distributor and retail levels, as well as by farmers, truckers and suppliers. Rather than contributing to the state's economy, these individuals then become a burden to the state through unemployment benefits paid by all state taxpayers — drinkers and non-drinkers alike. Finally, beer is already among the most highly taxed consumer categories, with more than 40 cents of each beer dollar attributable to taxes, 68 percent higher than the average consumer product.

Why use the blunt weapon of taxes, which is unfair and economically damaging to all citizens regardless of whether or not they drink, when effective, focused policy alternatives are working well? According to the Partnership for a Drug-Free America, all types of teen alcohol use in 2005 were significantly down from 1998, and other well-known government data show the lowest levels of underage drinking since surveys began tracking it decades ago. It's not a difficult decision to reject excise taxes.

AP Photo/Joel Page

AP Photo/Al Behrman

To Drink or Not to Drink

Students sip wine in a dining hall at Colby College in Waterville, Maine, which serves beer and wine to students 21 and older to teach them about responsible drinking (top). Members of Phi Delta Theta fraternity hit the books at the University of Cincinnati. It's one of 11 national fraternities that bar alcohol in chapter houses (bottom).

Continued from p. 663

While some fraternity members may bring their heavy drinking habits from high school, many others acquire them in the fraternity. "For students who do not already drink heavily when they begin college, joining a Greek organization is a sure way to start," writes Wechsler. In his study, three-quarters of fraternity and sorority residents who had not binged in high school became binge drinkers in college. [44]

In the past decade, fraternities and college administrators have taken steps to curb excessive drinking within the Greek system. Most sororities have been dry for decades, but not fraternities.

But that is beginning to change. Eleven of the 68 national fraternities active in the U.S. have gone dry, including Phi Delta Theta, Phi Kappa Sigma, Delta Sigma Phi and Theta Chi. They allow no alcohol in chapter houses, even during parties and even among upperclassmen of legal drinking age. Local chapters that want to serve alcohol at parties have to hold those events elsewhere. Often they will rent out the back room of a bar.

In part, rising insurance premiums have triggered the change. A study by an insurer of fraternities found that alcohol was involved in:

- 95 percent of roof/window falls;
- 94 percent of fights;
- 93 percent of sex-abuse incidents;
- 88 percent of fatalities;
- 87 percent of auto incidents. [45]

Another reason to go dry is to return the fraternity to its roots. Ron Binder, director of Greek Affairs at Bowling Green State University in Ohio and president of the Association of Fraternity Advisors, says fraternities and sororities were founded on four core values: scholarship, service, leadership and brotherhood. "What I've seen in the past 10 years is a renewed focus on those values," he says.

Initially, many fraternities that went dry saw their membership drop, but membership has since rebounded, and the type of member they attract "has changed pretty dramatically," says Binder. "They're attracting people whose sole focus isn't social."

College administrators sometimes take the matter into their own hands. On July 1, Rensselaer Polytechnic Institute in Troy, N.Y., began severely curtailing drinking at Greek houses. Alcohol is allowed only in the rooms of students 21 years of age or older and forbidden in common areas. All house parties must be alcohol-free.

"They just kind of popped it on us," said Rory Arredondo, a Sigma Alpha Epsilon brother. "It's going to kill Greek life." [46]

But imposing an alcohol-free policy on fraternities is not an option for many colleges. Only about a third of Greek societies have on-campus residences owned by the college. The rest are privately owned and are often located off campus, raising questions about how far the university can extend its reach.

The University of Nebraska's privately owned Greek houses must be alcohol-free because they admit freshmen and therefore are considered part of campus housing. The university began serious enforcement in 1998, and by 2000 half of all fraternities were on some form of judicial sanction. One fraternity lost its housing status and ended up closing.

At that point, "our Greek leaders recognized that things were going to have to change; it was getting ugly," says Workman of the university's Office of Student Involvement. Funded by a grant from the U.S. Department of Education, the school and its fraternities have been working to change the drinking culture.

Other schools are not going quite so far as to ban alcohol in fraternity houses but are tightening up enforcement of rules that govern party size, underage drinking, noise and security.

There are some signs that these changes are having an impact on drinking, if only a small one. The percentage of residents of fraternities and sororities who binge drink was slightly lower in 2001 than in 1993, according to Harvard's "College Alcohol Study." And the study found that fewer students are attending fraternity and sorority parties, and when they do, the percentage who binge drink is slightly lower.

However, students apparently are taking their heavy drinking elsewhere. The percentage of students attending off-campus parties has risen along with the percentage who binge drink when they get there. [47]

State Actions

States play an important role in the fight against underage and excessive drinking, passing laws, enforcing compliance and providing guidance to local communities. However, the number of laws, the severity of penalties and the level of enforcement vary from state to state, and — not surprisingly — so does the level of drinking.

Slightly more than 33 percent of college students binge drink in states with four or more laws restricting promotion and sales of high volumes of alcohol, according to one study. But in states with fewer laws, the binge-drinking rate was just over 48 percent. [48]

According to the Alcohol Policy Information System, a government Web site that monitors state alcohol policies, more and more states are passing laws designed to restrict underage drinking and service to intoxicated individuals. [49] For instance:

- 27 states have keg-registration laws, up from 20 in 2003. An identification number is attached to kegs exceeding a specified capacity (two-to-eight-gallon minimum depending on the state). The retailer records the purchaser's identifying information and may collect a refundable deposit. The intent is to make it difficult for underage youth to obtain kegs for parties.
- 28 states have happy-hour restrictions — such as prohibitions against free drinks, price discounts, unlimited drinks for a fixed price and giving alcoholic beverages as prizes — up from 27 states in 2003.
- 22 states have laws requiring beverage-server training, up from 15 in 2003; liquor-license holders, managers or servers must attend training to prevent alcohol sales to minors and intoxicated customers.
- 20 states have social-host liability laws, up from 16 in 2003; individuals (social hosts) can be held criminally responsible for underage drinking events on their property.

But just having a law on the books does not mean it is enforced or that its penalties are serious enough to actually matter. For instance, 47 states prohibit serving alcohol to someone obviously intoxicated. "But those laws are basically ignored in all states," says Jim Mosher, director of the Center for the Study of Law and Enforcement Policy at the Pacific Institute for Research and Evaluation. "Research shows that if you send in actors who feign intoxication, they will be served 70 percent of the time."

States need to send more undercover agents to bars and publicize the crackdowns, Mosher says. "This is particularly important in college communities where we see bars conducting these very questionable sales practices." But alcoholic-beverage control agencies in most states are underfunded and understaffed.

In addition, the fines for selling alcohol to intoxicated customers or to minors are often paltry. "Many states haven't adjusted their fines in 30 years," says the University of Florida's Wagenaar. "The fines can be just $100, or maybe $200 for a second offense."

But when states try to toughen penalties, the alcohol industry "often sends their lobbyists to state legislatures to oppose the actions," says Wagenaar. "So we have a slow process of change to modernize these regulations." ■

OUTLOOK

Student Support?

Colleges' efforts to curb alcohol abuse have produced both hopeful and worrisome results. On the plus side, the percentage of students abstaining from drink has increased, and binge drinking at fraternities has decreased. There are more "frequent" binge drinkers, however, and more binge drinking at off-campus parties. Moreover, the rate for female binge drinkers has risen slightly over the years, particularly at all-women colleges. And the percentage of African-American students who report binge drinking has risen significantly, although it is still half that of white students. [50] (*See graph, p. 662.*)

Colleges clearly need to enlist the support of students to reverse these trends. The latest Harvard "College Alcohol Survey" showed that the vast majority of students support some alcohol-control policies, such as clarifying the alcohol rules, providing more alcohol-free recreational and cultural opportunities and offering more alcohol-free residences — all measures supported by at least 89 percent of students. [51]

But, not surprisingly, support declines when restricting access to alcohol is proposed. For instance, only 56 percent of the students surveyed support cracking down on drinking in Greek houses, 60 percent support prohibiting kegs on campus and 63 percent support stricter enforcement of campus alcohol rules. [52] Yet, supporters point out, those are still majorities of the students surveyed.

Sometimes the minority, however, will "fight for their right to party." Riots or public disturbances occurred at several schools when alcohol restrictions were tightened, including the University of Colorado, Syracuse and Michigan State.

College administrators are struggling to convert the heavy-drinking minority to the majority view. The most effective alcohol policies may be those crafted in collaboration with students and alumni, according to Harvard's Wechsler. "Students are key contributors to the success of any prevention efforts," he says. [53]

At Florida State, for example, the social norms marketing campaign is not a top-down program. Students submitted proposed ads, says Coburn, which she feels made them more effective.

Similarly, the University of Nebraska's ambitious NU Directions program to reduce high-risk drinking tries to involve students at every step. The university held a series of meetings between students, neighbors and landlords in order to improve relations between students and town residents, and the university regularly holds discussion groups for students on alcohol policies.

Wechsler advises colleges to include students in all efforts, such as helping to develop campus codes of conduct, joining alcohol task forces and campus-community coalitions and serving on judicial review boards that adjudicate alcohol infractions. Most important, Wechsler advises administrators not to give up.

"The problem of college binge drinking took decades to develop," he said. "You won't get rid of it overnight." [54] ■

About the Author

Barbara Mantel is a freelance writer in New York City whose work has appeared in *The New York Times*, the *Journal of Child and Adolescent Psychopharmacology* and *Mamm Magazine*. She is a former correspondent and senior producer for National Public Radio and has won several journalism awards, including the National Press Club's Best Consumer Journalism Award and Lincoln University's Unity Award. She holds a B.A. in history and economics from the University of Virginia and an M.A. in economics from Northwestern University.

Notes

1 Quoted in Christine Vovakes, "Chico's softball gets ax," *Sacramento Bee*, March 31, 2006, p. B1.

2 *Ibid.*

3 For previous coverage in *CQ Researcher*, see Karen Lee Scrivo, "Drinking on Campus," March 20, 1998, pp. 241-264; David Masci, "Preventing Teen Drug Use," March 15, 2002, pp. 217-241; Sarah Glazer, "Preventing Teen Drug Use," July 28, 1995, pp. 657-680; Charles S. Clark, "Underage Drinking," March 13, 1992, pp. 217-240; J. Rosenblatt, "Teen-Age Drinking," in *Editorial Research Reports*, May 15, 1981, available at *CQ Researcher Plus Archive*, CQ Electronic Library, http://library.cqpress.com.

4 Henry Wechsler, *et al.*, "Trends in College Binge Drinking During a Period of Increased Prevention Efforts," *Journal of American College Health*, March 2002, p. 207.

5 www.duke.edu/~amwhite/College.

6 Wechsler, *et al.*, *op. cit.*, p. 210.

7 *Ibid.*, p. 211.

8 Ralph Hingson, *et al.*, "Magnitude of Alcohol-Related Mortality and Morbidity Among U.S. College Students Ages 18-24," *Annual Review of Public Health*, 2005, p. 265.

9 www.duke.edu/~amwhite/College.

10 Aaron White, *et al.*, "Many College Freshmen Drink at Levels Far Beyond the Binge Threshold," *Alcoholism: Clinical and Experimental Research*, June 2006, p. 1008.

11 National Institute of Alcohol Abuse and Alcoholism, "A Call to Action," April 2002, p. 8.

12 *Ibid.*, p. 2.

13 "Harvard Study of Social Norms Deserves 'F' Grade for Flawed Research Design," Higher Education Center for Alcohol and Other Drug Abuse and Violence Prevention, p. 2.

14 John D. Clapp, *et al.*, "A Failed Norms Social Marketing Campaign," *Journal of Studies on Alcohol*, May 2003, p. 409.

15 David Kesmodel, "Schools Use Web to Teach About Booze," *The Wall Street Journal*, Nov. 1, 2005.

16 www.duke.edu/~amwhite/College.

17 Wechsler, *et al.*, "Colleges Respond to Student Binge Drinking: Reducing Student Demand or Limiting Access," *Journal of American College Health*, January/February 2004, p. 161.

18 "Guest Editorial: College sports must end ties with alcohol," *NCAA News Comment*, Oct. 12, 1998, www.ncaa.org/news/1998/19981012/comment.html.

[19] Campaign for Alcohol-Free Sports TV, http://cspinet.org/booze/CAFST/index.htm.

[20] Center on Alcohol Marketing and Youth, "Alcohol Advertising on Sports Television, 2001 to 2003," p. 12.

[21] alcoholstats.com, Anheuser-Busch Companies, www.alcoholstats.com/mm/docs/2754.pdf.

[22] Leslie B. Snyder, *et al.*, "Effects of Alcohol Advertising Exposure on Drinking Among Youth," *Archives of Pediatrics and Adolescent Medicine*, January 2006, p. 18.

[23] Meichun Kuo, *et al.*, "The Marketing of Alcohol to College Students," *American Journal of Preventive Medicine*, 2003, p. 210.

[24] Christina Hoag, "More colleges are turning off tap for booze advertising," *The Miami Herald*, Dec. 12, 2005, p. A1.

[25] Mark Edward Lender and James Kirby Martin, *Drinking in America* (1987), pp. 2, 9.

[26] "The History of the NIAAA," National Institute of Alcohol Abuse and Alcoholism, June 2002, p. 1.

[27] David Musto, "Alcohol in American History," *Scientific American*, April 1996, p. 78.

[28] *Ibid.*, p. 81.

[29] Lender and Martin, *op. cit.*, p. 144.

[30] Robert Straus and Selden D. Bacon, *Drinking in College* (1953), p. 100.

[31] *Ibid.*, p. 103.

[32] Musto, *op. cit.*, p. 78.

[33] Alexander Wagenaar and Traci Toomey, "Effects of Minimum Drinking Age Laws: Review and Analyses of the Literature from 1960 to 2000," *Journal of Studies on Alcohol*, Supplement No. 14, 2002, p. 219.

[34] Pam Belluck, "Vermont Considers Lowering Drinking Age to 18," *The New York Times*, April 13, 2005, p. A13.

[35] George Mason University, "The 2000 College Alcohol Survey," March 2001, p. 13.

[36] For background, see Kathy Koch, "Drunken Driving," *CQ Researcher*, Oct. 6, 2000, pp. 793-808.

[37] www.beeresponsible.com/home.html.

[38] *Ibid.*

[39] The Marin Institute, "Alcohol Industry 'Responsibility' Advertising," p. 1.

[40] Gina Agostinelli and Joel W. Grube, "Alcohol counter-advertising and the media: a review of recent research," *Alcohol Research and Health*, winter 2002, p. 18.

[41] Wechsler, *et al.*, 2002, *op. cit.*, p. 208.

[42] Henry Wechsler and Bernice Wuethrich, *Dying to Drink* (2002), p. 35.

[43] *Ibid.*, p. 38.

[44] *Ibid.*, p. 37.

[45] *Ibid.*, p. 43.

FOR MORE INFORMATION

Alcohol Policy Information System (APIS), www.alcoholpolicy.niaaa.nih.gov. An online government resource that provides detailed information on state and federal alcohol-related policies.

American Beverage Licensees, 5101 River Rd., Suite 108, Bethesda, MD 20816; (301) 656-1494; www.ablusa.org. A trade association for nearly 20,000 U.S. retail liquor license holders, including bars, taverns, restaurants, casinos and package stores.

Association of Fraternity Advisors, 9640 North Augusta Dr., Suite 433, Carmel, IN 46032; (317) 876-1632; www.fraternityadvisors.org. An international organization providing resources, recognition and support for campus fraternity and sorority advisers.

Beer Institute, 122 C St., N.W., Suite 350, Washington, DC 20001; (202) 737-2337; www.beerinstitute.org. A trade association that represents brewers before Congress, state legislatures and public forums across the country.

Center on Alcohol Marketing and Youth, Health Policy Institute, Georgetown University, 3300 Whitehaven St., N.W., Suite 5000, Washington, DC 20057; (202) 687-1019; www.camy.org. Monitors the alcohol industry's marketing practices.

The Century Council, 1310 G St., N.W., Suite 600, Washington, DC 20005; (202) 637-0077; www.centurycouncil.org. Funded by American distillers, a nonprofit organization dedicated to fighting drunken driving and underage drinking.

College Drinking: Changing the Culture, www.collegedrinkingprevention.gov. A government Web site providing comprehensive research-based information on issues related to alcohol abuse and binge drinking among college students.

Distilled Spirits Council of the United States, 1250 I St., N.W., Suite 400, Washington, DC 20005; (202) 628-3544; www.discus.org. A trade association representing producers and marketers of distilled spirits and importers of wine sold in the United States.

Higher Education Center for Alcohol and Other Drug Abuse and Violence Prevention, 55 Chapel St., Newton, MA 02458; (800) 676-1730; www.higheredcenter.org. Funded by the U.S. Department of Education; provides support to institutions of higher education in their efforts to address alcohol and other drug problems.

National Center on Addiction and Substance Abuse at Columbia University, 633 Third Ave., 19th Floor, New York, NY 10017; (212) 841-5200; www.casacolumbia.org. Studies and combats substance abuse in all sectors of society.

National Social Norms Resource Center, Social Science Research Institute, Northern Illinois University, Dekalb, IL 60115; (815) 753-9745; www.socialnorms.org. Supports, promotes and provides technical assistance in the application of the social norms approach to a broad range of health, safety and social-justice issues.

Pacific Institute for Research and Evaluation, 11710 Beltsville Dr., Suite 125, Calverton, MD 20705; (301) 755-2700; www.pire.org. A nonprofit organization focusing on individual and social problems associated with the use of alcohol and other drugs. The organization's Prevention Research Institute is in Berkeley, Calif.

[46] Kenneth Aaron, "College restricts Greek lifestyle," *The* [Albany, N.Y.] *Times Union*, April 15, 2006, p. A1.

[47] Wechsler, *et al.*, 2002, *op. cit.*, p. 212.

[48] Toben F. Nelson, *et al.*, "The State Sets the Rate," *American Journal of Public Health*, March 2005, p. 443.

[49] Alcohol Policy Information System, www.alcoholpolicy.niaaa.nih.gov.

[50] Wechsler, *et al.*, *op. cit.*, p. 208.

[51] Wechsler, *et al.*, *op. cit.*, p. 213.

[52] *Ibid.*

[53] Wechsler and Wuethrich, *op. cit.*, p. 227.

[54] *Ibid.*, p. 237.

Bibliography

Selected Sources

Books

Lender, Mark Edward, and James Kirby Martin, *Drinking in America: A History*, The Free Press, 1987.
Professors at Kean University in New Jersey (Lender) and the University of Houston (Martin) describe drinking in America, from Colonial times through the 1980s.

Seaman, Barrett, *Binge: What Your College Student Won't Tell You*, John Wiley & Sons, 2005.
A retired reporter and editor at *Time*, who spent two years investigating campus life, describes students who are overextended, isolated by technology, drink too much and study too little.

Wechsler, Henry, and Bernice Wuethrich, *Dying to Drink: Confronting Binge Drinking on College Campuses*, Rodale, 2002.
The director of the "College Alcohol Study" at Harvard's School of Public Health (Wechsler), and a science writer (Wuethrich) warn that campus drinking is taking a bigger toll than the public realizes and offer some possible solutions.

Articles

Butler, Katy, "The Grim Neurology of Teenage Drinking," *The New York Times*, July 4, 2006, p. F1.
Mounting evidence suggests that drinking alcohol causes more damage to the developing brains of teenagers than was previously thought.

Horovitz, Bruce, Theresa Howard and Laura Petrecca, "Alcohol Makers on Tricky Path in Marketing to College Crowd," *USA Today*, Nov. 17, 2005, p. B1.
Industry watchdogs, lawmakers, parents and college administrators are scrutinizing how alcohol companies market to college students.

Kesmodel, David, "Schools Use Web to Teach About Booze," *The Wall Street Journal*, Nov. 1, 2005.
Colleges trying to curb drinking are increasingly requiring first-year students to take an online class about alcohol.

Roan, Shari, "Threat Behind the Party-Girl Image," *Los Angeles Times*, May 8, 2006, p. F4.
Recent surveys suggest young women today are drinking more and earlier than previous generations.

Thornburgh, Nathan, "Taming the Toga," *Time*, Feb. 20, 2006, p. 52.
As campuses fight boorish behavior, the nation's largest fraternity seeks a manners makeover.

Reports and Studies

"Blueprint for the States: Policies to Improve the Ways States Organize and Deliver Alcohol and Drug Prevention and Treatment," Join Together, June 2006.
A Boston University program dedicated to developing community-based alcohol- and drug-abuse prevention and treatment programs describes how states can raise funds and improve delivery of substance-abuse prevention and treatment.

"A Call to Action: Changing the Culture of Drinking at U. S. Colleges," *National Institute on Alcohol Abuse and Alcoholism*, April 2002.
The institute's Task Force on College Drinking reports on the consequences of college drinking and recommends research on the best way to change the drinking culture on college campuses.

Hingson, Ralph, *et al.*, "Magnitude of Alcohol-Related Mortality and Morbidity Among U.S. College Students Ages 18-24: Changes from 1998 to 2001," *Annual Review of Public Health*, April 2005, pp. 259-279.
Alcohol related deaths and injuries among college students increased between 1998 and 2001.

Kuo, Meichun, *et al.*, "The Marketing of Alcohol to College Students," *American Journal of Preventive Medicine*, 2003; 25(3): 204-211.
Regulating sale prices, local promotions and advertisements may help reduce binge drinking among college students.

Wagenaar, Alexander C., and Traci L. Toomey, "Effects of Minimum Drinking Age Laws: Review and Analysis of the Literature from 1960 to 2000," *Journal of Studies on Alcohol*, Supplement No. 14: 206-225, 2002.
Raising the legal age for purchase and consumption of alcohol to 21 has been the most successful effort to date in reducing drinking among teenagers.

Wechsler, Henry, *et al.*, "Trends in College Binge Drinking During a Period of Increased Prevention Efforts," *Journal of American College Health*, March 2002.
Researchers summarize the results of four national surveys of drinking patterns on college campuses conducted by the Harvard School of Public Health's "College Alcohol Study."

Ziegler, D. W., *et al.*, "The Neurocognitive Effects of Alcohol on Adolescents and College Students," *Preventive Medicine*, 40 (2005) pp. 23-32.
Underage alcohol use is associated with brain damage and neurocognitive deficits, with implications for learning and intellectual development.

The Next Step:

Additional Articles from Current Periodicals

Alcohol Abuse on Campus

The Associated Press, "Lethal Drinking Stalks College Campuses," *Los Angeles Times*, Nov. 28, 2004, p. A26.
Alcohol poisoning and drunken driving have been blamed for several recent deaths on college campuses.

The Associated Press, "Will Hard-Partying Freshmen Recognize A Need to Change?" *Charlotte Observer*, June 17, 2005, p. B8.
The Research Triangle Institute plans to study 250 East Carolina University students annually for five years.

Dotinga, Randy, "Quandary For Colleges: How to Battle Binge Drinking," *The Christian Science Monitor*, Jan. 18, 2005, p. 11.
Students and college administrators are unsure of what strategies are best for preventing excessive student drinking.

Gegax, T. Trent, "An End to 'Power Hour,' " *Newsweek*, June 6, 2005, p. 28.
Minnesota and North Dakota passed laws to stop "power hour," a post-midnight drinking spree for students just turning 21, a practice common on college campuses.

Hoover, Eric, "New Data Supports 'Social Norms' Approach to Moderating Student Drinking," *The Chronicle of Higher Education*, Aug. 12, 2005, p. 36.
Officials from six colleges said social norms programs help change student's perceptions of drinking behavior.

Sink, Mindy, "Drinking Deaths Draw Attention to Old Campus Problem," *The New York Times*, Nov. 9, 2004, p. A16.
A freshman at the University of Colorado and a Colorado State sophomore died of alcohol poisoning.

Williams, Ed, "Just How Bad is College Drinking?" *Charlotte Observer*, June 18, 2006, p. A23.
Roughly 23 percent of college students engage in the frequent binge drinking that accounts for 68 percent of the alcohol consumed on college campuses.

Alcohol Policies

Canfield, Clarke, "Maine College Uncorks A Wine Course," *Chicago Tribune*, March 25, 2005, p. 13.
Students 21 and older at Colby College get together on Friday nights to learn about and drink wine.

Gold, Scott, "After Student's Death, Campus Tries to Dry Up," *Los Angeles Times*, Dec. 18, 2004, p. A28.
University of Oklahoma President David L. Boren banned alcohol in residence halls and fraternity houses.

Hefler, Jan, "Family to Sue College Over Son's Death," *The Philadelphia Inquirer*, June 6, 2006, p. B1.
The parents of a College of New Jersey freshman are suing the college for not enforcing drinking laws.

Stowe, Stacey, "Students Accept Drinking Rules, But the Alumni Strike Back," *The New York Times*, Nov. 19, 2005, p. B1.
Yale University alumni are angry after the school banned drinking at football games.

Winchester, Donna, "Student Binge Drinking on the Rise at Florida School," *The Philadelphia Inquirer*, Sept. 25, 2005, p. A3.
The University of Florida's new president is imposing academic sanctions for off-campus alcohol violations.

Sports and Alcohol

The Associated Press, "Cal State Bans Alcohol at Sports Events," *Los Angeles Times*, Jan. 13, 2006, p. D7.
California's state university system is banning alcohol from basketball games and other intercollegiate athletic events.

Crowe, Jerry, "Internet Propels Athlete Hazing Issue to Forefront," *Los Angeles Times*, May 19, 2006, p. D1.
College sports programs nationwide are facing discipline after online pictures showed athletes engaged in drinking.

Lipka, Sara, "Embattled Duke Lacrosse Players Abused Alcohol and Had Little Oversight, Reports Say," *The Chronicle of Higher Education*, May 12, 2006, p. 44.
Members of Duke University's men's lacrosse team frequently abused alcohol.

CITING *CQ RESEARCHER*

Sample formats for citing these reports in a bibliography include the ones listed below. Preferred styles and formats vary, so please check with your instructor or professor.

MLA STYLE

Jost, Kenneth. "Rethinking the Death Penalty." CQ Researcher 16 Nov. 2001: 945-68.

APA STYLE

Jost, K. (2001, November 16). Rethinking the death penalty. *CQ Researcher, 11*, 945-968.

CHICAGO STYLE

Jost, Kenneth. "Rethinking the Death Penalty." *CQ Researcher*, November 16, 2001, 945-968.

Researcher PLUS Archive
New!

CQ Researcher

Published by CQ Press, a division of Congressional Quarterly Inc.

cqresearcher.com

Treatment of Detainees

Are suspected terrorists being treated unfairly?

The Supreme Court recently struck down the Bush administration's system for holding and trying detainees at the U.S. Naval base at Guantánamo Bay, Cuba. The administration had maintained that the Geneva Conventions did not protect alleged terrorists captured in Afghanistan and other battlefields in the five-year-old war on terror, and critics say that policy led to the use of abusive interrogation methods, such as "water-boarding" and sleep deprivation. The critics, including top military lawyers, successfully argued that the United States was violating the laws of warfare. They also opposed military commissions the administration has proposed for conducting detainee trials. Bush said the war on terrorism required the commissions' streamlined procedures, which deny some rights guaranteed by the conventions. The court's decision leaves Congress with two options: require detainees to be tried under the military's existing court-martial system or create a new, legal version of the administration's commissions.

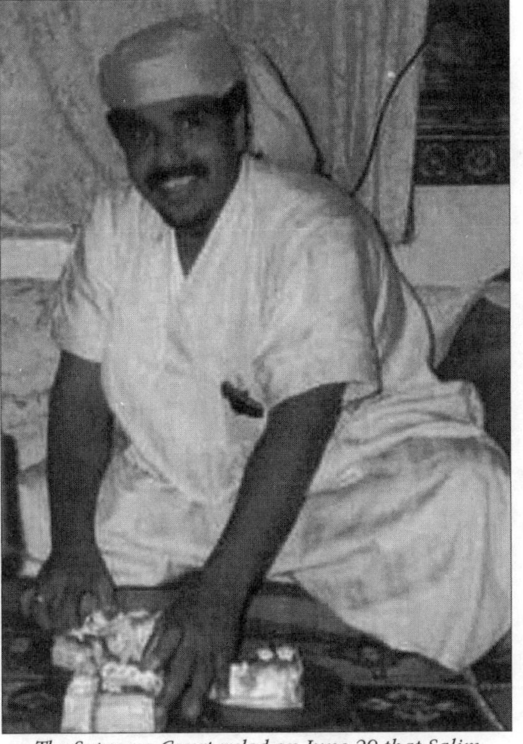

The Supreme Court ruled on June 29 that Salim Ahmed Hamdan, a prisoner at Guantánamo Bay, and other terrorism suspects are protected by the Geneva Conventions and that President Bush had exceeded his authority in establishing military commissions for detainees' trials.

INSIDE

THIS REPORT

CQ Researcher • Aug. 25, 2006 • www.cqresearcher.com
Volume 16, Number 29 • Pages 673-696

CQ PRESS

RECIPIENT OF SOCIETY OF PROFESSIONAL JOURNALISTS AWARD FOR EXCELLENCE ◆ AMERICAN BAR ASSOCIATION SILVER GAVEL AWARD

Treatment of Detainees

The Issues

Background

Current Situation

Outlook

Sidebars and Graphics

For Further Research

Cover photograph: AP Photo/Prof. Neal Katyal, Georgetown University

CQ Researcher

Aug. 25, 2006
Volume 16, Number 29

Managing Editor: Thomas J. Colin

Assistant Managing Editor: Kathy Koch

Associate Editor: Kenneth Jost

Staff Writers: Marcia Clemmitt, Peter Katel

Contributing Writers: Rachel S. Cox, Sarah Glazer, Alan Greenblatt, Patrick Marshall, Tom Price

Design/Production Editor: Olu B. Davis

Assistant Editor: Melissa J. Hipolit

CQ Press

A Division of Congressional Quarterly Inc.

Senior Vice President/Publisher: John A. Jenkins

Director, Library Publishing: Kathryn C. Suárez

Director, Editorial Operations: Ann Davies

Congressional Quarterly Inc.

Chairman: Paul C. Tash

Vice Chairman: Andrew P. Corty

President/Editor in Chief: Robert W. Merry

CQ Researcher (ISSN 1056-2036) is printed on acid-free paper. Published weekly, except March 24, July 7, July 14, Aug. 4, Aug. 11, Nov. 24, Dec. 22 and Dec. 29, by CQ Press, a division of Congressional Quarterly Inc. Annual full-service subscriptions for institutions start at $667. For pricing, call 1-800-834-9020, ext. 1906. To purchase a *CQ Researcher* report in print or electronic format (PDF), visit www.cqpress.com or call 866-427-7737. Single reports start at $15. Bulk purchase discounts and electronic-rights licensing are also available. Periodicals postage paid at Washington, D.C., and additional mailing offices. POSTMASTER: Send address changes to *CQ Researcher*, 1255 22nd St., N.W., Suite 400, Washington, DC 20037.

Treatment of Detainees

By Peter Katel and Kenneth Jost

The Issues

"Killers," President George W. Bush has called the prisoners being held by the United States at Guantánamo Bay — murderers of civilians who don't deserve to be treated under the international laws of war. "These are terrorists," Bush declared in 2002. "They know no countries." [1]

But the top lawyers from the Army, Navy, Air Force and Marines disagree with their commander in chief. When the Senate Armed Services Committee asked them on July 16 if Congress should endorse the controversial trial and detention system created by Bush for enemy combatants, they answered no — emphatically.

"Clearly, we need a change," declared Major Gen. Jack Rives judge advocate general of the Air Force. His colleagues agreed.

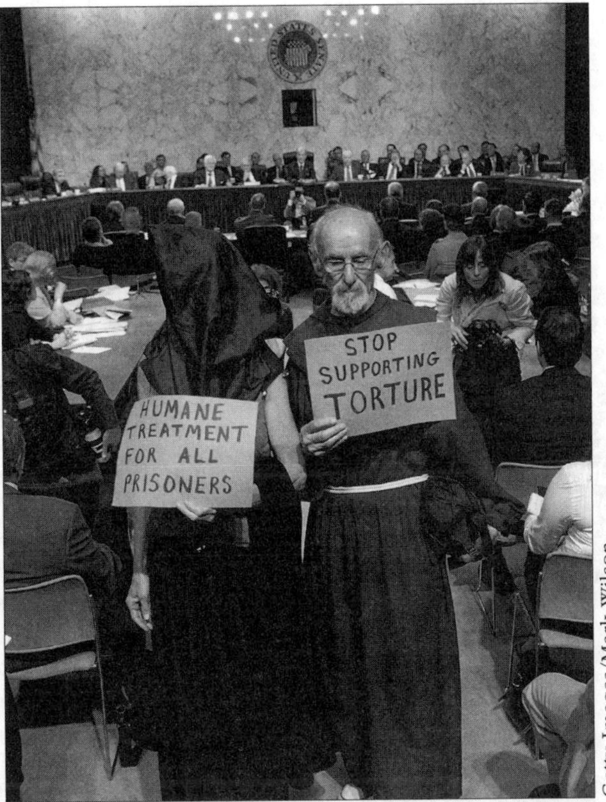

Getty Images/Mark Wilson

Protesters call for changes in U.S. policies on the treatment of suspected terrorists during a Senate Armed Services Committee hearing on July 13, 2006.

In fact, military attorneys have argued for the past several years against the administration's refusal to apply the Geneva Conventions to the war on terrorism. The conventions are the set of treaties governing military conduct in wartime, including the treatment of prisoners and civilians.

Until the Supreme Court ruled in late June, the Bush administration had maintained that the conventions did not apply to prisoners captured in Afghanistan and other battlefields in the war on terrorists. That led to the use of interrogation methods, such as threatening prisoners with guard dogs, near-drowning by "waterboarding," sleep deprivation and forcing prisoners into painful "stress positions."

For the past two years, the abuse of detainees held at Bagram Air Base, in Afghanistan, Abu Ghraib prison in Iraq and the U.S. Naval Station at Guantánamo Bay, Cuba, have generated international outrage. Yet military lawyers, politicians and other critics of U.S. policies had largely failed to get Bush and his top legal-affairs and military appointees to change policies on treatment of these prisoners, whom Bush defined as "unlawful combatants." [2]

In behind-the-scenes battles within the administration, military lawyers argued that the United States was violating the laws of warfare in seeming to condone abuse and torture of detainees. The lawyers also opposed the system of military courts proposed by Bush for war-on-terrorism prisoners at Guantánamo that denied many rights that the conventions grant even to irregular fighters who don't wear any country's uniform. [3]

"I'd only say I wish they'd taken our advice," says William H. Taft, IV, chief legal adviser to Secretary of State Colin Powell during President Bush's first term. [4]

Critics could be ignored or overruled — but not the U.S. Supreme Court.

In its landmark June 29 decision, the justices ruled, 5-3, that prisoners being held in the fight against the al Qaeda terrorist organization are entitled to the protections afforded by the Geneva Conventions. The suit challenging the administration was brought on behalf of Salim Ahmed Hamdan, a Yemeni prisoner at Guantánamo who was Osama bin Laden's driver. [5]

"We fought very hard to get him a fair trial," Hamdan's military-appointed lawyer, Navy Lt. Cmdr. Charles Swift, told the Senate Judiciary Committee. He argued that the military's existing court-martial system — rather than tribunals known as military commissions — would suit that aim perfectly. *

Military lawyers and their congressional supporters argue that American lives may depend on whether the United States upholds Geneva standards for all detainees. "We will have more wars, and there will be Americans who will be taken captive," Arizona Republican Sen. John McCain, who was tortured during his five-and-a-half years as a prisoner of war in North Vietnam, told the Senate Armed Services Committee. "If we somehow carve out exceptions to treaties . . . then it will make it very easy for our enemies to do the same in the case of American prisoners."

---

* The lawsuit, *Hamdan v. Rumsfeld*, has delayed trials of other alleged terrorists.

Many Detainees Not Linked to Hostile Acts

More than half of the detainees at Guantánamo Bay have no history of hostile acts against the United States or its allies, according to an analysis of government data by lawyers for detainees (left). Nearly three-quarters of the detainees whom the U.S. government has characterized as "associated with" the al Qaeda terrorist network have not committed hostile acts against the United States or its allies.

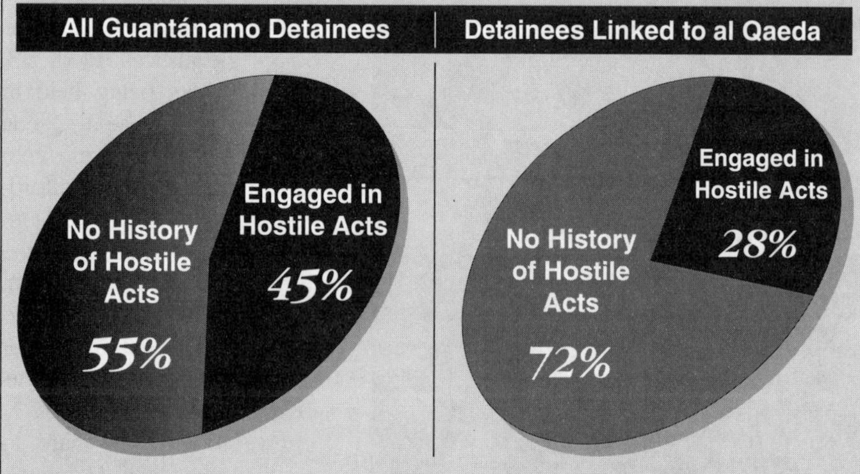

Source: "Report on Guantánamo Detainees, A Profile of 517 Detainees Through Analysis of Department of Defense Data," Seton Hall University School of Law

Sen. Saxby Chambliss, R-Ga., responded, "It certainly irritates me to no end to think that we have to continue to do what's right at all times when the enemy that we're fighting is going to be cruel and inhuman to American men and women who wear our uniform [if] they might fall into their hands."

While the Supreme Court did not address the government's right to hold war-on-terror prisoners "for the duration of active hostilities," it ruled that Bush had exceeded his authority in establishing the commissions. Only Congress has the power to decide that the standard military justice system couldn't be used, the court majority wrote. The decision leaves lawmakers with two basic options: require detainees to be tried under the existing court-martial system, or bow to the administration's wishes and create a new, legal version of the commissions. [6]

Retaining the commissions would, in effect, undercut the high court's ruling that Common Article 3 of the Geneva Conventions covers Guantánamo detainees. The provision requires that a prisoner on trial — even someone not fighting for a specific nation — be judged by a "regularly constituted court" that provides "all judicial guarantees which are recognized as indispensable by civilized peoples." And it prohibits "humiliating and degrading treatment" and well as "cruel treatment and torture." [7]

The high court's reasoning didn't sit well with some lawmakers.

"Where I'm from in South Dakota," Republican Sen. John Thune told his Armed Services colleagues, "when you talk about humiliating or degrading or those types of terms, in applying them to terrorists . . . people in my state would [not] be real concerned that we might be infringing on [the terrorists'] sense of inferiority."

But Sen. Lindsey Graham, R-S.C., resisted any implication that critics of the commission system want to coddle terrorists. "All the people who are out there ranting and raving [that] having . . . some basic due process cripples us in the war effort, you're flat wrong," said Graham, a colonel in the Air Force Reserve and a judge on the Air Force Court of Criminal Appeals. [8]

The debate over whether the rules of traditional warfare apply in the war on terrorists began in the months following the 9/11 terrorist attacks on the World Trade Center and the Pentagon. Then-White House Counsel Alberto Gonzales summed up the administration's mind-set in a Jan. 25, 2002, memo to Bush: "The war against terrorism is a new kind of war," wrote Gonzales, now the nation's attorney general. "The nature of the new war places a high premium on . . . the ability to quickly obtain information from captured terrorists and their sponsors in order to avoid further atrocities against American civilians, and the need to try terrorists for war crimes." [9]

Taft and then-Secretary of State Powell were among a handful of officials who rejected Gonzales' approach. [10]

But Gonzales and other officials carried the day. At about the time he wrote his memo, the first prisoners were being shipped to Guantánamo. By mid-2006, the camp held about 450 detainees, according to the Department of Defense (DOD). The military itself conceded that some of the Guantánamo prisoners didn't belong there. The DOD says about 80 men have been released and another 230 transferred to their countries of origin, in most cases after Combatant Status Review Tribunals determined they hadn't fought the United States and had no other connections to terrorism, or did not pose a significant threat. [11]

The tribunals were set up after the Supreme Court ruled in 2004 that the

Guantánamo prisoners could use habeas corpus petitions to challenge their detentions. [12]

That ruling landed the first major legal blow against the administration's detention policies. Only a month before, the scandal over prisoner abuses at Abu Ghraib had exploded, followed by leaked memos in which officials discussed how to avoid defining some interrogation methods as torture. By the end of 2004, the administration was forced to back down from a narrow definition of "torture" fashioned by a top Justice Department lawyer — that the term applied only to methods so extreme that they caused "organ failure" or the equivalent. [13]

Following that administration retreat, Congress at the end of 2005 passed the Detainee Treatment Act, sponsored by McCain, which prohibits "cruel, inhuman or degrading" treatment of any captive in American hands. A provision limiting court enforcement complicated the law's practical effect. [14]

The Supreme Court's *Hamdan* ruling further undermined the administration's detention and trial system for enemy fighters and terrorists. Captured in Afghanistan in 2001, Hamdan had acknowledged serving as a driver for al Qaeda leader Osama bin Laden. But the government charged him with participating in al Qaeda's conspiracy to kill Americans, which he denies. [15]

To the administration, Hamdan was exactly the kind of prisoner the new rules were designed to deal with — both an intelligence source and an alleged war criminal.

But military lawyers say Gonzales and other civilians blur the lines between intelligence gathering and war-crimes prosecution.

"That confusion has created all kinds of problems," says former Navy Judge Advocate General John D. Hutson, dean of Franklin Pierce Law Center in Manchester, N.H. For one thing, he argues, the administration hasn't distinguished among prisoners who clearly have valuable intelligence, those who had terrorist links but didn't possess any secrets and those who had neither.

But even an established connection to al Qaeda may mean less than the government alleges, according to Hutson. "Hamdan — we can pretend he was something else, but the reality is, he was a driver," Hutson says. "He is no more and no less a war criminal than Hitler's driver. To prosecute him for conspiracy is a very problematic proposition."

The charges against Hamdan have been described only in general terms, but an Air Force lawyer who works with the commission told *The New York Times* that the evidence, including photographs and Hamdan's statements to interrogators, added up to a "solid" case. [16]

As for other detainees, the Defense Department says they include former terrorist trainers, operatives and bomb makers who have provided "valuable insights" into al Qaeda methods and personnel. [17]

Meanwhile, the conflict over detention and trial has put military lawyers at odds with their civilian leaders. Swift, for example, told the Armed Services Committee the commissions' rules made a mockery of judicial fairness by allowing defendants to be kept out of the courtroom and barred from seeing at least some of the evidence against them.

To those who argue that following Geneva Convention rules would compromise America's defenses, Swift said: "Given the handcuffs put on its counsel, the accused is really the only one that can dispute the evidence against him.

Where Are the Detainees?

About 14,000 detainees are being held by the United States, but the number fluctuates, especially following major offensives. Many prisoners captured in battle initially are held at bases in combat zones and are not included in the detainee figures below.

Locations of Detention Facilities	No. of Detainees
Afghanistan	
Bagram Air Force Base	**500**
Kandahar	**100 to 200**
Cuba	
Guantánamo Bay	**450**
Since the detention camp was opened, about 310 prisoners have been freed or transferred to their home countries or to other nations.	
Iraq	**12,800**
The majority of the prisoners captured in Iraq and Afghanistan are held at Abu Ghraib prison, Camp Bucca and various facilities around Baghdad airport.	
Other Locations	**30**
Human Rights Watch says more than two-dozen high-value detainees, sometimes called "ghost prisoners," are in CIA custody in undisclosed locations outside the United States.	

Sources: Department of Defense, Human Rights Watch

Without knowing what that evidence is, the accused is left undefended."

As the political, legal and military communities ponder how to treat prisoners, these are some of the major issues being debated:

Should Congress require wartime detainees to be treated according to the Geneva Conventions?

The *Hamdan* decision brought Congress face-to-face with a fundamental choice: Whether to create a system for imprisoning and trying detainees based on the Geneva Conventions.

The Supreme Court seemingly decided the issue when it rejected the administration's assertion that Common Article 3 of the conventions does not apply to Guantánamo detainees. "That reasoning is erroneous," the majority opinion said. "Common Article 3 . . . is applicable here." [18]

Moreover, military lawyers have testified that Common Article 3 has served as the minimum standard for decades on how troops must treat all prisoners. In fact, U.S. military personnel are required to meet an even higher threshold, treating all prisoners as uniformed prisoners of war representing a nation, Thomas J. Romig, a former Army judge advocate general, told the Senate Armed Services Committee. "And at that standard, you're never going to violate Common Article 3," he said.

Under the Geneva Conventions POWs must be allowed to keep their personal property, exercise and receive regular medical care. Common Article 3, on the other hand, imposes what military lawyers consider the bare essentials of how to treat an enemy, even a terrorist. [19]

But defining those bare essentials has become the biggest point of dispute between the administration and its critics.

"Common Article 3 is written in such generalities, it's almost like taking a blank piece of paper," says Andrew C. McCarthy, a former federal prosecutor who helped mount the case against the terrorists who tried to blow up the World Trade Center in 1993. " 'Judicial guarantees,' which are recognized as indispensable by civilized peoples — what does that mean? What does Common Article 3 tell you about whether you need to give terrorist defendants access to national-security secrets during trial? Is that indispensable to civilized peoples? Who knows?"

Variations on that theme have become a major feature of debates on detainee treatment. Daniel Dell'Orto, principal deputy general counsel at the Pentagon, told the House Armed Services Committee: "I don't want a soldier when he kicks down a door in a hut in Afghanistan searching for Osama bin Laden to have to worry about whether — when he does so and questions the individuals he finds inside, who may or may not be bin Laden's bodyguards, or even that individual himself — he's got to advise them of some rights before he takes a statement."

Former Navy Judge Advocate General Hutson says: "Yes, Common Article 3 is vague in some sense, I suppose, but life, and particularly law, are replete with vague terms: obscenity, probable cause, torture. If we need to explain what we believe those terms mean, then we should do it. We're just using vagueness as an excuse to avoid Common Article 3 and the Geneva Conventions."

But Hutson noted during an appearance before the Senate Armed Services Committee on July 13, "nobody — certainly not me" had argued that troops on a search mission should be required to give Miranda warnings.

As for how to define various terms in Common Article 3, Air Force Maj. Gen. Rives added that the provision has been incorporated into military law for more than 50 years with no objections raised.

Washington lawyer David B. Rivkin Jr., a former lawyer in the Reagan and George H.W. Bush administrations, zeroes in on Common Article 3's opening sentence, which specifies that it applies to conflicts occurring only in the countries that signed the convention. "Not every country has signed," Rivkin says, arguing that the restriction would make enforcement unmanageable. "So if you capture al Qaeda personnel in Afghanistan, which is a party to the Geneva Conventions, you have one set of rules, and if you make a capture in Somalia — I don't know if Somalia signed — then Common Article 3 doesn't apply. Does that make any sense?"

But Katherine Newell Bierman, a former Air Force captain who is now counterterrorism counsel for Human Rights Watch (HRW), says no such geographic limitation would exist if Congress simply adopted the protections of Common Article 3 in a statute.

Bierman notes that nothing in the provision requires every prisoner to be granted a trial. "But if you're going to sentence them, there has to be a fair trial," she says. What that means, she says, amounts to nothing more extravagant than giving the defendant a chance to defend himself, not forcing him to incriminate himself and ensuring he's not tortured — the elements of what an ordinary citizen would consider a fair trial.

Administration supporters insist that such seemingly simple notions of justice conflict with the plain reality that definitions of elementary matters vary widely from country to country. For instance, says Kris Kobach, a former Justice Department lawyer who now teaches at the University of Missouri School of Law, " 'Cruel and unusual punishment' can mean one thing in the United States, where we're trying to decide whether it's cruel to put someone to death by virtually pain-free lethal injection, whereas in another country the question is whether public caning is cruel. This is a war in which very different cultures are involved."

Should Common Article 3 apply to CIA prisoners held in undisclosed locations in other countries?

Although attention has focused on detainees held by the military, there is also concern about prisoners being held in secret by the Central Intelligence Agency (CIA). Human Rights Watch (HRW) says media reports indicate that 30 such "ghost" detainees are being held, including high-ranking alleged terrorists. Government officials have confirmed some of the detentions. [20]

Getty Images/Mark Wilson

Top military lawyers, or judge advocate generals (JAGs), testify before a Senate Armed Services Committee hearing on military tribunals for Guantánamo Bay detainees, on July 13, 2006. From left: Maj. Gen. Scott C. Black (Army), Rear Adm. James E. McPherson (Navy), Maj. Gen. Jack L. Rives (Air Force), Brig. Gen. Kevin M. Sandkulher (Marine Corps) and former JAGs Thomas J. Romig (Army) and John D. Hutson (Navy).

Administration critics say flatly that prisoners of the United States should not be held incommunicado but should be put on trial if they're believed to have committed crimes. "Secret detention is the gateway to torture," said Reed Brody, a special counsel for HRW, arguing that the Geneva Conventions on both POWs and detained civilians require International Red Cross access to all prisoners. [21]

But administration advocates argue that the relevance of the conventions to CIA prisoners detained as terrorists isn't clear.

"We're testing our definitions," the University of Missouri's Kobach says. "We have two categories that we know: traditional soldiers who become POWs when we capture them and garden-variety criminals who become defendants in civilian courts when we capture them. Terrorists fit somewhere in between. They're committing offenses against laws of war and terrorist acts that transcend normal criminal acts."

Kobach acknowledges that he could make the argument that even CIA prisoners are entitled to military trials, but he said that the *Hamdan* decision doesn't provide guidance on whether alleged terrorists who are not being held by the Defense Department should get the same treatment. One common factor with the Guantánamo prisoners is that they have all been apprehended by the U.S. military," he says. "If someone has been apprehended by a foreign government, it wouldn't necessarily flow that he should go to Guantánamo."

"Ghost" detainees took center stage in 2004 following the disclosure of photographs of detainees being abused at Abu Ghraib prison in Iraq. On Sept. 9 — some five months after the prison abuse came to light — an Army general told the Senate Armed Services Committee that "dozens, perhaps up to 100" CIA detainees had been imprisoned secretly. [22]

At least one CIA prisoner died in custody at Abu Ghraib, apparently from a rifle butt blow to the head while in custody. The injury went undiscovered because he didn't get a medical screening when brought to the prison, as did prisoners held by the military. [23]

"Water-boarding," a form of torture that simulates drowning, reportedly was used on Khalid Shaikh Muhammed, a Pakistani whom the government's "9/11 Commission" called the "principal architect" of the 9/11 attacks. [24] No trials have been reported scheduled for Shaikh Muhammed or for any other spy-agency prisoner.

"There's some interagency discussion about what you do with these people long term once their intelligence value has been fully exploited," a U.S. intelligence official told the *Los Angeles Times* in 2004. "The CIA is an intelligence collection and analysis organization. This isn't the bureau of prisons." [25]

Bierman of HRW says putting the alleged terrorists on trial would solve the problem. "Anybody subject to the laws of war — and all these people are subject — should be prosecuted in fair trials," she says. "Prosecuting these guys would be a step ahead of hiding them and torturing them. The whole idea of socking them away is that these are people the law doesn't even reach. That is so fundamentally abhorrent to our values."

Rivkin agrees the status of CIA detainees should be "regularized." But his reasoning differs sharply from that of human-rights advocates. Creating a standard detention-and-trial process would cut down on lawsuits aimed at forcing disclosures of prisoners' whereabouts, he says. "Who needs that crap?"

That view flows out of Rivkin's analysis that even Common Article 3 doesn't require POW-style detention —

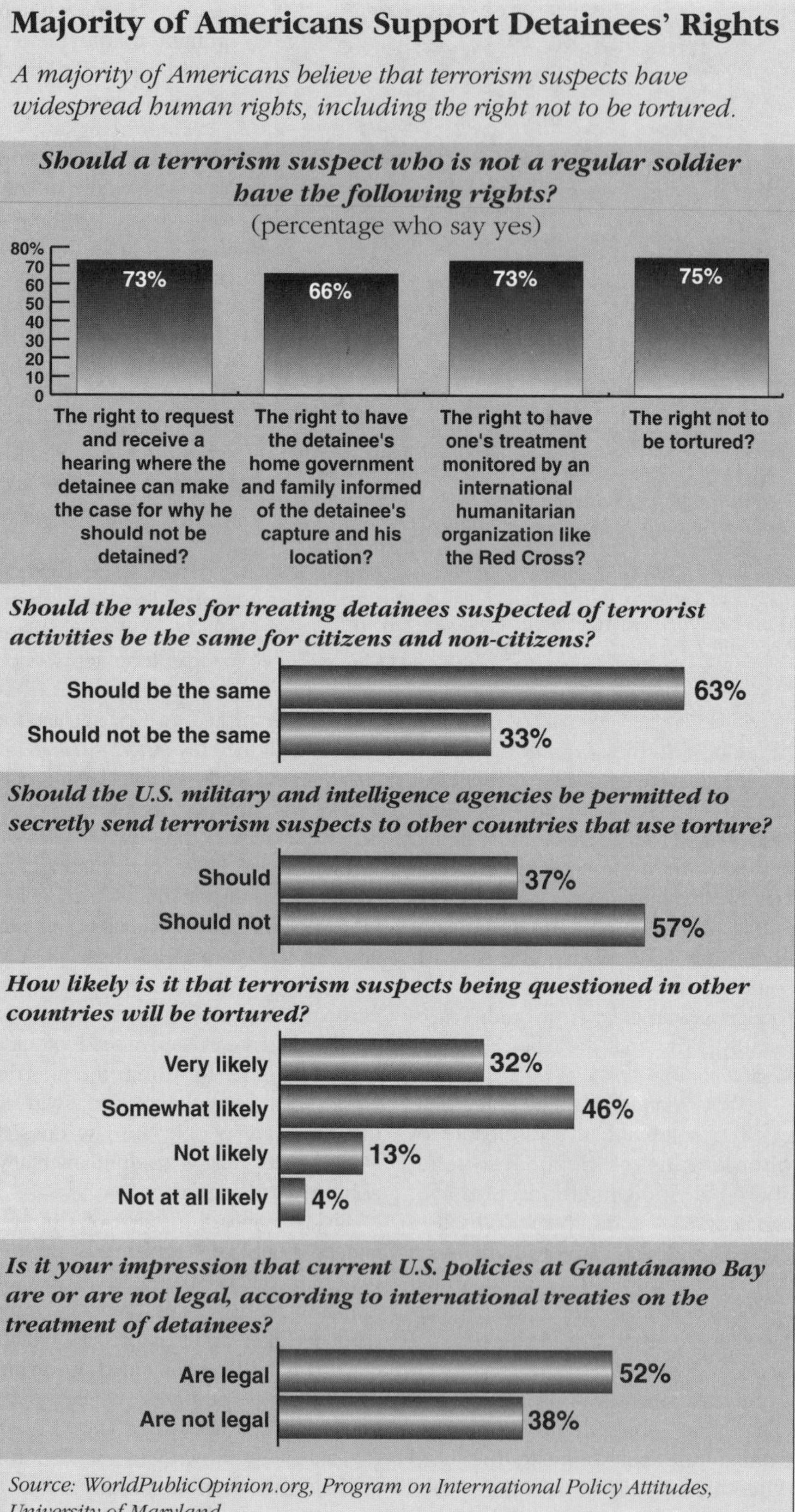
Majority of Americans Support Detainees' Rights
A majority of Americans believe that terrorism suspects have widespread human rights, including the right not to be tortured.
Should a terrorism suspect who is not a regular soldier have the following rights?
(percentage who say yes)
80%
70
60
50
40
30
20
10
0
73%
66%
73%
75%
The right to request and receive a hearing where the detainee can make the case for why he should not be detained?
The right to have the detainee's home government and family informed of the detainee's capture and his location?
The right to have one's treatment monitored by an international humanitarian organization like the Red Cross?
The right not to be tortured?
Should the rules for treating detainees suspected of terrorist activities be the same for citizens and non-citizens?
Should be the same
63%
Should not be the same
33%
Should the U.S. military and intelligence agencies be permitted to secretly send terrorism suspects to other countries that use torture?
Should
37%
Should not
57%
How likely is it that terrorism suspects being questioned in other countries will be tortured?
Very likely
32%
Somewhat likely
46%
Not likely
13%
Not at all likely
4%
Is it your impression that current U.S. policies at Guantánamo Bay are or are not legal, according to international treaties on the treatment of detainees?
Are legal
52%
Are not legal
38%
Source: WorldPublicOpinion.org, Program on International Policy Attitudes, University of Maryland

with food parcels from the Red Cross, and notification to detainees' families of where they are being held, among other provisions. "No, you do not have to tell the world where they are," he says. "You don't have to give them rights to which they are not entitled. It's not bad to have people disoriented, and it's not useful to tell the bad guys who we've captured. Let them wonder if the guy is alive or dead."

But Eugene R. Fidell, president of the National Institute of Military Justice, argues that imposing the Common Article 3 standard even on intelligence agencies someday might protect captured CIA officers from extreme abuse.

Practicality aside, Fidell says that because Common Article 3 imposes a minimum set of standards, it must be the baseline for treatment of all detainees, regardless of who holds them. "You can't say, 'Anybody in uniform, fine,' but if the CIA is holding them, the sky's the limit" regarding abuse.

Should the U.S. outlaw "extraordinary rendition"?

Another variant of CIA detention — "extraordinary rendition" — came to light in 2004. The secret procedure involves the seizure of terrorism suspects, usually outside the United States, by U.S. intelligence agents, who ship them to countries reputed to use torture during interrogations. [26]

Ex-CIA officer Michael Scheuer told *The New Yorker's* Jane Mayer that extraordinary rendition began during the Clinton administration, when the threat from bin Laden and associated terrorists first arose. The program expanded after 9/11, when government lawyers created a loophole in a requirement that war-on-terrorism prisoners be treated humanely: Only the military had to comply, not intelligence agencies. [27]

On the CBS news program "60 Minutes II," Scheuer said that countries receiving the suspects were supposed to assure the United States that the prisoners wouldn't be tortured. But no one took the assurances seriously, he said. The bottom line, he said, was that "extraordinary rendition" had produced "very useful" information. Asked if he condoned the use of torture, he replied, "It's OK with me. I'm responsible for protecting Americans." [28]

Only a few "rendered" prisoners have emerged from foreign prisons. Khaled al-Masri, a German of Kuwaiti origin, and Maher Arar, a Canadian citizen from Syria, say they were released after managing to prove their innocence. Both sued the United States for allegedly violating their rights, but the suits were dismissed after government lawyers said the trials would expose official secrets. [29]

Rendition is a long-established procedure for turning wanted people over to governments asking for them, says former State Department adviser Taft. He says rendition can be carried out without violating any laws or policies against delivering people to torturers. If another country asks for a citizen to be sent back because he's wanted for questioning or trial, "Before we would transfer anybody in those circumstances, we ensure that we are confident that they will be treated properly," he says. He adds that he wasn't involved in any extraordinary rendition cases and knows nothing of them beyond media reports.

If the requesting country has a spotty human-rights record, the State Department can ask to see the prisoner routinely, Taft says. And some countries are off-limits. "I would think that for every person who is bundled off — there should be confidence they will not be treated improperly," he says. "I thought that was the process."

Advocates of the Bush administration approach to counterterrorism acknowledge that human-rights protections may not be assured for terrorism suspects — but they say imposing such a rule would be impractical. "This is one area where Congress is not particularly entitled to the right to oversight," Rivkin says. "It just gets too much into the regulation of foreign policy and intelligence operations."

The process by which American officials evaluate the trustworthiness of other countries' pledges not to mistreat suspects is "too delicate and imprecise to try to reduce to writing," Rivkin says.

But administration critics argue that the Supreme Court's *Hamdan* ruling left no wiggle room about standards for prisoner treatment. "The language of the decision guarantees minimum Geneva Convention Common Article 3 rights to all detainees," says Neal Katyal, Hamdan's co-counsel, a professor at Georgetown Law School. He argues, moreover, that military-justice standards demand humane treatment across the board.

Attorney General Gonzales told the House Judiciary Committee in April that the United States is committed by treaty to not sending people to countries where their human rights would be violated. The 1987 Convention Against Torture and Other Cruel, Inhuman or Degrading Treatment or Punishment, which the Senate ratified in 1990, commits the U.S. not to "expel, return or extradite a person to another State where there are substantial grounds for believing that he would be in danger of being subjected to torture."

But in practice U.S. observance of the treaty is a "farce," says Joseph Margulies, a professor at Northwestern University Law School who is among the lead lawyers for Guantánamo detainees challenging their confinement. He cites the U.S. reliance on declarations by other countries that they won't torture prisoners.

Even some hard-line administration supporters are troubled by the possibility that the United States might wink at the prohibition. If the government doesn't believe that the prohibition against torture should apply to accused terrorists sent to their home countries, ex-prosecutor McCarthy says, officials should say so publicly. "Or else, we should stop doing it."

A critic of the administration's overall detainee policy takes that reasoning even further. Former Navy JAG Hutson favors outlawing extraordinary rendition. But, he adds, "If you're going to torture, you ought to, at least, have the moral courage to do it yourself. Don't send them to Saudi Arabia. It's even worse to contract it out to have it done by someone else." ■

AP Photo/WRAL-TV (left)/U.S. District Court

Former CIA contractor David A. Passaro (left) faces up to 11 years in prison after being convicted on Aug. 17, 2006, of beating Afghan farmer Abdul Wali (right) in June 2003 during questioning about rocket attacks at a remote base in Afghanistan; Wali died two days later.

BACKGROUND

Laws of War

The Constitution designates the president as "commander in chief of the Army and Navy of the United States." But the power to "make rules concerning captures on land and water" is reserved for Congress. Throughout history, Congress has passed laws governing trials before military courts or tribunals, but presidents or military commanders have sometimes skirted the required procedures. [30]

A full year before the Declaration of Independence, the Continental Congress in 1775 passed 69 "Articles of War" to regulate Army conduct. As commander in chief during the Revolutionary War, Gen. George Washington used the powers provided to convene tribunals to try suspected spies. In the most notable instance, Washington convened a board of 14 officers to try a captured British spy, Major John Andre, Gen. Benedict Arnold's infamous co-conspirator. The board found Andre guilty and recommended a death sentence, which Washington approved.

As a general in the War of 1812 and again in the first Seminole War (1817-1818), Andrew Jackson drew criticism for his broad view of his powers as a military commander. (He was elected president in 1828.) In 1818, Jackson faced a censure motion in Congress for having two British subjects tried and sentenced to death for inciting the Creek Indians against the United States. Although the House of Representatives rejected the censure motion, House and Senate committees strongly criticized his actions.

During the Civil War and again during World War II, the Supreme Court was called on to resolve challenges to presidential orders for trials of enemy belligerents. The Civil War provoked intense conflicts over the use of military trials during wartime. To enable the military to summarily arrest Confederate spies and sympathizers, President Abraham Lincoln suspended habeas corpus shortly after the war broke out in April 1861. A month later, Chief Justice Roger B. Taney, in his role as a circuit justice, ruled the action unconstitutional, but Lincoln ignored the decision. Over the next two years, hundreds of people suspected of aiding the secessionists were arrested and tried by ad hoc military tribunals, which sometimes ignored judicial orders to release the prisoners.

Congress passed a law sanctioning the suspension of habeas corpus in 1863 and adopted various rules for military tribunals, but their authority outside war zones remained doubtful. The Supreme Court dodged the issue in 1864, but after the war had ended, however, it ruled that martial law could not be imposed outside war theaters if civil courts were "open and their process unobstructed." The 1866 decision in *Ex parte Milligan* ordered the release of a prominent Southern sympathizer, Lambdin Milligan, who had been convicted of conspiracy by a military tribunal and sentenced to death. [31]

In the meantime, military tribunals had been used in two other high-profile cases: the May 1865 trial of the Lincoln assassination conspirators and the August 1865 trial of Capt. Henry Wirz, the Confederate commander of the notorious Andersonville prison camp in Americus, Ga., where nearly 13,000 prisoners died. Speedy convictions and executions resulted in both cases. Military tribunals continued to be used in the South during the early years of Reconstruction. [32]

Like Lincoln, President Franklin D. Roosevelt tested the limits of the president's powers during World War II. And, as in the Civil War, the Supreme Court erected no obstacle to Roosevelt's actions. In 1943 and 1944, the court upheld the curfew and then the internment of Japanese-Americans on the West Coast. [33] A more direct confrontation with the judiciary, however, came in 1942 with the trial of eight German saboteurs. They were speedily brought to trial before a military commission specially convened by Roosevelt that deviated from prescribed procedures in several respects.

The saboteurs, who had come ashore in June 1942 in Florida and New York from German submarines, were rounded up after one turned informant. Roosevelt's order creating a seven-member commission to try the men authorized the tribunal to admit any "probative" evidence and to recommend a death sentence by a two-thirds vote instead of the normal unanimous verdict.

Seven of the men filed habeas corpus petitions, but the Supreme Court — also departing from regular procedure — rejected their pleas in a summary order issued on July 31, only two days after hearing arguments in the case, known as *Ex parte Quirin*. The court issued a full opinion on Oct. 29 — after six of the men had been executed. The justices unanimously ruled that the offenses fell within the tribunal's jurisdiction. They also upheld the procedures used: Some justices said they complied with the Articles of War; others said the Articles did not apply. [34]

The court again blinked at departures from standard military procedures in its 1946 decision upholding the war-crimes conviction of Gen. Tomoyuki Yamashita, the Japanese commander in the Philippines. Rushed to trial in late October 1945 on charges of failing to prevent wartime atrocities, Yamashita was found guilty and sentenced on Dec. 7 to death by hanging.

Yamashita filed a habeas corpus petition, but the high court rejected his request on Feb. 2, 1946, upholding the military commission's jurisdiction and procedures. In stinging dissents, however, Justices Frank Murphy and

Continued on p. 684

Chronology

1860s-1946

Conflicts arise among the three branches of government over the treatment of captured enemy soldiers and spies and respect for civil liberties vs. national-security concerns.

1861
President Abraham Lincoln suspends habeas corpus, defying the Supreme Court and setting the stage for military trials of hundreds of accused Confederate agents.

1866
U.S. Supreme Court orders release of a Confederate sympathizer who had been sentenced to death, on the grounds that martial law can't be applied outside theaters of war as long as civilian courts are functioning.

1942
Supreme Court upholds military tribunal convictions of eight German saboteurs; six are executed.

1946
Gen. Tomoyuki Yamashita is executed after a quick — and some say unfair — military commission trial finds him guilty of not stopping atrocities by Japanese troops in the Philippines.

1949-1971

In the wake of World War II atrocities, greater protection is offered for prisoners and civilians.

1949
Geneva Conventions are revised to apply prisoner of war (POW) standards to prisoners in conflicts that aren't wars between nation-states.

1950
Congress enacts the Uniform Code of Military Justice, which grants defendants rights equal to those enjoyed by defendants in civilian courts and adopts the standards of Geneva's Common Article 3. The provision requires prisoners on trial — even those not fighting for a specific nation — to be judged by a "regularly constituted court."

1966
U.S. military command in Vietnam grants POW status to captives from the Vietcong guerrilla army.

1971
The massacre of 400-500 Vietnamese civilians in the village of My Lai leads to courts-martial for two officers; one is convicted and one acquitted.

2000s

Attacks on the World Trade Center and the Pentagon on Sept. 11, 2001, prompt the Bush administration to set up controversial special courts to try accused terrorists and "unlawful combatants."

Nov. 13, 2001
President George W. Bush signs an executive order establishing military commissions to try accused members and supporters of the al Qaeda terrorist network.

2002
Two groups of Guantánamo detainees file habeas corpus petitions challenging their confinement.

July 2003
A military commission rules that Salim Ahmed Hamdan, a driver for Osama bin Laden captured in Afghanistan, is eligible for trial; he is later charged with conspiracy.

April 27, 2004
CBS News' "60 Minutes II" televises photographs of U.S. troops abusing prisoners at Abu Ghraib prison.

June 28, 2004
U.S. Supreme Court rules, in *Rasul v. Bush*, that Guantánamo prisoners can go to court to demand they be freed.

Oct. 21, 2004
The first in a stream of internal government documents concerning treatment of detainees are released to the American Civil Liberties Union by the government.

December 2005
Congress passes the Detainee Treatment Act, prohibiting torture and mistreatment of prisoners while limiting detainees' right to challenge their detentions.

June 29, 2006
Supreme Court rules in *Hamdan v. Rumsfeld* that the president exceeded his authority in establishing military commissions.

July 13, 2006
Top military legal officers tell congressional committees that lawmakers shouldn't endorse the administration's military commission system.

Aug. 2, 2006
Attorney General Alberto R. Gonzales argues that Congress shouldn't ban coerced testimony in military trials of accused terrorists.

Aug. 17, 2006
Former CIA contract interrogator David A. Passaro faces up to 11 years in prison after being convicted of beating Afghan farmer Abdul Wali, who died two days later.

Geneva Conventions Protect Prisoners

Warfare has changed radically since the first of four Geneva Conventions was adopted in 1864. Well-ordered lines of uniformed infantrymen with rifles at the ready have given way to vast, highly mobile armies and atomic weapons as well as terrorists and stateless paramilitary groups.

The changes have strained the international treaties governing the military's treatment of combatants and civilians.

The Bush administration says the Geneva Conventions don't cover prisoners captured during the wars in Afghanistan and Iraq. "In my judgment, this new paradigm [in warfare] renders obsolete Geneva's strict limitations on questioning of enemy prisoners," Attorney General Alberto Gonzales advised the president in 2002. [1]

Gary Solis, former director of the law of war program at the U.S. Military Academy at West Point, dismisses Gonzales' view. "The Geneva conventions do apply to today's warfare," says the retired Marine Corps lieutenant colonel. "You just have to have half a brain to apply them."

The U.S. Supreme Court also stepped into the debate, ruling on June 29, 2006, in *Hamdan v. Rumsfeld* that U.S. plans to prosecute Salim Ahmed Hamdan and other detainees being held at the U.S. Naval Station in Guantánamo Bay, Cuba, violated the conventions.

The conventions grew out of the horrors witnessed in 1859 by Henri Dunant, a Swiss merchant, after a battle between Austrian and French forces during the Austro-Sardinian War. After Dunant saw the more than 40,000 soldiers who had been left dead or dying on the battlefield near Solferino, Italy, he organized volunteers to help both sides. [2]

Dunant went on to found the International Committee for Relief to the Wounded, which later became the International Committee of the Red Cross (ICRC). In 1864, Dunant convinced the Swiss government to hold a diplomatic conference to lay down rules for the treatment of battlefield casualties. [3]

Ten European governments sent representatives to the conference and adopted the Geneva Convention for the Amelioration of the Condition of the Wounded in Armies in the Field, more commonly known as the first Geneva Convention. [4] It protects wounded soldiers on the battlefield and the medical personnel attending to them. [5]

The second convention, adopted in 1929, required prisoners of war to be humanely treated, properly fed and quartered in conditions comparable to those used by their captors.

And following the Holocaust and other atrocities committed against civilians in World War II, a third convention was created in 1949, protecting non-combatants and their property from harm. Protections given to ground troops in the first convention were also extended to wounded and shipwrecked sailors.

"In 1949, we had a unity in the world that we hadn't seen before and we're not likely to see again," Solis says. "The world

Continued from p. 682

Wiley Rutledge strongly attacked, among other things, the validity of the charges, the limited time for Yamashita to prepare a defense and the sufficiency of the evidence against him. [35] He was hanged on Feb. 23.

'Military Justice'

Two major legal reforms adopted after the war fundamentally changed the laws of war. The Geneva Conventions extended previous POW protections to combatants in conflicts other than those between nation-states. The Uniform Code of Military Justice (UCMJ), approved by Congress in 1950, brought civilian-like procedures and protections into a system previously focused on discipline and command authority.

The widespread atrocities committed during World War II against civilians, combatants and POWs led humanitarian groups to strengthen the protections for wartime captives initially established by the Geneva Convention of 1929. The resulting four accords — signed in Geneva in 1949 — outlined provisions for treating "the wounded and sick" on the battlefield or at sea, prisoners of war and civilians. Each accord also included Common Article 3, which extends basic protections against violence, humiliating or degrading treatment and summary punishment to non-traditional conflicts such as civil wars or conflicts in which at least one side is not a nation-state. The Senate ratified the four treaties in 1954.

One purpose of the UCMJ was to establish a uniform system of military justice for what were then three services: Army, Navy and Coast Guard. But it was also intended to respond to criticism of the Army and Navy justice systems as unfair to service members accused of offenses. Harvard law Professor Edmund Morgan, who headed the committee that drafted the proposed code, said it was designed to "provide full protection of the rights of persons subject to the code without undue interference with appropriate military discipline and the exercise of appropriate military functions." Morgan's draft was introduced in Congress in February 1949 and formed the principal basis for the final version approved by Congress in May 1950. [36]

Another development would become crucial to the present debate over detainees. U.S. law and the military code of conduct embraced Common Article 3, as the Supreme Court majority noted in its *Hamdan* decision. [37]

was united in its abhorrence of the actions of the Nazis and the Japanese."

In 1977, the conventions were amended with two additional protocols to cover the use of modern weapons and protect victims of internal conflicts. [6]

In 2005, another protocol was added permitting the use of a hollow, red diamond symbol in addition to the traditional cross and crescent emblems of the Red Cross. This protocol was instrumental in bringing Israel into the international humanitarian movement because Magen David Adom, Israel's rescue service, refused to work under the cross or crescent, the Red Cross symbol used in Muslim countries. [7]

The most controversial part of the conventions of late has been Common Article 3, which appears in each of the four conventions and was cited in the *Hamdan* case. It protects noncombatants from violence, cruel treatment, degradation and torture; prevents the taking of hostages; and ensures prisoners the right of a fair trial by a "regularly constituted court." [8]

The burden of enforcing the conventions falls on signatory nations and international organizations like the ICRC, which performs regular inspections of POW camps. The conventions became federal law in the United States after they were signed and ratified by Congress.

Despite their role in dictating foreign policy today and their importance to domestic and international law, the Geneva Conventions (GC) are only as strong as the member nations want them to be.

"If you approach the GC's in such a way as to find loopholes, and to work around them, then you can do it," Solis says. "Geneva depends on the good will of those who adopt it. . . . No law is going to deter the lawless."

— Nicholas Sohr

[1] Gail Gibson, "Abuse scandal puts Gonzales in spotlight," *The Houston Chronicle*, May 23, 2004.

[2] Michael Tackett, "Abuses in Iraq highlight standards for treatment," *Chicago Tribune*, May 12, 2004.

[3] Maria Trombly, "A Brief History of the Laws of War," *Reference Guide to the Geneva Conventions*, July 31, 2006, www.genevaconventions.org.

[4] Tackett, *op. cit.*

[5] Office of the United Nations High Commissioner for Human Rights, www.ohchr.org/english/.

[6] For background, see Kenneth Jost, "International Law," *CQ Researcher*, Dec. 17, 2004, pp. 1049-1072, and David Masci, "Ethics of War," *CQ Researcher*, Dec. 13, 2002, pp. 1013-1032.

[7] Alexander G. Higgins, "Red Cross changes emblem," *The Seattle Times*, Dec. 8, 2005.

[8] For full text of Common Article 3, see "Protection of victims of non-international armed conflicts," International Committee of the Red Cross, Dec. 31, 1988. www.icrc.org/Web/Eng/siteeng0.nsf/iwpList104/6D73335C674B821DC1256B66005951D1.

However, the United States exceeded that minimum treatment threshold during the Vietnam War. In 1966, the U.S. Military Assistance Command in Vietnam ordered enemy captives to be granted prisoner of war status, even if they belonged to the guerrilla force known as the Vietcong (which fought alongside the regular North Vietnamese Army). Vietcong captured performing "terrorism, sabotage or spying" operations were classified as civilian defendants and were to be treated under the Geneva Conventions. [38]

Military justice also demands punishment for war crimes committed by one's own troops. In the Vietnamese hamlet of My Lai in 1968, U.S. soldiers massacred some 400-500 civilians. Lt. William Calley, the senior officer on scene, was convicted of murder and sentenced to life at hard labor, though the sentence was later reduced to 10 years, and Calley was freed on parole. Calley's commanding officer, Capt. Ernest Medina, was acquitted on charges of failing to control the troops under him because prosecutors couldn't prove that he knew what the soldiers were doing. Two other officers were acquitted of lesser charges. [39]

After Vietnam, new questions about detainees grew out of American support for U.N. "peacekeeping missions." In 1993, efforts by Special Operations troops to capture warlord Mohammed Farah Aidid in Mogadishu, Somalia, went terribly wrong. The U.S. action — depicted in the book and movie "Black Hawk Down" — led to the deaths of 18 Americans. One of the dead soldiers was dragged through the city.

The U.N.'s peacekeeper role in civil conflicts has turned the world organization into an enforcer of the international laws of war. U.N. tribunals have been established to try war-crimes cases arising from massacres during the 1990s and early 2000s in the former Yugoslavia, Rwanda and Sierra Leone. As the new century opened, military justice was coming to be seen as the leading source of law in regions torn by conflict involving irregular forces. [40]

'War on Terror'

Within weeks of the 9/11 terrorist attacks on the World Trade Center and the Pentagon, President Bush and other administration officials came to view the capture and detention of al Qaeda members and adherents as critical to the president's "war on terror." A month after the 9/11 attacks, an executive order signed by Bush on Nov. 13, 2001, calling for "enemy combatants" to be detained outside the

United States and tried outside regular civilian or military courts, provoked immediate criticism and legal challenges. But the administration vigorously defended its plans and resisted changes, even after adverse court rulings. [41]

Bush's order directed that al Qaeda members, other terrorists and any others who had "harbored" them were to be "placed in the custody of the secretary of Defense," tried by military commissions to be created under newly written rules and regulations and denied any right to "seek the aid of" any U.S. court or international tribunal. Administration officials said the national terrorism emergency required special procedures, but the order drew immediate criticism from a variety of sources, including military lawyers, civil libertarians, constitutional scholars and members of Congress from both parties.

Getty Images/Joshua Roberts

Georgetown University Law Professor Neal Katyal, left, and Navy Lt. Commander Charles Swift, lawyers for Guantánamo Bay detainee Salim Ahmed Hamdan, address the media following the Supreme Court's ruling against the Bush administration's proposed military tribunals on June 29, 2006. The court ruled the tribunals violate both American military law and the Geneva Conventions.

Late in December, Defense Secretary Donald H. Rumsfeld announced that detainees from Afghanistan would be transported to Guantánamo — "the least worst place," he called it — but that no trials would be held there. The Pentagon first issued procedures for the tribunals in March 2002 in so-called Order No. 1, with still no trial site specified. More detailed rules continued to come out through 2003, but the delays also reflected the administration's decision to give priority to interrogating detainees, not trying them.

With criticism of the procedures continuing, the administration in early 2002 also began facing court challenges. Two groups of Guantánamo detainees filed habeas corpus petitions in federal court in Washington, D.C., in February and May, generally denying involvement with al Qaeda and challenging their detention without trial or even charges. The administration argued not only that federal courts had no authority over Guantánamo since it was outside the United States but also that the president's war powers justified his actions. Two more habeas petitions were filed in June by two U.S. citizens — José Padilla and Yaser Hamdi — who were being held as enemy combatants, also without charges, at a naval brig in Charleston, S.C.

After lower-court proceedings, the cases reached the Supreme Court, which handed the administration limited but unmistakable setbacks on June 28, 2004. In the consolidated Guantánamo cases, the court ruled, 6-3, that federal courts could exercise jurisdiction over Guantánamo prisoners' challenges. The majority noted that unlike the situation that prompted a contrary ruling in 1950, the government had virtual control over the Guantánamo base. [42]

The ruling in *Rasul v. Bush* settled only the jurisdictional issue and left all other questions for further development in lower courts. In the *Hamdi* and *Padilla* cases, the court upheld the president's authority to detain a U.S. citizen as an enemy combatant but also required some form of hearing before "a neutral decision-maker." [43]

In the meantime, Hamdan had been designated as eligible for trial by a military commission in July 2003, and a single charge of "conspiracy" was filed a year later, in July 2004.

The charging document accused Hamdan of "willingly and knowingly" joining al Qaeda in order to commit terrorism; it specified as "overt acts" his serving as bin Laden's driver, delivering weapons and receiving arms training. Hamdan's trial opened at Guantánamo on Aug. 28 — the first of the military commission proceedings — even as his lawyers were pressing his habeas corpus petition.

An initial ruling granting Hamdan's petition put the trial on hold while the government appealed. The federal appeals court in Washington reversed the ruling in July 2005. His lawyers then appealed to the Supreme Court, which heard his case in March 2006.

Congress then entered the picture by passing the Detainee Treatment Act, which Bush signed on Dec. 30, 2005. Although its anti-torture provision received most of the attention, the act also curtailed judicial review of the Guantánamo cases. In two sections, the law limited review of decisions by the Combatant Status Review Tribunals. The new law also barred federal courts from hearing habeas corpus petitions filed by the Guantánamo detainees, but it did not say whether that provision applied to

Continued on p. 688

Military Lawyers Endorse Geneva Rules

The sight of uniformed officers arguing that detainees deserve more legal rights may cause some observers to wonder if the military has gone soft. But retired Air Force Col. Katherine Newell Bierman is among those who argue that treating prisoners humanely — aside from being legally required — simply makes good sense militarily.

"It's common-sense war fighting," says Bierman, now counterterrorism counsel for the advocacy group Human Rights Watch. "If you don't have some control over how your people are behaving, you lose discipline."

For Bierman as well as many active-duty military lawyers, the Geneva Conventions provide that control.

"When we train Marines, and soldiers, sailors and airmen, when we talk about handling people that we grab or get on the battlefield, we're normally talking in context of the Geneva Conventions regarding prisoners of war," Brig. Gen. Kevin Sandkuhler, the Marine Corps' top legal officer, told the Senate Armed Services Committee in July.

Administration officials suggest the military attorneys are making the classic soldier's mistake of fighting today's war with yesterday's doctrines. Attorney General Alberto R. Gonzales, testifying at a later hearing, echoed Republican lawmakers' comments that Geneva language such as "humiliating and degrading treatment," aren't adequately defined. "I wonder, given the times that we currently live in and given this new enemy and this new kind of conflict, whether all of the provisions continue to make sense," Gonzales said, adding that he wasn't "in any way suggesting a retreat from the basic principles of Geneva, in terms of the humanitarian treatment."

In early 2006, recently retired generals began leveling attacks at Defense Secretary Donald H. Rumsfeld and, in some cases, at the Iraq war itself. "It speaks volumes that guys like me are speaking out from retirement about the leadership climate in the Department of Defense," said retired Maj. Gen. John Batiste, who led an infantry division in Iraq in 2004-2005. "I think we need a fresh start," he said. [1]

Another Iraq war veteran, retired Army Maj. Gen., Charles H. Swannack Jr., said Rumsfeld had "culpability" for abuse and torture at Abu Ghraib prison in Iraq. [2]

The attacks on Rumsfeld by retired generals, combined with criticism of the administration's detainee policy from military lawyers, led a noted constitutional scholar to remark half-jokingly that military-civilian relations had undergone a drastic change.

"For the first time in our nation's history, a military takeover of the government would move the country slightly to the left," Walter Dellinger quipped at a July 26 discussion of the *Hamdan* decision sponsored by the liberal American Constitution Society for Law and Policy. Dellinger, now a professor at Duke University law school, was acting solicitor general under President Bill Clinton.

A conservative fellow panelist, a former lawyer during the Reagan and George H.W. Bush administrations, David B. Rivkin Jr., challenged military lawyers' oft-stated insistence that humane detention policies help assure civilized treatment of American military prisoners. "It is rubbish to talk about how our POWs will be mistreated" if the U.S. does not abide by the Geneva Conventions, he said, citing a consistent pattern of abuse and torture of U.S. POWs since World War II, including Korea and Vietnam. "The notion that the head cutters and the torturers are going to be motivated to behave better if we accord them Geneva treatment is laughable."

Meanwhile, criticism of administration detainee policies has emerged among civilians as well as the military. William H. Taft IV, a former legal adviser to Secretary of State Colin Powell, was among the first internal critics of prisoner policy when it was developed in 2001-2002. Powell himself warned then-Counsel to the President Gonzales that not applying Geneva Conventions standards to the detainees would "reverse over a century of U.S. policy and practice in supporting the Geneva Conventions and undermine the protections of the law of war for our troops, both in this specific conflict and in general." [3]

Another civilian critic, former Navy general counsel Alberto J. Mora, urged the administration to stop the mistreatment of prisoners at Guantánamo. "I was appalled by the whole thing," Mora told Jane Mayer of *The New Yorker* after resigning. "It was clearly abusive, and it was clearly contrary to everything we were ever taught about American values." [4]

Military lawyers, for their part, also cite professional pride in advocating adherence to the Geneva rules. "When we get a conviction, we can say forthrightly that we won because we had the best evidence — as opposed to, 'The [defendant] wasn't in the courtroom and didn't get to see any of the evidence against him,' " says Hardy Vieux, a former Navy JAG lawyer who serves on the board of the nonprofit National Institute of Military Justice.

Among institute members, virtually all of them former military lawyers, "We're unanimous" in supporting a return to Geneva Convention rules, says Vieux. "I don't know of a dissenting voice."

---

[1] Thomas E. Ricks, "Rumsfeld Rebuked by Retired Generals," *The Washington Post*, April 13, 2006, p. A1.

[2] Peter Spiegel, "Another Retired General Joins Battalion of Rumsfeld Critics," *Los Angeles Times*, April 14, 2006, p. A5.

[3] Quoted in Colin L. Powell, "Memorandum To: Counsel to the President; Assistant to the President for National Security Affairs," Jan. 26, 2002. See also, William H. Taft IV, "Memorandum, to: Counsel to the President," Feb. 2, 2002; The memos, along with other internal administration documents concerning U.S. policy toward detainees, are available at www.nytimes.com/ref/international/24MEMO-GUIDE.html.

[4] Jane Mayer, "The Memo; how an internal effort to ban the abuse and torture of detainees was thwarted," *The New Yorker*, Feb. 27, 2006, p. 32. Mora's 22-page memo to the Navy's inspector general is available at www.newyorker.com/images/pdfs/moramemo.pdf.

Continued from p. 686

pending cases such as Hamdan's.

In ruling in Hamdan's case on June 29, the court held that the Detainee Treatment Act did not eliminate the court's jurisdiction over the case and that the military commissions established by Bush violated both the Uniform Code of Military Justice and the Geneva Conventions. In separate opinions, Justices John Paul Stevens and Anthony M. Kennedy faulted several departures in the tribunal rules from regular court-martial procedures, including provisions to exclude the accused from portions of a trial, to allow hearsay evidence and to use non-lawyer judges who would not be appointed by the judge advocate general. In a brief concurrence, Justice Stephen G. Breyer added, "Nothing prevents the president from returning to Congress to seek the authority he believes necessary." ■

Getty Images/Jim Watson

President George W. Bush answers questions on the treatment of detainees at Guantánamo Bay during a joint press conference with Japanese Prime Minister Junichiro Koizumi at the White House on June 29, 2006, following the Supreme Court's rejection of the administration's trial and detention system.

CURRENT SITUATION

Allowing Coercion?

The Bush administration, Senate and House committees and military and civilian lawyers of all stripes are arguing over whether testimony obtained under duress should be allowed in military trials of alleged terrorists.

A series of congressional hearings in the weeks following the *Hamdan* decision have been marked by administration attempts to preserve military commissions as they were first established by presidential order. After bad reviews from lawmakers and military lawyers, administration officials have been proposing commissions modeled more closely on courts-martial — but with permissive evidence rules that would allow coercive interrogations. [44]

"As we talk about whether or not coerced testimony should come in," Gonzales told the Senate Armed Services Committee on Aug. 2, "our thinking is that if it's reliable and if it's probative, as determined by a certified military judge, that it should come in. If you say that coerced testimony cannot come in, everyone is going to claim evidence has been coerced. Then we'll get into a fight with respect to every prosecution as to what is, in fact, coerced or what is not coerced." [45]

Maj. Gen. Scott C. Black, the Army's judge advocate general, opposed the use of coercion. "I don't believe that a statement that is obtained under coercive — under torture, certainly, and under coercive measures — should be admissible," he told the Senate Judiciary Committee on Aug. 2, 2006. [46]

On the same day, Attorney General Gonzales was explaining the administration's position. At a Senate Armed Services Committee hearing, Sen. McCain asked Gonzales if statements obtained through "illegal, inhumane treatment should be admissible."

After a long pause, Gonzales haltingly replied: "The concern that I would have about such a prohibition is, What does it mean? . . . If we could all reach agreement about the definition of cruel, inhumane and degrading treatment, then perhaps I could give you an answer. . . . Depending on your definition of something as degrading, such as insults, I would say that information should still come in." [47]

McCain called the proposal to use coercion a "radical departure" from standards of military conduct. And, he said, "We must remain a nation that is different from, and above, our enemies."

The exchanges showed that the question of whether torture or rough treatment is permissible remains very much alive, despite the Supreme Court's *Hamdan* decision, which ruled that Common Article 3 should apply to Guantánamo detainees. Even lawyers who support the Common Article 3 standard agreed that Congress isn't bound to uphold it.

"Sure, Congress could effectively disavow Common Article 3 by passing an inconsistent law," says military law expert Fidell. Constitutional scholar Laurence H. Tribe of Harvard Law School writes, however, that doing so

Continued on p. 690

At Issue:

Should detainee trials before military commissions be based on courts-martial?

EUGENE R. FIDELL
PRESIDENT, NATIONAL INSTITUTE OF MILITARY JUSTICE

FROM TESTIMONY BEFORE THE SENATE ARMED SERVICES COMMITTEE, JULY 19, 2006

yes

The National Institute of Military Justice believes that the highest priority for military justice is the achievement of public confidence in the administration of justice. The institute's basic approach is to strongly tilt military commissions in the direction of general courts-martial, our felony-level military court.

[T]here's no question that Congress cannot legislate every jot and tittle of the system . . . there is always going to be some presidential rulemaking. The president [should have the] power to depart from the Uniform Code of Military Justice (UCMJ) model [by stating] with particularity those facts that render it impracticable to follow the general court-martial model on any particular point — not a blanket presidential determination that general court-martial rules are impracticable across-the-board.

The president will not have satisfied the requirement if his justification is filled with vague generalities. Our proposal requires that Congress be notified of any determination of impracticability. Congress should stand ready to review determinations and intervene with legislation. And the president's determination that some rule is impracticable [would be] subject to judicial review for abuse of discretion or on the ground that it is contrary to law.

Congress could take certain things off the table — for example, the right to select your own uniformed defense counsel. Congress could conclude that that is part of the deluxe version of military justice that need not be extended to enemy combatants in the context of a military commission.

Congress might also conclude that some provisions are so critical to public confidence in the administration of justice that they should be placed beyond the president's power to make exceptions. Congress has already said that we don't want coerced testimony in a court-martial. I can't imagine that Congress would take a different position in a military commission.

"Public confidence in the administration of justice" is not another way of saying we have 100 percent assurance that every person who is charged will be convicted. Rather it is a shorthand way of summarizing all of those deeply held values that reflect the commitment of the Founders to due process of law and fundamental fairness. This sounds like an obvious proposition, but it bears repeating because there are those who believe the military commission system rules must ensure convictions. I believe they must ensure fairness. If that means some who are guilty may not ultimately be convicted, that is the price we pay for having a legal system.

JAMES J. CARAFANO
SENIOR RESEARCH FELLOW, THE HERITAGE FOUNDATION

FROM TESTIMONY BEFORE THE SENATE ARMED SERVICES COMMITTEE, JULY 19, 2006

no

President Bush was right to argue that the concerted effort to destroy the capacity of transnational groups who seek to turn terrorism into a global corporate enterprise ought to be viewed as a long war. The Uniform Code of Military Justice (UCMJ) is not at all appropriate for the long war [because it] puts the protection of the right of the individual foremost, and then adds in accommodations for national security and military necessity.

For example, the UCMJ requires informing servicemen suspected of a crime of their Miranda rights. The exercise of Miranda rights is impractical on the battlefield. Hearsay evidence is prohibited in a court-martial. On the battlefield, reliable hearsay may be the only kind of evidence that can be obtained about the specific activities of combatants. Likewise, overly lenient evidentiary rules make sense when trying a U.S. soldier for a theft committed on base, but not when someone is captured on the battlefield and is being tried for war crimes committed prior to capture, perhaps in another part of the world.

Rather than amend court-martial procedures to address security concerns, it would be preferable to draft military commissions that put the interests of national security first, and then amend them to ensure that equitable elements of due process are included in the procedures.

After Sept. 11, the Bush administration's critics framed a false debate that indicated citizens had a choice between being safe and being free, arguing that virtually every exercise of executive power is an infringement on liberties and human rights. The issue of the treatment of detainees at Guantánamo Bay has been framed in this manner. It is a false debate. Government has a dual responsibility to protect the individual and to protect the nation. The equitable exercise of both is guaranteed when the government exercises power in accordance with the rule of law.

In wartime it's the courts' job to interpret the war, it's the president's job to fight the war and essentially it's the Congress' job to provide the president the right kinds of instruments to do that.

If we respect the purposes of the Geneva Conventions and want to encourage rogue nations and terrorists to follow the laws of war, we must give humane treatment to unlawful combatants. However, we ought not to reward them with the exact same treatment we give our own honorable soldiers. Mimicking the UCMJ sends exactly the wrong signal.

Continued from p. 688

would effectively require the United States to jettison all the other Geneva Conventions as well.

"Unless Congress is prepared to step up to the plate and say it is knocking Geneva out of the park, Geneva should be deemed to remain in place and therefore binding," Tribe wrote to David Remes, a Washington lawyer representing Guantánamo detainees who are challenging their detention (*see below*). [48]

Even before details of the administration proposal began to filter into the press, officials had made clear their opposition to using military-justice standards in terrorism trials for non-citizens.

"Full application of court-martial rules would force the government either to drop prosecutions or to disclose intelligence information to our enemies in such a way as to compromise ongoing or future military operations, the identity of intelligence sources and the lives of many," Dell'Orto, the Pentagon deputy general counsel, told the House Judiciary Committee on July 12. "Military necessity demands a better way."

Administration critics argue that the practicalities of the matter run in the other direction. A congressionally approved version of the military commission would be held up by court challenges, they said. "If . . . after more litigation we find ourselves right back here in four or five more years after we've litigated, then what are we going to end up with?" Lt. Cmdr. Swift, Hamdan's lawyer, asked the Senate Judiciary Committee on July 11. "Neither side will ever get a fair trial, and both Mr. Hamdan and the United States deserve one."

Legally speaking, says Hamdan's co-counsel Katyal, objections that court-martial procedures are too protective of defendants' rights to function effectively in terrorism cases ring hollow. In fact, Katyal told Senate Armed Services members, courts-martial can be closed to keep national-security matters secret, witnesses' identities can be hidden and officers who act as juries can be required to possess security clearances.

Meanwhile, the administration is discussing the possibility of allowing detainees to face life imprisonment or death based on evidence that was never disclosed to the accused at trial. [49]

Beyond the arguments over commissions vs. courts-martial looms a debate over the extent of the president's power. For instance, last December when Bush signed the Detainee Treatment Act banning torture of prisoners in U.S. military custody, he included a "signing statement" that suggested he was not bound by it. Indeed, Gonzales recently suggested that Bush might be inclined to retain his unilateral approach to terrorist crimes regardless of what Congress does. [50]

A July 18 exchange between Gonzales and Sen. Russell Feingold, D-Wis., made clear the president's views on the limits of congressional power. Feingold asked if Gonzales saw the Supreme Court as having ruled that "the president has to obey the statutes we write."

Gonzales replied: "Of course, we have an obligation to enforce the laws passed by the Congress. But the president also takes an oath, senator, to preserve, protect and defend the Constitution. And if, in fact, there are constitutional rights given to the president of the United States, he has an obligation to enforce those rights."

Other Prisoner Suits

Hamdan is only one of dozens of Guantánamo detainees who have challenged the United States' power to try or to hold them. While Hamdan awaits a government decision on what to do following the Supreme Court's June 29 decision, the rest of the lawsuits are pending in federal appeals court in Washington.

Lawyers for about 65 prisoners held as "unlawful combatants" — but not yet charged with a crime like Hamdan — have filed habeas corpus petitions seeking to have their detentions ruled illegal.

The prisoners argue that the government hasn't proved that any of them fought for al Qaeda or the Taliban. The government has cited decisions by Combatant Status Review Tribunals concluding that the prisoners involved had indeed been fighters. Shortly after the tribunals began, Army Maj. Gen. Geoffrey D. Miller, then in command at Guantánamo said, "I have found no innocent people" at the camp. [51]

During the tribunal hearings, which began in 2004, prisoners appearing before the panels of three military officers had neither lawyers — nor access to the evidence against them. Defense lawyer Remes calls the panels "pseudo-tribunals" designed to give a false impression that evidence had been fully and fairly evaluated in each detainee's case.

At the district court level, the habeas suits have produced contradictory rulings by the two judges who considered the cases. In January 2005, U.S. District Judge Richard J. Leon ruled that courts had little room to challenge the president's right to hold enemy prisoners." Any [judicial] role must be limited when, as here, there is an ongoing armed conflict and the individuals challenging their detention are non-resident aliens." [52]

Less than a month later, Judge Joyce Hens Green reached the opposite conclusion. "Although this nation unquestionably must take strong action under the leadership of the commander in chief to protect itself," she wrote, "that necessity cannot negate the existence of the most basic fundamental rights." [53]

The Guantánamo habeas suits began in 2004, two years after Hamdan's case began. Though *Hamdan* focused on the legality of the military commissions, the Supreme Court's June decision has become an issue in the habeas cases. The Court of Appeals for the District of Columbia Circuit has ordered lawyers on both sides to present written arguments on how the *Hamdan* decision affected the habeas cases.

Government lawyers argued that *Hamdan's* upholding of Common Article 3 wasn't relevant to the habeas prisoners. The Geneva Convention doesn't grant any rights that an individual can go to court to demand, the government said. [54]

Moreover, the prisoners' challenges now have to be started over in the appeals court, which has "exclusive jurisdiction" under the Detainee Treatment Act of 2005, the government lawyers argued.

The prisoners' lawyers maintained that the *Hamdan* decision makes clear that the prisoners can challenge their detentions on the grounds that they violate the Geneva Conventions. The Supreme Court ruled that the conventions can be enforced by American courts, the lawyers said. Remes says habeas litigation could drag on for years. If the appeals court does not rule soon, he warns, the U.S. Supreme Court may not be able to decide the cases until late 2007. "By that time," Remes says, "the men at Guantánamo will have been there for more than five-and-a-half years." ■

OUTLOOK

'Blistering Fight'

The uncertainty surrounding the future of the war on terrorists makes for hesitancy on all sides about predicting the fate of Guantánamo detainees, and of detainee policy in general.

"We're still in mid-chapter," says military-law expert Fidell. "Our national course in constitutional law is not yet finished."

Ex-prosecutor McCarthy says conflict could arise over whether Common Article 3 creates rights that people in U.S. custody can claim — as opposed to rights that a foreign government would demand for its detained citizens.

"Pro-international law people are arguing that the Supreme Court crossed the Rubicon and made provisions of a treaty judicially enforceable by individuals," McCarthy says. "People on my side of the fence say that the Supreme Court didn't address that issue." The dispute is likely to come to a head in a "blistering fight," he says.

Margulies, who represents some Guantánamo detainees, raises the question of whether Guantánamo prisoners taken in Afghanistan could be held even after combat ended there.

"Could Congress define the conflict in such a way that even if Afghanistan, a sovereign state, orders the United States to leave or the conflict moves to a different place, you can still hold a guy who's picked up in Afghanistan?" he asks. Margulies says the answer is no but acknowledges that others may differ.

Former Justice Department official Kobach agrees that the question of how to define the end of conflict is likely to wind up in court. "If 20 years from now we're still engaged in a worldwide battle against the same enemy organizations, a case might be brought arguing that the war itself is over and the detainees should be released," he says. "I don't think it will fly."

For all the cloudiness obscuring views of the future, advocates on all sides of the divide over how to fight terrorists speak unequivocally about the dangers of taking the wrong path.

Former Reagan and George H.W. Bush administration lawyer Rivkin argues that granting treatment decreed by the Geneva Conventions to terrorists and other "unlawful combatants" would be a major step down the wrong road. "We have a civilization that is besieged by a bunch of barbarians and bad people," he says. "We are dealing with a grave threat to everything, to civilized law and order, to democracy. Much of the rest of the world has abandoned the stigmatization and de-legitimization of unlawful combatants. For us to say, 'We're to treat everyone the same, everyone's going to get the gold standard, everyone's going to get courts-martial,' given where the rest of the world is, would just complete this transformation. It would be unimaginably bad."

Meanwhile, detainees' advocates worry about continued Republican dominance in Washington and its likely effect on Supreme Court makeup.

If 86-year-old Justice John Paul Stevens — a member of the *Hamdan* majority — stays on the bench through the end of the Bush presidency, and the next president is a Democrat, "The Supreme Court will probably not shift to the right," says detainee lawyer Remes."

But if Stevens retires soon and Bush gets to pick his successor, "The Guantánamo prisoners could be dead meat," Remes says. "You could have a Supreme Court majority that would uphold unlimited, unreviewable executive power. That would be a sad day for America." ■

Notes

[1] Quoted in Richard A. Serrano, "Officials Agree on Prisoners' Status," *Los Angeles Times*, Jan. 29, 2002, p. A9.

[2] *Ibid.*; for Bush's definition of prisoners, see David E. Sanger, "President Defends Military Tribunals in Terrorist Cases," *The New York Times*, Nov. 30, 2001, p. A1.

[3] A virtual library of books, reports and articles exists on treatment of detainees in the war on terrorists. Selected examples include, "Article 15-6 Investigation of the 800th Military Police Brigade," [Taguba Report on Abu Ghraib], 2004 [undated], www.fas.org/irp/agency/dod/taguba.pdf; Tim Golden, "In U.S. Reports, Brutal Details of 2 Afghan Inmates' Deaths," *The New York Times*, May 20, 2006, p. A1. For a response to critics of U.S. detention practices, see Kenneth Anderson, "An American Gulag? Human rights groups test the limits of moral equivalency," *The Weekly Standard*, Jan 13, 2005. A voluminous file of government documents involving interrogations was released to the American Civil Liberties Union and can be found at www.aclu.org/safefree/torture/torturefoia.html#.

[4] William H. Taft, IV, "Memorandum To:

Counsel to the President," Feb. 2, 2002; Colin L. Powell, "Memorandum To: Counsel to the President; Assistant to the President for National Security Affairs," Jan. 26, 2002. The memos, along with other internal administration documents concerning U.S. policy toward detainees, are available at www.nytimes.com/ref/international/24MEMO-GUIDE.html.

[5] The case is *Hamdan v. Rumsfeld*, 05-184 (2006). For an analysis of the court decision, see Kenneth Jost, *Hamdan v. Rumsfeld*, CQ Electronic Library, *CQ Supreme Court Collection* (2006), at http://library.cqpress.com/scc/scyb05-421-18449-991165. Only eight justices participated in the decision; Chief Justice John Roberts recused himself.

[6] *Ibid.*

[7] "Geneva Convention relative to the treatment of prisoners of war," adopted Aug. 12, 1949, available at www.unhchr.ch/html/menu3/b/91.htm.

[8] For background on Graham's career, see Maura Reynolds, "Senate Insider on Military Justice," *Los Angeles Times*, July 13, 2006, p. A20.

[9] Alberto R. Gonzales, "Memorandum for the President," Jan. 25, 2002, p. 1. The memo is one of a series of internal Bush administration documents, some leaked and some officially released through a Freedom of Information Act lawsuit by the American Civil Liberties Union. The leaked documents are collected on Web sites of several research and news organizations, including *The New York Times*. See "A Guide to the Memos on Torture," [undated] www.nytimes.com/ref/international/24MEMO-GUIDE.html.

[10] For detailed explanations of their opposition, see William H. Taft, IV, "Memorandum To: Counsel to the President," Feb. 2, 2002; Colin L. Powell, "Memorandum To: Counsel to the President; Assistant to the President for National Security Affairs," Jan. 26, 2002, www.nytimes.com/ref/international/24MEMO-GUIDE.html.

[11] The Defense Department maintains updated statistics and other information at the "Detainee Affairs" section of the Pentagon Web site, www.defenselink.mil/home/features/Detainee_Affairs. For a critical analysis of the tribunal rulings, see Mark Denbeaux, Joshua Denbeaux, *et al.*, "Report on Guantánamo Detainees," Seton Hall University School of Law, Feb. 8, 2006, http://law.shu.edu/news/guantánamo_report_final_2_08_06.pdf.

[12] The case was *Hamdi v. Rumsfeld*, 542 U.S. 547 (2004). The Pentagon announced formation of the tribunals about a week after the Supreme Court decision. See John Hendren, "Pentagon Sets Review of Detainees," *Los Angeles Times*, July 8, 2004, p. A13.

[13] For the article that broke the Abu Ghraib story, see Seymour Hersh, "Torture at Abu Ghraib," *The New Yorker*, May 10, 2004, www.newyorker.com/fact/content/?040510fa_fact. For the "organ failure" definition, see "Memorandum for Alberto R. Gonzales, Counsel to the President," Aug. 1, 2002, http://fl1.findlaw.com/news.findlaw.com/nytimes/docs/doj/bybee80102mem.pdf. For the Supreme Court decision, see Charles Lane, "Justices Back Detainee Access to U.S. Courts," *The Washington Post*, June 29, 2004, p. A1. For the torture policy revision, see R. Jeffrey Smith and Dan Eggen, "Justice Expands 'Torture' Definition," *The Washington Post*, Dec. 31, 2004, p. A1.

[14] For background on McCain, see "John McCain, CQ Politics in America Profile," CQ.com, updated April 2005.

[15] For background on Hamdan, see Jonathan Mahler, "The Bush Administration vs. Salim Hamdan," *The New York Times Magazine*, Jan. 8, 2006, p. 44.

[16] *Ibid.* The charge against Hamdan, undated and unsigned is available at www.defenselink.mil/news/Jul2004/d20040714hcc.pdf.\

[17] "Information from Guantánamo Detainees," JTF-GTMO (Joint Task Force-Guantánamo), March 4, 2005, www.defenselink.mil/news/Mar2005/d20050304info.pdf.

[18] *Hamdan v. Rumsfeld*, Supreme Court, 548 U.S.__(2006), pp. 67, 69.

[19] "Relative to the Treatment of Prisoners of War, Geneva, 12 August 1949," [Geneva Convention III], http://www.globalissuesgroup.com/geneva/convention3.html; "Text of Geneva Conventions Article 3," The Associated Press, http://seattlepi.nwsource.com/national/1151AP_Guantánamo_Geneva_Conventions.html.

[20] For an earlier, shorter list of CIA detainees, see "The United States 'Disappeared': The CIA's Long-Term 'Ghost Detainees,' Human Rights Watch, October 2004, www.hrw.org/backgrounder/usa/us1004. p. 37.

[21] "U.S.: Investigate 'Ghost Detainees," Human Rights Watch, Sept. 10, 2004, press release, http://hrw.org/english/docs/2004/09/10/usint9338_txt.htm.

[22] Gen. Paul J. Kern quoted in Eric Schmitt and Douglas Jehl, "Army Said C.I.A. Hid More Detainees Than It Claimed," *The New York Times*, Sept. 9, 2004, p. A1.

[23] Douglas Jehl and David Johnston, "C.I.A. Expands Its Inquiry Into Interrogation Tactics," *The New York Times*, Aug. 28, 2004, p. A10.

[24] For an account of "water-boarding" used on Shaikh Muhammed, see James Risen, David Johnston and Neil A. Lewis, "Harsh C.I.A. Methods Cited in Top Qaeda Interrogations," *The New York Times*, May 12, 2004, p. A1; for a characterization and account of Shaikh Muhammed's role in the 9/11 plot, see *The 9/11 Commission Report* (2004), pp. 145-180.

[25] Quoted in Greg Miller, "It's a Tough Time to be the Intelligence Chief," *Los Angeles Times*, Feb. 20, 2004, p. A23.

About the Authors

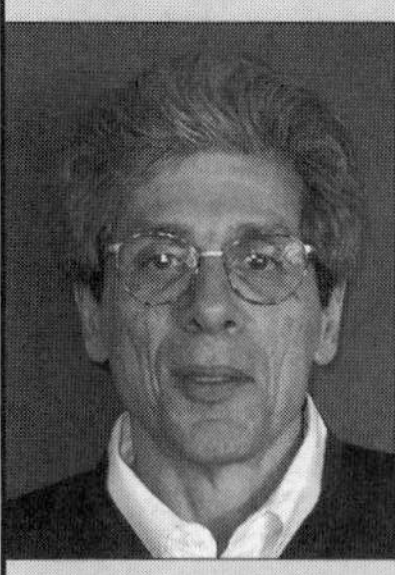

Peter Katel is a *CQ Researcher* staff writer who previously reported on Haiti and Latin America for *Time* and *Newsweek* and covered the Southwest for newspapers in New Mexico. He has received several journalism awards, including the Bartolomé Mitre Award for coverage of drug trafficking from the Inter-American Press Association. He holds an A.B. in university studies from the University of New Mexico. His recent reports include "Immigration Reform," "War on Drugs" and "Whistleblowers."

Associate Editor **Kenneth Jost** graduated from Harvard College and Georgetown University Law Center. He is the author of the *Supreme Court Yearbook* and editor of *The Supreme Court from A to Z* (both *CQ Press*). He was a member of the *CQ Researcher* team that won the 2002 ABA Silver Gavel Award. His recent reports include "Presidential Power" and "Transgender Issues."

[26] For the first U.S. journalistic reports, see Jane Mayer, "Outsourcing Torture: the secret history of America's 'extraordinary rendition' program," *The New Yorker*, Feb. 14, 2005, p. 106; Craig Whitlock, "A Secret Deportation of Terror Suspects," *The Washington Post*, July 25, 2004, p. A1; Megan K. Stack and Bob Drogin, "Detainee Says U.S. Handed Him Over For Torture," *Los Angeles Times*, Jan. 13, 2004, p. A1.

[27] *Ibid.*

[28] "CIA Flying Suspects to Torture?" CBS' "60 Minutes II," March 6, 2005, partial transcript available at http://cbs5.com/minutes/sixtyminutes_story_065094819.html.

[29] Scott Shane, "Invoking Secrets Privilege Becomes a More Popular Legal Tactic by the U.S.," *The New York Times*, June 4, 2006, p. A32.

[30] Background drawn in part from Louis Fisher, *Military Tribunals and Presidential Power: American Revolution to the War on Terrorism* (2005). See also briefs by the following "friends of the court" in *Hamdan v. Rumsfeld:* Military Historians; Former Attorneys General; Citizens for Common Defense, posted at www.hamdanvrumsfeld.com/briefs (last visited July 2006).

[31] The citation is 71 U.S. 2 (1866). The earlier decision is *Ex parte Vallandingham*, 68 U.S. 243 (1864).

[32] Four of the eight Lincoln conspirators were sentenced to death and were hanged on July 7, 1865; Wirz was hanged on Nov. 10, 1865.

[33] The ruling in the curfew case is *Hirabayashi v. United States*, 320 U.S. 81 (1943); the ruling in the internment case is *Korematsu v. United States*, 323 U.S. 214 (1944). For background, see David Masci, "Reparations Movement," *CQ Researcher*, June 22, 2001, pp. 529-552.

[34] The citation is 317 U.S. 1 (1942). For a full account, see Louis Fisher, *Nazi Saboteurs on Trial: A Military Tribunal and American Law* (2003). For background, see C. E. Noyes, "Sabotage," *Editorial Research Reports, 1941* (Vol. I), available at *CQ Researcher Plus Archives*, CQ Electronic Library, http://library.cqpress.com.

[35] The decision is *In re Yamashita*, 327 U.S. 1 (1946).

[36] See Edmund M. Morgan, "The Background of the Uniform Code of Military Justice," *Military Law Review*, Vol. 28 (April 1965).

[37] *Hamdan v. Rumsfeld, op. cit.*, p. 68, n. 3.

[38] For a summary of the Vietnam policy, see Jennifer Elsea, "Treatment of 'Battlefield Detainees' in the War on Terrorism," Congressional Research Service, Sept. 17, 2003, pp. 31-32.

[39] For a detailed account of the My Lai massacre and aftermath, see Maj. Tony Raimondo, "The My Lai Massacre: A Case Study," School of the Americas, Fort Benning, Ga. [undated]; http://carlisle-www.army.mil/usamhi/usarsa/HUMANRT/Human%20Rights%202000/my-lai.htm. For legal details of the *Medina* case, see Fisher, *op. cit., Military Tribunals and Presidential Power*, pp. 153-153.

[40] In establishing the tribunals, U.N. member states aimed explicitly to restore or create the rule of law by establishing accountability for war crimes and crimes against humanity. The sites for the Rwanda, Sierra Leone and former-Yugoslavia tribunals are: Rwanda, http://69.94.11.53/default.htm; Sierra Leone, www.sc-sl.org/; former Yugoslavia, www.un.org/icty/.

[41] For an overview, see Fisher, *op. cit.*, pp. 168-252; for Fisher's critical assessment, see pp. 253-260.

[42] The earlier case is *Johnson v. Eisentrager*, 339 U.S. 763 (1950).

[43] The decisions are *Rasul v. Bush*, 542 U.S. 466 (2004), and *Hamdi v. Rumsfeld*, 542 U.S. 507 (2004). The other U.S. citizen case, *Rumsfeld v. Padilla*, 542 U.S. 426 (2004), was dismissed on the grounds it had been filed in the wrong federal court.

[44] For reports on Senate hearings concerning the debate, see R. Jeffrey Smith, "Top Military Lawyers Oppose Plan for Special Courts," *The Washington Post*, Aug. 3, 2006, p. A11; and Kate Zernike, "White House Asks Congress to Define War Crimes," *The New York Times*, Aug. 3, 2006, p. A16.

[45] Committee testimony, Aug. 2, 2006.

[46] Smith, *op. cit.*

[47] *Ibid.*

[48] Tribe's July 11, 2006, letter, confirmed by his office, was made available by Remes.

[49] Jeffrey R. Smith, "On Prosecuting Detainees; Draft Bill Waives Due Process for Enemy Combatants," *The Washington Post*, July 28, 2006, p. A23.

[50] For background see Kenneth Jost, "Presidential Power," *CQ Researcher*, Feb. 24, 2006, pp. 169-192.

[51] Quoted in John Mintz, "Most at Guantánamo to Be Freed or Sent Home, Officer Says," *The Washington Post*, Oct. 6, 2004, p. A16. For a detailed look at the tribunals' operation, see Neil A. Lewis, "Guantánamo Prisoners Getting Their Day, but Hardly in Court," *The New York Times*, Nov. 8, 2004, p. A1.

[52] Quoted in Charles Lane and John Mintz, "Detainees Lose Bid For Release," *The Washington Post*, Jan. 20, 2005, p. A3.

[53] Quoted in Neil A. Lewis, "Judge Extends Legal Rights For Guantánamo Detainees," *The New York Times*, Feb. 1, 2005, p. A12.

[54] For an analysis of the government's claims, see Lyle Denniston, "Government: Detainee cases must start over," Scotusblog, Aug. 1, 2006 (includes a link to government brief), www.scotusblog.com/movabletype/archives/2006/08/government_deta_1.html.

FOR MORE INFORMATION

American Civil Liberties Union, 125 Broad St., New York, NY 10004; www.aclu.org. Obtains and disseminates government documents on detention and litigates on behalf of detainees.

Center for Constitutional Rights, 666 Broadway, 7th Floor, New York, NY 10012; (212) 614-6464; www.ccr-ny.org/v2/home. Played a key role in the filing of habeas corpus lawsuits by Guantánamo detainees.

Department of Defense, Public Affairs, 1400 Defense Pentagon, Washington, DC 20301; (703) 428-0711; www.defenselink.mil/home/features/DetaineeAffairs. Provides information on detainees and related matters.

The Heritage Foundation, 214 Massachusetts Ave., N.E., Washington, DC 20002; (202) 546-4400; www.heritage.org. Supports the administration's approach to the detention and trial of prisoners in the war on terror.

MacArthur Justice Center, Northwestern University School of Law, 375 E. Chicago Ave., Chicago, IL 60611; (312) 503-1271; http://macarthur.uchicago.edu. Has been active in representing Guantánamo detainees.

National Institute of Military Justice, 4801 Massachusetts Ave., N.W., Washington, DC 20016; (202) 274-4322; www.nimj.org/home. An organization of retired military lawyers that is participating in the debate on detainee treatment.

Bibliography

Selected Sources

Books

Fisher, Louis, *Military Tribunals & Presidential Power: American Revolution to the War on Terrorism*, University of Kansas Press, 2005.

A specialist at the Library of Congress on the power relationships between the three branches of government closely examines the development of the president's wartime authority in legal matters.

Margulies, Joseph, *Guantánamo and the Abuse of Presidential Power*, Simon & Schuster, 2006.

A law professor at the MacArthur Justice Center at Northwestern University Law School provides a non-legalistic narrative of his experiences in representing Guantánamo detainees.

Saar, Erik, and Viveca Novack, *Inside the Wire: A Military Intelligence Soldier's Eyewitness Account of Life at Guantánamo*, Penguin Press, 2005.

Confusion, ignorance and bigotry plagued the ranks of the military personnel who supervised and interrogated Guantánamo detainees, according to Saar, a former translator and interrogator, and *Time* reporter Novack.

Yoo, John, *The Powers of War and Peace*, University of Chicago Press, 2005.

A former top Justice Department lawyer in 2001-2003 explains how the government's detention policy grew out of the government's belief that presidents have greater power during wartime. Now a law professor at the University of California at Berkeley, Yoo helped craft the policy.

Articles

Golden, Tim, "After Terror, a Secret Rewriting of Military Law," *The New York Times*, Oct. 24, 2004, p. A1.

An investigative reporter digs into the legal and political origins of the detention and trial system centered at Guantánamo Bay.

Mahler, Jonathan, "The Bush Administration vs. Salim Hamdan," *The New York Times Magazine*, Jan. 8, 2006, p. 44.

A New York-based journalist who is writing a book about Hamdan traveled to Yemen to speak to the family of the man at the center of the Supreme Court's latest ruling on detainees.

Mayer, Jane, "The Memo; How an internal effort to ban the abuse and torture of detainees was thwarted," *The New Yorker*, Feb. 27, 2006, p. 32.

A Washington-based staff writer for *The New Yorker* details how the Navy's top civilian lawyer — now resigned — tried and failed to have mistreatment of detainees prohibited.

Rivkin, David B., Jr., and Lee A. Casey, "The Gitmo Decision," "Targeting Illegal Combatants," "Misreading Hamdan v. Rumsfeld," "Bush hatred and constitutional reality," *The Washington Times*, July 11-July 14, 2006.

Conservative lawyers who served in the Reagan and George H.W. Bush administrations lay out legal and political arguments for the present administration's detainee policy.

Weisman, Jonathan, and Michael Abramowitz, "White House Shifts Tack on Tribunals," *The Washington Post*, July 20, 2006, p. A3.

Two reporters track the administration's re-embrace of a harder line concerning detainee treatment following the Supreme Court's *Hamdan* decision.

Reports and Studies

"JTF-GTMO [Joint Task Force-Guantánamo] Information on Detainees — Information From Guantánamo Detainees," Department of Defense, March 4, 2005.

Detainees have provided valuable information on matters ranging from terrorist support structures to bomb-making techniques to the identities of al Qaeda operatives, according to the Pentagon.

"Report on Torture and Cruel, Inhuman and Degrading Treatment of Prisoners at Guantánamo Bay, Cuba," Center for Constitutional Rights, July 2006.

The liberal group uses notes by lawyers for detainees, government documents, press accounts and other sources to depict what it views as a pattern of treatment that violates international treaties and U.S. law.

"Situation of detainees at Guantánamo Bay," Report of the Chairperson of the Working Group on Arbitrary Detention, United Nations, Feb. 15, 2006.

Legal and physical treatment of detainees violate international treaties that the United States has signed, the U.N. panel concluded.

Elsea, Jennifer, "Treatment of 'Battlefield Detainees' in the War on Terrorism," Congressional Research Service, Sept. 17, 2003.

The CRS dispassionately examines the controversy surrounding detainee treatment in light of history, recent litigation and options facing Congress.

Gardner, Nile, and James J. Carafano, "The UN's Guantánamo Folly: Why the United Nations Report is Not Credible," The Heritage Foundation, Feb. 27, 2006.

Conservative commentators argue that the U.N. report on detainees (above) is politically biased.

The Next Step:

Additional Articles from Current Periodicals

Detainee Lawsuits

The Associated Press, "Judge Allows Former Guantánamo Detainees to Pursue Lawsuit Over Alleged Violation of Religious Rights," *The Miami Herald*, May 10, 2006.

Four British citizens who were detained at Guantánamo Bay after the U.S. invasion of Afghanistan are suing U.S. military officials for violating their religious rights.

The Associated Press, "L.A. Man Detained in Iraq Sues U.S.," *The Washington Post*, July 9, 2006, p. A9.

An Iranian-American filmmaker who spent two months in a prison in Iraq without being charged is suing U.S. military officials for violating his civil rights.

The Associated Press, "National Briefing Washington: Request Granted in Detainee Case," *The New York Times*, July 28, 2006, p. A25.

A federal appeals court granted a Bush administration request for a rare fourth round of legal filings in lawsuits brought by detainees at Guantánamo Bay.

Barakat, Matthew, "Judge Dismisses Ex-Detainee's Suit Against CIA," *The Philadelphia Inquirer*, May 19, 2006, p. A8.

A federal judge dismissed a lawsuit by Khaled al-Masri, a German citizen who says the CIA wrongfully held him in Afghanistan.

Detainee Legislation

Cloud, David S., and Sheryl Gay Stolberg, "Rules Debated For Trials of Detainees," *The New York Times*, July 27, 2006, p. A20.

Bush administration officials are debating a draft bill that establishes new rules for bringing terror detainees to trial.

Hedges, Michael, "Bush Poised to Accept Two Curbs on His Authority," *The Houston Chronicle*, July 14, 2006, p. A1.

The White House reportedly has agreed that trials for detainees at Guantánamo Bay would continue under established military procedures instead of wartime "commissions."

Smith, R. Jeffrey, "On Prosecuting Detainees: Draft Bill Waives Due Process for Enemy Combatants," *The Washington Post*, July 28, 2006, p. A23.

A bill under consideration by the Bush administration would allow U.S. military personnel to impose the death penalty based on evidence never disclosed to the accused.

Smith, R. Jeffrey, "War Crimes Act Changes Would Reduce Threat of Prosecution," *The Washington Post*, Aug. 9, 2006, p. A1.

Political appointees, CIA officers and former military personnel could not be prosecuted for subjecting detainees to humiliating treatment under new amendments to a war-crimes law.

Spiegel, Peter, and Richard B. Schmitt, "New Plan is Proposed for Detainees," *Los Angeles Times*, Aug. 3, 2006, p. A15.

A new Bush administration plan for prosecuting accused terrorists would give detainees some additional legal rights but still allow the use of coerced confessions.

Interrogation Techniques

The Associated Press, "CIA Contractor Goes to Trial in Abuse Case," *The New York Times*, Aug. 8, 2006, p. A14.

Former CIA contract interrogator David Passaro is on trial for beating an Afghan farmer with a metal flashlight; Abdul Wali later died.

El-Magd, Nadia Abou, "Visiting Egypt, Gonzales Defends Prisoner Transfers," *St. Louis Post-Dispatch*, July 2, 2006, p. A5.

Attorney General Alberto Gonzales defended the transfer of terrorism suspects for incarceration and interrogation.

Schmitt, Eric, "Banned Tactic Used in Detainee Interrogations, Pentagon Says," *The Houston Chronicle*, June 17, 2006, p. A21.

U.S. Special Operations troops utilized unauthorized interrogation techniques against detainees in Iraq in early 2004.

Schmitt, Eric, "Pentagon Rethinking Manual With Interrogation Methods," *The New York Times*, June 14, 2006, p. A21.

The Pentagon is expected to drop a classified set of interrogation techniques from a new Army field manual.

Citing *CQ Researcher*

Sample formats for citing these reports in a bibliography include the ones listed below. Preferred styles and formats vary, so please check with your instructor or professor.

MLA Style

Jost, Kenneth. "Rethinking the Death Penalty." CQ Researcher 16 Nov. 2001: 945-68.

APA Style

Jost, K. (2001, November 16). Rethinking the death penalty. *CQ Researcher, 11*, 945-968.

Chicago Style

Jost, Kenneth. "Rethinking the Death Penalty." *CQ Researcher*, November 16, 2001, 945-968.

CQ Researcher

Published by CQ Press, a division of Congressional Quarterly Inc.

cqresearcher.com

Stem Cell Research

Is President Bush blocking important medical research?

President George W. Bush used his veto power for the first time on July 19, stopping a bill that would have increased federal funding for research on embryonic stem cells (ESCs). The cells might provide cures for diseases ranging from Alzheimer's to diabetes. ESCs are thought to have more disease-treating potential than similar cells found in adults, but they are controversial because harvesting them destroys a human embryo. The federal government supports research on several ESC cultures derived prior to 2001 from embryos created during in vitro fertilization (IVF) but not used. But the government won't pay to expand the research to other cell lines, which many scientists urge. Bush and other conservatives say morality forbids destroying additional embryos, regardless of the cells' treatment-producing potential. But ESC-research supporters argue the cells' life-saving potential outweighs qualms over destruction of IVF embryos, most of which eventually will be discarded.

Actor Christopher Reeve became a tireless crusader for increased funding for stem cell research after a riding accident in 1995 left him paralyzed from the neck down. He died in 2004.

INSIDE THIS REPORT

CQ Researcher • Sept. 1, 2006 • www.cqresearcher.com
Volume 16, Number 30 • Pages 697-720

CQ PRESS

RECIPIENT OF SOCIETY OF PROFESSIONAL JOURNALISTS AWARD FOR EXCELLENCE ◆ AMERICAN BAR ASSOCIATION SILVER GAVEL AWARD

STEM CELL RESEARCH

Cover photograph: Getty Images/Mark Wilson

CQ Researcher

Sept. 1, 2006
Volume 16, Number 30

MANAGING EDITOR: Thomas J. Colin

ASSISTANT MANAGING EDITOR: Kathy Koch

ASSOCIATE EDITOR: Kenneth Jost

STAFF WRITERS: Marcia Clemmitt, Peter Katel

CONTRIBUTING WRITERS: Rachel S. Cox, Sarah Glazer, Alan Greenblatt, Barbara Mantel, Patrick Marshall, Tom Price, Jennifer Weeks

DESIGN/PRODUCTION EDITOR: Olu B. Davis

ASSISTANT EDITOR: Melissa J. Hipolit

CQ PRESS

A Division of Congressional Quarterly Inc.

SENIOR VICE PRESIDENT/PUBLISHER: John A. Jenkins

DIRECTOR, LIBRARY PUBLISHING: Kathryn C. Suárez

DIRECTOR, EDITORIAL OPERATIONS: Ann Davies

CONGRESSIONAL QUARTERLY INC.

CHAIRMAN: Paul C. Tash

VICE CHAIRMAN: Andrew P. Corty

PRESIDENT/EDITOR IN CHIEF: Robert W. Merry

CQ Researcher (ISSN 1056-2036) is printed on acid-free paper. Published weekly, except March 24, July 7, July 14, Aug. 4, Aug. 11, Nov. 24, Dec. 22 and Dec. 29, by CQ Press, a division of Congressional Quarterly Inc. Annual full-service subscriptions for institutions start at $667. For pricing, call 1-800-834-9020, ext. 1906. To purchase a *CQ Researcher* report in print or electronic format (PDF), visit www.cqpress.com or call 866-427-7737. Single reports start at $15. Bulk purchase discounts and electronic-rights licensing are also available. Periodicals postage paid at Washington, D.C., and additional mailing offices. POSTMASTER: Send address changes to *CQ Researcher*, 1255 22nd St., N.W., Suite 400, Washington, DC 20037.

Stem Cell Research

BY MARCIA CLEMMITT

THE ISSUES

For the first time in his five-and-a-half years in office, President George W. Bush used his veto power on July 19, rejecting a bill Congress sent him on the grounds that it trespassed "a moral boundary that our decent society needs to respect." [1]

The Stem Cell Research Enhancement Act would have expanded federal funding for research on so-called embryonic stem cells (ESCs), which are derived from human embryos left over from in vitro fertilization (IVF) treatments. [2]

In August 2001, eight months after he first took office, Bush had restricted federal funding to ESC lines that had already been harvested from the embryos, despite biologists' insistence that ESC research is vital to understanding how humans develop and to curing or treating devastating degenerative illnesses like juvenile diabetes and Parkinson's disease.

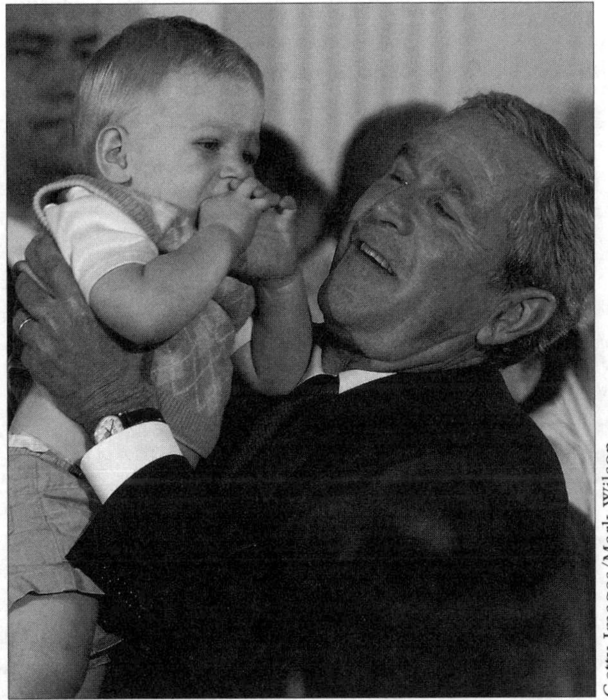

Getty Images/Mark Wilson

President Bush holds a "snowflake" baby during a July 19 ceremony for children born from unused frozen embryos that were given up for "adoption" by the couples who created them. Bush said he vetoed a bill calling for expanded funding for stem cell research because it would have supported "the taking of innocent human life in the hope of finding medical benefits for others." A majority of Americans say the potential benefits of such research outweigh the concerns.

But the use of donated frozen embryos — called blastocysts — for research outrages many conservative Christians. They say the embryos, which must be destroyed to harvest ESCs, have the same moral status as adult humans and must not be used in research to which they, obviously, cannot consent.

Bush explained his veto at a White House event highlighting a group of so-called snowflake kids, children born from unused IVF embryos that were given up for "adoption" by the couples that created them. The bill would have supported "the taking of innocent human life in the hope of finding medical benefits for others," Bush said. [3]

Named by the California-based Nightlight Christian Adoptions agency to highlight the uniqueness of each frozen embryo, the snowflake children also visited members of Congress this summer.

"Yesterday, Hannah Strege, the first known snowflake embryo adoption, told a small group of us, 'Don't kill the embryos, we are kids and we want to grow up, too,' " Rep. Chris Smith, R-N.J., said as he urged his colleagues to uphold Bush's veto. "How come a 7-year-old gets it and we don't?" [4]

According to California's Rand Corporation, 400,000 frozen blastocysts have been stored since the late 1970s, and the couples who created them are no longer likely to use them. [5]

Thus, say ESC-research supporters, conducting lifesaving medical research on ESCs harvested from the embryos is justified because the blastocysts are otherwise slated for eventual destruction.

Anti-abortion members of Congress disagree. "This last week, the 108th baby was born through . . . Operation Snowflake," said Sen. Tom Coburn, R-Okla., so suggesting that research or destruction are the only options is "a false choice." [6]

This summer, the House, which passed the vetoed legislation by a 238-194 margin in 2005, failed to muster the two-thirds majority vote needed to override the presidential veto.

The story did not end there, however. For one thing, some states are now putting up their own money to fund in-state ESC research. In November 2004, for example, California voters agreed to a $3-billion state investment in ESC research over 10 years. And on July 20, 2006, the day after Bush vetoed the federal funding expansion, California Gov. Arnold Schwarzenegger (R) added $150 million from state general funds to the ESC pot. *(See chart, p. 704.)*

Other states — including New Jersey, Wisconsin, New York and Illinois — also are actively building ESC research capacity.

Stem cell research is also moving forward abroad. In July, the European Union voted to allow EU funds to be used for ESC research. And along with Japan, Israel, Australia, Canada and several European nations, the burgeoning high-tech economies of Singapore, Taiwan, China and South Korea are quickly jumping into the game.

"Asia has never dominated [any field in] cutting-edge biology," said Chunhua Zhao, director of Beijing's

Support for Research Is Growing

Fifty-six percent of Americans believe the potential benefits of embryonic stem cell research outweigh concerns about the destruction of human embryos involved in the research, up from 43 percent in 2002. At the same time, the percentage who said they didn't know about the issue dropped by 7 percentage points, reflecting the growing interest and awareness in stem cell research.

Attitudes About Embryonic Stem Cell Research

It is more important to . . .

	March 2002	August 2004	December 2004
Conduct research	43%	52%	56%
Protect embryos	38	34	32
Don't know	19	14	12

Source: The Pew Research Center For The People & The Press, May 23, 2005; survey results are based on telephone interviews with a nationwide sample of 2,000 adults age 18 and older.

National Center for Stem Cell Research. "This could be our chance." [7]

State and national governments are drawn to ESCs both by medical promise and as a way to bolster their economies through biotech-industry development. ESCs — which can be used to form any of the more than 220 cell types in the human body — hold secrets to how life develops as well as the tantalizing promise of treatments that could change the face of medicine.

The ultimate in medical research would be "a disease in a dish," where degenerating cells themselves could be observed and treatments tested as a condition like Parkinson's develops, says Christopher Scott, executive director of the Program in Stem Cells and Society at Stanford University's Center for Biomedical Ethics.

"The ultimate treatment is to put somebody back to normal," says Alan Leshner, CEO of the American Association for the Advancement of Science (AAAS). In "any disease or injury where tissue is being depleted, or has been damaged or removed, you would like to put a bridge there and make it grow back." ESCs may work as such bridges, Leshner says.

Many scientists say current federal funding restrictions, along with the limited number of ESC lines available, are slowing development of important science and may also put the United States at risk of losing its premiere position in biomedical research.

As a result, only a few U.S. labs can conduct significant ESC studies, and such isolated efforts aren't enough to tackle the huge and highly significant field, cell biologists say.

"I'm a tenured professor at Harvard, where I have a president who backs my freedom of inquiry — and puts money behind it," said Douglas Melton, co-director of the Harvard Stem Cell Institute. "If I'd been at a [less well-funded] state college, it would have been a different story. . . . The bottom line here is that it's unlikely that one person or one lab will solve a problem as big as degenerative disease," he said. [8]

"It takes a community . . . to solve a big problem. If you were trying to solve cancer at [only] two places, no one would think that was enough," Melton said.

Some scientists also argue that scientists and private companies are more likely to bypass ethical, financial and scientific standards for gain without the National Institutes of Health (NIH) acting as a central arbiter of the research agenda.

For example, *Science* magazine reported last month on a private clinic, the Preventive Medicine Center, in Rotterdam, Netherlands, which advertises $23,000 treatments that the clinic claims can create "often spectacular" improvements for patients with incurable neurological diseases like Parkinson's and multiple sclerosis. [9]

Such reports suggest that without a strong federal infrastructure in the United States stem cell science could become a kind of medical Wild West, with doctors touting "cures" that aren't backed up by evidence, said stem cell pioneer Irving Weissman of Stanford University. Some clinics are "preying on desperate patients. . . . It's a horrible disservice" and may tarnish the field's reputation. [10]

But opponents argue that NIH has no business funding ESC research. As soon as an egg is fertilized, the resulting embryo deserves the full respect that's accorded to a child or adult, putting ESC research off-limits for an ethical society, they contend.

"Personally, I would not consent to having my body's resources exploited and my life ended in order to provide benefits to other people's bodies and lives," said David Gushee, professor of moral philosophy at the "Christ-centered" Union University in Jackson, Tenn. "At least, I would want to have the opportunity to make such a decision for myself [but] embryos . . . are not able to speak up for themselves." [11]

The argument that most frozen IVF embryos are slated to die anyway doesn't hold water, according to Gushee. "People on death row are going to die anyway. So why not experiment on them, even if those experiments involve killing them? After all, we might as well get some good use out of them. The same thing could be said for, say, millions of people with terminal illnesses, or in nursing homes in their very last days." [12]

Most opponents of ESC research take pains to say that they're not opposed to stem cell research generally. In fact, most tout what they say are treatment advances attained not with ESCs but through research on so-called adult stem cells (ASCs), which are found in infants' umbilical cord blood as well as throughout the bodies of all humans beyond the blastocyst stage.

The FDA has approved nine treatments developed using adult stem cells. But ASC supporters claim more than 60 treatments have proven effective although only small, unverified trials have been conducted using the treatments. "Adult stem cells have been shown to be safe. Adult stem cells have been shown to treat a whole host of conditions," said Rep. Dave Weldon, R-Fla. [13]

Meanwhile, public and congressional opinion continues to shift, apparently toward a more favorable view of ESC research, some analysts say.

"Even though President Bush was adamant about vetoing the bill, the fact that so many members of his party were willing to vote for it speaks volumes," says Joanne Carney, director of the AAAS' Center for Science, Technology and Congress. "I don't think you can take lightly" the fact that congressional support has grown, even among Republicans.

Sean Tipton, president of the Coalition for the Advancement of Medical Research and public-affairs administrator at the American Society for Reproductive Medicine, agrees that public sentiment is shifting in favor of ESC research.

Many Nations Permit ESC Research

More than 30 nations have explicit policies permitting at least some research into embryonic stem cells (ESCs).

Research Policies on Embryonic Stem Cells (ESC)
(As of mid-2006)

Permissive or Flexible Policy
Australia, Belgium, Brazil, Canada, China, Czech Republic, Denmark, Estonia, Finland, France, Greece, Hong Kong, Hungary, Iceland, India, Iran, Israel, Japan, Latvia, Netherlands, New Zealand, Russia, Singapore, Slovenia, South Africa, South Korea, Spain, Sweden, Switzerland, Taiwan, Thailand, United Kingdom
Tightly Restricted
Germany, Italy, United States
Banned
Austria, Ireland, Lithuania, Norway, Poland

Sources: Minnesota Biomedical and Bioscience Network, Aug. 28, 2006; The Century Foundation, 2006

Radio talk-show appearances to discuss ESC research in July 2006 and in August 2001 "were very, very different experiences," Tipton says. "People are understanding it more and are much more favorably disposed." In 2001, many listeners who called in vented anger about the research, but this year "we didn't get one hostile call" on Wisconsin Public Radio, Tipton says. "As bad as it got was, 'We wish we didn't have to destroy the embryos.' "

As scientists push for expanded funding for stem cell research and opponents cite their ethical concerns, here are some of the questions being discussed:

Is conducting medical research on unused embryos from fertility clinics immoral?

In the past year, Congress has debated whether the federal government should fund ESC research with excess IVF embryos.

Backers argue that the research is justified because of the potential for finding cures for diseases like diabetes and sickle-cell anemia. But several religious groups, including Catholics and some evangelical Christians, consider the blastocysts to have the same status as fully developed human beings and oppose the research on those grounds. Other denominations support ESC research. (*See sidebar, p. 705.*)

Embryos should be protected because they are "that which we all once were," said Kevin T. Fitzgerald, a Jesuit priest who is a bioethicist and professor of oncology at Georgetown University Medical School. [14]

Over the years, conservative lawmakers increasingly have expanded legal protections to earlier stages of human development, including a fertilized egg, or zygote. To many conservative Christians, that protection is a point of religious faith. "The fact that Jesus became a human being at the moment of conception reinforces that all stages of human life have inherent value," said Nancy Jones, an associate professor of pathology at Wake Forest University School of Medicine. [15]

Indeed, according to Gilbert Meilander, a professor of Christian ethics at Indiana's Valparaiso University and a member of President Bush's Council on Bioethics, advances in medicine are putting mankind in danger of forgetting potentially higher values. "So great is our modern concern to overcome suffering, we may almost forget that there are perspectives" — such as Stoic philosophy and some Christian theologies — that put other principles first, Meilander said. [16]

Using embryos that can't consent to research is equivalent to forcibly drafting any other human being to be an experimental research subject, he said. A military draft is sometimes needed "to save our society," he said. But "the fact that we do not ordinarily conscript" experimental subjects indicates that, however much we value research, we do not think of it as an "obligation" equivalent to national defense. [17]

"The vulnerability that ought to concern us most is not our own vulnerability to illness and suffering but, rather, the vulnerability of those whose very helplessness might make them seem all too readily available to us . . . in our never-ending struggle to make progress," Meilander said. [18]

Some argue that it's inappropriate to use tax dollars to fund research that a significant number of taxpayers oppose. "I believe it is morally wrong to take the tax dollars of millions of pro-life Americans, who believe that life is sacred, and use it to fund the destruction of human embryos for research," said Rep. Mike Pence, R-Ind., who voted to sustain Bush's veto. [19]

In July, a *USA Today*/Gallup poll found that 36 percent of Americans approved of Bush's veto of the ESC funding bill, and 61 percent said that he vetoed the legislation because of his personal moral beliefs, not politics. [20]

Supporters of expanding ESC funding dispute the idea that a blastocyst — even one that is not implanted in a woman's uterus — has the same ethical status as a further-developed human.

"An embryo in a dish is more like a set of instructions or blueprint for a house," said Arthur Caplan, professor of medical ethics at the University of Pennsylvania. "It can't build the house. For the cells to develop into a human being requires an interactive process in the uterus between the embryo and the mother." [21]

"If you were to leave that fertilized blastocyst in the petri dish and provide it with nutrients and go away for a trip to the beach, you won't come back and find your son or daughter in the petri dish," said Gary Pettett, a neonatologist at the Center for Practical Bioethics in Kansas City, Mo. "It will reach a stage where it will simply die." [22]

In 1994, a National Institutes of Health panel deemed ESC research permissible "because, although embryos deserve respect, they are not morally equivalent to human beings," according to policy analysts Jonathan Moreno and Sam Berger of the progressive Center for American Progress. [23]

The panel's conclusion: Rather than being an all-or-nothing proposition, full human status accrues to an embryo over time, as it develops more qualities that distinguish humans. "Arguing that . . . a collection of cells in a petri dish are morally equivalent to a living person or even a developing fetus, fails to recognize the emergent character of human life and personhood," Moreno and Berger say. [24]

Evidence exists that most people view early-stage embryos in at least slightly different terms, says Philip Nickel, an assistant professor of philosophy at the University of California at Irvine. For example, while it's well known that "many embryos are shed naturally, in very early abortions and miscarriages," no one makes an effort to save or grieve for them, as frequently happens with later-stage fetuses. This shows that "people do view embryos as somewhat different from people, even though they may not realize it," he says.

"Different religions take different views on it," says the AAAS' Leshner. "But what has happened recently is that people have realized that there are some 400,000" unused IVF embryos, many of which "will be discarded anyway.

"People have said, 'Wouldn't a better use be to take for research the ones that we aren't going to implant?' " he says. "I would rather save lives and not worry about angels on the head of a pin."

ESC research crosses a "particular ethical line" that "looms large only for a narrow segment of the population," *The New York Times* editorialized last year. "It is not deemed all that critical by most Americans or by most religious perspectives." Bush's determination to ban funding is "based on strong religious beliefs on the part of some conservative Christians." But, while "such convictions deserve respect . . . it is wrong to impose them on this pluralistic nation." [25]

"What we have before us is an opportunity to move forward on stem cell research with very strict ethical guidelines" by bringing it under the umbrella of federally funded research, said Sen. Richard Durbin, D-Ill. "We have a choice: Will we take these thousands of stem cells [and discard them] as waste and surplus . . . or use them in a laboratory to give a 12-year-old girl suffering from juvenile diabetes a chance for a normal, happy life?" [26]

Does research on adult stem cells hold as much promise as embryonic stem cell research?

Lawmakers who support Bush's veto argue that research on adult stem cells is not only the moral approach but also the more scientifically fruitful. ESC-research backers, however, say that most scientists believe that research on all kinds of stem cells is required.

ASCs "hold more promise for helping patients with diseases and injuries" than ESCs, said David Prentice, a senior fellow at the conservative Family Research Council and a former professor of life sciences at Indiana State University. "Their normal function is repair, and we're seeing more and more examples of their utility." [27]

According to Sen. Sam Brownback, R-Kan., "There are 72 clinical human trials using adult cord [blood stem cell] research," while ESC research has not reached the clinical trial stage. "Here is a gentleman I hosted at a hearing about Parkinson's disease," Brownback said, holding up a photograph. He had "adult stem cells put back in his . . . brain. . . . He was Parkinson's-free for five years. We had trouble getting him in to testify. He was out doing African safaris and things." [28]

Indeed, said Brownback, the 70th peer-reviewed study showing the medical effectiveness of ASCs was published in June. "I want you to see where we're seeing successes without bioethical questions," he said, pointing to an 18-year-old spinal-injury patient who said that feeling was restored to her hip after an ASC transplant. [29]

"During the past 30 years, there have been more than 50 clinical applications in humans of adult stem cells, primarily from blood and bone marrow," said Andrew Lustig, a professor of religion at Davidson College in North Carolina. "In addition, recent animal studies and several human clinical trials have achieved promising results in repairing damaged organs and in 'tweaking' specific types of adult stem cells into other sorts of tissue." [30]

But many scientists say that ESC opponents overstate the achievements of ASCs.

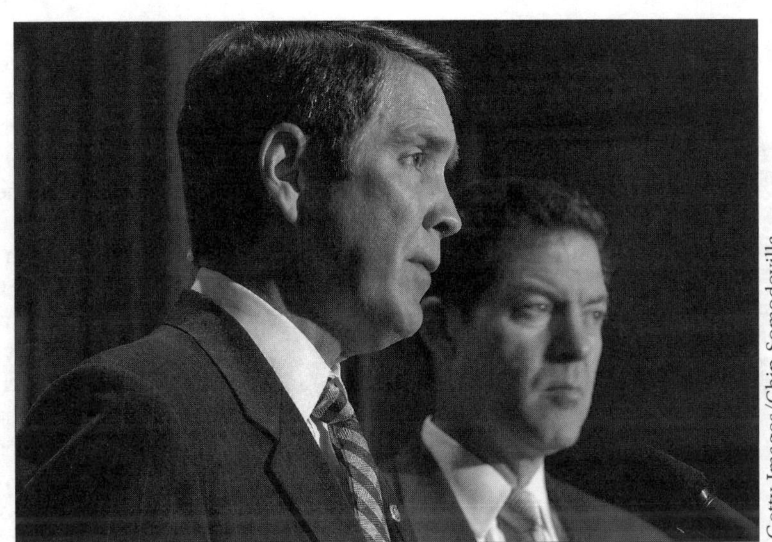

Getty Images/Chip Somodevilla

Senate Majority Leader Bill Frist, R-Tenn., left, supports the Stem Cell Research Enhancement Act (HR 810) while Sen. Sam Brownback, R-Kan., opposes it. Three years ago, Brownback proposed criminalizing embryonic stem cell research.

Some ASC-based treatments have been developed, but the cells remain very difficult to work with, says Scott of Stanford's Program in Stem Cells and Society. ASCs "have a bunch of problems," including being hard to keep alive in the lab, he says.

After ASCs are removed from a patient's body, they often must be propagated in tissue culture for long periods of time before transplantation back into the patient. That's "impractical from a clinical standpoint and can lead to potentially damaging changes" in the cells, said Mehmet C. Oz, a professor of surgery at Columbia University. Harvesting ASCs may "often require damage to the host organ, which is awkward if they are to be used clinically for regeneration of the same organ!" [31]

While most ASC advocates claim 65 or more proven ASC-derived treatments, the U.S. Food and Drug Administration has approved ASC treatments for only nine conditions, including anemia, according to Shane Smith of the Children's Neurobiological Solutions Foundation in Santa Barbara, Calif., William Neaves of the Stowers Institute for Medical Research in Kansas City, Mo., and Steven Teitelbaum, a professor of pathology and immunology at Washington University in St. Louis. [32]

Most ASC-related treatments "remain unproven and await validation," while some, "such as those for Parkinson's or spinal-cord injury, are simply untenable," wrote Smith, Neaves and Teitelbaum. They noted that a list of 60-plus therapies assembled by Prentice is not based on peer-reviewed scientific studies but on "various case reports, a meeting abstract, a newspaper article and anecdotal testimony before a congressional committee." [33]

"We really are limited in our ability to use adult cells," says William Brinkley, dean of the graduate school of biomedical sciences at Baylor College of Medicine in Houston. "People tend to overinterpret" very small-scale clinical results on ASCs, says Brinkley. "The tendency is to say, 'We think there's lots of potential.' But there's not much data." Data from most of the small trials cited by ASC supporters has never been verified by other labs.

Since ASC research began long before ESC studies and has had more funding, comparisons of the two aren't meaningful, according to Stanford's Scott. "ASC and ESC are on different time lines," Scott says. "ASC understanding has a 20-year history, beginning from bone marrow, and, as a result, science knows more about ASCs. ESCs only became part of the science in 1998."

"And in that time," he adds, "we've been doing it with one hand tied behind our back" because of federal funding restrictions. "That makes it kind of hard to compare them competitively."

States, Foundations Provide Research Funding

A growing number of foundations and states are providing funding for research on human embryonic stem cells (ESCs) in response to President Bush's July 19 veto of stem cell funding legislation.

Non-Federal Funders of ESC Research

State commitments	
California	$3 billion over 10 years
Connecticut	$100 million over 10 years
Illinois	$15 million
Maryland	$15 million this year, to start
New Jersey	$5 million
Wisconsin	$5 million to attract companies

Upcoming ballot issues	
Florida	2008
Missouri	2006
New Jersey	2006
New York	2006

Private Donations That Include Support for ESC Research

Donor	Amount	Recipient
Mayor Michael Bloomberg	$100 million	Johns Hopkins University
Starr Foundation	$50 million	Rockefeller U., Cornell U., Sloan Kettering Cancer Center
Broad Foundation	$25 million	U. of Southern California
Ray and Dagmar Dolby	$16 million	U. of California, San Francisco
Sue and William Goss	$10 million	U. of California, Irvine
Stowers Medical Institute	$10 million	Kevin Eggan, Chad Cowan, Harvard University
Leon D. Black	$10 million	Mount Sinai School of Medicine
Private individuals	Nearly $40 million	Harvard Stem Cell Institute

Source: The Century Foundation, 2006; Science, *July 28, 2006*

Research on both cell types is necessary because ASC and ESC research "inform each other extensively," says Melton, of the Harvard Stem Cell Institute. As a result, "the adult vs. embryonic distinction is not something that scientists think about very much."

"From a biologist's point of view, you can't separate them," Scott agrees. "What you discover today about adipose tissue" — fat, in which some versatile stem cells have been found — "may tell you something tomorrow about ESCs."

For example, scientists hope to learn enough about how ESCs turn into ASCs to be able to manipulate ASCs into regaining the potential they once had to produce any kind of tissue. In fact, a paper in the Aug. 25 issue of *Cell*, the bible of cell biology, claims that scientists at Japan's Kyoto University have accomplished just such a feat with mouse ASCs. [34]

The prospect excites scientists "since it reveals a roadmap by which ESCs might be obtained . . . without having to obtain them from embryos," said John Lough, a stem cell researcher at the Medical College of Wisconsin. "Ethical dilemmas would largely be defused," and cell-based treatments could be freely pursued. [35]

But finding the right genetic pathways to trigger an ASC-to-ESC conversion requires research on ESCs, not just ASCs, says Scott. "So if you can't work with embryonic cells, then you'll never get to the point where you don't need them."

The bottom line for many scientists is that only ESCs — called pluripotent because they are capable of developing into every type of body cell — offer a research window into the "earliest story of human development." In other words, only pluripotent cells can explain how an undifferentiated clump of cells develops into a complex organism, says Terry Devitt, a University of Wisconsin science writer who specializes in stem cells.

"When the history is written in 100 years, probably the most important upshot" of ESC research "will be what we learn about the very earliest stages of human development," Devitt says. "If you understand that, it may be possible to understand what happens when things go wrong and perhaps develop prevention strategies. That would be a much better way" to treat disease than techniques like cellular transplants.

Are Bush administration policies on ESC research crippling U.S. biomedical research?

Opponents of the Bush administration's limited ESC funding argue that the resulting lack of a federal infrastructure to support the research may cause long-term damage to American biomedicine. But ESC opponents argue that limiting the research ensures that science is used for ethical purposes only.

Far from crippling American biomedical research, Bush's veto strengthens the enterprise by maintaining its ethical core, said the Family Research Council's Prentice. "It's important to continue to hold the ethical line that no human life, at any age, should be used as raw material or be under the threat of government-sanctioned destruction," Prentice said. "My colleagues and I are

Religious Views Vary on Stem Cell Research

Polls indicate that a majority of Americans favor embryonic stem cell (ESC) research. However, 29 percent of Americans said they either "somewhat" or "strongly" oppose it, and 57 percent of the opponents based their opposition on religious principles, according to a 2005 poll by the pro-ESC research group Research America. [1] The following sampling reflects the wide range of religious views on the morality of ESC research:

Religious Groups That Generally Approve of ESC Research

- **United Methodist Church** — At its 2004 general conference, the church, of which President George W. Bush is a member, approved ESC research using excess embryos from in vitro fertilization (IVF). "Given the reality that most, if not all, these excess embryos will be discarded, we believe that it is morally tolerable to use existing embryos for stem cell research purposes. This position is a matter of weighing the danger of further eroding the respect due to potential life against the possible, therapeutic benefits that are hoped for from such research." [2]
- **Committee on Jewish Law and Standards of the United Synagogue of Conservative Judaism** — The committee in 2003 "overwhelmingly" approved ESC research. Research on cells from excess frozen IVF embryos slated for discard is permissible "for research into creating cures for a number of human ailments," and the synagogue should "publicly advocate" for use of the cells "in all appropriate ways," the group said. [3]
- **General Convention of the Episcopal Church** — A task force to the 2003 convention concluded that making research use of embryos that would otherwise be discarded is "in keeping with our call to heal the afflicted." [4]
- **Islam** — Among Muslims as among Christians, beliefs vary. Some Islamic groups and scholars support ESC research. For example, IVF is permissible in Islam as long as the embryo is implanted into the mother whose egg was used to create it, not a surrogate mother, wrote Muzammil Siddiqi, past president of the Islamic Society of North America. And, while an embryo outside the womb "has the potential to grow into a human being, it is not yet a human being," according to Muslim law, Siddiqi wrote. That being the case, "there is nothing wrong in doing this research, especially if the research has a potential to cure diseases," if the embryo used would otherwise simply be wasted. [5]

Religious Groups Opposed to ESC Research

- **Christian Coalition of America** — The conservative grassroots political group calls ESC studies "unethical research resulting in the killing of human embryos." [6]
- **U.S. Conference of Catholic Bishops** — It called the Clinton administration's 2000 decision to fund ESC research at the National Institutes of Health both immoral and illegal. It also criticized President George W. Bush's 2001 partial funding of ESC research on cell lines already in existence, calling it an "accommodation" of the "morally unacceptable" act of killing IVF embryos to obtain the cells. [7]
- **Southern Baptist Convention** — At its 2005 annual meeting, the convention declared that ESC research "currently requires the destruction of human embryos," and "it is never morally acceptable to prey on some humans to benefit others." [8]

---

[1] "Taking Our Pulse: The PARADE/Research! America Health Poll," Charlton Research Company, 2005.

[2] "Religions Have Sound Moral Reasons to Favor Expanded Funding for Embryonic Stem Cell Research," Religious Coalition for Reproductive Choice, www.rcrc.org/news/views/stemcells.cfm.

[3] "Stem Cell Research and Education," United Synagogue of Conservative Judaism, 2003, www.uscj.org.

[4] "Stem Cell Research: Religious Groups Weigh In," beliefnet, www.belief.net.

[5] Muzammil Siddiqi, "An Islamic Perspective on Stem Cell Research," Islam101, www.islam101.com.

[6] "Christian Coalition Urges Senate to Delay Embryonic Stem Cell Vote," press release, Christian Coalition of America, Aug. 22, 2005, www.cc.org.

[7] "Stem Cell Research: Religious Groups Weigh In," *op. cit.*

[8] Resolution No. 2: On Stem Cell Research, Southern Baptist Convention, Annual Meeting 2005, www.sbcannualmeeting.net.

pro-science, and that's why we want to see the ethical science flourish." [36]

Despite federal restrictions, ESC research thrives in the United States, said Rep. Roger Wicker, R-Miss. "Embryonic stem cell research is legal in America, and nothing in the administration's current policy affects that legality; 400 [ESC] lines are currently" used for studies "in the private sector and by the federal government." [37]

"It is false to suggest that medical breakthroughs come only through government research," said Wicker. "Private researchers discovered penicillin and the polio vaccine" and "conducted the first kidney and lung transplants . . . without federal dollars." [38]

The United States currently leads the world in ESC research, said Rep. Cliff Stearns, R-Fla. "A recent [issue of] *Nature* states that U.S. scientists contributed 46 percent of all stem cell publications since 1998. Germany comes in second, representing 10 percent of studies, and the remaining 44 percent derive from between 16 other countries." [39]

Even those who hope to expand federal funding note that current state efforts — undertaken to compensate for federal restrictions — are providing more ESC funds than NIH probably could, even without the Bush restrictions.

"The day after the veto, California put in $150 million," says Tipton of the American Society for Reproductive Medicine. "So in some ways it turned out to be a good thing."

And while the formerly large U.S. lead in ESC research publications is slipping, the situation is "not, Oh my God! The sky is falling!" says Harvard's Melton. "It's not the case that scientists are all calling their travel agents" to relocate in countries more hospitable to ESC research, he said.

Nevertheless, while the number of stem cell papers "is ever rising, the U.S. proportion is steadily declining," Melton says. "That's definitely a trend."

ESC papers with U.S. authors held "relatively constant at approximately 40 percent from 1999 to 2002," but "dropped to 30 percent in 2003 and remained at this lower level in 2004," according to a September 2005 study by Princeton University doctoral candidate Aaron Levine. [40]

And while the unprecedented rise in state biomedical funding — virtually all to support ESC research — is "better than nothing," there are "very good reasons" why research should remain a federal responsibility, says Tipton.

NIH "understands grant review," and there's widespread confidence that its funding generally goes to scientists best suited for the job, Tipton says. "With the states doing it, this little sliver of money will go to the best scientist in Illinois, for example. But what if the best scientist for that study is actually in Texas?"

Federal funding rules prohibit the use of federally subsidized equipment or employees in research on non-federally-approved cell lines. And Harvard, for example, "already has spent hundreds of thousands of dollars on lawyers and accountants" to make sure its records clearly demonstrate the university is abiding by that rule, says Melton.

One university lab even "has police tape down the middle to remind students and staff not to mingle equipment," says Stanford's Scott. Stanford itself is building an off-campus lab for non-federal funding. "That's really inefficient," he says.

State-by-state funding is raising new, time-consuming questions, since the new laws aren't necessarily clear, Melton says. For example, "we have already had confusing conversations with California" about whether California-funded personnel and lab materials can participate in research outside the state, at Harvard.

Clarity about how the overall stem cell research portfolio is progressing also will wane, says Tipton. "With NIH, everything goes in a peer-reviewed journal, and there's access to the list of who's doing what." But private foundations and companies funding research "have different incentives" for announcing findings or a new study, he says. For example, a foundation may tout a study in order to increase donations or a company may tout one "because it will help their stock price."

"What worries me most is the generational brain drain," says Tipton. "The lifeblood of an academic career is NIH funding. It leads to scientific status." If students find they can't get that funding to study ESCs, "they'll choose another field, where you don't have to fight all this."

If younger American scientists desert the ESC field, the United States could lose its technological edge in biomedicine to other countries, says Daniel Perry, executive director of the Alliance for Aging Research.

Will that matter? "Does it matter that we lost the semiconductor and computer industries to Japan, and now we buy their [electronics]?" he asks. Today, countries including Australia, France, Israel, and Singapore "are seeing a chance to steal a march on the United States for bragging rights and attracting venture capital" to ESC research, Perry says. ■

BACKGROUND

Cell Search

As much as a hundred years ago, doctors knew there was something special about bone marrow — the blood-making tissue found in the center of large bones. Physicians attempted to cure patients with anemia and leukemia by feeding them bone marrow. [41] The marrow-by-mouth treatment didn't work, but the physicians were onto something big: stem cells. [42]

Stem cells are very basic cells in humans and animals that when needed can renew themselves indefinitely and repeatedly produce at least one kind of highly specialized cell, such as a muscle, skin, blood, brain or intestinal cell.

Such regeneration occurs most vividly when a salamander grows a torn-off tail or a deer drops its antlers and grows a full new rack. But regeneration routinely occurs in humans, too, at least in some organs. For example, skin cells regenerate skin that has been wounded, and the human liver regenerates itself after part of it has been removed by surgery.

Of the two kinds of stem cells — embryonic and adult — ESCs are the more versatile, capable of becoming any of the more than 200 types of tissue that make up a human body.

A human's development begins with a single cell, or zygote, which forms after an egg is fertilized by a sperm. After about five days, the zygote develops into a ball of around 150 cells, called a blastocyst, a very early-stage embryo. So far as we know today, pluripotent cells are found only in the center of the blastocyst.

After ESCs differentiate into the many cell types that make up the fetus, most lose the power to become different kinds of cells. However, because cell systems like blood and skin need to be regenerated repeatedly, some cells with limited regenerating power — ASCs — remain. Found in all humans and animals that are past the blastocyst stage, ASCs come in many varieties and exist in organs throughout the body, such as the skin

Continued on p. 708

Chronology

1980s-1990s

Scientists deepen their understanding of embryonic and adult stem cells as political and public anxiety grows over medical research involving embryos and fetuses. In vitro fertilization (IVF) is launched in the United States as an unregulated business.

1981

Researchers isolate mouse embryonic stem cells (ESCs). . . . The first IVF clinics open in the United States.

1995

Primate ESCs from rhesus macaque monkeys are isolated. . . . Congress passes the Dickey amendment, banning federal funds for research involving creation or destruction of human embryos.

1996

U.S. IVF birth rate reaches 20,000.

1997

Dolly the sheep is cloned by scientists at the Roslin Institute in Edinburgh, Scotland.

1998

Scientists at the University of Wisconsin and Johns Hopkins University isolate human ESCs for the first time. . . . American scientist Richard Seed announces plans to open a human-cloning clinic, but his effort fails.

1999

President Bill Clinton's National Bioethics Advisory Commission recommends that federally funded scientists be allowed to extract cells for ESC research from embryos left over from IVF treatments but not create embryos expressly for research.

2000s

Stem cell research moves ahead around the world. Federal funding of ESC research is limited in the United States.

2000

Actor Michael J. Fox, who has Parkinson's disease, pleads for more U.S. funding of ESC research in a column in *The New York Times*. . . . Clinton administration announces that the National Institutes of Health (NIH) will not fund scientists to derive ESC cultures from embryos but will fund research on ESCs harvested with non-federal funds. . . . An expert panel advises the British government to allow cloning for research into medical treatments but not reproduction.

2001

Pro-life groups sue the U.S. government to stop ESC research funding. . . . Pope John Paul II and the conservative Christian group Focus on the Family condemn ESC research, but the United Church of Christ supports federal ESC funding. . . . After putting NIH funding for ESC research on hold, newly elected President George W. Bush announces that the federal government will fund studies only on ESC lines that already exist. Eventually, most of the 60-to-70 lines the administration says exist are found to be unavailable or unsuitable for research. . . . About 40,000 IVF babies are born in the United States.

2002

Former first lady Nancy Reagan supports ESC research, which she says might provide a cure for Alzheimer's disease. Her husband, former President Ronald Reagan, suffered from the disease.

2003

Analysts at the Rand Corporation report that as of 2002 about 400,000 unused embryos had been frozen and stored at U.S. IVF clinics since the late 1970s.

2004

New Jersey and California launch state ESC-research initiatives. . . . The world's first publicly funded stem cell "bank" for researchers opens in Britain. . . . South Korean scientists announce they cloned a human but admit a year later that the claim was based on faked data.

2005

House of Representatives passes legislation expanding federally funded ESC research to include cell lines newly derived from donated, leftover IVF embryos. . . . Connecticut, Illinois, New Jersey and Maryland join the list of states funding ESC research.

2006

Congress passes legislation to expand federal ESC-research funding, but President Bush vetoes the bill. . . . The Nightlight Christian Adoption agency says more than 100 babies have been born from leftover IVF embryos "adopted" by other couples. . . . California Gov. Arnold Schwarzenegger (R) pledges an additional $150 million for ESC research in the state. . . . The European Union votes to allow EU general research funds to pay for ESC studies. . . . Biologists claim to have developed a technique for establishing colonies of human embryonic stem cells from an early human embryo without destroying it. But critics immediately question the new method, reported by California-based Advanced Cell Technology on Aug. 23.

The Research Breakthrough That Wasn't

South Korean biologist Woo Suk Hwang became a sensation in the biotech world when he reported dramatic breakthroughs in stem cell research. But the hero had crashed to Earth by New Year's 2006, when a South Korean scientific panel declared that Hwang had falsified his data.

In a 2004 paper in the respected journal *Science*, Hwang reported producing the first stem cell line from a cloned human embryo. Then, in 2005, he reported the creation of 11 patient-specific human stem cell lines. Such lines are among the Holy Grails of stem cell science because — if and when stem cell therapies are developed — patient-specific cells could be transplanted into a patient's body to regenerate tissue without rejection by the immune system. Hwang claimed that his 11 lines matched patients with spinal-cord injury, diabetes and an immune-system disorder. [1]

But the triumph for South Korea's fledgling biotech efforts soon began unraveling. On June 1, a young scientist anonymously reported to investigative journalists at Seoul's Munhwa Broadcasting Corp. (MBC) that there were problems with Hwang's research, ranging from coercion of junior female scientists to donate eggs to the project to actual faking of data. [2]

Eventually, MBC reported the fraud allegations about Hwang, who was enjoying almost rock-star status. The report triggered a public outcry against MBC as well as a full-scale investigation by Seoul National University. On Dec. 29, 2005, university investigators announced they had found no evidence in Hwang's lab that any of the 11 cloned cell lines even existed. [3]

The finding sent shock waves through the international scientific community as well as through South Korea. In its rush to report Hwang's exciting firsts, had *Science* — published by the American Association for the Advancement of Science — and the peer reviewers who OK'd the paper overlooked evidence of fraud? Editor-in-chief Donald Kennedy insisted that the answer is no. "Peer review cannot detect [fraud] if it is artfully done." [4]

Nevertheless, a desire to rush hot, new discoveries into print before other scientists have a chance to reproduce them in their own labs contributed to the mess, said Katrina Kelner, *Science's* deputy managing editor for life sciences. "A culture that wanted to see things reproduced before making a big deal out of them would probably be a healthier culture." [5]

In its eagerness to become a stem cell powerhouse, the South Korean government and academic community skipped safeguards that might have kept a hot-dogging scientist like Hwang in check, said some analysts.

"For the Korean government, Hwang was sort of the short-cut [to the] biotech revolution," said University of Vienna stem cell expert Herbert Gottweis. "There was this desire to move ahead rapidly, and Hwang was supposed to be the person to pull this cart." [6]

High expectations created reluctance to rein in a scientist who promised results, said Jang Sung Ik, editor of *Environment and Life*, a Korean journal. "The government is most responsible," he said. "It gave people an impression that Hwang's technology was a goose that lays golden eggs." [7]

Continued from p. 706

and liver. Current science indicates that each ASC can develop into only a limited number of cell types.

More than 50 years ago, in the earliest therapeutic use of stem cells, scientists injected bone marrow into the bloodstreams of mice to cure them of blood-depleting illnesses like radiation sickness. At the time, no one knew that ASCs in the injected marrow created new blood. Instead, it was widely believed that some chemical in the marrow must spur blood to renew itself. A series of experiments during the 1950s eventually revealed the existence of hematopoietic — blood-making — ASCs in marrow.

Since then, knowledge of stem cells has advanced slowly, despite intense scientific interest.

According to Sean Morrison, associate professor of cell biology at the University of Michigan, scientists seek to find, grow and study ESCs and ASCs in tissue cultures for three main purposes:

- To determine if transplanted stem cells might replace cells damaged or destroyed by physical injury, such as to the spinal cord, and diseases, such as diabetes and Parkinson's.
- To gain insight into the way bodies develop and the ways in which development can go wrong when diseases such as cancer strike.
- To explore whether stem cell cultures of cells that bear the genetic stamp of certain diseases might be grown in the lab, where scientists could use them to test potential new treatments. [43]

Basic research on stem cells provides "the first window into the very earliest story of human development," says Wisconsin's Devitt.

Although news headlines occasionally tout stem cell advances as if major, new cures were on the doorstep, stem cell science actually is in its early infancy. Until very recently, the study of ASCs, for example, "was in the bird-watching phase," says Stanford's Scott. "If you could spot stem cells, it was a big deal, like a birdwatcher yelling, 'Hey, I saw a yellow flycatcher!' "

Scientists probably don't have anything like a full catalog of the body's ASCs. "They're damnably hard to find in the body" because they're scattered about among other cells, and "there aren't very many" in any one place, says Scott.

The result: Scientists have known

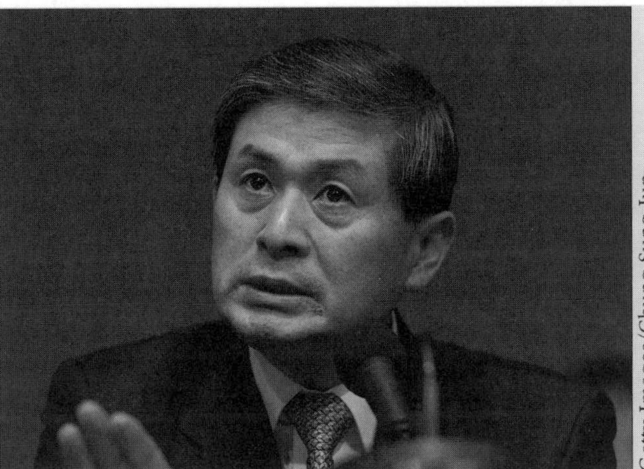
Getty Images/Chung Sung-Jun

South Korean stem cell scientist Woo Suk Hwang.

Stem cell scientists worry the Hwang debacle might further taint the image of their field among the public and lawmakers.

"It has to raise, in the public's mind, the question as to whether there's legitimacy to this kind of science," said Douglas Melton, director of the Stem Cell Institute at Harvard University. "Fortunately, stem cell research is not dependent on one discovery," and Hwang's claimed work was a technical accomplishment only, not a paradigm-changing scientific finding.[8]

"I'd like to tell you I suspected something; I didn't," said Melton, when asked whether he had been skeptical. "When his papers were published, I read them carefully. I was impressed by the speed and the efficiency with which he'd cloned a human embryo. We hadn't done those experiments ourselves. So I didn't know how difficult it would be. . . . I met Dr. Hwang . . . several times. He didn't seem nutty, squirrelly or deceptive or anything like that," Melton said.[9]

Hwang was fired from his job and in May 2006 was indicted for fraud, embezzlement and bioethics-law violations.[10] But his supporters in the public were reluctant to give up. On weekends throughout the spring, pro-Hwang rallies in downtown Seoul drew crowds numbering in the thousands. One man protested the university's fraud allegations against Hwang by burning himself to death.[11]

[1] Woo Suk Hwang, *et al.*, "Evidence of Pluripotent Human Embryonic Stem Cell Line Derived from a Cloned Blastocsyst," *Science*, March 12, 2004, p. 1669, retracted Jan. 12, 2006; Woo Suk Hwang, *et al.*, "Patient-Specific Embryonic Stem Cells Derived from Human SCNT Blastocysts," *Science*, June 17, 2005, p. 1777, retracted Jan. 12, 2006.

[2] Sei Chong and Dennis Normile, "How Young Korean Researchers Helped Unearth a Scandal," *Science*, Jan. 6, 2006, p. 22.

[3] *Ibid.*

[4] Quoted in Jennifer Couzin, "And How the Problems Eluded Peer Reviewers and Editors," *Science*, Jan. 6, 2006, p. 23.

[5] Quoted in *ibid.*

[6] Quoted in Choe Sang-Hun, "Lesson in South Korea: Stem Cells Aren't Cars or Chips," *International Herald Tribune*, Jan. 11, 2006.

[7] Quoted in *ibid.*

[8] Quoted in Claudia Dreifus, "At Harvard's Stem Cell Center, the Barriers Run Deep and Wide," *The New York Times*, Jan. 24, 2006.

[9] *Ibid.*

[10] Lee Hyo-sik, "Hwang Woo-suk Indicted for Fraud," *The Korea Times*, May 12, 2006, http://times.hankooki.com.

[11] "Hwang Love Persists," *Science*, April 14, 2006.

of ASCs' existence for decades, "but we still know very little about them," says Baylor's Brinkley.

As for ESCs, stem cells from a mouse blastocyst were first isolated and grown in the laboratory in 1981. Primate ESCs from rhesus monkeys were isolated in 1995. In 1998, scientists at the University of Wisconsin and Johns Hopkins University both isolated and grew human ESCs.

Today, science is learning ever more about ESCs and ASCs, with constant surprises along the way. For example, while ASCs in bone marrow were long believed capable of creating only new blood cells, "it now looks as if some cells in bone marrow may be able to make different" tissues, says Stephen Emerson, a professor of stem cell medicine and transplant immunology at the University of Pennsylvania. In fact, "most everywhere in the body" a few stem cells may lurk that are not as "tissue limited" as previously thought, he says.

ASCs also are playing a major role in unraveling the mysteries of cancer. For years, biologists puzzled over a "bizarre situation" — cancer frequently returned, even when doctors thought a therapy had destroyed all the cancerous cells, Emerson says.

Then biologists discovered that in any cancerous outbreak a handful of cancer cells pump out a particular protein that fights off chemotherapy treatments — and that the same protein pump exists in stem cells. "We now know that cancer is a disease of tissue-specific" — adult — "stem cells," says Emerson. "And it means we need to change our whole way of treatment."

Fetal Attraction

The potential of stem cells to unravel medical mysteries has long fascinated scientists, but it didn't catch the attention of policymakers and the public until 1998, when researchers first isolated human ESCs.

The excitement wasn't just about the biological advance, however. Lawmakers became involved because of where the ESCs came from. James Thomson, of the University of Wisconsin, isolated his ESCs from a blastocyst — an approximately six-day-old embryo — left over from an in vitro fertilization procedure.

Obtaining ESCs from donated, frozen, leftover embryos might not have raised much opposition if scientists had not also been exploring cloning technologies. Cloning is the process of

Couples Reluctant to Abandon Their Frozen Embryos

A majority of Americans favor conducting embryonic stem cell (ESC) research on cells harvested from donated, unused frozen embryos at in vitro fertilization (IVF) clinics.

But the question becomes more pressing for the couples whose unused embryos are being stored in IVF clinic freezers. Meanwhile, some ethicists argue that the virtually unregulated IVF business in the United States raises at least as many moral dilemmas as ESC research.

In 2003, analysts at the Rand Corp., a California think tank, estimated that as of 2002 nearly 400,000 IVF embryos — or blastocysts, fertilized eggs that have developed for six or fewer days — had been stored in IVF clinic freezers around the country. [1]

The IVF process often produces more embryos than a couple can use, and in the United States deciding what to do with the extra embryos is up to the couples who produced them. And with greater use of IVF technologies, the number of frozen embryos seems destined to grow. In 2003, for example, 123,000 IVF procedures were performed in the United States to help some of the estimated one-in-seven couples who have difficulty conceiving. [2]

Options for couples with unused frozen embryos include donating them to help other infertile couples have children; making them available for biomedical research, mainly for harvesting ESCs; or designating that they be discarded. But, according to the Rand analysts, most couples simply do nothing.

Of the 400,000 embryos frozen over two-plus decades, 88.2 percent were being held for family building, while 2.8 percent — 11,000 — were designated for research, 2.3 percent had been donated for other patients' fertility treatments and 2.2 percent designated to be discarded. About 4.5 percent of the embryos were being retained in storage because clinics had lost track of the couples or because death, divorce or abandonment had made it unclear who controlled the embryos. [3]

The produce-and-hold strategy most couples adopt for their embryos typifies a general, largely unspoken unease about these tiny byproducts of the IVF process, some analysts say.

Some ESC-research opponents argue that U.S. IVF clinics should more tightly control the number of embryos produced. European IVF clinics create fewer excess embryos, a pattern U.S. IVF doctors should follow, Sen. Tom Coburn, R-Okla., suggested in July. "We create about four times as many" embryos for fertility procedures "as the rest of the world," which is "overdoing" it, he said. [4]

In general, however, both anti-abortion and pro-choice forces keep mum on the subject of IVF.

IVF remains unregulated and, largely, undiscussed even by those most closely involved in it because it "touches two fatal third rails" in American life and politics, says Arthur Caplan, a professor of medical ethics at the University of Pennsylvania.

Pro-abortion people leave IVF alone because they don't want to interfere with their top principle — reproductive choice — says Caplan. Meanwhile, pro-life people are eager to promote family life and so are also reluctant to say "stop making embryos" or to "acknowledge that embryos die all the time for the purpose of making babies," Caplan says.

As the years wear on and more frozen embryos accumulate in IVF clinics, however, unease about their fate grows among fertility patients and clinic operators.

"I created these things, I feel a sense of responsibility for them," an IVF patient told *Mother Jones* magazine. "Describing herself as

---

creating a genetically identical copy of an existing organism by removing the nucleus of an egg cell and replacing it with a cell, such as a skin cell, from the organism to be duplicated. [44]

If it turns out that ESCs can provide actual tissues that can be transplanted to repair diseased or injured organs, a cloned human embryo could supply ESCs that would be an exact genetic match for the patient. ESCs from the clone would make the treatment work because, unlike ESCs from another donor, they would not be rejected by the patient's immune system.

But implementing such cures would require cloning embryos for the sole purpose of destroying them. That led conservative Christians to oppose embryonic stem cell studies as soon as the first human ESCs were isolated. Other critics also voiced concern that women might be coerced into donating the millions of human eggs that might be demanded for clone creation, if stem cell-based therapies proved to be effective.

Debate over ESC research takes place as a growing number of state and federal laws declare that "independent personhood" exists at earlier and earlier stages of development.

At least 36 state laws criminalize fetal homicide, and in at least 15 states fetal-homicide laws "apply to the earliest stages of pregnancy" — immediately after fertilization — according to the National Conference of State Legislatures. [45]

In Alabama, for example, legislation that took effect on July 1, 2006, designates full victim rights to "an unborn child in utero at any stage of development, regardless of viability," according to the National Right to Life Committee. [46]

In response to worries that scientists might clone human embryos for research purposes, Congress in 1996 passed the so-called Dickey Amendment, banning the use of federal funds for research involving creation or destruction of human embryos. [47]

Following the 1998 breakthrough that allowed scientists to grow stem cell cultures — derived from early-stage embryos — in the lab, the Clinton administration, backed by the science community, wanted NIH to fund ESC research.

In 1999, the U.S. Department of Health and Human Services (HHS) declared that, while the Dickey Amendment prohibited spending federal dollars

staunchly pro-choice, this patient found that she could not rest until she located a person — actually, two people — willing to bring her excess embryos to term," the magazine reports. [5]

In fact, "ambivalence" and "personal connection" seem to be the best descriptions of fertility patients' feelings toward the embryos they created. For instance, in one study, seven-out-of-eight couples who at the beginning of the IVF process planned to donate their embryos for research ultimately decided they would rather use them themselves or designate them to be thawed and destroyed. In the same study, "nearly all" the couples who initially planned to donate their embryos for use by another infertile couple later decided not to do so.

On the other hand, more than half the couples who originally said they'd discard their unused embryos also changed their minds, deciding instead to donate or use them. In total, 71 percent of couples changed their original decisions about how to handle the excess blastocysts. [6]

Several studies abroad suggest that giving up one's own genetically related embryos for use by other infertile couples is one of the hardest decisions.

In Denmark, where embryos may be stored for a couple's own use for only two years, 60 percent of surveyed couples with frozen embryos said they would donate them for research, but only 29 percent were willing to donate them to other infertile couples. [7]

In an Australian study, 18.8 percent of couples chose to discard their embryos, compared to only 5.9 percent who donated them to other couples. [8]

Unlike in most other countries, IVF is unregulated in the United States, and embryos can be stored indefinitely, sharpening the dilemma about what to do with them for clinic operators as well as patients.

Clinics are afraid to dispose of embryos on their own, even when they've been unable to contact the parents for years. "Nobody does it," said Alan DeCherney, a reproductive endocrinologist at the National Institutes of Health. [9]

"I have thousands of embryos from patients who have been through this program for . . . 10-, 12-plus years, changing addresses, never called back, never paid storage fees — you can't track them down," said Vicken Sahakian of the Pacific Fertility Center in Los Angeles. His "biggest nightmare" — trying to retire but being unable to sell his practice because "People do not want to inherit embryos. . . . I have embryos that have been here since 1992." [10]

[1] "How Many Frozen Human Embryos Are Available for Research," Research Brief, *RAND Law and Health*, 2003. The Rand estimate is the most current and most widely accepted.

[2] Liza Mundy, "Souls on Ice," *Mother Jones*, July/August 2006, pp. 39-45.

[3] *Ibid.*

[4] *Congressional Record*, Senate, July 17, 2006, p. S7583.

[5] Mundy, *op. cit.*

[6] *Ibid.*

[7] S. Bangboll, A. Pinborg, C. Yding Anderson, and A. Nyboe Andersen, "Patients' Attitudes Towards Donation of Surplus Cryopreserved Embryos for Treatment or Research," *Human Reproduction*, Aug. 13, 2004, http://humrep.oxfordjournals.org.

[8] Neroli Darlington and Phillip Matson, "The Fate of Cryopreserved Human Embryos Approaching Their Legal Limit of Storage," *Human Reproduction*, September 1999, http://humrep.oxforjournals.org.

[9] Quoted in Mundy, *op. cit.*

[10] Quoted in *ibid.*

to harvest ESCs from embryos, federally funded research could be conducted on cell lines that had been derived with other funds.

Limited Cell Lines

When President Bush took office in January 2001, the NIH had just begun to establish a research portfolio for ESCs, based on the 1999 HHS ruling, but the new president's conservative Christian base vehemently opposed that effort. Under heavy pressure from both sides of the ESC divide — and with federal funding on hold until a decision was announced — Bush eventually unveiled a plan that didn't fully satisfy either group.

On Aug. 9, 2001, Bush announced that NIH would begin funding ESC research, but only on stem cell lines that had been harvested and established before that date. After a quick international survey, the administration announced that about 66 lines worldwide met that criterion.

In the past five years, NIH has funded about $90 million in ESC research, a tiny segment of the agency's full research portfolio. [48] In fiscal 2003, for example, NIH spent less than one-tenth of 1 percent of its research budget on ESC studies — $25 million out of a total of around $28 billion. [49]

Part of the reason for the limited federal support is that, in the end, only about 20 ESC lines were available, not the 60-to-70 that the administration had estimated.

In addition, even some of those presidentially approved lines didn't pass muster with many researchers, says Harvard's Melton.

Nevertheless, "anyone who says that the presidential lines are useless is wrong," Melton says. "They are useful because they allow people to begin." Melton's lab is producing its own non-presidentially approved ESC lines, of which "a couple of thousand" batches have been sent out to scientists around the world, he says.

The administration's count was wrong because it "just asked people all over the world if they had" previously derived ESC lines, "and people said yes, even if they were just starting, or just intending" to grow the cultures, "even if they hadn't unthawed the embryos yet," Melton says. Many small players, such as biotech companies and labs in developing countries like India, promised lines "so they could say they were suppliers."

As a result, many of the presidentially approved lines have no descriptive information published in peer-reviewed journals, says Melton. "Do [the cells] have enough chromosomes? We don't know." Scientists are reluctant to pursue research on cell cultures "when they don't know what they are and whether they're good. And the way in which these were collected means we don't know that."

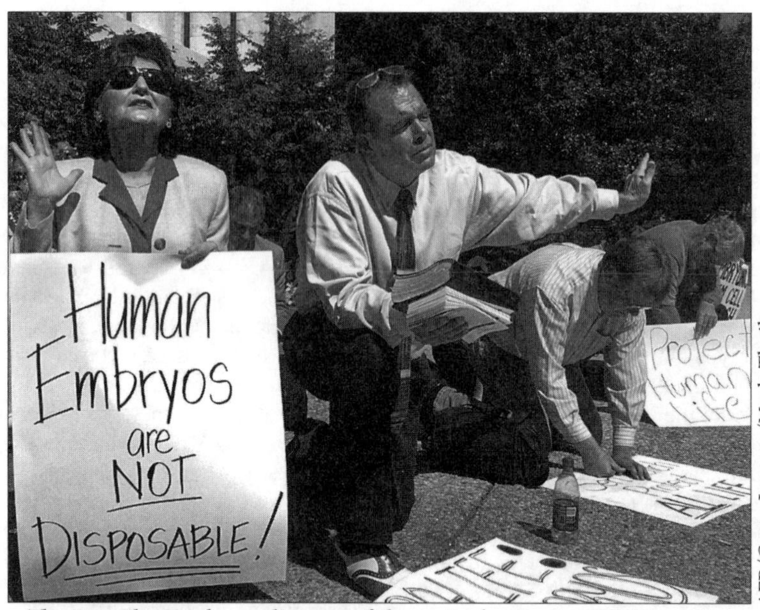

AFP/Getty Images/Mark Theiler

The Rev. Flip Benham, director of the anti-abortion group Operation Save America (formerly Operation Rescue) leads protesters on Capitol Hill against President George W. Bush's 2001 decision to allow some stem cell research, although he restricted federal funding to ESC lines that had already been harvested from the embryos.

Action by States

With most scientists agreeing with Melton that "there will always be more stem cell lines needed," some states have jumped into the ESC fray, announcing they'll fund in-state research on their own.

In May 2004, then-Gov. James McGreevey, D-N.J., was the first to respond, committing $9.5 million to create a new stem cell institute.

Then, in November, California voters approved a ballot proposition dedicating $3 billion in funding over 10 years to build and support an infrastructure for ESC studies. Other states, including Connecticut, Illinois, Massachusetts, New York, Maryland, Washington and Wisconsin, also have launched or are considering initiatives. [50]

States with strong traditions in academic medicine or with burgeoning biotech sectors are most likely to jump in. "Some states hope to benefit economically by encouraging the development of the stem cell equivalent of Silicon Valley within their borders," says Princeton's Levine.

The state efforts, if they persist, likely will direct more funding toward ESCs than NIH could, even if federal funding were not restricted. However, analysts say that supporting research involves more than funneling in dollars.

With state funding, "a lot of science will get done, but it won't be coordinated as well," says Leshner of AAAS. For example, "you won't have standard ethical regulations." And while the state approach is "very clever," it's still untried and involves "reproducing an infrastructure that we would prefer not to reproduce."

State money will be helpful, but NIH is a better venue for the research, says Perry, of the Alliance for Aging Research. "We would want this to be done with informed consent" — by embryo donors and clinical-trial patients — "and without financial incentives" that might taint reporting of results, he says. "NIH has the reputation for assuring that."

Anti-ESC groups have their own reasons for criticizing the state efforts.

California Gov. Arnold Schwarzenegger "is supposed to be a Republican, so I don't understand his thinking here," said Dana Cody, executive director of the Life Legal Defense Foundation. The millions in research funds that Schwarzenegger has promised are "coming out of the taxpayers' pocket for something that is questionable at best."

Besides state dollars, private donations also support ESC research at a handful of elite institutions, including Cornell University, the University of California and Mount Sinai School of Medicine in New York. Nearly $40 million in individual private grants back ESC research at Harvard's Stem Cell Institute. [51]

In one of the newest developments, some scientists and ethicists think they see a way out of the dilemma that pits potentially life-saving research against destruction of blastocysts: developing methods of obtaining ESCs without destroying embryos.

Interest is high in potential alternative methods to derive ESCs, but no method has yet been proven in the lab. Last year, the President's Council on Bioethics published a white paper outlining four ways that ESC-like cells might be derived without destroying embryos. One possibility involves deriving cells from blastocysts that are found to be "organismically dead," because they've lost the capacity for the integrated, continued cell division and

Continued on p. 714

At Issue:

Does embryonic stem cell research amount to murder?

SEN. SAM BROWNBACK, R-KAN.
EXCERPTED FROM THE CONGRESSIONAL RECORD, JUNE 29, 2006

yes

The differences over embryonic stem cells come down to the basic view of the youngest of human life. I view human life as sacred at all of its stages and all of its places. Period. It is unique. It is beautiful, it is a child of the living God. It deserves our respect and protection under law at the very earliest stages of life.

We can try to divide it under law. We can say it is property at this stage of life; it is not worth living at that stage. All of those, I think, are false distinctions. Life is sacred, period, because it is human. That is the point of view from which I think a lot of Americans come.

In our jurisprudence system, they are either a person or a piece of property.

What is the youngest of human life? Is it person or property? We have had this debate before in this country. We have looked at it; we have drawn distinctions. At points in time, even in our Constitution, we have said a person was only three-fifths of a person, and yet we knew at that time: How can you be three-fifths of a person? That didn't stand the test of time and reason then, and it doesn't stand the test in this country now.

Some will say that the youngest of human life is property and at some point in development it becomes a person. Yet in our jurisprudence system, we don't recognize the transition that goes from property to personhood, and if, so, where would you draw that line? When would it happen?

The biology is quite clear on this point. If you start out a person, you end up a person. If you start out a human being, you don't become a plant. If you start out a human being, you don't become a desk. If you start out a human, you end up a human.

The biology on this is clear. If you are a human embryo and you are given nurture, you end up, by anybody's definition, a full-scale human being.

At one time, we have all started out as an embryo. Whether you are Sam Brownback or anybody else in this room, we all started out being a human embryo. If you destroy us at the earliest stage, you never end up with us at this stage.

SEN. BYRON DORGAN, D-N.D.
EXCERPTED FROM THE CONGRESSIONAL RECORD, JULY 10, 2006

no

It has been just over one year now since the U.S. House of Representatives passed legislation called the Stem Cell Research Enhancement Act, with very broad bipartisan support.

Those of us in the Senate and those across this country who have lost loved ones to some dread disease — Alzheimer's, Parkinson's, heart disease, diabetes — understand that the urgency to do the research to find the cures for these diseases really must be pre-eminent. So many in this country are very concerned that we move forward on stem cell research and try to find ways to unlock the mysteries of juvenile diabetes, ALS [amyotrophic lateral sclerosis], Parkinson's, Alzheimer's and so many more.

There are now more than 1 million people living among us who were born as a result of in vitro fertilization. At IVF clinics, more eggs are fertilized than are actually implanted and used. There are roughly 400,000 embryos that are now cryogenically frozen at these clinics. Somewhere between 8,000 and 10,000 each year are simply discarded.

Those who say that the use of those embryos for research is the equivalent of murder, I believe also probably say the same of the discarding of embryos that are not going to be used — that it represents 8,000 or 10,000 murders a year.

I don't believe that. Those embryos can never and will never become a human being, unless implanted into a uterus.

The question is: Can we use these embryos to create stem cell lines to try to find cures to dread diseases?

I believe that we ought to proceed with thoughtful, ethical guidelines on stem cell research. I understand that is a controversial position for some. In fact, in the last campaign for office for me, my opponent ran a television advertisement. In it was a fellow who was sitting around a campfire with some children. One of the children said: Tell us a scary story.

And the campfire leader said: Well, there is a man named Dorgan who has a plan to put embryos inside the womb of a mother and grow them for body parts to be harvested later.

I am mindful that there should be solid ethical guidelines for the research. But I don't believe this is about harvesting body parts. This is about giving life. This is about giving hope. It is about giving life, providing opportunity for those who are suffering from dread diseases.

Continued from p. 712

differentiation needed to produce a viable fetus. [52]

Another suggested method — altered nuclear transfer, or ANT — would be a twist on cloning. An unfertilized egg cell would be implanted with DNA that lacks a few of the elements needed to develop into a full organism.

But analysts who object to ESC research are generally skeptical that alternate methods would withstand their ethical objections either.

ANT, for example, would deliberately create an embryo that develops normally to a certain point but which scientists would deliberately prevent "from developing fully." Deliberately creating such a stunted embryo is itself an unallowable act, said Assistant Professor of Theology Jose Granados of Catholic University and Malcolm Byrnes, a biochemistry professor at Howard University College of Medicine. [53]

On Aug. 23, 2006, the Massachusetts biotech company Advanced Cell Technologies announced that it had created an ESC line from only one cell removed from an embryo, a process that the company argues would bypass ethical objections because it allows the original embryos to survive. The method hasn't yet been verified by another lab, however. And some ESC opponents argue that it may not pass their ethics test because it is possible that the single removed cell could itself develop into a complete human being, making non-consensual research on the cell immoral. [54] ■

CURRENT SITUATION

Shift in Congress

Many members of Congress, including Republicans, have warmed up to federally funded ESC research, perhaps in response to appeals from groups such as the Christopher Reeve Foundation, which advocates for research on spinal injury, and juvenile diabetes and Parkinson's disease groups.

"There's been a very slow, deliberate change in the House and the Senate," says Stanford's Scott. "Three years ago, Sen. Brownback proposed criminalizing the research, and that bill won big in the House and got 47 votes in the Senate," Scott says.

By May 2005, however, Congress had passed legislation to expand federal funding to include research on any ESCs that were derived from donated, leftover IVF embryos. The Stem Cell Research Enhancement Act of 2005 (HR 810), sponsored by Reps. Michael Castle, R-Del., and Diane DeGette, D-Colo., passed on nearly "the same vote as the Brownback bill, but in the opposite direction," Scott says.

The change "is a good example of how public discourse has moved the debate," says Caplan of the University of Pennsylvania. "Even to a conservative Congress, the groups that have really mattered are the patient groups. They backed off the pro-life forces."

After the House passed HR 810, Senate Majority Leader Bill Frist, R-Tenn., promised to bring the bill to a vote in the Senate. But after trying to craft a more limited measure, Frist, who had previously opposed federal funding, unexpectedly announced in July 2005 that he supported the bill.

"I personally believe human life begins at conception," said Frist, a heart-lung transplant surgeon who is considering a run for the presidency in 2008. "But it isn't just about faith; it's a matter of science." [55]

In late June 2006, Frist introduced HR 810 and two other stem cell bills for Senate consideration.

Congressional Republican leaders intended to pass and send to Bush all three bills: HR 810 and two others — one supporting research into methods of obtaining ESCs without destroying embryos and one outlawing "fetal farms," where human embryos would be created for the purpose of harvesting tissue for transplant.

The idea was to give the president a "safe haven" to signal his support for research by signing the stem cell alternative bill, says Carney, of the AAAS Center for Science, Technology and Congress. Then, Bush could maintain his pro-life credentials by vetoing the funding-expansion bill and signing the bill outlawing fetal farming.

The Senate quickly passed all three bills. But the leadership plan went awry when the House failed to pass the alternative-methods bill. So in the end, Bush was only able to sign the bill outlawing fetal farming and veto the funding-expansion measure.

With ESC research growing in popularity among voters, GOP House leaders facing a potentially tough election this November scheduled a vote on overriding Bush's veto, but it came 51 votes short of passage, and the funding restrictions stand.

Supporters of the legislation to expand funding of ESC research argue that President Bush is denying hope to people with degenerative diseases like Parkinson's and juvenile diabetes. Bush is "putting himself in the company of people . . . who told Galileo it was heresy to claim that the Earth revolved around the sun," said Sen. Tom Harkin, D-Iowa. [56]

Cell Cultures

While the United States and a few other countries deny federal funding to most ESC research, many other nations support it, although not without controversy.

In 1997, the Council of Europe adopted a Convention on Biomedicine and Human Rights, allowing ESC research but banning procedures such as the creation of embryos for research purposes. By 2006, 32 of the Council's 46 members had signed the treaty. [57]

Individual nations have taken a variety of stances toward ESCs. Austria, Ireland, Lithuania and Poland have banned the research outright. But many countries, including Australia, Brazil, Canada, Denmark, Finland, France and Spain allow research using unused IVF embryos.

After contentious debate, the European Union (EU) on July 24 agreed to allow money from EU's general research budget to fund ESC research on unused IVF embryos. Several predominantly Catholic countries, including Malta, Lithuania, Poland and Slovakia, had loudly opposed the plan. It won the day, however, when Italy, Slovenia and Germany agreed to support the proposal after first opposing it. [58]

Germany has particular qualms about ESC research, based on its history of Nazi genetic experiments conducted on non-consenting subjects. "The protection of human dignity, the right to life, needs to be properly entrenched," said Germany's research minister, Annette Schavan. "There should be no financial incentives for the destruction and killing of embryos." [59]

Countries that support ESC studies argued that scientific progress demands the research. "It is morally unacceptable to withhold these advances from patients, because it offers potentially tremendous advantages to European citizens," said British science minister David Sainsbury. [60]

Since most research in Europe is paid for by individual countries, however, and not by the EU, it's not clear that the EU funding will do much to drive the research forward.

Meanwhile, many Asian nations, including traditional scientific powerhouse Japan and newcomers like South Korea, Singapore, Taiwan and China, are pushing ESC studies. China, for example, has about 30 stem cell research teams, and the number continues to grow. [61]

Unlike in the United States and Europe, research regulations are looser in some Asian countries, such as China. And some U.S. scientists are noticing: A growing number of foreign-trained Chinese scientists are leaving U.S. and European jobs to work in China. [62]

"Most major teams" in Chinese ESC research now have U.S.- or European-trained scientists in senior roles, said Sheng Hui Zhen, an ESC researcher at Shanghai Second Medical University. Sheng, who spent 11 years at NIH before going to Shanghai in 1999, leads a 50-person team hoping to create human ESCs by inserting the nuclei from human skin cells into rabbit eggs. [63]

That research program would be banned in many countries, including the United States, because it raises the specter of creating chimera — human-animal hybrids. But Sheng said the project's aim is only to create human ESCs without the need to create and destroy human embryos.

"My Chinese lab does not have everything my NIH lab had," said Sheng. "But here I can work on this important problem, and there I couldn't." [64] ■

OUTLOOK

Long Road Ahead

Stem cells are a political issue and could figure in November's mid-term elections.

"I've heard from candidates for sheriff, quite literally, who say that they're interested and that, 'It'll do well for me politically if I can be associated with it,' " says Tipton of the Coalition for the Advancement of Medical Research.

Nevertheless, with other hot issues like the Iraq war predominating, stem cell research "won't play a major role across the board in the next election," says the University of Pennsylvania's Caplan. "But in parts of the country where biotech is part of the economy" — such as Missouri and Wisconsin — "or places where being pro- or anti-science counts, like Massachusetts, Connecticut and Florida, it will be an issue."

Despite occasional newspaper-headline hype suggesting that patient-specific stem cell treatments or "organ farming" are right around the corner, stem cell science is in its infancy, with such developments decades down the road, biologists say.

There will be "major advances over the next few years" stemming from our new understanding that ASCs are the root of cancers, says Emerson of the University of Pennsylvania.

When it comes to ASC-based therapies for other conditions, however, "it's very early. Bone-marrow stem cells are the only ones that have worked" so far, he says.

If ESC research restrictions are removed, biologists say that studies would profit from having as many lines as possible available. As long as creation of those lines depends on donation of unused IVF embryos, however, the number would be limited. For example, about 11,000 unused IVF blastocysts have been designated as available for research by the couples who created them, but only about 275 ESC lines, at most, could be created from those embryos, given the trickiness of the process.

Today, we still don't know many basic facts about ESCs, says Emerson. For example, "we don't yet know how to make single tissues" out of ESC cultures but can only coax a culture to develop into several different kinds of cells, perhaps with one type predominating.

Nevertheless, "I'm optimistic that, within a decade, if you call me up and say, 'I need toenail cells, heart cells, I can give them to you," says Harvard's Melton. "But not today."

The bottom line: "We're years away from going into human clinical trials of ESC-based therapies," says Melton.

The first practical application to emerge from ESC research will be far less glamorous-sounding, say cell researchers. ESC cultures will provide a new way to conduct so-called "high throughput" drug screening — quick, accurate testing of many new drug candidates on the exact cells that the drugs are intended to affect, something that's not possible today.

When scientists learn to securely direct development of a cell culture, they can develop a "disease in a dish" — a cell culture that, for example, includes only the brain cells that become defective when Parkinson's disease prevents a patient from producing required amounts of dopamine, says Melton.

Such disease-in-a-dish cultures will bypass much of the animal testing and clinical testing in humans that's done on drugs today, thus eliminating risk to those research subjects and targeting the trial more precisely on the exact cells that drug developers hope to treat.

"These would be drugs that would slow the generation of defective cells," not the tissue-based total cures that are sometimes hyped, but they are still very important drugs, says Melton. ■

Notes

[1] Susan Ferrechio and Elizabeth B. Crowley, "Bush Cites 'Decent Society' in Vetoing Bill Broadly Supported by Congress," *CQ Today*, July 19, 2006.

[2] For background, see Adriel Bettelheim, "Embryo Research," *CQ Researcher*, Dec. 17, 1999, pp. 1065-1088.

[3] Quoted in *ibid.*

[4] *Congressional Record*, House, July 19, 2006, p. H5444.

[5] "How Many Frozen Human Embryos Are Available for Research?" Research Brief, *RAND Law and Health*, 2003.

[6] *Congressional Record*, Senate, July 17, 2006, p. S7583.

[7] Quoted in Dennis Normile and Charles C. Mann, "Asia Jockeys for Stem Cell Lead," *Science*, Feb. 4, 2005, p. 660.

[8] Quoted in Claudia Dreifus, "At Harvard's Stem Cell Center, the Barriers Run Deep and Wide," *The New York Times*, Jan. 24, 2006.

[9] Martin Enserink, "Selling the Stem Cell Dream," *Science*, July 14, 2006, p. 160.

[10] Quoted in *ibid.*

[11] David P. Gushee, "The Stem Cell Veto," The Center for Bioethics and Dignity, July 20, 2006, www.cbhd.org.

[12] *Ibid.*

[13] *Congressional Record*, House, July 13, 2006, p. H5218.

[14] "An Interview with Kevin T. Fitzgerald," *Student Pugwash USA*, www.spusa.org.

[15] Nancy L. Jones, "The Stem Cell Debate: Are Parthenogenic Human Embryos a Solution?" Center for Bioethics and Human Dignity, June 2, 2003, www.cbhd.org.

[16] Gilbert Meilander, "Bioethics and Human Nature: Exploring Some Background Issues," Pew Forum on Religion and Public Life, Dec. 7, 2004, http://pewforum.org.

[17] *Ibid.*

[18] *Ibid.*

[19] Quoted in "Pence Applauds Bush Veto, Votes to Sustain," press release, office of Rep. Mike Pence, July 19, 2006, http://mikepence.house.gov.

[20] *USA Today*/Gallup national poll of 1,005 adults, July 21-23, 2006, www.pollingreport.com.

[21] Quoted in Patricia Schudy, "An Embryo by Any Other Name: The Battle Over Stem Cell Research Begins With Language," *National Catholic Reporter*, Aug. 26, 2005.

[22] Quoted in *ibid.*

[23] Jonathan Moreno and Sam Berger, "Taking Stem Cells Seriously," *American Journal of Bioethics*, May-June 2006, http://ajobonline.com.

[24] *Ibid.*

[25] "The President's Stem Cell Theology," editorial, *The New York Times*, May 26, 2005.

[26] *Congressional Record*, Senate, July 18, 2006, p. S7654.

[27] Quoted in "Ethical Alternatives Q & A" *National Review Online*, July 19, 2006, http://article.nationalreview.com.

[28] *Congressional Record*, Senate, July 17, 2006, pp. S7592, S5793.

[29] Quoted in John Reichard, "Stem Cell Wars: Of Mice and Men," *CQ Healthbeat*, June 20, 2006.

[30] Andrew Lustig, "Cloning for Dollars: Morality and the Market for Stem Cells," *Commonweal*, June 17, 2005.

[31] Mehmet C. Oz, "Demystifying Stem Cells," *Saturday Evening Post*, November-December 2004.

[32] Shane Smith, William Neaves and Steven Teitelbaum, "Adult Stem Cell Treatments for Diseases?" letter to the editor, *Science*, July 28, 2006, p. 439.

[33] *Ibid.*

[34] Kazutoshi Takahashi and Shinya Yamanaka, "Induction of Pluripotent Stem Cells from Mouse Embryonic and Adult Fibroblast Cultures by Defined Factors," *Cell*, Aug. 25, 2006, p. 1.

[35] "Stem Cell Work Could Heal Ethical Rift," *Milwaukee Journal Sentinel*, Aug. 11, 2006, www.jsonline.com.

[36] "Ethical Alternatives Q & A," *op. cit.*

[37] *Congressional Record*, July 19, 2006, *op. cit.*, H5437.

[38] *Ibid.*

[39] *Ibid*, p. H5448.

[40] Aaron Levine, "Trends in the Geographic Distribution of Human Embryonic Stem-Research," *Politics and the Life Sciences*, Sept. 14, 2005, p. 41.

[41] "History of Marrow and Blood Cell Transplants," National Marrow Donor Program, www.marrow.org/NMDP/history_of_transplants.html.

[42] For background, see Ann B. Parson, *The*

About the Author

Staff writer **Marcia Clemmitt** is a veteran social-policy reporter who previously served as editor in chief of *Medicine and Health* and staff writer for *The Scientist*. She has also been a high-school math and physics teacher. She holds a liberal arts and sciences degree from St. John's College, Annapolis, and a master's degree in English from Georgetown University. Her recent reports include "Climate Change," "Controlling the Internet," "Pork Barrel Politics" and "Cyber Socializing."

Proteus Effect: Stem Cells and Their Promise (2006) and "Stem Cell Information," National Institutes of Health, http://stemcells.nih.gov.

43 Sean J. Morrison, written testimony, Ad Hoc Congressional Hearing on Stem Cell Research, May 16, 2005, www.lifesciences.umich.edu/research/featured/sjmtestimony.pdf.

44 For background, see Brian Hansen, "Cloning Debate," *CQ Researcher*, Oct. 22, 2004, pp. 877-900.

45 "Fetal Homicide," National Conference of State Legislatures, June 2006, www.ncsl.org/programs/health/fethom.htm.

46 "State Homicide Laws That Recognize Unborn Victims," National Right to Life Committee, June 16, 2006, www.nrlc.org.

47 For background, see "Stem Cells and Public Policy," Century Foundation, 2006.

48 Jodi Rudoren, "Stem Cell Work Gets States' Aid After Bush Veto," *The New York Times*, July 25, 2006.

49 "Fact Sheet on Embryonic Stem Cell Research," U.S. Department of Health and Human Services, July 14, 2004.

50 Aaron Levine, "The Rise of State-Sponsored Stem Cell Research in the United States," unpublished paper, 2006. The author is a doctoral student at Princeton University.

51 "States, Foundations Lead the Way After Bush Vetoes Stem Cell Bill," *Science*, July 28, 2006, p. 420.

52 Bonnie Steinbrook, "Alternative Sources of Stem Cells," *The Hastings Center Report*, winter 2005, p. 24.

53 John Reichard, "Split Among Abortion Rights Foes Over Santorum-Specter Stem Cell Bill?" *CQ Healthbeat*, June 19, 2006.

54 Gareth Cook, "Stem Cell Method Preserves Embryo," *The Boston Globe*, Aug. 24, 2006.

55 Quoted in Kate Schuler, "Senate Deal Clears Way for Debate on Three Stem Cell Measures," *CQ Weekly*, July 10, 2006, p. 1904.

56 "Statement of Senator Tom Harkin on the President's Veto of HR 810," press release, July 19, 2006, http://harkin.senate.gov.

57 For background, see "Stem Cells and Public Policy," *op. cit.*

58 For background, see Dan Bilefsky, "EU to Fund Stem Cells," *International Herald Tribune*, July 25, 2006.

59 Quoted in *ibid.*

60 Quoted in *ibid.*

61 Normile and Mann, *op. cit.*

62 *Ibid.*

63 Quoted in *ibid.*

64 *Ibid.*

FOR MORE INFORMATION

Alliance for Aging Research, 2021 K St., N.W., Suite 305, Washington, DC 20006; (202) 293-2856; www.agingresearch.org. Promotes research into the aging process, including medical research on stem cells.

American Society for Cell Biology, 8120 Woodmont Ave., Suite 750, Bethesda, MD 20814-2762; (301) 347-9300; www.ascb.org. Provides information and education about stem cell science.

American Society for Reproductive Medicine, 1209 Montgomery Highway, Birmingham, AL 35216-2809; (205) 978-5000; www.asrm.org. Provides information on issues including in vitro fertilization and stem cell science.

Bedford Stem Cell Research Foundation, P.O. Box 1028, Bedford, MA 01730; (617) 623-5670; www.bedfordresearch.org. Conducts biomedical research in fields that supporters believe are insufficiently supported by the federal government, such as stem cells.

California Institute for Regenerative Medicine, www.cirm.ca.gov. A new California state agency that will make grants and provide loans for stem cell research.

Center for Bioethics and Human Dignity, 2065 Half Day Road, Bannockburn, IL 60015; (847) 317-8180; www.cbhd.org. Provides information and education about Christian perspectives on biomedical issues including stem cells.

Center for Genetics and Society, 436 14th St., Suite 700, Oakland, CA 94612, (510) 625-0819; http://genetics-and-society.org/. Advocates for the responsible use of new biomedical knowledge and technologies, opposing applications that members believe would objectify human beings.

Christopher Reeve Foundation, 636 Morris Turnpike Suite 3A, Short Hills, NJ 07078; (800) 225-0292; www.christopherreeve.org. Advocates for stem cell research and other efforts to cure spinal-cord injuries.

Coalition for the Advancement of Medical Research, 2021 K St., N.W., Suite 305, Washington, DC 20006; (202) 293-2856; www.stemcellfunding.org. Advocacy group that promotes stem cell research.

Genetics Policy Institute, 701 8th St., N.W., Suite 400, Washington, DC 20001; (888) 791-3889; www.genpol.org. Advocates for public policies to promote responsible use of therapeutic cloning and stem cell science.

Geron Corp., 230 Constitution Dr., Menlo Park, CA 94025; (650) 473-7700; www.geron.com. Holds patents on embryonic stem cell research findings and hopes to commercialize therapies for cancer and degenerative conditions based on them.

Institute for Ethics and Emerging Technologies, Williams 229B, Trinity College, 300 Summit St., Hartford, CT 06106; (860) 297-2376; http://ieet.org/. Supports the examination by philosophers and ethicists of the social implications of new technologies such as stem cell therapies.

International Society for Stem Cell Research, 60 Revere Dr., Suite 500, Northbrook, IL 60062; (847) 509-1944; www.isscr.org. Provides information to the public and to doctors and scientists on stem cell research and its applications.

National Institutes of Health, Stem Cell Information, 9000 Rockville Pike, Bethesda, MD 20892; e-mail: stemcell@mail.nih.gov; http://stemcells.nih.gov/. The federal government's central information bank on stem cells and federal stem cell policy and research funding.

President's Council on Bioethics, 1801 Pennsylvania Ave., N.W., Suite 700, Washington, DC 20006; (202) 296-4669; www.bioethics.gov. Advises the Bush administration on bioethical issues including stem cells.

Bibliography

Selected Sources

Books

Parson, Ann B., *Proteus Effect: Stem Cells and Their Promise for Medicine*, Joseph Henry Press, 2006.
A journalist recounts the scientific history that led to current discoveries about stem cells, beginning with 18th-century natural philosophy and giving full accounts of the 20th- and 21st-century experiments leading to the current view of stem cells' potential for producing medical treatments.

Ruse, Michael, and A. Christopher Pynes, eds., *The Stem Cell Controversy: Debating the Issues*, Prometheus Books, 2006.
Philosophy professors at Florida State and Western Illinois universities assemble essays by biologists, doctors, theologians and others that lay out the main ethical, scientific and public-policy issues at stake in the stem cell debate.

Scott, Christopher Thomas, *Stem Cell Now: From the Experiment That Shook the World to the New Politics of Life*, Pi Press, 2005.
A biologist who is executive director of Stanford University's Program in Stem Cells and Society explains the history and possibilities of stem cell research and the political and ethical controversies that surround it.

Articles

Arnold, Wayne, "Science Haven in Singapore," *The New York Times*, Aug. 17, 2006, p. C1.
In hopes of becoming a biotech powerhouse, Singapore is luring U.S. stem cell researchers to its new labs.

Cook, Gareth, "Stem-cell Method Preserves Embryo," *The Boston Globe*, Aug. 24, 2006, p. A1.
A Massachusetts biotech company says it can grow embryonic stem cell cultures without destroying embryos.

Fitzpatrick, William, "Surplus Embryos, Nonreproductive Cloning, and the Intend/Foresee Distinction," *The Hastings Center Report*, May 2003, p. 29.
An assistant professor of philosophy at Virginia Tech University outlines the ethical issues that distinguish embryo creation and destruction in the course of in vitro fertilization procedures from embryo creation and destruction related to stem cell and cloning research.

Kolata, Gina, "Embryonic Cells, No Embryo Needed: Hunting for Ways Out of an Impasse," *The New York Times*, Oct. 11, 2005, p. F1.
Scientists and ethicists seek methods to produce embryonic stem cell lines without transgressing the moral boundaries of conservative Christian opponents.

Vergano, Dan, "U.S. Stem Cell Researchers Sense a Chill," *USA Today*, July 26, 2006, p. 8D.
With federal funding for embryonic stem cell research severely restricted in the United States, biologists say that promising studies have been put on indefinite hold.

Reports and Studies

"Ethical Issues in Human Stem Cell Research," National Bioethics Advisory Commission, September 1999.
A panel appointed to advise the Clinton administration lays out the background and arguments that led it to recommend federal funding of research on embryonic stem cells.

"Guidelines for Human Embryonic Stem Cell Research," Institute of Medicine Board on Health Sciences Policy, The National Academies Press, 2005.
An expert panel describes current U.S. regulations pertaining to stem cell research and recommends regulatory steps for governments and research institutions that would facilitate future research while protecting the rights of humans involved in studies, such as egg donors.

"Monitoring Stem Cell Research," President's Council on Bioethics, January 2004.
A panel appointed to advise the Bush administration examines the history and potential of stem cell research and its moral and social significance.

"Stem Cells and Public Policy," The Century Foundation, 2006.
The progressive public-policy foundation offers a primer on stem cell science and current events and controversies, including a summary of stem cell regulation and funding systems in the United States and abroad.

Parens, Erik, and Lori P. Knowles, "Reprogenetics and Public Policy," The Hastings Center, 2003.
The report examines ethical issues connected with the largely unregulated proliferation of reproductive technologies and research involving use and storage of embryos outside a uterus, including stem cell research and technologies such as pre-implantation diagnosis to weed out embryos at risk for genetically based diseases in in vitro fertilization procedures.

Simpson, John M., "Affordability, Accessibility and Accountability in California Stem Cell Research," The Foundation for Taxpayer and Consumer Rights, January 2006.
California's taxpayer-supported stem cell research initiative raises questions about who should have patents to, profit from and have access to whatever medical therapies the initiative ultimately develops.

The Next Step:

Additional Articles from Current Periodicals

Adult Stem Cells

Ackerman, Todd, "Scientists See Value in Both Embryonic, Adult Stem Cells," *The Houston Chronicle*, July 20, 2006, p. A6.

Scientists say both embryonic and adult stem cell research are important, criticizing President Bush for calling into question the "hype" surrounding embryonic stem cells.

Manier, Jeremy, and Judith Graham, "Experts Rip Rove Stem Cell Remark," *Chicago Tribune*, July 19, 2006, p. 1.

Most stem cell research scientists say the argument by presidential adviser Karl Rove that adult stem cells show far more promise than embryonic stem cells is entirely inaccurate.

Bush's Veto

Alter, Jonathan, "It Was the Veto of a Lifetime," *Newsweek*, July 31, 2006, p. 40.

Alter argues that Bush's religious arrogance and obsession with his conservative base led him to commit a political blunder and veto a modest stem cell bill.

Hines, Cragg, "Stem Cell Redux: The Veto and Passionate Responses," *The Houston Chronicle*, July 23, 2006, p. 3.

Hines shares various *Chronicle* readers' responses to Bush's stem cell bill veto.

King, Warren, "Stem-Cell Fight Isn't Over," *The Seattle Times*, July 25, 2006, p. B1.

Democratic U.S. Sens. Patty Murray and Maria Cantwell, both of Washington, pledged to work for new stem cell legislation after Bush's veto.

Klein, Rick, "Bush Vetoes Stem-Cell Research Bill," *The Boston Globe*, July 20, 2006, p. A2.

President Bush used his first veto since taking office in 2001 to reject a bill to expand federal funding for embryonic stem cell research.

Talev, Margaret, "Stem-Cell Politics Turning Personal," *The Miami Herald*, July 19, 2006, p. A1.

Senators from both parties revealed their own family struggles with incurable illnesses in passing a stem cell research bill, hoping to pressure Bush into changing his mind.

Fraud in South Korea

"Fraud Trial Begins for Stem Cell Scientist," *Los Angeles Times*, June 21, 2006, p. A17.

The trial began today for South Korean scientist Woo Suk Hwang, accused of accepting $2.1 million in private donations based on the outcome of falsified research and embezzling $831,000 in private and government research funds.

The Associated Press, "Disgraced Korean Cloning Scientist Indicted," *The New York Times*, May 12, 2006, p. A12.

Prosecutors in South Korea indicted scientist Woo Suk Hwang on embezzlement and bioethics law violations linked to faked stem cell research.

Lemonick, Michael D., "The Rise and Fall of the Cloning King," *Time*, Jan. 9, 2006, p. 40.

South Korean scientist Woo Suk Hwang became a national hero after claiming the first therapeutic cloning of a human embryo and the first cloning of a dog.

State Funding

Franck, Matthew, "Women's Risk Is Stem-Cell Issue," *St. Louis Post-Dispatch*, Aug. 7, 2006, p. B1.

Religious groups that oppose abortion and some women's health advocates that are pro-choice in Missouri are teaming up to fight a proposed constitutional amendment protecting stem cell research.

Romney, Lee, "State Takes Lead in Stem Cell Efforts," *Los Angeles Times*, July 21, 2006, p. B1.

Republican California Gov. Arnold Schwarzenegger requested $150 million be loaned to the state's voter-approved stem cell research institute, making the state the nation's top public funder of such research.

Rudoren, Jodi, "Stem Cell Work Gets States' Aid After Bush Veto," *The New York Times*, July 25, 2006, p. A1.

Several states have pledged money to fund stem cell research after Bush vetoed legislation to expand federally financed embryonic stem cell research.

Citing *CQ Researcher*

Sample formats for citing these reports in a bibliography include the ones listed below. Preferred styles and formats vary, so please check with your instructor or professor.

MLA Style

Jost, Kenneth. "Rethinking the Death Penalty." CQ Researcher 16 Nov. 2001: 945-68.

APA Style

Jost, K. (2001, November 16). Rethinking the death penalty. *CQ Researcher, 11*, 945-968.

Chicago Style

Jost, Kenneth. "Rethinking the Death Penalty." *CQ Researcher*, November 16, 2001, 945-968.

CQ Researcher

Published by CQ Press, a division of Congressional Quarterly Inc.

cqresearcher.com

Sex Offenders

Will tough, new laws do more harm than good?

In response to horrific sex crimes against children, Congress and the states have passed hundreds of new laws in recent years to crack down on offenders. In addition to much longer sentences and more rigorous tracking of sex criminals upon release, some of the new laws place limits on where offenders can live, banning them from neighborhoods surrounding schools, parks and playgrounds. But critics warn the laws may prove counterproductive, driving sex offenders further underground. They also point out that most perpetrators are family members or other acquaintances of victims, so the new laws may shift resources away from treatment programs that could help more. Moreover, experts note sex offenders' low recidivism rates and a dramatic drop in child sexual-abuse cases. But with the media giving heavy coverage to the worst cases of abduction and abuse, it's no wonder that lawmakers are willing to approve any punishment or tracking technique that promises to prevent crimes against children.

Registered sex offender John Evander Couey confessed last year to kidnapping and killing 9-year-old Jessica Lunsford, of Homosassa, Fla.

INSIDE THIS REPORT

CQ Researcher • Sept. 8, 2006 • www.cqresearcher.com
Volume 16, Number 31 • Pages 721-744

CQ PRESS

RECIPIENT OF SOCIETY OF PROFESSIONAL JOURNALISTS AWARD FOR EXCELLENCE ◆ AMERICAN BAR ASSOCIATION SILVER GAVEL AWARD

Cover photograph: Getty Images/Citrus County Sheriff's Department

CQ Researcher

Sept. 8, 2006
Volume 16, Number 31

MANAGING EDITOR: Thomas J. Colin

ASSISTANT MANAGING EDITOR: Kathy Koch

ASSOCIATE EDITOR: Kenneth Jost

STAFF WRITERS: Marcia Clemmitt, Peter Katel

CONTRIBUTING WRITERS: Rachel S. Cox, Sarah Glazer, Alan Greenblatt, Barbara Mantel, Patrick Marshall, Tom Price, Jennifer Weeks

DESIGN/PRODUCTION EDITOR: Olu B. Davis

ASSISTANT EDITOR: Melissa J. Hipolit

CQ PRESS

A Division of Congressional Quarterly Inc.

SENIOR VICE PRESIDENT/PUBLISHER: John A. Jenkins

DIRECTOR, LIBRARY PUBLISHING: Kathryn C. Suárez

DIRECTOR, EDITORIAL OPERATIONS: Ann Davies

CONGRESSIONAL QUARTERLY INC.

CHAIRMAN: Paul C. Tash

VICE CHAIRMAN: Andrew P. Corty

PRESIDENT/EDITOR IN CHIEF: Robert W. Merry

CQ Researcher (ISSN 1056-2036) is printed on acid-free paper. Published weekly, except March 24, July 7, July 14, Aug. 4, Aug. 11, Nov. 24, Dec. 22 and Dec. 29, by CQ Press, a division of Congressional Quarterly Inc. Annual full-service subscriptions for institutions start at $667. For pricing, call 1-800-834-9020, ext. 1906. To purchase a *CQ Researcher* report in print or electronic format (PDF), visit www.cqpress.com or call 866-427-7737. Single reports start at $15. Bulk purchase discounts and electronic-rights licensing are also available. Periodicals postage paid at Washington, D.C., and additional mailing offices. POSTMASTER: Send address changes to *CQ Researcher*, 1255 22nd St., N.W., Suite 400, Washington, DC 20037.

Sex Offenders

BY ALAN GREENBLATT

THE ISSUES

Kerry Skora thinks there are worse things than being known as a murderer.

Sex offenders still face penalties after they serve their sentences — including some that don't even apply to murderers. That's why Skora didn't want to be labeled as a sex offender when he was released from an Illinois prison this year after serving 15 years for a murder he committed at age 19. But because his victim was 16, that's how state law categorized him, even though his crime did not involve sex.

And in Illinois sex offenders have to register their whereabouts with police and are not allowed to live within 500 feet of schools or other public places where children gather — making it hard to find a place to live. Miami Beach, Iowa City and many other cities and states have similar laws.

Getty Images/Citrus County Sheriff's Department

Jessica Lunsford's death last year led some two-dozen states to enact versions of "Jessica's Law," which requires more thorough tracking of sex offenders and stricter sentences. Congress also enacted a law this year that will prod states to track sex offenders more closely. Contrary to popular belief, sex offenders have relatively low recidivism rates, and family members, not strangers, are responsible for most reported sex crimes against children.

"It's more like banishment than a zoning restriction," says Roxanne Lieb, executive director of the Washington State Institute for Public Policy. "There isn't any other group in society where we banish them. You could commit a double murder and come back and live somewhere, or be a three-time drug dealer, but not a sex offender."

The Illinois legislature agreed with Skora's complaint that it was unfair to tar him as a sex offender just because his victim was a minor. The state created a new registry for non-sexual violent criminals. The fact that sex offenders are subject to even more intense scrutiny than murderers demonstrates just how seriously lawmakers are taking the problem of sex crimes against children.

It's not hard to figure out their motivation. Sex crimes against children are among the most heinous imaginable. "Surely there can be no crime that inspires greater anguish among the general public than sexual crimes, especially violent sexual offenders," writes Karen J. Terry, an associate professor at the City University of New York's John Jay College of Criminal Justice. [1]

The media have made several especially terrifying crimes into continuing national nightmares, vividly and repeatedly portraying both the victim and the crime. A case in point is the rape and murder of 6-year-old Colorado beauty queen JonBenet Ramsey a decade ago. After an Atlanta, Ga., man, John Mark Karr, said he killed the child, he was arrested in Thailand and brought back to the United States. However, police said his DNA didn't match that found in her underwear, and he was not charged.

But there have been numerous other high-profile cases that have shocked the public and prompted increased legislative action. Last year, 9-year-old Jessica Marie Lunsford was abducted from her Florida home by a convicted sex offender, sexually assaulted and buried alive. Since then, two-dozen states have enacted versions of "Jessica's Law," which requires more thorough tracking of released sex offenders through means such as DNA samples, ankle bracelets and GPS (global positioning system).

California voters are expected to approve a particularly strict version of the law in November. Congress also enacted a law this year that will prod states to track sex offenders more closely.

"When you have someone taking a 9-year-old child and burying her alive, it just calls out for a legislative response," says Lieb.

What is particularly troubling about a case such as Jessica's, say those calling for stricter laws, is that her alleged assailant had a long criminal record, including sexual offenses. (The trial of John Evander Couey has not been able to proceed because it was impossible to seat an impartial jury in the county in which the crime occurred.)

"Whatever it takes to track these sex offenders must be done, because rehabilitation tends not to happen," says Stacie D. Rumenap, executive director of Stop Child Predators, which lobbies for passage of Jessica's Law in every state.

Child Sexual Abuse Dropped Significantly

The rate of identified sexual abuse of children in the United States fell by 50 percent from 1991 to 2004. David Finkelhor, director of the Crimes Against Children Research Center, thinks the declines may be linked to greater awareness about child maltreatment, improved parenting and more effective treatment for family and mental health problems, including psychiatric medications.

Child Sexual-Abuse Rates in the United States
(based on substantiated reports)

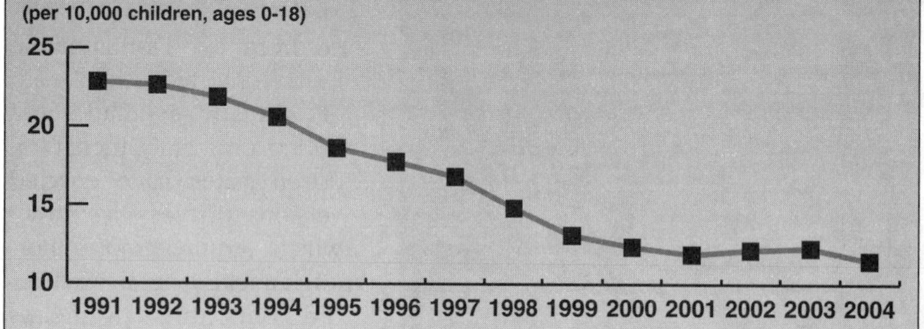

Note: The data come from state child-protection agencies and cover offenses against children committed primarily by parents and other caretakers; they do not typically cover sex crimes against children committed by strangers.

Source: Crimes Against Children Research Center, University of New Hampshire, 2006

But Terry and other experts on deviancy dispute the frequently heard claim that sex offenders have a particularly high rate of recidividism. Tracking every sex offender — or even, as in Skora's case, many nonsexual offenders — is a distraction, they argue, from concentrating attention on those who are most dangerous and most likely to commit more crimes.

"We have 41,000 names on our [sex offenders] registry," said Allison Taylor, executive director of the Texas Council on Sex Offender Treatment. "If we could take our money and focus it on the 10 percent or so who are most likely to re-offend, we could make great progress." [2]

Although a Gallup Poll last year found that more Americans are "very concerned" about child molesters than violent crime in general or even terrorism, the rates of sex crimes against children have actually dropped significantly since the early 1990s. [3] What's more, such crimes are far more likely to be committed by a family member or someone else previously known to the victim than by a stranger. (*See chart, p. 728.*)

In fact, strangers are responsible for only 7 percent of reported cases of juvenile sex crimes, according to the Justice Department. Thirty-four percent are victimized by their own families, and 59 percent of cases occur among friends. [4] According to the National Center for Missing and Exploited Children, only about 115 out of 260,000 children kidnapped each year are snatched by strangers. [5]

"We're doing a disservice, essentially, with most of the legislation we're seeing right now around sex offenders," says Alisa Klein, public-policy consultant with the Association for the Treatment of Sex Offenders. "We're creating this myth that if we just know who the identified sex offenders are, you can keep your children safe."

Some of the layers of sex-offender laws passed over the past decade do seem to conflict with each other. For instance, the recent rigid zoning restrictions are leading some sex offenders to lie about their whereabouts or to drop off law enforcement's radar entirely, undercutting the effectiveness of registration and community-notification requirements.

But once anti-sex-offender legislation comes to a vote following an emotionally charged crime, the voices of skeptics are barely heard. "Everyone knew some parts of the bill were flawed," says Republican Georgia state Rep. John Lunsford, referring to the state's new zoning restrictions passed in April, parts of which have already been found to be unconstitutional. "Once it reached the floor, you were either voting for the perverts or voting for your constituency."

Tough, new sex-offender laws tend to pass unanimously, or nearly so. If there are flaws in some of the approaches, advocates for the get-tough approach say, that is only more reason to keep working to strengthen them. If many sex offenders are slipping between the cracks, for instance, that makes it all the more necessary to ensure compliance through GPS or other methods.

The new federal law makes failure to register a felony and offers states money to buy GPS systems. "We track library books better than we do sex offenders," complained Republican Florida Rep. Mark Foley, one of the bill's sponsors. [6]

And if most sex offenders are family members or other close acquaintances of children, that's still no reason not to try to protect children against violent and predatory criminals, such as the one who killed Jessica Lunsford.

"It's not about the overall rate, it's about wanting to make sure that events like this don't occur," says Lieb.

As the debate about the best way to prevent child molestation rages on, here are some of the questions people are debating:

Should sex offenders be allowed to live near children?

In May, Jim L'Etoile lost his job as director of California's Parole and Community Services Division because of his handling of sex offenders. It's not that he lost track of too many of them, or that they committed new crimes under his supervision. His mistake was placing 23 "high-risk" sex offenders — those considered most likely to commit repeat crimes — in hotels and motels within a few miles of Disneyland.

That placement showed "a total lack of common sense," says Democratic state Rep. Rudy Bermudez, a former parole officer. "When you place high-risk sex offenders where children are, you're almost violating the laws by putting children in harm's way."

Communities around the country don't want sex offenders living anywhere near children. They may not have attractions as glamorous as Disneyland, but 17 states and dozens, if not hundreds, of local governments have banned registered sex offenders from living near public places where children can be expected to gather, such as schools.

"I've had folks say, 'I don't want them anywhere in my town,' " says Charles Olney, a researcher at the U.S. Department of Justice's Center for Sex Offender Management. "Everyone wants these folks somewhere else."

As Democratic Miami Beach Mayor David Dermer puts it, "If you have a child, do you want a registered sex offender living next to you? Do you feel comfortable with that?"

His city passed an ordinance last year to block sex offenders from living within 2,500 feet of any school, public bus stop, day-care center, park "or other place where children regularly congregate." For all practical purposes, no sex criminals can live anywhere in the city.

Few Sex Offenders Rearrested for Sex Crimes

Less than 4 percent of the sex offenders released from prison in the U.S. in 1994 were reconvicted of a new sex crime within three years of their release. Sexual assault is considered an underreported crime, however, and actual recidivism rates may be higher than indicated below. Studies of released sex offenders over longer periods of time show greater recidivism rates.

	Percentage of Released Sex Offenders		
Recidivism Measure	**Child molesters**	**Rapists**	**Statutory Rapists**
Within 3 years following release:			
Rearrested for any new sex crime	5.1%	5.0%	5.0%
Reconvicted for any new sex crime	3.5%	3.2%	3.6%
Total Released	**4,295**	**3,115**	**443**

Source: "Recidivism of Sex Offenders Released From Prison in 1994," Bureau of Justice Statistics, November 2003

"The whole city is basically covered by this," Dermer says. "As far as I'm concerned, it worked well."

Others worry that so-called proximity restrictions amount to an unfair extra dose of punishment brought against offenders who already have served their sentences. A federal judge has blocked a portion of Georgia's law, finding it unconstitutional to force sex offenders to move — even if the crimes they committed occurred many years earlier — when school bus stops are rerouted close to their homes.

Because of such concerns, 11 of the 17 states with proximity laws offer exemptions to those who lived within the buffer zones before the new laws were passed, according to Wayne A. Logan, a law professor at the College of William and Mary.

Even critics of the residency restrictions agree that convicted sex offenders should not be allowed to work in jobs, such as teaching, that would bring them into close proximity with children. It's dangerous when predators are able to establish relationships with children and build a level of trust that they can exploit. Most sex crimes, after all, are perpetrated by someone known to the victim. (*See chart, p. 728.*)

But offenders' ability to establish such relationships has nothing to do with where they live, critics of the restrictions say. Criminals don't have to live near arcades or playgrounds to visit them. "Schools, parks and playgrounds aren't a factor in most sex-abuse cases," says Jill S. Levenson, a human-services professor and researcher at Lynn University, in Fort Lauderdale, Fla., who has coauthored studies of sex-offender residency restrictions.

"It sounds good in theory," Levenson continues, "but the big problem with residency restrictions, aside from the fact that there's no evidence that they work, is that they push sex offenders from cities into rural areas so they're more difficult to track and monitor and are farther from social services and psychiatric services." Those are factors associated with increased recidivism, not lower recidivism, Levenson says.

"When you ostracize these individuals, they're taken away from social-network support, job opportunities and family," says Logan, who is preparing

Sex Abuse Still Haunts Catholic Church

The Rev. Francisco Xavier Ochoa, a Catholic priest in Santa Rosa, Calif., confessed to local church officials on April 28 that he had kissed a 12-year-old boy and offered him $100 to do a striptease. Ochoa also admitted to other incidents with boys elsewhere in earlier years. But in defiance of California law, church authorities failed to report Ochoa immediately to the police, instead waiting until May 1. In the meantime, Ochoa fled to Mexico.

"I made an error in judgment by waiting to report Rev. Ochoa's admissions," Bishop Daniel Walsh wrote in an August letter to parishioners. "I should have acted immediately and not delayed."

The bishop's apology didn't satisfy the Sonoma County Sheriff's Department, which recommended on Aug. 25 that criminal charges be filed against Walsh. It would be the first time a U.S. Catholic Church official faces criminal prosecution for failing to report sexual abuse. [1]

The Catholic Church has arguably been damaged more by child sex-abuse scandals than any other institution in American life. The scandal appeared to peak in 2002, when the U.S. Conference of Catholic Bishops announced a sweeping set of reform measures intended to curb abuse and protect children. [2]

Since that time, legal settlements with victims of priestly abuse have forced dioceses in Tucson, Spokane and Portland, Ore., to declare bankruptcy, while many other dioceses have sold property to pay the bills. Abuse-related church expenses peaked last year at $467 million. [3]

The 2002 reforms call for priests and other parish officials, as well as the laity and children, to undergo regular training in spotting and preventing sexual abuse of children. The program includes educational videos, workshops and the development of a common language and policy for confronting people whose behavior is questionable, such as saying, "It's parish policy not to give long, lingering hugs to small children."

These efforts are subject to regular audits, and "the church urges that anyone who has been abused by a priest or deacon or person of authority report the abuse immediately and that the person be removed from their position," says Sister Mary Ann Walsh, spokeswoman for the bishops' conference.

"The church has addressed the problem very aggressively," she said. "We're horrified by it."

But critics of the church complain that Catholic leaders, while paying lip service to the problem, have failed to live up to their own promises. "The gap between what the bishops say publicly and what they do privately has never been greater," says David Clohessy, national director of the Survivor Network of Those Abused by Priests. "The reforms they've adopted since 2002 are essentially like speed limits, but no cops."

Several recent incidents suggest the church has not learned from the earlier round of scandals, in which its leadership allowed known molesters to continue working with children. In Chicago, the Rev. Daniel McCormack was allowed to continue in his ministry for four months after allegations surfaced that he had abused three boys. After a stinging audit, Cardinal Francis George said in March that he was "most truly sorry . . . for the tragedy of allowing children to be in the presence of a priest against whom a current accusation of sexual abuse has been made." [4]

a book on offender-registration laws. In one instance, 21 sex offenders wound up grouped together in a cheap motel outside of Cedar Rapids, Iowa, because they had been, in effect, banished from within the city limits. [7] The fact that some sex offenders are being forced either into homelessness or into living arrangements with their ostracized peers may make them less likely to stay on the straight-and-narrow.

"Yes, it's an inconvenience — some folks will have to move," said Republican state Rep. Jerry Keen, majority leader of the Georgia House and sponsor of the state's proximity law. "But if you weigh that argument against the overall impact, which is the safety of children, most folks would agree this is a good thing." [8]

The foundation for residency restrictions on sex offenders was laid more than a decade ago, in 1994, when Congress required states to compel convicted sex offenders to register their addresses with local police. The requirement helped parole and probation officers supervise and monitor their charges. Two years later, "Megan's Law" required communities to provide citizens with information on sex offenders in their midst. The law was named in honor of Megan Kanka, a 7-year-old New Jersey child raped and murdered in 1994 by a convicted sex offender who lived across the street, Jesse Timmendequas.

But some critics of the proximity laws — including some prosecutors and law-enforcement officials — are now worried that the buffer-zone approach also may erode the effectiveness of the registry and community-notification requirements. If it becomes too difficult for sex offenders to find an affordable place to live, they may change residences without notifying authorities, register false addresses or simply disappear, making it harder for law enforcement to do its job.

In Chicago, for example, more than 75 percent of the addresses given by 81 sex offenders were found to be bogus. [9] In Iowa, the number of sex offenders who are unaccounted for on the state's list of 6,000 offenders has doubled since a statewide residence law took effect last September. [10] "The truth is that we're starting to lose people," said Don Vrotsos, chief deputy of the Dubuque County sheriff's office. [11]

That same week, New Hampshire's attorney general released an audit saying the church had failed to make sure all those who work with children pass criminal background checks. To get the state to agree to drop a criminal investigation, the church had to agree to conduct the background checks. And the church has lobbied hard against legislation in several states to extend the statute of limitations for bringing sex-abuse complaints. [5]

Even the National Review Board, a lay committee created in 2002 to investigate sex abuse, has sharply criticized church leaders. The board's chairman, a former governor, compared bishops to the mafia, while a former leader said the bishops had "manipulated" the group and had been far from forthcoming. [6]

At the local level, church officials say that the new policies and education programs are starting to take root. "I don't tend to use superlatives very often, but I think this is a program that is going to change lives," says Helen Osman, communications director for the diocese of Austin, describing the church's education efforts for children. "As far as sexual abuse, no one has reported anything to us."

AP Photo/Nick Ut

Former Los Angeles Catholic priest Michael Wempe, right, was sentenced in May to three years in prison for child abuse.

Meanwhile, critics charge that the bishops remain impervious to outside oversight, relying too heavily on self-audits by dioceses to ensure compliance with the church's own rules and legal settlements, such as the one in New Hampshire that required thorough background checks.

"As long as there is that structure, with no checks and balances," says Clohessy, "with no oversight and no consequences for wrongdoing, there will continue to be sex crimes and cover-ups."

[1] John Cote, "Catholic Bishop May Face Jail," *San Francisco Chronicle*, Aug. 26, 2006, p. B1.

[2] For background, see Kenneth Jost, "Sexual Abuse and the Clergy," *CQ Researcher*, May 3, 2002, pp. 393-416.

[3] Rachel Zoll, "Costs Soar as Clergy Sex Abuse Cases Rise," Associated Press, March 31, 2006.

[4] T.R. Reid, "Catholic Leaders Fight Legislation on Suits," *The Washington Post*, April 1, 2006, p. A10.

[5] *Ibid.*

[6] Joe Feuerhard, "Review Board Head Charges Bishops 'Manipulated' Sex Abuse Panel and Withheld Information," *National Catholic Reporter Online*, May 11, 2004.

The Iowa County Attorneys Association has called for a repeal of the banishment law.

"You have to be very careful with those sorts of laws because we don't know if they're going to help, and they may hurt," says Carlos Cuevas, an assistant professor at Northeastern University's College of Criminal Justice.

Should sex offenders receive harsher punishments?

James Jenkins says he's "all for castration for certain sex offenders. It would do a lot to prevent recidivism and [reduce] the amount of money we have to spend on treatment centers."

Jenkins should know. He was sent to a sex-offender treatment center after he molested three young girls. Before being sent to the institution, Jenkins castrated himself with a razor. "Castration has done precisely what I wanted it to do," Jenkins said. "I have not had any sexual urges or desires in over two years. My mind is finally free of the deviant sexual fantasies I used to have about young girls." [12]

Eight states allow either for chemical or surgical castration. It's one sign among many that over the past decade states and local communities have decided they need to toughen their laws against sex offenders.

In the wake of the community-notification requirements passed a decade ago, nearly half the states now have passed versions of Jessica's Law, which requires more aggressive tracking of sex offenders through use of GPS (global positioning system) technology.

"You see the continual need for more pieces of the pie — tougher law enforcement and greater community awareness," says Rumenap, of Stop Child Predators. "We need to keep our children safe."

Anti-sex-offender laws rarely encounter much political resistance. Both houses of the Washington state legislature, for instance, earlier this year passed mandatory 25-year prison sentences for some sex offenders without a dissenting vote.

"In Oklahoma, we have no sympathy for those who would harm our children. We've increased penalties across the board for all forms of sex abuse against children," says Democratic Gov.

Most Victims Know Their Attacker

The vast majority of sexual-assault victims are attacked by family members or acquaintances, not strangers.

Offenders (by percentage)

Victim Age	Family member	Acquaintance	Stranger
All victims	26.7%	59.6%	13.8%
Juveniles	34.2	58.7	7.0
0-5 years old	48.6	48.3	3.1
6-11	42.4	52.9	4.7
12-17	24.3	66.0	9.8
Adults			
18-24	9.8	66.5	23.7
24 +	12.8	57.1	30.1

Source: "Sexual Assault of Young Children as Reported to Law Enforcement: Victim, Incident, and Offender Characteristics," Bureau of Justice Statistics, U.S. Department of Justice, July 2000

Brad Henry, who signed a law in June imposing the death penalty on certain repeat offenders who have abused children.

Oklahoma became the fifth state to impose the death penalty for sex crimes against children. (South Carolina had enacted its law one day earlier.)

The U.S. Supreme Court ruled in 1977 that the death penalty was disproportionate in cases involving the rape of adults, and thus amounted to "cruel and unusual punishment," which is banned by the Eighth Amendment. The court has not ruled on a death-penalty case involving an offense against a child. [13]

Lieb, of the Washington State Institute for Public Policy, says the new laws serve an important purpose — not just by imposing harsher sentences but in raising public awareness about sex crimes. "Personally, I think it's a very valuable change in our society. It's recognition of the harm," she says. "There's no doubt, looking at sex offenders who have committed horrific crimes and gotten out, the thing you would most wish for is that they got a longer sentence."

But Lieb questions laws that raise the level of punishment for sex offenses above those for murder, as in Washington. "There's been research that shows if you set mandatory sentences too high, then prosecutors won't file those charges, and judges and juries won't convict," she says.

It's not only a question of whether the legal system will apply the most rigorous penalties, says R. Karl Hanson, a psychologist and a corrections researcher with Public Safety and Emergency Preparedness Canada, that country's main public safety agency. Victims invariably find the court process a challenge, he says, and they are sometimes especially reluctant to press charges when the perpetrator is a relative or someone known to them, as is the case more often than not. Studies from the 1990s showed that 73 percent of molestation victims don't report the crime if the perpetrator is a relative or step-parent, while 70 percent don't report an acquaintance. [14] Children sometimes fear further harm as a result of reporting.

"The consequences may be harsher than the victim wants," Hanson says. "Many victims of sexual assault don't necessarily want a big punishment — they just want it to stop. Sometimes they're afraid to disclose the crime because it's their uncle who will have to go away forever."

Becky Rogers Martin, a Republican state representative in South Carolina, also has concerns that police and prosecutors may not enforce laws that they don't believe fit the crime. "Lots of times we'll put in real strict penalties so that even if they're cut down they'll still serve real time," she says. "But our concern was that if we made it so strict, they wouldn't take it seriously."

Others warn that longer sentences or even the death penalty won't act as a successful deterrent to crime. "People think it's effective because they confuse deterrence with retribution," says Murray A. Straus, a sociologist at the University of New Hampshire. "That doesn't mean that punishment never works as a deterrent. It does — but it has a very high failure rate."

"Offenders are going to become more aware that society doesn't want to deal with them on the street," says Christopher J. Murphy, deputy chief of the adult probation and parole department in Montgomery County, Pa. "But the majority of sex offenders that I've dealt with didn't think they were going to be caught to begin with."

Many criminologists also are concerned that contemporary laws dealing with sex offenders often lump them together broadly as a group. In some cases, men who were teenagers when found guilty of statutory rape may be subjected to the same kinds of living restrictions and community-notification requirements as older men who repeatedly molested young children. Even putting aside the question of fairness, they say, this amounts to a wasteful dilution of effort. Keeping track of hundreds of sex offenders is hard.

"We tend to put all sex offenders under one umbrella, and these laws are applied to them equally," says Terry, of the John Jay College of Criminal Justice.

"We often apply the resources to the punishment rather than to the treatment," she continues. "Personally, I think that there should be more of a focus on treatment."

AFP/Getty Images/Tim Sloan

President George W. Bush shakes hands with John Walsh after signing the Adam Walsh Child Protection and Safety Act on July 27; Mrs. Walsh is at left. Six-year-old Adam was murdered in 1981 after being abducted from a suburban shopping mall in Florida. John Walsh later became host of "America's Most Wanted" and a leader in the push for victims' rights.

Can sex offenders be rehabilitated?

Many of the most disturbing violations of children in recent times have been perpetrated by repeat offenders. The suspect in the case of Jessica Lunsford, the Florida girl whose kidnap, rape and murder has prompted half the states to pass stricter tracking requirements, is a previously convicted sex offender who had failed to register with police.

The idea that someone could molest children and then be set free to commit the same crime again — or an even more violent crime — is a central motivation behind the current push toward more stringent punishments and tracking.

"The problem with this type of crime is that the rate of recidivism is high," contends Rumenap, of Stop Child Predators.

Referring to "To Catch a Predator," the NBC "Dateline" series that investigates men who use the Internet to troll for minors, Rumenap says, "That show has been on five or six times, and they're getting some of the same sex offenders showing up time and again."

Determining the true rate of recidivism among sex offenders, though, is one of the most contentious points within the policy debate surrounding the issue. Some studies indicate that rates of recidivism among sex offenders are actually lower than for people who commit other violent crimes or property crimes.

A study by the Justice Department's Bureau of Justice Statistics found that only 5.3 percent of sex offenders (defined as men who had committed rape or sexual assault) were rearrested for another sex crime within three years after their release from prison in 15 states. That was far below the 68 percent rearrest rate for non-sex offenders, 25 percent of whom were resentenced to prison for new crimes. [15]

A broader and widely cited Canadian study found that within five years of release 14 percent of sex offenders were brought up on new charges for a sexual offense. After 20 years of release, 73 percent of sex offenders had not been charged with another sexual offense. [16]

"It's hard to argue that all sex offenders will inevitably re-offend," says psychologist Hanson, coauthor of the Canadian study. "On average, the overall recidivism rate is lower than for general offenders, but they are more at risk for committing new sex offenses."

Ernie Allen, president of the National Center for Missing and Exploited Children, disputes the idea that recidivism studies prove that sex offenders are relatively unlikely to strike again. Just because they aren't brought up again on charges doesn't mean they haven't perpetrated more crimes, he argues.

"Recidivism research measures crimes reported to law enforcement that result in arrest and conviction," Allen writes. "But according to the Justice Department, crimes against children are the most underreported of all crimes. Researchers estimate that one-in-five girls and one-in-10 boys will be sexually victimized in some way before they reach adulthood. Yet only one-in-three will tell anybody about it." [17]

Even those who believe that most sex offenders are unlikely to strike again concede that such criminals will never entirely shed their destructive impulses. But they say that the behavior of many sex offenders can be managed, just as incurable diseases such as diabetes can be managed.

"We don't talk about it in terms of a cure," says Levenson, of the Center for Offender Rehabilitation and Education. "Some may always be attracted to children, but they can certainly learn to control that and not act on it."

Hanson says crunching the data from 17 different studies about sex-offender management shows a five-year recidivism rate of 10 percent for those who had undergone some form of treatment, compared with a 17 percent rate for those who hadn't. "The evidence suggests that those offenders who go to treatment are less likely to re-offend than those who don't," he says. "That may be partly because the more cooperative offenders are more likely to go."

Trying to sort out which criminals are going to be more compliant is just one of the tricks involved in successful sex-offender management. Criminologists say that sex offenders are more

Many Victims Are Under Age 6

One of every seven victims of sexual assault (14 percent) reported to law-enforcement agencies was under age 6, and more than a third of all victims were under 12.

Ages of Sexual-Assault Victims
(1991-1996)

Victim Age	All sexual assault	Forcible rape	Forcible sodomy	Sexual assault with object	Forcible fondling
0-5	14.0%	4.3%	24.0%	26.5%	20.2%
6-11	20.1	8.0	30.8	23.2	29.3
12-17	32.8	33.5	24.0	25.5	34.3
18-24	14.2	22.6	8.7	9.7	7.7
25-34	11.5	19.6	7.5	8.3	5.0
34+	7.4	12.0	5.1	6.8	3.5

Source: "Sexual Assault of Young Children as Reported to Law Enforcement: Victim, Incident, and Offender Characteristics," Bureau of Justice Statistics, U.S. Department of Justice, July 2000

heterogeneous than other types of violent criminals, with a wider range of age and education.

They also vary widely in terms of their tendencies toward violence. For that reason, management programs need to be tailored to take into account particular offending patterns and proclivities. A program that works for a middle-aged offender, for instance, won't work for a teenager.

"If you have sex offender-specific treatment, it can work, for those offenders who want to take advantage of it," says Murphy, the Pennsylvania probation official. "Unfortunately, you don't know which ones are which." ■

BACKGROUND

Cycles of Concern

Throughout the 20th century, the legal and political response to sex offenders has evolved through a series of cycles. At certain junctures, horrific crimes have sparked stepped-up efforts to combat the problem. Over time, however, as tensions ease, more liberal approaches come into fashion, such as a greater focus on rehabilitation. But then some new and shocking event shakes society's complacency, and tougher laws again sweep the land.

A series of "Jack the Ripper" serial-murder cases in several states drew public attention during the early 1900s, some of which involved child molestation. The killings led to a widespread belief that sex crimes were perpetrated by a deviant person from outside the community. "It is always the crime of a mentally unbalanced, feeble-minded person," editorialized *The New York Times* in 1915. "Moral degenerates are easily discoverable without waiting until acts of violence put them in the category of harming children." [18]

Reflecting such concerns, police began to investigate men with suspicious collections of photographs of children, believing they might mark a potential "ripper." And most states between 1905 and 1915 passed new laws for sex offenders that imposed open-ended sentences. By 1921, New York state permitted offenders considered mentally defective to be imprisoned for life (overseen by a doctor rather than a warden), regardless of whether they had been convicted of a crime.

"Failure to require actual conviction on a specific charge reflected the therapeutic assumption that no real harm could come from merely being diagnosed and treated medically, and the social assumption that merely being charged demonstrated that a person was a troublemaker of some kind," writes Philip Jenkins, a historian and religious-studies professor at Pennsylvania State University, in his 1998 book *Moral Panic.* [19]

The twin mixing of civil and criminal penalties and penology with treatment would remain the legal model for decades. The social and political climate shifted during the 1920s, however, and by the end of the decade charges of offenses against morality and chastity had plummeted. Police and the media turned their attention to Prohibition and the culture of gangsters, while a National Commission on Law Observance and Enforcement barely mentioned sex crimes in its 1931 report on pressing criminal-justice issues.

The period's relative quiet was disturbed by the 1934 apprehension of Albert Fish, who was charged with the murder, mutilation and cannibalism of Grace Budd, a 12-year-old from White Plains, N.Y. Fish had experimented with numerous perverse activities, which he recorded in his diaries. His shocking trial exposed the public to the outer reaches of sexual deviancy, engendering the sense that dangerous perverts were on the loose and waiting to strike. Fish's execution preceded by three months that of Bruno Hauptmann, who had kidnapped and killed the infant son of aviation pioneer Charles Lindbergh. Their stories often jostled for space on the front pages of the nation's newspapers

Continued on p. 733

Chronology

1940s-1970s

Ineffective civil-commitment statutes lead to a backlash against tough sex-offender laws.

1949
During "horror week" in November, three young girls across the country are raped and murdered or left to die. In response, 15 states establish commissions to study the sex-offender problem.

1955
After nearly 20 states pass laws allowing sexual-psychopaths to be held indeinitely, the population of state mental hospitals reaches 550,000, more than double the total 25 years earlier.

1974
Congress passes the Child Abuse Prevention and Treatment Act, mandating the reporting and investigation of abuse allegations.

1975
U.S. Supreme Court rules there is no constitutional basis for confining mental patients unless they present an immediate danger to themselves or their communities.

1980s-1990s

Sex crimes, particularly those against children, re-emerge as a major legislative concern.

1981
Two members of Congress are accused of having sex with teenage congressional pages.

1982
Wayne B. Williams is convicted for two out of a string of 23 murders of children that shocked Atlanta from 1979 to 1981.

1990
Washington state passes a law that becomes a model for other states, requiring dangerous sex offenders to register with police and reopening the possibility of civil commitment following prison sentences. . . . After six years of criminal trials in California, there are no convictions in the McMartin preschool case, in which a teacher and administrator had been accused of ritual sex abuse involving hundreds of children despite a lack of physical evidence.

1992
The number of reported child sex-abuse cases peaks at about 150,000.

1993
Polly Klaas and Jacob Wetterling, pre-teens who were abducted and either killed or presumed dead, spark massive public interest, leading to the pictures of missing children appearing on milk cartons and further legislation against sex offenders.

1994
As part of a larger crime bill, Congress passes the Jacob Wetterling Act, requiring sex offenders to register their whereabouts with police. . . . New Jersey becomes the first state to pass "Megan's Law," requiring community notification when a sex offender lives in the area; it honors murdered 7-year-old Megan Kanka.

1996
Congress passes a federal version of Megan's Law requiring all states to enact sex-offender registries or forfeit law-enforcement grants. . . . California requires chemical castration of offenders twice convicted of child molestation. . . . JonBenet Ramsey, a 6-year-old beauty queen, is found murdered and sexually assaulted in her home in Boulder, Colo., on Dec. 26.

2000s

Congress and the states crack down further on sex offenders, despite declining rates of such crimes.

2002
Bringing a year of scandal to a close, the U.S. Conference of Catholic Bishops adopts sweeping new sex-abuse prevention policies that mandate education in each diocese and call for tougher action against priests accused of pedophilia or other sex offenses involving children.

2005
Jessica Lunsford, a 9-year-old Florida girl, is abducted, sexually assaulted and buried alive. In response, two-dozen states enact "Jessica's Law," requiring stricter tracking of convicted sex offenders. . . . In all, states pass more than 100 new sex-offender laws, the most ever in a given year.

2006
U.S. marshals lead a 27-state dragnet from April 17-23 that nabs 1,102 wanted sex offenders. . . . On June 9 Oklahoma becomes the fifth state to approve the death penalty for sex offenders. . . . A U.S. district judge rules on June 29 that portions of Georgia's residence-restriction law, passed in April, are unconstitutional. . . . President Bush on Aug. 27 signs the Adam Walsh Act, requiring sex offenders to provide DNA samples and states to maintain offender registries on the Internet and impose criminal penalties for offenders who fail to register. . . . On Nov. 7 California voters are expected to approve a strict version of Jessica's Law, imposing mandatory minimum sentences on convicted sex offenders.

Online Predators Worry Experts

Kids who spent this past summer camping at Island Lake in Starrucca, Pa., were encouraged to write about their experiences online but not to say exactly where they were. Camp officials were worried about Internet sex predators.

Many camps have banned the use of their names or logos from Web pages and blogs set up by campers. Some even ban digital cameras from their grounds. "The information that kids share today often is personal and private information that allows predators to track them down," said Peg Smith, chief executive officer of the American Camp Association. [1]

Of course, children and youth don't have to go away to camp to make their presence known on the Internet. Social-networking sites such as MySpace and Facebook have loads of information about millions of children and youths — their names, their photographs, their diaries and pet peeves and favorite songs — even their eating habits and relative tendency to motion sickness. [2]

All of that is rich material for sex predators, who typically try to "groom" potential victims by getting to know them and building up trusting relationships. "The social-networking sites have become, in a sense, a happy hunting ground for child predators," says Rep. Michael G. Fitzpatrick, R-Pa.

Fitzpatrick's Deleting Online Predators Act passed the House, 410-15, on July 26. [3] The bill would ban access to chat rooms and a variety of online forums in public schools and libraries. Some groups, such as the American Library Association, say that it could have the effect of blocking students from finding information on legitimate sites, such as Yahoo, that host legitimate social forums.

Congress has tried for years to fashion laws that would protect children from the perils of the Internet. The Communications Decency Act of 1996 made it a crime to transmit "patently offensive" material over the Internet in a way that would be accessible to minors. The Supreme Court struck the law down the next year on free-speech grounds, however.

But the court in 2003 upheld the Children's Internet Protection Act of 2000, which requires libraries that accept federal funds to install anti-pornography filtering software. "The interest in protecting young library users from material inappropriate for minors is legitimate," Justice Anthony Kennedy wrote. [4]

Justice Department officials have grown particularly concerned about Internet pornography because, says a senior counsel at the Department of Justice, "the price of admission" for access to some pornography sites may be images of child sex abuse that in many cases may be homemade — suggesting that "mere possession of child porn may indicate a dangerous person."

Internet companies had resisted calls from the Bush administration that they share more information about their users with law-enforcement agencies, citing privacy concerns. But five leading Internet service providers, including AOL, Yahoo and Microsoft, announced in June that they will jointly build a database of child-pornography images and develop tools to help law enforcement prevent their distribution. [5]

A large percentage of those who possess illicit images of children, says the Justice official, who asked not to be named, may actually be offenders or contact children. "The Internet is a wonderful connector," he says, "but it brings dark alleys and dangerous places into your home, putting deviants together with their prospective victims."

As part of its Project Safe Childhood initiative, the Justice Department has stepped up its investigation and coordination of "enticement cases" in which predators contact children through the Internet and arrange to meet with them in person. NBC has broadcast an occasional series called "To Catch a Predator" that has resulted in nearly 100 arrests. [6]

According to a study released last month by the University of New Hampshire's Crimes Against Children Research Center, about 13 percent of children ages 10 to 17 have been solicited online for sexual activity or conversations. That was down from a total of 19 percent five years earlier. Researchers attributed the drop to warnings and education campaigns.

But "the most serious kinds of sexual solicitations, those in which solicitors make offline contact with young children, did not decline." [7]

Larry D. Rosen, a psychologist at California State University-Dominquez Hills and an expert on Internet socializing, says that sites such as MySpace are not "inherently scary or dangerous," but can, in fact, be healthy ways for teens to develop a sense of community and their own identity.

The major issue he found in a recent study is that "parents simply ignore their children's activities on MySpace. This is particularly striking, given that through the media parents are convinced that MySpace is ripe with sexual predators." [8]

---

[1] Pam Belluck, "Young People's Web Postings Worry Summer Camp Directors," *The New York Times*, June 22, 2006, p. A16.

[2] For background, see Marcia Clemmitt, "Cyber Socializing," *CQ Researcher*, July 28, 2006, pp. 625-648.

[3] Kathryn A. Wolfe, "Minors' Use of Social Web Sites at Schools and Libraries Targeted," *CQ Weekly*, July 31, 2006, p. 2125.

[4] Jan Crawford Greenburg, "Justices Back Porn Filters at Libraries," *Chicago Tribune*, June 24, 2003, p. 1.

[5] The Associated Press, "Internet Firms to Step Up Child-Porn Fight," *Los Angeles Times*, June 27, 2006, p. C7.

[6] Julia Rawe, "How Safe is MySpace?" *Time*, July 3, 2006, p. 34.

[7] "Youth Online Exposed to More Porn But Fewer Sexual Solicitations, According to New Study," University of New Hampshire press release, Aug. 9, 2006.

[8] Larry D. Rosen, "Adolescents in MySpace: Identity Formation, Friendship and Sexual Predators," June 2006; www.csudh.edu/psych/Adolescents%20in%20MySpace%20-%20Executive%20Summary.pdf.

Continued from p. 730

and "may have encouraged readers to see the generalized danger to children in sexually explicit terms," Jenkins writes. [20]

The Fish case and several other notorious crimes over the next decade put sex offenders squarely back on the radar of both media and law enforcement. In the years following World War II, 15 states established commissions to study the problem. In a widely quoted article — "How Safe Is Your Daughter?" — FBI Director J. Edgar Hoover asserted, "The most rapidly increasing type of crime is perpetrated by degenerate sex offenders," and his agency distributed posters urging children to be wary of strangers and not to accept rides from them. [21] A third of Americans surveyed agreed with the proposition that "prison is too good for sex criminals. They should be publicly whipped or worse." [22]

AP Photo

Twelve-year-old Polly Klass was murdered after being kidnapped at knife-point from her home in Petaluma, Calif., by Richard Allen Davis, who is now awaiting execution at San Quentin Prison.

More than half the states passed so-called sexual-psychopath statutes allowing dangerous offenders to be held for treatment for indeterminate periods (the Pennsylvania statute authorized a sentence of "one day to life"). [23] "The sexual psychopath gets locked up, and that's the end of it," said a Wisconsin administrator. [24] The statutes assumed that psychopaths were compulsive and would progress naturally from one type of crime to something worse, so they were broadly defined. Swept into the dragnet were not just rapists and molesters but also those charged with "public masturbation (without indecent exposure)"; "the following of a white female by a Negro"; and "a non-aggressive homosexual convicted of passing bad checks." [25]

No Constitutional Basis

Although sexual-psychopath laws continued to be passed into the 1960s, they drew increasing criticism for being overly broad and for violating ordinary rules of due process. A consultant for New Jersey's sex-offender commission said that prosecutors came to view them "merely as a useful tool to be employed or avoided in accordance with their own convenience." [26]

Sexual-psychopath laws soon became completely ineffective or were nullified in most of the states that had passed them. (Only about 200 offenders a year were committed annually by the end of the 1950s. [27]) Sociologist Edwin H. Sutherland wrote in 1950, "The concept of the 'sexual psychopath' is so vague that . . . the states which have enacted such laws make little or no use of them." [28]

In a backlash against the earlier panic, judges and legislators during the 1960s and early '70s sharply curtailed forced civil commitments and indeterminate sentencing for several psychopaths. Many media accounts of sex crimes turned their focus to miscarriages of justice or racial bias.

This shift in attitudes was exemplified by sociologists who began to claim that rape was an overreported phenomenon and that women seldom resisted their assailants, instead filing complaints only after they'd been jilted or abandoned. And the professional literature of the era also downplayed the damaging effects of molestation on children. "In every way," Jenkins writes, "scholarship of this era presented the plight of the abuse victim in language that seems stunningly callous to modern ears." [29]

The courts began to afford more protection to defendants. In the famous *Miranda* case, which involved a sex offender, the Supreme Court found in 1966 that police had to respect the due-process rights of defendants or forfeit evidence they'd acquired. In subsequent years, courts rejected indeterminate sentencing, the confinement of mental patients who posed no immediate danger to themselves or others and sexual-psychopath statutes that set an impossibly high bar for release.

Mandatory Reporting

But even as the courts were reflecting the notion that child molestation was not a significant problem, the broader societal pendulum was once again swinging back toward fear about the issue. The feminist movement joined with conservatives to draw attention to problems of rape, incest and child abuse, generating renewed media interest and prompting legislative action. In 1974, Congress passed the Child Abuse Prevention and Treatment Act, which mandated the reporting and investigation of abuse allegations and provided matching funds to states that identified abused children and prosecuted abusers. This led to the creation of an infrastructure of agencies, both public and private, devoted to investigating mistreatment.

The advent of mandated reporting swelled abuse statistics. States began to ease physical-evidence requirements, and the number of reported rapes — which had been 22,467 in 1965 — quadrupled to more than 100,000 by 1990. [30] The media also began to report that huge numbers of children — as many as 100,000 — were caught up in pornography rings. Although the figures were largely uncorroborated, increased attention to child pornography and abuse meant that actual incidents were more likely to be reported, which in turn stimulated further investigation and legislation. Sex-abuse claims increased by a factor of 18 between 1976 and 1985, while various surveys indicated that upwards of 20 percent of Americans had been sexually abused as children.

States throughout the 1980s made it easier for children to testify in abuse cases, lifting the obligation that victims — or survivors, as they were becoming known — had to face defendants against whom they were testifying. In a series of rulings in the early 1990s, the Supreme Court made clear that it would favor child protection over established constitutional assumptions about the rights of defendants. In 1992, the court ruled that hearsay testimony offered by doctors, police or family could be offered in lieu of forcing a child to testify. [31]

Studies of treatment programs conducted in the 1970s and '80s found no evidence of reduced recidivism. But therapists and others dealing with sex offenders made important strides during the 1980s, developing cognitive-behavioral therapy programs and relapse training. "Offenders were finally trained to recognize and manage their fantasies and behavior that could not be cured," writes Terry, of the John Jay College of Criminal Justice. [32] In the 1990s, the use of polygraphs also strengthened sex-offender management, offering insights into offenders' honesty (or lack thereof) about their behavior between sessions.

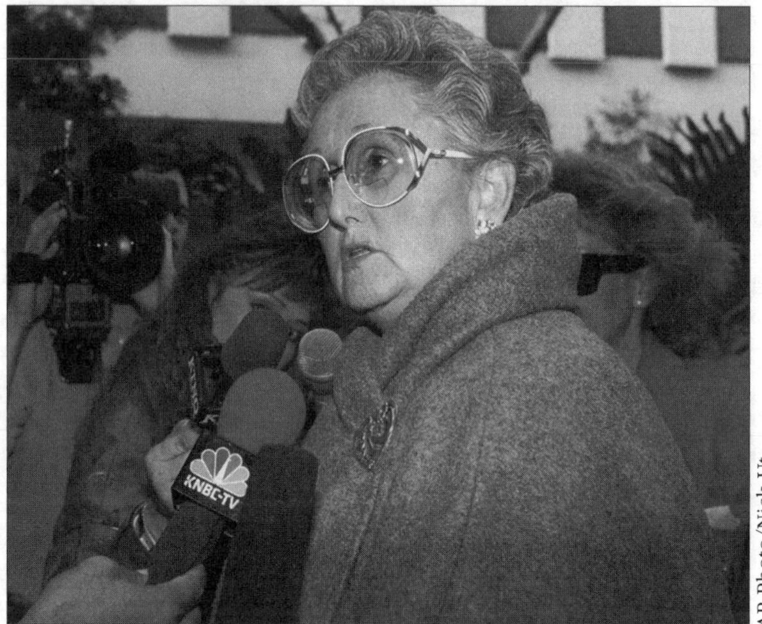

AP Photo/Nick Ut

Peggy McMartin Buckey was cleared in the infamous McMartin preschool case in 1990 after testimony indicated false allegations of an abusive sex ring at the Los Angeles school had been the result of inappropriate coaching of witnesses by police and social workers.

However, shocking cases garnered much more public attention than rehabilitation methods. In the infamous McMartin preschool case in Manhattan Beach, Calif., sensational allegations of satanic sex rituals at the school ultimately proved false. As the case dragged on throughout the 1980s, it became clear that the allegations had been the result of inappropriate coaching of testimony by police and social workers after initial complaints had been brought by a delusional woman. Fear of satanic and ritual sex rings led to other instances in which children who had been coached began, as with the Salem witch trials of the 17th century, to direct charges against investigators once they ran out of other adults they could plausibly accuse. [33] (The validity of repressed or "recovered" memories of abuse that emerged under therapeutic intervention also came into question. [34])

"Part of the problem is that you had really little kids — 3, 4 and 5 years old — and people interviewing them who had almost no awareness of children's suggestibility," says John E.B. Myers, director of the criminal-justice program at the University of the Pacific's McGeorge School of Law.

But other cases were real enough and again focused attention on "stranger danger." In 1989, Earl K. Shriner assaulted and mutilated a 7-year-old boy in Washington state. Shriner had a long criminal record and, while in prison, had designed a van he intended to use for abducting, torturing and killing children. After it became clear that authorities had released an offender who clearly meant to do more harm, the legislature, under enormous pressure to act, in 1990 required dangerous sex offenders to register with police. The law also allowed the state to detain an offender past his release date pending a hearing on civil commitment. (As a *New York Times* headline explained, "Strategy on Sex Crimes Is Prison, Then Prison." [35])

The Washington law drew questions about its constitutionality but nonetheless became a model for at least 16 other state laws, as well as federal legislation enacted in 1994. Before 1994, only five states required sex offenders to register their addresses.

That year, 7-year-old Megan Kanka was raped and strangled. Within weeks, the New Jersey legislature had passed a statute modeled on Washington state's, with the added requirement that police notify neighbors and schools about high-risk offenders in their community. "Megan's Law" had been passed in 35 other states by the time Congress enacted its version in 1996. ■

Average Molester Serves Three Years

Convicted child molesters who were released from prison in 1994 were sentenced to about seven years in prison, on average, but served an average of about three years. Rapists and sexual assaulters served slightly longer before release.

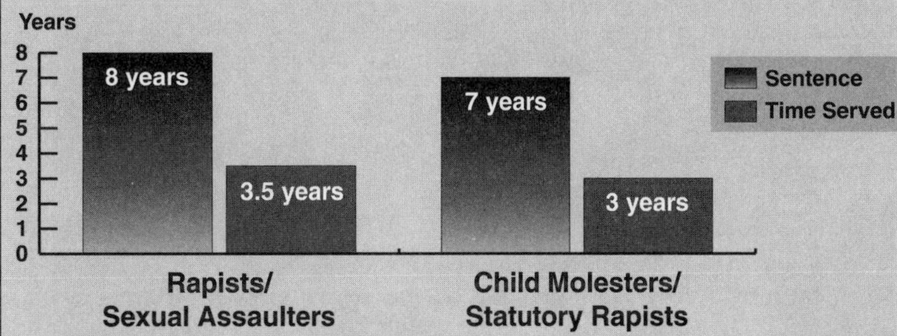

Note; The data are based on 9,691 rapists and 4,295 molesters released in 1994 in 15 states (Ariz., Calif., Del., Fla., Ill., Md., Mich., Minn., N.J., N.Y., N.C., Ohio, Ore., Texas, Va.)

Source: "Recidivism of Sex Offenders Released From Prison in 1994," Bureau of Justice Statistics, November 2003

CURRENT SITUATION

New Legislation

The pace of sex-offender legislation has never been quicker than it is today. In 2005, 45 states passed more than 150 sex-offender laws, according to the National Conference of State Legislatures. That was the most ever passed in a single year and twice the amount of legislation in 2004.

States have kept up the pace, joined by federal lawmakers. Congress this summer passed the Adam Walsh Child Protection and Safety Act, requiring states to maintain publicly accessible offender registries on the Internet, in effect creating a national registry. The new law also requires that sex offenders provide DNA samples and be subject to more frequent in-person verification of their homes and workplaces. Offenders who don't register or update their information are subject to 10-year prison terms, and those who commit violent crimes while registered face five-year minimum sentences. The law also imposes a 30-year minimum sentence for those who have sex with a child younger than 12. [36]

President Bush signed the bill into law on July 27, the 25th anniversary of the murder of the 6-year-old boy, who was abducted while shopping with his mother in Hollywood, Fla. His killer has never been found. Adam was the son of John Walsh, who became a victims'-rights advocate and host of the TV show "America's Most Wanted." "This may be the toughest piece of child-protection legislation in 25 years," Walsh said.

The U.S. Department of Justice has also made fighting sex offenders a top priority. The Adam Walsh Act authorized the department's Project Safe Childhood program, launched earlier this year, which seeks to combat Internet predators by providing grants to states and coordinating federal, state and local law enforcement agencies. "This is an area where effective government is not an option — we *must* be effective," says a DOJ senior counsel.

As part of an annual dragnet in April, the U.S. Marshals Service rounded up 1,102 people wanted for violent sex crimes or for failing to register as a sex offender. The operation "targeted the worst of the worst," said U.S. Attorney General Alberto R. Gonzales. [37]

At the state level, the signature sex-offender law of the last two years is Jessica's Law, after Jessica Lunsford, a 9-year-old Florida girl who was abducted, raped and buried alive in 2005.

AFP/Getty Images/Patrick Davison

Getty Images/Paula Bronstein

False Confession in Ramsey Case

The sensational sexual assault and murder of 6-year-old beauty queen JonBenet Ramsey, of Boulder, Colo., in December 1996 focused suspicion on her parents, John and Patricia, holding a reward poster. John Mark Karr, a teacher from Atlanta, Ga., confessed to the crime after his recent arrest in Thailand, but DNA testing indicated he was not the killer, and he was not charged.

Two-dozen states have passed versions of Jessica's Law, which generally imposes mandatory minimum sentences of 25 years on some categories of offenders and requires those who have committed specific sex crimes to wear satellite-tracking devices for life.

California voters are expected to overwhelmingly pass a strict version of Jessica's Law in November. In addition to a minimum-sentencing requirement (25 years for child rapists) and satellite tracking, the measure would bar offenders from living within 2,000 feet of schools and increase prison terms for a variety of crimes, including possession of child pornography and Internet luring.

A Florida State University study released this year of more than 75,000 offenders placed on home confinement found that those who were tracked by GPS were 90 percent less likely to abscond or re-offend, compared with those who were not electronically monitored. [38]

"We will not mess around with those who mess with our children," Gov. Arnold Schwarzenegger, R-Calif., said in June. "We will find them. We will put them in jail. And we will keep them there." [39] Schwarzenegger's opponent for re-election, Democratic state Treasurer Phil Angelides, has also endorsed the initiative.

The California Legislative Analyst's Office has estimated that Jessica's Law could cost the state $200 million annually after 10 years because of the cost of electronic monitoring and extra parole officers. "It costs an awful lot of money, and it's going to have virtually no effect," said Ron Kokish, a spokesman for the California Coalition on Sexual Offending, a group of treatment providers, public defenders and probation officers. [40]

Such groups have had a hard time getting heard in most legislative debates. In Prince George's County, Md., the public-defender's office lobbied against

Continued on p. 738

At Issue:

Should California voters approve Jessica's Law?

STACIE D. RUMENAP
EXECUTIVE DIRECTOR, STOP CHILD PREDATORS

WRITTEN FOR *CQ RESEARCHER*, SEPTEMBER 2006

yes

With more than 560,000 registered sex offenders in the United States (over 100,000 of them living in California) it should come as no surprise that one-in-five girls and one-in-10 boys are sexually exploited.

In Florida last year a registered sex offender with arrests for sexual assault and fondling a minor was accused of abducting, molesting and burying alive 9-year-old Jessica Lunsford. In Idaho, a twice-convicted registered sex offender was charged with kidnapping and molesting 8-year-old Sasha Groene, molesting and murdering her brother and killing the rest of the family. And these are just a couple of examples of the horrific crimes committed against our nation's children.

As these examples make clear, sex offenders are often released back into society too soon. According to the Justice Department's Bureau of Justice Statistics, the average sentence imposed on a child molester released in 1994 was seven years, although the average offender was released after serving only three — despite the fact that sex offenders are four times more likely than other criminals to commit a sexual offense.

Fortunately for the voters of California, they have the opportunity to protect their children by voting "yes" this November on Proposition 83, "Jessica's Law." Proposition 83 increases penalties for violent sex offenders to 25 years to life in prison and requires lifelong tracking of sex offenders upon release — with costs of the monitoring system paid by the offender. Proposition 83 also bans sex offenders from living within 2,000 feet of any school or park and allows prosecutors to classify possession of child pornography as a felony.

Some critics may argue that mandatory sentencing takes away judicial discretion. As recent court cases demonstrate, however, such discretion is not always in the public's best interest.

In Vermont this past January, Judge Edward Cashman came under fire for handing out a light sentence to a man who confessed to repeatedly raping a young girl over a four-year period. More recently, Judge Kristine Cecava of Nebraska placed a five-foot-one-inch man convicted of sexually assaulting a 12-year-old girl on probation rather than giving him prison time because she was afraid of what might happen to him in jail.

At the very least, mandatory sentencing ensures that judicial indiscretion will not put predatory criminals immediately back on the streets.

We cannot afford another Jessica Lunsford tragedy. It is time for California to join the 24 states that have already passed Jessica's Law by voting "yes" on Proposition 83.

CARLEEN R. ARLIDGE
PRESIDENT, CALIFORNIA ATTORNEYS FOR CRIMINAL JUSTICE

EXCERPTED FROM *CALIFORNIA VOTER INFORMATION GUIDE*, AUG. 14, 2006

no

Proposition 83 would cost taxpayers an estimated $500 million but will not increase our children's safety. Instead, by diluting law-enforcement resources, the initiative would actually reduce most children's security while increasing the danger for those most at risk.

The initiative proposes to monitor every registered sex offender on the misguided theory that each is likely to re-offend against strangers. But law-enforcement experience shows that when sex registrants re-offend, their targets are usually members of their own household. This proposition would do nothing to safeguard children in their own homes, even though they are most at risk.

Second, the proposition would not focus on the real problem — dangerous sex offenders — but would instead waste limited resources tracking persons who pose no risk. The new law would create an expensive tracking system for thousands of registrants who were convicted of minor, non-violent offenses, perhaps years or decades ago. Law-enforcement's resources should be directed toward high-risk individuals living in our neighborhoods.

Proposition 83 would have other dangerous, unintended consequences. The proposition's monitoring provisions would be least effective against those posing the greatest danger. Obviously, dangerous offenders would be the least likely to comply, so the proposed law would push the more serious offenders underground, where they would be less effectively monitored by police. In addition, by prohibiting sex offenders from living within 2,000 feet of a park or school, the initiative would force many offenders from urban to rural areas with smaller police forces. A high concentration of sex offenders in rural neighborhoods will not serve public safety.

Prosecutors in the state of Iowa know from sad experience that this type of residency restriction does not work. In 2001, Iowa adopted a similar law, but now the association of county prosecutors says that it does not provide the protection that was originally intended and that the cost of enforcing the requirement and unintended effects on families of offenders warrant replacing the restriction with more effective protective measures.

Residency restrictions do not reduce sex offenses against children or improve children's safety. Residency restrictions will not be effective against 80 to 90 percent of the sex crimes against children because those crimes are committed by a relative or acquaintance of the child. Residency restrictions cause sex registrants to disappear from the registration system.

The laws also cause unwarranted disruption to the innocent families of ex-offenders.

Continued from p. 736

state legislation requiring GPS tracking and bans on rapists and child molesters from school grounds. The office had no success with its arguments that the GPS technology is uncertain and that it may not be practical to notify churches and schools every time an offender moves. "The problem I'm having is that this is such an emotional issue," said Public Defender Brian C. Denton. "I mean, no one's for sex offenders." [41]

Another popular type of legislation, however, appears to be attracting increasingly louder criticism. Seventeen states and numerous localities have passed such laws, which prohibit sex offenders from living near schools, parks, playgrounds and other places where children congregate.

For supporters, it only makes sense to try to protect children from sexually violent predators. 'This is something that is taking root all over the country," said state Rep. Keen, sponsor of a Georgia proximity law enacted in April. "People are putting a premium on the safety of kids." [42]

But critics say residency-restriction laws are counterproductive. In states where they have taken effect, such as Iowa, there is already evidence that sex offenders are no longer registering. (Groups that follow the issue generally estimate that approximately 100,000 of the 550,000 known sex offenders nationwide have absconded, or gone missing.) The Iowa County Attorneys Association favors repeal of the law.

Getty Images/Jeff Topping

A newly installed facial-recognition camera linked to a Sheriff's Department database of registered sex offenders monitors Royal Palms Middle School, near Phoenix, Ariz., in December 2003. The school removed its two cameras last year after no suspects were spotted entering the school after two years.

In addition to the problem of offenders who abscond, critics say, offenders who comply but are forced to move because their homes are located too near to schools or other facilities that serve children often must go to rural areas with fewer support services. "We know that for people who have a tendency to violence, if they have no support or basic comforts, that really creates an incredibly heightened risk for re-offense," says Klein of the Association for the Treatment of Sex Offenders.

Vigilantism also has been a problem. Last Easter, a Canadian man shot two registered sex offenders in their Maine homes after tracking them down via the state's sex-offender registry Web site. One had been convicted as a sexual predator. The other was 17 when he was arrested for being in a relationship with a 15-year-old girl. The state temporarily took down its registry after the shootings. [43]

Where to Put Ex-Offenders?

With sex offenders facing either legal banishment or, in many cases, community ostracism and protests, it's become tough to know where to put them once they get out of prison. In Colorado, there has been talk of creating a separate town for sex offenders. In Solano County, east of the San Francisco Bay area, California corrections officials have resorted to letting a few sex offenders sleep on cots in a parole office due to a lack of other options. [44]

Perhaps the most controversial approach has been the revival in some states of permanent or semi-permanent civil commitment — holding offenders involuntarily in mental institutions and similar facilities. In an echo of the sexual-psychopath laws of the 1930s, 17 states now allow prisoners to be held for evaluation and treatment after serving their sentences. At the end of 2004, nearly 3,500 prisoners nationwide were being held, according to the Washington State Institute for Public Policy.

Civil commitment is expensive, costing in the neighborhood of $100,000 per year per inmate. In January, Gov. Tim Pawlenty, R-Minn., proposed borrowing $44.6 million to build a 400-bed locked residential building. [45] Republican New York Gov. George E. Pataki has proposed turning an upstate, rural prison into a civil-commitment facility, with a $130 million price tag. [46]

In addition to cost concerns, civil-commitment laws have drawn frequent legal challenge. The U.S. Supreme Court upheld a Kansas law in 1997, saying the state can commit individuals who are likely to engage in predatory acts of violence due to mental abnormality or personality disorder. But the court narrowed states' latitude in 2002, saying they must prove offenders have "serious difficulty" controlling their behavior before they can be committed. [47]

AP Photo/Jeff Roberson

Kerry Skora served 15 years for murder but was labeled as a sex offender after his release because his victim had been a minor. Skora's complaint about the policy led the Illinois legislature to create a new registry for non-sexually violent criminals.

Several other recent sex-offender laws have drawn legal scrutiny. A U.S. district judge found a portion of the Georgia residency-restriction law unconstitutional in June. Iowa's proximity law also was struck down by a district judge in 2004, but an appeals court subsequently ruled that sex-offenders' rights were superseded by the state's compelling interest in protecting its citizens.

In general, concern about citizens' safety has led courts to be tolerant of recent crackdown laws. Some of the laws would seem to violate the Constitution's ex post facto clause — which prohibits laws that impose new punishments for crimes committed prior to the law's passage — such as requiring men who committed sex crimes years earlier to wear satellite-tracking ankle bracelets. Others would seem to violate the double-jeopardy rule — meaning the state can't punish an offender twice for the same crime — such as subjecting an offender to a sanity hearing and civil commitment after his prison term. In general, the courts have held that such laws are regulatory, rather than punitive, and within the state's charge of maintaining public safety.

The return to indefinite civil commitment troubles Lieb, of the Washington State Institute for Public Policy, who has favored other tough, new punishments. "When I read historical articles, in some ways it's disturbing," she says. "You see the same thing going on. It's taught me a certain amount of patience."

Opponents of the contemporary crackdown, however, are happy that the Adam Walsh Act calls for the attorney general to study different containment and treatment methods. They hope that a thorough look at modern treatment techniques will reveal the value of providing programs to offenders who can benefit from them. For instance, juvenile offenders have lower recidivism rates than adult offenders if they undergo treatment, but they tend increasingly to be lumped in with the adults under many of the new laws.

Treatment programs tend to be underfunded, particularly in prison settings. Many officials are skeptical of them, recalling their poor record in early studies and noting that some of the most notorious offenders were treatment failures. In the current environment, though, treatment and rehabilitation are bound to be greeted with more skepticism than stricter punishment.

Approximately 60 to 70 percent of sex offenders are given either probation or a combination of jail and probation, with nearly 90 percent of those required to participate in treatment. But there aren't enough programs to go around and even fewer available in prisons, reports John Jay College criminologist Terry. "The politicians, community and media alike tend to focus only on the risk-management failures of this group of offenders, thereby presenting the supervision agencies as largely ineffective," she writes. [48]

New York Assembly Speaker Sheldon Silver, for instance, proposed legislation this year to require at least two years of treatment for all prisoners incarcerated for a felony sex offense and continued treatment upon release. That measure failed. But the legislature expanded the categories of offenders whose registration information had to be made available to the public while greatly extending the length of time offenders would have to remain on registries. Lawmakers also increased penalties for sexual assaults against children and lengthened the statute of limitations on sex crimes. ■

OUTLOOK

Tougher Laws?

The rate of reported sex crimes against children continues to be low compared to the levels reached 15 years ago. Experts say the tougher laws could be starting to have an effect — either through deterrence or by simply keeping more offenders behind bars or under surveillance. In addition, there has been a 400 percent increase in sex-offender convictions over the past decade. Sex crimes against adults are stable. The attention paid to sex crimes in the wake of high-profile cases has made communities more aware and perhaps more vigilant in keeping children safe.

For some, that's not entirely a good thing. Aside from the incidents of vigilante violence — like Connecticut man charged with stabbing his 2-year-old daughter's alleged molester on Aug. 29 — some observers worry that people are not equipped to deal with the amount of information now available about sex offenders in their midst. The number of Internet searches looking for neighboring sex offenders, for instance, spikes every year around Halloween (several states have made it illegal for registered offenders to hand out candy).

"If I read [online] there's a sex offender in the community, give me some guidance on what I ought to be doing about it," says Fred Berlin, an associate professor of psychiatry at Johns Hopkins University who has been treating sex offenders for 25 years. "That's not happening in a universal way."

Others worry that since sex crimes are overwhelmingly perpetrated by people previously known to the child, all of these laws that try to insulate children from strangers will have the unwarranted effect of making parents feel falsely secure. Moreover, most sex crimes perpetrated by strangers are the work of first-time offenders, against whom background checks, registries and residence restrictions offer no protection.

"Teaching our children about stranger danger sends them the wrong message if that's the only message we give," said Robert Schilling, lead detective in the Seattle Police Department's Sex and Kidnapping Offender unit. "Parents get the idea that Internet predators and strangers in the bushes are who sex offenders are. They don't realize that is one out of thousands. The message has to change." [49]

But fear of sex crimes is likely to extend the push for increasingly strict laws. In California, for instance, the number of forcible rapes dropped by nearly 23 percent from 1999 to 2004 while other sex felonies remained flat, according to the state attorney general's office. Nevertheless, California voters are expected to overwhelming approve one of the toughest sex-offender laws in the nation come November.

"The benefit of having laws like these in all 50 states is that there's no place for sex offenders to hide," says Rumenap, of Stop Child Predators.

The current cycle of anti-sex-offender lawmaking, which extends back for more than 20 years, is already longer than any other such cycle during the 20th century and shows no signs of abating. "There's certainly a movement for longer sentences, often life sentences," says John Jay College criminologist Terry. "Instead of cognitive-behavioral treatment, we're moving toward more chemical castration. There's a move in many states toward civil-commitment laws where they don't already have them."

Beyond the debate about the wisdom and effectiveness of sex-offender legislation, which will certainly be gauged carefully in the coming years, it's clearly one issue that will not go away. "It's not likely state policymakers are going to come up with a solution that will eliminate these problems," says Lieb, of the Washington State Institute for Public Policy. ■

About the Author

Alan Greenblatt is a staff writer at *Governing* magazine. He previously covered elections, agriculture and military spending for *CQ Weekly*, where he won the National Press Club's Sandy Hume Award for political journalism. He graduated from San Francisco State University in 1986 and received a master's degree in English literature from the University of Virginia in 1988. His recent *CQ Researcher* reports include "The Partisan Divide" and "Media Bias."

Notes

[1] Karen J. Terry, *Sexual Offenses and Offenders* (2006), p. xv.

[2] Mark Memmott, "Girl's Death Raises Question About Tracking of Sex Offenders," *USA Today*, March 25, 2005, p. 4A.

[3] "The Greatest Fear," *The Economist*, Aug. 26, 2005, p. 24.

[4] Howard N. Snyder, "Sexual Assault of Young Children as Reported to Law Enforcement: Victim, Incident, and Offender Characteristics," Bureau of Justice Statistics, U.S. Department of Justice, July 2000, p. 10; available at www.ojp.usdoj.gov/bjs/pub/pdf/saycrle.pdf.

[5] Tara Bahrampour, "Discovering a World Beyond the Front Yard," *The Washington Post*, Aug. 27, 2006, p. C1.

[6] Wendy Koch, "States Get Tougher With Sex Offenders," *USA Today*, May 24, 2006, p. 1A.

[7] Lee Rood, "Residency Law Creates Clusters of Sex Offenders," *Des Moines Register*, January 29, 2006, p. 1A.

[8] Jenny Jarvie, "Suit Targets Sex Offender Law," *Los Angeles Times*, July 2, 2006, p. A24.

[9] Charles Sheehan, "Sex Offenders Slip Away," *Chicago Tribune*, March 31, 2006, p. 1.

[10] Ellen Perlman, "Where Will Sex Offenders Live?" *Governing*, June 2006, p. 54.

[11] Monica Davey, "Iowa's Residency Rules Drive Sex Offenders Underground," *The New York Times*, March 15, 2006, p. A1.

[12] Candade Rondeaux, "Can Castration Be a Solution for Sex Offenders?" *The Washington Post*, July 5, 2006, p. B1.

[13] Adam Liptak, "Death Penalty in Some Cases of Child Sex Is Widening," *The New York Times*, June 10, 2006, p. 9. The case is *Coker v. Georgia*, 433 U.S. 584 (1977).

[14] Terry, *op. cit.*, p. 17.

[15] Patrick A. Langan, Erica L. Schmitt and Matthew R. Durose, "Recidivism of Sex Offenders Released From Prison in 1994," Bureau of Justice Statistics, November 2003; www.ojp.usdoj.gov/bjs/pub/pdf/rsorp94.pdf.

[16] Andrew J.R. Harris and R. Karl Hanson, "Sex Offender Recidivism: A Simple Question," Public Safety and Emergency Preparedness Canada User Report 2004-03; available at http://ww2.psepc-sppcc.gc.ca/publications/corrections/pdf/200403-2_e.pdf.

[17] Ernie Allen, "We Need Stronger Tools for Tracking Sex Offenders," *The Washington Post*, Sept. 14, 2005, p. A30.

[18] Quoted in Philip Jenkins, *Moral Panic* (1998), p. 37.

[19] *Ibid.*, p. 37.

[20] *Ibid.*, p. 50.

[21] J. Edgar Hoover, "How Safe Is Your Daughter?" *American Magazine*, July 1947, p. 32.

[22] Elizabeth H. Pleck, *Domestic Tyranny* (1987), p. 121.

[23] Terry, *op. cit.*, p. 28.

[24] Quoted in Gladys Schultz, *How Many More Victims?* (1965), p. 210.

[25] Jenkins, *op. it.*, p. 86.

[26] Paul Tappan, *The Habitual Sex Offender* (1950), p. 15.

[27] Jenkins, *op. cit.*, p. 86

[28] Edwin H. Sutherland, "The Diffusion of Sexual Psychopath Laws," *American Journal of Sociology 56*, 1950, p. 142.

[29] Jenkins, *op. cit.*, p. 103.

[30] *Ibid.*, p. 127.

[31] David G. Savage, "Justices Shield Child Victims in Abuse Cases," *Los Angeles Times*, Jan. 16, 1992, p. A3.

[32] Terry, *op. cit.*, p. 142.

[33] Jenkins, *op. cit.*, p. 166.

[34] Terry, *op. cit.*, p. 33.

[35] Robb London, "Strategy on Sex Crimes Is Prison, Then Prison," *The New York Times*, Feb. 8, 1991, p. B16.

[36] Seth Stern, "Law Enacted to Strengthen Penalties Against Child Molesters," *CQ Weekly*, July 29, 2006, p. 2116.

[37] The Associated Press, "1,102 Sex Offenders Rounded up in 27-State Dragnet," *The Washington Post*, April 28, 2006, p. A2.

[38] Wendy Koch, "More Sex Offenders Tracked by Satellite," *USA Today*, June 7, 2006, p. 3A.

[39] John Maurelius, "Governor Pushes Anti-Crime Agenda," *The San Diego Union-Tribune*, June 30, 2006, p. B1.

[40] Jordan Rau, "A Bid to Toughen Stance on Sex Offenses," *Los Angeles Times*, Feb. 19, 2006.

[41] Matthew Mosk, "A Lone Voice Against Sex Offender Bill," *The Washington Post*, March 25, 2006, p. B1.

[42] Jarvie, *op. cit.*

[43] Judy Harrison, "2 men slain in Milo, Corinth; Suspect from Canada kills himself in Boston," *Bangor Daily News*, April 17, 2006, p. A1.

[44] Jenifer Warren, "Sex Offender Housing Scarce," *Los Angeles Times*, May 31, 2006, p. A1.

[45] John Q. La Fond and Bruce J. Winick, "Doing More Than Their Time," *The New York Times*, May 21, 2006, p. 14:23.

[46] "A Place for Sex Offenders," *The New York Times*, Jan. 22, 2006, p. 14:11.

[47] Jan Crawford Greenburg, "Justices Set Higher Bar for Detention," *Chicago Tribune*, Jan. 23, 2002, p. 8. The cases are *Kansas v. Hendricks*, 521 U.S. 346 (1997) and *Kansas v. Crane*, 534 U.S. 407 (2002).

[48] Terry, *op. cit.*, p. 142.

[49] Natalie Singer, "'Stranger Danger' Emphasis Misguided," *Seattle Times*, May 23, 2006, p. B1.

FOR MORE INFORMATION

Association for the Treatment of Sex Offenders, 4900 S.W. Griffith Dr., Suite 274, Beaverton, OR 97005; (503) 643-1023; www.atsa.com. A nonprofit, interdisciplinary organization that fosters research, develops practice guidelines and promotes professional education in the field of sex-offender evaluation and treatment.

Bureau of Justice Statistics, U.S. Department of Justice, 810 Seventh St., N.W., Washington, DC 20531; (202) 307-0765; www.ojp.usdoj.gov/bjs/welcome.html. A primary source for crime statistics; collects, analyzes and publishes information on crime and criminal offenders.

Center for Sex Offender Management, 8403 Colesville Rd., Suite 720, Silver Spring, MD 20910; (301) 589-9383; www.csom.org. A group supported by the U.S. Department of Justice that works to improve means of managing adult and juvenile sex offenders who are not incarcerated.

National Center for Missing and Exploited Children, 699 Prince St., Alexandria, VA 22314; (202) 274-3900; www.missingkids.org. A nonprofit group that works to prevent child abduction and sexual exploitation.

Stop Child Predators, 601 Thirteenth St., N.W., Suite 930 South, Washington, DC 20005; (202) 234-0090; www.stopchildpredators.org. An advocacy group promoting more diligent tracking of sex offenders and greater protection of victims' rights.

Bibliography

Selected Sources

Books

Jenkins, Philip, *Moral Panic: Changing Concepts of the Child Molester in America*, Yale University Press, 1998.
A Pennsylvania State University historian shows how periods of concern have been followed by periods of neglect throughout the 20th century.

La Fond, John Q., *Preventing Sexual Violence: How Society Should Cope With Sex Offenders*, American Psychological Association, 2005.
A University of Missouri law professor says laws enacted since 1990 are based on false assumptions and present data in an effort to persuade professionals in the field to focus on risk-management programs.

Terry, Karen J., *Sexual Offenses and Offenders: Theory, Practice, and Policy*, Wadsworth, 2006.
A John Jay College criminologist offers a comprehensive survey of current data and policy regarding sex offenders.

Articles

"The Greatest Fear," *The Economist*, Aug. 26, 2006, p. 24.
The British magazine concludes that American fear of sex crimes is disproportionate.

Koch, Wendy, "States Get Tougher With Sex Offenders," *USA Today*, May 24, 2006, p. 1A.
Both Congress and the states are working on stricter penalties for sex offenders.

Jarvie, Jenny, "Suit Targets Sex Offender Law," *Los Angeles Times*, July 2, 2006, p. A24.
A U.S. district judge rules that part of a Georgia law restricting where sex offenders can live is unconstitutional.

Liptak, Adam, "Death Penalty in Some Cases of Child Sex Is Widening," *The New York Times*, June 10, 2006, p. 9.
Oklahoma and South Carolina join three other states in imposing the death penalty on repeat sex offenders.

Perlman, Ellen, "Where Will Sex Offenders Live?" *Governing*, June 2006, p. 54.
State and local laws are making it harder for sex criminals to find places to live, which in turn hampers law enforcement's ability to do its job effectively.

Rau, Jordan, "A Bid to Toughen Stance on Sex Offenses," *Los Angeles Times*, Feb. 19, 2006, p. B1.
California voters will decide whether to stiffen penalties against sex offenders, but the experience of other states with similar laws cautions against certain success.

Rondeaux, Candace, "Can Castration Be a Solution for Sex Offenders?" *The Washington Post*, July 5, 2006, p. B1.
A sex criminal who castrated himself argues that the method eliminates unhealthy sexual desires, but others wonder whether it's effective or constitutional.

Stern, Seth, "Law Enacted to Strengthen Penalties Against Child Predators," *CQ Weekly*, July 29, 2006, p. 2116.
President Bush signs a law that creates a national sex-offender registry and toughens penalties for sex crimes against children.

Turner, Joseph, "Bill Ups Required Sex Felon Sentence," *The* [Tacoma] *News Tribune*, March 5, 2006, p. B1.
The Washington state legislature unanimously approves longer sentences for sex offenders.

Reports and Studies

Finkelhor, David, and Lisa M. Jones, "Explanations for the Decline in Child Sexual Abuse Cases," Juvenile Justice Bulletin, Office of Juvenile Justice and Delinquency Prevention, U.S. Department of Justice, January 2004.
The authors, from the Crimes Against Children Research Center at the University of New Hampshire, say multiple factors are involved in a 40 percent reduction in child sex-abuse cases between 1992 and 2000, including a particular focus on preventing this form of child maltreatment.

Harris, Andrew J.R., and R. Karl Hanson, "Sex Offender Recidivism: A Simple Question," Public Safety and Emergency Preparedness Canada User Report 2004-03.
Data from 10 follow-up studies of adult, male sex offenders indicate that most do not reoffend sexually and that first-time offenders are much less likely to sexually re-offend than those with previous sex crime convictions.

Langan, Patrick A., Erica L. Schmitt and Matthew R. Durose, "Recidivism of Sex Offenders Released From Prison in 1994," Bureau of Justice Statistics, November 2003.
A study of 9,691 prisoners released from prisons in 15 states in 1994 finds that 5.3 percent of them were rearrested for another sex crime within three years of release.

Snyder, Howard N., "Sexual Assault of Young Children as Reported to Law Enforcement: Victim, Incident, and Offender Characteristics," Bureau of Justice Statistics, U.S. Department of Justice, July 2000.
Crimes against juveniles represent a large majority of sex-abuse cases handled by law enforcement. One-in-seven victims is under age 7, and more than a third of cases involved a victim under 12.

The Next Step:

Additional Articles from Current Periodicals

Catholic Church

Dooley, Tara, "Fewer Church Abuse Claims Found," *The Houston Chronicle*, March 31, 2006, p. B3.
Allegations of sexual abuse of minors by U.S. Catholic Church clergy in 2005 decreased by more than 300 claims.

Fisher, Ian, and Laurie Goodstein, "Vatican Disciplines Founder of Order Over Abuse Charges," *The New York Times*, May 20, 2006, p. A6.
The Vatican forced the Rev. Marcial Maciel Degollado, 86, one of the most prominent priests to be accused of sexual abuse, to give up his public ministry.

O'Reilly, David, "Bishops: We're Not Blocking Legislation," *The Philadelphia Inquirer*, Aug. 14, 2006, p. A1.
Pennsylvania's Catholic bishops say their passive approach toward sex-abuse bills does not mean they oppose the laws.

Internet Predators

Dardick, Hal, "Bills Seek Crackdown on Internet Predators," *Chicago Tribune*, July 29, 2006, p. 15.
A bill in the Illinois House would make it a felony for anyone 17 or older to discuss sex acts on the Internet with a minor.

Eichenwald, Kurt, "From Their Own Online World, Pedophiles Extend Their Reach," *The New York Times*, Aug. 21, 2006, p. A1.
Pedophiles connect with other pedophiles on the Internet to seek tips for getting near children.

Tougher Sentences

Brundrett, Rick, "Child-Sex Clause Draws Criticism," *Charlotte Observer* (North Carolina), July 9, 2006, p. Y7.
Critics of South Carolina's version of Florida's Jessica's Law say it would allow suspects in consensual relationships to claim they didn't know their victims were underage.

Clark, Lesley, "Bush Signs Law to Track Child Predators," *The Miami Herald*, July 28, 2006, p. A3.
President Bush signed a new law that requires convicted sex offenders to be listed on a national registry.

Doan, Lynn, "Twenty-Five Suspected Molesters May Face Deportation," *Los Angeles Times*, Aug. 25, 2006, p. B5.
Federal agents are cracking down on foreign nationals who prey on children.

Franck, Matthew, "Offender Bill Requires No Warrant," *St. Louis Post-Dispatch*, Feb. 23, 2006, p. D1.
A Missouri bill would permit police seeking a missing child to search a sex offender's home without a warrant.

Jenkins, Chris L., "Sex-Predator Laws Widen State Powers," *The Washington Post*, April 25, 2006, p. B5.
Virginia Gov. Timothy Kain signed several bills that will toughen the punishment and monitoring of sex offenders.

Luscombe, Richard, "Florida's Tough Stand Against Child Molesters," *The Christian Science Monitor*, May 4, 2005, p. 2.
Florida Gov. Jeb Bush signed "Jessica's Law" to provide for satellite tracking of sex offenders in the state.

Thomas, Ralph, "Father Calls For Stricter Laws," *The Seattle Times*, Jan. 13, 2006, p. B1.
Mark Lunsford, whose daughter Jessica was raped and killed last year, is urging states to pass tough anti-sex-crime laws.

Waddell, Lynn, "Iris Scans: Keeping an Eye on Sex Offenders," *Newsweek*, July 24, 2006, p. 8.
Law enforcement can now keep track of sex offenders with the Sex Offender Registry and Identification System (SORIS).

Zoning Restrictions

Warren, Jennifer, "State Is Ordered to Screen Sex Offenders Before Parole," *Los Angeles Times*, June 17, 2006, p. B9.
Gov. Arnold Schwarzenegger ordered California's corrections department to ensure released sex offenders are not housed near schools.

Jarvie, Jenny, "Georgia Sex-Offender Rules Create Stir," *The Seattle Times*, July 3, 2006, p. A5.
U.S. District Judge Clarence Cooper temporarily blocked a Georgia law signed in April that prohibits sex offenders from living within 1,000 feet of a school-bus stop.

CITING *CQ RESEARCHER*

Sample formats for citing these reports in a bibliography include the ones listed below. Preferred styles and formats vary, so please check with your instructor or professor.

MLA STYLE

Jost, Kenneth. "Rethinking the Death Penalty." CQ Researcher 16 Nov. 2001: 945-68.

APA STYLE

Jost, K. (2001, November 16). Rethinking the death penalty. *CQ Researcher, 11*, 945-968.

CHICAGO STYLE

Jost, Kenneth. "Rethinking the Death Penalty." *CQ Researcher*, November 16, 2001, 945-968.

CQ Researcher

Published by CQ Press, a division of Congressional Quarterly Inc.

cqresearcher.com

Voting Controversies

Can all citizens vote — and are all votes counted?

Vote-counting controversies in both the 2000 and 2004 presidential elections have left a cloud of concern hanging over the upcoming November 2006 congressional vote as well as the not-so-far-off 2008 presidential election. The issues range from the trustworthiness of electronic, touch-screen voting machines to fears that laws requiring more stringent verification of citizens' identities would disenfranchise minority voters. Some computer experts insist that touch-screen machines are vulnerable to hackers and that "paper trails" are needed to ensure that the vote counts can be verified if challenged. But the devices are so popular with election officials that up to 40 percent of voters will use touch-screen machines this year, many of which will not produce backup paper print-outs. Meanwhile, scrutiny of the entire voting process, from voter registration to ballot counting is intensifying in courthouses and statehouses across the country.

A Miami woman votes during the 2004 presidential election. The reliability of touch-screen and electronic voting machines is an issue in the upcoming November elections.

INSIDE THIS REPORT

CQ Researcher • Sept. 15, 2006 • www.cqresearcher.com
Volume 16, Number 32 • Pages 745-768

CQ PRESS

RECIPIENT OF SOCIETY OF PROFESSIONAL JOURNALISTS AWARD FOR EXCELLENCE ◆ AMERICAN BAR ASSOCIATION SILVER GAVEL AWARD

THE ISSUES

BACKGROUND

CURRENT SITUATION

OUTLOOK

SIDEBARS AND GRAPHICS

FOR FURTHER RESEARCH

Cover photograph: Getty Images/G. De Cardenas

CQ Researcher

Sept. 15, 2006
Volume 16, Number 32

MANAGING EDITOR: Thomas J. Colin

ASSISTANT MANAGING EDITOR: Kathy Koch

ASSOCIATE EDITOR: Kenneth Jost

STAFF WRITERS: Marcia Clemmitt, Peter Katel

CONTRIBUTING WRITERS: Rachel S. Cox, Sarah Glazer, Alan Greenblatt, Barbara Mantel, Patrick Marshall, Tom Price, Jennifer Weeks

DESIGN/PRODUCTION EDITOR: Olu B. Davis

ASSISTANT EDITOR: Melissa J. Hipolit

A Division of Congressional Quarterly Inc.

SENIOR VICE PRESIDENT/PUBLISHER: John A. Jenkins

DIRECTOR, LIBRARY PUBLISHING: Kathryn C. Suárez

DIRECTOR, EDITORIAL OPERATIONS: Ann Davies

CONGRESSIONAL QUARTERLY INC.

CHAIRMAN: Paul C. Tash

VICE CHAIRMAN: Andrew P. Corty

PRESIDENT/EDITOR IN CHIEF: Robert W. Merry

CQ Researcher (ISSN 1056-2036) is printed on acid-free paper. Published weekly, except March 24, July 7, July 14, Aug. 4, Aug. 11, Nov. 24, Dec. 22 and Dec. 29, by CQ Press, a division of Congressional Quarterly Inc. Annual full-service subscriptions for institutions start at $667. For pricing, call 1-800-834-9020, ext. 1906. To purchase a *CQ Researcher* report in print or electronic format (PDF), visit www.cqpress.com or call 866-427-7737. Single reports start at $15. Bulk purchase discounts and electronic-rights licensing are also available. Periodicals postage paid at Washington, D.C., and additional mailing offices. POSTMASTER: Send address changes to *CQ Researcher*, 1255 22nd St., N.W., Suite 400, Washington, DC 20037.

Voting Controversies

BY PETER KATEL

THE ISSUES

Suspense is building as Americans prepare to vote in critical midterm congressional elections on Nov. 7. With the Bush administration facing increasing criticism over the Iraq war, some experts are saying the Republican Party could lose both its House and Senate majorities.

Politics explains only part of the tension. Many experts and everyday Americans question whether the nation's electoral system can deliver reliable results.

The concern largely stems from controversies surrounding the cliffhanger 2000 and 2004 presidential elections, which sparked a wave of legal, procedural and technological changes in Congress, statehouses and the 9,500 voting jurisdictions that conduct U.S. elections.

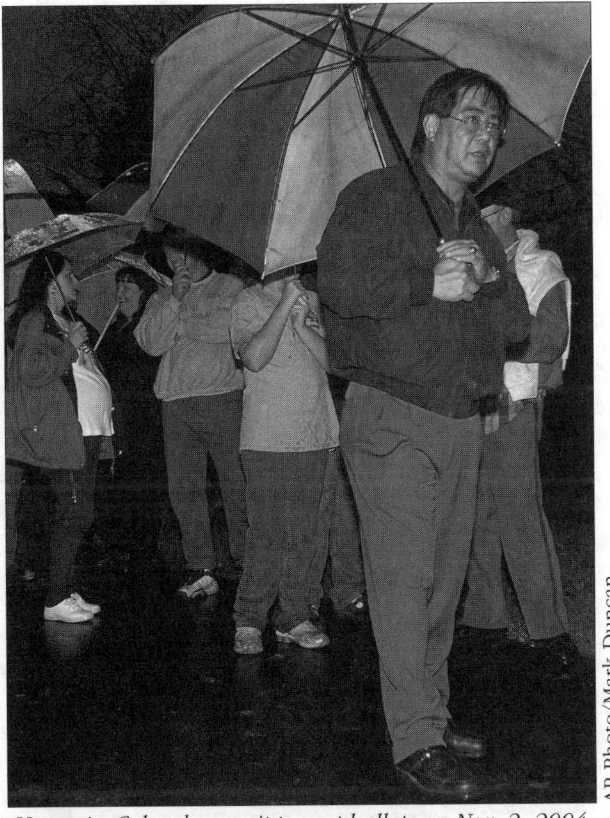

AP Photo/Mark Duncan

Voters in Columbus wait to cast ballots on Nov. 2, 2004. Some Ohio voters waited in line up to 10 hours. Problems in the 2000 and 2004 presidential elections have left a cloud of concern over the upcoming November congressional elections.

Some election-reform advocates warn that critical issues have been left unresolved, among them questions about the reliability of computerized voting machines and the possibility that some voter-identification laws effectively block minorities and poor people from voting.

The election system "is ripe for another crisis in 2006," warned Robert Pastor, director of American University's Center for Democracy and Election Management." [1]

Pastor spoke last February at a conference sponsored by the American Enterprise Institute and the Brookings Institution, two of the many think tanks, research centers, foundations and blue-ribbon commissions that have mobilized over the past six years to recommend electoral-system improvements. Their work is taking place against the backdrop of the bitter partisan split that has defined the country's politics for most of the decade, especially since the terrorist attacks of Sept. 11, 2001.

"There is a sense since 9/11 — and it's more severe since the Iraq war — that there's a tremendous amount at stake here for our country and the world," says historian Alexander Keyssar, a specialist in elections at Harvard University's John F. Kennedy School of Government. "There is a sense of dramatically heightened stakes." In such an atmosphere, he adds, "Whether elections express the will of the people becomes a much sharper and more important issue."

In 2000, the U.S. Supreme Court stepped in to order an end to recounting in Florida — the state that clinched George W. Bush's victory over the Democratic candidate, Vice President Al Gore. By the time the court ruled, dramatic images had been beamed around the world of vote counters peering at the "hanging chads" on ballots from punch-card voting machines.

Congress responded by passing the Help America Vote Act (HAVA) of 2002, which earmarked $650 million for states to replace old-style machines, such as Florida's, with computerized devices and to train poll workers and update voter databases. [2] But despite many technological changes, the presidential election of 2004 also came down to the votes of a single state — Ohio — where Election Day foul-ups and irregularities marred voters' confidence in the outcome. (*See sidebar, p. 756.*)

For Democrats, the Ohio problems centered on practices that they said led to thousands of would-be voters — mostly African-Americans — being prevented from registering or blocked from casting their votes. "We can live with winning and losing," the Rev. Jesse Jackson said later. "We cannot live with fraud and stealing." [3]

"Jackson owes every election official in Ohio an apology," responded Keith Cunningham, vice president of the Ohio Association of Election Officials. "His accusations are outrageous, preposterous and baseless." [4]

However, Jackson's charges echoed the country's long history of keeping black people from voting. The Voting Rights Act of 1965 made racial exclusion illegal, but Keyssar says discrimination against black voters is tempting. "African-American voters are a very easily identifiable and locatable group of voters whose partisan preferences are reasonably clear."

Such charges are key parts of lawsuits in Indiana and several of the other 22 states that have enacted new voter-identification laws that expanded on a HAVA provision that allows first-time registrants to enroll by mail. The Democratic Party and the American Civil Liberties Union (ACLU) argued that fees for the voter-ID cards now required under the new laws are dangerously reminiscent of poll taxes used throughout the South to bar blacks from voting during the Jim Crow era. [5]

"It's 100 percent untrue," says Robert Vane, communications director of the Indiana Republican Party. "The Democrats' greatest fear is that black folks will start taking a long look at the Republican Party. They're dredging up all these crazy claims as their best ammo in that desperate fight."

Underlying much of the election-law litigation are GOP charges of large-scale election fraud aimed at expanding the ranks of likely Democratic voters. The Republicans allege widespread multiple voting by individuals as well as voting by convicted, unpardoned felons and non-citizens. Democrats and their allies deny the charges and say Republicans are stoking alarmism in order to build support for restricting access to the polls. [6]

"You hear all the time [from Democrats] that illegal elections are going on all over the country," says Randy Pullen, a Republican national committeeman from Phoenix, Ariz., sarcastically repeating Democratic accusations — " 'They stole the election in Florida, they stole the election in Ohio.' " In the end, he says, the Democrats cry fraud but resist attempts to curb it.

But fraud takes on a different meaning to Democrats. For them, electoral trickery includes manipulating vote counts, blocking eligible voters from casting ballots and raising obstacles to efforts by private organizations such as the League of Women Voters to register voters.

Justin Levitt, associate counsel of the Brennan Center for Justice at New York University, says there is no evidence of systematic fraud, as Republicans allege. "Eligible citizens should be allowed to vote, and we should be facilitating that process rather than putting down hurdle after hurdle," he says. "It's striking that governments are putting in new restrictions because government doesn't trust the people." The Brennan Center — named after the late liberal Supreme Court Justice William J. Brennan — is litigating challenges to voter-identification laws in five states.

The need for identification requirements also ranked high on the priority lists of two blue-ribbon panels that examined the election system following the 2000 and 2004 elections. The report of the National Commission on Federal Electoral Reform, chaired by former presidents Democrat Jimmy Carter and Republican Gerald R. Ford, became the basis for HAVA in 2002. Then, in 2004, Carter co-chaired the almost identically named Commission on Federal Electoral Reform with ex-Secretary of State James A. Baker III, a Republican. [7]

HAVA required first-time voters registering by mail to present proof of identity either when registering or voting. But some states have gone further — Arizona became the first in the country to require definitive proof of U.S. citizenship for registration. [8]

The Carter-Baker commission recommended a similar measure nationwide. But the commission also urged states to seek out minorities, the old and the poor to make sure that they aren't kept from voting. [9]

Meanwhile, the spread of computer voting machines has sparked debate among citizen activists and scientists as well as technology experts. [10] (*See sidebar, p. 750.*)

HAVA encouraged the spread of computerized voting by offering states $325 million to buy modern machines. But local governments' growing adoption of entirely paperless direct recording electronic (DRE) touch-screen devices — cousins to automatic teller machines (ATMs) — has sparked a firestorm of opposition, in large part because they do not all produce paper records that can be used to verify a machine-vote recount.

Still, some election-law experts caution against hyping computer dangers. "There is reason to be concerned," says Richard L. Hasen, a professor at Loyola Law School in Los Angeles who runs a widely consulted election-law blog. "But this is true with all voting machines. We've had voting fraud long before we had computers."

Purely technological problems may prove less serious, in the end, than deliberate interference with the election process. Tracy Campbell, a University of Kentucky historian specializing in election fraud, says political passion can fuel a determination to win by any means necessary, including fraud.

"With so much on the line in an election, especially when partisan rancor is so extreme, you've got to expect people to think, 'What I'm doing is defending the Republic, and my opponents are trying to destroy it,'" She says. "There's now a patriotic, almost religious, fervor to it."

As Election Day 2006 approaches, these are some of the questions being asked by lawmakers, politicians and voters:

Do new registration and voting requirements pose unfair barriers to minorities?

Nowhere are the political battle lines drawn more clearly than over the question of who can register and vote. "Without exception," says election-law scholar Hasen, "these laws have been promoted and passed by Republican-dominated legislatures and opposed by Democrats. I don't think that's a coincidence."

A total of 22 states now require voters to present identification at the polls — up from 11 in 2000. Although HAVA does not impose a nationwide ID standard for registering and voting, the law does require all first-time voters who have registered by mail — often by providing a photocopy of a driver's license — to present an ID when they vote. [11]

New Voter-ID Rules in 26 States

More than half of the states have implemented the minimum voter-ID requirements called for under the 2002 Help America Vote Act (HAVA). Indiana is the only state that requires all voters to show a state or U.S. government-issued photo ID.

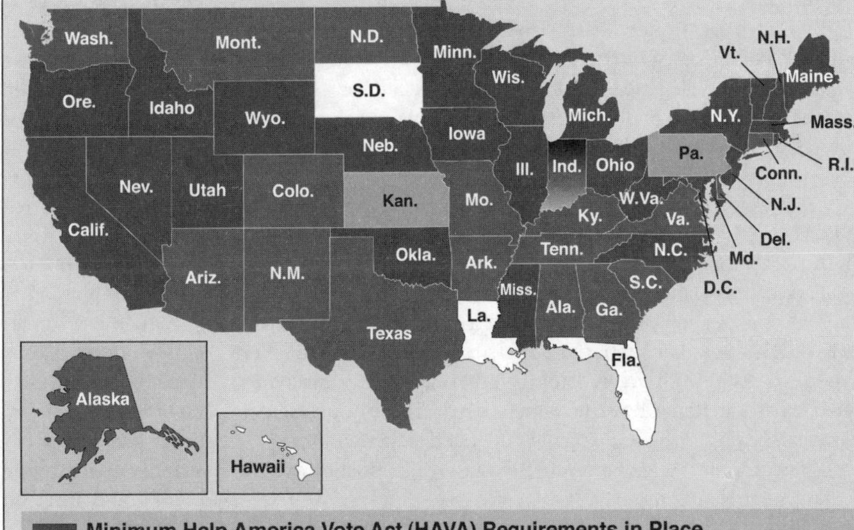

Minimum Help America Vote Act (HAVA) Requirements in Place
(Verification required of first-time voters who register by mail and did not provide verification with their registration application)

Some Form of Verification Required for All Voters
(photo and non-photo verification accepted)

Some Form of Verification Required of All First-Time Voters

State or U.S. Government-Issued Photo ID Required to Vote

Photo Identification Requested of All Voters
(Voters without verification can sign affidavits and cast regular ballots)

Source: electionline.org, "What's Changed, What Hasn't and Why, 2000-2006," February 2006

In 2005, the Carter-Baker commission called for tougher voter-identification requirements by recommending a nationwide, universal voter ID to guard against multiple voting — which Republicans insist is widespread and most Democrats say is minor. The partisan divide on the issue even reached into the ranks of the bipartisan panel. "The commission is divided on the magnitude of voter fraud," the 20-member panel reported, while noting that even small-scale fraud can tip the scales in a close election. [12]

Republican Party activists complain there is evidence of widespread election fraud and argue that if mundane tasks such as renting a movie require an ID so should an activity as important as voting. Democrats and their allies call allegations of widespread voter fraud "rhetoric" that camouflages a strategy of ensuring that likely Democratic voters are kept off the rolls or out of the polls.

In fact, says Levitt, of the Brennan Center for Justice, GOP proof of systematic fraud is so thin that no possible goal besides disenfranchising poor and minority-group votes could explain the Republican demand for voter IDs. "When you add up the documented cases of people misrepresenting their identity at polls," he says, "the chances that someone will commit fraud that can be stopped by the use of an ID card are almost the same as getting hit and killed by lightning."

Jason Torchinsky, a lawyer for the American Center for Voting Rights and a former attorney for the 2004 Bush campaign, says the same about the Democrats. "They don't really have any studies or evidence to back their assertion" that Republicans are using fraud allegations to bar minorities from voting, Torchinsky says.

Levitt later countered with a 2005 report by the League of Women Voters of Ohio and the Coalition on Homelessness and Housing of Ohio. It found four cases of fraudulent voting in the 2002 and 2004 general elections in Ohio, in which more than 9 million votes were cast — making a lightning strike more likely than a fraudulent vote, researchers calculated. [13]

But Jonathan Bechtle, director of the voter-integrity project at the conservative Evergreen Freedom Foundation in Olympia, Wash., says documented fraud cases inevitably understate the magnitude of the problem. "There aren't a lot of those [because] prosecutors put a low priority on them," he says. He noted that in Washington — where Democratic Gov. Christine Gregoire won the election by 129 votes in 2004 — more than 3,000 people were found to be registered twice, but only eight have been charged with fraudulent voting. A GOP attempt to overturn the election failed in court. [14]

Opponents of tougher ID requirements cite a 2005 University of Wisconsin study that found only 45 percent of African-American men and 51 percent of black women in Wisconsin had valid driver's licenses — the most common form of identification. Similarly, only 54 percent of Hispanic men and 41 percent of the women had licenses. [15]

Driver's licenses are closely linked to socioeconomic status and age, the

Continued on p. 752

Would a 'Paper Trail' Eliminate Vote-Counting Fraud?

Primary elections in Ohio last May provided an object lesson in what can go wrong with an election — even when high-tech voting machines produce paper backup records.

In Cuyahoga County (Cleveland), nearly 10 percent of the rolls of paper on which results were printed out were "destroyed, blank, illegible, missing, taped together or otherwise compromised," the San Francisco-based Election Science Institute (ESI) reported to the County Commission last August in a 234-page report. [1]

"Discrepancies between paper record and the electronic record were . . . pervasive," ESI said. "One likely result is diminished public confidence in a close election." [2]

Paradoxically, the election system that ESI examined had been upgraded in recent years precisely to assure reliability. Ohio is one of 25 states that require a paper record of each vote, even when voters use direct recording electronic (DRE) machines, such as those that Cleveland voters used. These touch-screen devices weren't designed originally to need paper. [3]

But computer scientists, activists and some politicians saw a flaw in that design.

Without a paper ballot, "You cannot assume that what you put in is what you get out," says Richard A. Celeste, a former governor of Ohio who co-chaired a study of voting-machine technology for the National Research Council of the National Academies. "You need ways to monitor and audit results." [4]

The drive for paper backup follows a nationwide switch to electronic voting machines. In the Help America Vote Act of 2002 (HAVA), Congress authorized handing out $325 million to states so they could replace old-fashioned punch-card and lever-action machines. Lawmakers were responding to the presidential election crisis of 2000, when Florida vote-counters tried to determine who won by examining paper ballots for "hanging chads." [5]

Many states and local governments turned to optical-scan machines, which "read" voters' markings on a paper ballots and count the results. By its nature that system comes with its own paper backup.

In congressional elections this November, about 40 percent of U.S. voters will be making their choices on optical-scan devices, and a roughly equal share of voters will be using DREs. [6]

Michael Shamos, a computer scientist and lawyer at Carnegie-Mellon University in Pittsburgh, Pa., says paper records aren't necessarily more reliable than computer memories. "If the machine cannot be trusted — which is the working hypothesis of paper-trail proponents — then it cannot be trusted to deal with the paper trail safely," he writes. [7]

Nonetheless, says Aviel D. Rubin, a computer-science professor at Johns Hopkins University, if election results are challenged in a precinct that uses paperless computers, "There's nothing to count." Rubin and others have been pressing that argument even as DRE electronic voting machine sales have boomed. Revenues of the four industry leaders and three smaller firms total from $350 million to $550 million a year, estimates Michael Kerr, director of the International Technology Association of America's Election Technology Council, the trade group for voting-machine manufacturers.

DRE advocates say the machines all but eliminate the problems of unreadable or incorrectly marked ballots, known in the election trade as residual votes and undervotes. "DREs provide dramatic improvements" over mechanical systems, Kerr says. As for paper-printout requirements, "I don't think we have any particular opinion."

Other DRE defenders are quick to point out that the machines are not known to have altered the results of any elections. "There were no substantiated reports from any state of compromised elections due to security flaws that involved computer hacking or similar attacks in 2004," the Congressional Research Service reported, though acknowledging that some computer fraud can't be spotted. [8]

However, a Government Accountability Office report last year found that some electronic voting machines did not encrypt votes or audit logs, making it possible to alter the files "so that the votes for one candidate could be recorded for a different candidate" without being detected. [9]

HAVA does require an elementary level of hard-copy backup — a requirement that every voting machine produce a "permanent paper record with manual audit capacity." [10] But Rubin and other DRE critics say the gold standard is a "voter-verified paper audit trail (VVPAT)."

This system was the brainchild of Rebecca Mercuri, president of Notable Software, a Hamilton Township, N.J., consulting and forensic-investigation firm. In a VVPAT system, the voters don't "cast" their vote until they have seen a paper printout of the choices made on the touch screen. If the printout is wrong, that printout is voided, and the voting process begins again. "By that casting action, the ballot is verified," Mercuri says. "Now it is the ballot of record."

Rep. Rush Holt, D-N.J., has proposed a bill to require VVPAT systems nationwide, which is awaiting House Administration Committee action.

Mercuri supports Holt's bill. But she and many other VVPAT advocates make no secret of their view that the paper trail is merely a stopgap. They argue that computer memories are too vulnerable to tampering and breakdown to be entrusted with elections. "Abolish DREs entirely," urges journalist Ronnie Dugger of Cambridge, Mass., who wrote the first account of potential problems with computerized voting in 1988. "There should be no vote counting by secret and invisible ballots." [11]

As Cleveland's troubles in its primary elections in May would seem to indicate, even VVPATs don't offer a completely reliable backstop. Mercuri, Rubin and others say optical-scan systems offer far more protection against technological problems and high-tech fraud.

But the manufacturer of Cleveland's DRE machines, Diebold Election Systems Inc. of Allen, Texas, didn't take the ESI report lying down. The company blamed problems on poll workers and accused ESI of shoddy work. "There would seem to be apparent weakness in the skills of ESI or the investigatory methodology employed by them," Michael E. Lindroos, the company's vice president, wrote to county commissioners on Aug. 16 [12] ESI countered that technical data it had requested was still not forthcoming and that flaws and questions identified during the investigation hadn't been resolved. [13]

None of the give-and-take satisfied William Ritter, a high-school history teacher who had run for the Democratic nomination for the state House of Representatives. Between the first unofficial count and the official count two weeks later, Ritter went from winner by 115 votes to loser by 178.

Given all the vote discrepancies, Ritter asks, "How can they tell me I lost?"

'Paper Trails' Required by Many States

The majority of states that utilize direct recording electronic (DRE) voting machines require the use of voter-verified paper audit trails (VVPATs) or paper ballots. But 18 states that have DRE voting systems do not require paper audit trails.

Use of Voter-Verified Paper Audit Trails, 2006

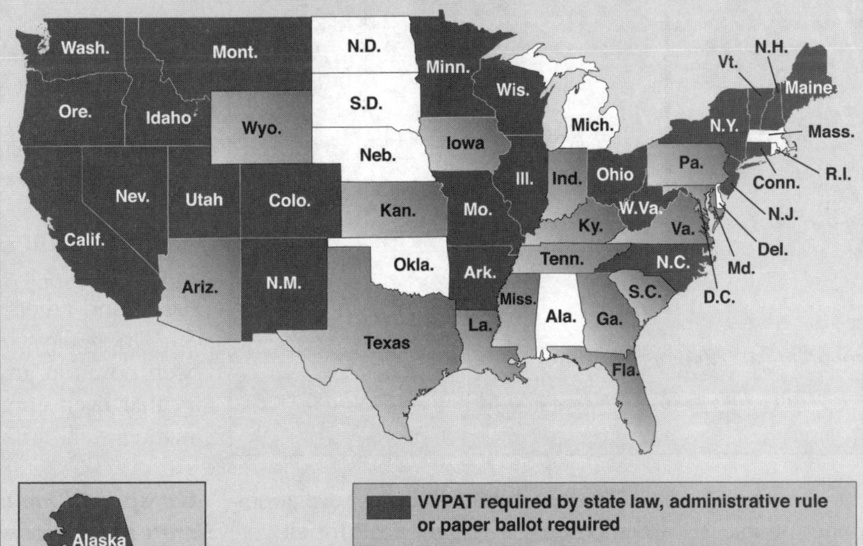

Source: electionline.org, "What's Changed, What Hasn't and Why, 2000-2006," February 2006

[1] Quoted in "DRE Analysis for May 2006 Primary, Cuyahoga County, Ohio," August 2006, p. 6, http://bocc.cuyahoga-county.us/GSC/pdf/esi_cuyahoga_final.pdfreport.

[2] *Ibid.*, p. 7.

[3] For details on paper-trail states, see "Election Reform: What's Changed, What Hasn't and Why, 2000-2006," electionline.org, February 2006, pp. 10-12, www.electionline.org/Portals/1/ Publications/2006.annual.report.Final.pdf.

[4] The study is Celeste *et al.*, "Asking the Right Questions About Electronic Voting," National Research Council of the National Academies, 2006, p. 42. www.nap.edu/catalog/11449.html.

[5] For details on HAVA spending, see "Building Confidence in U.S. Elections," Commission on Federal Election Reform, September 2005, p. 25, www.american.edu/ia/cfer/report/full_report.pdf.

[6] For detailed estimate showing 38.2 percent of voters expected to use DREs, and 41.2 percent expected to use optical-scan devices, see "Election Reform," *op. cit.*, pp. 10-12.

[7] Michael Shamos, "Paper v. Electronic Voting Records, An Assessment," School of Computer Science, Carnegie-Mellon University, http://euro.ecom.cmu.edu/people/faculty/mshamos/paper.htm.

[8] Eric A. Fischer and Kevin J. Coleman, "The Direct Electronic Voting Machine (DRE) Controversy: FAQs and Misperceptions," Congressional Research Service, Dec. 14, 2005, p. 5.

[9] "Elections: Federal Efforts to Improve Security and Reliability of Electronic Voting Systems Are Under Way, but Key Activities Need to Be Completed," Government Accountability Office, October 2005, pp. 2-3; www.gao.gov/new.items/d05956. pdf#search=%22GAO-05-956%22.

[10] Quoted in, "Building Confidence in U.S. Elections," *op. cit.*

[11] For the article, see Ronnie Dugger, "Annals of Democracy; Counting Votes," *The New Yorker*, Nov. 7, 1988; the article has been posted on the Web at www.csl.sri.com/users/neumann/dugger.html.

[12] Michael E. Lindroos, letter to Cuyahoga County Commissioners, Aug. 16, 2006, www.cuyahogacounty.us/bocc/GSC/pdf/elections/Diebold_letter_081606.pdf.

[13] Election Science Institute, "Board Meeting Statement," undated, http://electionline.org.

Most Americans Will Vote by Computer

About 80 percent of U.S. voters will use optical-scanning or electronic (touch screen) equipment in November — almost twice as many voters as in 2000.

Voting System Usage as Percentage of Registered Voters

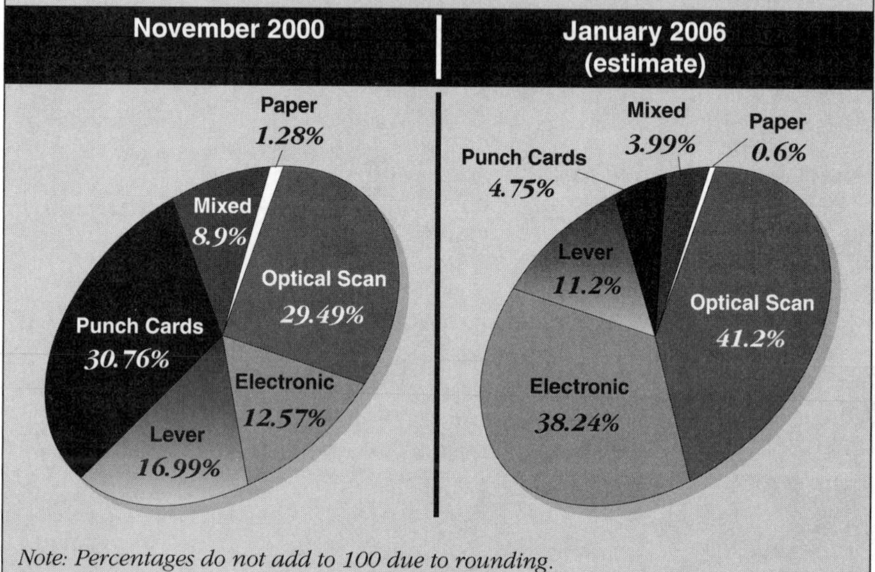

Note: Percentages do not add to 100 due to rounding.

Source: electionline.org, "What's Changed, What Hasn't and Why, 2000-2006," February 2006

Continued from p. 749

study concluded. Among people 65 and older in Wisconsin, 23 percent — 177,399 residents — lacked a license or other photo ID.

The study helped convince Wisconsin's Democratic Gov. Jim Doyle to veto three bills that would have required all voters to show a photo ID at the polls. "If Republicans keep sending me a bill over and over that disenfranchises 177,000 seniors, my only choice is to veto it," he said in June. [16]

Nevertheless, Wisconsin's 2004 general election revealed deep flaws throughout the state's voter-registration system, according to the state's nonpartisan Legislative Audit Bureau. Counts were mistaken, registration lists outdated and, in Milwaukee, dozens of discrepancies were found between the numbers of votes cast and the number of voters who signed in to vote. [17]

To Republicans, those revelations demonstrate an urgent need for all voters to prove their identity. "I guarantee you, the election in Wisconsin was stolen," says Pullen of the Republican National Committee. "How do you steal elections? You get people not qualified to vote and get them credentials to vote."

Yet new voter-ID laws — as well as the Carter-Baker commission's ID proposal — don't toughen identification requirements for absentee voters. Critics say the effect would be discriminatory. "Whites are about twice as likely as African-Americans to vote via absentee ballot, and . . . absentee ballots are widely acknowledged to be more susceptible to fraud than ballots cast at the polls," Spencer Overton, an election-law specialist at George Washington University law school and a commission member, said in dissenting from the panel's ID recommendation. [18]

Backers of tougher ID requirements, including an Indiana federal judge who upheld that state's identification law, say that absentee voting — with its easier criteria — offers an alternative for the elderly and others for whom the new standards would be a hardship. [19]

Election-law expert Hasen, argues that the only way out of the partisan debate is to make voter ID and registration an entirely government-funded service. Both Democrats who want to expand voter rolls would be satisfied and so would Republicans intent on guarding against fraud. "As students graduated from high school," Hasen says, "the government could provide them a voter ID."

Levitt says that a free ID system open to all Americans would overcome his objections to existing identification laws. But, he adds, the universal-ID process recommended by Hasen and others is "entirely theoretical." In reality, he says, "There has been no effort anywhere in the country that even comes close to approximating such an outreach."

Are special measures needed to keep non-citizens from voting?

Rep. Henry J. Hyde, R-Ill., has proposed legislation to make proof of citizenship a prerequisite to voter registration. "We have an awful lot of non-citizens who are voting," he told the House Administration Committee in June. [20]

So far, only Arizona demands proof of citizenship for registration, and it is being challenged in U.S. District Court.

Hyde isn't the first to propose a nationwide proof-of-citizenship requirement. The Carter-Baker commission's voter-ID proposal would extend the reach of a new law that will require states to verify the citizenship of everyone who applies for a new or a renewed driver's license. The Real ID Act of 2005 requires that by 2008 voters must prove their citizenship or legal residence by presenting documents such as passports and birth certificates. States would be required to check a national immigration database and to share information on applicants with each other.

Under the Carter-Baker proposal, state governments would also seek out elderly people and others who lack driver's licenses and issue them identification cards, thereby ensuring that they don't lose the right to vote for lack of a license. [21]

But the Real ID Act may not take effect on schedule. State governments are campaigning to postpone the 2008 effective date, and the National Governors' Association, National Conference of State Legislatures and the American Association of Motor Vehicle Administrators reported in May that complying with the law will take eight years. [22]

A governor's commission in Virginia reported that bringing its license system up to the law's standard would cost $169 million and that operating costs would run up to $63 million a year. Federal start-up funds for all states total no more than $40 million. [23]

Paul Bettencourt, voter registrar for Harris County, Texas, which includes Houston, didn't put a price tag on a data-centralization proposal he made to the House Administration Committee in June. He advocated combining driver's-license information — some of which includes citizenship data — from all states, then cross-checking that information against the passport list, immigration records or Social Security files.

At the moment, Bettencourt said, barriers against non-citizen voting are so low that the federal government should take action immediately. A review in Houston last year found 35 cases in which foreign citizens had applied for or received voter-registration cards. In those cases, Bettencourt's office had been tipped off by citizens who knew about the illegal registrations. Otherwise, he said, "We have no real way to stop a foreign citizen from voting." [24]

And, he added, in Houston elections only a handful of votes regularly stand between the winner and the loser.

Opponents of the proof-of-citizenship proposal argue that it would entail far more complications than most people realize. "In the last year, almost 3,000 Missourians have been unable to receive birth certificates because the Vital Statistics Division has been unable to locate a record of birth," Wendy Noren, county clerk in Boone County, Mo., which includes Columbia, told the House Administration Committee. "In many cases, the birth was never registered, and in others the information an individual has does not match their records. Voters whose births were never registered can wait up to a year to register a delayed birth record." [25]

But proof-of-citizenship advocates argue that if registration supervisors could access the immigration databases through which citizenship status is checked, much of the problem can be solved.

Bechtle, at the Evergreen Freedom Foundation, says that in the current data environment critics of a proof-of-citizenship requirement can't be refuted when they say there's no evidence that non-citizen voting amounts to a major problem. "A lot of that is because it's been difficult to show who's a non-citizen and who isn't," he says.

Daniel Tokaji, an election-law specialist at Ohio State University's Moritz College of Law, is among those who say advocates of proof-of-citizenship voting can cite only scattered episodes of non-citizens registering or voting.

He also argues that the poor and elderly wouldn't be the only people to suffer discriminatory treatment. "There is always a risk that the requirement will be applied in a discriminatory manner — that whites won't be required to show proof but that brown-skinned people, or yellow-skinned people or people with accents will," Tokaji says. He adds that he'd have to rely on his birth certificate to definitively prove citizenship — and he doesn't know where it is.

Patrick J. Rogers, an Albuquerque, N.M., lawyer and a director of the American Center for Voting Rights Legislative Fund, acknowledged before the U.S. House Administration Committee that he couldn't "quantify or even begin to quantify the magnitude of the problem."

But Rogers cited a 1996 California congressional race between Democrat Loretta Sanchez and Republican Robert Dornan in which the *Los Angeles Times* found that 85 people who were legal residents of the United States but not citizens had voted (questionable votes weren't enough to overturn Sanchez's 984-vote victory margin). [26]

Likewise, Pullen, the Arizona Republican activist, argues that so many immigrants have crossed the border illegally that it would be surprising if they weren't voting. "We know we have these problems," he says. "Just because we don't have a lot of statistics doesn't mean it's not going on."

Can electronic voting machine results be trusted?

The spectacle of poll workers squinting to examine "hanging chads" after the 2000 presidential election in Florida sparked a nationwide call to upgrade voting machines.

By the 2004 election, about 35 percent of the nation's voters were using optical-scan machines, which record voters' choices marked on paper ballots. About 29 percent of voters were using voting computers, mostly touch-screen machines known as direct recording electronic (DRE) devices, some of which do not provide paper printouts of votes. [27]

Both methods are still growing in popularity. In the upcoming 2006 elections, about 80 percent of the electorate will vote on optical-scan and DRE machines. The remaining 20 percent will use old-style punch cards, lever machines and paper ballots. [28]

But if the specter of hanging chads has been nearly eliminated, the surge in electronic voting has given rise to concerns that local governments don't have the expertise to operate the machines and protect them from hackers. "Some electronic voting systems did not encrypt cast ballots or system audit logs, and it was possible to alter both without being detected," the Government Accountability Office (GAO) reported last year. "It was possible to alter the files . . . so that the votes for one candidate could be recorded for a different candidate." [29]

Today, a growing chorus of citizen activists, computer scientists and voting officials insist the computer voting machines are inherently dangerous to the election process.

"I'm not big fan of what I call faith-based voting," says Ion Sancho, the election supervisor of Leon County, Fla., which includes the state capital, Tallahassee. "If you're using electronic voting, it comes down to that: the supervisor of elections says it works; the voting machine company says it works. But I believe voting should be an audited process."

Michael Shamos, a computer-science professor at Carnegie-Mellon University in Pittsburgh, argues that such objections amount to anti-technology bias. "There are zero incidents of tampering" with DREs, he says. "Yet we still have notorious incidents of tampering with paper ballots, because it's so easy." Shamos is also a lawyer who has testified as an expert witness for state and county governments responding to lawsuits challenging use of DREs.

DRE critics typically explain the absence of reported DRE tampering by noting that it can be accomplished with no one the wiser. "There is no transparency," says computer-science Professor Aviel D. Rubin of Johns Hopkins University in Baltimore, a prominent DRE critic and author of the just-published *Brave New Ballot: The Battle to Safeguard Democracy in the Age of Electronic Voting*. "You cannot observe the machine and tell what's going on inside. And you cannot observe the counting of votes." Consequently, he wrote recently, "suspicion that software has been manipulated to alter vote results is inevitable — and virtually impossible to disprove conclusively." [30]

Meanwhile, a handful of episodes with DREs raised questions of sheer technological reliability — or of poll-workers' competence to keep them running. In North Carolina, the results of the 2004 election for agriculture commissioner remained in doubt three months after the voting because a misprogrammed DRE manufactured by Unilect Corp. of Dublin, Calif., lost 4,000 votes in one county. In Pennsylvania, Unilect machines showed a higher-than-normal error rate during the November 2004 primaries. (As a consultant for the state, Shamos tested the Unilect device and recommended against its use.) [31]

The problems in Pennsylvania and North Carolina added to the calls for DREs to be modified to provide a printed version of the electronically recorded vote, or so-called voter-verified paper audit trails (VVPATs). In theory, the paper record could be used to check machines' vote totals to settle any challenges. [32] As of early 2006, 25 states required VVPATs or the use of paper ballots only.

The use of printers has turned some early critics of DREs into believers. "That paper trail is being created right then and there as you're voting," says Republican committeeman Pullen, a CPA. "You can see what's being recorded, and the paper can be matched up against votes."

But some DRE opponents argue that paper trails provide only a false sense of security. One objection, says Holly Jacobson of Seattle, Wash., co-director of the Berkeley, Calif.-based advocacy group Voter Action — which is challenging DREs in five states — is that the paper trails consist of rolls of thermal paper, which deteriorate with handling.

A deeper objection is that if a machine has been misprogrammed and isn't recording votes correctly, a printer would simply be printing out the inaccurate product of the machine's instructions. "If there's a discrepancy, it's going to depend on who has the best counsel," says Jacobson. "We know that DREs don't record votes properly."

Rubin says some computer voting machines can be reprogrammed within two minutes by a skilled hacker. In Florida, Leon County rejects DRE machines, with the exception of three reserved for disabled voters whose handicaps prevent them from using other devices. Sancho says his distrust in DREs was confirmed after computer scientists he authorized to test the security of his county's optical-scan devices last year took "less than an hour" to alter a memory card so votes were switched from one candidate to another. "Only by comparing the physical paper ballot to the electronically recorded total can you test for this security violation — but you don't have a paper ballot with a touch screen," Sancho says.

Donald F. Norris, director of the Maryland Institute for Policy Analysis and Research at the University of Maryland, Baltimore County, argues that critics are wrongly focusing on hardware instead of security measures. Computer scientists are "very smart, and they're absolutely right when they say you can hack into a computer," he says. But, "they don't look at the system in place around these machines to ensure that nothing like that can or does happen — a system to ensure that only the right voting software is loaded onto machines and done securely, that the machines are secured before Election Day, after Election Day."

Paper ballots, Norris says, "were much more easily tampered with." ■

BACKGROUND

Democratic Experiment

Free and fair elections arrived relatively late on the American scene — both as an ideal and in reality. [33]

But in Colonial America, no less a figure than George Washington

Continued on p. 756

Chronology

1600s-1860

Voting procedures evolve amid political conflicts.

1758
George Washington is elected to the Virginia House of Burgesses after buying liquor for voters.

1788
The Constitution is enacted, including an infamous provision in which five slaves were counted as three people — to boost congressional representation of the South.

1850s
Election fraud becomes institutionalized in New York and other cities.

1860
Abraham Lincoln wins the presidency — despite being left off the ballots in 10 Southern states.

1860s-1888

African-American voting power briefly emerges during the post-war Reconstruction era.

1868
Murderous violence against black voters mars the election campaign for Louisiana governor.

1876
Rutherford B. Hayes of Ohio is declared victor over Samuel Tilden of New York in a presidential race that becomes a lowpoint of voting fraud in the United States.

1888
Widespread fraud also mars the presidential contest between Democrat Grover Cleveland of New York and Republican Benjamin Harrison of Indiana.

1890s-1964

Procedural and technological changes set the direction of today's electoral process.

1890s
Government-printed "Australian ballots" become the norm, ending the era of ballots produced by parties.

1920
A constitutional amendment grants women the right to vote.

1957
President Dwight D. Eisenhower signs the first law barring racial discrimination in voting, but the law lacks enforcement power.

1960
Democrat John F. Kennedy is elected president after Richard M. Nixon refrains from challenging apparent voting fraud.

1964-1990s

Civil rights movement finally breaks down the barriers against African-American voting.

1964
Civil Rights Act bans discrimination in voter registration.

Aug. 6, 1965
President Lyndon B. Johnson signs the Voting Rights Act, which outlaws all the practices traditionally used to keep black citizens from voting.

1971
The 26th Amendment lowers the voting age from 21 to 18.

1984
Congress passes the Polling Place Accessibility for the Elderly and Handicapped Act.

1993
"Motor Voter" law allows citizens to register to vote while obtaining their driver's licenses.

2000s

Flaws in the first two presidential elections of the decade spark reforms.

Dec. 12, 2000
U.S. Supreme Court orders an end to vote recounting in Florida's presidential election, effectively ensuring George W. Bush's victory over Vice President Al Gore.

August 2001
National Commission on Federal Election Reform recommends adoption of more reliable and accurate voting machines.

Oct. 29, 2002
President Bush signs Help America Vote Act (HAVA), which provides money to states to buy modern voting machines.

November 2004
President Bush defeats Sen. John Kerry, D-Mass., in the presidential election, which again hangs on the outcome in a single state — Ohio — where widespread voting problems are reported.

September 2005
Another bipartisan commission recommends more electoral-system changes, including a nationwide voter-registration system.

April 14, 2006
A federal judge upholds Indiana's photo-ID requirement for voting.

July 27, 2006
President Bush signs an extension of the Voting Rights Act.

Did Voting Glitches Defeat Kerry in Ohio?

The 2004 presidential election in Ohio, which decided the contest in favor of President George W. Bush, was disputed before, during and after the state's voters went to the polls.

Its repercussions continue. Some Democrats still contend that Republicans in the state engineered a massive fraud. Republicans and even other Democrats dispute the idea, but there is agreement that problems were widespread and resulted in disenfranchisement of some voters. Researchers say the problems of 2004 should inspire a new wave of voting reforms, though substantive changes are unlikely before the 2008 elections.

"The level of science in this country is sufficient to address the issues," says Steven Hertzberg, project director of the San Francisco-based Election Science Institute, a nonpartisan advocacy organization devoted to improving the election process. "But we need to roll up our sleeves as a nation and face the challenges head on. And we're not doing that right now."

Bush defeated Sen. John Kerry, D-Mass., in the 2004 election in Ohio by more than 118,000 votes. Nationally, Bush won by more than 3 million votes. But if Kerry had taken Ohio, he would have had enough Electoral College delegates to win the election. [1]

Both parties had identified Ohio as a key "battleground" state well in advance of the election, and both mounted ambitious efforts to register new Ohio voters. Prior to the election, Ohio Secretary of State J. Kenneth Blackwell — who also chaired Bush's Ohio re-election campaign — made a series of decisions that Democrats charged were intended to suppress votes for Kerry. [2] One of the most controversial — later rescinded — required voter-registration applications to be printed only on paper of a certain weight.

During the election itself, several problems were encountered. In one county, 25 electronic voting machines transferred an "unknown number" of Kerry votes to Bush, according to a Democratic report on the election. In another, elections officials locked reporters and election observers out of a building where votes were counted, citing a non-existent FBI warning about a potential terrorist threat. In many precincts, long lines caused voters to wait as long as 10 hours to vote. [3]

Kerry himself never charged that Republicans tried to steal the Ohio election. But Rep. John Conyers of Michigan, the senior Democrat on the House Judiciary Committee, concluded — based on a report by the panel's Democratic staff — that "numerous, serious election irregularities in the Ohio presidential election" resulted in "a significant disenfranchisement of voters." [4]

Republicans dismissed the report as partisan and inaccurate. Kerry himself conceded defeat in Ohio and nationally. But other Democrats continued to contest the election.

Harper's, in September 2005, published an article — "None Dare Call it Stolen" — that attributed most of the Ohio election problems to "Republican chicanery" and said that "the evidence that something went extremely wrong last fall is copious." [5] *Rolling Stone* published a story by Robert F. Kennedy, Jr. in June 2006 in which the author wrote: "Across the country, Republican election officials and party stalwarts employed a wide range of illegal and unethical tactics to fix the election," though the story focused on problems in Ohio. [6]

The online magazine *Salon.com* published a rebuttal of the Kennedy story two days later that said, "the evidence he cites isn't new and his argument is filled with distortions and blatant omissions." [7]

But Democrats continue to stoke controversy over the 2004 election — including Kerry. On Aug. 29, he sent an e-mail to Democratic campaign donors, soliciting money for Ohio's Democratic gubernatorial candidate, Ted Strickland, charging that Blackwell "used the power of his state office to try to intimidate Ohioans and suppress the Democratic vote." [8]

A Blackwell spokesman told The Associated Press that "the historical record contradicts Sen. Kerry." [9] However, Blackwell announced on Aug. 30 that he would delay the scheduled destruction of ballots from the 2004 election in response to pressure from politicians, statisticians and lawyers who are conducting another investigation of the election. [10]

Voting reform has been an issue in Ohio's elections and in its legislature since 2004. In 2005, voters rejected four amendments to the state constitution — pushed by liberal activists — that would have overhauled the state's election system, including stripping the secretary of state of his role supervising elections. [11] In February, Ohio Gov. Bob Taft, a Republican, signed a law opposed by many Democrats that would require voters to show identification at the polls and make it more difficult to place issues on the ballot or challenge elections. [12]

Continued from p. 754

bought gallons of rum, brandy, wine and beer for voters to improve his chances of election to the Virginia House of Burgesses in 1758. He was elected. Although the concept of democratic elections as it's now understood didn't exist, Washington's fellow delegates nonetheless soon prohibited such tactics.

Following the American Revolution, voting was limited in most states to white men with property. The latter restriction began disappearing early in the 19th century. But the horrors of slavery and its Jim Crow aftermath would haunt American electoral politics until well into the 20th century.

Throughout the country, meanwhile, politicians and their backers developed methods of electoral fraud that would stand the test of time, such as organizing squads of "repeaters" to cast ballots in precinct after precinct. The even simpler ploy of ballot-box stuffing began in the 1800s, along with requiring city employees to do election work for the city's political bosses — a method fine-tuned by New York's Tammany Hall machine.

AP Photo/The Plain Dealer, John Kuntz

Cuyahoga County Board of Elections Director Michael Vu collects computer tapes from voting machines in Cleveland on May 3, 2006. The state hired an independent firm to audit the May results after investigators found irregularities in the 2004 presidential election in Ohio.

Cuyahoga County (Cleveland), the state's largest, has become a petri dish for voting reform. In the 2004 election, according to the Conyers report, more than 10,000 Cuyahoga citizens were unable to vote because of voter-registration errors, and 8,099 provisional ballots out of 24,472 were ruled invalid after the election, the highest such proportion in the state. [13]

The county's Board of Commissioners decided to audit Cuyahoga's election system this year after its Board of Elections asked the commissioners to purchase 900 additional voting machines. Before purchasing the new machines, the county employed Hertzberg's organization to study the operations of its voting machines, poll workers and elections officials during the county's May 2006 primary election.

The county uses an electronic voting system built by Diebold that also produces paper ballots voters can verify at the polls. But in its audit, the Election Science Institute found that the vote totals recorded on individual ballots, ballot summaries, the voting machines' internal memories and on memory cards did not match.

"Relying on this system in its present state should be viewed as a calculated risk in which the outcome may be an acceptable election, but there is a heightened risk of unacceptable cost," Hertzberg's report said. Left unchanged, the county's election system could result in "diminished public confidence in a close election," the report found. [14]

Diebold has attacked the report and the institute's methodology, calling it "intentional and willful defamation" of the company. [15] But county officials accepted the report's findings.

"We were concerned by it," said Dennis Madden, Cuyahoga County's administrator. "It brought up a lot of discrepancies, potentially, with the voting units themselves and the staff that were operating them. Some of the discrepancies were astonishing."

Hertzberg says the county's voting problems may have been the fault of poll workers and elections officials, not Diebold's machines. Either way, he says, they can be corrected. (Madden said that many of the problems have been addressed.)

The report has prompted positive changes elsewhere in Ohio, Hertzberg said. Franklin County, for example, has decided to release all its voting data to the public after elections, hire an independent firm to handle ballot recounts and randomly test its electronic voting machines on Election Day.

Meanwhile, Madden said the Board of County Commissioners decided to buy the new voting machines and may audit the general election.

— Alex Wayne

[1] "2004 Election Results," Federal Elections Commission, www.fec.gov/pubrec/fe2004/tables.pdf.

[2] "Preserving Democracy: What Went Wrong in Ohio," Status Report of the House Judiciary Committee Democratic Staff, Jan. 5, 2005.

[3] *Ibid.*

[4] *Ibid.*

[5] Mark Crispin Miller, "None Dare Call it Stolen," *Harper's*, August 2005.

[6] Robert F. Kennedy, Jr., "Was the 2004 Election Stolen?" *Rolling Stone*, June 1, 2006.

[7] Farhad Manjoo, "Was the 2004 election stolen? No." *Salon.com*, June 3, 2006.

[8] Sen. John Kerry, "Battleground Ohio," Aug. 29, 2006.

[9] David Hammer, "Kerry revives 2004 allegations in Ohio fundraising e-mail," The Associated Press, Aug. 28, 2006.

[10] Ian Urbina, "Ohio to Delay Destruction of Presidential Ballots," *The New York Times*, Aug. 31, 2006.

[11] Jim Provance, "Ohioans cast off election reforms; amendments lose by wide margins," *Toledo Blade*, Nov. 9, 2005.

[12] Jim Provance, "New law requires Ohio voters to show identification at polls," *Toledo Blade*, Feb. 1, 2006.

[13] Status Report of the House Judiciary Committee Democratic Staff, *op. cit.*

[14] "Analysis of May 2006 Primary Election, Cuyahoga County, Ohio," Election Science Institute, Aug. 15, 2006.

[15] Michael E. Lindroos, letter to Cuyahoga County Commissioners, Diebold Election Systems Inc., Aug. 16, 2002.

In the nation's early days, slaves were denied the vote mainly to protect the power of the white population in the South, which had the most slaves. But under the infamous "three-fifths compromise," the South could take political advantage of its large, disenfranchised slave population by counting every five slaves as three people, thereby boosting the number of Southern congressional seats on the backs of people who enjoyed virtually no rights, much less the right to vote. [34]

The political disenfranchisement of African-Americans, especially in the South, didn't end when slavery was abolished. The white Southern political class used every means, including murder, to prevent black people from voting for Lincoln's Republican Party.

"It has been charged that the white man's party intends to achieve success by intimidation," an anonymous member of a New Orleans organization called the White League told a congressional committee investigating the 1868 election for Louisiana governor. "This is strictly true. We intend to succeed by intimidation." During the six-month run-up to the election, more than

1,000 black people were killed in Louisiana.[35]

The fate of Reconstruction hung in the balance in the fraud-plagued 1876 presidential race between Republican Rutherford B. Hayes of Ohio and Democrat Samuel J. Tilden of New York. Southern whites intimidated black voters into staying away from the polls, where the ex-slaves would have voted Republican in hopes of keeping Reconstruction alive.

But in Florida and Louisiana, Republicans still controlled canvassing boards, which retaliated for suppression of the black vote by throwing out Democratic votes. Meanwhile, in New York, Indiana and Ohio, Democrats carried out repeat-voting operations in order to boost their party's showing.

Congress appointed a commission with a one-vote Republican majority that eventually voted along party lines to award a majority of electoral votes to Hayes. Meanwhile, white Southerners' opposition to Hayes had eroded somewhat under the expectation that he would withdraw federal troops from the South, thereby ending Reconstruction — which he did, in 1877.

The presidential race of 1888 between Democratic incumbent Grover Cleveland of New York and Republican Benjamin Harrison of Indiana precipitated a similar crisis.

Again, Southern Democrats suppressed black Republican votes for Harrison, and New York saw considerable vote-rigging on behalf of Harrison. And repeat voting was plentiful in Harrison's home state of Indiana. Harrison ended up losing the national popular vote by more than 60,000 votes but winning in the Electoral College.

Meanwhile, terror campaigns against black voting intensified in the South. "Go to the polls tomorrow, and if you find the negro out voting, tell him to leave the polls, and if he refuses, kill him," Alfred Moore Waddell, a former House member told a rally in Wilmington, N.C., in 1898, on the eve of congressional elections. Afterwards, a mob of whites descended on black neighborhoods, killing as many as 300 people. The rampage set the stage for a state constitutional amendment in 1900 that formally disenfranchised African-Americans. By putting the law on their side, white politicians hoped to reduce their reliance on mob violence.[36]

Civil Rights Movement

When the civil rights movement began gathering strength in the late 1950s and early '60s, voting rights soon topped the agenda. In the South especially, the old Jim Crow tradition of barring African-Americans from the polls through taxes, literacy tests and intimidation was alive and well.

In 1964, "Mississippi Freedom Summer," sponsored by a coalition of civil rights organizations, sent hundreds of volunteers to the Deep South state where resistance to blacks' rights ran strongest. Registering voters was among the project's top goals. The level of fear and hatred the civil rights workers inspired became tragically clear when segregationists murdered three young activists — two white men from New York and one black man from Mississippi.[37]

The killings helped galvanize support for legislation to finally stamp out the systematic political exclusion of African-Americans, particularly in the South. On Aug. 6, 1965, President Lyndon B. Johnson — a Texas native who considered himself a Southerner — signed the Voting Rights Act, which banned poll taxes, literacy tests and similar tactics. States with histories of discrimination were required to obtain Justice Department "preclearance" before making any changes in election law that might circumvent the new law.

That supervisory authority from Washington had been due to expire this year, but many Republicans opposed extending those provisions. The rebellion was centered in the House, where GOP lawmakers said they objected mainly to the law's requirement that ballots be bilingual in precincts with substantial numbers of foreign-language voters. Longstanding resentment of Justice Department supervisory authority also played a part.

Republican Rep. Jack Kingston of Georgia noted that his state has nine elected black officials. Even so, he said, "If you move a polling place from the Baptist church to the Methodist church, you've got to go through the Justice Department."[38]

But voting-rights advocates said the Republicans were ducking evidence of recent voting-rights violations in Southern states including Georgia and Texas. "These are not states that can say their hands are clean," said Barbara Arnwine, executive director of the Lawyers' Committee for Civil Rights Under Law.[39]

In the end, the law and its preclearance procedures passed both chambers. "By reauthorizing this act, Congress has reaffirmed its belief that all men are created equal," Bush said in signing the legislation on July 27 at a White House ceremony with veteran leaders of the civil rights movement in attendance.[40]

Reform Attempts

Recent controversies over disparities between results in the popular vote and the Electoral College recall earlier crises, although voting in the 19th century had little resemblance to today's methods.[41]

Secret voting didn't become the rule until the late 19th century. Voters expressed their choices out loud during the Colonial period and later in some states.

The paper ballots that replaced voice voting were printed by political parties and showed only their candidates. The shape and color of ballots signaled the voter's preferences. The crisis of 1876 spurred introduction of the so-called Australian ballot — a government-printed form that a voter marked in secret. In

1888, Massachusetts inaugurated the national trend of uniformly printed, secretly marked ballots. By the early 1900s, all but three states had followed suit.

During the same period, a machine was developed that eliminated paper ballots — and ended ballot-box stuffing. In 1896, Rochester, N.Y., unveiled a lever-action voting machine, which gradually became the national standard. By the mid-20th century, nearly two-thirds of voters were pulling levers.

In 1960, the American electorate was closely divided between Democrat John F. Kennedy and Republican Richard M. Nixon. Indeed, the popular vote outcome showed Kennedy ahead of Nixon by a mere 118,000 votes of 68 million cast, a 0.2 percent margin of victory. But in the Electoral College, Kennedy enjoyed a far more comfortable 303-219 victory.

A slight change in the razor-thin popular vote margin might have prompted Southern electors in the Electoral College to desert Kennedy, but Nixon refrained from challenging the results outright. Other top Republicans, convinced that their party had been robbed, launched challenges in two bastions of Democratic machine politics — Illinois and Texas.

Recounts in some Chicago-area precincts showed Nixon picking up more than 900 votes, according to Democrats, and more than 4,000, according to Republicans. Examination of results in Texas showed a series of suspicious counts. But recounts were stopped dead in both states — halted by judges who dismissed Republican lawsuits challenging the results.

University of Kentucky historian Campbell traces the Watergate scandal to Nixon's suspicion — based on his 1960 experience — that Democrats in 1972 would return to their old methods to, as he saw it, steal the election. Hence his order to establish the "plumbers," who broke into the Democratic National Committee headquarters, which eventually led to Nixon's downfall. [42]

In the 1980s, some local governments switched from lever machines to early models of DRE machines. In 1988, journalist and historian Ronnie Dugger anticipated much of the present debate over touch-screen machines, warning in *The New Yorker* that the new-generation machines made vote-count manipulation relatively easy. [43]

Getty Images/National Archive/Newsmakers

President Lyndon B. Johnson presents one of the pens used to sign the Voting Rights Act of 1965 to James Farmer, director of the Congress of Racial Equality, on Aug. 6, 1965.

Crisis in Florida

Controversy erupted again in 2000, when voters were closely divided between presidential candidates Bush and Gore. The controversies, accusations and suspicions came to a head in one state — Florida. With the rest of the country's votes at nearly 50-50, Florida and its 25 electoral votes held the key to victory. But Florida's results yielded more questions than certainty.

On Nov. 8, one day after the vote, Secretary of State Katherine Harris (who had campaigned for Bush in the New Hampshire Republican primary) announced that Bush held a lead of 1,784 votes, with 14 counties not yet having provided rechecked results. But The Associated Press surveyed 66 of the state's 67 counties and reported that Bush's margin amounted to no more than 229 votes.

"Hanging chads" — a term that attained instant notoriety — accounted for some of the uncertainty. For days, election officials in Broward County (Fort Lauderdale) peered at punch-card voting machine ballots on which voters hadn't completely perforated the paper, making their intentions unclear.

The chad examination proved a TV-friendly story. But the votes that really counted for Bush came from absentee ballots. According to Harris' office, Bush owed his final 537-vote lead to 1,575 mailed-in ballots from overseas absentee voters — most of them military personnel, with Florida mailing addresses and Republican voting records — who were serving overseas. (An additional 836 of the military absentees voted for Gore.)

A *New York Times* investigation in early 2001 concluded that 680 of the absentee votes didn't meet Florida's standards for acceptance because of late postmarks and other deficiencies, but were accepted in heavily Republican counties. Gore decided not to challenge these votes to avoid the appearance of disenfranchising members of the armed forces. [44] If those absentee voters had been excluded, Gore would have carried Florida by 200 votes.

Another Gore decision might have changed history. After first advocating a statewide recount, he backed off and settled for a recount in only four Democratic counties. After an exhaustive, 10-month examination of the 175,010 ballots that had been rejected in the recounts, a team of statisticians working on behalf of eight news organizations concluded that a statewide recount that took those votes into account could have yielded — under one computation method — a 107-vote margin of victory for Gore. But the four-county recount would have focused on a smaller group of 43,000 ballots. If those had been examined, Bush would still have been the victor, the consortium concluded. [45]

In any event, the 36-day Florida conflict came to a halt on Dec. 12, 2000, when the U.S. Supreme Court ruled in a 5-4 decision that a partial recount ordered by Florida's high court violated the constitution's Equal Protection clause. With that, the election was over, and Harris' official results — showing the 537-vote lead — would stand. [46]

Despite the spotlight thrown on election defects by the Bush-Gore confrontation in Florida, the presidential race four years later also came down to the results from one battleground state plagued by allegations of voting irregularities, most aimed at supporters of Bush, who was running for reelection against Democrat John Kerry.

Ohio events that troubled Democrats included the performance of electronic voting machines in one county that switched votes from Kerry to Bush, and voting procedures elsewhere that forced voters to stand in line up to 10 hours to cast ballots. Though Kerry himself never charged election fraud, some — but not all — Democrats charged that the Ohio election demonstrated a strategy to reduce Democrats' voting strength. (*See sidebar, p. 756.*) ■

Getty Images/Robert King

Demonstrators in Tallahassee on Dec. 13, 2000, protest the U.S. Supreme Court decision ending a recount of the disputed Florida vote. The ruling meant victory for George W. Bush and defeat for Vice President Al Gore.

CURRENT SITUATION

Key Cases

Courts around the country are forcing key last-minute rules changes, some of which will affect eligibility to vote on Nov. 7. Two of the most influential decisions were handed down in Ohio and Florida.

U.S. District Judges Patricia Seitz of Miami and Kathleen O'Malley of Cleveland ruled in late August and September, respectively, that tough, new rules restricting registration efforts by private organizations like the League of Women Voters were unconstitutional.

In Florida, Seitz issued a preliminary injunction on Aug. 28 blocking enforcement of a state law that took effect this year calling for fines of up to $5,000 per voter-registration form if forms were submitted more than 10 days after collection, missed a submission deadline or were not submitted at all. If an organization couldn't pay, the member who personally collected the applications in question would be responsible.

"The law's combination of heavy, strict . . . fines is unconstitutional as it chills plaintiffs' First Amendment speech and association rights," Seitz ruled. [47]

Florida's secretary of state and the state election division — in charge of enforcing the law — immediately said they would appeal. The League of Women Voters, one of the plaintiffs, said it would resume its voter registration campaign, which it had suspended because of the law.

Four days later, on Sept. 1, Judge O'Malley rejected provisions of a new Ohio election law that set *criminal* penalties if registration canvassers do not personally deliver forms they collect to the secretary of state's office. In the past, canvassers have relied on their organizations to submit the forms. Ohio Secretary of State J. Kenneth Blackwell — the Republican candidate for governor — said he wouldn't appeal the order. O'Malley said she ruled quickly because she wanted to allow registration workers to sign up voters over the Labor Day weekend. [48]

Besides voter-registration cases, several other election-related legal matters are pending around the country. In Arizona, for instance, state officials are fighting a lawsuit challenging requirements that registration applicants prove their citizenship and that prospective voters prove their identities.

"The citizens of Arizona were victorious in retaining their inherent right to properly establish sufficient proof of citizenship when registering to vote," GOP Secretary of State Janice K. Brewer said in June after plaintiffs — including the Mexican-American Legal Defense and Education Fund, the Inter Tribal Council of

Continued on p. 762

At Issue:

Are elections nationwide open to systematic voter fraud?

JASON TORCHINSKY
AMERICAN CENTER FOR VOTING RIGHTS

WRITTEN FOR *CQ RESEARCHER*, SEPTEMBER 2006

yes

Most U.S. elections are decided fairly and openly without the unfortunate taint of voter fraud, but the possibility of fraud still exists, and Americans are concerned.

Among the problems that open the system up to the potential for fraud are voter-registration lists that include voters who have moved, passed away or are not citizens and organizations and individuals submitting fraudulent voter registrations.

From a law-enforcement perspective, the Department of Justice has indicted 95 people in the past four years for felony election crimes. In Wisconsin, several convictions came out of the 2004 election after FBI and local prosecutors determined that, in Milwaukee County alone, more than 200 ballots were illegally cast by persons who had been convicted of felonies, and more than 100 ballots were cast by people who voted twice, used false names or voted in the name of someone who was dead. But these represent just a small percentage of fraud reports that ever turn into investigations, let alone indictments.

Two federal laws are designed to address the problems that have been identified, but they are often not fully enforced. The National Voter Registration Act and the Help America Vote Act both require state officials to keep their voter lists up-to-date and remove the names of voters who have moved, died or otherwise become ineligible to vote. Too often, this part of federal law is ignored by state officials, or state officials attempting to clean up voter rolls are sued by interest groups who want to stop them. HAVA also requires certain proof of identity in order to register to vote, but states have failed to vigorously enforce these requirements.

Others have alleged that electronic voting machines increase the likelihood of fraud. However, to date, there has not been a documented incident of voter fraud occurring as a result of tampering with electronic voting machines. Furthermore, the trend towards all-mail elections opens up additional possibilities for fraud, as the Brennan Center for Justice has noted repeatedly in briefs and public statements about the potential for fraud created by absentee ballots.

Many of the problems and the perceptions arising from them could be avoided if existing laws were fully implemented and states adopted commonsense reforms. These include ideas such as voter identification, verification of voter registrations and other simple measures that will allow free and fair elections to continue while addressing concerns about fraud.

JUSTIN LEVITT
ASSOCIATE COUNSEL, BRENNAN CENTER FOR JUSTICE, NEW YORK UNIVERSITY SCHOOL OF LAW

WRITTEN FOR *CQ RESEARCHER*, SEPTEMBER 2006

no

In November, used-car dealers will announce huge holiday sales. There will also be a ruckus about voter fraud. In either case, it's sound policy not to buy the hype.

Consider the facts. There is no reliable evidence showing a widespread wave of fraud by American voters. No credible documentation suggests an epidemic of individuals voting multiple times, voting as someone else or voting despite knowing they're ineligible.

For those who nevertheless believe in voter fraud — incontrovertibly believe, as if Tinkerbelle's life hung in the balance — such facts are no impediment. Voter fraud, they say, is simply difficult to trace.

It is more likely, however, that mass voter fraud just does not exist. Most voters offer their legitimate signatures and sworn oaths with the gravitas this hard-won civic right deserves. Moreover, one act of voter fraud risks five years in prison and a $10,000 fine — but yields at most one incremental vote. Few rational individuals would buy in at that price.

To be sure, some ineligible voters do cast ballots, a few of which are fraudulent. New statewide databases have the potential to make this even rarer. But even without new technology, voter fraud is shown to happen approximately 0.00004 percent of the time — about as often, actually, as Americans are struck by lightning.

Like death by lightning, the few voter-fraud stories do make vivid anecdotes. Many survive long after being debunked. Researchers have visited homes on supposedly vacant lots and have interviewed citizens demonstrably not deceased.

Fraud mongers with a policy agenda, however, throw these anecdotes (true and false) in with vote buying, official misconduct and other election improprieties — all under the misleading label of "voter fraud."

The rhetorical sloppiness is both distracting and dangerous. The "voter fraud" bogeyman is used to justify solutions that don't really work for a problem that doesn't really exist. Restrictive rules — like identification requirements — then sprout like weeds, becoming unnecessary and unlawful impediments to the exercise of a fundamental constitutional right. Meanwhile, the list of real problems grows: flyers spread misinformation; voting machines register inaccurate tallies; election officials misunderstand eligibility rules; actual voters are mistakenly purged.

Americans deserve policies grounded in facts, not hysteria. Our elections are prone to serious concerns that we must address. Voter fraud is nowhere near the top of that list.

Continued from p. 760

Arizona, the ACLU and the League of Women Voters — lost their request for a Temporary Restraining Order against enforcement of the provisions. But the underlying case was still pending before U.S. District Judge Roslyn O. Silver. [49]

In Georgia and Indiana, meanwhile, two challenges to new voter-ID requirements produced contradictory rulings. U.S. District Judge Sarah Evans Barker upheld Indiana's new photo ID requirement, which had been challenged by the Democratic Party and other organizations arguing that some voters would be excluded from the polls. The Democrats have appealed. Such a law was overturned in Georgia last year, only to be replaced by a similar requirement this year — which has again been challenged in federal court. [50]

In Missouri, a state circuit judge is considering a Democratic Party challenge to a photo-ID requirement. As in other states, arguments center on fraud prevention and voter exclusion. [51]

In Pennsylvania, a Democratic governor, Ed Rendell, vetoed a voter-ID bill passed by the Republican-controlled legislature, calling the proposal a "ruse" to deny voting rights to elderly and poor citizens. Existing law requires only that citizens voting in a precinct for the first time present identification. [52]

And in Albuquerque, N.M., the ACLU has sued to block a referendum-approved city ordinance that would require voters to present photo IDs. The lawsuit challenges the ordinance as discriminatory. Stepping into the case to defend the ordinance, a Republican secretary of state joined two citizens, one of whom said he found his 13-year-old son had fraudulently been signed up to vote, and another who told of being turned away from the polls because someone else had voted using his name. [53]

Meanwhile, lawsuits in Arizona, Colorado, California, Florida, Georgia Texas, Ohio and Pennsylvania are challenging use of DRE machines, alleging poor performance, vulnerability to fraud, failure to provide backup paper records or related issues. [54]

David Bear, a spokesman for Diebold Election Systems of Ohio, the dominant manufacturer in the field, said his company's technology "has proven to be more accurate" than punch-card machines. He rejected reports of vulnerability to software manipulation, calling them "what-if scenarios." [55]

And in Ohio a lawsuit filed in U.S. District Court in Cleveland on Aug. 29 is one of three to challenge the legality of identification standards, including an Ohio requirement that foreign-born prospective voters prove citizenship. The suit was filed by election-law expert Tokaji and lawyers for the American Civil Liberties Union on behalf of 19 naturalized Americans. It may not get much opposition, however. A spokesman for Ohio Secretary of State Blackwell called the proof-of-citizenship requirement "unenforceable," and said his office will try to settle the case. [56]

Purging Voter Rolls

A HAVA requirement that states maintain centralized databases of all registered voters is proving problematic in some places, despite the rule's seemingly simple and commonsense nature. It is up to each state to decide how to fulfill the requirement.

In Washington state, the legislature ordered the secretary of state to purge voters from the rolls if their identifying information — first or last names, for instance — didn't match up with driver's license records and entries in other databases. As a result, about 55,000 names were dropped from the state's new centralized list in May. The secretary of state's office said they represented duplicate registrations and convicted felons barred from voting. [57]

But on Aug. 1, U.S. District Judge Ricardo S. Martinez granted a preliminary injunction halting further enforcement of the law after the Washington Association of Churches, a labor union and antipoverty organizations challenged it. State law only requires that prospective voters be persons over age 18 who have not been deprived of the right to vote — through a felony conviction, for instance. State officials hadn't shown how a data mismatch "is material in determining whether that person is qualified to vote," Martinez ruled. [58]

Voter roll purging has also run up against problems in Kentucky, where Attorney General Gregory D. Stumbo, a Democrat, is challenging methods used by Secretary of State Trey Grayson to purge about 8,000 names from the voter list. Grayson said those voters were also registered in Tennessee and South Carolina. [59]

Under pressure from Stumbo, Grayson's office notified the purged voters that they'd been removed from the rolls. But, Stumbo insisted, "This in no way excuses the illegality of purging voters in the first place." [60]

The Brennan Center has attempted a nationwide survey of methods used by all states in assembling centralized voter registries, but found that many states have only just begun the process. "We may find out over the next couple of months that the problem is very severe indeed," associate counsel Levitt says.

In their survey, Levitt and his colleagues found seven states — including Washington state — that have been dropping names whose information didn't match up with other state records. The center opposes this so-called "no-match" approach. Name changes in marriage or divorce are one problem, the center says, and so is the frequency with which data on file have been incorrectly entered.

The other six states using the "no-match" purge method are Pennsylvania, Maryland, South Dakota, Texas, Virginia and Iowa. In the latter state, John Hedgecoth, a spokesman for the secretary of state's office, said officials had found that only 115 names among 2,098,778 voters that failed match tests. "It's a good system," he said. [61] ■

OUTLOOK

Partisan Muddle

The country's political divide will continue to set the tone of debates over election administration, say election-law experts, who see only the dimmest outlines of a future in which the public trusts the way elections are conducted and accepts the results.

The left-right political fault line running through the country shows little sign of narrowing over the next 10 years, they say, particularly if virtually all election systems continue to be supervised by officials who are political partisans.

Hasen, the Loyola Law School election-law specialist, sees only one possibility that partisan election management could change. "It depends on whether we have another meltdown like *Bush v. Gore*," he says, referring to the 2000 election crisis. "That could provide short-term pain and long-term gain. Otherwise we'll muddle through in a partisan way. If the 2000 debacle and what's come since have not motivated lawmakers to move beyond partisan positions, I'm not sure what will."

Ohio State law Professor Tokaji agrees. "The parties realize that every vote matters. There will be some folks who are seeking to impose barriers to voting in the name of protecting electoral integrity. There will be others seeking to remove barriers and expand access."

When it comes to the voting-technology debate, however, warnings about dangers to electoral system integrity from computer voting machines are likely to come mainly from the left, as they do today, he says. He puts those fears on an equal plane with warnings from the right about voter fraud. "I tend to think that fraud is not nonexistent," Tokaji says, "but that both sides are exaggerating the threat of electoral manipulation."

Shamos, the Carnegie-Mellon computer voting specialist, offers a sharper view of the future of computer-voting criticism. "In 10 years, the only peep you will be hearing about it will be from the confirmed insane. We will have had enough experience with electronic voting that we will rely on it."

Getty Images/Robyn Beck

President George W. Bush and Democratic presidential candidate Sen. John Kerry participate in their final televised debate, in October 2004, before the controversial November election.

From a Republican perspective, Pullen, the Arizona businessman and GOP committeeman, says he's hopeful that "we will have a sane, rational electoral system whereby people who are qualified to vote can prove they're qualified and vote."

Scholars of American elections argue that the historical context, as well as more recent developments, offer few grounds for expecting election peace and tranquility.

"I don't think that we're just seeing a little period of tumult," Harvard historian Keyssar says. "It's clear — from things like voter-IDs and lawsuits around that and around technology — that political professionals see these as things that can turn elections. The general partisan balance in the country and in many states is sufficiently close that 2 or 3 or 4 percent can be the difference between winning and losing. We really don't know how many people will not vote if there are photo IDs. Suppose it's 4 percent?"

University of Kentucky historian Campbell argues that an era of harmonious elections is as far-off as a society free of racial distinctions. The interests at stake and the passions at play in American elections show no signs of diminishing, he says.

"I live in a state where violence and elections have gone hand in hand," Campbell says. "During the Depression, a small newspaper headline would say, 'Eight killed in Election Day violence.' And, speaking as a historian, that's not a long time ago."

Bechtle, voting-integrity director for the conservative Evergreen Freedom Foundation, hopes citizen pressure will force continued reform. "After 2000, HAVA was a step in the right direction, and that was because of public concern," he says. "I think that a continuing lack of public confidence in elections will drive some more good reforms, giving us 10 years of a continuing pattern of reform."

But Bechtle acknowledges the possibility of another outcome. "I can also see public confidence continuing to fall because of continued close elections. We're at a place — a crisis point — where we could go either way." ■

Notes

[1] Pastor's complete remarks at the AEI-Brookings Election Reform Project Launch, Feb. 8, 2006, can be seen and heard at http://media.brookings.edu/MediaArchive/20060208_ElectionReform_p3_Pastor.wmv.

[2] See "New Voting Standards Enacted," *2002 CQ Almanac*, pp. 14-3 — 14-6.

[3] Sam Howe Verhovek, "For Some, the Race Remains Far From Over," *Los Angeles Times*, Dec. 12, 2004, p. A28.

[4] *Ibid.*

[5] Richard D. Walton, "Law upheld: Voters need photo ID," Indianapolis Star, April 15, 2006, p. A1. For background on Jim Crow laws, see L. Wheildon, "Negro Segregation," in *Editorial Research Reports*, 1947, available in *CQ Researcher Plus Archives*, http://library.cqpress.com.

[6] For more details on nationwide ID requirements, see "Election Reform Since November 2000: What's Changed, What Hasn't and Why, 2000-2006," electionline.org, February 2006, pp. 5, 14-15; www.electionline.org/Portals/1/Publications/2006.annual.report.Final.pdf.

[7] For details of the Carter-Ford commission's recommendations, see "To Assure Pride and Confidence in the Electoral Process," National Commission on Federal Electoral Reform, July 31, 2001, pp. 70-71; www.tcf.org/Publications/ElectionReform/99_full_report.pdf. For details of the Carter-Baker commission's recommendations, see, "Building Confidence in U.S. Elections," Commission on Federal Election Reform, September 2005; www.american.edu/ia/cfer/report/full_report.pdf. Also see Kathy Koch, "Election Reform," *CQ Researcher*, Nov. 2, 2001, pp. 897-920, and Mary H. Cooper, "Voting Rights," *CQ Researcher*, Oct. 29, 2004, pp. 903-922.

[8] For details of Arizona's law, see Matthew Benson and Robbie Sherwood, "Lawsuit Questions Legality of ID Rules," *Arizona Republic*, May 10, 2006, p. B1.

[9] "Building Confidence in U.S. Elections," *op. cit.*, pp. 18-20.

[10] For additional information on the computer controversies, see Monica Davey, "New Fears of Security Risks in Electronic Voting Systems," *The New York Times*, May 12, 2006, p. A23; Viveca Novak, "The Vexations of Voting Machines," *Time*, May 3, 2004, p. 42.

[11] "Building Confidence in U.S. Elections," *op. cit.*, p. 18.

[12] *Ibid.*, pp. 18-19.

[13] For detailed statistics, see "A Joint Report on Election Reform Activities in Ohio," Coalition on Homelessness and Housing in Ohio, League of Women Votes of Ohio, June 14, 2005; www.cohhio.org/alerts/Election%20Reform%20Report.pdf.

[14] For details of the Washington governor's election aftermath, see David Postman, "It's over: Rossi loss in court, ends fight," *The Seattle Times*, June 7, 2005, p. A1; *Seattle Times Staff*, "Toss out felon vote, Gregoire still wins," *The Seattle Times*, May 22, 2005, p. A1; Keith Ervin, "2 fined for casting ballots for their deceased spouses," *The Seattle Times*, June 3, 2005, p. A12; Keith Ervin, "6 accused of casting multiple votes," *The Seattle Times*, p. B4; Emily Heffter, "5,224 dead are registered to vote," *The Seattle Times*, Feb. 2, 2006, p. B1.

[15] John Pawasarat, "The Driver's License Status of the Voting Age Population in Wisconsin," Employment and Training Institute, University of Wisconsin-Milwaukee, June, 2005, pp. 1-2, www.uwm.edu.

[16] Quoted in Steven Walters, "Doyle not shy in use of veto pen," *Milwaukee Journal-Sentinel*, June 4, 2006, p. A1.

[17] For background see, Greg J. Borowski and Stacy Forster, "Progress is slow in voting reforms," *Milwaukee Journal Sentinel*, Oct. 31, 2005, p. A1; Ryan J. Foley, "Auditors find errors in voter registration procedures," The Associated Press, Sept. 16, 2005.

[18] For more details see Spencer Overton, "Dissenting Statement," 2005, www.carterbakerdissent.com.

[19] The judge was U.S. District Judge Sarah Evans Barker. For details, see Richard D. Walton, "Law Upheld: Voters Need Photo ID," *Indianapolis Star*, April 15, 2006, p. A1.

[20] Elizabeth B. Crowley, "House Administration Committee on Immigration Foreshadows Summer Rhetoric," *CQ Today*, June 22, 2006.

[21] "Building Confidence in U.S. Elections," *op. cit.*, pp. 19-20.

[22] Pam Belluck, "Mandate for ID Meets Resistance From States," *The New York Times*, May 6, 2006, p. A1.

[23] *Ibid.*

[24] Testimony, House Administration Committee, June 22, 2006.

[25] *Ibid.*

[26] For details of the Sanchez-Dornan race, see Peter M. Warren, "'Unlawful' Votes Fail to Change Outcome," *Los Angeles Times*, April 10, 1997, p. B1.

[27] Statistics are from "Elections: Federal Efforts to Improve Security and Reliability of Electronic Voting Systems Are Under Way, but Key Activities Need to Be Completed," Government Accountability Office, September 2005, pp. 7-14, www.gao.gov.

[28] Estimates from various sources differ only slightly. For detailed statistics see "Election Reform," *op. cit.*, p. 11; "69 Million Voters will use Optical Scan Ballots in 2006," Election Data Services, Feb. 6, 2006, www.electiondataservices.com.

[29] Government Accountability Office, *op. cit.*

[30] Aviel Rubin, "Pull the Plug," *Forbes*, Sept. 9, 2006; www.forbes.com/forbes/2006/0904/040.html.

[31] For details of the North Carolina episode, see Gary D. Robertson, "Months Later, N.C. Official Admits Defeat," The Associated Press, Feb. 5,

About the Author

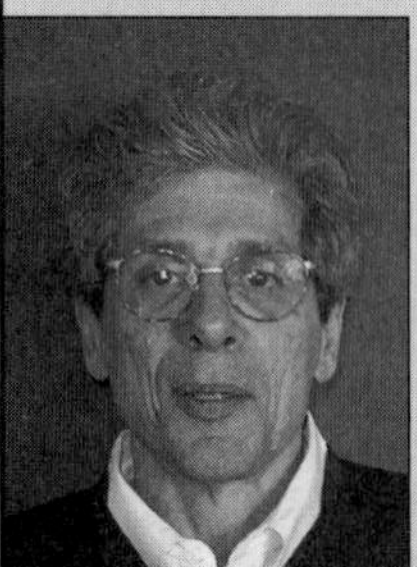

Peter Katel is a *CQ Researcher* staff writer who previously reported on Haiti and Latin America for *Time* and *Newsweek* and covered the Southwest for newspapers in New Mexico. He has received several journalism awards, including the Bartolomé Mitre Award for coverage of drug trafficking from the Inter-American Press Association. He holds an A.B. in university studies from the University of New Mexico. His recent reports include "Immigration Reform" and "Treatment of Detainees."

2005; Lynn Bonner, "Judge cancels new election for agriculture commissioner," *The News & Observer* (Raleigh, N.C.), Jan. 13, 2005, p. B1. For details of the Pennsylvania events, see Bill Toland and Tom Barnes, "State Dumps Voting System," *Pittsburgh Post-Gazette*, April 8, 2005, p. C1; Marc Levy, "Unilect voting machine remains barred in Pa.," The Associated Press, April 29, 2005. Both states' experiences are summarized in "Election Reform," *op. cit.*, pp. 9-10.

[32] "Election Reform," *op. cit.*, pp. 9-12.

[33] Unless otherwise indicated, information in this section is drawn from Tracy Campbell, *Deliver the Vote: A History of Election Fraud, an American Political Tradition: 1724-2004* (2005).

[34] For background, see B. Putney, "Civil and Social Rights of the Negro," *Editorial Research Reports*, 1939, available in *CQ Researcher Plus Archives*, http://library.cqpress.com.

[35] Quoted in Campbell, *op. cit.*, p. 61.

[36] Quote in *ibid*, p. 105.

[37] For more detail on Mississippi Freedom Summer and the voting-rights campaign in general, see Taylor Branch, *Pillar of Fire: America in the King Years, 1963-65* (1999), pp. 320-362. Also see Richard L. Worsnop, "Racism in America," in *Editorial Research Reports*, 1964, available in *CQ Researcher Plus Archives*, http://library.cqpress.com.

[38] Quoted in Charles Babington, "GOP Rebellion Stops Voting Rights Act," *The Washington Post*, June 22, 2006, p. A7

[39] Quoted in *ibid.*

[40] Quoted in Hamil R. Harris and Michael Abramowitz, "Bush Signs Voting Rights Act Extension," *The Washington Post*, July 28, 2006, p. A3.

[41] Information in this sub-section also draws from Roy G. Saltman, "Independent Verification: Essential Action to Assure Integrity in the Voting Process," Report submitted to National Institute of Standards and Technology, Aug. 22, 2006, www.votetrustusa.org.

[42] Ronnie Dugger, "Annals of Democracy; Counting Votes," *The New Yorker*, Nov. 7, 1988, posted at www.csl.sri.com/users/neumann/dugger.html.

[43] Campbell, *op. cit.*, pp. 259-260.

[44] For a summary of the absentee-ballots issue, see Ford Fessenden and John M. Broder, "Study of Disputed Florida Ballots Finds Justices Did Not Cast the Deciding Vote," *The New York Times*, Nov. 12, 2001, p. A1.

[45] *Ibid.*

[46] The case is *Bush v. Gore*, 531 U.S. 98 (2000). For analysis, see, Kenneth Jost, "Bush V. Gore," *CQ Supreme Court Collection*.

FOR MORE INFORMATION

American Center for Voting Rights Legislative Fund, 13807 Beechwood Point Rd., Midlothian, VA 23112; www.ac4vr.com. Advocates and litigates for tougher voter identification standards.

Black Box Voting, 330 S.W. 43rd St., Suite K, PMB 547, Renton, WA 98055; (206) 335-7747; www.blackboxvoting.org. A pioneering anti-electronic voting machine group provides information, advice for activists.

Brennan Center for Justice, NYU School of Law, 161 Avenue of the Americas, 12th floor, New York, NY 10013; (212) 998-6730; www.brennancenter.org. Litigates against what it views as discriminatory practices that limit voting rights.

Election Law Blog, http://electionlawblog.org; rickhasen@lls.edu. Widely read, nonpartisan blog by one of the country's top election-law experts.

electionline.org, 1101 30th St., N.W., Suite 210, Washington, DC 20007; (202) 338-9860; www.electionline.org. Provides detailed, nonpartisan reporting on election news and issues nationwide.

Election Technology Council, Information Technology Association of America, 1401 Wilson Blvd., Suite 1100, Arlington, VA 22209; (703) 522-5055; www.electiontech.org. Computerized voting machine industry trade association; provides information on security and reliability of the devices.

www.votingmachinesprocon.org. Provides links to top sources on both sides of the debate over touch-screen electronic voting machines.

Voter Action, 1604 Solano Ave., Berkeley, CA 94707; (206) 723-1941; www.voter-action.org. Litigates against touch-screen electronic voting machines.

[47] Quoted in Jay Weaver, "Ruling helps voter registration groups," *The Miami Herald*, Aug. 29, 2006. See also Alisa Ulferts, "Judges rejects 'chilling' voter registration law," *St. Petersburg* [Florida] *Times*, Aug. 29, 2006, p. A1.

[48] For details see, M. R. Kropko, "Judge throws out voter registration rules," The Associated Press, Sept. 2, 2006.

[49] Quoted in Matthew Benson, "Request to Halt ID Rules Rejected," *The Arizona Republic*, June 20, 2006, p. 1B. See also Paul Davenport, "Judge hears challenge to state's voter ID requirement," The Associated Press, Aug. 30, 2006.

[50] For details see Carlos Campos, "Fight over photo ID resumes," *Atlanta Journal-Constitution*, Sept. 2, 2006, p. D1; Mary Beth Schneider, "Dean to fight voter ID statute," *Indianapolis Star*, May 5, 2006, p. B1.

[51] Kelly Wiese, "Hearing held in photo ID lawsuits," The Associated Press, Aug. 22, 2006.

[52] For more details see The Associated Press, "Rendell vetoes GOP's voter ID legislation," March 15, 2006.

[53] For more details see Lloyd Jojola, "ACLU Challenges Voter ID Measure," *Albuquerque Journal*, Oct. 28, 2005, p. B1; The Associated Press, "Secretary of State Candidate Opposes ACLU Lawsuit," June 14, 2006.

[54] Carlos Campos, "Touch vote machines take a hit," *Atlanta Journal-Constitution*, Sept. 2, 2006, p. D2; Deborah Hastings, "Electronic voting machines come under legal attack from activists," The Associated Press, July 13, 2006.

[55] *Ibid.*

[56] Quoted in Michael O'Malley, "Foreign-born file election suit," *Plain Dealer* [Cleveland], Aug. 30, 2006, p. B1.

[57] For details see Andrew Garber, "State purges 55,000 dead and duplicate voters from database," *Seattle Times*, May 13, 2006, p. B1.

[58] Gene Johnson, "Judge bars Wash state from enforcing voter registration rule," The Associated Press, Aug. 2, 2006.

[59] "Attorney general's office says voter purge lacked proper approval," The Associated Press, Aug. 7, 2006.

[60] "Attorney General Greg Stumbo Voices Concern Regarding Voter Purge Effect on Primary Election," States News Service, Aug. 10, 2006.

[61] Mike Glover, "Study sees flaws in voter registration system," The Associated Press, March 9, 2006.

Bibliography

Selected Sources

Books

Campbell, Tracy, *Deliver the Vote: A History of Election Fraud, an American Political Tradition, 1743-2004*, Carroll & Graf, 2005.
In a narrative written for a general audience, a University of Kentucky historian pulls back the curtain on America's long and often brutal tradition of fixed elections.

Fund, John, *Stealing Elections: How Voter Fraud Threatens Our Democracy*, Encounter Books, 2004.
In a book published on the eve of the 2004 elections, a conservative columnist for *The Wall Street Journal* argues for stronger measures to verify voters' identities — and also stronger oversight of electronic voting machines.

Miller, Mark Crispin, *Fooled Again: How the Right Stole the 2004 Election and Why They'll Steal the Next One Too (Unless We Stop Them)*, Basic Books, 2005.
A left-of-center journalist argues that the Republicans combined trickery with the use of such legal techniques as absentee voting to win the 2004 election.

Keyssar, Alexander, *The Right to Vote: The Contested History of Democracy in the United States*, Basic Books, 2001.
In an account rich with detail and analysis, a Harvard University historian tells the story of voting rights in America — a far more complicated tale than most Americans realize.

Rubin, Aviel D., *Brave New Ballot: The Battle to Safeguard Democracy in the Age of Electronic Voting*, Morgan Road Books, 2006.
A computer scientist chronicles the fight by him and others against paperless electronic voting.

Articles

Eggen, Dan, "Politics Alleged in Voting Cases; Justice Officials Are Accused of Influence," *The Washington Post*, Jan. 23, 2006, p. A1.
Bush administration appointees in the Justice Department approved tighter voter-ID laws, prompting some colleagues to call the moves politically motivated.

Marimow, Ann E., "La Plata Pressured to Change Voting Rule," *The Washington Post*, Nov. 15, 2005, p. B5.
A Maryland town's voter-identification rule is challenged as discriminatory.

Pryne, Eric, "GOP admits it erred in challenging some voters' registration. But party says it stands behind most complaints," *Seattle Times*, Nov. 5, 2005, p. A1.
A purge of voter rolls in Washington state leads to a partisan battle over alleged voter exclusion.

Stone, Andrea, "Analysis finds e-voting machines vulnerable," *USA Today*, July 27, 2006, p. A1.
A leading voting-rights advocacy organization reports on an in-depth examination of the vulnerabilities of electronic voting machines.

Wallsten, Peter, "Parties Battle Over New Voter ID Laws," *Los Angeles Times*, Sept. 12, 2006, p. A1.
State voter-ID laws spark partisan litigation nationwide that appears far from its final resolution.

Whoriskey, Peter, "Election Whistle-Blower Stymied by Vendors," *The Washington Post*, March 26, 2006, p. A7.
A county election supervisor in Florida reports that voting-machine manufacturers won't deal with him after criticizing some of their products.

Reports and Studies

"Building Confidence in U.S. Elections," Commission on Federal Election Reform, September 2005.
A bipartisan commission headed by a Democratic ex-president and a Republican ex-secretary of State recommends measures including nationwide registration of all citizens using driver's licenses, with special measures for those who don't drive. Also recommended: voter-verified paper audit trails on touch-screen electronic voting machines.

"Elections: Federal Efforts to Improve Security and Reliability of Electronic Voting Systems Are Under Way, but Key Activities Need to Be Completed," Government Accountability Office, September 2005.
A nonpartisan examination finds gaps in the supervision of voting machines during elections, including their security features and basic operability.

"A Blueprint for Change: Recommendations on Election Reform for States," Evergreen Freedom Foundation, 2006.
A conservative think tank recommends election-reform measures including stricter voter-identification requirements and voter-verified paper audit trails for computer voting machines.

Levitt, Justin, *et al.*, "Making the List: Database Matching and Verification Processes for Voter Registration," Brennan Center for Justice, March 24, 2006.
A voting-rights advocacy and litigation group examines the ways in which it says registered voters can be dropped from statewide voter rolls as states match data from various databases.

The Next Step:

Additional Articles from Current Periodicals

Electronic Voting

The Associated Press, "Oregon May Run Afoul of Voter Law," *The Seattle Times*, March 21, 2006, p. B4.

Oregon is in danger of violating the federal 2002 Help America Vote Act, which requires every polling place to have a machine that allows disabled people to vote independently and privately.

Benn, Evan S., "Paper Vote Records Vital," *The Miami Herald*, June 28, 2006, p. B2.

David Dill, a Stanford University computer science professor, discussed the importance of having a paper record attached to electronic voting machines.

Davey, Monica, "New Fears of Security Risks In Electronic Voting Systems," *The New York Times*, May 12, 2006, p. A23.

Election officials in Pennsylvania and California announced a potential security risk in their touch-screen voting machines, prompting other states to assess their machines.

Petersen, Nancy, and Marc Schogol, "Suburbs Slow in Tabulating Totals," *The Philadelphia Inquirer*, May 17, 2006, p. B9.

Roughly 100 of Philadelphia's 3,500 electronic voting machines malfunctioned on primary day.

Vogel, Steve, "Touch-Screen Machines Stir Election Anxiety in Md.," *The Washington Post*, Aug. 19, 2006, p. B1.

Gov. Robert L. Ehrlich Jr., R-Md., purchased touch-screen voting machines three years ago but now questions whether they can provide fair and accurate elections.

Fraud and Discrimination

The Associated Press, "Pennsylvania Democrats Contest Green Party Filings," *St. Louis Post-Dispatch*, Aug. 9, 2006, p. A5.

The Pennsylvania Democratic Party objected to signatures collected by three Green Party candidates, alleging that more than 69,000 signatures included fake names, unregistered voters and illegible signatures.

Garvin, Michael J., "Legislature Must Step in to Help Clerks Prevent Fraud," *The Philadelphia Inquirer*, May 31, 2006, p. B2.

Critics of absentee ballots delivered by messengers in New Jersey want the clerk's office to limit the number of applications that the office will accept from a single messenger in order to prevent fraud.

Goodman, Brenda, "Judge Blocks Requirement In Georgia For Voter ID," *The New York Times*, July 8, 2006, p. A10.

A judge blocked a Republican-sponsored effort to require Georgia voters to present government-issued photo identification cards before they can vote, saying it violated the state Constitution.

Johnson, Gene, "Judge Says State's New Voter-ID Law Too Stringent," *The Seattle Times*, Aug. 2, 2006, p. B2.

A federal judge in Seattle barred Washington state from enforcing a new law that prevents people from registering to vote if their names do not perfectly match identifying information in other government databases.

Jonsson, Patrik, "Struggle Over Voter IDs Evokes a Bitter Past," *The Christian Science Monitor*, May 9, 2005, p. 2.

South Carolina and dozens of other states want to demand that registered voters flash a picture ID to vote, but critics say the measures are reminiscent of poll taxes and techniques used to keep blacks from voting.

Page, Clarence, "Tinkering With Voting Rights," *Chicago Tribune*, June 25, 2006, p. C7.

When moving to renew the 1965 Voting Rights Act, congressional Republicans debated the law's special requirements for the states of the old, segregated South.

Williams, Joseph, "Voting Act Overshadows Race Debate," *The Boston Globe*, July 31, 2006, p. A2.

Democrats are debating whether mostly black voting districts in cities like Petersburg, Va. — which helped elect the state's first African-American House member in more than 100 years — should be diluted to spread around liberal voters and help elect more Democrats to Congress.

Citing *CQ Researcher*

Sample formats for citing these reports in a bibliography include the ones listed below. Preferred styles and formats vary, so please check with your instructor or professor.

MLA STYLE

Jost, Kenneth. "Rethinking the Death Penalty." CQ Researcher 16 Nov. 2001: 945-68.

APA STYLE

Jost, K. (2001, November 16). Rethinking the death penalty. *CQ Researcher, 11*, 945-968.

CHICAGO STYLE

Jost, Kenneth. "Rethinking the Death Penalty." *CQ Researcher*, November 16, 2001, 945-968.

CQ Researcher

Published by CQ Press, a division of Congressional Quarterly Inc.

cqresearcher.com

Abortion Showdowns

Will the latest anti-abortion moves succeed?

South Dakota has become the latest battlefield in the abortion wars. A Nov. 7 referendum will let voters approve or reject a new law aimed at banning virtually all abortions in the state. South Dakota legislators passed the law earlier this year in a direct challenge to the Supreme Court's landmark 1973 decision, *Roe v. Wade*, which legalized abortion during most of a woman's pregnancy. Abortion-rights advocates in South Dakota forced a referendum on the measure, which would allow abortions only if necessary to protect a woman's life. The balloting is the first popular vote on an abortion ban since Oregon voters rejected such a measure in 1990. Meanwhile, the Supreme Court is set to hear arguments on Nov. 8 in the Bush administration's defense of the federal law banning what opponents call "partial-birth abortions." The high court struck down a state ban in 2000, but anti-abortion groups hope two new justices may change the outcome this time around.

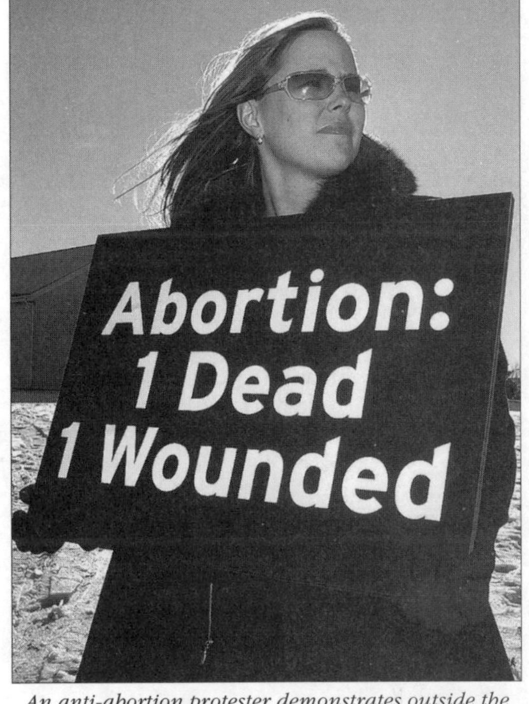

An anti-abortion protester demonstrates outside the Planned Parenthood abortion clinic in Sioux Falls, S.D., on Jan. 4, 2006.

INSIDE THIS REPORT

CQ Researcher • Sept. 22, 2006 • www.cqresearcher.com
Volume 16, Number 33 • Pages 769-792

CQ PRESS

RECIPIENT OF SOCIETY OF PROFESSIONAL JOURNALISTS AWARD FOR EXCELLENCE ◆ AMERICAN BAR ASSOCIATION SILVER GAVEL AWARD

Cover photograph: *Argus Leader*/Cory Myers

CQ Researcher

Sept. 22, 2006
Volume 16, Number 33

MANAGING EDITOR: Thomas J. Colin
ASSISTANT MANAGING EDITOR: Kathy Koch
ASSOCIATE EDITOR: Kenneth Jost
STAFF WRITERS: Marcia Clemmitt, Peter Katel
CONTRIBUTING WRITERS: Rachel S. Cox, Sarah Glazer, Alan Greenblatt, Barbara Mantel, Patrick Marshall, Tom Price, Jennifer Weeks
DESIGN/PRODUCTION EDITOR: Olu B. Davis
ASSISTANT EDITOR: Melissa J. Hipolit

CQ PRESS
A Division of Congressional Quarterly Inc.

SENIOR VICE PRESIDENT/PUBLISHER: John A. Jenkins
DIRECTOR, LIBRARY PUBLISHING: Kathryn C. Suárez
DIRECTOR, EDITORIAL OPERATIONS: Ann Davies

CONGRESSIONAL QUARTERLY INC.
CHAIRMAN: Paul C. Tash
VICE CHAIRMAN: Andrew P. Corty
PRESIDENT/EDITOR IN CHIEF: Robert W. Merry

CQ Researcher (ISSN 1056-2036) is printed on acid-free paper. Published weekly, except March 24, July 7, July 14, Aug. 4, Aug. 11, Nov. 24, Dec. 22 and Dec. 29, by CQ Press, a division of Congressional Quarterly Inc. Annual full-service subscriptions for institutions start at $667. For pricing, call 1-800-834-9020, ext. 1906. To purchase a *CQ Researcher* report in print or electronic format (PDF), visit www.cqpress.com or call 866-427-7737. Single reports start at $15. Bulk purchase discounts and electronic-rights licensing are also available. Periodicals postage paid at Washington, D.C., and additional mailing offices. POSTMASTER: Send address changes to *CQ Researcher*, 1255 22nd St., N.W., Suite 400, Washington, DC 20037.

Abortion Showdowns

BY KENNETH JOST AND KATHY KOCH

THE ISSUES

Sally Gramm and Leila Huisken take up their positions on the sidewalk outside the Planned Parenthood clinic in Sioux Falls, S.D., on a chilly, overcast Monday morning in mid-September. They carry placards from the American Life League: "Face It. Abortion Kills," the signs read. The message appears above the face of a newborn baby.

"We'd like to close this place," says Huisken, a retired pharmacy technician from nearby Brookings and mother of three adopted children. "Maybe some people don't even know that this place exists or what it does."

The clinic, housed in a nondescript one-story building on a major artery in Sioux Falls' western outskirts, is the only facility for elective abortions in the entire state of South Dakota. Almost all of the state's abortions — there were 814 in 2004 — are performed inside, most of them on Mondays.

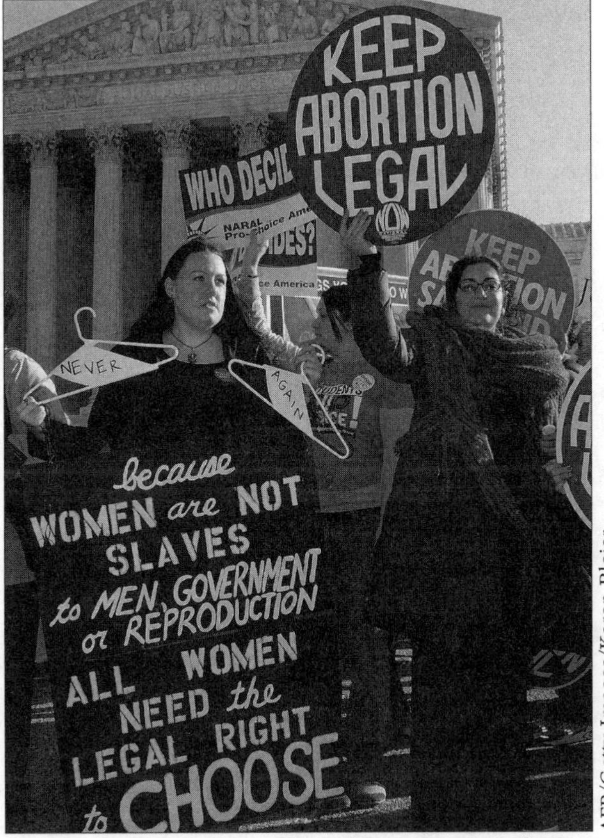

AFP/Getty Images/Karen Bleier

Pro-choice activists at the U.S. Supreme Court last November oppose the nomination of conservative Justice Samuel A. Alito. This November, the court will hear arguments in the Bush administration's defense of the law banning "partial-birth abortions." And in South Dakota, a referendum will decide the fate of a new law that would ban virtually all abortions in the state.

The patients who come for what the clinic calls "abortion care" are typically nervous or scared as they arrive and relieved as they leave, according to the physician who has flown in from Minneapolis for a relatively light day of eight procedures. The doctor — who declines to give her name for fear of harassment or retaliation — says several of the patients appear surprised that the procedure is physically less difficult than expected. *

Emotionally, however, the experience is taxing. "Many women are sad that they feel they have to make this decision at this time," the doctor, a two-year veteran of the Minneapolis-Sioux Falls commute, says. "We see tears sometimes."

The doctor is one of four Minnesota physicians who service the South Dakota clinic. No South Dakota doctor performs elective abortions on a regular basis: Some refuse out of conviction, others out of fear of social or professional ostracism. But Kate Looby, Planned Parenthood's South Dakota director, offers no apologies for the clinic's practice.

"What we primarily do here is family planning," Looby explains. "There is nothing to be shy about that. We also provide abortion care from this location, and I don't feel there's anything to be shy about that as well."

If anti-abortion forces in South Dakota have their way, however, the clinic's abortion-care services will be shut down after Nov. 7. That's when South Dakota voters decide in a referendum whether to retain the state's law making abortion a felony in the state unless the procedure is necessary to save the life of the mother. [1] The law — passed in February — has not gone into effect, pending the outcome of the referendum.

Abortion-rights advocates opposed the bill as it moved through the legislature and then gathered more than 38,000 signatures in order to force the referendum. They say the law goes too far even for a pro-life, "red" state like South Dakota.

"There's no exception for rape or incest and no exception for the woman's health," says Jan Nicolay, a former state representative and one of the co-chairs of the benignly titled South Dakota Campaign for Healthy Families. "I think every state is anti-abortion, but this is not the way you go at it."

The clinic itself answers the protesters' messages with a banner that hangs on the outside wall big enough for pedestrians and motorists to read at a glance: "These doors will stay open."

In a former industrial warehouse on the opposite side of town, Leslee Unruh is managing the Vote Yes for Life campaign aimed at winning approval of the abortion ban — listed

* Miriam McCreary, another Minnesota physician, has previously granted interviews about abortions she performed at the South Dakota clinic in the past. See "Abortion doctor says she has no doubts about her work," The Associated Press, April 4, 2006.

Many States Now Restrict Abortions

In the past decade, many states have imposed restrictions on abortion, such as banning so-called partial-birth abortions, limiting public funding of abortions and requiring pre-abortion counseling, waiting periods and parental notification or consent for minors to obtain an abortion. The most restrictive states are in the South, Midwest and West. Other states, primarily on the East and West coasts, have introduced laws protecting a woman's right to obtain an abortion.

How States Deal With Abortion

Sources: Melody Rose, Safe, Legal and Unavailable? Abortion Politics in the United States, *CQ Press, 2007*

as Referred Law 6 on the ballot. Unruh, who had an abortion herself in her 20s and now runs a support center for other "post-abortive women," is centering the campaign on the slogan, "Abortion hurts women."

"It wasn't healthy for me to have an abortion," Unruh says. "It's a very unhealthy thing to do emotionally and physically." She says she was married and already had children when she decided to terminate the pregnancy, but turns aside more detailed questions.

Abortion-rights advocates say it is one of medicine's safest procedures and that for most women there are no negative psychological effects. "The risk of death from abortion is lower than that from a shot of penicillin," says Nancy Keenan, president of NARAL-Pro-Choice America. "But the other side won't talk about that. They don't want people thinking about women being forced to go back to the days of seeking abortions down back alleys."

The South Dakota referendum comes as anti-abortion groups continue making gains in legislative arenas and see signs of diminishing support for abortion rights in public-opinion polls. (*See graph, p. 776.*) They also hope that President George W. Bush's two appointees to the Supreme Court — Chief Justice John G. Roberts Jr. and Justice Samuel A. Alito Jr. — will narrow the court's abortion-rights rulings, including the landmark 1973 decision legalizing abortion, *Roe v. Wade*, and vote to uphold abortion restrictions passed by Congress or state legislatures. [2]

"Most Americans are against most abortions," says Douglas Johnson, legislative director of the National Right to Life Committee. "There's never been anything approaching majority opinion for the actual policy embodied in *Roe v. Wade*, which is legal abortion for any reason up to provable viability and then for health, including mental health, after viability."

Abortion-rights groups, however, stress that a majority of Americans continue to support what they call "a woman's right to choose" and to oppose overturning *Roe v. Wade.* They also say that pro-life groups are experiencing a public backlash because of their opposition to eased access to contraception and their stance on right-to-die issues, including the Terri Schiavo case. [3]

"It's no longer just a debate about abortion," says Keenan. "These attacks on women's reproductive health have gone too far." The Schiavo case represented a turning point, she adds. "The American public is saying, 'Enough of these politicians being involved in our private decisions.' "

Meanwhile, the number of abortions performed in the United States is continuing to decline from a peak of 1.6 million in 1990. About 1.3 million abortions were performed in 2003, the most recent year for which statistics are available, according to the Guttmacher Institute, a respected research center affiliated with Planned Parenthood. The abortion rate has similarly been falling. In 2003, there were 20.8 abortions per 1,000 women of normal childbearing age (15-44), according to the institute. [4] (*See graph, p. 773.*)

Abortion-rights advocates cite the decline as evidence that sex education and access to contraception can help reduce the number of abortions. But they also worry that the decline may be due in part to restrictive state laws on abortion and a decline in the number of abortion providers. And some anti-abortion advocates do say that restrictive state laws have served their purpose by making abortions harder to obtain. (*See sidebar, p. 774.*)

In South Dakota, supporters of the abortion ban appear to be behind, according to the one nonpartisan poll on the referendum commissioned by news organizations and published in late July. The poll, conducted by Mason Dixon Polling and Research for KELO-TV and the *Argus Leader* of Sioux Falls, showed 47 percent of respondents opposed to the measure, 39 percent in favor and 14 percent undecided. [5]

The South Dakota vote will come on the day before the Supreme Court hears its first abortion case since Alito joined the court in late January. The Bush administration is urging the court to reinstate a law Congress passed in 2003 to prohibit the late-pregnancy procedure that anti-abortion groups call a "partial-birth abortion." (*See sidebar, p. 780.*)

Three federal appeals courts have ruled the law unconstitutional, citing the high court's 2000 ruling striking down a similar Nebraska statute. The justices agreed to hear the government's appeals in two of the cases, with arguments scheduled back to back on Nov. 8.

As the opposing groups prepare for the closely watched showdowns in South Dakota and in Washington, here are some of the major questions being debated:

Abortion Rate Has Been Dropping Since 1981

The rate of abortions performed in the United States each year climbed dramatically after Roe v. Wade *legalized the practice in 1973, peaking in 1981 at 29 abortions for every 1,000 women of child-bearing age, or 1.57 million abortions. Since then, the rate has declined to 21 abortions per 1,000, or 1.28 million abortions.*

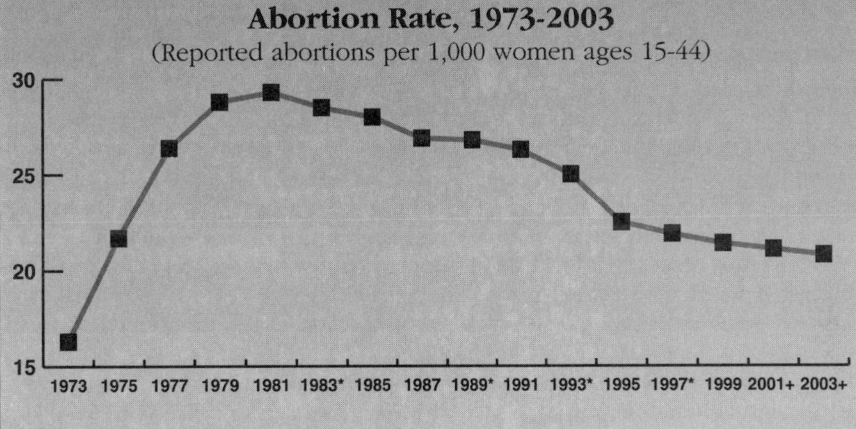

* *Based on estimates*

\+ *Preliminary*

Source: Lawrence B. Finer and Stanley K. Henshaw, "Estimates of U.S. Abortion Incidence, 2001-2003," Guttmacher Institute, Aug. 3, 2006

Should states ban abortions to try to overturn Roe v. Wade?

After more than 20 years in the pro-life movement, Unruh of the Vote Yes for Life Campaign is fed up with politicians who run on anti-abortion platforms but fail to deliver afterwards. "We have a problem in this country that people win elections with this issue, and people like me are tired of that," Unruh says. "I'm sick of the politics that surrounds the issue."

As the prime mover behind the South Dakota abortion ban, Unruh is directing the campaign aimed at winning approval of the law in the statewide referendum on Nov. 7. But she is waging the fight without support from the nation's major anti-abortion groups: the National Right to Life Committee (NRLC) and Americans United for Life.

Both groups opposed the ban when it was passed. NRLC issued a terse statement on the day Gov. Michael Rounds, a Republican, signed the bill into law. "Currently, there are at least five votes, a majority on the U.S. Supreme Court, to uphold *Roe v. Wade*," spokeswoman Cristina Minniti said while declining to make any of the group's officials available for questioning. [6]

Today, NRLC continues to decline requests to comment on the ban. Meanwhile, Clarke Forsythe, senior counsel at Chicago-based Americans United for Life, calls the ban "premature," noting that only two current justices — Antonin Scalia and Clarence Thomas — have voted to overturn *Roe*.

"You can't count to five on the Supreme Court," Forsythe says. "You can't even count beyond two." The ban "was a move of high risk and low odds," he says, "but then instead of immediately going into court, they have encountered the unanticipated circumstance of the [referendum] process."

Unruh dismisses the naysayers within her own camp. "Most other pro-life groups are behind us," she says. "Individuals across the nation are supportive."

In fact, some pro-life groups, including the Washington-based Concerned Women for America and Family Research Council, are lending at least verbal support to the South Dakota ban. "The purpose of government

Continued on p. 776

States Restrict Access to Abortion

On a sweltering July morning in Jackson, Miss., a short woman with curly brown hair wearing a violet T-shirt and shorts joined pro-life activists protesting outside Mississippi's last remaining abortion clinic.

"It would really please the Lord God if Mississippi becomes the first abortion-free state," she told the group. "Then all he'd have to worry about are the other 49." [1]

The speaker was Norma McCorvey — the once-anonymous "Jane Roe," lead plaintiff in the landmark class-action lawsuit *Roe v. Wade* that legalized abortion in the United States. Since being born again in 1995, McCorvey has been an anti-abortion activist.

Both pro-life and pro-choice protesters descended on the Jackson clinic this summer, staging weeks of contentious rallies in an effort to make Mississippi a key state in the fight over access to abortion. However, abortion-rights groups say a quieter, more far-reaching battle over access has been raging in statehouses across the country, where anti-abortion forces have been working since the early 1990s to enact hundreds of laws restricting abortion. Pro-choice advocates say abortions are now particularly difficult for poor, rural and young women to obtain, or women in especially restrictive states.

Legislators have created "a gauntlet that women have to traverse before they can access abortion," says Jackie Payne, director of government relations at the Planned Parenthood Federation, which runs 860 women's health clinics nationwide.

Partly as a result of the state restrictions, the United States has fewer abortion clinics today than at any time since *Roe* was decided in 1973. In addition to Mississippi, South Dakota has only one abortion clinic. Between 1996 and 2000, the number of abortion providers nationwide fell by 11 percent, and today more than a third of American women of childbearing age live in the 87 percent of U.S. counties that lack an abortion provider. [2]

But pro-life advocates reject the notion that state laws have dramatically reduced abortion access, pointing out that 1.3 million abortions are still performed in the United States each year. "It's just not credible to claim that pro-lifers have been able to make abortions illegal," says Cathy Cleaver Ruse, senior fellow for legal studies at the Family Research Council.

Anti-abortion advocates do concede, however that their push for greater state restrictions on abortion gained momentum after the Supreme Court's 1992 decision in *Planned Parenthood of Southeastern Pennsylvania v. Casey*, which said states could regulate abortion if they did not place "significant obstacles" in the path of women seeking abortions. With that opening, states enacted 299 laws in the 1990s limiting access to abortion and dramatically changing abortion politics. [3]

"*Casey* helped us to focus our attention and build our movement" at the grass-roots level, says Wendy Wright, president of the anti-abortion group Concerned Women for America. It also "helped prepare us" for the coming battle over abortion bans that will shift to the states if *Roe* is overturned, she says.

Mississippi has led the pack, enacting more pro-life laws than any other state. Today, more than 30 states require patients to receive pre-abortion counseling, 24 states require a waiting period — usually 24 hours — between counseling and the procedure, 12 states have banned so-called partial-birth abortions, 32 states limit Medicaid funding of abortions and 34 states require parental notification or consent for minors to obtain an abortion. [4]

Sondra Goldschein, an attorney for the Reproductive Freedom Project at the American Civil Liberties Union in New York, says that especially for poor women and minors, the level of access is "comparable to the access when abortion was illegal."

The limits on Medicaid funding have had the greatest impact on poor women, says Smith. "One-fifth of the women who would have had abortions ended up carrying the fetus to term" because they cannot afford the procedure, she says. The mandatory waiting periods also force some women to travel long distances, pay for overnight child care and a hotel room and take time off from work. "This makes it harder for poor or rural women to obtain services."

A recent report by the pro-choice Guttmacher Institute found that since the mid-1990s a widening gap has developed between poor women and higher-income women: Unplanned-pregnancy rates among poor women have increased by 29 percent while wealthier women's rates dropped 20 percent. Thus, the report concluded, a poor woman today is four times as likely to experience an unplanned pregnancy as a higher-income woman. [5]

"They keep going back and trying to make it harder and harder to get an abortion, such as requiring notification and/or consent from both parents for a minor to get an abortion," Goldschein says.

Although restrictive measures have been introduced in Congress, most of the action has been in the states. In 2005, about 500 anti-abortion bills were introduced in the states, of which 26 were enacted, says Vicky Supporter, president of the National Abortion Federation (NAF), a group of 400 U.S. abortion providers.

"We are worried that in some states the goal really is to make abortion inaccessible," says Judith Waxman, vice president for health and reproductive rights at the National Women's Law Center.

Tanya Britton, president of Pro-Life Mississippi, makes no bones about that being her group's goal: "We'd like to see the Jackson clinic closed down, so Mississippi can be 100 percent pro-life."

Britton strongly disagrees that limiting abortion access disproportionately harms poor women, as does Ruse. "Abortion hurts women — all women," says Ruse. "It is a tragedy that minority women experience abortion at higher rates than white women today. Pro-life African-Americans see this as a form of racial genocide."

Other pro-life advocates deny that state restrictions on abortion unduly block access. "Our legislation just nibbles around the edges," says Wright. "*Roe* gave the pro-choice folks the entire pie: abortion on demand in all nine months. So they will go to the mat to oppose even the most common-sense legislation, such as allowing women to get full information before they get an abortion."

Ruse agrees, noting that because *Roe* prohibited states from banning abortion outright, they can enact only "very limited" regulations — such as parental involvement, waiting periods and informed consent — "none of which impinges on access" unless a judge refuses to exempt a minor from parental-notification rules. "But minors do get abortions without their parents' knowledge. It happens quite readily."

Rose Afriyie, right, a field organizer for the National Organization for Women, leads demonstrators in Jackson, Miss., on July 17, 2006, against attempts to close the state's only abortion clinic.

Even if, as Ruse says, state restrictions have not limited access to abortion per se, they have helped reduce the number of abortions performed each year, says Michael J. New, assistant professor of political science at the University of Alabama and a visiting health-policy fellow at the conservative Heritage Foundation. "These laws are having a real impact," he concluded after analyzing abortion data from all 50 states. [6] Abortion rates declined in states with more pro-life laws, he found, particularly in states that limited Medicaid funding or required informed consent and parental notice. "State legislation was a key factor in the 18 percent decline in the number of abortions performed in the United States between 1990 and 1999," he wrote. [7]

In addition to state restrictions, say abortion-rights advocates, access is declining because most young doctors today do not learn how to perform abortions. That's because fewer hospitals — where most doctors are trained — provide abortions, either because of fear or because they are operated by pro-life entities like the Catholic Church, they say. [8]

"In most of the country, finding a doctor qualified to perform an abortion cannot be assured," says Lois Backus, executive director of Medical Students for Choice (MSFC), based in Oakland, Calif., which is pushing medical schools to train students in the procedure. "The direst need is in the Midwest and Southeast, where the pro-life movement has gained political strength." (*See map, p. 772.*)

According to the pro-choice advocacy group NARAL, there are five or fewer abortion providers in eight states: Kentucky, Mississippi, Nebraska, North Dakota, South Dakota, Utah, West Virginia and Wyoming. And in 10 states, more than 95 percent of the counties have no provider: Arkansas, Kansas, Kentucky, Mississippi, Missouri, Nebraska, North Dakota, Oklahoma, South Dakota and West Virginia. Only Hawaii has an abortion provider in every county.

"Many providers have been driven out of business or are too scared to provide services," says Goldschein.

But Ruse — noting that clinic violence has dramatically declined since Congress outlawed it in the 1990s — insists that restrictive state laws, fear of violence and lack of training have nothing to do with the disappearance of providers. "Most people in the healing profession do not want to go into the business of killing," she says. That sentiment has grown among physicians and pregnant women since ultrasound technology became common in the 1990s, she says.

"People began to see that the baby had fingerprints, legs, arms and brainwaves. It wasn't just a clump of cells," adds Wright. "Ultrasound did what we had been trying to do: explain that this was a human being that was being destroyed."

In the final analysis, says Wright, pro-life groups have succeeded in the statehouses because they made their case "at the grass-roots level, using everyday language, while the other side has been making its case in the courts, using legal arguments." Moreover, "80 percent of the American public" supports the "common sense" restrictions pro-life groups have advocated, she adds.

Pro-choice advocates have fought the anti-abortion efforts "every step of the way," says Goldschein, while also pushing for their own "common sense" measures designed to prevent the need for abortions: increasing access to birth control, comprehensive sex education and emergency contraception. "We are trying to get legislators to come together on issues that both sides can agree on," she says.

Susan Hill, who owns the beleaguered Jackson clinic, is optimistic that ultra-extremist groups like those that vowed to shut down the clinic in July will end up arousing abortion-rights advocates. During the rallies, many Jackson residents Hill had never seen before showed up to support the clinic, she says.

"When people get to the brink and realize they might lose their only access to abortion in the state," she adds, "the pro-choice people begin to fight back."

---

1 Michelle Goldberg, "Abortion under siege in Mississippi," *Salon.com*, Aug. 1, 2006.

2 Lawrence B. Finer and Stanley K. Henshaw, "Abortion Incidence and Services in the United States in 2000," *Perspectives on Sexual and Reproductive Health*, January/February 2003; www.guttmacher.org/pubs/journals/3500603.html.

3 "An Overview of Abortion Laws," Guttmacher Institute, Sept. 1, 2006.

4 *Ibid.*

5 Heather Boonstra, *et al.*, "Abortion in Women's Lives," Guttmacher Institute, 2006.

6 Michael J. New, "States Save Lives," *National Review Online*, Jan. 30, 2006.

7 Michael J. New, "Using Natural Experiments to Analyze the Impact of State Legislation on the Incidence of Abortion," Heritage Foundation, Jan. 23, 2006, www.heritage.org/Research/Family/cda06-01.cfm.

8 "The Provider Shortage," Medical Students for Choice, www.ms4c.org/issueshortage.htm.

Continued from p. 773

is to defend and protect — to protect life," says Wendy Wright, president of Concerned Women. "And if you don't have the fundamental right to live, you don't have any rights at all." But Wright declines to answer questions about whether the South Dakota ban is a wise strategy for the right-to-life movement or what impact a potential defeat would have.

Opponents of the ban profess confidence that the strategy will, in fact, backfire. "They've been gunning at *Roe v. Wade* for 33 years," says Lindsay Roitman, campaign manager for the South Dakota Campaign for Healthy Families. "They have taken this as their opportunity. They're going to find that they don't have the support of the majority."

"The Right to Life Web site doesn't even mention the South Dakota ban," says Keenan, of NARAL Pro-Choice America. "They know that [the South Dakota ban supporters] are out of step with mainstream America."

Some abortion-rights advocates appear less certain about the Supreme Court's likely ruling on an abortion ban, however, than anti-abortion groups that view a reversal of *Roe* as unlikely. "I'm hoping that South Dakota is not going to make it there," says Priscilla Smith, a lawyer with the New York-based Center for Reproductive Rights.

"I don't think that they have the votes for an outright overturning of *Roe*, but we could be one vote away," she says — counting Roberts, Scalia, Thomas and Alito as potential votes to discard the precedent. "If we lose one more vote, I'd be very, very concerned. I'm very concerned now."

Critics of the *Roe* decision stress that reversing the ruling would not ban abortions nationwide but would only allow each state discretion to regulate or restrict the procedure as it thinks best. "In our view, it would be a big step in the right direction if the unelected judges would remove the judicial legislation and allow the elected legislators to address the issue," says Johnson, the NRLC lobbyist.

Pro-Life Supporters Picked Up Support

The number of pro-life Americans rose 11 percentage points in the last decade while abortion-rights advocates dropped eight points.

What is your stance on abortion?

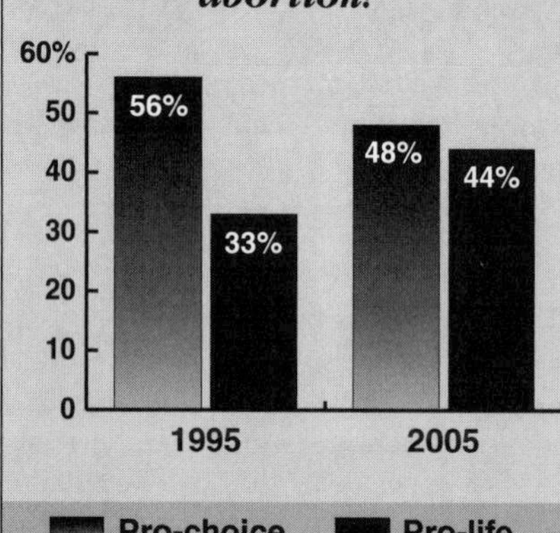

Source: Gallup Poll, "Americans Closely Divided Into Pro-Choice and Pro-Life Camps," May 12, 2005

Abortion-rights advocates say allowing each state to write its own abortion laws with no constitutional restraints would be unfair for women. "It's a social-justice issue," says Looby of Planned Parenthood in South Dakota. "We'll have this patchwork of states where you can get legal abortions, but in many states you won't. Wealthy women will be able to access safe and legal abortion care, and poor women will not."

"There would be variations in jurisdictions at least for some period of time," Johnson concedes. "We'd keep working for the day when the unborn would be protected," he adds. "But I'm not sure where you would find a majority in support of a policy as permissive or as unrestrained as *Roe v. Wade*."

Should the U.S. Supreme Court uphold the federal 'partial-birth abortion' ban?

Marvin Buehner, a Rapid City, S.D., obstetrician, acknowledges ambivalence about abortion, especially about the procedure that opponents have labeled a partial-birth abortion.[7] "Everyone knows what a grisly procedure it is," says Buehner.

But Buehner quickly adds that he opposes the law Congress passed in 2003 to prohibit the procedure. "Since I don't do the procedure, I can't comment on how appropriate it is," he explains. "But I can tell you that eliminating a single procedure is not good medicine; it's not good policy."

Congress and more than 31 states that enacted similar bans disagree. But the Supreme Court ruled in 2000 that Nebraska's law — typical of the state statutes — was unconstitutional. And three federal appeals courts have similarly ruled the federal law invalid even though Congress tried to craft it to meet the high court's objections.

All of the courts say the bans are invalid because their language applies not only to what doctors generally call a "dilation and extraction," procedure, or D&X, but also to the more commonly used abortion procedure: a "dilation and evacuation," or D&E. The laws are also defective, the courts say, because they do not allow the procedure if doctors believe it necessary to protect the woman's health.

Anti-abortion groups say the court rulings are wrong. "We don't think there's anything in the Constitution that prevents the legislature from protecting the unborn in general and nothing that prevents it from banning this brutal procedure," says Johnson. "We agree with the congressional finding that there isn't any need to mostly deliver a premature infant and stab her with a surgical device."

Abortion-rights groups hope the Supreme Court will adhere to its previous ruling after the justices hear arguments on Nov. 8. "Congress was thumbing its nose at the Supreme Court and ignoring precedent from just six years ago that protected women's health — just as the court has done for the past 30 years," says Smith of the Center for Reproductive Rights, who will argue one of two abortion cases before the high court.

In passing the "partial-birth abortion" law, Congress said the procedure is never medically necessary and is harmful to women's health. Government lawyers argue the court should defer to those findings, which they say are supported by "substantial evidence."

Forsythe, who helped prepare a supporting brief for Americans United for Life, agrees. "Medical evidence is clear that there are recognizable, established medical alternatives to D&X, or partial-birth abortion," says Forsythe. "And there are still no empirical data demonstrating its safety or effectiveness."

Roger Evans, Planned Parenthood's senior director for public-policy litigation, says there is "no substance" to the opponents' arguments. "That is ideological poppycock, totally unsupported by the medicine," Evans says. "The judges who have heard testimony on the subject have consistently concluded that it is a safer method of abortion for many women and that it is a medically necessary method of abortion for women in some circumstances."

Evans adds that the failure to include a health exception is especially problematic because of the law's potential application to commonly used D&E procedures. "This ban would endanger women's health more or less every day of the week all across the country," he says.

Forsythe counters that under the broad definition of women's health established in Supreme Court precedents, any health exception would create a massive loophole. "If you prohibit partial-birth abortion except for emotional well-being, your exception has gutted the law," he says.

When the court struck down the Nebraska law in 2000, dissenting justices described the procedure in graphic terms and registered their disapproval. Justice Anthony M. Kennedy depicted the procedure as "abhorrent," while Thomas suggested it was close to "infanticide."

Anti-abortion advocates say those views mirror those of the American public. "The court should uphold the ban because it's a barbaric procedure that most Americans reject," says Cathy Cleaver Ruse, senior fellow for legal studies at the Family Research Council in Washington.

Abortion-rights advocates believe opponents have misled the public by suggesting the procedures are performed after a fetus can live on its own. "None of these are post-viability," says Smith, "which is one of the big misconceptions."

Still, Smith and Evans say they face an uphill fight before the Supreme Court in seeking to strike down the federal law because of the two new appointments since 2000: Roberts and Alito. "I have a tough row to hoe," says Smith.

For their part, anti-abortion groups profess cautious optimism. "I think you'll get five justices to uphold the statute," says Forsythe.

Should states try to increase access to abortion?

Susan Hill has noticed something peculiar at the abortion clinic she runs in Raleigh, N.C. "In the last three or four years, our parking lot has been full of out-of-state license tags," says Hill, who owns four other clinics in the South. "It's because all the surrounding states have imposed restrictions."

Abortion-rights advocates like Hill say state limits on abortions have made them increasingly difficult to obtain — particularly for poor, rural or young women and those living in Southern, Midwestern and some Western states. According to the Guttmacher Institute, there are fewer abortion clinics in the United States today than at any time since *Roe v. Wade* legalized abortions in 1973. Mississippi has a lone abortion clinic still operating, owned by Hill, and overall only 13 percent of U.S. counties have an abortion facility. Nationwide, the number of abortion providers has declined by 37 percent since 1982. [8] (*See sidebar, p. 774.*)

Pro-life advocates contend the access problem is a myth. "Each year 1.3 million abortions are performed in the United States — the highest abortion rate in the Western world," says the Family Research Council's Ruse. "Doesn't sound like an access problem to me."

Pro-choice advocates say abortion clinics and doctors have disappeared not only because of the new state restrictions but also because of intimidation (and even murder) of providers and the aging of abortion doctors. Today, 57 percent of abortion doctors are over 50, and most young doctors are not being trained in the procedure. [9]

Anti-abortion forces "have been chipping away" at *Roe* for 10 years by waging a quiet, "incrementalist attack in state legislatures that has gone largely unnoticed" by the public, says Sondra Goldschein, state strategies attorney for the New York-based ACLU Reproductive Freedom Project. In some counties "providers have been driven out of business or are too scared to provide services."

But Ruse counters that American women can obtain abortions during all nine months of pregnancy if a doctor determines that a late-term abortion "is necessary for the 'well-being' of his patient." And, she adds, "Even financial considerations have been deemed to 'endanger' the mother's health."

Finally, she says, many state laws — such as those that would ban or limit partial-birth abortions — have been unenforceable because they have been challenged in court.

Among other things, states have mandated pre-abortion counseling and waiting periods, limited public funding of abortions for poor women, required parental notification and/or consent before a minor can obtain an abortion and allowed religiously affiliated providers — sometimes the only hospital in a region — to refuse to provide or fund abortions. Moreover, say abortion-rights advocates, some state Medicaid programs refuse to fund abortions for poor women impregnated through rape, incest or when the mother's life is in danger — which is allowed under federal law (the so-called Hyde Amendment).

As a result, they say, a two-tiered system is emerging. While abortion remains technically legal for all, only wealthier, urban women have convenient access to safe, early abortions but poor, rural and young women must first overcome multiple hurdles.

"Already, for poor women there are so many hoops they have to jump through, they are not able to enjoy their constitutional rights," says Judith Waxman, vice president for health and reproductive rights at the National Women's Law Center. Today, 35 percent of Medicaid-eligible women who would obtain an abortion but cannot afford one end up carrying the baby to full term, she says.

To correct the inequities, "States should try to increase abortion access," says Jackie Payne, director of government relations at Planned Parenthood, which runs 860 women's health clinics nationwide. "It's a legal, appropriate medical procedure."

Policymakers should restore public funding for abortions for low-income women and repeal state restrictions that delay abortions and endanger women's health, Payne says. And to reduce the need for abortions in the first place, she says, lawmakers should fund comprehensive sex education and make birth control more available and affordable. And more states should follow the lead of Hawaii — which recently codified the constitutionality of abortion in that state — and California, which prohibits anyone from interfering with a woman's access to abortion, she says.

But pro-life groups strongly oppose most such measures. As for restoring Medicaid funding of abortions, Ruse says, "Most Americans — whether or not they think abortion ought to be legal — think abortion is morally wrong and they do not want to be forced to pay for it with their tax dollars."

As for poor women, "No compassionate person wants to see a woman suffer through the personal tragedy of abortion," she says. "There are life-giving alternatives that serve not only the best interest of the child but also that of the mother."

"I've never met a woman who is happy that she killed her child," says Tanya Britton, president of Pro-Life Mississippi. "To increase access will only increase suffering among women who have been abandoned by their partners [or] coerced into an abortion."

Wright, of Concerned Women for America, says the fact that 87 percent of U.S. counties lack abortion providers is not a problem. "Abortion is not like groceries that people need frequently and nearby," she says. "And many, if not most, U.S. counties are lightly populated, so this is a ridiculous standard."

And rolling back state restrictions, she says, would undo "very popular state regulations that protect patients and force health-care workers to commit what they believe to be murder." It would also "make it easier for unscrupulous abortion providers" to begin offering the procedure, "causing greater risks to women."

Britton, who is also a nurse, says, "I've seen women die or lose their uteruses after having abortions. I've seen enough of that to know that this is not something states should be encouraging."

But NARAL's Keenan says, "Legal abortion has brought about significant improvements in women's health," citing a drop in the abortion-related death rate from 4.1 deaths per 100,000 abortions in 1973 when the procedure was legalized to 0.6 deaths in 1997. The American Medical Association's Council on Scientific Affairs attributes much of the decline to the shift from illegal to legal abortions, according NARAL's fact sheet on the safety of abortions. [10]

"Legal abortion entails half the risk of death involved in a tonsillectomy and one-hundredth the risk of death involved in an appendectomy," says the fact sheet, which also cites four scientific studies showing that abortions cause no long-term negative psychological effects for most women.

By exaggerating the dangers of abortions, says Keenan, pro-life groups "disregard the science and insist on talking about 'late-term abortions,' which are a minuscule portion of the abortions performed today. It's part of their attack on science."

But clinic operator Hill says states should ensure that each state has at least one provider because traveling several states away to get an abortion increases women's health risks. If a woman has post-surgical complications, she says, "her doctor needs to be near her home — not five states away."

Moreover, she concludes, "If you limit access, women won't stop having abortions. They'll just go underground, like they did before *Roe*," increasing the dangers from botched abortions.

Or, she says, remembering the out-of-state license plates in her parking lot, "women will just travel to a different place." ■

BACKGROUND

Out of the Shadows

Abortion was a common but illegal procedure in the United States — and a taboo subject — in the decades before a reform movement emerged in the 1950s to make it a national issue. The Supreme Court's landmark 1973 decision, *Roe v. Wade*, gave women a qualified constitutional right to abortion but produced a powerful and lasting backlash. Since then, anti-

Continued on p. 780

Chronology

1800s *State and federal laws criminalize abortion.*

1900-1950

Illegality of abortions leads to deaths caused by unsafe, clandestine procedures.

1950s-1960s

Clergy and physicians' groups seek to legalize abortion.

1959
American Law Institute (ALI) endorses a model reform law that would permit a physician to perform a "therapeutic" abortion if the woman's health were threatened, the fetus had a grave defect or in cases of rape or incest.

1967
Colorado enacts ALI-style law; North Carolina and California follow suit.

1970s *States begin overturning their anti-abortion laws as public opinion shifts.*

1970
New York repeals its abortion ban.

1971
Hawaii and Washington repeal their abortion bans.

1973
U.S. Supreme Court's *Roe v. Wade* decision recognizes a woman's right to an abortion. The ruling allows the government to regulate abortion procedures during the second trimester of pregnancy to protect the woman's health or safety; abortions can be banned only in the final trimester.

1976
Congress bans Medicaid funding for abortions for poor women unless needed to save the woman's life.

1980s *Supreme Court strikes down waiting periods and "informed consent" provisions in abortion laws.*

1990s-2000s

Abortion policy swings back and forth after a Supreme Court ruling on Pennsylvania's abortion law; conservative appointments to Supreme Court raise possibility* Roe v. Wade *could be overturned.

1990
Oregon voters reject abortion ban.

1992
Supreme Court's *Planned Parenthood of Southeastern Pennsylvania v. Casey* ruling upholds all but one of the challenged provisions of Pennsylvania's abortion restrictions, opening door to stricter state regulation of abortions. But three justices reaffirm "the essential holding" of *Roe.*

June 2000
Supreme Court votes 5-4 in *Stenberg v. Carhart* to strike down Nebraska's "partial-birth abortion" ban, citing its overbreadth and failure to include a health exception for the mother.

November 2002
Republicans gain control of Senate, cheering anti-abortion supporters.

Nov. 5, 2003
President George W. Bush signs federal "partial-birth abortion" ban.

July 8, 2005
Federal appeals court in St. Louis holds federal "partial-birth abortion" ban unconstitutional.

Sept. 29, 2005
Senate confirms federal judge John Roberts Jr. as chief justice of the U.S.

January 2006
Supreme Court, in interim decision, says New Hampshire parental-notification statute must include emergency exception or be struck down. . . . Federal appeals courts in New York and San Francisco rule federal "partial-birth abortion" ban unconstitutional. . . . Senate confirms federal judge Samuel A. Alito Jr. to succeed retiring Supreme Court Justice Sandra Day O'Connor.

February 2006
Supreme Court agrees to hear two cases challenging the federal "partial-birth abortion" ban.

March 2006
Gov. Michael Rounds, R-S.D., signs bill banning abortions in South Dakota except to save life of mother; opponents launch successful drive to put a referendum on the law on the Nov. 7 ballot.

Nov 7, 2006
South Dakota to vote on whether to retain its state abortion ban.

Nov. 8, 2006
Supreme Court to hear arguments in cases challenging federal "partial-birth abortion" ban.

'Partial-Birth Abortion' Case Divides Doctors

When Congress passed the Partial-Birth Abortion Ban Act of 2003, lawmakers declared that the controversial procedure is never medically necessary and poses significant health risks for the patient.

But many medical experts disagree. Those disagreements will be pivotal issues for the Supreme Court when it hears the Bush administration's arguments in November for saving the law, which three federal courts have deemed unconstitutional. The courts said the law is too broad, potentially applying not only to what some doctors call a "dilation and extraction" procedure (D&X) but also to the more commonly used abortion procedure: a "dilation and evacuation" (D&E).

The law itself begins by graphically defining "partial-birth abortion" as a procedure in which a physician "vaginally delivers a living, unborn child's body" until "the entire head" or "any part of the baby's trunk past the navel" is outside the body and then kills the "partially delivered infant" by "an overt act (usually the puncturing of the back of the child's skull and removing the baby's brains)." [1]

"The law is crudely written and misleading," says David Grimes, a physician and a member of the National Medical Committee of the Planned Parenthood Federation of America. "It's not an 'unborn child,' an 'infant' or a 'baby.' At that point it's a fetus."

Six obstetricians, along with the National Abortion Federation, are joining in a friend-of-the-court brief urging the Supreme Court to strike down the federal ban. The brief rejects the term partial-birth abortion, instead referring to the banned procedure as an "intact D&E" — the technique used in the vast majority of second-trimester abortions.

The term partial-birth abortion is not "medically recognized," says Stephen Chasen, associate professor at Cornell Medical College in New York City and one of the six obstetricians. "It clearly wasn't introduced by physicians who perform abortions."

On the opposite side, the American Association of Pro Life Obstetricians and Gynecologists and four physician members of Congress are urging the high court to uphold the ban. Their legal brief also avoids using the term partial-birth abortion, referring to the banned procedure as a "D&X."

Despite the difference in terminology, Elizabeth Shadigian, the association's president and a clinical associate professor at the University of Michigan Medical School in Ann Arbor, says the term D&X accurately denotes a procedure different from a standard D&E, in which the doctor dismembers the fetus inside the womb and removes the fetal parts piece by piece.

"It's not just a variation of the D&E," says Shadigian. "That's what the other side says. It's not."

Congress included in the law 29 paragraphs of "findings" that challenge the Supreme Court's decision striking down a similar Nebraska law in 2000. [2] Congress "is entitled to reach its own factual findings," the act declares.

Chasen, however, says Congress got it wrong on both of the critical points: medical necessity and safety. But he argues mainly that the line between the two procedures is murky at best. "It goes into the operating room as a D&E," Chasen says. "It's an intraoperative judgment about the most appropriate procedure."

The reduced use of instruments inside the woman's body makes the intact D&E safer for the woman, Chasen contends. "Every time I put a forceps in a uterus — open it, close it, pull — I'm risking damage," he says. The procedure also takes less time and reduces the possibility of leaving fetal parts inside the woman's body, he says.

Shadigian counters that a D&X, as she calls the procedure, risks various complications, including laceration of the cervix and future pre-term births. She further contends that no medical studies have proven the procedure safe.

Chasen coauthored a medical-journal article based on an examination of more than 380 abortion patients that reported similar outcomes for the standard and intact D&E procedures. Shadigian contends the study did not produce statistically valid conclusions. [3]

As to the need for the procedure, Shadigian says there is "no evidence" of any maternal or fetal condition that requires a D&X instead of the standard D&E. Chasen responds that the safety advantages of an intact D&E for some patients — for example, in cases of fetal anomalies — show the need for the procedure.

In contrast to other supporters of the ban, Shadigian does not contend that a "partial-birth abortion" is distinctively "gruesome and inhumane" — as Congress declared. "Of course, it's grisly. It's killing a life," Shadigian says. "But it's not necessarily more grisly than a D&E, pulling a baby apart limb by limb. Both are grisly."

For his part, Chasen distances himself in the operating room from any feelings about the procedure. "However you do it, it's not an aesthetic procedure. It's not a pleasant procedure," he says. "It's not really something I should be considering. It's not something that I do consider."

---

[1] The law, PL 108-105 (Nov. 5, 2003), has been codified as 18 U.S.C. §1531 (http://caselaw.lp.findlaw.com/casecode/uscodes/18/parts/i/chapters/74/sections/section%5F1531.html). The text of the act, including the congressional findings, can be found in briefs filed in the Supreme Court cases: *Gonzales v. Carhart*, 05-380; and *Gonzales v. Planned Parenthood*, 05-1382 (www.supremecourtus.gov).

[2] The case is *Stenberg v. Carhart*, 530 U.S. 914 (2000).

[3] Stephen T. Chasen, *et al.*, "Dilation and Evacuation at ≥ 20 Weeks: Comparison of operative techniques," *American Journal of Obstetrics and Gynecology*, Vol. 190, 1180-1183 (2004).

Continued from p. 778

abortion groups have won passage of numerous state and federal restrictions on abortion procedures and access but have failed in their efforts to completely overturn the *Roe* decision. [11]

States and the federal government enacted laws to criminalize most abortions in the 19th century, partly to protect women's health and partly to seek to control sexual conduct. Despite those laws, experts estimated anywhere from

200,000 to 1.3 million illegal abortions were performed in the United States annually as of the early 1950s. The famed sex researcher Albert Kinsey reported in his study *Sexual Behavior in the Human Female* that nine out of 10 premarital pregnancies ended in abortion and that 22 percent of married women had an abortion while married.

A nascent reform movement formed in the 1950s and gained momentum in the 1960s, driven by clergy and physicians' groups concerned about deaths among women after self-induced or clandestine abortions performed in unsafe conditions. [12]

The American Law Institute (ALI), a prestigious legal-reform group, endorsed a model reform law in 1959 that would permit a physician to perform a "therapeutic" abortion if the woman's physical or mental health were threatened, the fetus had a grave defect or the pregnancy had resulted from rape or incest. Colorado enacted an ALI-style law in 1967, followed by North Carolina and California. In 1970, New York went further by repealing outright its abortion prohibition; Hawaii and Washington followed suit the same year. A year later, a national poll showed that more than half of those surveyed supported legalizing abortion.

Meanwhile, abortion-reform advocates were claiming in court cases that laws banning or severely restricting the procedure violated women's constitutional rights to privacy and equal protection. The Supreme Court took up the issue in challenges to two state laws: Texas' virtually complete ban and Georgia's "reform" statute allowing abortions when approved by two doctors other than the woman's personal physician. The 7-2 decision in *Roe v. Wade* — issued on Jan. 22, 1973 — invalidated all existing abortion laws by recognizing a woman's privacy right, in consultation with her physician, to decide whether to terminate a pregnancy. The ruling allowed the government to regulate abortion procedures during the second trimester of pregnancy to protect the woman's health or safety. Abortions could be banned only in the final trimester — after the fetus was deemed "viable" or capable of living on its own.

Getty Images/Alex Wong

President George W. Bush signs the Partial-Birth Abortion Act on Nov. 5, 2003, joined by, from left, Sen. Orrin Hatch, R-Utah, Rep. F. James Sensenbrenner, R-Wis., Sen. Rick Santorum, R-Pa., and Rep. James Oberstar, D-Minn.

By the end of the year, the court's ruling was being credited with having made abortion procedures safer and less stigmatizing. Over the next decade, the number of abortions in the United States roughly doubled before plateauing somewhat above 1.5 million per year in the mid-1980s, according to Guttmacher Institute statistics. [13] (*See graph, p. 773.*) The actual availability of abortion services was uneven, however, because of the costs of the procedure and restrictive laws passed in many states. [14]

Among the most important restrictions were laws enacted by Congress and in most of the states that barred public funding for abortions for poor women. Congress first banned federal funding for abortions for Medicaid recipients in 1976 in a provision called the Hyde Amendment after its principal House sponsor, Rep. Henry J. Hyde, R-Ill. The law has remained on the books ever since; in its current form, it prohibits federal funding unless the pregnancy is the result of rape or incest or if the procedure is necessary to save the life of the woman. Despite constitutional challenges, the Supreme Court has upheld the laws. A funding restriction "places no obstacles — absolute or otherwise — in a pregnant woman's path to an abortion," the court said in upholding a state ban in 1977. [15]

Through the 1980s, the court struck down some other restrictions, including waiting periods and "informed consent" provisions. Four Supreme Court appointments by the avowedly pro-life President Ronald Reagan, however, encouraged anti-abortion groups to hope that the court would be more deferential to state regulations or even overturn *Roe* altogether. The court in 1990 did vote narrowly to uphold parental-notification laws for minors as long as a judge could exempt minors who can show they would be in danger if they notify their parents. [16]

Two years later — after two appointments by President George H. W. Bush — the court gave anti-abortion groups a partial victory that left them largely disappointed and abortion-rights advocates relieved. The 1992 ruling in *Planned Parenthood of Southeastern Pennsylvania v. Casey* upheld all but one of the challenged provisions of Pennsylvania's abortion restrictions, including waiting-period and informed-consent provisions; it struck down only a spousal-notification requirement. [17]

In a pivotal plurality opinion, however, three justices — Sandra Day O'Connor, Anthony M. Kennedy and David H. Souter — said they were reaffirming "the essential holding" of *Roe*. Significantly, the opinion jettisoned *Roe*'s trimester framework for a single test: Abortion regulations were to be upheld unless they imposed "an undue burden" on a woman's decision. The new test opened the door to more legislative efforts to regulate abortion procedures and more court battles over those regulations.

Policy Swings

Abortion policy swung back and forth in the decade after the Supreme Court's ruling in *Casey*. Abortion-rights supporters won significant gains after Bill Clinton's election as president in 1992 but lost control of the agenda after Republicans gained control of the House of Representatives in the 1994 elections. Anti-abortion forces gained dominant influence after Bush's election in 2000 and the GOP's takeover of the Senate after the 2002 midterm elections. Bush reversed Clinton's pro-choice policies and in 2003 signed a "partial-birth abortion" ban similar to bills Clinton had vetoed.

Clinton's election brought a pro-choice president to the White House for the first time since *Roe v. Wade*. (Democrat Jimmy Carter favored abortion rights but also supported restrictions on Medicaid funding for abortions.) Two days after taking office in 1993, Clinton signed executive orders reversing three anti-abortion policies from the Reagan-George H.W. Bush era, including a ban on abortion counseling at federally funded family-planning clinics. Over the next two years, Clinton also strengthened the Supreme Court's pro-choice bloc by appointing two abortion-rights supporters: Ruth Bader Ginsburg, who replaced Byron R. White, a dissenter in *Roe*, and Stephen G. Breyer, who succeeded Harry A. Blackmun, author of the *Roe* decision.

Meanwhile, Congress in 1994 passed a law — the Freedom of Access to Clinic Entrances Act — aimed at countering anti-abortion groups' tactics of blockading women's clinics where abortions were performed. Passage of the law came after a year marked by the assassination of physician David Gunn outside an abortion clinic in Pensacola, Fla., and a wave of other violence, including one bombing, 12 arsons and 66 blockades. The National Abortion Federation credited the new law with virtually eliminating clinic blockades, but other incidents of disruption or violence spiked again in the late 1990s and early 2000s, according to the group's statistics.

By the mid-'90s, anti-abortion groups were lobbying effectively for laws to ban what they termed "partial-birth abortions." The GOP-controlled House and the Democratic-controlled Senate twice approved a federal ban on the procedure — in 1996 and 1997 — but Clinton vetoed each of the bills because they lacked a health exception. Supporters lacked the two-thirds majority in the Senate needed to override the vetoes. Anti-abortion groups made substantial headway with state legislatures, however. By the end of the decade, some 30 states had banned the procedure.

Emboldened in part by the 1992 *Casey* decision, states in the 1990s enacted scores of other laws regulating abortion procedures, such as those requiring waiting periods, informed consent and parental notice before abortions could be obtained. All told, the abortion-rights group NARAL counted 262 "anti-choice" measures enacted from 1995 through 2000. Women's reproductive rights "are more restricted than they were in 1973," NARAL lamented in its 2001 annual report. Today, anti-abortion groups credit the laws with helping to drive down the number and the rate of abortions in the last years of the decade. "State legislation certainly played a factor," says Forsythe, of Americans United for Life.

Anti-abortion groups suffered a setback in June 2000, however, when the Supreme Court struck down, by a 5-4 vote, Nebraska's partial-birth abortion ban. For the majority, Breyer said the measure created "an undue burden on a woman's right to make an abortion decision" because it could be construed to prohibit the commonly used dilation and extraction (D&X) procedure and because it failed to include a health exception. In a pivotal concurring opinion, O'Connor suggested that a more carefully drawn statute might pass constitutional muster.

The close division on the court focused attention on the 2000 presidential race, in which Republican George W. Bush embraced anti-abortion positions and Democrat Al Gore took abortion-rights stands. Pro-life groups cheered Bush's election, and the president repaid their support once in the White House. In January 2001 — only two days after taking office — Bush reinstated a Reagan-era policy barring U.S. funds for international family-planning organizations that promoted abortion. Over the next two years, Bush lent his support to other initiatives pushed by anti-abortion groups, but several legislative proposals — including a federal "partial-birth abortion" ban — died in the Democratic-controlled Senate.

Republican gains in the 2002 midterm elections broke the logjam in the Senate. Anti-abortion groups counted eight of the 10 new senators as "pro-life." Under Republican control, the Senate passed the "partial-birth abortion" ban on March 13, 2003, by a 64-33 margin.

Abortion-rights supporters had to content themselves with one symbolic amendment affirming support for *Roe v. Wade.* The House passed its own version — without the *Roe v. Wade* provision — by a 282-139 vote on June 4.

Supporters in both chambers insisted they had cured the constitutional defects the Supreme Court had cited in striking down the state law by defining the banned procedure more precisely and making congressional "findings" that the procedure was never medically necessary. Opponents called the definition too broad and the congressional findings unpersuasive. The debate continued as the House and the Senate completed action in October, and Bush signed the bill into law on Nov. 5.

AP Photo/Dirk Lammers

Pro-choice activists introduce a petition drive last March 24 to put South Dakota's abortion ban before the voters in November. The law would ban all abortions except to save a woman's life, with no exceptions for rape or incest. Former state Rep. Jan Nicolay is at right.

Within hours, opponents went into federal courts in New York and San Francisco and won injunctions blocking the law from going into effect.

Eyes on the Courts

Over the next two years federal courts uniformly ruled the federal "partial-birth abortion" ban unconstitutional. The rulings set the stage for a showdown on the law before a Supreme Court with two new justices with a history of opposition to *Roe v. Wade.* Meanwhile, anti-abortion groups made progress on other fronts, winning passage of new abortion restrictions in many states.

The federal law was challenged in separate suits filed by Planned Parenthood in San Francisco, the National Abortion Federation in New York and Dr. LeRoy Carhart, the Nebraska physician who had challenged that state's law in the earlier Supreme Court case. After lengthy trials, judges in each of the cases issued detailed rulings in 2004 declaring the laws unconstitutional and faulting in particular the congressional fact-finding as biased.

Federal appeals courts in San Francisco, New York and St. Louis all agreed. The three-judge panels were unanimous in the Nebraska and San Francisco decisions. In the New York case, however, one judge concurred reluctantly because of the Supreme Court precedent, and another dissented. A woman's right to terminate a pregnancy does not permit "destruction of a child that is substantially outside her body," the dissenting judge wrote. [18]

The appeals court decisions emerged as the Supreme Court was undergoing its first changes in membership since Breyer's appointment in 1994. Bush's selection of Roberts to succeed Chief Justice William H. Rehnquist and Alito to succeed O'Connor galvanized groups on both sides of the abortion issue. Roberts had criticized *Roe v. Wade* while serving as a White House and Justice Department lawyer in the Reagan administration and signed a brief calling for overturning *Roe* while deputy solicitor general under the first President Bush. Alito had claimed credit for opposing abortion rights while in the solicitor general's office during the Reagan administration. Alito also voted as a federal judge in 1991 to uphold all parts of the Pennsylvania law challenged in the *Casey* decision — including a spousal-notification provision that was the only part of the law rejected by the Supreme Court.

Abortion-rights groups cited Roberts' and Alito's past views as evidence that either or both would vote to narrow or even overturn *Roe v. Wade* if confirmed. Both nominees testified before the Senate Judiciary Committee that they would respect precedent but stopped short of promising not to overturn either *Roe* or *Casey.* Anti-abortion and other conservative groups backed both nominees, praising them as advocates of judicial restraint and criticizing abortion-rights groups for seeking to impose a litmus test for confirmation. In the end, the Republican-controlled Senate confirmed both men: Roberts won the support of half the Democratic senators in his 78-22 confirmation on Sept. 29, 2005; Alito prevailed on a nearly party-line 58-42 vote on Jan. 31, 2006.

With Alito's confirmation pending, the court itself issued what appeared to be a temporizing decision in a challenge to New Hampshire's parental-notification statute. With unaccustomed unanimity, the justices said the law could not be enforced to require a physician to notify a minor's parents before performing an abortion if a delay would endanger the girl's health. But the court also said the law need not be struck down in its entirety on that ground. Abortion-rights

At the Empire Mall, Few Embrace Abortion Ban

South Dakota is regarded as one of the stronger pro-life states. [1] But as voters brace for an intense battle over a proposed state abortion ban, early indications suggest that supporters of the ban are behind.

Opponents of the ban appear to be holding on to self-identified pro-choice voters and adding anti-abortion voters who agree with those who say the ban goes too far. The ban was approved by the legislature early this year but was then blocked pending a statewide referendum on Nov. 7.

At the Empire Mall in Democratic-leaning Sioux Falls in mid-September, pro-choice sentiments are the most common comments among an unscientific sample of some 20 people of all ages and divided roughly equally among men and women. Among likely voters, only three people tell a reporter they are certain to vote in favor of the ban. The comments tend to corroborate a professional statewide poll in late July showing supporters of the ban trailing opponents.

"I'm going to vote no," says Ralph Wermers, an Air Force retiree. "It's a woman's right to make up her mind. It's not politicians who can make that decision for a woman."

Tony Gross, 20, a jewelry store clerk, is also inclined to oppose the ban, but "if they'd allow [exceptions] for incest or rape, I guess I'd be more for banning abortion," he says.

Josh Merkley, an analyst with a communications company, says his views changed from noncommittal to pro-life after his wife Joanie became pregnant with their first child. "Having kids was part of my change," Merkley says. "Once you see the miracle of life, you realize what life's all about."

Mike Pagones, a student at a local technical college, agrees. "I feel it's wrong to destroy a human life that's already formed," he says.

In a troubling sign for supporters of the ban, four other people — two couples — all said they support the law but are not registered or do not intend to vote.

The visibility of the issue has receded since the bill quickly moved through the South Dakota legislature in February, and Republican Gov. Michael Rounds signed it into law on March 6. Republicans outnumber Democrats in the state and control both chambers of the state legislature. But partisan lines have blurred somewhat on the issue.

State Rep. Kathy Miles, a Sioux Falls Democrat, is one of the cochairs of the Vote Yes for Life campaign. Former state Rep. Jan Nicolay, a Republican, cochairs the South Dakota Campaign for Healthy Families, the coalition opposing the ban.

The ban makes it a felony, punishable by up to five years in prison, to perform an abortion unless the procedure is intended "to prevent the death of a pregnant mother." The law precludes any prosecution of the pregnant woman.

The law does not permit abortions for rape or incest victims or to safeguard a woman's health. But supporters say that Section 3 of the act — which, in effect, exempts emergency contraception or so-called "morning after" pills from the ban — allows rape or incest victims to avoid pregnancy. "If they have been raped, they have time to go to the doctor and make that decision for themselves," says Leslee Unruh, manager of the Vote Yes campaign.

But Wermers mocks the argument. "You can't get an abortion till you know if you're pregnant," he says. "And when you do, you can't get an abortion."

Unruh and Lindsay Roitman, campaign manager of the Healthy Families coalition, both plan media campaigns as the election nears, and both expect to win.

"The key to this election is to get education to the people who don't understand what this issue is all about," says Unruh. "They don't know that abortion hurts women. They don't know that the abortion industry hurts women like myself."

"We have the facts. We have the message," counters Roitman. "We are every bit in favor of reducing the amount of abortions in South Dakota and in the nation, but this is not the way to do it."

[1] According to a SurveyUSA News Poll in August 2005, 49 percent of South Dakota adults are pro-life and 47 percent are pro-choice. Among the states, South Dakota ranks 11th from the top in pro-life sentiment.

supporters cheered what they viewed as a reaffirmation of the need for a health exception in any abortion regulations. Anti-abortion groups emphasized instead the court's apparent holding that an abortion statute can stay on the books even if one or more parts cannot be constitutionally enforced. [19]

Meanwhile, anti-abortion groups began the new year generally pleased with their legislative accomplishments in Washington and in state capitals. Besides the "partial-birth abortion" ban, Congress in 2004 also passed and President Bush signed the Unborn Victims of Violence Act, which makes it a federal crime to injure or kill "any child in utero," regardless of its gestational age. [20]

"We've seen some very important victories at the federal level in the last few years," says Johnson of the National Right to Life Committee.

Meanwhile, anti-abortion regulations have been enacted in a majority of states. States have passed parental-involvement laws, informed-consent laws and laws regulating abortion-clinic procedures. They also limited public funding for abortions — including South Dakota, which provided coverage only in life-saving situations. [21]

The step-by-step legislative strategy, however, left some anti-abortion legislators dissatisfied. In South Dakota, the legislature in 2005 banned abortions in a move aimed directly at forcing the Supreme Court to reconsider *Roe v. Wade*. Gov. Rounds vetoed the measure, however, explaining that as written the bill would leave South Dakota with no abortion law if federal courts struck it down.

Continued on p. 786

At Issue:

Should the Roe v. Wade *decision be overturned?*

MARY SPAULDING BALCH
STATE LEGISLATIVE DIRECTOR, NATIONAL RIGHT TO LIFE COMMITTEE

WRITTEN FOR *CQ RESEARCHER*, SEPTEMBER 2006

yes

The heart is beating less than three weeks after fertilization, and brain waves can be detected in the sixth week. By the seventh week, the unborn child is kicking and swimming inside the womb. Pain receptors, which begin to appear by four or five weeks, are present throughout the body by 18 weeks. When an unborn child is injected by a needle, stress hormones are released just as when adults feel pain.

As the executive director of the National Coalition of Abortion Providers, Ron Fitzsimmons acknowledges that abortion "is a form of killing. You're ending a life." Fifty-six percent of Americans believe abortion should be legal, at most, when pregnancy results from rape or incest or when it threatens the life of the mother. Yet less than 7 percent of the roughly 1.3 million U.S. abortions each year are performed for these reasons.

What stands in the way of democratically adopted limitation or regulation of abortion is the U.S. Supreme Court decision in *Roe v. Wade* and its companion case *Doe v. Bolton*. Together, these decisions mean that abortion must be legal effectively on demand for the full nine months of pregnancy; right up until the umbilical cord is cut.

Indeed, applying *Roe* and *Doe*, the court has struck down efforts to prevent even "partial-birth abortion," in which the child is delivered out of the uterus up to the neck, then surgical scissors are stuck into the skull and the brain is suctioned out — abortions that occur at least 3,000 to 5,000 times a year.

Because of *Roe v. Wade*, abortions must be permitted as a method of birth control and for sex selection. There can be no legal requirement that the father even be notified before his unborn child is aborted. In the case of a minor girl, while virtually any other surgery requires parental consent, any requirement that the parents even be notified of their daughter's planned abortion must yield if a judge, having heard only one side, considers abortion is in her "best interests." In America, for every 1,000 live births, there are 319 abortions — 3,500 a day, one every 24 seconds. There have been over 47 million since *Roe v. Wade* in 1973.

Reversal of *Roe* would not itself decide which abortions would be legal, or under what circumstances or regulations. Instead, reversal of *Roe* would allow the people and their elected representatives to decide whether and to what extent they want to maintain the current regime of unlimited abortion throughout pregnancy, the most extreme policy on abortion of any nation in the world.

NANCY KEENAN
PRESIDENT, NARAL PRO-CHOICE AMERICA,

WRITTEN FOR *CQ RESEARCHER*, SEPTEMBER 2006

no

The U.S. Supreme Court's decision in *Roe v. Wade* embodies the essential American values of freedom and privacy. More than 30 years after it was decided, *Roe* remains a pillar of constitutional law that supports the health and well-being of women and their families.

The Supreme Court's acknowledgement of a zone of privacy, which began well before its decision in *Roe*, recognizes a fundamental principle: Certain decisions are so personal and life-altering that they must be made by individuals and their families, not by politicians. In his *Roe* opinion, Chief Justice Harry Blackmun wrote: "This right of privacy . . . is broad enough to encompass a woman's decision whether or not to terminate her pregnancy. The detriment that the State would impose upon the pregnant woman by denying this choice altogether is apparent."

In 1992, in *Planned Parenthood v. Casey*, the court reaffirmed *Roe's* central holding: "Our precedents 'have respected the private realm of family life which the state cannot enter.' These matters, involving the most intimate and personal choices a person may make in a lifetime, choices central to personal dignity, are central to the liberty protected by the Fourteenth Amendment."

Many observers — often anti-choice advocates — wrongly claim that if the court were to reverse this landmark decision, the issue would simply return to the states. What they are doing is attempting to downplay to a pro-choice American public the enormity of the impact of overturning *Roe*. Congress already has demonstrated its eagerness to undermine the legal foundations of *Roe* and to impose abortion restrictions even on states that have opted not to impose them.

Without *Roe* to prevent it, an anti-choice Congress could pass a nationwide ban on abortion. And if the issue did return to the states, scores of American women would lose their right to choose. In addition to the more than a dozen pre-*Roe* abortion bans that remain on the books and might become enforceable, this year alone even with *Roe* in place, 14 states considered new near-total bans on abortion — and South Dakota enacted one.

Basic rights are too important to give to some people and not to others. What if some states did not guarantee the right to vote to everyone? Or free speech, or the freedom of religion? *Roe* is not just about abortion. It is about personal freedom and personal responsibility and the ability to decide private family issues — without intrusion from politicians and the government. Our Constitution guarantees this right to every woman — no matter where she lives.

Continued from p. 784

With anti-abortion groups in other states watching the developments, the South Dakota legislature approved a revised measure in February 2006, and Rounds signed it into law on March 6. Less than three weeks later, opponents from within the state held a March 24 news conference to announce the launch of a petition drive to put the ban before the public in a statewide referendum on Nov. 7. ■

CURRENT SITUATION

Bans and Exceptions

Supporters of South Dakota's ban on abortions are using the availability of emergency contraception — long opposed by pro-life groups — to counter criticisms by abortion-rights advocates that the law makes no exceptions for rape and incest victims. [22]

The potentially critical issue focuses on a section of the law that exempts from the proposed ban any "contraceptive measure" that is "administered prior to the time when a pregnancy could be determined through conventional medical testing." The legalistic phrasing refers to the so-called Plan B emergency contraception or "morning after" pill, which the Food and Drug Administration (FDA) approved for over-the-counter sale to adults in late August despite opposition from anti-abortion groups and social conservatives.

"Referred Law 6 provides options for rape and incest victims," the Vote Yes for Life campaign's printed cards read. South Dakota's proposed ban "preserves" the rights of women who are sexually assaulted "to seek medical attention to prevent pregnancy after the incident," the card says.

Opponents of the ban say emergency contraception is an unrealistic option for rape or incest victims who become pregnant. Many victims "are too ashamed or afraid to come forward in time to prevent the pregnancy," says Maria Bell, an obstetrician-gynecologist and one of the cochairs of the anti-ban campaign. Bell and other opponents of the ban also point out that emergency contraception is not widely available in South Dakota.

The potential importance of the rape-incest exception issue stems from a secondary finding of the KELO-TV/*Argus Leader* poll in July that showed opponents of the ban with an 8 percentage point lead over supporters. The same respondents said by a 59 percent to 29 percent margin that they would support the ban if it included exceptions for rape and incest — a 30-point swing over the issue. The "no exception" voters could hold the key to the ban's fate, according to Brad Coker, managing director of the Mason-Dixon polling firm, which conducted the survey. [23]

Supporters of the ban say the issue is being exaggerated because rape and incest victims comprise a small percentage of abortion cases in South Dakota or nationwide. At the same time, many are arguing strongly against abortions in cases of rape or incest.

"A life is a life no matter how it gets there," Megan Barnett, who became pregnant following a rape and declined emergency contraception or an abortion, told the South Dakota Right to Life's annual convention in Sioux Falls on Sept. 9. Barnett is the niece of Dana Randall, an Aberdeen financial planner and president of the organization.

South Dakota appears to offer a close-to-ideal testing ground for the broadest possible restrictions on abortion. Even before the proposed ban began moving through the state legislature, South Dakota already had some of the most restrictive abortion regulations of any state. Informed-consent laws require that patients hear a state-prescribed script on the relative risks of abortion and childbirth and be offered a booklet on fetal development at least 24 hours before the procedure. Abortions cannot be performed in a clinic after the 14th week of pregnancy.

Politically, registered Republicans outnumber registered Democrats 48 percent to 38 percent. Republicans control both chambers of the state legislature by comfortable margins. GOP voters flexed their muscles on the abortion issue in a June primary election by defeating four Republican lawmakers who had voted against the ban. [24]

The state's religious make-up also provides fertile ground for anti-abortion causes, according to the Polis Center's Project on Religion and Urban Culture at Indiana University/Purdue University. [25] About 35 percent of South Dakota's religious adherents are Catholic and another 23 percent are Lutheran — both faiths strongly associated with pro-life causes. Evangelical and other conservative Christian denominations comprise another 20 percent of religious adherents. Mainline Protestant denominations more favorable to abortion rights constitute about 15 percent of believers.

Despite the favorable terrain, supporters of the abortion ban appear to face an uphill fight as the Nov. 7 election nears. As of mid-September, Unruh of the Vote Yes campaign was calling the contest a "dead heat" but offered no polling data to contradict the KELO-TV/*Argus Leader*'s results. Roitman of the Healthy Families campaign said their telephone surveys correspond to the news organizations' poll. And Rick Knobe, a radio talk-show host on KSOO in Sioux Falls, said two call-in polls on his program in May and August both produced 2-to-1 results against the ban.

"I'm optimistic that the South Dakota ban will be defeated in the referendum," says Keenan, who hails from neighboring Montana. "South Dakotans are very much like Montanans. It's a very libertarian state, and the folks there feel that politicians should stay out of their business. Within the first hour after South Dakota banned abortion, our Web site got 450 hits from people who had never been to the site before," she says. [26]

Legal Arguments

Justice Department lawyers are urging the Supreme Court to defer to Congress and uphold the federal ban on "partial-birth abortions," while opponents say the court should follow its six-year-old precedent and strike down the 2003 law.

Lawyers on both sides are focusing their arguments on three justices: Kennedy, who dissented when the court struck down Nebraska's "partial-birth abortion" ban in 2000; and Roberts and Alito, conservatives who both criticized abortion-rights rulings as Reagan administration lawyers but made qualified promises to respect the court's precedents during their confirmation hearings in late 2005 and early 2006, respectively.

The votes of the other six justices are presumed to be set. Four liberal justices who voted to strike down the Nebraska law — John Paul Stevens, Souter, Ginsburg and Breyer — are deemed all but certain to vote to invalidate the federal statute. Conservatives Scalia and Thomas, who would have upheld the Nebraska law, are expected to vote the same way on the federal ban.

Briefs filed by the solicitor general's offices in the two cases — both set for argument on Nov. 8 — argue that Congress had "substantial evidence" for two factual findings aimed at circumventing the court's ruling on the Nebraska law. In the act's opening section, Congress specified that a partial-birth abortion "is never medically necessary" and in fact "poses serious risks" to a woman's health or "in some circumstances" to her life.

"Congressional findings on constitutionally relevant factual issues are entitled to great deference," the briefs read. The briefs say that Congress reached its conclusion after hearing testimony from many doctors, so the court should respect the lawmakers' judgment even if medical opinion is divided. [27]

In their brief in the Nebraska case challenging the federal law, lawyers for the Center for Reproductive Rights argue that medical evidence since 2000 "has strengthened this Court's finding that banning intact D&Es endangers women's health." The center also argues that evidence shows "the significant safety advantages of intact D&Es."

On both points, the center contends, justices should make their own independent judgment instead of deferring to Congress. "This Court should not defer to Congress's unreasonable findings that restrict a fundamental right," the brief says. [28]

The opposing briefs also sharply disagree on the breadth of the federal law. The government contends that the act's definition applies only to a rarely used and "disfavored" procedure. The center's lawyers counter that the act "does not clearly distinguish" between an intact D&E and the commonly used D&E procedure in a way that would allow doctors to comply with the ban.

In a final disagreement, the government urges the court to overturn the earlier ruling if its efforts to distinguish the federal statute from the Nebraska ban are rejected. The center's lawyers say the government shows no justification for "jettisoning" a recent precedent.

In the Planned Parenthood case, lawyers are presenting an additional issue for the justices to consider: whether the court can leave the federal law on the books while in effect adding a judicially crafted health exception. The government argues that the law need not be invalidated in its entirety because it would not "impose an undue burden" on women "in a large fraction of its applications."

But lawyers for Planned Parenthood will argue in their brief, due Sept. 27, that adding a health exception would contradict Congress' action in rejecting just such a provision. "It's 180 degrees opposite to legislative intent," says Planned Parenthood lawyer Evans. [29]

The two cases have attracted more than two dozen amicus briefs from groups and individuals on both sides. Two anti-abortion groups urge the court to reconsider or overrule the 1973 decision in *Roe v. Wade*, but court watchers agree the justices are virtually certain to spurn the suggestion. A decision is due by the end of June 2007— and unlikely to come much sooner.

Meanwhile, anti-abortion groups are making a final push for congressional approval of a bill to make it a federal crime to take minors across state lines to circumvent state parental-notification and consent laws. Supporters say the Child Interstate Abortion Notification Act will strengthen state laws, while opponents say it will impede access to abortions for some teens in crisis pregnancies.

The House and the Senate passed slightly different versions of the bill in April and July, respectively, both by nearly 2-to-1 margins. Senate Democrats, however, are using a parliamentary maneuver to block a conference on the measure. If approved and signed by Bush, the bill would be the only major abortion-related measure to emerge from the current Congress. [30] ■

OUTLOOK

Continuing Battles

After more than three decades, the abortion wars show no signs of subsiding — in South Dakota or the United States as a whole. Anti-abortion forces are making gains, but failing to win decisive victories. Abortion-rights advocates are constantly on the defensive but holding on to their most important victory: the Supreme Court's recognition of a woman's qualified constitutional right to choose an abortion subject to some degree of government regulation.

Advocates and partisans on opposing sides depict the present situation in stark terms — for opposite reasons. "Every 20 seconds in America a child is killed — over 4,000 a day," claims Tom Rooney, executive pastor of the First Assembly of God in Sioux Falls. "That's a horrible thing to think about, and it breaks my heart."

Rooney's church is within sight of the Planned Parenthood clinic on the opposite side of the street. Rooney sometimes joins the sidewalk vigils outside the clinic. The church's marquee urges passersby, "Pray for Life. Vote for Life on Nov. 7."

Inside the clinic, meanwhile, the itinerant Minnesota doctor worries that women — especially the young and the poor — have fewer reproductive options as access to contraception is limited and access to abortion impeded. If the ban passes, she fears South Dakota women would resort to illegal abortions, at greater risk.

"Those who have resources to go elsewhere would travel out of state," the doctor says. "Those who don't would seek other alternatives, and those alternatives might be very unsafe. That would be true for the most vulnerable women of South Dakota, particularly those who are young and poor."

Hardly anyone — except Vote Yes for Life campaign manager Unruh — expects the South Dakota ban ever to go into effect, however, even if South Dakota voters approve it. A court challenge is certain, and the major national anti-abortion groups acknowledge that they lack the votes on the Supreme Court to overturn outright either *Roe v. Wade* or its 1992 modification in *Planned Parenthood v. Casey.*

The outcome of the pending Supreme Court cases on the federal "partial-birth abortion" ban is harder to predict. Anti-abortion groups are counting on Roberts and Alito to vote to uphold the federal law and for Kennedy as well as Scalia and Thomas to adhere to their dissenting views from the 2000 decision to strike down the Nebraska ban. Abortion-rights groups fear that their opponents are handicapping the cases correctly.

The immediate impact of upholding the federal law is uncertain, however. Abortion providers and abortion-rights supporters say the procedure — strictly defined — is rare. "I've never done the procedure or seen the procedure," says Rapid City obstetrician Buehner.

In their brief, the opponents of the law warn that the congressional definition of the procedure will potentially cover many standard D&E abortions. Even if the court upholds the law, however, the justices might interpret it for future application in a way that avoids that result.

Still, a ruling to uphold the federal ban could have a broader meaning for future cases. It could weaken the requirement to include health exceptions in any abortion regulations and validate anti-abortion groups' efforts to directly regulate the abortion procedure itself — opening up new avenues for legislative restrictions.

On both sides, advocates acknowledge obstacles for their views but profess confidence that the trend is favorable for their side, not the other. If judicial limitations were eased, Forsythe says, states would enact policies "much more restrictive of abortion than exist today." Abortion-rights supporters, meanwhile, say that despite passage of abortion restrictions, most Americans still favor legal protections for a woman's right to choose. "I am optimistic that the American public will not want to turn the clock back to pre-*Roe* days and will insist that access to abortions remains available," says Waxman, of the National Women's Law Center in Washington. ■

About the Authors

Associate Editor **Kenneth Jost** graduated from Harvard College and Georgetown University Law Center. He is the author of the *Supreme Court Yearbook* and editor of *The Supreme Court from A to Z* (both *CQ Press*). He was a member of the *CQ Researcher* team that won the 2002 ABA Silver Gavel Award. His recent reports include "Presidential Power" and "Transgender Issues."

Kathy Koch, *CQ Researcher*'s assistant managing editor, previously served as a *Researcher* staff writer covering education and social issues. She also has covered environmental legislation for *CQ Weekly*, reported for newspapers in South Florida and freelanced in Asia and Africa for several U.S. newspapers, including *The Christian Science Monitor* and *USA Today*. She graduated in journalism from the University of North Carolina at Chapel Hill.

Notes

[1] For the text of the law, see http://legis.state.sd.us/sessions/2006/bills/HB1215enr.htm. For the South Dakota secretary of state's ballot pamphlet, including a description of the law and opposing arguments, see www.sdsos.gov/electionsvoteregistration/electvoterpdfs/2006SouthDakotaBallotQuestionPamphlet.pdf.

[2] For background, see Marcia Clemmitt, "Birth-Control Debate," *CQ Researcher*, July 24, 2005, pp. 565-588, Sarah Glazer, "*Roe v. Wade* at 25," *CQ Researcher*, Nov. 28, 1997, pp. 1033-1056,

and Kenneth Jost, "Abortion Debate," *CQ Researcher*, March 21, 2003, pp. 249-272.

[3] For background, see Kenneth Jost, "Right to Die," *CQ Researcher*, May 13, 2005, pp. 421-444.

[4] Lawrence B. Finer and Stanley K. Henshaw "Estimates of U.S. Abortion Incidence, 2001-2003," Guttmacher Institute, Aug. 3, 2006.

[5] "Poll shows distaste for proposed SD abortion ban," The Associated Press, July 31, 2006. The telephone survey of 800 registered voters was conducted July 24-26 and had a margin of sampling error of plus or minus 3.5 percentage points.

[6] Monica Davey, "South Dakota Bans Abortion, Setting Up a Battle," *The New York Times*, March 7, 2006, p. A1.

[7] For information and views from opposing perspectives, see Web sites maintained by the National Right to Life Committee (www.nrlc.org); and jointly by the Center for Reproductive Rights, National Abortion Federation and Planned Parenthood (www.federalabortionban.org).

[8] See Lawrence B. Finer and Stanley K. Henshaw, "Abortion Incidence and Services in the United States in 2000," *Perspectives on Sexual and Reproductive Health*, January/February 2003; www.guttmacher.org/pubs/journals/3500603.html.

[9] "The Provider Shortage," Medical Students for Choice, www.ms4c.org/issueshortage.htm.

[10] "The Safety of Legal Abortions and the Hazards of Illegal Abortion," NARAL Pro-Choice America Foundation, www.prochoiceamerica.org.

[11] For a compact chronology through 1996, see Rickie Solinger (ed.), *Abortion Wars: A Half Century of Struggle, 1950-2000* (1998), pp. xi-xvi.

[12] Heather Boonstra, *et al.*, "Abortion in Women's Lives," Guttmacher Institute, 2006.

[13] Finer and Henshaw, *op. cit.*

[14] *The New York Times*, Dec. 31, 1973, p. 14.

[15] The case is *Maher v. Roe*, 432 U.S. 464 (1977). The court similarly upheld the federal funding restriction in *Harris v. McRae*, 448 U.S. 297 (1980).

[16] The decisions are *Hodgson v. Minnesota*, 497 U.S. 417 (1990), and *Ohio v. Akron Center for Reproductive Health*, 497 U.S. 502 (1990).

[17] The case is 505 U.S. 833 (1992).

[18] The cases are *Carhart v. Gonzales* (CA8 July 8, 2005), *Planned Parenthood v. Gonzales* (CA9 Jan. 31, 2006), *National Abortion Federation v. Gonzales* (CA2 Jan. 31, 2006).

[19] The decision is *Ayotte v. Planned Parenthood* (Jan. 18, 2006).

[20] James Gerstenzang, "Bush Signs Anti-Violence Law That Extends Into the Womb," *Los Angeles Times*, April 2, 2004, p. A20.

FOR MORE INFORMATION

American Association of Pro-Life Obstetricians and Gynecologists, 339 River Ave., Holland, MI 49423; (616) 546-2639; www.aaplog.org. Provides information to support obstetrician-gynecologists who take pro-life positions.

American College of Obstetricians and Gynecologists, 409 12th St., S.W., P.O. Box 96920, Washington, DC 20090-6920; (202) 638-5577; www.acog.org. The nation's leading group of professionals providing health care for women.

Americans United for Life, 310 S. Peoria, Suite 300, Chicago, IL 60607; (312) 492-7234; www.aul.org. A nonprofit public-interest law firm that provides legal protection to unborn children.

Center for Reproductive Rights, 120 Wall St., New York, NY 10005; (917) 637-3600; www.crlp.org. Provides legal assistance to protect reproductive freedom.

Concerned Women for America, 1015 15th St., N.W., Suite 1100, Washington, DC 20005; (202) 488-7000; www.cwfa.org. Advocates Biblical principles in public policy.

Family Research Council, 801 G St., N.W., Washington, DC 20001; (202) 393-2100; www.frc.org. Formulates public policy that values human life starting at conception.

Guttmacher Institute, 120 Wall St., New York, NY 10005; (212) 248-1111; www.guttmacher.org. An affiliate of the Planned Parenthood Federation of America that provides research aimed at protecting reproductive choices.

NARAL Pro-Choice America, 1156 15th St., N.W., Suite 700, Washington, DC 20005; (202) 973-3000; www.naral.org. Lobbies for abortion-rights legislation.

National Abortion Federation, 1755 Massachusetts Ave., N.W., Suite 600, Washington, D.C. 20036; (202) 667-5881; www.prochoice.org. An association of abortion providers that sets quality standards for clinics, trains operators and monitors clinic violence.

National Right to Life Committee, 419 7th St., N.W., Suite 500, Washington, DC 20004-2293; (202) 626-8800; www.nrlc.org. The nation's largest anti-abortion group.

Planned Parenthood Federation of America, 434 West 33rd St., New York, NY 10001; (212) 541-7800; www.ppfa.org. Provides information about reproductive health and operates health centers offering low-cost abortions.

[21] Maile R. Smith, "Abortion and the Protection of the Unborn: A Survey of Federal and State Law," in Americans United for Life, Defending Life 2006 (www.unitedforlife.org). "Fetal Protection, 2003-2004 Legislative Chronology," *Congress and The Nation Online Edition, CQ Electronic Library*, http://library.cqpress.com.

[22] Here are links to the Web sites for the opposing campaigns: Vote Yes for Life, www.Voteyesforlife.com; South Dakota Campaign for Healthy Families, www.sdhealthyfamilies.org.

[23] For coverage, see Megan Myers, "Rape victims speak out on abortion," *Argus Leader* (Sioux Falls), Sept. 14, 2006.

[24] South Dakota Secretary of State's office; www.sdsos.gov/electionsvoteregistration/pastelections_electioninfo06_primaryvoterregistrationtotals.shtm.

[25] www.religionatlas.org/religion_region/MIDWEST/SdAd.htm. The Polis Center is part of the Indiana University School of Liberal Arts

[26] "The Safety of Legal Abortions and the Hazards of Illegal Abortion," NARAL Pro-Choice America Foundation, www.prochoiceamerica.org.

[27] The government's briefs can be found on the Web site of the Office of the Solicitor General: *Gonzales v. Carhart*, www.usdoj.gov/osg/briefs/2005/3mer/2mer/2005-0380.mer.aa.html; *Gonzales v. Planned Parenthood*, www.usdoj.gov/osg/briefs/2005/3mer/2mer/2005-1382.mer.aa.html.

[28] The center's brief in *Gonzales v. Carhart* can be found on its Web site: www.reproductiverights.org/crt_pba.html.

[29] See Planned Parenthood Web site, www.plannedparenthood.org.

[30] See "Abortion: Transporting Minors," *CQ Weekly*, Sept. 4, 2006, p. 2307.

Bibliography

Selected Sources

Books

Balkin, Jack (ed.), *What* Roe v. Wade *Should Have Said: The Nation's Top Legal Experts Rewrite America's Most Controversial Decision*, New York University Press, 2005.

Eleven law professors write how they would have decided the *Roe v. Wade* abortion case. Balkin, a professor at Yale Law School, provides an introductory essay.

Garrow, David J., *Liberty and Sexuality: The Right to Privacy and the Making of* Roe v. Wade, Macmillan, 1994 [updated edition with epilogue published by University of California Press, 1998].

A professor at Emory Law School and an unabashed abortion-rights advocate has produced a definitive history of the Supreme Court's decisions on reproductive rights. Includes voluminous notes, 30-page bibliography.

Hull, N.E.H., Williamjames Hoffer and Peter Charles Hoffer (eds.), *The Abortion Rights Controversy in America: A Legal Reader*, University of North Carolina Press, 2004.

The compilation includes excerpts from primary sources from the criminalization of abortion in the 19th century through the anti-abortion movement that began in the 1970s. Hull and Peter Hoffer are coauthors of an excellent overview of the issue: *Roe v. Wade: The Abortion Rights Controversy in America* (Kansas University Press, 2001).

Palmer, Louis J. Jr., *Encyclopedia of Abortion in the United States*, McFarland, 2002.

The 420-page volume comprehensively covers abortion and related topics, including individual entries for all 50 states on abortion laws and statistics. Palmer is an attorney for the West Virginia Supreme Court of Appeals.

Rose, Melody, *Safe, Legal, and Unavailable? Abortion Politics in the United States*, CQ Press, 2007.

An associate professor of political science at Portland State University (Ore.) provides an up-to-date overview of the abortion controversy with a major focus on restrictions to abortion access at the state and federal levels.

Solinger, Rickie (ed.), *Abortion Wars: A Half Century of Struggle, 1950-2000*, University of California Press, 1998.

Essays by 21 contributors examine the abortion controversy from an abortion-rights perspective. Independent historian Solinger is also the author of a recent primer, *Pregnancy and Power: A Short History of Reproductive Politics in America* (Reed Elsivier, 2005).

For earlier works, see Bibliography in Kenneth Jost, "Abortion Debates," CQ Researcher, *March 21, 2003, pp. 249-272.*

Articles

Gorney, Cynthia, "Reversing *Roe*," *The New Yorker*, June 26, 2006, pp. 46-55.

A veteran journalist travels across South Dakota to take the mood of the people as activists try to put the state's controversial anti-abortion law on the November ballot. Gorney teaches writing and reporting at the University of California, Berkeley.

Lopez, Kathryn Jean, "Pro Life Generation?" *National Review Online*, Sept. 13, 2006.

Jonathan Tonkowich, a student at Thomas Aquinas College, created Wash for Life to bring together pro-life youth groups nationwide to raise money for local crisis-pregnancy centers. Lopez says he typifies younger Americans now supporting pro-life policies.

Stevens, Allison, "What the Left Didn't Do," *American Prospect*, July 5, 2006.

Pro-abortion forces are criticized in this left-leaning magazine for being outmaneuvered in the states by better-organized, more passionate pro-life advocates.

Reports and Studies

Burke, Denise M., (editor-in-chief), *Defending Life 2006: Proven Strategies for a Pro-Life America*, Americans United for Life, 2006.

The 520-page "state-by-state legal guide to abortion, bioethics and the end of life" also includes several pro-life essays. Burke is the organization's legal director.

NARAL Pro-Choice America, "Who Decides? The Status of Women's Reproductive Rights in the United States," January 2006.

The abortion-rights advocacy group's 15th compendium of state abortion laws details what it calls the "further erosion" of *Roe v. Wade.*

National Right to Life Committee, "NRL News," monthly series (www.nrlc.org/news).

The anti-abortion group's monthly newsletter provides up-to-date information and perspective on legislative and legal developments.

New, Michael J., "Using Natural Experiments to Analyze the Impact of State Legislation on the Incidence of Abortion," Heritage Foundation, Jan. 23, 2006, www.heritage.org/Research/Family/cda06-01.cfm.

A visiting health-policy fellow at the conservative Heritage Foundation says state laws limiting abortions were a key factor in the 18 percent decline in the number of abortions performed between 1990 and 1999.

The Next Step:

Additional Articles from Current Periodicals

"Partial-Birth Abortions"

Egelko, Bob, " 'Partial Birth' Abortion Ban Held Unconstitutional," *The San Francisco Chronicle*, Feb. 1, 2006, p. A4.
Federal appeals courts in New York and San Francisco declared the federal government's attempt to outlaw "partial-birth abortion" unconstitutional.

Henderson, Stephen, "Supreme Court Could Change How Abortion Laws Are Challenged," *The Philadelphia Inquirer*, April 2, 2006, p. A3.
When it reviews the Partial Birth Abortion Ban Act this fall, the Supreme Court could make it easier for states to enact stringent restrictions on abortion without fear that courts will overturn them.

Preston, Julia, "Appeals Court Voids Ban on 'Partial Birth' Abortions," *The New York Times*, July 9, 2005, p. A11.
The U.S. Court of Appeals for the Eighth Circuit, in St. Louis, upheld a ruling by a lower court judge striking down the Partial Birth Abortion Ban Act.

Public Opinion

Benac, Nancy, "Americans Hold Firm To Views on Abortion," *St. Louis Post-Dispatch*," March 13, 2006, p. A3.
A solid majority of Americans believe the courts should uphold *Roe v. Wade*, the 1973 decision allowing abortion, but they also support some limits on when abortions can be performed.

Ehrich, Tom, "Where Does God Stand on Abortion?" *USA Today*, Aug. 14, 2006, p. A11.
The debate between religions over whether abortion should be legal or not is shaded in gray.

Sowti, Naseem, "Abortion: Just the Data," *The Washington Post*, July 19, 2005, p. F1.
The number of U.S. women having abortions continues its decades-long decline, reaching its lowest level since 1976.

Tierney, John, "Men's Abortion Rights," *The New York Times*, Jan. 10, 2006, p. A25.
Most Americans think a husband should be notified before an abortion.

State Laws

"Petitioning For Reason," *The Houston Chronicle*, April 13, 2006, p. B8.
Pro-life South Dakotans are gathering signatures to fight the state's abortion ban because they believe women should have a choice in cases of rape or incest.

Alford, Jeremy, "Louisiana Governor Plans to Sign Anti-Abortion Law," *The New York Times*, June 7, 2006, p. A18.
Gov. Kathleen Babineaux, D-La., will sign into law a bill that would permit abortion only in cases where the woman's life was threatened by her pregnancy.

Biskupic, Joan, "Abortion Foes Gain on New Front," *USA Today*, Feb. 8, 2006, p. A1.
Several states have introduced legislation requiring doctors to tell women seeking abortions that their fetuses might feel pain during the procedure.

Elliott, Janet, "State Rules Sought on Doctors, New Abortion Laws," *The Houston Chronicle*, July 13, 2006, p. B2.
Texas state Rep. David Swinford, R-Amarillo, has asked the state's attorney general to decide if physicians can be criminally charged for performing late-term abortions or abortions on minors based on laws passed in 2003 and 2005.

Klas, Mary Ellen, "Doctors Must Tell Women of Abortion Risk, Court Says," *The Miami Herald*, April 7, 2006, p. A1.
The Florida Supreme Court upheld a state law that requires doctors to tell women about the risks of an abortion.

Nussbaum, Paul, "Unpredictable Lines in South Dakota Abortion Fight," *The Philadelphia Inquirer*, July 9, 2006, p. A1.
For the first time in 33 years, voters in South Dakota will decide this fall whether to outlaw abortion in their state.

Ostrom, Carol M., "Prescriptions Must Be Filled Under Newly Adopted Rule," *The Seattle Times*, Sept. 1, 2006, p. B1.
A pharmacist who personally objects to filling a prescription for emergency contraception would be required to fill it under a rule adopted by the Washington Board of Pharmacy.

CITING *CQ RESEARCHER*

Sample formats for citing these reports in a bibliography include the ones listed below. Preferred styles and formats vary, so please check with your instructor or professor.

MLA STYLE

Jost, Kenneth. "Rethinking the Death Penalty." CQ Researcher 16 Nov. 2001: 945-68.

APA STYLE

Jost, K. (2001, November 16). Rethinking the death penalty. *CQ Researcher, 11*, 945-968.

CHICAGO STYLE

Jost, Kenneth. "Rethinking the Death Penalty." *CQ Researcher*, November 16, 2001, 945-968.

In-depth Reports on Issues in the News

Are you writing a paper?

Need backup for a debate?

Want to become an expert on an issue?

For 80 years, students have turned to *CQ Researcher* for in-depth reporting on issues in the news. Reports on a full range of political and social issues are now available. Following is a selection of recent reports:

Civil Liberties
Voting Controversies, 9/06
Right to Die, 5/05
Immigration Reform, 4/05
Gays on Campus, 10/04

Crime/Law
Sex Offenders, 9/06
Treatment of Detainees, 8/06
War on Drugs, 6/06
Domestic Violence, 1/06
Death Penalty Controversies, 9/05

Education
Academic Freedom, 10/05
Intelligent Design, 7/05
No Child Left Behind, 5/05
Gender and Learning, 5/05

Environment
Nuclear Energy, 3/06
Climate Change, 1/06
Saving the Oceans, 11/05
Endangered Species Act, 6/05
Alternative Energy, 2/05

Health/Safety
Rising Health Costs, 4/06
Pension Crisis, 2/06
Avian Flu Threat, 1/06
Domestic Violence, 1/06
Disaster Preparedness, 11/05

International Affairs/Politics
Change in Latin America, 7/06
Pork Barrel Politics, 6/06
Future of European Union, 10/05
War in Iraq, 10/05

Social Trends
Blog Explosion, 6/06
Controlling the Internet, 5/06

Terrorism/Defense
Port Security, 4/06
Presidential Power, 2/06

Youth
Drinking on Campus, 8/06
National Service, 6/06
Teen Spending, 5/06
Bullying, 2/05

Upcoming Reports

Biofuels, 9/29/06
National Parks, 10/6/06
Elder Care, 10/13/06
Ecotourism, 10/20/06
Middle East Update, 10/27/06

ACCESS

CQ Researcher is available in print and online. For access, visit your library or www.cqresearcher.com.

STAY CURRENT

To receive notice of upcoming *CQ Researcher* reports, or learn more about *CQ Researcher* products, subscribe to the free e-mail newsletters, *CQ Researcher Alert!* and *CQ Researcher News*: www.cqpress.com/newsletters.

PURCHASE

To purchase a *CQ Researcher* report in print or electronic format (PDF), visit www.cqpress.com or call 866-427-7737. Single reports start at $15. Bulk purchase discounts and electronic-rights licensing are also available.

SUBSCRIBE

A full-service *CQ Researcher* print subscription—including 44 reports a year, monthly index updates, and a bound volume—is $688 for academic and public libraries, $667 for high school libraries, and $827 for media libraries. Add $25 for domestic postage.

CQ Researcher Online offers a backfile from 1991 and a number of tools to simplify research. For pricing information, call 800-834-9020, ext. 1906, or e-mail librarysales@cqpress.com.

CQ RESEARCHER ***PLUS*** *ARCHIVE*

GET ONLINE ACCESS TO VITAL ISSUES FROM 1923 TO THE PRESENT

CQ Researcher Plus Archive delivers fast, online access to every *CQ Researcher* report from 1991 to the present, *PLUS* lets you explore the complete archive of *Editorial Research Reports** from 1923-1990. Search and browse more than 3,600 in-depth reports.

Loaded with handy online features, *CQ Researcher Plus Archive* provides the trustworthy reporting and the advanced online functionality today's researchers demand. The new "Issue Tracker" feature provides quick links to past and present reports on the specific topics you need.

For a free trial, visit http://library.cqpress.com/trials.

For pricing information, call 1-800-834-9020, ext. 1906 or e-mail librarymarketing@cqpress.com.

**Editorial Research Reports*, the predecessor to *CQ Researcher*, provides the same expert, nonpartisan reporting on the vital issues that have shaped our society.

CQ Press • 1255 22nd Street, NW, Suite 400 • Washington, DC 20037

CQ Researcher

Published by CQ Press, a division of Congressional Quarterly Inc.

cqresearcher.com

Biofuels Boom

Can ethanol satisfy America's thirst for foreign oil?

Energy companies across the Midwest are building new plants to convert locally grown corn into ethanol. The construction spurt is the most visible evidence of expanded interest in renewable fuels, which politicians increasingly believe can begin to wean America from its voracious appetite for foreign oil. Ethanol, the only renewable fuel being produced in the United States in any significant quantity, is being aggressively promoted as a key ingredient in the quest for energy security. But before competing head-to-head with gasoline, it will have to overcome major hurdles. Not only is it more expensive to produce, but some studies say it takes more energy to process corn into ethanol than the fuel delivers. Experts believe a more viable long-term ethanol source could be switchgrass or other so-called cellulosic biomass. The current biofuels boom also bodes well for other renewables, including biodiesel, which has achieved popularity in Europe.

An ethanol plant near Lena, Ill., is one of 128 U.S. plants producing 4.5 billion gallons of ethanol a year from corn. Production will rise by about 50 percent when plants now under construction go online.

INSIDE THIS REPORT

CQ Researcher • Sept. 29, 2006 • www.cqresearcher.com
Volume 16, Number 34 • Pages 793-816

CQ PRESS

RECIPIENT OF SOCIETY OF PROFESSIONAL JOURNALISTS AWARD FOR EXCELLENCE ◆ AMERICAN BAR ASSOCIATION SILVER GAVEL AWARD

CQ Researcher

Sept. 29, 2006
Volume 16, Number 34

CQ Researcher (ISSN 1056-2036) is printed on acid-free paper. Published weekly, except March 24, July 7, July 14, Aug. 4, Aug. 11, Nov. 24, Dec. 22 and Dec. 29, by CQ Press, a division of Congressional Quarterly Inc. Annual full-service subscriptions for institutions start at $667. For pricing, call 1-800-834-9020, ext. 1906. To purchase a *CQ Researcher* report in print or electronic format (PDF), visit www.cqpress.com or call 866-427-7737. Single reports start at $15. Bulk purchase discounts and electronic-rights licensing are also available. Periodicals postage paid at Washington, D.C., and additional mailing offices. POSTMASTER: Send address changes to *CQ Researcher*, 1255 22nd St., N.W., Suite 400, Washington, DC 20037.

THE ISSUES

BACKGROUND

CURRENT SITUATION

OUTLOOK

SIDEBARS AND GRAPHICS

FOR FURTHER RESEARCH

Cover photograph: Getty Images/Scott Olson

Biofuels Boom

By Adriel Bettelheim

The Issues

No doubt few Wall Street investors or members of Congress can locate Edmonds County, S.D., on a map. The sparsely populated area in the north of the state has a population of around 4,000 residents that has been declining for years.

To make matters worse, the most recent corn crop was poor. But that didn't stop Glacial Lakes Energy from coming to town. The company recently raised $95 million in three days to help finance a new processing plant near the tiny town of Mina to convert locally grown corn into ethanol fuel.

"People asked us, 'Why are you going into that area?' So you begin to question yourself," Glacial Lakes' Chairman Jon T. Anderson said at a groundbreaking ceremony in September. But, he said, the potential to be a player in domestic energy production persuaded the company to forge ahead (along with the help of generous federal subsidies). "The optimism is here," he said. [1]

AFP/Getty Images/Karen Bleier

A gas station in Arlington, Va., offers biodiesel and E85 — a blend of 85 percent ethanol and 15 percent gasoline — in May 2006. Concerns over air quality, climate change and U.S. dependence on foreign oil are sparking new interest in ethanol and other agriculture-based alternative fuels. But some economists say it takes more energy to produce ethanol than it delivers, when transportation and other costs are considered.

Ethanol plants are springing up across the Midwest, the most visible evidence of a broad effort to increase supplies of renewable fuels. Politicians at the federal and local levels believe renewables, or "biofuels," will gradually reduce U.S. demand for gasoline and other petroleum products.

Enthusiasm for alternative fuels until recently was largely confined to the environmental community and commodities growers. But a number of factors — discontent over the Iraq war, jittery global energy markets, uncertainty over future supplies of crude oil and recent $3 per gallon pump prices — have dramatically changed policymakers' outlook, intensifying efforts to develop a homegrown alternative to fossil fuels. Ethanol is on the leading edge, thanks both to the abundance of corn and to more than two decades of federal tax breaks and subsidies to encourage its production. The clean-burning fuel has the added virtue of not emitting carbon dioxide, a "greenhouse" gas implicated in global warming. [2]

In his State of the Union address on Jan. 31, Bush — a former Texas oil wildcatter who has long said that increased domestic oil and gas production will help satisfy the nation's energy needs — hailed ethanol and other renewables as an environmentally friendly tonic that will "make dependence on Middle East oil a thing of the past." [3]

Bush's remarks came after Congress passed an energy bill that ordered refiners to use 7.5 billion gallons of renewable fuels annually by 2012. And with crude oil — which exceeded $70 per barrel this summer — expected to remain above $50 per barrel into the foreseeable future, some farm-state lawmakers are suggesting that the United States should aim to produce 25 percent of its energy needs from farmland and forests by 2025.

"Anyone at a gas pump today knows that we need to act now," says Rep. Gil Gutknecht, R-Minn., one of Congress' most enthusiastic promoters of renewable fuels. "Support for renewable fuels is good for the environment, cycles more money through our rural economy and reduces our dependence on foreign powers and big oil."

The trend bodes particularly well for Gutknecht and other Corn Belt officials, where 95 percent of the raw material for ethanol is produced. The nation's 128 ethanol distillation plants are concentrated in Iowa, Nebraska, Minnesota and South Dakota, mostly to reduce corn-shipping costs. But the ethanol boom also is drawing in new players, including outside investors who sense the nation is beginning to view agriculture not only as a source of food but also as a long-term provider of energy security.

So far 21 states already have ethanol plants, and with new plants being planned, annual production would increase from today's 4.5 billion gallons to more than 7 billion gallons. (*See map, p. 796, and chart, p. 797.*) By decade's end, some government analysts predict ethanol production will exceed 10 billion gallons — double current levels. [4]

Yet there is considerable skepticism about whether renewable fuels

Ethanol Produced in 21 States

Ethanol is produced at 128 distillation plants throughout the country. To hold down shipping costs, most of the plans are in the states that grow the most corn.

Number of Ethanol Plants

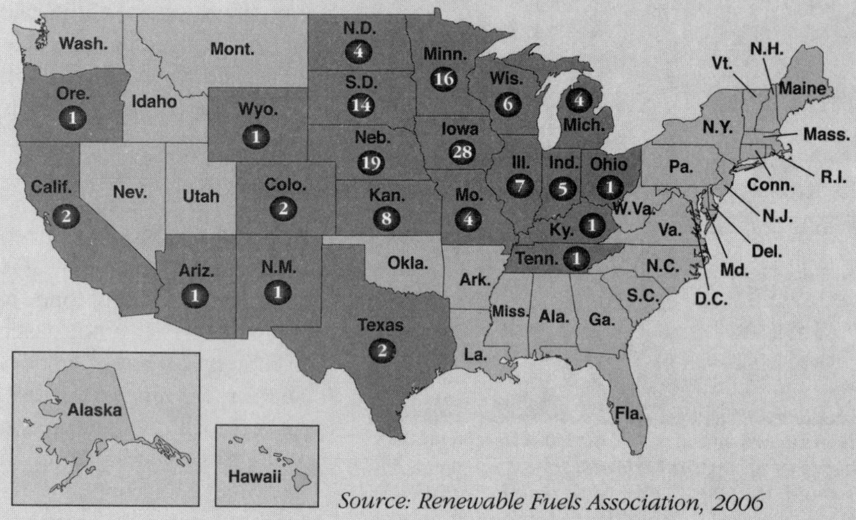

Source: Renewable Fuels Association, 2006

can really reduce the nation's dependence on oil without an accompanying decline in overall energy consumption. If Americans keep consuming more and more energy — commuting longer distances, taking the kids to soccer practice, and so on — even big gains in renewable production won't keep us from having to look abroad.

Many experts think raising fuel-efficiency standards would make a bigger dent than increasing supplies of fuels not everyone wants. Agriculture-based fuels accounted for only six-tenths of a percent of total energy consumption in 2004. Moreover, they have achieved lower-than-expected market penetration over the past quarter-century because of generally low fossil fuel and electricity prices.

Producers continue to rely on generous federal and state subsidies that critics contend are distorting markets and diverting research money from the development of other potential energy sources, such as solar and geothermal. Energy analysts predict it will be difficult to justify continued federal aid for renewable fuels if oil markets stabilize and gas prices fall, providing consumers with cheap and plentiful energy.

Oil prices dipped briefly below $60 in late September for the first time in six months, and natural-gas prices reached their lowest level in more than two years.

"One of the best alternatives to using gasoline is to conserve energy, but you don't get re-elected forcing voters to buy a smaller car," says Kevin Book, senior energy analyst for Friedman Billings Ramsey, an Arlington, Va., investment bank. "Everyone from a farm state loves ethanol. So does everyone with research interests, 35 governors and a substantial majority of the House and Senate. They see this as solving a shortage of refined product."

Others question ethanol's actual energy value as a fuel. Several scientific studies have concluded that — when the costs of growing, harvesting, transporting and processing the crop are thrown into the calculations — it ultimately takes more energy to make ethanol from corn than is derived from burning the fuel. Because ethanol's energy output when burned is only about two-thirds that of gasoline, researchers at the Polytechnic University of New York have estimated the nation's entire corn crop would supply only 3.7 percent of the country's transportation needs. Ethanol-industry backers strenuously dispute the notion that their fuel produces a negative return, saying critics are overstating production costs and making widely varying assumptions about farming practices. [5]

Many energy experts and scientists contend that a more energy-efficient solution is to produce ethanol from switchgrass, wood chips, crop residues or other widely available forms of cellulose, as is the norm in other countries. Advocates of this approach note that Brazil — the world's leading ethanol producer — has met its demand for transportation fuels by using sugar cane.

But there are technological challenges in converting cellulose from trees and grass into sugar to start the ethanol-production process. Committing to another feedstock, or source, instead of corn also would undercut the current boom in corn-based ethanol production and possibly alienate an important political constituency in farm states.

For now, policymakers are straddling the line, continuing strong support for corn-based ethanol while backing research into alternative methods of producing the product and other biofuels. Congress is considering various proposals to increase federally financed research-and-development efforts at government and university labs and to require oil companies to blend more ethanol with their transportation fuels.

Republicans in Congress are trumpeting their promotion of biofuels in the run-up to the 2006 elections in the hope of bolstering their environmental credentials and demonstrating concern over the reliance on foreign oil.

Meanwhile, the Big Three U.S. automakers have pledged to double production of "flexible fuel" vehicles capable of running on ethanol and other biofuels by 2010. Automakers are poised to benefit from the trend, because companies that produce flexible-fuel vehicles receive extra credit toward meeting federal fuel-efficiency standards for their fleets, regardless of what fuel the vehicles actually burn.

Though ethanol is the only renewable fuel being produced in any significant quantities, other products stand to benefit from the push to expand supplies. One is biodiesel — produced from animal fat or vegetable oil — which works in diesel engines without the need for modifications and is more energy efficient than ethanol. The U.S. Postal Service and the Pentagon, as well as many state governments, are directing their bus and truck fleets to incorporate biodiesel into their fuel base. Country singer Willie Nelson has started a biodiesel-fuel company and is promoting use of "BioWillie" fuel by long-haul truckers. Biodiesel fuel is heavily promoted by soybean growers, who now provide about 90 percent of the raw material for biodiesel.

Energy analysts also suggest that biogas, or methane, can be produced on farms from the decomposition of animal wastes, and that hydrogen could power cars outfitted with special fuel cells. [6] These alternatives, however, are still in early stages of development and deemed years away from large-scale commercial applications.

The push to increase supplies of renewable fuels has overshadowed efforts to tamp down energy demand, such as tightening fuel-efficiency standards for passenger cars. Focusing on the demand side of the equation has merit, in the view of many experts, because the average number of miles driven by every American over age 16 has risen 60 percent — from about 7,500 miles per year in 1970 to about 12,000 in 2004 — a reflection of rising incomes, Americans' tendency to live farther from city centers and consumers' penchant for using sport-utility vehicles, trucks and minivans.

A 2002 study by the National Academies of Sciences concluded that federal fuel-efficiency standards had succeeded in lowering national energy consumption by 2.8 million barrels of oil a day. And the Congressional Budget Office has estimated that raising the standards by a relatively modest 3.8 miles per gallon for cars and light trucks — the classification that includes most SUVs and minivans — would lower the average rate of gas consumption for light trucks by 15 percent and for cars by 12 percent.

But encouraging Americans to buy more fuel-efficient cars is a politically risky proposition, especially since many consumers in recent years took advantage of low-cost financing deals offered by domestic automakers for less fuel-efficient cars. The experts say current efforts to increase fuel supplies are more realistic than prodding drivers to give up their current vehicles and will, over time, still bring a more conservation-centric ethic to policymaking.

"The most important thing for people to realize is the environmental impact of not doing anything, which is global warming," says Joseph Romm, executive director of the Arlington, Va.-based Center for Energy and Climate Solutions and a former energy official in the Clinton administration. "Corn ethanol isn't the endgame, but we need a fuel to replace gasoline that doesn't

Ethanol Production to Increase by 50 Percent

Iowa, Nebraska and Illinois produce more than half the ethanol made in the United States. Production will rise by about 50 percent when distillation plants under construction go online.

Ethanol Production Capacity by State, April 2006

State	Currently Operating Million gal/yr	%	Under Construction Million gal/yr	Total Million gal/yr	%
Iowa	1,218	27%	480	1,698	25%
Nebraska	553	12	504	1,057	16
Illinois	724	16	107	831	12
S.D.	585	13	238	823	12
Minn.	536	12	58	594	9
Indiana	102	2	290	392	6
Wis.	188	4	40	228	3
Mich.	50	1	157	207	3
Kansas	167	4	40	207	3
Missouri	110	2	45	155	2
Others	253	6	271	524	8
U.S. Total	4,486	100	2,230	6,716	100

Note: Percentages do not add to 100 due to rounding.

Source: Congressional Research Service, "Agriculture-Based Renewable Energy Production," May 18, 2006

use so much carbon, and improving the process of conversion on the cellulosic side is a critical task at this point." [7]

As policymakers mull ways to change America's energy-consumption habits and ponder the merits of alternative fuels, here are some questions they are asking:

Can renewable fuels lessen U.S. dependence on foreign oil?

"I believe all Americans want to see a homegrown, renewable fuel play a bigger role in meeting our transportation fuel needs, particularly in light of the recent run-up in gasoline prices we have all endured," said Energy Secretary Samuel W. Bodman during a May appearance in Indianapolis to tout a network of filling stations that dispense E85, a fuel consisting of 85 percent ethanol.

Bodman and many other policymakers sense that Americans are weary of depending on foreign leaders in politically volatile countries to feed their energy needs. Likewise, surging gas and home heating oil prices are intensifying economic anxiety among middle-class consumers, who also are grappling with higher health-care and housing costs. The notion of turning to American farms for price relief is appealing because it would promote energy security and invigorate rural economies.

Efforts to turn that vision into reality are under way in places like the Argonne National Laboratory near Chicago, where the Department of Energy is collaborating on biofuels research with agricultural giant Archer Daniels Midland Corp., the energy conglomerate BP PLC and other businesses. Among the projects is one to design new refineries that can process biomass from crops, grasses and trees and convert it into ethanol and other chemicals at a lower cost than the traditional petroleum-refining process. The Energy Department hopes to use advances in biotechnology to maximize crop yields and optimize the fermentation process that converts plant sugars into ethanol.

But experts say renewable fuels, and ethanol in particular, will have to overcome some significant hurdles to replace imported oil in a meaningful way. Despite the industry's rapid growth, ethanol still accounts for only a small fraction of total U.S. fuel consumption: In 2005, the industry produced 3.9 billion gallons, or approximately 2 percent of national fuel use. Though that share is certain to rise because of federal mandates and subsidies, the product is handicapped by the fact that the fuel is more costly to produce than gasoline — and difficult to obtain outside of the Midwest. [8]

AP Photo/Chris Park

With two gas tanks to fill, a Hummer owner turns to biodiesel at a filling station in San Diego, Calif. The station sells alternative fuels in addition to gasoline, but drivers in many states have a hard time finding alternative fuels.

E85, the most aggressively promoted ethanol fuel, is available at more than 850 gas stations. States and agricultural interests are offering loans and other incentives to more station owners to expand its availability. But because cars must be specially engineered to run on the fuel, consumer demand remains relatively low, leaving station operators reluctant to install pumps and underground storage tanks that can cost as much as $200,000. Their ambivalence is partly influenced by oil companies, which are reluctant to support alternative fuels. Ethanol producers rely on the oil companies because they must add their product to gasoline. As a result, at the end of the 2006 summer driving season ethanol fuel could not be found anywhere in the Northeast or New England and was on sale at only a single filling station in California. [9]

"Most of the people who have flexible-fuel vehicles don't have any kind of realistic, practical access [to renewable fuels]," said Don MacKenzie, a vehicles engineer with the Union of Concerned Scientists. [10]

Moving the fuel from the Farm Belt to major coastal population centers is another significant challenge. Producers must ship ethanol in small quantities by train, truck or barge because the compound attracts water molecules that corrode pipelines, posing the risk of groundwater contamination. Though there is talk about building fully dedicated ethanol pipelines, energy companies are taking a wait-and-see approach because the market has not fully developed. Alternatively, they could build processing plants closer to lucrative markets, but that would only be economical if enough corn could be obtained nearby.

"There are costs involved in requiring physical volumes [of fuel] to move where they would otherwise not economically go," notes Lawrence Goldstein, president of the Petroleum Industry Research Foundation, a New York consultancy.

Ethanol's market potential is also heavily influenced by the price of raw material. Many analysts predict the cost of producing ethanol will rise in coming years as more processing plants come online and drive up demand for corn. E85 currently sells for less than regular unleaded gas because the government gives producers a 51-cent tax credit for every gallon they produce, allowing the companies to sell the fuel below cost. The government also insulates domestic producers from overseas competition by levying a 54-cent-per-gallon tariff and a 2.5 percent duty on imported ethanol — policies that keep Brazil's cheaper ethanol off U.S. markets.

But if corn rises above recent levels of $2 per bushel and drives up producers' costs, the fuel might lose its price advantage. That prospect has led some farm-state lawmakers to promote new uses for the fuel, such as mandating that utilities use renewable sources to produce a certain percentage of their electricity.

Even if U.S. energy policies continue to favor renewable fuels, their long-term prospects will be heavily influenced by events overseas. Major oil-producing nations are capable of adjusting production levels to influence the price they receive for crude oil, often to the detriment of alternative fuels. Such was the case in the 1980s, after the Carter administration, responding to spiking crude-oil prices in the mid-1970s, launched a major round of government-funded research to develop conservation technologies and alternative fuels. Middle Eastern members of the Organization of Petroleum Exporting Countries (OPEC) oil cartel, faced with declining demand and more worldwide competition from non-OPEC producers, decided to step up oil production in 1985 and 1986, dramatically lowering the price refiners paid for imported crude. The re-emergence of cheap petroleum weakened political support for alternative fuels just as Ronald Reagan's administration adopted a market-based approach to energy and scaled back subsidies for alternative fuels. Reagan eventually killed the Carter initiative.

A variation of that scenario could play out today if imported oil prices drop further, resulting in a glut of ethanol larger than the levels Congress ordered refiners to blend in their products. Producers and farmers could be crippled by oversupply and unable to recoup their costs.

"There's really no mechanism that would protect this industry from excess supply," says Daniel Welt, a credit analyst for Standard & Poor's Corp. "For an industry to be viable long-term, it should be able to weather the entire commodity cycle, not just the top of the commodity cycle." [11]

Promoters of alternative fuels remain confident that nationwide demand will increase as more ethanol plants begin operations and that the continuation of government incentives will make biodiesel and other alternative fuels economically viable, too.

"The potential for the ethanol industry to continue to build infrastructure and become a substantial volume of our domestic motor-fuels supply is enormous, and if we truly are working toward energy independence, then we must continue moving forward," said Chris Standlee, executive vice president of Abengoa Bioenergy Corp. and vice chair of the Renewable Fuels Association, a Washington, D.C., trade group. [12]

Is corn the best raw material for deriving ethanol?

To understand corn's dominant position in the renewable-fuel industry, one has to first consider its status as the nation's commodity of choice. Modern crop science and genetic engineering have turned today's corn plant into an unusually hearty specimen that grows in a variety of regions. Farmers raised a record 12 billion bushels in 2004, and with even bigger yields forecast, they are finding more and more markets and commercial applications. Corn already is the leading feed grain for cattle and dairy cows, pigs and chickens. Corn sweetener has become a mainstay of sodas, ice cream, canned fruit and other popular foods, and byproducts are used to manufacture textiles, plastics and petroleum products.

Using corn to make fuel has enormous appeal for growers and processors because it gives them a role in debates over energy policy and national security and allows them to make the case that their product is essential to achieving energy independence. "If we were to get serious about renewables, the extent of the demand engulfs anything that agriculture has seen in food and fiber," notes Purdue University economist Wallace Tyner. [13]

The industry's efforts have been helped by the recent decisions of two dozen states to ban MTBE, a rival fuel additive that has been implicated in groundwater pollution. Groups such as the National Corn Growers Association are trying to improve corn's market position through a variety of steps, such as lobbying for requirements that all gasoline sold in the United States contain a 10 percent blend of non-imported renewable fuels by 2010.

"Our nation's farmers are the best in the world at growing corn, which means that we must continually grow existing markets and discover new ones for our product," says Bruce Noel, chairman of the growers association's ethanol committee. "The ethanol market is the single most successful and fastest-growing value-added market for farmers."

But some nagging questions trouble the industry's efforts. Some economists and energy analysts question whether the intensifying push to use corn as a fuel will gradually deplete supplies needed for more traditional uses, potentially driving up food prices. Last year, about 14 percent of the nation's corn went into ethanol production, compared with 11 percent four years ago. This year, the volume of corn for

Fossil Fuels Dominate Energy Consumption

Renewable-energy sources — including hydroelectric power, wood, waste, ethanol and biodiesel — accounted for only 6 percent of all energy consumed in the United States in 2004. Comparitively, fossil fuels — including oil, coal and natural gas — supplied nearly 90 percent of all energy consumed.

U.S. Energy Production and Consumption, 2004

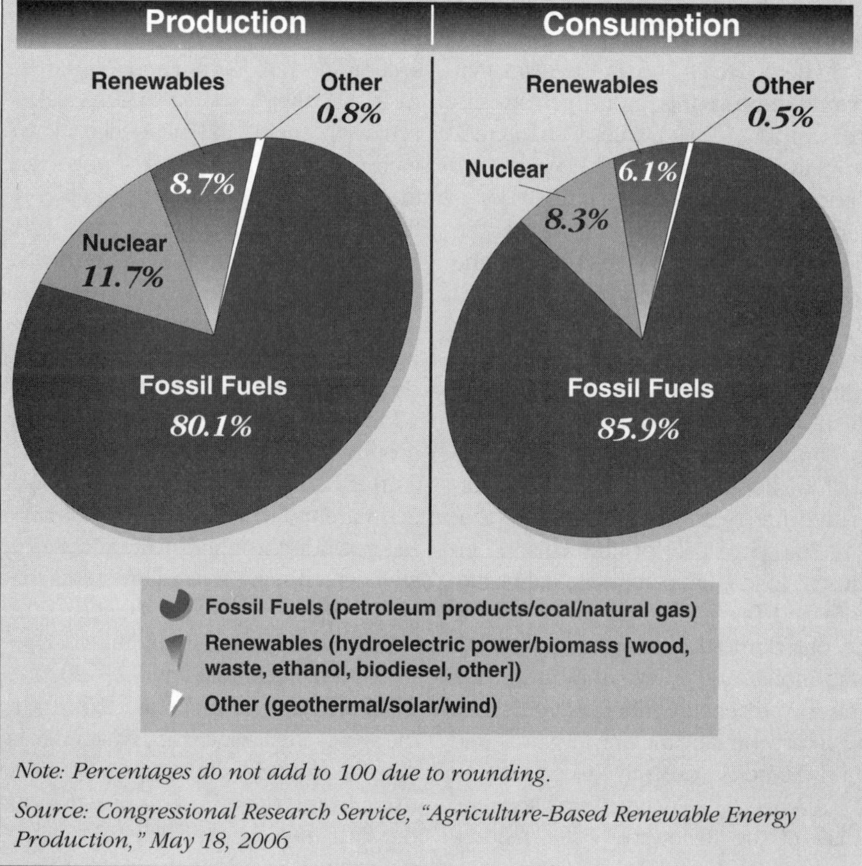

Note: Percentages do not add to 100 due to rounding.

Source: Congressional Research Service, "Agriculture-Based Renewable Energy Production," May 18, 2006

ethanol could rise to 19 percent, according to Department of Agriculture estimates. [14]

There also is a growing body of evidence suggesting that ethanol production consumes more energy than the finished fuel contains, which some critics say points to the need for alternative fuel sources.

"People tend to think of ethanol and see an endless cycle: Corn is used to produce ethanol, ethanol is burned and gives off carbon dioxide and corn uses the carbon dioxide as it grows. But that isn't the case. Fossil fuel actually drives the whole cycle," says University of California-Berkeley engineering Professor Tad Patzek. "Taking grain apart, fermenting it, distilling it and extruding it uses a lot of fossil energy. We are grasping at a solution that is by far the least efficient." [15]

Scientists like Patzek have been debating the costs-benefits of ethanol production for years. For instance, a study by Alexander Farrell — another engineering professor at Patzek's school — reached the opposite conclusion.

And University of Minnesota researchers this summer released a comprehensive analysis of the energy needed to grow corn and soybeans and convert them into biofuels. Writing in the *Proceedings of the National Academies of Sciences*, they concluded that both corn-based ethanol and biodiesel produced from soybeans generate more energy than is needed to produce them. However, while biodiesel from soybeans returns 93 percent more energy than is used to produce it, corn-based ethanol provides only 25 percent more energy. [16]

David Tilman, a coauthor of the study, says ethanol is a good first-generation fuel but eventually could be superceded by commodities that deliver better energy and environmental returns. He points to switchgrass, mixed prairie grasses, woody plants and other cellulose sources that cost less than corn because they can be produced on marginally productive land and require less fertilizer and pesticide. Tilman's findings are echoed by the Union of Concerned Scientists, which estimates corn ethanol reduces greenhouse gas emissions by only 10 to 20 percent per unit of energy delivered, compared to as much as 80 to 90 percent for cellulosic ethanol.

But development of a cellulose-based ethanol industry is years away because of technical challenges in converting the crops into fermentable sugar. Although pilot plants have been established, only a single commercial facility, in Ottawa, Canada, is in operation — using wheat straw. The U.S. Department of Energy estimates using enzymes to break down cellulosic raw material costs 30 to 50 cents per gallon compared to a few cents for corn-based ethanol. If new technology brings cellulosic enzyme costs down to less than 5 cents per gallon, it would have a distinct price advantage over corn-based ethanol. But experts say such breakthroughs may be a decade away. [17]

Meanwhile, officials predict biotechnology advances will continue to improve corn-crop yields, and next-generation processing plants will convert raw materials into fuel more efficiently. Farmers will shift acreage to corn from less profitable crops like soybeans and cotton. And corn growers say because long-term demand for corn as livestock feed is expected to be relatively flat, the net result will be abundant harvests that will satisfy the need for both food and fuel at a reasonable price.

"The increased use of ethanol in our nation's fuel supply is not the singular answer for America's dangerous dependence on foreign oil. However, ethanol is already playing an important role in our nation's overall energy policy and will play an integral part in finding a long-term energy-security solution," says the growers association's Noel.

Getty Images/Scott Olson

Hybrid corn growing near Freeport, Ill., produces about 4 percent more ethanol than other varieties. A bushel of corn produces about 2.7 gallons of ethanol. Congress this year mandated that refiners use 7.5 billion gallons of renewable fuels annually by 2012.

Should the federal government be doing more to promote the ethanol industry?

President Bush's State of the Union endorsement of renewable fuels and his goal of reducing the nation's need for imported oil by 5 million barrels a day by 2025 have unleashed a variety of new government-sponsored initiatives to promote renewable-energy research and development.

His fiscal 2007 budget request sought $359.2 million for the Department of Energy's Renewable Energy Program — a 30.5 percent, increase over 2006 funding levels — and there are indications Congress will meet or exceed the request. The administration also is contributing $160 million over the next three years to build cellulosic biorefineries to make ethanol from corn stalks, wheat straw, switchgrass or other commonly available biomass.

But the far bigger contribution to renewable-energy development comes in the form of tax credits, mandates and subsidies that have been included in energy and farm bills and as amendments to the Clean Air Act for more than a decade. For example, the energy bill Congress passed last year included tax breaks for ethanol, biodiesel, solar, geothermal and other renewable-energy sources totaling $3.4 billion over 10 years. [18]

Such assistance tends to trigger intense debates over the viability of renewable fuels. Critics — including fiscal conservatives and groups opposed to government waste — fear the future of alternative products will be influenced by political considerations instead of market realities and that many of the most heavily subsidized products will never turn a profit or be able to compete head-to-head with fossil fuels. Moreover, the generous taxpayer assistance is benefiting big corporations, not just small refiners and family farmers. Agriculture giant Archer Daniels Midland's earnings for the quarter that ended June 30 more than doubled because of increased demand for crop-based fuels, while its revenues rose 1 percent, to $9.6 billion.

"If ethanol is to succeed as a motor fuel, it will have to be the cheapest ethanol globally available," says Ben Lieberman, a senior economic-policy analyst at the conservative Heritage Foundation. "Consumers would benefit if the market, not special-interest politics, decided how much ethanol to use and where it should come from." Lieberman believes Congress should repeal laws that levy tariffs and duties on cheap foreign ethanol instead of continuing to subsidize the domestic ethanol industry.

But ethanol advocates point out that government subsidies for renewable energy comprise only a fraction of the tax breaks and subsidies extended to the fossil fuel industry. Congress in recent years has promoted oil and gas development, including, for example, a provision in the 2004 corporate tax bill that made domestic drilling eligible for a 3-percentage-point reduction in the top tax rate for manufacturing — from 35 percent to 32 percent. And last year's energy bill allowed oil and gas companies to pay lower royalty fees for marginally productive wells and reduced royalty payments for gas wells in shallow waters in the Gulf of Mexico. It also allowed electric utilities to write off billions of dollars' worth of air-pollution equipment on older power plants and accelerated to 15 years — from 20 years — the depreciation period for property used in the transmission of electricity. [19]

Renewable-fuel proponents say subsidies for the industry are in the national interest because they help create a homegrown industry that over time will insulate Americans from global energy price shocks. Thus Congress and presidential administrations must continue with long-term funding commitments to help their industry compete, they argue.

"As the industry expands outside the traditional Corn Belt, more and more Americans will be able to invest in and realize the benefits of a stronger energy future," says Bob Dinneen, president of the Renewable Fuels Association.

But some in the Bush administration are struggling with competing impulses to prop up renewable fuels and at the same time subject them to market forces. Energy Secretary Bodman this summer broached the idea of scrapping the 51-cent-per-gallon ethanol production tax credit if the industry grows larger and fuel supplies are plentiful.

"The question to me that I think deserves a discussion is the nature of the subsidy, how long it should stay," Bodman said during a June telephone news conference. "Right now it's geared to stay for another four years through the year 2010. . . . And what happens after that, and what kind of a picture should we be working on? To me those are the key questions and the areas that will, I think, determine the ultimate volumes of ethanol available to our taxpayers."

Though political support for the tax credit is likely to remain strong, Bodman's comments reflect the unease felt in some quarters over how long the government should prop up a growing industry — and what federal policymakers should do if demand for ethanol doesn't match supplies. There is pressure within the energy community to spread the wealth and expand government support for other renewable resources, including wind, solar and geothermal energy.

The popularity of renewable fuels also is triggering a debate over the manner in which Congress awards funding for research into renewable energy. Lawmakers increasingly are "earmarking" funds for specific projects in their states and districts, particularly in the areas of biomass, hydrogen and wind energy research. Because of spending caps, the designations — which usually go to colleges and universities or government labs in home districts — result in corresponding cuts to the size of government grants awarded competitively to researchers from elsewhere in the country. [20] An analysis by the American Academy for the Advancement of Science (AAAS) found that energy-research earmarks in the fiscal 2006 spending bills more than doubled — to $266 million — over 2005 levels. [21]

"With the fiscal situation unlikely to get better in the fiscal 2007 budget, congressional appropriators will have to square demands for earmarked funds against tight spending targets once again," the AAAS noted. "With the Bush administration unlikely to expend political capital against earmarking, the push for earmarking the R&D budget will not abate in 2007." ■

Background

Alcohol Fuels

The earliest efforts to promote alternative fuels in the United States did not take place in the Midwest, but in New Hampshire. Mill owner Samuel Morey, who was fond of tinkering with steam engines, developed a rudimentary internal combustion engine in 1823 that ran on ethanol and turpentine. It soon proved popular with farmers, who maintained stills on their land to turn crop waste into lamp oil and other kinds of fuel for household use. German engineer Nicholas Otto developed a more refined version of Morey's invention in 1860, again using ethanol as the propellant. By mid-century, grain alcohol had become a major illuminating fuel in the United States. [22]

The Civil War, however, abruptly put an end to ethanol use. The Union placed a $2-per-gallon excise tax on ethanol to pay for war costs. Americans quickly switched to cheaper kerosene, leaving ethanol in the shadows for most of the remainder of the 19th century. Commercial prospects for the fuel only began to revive in 1896, when Henry Ford used pure ethanol to power his first automobile, called the quadricycle. A little over a decade later, Ford began producing the widely popular Model T, which was a flexible-fuel vehicle, meaning it could run on ethanol, gasoline or a combination of the two. However, ethanol's market potential from the beginning of the 20th century on would be influenced more by U.S. government policies and global events than by homegrown technologies.

In 1906 Congress decided to lift the excise tax it had imposed half a century earlier, allowing ethanol to compete head-to-head with gasoline. The outbreak of World War I intensified demand for all fuels, prompting ethanol demand to peak at 50 to 60 million gallons annually. But in 1919, a year after the war's end, Prohibition put an end to widespread distribution, leaving gasoline the fuel of choice. Though some refiners continued to use ethanol to increase gasoline's octane rating and eliminate engine knocking, many in the oil industry worried they were turning filling stations into speakeasies and decided to instead add lead to motor fuels to boost the octane.

The end of Prohibition and the outbreak of World War II again revived ethanol's fortunes. During the 1930s, more than 2,000 filling stations in the Midwest sold a gasoline blended with 6 to 12 percent ethanol, known as gasohol. Non-fuel wartime manufacturing needs further drove up demand. But the fuel's fortunes took another nosedive at the end of the war, when demand for fuels fell sharply, accompanied by low gasoline prices. From the late 1940s to the late 1970s, virtually no commercial ethanol fuel could be purchased in the United States.

Continued on p. 805

Chronology

1900-1960s

Fuel demand surges during the world wars, but renewables can't compete with fossil fuels.

1908
Ford's Model T becomes the first mass-produced vehicle capable of running on gasoline, ethanol or a combination of the two.

1917-1918
Wartime demand for ethanol surges to 60 million gallons per year.

1919
Prohibition squelches ethanol's commercial viability. In the next decade, oil companies toy with using it to eliminate knocking in engines and raise the octane rating, but turn to lead instead, fearing gas stations will become speakeasies.

1930s
The end of Prohibition revives ethanol's place in the market. More than 2,000 gas stations in the Midwest begin selling gasohol, a blend consisting of between 6 percent and 12 percent ethanol.

1941-1945
World War II again drives up demand for fuel, but increased use of ethanol is largely for non-fuel, manufacturing purposes.

1945-1970s
Low fuel prices through the 1960s again drive down ethanol's attractiveness as a fuel.

1970s

The Arab oil embargo, the fall of the shah of Iran and increased environmental awareness spark interest in alternative fuels.

1974
The first legislative effort to promote ethanol as a fuel — the Solar Energy Research, Development and Demonstration Act — leads to widespread research into ways of converting cellulose into fuel.

1975
The government begins to phase out the use of lead as a fuel additive, making ethanol more attractive as a substitute to boost octane.

1979
Amoco Oil Co. begins selling alcohol-blended fuels and is quickly followed by other major oil companies. Congress approves spending some $1 billion on biomass-related projects.

1980s

Congress extends subsidies and tax breaks to spur renewable-fuel production. But market forces discourage widespread use of renewables.

1984
There are 163 ethanol plants in the United States — a response to tax benefits and government-backed loans approved by Congress the previous four years.

1985-1986
The Organization of Petroleum Exporting Countries (OPEC), responding to lower U.S. demand and competition from non-OPEC oil producers, cuts prices. Ethanol producers, in turn, begin receiving very low prices for their products, despite a 60-cent-per-gallon production credit, and many go out of business. In Denver, ethanol is used for the first time as an oxygenate in the winter to tamp down carbon monoxide emissions.

1987
The Austrian company Gaskoks acquires South African technology and opens the first commercial biodiesel plant.

1990s-Present

States and the federal government mandate that fleet vehicles use more renewable fuels. Tight oil supplies and occasional supply disruptions spur more interest in alternative fuels.

1998
The ethanol subsidy is extended through 2007, but its size is gradually reduced, from 54-cents-per-gallon to the current 51-cents-per-gallon.

1999-2000
Some states ban use of the fuel additive MTBE because it is showing up in groundwater. The Environmental Protection Agency (EPA) in 2000 recommends the product be phased out nationally.

2004-2005
Violence in the Middle East, a standoff over Iran's nuclear program, rising anti-American sentiment in Venezuela and surging energy demand from China and India raise new concerns about American energy security and the continuity of supplies. Hurricanes Katrina and Rita knock out about 5 million barrels of refining capacity in summer 2005. Congress mandates that refiners use 7.5 billion gallons of renewable fuels annually by 2012.

2006
President George W. Bush promotes renewable fuels and other alternative sources of energy, saying America must be weaned from its appetite for foreign oil.

Drivers Can't Find Enough Ethanol Stations

With great fanfare, Gov. Mitch Daniels announced plans recently to designate the hamlet of Reynolds, Ind., as "BioTown USA" and make it the first community in the United States to meet all its needs with renewable energy.

"We are taking challenges and turning them into opportunities by developing homegrown, local energy production," the first-term Republican governor declared. State officials recruited General Motors to provide free, two-year leases on 20 ethanol-burning cars and generous discounts to locals who purchased flexible-fuel vehicles capable of running on gasoline or E85 — a fuel consisting of 85 percent ethanol. Officials also encouraged the local filling station to install pumps dispensing E85 and biodiesel fuel. [1]

But a year later, the 550 residents of Reynolds are trying to make sense of their unique status. Though residents wound up buying 135 ethanol-burning cars, operators of the filling station balked at the half-million-dollar estimated cost of installing the necessary pumps and decided to sell the business. Drivers determined enough to travel 80 miles to Indianapolis could find ethanol on sale at only two filling stations — but for not much less than regular gas because of a sharp spike in prices for the alternative fuel.

AP Photo/John Harrell

Hog farmer William Schroeder of Reynolds, Ind., may sell the waste generated from his 20,000 hogs for use in the "BioTown USA" experiment. Gov. Mitch Daniels wants Reynolds to be the first U.S. community to meet all its needs with renewable energy.

"We need the alternatives to get away from the foreign oil," said insurance agent Gary Dedaker, who owns two flexible-fuel trucks but has not yet been able to use ethanol. "As we get more plants, I think prices will go down." [2]

The experience in Reynolds is being mirrored elsewhere in the Midwest. Though E85 is available at more than 850 service stations nationwide, drivers cannot find enough of it in contiguous locations to make it a viable alternative to gasoline. Those who can often don't buy ethanol-based fuels unless they are significantly cheaper than regular gasoline, because ethanol only delivers three-quarters as much energy per gallon, meaning more frequent fill-ups. [3]

The availability raises serious questions about how much federal and state governments have to spend to create an adequate infrastructure for ethanol. Iowa, the nation's biggest corn producer, this year began giving retailers a 25-cent-per-gallon tax credit for selling E85, and is paying as much as half the cost of installing necessary pumps. In Illinois, Democratic Gov. Rod Blagojevich has proposed spending $30 million to add 900 pumps by 2011. Even if that works, huge gaps remain. Ethanol is unavailable on most of America's two coasts and in New England.

Analysts say motorists frequently don't know enough about the availability of the fuel — and, in some cases, whether their vehicles can burn it — to generate sustained demand. Without steady business, even filling station owners in the heart of the Corn Belt are taking a wait-and-see approach, installing pumps when they do largely to support local corn growers. Promotional efforts remain scattershot. In June, Ford Motor Co. and VeraSun Energy, a large ethanol producer, christened 300 miles of interstate between Chicago and St. Louis the "Midwest Ethanol Corridor." Some automakers are giving away $1,000 of free fuel to purchasers of flexible-fuel vehicles.

Part of the problem is timing. Federal and state mandates have prompted refiners in recent years to stop using the chemical MTBE as a fuel additive and instead look to ethanol as a replacement. That drove up demand for the product and raised prices for fuels like E85. Retailers say the result was that ethanol sales tended to rise when gasoline prices crested above $3 per gallon. Below that, customers usually stuck with traditional fossil fuels. During the peak summer driving season, with prices for unleaded regular hovering around $3, ethanol typically was selling for about 40 cents per gallon less, according to spot checks conducted in the Midwest.

Many residents in rural communities in the heartland remain optimistic the home-grown fuel will become commercially viable. In Biotown USA, they are even contemplating other sources of energy production, including burning methane gas from the town's sewer system and nearby hog farms to create electricity for homes and businesses.

"We're addicted to oil," says Charlie Van Voorst, Reynolds' town council president. "It would be nice if we were addicted to ethanol."

[1] For background, see J. K. Wall, "Ethanol Test Town Has . . . No Ethanol," *The Indianapolis Star*, Aug. 27, 2006.

[2] *Ibid.*

[3] See Alexei Barrionuevo, "Fill Up on Corn If You Can," *The New York Times*, Aug. 31, 2006, p. C1.

Continued from p. 802

The 1973 Arab oil embargo ushered in a new era for renewable fuels. [23] Energy costs surged in the aftermath of the embargo as the cost of imported crude oil roughly tripled. Making matters worse, federal price controls kept the price of domestic production below market prices. The policy, designed to insulate consumers from some price increases, instead discouraged oil companies from making fuel at home and intensified the nation's reliance on imported oil. The fall of the shah of Iran in 1979 and the Iranian Revolution subsequently reduced the flow of Iranian oil to world markets, creating more supply disruptions and spurring Carter administration efforts to promote conservation, including the first fuel-economy standards. [24] Oil companies, led by Amoco, began selling alcohol-blended fuels, and Congress began supporting research into alternative fuels.

From 1980 to 1984, Congress enacted a series of tax breaks to ethanol producers and blenders and also placed a tariff on imported ethanol. The number of ethanol plants increased to 163 by 1984, and tax writers in the House and Senate increased the ethanol production subsidy to 60 cents per gallon. Officials in Denver, Colo., christened a new use for the product by mandating that ethanol-containing oxygenated fuels be used in wintertime to control carbon monoxide emissions.

But world events again intruded on ethanol's fortunes. Faced with declining market share and revenues, the OPEC oil cartel increased production in the mid-1980s, thus lowering the price of its products. In 1985 and 1986, refining costs for imported oil plunged from $27 per barrel to $14 per barrel, leaving ethanol unable to compete.

And though imported crude prices shot up again during the first Gulf War, OPEC continued to assure long-term demand by boosting production whenever there was a loss of supplies.

Despite tough market conditions in the 1990s, Washington policymakers continued to support the ethanol industry by requiring that certain car fleets purchase alternative-fuel vehicles, mandating wintertime use of oxygenated fuels and exempting alternative fuels from some excise taxes. The ethanol production tax credit was extended several times, though gradually reduced to the current 51-cents-per-gallon level. Enthusiasm for the fuel extended to states, which began banning the rival fuel additive MTBE over concerns that it was contributing to widespread groundwater contamination.

Ethanol Production Grows Rapidly

U.S. ethanol production began after the 1970s energy crises and rose steadily, sparked by the Energy Tax Act of 1978, which gave ethanol a partial exemption from the motor fuels excise tax, and the Clean Air Act Amendments of 1990, which favored ethanol blended with gasoline. New government incentives are expected to spur continued production growth through at least 2010.

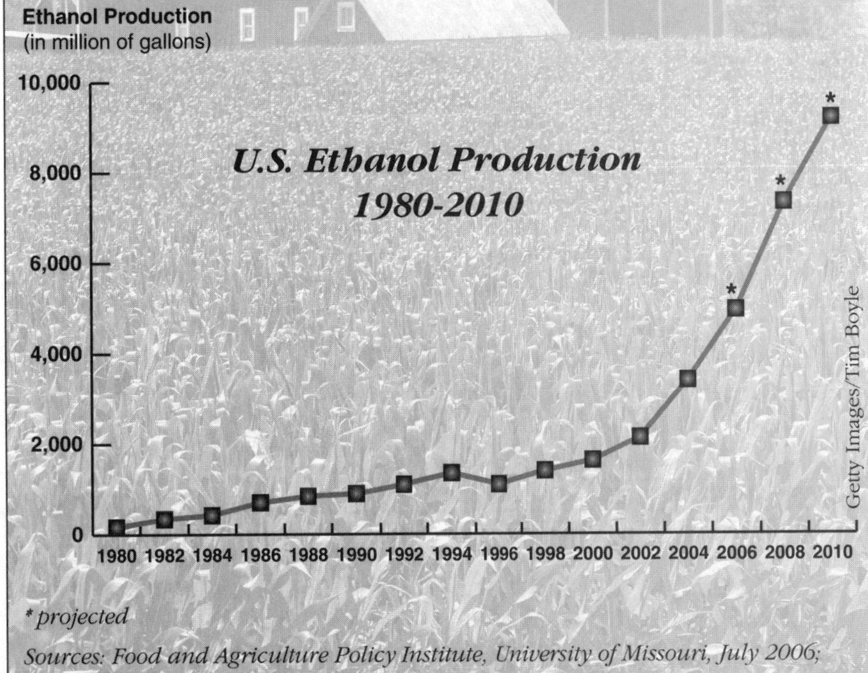

* projected

Sources: Food and Agriculture Policy Institute, University of Missouri, July 2006; Renewable Fuels Association

Biodiesel

Like ethanol, biodiesel's roots extend back to the 19th century. Rudolf Diesel introduced the first diesel engine — an iron cylinder with a flywheel in the base — in Germany in 1893, using peanut oil to power the device. He predicted in a 1912 speech that vegetable-oil fuels would become as prevalent as gasoline. But by the 1920s, manufacturers were designing diesel engines to run on lower viscosity fossil fuels, which were cheaper than biofuels.

Interest in biodiesel didn't re-emerge until the late 1970s in South Africa, where chemists processed and refined sun-

Getty Images/Andre Vieira (both)

From Cane to Car

Abundant supplies of sugar cane have made Brazil the world's biggest ethanol producer. This distillation plant is in prosperous São Paulo state (top). Wielding machetes, Brazilian cane cutters take down the last stalks in a field (bottom).

flower oil. The Austrian company Gaskoks acquired the technology and established the first biodiesel pilot plant in 1987. Throughout the 1990s, production gradually expanded through Europe as bus and truck fleets modified their vehicles to run on the fuel and automakers including Renault and Peugeot developed vehicles that could run on diesel fuel blended with up to 30 percent biodiesel. Since 1999, annual U.S. production of the fuel has increased 75-fold — from less than 1 million gallons in 1999 to about 75 million gallons in 2005, made almost entirely from soybeans. The National Biodiesel Board, a trade group, says as of mid-2006 there were 65 companies producing the fuel and another 50 either building or contemplating plants.

Government biodiesel supports are similar to those for ethanol and include a production tax credit of $1 per gallon used in the blending of petroleum-based diesel fuel. Manufacturers producing less than 60 million gallons a year are entitled to a small-producer income tax credit of 10 cents per gallon for the first 15 million gallons. Despite the support, the outlook for continued support for biodiesel is murky; the production tax credit expires in 2008, leaving little time for the industry to develop. In addition, vegetable-oil feedstocks like soybeans, sunflower or rapeseed are less abundant than corn and other sources of ethanol. And biodiesel suffers from a limited ability to substitute for oil imports, even if market conditions warrant it. A hypothetical federal mandate that biodiesel make up 1 percent of current vehicle diesel fuel use would exhaust most available vegetable oils and animal fats and require manufacturers to find an additional 1.3 billion pounds of oil.

"The bottom line is that a small increase in demand for fats and oils for biodiesel production could quickly exhaust available feedstock supplies and push vegetable-oil prices significantly higher due to the low elasticity of demand for vegetable oils in food consumption," the Congressional Research Service concluded in a recent report. "At the same time, it would begin to disturb feed markets." [25] ■

CURRENT SITUATION

Blocked by 'Pork'

Though the Bush administration and Congress have expressed strong support for renewable fuels, government efforts to spur production are highly contingent on the annual congressional appropriations process. And proposed cuts in fiscal 2007 spending are hampering efforts by the Environmental Protection Agency (EPA) to finalize the rule that actually would expand use of the products in gasoline. On Sept. 7 the EPA officially proposed a rule requiring that 3.71 percent of gasoline demand in 2007 come from renewable sources. In keeping with the goals of last year's energy bill, the agency also said it wants to cut petroleum use by 3.9 million gallons by 2012 and correspondingly reduce greenhouse-gas emissions by 14 million tons annually. [26]

House and Senate appropriators, however, refuse to match the administration's request for $11.4 million to implement the regulation, in part because their versions of the fiscal 2007 Interior-Environment spending bill contain hundreds of millions of dollars for earmarked projects directed at their home states and districts. William Wehrum, the EPA's acting chief of air and radiation, says tight budgets have forced the agency to adjust its agenda accordingly, including delaying regulations designed to curtail emissions from locomotive and marine-diesel engines. Though renewable-fuel standards remain high on EPA's to-do list, Wehrum warns, "What we may or may not do in the future depends on what Congress eventually appropriates." Final spending figures are not expected until after the November elections.

Any delays in setting a nationwide target for ethanol use raise concerns within some quarters of the energy industry because they could give rise to a patchwork of state ethanol standards that would complicate oil companies' ability to efficiently deliver fuels. As of mid-2006, six states had set their own standards for blending ethanol with other fuels, and at least 16 others were considering similar moves, according to the Renewable Fuels Association.

Oil companies predict they will encounter bottlenecks and periodic shortages as they try to ship ethanol-blended gasoline to certain regions. The gloomy scenario is reminiscent of the one the industry predicted when it argued against the use of so-called boutique fuels — gasoline blends designed to improve air quality in some parts of the country. However, oil companies say ethanol standards pose a bigger problem because political support for the fuel is intense, and anticipated usage will dwarf that of other alternative fuels. [27]

"If every gallon has to have 5 percent or 10 percent ethanol, that is a problem that absolutely has to be addressed," says Edward Murphy, group director for downstream and industry operations at the American Petroleum Institute, a trade group representing oil companies.

But many are skeptical of the oil companies' claims. The Renewable Fuels Association's Dinneen says blending ethanol with gasoline does not require a special grade of gas from refiners and does not add to the complexity of the fuel-distribution system. State regulators, however, argue that legislatures have a right to set fuel standards, whether to promote cleaner air, local agriculture or both.

Ethanol Comes With a High Price Tag

Corn-based ethanol produces less energy per gallon and is the most expensive alternative fuel, costing 52 cents more per gallon than gasoline.

Energy and Price Comparisons for Alternative Fuels
(as of February 2006)

Fuel Type	BTUs per gallon*	GEG**	Average Price ($/GEG)
Gasoline	125,071	1.00	$2.23
Ethanol (E85)	90,383	0.72	$2.75
Diesel Fuel	138,690	1.11	$2.31
Biodiesel	138,690	1.11	$2.38
Propane	91,333	0.74	$2.68

** A Btu (British thermal unit) is a measure of the heat content of a fuel and indicates the amount of energy contained in the fuel.*

*** Gasoline-equivalent gallon (GEG) is the amount of BTUs in a gallon of fuel, compared to the BTUs in a gallon of gasoline.*

Source: Congressional Research Service, "Agriculture-Based Renewable Energy Production," May 18, 2006

New Technologies

While regulators sort out options for renewable-fuel standards, the Big Three automakers are getting on the ethanol bandwagon by accelerating plans to roll out flexible-fuel vehicles. General Motors Corp., Ford Motor Co. and DaimlerChrysler's Chrysler Group jointly announced on June 28 they will double production of cars and trucks capable of running on ethanol blends and other biofuels by 2010. The companies to date have produced about 5 million flexible-fuel vehicles; the commitment would lead to 2 million annually by decade's end. General Motors also has plans to produce hydrogen fuel cell-powered vehicles as soon as 2011. The company says it will use up to $9 billion freed up as part of a recent corporate restructuring to fund the efforts. [28]

Europeans Embrace Biofuels

While the United States is just beginning to view biofuel as a viable alternative to petroleum, Europeans already are embracing ethanol and biodiesel as mainstays at the gas pump. Indeed, the popularity of agriculture-based fuels is forcing European Union (EU) members increasingly to look abroad to satisfy demand for both raw materials and finished product.

With robust economic growth between 1985 and 2004, European demand for transportation fuels rose by nearly 50 percent, forcing governments to import more oil. But two factors prompted governments to seek a clean-burning alternative that could provide some measure of energy security: concerns about possible supply disruptions and Kyoto Protocol mandates to reduce greenhouse-gas emissions. [1]

In 2003, the European Commission set a voluntary goal of deriving at least 2 percent of energy needs from biofuels by the end of 2005 and growing that share by 0.75 percent each year until the end of 2010.

Most of the activity has centered on expanding supplies of biodiesel, which is manufactured primarily from rapeseed oil but also from animal fats and even left-over restaurant grease. Total European rapeseed production this year is projected at 15.3 million tons, with the highest yields coming from Poland and the Baltic states. Oilseed-crushing plants are being built throughout the continent. But agriculture experts say future production is constrained by a lack of suitable land for growing and the high cost of growing and processing raw materials. As a result, Europe is looking abroad for raw materials and a more diverse mix of alternative fuels. [2]

EU nations have built a burgeoning ethanol trade with Pakistan, which in recent years has accounted for 20 percent of Europe's ethanol imports. Other ethanol-exporting countries include Guatemala, Peru, Bolivia, Ecuador, Nicaragua and Panama, as well as South Africa, the Republic of Congo and Egypt. The raw materials, or feedstocks, used to create ethanol run the gamut — from molasses (Pakistan) to sugar cane (Latin America and South Africa) to sugar beets, wheat, corn and rye (Europe).

Trade in biodiesel has not evolved yet because there is no significant production outside of Europe. But to relax pressure on domestic rapeseed-oil production, European biodiesel producers are importing other raw materials, such as palm oil from Malaysia. And because Europe doesn't produce large amounts of soybeans — another biodiesel raw material — it is turning to Brazil, whose crop is desirable because of its high protein and oil content and the country's long growing seasons.

But Europeans are wary of becoming too reliant on overseas markets for their alternative fuels. Researchers are developing new technologies to convert cellulose fibers into ethanol. Royal Dutch Shell and the German biodiesel innovator Choren Industries also are pioneering a gasification process that converts wood or grass into carbon monoxide and hydrogen, then uses catalysts to chemically reassemble the gases into a diesel fuel.

"Second-generation biofuels require further technology development that may take another 10 years or so," said Andre Faiij, an associate professor at Copernicus University at Utrecht University in the Netherlands, who studies energy supplies. "The new generation of technologies emerging will really tip the balance." [3]

[1] For background see Mary Cooper, "Global Warming Treaty," *CQ Researcher*, Jan. 26, 2001, pp. 41-64. The treaty, which the U.S. did not ratify, went into force on Feb. 15, 2005.

[2] See "European Union Biofuels Policy and Agriculture: An Overview," Congressional Research Service Report No. RS22404, March 16, 2006.

[3] Quoted in Christopher Knight, "New Alchemy: Grass Into Fuel," *International Herald-Tribune*, Sept. 18, 2006, p. 12.

The domestic automakers see flexible-fuel vehicles as a way of enhancing their environmental credentials and competing with Asian rivals, particularly Toyota Motor Corp. and Honda Motor Co., which have capitalized on the burgeoning market for hybrid autos that run on a combination of electric and gas-powered engines. Energy analyst Book notes that flexible-fuel vehicles are considerably cheaper to make than hybrids, which require the use of advanced electronic systems and, usually, an extensive redesign of the vehicle.

"It costs carmakers just a few hundred dollars to turn a regular car into a flexible-fuel vehicle," Book says. "The people who are worried about their energy costs aren't going to pay thousands of dollars extra for a hybrid. For the [maximum] publicity yield, committing to flexible-fuel vehicles is the best bargain."

The car industry isn't alone in adapting technology to promote ethanol. Agriculture companies are beginning to genetically tweak the corn plant so that it can begin to convert itself into the fuel, by adding an enzyme that currently has to be introduced at ethanol-processing plants. The companies also are trying to reduce the amount of lignin in corn, the substance that enables plants to stand upright but which can block conversion of cellulose into ethanol. [29]

Companies such as Monsanto and Pioneer HiBred, a subsidiary of DuPont, say the work represents an extension of ongoing genetic engineering designed to boost agricultural yields and make plants resistant to pests and herbicides. In the case of ethanol, officials say crop science can be used to increase the fermentable starch content of certain corn plants, potentially increasing their production potential 2 percent to 5 percent over other varieties. [30]

Perhaps the most dramatic genetic modification has arisen from research by agriculture giant Syngenta that yielded a technique for coaxing corn into making amylase, an enzyme that breaks down starch into sugar, which is then fermented into ethanol. Syngenta inserted

Continued on p. 810

At Issue:

Should the government continue to promote ethanol as an alternative to imported oil?

SEN. RICHARD G. LUGAR, R-IND.
CHAIRMAN, FOREIGN RELATIONS COMMITTEE

FROM SPEECH TO THE BROOKINGS INSTITUTION, MARCH 13, 2006

yes

For decades, the energy debate in this country has pitted so-called pro-oil realists against idealistic advocates of alternative energy. The pro-oil commentators have attempted to discredit alternatives by saying they make up a tiny share of energy consumed and that dependence on oil is a choice of the marketplace. They assert that our government can and should do little to change this. They have implied that those who have bemoaned oil dependency do not understand that every energy alternative comes with its own problems and limitations.

Indeed, advocates of alternative energy must resist the rhetorical temptations to suggest that energy problems are easily solved. They are not. Relieving our dependence on oil in any meaningful way is going to take much greater investments of time, money and political will. There is no silver-bullet solution. . . .

We have entered a different energy era that requires a much different response than in past decades. What is needed is an urgent national campaign led by a succession of presidents and congresses who will ensure that American ingenuity and resources are fully committed to this problem.

We could take our time if this were merely a matter of accomplishing an industrial conversion to more cost-effective technologies. Unfortunately, U.S. dependence on fossil fuels and their growing scarcity worldwide have already created conditions that are threatening our security and prosperity and undermining international stability. In the absence of revolutionary changes in energy policy, we are risking multiple disasters for our country that will constrain living standards, undermine our foreign policy goals and leave us highly vulnerable to the machinations of rogue states. . . .

As alternative fuels become more competitive, oil and gas producers have strong incentive to drop prices to kill the competition. Investors need to know that alternative-energy initiatives will continue to be competitive. A revenue-neutral $35-per-barrel price floor on oil would provide the security investors need. At this price, alternative fuels like cellulosic ethanol, shale and tar sands oil and diesel could still compete with regular gasoline.

Long-term energy security also requires the use of clean energy. As long as we continue to consume fuels that do not burn cleanly or cannot have their damaging gases sequestered, we will continue to pay environmental costs and will remain vulnerable to a climate-change-induced disaster.

JERRY TAYLOR
SENIOR FELLOW IN ENERGY POLICY AND ENVIRONMENTAL PROTECTION, CATO INSTITUTE, WWW.CATO.ORG

no

When politicians talk about energy independence, the conversation quickly turns to renewable energy. And rightly so. The U.S. consumes a bit beyond 20 million barrels of oil every day, but it produces only about 5 million barrels a day. At present, there is no way to achieve self-sufficiency regardless of how carefully we pinch our gasoline pennies or how aggressively we unleash the domestic oil industry.

Accordingly, if we want to achieve energy independence, it's going to mean giving up oil and moving to something else. Conservatives often talk about nuclear energy as the best prescription for energy independence. Liberals, on the other hand, rhapsodize about the glories of solar and wind power. But no matter how you feel about those technologies, they have virtually no impact on energy independence or the price of gasoline.

We use oil primarily to make transportation fuels and chemicals, whereas we use nuclear, solar and wind power to generate electricity. Until we achieve some fairly arresting breakthroughs in battery-powered technology, most of the alternative fuels we're betting on to break our so-called oil addiction are placebos.

Unfortunately, there is nothing on the horizon that comes close to gasoline as far as cost and performance are concerned. Consider the fact that taxes in Europe put gasoline prices at $5 to $8 per gallon. If alternatives to gasoline had economic merit, they would surely have arisen in Europe.

Ethanol made out of corn is probably the closest thing we have to a domestic alternative to gasoline. But no matter how nice "growing our own fuel" might be in theory, it's uneconomically expensive. Even after 30 years of lavish federal subsidy, ethanol (defined as fuel that is nine parts gasoline and one part ethanol) has only managed to capture a bit more than 3 percent of the automotive-fuels market.

One might think the current run on gasoline prices would have narrowed the cost gap, but one would be wrong. It takes a tremendous amount of energy to grow corn and a lot of energy to distill it into ethanol and get it into the market. Accordingly, rising energy prices have made ethanol more expensive.

Technological breakthroughs in the ethanol business are, of course, possible. And beyond harnessing oil and plants for fuel, we can move cars by compressed natural gas, hydrogen (via fuel cells), coal (by turning the black rock into liquid hydrocarbons) and, of course, with electricity.

For the time being, however, cheap fuel means gasoline. Mandating a switch — given current technology — would increase, not decrease, pump prices.

Continued from p. 808

three genes from a microbe called archaea that lives on the sea floor, allowing the corn to make its own amylase. Officials say that because the deep-sea organism lives near hot-water vents, the ethanol plants processing the corn can operate at higher temperatures, increasing efficiency.

Similar efforts by Monsanto are aimed at producing a drought-resistant strain of switchgrass that has higher yields and can break down faster in ethanol production. Officials like the long-term potential of switchgrass and other inexpensive types of biomass because they require less fertilizer and irrigation than conventional corn.

Environmentalists increasingly worry, however, that genetically altered corn or soybeans will cross-pollinate in the wild and add undesirable traits to crops intended for food. Margaret Mellon, director of the food and environment program at the Union of Concerned Scientists, questions whether consumers will wind up eating products made from corn with extra enzymes, possibly derived from exotic microbes. Such a scenario took place in 2000, when StarLink corn, a product made by Aventis CropScience only for livestock use, ended up in human food products, prompting widespread recalls and disrupted exports.

Syngenta dismisses such concerns, saying enzymes like amylase are safe and are found naturally in saliva. But to play it safe, the company is seeking approval of its corn for both human and animal uses in the United States, Europe, South Africa and elsewhere. ■

AP Photo/Dennis Poroy

Singer Willie Nelson inaugurates his first "BioWillie" filling station in San Diego on Feb. 8, 2006. He launched his biodiesel fuel company in 2004 "to do something useful towards eliminating America's dependence on foreign oil, help put the American family farmer back to work and clean up the environment we live in." BioWillie fuel is a blend of 20 percent soybean-based biodiesel fuel and 80 percent commercial diesel.

OUTLOOK

Environmental Risks?

The debate over long-term use of renewable fuels increasingly involves concerns that expanded production will stretch the nation's agricultural resources thin, pose environmental risks and unleash other unintended side effects.

For instance, recent studies show that even if the entire U.S. corn crop were diverted to ethanol production, it would only provide enough fuel to replace about 12 percent of gasoline demand. Thus, alternative-fuels proponents face a fundamental dilemma: Making the products truly competitive with fossil fuels would require diverting existing crops from food or feed, cutting agricultural exports, finding new raw materials and possibly replacing some low-margin crops that don't play a role in the energy cycle.

"There will be some costs, there is no question about that," said Keith Collins, the Department of Agriculture's chief economist. "But it can be manageable, given the objective of reducing foreign oil imports." [31]

Collins estimates the nation's farmers will have to plant 90 million acres of corn by 2010 in order to fulfill demand for ethanol and livestock feeds and continue to satisfy export markets. He predicts the thirst for ethanol will remain strong as long as crude oil prices remain above $50 per barrel and corn prices do not rise considerably, because subsidies and improving economics of production ensure ethanol will produce a desirable rate of return. In the unlikely event crude prices dip below about $30 per barrel, Collins says there will be no incentive to produce ethanol at levels that exceed the congressionally mandated 7.5-billion gallon renewable-fuel standard.

But sustained demand for ethanol doesn't necessarily guarantee benefits for all sectors of American agriculture. If Collins' estimates about ethanol demand are correct, farmers would have to plant about 10 million acres more of corn than the average planted in 2005 or 2006. They would not undertake such a significant expansion unless corn prices rise to around $3.10 to $3.20 per bushel — near the record high. But those higher prices would likely reduce the attractiveness of American corn on export markets and threaten livestock producers, whose largest single expense is feed costs. Some of those producers, worried about higher operating expenses, already are broaching the idea of a "circuit breaker" mechanism that would temporarily suspend ethanol mandates and incentives if corn supplies get tight, for instance, during a widespread drought.

"We're not throwing a brick through the windshield of the ethanol industry or corn growers," says Kirk Ferrell, vice president of public policy for the National Pork Producers Council. "But we're saying these are concerns we need to look at." [32]

Some producers and their representatives in Congress advocate increasing production by growing corn on farmland that is sitting idle in conservation programs, exempting only the most environmentally sensitive land. The federal Conservation Reserve Program has 36 million acres set aside, and preliminary Agriculture Department estimates conclude between 4.3 million and 7.2 million acres of that amount could be used to grow corn for ethanol or soybeans for biodiesel in a sustainable way. House Agriculture Committee Chairman Robert W. Goodlatte, R-Va., who represents a poultry-growing district, and like-minded lawmakers are expected to explore the prospect when they begin a planned reauthorization of farm programs in 2007.

But placing more acres of corn into production concerns environmentalists, who blame agricultural runoff from Midwestern farms that runs down the Mississippi River for polluting the Gulf of Mexico. The advocacy organization Environmental Working Group says fertilizer-rich agricultural runoff carried into the Gulf has created a "dead zone" of oxygen-robbing algae blooms the size of New Jersey — ranging from 5,000 to 8,000 square miles — that has obliterated all marine life. The group is calling for more careful spending of agriculture subsidies, along with wetland restoration and the planting of more streamside buffers of grass and trees to absorb runoff.

But such concerns sometimes take a back seat in the political race to nurture the ethanol industry. In one sign of the enthusiasm for alternative fuels, the Center for American Progress, a liberal think tank based in Washington, has recommended that the United States produce 25 percent of liquid fuel consumption from renewable resources by 2025, putting it squarely in a camp with Republican farm-state lawmakers like Gutknecht and Goodlatte.

Unlike ethanol, biodiesel poses fewer immediate dilemmas, if only because the industry still is in a nascent state. The industry's long-term viability is highly dependent on the cost of feedstocks; it currently costs about $1.95 to produce a gallon of biodiesel from soybean oil, making it hard to compete with traditional diesel fuel. But government incentives and higher fuel prices are making the industry more profitable, raising more questions about whether agricultural supplies can keep up demand. Agriculture Department economist Collins says biodiesel is expected to account for 2.6 billion pounds, or 13 percent, of total soybean oil use this year — the amount extracted from 229 million bushels of soybeans — or 8 percent of domestic production.

Analysts and politicians predict economic analyses and cost-benefit considerations will play an increasingly prominent role in the next phase of the debate over renewable fuels. Optimistic market-watchers hope the increased popularity of ethanol, biodiesel and other products will place pressure on oil and gas producers to keep their prices low. But most suspect that volatile oil markets will continue to force Congress and future presidents to make tough policy choices in the years ahead.

Violence in the Middle East, anti-American sentiment in Venezuela, nuclear tensions in Iran and political upheaval in Nigeria and other oil-producing regions already have changed the way politicians approach energy policy, and how they view agriculture.

"Energy," says ethanol proponent Sen. Richard Lugar, R-Ind., "is the albatross of U.S. national security." ■

Notes

[1] See Russ Keen, "Ethanol Plant Digs In," *Aberdeen* (S.D.) *American News*, Sept. 22, 2006, p. A1.

[2] For background see Marcia Clemmitt, "Climate Change," *CQ Researcher*, Jan. 27, 2006, pp. 73-96.

[3] For background see Jennifer Weeks, "Domestic Energy Development," *CQ Researcher*, Sept. 30, 2005, pp. 809-832; and Mary H. Cooper, "Energy Security," *CQ Researcher*, Feb. 1, 2002, pp. 73-96.

[4] For background see John Cochran, "Fuel From the Farm," *CQ Weekly*, Aug. 7, 2006, pp. 2166-2174.

[5] See James Jordan and James Powell, "The False Hope of Biofuels," *The Washington Post*, July 2, 2006, p. B7.

About the Author

Adriel Bettelheim, regulatory editor at *CQ Weekly*, previously covered telecommunications, science and technology for the magazine. He also has been Washington correspondent for *The Denver Post*, a business reporter for the *Syracuse Herald-Journal* and a member of the *CQ Researcher* team that won the Society of Professional Journalists Award for Excellence for a 10-part series on health care. He is author of *Aging in America A to Z* (CQ Press, 2001). He graduated from Case Western Reserve University with a bachelor's degree in chemistry.

[6] For background see Mary H. Cooper, "Alternative Fuels," *CQ Researcher*, Feb. 25, 2005, pp. 173-196.
[7] See Roel Hammerschlag, "Ethanol's Energy Return on Investment: A Survey of the Literature 1990-present," *Environmental Science and Technology*, Vol. 40, No. 6, pp. 1744-1750.
[8] For background see "Agriculture-Based Renewable Energy Production," Congressional Research Service Report RL 32712, May 18, 2006.
[9] See Alexei Barrionuevo, "Fill Up on Corn if You Can," *The New York Times*, Aug. 21, 2006, p. C1.
[10] Quoted in Josh Goodman, "Pumping Corn," *Governing*, September 2006, pp. 47-49.
[11] See "Ethanol Industry Could Face Oversupply, Analysts Say," The Associated Press, June 16, 2006.
[12] Testimony before Senate Energy and Natural Resources Committee, June 19, 2006.
[13] Quoted in Cochran, *op. cit.*
[14] See H. Josef Hebert, "Study: Ethanol Won't Solve Energy Problems," The Associated Press, July 10, 2006.
[15] Quoted in Elizabeth Svoboda, "UC Scientist Says Ethanol Uses More Energy Than It Makes," *San Francisco Chronicle*, June 27, 2005, p. A4.
[16] See Jason Hill, *et al.*, "Environmental, Economic and Energetic Costs and Benefits of Biodiesel and Ethanol Biofuels," *Proceedings of the National Academies of Science*, Vol. 103, No. 30, July 25, 2006, pp. 11206-11210.
[17] See Department of Energy, Energy Efficiency and Renewable Energy Biomass Program, "Cellulase Enzyme Research," www1.eere.energy.gov/biomass/cellulase_enzyme.html.
[18] For background see "Renewable Energy: Tax Credit, Budget and Electricity Production Issues," Congressional Research Service Report IB 10041, May 25, 2006.
[19] For background see "Petroleum and Ethanol Fuels: Tax Incentives and Related GAO Work," General Accounting Office Report B 286311, Sept. 25, 2000.
[20] For background see Marcia Clemmitt, "Pork Barrel Politics" *CQ Researcher*, June 16, 2006, pp. 529-552.
[21] See "R&D Earmarks Hit New Record of $2.4 Billion, Up 13 Percent," *R&D Funding Update*, American Academy for the Advancement of Science, Jan. 4, 2006, p. 5.
[22] Portions of this section adapted from "Energy Kid's Page," Energy Information Administration; Ethanol Timeline available at www.eia.doe.gov/kids/histories/timelines/ethanol.html.
[23] For background see R. C. Schroeder, "Arab Oil Money," in *Editorial Research Reports 1974* (Vol. I), available at *CQ Researcher Plus Archive*, CQ Electronic Library, http://library.cqpress.com.
[24] For background see D. Teter, "Iran between East and West," in *Editorial Research Reports 1979* (Vol. I); "Auto Research and Regulation," in *Editorial Research Reports 1979* (Vol. I), and M. Leepson, "Synthetic Fuels," in *Editorial Research Reports 1979* (Vol. II); all available at *CQ Researcher Plus Archive*, CQ Electronic Library, http://library.cqpress.com.
[25] See "Agriculture-Based Renewable Energy Production," Congressional Research Service Report RL 32712, May 18, 2006, pp. 17-23.
[26] See Manu Raju, "Tight Budget Has EPA Hamstrung on Finalizing Renewable Fuels Language," *CQ Today*, Sept. 6, 2006, www.cq.com.
[27] See Jeff Tollefson, "Oil Companies Fret About Ethanol Mandates," *CQ Today*, June 19, 2006, www.cq.com.
[28] See "Big Three to Make More Biofuels Cars," The Associated Press, June 29, 2006.
[29] See Andrew Pollack, "Redesigning Crops to Harvest Fuel," *The New York Times*, Sept. 8, 2006, p. D1.
[30] For background see David Hosansky, "Biotech Foods," *CQ Researcher*, March 30, 2001, pp. 249-272.
[31] Testimony before Senate Committee on Environment and Public Works, Sept. 6, 2006.
[32] Quoted in Cochran, *op. cit.*

FOR MORE INFORMATION

Alliance of Automobile Manufacturers, 1401 I St., N.W., Suite 900, Washington, DC 20005; (202) 326-5500; www.autoalliance.org. A coalition of nine car and light-truck manufacturers, including the Big Three U.S. automakers, that promotes the companies' efforts at developing alternative-fuel vehicles, hybrids and new fuel cells.

Alliance to Save Energy, 1850 M St., N.W., Suite 600, Washington, DC 20036; (202) 857-0666; www.ase.org. Advocates expanded federal policies to promote energy efficiency.

American Petroleum Institute, 1220 L St., N.W., Washington, DC 20005; (202) 682-8000; www.api.org. The oil and natural gas industry's lobbying arm in Washington, lobbies on fuel standards, climate change and exploration and production issues.

Archer Daniels Midland Co., 4666 Faries Parkway, Decatur, IL 62526; (800) 637-5843; www.admworld.com. The agriculture giant is the biggest domestic ethanol producer.

Environmental Working Group, 1436 U St., N.W., Suite 100, Washington, DC 20009; (202) 667-6982; www.ewg.org. Analyzes government data and scientific studies to expose environmental threats and to find solutions.

National Biodiesel Board, 3337a Emerald Land, Jefferson City, MO 65110; (800) 841-5849; www.biodiesel.org. National trade association representing the biodiesel industry and coordinating body for R&D efforts.

National Corn Growers Association, 122 C St., N.W., Suite 510, Washington, DC 20001; (202) 628-7001; www.ncga.com. Lobbying group that represents corn producers and heavily promotes the use of corn-based ethanol.

Petroleum Industry Research Foundation, 3 Park Ave., 26th floor, New York, NY 10016; (212) 686-6470; www.pirinc.org. Studies energy economics with a special emphasis on oil.

Renewable Fuels Association, 1 Massachusetts Ave., N.W., Suite 820, Washington, DC 20001; (202) 289-3835; www.ethanolrfa.org. The chief lobbying group for the U.S. ethanol industry.

Union of Concerned Scientists, 2 Brattle Square, Cambridge, MA 02238; (617) 547-5552; www.uscusa.org. Nonprofit of scientists and citizens that promotes environmentally sound policies in energy, global warming and vehicles.

U.S. Department of Energy, Energy Efficiency and Renewable Energy Program, Mail Stop EE-1, Department of Energy, Washington, DC 20585; (202) 586-9220; www1.eere.energy.gov. Promotes much of the government's renewable-energy research, including next-generation vehicles and fuel technologies.

Bibliography

Selected Sources

Articles

Brubaker, Harold, "Fresh Energy," ***Philadelphia Inquirer*****, Aug. 27, 2006, p. E1.**

Projects at farms and laboratories across the country to develop ethanol from plants and biomass other than corn are giving experts high hopes for cellulosic ethanol, which has been billed as "just around the corner" since the 1990s.

Cochran, John, "Fuel From the Farm," ***CQ Weekly*****, Aug. 7, 2006, pp. 2166-2174.**

The desire to achieve greater energy independence has bolstered the political prospects of the already influential U.S. corn lobby.

Goodman, Josh, "Pumping Corn," ***Governing*****, September 2006, pp. 47-49.**

Farmers can turn almost any crop into fuel, but the article questions whether they can make any money without government help.

Hill, Jason, ***et al.*****, "Environmental, Economic and Energetic Costs and Benefits of Biodiesel and Ethanol Biofuels,"** ***Proceedings of the National Academy of Sciences*****, July 25, 2006, pp. 11206-11210.**

University of Minnesota researchers evaluate whether renewable transportation biofuels yield more energy than the energy invested in their production. The study concludes biodiesel is more energy efficient than ethanol and projects how well existing corn and soybean production would satisfy future demand.

Miller, James P., "Ethanol Fever Cooling Off," ***Chicago Tribune*****, Aug. 27, 2006, p. C5.**

The gold-rush mentality surrounding ethanol is prompting investors to take a harder look at the rush to capitalize on ethanol's promise.

Pollack, Andrew, "Redesigning Crops To Harvest Fuel," ***The New York Times*****, Sept. 8, 2006, p. C1.**

Agricultural scientists are genetically modifying corn and other crops to make it easier to convert them into transportation fuels.

Reel, Monte, "Brazil's Road to Energy Independence," ***The Washington Post*****, Aug. 20, 2006, p. A1.**

Brazil's domestically produced ethanol from sugar cane and even natural gas have supplanted gasoline as preferred transportation fuels.

Reports

"Agriculture-Based Renewable Energy Production," Congressional Research Service Report No. RL32712, May 18, 2006, Washington, D.C.

Congress' research arm provides an overview of the history and status of leading, farm-based renewable fuels, with a legislative summary of congressional efforts to promote each product.

"Alternative Fuels and Advanced Technology Vehicles," Congressional Research Service Report No. RL33564, July 20, 2006.

Congress' research arm reviews congressional efforts to provide incentives for the development and commercialization of alternative fuels and advanced-technology vehicles.

"Energy Policy: Conceptual Framework and Continuing Issues," Congressional Research Service Report No. RL31720, May 11, 2006, Washington, D.C.

The report provides short-term and longer-term policy options in response to rising prices for imported oil and a history of energy policy since the 1970s Arab oil embargo.

"Ethanol: Frequently Asked Questions," Union of Concerned Scientists, 2006.

An advocacy group that supports increased use of alternative energy provides a guide to supply-and-demand issues concerning America's most abundant renewable fuel.

"Meeting Energy Demand for the 21st Century," General Accounting Office Report GAO-05-414T, March 16, 2005, Washington, D.C.

Plentiful, inexpensive energy has been the backbone of much of America's prosperity. But the GAO says U.S. energy systems are increasingly showing signs of strain and instability.

"Update on Ethanol," Petroleum Industry Research Foundation, July 2006.

A nonpartisan research foundation explains why further ethanol-promotion efforts raise costs for consumers and taxpayers.

Lieberman, Ben, "How the Energy Bill Boosted Prices at the Pump," Heritage Foundation WebMemo No. 1053, April 28, 2006, www. heritage.org.

A conservative policy analyst asserts that the 2005 energy bill's ethanol mandate had counterproductive consequences for the gasoline market.

The Next Step:

Additional Articles from Current Periodicals

Biodiesel

Cline, Erin, "Soybean Tops Corn in Fuel Study, But It's No Gas," ***Los Angeles Times*****, July 15, 2006, p. A21.**
Soybean-derived biodiesel yields a 93 percent return on the energy investment used in production, compared with a 25 percent return for corn-grain ethanol.

Popper, Helen, "Argentina Expects Big Gain From Soy Use," ***The Houston Chronicle*****, Sept. 12, 2006, p. 10.**
Soy farmers in Argentina, the world's top soy-oil exporter, want to expand acreage and yields as demand for biodiesel surges in Europe.

Scherer, Ron, "Do-It-Yourselfers Turn Diner Grease Into Biodiesel Fuel," ***The Christian Science Monitor*****, July 18, 2006, p. 1.**
Entrepreneurs are turning their basements and garages into mini-oil refineries, converting cooking oil into diesel fuel.

Unmacht, Eric, "Faced With Soaring Oil Prices, Indonesia Turns to Biodiesel," ***The Christian Science Monitor*****, July 5, 2006, p. 14.**
Indonesia and Malaysia control nearly 85 percent of the production of crude palm oil, which can be used to make biodiesel.

Wald, Matthew L., "A Petroleum Alternative, But U.S. Says It's Illegal," ***The New York Times*****, July 23, 2006, p. 2.**
Modifying a car or truck to run on vegetable oil is illegal because the Environmental Protection Agency requires that motor vehicles be certified before they are sold.

Ethanol

Barrionuevo, Alexei, "Oodles of Corn But Little E-85," ***The Houston Chronicle*****, Aug. 31, 2006, p. 4.**
Car companies, farmers and politicians love to promote the corn-based fuel blend of 85 percent ethanol and 15 percent gasoline as a way out of American's oil addiction, but it is still unavailable at most of U.S. service stations.

Freiderich, Steven, "Pulp Mill May Find Salvation in Ethanol," ***The Seattle Post-Intelligencer*****, Sept. 5, 2006, p. C2.**
The Weyerhaeuser pulp mill in Cosmopolis, Wash., is in danger of closure, but community leaders say the mill could be converted to create ethanol.

Melcer, Rachel, "In Search of The Perfect Kernel Area Scientists Are Trying to Find Plants That Will Yield the Highest Amount of Ethanol," ***St. Louis Post-Dispatch*****, Aug. 25, 2006, p. B1.**
Scientists in the Midwest are working to identify corn hybrids that produce the most ethanol per bushel and improve marketable byproducts such as cooking oil and animal feed.

Miller, James P., "Ethanol Fever Cooling Off," ***Chicago Tribune*****, Aug. 27, 2006, p. C5.**
Despite rising demand for ethanol, soaring prices and Wall Street's support, some analysts believe share prices are topping out.

Reel, Monte, "Brazil's Road to Energy Independence," ***The Washington Post*****, Aug. 20, 2006, p. A1.**
Ethanol has replaced about 40 percent of Brazil's gasoline consumption, causing U.S. lawmakers and venture capitalists to begin visiting Brazil for energy solutions

Royse, David, "First Ethanol Pump Opens," ***Orlando Sentinel*****, Sept. 14, 2006, p. B5.**
A gas station in Tallahassee becomes the first in Florida to sell the ethanol-blend fuel E-85.

Woodyard, Chris, "Honda Sees Possible Ethanol Breakthrough," ***USA Today*****, Sept. 15, 2006, p. B4.**
Honda has developed a new and more-efficient process to develop ethanol, using a microorganism developed in Japan to convert sugar in plants into the alternative fuel.

Foreign Oil

Hall, Kevin G., "Find Oil Substitute," ***The Philadelphia Inquirer*****, June 8, 2006, p. D1.**
Former Federal Reserve Chairman Alan Greenspan testified that the United States must quickly develop alternative-energy sources to reduce its dependence on foreign oil.

Lazarus, David, "Finding Oil Not the Answer," ***The San Francisco Chronicle*****, Sept. 10, 2006, p. F1.**
Energy experts say Chevron's new oil find in the Gulf of Mexico is not going to ease U.S. dependence on foreign oil.

Thomas, Ken, "Big Three Automakers Push Lawmakers on Ethanol Fuels," ***St. Louis Post-Dispatch*****, May 19, 2006, p. B3.**
Leaders of General Motors, Ford and DaimlerChrysler's Chrysler Group pressed Congress to help make ethanol fuels more widely available to reduce U.S. dependence on foreign oil.

Foreign Production and Use of Ethanol

Casey, Michael, "Asia Plants Seeds of Reduced Oil Dependence," ***The Washington Post*****, May 7, 2006, p. A17.**
Countries throughout Asia are testing various crops, including coconut, castor oil and cow dung, for fossil-fuel alternatives such as ethanol and biodiesel.

Cowell, Alan, "Sweden and U.S. Agree About the Oil Dependency Problem, but for Different Reasons," ***The New York Times*****, Feb. 5, 2006, p. 12.**
Sweden, a model for alternative-energy solutions because of

its abundant natural water supply and vast farmland, wants to follow the example of Brazil and reduce the region's reliance on expensive imported oil by using its sugar industry to produce ethanol.

Sample, Ian, "A Sweet Solution to Fuel Troubles," *The Guardian* (London), Feb. 16, 2006, p. 1.
Gas stations across southeast England are increasingly selling bioethanol, preceding government moves to press companies to produce the alternative fuel.

Smith, Craig S., "A Wine of Character, But How Many Miles to a Gallon?" *The New York Times*, Oct. 6, 2005, p. A4.
France has begin distilling some of its higher-rated wines into ethanol because a worldwide glut of wine has greatly decreased the price of quality French wine, causing winemakers to look for other sources of income from their product.

Going Green

Baker, David R., "Biodiesel Puts On A Suit," *The San Francisco Chronicle*, July 2, 2006, p. F1.
Biodiesel is starting to make inroads in industries that consume large amounts of fuel, such as the Phil Foster Ranch in San Benito County, Calif., which uses the fuel to till land and haul vegetables to market.

Crouch, Elise, and Shane Graber, "MoDOT Aims to Save With New Hybrid Bucket Trucks," *St. Louis Post-Dispatch*, Aug. 7, 2006, p. B3.
The Missouri Department of Transportation will be replacing two-thirds of its bucket trucks, which lift maintenance workers to install signs and traffic signals, with hybrid bucket trucks that use 50 percent less fuel.

Herman, Valli, "Vegetable Juice," *Los Angeles Times*, Aug. 5, 2006, p. E1.
Lovecraft Biofuels in Silver Lake, Calif., is an auto shop that specializes in converting cars, especially diesel-powered Mercedes built from 1975 to 1989, to run on 100 percent vegetable oil, including used restaurant grease.

Thomas, Ken, "Toyota Plans to Develop Easily Recharged Hybrid," *The Houston Chronicle*, July 19, 2006, p. 3.
Toyota Motors is "strongly considering" a program to develop vehicles capable of running on the ethanol-blend fuel E-85 and also plans to pursue development of a plug-in hybrid vehicle.

Switchgrass

Brubaker, Harold, "Fresh Energy," *The Philadelphia Inquirer*, Aug. 27, 2006, p. E1.
Government scientists are studying how to get the most out of switchgrass, a tall grass, as a renewable fuel.

Gillis, Justin, "Fill 'Er Up With Plant Waste," *Pittsburgh Post-Gazette*, June 25, 2006, p. A3.
The United States wants to devote millions of acres to growing special energy crops like switchgrass that can be turned into liquid fuel.

"Renaissance Deferred; The Mississippi Delta," *The Economist*, May 13, 2006.
The Mississippi Delta could become the first bio-refinery in the United States to use switchgrass, plus wood chips, to make fuel.

U.S. Energy Policy

Brownstein, Ronald, "All Revved Up, Going Nowhere on Energy Policy," *Los Angeles Times*, April 30, 2006, p. A4.
U.S. lawmakers have considered using renewable energy to reduce the nation's dependence on foreign oil, but each party has derailed the most ambitious proposals of the other.

Clayton, Mark, "U.S. To Cut Funds For Two Renewable Energy Sources," *The Christian Science Monitor*, Sept. 15, 2006, p. 2.
The Bush administration's fiscal 2007 budget calls for the elimination of hydropower and geothermal research, declaring them "mature technologies" that need no further funding.

Tomich, Jeffrey, "Blagojevich Will Unveil Fuel Substitution Plan," *St. Louis Post-Dispatch*, Aug. 22, 2006, p. D1.
Gov. Rod Blagojevich, D-Ill., will unveil a proposal to slash the state's petroleum consumption in half over the next decade by using fuels made from coal, corn and soybeans.

Citing *CQ Researcher*

Sample formats for citing these reports in a bibliography include the ones listed below. Preferred styles and formats vary, so please check with your instructor or professor.

MLA Style

Jost, Kenneth. "Rethinking the Death Penalty." CQ Researcher 16 Nov. 2001: 945-68.

APA Style

Jost, K. (2001, November 16). Rethinking the death penalty. *CQ Researcher, 11*, 945-968.

Chicago Style

Jost, Kenneth. "Rethinking the Death Penalty." *CQ Researcher*, November 16, 2001, 945-968.

CQ Researcher

Published by CQ Press, a division of Congressional Quarterly Inc.

cqresearcher.com

National Parks Under Pressure

Should conservation or recreation take precedence?

The National Park System is threatened by pollution, invasive species, climate change and encroaching development. Moreover, budget constraints are making the national parks and other units in the system not only more dangerous to visitors but also less satisfying and less educational, some observers warn. To compensate for funding shortfalls, parks are raising entrance fees, soliciting corporate donations and cutting ranger programs. Underlying the challenges is a fundamental struggle between recreational users — such as snowmobilers and jet skiers — and traditionalists who say preserving the parks' tranquility and fragile resources should always remain the paramount mission. Meanwhile, "gateway communities" say park officials should take their economic survival into account as they try to keep the parks meaningful for 274 million visitors a year and preserve natural values for future generations.

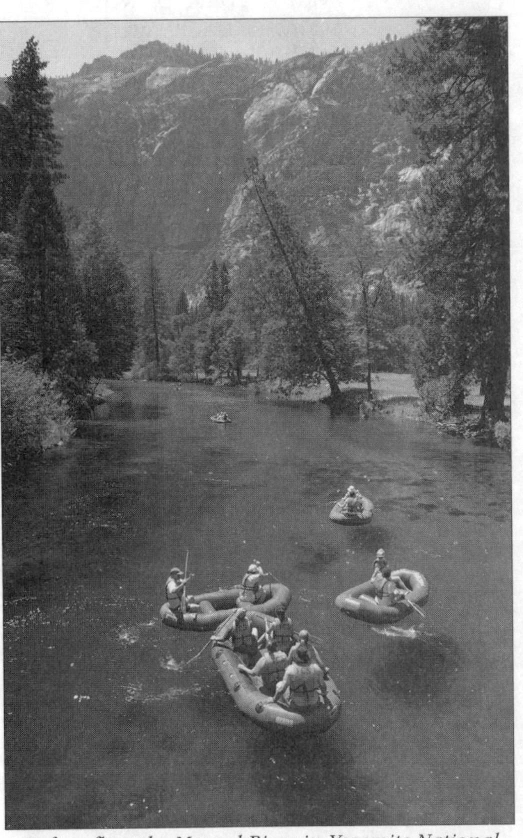

Rafters float the Merced River in Yosemite National Park, which is struggling to accommodate visitors while protecting natural resources.

INSIDE THIS REPORT

CQ Researcher • Oct. 6, 2006 • www.cqresearcher.com
Volume 16, Number 35 • Pages 817-840

CQ PRESS

RECIPIENT OF SOCIETY OF PROFESSIONAL JOURNALISTS AWARD FOR EXCELLENCE ◆ AMERICAN BAR ASSOCIATION SILVER GAVEL AWARD

NATIONAL PARKS UNDER PRESSURE

Cover photograph: Getty Images/David McNew

CQ Researcher

Oct. 6, 2006
Volume 16, Number 35

MANAGING EDITOR: Thomas J. Colin

ASSISTANT MANAGING EDITOR: Kathy Koch

ASSOCIATE EDITOR: Kenneth Jost

STAFF WRITERS: Marcia Clemmitt, Peter Katel

CONTRIBUTING WRITERS: Rachel S. Cox, Sarah Glazer, Alan Greenblatt, Barbara Mantel, Patrick Marshall, Tom Price, Jennifer Weeks

DESIGN/PRODUCTION EDITOR: Olu B. Davis

ASSISTANT EDITOR: Melissa J. Hipolit

CQ PRESS

A Division of Congressional Quarterly Inc.

SENIOR VICE PRESIDENT/PUBLISHER: John A. Jenkins

DIRECTOR, LIBRARY PUBLISHING: Kathryn C. Suárez

DIRECTOR, EDITORIAL OPERATIONS: Ann Davies

CONGRESSIONAL QUARTERLY INC.

CHAIRMAN: Paul C. Tash

VICE CHAIRMAN: Andrew P. Corty

PRESIDENT/EDITOR IN CHIEF: Robert W. Merry

CQ Researcher (ISSN 1056-2036) is printed on acid-free paper. Published weekly, except March 24, July 7, July 14, Aug. 4, Aug. 11, Nov. 24, Dec. 22 and Dec. 29, by CQ Press, a division of Congressional Quarterly Inc. Annual full-service subscriptions for institutions start at $667. For pricing, call 1-800-834-9020, ext. 1906. To purchase a *CQ Researcher* report in print or electronic format (PDF), visit www.cqpress.com or call 866-427-7737. Single reports start at $15. Bulk purchase discounts and electronic-rights licensing are also available. Periodicals postage paid at Washington, D.C., and additional mailing offices. POSTMASTER: Send address changes to *CQ Researcher*, 1255 22nd St., N.W., Suite 400, Washington, DC 20037.

National Parks Under Pressure

BY TOM ARRANDALE

THE ISSUES

On a steep mountain road in Wyoming's Yellowstone National Park, biologist Emily Almberg is telling a group of tourists how wolves have returned to the huge park. Suddenly, in the grassy meadow along Antelope Creek, two wolf pups pop up, stretch and yawn and begin chasing one another.

Almberg cranks her tripod-mounted Nikon telescope down to eye level for a 4-year-old boy from Libertyville, Ill. "Do you have a dog at home?" she asks. "When you come home, does it ever lick you in the face?"

Face licking is a greeting and a way of asking for food, Almberg explains. "That's what wolf pups do when the adults arrive," she says. "They lick the adults to get them to spit out the meat they've carried back from a carcass to feed their pups."

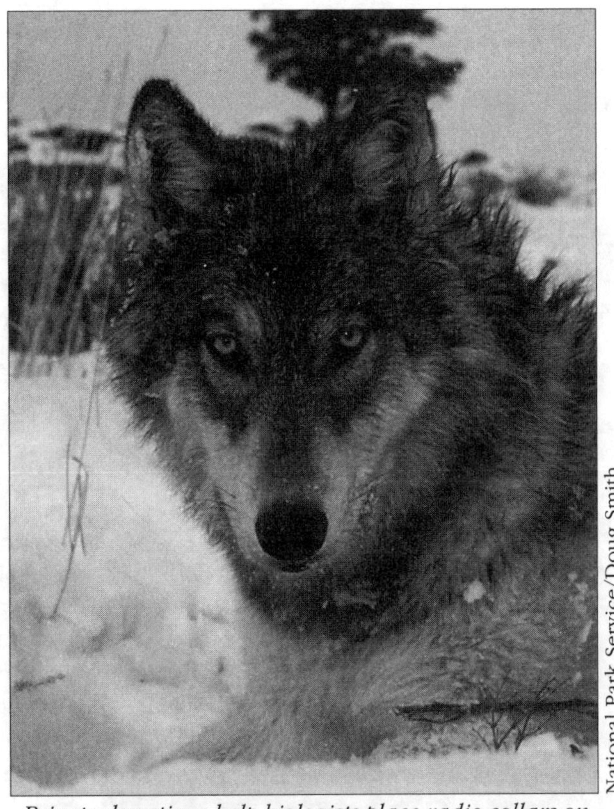

National Park Service/Doug Smith

Private donations help biologists place radio collars on the wolves at Wyoming's Yellowstone National Park and monitor wolf-pack movements. Budget shortages are forcing national parks around the country to seek private and corporate funding not only to continue scientific research but also to accommodate the parks' 274 million annual visitors, while at the same time preserving treasured lands for future generations.

To many Americans, the chance to glimpse and learn about wolves, grizzly bears, moose, elk and other wildlife defines why protecting U.S. national parks is so important. Yellowstone's estimated 150 wolves draw visitors from around the world and often star in TV nature documentaries. For biologists like Almberg, the Yellowstone Wolf Project has been an unprecedented opportunity to study wolves in the wild.

But Yellowstone no longer can afford to pick up the tab for one of the world's most celebrated biological experiments. The federal government pays three staff biologists, but wolf-project managers must raise $250,000 a year from private foundations and businesses to place radio collars on the wolves, monitor pack movements and station biologists along park roads where visitors gather to watch the wolves.

"It's tragic that the premier endangered-species effort in the United States right now has to go to private donors, hat in hand," says Tim Stevens, Yellowstone program manager for the National Parks Conservation Association (NPCA).

All around the country, America's beloved national parks are falling on hard times. The Park Service is still among the most widely respected government agencies, but the NPCA says federal funding now falls $800 million a year short of what the parks need to accommodate 274 million visitors a year — two-thirds more than in 1970 — and at the same time fulfill the historic mandate to keep the nation's most treasured lands "unimpaired for the enjoyment of future generations."

Now environmental organizations, retired park superintendents and rangers have begun speaking out against budget restrictions and subtle management pressures they contend undercut that mission.

"For the last [several] presidential administrations, the Park Service hasn't received the funding that would be needed to do the three things national parks were created to do — provide a quality visitor experience, protect resources for the future and have a productive relationship with park interest groups," says Rick Smith, a former superintendent at Carlsbad Caverns-Guadalupe Mountains National Park.

The Park Service receives about $2.5 billion a year — up from $1.7 billion in 1997 — to manage 84 million acres in 390 park units, which include 58 national parks and a growing number of historic sites, battlefields and public recreation areas. It employs 20,000 rangers, interpreters, biologists, historians, archeologists, clerks, maintenance workers and other staff.

But funding hasn't kept up with the Park Service's expanding responsibilities, say service supporters, including a $5 billion maintenance backlog and implementation of anti-terrorism plans — despite a 35 percent increase in anti-terrorism funds since 2000. And because Congress added new units to the system without providing additional maintenance funds, campgrounds, toilets, trails, visitor centers, historic lodges and headquarters buildings have fallen into disrepair, according to Park Service advo-

Most-Popular Attractions Are in the East

Seven of the 10 most-popular National Park Service units are in the Eastern United States (top). Four times more people visit the Blue Ridge Parkway than the Grand Canyon, for example. But most of the most popular national parks are in the West (bottom).

Park Unit	Location	Visits in 2005
The 10 Most-Visited Units in the National Park System		
Blue Ridge Parkway	N.C., Va.	17,882,567
Golden Gate National Recreation Area	San Francisco	13,602,629
Great Smoky Mountains National Park	N.C., Tenn.	9,192,477
Gateway National Recreation Area	New York City	8,294,353
Lake Mead Nat. Recreation Area	Nev., Ariz.	7,692,438
George Washington Memorial Parkway	Washington, D.C., Va.	7,284,165
Natchez Trace Parkway	Miss., Ala., Tenn.	5,482,282
Delaware Water Gap National Recreation Area	N.J., Pa.	5,052,264
National World War II Memorial	Washington, D.C.	4,410,379
Grand Canyon National Park	Ariz.	4,401,522
The 10 Most-Visited National Parks		
Great Smoky Mountains	N.C., Tenn.	9,192,477
Grand Canyon	Ariz.	4,401,522
Yosemite	Calif.	3,304,144
Olympic	Near Seattle	3,142,774
Yellowstone	Wyo., Mont., Idaho	2,835,651
Rocky Mountain	Colo.	2,798,368
Zion	Utah	2,586,665
Cuyahoga Valley	Ohio	2,533,827
Grand Teton	Wyo.	2,463,442
Acadia	Maine	2,051,484

Source: National Park Service

cates. They point to such problems as washed out trails at Mount Rainier National Park in Washington, decaying fortifications at Florida's Dry Tortugas National Park and collapsing ancient structures at New Mexico's Chaco Culture National Historical Park. [1]

What's more, a recent Government Accountability Office (GAO) report said funding for daily park operations comes nowhere near the amount needed to keep pace with fixed costs. [2] "Looking at federal dollars, they're not going up," Yellowstone Superintendent Suzanne Lewis told the Cody, Wyo., Chamber of Commerce in September. "In the National Park Service, we've been fortunate; our budget hasn't nosedived. But every year we tend to get a little bit of money that will not quite cover the fixed costs for another year."

Faced with skyrocketing fuel and utility costs and a new, more generous retirement system for younger employees, superintendents at national parks around the country have had to cut education, maintenance activities and visitor and resource protection, the GAO report said. For example, Maine's Acadia closed seven restrooms during the popular winter season, Shenandoah in Virginia shut down a visitor center and Grand Canyon canceled 12 daily interpretative programs.

Moreover, Bryce Canyon National Park in Utah curtailed backcountry patrols, despite suspicions of wildlife poaching, and Yellowstone eliminated six law-enforcement rangers. "Visitors and resources at national parks will be put at greater risk this summer than in the past," said a Coalition of National Park Service Retirees report. [3]

Faced with such fiscal challenges, the Park Service is developing a systemwide scorecard for measuring how parks are performing, and some parks are devising business plans and setting priorities for the next five years at current budget levels. But, worries Blake Selzer, chief budget analyst for the NPCA, "are they only just looking at ways to operate parks at a bare-bones minimum?"

In addition to the budget cutbacks, environmental threats — including climate change, air and water pollution, invasive species and encroaching development — are taking a toll on the parks. By 2030, scientists warn, global warming could melt the remaining glaciers in Montana's Glacier National Park and the snow-capped peaks at Washington state's Mt. Rainier National Park and others; dry up lakes and flood shorelines at popular national recreation areas; and kill the ancient trees at California's Joshua Tree National Park. [4]

"A disrupted climate is the single greatest threat" to ever face national parks in the Rocky Mountains, along the Pacific Coast and in Southwestern deserts, said a report by the Natural Resources Defense Council and the Rocky Mountain Climate Organization. [5]

More immediately, cars, trucks and industrial smokestacks are throwing vast pollution clouds over the Grand Canyon and Great Smoky Mountains, while pollution surpasses federal air-quality standards in 150 of the park system's 390 units, according to the NPCA. [6] "Air pollution threatens the very essence of what Americans value most about our national parks," said Mark Wenzler, NPCA's clean-air director.

Water pollution also threatens the system's rivers, wetlands, beaches and marine sanctuaries, while non-native species endanger the system's 398 threatened or endangered plants and animals. For example, South American boa constrictors and Burmese pythons — apparently released by pet owners — now thrive in the Everglades, and lake trout illegally released in Yellowstone Lake are preying on native cutthroat trout.

Meanwhile, new homes, roads and businesses around Yellowstone and Glacier parks are cutting wildlife off from traditional migration routes; subdivisions are going up right on the edge of West Virginia's New River Gorge National River; 6,000 new homes may be permitted near Everglades National Park, and 20,000 homes, several golf courses and a giant landfill for Los Angeles' trash are planned near Joshua Tree National Park, northeast of Palm Springs. [7]

As park officials try to cope with the multitude of pressures, government officials and advocates for the national parks are asking:

Number of Park Visitors Levels Off

The number of people visiting national parks grew steadily after World War II but leveled off in the last 10 years, despite population growth and the addition of new park units. Higher gas prices and entrance fees may have kept visitors away.

Source: National Park Service

Should visitors and donors bear more of the costs of running the parks?

With federal budgets expected to remain tight, the Park Service is seeking other resources to cover costs — raising serious questions about whether it's appropriate for the service to cash in on the national parks' popularity by charging higher fees and courting corporate and charitable sponsors.

Although entrance to many historic sites and small park units is still free, other less popular sites now charge $5-$10, and most large parks charge $20 per car for a one-week pass. Last year, however, Yellowstone, Glacier, Grand Teton and Grand Canyon national parks raised their weekly fees to $25. That's still a bargain compared to what vacationers pay for a day at Disneyland or other major leisure destinations, but the Park Service's growing reliance on fees could eventually price some Americans out of their national parks, say critics. And, since individual parks now can keep most of their receipts to build and maintain their own facilities, critics worry that managers will feel compelled to court increasing numbers of visitors by investing in facilities at the expense of protecting natural and cultural resources.

In fiscal 2005, the agency collected $160 million in entrance fees at 151 park units, plus additional charges for campgrounds and other facilities. Hospitality companies paid another $47 million in franchise fees to operate more than 600 lodges, restaurants, souvenir shops, gasoline stations, campgrounds, river rafting trips, horseback rides and other services. Parks require those businesses to plow the bulk of those concession revenues back into improving the park-owned facilities they operate.

In fact, the Interior Department's initiatives to collect visitors' fees to supplement park budgets have been stirring controversy since they were initiated a decade ago. Three years ago, for instance, Yellowstone began charging adults $15 for popular day hikes led by park rangers through some geyser basins, lakes and backcountry valleys.

Tourism and recreation-industry groups support visitors' fees, pointing out that those who drive recreation vehicles and other outdoor equipment welcome the chance to help pay for the facilities they're using. "The cost of many things should be borne by the people who are the direct beneficiaries," says Derrick A. Crandall, president of the American Recreation Coalition, which represents travel businesses, recreation organizations, campgrounds, marinas, hotels and manufacturers of snowmobiles, off-road and recreational vehicles and small watercraft.

Getty Images/David McNew

Several golf courses, 20,000 homes and a giant landfill for trash from Los Angeles are planned near California's Joshua Tree National Park. In the next three decades, the park's ancient trees could be killed by global warming, scientists warn.

In 1996, Congress approved a "fee demo" program, which allowed national parks and other public lands to keep 80 percent of their fee receipts and plow them back into infrastructure improvements. Most participating parks doubled their entrance fees, and in fiscal 2006 the Park Service is expected to generate more than $137 million in fees that park managers can use for maintenance and construction. During the last decade, more than $1 billion, mostly from entrance fees, has been poured back into the parks to upgrade and replace aging facilities, of which $473 million went towards maintenance, $228 million to rehabilitate historic structures, maintain cultural landscapes and protect museum collections, $103 million to improve visitor centers and exhibits and $123 million to upgrade campgrounds, trails and backcountry facilities.

For instance, Yosemite National Park used fee receipts to build a visitor-center theater, replace leaky sewer lines, install new campground picnic tables and fire rings and expand its shuttle-bus fleet. Yellowstone spent $8.6 million to expand and refurbish a 1958 visitor-education center with state-of-the-art models and computer-generated exhibits on volcanic geology, which forms the park's unique geysers.

Dedicating the center on Aug. 25, 2006, Secretary of the Interior Dirk Kempthorne noted that it was built with funds contributed by 20 million Yellowstone visitors between 1997 and 2005. "To put it a different way, each visitor contributed 43 cents," Kempthorne said. "It's amazing what pocket change will do."

In some Western states, local hunters, fishermen and other groups have protested when the U.S. Forest Service began raising fees and imposing new charges at national forest facilities. But a 2003 Park Service survey found that 80 percent of park visitors thought entrance fees were "just about right" and that 92 percent preferred that their money stay in the parks they had visited. Economists contend that keeping a share of fees gives managers a direct incentive to keep facilities repaired and attractive. "They're getting into it, because they know they get to spend the money themselves instead of just sending it back to Congress," says Holly Fretwell, a Montana State University economist.

In 2004 Congress extended the fee demo program another 10 years, and revenues are climbing. In its fiscal 2007 budget, the Park Service predicts that visitor fees will generate almost $165 million a year — 29 percent more than two years ago.

For some parks, however, the fees have not produced much income. For instance, when the federal government created Great Smoky Mountains National Park by buying privately owned forests, Tennessee prohibited entrance fees so motorists could drive on park highways for free. And small units with relatively few visitors do not collect much.

The NPCA backs the fee demo concept. But some environmentalists worry that the program creates incentives for empire-building park managers to invest in infrastructure to attract more fee-paying visitors, damaging natural and cultural resources in the process. Park

Service policy also prohibits using fee demo revenues to cover operating costs. As a result, notes NPCA budget expert Selzer, some heavily traveled parks have applied fee demo receipts to building new facilities, but Congress hasn't provided sufficient funds for the salaried staffs needed to run them.

"They're taking in a lot of money," says Smith, the retired superintendent, but "by and large it ends up being put into bricks and mortar, and in many parks, infrastructure is not the problem."

Another concern about entrance fees, says former Shenandoah National Park Superintendent Bill Wade, who chairs the retirees' group, is that "The more you rely on recreation fees, the more you're pricing some people out of the market. I think entrance fees ought to be ended altogether."

Yellowstone Superintendent Lewis notes that park attendance declined barely 1 percent after the $5-per-car fee increase was imposed last year. "We're really still getting a bargain," Stevens, the NPCA's Yellowstone representative, concurs. "But there may be a tipping point, and we don't want to make parks inaccessible to any Americans."

In Yellowstone, Stevens adds, the park has crossed that line by charging adults $15 for the popular day hikes that rangers lead to backcountry lakes, and across wild valleys on trails that lead away from crowded roads and visitor facilities. "That's part of the whole national park experience," but even with discounts for children, "for my family that would be $50, and we probably couldn't afford that," Stevens says.

Parks also depend increasingly on donations from foundations and wealthy citizens. The National Park Foundation, chartered by Congress in 1967, collects $30 million a year from foundations and large corporations such as Unilever, American Airlines, Ford Motor Co., and the Discovery Channel. In addition, 150 "friends" groups affiliated with individual parks raise another $17 million a year, and 65 nonprofit associations pass along another $26 million in receipts from book stores they run in the parks. And through the service's Volunteers in the Parks program, 122,000 citizens work 4.5 million hours a year helping rangers greet visitors and distribute maps and information. [8]

Then-Yellowstone Superintendent Michael Finley helped set up the Yellowstone foundation in 1995, making it the first organization created to raise funds for a specific national park. Now, similar partner organizations are helping to upgrade facilities and keep some of the country's most popular parks running. For instance, the Friends of Acadia raised $9 million to restore 130 miles of trails inside Acadia National Park, and private education groups created an environmental learning center at Indiana Dunes National Lakeshore.

The Yellowstone foundation contributed $1 million for the park's recently reconstructed Canyon Visitor Center and just finished raising $15 million to supplement $11 million in federal funding for the new visitor center at Old Faithful Geyser. In all, the foundation has raised more than $36 million for programs "that would not be likely to get congressional allocations," says Michael Cary, the organization's president.

For the wolf project, the foundation pays for collaring devices, staff members to track wolves' movements from helicopters and graduate students to study how predators affect elk and bison populations. Primarily, "we fund the science," Cary says, "and there's a lot of good scientific information being generated."

In May, the Park Service backed off from a proposal allowing employees to actively solicit donations from visitors and the private sector, including from park concessions. Critics had argued the policy might pave the way for corporate donors to display commercial logos on kiosks and other park structures. "There will be few places in the common areas of national parks . . . off-limits to the Nike swoosh or the McDonald's arches," contended Public Employees for Environmental Responsibility, a whistle-blowers' organization representing government workers. [9]

The Park Service retirees' group shares concern about parks getting too close to private benefactors. "The less the national parks rely on public funds, the greater the risk that they'll be less national and less public," Wade says. Adds former Carlsbad Superintendent Smith: "We shouldn't turn parks and park superintendents into beggars and panhandlers. The parks are for the American people, and they deserve public funding."

Is recreation compatible with keeping parks 'unimpaired'?

The 1916 National Park Service Organic Act directed the agency to keep parks "unimpaired" while still accommodating human visitors. But the continuing funding shortages are intensifying the debate over whether the Park Service's concern about conserving natural resources has pushed aside its obligation to give ordinary Americans opportunities to enjoy the parks.

That debate has come into clear — and noisy — focus as the service considers allowing snowmobiles, off-road vehicles and small personal watercraft to explore areas previously unreachable except by foot or horseback. As motorized vehicles have become more popular, the Park Service has encouraged snowmobiles on Yellowstone's unplowed roads during winter months and has tolerated jet skis on heavily used recreation-area waters.

But the noisy vehicles spew exhaust fumes and can erode trails, tear up beaches and other wild areas. The federal Wilderness Act of 1964 bars motor-driven vehicles from the nation's protected wilderness, including the backcountry in national parks. But even in developed park areas, rangers and conservationists contend the machines have begun disrupting the silence and

Funding Rose for Park Operations

The amount of money allocated to run the national parks increased by nearly $700 million over the past decade. But Park Service officials and outside observers say current funding isn't keeping up with personnel and infrastructure needs.

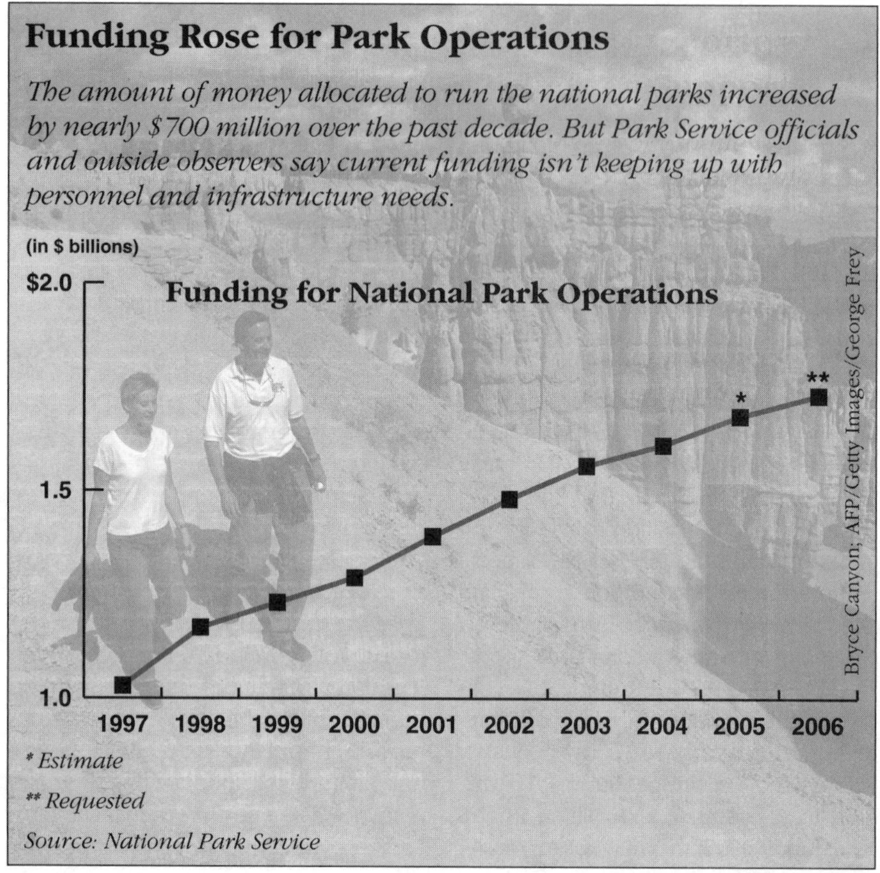

* Estimate

** Requested

Source: National Park Service

natural conditions of the parks. In 2000, as the Clinton administration moved to strengthen the Park Service's focus on conservation, the agency proposed phasing snowmobiles out of Yellowstone and barring jet skis from national park waters.

Most of Yellowstone remains impassable to automobiles in winter, except for a single road the Park Service keeps open to two isolated Montana communities. Starting in the 1950s, tourists began riding multi-passenger over-snow coaches over unplowed park roads; and snowmobiles began roaring into the park in 1963. Businesses in gateway communities promoted the sport to generate winter customers, and by the 1990s some 1,400 motorized sleds were entering the park on peak winter days. Winter visitors were spending $30 million a year in West Yellowstone, Mont., the most popular park entrance for snowmobilers. [10]

By the mid-1990s, the Park Service had become concerned that growing snowmobile traffic was causing air pollution and road overcrowding while disturbing the park's elk and bison. Prodded by a lawsuit by the Fund for Animals, Yellowstone Superintendent Finley proposed in November 2000 to exclude snowmobiles from the park after three more winters. Snowmobile manufacturers promptly challenged the decision in court, and several contending lawsuits were filed over the following years.

Eventually, the park set a limit of 720 snowmobiles a day through the upcoming 2006-2007 winter and required snowmobilers to hire trained guides and use clean-burning, four-stroke engines. The plan bars snowmobiles from park roads at night and sets 14 miles of side roads aside for the big snow coaches. Legal disputes remain on hold, and Yellowstone planners are now working on a permanent snowmobile policy that's likely to face additional court challenges.

Meanwhile, other park-system units are struggling through similar controversies. After settling an environmental group's lawsuit in 2002, the service permanently closed five seashore and recreation areas to personal watercraft and moved to keep them out of 16 other units while park managers assessed their impact. Ten units were reopened in 2005, and in May the craft were permitted again at Gulf Islands National Seashore off the Florida and Mississippi coasts and in September at Cape Lookout National Seashore in North Carolina.

Park managers in both units wanted to continue banning jet skis but were overruled by President George W. Bush's first secretary of the Interior, Gale Norton, according to *National Parks Traveler* magazine. [11] Recreation interests contended the Clinton-administration rule had needlessly harmed gateway towns and motorized-equipments sales without proving the parks were being damaged.

The jet ski deliberation process "has been delayed too long, and in the meantime millions of Americans have been denied access to their national parks, thousands of small businesses have suffered and thousands of jobs have been lost," Maureen Healey, director of the Personal Watercraft Industry Association, said recently. [12]

Just before Bill Clinton left office in 2001, the Park Service rewrote its official 280-page operations manual, reaffirming that conservation is the service's top priority, even if it requires limiting access. Recreation users have challenged that focus, arguing that Clinton-era policies excluded millions of Americans from enjoying their national parks with motorized vehicles.

"The 2001 policies were driven by a belief that the American public is loving the parks to death, and we do not share that belief," says Crandall, of the American Recreation Coalition. As Crandall told Park Service Director Fran

Mainella in February, the group is concerned that the revised operations manual sets out a "simplistic, single-focused mission" that ignores the agency's long history of building roads, visitor centers, lodging and other infrastructure "that has long enhanced visitation to the parks while providing protection for park features and qualities." [13]

William P. Horn, an assistant Interior secretary during the Reagan administration, contends the revisions misinterpret the 1916 Organic Act. "Congress has never intended that parks be managed as biospheres under glass or managed in an exclusionary manner," Horn told the Senate National Parks Subcommittee in 2005. "In contrast, imagine today trying to build a fraction of Yellowstone's road system or even one of its historic hotels or lodges. It is an absolute certainty that impairment, especially the very-low-impact threshold [allowed] in the Clinton-era policies, would be the basis for objections."

In Crandall's view, current management policies overlook the different purposes of the various parks, historic sites and recreation areas. In 2005, the nation's 58 national parks drew 63 million visitors — less than a quarter of the total that year for all Park Service units. Seventeen national recreation areas and 10 national seashores attracted roughly as many, mostly from nearby metropolitan areas. Virginia's Blue Ridge Parkway and San Francisco's Golden Gate National Recreation Area are by far the most heavily visited units; only two national parks, Grand Canyon and Great Smoky Mountains, ranked in the top 10 most-visited units in 2005. (*See chart, p. 820.*)

"Not every unit is a Grand Canyon, a Yellowstone or a Grand Teton," Crandall says. Even in such natural parks, he adds, "90-plus percent of visitors never get beyond an eighth of a mile from the paved surface of the road system." By giving conservation priority over recreation opportunities throughout all 390 units, the Clinton policies "reduce the value of the system to the American public by providing fewer opportunities for physical, mental and spiritual fulfillment."

In 2005, Paul Hoffman, then the Interior Department's deputy assistant secretary for fish, wildlife and parks, drafted a new version of the management manual giving recreation equal standing with conservation. A former aide to Vice President Dick Cheney, Hoffman had also been director of the Chamber of Commerce in Cody, a gateway community leading to Yellowstone.

The park retirees' group leaked Hoffman's draft to the press and claimed it would open the parks to inappropriate commercial uses. Jon Catton — a leading critic of snowmobiles in Yellowstone — says Hoffman apparently went through the manual line-by-line and removed key phrases giving park officials authority to find that noise, air pollution and wildlife impacts from motorized recreation unacceptably impair the parks.

Park Service officials quickly disowned Hoffman's proposals and issued yet another revised manual, allowing recreation only at levels that never imperil natural or cultural values.

Should "gateway communities" help decide how national parks are managed?

While all Americans have a stake in park-management decisions, nearby communities feel the consequences most acutely. "We're a big player in any community," says Yellowstone Superintendent Lewis, who previously ran Glacier National Park and Chattahoochee National Recreation Area, near Atlanta. "The wildlife doesn't stop at the park boundary. The visitors don't stop at the park boundary. Nothing stops at the park boundary."

Superintendents often come under pressure to take local interests into account when they decide whether recreation activities will impair natural or cultural resources.

Since Yellowstone became the first national park in 1872, towns near national parks have catered to tourists arriving first by railroad and then automobile. In addition to providing motels, restaurants and gas stations for tourists, neighboring communities share the costs of police and fire protection and medical care with the parks. In turn, some parks help maintain and plow nearby scenic highways.

Visitors spent $10.3 billion in gateway communities in 2005, supporting 211,000 jobs paying $3.9 billion in wages and salaries, according to a 2006 Park Service study. [14] Park visitors have long been crucial economic mainstays for gateway communities like Gatlinburg, Tenn. (Great Smoky Mountains National Park); Bar Harbor, Maine (Acadia); Estes Park, Colo. (Rocky Mountain) and Springdale, Utah (Zion). And many communities have grown even more reliant on park tourism in recent decades as mining, logging and ranching opportunities have declined.

What's more, Lewis told the Cody chamber, Yellowstone's own 400-person payroll "runs upwards of $20 million a year, and all of these people live and shop and interact in these local communities" at park entrances.

"There is a very significant, tight, symbiotic relationship" between the Park Service and adjacent towns and counties, says Bill Murdock, a county commissioner in Gallatin County, Mont., on Yellowstone's northwest border. But too often the parks have "taken those communities for granted."

Park Service officials agree that some superintendents haven't spent enough time talking with surrounding communities. "In the past we had an attitude that we just want to run the parks," says Stephen P. Martin, deputy director for operations.

Conflicts have escalated — particularly around big parks — since the Park Service began giving higher priority to protecting natural resources in the 1960s. Nearby communities sometimes feel they're losing out, for instance when park decisions ban or limit motorized snowmobiles and jet skis that gateway businesses sell, maintain and rent to vacationers. And 10 years after federal biologists brought wolves back into Yellowstone, ranchers, big-game outfitters and county commissioners complain the predators kill livestock and reduce elk herds as they move outside the park.

The Park Service has also worked with federal and state livestock agencies to cull 1,000 bison from Yellowstone's expanding herds because ranchers' fear they carry the livestock disease brucellosis. And businesses in California gateway communities complain that Yosemite's long-debated plans to limit traffic and possibly visitor numbers in the Yosemite Valley "have left a significant portion of the public searching for a more convenient alternative for vacations and getaways," Bob Warren, chairman of the National Alliance of Gateway Communities, told Congress in May. [15]

Legislation proposed by Rep. George Radanovich, a California Republican whose district lies near Yosemite, would require the Park Service to give gateway communities formal roles in park-management decisions. The measure has gone nowhere, but in revising its systemwide management policies in August, the service instructed park superintendents to engage more regularly with gateway communities as well as other groups with interest in park operations.

"Some superintendents are better at that than others," points out Martin. Yellowstone's Lewis, for instance, "has been very accessible to gateway communities," says Gene Bryan, director of the Cody Chamber of Commerce. "We don't always agree, but we can sit and talk and not be disagreeable."

In Cody, West Yellowstone and other gateway towns, business leaders are counting on continued snowmobile access to Yellowstone to keep winter visitors coming. Murdock and Bryan agree that tighter regulation is required, including clean-running sleds and limits on the number of visitors. Some established West Yellowstone operations already have begun upgrading rental fleets and offering snowcoach tours as alternatives to snowmobiles. "We're not asking for throwing the park wide open," Bryan says. "None of us who have been in this business very long wants to do anything to harm the very reason we live here."

At some other national parks, local governments have worked closely with park administrators on mutually beneficial projects, such as traffic management. Environmental groups realize that over the long term, wild and natural landscapes are gateway regions' economic salvation. People increasingly are moving into communities near national parks and other natural lands — precisely because the parks offer compelling scenery, fascinating wildlife and undeveloped lands where they can hunt, fish, hike or ride horses or motorized off-road vehicles.

"More and more gateway communities are finding that adjoining parks, wildlife refuges or wilderness areas can be powerful economic assets," wrote three land-conservation advocates in a 1997 book on gateway towns. [16]

Between 1970 and 2000, the population in 20 counties surrounding Yellowstone National Park grew 62 percent, and "demographers believe that this rapid migration will continue in areas . . . rich in natural amenities," noted a 2005 study by the Sonoran Institute and Montana State University. [17] A separate National Parks Conservation Association report on six Yellowstone gateway counties found that the region's wild landscapes "do far more than simply draw tourists in large numbers. Much of the area's success is driven by the region's spectacular setting, abundant wildlife, easy access to outdoor recreation and small, friendly towns." [18]

That success, however, threatens to encircle parks with resorts and subdivisions that cut off wildlife-migration corridors along park boundaries. Long-term land-use decisions by local governments could be critical to preserving Yellowstone's ecosystem, says Murdock, the Montana county commissioner. "The elk don't stop at the park boundary when they migrate, nor do the grizzlies or the wolves," he says.

Because of that interdependence, "it's very, very important that the communities understand what the park can and cannot do with its resources — and [understand] what the connection is between the community and the value of living in the community relative to keeping those resources healthy," Lewis told Cody business leaders."

The NPCA has proposed that the Park Service participate in land-use planning around gateway communities. Meanwhile, as they implement the revised management policies, park superintendents will try to step up their outreach to adjacent communities while maintaining their "fundamental mission of long-term conservation of resources," says NPCA President Kiernan. "You can do both." ■

BACKGROUND

Promoting the Parks

Protecting a national park against development was a new idea in 1872 when Congress set Yellowstone National Park aside at the headwaters of the Yellowstone River "as a public park or pleasuring ground for the benefit and enjoyment of the people." Ever since, the government has been trying to balance promoting recreation with preserving the parks' natural resources. [19]

The federal government assigned the U.S. Army to manage the park in 1886 to bring rampant wildlife poaching under control and protect natural features. To attract vacationing passengers, Western railroads began advertising the scenic wonders

Continued on p. 828

Chronology

1860s-1890s

Federal government begins setting aside scenic public lands.

1864
President Abraham Lincoln gives Yosemite Valley to California "for public use, resort and recreation."

1872
President Ulysses S. Grant establishes world's first national park at Yellowstone.

1886
U.S. Army assigned to Yellowstone to protect natural features and arrest poachers. Congress passes the Lacy Act, strengthening federal control of national park resources.

1890
Congress sets aside Yosemite National Park.

1900s-1950s

Federal government creates National Park Service and dramatically increases national park acreage.

1906
President Theodore Roosevelt signs the Antiquities Act, authorizing presidents to proclaim federal lands as natural and historic monuments. The size of the national parks doubles during his tenure.

1913
Over conservationist John Muir's objections, Congress approves damming Yosemite's Hetch Hetchy Valley to supply water to San Francisco.

1916
President Woodrow Wilson signs Organic Act, creating National Park Service.

1919
The East's first national park — Lafayette, later renamed Acadia — is created in Maine.

1926
Congress authorizes Great Smoky Mountains National Park.

1933
Park Service is given responsibility for national battlefields and historic sites.

1956
Park Service launches Mission 66, a 10-year, $1 billion project to upgrade park facilities for Park Service's 50th anniversary in 1966.

1960s-1990s

Park Service expands, switches from managing wildlife to "natural regulation" of ecosystems.

1963
Park Service stops controlling elk and bison herds in Yellowstone, allows natural regulation instead; policy eventually expands to other park ecosystems.

1964
Wilderness Act protects wild landscapes in national forests and on public lands around national parks.

1980
President Jimmy Carter signs landmark Alaska Lands law, increasing Alaska's national park acreage sixfold.

1988
Wildfires burn nearly a third of Yellowstone, testing the service's resolve to let natural forces regulate park ecosystems.

1995
Wolves are returned to Yellowstone National Park.

2000s

Conflicts continue between conservation and recreation.

2000
Yellowstone National Park proposes banning snowmobiles.

2001
President Bill Clinton uses Antiquities Act to create new monuments. . . . Park Service strengthens policy of giving conservation priority over recreation. . . . President George W. Bush names Gale Norton as Interior secretary and Fran Mainella as Park Service director.

2004
After court battles, Yellowstone allows snowmobiles temporarily, through winter 2006-2007; rule limits numbers, requires guided tours and cleaner engines.

2005
Critics claim proposed Interior policy could allow commercial development and motorized recreation to ruin the parks' resources.

2006
Norton and Mainella resign. Former Idaho Gov. Dirk Kempthorne becomes Interior secretary; Mary Bomar becomes Park Service director. . . . Park Service maintains 2001 focus on conservation. Kempthorne promises to develop 10-year Centennial Challenge program to improve the system by the agency's 100th anniversary in 2016.

'We Have to Be Relevant to the Kids'

When she was a child in suburban Ohio, Suzanne Lewis remembers playing in the nearby woods all the time.

"But we don't tell our kids to go play in the woods after school anymore," says Lewis, who grew up to become superintendent of the National Park System's crown jewel, Yellowstone National Park.

As a result, "We've got a lot of kids today who aren't comfortable in the outdoors," she continues, a condition some researchers have dubbed "nature-deficit syndrome." Researchers recently have found that the symptoms of attention deficit hyperactivity disorder in children can be alleviated if they spend less time watching television or playing video games and more time outdoors. [1]

The trend away from outdoor activities for children worries Lewis and other Park Service officials. "Who is going to come to the national parks?" Lewis asked in a recent speech to the Cody, Wyo., Chamber of Commerce. "And when they do come, what will be their comfort level in these parks and what will they want from these wild places?" For the future of the National Park System "that's a very, very significant question."

Indeed, the total number of park visitors has leveled off in the last decade — even at Yellowstone — even though more park units have been added and the U.S. population has grown.

While Lewis attributes this year's decline to summer gasoline prices that topped $3 a gallon, some Park Service officials are beginning to worry that the national treasures they manage are losing their allure to new generations of Americans.

"The thing I am most concerned about is the demographics of who's coming to the parks — and who's going to come in the future," she told the Cody chamber.

Visits to the national park system grew steadily after World War II, peaking at 287 million in 1987. In the last 20 years, however, despite the addition of 80 new units to the system and a 23 percent increase in the nation's population to nearly 300 million people, park visitation had fallen to 274 million in 2005.

New Mexico Tourism Secretary Michael Cerletti blamed the falloff on fee increases and overcrowding. Plus, he said in April testimony to Congress, people aren't visiting the parks because they find them overcrowded, the facilities degraded and the interpretive programs boring.

But recreation-industry officials argue that policies designed to protect the parks from crowds and noise — such as higher entrance fees and restricting snowmobiles, jet skis and off-road vehicles — have discouraged visitors.

"Fewer Americans are visiting and benefiting from our parks, and the failure to deliver these benefits to urban Americans, youth, senior citizens, the disabled and Americans of diverse ethnicity should be of particular concern," the American Recreation Coalition told Secretary of the Interior Dirk Kempthorne in a letter in August.

The Park Service has focused too much on preserving natural conditions and lost touch with modern-day Americans who have grown up watching television, using computers and cell phones and enjoy riding motorized equipment and camping out in trailers and recreation vehicles, say tourism- and recreation-equipment manufacturers.

"Gone are the days of taking the station wagon for a two-week camping trip to a national park," Bob Warren, a Northern California tourism official, told an April congressional hearing on park-visitation trends. "Hiking, cookouts, sleeping in tents and

Continued from p. 826

of Yellowstone and helped convince Congress to protect other natural areas as national parks, including the Yosemite, Sequoia and General Grant parks in California. President Theodore Roosevelt, an ardent outdoorsman who frequently visited the parks, doubled the nation's park acreage during his administration, and Congress in the 1906 Antiquities Act authorized presidents to protect threatened lands by declaring them national monuments.

In 1913, however, in a portent of future conflicts between using park resources and preserving them, Congress approved damming the Hetch Hetchy Valley inside Yosemite to supply water to San Francisco, despite the objections of Sierra Club founder John Muir.

The tension between preservation and development continued after Congress established the National Park Service in 1916. The Organic Act declared that the fundamental purpose of the parks was "to conserve the scenery and the natural and historic objects and the wildlife therein and to provide for the enjoyment of the same in such manner and by such means as will leave them unimpaired for the enjoyment of future generations." Although that mission remains on the books, how the Park Service applies it has evolved over the last nine decades.

President Woodrow Wilson appointed Stephen T. Mather, a Chicago borax manufacturer who had campaigned for the Organic Act, as the first Park Service director. He served until 1929, when his longtime aide Horace Albright took over. Both worked to solidify public support for the parks by encouraging tourists to visit and by courting influential businessmen and conservation leaders.

While Mather rejected a plan to string a cable car across the Grand Canyon, he and Albright encouraged more park visitors by building roads, campgrounds and large, rustic lodges and restaurants. The service granted concessions to private businesses to

watching deer is just not stimulating enough for those who have grown up with constant and instant multimedia stimulation. Their definition of an outdoor experience includes jet skis, ATVs [all-terrain vehicles], motorcycles and jet boats — all part of activities that are largely prohibited in national parks."

Currently, the nation's 58 national parks draw 23 percent of the system's visitors, while units near major metropolitan areas — created primarily for recreation — now attract just as many.

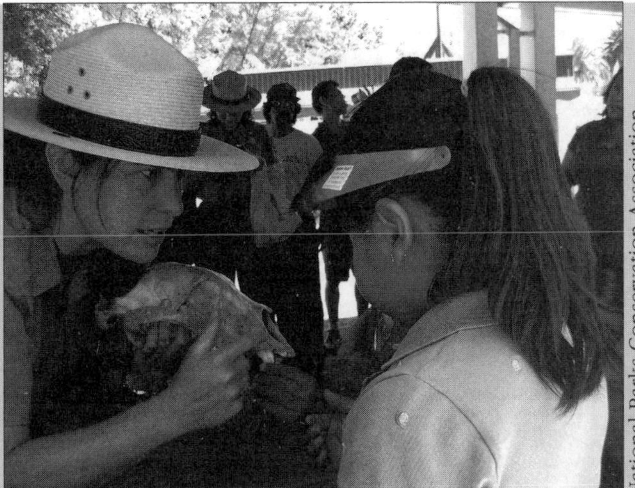

National Parks Conservation Association

Yosemite Ranger Adrienne Freeman shows off an animal skull during National Parks Family Day. Budget cutbacks have forced many parks to reduce ranger staffs and programs.

However, Laura Loomis, director of visitor experience at the National Parks Conservation Association, notes that surveys show that 95 percent of visitors say they've enjoyed the time they spent in the parks. "Overall, they're in support of staying the course and keeping the parks the same," she says.

Others question the claim that visitation is off, pointing out that visitors to the Gulf Islands National Seashore dropped 2.5 million during the extraordinary 2005 hurricane season — accounting for three-quarters of that year's nationwide decline. [2]

Some critics say the tradition-bound Park Service has been slow to adapt to social and economic changes. "There is a tremendous value in the legacy and esprit de corps in the service," says recreation coalition Director Derrick A. Crandall. But "many recent superintendents have been too much focused backward and not enough on changes" in the public who visits parks. Crandall admires some business-minded managers of popular parks who "are not quite as wedded to the past."

Advocates of the Park Service, on the other hand, attribute dropping attendance to high gasoline prices, fears of terrorism and economic changes that leave families with less time for extended vacations in the parks.

In any case, says Lewis, parks must adapt to the changing interests and expectations of modern park visitors in addition to preserving natural experiences. Yellowstone's recently redesigned Canyon visitor center, for example, features state-of-the-art educational displays depicting the volcanic geology beneath that park. "We have to be relevant to the kids," Lewis says. "We can't tell them not to bring their Ipods."

[1] Frances E. Kuo and Andrea Faber Taylor, "A Potential Natural Treatment for Attention-Deficit/Hyperactivity Disorder: Evidence From a National Study," *American Journal of Public Health*, www.ajph.org/cgi/content/abstract/94/9/1580. For background on attention deficit disorder, see Kathy Koch, "Rethinking Ritalin," *CQ Researcher*, Oct. 22, 1999, pp. 905-928.

[2] Kurt Repanshek, "Keeping Track of Visitors No Easy Task," *National Parks Traveler*, Oct. 2, 2006, www.nationalparkstraveler.com.

run lodges, cabins, stores, restaurants and gasoline stations inside the parks.

Visitors have paid fees to enter national parks since Mount Rainier National Park began charging an entrance fee in 1908. When the Park Service was created in 1916, seven of the system's 14 units already charged entrance fees to drive an automobile into the park, including $10 a year at Yellowstone and $2 a year at Glacier and Mesa Verde national parks. Mather thought the agency could finance all park operations and improvements from concession revenues and entrance fees.

But in 1918 Congress directed the Park Service to deposit revenues directly into the federal Treasury. "This broke the link between park revenues and park spending, and expenditures have become political footballs ever since," conservative economists Donald R. Leal and Montana State University's Fretwell argued in a 1997 study for the Property and Environment Research Center, which contends that private interests provide the most effective incentives for environmental protection. [20]

The Park Service expanded its political base when Congress created Acadia National Park in Maine and Great Smoky Mountains National Park in the Southeast. In the 1930s, President Franklin D. Roosevelt doubled the system by giving the Park Service control over national monuments, battlefields, historic sites and national shrines and parks in Washington, D.C.

During World War II, park funding was constricted, leaving the service with a backlog of facilities in disrepair just as tourism boomed with the nation's postwar prosperity. In the 1950s, Director Conrad Wirth responded with his crash "Mission 66" initiative to make the parks more accessible by 1966, the 50th anniversary of the Organic Act. The project built or improved 2,000 miles of roads and constructed 114 visitor centers, many with cafeterias, souvenir shops and auditoriums.

The tourism industry and philanthropists continued playing important roles in expanding and popularizing the park system. John D. Rockefeller Jr. contributed $25 million of his own fortune, providing land for Grand Teton, Great Smoky Mountains, Shenandoah and Yosemite.

In keeping with prevailing feelings about wildlife, the Park Service promoted picturesque wildlife — like elk and deer — but eliminated predatory wolves and mountain lions from Yellowstone. Rangers there also allowed tourists to feed black bears begging for handouts along roadsides and erected bleachers where visitors gathered to watch grizzlies feed at open garbage dumps.

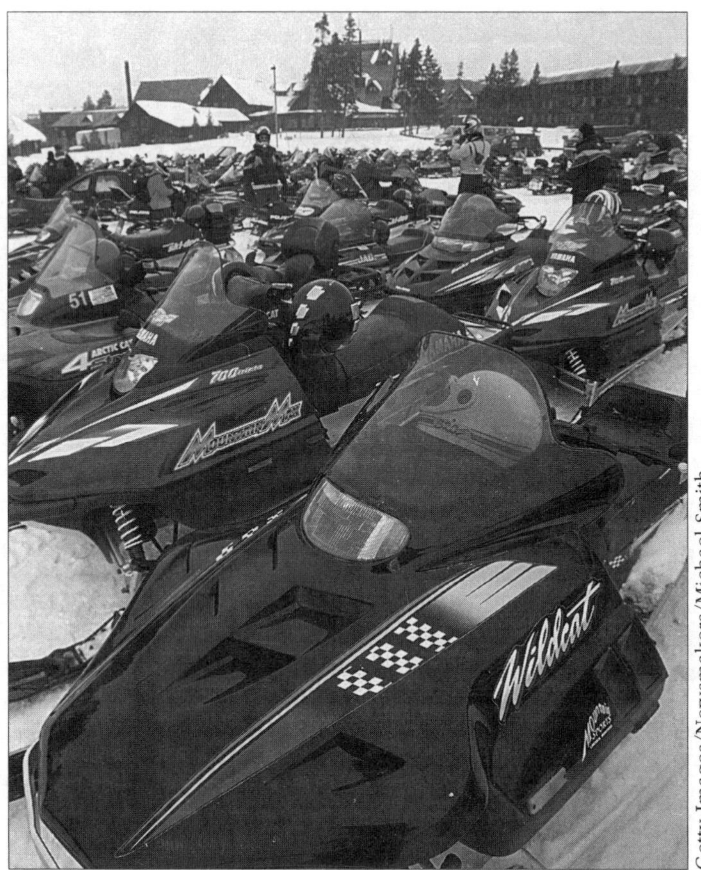

Getty Images/Newsmakers/Michael Smith

Snowmobiles await riders in Yellowstone National Park. Concern that growing snowmobile traffic was causing air pollution and disturbing wildlife prompted the Park Service to set a limit this year of 720 snowmobiles per day and require snowmobilers to hire trained guides and use clean-burning, four-stroke engines.

Conserving the Parks

Public attitudes about wilderness began shifting in the 1950s and early '60s. The Sierra Club and other environmental groups rallied to the park system's defense to block construction of a dam in Dinosaur National Monument and others on the Colorado River inside the Grand Canyon. The Park Service continued to struggle with the growing tension between recreation and preservation.

With natural predators eliminated, Yellowstone's plentiful elk population threatened to denude the park's northern range. But public outcry forced rangers to stop shooting the elk to cull the herd to sustainable levels. Zoologist A. Starker Leopold, son of legendary wilderness advocate Aldo Leopold, recommended that the Park Service shift away from artificially manipulating wildlife and natural conditions. The 1963 Leopold report proposed letting natural forces run their course as much as possible inside park boundaries in order to "maintain a vignette of primitive America."

Stewart L. Udall, the conservation-minded Interior secretary during the Kennedy and Johnson administrations, embraced the report and pushed the Park Service to stress conservation. Congress reinforced the effort over the following decade by enacting laws setting out national goals for cleaning up air and water pollution and saving endangered species. Since then, superintendents, biologists and rangers have embraced a preservationist view of their work. Following the new philosophy, Yellowstone closed its dumps in the 1960s, fined tourists for feeding bears and let elk and bison herds expand and migrate outside the park in winter.

On Dec. 2, 1980, during his lame-duck tenure, President Jimmy Carter signed the landmark Alaska Lands legislation into law, culminating an intense, nine-year congressional battle. While restricting development on more than 100 million acres of land in Alaska, the massive bill also expanded three existing Alaskan national parks and created 10 new parks — increasing the state's national park acreage sixfold, from 7.5 million acres to 43.6 million acres.

Dubbed the "conservation vote of the century" by environmentalists, the bill more than doubled the size of the country's national park and wildlife refuge systems and nearly tripled the amount of U.S. territory designated as wilderness. [21]

Six weeks later, Ronald Reagan was inaugurated, and his administration took a decidedly different tack on park conservation. His Interior secretary, James Watt, disdained the preservation trend. Watt snowmobiled through Yellowstone, proclaimed himself bored while rafting through the Grand Canyon and scoffed at hikers and other environmentalists. Watt forced the Park Service to transfer managers after they resisted hunting in some of the new Alaskan national parks and others who tried to restrict Glacier Bay boat tours that disturbed endangered humpback whales. [22]

But while Watt pushed other Interior agencies to accelerate logging and oil and gas drilling, the Park Service

Can Cell Phones and Wilderness Coexist?

For generations, Americans visited their national parks to get away from it all. That experience didn't include receiving instant BlackBerry messages from the office, nor could visitors overhear others ordering pizza by cell phone while watching — and trying to hear — geysers erupt in Yellowstone National Park's remote thermal basins.

Today, however, as wireless technologies have changed how millions of Americans live, the National Park Service is deciding whether visitors should be able to stay in touch with the outside world — and possibly ruin the solitude and scenic vistas that others hope to find when they cross national park boundaries.

Two years ago, environmental groups and Wyoming historic preservation officials complained that a 100-foot-tall tower was marring the landscape within sight of Yellowstone's Old Faithful geyser. Park officials lopped 20 feet off the structure last year — and coated the steel with vinegar and water to dull its shine. They also began studying whether blanketing Yellowstone with wireless service is compatible with keeping the national parks unimpaired.

Yellowstone Superintendent Suzanne Lewis said the park's challenge "is how to respond appropriately to visitor expectations" for convenient wireless service while still "protecting the historic, rustic, outdoor experience of a visit to the world's first national park."

Cell towers have been installed in the Grand Canyon, Everglades and Yosemite national parks and other units, pursuant to the Telecommunications Act of 1996, which ordered government agencies to allow cell companies to build towers on federally owned lands. But Sen. Lamar Alexander, R-Tenn., has blocked a proposal to build three 120-foot towers inside Great Smoky Mountains National Park, and cell projects in other parks have begun encountering similar opposition.

National Parks Conservation Association

Park officials lopped 20 feet off a cell phone tower in Yellowstone park last year after preservationists complained it was marring the view of Old Faithful geyser.

Yellowstone imposed a moratorium on new towers in 2004 and is reviewing wireless technologies used inside the park — including two-way radios, Web cams, seismic monitors and radio collars on wolves and grizzly bears. The assessment likely will set a precedent for how other parks respond when cellphone companies propose building new towers to expand service coverage.

Yellowstone rangers still communicate with handheld radios, a 1930s-era technology that involves "many dead zones where they can't receive communications," says Eleanor Clark, Yellowstone's chief of planning. After the first cell towers were installed in the mid-1990s, some park rangers began carrying cell phones, but they only work in 5 percent of Yellowstone's 2.2 million acres. "We know where to stop to get reception," says Stephen Swanke, Yellowstone's assistant chief ranger.

With better cell coverage, Yellowstone visitors could summon help by dialing 911, and park staff could stay in closer touch while on backcountry patrols. But environmentalists are urging the park to consider giving rangers satellite phones instead or perhaps limiting public cell access to 911 emergency calls. Cell phones may make visitors feel safer, but they could also encourage "reckless behavior based on a false sense of security" if visitors grow overconfident when they wander through active thermal areas or hike into backcountry grizzly-bear habitat, says Amy E. McNamara, the national parks director for the Greater Yellowstone Coalition.

Tim Stevens, the National Parks Conservation Association's Yellowstone program director, says the park should consider tearing down the Old Faithful cell tower and remind visitors they shouldn't enter a wild and natural park expecting all the modern-day conveniences.

"It's not like spending a day in the city," Stevens says. "There are plenty of people who would rather protect the silence and solitude of Yellowstone Park."

continued its shift toward standing aside while natural forces took their course, for instance by maintaining a policy of allowing many lightning-sparked wildfires to burn themselves out. In 1988, however, Yellowstone Superintendent Bob Barbee came under intense criticism when fires burned across more than a third of the park's 2.2 million acres, threatening the historic Old Faithful Inn, coming close to gateway towns and forcing visitors to evacuate.

In the 1990s, funding problems continued to plague the parks, and a $34 million shortfall in 1993 led the service to close campgrounds and eliminate other services. Congress created the fee demo program in 1996, and in 2000 the Park Service began selling $50-a-year National Parks Passes that allow access to all units. But President Clinton's

National Park Service (All)

The Great Outdoors, from East to West

The National Park Service manages 84 million acres in 390 park units, including 58 national parks ranging from Dry Tortugas in Florida (top) to Acadia in Maine (middle) to Mesa Verde in Colorado (bottom). The park system also includes a growing number of historic sites, battlefields and public recreation areas and employs 20,000 rangers, interpreters, biologists, historians, archeologists, clerks, maintenance workers and other staff.

Interior secretary, Bruce Babbitt, a former Arizona governor who later led the League of Conservation Voters, reaffirmed the federal commitment to keeping park lands wild and pristine, protecting and, if possible, restoring ecosystems.

Over the objections of neighboring states, Babbitt in 1995 approved transplanting Canadian wolves into Yellowstone to help keep elk and bison in check. After 1997 floods washed away two popular Yosemite campgrounds, Babbitt approved a long-term plan to restore natural woodland habitat and native aquatic species along the Merced River.

Before Babbitt left office, he and Park Service scientists helped negotiate a comprehensive federal-state plan that attempts to rescue Everglades National Park and three nearby parks by partially restoring natural water flows that federal flood-control projects had diverted from the Everglades. [23] During the Clinton administration's final year, the Park Service set the stage for recent controversies when it barred snowmobiles and jet skis from certain parks and redrafted its management manual to give park superintendents a strengthened hand to restrict recreation in order to protect natural and cultural resources.

Many of Babbitt's decisions were controversial, particularly in the recreation industry and gateway communities. But in those years, the agency had shifted its goal to embrace more actively protecting park resources. In 1999, the Park Service launched a five-year "Natural Resources Challenge" to strengthen scientific research, inventory native ecosystems, monitor natural conditions and control invasive species.

"For most of the 20th century, we have practiced a curious combination of active management and passive acceptance of natural systems and processes, while becoming a superb visitor-services agency," the Park Service declared in a plan signed by Robert Stanton, Clinton's Park Service director, authorizing the challenge effort.

Continued on p. 834

At Issue:

Are Park Service policies keeping people out of the parks?

yes

DERRICK A. CRANDALL
PRESIDENT, AMERICAN RECREATION COALITION

FROM LETTER TO NATIONAL PARK SERVICE DIRECTOR FRAN MAINELLA, FEB. 17, 2006

The 2001 version of NPS [National Park Service] management policies was developed under Interior [Department] leadership that repeatedly expressed concerns about visitors "loving the parks to death" and suggested the likelihood of continuing large increases in park visitation.

We believe that philosophy was based on a false premise. In fact, recent data suggest that visitation to the National Park System is not increasing. Visitation in 2005 was down 2.1 percent for the year, and visitation to the small portion of the 388-unit system comprised of national parks has been stable or trending downward for several years. We have real fear that the mental, physical and spiritual benefits of visits to our National Park System will be realized by a declining portion of the public — and that the system will have little meaning for some of the U.S. population cohorts experiencing the fastest growth — ethnic minorities, urban residents and young people.

We believe that the 2001 policies erred in responding favorably to an understandable desire among some park managers and park advocates for a simplistic, single-focused mission. [The manual] does not reflect the direction of the Organic Act and ignores the management precedents of the agency's most respected early leaders. The vision of those leaders resulted in design and construction of infrastructure that has long enhanced visitation to the parks while providing protection for park features and qualities.

The mission of the agency cannot be effectively implemented through appropriations alone. We feel increased attention can and should be placed upon using fees to increase agency resources. We firmly believe that increased use of technology to educate, interpret for and manage visitors — often through partnerships — is a preferred course for the National Park Service.

The extraordinary diversity of the National Park System must be reflected in the operations of these units. Man-altered environments like Lake Mead, much of Golden Gate National Recreation Area and the National Mall, for example, must be managed much differently than park units with extensive wilderness and backcountry zones. These are the units that many Americans will first encounter when they visit the National Park System and play a special role in creating an understanding of the value of the priceless outdoor legacy we enjoy today.

no

DENIS GALVIN
RETIRED DEPUTY DIRECTOR, NATIONAL PARK SERVICE

ON BEHALF OF THE NATIONAL PARK CONSERVATION ASSOCIATION, FROM TESTIMONY BEFORE THE HOUSE SUBCOMMITTEE ON NATIONAL PARKS, FEB. 15, 2006

What is needed is for a broad constituency of interests that are engaged with the National Park Service — recreation, tourism, gateway communities, conservation, preservation and regular "good citizens" — to step up their support for their national parks as they are, and as they are intended to be: preserved unimpaired for future generations to enjoy.

Nearly 300 million people visited the parks last year, and we know from surveys that they "enjoyed" them. NPS concessionaires grossed over $1 billion in 2004; surrounding gateway communities and businesses grossed over another $11 billion attributable to national park visitors.

Despite this, there are those who suggest that NPS management of the parks is too restrictive, or that the parks are locked up, or lack access. Nothing could be further from the truth.

The national parks do not have to sustain all recreation; that is why we have various other federal, state, local and private recreation providers. The NPS mission is different from that of state park agencies, or of county or city park agencies. Together, these agencies provide for many forms of public recreation — but not all forms of recreation are appropriate in national parks.

There is no credible debate over whether parks should be used by the American people; the debate centers on how the use occurs, or sometimes when or where.

For the NPS professionals, conserving the parks unimpaired for future generations is synonymous with offering park visitors a high-quality experience. Scenic vistas should be clear, natural sounds should dominate over man-made noises, native wildlife should be abundant and visible for visitors, historic sites such as battlefields should look like they did when the historic events occurred, park visitor facilities should not be so located as to disturb the natural scene or the cultural landscape.

Preservation is the key to continued success of the NPS in fulfilling its statutory mandate, and also to sustaining the core destinations that fuel the tourism industry.

Continued from p. 832

"In the 21st century, that management style clearly will be insufficient to save our natural resources." [24] ■

CURRENT SITUATION

Budget Woes

Six years into the Bush administration, debate continues over whether the National Park Service has been able to give the national parks the protection they require. [25]

In tough fiscal times during the Reagan administration, the service's sterling reputation with the American public helped fend off debilitating funding cuts. But since 2001, managers have been handling ever more difficult responsibilities with shrinking budgets, sometimes under what Park Service veterans say has been unprecedented political duress.

"We certainly did better during the Reagan administration than anybody else in Interior, but that's not the case now," says former Superintendent Smith. Former Secretary Norton, her deputy Steven Griles and NPS Director Mainella were regarded within the service as sympathetic to recreation interests and distrustful of longtime agency employees. Like Watt, a former mentor, Norton took a snowmobiling trip through Yellowstone. The administration also declared that the Park Service would focus on catching up with a much-discussed backlog in repairing lodges, campgrounds, restrooms and other visitor facilities.

Since fiscal 2002, the Park Service has poured $4.9 billion into deferred maintenance work on nearly 6,000 facilities, according to the agency's fiscal 2007 budget proposal. For fiscal 2007, the Park Service has asked Congress for $393.5 million for maintenance, $229.3 million for new facilities and $210 million in highway funds to upgrade park roads. The budget request included $10 million a year for routine repairs to keep facilities from deteriorating. Overall, with funds expected through 2009, park assets "will be brought into acceptable condition," according to the agency's fiscal 2007 Park Service budget, nicknamed the Green Book. [26] But in 2005, the Congressional Research Service (CRS) said there was still a $7.1 billion backlog of repairs through 2004. [27]

At the same time, the White House and Congress have slashed federal funding for daily park operations well below what superintendents say they need. Between fiscal 2001 and 2005, the amounts allocated for daily operations rose by $100 million — to more than $1 billion a year, but that doesn't keep up with inflation, according to the CRS.

"The Park Service has been something of a thorn in the side of this administration," says Smith. And although current officials talk guardedly about funding cuts, in the past year retired park managers have gone public with complaints that Congress and Interior Department superiors are meddling in Park Service efforts to preserve threatened national parks. In 2003, more than 500 retired park officials formed the Coalition of National Park Service Retirees, which has harshly criticized the way the administration is trying to change how the parks are managed.

By speaking out, says John Varley, a former Yellowstone Resources Center director who retired in 2005, the retirees demonstrate the dismay within current Park Service ranks about budget cuts and political interference they contend have kept the agency from protecting the parks against serious threats.

Ecological Integrity

In recent decades, it has become clear that even the largest parks are not big or isolated enough to be immune from environmental damage, particularly from air and water pollution, invasive species and human development.

Serious ecological problems are threatening the park system's biodiversity, particularly the 398 threatened or endangered species of plants and animals. "The mission to preserve parks unimpaired includes the ecological integrity of park resources," the NPS' Science Advisory Committee declared in a 2004 study. "National parks with decreased biological diversity and diminished natural systems can in no way be considered unimpaired." [28]

A recent NPCA study also found that the air in California's Sequoia and Kings Canyon national parks violated federal ozone standards for an average of 61 days a year, making hiking, biking and rock climbing potentially hazardous. Yellowstone and Grand Teton national parks are threatened by emissions from new coal-fired power plants and 8,700 oil and gas wells being drilled in surrounding regions, while a new power plant 50 miles west of Kentucky's Mammoth Cave National Park will increase mercury concentrations already found in the park's endangered Indiana bats. [29]

Preserving ecosystems inside parks is also complicated by exotic plants and animals. Feral pigs run through the Great Smoky Mountains National Park and park units in Hawaii. The service now deploys 16 mobile exotic-plant management teams, including experts trained to tackle tamarisk in the Rio Grande Valley, leafy spurge in Great Plains parks and lygodium, an Old World climbing fern that's killing native trees in the Everglades.

Michael Soukup, the service's longtime associate director for natural stewardship and research, sees invasive species and housing developments surrounding park boundaries as the most severe threats. Moreover, he adds, global climate change and loss of habitat overseas may be changing park ecosystems. Migratory birds are losing South American wintering grounds, he says, and "it will be sad if our parks don't have some of their songbirds in the future." If concerns about global warming are realized, Soukup adds, "there will be some big changes afoot that will affect the distribution of wildlife."

The Clinton administration's Natural Resource Challenge called for funding to be channeled into improving scientific research in the system's natural parks. The challenge is conducting inventories of ecological resources, monitoring for changes and improving environmental conditions. The service now is working with biologists from universities and other government agencies to study all the birds, mammals, reptiles, amphibians, fish and plants in the parks.

The initiative expanded efforts to remove invasive species that threaten native wildlife and created 13 research learning centers for scientists conducting studies in parks around the country. The Bush administration has continued funding the Natural Resource Challenge and has proposed spending an additional $1 million for fiscal 2007 to establish the last two of 32 networks for monitoring the vital signs of park ecosystems.

Fear and Whistleblowers

The Natural Resource Challenge "is having an enormous impact," says Soukup, but "it's going to take a long time to realize the full importance of what it accomplishes."

But while the 1999 initiative proposed doubling natural-resource spending from $85 million to $170 million a year, Varley says funding has begun drying up. Inside the parks, experts say budget cuts are taking a toll on biological research and resource-management programs. [30]

For instance, Yellowstone has kept its wolf program funded through private support, "but most projects don't have that charisma," says Varley. While the agency focuses on protecting endangered species and controlling invasive pests, "You have smaller programs that just vanish — any programs on bats, for example. They're not on anybody's radar screen, but they're a good indicator species for environmental quality."

In the short term, most wildlife "is resilient enough that it's not going to hell in a handbasket tomorrow," Varley says. For the long term, however, he fears funding cutbacks will prevent park scientists from spotting ecological trends before they become dire threats. "You can't measure that from one year to the next," he says. Consistent monitoring year after year "is the only way you can figure out there's a problem for grizzlies, wolves and elk — and for bats and songbirds. You can't go back in time and get the numbers, so you don't know what's increasing or decreasing."

In some cases, park managers have felt subtle pressure not to speak publicly about resource threats for fear of retribution. For example, the White House does not accept that global warming is a major threat, Varley says, "but anybody who's been in the park and worked in the field believes it's real. I was never asked not to say anything, but I never tested it. If I couldn't tell the truth, I didn't speak. I was too close to retirement."

Meanwhile, Varley adds, "I don't know anybody [inside the Park Service] who's talking. This cast of [Bush administration] characters knows Old Testament vengeance."

In one incident, Hoffman, author of the controversial manual revision, reportedly challenged Death Valley National Park Superintendent J. T. Reynolds' policy of keeping off-road enthusiasts from driving jeeps up steep canyons. Then in 2005, after Reynolds criticized Hoffman's proposed manual revisions, the service conducted three investigative reviews of how Death Valley is managed but found no significant problems. At the Mojave National Reserve, a new California unit that allows hunting, Hoffman questioned Superintendent Mary Martin, who resisted pressure from Hoffman and congressional staffers to reopen artificial water "guzzlers' to attract game animals for hunters. Martin eventually transferred to become superintendent of Lassen Volcano National Park and the guzzler decision is still disputed. [31]

The National Parks Conservation Association came to Reynolds' defense by giving him its 2005 Stephen T. Mather Award for protecting national parks. Most current employees feel compelled to keep silent to protect their jobs, but Smith says some high-ranking officials, including park superintendents, have been quietly passing tips along to the retiree group's whistleblowers. [32]

Over time, Park Service veterans are beginning to worry that tight budgets and political pressures are producing a "not very attractive" evolutionary change in park managers, Smith says. Now an official can rise through the Park Service ranks "if your park makes money because you're able to collect fees or you're a great fund-raiser, or if your park has a congressman or congresswoman on an appropriations committee you get palsy-walsy with," he says. "I would prefer a park manager who has real dedication to preserving and protecting the resource." ■

OUTLOOK

Back to Basics?

On Aug. 25, as the Park Service celebrated the 90th anniversary of the Organic Act, new possibilities seemed to be in the crisp Yellowstone air as Kempthorne traveled to the park to dedicate its new Canyon Visitor and Education Center. He announced a new 10-year Centennial Challenge initiative "to prepare national parks for another century of conservation, preservation and enjoyment" before the 100th anniversary in 2016.

"The challenge facing the National Park Service — at Yellowstone and all our parks — is to conserve what is timeless while keeping pace with the modern needs and expectations of the American people," Kempthorne said, citing the Mission 66 project as a precedent. In an accompanying message, the president directed the service to set performance goals and signature projects for improving the parks "that continue the . . . legacy of leveraging philanthropic partnerships and government investments for the benefit of national parks and their visitors." [33]

The administration has given the Park Service until May 31, 2007, to figure out how that will be accomplished. Deputy Director Martin says the agency will need additional appropriations and revenues from fees and private contributions. "Fee demo will be part of it, but it can't be all of it," Martin says. "It's not enough to meet the fundamental missions of the parks."

In September, Sen. Craig Thomas, R-Wyo., chairman of the Senate Subcommittee on National Parks, joined with Hawaii's Sen. Daniel Akaka, the committee's ranking Democrat, to circulate a draft letter to Bush among Senate colleagues calling for increases in park operating budgets. Taking note of President Dwight D. Eisenhower's $1 billion Mission 66 program, the draft letter called for "a proportional investment in our national parks as we embark on their 100th anniversary." [34]

In the House, Rep. Mark Souder, an Indiana Republican, has been pushing a proposed National Park Centennial Act to create a federal income tax check-off allowing Americans to donate tax refunds to park system funding. NPCA President Kiernan welcomed the administration's plan but cautioned that it won't be enough to repair and build facilities, nor will it cover operating funds. In the four decades since Mission 66 was completed, "we've learned a lot about what it means to protect the natural and cultural resources in the parks," Kiernan says. "We need to do this in a very sensitive way."

Meanwhile, the parks still struggle to balance conflicting missions. On Aug. 31, NPS Director Mainella signed updated management policies that she says "make clear the National Park Service's desire for people to visit and enjoy their national parks" while steering the agency toward "cooperative conservation and civic engagement in our decision-making." The revisions encourage park superintendents to reach out to gateway communities and other interested groups "trying to move to the center so we can make long-term sustainable decisions," says NPS Deputy Director Martin, a former Grand Teton superintendent.

"But it's a two-way street," Mainella continues. "The outside groups need to understand what our fundamental mission is and come up with solutions that work for the mutual benefit of everybody."

The new version of the management manual maintains the 2001 directive giving conservation top priority, leaving it up to park managers to make tough calls balancing recreation with preservation. Catton, the Montana snowmobile critic, expects park managers will still come under pressure to define potential impacts in ways that subtly bypass the 1916 Organic Act's ban on impairing park resources.

Recreation interests and some gateway communities "will continue the pressure on the Park Service and in some cases on individual park superintendents," says retired Shenandoah Superintendent Wade. "It's going to come down to how the management policies are implemented."

Meanwhile, environmentalists keep pushing the parks for more stringent preservation. California advocates are in court demanding that Yosemite limit visitor numbers as it redesigns roads and facilities damaged by Merced River floods nine years ago. In 2007, more legal challenges will be likely as Yellowstone planners try to settle on a permanent snowmobile policy.

"We need to be brave enough to recognize that park resources have limits," says Yellowstone's Lewis. "Those limits aren't intended to have negative impacts on the economies of these local communities," but accepting them will be essential for "making those resources last for a long, long time." ■

About the Author

Tom Arrandale is a freelance writer in Livingston, Mont., reporting on environmental, natural resource and wildlife issues. He is a columnist for Congressional Quarterly's *Governing* magazine and has written for *Planning Magazine*, *High Country News* and *Yellowstone Journal*. He authored *The Battle for Natural Resources* (CQ Press, 1983). He serves on the Livingston Historic Preservation Commission and Board of Adjustment. He visits Yellowstone National Park regularly to hike, snowshoe and photograph wildlife. He graduated from Dartmouth College with a history degree and from the University of Missouri with a master's degree in journalism.

Notes

[1] "The Burgeoning Backlog," National Parks Conservation Association, May 2004.

[2] Government Accountability Office, "National Park Service, Major Operations Funding Trends and How Selected Park Units Responded to Those Trends for Fiscal Years 2001 through 2005," March 2006.

[3] Coalition of National Park Service Retirees, "Reality Check: What Visitors to America's National Parks Will Experience During Summer 2006," June 15, 2006.

[4] For background see Marcia Clemmitt, "Climate Change," *CQ Researcher*, Jan. 27, 2006, pp. 73-96; Stephen Saunders and Tom Easely, "Losing Ground, Western National Parks Endangered by Climate Disruption," Natural Resources Defense Council (NRDC) and the Rocky Mountain Climate Organization, July 2006, p. v.

[5] *Ibid.*, NRDC.

[6] "Turning Point," National Parks Conservation Association, August 2006.

[7] See Benjamin Spillman, "Developers Covet Areas Surrounding National Parks," *USA Today*, March 21, 2006.

[8] Kurt Repanshek, "Life in America's National Parks," *National Parks Traveler*, www.nationalparkstraveler.com, Nov. 15, 2005.

[9] Public Employees for Environmental Responsibility, "Comments on Proposed Rewrite Director's Order #21 Donations and Fundraising," Nov. 30, 2005.

[10] Michael Lanza, "Still Buzzing," *Backpacker*, February 2006, p. 71.

[11] Kurt Repanshek, "Jet Skis in the Parks: Congresswoman Miller Wants Them," *National Parks Traveler*, www.nationalparkstraveler.com, Feb. 4, 2006.

[12] Press release, May 4, 2006.

[13] Derrick A. Crandall, letter to National Park Service Director Fran Mainella. Feb. 17, 2006.

[14] "National Park Service Social Science Program, FY 2005 Money Generation Model Briefing Statement," March 2006.

[15] Prepared testimony, Senate Subcommittee on Public Lands and Forests, May 10, 2006.

[16] Jim Howe, Ed McMahon and Luther Probst, *Balancing Nature and Commerce in Gateway Communities* (1997), p. 6.

[17] Patricia Gude, "Yellowstone 2020, Creating our Legacy," Sonoran Institute, 2005.

[18] "Gateways to Yellowstone, Protecting the Heart of Our Region's Thriving Economy," National Parks Conservation Association, May 2006.

[19] For background, see Rachel S. Cox, "Protecting the National Parks," *CQ Researcher*, June 16, 2000, pp. 521-544, and Richard L. Worsnop, "National Parks," *CQ Researcher*, May 28, 1993, pp. 457-480.

[20] Donald R. Leal and Holly L. Fretwell, "Back to the Future to Save Our Parks," *PERC Policy Series Issue No. PS-10*, Property and Environment Research Center, June 1997.

[21] For background see "Alaska Lands," *1980 Congress and the Nation, Vol. V*, pp. 577-583, or online at http://library.cqpress.com/catn/.

[22] For background see Tom Arrandale, "Access to Federal Lands," in *Editorial Research Reports 1981* (Vol. II), available at *CQ Researcher Plus Archive*, CQ Electronic Library, http://library.cqpress.com.

[23] See Michael Grunwald, *The Swamp, The Everglades, Florida, and the Politics of Paradise* (2006). See also David Hosansky, "Reforming the Corps," *CQ Researcher*, May 30, 2003, pp. 497-520, and Mary H. Cooper, "Water Quality," *CQ Researcher*, Nov. 24, 2000, pp. 953-976.

[24] "The Natural Resources Challenge, The National Park Service's Action Plan for Preserving Natural Resources," National Park Service, August 1999, p. 2.

[25] For background, see Mary H. Cooper, "Bush and the Environment," *CQ Researcher*, Oct. 25, 2003, pp. 865-896.

[26] "Budget Justifications and Performance Information, Fiscal Year 2007, Overview," National Park Service.

[27] Carol Hardy Vincent, "National Park Management," Congressional Research Service, March 11, 2005.

[28] "National Park Service Science in the 21st Century," National Parks Science Committee, March 2004, p. 3.

[29] "Turning Point," *op. cit.*

[30] For background, see Marcia Clemmitt, "Budget Deficit," *CQ Researcher*, Dec. 9, 2005, pp. 1029-1052.

[31] See Michael Shnayerson, "Who's Ruining Our National Parks," *Vanity Fair*, June 2006.

[32] For background, see "Peter Katel, "Protecting Whistleblowers," *CQ Researcher*, March 31, 2006, pp. 265-288.

[33] "Memorandum for the Secretary of the Interior," President George W. Bush, Aug. 24, 2006.

[34] Quoted in Noelle Straub, "Thomas urges Bush's help on national parks," *Billings Gazette*, Sept. 9, 2006, p. 7B.

FOR MORE INFORMATION

American Recreation Coalition, 1225 New York Ave., N.W., Suite 450, Washington, DC 20005-6405; (202) 682-9530; www.funoutdoors.com. Fosters public/private partnerships to enhance and protect outdoor recreational opportunities.

Coalition of National Park Service Retirees, 5625 North Wilmot, Tucson, AZ 85750; (520) 615-9417; www.npsretirees.org. Former National Park Service employees work to improve parks funding and other aspects of parks management.

National Parks Conservation Association, 1776 Massachusetts Ave., N.W., Suite 200, Washington, DC 20036-6404; (202) 223-6722; www.npca.org. A citizens' interest group that seeks to protect national parks.

National Park Foundation, 1101 17th St., N.W., Suite 1102, Washington, DC 20036-4704; (202) 785-4500; www.nationalparks.org. Chartered by Congress and chaired by the Interior secretary; encourages private-sector support of the National Park System.

National Park Service, U.S. Department of the Interior, 1849 C St., N.W., Washington DC 20240; (202) 208-3100; www.doi.gov. Cares for the nation's nearly 400 national parks, historic monuments and recreation sites.

Public Employees for Environmental Responsibility, 2000 P St., N.W., Suite 240, Washington, DC 20036; (202) 265-7337; www.peer.org. An alliance of local, state and federal scientists, law-enforcement officers, land managers and other professionals dedicated to upholding environmental laws and values.

Sonoran Institute, 7650 E. Broadway, Suite 203, Tucson, AZ 85710; (520) 290-0828; www.sonoran.org. Works with communities to conserve and restore important natural landscapes in Western North America.

Yellowstone Park Foundation, 222 East Main St., Suite 301, Bozeman, MT 59715; (406) 586-6303; www.ypf.org. Works with the National Park Service to protect, preserve and enhance the natural and cultural resources and the visitor experience at Yellowstone National Park.

Bibliography

Selected Sources

Books

Chase, Alston, *Playing God in Yellowstone, The Destruction of America's First National Park*, Atlantic Monthly Press, 1986.
A Montana-based writer with a long association with Yellowstone National Park takes a critical look at how park officials shifted away from actively managing park wildlife to adopt "natural regulation" policies.

Grunwald, Michael, *The Swamp: The Everglades, Florida, and the Politics of Paradise*, Simon & Schuster, 2006.
Washington Post reporter Grunwald traces the history of development in South Florida's unique Everglades system, including how preserving Everglades National Park spurred comprehensive change in government water policy.

Howe, Jim, Ed McMahon and Luther Probst, *Balancing Nature and Commerce in Gateway Communities*, Island Press, 1997.
Conservation experts from the Conservation Fund and the Sonoran Institute summarize case studies of how gateway communities prosper because of proximity to wild landscapes in national parks.

Rettie, Dwight F., *Our National Park System*, University of Illinois Press, 1995.
A former chief of the National Park Service's Policy Development Office provides an insider's look at the agency's organization and argues for a more coherent vision for managing the national parks.

Sellers, Richard West, *Preserving Nature in the National Parks, A History*, Yale University Press, 1997.
A historian with the National Park Service discusses the history of the service and traces the continuing conflict between encouraging tourism and managing resources scientifically.

Articles

Lanza, Michael, "Still Buzzing," *Backpacker*, February 2006.
The magazine's Northwest editor looks at the continuing fight over snowmobiles in Yellowstone National Park and sees room for both the machines and quieter, non-motorized recreation.

Mitchell, John G., "Our National Parks in Peril," *National Geographic*, October 2006, p. 68.
The author says "veiled hostility" directed at national parks by high-level political appointees has not only rattled the morale of many career professionals but also assaulted the legal and regulatory fabric that has held the National Park System together for 90 years.

Schnayerson, Michael, "Who's Ruining Our National Parks?" *Vanity Fair*, June 2006.
Contributing Editor Schnayerson provides a critical report on the role of Paul Hoffman, an Interior Department political appointee, in a controversial effort to rewrite national park policies to favor recreation over conservation.

Reports and Studies

National Park Service, U.S. Department of the Interior, *Budget Justifications and Performance Information*, Fiscal Year 2007.
The Park Service's "Green Book" outlines funding trends and goals for the agency's annual operations.

National Park Service, U.S. Department of the Interior, *Management Policies, the Guide to Managing the National Park System*, Aug. 31, 2006.
The final 2006 revision of the service's manual maintains most of the Clinton administration's 2001 changes affirming that keeping parks unimpaired remains the overriding objective in managing national parks.

National Parks Conservation Association, *Endangered Rangers*, March 2004.
The advocacy group traditionally closely aligned with the National Park Service outlines how it believes federal budget cuts are damaging the national parks.

National Parks Conservation Association, *Gateway to Glacier*, 2003; *Gateways to Yellowstone*, May 2006; *National Treasures and Economic Engines, The Economic Impact of Visitor Spending in California's National Parks*, undated.
The park advocacy group's regional offices contend that the ecological attractions of Western national parks serve as the chief economic assets for gateway communities and counties.

The Trade Partnership, *Analysis of the Economic Impact of the Ban on Use of Personal Watercraft by the National Park Service*, February 2006.
Commissioned by personal-watercraft manufacturers, the study says restrictions on using jet skis in national parks cost the country $567 million and 3,300 jobs a year but offer few environmental benefits.

U.S. Government Accountability Office, *National Park Service, Major Operations Funding Trends and How Selected Park Units Responded to Those Trends for Fiscal Years 2001 through 2005*, March 2006.
The report to Congress lays out trends in overall Park Service operating funds and outlines how 12 park units cut operations or shifted priorities because of fiscal cutbacks.

The Next Step:

Additional Articles from Current Periodicals

Animals in National Parks

Dean, Cornelia, "Home on the Range: A Corridor for Wildlife," *The New York Times*, May 23, 2006, p. F1.
A collaborative group of researchers, conservationists, government officials and others are working to mitigate the effects of development on wildlife in national parks.

Flinn, John, "Winter's Wonderland For Wolf-Spotters," *The San Francisco Chronicle*, Feb. 5, 2006, p. F6.
Since Yellowstone National Park reintroduced wolves 11 years ago, the park has become the premier venue in North America for viewing wild wolves.

Johnson, Kirk, "Plan to Thin Elk Herd Raises Ire in the Rockies," *The Houston Chronicle*, May 28, 2006, p. A6.
Elk overpopulation in Rocky Mountain National Park has led administrators to propose a 20-year elk herd reduction program that would involve shooting hundreds of the animals.

Riccardi, Nicholas, "Regulated Bison Hunting Debated," *The Houston Chronicle*, Feb. 26, 2006, p. A2.
Montana authorized its first legal hunt of a herd of 4,000 buffalo that roam outside of Yellowstone National Park, where hunting is banned, into areas where they are not welcome.

Robbins, Jim, "Treating Wolves As 'Pests,' " *Pittsburgh Post-Gazette*, March 12, 2006, p. A11.
Wyoming ranchers want permission to kill wolves without restrictions, but the federal government objects because the wolves in Wyoming are descendants of those reintroduced into Yellowstone National Park in 1994.

Development in National Parks

Harkavy, Jerry, "Maine Struggles With Supersized Proposal Near North Woods," *Chicago Tribune*, Oct. 16, 2005, p. 50.
Some Maine residents want to develop the entrance area of the North Woods — the largest unprotected forest east the Mississippi — with house lots, resorts and a golf course, but others want a national park there.

Kowal, Jessica, "Parking Lot is Bargaining Chip As Quileute Tribe Battles for Land," *The Seattle Times*, July 30, 2006, p. B7.
The Quileute Indian tribe in Washington wants the National Park Service to give it 750 acres of higher land from neighboring Olympic National Park because half of the tribe's reservation is in a flood plain.

Squatriglia, Chuck, "Judge Blocks Park Service Merced River Plan, Environmentalists Cheer," *The San Francisco Chronicle*, July 21, 2006, p. B3.
A federal judge struck down Yosemite National Park's plan to protect 81 miles of the Merced River, saying it doesn't adequately limit development and recreation.

Environmental Problems

Kay, Jane, "Climate Change Seen Hurting National Parks," *The San Francisco Chronicle*, July 26, 2006, p. B1.
Coastal national parks, including Point Reyes National Seashore and Golden Gate National Recreation Area, are in danger of eroding because of global warming.

Wilson, Janet, "On a Clear day, You Can't See the Pollution," *Los Angeles Times*, May 23, 2006, p. A5.
National Park Service data show that ozone pollution worsened significantly between 1995 and 2004 in 10 national parks.

Snowmobiles in National Parks

Bohrer, Becky, "Yellowstone Officials Study What Kind of Vehicles to Allow in Winter," *The Philadelphia Inquirer*, April 2, 2006, p. A17.
National Park Service officials are studying whether more snowmobiles or mass-transit snow coaches should be allowed on the winter roads of Yellowstone and Grand Teton national parks.

Kenworthy, Tom, "Yellowstone Visitors Take it Slower," *USA Today*, Feb. 16, 2006, p. A3.
A growing number of visitors to Yellowstone National Park are opting to view the surroundings from snowcoaches — vans on treads that travel over snow-covered roads — instead of noisy snowmobiles.

CITING *CQ RESEARCHER*

Sample formats for citing these reports in a bibliography include the ones listed below. Preferred styles and formats vary, so please check with your instructor or professor.

MLA STYLE

Jost, Kenneth. "Rethinking the Death Penalty." CQ Researcher 16 Nov. 2001: 945-68.

APA STYLE

Jost, K. (2001, November 16). Rethinking the death penalty. *CQ Researcher, 11*, 945-968.

CHICAGO STYLE

Jost, Kenneth. "Rethinking the Death Penalty." *CQ Researcher*, November 16, 2001, 945-968.

CQ Researcher

Published by CQ Press, a division of Congressional Quarterly Inc.

cqresearcher.com

Caring for the Elderly

Who will pay for care of aging baby boomers?

Nearly 70 percent of those turning 65 this year will need long-term care (LTC) in their lifetimes; 20 percent will need it for five years or longer. But — unlike most other industrialized nations — the United States has no public or private insurance infrastructure to pay for LTC. Those needing years of care will have to impoverish themselves before Medicaid will pay for it. But state officials say Medicaid — intended as a health-care safety net for poor children — could be bankrupted by rising LTC costs as the baby-boom generation ages, and the number of people over age 85 soars from around 5 million to 21 million by 2050. Meanwhile, understaffing, low pay and poor working conditions at nursing homes put residents at risk of life-threatening malnutrition and bed sores. As an alternative, states and nonprofits are offering more home- and community-delivered care, but LTC experts say the alternatives may not be any safer.

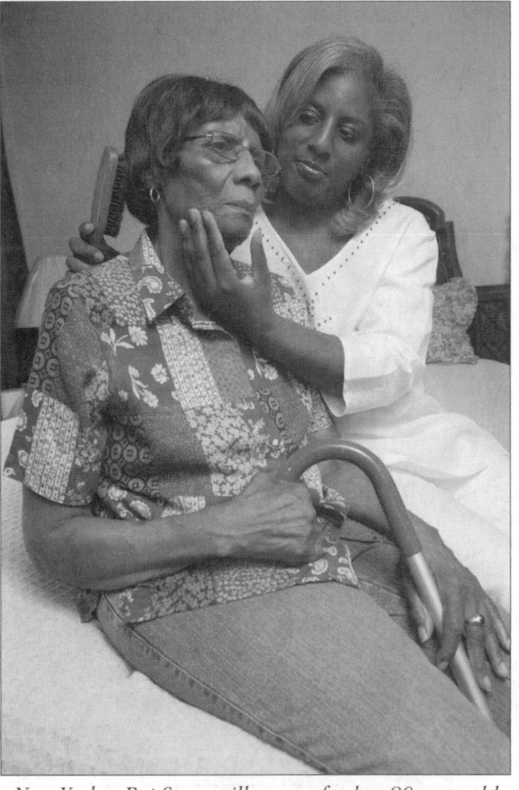

New Yorker Pat Somerville cares for her 80-year-old mother, Lena, who suffers from Alzheimer's disease. Over the past 20 years, elder care gradually has shifted from nursing homes to home-based care and assisted-living centers.

INSIDE THIS REPORT

CQ Researcher • Oct. 13, 2006 • www.cqresearcher.com
Volume 16, Number 36 • Pages 841-864

RECIPIENT OF SOCIETY OF PROFESSIONAL JOURNALISTS AWARD FOR EXCELLENCE ◆ AMERICAN BAR ASSOCIATION SILVER GAVEL AWARD

THE ISSUES

BACKGROUND

CURRENT SITUATION

OUTLOOK

SIDEBARS AND GRAPHICS

FOR FURTHER RESEARCH

Cover photograph: United Hospital Fund, New York

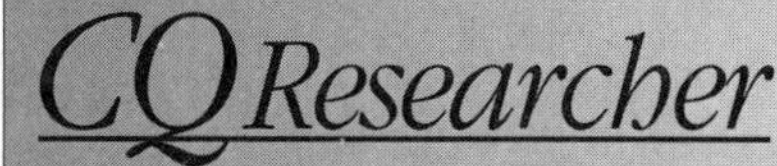

Oct. 13, 2006
Volume 16, Number 36

MANAGING EDITOR: Thomas J. Colin
ASSISTANT MANAGING EDITOR: Kathy Koch
ASSOCIATE EDITOR: Kenneth Jost
STAFF WRITERS: Marcia Clemmitt, Peter Katel
CONTRIBUTING WRITERS: Rachel S. Cox, Sarah Glazer, Alan Greenblatt, Barbara Mantel, Patrick Marshall, Tom Price, Jennifer Weeks
DESIGN/PRODUCTION EDITOR: Olu B. Davis
ASSISTANT EDITOR: Melissa J. Hipolit

A Division of Congressional Quarterly Inc.

SENIOR VICE PRESIDENT/PUBLISHER: John A. Jenkins
DIRECTOR, LIBRARY PUBLISHING: Kathryn C. Suárez
DIRECTOR, EDITORIAL OPERATIONS: Ann Davies

CONGRESSIONAL QUARTERLY INC.
CHAIRMAN: Paul C. Tash
VICE CHAIRMAN: Andrew P. Corty
PRESIDENT/EDITOR IN CHIEF: Robert W. Merry

CQ Researcher (ISSN 1056-2036) is printed on acid-free paper. Published weekly, except March 24, July 7, July 14, Aug. 4, Aug. 11, Nov. 24, Dec. 22 and Dec. 29, by CQ Press, a division of Congressional Quarterly Inc. Annual full-service subscriptions for institutions start at $667. For pricing, call 1-800-834-9020, ext. 1906. To purchase a *CQ Researcher* report in print or electronic format (PDF), visit www.cqpress.com or call 866-427-7737. Single reports start at $15. Bulk purchase discounts and electronic-rights licensing are also available. Periodicals postage paid at Washington, D.C., and additional mailing offices. POSTMASTER: Send address changes to *CQ Researcher*, 1255 22nd St., N.W., Suite 400, Washington, DC 20037.

Caring for the Elderly

BY MARCIA CLEMMITT

THE ISSUES

When 87-year-old Germaine Morsilli entered Hillside Health Center nursing home in Providence, R.I., in 2000, she could still take care of many of her own needs. But dementia caused the retired factory worker to forget to eat so often that she was in danger of malnutrition.

Morsilli took a turn for the worse in 2002, when she fell and fractured her left hip while dancing to Christmas music. Bedridden for several months, Morsilli developed serious bedsores. Nearly a year later, health department inspectors found her lying on urine-soaked sheets, and at high risk of infection.

The inspectors gave Hillside time to correct the many problems they found. But in February 2004 Morsilli's worsening bedsores prompted health officials to declare her in "immediate jeopardy" and transfer her to another home. But they still did not close Hillside, despite repeated observations of similar poor care for other residents.

Morsilli's daughter later said she wished she had moved her mother sooner but, like the state, she'd hoped Hillside would do better. Besides, she said, "you don't know how much worse the next nursing home might be." [1]

Morsilli died soon after she was moved, and in May 2004 Hillside's owners closed the facility, leaving $82,250 in state fines unpaid.

Stories of horrific conditions in nursing homes have made headlines for decades, and probably contributed to a growing trend in long-term care (LTC) for the elderly. Over the past 20 years, elder care has been gradually shifting from nursing homes to home-based care and assisted-living centers, which offer less direct patient care than nursing homes.

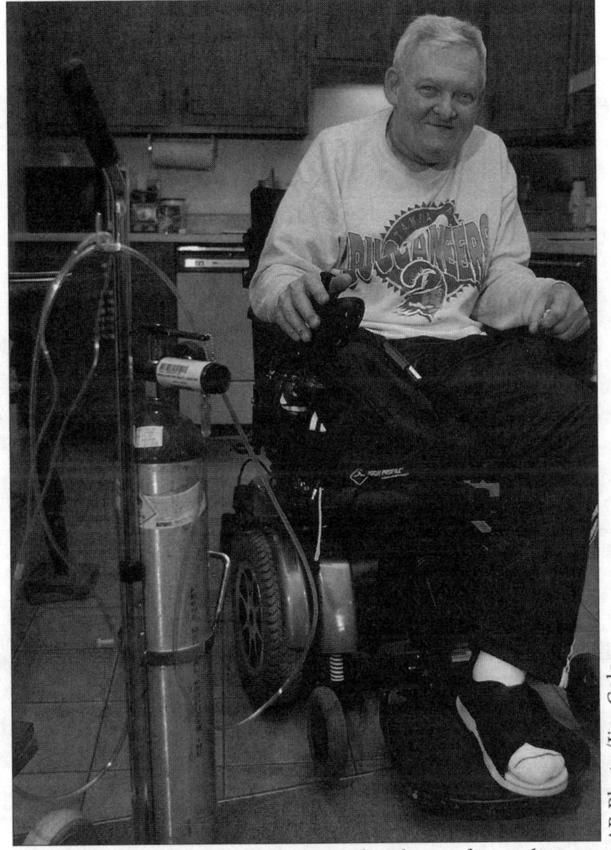

AP Photo/Jim Cole

Dick Peterson needs daily care, but he prefers to live at home in Concord, N.H., rather than in a nursing home. While more elderly Americans are being cared for outside of nursing homes, they may not be getting better care. Assisted-living facilities do not follow the federal standards set for nursing homes, and home-based care is difficult to monitor.

"Nursing-home use rates for people 85 years and older are half of what they were 25 years ago," says Lisa Alecxih, vice president of the Falls Church, Va.-based Lewin Group consultancy. Altogether, about 6 million elderly Americans use some form of LTC, including around half of those age 85 or older. [2]

Perhaps because the more able-bodied seniors are being cared for at home and in assisted-living centers, a larger proportion of nursing-home residents today are the most vulnerable elders — those with dementia or other debilitating conditions. From 1999 to 2005, the percentage of nursing-home residents with dementia, including Alzheimer's disease, grew from 41.4 percent to 45.4 percent, according to Charlene Harrington, a professor of sociology and nursing at the University of California in San Francisco. [3] Those with other psychiatric diagnoses rose from 13.8 percent to 19.7 percent of residents.

With the federal government paying more attention to specific care-quality issues — such as the number of residents who spend most of their time in bed — nursing-home care has improved recently by some measures, says Harrington. The percentage of residents spending most of their time in bed dropped by more than a third between 1999 and 2005, and the percentage of residents kept in physical restraints also dropped by more than a third, partly because some states have outlawed the practice. [4]

Overall, however, care quality still is not only deficient but getting worse. In 2005, for example, nearly 35 percent of nursing homes violated food-sanitation standards, and quality-of-care violations rose from 21 percent to 29.5 percent of all nursing homes. [5]

And while more seniors are being cared for outside of nursing homes, there's little reason to believe they are getting better-quality care. Assisted-living facilities do not have to comply with the same quality standards that Congress set for nursing homes in 1987, and it's very difficult to monitor quality in home-based care.

For example, in a Tucson, Ariz., assisted-living center an elderly woman

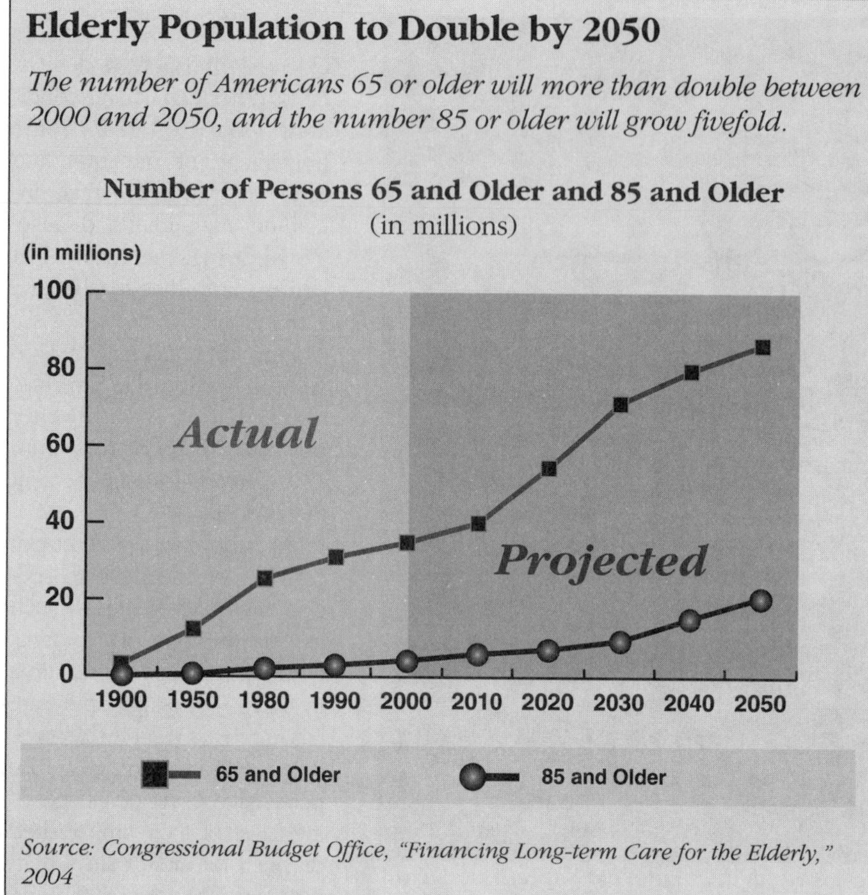

Source: Congressional Budget Office, "Financing Long-term Care for the Elderly," 2004

died in December 2005 after she was given her husband's medication instead of her own for 38 days. [6]

"To me, assisted living's problems are the same as in nursing homes," says Toby Edelman, a senior policy attorney at the Center for Medicare Advocacy. Consumers do not know that there are no federal quality standards for assisted-living facilities, she says, and state regulators "are all over the place" — some relatively vigilant, some not.

The root of the quality problems, many agree, is a long-running — and worsening — shortage of trained staff. LTC "is a quintessential person-on-person service, and I think in the long run the staffing issue is going to swamp everything else," says Joshua M. Wiener, program director for aging, disability and LTC at the North Carolina-based nonprofit research organization RTI International.

But today's LTC manpower problems are nothing compared to the "huge shortages of manpower" expected when the over-85 population swells from 4.2 million in 2000 to a projected 21 million by 2050, says James Tallon, president of the United Hospital Fund (UHF) of New York and chairman of the Kaiser Commission on Medicaid and the Uninsured. [7]

To train and retain more and better staff, "there will need to be a shifting of resources into the sector," says Christine Bishop, a professor at Brandeis University's Heller School of Social Policy and Management.

Meanwhile, "you've got the perfect political crime going on," says Leonard Fishman, president of Boston's Hebrew SeniorLife elder-care system. "Elected officials get up on their soapboxes and complain about LTC quality. But when their own reports tell them you need more staffing — which means more money — they won't do it."

Americans spent $135 billion for LTC in 2003 — of which Medicaid paid $47.3 billion, individuals paid $44 billion, Medicare paid for $33.6 billion and private insurance paid $5.6 billion. [8] (See graph, p. 846.)

Aside from finding the money for higher-quality care, paying for any care at all will be an enormous challenge as the elderly make up an increasingly larger share of the population. A nursing home costs $72,000 a year, on average, but can run much higher in some metropolitan areas. Home health care can run as high as $25,000 a year for four hours of care a day, while assisted living — which often provides no special services — averages $20,000 to $30,000 a year, according to Molly O'Malley, senior policy analyst for the nonprofit Kaiser Family Foundation (KFF).

And although LTC can cost as much as hospital and physician care, in the U.S. system the two are treated differently. Medical care is paid through insurance, which spreads the largely unpredictable risk of illness over a large group and protects those unlucky enough to become ill from shouldering all the costs. But only a handful of Americans carry private LTC insurance, and Medicaid — the federal program that pays for nursing-home care — is a welfare program that requires people to impoverish themselves before they can get public help.

Some analysts say the government should establish a mandatory public LTC insurance program — modeled on Social Security — to spread the risk across the population. "If elderly people smoke and go to the hospital, we pay" through Medicare, says Richard Kaplan, a professor of tax law at the University of Illinois College of Law. "But if somebody doesn't smoke but gets the 'wrong' disease, such as Alzheimer's, they bear the burden themselves. We're discriminating in favor of the diseases people might have prevented themselves."

Others say a tax-supported program is not feasible in today's budgetary and political climates. "If we continue to take it back to that discussion, it'll be wheel-spinning," says Mark Meiners, director of George Mason University's Center for Health Policy, Research and Ethics. It's more realistic to help people share the risk by strongly encouraging them to purchase private LTC insurance, he says.

Whether we opt for one of those plans or a hybrid, serious debate over our LTC future should begin today, analysts agree.

But LTC is easy to ignore, says Kaplan. "We don't have a Hurricane Katrina," he says. "The situation is cataclysmic, but it's cataclysmic one family at a time." When a loved one develops Alzheimer's disease, "each family is devastated emotionally and financially," but "until there is a critical mass of interest there won't be a policy," and each family "thinks that they're the only ones."

As families, lawmakers and advocates for the elderly debate how to pay for and ensure the quality of long-term care, here are some of the questions being asked:

10 Million Americans Need Long-Term Care

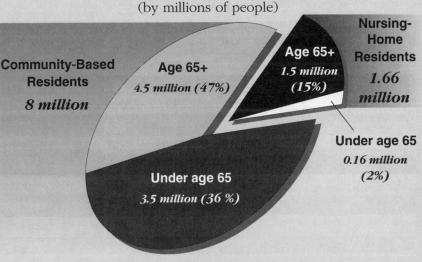

Nearly 10 million Americans — 62 percent of whom were 65 or older — needed long-term-care services in 2000; the other 38 percent were disabled. More than 80 percent lived in their homes and communities, rather than in nursing homes.

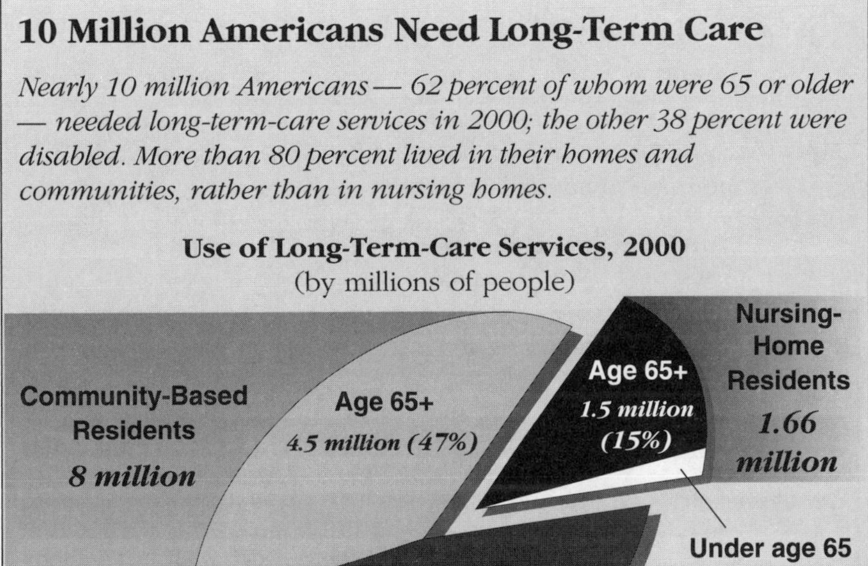

Source: The Henry J. Kaiser Family Foundation, Kaiser Commission on Medicaid Facts, July 2006

Should the government establish a mandatory insurance program for long-term care?

Just as homeowners know they need to insure their homes against fire, virtually everyone agrees that insurance should protect Americans against at least some long-term-care costs. It is much more likely, however, that people will need long-term care than that their homes will catch fire.

While LTC insurance is generally considered expensive, economists point out that it is not expensive if you are one of the unlucky ones who end up needing it for an extended period of time. For instance, the average person turning 65 in 2005 will spend $47,000 for long-term care over their lifetime. But that average masks a huge, unpredictable difference among people. Only 58 percent will spend anything on LTC, while another 19 percent will spend less than $10,000. However, an unlucky 5 percent will spend $250,000 or more. (*See graph, p. 854.*)

"This is not something that people can save for," says Brandeis' Bishop, arguing that either public or private LTC insurance is crucial.

Yet private LTC insurance can be expensive, costing on average $1,600 a year for an individual policy or $600 for an employer-based policy. [9] The high cost prompts some LTC advocates to argue that the federal government should require and subsidize an LTC insurance program. Others say similar federal initiatives — such as Medicare — have been poorly managed and wasteful and that private LTC insurance alone can do the job.

Private LTC insurance "is affordable for only 10 percent to 20 percent" of the elderly, making "federal involvement . . . essential" to "assure access to long-term care without making families face impoverishment," said a long-term-care study panel of the National Academy of Social Insurance. [10]

A federal program could operate in two ways, according to the panel. Like Social Security, it could guarantee "everyone access to a basic, limited, long-term-care benefit" financed by a special tax and supplemented by private insurance for higher-income people and additional public assistance for lower-income people. Or the federal government could expand current Medicaid LTC coverage by guaranteeing government assistance to pay LTC costs to anyone, once they had spent their own resources down to a nationally established minimum. People who wanted to protect more of their assets could buy private LTC insurance as a supplement. [11]

Government Pays for Most Long-Term Care

Sixty percent of all long-term-care expenditures for the elderly — $80.9 billion — were paid for by Medicaid and Medicare in 2004. Out-of-pocket expenditures by the elderly — mainly for institutional care — amounted to about $44 billion.

Who Pays for Long-Term Care for the Elderly
(in $ billions, 2004)

Payment Source	Institutional Care	Home Care	Total
Medicaid	$36.5	$10.8	$47.3
Medicare	15.9	17.7	33.6
Private Insurance	2.4	3.3	5.6
Out of Pocket	35.7	8.3	44.0
Other	2.0	2.5	4.4
Total	**$92.4**	**$42.5**	**$134.9**

Note: Numbers do not add exactly due to rounding.

Source: Congressional Budget Office, "Financing Long-term Care for the Elderly," 2004

"Other countries have demonstrated that either approach — or a hybrid of the two — can target benefits to those in greatest need, retain personal responsibility through cost sharing and control costs," said the panel. [12]

"The debate about the aged is a social-insurance debate," not a matter for private markets to handle, says Tallon, of the Kaiser Commission on Medicaid and the Uninsured. "No market will be as successful as mandatory resource pooling."

"Most people don't think about LTC until it affects them. Then they ask, 'Where is the government?' " says Kaplan, at the University of Illinois. Still, the idea of a dedicated payroll tax to fund LTC coverage remains generally unpopular, he says, adding that he doubts whether even Medicare, with its payroll-tax financing, would be enacted in today's anti-tax atmosphere.

Nevertheless, says Kaplan, because needing LTC is a risk, not a certainty, and is expensive, "it is a classic instance of what should be covered by social insurance," like Medicare or Social Security.

Kaplan argues that the private LTC insurance industry's track record so far doesn't offer much hope that it will be a viable financing vehicle in the future. Many smaller companies in the field have gone out of the business, for example. "That leaves a question in people's minds about whether the insurance companies will even be around" when care is needed, decades down the line, says Kaplan. Even mammoth TIAA-CREF — which manages financial planning for the education and nonprofit communities — entered and then left the private LTC insurance business, he points out.

"And other companies have raised rates even on existing policies," making the private LTC insurance market unstable and scaring away people who might otherwise buy coverage, Kaplan says.

Opponents of government action say existing government insurance initiatives, such as Medicare, are themselves on the brink of failure and that no more such programs should be attempted. To see the futility of expanding the government's presence into LTC, "you have to look 20 years ahead, when Medicare and Social Security will be in the last stages of collapse, and Medicaid will be history," says Stephen A. Moses, president of the Seattle-based Center for Long-Term Care Reform, who advocates more private financing of LTC.

The bottom line, says RTI's Wiener, is that "Congress and the president are not open to anything that would expand the government role."

Meanwhile, private LTC insurance sales are flat. About 95 percent of people between the ages of 45 and 64 with annual incomes over $20,000 are uninsured for LTC — unchanged since 2003, according to the Long Term Care Group, an El Segundo, Calif., company that provides administrative services to the LTC insurance industry. Among people age 65 and over, about 85 percent lack coverage, an increase from the 82 percent who lacked coverage in 2003. [13]

"Sales have not gone up," and insurers are reaching "only about 5 to 10 percent of the potential market," says Jodi Anatole, vice president for LTC for the MetLife insurance company.

Thus, "if you're not going to expand Medicare [to insure LTC], then you need to do something to make private insurance more palatable," says Kaplan. "LTC insurance is all over the map on benefits," he explains, making it hard for potential buyers even to figure out what a plan offers. If the government stepped in to require that policies be sold in standardized packages, "insurers could compete on price," potentially enticing more consumers to buy, he says.

Many analysts say neither an all-public nor an all-private LTC financing system will work and that hybrid solutions are needed. "A social-insurance program wouldn't solve the whole problem," says William J. Scanlon, a research professor at Georgetown University's Institute for Health Care Research and Policy. That's because no

Caring for Elderly Is a Global Challenge

Most industrialized countries have a significantly larger proportion of elderly citizens than the United States. As a result, they have enacted insurance systems to cover all long-term-care (LTC) costs and focused on making housing senior-friendly.

For example, in 2003 people 65 and older were about 12 percent of the U.S. population but nearly 19 percent of the population in Japan and Italy. In most European countries 15 percent or more were 65-plus. [1]

"Germany, Japan, the Netherlands, Luxembourg — all have social insurance for LTC," says Joshua M. Wiener, program director for aging, disability and LTC at RTI International, a North Carolina-based nonprofit research organization. "If you look across the world, wherever they have programs and services for LTC, it's overwhelmingly a government responsibility."

When Japan launched its universal government-funded LTC program in 2000, many doubted the government's ability to fund it. But, "many Japanese have now accepted the important role" of the program in easing burdens on elders and their families, said Tatsuo Honda, director of the department of planning at Japan's National Institute of Population and Social Security Research. [2]

While national insurance programs in many countries help spread financial risk, they now must grapple with the need to control costs, even as elderly populations keep growing.

Some advocates of private LTC insurance doubt public programs can ever hold down spending. "Has anyone run the numbers for the difference between promises made through Japan's social-insurance programs . . . and the country's ability to keep those promises?" asks Stephen A. Moses, president of the Seattle-based Center for Long-Term Care Reform, which advocates private LTC. [3]

"In the absence of a private market for services in which supply and demand set prices and determine priorities, governments are hopelessly at a loss to decide the best services to offer and the proper prices to charge for them," Moses says.

Cost-control initiatives are only in their infancy, and many focus on keeping elderly people healthier longer and providing more options for them to remain at home.

For example, Germany recently cut elders' use of more expensive medical institutions like nursing homes by paying for home-based care, including paying family members and friends for their assistance. [4] The Netherlands is stressing home-based care and is mulling incentives to encourage patients and health providers to opt for more cost-efficient care when possible. [5]

New Zealand and Japan are among the nations beefing up preventive-health services, such as exercise and nutrition programs for elders who still need only minor assistance. [6] Japan's program also provides recipients with a once-in-a-lifetime subsidy to modify their existing homes so they can remain there longer, even with disabilities, said Honda. [7]

Housing that helps seniors feel independent and integrates their lives with overall community life is important to keeping seniors healthier longer, according to some analysts. "If you go to northern Europe" — mainly Scandinavia — "and talk about elder care, you hear about it as a housing issue," says Leonard M. Fishman, president of the Hebrew SeniorLife elder-care system in Boston. Higher-quality, more efficient elder care can be attained if elders can live on their own in housing clustered near senior services that provide both care and opportunities to stay active in community life, he says.

In Finland, senior buildings in urban areas are called "service homes," says Fishman. "The first floor has a dining room, lecture halls, rooms for doctors to come in and conduct exams. Then, on the floors above are housing units" designed to help preserve elders' independence, with rooms where "it's easy to roll your wheelchair into the showers," for example.

Perhaps most important, most senior housing in northern Europe has "dining facilities that are open to the public," where neighbors frequently join residents for dinner, Fishman says. Linking elder housing to the community at large helps ensure that the elder facility maintains high quality and that residents don't lapse into learned helplessness that worsens their health, Fishman says. "Every decent institution has its windows and doors open."

---

1 "Older Americans 2004: Key Indicators of Well-Being," Federal Interagency Forum on Aging-Related Statistics, www.agingstats.gov.

2 Quoted in "Interview With Mr. Tatsuo Honda," *Long-Term Care Trends*, AARP, Aug. 25, 2006, www.aarp.org.

3 Stephen A. Moses, "Kaigo-Jigoku (LTC Hell) and What Japan's Doing About It: Valuable Lessons for the U.S. and Vice Versa," www.centerltc.com.

4 *Proceedings*, AARP International Forum on Long-Term Care, AARP Global Aging Program, 2003, p. 4, www.aarp.org/international.

5 *Ibid.*, p. 5.

6 *Ibid.*, p. 9.

7 "Interview with Mr. Tatsuo Honda," *op. cit.*

---

government-sponsored program could guarantee more than a very basic level of care universally, and many people expect far more, Scanlon says.

He suggests developing a plan similar to retirement financing, where Social Security provides basic support, and employer-sponsored retirement plans and personal savings add extra layers of funds.

Alternatively, the government might "say to everybody, 'You should have a year's worth of [private] LTC coverage,' " says George Mason University's Meiners. People could get public subsidies if they needed more, he says.

Are government and private industry doing enough to promote high-quality LTC?

Since Congress mandated improvements in nursing-home quality in 1987, federal, state and industry initiatives have aimed to make LTC safer. But while most experts agree that some of the

Medicaid Spending Tripled on Long-Term Care

Medicaid spending on long-term care was $95 billion in 2005, nearly triple the 1991 amount. The portion spent on home- and community-based care has risen steadily during the period, to 37 percent of total expenditures.

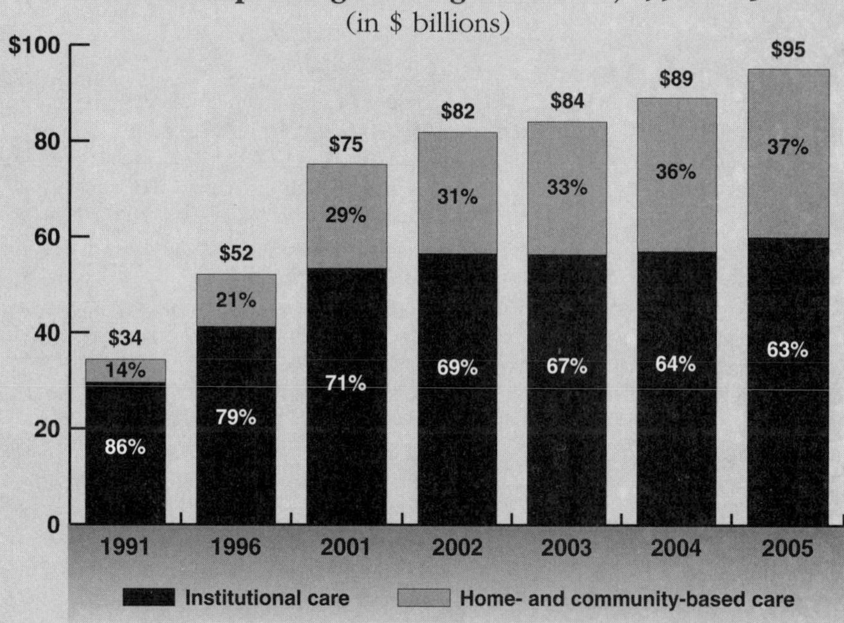

Source: The Henry J. Kaiser Family Foundation, "Kaiser Commission on Medicaid Facts," July 2006

most egregious problems — such as fatal fires — are less frequent today, critics say serious problems still exist. Moreover, the critics say the problems could worsen as nursing homes are replaced by largely unregulated home- and community-based care and assisted-living facilities.

Before Congress passed the Omnibus Budget Reconciliation Act of 1987 (OBRA), conditions in nursing homes "were pretty darned bad," says Edward Miller, an assistant professor of public policy at Brown University. "No matter how bad they are now, they were a heck of a lot worse."

New regulations "have improved quality in measurable ways," such as reducing the number of patients placed in restraints, Bishop and three Brandeis colleagues wrote in a 2005 report to the National Commission for Quality Long-Term Care. Furthermore, they wrote, national standards have become "ever more demanding," covering issues ranging from basic safety concerns to pain treatment. [14]

In addition, the Bill Clinton and George W. Bush administrations have pushed to post information about the quality of care at various nursing homes on the government's Nursing Home Compare Web site, says Wiener. *

Perhaps as a result of all these efforts, the most recent data show that the average number of nursing-home deficiencies cited by state inspectors dropped in 2005, says the University of California's Harrington. After increasing from 5.7 deficiencies per nursing home to 9.2 between 1999 and 2004, deficiencies dropped to 7.1 per nursing home in 2005. [15]

But Harrington fears that the statistics indicate only that state inspectors are "issuing fewer citations" rather than that homes are better. "It is unlikely that quality has improved," she says.

Other critics agree. "Even where we see progress, we worry that some of it may be artificial," says Georgetown's Scanlon. "Our ability to detect problems" is not uniform across the country.

In fact, state inspectors say they are not well trained and have told Congress they are pressured to understate problems because the LTC industry has political clout with state lawmakers, says Janet C. Wells, director of public policy at the National Citizens' Coalition for Nursing Home Reform. "Study after study shows that surveyors are undercoding" — or understating the severity of deficiencies, she says.

"There is no ambiguity in problems that we do find," Scanlon says. For example, 10 to 15 percent of all nursing homes — between 1,500 and 2,000 homes nationwide, serving perhaps 200,000 residents — are cited persistently for deficiencies. That fact alone means that, "putting all gray areas aside, we've got a problem." Likewise, the Brandeis analysts cited "the continued presence of quality deficiencies" and the slow pace of adoption of "state-of-the-art care processes." [16]

Meanwhile, the jury is still out on initiatives like Nursing Home Compare. Adequate information on how to buy quality doesn't yet exist, says Wells. For example, the government is only in the earliest stages of collecting staffing information about individual homes.

"A family should know staffing data when they consider a home," Wells says. "Currently, we don't have it."

* The site is www.Medicare.gov/NHCompare.

The biggest barrier to delivering high-quality LTC is retaining good workers, which is nearly impossible today, say many analysts. To keep trained staff, they need higher pay and health insurance, says RTI International's Wiener. Furthermore, "there's no career path" for direct-care workers like nursing assistants. "People don't have control over their work. The conventional wisdom is that wages get people in the door, but to keep them you need to redesign the job."

Turnover ranges from 50 percent to more than 100 percent annually in LTC jobs, says Miller. "We are woefully understaffed in gerontology at all levels," including registered nurses and even nursing-home administrators, he says. Among administrators, for example, very few are certified, and without qualified leadership quality initiatives are harder to sustain, he adds.

Retirement of older workers and potential limits on immigration could worsen the problem. "We have been heavily dependent on an immigrant work force," says Fishman, of Boston's Hebrew SeniorLife System. And, "when you look at the number of people retiring in this field, I think that's going to be a train wreck," he says.

"We need to quasi-professionalize these front-line workers" in line with quality-improvement models that have worked in other service industries like banking, says Bishop. Unionization also could help, she says. "Unionization gives workers more of a voice," she says, often resulting in better treatment for the industry, such as higher government reimbursement.

Many people view home care or assisted-living facilities as offering superior quality, but watchdogs caution that care quality outside of nursing homes may be even worse. Unlike a decade ago, many people with serious disabilities, including dementia, now reside in assisted-living centers, says Edelman, at the Center for Medicare Advocacy. But those facilities haven't increased their staffs to meet the higher needs of this population since they aren't required to meet the same federal standards as nursing homes, she says.

"In a nursing home, at least there's an R.N. on the day staff," she points out.

Home-based services are delivered all over the community on hard-to-predict schedules, "so we do less monitoring," which could leave problems undiscovered, says Georgetown University's Scanlon.

Dementia is an unsolved quality problem in all venues, says Stephen McConnell, vice president for advocacy and public policy at the Alzheimer's Association. Health care "costs Medicare three times as much for a person with dementia," presumably a strong incentive to manage it well, says McConnell.

But many elderly patients aren't being screened for dementia in Medicare's new chronic-care initiatives, which are intended to keep seniors healthier longer, he says. In addition, doctors aren't paid for long-enough office visits to communicate adequately with both dementia patients and their family caregivers, he says. These failures to take dementia into account gravely diminish care quality.

"If you manage diabetes, for example, and don't recognize dementia, your diabetes management will fail," McConnell says.

Are the government and private industry doing enough to promote home- and community-based care?

State and federal officials are trying to provide more elder-care services in homes and neighborhoods, where it is significantly cheaper than in nursing homes. Home care costs up to $25,000 a year for four hours of care per day, compared to $72,000 a year for the average nursing home.

But critics worry that states' home-and-community-based-services initiatives (HCBS) focus too much on cutting costs and do not offer counseling and consumer information to help family caregivers.

Over the past decade, Medicaid LTC expenditures have shifted away from nursing homes and toward HCBS. According to the Kaiser Commission on Medicaid and the Uninsured, in 1994 about 61 percent of Medicaid LTC spending went to nursing homes while 19 percent went to HCBS home-health agencies and personal-care assistants. By 2004, nursing homes' share of LTC expenditures had shrunk to 51 percent, while 36 percent went to HCBS. [17]

"Other options are there, they're viable, and people are using them," says the Lewin Group's Alecxih.

Much of the shift involves care of younger physically or mentally disabled people, says RTI International's Wiener. Currently, about two-thirds of Medicaid LTC spending goes to institutions and about one-third to home-based services — but only 20 percent of that third goes toward caring for the elderly.

"There has been a revolution in favor of HCBS" for those with intellectual disabilities, Wiener says. In some areas, such as Washington state, home care "is the dominant form of care" — even for the elderly.

Last year nearly three-quarters of the states added new HCBS services or expanded eligibility for their HCBS programs, according to the Kaiser Family Foundation's O'Malley.

But their efforts fall short in some key areas, say some advocates. Besides a shortage of workers" for HCBS, "turnover rates are high, and there are job vacancies. . . . Some areas like Wisconsin and the District of Columbia would like to expand HCBS but can't find enough workers," says Wiener.

It would help enormously if states provided databases or statewide information centers to help elderly residents and their families find people who provide home-care or community services, such as adult day care, transportation or respite care, says Susan C. Reinhard, director of the Center for State Health Policy at Rutgers University.

"Information is a big deal" when it comes to sustaining the elderly in their own homes rather than moving them to institutions, says Penny Feldman, vice president for research and evaluation at the Visiting Nurse Service of New York. "We pay a lot of lip service to it but don't do much."

People can better "age in place" if they have power and a voice in changes, according to advocates. "We are so used to taking a very paternalistic approach to these services," says Fredda W. Vladeck, director of the United Hospital Funds' Aging in Place Initiative. For instance, younger seniors could help drive older seniors to shopping and doctors' appointments, and seniors could form "social-action groups" to petition city governments to change a bus route, Vladeck says. "The more you empower seniors to take some ownership of this, the better," but that goal may take more than a generation to realize, she says.

Hebrew SeniorLife

A staff expert in exercise physiology gives residents a workout at the Jack Satter House, an apartment facility for seniors in Revere, Mass., operated by Hebrew SeniorLife, which specializes in improving the quality of life for elderly people in the Greater Boston area.

Family caregivers also need to be brought into the discussion, say advocates. "In the material out there on HCBS, there is very little reference to families or friends," says Carol Levine, director of the United Hospital Fund's Families and Health Care Project. Yet, "who do they think is going to do the caring?" asks Levine, a caregiver for her husband, who was severely injured in a 1990 car accident.

Hired "aides can't be there 24 hours a day," she continues, citing a recent study showing that family members contribute 80 percent of the labor involved in home care for stroke victims, even those with paid helpers.

Nevertheless, Levine says, families "are almost always left out of policy discussions," have little access to respite services for needed breaks and are seldom given any training. That's in major contrast to the United Kingdom, for example, where family caregivers are entitled by law to take time off from work and to receive an official assessment of their assets and needs as caregivers, Levine says.

Social-service workers with the ill and elderly "have figured this out," she says. "But the medical side is still resistant" to actively engaging families in discussions about care.

"There is the idea that everybody in nursing homes can just end up in HCBS, but that's wrong," says McConnell, of the Alzheimer's Association. "We're a bit of a lone voice in the disability community, but we believe very strongly that when dementia reaches a certain point" — such as "when a wife's health fails from the strain of caring for her husband" — institutional care is necessary.

By pushing too hard for home care, "in some cases we're just shifting the cost to families," McConnell says. "And families already do a lot." ■

BACKGROUND

Family Matters

Elder care is a relatively new problem in history, largely because as late as 1900 few people lived to retirement age, and average life expectancy was 47. [18] But with people over age 85 today making up the fastest-growing population in industrialized countries, worries about how to provide seniors with health care and other assistance are becoming increasingly acute. [19]

One of the most hotly debated issues in the United States is how to balance individual responsibility with society's responsibility to care for those who've worked a lifetime but now face limited incomes and frailty. In addition, ensuring quality of care for elders is a perennial concern.

In the Middle Ages church law held children responsible for caring for their parents, based on the Bible's commandments to honor one's parents. The church also forbade others in the community from turning away poor, elderly parents seeking help. [20]

But when Protestant reformers like John Calvin and Martin Luther split the Catholic Church, they diluted the influence of church law. In 1601, England's so-called Elizabethan Poor Law first outlined society's legal obligations to manage poverty: Poor, elderly parents were expected to live with their children, and the community would assist the parents only after

Continued on p. 852

Chronology

1950s-1960s

Lawmakers seek to ensure nursing-home residents' safety after fires at several nursing homes kill patients, and the federal government begins paying for nursing-home care.

1954
First national inventory of nursing homes finds many safety and quality-of-care problems.

1960
Senate report says 44 percent of nursing homes do not meet basic safety standards.

1965
Congress enacts Medicare — which covers only short, post-hospitalization nursing-home care — and Medicaid, through which states may cover long-term nursing-home care for the poor.

1970s-1980s

Demand for long-term care (LTC) grows as elderly population swells. Some older nursing homes close as government tightens safety rules.

1970
The number of Americans age 85 or over — those most likely to need LTC — reaches 1 million.

1971
Federal officials establish national standards for nursing-home safety. President Richard M. Nixon beefs up safety enforcement, convenes the first White House Conference on Aging.

1975
Twelve consumer groups form National Citizen's Coalition for Nursing Home Reform to promote safe, high-quality care.

1981
Congress gives states the option of covering more home- and community-based LTC services under Medicaid.

1987
Congress establishes training and national minimum-staffing standards for nursing homes in the Omnibus Budget Reconciliation Act of 1987.

1990s

Interest grows in Medicaid-paid home- and community-based care; federal government begins developing quality measures for LTC. Four states establish experimental LTC Partnerships, promising LTC insurance purchasers that after their private benefits are exhausted they may access Medicaid LTC without divesting themselves of assets.

1993
Fearing that LTC Partnerships benefit only high-income people, Congress limits them to four states.

1994
Medicaid spends $8.4 billion on home-delivered services.

1996
Congress allows taxpayers to deduct private LTC insurance premiums from their taxes and makes it a crime to give away assets in order to quality for Medicaid LTC.

1999
A new series of government reports finds continuing quality problems in nursing homes, including tying up and drugging residents to control them.

2000s

Quality concerns continue as the elderly population grows faster than younger age groups; LTC staffing shortages loom.

2000
Congress creates a small program of state grants to offer paid respite services and other help to family caregivers. Over-85 population rises to 4.2 million.

2002
Private LTC insurance is made available to federal employees. The federal government launches its Nursing Home Compare Web site, reporting individual homes' scores on quality measures.

2003
Medicaid pays $86.3 billion for LTC — 47.4 percent of the total amount Americans spent for long-term care.

2004
Medicaid spends $31.6 billion on home-delivered care, 36 percent of its LTC budget. Private LTC insurance pays about 4 percent of total LTC costs.

2006
The Deficit Reduction Act tightens financial-eligibility requirements for Medicaid LTC, makes it easier for states to offer Medicaid-paid home-based care and lifts the ban on states establishing LTC Partnerships. . . . Nursing-home care costs, on average, about $70,000 a year. . . . Thirty-eight states expand Medicaid coverage of home-delivered LTC services.

2050
The number of Americans age 65 or older will top 86 million — more than double the number in 2000.

They Work Hard for a Living

After caring for his dying mother, Thomas E. Gass, a former Catholic seminarian and halfway-house director, decided to translate his family experience into a new job as a nursing-home aide. [1]

A worker shortage plagues long-term care (LTC), and it is expected to worsen over the next few decades. Hard work, low pay and bad working conditions would make it hard to retain enough qualified workers even if the elderly population wasn't about to explode, analysts say.

The need for paid caregivers will increase by 39 percent between 2000 and 2010, but the population of 18-to-55-year-old women, who make up most of the LTC work force, will increase by only 1.25 percent over the period, according to the Bureau of Labor Statistics. Most workers in nursing homes and home-health agencies earn little more than the minimum wage, and few receive any benefits like health insurance. [2]

The work can be frustrating, dirty and sad, according to Gass' 2005 book about his experiences, *Nobody's Home: Candid Reflections of a Nursing Home Aide*.

Along with one other aide, Gass had three hours each morning to ready the 26 residents on his hall for breakfast. "On average, we are allowed 15 minutes to get each resident out of bed, toileted, dressed, coifed and wheeled or walked to breakfast. Every morning is a head-on collision against time," he wrote. "As a relatively well-paid aide, my cut is $6.90 an hour." [3]

One resident, Skooter, "is a graduate of Cambridge in his late eighties," wrote Gass. "He usually plays with his morning bowel movement, lightly smearing it on the bed sheets, the bed rails and himself. Sometimes he rubs it in his eyes. Nonetheless, he carries the bearing of a gentleman, always courteous and willing to help as best he can." [4]

Despite low pay and non-existent benefits, a good "direct care" worker needs to be patient, strong and perceptive to an unusual degree. "She's kind, she's empathetic, she's safe, and those are the attributes we look for," said Christie Overmyer, a supervisor at the Presbyterian SeniorCare facility in Oakmont, Pa., describing nurse's aide Barbara Bedillion. [5]

"I've always been a little sentimental about seeing my residents as individuals, always trying to do for them what I would want them to do for me, if our places were reversed," said Bedillion. But at 58, Bedillion, who's been on the job for 15 years, is one of the lucky ones. Presbyterian SeniorCare is among the elder-care facilities trying to reverse the industry trend of high staff turnover by improving the lives of its workers. Starting pay at the facility is $10.25 an hour, and workers who remain on the job for several years become eligible for health insurance and paid vacation. [6]

Experts know how to improve working conditions and retain LTC workers. Just treating them with the respect their front-line status deserves keeps many on the job, and research has "underscored the importance of including nursing assistants in care planning," according to Robyn I. Stone, executive director of the American Association of Homes and Services for the Aging's Institute for the Future of Aging Services, and Joshua M. Wiener, of RTI International, a North Carolina research organization. For example, they said, one study found that nursing homes in which supervisors accepted nursing assistants' advice or discussed care plans with the aides had turnover rates

Continued from p. 850

their children had used up their financial means. [21]

The American Colonies adopted the Poor Law. But other aspects of 18th- and 19th-century life also contributed to sustaining the principle that families should care for their own, according to Alvin Schorr, a liberal social reformer and long-time federal bureaucrat who also served as dean of the New York University School of Social Work. [22]

For example, farms and businesses generally were family-owned enterprises, and parents usually continued to control those properties until they died, wrote Schorr. So children were bound to their parents "in an economic unit by more than filial feeling or social pressure." Parental ownership gave adult children a strong monetary incentive to shoulder as much parental care as they could, according to Schorr. [23]

After the Colonies became the United States, Northeastern states — with a strong English Puritan tradition — required children to take responsibility for elderly parents, according to Schorr. But states to the south and west did not. As the economy shifted away from family-controlled enterprises, it grew less clear that adult children would shoulder the care for their elderly parents, Schorr wrote.

Economic changes aside, as the elderly population grew during the 20th century its burgeoning numbers helped turn elder care into a major issue. In 1900, only about 100,000 Americans were over 85. By 2000, that population had grown to 4.2 million; by 2050 it is expected to jump fivefold — to about 21 million. [24]

Among those turning 65 this year, nearly 70 percent will need some form of LTC, according to health policy professors Peter Kemper, of Pennsylvania State University, Harriet L. Komisar of Georgetown University and the Lewin Group's Alecxih. Twenty percent will need at least five years of LTC, while 31 percent won't need any, according to the analysis. [25]

But since no one can confidently predict his own need for LTC and because it is so expensive, most economists believe insurance — not savings — should pay for it.

Think of it like fire insurance, says Kemper. "There is a risk of your

one-third lower than those without such practices. [7]

Better pay and benefits also help. For example, turnover rates in California declined after the Service Employees International Union organized 46,000 home-care workers in that state to bargain collectively for better wages and benefits. Full-time wages rose from around $6.15 an hour to between $8.45 and $10.50 an hour, according to a paper in the liberal journal *NewPolitics* by Brandynn Holgate and Jennifer Shea, doctoral candidates at the University of Massachusetts in Boston. Workers also got access to health insurance, transportation reimbursement and training. [8] Not surprisingly, turnover declined. For example, in San Francisco County, where wages doubled from $5 to $10 an hour between 1997 and 2002, the percentage of workers who stayed on their jobs for over a year increased from 39 percent to 74 percent. [9]

Cornell University Press

Former seminarian Thomas Gass, pictured with his pet falcon, writes about his work as a $6.90-an-hour nursing-home aide.

Change doesn't come easy, however, and efforts to give care workers more responsibility and respect sometimes run afoul of managers, such as registered nurses, who cling to the status quo.

For instance, the Green House Project — an experimental nursing home that originated in Tupelo, Miss. — rejected the traditional nurses'-aide model in favor of "universal workers," who receive more training, carry out a wider range of tasks and have much more decision-making autonomy than traditional workers. The new role pleased the staff but ran into initial resistance among nurses, dietitians and other clinicians accustomed to being boss, according to Green House founders. [10]

However, based on promising results from Mississippi, the Green House model is spreading to other states. [11]

---

[1] Thomas Edward Gass, *Nobody's Home: Candid Reflections of a Nursing Home Aide* (2005), p. 1.

[2] *Occupational Outlook Handbook*, 2006-2007, Bureau of Labor Statistics.

[3] *Ibid.*, p. 13.

[4] *Ibid.*

[5] Quoted in Gary Rotstein, "Nursing Home Aide Has Empathy," *Pittsburgh Post-Gazette*, May 17, 2006.

[6] *Ibid.*

[7] Robyn I. Stone and Joshua M. Wiener, "Who Will Care for Us? Addressing the Long-Term Care Workforce Crisis." Urban Institute, posted to the Web Oct. 26, 2001, www.urban.org.

[8] Brandynn Holgate and Jennifer Shea, "SEIU Confronts the Home Care Crisis in California," *NewPolitics*, Summer 2005, www.wpunj.edu/newpol/issue41/.

[9] *Ibid.*

[10] Judith Rabig, William Thomas, Rosalie A. Kane, Lois J. Cutler and Steve McAlilly, "Radical Redesign of Nursing Homes: Applying the Green House Concept in Tupelo, Mississippi," *Practice Concepts*, The Gerontological Society of America, 2006, p. 533.

[11] *Ibid.*, p. 539.

house burning down, but it's a relatively low probability. If it does burn down, though, you need a heck of a lot of money to pay for it," he says. "You can't expect everybody to have enough money in the bank. That's unreasonable. What insurance does is say that, on average, the cost of financing fires across a whole group is a pretty small amount [per person], so let everybody in the group pay that," and everyone will be shielded from substantial loss.

Unlike fire risk, LTC risk "is largely uninsured," says Kemper. Instead, the burden is borne in large part by individual "families providing care for elderly relatives," he says — a private responsibility that "is distributed very unequally."

Who Pays?

In Japan, Canada and most of Europe, governments have mandated nation- or province-wide LTC insurance programs financed in part with public funds. In the demographically younger United States, however, the question of whether LTC costs should be borne individually or across society has not even been openly debated, so the U.S. LTC system has developed by default.

Home-based care has been the "backbone of long-term care in this country," and family and friends provide about 80 percent of that care for free, says Kaplan of the University of Illinois. But providing that $306 billion worth of home-based care has become increasingly difficult as women join the work force, and adult children move away from their parents, he says. [26]

Americans spent $182 billion for LTC in 2003, of which Medicaid paid 47.4 percent, individuals paid 20.6 percent, Medicare paid for 17.8 percent and private insurance paid for 8.7 percent. [27]

However, 40 percent to 43 percent of all U.S. Medicaid expenditures went to non-elderly disabled people while elder care accounted for only 27 percent to 30 percent, according to an analysis by Bruce C. Vladeck, a former federal Medicare and Medicaid chief who is professor of health policy at New York City's Mount Sinai Medical Center. (He is married to the United Hospital Fund's Vladeck.) [28]

How Much Will You Spend on LTC?

Nearly 60 percent of seniors will have to pay for long-term care during their lifetimes, at an average cost of $47,000. But while nearly 20 percent of those will pay less than $10,000, an unlucky 16 percent will have to spend more than $100,000.

What Seniors Will Pay for Long-Term Care

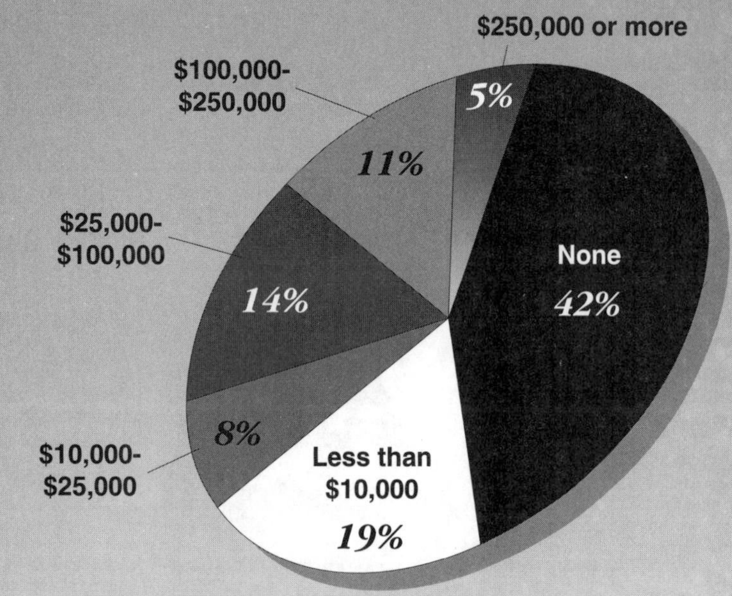

Note: Percentages do not add to 100 due to rounding.

Source: Peter Kemper, et al., *"Long-Term Care Over an Uncertain Future: What Can Current Retirees Expect?"* Inquiry, *winter 2005/2006.*

But Medicaid is a welfare program, not an insurance program. To qualify for LTC under Medicaid, an elderly person must either be too poor to afford LTC on their own or must "spend down" their income and assets to qualify.

"We've got a system where people routinely impoverish themselves" to pay for elder care, and "nobody likes that," says RTI International's Wiener, who favors a hybrid LTC system with government participation.

Medicaid's rules allow adult children to routinely commit what Moses, of the Center for Long-Term Care Reform, calls "financial abuse" on their elderly parents. The children hire lawyers to deplete the parents' estates of enough assets to make them eligible for Medicaid while preserving the children's inheritance in financial trusts, he explains. Moses advocates the voluntary purchase of private insurance, with the government's role confined to helping the very poor pay for LTC.

So far, Washington has taken no significant action on LTC financing. Federal taxpayers are permitted to deduct premiums for private LTC insurance. But under current rules, a person with an adjusted gross income of $40,000 must have $3,000 in deductible medical expenses before he can claim any deduction for LTC premiums or any other medical expenses, according to Karen M. Ignagni, president of the industry association America's Health Insurance Plans. With such a high threshold, it's not surprising that "fewer than 5 percent of all tax returns" take these deductions, she said. [29]

Aging in Place

Throughout American history, lawmakers and advocates for the elderly have paid more attention to the quality of elder care than to financing it. As far back as Colonial times, local governments and charities ran poorhouses for those who couldn't care for themselves, often the elderly and the disabled.

Some 18th-century towns also offered "outdoor relief," a kind of community-based care as an alternative to literally going into the poorhouse. Home-based care also has a long history. As far back as 1909, the Metropolitan Life Insurance Co. offered coverage for nursing services delivered in patients' homes.

But many small, local LTC institutions couldn't cope with the scale of poverty that arrived in the 20th century, particularly during the Great Depression of the 1930s. State and federal governments assumed responsibility for elder-care financing, and eventually lawmakers tried to ensure that LTC institutions met basic quality and safety standards.

In the 1940s and '50s, for example, a number of fatal nursing-home fires led to an intensive national effort to develop state licensing standards for nursing homes. [30] After a 1960 Senate report found that 44 percent of nursing homes failed to meet minimum safety standards, Congress passed the Kerr-Mills Act, which gave states more federal matching funds to care for the poor and elderly and the "medically needy," whose severe health conditions drive them into poverty. [31]

In the early 1970s, shocking accounts of nursing-home abuses were brought to Congress' attention by a

Continued on p. 856

Turning Home Equity into Long-Term Care

The need for long-term care (LTC) most often hits late in life, when savings run low and many people live on fixed incomes. Most older people own their own homes, however, and some policymakers favor encouraging them to use their home equity to help pay for in-home care.

Eighty percent of those over age 65 own their homes, and nearly three-quarters have paid off their mortgages. Moreover, home equity is the major asset for most seniors: The median net worth of those age 75 and older is around $100,000, but only $19,000 of that is in non-housing assets like investments. [1]

Seniors' limited incomes and high home equity — and their preference for at-home LTC — lead some advocates to urge them to use so-called reverse mortgages — also called home-equity conversion mortgages — to pay for at-home care.

A senior over age 62 can qualify for a reverse mortgage by owning a home that is fully or nearly paid off.

Here's how it works: A bank lends money to the homeowner, either as fixed monthly cash payments or as a line of credit the homeowner can draw on. As long as homeowners remain in their house, they don't have to make any payments on the loan. After the homeowner either dies or sells the house, the bank recoups the payments made to the homeowner, plus the interest and finance charges due on the loan from the proceeds of the house sale.

Fifty-nine percent of older households — 14.2 million households — have sufficient housing assets to qualify for reverse mortgages, but about 3.8 million of those households have non-housing assets of $275,000 or more, which would make them unlikely to need a reverse mortgage, according to Georgetown University's Long-Term Care Financing Project. [2]

Tapping into home equity can give seniors "the purchasing power they need" to buy either LTC insurance or home-based "services they need to stay in their homes and out of nursing facilities," said Thomas Scully, former chief of the Medicare and Medicaid programs. [3]

A 2005 study funded by the federal Centers for Medicare and Medicaid Services "shows that reverse mortgages have significant potential to help many seniors," said James Firman, president and CEO of the National Council on Aging (NCOA), which published the study. [4]

But the mortgages can't help everyone, and they aren't the most efficient or effective financial tools, say many analysts. For example, the NCOA study cites "the need for strong consumer safeguards and lower transaction costs" to attract more users, said Firman. [5]

Reverse-mortgages "are very high-fee transactions," says Stephen I. Golant, a University of Florida professor of geography who studies elder housing issues. "A home may be worth $100,000, but you may get only $50,000 out of that, after fees and interest. That's a high price to pay for the privilege of remaining in your home."

Since many seniors' homes have relatively low value, they still couldn't borrow enough money through a reverse mortgage to cover major episodes of LTC, according to independent health-policy consultant Mark Merlis, who wrote the Georgetown study. Forty-four percent of potential reverse-mortgage users could pay for 25 months of home care, the median length of time people use home-based LTC. But only 2 percent of likely reverse-mortgage purchasers would get enough from their loans to cover 51 months or more of home-based LTC, the amount used by 25 percent of people who use home care, Merlis wrote. [6]

And for many people, reverse mortgages may not be the best way to turn home equity into cash, say other analysts.

A better option for many seniors might be selling their houses and reinvesting the proceeds in a low-fee, income-producing fund that could help pay the rent in less expensive housing. "A significant share of older people . . . should not be encouraged to stay put," Golant says, because their old homes are too expensive, too big and too difficult to keep up. "It would probably be much better to have at least some older people in group housing or concentrated housing" near necessary services, such as grocery stores. That also would hold caregivers' travel costs down because they could visit several households at once, he adds.

There's one catch, however: Affordable housing is scarce, and senior-friendly housing is hard to find. "When it comes to adapting current housing, such as by adding grab bars [in bathrooms], we hear about it ad nauseam, but outside of the work of a few foundations, most of these simple things aren't being done," says Penny H. Feldman, vice president for research and evaluation at the Visiting Nurse Service of New York. Neither has affordable assisted living been made available in line with the demand, says Golant.

Affordable senior housing "is not that expensive," says Leonard Fishman, president of Hebrew SeniorLife, an elder-care system in Boston. "There's no big constituency demanding it, but it would be hard to find a more cost-effective change you can make."

But before the nation considers investing in affordable housing for seniors, says Golant, it needs to have a sensitive public-policy debate about two questions: "What's the best way for older people to translate their housing wealth into providing for their LTC? And should adult children expect to have their parents' houses passed on as part of their inheritance?"

---

[1] "Demographic Profile: Americans 65+," Mature Market Institute, MetLife, 2004.

[2] Mark Merlis, "Home-Equity Conversion Mortgages and Long-Term Care," Georgetown University Long-Term Care Financing Project, March 2005, www.ltc.georgetown.edu.

[3] Quoted in "Program Promotes Reverse Mortgages to Pay LTC," *Nursing Homes*, March 2004.

[4] "NCOA Study Shows Reverse Mortgages Can Help Seniors Pay for Long-Term Care at Home," press release, National Council on Aging, Jan. 26, 2005.

[5] *Ibid.*

[6] Merlis, *op. cit.*, p. 12.

Continued from p. 854

group of young female volunteers organized by consumer advocate Ralph Nader. The young women took jobs in or visited nursing homes in Washington, D.C., Connecticut, Maryland, New Jersey, New York and Virginia. "What we found in our study," the project's director told the Senate Special Committee on Aging, "was horrifying, disillusioning, heartbreaking and totally inexcusable." [32]

In 1971, six years after the Medicare and Medicaid programs were established, the federal government published national fire and safety standards that all nursing homes paid by Medicare and Medicaid were required to meet. The standards were four years in the making, and between 1969 and 1971 about 1,500 older nursing homes closed in expectation that they would not be able to meet the coming standards.

Since then, while worries about LTC quality have never disappeared, concern has gradually shifted from fire- and safety-code violations to quality of care. For example, a "litany of nursing-home abuses" laid out at a 1974 Senate hearing included improper use of physical restraints on patients and poor management of medications. [33]

In 1987, the Omnibus Budget Reconciliation Act mandated new minimum national standards for staffing nursing homes and training their staff. The bill also called for standardized assessments of the health and needs of nursing-home residents and stated that facilities should help residents attain "the highest practicable physical, mental and psychosocial well-being." [34]

Nevertheless, reports of quality problems in nursing homes persist. For example, a series of government reports between 1999 and 2003 provided "additional startling documentation of ongoing quality failures and continued public dissatisfaction," says a report to the National Commission for Quality Long-Term Care. [35]

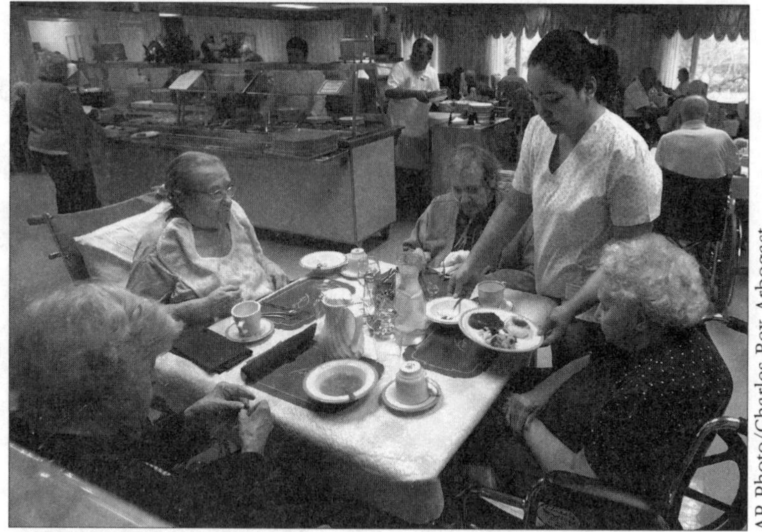

AP Photo/Charles Rex Arbogast

Residents at a Chicago nursing home have the luxury of ordering their meals from a menu. While care at nursing homes has improved by some measures, more than a third violated food-sanitation standards in 2005, and quality-of-care violations rose from 21 percent to 29.5 percent of all nursing homes.

At least partly in reaction to such longstanding complaints, the past 25 years have seen a gradual shift away from nursing home care into assisted living and home-based care. Among those age 85 and older, there are about the same number living in nursing homes today as 20 years ago, even though the over-85 population has doubled, says the Lewin Group's Alecxih.

Residents in assisted-living facilities today tend to have about the same level of disability as nursing-home residents had in past decades. "We have a million beds in assisted living today compared to a million-and-a-half in nursing homes, and many in the nursing homes are short-term patients, just off a hospital stay, not long-term residents," says Georgetown's Scanlon.

Various types of home-based care also are growing. For example, about 920,000 Medicaid beneficiaries receive care through state home-and-community-based services (HCBS) programs, 722,000 obtain care from home-health agencies and 683,000 receive personal, non-health assistance paid for by Medicaid. But, of course, many of these beneficiaries are non-elderly. [36]

Falling nursing-home occupancy rates could conceivably create what RTI International's Wiener calls a "market moment." Nursing homes "are more hungry for residents and could conceivably make quality improvements to attract them," he says.

Or low occupancy could have the opposite effect, creating some horrendous — and formerly unheard of — quality breaches, says Wells, at the National Citizens' Coalition for Nursing Home Reform. "While occupancy drops, facilities stay open, and that's where you may get the most horrible cases of abuse," she says. "To fill beds, they bring in people who are unsuitable residents, people with violent criminal histories, mental illness, sexual predators."

In Illinois, for example, more than 1,000 parolees, including sex offenders, were found to be among the state's 100,000 nursing-home residents this year, after a new law required criminal background checks of all residents. The law was prompted by an incident in which a convicted rapist groped a 77-year-old fellow resident in a Homewood, Ill., home. [37]

Continued on p. 858

At Issue:

Should the federal government establish a mandatory long-term-care insurance program?

The Long-Term Care Study Panel, National Academy of Social Insurance

Judy Feder (L)
Co-Chair; Dean, Georgetown Public Policy Institute

Sheila P. Burke (R)
Co-Chair; Chief Operating Officer, Smithsonian Institution

From "Developing a Better Long-Term Care Policy," November 2005

yes

Transforming long-term care ultimately requires fundamental reform of its financing and a substantial commitment of federal resources. Because the need for long-term care is a risk, not a certainty, it should be handled like other unpredictable and potentially catastrophic events — that is, through insurance.

Private long-term-care insurance, while growing, is affordable for only 10 to 20 percent of the elderly. To assure access without making families face impoverishment, federal involvement is therefore essential.

Creating an effective system requires a substantial new commitment of public resources, and — if benefits are to be adequate in all states — they must be federal resources. Expanded federal financing for long-term care could take a variety of forms and need not eliminate personal responsibility.

One approach, modeled on Social Security, would provide everyone access to a basic, limited, long-term-care benefit. Social insurance for long-term care could provide the same kind of basic protection. Individuals with sufficient income and assets could purchase private insurance to supplement the public program, while a safety-net program could help low-income people unable to afford private supplemental insurance.

Another approach would establish a national floor of income and asset protection that would reform or replace Medicaid. Such a program would assure everyone access to affordable, quality, long-term care without having to give up their life savings, as Medicaid requires today.

Other countries have demonstrated that either approach — or a hybrid of the two — can target benefits to those in greatest need, retain personal responsibility through cost-sharing and control costs. Analysis by the Organization for Economic Cooperation and Development in 19 countries finds a growing number [of nations] with universal public plans for financing long-term care.

Public protection does not imply the absence of private obligations, nor does it imply unlimited service or exploding costs. It aims to strike a fairer balance between public and private financing — relating personal contributions to ability to pay and targeting benefits to those in greatest need.

Stephen A. Moses
President, Center for Long-Term Care Reform

From speech to insurers, posted at www.centerltc.com/speakers/what_i_believe_about_ltc.htm, Feb. 28, 2006

no

The personal tragedy of long-term care for individuals and families can be substantially relieved if people are able to pay privately for high-quality personal and respite care. The social tragedy of long-term care for America's aging population can be entirely averted by changing public policy so that fewer people end up dependent on underfinanced public welfare programs.

Friends and families provide most long-term care at no charge, but under enormous financial and emotional stress. The vast majority of all formal, compensated long-term-care services are paid for by Medicaid (welfare) or Medicare (social insurance). I believe that Medicaid routinely pays less than the cost of providing long-term care and that Medicare is slowly ratcheting down its reimbursement, while both programs impose heavier and heavier regulation on providers.

We're in [this mess] because 40 years ago the government started paying for nursing-home care without limiting its free and subsidized services to people in financial need. By making nursing-home care free, for all intents and purposes, the government impeded the development of a private market place for home- and community-based services. By subsidizing long-term care for middle- and upper-class Americans, the government impeded the development of a private insurance market to help pay for the kinds of services people prefer.

By becoming a single buyer of long-term care, the government artificially increased the demand for and the price of care beyond its ability to pay adequately. The resulting cost containment caused quality of care to decline and led directly to the overregulation that tied nursing homes and home-health agencies in bureaucratic knots.

If too much government financing has caused excessive dependency on inadequately financed institutional care, then the answer must lie in targeting scarce government resources to a smaller number of people truly in need.

When government programs have fewer people to serve, they will be better able to provide adequate reimbursement of higher quality. If they cannot ignore the risk and cost of long-term care, most people will save, invest and insure and thus be able to purchase red-carpet access to care in the private marketplace. When the government stops giving away what the long-term-care insurance industry and reverse-mortgage lenders are trying to sell, more people will buy those products.

Continued from p. 856

On the brighter side, LTC activists in recent years have developed several new types of elder facilities that may improve care. One such undertaking, called Green House homes, has shown promise in Mississippi. Self-contained houses accommodate about 10 residents cared for by nursing aides with advanced training and a visiting medical-support team. [38] Each house provides shared living space near residents' individual quarters, which has "worked well," according to a group of analysts that included the creators of the Green House concept, gerontologists Judith Rabig and William Thomas.

"Many elders stopped using wheelchairs because they were able to navigate the short distances in the house," and staff absenteeism and turnover is lower than in other nursing facilities, wrote Rabig and Thomas. [39] Additional Green House projects are planned in at least 10 states. [40] ■

CURRENT SITUATION

Deficit Reduction Act

Experts in LTC financing hope more Americans will buy private LTC insurance now that Congress has made it tougher to get Medicaid to pick up the tab for long-term care.

Last February President Bush signed into law the Deficit Reduction Act (DRA), which included the most significant provisions ever aimed at boosting home-delivered care and the private LTC insurance market. Skeptics say, however, that while the law is designed to help trim government LTC spending, no one knows yet to what extent it will ultimately reshape the LTC landscape.

Passed in response to governors' warnings that rising Medicaid costs threaten to swamp their budgets, the law is expected to cut federal Medicaid spending by $43.2 billion between 2006 and 2014. At least $6.4 billion of that will come from tightening eligibility rules for LTC. [41]

"The DRA was the culmination of a decade of major work for me," says Moses, of the Center for Long-Term Care Reform. He has been one of the strongest voices urging lawmakers to make it harder for people to qualify for Medicaid-funded LTC because it would spur development of a strong, private LTC insurance market. "It's a virtual miracle that we got as much as we did" in the DRA, "though it doesn't go far enough," he says.

The law is designed to discourage people from counting on Medicaid to pay their LTC costs. Among other changes, the DRA bars anyone with more than $500,000 in home equity from qualifying for Medicaid nursing-home benefits. In the past, people were permitted to retain unlimited equity in their primary residence but had to exhaust other assets before qualifying for Medicaid LTC.

The law also imposes a much stiffer penalty on people who get rid of money or other assets, presumably in an effort to "spend down" to qualify for Medicaid LTC. States will now scrutinize the past five years — rather than three years — of seniors' financial transactions prior to Medicaid application for evidence of a spend-down, such as gifts to children or charities or sale of a car or summer cottage at below-market price to a relative. The new restrictions mean that applicants — even those who did not intentionally draw down their assets — will become ineligible for LTC payments for months or even years at the very time that they need to be admitted to a nursing home, say critics of the new rules.

People who help out in family emergencies and then suddenly find themselves needing assistance themselves, for example, are heavily penalized under the new law, said New York elder-care attorney Bernard A. Krooks. [42] For example, he said, a grandmother who pays $30,000 in vital bills over several years for a grown daughter with chronic-fatigue syndrome who's supporting two young children herself suffers a heart attack and a debilitating stroke. Two years later, after she's depleted all her financial assets and must turn to Medicaid, she finds that she is ineligible for many months because of the aid she gave her family within the last five years, Krooks said.

The law "suggests that the elderly can predict their medical and financial circumstances five years into the future," he said, and "will punish unwitting elders who have helped their families . . . and then experience medical events such as a stroke, hip fracture or Alzheimer's disease." [43]

The tougher eligibility rules are based on the argument that the Medicaid LTC benefit discourages people from buying private LTC insurance, even when they can afford it.

Jeffrey Brown, an assistant professor of finance at the University of Illinois at Urbana-Champaign, calls Medicaid "an implicit tax on LTC insurance" because buyers of LTC insurance end up being ineligible for government Medicaid benefits that uninsured people at the same wealth level can obtain. "Most insurance doesn't take something away from you when you buy it," he says.

"We have a lot of people on Medicaid for LTC who would have, could have and should have been able to pay, had they taken the steps to do so," says Moses.

He acknowledges that there is "little empirical research" showing how many people illegitimately spend down money to qualify for Medicaid LTC. The phenomenon is "driven by adult children" of cognitively impaired parents who "hate to see their inheritance consumed" paying for private LTC, so they transfer and conceal their parents' assets so Medicaid will pay instead, Moses says.

Others disagree. The DRA provisions that tighten eligibility "won't make much difference" because "half a dozen studies show there is not much of this going on," says RTI International's Wiener.

A September 2005 report by the Government Accountability Office (GAO) found insufficient data to determine how much asset transfer occurs. In 2002, however, 22 percent of elderly households — about 6 million — reported that they'd transferred cash in the past two years, the GAO found. [44]

Most of the asset transfers occurred in higher-income households. While only about 10 percent of the lowest-income third of households were found to have transferred cash — in an average amount of $4,000 — more than 30 percent of the richest third had transferred cash — averaging more than $12,000 per household. And households with disabled elders, with the highest risk of needing LTC, "were less likely to transfer cash" than households with non-disabled elders, said the GAO. [45]

LTC Carrots

In response to longstanding pleas from state governments and disability advocates, the DRA allowed states to expand Medicaid coverage of home- and community-based elder care and simplified those procedures. It also stepped up a long-stalled initiative using positive reinforcement to entice people to buy private LTC insurance.

Most analysts agree that bolstering Medicaid programs offering home-and-community-based services (HCBS) will be good for many elderly and disabled people, but few studies give hard data.

But home-based care is generally more expensive than assisted living, and HCBS programs will only be as large as states can afford, some warn. The initiative "isn't going to go very far, because there isn't enough money," predicts Moses.

According to the disability community, many nursing-home residents could be moved back into their homes if more home-delivered services were available. But skeptics, like the United Hospital Fund's Tallon, say that might not be true for the elderly, given the current level of frailty among most nursing-home residents. "I'm not a great believer that most people in nursing homes don't belong there," he says.

The DRA also lifted a longstanding moratorium on long-term care partnerships — state programs that allow people to receive Medicaid LTC benefits without impoverishing themselves if they purchase private LTC insurance. Established in the late 1980s as a private research initiative, the partnerships were limited by Congress in 1993 to four states — California, Connecticut, Indiana and New York — because lawmakers feared that only wealthy people would benefit from the program because they are the only ones who can afford the high cost of LTC insurance.

Under the DRA, states now may offer Medicaid LTC coverage to consumers who exhaust their private LTC benefits. Such policyholders may retain assets worth the dollar value of their LTC policy. "The program has the merit of getting LTC insurance onto everybody's radar screen," says George Mason's Meiners, a key architect of the original partnership program. About 20 states reportedly are interested in establishing similar programs, but, "We aren't at a stage where you just turn a switch."

Moreover, the data on whether the partnerships work is "inconclusive," according to the National Conference of State Legislatures. So far, only 251 participants in the four states have exhausted their private coverage, and only 119 have accessed Medicaid — numbers too small to draw conclusions. Officers of Connecticut's program estimate it has saved the state $2.8 million. [46]

But MetLife's Anatole says the LTC insurance industry, which "pushed very hard" for the partnerships, is excited about the LTC insurance-education funding in the DRA law. Partnerships "may not be the be-all and end-all," but statistics show that insurers with a strong focus on LTC coverage have had stronger sales in the four partnership states, she says. ■

OUTLOOK

Higher and Higher

With the elderly population swelling, the cost of providing LTC in coming decades undoubtedly will rise dramatically. But it is difficult to predict how existing LTC delivery and financing systems may change to accommodate the deluge.

In the short run, Congress is expected to do little to address LTC financing and quality issues, although a few small but meaningful measures could be enacted in the next year or so.

A bill offering respite services for family caregivers of the elderly and ill of all ages has "lots of bipartisan support," says the Alzheimer's Association's McConnell. Expanding respite opportunities for families "plays right into the home-based-care trend, and it's not that expensive," he says.

The United Hospital Fund's Vladeck also predicts that some cities will experiment with NORCs — "naturally occurring retirement communities" — where seniors get help retooling their communities to facilitate "aging in place." [47] Advocates expect a nationwide NORC demonstration to be part of an eventual reauthorization of the Older Americans Act, which governs most of the country's programs for the elderly outside of Medicare, Medicaid and Social Security. It has been awaiting reauthorization for several years.

Eventually, however, sheer demographics will rivet Americans' attention to LTC. "The numbers . . . coming through the pipeline are pretty forbidding," says Georgetown University's Scanlon. And, as for LTC, "40 percent of the elderly think Medicare covers it, so there's a shock factor" when people discover that it doesn't.

Americans are "in denial of disability," says Kaplan of the University of Illinois, who favors an expansion of Medicare to include LTC. "But I don't have any fantasies about that happening any time soon. I don't know that Medicare itself would be enacted today."

Between 2000 and 2040, the share of the population age 65 and over will rise from 12.6 percent to 20.5 percent, according to the nonpartisan Congressional Budget Office. And since 55 percent of those age 85 and older have chronic physical impairment that makes it difficult to perform fundamental tasks required to live independently, like cooking or bathing, LTC spending is expected to reach $484 billion annually by 2040 — or about 2 percent of the nation's gross domestic product. [48]

Nevertheless, says UHF's Tallon, "When we're talking about health and health care, it's very hard to predict the future."

In the short term, he says, it's more important to recognize that "there is unmet need now" for LTC services. Thus, he suggests that policymakers put aside for now the debate on future LTC costs and ask instead, "Can you provide good LTC services today? If you can, that's the best step for the future." ■

About the Author

Staff writer **Marcia Clemmitt** is a veteran social-policy reporter who previously served as editor in chief of *Medicine and Health* and staff writer for *The Scientist*. She has also been a high-school math and physics teacher. She holds a liberal arts and sciences degree from St. John's College, Annapolis, and a master's degree in English from Georgetown University. Her recent reports include "Climate Change," "Controlling the Internet," "Pork Barrel Politics" and "Cyber Socializing."

Notes

1 Quoted in Jennifer Levitz, "Resident #1," *Providence Journal*, Aug. 22, 2004.
2 Ellen O'Brien, "Long-Term Care: Understanding Medicaid's Role for the Elderly and Disabled," Kaiser Commission on Medicaid and the Uninsured, November 2005, p. 1.
3 Charlene Harrington, "Nursing Facilities, Staffing, Residents, and Facility Deficiencies, 1998 Through 2004," www.pascenter.org/documents/.
4 *Ibid.*
5 *Ibid.*
6 Jane Erikson, "Several Elder-Care Facilities Fined for Violations," *Arizona Daily Star*, Sept. 3, 2006.
7 "Older Americans 2004: Key Indicators of Well-Being," Federal Interagency Forum on Aging-Related Statistics, www.agingstats.gov.
8 Financing Long-Term Care for the Elderly, Congressional Budget Office, April 2004.
9 Marc A. Cohen, "Long-Term Care Insurance: Market Trends," address delivered to a Munich America Reassurance Co. conference, April 20, 2006.
10 "Developing a Better Long-Term Care Policy: A Vision and Strategy for America's Future," National Academy of Social Insurance, November 2005, p. iv.
11 *Ibid.* For background, see Mary H. Cooper, "Social Security Reform," *CQ Researcher*, Sept. 24, 2004, pp. 781-804; and Adriel Bettelheim, "Medicare Reform," *CQ Researcher*, Aug. 22, 2003, pp. 673-696.
12 *Ibid.*
13 "The Index of the Long Term Care Uninsured," Long Term Care Group, Inc., www.ltcg.com/INDEX%20of%20Long%20Term%20Care.pdf.
14 John Capitman, Walter Leutz, Christine Bishop and Rosemary Casler, "Long-Term Care Quality: Historical Overview and Current Initiatives," National Quality Forum, 2005, www.qualitylongtermcarecommission.org/reports/pdfs.
15 Harrington, *op. cit.*
16 Capitman, *et al., op. cit.*, p. 1.
17 O'Brien, *op. cit.*
18 *Ibid.*
19 For background, see Capitman, *et al., op. cit.*; and Karen Buhler-Wilkerson, *No Place Like Home: A History of Nursing and Home Care in the United States* (2003).
20 Alvin Schorr, "Thy Father and Thy Mother: A Second Look at Filial Responsibility and Family Policy," Government Printing Office, 1980, p. 7.
21 *Ibid.*
22 *Ibid*, p. 8.
23 *Ibid.*
24 "Older Americans 2004: Key Indicators of Well-Being," Federal Interagency Forum on Aging-Related Statistics, www.agingstats.gov.
25 Peter Kemper, Harriet L. Komisar and Lisa Alecxih, "Long-Term Care Over an Uncertain Future: What Can Current Retirees Expect?" *Inquiry*, winter 2005-2006, p. 335.
26 Carol Levine, director, Families and Health Care Project, United Hospital Fund, New York.
27 O'Brien, *op. cit.*, p. 4.
28 Bruce C. Vladeck, "Where the Action Really Is: Medicaid and the Disabled," *Health Affairs*, January/February 2003, p. 92.
29 Karen M. Ignagni, testimony before House Energy and Commerce Subcommittee on Health, April 27, 2005.
30 For background, see R. McNickle, "Older People," *Editorial Research Reports 1949* (Vol. II), available at CQ Researcher Plus Archive, at CQ Electronic Library, http://library.cqpress.com.
31 Capitman, *et al., op. cit.*, p. 11. Also see H. B. Shaffer, "Nursing Homes and Medical Care," *Editorial Research Reports 1963* (Vol. II), available at CQ Researcher Plus Archive, CQ Electronic Library, http://library.cqpress.com.

[32] For background, see H. B. Shaffer, "Plight of the Aged," *Editorial Research Reports 1971* (Vol. II), available at CQ Researcher Plus Archive, CQ Electronic Library, http://library.cqpress.com.
[33] Capitman, *op. cit.*, p. 13.
[34] *Ibid.*; see also R. K. Landers, "The Elderly in an Aging America," *Editorial Research Reports 1988* (Vol. II), available in *CQ Researcher Plus Archives*, CQ Electronic Library, http://library.cqpress.com.
[35] *Ibid.*, Capitman.
[36] O'Brien, *op. cit.*, p. 14.
[37] Lori Rackl and Chris Fusco, "Background Checks Find 1,000 Felons in Nursing Homes," *Chicago Sun-Times*, July 21 2006, p. 6.
[38] Judith Rabig, William Thomas, Rosalie A. Kane, Lois J. Cutler and Steve McAlilly, "Radical Redesign of Nursing Homes: Applying the Green House Concept in Tupelo, Mississippi," *Practice Concepts*, The Gerontological Society of America, 2006, p. 533.
[39] *Ibid.*, p. 538.
[40] *Ibid.*, p. 539. The states are New York, Ohio, Arizona, Georgia, Nebraska, North Carolina, Florida, Michigan, Kansas and Hawaii.
[41] "Deficit Reduction Act of 2005: Implications for Medicaid," Kaiser Commission on Medicaid and the Uninsured, February 2006.
[42] Bernard A. Krooks, testimony delivered to the House Energy and Commerce Health Subcommittee, April 27, 2005.
[43] *Ibid.*
[44] "Transfers of Assets by Elderly Individuals to Obtain Long-Term Care Coverage," Government Accountability Office, September 2005.
[45] *Ibid.*
[46] Matthew Gever, "Long-Term Care Partnerships Could Bloom Again Under the DRA," National Conference of State Legislatures, www.mcsl.org.
[47] For background, see H. B. Shaffer, "Housing for the Elderly," *Editorial Research Reports 1959* (Vol. I), available at CQ Researcher Plus Archive, CQ Electronic Library, http://library.cqpress.com.
[48] Congressional Budget Office, *op. cit.*

FOR MORE INFORMATION

AARP, 601 E St., N.W., Washington, DC 20049; (888) 687-2277; www.aarp.org. Formerly known as the American Association for Retired Persons, the organization conducts policy research and offers consumer information on long-term care.

Alzheimer's Association, 225 N. Michigan Ave., 17th Fl, Chicago, IL 60601-7633; (800) 272-3900; www.alz.org. Supports research on dementia and provides information about how long-term-care policies affect dementia sufferers and their families.

American Association of Homes and Services for the Aging, 2519 Connecticut Ave., N.W., Washington, DC 20008; (202) 783-2242; www.aahsa.org. Provides aging services to the elderly and conducts research on long-term care.

Center for Long-Term Care Reform, 2212 Queen Ave. North, #110, Seattle, WA 98109; (206) 283-7026; www.centerltc.com. Supports private long-term-care insurance and other private financing options for long-term care.

Family Caregivers Alliance, 180 Montgomery St, Suite 1100, San Francisco, CA 94104; (415) 434-3388; www.caregiver.org. Promotes development of programs at the local, state and national levels to support informal caregivers.

Kaiser Family Foundation, 1330 G St., N.W., Washington, DC 20005; (202) 347-5270; www.kff.org. Conducts and disseminates research on national health-care issues, including Medicaid and long-term care.

Medicaid Commission, Hubert H. Humphrey Building, 200 Independence Ave., S.W., Suite 450G, Washington, DC 20201; http://aspe.hhs.gov. Congress asked this expert panel to recommend policies by December 2006 that ensure long-term financial stability in Medicaid.

National Association for Home Care and Hospice, 228 Seventh St., S.E., Washington, DC 20003; (202) 547-7424; www.nahc.org. Provides information and advocacy on how long-term-care policies affect providers of home-delivered care.

National Citizens' Coalition for Nursing Home Reform, 1828 L St., N.W., Suite 801, Washington, DC 20036; (202) 332-2276; www.nccnhr.org. Advocates for better-quality nursing-home care and provides information about choosing nursing homes.

National Senior Citizens' Law Center, 1101 14th St., N.W., Suite 400, Washington, DC 20005; (202) 289-6976; www.nsclc.org. Advocates and litigates on behalf of low-income seniors and people with disabilities and provides consumer and policy information on long-term-care options.

United Hospital Fund, Empire State Building, 23rd Floor, 350 Fifth Ave., New York, NY 10118; (212) 494-0700; www.uhfnyc.org. Provides research and grant funding on health-care issues, including family caregiving and aging-in-place initiatives.

Bibliography

Selected Sources

Books

Buhler-Wilkinson, Karen, *No Place Like Home: A History of Nursing and Home Care in the United States*, The Johns Hopkins University Press, 2003.

A professor of community health at the University of Pennsylvania traces the history of home-delivered health care in the United States, comparing its relatively limited use to the much wider spread of residential health-care institutions.

Levine, Carol, and Thomas H. Murray, eds., *The Cultures of Caregiving: Conflict and Common Ground Among Families, Health Professionals, and Policy Makers*, The Johns Hopkins University Press, 2004.

Murray, a bioethicist, and Levine, an advocate for family caregivers, assemble data, personal stories and essays that demonstrate the varying perspectives of family caregivers, medical personnel and health-care administrators.

Gass, Thomas Edward, *Nobody's Home: Candid Reflections of a Nursing Home Aide*, ILR Press, 2005.

Gass describes the daily routines of his work and reflects on how quality of life could be improved for nursing-home residents.

Mezey, Mathy Doval, Barbara J. Berkman, Christopher M. Callahan and Ethel L. Mitty, eds., *The Encyclopedia of Elder Care*, Prometheus Books, 2004.

Professors of medicine and nursing at various universities provide advice on health care for seniors and articles about the financing and delivery of long-term care for elderly people.

Articles

"Nursing Home Guide," *Consumer Reports*, www.consumerreports.org/cro/health-fitness/nursing-home-guide/0608_nursing-home-guide.htm, September 2006.

The nonprofit consumer-research group provides state-by-state listings of nursing homes that are likely to provide the best and the worst care; discusses how to choose high-quality long-term care; and analyzes how the federal government's Web site on nursing-home quality falls short.

Peck, Richard L., "Turning LTC Upside Down," *Nursing Homes*, www.nursinghomesmagazine.com/Past_Issues.htm?ID=4180, June 2005.

In an interview, Leonard Fishman, former president of the American Association of Homes and Services for the Aging, describes current efforts to create a new continuum of senior-housing options to avoid institutionalization and improve elders' quality of life.

Reports and Studies

"Financing Long-Term Care for the Elderly," Congressional Budget Office, April 2004.

Congress' nonpartisan budget-analysis office analyzes trends in population aging, disability and long-term-care service delivery and discusses what they mean for future long-term-care costs in the United States.

Burke, Sheila P., Judith Feder and Paul N. Van de Water, eds., "Developing a Better Long-Term Care Policy: A Vision and Strategy for America's Future," National Academy of Social Insurance, November 2005.

Experts on public social-insurance programs discuss why the United States needs social insurance to finance future long-term-care needs.

Capitman, John, Walter Leutz, Christine Bishop and Rosemary Casler, "Long-Term Care Quality: Historical Overview and Current Initiatives," National Quality Forum, 2005.

Professors of public policy at Brandeis University examine how standards for long-term-care quality have changed over the years and what steps federal and state governments have taken to measure and improve quality.

Johnson, Richard W., and Joshua M. Wiener, "A Profile of Frail Older Americans and Their Caregivers," The Retirement Project, Urban Institute, February 2006.

Analysts from a liberal-leaning think tank describe the demographic, financial and health-related characteristics of Americans who need long-term care and the friends and family who provide unpaid care for them.

O'Brien, Ellen, "Long-Term Care: Understanding Medicaid's Role for the Elderly and Disabled," Kaiser Commission on Medicaid and the Uninsured, November 2005.

A nonprofit research organization that studies health policy for low-income people describes Medicaid's role in paying for and delivering long-term care, including how state long-term-care programs vary.

Wunderlich, Gooloo S., and Peter O. Kohler, eds., "Improving the Quality of Long-Term Care," National Academies Press, 2001.

An expert panel from the Institute of Medicine examines quality-of-care problems in nursing homes, home-health agencies and other long-term-care providers and proposes methods for beefing up staffing and setting and enforcing quality standards.

The Next Step:

Additional Articles from Current Periodicals

Assisted Living

Benn, Evan S., "Senior's Work Gets Notice-and $100,000," ***The Miami Herald*****, Sept. 6, 2006, p. B5.**

Conchy Bretos has spent the past decade helping public-housing groups provide poor seniors in Miami, Fla., with assisted-living services.

Bernstein, Elizabeth, "Assisted-Living Help Reaches Out to Elderly," ***Chicago Tribune*****, June 3, 2006, p. 8.**

Companies that run assisted-living or nursing homes are increasingly offering an array of non-medical services to elderly people who want to remain in their homes.

Bretting, Sandra, "Suburbs See Growing Need For Assisted Living," ***The Houston Chronicle*****, Sept. 16, 2006, p. 1.**

Aging residents of Houston's established master-planned communities, which were created 15-35 years ago, are now in the market for assisted-living facilities.

Dilanian, Ken, "Troubled Care Facility Closes," ***The Philadelphia Inquirer*****, April 26, 2006, p. A1.**

Pennsylvania regulators closed the St. James Retirement and Rehabilitation Center after the suspicious death of a resident.

Kornblum, Janet, "Assisted-Living Facility Gets Technology Assist," ***USA Today*****, July 6, 2006, p. D1.**

Assisted-living facilities that electronically measure and monitor residents 24 hours a day represent the future.

Pristin, Terry, "Hot Niche in the Rental Market: Housing for the Elderly," ***The New York Times*****, Feb. 15, 2006, p. C6.**

The commercial real estate sector known as senior housing was in trouble a few years ago, but now it's thriving.

Stewart, Janet Kidd, "Assisted-Living Costs Trigger Sticker Shock," ***Orlando Sentinel*****, June 18, 2006, p. G5.**

The cost of a one-bedroom unit in an assisted-living facility rose 7 percent from 2005, to $32,294.

Nursing Homes

The Associated Press, "Nonchain and Nonprofit Nursing Homes Receive Edge on Care in Report," ***St. Louis Post-Dispatch*****, Aug. 7, 2006, p. A2.**

Nonprofit nursing homes provide residents better care than those operated for profit, according to a nationwide study.

Babwin, Don, "Nursing Home Residents Getting More Say in How They Live," ***The Washington Post*****, March 5, 2006, p. A11.**

A growing number of nursing homes are encouraging residents to make their own decisions, like when to go to sleep or take a shower, instead of having nurses decide.

Clemetson, Lynette, "U.S. Muslims Confront Taboo on Nursing Homes," ***The New York Times*****, June 13, 2006, p. A1.**

Several Muslim families in the United States are trying to reconcile their Islamic religious teachings on caring for elderly relatives with the modern realities of their hectic American lives.

Taylor, Liz, "Culture Change is on the Horizon For Long-Term Health Care," ***The Seattle Times*****, Aug. 14, 2006, p. D6.**

Nursing homes are beginning to undergo a "culture change," instituting "person-directed care" to improve the quality of their health care.

Nursing-Home Deficiencies

Fallik, Dawn, "Wrong Dosages Administered Daily," ***The Philadelphia Inquirer*****, July 21, 2006, p. A1.**

At least 1.5 million Americans annually are harmed from medication mistakes, mostly in nursing homes.

Pear, Robert, "Nursing Homes Inspections Miss Violations, Report Says," ***The New York Times*****, Jan. 16, 2006, p. A9.**

State inspectors ensuring that nursing homes meet quality-of-care federal standards to participate in Medicaid and Medicare often overlook serious deficiencies, including life-threatening conditions, according to a Government Accountability Office report.

Vigil, Delfin, "Bad Marks For Nursing Homes," ***The San Francisco Chronicle*****, Aug. 7, 2006, p. B2.**

Two of the 12 nursing homes nationwide with the poorest performance records in recent years are in the San Francisco Bay Area, according to a *Consumer Reports* investigation.

Citing *CQ Researcher*

Sample formats for citing these reports in a bibliography include the ones listed below. Preferred styles and formats vary, so please check with your instructor or professor.

MLA Style

Jost, Kenneth. "Rethinking the Death Penalty." CQ Researcher 16 Nov. 2001: 945-68.

APA Style

Jost, K. (2001, November 16). Rethinking the death penalty. *CQ Researcher, 11*, 945-968.

Chicago Style

Jost, Kenneth. "Rethinking the Death Penalty." *CQ Researcher*, November 16, 2001, 945-968.

CQ Researcher

Published by CQ Press, a division of Congressional Quarterly Inc.

cqresearcher.com

Ecotourism

Does it help or hurt fragile lands and cultures?

In the booming global travel business, ecotourism is among the fastest-growing segments. Costa Rica and Belize have built national identities around their celebrated environmental allure, while parts of the world once all but inaccessible — from Antarctica to the Galapagos Islands to Mount Everest — are now featured in travel guides, just like Manhattan, Rome and other less exotic destinations. Advocates see ecotourism as a powerful yet environmentally benign tool for sustainable economic development in even the poorest nations. But as the trend expands, critics see threats to the very flora and fauna tourists flock to visit. Moreover, traditional subsistence cultures may be obliterated by the ecotourism onslaught, replaced by service jobs that pay native peoples poverty wages. Meanwhile, tour promoters are using the increasingly popular "green" label to lure visitors to places unable to withstand large numbers of tourists.

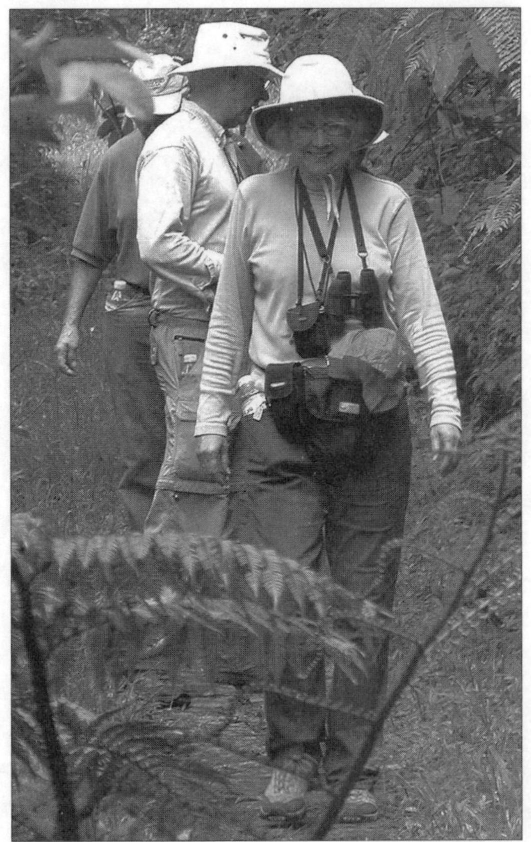

Ecotourists seek sightings of the rare Indri lemur in Madagascar's Perinet Reserve rain forest.

INSIDE THIS REPORT

CQ Researcher • Oct. 20, 2006 • www.cqresearcher.com
Volume 16, Number 37 • Pages 865-888

CQ PRESS

RECIPIENT OF SOCIETY OF PROFESSIONAL JOURNALISTS AWARD FOR EXCELLENCE ◆ AMERICAN BAR ASSOCIATION SILVER GAVEL AWARD

THE ISSUES

BACKGROUND

CURRENT SITUATION

OUTLOOK

SIDEBARS AND GRAPHICS

FOR FURTHER RESEARCH

Cover photograph: Terra Incognita Ecotours/Gerard "Ged" Caddick

CQ Researcher

Oct. 20, 2006
Volume 16, Number 37

MANAGING EDITOR: Thomas J. Colin

ASSISTANT MANAGING EDITOR: Kathy Koch

ASSOCIATE EDITOR: Kenneth Jost

STAFF WRITERS: Marcia Clemmitt, Peter Katel

CONTRIBUTING WRITERS: Rachel S. Cox, Sarah Glazer, Alan Greenblatt, Barbara Mantel, Patrick Marshall, Tom Price, Jennifer Weeks

DESIGN/PRODUCTION EDITOR: Olu B. Davis

ASSISTANT EDITOR: Melissa J. Hipolit

CQ PRESS

A Division of Congressional Quarterly Inc.

SENIOR VICE PRESIDENT/PUBLISHER: John A. Jenkins

DIRECTOR, LIBRARY PUBLISHING: Kathryn C. Suárez

DIRECTOR, EDITORIAL OPERATIONS: Ann Davies

CONGRESSIONAL QUARTERLY INC.

CHAIRMAN: Paul C. Tash

VICE CHAIRMAN: Andrew P. Corty

PRESIDENT/EDITOR IN CHIEF: Robert W. Merry

CQ Researcher (ISSN 1056-2036) is printed on acid-free paper. Published weekly, except March 24, July 7, July 14, Aug. 4, Aug. 11, Nov. 24, Dec. 22 and Dec. 29, by CQ Press, a division of Congressional Quarterly Inc. Annual full-service subscriptions for institutions start at $667. For pricing, call 1-800-834-9020, ext. 1906. To purchase a *CQ Researcher* report in print or electronic format (PDF), visit www.cqpress.com or call 866-427-7737. Single reports start at $15. Bulk purchase discounts and electronic-rights licensing are also available. Periodicals postage paid at Washington, D.C., and additional mailing offices. POSTMASTER: Send address changes to *CQ Researcher*, 1255 22nd St., N.W., Suite 400, Washington, DC 20037.

Ecotourism

By Rachel S. Cox

The Issues

A week-long cruise to the fabled Galapagos Islands last summer took members of the Sturc family of Washington, D.C., back into history. As they clambered out of their rubber landing raft, boobies and penguins, iguanas and sea lions greeted them as nonchalantly as their forebears had greeted British naturalist Charles Darwin when he arrived in 1835 to collect evidence that led to his theory of natural selection.

"It was beautiful in a very stark way," Susan Sturc recalls. "We were impressed at how clean everything was. There was no trash anywhere." But, she adds, the islands 600 miles off the coast of Ecuador were "not as untouched as I had thought they would be. I was surprised at how much development there was. I thought it would be pristine."

Terra Incognita Ecotours/Gerard "Ged" Caddick

Marine iguanas show little fear of visitors to the Galapagos Islands, where the Ecuadorian government tightly controls tourism. Ecotourism supporters say such "sustainable" travel brings environmental and economic benefits to isolated communities, but critics warn that even well-managed ecotourism can destroy the very attractions it promotes.

The Sturcs' experience typifies the paradox of ecotourism, a relatively new and increasingly popular form of tourism that The International Ecotourism Society defines as "responsible travel to natural areas that conserves the environment and improves the well-being of local people."

To its supporters, ecotourism offers a model with the potential to remake the travel industry, bringing environmental and economic benefits to destination communities while providing tourists with more meaningful experiences than conventional tourism offers. But critics warn that the environmental and social changes that accompany even well-managed ecotourism threaten to destroy the very attractions it promotes.

Over the last 25 years, travelers have enjoyed expanding opportunities to visit locations once considered impossibly remote. Even Antarctica is now visited by more than 10,000 travelers per year. Tourism in general is considered by many to be the world's largest industry, and one of the fastest growing. Indeed, eco/nature tourism is growing three times faster than the tourism industry as a whole, according to the World Tourism Organization. [1]

Tourism activist Deborah McLaren, the founder of Indigenous Rights International, says many tourists are no longer interested in the fantasy tourism culture of "sand, sun, sea and sex" offered by packaged tours to beach resorts and cruise ships. [2] Many travelers now prefer what the industry calls "experiential" tourism — encounters with nature, heritage and culture. Many also want a sense of adventure and discovery or philanthropic activities, such as restoring historic buildings or teaching. [3]

While ecotourism has brought new income to isolated parts of the world, it has come at a price, critics say. When archeologist Richard Leventhal, director of the Museum of Archaeology and Anthropology at the University of Pennsylvania, began his field work in 1972 in Cancun, Mexico, grass huts bordered the island's white-sand beaches. Today, Cancun's 20,000 hotel rooms attract more than 2.6 million visitors a year, and a sprawling shanty town houses the 300,000 workers drawn to the new industry. [4]

"Ecotourism has brought a lot of attention to a lot of places that wouldn't have gotten it otherwise," Leventhal observes. "That's generally good, because the economies are so fragile." But "tourism is one of the most fickle stimuli that exist. A hurricane comes, and the tourists are gone."

"Ecotourism is not the cost-free business option that its supporters suggest," argues Rosaleen Duffy, a senior lecturer at the Centre for International Politics at Manchester University in England. "Because ecotourism often takes place in relatively remote areas and small communities, the effects of establishing a small-scale hotel or food outlet can have the same impact as building a Hilton in a large town or city." [5]

As a Maya scholar, Leventhal has worked closely with communities

Hotels Going 'Green' Around the World

Many tourism companies are trying to reduce their impact on the environment — and save money — by cutting consumption of water, energy and other resources and improving the disposal of waste.

Hotel "Greening" Success Stories

Hilton International

The chain saved 60 percent on gas costs and 30 percent on both electricity and water in recent years, cutting waste by 25 percent. Vienna Hilton and Vienna Plaza reduced laundry loads by 164,000 kilograms per year, minimizing water and chemical use.

Singapore Marriott and Tang Plaza Scandic

Efforts to save some 40,000 cubic meters of water per year have reduced water use by 20 percent per guest. The chain pioneered a 97 percent "recyclable" hotel room and is building or retrofitting 1,500 rooms annually.

Sheraton Rittenhouse Square, Philadelphia

Boasts a 93 percent recycled granite floor, organic cotton bedding, night tables made from discarded wooden shipping pallets, naturally dyed recycled carpeting and nontoxic wallpaper, carpeting, drapes and cleaning products. The extra 2 percent 'green' investment was recouped in the first six months.

Inter-Continental Hotels and Resorts

Each facility must implement a checklist of 134 environmental actions and meet specific energy, waste and water-management targets. Between 1988 and 1995, the chain reduced overall energy costs by 27 percent. In 1995, it saved $3.7 million, reducing sulfur dioxide emissions by 10,670 kilograms, and saved 610,866 cubic meters of water — an average water reduction of nearly 7 percent per hotel, despite higher occupancies.

Forte Brighouse, West Yorkshire, United Kingdom

Energy-efficient lamps reduced energy use by 45 percent, cut maintenance by 85 percent and lowered carbon emissions by 135 tons. The move paid for itself in less than a year.

Hyatt International

Energy-efficiency measures in the United States cut energy use by 15 percent and now save the chain an estimated $15 million annually.

Holiday Inn Crowne Plaza, Schiphol Airport, Netherlands

By offering guests the option of not changing their linens and towels each day, the hotel reduced laundry volume, water and detergent — as well as costs — by 20 percent.

Source: Lisa Mastny, "Traveling Light, New Paths for International Tourism."

throughout Central America, especially in Belize — considered a leading ecotourism success story similar to nearby Costa Rica. "What I always ask," he says, "is, 'Does it really benefit local people?' "

Development economists call the problem "leakage." Studies have shown that up to half of the tourism revenue entering the developing world reverts to the developed world in profits earned by foreign-owned businesses, promotional spending abroad or payments for imported labor and goods. [6]

And, as "ecotourism" has become a popular gimmick in travel marketing, another sort of leakage has emerged. "Ten years ago, I could tell you what ecotourism was," Leventhal says. "Today, everyone's trying to claim it, because it's a hook people really like."

Ron Mader, a Mexico-based travel writer and founder of the ecotourism Web site Planeta.com, agrees. "Look at national travel Web sites," he says. "Even Cancun has a page on ecotourism," with a picture of a contented drinker lounging at a pool bar, suggesting that just getting a sunburn is "practicing ecotourism."

Partly to clarify such public misperceptions, some ecotourism advocates support creation of a certification system reflecting a destination's environmental and cultural sensitivity. Conservation groups like the Rainforest Alliance and Conservation International see the plan as a way to encourage responsible ecotourism and sound environmental practices.

"'Eco-travel' can come in many shades of green," senior editor Rene Ebersole writes in *Audubon* magazine. "Without a global certification label — something as recognizable as, say, the [U.S. Department of Agriculture] 'Organic' sticker on produce — it's hard to be sure" which trips qualify as genuine ecotourism. [7]

Critics contend, however, that ecotourism certification will further diminish the involvement of indigenous people and exacerbate many of the problems ecotourism already creates for its communities. "It really pits people against each other," says McLaren.

Conservation International and other major non-governmental conservation organizations (NGOs) say ecotourism can give indigenous people a stake in protecting their environment, with income from tourism compensating for the loss of traditional lifeways, such as hunting and slash-and-burn agriculture.

"Carefully planned and implemented tourism can . . . offer a powerful incentive to conserve and protect biodiversity," says Conservation International. "People who earn their living from ecotourism are more likely to protect their natural resources and support conservation efforts." [8]

But Luis Vivanco, an anthropology professor at the University of Vermont who has studied the effects of ecotourism in Costa Rica, is skeptical. "For elites and people with the ability to make money, it's a great opportunity," he says. But in real life, "ecotourism is redefining people's lives and landscapes. It's impossible not to wonder if they could be destroying what they love."

As conservationists, tourism operators, development banks and anthropologists evaluate ecotourism, here are some of the key questions in the debate:

Does ecotourism threaten fragile ecosystems?

Traveling in Nepal in the early 1980s, Steve Powers, a tour operator in Long Beach, N.Y., witnessed the effects of uncontrolled tourism. "Nepal was a prime example of how not to do tourism in the Third World," he says. "The government policy was to let everybody in with no controls. Tourists just trashed the trekking sites, and backpackers living on $2 a day really weren't benefiting the community."

Even the native porters contributed to the problem. He remembers seeing them conscientiously collect all the trash at a campsite, then dump it in a river.

By 2003, more than 25,000 trekkers were visiting the Khumbu Valley near Mt. Everest. Much of the area that Sir Edmund Hillary described as being superbly forested in 1951 had become "an eroding desert." [9]

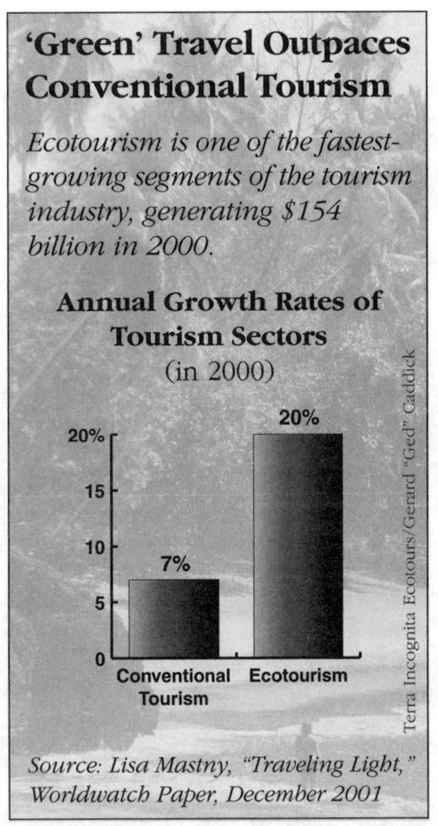

'Green' Travel Outpaces Conventional Tourism
Ecotourism is one of the fastest-growing segments of the tourism industry, generating $154 billion in 2000.
Annual Growth Rates of Tourism Sectors
(in 2000)
20%
15
10
5
0
7%
20%
Conventional Tourism
Ecotourism
Terra Incognita Ecotours/Gerard "Ged" Caddick
Source: Lisa Mastny, "Traveling Light," Worldwatch Paper, December 2001

The main culprit in the area's massive deforestation was the tourists, and the demand they created not only for fuel to warm themselves and their porters but also to build the "teahouses" where they stayed.

"Do tourists who come here consider what their need for hot water costs in terms of wood?" asked Gian Pietro Verza, field manager at an Italian environmental research station near a Sherpa village. "One trekker can consume an average of five times more wood per day than an entire Sherpa family uses — and the porters and guides they bring with them need firewood, too." [10]

Other ecotourism skeptics tell the story of Brazil's first "eco-resort," Praia do Forte, a 247-room hotel whose developer bought thousands of acres of rain forest on a spectacular beach, then leveled much of the forest to build his hotel. [11]

In Africa, uncontrolled "nature" tourism has been linked to a decline in cheetah survival rates. As tourists clamor to watch the cats up close, according to Costas Christ, Sr., director of ecotourism at Conservation International, they frighten the cheetahs and their young away from hard-won kills, the food is scavenged by hyenas and the cubs go hungry. [12]

The Third World Network, a Malaysia-based coalition that supports development in developing countries, recently reported that tourism was destroying the "World's Eighth Wonder" — the Banaue rice terraces, a UNESCO World Heritage site in the northern Philippines. The group said timber cutting in the Banaue watershed to provide wood for handicrafts for tourists was reducing water flow to the terraces and encouraging giant earthworms to bore deeper into their banks.

In addition, a recent study by the Tebtebba Foundation, a Philippines-based indigenous peoples' advocacy and research center, found the terraces also were being damaged by the water demands of hotels, lodges and restaurants, as well as the conversion of rice paddies into lots for lodges and shops. At the same time, the study said, rice farmers are giving up their traditional livelihoods to take jobs in tourism. [13]

Similarly, the development in the Galapagos Islands that surprised ecotourist Susan Sturc reflected social changes brought about by increased tourism. The Ecuadorian government tightly controls Galapagos tourism, limiting the number of cruise ships, requiring visitors' groups to be accompanied by guides and prohibiting the carrying of food onto the islands. [14]

Nonetheless, the influx of tourists has attracted many Ecuadorians from the mainland who seek better economic opportunities. Between 1974 and 1997 the population of the Galapagos grew by almost 150 percent, and today there are about 27,000 year-round residents. In 2004, a study about the future of the Galapagos warned "tourism is the main economic driver, yet the migration it induces threatens the future of tourism." [15]

These and many other environmental impacts are being addressed by governments and NGOs. Tour operator Powers helped to establish Nepal's Kathmandu Environmental Education Project, now being run by Nepalis. It educates both tourists and locals by conducting eco-trekking workshops, encouraging trekking companies to be environmentally responsible and even paying porters for the trash they bring home. "It's better now," he says, but finding funds for such educational efforts is a perennial problem.

Powers believes organizations like the American Society of Travel Agents (ASTA) can help educate businesses, especially since its code of conduct includes respecting destination cultures and environments. But in-country operators — the local hotels and guides with whom travel agents arrange tours — also should be held accountable, he says.

But defining and measuring practices that promote environmental sustainability is a very new field, says David Weaver, a professor of tourism management and an ecotourism expert at the University of South Carolina in Columbia. "We're working to pin down the variables and criteria you would need to measure to determine whether an operation is sustainable," he says, but "we still have a long way to go. There aren't a lot of mature programs, and a lot of it is learn as you go."

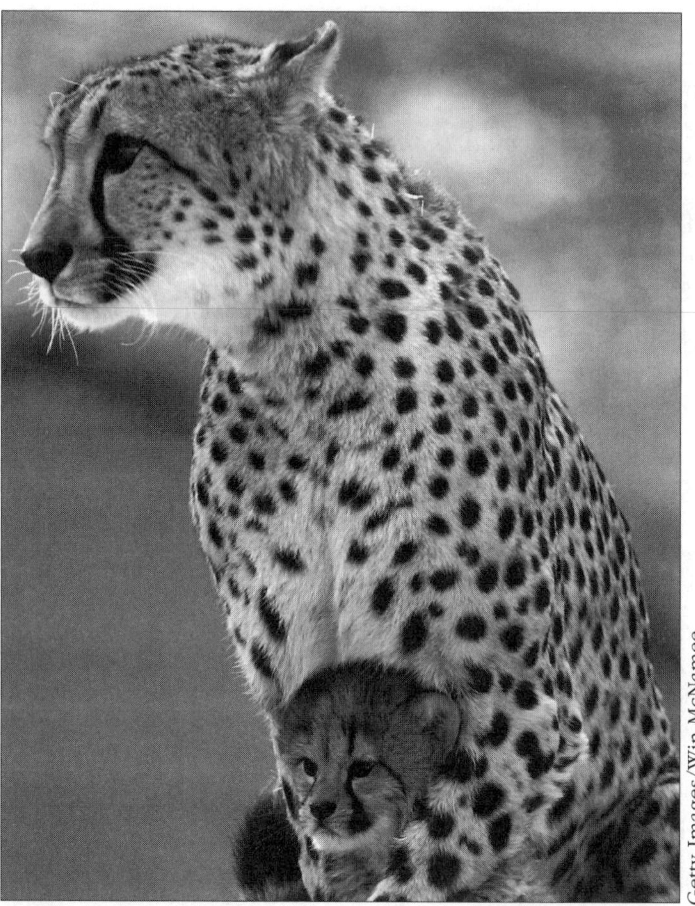

Getty Images/Win McNamee

Declining survival rates of African cheetahs have been linked to heavy tourism in game preserves. According to Conservation International, clamoring tourists frighten adult cheetahs and their young away from their kills, allowing hyenas to scavenge the food and forcing cubs to go hungry.

For instance, a recent study of Magellanic penguins nesting at Punta Tombo, in Argentina, found that the birds adjusted relatively quickly to tourists. To study stress in the birds, researchers measured their number of head turns when humans approached and the level of stress-related hormones they secreted.

Greg Wetstone, U.S. director for the International Fund for Animal Welfare, calls the findings encouraging. "We still have a lot to learn, but this study reinforces the sense that responsible ecotourism can be a low-impact way to create economic pressure for protecting threatened wildlife." The study's authors cautioned, however, that "long-term consequences are much harder to document, especially in long-lived animals." [16]

Ecotourism consultant Megan Epler Wood, the first executive director of the Ecotourism Society (now The International Ecotourism Society), sees the problem of managing environmental effects more in terms of money than methodology. "With the participation of large conservation agencies, it has been shown that as long as an ecotourism project is appropriately planned, zoning the infrastructure well away from protected areas, people can visit without harming," she says.

But even in the United States, Epler Wood notes, the National Park Service has trouble implementing new methodologies because of funding gaps, a situation that is even more dire in developing countries. [17] "You may have one or two staff overseeing hundreds or thousands of acres," she says. The idea of them controlling and managing so much requires a budgetary level that many can't approach."

Even the best-managed ecotourism facility can pave the way for less-benevolent permanent development, say other observers. In the remote Canadian province of Newfoundland, for instance, the tourism infrastructure gradually improved as the fishing industry gave out. "There has always been the hook and bullet crowd," says Larry Morris, president of the Quebec-Labrador Foundation/Atlantic Center for the Environment. "Now it's 'non-consumptive use.' "

The sophistication of the outfitters has increased dramatically, Morris notes, and the province is capitalizing on concerns about global warming by promoting itself as a reliable destination for snow lovers. Now some of the visitors are purchasing permanent homes — a trend the industry labels "amenity migration." The province just got its first gated community, in Deer Lake, and its "wilderness cottages" — next to a new golf course — are attracting buyers from the United Kingdom.

The University of South Carolina's Weaver suggests that environmental damage caused by ecotourism can be diminished if it is practiced in areas that are already heavily altered. In downtown Austin, Texas, for instance, crowds gather every night at the Congress Street Bridge between March and November to watch up to 1.5 million Mexican free-tailed bats — North America's largest urban bat colony — emerge from their nests in deep crevices.

"You can have very high-quality ecotourism in highly disturbed areas," he says. "People go to see whooping cranes in the stubble of farmers' fields in Saskatchewan."

Others view peregrine falcons roosting in Pittsburgh skyscrapers, and even in the much-maligned New Jersey Meadowlands — just five miles from Manhattan — a bird-watching and fishing guidebook now promotes ecotourism. [18]

"The perception that [ecotourism] is a threat comes mostly from indigenous groups," says anthropologist Vivanco. "When you don't have control over tourism in your community, things leave." About five years ago, he points out, "bioprospecting" — in which pharmaceutical companies send people into the rain forest to see if they can find useful plants — became identified as ecotourism.

"Indigenous groups felt that things were being taken from them," he says, and it made them "very politicized," even though the evidence of biological theft was mostly anecdotal. "There is the notion that this is yet another effort to bring us into the modern world, to get control of our land — the latest version of the white man telling us what we should do with our land."

Some indigenous peoples involved with ecotourism projects are simply calling it quits. In Santa Maria, Costa Rica, where for several years Vivanco took his students on field trips, the community-based tourism project that sent paying guests to stay in local homes began to arouse resentment because not all families got guests. Recently, the villagers decided to end the program. "People are saying, 'We've had enough. It's causing division in the community,' " Vivanco says. "Their own conflicts play out in tourism."

Does ecotourism offer a realistic alternative to more traditional commercial development?

In the early 1990s, archeologist Leventhal worked with a group of Mayan Indians studying the future of their communities in southern Belize. At the time Belize — following Costa Rica's lead — was in the process of transforming itself into a major ecotourism destination. The group went on a tour of Mexico's popular Yucatan Peninsula.

"They were fascinated by being waited on by other Maya," Leventhal recalls. But not all the encounters were positive. When they'd walk into the big hotels, the Mayan security guards would immediately stop them.

"They really understood the impact of tourism," Leventhal says. "Yes, it brought money in, but they got very worried about certain aspects of it. They got involved with the idea that these were their cousins. Living in a subsistence economy in their own villages, they basically controlled the show. They didn't need to borrow money. When you borrow money, you have to pay it back." In the end they rejected ecotourism.

A 1999 study commissioned by the environmental group Greenpeace and conducted by American resource economist Christopher LaFranchi, however, suggests that while ecotourism may not be perfect, it is far more advantageous for indigenous peoples than "industrial" options such as logging and plantation-style agriculture. The study compared such traditional development tactics with small-scale development options, including ecotourism in the forest lands of the Marovo lagoon area in the Solomon Islands. It found negative long-term repercussions despite "rapid and considerable cash returns available from abruptly selling the forest for logging" and potential governmental revenues derived from taxing the timber industry.

"The rapid exploitation of tropical forests, although very profitable for international timber companies, has produced only limited long-term economic gain for the nations of the Pacific, and at great environmental and social cost," the study said. [19]

In comparing the costs and benefits of exploiting the reef and forest resources of the area, the study found that "the economic benefits of the small-scale options considerably exceed those of the industrial options. Moreover, they leave landowners in more direct control of their resources, distribute benefits more equitably and do not expose them to the high risks of fluctuations in international commodity markets." [20]

The present value of industrial options — mainly logging and palm oil — to landowners was estimated at $8.2 million, while small-scale options were valued at $29 million.

Tourism Professor Weaver calls this advantage the "one shot" angle. With traditional development, he says, "You get a lot of money in a limited time, but then it's done. With ecotourism, it's never exhausted."

Within the world of international aid agencies and development banks, says ecotourism consultant Epler Wood, ecotourism is "increasingly gaining credibility as a development tool because of its clear economic statistics and because there aren't that many other tools." Proposed development projects must now be sustainable, she says.

'Green' Certification on the Rise

Tourism companies increasingly are participating in voluntary certification programs that provide a seal of approval to businesses that demonstrate environmentally or socially sound practices.

Selected Tourism-Certification Efforts Worldwide

Green Globe 21 — Has awarded logos to some 500 companies and destinations in more than 100 countries. Rewards efforts to incorporate social responsibility and sustainable resource management into business programs. But may confuse tourists by rewarding not only businesses that have achieved certification but also those that have simply committed to undertake the process.

ECOTEL® — Has certified 23 hotels in Latin America, seven in the United States and Mexico, five in Japan and one in India. Assigns hotels zero to five globes based on environmental commitment, waste management, energy efficiency, water conservation, environmental education and community involvement. Hotels must be reinspected every two years, and unannounced inspections can occur at any time. A project of the industry consulting group HVS International.

European Blue Flag Campaign — Includes more than 2,750 sites in 21 European countries; being adopted in South Africa and the Caribbean. Awards a yearly ecolabel to beaches and marinas for their high environmental standards and sanitary and safe facilities. Credited with improving the quality and desirability of European coastal sites. Run by the international nonprofit Foundation for Environmental Education.

Certification for Sustainable Tourism, Costa Rica — Has certified some 54 hotels since 1997. Gives hotels a ranking of one to five based on environmental and social criteria. Credited with raising environmental awareness among tourism businesses and tourists. But the rating is skewed toward large hotels that may be too big to really be sustainable.

SmartVoyager, Galapagos, Ecuador — Since 1999, has certified five of more than 80 ships that operate in the area. Gives a special seal to tour operators and boats that voluntarily comply with specified benchmarks for boat and dinghy maintenance and operation, dock operations and management of wastewater and fuels. A joint project of the Rainforest Alliance and a local conservation group.

Green Leaf, Thailand — Had certified 59 hotels as of October 2000. Awards hotels between one and five "green leaves" based on audits of their environmental policies and other measures. Aims to improve efficiency and raise awareness within the domestic hotel industry.

Source: Lisa Mastny, "Traveling Light, New Paths for International Tourism."

"The economic growth potential is on a par with textiles. The reception is growing, and all the statistics have been clearly presented."

Often, she points out, the poorest countries stand to gain the most from ecotourism. Many studies show that traditional development strategies "have created a gap between rich and poor and between urban and rural," she explains. "Rural people have been left out of grand development schemes. But as long as they are an ecotourism attraction, rural people can get a nice growth trend."

Ecotourism has other advantages over traditional development schemes, she adds. Start-up takes a much lower investment and, thanks to the Internet, projects can be marketed directly to consumers, allowing the benefits to be delivered directly to the producer.

"It's very viable," says Benjamin Powell, a managing partner of Agora Partnerships, an American NGO that promotes Nicaraguan entrepreneurship. "Certain countries have completely branded themselves as ecotourism destinations to great effect. If it is done right, people are often willing to pay, and it often does trickle down to the locals."

Traditionally, institutional and cultural barriers have prevented native people from owning local businesses. Besides lacking a cultural tradition of entrepreneurship, Powell explains, "Most aspiring entrepreneurs in poor countries are caught in a development blind spot: They're too big for microfinance, yet too small for traditional lending."

Powell promotes the advantages to small investors of small investments in local businesses. "From an investment perspective, you have more leverage if you invest in a local operation because you can put some corporate-responsibility standards in place," he says. "There's no correlation with the stock market at all. It's a very specific market, very local. It's not affected by anything macro. But still, it is very risky."

Should ecotourism businesses and programs be certified?

As ecotourism has become highly marketable, numerous schemes have sprung up that offer a "green" imprimatur for businesses. Some certification proposals require high standards while others set the bar lower; some are operated for profit, others are run by nonprofit organizations; some can be purchased, others are awarded.

"We're seeing nearly 100 different programs," says Katie Maschman, a spokeswoman for The International Ecotourism Society. Some programs are worldwide, national or regional in scope and others relate to specific resources, such as Blue Flag certification for healthy beaches. Other examples include the worldwide program Green Globe 21 and the World Wildlife Fund's PAN Parks network in Europe. The American Hotel & Lodging Association lets its most energy-efficient members display a Good Earthkeeping logo. The association estimates 43 million domestic travelers each year are "environmentally minded."

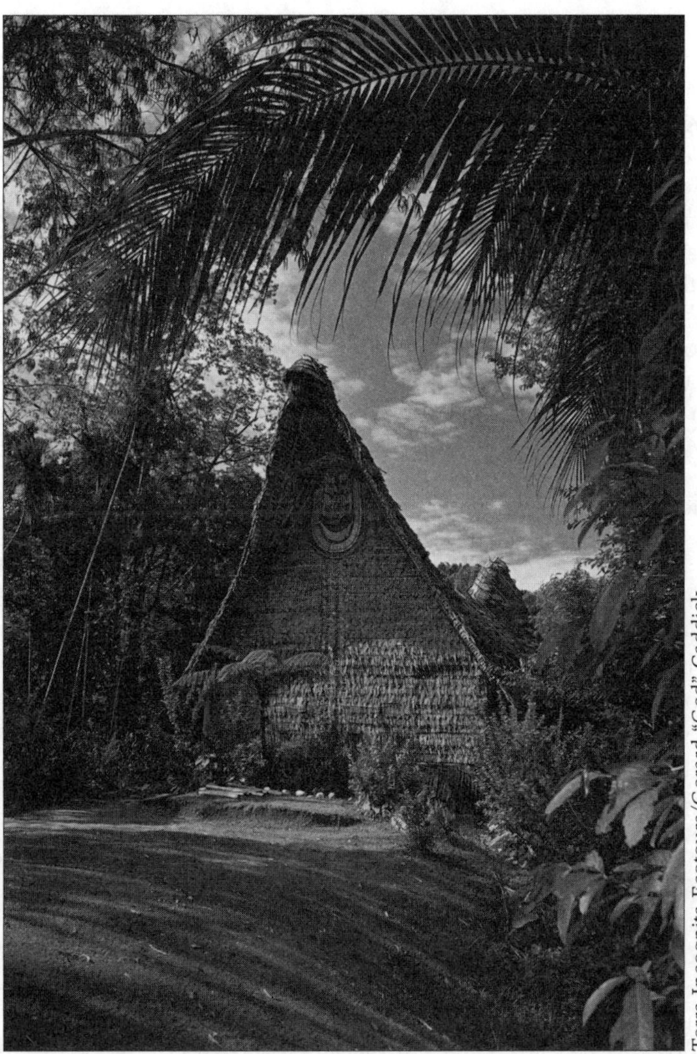
Terra Incognita Ecotours/Gerard "Ged" Caddick

The Karawari Lodge in Papua New Guinea's East Sepik Province sits on the edge of a lowland rain forest in one of the country's most remote regions. Visitors can explore the area's varied flora and fauna and visit villages on the Karawari River.

In recent years, the Rainforest Alliance and the ecotourism society have spearheaded an effort to regularize certification, supported by the Inter-American Development Bank, foundations and other development groups. Now they are studying how to develop and judge standards and certify eco-ventures that practice sustainable tourism, inspired by successful certification programs in other industries — such as the Forest Stewardship Council's approval of sustainably harvested lumber and the fair trade movement's certification of "green" coffee beans and bananas.

Advocates argue that a more coherent certification system is the only way to protect the market advantages of genuine ecotourism and encourage development of sustainable practices in the broader marketplace.

But critics say certification programs now being discussed raise more questions than they answer. For one thing, deciding who qualifies is not a simple matter. At an ecolodge in Australia, for example, visitors can buy packets of seeds to feed the colorful, parrot-like lorikeets, which will then flock around and alight on tourists' arms and heads.

"It's a paradox that this park lodge has advanced accreditation," says tourism professor Weaver. "They do a lot of fantastic things," but the bird feeding is a "demonstrable ecological problem." It keeps a lot of weak birds alive, which spreads diseases, he explains, and when the birds, gorged on seeds, return to the wild and defecate, weeds and other invasive species are introduced.

Nonetheless, a good ecolabel or certification "would give the public some confidence in what they're buying," Weaver says.

The difficulties lie in deciding how such a system would be monitored, he says, and what penalties should be levied for violations. To Planeta.com founder Mader, certification based on sustainability does not address questions many travelers are concerned about. "Most of the travelers I talk to would love certification if it would tell them where there's a clean bathroom," he says. Mader sees a far greater need for certification in safety- and service-related areas such as scuba diving, rock climbing or massage therapy.

Certification efforts so far have been "prioritized far too ahead of the curve, before we have reliable information, let alone communication," Mader argues. "In countries that are developing rural travel, there are usually six to 12 state or federal entities involved — none of whom ever want to talk to one another. The tourism section and the environmental, labor, agriculture and forestry sections each want to protect its place in the pipeline. Communication that could improve the marketability of the ecotourism product is all too rare. They're not sharing information, and none is very transparent or public."

McLaren, of Indigenous Rights International, questions the parallel being drawn between products like lumber and ecotourism. "It's really hard, because tourism is a service instead of a product. You can follow the trail from farm to market with a potato, but it's much more difficult to certify all these different parts" of tourism.

McLaren says the certification process so far looks to some observers like "another grab at money and control" that has left the local communities out of the process.

"We need to talk to the businesses," says Mader, echoing her concern. "There's a lot of discussion at the consultancy level, but at the operator level we're just not speaking their language."

Martha Honey, executive director of The International Ecotourism Society and a leader of the certification effort, says that while many certification programs came into being without consultation with indigenous people, those involved in current efforts are "extremely concerned about and sensitive to" the issue. Last September, she notes, the first meeting in an effort to bring indigenous peoples to the table was held in Quito, Ecuador, and future meetings are scheduled in Fiji and Norway. She cites as a possible model the Respecting Our Culture program in Australia, run by indigenous peoples through a program called Aboriginal Tourism Australia.

Critics of certification also worry that it will be too costly. "The field is not ready for certification," says Epler Wood. "There's no identifiable market for it, and without a market driver you get a lot of investment in systems that are not selling with the public."

"Ecotourism is a small, micro-business phenomenon," she continues. "The profit margins barely justify staying in business." While certification could have a viable role in developing a bigger market, she says, until the companies are more stable and profitable, they cannot afford it.

Honey agrees that cost is an issue. "Certification cannot be so expensive that it sets the bar too high for small-scale operators," she says, but she feels the problem is surmountable. One solution would be scaled fees, with larger operators paying more. Another might be government subsidies drawn from revenues such as airport taxes or "negative taxes" on less eco-friendly businesses, such as the cruise industry.

Honey explains that existing certification programs failed to develop a large market because most of them had virtually no marketing budget. And, she says, what marketing they did was misdirected. The key to greater success, she believes, is to market the label not to travelers — the ultimate consumers — but to the tourist industry's equivalent of dealers or middle men — tour operators who stand to save money by not having to investigate individual accommodations and attractions for themselves.

Honey also argues that a reliable certification program also would be extremely useful to guidebook publishers, national parks — which must evaluate the reliability of concessionaires — and development agencies like the U.N. Development Programme, the U.S. Agency for International Development and the World Bank.

But Xavier Font, a lecturer in tourism management at Leeds Metropolitan University in England, says "certification is most suited to those countries with well-established infrastructures and the finances to support industry to reduce its negative impacts. It is not the best tool for livelihood-based economies or sectors, be it tourism, forestry, agriculture or any other at the center of attention of certification today." [21]

Brian Mullis, president of Sustainable Travel International, a nonprofit organization that is developing the first certification program in North America, disagrees. "Having spent a good part of the last four years looking at the problem," Mullis says, "I don't think it is premature. At the end of the day, the only way sustainable travel can really be defined is to have verification that companies are doing what they say they're doing.

"More and more consumers are supporting businesses that define themselves as green," he continues. "But if they're not doing what they say they're doing, it doesn't really matter what they say." ■

BACKGROUND

Tourism Is Born

Travel for pleasure came on the world scene with the emergence of wealth and leisure. Affluent Greeks and Romans vacationed at thermal baths and visited exotic locales around Europe and the Mediterranean. The first guidebook for travelers is credited to the French monk Aimeri de Picaud, who in 1130 wrote a tour guide for pilgrims traveling to Spain. In the 18th and 19th centuries, European and British aristocrats as well as wealthy Americans took the "grand tour" of continental Europe's natural and cultural attractions, including the Swiss Alps, and health spas became popular destinations. [22]

Until the Industrial Revolution, travel had more to do with its etymological root — the French word for "work," travailler — than with pleasure. The development of railroads, steamships and, later, the automobile and airplane, made travel easier and faster. The Englishman Thomas Cook set up a travel agency in 1841 and organized tourist excursions by train to

Continued on p. 876

Chronology

1860s-1960s
Interest in nature travel grows after first being limited largely to the wealthy.

1916
U.S. National Park Service is founded.

1920s
"Bush walker" movement in Australia increases the popularity of wilderness excursions.

1953
Sir Edmund Hillary and Tenzing Norgay are the first to climb Mount Everest.

1970s
Tourism spreads into remote and fragile regions after wide-bodied jets make travel cheaper.

1970
First cruise ship visits Antarctica. . . . First Earth Day on April 22 signals birth of environmental movement.

1980s
Environmental and cultural impact of tourism sparks concern.

1980
Manila Declaration on World Tourism declares that "tourism does more harm than good" to people and societies in the Third World. . . . Ecumenical Coalition on Third World Tourism takes shape to fight such negative impacts as poverty, pollution and prostitution.

1989
Hague Declaration on Tourism calls on states "to strike a harmonious balance between economic and ecological considerations."

1990s
Ecotourism is promoted as a "win-win" for economic development and the environment. Tourism increases 66 percent in 10 years on the Galapagos Islands.

1990
The Ecotourism Society (later renamed The International Ecotourism Society) is founded.

1992
First World Congress on Tourism and the Environment is held in Belize.

1995
Conde Nast Traveler magazine publishes its first annual "Green List" of top ecotourism destinations.

1996
World Tourism Organization, World Travel & Tourism Council and Earth Council draft Agenda 21 for the travel and tourism industry, outlining key steps governments and industry need to take for sustainability.

1997
Governments and private groups from 77 countries and territories pledge in the Manila Declaration on the Social Impact of Tourism to better involve local communities in tourism planning and to address social abuses.

1999
World Bank and World Tourism Organization agree to cooperate in encouraging sustainable tourism development.

2000s
"Sustainable travel" is embraced by governments and the travel industry. The number of tourists visiting Antarctica tops 10,000 a year.

2000
Mohonk Agreement sets out terms for international ecotourism certification. . . . One-in-five international tourists travels from an industrial country to a developing one, compared to one-in-13 in the mid-1970s.

2002
U.N. celebrates International Year of Ecotourism; more than 1,000 participants at World Ecotourism Summit approve Quebec Declaration on Ecotourism — stressing the need to address tourism's economic, social and environmental impacts.

2003
The once heavily forested base of Mt. Everest has become an "eroding desert" due to 10,000 trekkers a year burning trees for fuel.

2004
A study about the Galapagos Islands warns that tourism-induced human migration "threatens the future of tourism."

2005
Between 1950 and 2004, the number of tourist arrivals worldwide grows by more than 3,000 percent — from 25 million arrivals to some 760 million in 2004.

2006
International tourist travel jumps 4.5 percent worldwide in the first three months. The fastest-growing destinations are Africa and the Middle East, each rising about 11 percent.

Taking the Guilt Out of Ecotravel

Travel — even by the most dedicated ecotourists — invariably takes a toll on the environment. But now environmentally sensitive travelers are finding ways to compensate.

When the World Economic Forum sponsored a meeting of its Young Global Leaders Summit this year in Vancouver, British Columbia, the forum offered attendees the opportunity to "offset" the negative environmental effect of the emissions generated by their plane flights by contributing to the rehabilitation of a small hydropower plant in Indonesia.

Concerns about the negative impact of their own airplane emissions also prompted conservationists and community-development activists who gathered in Hungary in April 2006, to offset their emissions by planting trees on a Hungarian hillside.

Airplanes contribute 3 to 5 percent of global carbon dioxide emissions — 230 million tons in the United States alone in 2003 — and air transport is one of the world's fastest-growing sources of emissions of carbon dioxide and other so-called greenhouse gases, according to the Worldwatch Institute. [1]

The only sure-fire way to eliminate negative environmental impacts is to stay home — an option some travel writers actually are promoting. [2] But short of that, say those promoting ecotourism, travelers can "give back" to Mother Nature by donating "carbon offsets."

At the Web site for ClimateCare.org, a British organization started in 1998, travelers can learn how many tons of carbon dioxide their trip will produce and donate money to underwrite renewable-energy projects, energy-efficiency improvements and reforestation efforts in developing countries to produce a comparable reduction in carbon emissions. A round trip between New York and Chicago, for example, produces the equivalent of 0.27 tons of CO_2, which the organization translates into a $3 donation per traveler to renewable-energy projects.

A 2004 German program, atmosfair (www.atmosfair.de/index.php?id=08L=3) converts carbon emissions into euros, then contributes donated sums to climate-protection projects in India and Brazil. Its installation of solar power instead of diesel- and wood-fired equipment in 10 industrial kitchens in India, for example, will save roughly 570 tons of CO_2 — the equivalent of 2,000 round-trip flights between New York and Chicago.

The Portland, Ore.-based Better World Club claims it's "the first travel company in the world to offer a carbon-offset program." Its TravelCool! Program offers offsets in $11 increments, which it equates to roughly one ton of CO_2, or a tenth of the emissions produced annually by the typical automobile. The funds collected have helped replace old oil-burning boilers in Portland public schools.

The Web site nativeenergy.com, based in Charlotte, Vt., will calculate all the carbon dioxide emissions from an entire vacation, including hotel stays. The Native American group supports American Indian and farmer-owned wind, solar and methane projects. Contributions to offset automobile and other travel emissions can be made in the form of regular monthly contributions.

[1] Lisa Mastny, "Traveling Light: New Paths for International Tourism," Worldwatch Paper 159, December 2001, p. 29; and Esther Addley, "Boom in green holidays as ethical travel takes off, *The Guardian*, July 17, 2006; and P. W. McRandle, "Low-impact vacations (Green Guidance)," *World Watch*, July-August 2006.

[2] See Ian Jack and James Hamilton-Paterson, "Where Travel Writing Went Next," *Granta*, Summer 2006.

Continued from p. 874

temperance rallies in the English Midlands. By the mid-1850s he was offering railway tours of the Continent.

In the United States, the American Express Co. introduced Travelers Cheques and money orders, further easing the logistics of tourism. By the end of the 19th century, the tourism industry had fully emerged, complete with guidebooks, packaged tours, booking agents, hotels and railways with organized timetables. [23]

Earlier, the dawning of the Romantic era in around 1800 had fired a new passion for the exotic among Europeans and an upwelling of scientific curiosity that fueled journeys of exploration and discovery. Beginning in 1799, Alexander von Humboldt, a wealthy German, spent five years exploring in the uncharted reaches of Central and South America, gathering data and specimens. Three decades later, a young British aristocrat keen on biology, Charles Darwin, sailed to the Galapagos Islands and developed the foundations of his revolutionary theory of evolution. [24]

Armchair adventurers avidly sought reports of explorers supported by the British Royal Geographic Society, founded in 1830. Among them were the legendary missionary/explorer David Livingstone in Africa and the man who went to find him, journalist Henry Stanley, in the mid-19th century; Antarctic explorers Robert Scott, the British naval officer who perished on his journey to the South Pole, and Ernest Shackleton in the early 20th century; and Sir Edmund Hillary, the New Zealander who in 1953, with his Nepalese guide Tensing Norgay, first climbed Mt. Everest.

By the late 19th century, the beauty of unspoiled nature was attracting more and more ordinary visitors. In the United States, Congress set aside more than 2 million acres in 1872 to create Yellowstone National Park, the world's first national park. Reserving public lands for "public use, resort and recreation," became a guiding principle of the National Park Service, established in 1916.

Private tourism promoters also played a large role in the creation and expansion of the National Park System, with the Northern Pacific Railroad urging the creation of Yellowstone as a draw for its passengers. The railroads later played similar roles in promoting the creation of Sequoia and Yosemite (1890), Mount Rainier (1899) and Glacier (1910) national parks. [25]

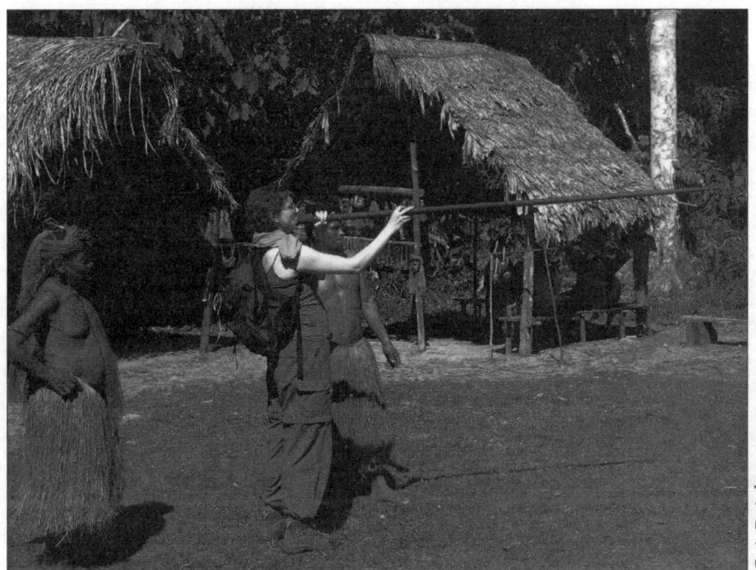

G.A.P Adventures

Watched by local experts, an ecotourist gives a blowgun a try in Peru's Amazon rain forest. Tour groups now flock to the Amazon for trips up the river and forays into the forest in search of the region's animals and colorful birds.

Beginning in Australia in 1879, other countries also set aside protected areas for parks, including Mexico (1898), Argentina (1903) and Sweden (1909). The Sierra Club began its Outings program in 1901 with an expedition for 100 hikers, accompanied by Chinese chefs, pack mules and wagons, to the backcountry wilderness of the Sierra Nevada Mountains. The trips not only provided healthful diversion for the members but also encouraged them to "become active workers for the preservation of the forests and other natural features" of the area.

The political implications behind the early trips would continue to motivate nonprofit organizations to sponsor travel outings in the years ahead.

In the 1950s, big-game hunters began flocking to luxury safari lodges in Kenya, South Africa and, later, Tanzania. The creation of national parks and wildlife sanctuaries by Kenya's British colonial government, however, forced the nomadic Maasai people from their ancestral lands. The resulting resentments led to poaching and vandalism, problems that to this day complicate conservation efforts.

Rise of Ecotourism

The powerful combination of the labor movement and 20th-century industrialization brought tourism within reach of a vast, new universe — the burgeoning population of middle-class wage earners seeking diversion for their annual vacations.

In 1936, the International Labor Organization called for a week's paid vacation every year. A 1970 ILO convention expanded the standard to three weeks with pay.

But it was the rise of the aviation industry after World War II that sparked mass, intercontinental tourism. In 1948 Pan American World Airways introduced tourist class, and the world suddenly grew smaller. In 1957 jet engines made commercial travel faster still.

The introduction of wide-bodied jets in the 1970s made international travel between developed and developing nations practical for holiday travelers. By 1975, international tourist arrivals had surpassed 200 million annually — and double that number by 1990. [26]

In the mid-1970s, 8 percent of all tourists were from developed countries traveling on holidays to developing countries. By the mid-1980s the number had jumped to 17 percent.

Developing countries and international aid institutions initially welcomed the burgeoning source of foreign exchange sparked by the spurt in tourism. The World Bank's first tourism-related loan was made in 1967 for a hotel in Kenya that was partly owned by a subsidiary of Pan American Airways. In the 1970s the bank loaned about $450 million directly to governments for 24 tourism projects in 18 developing countries, and other international aid and lending institutions followed suit.

But the bank's support of conventional tourism and large hotel projects provoked criticism that it encouraged indebtedness while failing to address the problems of poverty in Third World countries. Concern about the environmental effects of resort development, along with a string of financial failures, caused the bank to close down its Tourism Projects Department in 1979.

As the emergence of the environmental movement in the 1960s and '70s pushed international aid agencies to re-examine their commitments, other forces were also pushing the development of a less intrusive, more eco-friendly form of travel.

Despite setbacks among local operators and growing discontent among indigenous peoples, by the turn of the millennium the notion that tourism could be both more lucrative and less resource-intensive than heavy industry or plantation-style monoculture was

G.A.P Adventures

Terra Incognita Ecotours/Gerard "Ged" Caddick

G.A.P Adventures

Mixing People and Nature

Penguins in Antarctica show no fear of humans (top); tourists in Baja, Calif., watch a blue whale (middle); and a visitor gets acquainted with giant turtles in the Galapagos Islands (bottom).

gaining currency in the international community. In 1998 it was reported to be the only economic sector in which developing countries consistently ran a trade surplus. It represented roughly 10 percent of developing-world exports and accounted for more than 40 percent of the gross domestic product in some countries. [27]

In 2002, more than 1,000 participants from 132 countries gathered in Quebec, Canada, to attend the World Ecotourism Summit, organized by the U.N. Environment Programme and the World Tourism Organization. In adopting the Quebec Declaration on Ecotourism, they embraced "the principles of sustainable tourism, concerning the economic, social and environmental impacts of tourism" — which would come to be seen as the "triple bottom line" in development circles.

The declaration also pointed out that ecotourism differed from the broader concept of "sustainable tourism" by four key characteristics:

- contribution to the conservation of natural and cultural heritage;
- inclusion of local and indigenous communities;
- interpretation of natural and cultural heritage; and
- affinity for independent and small-group travelers. [28]

The summit also boosted ecotourism certification efforts by endorsing "the use of certification as a tool for measuring sound ecotourism and sustainable tourism" while also stressing that certification systems "should reflect regional and local criteria." [29]

Giving native peoples a stake in conservation outcomes was a prime force behind the development of ecotourism, says Harold Goodwin, director of the International Centre for Responsible Tourism at the University of Greenwich in England. To win the support of indigenous peoples, international conservation organizations began creating environmentally responsible tourist accommodations near private conservation

Making Sure Your Travel Is Really 'Green'

The term ecotourism is used so loosely by marketers these days that tourists may be getting "ecotourism lite," not a truly "green" experience, says Katie Maschman, a spokeswoman for The International Ecotourism Society.

"It's great to see ecotourism principles incorporated from a mass-tourism perspective," Maschman says, "but there is a lot of green-washing going on. A hotel simply advertising that they only change the sheets every three days does not, by any means, suggest they've given it real attention."

Research is vital to planning a trip that minimizes negative environmental and cultural impacts, experts say. And while a variety of Web sites and guidebooks focus on "green" travel, nothing substitutes for direct questioning of tour and facility operators and of other travelers. [1]

"The best thing to do is to ask to speak to former clients," says Steve Powers, of Hidden Treasure Tours, in Long Beach, N.Y. Like many other tour packagers, Powers tries to support small, grassroots programs. But it can be difficult to determine whether operators at a far-off destination are actually doing what they say.

A tourist also can ask travel companies for their policies, which may already be codified and thus easily communicated. "If you want to book a tour," says Ron Mader, founder of the ecotourism Web site planeta.com, "ask [tour operators] if they support conservation or local development projects. Many agencies and operators are very proud of their environmental conservation and community-development work." [2]

Helpful Web sites featuring ecotourism destinations are operated by nonprofit organizations, travel marketers and for-profit online travel clubs and information exchanges, including www.sustainabletravelinternational.org, ecoclub.com, responsibletravel.com, eco-indextourism.org, ecotourism.org, ecotour.org, tourismconcern.org, travelersconservationtrust.org, and visit21.net.

Travel-award programs are another good source of ideas, such as the Tourism for Tomorrow awards of the World Travel & Tourism Council at www.tourismfortomorrow.com; the annual ecolodge award of the International Ecotourism Club, available at ecoclub.com; and the First Choice Responsible Tourism Awards from responsibletravel.com.

In addition to consulting those and similar sites, adding terms such as "green travel" or "ecotourism" to a country- or destination-based Internet search can bring results.

Here are the questions experts say travelers should ask their tour firm or the operator of the destination:

- Do you have an ethical ecotourism policy?
- What steps have you taken to reduce waste and water use?
- Do you practice recycling?
- How do you minimize damage to wildlife and marine environments?
- What community members do you employ and do they have opportunities for advancement? What local products do you purchase, and do you use local produce whenever possible? What community projects are you involved in?
- Do you donate to community organizations and/or conservation programs?
- What energy-saving activities do you practice?
- Are your buildings built with locally available materials?
- Do you use environmentally friendly products?

[1] P. W. McRandle, "Low-impact Vacations (Green Guidance)," *World Watch*, July-August 2006; and Esther Addley, "Boom in Green Holidays as Ethical Travel Takes Off," *The Guardian*, July 17, 2006.

[2] Quoted in Clay Hubbs, "Responsible Travel and Ecotourism," *Transitions Abroad*, May/June 2001, www.transitionsabroad.com/publications/magazine.

areas that would provide some income to native peoples. Foundations were established to return earnings to the community in the form of water projects and other physical improvements, educational opportunities, even clinics and health services. Besides being altruistic, the program had practical outcomes as well.

"You have to give the local community economic benefits so they don't poach," Goodwin says.

Ecotourism also opened up new marketing possibilities, Goodwin says. Costa Rica, for example, unable to compete in the world tourism market on the quality of its beaches, began promoting its rich, unspoiled biodiversity as an attraction — with great success. Belize followed suit.

Ecotourism also introduced a new type of competition, he says, because "there are only so many places to go and things to do," and only so much elasticity in pricing. Introducing the values of environmentalism, conservation and education, he says, "avoids competing on price. You can compete on interpretation."

But many of the first small, local ecotourism endeavors that sprang up in the 1990s failed because there was a disconnect between the international market and the local entrepreneurs, Goodwin says. Those that succeeded, however, transformed their surroundings.

"In the early 1990s, everybody was talking about ecotourism," says anthropologist Vivanco, who did his field research at that time near the private Monte Verde Cloud Forest Preserve, considered the jewel in the crown of Costa Rica's extensive park system. "Over 10 years ago, there were about 45,000 to 50,000 tourists a year in an area of about 3,500 to 4,000 inhabitants," he says. But as the number of visitors increased and new facilities went up, hundreds of Costa Rican workers moved to the area, creating a negative environmental impact on the fringe of the preserve — a problem that has afflicted ecotourism sites as remote as the Galapagos Islands.

"Nowadays, there are at least 140,000, and as many as 200,000 visitors, "and it's grown up in a completely unmanaged way at the edge of the park," he says.

"The population explosion has an impact on their whole way of life," Vivanco continues. "Class differences emerged that didn't exist before. Locally, many people were saying, 'It's a bit out of hand, we need to get greater control.' " ■

AFP/Getty Images/Romeo Gacad

Tourism is threatening the Philippines' ancient Banaue rice terraces, created 2,000 years ago by Ifugao tribesmen. The naturally irrigated paddies are endangered by deforestation to supply wood for tourist handicrafts and by the water demands of hotels and restaurants.

fastest-growing areas for international travel in the first quarter of 2006 were Africa and the Middle East, with estimated increases of 11 percent each. [36]

For example, Wildland Adventures conducts tours to Central America, the Andes, Africa, Turkey, Egypt, Australia, New Zealand and Alaska. The Seattle-based tour operator created the nonprofit Traveler's Conservation Trust, which contributes a portion of the firm's earnings to community-improvement projects and conservation organizations in the countries they visit.

In the Ecuadorian Amazon rain forest, Yachana, an eco-lodge constructed in 1995 by the Foundation for Integrated Education and Development, attracts nearly 2,000 visitors a year — but limits the number to 40 at a time — who reach the lodge by canoe. Visitors spend time with indigenous families, participate in traditional rituals and visit the foundation's model farm and tree nursery. The lodge has generated more than $3.5 million for the foundation's programs in conservation, poverty reduction, health care and community development.

CURRENT SITUATION

Global Presence

Growing awareness of the environmental costs of travel, such as its contribution to global warming, increasingly affects travel decisions. More than three-quarters of U.S. travelers "feel it is important their visits not damage the environment," according to a study by the Travel Industry Association of America and *National Geographic Traveler* magazine. The study estimated that 17 million U.S. travelers consider environmental factors when deciding which travel companies to patronize. [30]

A survey by the International Hotels Environmental Initiative found that more than two-thirds of U.S. and Australian travelers and 90 percent of British tourists consider active protection of the environment — including support of local communities — to be part of a hotel's responsibility. [31] Another industry study found that 70 percent of U.S., British and Australian travelers would pay up to $150 more for a two-week stay in a hotel with a "responsible environmental attitude." [32]

Overall, the travel industry employs 200 million people, generates $3.6 trillion in economic activity and accounts for one in every 12 jobs worldwide. [33] Between 1950 and 2004, the number of tourist arrivals worldwide grew by more than 3,000 percent — from 25 million arrivals in 1950 to some 760 million in 2004. [34]

Moreover, travelers' destinations have shifted, with visits to the developing world increasing dramatically while travel to Europe and the Americas has dropped. By 2000, one-in-five international tourists from industrial countries traveled to a developing nation, compared to one-in-13 in the mid-1970s. [35] The

International Development

"Nearly every country with national parks and protected areas is marketing some type of ecotourism," according to the Center on Ecotourism and Sustainable Development. "Lending and aid agencies are funneling hundreds of millions of dollars into

Continued on p. 882

At Issue:

Will improved certification make ecotourism more marketable?

MARTHA HONEY
EXECUTIVE DIRECTOR, THE INTERNATIONAL ECOTOURISM SOCIETY

WRITTEN FOR *CQ RESEARCHER*, OCTOBER 2006

yes

Reputable "green" certification programs that measure environmental and social impacts will promote ecotourism — but it will take time to educate consumers. It took some 30 years to build the U.S. market for certified organic foods, and now consumer demand for organics is booming. In tourism, AAA and 5 Star quality-certification programs for hotels and restaurants have been around for nearly a century and are part of the "fabric" of the tourism industry.

U.S. consumers want to travel responsibly. But they are not yet actively asking for "green" certification, in part because there is no national program.

Around the world, my colleague Amos Bién notes there are some 60 to 80 "green" tourism-certification programs, but most are less than 10 years old. Costa Rica's Certification for Sustainable Tourism (CST) program, launched in 1998, awards one to five green leaves to hotels and tour operators. Lapa Rios Ecolodge is one of only two hotels there to have earned five leaves. Owner Karen Lewis sees a link between certification, improved sustainability and increased marketability. "Certification is the best internal audit out there, for any owner and/or management team," she says.

Adriane Janer, of EcoBrazil, who has been involved in creating Brazil's new Sustainable Tourism Program, says "certification has been very successful in improving quality and reliability of products and services." In Guatemala, the Green Deal program principally certifies small businesses at a minimal cost of $300. In Costa Rica, certification is free, and the CST cannot keep up with all the hotels wanting to be audited.

In tourism, as in retailing, we're beginning to see the successful use of "retailers" — tour operators — who are choosing to use certified hotels and other "green" supplies. The Dutch tour operators association, which represents over 850 travel companies, requires all members to use hotels and other businesses that have a credible sustainability policy. In Costa Rica, seven leading tour operators are giving preference to CST-certified hotels, and at least two are hoping within three years to be using only certified hotels.

Indeed, without certification, the danger of 'greenwashing' — businesses that use "eco" language in their marketing but don't fit any of the criteria of ecotourism — greatly increases. Certification provides a necessary tool to separate the wheat from the chafe, the genuine ecotourism businesses from the scams and the shams.

As Glenn Jampol, owner of the Finca Rosa Blanca Inn, the other Costa Rican hotel to have earned five green leaves, puts it, "I envision a day when guests will routinely check for Rosa Blanca's green leaf rating as well as our star rating."

RON MADER
FOUNDER, PLANETA.COM

WRITTEN FOR *CQ RESEARCHER*, OCTOBER 2006

no

Indigenous peoples, tour operators and others claim that many certification programs for ecotourism and sustainable travel do not deserve support. I agree.

Certification has a number of serious problems, starting with the lack of consumer demand. Moreover, most stakeholders have been left out of the process, including indigenous people, community representatives and owners of travel businesses. When invited to participate, many of these leaders opt out, reminding organizers they have other priorities.

Stakeholders around the world confided during the International Year of Ecotourism that certification does not enhance business. In fact, some leading tour operators believe certification and accreditation schemes are a scam that creates a cottage industry for consultants.

In short, ecotourism certification is not a "market-driven" option.

Said one tour operator during the Ethical Marketing of Ecotourism Conference: "First, get consumers to care, then worry about rating and certification. Doing it any other way is not only putting the cart before the horse, it is putting the wheel before the cart, the spoke before the wheels."

Much more effective are industry awards. They are conducted in the public eye and cost a fraction of formal certification programs. Likewise, an investment in Google ads pays better dividends than certification.

In 2006 Planeta.com invited tourism professionals — particularly those at the forefront of ecotourism — to participate in a candid review of tourism promotion. Respondents gave government marketing campaigns around the world a low mark. Comments indicate that in-country and outbound travel operators do not know the PR agencies that represent the country.

These are alarming results for those interested in ecotourism and responsible travel as they indicate that rather than promoting what's available, the promotion departments are seen as an obstacle, particularly for small- and medium-sized in-country businesses.

If our collective goal is to improve the marketing of ecotourism, the solution is simply to improve the dialogue among operators and national tourism campaigns. The reality is that by far the most "eco" and "community-focused" services are the ones that receive the least promotion.

While little or no consumer demand may exist for certified "eco" vacations, we should not accept the status quo. The emphasis needs to be placed on evaluating the industry and offering training and promotion for local providers who strive toward sustainability and ecotourism.

Continued from p. 880

projects that include ecotourism; major environmental organizations are sponsoring ecotourism projects and departments; and millions of travelers are going on ecotours."

"It's absolutely excellent," says ecotourism consultant Epler Wood. "I used to tell people I was a consultant on ecotourism, and they'd give me a blank stare. Now they are, like, 'Wow, you are so lucky.' It's been one of our greatest goals to make it an accepted, mainstream profession."

Moreover, many of the basic tenets of ecotourism are being embraced by the international development world as goals for economic development generally. In choosing which development projects to fund, the new "triple bottom line" adds environmental and social/cultural effects to the long-standing criterion of profitability — at least on paper.

At a tourism policy forum at George Washington University in October 2004 — the first of its kind — Inter-American Development Bank (IDB) President Enrique Iglesias and World Bank Vice President James Adams joined delegates from donor agencies, developing countries and academia in endorsing tourism's potential as a sustainable-development strategy. They also agreed, however, that the complex nature of the industry presents special challenges.

The IDB, after being involved with tourism projects for 30 years, has changed its focus from big infrastructure projects to more community-based projects, Iglesias said. Adams reported the World Bank had undertaken approximately 100 projects, including tourism in 56 countries — 3 percent of the bank's total investment. [37]

USAID Administrator Andrew Natsios similarly stressed the need for community involvement to ensure tourism is sustainable. "Properly planned tourism requires good natural-resource management and good local governance to protect and enhance the resources on which it depends," he said. [38]

Until recently, says Epler Wood, ecotourism funds typically were funneled through conservation-oriented NGOs, which often lacked the business experience needed to make new enterprises succeed. Another handicap was the paucity of small-scale loans. In 1995, she recalls, the International Finance Corp., profit-making arm of the World Bank, was investing no less than $500 million per project. Now, she says, they're down to about $1 million — still high for community-based ecotourism undertakings. And they're looking for partners with expertise in business development, not conservation.

"We're at the very beginning phase in a new era of enterprise development," Epler Wood says. "It's still a new paradigm. Economic growth still gets the big players and the big money, while the environmental and humanitarian development goals tend to be evaluative afterthoughts, instead of being integral to the projects."

But, she says, the big players are taking an interest. "The donor architecture is still not quite built to accommodate the potential of ecotourism as a sustainable-development tool. It's a very big, slow-moving world, but you do see change happening within it."

Variations on a Theme

As ecotourism joins the tourism mainstream, it is spinning off numerous new tourism genres. In Europe, especially, so-called pro-poor tourism, responsible tourism and ethical tourism aim to extend the benefits of tourism to developing countries while improving its effects on destination communities and the environment.

Evidence is mounting that travelers are embracing the concept's values. In England this past summer, ethical holidays reportedly were the fastest-growing travel sector. According to a recent survey, by 2010 the number of British visitors going on "ethical" holidays outside England will have grown to 2.5 million trips a year, or 5 percent of the market. The Web site ResponsibleTravel.com has seen bookings double in the last year. [39]

Other variations of ecotourism are viewed less favorably by ecotourism advocates. Adventure travel to exotic and often physically challenging destinations — "ecotourism with a kick," ecotourism society executive director Honey calls it — has been a particularly fast-growing style of nature tourism.

Adventure travel proponents argue that adventurers, like ecotravelers, have an interest in protecting the resources they enjoy, but critics blame them for a wide range of damaging intrusions — helicopter trips causing noise and air pollution while taking skiers to pristine mountain tops; growing numbers of tourists struggling to ascend Mt. Everest (and risking their lives and the lives of others in the process); polar bear watchers who ride bus-like vehicles on monster-truck tires along the south shore of Hudson Bay in Manitoba in the fall, dangerously stressing the bears when they should be building up fat reserves for the long winter season. [40]

"Whereas nature, wildlife and adventure tourism are defined solely by the recreational activities of the tourist," Honey explains, "ecotourism is defined as well by its benefits to both conservation and people in the host country."

'Green' Chic

An essay in *The New York Times* fall travel magazine, "Easy Being Green," portrays ecotourism as the latest fashion trend. "In luxury resorts, eco is the flavor du jour," proclaims author Heidi S. Mitchell. [41]

"There has been a real movement toward high-end ecotourism," Honey said. A 2004 survey found that 38 percent would be willing to pay a premium to patronize travel companies that use sustainable environmental practices. [42]

But as green travel goes upscale, environmentalists worry that the original goals of environmental conservation paired with community betterment will be lost under a misleading "greenwash."

"Ecotourism has been watered down from the beginning," says Planeta.com founder Mader. "The NGOs have watered it down. They're even participating in Antarctic travel."

But others, like Honey, see the upscale trend as a sign that environmental sustainability — a key aspect of ecotourism — is having a real effect on the travel industry as a whole. In a less glamorous example, the Rainforest Alliance, with support from the Inter-American Development Bank, is working with small- and medium-sized travel businesses in Latin America to improve sustainable practices, whether or not the businesses meet all the requirements of classic ecotourism.

In Costa Rica, Guatemala, Belize and Ecuador, more than 200 tourism operations in or near sensitive or protected areas are receiving training in the "best practices" of sustainable tourism, including waste management and water and electricity conservation, as well as such social factors as paying adequate salaries and including local and indigenous people in decision-making.

Businesses that adopt best practices become eligible for certification by existing national programs and gain access to marketing networks and trade-show appearances organized by the Rainforest Alliance. The program has had two benefits, says Alliance marketing specialist Christina Suhr: "It has let people know what we do, and they have gained confidence in us." ■

Terra Incognita Ecotours/Gerard "Ged" Caddick

Visitors can come within a few yards of wild mountain gorillas in Volcanoes National Park, on the Rwanda side of the Virunga Volcanoes. "I just about burst open with happiness every time I get within one or two feet of them," said naturalist Dian Fossey, who studied the gorillas for years.

OUTLOOK

Setting Limits

The latest worry for travelers who care about the Earth's environment is global warming, especially since air transport is one of the world's fastest-growing sources of emissions of carbon dioxide and other greenhouse gases. If global warming continues unabated, many of the attractions most favored by eco-travelers will be among the most vulnerable. A report for the United Kingdom's World Wide Fund for Nature warned of soaring temperatures, forest fires and other consequences that could drive wildlife from safari parks in Africa, damage Brazil's rain forest ecosystems and flood beaches and coastal destinations worldwide. [43]

Some observers say the costs of global travel in environmental damage, cultural homogenization and economic displacement are so serious that would-be travelers should just stay home.

"The more we flock to view the disappearing glaciers, the faster they will vanish," mused novelist James Hamilton-Paterson. [44]

Similarly, travel writer Anneli Rufus observes ruefully, "Colonialism isn't dead. Colonialism is alive and well every time you travel from the First World to the Third and come home bearing photographs of sharks and storms and slums . . . and then you tell your friends and co-workers, 'Oh man, it was so great, you gotta go.' "

But the quandary Rufus faces as she considers ending her travel writing is common to affluent travelers visiting poor countries: "Am I saving some tribe from extinction by not looking for it, much less telling you about it? Or am I starving some shopkeeper by not buying his sandals? Both. Neither. I am out of that [travel writing] game now." [45]

But indigenous-rights activist McLaren feels that the interpersonal connections and first-person impressions derived from independent travel are more important than ever. "In an age where the media dominates and shapes our views of the world," she writes, "it is imperative to utilize tourism as a means to effectively communicate with one another. In fact, there is no better way to understand the global crisis that we face together than through people-to-people communication." [46]

McLaren finds hope in the growing number of successful projects that blend tourism, environmentalism and sustainability, like Elephant Valley eco-resort in India. "There are lots of good examples, though not everybody calls them ecotourism," McLaren says. "A lot of workable projects tend to be more regional, more of public-private partnerships. Elephant Valley, she says, is "a beautiful, low-impact place. Money is really being used to conserve the area, employ local people, produce food, teach about sustainability and work with schools in the region."

In Tasmania, ecotourism has been proposed as an alternative to logging in Australia's largest temperate rain forest, the Tarkine. [47]

In the Patagonia region of southern Chile, environmentalists are seeking to block plans to build a series of hydroelectric dams that would flood thousands of acres of rugged, pristine lands that, they say, could better serve as ecotourism attractions and ranchland. [48]

And in Puerto Rico, environmentalists and other groups are fighting the proposed development of resorts and residential complexes in one of the territory's "last remaining pristine coastal areas," seeking to preserve it "for wildlife, the citizens of Puerto Rico and ecotourism." According to the Waterkeeper Alliance, an organization leading the fight, the developments threaten local water supplies and also mean that "tourists who flock to Puerto Rico to enjoy its cultural and natural resources . . . will have one less reason to visit the island." [49] ■

Notes

[1] The International Ecotourism Society, Fact Sheet, June 2004, p. 2.

[2] Deborah McLaren, "Rethinking Tourism," Planeta Forum, updated June 16, 2006, www.planeta.com/planeta/97/1197rtpro.html; Martha Honey, *Ecotourism and Sustainable Development: Who Owns Paradise?* (1999), p. 9.

[3] A 2003 study by the Travel Industry Association of America and *National Geographic Traveler* found that 55.1 million U.S. travelers could be classified as "geo-tourists" interested in nature, culture and heritage tourism; see "The International Ecotourism Society, *op. cit.*

[4] Jacob Park, "The Paradox of Paradise," *Environment*, October 1999. For a detailed discussion of the environmental costs of resort development, see Polly Patullo, *Last Resorts: the Cost of Tourism in the Caribbean* (1996).

[5] Rosaleen Duffy, *A Trip Too Far: Ecotourism, Politics & Exploitation* (2002), pp. x-xii.

[6] Lisa Mastny, "Traveling Light," *Worldwatch Paper 159*, Worldwatch Institute, 2001, p. 10.

[7] Rene Ebersole, "Take the High Road," *Audubon Travel Issue*, July-August 2006, p. 39.

[8] Conservation International Web site; www.conservation.org/xp/CIWEB/programs/ecotourism/.

[9] Finn-Olaf Jones, "Tourism Stripping Everest's Forests Bare," *National Geographic Traveler*, Aug. 29, 2003.

About the Author

Rachel S. Cox is a freelance writer in Washington, D.C., who writes about health, design and environmental issues for *The Washington Post* and other publications. She previously served as associate editor of *Historic Preservation* magazine. She holds a B.A. in English from Harvard University and studied architectural history at the University of California, Los Angeles. Her last report for *CQ Researcher* explored the "Home Schooling Debate."

Statement of Ownership Management, Circulation

Act of Aug. 12, 1970: Section 3685, Title 39, United States Code

Title of Publication: CQ Researcher. Date of filing: September 15, 2006. Frequency of issue: Weekly (Except for 3/24, 7/7, 7/14, 8/4, 8/11, 11/24, 12/22, 12/29/06). No. of issues published annually: 44. Annual subscription price for libraries, businesses and government: $660. Location of known office of publication: 1255 22nd Street, N.W., Suite 400, Washington, D.C. 20037. Names and addresses of publisher and managing editor: Publisher, John A. Jenkins, CQ Press, A Division of Congressional Quarterly, 1255 22nd Street, N.W., Suite 400, Washington, D.C. 20037; Managing Editor, Thomas J. Colin, 1255 22nd Street, N.W., Washington, D.C. 20037. Owner: Congressional Quarterly, Inc., 1255 22nd Street, N.W., Suite 700, Washington, D.C. 20037; Times Publishing Co., P.O. Box 1121, St. Petersburg, Fla. 33731. Known bondholders, mortgagees and other security holders owning or holding 1 percent or more of total amount of bonds, mortgages or other securities: none.

Extent and Nature of Circulation	Average Number of Copies of Each Issue During Preceding 12 months	Actual Number of Copies of Single Issue Published Nearest to Filing Date
A. Total number of copies printed *(Net press run)*	2,579	2,234
B. Paid and/or requested circulation		
(1) Mailed outside-county mail subscriptions stated on Form 3541	2,154	2,009
(2) Mailed in-county subscriptions stated on Form 3541	25	25
(3) Sales through dealers and carriers, street vendors, counter sales, and other non-USPS paid distribution	25	25
(4) Other classes mailed through the USPS		
C. Total paid and/or requested circulation	2,204	2,059
D. Free distribution by mail (Samples, complimentary, and other free copies)		
(1) Outside-county as stated on Form 3541		
(2) In-county as stated on Form 3541		
(3) Other classes mailed through the USPS	75	75
(4) Free distribution outside the mail (Carriers or other means)		
E. Total free distribution	75	75
F. Total distribution	2,279	2,134
G. Copies not distributed	300	100
H. Total	2,579	2,234
I. Percent paid and/or requested circulation	88%	95%

FOR MORE INFORMATION

Center on Ecotourism and Sustainable Development, 1333 H St., N.W., Suite 300, East Tower, Washington, DC 20005; (202) 347-9203; www.ecotourismcesd.org. Designs, monitors, evaluates and seeks to improve ecotourism practices and principles.

Conservation International, 1919 M St., N.W., Suite 600, Washington, DC 20036; (202) 912-1000; www.conservation.org. Seeks to protect endangered plants and animals around the world.

EplerWood International, www.eplerwood.com. Consultancy that offers insights into the challenges and opportunities of ecotourism from specific projects to broader economic and organizational issues.

The International Ecotourism Society, 1333 H St., N.W., Suite 300, East Tower, Washington, DC 20005; (202) 347-9203; www.ecotourism.org. Works to foster responsible travel to natural areas that conserves the environment and improves the well-being of local people.

Planeta.com, www.planeta.com. An ecotourism Web site featuring news, blog articles and links to other relevant Internet sites.

Transitions Abroad, P.O. Box 745, Bennington, VT 05201; (802) 442-4827; www.transitionsabroad.com. Web site offering information on working, studying, traveling and living abroad.

World Tourism Organization, Calle Capitan Haya, 42, 28020 Madrid, Spain; (34) 91 567 9301; www.unwto.org. United Nations agency that promotes economic development through responsible, sustainable tourism.

[10] *Ibid.*

[11] Simon Davis, "So Can Tourism Ever Really Be Ethical?" *The* [London] *Evening Standard*, July 19, 2006, p. 51.

[12] Costas Christ Sr., "A Road Less Traveled," Conservation International Web site; www.conservation.org/xp/frontlines/partners/focus32-1.xml.

[13] Maurice Malanes, "Tourism Killing World's Eighth Wonder," Third World Network, www.twnside.org.sg/title/mm-cn.htm.

[14] An exception to the low-impact policy was recently permitted, allowing small kayaking groups to camp in preapproved sites on some islands.

[15] Juliet Eilperin, "Despite Efforts, Some Tours Do Leave Footprints," *The Washington Post*, April 2, 2006, p. A1.

[16] Juliet Eilperin, "Science Notebook," *The Washington Post*, Jan. 30, 2006, p. A5.

[17] For background, see Thomas Arrandale, "National Parks Under Pressure," *CQ Researcher*, Oct. 6, 2006, pp. 817-840.

[18] Janet Frankston, "State to push unlikely site for eco-tourists: the Meadowlands," The Associated Press, Aug. 8, 2006.

[19] Christopher LaFranchi and Greenpeace Pacific, "Islands Adrift: Comparing Industrial and Small-Scale Economic Options for Marovo Lagoon Region of the Solomon Islands," Greenpeace, 1999, p. 4; www.greenpeace.org/international.

[20] *Ibid.*

[21] Xavier Font, "Critical Review of Certification and Accreditation in Sustainable Tourism Governance," www.Planeta.com.

[22] Unless otherwise noted, background drawn from Honey, *op. cit.*, pp. 7-8.

[23] Mastny, *op. cit.*, p. 10.

[24] For background, see Marcia Clemmitt, "Intelligent Design," *CQ Researcher*, July 29, 2005, pp. 637-660.

[25] Rachel S. Cox, "Protecting the National Parks," *CQ Researcher*, June 16, 2000, p. 521-544.

[26] Mastny, *op. cit.*, p. 13.

[27] *Ibid.*

[28] See "Ecotourism: a UN Declaration," *The Irish Times*, Aug. 5, 2006.

[29] Martha Honey, "Protecting Eden: Setting Green Standards for the Tourism Industry," *Environment*, July-August, 2003.

[30] *Ibid.* For background, see Marcia Clemmitt, "Climate Change," *CQ Researcher*, Jan. 27, 2006, pp. 73-96.

[31] Zoe Chafe, "Consumer Demand and Operator Support for Socially and Environmentally Responsible Tourism," CESD/TIES Working Paper No. 104, Center on Ecotourism and Sustainable Development and The International Ecotourism Society, revised April 2005, p. 4.

[32] *Ibid.*, p. 6.

[33] Mintel report cited in The International Ecotourism Society, Ecotourism Fact Sheet, "Eco and Ethical Tourism-UK," October 2003.

[34] Mastny, *op. cit.*, and "Ecotourism Fact Sheet," The International Ecotourism Society and World Tourism Organization, *World Tourism Barometer*, January 2005, p. 2.

[35] Martha Honey, *Ecotourism and Sustainable Development: Who Owns Paradise?* (1999), p. 8.

[36] World Tourism Organization, news release, *op. cit.*

[37] Cited in www.dantei.org/wto.forum/background-papers.html

[38] Theodoro Koumelis, "WTO Policy Forum: Tourism is top priority in fight against poverty," Oct. 22, 2004, TravelDailyNews.com.

[39] Simon Davis, "So Can Tourism Ever Really Be Ethical?" *The* [London] *Evening Standard*, July 19, 2006, p. A51."

[40] Mark Clayton, "When Ecotourism Kills," *The Christian Science Monitor*, Nov. 4, 2004, p. 13.

[41] Heidi S. Mitchell, "Easy Being Green," *The New York Times Style Magazine*, fall travel 2006, Sept. 24, 2006, p. 14.

[42] Christopher Solomon, "Where the High Life Comes Naturally," *The New York Times*, May 1, 2005, Sect. 5, Travel, p. 3.

[43] Mastny, *op. cit.*, p. 29. The report is by David Viner and Maureen Agnew, "Climate Change and Its Impact on Tourism," 1999.

[44] James Hamilton-Paterson, "The End of Travel," *Granta*, summer 2006, pp. 221-234.

[45] Anneli Rufus, "There's No Such Thing as Eco-Tourism," AlterNet; posted Aug. 14, 2006; www.alternet.org/story/40174/.

[46] McLaren, *op. cit.*

[47] Leisa Tyler, "Next Time You're In . . . Tasmania," *Time International*, Dec. 27, 2004, p. 120.

[48] Larry Rohter, "For Power or Beauty? Debating the Course of Chile's Rivers," *The New York Times*, Aug. 6, 2006, p. 3.

[49] Waterkeeper Alliance Web site, "Marriott and Four Seasons: Do Not Disturb PR"; www.waterkeeper.org/mainarticledetails.aspx?articleid=262.)

Bibliography

Selected Sources

Books

Buckley, Ralf, ed., *Environmental Impacts of Ecotourism*, CABI Publishing, 2004.

This collection of articles analyzes the cost of various types of ecotourism and what is being done to mitigate negative impacts of the industry.

Duffy, Rosaleen, *A Trip Too Far: Ecotourism, Politics and Exploitation*, Earthscan, 2002.

Based on her field work in Belize, a senior lecturer at the Centre for International Politics at the University of Manchester in England critiques positive assumptions about ecotourism by examining its place in the complex web of "green capitalism."

Honey, Martha, *Ecotourism and Sustainable Development: Who Owns Paradise?* Island Press, 1999.

Using a clear, engaging writing style, Honey outlines the history and development of ecotourism, including a country-by-country study of the industry.

Weaver, David B., ed., *The Encyclopedia of Ecotourism*, CABI Publishing, 2001.

Papers by leading experts cover a range of ecotourism issues — from defining the term and its impact on host destinations to the practicalities of business planning and management.

Articles

Boynton, Graham, "The Search for Authenticity," *The Nation*, Oct. 6, 1997.

Paradoxes and compromises emerge when tourists search for "the real thing" in the developing world.

Duffy, Rosaleen, ed., "The Politics of Ecotourism and the Developing World," *Journal of Ecotourism*, Vol. 5, Nos. 1 and 2, September 2006.

An ecotourism scholar explores the range of issues raised by the politics of ecotourism in the developing world — from abstract theories to specific cases.

Ebersole, Rene, "Take the High Road," *Audubon Travel Issue*, July-August 2006, p. 39.

Without a globally recognizable certification label, travelers cannot be sure which trips and hotels qualify as genuinely ecologically friendly.

Honey, Martha, "Protecting Eden: Setting Green Standards for the Tourism Industry," *Environment*, July-August, 2003.

The writer provides an excellent overview of the background and rationale for creating a regularized certification program for ecotourism.

Jones, Finn-Olaf, "Tourism Stripping Everest's Forests Bare," *National Geographic Traveler*, Aug. 29, 2003.

As of 2003, more than 25,000 trekkers were visiting the Khumbu Valley near Mt. Everest, turning into "an eroding desert" much of the area described by Sir Edmund Hillary in 1951 as being superbly forested.

Nicholson-Lord, David, "The Politics of Travel: Is Tourism Just Colonialism in Another Guise?" *The Nation*, Oct. 6, 1997.

The writer offers a negative take on the cultural, political and economic conundrums posed by ecotourism.

Vivanco, Luis A., "The Prospects and Dilemmas of Indigenous Tourism Standards and Certification," in R. Black and A. Crabtree, eds., *Quality Control and Ecotourism Certification*, CAB International, in press.

An anthropologist examines ecotourism certification from the point of view of native peoples.

Reports and Studies

Chafe, Zoe, "Consumer Demand and Operator Support for Socially and Environmentally Responsible Tourism," *CESD/TIES Working Paper No. 104*, Center on Ecotourism and Sustainable Development/The International Ecotourism Society, revised April 2005.

Statistics and trends are presented from a range of studies focusing on the U.S., Europe, Costa Rica and Australia.

Christ, Costas, Oliver Hillel, Seleni Matus and Jamie Sweeting, "Tourism and Biodiversity: Mapping Tourism's Global Footprint," Conservation International, 2003, p. 7.

The authors document the overlap between biodiversity "hotspots" and tourist destinations, making a case for carefully managed, sustainable tourism.

LaFranchi, Christopher, and Greenpeace Pacific, "Islands Adrift? Comparing Industrial and Small-scale Economic Options for Marovo Lagoon Region of the Solomon Islands," Greenpeace, March 1999; www.greenpeace.org/international/press/reports/islands-adrift-comparing-indu.

An analysis of the subsistence-based economy of a small but biologically rich region illuminates the complex issues that arise when ecotourism is chosen over more conventional, extractive development routes.

Mastny, Lisa, "Traveling Light: New Paths for International Tourism," Worldwatch Paper 159, Worldwatch Institute 2001.

A well-documented study examines the environmental implications of global travel in light of the massive economic forces it entails and considers the challenges and opportunities of achieving sustainable travel.

The Next Step:

Additional Articles from Current Periodicals

Consequences of Ecotourism

Clayton, Mark, "When Ecotourism Kills," *The Christian Science Monitor*, Nov. 4, 2004, p. 13.
Evidence is growing that some ecotourism efforts morph into organizations more concerned with profit than animals, harming wildlife in the process.

Dickerson, Marla, "Cruise-Ship Visitors Altering Belize," *The Philadelphia Inquirer*, April 2, 2006, p. A15.
The increased number of cruise ships arriving in Belize is upsetting longtime tour operators, who say the hordes of new visitors endanger Belize's niche as an ecotourism paradise.

Eilperin, Juliet, "Despite Efforts, Some Tours Do Leave Footprints," *The Washington Post*, April 2, 2006, p. P1.
Some ecotourism companies that visit the Galapagos Islands in Ecuador are not always so careful about protecting the ecosystem they market to their clients.

Gilden, James, "Cost of Air Travel Measured in Terms of Pollution, Not Dollars," *Los Angeles Times*, Sept. 17, 2006, p. L2.
The online travel agencies Expedia and Travelocity are helping to fund clean-energy projects and reforestation to appease "green" consumers.

Eco-Resorts

Bear, David, "Eco Trips," *Pittsburgh-Post Gazette*, Aug. 27, 2006, p. E1.
Eco-resorts offer outdoor activities and comfortable accommodations in scenic or still-wild settings.

Sell, Shawn, "10 Great Places to Tread Lightly on Earth," *USA Today*, Aug. 20, 2004, p. D3.
The writer profiles his favorite "green" hotels.

Solomon, Christopher, "Where the High Life Comes Naturally," *The New York Times*, May 1, 2005, p. 3.
High-end ecotourism options are expanding, with companies offering wealthy visitors close encounters with nature, gourmet food and luxurious accommodations.

Ecotourism in the United States

Carmody, Kevin, "Texas Ranchers Thwart Development Through Ecotourism," *Chicago Tribune*, Jan. 16, 2005, p. P5.
Ranching clans in Texas' Davis Mountains have started capitalizing on expanded ecotourism opportunities in the region to make extra income.

Simmons, Ann M., "Logging Visits Rather Than Trees," *Los Angeles Times*, March 20, 2005, p. B1.
With the timber industry in decline, Shasta County, Calif., hopes to improve its economy by becoming an ecotourism destination.

Talcott, Christina, "In West Virginia, Eco-Tourism Is Becoming Second Nature," *The Washington Post*, Aug. 26, 2005, p. T29.
West Virginia's ecotourism pioneers are taking cues from places like Costa Rica to make sure the mountains, trees and clean rivers that tourists are coming to see now will be around in the future.

Global Ecotourism

Higgins, Michelle, "If It Worked For Costa Rica . . .," *The New York Times*, Jan. 22, 2006, p. 10.
The success of Costa Rica and Ecuador in luring travelers to mountain treks and jungle safaris is encouraging several other regions worldwide to try ecotourism as a strategy for economic growth.

Jackson, Kristin, "Where The Wild Things Are," *The Seattle Times*, Feb. 19, 2006, p. K1.
A handful of native villages that dot the coast of the Great Bear Rainforest in British Columbia are turning to ecotourism as part of their economic future.

Stoddard, Ed, "Tired of Hunting Lions? Try Going on Frog Safari," *The Houston Chronicle*, Feb. 20, 2005, p. A25.
Alwyn Wentzel hopes to introduce a new concept in ecotourism — frog safaris in the Amazulu Game Reserve in South Africa's KwaZulu-Natal Province.

CITING *CQ RESEARCHER*

Sample formats for citing these reports in a bibliography include the ones listed below. Preferred styles and formats vary, so please check with your instructor or professor.

MLA STYLE

Jost, Kenneth. "Rethinking the Death Penalty." CQ Researcher 16 Nov. 2001: 945-68.

APA STYLE

Jost, K. (2001, November 16). Rethinking the death penalty. *CQ Researcher, 11*, 945-968.

CHICAGO STYLE

Jost, Kenneth. "Rethinking the Death Penalty." *CQ Researcher*, November 16, 2001, 945-968.

CQ Researcher

Published by CQ Press, a division of Congressional Quarterly Inc.

cqresearcher.com

Middle East Tensions

Are there any hopeful signs?

United Nations peacekeepers are maintaining a fragile peace in south Lebanon after last summer's devastating 34-day war between Hezbollah and Israel. Elsewhere in the Middle East, the climate of confrontation makes prospects for peace appear grim. In the region's longest-running conflict, Israel and the Palestinians remain locked in disagreement over creation of a permanent homeland for the Palestinians, and armed skirmishes between rival Palestinian parties are complicating efforts to restart peace negotiations with Israel. In addition, the Bush administration is leading an international boycott of one of those parties — Hamas — for its refusal to recognize Israel and renounce violence. In Lebanon, many fear the truce between Israel and the Hezbollah militia won't last. Hezbollah's main patron, Iran, is defying American and European efforts to ensure that its nuclear-power development is limited to peaceful purposes. And in Iraq, U.S. forces remain bogged down after more than three years of fighting.

Supporters of the Islamic resistance organization Hamas vow never to recognize Israel during an Oct. 6 rally in the Gaza Strip.

Inside This Report

CQ Researcher • Oct. 27, 2006 • www.cqresearcher.com
Volume 16, Number 38 • Pages 889-912

CQ Press

Recipient of Society of Professional Journalists Award for Excellence ◆ American Bar Association Silver Gavel Award

THE ISSUES

BACKGROUND

CURRENT SITUATION

OUTLOOK

SIDEBARS AND GRAPHICS

FOR FURTHER RESEARCH

Cover photograph: AFP/Getty Images/Abid Katib

CQ Researcher

Oct. 27, 2006
Volume 16, Number 38

MANAGING EDITOR: Thomas J. Colin

ASSISTANT MANAGING EDITOR: Kathy Koch

ASSOCIATE EDITOR: Kenneth Jost

STAFF WRITERS: Marcia Clemmitt, Peter Katel

CONTRIBUTING WRITERS: Rachel S. Cox, Sarah Glazer, Alan Greenblatt, Barbara Mantel, Patrick Marshall, Tom Price, Jennifer Weeks

DESIGN/PRODUCTION EDITOR: Olu B. Davis

ASSISTANT EDITOR: Melissa J. Hipolit

CQ PRESS

A Division of Congressional Quarterly Inc.

SENIOR VICE PRESIDENT/PUBLISHER: John A. Jenkins

DIRECTOR, LIBRARY PUBLISHING: Kathryn C. Suárez

DIRECTOR, EDITORIAL OPERATIONS: Ann Davies

CONGRESSIONAL QUARTERLY INC.

CHAIRMAN: Paul C. Tash

VICE CHAIRMAN: Andrew P. Corty

PRESIDENT/EDITOR IN CHIEF: Robert W. Merry

CQ Researcher (ISSN 1056-2036) is printed on acid-free paper. Published weekly, except March 24, July 7, July 14, Aug. 4, Aug. 11, Nov. 24, Dec. 22 and Dec. 29, by CQ Press, a division of Congressional Quarterly Inc. Annual full-service subscriptions for institutions start at $667. For pricing, call 1-800-834-9020, ext. 1906. To purchase a *CQ Researcher* report in print or electronic format (PDF), visit www.cqpress.com or call 866-427-7737. Single reports start at $15. Bulk purchase discounts and electronic-rights licensing are also available. Periodicals postage paid at Washington, D.C., and additional mailing offices. POSTMASTER: Send address changes to *CQ Researcher*, 1255 22nd St., N.W., Suite 400, Washington, DC 20037.

Middle East Tensions

BY PETER KATEL

THE ISSUES

When Paul Salem and Gerald Steinberg look at the devastation in southern Lebanon caused by last summer's brief war between Israel and Hezbollah, they see two different realities.

Salem, a Harvard-educated Lebanese political scientist who drove through the area shortly after the 34-day war, says, "I've been through towns where there is not a single house left." The devastation makes only one conclusion possible, says Salem, director of the Beirut-based Middle East Center of the Carnegie Endowment for International Peace. "Clearly, this was largely deliberate," he says. "The Israelis wiped out huge areas" in order to create a "no-man's-land" along Lebanon's border with Israel.

From the Israeli side, Steinberg, a strategy and diplomacy specialist at Bar-Ilan University, points out a few things missing from Salem's description. "The entire area was combed with underground structures — missile-storage sites and bunkers — used against Israeli troops," Steinberg says. "I wouldn't say there was a leveling of villages. It was much more a destruction of infrastructure."

The fighting between Israel and the Lebanese Hezbollah militia erupted on July 12 after Hezbollah fighters crawled through a tunnel to the Israeli side, killed three Israel Defense Force (IDF) soldiers and captured two others. Israel retaliated the next day by bombing the Beirut airport and Hezbollah's television station, followed by a month of bombing throughout south Lebanon and an attack by ground troops. [1] Hezbollah responded by launching 3,790 rockets into Israel, many fired from mobile units located in villages and residential areas.

By the time a United Nations-sponsored cease-fire took effect on Aug. 14, at least 1,110 Lebanese and 42 Israeli civilians had died, along with 118 Israeli troops and an undisclosed number of Hezbollah fighters. Moreover, an estimated 940,000 Lebanese were displaced and 150,000 houses and apartments destroyed. [2]

AFP/Getty Images/Thomas Coex

A Lebanese woman stands amid the rubble of her home following the 34-day war that erupted in July between Israel and the Lebanese Islamic group Hezbollah. The conflict, which killed at least 1,300 people, destroyed 150,000 houses and apartments and left 940,000 Lebanese homeless, is only one of many flash points in the Middle East.

Today, about a million unexploded cluster bombs — designed to explode into flesh-ripping fragments — still litter the Lebanese countryside, say U.N. experts. An IDF artilleryman called Israel's use of cluster bombs "insane and monstrous" — to which the IDF responds they are legal under international law. [3]

Early in the fighting, Secretary of State Condoleezza Rice had optimistically depicted the conflict as "the birth pangs of a new Middle East." [4] But her rosy prediction was premature, at best. Permanent peace between Israel and its Muslim neighbors appears a distant hope, as does peace between the Middle East's many other longtime adversaries, including secular and religious Arab nationalists and Shiite and Sunni Muslims.

Both before and after the Lebanon war, Palestinian guerrillas have been firing rockets into Israel from the Gaza Strip, the formerly Israeli-occupied territory that Israel withdrew from last year. IDF retaliation in late October alone killed 26 Palestinians, including three civilians.

Some experts argue that Hezbollah's success in withstanding the Israeli offensive in Lebanon may embolden the Palestinians to fortify the Gaza Strip, just as Hezbollah fortified a buffer zone in southern Lebanon after Israel withdrew from it in 2000, after a long occupation. "We will not [allow] the transformation of the Gaza Strip into south Lebanon," Israeli Defense Minister Amir Peretz said on Oct. 15, warning of heavier military action if the attacks from Gaza persist. [5]

Continued on p. 893

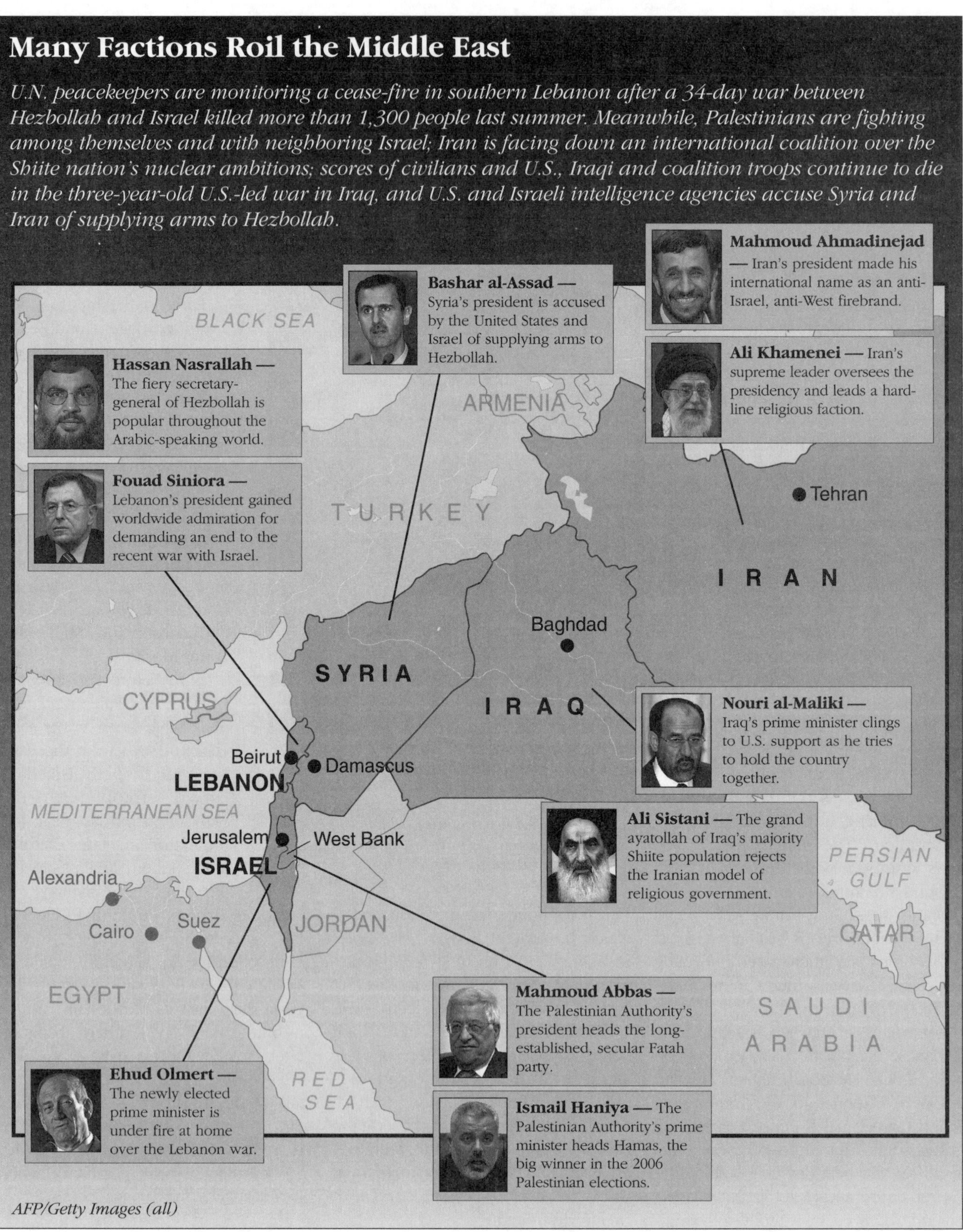

Many Factions Roil the Middle East
U.N. peacekeepers are monitoring a cease-fire in southern Lebanon after a 34-day war between Hezbollah and Israel killed more than 1,300 people last summer. Meanwhile, Palestinians are fighting among themselves and with neighboring Israel; Iran is facing down an international coalition over the Shiite nation's nuclear ambitions; scores of civilians and U.S., Iraqi and coalition troops continue to die in the three-year-old U.S.-led war in Iraq, and U.S. and Israeli intelligence agencies accuse Syria and Iran of supplying arms to Hezbollah.
Mahmoud Ahmadinejad — Iran's president made his international name as an anti-Israel, anti-West firebrand.
Bashar al-Assad — Syria's president is accused by the United States and Israel of supplying arms to Hezbollah.
Hassan Nasrallah — The fiery secretary-general of Hezbollah is popular throughout the Arabic-speaking world.
Ali Khamenei — Iran's supreme leader oversees the presidency and leads a hard-line religious faction.
Fouad Siniora — Lebanon's president gained worldwide admiration for demanding an end to the recent war with Israel.
Nouri al-Maliki — Iraq's prime minister clings to U.S. support as he tries to hold the country together.
Ali Sistani — The grand ayatollah of Iraq's majority Shiite population rejects the Iranian model of religious government.
Mahmoud Abbas — The Palestinian Authority's president heads the long-established, secular Fatah party.
Ehud Olmert — The newly elected prime minister is under fire at home over the Lebanon war.
Ismail Haniya — The Palestinian Authority's prime minister heads Hamas, the big winner in the 2006 Palestinian elections.
BLACK SEA
ARMENIA
TURKEY
Tehran
IRAN
Baghdad
SYRIA
IRAQ
CYPRUS
Beirut
Damascus
LEBANON
MEDITERRANEAN SEA
Jerusalem
West Bank
ISRAEL
Alexandria
Cairo
Suez
JORDAN
EGYPT
PERSIAN GULF
QATAR
SAUDI ARABIA
RED SEA

AFP/Getty Images (all)

Continued from p. 891

Palestinians are also fighting among themselves to the point that they are "now on the verge of civil war," says Robert Malley, Middle East-North Africa program director for the International Crisis Group, an influential Brussels-based nonprofit that is promoting a new, comprehensive, Arab-Israeli peace plan. "What is being created in Palestine today is a failed state even before the Palestinians have a state." [6] During the Clinton administration, Malley served as special assistant to the president for Arab-Israeli Affairs.

Street fighting broke out in the Palestinian territories (the lands that Israel seized from Jordan and Egypt in a 1967 war) recently between loyalists of the long-established secular Fatah party, led by Palestinian Authority President Mahmoud Abbas, and fighters for the Islamic resistance organization Hamas, which adopted electoral politics and won a parliamentary majority in 2005, led by Prime Minister Ismail Haniya.

On the Israeli side, where memories of suicide-bombing campaigns by Hamas and other organizations remain vivid — 415 civilians were killed and more than 2,000 injured in 2000-2002 alone — skepticism about the prospects for peace between the Palestinians and Israel runs so deep that some welcome a Palestinian civil war. [7]

"This is what happened in America," says Efraim Inbar, director of the Begin-Sadat Center for Strategic Studies at Bar-Ilan University. "Sometimes civil wars are necessary to establish central authority."

For its part, the administration of President George W. Bush continues to support statehood for Palestinians displaced by Israel's creation. Secretary of State Rice declares that her own life story leads her to discount skepticism about peace between Israel and the Palestinians. After all, if the history of U.S. race relations were any guide, she told the American Task Force on Palestine on Oct. 11, "I should never have grown up in segregated Birmingham, Alabama, to become the secretary of State of the United States of America." [8]

Adding to regional tensions, Iran is embroiled in a standoff with the United States and much of the rest of the international community over its alleged development of nuclear weapons. The Bush administration and the European Union have demanded that Iran suspend its uranium-enrichment program until international inspectors can determine whether it is being used to produce fuel for nuclear weapons rather than nuclear reactors. Experts say Iran is less than 10 years away from being able to produce nuclear weapons. [9]

The confrontation with Iran had been intensifying when the Lebanon war erupted — a conflict an administration official (who asked to remain anonymous) called a "proxy war" between the United States (represented by Israel) and Iran (represented by Hezbollah). "The Israeli defense establishment . . . regards Hezbollah as a frontal commando unit of the Iranian Revolutionary Guards," writes Ze'ev Schiff, a widely read defense expert who is chief military correspondent for the Israeli daily *Haaretz*. [10]

Other Israelis see a more nuanced relationship. "Iran doesn't make 100 percent of Hezbollah's decisions," says retired Maj. Gen. Shlomo Gazit, a former director of Israeli military intelligence.

Virtually everyone agrees, however, that Iran helped to create Hezbollah ("Party of God") in 1982, when the newly triumphant revolutionary — and zealously anti-Israel and anti-American — Shiite Muslim government in Tehran helped south Lebanon's majority Shiite population resist an Israeli occupation. Israel maintained a nine-mile deep security zone along the Lebanon-Israel border until 2000. [11]

Western governments and independent scholars also agree that Hezbollah gets most of its advanced weapons from Iran and Syria, although Iran denies providing military aid in the recent conflict with Israel. [12]

Israel, meanwhile, enjoys such strong U.S. support that many believe the Bush administration refused to join a worldwide call for a cease-fire early in the war with Hezbollah to allow Israel to score a decisive victory — an outcome that Bush hoped would resonate in Iran. (*See sidebar, p. 900.*)

"The root cause of the problem," Bush said on July 28, is a Hezbollah "armed and willing to fire rockets into Israel [and which], I firmly believe, is backed by Iran and encouraged by Iran." [13]

In any event, the war's effects on Iran are widely disputed. "Iran was undoubtedly strengthened by the war," says Ali Ansari, a historian of Iran and the Middle East at the University of St. Andrews in Fife, Scotland. "It has made Iran bolder, and the more emboldened it is the more reckless it is going to be. This has made the nuclear standoff more difficult to resolve. Unless you have an amazingly bold act of leadership by someone in the U.S., we are on a steady spiral downward."

But in the view of David Mack, a former deputy assistant secretary of State, "Iranians are the big losers. Iran did see the buildup of a [Hezbollah] missile capability that could serve as a deterrent to Israelis or ourselves. But now "most of that deterrent has been shot off in the general direction of Israel," says Mack, acting director of the Middle East Institute, a Washington think tank.

That reading is so widely shared that Hassan Nasrallah, Hezbollah's charismatic secretary-general, made a point of contradicting it. "What we offered in the war was a very small part of our resources," Nasrallah told hundreds of thousands of cheering, flag-waving supporters in Beirut on Sept. 22. "Today . . . I say to the enemy that the resistance has more — pay attention, underline the word 'more,' — than 20,000 rockets!" [14]

Less than a month earlier, Nasrallah had taken a far less bellicose stance, acknowledging that Hezbollah's recent war with Israel had brought grief to all Lebanese. "If I knew the process of capturing [the Israeli soldiers], even with a 1 percent probability, would lead to a war like this, and then if you asked me would you go and capture them, my answer would be, of course, no — for humanitarian, moral, social and security reasons." [15]

Despite the war's heavy civilian toll, Hezbollah retained its strongholds in southern Lebanon and south Beirut and prevented Israel from breaking the militia as a military threat. [16] Israelis, who tie their national survival to a powerful military, excoriated newly elected Prime Minister Ehud Olmert for his administration's poor showing.

U.S. Embassy via Getty Images/Matty Stern

U.S. Secretary of State Condoleezza Rice meets in Jerusalem with Israeli Defense Minister Amir Peretz on her first Middle East tour since hostilities between Israel and Hezbollah ended. Rice has pushed for more cooperation between the Israelis and Palestinians, but tension remains high between the two groups, as it does among warring Palestinian factions.

"In Damascus, Gaza, Tehran and Cairo . . . people are looking with amazement at the IDF that could not bring a tiny guerrilla organization to its knees for more than a month," wrote *Haaretz* columnist Reuven Pedatzur, a military expert and former Israeli fighter pilot. "What happened to this mighty army?" [17]

Public protests, many featuring IDF reservists who had fought in Lebanon, forced Olmert's cabinet to appoint a committee to investigate the government's handling of the war. [18]

Strikingly, many Arabs — who for the first time viewed a war with Israel live on satellite TV — also say the war damaged Israel's military image.

"Hezbollah showed that you don't have to lose to the Israeli army," says the Carnegie Endowment's Salem. "That has a general impact on public opinion in the Arab world. It shows you can fight Israel. Hezbollah showed them how to do it."

As turmoil continues throughout the Middle East, these are some of the questions being debated:

Did the Lebanon war open the door to reduced hostilities between Hezbollah and Israel?

The war between Hezbollah and Israel last summer ended with the dispatch of a U.N. military force to help the Lebanese army maintain a cease-fire. [19]

Just how that mission was to be accomplished by the U.N. contingent — authorized to expand from 2,000 troops to 15,000 — remains hazy. "We will advise, help and assist the Lebanese forces," said Col. Rosario Walter Guerrisi, commander of an Italian unit that is part of the U.N. force. He said his troops were not authorized, however, to conduct searches or stop vehicles seen carrying weapons. [20]

Guerrisi's comments prompted Secretary of State Rice to note with concern: "I would hope that Unifil [United Nations Interim Force in Lebanon] would interpret its mission in a way that allows it to really do what it is supposed to do, which is not to allow a return to the status quo . . . in the south," when Hezbollah sparked the war with Israel. [21]

For their part, Hezbollah supporters said they will accept Unifil only if it takes no action against the Shiite militia. "The people here will fight against anybody who tries with force to take Hezbollah's weapons away," said Ibrahim Noureddin, a resident of Burj Qalawiyah. Israel hit the village heavily this year and five other times since 1972, residents said. [22]

In Israel, some analysts say Unifil's narrowly defined mission is enabling Hezbollah to restore its military strength. "It's a question of time and of the extent to which the Lebanese army will do something [to prevent such a buildup], which I doubt very much," says the Begin-Sadat Center's Inbar. Fear of reviving Lebanon's 1975-90 civil war might discourage Lebanese forces from challenging Hezbollah, he argues. "The Lebanese political system doesn't want another civil war," Inbar says. "If that's the choice, they prefer a war with Israel."

But in Beirut, the Carnegie Endowment's Salem argues that the presence of U.N. and Lebanese army forces could help stabilize the restive border region, which has been under virtual Hezbollah control since the 1980s.

Salem also points out that Hezbollah didn't come away unscathed. "They probably have a lot of missiles left, but their strategy and tactics — the way they hide and fight — are a surprise to Israel no longer. You can only surprise once."

Moreover, Salem says, "Their constituency has taken such a staggering blow that Hezbollah cannot get them into war anytime again soon."

Indeed, some observers think the sheer enormity of the destruction witnessed recently by Salem could encourage Hezbollah to enter into détente with Israel. And Israel's own political instability could encourage an end to violence.

But the Middle East Institute's Mack argues those conditions are the very opposite of what's needed. "Détente is usually achieved by strong governments negotiating with one another, like the U.S. and Soviet governments under President Reagan," he says.

Such negotiations might have led to Hezbollah's disarmament, Mack says, but "all that work still has to be done. Hezbollah may not have armed units parading around the villages in the south — which was obviously an undesirable situation — but they still bear arms, they are still very much involved in the politics of south Lebanon."

Nonetheless, says former military intelligence chief Gazit, now at the Jaffee Center for Strategic Studies at Tel Aviv University, "I don't expect military operations [by Hezbollah] in the foreseeable future." Hezbollah saw its strategy of harassing Israel with rocket fire undone by the massive Israeli response, he explains.

"Hezbollah has to re-evaluate," and Hezbollah knows it, Gazit continues, referring to Nasrallah's regret about sparking Israel's massive retaliation. "A high-ranking military figure saying such words — if he's not sincere then he must be crazy." And Gazit doesn't consider Nasrallah crazy.

Should the United States do more to mediate the Israeli-Palestinian struggle?

The nearly century-old conflict between Israel and the Palestinians lies at the root of all troubles in the Middle East, many observers believe. Some say the United States is too supportive of Israel and has lost the ability to be an honest peace broker in the conflict. Others contend the Bush administration is doing all it can by working with moderate Palestinians and is right to refuse talks with Hamas until it rejects terrorism.

"The entire U.S. relationship with the Muslim world stems from the fact that the United States supports a continuing [Israeli] colonization of Palestinian territory on the West Bank," says the Carnegie Endowment's Salem. "It's a straightforward injustice."

Some Israelis agree the conflict between Israel and the Palestinians helps to fuel rage at Israel and its Western allies throughout the Muslim world. "There's a genuine case to be made for its radicalizing effects," says Daniel Levy, a former adviser to Israel in the 1995 negotiations that led to a groundbreaking agreement on Palestinian self-government in the occupied territories. The fact that the Palestinians lack a state of their own "is genuinely viewed as wrong by many Arabs and Muslims, who don't [necessarily] harbor deep-seated prejudices against Jews. They are angry about this."

Thus, the argument goes, if the United States would just help resolve the Israeli-Palestinian problem, it would go a long way toward lessening the rampant anti-Americanism in the Middle East and beyond.

But more conservative Israelis and their supporters have argued for years that calling the conflict a "root cause" of terrorism, instability and anti-Americanism amounts to blaming Israel for everything bad that happens in the Middle East. In fact, they say, the real root causes lie with Middle Eastern despots who violate human rights and deny their citizens an opportunity to better their lives.

"The repression, humiliation and violence that are the daily portion of people living under autocratic regimes nurture rage and fanaticism," commented Joshua Muravchik, a neoconservative analyst at the American Enterprise Institute (AEI). [23]

In the wake of the Sept. 11, 2001, terrorist attacks on the World Trade Center and the Pentagon by al Qaeda terrorists, Muravchik applauded the U.S.-led invasion of Afghanistan. Today, however, even critics of Bush's military approach tend to agree that only the United States has the power to help bring about positive change in the Middle East conflict. But most advocate using negotiation, not invasion, to break the Israeli-Palestinian deadlock.

Theoretically, says Levy, director of the Middle East Policy Initiative sponsored by the New America and Century foundations, both sides of the conflict should be able to negotiate an agreement on their own. But as a practical matter, there won't be any negotiations without outside pressure, he says. "The thing that most pains me is that I rarely remember an occasion so crying out for leadership — but it's just not there," Levy says.

Too many Bush administration officials think Iran, Lebanon and other issues can be resolved "without worrying about Israel-Palestine," Levy says. He partly blames the administration's courting of evangelical Christians for its reluctance to publicly link Israel with the broader regional conflict. Evangelicals and other religious conservatives oppose any action that might be interpreted as pressuring

U.S.-Iran Relations Remain Complicated

It might come as a shock to many Americans that the ex-president of a country where the United States is still called the "Great Satan" declares his affection for Thomas Jefferson and espouses peaceful coexistence between East and West.

"The Orient . . . can engage in a historic dialogue with Europe and the United States" that . . . could promote "moderation and tranquility," Mohammed Khatami told an audience at Washington's National Cathedral on Sept. 7. [1]

A moderate senior cleric who was president from 1997-2005, Khatami represents one dimension of the half-century-old U.S.-Iran relationship, now at one of its lowest points. The public side of U.S.-Iran relations has been ugly — and seemingly getting worse — ever since the 1979 Iranian revolution. A week before Khatami's address, President Mahmoud Ahmadinejad had defied an Aug. 31 deadline set by the United States and the European Union to suspend uranium-enrichment efforts pending a determination that Iran is not producing weapons-grade material.

A century of foreign manipulation in Iranian affairs simmers beneath Ahmadinejad's stance and his provocative rhetoric about the United States and Britain: "If the governments of the United States or the United Kingdom, who are permanent members of the Security Council, commit aggression, occupation, and violation of international law, which of the organs of the U.N. can take them to account?" Ahmadinejad asked in a speech to the U.N. General Assembly on Sept. 19. "If they have differences with a nation or state, they drag it to the Security Council, and its claimants arrogate to themselves simultaneously the roles of prosecutor, judge and executioner. Is this a just order? Can there be a more vivid case of discrimination and more clear evidence of injustice?" [2]

Ahmadinejad's harsh words echoed widely shared Iranian resentment that in 1953 the Central Intelligence Agency — with Britain's aid — helped topple Iran's Prime Minister Mohammed Mossadeq after he proposed nationalizing Iran's oil industry. "To this day," writes Ray Takeyh, a historian at the Council on Foreign Relations, "many Iranians believe that an opportunity to forge a new independent and non-aligned foreign policy, employ natural resources for national development and build a democracy were all lost due to the machinations of a rapacious superpower." [3]

Following the coup, the United States built a close relationship with the shah (emperor) of Iran, Mohammed Reza Pahlevi. As early as 1960, a British diplomat reported to London: "American assistance has equipped with American weapons and dressed in American [style] uniforms an army of 200,000 men; peopled the administration with American advisers; sprinkled the country with American projects. All this is profoundly disturbing to traditional ways of life in Iran." [4]

For their part, Americans have been equally disturbed by events since the 1979 revolution that toppled the shah, including the holding of 52 U.S. Embassy personnel as hostages in Tehran in 1979-81; Iranian patronage of Hezbollah, which killed 241 Marines in Beirut in 1983 and Ahmadinejad's anti-Israel rhetoric and denial of the Holocaust.

Yet officials of both governments have cooperated. A nascent covert relationship hit a major snag, however, in 1986, when an Iranian official leaked word of the Reagan administration scheme for using profits from illegal arms sales to Iran to illegally aid a guerrilla army in Nicaragua, setting off a scandal that rocked the Reagan administration.

"Regardless of questions over the wisdom of the arms-for-hostages negotiations," writes former Bush administration official

Israel because they believe the Jews' return to Israel signals the return of the Messiah and the beginning of the End Times — an apocalyptic battle between good and evil. Hence, attempts to create a separate Palestinian state are seen as blasphemy or worse. [24]

But another Israeli analyst, Inbar of the Begin-Sadat Center, says trying to encourage talks with the Palestinians is futile — even if the United States could use its influence. "The Americans have difficulties in Iraq, so what can they do in Palestine?" he asks. "In Iraq, they're ready to shoot the bad guys, but I don't think the Europeans or Americans are ready to come to Palestine and shoot the bad guys."

In any event, he adds, referring to fighting among Palestinians, "There is nobody [among the Palestinians] you can negotiate with who will deliver. It's a total mess."

Manuel Hassassian, the Palestinian Authority's ambassador to the United Kingdom, concedes that the Palestinian civil conflict could lead to all-out civil war. A supporter of Authority President Abbas, Hassassian blames Hamas for the fighting among Palestinians but argues against using the Palestinians' political breakdown as an excuse by the United States to walk away from efforts to forge an agreement with Israel.

Nevertheless, Hassassian has no hope that Washington will step in, at least for now. Instead, he's pinning his hopes on British Prime Minister Tony Blair, now serving his final months in office. While Blair is willing to step in, the failure of the two main Palestinian parties to form a "national unity" government is a major obstacle to progress. In addition, Palestinian fighters are still holding Gilad Shalit, the Israeli soldier whose June 25 capture launched last summer's fighting.

"Mr. Blair wants to reinvigorate the peace process," Hassassian says. "He will put pressure on President Bush and the Israelis if two things take place — a release of Shalit in exchange for political prisoners and the formation of a national unity government."

Michael Rubin, a resident scholar at the American Enterprise Institute, "the episode represented a serious, sensitive and covert attempt to reach out to the Iranian government." [5]

For Rubin, the so-called Iran-Contra scandal also displayed what he called the strength of the hard-line clerical faction run now by Supreme Leader Ali Khamenei. The considerable level of dissent in Iran "doesn't change the overall philosophy of the regime," Rubin says. "Ultimately, the power center is with Khamenei; that's stable."

After Iran-Contra, "Not too many American officials were willing to assume risks and move forward with provocative ideas," writes Takeyh, who is nonetheless optimistic about chances for eventual U.S.-Iranian coexistence. [6]

Some of that optimism may stem from a strong current of pro-American sentiment still to be found in Iran. After the Sept. 11 terrorist attacks, for instance, hundreds of Iranians held a candlelight vigil in Tehran in honor of the U.S. victims. And a letter from Tehran Mayor Morteza Alviri to Mayor Rudolph W. Giuliani said, "Tehran's citizens express their deep hatred of this ominous and inhuman move," which was "not just against New Yorkers but against all humanity." [7]

The Iranian government even offered to join the Bush administration's war against terrorism, provided it did not "[turn] a blind eye" to what it called Israel's acts of terror in Gaza and the West Bank. Within months, however, the relationship chilled again after President Bush called Iran part of the infamous "axis of evil."

Even after that, Iranian officials reportedly indicated in 2003 that they were interested in opening "comprehensive negotiations" to settle all problems between Iran and the United States. "Unfortunately, the administration's response was to complain that the Swiss diplomats who passed the document from Tehran to Washington were out of line," wrote Flynt Leverett, formerly the National Security Council's senior director for Mideast Affairs. [8]

"By continuing to reject a grand bargain with Tehran, the Bush administration has done nothing to increase the chances that Iran will accept meaningful, long-term restraints on its nuclear activities," Leverett wrote in a follow-up piece. [9]

However serious the reported offer might have been, it wasn't enough to lower the barrier created by a quarter-century of bad history.

"We don't talk to each other," R. Nicholas Burns, under secretary of State for political affairs, said in September. "I've been an American diplomat for 25 years this coming February. And I have never met an Iranian diplomat." [10]

[1] See "Lecture by Former Iranian President Mohammed Khatami," Sept. 7, 2006; www.cathedral.org/cathedral/programs/lecture060907.shtml. For Khatami reference to Jefferson, see Robin Wright, "War Backfiring on U.S., Khatami Says," *The Washington Post*, Sept. 6, 2006, p. A4.

[2] See "Iranian President Ahmadinejad Delivers Remarks to the U.N. General Assembly, New York," Sept. 19, 2006, Newsmaker Transcripts, cq.com.

[3] Quoted in Ray Takeyh, *Hidden Iran: Paradox and Power in the Islamic Republic* (2006), p. 84.

[4] Quoted in Ali M. Ansari, *Confronting Iran: The Failure of American Foreign Policy and the Next Great Conflict in the Middle East* (2006), p. 45.

[5] Michael Rubin, "Can Iran Be Trusted," American Enterprise Institute, September 2006, p. 1, http://aei.org/publications/pubID.24854,filter.all/pub_detail.asp.

[6] Takeyh, *op. cit.*, p. 108.

[7] John Ward Anderson, "Overtures From Iran: A Mixed Message; Washington Wary Of Offers to Assist," *The Washington Post*, Sept. 19, 2001, p. A10.

[8] For details, see Flynt Leverett, "The Gulf Between Us," *The New York Times*, Jan. 24, 2006, p. A21.

[9] For details, see Flynt Leverett, "The Race for Iran," *The New York Times*, June 17, 2006, p. A21.

[10] For a transcript of Burns' remarks, see "The Charlie Rose Show," Sept. 27, 2006.

Shalit's kidnappers have been demanding the release of hundreds of Palestinian prisoners held by Israel, including about 400 women and minors. Israel has never shown reluctance to hit back hard at Palestinians it believes are involved in terrorism. Since 2000 alone, the Israeli policy of "targeted killings" has resulted in the deaths of more than 200 people Israel says were terrorists. But others are killed along the way. The bombing of a house to kill a senior Hamas leader in 2002 also killed 16 civilians who weren't targets, including nine children. [25]

An American supporter of the Palestinian cause doubts the Bush administration's commitment to mediating the conflict between Israel and the Palestinians. "I don't trust our government to do it," says Mark Perry, co-director of the Conflicts Forum, which advocates negotiations between Western governments and Islamist radicals, including Hezbollah, Hamas and other groups that have attacked Israeli civilians.

"The Bush administration says these groups can't have one foot in democracy and one foot in terrorism," Perry says, referring to the fact that the U.S. government classifies both groups as terrorist organizations. "That is to say, you have to accept Israel and its violence or you're a terrorist organization."

Is Iran a threat to the West?

Iran's pursuit of nuclear power, coupled with defiance of efforts to ensure that the effort has strictly peaceful intentions, has prompted enormous concern that a government with a track record of support for terrorism could possess nuclear weapons.

Largely for that reason, President Bush defined Iran in 2002 as a member of the "axis of evil" (along with Kim Jong-il's North Korea and Saddam Hussein's Iraq). [26]

The administration's tough line on Iran hardened even more after 2005, when Iranians elected Mahmoud Ahmadinejad to replace Muhammed Khatami as president. Ahmadinejad, who has vowed to wipe Israel off the map and questioned whether the Holocaust occurred, seemed uninterested in promoting dialogue with the United States. Instead, he defied international attempts to supervise his country's nuclear research, which he insists is purely for peaceful purposes.

In Israel and Washington, a powerful chorus of Iran hawks now dismisses Ahmadinejad's talk of peaceful objectives.

"The problem isn't necessarily that they would drop nuclear weapons," says Michael Rubin, an Iran specialist who served on Defense Secretary Donald Rumsfeld's staff in 2002-2004. "Ultimately, Iran is committed to exporting revolution. They've struck at American targets before by proxy," he continues, citing Iran's support for Hezbollah (which blew up the U.S. Marine barracks in Beirut in 1983, killing 241 soldiers). Rubin, a resident scholar at the conservative American Enterprise Institute, speaks Farsi and lived in Iran while researching his doctorate in history.

Iran's most dangerous trait is overconfidence, says Rubin. "Many Iranians in power centers tend not to accurately understand the frustration in Washington, the hardening of attitudes in Washington," he says. "Whether or not we want military action, if Iran pushes us too hard we may be pushed into a position in which we have to push back."

Critics of the Bush administration, however, say hawks are turning challenge into a crisis. "Iran certainly is a huge problem for a lot of our strategic interests in the Middle East, but I don't think it is a strategic threat," says Mack of the Middle East Institute. Mack takes his cue from the views of U.S.-allied Sunni Arab governments — such as Egypt, Jordan and Saudi Arabia — who have long worried that Shiite Iran could destabilize the region.

Iran's neighbors, Mack says, worry about Iranian nuclear development but have always thought that the way to contain Iran's ambitions for military and political hegemony is to lure them into a web of economic relations. They prefer to see Iran "trading with them and with the rest of the world," says Mack.

But Israelis take a less benign view of Iran, seeing it as a "regional and global" threat, says political scientist Steinberg, of Israel's Bar-Ilan University. "Iran is a revolutionary power that seeks to play a major role on the world stage and promote radical Shiite Islam in the process." The threat is all the greater, he says, because Israel has no diplomatic options with Iran, so there is no way to negotiate with them. Moreover, points out Steinberg, "There is such a strong Iranian commitment to the destruction of Israel."

Ansari, of the University of St. Andrews and author of a new book on the Iran-U.S. standoff, contends that Iran "represents a greater threat to its own people," partly because of the repression that's been imposed on the Iranian people. The Iranian government regulates women's attire and journalistic expression and has vetoed candidates for public office.

"If the Iranians back down [on the nuclear-development standoff], then the government falls," he continues. "They staked everything on this crisis. They need a national crisis, with this great righteous indignation. If they back down on this, they haven't got anything else to stand on. People in the West know this, so the potential for confrontation becomes greater." ■

BACKGROUND

New Middle East

Shortly after the dawn of the 20th century, Jewish immigration to the Middle East took on major proportions. Starting in 1904, Jews escaping Russia's anti-Semitic pogroms (massacres) began creating a state-within-a-state in a region of the Ottoman Empire known as Palestine. Jews who began calling in the 19th century for Jews to settle in "Zion," their historic homeland, argued that Europe had never accepted their presence and never would. The Zionists based their claim to Palestine on the Jews' ancient presence there, which had ended when the Romans destroyed Jerusalem and dispersed most of the Jews in 70 A.D.

The nascent state grew even stronger following a third wave of immigration after World War I, when Great Britain took over Palestine under a mandate from the League of Nations, the predecessor of the United Nations. Under the so-called Balfour Declaration of 1917, Britain had committed itself to allowing establishment of a Jewish "national home" in Palestine, with the proviso that "nothing shall be done which may prejudice the civil and religious rights of existing non-Jewish communities in Palestine." The measure was endorsed by France, Italy, Japan and, in principle — unanimously — by Congress in 1922. [27]

Following the murder of 6 million Jews by the Nazis in World War II, thousands of Holocaust survivors flooded into Palestine, many joining the ranks of a determined and effective underground army — the Haganah. Its actions, and Palestinian Arab resistance to growing Zionist strength, brought the United Nations to vote for creation of separate countries for Arabs and Jews.

But after Israel declared itself an independent nation on May 14, 1948, the Arab League went to war to reclaim all of Palestine. Israel defeated the league in what Israelis call the "War of Independence." Palestinians call it "the catastrophe" ("Naqba") because it led to the departure or expulsion of hundreds of thousands of Arabs from the new country of Israel

Continued on p. 900

Chronology

1917-1945
Ottoman Empire collapses and is divvied up between World War I victors.

1917
British Foreign Secretary Arthur Balfour commits the British government to support a Jewish homeland in Palestine, with the rights of Arabs respected.

1926
Lebanon, which had been administered by France, formally gains sovereignty and later devises a power-sharing system among its religious/ethnic communities.

1945
Discovery of the vast extent of the Nazi mass murder of Jews intensifies Zionists' fight for a Jewish homeland.

1948-1967
Founding of Israel opens a new era in the Middle East — one largely defined by war.

May 14, 1948
Israel declares itself a nation, then defeats Arab neighbors, who vow to destroy Israel.

1953
Central Intelligence Agency helps overthrow Iranian prime minister who wants to nationalize the country's oil resources.

1964
Palestinian exiles create the Palestine Liberation Organization (PLO) to reclaim their homeland by force.

June 7, 1967
Israeli troops enter East Jerusalem in the "Six-Day War."

1972-1979
Era of large-scale anti-Israeli terrorism begins.

Sept. 5, 1972
PLO gunmen seize 11 Israeli athletes at Munich Olympic Games; all the athletes die in a rescue attempt.

1975
Civil war begins in Lebanon.

1979
Shah of Iran is overthrown; militants take U.S. Embassy personnel hostage.

1982-1990
Israel invades Lebanon, sparking the birth of Hezbollah.

1982
Israel invades Lebanon to fight Palestinian guerrillas.

1983
Hezbollah terrorists bomb Marine barracks in Beirut, killing 241.

1986
Reagan administration's covert dealings with Iran spark a scandal.

1993-2000
Peace process between Israel and Palestinians makes major progress but then falters.

1993
Israeli Prime Minister Rabin and PLO leader Arafat sign "Oslo Accords" for Palestinian self-rule.

1995
Jewish terrorist assassinates Rabin.

2000
Israel's occupation of Lebanon ends.

2001-2006
Anti-West sentiment in Middle East goes global when Arab terrorists attack the United States on Sept. 11, 2001; similar attacks follow in Europe, Asia.

Oct. 8, 2001
U.S.-led coalition invades Afghanistan to topple the Taliban regime.

2002
President George W. Bush names Iran as part of "axis of evil."

March 20, 2003
United States and allies invade Iraq to topple Saddam Hussein.

Feb. 14, 2005
Former Prime Minister Rafiq Hariri of Lebanon is assassinated.

June 25, 2005
Populist Mahmoud Ahmadinejad is elected president of Iran.

Jan. 26, 2006
Hamas wins a decisive majority in the Palestinian parliament.

June 25, 2006
Palestinian guerrillas capture Israeli soldier, demand release of captured Palestinians.

July 12, 2006
Hezbollah guerrillas capture two Israeli soldiers, setting off war in south Lebanon.

Sept. 19, 2006
Ahmadinejad challenges the right of the U.S. and other Western powers to oversee Iranian nuclear development.

Comments on 'Israel Lobby' Raise Furor

Two prominent American political scientists have raised a furor in academic and foreign-policy circles by arguing George W. Bush and other American presidents have made decisions about the Middle East — including the war in Iraq — based on what's best for Israel, not the United States.

Critics say the professors perpetuate the centuries-old anti-Semitic charge that Jews manipulate governments to their advantage while others pay the price.

Supporters claim that Stephen M. Walt of Harvard and John J. Mearsheimer of the University of Chicago are being tarred because they dared to open debate on a subject considered taboo in respectable circles. "For many American Jews, there is no daylight in their thinking between American interests and Israel's interest," said historian Tony Judt of New York University, a Jewish critic of Israeli policy. "The two have blended. If you talk about the problem of our relations with Israel, people can only assume you have another agenda."

Judt spoke at a heated debate in New York City on Sept. 28, where Mearsheimer denied any anti-Jewish bias in his *London Review of Books* article of March 23. "I don't think a case can be made that the piece is anti-Semitic," he said. "People sometimes . . . think we're talking about a cabal or all-powerful conspiracy. That is not what we are talking about. We are talking about an organized interest group . . . that works assiduously on behalf of Israel. There is absolutely nothing wrong with that." [1]

But Walt and Mearsheimer call the "Israel Lobby" far more powerful than its counterparts. "This situation has no equal in American political history," they write. "The overall thrust of U.S. policy in the [Mideast] region is due almost entirely to U.S. domestic politics, and especially to the activities of the 'Israel Lobby.' Other special-interest groups have managed to skew U.S. foreign policy in directions they favored, but no lobby has managed to divert U.S. foreign policy as far from what the American national interest would otherwise suggest."

Many critics ridiculed Mearsheimer and Walt's views. They "think that a population of 5 million Jews — less than 2 percent . . . of the U.S. population — is somehow able to bully and confuse 295 million non-Jews into consistently acting against their own true interests," Alan Dershowitz, a law professor at Harvard Law School, wrote in a 44-page rejoinder. [2]

Mearsheimer and Walt include Christian evangelicals and other non-Jews in their definition of the lobby. [3] In any event, no one disputes that Israel enjoys a favored place in U.S. foreign policy. Since 1976, Israel has been biggest recipient of U.S. domestic and military aid, according to the Congressional Research Service. In 1998, the United States readjusted its aid package to Israel, increasing military aid from $1.8 billion a year to $2.4 billion annually over the next 10 years while eliminating $1.2 billion a year in economic support. [4]

Critics also fault Mearsheimer and Walt's view of the Israel lobby as far more extensive than the influential American Israel Public Affairs Committee (AIPAC). AIPAC is part of a "a loose coalition" of administration officials, columnists, think tanks and other people and institutions "who actively work to shape U.S. foreign policy in a pro-Israel direction" even if they disagree on some issues, according to the political scientists.

By that broad definition, critics say, Israel supporters who favor peace with Palestinians work hand-in-hand with pro-Israel hawks who distrust the Palestinians and view peace as a mirage, at least for the foreseeable future. "You're talking about two very different kinds of constituencies," former U.S. diplomat Dennis Ross told Mearsheimer during the New York debate. "So how can they both be part of the Israel lobby?"

Continued from p. 898

— the root of the present-day conflict between the Palestinians and the Jewish state. [28]

Lebanon also emerged from the Ottoman Empire. But Israel's northern neighbor had enjoyed autonomous status after France extended protection to the French-oriented Maronite Christian community, a major force in a tiny country with the most religiously diverse population in the Middle East. After the Ottoman collapse, France supervised the creation of a Greater Lebanon consisting of several Ottoman provinces, including territory that was historically part of Syria. Lebanon gained sovereignty in 1926.

In 1943, Lebanon's ethnic and religious populations — Maronite and Greek Catholics, Greek Orthodox, Armenians and Sunni, Shiite and Druze (a Shiite offshoot) Muslims — cobbled together a National Pact. Basically power would be shared based on each group's percentage of the population and its historic role.

Persia (as Iran was known until the early 20th century) — never belonged to the Ottoman Empire, nor are its people Arabs. It has the Muslim world's only Shiite religious government. In 1905, the Persian Empire transformed itself into a quasi-democracy after a revolution forced the shah (emperor) to adopt a constitution and establish a "consultative assembly." Persia's oil reserves, discovered several decades earlier, at that point were controlled by the British.

Early Conflicts

Israel's founding opened the series of Middle Eastern wars that continues to this day. The 1948 war of independence, in which Israel defeated the Arab League — Egypt, Syria, Lebanon, Transjordan (now Jordan), Iraq, Saudi Arabia and Yemen — was followed by the Six-Day War of 1967 and the Yom Kippur War of 1973. After the Six-Day War against the region's major Arab countries — led by

Mearsheimer said he and Walt acknowledged that members of the lobby disagree about many issues but "make a significant effort in their daily lives to advance Israel's interests."

Others have advanced a deeper critique of the professors' notion of a "national interest" that can be influenced by lobbies. "Policy in the modern American system is not determined by a council of the learned and the disinterested," wrote Dmitri K. Simes, founding president of the Nixon Center think tank. "Fundamental to our democracy is the notion that those with an interest in shaping decisions should organize, advise and advocate — and anyone who wants a role needs a lobby." Simes added that abandoning Israel "would embolden the Jewish state's enemies and other extremists, destabilizing the whole region." [5]

But Simes also defended Mearsheimer and Walt against the accusation of anti-Semitism and argued that America's Israel policy gets too little scrutiny. [6]

Martin Indyk, a former U.S. ambassador to Israel, said Mearsheimer and Walt's standard for defining members of the Israel lobby shows up when they state their case about the lobby and the Iraq war. "They take neoconservatives, who were definitely in favor of the war, but because they happen to be Jewish, they're named as part of the lobby," Indyk said during the debate. He was referring to a faction made up largely of Jewish political writers and activists who started out as socialists or Democrats and turned to the right in the 1960s and '70s. [7]

Indyk, who heads the Brookings Institution's Saban Center for Middle East Studies, recalled that he had called publicly for Congress to reduce foreign aid to Israel in order to help rebuild Lebanon. How does advocating reducing aid for Israel fit the Mearsheimer-Walt theory? Indyk asked, his voice dripping with contempt. Mearsheimer didn't respond directly.

Mearsheimer and Walt call "pressure from Israel and the lobby" a "critical element" in the Bush administration's decision to invade Iraq. "The war was motivated in good part by a desire to make Israel more secure," they write.

Some members of the Israeli foreign-policy establishment rebutted the idea of an Israeli push for war with Iraq. Shlomo Ben-Ami, a former foreign minister and a member of Israel's peace camp, noted in the debate that Israeli policymakers had viewed Iran as posing a bigger threat to Israel than Saddam Hussein's Iraq. Moreover, he said, the Bush administration's rationale that toppling Hussein would spur the birth of Middle Eastern democracy was a "neoconservative fantasy." He added, "Democracy in the Middle East right now is bound to create instability, and nobody [in Israel] is interested in that."

---

[1] John J. Mearshimer and Stephen M. Walt, "The Israel Lobby," *London Review of Books,*, March 23, 2006, www.lrb.co.uk/v28/n06/mear01_.html. For the full version of the paper, see Mearshimer and Walt, "The Israel Lobby and U.S. Foreign Policy," March 2006, http://ksgnotes1.harvard.edu/Research/wpaper.nsf/rwp/RWP06-011/$File/rwp_06_011_walt.pdf. For a video recording of the New York debate, see www.scribemedia.org/2006/10/11/israel-lobby.

[2] For the full text of Dershowitz' response, see Alan Dershowitz, "Debunking the Newest — and Oldest — Jewish Conspiracy, a Reply to the Mearsheimer-Walt 'Working Paper,' " Harvard Law School, April 2006, www.ksg.harvard.edu/research/working_papers/dershowitzreply.pdf.

[3] For background on evangelicals' support of Israel, see Nicole Gaouette, "Evangelical Christians Support Israel," in "Middle East Peace," *CQ Researcher*, Jan. 21, 2005, p. 68.

[4] For details, see Carol Migdalovitz, "Israel: Background and Relations with the United States," Congressional Research Service, updated Aug. 31, 2006, pp. 17-18, www.fas.org/sgp/crs/mideast/IB82008.pdf.

[5] Dmitri K. Simes, "Unrealists," *The National Interest*, June 1, 2006.

[6] *Ibid.*

[7] For background, see Stephen Schwartz, *Is It Good for the Jews: The Crisis of America's Israel Lobby* (2006), pp. 44-74; 96-128.

Syria and Egypt — Israel occupied lands now known as the Palestinian territories — the West Bank (of the Jordan River) and the Gaza Strip, which runs along the Mediterranean.

During the second half of the 20th century, nationalism was rising among Palestinian Arabs, who demanded their homeland back. By 1964, a group of exiles that included Fatah leader Yasser Arafat founded the Palestine Liberation Organization (PLO), bringing together religiously oriented political activists and left-wing Arab nationalists. The following year, they declared an armed struggle against Israel to reclaim the formerly Arab lands.

Awaiting the day when they could retake their old homeland, the Palestinians set up states-within-states in neighboring Lebanon and Jordan. Alarmed at the possibility of losing control of his country, Jordan's King Hussein launched a massive attack on them. Thousands were killed in a bloody episode that became known as "Black September." PLO members and their sympathizers fled to Lebanon.

Though powerless to defeat Israel, Palestinians took their fight to the international arena. Most notoriously, a PLO terrorist cell named Black September kidnapped 11 Israeli athletes at the 1972 Olympic Games in Munich, Germany; all died during a rescue attempt.

In Lebanon, the PLO lent its strength to the growing Palestinian state-within-a-state, exacerbating already strained relations with Lebanon's religious and ethnic communities. In 1975, civil war broke out in which the Palestinians joined a Muslim coalition fighting a Christian alliance. The war persisted on and off for 15 years.

Meanwhile, in neighboring Iran, the public grew increasingly bitter over British control of their oil resources. After World War II, as the British Empire was fading, the United States became the dominant Western power in the Middle East, where Washington depended on keeping petroleum flowing to the booming U.S. market. When

Iranians in 1951 elected a prime minister, Mohammed Mossadegh, who pushed to nationalize Iran's oil production, the CIA — aided by the British — launched a coup and helped to install a prime minister more friendly to the West. For many Iranians, the 1953 coup marked the emergence of the United States as an imperialist force bent on controlling an oil-rich but independent nation.

Iran's monarch, Shah Mohammad Reza Pahlavi maintained friendly relations with Israel. But the monarchy's corruption, repression and ties to the West — as well as the shah's efforts to expand women's rights — did not sit well with traditional clerics.

AFP/Getty Images/Ali Dia

U.N. soldiers install barbed wire around their camp in the southern Lebanese village of Blat, where they are working alongside Lebanese troops to enforce a cease-fire between Hezbollah and Israel. By the time the United Nations-sponsored cease-fire took effect on Aug. 14, at least 1,110 Lebanese and 42 Israeli civilians had died, along with 118 Israeli troops and an undisclosed number of Hezbollah fighters.

War and Revolution

On Jan. 16, 1979, a revolution that united left-wing students, conservative bazaar merchants and clerics toppled the shah. The Ayatollah Ruhollah Khomeini became the revolution's leader after he returned from exile. The ayatollah — a Shiite honorific title meaning "Sign of God" — helped transform Iran into a state dominated by authoritarian clerics claiming divine inspiration.

Iran's new ideology — including virulent hostility toward the United States — hit home on Nov. 4, 1979. Militant Iranian students — angered by the U.S. government's decision to allow the ousted shah to enter the United States for cancer treatment — seized the American Embassy in Tehran, taking some 90 Americans hostage. *

President Jimmy Carter — whose diplomatic efforts to free the hostages also failed — had brokered an historic peace treaty between Israel and its biggest neighbor, Egypt, just months before the Iranian hostage-taking.

Meanwhile, the civil war in Lebanon was intensifying along with the strength of the Palestine Liberation Organization (PLO). For Israel, that development spelled danger, a presentiment that was confirmed in 1981, when Lebanon-based Palestinians fired rockets into Israel.

Israel responded by invading Lebanon the next year, ostensibly to stop the attacks. But Israeli leaders soon revealed their real goal: to eliminate the PLO from Lebanon altogether. In effect, Israel sided with the Christian militias battling the PLO and other Muslim forces in Lebanon's civil war. Israeli troops pushed through southern Lebanon to Beirut, besieging the city to force a PLO evacuation. After a Christian militia leader was assassinated, the Israelis moved into the Palestinians' west Beirut stronghold.

Israeli forces then eased the way for Christian militias to enter the Palestinian refugee camps of Sabra and Shatila, where the militias massacred as many as 3,000 civilians. Defense Minister Ariel Sharon was forced out of office for approving the militias' entry into the camps. Ever since, Sabra and Shatila have been rallying cries for critics and enemies of Israel.

Israel pushed the PLO into exile in Tunisia, leaving an opening for a new Muslim force in Lebanon. Iran stepped into the breach, helping to form Hezbollah, a political movement and militia representing Iran's religious compatriots — the downtrodden, rural Shiites of southern Lebanon.

Even though Israel withdrew in 1985 to a buffer zone in southern Lebanon, the country's civil war continued. President Reagan sent U.S. Marines as peacekeepers but pulled them out after a Hezbollah truck bomb blew up their barracks, killing 241 Americans.

---

* After holding 52 of the hostages for 444 days, the students freed them in January 1981 in a deal negotiated with incoming President Ronald Reagan. In return, the United States released to Iran about $5 billion in Iranian assets held abroad that Washington had frozen. By then, a daring helicopter raid launched by Reagan's predecessor, Jimmy Carter, to free the hostages had failed because of a raging sandstorm.

Eventually, Syria helped bring the Lebanese civil war to an end — but at a high price: Syria retained a military presence in Lebanon and dominated Lebanese affairs. It also supported Hezbollah, which began a sustained guerrilla campaign against Israeli troops and their Christian allies in southern Lebanon. Although Syria is not a majority-Shiite country, Hezbollah was seen as a natural ally because it was ferociously anti-Israel and supported Syria's dominance of Lebanese politics.

Meanwhile, large-scale, conventional war had broken out to the east after Iraqi dictator Saddam Hussein attacked the new Iranian regime — hoping to seize oil-rich territory and humble a historic rival. The eight-year war, in which the U.S. leaned toward Iraq, ended in 1988. Approximately 1 million people were killed, including thousands of Iranians and Iraqi Kurds, after Hussein attacked them with poison gas. In military terms, Iraq won.

The victory emboldened Hussein to invade another neighbor — tiny, oil-rich Kuwait — in 1990. The move alarmed both the United States and Saudi Arabia, Kuwait's neighbor and America's strategic, oil-supplying ally. President George H. W. Bush organized a multinational coalition to liberate Kuwait, a goal accomplished in the so-called "100-hour war."

But Bush decided not to send forces into Baghdad to topple Hussein. He and one of his top advisers, Brent Scowcroft, later wrote that they had feared American forces becoming "an occupying power in a bitterly hostile land." [29]

Hope, Despair

In 1993, as President Bill Clinton looked on, Arafat — then the undisputed leader of the Palestinians — shook hands with Israeli Prime Minister Yitzhak Rabin in the Rose Garden of the White House, marking their signing of the historic Oslo Agreement. The pact enabled Arafat to return to the Israeli-occupied Palestinian territories for the first time in 27 years, establishing the Palestinian Authority as a proto-government. [30]

Two years later, in 1993, a Jewish extremist assassinated Rabin, and Palestinian terrorists killed 54 Israelis with bombs, stalling the peace process.

In Iran, a political crisis led to election of reformist Khatami as president in 1997. Although conservative clerics still held ultimate control, hopes rose for restoration of relations with the United States.

Those hopes rose after Khatami, in a 1998 interview on CNN, condemned terrorism "in all its forms and manifestations." And he insisted that the 1979-80 hostage crisis grew out of a revolutionary climate from the past. "Today," he said, "our new society has been institutionalized . . . and there is no need for unconventional methods of expression." [31]

Clinton administration officials noted, however, that Khatami hadn't ended support for terrorism and the development of weapons of mass destruction. "We will . . . judge what is significant, based on actions, not words," State Department spokesman James Rubin declared. [32]

In southern Lebanon, years of low-intensity warfare between the Israeli occupiers and Hezbollah militia were taking a political toll in Israel — especially since most Israelis saw the conflict with Palestinians in the Israeli-occupied West Bank and Gaza Strip as a more pressing concern. Finally, in 2000, after 18 years of occupation, the Israeli government released Lebanese prisoners and exited Lebanon. Syrian forces remained.

A year later, the 9/11 attacks radically changed the Middle East equation. President Bush declared the United States would use all its power against radical Islamists, starting with a coalition-led invasion of Afghanistan to oust the ultraconservative Taliban regime, which was harboring al Qaeda leader Osama bin Laden, architect of the terrorist attacks.

The Taliban's hostility to Iran's Shiites prompted Iran to quietly help the United States in the invasion. For similar reasons, Iran did not oppose the 2003 overthrow of Iraq's Hussein, a hated enemy whose opponents included a domestic Shiite majority. [33]

In Lebanon, the civil-war scars were finally healing and Rafik Hariri, an energetic and popular prime minister, was overseeing the rebuilding of Beirut and the rebirth of the nation's tourism industry. But in 2005, after the end of his term, Hariri was assassinated by a car bomb, which many Lebanese blamed on Syria, given his opposition to Syrian control. Within months, Syrian troops had been forced out of Lebanon by a popular movement that did not include Hezbollah.

Another sign of hope appeared on the Israeli-Palestinian front. Sharon, who had returned from political obscurity to become prime minister in 2001, pushed through a plan to withdraw the Israeli presence from the Gaza Strip. The withdrawal was completed in September 2005, but optimism about the future was tempered by Israel's retention of control of the main border crossings between Gaza and Israel and Gaza and Egypt. That severely limited the commerce on which Gaza's economic future depended, but Israel said it was worried about weapons and fighters entering Gaza through Egypt. [34]

Secretary of State Rice later traveled to Jerusalem to broker a deal to reopen the Rafah border crossing between Gaza and Egypt, placing it under Palestinian control. [35]

That same year, firebrand Ahmadinejad was elected president of Iran, succeeding the reformist Khatami. ■

CURRENT SITUATION

New 'Peace Process'?

Since the war in Lebanon ended, Secretary of State Rice has been encouraging more cooperation between the Israelis and Palestinians. But even that modest objective has eluded her as tensions rise between Israel and the Palestinians and among the Palestinians themselves.

In a trip to the region in early October, Rice sought to reactivate the stalled Gaza border deal she helped put in place last year. But even the reactivation plan — which President Abbas' U.S. adviser Edward Abington called "pretty minimalist" — never fully took effect. [36] In fact, Rice's goals were so modest that one Israeli expert speculated her border agenda concealed a more strategic goal — convincing President Bush that his policies aren't working.

"Maybe, just maybe, she was going in order to report back to the president: 'Mr. President, I tried to get movement on building our alliances in the region. If you don't give me a mandate on the Israel-Palestine question, I don't think I can deliver.' " [37]

Levy and other critics of current policy reject conditions set by the Bush administration and its fellow members of the Middle Eastern "quartet" (the United Nations, the European Union and Russia) for allowing Hamas access to its own funds overseas: renunciation of violence, recognition of Israel's right to exist and acceptance of all previous agreements between Israel and the Palestinian Authority.

Secretary Rice has said repeatedly that Hamas can't expect to be treated as a governing party while holding onto its original guerrilla identity. "Either you are a peaceful political party or a violent terrorist group — but you cannot be both," Rice said in her Oct. 11, 2006, speech to the American Task Force on Palestine. [38]

Rice was speaking in an atmosphere still dominated by memories of last summer's Hezbollah-Israeli war, in which U.S. support for Israel was seen in the Arab street as a dramatic departure from America's historic role as a relatively unbiased broker in the conflict and as part of new, worldwide, anti-Muslim crusade being waged by the United States. [39]

Critics of the Bush administration argue that the conditions set out by Rice prevent Hamas from accepting a long-term cease-fire. "They are not prepared to recognize Israel or accept Israel, but they are inching toward the notion that they are going to have to live in a two-state reality," Malley, of the International Crisis Group, told the New America Foundation. "They believe that without compromising their basic ideology they can reach an accommodation with Israel that would entail greater freedom, greater economic prosperity and greater control over land."

But for now, at least, few think the Bush administration and its international partners are ready to drop the conditions on dealing with Hamas. And U.S. support for Abbas' Fatah party has further embittered Hamas. In mid-October, a Hamas spokesman accused the Bush administration of trying to use Fatah as a stooge in its "crusade" against Muslims. "They want tools for this war," he said. [40]

AFP/Getty Images/Marwan Naamani

Farmer Ali Wansa lost his leg when an Israeli cluster bomb exploded as he was working on his land in southern Lebanon. Since the month-long war between Israel and Hezbollah ended on Aug. 14, more than 20 people — including five bomb-disposal experts — have been killed and another 100 wounded by the controversial devices. About a million undetonated cluster bombs — designed to explode into flesh-ripping fragments — still litter the Lebanese countryside, according to U.N. experts.

Iran's Nuclear Challenge

The detonation of a nuclear device by North Korea on Oct. 9 added another layer of complication and danger to the standoff over Iran's nuclear ambitions by encouraging its defiance.

"'It looks like the message of North Korea's test for Iran was that it can

Continued on p. 906

At Issue:

Is U.S. support for Israel the main obstacle to peace in the Middle East?

HUSSEIN IBISH
SENIOR FELLOW, AMERICAN TASK FORCE ON PALESTINE

WRITTEN FOR *CQ RESEARCHER*, OCTOBER 2006

yes

U.S. support for Israel is like "friends who let friends drive drunk." They are both central players in a dangerous and potentially destructive scenario. U.S. support for Israel per se is not problematic, but the American approach for at least the past decade has been fundamentally flawed in at least two crucial ways that have undoubtedly helped prolong the conflict.

First, American support for Israel is, in effect, unconditional. Our aid and diplomatic support are not contingent on Israel's cooperation with stated American policy goals, including the creation of a Palestinian state. This is most dramatically illustrated by Israel's ongoing settlement activity, every element of which complicates — and in the long run may preclude — an end to the conflict based on two states living side-by-side in peace.

By making our support for Israel effectively independent of their actions that undermine U.S. policies, we hand our Israeli friends the political equivalent of a bottle of bourbon and the keys to the Corvette, with hearty wishes to have a good time. Making support for Israel conditional on their cooperation in the quest for peace would be a boon not just to Americans but to Israelis as well. It is plainly an indispensable requirement for realizing the only viable solution to the conflict.

Second, American support for Israel, especially in Congress, is often framed as exclusive of support for — or acknowledgement of the legitimate rights of — Palestinians and other Arabs. Too many American leaders have accepted the false notion of a zero-sum relationship between Israel and the Palestinians and speak and act as if anything good for one is by definition bad for the other.

If the United States is going to be a force for resolving the conflict in the interests of all parties rather than prolonging it by unconditionally supporting one side over the other, it is imperative that American leaders recognize that we can — and must — be friends to both Israel and the Palestinians simultaneously. This is possible not least because the future of both peoples depends on an end to the conflict based on the creation of a Palestinian state in the occupied territories living alongside Israel in peace.

Sincere friends of both Israel and Palestine should work together to ensure that American policies push both peoples in this direction, for their own good and ours.

DAVID ELCOTT
EXECUTIVE DIRECTOR, ISRAEL POLICY FORUM

WRITTEN FOR *CQ RESEARCHER*, OCTOBER 2006

no

I am a passionate advocate of maximizing Jewish impact on American policies — from foreign affairs to immigration, from human and civil rights to church-state separation.

Those who argue that the pro-Israel lobby has forced American governments to support policies detrimental to our interests or to the forces of peace are wrong.

We function within a democratic framework, which we hope reflects what Americans actually support. There is a vigorous history of popular support for Israel and a belief that, while Israel must do its part to bring peace, the major obstacle to peace is not Israel. Americans identify with the State of Israel and see it as an ally. The attacks on Israel this summer only deepened these beliefs. Pro-Israel groups may well nurture those views, but there is a bedrock support for Israel.

In comparison, huge investments in public relations and a close relationship with the Bush family have not changed negative American public opinion about Saudi Arabia.

Our organization advocates on behalf of Israel. There are times that we join our pro-Israel allies, and there are times that we do not. We differed most recently over how much leverage to give President Bush in diplomacy with Palestinians. While American Jews overwhelmingly support a two-state solution, many do not. There are Jewish leaders who advocate dismantling the settlements and ending targeted assassinations and unnecessary incursions into Palestinian territory. Our community is diverse. Claims that there is a monolithic Jewish machine controlling American policy says more about the critic than about the Israel lobby.

It is false to claim that the United States will not negotiate with Hamas because of the American Israel Public Affairs Committee (AIPAC), or that it is unwilling to talk to Syria because of the Israel Policy Forum. I only wish we had the clout attributed to us.

Looking at the full scope of global U.S. behavior, the way America supports Israel is determined by this government's world view. If you do not agree with its policies, speak to the White House, not the Israel lobby.

But this is clear: If anyone had the unequivocal answer on how to provide for a secure Israel next to a safe Palestine, the pro-Israel lobby would be in full-throated support. Until that day, those of us who advocate in Washington for Israel will persevere even as we may disagree over some of the specifics. That is our job and the right of citizenship we uphold. And that is ultimately very good for America.

Continued from p. 904

also continue its program . . . if they act forcefully and confrontationally," said Saeed Leylaz, an economist and political analyst in Tehran. [41]

Although the U.N. Security Council on Oct. 14 banned North Korea from importing materials to make weapons of mass destruction and also barred importation of luxury goods, China's ambassador to the U.N. said China would not search ships bound for North Korea. [42] "Inspections yes, but inspection is different than interdiction and interception," he said. China fears destabilization of North Korea, a neighbor, could have serious repercussions in China. [43]

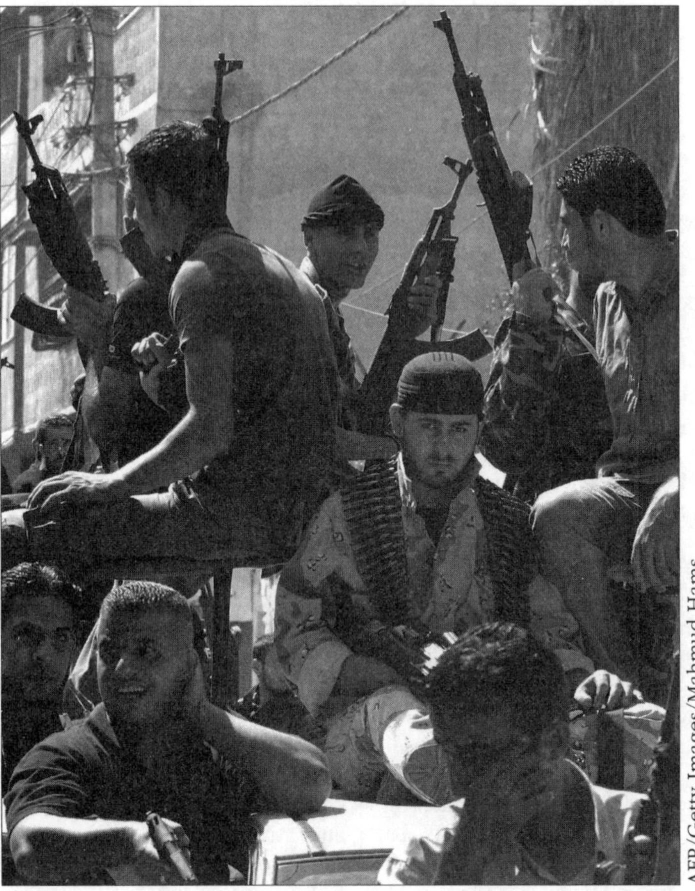

AFP/Getty Images/Mahmud Hams

Palestinian security forces patrol Gaza City on Oct. 2, 2006, following a deadly clash between police loyal to Palestinian Authority President Mahmoud Abbas and militia loyal to the Hamas-led government. Feuding between Abbas' Fatah movement and Hamas, which took power in March, threatens efforts to create a national unity government.

Whatever example North Korea may set for Iran, the Islamic republic was already inclined to defy Western attempts to supervise and limit nuclear research and development. Iran ignored the Security Council's Aug. 31 deadline on halting uranium enrichment while the International Atomic Energy Agency (IAEA) — the U.N. nuclear watchdog — determined if the process was aimed at producing weapons-grade material. On the deadline day, President Ahmadinejad said Iran "will not accept for one moment any bullying, invasion and violation of its rights." [44]

Those rights, he told the U.N. General Assembly on Sept. 19, include development of nuclear power. "All our nuclear activities are transparent, peaceful and under the watchful eyes of the IAEA inspectors," he said. [45] But the atomic agency says Iran has denied inspectors access to records as well as permission to take uranium samples. [46]

Because Iran has paid no price for defying Washington and the United Nations, the Ahmadinejad government would see no reason not to maintain its stance, says the American Enterprise Institute's Rubin. "Sincere as Bush may be, he has no credibility in the world. His rhetoric time and time again has proven empty."

But just as Hezbollah misjudged Israel's response to a cross-border raid, Iran risks misjudging how far the United States can be pushed. "They're going to keep pushing until we push back," Rubin says, referring to military action against Iranian nuclear installations. Only "regime change" — from within — could ensure that Iranian nuclear ambitions remain peaceful, he says.

North Korea's nuclear test on Oct. 9 was a further indication the superpowers' decades-old efforts to prevent further nuclear proliferation appear to be breaking down, say experts. [47] And Asian and Middle Eastern countries are especially likely to want the most destructive weaponry available.

"Nuclear weapons can be attractive for the security benefits," said Daniel Pinkston, director of the East Asia Nonproliferation Program at the private Monterey Institute for International Affairs. "Unless you can resolve the security dilemma, you aren't going to resolve the problem." [48]

Rubin and other experts say Iran's apparent nuclear ambitions will likely encourage Egypt and Saudi Arabia to follow suit. Meanwhile, Israel, which is believed to have had nukes for years, views Iran's plans as a threat.

"Israeli experts are divided between those who feel [an] Iranian nuclear weapon is one that Israel cannot live with, and those who feel that Israel needs to increase its deterrence but that a pre-emptive strike against Iranian nuclear capability is not feasible," says Steinberg of Bar-Ilan University. The first camp is expanding, however, because Israelis don't think U.S. action against Iran is likely. "The view is the president is weak and isolated, and that in the military and Congress there is not much support for taking on another major Islamic country." ■

OUTLOOK

Waning Washington?

For nearly 80 years, instability has been a constant in the Middle East — a primary source of the world's oil and the cradle of the globe's three great monotheistic religions. And since 1979, the tempo of revolution, war, invasion and assassination has quickened.

Although experts on the area agree there probably won't be any dramatic changes in a political way of life marked by violence and abrupt transformation, they differ on where the big shifts will take place during the next 10 years, and what new forces may emerge.

Some regional leaders worry about the "internationalization" of the Iraq war. Nouri al-Maliki, Iraq's embattled prime minister, told a news conference on Oct. 25 that "friendly and neighboring countries" should stop meddling in his country's affairs. He was apparently referring to Iran, which has ties to at least one of Iraq's Shiite militias, and to Syria, which Sunni Muslim terrorists have long been reported to use as a crossing point into Iraq. And neighboring Saudi Arabia, which has a restive Shiite minority, is worried enough about spillover from Shiite-majority Iraq to have arranged a joint call for peace by Sunni and Shiite Iraqi clerics, some of whose followers are killing each other.

Richard Haass, president of the Council on Foreign Relations, sees Washington's power in the region waning because it is bogged down in the Iraq war, unable to broker peaceful coexistence between Israel and the Palestinians and under fire from Islamist radicals — some of whom, ironically, have been empowered by elections encouraged by the Bush administration. Within the region, he says, Iran's rise appears unstoppable. [49]

And the sudden proliferation of Arab satellite TV channels works to America's disadvantage as well, he writes. "Much of the content — scenes of violence and destruction in Iraq; images of mistreated Iraqi and Muslim prisoners; suffering in Gaza, the West Bank and now Lebanon — has further alienated many people in the Middle East from the United States. As a result, governments in the Middle East now have a more difficult time working openly with the United States." [50]

Haass also sees little chance of peace between Israel and the Palestinians in the foreseeable future, due in part to their political fragmentation.

Hassassian, the Palestinian ambassador to Great Britain, agrees that short-term possibilities for peace are slender but sees peace as inevitable in the longer run. "There will be no military solution to this," he says. "How long can Israel maintain its garrison state and live with a siege mentality? Otherwise, the only way to get rid of the Palestinians is genocide."

For Israeli strategists, the Palestinians make up only one element in a panorama of potential crises. In fact, Schiff, the *Haaretz* military correspondent, argues in a recent analysis that Israel should reorder its list of top issues. "Israel has become quite successful at countering and coping with [Palestinian] suicide attacks," he writes. "Given the much more existential danger that Iran represents, Israel should make Iran its top priority." [51]

But other potential dangers also loom. For instance, says retired Gen. Gazit, the 25-year rule of 78-year-old Egyptian President Hosni Mubarak will be ending at some point in the not-too-distant future. "Will there be another military leader and a cold peace — but one that works?" Gazit asks, referring to the present state of affairs. Or could the Egyptian government take an Islamist turn, creating a government with a religiously based hatred of Israel? he asks.

Salem, the Carnegie Endowment's Beirut-based Middle East program director, finds the same level of uncertainty pervading the future of the entire Middle East. "If things continue as they are, we have a very, very tense region," he says, characterized by "a nuclear Iran, a failed American presence in Iraq with perhaps 10 years of civil war there, Israel embattled and basically a fortress, and Egypt trying to become nuclear. A region essentially in deep turmoil — that's a situation that can go on for several decades."

Alternatively, he says, "The U.S. administration and Israel have realized, to some degree, the limitations of military power and black-and-white solutions." That might make them more willing to accept middle-of-the-road solutions that don't promise ultimate peace but could ease the way for a less threatening future, Salem says. The key would be an agreement with Iran that rewarded a no-nuclear-weapons commitment with trade or other benefits.

But Steinberg of Bar-Ilan University says Israelis tend to hope that the Lebanon war — whatever else it may have done — showed the rest of the region "that Israel has clear red lines and will act disproportionately to defend its interests." ■

Notes

[1] The captured soldiers are Ehud Goldwasser and Eldad Regev. For more details of their capture and the war's beginning see Anthony Shadid and Scott Wilson, "Hezbollah Raid Opens 2nd Front for Israel," *The Washington Post*, July 13, 2006, p. A1.

[2] For more details on the war's effects in both countries, see Anthony Cordesman, "Preliminary 'Lessons' of the Israeli-Hezbollah

War," Center for Strategic and International Studies, Sept. 11, 2006, p. 9, www.csis.org/media/csis/pubs/060911_isr_hez_lessons.pdf; and Jeffrey B. White, "Military Implications of the Israeli-Hizballah War in Lebanon," in "Lessons and Implications of the Israel-Hizballah War: A Preliminary Assessment," Washington Institute for Near East Policy, October 2006, p. 41, www.washingtoninstitute.org/templateC04.php?CID=251.

[3] For details on the cluster bomb issue, see Meron Rapoport, "IDF commander: We fired more than a million cluster bombs in Lebanon," *Haaretz*, Sept. 9, 2006; Michael Slackman, "Israeli Bomblets Plague Lebanon," *The New York Times*, Oct. 6, 2006, p. A1; Anthony Shadid, "In Lebanon, a War's Lethal Harvest," *The Washington Post*, Sept. 26, 2006, p. A1.

[4] For a transcript of Rice's remarks, see "Special Briefing on Travel to the Middle East and Europe," State Department, July 21, 2006, www.state.gov/secretary/rm/2006/69331.htm. Lebanon's population stands at an estimated 3.8 million, roughly half the population of the Washington, D.C.-Baltimore metropolitan area. For details see "CIA Factbook: Lebanon," updated Oct. 5, 2006, www.cia.gov/cia/publications/factbook/geos/le.html#People; and "Population Change and Distribution, Census 2000 Brief," U.S. Census Bureau, April 2001, www.census.gov/prod/2001pubs/c2kbr01-2.pdf.

[5] For details on Gaza events see The Associated Press, "Israel Meets Rockets with Strikes in Gaza," *Los Angeles Times*, Oct. 15, 2006, p. A14; Ken Ellingwood, "9 Slain As Gaza Clashes Continue," *Los Angeles Times*, Oct. 14, 2006, p. A4; Gideon Alon, "Peretz: IDF will strike all Gaza militants, whatever their affiliation," *Haaretz*, Oct. 16, 2006.

[6] For details on the peace plan proposal, see "The Arab-Israeli Conflict: To Reach a Lasting Peace," International Crisis Group, Oct. 5, 2006, www.crisisgroup.org/library/documents/middle_east___north_africa/arab_israeli_conflict/58_the_arab_israeli_conflict___to_reach_a_lasting_peace.pdf.

[7] For details of the post-2000 wave of suicide bombings see "Erased in a Moment: Suicide Bombing Attacks Against Israeli Civilians," Human Rights Watch, October 2002, p. 1, www.hrw.org/reports/2002/isrl-pa/ISRAELPA1002.pdf.

[8] For details see "Helping Palestinians Build a Better Future," Secretary of State Condoleezza Rice, Oct. 11, 2006, www.state.gov/secretary/rm/2006/73895.htm.

[9] A vast quantity of background material is available on the Iranian nuclear standoff. For an introduction, see Scott D. Sagan, "How to Keep the Bomb From Iran," *Foreign Affairs*, September-October 2006, p. 45; Mark Silva, "Iran Gets Overture from U.S.," *Chicago Tribune*, June 1, 2006, p. A1. For recent estimates on Iranian weapons capability, see Alissa J. Rubin, "Confront North Korea; Iran Unfazed by Outrage Over North Korea's Test," *Los Angeles Times*, Oct. 11, 2006, p. A11.

[10] Ze'ev Schiff, "Israel's War With Iran," *Foreign Affairs*, November-December 2006. For details of the proxy war analysis, see Doyle McManus, "Iran Is Bush's Target in Lebanon," *Los Angeles Times*, July 30, 2006, p. A1.

[11] For an introduction to the Iran-Hezbollah history see Ray Takeyh, *Hidden Iran: Paradox and Power in the Islamic Republic* (2006), pp. 200-206.

[12] For details of the denial see The Associated Press, "Iran denies giving aid to Hizbullah," *Jerusalem Post*, July 28, 2006, www.jpost.com/servlet/Satellite?pagename=JPost/JPArticle/ShowFull&cid=1153292020585.

[13] Quoted in McManus, *op. cit.*

[14] For transcript of Nasrallah's speech see "Hezbollah leader addresses 'victory rally' in Lebanon," BBC Middle East Monitoring — Political, Sept. 23, 2006. For an account of the event, see Anthony Shadid, "Hezbollah Chief Defiant at Huge Rally," *The Washington Post*, Sept. 23, 2006, p. A1.

[15] Quoted in Borzou Daragahi, "Hezbollah Chief Indicates Regret for Kidnappings," *Los Angeles Times*, Aug. 28, 2006, p. A4.

[16] For more technical military details of the war see White, *op. cit.*

[17] Quoted in Doug Struck and Tal Zipper, "War Stirs Worries in Israel About Military," *The Washington Post*, Aug. 20, 2006, p. A13. For background on Pedatzur see Ariel Center for Policy Research, www.acpr.org.il/people/rpedatzur.html.

[18] Quoted in Steven Erlanger, "Reservists in Israel Protest Conduct of Lebanon War," *The New York Times*, Aug. 22, 2006, p. A11. For details of the investigative committee formation, see Ken Ellingwood, "Israeli Government Panel to Probe War," *Los Angeles Times*, Sept. 18, 2006, p. A4.

[19] For details on the U.N. force's mission see Michael Slackman, "U.N. Force is Treading Lightly on Lebanese Soil," *The New York Times*, Sept. 25, 2006. p. A1; and Anthony Shadid, "Lebanon Peacekeepers Met With Skepticism," *The Washington Post*, Sept. 20, 2006, p. A12.

[20] Quoted in Slackman, *ibid.*

[21] Quoted in Thom Shanker, "U.N. Peacekeepers Have 'Robust' Mandate, Rice Says," *The New York Times*, Sept. 26, 2006, p. A11.

[22] Quoted in Slackman, *op. cit.*, Sept. 26, 2006.

[23] The full text is available at Joshua Muravchik, "Freedom and the Arab World," *The Weekly Standard*, Dec. 31, 2001, p. 15.

[24] See Nicole Gaouette, "Evangelical Christians Support Israel," in "Middle East Peace," *CQ Researcher*, Jan. 21, 2005, pp. 53-76.

[25] For details on the Palestinian demand, see Greg Myre, "Israeli Leader Defends Incursion Into Gaza," *The New York Times*, July 11, 2006, p. A13. For details on the "targeted killing" policy, see Daniel Byman, "Targeted Killing, American Style; Israel's experience in taking out terrorists offers lessons for the United States," *Los Angeles Times*, Jan. 20, 2006, p. B13.

[26] Bush used the "axis of evil" term in his 2002 State of the Union address. For the entire speech see "President Delivers State of the Union Address, The White House, Jan. 29, 2002, www.whitehouse.gov/news/releases/2002/01/20020129-11.html.

[27] This section is drawn from Reinhard Schulze, *A Modern History of the Islamic World* (2002); Thomas L. Friedman, *From Beirut to Jerusalem*

About the Author

Peter Katel is a *CQ Researcher* staff writer who previously reported on Haiti and Latin America for *Time* and *Newsweek* and covered the Southwest for newspapers in New Mexico. He has received several journalism awards, including the Bartolomé Mitre Award for coverage of drug trafficking from the Inter-American Press Association. He holds an A.B. in university studies from the University of New Mexico. His recent reports include "Immigration Reform," "War on Drugs" and "Whistleblowers."

(1989); Ali M. Ansari, *Confronting Iran: The Failure of American Foreign Policy and the Next Great Conflict in the Middle East* (2006); and Walter Laqueur, *A History of Zionism* (2003). See also "The British Task in Palestine," *Editorial Research Reports, Vol. III*, Sept. 10, 1929, available in *CQ Researcher* Plus Archive, http://library.cqpress.com.

[28] The extent to which Palestinians were forced out or, as traditional Israeli history said, fled, has been furiously debated in Israel since the late 1980s, when a new generation of historians cast doubt on the conventional narrative. For details see Daniel Williams, "New Conflicts of Historic Interest Rack the Heart of the Holy Land," *Los Angeles Times*, May 14, 1989, Part 5, p. 2; Joel Greenberg, "Israel's History, Viewed Candidly, Starts a Storm," *The New York Times*, p. A8, April 10, 1998.

[29] Quoted in George [H. W.] Bush and Brent Scowcroft, *A World Transformed* (1998), p. 489.

[30] For background, see Gaouette, *op. cit.*

[31] Quoted in "Iranian President Favors People to People Dialogue," CNN Worldview, Jan. 7, 1998.

[32] Quoted in "White House Disappointed With Khatami's Remarks," CNN Newsday, Jan. 8, 1998.

[33] For details about Iran and Afghanistan see Barbara Slavin, "Events in Mideast, Afghanistan strain U.S.-Iran Ties," *USA Today*, Jan. 11, 2002. For details about Iran and the invasion of Iraq see Karl Vick, "Few Signs Emerge of U.S.-Iran Thaw," *The Washington Post*, May 3, 2003, p. A13. Also see Kenneth Jost, "Rebuilding Afghanistan," *CQ Researcher*, Dec. 21, 2001, pp. 1041-1064; and David Masci, "Reform in Iran," *CQ Researcher*, Dec. 18, 1998, pp. 1097-1120.

[34] For details of the final Israeli withdrawal, see Scott Wilson, "Israel Lowers Its Flag in Gaza as Last Troops Withdraw," *The Washington Post*, Sept. 12, 2005, p. A14.

[35] For details of the border agreement, see Laura King and Tyler Marshall, "Rice Brokers a Deal to Open Crossing on Gaza-Egypt Border," *Los Angeles Times*, Nov. 16, 2005, p. A3; Scott Wilson, "Israelis Hand Off Gaza Crossing," *The Washington Post*, Nov. 26, 2005, p. A1; and Greg Myre and Steven R. Weisman, "Deal Is Reached on Easing Gaza Crossings," *The New York Times*, Nov. 16, 2005, p. A10.

[36] Quoted in Barbara Slavin, "Rice will try to get Arab allies to join efforts against Iran," *USA Today*, Oct. 2, 2006, p. 11A.

FOR MORE INFORMATION

American Task Force on Palestine, 815 Connecticut Ave., Suite 200, Washington, DC 20006; (202) 887-0177; www.americantaskforce.org. The major U.S. advocate for a Palestinian state that coexists peacefully with Israel.

B'Tselem, 8 HaTa'asiya St. (4th Floor), P.O. Box 53132, Jerusalem 91531, Israel; (972-2) 673-5599; www.btselem.org/English. Israel's leading human-rights organization focuses on treatment of Palestinians in the occupied territories.

Conflicts Forum, (202) 470-1114; www.conflictsforum.com. Advocates dialogue with radical Islamist organizations, including Hamas and Hezbollah.

Jaffee Center for Strategic Studies, Tel-Aviv University, Ramat Aviv, Tel-Aviv 69978, Israel; (972-3)-640-9926; www.tau.ac.il/jcss. A leading Israeli think tank focusing on the Middle East.

Jerusalem Media & Communications Centre, Khalil El Sakakeeni St., PO Box 25047, East Jerusalem 97300; (972-2)583-8266; www.jmcc.org. A news and research service run by Palestinian journalists that focuses on the occupied territories.

Middle East Institute, 1761 N St., N.W., Washington, DC 20036; (202) 785-1141; www.mideasti.org. A Washington think tank founded in 1946 that publishes studies, sponsors conferences and conducts language training.

Middle East Media Research Institute, P.O. Box 2783, Washington, DC 20038; (202) 955-9070; http://memri.org. Disseminates translations of media coverage from Arabic, Farsi and Turkish.

Saban Center for Middle East Policy, The Brookings Institution, 1775 Massachusetts Ave., N.W., Washington, DC 20036; (202) 797-6462; www.brook.edu/fp/saban/sabancenter_hp.htm. A think tank headed by a former U.S. ambassador to Israel focuses on conflict resolution and economic development.

[37] Levy spoke at an Oct. 13, 2006, forum at the New America Foundation, where he heads the Middle East program.

[38] Rice, *op. cit.*

[39] For a detailed version of this argument from a Western critic, see Henry Siegman, "How Bush's Backing Endangers Israel," *The Financial Times* (London), Sept. 15, 2006, p. A11.

[40] For details on the further deterioration of the Hamas-Fatah relationship, see Diaa Hadid, "Hamas: Fatah acting as U.S. Stooge," The Associated Press, Oct. 15, 2006.

[41] For details see Nazila Fathi, "Iran Defies Call to Drop Nuclear Plans," *The New York Times*, Oct. 13, 2006, p. A13.

[42] For details see Colum Lynch and Glenn Kessler, "U.N. Votes to Impose Sanctions on N. Korea," *The Washington Post*, Oct. 15, 2006, p. A1.

[43] For details of the Chinese position, see Thom Shanker and David E. Sanger, "North Korean Fuel Identified as Plutonium," *The New York Times*, Oct. 17, 2006, p. A9.

[44] Quoted in Alissa J. Rubin and Maggie Farley, "U.N. Nuclear Agency Faults Iran," *Los Angeles Times*, Sept. 1, 2006, p. A4.

[45] For full text of speech see "Iranian President Ahmadinejad Delivers Remarks to the U.N. General Assembly, New York," Sept. 19, 2006, Newsmaker Transcripts, www.cq.com.

[46] *Ibid.*

[47] For background, see Mary H. Cooper, "Nuclear Proliferation and Terrorism," *CQ Researcher*, April 2, 2004, pp. 297-320.

[48] Quoted in Alissa J. Rubin, "Confront North Korea; A New Global Nuclear Order," *Los Angeles Times*, Oct. 15, 2006, p. A1.

[49] For more details, see Richard Haass, "The New Middle East," *Foreign Affairs*, November-December 2006.

[50] *Ibid.*

[51] Schiff, *op. cit.*

Bibliography

Selected Sources

Books

Ansari, Ali M., *Confronting Iran: The Failure of American Foreign Policy and the Next Great Conflict in the Middle East*, Basic Books, 2006.

A historian at Scotland's University of St. Andrews analyzes the U.S.-Iran relationship, concluding that the odds don't favor peace.

Clawson, Patrick, and Michael Rubin, *Eternal Iran: Continuity and Chaos*, Palgrave Macmillan, 2005.

Washington think-tank analysts examine Iranian history and also take a downbeat look at U.S.-Iran relations.

Friedman, Thomas L., *From Beirut to Jerusalem*, Farrar Straus Giroux, 1989 (updated 1996).

This fast-moving memoir by the Pulitzer Prize-winning *New York Times* correspondent (now columnist) who covered the 1982 Israeli invasion of Lebanon serves as a good introduction to the region.

Khalidi, Rashid, *The Iron Cage: The Story of the Palestinian Struggle for Statehood*, Beacon Press, 2006.

The director of Columbia University's Middle East Institute has won praise for his dispassionate view of the Palestinians' long and so-far-unsuccessful fight for a country of their own.

Schulze, Reinhard, *A Modern History of the Islamic World*, New York University Press, 2002.

A historian at the University of Berne in Switzerland provides a detailed chronicle of modern Islamic historic.

Articles

Fallows, James, "Will Iran Be Next?" *The Atlantic Monthly*, December 2004.

A journalist (and former speechwriter for President Jimmy Carter) organizes an Iran war game among former military and intelligence officials. They conclude that Iran is indeed developing nuclear weapons but that a U.S. military strike would be disastrous.

Halevy, Efraim, "Romancing Iran," *The New Republic*, Aug. 14, 2006, p. 9.

A former chief of Mossad, Israel's foreign intelligence agency, analyzes Iran's role in the Lebanon war.

Salem, Paul, "The Future of Lebanon," *Foreign Affairs*, November-December 2006.

A Lebanese political scientist analyzes the ways in which the 2006 truce that ended the war can endure.

Shadid, Anthony, "Inside Hezbollah, Big Miscalculations; Militia leaders Caught off Guard by Scope of Israel's Response in War," *The Washington Post*, Oct. 8, 2006, p. A1.

One of America's leading journalistic specialists on the Middle East tells the inside story of the Hezbollah misjudgments behind the 2006 war.

Slackman, Michael, "Who Killed Rafik Hariri? Searching for the Truth in the Middle East," *The New York Times*, Dec. 18, 2005, Sect. 4, p. 5.

A *New York Times* correspondent reports on the difficulty of investigating the assassination of a Lebanese politician-businessman who had aroused the Syrian government's anger.

Vick, Karl, and Dafna Linzer, "Iran Shifts Stance on Nuclear Dialogue," *The Washington Post*, May 24, 2006, p. A1.

Two correspondents report on an optimistic current that was soon dispelled.

Wagner, Matthew, "Purity of Arms," *The Jerusalem Post*, Sept. 27, 2006.

A detailed report investigates Israeli soldiers' and civilians' varied views of the Israeli Defense Force's conduct in Lebanon.

Wright, Robin, "Arabs Pressure Rice on U.S. Peace Efforts," *The Washington Post*, Oct. 4, 2006, p. A4.

A longtime Middle East diplomacy correspondent reports on tough sledding for Secretary of State Condoleezza Rice during her October 2006 trip to the Middle East.

Reports

***Fatal Strikes: Israel's Indiscriminate Attacks Against Civilians in Lebanon*, Human Rights Watch, August 2006.**

The non-governmental organization considered the most reliable, dispassionate investigator of human-rights abuses concludes Israeli forces did little to distinguish between civilian and military targets in last summer's war. Some Israelis and supporters called the report biased.

Migdalovitz, Carol, "Israeli-Arab Negotiations: Background, Conflicts, and U.S. Policy," Congressional Research Service, updated Sept. 1, 2006.

A Middle East expert for Congress' research and analysis agency documents the status and context of efforts to find a peaceful solution to the region's longest-running conflict.

Mearsheimer, John J., and Stephen M. Walt, *The Israel Lobby and U.S. Foreign Policy*, March 2006.

A controversial study by political scientists at the University of Chicago and Harvard concludes that a loosely organized coalition of pro-Israel advocates has bent U.S. foreign policy in a pro-Israel direction, against the best interests of the United States. The report has been fiercely praised and attacked.

The Next Step:

Additional Articles from Current Periodicals

Iran and Human Rights

Applebaum, Anne, "A Web Witness to Iranian Brutality," ***Pittsburgh Post-Gazette*****, Jan. 22, 2006, p. H4.**
Two sisters created an online archive to document the thousands of victims of Iran's Islamic regime.

Boustany, Nora, "Iranian Ex-Lawmaker Alleges Torture," ***The Washington Post*****, Sept. 27, 2006, p. A20.**
Ali Akbar Mousavi Khoini, a former Iranian lawmaker who has been jailed without charges in Tehran, alleged torture and other harsh treatment.

Dareini, Ali Akbar, "Iran Allows Media to Tour a Prison Known for Abuses," ***The Houston Chronicle*****, June 28, 2006, p. A27.**
Iran allowed international media to view the women's section of the infamous Evin prison, from which stories have emerged of torture, forced confessions and floggings.

Ghaemi, Hadi, "For Iran, the Man Is the Message," ***The New York Times*****, June 29, 2006, p. A25.**
Saeed Mortazavi, Tehran's prosecutor general and a notorious human-rights violator, was a member of Iran's delegation to the opening session of the new United Nations Human Rights Council.

Holmes, Kristin E., "Concern Rises Over Baha'is in Iran," ***The Philadelphia Inquirer*****, May 6, 2006, p. B4.**
Baha'i officials believe 200 Iranians have died as a result of persecution because they believe in a faith the Iranian government doesn't like.

Israel-Lebanon War

Cody, Edward, "With Fatal Blasts, War Invades Quiet Enclave of Beirut," ***The Washington Post*****, Aug. 9, 2006, p. A11.**
Lebanon's war invaded a quarter in southern Beruit where Christian and Muslim neighbors thought they were safe from the fighting between Hezbollah and Israel.

Greenberg, Joel, "As Battles Grind On, Support For War is Starting to Fade," ***Chicago Tribune*****, Aug. 11, 2006, p. C6.**
The first cracks in the consensus of support for a military campaign widely seen by Israelis as a justified response to an unprovoked attack are starting to form, as some want the fighting to end.

Palestinians

Allam, Hannah, "Refugee Camp Breeds Fears of Militancy," ***The Miami Herald*****, Oct. 8, 2006, p. A16.**
Ever since Hezbollah declared victory over Israel, militants in Lebanon's largest Palestinian refugee camp, in the port city of Sidon, have grown more aggressive in their calls for armed action against Israel.

Erlanger, Steven, and Greg Myre, "Palestinian Reports Unity Deal With Hamas to End Aid Cutoff," ***The New York Times*****, Sept. 12, 2006, p. A1.**
Mahmoud Abbas, president of the Palestinian Authority, announced he had reached a tentative agreement with Hamas, the militant Islamic group, to form a national unity government.

Katz, Gregory, "Western Aid Cutoff Ravages Gaza Strip," ***The Houston Chronicle*****, April 30, 2006, p. A1.**
The U.S.-led cutoff of millions of dollars of aid to the occupied territories is crippling hospitals, piling streets with trash and halting paychecks.

Mitnick, Joshua, "Palestinian Charities Help Hamas Endure," ***The Christian Science Monitor*****, Oct. 16, 2006, p. 7.**
Foreign donations to Islamic aid groups are reaching Hamas' network of social-welfare affiliates even though the Western boycott has rendered the Hamas government powerless.

Nessman, Ravi, "Gaza's Dreams of a Year Ago Gone," ***The Houston Chronicle*****, Sept. 24, 2006, p. A27.**
With the Palestinian Authority on the brink of collapse, worsening poverty and the threat of an explosion of internal violence, Gaza is facing disaster.

Warwick, Ned, "A Powder Keg Awaiting the Match," ***The Philadelphia Inquirer*****, Oct. 8, 2006, p. A2.**
With 60 percent of Gaza's work force unemployed and two rival political organizations jousting for power, the volatile region has reached the point of desperation.

CITING *CQ RESEARCHER*

Sample formats for citing these reports in a bibliography include the ones listed below. Preferred styles and formats vary, so please check with your instructor or professor.

MLA STYLE

Jost, Kenneth. "Rethinking the Death Penalty." CQ Researcher 16 Nov. 2001: 945-68.

APA STYLE

Jost, K. (2001, November 16). Rethinking the death penalty. *CQ Researcher, 11*, 945-968.

CHICAGO STYLE

Jost, Kenneth. "Rethinking the Death Penalty." *CQ Researcher*, November 16, 2001, 945-968.

CQ Researcher

Published by CQ Press, a division of Congressional Quarterly Inc.

cqresearcher.com

Understanding Islam

Is Islam compatible with Western values?

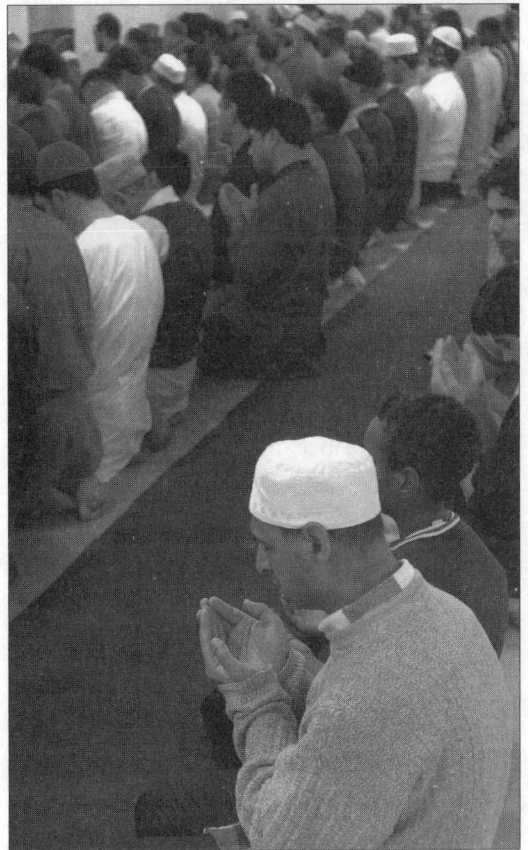

Muslim men pray at a mosque in suburban Annandale, Va., during Ramadan in October 2006.

With more than 1 billion adherents, Islam is the world's second-largest religion after Christianity. Within its mainstream traditions, Islam teaches piety, virtue and tolerance. Ever since the Sept. 11, 2001, terrorist attacks in the United States, however, many Americans have associated Islam with the fundamentalist groups that preach violence against the West and regard "moderate" Muslims as heretics. Mainstream Muslims and religious scholars say Islam is wrongly blamed for the violence and intolerance of a few. But some critics say Muslims have not done enough to oppose terrorism and violence. They also contend that Islam's emphasis on a strong relationship between religion and the state is at odds with Western views of secularism and pluralism. Some Muslims are calling for a more progressive form of Islam. But radical Islamist views are attracting a growing number of young Muslims in the Islamic world and in Europe.

Inside This Report

CQ Researcher • Nov. 3, 2006 • www.cqresearcher.com
Volume 16, Number 39 • Pages 913-936

CQ Press

Recipient of Society of Professional Journalists Award for Excellence ◆ American Bar Association Silver Gavel Award

UNDERSTANDING ISLAM

Cover photograph: Getty Images/Stefan Zaklin

CQ Researcher

Nov. 3, 2006
Volume 16, Number 39

MANAGING EDITOR: Thomas J. Colin

ASSISTANT MANAGING EDITOR: Kathy Koch

ASSOCIATE EDITOR: Kenneth Jost

STAFF WRITERS: Marcia Clemmitt, Peter Katel

CONTRIBUTING WRITERS: Rachel S. Cox, Sarah Glazer, Alan Greenblatt, Barbara Mantel, Patrick Marshall, Tom Price, Jennifer Weeks

DESIGN/PRODUCTION EDITOR: Olu B. Davis

ASSISTANT EDITOR: Melissa J. Hipolit

A Division of
Congressional Quarterly Inc.

SENIOR VICE PRESIDENT/PUBLISHER: John A. Jenkins

DIRECTOR, LIBRARY PUBLISHING: Kathryn C. Suárez

DIRECTOR, EDITORIAL OPERATIONS: Ann Davies

CONGRESSIONAL QUARTERLY INC.

CHAIRMAN: Paul C. Tash

VICE CHAIRMAN: Andrew P. Corty

PRESIDENT/EDITOR IN CHIEF: Robert W. Merry

CQ Researcher (ISSN 1056-2036) is printed on acid-free paper. Published weekly, except March 24, July 7, July 14, Aug. 4, Aug. 11, Nov. 24, Dec. 22 and Dec. 29, by CQ Press, a division of Congressional Quarterly Inc. Annual full-service subscriptions for institutions start at $667. For pricing, call 1-800-834-9020, ext. 1906. To purchase a *CQ Researcher* report in print or electronic format (PDF), visit www.cqpress.com or call 866-427-7737. Single reports start at $15. Bulk purchase discounts and electronic-rights licensing are also available. Periodicals postage paid at Washington, D.C., and additional mailing offices. POSTMASTER: Send address changes to *CQ Researcher*, 1255 22nd St., N.W., Suite 400, Washington, DC 20037.

Understanding Islam

BY KENNETH JOST

THE ISSUES

Aishah Azmi was dressed all in black, her face veiled by a *niqab* that revealed only her brown eyes through a narrow slit.

"Muslim women who wear the veil are not aliens," the 24-year-old suspended bilingual teaching assistant told reporters in Leeds, England, on Oct. 19. "Integration [of Muslims into British society] requires people like me to be in the workplace so that people can see that we are not to be feared or mistrusted."

But school officials defended their decision to suspend Azmi for refusing to remove her veil in class with a male teacher, saying it interfered with her ability to communicate with her students — most of them Muslims and, like Azmi, British Asians.

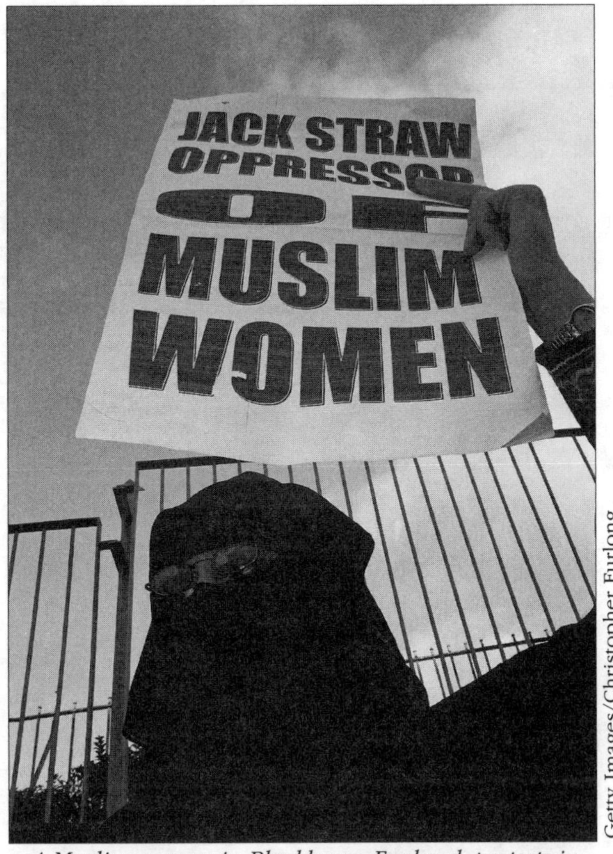

A Muslim woman in Blackburn, England, protests in October 2006 against criticism of face veils by House of Commons leader Jack Straw. Disputes over veils have erupted in several European countries, as well as the United States, reflecting the increasingly strained relations between Islam and the West.

"The school and the local authority had to balance the rights of the children to receive the best quality education possible and Mrs. Azmi's desire to express her cultural beliefs," said local Education Minister Jim Dodds. [1]

Although an employment tribunal rejected Azmi's discrimination and harassment claims, it said the school council had handled her complaint poorly and awarded her 1,100 British pounds — about $2,300.

Azmi's widely discussed case has become part of a wrenching debate in predominantly Christian England over relations with the country's growing Muslim population.

In September, a little more than a year after subway and bus bombings in London claimed 55 lives, a government minister called on Muslim parents to do more to steer their children away from violence and terrorism. Then, in October, a leaked report being prepared by the interfaith adviser of the Church of England complained that what he called the government's policy of "privileged attention" toward Muslims had backfired and was creating increased "disaffection and separation." [2]

The simmering controversy grew even hotter after Jack Straw, leader of the House of Commons and former foreign secretary under Prime Minister Tony Blair, called full-face veils "a visible statement of separation and difference" that promotes separatism between Muslims and non-Muslims. Straw, whose constituency in northwestern England includes an estimated 25 percent Muslim population, aired the comments in a local newspaper column.

Hamid Qureshi, chairman of the Lancashire Council of Mosques, called Straw's remarks "blatant Muslim-bashing." [3]

"Muslims feel they are on center stage, and everybody is Muslim-bashing," says Anjum Anwar, the council's director of education. "They feel very sensitive."

Britain's estimated 1.5 million Muslims — comprising mostly Pakistani or Indian immigrants and their British-born children — are only a tiny fraction of Islam's estimated 1.2 billion adherents worldwide. But the tensions surfacing in the face-veil debate exemplify the increasingly strained relations between the predominantly Christian West and the Muslim world.

The world's two largest religions — Christianity has some 2 billion adherents — have had a difficult relationship at least since the time of the European Crusades against Muslim rulers, or caliphs, almost 1,000 years ago. Mutual suspicion and hostility have intensified since recent terrorist attacks around the world by militant Islamic groups and President George W. Bush proclaimed a worldwide "war on terror" in response to the Sept. 11, 2001, attacks in the United States. [4]

Bush, who stumbled early on by referring to a "crusade" against terrorism, has tried many times since then to dispel perceptions of any official hostility toward Islam or Muslims generally. In Britain, Blair's government has carried on a 40-year-old policy of "multiculturalism" aimed at promoting cohesion

Continued on p. 917

The Muslim World

Islam is the world's second-largest religion (after Christianity), with an estimated 1.2 billion adherents. Some 40 nations from Senegal in West Africa to Indonesia in Southeast Asia either are virtually all Muslim or have Islamic majorities. Another 14 nations have substantial Muslim minorities. Indonesia has the world's largest Muslim population — 215 million people — followed by India, with approximately 150 million. In addition, several million Muslims live in nations of the Islamic diaspora (insert). From 1997 to 2002, Islam grew by nearly 7 percent; Christianity grew slightly less than 6 percent.

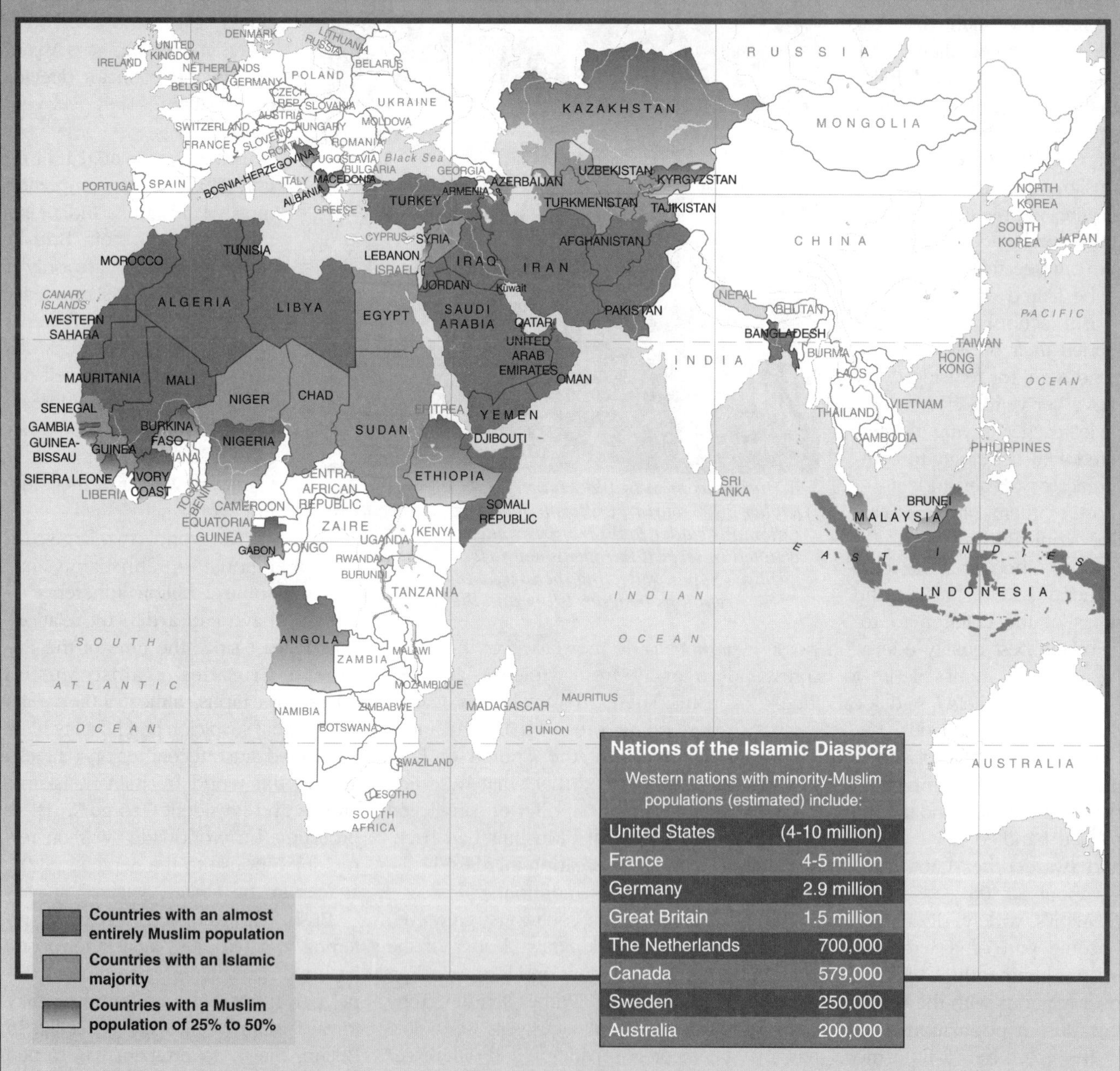

Nations of the Islamic Diaspora

Western nations with minority-Muslim populations (estimated) include:

United States	(4-10 million)
France	4-5 million
Germany	2.9 million
Great Britain	1.5 million
The Netherlands	700,000
Canada	579,000
Sweden	250,000
Australia	200,000

Sources: Paul Grieve, Islam: History, Faith and Politics: The Complete Introduction, *2006; Central Intelligence Agency,* The World Factbook, *2006.*

Continued from p. 915

among the country's various communities, Muslims in particular.

Despite those efforts, widespread distrust of Islam and Muslims prevails on both sides of the Atlantic. In a recent poll in the United States, 45 percent of those surveyed said they had an unfavorable view of Islam — a higher percentage than registered in a similar poll four years earlier. (*See chart, p. 920.*)

British Muslim leaders also say they feel increasingly hostile anti-Muslim sentiments from the general public and government officials. "Muslims are very fearful, frustrated, upset, angry," says Asghar Bukhari, a spokesman for the Muslim Public Affairs Committee in London. "It's been almost like a mental assault on the Muslim psyche here."

As the face-veil debate illustrates, the distrust stems in part from an array of differences between today's Christianity and Islam as variously practiced in the so-called Muslim world, including the growing Muslim diaspora in Europe and North America. (*See map, p. 916.*)

In broad terms, Islam generally regards religion as a more pervasive presence in daily life and a more important source for civil law than contemporary Christianity, according to the British author Paul Grieve, who wrote a comprehensive guide to Islam after studying Islamic history and thought for more than three years. [5] "Islam is a system of rules for all aspects of life," Grieve writes, while Western liberalism limits regulation of personal behavior. In contrast to the secular nation-states of the West, he explains, Islam views the ideal Muslim society as a universal community — such as the *ummah* established by the Prophet Muhammad in the seventh century.

Those theological and cultural differences are reflected, Grieve says, in Westerners' widespread view of Muslims as narrow-minded and extremist. Many Muslims correspondingly view Westerners as decadent and immoral.

How American Muslims View the Issues

Most Muslim voters in America oppose terrorist attacks and say they harm U.S. Muslims. More than half worry President Bush's "war on terror" has become a war on Islam.

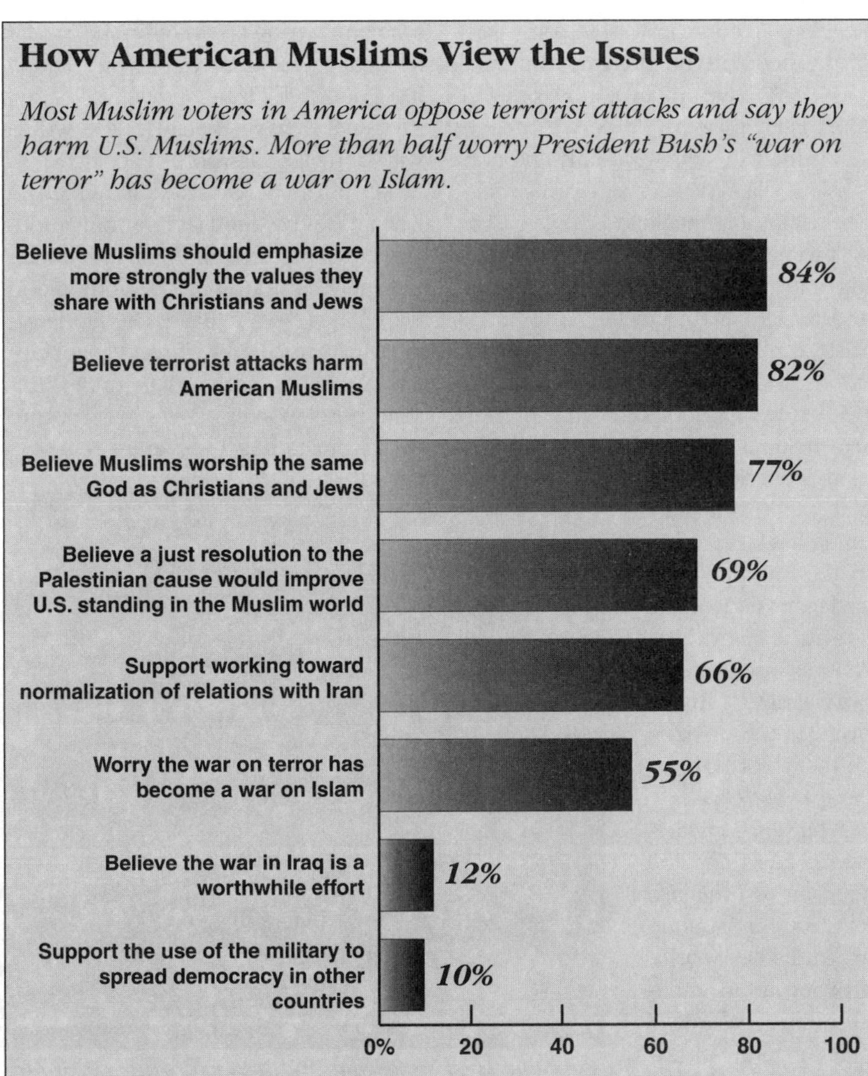

Source: Council on American-Islamic Relations, October 2006

The differences also can be seen in the debates over the role Islam plays in motivating terrorist violence by Islamic extremist groups such as al Qaeda and the objections raised by Muslims to what they consider unflattering and unfair descriptions of Islam in the West.

Muslim leaders generally deny responsibility for the violence committed by Islamic terrorists, including the 9/11 terrorist attacks in the United States and subsequent attacks in Indonesia, Spain and England. "Muslim organizations have done more than ever before in trying to advance community cohesion," Anwar says. They also deny any intention to deny freedom of expression, even though Muslims worldwide denounced a Danish cartoonist's satirical portrayal of Muhammad and Pope Benedict XVI's citation of a medieval Christian emperor's description of Islam as a violent religion.

For many Westerners, however, Islam is associated with radical Muslims — known as Islamists — who either advocate or appear to condone violence and who take to the streets to protest unfavorable depictions of Islam. "A lot of traditional or moderate Islam is inert," says Paul Marshall, a senior fellow at Freedom House's Center for

Religious Freedom in Washington. "Many of the people who disagree with radicals don't have a developed position. They keep their heads down."

Meanwhile, many Muslims and non-Muslims alike despair at Islam's sometimes fratricidal intrafaith disputes. Islam split within the first decades of its founding in the seventh century into the Sunni and Shiite (Shia) branches. The Sunni-Shiite conflict helps drive the escalating insurgency in Iraq three years after the U.S.-led invasion ousted Saddam Hussein, a Sunni who pursued generally secularist policies. [6] "A real geopolitical fracturing has taken place in the Muslim world since the end of the colonial era," says Reza Aslan, an Iranian-born Shiite Muslim now a U.S. citizen and author of the book *No god but God.*

The tensions between Islam and the West are on the rise as Islam is surging around the world, growing at an annual rate of about 7 percent. John Voll, associate director of the Prince Alwaleed bin Talal Center for Christian-Muslim Understanding at Georgetown University, notes that the growth is due largely to conversions, not the high birth rates that are driving Hinduism's faster growth.

Moreover, Voll says, Muslims are growing more assertive. "There has been an increase in intensity and an increase in strength in the way Muslims view their place in the world and their place in society," he says.

Teaching assistant Azmi's insistence on wearing the *niqab* exemplifies the new face of Islam in parts of the West. But her choice is not shared by all, or even, most of her fellow Muslim women. "I don't see why she needs to wear it," says Anwar. "She's teaching young children under 11." (Azmi says she wears it because she works with a male classroom teacher.)

Muslim experts generally agree the Koran does not require veils, only modest dress. Observant Muslim women generally comply with the admonition with a head scarf and loose-fitting attire. In particularly conservative cultures, such as Afghanistan under Taliban rule, women cover their entire bodies, including their eyes.

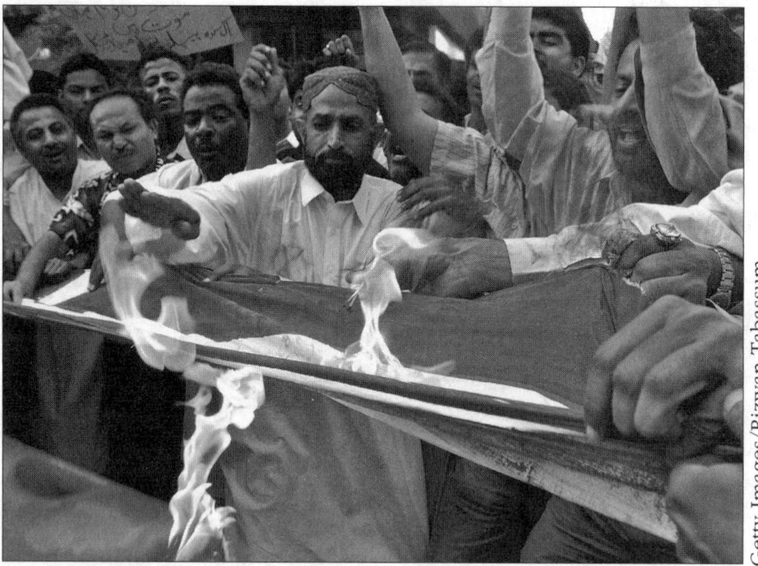

Getty Images/Rizwan Tabassum

Pakistani Muslims torch a Danish flag during a February 2006 protest in Karachi to denounce a Danish cartoonist's satirical depictions of the Prophet Muhammad. First published in September 2005, the cartoons provoked protests from Muslims throughout the world.

Still, despite the varying practices, many Muslim groups see a disconnect between the West's self-proclaimed tolerance and its pressure on Muslims to conform. "It's a Muslim woman's right to dress as she feels appropriate, given her religious views," says Ibrahim Hooper, director of communications for the Council on American-Islamic Relations in Washington. "But then when somebody actually makes a choice, they're asked not to do that."

Indeed, in Hamtramck, Mich., a judge recently came under fire for throwing out a small-claims case because the Muslim plaintiff refused to remove her full-face veil. (*See sidebar, p. 924.*)

As the debates continue, here are some of the questions being considered:

Is Islam a religion that promotes violence?

Within hours of the London subway and bus bombings on July 7, 2005, the head of the Muslim World League condemned the attacks as un-Islamic. "The heavenly religions, notably Islam, advocate peace and security," said Abdallah al-Turki, secretary-general of the Saudi-funded organization based in Mecca. [7]

The league's statement echoed any number of similar denunciations of Islamist-motivated terrorist attacks issued since 9/11 by Muslims in the United States and around the world. Yet many non-Muslim public officials, commentators, experts and others say Muslims have not done enough to speak out against terrorism committed in the name of their religion.

"Mainstream Muslims have not stepped up to the plate, by and large," says Angel Rabasa, a senior fellow at the Rand Corp., a California think tank, and lead author of a U.S. Air Force-sponsored study, *The Muslim World after 9/11.* [8]

Muslim organizations voice indignant frustration in disputing the accusation. "We can always do more," says Hooper. "The problem is that it never seems to be enough. But that doesn't keep us from trying."

Many Americans, in fact, believe Islam actually encourages violence among its adherents. A CBS poll in April 2006 found that 46 percent of those surveyed believe Islam encourages violence more than other religions. A comparable poll four years earlier registered a lower figure: 32 percent. [9]

Those perceptions are sometimes inflamed by U.S. evangelical leaders. Harsh comments about Islam have come from religious leaders like Franklin Graham, Jerry Falwell, Pat Robertson and Jerry Vines, the former president of the Southern Baptist Convention. Graham called Islam "a very evil and wicked religion," and Vines called Muhammad, Islam's founder and prophet, a "demon-possessed pedophile." Falwell, on the CBS news magazine "60 Minutes" in October 2002, declared, "I think Muhammad was a terrorist." [10]

Mainstream Muslims insist Islam is a peaceful religion and that terrorist organizations distort its tenets and teachings in justifying attacks against the West or other Muslims. But Islamic doctrine and history sometimes seem to justify the use of violence in propagating or defending the faith. The dispute revolves around the meaning of *jihad*, an Arabic word used in the Koran and derived from a root meaning "to strive" or "to make an effort for." [11] Muslim scholars can point to verses in the Koran that depict *jihad* merely as a personal, spiritual struggle and to others that describe *jihad* as encompassing either self-defense or conquest against non-believers.

Georgetown historian Voll notes that, in contrast to Christianity, Islam achieved military success during Muhammad's life and expanded into a major world empire within decades afterward. That history "reinforces the idea that militancy and violence can, in fact, be part of the theologically legitimate plan of the Muslim believer," says Voll.

"Islam, like all religions, has its historical share of violence," acknowledges Stephen Schwartz, an adult convert to Islam and executive director of the Center for Islamic Pluralism in Washington. "But there's no reason to single out Islam."

Islam Is Second-Largest Religion

Twenty-one percent of the world's 6 billion population, or 1.2 billion people, are Muslims. Christianity is the largest denomination, with 33 percent of the population, or 2 billion people.

Major World Religions

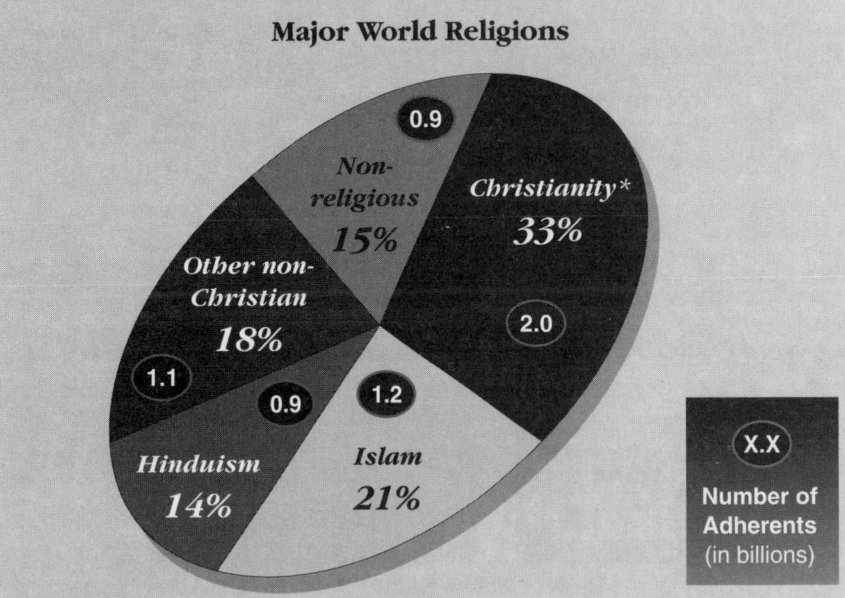

** Includes Roman Catholic, Protestant, Eastern Orthodox, Pentecostal, Anglican, Evangelical and other sects.*

Totals do not add to 100 percent due to rounding.

Sources: www.adherents.com; Angel M. Rabasa, et. al., *"The Muslim World After 9/11"; Encyclopedia Britannica online*

Modern-day jihadists pack their public manifestos with Koranic citations and writings of Islamic theologians to portray themselves as warriors for Allah and defenders of true Islam. But Voll and others stress that the vast majority of Muslims do not subscribe to their views. "You have a highly visible minority that represents a theologically extreme position in the Muslim world," Voll says.

In particular, writes Seyyed Hossein Nasr, a professor of Islamic studies at George Washington University, Islamic law prohibits the use of force against women, children or civilians — even during war. "Inflicting injuries outside of this context," he writes, "is completely forbidden by Islamic law." [12]

Rabasa says, however, that Muslims who disapprove of terrorism have not said enough or done enough to mobilize opposition to terrorist attacks. "Muslims see themselves as part of a community and are reluctant to criticize radical Muslims," he says.

In addition, many Muslims are simply intimidated from speaking out, he explains. "Radicals are not reluctant to use violence and the threat of violence," he says. Liberal and moderate Muslims are known to receive death threats on their cell phones, even in relatively peaceful Muslim countries such as Indonesia.

Voll also notes that Islamic radicals have simply outorganized the moderates. "There is no moderate organization that even begins to resemble

Negative Impressions of Islam Have Increased

The percentage of Americans with a favorable view of Islam dropped from 30 percent in 2002 to 19 percent in April 2006. There was a similar increase in the percentage who believe Islam encourages violence more than other religions.

What is your impression of Islam?

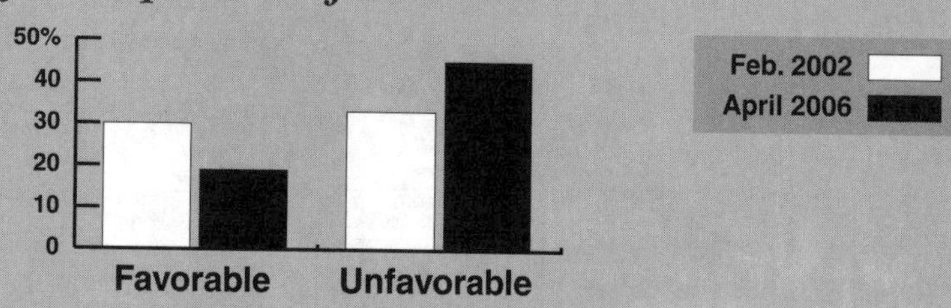

Compared with other religions, Islam encourages violence . . .

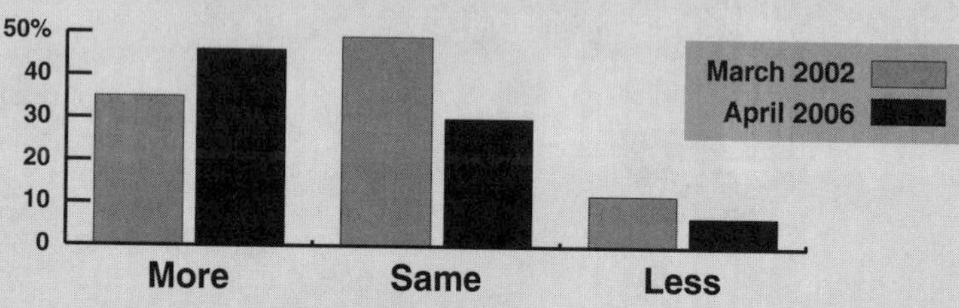

What is your impression of . . . ?

	Favorable	Unfavorable	Don't Know
Protestantism/other Christians	58%	12%	30%
The Catholic religion	48	37	15
The Jewish religion	47	16	37
Christian fundamentalist religions	31	31	38
The Mormon religion	20	39	41
Islam	19	45	36
Scientology	8	52	40

Do you know more or less about Islam now than you did five years ago?

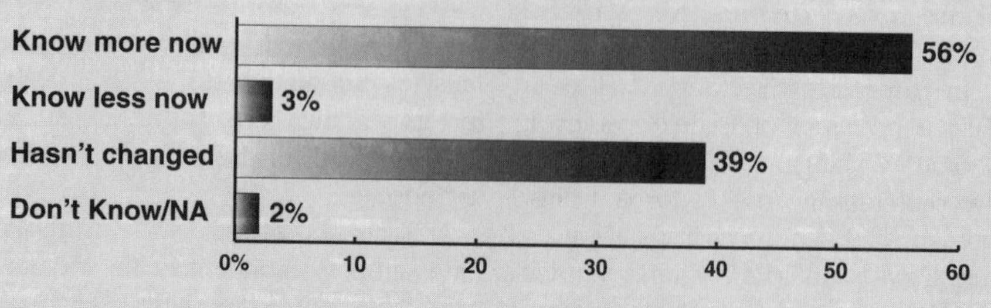

Sources: CBS News Poll, April 2006; Gallup Poll, 2002

some of the radical organizations that have developed," he says.

In Britain, Bukhari of the Muslim Public Affairs Committee criticizes Muslim leaders themselves for failing to channel young people opposed to Britain's pro-U.S. foreign policy into nonviolent political action. "Children who could have been peaceful react to that foreign policy in a way that they themselves become criminals," he says.

The Council on American-Islamic Relations' Hooper details several anti-terrorism pronouncements and drives issued following the London bombings by various Muslim groups and leaders in Britain and in the United States, including *fatwas*, or legal opinions, rejecting terrorism and extremism. [13]

For his part, Omid Safi, an associate professor of Islamic studies at the University of North Carolina in Chapel Hill, points out that virtually every Muslim organization in the United States issued condemnations of violence almost immediately after the 9/11 terrorist attacks. [14]

"How long must we keep answering this question?" Safi asks in exasperation. But he concedes a few moments later that the issue is more than perception. "Muslims must come to terms with our demons," he says, "and one of those demons is violence."

Is Islam compatible with secular, pluralistic societies?

In 2003, Germany's famed Deutsche Oper staged an avant-garde remake of Mozart's opera "Idomeneo," which dramatizes the composer's criticism of organized religion, with a scene depicting the severed heads of Muhammad, Jesus, Buddha and Poseidon. That production was mounted without incident, but the company dropped plans to restage it in November 2006 after police warned of a possible violent backlash from Muslim fundamentalists.

The cancellation prompted protests from German officials and artistic-freedom advocates in Europe and in the

United States, who saw the move as appeasement toward terrorists. Wolfgang Bornsen, a spokesman for conservative Chancellor Angela Merkel, said the cancellation was "a signal" to other artistic companies to avoid any works critical of Islam. [15]

The debate continued even after plans were discussed to mount the production after all — with enhanced security and the blessing of German Muslim leaders. "We live in Europe, where democracy was based on criticizing religion," remarked Philippe Val, editor of the French satirical magazine *Charlie Hebdo*. "If we lose the right to criticize or attack religions in our free countries . . . we are doomed." [16]

As with the issue of violence, Islam's doctrines and history can be viewed as pointing both ways on questions of pluralism and tolerance. "There are a great many passages [in the Koran] that support a pluralistic interpretation of Islam," says the Rand Corp.'s Rabasa. "But you also find a great many that would support an intolerant interpretation."

"Intellectual pluralism is traditional Islam," says Schwartz at the Center for Islamic Pluralism. An oft-quoted verse from the Koran specifically prohibits compulsion in religion, he says. Voll and other historians agree that Muslim countries generally tolerated Christians and Jews, though they were often subject to special taxes or other restrictions.

"Islam is the only major religious system that has built-in protections for minorities," says Hooper at the Council on American-Islamic Relations. "You don't see the kind of persecutions of minorities that we often saw in Europe for hundreds of years. Many members of the Jewish community fled to find safety within the Muslim world."

Even so, Islam's view of religion and politics as inseparable creates difficult issues. Outside the Arab world, most Muslims live in practicing democracies with fair to good human-rights records. But some Muslim countries — Arab and non-Arab — have either adopted or been urged to adopt provisions of Islamic law — *sharia* — that are antithetical to modern ideas of human rights, such as limiting women's rights and prescribing stoning or amputations as criminal penalties.

Muslims participating in a society as a minority population face different issues, according to author Grieve. "Islam is difficult to accommodate in a determinedly secular Western society where almost all views are equally respected, and none is seen as either right or wrong," he writes. [17]

The tensions played out in a number of controversies in recent years were provoked by unflattering depictions of Islam in Europe. A Danish cartoonist's satirical view of Muhammad provoked worldwide protests from Muslim leaders and groups after they were publicized in early 2006. Scattered violence resulted in property damage and more than 30 deaths.

Somewhat similarly, Pope Benedict XVI drew sharp criticism after a Sept. 12, 2006, lecture quoting a medieval Christian emperor's description of Islam as "evil and inhuman." Along with verbal denunciations, protesters in Basra, Iraq, burned an effigy of the pope. Within a week, he disclaimed the remarks and apologized.

Freedom House's Marshall says such controversies, as well as the cancellation of the opera in Berlin, strengthens radical Muslim elements. "Bending to more radical demands marginalizes the voices of moderate Muslims and hands over leadership to the radicals," he says.

Many Muslims in European countries, however, view the controversies — including the current debate over the veil in England — as evidence of pervasive hostility from the non-Muslim majorities. "There is a growing hatred of Muslims in Britain, and anybody who bashes Muslims can only get brownie points," says Bukhari of the Muslim Public Affairs Committee.

"These are not friendly times for Western Muslims," says Safi, at the

Basic Tenets of Islam

Islam is the youngest of the world's three major monotheistic religions. Like the other two, Judaism and Christianity, Islam (the word means both "peace" and "submission") holds there is but one God (Allah). Muslims believe God sent a number of prophets to teach mankind how to live according to His law. Muslims consider Jesus, Moses and Abraham as prophets of God and hold the Prophet Muhammad as his final and most sacred messenger. Many accounts found in Islam's sacred book, the Koran (Qur'an), are also found in sacred writings of Jews and Christians.

There are five basic pillars of Islam:

- **Creed** — Belief in God and Muhammad as his Prophet.
- **Almsgiving** — Giving money to charity is considered a sacred duty.
- **Fasting** — From dawn to dusk during the month of Ramadan.
- **Prayer** — Five daily prayers must be given facing Mecca, Islam's holiest city.
- **Pilgrimage** — All Muslims must make a *hajj* to Mecca at least once during their lifetime, if they are physically able.

University of North Carolina. "Whenever people find themselves under assault, opening their arms and opening their hearts is difficult."

Does Islam need a "reformation"?

If Pakistan's Punjab University expected a chorus of approval when it decided to launch a master's program in musicology in fall 2006, it was in for a surprise. At the Lahore campus, the conservative Islamic Assembly of Students, known as I.J.T., rose up in protest.

Handbills accused school authorities of forsaking Islamic ideological teachings in favor of "the so-called enlightened moderation" dictated by "foreign masters." Undeterred, administrators opened the program for enrollment in September. When fewer students applied than expected, they blamed the poor response in part on the I.J.T. campaign. [18]

The episode reflects how Islam today is evolving differently in the West and in some parts of the Muslim world. Many Muslim writers and scholars in the United States and Europe are calling for Islam to adapt to modern times by, for example, embracing pluralism and gender equality. Introducing a collection of essays by "progressive" Muslims, the University of North Carolina's Safi says the movement seeks to "start swimming through the rising waters of Islam and modernity, to strive for justice in the midst of society." [19]

In much of the Muslim world, however, Islam is growing — in numbers and intensity — on the strength of literal interpretations of the Koran and exclusivist attitudes toward the non-Muslim world. "In the Muslim world in general, more extreme or reactionary forms of Islam are getting stronger — in Africa, Asia and the Middle East," says Freedom House's Marshall, who has previously worked on issues pertaining to persecution of Christians around the world.

Islamist groups such as I.J.T. talk about "reforming" or "purifying" Islam and adopting Islamic law as the primary or exclusive source of civil law. In fact, one version of reformed Islam — Wahhabism * or the currently preferred term Salafism — espouses a literalistic reading of the Koran and a puritanical stance toward such modern practices as listening to music or watching television. It has been instituted in Saudi Arabia and has advanced worldwide because of financial backing from the oil-rich kingdom and its appeal to new generations of Muslims.

"The Salafi movement is a fringe," says the Rand Corp.'s Rabasa. "But it's growing because it's dynamic and revolutionary, whereas traditional Islam tends to be conservative. It has this appeal to young people looking for identity."

But the Center for Islamic Pluralism's Schwartz, an outspoken critic of Salafism, says many Muslims are rejecting it because of its tendency to view other branches of Islam as apostasy. "People are getting sick of this," he says. "They're tired of the social conflict and upheaval."

Voll at the Center for Christian-Muslim Understanding also says some Muslim legal scholars are disputing literalistic readings of *sharia* by contending that the Islamic law cited as divinely ordained is actually "a human construct subject to revision."

Some Western commentators refer to a "reformation" in calling for a more liberal form of Islam. Nicholas D. Kristof, a *New York Times* columnist who focuses on global human-rights issues, sees "hopeful rumblings . . . of steps toward a Muslim Reformation," especially on issues of gender equality. He notes that feminist Muslim scholars are reinterpreting passages in the Koran that other Muslims cite in justifying restrictions on women, such as the Saudi ban on women driving. [20]

* Wahhabism originated in the Arabian peninsula in the late 1700s from the teachings of Arabian theologian Muhammad ibn Abd al Wahhab (1703-1792).

Safi says he avoids the term reformation because it has been adopted by Salafists and also because it suggests a need to break from traditional Islam. He says "progressive" Muslims return to the Prophet's vision of the common humanity of all human beings and seek "to hold Muslim societies accountable for justice and pluralism."

Rabasa also says reformation is historically inappropriate as a goal for liberal or progressive Muslims. "What is needed is not an Islamic reformation but an Islamic enlightenment," says Rabasa. The West's liberal tradition, he notes, was produced not by the Reformation but by the Enlightenment — the 18th-century movement that used reason to search for objective truth.

Whatever terms are used, the clash between different visions of Islam will be less susceptible to resolution than analogous disputes within most branches of Christianity because Islam lacks any recognized hierarchical structure. Islam has no pope or governing council. Instead, each believer is regarded as having a direct relationship with God, or Allah, with no ecclesiastical intermediary.

"In the face of contemporary Islam, there is absolutely the sense of an authority vacuum," says Safi. Islam's future, he adds, "is a question that can only be answered by Muslims." ■

BACKGROUND

Two Faces of Islam

Islam began as the faith of a small community of believers in Arabia in the seventh century and grew within a matter of decades to be the dominant religion of a powerful empire. The Muslim world expanded

Continued on p. 924

Chronology

Before 1900

Islam grows from origins in 7th-century Arabia to become dominant religion of a global empire but recedes as European nations become colonial powers in 18th, 19th centuries.

1900-1970

Muslim world throws off European rule.

1932
Kingdom of Saudi Arabia formed, adopts radical Islamist branch of Wahhabism as state religion.

1947-48
Pakistan becomes world's first avowedly Islamist state following Indian independence, partition. . . . Indonesia gains independence to become world's most populous Muslim nation. . . . Israel established, displacing Palestinians and creating lasting conflict with Arabs, Muslims.

1952
Col. Gamal Abdel Nasser gains power in Egypt, adopts secular Arab socialism as platform.

1965
Immigration and Naturalization Services Act of 1965 abolishes national-origins quota system in U.S., opening door for more Muslim immigrants.

1970s-1980s

Radical Islam advances in Muslim world despite resistance, reluctance by conservative regimes.

1979
Iranian Revolution ousts U.S.-backed Reza Shah Pahlavi, brings Ayatollah Ruholla Khomeini to power as head of Islamist regime.

1987
Osama bin Laden, a wealthy Saudi expatriate, forms al Qaeda terrorist network as "base" for Islamic crusade.

1989
Islamic National Front gains power in Sudan, triggering long civil war against Christian south.

1990s

Islamist movements have gains, setbacks.

1990-91
U.S.-led invasion drives Saddam Hussein's Iraq out of Kuwait; U.S. forces use Saudi Arabia as staging area, angering bin Laden.

1991
Algerian military cancels scheduled parliamentary run-off to thwart possible victory by Islamic Salvation Front.

1996
Islamist Taliban movement gains power in Afghanistan.

2000-Present

Islamist movement advances; U.S. declares "war on terror" after 9/11 attacks.

Sept. 11, 2001
Terrorist attacks on the World Trade Center and the Pentagon kill nearly 3,000. President George W. Bush declares war on "global terrorism," wins international support for invasion of Afghanistan over its role in harboring bin Laden, al Qaeda; Arabs, Muslims targeted in domestic crackdown.

2002
Islamic Justice and Development Party wins parliamentary majority in secular Turkey.

2003
U.S.-led invasion ousts Iraq's Hussein but fails to bring order as insurgency grows into civil war between majority Shiites and long-dominant Sunnis.

2004
France bans wearing of religious garb, including Muslim head scarves, by public school pupils. . . . Terrorist bombing of Madrid subway kills 190 people. . . . Dutch filmmaker Theo Van Gogh slain, apparently over film critical of Islam's treatment of women.

2005
Shiites gain upper hand in Iraqi parliamentary elections; banned Muslim Brotherhood makes gains in Egyptian assembly. . . . More than 50 people killed in terrorist subway, bus bombings in London. . . . Taliban resurgent in Afghanistan. . . . Muslims riot in France.

2006
Danish cartoonist's satirical depictions of Prophet Muhammad provoke protests, violence in much of Muslim world. . . . Militant Hamas wins majority in Palestinian elections, displacing more moderate Palestine Liberation Organization. . . Pope Benedict XVI draws fire for quoting medieval emperor's criticism of Islam. . . . German opera company cancels production of opera with satirical depiction of Islam, other faiths. . . . British officials criticize Muslim veil (*niqab*) as separatist.

U.S. Muslims Feel 'Under a Spotlight'

A taxicab board in Minneapolis vetoes a plan to make it easier for Muslim drivers to refuse on religious grounds to transport passengers carrying alcoholic beverages.

A local school board member in Ohio objects when a high-school principal allows two Muslim students to be excused during lunchtime as they fasted during Ramadan.

A judge in Michigan dismisses a Muslim woman's complaint against a car rental company because she refuses to remove her veil while testifying. [1]

The United States' rapidly growing Muslim population is presenting American society with a host of new issues. At the same time, many Americans anxious about terrorism are distrustful or fearful of Muslims around the world and here at home.

Government officials from President George W. Bush on down have tried to dispel Americans' concerns about U.S. Muslims generally. But government action against alleged Islamist terrorist cells or Muslim charities suspected of funding terrorists has created widespread feelings of official harassment or persecution among American Muslims.

"They really feel they're completely under a spotlight," says author Geneive Abdo, author of the new book *Mecca and Main Street*. Muslims "went from being a virtually invisible minority [before 9/11] to being completely the focus of attention" ever since. [2]

In fact, Muslims are barely mentioned in most accounts of the building of America, even though Arab explorers may have reached the New World seven centuries before Columbus. Many of the African slaves transported to the English Colonies brought their Muslim faith with them, as did some of the Arab immigrants who came to the United States from the Ottoman Empire in the late 19th and early 20th centuries. [3]

Muslims did not begin immigrating in substantial numbers, however, until after the 1965 Immigration Act, which abolished national quotas favoring northern European countries. Today, a survey by Georgetown University's Center for Muslim-Christian Understanding and the polling firm Zogby International indicates that about two-thirds of the country's more than 4 million Muslims immigrated to this country. [4] But Islam is the country's fastest-growing religion also in part because of an increasing number of conversions by Americans of other faiths.

In contrast to Europe — where Muslim immigrants have been predominantly lower-income — the United States has been receiving a larger proportion of well-educated, higher-income professionals and managers. Overall, about 62 percent of American Muslims have a college degree, according to a survey by the Council on American-Islamic Relations (CAIR), while 43 percent have household incomes above $50,000. [5]

The demographics make American Muslim communities a generally inhospitable environment for radical Islamists, observers say. "What we have here among Muslim-Americans is a very conservative success ethic," says John Zogby, president of Zogby International in Utica, N.Y., whose polling firm surveys the Muslim-American community. [6]

American Muslims have been becoming more observant for several years. Abdo cites a survey indicating that mosque attendance doubled from 1994 to 2000. From her own reporting, Abdo says Muslims generally and younger Muslims in particular have become more pious since 9/11 and more assertive in speaking up for Islam in the face of public criticism or ignorance. Still, the CAIR survey found that only 31 percent of those questioned — slightly less than one-third — attend mosque weekly, while 27 percent said they attend seldom or never.

With their growing numbers and the growing sense of being under siege, Muslims have been increasingly active politically in the years since 9/11. Muslim and Arab political action committees have been increasing campaign contributions, and a

Continued from p. 922

over the next 1,000 years, eventually stretching from Spain and western Africa east to China, the Indian subcontinent and Indonesia, but most of that world came under European domination in the 1700s and 1800s. The 20th century opened with roiling debates within Islam between secular nationalists and Islamic fundamentalists over how best to regain a measure of the glories of times past. [21]

Muhammad (c. 570-632) was a respected businessman in the commercial and religious center of Mecca when, according to Islamic belief, he received the divine revelation now preserved in the Koran. The central monotheistic message — "there is no god but Allah" — incorporated beliefs of Judaism and Christianity and challenged the prevailing polytheism as well as the wealth and status of Mecca's power structure.

Facing possible assassination, Muhammad accepted an invitation in 622 to serve as a judge in Medina, 400 kilometers to the north. There, the Prophet became — as historian Voll describes it — the leader of the *ummah*, or community, "in all matters of life," both religious and temporal. By the time of his death in 632, the new Muslim community was successfully established. Mecca had been defeated and incorporated into the *ummah* in important ways. Today, observant Muslims are called to undertake a pilgrimage, or *hajj*, to Mecca at least once in their lives.

Within barely three decades, the Muslim community became a major global empire by conquering the Persian Empire to the east and the Syrian territories of the Byzantine Empire to the west. But the rapid expansion ended with a civil war (656-661) that split Islam into two traditions that, as

growing number of Arab-Americans have been seeking elective office: 49 in 2004, 52 in 2006, according to the Arab-American Institute. Keith Ellison, a black attorney who converted to Islam as a college student, is highly favored to be elected on Nov. 7 as a Democrat in Minnesota's 5th Congressional District, becoming the country's first Muslim member of Congress. [7]

Getty Images/Stefan Zaklin

Muslim friends dine at an Afghan restaurant in Alexandria, Va., in October 2006 after daytime fasting during the Islamic holy month of Ramadan.

President Bush's role in the war on terror and the Iraq conflict appears to have cost him heavily among Muslim-Americans. A plurality of Muslims supported Bush over Al Gore in the 2000 presidential election, but Muslims heavily favored Democrat John Kerry over Bush in 2004, according to the Georgetown-Zogby survey. In its more recent poll, CAIR found that 42 percent of those surveyed identified as Democrats compared to 17 percent as Republicans.

Muslims' growing visibility and assertiveness produces a reflexive defensiveness among many public officials, commentators and private citizens. "We are a Christian nation, not a Muslim nation," school board member Jennifer Miller in Mason, Ohio, said when complaining about the Mason High School principal's decision to accommodate the two Muslim students' wishes to be excused from the lunchroom during Ramadan.

Muslim and Arab-American groups also continue to report increases in anti-Muslim incidents. But Reza Aslan, an Iranian-American author, plays down their importance. "They're obviously a problem," says Aslan, "but they're not representative of the larger perception of Muslim or Islam among Americans."

"There's always going to be a sector of American society that is unaccepting not only of Muslims but of any group that is 'the other,' " Aslan continues. "It's going to take a while for Americans to recognize Islam not as a religion of the other but as part of the country's rich, pluralistic religious experience."

[1] See Oren Dorell, "Cabbies, culture clash at Minn. airport," *USA Today*, Oct. 11, 2006, p. 3A; Michael D. Clark, "Room for Fasting Muslims Raises Furor at School Board," *Cincinnati Enquirer*, Oct. 26, 2006, p. 1A; Zachary Gorchow, "Veil Costs Her Claim in Court," *Detroit Free Press*, Oct. 22, 2006, p. 1.

[2] Interview with Madeleine Brand, "Day to Day," National Public Radio, Sept. 11, 2006.

[3] Some historical background drawn from Geneive Abdo, *Mecca and Main Street: Muslim Life in America After 9/11* (2006). See also Mary H. Cooper, "Muslims in America," *CQ Researcher*, April 30, 1993, pp. 361-384.

[4] Project MAPS/Zogby International, "Muslims in the American Public Square: Shifting Political Winds and Fallout from 9/11, Afghanistan, and Iraq," October 2004 (www.projectmaps.com/AMP2004report.pdf). Project MAPS — "Muslims in the American Public Square" — was a project of the Center for Muslim-Christian Understanding, Georgetown University, funded by the Pew Charitable Trusts.

[5] Council on American-Islamic Relations, "American Muslim Voters: A Demographic Profile and Survey of Attitudes," Oct. 24, 2006; www.cair.com/pdf/American_Muslim_Voter_Survey_2006.pdf.

[6] Quoted in Alexandra Marks, "Radical Islam finds US to be 'sterile ground,'" *The Christian Science Monitor*, Oct. 23, 2006, p. 1.

[7] See Claude R. Marx, "American Arabs and Muslims Begin to Flex Political Muscles," Jewish Telegraphic Agency, Oct. 25, 2006.

Voll relates, live on to this day. The mainstream or Sunni tradition — sunna refers to the life and sayings of the Prophet — traces its origins to the first four "rightly guided" *khalifahs* (caliphs), successors to Muhammad. Sunni Muslims combine an emphasis on consensus and piety with a pragmatic focus on governmental stability.

The Shia tradition — shi'ah is Arabic for faction or party — begins with Ali, a cousin of Muhammad who became the leader of a breakaway group of mutinous troops and others in Medina in 656. Ali — viewed by his supporters as Muhammad's rightful successor — prevailed militarily, only to be murdered five years later. Shi'a Islam reflects a belief in a divinely guided imam, or leader, with authority unbound by human consensus or pragmatic reasons of state.

The Muslim world expanded initially through military conquest and later through global trade. During the golden age of Islam (750-1300), Islamic civilization dominated in art, architecture, mathematics and other fields as Christian Europe languished during the so-called Dark Ages before 1000. Over the next 500 years, the rising states of Europe waged war against Muslim rule — most famously in the seven Christian Crusades fought between 1095 and 1291 — in an unsuccessful effort to free the Holy Land from rule by Muslim "infidels."

To more tangible effect, the Mongols began their conquest of the Islamic states early in the 13th century. Later, the Christian reconquest of Spain ended Muslim rule on the Iberian Peninsula in 1492, while Christian forces stopped the Muslim Ottoman Empire's advance from the Balkans at the gates of Vienna in the 16th and 17th centuries. Even as Muslim military might receded, however, Muslim merchants were gaining converts for Islam in Africa, central Asia and India.

Most of the Muslim world came under European control in the 1700s and 1800s, but Islam remained the dominant religion and most important source of resistance to European expansion. The decline of Muslim power provoked self-examination and calls for reform. One of the Islamic "reformers" was Muhammad ibn Abd al-Wahhab (1703-1792), an Arabian theologian who preached a strict interpretation of the Koran. Wahhab allied himself with a prince, Muhammad Ibn Saud, whose family would unite the Arabian Peninsula two centuries later. In contrast to Wahhab, reformers in the late 19th century such as Muhammad Abduh in Egypt and Sayyid Ahmad Khan in India sought to integrate Islam with modernity by showing that faith and reason were compatible and that Islam and the West were not necessarily in conflict.

World War I marked the end of one era in the history of Islam and the beginning of another. The Ottoman Empire, allied with Germany, was defeated, occupied and dismembered. At the heart of the former empire, the Turkish nationalist Mustafa Kemal Ataturk established a new, avowedly secular state while the Muslim lands to the east were divided into French and British protectorates. Nationalism helped drive opposition to European colonial rule among Muslims in India, Indonesia and elsewhere.

As Voll recounts, other emerging movements advocated a more all-encompassing adoption of Islam in modern society, including the Muslim Brotherhood, established in Egypt by Hasan al-Banna (1906-1949), and the Jama'at-I Islami (Islamic Society), founded in India in 1941 under the leadership of Mawlana Abu al-Ala Mawdudi (1903-1979). These movements criticized the secularism of Western life and called for applying Islam to economics and politics as well as to individual religious life.

Islamist Movements

The Muslim world threw off European rule after World War II and gained control of its own destiny for the first time in several centuries. Many majority-Muslim countries followed a secular path, several under leaders who combined socialist programs with authoritarian practices. Oil-rich Saudi Arabia, however, adopted Wahhabism as the state religion and followed its dictates by imposing a pervasive web of social controls. Strict Islamist movements contended with secular regimes elsewhere but gained power in only two: Iran (1979) and Sudan (1989). Meanwhile, the establishment of Israel in 1948 — with the strong support of the United States and its European allies — created a deep estrangement between the Muslim world and the West.

Two of the most populous Muslim-majority countries gained their independence shortly after World War II. Muslims joined in the resistance to British rule in India that brought independence in 1947 along with the partition of the subcontinent into a secular, predominantly Hindu India and a separate, majority-Muslim Pakistan. A year later, an Indonesian independence movement led by the nationalist leader Sukarno threw off Dutch colonial rule, but he elevated nationalism and socialism over Islamism during his nearly two decades in power. Islam played a larger role in Pakistan as the source of national identity, but the government defined its policies in largely secular terms through the 1950s and '60s.

Egypt, partially independent since 1922, won full independence from Britain after World War II. Col. Gamal Abdel Nasser came to power in a military coup in 1952 and disappointed Islamist supporters by espousing a largely secularized Arab socialism. Nasser banned the Muslim Brotherhood in 1954 after an attempted assassination and imprisoned many of its members. Among those jailed was Sayyed Qutb, a U.S.-educated author whose anti-Western Islamic manifestos continued to inspire radical Islamist movements even after his execution in 1966 for attempting to overthrow the state.

Iran provided a different model of a secular, majority-Muslim country through the 1970s. The United States and Britain helped install Reza Shah Pahlavi on the Peacock Throne in 1941 and used him in 1953 to engineer the ousting of Prime Minister Mohammed Mossadegh, who had called for nationalizing the Anglo-Iranian Oil Co. Combined with U. S. and British aid, Pahlavi's Westernizing policies helped spur economic growth. But his support for women's rights and his good relations with Israel angered Islamic fundamentalists and — along with his harsh, autocratic practices — led to his downfall in the 1979 Iranian Revolution that propelled the Ayatollah Ruholla Khomeini to power as head of an Islamist regime.

The Iranian Revolution marked the beginning of a new era that, as historian Voll explains, saw political Islam move from militant, often-underground opposition into the mainstream of political life in many majority-Muslim countries. Many Muslims — significantly including well-educated professionals — came to view such Islamization of state and society as a more promising path for the Muslim world than the leftist ideologies and nationalist state policies that had held sway in the postwar era. As Islamist parties formed, however, they met resistance from conservative monarchies and regimes that had relied on traditional Islam for support but viewed more radical Islam as a challenge.

Islamization, including the adoption of *sharia*, advanced in many parts of the Muslim world from the 1970s on, despite the resistance or reluctance of conservative regimes. [22] Egyptian President Anwar Sadat promised to adopt *sharia* but angered fundamentalists by signing a peace treaty with Israel in 1979. Two years later, he was assassinated by members of the Muslim Brotherhood. His successor, Hosni Mubarak, has tried alternately to co-opt the organization with partial Islamization or to suppress it with mass arrests. In Pakistan, President Muhammad Zia al-uh-Haq instituted strict enforcement of Islamic law during his 11-year dictatorship before his death in 1988 in a still unexplained plane crash. The government has been largely secular since, but — as author Grieve writes — has "trotted out" *sharia* as "a diversion" from recurrent crises. [23]

Getty Images/Joel Robine

Islamic-inspired head coverings are displayed at a shop near Paris. France banned the wearing of "conspicuous" religious symbols — such as Muslim head scarves, Jewish skullcaps and large Christian crosses — in public schools, but the measure is seen as aimed primarily at creeping fundamentalism among France's 5 million Muslims.

A military coup brought the Islamic National Front to power in Sudan in 1989, ushering in pervasive Islamization despite opposition from most Muslims and a bloody civil war aimed at the Christian minority in the country's south. The fundamentalist Taliban movement pursued a similar policy of thorough Islamization during the five years it effectively controlled Afghanistan (1996-2001), but only three countries formally recognized the regime: Pakistan, Saudi Arabia and United Arab Emirates.

In the most important setback for Islamist movements, the Islamic Salvation Front in Algeria appeared on the verge of winning a majority in a second round of balloting for the national parliament in 1992, but the military suspended the election after the front's strong showing in the first round in December 1991. The move touched off a civil war that claimed an estimated 200,000 lives before the front's military wing surrendered in 2002.

Iran instituted *sharia* to some extent but also left elements of the old civil-justice system in place. Electoral victories by secularizing reformers in the 1990s further slowed Islamization. Despite setbacks, however, the advance of Islamization could be seen across the Muslim world, even in such traditionalist countries as Indonesia and Malaysia.

'War on Terror'

The 9/11 terrorist attacks on the United States came after a decade of growing militancy by Islamic extremist groups and ushered in a period of increased tensions between Muslims worldwide and the United States and its allies in Europe and in the Middle East. Muslims in the United States complained of harassment and discrimination in the immediate aftermath of the attacks, despite efforts by President Bush to dispel anti-Muslim attitudes. Increased Muslim immigration in Europe fueled conflicts in several countries, including England, France and the Netherlands. The United States, meanwhile, initially found support within the Muslim world for its invasion of Afghanistan but encountered widespread opposition from Muslim populations and leaders after the invasion of Iraq in 2003.

The Sept. 11 attacks were readily traced to the terrorist organization al Qaeda, led by the wealthy Saudi expatriate Osama bin Laden. Bin Laden had fought with other Islamic militants to drive the Soviet Union from Afghanistan and then turned his attention to the United States and his former homeland after the Saudi government agreed to allow "infidel" U.S. troops to use the country — home to Islam's holiest sites — as a staging area for the 1991 Persian Gulf War. With backing from the United Nations and quiet support from some Muslim countries, the United States responded to the 9/11 attacks by launching an invasion to oust Afghanistan's Islamist Taliban regime for its role in harboring al Qaeda. [24]

Within the United States, meanwhile, Muslims bore the brunt of a crackdown aimed at ferreting out terrorists, potential terrorists or terrorist sympathizers. Government investigators asked hundreds of foreign Muslims legally in the United States to submit to voluntary questioning about terrorists in or outside the United States. Later, immigration officials moved to track down Muslim immigrants who had failed to comply with deportation orders issued before the attacks. The Council of American-Islamic Relations accused the government of "sacrificing the civil rights of Arabs and Muslims in the name of fighting terrorism." At the same time, the group blamed "anti-Muslim agitation on television and radio" for what it described as "the worst" wave of anti-Muslim hate crimes in U.S. history. [25]

The U.S.-led invasion of Iraq in 2003 ousted the dictatorial Saddam Hussein but left the United States in the middle of a sectarian dispute between the country's long dominant Sunni minority and the Shiite majority, which had suffered under Hussein's rule. The Sunni-Shiite conflict provided the backdrop for difficult political negotiations in the writing of a new constitution and contentious campaigning in the run-up to the January 2005 parliamentary elections, where Shiites emerged with a near majority. Armed Sunni and Shiite militias continued battling for control after the election even after the leading Shiite cleric, Grand Ayatollah Ali al-Sistani, called in July 2006 for all Iraqis "to exert maximum effort to stop the bloodletting."

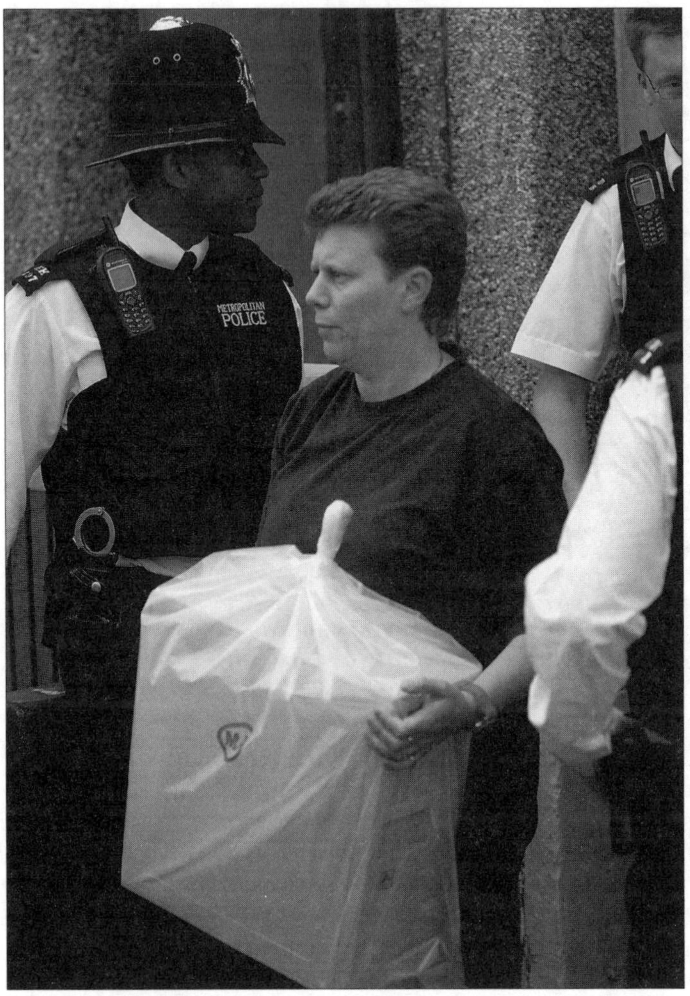

Getty Images/Chris Jackson

A police officer removes a computer from a house in London on Aug. 11, 2006, following the arrest of 24 men, mostly Muslim fundamentalists, believed to be involved in a plot to blow up planes flying from Britain to the United States. Police said the men had ties to the al Qaeda terrorist network.

In Europe, meanwhile, ethnic and religious tensions were surfacing as increased immigration from Muslim countries and high birthrates combined to make Islam the fastest-growing religion on the continent. [26] Increased religiosity in Europe's 15-million-strong Muslim community — as measured by construction of mosques or attendance at prayers — coincided with widespread feelings of alienation, especially among young, native-born Muslims. In France — with more than 5 million Muslims — riots erupted in the mostly Muslim suburbs of Paris and other French cities in October 2005 amid complaints of high unemployment and frequent discrimination. The burgeoning new minority is also challenging European concepts of national and personal identity, as when France banned Muslim girls from wearing head scarves in schools in 2004.

In addition to generalized grievances, Europe also fell victim to terrorist attacks by Islamists. The bombing of three Madrid train stations at rush hour in March 2004 left 190 people dead and more than 1,200 injured; a year and three months later coordinated bombings of three subway trains and a bus in London killed 52 people plus the four bombers. In the Netherlands, meanwhile, the Dutch filmmaker Theo Van Gogh was slain in November 2004 by a 26-year-old Moroccan after he had directed a film critical of Islam's treatment of women. And in August 2006 police in England arrested 24 people, nearly all of them Muslims, on charges of plotting to detonate explosives aboard aircraft destined for the United States.

Within the Muslim world, Islamic groups were making significant gains in several countries, according to historian Voll. [27] In Turkey, the Islamic Justice and Development Party won an outright majority in the parliament in 2002. In Egypt, the still-illegal Muslim Brotherhood won almost a quarter of the seats in 2005. In Iran, Mahmoud Ahmadinejad, a non-cleric who emphasized populist issues of poverty and economic justice, was elected president in 2005 with the support of the country's more conservative clergy. The United States found itself facing a resurgent Taliban in Afghanistan along with the escalating conflicts between Sunni and Shiite groups in Iraq. And in January 2006 the militant Palestinian group Hamas won an unexpected and resounding victory in elections for the Palestinian Legislative Council, defeating the more moderate Palestine Liberation Organization.

Many Muslims in the United States and elsewhere viewed the trends as a backlash against the widespread perception that the U.S.-proclaimed war on terror amounted to a war against Islam. "More and more you're seeing moderate Muslims being pushed away from the movement toward progressivism and moving toward the other camp," says author Aslan. ■

Continued on p. 930

At Issue:

Should Islam liberalize its view of women's rights?

OMID SAFI
ASSOCIATE PROFESSOR, ISLAMIC STUDIES, UNIVERSITY OF NORTH CAROLINA CO-CHAIR, STUDY OF ISLAM SECTION, AMERICAN ACADEMY OF RELIGION

WRITTEN FOR *CQ RESEARCHER*, OCTOBER 2006

yes

This loaded and misguided question suggests that Islam must change fundamentally to recognize the rights of women. Instead, I would suggest that a profound reading of the Koran leads one to conclude that God has formed both men and women already in full possession of humanity at every layer: physically, emotionally, intellectually and spiritually. Humanity's God-given capacity to bear the divine covenant is shared by men and women, Muslim and non-Muslim.

The Islamic tradition historically has cultivated such a beautiful understanding. But local and cultural gender roles have shaped Islamic thought and practice in some domains — particularly in Islamic law — and the patriarchal prejudices of pre-modern societies have crept into historical interpretations of Islam. So when we encounter statements suggesting women are deficient in reason and intellect — statements that we also find in the pre-modern Jewish, Christian and Greek traditions — we must ask whether these understandings reflect God's call for humanity and the example of the Prophet Muhammad or whether they reflect the patriarchies of human societies.

The Koran and Islamic law in many ways were centuries ahead of developments elsewhere regarding women's rights. Muslim women had the right to own and inherit property, manage their own finances and pray to God directly without using male intermediaries. Yet today much work remains to be done in Muslim communities with respect to gender issues. In Iran and Saudi Arabia women are told they must cover their hair this way or that way, and in Turkey, France and Great Britain they are told not to cover themselves this way or that way. Where is the recognition that women must come to God on their own terms? That seems to be the challenge of our day with respect to Islam and women's rights.

The emerging women's rights movement in Islam insists that a proper understanding of Islam will recognize men and women as spiritual and social equals. To be successful, it must insist on its own religious legitimacy and tap into the rich reservoirs of Islamic sources. In other words, it is not a matter of "restoring" or "giving back" women's rights, it is a matter of recognizing that women are divine creations intended to fully possess rights and privileges. The manifestations of patriarchy — both inside and outside of religious traditions — that have robbed humans of their vitality and moral agency must be dismantled.

STEPHEN SCHWARTZ
EXECUTIVE DIRECTOR, CENTER FOR ISLAMIC PLURALISM

WRITTEN FOR *CQ RESEARCHER*, OCTOBER 2006

no

Islam need not liberalize its view of women because problems of women's rights are not inherent to Islam. While Islam unfortunately is perceived in the West as a bastion of female oppression, this results from the conjunction of differing perspectives on the religion.

There are many ways to be Muslim, just as there are many ways to be Christian, Buddhist or Jewish. Although Islamic prayer is performed in Arabic and the Koran was delivered in Arabic, Islamic practice and culture are not restricted to an Arab paradigm. While the worst anti-female practices are maintained in the Arabian peninsula and its near neighbors, so-called honor killings have been exported to the non-Muslim world by uneducated people. But honor killings are also known to occur among non-Muslims.

Moreover, Arab customs are subject to change. A women's protest movement centered in Jiddah — near the holy cities of Mecca and Medina — opposes mandatory face covering and other forms of intimidation by the Saudi-Wahhabi religious militia or *mutawwa*. The women point out that they never covered their faces in the past, do not wish to do so now and say the *mutawwa* should return to their place of origin in eastern Arabia.

If women in the region of Mecca and Medina reject oppressive practices, how can such practices be considered Islamic? Similarly, the vast majority of young Bosnian Muslim women — who served as soldiers or mobilized civilians in the war of the 1990s in which 250,000 Muslims died — refuse to cover their hair, much less their faces.

Islam settled in the Eastern world, where progress has always been slow. But Islam also contrasts with other traditions in its early empowerment of women. Islam allowed women to divorce from the beginning, while divorce is still obstructed for Catholic and Orthodox Jewish women. Islam also abolished female infanticide — one of the first Islamic "reforms" among peninsular Arabs.

Muslim women never suffered bound feet or the common Indian habit of sari death. Capitalist democracies in Korea, Japan and East Asia do not encourage women to have political or media careers, while Muslim countries — even some of the most extreme — have female political leaders such as Tansu Ciller in Turkey. Israeli Arabs have *sharia* courts with women judges.

Social problems in Islamic countries reflect local culture and history, not the Islamic faith.

Continued from p. 928

CURRENT SITUATION

Muslim Identities

Muslims around the world are returning to their normal routines following Ramadan, the Islamic calendar's holiest month, traditionally marked by dawn-to-dusk fasting, daily prayers and self-examination. The apparent worldwide increase in observances of Ramadan corresponds with Islam's increasing visibility and importance in the Muslim world and elsewhere — and the increasingly cacophonous debate over the role and meaning of Islam in the modern world.

"There is a very open and public debate in many cases about who speaks for Islam throughout the [Muslim world]," says Dale Eickelman, a professor of anthropology and human relations at Dartmouth College, in Hanover, N.H. "Even in areas where there are repressive regimes, this debate has become increasingly public."

"Within the greater Middle East there is now a much greater emphasis on Islam as the primary source of identity," says Freedom House's Marshall. From his travels, Marshall says he sees the change not only in avowedly Islamist countries such as Saudi Arabia, Sudan and Iran but also in more secular Egypt, the most populous Arab nation and the historic seat of Islamic learning. "Each time I go there, the number of women who are completely covered up is increasing," he says.

Egypt's authoritarian President Mubarak continues to have a difficult relationship with the Muslim Brotherhood, which won 88 seats in the national parliament in 2005 despite being officially banned since 1954. In October, Mohammed Mahdi Akef, the leader of the Brotherhood, said the government barred him from traveling to Saudi Arabia for Islamic rituals. "They promised to let me travel but then banned me," Akef told The Associated Press. "It's nonsense." [28]

Meanwhile, religious officials and Egyptians generally appear to be less tolerant of opposing religious views. As noted in *The New York Times*, religious officials moved in three recent cases either to condemn or seek criminal prosecutions of people or publications for promoting unpopular religious views. "The people, of course, oppose anybody who talks about things that violate religion," remarked Sheik Omar el-Deeb, deputy in charge of Al Azhar, the famed Islamic seminary and university founded in the 10th century. [29]

The religious resurgence among Muslims coincides with increased religiosity elsewhere in the world — including in the United States, according to historian Voll. Eickelman also notes historical parallels to the role that religion played in the Solidarity movement in Poland and in the liberation-theology movements in Latin America in the 1980s.

As in those historical examples, Islam's present-day appeal in majority-Muslim countries stems in large part from the failures of established governments, Eickelman says. Secular authorities "have not been seen to be concerned" with improving the standard of living or reducing economic inequality, he says. "It's not clear that religious authorities can do better," Eickelman adds, but Muslim publics are increasingly willing to give them a chance.

Other experts stress that Islamist movements are — in contrast to their negative image in the West — neither monolithic nor necessarily anti-democratic. Established regimes, not Islamists, are the major impediments to democratic reform, according to Amr Hanzawy, an Egyptian and a senior fellow at the Carnegie Endowment for International Peace. Islamist groups are eager to participate in politics, he says, both to capitalize on their popular appeal and to gain protection from repression. [30]

As in Egypt, secular governments elsewhere are resisting the Islamist advance. In Syria, the government of President Bashar al-Assad bans the Muslim Brotherhood, which is allied with the secular opposition in calling for political reforms. In Tunisia, the government of President Zine Al-Abidine Ben Ali is conducting a campaign against Islamic head scarves, calling them "sectarian."

Any efforts to contain the religious impulse — whether by existing regimes or from Western governments or groups — appear unlikely to succeed, according to many experts. "Anybody trying to secure an audience in the Muslim-majority world would want to indicate a respect for Islam," says Eickelman. "You have to have answers on how to make society better — and better for religious reasons."

Religious Clashes

Suspended Muslim teaching assistant Aishah Azmi is still fighting for the right to wear a veil in her classroom but with little public support in England. Meanwhile, the veil controversy is sparking debate in other Western countries, including the United States — adding to tensions created by other clashes between Islam and the non-Muslim world.

The Muslim Member of Parliament (MP) from Azmi's constituency is among those urging her not to appeal an unfavorable ruling by an employment tribunal on her suspension. The tribunal rejected Azmi's claim that the local school council in northern England discriminated against her by suspending her for refusing to take off the veil in class, although it awarded her about $2,300 because the council had "victimized" her.

MP Shahid Malik said that local Muslim parents have told him they would not send their children to schools where women teachers wore the veil. "I would appeal to Mrs. Azmi just to let this thing go," Malik said the day after the ruling. "There is no real support for it." [31]

Reefat Drabu, the chair of social and family affairs at the Muslim Council of Britain, declared that Azmi's position was making things harder for Muslim communities in Britain. He said publicity about the case since September has led to "more attacks on Muslim women" and mosques and "a continuous hammering of Muslims throughout the country."

Azmi herself was avoiding additional comment after talking with reporters on the day of her decision. Nick Whittingham, her lawyer, said she was tired and feeling pressure after the verdict. "I expect she wishes it would all go away," he said. Still, Whittingham said he was exploring grounds for an appeal and considering seeking additional legal aid to take the case further, even possibly to the European Court of Human Rights.

Muslim leaders noted that wearing the veil is generally not considered obligatory and that only about 5 percent of Muslim women in Britain do. But an encouraging sign for women who choose to wear the veil emerged in a poll that showed a generation gap on the issue: 65 percent of Britons over age 65 expressed discomfort with the veil but only 31 percent of 18-24 year olds. [32]

Meanwhile, the controversy in Britain focused attention on similar episodes elsewhere in Europe. Jan Creemers, mayor of the small Belgian town of Maaseik, banned the *niqab* earlier in 2006 — and reportedly won the backing of most of the town's Moroccan Muslim population. Other Belgian towns followed suit. Italy's anti-terrorist laws have the effect of a ban by prohibiting hiding one's face. [33]

In addition, France effectively bars Muslim public school pupils from wearing even the less obtrusive head scarf under a law that bans religious accessories. Several states in Germany bar schoolteachers from wearing head scarves.

Getty Images/Wissam al-Okaili

Iraqi youngsters inspect the remnants of a car bomb that killed nine people and wounded 27 in a largely Shiite area of Baghdad on Oct. 9, 2006. Fighting between Sunni and Shiite Muslims is helping to drive the escalating insurgency in Iraq three years after the U.S.-led invasion ousted Saddam Hussein.

The issue flared in the United States when a state district judge in Michigan threw out a Muslim woman's court case because she refused to remove her veil when she testified. Judge Paul Paruk told Ginnah Muhammad that he needed to see her face in order to judge her veracity.

Meanwhile, the Vatican appears to be making progress toward healing the rift that Pope Benedict XVI created on Sept. 12 with a lecture that included a medieval Christian emperor's critical comment about Islam. [34] The quotation was part of what amounted to a contemporary interfaith dialogue between the Byzantine emperor Manuel II Paleologus and a Persian Muslim.

As Benedict recounted, the emperor described Islam in blunt terms: "Show me just what Muhammad brought that was new, and there you will find things only evil and inhuman, such as his command to spread by the sword the faith he preached." News accounts of the speech provoked outrage in much of the Muslim world and forced Benedict to dissociate himself from the criticism. The views, he said, "were a quotation from a medieval text which does not in any way express my personal thought."

The pope also met in the Vatican with representatives of all Muslim nations that had diplomatic representation. By late October, the efforts at rapprochement appeared to be bearing fruit. In a letter to the pope, 38 Muslim leaders accepted his explanation and welcomed his call for dialogue between Christians and Muslims. ■

OUTLOOK

Misunderstandings?

When France moved to ban head scarves from public schools in 2004, Britain's Labor government pointedly dissociated itself from any limits on religious attire. "In Britain we are comfortable with the expression of religion," Foreign Office Minister Mike O'Brien said. "Integration does not require assimilation." [35]

Two years later, however, Prime Minister Tony Blair joined in criticizing the wearing of the Muslim veil as a "sign of separation." And Blair's government — concerned about the homegrown Islamist extremists blamed for the London subway and bus bombings in 2004 and a foiled airplane sabotage plot last August — is quietly funding an Islamic Web site appealing for moderation and distributing CDs promoting moderation to Muslim students at universities.[36]

Among Muslims and non-Muslims alike, many Britons view the recent pronouncements from government officials on the veil issue as divisive. "If we go and demonize a substantial section of our own population, my advice would be to watch out," says Roger Ballard, an anthropologist affiliated with the University of Manchester who has studied the Pakistani Muslim community in Pakistan and England.

Bukhari of the London-based Muslim Public Affairs Committee says the criticisms amount to a "vilification" of Muslims from some quarters — due in part to the separation between Britain's Muslim and non-Muslim communities. "If you don't know a Muslim, you don't hang around with Muslims, then you have no one to rely on for your perceptions of Muslims besides the media," he says.

"Both the Muslim community and the non-Muslim community need to communicate with each other about each other," says Anwar with the Lancashire Council of Mosques. "I'm not very keen on this word 'tolerate.' I prefer understanding."

A combination of historical and contemporary circumstances, however, makes understanding Islam difficult both for the non-Muslim West and for Muslims themselves.

Historically, the three "religions of the book" — Judaism, Christianity and Islam — may share a common heritage, but they have engaged in theological, cultural and political disagreements and conflicts through much of the past 14 centuries. Islam and Christianity came to hold sway over different parts of the globe — the Muslim world and the Christian West — while Islam and Judaism have been drawn into a deadly conflict in their common homeland because of the Israeli-Palestinian dispute.

Mutual fears and recriminations have intensified since the 9/11 attacks and the proclaimed war on terror, according to British author Grieve. "To rise up with this nationalist fury was to completely misunderstand the event," he says.

Muslims reacted with understandable defensiveness, Grieve continues. "Islam in the current world situation has taken on this combative stance," he says. "It explains to them why their life is not just right."

Foreign-policy issues appear certain to be a continuing source of division, at least for the short term. Most notably, the Israeli-Palestinian dispute is "an open wound, a symbol for Muslims of the fundamental injustice of the region," according to progressive Muslim scholar Safi at the University of North Carolina. The Iraq insurgency may pit Sunnis against Shiites, but the vast majority of Muslims in the region appear united in wanting the United States to withdraw.

In Britain — as in many other parts of Europe — many Muslims expect divisions to increase. "Nothing's going to change," says Bukhari. "It's only going to get worse."

Prospects for successful integration may be better in the United States. "Attitudes toward Muslims in America are more accepting than in Europe," says author Aslan.

But Anwar says Muslims must also engage in self-examination. "As a Muslim community, we need to look at extremism internally," she says. "Are we really living our faith to the high standards we impose, or have we separated the religion from the faith?

"If Muslims started to live the faith as it is, then we can make a difference," Anwar continues. "The United Kingdom is a very fertile land, and it can take on new philosophies. But it has to be give-and-take. It will take time, but it will happen." ■

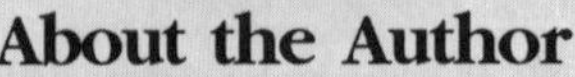

About the Author

Associate Editor **Kenneth Jost** graduated from Harvard College and Georgetown University Law Center. He is the author of the *Supreme Court Yearbook* and editor of *The Supreme Court from A to Z* (both *CQ Press*). He was a member of the *CQ Researcher* team that won the 2002 ABA Silver Gavel Award. His recent reports include "Democracy in the Arab World" and "Religious Persecution."

Notes

[1] Coverage from these London newspapers, all on Oct. 20, 2006: Andrew Norfolk, " 'I won't be treated as an outcast,' says Muslim teacher in veil row," *The Times*; Ian Herbert, "Teaching assistant 'victimised' for wearing veil, tribunal rules," *The Independent*; Martin Wainwright, "Tribunal dismisses case of Muslim woman ordered not to teach in veil," *The Guardian*. See also Jake Morris, "The Great Veil Debate," *The Mirror*, Oct. 14, 2006, p. 9.

[2] Jonathan Wynne-Jones, "Drive for multi-faith Britain deepens rifts, says Church," *Daily Telegraph*, Oct. 8, 2006.

[3] See David Harrison, "Government policy on multiculturalism has been left in tatters," *The* [London] *Daily Telegraph*, Oct. 8, 2006. Other accounts of controversy taken from various English newspapers in October 2006. For coverage in a U.S. newspaper, see Alan Cowell, "British Leader Stirs Debate With His Call to Raise Veils," *The New York Times*, Oct. 7, 2006, p. A8.

[4] For background, see these *CQ Researcher* reports: Peter Katel, "Global Jihad," Oct. 14, 2005, pp. 857-880; David Masci and Kenneth Jost, "War on Terrorism," Oct. 12, 2001, pp. 817-848.

[5] Paul Grieve, *Islam: History, Faith and Politics: The Complete Introduction* (2006), pp. 21-22.

[6] For background, see Pamela M. Prah, "War in Iraq," *CQ Researcher*, Oct. 21, 2005, pp. 881-908; and David Masci, "Rebuilding Iraq," *CQ Researcher*, July 25, 2003, pp. 625-648.

[7] For the full text of his remarks, see www.aljazeera.com/me.asp?service_ID=8831.

[8] Angel M. Rabasa, *et al.*, *The Muslim World after 9/11* (2004).

[9] CBS News, "Poll: Sinking Perceptions of Islam," April 12, 2006 (www.cbsnews.com). The telephone survey of 899 adults was conducted April 9-12; the sampling error was plus or minus three percentage points. The February 2002 survey was by Gallup.

[10] Laurie Goodstein, "Seeing Islam as 'Evil' Faith, Evangelicals Seek Converts," *The New York Times*, May 27, 2003, p. A1; The Associated Press, "Threats and Responses; Muhammad a Terrorist to Falwell," *The New York Times*, Oct. 4, 2002, p. A17.

[11] See Sohail H. Hashmi, "Jihad," in *Encyclopedia of Religion and Politics* (2d ed.), 2006 [forthcoming].

[12] Seyyed Hossein Nasr, "Islam and the Question of Violence," *Al-Serat: A Journal of Islamic Studies*, Vol. XIII, No. 2, available at www.al-islam.org/al-serat/IslamAndViolence.htm.

[13] See Noreen S. Ahmed-Ullah, "Muslim Decree to Oppose Terrorism," *Chicago Tribune*, July 28, 2005, p. C12; Laurie Goodstein, "From Muslims in America, a New Fatwa on Terrorism," *The New York Times*, July 28, 2005, p. A14.

[14] Safi has collected some of the post-9/11 statements at http://groups.colgate.edu/aarislam/response.htm.

[15] Account drawn from Judy Dempsey and Mark Landler, "Opera Canceled Over a Depiction of Muhammad," *The New York Times*, Sept. 27, 2006, p. A1; Craig Whitlock, "Fear of Muslim Backlash Cancels Opera," *The Washington Post*, Sept. 27, 2006, p. A24.

[16] Quoted in Jeffrey Fleishman, "Europe Raising Its Voice Over Radical Islam," *Los Angeles Times*, Oct. 16, 2006, p. A4.

[17] Grieve, *op. cit.*, p. 318.

[18] See "Punjab University to Start Masters in Musicology Despite Protests," *Financial Times Global News Wire*, Sept. 17, 2006; "Pakistani students campaign against dance, music, theatre," Indo-Asian News Service, June 3, 2006. See also Aryn Baker, "No Dates, No Dancing," *Time*, Oct. 8, 2006.

FOR MORE INFORMATION

Center for Islamic Pluralism, (202) 232-1750; www.islamicpluralism.org. A think tank that opposes the radicalization of Islam in America.

Center for Muslim-Christian Understanding, Georgetown University, 37th & O Sts., N.W., Washington, DC 20057; (202) 687-8375; www.cmcu.net. Dedicated to achieving a better understanding between Islam and Christianity and between the Muslim world and the West.

Center for Religious Freedom, 1319 18th St., N.W., Washington, DC 20036; (202) 296-5101; www.freedomhouse.org/religion. Defends against religious persecution of all groups throughout the world.

Center for the Study of Islam and Democracy, 1050 Connecticut Ave., N.W., Suite 1000, Washington, DC 20036; (202) 772-2022; www.islam-democracy.org. Studies Islamic and democratic political thought and merges them into a modern Islamic democratic discourse.

Council on American-Islamic Relations, 453 New Jersey Ave., S.E., Washington, DC 20003; (202) 488-8787; www.cair.com. Works to enhance understanding of Islam and empower American Muslims.

Pew Forum on Religion & Public Life, 1615 L St., N.W., Suite 700, Washington, DC 20036-5610; (202) 419-4550; www.pewforum.org. The nonpartisan forum "seeks to promote a deeper understanding of how religion shapes the ideas and institutions of American society."

[19] Safi, *op. cit.*, p. 2.

[20] Nicholas D. Kristof, "Looking for Islam's Luthers," *The New York Times*, Oct. 15, 2006, sec. 4, p. 13.

[21] Background drawn from John O. Voll, "Islam," in Robert Wuthnow (ed.), *Encyclopedia of Politics and Religion* (2d ed.) (forthcoming December 2006).

[22] Some background drawn from Paul Marshall (ed.), *Radical Islam's Rules: The Worldwide Spread of Extreme Shari'a Law* (2005); Grieve, *op. cit.*

[23] *Ibid.*, p. 170.

[24] For background see David Masci and Kenneth Jost, "War on Terrorism," *CQ Researcher*, Oct. 12, 2001, pp. 817-848.

[25] Council on American-Islamic Relations, "American Muslims: One Year After 9-11," 2002, pp. 1-2.

[26] Some background drawn from David Masci, "An Uncertain Road: Muslims and the Future of Europe," Pew Forum on Religion and Public Life, October 2005 (www.pewforum.org).

[27] Voll, *op. cit.*

[28] "Muslin Brotherhood head says Egypt bars him from travel to Saudi Arabia," The Associated Press, Oct. 11, 2006.

[29] See Michael Slackman, "A Liberal Brother at Odds With the Muslim Brotherhood," *The New York Times*, Oct. 21, 2006, p. A4.

[30] See "Engagement or Quarantine: How to Deal with the Islamist Advance," Carnegie Endowment for International Peace, June 28, 2006 (synopsis at www.carnegieendowment.org).

[31] Quoted in Paul Stokes, "Muslim MP tells veiled class assistant to give up fight," *The Daily Telegraph* [London], Oct. 21, 2006, p. 8. Other background and quotes drawn from Paul Malley, "Top MPs in warning to Muslim," *Daily Star*, Oct. 21, 2006, p. 2; Huw Thomas, "Veil hang-ups may pass," *The Times Educational Supplement*, Oct. 27, 2006, p. 21.

[32] Cited in *ibid.*

[33] "Muslim Veils Spark Debate in Europe," Voice of America English Service, Oct. 21, 2006.

[34] See "Visit to Turkey a stern test for Vatican after Muslim outrage," *Irish Times*, Oct. 23, 2006.

[35] Shola Adenekan, "British criticism of headscarf ban," BBC News, Feb. 10, 2004.

[36] See Patrick Hennessy and Melissa Kite, "Al-Qaeda is winning the war of ideas, says Reid," *The Sunday Telegraph* [London], Oct. 22, 2006, p. 1.

Bibliography

Selected Sources

Books

Abdo, Geneive, *Mecca and Main Street: Muslim Life in America After 9/11*, Oxford University Press, 2006.

Author-journalist Abdo combines first-hand reporting in Muslim communities in the United States with broad background knowledge of Islam to produce an insightful portrait of American Muslims five years after the 9/11 terrorist attacks. Includes five-page bibliography.

Aslan, Reza, *No god but God: The Origins, Evolution, and Future of Islam*, Random House, 2005.

An Iranian-American Muslim recounts the history of Islam from the pre-Islamic era in Arabia to what he describes as the current "Islamic Reformation" under way in much of the Muslim world. Aslan is a fellow at the University of Southern California and Middle East expert for CBS News. Includes glossary, notes and six-page list of works consulted.

Grieve, Paul, *A Brief Guide to Islam: History, Faith and Politics: The Complete Introduction*, Carroll and Graf Publishers, 2006.

Grieve, a British author, studied Islam for three years while researching his second novel and turned his research into a comprehensive guide to the history of Islam, its doctrines and practices, and Islam's relations with the non-Muslim world. Includes 14-page glossary and other reference materials.

Lippman, Thomas W., *Understanding Islam: An Introduction to the Muslim World* (3d revd. ed.), 2002.

Lippman, a longtime newspaper correspondent in the Middle East, provides a well-organized primer on Islam's beliefs and practices, Muhammad's life and teachings, the Koran, law and government under Islam and Islam's history to present times. Includes compact glossary, bibliography.

Marshall, Paul (ed.), *Radical Islam's Rules: The Worldwide Spread of Extreme Shari'a Law*, Freedom House's Center for Religious Freedom, 2005.

Eight contributors examine the adoption or advance of "extreme" shari'a law in Saudi Arabia, Iran, Pakistan, Sudan, Nigeria, Malaysia, Indonesia and Afghanistan. Includes chapter notes. Marshall, a senior fellow at the Center for Religious Freedom, is also co-author with Roberta Green and Lela Gilbert of *Islam at the Crossroads: Understanding Its Beliefs, History, and Conflict* (Baker Books), 2002.

Rabasa, Angel M., *et al.*, *The Muslim World After 9/11*, RAND, 2004.

Eight contributors examine the political role and impact of Islam in the Muslim world, region by region. Includes glossary, 11-page bibliography and other reference material.

Safi, Omid (ed.), *Progressive Muslim: On Justice, Gender, and Pluralism*, Oneworld, 2003.

Fourteen contributors articulate the views of progressive Muslims on contemporary Islam, gender justice and pluralism. Safi is associate professor of Islamic studies at the University of North Carolina-Chapel Hill. Includes chapter notes, eight-page list of recommended readings.

Schwartz, Stephen, *The Two Faces of Islam: Saudi Fundamentalism and Its Role in Terrorism* (2d ed.), Doubleday, 2003.

Schwartz, a former journalist and now executive director of the Center for Islamic Pluralism, writes a strongly critical account of the origins of the radical form of Islam called Wahhabism and Saudi Arabia's role in its advance in the United States and around the world. Includes notes, bibliography.

Schulze, Reinhard, *A Modern History of the Islamic World*, New York University Press, 2002.

Schulze, a professor of Islamic studies at the University of Berne, provides a comprehensive account of the history of the Islamic world from the rise of nationalism and independence movements in the early 20th century through the reassertion of Islamic ideologies beginning in the 1970s. Includes notes, chronology, glossary, 26-page bibliography.

Articles

Voll, John O., "Islam," in Robert Wuthnow (ed.), *Encyclopedia of Politics and Religion* (2d ed.), CQ Press, 2006 [forthcoming].

The director of the Center for Muslim-Christian Understanding at Georgetown University provides an overview of the history and beliefs of Islam from its seventh-century origins to the present.

Reports and Studies

Council on American-Islamic Relations, "The Status of Muslim Civil Rights in the United States 2006: The Struggle for Equality," 2006.

The report by the Washington-based council notes a 30 percent increase in reported anti-Muslim incidents in 2005 over the previous year along with poll results indicating widespread negative perceptions of Muslims among Americans.

On the Web

"Islam and Islamic Studies Resources," a Web site maintained by Prof. Alan Godlas of the University of Georgia's Department of Religion (www.uga.edu/islam), provides a comprehensive and well-organized compendium of information and material on Islam.

The Next Step:

Additional Articles from Current Periodicals

Head Scarves and Veils

"Australia Fury At Cleric Comments," BBCNews.com, Oct. 26, 2006.

Australia's most senior Muslim cleric raised hackles when he said women who did not cover their bodies were like "uncovered meat" to cats and invite sexual assault.

"The Islamic Veil Across Europe," BBCNews.com, Oct. 6, 2006, http://news.bbc.co.uk/2/hi/europe/5414098.stm.

This Web page provides a country-by-country summary of what is happening in Russia and six European countries regarding hard scarves or veils worn by Muslim women.

Ambah, Faiza Saleh, "Saudi Women Rise in Defense of the Veil," *The Washington Post*, June 1, 2006, p. A12.

Many women in conservative Saudi Arabia embrace veils as a form of protection and an integral part of their religion.

Fraser, Suzan, "Court tries, acquits Turkish archaeologist for her view on head scarves," Associated Press, Nov. 1, 2006.

A Turkish court acquitted a 92-year-old archaeologist on Nov. 1 on charges of insulting "Turkishness" for writing that Islamic-style head scarves were first worn 5,000 years ago by Sumerian priestesses initiating young men into sex. The predominantly Muslim country has strict secular regulations that bar head scarves in schools and in public offices, but Turkish women are increasingly veiling themselves in a show of religious piety.

Sciolino, Elaine, "Ban on Head Scarves Takes Effect in a United France," *The New York Times*, Sept. 3, 2004, p. A8.

A new French law bans Muslim head scarves, Jewish skullcaps and large Christian crosses but was aimed primarily at perceived creeping fundamentalism among France's 5 million Muslims.

Islamic Reformation

Aslan, Reza, "A Coming Islamic Reformation," *Los Angeles Times*, Jan. 28, 2006, p. B17.

Osama bin Laden's militantly individualistic and anti-institutional movement can be paralleled to several aspects of the Christian Reformation.

Diehl, Jackson, "In Iran, Apocalypse vs. Reform," *The Washington Post*, May 11, 2006, p. A27.

Iran holds some of the world's most progressive Islamic scholars, who believe democracy, human rights and equality for women are compatible with the Koran.

Kristof, Nicholas D., "Looking for Islam's Luthers," *The New York Times*, Oct. 15, 2006, p. 13.

The author sees threads of reform in the Islamic world.

Murphy, Brian, "Taking Intolerance From Texts," *The Miami Herald*, Nov. 27, 2005, p. A23.

Muslim activists are seeking to rewrite Muslim textbooks that promote prejudice and glorify violence.

Rushdie, Salman, "The Right Time for An Islamic Revolution," *The Washington Post*, Aug. 7, 2005, p. B7.

Islam needs a reform movement to bring Islam's core concepts into the modern age.

Muslims in America

Abdo, Geneive, "America's Muslims Aren't as Assimilated as You Think," *The Washington Post*, Aug. 27, 2006, p. B3.

U.S. Muslims are increasingly alienated from mainstream life, choosing an Islamic identity over an American one.

Bahadur, Gaiutra, "Muslims Balance Between Cultures," *The Philadelphia Inquirer*, Aug. 7, 2005, p. B1.

Experts say the American tradition of assimilation makes Muslim immigrants and their children less likely recruits for terrorist organizations.

Cooper, Candy J., "For Muslim Women, Marriage's Delicate Dance," *The New York Times*, Jan. 8, 2006, p. 1.

Young, affluent, educated Muslim women in America are caught between forward-thinking ideas and arranged marriages.

Elliott, Andrea, "Five Years After 9/11, Muslims Moving to U.S. in Droves," *The Houston Chronicle*, Sept. 10, 2006, p. A14.

More than 40,000 Muslims were admitted into the United States in 2005, the highest number since Sept. 11, 2001.

Citing *CQ Researcher*

Sample formats for citing these reports in a bibliography include the ones listed below. Preferred styles and formats vary, so please check with your instructor or professor.

MLA Style

Jost, Kenneth. "Rethinking the Death Penalty." CQ Researcher 16 Nov. 2001: 945-68.

APA Style

Jost, K. (2001, November 16). Rethinking the death penalty. *CQ Researcher, 11*, 945-968.

Chicago Style

Jost, Kenneth. "Rethinking the Death Penalty." *CQ Researcher*, November 16, 2001, 945-968.

CQ Researcher

Published by CQ Press, a division of Congressional Quarterly Inc.

cqresearcher.com

Video Games

Do they have educational value?

More than three-quarters of American youths have video-game consoles at home, and on a typical day at least 40 percent play a video game. Some academic scholars claim playing games is good for literacy, problem-solving, learning to test hypotheses and researching information from a variety of sources. Others say gaming may be good for understanding technical information but not for reading literature and understanding the humanities. Enthusiasts claim gaming is preparing young people for the knowledge-based workplace. Critics worry that it's making kids more socially isolated, less experienced in working with others and less creative. Experts remain divided about whether addiction to games is widespread and whether violent games produce violent behavior. Increasingly, researchers are studying why games are so engrossing, and some are urging educators to incorporate games' best learning features into school programs.

Multiplayer fantasy games like "World of Warcraft" allow players to assume the role of characters like this blood elf.

INSIDE THIS REPORT

CQ Researcher • Nov. 10, 2006 • www.cqresearcher.com
Volume 16, Number 40 • Pages 937-960

RECIPIENT OF SOCIETY OF PROFESSIONAL JOURNALISTS AWARD FOR EXCELLENCE ◆ AMERICAN BAR ASSOCIATION SILVER GAVEL AWARD

VIDEO GAMES

Cover photograph: Blizzard Entertainment/World of Warcraft

CQ Researcher

Nov. 10, 2006
Volume 16, Number 40

MANAGING EDITOR: Thomas J. Colin

ASSISTANT MANAGING EDITOR: Kathy Koch

ASSOCIATE EDITOR: Kenneth Jost

STAFF WRITERS: Marcia Clemmitt, Peter Katel

CONTRIBUTING WRITERS: Rachel S. Cox, Sarah Glazer, Alan Greenblatt, Barbara Mantel, Patrick Marshall, Tom Price, Jennifer Weeks

DESIGN/PRODUCTION EDITOR: Olu B. Davis

ASSISTANT EDITOR: Melissa J. Hipolit

CQ PRESS

A Division of Congressional Quarterly Inc.

SENIOR VICE PRESIDENT/PUBLISHER: John A. Jenkins

DIRECTOR, LIBRARY PUBLISHING: Kathryn C. Suárez

DIRECTOR, EDITORIAL OPERATIONS: Ann Davies

CONGRESSIONAL QUARTERLY INC.

CHAIRMAN: Paul C. Tash

VICE CHAIRMAN: Andrew P. Corty

PRESIDENT/EDITOR IN CHIEF: Robert W. Merry

CQ Researcher (ISSN 1056-2036) is printed on acid-free paper. Published weekly, except March 24, July 7, July 14, Aug. 4, Aug. 11, Nov. 24, Dec. 22 and Dec. 29, by CQ Press, a division of Congressional Quarterly Inc. Annual full-service subscriptions for institutions start at $667. For pricing, call 1-800-834-9020, ext. 1906. To purchase a *CQ Researcher* report in print or electronic format (PDF), visit www.cqpress.com or call 866-427-7737. Single reports start at $15. Bulk purchase discounts and electronic-rights licensing are also available. Periodicals postage paid at Washington, D.C., and additional mailing offices. POSTMASTER: Send address changes to *CQ Researcher*, 1255 22nd St., N.W., Suite 400, Washington, DC 20037.

Video Games

By Sarah Glazer

The Issues

On a hot summer afternoon, eight teenagers gathered in the darkened basement of the Bronx Central Library to play the top-selling football video game "Madden NFL." The Madden tournament in the Bronx, complete with prizes, is part of a growing effort at libraries across the country to lure a client who rarely darkens the door of a public library — the adolescent boy.

"If it wasn't for the gaming stuff dragging me in that first time, I would have gone maybe once in the past two years," says Ian Melcher, 17, a gamer in Ann Arbor, Mich., who had just checked out two calculus books. "I realized the library was pretty cool and had other things I was interested in."

To persuade skeptical libraries to put video games on the shelf next to books, young librarians who grew up on games are drawing support from a surprising source — academic researchers. They claim that playing video games is practically a requirement of literacy in our digital age.

To many parents and baby boomers, playing video games looks like mindless activity. Yet the knowledge built into "Madden," for example, employs a playbook the size of an encyclopedia. To win, players must have a sophisticated understanding of strategy and make split-second decisions about which play to choose.

"Games stress taking your knowledge and applying it. That's pretty crucial in the modern world," says University of Wisconsin Professor of Reading James Gee, author of the 2003 book *What Video Games Have to Teach Us about Learning and Literacy.*

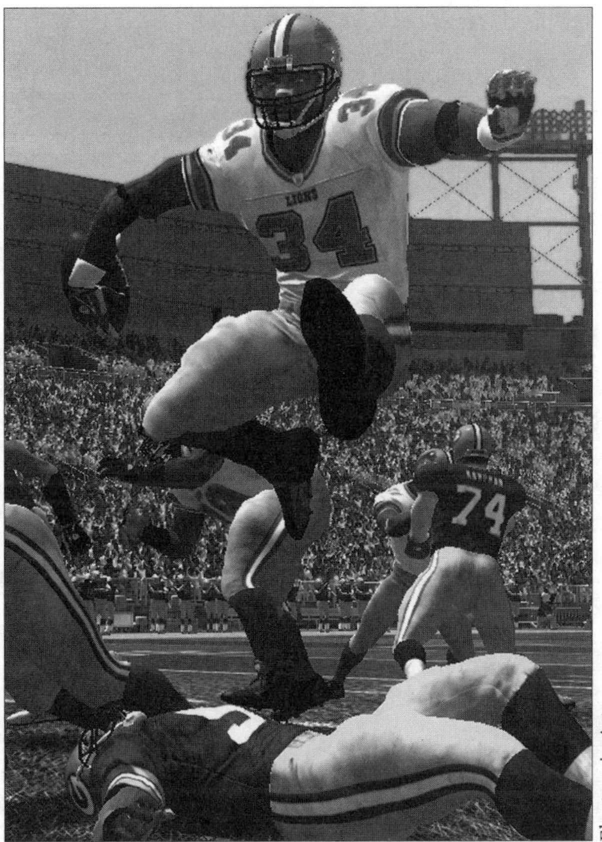

Electronic Arts

Detroit Lions running back Kevin Jones goes airborne for extra yardage in the 2007 edition of the popular video game "Madden NFL." Some scholars claim video and computer games help literacy, but others say they don't assist with reading literature or understanding the humanities. Experts also remain divided about whether addiction to games is widespread and whether some games produce violent behavior.

Indeed, the argument that video and computer games are superior to school in helping children learn is gaining currency in academic circles. CLaimed benefits include improved problem-solving, mastery of scientific investigation and the ability to apply information learned to real-life situations. Some of the more complex games, especially multiplayer games like "World of Warcraft" — played online simultaneously with thousands of players — lead some teens to engage in esoteric, online conversations about strategy and to create their own literary spin-offs or so-called fanfiction.

"Many video games require players to master skills in demand by today's employers," concluded a report released in October by the Federation of American Scientists, citing complex decision-making and team building. The organization urged the federal government to invest in research and development of educational games for K-12 students and for adult work-force training. [1]

Science writer Steven Johnson, who popularized the pro-game argument in his 2005 book *Everything Bad is Good for You,* argues that when a child enters the world of a computer game, he is "learning the scientific method" as he tries out multiple hypotheses. [2] For instance, today's youngsters don't first sit down and read a rule book, the way baby boomers did. They start pushing buttons to see what happens.

That willingness to learn from failure uniquely prepared members of the dot-com generation, giving them an advantage as entrepreneurs and creative thinkers in the new economy, argue business experts John C. Beck and Mitchell Wade in their 2004 book *Got Game.* "A kid in the classroom has to worry about looking like an idiot. In a game, they're raising their hand all the time, and true learning comes from failing," concurs Dmitri Williams, assistant professor of speech communication at the University of Illinois at Urbana-Champaign. "When you strip away all the explosions, blood, magic coins, princesses and castles, video games are problem-solving tasks —

Sports and Multiplayer Games Most Popular

The 10 highest-selling video games are either about major-league sports, auto racing or "Star Wars," which largely appeal to boys; most are rated suitable for the entire family. Among computer games, four of the top 10 are "Sims" games, which also appeal to girls, and several are warfare games. Multiplayer games like "World of Warcraft" — which has 6 million players — are heavily female.

Top 10 Video Games, 2005

Rank	Title	Rating*
1.	Madden NFL 06 (PlayStation version)	E
2.	Gran Turismo 4	E
3.	Madden NFL 06 (Xbox version)	E
4.	NCAA Football 06	E
5.	Star Wars: Battlefront II	T
6.	MVP Baseball 2005	E
7.	Star Wars Episode III: Sith	T
8.	NBA Live 06	E
9.	Lego Star Wars	E
10.	Star Wars: Battlefront II	T

Top 10 Computer Games, 2005

Rank	Title	Rating*
1.	World of Warcraft	T
2.	The Sims 2: University Expansion Pack	T
3.	The Sims 2	T
4.	Guild Wars	T
5.	Roller Coaster Tycoon 3	E
6.	Battlefield 2	T
7.	The Sims 2 Nightlife Expansion Pack	T
8.	MS Age of Empires III	T
9.	The Sims Deluxe	T
10.	Call of Duty 2	T

** T = Teens (suitable for ages 13 and older)*

E = Everyone (suitable for ages 6 and older)

Source: Entertainment Software Assn., "2006 Sales, Demographic and Usage Data"

puzzles. There's some irony in the fact that kids are bored at school but rush home to solve these games where they learn math and history."

As evidence that kids are willing to master language and concepts usually considered over their head, Johnson describes an hour spent teaching his nephew to play the urban planning-style game "SimCity." While Johnson was trying to figure out how to save a dying industrial neighborhood, the 7-year-old piped up, "I think we need to lower industrial tax rates." [3]

"SimCity" creator Will Wright says the youngster probably didn't understand tax rates any more than baby boomers understood mortgages when they played "Monopoly" as kids. But he thinks games teach something else. "The ability to reverse-engineer in your head a model of some arbitrarily complex thing is an incredibly valuable skill that you can apply to almost anything in this world," he says, whether that's doing your taxes, programming a new cell phone or predicting the effect of global warming.

Despite the worries of baby-boomer parents, there's no evidence that video gaming is replacing reading among teens. According to a Kaiser Family Foundation survey, reading for pleasure has remained steady in the past five years even as video-gaming time has risen. [4]

But what about teens who seem to spend most of their leisure time on games? Heavy gamers — more than an hour a day — actually spend more time reading for pleasure (55 minutes daily) than teens who play no video games at all (41 minutes), according to the Kaiser survey. And Kaiser found only 13 percent of adolescents were heavy gamers.

Nevertheless, the persistent anecdotes about teens and adults who skip meals, classes and even work to indulge in hours of video-gaming has led some to worry the games are addictive. Clinics have even sprung up claiming to treat "Internet addiction disorder."

But many psychologists remain skeptical. "There's hardly anyone I would class as a genuine video-game addict," says Professor of Gambling Studies Mark Griffiths of Nottingham Trent University in Nottingham, England. Few players, he says, meet a strict definition of addiction, which includes withdrawal symptoms and a preoccupation so single-minded that every other aspect of life is neglected.

Experts are also divided over whether graphic violence in games like "Grand Theft Auto" has any lasting negative effects on players' behavior, despite a few cases in which a teen's murderous frenzy has been blamed on games by the victim's parents. Recent studies indicate that the younger a player is, the more likely he is to be negatively affected by video violence and the longer lasting the effect. (*See sidebar, p. 948.*)

Concerns about both addiction and violence have led to efforts to curb online role-playing games like "World of Warcraft" and "Lineage II." Last year, the Chinese government imposed penalties on gamers who spend more than three hours playing a game by reducing the abilities of their characters. All the biggest online game operators said they would adopt the new system. The measures were designed to combat addiction in a country where more than 20 million Chinese play games regularly, mainly in net cafes. In one case, a player killed a fellow player who had stolen his virtual sword. (The penalties were later rescinded after widespread protests.)

Aside from worries about addiction and violence, not all scholars are equally enthusiastic about the learning value of video games on the market. In most games, the content is "garbage," according to Harvard Graduate School of Education Professor Christopher Dede, "in the sense that it deals with imaginary situations that are not close to the knowledge and skills people need for the 21st century. To claim that learning magic spells is good preparation for the knowledge-based workplace is just plain silly."

Dede is among those interested in adapting one of the most popular offshoots of gaming — virtual worlds — to educational aims. Player create characters (or avatars) who enter a virtual world. Hundreds of thousands of teenagers now participate in virtual worlds like There.com and Second Life, where they can create a character, buy clothes and real estate and meet other players' avatars. (*See sidebar, p. 952.*)

In "River City," created by Dede's team at Harvard, players try to figure out the cause of a mysterious epidemic in a 19th-century town. Researchers found that middle-schoolers using "River City" improved their biological knowledge and science skills more than peers taught more traditionally. [5]

Another sign of university interest: Colleges now offer courses in "Second Life." Starting this fall, teens entering There.com will be able to take classes in areas like copyright law taught by university professors.

But some advocates worry that all this high-level learning will be limited to middle-class kids, who have access to fancier, faster hardware and to educated parents who can guide their choice of games — creating a new equity gap on top of the existing reading gap between income groups.

While 83 percent of young people ages 8-18 have a video console at home, they may not be using them the same way. [6] A recent study of Philadelphia libraries with computers found that middle-class 12-13-year-olds typically used computers to increase their knowledge, by looking up — for example — Christopher Columbus on the encyclopedia site Encarta. But those from low-income neighborhoods were more likely to play "Magic School Bus," a game for 9-year-olds. [7]

The difference can be traced to the lack of guidance from a parent or other adult, which is as crucial for good games as for good books, says the University of Wisconsin's Gee. "Giving a kid a book [or game] is okay, but with no adult to

Most Gamers Are Males

Sixty-two percent of video-game players are males between 18 and 49, and fully one-quarter are at least 50.

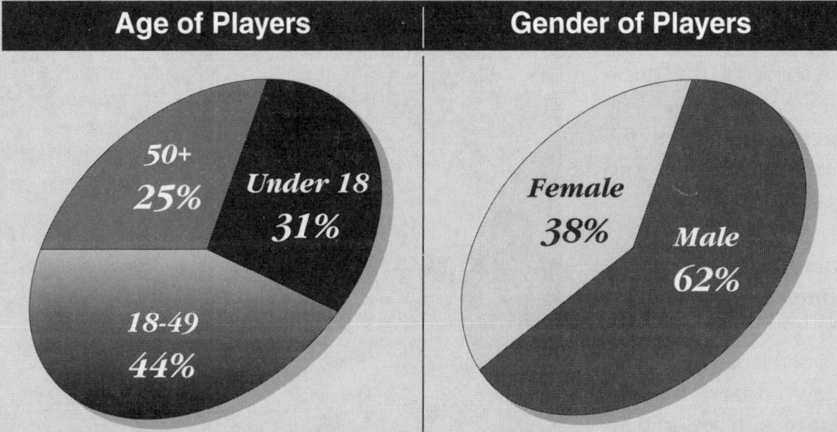

Gamers at a Glance

- *The average gamer is 33 years old.*
- *Women over 17 represent a larger portion of the game-playing population (30 percent) than boys under 18 (23 percent).*
- *69 percent of U.S. heads of households play computer/video games.*
- *The average age of the most frequent game purchaser is 40.*
- *Adult gamers have been playing for an average of 12 years.*
- *Among the most frequent gamers, adult males average 10 years of playing, females, eight years.*

CQ Press/Joe King-Shaw

Source: Entertainment Software Association

mentor the child and talk about the material it isn't very helpful," he says.

As video games increasingly become a fact of life in the lives of children and adults, here are some of the questions being debated by parents, academics, the gaming industry and players themselves:

Does playing video games improve literacy?

For the past year, nearly two-dozen 8-to-13-year-olds from low-income neighborhoods in Madison, Wis., have gathered after school to play the best-selling game "Civilization," under the watchful eyes of University of Wisconsin researchers. Players rule a society from 4,000 B.C. to the present, building cities, trading, gathering natural resources and waging war. A single game requires about 20 hours to play; achieving high-level mastery requires 100 hours or more.

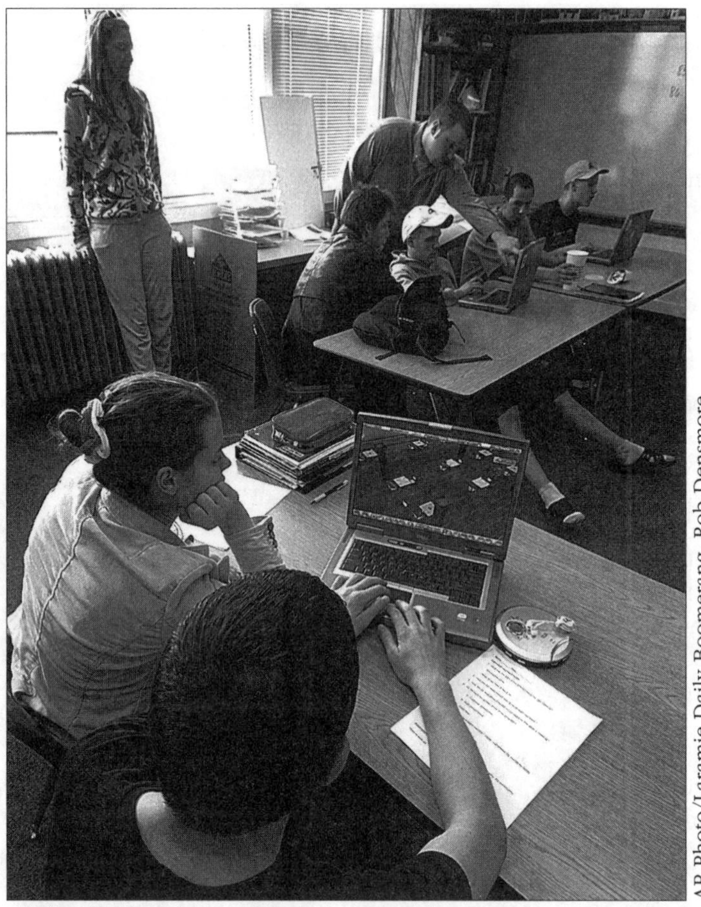

AP Photo/Laramie Daily Boomerang, Rob Densmore

High-school students in Laramie, Wyo., play "Restaurant Empire," a video game that teaches them about the restaurant industry, in March 2006. Researchers are increasingly urging educators to incorporate games' best learning features into school programs.

The children encounter words like "monarchy" and "monotheism" for the first time — but more important, they have to figure out how those and other factors, like natural resources, help a civilization survive or fail, says Kurt Squire, an assistant professor of educational communications and technology, who is directing the study.

"We found when they're expert gamers, they can tell you the differences between civilizations, what technologies they would need, what resources they'd need," he says. To Squire, the game's lifelike simulation is a powerful twist on the progressive-education adage, learning by doing.

Students remember only 10 percent of what they read and 20 percent of what they hear but almost 90 percent if they do the job themselves, even if only as a simulation, according to research cited by the Federation of American Scientists. [8] The University of Wisconsin's Gee even claims that the mind works like a video game in that "effective thinking is more like running a simulation" than forming abstract generalizations. [9]

An academic camp led by Gee argues video games foster a more sophisticated kind of literacy than the simple decoding of words. Video games foster creative thinking — producing "gaming literacies" in the words of Katie Salen, a designer at Parsons The New School for Design in New York City. Gamers not only follow the rules "but push against them, testing the limits of the system in often unique and powerful ways," she says. [10]

Digital literacy also means learning to take information from multiple sources, including Web sites and other players, rather than from one authoritative source like a teacher or textbook.

But Harvard's Dede says that while games may be powerful learning tools, their content leaves much to be desired, and so far no research backs up the claim that games teach kids to think like scientists. To produce those results, he argues the engaging qualities of games must be married to scientific content.

Dede developed "River City" to teach basic science skills, such as forming a hypothesis. After 7,000 middle-school students tested the game-like simulation, they improved their scientific-inquiry skills and increased their knowledge of biology at twice the rate of peers using traditional hands-on labs. [11]

But hard data like Dede's is scant, and most studies have been done with only small numbers of children. The Federation of American Scientists, while enthusiastic about games' learning potential, noted that while kids "seem to do better," the research suffers from a lack of concrete measures of learning. [12]

"We don't have anywhere near sufficient evidence about whether playing computer games helps literacy," says Justine Cassell, professor of communication studies and computer science at Northwestern University. On the other hand, she adds, "There's no evidence that computers hurt literacy."

A computer game Cassell has developed for toddlers with a clown-like character can — much like an imaginary friend — help them develop sophisticated language earlier because they must explain what's happening to an absent person. (For example, toddlers get more precise on the phone, saying, "John went to the store" instead of "He went there.") Teens, she says, have a similar experience when blogging because they learn to write like journalists for an unseen audience.

The more than 4 million players of "Lineage" compete against one another for castles in a virtual kingdom of wizards, elves and knights. These "castle sieges" engage players in complex arguments online about strategy, according to University of Wisconsin researcher Constance Steinkuehler. [13]

Steinkuehler found players' online posts typically written at a 12th-grade reading level or above and often involve scientific reasoning. "I've watched kids who, in an effort to 'cheat' the game, gather data, build simple mathematical models and argue about those models," which, she adds, educators say "is extremely difficult to get high-schoolers to do."

Parents often despair because their teen is "not sitting on a couch reading a storybook, which is what we think literacy is," says Gee. But "the kids' version of literacy is better for a modern-world understanding of technical language," Gee maintains.

In the best games, players must master a specialized game vocabulary, consulting Web pages for hints on winning that probably use syntax far more complex than their reading in school, Gee argues. "I believe firmly the key to school success is handling technical language," he says.

To see how complex the language can get, Gee suggests looking at a Web site offering hints on playing "Yu-Gi-Oh" (both a video and card game). A typically impenetrable sentence reads, "The effect of 8-Claws Scorpion is a Trigger Effect that is applied if the condition is correct on activation." Seven-year-olds are reading sentences like this, even though its complexity won't be matched in the classroom until middle or high school, Gee says.

But can games produce the kind of literacy we most value? The technical material highlighted by enthusiasts is closer to technical manuals than novels and "more likely to appeal to techies than to dreamers, humanists and conversationalists" and to boys rather than girls, worries Harvard Professor of Cognition and Learning Howard Gardner. Immersing oneself in long novels like *Madame Bovary*, in poetry or in a philosophical text involves a skill many game enthusiasts disparage — linear thinking over many pages. That's "an entirely different mental faculty than is exploited when one surfs the Web from one link to another," Gardner argues.

Moreover, even a good video game can't compete with a great teacher, asserts former teacher Joan Almon, coordinator of the Alliance for Childhood in College Park, Md. "It bothers me that people are using these as the great way of learning. They're a modest alternative to very bad teaching," she says.

In its recent report, however, the Federation of American Scientists urges teachers to change from their "tell and test" method — which encourages passive learning — to incorporating the highly interactive, challenge-reward environment of video games. Game developers have incorporated the best learning features recognized by cognitive science, the report says, including:

- tons of practice;
- continual monitoring and feedback on the player's progress;
- encouragement to seek out information on the game strategy from other gamers, friends and Web sites; and,
- bridging the gap from what's learned to real situations. [14]

Some enthusiasts point out that the Internet is already allowing teenagers to become online creators on a huge scale via blogs, music and mini-films known as *machinima* — often inspired by games. Players have posted several-hundred-thousand stories ranging from 10-page plots to small novels as part of the best-selling computer game of all time, "The Sims," where players create their own family and play virtual house.

Some of that interaction could even raise the level of public discourse. In

Gamers Are Not Isolated, Obsessed

Contrary to the stereotype, gamers are not socially isolated people glued to their PlayStations, Xboxes or computers. Players say they spend more than three times as much time each week (23.4 hours) exercising, playing sports, volunteering, attending cultural activities or reading than they spend playing games (6.8 hours).

Percent of gamers who say they:

Exercise or play sports at least 20 hours a month	79%
Volunteer at least 5.4 hours per month	45%
Regularly read books or daily newspapers	93%
Attend concerts, museums, theater	62%
Play games with others in person at least 1 hr/wk	51%
Play games with others online at least 1 hr/wk	25%

CQ Press/Joe King-Shaw

Source: Peter D. Hart Research Associates, 2004

'Sims' Inventor Exploring New Frontiers in Creativity

The creator of the most popular PC game of all time is lanky, bespectacled and surprisingly bookish. Will Wright is already famous for creating "The Sims," akin to playing house, which has sold close to 60 million copies. [1] He's also famous for designing one of the most creative games, "SimCity," an urban-planning game so sophisticated it was later used to train city planners.

But the game world is most excited about the new game — "Spore" — that Wright is developing to be released next year by Entertainment Arts. It started out as a game about extraterrestrial life. But in preparation, Wright says, he read 100 books, including many about biology, which led him to a fascination with evolution, the current game's theme.

In "Spore," players create characters who progress from a one-celled organism to an entire race of creatures using principles of evolution. Will your creature be an herbivore or a carnivore? Will you give it two limbs or 5? And will it survive with the claws you've picked out? (If not, go back and pick something different.) Once you've created a creature, you'll move on to creating tribes, communities and planets. Wright estimates it would take 70 years to visit every planet in "Spore."

But the most revolutionary part of "Spore," may be players' ability to access other gamers' creations for their own play. Once players' creations are uploaded onto Spore's server, they can even request their friends' creations.

As a child, Wright was drawn to taking things apart, which got him interested in robots and ultimately computers, he said in an interview at his studio in Emeryville, Calif. Yet Wright, 46, considers himself part of the generation that grew up reading manuals. By contrast, today's kids press buttons in a game to see what happens — a practice he says leads to more creativity. It also gives kids an early experience with testing models in a simulated environment, an important skill as science and other fields increasingly revolve around simulation, he believes.

Wright challenges the basic notion that it's more educational to read a book than to play a game. "You can step back and see that our natural mode of interacting with the world is not to sit back passively, observe it as a movie or book would present it, but to interact with it and actually have effects on the system and study the effects," he says. Play was probably the first educational activity, he suggests, which permitted us to parse out patterns in the world around us.

"I think you can do that to a limited degree with storytelling but not nearly as deeply as with an interactive experience," Wright says. "Yeah, *Harry Potter* is a great universe and all that, but you can't take the stuff you know about Harry Potter's universe and apply it anywhere else."

a study of an international Internet community of 3,000 teens, Northwestern's Cassell found, "the boys came to talk like the girls in a way that would make many of us happy," such as incorporating language that synthesized the ideas of others, and younger teens adopted the language of older teens.

Thanks to the Internet, teens are "no longer just media consumers" but are producing content, which is good for literacy, says Cassell. "We know that media creation — in whatever medium — is good for children's imagination and good for their ability to create a text for someone else."

Are video games addictive?

Jeffrey Stark, a high-school student from Ontario, Canada, claimed his compulsive playing of the sword-and-sorcery game "EverQuest" ruined his life. He went for a week without bathing or eating a proper meal and stopped going to school for a semester. [15]

Similarly, a 30-year-old registered nurse who plays "EverQuest" with her husband said, "We spend hours — hours! — every single day playing this damn game. My fingers wake me, aching, in the middle of the night. I have headaches from the countless hours I spend staring at the screen. I hate this game, but I can't stop playing. Quitting smoking was never this hard." [16]

About 40 percent of players of multiplayer online games like "EverQuest" say they consider themselves "addicted." [17] Some players call the game "Evercrack." "EverQuest" is an early version of a so-called massively multiplayer online role-playing game (MMORPG), where players create a character who enters a fantasy world and interacts with other players. Online sites like EverQuest Widows, the Yahoo group WOW Widows for spouses of the more than 6 million players of the online "World of Warcraft," and gamewidow.com attest to the despair of gaming spouses and significant others. [18]

In South Korea, the epicenter of online gaming, game addiction reportedly claimed 10 lives in 2005, mainly by cutting off circulation when sitting for hours at the screen. In April, the South Korean government launched a game-addiction hotline, and hundreds of hospitals and private clinics treat the addiction, said to afflict an estimated 2.4 percent of Koreans ages 9-39. [19]

Europe's first clinic for video-game addicts opened in the Netherlands in 2005, and several psychologists treat Internet addicts in the United States. Since starting the Computer Addiction Services program at McLean Hospital — a noted psychiatric facility in Belmont, Mass. — in 1995, Harvard psychologist Maressa Hecht Orzack has treated many gamers who she said were neglecting their jobs, schoolwork and families. "They have withdrawal symptoms. They can't wait to get back on [the

Players are starting to use his games increasingly for self-expression, not just entertainment, Wright observes, which could help explain their enduring popularity. A feature added to "The Sims" that allows players to write stories in the game and save them on a Web page resulted in several-hundred-thousand short stories, novels and biographical accounts that players "were pouring their heart and soul into," says Wright. Fans "form a very tight community around these games," he observes, as they browse one another's stories, download content and create new elements. A moviemaking feature in "Sims2" led to tens of thousands of movies being created by players.

www.will-wright.com

Will Wright, creator of "The Sims," loved to take things apart as a child.

"Spore" will give players unprecedented room for creation. In "The Sims," players can manipulate the face, but it's still a two-legged creature, Wright points out. "This is designing content in a different way that allows the player to have all the freedom," he says. But when this visitor played a preview of the game, it was apparent even the most imaginative designers set limits, suggesting that creativity inside a game isn't the same as creativity outside — a major concern of some educators.

First there's the aesthetic style — cute creatures familiar to young watchers of Pixar movies and reminiscent to older viewers of Flintstone dinosaurs. What if one wanted to create something more frightening?

"Within 'Spore' we offer a series of editors that serve as creative toolkits for making everything from creatures and vehicles to plants and buildings," says Executive Producer Lucy Bradshaw. "What these look like is up to the player. So, I might do something cute and cuddly and sort of Teddy Bear-ish, or I might make a really frightening creature with spindly spider legs and an angry-looking beak that looks like it came out of a horror film. It's all about my personal aesthetic. We want Moms to enjoy this just as much as their 15-year-old sons!"

---

1 "How to Create a Game About Creating a Universe," *Computer Gaming World*, June 2006, p. 70.

game] again," she said, adding that the games "are made to be addictive." [20]

But some prominent addiction experts say even those who play games excessively rarely meet all the characteristics of addiction — such as developing physical withdrawal symptoms like sweating (true for gambling), needing to play more and more to get the same kick and being preoccupied to the point it is destructive to one's livelihood and family. Even though some psychologists talk about "Internet addiction disorder," the American Psychiatric Association has not recognized it in its official handbook, the *Diagnostic and Statistical Manual of Mental Disorders.*

Psychologist and gambling studies professor Griffiths, at Nottingham Trent University, found in a study that one-in-20 British children reported playing more than 30 hours a week. But Griffiths says very few of those children — or the population generally — meet all of the criteria for addiction. "It's quite clear when a parent rings me and says, 'My little Johnny is addicted,' it's hard to fulfill more than one or two of the criteria," he says. "Their real concern is the vast amount of time they're playing. The real question is: To what extent is it having a negative effect on their life?"

For a 38-year-old man with three children and a good job, playing 14 hours daily will negatively affect his livelihood and family. But for an unemployed 23-year-old with no partner or children, the same amount of time "has nothing but positive effects" if it brings him into a social network and raises self esteem, says Griffiths.

Even if they're not technically addicted, users of multiplayer online role-playing games who play on average 20 hours a week tend to describe their game play as "obligation, tedium and more like a second job than entertainment," according to Stanford University researcher Nick Yee. [21]

For example, if a player wants to engage in pharmaceutical manufacturing, one of many possible career choices in "Star War Galaxies," it takes about three to six weeks of normal game play to acquire the abilities to be competitive. Most such games — which get harder as the player becomes more skilled — use designs based on behavioral conditioning, according to Yee, which conditions players to work harder and faster as they improve, creating a kind of digital treadmill of which players are often unaware. [22]

The work required to advance a character's abilities is so time-consuming that companies like TopGameSeller, based in Shanghai, China, offer services to bring one's character up to a more advanced level. Bringing a character in "World of Warcraft" to a higher level. can cost up to $1,488. "We assign two or three expert players to your character to do the leveling," the company promises on its Web site (www.topseller.com), which largely involves "simply killing monsters over and over."

Even Griffiths notes that magazines often rate games on their "addictiveness" as a positive attribute. "It's quite clear that the reward systems in video gaming are similar to gambling," he says. "I don't pick up a video game unless I know I have six hours to burn. If I start now, I'll still be playing at 10 p.m. As soon as you've beaten the high score, you want to beat it again."

Many parents worry that video games are displacing other activities like socializing, creative play and reading. But recent surveys show that teen reading has not declined, even as video-gaming hours have risen. And researchers like Yee find that online gaming takes on a social cast, as players communicate over typed chat.

In any case, game enthusiasts and critics alike say parents must set limits, as with any activity.

Do video games prepare young people for the future job market?

"You play 'World of Warcraft'? You're hired!" Someday those words may be spoken by employers — if they're not already — two technology experts wrote in *Wired*, praising multiplayer games for teaching important workplace skills. [23]

In "Warcraft," players band together in guilds to share knowledge and manpower in a "quest," such as slaying monsters. To run a large guild, a master must be able to recruit new members, create apprenticeship programs, orchestrate group strategy and settle disputes. One young engineer at Yahoo used to worry about whether he could do his job. "Now I think of it like a quest," he said. "By being willing to improvise, I can usually find the people and resources I need to accomplish the task." [24]

Indeed, becoming a guild master "amounts to a total-immersion course in leadership," argue John Seely Brown, former director of Xerox's Palo Alto Research Center, and Douglas Thomas, an associate professor of communication at the University of Southern California's Annenberg School for Communications. [25]

Business experts Beck and Wade came to similar conclusions after surveying 2,100 young professionals, mainly in business. In their book *Got Game*, they claim those with extensive gaming experience were better team members, put a high value on competence and had more potential to be superior executives. Perhaps most important, they argue, gamers understand that repeated failure is the road to success. They found that 81 percent of those under age 34 had been frequent or moderate gamers. [26]

In their most provocative assertion, Beck and Wade claim the dot-com phenomenon was "structured exactly like a video game" in that it called for entrepreneurial skills and a fearlessness toward failure in a generation that grew up gaming. Among the rules learned from gaming were:

- If you get there first, you win;
- Trial and error is the best and fastest way to learn;
- After failure, hit the reset button; don't shrink away. [27]

As Stanford researcher Yee has discovered, many players view playing multiplayer online games as work. Players in "Star War Galaxies" who pick pharmaceutical manufacturing as a career must decide how to price and brand their products, how much to spend on advertising and whether to start a price war with competitors or form a cartel with them. Once players acquire the skills to be competitive in the market, their business operations require a daily time commitment. [28]

Yet today's schools, obsessed with reading and writing, are preparing children for jobs that soon will be outsourced oversees, claims David Williamson Shaffer, associate professor of learning science at the University of Wisconsin-Madison. "The only good jobs left will be for people who can do innovative and creative work," he writes, arguing that video games that teach professional-level language can accomplish that task better than traditional schooling. [29]

A Federation of American Scientists report recently endorsed that view, urging government, industry and educators to take advantage of video-game features to "help students and workers attain globally competitive skills." [30] It said video games could increase the speed at which expertise is acquired, improve players' ability to apply learning and improve decision-making — all important for the coming "conceptual economy."

Already gamers are running political campaigns, negotiating treaties and building environmentally sensitive communities, the report notes. [31] Ashley Richardson was a middle-schooler when she ran for president of Alphaville, the largest city in the popular multiplayer game, "The Sims Online." She debated her opponent on National Public Radio in her campaign to control a government with more than 100 volunteer workers, which made policies affecting thousands of people. [32]

By contrast, students who pass typical school tests often can't apply their knowledge to real-life problems, according to research cited by Shaffer. Students who can write Newton's laws of motion down on a piece of paper still can't use them to answer a simple problem like, "If you flip a coin into the air, how many forces are acting on it at the top of its trajectory?" [33]

Shaffer has designed games that teach middle- and high-school students to think like professionals in solving real-life problems. Students who play urban-planning or science games developed by Shaffer soon develop more sophisticated, professional-level language in those areas, he reports. For example in one game, students help the Chicago Transportation Authority choose what type of seats to put on new buses. "Before playing the game, a player was likely to say, 'I'd choose this seat because it looks comfortable,' " says Shaffer. "Afterwards, the same player says, 'I'd

Continued on p. 948

Chronology

1950s-1960s

Pinball becomes popular among young adults. Early video games are included on computers used by computer students.

1958
Government physicist William A. Higinbotham invents first computer game — electronic Ping Pong.

1961
MIT student Steve Russell creates the rocket-ship game "Spacewar!" Loaded into computers used in tech courses, it exposes computer-science students to the first video game.

1970s

First commercial video games are marketed to families and young singles in arcades.

1972
Magnavox introduces Odyssey, first home video-game console.

1976
Computer game "Adventure" first allows players to control characters' behavior.

1977
Atari introduces first video home console with plug-in cartridges.

1980s

Video-game popularity spikes with Atari in early 1980s; Atari goes bust and industry collapses; Nintendo revives industry at end of decade.

1980
"Pac-Man" is introduced.

1982
Atari sells almost 8 million units. . . . Surgeon general says games create taste for violence.

1984
Warner sells Atari as sales wane.

1985
Popular games "Tetris," "Where in the World is Carmen Sandiego?" and "Super Mario Bros" are introduced.

1989
Nintendo introduces Game Boy; "SimCity," popular urban-planning computer game, is released.

1990s

"First-person shooter" games introduce realistic violence; as sales spike, juvenile violence declines. Multiplayer online games, complex PC games are introduced.

1991
"Civilization," a history game that takes hours to play, is introduced.

1992
"Wolfenstein 3D" is introduced — the first first-person shooter game.

1993
Introduction of "Doom," with more blood and gore.

1994
Sony PlayStation is introduced.

1997
"Grand Theft Auto," a gang-member survival game, is introduced.

1999
"EverQuest," early online multiplayer game, is introduced.

2000s

Concern about excessive game violence and potential for game addiction leads to calls for curbs; number of female gamers rises.

2000
"The Sims," a game about relationships popular with girls, is introduced; becomes best-selling computer game of all time.

2002
Microsoft launches Xbox Live, the first online multiplayer console network. . . . U.S. Army launches "America's Army" to recruit and train soldiers.

Nov. 9, 2004
"Halo2," sci-fi game, creates biggest-grossing media day in history.

2004
The parents of British teenager Steven Pakeerah, murdered by a friend in England, blame his killer's obsession with violent games.

2005
Chinese government penalizes gamers who play for more than three hours. . . . American Psychological Association calls on companies to reduce violence in video games for children and teens. . . . Sen. Hillary Rodham Clinton, D-N.Y., introduces bill to ban rentals, sales of Mature or Adult Only games to minors.

October, 2006
MacArthur Foundation announces grant of $50 million over five years to research how people learn from video games, other digital media. . . . Federation of American Scientists recommends federal research on educational potential of video games.

Do Video Games Make Kids More Violent?

After 14-year-old Stefan Pakeerah was savagely murdered in England by a friend, his parents claimed the murderer had been obsessed by the violent computer game "Manhunt," which awards points for savage killings. Warren Leblanc, 17, who pleaded guilty in 2005 to the murder, had beaten Stefan with a hammer and stabbed him repeatedly after luring him to a local park, the press reported.

Stefan's parents blamed the game and asked retailers to stop selling it. "It's a video instruction on how to murder somebody; it just shows how you kill people and what weapons you use," Patrick Pakeerah said last year, after several major British retailers agreed to stop selling the game. [1]

There is substantial debate among psychologists over whether violent behavior can be blamed on video games, since game players are often exposed to violence from other sources, such as TV or their own lives. Although few long-term studies have been done to see if the effects are long-lasting, many U.S. psychologists are alarmed. Last year, the American Psychological Association adopted a resolution recommending that all violence be reduced in video games marketed to children and youth. The policy decision came after an expert committee reviewed research indicating that exposure to video-game violence increases youths' aggressive thoughts and behavior and angry feelings. [2]

In violent scenes, the committee noted, perpetrators go unpunished 73 percent of the time — teaching children that violence is an effective way to resolve conflict. Some studies also suggest that the active participation peculiar to video games may influence learning more than the kind of passive observation involved in watching TV, the panel pointed out.

"Playing video games involves practice, repetition and being rewarded for numerous acts of violence, which may intensify the learning," said Elizabeth Carll, a New York psychologist who co-chaired the committee. "This may also result in more realistic experiences, which may potentially increase aggressive behavior." [3]

Mark Griffiths, a psychologist at Nottingham Trent University in Nottingham, England, agrees. "I've concluded the younger the person, the more likely there is to be an effect," he says. "If children watch or play video games, right afterwards they will mimic what they see on the screen."

But Griffiths is more skeptical about the lasting effects of video-game violence, especially in older teens and adults. "Video games may have a contributory effect, but overall the evidence is quite slim," he says. "I think there's a predisposition of people who play violent video games to violence anyway. Youthful offenders play more violent video games [than average]. My guess is these people already have problems to start with and seek out that kind of game — not that they become more violent as a result of playing those games."

Another leading researcher at the other end of the spectrum, Iowa State University psychologist Craig Anderson, finds some effects persist in young children. In a recent study of third-, fourth- and fifth-graders, he found that those who played more video games than their peers early in the school year became more verbally and physically aggressive over the course of the year. He describes exposure to violent video games as a "risk factor" — one of many — that could contribute to this behavior. [4]

Seven states limit or ban the sale of violent video games to minors. But most such laws have been overturned after legal challenges by the game industry, usually as unconstitutional in-

Continued from p. 946

choose this one because you get more seats on the bus, it's less expensive and has a higher safety rating.' These were exactly the criteria the bus company was looking at."

Indeed, simulation games have long proven to be effective in training people for a variety of skills, including performing surgery. More than 6 million people have registered to play "America's Army," a game released by the military in 2002 to teach military skills; 3 million completed the basic combat-training course and 3 million completed the three-lecture medic course. [34] And some soldiers in Iraq say playing video games gave them the skills they needed for real battles. [35]

Simulations might be a powerful technique, but they are not the same as real life, observes Harvard's Gardner. "I am happy to have medical students or airplane pilots in training learn as much as they can from simulations — but I also want them to have some real, high-stakes experience," he says. And these are two areas where simulation makes sense, he notes. "I don't think it makes sense for many professions, ranging from poet to priest."

The biggest success stories involve skills associated with science, technology or engineering. "I want my children — indeed all young people — to learn how to think like a historian, a philosopher, an economist, a literary critic," says Gardner. "I want to stimulate their imaginations to create their own worlds, not just that conjured up by the makers of 'World of Warcraft.' "

Some critics worry that the game-playing 20-something generation never gained some of the socialization skills and creativity needed in the workplace. The Alliance for Childhood's Almon doubts that chatting online in a multi-player game can substitute for face-to-face interaction.

"We've been told by one software company that they have to spend so much time teaching the young 20s how to work with others because they've grown up in isolation," she says. The way children traditionally developed those problem-solving skills was by creating their own play situa-

fringements on free speech. None of the laws is currently being implemented, according to the Child-Responsible Media Campaign, which advocates restrictions. [5]

Sen. Hillary Rodham Clinton, D-N.Y., introduced a bill in Congress last year that would make it illegal to rent or sell a video game with Mature or Adult Only ratings to minors. Clinton, who said she was disturbed by the sexually explicit content of "Grand Theft Auto," as well as the violence, cited findings that boys as young as 9 often could buy Mature-rated games. [6] But Clinton's bill also could run into constitutional problems, say even those who advocate restrictions. [7]

"Grand Theft Auto: Vice City," which debuted in 2002, drew criticism for its violence. Players can steal vehicles, engage in drive-by shootings and robberies and buy weapons ranging from submachine guns to hand grenades. Members of gangs also engage in shoot-outs.

Courts have been skeptical of a link between video games and violence. For example, a district court in Michigan blocked implementation of a state ban on sales of violent video games to minors. The decision reflected concern that Anderson's studies had "not provided any evidence that the relationship between violent games and aggressive behavior exists. It could just as easily be said that the interactive element in video games acts as an outlet for minors to vent their violent or aggressive behavior, thereby dimming the chance they would actually perform such acts in reality," the court declared. [8]

Yet game-industry spokesmen also point out that juvenile-crime statistics dropped sharply as the violence in video games crested and have not spiked since. (The breakthrough in realistic video-game violence can be traced to the 1992 release of "Wolfenstein 3 D," the first major "first-person shooter" game, where the player saw the game world through the eyes of the character and enemies fell and bled on the floor.)

"Just as violent video games were pouring into American homes on the crest of the personal-computer wave, juvenile violence began to plummet," according to University of Pennsylvania criminologist Lawrence Sherman. "Juvenile murder charges dropped by about two-thirds from 1993 to the end of the decade and show no signs of going back up. If video games are so deadly, why has their widespread use been followed by reductions in murder?" [9]

---

[1] BBC News, "Manhunt Game Withdrawn by Stores," Feb. 18, 2005; http://news.bbc.co.uk. See also "Grand Theft Auto Sparks Another Lawsuit," *GameSpot*, retrieved Aug. 18, 2006.

[2] American Psychological Association press release, "APA Calls for Reduction of Violence in Interactive Media Used by Children and Adolescents," Aug. 17, 2005; www.apa.org/releases.

[3] Quoted in *Ibid.*

[4] Douglas A. Gentile and Craig A. Anderson, "Violent Video Games: The Effects on Youth, and Public Policy Implications," in N. Dowd, *et al., Handbook of Children, Culture and Violence* (2006), p. 231 (from page proofs.)

[5] Washington, Illinois, Michigan, California, Minnesota, Oklahoma and Louisiana have passed laws restricting the sale of violent games to minors. See www.medialegislation.org. Also see Gentile and Anderson, *op. cit.*, p. 240. In the past five years, U.S. courts have ruled at least eight times that computer games and video games are protected speech under the First Amendment, according to the Entertainment Software Association; on Oct. 11, 2006, a U.S. district judge in Oklahoma issued a preliminary injunction halting implementation of Oklahoma's law, calling the act's language unconstitutionally vague.

[6] News release, "Sens. Clinton, Lieberman and Bayh Introduce Legislation to Protect Children from Inappropriate Video Games"; http://clinton.senate.gov.

[7] The Child-Responsible Media Campaign; www.medialegislation.org.

[8] Entertainment Software Association, "Essential Facts about Video Games and Court Rulings;" www.theesa.com.

[9] Quoted in John C. Beck and Mitchell Wade, *Got Game* (2004), pp. 53-54.

---

tions with one another, which were "extremely complex, nuanced and filled with social learning, problem-solving and creativity," she says. But children don't do that much independent play anymore, she observes.

Some enthusiasts counter that video games can turn gamers into little scientists who have to figure out the rules on their own. Simulation games like "The Sims" help in mastering sciences that utilize computer-based simulation, including biology and cognitive science, suggests the University of Wisconsin's Gee. [36]

But Harvard's Dede is skeptical. "Do kids learn some things about taking a confusing situation and puzzling about it? Sure. But we wouldn't need schooling if learning was as simple as just putting people into experience and letting them figure it out," he says. "That's just as true for gaming experiences as for real-world experiences." The key is to adapt the methods developed for entertainment to educational games so they can be "a powerful vehicle for education." ■

BACKGROUND

Pinball Precursor

Pinball was the mechanical precursor of video games, say some historians, rousing many of the same fears that video games do today. In the 1930s, New York Mayor Fiorello La Guardia smashed pinball machines with a sledgehammer and banned them — a ban that was only lifted in the 1970s. [37]

In 1958, William A. Higinbotham, a physicist at Brookhaven National Laboratory on Long Island, invented a game of electronic Ping-Pong. Although the game was dismantled the next year — its components were needed for other projects — it was remembered by a future editor of *Creative Computing* magazine, David Ahl, who had seen the game during a high school visit. He dubbed Higinbotham the grandfather of video games. [38]

However, Massachusetts Institute of Technology (MIT) student Steve Russell is generally considered the inventor of video games. In 1961, he created a rocketship game called "Spacewar!," which could be played on one of MIT's computers. The manufacturer of the computer, Digital Equipment Corp., began shipping its computers pre-loaded with the game, exposing computer-science students across the country to "Spacewar." [39]

AP Photo/Lenny Ignelzi

Software engineer Tammy Yap designs video games at Midway Home Entertainment in San Diego. Some experts blame girls' lower interest in video games on the scarcity of sympathetic female characters and game designers.

In 1972, Magnavox introduced "Odyssey," the first home video-game console, which Magnavox marketed as a family game. Until the early 1980s manufacturers also marketed arcade games to single adults as having sex appeal.

Slow adoption of video games through the 1970s culminated in the 1977 introduction of Atari — the first video-game console to use plug-in cartridges rather than built-in games. Atari became one of the most successful introductions in history, selling about 3 million consoles a year. Atari was considered wildly popular in the early 1980s until its manufacturer collapsed. [40]

Nintendo revived the industry in the late 1980s, and since then a wide variety of consoles and games have been introduced, including Sony's PlayStation and Microsoft's Xbox. A variety of other games have been designed for personal computers. As computer animation permitted film-like dramas with original scripts and music, computer games became increasingly sophisticated, bearing little resemblance to the black and white blips of Higinbotham's original game.

The late 1980s were a crucial turning point in the social history of video games, according to Williams, at the University of Illinois. Games began moving from bars, nightclubs and arcades to homes as prices dropped, houses expanded and Americans had more disposable income. Driven by Nintendo's marketing, games became the province of children for the next 10 years. [41]

Video games also ushered in a new generation of young people "comfortable and techno-literate enough to accept personal computers, electronic bulletin boards, desktop publishing, compact disks and the Web," he writes, and pushed the development of microprocessors, broadband networks and display technologies. [42]

Today half of all Americans 8-18 have a video-game player in their bedrooms. [43] They also have less contact with people they know (within the family) but more contact with unknown people from a variety of backgrounds, particularly with the rise of multiplayer games, Williams points out. That gives a 12-year-old boy access to the knowledge of a 40-year-old lawyer playing the same game (and vice versa) but also rouses fears about whom children are meeting online. [44]

Besides worrying that children might meet potential predators online, adults also were concerned about the violent content of video games. In 1982, Surgeon General C. Everett Koop claimed that video games were hazardous, creating aberrant behavior and increasing a taste for violence. Nearly 25 years later, researchers still have not found definitive proof of long-lasting negative effects from video violence, or of the predicted increase in withdrawal and social isolation, according to Williams. But these worries survive.

Meanwhile, video games long ago became more than child's play. Today, the average age of video gamers is 33, a quarter of gamers are over 50 and only 31 percent are under 18, according to the Entertainment Software Association. [45]

Equity Gap?

With video-game consoles in 83 percent of the homes of the under-18 crowd, one would expect the benefits of gaming to be pervasive. [46] But surveys suggest that low-income children aren't getting the same access to technology as their middle-class peers — a video-gaming "equity gap" that resembles the so-called digital divide between those with and without Internet access. Although 87 percent of teens use the Internet, those who don't are generally from lower-income households with limited access to high-tech hardware and are disproportionately African-American. [47]

That could mean they lack access to some of the more complex games played on computers and online. Convinced of games' educational potential, Global Kids, a nonprofit that provides education on international issues to urban youth, has obtained a Microsoft grant to teach disadvantaged New York City teens to design and play games.

"Some of these kids don't know how to move a cursor into a Web browser," says Global Kids' Online Leadership Director Barry Joseph. Paradoxically, most attend schools with plenty of computer equipment — courtesy of Clinton-era funding. But many of the students are not connected to the Internet because teachers are often unfamiliar with the technology, Joseph says.

"Middle-class homes have multiple gaming consoles, broadband and adults familiar enough with systems to encourage young people" to play games with learning potential, Joseph says. By contrast, lower-income kids may only have access to a computer at the school library, where daily time is limited to 10 minutes, mandatory filters block the ability to blog and computers have no capacity to store kids' creations, notes MIT's Director of Comparative Media Studies Henry Jenkins.

However, surveys about access may not tell the real story about who's benefiting from technology. "Some folks are using the technology in new ways; others are less digitally savvy and are just playing Gameboy. That may be the real divide in who has positive effects," says Connie Yowell, director of educational grant-making at the MacArthur Foundation, which is helping Global Kids and other groups study how young people are using technology.

Gender Gap Narrows

Boys between 8 and 18 spend more than twice as much time playing video games as girls, according to a recent Kaiser Family Foundation survey. [48] Some have blamed girls' lower interest on the scarcity of sympathetic female characters and game designers.

"Games were built by boys for boys," Northwestern's Cassell found in 1997 when she co-edited *From Barbie to Mortal Kombat*, a book of scholarly essays on the gender slant of video games. [49]

But Cassell and other experts say the gender gap has been narrowing. Today, women over 18 represent 30 percent of U.S. gamers — a greater proportion than do boys 17 and under (23 percent). [50] "Boys may be playing more traditional video games," Cassell says, "but girls are playing more 'Sims,' " which is akin to playing house.

And virtual worlds are much more popular among females. Females make up the majority of the 400,000 subscribers to There.com, a virtual world where participants can create a character to interact with others, according to Michael K. Wilson, CEO of Makena Technologies, the company behind the site. Socializing and shopping seem to be two major draws for teenage girls, he says.

"It's very clear to us that teens are very interested in shopping. There.com is the holy grail of shopping sites. You can try on a dress [or your avatar can] and ask friends how you look in it," says Wilson. There.com has also experimented with Nike and Levi Strauss & Co. to turn that click on a product into a real-world purchase.

In Second Life, another virtual world, companies like Reebok and Amazon have set up shops to sell real-world versions of their products as well as virtual ones. [51]

Another magnet drawing women has been the rise in so-called casual games — which may take as little as 10 minutes to play, such as Solitaire, mahjong and some short action games. In the past few years, thousands of such games have sprung up on the Internet and game consoles.

The typical casual game players are women in their 40s, one of the fastest-growing sectors of the industry, according to the International Game Developers Association. From almost nothing in 2002, casual games grew to a $600 million business by 2004, and by 2008 industry experts expect to see $2 billion in U.S. sales alone. [52]

Female gamers spend an average of two hours more per week playing video games than a year ago, for an average of 7.4 hours a week, according to the Entertainment Software Association. While male gamers still spent more daily time than females on video games in 2003, the gap had narrowed from 18 minutes to six minutes by 2004. [53]

Males still comprise the majority of those who play online, but the games played most often online — puzzle board and trivia games — are among those most favored by females. [54]

Nevertheless, many young girls don't think they're good at games, Cassell says, because they buy the traditional definition that "real" video games involve action or sports. In the late 1990s, many experts feared the gender gap in game playing would further widen the gender gap in access to technology and science generally. But that may be changing as girls become a major presence in games and virtual worlds that emphasize interaction and creativity over competition.

And some researchers, like Harvard's Dede, find girls are just as interested in a game involving science if it minimizes the things that bore them — like scoring points and violence — and stresses personal interaction instead. For instance, girls trying to discover the cause of a mysterious epidemic in the "River City" simulation game approach the problem differently from boys. "Girls on balance try to establish a relationship with the residents of this virtual town," through the characters they create, and use those relationships to solve the mystery, Dede says.

"Typically, research shows girls aren't interested in science," notes "River City" Project Director Jody Clarke, particularly in middle school, the age the Harvard team is observing.

Entering the New Virtual World of Education

Students enrolled in "Law in the Court of Public Opinion" at the Harvard Extension School in fall 2006 log onto their computers every Thursday evening and send animated versions of themselves into a virtual classroom. There, a so-called avatar — another animated persona — representing Law Professor Charlie Ness (looking about 20 years younger) teaches the course in real time, using Ness' real voice. An avatar representing Ness' daughter Rebecca, a computer expert, occasionally flies down from the ceiling to help teach the course.

Harvard is one of several universities that have begun entering game-like virtual worlds to reach a wider audience. The audience is large and growing at a rate of 10-20 percent a month by some estimates. [1]

Ness teaches his course in the virtual world of Second Life, which boasts more than 1 million inhabitants. [2] Participants enter the Second Life fantasy world to meet people and buy and sell virtual real estate, clothes and other goods. (Linden Labs, the company behind Second Life, makes most of its money leasing virtual land to tenants.) In spring 2006, the 20 courses offered in Second Life included "Theatre and Culture," from Case Western Reserve University, and Stanford University's "Critical Studies in New Media."

Second Life's virtual library offers monthly book discussions, talks by authors (as avatars, of course) and a reference service. It was created because of college students' tendency to use online resources instead of brick-and-mortar libraries, according to Lori Bell, director of innovation at the Alliance Library System in East Peoria, Ill., which helped create the virtual library. As for being in virtual worlds, she observes, "The library needs to be there or we're going to start losing people."

So far, 2,000-3,000 people a day visit the library, according to Bell. "We get a lot of people coming because it's a safe place." Elsewhere in Second Life, she notes, "There's a lot of sex, gambling and adult places. The library is somewhere you don't have to buy anything, you don't have people hitting on you, and people are friendly."

Much like the real world, people enter a virtual universe for a variety of reasons, and education is not necessarily at the top of the list. Lauren Gelman, associate director of the Stanford Law School's Center for Internet and Society, says when she first entered the popular virtual world of There.com — with 400,000 subscribers between ages 13 and 26 — "the first thing that happened is I got propositioned." With islands populated by avatars in bikinis, she says, "It's a very Club Med kind of environment."

This fall, Gelman became dean of a virtual university in There.com — the State of Play Academy — which will offer courses by experts in technology-related areas of law such as copyright, patents and trade secrets. [3] Eventually, the academy might even offer a degree-like certificate, Gelman says.

Students who come to these classes are expected to bring a better grasp of technology than the law professor, permitting a two-way transfer of information. "Sometimes I'll be the teacher and sometimes the student," says Gelman, who teaches a course on technology and law at Stanford.

The power of virtual worlds to project situations in 3-D means students can "experience" what they're learning. To train health-care professionals in how to deal with bioterrorism and natural disasters, for example, Idaho State University provides simulations in Second Life of earthquakes and fires, injured victims and how to treat them. [4] Recently, the library invited residents to heckle Tudor King Henry VIII of England and ask his wife Ann Boleyn what it felt like to be beheaded. Two librarians acted out the roles as avatars in full 16th-century dress.

This summer, teens in Second Life participated in a virtual summer camp aimed at building awareness of global issues like sex trafficking, sponsored by Global Kids, a New York-based group that teaches urban youth about leadership and global citizenry. [5] "We take real-world issues and do something about it in a way you could never do in real life," says Barry Joseph, online leadership director at Global Kids. "In Second Life, you can click on someone's 'Save Darfur' green wrist band and get information about what's going on right now in Darfur."

The argument that kids learn better in the video universe has been a major influence on pioneers like Gelman. "If we know there's educational value in that kids think differently when they navigate these worlds, could we put it to better use to teach them substantive stuff while they're sitting in front of 'World of Warcraft' for 10 hours on a Saturday?" asks Gelman. "It could be at the cusp of something completely revolutionary in education — or it might not work."

[1] Richard Siklos, "A Virtual World But Real Money," *The New York Times*, Oct. 19, 2006. According to the Second Life Web site, $7.4 million changed hands in September.

[2] http://secondlife.com. Regular users — those who logged on in the last 30 days — totaled 427,838 in mid-October 2006.

[3] http://stateofplayacademy.com/

[4] http://www.isu.edu/irh/IBAPP/second_life.shtml.

[5] www.globalkids.org.

But "we're finding girls are interested in open-ended exploration and engaging with teams, so they're doing science differently," she says. Similarly, multiplayer online games that are drawing female players are designed around open-ended exploration that allows team-like player networks to develop, she says.

"I ask girls whether they're good at computers and they say 'No' even though they are," says Northwestern's Cassell, noting their growing presence in games and blogging. "The traditional definition of a game excludes the kinds of things girls like. It's not true that girls don't like games." ■

Continued on p. 954

At Issue:

Do video games significantly enhance literacy?

JAMES PAUL GEE
***TASHIA MORGRIDGE PROFESSOR OF READING, UNIVERSITY OF WISCONSIN AUTHOR,* WHAT VIDEO GAMES HAVE TO TEACH US ABOUT LEARNING AND LITERACY**

WRITTEN FOR *CQ RESEARCHER*, NOVEMBER 2006

yes

Popular culture today often involves quite complex language, and that matters because the biggest predictor of children's school success is the size of their early vocabularies and their abilities to deal with complex language.

Consider, for example, a typical description of a "Pokemon" ("pocket monsters" found in video games, cards, books, movies and television shows): "Bulbasaur are a combination of Grass-type and Poison-type Pokémon. Because they are Grass-type Pokémon, Bulbasaur have plant-like characteristics." Or consider this from a Web site for "Yu-Gi-Oh" (another card, game, book, movie phenomenon): "The effect of '8-Claws Scorpion' is a Trigger Effect that is applied if the condition is correct on activation." Lots of low-frequency words here; complex syntax, as well. Children as young as 6 and 7 play "Pokemon" and "Yu-Gi-Oh." To play they have to read — and read complex language.

The biggest barrier to school success is the child's ability to deal with complex "academic" language, the sort of language in textbooks. Such language starts to kick in about fourth grade and ever increases thereafter in school. Children who learn to decode, but can't read to learn in the content areas later on, are victims of the well-known "fourth-grade slump." Worse yet, research shows that even children who can pass tests in the content areas often can't apply their knowledge to real problem-solving.

Without lots of practice, humans are poor at learning from words out of their contexts of application. Good video games put young people in worlds composed of problems to be solved. They almost always give verbal information "just in time" — when players need and can use it — and "on demand," when the player asks for it. They show how language applies to the world it is about.

Research suggests that people really know what words mean only when they can hook them to the sorts of actions, images or dialogues to which they apply. That is why a game manual or strategy guide makes much more sense after someone has played a game for awhile than before. So, too, science textbooks, cut off from the images and actions science is about, are like a technical game manual without any game.

But, a warning: Good video games — good commercial ones like "Civilization 4" and good "serious games" made around academic content — will not work by themselves. Mentors are needed to encourage strategic thinking about the game and the complex language connected to them.

HOWARD GARDNER
HOBBS PROFESSOR OF COGNITION AND EDUCATION, HARVARD GRADUATE SCHOOL OF EDUCATION

WRITTEN FOR *CQ RESEARCHER*, NOVEMBER 2006

no

It's difficult to argue with many of Gee's points, and the jury is still out on others. Yet I'd point to several biases in the cited examples. 1) They are oriented toward competition (despite the fact that some also entail cooperation); 2) The literacy highlighted is that used in technical manuals; 3) These games, and the epistemology underlying them, are more likely to appeal to boys rather than to girls, and to "techies" rather than dreamers, humanists and conversationalists; 4) They foreground simulation, a very powerful technique, but it's not the same as real life.

I am happy to have medical students or future airplane pilots train on simulations — but they also require real, high-stake experience. Patients have feelings; simulacra and robots don't. And note that these are two areas where simulation makes sense. In many other professions, from poets to priests, they don't.

Which leads to the most important point. Literacy is far more than expertise in technical manuals or even in understanding science and technology, important as they are. It entails the capacity to immerse oneself and, ultimately, to love long, imaginative pieces of fiction, such as *Madame Bovary* or *One Hundred Years of Solitude*; poring over difficult philosophical texts and returning time and again to key passages (Kant, Wittgenstein); and spending time and exercising emotional imagination with challenging poets (Gerard Manley Hopkins, Jorie Graham).

Literacy involves linear thinking over many pages — an entirely different mental faculty than is exploited when one surfs the Web from one link to another, often randomly encountered one. I want all young persons to learn how to think like a historian, a philosopher, an economist, a literary critic (four very different "frames of mind"). I want to stimulate their imaginations to create their own worlds, not just that conjured up by the makers of "World of Warcraft."

In sum, the treasures and skills entailed in the video games of today are impressive, but they still represent only a very partial sampling of the kinds of minds that young people have and the kinds that can and should be cultivated. Some can be cultivated in front of a screen. But too much time there is not healthy on any criterion — and any slice of life — no matter how engrossing — is only partial at best. So two cheers for Jim Gee — but two cheers as well for Mark Hopkins * on one end of a log, and an eager questioner and listener on the other.

** A 19th-century president of Williams College.*

Continued from p. 952

CURRENT SITUATION

Big Business

Today, about half of all Americans play computer and video games, according to the Entertainment Software Association (ESA), and Americans spend more money on video games each year than they do going to the movies. [55] Americans also spend more time playing video games than watching rented videos. [56]

In the past 10 years, U.S. video-game sales have almost tripled to $7 billion last year — after peaking at $7.4 billion in 2004 — representing nearly 230 million computer and video games. [57]

In fact, the largest-grossing one-day media sale ever occurred on Nov. 9, 2004, when stores sold $125 million worth of "Halo 2" games — the eagerly awaited sequel to the hit Xbox game "Halo", in which individual players defend Earth against alien invaders. [58]

Today, the personal computer is the most popular game machine, contrary to earlier industry predictions that game consoles would dominate. Until recently, Microsoft hadn't marketed games as a core part of its computer. But now it plans to make games easier to install and will emphasize that in its marketing.

Hundreds of millions of people around the world use computers that run the Windows operating system, and about half of them play games, according to Microsoft surveys. The driving force, most analysts say, are subscription-based online multiplayer games played on computers. Games like "World of Warcraft" are expected to take in more than $2 billion worldwide. [59]

Teens have been a big contributor to this growth, with 81 percent of teens — 17 million people — using the Internet to play games online, according to the Pew Internet & American Life Project. That's a 52 percent jump since 2000. [60]

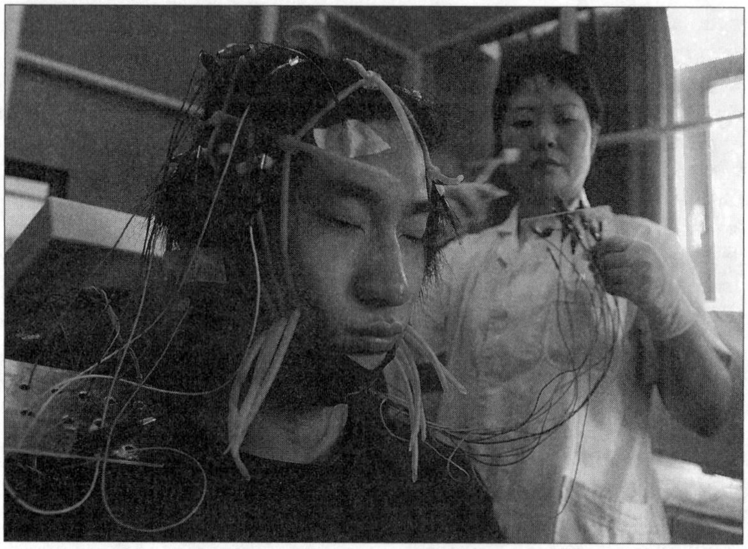

Getty Images/Cancan Chu

A young man receives an electroencephalogram at a clinic for video-game "addicts" in Beijing in July 2005. Such clinics have opened in several countries, but many psychologists question whether game playing can lead to true addiction.

Social Networking

With 81 percent of all teens playing online video games — up from 66 percent in 2000 — online games have become a widespread form of social networking, according to Amanda Lenhart, senior research specialist at the Pew Internet & American Life Project. [61]

"As with all things on the Internet, it's possible to meet all sorts of people," says Lenhart. "I've heard from a law-enforcement officer about a person who was preyed upon by somebody they met in a game. But the vast majority of people I've talked to have not mentioned any trouble with that sort of thing."

Virtual worlds help teens with two crucial developmental issues — developing an identity and interacting with peers, says Northwestern's Cassell. "That's why they're so popular. They're all about trying on different identities and manifestations," she says.

Although multiplayer games and virtual worlds are clearly places for social networking, they have not become the target of legislation, as have other networking spaces like Myspace.com. [62] Rep. Fred Upton, R-Mich., and others in Congress have proposed restricting children's access to social-networking Web sites. Due to such efforts, as well as entertainment-industry threats to tighten copyright restrictions on kids' variations of games or movies, MIT's Jenkins fears that authorities will "shut down [digital media] before we understand them." [63]

Meanwhile, age, ethnic and social stratifications are breaking down as youngsters play online with older people from cultures around the world. "This is social broadening, which can be scary" to society, says the University of Illinois' Williams. While mixing is positive for diversity, the bonds are different than with a face-to-face friend. "An online friend can console you but can't drive you to the hospital," he points out.

Libraries Log On

One Friday night each month, nearly 100 Michigan teenagers gather at the Ann Arbor District Library to compete in the Nintendo racing game "Mario Kart." "It's just like story-time, only noisier and smellier," says the library's technology manager, Eli Neiburger.

Libraries increasingly are offering such gaming events, and younger librarians are trying to persuade colleagues that video games are a legitimate part of libraries' mission. A new Young Adult Library Services Association task force is examining whether to recommend video games for teens alongside its annual list of recommended books.

When kids ask, "What can I read?" librarians should give the answer a gaming spin, advises task force member Beth Gallaway, a trainer/consultant for youth services at the Metrowest Massachusetts Regional Library System in Waltham. "No matter what kind of game kids are playing, they come in genres just like the books we're so familiar with — science fiction, fantasy — and you can pull out these elements from the game," she says.

"There seems to be a lot of interest right now," says Christopher Couzes, director of institutional marketing at Baker and Taylor in Charlotte, N.C., which sells books and other media to libraries. But so far, only about 200 libraries have purchased video games from his firm.

According to the University of Wisconsin's Squire, nearly every student he's met who has played a content-rich game like "Civilization" has checked out a library book on a related topic. But those mind-teaser games are not the games libraries are purchasing. "Libraries want to bring in titles that are popular and that circulate," says Couzes, such as sports games and the popular "Mario Brothers."

Saying Less?

Although no one knows for sure whether the rising use of video gaming is affecting national literacy and problem-solving abilities, the percentage of U.S. college graduates with proficient English literacy has declined — from 40 percent in 1992 to 31 percent in 2003. [64]

Citing that decline, longtime technology critic Jeremy Rifkin, founder of the Foundation on Economic Trends, blames the increasing use of video games and other electronic media like TV and text messaging. "The human vocabulary is plummeting all over the world, making it more difficult to express ourselves," he says. "It appears that we are all communicating more, but saying less." [65]

However, science writer Johnson observes IQ scores in most developed countries have increased over the past century. He also notes the rate of increase has accelerated in the past 30 years and attributes the rise to the increasing cognitive labor in our mental diet. Compared to the simple children's games of a century ago, today's 10-year-old must master "probing and telescoping through immense virtual worlds," switching from instant-messaging to e-mail and troubleshooting new technologies, Johnson writes. The fact that the U.S. lags behind other countries in educational assessments just shows that students are getting their IQ advantage outside of school, he argues. [66]

A Federation of American Scientists report recently called on the federal government to research the education and work-force-training potential of video games. The report followed a yearlong evaluation and conference sponsored by the National Science Foundation, which is funding projects to develop educational science games, including multiplayer online games. [67]

While video games could improve learning and motivation, the scientists' report said most commercial games probably will not accomplish those goals, and more educational games should be developed. More research is needed to understand exactly which features of games are important for learning, it said.

High costs and an uncertain market make production of purely educational games too risky for private industry to develop, the federation report said. While some classrooms already use games like "Civilization" for history, "SimCity" for urban planning and "Roller Coaster Tycoon" for physics, schools are unwilling to abandon textbooks and traditional teaching for games whose effectiveness is unknown. The scientists urged educators to develop educational materials around content-rich games like "Civilization" and develop tests to find out what students learn in games. ■

OUTLOOK

Testing the Hypothesis

As video games become more sophisticated and broaden their audience, some cultural observers say it's time to look beyond fears of lurking pedophiles and rotting brains and conduct research to find out what's genuinely good and bad about games.

In October the MacArthur Foundation announced it was committing $50 million to understanding how video games and other digital media affect learning by young people. [68] The foundation is giving grants to game enthusiasts like Wisconsin's Gee and Global Kids' Joseph, as well as to skeptics like Harvard's Gardner.

Unlike school, games are producing "kid-driven learning," says Yowell, noting the foundation will fund innovations based on "what we learn from the kids." MacArthur's hypothesis is that digital media *do* affect how children learn. "That has huge implications for parents, teachers and policymakers, and we need to understand that," Yowell says.

Edward Castronova, an associate professor of telecommunications at Indiana University, will use his $240,000 grant to build an online game around Shakespeare's plays, then study how kids' alter-egos dressed in 17th-century costumes learn the bard's words and change their social behavior while living in a very different society. [69]

Some of the enthusiasts' biggest claims will be tested with MacArthur-funded research. Do kids experience failure differently in games? Are they problem-solving differently? What's the effect of giving kids immediate feedback in a game? How do you test what they've learned in a game?

MacArthur grantees will also be asking some of the critics' questions, such as: What's being lost with all the time spent playing? Are players socially isolated? Are they daydreaming less? "We're agnostic," says Yowell.

At least one grant, to Gardner, will examine how kids make ethical decisions about what they share publicly about themselves and their creations. In virtual worlds and multiplayer games, "If I get to pretend to be someone else, what does that mean about how I make ethical decisions?" Yowell asks.

Increasingly, much of our national political debate comes down to disagreements over whether a model is accurate: Will the Earth really suffer from global warming? Did the Iraq war reduce terrorism or stimulate more of it? Since games are all about testing models, they could provide a test-bed for citizenship. Increasingly, they're also about collecting information from many sources — not just rote memorization from a central source.

The big question, enthusiasts say, is whether educators will adapt those techniques to make school as engaging and complex as the best video games. But can games move beyond blood and monsters to become socially positive? Global Kids thinks so and has developed a game about poverty set in Haiti. In a family's struggle to survive, the player has to choose between sending the children to school (and going into debt) or sending them out to work and reaping short-term additional income. [70]

Yet will these kinds of games fly with children who've grown up on the thrills of "Grand Theft Auto"? It's hard to predict, especially as games become ever more realistic and enthralling in this fast-changing industry.

One of the more futuristic visions foresees virtual characters who can respond emotionally to players. "Laura," a computerized exercise trainer developed at MIT, provides empathetic verbal and facial feedback. To technology critic Rifkin, it's hard to know whether to see such attempts as "sadly pathological . . . or whether to be truly frightened." [71]

Ultimately, says MIT's Jenkins, video games are not simply an add-on to mainstream education but a "basic paradigm shift" in how kids learn — one that's here to stay. Parents will have to be actively involved in the digital world to understand it and offer guidance, he says — whether it's questioning the ethics in Second Life or steering kids to the fanfiction sites where they can learn to become better writers.

His advice to parents: Sit down and play a game with your kids. [72] ■

About the Author

Sarah Glazer, a New York freelancer, is a regular contributor to the *CQ Researcher*. Her articles on health, education and social-policy issues have appeared in *The New York Times*, *The Washington Post*, *The Public Interest* and *Gender and Work*, a book of essays. Her recent *CQ Researcher* reports include "Increase in Autism" and "Gender and Learning." She graduated from the University of Chicago with a B.A. in American history.

Notes

1 Federation of American Scientists (FAS), "Summit on Educational Games 2006," October 2006; www.fas.org.

2 Steven Johnson, *Everything Bad is Good For You* (2006), p. 45.

3 *Ibid.*, p. 31

4 Kaiser Family Foundation, "Generation M," 2005; www.kff.org. The survey was among children ages 8-18.

5 C. Galas and D.J. Ketelhut, "River City," *Leading with Technology*, 2006, pp. 31-32; http://muve.gse.harvard.edu/rivercityproject/research-publications.htm.

6 Kaiser Family Foundation, *op. cit.*

7 Susan B. Newman and Donna Celano, "The Knowledge Gap," *Reading Research Quarterly*, April/May/June 2006, pp. 176-201; www.reading.org/publications/journals/rrq.

8 FAS, *op. cit.*

9 James Paul Gee, "Reading, Specialist Language Development, and Video Games," unpublished paper, p. 36.

10 MacArthur Open Forum, "Dialogue 2: Gaming Literacies"; http://community.macfound.org.

11 Galas and Ketelhut, *op. cit.*

12 Federation of American Scientists, *op. cit.*, p. 43.

13 Constance A. Steinkuehler, "Massively Multiplayer Online Video Gaming as Participation in A Discourse," *Mind, Culture and Activity*, 2006, 13 (1), pp. 38-52.

14 FAS, *op. cit.*

15 Julia Scheeres, "The Quest to End Game Addiction," *Wired News*, Dec. 5, 2001; www.wired.com.

16 Nick Yee, "The Labor of Fun: How Video Games Blur the Boundaries of Work and Play," *Games and Culture*, January 2006, pp. 68-71. This and other articles/surveys by Yee are at www.nickyee.com/daedalus.

[17] www.nickyee.com/daedalus.

[18] http://games.groups.yahoo.com/group/WOW_widow/; Scheeres, *op. cit.*

[19] Anthony Faiola, "Experts Fear Epidemic of Gaming Addiction," *The Miami Herald*, June 4, 2005, p. A25.

[20] Gregory M. Lamb, "Are Multiplayer Games More Compelling, More Addictive?," *The Christian Science Monitor*, Oct. 13, 2005, p. 13.

[21] Yee, *op. cit.*, p. 68.

[22] *Ibid.*

[23] John Seely Brown and Douglas Thomas, "You Play World of Warcraft? You're Hired," *Wired*, April 2006, p. 120.

[24] *Ibid.*

[25] *Ibid.*

[26] John C. Beck and Mitchell Wade, *Got Game* (2004), p. 10.

[27] *Ibid.*, p. 42.

[28] Yee, *op. cit.*, p. 69.

[29] David Williamson Shaffer, *How Computer Games Help Children Learn* (2006).

[30] Federation of American Scientists, press release, "Study Recommends Fix to Digital Disconnect in U.S. Education and Workforce Training," Oct. 17, 2006; www.fas.org.

[31] Federation of American Scientists, "Summit on Educational Games 2006," *op. cit.*, p. 14.

[32] Henry Jenkins, *et al.*, "Confronting the Challenges of Participatory Culture," John D. and Catharine T. MacArthur Foundation, 2006, p. 5; www.digitallearning.macfound.org.

[33] *Ibid.*

[34] Federation of American Scientists, "Summit on Educational Games 2006," *op. cit.*, p. 12.

[35] Jose Antonio Vargas, "Virtual Reality Prepares Soldiers for Real War," *The Washington Post*, Feb. 16, 2006, p. A1.

[36] James Gee, *What video games have to teach us about learning and literacy* (2003), p. 48.

[37] Chris Suellentrop, "Playing With Our Minds," *Wilson Quarterly*, summer 2006, pp. 14-21.

[38] *Ibid.*

[39] *Ibid.*

[40] Beck and Wade, *op. cit.*, p. 8.

[41] Dmitri Williams, in P. Vorderer and J. Bryant, eds., *Playing Computer Games* (2006) in press; https://netfiles.uiuc.edu/dcwill/www/.

[42] *Ibid.*, p. 6.

[43] Kaiser Family Foundation, press release, "Media Multi-Tasking Changing the Amount and Nature of Young People's Media Use," March 9, 2005.

[44] For background see Brian Hansen, "Cyber-Predators," *CQ Researcher*, March 1, 2002, pp. 169-192.

FOR MORE INFORMATION

Federation of American Scientists, 1717 K St., N.W., Suite 209, Washington, DC 20036; (202) 546-3300; www.fas.org. Scientists' organization that has called on the federal government to use video games to strengthen education.

Games, Learning and Society, University of Wisconsin, Teacher Education Bldg., 225 North Mills St., Madison, WI 53706; (608) 263-4600; http://website.education.wisc.edu/gls/research.htm. Studies the learning potential of video games.

Global Kids, Inc., 561 Broadway, New York, NY 10012; (212) 226-0130; www.globalkids.org. Educates urban youth on international issues and is teaching disadvantaged teens to design and play games.

Kaiser Family Foundation, 2400 Sand Hill Rd., Menlo Park, CA 94025; (650) 854-9400; www.kff.org. Conducts surveys on media use by youth and teens.

MacArthur Foundation, 140 S. Dearborn St., Chicago, IL 60603; (312) 726-8000; www.macfound.org. Provides grants for research on the learning potential of video games and other digital media.

www.nickyee.com/daedalus. The research findings of Stanford researcher Nick Yee, who has surveyed more than 35,000 players of online multiplayer games.

Pew Internet & American Life Project, 1615 L St., N.W., Suite 700, Washington, DC 20036; (202) 419-4500; www.pewinternet.org. Surveys youth media use.

[45] Entertainment Software Association; www.theesa.com. See "Facts and Research."

[46] Kaiser Family Foundation, "Generation M: Media in the Lives of 8-18 Year Olds: Executive Summary," March 2005; www.kff.org.

[47] Pew Internet & American Life Project, "Teens and Technology: Youth are Leading the Transition to a Fully Wired and Mobile Nation," July 27, 2005; www.pewinternet.org. For background see Kathy Koch, "Digital Divide," *CQ Researcher*, Jan. 28, 2000, pp. 41-64.

[48] Kaiser Family Foundation, *op. cit.*, March 9, 2005, p. 17. Boys spend an average of 1 hour 12 minutes a day compared to girls' 25 minutes.

[49] Justine Cassell and Henry Jenkins, eds., *From Barbie to Mortal Kombat: Gender and Computer Games* (1998).

[50] Entertainment Software Association, "Facts and Research"; www.theesa.com.

[51] Richard Siklos, "A Virtual World But Real Money," *The New York Times*, Oct. 19, 2006.

[52] International Game Developers Association, "2006 Casual Games White Paper"; www.igda.org/casual.

[53] *Ibid.*

[54] *Ibid.*

[55] Suellentop, *op. cit.*, pp. 16-17.

[56] Beck and Wade, *op. cit.*, p. 3.

[57] The NPD Group, Point-of-Sale Information.

[58] Kurt Squire, "From Content to Context," presentation made at Serious Games Summit, Feb. 24, 2004, p. 2.

[59] Seth Schiesel, "The PC Embraces Its Gaming Abilities," *The New York Times*, July 18, 2006, Arts Section, pp. 1, 4.

[60] Pew Internet & American Life Project, *op. cit.*

[61] *Ibid.*

[62] For background see Marcia Clemmitt, "Cyber Socializing," *CQ Researcher*, July 28, 2006, pp. 625-648.

[63] MacArthur Foundation Webcast of briefing, "Building the Field of Digital Media Learning," Oct. 19, 2006; www.macfound.org.

[64] National Center for Education Statistics, "A First Look at the Literacy of America's Adults in the 21st Century," Dec. 15, 2005; http://nces.ed.gov.

[65] Jeremy Rifkin, "Virtual Companionship: Our Lonely Existence," *International Herald Tribune*, Oct. 12, 2006, p. 8.

[66] Steven Johnson, *Everything Bad is Good for You* (2006), pp. 142-144.

[67] Federation of American Scientists, "Summit on Educational Games 2006," *op. cit.*

[68] MacArthur Foundation press release, "MacArthur Investing $50 Million in Digital Learning," Oct. 19, 2006; www.macfound.org.

[69] Daniel Terdiman, "Shakespeare Coming to a Virtual World," *The New York Times*, Oct. 19, 2006.

[70] "Ayiti — the Cost of Life"; thecostoflife.org and www.holymeatballs.org.

[71] Rifkin, *op. cit.*

[72] MacArthur Foundation Webcast, *op. cit.*

Bibliography

Selected Sources

Books

Beck, John C. and Mitchell Wade, *Got Game: How the Gamer Generation is Reshaping Business Forever*, Harvard Business School Press, 2004.
Two business experts argue video games provide the kind of leadership, entrepreneurship and team-building skills needed for today's workplace.

Gee, James Paul, *What Video Games Have to Teach Us About Learning and Literacy*, Palgrave Macmillan, 2003.
An education professor at the University of Wisconsin-Madison argues that video games provide an intricate learning experience in a modern world where print literacy is not enough.

Johnson, Steven, *Everything Bad is Good for You*, Riverhead Books, 2006.
Science writer argues that gamers are learning the scientific method when they try to figure out the "physics" of a game.

Prensky, Marc, *Don't Bother Me Mom-I'm Learning!* Paragon House, 2006.
In this enthusiastic book, the founder of an e-learning company urges parents (whom he calls "digital immigrants") to start engaging with digital natives — kids who've grown up with games as a positive learning experience.

Articles

Brown, John Seely and Thomas Douglas, "You Play World of Warcraft? You're Hired!" *Wired*, April 2006, p. 120.
Skills learned in multiplayer games like "World of Warcraft" are training young people for workplace leadership roles.

Rauch, Jonathan, "Sex, Lies, and Videogames," *The Atlantic Monthly*, November 2006.
The future of video-game technology includes interactive dramas and Spore, a game coming out next year, that will give players new scope in designing new worlds.

Rifkin, Jeremy, "Virtual Companionship," *International Herald Tribune*, Oct. 12, 2006, p. 8.
Technology critic worries that the nation is becoming less literate as video games proliferate, and expresses disgust at futuristic interactive computer characters.

Shaffer, David Williamson, *et al.*, "Video Games and the Future of Learning," *Phi Delta Kappan*, October 2005, pp. 105-111.
University of Wisconsin educational researchers argue that video games offer "learning by doing" on a grand scale and that schools need to catch up.

Siklos, Richard, "A Virtual World But Real Money," *The New York Times*, Oct. 19, 2006.
The popularity and economies of virtual worlds like Second Life are growing rapidly.

Suellentrop, Chris, "Playing with Our Minds," *Wilson Quarterly*, summer 2006, pp. 14-21.
A *New York Times* columnist suggests games do not permit innovation because they force players to play within the system.

Tompkins, Aimee, "The Psychological Effects of Violent Media on Children," Dec. 14, 2003, *AllPsych Journal*, http://allpsych.com.
So far, research on the effect of violent video games and other media on children only shows evidence of short-term effects.

Wright, Will, "Dream Machines," *Wired*, April 2006, pp. 111-112.
The creator of "The Sims," the best-selling PC game of all time, argues that gamers are learning in a "totally new way" and "treat the world as a place for creation." As guest editor, he invited other authors to write about the future and impact of video games for this special issue.

Reports

Federation of American Scientists, *Summit on Educational Games: Harnessing the Power of Video Games for Learning*, 2006; www.fas.org.
After a yearlong study, the federation recommended that the federal government fund research into the most effective educational features of video games and help develop new educational games.

Jenkins, Henry, *et al.*, *Confronting the Challenges of Participatory Culture*, 2006, MacArthur Foundation; www.digitallearning.macfound.org.
MIT's Jenkins and other technology experts argue that involvement in digital media has given young people new skills and new scope for creativity, and they urge schools to do more to foster "media literacies."

Kaiser Family Foundation, "Generation M: Media in the Lives of 8-18 Year-olds," 2005; www.kff.org.
More than 80 percent of adolescents have a video console player at home, and the amount of time spent playing video games has increased in the past five years.

Pew Internet & American Life Project, *Teens and Technology*, July 27, 2005; www.pewinternet.org.
The vast majority of U.S. teens use the Internet and 81 percent of those play games online.

The Next Step:

Additional Articles from Current Periodicals

Addiction and Video Games

Brody, Leslie, "Can You Be a Video-Game 'Addict?' " *The Seattle Times*, Aug. 19, 2006, p. C2.
Experts debate whether an obsession with video games can actually be labeled an addiction.

Curley, Fia, "Video-Game Addicts Log In At Detox Clinic," *The Houston Chronicle*, June 18, 2006, p. 4.
An addiction center in the Netherlands is opening Europe's first detox clinic for video-game addicts.

Benefits of Video Games

Ault, Alicia, "Turn On, Tune Out, Get Well?" *The Washington Post*, Oct. 4, 2005, p. F1.
Some physicians and psychiatrists believe video games can be used as tools to boost fitness and knowledge.

Marriott, Michel, "We Have to Operate, But Let's Play First," *The New York Times*, Feb. 24, 2005, p. G4.
James Clarence Rosser Jr. believes the manual dexterity that video games require also makes for a good surgeon.

Snider, Mike, "Video Games Actually Can Be Good For You," *USA Today*, Sept. 27, 2005, p. D7.
Video games can help children and adults diagnosed with attention-deficit disorder (ADD) learn to focus.

Industry Trends

Achen, Paul, "Colleges Tap Into Video Gaming," *The Houston Chronicle*, Feb. 16, 2005, p. B2.
A growing number of colleges are offering classes in video-game design as a result of a booming video-game industry.

Marriott, Michel, "Weaned on the Video Console," *The New York Times*, Oct. 28, 2004, p. G1.
A growing number of video-game makers are aiming at children as young as 3.

Vargas, Jose Antonio, "Taking the Controllers," *The Washington Post*, Aug. 6, 2005, p. C1.
The Urban Video Game Academy is teaching minority teens about game design to expose them to the possibility of careers in the multibillion-dollar field.

Learning and Video Games

Dunnewind, Stephanie, "Critics Doubtful Video Games Really 'Educational' Tool For Toddlers," *Chicago Tribune*, Dec. 23, 2004, p. 2.
Many child-development experts are skeptical that preschool video games are actually educational.

Feller, Ben, "Video Games Can Add Zest to Learning, Scientists Say," *Chicago Tribune*, Oct. 18, 2006, p. C13.
Scientists called for federal research into how video games can be converted into serious learning tools for schools.

Yi, Matthew, "Playing Games in School," *The San Francisco Chronicle*, Feb. 20, 2006, p. E1.
Video games are becoming increasingly popular among teachers in physical education, social studies and history.

Violence and Video Games

Brown, Sylvester Brown Jr., "Some Video Games Make a Point With Their Violence," *St. Louis Post-Dispatch*, July 2, 2006, p. D1.
Some experts say video games like "Darfur is Dying" can be used to raise humanitarian awareness.

Glasser, Debbie, "Violence Not Child's Play," *The Miami Herald*, Feb. 24, 2005, p. W19.
Children with a preference for violent video games demonstrated lower empathy than their peers.

Gledhill, Linda, "Governor Signs Bills Aimed At Teen Behavior," *The San Francisco Chronicle*, Oct. 8, 2005, p. A1.
Gov. Arnold Schwarzenegger, R-Calif., signed a bill that bans the sale or rental of extremely violent video games to children under 18 without parental approval.

Leland, Elizabeth, "Gaming to the Max," *Charlotte Observer*, May 1, 2005, p. E1.
Max Aberle spends several hours a day in front of the television destroying bad guys on video games, exemplifying the new American childhood.

CITING *CQ RESEARCHER*

Sample formats for citing these reports in a bibliography include the ones listed below. Preferred styles and formats vary, so please check with your instructor or professor.

MLA STYLE

Jost, Kenneth. "Rethinking the Death Penalty." CQ Researcher 16 Nov. 2001: 945-68.

APA STYLE

Jost, K. (2001, November 16). Rethinking the death penalty. *CQ Researcher, 11*, 945-968.

CHICAGO STYLE

Jost, Kenneth. "Rethinking the Death Penalty." *CQ Researcher*, November 16, 2001, 945-968.

CQ Researcher

Published by CQ Press, a division of Congressional Quarterly Inc.

cqresearcher.com

Privacy in Peril

Will Congress strengthen privacy safeguards?

The proliferation of massive Internet-accessible databases is making corporate and government electronic snooping possible on a scale unprecedented in U.S. history. In the past year Americans have been buffeted by revelations that the government is conducting warrantless spying on citizens' phone calls, that corporate directors are hiring detectives who use false identities to access private phone records, and that thousands of credit-card numbers held in commercial databases have been lost or stolen. Privacy advocates warn that growing access to huge amounts of personal data — from Social Security numbers to health information — are virtually eliminating the concept of personal privacy. If the current Congress does not act this year on President Bush's request for expanded authority to wiretap citizens, the incoming Democrat-led Congress is not expected to approve it. The new Congress, however, is expected to consider requiring businesses and government to take stronger action to protect personal data.

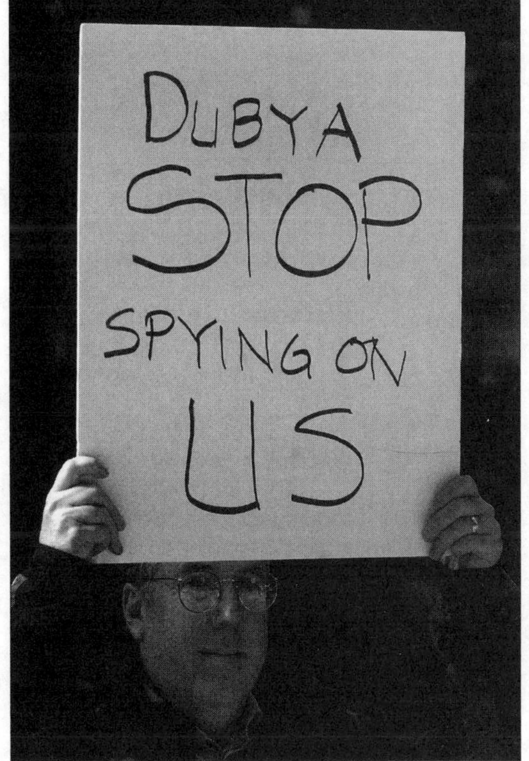

A MoveOn.org demonstrator in Chicago last Feb. 22 protests President Bush's use of warrantless domestic wiretaps in fighting the war on terrorism.

INSIDE THIS REPORT

CQ Researcher • Nov. 17, 2006 • www.cqresearcher.com
Volume 16, Number 41 • Pages 961-984

CQ PRESS

RECIPIENT OF SOCIETY OF PROFESSIONAL JOURNALISTS AWARD FOR EXCELLENCE ◆ AMERICAN BAR ASSOCIATION SILVER GAVEL AWARD

THE ISSUES

BACKGROUND

CURRENT SITUATION

OUTLOOK

SIDEBARS AND GRAPHICS

FOR FURTHER RESEARCH

Cover photograph: Getty Images/Tim Boyle

CQ Researcher

Nov. 17, 2006
Volume 16, Number 41

MANAGING EDITOR: Thomas J. Colin
ASSISTANT MANAGING EDITOR: Kathy Koch
ASSOCIATE EDITOR: Kenneth Jost
STAFF WRITERS: Marcia Clemmitt, Peter Katel
CONTRIBUTING WRITERS: Rachel S. Cox, Sarah Glazer, Alan Greenblatt, Barbara Mantel, Patrick Marshall, Tom Price, Jennifer Weeks
DESIGN/PRODUCTION EDITOR: Olu B. Davis
ASSISTANT EDITOR: Melissa J. Hipolit

A Division of Congressional Quarterly Inc.

SENIOR VICE PRESIDENT/PUBLISHER: John A. Jenkins
DIRECTOR, LIBRARY PUBLISHING: Kathryn C. Suárez
DIRECTOR, EDITORIAL OPERATIONS: Ann Davies

CONGRESSIONAL QUARTERLY INC.

CHAIRMAN: Paul C. Tash
VICE CHAIRMAN: Andrew P. Corty
PRESIDENT/EDITOR IN CHIEF: Robert W. Merry

CQ Researcher (ISSN 1056-2036) is printed on acid-free paper. Published weekly, except March 24, July 7, July 14, Aug. 4, Aug. 11, Nov. 24, Dec. 22 and Dec. 29, by CQ Press, a division of Congressional Quarterly Inc. Annual full-service subscriptions for institutions start at $667. For pricing, call 1-800-834-9020, ext. 1906. To purchase a *CQ Researcher* report in print or electronic format (PDF), visit www.cqpress.com or call 866-427-7737. Single reports start at $15. Bulk purchase discounts and electronic-rights licensing are also available. Periodicals postage paid at Washington, D.C., and additional mailing offices. POSTMASTER: Send address changes to *CQ Researcher*, 1255 22nd St., N.W., Suite 400, Washington, DC 20037.

Privacy in Peril

BY MARCIA CLEMMITT

THE ISSUES

When Thelma Arnold of Lilburn, Ga., used AOL's search engine last year, she certainly hoped the information she was looking for would stay private. After all, in addition to seeking help in buying school supplies for Iraqi children, she wanted to know what to do about a "dog that urinates on everything" and where to find single men over 60.

Unfortunately for Arnold, AOL had posted details of her searches on the Internet last summer, along with 20 million other queries submitted to AOL by some 657,000 customers. * Although AOL had replaced the searchers' names with numbers to protect their identities, many of the queries included personal information, such as Social Security numbers and date of birth.

AP Photo/*The Record*, Peter Willott

Police inversigators discovered that before killing his wife, business consultant Justin Barber of Jacksonville, Fla., at left, searched the Internet for famous murder cases and ways to avoid extradition. He was convicted in June 2006 and sentenced to life in prison. Privacy advocates warn that while personal information can help solve crimes, its misuse by criminals and corporations violates citizens' privacy on a vast scale.

Within days, Arnold got a phone call from a *New York Times* reporter, who read her a list of search terms and asked if she was customer number 4417749. Arnold confirmed that she was. Her searches for "landscapers in Lilburn, Ga.," as well as for several people with her last name, helped the reporter figure out her identity.

"My goodness, it's my whole personal life," she said. "I had no idea someone was looking over my shoulder." [1]

As computer databases and electronic-surveillance technologies continue to proliferate, governments and businesses are finding more and more opportunities to develop detailed dossiers on anyone who buys a product, signs up for a government program or logs onto a computer. National-security and law-enforcement agencies say they need the information to head off terrorism and fight crime, while businesses seek purchasing data in order to better target their marketing efforts. The growing demand for and increasing supply of personal information available today make for what privacy advocates call a "perfect storm" of privacy breaches.

Eventually, says James P. Nehf, a professor at the Indiana University School of Law, "Our movements will be tracked so that people will know where you've been and what time of day you were there" through machine-readable chips in driver's licenses and passports and even implanted in our bodies.

If, as is likely, "all this information that's picked up goes into a database" where it's linked with other personal information on file, "the potential for abuse is enormous," he says. Such databases will make identity theft easy and devastating and threaten the speedy approach "of a Big Brother society."

Today, data-gathering is ubiquitous. The Electronic Privacy Information Center estimates that Londoners are photographed more than 300 times a day by more than 1.5 million surveillance cameras throughout the city. [2] Within a few years, all new cars will be equipped with "black boxes" that record data like speed, steering-wheel movement and how hard brakes are pressed; 64 percent of 2005 cars had them. [3]

In September the social-networking Web site Facebook faced a user revolt after it began instantly reporting any changes in members' pages to all their Facebook "friends." [4] In 2005, Walt Disney World's Florida theme parks began fingerprint scans for all visitors to prevent ticket sharing. [5]

Beginning in 2008, the Real ID Act enacted by Congress last year will require states to electronically link all driver's licenses to personal information in a database accessible to all other states. The new database will make all other existing databases "look minuscule by comparison," says Nehf.

With so many public and private databases cropping up, privacy advocates say opportunities are rife for government to buy or subpoena unprecedented amounts of personal

* AOL said it posted the information to help researchers studying consumers. Cynics speculated that AOL wanted to show that it was competing with Google and other popular search engines.

Most States Require Notification After ID Theft

More than 200 major cases of identity theft have been reported in the United States since 2005. Since California passed the first breach-notification law in 2003, 31 states have adopted breach laws.

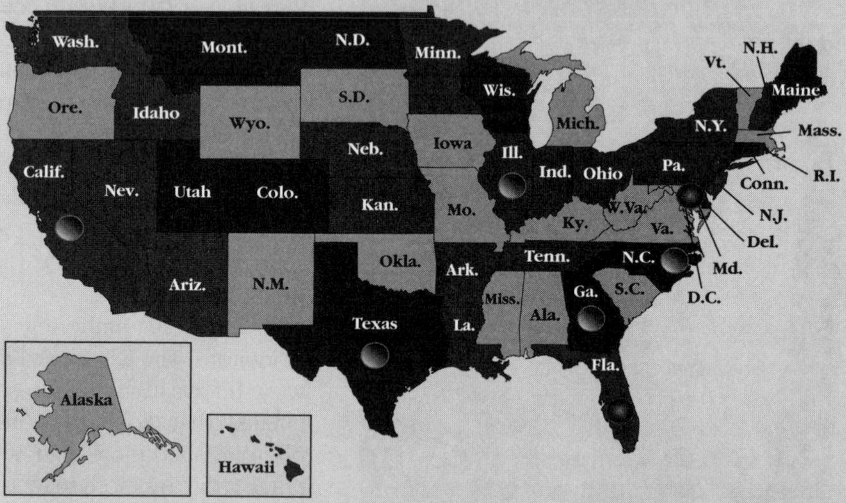

States with no breach-notification laws (18)

States with breach-notification laws applying to any agency or company (21)

States with breach-notification laws that do not apply to public agencies (11)

Major security breaches since 2005:

Between 500,000 and 2 million people affected

More than 2 million people affected

Source: Stateline.org, "States Failing to Secure Personal Data," July 12, 2006

information and for private companies and individuals to buy or steal it.

The potential for abuse is significant, explains Illinois Attorney General Lisa Madigan. Earlier this year she sued several so-called data brokers, or aggregators, for allegedly selling fraudulently obtained cellular-phone records that reveal not only whom phone owners spoke with but also their location. (*See sidebar, p. 972.*)

"Imagine that you are a victim of domestic violence" who has "found the courage and the means to flee" an abusive spouse, said Madigan. With cell-phone records available for sale by shady data brokers, "your abuser . . . will know when you pick the kids up at school and when you get home. Now he can find you." [6]

At the same time, other experts say the vast, new databases also help solve crimes and streamline business transactions. In fact, the same kind of cell-phone records that can enable a stalker to track a victim have also helped to catch wanted criminals, including kidnapping suspects. [7]

Cell-phone records, for instance, quickly helped North Dakota police focus on Alfonso Rodriguez as a suspect in the 2003 kidnapping and murder of University of North Dakota student Dru Sjodin. Rodriguez was sentenced to death in September. And in Maryland, investigators are narrowing down leads in the mysterious 2003 death of Maryland Assistant U.S. Attorney Jonathan Luna, using cell-phone records and data from his EZ-Pass toll card.

Internet searches for terms like murder, missing corpse and presumed dead led Florida police to business consultant Justin Barber, convicted in June for the 2002 murder of his wife, April. [8] Google searches for words like neck and snap also led North Carolina investigators to computer consultant Robert Petrick, who was convicted in November 2005 for the 2003 murder of his wife, Janine. [9]

Last spring, Congress began investigating companies and individuals who obtain personal information by "pretexting" — or claiming to be someone they're not. The practice came under scrutiny last summer, when a scandal erupted at Hewlett Packard (HP). Private investigators hired by the computer giant to determine who leaked secret information apparently used pretexting to obtain journalists' and board members' phone records.

Although the House Energy and Commerce panel held hearings about the HP scandal in September, it had already, in fact, overwhelmingly approved a bill to outlaw pretexting last spring. But the measure has stalled, despite the new media attention from the HP affair.

Also stalled are Bush administration efforts to get Internet companies, phone companies and Web sites to retain consumer information — including lists of Web sites visited — that might help fight child pornography and other crimes. While some lawmakers introduced measures to mandate such data retention, others proposed banning it. Meanwhile, the European Union in December 2005 required companies operating in Europe to retain such information.

In perhaps the year's highest-profile privacy-related controversy, the Bush administration asked for expanded anti-terrorism powers to wiretap Americans' overseas phone calls and e-mails without seeking warrants. Despite vocal opposition from privacy advocates and congressional Democrats, both the House and Senate considered legislation expanding the president's wiretapping powers, and the full Senate approved a bill in September.

As the means and motives for collecting personal data proliferate, some privacy advocates and even some businesses — including computer companies such as Microsoft, Intel and eBay — have called for federal privacy-protection legislation. The United States needs "a national data-protection office, like every other country in the industrialized world," said Simson L. Garfinkel, a postdoctoral fellow at Harvard's Center for Research on Computation and Society. [10]

Regardless of whether Congress acts to curb information gathering and sharing, technology eventually will allow agencies and corporations to track individuals' activities by linking data such as cell-phone records and surveillance videos to credit-card numbers, voting records and Internet search queries. Once those databases are integrated — as they will be — "your life will be pretty much an open book," says Nehf.

With computer databases swelling and electronic-surveillance technology evolving rapidly, here are some of the questions lawmakers and privacy advocates are asking:

Hackers Have Easy Access to Personal Data

More than 97 million records containing Americans' personal information have been involved in security breaches at universities, corporations and government agencies since 2005.

Selected Recent Data Breaches in the United States

Name	Date Made Public	Nature of Breach	No. of Records Involved
Starbucks Corp.	Nov. 3, 2006	Two laptops with employees' addresses and Social Security numbers were lost.	60,000
University of Minnesota	Sept. 8, 2006	Two computers stolen containing information on students from 1992-2006.	13,084
Circuit City, Chase Card Services	Sept. 7, 2006	Five computer data tapes were lost containing cardholders' personal information.	2.6 million
University of Tennessee	July 7, 2006	Hacker accessed computer data on past and current employees.	36,000
Texas Guaranteed Student Loan Corp.	May 30, 2006	A subcontractor's worker lost a computer with borrowers' data.	1.7 million
Dept. of Veterans Affairs	May 22, 2006	A laptop containing data on all U.S. veterans was stolen.	28.6 million
Vermont State Colleges	March 24, 2006	Laptop stolen containing data of students, faculty and staff.	14,000
General Electric	Sept. 25, 2005	Laptop containing Social Security numbers of GE employees stolen.	50,000
CardSystems	June 16, 2005	Hacking	40 million

Source: Privacy Rights Clearinghouse, "A Chronology of Data Breaches"

Should Congress make warrantless wiretapping easier?

Late last year, reporters discovered that President George W. Bush had authorized government agencies to wiretap Americans without first obtaining warrants, arguing the power to quickly authorize such surveillance was vital to fighting terrorism. Despite an outcry by civil-liberties advocates who said the wiretaps were illegal, Congress this year has considered giving the president expanded wiretapping powers.

Following the Democrats' Nov. 7 electoral takeover of both houses of Congress, Bush said he still hopes to sign a bill giving him broader discretion to wiretap U.S. residents suspected of terrorist ties. Presumptive House Speaker Rep. Nancy Pelosi, D-Calif., however, said it's possible the White House and congressional Democrats will reach common ground on wiretapping but that Democrats will insist on some kind of judicial oversight of each individual case rather than the blanket approval the White House seeks. [11]

Wiretap opponents say snooping on Americans without adequate judicial oversight compromises their privacy and violates their Fourth Amendment constitutional protections against government searches without reasonable "cause" for such a search being shown first. About 30 lawsuits have been filed around the country challenging the searches "on constitutional grounds," says Nancy Libin, staff counsel at the Center for Democracy and Technology (CDT).

Revelations that the government had wiretapped dissidents' conversations during the turbulent 1960s and '70s led Congress in 1978 to pass the Foreign Intel-

Smile, Your Employer May Be Watching

After 14 years at Weyco, an insurance consulting firm near Lansing, Mich., Anita Epolito was summarily fired last year for a reason she never expected — smoking cigarettes. Her boss had given employees 15 months to quit smoking and then in January 2005 began firing workers if random screenings showed they still used nicotine.

But Epolito says the smoking was just a "smoke screen" obscuring the true issue. "This is about privacy," said Epolito. "This is about what you do on your own time that is legal, that does not conflict with your job performance."

But her boss, Howard Weyers, said the policy was about smokers who develop illnesses that drive up the cost of health insurance. The random nicotine tests are perfectly legal and in the best interests of his business, Weyers said, adding, "I'm not going to bend from the policy." [1]

Many other kinds of worker-surveillance methods — both electronic and more low-tech — are available to employers today. Software can monitor anything sent from workplace computers, including Internet browsing, chat room comments and even e-mails sent from workers' private e-mail accounts accessed on office computers. Keystroke loggers can record everything typed on a workers' computer, including deleted material. In some companies, so-called smart ID cards track employees' location throughout the workplace, including how long they spend in the bathroom. And while lie-detector tests are banned in hiring, lengthy psychological tests are permitted and frequently used.

The number of employers who snoop on workers is increasing, according to periodic surveys by the American Management Association (AMA). In 2005, 76 percent of employers told the AMA they monitored workers' Web connections. (*See graph, p. 967.*) [2]

While older workers often bristle at surveillance, those in their teens and 20s take it in stride, says Camille Hebert, a professor at Ohio State University's Moritz College of Law. "I'm 47 and have never taken a drug test," she says. "My 21-year-old has taken a test several times. After a while, it seems normal."

Some scholars of workplace behavior say excessive snooping could backfire on employers. Workers who feel their privacy is being invaded are more likely to withhold information from employers and, generally, lose their commitment to the organization, argue Bradley J. Alge, an associate professor of management at Purdue University, and Jerald Greenberg, a professor of management at Ohio State University. Loss of commitment leads to behaviors like increased absenteeism, "checking out" during meetings and being less willing to exercise creativity on the job, Alge and Greenberg write. Monitoring perceived as unjust by workers "can have particularly dire consequences . . . potentially undermining the very safety and security the monitoring system is designed to ensure in the first place." [3]

As surveillance technologies like video cameras and computer-keystroke monitors become cheaper and more effective, employers are increasingly viewing worker surveillance as a key cost-containment strategy. [4]

Although the Constitution prohibits government agents from searching citizens' homes without a warrant showing "cause," no such protection exists for employees. Courts generally give employers broad latitude to monitor workers, arguing that they have the right to ensure that people they hire perform their jobs

ligence Surveillance Act (FISA), which set up a secret panel of judges empowered to review government requests for security-related domestic surveillance. The FISA court fast-tracks government requests for surveillance warrants in national-security cases, although information gleaned from such surveillance can not be shared with agents working on criminal cases. The law also allows the government to wiretap citizens without a warrant for a limited number of days in certain circumstances.

Attorney General Alberto R. Gonzales contends that expanded power to wiretap Americans making overseas phone calls is crucial because the nation is at war against terrorists. "The terrorist-surveillance program is an essential element of our military campaign against al Qaeda," he told the Senate Judiciary Committee. [12] Obtaining FISA warrants currently takes too long and requires the government to submit too much information, and the warrantless wiretaps allowed are too restrictive, he contends.

Enabling the president to authorize speedy and long-term wiretapping on American soil "allows us to collect more information regarding al Qaeda's plans, and, critically, it allows us to locate al Qaeda operatives, especially those already in the United States and poised to attack," said Gonzales. "We cannot defend the nation without such information, as we painfully learned on Sept. 11."

Intelligence and military professionals, not courts, are best suited to decide who should be wiretapped, he said. "The optimal way to achieve the speed and agility necessary to this military-intelligence program . . . is to leave the decisions about particular intercepts to the judgment of a professional intelligence officer," said Gonzales. If an intelligence officer is required to navigate through the FISA procedures, "there would be critical holes in our early-warning system."

Historically, presidents have been allowed to conduct warrantless surveillance against wartime enemies on home soil, said Douglas W. Kmiec, a professor of constitutional law at Pepperdine University. "Neither Congress nor the president has required the armed forces to seek a battlefield warrant to conduct visual electronic surveillance,"

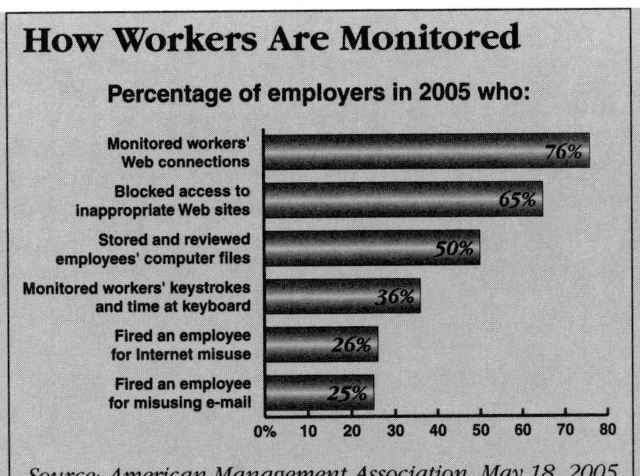

as well as possible, says Hebert. In essence, "employers can do whatever they want," she says.

Worker privacy is "not a very coherent area of the law," she adds. "There is no federal statute that provides for privacy protection." Instead, some protection is offered by a variety of more general federal laws, such as those covering wiretapping, and state laws that govern the way drug tests are given, for example. However, courts do uphold a few strong privacy standards, such as banning cameras in places where workers may disrobe. A federal law bans the use of lie-detector tests for general screening, allowing polygraphs only when some specific wrongdoing is suspected.

Otherwise, courts and legislators generally maintain that "if an employer hires you, they have a right to have you be on time and be efficient," which a business may conclude requires monitoring, says Hebert.

From time to time Congress considers strengthening safeguards on worker privacy. In 2000, for example, Rep. Charles Canady, R-Fla., and Sen. Charles Schumer, D-N.Y., introduced a measure that would have allowed workers to sue employers who didn't notify them that their electronic communications were being monitored. "Everybody has the right to know when they're being watched," said Schumer. [5] However, although House and Senate panels debated the bills, they never made it to the floor. [6]

In the 1970s, Congress created a panel to examine whether consumers and workers needed privacy protections. Setting the tone for today's hands-off approach on workplace privacy, the Privacy Protection Study Commission concluded that employers set workplace policies — including privacy standards. And, because workers are free to work for an employer or not, they are generally obligated to abide by the boss' rules.

[1] "Whose Life Is It Anyway?" CBS News, Oct. 30, 2005, www.workrights.org/in_the_news?in_the_news_cbs60minutes.html.

[2] "2005 Electronic Monitoring and Surveillance Survey: Many Companies Monitoring, Recording, Videotaping — and Firing — Employees," American Management Association, May 18, 2005, www.amanet.org.

[3] Bradley J. Alge, Jerald Greenberg and Chad T. Brinsfeld, "An Identity-Based Model of Organizational Monitoring: Integrating Information Privacy and Organizational Justice," *Research in Personnel and Human Resources Management*, 2006, pp. 71, 120.

[4] For background see "Privacy in the Workplace," *Editorial Research Reports*, 1986, and Patrick G. Marshall, "Your Right to Privacy," *CQ Researcher*, Jan. 20, 1989, both available at *CQ Researcher* Plus Archive, www.cqpress.com; and Richard L. Worsnop, "Privacy in the Workplace," *CQ Researcher*, Nov. 19, 1993, pp. 1009-1032.

[5] Quoted in "Congressional Alert: Bill S. 2898, HR 4908," *The Internet Party* blog; www.theinternetparty.org/congress/index.php?section_type=con&cat_name=Privacy&td=20011015162238&page_sort=3.

[6] "Workplace Privacy," Electronic Privacy Information Center, www.epic.org/privacy/workplace.

said Kmiec. "The Civil War is . . . the main historical battle fought on our soil, and there is no history suggesting that any search or observation of Confederate forces . . . was subject to a warrant requirement." [13]

There's no reason to imagine that the power to wiretap without a warrant would be misused for political purposes, said Robert F. Turner, associate director of the University of Virginia School of Law's Center for National Security Law. President Bush's critics "have done a grave disservice to our nation in drawing comparisons with President [Richard M.] Nixon's 'enemies list' and suggesting there is something evil about the program," he said, referring to a "watch list" of political opponents maintained by Nixon. [14]

Most Americans would gladly trade some privacy to help defeat terrorists, Turner continued. "I find it unimaginable that many rational Americans who are not intentionally assisting foreign terrorists would favor a policy by which the [National Security Agency] would ignore communications between known or suspected al Qaeda operatives abroad and . . . people within this country," he said. "They would be asserting that their privacy interests are of greater importance than the right to exist of perhaps tens- or hundreds-of-thousands of their fellow citizens."

But opponents of expanded wiretapping power say allowing a single government branch to breach Americans' privacy without sufficient oversight is a recipe for abuse. "This is not a debate about whether we ought to be wiretapping terrorists. The government had better be," says the Center for Democracy and Technology's Libin. "It's a debate over whether there should be checks" on the wiretapping power.

It's even more important to retain such checks in national-security cases than in criminal cases, where "you have a trial at the end that acts as a check" with public exposure of evidence, she says, whereas terrorism cases often are handled in secret military tribunals. " 'Trust us' is not the principle on which our country was founded."

She notes that since the FISA court was established, it has reviewed about 20,000 requests for FISA warrants and rejected only four — all in 2002. In that year, the Bush administration began

Wiretapping Spikes After Sept. 11

About 20,000 national-security wiretaps on Americans' phone calls and e-mails have been approved since 1979 by the court established by the Foreign Intelligence Surveillance Act (FISA). The number increased significantly after the Sept. 11, 2001, terrorist attacks.*

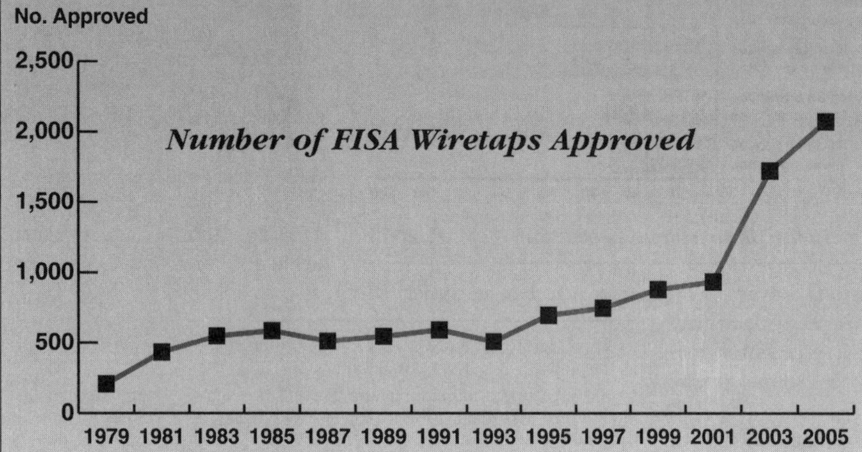

** The total does not include warrantless eavesdropping on the international calls of several thousand people in the United States.*

Source: Electronic Privacy Information Center

bypassing the court and using warrantless wiretapping of U.S. residents.

Harold Hongju Koh, dean of Yale Law School, argues that proposed legislation to expand presidential wiretapping power "would make matters far worse by giving Congress' blanket pre-authorization to a large number of unreasonable searches and seizures." (*See "At Issue," p. 977.*) Further, he added, the wiretapping bill approved by the Senate this fall "ratifies an illegal ongoing program without demanding first a full congressional review of what is now being done and more executive accountability going forward." It also would provide "neither the congressional oversight nor the judicial review that this program needs to restore . . . confidence in our constitutional checks and balances." [15]

Kenneth Gormley, professor of constitutional law at Pittsburgh's Duquesne University, said unless the government adheres to the Bill of Rights' ban on unreasonable government searches, officials would be destroying the very democracy they claim to be protecting from terrorists. [16]

The president's wiretapping program and congressional proposals to authorize it are vague enough to allow many abuses, say critics. "If, as they claim, the Bush administration can ignore FISA's express prohibition of warrantless wiretapping, can the government also eavesdrop on purely domestic phone calls?" asked Vermont Sen. Patrick J. Leahy, the top-ranking Democrat on the Senate Judiciary Committee and its incoming chairman. "Can it search or electronically bug an American's home or office?" [17]

Since combating terrorism is neither a declared war nor a time-limited activity, extra presidential powers granted in that context would essentially be eternal, Gormley pointed out. "When does this emergency cease?" he asked. Are "we prepared to say that the president may unilaterally suspend the Constitution for an indefinite period of time in order to deal with emergencies that have no ending point?"

Wiretapping under a FISA warrant is as effective as warrantless wiretapping, *The New York Times* editorialized last January. "The nation's guardians did not miss the 9/11 plot because it takes a few hours to get a warrant to eavesdrop on phone calls and e-mail messages," the paper said. "They missed the plot because they were not looking. Nothing prevented American intelligence from listening to a call from al Qaeda to the United States, or a call from the United States to al Qaeda, before Sept. 11, 2001, or since."

FISA "simply required the government to obey the Constitution in doing so," the editorial continued. "And FISA was amended after 9/11 to make the job much easier." [18]

Should companies be required to save data on customers' phone calls and Web searches?

To aid law enforcement, especially in child-pornography cases, President Bush has asked Internet and phone companies to save information on customers' Internet searches and phone calls. Attorney General Gonzales told the Senate Banking Committee that data retention "helps us make cases" against child pornographers and sex predators. "We have to find a way for Internet service providers (ISPs) to retain information for a period of time so we can go back with a legal process to get them." [19]

Although the Bush administration hasn't specifically mentioned the war on terrorism as a rationale for asking companies to retain Web-search data, the European Union (EU) directed telecommunications companies and ISPs in Europe to retain such data in order to put "a vital tool against terrorism and serious crime" in the hand of law-enforcement agencies," said British Home Secretary Charles Clarke. "Modern criminality crosses borders and seeks to exploit digital technology." [20]

Privacy advocates, however, argue that while such databases might help police they also could endanger privacy by allowing others, such as divorce lawyers, to conduct "fishing" expeditions into personal information. "If you have a huge database, then it becomes a huge target," says Indiana University's Nehf. "Unauthorized access by computer hacking," for example, is a huge problem now, but once the information is available, businesses, law-enforcement agencies, attorneys in civil cases and others "will start wanting to use it for 85 different purposes," he says.

However, state attorneys general agree with Gonzales that access to computer searches is critical for law enforcement. Last June, 49 attorneys general asked Congress to require ISPs to retain more data, citing the "growing crisis of Internet-based sex crimes against children and, in particular, the problem of insufficient data-retention policies" by ISPs.

"While law enforcement is doing more to catch online predators, their investigations often tragically dead-end at the door of [ISPs] that have deleted information critical to determining a suspect's name and physical location," the National Association of Attorneys General wrote in a letter to Congress. Although the group declined to specify how long subscriber information and content should be retained, "it is clear that something must be done," it said. [21]

Retaining phone records is especially important now that many phone companies are adopting flat-rate billing rather than charging by the call, according to the International Association of Chiefs of Police. Migration to flat-rate billing "has substantially eroded" law enforcement's ability to lawfully obtain telephone records "critical to the identification, detection and prevention" of terrorist and criminal conspiracies, the group said in a resolution endorsed in October. [22]

The EU's data-retention directive would also help music and media companies fight music and video theft. "We would appreciate your support in ensuring that this becomes an effective instrument in the fight against piracy," said the Creative and Media Business Alliance, whose members include such companies as EMI, SonyBMG and TimeWarner. [23]

But opponents argue that additional data retention threatens consumers' privacy and would turn phone and Internet companies into unofficial government agents. The government has asked ISPs to retain all of their records "just in case, someday, somehow, for some reason, the government may want them in some future case," said Mark Rasch, chief security counsel of the Omaha-based computer firm Solutionary. The proposal "represents a dangerous trend of turning private companies into proxies for law enforcement or intelligence agencies against the interest of their clients or customers." [24]

ISPs create short-term records of "virtually everything that virtually everyone does virtually," said Rasch, from blog posting and shopping online to editing a MySpace account or downloading music. But those records are frequently purged because they serve no real function for the ISP, he said.

Moreover, law-enforcement agencies already have the right to demand that ISPs retain specific records for between three and six months, he pointed out.

If such records are retained indefinitely, all Internet travels will become fair game for "criminal or civil subpoena, investigative demand, national security letter, grand jury subpoena, search warrant [and] administrative demand" in matters ranging from criminal investigations to divorce, according to Rasch. "If records exist, they will be subpoenaed, stolen, lost or hacked."

Furthermore, the Center for Democracy and Technology worries that ISPs, to recoup some of the expense of storing all that new data, "might be tempted to use the stored information for a range of currently unanticipated purposes," exposing customers to additional privacy threats. [25]

A list of an individual's Internet browsing — called a clicktrail — is "the equivalent of being tailed everywhere you go," undermining one's ability to remain anonymous, because analysts of that data "are likely to identify you," according to William McGeveran a fellow at Harvard Law School's Berkman Center for Internet and Society. [26]

Data retention could also breach the privacy of police work, according to Peter P. Swire, a law professor at Ohio State University. "Commercial ISPs would retain detailed records of communications to and from the FBI or the local police department," becoming "a honey pot for attacks" from ISP employees working for or bribed by criminals or from outside hackers, Swire said. "Organized-crime groups . . . might find it irresistible to place a spy in ISPs in cities where they operate." [27]

Other critics argue that businesses already save too much information. For example, companies like Google and MSN archive search-engine queries, as Thelma Arnold discovered when a reporter tracked her down in Lilburn, Ga.

"Search engines can only regain the trust of the public if they delete the search queries as soon as they get them," said British technology reporter Andrew Orlowski. In many cases, "these questions . . . would only have been made with the assumption that no one would ever see them. So what business do . . . organizations have hoarding this information?" [28]

Should Congress criminalize pretexting?

Obtaining access to confidential information by pretending to be another person — or pretexting — became news this year when investigators for HP used the tactic to obtain phone records of board members and journalists.

A pending House bill would ban pretexting to obtain phone records and require phone companies to do more to prevent the practice. Supporters of the measure say it's needed because some lawyers believe pretexting is legal. But opponents say it would unfairly increase phone companies' privacy-protection responsibilities. Others say lawmakers should spend their energy developing a broader consumer-privacy law.

"Even though most experts agree" that pretexting is already illegal under state and federal laws, the HP case indicates that there is "confusion in the highest echelons of corporate America and among their legal counsel" about that fact, said Rep. Dianne DeGette, D-Colo. [29]

The legislation also pressures phone companies to do more to safeguard customers' data, supporters say. Without the bill, it's too easy for scam artists to get the personal phone logs of others, said Rep. Jan Schakowsky, D-Ill. [30]

"We are putting obligations on you to protect our constituents' privacy," Rep. Jay Inslee, D-Wash., told telephone executives at a Sept. 29 House Commerce Subcommittee on Oversight and Investigations hearing. "It's entirely appropriate . . . to have a more uniform system so that we can have the highest level of anti-pretexting technologies in use. That is a fair obligation on the industry." [31]

A new law would help clarify "the illegality of this practice," Joel Winston, the Federal Trade Commission's associate director for privacy protection, told the subcommittee. Moreover, he added, the law should apply not only to the pretexters but also to anyone who solicits their services "when they know or should know that fraudulent means are being deployed." [32]

However, private investigators, corporate boards and others who want to access phone records now legally accessible only to law-enforcement agencies armed with a judicial warrant, argue that sometimes their need for information trumps privacy worries.

Rep. Ed Whitfield, R-Ky., told fellow subcommittee members that after one of the panel's hearings on the HP pretexting scandal, two legislators warned him that corporate boards "should have the right to determine who's leaking information." [33]

Jimmie Mesis, editor in chief of *PI Magazine*, said banning pretexting would cripple the ability of private investigators to solve important cases. He said he had warned private detectives to stop "blatantly" advertising that they can obtain unpublished numbers or phone records or risk a new law that "will eventually prevent us from using an amazing investigative resource." [34]

Although phone companies oppose pretexting and have sued pretexters, they are reluctant to endorse a new law because they think consumers would find tougher security measures inconvenient. Customers "don't want another password," said Tom Meiss, associate general counsel of Cingular Wireless. "Ironically, the stronger you make the security, the more likely it is that people are going to get locked out" of their own accounts. That would just play into pretexters' plans, he said, because many pretexters get the records by telling customer-service representatives they are customers who have forgotten their passwords. [35]

Many legal scholars and privacy advocates point out that pretexting is already clearly illegal and that many other privacy issues deserve lawmakers' attention but are not being addressed by current laws or regulations.

"Congress might pass a law making [pretexting for phone records] illegal, but it's already illegal, so I don't think that gets you very far," says Nehf. ■

BACKGROUND

Behind Closed Doors

In the days before the telegraph and telephone, privacy was defined as the right to be free from unreasonable intrusions into one's own home. But with people's lives increasingly dominated by electronics, the question of what is private has become harder to answer. For example, once a customer enters a credit-card number into a database that belongs to a commercial business, who owns that information — the customer or the business owner? Or has the customer made it public record by giving it away? [36]

Starting in the 15th century, the British government began challenging citizens' views that their homes were effectively their castles — where privacy was sacrosanct — by authorizing government agents to search homes and businesses if they suspected the owners of criminal activity, heresy or political dissent.

Eventually, England began regularly issuing "general warrants" authorizing searches of houses and businesses without any proof that owners had done anything wrong and without even naming the object of the search.

By the mid-18th century, however, English citizens fed up with general warrants successfully sued government agents for trespassing. In one case, England's Court of Common Pleas found that the defendants had no right to use the warrants, asserting "there is no law in this country to justify the defendants in what they have done. If there was, it would destroy all the comforts of society." [37]

At about the same time, the American colonists were outraged by similar general warrants — so-called writs of assistance — issued to British customs officers searching for smuggled goods. The writs had no time limit, allowed officers to search anyplace they wanted without responsibility for damages and could be transferred from officer to officer.

The writs were among the grievances the colonists listed when they declared their independence from England in 1776. The Constitution's Fourth Amendment — citizens' primary pro-

Continued on p. 972

Chronology

1890s-1960s

Law-enforcement agencies raise privacy concerns when they wiretap phones.

1895
New York City police looking for criminal evidence figure out how to wiretap telephones.

1928
Supreme Court declares in *Olmstead v. United States* that warrantless police wiretaps don't violate the Constitution's ban on "unreasonable searches and seizures."

1956
FBI launches COINTELPRO counterintelligence program to keep tabs on the Communist Party and other dissident groups.

1967
Supreme Court in *Katz v. United States* overturns *Olmstead*, requiring warrants before police can wiretap.

1970s-1980s

Government surveillance in national-security matters draws scrutiny, and personal information begins to migrate into computer databases.

1972
Supreme Court in *United States v. United States District Court* requires warrants for wiretapping in national-security cases.

1974
Privacy Act requires federal agencies to safeguard privacy when they collect personal information; attempts to extend privacy requirements to commercial businesses fail.

1976
The so-called Church committee concludes that from World War I through the 1970s U.S. presidents have claimed national-security reasons for spying on political enemies.

1978
Foreign Intelligence Surveillance Act creates a special court to secretly assess government requests for national-security wiretaps.

1986
Electronic Communications Privacy Act prohibits warrantless government wiretaps of electronic communications.

1990s

The booming Internet and cell-phone industries make more private data vulnerable to computer hacking and other misuse. Australia, Canada, New Zealand and most European countries enact wide-ranging consumer-privacy laws.

1995
European Union adopts a privacy directive establishing a minimum standard of data-privacy protection across Europe.

1999
A woman is shot to death in New Hampshire after a business obtains her personal data by trickery and sells it to a stalker. . . . The Gramm-Leach-Bliley law makes it a federal crime to obtain financial records by pretexting — claiming a false identity.

2000s

Terrorism fears and burgeoning electronic technology increase government-surveillance initiatives. Data aggregators sell personal information gained from multiple public and private sources.

2001
Terrorist attacks on Sept. 11 shift attention from privacy protection to national security. . . . USA Patriot Act passed on Oct. 25, giving government sweeping surveillance powers.

2005
Atlanta-based data aggregator ChoicePoint sells data on 163,000 people to a crime ring and later faces a $15 million fine. . . . Computers are hacked at CardSystems Solutions, which manages credit-card money transfers, potentially exposing financial data on 40 million people. . . . AT&T is accused of helping the Bush administration wiretap Americans' phone calls without warrants. . . . Real ID Act requires nationally standardized driver's licenses to be electronically linked to personal data and available to all states. . . . Congress reauthorizes Patriot Act but with new surveillance limits.

2006
Federal judge strikes down National Security Agency domestic-surveillance program, but its wiretaps continue under appeal. . . . Congress considers increasing the president's power to order wiretaps. . . . AOL posts 650,000 supposedly anonymous search-engine queries online, but researchers identify customers using Social Security and credit-card numbers in the data. . . . A Department of Veterans Affairs laptop computer with veterans' personal data is stolen. . . . Investigators working for computer giant HP in a leak investigation use pretexting to get journalists' and board members' phone records.

Attacks on Privacy Getting More Ingenious

Companies are creating increasingly ingenious ways to monitor consumers' buying habits. Many supermarkets and drug stores, for instance, now offer discounts on certain products to those who sign up for the stores' frequent-buyer cards. But to get that card — and a few bucks off on their purchases — customers must give the store their names, addresses and phone numbers. The store's computers then track the buyers' purchasing preferences and sell the information to other marketers.

But besides collecting data for commercial purposes, a growing number of companies — legitimate and illegitimate — are in the business of selling personal information. These data aggregators (also called data brokers or information resellers) sometimes collect information under false pretenses — known as pretexting — and sell it to all comers. Law-enforcement agencies around the country have recently tried to shut down such companies.

In March, for example, Florida Attorney General — now governor-elect — Charlie Crist charged the Global Information Group with pretexting to obtain customer phone records. [1] Between Sept. 14 and Oct. 19, 2005, the company allegedly made more than 5,100 calls to Florida Verizon Wireless customers, attempting to obtain confidential information "through deceit, either by impersonating a customer or employee, or otherwise convincing the customer-service representative to provide private information . . . without the customer's consent or knowledge," the lawsuit claims. [2]

"Why do these people sell this data — and, apparently, sell it to anyone? Frankly, greed is the name of the game," said information-security consultant Robert Douglas, CEO of PrivacyToday.com. Individuals ranging from lawyers and private investigators to vengeful ex-spouses, obsessed stalkers or identity thieves will pay top dollar for personal data, he said. [3]

Beyond the underworld of information thieves there is the fast-growing world of large, legitimate data aggregators. Companies such as ChoicePoint, Acxiom and InfoUSA assemble for resale detailed personal profiles from government sources including birth and death records, property records, voter registrations and court files, publicly available information like telephone and business directories and proprietary sources such as credit files and product-warranty questionnaires.

Law-enforcement agencies and government offices buy information from data aggregators, according to the Government Accountability Office (GAO). In fiscal 2005, for example, the Justice, Homeland Security and State departments, as well as the Social Security Administration, spent $30 million buying personal information from resellers, according to GAO. The agencies used the information for purposes like tracking down potential witnesses and making sure that people are entitled to the government benefits they receive. [4]

It's far cheaper for government to use commercially aggregated data, Consumer Data Industry Association President Stuart Pratt told the House Judiciary Committee in April. "One commercial database provider charges just $25 for an instant comprehensive search of . . . more than 100 million criminal records across the United States," said Pratt. "An in-person, local search of one local courthouse for felony and misdemeanor records takes three . . . days and costs $16 [in] courthouse fees," adding up to a $48,544 tab for an in-person search of every county courthouse nationwide. [5]

But critics say that as commercial — but largely unregulated — data aggregators replace public records as the preferred information source for business and government, oversight is needed to protect individuals' privacy.

For example, 41 states allow some people accused or convicted of crimes to expunge their criminal records under certain circumstances. But removing a crime from one's record is much more difficult now that private companies serve as key providers of public data. Unlike government offices, private companies are not legally required to ensure the accuracy of their data. Consequently, many databases "are updated only fitfully, and expunged records now often turn up in criminal background checks ordered by employers and landlords." [6]

For the interconnected world of government and commercial data keeping, a new legal framework to protect personal information is needed, say some analysts.

In the case of criminal-record expungement, for example, "the solution . . . is for states . . . to require" commercial data brokers "to promise that they will delete records when they are expunged" from the public records, according to Daniel J. Solove, an associate professor of law at The George Washington University." [7]

[1] "Crist Charges Second Data Broker Over Sale of Phone Records," press release, Office of the Attorney General of Florida, Feb. 24, 2006, http://myfloridalegal.com.

[2] *Florida v. Global Information Group, Inc.*, http://myfloridalegal.com/webfiles.nsf/WF/MRAY-6M9RY3/$file/Global_Complaint.pdf.

[3] Testimony before House Committee on Energy and Commerce, Feb. 1, 2006.

[4] Linda D. Koontz, "Personal Information: Agencies and Resellers Vary in Providing Privacy Protections," Government Accountability Office, April 4, 2006.

[5] Testimony before House Judiciary Subcommittees on Commercial and Administrative Law and on the Constitution, April 4, 2006.

[6] Adam Litpak, "Expunged Criminal Records Live to Tell Tales," *The New York Times*, Oct. 17, 2006.

[7] Daniel J. Solove, "The Reincarnation of Expunged Criminal Records," *Concurring Opinions* blog, Oct. 17, 2006; www.concurringopinions.com.

Continued from p. 970

tection against unreasonable government searches — banned general search warrants.

Electronic Intrusion

As technologies advanced, however, the meaning of a guarantee against "unreasonable searches" became murkier. When private information is transmitted long distances over a wire, for instance, it is unclear whether it remains protected private information. [38]

In the second half of the 19th century, some states made it a crime for a telegraph company to disclose a telegram's contents to anyone but its authorized recipient. And in 1877, Western Union President William Orton resisted a congressional subpoena seeking telegrams for evidence in an investigation of voting irregularities.

The subpoena asked his company "to become spies and . . . informers against the customers who have reposed in us the gravest confidence concerning both their official and their private affairs," Orton said. [39] After being declared in contempt of Congress and arrested, however, he gave in and handed over 30,000 telegrams. To avoid similar future troubles, Western Union reduced the amount of time it kept copies of messages.

By the late 1880s, a new technology — the telephone — was transmitting a million messages a day in the United States. Original users of the telephone had little expectation of confidentiality, though, because initially four or more neighbors shared the same "party line," and operators knew exactly who was talking to whom, since the operators placed most calls manually.

Meanwhile, police agencies were quick to see the telephone's potential for evidence gathering, and by the 1890s police had figured out how to "tap" phones. The public remained largely unaware of this development until a 1916 investigation into New York public utilities turned up evidence of the taps, which were being used to keep tabs on resident aliens who might be spying for enemy governments during World War I.

The government had set up "a complete central-office switchboard . . . in the New York Custom House, with taps running into it from all parts of the city. Every time a suspected alien lifted his receiver a light showed . . . and a stenographer . . . took a record of the conversation." [40]

Discovery of the taps triggered public outrage, and the telephone company ended its cooperation with the government. But police wiretapping continued unchecked.

By the 1920s, most U.S. phone calls were placed by automatic switchboards, not live operators, and the public began to expect that telephone conversations were confidential. But as more and more conversations about activities — legal and illegal — began traveling over telephone lines, police saw more reason to wiretap. Eventually, the Supreme Court was asked to consider whether the Fourth Amendment restricted wiretapping.

During Prohibition, Seattle police Lt. Roy Olmstead was arrested for bootlegging. But because federal agents had not sought a warrant before tapping phones at his home and the homes of three associates, he claimed the taps violated his constitutional protection against warrantless searches. But a 5-4 Supreme Court decision in 1928 held that the taps were not an "unreasonable search" under the Constitution. [41]

"There was no searching. There was no seizure," wrote Chief Justice William Howard Taft for the majority. "The evidence was secured by the sense of hearing and that only."

In a strong and seemingly prescient dissent, Justice Louis D. Brandeis protested that "subtler and more far-reaching means of invading privacy have become available to the government. . . . The progress of science . . . is not likely to stop with wiretapping. Can it be that the Constitution affords no protection against such invasions of individual security?" Surely, Brandeis continued, the Constitution protects against "every unjustifiable intrusion by the Government upon the privacy of the individual, whatever the means employed." [42]

For nearly four decades, the court's declaration that warrantless wiretaps were constitutional held sway. By 1967, however, with the world firmly entrenched in the electronic era, the court came around to Brandeis' view. In *Katz v. United States* the court ruled that FBI agents had violated the Fourth Amendment by not requesting a judicial warrant before installing a listening device on a phone booth to record calls made by Charles Katz, a small-time Los Angeles gambler.

The *Katz* decision reflected how advancing technology had changed the concept of privacy. No longer did invasion of privacy require intrusion into one's home or a sealed letter. "Once it is recognized that the Fourth Amendment protects people — and not simply 'areas' — against unreasonable searches and seizures, it becomes clear that the reach of that Amendment cannot turn upon the presence or absence of a physical intrusion into any given enclosure," said the court majority in *Katz*. [43]

National Security

For nearly as long as there have been telephones, government agencies have argued that national security requires eavesdropping on electronic communications. The FBI, NSA and other executive-branch agencies say they need secrecy and know more than the courts about security threats so they should be free to conduct surveillance — including of American citizens — without seeking warrants.

In the 1950s and '60s, the FBI, under orders from Director J. Edgar Hoover, set up a nationwide counterintelligence program — COINTELPRO — to investigate dissident political organizations ranging from the Communist Party to the Black Panthers. Eventually, COINTELPRO expanded to spy on the Ku Klux Klan and anti-war groups such as Students for a Democratic Society.

Meanwhile, NSA's "Project Shamrock" searched for key words in every telegram sent into or out of the United States in search of communist sympathizers — another example of massive domestic surveillance conducted without a judicial warrant.

By the early 1970s, worries were growing about how such programs compromised Americans' privacy. And in 1971, U.S. Court of Appeals Judge Damon J. Keith ruled in the Michigan criminal trial of the White Panther Party that national-security concerns were not an adequate justification for warrantless wiretapping of Americans. [44]

In the case, which involved the bombing of CIA offices in Ann Arbor, the government claimed that the president and attorney general had the power "to authorize without judicial warrant electronic surveillance in 'national security' cases and to determine unilaterally whether a given situation is a matter . . . of national security," wrote Keith. [45]

But "we are a country of laws and not of men," Keith said. "If the president is given power to delegate who shall conduct wiretaps, the question arises whether there is any limit on this power."

ACLU/ALA

A poster sponsored by the American Civil Liberties Union and the American Library Association condemns so-called third-party searches permitted by the 2001 USA Patriot Act. The controversial law allowed the government to obtain data on which books patrons checked out and prohibited librarians from revealing that a search had occurred. Protests by privacy activists led Congress in 2005 to tighten the requirements for such searches.

In 1972, the Supreme Court unanimously upheld Keith's ruling. "We cannot accept the government's argument that internal security matters are too subtle and complex for judicial evaluation," wrote Justice Lewis F. Powell. [46]

In 1976, the Senate launched an investigation of national-security surveillance. The Select Committee to Study Governmental Operations with Respect to Intelligence Activities — known as the Church committee after its chairman, Sen. Frank Church, D-Idaho — examined millions of pages of documents and concluded that abusive domestic spying by federal agencies went as far back as World War I.

"The constitutional system of checks and balances has not adequately controlled intelligence activities," the committee's report said. "Too many people have been spied upon by too many government agencies, and too much information has been collected. . . . The government has often undertaken the secret surveillance of citizens on the basis of their political beliefs, even when those beliefs posed no threat of violence or illegal acts on behalf of a foreign power." [47]

To prevent such abuses in the future, the Supreme Court and members of Congress declared that lawmakers should set up a system for issuing national-security warrants. The 1978 Foreign Surveillance Intelligence Act (FISA) established the Foreign Surveillance Intelligence Court (FISC) — a secret panel of judges empowered to review government requests for security-related domestic surveillance.

FISA fast-tracks government requests for warrants for national-security surveillance on the condition that information gained through FISA warrants not be shared with agents working on criminal cases. Since the Sept. 11, 2001, terrorist attacks, Congress has amended the law five times at the request of both Congress and the administration. Among other things, the changes:

- Permit extending wiretaps to other phones a suspect may be using, even if the phone owners are not under investigation;
- Lengthen the time warrants are valid for both wiretaps and physical searches;
- Allow surveillance of e-mails under the same wiretapping warrant;
- Allow FISA wiretapping for a broader range of investigations by allowing foreign-intelligence gathering to be only "a significant

Tips on Protecting Your Privacy

Many experts argue that surveillance and database technologies have proliferated to such an extent that Americans have little privacy left to protect. Nevertheless, here are some ways consumer and advocacy groups say citizens can protect their personal information:

Be on the lookout for pretexting. Many unscrupulous individuals and businesses try to get private information under false pretenses, says the Federal Trade Commission (FTC). To avoid being victimized, never give out your Social Security number, mother's maiden name, bank account numbers or other personal information to a telephone caller or e-mailer, no matter who they claim to be, says the FTC.

"Pretexters may pose as representatives of survey firms, banks, Internet service providers and government agencies" to get you to reveal your data. But "legitimate organizations with which you do business have the information they need and will not ask you for it." [1]

The FTC also advises consumers to ask banks and other companies that gather personal information what measures they take to prevent pretexting.

Don't use your Social Security number (SSN) or birth date as a password. The technology magazine *Wired* says both are too easily discovered to make for good security, and using them as passwords only makes it easier for someone to steal them. Insist that your health-insurance provider and phone companies allow you to use a customer-designated password, and use different passwords for different accounts, the magazine advises. [2]

Use unique passwords. Thieves can easily discover passwords like a pet's name or consecutive numbers, says the Privacy Rights Clearinghouse, "Think of a favorite line of poetry, like 'Mary had a little lamb.' Use the first or last letters to create a password. Use numbers to make it stronger. For example, MHALL, or better yet, MHA2L." [3]

Use a prepaid disposable cell phone. If you're worried about your phone records becoming available to third parties, such as stalkers, buy a disposable phone and add calling minutes through the phone company rather than through a Web site, which might track your computer's address. [4]

Use a Web-accessible e-mail account for personal e-mails. While employers may still be able to read your e-mails if you access the account from a workplace computer, they won't be automatically stored in the company's main computer server, says the Center for Democracy and Technology (CDT). All mail sent through your workplace e-mail is stored there, even if you access your work e-mail from a home computer. [5]

Clear your computer's memory cache frequently. While keeping a cache of recently visited Web pages makes it easier to call the pages up again, failing to periodically erase it can have "grave implications for personal privacy," especially if you share a computer, says CDT. Go to the "preferences" folder in your Internet browser and click "empty cache" to delete your browsing list. In Internet Explorer, call up "Internet options" from the "tools" menu, and then click "clear history." [6]

Ask your bank how much personal data it shares about you. The Federal Reserve Board (FRB) points out that banks, insurance companies and other financial-services companies can share customer information with other businesses, but they must first send privacy notices to customers offering them a chance to opt out. If you didn't opt out when you received your privacy notification, "it's not too late," says the FRB. "You can always change your mind." Just call the company for instructions on opting out of future data-sharing. [7]

Use other "opt-out" tools to protect your information. To limit the number of preapproved credit-card offers you receive, opt out of credit-reporting bureaus' marketing lists at www.optoutprescreen.com or call 888-5OPTOUT. To opt out of calls from nationwide marketers, contact the FTC's National Do Not Call Registry at www.donotcall.gov or call (888) 382-1222. [8]

---

[1] "Pretexting: Your Personal Information Revealed," *Facts for Consumers*, Federal Trade Commission, www.ftc.gov.

[2] Kim Zetter, "Protect Yourself From Pretexting," *Wired News*, Sept. 14, 2006; www.wired.com.

[3] "Coping With Identity Theft: Reducing the Risk of Fraud," *Fact Sheet 17*, Privacy Rights Clearinghouse, September 2006, www.privacyrights.org.

[4] *Ibid.*

[5] "Getting Started: Top Ten Ways to Protect Privacy Online," Center for Democracy and Technology, www.cdt.org.

[6] *Ibid.*

[7] "Privacy Choices for Your Personal Financial Information," Federal Reserve Board, www.federalreserve.gov/pubs/privacy/.

[8] Privacy Rights Clearinghouse, *op. cit.*

---

purpose" rather than "the purpose" of the investigation;

- Protect from legal liability anybody who helps with FISA wiretapping. [48]

By 2005 the FISA court had granted some 20,000 warrants during its 27-year existence. It had turned down government requests for warrants only four times — in 2002. Last year the court approved 2,072 warrant requests — the highest annual total ever and 18 percent more than in 2004. [49]

Yet in December 2005 *The New York Times* reported that since early 2002 President George W. Bush had secretly authorized the NSA to bypass the FISA court and conduct warrantless eavesdropping on U.S. citizens' international telephone calls and e-mails. Through the end of 2005, several thousand people in the United States had had their international communications monitored, with about 500 Americans under surveillance at any given time, government officials told the paper. [50]

The administration says the program has been successful in slowing terrorists. For example, officials said, it helped uncover a plot by a naturalized citizen in Ohio, Iyman Faris, who pled guilty in 2003 to plotting to destroy the Brooklyn Bridge. [51]

In August 2006, however, a U.S. district judge ruled that the NSA eavesdropping program was unconstitutional. The government has appealed the decision, and a court has said the eavesdropping may continue while the appeal proceeds. [52]

Another post-9/11 security measure — the USA Patriot Act — allowed government agents to obtain personal records held by "third parties," such as library records of what books an individual has borrowed, and prohibited anyone — librarians, for instance — from revealing that such a search had occurred. [53]

When Congress reauthorized the measure in 2005, it barred third-party searches without the approval of top FBI officials and required the Justice Department's inspector general to audit each search request. Congress also recommended that citizens be able to challenge the search orders in court. [54]

Database Era

Before the computer age, privacy advocates worried most about concentrations of personal information at government agencies. But with computers came a new age of information gathering, with government agencies and private businesses accumulating, analyzing, sharing and selling personal information of all kinds.

We are in a period of "surveillance creep" — where personal information is demanded not by a policeman's knock on the door but through various kinds of "soft surveillance," in which people are persuaded to give up their privacy on the grounds that it's in the best interests of themselves and society, according to Gary T. Marx, a professor emeritus of sociology at the Massachusetts Institute of Technology.

For example, more buildings now post signs stating that "in entering here you have agreed to be searched," says Marx. In the Justice Department's "Watch Your Car" auto-theft-prevention program, owners place decals on their cars inviting police anywhere to stop the car if it is driven late at night.

"There is a chilling and endless-regress quality in our drift into a society where you have to provide ever-more-personal information in order to prove that you are the kind of person who does not merit even more intensive scrutiny," he contends. [55]

Private information that allows government and business to profile and track individuals is being collected in a variety of new ways and used for many purposes. For example, Illinois' E-Z Pass — an electronic card that allows drivers to pass quickly through highway toll booths — has taken center stage in some family-court cases. Divorce attorneys subpoena E-Z Pass records to see if travel patterns demonstrate that a spouse had an extramarital affair or spends too much time on the road to be awarded child custody. [56]

"When a guy says, 'Oh, I'm home every day at 5, and I have dinner with my kids every single night,' you subpoena his E-Z Pass, and you find out he's crossing that bridge every night at 8:30. Oops!" said Philadelphia lawyer Lynn Gold-Bikin. [57]

Now even more extensive databases are coming. Under the 2005 Real ID Act, states must issue standardized driver's licenses with digital photographs and machine-readable chips beginning in 2008. States must verify that all license holders are in the country legally, retain the proofs of identity on file for up to a decade and maintain all license information in a database accessible to all other states.

"The average person does not see the privacy consequences" of the massive, interconnected databases that will result, said James W. Harper, director of information studies at the libertarian Cato Institute. "The one that I prioritize most is the likelihood that Real ID will be used for tracking and surveillance. That's not an immediate concern, but down the line you can be sure it will be used that way." [58]

In the early 1970s, when the era of databases was just beginning, Sen. Samuel J. Ervin, D-N.C., proposed enacting a comprehensive privacy bill that would apply to both the government and the private sector. Businesses objected, however, claiming it would be expensive and was unnecessary.

In the end, the Privacy Act of 1974 applied only to federal agencies. Companies were allowed to self-regulate based on a consensus list of Fair Information Practice Principles (FIPP) that business, government and privacy advocates developed. The principles are designed to make sure agencies collect only the information needed for a specific purpose and to ensure citizens' access to the data collected about them so they can check it periodically for accuracy. [59]

As a result of the Privacy Act's limitations — and unlike most industrial nations — the United States has no comprehensive privacy law today. A piecemeal collection of state and federal laws does set data-handling standards for certain industries, however.

For instance, the Health Insurance Portability and Accountability Act of 1996 (HIPAA) established some privacy safeguards for medical records. The Gramm-Leach-Bliley Act of 1999 sets customer-notification standards and outlaws pretexting for financial records.

Meanwhile, private databases continue to grow, filled with information used by both businesses and government.

Such large databases of personal information speed up business, to everyone's benefit, according to technology writer Declan McCullagh, chief political correspondent for the tech-news Web site News.com. [60] "A few decades ago, applying for credit meant an in-person visit. . . . If the loan officer didn't know you personally, he or she would contact your references and . . . eventually make a decision a few weeks later.

Continued on p. 978

At Issue:

Should Congress expand the president's authority to wiretap Americans to combat terrorism?

STEVEN G. BRADBURY
ACTING ASSISTANT ATTORNEY GENERAL

TESTIMONY BEFORE THE SENATE COMMITTEE ON THE JUDICIARY, JULY 26, 2006

yes

Foreign-intelligence surveillance is a critical tool in our common effort to prevent another catastrophic terrorist attack on the United States. The enemies we face operate in obscurity, through secret cells that communicate globally while plotting to carry out surprise attacks from within our own communities.

The past 28 years since the enactment of the Federal Intelligence Surveillance Act (FISA) have seen perhaps the greatest transformation of modes of communication of any period in history. At that time, Congress did not anticipate the technological revolution that would bring us global high-speed fiber-optic networks, the Internet, e-mail and disposable cell phones.

Innovations in communications technology have fundamentally transformed how our enemies communicate, and therefore how they plot and plan their attacks. Meanwhile, the United States confronts the threat of al Qaeda with a legal regime designed for the last century and geared more toward traditional case-by-case investigations.

In times of national emergency and armed conflict involving an exigent terrorist threat, the president may need to act with agility and dispatch to protect the country by putting in place a program of surveillance targeted at the terrorists and designed to detect and prevent the next attack. Article II of the Constitution gives the president authority to act in this way to defend the nation.

[Legislation] sponsored by Judiciary Committee Chairman Arlen Specter, R-Pa., would create for the first time an innovative procedure whereby the president will be able to bring such a surveillance program promptly to the FISA court for a judicial determination that it is constitutional and reasonable. *

Chairman Specter's bill includes several important reforms to update FISA for the 21st century. The bill would change the definition of "agent of a foreign power." Occasionally, a foreign person who is not an agent of a foreign government or a suspected terrorist will enter the United States in circumstances where the government knows that he possesses potentially valuable foreign-intelligence information, and the government currently has no means to conduct surveillance of that person under FISA.

The chairman's legislation would limit the amount of detail required for applications for FISA warrants. And, very importantly, the "emergency authorization" provisions would be amended to permit emergency surveillance for up to seven days, as opposed to the current three days.

HAROLD HONGJU KOH
DEAN, YALE LAW SCHOOL

TESTIMONY BEFORE THE SENATE COMMITTEE ON THE JUDICIARY, FEB. 28, 2006

no

For nearly 30 years, the Foreign Intelligence Surveillance Act of 1978 (FISA) has guaranteed compliance with constitutional requirements by providing a comprehensive, exclusive statutory framework for electronic surveillance. Yet apparently, the National Security Agency (NSA) has violated these requirements repeatedly by carrying on a sustained program of secret, unreviewed, warrantless electronic surveillance of American citizens and residents.

Unfortunately, [legislation] sponsored by Judiciary Committee Chairman Arlen Specter, R-Pa., would not improve the situation. *

The proposed law would simply amend FISA to increase the authority of the president to conduct surveillance, based on a showing of "probable cause" that the entire surveillance program — not any particular act of surveillance — will intercept communications of a foreign power or agent, or anyone who has ever communicated with a foreign agent.

While perhaps legalizing a small number of reasonable searches and seizures, the statute would make matters far worse, giving Congress' blanket pre-authorization to a large number of unreasonable searches and seizures, and providing neither the congressional oversight nor the judicial review that this program needs.

We must not forget the historical events that led to enactment of the 1978 FISA statute. When American ships were attacked in the Gulf of Tonkin in 1964, President [Lyndon B.] Johnson asked Congress for a resolution that gave him broad freedom to conduct a controversial, undeclared war in Indochina. That war traumatized our country and triggered a powerful antiwar movement. It soon came to light that to support the war effort, three government agencies — the FBI, the CIA and the NSA — had wiretapped thousands of innocent Americans suspected of committing subversive activities against the U.S. government.

To end these abuses, Congress passed FISA, which makes it a crime for anyone to wiretap Americans in the United States without a warrant or a court order.

Drafted with wartime in mind, FISA permits the attorney general to authorize warrantless electronic surveillance in the United States for only 15 days after a declaration of war, to give Congress time to pass new laws to give the president any new wiretap authority he may need to deal with the wartime emergency.

In short, FISA was based on simple, sensible reasoning: Before the president invades our privacy, his lawyers must get approval from someone who does not work for him.

** The proposed legislation is S2453.*

Continued from p. 976

. . . It was a slow, painful process that was hardly consumer-friendly.

"Today, not only can you get a loan nearly instantly, you'll pay less for it than in countries that prevent the free flow of information," McCullagh continues. Economist Walter Kitchenman, of Purchase Street Research in New York, estimates that U.S. mortgage rates are up to two full percentage points lower than they would be otherwise, thanks to information sharing among financial firms. ■

CURRENT SITUATION

Spying Bills Stall

Congress has been considering bills this year that would give the president more leeway to wiretap Americans without a warrant and outlaw the use of a false identity to obtain phone records. A group of high-tech companies has also been pushing for a wide-reaching consumer-privacy law.

Both the Senate and the House considered — but did not pass — bills to make it easier for the president to eavesdrop on international phone calls and Internet messages in order to combat terrorism. Despite repeated amendments to FISA procedures since September 2001, administration officials say the federal framework of issuing national-security warrants still doesn't work for anti-terror efforts.

"Frankly, I don't think anyone can make the claim that the FISA statute was designed to deal with 9/11 or to deal with a lethal enemy who likely already had armed combatants inside the United States," CIA Director Gen. Michael V. Hayden told the Senate Judiciary Committee in July. [61]

Several lawmakers agreed, proposing bills that would give the president wider eavesdropping latitude. For example, a bill introduced in the House by Rep. Heather Wilson, R-N.M., would reduce the amount of information federal agents must give to the FISC before the court issues a warrant. The measure also would expand the amount of time the president may conduct surveillance before obtaining a warrant and would allow warrantless surveillance after any "armed attack" on the United States.

"You can't get the information for probable cause . . . fast enough" to meet current FISC requirements, Wilson said at a House Intelligence Committee hearing in July. [62]

Privacy advocates say the FISA system does not need such a broad overhaul and argue that many proposed changes leave too much room for interpretation and unchecked action by the president. For example, allowing warrantless surveillance in cases of "armed attack" against the United States rather than only during wartime opens the possibility that a president could snoop on U.S. citizens for months if a U.S. embassy abroad were attacked, says the Center for Democracy and Technology's Libin.

This is not to say that FISA shouldn't be "streamlined" to keep up with current developments, she says. For example, a bipartisan bill sponsored by Sens. Dianne Feinstein, D-Calif., and Arlen Specter, R-Pa., would allow wiretapping without a warrant in some emergency cases for seven days rather than 72 hours as is currently allowed. The extension would give the government more time to demonstrate that it needs a warrant in complex terrorism investigations. "By all means, let's have a discussion about whether changes like that are needed," Libin says.

This year, Congress also failed to pass several consumer-privacy proposals. The full House failed to consider the House Energy and Commerce Committee's bipartisan bill to outlaw pretexting to obtain phone records. "There are people who think the phone record is not your personal property, it is the company's property," said Commerce Committee Chairman Rep. Joe L. Barton, R-Texas, in explaining why the measure did not progress. [63] If the records belong to the company, companies do not want responsibility for protecting their confidentiality, as the Commerce-passed bill would do, he said.

Congress also failed to pass data-retention requirements for Internet service providers. Colorado Rep. DeGette sponsored legislation similar to the administration's request: It required Internet companies to retain records of customer Web searches for at least a year in order to help solve child-pornography cases.

Neither did Congress pass legislation on the "other side" of the privacy question proposed by Rep. Edward J. Markey, D-Mass., the top-ranking Democrat on the House Telecommunications and Internet Subcommittee. In the wake of numerous incidents in which data thieves stole personal information from companies, Markey's bill would "prevent the stockpiling of private citizens' personal data" by requiring Web-site owners to quickly destroy any identifiable personal information such as credit-card numbers. [64]

Most observers expect the new Democrat-led Congress next year to push harder for consumer-privacy measures, but with a crowded agenda and different White House priorities it is unclear how much the 110th Congress will be able to accomplish.

States Act

Legal analysts say a comprehensive privacy law is needed, rather than today's piecemeal approach.

Lawmakers must examine the many types of electronic data-sharing — from business transactions to personal shopping to instant messaging and chat-room conversations — and decide what level of privacy protections are required for the various modes, says Ric Simmons, an assistant professor at Ohio State University's Moritz College of Law. "Not everything deserves the same level of protection," he adds, but with sound technical advice lawmakers should be able to create a comprehensive outline of what needs to be protected at what level and why.

Such comprehensive privacy-protection standards should cover all business sectors, says Center for Democracy and Technology Deputy Director Ari Schwartz. "The current model — that every sector's data has to have its own standard — doesn't work," he says. Businesses aren't yet talking about it publicly, Schwartz says, but in private some companies now favor standards, and leading lawmakers on key committees are interested in broad consumer-privacy protections. "We're going to have much more serious debate of a consumer-privacy law" in the near future.

States and businesses are helping create momentum for consumer-privacy regulation, especially after a series of highly publicized data breaches in the past few years raised fears among lawmakers and advocacy groups that the immense personal databases companies are amassing are not being adequately protected from hackers and data and identity thieves.

As a result, companies now face lawsuits and a patchwork of state laws. Beginning with California, 32 states have enacted laws requiring companies to notify consumers when their information is compromised; 22 of the laws apply to government agencies as well as to private companies. Lawmakers in California, Illinois, Florida and Washington also have introduced bills banning the sale and acquisition of cell-phone records. [65]

Other states are suing to block Web sites from selling records and are prosecuting companies that gain records on false pretenses. In January, Illinois became the first state to sue a rogue data-collection company when Attorney General Madigan sued Florida-based 1st Source Information Specialists. [66]

Perhaps because of the widely divergent maze of state laws that has emerged, a group of high-tech companies — including eBay, Google, HP, Intel, Microsoft, Oracle, Sun Microsystems and Symantec — recently reversed their long-held opposition to federal consumer-privacy laws and formed the Consumer Privacy Legislative Forum to help enact a multisector nationwide privacy law.

A May 2006 survey revealed that 94 percent of Americans view identity theft as a serious problem, and only 24 percent think businesses are doing enough to protect their information. [67] "The time has come . . . to consider comprehensive harmonized federal privacy legislation to create a simplified, uniform but flexible legal framework," said the forum. [68]

In the meantime, insurance companies, state agencies and universities — largely at the behest of state legislatures — already are tightening controls on personal data, mainly by ending the use of Social Security numbers as all-purpose passwords, says Indiana University's Nehf. "The easy days of having one number" to access multiple databases "are going away," he says.

Several Democrat-sponsored privacy bills are waiting in the wings and are likely to be considered by the new Democratic Congress, according to Libin. For example, a bill cosponsored by Vermont's Sen. Leahy, incoming chairman of the Senate Judiciary Committee, and current Chairman Specter would allow individuals to access and correct personal information held by commercial data brokers and require private and public organizations holding personal data to establish privacy-protection policies.

A bill introduced by Specter and Sen. Feinstein would "streamline the FISA apparatus" without giving the president expansive new wiretapping powers, as Republican-sponsored legislation would do, Libin says. Specter "hasn't been touting that bill" in this Congress, but its chances would greatly improve in a Democrat-led Senate, she says. In addition, some Democratic leaders have already vowed to hold oversight hearings on the NSA's surveillance of U.S. citizens. ■

OUTLOOK

Good-bye Privacy?

Some scholars predict that as new means of electronic data-gathering continue to proliferate, the concept of "private" data will disappear. Computer databases and electronic-surveillance devices such as radio-frequency identification devices (RFIDs) — machine-readable chips already being implanted in everything from supermarket products to pets and people — are spreading so rapidly that privacy will soon be an alien concept, say some scholars.

Surveillance technologies are already so ubiquitous, said Hal Varian, professor of information at the University of California, Berkeley, that privacy "is a thing of the past. Technologically, it is obsolete." As humanity adjusts, however, "social norms and legal barriers will dampen out the worst excesses." [69]

Michael Dahan, a professor at Israel's Sapir Academic College, predicts that by 2020 — just 14 years from now — every newborn child in industrialized countries will be implanted with a machine-readable chip that can track that person from a distance. "Ostensibly, providing important personal and medical data may also be used for tracking and surveillance."

Others argue that as privacy vanishes in a world with vast databases containing everything known about each individual, people will come to value privacy more. "Privacy will be seen more and more as a basic human right, and there will be growing pressure to define this in an international . . . convention and to have states enforce it," said Robert

Shaw, policy adviser for the International Telecommunication Union. [70]

Still others are skeptical. Young people currently seem to have less interest in privacy than older generations, as they post personal revelations on Web sites like MySpace, some scholars point out.

"Historians have said that 300 and 400 years ago, nobody had any privacy," says Indiana University's Nehf. "Today we value it. But it might be that in another 100 years we will have lost it again as a value." ■

Notes

[1] For background, see Michael Barbaro and Tom Zeller, Jr., "A Face Is Exposed for AOL Searcher No. 4417749," *The New York Times*, Aug. 9, 2006.

[2] Peter Monaghan, "Watching the Watchers," *Chronicle of Higher Education*, March 17, 2006; http://chronicle.com.

[3] "New Rule: Car Buyers Must Be Told About 'Black Boxes,' " *CNN Money*, Aug. 22, 2006; www.cnn.com/2006/AUTOS/08/21/event_data_recorder_rule/index.html.

[4] For background, see Danah Boyd, "Facebooks' 'Privacy Trainwreck': Exposure, Invasion, and Drama," *Apophenia Blog*, Sept. 8, 2006; www.danah.org/papers/FacebookAndPrivacy.html.

[5] "Disney World Mandates Fingerprint Scans," *NetWorkWorld Weblogs*, July 18, 2005; www.networkworld.com/weblogs/layer8/009514.html.

[6] Testimony before House Committee on Energy and Commerce, Feb. 1, 2006.

[7] Tresa Baldas, "High-Tech Evidence: A Lawyer's Friend or Foe?" *The National Law Journal*, Aug. 24, 2004; www.law.com.

[8] "Against Jury's Recommendation, Judge Spares Justin Barber Death Penalty for Wife's Murder," "Court TV News," Sept. 15, 2006; www.courttv.com.

[9] "Patrick Googled 'Neck,' 'Snap,' Among other Words, Prosecutor Says," *WRAL.com*, Nov. 9, 2005; www.wral.com.

[10] Quoted in Monaghan, *op. cit.*

[11] Michael Abramowitz and Jonathan Weisman, "Bush Meets With Pelosi; Both Pledge Cooperation," *The Washington Post*, Nov. 10, 2006, p. A1.

[12] Testimony before Senate Committee on the Judiciary, Feb. 6, 2006; http://judiciary.senate.gov.

[13] *Ibid.*

[14] *Ibid.*; for background on Nixon's enemies list, see "List of White House 'Enemies' and Memo Submitted by Dean to the Ervin Committee," *Watergate and the White House, Vol. 1, Facts on File*, pp. 96-97; http://web.archive.org/web/20030621235432/www.artsci.wustl.edu/~polisci/calvert/PolSci3103/watergate/enemy.htm.

[15] *Ibid.*

[16] *Ibid.*

[17] Remarks to 16th Annual Conference on Computers, Freedom & Privacy, May 3, 2006; http://leahy.senate.gov.

[18] "Spies, Lies and Wiretaps," *The New York Times*, Jan. 29, 2006.

[19] Quoted in "Gonzales Calls for ISP Data Retention Laws," *The Register*, Sept. 20, 2006; www.theregister.co.uk.

[20] Quoted in Jo Best, "Europe Passes Tough New Data Retention Laws," *C/Net News.com*, Dec. 14, 2005; http://news.com.com.

[21] Letter to congressional leaders, National Association of Attorneys General, June 21, 2006; www.naag.org.

[22] International Association of Chiefs of Police, resolution adopted at 113th annual conference, Oct. 17, 2006; www.politechbot.com.

[23] Quoted in Graeme Wearden and Karen Gomm, "Entertainment Industry 'Trying to Hijack Data Retention Directive,' " *ZDNet.UK*, Nov. 24, 2005; www.zdnet.co.uk.

[24] Mark Rasch, "Retain or Restrain Access Logs?" *Security Focus* blog, www.securityfocus.com/print/columnists/406.

[25] Nancy Libin and Jim Dempsey, "Mandatory Data Retention — Invasive, Risky, Unnecessary, Ineffective," Center for Democracy and Technology, June 2, 2006; www.cdt.org.

[26] William McGeveran, "Some Objections to DOJ's Data Retention Proposal," *Harvard Law School Info/Law* blog, June 5, 2006; http://blogs.law.harvard.edu.

[27] Peter P. Swire, "Is Data Retention Secure?" *Federal Computer Week*, June 12, 2006; www.fcw.com.

[28] Andrew Orlowski, "Google Vows: We'll Keep Hoarding Your Porn Queries," *The Register*, Aug. 12, 2006; www.theregister.co.uk.

[29] Quoted in "House Energy and Commerce Subcommittee on Oversight and Investigations Holds Hearings on Hewlett-Packard Pretexting Scandal," *Congressional Quarterly Congressional Transcripts*, Sept. 29, 2006.

[30] Quoted in Roy Mark, "Telecoms Refuse to Endorse Pretexting Bill," *internetnews.com*, Sept. 29, 2006; www.internetnews.com/bus-news/article.php/3635241.

[31] Quoted in *ibid.*

[32] Testimony before House Energy and Commerce Subcommittee on Oversight and Investigations, Sept. 29, 2006.

[33] Quoted in "House Energy and Commerce Subcommittee on Oversight and Investigations Holds Hearings on Hewlett-Packard Pretexting Scandal," *op. cit.*

[34] Quoted in Chris Jay Hoofnagle, testimony before California State Assembly Committee on Public Safety, March 7, 2006; www.epic.org.

[35] Quoted in "House Energy and Commerce Subcommittee on Oversight and Investigations Holds Hearing on Hewlett-Packard Pretexting Scandal," *op. cit.*

[36] For background, see Susan W. Brenner, "The Fourth Amendment in an Era of Ubiquitous Technology," Dec. 13, 2005; www.olemiss.edu/depts/law_school/ruleoflaw/pdf/01-BRENN.pdf; Robert Ellis Smith, "Ben Franklin's Web Site; Privacy and Curiosity from Plymouth Rock to the Internet," *Privacy Journal* (2004); J. Hamer, "Rights to Privacy," *Editorial Research Reports*, 1974, in *CQ Researcher* Plus Archive; www.cqpress.com.

[37] Chief Justice of the Common Pleas, Charles Pratt, First Earl Camden, *Entick v. Carrington*, 2 Wils. K. B. 275,291. Quoted in *ibid.* For background, see www.constitution.org/trials/entick/entick_v_carrington.htm.

About the Author

Staff writer **Marcia Clemmitt** is a veteran social-policy reporter who previously served as editor in chief of *Medicine and Health* and staff writer for *The Scientist*. She has also been a high-school math and physics teacher. She holds a liberal arts and sciences degree from St. John's College, Annapolis, and a master's degree in English from Georgetown University. Her recent reports include "Climate Change," "Controlling the Internet," "Pork Barrel Politics" and "Cyber Socializing."

[38] For background, see H. B. Shaffer, "Eavesdropping Controls," *Editorial Research Reports*, 1956; H. B. Shaffer, "Wiretapping in Law Enforcement," *Editorial Research Reports*, 1961, and J. Kuebler, "Wiretapping and Bugging," *Editorial Research Reports*, 1967, all in *CQ Researcher* Plus Archive; www.cqpress.com.

[39] Quoted in Brenner, *op. cit.*

[40] "Tapping the Wires," *The New Yorker*, June 18, 1938; www.spybusters.com/History_1938_Tapping_Wires.html.

[41] *Olmstead v. United States*, 277 U.S. 438 (1928).

[42] Louis D. Brandeis, Dissenting Opinion, *Olmstead v. United States*, 277 U.S. 438 (1928); www.law.cornell.edu/supct/html/historics/USSC_CR_0277_0438_ZD.html.

[43] *Katz v. United States*, 389 U.S. 347, 348 (1967).

[44] The case was *U.S. v. Sinclair.*

[45] Quoted in Spencer Overton, "No Warrantless Wiretaps of Citizens," *blackprof.com blog*, Dec. 18, 2005; www.blackprof.com.

[46] *United States v. United States District Court* 407 U.S. 297 (1972).

[47] "Final Report of the Select Committee to Study Governmental Operations With Respect to Intelligence Activities," April 26, 1976; www.icdc.com/~paulwolf/cointelpro/churchfinalreportIIa.htm.

[48] "Amendments to the Foreign Intelligence Surveillance Act," Congressional Research Service, July 2006; www.fas.org/sgp/crs/intel/m071906.pdf. The FISA amendments were included in the Patriot Act of 2001, the Fiscal Year 2002 Intelligence Authorization Act, the Homeland Security Act of 2002, the Intelligence Reform and Terrorism Prevention Act of 2004, and the USA Patriot Improvement and Reauthorization Act of 2005.

[49] Foreign Intelligence Surveillance Act Orders, 1979-2005; Electronic Privacy Information Center; www.epic.org/privacy/wiretap/stats/fisa_stats.html.

[50] James Risen and Eric Lichtblau, "Bush Lets U.S. Spy on Callers Without Courts," *The New York Times*, Dec. 16, 2005, p. A1.

[51] *Ibid.*

[52] Grant Gross, "NSA Wiretapping Program Can Continue," *InfoWorld*, Oct. 4, 2006; www.infoworld.com/article/06/10/04/HNnsasurveillance_1.html.

[53] For background, see Kenneth Jost, "Civil Liberties Debates," *CQ Researcher*, Oct. 24, 2003, pp. 893-916.

[54] "Print Shop," House Committee on the Judiciary; http://judiciary.house.gov/Printshop.aspx?Section=232.

[55] Quoted in Monaghan, *op. cit.*

[56] Tresa Baldas, "High-Tech Evidence: A Lawyer's Friend or Foe?" *The National Law Journal*, Aug. 24, 2004; www.law.com.

[57] Quoted in *ibid.*

[58] Quoted in Mike Stuckey, "Where Rubber Meets the Road in the Privacy Debate," MSNBC.com, Oct. 20, 2006; www.msnbc.com.

[59] "Fair Information Practice Principles," Federal Trade Commission; www.ftc.gov/reports/privacy3/fairinfo.htm.

[60] Declan McCullagh, "Database Nation: The Upside of 'Zero Privacy,' " *Reason*, June 2004.

[61] Quoted in "Senate Judiciary Committee Holds Hearing on Foreign Intelligence Surveillance," *Congressional Quarterly Congressional Transcripts*, July 26, 2006; www.cq.com.

[62] Quoted in "House Intelligence Committee Holds Hearing on Foreign Intelligence Surveillance Act," *Congressional Quarterly Congressional Transcripts*, July 27, 2006; www.cq.com.

[63] Quoted in "House Energy and Commerce Subcommittee on Oversight and Investigations Holds Hearing on Hewlett-Packard Pretexting Scandal," *op. cit.*

[64] Quoted in Bill Brenner, "Security Blog Log: Data Storage Bills Go To Extremes," *Search Security.com*, May 21, 2006; http://searchsecurity.techtarget.com.

[65] *Stateline.org*; www.stateline.org/live/ViewPage.action?siteNodeId=137&languageId=1&contentId=126215#map.

[66] John Gramlich, "States, Feds, Go After Online Records Brokers," *Stateline.org*, Feb. 4, 2006; www.stateline.org.

[67] For background, see Peter Katel, "Identity Theft," *CQ Researcher*, June 10, 2005, pp. 517-540.

[68] Peter P. Swire, testimony before House Energy and Commerce Subcommittee on Commerce, Trade and Consumer Protection, June 20, 2006.

[69] Quoted in *Future of the Internet II*, Pew Internet & American Life Project, 2006.

[70] Quoted in *ibid.*

FOR MORE INFORMATION

American Civil Liberties Union, 1333 H St., N.W., 10th Floor, Washington, DC 20005; (202) 544-1681; www.aclu.org/. Advocates for protection of individuals' privacy and other rights.

ARMA International, 13725 W. 109th St., Suite 101, Lenexa, KS 66215; (913) 341-3808; www.arma.org. An organization for information-management professionals that develops standards for privacy protection.

Berkman Center for Internet and Society at Harvard Law School, Baker House, 1587 Massachusetts Ave., Cambridge, MA 02138; (617) 495-7547; http://cyber.law.harvard.edu. Investigates legal, technical and social issues surrounding the Internet, including privacy.

Center for Democracy and Technology, 1634 I St., N.W., Suite 100, Washington, DC 20006; (202) 637-9800; www.cdt.org. Advocates preservation of privacy and other constitutional freedoms in the developing digital world.

Consumer Data Industry Association, 1090 Vermont Ave., N.W., Suite 200, Washington, DC 20005-4905; (202) 371-0910; www.cdiaonline.org. Represents businesses involved in database aggregation, such as credit agencies and security firms.

Electronic Frontier Foundation, 454 Shotwell St., San Francisco, CA 94110; (415) 436-9333; www.eff.org. Advocates for and litigates on technological issues involving privacy, free speech, freedom to innovate and consumer rights.

Electronic Privacy Information Center, 1718 Connecticut Ave., N.W., Suite 200, Washington, DC 20009; (202) 483-1140; www.epic.org. Provides information and advocacy on privacy as a civil right.

Pew Internet & American Life Project, 1615 L St., N.W., Suite 700, Washington, DC 20036; (202) 419-4500; www.pewinternet.org. Provides data and analysis on social issues surrounding Internet usage, such as threats to privacy.

Privacy International, 2nd Floor, Lancaster House, 33 Islington High St., London N1 9LH UK; 44 7947 778247; www.privacy.org. Advocates for privacy rights and tracks privacy issues worldwide.

Bibliography

Selected Sources

Books

Lane, Frederick, *The Naked Employee: How Technology Is Compromising Workplace Privacy*, American Management Association, 2003.
A technology writer describes the growth of employer surveillance of workers, a trend he says federal law allows to proceed unchecked.

O'Harrow, Robert, *No Place To Hide: Behind the Scenes of Our Emerging Surveillance Society*, Free Press, 2005.
A *Washington Post* technology reporter describes the burgeoning public and private use of surveillance and data-storage technologies.

Rosen, Jeffrey, *The Naked Crowd: Reclaiming Security and Freedom in an Anxious Age*, Random House, 2005.
A George Washington University law professor uses sociological and psychological descriptions of how people respond to unsettling events to explore how the terrorist attacks of 2001 changed Americans' attitudes toward privacy and security.

Smith, Robert Ellis, *Ben Franklin's Web Site: Privacy and Curiosity from Plymouth Rock to the Internet*, Privacy Journal, 2004.
The editor of the *Privacy Journal* newsletter recounts the social history of privacy in America, including chapters on how Americans have viewed privacy in relation to sex, government snooping and tabloid-press invasions of celebrities' privacy.

Solove, Daniel J., *The Digital Person: Technology and Privacy in the Information Age*, New York University Press, 2004.
An associate professor of law at The George Washington University argues that ignorance of and indifference to the collection of personal data by businesses and public agencies are the main barriers to creating a legal framework to protect privacy.

Articles

"AT&T Whistle-Blower's Evidence," *Wired News online*, May 17, 2006; www.wired.com/news/technology/1,70908-0.html.
An AT&T technician explains what he observed in the company's San Francisco offices to convince him that the phone company was illegally cooperating with the National Security Agency's warrantless surveillance program.

Meredith, Peter, "Facebook and the Politics of Privacy," *Mother Jones*, Sept. 14, 2006; www.motherjones.com.
In an interview, a University of California student explains his privacy concerns about Facebook's new "news feed" feature.

Richtel, Matt, and Miguel Helft, "An Industry Is Based on a Simple Masquerade," *The New York Times*, Sept. 11, 2006, p. C1.
Some small companies gather personal data by tricking telephone companies and other holders of consumer records, but awareness of these fraudulent businesses is growing.

Risen, James, and Eric Lichtblau, "Bush Lets U.S. Spy on Callers Without Courts," *The New York Times*, Dec. 16, 2005, p. A1.
Federal officials reveal that President Bush authorized warrantless wiretaps of some Americans' international phone calls and e-mails, beginning in 2002.

Sullivan, Bob, "Who's Buying Cell Phone Records Online? Cops," MSNBC.com, June 20, 2006, www.msnbc.msn.com.
Shady data brokers claim that police agencies, including the FBI, are among their customers.

Reports and Studies

"Digital Search and Seizure: Updating Privacy Protections to Keep Pace with Technology," Center for Democracy & Technology, February 2006.
A privacy-advocacy organization argues that due to new developments in information storage and surveillance technology, new regulations are needed to allow government surveillance without swamping civil rights.

"Privacy and Human Rights 2005," Electronic Privacy Information Center and Privacy International, 2006.
In the current edition of this annual report, two privacy-advocacy groups describe the privacy landscape in more than 60 countries, including new legislation, emerging technology issues and post-9/11 security concerns that are leading some governments to forgo privacy protections.

Anderson, Janna Quitney, and Lee Rainie, *The Future of the Internet, II*, Pew Internet & American Life Project, September 2006; www.pewinternet.org/pdfs/PIP_Future_of_Internet_2006.pdf.
Internet analysts and Internet-business leaders predict that by 2020 Internet information gathering and electronic surveillance will facilitate many government and business functions but will also threaten personal privacy.

Brenner, Susan W., "The Fourth Amendment in an Era of Ubiquitous Technology," December 2005; www.olemiss.edu/depts/law_school/ruleoflaw/pdf/01-BRENN.pdf.
A professor of law and technology at Ohio's University Dayton School of Law explains how then-current technologies helped shape legal interpretations of privacy from the 12th century to the present.

The Next Step:

Additional Articles from Current Periodicals

Government Surveillance

Dlouhy, Jennifer A., "Bush Seeks Broad New Spying Powers," *The Seattle Post-Intelligencer*, July 27, 2006, p. A4.
Bush administration officials are endorsing legislation that would allow the executive branch to conduct electronic surveillance to gather intelligence for up to a year without a court order.

Goldenberg, Suzanne, "Hitchens Joins Authors Seeking U.S. Wiretapping Ban," *The Guardian* (London), Jan. 18, 2006, p. 17.
The American Civil Liberties Union and the Centre for Constitutional Rights filed separate lawsuits yesterday accusing the president of violating the Constitution by eavesdropping without a warrant.

Zajac, Andrew, "State Secrets Privilege Slams Door On Civil Suits," *Chicago Tribune*, May 24, 2006, p. 1.
Several AT&T customers are accusing the telephone company of invading its customers' privacy by sharing phone records with the National Security Agency.

Privacy Breaches

The Associated Press, "AOL is Sued Over Privacy Breach," *Los Angeles Times*, Sept. 26, 2006, p. C2.
Three customers have sued AOL for making records of their Internet searches available online.

Doan, Lynn, "College Door Ajar For Online Criminals," *Los Angeles Times*, May 30, 2006, p. A1.
Security breaches at university computer systems are exposing the personal information of thousands of students, alumni, employees and applicants.

Kruse, Michael, "Too Much Of An Open Facebook," *St. Petersburg Times*, Sept. 18, 2006, p. E1.
College students raised a ruckus after Facebook.com, a social-networking site, debuted a new feature that tracks users' actions.

Lazarus, David, "Shifting Sands in Data Link," *The San Francisco Chronicle*, Feb. 25, 2005, p. C1.
Data broker ChoicePoint is in hot water after scammers operating behind fictitious businesses stole the names, addresses and Social Security numbers of nearly 145,000 people from their database.

Menn, Joseph, "Some Big Consumer Data Firms Fear Tough State Rules," *The Seattle Times*, Dec. 27, 2005, p. C1.
Information brokers like ChoicePoint and LexisNexis are supporting proposed federal rules to safeguard personal information because a growing number of states are requiring stricter privacy-protection standards.

Nogunchi, Yuki, "George Mason Officials Investigate Hacking Incident," *The Washington Post*, Jan. 13, 2005, p. E1.
A hacker entered a George Mason University computer, compromising students' names, Social Security numbers, university identification numbers and photographs.

Zeller, Tom Jr., "Breach Points Up Flaws in Privacy Laws," *The New York Times*, Feb. 24, 2005, p. C1.
A recent privacy breach at the data-collection giant ChoicePoint has exposed the patchwork of sometimes conflicting state and federal rules that govern consumer privacy and commercial data vendors.

Real ID Act

Belluck, Pam, "Mandate For ID Meets Resistance From States," *The New York Times*, May 6, 2006, p. A1.
States oppose as too expensive a new anti-terrorism law that requires them to use sources like birth certificates to verify that people applying for or renewing driver's licenses are legal residents.

Fears, Darryl, "ID Program Will Cost States $11 Billion, Report Says," *The Washington Post*, Sept. 22, 2006, p. A4.
State motor-vehicle officials estimate it would cost more than $11 billion over five years to implement the technology required by the Real ID Act.

Texeira, Erin, "New Driver's License Law Slammed," *The Houston Chronicle*, May 12, 2005, p. A9.
Immigrants' advocates say the Real ID Act is anti-immigrant because it requires states to verify that people who apply for a driver's license are in the country legally and makes it harder for immigrants to gain amnesty.

CITING *CQ RESEARCHER*

Sample formats for citing these reports in a bibliography include the ones listed below. Preferred styles and formats vary, so please check with your instructor or professor.

MLA STYLE

Jost, Kenneth. "Rethinking the Death Penalty." CQ Researcher 16 Nov. 2001: 945-68.

APA STYLE

Jost, K. (2001, November 16). Rethinking the death penalty. *CQ Researcher, 11*, 945-968.

CHICAGO STYLE

Jost, Kenneth. "Rethinking the Death Penalty." *CQ Researcher*, November 16, 2001, 945-968.

In-depth Reports on Issues in the News

Are you writing a paper?

Need backup for a debate?

Want to become an expert on an issue?

For 80 years, students have turned to *CQ Researcher* for in-depth reporting on issues in the news. Reports on a full range of political and social issues are now available. Following is a selection of recent reports:

Civil Liberties
Voting Controversies, 9/06
Right to Die, 5/05
Immigration Reform, 4/05
Gays on Campus, 10/04

Crime/Law
Sex Offenders, 9/06
Treatment of Detainees, 8/06
War on Drugs, 6/06
Domestic Violence, 1/06
Death Penalty Controversies, 9/05

Education
Academic Freedom, 10/05
Intelligent Design, 7/05
No Child Left Behind, 5/05

Environment
Biofuels Boom, 9/06
Nuclear Energy, 3/06
Climate Change, 1/06
Saving the Oceans, 11/05
Endangered Species Act, 6/05
Alternative Energy, 2/05

Health/Safety
Rising Health Costs, 4/06
Pension Crisis, 2/06
Avian Flu Threat, 1/06
Domestic Violence, 1/06

International Affairs/Politics
Understanding Islam, 11/06
Change in Latin America, 7/06
Pork Barrel Politics, 6/06
Future of European Union, 10/05
War in Iraq, 10/05

Social Trends
Video Games, 11/06
Blog Explosion, 6/06
Controlling the Internet, 5/06

Terrorism/Defense
Port Security, 4/06
Presidential Power, 2/06

Youth
Drinking on Campus, 8/06
National Service, 6/06
Teen Spending, 5/06

Upcoming Reports

Enviromental Activism, 12/1/06
The New Philanthropy, 12/8/06
Patent Law Disputes, 12/15/06
Prison Health Care, 1/5/07
Factory Farms, 1/12/07
The Catholic Church, 1/19/07

ACCESS

CQ Researcher is available in print and online. For access, visit your library or www.cqresearcher.com.

STAY CURRENT

To receive notice of upcoming *CQ Researcher* reports, or learn more about *CQ Researcher* products, subscribe to the free e-mail newsletters, *CQ Researcher Alert!* and *CQ Researcher News*: www.cqpress.com/newsletters.

PURCHASE

To purchase a *CQ Researcher* report in print or electronic format (PDF), visit www.cqpress.com or call 866-427-7737. Single reports start at $15. Bulk purchase discounts and electronic-rights licensing are also available.

SUBSCRIBE

A full-service *CQ Researcher* print subscription—including 44 reports a year, monthly index updates, and a bound volume—is $688 for academic and public libraries, $667 for high school libraries, and $827 for media libraries. Add $25 for domestic postage.

CQ Researcher Online offers a backfile from 1991 and a number of tools to simplify research. For pricing information, call 800-834-9020, ext. 1906, or e-mail librarysales@cqpress.com.

CQ RESEARCHER PLUS ARCHIVE

GET ONLINE ACCESS TO VITAL ISSUES FROM 1923 TO THE PRESENT

CQ Researcher Plus Archive delivers fast, online access to every *CQ Researcher* report from 1991 to the present, *PLUS* lets you explore the complete archive of *Editorial Research Reports** from 1923-1990. Search and browse more than 3,600 in-depth reports.

Loaded with handy online features, *CQ Researcher Plus Archive* provides the trustworthy reporting and the advanced online functionality today's researchers demand. The new "Issue Tracker" feature provides quick links to past and present reports on the specific topics you need.

For a free trial, visit http://library.cqpress.com/trials.

For pricing information, call 1-800-834-9020, ext. 1906 or e-mail librarymarketing@cqpress.com.

**Editorial Research Reports*, the predecessor to *CQ Researcher*, provides the same expert, nonpartisan reporting on the vital issues that have shaped our society.

CQ Press • 1255 22nd Street, NW, Suite 400 • Washington, DC 20037

CQ Researcher
Published by CQ Press, a division of Congressional Quarterly Inc.
cqresearcher.com

The New Environmentalism

Can new business policies save the environment?

Concern about the environment is intensifying, but new efforts to reduce pollution and save energy differ from past environmental movements. Unable to get much satisfaction from the Republican-dominated federal government, environmental activists have set their sights on businesses — trying to influence corporate behavior and even forming partnerships with companies to confront environmental challenges. A growing number of businesses — including Wal-Mart, the world's biggest retailer — are concluding that saving the environment is good for the bottom line. But some conservative critics charge that such actions actually dilute companies' primary purpose — to increase shareholder value. Meanwhile, in the absence of federal action, state and local governments are instituting policies aimed at weaning industry from fossil fuels. And some environmentalists are even rethinking nuclear power.

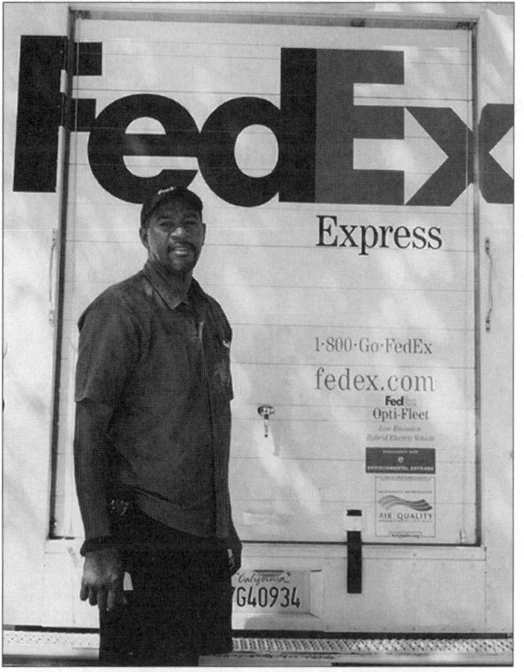

Hybrid delivery trucks that reduce fuel use and exhaust emissions by more than a third are part of FedEx's wide-ranging efforts to improve the environment and save energy.

Inside This Report

CQ Researcher • Dec. 1, 2006 • www.cqresearcher.com
Volume 16, Number 42 • Pages 985-1008

Recipient of Society of Professional Journalists Award for Excellence ◆ American Bar Association Silver Gavel Award

THE NEW ENVIRONMENTALISM

Cover photograph: FedEx

CQ Researcher

Dec. 1, 2006
Volume 16, Number 42

MANAGING EDITOR: Thomas J. Colin

ASSISTANT MANAGING EDITOR: Kathy Koch

ASSOCIATE EDITOR: Kenneth Jost

STAFF WRITERS: Marcia Clemmitt, Peter Katel

CONTRIBUTING WRITERS: Rachel S. Cox, Sarah Glazer, Alan Greenblatt, Barbara Mantel, Patrick Marshall, Tom Price, Jennifer Weeks

DESIGN/PRODUCTION EDITOR: Olu B. Davis

ASSISTANT EDITOR: Melissa J. Hipolit

CQ PRESS

A Division of
Congressional Quarterly Inc.

SENIOR VICE PRESIDENT/PUBLISHER: John A. Jenkins

DIRECTOR, LIBRARY PUBLISHING: Kathryn C. Suárez

DIRECTOR, EDITORIAL OPERATIONS: Ann Davies

CONGRESSIONAL QUARTERLY INC.

CHAIRMAN: Paul C. Tash

VICE CHAIRMAN: Andrew P. Corty

PRESIDENT/EDITOR IN CHIEF: Robert W. Merry

CQ Researcher (ISSN 1056-2036) is printed on acid-free paper. Published weekly, except March 24, July 7, July 14, Aug. 4, Aug. 11, Nov. 24, Dec. 22 and Dec. 29, by CQ Press, a division of Congressional Quarterly Inc. Annual full-service subscriptions for institutions start at $667. For pricing, call 1-800-834-9020, ext. 1906. To purchase a *CQ Researcher* report in print or electronic format (PDF), visit www.cqpress.com or call 866-427-7737. Single reports start at $15. Bulk purchase discounts and electronic-rights licensing are also available. Periodicals postage paid at Washington, D.C., and additional mailing offices. POSTMASTER: Send address changes to *CQ Researcher*, 1255 22nd St., N.W., Suite 400, Washington, DC 20037.

The New Environmentalism

BY TOM PRICE

THE ISSUES

Across the globe, evidence abounds of a rising concern for protecting the planet.

But the new concern about the environment is not your father's environmental movement. Corporate executives, investors, conservative Christians, labor unions and others not traditionally associated with the cause have joined the intensifying campaign to save the Earth. There's even a handful of environmentalists who are promoting nuclear power.

Getty Images/Thomas Cooper

Huge windows reduce energy bills at the experimental Wal-Mart Super Store that opened in Aurora, Colo., in November 2005. The eco-friendly store uses recycled materials for construction and solar and wind power to supplement standard power sources. Wal-Mart and many other businesses are jumping on the conservation bandwagon, joining environmental groups they once fought with.

• Environmental Defense, a leading advocacy group, hires a director of corporate partnerships and begins helping businesses "go green." Among the many fruits of these collaborations: fuel-efficient hybrid FedEx delivery trucks, reusable UPS shipping envelopes and measures to cut greenhouse-gas emissions at DuPont facilities that saved the company $325 million in one year. [1]

• The National Association of Evangelicals — known for conservative politics — proclaims a "sacred responsibility to steward the Earth," urging governments to "encourage fuel efficiency, reduce pollution, encourage sustainable use of natural resources and provide for the proper care of wildlife and their natural habitats." [2]

• British chemist and environmentalist James Lovelock — famous for arguing that Earth acts as a self-sustaining organism — says building more nuclear power plants is "the only green solution" to the threat of global warming. [3]

In the burgeoning, new environmental movement, a growing number of people are perceiving threats to the environment, businesses are jumping on the conservation bandwagon and environmentalists are joining hands with groups they once crossed swords with.

"We're seeing the environmental movement getting deeper and broader at the same time," says Rainforest Action Network Executive Director Michael Brune. "We're seeing an increase in straight-up, old-school, traditional grassroots activists wanting to get involved. We're also seeing genuine interest from the business community, evangelicals, labor and other non-traditional allies."

In the words of Oklahoma State University sociology Professor Riley Dunlap, who has studied public opinion about the environment for 40 years and is the Gallup Organization's environmental scholar, "These local government initiatives, state initiatives, corporate initiatives represent a different kind of environmentalism."

The broadening consensus has been spurred mainly by concerns that global warming poses a real and potentially catastrophic threat to life on Earth but that a conservative federal government refuses to act.

"There's undoubtedly a buzz about global warming that wasn't there a year ago," says David Yarnold, executive vice president of Environmental Defense. "The sense of urgency has grown. And the more people learn about climate change, the more they want to know what they can do."

In a July poll by the Pew Research Center, 70 percent of Americans said there is "solid evidence" for global warming, and 74 percent said it constitutes a serious or somewhat serious problem. In a measure of public confusion about the topic and what should be done, however, 59 percent who believed in global warming thought human activity is the cause, while 30 percent blamed natural climate patterns. [4]

In another poll last January, Pew found that nearly 60 percent of Americans wanted the federal government to make energy and the environment top priorities, the highest percentage since 2001. [5] A Harris Poll last year found three-quarters of Americans feel "protecting the environment is so important that requirements and standards cannot be too high, and continuing environmental improvements must be made regardless of cost." [6]

Public Support for Environment Is Up

Support for the environment is up after taking a big dip beginning in 2000. Pro-environment respondents outnumbered pro-economy respondents by 17 percentage points in 2005 and 15 points this year.

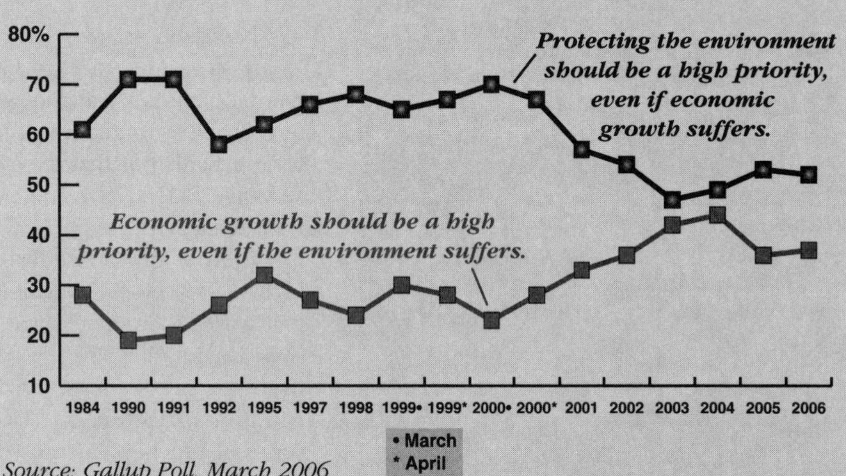

Source: Gallup Poll, March 2006

Despite pubic support, "there's been an appalling vacuum of leadership coming from within the [Washington] Beltway — on both sides of the aisle," Brune says. "The current administration and [Republican-controlled] Congress can't be accused of being environmental leaders, but even most Democrats haven't been stepping up and showing an appropriate level of response to the environmental threats we face."

In the absence of action in Washington, he adds, "You're seeing a lot of others trying to show leadership."

Although environmentalists were heartened by the Democratic capture of Congress in the November 2006 elections, they're not expecting revolutionary changes in federal policies. President George W. Bush has two more years in office, Democrats hold only a slim majority in the Senate and not all Democrats are environmentalists. For instance, Rep. John D. Dingell, D-Mich. — the presumptive chair of the Energy and Commerce Committee, whose district includes Detroit — has opposed raising automobile gas-mileage requirements.

The most that U.S. Greenpeace Executive Director John Passacantando expects out of the Democrats are "some baby steps." So environmentalists aren't about to change the strategy they've developed since Republicans seized control of Congress in 1994: influencing corporations and state and local governments.

Environmental Defense presents itself to businesses essentially as a consulting firm, offering advice on how they can increase profits by adopting green business practices. The more aggressive Rainforest Action Network (RAN) also enters partnerships — but usually only after businesses succumb to public protests.

"We're not as confrontational as some other groups," says Gwen Ruta, Environmental Defense's corporate partnership director. "We've had pretty good success in going to companies in the spirit of cooperation and saying, 'This is what we want to do.' "

RAN usually stages public demonstrations to "get on the radar screen," says Ilyse Hogue, who manages the organization's campaign to promote green banking, or socially responsible investing. Once a bank agrees to work with her organization, she says, "the intellectual capital at these institutions is so vast that it's fun to participate in the dialogue. These are very bright people who just never really looked at these issues."

Investors also are pressuring companies to adopt green business practices, using tactics such as proposing policy resolutions at shareholders' meetings or investing only in corporations with positive environmental records. How-to guides to shareholder activism have been published both by Friends of the Earth and a partnership of the As You Sow Foundation and Rockefeller Philanthropy Advisors. [7]

"Not to engage the private sector is to miss a huge opportunity to have a positive impact on global warming," says Rockefeller Senior Vice President Doug Bauer.

Some investors band together to increase their clout. Through the Carbon Disclosure Project, for instance, major global investors each year ask about 2,000 companies — including the world's largest 500 — to reveal their impact on greenhouse-gas emissions. In 2006, 225 investors with $31.5 trillion in assets made the request — up from 143 investors the year before. Nearly three-quarters of the largest 500 companies responded this year, up from just under 50 percent in 2005. [8]

The project aims to spur companies to reduce emissions after they've compiled the information needed for the report. Wal-Mart's experience indicates that's happening. In preparing its report, Wal-Mart discovered that refrigerants used in its grocery stores caused more of the company's "greenhouse-gas footprint" than its truck fleet did. Wal-Mart said it is acting on that discovery. *(See sidebar, p. 990.)*

Complaining that the federal government is not acting effectively, cities and states are adopting their own environmental-protection programs — forcing nationwide companies to cope with a patchwork of environmental regulations.

Nearly half the states are requiring that power plants use at least some renewable fuels, and California just mandated cuts in motor vehicles' carbon dioxide emissions. If that law withstands the auto industry's challenges, other states are prepared to act. Meanwhile, just as they did in striving to reduce acid rain, Northeastern states are establishing a consortium to set limits on greenhouse-gas emissions, distribute emission allowances to plants and permit cleaner plants to sell their allowances to dirtier facilities. Western states are crafting a similar agreement. [9]

Gov. Arnold Schwarzenegger, R-Calif., reached across the Atlantic to explore global-warming strategies with British Prime Minister Tony Blair. Former President Bill Clinton is discussing emission-reduction efforts with leaders of the world's 22 largest cities. [10]

Labor unions — which in the past clashed with environmentalists — have joined the new movement through the Apollo Alliance for Good Jobs and Clean Energy. [11] Named for the project that put man on the moon, the alliance promotes both jobs and the environment through government incentives for high-mileage autos, clean and efficient manufacturing, green buildings, renewable energy, public transportation and hydrogen-fuel technology. [12]

Environmentalism has become such a popular topic that it turned former Vice President Al Gore into a best-selling author and movie star while inspiring a real movie star — Leonardo DiCaprio — to try to take environmentalism to television. Gore's book about the threat of global warming, *An Inconvenient Truth*, made *The New York Times* best-seller list, and his movie of the same name was a surprise box-office hit. DiCaprio is teaming up with "Survivor" producer Craig Piligian to create a "reality" television show in which a down-and-out American town gets re-made into a healthy green community. DiCaprio and Piligian are shopping the concept, tentatively titled "E-topia," to networks and sponsors. Instead of just upgrading a wardrobe or a room, as other such shows do, "E-topia" will "take an American town that has been destroyed and bring it back to its former glory and then some," Piligian said. "This town will be reborn as the prototype for the future." [13]

As activists and business executives confront environmental challenges, here are some of the questions they're trying to answer:

Most CEOs Support Sustainability

The percentage of corporate chief executives in 43 countries who support sustainability has increased nearly 20 percentage points from 2003 to 2005.

CEOs who say environmental sustainability is important to profits

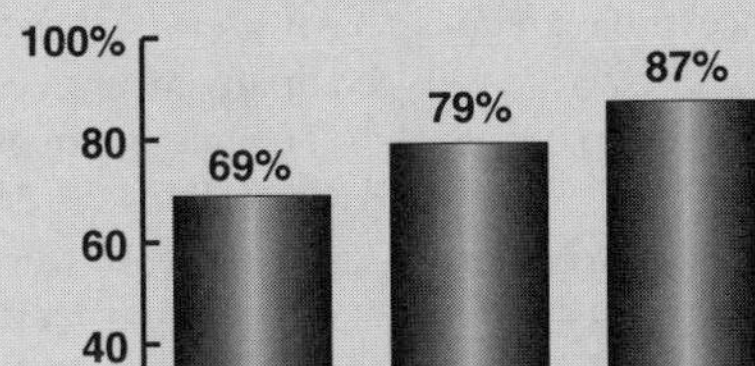

Source: PricewaterhouseCoopers

Is going "green" good for the corporate bottom line?

A growing number of companies are adopting environmental-protection policies they say are good for business. Some conservative critics contend, however, that such actions actually dilute companies' primary — some say only — purpose: to increase shareholder value.

Corporate executives say they implement green practices for a variety of reasons: to attract more customers, cut costs, drive up the value of their companies' stock, recruit and retain high-quality employees and assure their companies' long-term health.

"Increasingly, suppliers and customers are demanding greater devotion to the environment," says Douglas Pinkham, president of the Public Affairs Council, the professional association for public affairs officers. Employees prefer environmentally friendly corporations because "nobody wants to work for a company that's known as an environmental pirate."

But companies are not going green "just because it helps their reputation," Pinkham adds. "Companies are saying we can make a buck by being environmentally sustainable."

And that goes beyond short-term profit-and-loss calculations, says business consultant Margery Kraus. "I heard an executive comment once that you can't have a successful business in a failed world," explains Kraus, head of APCO Worldwide, an international consulting firm. "I think that says it all." (*See "At Issue," p. 1001.*)

According to Oklahoma State's Dunlap, American businesses are beginning to practice "what people in Europe call ecological modernization."

"You don't hear much talk about business vs. environment there," Dunlap explains. "They've adopted the approach that what's good for the environment is good for the economy, and I think we're seeing America kind of struggling to do the same.

Wal-Mart Sets Ambitious 'Green' Goals

Wal-Mart, the world's largest retailer, wants to be the greenest as well. President and Chief Executive Officer Lee Scott laid out the corporation's ambitious long-term goals a year ago: to use only renewable energy, to create no waste and to sell products that "sustain our resources and environment."

He also established specific short-term goals:

- increase truck fuel efficiency by 25 percent in three years and 100 percent in 10;
- cut store energy consumption by 30 percent and reduce facility greenhouse-gas emissions by 20 percent in seven years;
- reduce solid waste at stores by 25 percent in three years;
- establish a program within 18 months that gives preference to suppliers that "aggressively" reduce their greenhouse-gas emissions, and
- increase sales of organic food and other environmentally friendly products.

"Environmental problems are *our* problems," Scott told employees at the company's Bentonville, Ark., headquarters. Solving them is good for humanity, he said, and it's good for business. [1]

During 2005, Wal-Mart opened two experimental stores — in McKinney, Texas, and Aurora, Colo. — to test green technology.

Highly efficient light-emitting diodes — or LEDs — illuminate exterior signs and interior display cases. Heating systems burn cooking oil and motor oil from the stores' restaurants and auto repair shops. Heat is recovered from refrigerators and freezers, and solar collectors and wind turbines supply electricity. Doors were installed on refrigerated cases that usually are left open, and their lights brighten and dim as shoppers open and close the doors. The restrooms have water-conserving sinks, and the men's rooms use waterless urinals. Countertops are made with recycled glass and concrete.

Outside, drought-tolerant vegetation cuts the water needed for irrigation. Food waste is composted and sold. Roads are paved with recycled materials, and concrete is mixed with fly ash from burned coal and slag from steel production. [2]

Some of the innovations were immediate hits, the company reported in a one-year review, while others "still need to be refined." Some of the earliest successes — the lighting, landscaping, sinks and urinals — will begin showing up in other Wal-Marts in 2007. The company hopes the other innovations will prove themselves over the next two years.

"Due to our size and scope, we are uniquely positioned to have great success and impact in the world, perhaps like no company before us," Scott said.

Seemingly small changes, when Wal-Mart makes them, can save millions of dollars.

Because its truck fleet travels a billion miles a year, for instance, raising fuel efficiency by just one mile per gallon would save the company more than $52 million annually at current fuel prices, Scott said. Meeting his goal of doubling efficiency by 2015 would jump that savings to $310 million.

If the company could sell one compact fluorescent light bulb to each of the 100-plus million shoppers who walk into Wal-Mart stores every week, those customers' electric bills would drop a collective $3 billion. If the company succeeds in encouraging green practices by its 60,000 suppliers and 1.3 million employees, environmental benefits will ripple around the world. [3]

Known primarily for its low prices, Wal-Mart confronts a stiff challenge in selling green products that often cost more than their non-green counterparts.

"In the old days, it was easy to blame industry for 'greenwashing,' " or trying to appear more environmentally active than they really are. "But I'm increasingly convinced that we're seeing industries realize they have to integrate environmental concerns into their bottom line if they're to be successful."

A 2005 PricewaterhouseCoopers survey of chief executives in 43 countries found 87 percent saying environmental sustainability is important to company profits. That represented a rapid rise from 79 percent in 2004 and 69 percent in 2003. [14] (*See graph, p. 989.*)

Cost-saving is the most obvious benefit of greening a business. As Wal-Mart Chief Executive Lee Scott put it, when a company doesn't recycle, "We pay twice — once to get it, once to have it taken away." [15]

Wal-Mart expects to save $2.4 million a year by shrinking packaging for one private-label toy line, $26 million by cutting delivery-truck idle time and $28 million by recycling plastic in its stores. For really big savings, the giant retailer plans to reduce its stores' energy use by 30 percent and cut its trucks' fuel consumption by 25 percent in three years and 50 percent within 10 years. [16]

DuPont has already saved more than $3 billion by cutting energy use by 7 percent. [17] FedEx is deploying hybrid trucks that reduce fuel costs by more than a third. [18] PNC Financial Services Group is building green bank branches that use 45 percent less energy than standard structures. [19]

General Electric is betting billions that environmentalism sells as well as saves. In mid-2005, the global conglomerate launched its "Ecomagination" initiative to develop products and services that address environmental challenges. GE Chairman and CEO Jeff Immelt announced the company will produce improved technology in solar energy, hybrid locomotives, fuel cells, low-emission aircraft engines, light and strong materials, efficient lighting and water purification.

"We've seen that if a green product costs the same, it's a runaway success," Vice President Andrew Ruben says. "If it costs a little more, it can be successful. Above that, we've got to do things in a smarter way" to try to bring the price down. The company's goal is to price organic products no more than 10 percent above their conventional counterparts.

Environmentalists and organic-farming advocates give Wal-Mart's plan mixed reactions.

The company has consulted with the World Wildlife Federation, the Natural Resources Defense Council, Greenpeace and other environmental organizations. Environmental Defense, another Wal-Mart advisor, opened a Bentonville office so it could dispatch a representative to corporate headquarters at a moment's call.

Describing Wal-Mart's impact on the U.S. economy as "almost beyond calculation," Environmental Defense Executive Vice President David Yarnold said he and his colleagues "really believe that Wal-Mart can create a race to the top for environmental benefits." [4]

The Sierra Club refused to work with Wal-Mart because of concern about its labor policies, but Executive Director Carl Pope said Wal-Mart managers "deserve the chance to show that their business model is compatible with high standards, not just low prices." [5]

Nu Wexler, a spokesman for Wal-Mart Watch — which was created to challenge the company's business practices — said his organization is "encouraged by Wal-Mart's new environmental initiatives because they could, if implemented, change the way American businesses approach environmental sustainability." [6]

The Cornucopia Institute, an advocate for small organic farms, attacked the company for purchasing from "industrial-scale factory farms" and from China. Pressure to cut prices could destroy family farms and reduce some of the environmental benefits of organic farming, said Mark Kastel, Cornucopia's senior farm-policy analyst.

"Food shipped around the world — burning fossil fuels and undercutting our domestic farmers — does not meet the consumer's traditional definition of what is truly organic," Kastel said. [7]

Ronnie Cummins, national director of the Organic Consumers Association, questioned the authenticity of organic food grown in China, where "organic standards are dubious, and farm-labor exploitation is the norm." [8]

Wal-Mart replied that it would not compromise organic standards. [9] In addition, a spokesman said, "whenever possible, as with all fresh merchandise, we try to purchase fresh organic products from local suppliers for distribution to stores in their areas. This is good for the surrounding communities and helps to generate savings on distribution costs that we can pass on to our customers." [10]

---

[1] Lee Scott, presentation to Wal-Mart employees, Bentonville, Ark., Oct. 24, 2005; www.walmartstores.com/Files/21st%20Century%20Leadership.pdf.

[2] "Experimental Wal-Mart Stores One Year Later," Wal-Mart; www.walmartfacts.com/FactSheets/11132006_Experimental_Stores.pdf.

[3] Marc Gunther, "The Green Machine," *Fortune*, Aug. 7, 2006. p. 42. Michael Barbaro, "Wal-Mart Effort on Health and Environment Is Seen," *The New York Times*, June 22, 2006, p. 2.

[4] "Environmental Defense Will Add Staff Position in Bentonville, Arkansas," Environmental Defense, July 12, 2006; www.environmentaldefense.org/pressrelease.cfm?ContentID=5322.

[5] Abigail Goldman, "Wal-Mart goes 'green,' " *Los Angeles Times*, Nov. 13, 2006.

[6] *Ibid.*

[7] Mark Kastel, "Wal-Mart Declares War on Organic Farmers, the Cornucopia Institute, Sept. 28, 2006; www.cornucopia.org/WalMart_News_Release.pdf.

[8] Ronnie Cummins, "Open Letter to Wal-Mart," the Organic Consumers Association, July 4, 2006; www.organicconsumers.org/2006/article_1009.cfm.

[9] Tom Daykin, "Wal-Mart threatens farmers, report says," *The Milwaukee Journal Sentinel*, Sept. 28, 2006.

[10] Mya Frazier, "Critics' latest beef with Wal-Mart is . . . organics?" *Advertising Age*, Oct. 16, 2006, p. 47.

GE will invest $1.5 billion in research and development in those technologies by 2010 — up from $700 million in 2004 — "and we plan to make money doing it," Immelt said. Moreover, the company intends to double its revenues in those areas, from $10 billion in 2004 to at least $20 billion in 2010 and substantially more later. [20]

Potlatch Corp. Public Affairs Vice President Mark Benson isn't as precise about his forest-products company's future earnings, but he agrees it makes sense to prepare for a green marketplace. Potlatch seeks to distinguish itself from competitors by complying with all of the American Forest and Paper Association's environmental guidelines and then earning certification from the environmental movement's Forest Stewardship Council as well. As a result, Benson says, "we've positioned ourselves so, if that [green] market takes off, we're going to be there to serve it."

Retailers are discovering that "dedication to the environment makes them more attractive to consumers — especially if they're trying to appeal to an upscale audience," Pinkham says. Potlatch's policies also may make it more attractive to green investors, a group that is growing in numbers and influence, Benson says.

Assets devoted to so-called socially responsible investing (SRI) — of which green investing is a part — have grown slightly faster than other kinds of investing over the last decade, according to the Social Investment Forum, the SRI industry's trade association. SRI investments now represent 9.4 percent of all professionally managed assets tracked in Nelson Information's *Directory of Investment Managers*. [21]

Among SRI investors, 37 percent consider companies' environmental records when making investment decisions, the forum reported. Many also attempt to influence corporate environmental policy by introducing resolutions at shareholders' meetings.

Investors are proposing a growing number of resolutions, according to a report from the As You Sow Foundation and Rockefeller Philanthropy Advisors. Investors' proposals have addressed the environment more than any other issue in recent years, the report said, and the number of environmental resolutions proposed has increased faster than most other topics. [22]

But not everyone is bullish on green business.

Jerry Taylor, a senior fellow at the libertarian Cato Institute, suggests that talk of consumers' and companies' concern about the environment is overblown. "Public demands have always been for bigger and bigger and bigger homes," he notes. "How do you square that with the rise of environmentalism? And if consumers are looking at more fuel-efficient cars, I think that has more to do with the price of gas than anything else." If gas prices drop, Americans might go right back to their big SUVs, he says.

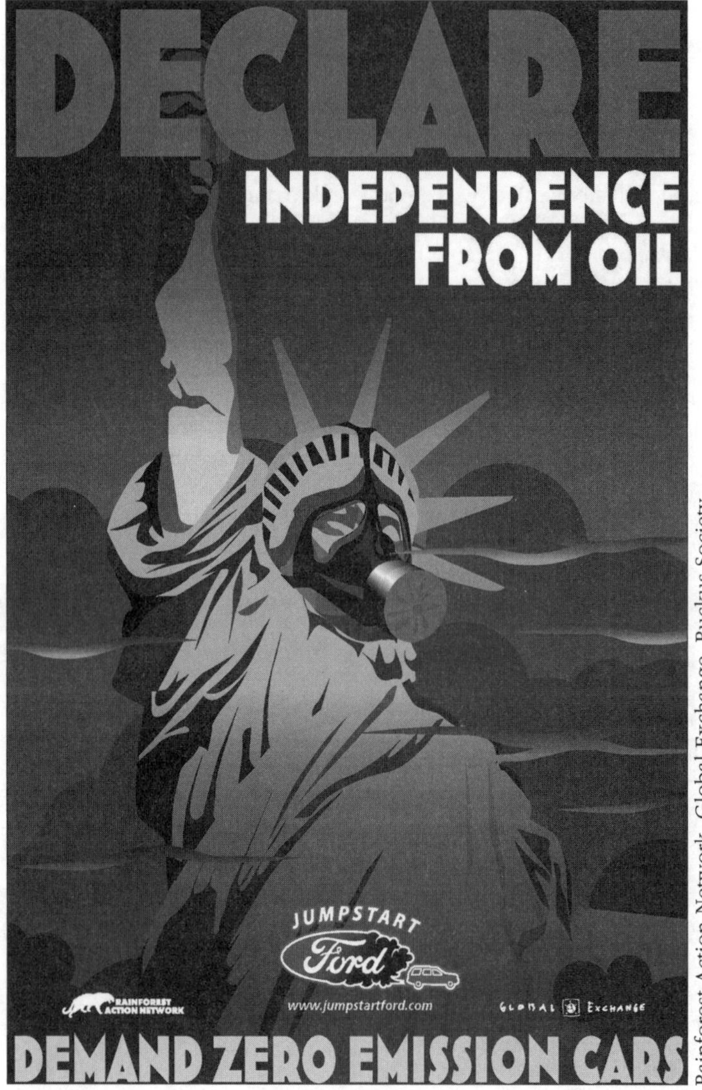

DECLARE
INDEPENDENCE
FROM OIL
JUMPSTART
Ford
RAINFOREST ACTION NETWORK
www.jumpstartford.com
GLOBAL EXCHANGE
DEMAND ZERO EMISSION CARS

Rainforest Action Network, Global Exchange, Ruckus Society

The Rainforest Action Network's Jumpstart Ford campaign urges Ford and other corporations to reduce their dependence on oil. The campaign claims Ford has the worst fleetwide fuel efficiency and the highest average vehicle greenhouse-gas emissions of major U.S. automakers.

Businesses may find conservation economical now, he adds, but if energy prices drop, companies might find it less expensive to use more energy than to buy energy-efficient equipment, he says. Competition could force companies to enlarge packaging to catch consumers' eyes, he says, even if that uses more materials.

While executives contend they adopt green policies to boost the bottom line, Competitive Enterprise Institute President Fred Smith Jr. charged the policies usually are intended "to appease [a business's] critics, to apologize for past mistakes, to bribe its opponents."

"The modern firm solves one — but only one — of the major problems of mankind: the creation of wealth," Smith said. "That wealth then allows individuals in their various roles the opportunity to protect values they care about." [23]

Is more federal action needed to encourage energy efficiency?

Almost everyone agrees Americans would be better off if they used energy more efficiently. Even those who don't fear global warming see benefits in reducing U.S. dependence on energy sources from unstable regions of the world, such as the Middle East. Most also agree that only federal action could spur significant gains in efficiency.

But there is disagreement over whether the desire for efficiency warrants government intervention and which measures would be most effective. Most environmental organizations advocate government mandates. Many businesses prefer incentives for voluntary action.

"We cannot solve these issues without the active participation of the federal government," says the Rainforest Action Network's Brune.

"There is no substitute for having clear national goals," Sierra Club spokesman Eric Antebi agrees. "It's great to have over 300 mayors doing their part. It's critical that states are taking the lead. But there are still too many gaps."

"There are some places where voluntary business actions will offer the greatest opportunities," says Denis Hayes, president and CEO of the Bullitt Foundation, and one of the key organizers of the first Earth Day. "But it's nice to have a regulatory basement beneath which you're not allowed to sink."

U.S. energy consumption is like a giant ocean liner that can't change direction quickly, says Americans for Balanced Energy Choices Executive

Director Joe Lucas. "We don't want draconian measures," says Lucas, whose advocacy group is funded by coal producers and consumers. "Don't force the ocean liner to do a U-turn immediately."

The federal government should continue to fund efforts to develop technologies that burn coal more efficiently and with fewer emissions, he says. And the government should offer incentives for farmers and foresters to adopt practices that absorb more greenhouse gases from the atmosphere.

Similarly, the auto industry opposes higher fuel-efficiency standards but favors tax breaks for those who buy fuel-efficient cars. "Competition among the automakers will drive this process far better and with fewer disruptions to the marketplace than any regulations that can be adopted," said Frederick Webber, president and CEO of the Alliance of Automobile Manufacturers. [24]

American businesses and individuals have become much more energy efficient since the emergence of the modern environmental movement and the 1973 Arab oil embargo. Today coal emits 70 percent less pollution per unit of energy produced than it did 30 years ago, Lucas says. Compared with the growth in gross domestic product, the United States puts a declining amount of greenhouse gases into the air, he adds.

America's new cars and light trucks average about 24 miles per gallon now, up from 15 in 1975. The typical refrigerator uses less than half as much electricity as its counterpart in 1972. [25]

Population growth, economic expansion and consumer tastes, however, have driven total energy consumption up by a third since 1973, and it is expected to jump another 30 percent by 2025. [26] Americans burned 75 percent more coal in 2005 than in 1980, and the coal industry says consumption will increase more than 30 percent over the next two decades. [27]

This doesn't surprise Joel Schwartz, a visiting fellow at the American Enterprise Institute (AEI), who doubts the need for, or effectiveness of, government regulations. "When you make things more efficiently," he explains, "you free up resources to make something else. Pound for pound, cars are more energy efficient now. Because of consumer demand, the efficiency benefits have gone into creating bigger cars that get about the same fuel economy."

If the United States did import less oil, Schwartz adds, "it would get used somewhere else. Developing countries would use that energy."

Nevertheless, environmentalists want the federal government to impose tougher restrictions on the use of fossil fuels. Cars began getting better gas mileage after federal corporate average fuel economy (CAFE) standards were enacted in 1975, they note. But the standard for passenger cars has not been raised since 1990, and the average fuel efficiency of cars and light trucks has actually declined since 1987. Over the last two decades, the auto industry has focused technology on getting heavier vehicles to run faster, and the growing American population has driven more miles.

The Union of Concerned Scientists wants CAFE standards increased to more than 40 miles per gallon (mpg) by 2015 and 55 mpg by 2025. Boosting mileage standards would not require U.S. auto companies to reinvent the wheel, the organization contends. For instance, Ford could apply existing technology to boost the Explorer SUV's fuel efficiency to 36 miles per gallon from 21. [28]

Environmental organizations also want restrictions on greenhouse-gas emissions, which are not regulated because they are not legally classified as pollutants under the Clean Air Act. [29] One often-advocated plan would assign every company an emissions allowance and let those that emit less sell their excess allowance to others. This so-called "cap-and-trade" scheme has been used successfully to reduce the sulfur emissions that cause acid rain.

Sens. John R. McCain, R-Ariz., and Joseph I. Lieberman, D-Conn., introduced legislation to do that in early 2005, and Maryland Republican Rep. Wayne T. Gilchrest did the same in the House. Neither bill got out of committee.

Recently some conservatives, concerned about U.S. reliance on imported oil, have suggested raising taxes on fossil fuels. "That's the way to get consumption down," said Alan Greenspan, former chairman of the Federal Reserve Board. "It's a national-security issue." Joining him have been such prominent conservative economists as Gregory Mankiw, former chairman of President Bush's Council of Economic Advisors, and Andrew Samwick, the council's former chief economist. [30]

While he doesn't agree that it's needed, Schwartz says a tax would be the most effective way to curb fossil-fuel use, as long as it were combined with other tax cuts so it didn't depress the economy.

Can the industrial world switch from fossil fuels to other forms of energy?

Environmentalists argue the only way to stop global warming is to stop burning fossil fuels. But switching from coal and oil is no easy task, and alternative energy sources have their own drawbacks — including damage to the environment.

"No energy source is perfect," says David Hamilton, director of the Sierra Club's global warming and energy program, using words echoed by Lucas, the coal-industry advocate.

For Hamilton, that means accepting the shortcomings of alternative fuels in the near term while conducting the research and development needed to make them work over the long haul. For Lucas, it means environmentalists have to accept that fossil fuels will be the world's primary energy source for the foreseeable future.

Eliminating coal and oil is "a pipe dream," that could occur only in "science-fiction land," Lucas says. "For the next 30 to 50 to 100 years, folks are going to have little choice but to use coal."

Currently, nearly 80 percent of the world's energy comes from burning fossil fuels. [31] In the United States, it's 86 percent. [32] Coal produces 52 percent of the electricity consumed in the United States, [33] and oil powers nearly all U.S. transportation. [34]

The coal producers and their customers project that America will continue to get a majority of its electricity from coal in 2025. They also say they will steadily reduce coal emissions during that time and will begin building "ultra-low-emissions plants" in the decade following 2025. Those plants could eliminate more than 99 percent of sulfur, nitrogen oxide and particulate emissions, along with 95 percent of mercury, they say. They also aim to be able to capture and sequester carbon dioxide, fossil fuels' primary contributor to global warming. [35]

The Rainforest Action Network's Brune acknowledges that "we have massive amounts of coal in the United States and around the world. If we want to extract every bit of fossil fuel, we could go for a couple hundred more years. But the planet wouldn't be able to survive."

Industry has not proven that it can capture and sequester greenhouse gases on a commercial scale, he says, and coal mining itself does terrible damage to the environment.

Even if factories could capture greenhouse gases in the future, Hamilton says, "scientists say we need to actually reduce emissions now, not just get on a path to reducing emissions in 10 years."

That would require a variety of methods for conserving and switching to alternative sources of energy, environmentalists say. "There is no silver bullet," Sierra Club spokesman Antebi says. "I heard someone say that you need silver buckshot.

"We're going to need to make our cars go further on a gallon of gas," he continued. "We're going to need solar and wind power and biofuels. We're going to need to design our buildings to operate more efficiently. We're going to need to clean up our power plants and use new technologies to reduce their impact on global warming."

Wind power has been the fastest-growing U.S. source of energy, jumping by 160 percent from 2000 to 2005. But it accounts for less than two-tenths of a percent of American energy consumption. [36] And it is not without its problems.

Jesse Ausubel, director of Rockefeller University's human-environment program, terms wind one of environmentalism's "false gods." To replace a typical, traditional power plant, he said, a windmill farm would have to cover 300 square miles. Other environmentalists oppose windmill farms because they endanger birds and can clutter the landscape. [37]

Similarly, U.S. use of ethanol — a fuel made from corn and other plants — increased by 145 percent from 2000 to 2005. Like wind power, however, it supplies a tiny fraction of America's energy — about a third of a percent. [38] Spurred by government incentives, annual ethanol production may more than double from 4.5 billion gallons now to more than 10 billion by 2010. [39] But that still would represent less than 1 percent of U.S. energy sources, and ethanol, too, carries environmental baggage. (*See sidebar, p. 996.*)

Despite problems posed by some alternative-energy sources, Hamilton says, "we're going to need almost every tool in the shed for a while.

"Scientists are saying we won't have the luxury to go back and stop global warming if we reach some of these biological tipping points," he continues. "We need to solve this problem now, and if we do we will then have the opportunity to make technological improvements later.

"You can always take the wind turbines down because some people think they're ugly. You can't take the carbon dioxide out of the air — it stays there for 200 years."

Many environmentalists place hope in solar energy, even though it currently produces less than a tenth of a percent of U.S. power. A handful of environmentalists are calling for more use of nuclear power. A growing number of environmental organizations are acknowledging that nuclear shouldn't be rejected out of hand. But most argue that nuclear's downsides will not be overcome in the foreseeable future.

Pro-nuclear environmentalists, such as British scientist Lovelock, contend it offers the only realistic alternative to fossil fuels. Other alternatives are "largely gestures," Lovelock said. "If it makes people feel good to shove up a windmill or put a solar panel on their roof, great, do it. It'll help a little bit, but it's no answer at all to the problem." [40]

Bruce Babbitt — Clinton administration Interior secretary and one-time head of the League of Conservation Voters — described nuclear power as "the lesser [evil] of the only two alternatives that are on the table right now. One is to fry this planet with continuing use and burning of fossil fuels, and the other is to try to make nuclear power work." [41]

Environmentalists can't "just say 'no way, no how,' " Environmental Defense's Yarnold says. "That's one reason some people look at a caricature of environmentalists and say, 'There they go again.' "

But he also says the nuclear industry must answer tough questions about reactor safety, waste disposal and weapons proliferation before new plants should be opened.

The industry might be able to address some concerns about safety, the Bullitt Foundation's Hayes says, "but the one I can't think of any way to make progress on is nuclear proliferation. I'm pretty terrified of a world in which 60 countries have nuclear stockpiles, and if they all have nuclear power I can't think of any way to avoid that." ■

Continued on p. 996

Chronology

1870-1900

Environmentalists organize, and Congress begins to act.

1870
Congress passes law to protect Alaska wildlife.

1872
Yellowstone becomes world's first national park.

1891
Congress empowers president to create national forests.

1900-1969

Teddy Roosevelt leads crusade to protect the environment. Modern environmental movement is born.

1901
President Theodore Roosevelt makes conservation a priority.

1906
Congress passes Antiquities Act; Roosevelt creates the first national monuments — Devil's Tower in Wyoming and Petrified Forest in Arizona.

1916
National Park Service created.

1962
Writer and biologist Rachel Carson warns of the dangers of pesticides in her landmark book *Silent Spring*.

1970-1979

Modern environmental movement soars into prominence; Congress responds with landmark laws.

1970
Some 20 million Americans celebrate first Earth Day. . . . Clean Air Act passed. . . . Environmental Protection Agency created.

1972
Clean Water Act passed; DDT is banned.

1973
Endangered Species Act passed.

1974
Safe Water Drinking Act enacted.

1975
Fuel-economy and tailpipe-emission standards are established.

1980-1987

Environmental activism slows, but Congress passes significant legislation, and international agreements target global environmental challenges.

1980
Superfund created to clean hazardous-waste sites. . . . Landmark Alaska Lands legislation sets aside more than 100 million acres, doubling U.S. parks and refuge acreage

1987
Two-dozen nations agree to phase out chlorofluorocarbons, which damage Earth's ozone layer.

1990-1999

Climate change becomes top global environmental issue.

1992
U.N. convention calls for greenhouse-gas reductions.

1994
Republican takeover of Congress diminishes environmentalists' power in federal government.

1995
Attack on acid rain launched.

1997
Kyoto Protocol mandates greenhouse-gas reductions; U.S. fails to ratify.

2000-2006

Republican control of Congress and White House further weakens environmentalists' voice. Environmentalists increase efforts to influence business. More businesses go "green."

2000
Republican George W. Bush wins White House; GOP holds Congress. . . . Thirty-five institutional investors with several trillion dollars in assets launch Carbon Disclosure Project to pressure corporations to address global warming.

2001
Vermont Sen. James Jeffords, an environmentalist, leaves Republican Party mid-year, giving Democrats control of Senate.

2002
GOP regains control of Senate.

2006
Environmentalists celebrate Democratic capture of Congress but don't expect great success while Bush occupies White House and Senate is nearly evenly divided. . . . Carbon Disclosure Project grows to 225 investors with $31.5 trillion in assets. . . . Tyson Foods warns meat prices to rise because ethanol production is driving up cost of corn.

The Promise — and Problems — of Ethanol

For environmentalists, ethanol wields a double-edged sword. It replaces oil-based fuels, reducing emissions of greenhouse gases and other pollutants. But it poses its own threats.

Tyson Foods, the world's largest meat processor, recently underscored one ethanol worry — that increased production of ethanol, almost all from corn, will drive up the price of that widely used grain. Rising corn prices will lead to higher chicken, beef and pork prices in 2007, the company announced in November.

"The American consumer is making a choice here," Tyson President and CEO Richard Bond said. "This is either corn for feed or corn for fuel. That's what's causing this." [1]

Critics also worry that devoting more land to expanded corn production could damage the environment by increasing harmful runoff of pesticides and fertilizers and by discouraging the preservation of land for conservation reserves, wetlands, wildlife preserves and wilderness. [2] According to Friends of the Earth, corn requires nearly six times more fertilizer and pesticide than most crops. [3]

Ethanol enjoys substantial government subsidies, in no small part because of farm-state lawmakers whose constituents grow corn. Ethanol production consumed about 14 percent of U.S.-grown corn in 2005 and was projected to run as high as 19 percent this year. America's entire corn crop would supply just 3.7 percent of the energy demanded by the U.S. transportation sector, however, researchers at the Polytechnic University of New York estimated. [4]

Corn ethanol contains less energy than gasoline, so an ethanol-fueled vehicle gets lower fuel efficiency. *Consumer Reports* magazine compared gasoline with an ethanol fuel burned in a Chevy Tahoe sport utility vehicle, a so-called "flexible fuel" model that can run on gasoline or a mixture of up to 85 percent ethanol and 15 percent gas. The ethanol blend delivered 27 percent lower gas mileage. [5]

According to a team of researchers from the University of California at Berkeley, corn ethanol can make a real, but relatively small, contribution to reducing greenhouse-gas emissions. They compared the energy in the ethanol with the fossil fuels used to make it — powering farm machinery and production equipment, for instance. The ethanol contained 20 percent more energy than was used to make it, and it reduced greenhouse-gas emissions by 13 percent. [6]

Most modern cars can run on a 10 percent ethanol blend, and about a third of U.S. motor fuel uses that mixture to reduce pollution. But only about 5 million of America's 230 million passenger vehicles can run on 85-percent ethanol, called E85, and many of them are gas-guzzlers like the Tahoe. [7] The United States had 70 percent more E85-dispensing service stations in August than it did at the beginning of last year, but that's still just 850 of 169,000 stations nationwide. [8]

Ethanol proponents hope other crops will prove to be more efficient energy sources.

Ethanol from sugarcane has eight times the energy of corn ethanol. [9] It delivers 40 percent of Brazil's automobile fuel, costs less than half as much as gasoline there and helps to generate electricity as well. [10] But the United States doesn't have much land suitable for the crop. In addition, federal laws keep sugar prices artificially high and restrict imports of cheaper sugar from overseas. [11]

Entrepreneurs and scientists are trying to produce ethanol from more economical plant matter, such as farm waste, municipal trash, grass, leaves and wood. Corn ethanol is made from the corn's starch. Ethanol also can be made — with greater difficulty — from

Continued from p. 994

BACKGROUND

Early Warnings

American environmentalists can trace their roots to distinguished writers — and some obscure bureaucrats — of the mid-19th century. [42]

Students still read Henry David Thoreau's *Walden* (published in 1854) and his other paeans to nature. In 1857, after the discovery of the California redwoods, poet James Russell Lowell proposed establishing a society for the protection of trees.

But even earlier, the U.S. commissioner of patents warned in 1849 about "the folly and shortsightedness" of wasting timber and slaughtering buffalo. Other commissioners of patents and of agriculture issued similar warnings about environmental destruction throughout the 1850s and '60s.

Congress had gotten the message by 1864, when it gave Yosemite Valley to California to establish a state park. Eight years later, it made Yellowstone the world's first national park.

During the 1870s, Congress passed legislation to protect fur-bearing animals in Alaska, fisheries in the Atlantic Ocean and Eastern lakes and trees on government lands. Environmental organizations also began to sink roots. Botanists and horticulturalists created the American Forestry Association (now known as American Forests), and New Englanders founded the Appalachian Mountain Club.

The 1890s also proved to be "green." Congress established Sequoia and General Grant (now part of Kings Canyon) national parks, and brought Yosemite back under federal control. Congress also gave the president power to create national forests, and President Benjamin Harrison issued a proclamation that created the first national wildlife refuge, in Alaska. In the private sector,

cellulose, which is the main component of plant-cell walls.

Not only can cellulosic ethanol be made from more materials, it also can reduce greenhouse-gas emissions by 67 to 89 percent, according to the U.S. Energy Department's Argonne National Laboratory.[12]

The economies of tropical and subtropical countries, with year-round growing seasons, could benefit from the growing demand for sugarcane ethanol. "The risk," Earth Policy Institute President Lester Brown warned, "is that economic pressures to clear land for expanding sugarcane production . . . in the Brazilian cerrado and Amazon basin . . . will pose a major threat to plant and animal diversity."[13]

The Rainforest Action Network is "very concerned about biofuel's impact on rain forests," Network Executive Director Michael Brune says. Ethanol can contribute to reducing fossil-fuel consumption, he says, but only as part of a comprehensive approach that includes more efficient motor-vehicle engines and clean generation of electricity.

"If we replaced gas-guzzling internal-combustion engines with a similar engine that uses biofuel, we'll just be replacing one problem with another," Brune says. "If we use more advanced auto technology and 'green' the electricity grid, then the impact of an appropriate use of biofuels would be revolutionary."

More Corn Used for Ethanol

Nearly 20 percent of the corn grown in the United States this year — a five-percentage-point increase over 2005 — was used for ethanol production. If the nation's entire corn crop were used for ethanol, it would supply just 3.7 percent of the energy needed for transportation alone.

Percentage of U.S. Corn Used for Ethanol Production

Year	Percentage
2005	14%
2006	19%

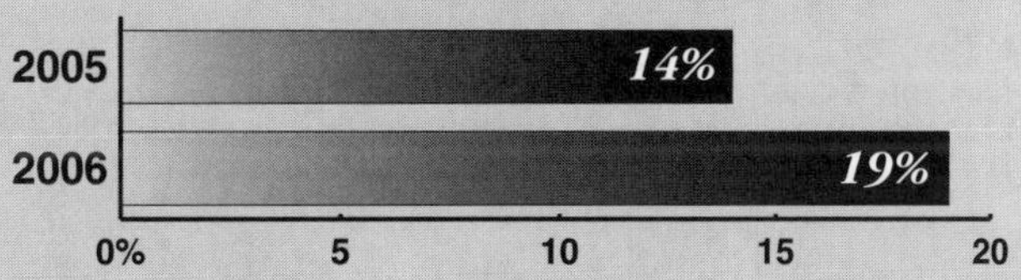

Source: Polytechnic University of New York

[1] Marcus Kabel, "Tyson Foods Sees Higher Meat Prices," The Associated Press, Nov. 13, 2006.

[2] Brad Knickerbocker, "Why the Next Congress Will Be 'Greener,' But Only by a Few Shades," *The Christian Science Monitor*, Nov. 15, 2006, p. 2.

[3] Mike Nixon, "Skepticism Rides along with Gasoline Ethanol Requirement," *St. Louis Daily Record*, July 15, 2006.

[4] Adriel Bettelheim, "Biofuels Boom," *CQ Researcher*, Sept. 29, 2006, pp. 793-816.

[5] "The Ethanol Myth," *Consumer Reports*, October 2006, p. 15.

[6] Elizabeth Douglass, "Report Challenges Claims about Ethanol," *Los Angeles Times*, Jan. 27, 2006, p. C2.

[7] Elizabeth Douglass, "A Future Without Oil?" *Los Angeles Times*, April 16, 2006, p. C1; "Annual Vehicle Distance Traveled in Miles and Related Data 2004," Federal Highway Administration, www.fhwa.dot.gov/policy/ohim/hs04/htm/vm1.htm.

[8] Alexei Barrionuevo, "An Alternative Fuel Is Scarce, Even in the Farm Belt," *The New York Times*, Aug. 31, 2006, p. C1.

[9] Jerry Taylor and Peter Van Doren, "California's Global Warming Dodge," *The Arizona Republic*, May 7, 2006.

[10] Marla Dickerson, "Homegrown Fuel Supply Helps Brazil Breathe Easy," *Los Angeles Times*, June 15, 2005, p. 1.

[11] "Sugar's sweet deal," *Sarasota Herald-Tribune*, Aug. 15, 2006, p. A10.

[12] Barbara McClellan, "Biofuel Crossroads," *Ward's Auto World*, Nov. 1, 2006, p. 30.

[13] Lester R. Brown, "Rescuing a Planet Under Stress," *The Futurist*, July 1, 2006, p. 18.

John Muir and some friends on the West Coast founded the Sierra Club to preserve wilderness. Back East, creation of the Massachusetts Audubon Society touched off the Audubon movement, which led to the National Association of Audubon Societies in 1905.

President Theodore Roosevelt (1901-1909), an avid outdoorsman, doubled the acreage in national parks and established 53 wildlife sanctuaries. Following congressional passage of the American Antiquities Act in 1906, Roosevelt created the first national monuments — Devil's Tower in Wyoming and Petrified Forest in Arizona. The early-20th century also spawned Western opposition to federal environmental-protection activities, notably when Western business and government representatives met at the Denver Public Lands Convention and demanded that federal lands be turned over to the states.

While most early 20th-century environmentalism focused on preserving pristine nature, public officials also began to take note of a growing side effect of urbanization — pollution of waters near big cities. Congress responded in 1910 by passing legislation that restricted dumping refuse into Lake Michigan in or near Chicago.

In something of a harbinger of current partnerships between environmental organizations and businesses, conservationists and sportsmen found allies within railroads and travel agencies. Together, they promoted creation of a federal bureau to look after the national parks. Congress responded in 1916 by establishing the National Park Service.

Three years later, supporters of the parks founded the National Parks Association (which was renamed the National Parks and Conservation Association in 1970). The organization sought to build public backing for the parks through educational activities and by encouraging Americans to visit.

The roaring '20s became better known for environmental exploitation than environmental protection, as Congress opened federal lands to mining and drilling for small fees, authorized federal hydroelectric projects and set the U.S. Army Corps of Engineers to dredging and damming inland waters.

In the 1930s, the Great Depression was worsened when poor agricultural practices contributed to massive dust storms that turned formerly bountiful farmland on the Plains into the Dust Bowl. In efforts to fight the Depression, President Franklin D. Roosevelt's New Deal policies created the Civilian Conservation Corps, through which unemployed workers planted trees, built roads, erected fire towers and carried out other public works.

The environmental costs of industrialization commanded increasing attention during the 1930s, '40s and '50s. Offshore oil drilling began. Smog episodes in St. Louis led to the nation's first smoke-control ordinance. Los Angeles established the first air-pollution control bureau. California adopted the first automobile-emissions standards. Congress passed laws — that would be strengthened after the '60s — to address water and air pollution.

The political and counter-culture ferment of the 1960s spurred interest in environmentalism that emphasized personal responsibility. This manifested itself in movements to encourage recycling, organic gardening and farming, cooperatives and purchases of "green" products.

Mimicking the violent political activists of the era, a few organizations and individuals began engaging in "ecoterrorism," destroying property that they viewed as encroaching on nature and setting booby traps to threaten loggers. Their legacy included trials and guilty pleas this year from alleged members of the Earth Liberation Front and Animal Liberation Front who were charged with firebombing ranger stations, corrals, lumber mill offices, ski resorts, slaughterhouse and federal plant-inspection facilities throughout the West between 1996 and 2001. [43]

Getty Images/Sandy Huffaker

The Kumeyaay wind farm on the Campo Indian Reservation serves 30,000 customers in San Diego. Wind power is the fastest-growing U.S. source of energy but accounts for less than two-tenths of a percent of American energy consumption. Replacing a typical, traditional power plant with wind power would require a 300-square-mile wind farm, according to one expert.

Era of Activism

Taking an entirely different tack, biologist Rachel Carson wrote *Silent Spring*, highlighting the dangers posed by DDT and other pesticides and foreshadowing the coming era of massive environmental activism.

That era was kicked off by the first Earth Day, on April 22, 1970. The event was conceived by Democratic Sen. Gaylord Nelson of Wisconsin as a way to "shake up the political establishment and force this issue onto the national agenda." [44] He modeled it after the teach-ins that built opposition to the Vietnam War on college campuses, and it succeeded beyond his wildest dreams.

An estimated 20 million Americans — including 10 million students from 2,000 colleges and 1,000 high schools — participated in a wide variety of activities throughout the country. There were marches, rallies, songfests, mock funerals for the internal-combustion engine, mock trials of polluters, trash pickup drives, protests against aircraft noise and polluting companies. New York City closed Fifth Avenue for Earth Day events. Congress shut down because so many members were out participating. Earth Day speakers ranged from famed anthropologist Margaret Mead to liberal Sen. Edward M. Kennedy, D-Mass., to conservative Sen. Barry Goldwater, R-Ariz., to Nixon administration Cabinet officers. [45]

At the same time, according to organizer Hayes, Attorney General John

R. Mitchell ordered the FBI to investigate the organizers of Earth Day. [46] In addition, a Georgia gubernatorial candidate called Earth Day a communist plot because it was held on Russian revolutionary Vladimir Lenin's birthday, and the Daughters of the American Revolution denounced it as "subversive." [47]

But lawmakers heard loud and clear that Earth Day was above all an expression of national will. Later in 1970, Congress passed the Clean Air Act, and President Richard M. Nixon established the Environmental Protection Agency. These were followed in subsequent years by a flood of landmark laws, including the Clean Water Act, the Endangered Species Act, the Marine Mammal Protection Act, the Safe Drinking Water Act, the Toxic Substances Control Act, the Resource Conservation and Recovery Act to regulate hazardous waste, fuel-economy standards, tailpipe-emission and lead-paint restrictions, bans on DDT, the phasing out of leaded gasoline, PCBs and ozone-destroying chlorofluorocarbons and a U.S.-Canada agreement to clean up the polluted Great Lakes.

The '70s also witnessed the birth of Green political parties, which eventually wielded significant influence in Europe but not in the United States. While the first Green parties were organized in New Zealand and Australia, the first Green Party candidate won election to a national legislature in Switzerland, in 1979. Green parties contributed to some of the movements that overthrew communist regimes in former Soviet-bloc countries. The German Green Party joined the governing coalition in 1998, and its leader served as foreign minister. Greens also have been mayors of Dublin, Rome and other major European cities.

In the United States, although Congress passed environmental legislation at a slower pace in the 1980s and '90s, some of the new laws were highly significant. The Superfund program began to clean up hazardous-waste sites in the '80s, for example, and the attack on acid rain began in the following decade.

Global warming has been the world's top environmental issue since the 1990s. Most — though not all — scientists believe that fossil-fuel emissions are causing the planet to heat up. Scientists can't make specific predictions about how much or how fast. Worst-case scenarios are truly catastrophic, forecasting drought, famine, floods, animal and plant extinctions, destruction of island and coastal communities — even massive human death.

The 1992 U.N. Framework Convention on Climate Change called on industrialized nations to reduce their emissions of "greenhouse gases," which are released when coal, oil and other fossil fuels are burned. The reduction was voluntary, however, and countries soon realized that the convention's goal — to stabilize emissions at 1990 levels by 2000 — would not be met.

The Kyoto Protocol, negotiated in 1997, set mandatory emissions reductions. But the United States — the world's largest greenhouse-gas emitter — has refused to ratify it, arguing that compliance would damage the economy. Critics warn that countries that have ratified may not meet the cuts because they aren't making sufficient changes in their consumption of fossil fuels. And rapidly industrializing countries — notably China and India — are expected to make major increases in their emissions. ■

CURRENT SITUATION

Democrats Take Over

Environmentalists celebrated the Democratic takeover of Congress on Nov. 7, 2006, and can point to growing signs of public support for environmental protection. But many environmental leaders remain focused on businesses for solutions to environmental problems, especially global warming.

Meanwhile, environmental groups are reporting recent increases in membership and financial contributions. The Sierra Club now has 800,000 members, a one-third rise in the last four years. [48] Between 2003 and 2006, membership jumped from 400,000 to 550,000 in the Natural Resources Defense Council and from 300,000 to 400,000 at Environmental Defense. Both reported substantial budget hikes as well. [49]

Overall, giving to environmental organizations increased by 7 percent from 2003 to 2004 and by 16.4 percent the next year — greater growth in both years than any other category of nonprofit organization tracked by the Giving USA Foundation. [50]

The Gallup Organization reports that the percentage of Americans who worry about the environment "a great deal" or "a fair amount" increased from 62 to 77 percent between 2004 and 2006. Since 1984, Gallup has asked Americans to choose between two sides in a mock debate: whether "protection of the environment should be given priority, even at the risk of curbing economic growth," or "economic growth should be given priority, even if the environment suffers to some extent." (*See graph, p. 1000.*)

The pro-environment side has always prevailed, usually by a large margin. After falling precipitously during the early years of the Bush administration — from a 43-percentage-point pro-environment margin in 2000 to 5 percentage points in 2003 and 2004 — the pro-environment gap began widening again. Pro-environment respondents outnumbered pro-economy respondents by 17 percent in 2005 and 15 percent this year. [51]

Despite such positive signs, environmental activists don't expect major legislation to work its way through the

Public Strongly Favors Action on Environment

Americans strongly favor environmental initiatives by both industry and government to cut pollution and increase energy efficiency.

Do you generally favor or oppose:

	Favor	Oppose
Expanding the use of nuclear energy	55%	40%
More strongly enforcing federal environmental regulations	79%	20%
Setting higher auto-emission standards	73%	25%
Setting higher emission and pollution standards for business and industry	77%	22%
Imposing mandatory controls on carbon-dioxide emissions and other greenhouse gases	75%	23%
Spending more government money on developing solar and wind power	77%	21%
Spending government money to develop alternate sources of fuel for cars	85%	14%

Source: Gallup Poll, 2006

House and Senate and survive presidential vetoes during the next two years. They also believe businesses are essential to the solutions, with or without government action.

Democratic congressional leaders tend to be more supportive of environmentalists' positions than Republicans. But Democrats didn't win large enough majorities to override vetoes or break GOP filibusters in the Senate. Indeed, the agenda Democratic leaders announced for the opening days of the next Congress, in 2007, does not include environmental legislation.

The loss of Republican power means environmentalists won't have to battle attempts to roll back environmental protections, such as California Rep. Richard Pombo's efforts to weaken the Endangered Species Act, sell national park land in Alaska, open the Arctic National Wildlife Refuge to oil drilling and increase drilling off the nation's coasts. Pombo, who chaired the House Resources Committee, was defeated.

Individual representatives and senators will introduce environmental bills, including some to address global warming. But, said Sierra Club Executive Director Carl Pope, "I don't think we're going to see, at a national level, major progress, because Bush is still going to be there." [52]

Environmentalists "can't wait for the federal government, which is why you're seeing all these other players take the first steps," Sierra Club spokesman Antebi says.

Focus on Business

Environmentalists are drawing more sympathy from corporate executives, Public Affairs Council President Pinkham says, because "we've reached a tipping point where most business people agree that global warming is an issue that can't be ignored. Even companies with doubts are coming to realize you can't sit on the sidelines."

Environmental organizations are working with companies on a wide range of environmental challenges. Some relationships are cooperative, others confrontational. Environmentalists seek to apply pressure by winning support from companies' customers, employees and investors. They also appeal to executives' sense of social responsibility.

"We attempt to appeal to the most core, basic values that remind us that we're all human, that we all need to live on a healthy Earth together, and that some of us have far more decision-making power than others," says the Rainforest Action Network's Hogue. "If you're the CEO of a major bank or a government official or a logging executive, you are a human being first, and you don't want to do anything that you can't explain in good faith to your children and grandchildren."

In addition to its partnerships with FedEx, UPS and DuPont, Environmental Defense has struck agreements with numerous firms, including Wegmans Food Markets and Bon Appétit Management Company on implementing health and environmental standards for farmed salmon, McDonald's on reducing antibiotics in chicken, Compass Group food services on limiting antibiotics in pork and chicken, Bristol-Myers Squibb on incorporating environmental considerations into pharmaceutical development and packaging, and with other companies on other topics.

Having negotiated accords on environmentally friendly lending policies

Continued on p. 1002

At Issue:

Are businesses better equipped than governments to address 21st-century environmental challenges?

MARGERY KRAUS
PRESIDENT AND CEO, APCO WORLDWIDE*

WRITTEN FOR *CQ RESEARCHER*, NOVEMBER 2006

yes

There is no doubt the environment is on people's minds: Used hybrid cars can fetch more than the original sticker price at resale; the *Oxford American Dictionary*'s word of the year for 2006 is "carbon neutral." However hip it may be, environmental responsibility is more than just the "flavor of the month," it is our future. And businesses not only can be the most efficient catalyst for creating a more sustainable planet but they also are increasingly expected to play that role.

A recent study conducted by APCO Worldwide reveals that the American public holds businesses to a higher standard on environmental issues than it does the U.S. government. There is a belief that business is less encumbered by politics and bureaucracy and has more resources to act and influence others to do so.

Today's progressive companies already know they have this responsibility and embrace it. Big corporations are larger than many nations. Major companies' global reach and standards allow them to directly impact environments beyond the boundaries of any one country. As they expand globally, businesses are able to build factories with proven technologies that often exceed the requirements of local governments.

Corporations have a tremendous opportunity to influence individual behavior. Employees can be offered incentives to use public transportation, recycle and contribute time to community environmental efforts. More broadly, businesses can sway consumer bases to adopt environmentally responsible behavior.

Finally, an increased number of businesses see sustainable products as a new part of their business. They are engineering or re-engineering those products to be recyclable and to incorporate recycled materials; they are employing clean production processes to create less waste and pollution.

Down the road, these forward-looking businesses will have a healthy, sustainable work force, clean water and quality of life that will enable them to have good employees and more consumers. Their ultimate incentive: You can't run a successful business in a failed world.

Obviously, safeguarding our environment is best accomplished by governments, businesses and individuals working together. However, businesses, especially multinational corporations, are well-positioned to take decisive leadership and have the infrastructure and resources to achieve measurable results — and consumers are expecting nothing less.

** The public-relations and strategic-communications firm represents many of the world's largest corporations.*

MICHAEL BRUNE
EXECUTIVE DIRECTOR, RAINFOREST ACTION NETWORK

WRITTEN FOR *CQ RESEARCHER*, NOVEMBER 2006

no

Businesses and governments both have a vital role to play in addressing environmental challenges. We are beginning to see strong policies from a select number of high-profile businesses on issues such as forest protection and climate change. Meanwhile, state and local governments are responding to widespread public support for environmental protection, compensating for a disturbing lack of leadership in the White House and Congress.

One test for either businesses or governments is to determine to which constituency they are the most loyal. Most companies are guided by the old business axiom, "The customer is always right." These businesses realize that not only do consumers want to do business with companies that exhibit strong environmental values but also their own employees want to feel good about their employer's environmental record. Indeed, it is this view that has helped Home Depot, Lowe's, FedEx Kinko's and others to work with Rainforest Action Network to help protect endangered forests, and for Citigroup, Bank of America, JP Morgan Chase and Goldman Sachs to take principled stands on climate change and forest protection.

Conversely, many officials in Washington are stuck in the past, guarding the status quo. Within the last few years, the federal government has failed to enact, protect or enforce strong environmental policies, as evidenced by the attempted rollback of the Forest Service's "Roadless Rule" and the gutting of the Clean Water Act. Our politicians have fallen into the trap of believing they must choose between prosperity and the environment. Consequently, neither political party has stood up to the corporations whose policies are destabilizing and devastating our environment.

By leveraging public opinion and consumer choice to publicly stigmatize companies that refuse to adopt responsible environmental policies, environmental organizations are able to positively influence corporations' policies. This tactic strengthens marketplace democracy and empowers the consumer. It also has created significant progress and dramatic successes for environmental preservation. It gives consumers the ability to influence companies, stepping in where government has failed.

The reality is there is a new voice of business that shows how it is possible to do well by doing good, earning profits while upholding environmental principles. These businesses have shown a strong interest in working with government to meet the pressing environmental challenges of the 21st century. It's time for officials in Congress and the White House to listen and get to work.

Continued from p. 1000

with Citigroup, JPMorganChase and Goldman Sachs, the Rainforest Action Network (RAN) now is running campaigns against Wells Fargo's investments in oil, coal, logging and mining operations. Among RAN's other campaigns to change corporate policies, it's pressing for revisions in Weyerhaeuser's logging practices and for increases in the fuel-efficiency of Ford vehicles.

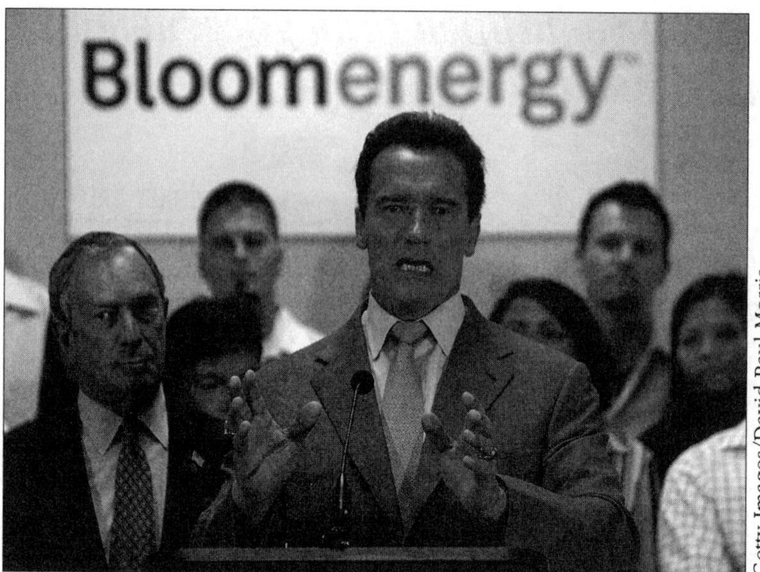

Getty Images/David Paul Morris

Gov. Arnold Schwarzenegger, R-Calif., discusses his environmental initiatives as New York City Mayor Michael Bloomberg looks on at fuel-cell maker Bloom Energy in Sunnyvale, Calif., on Sept. 21, 2006. The mayor announced he is launching a citywide greenhouse-gas inventory and appointing an environmental advisory board. California just mandated cuts in motor vehicles' carbon-dioxide emissions.

"You're seeing tremendous leadership from the private sector right now," Environmental Defense's Yarnold says. But environmentalists continue to press for government action because "businesses alone can't solve the global-warming problem."

Environmental groups want the federal government to require companies to meet environmental standards and to help them do so. New regulations are needed, environmentalists argue, not only to force recalcitrant companies to act but also to encourage corporations that want to act but can't afford to do more than their competitors.

"Many corporations, especially those active in international areas, are realizing they need to be more environmental and more progressive to stay competitive in the international arena," Oklahoma State University's Dunlap says. "A lot of American firms are caught in a bit of a dilemma. In some ways, they like having an administration that seems friendly to the market and keeping regulations minimal. On the other hand, they're not getting the incentives and the regulatory push to stay on the cutting edge."

Brune, of the Rainforest Action Network, describes companies that are "trying to lead by example and trying to pressure the government to wake up and step up to the plate."

The Sierra Club's Hamilton says he knows corporate executives "who have almost begged Congress to tell them what to do to reduce emissions, so they know how to plan for it. But companies are reluctant to take action on their own for fear of losing competitive advantage, because they don't know what is going to be required of them" when Congress finally does act.

"Businesses crave certainty," Yarnold explains. "Global businesses in particular crave certainty. To be operating in one regulatory environment in Europe and another in the United States is crazy. It's not good for business." Conflicts in state laws also will increase pressure for federal legislation, says Robert Brulle, an associate professor of sociology and environmental science at Drexel University, who is researching the 21st-century history of the environmental movement.

Environmentalists' top legislative goals are the cap-and-trading scheme for greenhouse gases and significant increases in vehicle fuel-economy standards. California Democrat Barbara Boxer, in line to chair the Senate Environment and Public Works Committee, said she plans "to roll out a pretty in-depth set of hearings on global warming. It isn't going to help any business, it isn't going to help anybody, if we do nothing" about the issue, she insisted.

Sen. McCain said he and Sen. Lieberman will re-introduce their global-warming bill and "absolutely" will push for a floor vote. McCain, a potential 2008 presidential candidate, also expressed optimism that President Bush would sign the legislation before he leaves the White House in January 2009.

"I think the president is coming around," McCain said. "He made a statement recently where he said that climate change is a significant issue. To tell you the truth, I'm worried more about [other] people in the administration than the president himself." [53]

In the past, Bush has said he agrees that human activity has contributed to climate change, but he has consistently rejected the idea of imposing mandatory curbs on carbon-dioxide emissions. Bush also has resisted calls to impose tougher standards on vehicle fuel economy, household appliances and building insulation — measures that could sharply reduce America's oil consumption.

Those Bush positions — plus opposition from other GOP lawmakers — lead other legislators to suggest that action is less likely than McCain predicts.

California Democrat Henry A. Waxman, incoming chair of the House Government Reform Committee, said environmentalists need to understand that "President Bush would veto any bill that ever got to him." [54] Oklahoma Republican James M. Inhofe, outgoing chair of the Senate Environment and Public Works Committee, expressed confidence that he can round up the 41 votes needed to sustain a filibuster against global-warming legislation.

Inhofe said he is seeing "an awakening" to his argument that harmful global warming is a myth. "People are realizing that [environmentalists] are saying things that are just flat not true," Inhofe said. [55]

Boxer, Inhofe's successor, acknowledged that passing legislation will be difficult. "Maybe I want to take the ball 50 yards," she said, "but I can take it only 30." [56]

OUTLOOK

Entrepreneurs in Spotlight

Environmentalists are counting on entrepreneurs to produce a future green world. Once governments impose restrictions on greenhouse-gas emissions, leaders of environmental organizations say, entrepreneurs will supply the technology that makes the restrictions work.

"It's going to look much the way it did during the information-technology gold rush at the advent of the Internet Age," Greenpeace Executive Director Passacantando says. "A whole new generation of entrepreneurs is going to lead us into the new era, and eventually we will have an economy that's built on low carbon-dioxide emissions or no carbon-dioxide emissions."

Environmental Defense's Yarnold sees hope in different pro-environment precedents — such as the restrictions on emissions that cause acid rain and deplete the ozone layer.

"Things were invented," he says. "Processes were created. People rise to the challenge. Investments get made. It creates economic activity. It creates jobs.

"Will there be solar panels made with nanotechnology? Are there chemical compounds that are better at conducting electricity than the materials we now have? I don't know. But I do know the circumstances under which those will be carried out. Efficient markets find low-cost, highly efficient solutions, and that's what will happen if the government puts a hard cap on carbon dioxide."

As Passacantando puts it, the choice of technologies "is not going to be Greenpeace's pick. It's going to be the entrepreneurs.' "

Environmentalists are most optimistic about conservation and renewable energies such as solar and wind.

"We have enough sunlight hitting the state of California every day to fulfill the country's energy needs," Oklahoma State's Brune says. "Enough wind flows through the Midwest to fulfill the country's energy needs. Both forms of energy are clean, create more jobs and have no greenhouse-gas emissions. Neither creates the environmental legacy of nuclear waste or the national-security problems associated with nuclear plants."

Some environmentalists acknowledge the possibility that new technology could make coal, oil and nuclear energy acceptable as well.

"There's great hope in low-carbon coal," Yarnold says, "and nuclear has to be on the table." Before new nuclear plants can be built, he adds, the industry must prove it can dispose of waste safely and prevent nuclear materials from being turned into weapons — obstacles that many environmentalists believe are insurmountable. Others caution that the transition away from fossil fuels won't be so simple. Envisioned solutions can be double-edged swords: windmill farms that deface the landscape and injure birds that fly too close; hydropower projects that dam waterways and injure fish; agriculture-based fuels that levy their own environmental costs and drive up the cost of food.

Critics from the left and the right warn against succumbing to pressure to take actions that don't really provide long-term solutions.

"You'll probably find that promises to do something about global warming will become more popular over time," the Cato Institute's Taylor says. "Politicians will make those promises, and voters will embrace politicians who make those promises. But the public doesn't seem to be willing to pay anything to reduce greenhouse gases. So politicians are going to find it's popular to propose programs but not popular to impose programs with costs, and I don't think greenhouse gases will be reduced much at all."

While Europe appears to be ahead of the United States in protecting the environment, Drexel University's Brulle says, Europe really is practicing "simulation of environmentalism. We have symbolic responses. But, when you look at carbon-dioxide emissions in Europe, they have not significantly gone down."

Brulle fears the United States will follow the same path. "We're not going to just stop using coal any more than we're going to destroy the economy of West Virginia," he says. Neither are Americans about to abandon a consumer culture that requires ever-higher energy consumption, he says.

"The way to reduce greenhouse-gas emissions now is to conserve big time, but I don't see any political will to do that," Brulle says. That leaves increased use of nuclear power as the only alternative for the foreseeable future, he argues.

"The question," he says, "is which is the worst poison. One will be absolutely fatal — climate change. One might be fatal, but is not always fatal — nuclear power.

"I'm not a fan of nuclear power, by any means. But, given the alternative of destroying the global ecosystem for thousands of years, we have to seriously consider putting nuclear power into the mix." ■

Notes

[1] "Corporate Innovation: Changing the Way Business Thinks About the Environment," Environmental Defense; environmentaldefense.org/corporate_innovation.cfm. See also Jia Lynn Yang, "It's Not Easy Being Green — But Big Business Is Trying," *Fortune*, Aug. 7, 2006.

[2] "For the Health of the Nation: An Evangelical Call to Civic Responsibility," National Association of Evangelicals, Oct. 7, 2004; www.nae.net/images/civic_responsibility2.pdf.

[3] Elizabeth Keenan, "Plugging Into Nuclear," *Time*, June 19, 2006, p. 46; Andrew C. Revkin, "Updating Prescriptions for Avoiding Worldwide Catastrophe," *The New York Times*, Sept. 12, 2006, p. F2. For background, see Marcia Clemmitt, "Climate Change," *CQ Researcher*, Jan. 27, 2006, pp. 73-96.

[4] Accessed at people-press.org/reports/display.php3?ReportID=280.

[5] Accessed at www.pewtrusts.com/pdf/pew_research_economy_012506.pdf.

[6] Accessed at www.harrisinteractive.com/harris_poll/index.asp?PID=607.

[7] Accessed at www.foe.org/camps/intl/corpacct/wallstreet/handbook/index.html and rockpa.org/wp-content/uploads/2006/06/Power%20of%20Proxy.pdf.

[8] The Carbon Disclosure Project, "The $31.5 Trillion Question: Is Your Company Prepared for Climate Change?" www.cdproject.net/viewrelease.asp?id=8/.

[9] Juliet Eilperin, "Cities, States Aren't Waiting For U.S. Action on Climate," *The Washington Post*, Aug. 11, 2006, p. A1.

[10] *Ibid.* See also Karen Matthews, "States To Lower Greenhouse Gas Emissions," The Associated Press, Oct. 16, 2006.

[11] Accessed at www.apolloalliance.org.

[12] Accessed at www.apolloalliance.org/strategy_center/a_bold_energy_and_jobs_policy/ten_point_plan.cfm. For background on hydrogen, see Mary H. Cooper, "Alternative Fuels," *CQ Researcher*, Feb. 25, 2005, pp. 173-196.

[13] Michael Schneider, "Leo's Green Builds Skein," *Daily Variety*, Oct. 17, 2006, p. 1.

[14] Karen Krebsbach, "The Green Revolution: Are Banks Sacrificing Profits for Activists' Principles?" *US Banker*, Feb. 6, 2005.

[15] Marc Gunther, "The Green Machine," *Fortune*, Aug. 7, 2006, p. 42.

[16] *Ibid.*

[17] Yang, *op. cit.*

[18] Accessed at fedex.com/us/about/responsibility/environment/hybridelectricvehicle.html?link=4.

[19] Steven Mufson, "As Power Bills Soar, Companies Embrace 'Green' Buildings," *The Washington Post*, Aug. 5, 2006, p. A1.

[20] General Electric, press release, "GE Launches Ecomagination to Develop Environmental Technologies"; http://home.businesswire.com/portal/site/ge/index.jsp?ndmViewId=news_view&ndmConfigId=1002373&newsId=20050509005663&newsLang=en&ndmConfigId=1002373&vnsId=681.

[21] "2005 Report on Socially Responsible Investing Trends in the United States," Social Investment Forum, Jan. 24, 2006; www.socialinvest.org/areas/research/trends/sri_trends_report_2005.pdf.

[22] "Proxy Season Preview — Spring 2006," As You Sow Foundation and Rockefeller Philanthropy Advisors; www.asyousow.org/publications/2006_proxy_preview.pdf.

[23] Carol Hymowitz, moderator, "Corporate Social Concerns: Are They Good Citizenship, Or a Rip-Off for Investors?" *The Wall Street Journal Online*, Dec. 6, 2005; http://online.wsj.com/public/article/SB113355105439712626.html?mod=todays_free_feature.

[24] Testimony before U.S. House Energy and Commerce Committee, May 2, 2006.

[25] Barbara Mantel, "Energy Efficiency," *CQ Researcher*, May 19, 2006, pp. 433-456.

[26] *Ibid.*

[27] The Coal Based Generation Stakeholders Group, "A Vision for Achieving Ultra-Low Emissions from Coal-Fueled Electric Generation," January 2005; www.nma.org/pdf/coal_vision.pdf.

[28] Mantel, *op. cit.*

[29] *Ibid.*

[30] Daniel Gross, "Raise the Gasoline Tax? Funny, It Doesn't Sound Republican," *The New York Times*, Oct. 8, 2006.

[31] Worldwatch Institute, *Vital Signs 2006-2007* (2006), p. 32.

[32] U.S. Energy Department, "Annual Energy Review 2005," Energy Information Administration, July 27, 2006, Table 1.3; www.eia.doe.gov/emeu/aer/pdf/pages/sec1_9.pdf.

[33] *Ibid.*, Table 8.4a; www.eia.doe.gov/emeu/aer/pdf/pages/sec8_17.pdf.

[34] *Ibid.*, Table 2.1e; www.eia.doe.gov/emeu/aer/pdf/pages/sec2_8.pdf.

[35] The Coal Based Generation Stakeholders Group, *op. cit.*

[36] "Annual Energy Review 2005," *op. cit.*, Table 1.3.

[37] Peter Schwartz and Spencer Reiss, "Nuclear Now! How Clean, Green Atomic Energy Can Stop Global Warming," *Wired*, February 2005.

[38] U.S. Energy Department, *op. cit.*, Table 10.1; www.eia.doe.gov/emeu/aer/pdf/pages/sec10_3.pdf.

About the Author

Tom Price is a Washington-based freelance journalist who writes regularly for *CQ Researcher*. Previously he was a correspondent in the Cox Newspapers Washington Bureau and chief politics writer for the *Dayton Daily News* and *The Journal Herald*. His most recent book, written with former congressman and ambassador Tony Hall, is *Changing The Face of Hunger: One Man's Story of How Liberals, Conservatives, Democrats, Republicans, and People of Faith Are Joining Forces to Help the Hungry, the Poor, and the Oppressed*. He is the author of two Washington guidebooks, *Washington, D.C., for Dummies*, and the *Irreverent Guide to Washington, D.C.* His work has appeared in *The New York Times*, *Time*, *Rolling Stone* and other periodicals. He earned a bachelor of science in journalism at Ohio University.

[39] Adriel Bettelheim, "Biofuels Boom," *CQ Researcher*, Sept. 29, 2006, pp. 793-816.
[40] Revkin, *op. cit.*, p. 2.
[41] Frank Clifford, "Alarmed by 'Cycle of Anti-Environmentalism,' *Los Angeles Times*, Nov. 15, 2005, p. B2.
[42] Unless otherwise noted, this "Background" section is based on "The Evolution of the Conservation Movement," Library of Congress; lcweb2.loc.gov/ammem/amrvhtml/conshome.html; Lorraine Elliott, "Environmentalism," *Encyclopaedia Britannica*, 2006; www.britannica.com/eb/article-224631; *History of the Environmental Movement*, Glen Canyon Institute; www.glencanyon.org/library/movementhistory.php; "History," U.S. Environmental Protection Agency; epa.gov/history/index.htm; Tom Arrandale, "National Parks Under Pressure," *CQ Researcher*, Oct. 6, 2006, pp. 917-840; Mary H. Cooper, "Environmental Movement at 25," *CQ Researcher*, March 31, 1995, pp. 273-296, and William Kovarik, "Environmental History Timeline," www.radford.edu/~wkovarik/envhist.
[43] The Associated Press, "3 Plead Guilty to Ecoterror Charges," *Los Angeles Times*, July 21, 2006, p. A19.
[44] "History of Earth Day," Earth Day Network; www.earthday.org/resources/history.aspx.
[45] Beverly Beyette, "Earth Observance: The Day Politics Stood Still," *Los Angeles Times*, May 23, 1985, p. 5-1. Joanne Omang, " 'Sun Day,' Slated in May," *The Washington Post*, Sept. 19, 1977, p. A20.
[46] Beyette, *op. cit.*
[47] The Associated Press, April 23, 1970 (Lenin's birthday); Dan Eggen, "Earth Day: From Radical to Mainstream," *The Washington Post*, April 22, 2000, p. B1 (Daughters of the American Revolution).
[48] Jerry Adler, "Going Green," *Newsweek*, July 17, 2006, p. 42.
[49] *Encyclopedia of Associations*, 2003 and 2006.
[50] *Giving USA 2006: The Annual Report on Philanthropy for the Year 2005*, published by the Giving USA Foundation.
[51] The Gallup Organization, 2006.
[52] Bettina Boxall, "Conservationist Clout," *Los Angeles Times*, Nov. 9, 2006. p. 27.
[53] Darren Samuelsohn, "Sen. McCain Pledges Push for 'Long-Overdue' Emissions Bill," *Environment and Energy Daily*, Nov. 17, 2006.
[54] *Ibid.*
[55] *Ibid.*
[56] Charles Babington, "Party Shift May Make Warming a Hill Priority," *The Washington Post*, Nov. 18, 2006, p. A6.

FOR MORE INFORMATION

American Enterprise Institute, 1150 17th St., N.W., Washington, DC 20036; (202) 862-5800; www.aei.org. Conservative think tank that studies environmental and other issues.

Bullitt Foundation, 1212 Minor Ave., Seattle, WA 98101-2825; (206) 343-0807; www.bullitt.org. Philanthropic organization working to protect, restore and maintain the natural environment of the Pacific Northwest.

Cato Institute, 1000 Massachusetts Ave., N.W., Washington, DC 20001; www.cato.org. Libertarian think tank that questions environmental-protection measures that interfere with free markets.

Ecomagination, ge.ecomagination.com. Web site where General Electric explains its plans to profit from making environmentally friendly products.

Environmental Defense, 257 Park Ave. South, New York, NY 10010; (212) 505-2100; www.environmentaldefense.org. The advocacy group forms partnerships with corporations to promote environmentally friendly business practices.

League of Conservation Voters, 1920 L St., N.W., Suite 800, Washington, DC 20036; www.lcv.org. Advocacy group that reports on government officials' actions on environmental issues.

Natural Resources Defense Council, 40 West 20th St., New York, NY 10011; www.nrdc.org. Advocacy group that studies and acts on a wide range of environmental issues, with special focus on wildlife and wilderness areas.

Pew Center on Global Climate Change, 2101 Wilson Blvd., Suite 550, Arlington, VA 22201; (703) 516-4146; www.pewclimate.org. Funded by Pew Charitable Trusts.

Rainforest Action Network, 221 Pine St., 5th Floor, San Francisco, CA 94104; (415) 398-4404; www.ran.org. The activist group protests corporate practices that harm the environment and helps design pro-environment business practices.

Resources for the Future, 1616 P St., N.W., Washington, DC 20036; www.rff.org. Independent scholarly organization that analyzes energy, environment and natural-resources issues.

Rockefeller Philanthropy Advisors, 37 Madison Ave., 37th Floor, New York, NY 10022; (212) 812-4330; www.rockpa.org. Studies and offers advice about shareholder activism by nonprofit organizations.

Sierra Club, 85 Second St., Second Floor, San Francisco, CA 94105; www.sierraclub.org. Founded in 1892 to protect wilderness but now active on many environmental issues.

Social Investment Forum, 1612 K St., N.W., Suite 650, Washington, DC 20006; (202) 872-5319; www.socialinvest.org. The socially responsible investing industry's trade association.

Wal-Mart Sustainability, www.walmartfacts.com/featuredtopics/?id=1. Web site where Wal-Mart showcases its efforts to become environmentally friendly.

Worldwatch Institute, 1776 Massachusetts Ave., N.W., Washington, DC 20036; (202) 452-1999; www.worldwatch.org. Studies environmental and economic trends.

Bibliography

Selected Sources

Books

Bailey, Ronald, ed., *Global Warming and Other Eco Myths: How the Environmental Movement Uses False Science to Scare Us to Death*, Prima Publishing, 2002.
In this collection of essays the writers argue that many warnings about threats to the environment are way overblown.

Gore, Al, *An Inconvenient Truth: The Planetary Emergency of Global Warming and What We Can Do About It*, Rodale Books, 2006.
Former Vice President Al Gore urges action on global warming in this book written to accompany his surprisingly popular movie of the same name.

Savitz, Andrew W., and Karl Weber, *The Triple Bottom Line: How Today's Best-Run Companies Are Achieving Economic, Social and Environmental Success — and How You Can Too*, Jossey-Bass, 2006.
A business consultant and a freelance writer offer practical advice on how companies can profit from responding to environmental and other public needs.

Articles

Adler, Jerry, "Going Green," *Newsweek*, July 17, 2006, p. 42.
Adler looks at how individual Americans are taking action to protect the environment.

Gunther, Marc, "The Green Machine," *Fortune*, Aug. 7, 2006, p. 42.
Gunther reports on Wal-Mart's ambitious plans to become the world's greenest retailer and increase profits at the same time.

Holstein, William J., "Saving the Earth, And Saving Money," *The New York Times*, Aug. 13, 2006, p. 9.
Gwen Ruta, director of corporate partnerships for Environmental Defense, explains how her organization works with businesses.

Hymowitz, Carol, moderator, "Corporate Social Concerns: Are They Good Citizenship, Or a Rip-Off for Investors?" *The Wall Street Journal Online*, Dec. 6, 2005. Available online at http://online.wsj.com/public/article/SB113355105439712626.html?mod=todays_free_feature.
Debaters about corporations' environmental responsibility included Benjamin Heineman Jr., then senior vice president of GE; Ilyse Hogue, director of the Rainforest Action Network's Global Finance Campaign; and Fred Smith Jr., president and founder of the Competitive Enterprise Institute.

Pollan, Michael, "Mass Natural," *The New York Times*, June 4, 2006, p. 15.
Pollan fears Wal-Mart's plan to become an organic grocer and its massive purchasing power and lust for low prices will hurt organic farmers and consumers.

Schwartz, Peter, and Spencer Reiss, "Nuclear Now! How Clean, Green Atomic Energy Can Stop Global Warming," *Wired*, February 2005.
The authors argue that nuclear power can end global warming and the other environmental degradations associated with extracting and burning coal and oil.

Reports and Studies

Coal Based Generation Stakeholders Group, "A Vision for Achieving Ultra-Low Emissions from Coal-Fueled Electric Generation," January 2005; www.nma.org/pdf/coal_vision.pdf.
The coal industry and its customers tell how they plan to meet America's energy and environmental needs by cleaning up their acts.

Friends of the Earth, "Confronting Companies Using Shareholder Power: A Handbook on Socially-Oriented Shareholder Activism;" www.foe.org/camps/intl/corpacct/wallstreet/handbook/index.html.
The environmental organization urges corporate shareholders to press their companies to adopt environmentally friendly practices.

Hayward, Steven F., "Index of Leading Environmental Indicators 2006," American Enterprise Institute, 2006; www.aei.org/books/bookID.854/book_detail.asp.
The think tank's annual analysis of environmental statistics contends Earth is in much better shape than leading environmental organizations say.

National Association of Evangelicals, "For the Health of the Nation: An Evangelical Call to Civic Responsibility," Oct. 7, 2004; www.nae.net/images/civic_responsibility2.pdf.
Conservative religious leaders admonish believers that faith requires acting to relieve social ills and to protect the environment.

Price, Tom, "Activists in the Boardroom: How Advocacy Groups Seek to Shape Corporate Behavior," Foundation for Public Affairs, 2006.
The author examines how advocacy organizations influence companies' policies through both confrontation and cooperation.

Worldwatch Institute, *State of the World 2006: A Worldwatch Institute Report on Progress Toward a Sustainable Society*, W. W. Norton, 2006.
The environmental group reports on developments important to environmental protection and sustainability, including renewable alternatives to oil and the special challenges posed by rapid economic development in China and India.

The Next Step:

Additional Articles from Current Periodicals

Alternative Energy

Gross, Daniel, "The Dot-Com Energy Boost," *The Washington Post*, July 23, 2006, p. B2.
Former leaders of the dot-com boom are now working to transform the energy industry by starting alternative-energy firms.

Martin, Glen, "When Kitchen Waste Isn't Wasted," *The San Francisco Chronicle*, Oct. 25, 2006, p. B1.
Eight tons of scraps from San Francisco's trendiest restaurants will be turned into biogas.

Voss, Stephen, and Matthew Carr, "Agency Pushes Alternative Energy," *The Houston Chronicle*, Nov. 8, 2006, p. 3.
Developed nations must promote alternative-energy use to avoid excessive energy costs, environmental damage and future supply disruptions, according to the International Energy Agency.

Yi, Matthew, "Despite Prop. 87 Defeat, Funds Are Assured," *The San Francisco Chronicle*, Nov. 9, 2006, p. A20.
Venture capitalists will continue to invest in the alternative-energy industry despite the defeat of California's Proposition 87, which would have taxed oil produced in the state to fund alternative-energy research.

Global Warming

Deutsch, Claudia, "Global Warming Subject for Directors at Big Companies," *The New York Times*, Sept. 21, 2006, p. C2.
Environmentalists say if corporate executives really understood the threat of global warming they would encourage their companies to prevent it.

Merzer, Martin, "Global Warming May Not Be Force in Storms," *The Miami Herald*, July 28, 2006, p. A1.
Studies that suggest hurricanes are growing stronger because of global warming may be incorrect.

Neikirk, William, "British Try to Nudge U.S. on Climate Policy," *Chicago Tribune*, Oct. 31, 2006, p. C10.
If left unchecked, global warming will eventually devastate economic growth, according to a major British report.

Simon, Stephanie, "Religious Right Getting Greener," *The Seattle Times*, Oct. 20, 2006, p. A7.
Scores of evangelical leaders believe Earth is facing a crisis in global warming and that God expects Christians to act.

Woodyard, Chris, "Global Warming Suit Hits Carmakers," *USA Today*, Sept. 21, 2006, p. B1.
California's attorney general has sued the six biggest-selling automakers, alleging their products foster global warming.

Young, Samantha, "Schwarzenegger Signs Law to Curb Greenhouse Gases," *St. Louis Post-Dispatch*, Sept. 28, 2006, p. A8.
Gov. Arnold Schwarzenegger, R-Calif., signed a global-warming initiative into law that imposes the nation's first cap on greenhouse-gas emissions.

Green Business

Goldman, Abigail, "Wal-Mart Goes 'Green,' " *Los Angeles Times*, Nov. 13, 2006, p. C1.
Wal-Mart is experimenting with environmentally friendly products and store construction at its Supercenter in Aurora, Colo.

Rice-Oxley, Mark, "Never Mind Altruism: 'Saving the Earth' Can Mean Big Bucks," *The Christian Science Monitor*, Oct. 25, 2006, p. 4.
The green-business market could be worth $1 trillion over the next five years, according to oil giant Shell UK.

Rifkin, Glenn, "Making a Profit and a Difference," *The New York Times*, Oct. 5, 2006, p. C5.
Business networks promoting the concept that local businesses can be both profitable and environmentally conscious are springing up throughout the country.

Rosenwald, Mike S., "Showcasing the Growth of the Green Economy," *The Washington Post*, Oct. 16, 2006, p. D1.
Businesses exhibited their products at the Green Festival in Washington, D.C.

Taylor, Denise, "Naturally, Everything On Sale at This Shop is Green," *The Boston Globe*, Aug. 21, 2005, p. 1.
The Dunia Ecostore in Boston sells everything from natural nail polish and recycled glass jewelry to organic-cotton baby clothes and non-toxic doggie water bowls.

CITING *CQ RESEARCHER*

Sample formats for citing these reports in a bibliography include the ones listed below. Preferred styles and formats vary, so please check with your instructor or professor.

MLA STYLE

Jost, Kenneth. "Rethinking the Death Penalty." CQ Researcher 16 Nov. 2001: 945-68.

APA STYLE

Jost, K. (2001, November 16). Rethinking the death penalty. *CQ Researcher, 11*, 945-968.

CHICAGO STYLE

Jost, Kenneth. "Rethinking the Death Penalty." *CQ Researcher*, November 16, 2001, 945-968.

CQ Researcher

Published by CQ Press, a division of Congressional Quarterly Inc.

cqresearcher.com

Philanthropy in America

Are Americans generous givers?

Billionaire investor Warren Buffett has a message for wealthy Americans: Give away your money. Last June Buffett announced he was donating 85 percent of his $44 billion fortune, most of it earmarked for a charitable foundation established by Microsoft co-founder Bill Gates and his wife, Melinda. Although Americans donated more than $7 billion for hurricane, tsunami and earthquake relief in 2005, the super-rich, in general, have not stepped up their donations to match the economy's growth. Some in the philanthropy community argue, in fact, that Americans' self-image as uniquely generous is overblown. Meanwhile, the foundations that are a mainstay of U.S. philanthropy need more public oversight, critics say. And some scholars question whether charitable organizations are funding medical and other services that the government should provide.

A tuberculosis sufferer and double amputee in South Africa tells Microsoft co-founder Bill Gates and his wife Melinda about the treatments he receives. Disease prevention in the Third World is a key priority of the $31 billion Gates Foundation.

INSIDE THIS REPORT

CQ Researcher • Dec. 8, 2006 • www.cqresearcher.com
Volume 16, Number 43 • Pages 1009-1032

CQ PRESS

RECIPIENT OF SOCIETY OF PROFESSIONAL JOURNALISTS AWARD FOR EXCELLENCE ◆ AMERICAN BAR ASSOCIATION SILVER GAVEL AWARD

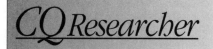

PHILANTHROPY IN AMERICA

Cover photograph: AP Photo/Sharon Farmer/Bill & Melinda Gates Foundation

Dec. 8, 2006
Volume 16, Number 43

MANAGING EDITOR: Thomas J. Colin

ASSISTANT MANAGING EDITOR: Kathy Koch

ASSOCIATE EDITOR: Kenneth Jost

STAFF WRITERS: Marcia Clemmitt, Peter Katel

CONTRIBUTING WRITERS: Rachel S. Cox, Sarah Glazer, Alan Greenblatt, Barbara Mantel, Patrick Marshall, Tom Price, Jennifer Weeks

DESIGN/PRODUCTION EDITOR: Olu B. Davis

ASSISTANT EDITOR: Melissa J. Hipolit

CQ PRESS

A Division of
Congressional Quarterly Inc.

SENIOR VICE PRESIDENT/PUBLISHER: John A. Jenkins

DIRECTOR, LIBRARY PUBLISHING: Kathryn C. Suárez

DIRECTOR, EDITORIAL OPERATIONS: Ann Davies

CONGRESSIONAL QUARTERLY INC.

CHAIRMAN: Paul C. Tash

VICE CHAIRMAN: Andrew P. Corty

PRESIDENT/EDITOR IN CHIEF: Robert W. Merry

CQ Researcher (ISSN 1056-2036) is printed on acid-free paper. Published weekly, except March 24, July 7, July 14, Aug. 4, Aug. 11, Nov. 24, Dec. 22 and Dec. 29, by CQ Press, a division of Congressional Quarterly Inc. Annual full-service subscriptions for institutions start at $667. For pricing, call 1-800-834-9020, ext. 1906. To purchase a *CQ Researcher* report in print or electronic format (PDF), visit www.cqpress.com or call 866-427-7737. Single reports start at $15. Bulk purchase discounts and electronic-rights licensing are also available. Periodicals postage paid at Washington, D.C., and additional mailing offices. POSTMASTER: Send address changes to *CQ Researcher*, 1255 22nd St., N.W., Suite 400, Washington, DC 20037.

Philanthropy in America

By Peter Katel

The Issues

In a world where wealth and conspicuous consumption often get big headlines, Warren Buffett's June 25 announcement made front pages around the world. Often called the world's second-richest man, the 76-year-old investment wizard from Omaha declared he would give away most of his $44 billion fortune.* And in keeping with his unassuming manner — he still lives in the same modest house he's been occupying for more than 40 years — he said most of the money would go to a foundation named for someone else. In fact, it's going to the vast foundation started by Microsoft co-founder Bill Gates and his wife Melinda.

Buffett, who has five children, pointedly rejected the standard rich man's practice of leaving most of his fortune to his family. "When your kids have all the advantages anyway . . . I would say it's neither right nor rational to be flooding them with money," he told *Fortune* magazine. . . . Dynastic mega-wealth would further tilt the playing field that we ought to be trying instead to level." [1]

AFP/Getty Images/Chris Kleponis

Billionaire investor Warren Buffett and his wife Susan arrive for a state dinner at the White House in February 2005. Buffett, who recently pledged to give away most of his $44 billion fortune, urges other wealthy Americans to more generously support philanthropic causes.

"Never in my career have I seen as much attention focused on philanthropy as in the two or three weeks after [Buffett's] announcement," says James A. Smith, a professor of philanthropy at Georgetown University's Public Policy Institute. "We had [the German newspaper] *Die Zeit*, here, and a film crew from Singapore."

Astounding as it was, Buffett's jaw-dropping donation was just the latest in a long line of recent mega-gifts, many from real-estate and high-tech billionaires. Many of the givers have been much younger than big donors of the past, like 19th-century steel magnate Andrew Carnegie. Even the 51-year-old Gates — who stoked his foundation with $21.8 billion — seems like an elder statesman next to improbably youthful billionaires like Google co-founders Sergey Brin and Larry Page — both 33 — whose philanthropic ventures include the $90-million Google Foundation. [2]

Still, many big givers today are older Americans like Buffett and currency trader George Soros, who specializes in political philanthropy. He has donated hundreds of millions of dollars beginning in the 1990s to pro-democracy and educational programs throughout the former Soviet bloc and poor countries (as well to justice-reform projects in the United States). Former President Bill Clinton — who turned 60 in August 2006 — got donors to pledge $2.5 billion last year to his foundation for programs to cut pollution and fight HIV/AIDS and other diseases. [3] On Nov. 30, Clinton announced that his foundation had persuaded anti-AIDS drugmakers to discount their prices by 45-60 percent to enable a new international consortium to treat 100,000 more children in 40 poor countries next year. In addition, Clinton and former President George H. W. Bush — who first teamed up to raise funds for tsunami relief efforts in Southeast Asia — raised $80 million after Hurricane Katrina for reconstruction projects in the U.S. Gulf Coast region. [4]

Last year U.S. corporations, foundations and individuals donated $260.3 billion — slightly below their all-time high of $260.5 billion at the height of the dot-com bubble in 2000. [5] Individuals gave $199 billion of the total. (*See graph, p. 1013.*) Although 67 percent of all American households give to charity, rich Americans have the biggest impact: Nine percent of households with incomes over $100,000

* Buffett structured his donation as a yearly gift of stock in his firm, Berkshire Hathaway Inc. The approximately $6 billion in shares not going to the Gates Foundation is being given to four philanthropic foundations that his children operate.

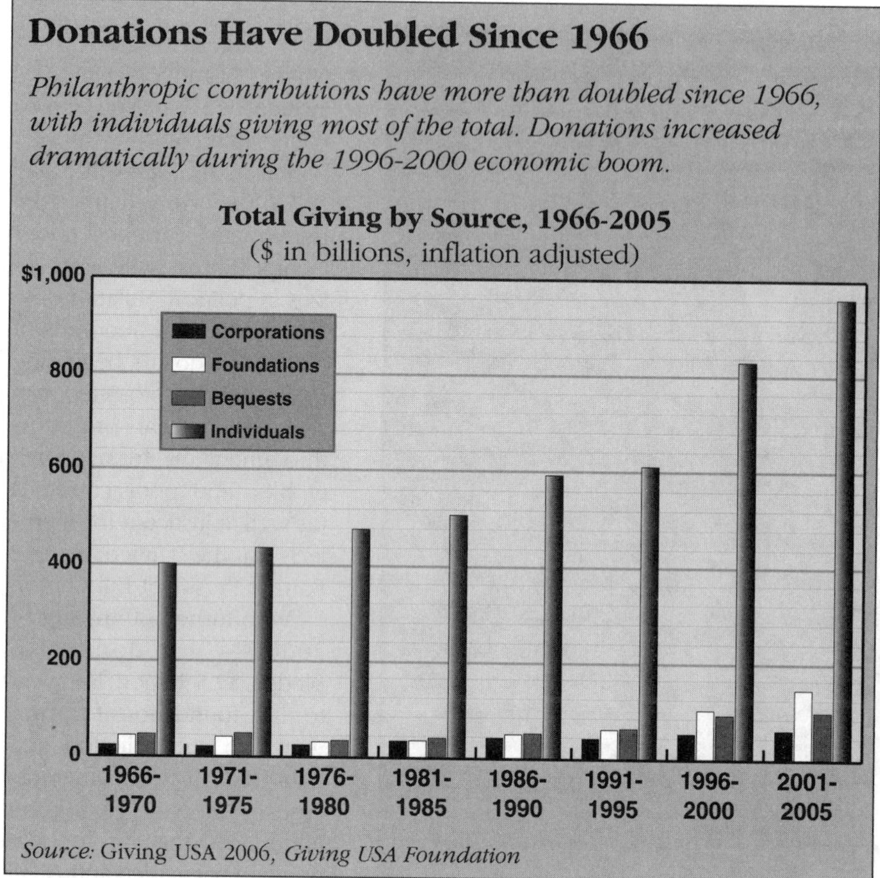

Donations Have Doubled Since 1966

Philanthropic contributions have more than doubled since 1966, with individuals giving most of the total. Donations increased dramatically during the 1996-2000 economic boom.

Source: Giving USA 2006, *Giving USA Foundation*

provided 43 percent of all charitable donations in 2003, according to the most recent data from the Giving USA Foundation. [6]

If donations following the tsunami, the India-Pakistan earthquake and Hurricanes Katrina, Rita and Wilma are excluded, however, charitable giving increased only nominally in 2005, from $245.22 billion to $252.99 billion — actually a 0.2 percent drop after adjusting for inflation. [7]

Viewed over the past 40 years, however, philanthropic contributions from Americans have soared. In 1965, total donations amounted to about $91 billion. Since then, inflation-adjusted donations have risen 185 percent.

Poor people who donate to charity give a greater percentage of their incomes than those in other income groups. That share runs as high as 4.7 percent for the poor (who favor religious causes) and no higher than 3.4 percent for the wealthy. But the better-off are more likely, as a group, to contribute in the first place. [8]

Historically, American philanthropy has compiled a record of achievement that no one disputes. Philanthropic foundations funded development of the Salk polio vaccine, drought- and plague-resistant strains of corn and wheat and modern medical-school curricula. Foundations also kept black colleges and universities alive throughout the Jim Crow era. [9]

"Individual American citizens have been for over 270 years the most generous people in the world — [particularly] to people we've never met," says Claire Gaudiani, a professor of philanthropic history at the George H. Heyman Jr. Center for Philanthropy and Fundraising at New York University and author of a book on American philanthropy. [10]

Philanthropy has woven itself so deeply into the fabric of American life that some observers, including many conservatives, say charities should provide many social services, instead of the government. But philanthropy's big players say charitable giving alone can't carry the ball.

"There's not a single problem that the Gates Foundation is confronting that we can solve with our own resources — or with our resources combined with those of other foundations," says Lowell Weiss, a senior program and advocacy officer at the foundation. "The problems we are confronting depend on [joint] government and private-sector participation."

Meanwhile, with Congress set to shift in January from Republican to Democratic control, some critics want the government to ratchet up its oversight to ensure that philanthropies are meeting their obligations to sponsor good works — and not underwriting high living by charity executives.

In recent years, the Senate Finance Committee under outgoing Chairman Charles E. Grassley, R-Iowa, has focused on exposing abuses by philanthropies and other nonprofit organizations. His Democratic successor, Sen. Max Baucus of Montana, is likely to take a different tack, says Steven Gunderson, president and CEO of the Council on Foundations. "I think Baucus will focus much more on the role of philanthropy in addressing social needs," Gunderson says.

Doubts about oversight of philanthropies intensified after 1995, when United Way Executive Director William Aramony was imprisoned for stealing from the organization. According to a recent poll, only 10 percent of Americans strongly agreed that charitable organizations handle donated money honestly and ethically. [11]

Many experts credit Americans' generosity to the U.S. tax system, which allows tax deductions for gifts. In additon, relatively low U.S. tax rates enable wealthy Americans to keep more of their money than people in higher-tax countries.

"Some other countries have higher tax rates, so some of the common good that we care for through philanthropy is cared for through the tax system," such as health care for all citizens, says Eugene Tempel, executive director of Indiana University's Center on Philanthropy.

By contrast, Americans in recent years have become increasingly interested in applying business principles and techniques to charitable giving. " 'Strategic philanthropy' is a term that's thrown around loosely," says Mark Kramer, founder of FSG-Social Impact Advisors, a nonprofit Boston consulting firm that advises foundations and governments on their projects and grants. "Increasingly, serious efforts are being made to be more accountable and to be able to demonstrate effectiveness." [12]

Modern philanthropists often cite the development of the New York public library system as a model of the public-private partnership. In 1901, retired steel baron Carnegie began paying for 39 free public libraries in New York City on the condition that the city government come up with operating funds. Carnegie eventually built 1,679 libraries nationwide — and many more worldwide. [13]

The self-made Scottish immigrant forged a philosophy of wealth that has guided Buffett and others. Carnegie argued that the rich owed a debt to society, and that paying it off demanded giving away much of what they had earned. The money should go to institutions and projects that give people at the bottom of the socioeconomic scale the chance to climb the ladder of success, he said.

"Man does not live by bread alone," Carnegie once wrote in explaining his support of libraries. . . . "There is no class so pitiably wretched as that which possesses money and nothing else."

Carnegie's philosophy lives on. In 1997, as he pledged $1 billion for U.N. human-services projects, CNN founder

Most Donations Come From Individuals

Individuals accounted for more than three-quarters of the $260 billion in U.S. charitable contributions in 2005 (top). Religious organizations received the largest share— more than a third of the total— followed by educational organizations (bottom).

Sources of Contributions, 2005 • Total: $260.3 billion
(in $ billions)

Bequests *$17.4 (6.7%)*
Individuals *$199.2 (76.5%)*
Foundations *$30.0 (11.5%)*
Corporations *$13.7 (5.3%)*

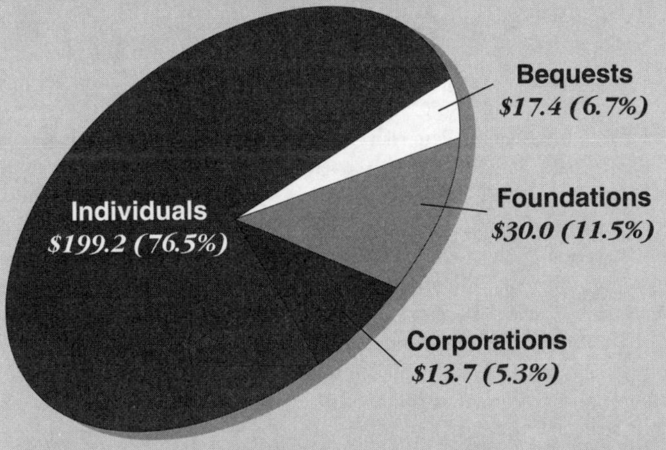

Recipients of Donations, by Type of Organization, 2005
Total: $260.3 billion
(in $ billions)

Foundations *$21.70 (8.3%)*
Other *$16.15 (6.2%)*
International affairs *$6.39 (2.5%)*
Environment and animals *$8.86 (3.4%)*
Religion *$93.18 (35.8%)*
Arts, culture and humanities *$13.51 (5.2%)*
Public/society benefit *$14.03 (5.4%)*
Human services *$25.36 (9.7%)*
Education *$38.56 (14.8%)*
Health *$22.54 (8.7%)*

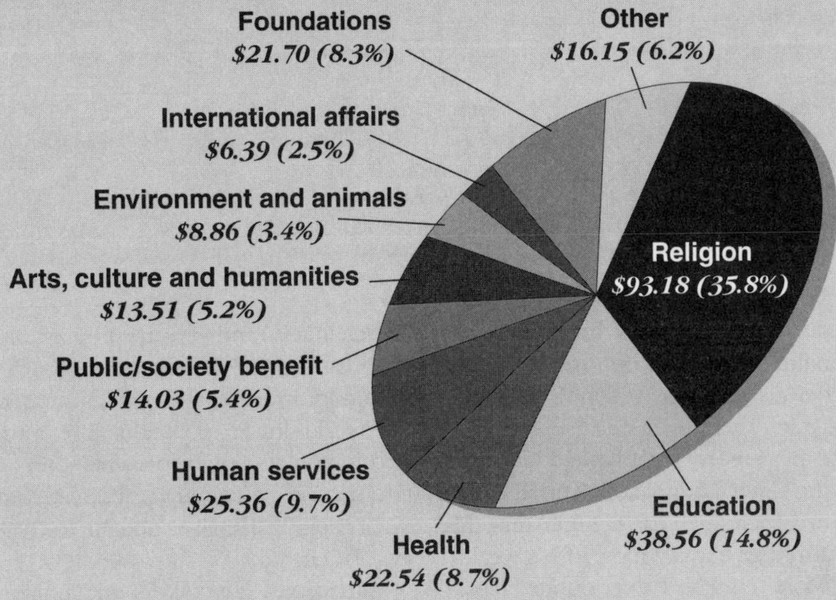

Note: Totals may not add to 100 percent due to rounding.

Source: Giving USA 2006, *Giving USA Foundation*

Watchdog Groups Spotlight Efficient Charities

Due diligence. That's the term used to describe the process of investigating the soundness of a company, typically before one buys or invests in it. In the business world, armies of analysts and shelves of publications offer just such determinations. Those wishing to give money to charity, however, have far less information to go on before writing their checks.

But resources do exist. Charity Navigator, a Mahwah, N.J.-based nonprofit, operates a free Web site designed to fill in some of the blanks. Executive Director Trent Stamp says his 11-person staff rates charities based on various criteria, including what percent of proceeds are spent on philanthropic work rather than administration and fundraising. The data all come from forms filed with the Internal Revenue Service (IRS).

"Our primary focus is as a donors' advocate," says Stamp. "Charities have their interest groups, charity recipients often have their interest groups and Congress has its groups, but there isn't anyone speaking for the rights of donors."

A similar organization, Ministry Watch, analyzes Christian charities. And the Better Business Bureau's Wise Giving Alliance gathers detailed information from hundreds of charities, granting seals of approval (for a fee) to organizations that meet its standards on finances and performance. More than 350 charities have earned the seal.

Unlike the Wise Giving Alliance, Charity Navigator does not seek information directly from the 5,000 organizations it evaluates. Relying solely on IRS data means not only that the same standards are applied to all charities, but that they are evaluated whether they welcome the scrutiny or not, Stamp says. "We want to keep an eye on people who don't necessarily want to participate in the process," he says.

The biweekly *Chronicle of Philanthropy* also keeps readers abreast of news about charities. And two organizations provide information on charities for a fee. Guidestar maintains a massive nonprofit database and a separate archive on charities. The American Institute of Philanthropy publishes a report on 500 charities.

Navigator began as the brainchild of philanthropists John and Marion Dugan, who found themselves stymied by a lack of data when searching for worthy charitable recipients. In 2001, the Dugans provided a start-up grant of $5 million to launch Navigator, which now receives money from foundations and corporate philanthropy programs at Cisco Systems Inc., and Tyco. [1]

However, using only financial data raises a question about whether charities that work to ensure efficient operations get unfairly downgraded for putting too much money into administration — a longstanding issue in the philanthropy world. "People want high-impact nonprofit organizations and no administrative costs," says Eugene Tempel, executive director of Indiana University's Center on Philanthropy. "They don't recognize that money needs to go into planning, administration and evaluation if you want effective programs."

Navigator tries to allow for reasonable administrative spending. It gives organizations a low score for "organizational efficiency" if they spend less than one-third of their budgets on services. These organizations "are simply not living up to their missions," the site says. Seven in 10 charities on the Navigator list spend at least 75 percent of their budgets on programs, and nine in 10 spend at least 65 percent. [2]

A former vice president of Teach for America, which recruits new college graduates to teach in poor neighborhoods and rural areas, Stamp has become a member of the philanthropy community's small corps of in-house critics. In a recent posting on his blog, he cites a recent survey showing declining public confidence in charities. [3]

"It's anything but surprising," he writes. "We're one Enron-like scandal away from an entire generation of donors taking their money and going home. As a sector, we can embrace these findings and push for real reforms in an effort to restore public trust, or we can stick our heads in the sand and hope it goes away."

[1] For background, see Robert Barker, "Charity Begins with a Fiscal Check-up," *BusinessWeek online*, Nov. 11, 2002, www.businessweek.com/magazine/content/02_45/b3807134.htm.

[2] Quoted in "Our Ratings Tables," Charity Navigator, undated, www.charitynavigator.org/index.cfm/bay/content.view/catid/2/cpid/48.htm.

[3] Trent Stamp, "Some Tasty Tidbits," Trent Stamp's Take [blog], Nov. 22, 2006, http://trentstamp.blogspot.com.

Ted Turner exhorted his fellow billionaires to strive to be America's most generous citizens. And he's been haranguing them ever since. Before Buffett announced his planned donation to the Gates Foundation, Turner called him a "Scrooge" for waiting until his death to give away most of his wealth.

More recently, Turner dubbed fellow communications tycoon Rupert Murdoch a tightwad. The chairman and CEO of News Corp. (holdings include the Fox TV channels and Twentieth Century Fox) has agreed to help finance a $3 million program to help cities around the world lower pollution. But Murdoch's contribution represents only a tiny fraction of his assets, estimated at $7.7 billion. [14] "He gives nothing to charity," Turner said. [15]

As citizens, lawmakers and philanthropists consider the role of charitable giving, here are some of the questions being asked:

Are Americans more generous than citizens of other countries?

The charitable impulse knows no borders. It is encouraged by virtually all the world's religions and predates the founding of the United States by millennia. Still, Americans tend to believe they are more generous than people in other countries.

Americans indeed are No. 1 in giving when charitable donations alone are considered. But when the value of volunteered work and cash and property gifts are calculated together, the United States ranks below the Netherlands and Sweden. (*See chart, p. 1016.*) In the Netherlands, the combined value of donated time and money amounted to 4.95 percent of gross domestic product (GDP) in 1995-2002. Sweden stood at 4.41 percent of GDP vs. the United States at 3.94 percent. [16]

Catholic Charities USA/Frank Methe

Catholic Charities volunteers clean out flooded houses in New Orleans after Hurricane Katrina. Thousands of volunteers flocked to the city to help, and Americans donated more than $5 billion for hurricane relief on the Gulf Coast in 2005.

Despite the universality of charitable giving, some scholars of philanthropy and members of the charity community point both to donations and to America's unparalleled record of philanthropically financed scientific and educational achievements to conclude that nowhere else has philanthropy been so widespread and so successful.

"We're by far the most charitable country on Earth," says Adam Meyerson, president of the Philanthropy Roundtable and former vice president for educational affairs at the conservative Heritage Foundation.

"We have a can-do spirit, a conviction that individuals can and should make a difference, a long tradition of neighbor helping neighbor, of not looking to government or the local nobleman to look out for us. That's part of why charity and philanthropy have been such a big part of the American experience."

But Pablo Eisenberg, a fellow at Georgetown University's Public Policy Institute, rejects that view. "A lot of it is myth," he says, arguing that Americans' philanthropy grows less out of their inherent generosity than out of the U.S. tax system. "Take away the tax deduction, and how much will people give, especially major donors? I'm willing to bet they wouldn't give half of what they give now. I agree it's probably good to have that incentive, but let's admit it's the incentive and not just the generosity."

But Meyerson points out that Carnegie, oilman John D. Rockefeller and the other pioneers of big-scale American philanthropy took up their roles before the advent of income-tax deductions for charitable contributions, in 1917; tax deductions for corporations' philanthropic donations were allowed in 1935.

"Massachusetts General Hospital, the Chicago Symphony, Stanford University — all of these great institutions of American life were started in the 19th century, before there were charitable tax incentives," says Meyerson.

Still, Eisenberg asks, how much philanthropy actually benefits the needy — as opposed to the well-endowed universities where the donors graduated? "The overwhelming number gave to universities, colleges, medical schools and hospitals," he says, citing surveys by *The Chronicle of Philanthropy* and Indiana University's Center on Philanthropy of major American donors. "They give to those institutions they know well, which saved their mother, which educated their kids and maybe an environmental group or two and cultural organizations that they know."

Some experts point out that comparisons between educational philanthropy in the United States and other societies often fail to account for the fact that other governments provide many educational services for which Americans must rely on themselves, financial aid or charity. In Western Europe, for instance, university education and health care are financed by much higher taxes than Americans pay — and cover all citizens.

"When you look at those types of things, the need for private philanthropy is quite different," says economist Patrick Rooney, research director at the Center on Philanthropy at Indiana University. "In Germany, even religion is financed through taxation. This is a whole different economy and set of values. While it's important to celebrate the generosity of Americans, we need to not get the horse riding too fast — this horse of righteous morality."

In fact, author Gaudiani argues that Europe's system of virtually free public universities loses much of its appeal on closer examination. The kinds of elementary and high schools available to low-income students in Europe do not prepare them for top-flight universities as well as the schools attended by wealthier students, says Gaudiani, who headed Connecticut College from 1988 to 2001.

Dutch Donate the Most to Charity

The Dutch give the most to philanthropic pursuits as a share of their country's gross domestic product (GDP), mostly in the form of volunteering. Americans donate the most cash and other property gifts.

Top 10 Countries in Philanthropy
(As a percentage of GDP, 1995-2002)

Country	All Private Philanthropy (volunteering and giving)	Country	Private Giving (cash and property gifts)
The Netherlands	4.95%	United States	1.85%
Sweden*	4.41	Israel	1.34
United States	3.94	Canada	1.17
Tanzania	3.78	Argentina	1.09
United Kingdom	3.70	Spain*	0.87
Norway	3.42	Ireland	0.85
France	3.21	United Kingdom	0.84
Germany	2.56	Uganda	0.65
Finland	2.43	Hungary	0.63
Canada	2.40	Tanzania	0.61

** Data on volunteering/giving to religious worship organizations not available.*

Source: Johns Hopkins Comparative Nonprofit Sector Project

Philanthropy scholars say that data on donations can provide material to both sides in the comparative-generosity debate. "When you look at [U.S.] giving as a share of GDP or national income, I'm struck by how stable it is — around 2 percent," says Smith of Georgetown's Public Policy Institute. "The fact that it hasn't moved would suggest we're not growing more generous."

But another conclusion is possible, says Smith, noting that the percentage of giving didn't drop following tax cuts the Bush administration pushed through Congress. Theoretically, as the tax obligations of rich people drop, they have less incentive to shelter earnings with tax-deductible contributions. "That would mean that we have sustained our levels of generosity even as the incentives for remaining generous have dropped," Smith says.

Do increases in private philanthropy lead to cuts in government funding for social programs?

A left-right divide underlies the debate on whether government or private charity is the best provider of social services. The conservative view that helping the unfortunate is a duty of charities — not government — has deep roots in American political culture.

For instance, when the Great Depression began to sweep the country, President Herbert Hoover declared that philanthropies — not the government — should relieve Americans' suffering. However, his hands-off policy wilted in the face of massive unemployment and hunger.

Franklin D. Roosevelt, Hoover's successor, reversed his policy. Roosevelt's New Deal became the liberals' rallying cry, with the government establishing employment and welfare programs ranging from the Civilian Conservation Corps to the Social Security system.

Now that memories of the Depression have faded and philanthropy is booming, the debate over government services vs. charity has revived. For conservatives, the billions of dollars pouring into philanthropies strengthen the case for shifting much of the burden of providing social services to charitable organizations.

President Bush has long insisted that faith-based organizations and charities do a better job of helping the needy than government-provided services. "Governments can hand out money," he told the first White House Conference on Faith-Based and Community Initiatives in 2004, "but governments cannot put love in a person's heart, or a sense of purpose in a person's life." [17]

Consistent with that view, Bush has pushed for cutting funding to such traditional anti-poverty programs as Medicaid, housing vouchers for low-income renters and community-development block grants. [18] He also called for eliminating a $93.5 million education program designed to promote small classes ("learning communities") in large high schools.

Rick Cohen, former director of the National Committee for Responsive Philanthropy, says the administration's main justification was that some major philanthropies had become active in the small-class movement. The administration's budget document said: "Non-federal funds for such purposes has [sic] become readily available through the Carnegie Corporation of New York and the Bill & Melinda Gates Foundation." [19]

Cohen, who now writes for *Nonprofit Quarterly*, argues that the administration overstates the level of service charities and other nonprofits can provide. "The reality is that they can supplement some of what government does, but shouldn't substitute for government," he says.

Some conservative philanthropy experts acknowledge that asking private organizations to replace the government is out of the question — for now. "At the moment," says Meyerson, of the Philanthropy Roundtable, "the philanthropic infrastructure is not there to replace large parts of what government currently does."

Along with other conservatives, he takes a long view and advocates a wide-ranging discussion on whether the federal government should end — or reduce its role in — such social services as providing legal representation for people without adequate funds and health care for the uninsured. The Federal Emergency Management Agency's (FEMA) monumentally botched response to Hurricane Katrina indicates that government services can be overrated, Meyerson says. "We can't say FEMA has been doing a distinguished job." [20]

Other voices in the nonprofit world, however, argue that so-called small-government conservatives disregard the fact that the federal government helps pay nonprofits to provide the services they offer. Although nonprofits get an average of 20 percent of their funding from private and corporate donations, about 31 percent comes from government, says Diana Aviv, executive director of Independent Sector, an alliance of charities, foundations and corporate philanthropy programs. Dues and fees provide most of the rest of nonprofit funding.

"We would need many, many Warren Buffets before we came near to the 31 percent of the nonprofit-sector budget that government funding supports," she says.

In fact, says Leslie Lenkowsky, director of graduate studies at Indiana University's Center on Philanthropy, ever since the Reagan administration the government has been pouring a growing amount of money into nonprofits because they deliver services more cheaply than the government.

Lenkowsky, a former CEO of the Corporation for National and Community Service, which encourages volunteerism, argues that liberals are more worried that federal funding of nonprofits increasingly takes the form of vouchers to service recipients, rather than grants to service providers. [21]

"When I get a Pell Grant" for higher education, Lenkowsky says, "I don't have to take it to the Ivy League, I can take it to a for-profit university; just as I can pick the hospital or day-care center I like. There's more competition, which means more uncertainty" for nonprofits. In the past, he says, many had mastered the bureaucracy of getting grants, hence assuring their organizations a secure existence.

Should Congress get tougher on charities?

A series of scandals that began in the mid-1990s focused attention on the almost complete lack of state and federal oversight of spending by philanthropic organizations. More recently, the *Los Angeles Times* in 2005 disclosed unusually high-end salaries, perks and insider deals at the J. Paul Getty Trust, considered one of the world's richest arts organizations.

"Charities shouldn't be funding their executives' gold-plated lifestyles," said Senate Finance Committee Chairman Grassley, as his panel prepared to consider reining in such spending. [22]

Some restrictions were eventually enacted in the Pension Protection Act of 2006, which doubles to $20,000 the amount foundation managers can be fined for "self-dealing" — making property deals or other advantageous arrangements with board or staff members and their relatives. The penalty would also double to 30 percent of the amount of money that foundations failed to distribute in grants, if the foundations didn't meet a requirement to distribute at least 5 percent of their assets each year. [23]

The legislation left intact, however, an IRS exemption allowing payments to foundation insiders who provide "reasonable and necessary" foundation work, such as investment advice. [24] Eisenberg of Georgetown University's Public Policy Institute says the exception effectively permits big fees to trustees for fundraising, investment guidance and legal work.

"One simple regulation — no self-dealing and no exceptions to self-dealing — would kill 100 percent of that," says Eisenberg, a former director of the foundation-supported anti-poverty organization, Center for Community Change, and a co-founder of the National Committee for Responsive Philanthropy.

At Georgetown Eisenberg directed a 2003 study of payments to trustees at large and small foundations. Researchers found that the 238 foundations surveyed paid insiders $44 million in 1998 (then the most recent year for which full records were available) for board membership and professional services. "The self-dealing provisions in IRS regulations have neither been a deterrent to large trustee fees nor served adequately as a tool by which to punish foundations and trustees guilty of providing excessive compensation," the report concluded. [25]

Tempel of Indiana University acknowledges that the Getty Trust scandal raises questions about how well some foundation boards run their organizations. "There may be other cases like that out there that we don't know about," he says. But Tempel believes — as do most foundation managers — that no new laws or regulations are needed. "There are regulations on the books that could use better enforcement, but there are few resources at the IRS to enforce them."

But philanthropy-community watchdogs say the present regulatory structure is nowhere near adequate. For one thing, says Trent Stamp, executive director of Charity Navigator, a New Jersey-based nonprofit that helps donors select charities, existing law delegates considerable enforcement authority to states, but many of today's philanthropies cross state lines.

"We are continuing to regulate nonprofits in a way that might have worked in 1954," he says, "but nonprofits are a big business that they weren't in 1954." And while the Securities and Exchange Commission (SEC) oversees for-profit organizations, he explained, influential nonprofit boards of directors investing billions of dollars in the stock market represent "a parallel universe that we are not paying attention to."

Stamp, in fact, advocates establishing an SEC counterpart to oversee the entire nonprofit sector. Short of that, philanthropies should have to justify keeping their tax-exempt status, he argues. "The IRS gives out tax-exempt status and doesn't see those charities ever again," except in a handful of cases, he says.

Lenkowsky agrees that the IRS only "lightly" keeps an eye on organizations to ensure that they still adhere to the standards for tax exemption. But he and others in the philanthropy community argue that stepped-up government oversight would cause more problems than it would solve.

"Let's get the nonprofit sector to take responsibility for its own behavior and to set its own standards," says Joel Fleishman, director of the Samuel and Ronnie Heyman Center for Ethics, Public Policy and the Professions at Duke University. "We don't need new legislation."

While Fleishman concedes that no amount of self-regulation can deal with willful violations of the law, he thinks nonprofit organizations themselves can deal with "inadvertent actions that amount to something less than the willful intention to defraud," such as excessive or improper compensation, or perks. ■

BACKGROUND

Biblical Roots

Since ancient times, charity has stood as a pillar of Judaism, Christianity and Islam. *The Book of Deuteronomy* (Deut. 26:12) instructs the faithful to tithe — donate 10 percent of their earnings — "to the stranger, to the fatherless, and to the widow, that they may eat within thy gates, and be satisfied." In the *New Testament*, Jesus tells his followers: "Sell that ye have, and give alms" (Luke 12:33). Every Muslim who can afford it is obligated to make a donation — the *zakat* — to charity. Islam's holy book, the *Koran*, tells the faithful: "Devote yourself to prayer [and] pay the *zakat*." (2:43). Countless Web sites help Muslims calculate what they should pay, depending on their occupations, incomes and assets.

In the United States, some wealthy early Americans embraced the admonition to share their wealth. In 1847, when businessman and former U.S. congressman Abbott Lawrence donated $50,000 to Harvard College, his brother Amos, a merchant and industrialist, told him his gift "enriches your descendants in a way that mere money never can do and is a better investment than any you have ever made." [26] Similarly, said 19th-century educator Horace Mann, inheriting a fortune saps "the muscles out of the limbs, the brain out of the head and virtue out of the heart." [27]

Charitable giving in the nation's early years was linked to helping to cure society's ills. For instance, activists collected donations from philanthropists to build reformatories for children being held in adult prisons. The first was the New York House of Refuge, built in 1825. Philadelphia and Boston soon followed suit, with a prominent Bostonian, Theodore Lyman, donating nearly $75,000 to build the first state reformatory, in Westborough.

Abolitionist ministers raised money to send escaped slaves to Canada, and some wealthy foes of slavery helped anti-slavery settlers move to Kansas in the early 1850s so they could vote against expansion of human bondage to the Western frontier.

The Civil War further spurred the growth of charities, as hundreds of noncombatants on both sides of the conflict formed organizations offering hospitality or medical care for soldiers and their families. Clara Barton, who went on to found the American Red Cross, began her public-health career tending to the war's wounded. But it was in the post-war era of vast industrial expansion that modern American philanthropy flowered. By the 1880s, railroads, steelworks and automated manufacturing were transforming American society — and creating enormous fortunes. Between the 1870s and 1916, the number of millionaires in America exploded from 100 to about 40,000. [28]

Carnegie helped lead the transition from charity to philanthropy, with its more ambitious goals than just helping the poor on an individual basis. As a young Scottish immigrant, the young Carnegie began work in the United States as a bobbin boy in a textile factory. He later gave away $350 million for projects aimed at helping people help themselves and at raising professional standards in various fields. In addition to building public libraries throughout the United States, he created a new medical-education system and established a pension system for college professors that spurred the development of pensions throughout the economy.

Carnegie also advocated taxing wealth, in part because it would encourage the wealthy to make big donations rather than see their assets taxed away. The wealthy should set an example of "unostentatious living," Carnegie argued. "The man who dies leaving behind him millions of available wealth, which was his to administer during life, will pass away 'unwept, unhonored, and unsung,' " he wrote. "Of such as these the public verdict will then be: 'The man who dies thus rich dies disgraced.' " [29]

The scale of the fortunes accumulated by the likes of Carnegie, Rockefeller and banker Andrew Mellon and others made plain that they couldn't simply give away money without a

Continued on p. 1020

Chronology

Early 1900s

Americans' charitable contributions expand after onset of Industrial Age.

1889
Steel tycoon Andrew Carnegie preaches that dying immensely wealthy is disgraceful.

1901
Oil magnate John D. Rockefeller suggests fellow millionaires establish foundations to ensure effectiveness of their donations.

1902-1931
Many of America's wealthiest citizens establish foundations.

1910
The Carnegie Foundation for the Advancement of Teaching publishes *Medical Education in the United States and Canada*, which transforms medical curriculum.

1913
Rockefeller Foundation established.

1932-1969

During the Great Depression, President Franklin D. Roosevelt establishes an active social role for government.

1949
President Harry S Truman declares a worldwide campaign against poverty.

1956
American philanthropies spend $535 million — 8 percent of all charitable spending — on foreign projects.

1968
Foundations direct nearly 20 percent of their grants to fight poverty and improve race relations.

1970s-1980s

Philanthropies are challenged to take over social programs.

Aug. 1, 1971
Ex-Beatle George Harrison mounts "Concert for Bangladesh" in New York's Madison Square Garden.

1973-74
Study of the nonprofit sector counts 6 million organizations receiving a total of $25 billion in donations and $23 billion in government funding.

1981
President Ronald Reagan urges more "voluntarism" and less government.

1985
Since Reagan became president, nonprofits have lost $30 billion in government funding.

1989
President George H. W. Bush declares that private charities, rather than government, should step up social-service work.

1990s

The dot-com boom fosters the first philanthropic ventures by a new class of young millionaires.

1992
Microsoft co-founder Bill Gates donates $12 million to the University of Washington.

1996
Billionaire financier George Soros pledges $100 million to set up Internet connections for regional Russian universities — part of hundreds of millions of dollars in democracy-building projects in the former Soviet Union and elsewhere.

1997
Desktop-publishing tycoon Paul Brainerd founds Social Venture Partners as a grant-making vehicle for himself and fellow high-tech success stories. . . . CNN founder Ted Turner commits $1 billion to the United Nations and challenges other billionaires to give their fortunes away.

1999-2000s

Bill Gates, Warren Buffett and Bill Clinton energize big-league philanthropy; newspaper exposés reveal foundation abuses.

1999
Bill and Melinda Gates kick their foundation into higher gear with a $6 billion contribution.

2001
Turner pledges $50 million to eradicate weapons of mass destruction.

2003
Newspapers in Massachusetts and California expose insider deals and lavish spending at some foundations.

2004
ebay founder Pierre Omidyar sets up a philanthropy dedicated to both nonprofit and for-profit ventures.

2005
Natural disasters in Asia and the U.S. Gulf Coast generate more than $7 billion in charitable donations.

June 25, 2006
Buffett announces he will give away 85 percent of his $44 billion fortune.

In Poor Nations, 'Philanthropy' Is Cost of Doing Business

In Kazakhstan Chevron Corp. spent $35 million last year to help build 430 new houses and a school for families displaced by expansion of the vast Tengiz oil field. [1]

In Nigeria's oil-rich Niger Delta, a Chevron-operated riverboat clinic provides free health care to 2,500 patients a month along the Benin and Escravos rivers.

In oil-rich Venezuela and Angola, Chevron is working with the Discovery Channel to install televisions, VCRs and satellite dishes in isolated rural classrooms and teach educators how to incorporate educational video programming into their curricula.

U.S.-based Chevron may be in the oil business, but last year it spent $73 million on social projects in many of the 180 countries where it operates. As part of the company's corporate-philanthropy arm, the projects are designed to create long-term, sustainable programs that serve specific local needs — indirectly benefiting the company's bottom line in the process. [2]

Stimulating economic growth and enabling communities to prosper "is fundamental to the broader success we seek to achieve as a business," says the company's annual Social Responsibility report. [3] For example, in HIV/AIDS-ravaged countries — including South Africa, Nigeria and Angola — the company runs voluntary testing, counseling and treatment programs for employees and their families, as well as awareness programs for the broader communities. [4]

"It's not being done for the intrinsic good that these programs bring, but to support our business goals and operations," says Chevron spokesman Alex Yelland. "We rely on a large, healthy employment pool, and a policy that supports our business operations, as well as being for the good of all, is helpful."

However, corporate philanthropy today is not only designed to achieve social benefits that indirectly benefit companies' bottom lines. Some charitable programs end up as investment opportunities. "There are actually business opportunities developing around social issues," says Mark Kramer, managing director of FSG-Social Impact Advisors, a Boston-based consulting firm for nonprofits. "You're beginning to see the merging of economic and social interests."

Microfinance projects — in which as little as a few dollars are loaned to very poor people to start or expand businesses — are a prime example, he says. Devised in 1976 by Bangladeshi economist Muhammad Yunus, microfinancing originated as a purely philanthropic enterprise, though it was designed to be self-supporting through interest payments. Then it attracted the attention — and dollars — of conventional investors. Citigroup set up a microfinance pilot program in Hyderabad, India, and the Netherlands-based venture-capital firm Goodwell has raised $10 million to invest in Indian microfinance operations. [5]

Continued from p. 1018

plan and hope to achieve meaningful results. "Let us erect a foundation, a trust, and engage directors who will make it a life work to manage, with our personal co-operation, this business of benevolence properly and effectively," said Rockefeller, the founder of the Standard Oil Co., in 1901. [30]

Many of the foundations created in the years immediately following Rockefeller's call are still operating today, including the Rockefeller Foundation, Rockefeller Institute for Medical Research (which later became Rockefeller University), the Carnegie Foundation for the Advancement of Teaching, Carnegie Endowment for International Peace and the Russell Sage Foundation.

New Directions

During the Great Depression, the Rockefeller Foundation and other big charitable organizations had limited success in preventing the ravages of unemployment and its ripple effects on health, housing and education.

President Hoover, who had built and directed pioneering famine-relief projects in post-World War I Western Europe and Russia, tried to enlist philanthropies in fighting the Depression's effects. In 1931, Hoover reminded Americans of the "God-imposed individual responsibility of the individual man and woman to their neighbors." [31]

In 1933 Roosevelt took office as president with a radically different agenda. Roosevelt believed the government should sustain unemployed workers "not as a matter of charity but as a matter of social duty." Under the New Deal forged during his presidency, government took responsibility for ensuring that the basic needs of citizens were met, effectively freeing philanthropies to pursue more far-reaching objectives. [32]

Although philanthropies had long worked hand in hand with the government, that relationship deepened during and after World War II, as American philanthropy became, in effect, an arm of U.S. foreign policy. In his inaugural speech on Jan. 20, 1949, President Harry S Truman declared a worldwide campaign against poverty in which the United States would furnish technical assistance and capital investment.

By 1956, U.S. donations for foreign philanthropic projects amounted to $535 million, or 8 percent of U.S. charitable spending. The Rockefeller and Ford foundations were especially active in international programs, along with religious organizations, such as the American Friends Service Committee, Church World Service and Catholic Relief Services.

Cooperation between the government and philanthropic organizations grew closer on the domestic front as well. In 1968, during the height of the civil-rights struggle, about 18 percent

It's all part of a philanthropy-business synthesis that as been emerging for years, says Kramer. In 2002, he co-authored an article with Harvard Business School Professor Michael Porter arguing that the traditional distinction between the profit motive and philanthropy was disappearing. "There is no inherent contradiction between improving competitive context and making a sincere commitment to bettering society," they wrote. "Improving education, for example, is generally seen as a social issue, but the educational level of the local work force substantially affects a company's potential competitiveness. The more a social improvement relates to a company's business, the more it leads to economic benefits as well." [6]

Apple Computer, for instance, has been donating computers to U.S. schools for years — a practice that helped them introduce new generations of users to Apple products, they pointed out. [7]

In a new wrinkle, however, partly to appease critics who claim their countries' resources are being pillaged, some developing countries have begun demanding that foreign companies — especially oil and mining companies — pay so-called "social bonuses" as a prerequisite to doing business. For instance, in 2004 the Angolan government sought and received a promise of $80 million from Chevron for school construction and other development projects if it wanted its lease extended on an offshore oil field. [8]

Chevron considers such bonuses as business expenses, not part of the company's philanthropic endeavors. "If you want to operate in Angola as an extractive industry, a 'social bonus' is going to be part and parcel of doing business," says Yelland.

---

1 For more details, see "Corporate Responsibility Report 2005," Chevron Corp., [undated], p. 17, http://chevron.com/cr_report/2005.

2 *Ibid.*, pp. 16-17, 3. For background, see Kathy Koch, "The New Corporate Philanthropy," *CQ Researcher*, Feb. 27, 1998, pp. 169-192.

3 *Ibid.*, p. 16.

4 For the complete policy, see "Policy 260, HIV/AIDS," 2005, http://chevron.com/social_responsibility/hiv_aids/docs/policy_260.pdf.

5 Yunus received a Nobel Prize this year for his creation of the microfinance model. For details, see "A Short History," Grameen Bank, www.grameen-info.org/bank/hist.html. For more on conventional investment in microfinance see Amy Yee, "A serious business not charity," *Financial Times* [London], Nov. 15, 2006, p. 12.

6 Michael E. Porter and Mark R. Kramer, "The Competitive Advantage of Corporate Philanthropy," *Harvard Business Review*, December 2002, p. 56.

7 *Ibid.*

8 For background on the Angola production deal, see "ChevronTexaco Awarded Extension of Block O Concession in Angola," press release, May 13, 2004, www.chevron.com/news/press/2004/2004-05-13.asp; "Angola Fact Sheet," Chevron Corp., updated November, 2006, http://chevron.com/operations/docs/angola.pdf. Also see John Reed, "A peace dividend is elusive as Angola embraces 'petro-diamond capitalism,' " *Financial Times* [London], Nov. 14, 2005, p. 15.

of foundation grants were going to programs aimed at poverty, race relations and urban problems. The Great Society programs of President Lyndon B. Johnson began channeling government funds to community social-service programs, including Community Action Boards in various cities. Money was being spent so fast that many wondered whether government money was undermining philanthropic independence and initiative.

Also in 1968, the Ford Foundation announced that it would invest part of its assets in minority-owned businesses and in low-income and racially integrated housing. "Never in the history of American philanthropy had anything comparable in scale and aggressiveness to the Ford Foundation's assault on the problem of race and poverty been seen," wrote Waldemar A. Nielsen, a philanthropy scholar and former Ford Foundation staffer. [33]

Rockers and Volunteers

The conservative era that began with President Ronald Reagan's election in 1980 fostered a view of the relationship between philanthropy and government different from the partnerships of the 1960s and '70s that grew out of the 1930s New Deal.

"Voluntarism is an essential part of our plan to give the government back to the people," Reagan said in 1981. [34]

Reagan wanted to cut back government social-service programs and let philanthropies pick up the slack. Indeed, Reagan's first budget included deep cuts in child welfare, day care, nutrition for the elderly, services for the mentally ill and developmentally disabled, food stamps, school lunches and aid to poor people with high energy bills.

But the notion that nonprofit organizations could fill the resulting gaps in services proved misguided, because the private groups depended heavily on government funding. In 1981-85 alone, nonprofit service providers' government receipts declined by $30 billion due to the Reagan budget cuts.

His successor, President George H. W. Bush, also thought that charities were better at helping the poor, the ill and the disabled. "The old solution, the old way, was to think that public money alone could end these problems," Bush said in his 1989 inaugural address. "We will turn to the only resource we have that in times of need always grows — the goodness and the courage of the American people.

"I have spoken of a thousand points of light, of all the community organizations that are spread like stars throughout the nation, doing good," he continued. "We will work hand in hand, encouraging, sometimes leading, sometimes being led, rewarding." [35]

Celebrities who support charitable efforts today are following in the footsteps of earlier entertainers, such as silent-film stars Douglas Fairbanks and Mary Pickford, who promoted the Red Cross during World War I. But new generations of music and movie stars have opted for somewhat deeper involvement.

In 1971, former Beatles lead guitarist George Harrison sparked the new age of celebrity involvement in campaigns against poverty and disease in poor nations when he organized the Concert for Bangladesh to benefit victims of flooding, famine and warfare in the newly independent nation. [36]

A long line of music and film stars have followed Harrison's example. In 1984 Irish rocker Bob Geldof recruited famous singers to help him record a song he'd co-written, "Do They Know It's Christmas?" — raising $10 million for famine relief in Ethiopia. The following summer, he organized "Live Aid" concerts in London and Philadelphia, which were televised worldwide and raised $80 million in pledges, also destined for Ethiopia. [37]

Also in 1985, singer Harry Belafonte used Geldof's model to assemble an all-star cast to record "We Are the World," a song written by Michael Jackson and Lionel Richie to raise funds for famine and hunger relief in Africa. The project drew in more than $40 million. [38]

More recently, Bono, frontman for the Irish band U2, has taken a different approach: Using his celebrity to focus public and government attention on poverty in Africa. Bono organized the "Live 8" concerts in Philadelphia and London last year, timed to coincide with a meeting of leaders of the G-8 — the world's eight industrial powers — to discuss aid to Africa and champion debt relief and effective aid in Africa. He also touts the work of Columbia University development-aid guru Jeffrey Sachs, who argues that ending deep poverty is a realistic worldwide goal.

Although Bono focuses more on encouraging foreign aid than individual philanthropy, his mastery of development issues and relentless lobbying of politicians and international institutions such as the World Bank have won him respect not usually accorded to entertainers who take up social causes. A new philanthropic venture shows that he has embraced the trend of business-savvy charity. The singer helped devise a multi-brand campaign in which Apple Computer, The Gap, Nike and American Express sell red-colored products (a red leather jacket from The Gap, for instance) and donate part of the revenue to projects fighting AIDS, malaria and other illnesses. [39]

Billionaires and Scandals

In a 1995 *Newsweek* interview with Bill Gates, the topic of giving away money never came up. Nor did Gates seem preoccupied by social problems. When one of the interviewers mentioned that many Americans lacked medical insurance, Gates shot back: "Don't joke around. Medical treatment across the board at every income level is dramatically better today than in the past." [40]

The only hint of Gates' future involvement in school reform came in the context of remarks he made about America's ranking in the global economy: "Our education system isn't as good as it needs to be. Our universities are very, very strong. The top 10 percent do pretty well, but . . . it's not as good as many, many other countries." [41]

Only three years earlier, Gates had made his first philanthropic donation — $12 million to the University of Washington in his hometown of Seattle to found a molecular biotechnology department. He also recruited a leader in the field to head the department.

"You've got to put in the same amount of work and exercise the same degree of judgment in giving money away as you do in making it," Gates told *Fortune*. [42]

None of today's other high-tech celebrity donors were even mentioned in the *Fortune* article, some because they weren't rich yet. For instance, Google founders Brin and Page were 19-year-old college students when the article appeared. [43]

Likewise, Paul Brainerd hadn't yet sold the desktop-publishing software company he founded, Aldus Corp., for $450 million. After that 1994 deal, Brainerd helped start Social Venture Partners, a philanthropic grant-maker that draws from the ranks of high-tech millionaires. And when Gates made his first big donation, Pierre Omidyar had not yet founded eBay, which cata-

Katrina Relief Efforts Received $5.3 Billion

Americans donated more than $5 billion for Gulf Coast hurricane relief.

U.S. Disaster-Relief Donations, 2005
(in $ billions, estimated)

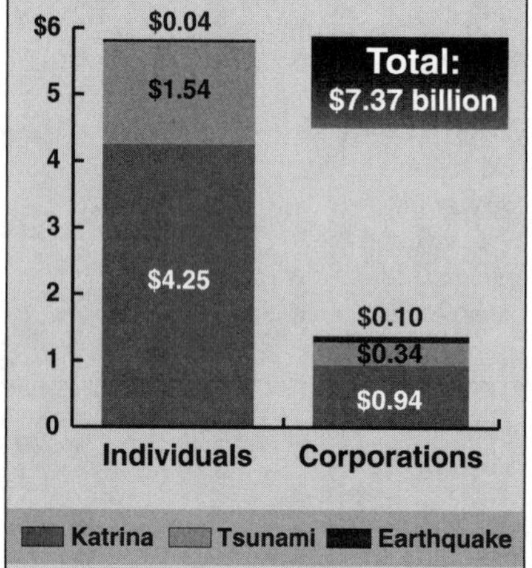

	Individuals	Corporations
Katrina	$4.25	$0.94
Tsunami	$1.54	$0.34
Earthquake	$0.04	$0.10

Total: $7.37 billion

Not shown: Foundation donations were $1.6 million

Source: Giving USA Foundation

pulted him into the billionaire class. In 2004, Omidyar set up the Omidyar Network, which funds nonprofits and invests in some for-profit businesses with socially responsible aims and methods.

"I really believe everyone has the power to make a difference," Omidyar told the *Financial Times* of London. "And by working together we can help make the world a better place." [44]

In the mid-1990s a series of scandals — primarily exposed by investigative journalists — focused a harsh glare on philanthropic foundations.

In 1995, the United Way's Aramony was sentenced to seven years in federal prison for diverting charitable donations to subsidize personal expenses — a case brought to light by *The Washington Post.* [45] Then in 2003 the *Boston Globe* reported that nonprofit foundations across the country were spending lavishly and promoting insider dealing. Some had bought private aircraft, while others had paid hundreds of thousands of dollars in fees to their trustees — some of them lawyers who also billed at their top rates for legal work. [46]

At about the same time, the *San Jose Mercury-News* reported that the James Irvine Foundation of San Francisco — well-known in California for its grants to colleges, social welfare programs and arts organizations — had paid its ex-president more than $700,000 a year, plus perks, at a time when economic recession had prompted the foundation to cut its grant making by $20 million. And some grant recipients and applicants had hired an executive-search firm owned by the president's wife, the newspaper reported. [47]

Then, in 2005, the *Los Angeles Times* began publishing details of high living by the $1.2 million-a-year president of the $9.6 billion J. Paul Getty Trust, one of the world's richest cultural organizations, named for the oil tycoon who bequeathed his estate to the trust, which received it in 1982. [48]

In October, California Attorney General Bill Lockyer named an outside overseer for the trust after concluding that its board had approved hundreds of thousands of dollars' worth of improper spending. Payouts included first-class travel costs for the wife of trust President Barry Munitz; initial installments of a $300,000 fee for a 25th-anniversary book on the trust by its outgoing board chairman and high-end perks for Munitz, including a $72,000 Porsche Cayenne SUV.

As the articles continued, Munitz resigned under pressure in February 2006, after repaying $245,000 and forgoing more than $2 million in severance benefits. [49] ■

CURRENT SITUATION

Legislative Outlook

The Council on Foundations' Gunderson is among the philanthropy world's best-placed players for analyzing what the new Congress may have in store for the nonprofit sector. A veteran of 16 years in the House as a Wisconsin Republican, Gunderson and his colleagues cultivated ties with prominent Democrats before the Nov. 7 elections.

Over the past year, council members have met with Sen. Max Baucus, D-Mont., incoming chairman of the Senate Finance Committee, and Reps. John Lewis, D-Ga., and Xavier Becerra, D-Calif., both members of the new majority on the House Ways and Means Committee. The two committees, which have jurisdiction over tax matters, are the key panels for philanthropy-related legislation.

"There was a consistent theme in what each of these individuals talked about," Gunderson says. It was: "We will work with you, the sector, to help grow philanthropy if you will partner with us to address issues of concern within our communities." For example, Baucus insisted that philanthropies focus attention on the problems of rural America. "We've offered to co-host a conference in Montana on that very topic," Gunderson adds.

Lenkowsky of Indiana University says he's been hearing talk for some time that lawmakers want to ensure that their constituents see the benefits of what foundations and other philanthropies do. Some have suggested, for example, assuring continuation of tax-exempt status for philanthropies that could demonstrate their work on behalf of low-income citizens.

That idea may resonate more with Republicans, however. Incoming Ways and Means Chairman Charles Rangel, D-N.Y., "has much more sympathy with the charitable sector" than his predecessor, Rep. Bill Thomas, R-Calif., a committee staffer told *The Chronicle of Philanthropy*. "He thinks there's a broad rationale for charitable tax exemption." [50]

Nevertheless, Gunderson acknowledges that the Democrats may get interested in tougher oversight if they perceive philanthropies as uninterested in producing palpable results for lawmakers' constituents. "There is always that risk," he says. "But if we start out with the premise that the mission of philanthropy is to enhance the common good, why would we not want to constructively participate with them?"

Indeed, before the election, Gunderson warned that the oversight issue remains potent. In an October speech to the National Association of State Charity Officials, he said, "If Capitol Hill doesn't believe we're serious about ethical conduct, we will see significantly more legislation coming from the Hill." [51]

Red Cross Shake-up

Following a string of upheavals — the resignations of two presidents in a row, revelations of failures in de-

Charitable Giving at a Glance

The 5 Largest Private Foundations
(As of May 1, 2006, based on total assets)

1. Bill & Melinda Gates Foundation ($31 billion)
2. The Ford Foundation ($11.6 billion)
3. J. Paul Getty Trust ($9.6 billion)
4. The Robert Wood Johnson Foundation ($9.0 billion)
5. Lilly Endowment ($8.6 billion)

The 5 Largest Corporate Grantmakers
(As of May 1, 2006, based on total given)

1. Wal-Mart Foundation ($154.5 million)
2. Aventis Pharmaceutical Health Care Foundation ($114.7 million)
3. Bank of America Foundation ($80.7 million)
4. Ford Motor Company Fund ($77.9 million)
5. The Wells-Fargo Foundation ($64.7 million)

The 5 Largest Nonprofit Organizations
(As of November 2005, based on total income)

1. YMCAs in the United States ($4.8 billion)
2. Catholic Charities USA ($3.2 billion)
3. Salvation Army ($3.1 billion)
4. American Red Cross ($3.1 billion)
5. United Jewish Communities ($2.9 billion)

The 5 Largest Gifts to Charity, 2005

1. Cornelia Scaife May ($404 million bequest to Colcom Foundation, others)
2. Bill & Melinda Gates ($320 million to Bill & Melinda Gates Foundation)
3. Eli & Edythe Broad ($300 million to the Broad Foundations and others)
4. George Soros ($240 million to Central European University and others)
5. T. Boone Pickens ($229 million to Oklahoma State University, others)

Sources: National Philanthropic Trust; Chronicle of Philanthropy; NonProfit Times

livering emergency aid and pressure from a powerful Senate committee — the American Red Cross has just proposed sweeping changes in the operation of America's most high-profile charity.

The country's premier disaster-response agency received more than $2.2 billion in donations after Hurricanes Katrina, Rita and Wilma in 2005, but operational problems have raised questions about how effectively that money was used. [52] In the past five years, many of the agency's problems have centered on conflicts between the presidents of the organization and its huge 50-member Board of Directors. In October, the board agreed — among other things — to reduce its own size to no more than 20 members by 2012. In addition, board members' role in day-to-day management would diminish, and internal auditing would be strengthened. [53]

The changes show how complicated the politics of philanthropy can become, even in an organization dedicated mainly to the straightforward task of relieving suffering after disasters. Politics can be even more tricky for the Red Cross because — while not a federal agency — it is chartered by Congress, and the president chooses the board chairman and seven other board members from among federal officials whose jobs involve working with the Red Cross. [54] That interlocking relationship — designed to ensure coordination between government agencies and the Red Cross — also guarantees a higher level of congressional interest when problems crop up.

"It's good news that the Red Cross' board recognized that a Band-Aid won't do, and that the American people expect the best from an organization that so many people have supported with time and money," Sen. Grassley said in a written statement responding to the proposed changes. Grassley, who will be stepping down as Finance Committee chairman in January because Republicans lost control of the Senate on Nov. 7, has taken the lead on Red Cross oversight. [55]

His investigation began after the 2001 resignation of Bernadine Healey, widely viewed as a divisive figure during her brief tenure as Red Cross president (1999-2001), who was forced out after repeatedly clashing with the board. Controversy erupted after it was revealed that she received a $1.9 million severance package. Then in 2005, President Marsha J. Evans resigned after three years, during which she, too, clashed with the board. Her severance package came to $780,000. [56]

In 2005, the Red Cross' internal problems became a national issue after a breakdown — visible to millions of TV watchers — in providing emergency aid to hurricane victims in New Orleans and the Gulf region. The Red Cross is supposed to work hand-in-hand with FEMA, but that relationship didn't materialize after the hurricanes, the Government Accountability Office (GAO) concluded earlier this year. [57]

Continued on p. 1026

At Issue:

Are tougher philanthropy laws needed?

RICK COHEN
FORMER EXECUTIVE DIRECTOR, NATIONAL COMMITTEE FOR RESPONSIVE PHILANTHROPY

WRITTEN FOR *CQ RESEARCHER*, DECEMBER 2006

yes

Nonprofits and the public need better protection against financial predators who misuse tax-exempt resources without suffering legal consequences. Current laws are not sufficient for today's nonprofit sector, where the number of nonprofits and foundations has doubled over the past two decades. The recent boom in nonprofit revenues and assets — philanthropy accounts for more than 5 percent of the nation's GDP — and new organizational structures that mix nonprofit and for-profit models and practices all point to a need to review and augment nonprofit-sector laws, which have not been comprehensively updated in nearly three decades.

Take, for example, philanthropic foundations — institutions that have no market accountabilities to speak of and are now collectively sitting on more than a half-trillion dollars. Half a dozen new laws are needed in this subsector alone. For instance, private foundations should be required to spend at least 6 percent of their assets — instead of the 5 percent they spend now. And they should not be allowed to count their often extravagant administrative expenditures toward their required payouts. Trustees should be prohibited from paying themselves five- and six-figure fees for their board service, and loopholes that allow foundation executives and trustees to engage in self-dealing and conflicts of interest should be closed. Meaningful standards need to be established for determining what constitutes excessive compensation and what should be done about it.

The opponents of additional government oversight say new laws will kill the goose that lays the golden egg. Apparently, preventing abuses, closing loopholes and mandating more accountability will drive away philanthropic donors and nonprofit workers. These same opponents, or their ideological predecessors, proclaimed the same doomsday scenario for philanthropy after the Tax Act of 1969. That prognostication didn't come to pass and neither will the panicked predictions of today's anti-regulatory leaders.

Tax-exempt funds are not the private funds of foundations and nonprofits. Tax-exempt resources are public funds entrusted to the stewardship of foundations and nonprofits for the public benefit. The media understands this, as reflected in its increasing coverage of accountability deficiencies. It is past time this sector's representatives get with the program.

What is needed? Three things: a new commitment to accountability by nonprofits and their associations, significant additional state and federal resources for oversight and new laws and regulations to address the growth and diversity of the nonprofit sector.

ADAM MEYERSON
PRESIDENT, THE PHILANTHROPY ROUNDTABLE

WRITTEN FOR *CQ RESEARCHER*, DECEMBER 2006

no

In January 2005, The Philanthropy Roundtable established the Alliance for Charitable Reform (ACR) as an emergency initiative to respond to legislative proposals on Capitol Hill that would affect private foundations and public charities. The mission of the ACR is to offer common-sense solutions for abuses in the charitable sector while protecting the freedom of donors and foundations to use their best judgment in carrying out their charitable objectives.

Government should vigorously enforce existing laws before announcing sweeping new ones. We recognize that new, narrowly targeted laws may be necessary to correct specific abuses not covered by current rules, and several provisions in new laws enacted in 2004 and 2006 are quite reasonable.

But most of the transgressions in our sector are violations of existing law. Some wrongdoers have already been subject to severe financial penalties and public humiliation, and their example is a powerful deterrent to future law-breakers. To catch more wrongdoers, state attorneys general and the Internal Revenue Service should devote more resources to policing charities and foundations — beginning with the excise tax revenues already assessed on foundations for this purpose.

There is no need to rewrite the fundamental public policy framework governing philanthropy, which historically has given private philanthropic organizations wide discretion in how they use their resources.

We expect that the big battle over philanthropic freedom will take place in 2007. We will do everything in our power to resist requirements for foundation accreditation, five-year reviews of tax-exempt status, arbitrary limits on trustee and staff compensation, federal micromanagement of the boards of private organizations, limits on the compensation of family members who sit on family foundation boards and other freedom-threatening measures proposed in the last three years by Senate Finance Committee and/or Joint Tax Committee staff.

As it becomes ever clearer that the Sarbanes-Oxley anti-corporate fraud law has imposed significant costs on small companies and is responsible for keeping new businesses from listing on American stock exchanges, it is also important to resist applying the Sarbanes-Oxley mindset to charities and foundations.

When existing laws are not being vigorously enforced, it makes no sense to add sweeping new regulations that will add costs and diminish freedom for the law-abiding majority without improving the likelihood that wrongdoers will be brought to justice.

Continued from p. 1024

"The agencies spent time during the response effort trying to establish operations and procedures, rather than focusing solely on coordinating services," the agency report said. [58]

In a written response in May, the Red Cross said the GAO had mischaracterized the agency's role under the federal emergency plan. Although in smaller-scale emergencies the Red Cross provides shelter and other necessities to victims, in massive emergencies like the Katrina disaster its primary function is "to help bring federal resources to state and local governments," the letter said. The Red Cross acknowledged, however, that the difference in the two roles caused "much confusion" after Katrina. [59]

Earlier, in March, the Red Cross dismissed three volunteers in the hurricane relief operation who had been accused by fellow volunteers of having diverted supplies. The Red Cross referred allegations of what it called "waste and abuse" to the FBI. [60]

Grassley praised the Red Cross for designing new procedures to encourage whistleblowers to step forward with reports of improprieties. "I want to make certain that the Red Cross also has in place reforms that will contribute to greater transparency and openness to the Congress and the public." [61]

Bonds for Vaccines

A bond issue on behalf of the Global Alliance for Vaccines and Immunization (GAVI) in London this month raised $1 billion to vaccinate children in the world's poorest countries against polio, hepatitis B, yellow fever and other preventable illnesses. The event not only linked philanthropy and business but also tightened the ties between philanthropy and government.

"It's a great example of how we're hoping to show people the way to bring in new resources from government," says Weiss, at the Bill & Melinda Gates Foundation.

The foundation committed an additional $1.5 billion to GAVI, an organization the foundation helped establish in 2000. [62] The bond issue, which will allow GAVI to expand its activities, was promoted by Gordon Brown, the United Kingdom's Chancellor of the Exchequer (the equivalent of the U.S. secretary of the Treasury). [63]

The program now will be able to immunize "500 million children against vaccine-preventable diseases before 2015, saving some 10 million lives," Gates and Brown wrote in the British newspaper *The Independent*, bringing the world "one step closer to eradicating polio." [64]

The funding scheme differs from traditional approaches to financing health initiatives in poor countries through grants, in that bond buyers expect a financial return — not just moral uplift. The five-year bonds were designed to yield about 0.32 percentage points more than equivalent U.S. Treasury bonds. Donor countries are helping to make the bond issue possible by pledging development aid to the countries where the immunizations will be carried out — pledges that amount to collateral on the bonds. [65]

Governments felt secure in making those pledges because the foundation had made an early leap into the mass-immunization program and was working to ensure that the money would be spent effectively, says Weiss. "New commitments to immunization are coming from governments in part because we were willing to be the first dollars in," he says.

Britain, Italy, France, Spain, Sweden and Norway made a total of $4 billion in commitments, along with the Gates Foundation. The United States — which has adopted a strategy of linking development aid to progress in fighting corruption and meeting other governance standards — was not among the pledging countries. [66]

Although the bond issue received virtually no news coverage in the United States, Brown and his colleagues showed a flair for grabbing headlines — at least in Europe. The bonds' first buyers were Pope Benedict XVI, the Archbishop of Canterbury, Britain's chief rabbi, the Muslim Council of Britain, the Hindu Forum of Britain and rock star development-aid advocates Bono and Geldof. [67] ■

OUTLOOK

Wealth Transfer?

The decades-long growth in American philanthropic contributions leads many experts to believe that U.S. donors' generosity will continue for the foreseeable future. In fact, some philanthropy scholars have predicted a major uptick in contributions as a result of the inter-generational "wealth transfer" from baby boomer parents to their children.

Paul Schervish, a sociologist and director of the Center on Wealth and Philanthropy at Boston College, co-authored a controversial study in 1999 that projected a minimum transfer of $41 trillion during the 55 years from 1998 to 2052. Of that amount, they calculated that about $6 trillion would be donated to philanthropies.

Defending the theory in a 2003 article, Schervish and a colleague wrote, "The $41 trillion estimate of wealth transfer is not affected by short-term economic fluctuations, and if wealth continues to grow in the next 51 years as it has in the past 51 years, the transfer amount will be less than a quarter of the total value of personally held wealth in 2052." [68] In other words, a philanthropy boom seems likely, because donors tend to give when they feel that their assets are secure.

But *The Chronicle of Philanthropy* recently quoted experts saying that the transfer had yet to show up in donation volume. And *The Journal of Gift Planning* published a symposium showing a range of views about the wealth-transfer theory. "I have far more confidence in the overall wealth-transfer figures . . . than in the amount projected to transfer to charity," said Kathyrn W. Miree, a consultant to nonprofits and foundations. [69]

Schervish acknowledges that gauging the future level of donations is tricky, even though his predictions about the family-to-family bequests appear to be panning out. "The wealth transfer and the growth in transfer is taking place," he says. The fact that it's not reflected in philanthropic donations, he explains, could reflect a drop in individuals' assets that makes them less willing to give, "or they're just not giving, or we're missing some other forms of giving."

In any event, most philanthropy experts predict the high-tech industry will continue to produce young success stories who will feel not only a moral obligation to spread their wealth but also a drive to produce fast results. "These are people in their 30s and 40s who are very impatient," says Fleishman of Duke University. "They'll say, 'I created an instant company, why can't we turn the same skills to solving persistent problems?' "

Former National Council on Responsive Philanthropy Director Cohen thinks a new donor class that rose to the top by developing new ways of doing business will likely create new forms of philanthropic development, such as eBay founder Omidyar's strategic focus on both nonprofit and for-profit beneficiaries.

But these new forms of philanthropy are likely to raise questions of where profit-taking stops and charity begins, and of who makes decisions about where to draw lines between business and philanthropy, Cohen says. As a result, "Questions of accountability and transparency are going to be even more troubling 10 years from now," he says.

Georgetown's Eisenberg agrees, pointing out that no one is establishing methods to examine accountability. "There's no debate, no discussion," he says. "We're supposed to be so happy that all these mega-wealthy folks are giving money. Everybody is patting each other on the ass. There are no critical faculties operating in philanthropy."

But Lenkowsky of Indiana University's philanthropy center thinks state attorneys general will become more aggressive in overseeing philanthropy, in part because the federal government has all but abandoned the field. Journalists, as well, are likely to keep digging, having seen the fruitful results of recent investigations of the Getty Trust and other foundations. "The big story of the last few years is not what Congress has enacted but that charitable organizations now wear, if not black hats, gray hats," he says.

Optimism remains, however, in part because of the greater sensitivity inculcated in today's high school and college graduates, many of whom have had to perform community-service projects as a prerequisite for graduation. "We are headed for a dramatic increase in giving" among that group, says New York University's Gaudiani. [70]

"The group under age 32 has done more volunteer work during its academic training than any other group in the nation's history," Lenkowsky says. "They are seeing what needs to be done, and as they graduate they have a much livelier commitment to making the world better." ■

Notes

[1] Quoted in Carol J. Loomis, "Warren Buffett Gives It Away," *Fortune*, July 10, 2006, p. 56. For details on the Buffett gift and its effects on the Gates Foundation's asset base, see Charles Pillar and Maggie Farley, "Buffett Pledges Billions to Gates," *Los Angeles Times*, June 26, 2006, p. A1; Timothy L. O'Brien and Stephanie Saul, "Buffett to Give Bulk of Fortune to Gates Charity," *The New York Times*, June 26, 2006, p. A1. For additional information on the Gates Foundation's assets and grants, see "Fact Sheet," Bill & Melinda Gates Foundation; www.gatesfoundation.org/MediaCenter/FactSheet.

[2] For details on the Google Foundation, see Katie Hafner, "Philanthropy Google's Way: Not the Usual," *The New York Times*, Sept. 14, 2006, p. A1. For details on the Gateses' first contributions, see Juan Forero, "$5 Billion Puts Gates Fund in First Place," *The New York Times*, Jan. 25, 2000, p. A14.

[3] For more details on Clinton, see Bethany McLean, "The Power of Philanthropy," *Fortune*, Sept. 18, 2006, p. 82. For more details on Soros, see his Open Society Institute Web site; www.soros.org. Also see Lee Hockstader, "U.S. Financier Gives Russia $100 Million for Internet Link," *The Washington Post*, March 16, 1996, p. A21; Mary Beth Heridan, " 'Oracle' Prefers Giving Away Millions," *Los Angeles Times*, Aug. 24, 1993, p. D8.

[4] For more details, see McLean, *ibid.*, p. 82. For additional details on the Bush-Clinton fund, see "Bush-Clinton Katrina Fund," http://bushclintonkatrinafund.org. For details of the new AIDS drug deal, see Celia W. Dugger, "Clinton Helps Broker Deal for Medicine to Treat AIDS," *The New York Times*, Dec. 1, 2006, p. A6.

[5] *Ibid.*, p. 30.

[6] For detailed statistics and analysis see *Giving USA 2006*, Center on Philanthropy at Indiana University, 2006, pp. 2-3, 56-77.

[7] The calculation assumes that post-disaster contributions were "new money" that wouldn't otherwise have been donated to charity. For details, see *ibid*, p. 11.

[8] For a detailed study, see Paul G. Schervish, "Explaining the Curve in the U-Shaped Curve," *Voluntas: International Journal of Voluntary and Nonprofit Organizations*, August 1995, p. 202, /www.bc.edu/research/swri/meta-elements/pdf/ucurve1.pdf. For further analysis, see Arthur C. Brooks, "Charitable Explanation," *The Wall Street Journal*, Nov. 27, 2006, p. A12.

[9] For details, see Roy E. Finkenbine, "Law, Reconstruction, and African American Education in the Post-Reconstruction South," and Gary R. Hess, "Waging the Cold War in the Third World," in Lawrence J. Friedman and Mark D. McGarvie, eds., *Charity, Philanthropy and Civility in American History* (2004), pp. 161-178; 329-330.

[10] See Claire Gaudiani, *The Greater Good: How Philanthropy Drives the American Economy and Can Save Capitalism* (2003).

[11] For more details, see "While a Third of Adults Think the Nonprofit Sector in the United States is Headed in the Wrong Direction, a Vast Majority of Households Have Donated to Charities in the Past Year," The Harris Poll, No. 33, April 27, 2006; www.harrisinteractive.com/harris_poll/index.asp?PID=657. See also Sharon Hoffman, "For U.S. charities, a crisis of trust," MSNBC.com, Nov. 21, 2006, www.msnbc.msn.com/id/15753760.

[12] For background, see Kathy Koch, "The New Corporate Philanthropy," *CQ Researcher*, Feb. 27, 1998, pp. 169-192.

[13] Robert H. Bremner, *American Philanthropy* (1988), p. 232. A higher number, 2,509, is cited in Gaudiani, *op. cit.*, p. 84. For more detail on the private-public partnership that Carnegie devised, see "The Carnegie Libraries," New York Public Library, undated, www.nypl.org/press/carnegielibraries.cfm.

[14] For details on Murdoch's assets, see Matthew Miller, "The Forbes 400," *Forbes*, Oct. 9, 2006, p. 194. Also see McLean, *op. cit.*, p. 82.

[15] Quoted in Aldo Svaldi, "Media mogul Turner takes a meaty poke at Murdoch," *Denver Post*, Nov. 16, 2006, p. C1.

[16] For the complete data, see "Private Philanthropy Across the World," the Comparative Nonprofit Sector Project, Center for Civil Society Studies, December 2005, www.jhu.edu/~cnp/pdf/comptable5_dec05.pdf.

[17] Remarks at the First White House National Conference on Faith-Based and Community Initiatives, June 1, 2004, http://usinfo.state.gov/usa/faith/s060104.htm.

[18] For more detail, see Ronald Brownstein, "Katrina's Aftermath; Floodwaters Lift Poverty Debate Into Political Focus," *Los Angeles Times*, Sept. 13, 2005, p. A1.

[19] Cohen's unsigned article on the Education Department cut and related administration moves is available on the National Coalition for Responsive Philanthropy Web site; www.ncrp.org/Bush_FY2007_Federal_Budget.asp. The administration's proposal is available in a White House budget document, "Major Savings and Reforms in the President's 2007 Budget," The White House, February 2006, p. 28, www.whitehouse.gov/omb/budget/fy2007/pdf/savings.pdf.

[20] For background, see Pamela M. Prah, "Disaster Preparedness," *CQ Researcher*, Nov. 18, 2005, pp. 981-1004.

[21] For background, see Sarah Glazer, "Faith-Based Initiatives," *CQ Researcher*, May 4, 2001, pp. 377-400.

[22] Quoted in Jason Felch and Robin Fields, "Senator Rebukes Getty," *Los Angeles Times*, June 23, 2005, p. B1.

[23] For details on the legislation, see "Analysis of Charitable Reforms & Incentives in the 'Pension Protection Act of 2006,' " Oct. 16, 2006; www.independentsecdor.org/programs/gr/Pension_Bill_Summary.pdf; "What Does the Pension Protection act of 2006 Mean for Private Foundations," Association of Small Foundations, Aug. 17, 2006; www.smallfoundations.org/legislative_update/pension_protection_act/pension_protection_act/file; "Self-Dealing: A Concise Guide for Foundation Board and Staff," Forum of Regional Associations of Grantmakers, 2006; www.ctphilanthropy.org/o/page-content/self_dealing_edie.pdf.

[24] For details see "Self-Dealing," *op. cit.*, p. 4; "Exceptions — self-dealing," Internal Revenue Service, undated; www.irs.gov/charities/foundations/article/0,,id=137700,00.html.

[25] Christine Ahn, Pablo Eisenberg and Channapha Khamvongsa, "Foundation Trustee Fees: Use and Abuse," Center for Public and Nonprofit Leadership, Public Policy Institute, Georgetown University, September 2003; http://cpnl.georgetown.edu/doc_pool/TrusteeFees.pdf.

[26] Quoted in Bremner, *op. cit.*, pp. 41-42. Unless otherwise indicated, material in this section is based on this book.

[27] *Ibid.*, p. 41.

[28] For more details, see Judith Sealander, "Curing Evils at Their Source: The Arrival of Scientific Giving," in Friedman and McGarvie, *op. cit.*, p. 218.

[29] http://alpha.furman.edu/~benson/docs/carnegie.htm.

[30] Quoted in Bremner, *op. cit.*, p. 111.

[31] Quoted in *ibid.*, p. 139.

[32] Quoted in *ibid.*, p. 144.

[33] Quoted in *ibid.*, p. 188.

[34] Quoted in *ibid.*, p. 206.

[35] For the full text of Bush's speech, see "Inaugural Address of George Bush," Jan. 20, 1989; www.yale.edu/lawweb/avalon/presiden/inaug/bush.htm.

[36] Caryn James, "Megastars Out to Save the World," *The New York Times*, Nov. 13, 2006, p. E1. George Harrison's project lives on in the form of the "George Harrison Fund for UNICEF," which aids children in Bangladesh as well as other regions afflicted by natural disaster and human cruelty. For more details, see www.unicefusa.org/site/c.duLRI8O0H/b.934081/k.20A2/The_George_Harrison_Fund_for_UNICEF__US_Fund_for_UNICEF.htm.

[37] For background, see, Mark Donnelly, "New Faces of Charity," *CQ Researcher*, Dec. 12, 1986, available at *CQ Researcher Plus Archives*, www.cqpress.com.

[38] For amount raised, see Robert Hilburn, "28th Annual Grammys a 'World'-Class Event," *Los Angeles Times*, Feb. 26, 1986, Part 5, p. 1.

[39] For background, see Peter Katel, "Ending Poverty," *CQ Researcher*, Sept. 9, 2005, pp. 733-760; and Josh Tyrangiel, "The Constant Charmer; the inside story of how the world's biggest rock star mastered the political game and persuaded the world's leaders to take on global poverty," *Time*, Dec. 26, 2005, p. 46. For information on the Red Brand campaign, see Candace Lombardi, "Red iPod supports AIDS charity," News.com[cnet], Oct. 19, 2006; Mike Hughlett and Sandra Jones, "One brand, but they're not the same," *Chicago Tribune*, Oct. 13, 2006, p. C1.

[40] For the full interview, see "Software Is My Life," *Newsweek*, Nov. 27, 1995, p. 73.

[41] *Ibid.*

[42] For more details, see Alan Farnham, "The Billionaires; How They Give Their Money Away," *Fortune*, Sept. 7, 1992, p. 92.

[43] For background on Google, see Adam Lashinsky, "Who's The Boss," *Fortune*, Oct. 2, 2006, p. 93, and Hafner, *op. cit.*, p. A1.

[44] For background on Omidyar and Brainerd, see Kristina Shevory, "When Charity Begins

About the Author

Peter Katel is a *CQ Researcher* staff writer who previously reported on Haiti and Latin America for *Time* and *Newsweek* and covered the Southwest for newspapers in New Mexico. He has received several journalism awards, including the Bartolomé Mitre Award for coverage of drug trafficking from the Inter-American Press Association. He holds an A.B. in university studies from the University of New Mexico. His recent reports include "Immigration Reform," "War on Drugs" and "Whistleblowers."

in a Circle of Friends," *The New York Times*, Oct. 9, 2005, Sect. 3, p. 1; and Fergal Byne, "Auction man: eBay made Pierre Omidyar billions overnight. Now he's starting to spend it," *Financial Times* [London], March 25, 2006, p. A16. See also the Omidyar Network's Web site, www.omidyar.net.

[45] Charles E. Shephard, "Power, Perks and Privileges in a Nonprofit World," *The Washington Post*, Feb. 16, 1992. For details of Aramony's sentencing, see Charles W. Hall, "Ex-United Way Chief Sentenced to 7 Years," *The Washington Post*, July 23, 1995, p. A1.

[46] Beth Healy, *et al.*, "Charity Begins at Home," Oct. 9, 2003, Nov, 9, 2003, Dec. 3, 2003, Dec. 17, 2003, Dec. 21, 2003, Dec. 29, 2003, *The Boston Globe*, p. A1 (all); www.boston.com/news/specials/nation.

[47] Eric Nalder, "CEO's Rewards at Nonprofit," *San Jose Mercury-News*, April 27, 2003, p. A1.

[48] "About the J. Paul Getty Trust," [undated] www.getty.edu/about/trust.html.

[49] Jason Felch, *et al.*, "State Names Monitor for Getty Trust," *Los Angeles Times*, Oct. 3, 2006, p. B1; Randy Kennedy and Carol Vogel, "President of Getty Trust Resigns Under Pressure," *The New York Times*, Feb. 10, 2006, p. A14; Jason Felch, *et al.*, "The Munitz Collection; Getty's Chief Executive Has Been Highly Compensated During a Time of Austerity," *Los Angeles Times*, June 10, 2005, p. A1.

[50] Quoted in Elizabeth Schwinn, "Congress' New Outlook," *The Chronicle of Philanthropy*, Nov. 23, 2006.

[51] For full text of Gunderson's speech, see Steve Gunderson, "A Delicate Balance: The Growth of Philanthropy and Its Regulation," Oct. 16, 2006, www.cof.org/Council/content.cfm?ItemNumber=7240&navItemNumber=2131.

[52] Statistic cited in "American Red Cross, Governance for the 21st Century, Report of the Board of Governors," October 2006, p. 14; www.redcross.org/static/file_cont5765_lang0_2176.pdf.

[53] For more details, see Suzanne Perry and Elizabeth Schwinn, "The Red Cross's new limitations on governance get mixed reviews," *The Chronicle of Philanthropy*, Nov. 9, 2006, p. 29. For the Red Cross board's own account of its proposals, see "American Red Cross, Governance for the 21st Century," *op. cit.*

[54] "American Red Cross," *ibid.*, p. 18.

[55] For Grassley's statement, see "Memorandum, To: Reporters and Editor[s]," U.S. Senate Committee on Finance, Sen. Chuck Grassley, of Iowa — Chairman, Oct. 20, 2006, www.senate.gov/~finance/press/Gpress/2005/prg103006.pdf.

FOR MORE INFORMATION

Center for the Advancement of Social Entrepreneurship, Fuqua School of Business, Duke University, Box 90120, Durham, NC 27708; (919) 660-7823; www.fuqua.duke.edu/centers/case/index.html. Sponsors research and offers an MBA program geared toward managing social-improvement projects.

Center on Philanthropy at Indiana University, 550 West North St., Suite 301, Indianapolis, IN 46202; (317) 274-4200; www.philanthropy.iupui.edu. Produces "Giving USA," a widely cited annual report on charitable donations.

Center on Wealth and Philanthropy, Boston College, McGuinn Hall 515, 140 Commonwealth Ave., Chestnut Hill, MA 02467; (617) 552-4070; www.bc.edu/cwp. Focuses on the moral aspects of philanthropy and intergenerational "wealth transfer."

Charity Navigator, 1200 MacArthur Blvd., 2nd Floor, Mahwah, N.J., 07430; (201) 818-1288; www.charitynavigator.org/index.cfm. A Web-based service that offers free evaluations of charities for donors investigating prospective beneficiaries.

Independent Sector, 1200 18th St., N.W., Suite 200, Washington, DC 20036; (202) 467-6100; www.independentsector.org/index.htm. Advocacy organization for non-profits supports legislation that provides incentives for donating.

National Committee for Responsive Philanthropy, 2001 S St., N.W., Suite 620, Washington, DC 20009; (202) 387-9177; www.ncrp.org. Encourages foundations and other donors to fight for economic and social justice.

Philanthropy Roundtable, 1150 17th St., N.W., Suite 503, Washington, DC 20036; (202) 822-8333; www.philanthropyroundtable.org. Serves politically conservative charities that tend to favor a reduced government role in social services.

[56] For details, see Jacqueline L. Salmon, "Red Cross Gave Ousted Executive $780,000 Deal," *The Washington Post*, March 4, 2006, p. A9; Jacquelin L. Salmon and Manny Fernandez, "Red Cross President Resigns Amid Conflict," *The Washington Post*, Oct. 27, 2001, p. A2.

[57] For details, see "Hurricanes Katrina and Rita: Coordination between FEMA and the Red Cross Should Be Improved for the 2006 Hurricane Season," Government Accountability Office, June 2006, pp. 1-2, www.gao.gov/new.items/d06712.pdf.

[58] *Ibid.*, pp. 12-13.

[59] The Red Cross response is included in the GAO report. For full text see, *ibid.*, pp. 26-30.

[60] For details, see "Red Cross Fires 3rd Volunteer Amid Inquiry," *The New York Times*, March 26, 2006; Adam Nossiter, "F.B.I. to Investigate Red Cross Over Accusations of Wrongdoing," *The New York Times*, March 31, 2006, p. A14.

[61] Quoted in "Memorandum," *op. cit.*

[62] Sebastian Boyd and John Glover, "Buying bonds to finance vaccines for the poor," *International Herald Tribune*, Nov. 8, 2006, p. A19.

[63] Johanna Chung and Andrew Jack, "Vaccines bond delayed by late investor interest," *Financial Times* [London], Oct. 14, 2006, p. 4.

[64] For the full text, see Gordon Brown and Bill Gates, "How to help the world's poorest children," *The Independent* [London], Nov. 7, 2006, http://comment.independent.co.uk/commentators/article1961419.ece.

[65] Boyd and Glover, *op. cit.*

[66] *Ibid.*, and see also Johanna Chung, "New bond raises Dollars 1 bn for child jabs," *Financial Times* [London], Nov. 8, 2006, p. 45.

[67] Chung, *op. cit.*

[68] John J. Havens and Paul G. Schervish, "Why the $41 Trillion Wealth Transfer Estimate Is Still Valid: A Review of Challenges and Questions," Boston College Social Welfare Research Institute, Jan. 6, 2003, www.bc.edu/research/swri/meta-elements/pdf/41trillionreview.pdf.

[69] For details, see Holly Hall, "Much-Anticipated Transfer of Wealth Has Yet to Materialize, Nonprofit Experts Say," *The Chronicle of Philanthropy*, April 6, 2006; and "Wealth Transfer: A Digest of Opinion and Advice," *Journal of Gift Planning*, 2nd Quarter, 2006; www.bc.edu/research/swri/meta-elements/pdf/jogpvol102.pdf.

[70] For background, see John Greenya, "National Service," *CQ Researcher*, June 30, 2006, pp. 577-600.

Bibliography

Selected Sources

Books

Bremner, Robert H., *American Philanthropy,* University of Chicago Press, 1988 (2nd edition).
Written for the lay reader, this survey of a centuries-old American tradition by a veteran historian provides an overview of events and persistent debates.

Brooks, Arthur C., *Who Really Cares: The Surprising Truth About Compassionate Conservatism*, Basic Books, 2006.
A professor at Syracuse University's Maxwell School of Public Affairs interprets a variety of data to show that religious, politically conservative Americans tend to be bigger givers to charity than liberals.

Gaudiani, Claire, *The Greater Good: How Philanthropy Drives the American Economy and Can Save Capitalism*, Owl Books, Henry Holt and Company, 2003.
A former college president turned philanthropy scholar praises American philanthropy.

Nasaw, David, *Andrew Carnegie*, Penguin Press, 2006.
A new biography of perhaps the single most influential person in the history of American philanthropy delves into the contradictions embodied in a ruthless business tycoon who advocated giving away of riches — and practiced what he preached.

Articles

Hafner, Katie, "Philanthropy Google's Way: Not the Usual," *The New York Times*, Sept. 14, 2006, p. A1.
A journalist specializing in the high-tech industry explores the business-oriented approach to philanthropy embraced by Google's young billionaire founders.

Katz, Stanley N., "What Does it Mean to Say that Philanthropy is 'Effective?' " *Proceedings of the American Philosophical Society, Vol. 149*, No. 2, June 2005, www.aps-pub.com/proceedings/1492/490201.pdf.
A Princeton University historian of philanthropy argues that foundations' growing emphasis on measurable, short-term results threatens basic research at universities long dependent on foundation grants.

Kramer, Mark R., "Foundation Trustees Need a New Investment Approach," *The Chronicle of Philanthropy*, March 23, 2006, p. 43.
A business veteran who now consults for philanthropies argues that foundations should look for investments that reflect their social missions, not ones that simply ensure financial return.

Nasaw, David, "Looking the Carnegie Gift Horse in the Mouth," *Slate*, Nov. 10, 2006, www.slate.com/id/2152830/.
The author of a new biography of Andrew Carnegie deplores widespread acceptance of the idea that society should have to depend on rich peoples' generosity for the solutions to critical problems.

Salmon, Jacqueline L., "With a Hefty Education Grant Come Equally Great Expectations," *The Washington Post*, Dec. 4, 2006, p. A1.
The Bill & Melinda Gates Foundation's mission to improve high schools is proving complicated and demanding.

Serwer, Andy, "The Power of Philanthropy, Robin Hood," *Fortune*, Sept. 18, 2006, p. 102.
The magazine's managing editor reports on a group of rich, young, hedge-fund executives who are applying business techniques to their donation strategy.

Smith, Douglas K., "Market Magic: Nonprofits could access needed capital by turning donors into investors," *Slate*, Nov. 13, 2006, www.slate.com/id/2152801/.
A management consultant lays out a way to restructure philanthropic donations as investments.

Reports and Studies

"Study on High Net Worth Philanthropy," Bank of America [prepared by the Center on Philanthropy at Indiana University], October 2006.
A research team found that wealthy donors tend to favor educational and cultural institutions as recipients.

Ahn, Christine, *et al.*, "Foundation Trustee Fees: Use and Abuse," The Center for Public and Nonprofit Leadership, Georgetown University, September 2003.
A research team finds wide differences among large and small foundations in whether and how much trustees are paid.

Hope, Hollis, *et al.*, "Philanthropy in the News: An Analysis of Media Coverage, 1990-2004," Foundationworks.
A detailed examination of press reports shows a steady increase in the volume of coverage, with most articles favorable and focused on big gifts and individual projects, rather than on analyses of goals and whether they're met.

Ostrower, Francie, and Marla J. Bobowick, "Nonprofit Governance and the Sarbanes-Oxley Act," The Urban Institute Center on Nonprofits and Philanthropy, Sept. 19, 2006.
Requiring nonprofits to meet new corporate-behavior legal standards would make more of a difference to small foundations, say two Urban Institute scholars, because large foundations have already adopted many of the norms.

The Next Step:

Additional Articles from Current Periodicals

Philanthropy and Business

Barbaro, Michael, "Candles, Jeans, Lipsticks: Products With Ulterior Motives," *The New York Times*, Nov. 13, 2006, p. F1.
Retailers are offering to donate a percentage of the cost of various items to a number of charities.

Cooperman, Alan, "Tsunami Aid Is Goodwill and Good Business," *The Washington Post*, Jan. 26, 2005, p. E1.
A growing number of companies are using "cause-related marketing" to increase business.

Meyerson, Bruce, "Corporate Giving Runs Risk of Abuse By Executives," *Charlotte Observer*, March 4, 2006, p. D3.
Corporate giving can lead to self-serving behavior by executives like former Fannie Mae chief executive Franklin Raines, who allegedly used charitable contributions to compromise the judgment of six board members.

Russell, Sabin, "Businesses Start 'Red' Campaign to Help Africa," *The San Francisco Chronicle*, Oct. 14, 2006, p. B1.
Companies participating in the PRODUCT RED campaign are pledging to donate a percentage of their profits to the Global Fund to Fight AIDS in Africa.

Urma, Viorel, "Giving at the Office," *The Philadelphia Inquirer*, Dec. 24, 2005, p. D1.
American companies are increasingly turning to philanthropy to advance their strategic interests abroad.

Philanthropy and Stars

Collins, Scott, and Randy Lewis, "Entertainers' Relief Efforts Get Off to a Slow Start," *Los Angeles Times*, Jan. 5, 2005, p. A10.
The unity displayed in relief efforts by the movie, TV and music industries after the terrorist attacks on Sept. 11, 2001, is missing in Hollywood's tsunami-relief efforts.

Freydkin, Donna, "Celebrity Activists Put Star Power to Good Use," *USA Today*, June 23, 2006, p. A1.
Americans are coming to expect charitable contributions from stars.

Heller, Karen, "Generous to a Fault," *The Philadelphia Inquirer*, Jan. 23, 2005, p. M3.
Celebrities should act with more modesty and grace when engaging in philanthropic activities.

Marks, Alexandra, "Celebrity 'Hyper-Agents' Transform Philanthropy," *The Christian Science Monitor*, Sept. 19, 2005, p. 13.
The new culture of philanthropy is being spurred in part by celebrity "hyper-agents" with the time, wealth, charisma and dedication to motivate others to help.

Rahimi, Shadi, "Celebrities Stay True to the AIDS Cause," *The New York Times*, Nov. 10, 2005, p. B1.
For more than two decades, Hollywood and the fashion world have stayed true to AIDS causes.

Salamon, Julie, "Celebrity Philanthropists Become Role Models," *The Houston Chronicle*, Jan. 10, 2005, p. 6.
Salamon argues that celebrities have a strong grip on people's imaginations, and on their wallets, and therefore provide a positive moral example when they give to help others.

Youths and Philanthropy

Fordyce, Kathleen, "Students in SHAPE Learn Philanthropy 101," *The Miami Herald*, Nov. 10, 2006, p. 36.
High-school students in South Florida's SHAPE program — Students Helping Achieve Philanthropic Excellence — pick a new cause each year and raise money, solicit grant proposals and then select organizations to help.

Gardner, Marilyn, "A Gift For an Entire Village," *The Christian Science Monitor*, Sept. 12, 2006, p. 17.
Villagers nursed Greg Mortenson back to health after a failed hiking trip to impoverished Pakistan, and now he builds schools there, placing a particular emphasis on educating girls.

Jayson, Sharon, "Generation Y Gets Involved," *USA Today*, Oct. 24, 2006, p. D1.
A growing amount of academic and market research suggests that people in their mid-20s and younger are civic-minded and socially conscious.

CITING *CQ RESEARCHER*

Sample formats for citing these reports in a bibliography include the ones listed below. Preferred styles and formats vary, so please check with your instructor or professor.

MLA STYLE

Jost, Kenneth. "Rethinking the Death Penalty." CQ Researcher 16 Nov. 2001: 945-68.

APA STYLE

Jost, K. (2001, November 16). Rethinking the death penalty. *CQ Researcher, 11*, 945-968.

CHICAGO STYLE

Jost, Kenneth. "Rethinking the Death Penalty." *CQ Researcher*, November 16, 2001, 945-968.

In-depth Reports on Issues in the News

Are you writing a paper?

Need backup for a debate?

Want to become an expert on an issue?

For 80 years, students have turned to *CQ Researcher* for in-depth reporting on issues in the news. Reports on a full range of political and social issues are now available. Following is a selection of recent reports:

Civil Liberties
Voting Controversies, 9/06
Right to Die, 5/05
Immigration Reform, 4/05
Gays on Campus, 10/04

Crime/Law
Sex Offenders, 9/06
Treatment of Detainees, 8/06
War on Drugs, 6/06
Domestic Violence, 1/06
Death Penalty Controversies, 9/05

Education
Academic Freedom, 10/05
Intelligent Design, 7/05
No Child Left Behind, 5/05

Environment
Biofuels Boom, 9/06
Nuclear Energy, 3/06
Climate Change, 1/06
Saving the Oceans, 11/05
Endangered Species Act, 6/05
Alternative Energy, 2/05

Health/Safety
Rising Health Costs, 4/06
Pension Crisis, 2/06
Avian Flu Threat, 1/06
Domestic Violence, 1/06

International Affairs/Politics
Understanding Islam, 11/06
Change in Latin America, 7/06
Pork Barrel Politics, 6/06
Future of European Union, 10/05
War in Iraq, 10/05

Social Trends
Privacy in Peril, 11/06
Video Games, 11/06
Blog Explosion, 6/06

Terrorism/Defense
Port Security, 4/06
Presidential Power, 2/06

Youth
Drinking on Campus, 8/06
National Service, 6/06
Teen Spending, 5/06

Upcoming Reports

Patent Law Disputes, 12/15/06
Prison Health Care, 1/5/07
Factory Farms, 1/12/07
The Catholic Church, 1/19/07

ACCESS

CQ Researcher is available in print and online. For access, visit your library or www.cqresearcher.com.

STAY CURRENT

To receive notice of upcoming *CQ Researcher* reports, or learn more about *CQ Researcher* products, subscribe to the free e-mail newsletters, *CQ Researcher Alert!* and *CQ Researcher News*: www.cqpress.com/newsletters.

PURCHASE

To purchase a *CQ Researcher* report in print or electronic format (PDF), visit www.cqpress.com or call 866-427-7737. Single reports start at $15. Bulk purchase discounts and electronic-rights licensing are also available.

SUBSCRIBE

A full-service *CQ Researcher* print subscription—including 44 reports a year, monthly index updates, and a bound volume—is $688 for academic and public libraries, $667 for high school libraries, and $827 for media libraries. Add $25 for domestic postage.

CQ Researcher Online offers a backfile from 1991 and a number of tools to simplify research. For pricing information, call 800-834-9020, ext. 1906, or e-mail librarysales@cqpress.com.

CQ RESEARCHER *PLUS* ARCHIVE

GET ONLINE ACCESS TO VITAL ISSUES FROM 1923 TO THE PRESENT

CQ Researcher Plus Archive delivers fast, online access to every *CQ Researcher* report from 1991 to the present, *PLUS* lets you explore the complete archive of *Editorial Research Reports** from 1923-1990. Search and browse more than 3,600 in-depth reports.

Loaded with handy online features, *CQ Researcher Plus Archive* provides the trustworthy reporting and the advanced online functionality today's researchers demand. The new "Issue Tracker" feature provides quick links to past and present reports on the specific topics you need.

For a free trial, visit http://library.cqpress.com/trials.

For pricing information, call 1-800-834-9020, ext. 1906 or e-mail librarymarketing@cqpress.com.

**Editorial Research Reports*, the predecessor to *CQ Researcher*, provides the same expert, nonpartisan reporting on the vital issues that have shaped our society.

CQ Press • 1255 22nd Street, NW, Suite 400 • Washington, DC 20037

CQ Researcher

Published by CQ Press, a division of Congressional Quarterly Inc.

cqresearcher.com

Patent Disputes

Does the system help or hurt innovation?

The U.S. patent system is designed to encourage technological innovation by granting inventors an exclusive right to profit from their discoveries. In recent years, however, many critics have complained that the system is actually impeding innovation. Critics say a hugely overburdened Patent and Trademark Office approves many dubious patents, some of which are used by so-called patent "trolls" to force companies using the patented devices into unjustified financial settlements. Meanwhile, a special federal appeals court created to handle patent cases is accused of misapplying the law and rewarding sometimes-abusive litigation. The Supreme Court is considering a case to tighten the standards for issuing patents, while Congress has been considering other proposed reforms. But the bills stalled because of a stalemate between high-tech industries supporting the measures and the pharmaceutical and biotechnology industries, which say the current system is working well to promote technological progress.

To settle a patent dispute that almost shut down BlackBerry wireless e-mail service this year, the manufacturer paid $612 million to a company claiming the popular device infringed five of its patents.

INSIDE

THIS REPORT

CQ Researcher • Dec. 15, 2006 • www.cqresearcher.com
Volume 16, Number 44 • Pages 1033-1056

CQ PRESS

RECIPIENT OF SOCIETY OF PROFESSIONAL JOURNALISTS AWARD FOR EXCELLENCE ◆ AMERICAN BAR ASSOCIATION SILVER GAVEL AWARD

THE ISSUES

BACKGROUND

CURRENT SITUATION

OUTLOOK

SIDEBARS AND GRAPHICS

FOR FURTHER RESEARCH

Cover photograph: AFP/Getty Images/Paul J. Richards

CQ Researcher

Dec. 15, 2006
Volume 16, Number 44

CQ PRESS

A Division of Congressional Quarterly Inc.

CQ Researcher (ISSN 1056-2036) is printed on acid-free paper. Published weekly, except March 24, July 7, July 14, Aug. 4, Aug. 11, Nov. 24, Dec. 22 and Dec. 29, by CQ Press, a division of Congressional Quarterly Inc. Annual full-service subscriptions for institutions start at $667. For pricing, call 1-800-834-9020, ext. 1906. To purchase a *CQ Researcher* report in print or electronic format (PDF), visit www.cqpress.com or call 866-427-7737. Single reports start at $15. Bulk purchase discounts and electronic-rights licensing are also available. Periodicals postage paid at Washington, D.C., and additional mailing offices. POSTMASTER: Send address changes to *CQ Researcher*, 1255 22nd St., N.W., Suite 400, Washington, DC 20037.

Patent Disputes

BY KENNETH JOST

THE ISSUES

The engineers at Teleflex Inc. thought their new, adjustable gas pedal was the proverbial better mousetrap — smaller, cheaper and sturdier than similar pedals being used to accommodate drivers of different heights.

The U.S. Patent and Trademark Office (PTO) agreed the pedal was both novel and useful — the major requirements to obtain a patent. In May 2001 the agency issued U.S. Patent No. 6,237,565 to the Pennsylvania manufacturer, giving it a presumptive 20-year legal monopoly over use of the device.

Armed with the patent, Teleflex filed a patent-infringement suit against one of its major competitors, KSR International, after the Canadian company landed a lucrative contract to supply a similar pedal assembly for General Motors trucks. KSR responded by contending that Teleflex's patent was invalid because the invention was "obvious" — nothing more than a combination of two familiar mechanisms that any automotive engineer could have devised.

In December 2003 a federal judge in Detroit agreed that Teleflex's patent was invalid because — in the words of the Patent Act — the invention would have been "obvious . . . to a person having ordinary skill . . . in the art to which [the invention] pertains." But the U.S. Court of Appeals for the Federal Circuit — the special Washington, D.C., court that handles all patent appeals — disagreed. Applying its own test for patentability, the appeals court said the invention was not "obvious" because there had been no "teaching, suggestion, or motivation" beforehand to combine the elements that Teleflex's engineers had put together. [1]

Now, this seemingly arcane business dispute is in front of the Supreme Court, where powerful industry groups have lined up on opposite sides of an issue that could have a significant impact on technological innovation in the United States.

Some of the biggest players in the high-tech industry are telling the justices the patent system gives too much legal protection to too many questionable inventions, contributing to costly litigation and legal gamesmanship and raising prices for businesses and consumers.

"The patent system is broken," says Chuck Fish, patent counsel for Time Warner, representing the Coalition for Patent Fairness — an ad hoc group that includes such high-tech companies as Microsoft, Dell, Intel, Cisco Systems and Oracle. Fish says the combination of poor-quality patents and abusive patent litigation has turned a system aimed at promoting innovation into one that results in "an innovation tax."

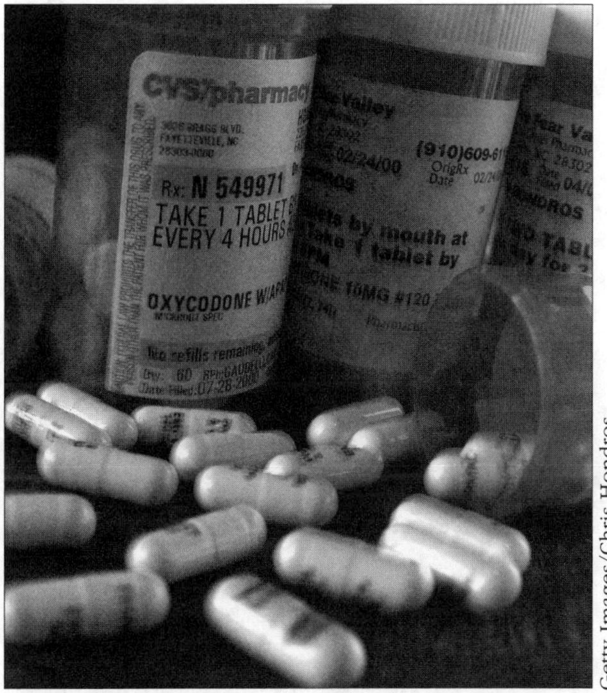

Getty Images/Chris Hondros

Drug manufacturers and biotechnology companies are resisting proposals by the high-tech industry to overhaul the U.S. patent system in order to make it easier to challenge patent applications. The pharmaceutical companies say making patents harder to obtain or enforce would reduce incentives for research and development, curtailing technological innovation.

On the opposite side, however, the pharmaceutical and biotechnology industries as well as bar associations representing patent attorneys warn that making it harder to obtain or enforce patents would reduce incentives for research and development, curtailing the technological innovations needed to keep the U.S. economy competitive in a global marketplace.

"We have the best patent system in the world, and we would not have the standard of living or quality of life that we have today but for our patent system," says Philip Johnson, chief patent counsel for Johnson & Johnson, the nation's fourth-largest pharmaceutical manufacturer. Reducing the value of patents or the certainty of enforcing them would have "an immediate impact on investment decisions and a long-term impact on the quality of innovation itself," Johnson says.

The rival industries have squared off in Congress as well over legislation designed to curb remedies in patent-infringement suits and to simplify the process of challenging patent applications. The high-tech industry supports the measures, but the pharmaceutical and biotechnology industries have been dragging their feet. House and Senate bills stalled in the last Congress but are expected to resurface early in the new 110th Congress in 2007. (*See "At Issue," p. 1049.*)

Patent Litigation Nearly Tripled

The number of patent-infringement suits filed rose by 270 percent since 1982, when Congress created a specialized court to handle all patent appeals. The increase reflects the rising number of patents approved and the growing recognition of the valuable property rights represented by a patent.

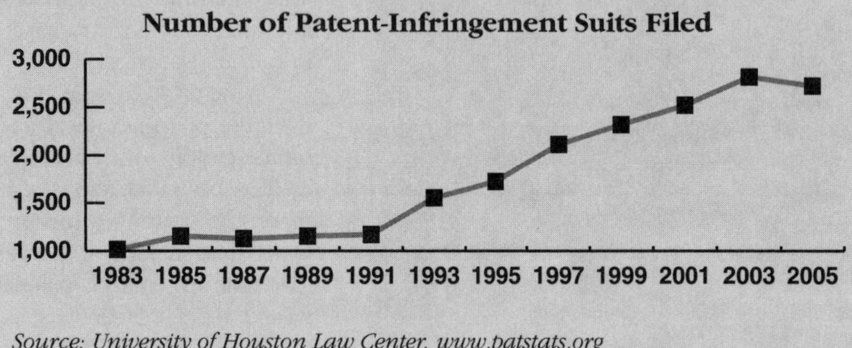

Source: University of Houston Law Center, www.patstats.org

Outside experts likewise disagree on how well the patent system is working. In a widely noticed book, two economics professors — Adam B. Jaffe of Brandeis University and Josh Lerner of the Harvard Business School — argue that "an alarming growth in legal wrangling" over patents in the past 20 years has resulted in "waste and uncertainty that hinder and threaten the innovative process." [2]

But Christopher Cotropia, an associate professor at the University of Richmond School of Law, says the patent system "is working better than most people say." Cotropia, who filed a brief supporting Teleflex in the Supreme Court case, adds, "When it's working well, we should have greater economic progress, and technology should be booming, and that seems to be happening."

For his part, Jon W. Dudas, director of the PTO and undersecretary of Commerce for intellectual property, also sees criticism of the system as overblown. "No, the patent system is not broken," Dudas says. "In fact, the patent system that we have in the United States is the model for the rest of the world."

Whether broken or not, the patent system is clearly straining under a sharp increase in both the number of patent applications and the number of patents issued. Since 1985 the number of applications has more than tripled, according to PTO statistics, while the number of patents issued jumped two-and-a-half times from 1985 to 2003, before falling for the past two years. (*See graph, p. 1040.*)

To cope with the surging workload, Dudas has continued hiring more examiners, a push initiated by his predecessor as PTO director, James Rogan. (*See graph, p. 1048.*) Despite the increase, the 4,800-plus patent examiners handle an average of 100 applications per year — double the caseload of their counterparts in some European countries.

Meanwhile, patent litigation has been increasing since 1982, when Congress created the Federal Circuit to handle all patent appeals. The number of patent suits nearly tripled between 1983 and 2004, according to the University of Houston Law Center. (*See graph above.*)

Some critics blame the litigation trend on what they say is the Federal Circuit's generally pro-patent orientation. Other legal experts — along with the judges themselves — deny that the court has been too favorably disposed to patent holders.

In any case, the Supreme Court's decision to hear the Teleflex case suggested to many observers that the justices shared the concern about a pro-patent bias at the Federal Circuit. The decision followed the high court's May 2006 ruling in another closely watched case admonishing the Federal Circuit against routinely upholding broad injunctions sought by patent holders in infringement suits. The ruling gave the popular online auction house eBay a new chance to avoid an injunction that could force it to shut down or significantly revamp its operations unless it reaches a licensing agreement with the patent holder who filed the suit. [3]

The eBay case made news just after lawyers had resolved a comparable patent dispute that had threatened to shut down the wildly popular BlackBerry wireless e-mail receiver. The Canadian maker of the device, Research in Motion (RIM), averted a court-ordered shutdown by agreeing to pay $612.5 million to a Virginia-based company, NTP, Inc., which claimed RIM had infringed five patents on which it owned rights.

The eBay and BlackBerry cases both focused attention on the increasing number of entrepreneurs — dubbed "patent trolls" by the critics — who acquire rights to patents from the inventor with the intention of licensing the patent to other companies rather than manufacturing the products themselves.

Critics say the practice amounts at best to speculation and in some cases comes close to extortion from companies that have incorporated, sometimes unwittingly, patented devices in their products. But the individuals and companies that acquire rights to patents say they serve a vital purpose by providing capital that financially strapped inventors need to develop and market their inventions. (*See sidebar, p. 1044.*)

As the Supreme Court deliberates on the Teleflex case and rival lobbying groups prepare for a new round of patent-reform proposals on Capitol Hill, here are some of the major questions being debated:

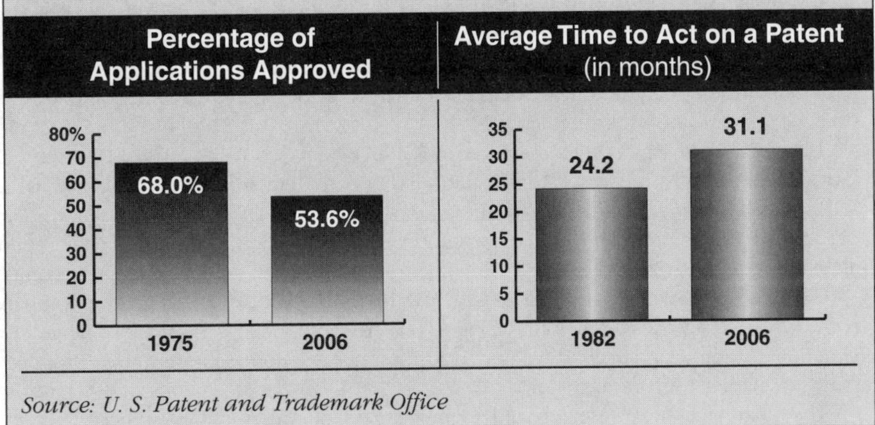

Should the standard for issuing patents be tightened?

Exhibit A: That American classic, the peanut-butter-and-jelly sandwich — the PB&J.

The patent office recently decided that it made a mistake in 1999 when it issued a patent for a sealed, crustless PB&J sandwich. The decision on U.S. Patent No. 6,004,596 grew out of a five-year-long patent-infringement fight between J. M. Smucker Co., the giant Ohio jam and jelly manufacturer, which owned rights to the PB&J sandwich patent, and Albie's Foods, a small Bay City, Mich., company that marketed its own empanada-like sealed, crustless sandwich, filled with meat. [4]

The PTO's Board of Patent Appeals and Interferences cited obviousness and indefiniteness issues in its Sept. 14 ruling rejecting the patent, which Smucker had claimed as legal protection for its Uncrustable thaw-and-serve PB&J sandwich. When Smucker learned in 2001 that Albie's had its own crustless, ready-to-serve filled sandwich, it hit its tiny rival with a cease-and-desist letter and then a patent-infringement suit.

With the patent board's ruling possibly ending the fight, Albie's attorney faults the patent examiner's initial decision, but he understands Smucker's reason for waging the battle. "They would want to monopolize this market," says Kevin Heinl, a veteran patent lawyer in Detroit. "The problem is, I don't think they've done anything that would rise to the level of invention." [5]

The episode contains many of the features cited by the patent system's critics: an ill-considered patent, a dubious infringement suit and a long and expensive legal fight. "We are now clogged with thousands and thousands of patents that never should have been issued because the costs of granting the coverage are not worth what limited contributions the invention represented," says Joshua Sarnoff, the head of the intellectual-property law clinic at American University's Washington College of Law.

"There are a fair number of low-quality patents out there — more than there should be," says Robert Merges, director of the University of California's Berkeley Center of Law and Technology.

Patent-law practitioners tend to view the problem with less concern. "The critics like to pick out one case or a handful of patents that they think are wrong and indict the entire system," says patent attorney Johnson. Mark Banner, a Chicago lawyer and former chair of the American Bar Association's intellectual-property section, says only that there are areas "on the fringes [that] need work."

PTO Director Dudas also discounts the issue somewhat. "I don't think there's a vast quality problem in the patent system," he says, noting that the approval rate for patent applications has fallen over the past six years and is now at a record low of 53.6 percent. (*See graphs above.*) The error rate — based on internal reviews — has also fallen to 3.5 percent, near a 30-year low.

The obviousness issue now before the Supreme Court tops the list of concerns among critics, especially those in the information-technology field. High-tech companies say they are particularly vulnerable to the threat — illustrated in the gas pedal and PB&J sandwich cases — that a patent issued for an "obvious" combination of existing elements can tie up another product using the same or similar technology. [6]

The Patent Act provision on obviousness — found in Section 103 — is aimed at weeding out patents sought for devices that would be "obvious" in the relevant field. But some patent-law experts say applying that test broadly could bar patent protection for advances that appear obvious

When Drug Patents Expire, Fighting Begins

The makers of brand-name and generic drugs frequently wrangle over patents before the U.S. Patent and Trademark Office (PTO) and in federal courts. But they are also waging significant side battles in Congress and at other federal agencies over procedures that generic drug makers say allow the major pharmaceutical companies to thwart competition with patent-protected medications.

The Generic Pharmaceutical Association (GPhA) wants Congress or the Food and Drug Administration (FDA) to rein in industry-backed "citizen petitions" at the agency that can delay or prevent the introduction of a non-brand-name medication after a patent has expired.

GPhA also wants Congress to pass a law to block brand-name drug companies from introducing so-called "authorized generics" during a protected 180-day period for a generic company to market the product.

The Pharmaceutical Research and Manufacturers of America (PhRMA) defends the regulatory filings as a legitimate device to keep unsafe drugs off the market. It says allowing brand-name companies to join in selling authorized generics lowers consumer prices.

Democratic lawmakers sponsored bills to deal with both issues in 2006, but they did not advance. Ranking FDA officials voiced concern about the industry-backed citizen petitions and instituted some internal changes in 2006 to try to control the practice. [1]

Pharmaceuticals provide the most visible example of the costs consumers pay for the patent system in the form of higher prices for products protected by a government-granted legal monopoly. Generic drug makers can provide lower-cost substitutes only if a patent expires or is ruled invalid by a court or the PTO. Major drug companies say patent protection is needed to enable them to invest millions of dollars over long periods to discover and win regulatory approval for new medicines.

Congress has passed several laws aimed at easing the way for generic drug companies to compete with brand-name medications, including a 1984 law that balanced pro-generic provisions with some additional protections for drug company patent holders.

The Hatch-Waxman Act — named after its chief sponsors, Sen. Orrin G. Hatch, R-Utah, and Rep. Henry A. Waxman, D-Calif. — gives the first company to seek FDA approval for a generic drug the exclusive right to market the non-branded medication for 180 days. The six-month exclusivity is seen as giving the generic company needed financial incentives to bring the drug to market. [2]

The FDA ruled in 2004 that the company that owns patent rights to a drug can also sell an unbranded version during the 180-day period. Generic drug makers say such "authorized generics" either reduce or kill the market for the generic firm. The big drug companies say the procedure lowers prices. [3]

Big drug companies' use of petitions to block new generics began to emerge as an issue in the late 1990s. The Clinton administration proposed a rule to revise procedures on citizen petitions in 1999, but the Bush administration withdrew it in 2003. FDA officials say nearly one-third of the 170 citizen petitions currently before the agency involve industry challenges to generic applications. [4]

In another fight, generic drug makers backed efforts by the Federal Trade Commission (FTC) to block brand-name companies from agreeing to pay cash settlements with individual generic firms in exchange for dropping patent challenges. The FTC claimed the settlements violated federal antitrust laws.

The federal appeals court in Atlanta rejected the argument in March 2005, and the Supreme Court declined to hear the case in late June 2006. A bipartisan group of senators critical of the drug industry in the past introduced a bill to curb the practice, but it expired with the end of the current Congress. [5]

[1] See Marc Kauffman, "Petitions to FDA Sometimes Delay Generic Drugs," *The Washington Post*, July 3, 2006, p. A1.

[2] The act is formally titled the Drug Price Competition and Patent Term Restoration Act of 1984.

[3] For background, see Peter Benesh, "Feds Look Into Battle Over Authorized Generics," *Investor's Business Daily*, Aug. 14, 2006, p. A7.

[4] Quoted in Kauffman, *op. cit.*

[5] The decision is *Schering-Plough Corporation v. Federal Trade Commission*, 402 F.3d 1056 (CA11 2005). For background, see Jeffrey Young, "Drug industry deals attracting attention," *The Hill*, June 28, 2006, p. 22.

only after the fact. "In hindsight, something could look quite unremarkable," says Johnson. " 'What's so special about that?,' people might ask."

The Federal Circuit sought to provide a more objective basis for judging obviousness with its "teaching, suggestion, or motivation" test. Under that test, a patent is to be upheld against a challenge for obviousness unless there was prior evidence from artisans in the field pointing in the direction of the invention at issue.

In the Supreme Court, KSR is arguing that the Federal Circuit went beyond the statute in creating the test and has applied it too rigidly so as to allow too many "obvious" patents to stay on the books. Teleflex and the business and patent-bar groups supporting its position say the test is a reasonable elaboration of the patent law and that the appeals court has applied it more flexibly than critics claim.

Whatever the outcome of the Supreme Court case, experts on both sides say the problem of poor-quality patents stems in part from limited resources. "For many years, the office was starved for resources," says Mike Kirk, executive director of the American Intellectual Property Law Association. "They had more work to do and no more resources to do it."

The increase in funds and staffing, however, has reduced that concern, Banner says. "The PTO now has the money it needs to do the jobs," he says. "Now it's time to deliver."

AP Photo/George Widman

A patent-infringement battle has raged for five years between giant Ohio jam and jelly manufacturer J. M. Smucker and tiny Albie's Foods, of Bay City, Mich. Smucker claimed that a meat-filled crustless sandwich sold by Albie's had infringed on Smucker's patented Uncrustable peanut-butter-and-jelly sandwich. In September a patent appeals board rejected the patent, but Smucker has until early 2007 to challenge the decision.

Should patent-infringement suits be limited?

Millions of Americans got a crash course in patent law in early 2006 when an infringement suit threatened to shut down BlackBerry wireless e-mail receivers nationwide. Device maker Research in Motion (RIM) averted the shutdown only by paying $612.5 million to a small patent-holding firm that had won a court fight even as a patent office re-examination was casting doubt on the patent at issue. [7]

NTP had claimed RIM's device was infringing a wireless e-mail technology patented by NTP but never developed. RIM insisted that it had developed its own technology and that NTP's patent was invalid anyway. But RIM lost a jury verdict in 2002 and in early 2006 failed to get a judge to overturn it. Facing a possible court-ordered injunction, RIM settled on March 3.

The outcome demonstrated the powerful legal tools enjoyed by patent holders under existing law. Patents are presumed valid in court even if being re-examined at the patent office. A challenger has to introduce "clear and convincing" evidence to invalidate a patent. A patent holder may be able to collect damages based on the value of the infringing product even if the patented device was only a small component. Moreover, damages may be tripled if the infringement is found to have been "willful" under a somewhat relaxed standard of evidence.

Most powerfully, a patent holder can obtain an injunction against the sale of the infringing product — a powerful inducement to settle even a dubious case. "Once they're threatening to shut down your product line, then everybody settles," says American University law Professor Sarnoff.

Critics — especially those in the high-tech industry — say the existing litigation rules are tilted too much toward patent holders. "The litigation system has become imbalanced over time," says Time Warner's Fish.

Others are less critical. "I don't think patentees are overcompensated," says the University of Richmond's Cotropia. PTO Director Dudas agrees. "The existing rules don't give patent holders too much [leverage]," he says.

The Supreme Court's decision in the eBay case may ease some of the concern about injunctions. The May 15 ruling came in a suit by another Virginia-based firm, MercExchange, which had charged eBay with violating a business-method patent for electronic marketing. A judge awarded MercExchange $30 million in damages after a jury found that the infringement was willful, but he refused a request for an injunction. On appeal, however, the Federal Circuit told the judge to reconsider because of what the court termed the "general rule" favoring injunctions in infringement cases.

The Supreme Court's 9-0 decision said judges in patent cases should apply the same, four-factor test used in other types of suits before issuing injunctions. Under that test, an injunction is issued only if monetary damages are an inadequate remedy, irreparable harm would result without an injunction, the balance of hardships favors the party seeking the injunction and the injunction would not hurt the public interest.

The eBay ruling "took away a very important weapon," says Berkeley law Professor Merges. "If you look at cases involving injunctions just in the last few months, you can see that it's already having effects."

Other issues are still on the table. Kirk, for example, acknowledges the call from the high-tech sector to make it harder to win triple damages for willful infringement. "There is nothing wrong fundamentally with the notion of having higher damages for a willful infringement," he says. "The problem is that it is difficult sometimes for a manufacturer to avoid an unnecessary charge of willfulness."

U.S. Patent Office Is Swamped

The U.S. patent office is straining to deal with a large increase in the number of patent applications and the number of patents issued. Since 1985 the number of applications has more than tripled and the number of patents issued jumped two-and-a-half times from 1985 to 2003, before falling for the past two years.

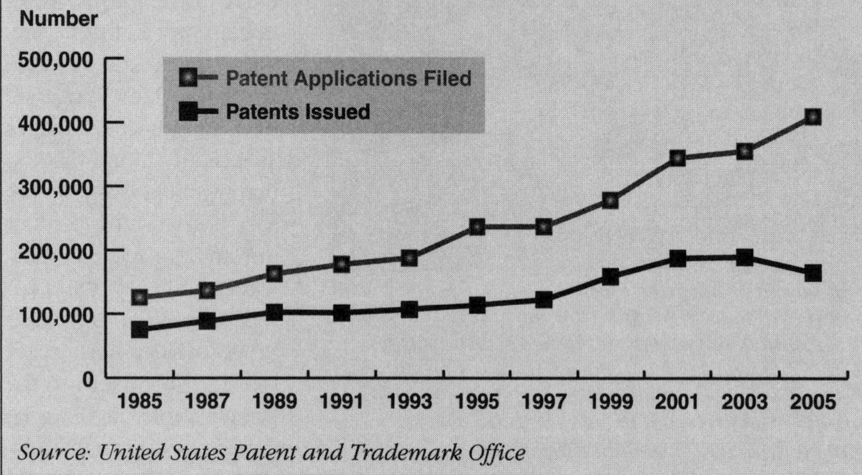

Source: United States Patent and Trademark Office

The computer industry also wants to limit potential damages in cases where the infringement involves only a small component of a multi-component system or product. The existing rule "greatly inflates" the potential remedy in high-tech cases, according to Brian Kahin, a senior fellow with the Computer and Communications Industry Association.

The pharmaceutical and biotech industries, however, worry that reducing the damages would lead to more infringement. "We don't want somebody's decision to infringe a patent to become just another business decision," says Hans Sauer, associate general counsel for intellectual property at the Biotechnology Industry Organization (BIO).

The high-tech industry also wants to limit the patent holder's discretion in choosing where to file an infringement case. The issue stems in large part from the emergence of a judicial forum perceived as highly favorable to patent holders in the unlikely location of Marshall, Texas. The federal court in the tiny East Texas town near the Louisiana border has had more patent suits this year than any other city except Los Angeles, and patent holders won in 78 percent of the cases, according to a patent-litigation tracking service.[8]

The computer industry wants to discourage "forum shopping" by requiring some connection between the place chosen and the underlying claim. "Plaintiffs should not be permitted to funnel cases into plaintiff-friendly courts," says Kahin.

But the pharmaceutical industry's Johnson minimizes the concern. "There is forum shopping, and there always will be forum shopping because of the nature of our court system," he says.

Should Congress overhaul the patent system?

Ever since then-Secretary of State Thomas Jefferson established the nation's patent system in 1790, the United States has followed the seemingly logical "first to invent" rule that patents are awarded to the first person to invent a new device or process. Today, however, every other country awards a patent to the first person to apply for a patent.

Even though timing disputes are relatively infrequent, many patent experts want the United States to change to a "first to file" rule in the interest of harmonizing U.S. patent laws with the rest of the world. But the idea draws opposition from universities and small-time inventors, who say it would encourage quickly submitted, poorer-quality applications and benefit large companies that can get to the patent office faster than home-workshop gadget makers.[9]

For members of Congress, the issue illustrates the political pitfalls in tackling a subject that in any event ranks low on the list of legislative priorities. In an unfamiliar area like patents, even a seemingly innocuous change can divide constituents and interest groups and risk unintended consequences.

Against those obstacles, the high-tech sector has been arguing on Capitol Hill for the past few years that the patent system is out of date and out of whack and that the problems are hurting the industry's ability to bring productivity-enhancing innovation to market. Along with needed changes in the courts and at the PTO, they say that Congress needs to rewrite some parts of the Patent Act, which has not undergone a major revision since 1952.

"Repairs are needed," says Time Warner's Fish. "Only a congressional overhaul can do all that is required."

The pharmaceutical and biotech industries counter that the patent system is working well for the most part and that they would be hurt by some of the changes sought by the information-technology (IT) industry. "The IT sector tends to have a different feeling about patents because their industry changes so rapidly that they're less focused on patents," says James C. Greenwood, president of BIO. "They want to weaken intellectual-property rights — which would be devastating to us."

The bills introduced in the House and Senate — HR 2795 in 2005 by Rep. Lamar Smith, R-Texas, and S 3818 in spring 2006 by Sens. Orrin G. Hatch, R-Utah, and Patrick J. Leahy, D-Vt. — included many provisions aimed at improving patent quality and making patent litigation less burdensome.

Both bills would have authorized a stronger "post-grant opposition" procedure that would allow third parties to contest a patent at the PTO instead of in court. Both bills would also tighten the procedures for awarding triple damages for "willful" infringement and to change the rules on "apportionment" to limit damages in cases where an infringing element is only a small component of the product. In addition, both bills included provisions to limit a patent holder's discretion in deciding where to file suit.

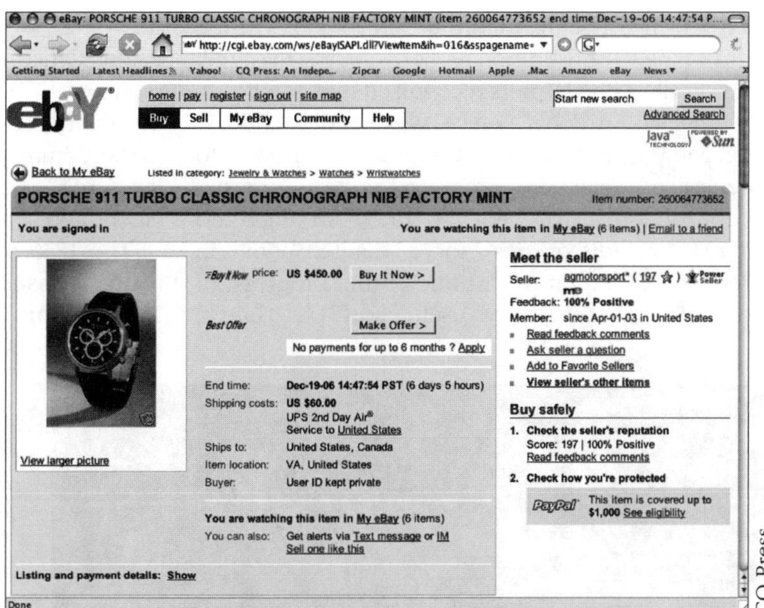

CQ Press

The Supreme Court ruled in May that a company that sued eBay for infringing its business-methods patents might not be entitled to an injunction forcing eBay to shut down or revamp its operations. The case focused attention on so-called "patent trolls," who acquire rights to patents solely to license the patent to other companies.

Some issues were dealt with in one but not both of the measures. The House bill, for example, would have given the PTO specific authority to limit "continuations" — amendments to a patent application submitted as the examination proceeds. The Senate bill included no comparable provision. Similarly, the House but not the Senate measure called for deleting a requirement — criticized by some as unnecessarily burdensome — that patent applicants specify the "best mode" for using the claimed invention.

For its part, the Bush administration is supporting the call for a post-grant opposition procedure and still studying other issues. But PTO Director Dudas agrees that Congress should consider revising the law. "It's absolutely healthy to have a debate on how to perfect patent law," he says.

The post-grant opposition procedure and changed apportionment rules appear to be the two biggest controversies, according to Kirk with the intellectual-property bar group. Both issues divide the rival industry groups because they would have a different impact on high-tech companies than they would have on the drug and biotech sectors.

Making it easier to challenge patents at the PTO could help high-tech companies reduce infringement suits for dubious claims on components or processes — as in the BlackBerry case, for example. But drug and biotech companies do not want to make it easier for companies, such as generic-drug manufacturers, to contest their patents.

Apart from the rival industries' positions, patent lawyers and experts disagree whether a new administrative procedure to contest patents would prove to be simpler and cheaper — or more complex and more expensive — than existing law, which channels those disputes into federal courts.

Similarly, a new "apportionment" rule that would limit damages when an infringing device is only a small part of a product or process would help some high-tech companies but could hurt the drug and biotech industries.

Kirk says the legislative stalemate might be broken if those two issues could be resolved. And leaders on both sides profess the desire to reach a compromise. "If we got together, we might find some common denominator," says Sauer at the biotech group.

"It does make sense to try to make it work well for everybody," says Ed Black, president of the Computer and Communications Industry Association.

"Something eventually will get passed," says the University of Richmond's Cotropia. "There's this general sentiment that things need to change in the patent system." ■

BACKGROUND

'The Useful Arts'

The United States' patent system dates to the first years of the republic, and legal disputes and policy debates over the scope of government-granted inventor protections go back almost as far. The patent office, which evolved from a part-time board to the present midsize agency, has generally expanded the availability of patents and their scope. With some exceptions, Congress has generally expanded patent protections, while courts have moved at times to tighten standards for patents or narrow patent-holders' rights and at other times to adopt more pro-patent policies. [10]

Renaissance Italy gave birth to the first true patent and the first patent statute. The Republic of Florence in 1421 issued a patent to the architect Filippo Brunelleschi for the ship that he designed to transport the marble to be used to construct his famed Duomo, or cathedral. A half-century later, Venice in 1474 passed a statute that gave the inventor of "any new and ingenious device" a 10-year monopoly; anyone copying the design without the inventor's consent was subject to a fine of 100 ducats and destruction of the device.

Getty Images

Model T maker Henry Ford led other carmakers in successfully contesting an infringement suit by George B. Selden, a New York inventor who had obtained a patent in 1895 for attaching an engine to a carriage. Selden's patent was invalidated in 1911 after a car built according to Selden's plans didn't work. Until then, carmakers had paid him royalties for every car they made.

By 1600, patent systems had spread to other European countries, including England. The Statute of Monopolies, enacted by Parliament in 1624, abolished the abused practice of commercial franchises granted by the crown but allowed a 14-year term for "letters patent" issued to the inventor of "any new manufacture within this Realm." The statute added a proviso that use of the patent could not be "contrary to law nor mischievous to the State."

Several American colonies followed the English model in establishing patent systems before the Revolution. At the Constitutional Convention in 1787, the framers recognized that a uniform, national system was needed and explicitly gave Congress the power to grant inventors and authors "the exclusive right" to their "writings and discoveries" for a "limited" time in order to "promote the progress of science and useful arts" (Art. I, sec. 8, cl. 8).

Exercising that authority, Congress passed the Patent Act of 1790, which provided for the issuance of patents for 14-year terms by a board composed of three Cabinet members: the secretaries of State and War and the attorney general. Congress responded to complaints about the cumbersome process with the Patent Act of 1793, which did away with the patent board and created an essentially clerical registration system.

The new system resulted in issuance of many questionable patents, prompting Congress in 1836 to revive an examination requirement. The Patent Act of 1836 also re-established the Patent Office as part of the State Department. The office was moved to the Interior Department in 1849 and to the Commerce Department in 1925. Its name was changed to the U.S. Patent and Trademark Office in 1975.

The 1836 act re-established novelty and utility as requirements for a patent. The Supreme Court added a third requirement with its first patent law decision, *Hotchkiss v. Greenwood* (1851). In rejecting a patent for doorknobs made of clay or porcelain, the court explained that an invention requires a "degree of skill and ingenuity." [11]

As the patent system matured over the next century, legal disputes were frequent. Samuel F. B. Morse and Alexander Graham Bell successfully defended their patents for the telegraph and the telephone against rival inventors. Thomas A. Edison, who was granted more than 1,000 patents in his lifetime, effectively established a monopoly in the nascent motion picture industry by vigorous enforcement of patents in the field. Later, Nikola Tesla fought an ultimately successful battle to invalidate Guglielmo Marconi's patent for inventing the radio in favor of his own. In another famous episode, Henry Ford led a group of four other carmakers in successfully contesting an infringement suit by George B. Selden, a New York lawyer and inventor who had obtained a patent in 1895 for attaching an internal combustion engine to a four-wheeled carriage. [12]

Over time, the Supreme Court shifted from a generally favorable attitude

Continued on p. 1044

Chronology

Before 1950

Congress creates patent system; legal, policy disputes ensue.

1790, 1793
Congress uses power granted in Constitution to pass first Patent Act in 1790; revises law in 1793 creating simplified registration system.

1836
Patent Act establishes independent patent office within State Department, re-establishes examination procedure, requires inventions to be novel and useful; office moved to Interior (1849), Commerce (1925).

1849
Abraham Lincoln is granted a patent for device to keep steamboats afloat in shallow water.

1851
Supreme Court says patented invention must entail "a degree of skill and ingenuity."

1930s-1940s
Supreme Court tilts against patent holders, says "flash of genius" required for invention.

1950-2000

Congress, Supreme Court broaden patent rights.

1952
Patent Act establishes "non-obviousness" requirement (Section 103): no patent if invention "obvious" to person skilled in pertinent art.

1966
Supreme Court, in first ruling on Section 103, bars patents for shock-absorbing plow shank and hold-down spray bottle.

1975
Reorganization brings new name: U.S. Patent and Trademark Office (PTO).

1980
Supreme Court allows patent for genetically engineered organism.

1981
Supreme Court allows patent for industrial process based on computer software.

1982
Congress cites need for uniformity in creating Federal Circuit Court of Appeals to hear all appeals in patent cases; 12-member court begins work in 1983, gains reputation as tilting toward patent holders. . . . Patent applications and litigation begin to rise sharply.

Mid-1990s
PTO begins losing ground to surge in applications; Congress exacerbates problem by diverting user fees to Treasury.

1999
Federal Circuit rules, in State Street Bank decision, business methods can be patented; decision brings quick surge in applications. . . . PTO grants patent for sealed, crustless peanut-butter-and-jelly sandwich (PB&J). . . . Congress passes American Inventors Protection Act, allowing outside parties limited participation in patent reexaminations. . . . "Patent troll" is coined as derogatory term for speculators in patent rights.

2000-Present

Increasing calls for patent reform from outside groups; backlog grows at patent office.

2001
George W. Bush administration ends diversion of PTO user fees; office begins hiring more examiners.

2003
PTO director acknowledges "crisis" at agency after backlog begins new rise. . . . Federal Trade Commission warns that "questionable patents" harm competition, hurt consumers; calls for more patent examiners to improve quality.

2004
National Research Council arm calls for stricter standards for patents, eased procedures to challenge patents at PTO. . . . Economists Jaffe and Lerner publish *Innovation and Its Discontents*, with sharp critique of patent system.

2005
Federal court in Marshall, Texas, becomes favored venue for patent holders to bring suit. . . . Congress takes up patent-reform bills backed by high-tech industry to tighten standards, curb litigation; measures stall in face of resistance by drug, biotech lobbies.

2006
Maker of BlackBerry wireless e-mail receiver averts shutdown with $612-million settlement in infringement case despite pending challenge to patent (March 3). . . . Supreme Court, in eBay case, reverses Federal Circuit decision favoring injunctions as normal remedy in infringement cases (May 15). . . . Patent appeals board rejects PB&J sandwich patent (Sept. 14). . . . Justices, in Teleflex gas-pedal case, voice discontent with Federal Circuit doctrine favoring patent applicants on obviousness issue (Nov. 28); decision in Teleflex case, two other patent disputes all due by end of June 2007.

'Trolls' Vacuum Up Patents, Demand Fees

Hundreds of colleges ranging from Harvard University to Truckee Meadows Community College in Reno, Nev., began receiving letters in 2002 demanding money — letters similar to others sent to porn-site operators.

What did the colleges and porn sites have in common? They both use streaming video. Acacia Research Corp. claims to hold five patents on the technology as well as dozens of other technology patents.

But Acacia doesn't actually make any products. Instead, it tries to collect fees from anyone who uses its inventions — including colleges, porn sites, newspapers and computer manufacturers — and sues those who refuse to pay up.

Many businesses figure it's cheaper to pay the licensing fees demanded by Acacia rather than risk a costly lawsuit and the possibility of being shut down if their company is found to be infringing a patent.

Critics call what Acacia does a legal form of extortion and call outfits like Acacia "patent trolls," after the mythical figures that waited underneath bridges to ambush travelers. They claim the trolls hinder or discourage innovation.

Defenders say the companies are simply asserting their lawful property rights against companies who might otherwise not pay independent inventors for their creations. [1]

"The patent troll is doing absolutely nothing the Constitution and the patent law prohibit," says Raymond P. Nero, an attorney who represents plaintiffs in such lawsuits. "The right to exclude is the essence of a property right."

Defenders say the patent troll problem is being exaggerated by big businesses that are urging Congress to change patent laws in ways that would hurt small inventors. "It's a clever bait-and-switch maneuver to blame the dastardly 'trolls' as a way to sneak in changes that hurt legitimate patent holders," says Nathan P. Myhrvold, chief executive officer of Intellectual Ventures, a company that has bought thousands of patents in recent years.

Jon W. Dudas, undersecretary of Commerce and director of the Patent and Trademark Office, calls the pejorative term "a clever name" but says it's "vastly too expansive" to describe any patent holder who does not develop and commercialize his invention as a patent troll. Some inventors prefer sticking to inventing rather than producing. Others try and fail to develop products using their creations, leaving them with the patent as their only asset. And middlemen have long helped small inventors commercialize their ideas in exchange for fees.

Making money on a patent through licensing is "a very old idea and something in the abstract that most economists would say is a positive aspect of a working market in intellectual property," says Adam B. Jaffe, an economist and dean of arts and sciences at Brandeis University.

Even the country's biggest businesses make money by licensing patents they don't use themselves. IBM, the nation's largest patent owner, earns more than $1.5 billion in licensing fees each year.

What concerns James Dabney, a New York City lawyer who defends companies in such patent-infringement lawsuits, is deep-pocketed investors who vacuum up big portfolios of patents and then wait until defendants have invested heavily in their

Continued from p. 1042

toward patents to a more critical view beginning in the 1930s. In one important decision, the court in 1941 rejected a patent for a car cigarette lighter that automatically turned off, saying the device lacked the "flash of genius" required for a separate patent. In another, the court in 1950 invalidated a patent for a precursor of the moving checkout counter in grocery stores. In a concurring opinion, Justice William O. Douglas famously wrote, "The Constitution never sanctioned the patenting of gadgets." [13]

The patent bar responded to the court's more critical attitude by drafting and lobbying for a new law, the Patent Act of 1952, with provisions more favorable to inventors and patent holders. In the most significant section, the act effectively superseded the "flash of genius" test by codifying what was intended to be an objective form of the "non-obviousness" requirement first set out in the 1851 *Hotchkiss* decision. Under the act, no patent could be issued if the subject matter would have been "obvious" at the time to "a person having ordinary skill in the art to which said subject matter pertains."

'Anything Made by Man'

Passage of the 1952 act ushered in a half-century of largely favorable developments for patent holders and applicants. The emerging biotechnology and information technology industries won major victories in the 1980s with Supreme Court decisions approving patent protections for genetically engineered organisms and computer-program applications. Congress' 1982 decision to consolidate all patent appeals in a newly created Federal Circuit Court of Appeals reflected an expectation that more uniform rulings would generally expand legal protections. The Federal Circuit, in fact, adopted pro-patent policies in a number of areas, including a controversial decision in 1999 to allow patents for business methods. Meanwhile, the patent office managed an ever-increasing number of patent applications by approving many seemingly questionable patents — such as the PB&J sandwich — and letting private litigants and courts sort out the disputes.

products before demanding licensing fees.

Intellectual Ventures, for instance, has scooped up thousands of patents since its founding by Myhrvold, Microsoft's former chief technology officer. Although it has not yet filed any lawsuits, observers fear it could prove to be the biggest troll yet, given its enormous portfolio of patents.

Ironically, one of the patent experts now employed at Intellectual Ventures is Peter Deitkin, the attorney credited with coining the patent-troll phrase in 1999 while working for Intel.

Getty Images

Nathan P. Myhrvold, founder of Intellectual Ventures, a patent-holding firm.

If a company is targeted by patent trolls, the stakes can be enormous. If found to be infringing, courts can issue injunctions requiring the defendant to stop manufacturing the product or offering the service. Plaintiffs can use the threat of such a shutdown to demand big payments.

"It's the legal equivalent of hostage taking," says Dabney. "Someone will pay a lot of money to avoid being killed."

That was the experience of Research in Motion (RIM), creator of the BlackBerry wireless e-mail device. A jury awarded $130 million to Virginia-based NTP, Inc., which held the patent. But to avoid having its BlackBerry service shut down, RIM had to pay NTP $612.5 million in March 2006.

In May 2006 the Supreme Court removed some of the value of such lawsuits when it ruled in a suit involving online retailer eBay that judges are not required to issue injunctions every time a company is found to infringe a valid patent. Since then, lower courts have issued fewer automatic injunctions, telling patent holders that don't produce goods that money damages are adequate compensation.

"That is good news for a lot of companies that have real investments," says Dabney. "And not so good news for people who have invested in patent litigation and are hoping to hit a quick score."

But many observers say the eBay decision does nothing to fix underlying patent-system problems exploited by trolls.

"I see patent trolls as a symptom rather than a disease," says Jaffe. "There are so many patents out there of dubious validity, and it's so expensive and risky to demonstrate that in court. So these so-called trolls can engage in what looks like blackmail rather than serious licensing activity."

— Seth Stern

[1] For a representative overview, see Nicholas Varchaver, "Who's Afraid of Nathan Myhrvold?" *Fortune*, July 10, 2006, pp. 111-118.

Initially, the Supreme Court continued to evince skepticism toward expansive patent protections. In its first interpretation of the "non-obviousness" standard of the 1952 act, the court in 1966 unanimously invalidated disputed patents for a shock-absorbing plow shank and a hold-down spray bottle, saying each device would have been "obvious" to someone "reasonably skilled in the prior art." The ruling in *Graham v. John Deere Co.* provided a laundry list of factors to consider in making obviousness determinations, but Justice Tom Clark signaled the court's general inclination by critically remarking on "the free rein often exercised by Examiners in their use of the concept of 'invention.' " [14]

In a pair of closely divided decisions a decade-and-a-half later, however, the court significantly expanded the scope of patent law, rejecting previous doctrines that had restricted protections for living organisms or mathematical formulas. In both cases, the patent office had rejected proposed patents only to be reversed by what was then the Court of Customs and Patent Appeals. While the justices divided somewhat across ideological lines, conservatives provided the critical votes in each of the rulings to extend patent protection.

In *Diamond v. Chakrabarty*, the court in 1980 held that a genetically engineered bacterium capable of breaking down crude oil "plainly qualifies" as patentable subject matter. The microbiologist's discovery, Chief Justice Warren E. Burger wrote for the majority, "is not nature's handiwork, but his own." As authority, Burger quoted a 1952 congressional committee report that called for extending patent protection to "anything under the sun that is made by man." [15]

A year later, the court in *Diamond v. Diehr* also ruled that a process for curing synthetic rubber that included computerized application of a mathematical formula was also eligible for patent protection. Distinguishing previous rulings barring patents for laws of nature, then-Associate Justice William H. Rehnquist said the patent had been sought for "an industrial process," not for a mathematical formula. [16]

Congress, meanwhile, was considering legislation to create a single, national appeals court to hear patent-related cases. In approving the new court in 1982, lawmakers said uniformity would reduce "forum-shopping" among regional appeals courts. Once the Federal Circuit was established in 1983, however, the immediate effect was also to increase the number of patents found, on appeal, to have been valid and infringed from less than 50 percent to more than 80 percent. The result was "a significant strengthening of the patent grant," according to the authors of a leading patent-law text. [17]

Over time, the 12-member court moderated its pro-patent orientation somewhat, but it continued to have a reputation as generally disposed toward upholding and permitting enforcement of patents. In one of its most controversial rulings, the Federal Circuit in 1999 essentially discarded a long-recognized "business-methods exception" in order to uphold a patent for an investment house's computerized system of valuing mutual funds. Signature Financial Group had licensed the system to many financial institutions, but Boston's State Street Bank sued to challenge the patent after licensing negotiations broke down. In upholding the patent, the court said an invention was eligible for protection if "it produces a useful, concrete and tangible result." The number of business-method patent applications quickly skyrocketed — from about 330 in 1995 to around 10,000 in 2001. [18]

The patent office meanwhile was suffering from an across-the-board surge in patent applications while dealing with a variety of chronic management problems — including low pay for overworked examiners — and new challenges, such as the need for computerization of patent rulings from the United States and other countries. The number of utility-patent applications more than tripled from 1985 to 2005 while the number of patents issued more than doubled. Patent examiners — with an average annual salary around $60,000 — were handling around 100 applications a year, nearly double the number assigned to their counterparts in the European Patent Office. [19]

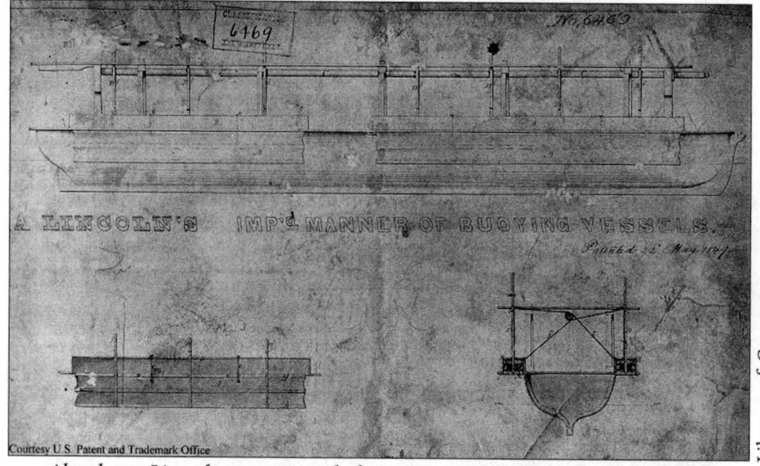

Courtesy U.S. Patent and Trademark Office

Library of Congress

Abraham Lincoln was awarded a patent in 1849 for his adjustable buoyant air chambers designed to keep steamboats afloat in shallow water. Lincoln's application — a rough drawing and 1,100-word description — was approved in less than three months. Lincoln is the only president ever to hold a patent. The device was never manufactured.

Patent litigation was also increasing. The number of patent suits rose from 811 in 1982 — the year before creation of the Federal Circuit — to 2,720 in 2005. The number of patent cases that survived preliminary challenges and reached juries also increased, from below 20 percent in the early 1980s to more than 70 percent in 2000. [20]

To supporters of the system, the trends reflected a sound recognition of the economic value of intellectual-property rights and the need to protect and enforce them. Some critics, however, warned the system was breeding more litigation than innovation. The patent system, wrote economists Jaffe and Lerner, "is generating waste and uncertainty that hinders and threatens the innovative process." [21]

Patents Re-examined

Criticism of the patent system intensified with the start of a new century, and a flurry of proposals emerged for overhauling the system. The head of the patent office himself acknowledged some of the criticisms, but critics said efforts at reform bore limited fruit. Congress took up reform proposals strongly backed by high-tech industries, but they languished in the face of opposition from the biotech and pharmaceutical industries. Meanwhile, the Supreme Court began taking a more active interest in patent law — seemingly in part to steer the Federal Circuit away from pro-patent rulings in some areas.

The Federal Trade Commission (FTC) joined critics of the system with a report in October 2003 warning that "questionable patents" can harm competition and innovation and raise costs for consumers. The report recommended a new administrative procedure to allow outside parties to challenge patents and a relaxed burden of proof to challenge patents in court. The consumer-protection agency also recommended making it easier to challenge patents as "obvious" and making it harder for patent holders to win triple damages for willful infringement. [22]

Six months later, the National Research Council, an arm of the National Academy of Sciences, weighed in with an April 2004 report echoing the call for third-party challenges and for stricter application of the non-obviousness standard for issuance of patents. The scientific body also called for more funding for the PTO. "The patent office needs additional resources to hire and train more examiners and to implement information technology that would boost its processing capabilities," the council said. [23]

Earlier, President Bush's first appointee to head the PTO had himself strongly warned about the agency's backlog in patent applications. "This is an agency in crisis, and it's going to get worse if we don't change our dynamic," Rogan, a former Republican congressman, told the *Los Angeles Times* in February 2003. [24]

In his two-year tenure in the post, Rogan tried to reduce the backlog by hiring more patent examiners and increasing fees for some applications. He also wanted to outsource some of the preliminary review of applications but dropped the idea in the face of strong opposition from Capitol Hill. Staffing increased under Rogan — thanks to a decision by Congress to allow the patent office to keep all fees collected instead of returning the surplus to the Treasury for general budget purposes, as had been done in the 1990s. Staffing continued to increase after Rogan left in December 2003 to take a job in Washington as a lawyer-lobbyist. But the backlog had not been reduced. In fact, the average time needed to act on a patent application increased from two years in 2002 to nearly 31 months today.

Congress, meanwhile, had been paying attention to the calls for reform in the FTC and National Academies' reports and from professional associations, experts and interest groups — most prominently, the high-tech industry. Lawmakers working on the issues in the 1990s had ended in 1999 with the American Inventors Protection Act, which encompassed only relatively minor changes. Among other provisions, it allowed outside parties limited participation in patent re-examinations at the PTO and required publication of patent applications from other countries.

The new calls for systemwide reforms produced broader bills in both the House and the Senate. With Republicans exercising disciplined control in the House, Smith's 2005 bill became the major legislative vehicle in the lower chamber. The Texas Republican's bill included limits on infringement suits and strengthened pre- and post-issuance review at the PTO.

High-tech industry groups were pleased, while the pharmaceutical and biotech industries warned against undermining a system that was working well. By late July, Smith had prepared a substitute bill that dropped the proposed limit on injunctions in infringement cases, leaving the high-tech industry disappointed. But the scheduled markup on the bill never took place. The bipartisan bill introduced in the Senate in spring 2006 by Republican Hatch and Democrat Leahy incorporated many provisions comparable to Smith's, but it too failed to advance.

The Supreme Court reduced the pressure for reform somewhat with its eagerly awaited eBay decision in May 2006. For several years, the justices had been showing an increased interest in patent cases — suggesting to many observers growing discontent with Federal Circuit rulings. In the eBay case, the justices confronted what seemed to be the Federal Circuit's nearly automatic rule for awarding patent holders injunctions after a finding of infringement. In seeking to overturn the injunction, the popular online auction house said it was facing a possible shutdown because of an arguably invalid patent.

The court ruled unanimously in *eBay Inc. v. MercExchange, L.L.C.*, that injunctions should be issued in infringement cases only if they met the normal rules for such sweeping court orders, including the need to balance the public interest against the potential harm to the patent holder. In concurring opinions, however, one group of three justices appeared to favor injunctions as the norm in infringement cases, while four others criticized routine use of injunctions. Justice Anthony M. Kennedy pointedly noted the rise of "an industry" that used patents not for producing and selling goods but "primarily for obtaining licensing fees." ■

CURRENT SITUATION

In the Spotlight

The patent office is gaining unaccustomed attention — and drawing unaccustomed criticism — for some of the patents it approves, even while it copes with a daunting backlog of pending applications and a continuing surge of new ones.

In one of the most publicized of current disputes, the head of the Internal Revenue Service (IRS) is echoing the criticism from many tax lawyers and preparers that the PTO should not issue business-method patents for tax-planning strategies. Granting patent protection could limit the use of legitimate tax-planning strategies and have "a negative impact on [taxpayers'] ability to comply with the tax law," IRS Commissioner Mark Everson told the House Subcommittee on Select Revenue Measures in July. [25]

Meanwhile, the patent bar is arguing against proposed rule changes that the PTO devised to try to speed applications and improve patent quality. One of the new rules would limit "continuations" — the ability to amend a patent application without losing the benefit of the original filing date. The other changes would limit the number of claims in a patent application and require greater disclosure by applicants.

Examiners Not Keeping Up With Applications

Skyrocketing patent applications have prompted the government to more than double the number of patent examiners in the past 12 years. Despite the increase, each of the 4,800-plus U.S. patent examiners handles an average of 100 applications per year — double the caseload of their counterparts in some European countries.

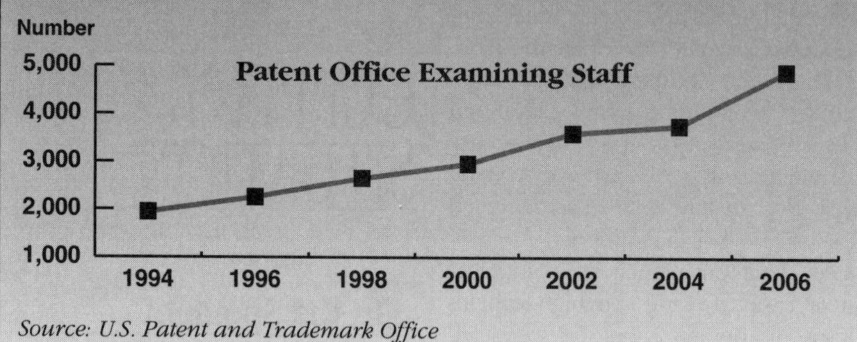

Source: U.S. Patent and Trademark Office

"Admittedly, the patent office has a very heavy burden," says Kirk of the intellectual-property bar group. "But these initiatives are not the right solution."

For its part, the PTO presents a rosy picture of its efforts to improve patent quality and improve the application process. In its most recent performance report, the office claims to have met numerical targets on six out of seven goals — including error and compliance rates, average costs and time for processing applications and use of electronic filing and processing. The office fell slightly short on one measure: the time before the first action on an application. The average time was 22.6 months instead of the targeted 22.0 months. [26]

PTO Director Dudas says the agency has turned the corner from what his predecessor, Rogan, described as a "crisis" in 2003. "The agency was facing a crisis at the time," Dudas says today. "The crisis that we were facing then, we have actually averted."

Dudas and others credit improved performance in part to increased funding, which results from increased filing fees and the Bush administration's decision to allow the office to retain all user fees. During the 1990s, Congress diverted about $740 million in user fees to the general federal budget.

Some observers are favorably impressed. "There are some real improvements at the administrative level," says the University of Richmond's Cotropia. Among other things, Cotropia credits managers with "pushing examiners a little more" and with instituting changes "to help the examiners do a better job."

Many patent lawyers and experts, however, are less sanguine. "Clearly the patent office needs to increase its productivity and output," says Banner, the Chicago lawyer. Sarnoff, the American University law professor, says the office suffers from "a historic failure of management."

The Government Accountability Office (GAO) also gives the agency mixed reviews. In a critical report in June 2005, the congressional watchdog agency found "systemic weaknesses" in the PTO's efforts to automate the processing of patent applications. Separately, the GAO credited the patent office with taking "a number of important and necessary actions to attract and retain qualified patent examiners" but also called on it to confront several "longstanding challenges" in human-resource policies — including communication, compensation criteria and training. [27]

Critics continue to focus in particular on the patent-quality issue. In a journal article earlier this year, two longtime patent lawyers contended that PTO statistics give a misleading picture of how many applications examiners are turning down. Cecil Quillen and Ogden Webster, both formerly with Eastman Kodak, say the statistics include a substantial number of continuations in the total number of applications — thus, lowering the percentage of applications shown as having been allowed. [28]

Whatever statistics are used, Berkeley law Professor Merges says examiners continue to have an institutional bias toward granting instead of disallowing a patent. "It's very difficult for them to do a better-quality check than they're currently doing," Merges says. "And it's difficult for them to get rid of a patent application except by granting it."

Sarnoff says the institutional bias reflects the PTO's view of patent applicants as the agency's "customers." "You have a captured agency," says Sarnoff. "You couldn't ask for a clearer statement."

"There's no question that the focus of the agency needs to be on the public at large," Dudas replies. "We certainly need to consider applicants, but applicants are just one constituency."

In the Courts

The Supreme Court appears poised to use the Teleflex gas-pedal case to make it somewhat easier to challenge a patent on grounds of obviousness — and to reverse the Federal Circuit for the second time in less than a year on a major patent law issue.

A majority of the justices were openly skeptical during oral arguments on

Continued on p. 1050

At Issue:

Should Congress significantly overhaul patent law?

CHUCK FISH
VICE PRESIDENT, CHIEF PATENT COUNSEL, TIME WARNER INC.

WRITTEN FOR *CQ RESEARCHER*, DECEMBER 2006

yes

The *American Heritage Collegiate Dictionary*'s definition of "overhaul" is: "to examine . . . carefully for needed repairs," and that is precisely what Congress should do. The review should be careful, because patents are important property rights and function differently for different industries. But there can be no reasonable dispute that repairs are needed, as serious problems affecting both patent use and granting have been well documented for years. The risk to future prosperity demands immediate and substantial congressional action.

Imbalances in the patent system are increasingly being exploited by actors who seek to extract licensing fees and fast out-of-court settlements from those who actually make and sell products and services. Given the lack of downside risk for patent plaintiffs, suing and threatening suit has become a cottage industry for those who seek only to litigate instead of create. Numbers of patent lawsuits remain at historically high levels, but no evidence suggests any related innovation gains. And the vast number of patent disputes that find their way to court is only the visible tip of the iceberg.

The costs of the shift in patent-litigation patterns are akin to an "innovation tax" on large and small companies offering new products who must pay unnecessary legal fees and settlements. Additionally, these same companies spend even more on pre-emptive defensive patenting and other strategies to avoid the innovation tax. All these costs represent funds diverted from productive research and development, and all are passed on in some form to consumers.

The all-too-apparent crisis in patent quality means Congress should overhaul the patent system and empower the U.S. Patent and Trademark Office (PTO) to help fix the problem. Evidence abounds — whether from internal PTO quality-review data, comparative studies or external expert analyses — that mistakes in granting patents happen much too frequently. Granting unworthy patents not only wastes public resources and harms unfortunate litigants and their customers but also can stifle true innovations by surrounding them with a thicket of baseless, trivial patents. The economic effects of patents with unclear boundaries and questionable inventiveness are staggering.

In short, demonstrably negative consequences flow from the U.S. patent system making patents too easy to assert and too easy to obtain. Although the courts and the PTO have begun some necessary changes, only a congressional overhaul can do all that is required. Innovation and economic growth are much too important to be left to the patent lawyers alone.

JAMES C. GREENWOOD
PRESIDENT AND CEO, BIOTECHNOLOGY INDUSTRY ORGANIZATION (BIO)

WRITTEN FOR *CQ RESEARCHER*, DECEMBER 2006

no

Developing biopharmaceuticals and other biotechnology products involves highly complex research, long development times, innovative manufacturing processes and rigorous pre-market approvals that only the most promising compounds accomplish successfully. Investing in this innovative research — which has the potential to deliver breakthrough cures, clean and sustainable energy and a safe and abundant food supply — is particularly risky and expensive. The Tufts Center for the Study of Drug Development recently reported that it costs approximately $1.2 billion over more than eight years to develop a new biotechnology therapy.

A company can invest this much time and money into the development of a new product only because the U.S. patent system provides a light at the end of the tunnel — protecting this invention from unauthorized use. The patent holder can use and license the invention as he sees fit, just as a landholder can use or lease his property. The patent holder also has the right to exclude others from using his property, just as a landholder is allowed to prevent others from using his land.

Most small biotech companies are founded on a single, core technology. The patents for this technology attract private investment to businesses that take years to be profitable. Without strong patents, these companies would not be able to attract the vast capital necessary to bring a breakthrough product, such as a life-saving medical therapy, to market.

Some of the proposals in the legislation introduced by Sens. Orrin G. Hatch, R-Utah, and Patrick J. Leahy, D-Vt., can help simplify the patent system without distressing the value of patent rights; however, several provisions of their bill would weaken the rights of patent holders and inject unpredictability into the patent system, thus reducing investment in innovation.

There are specific reforms that could improve the patent system for all stakeholders, especially the elimination of the "best mode" requirement and the often abused defense to patent infringement known as "inequitable conduct." Determining the validity of these subjective requirements and defenses is costly and time-consuming, and prevents prompt resolution of patent disputes.

BIO members are committed to supporting a patent system that protects the property rights of inventors, encourages investment and fosters innovation to improve the lives of people throughout the world. Any changes to this system must be fair and balanced so as not to undermine these essential traits, which have served our nation so well and have made the American economy the engine of worldwide innovation.

Continued from p. 1048

Nov. 28 of the "teaching, suggestion, or motivation" test that the Federal Circuit has crafted to help apply the statutory requirement of non-obviousness for patents. In the appeals court's most recent phrasing, a party challenging a patent as obvious must show some evidence that artisans in the field "would have been led to" make the same combination of elements that the patent holder claimed for its invention. [29]

Representing Teleflex, Washington attorney Thomas Goldstein met a barrage of derisive comments from justices as he tried to defend the Federal Circuit's ruling reversing a lower-court decision nullifying the company's patent. Justice Antonin Scalia called the appeals court's test "gobbledygook," while fellow conservative Samuel A. Alito Jr. said the test added nothing to the statutory provision. Chief Justice John G. Roberts Jr. called the test "worse than meaningless because it complicates the inquiry rather than focusing on the statute."

Earlier in the argument, liberal Justice Stephen G. Breyer — a critic of expansive patent protection in earlier decisions — professed an inability to understand the test. "I just don't understand what is meant by the term 'motivation,' " Breyer told New York attorney James Dabney, representing Teleflex's rival, KSR International. "Everybody has a motivation to look to the prior art."

Dabney had opened his argument by describing the Federal Circuit's test as "a judicially devised test that is fundamentally inconsistent" with the Patent Act provision. The act bars patents for any invention "obvious . . . to a person having ordinary skill in the [relevant] art."

Goldstein countered that the Federal Circuit's test was a practical guide to help prevent invalidating patents as obvious based on hindsight. "The right question," Goldstein said, was whether "it would have been apparent at the time of the invention to create this invention whether it's through a teaching, a suggestion, or a motivation."

Despite the justices' criticism of the Federal Circuit test, the arguments gave no clear signal on what standard, if any, the high court might elaborate as an alternative. In his briefs and arguments, Dabney argued for a broader definition that would find an invention obvious if an artisan "would have been capable of adapting extant technology to achieve a desired result."

Supporting KSR in the case, Deputy U.S. Solicitor General Thomas Hungar argued that patents should be upheld only if an invention was "sufficiently innovative." But Justice Ruth Bader Ginsburg, who had adopted pro-patent positions in earlier cases, called the government's test "vague." Justice David H. Souter also voiced concern that changing the Federal Circuit's test could result in "chaos" by casting doubt on thousands of patents issued over the years.

After arguments, Goldstein echoed Souter's worry that a ruling against Teleflex "would dramatically change the rules" on obviousness. But Dabney said the rules need to be changed to weed out invalid patents. Under existing rules, he said, "a court can't say no to a patent claim" except in limited circumstances.

The case is one of three patent disputes the court has on its calendar for the current term, which ends in June 2007. Earlier, the justices heard arguments in a dispute between two leading biotechnology companies that tests whether a company can challenge a patent as invalid even while paying the patent holder under a licensing agreement for the right to use the invention.

Virginia-based MedImmune wants to overturn a patent held by Genentech — the world's biggest biotechnology company — on an antibody-synthesis technology that MedImmune uses in its major product, Synagis, which treats respiratory infections in premature babies.

MedImmune, the industry's eighth-largest concern, is paying Genentech royalties under a licensing agreement but also contends Genentech's patent is invalid. It argues the Federal Circuit's decision barring its suit represented a departure from previous rulings that upheld a so-called "pay and sue" strategy. [30]

In a third case, the court will hear arguments in February in an effort by Microsoft to block a suit by AT&T, which claims the giant software company infringed a patent it holds on speech-recognition software. In addition to the validity of the patent, the case tests whether liability can be imposed for the foreign manufacture and sale of an infringing product. [31] ■

OUTLOOK

'The Knowledge Economy'

Alone among U.S. presidents, Abraham Lincoln has a patent in his name. U.S. Patent No. 6469 gave the future president legal protection for his design of adjustable buoyant air chambers to enable steamboats to stay afloat in shallow water.

Lincoln's "petition" to the commissioner of patents consisted of a page of drawings and an 1,100-word description of the claimed invention. The patent office granted the patent on May 22, 1849, barely two-and-a-half months after Lincoln's application.

Today, patent practice is crushingly more voluminous and numbingly more complex. Patents are now numbered in the millions — with about 1.5 million patents currently active. Patent applications are long and dense: 2,900 words for the adjustable gas pedal in the Teleflex case and almost as many — 2,300 — for the crustless PB&J sandwich.

Moreover, in an era of fast-paced technological change, the application process is excruciatingly slow. Today, it would take Lincoln about two-and-a-half years to get an answer.

Patent law is also vastly more complex than in Lincoln's time. The Supreme Court issued its first significant patent-law decision only in 1851 — some 60 years after the birth of the patent system. Today, patent-infringement suits number in the thousands each year, with litigation costs often in the millions. Microsoft, for example, says it spends more than $100 million annually defending infringement lawsuits, according to the company's chief patent counsel, Bart Eppanauer. [32] A specialized court handles all patent appeals, but the Supreme Court appears to think that the court needs closer supervision to get the rules right.

With so much at stake, it is no wonder that many patent experts say the system is broken. A wide range of critics — concentrated in the information-technology industries — are claiming that the combination of poor-quality patents and expensive litigation is hurting instead of promoting technological progress.

At the same time, some important vested interests — including the patent bar and the politically potent pharmaceutical industry — say the system is working well. Any changes to reduce the value of patents could hurt innovation and damage the U.S. economy and standard of living.

Prospects for significant changes in the short-term future are uncertain. The PTO is projecting a continuing 8 percent annual increase in applications. At that rate, any significant reduction in the backlog will be hard to achieve even if the office comes up with efficiency-enhancing procedures.

The time pressures militate against improvements in patent quality. In a typical case, a patent examiner is allowed only eight hours to search for "prior art" — the evidence used to determine whether the claimed invention is patentably novel or unpatentably obvious.

With three cases pending in its current term, the Supreme Court may redirect patent law somewhat on some issues, including the important question of obviousness. But Congress, not the courts, has the principal responsibility for deciding what level of proof is needed to challenge a patent in court or what rules are to be applied in awarding damages in infringement cases.

The rival interest groups claim to be interested in reaching agreement on legislative changes. "High-tech has some real problems," says Billy Tauzin, president of the Pharmaceutical Research and Manufacturers of America (PhRMA), "and we ought to be partners with them in a way that preserves protections but helps them deal with the real weaknesses that dramatically affect their ability to do business."

Time Warner's Fish confesses that he is "utterly ignorant" about the drug and biotech industries but says that high-tech companies have "the same interest at heart in strong property-rights protections." He adds, "Productive conversations are the ones between industry leaders trying to find changes that will be good for everybody."

Against that backdrop, PTO Director Dudas also stresses the importance of patent rights. "Nearly everyone's job in the United States today depends or is likely to depend on some form of intellectual property," he says.

"When you look at the technicalities of the law, sure it becomes boring or mesmerizing," Dudas continues. "But what it represents is the future of our economy. It is why the United States is growing in terms of gross domestic product. Intellectual property is the way to protect the knowledge economy." ■

Notes

[1] The decision is *Teleflex, Inc. v. KSR International Co.*, Jan. 6, 2005. The relevant section of the Patent Act is 35 U.S.C. section §103. For a detailed overview of the case, see Steve Seidenberg, "Patently Obvious: Supreme Court re-examines standards for non-obviousness," *Inside Counsel*, October 2006, IP section, p. 22 (www.insidecounsel.com).

[2] Adam B. Jaffe and Josh Lerner, *Innovation and Its Discontents: How Our Broken Patent System Is Endangering Innovation and Progress, and What to Do About It* (2004), p. 2. Jaffe is professor of economics and dean of arts and sciences at Brandeis, in Waltham, Mass.; Lerner is professor of investment banking at Harvard Business School, located in Allston, Mass.

[3] The decision is *eBay Inc. v. MercExchange, L.L.C.*, 547 U.S. — (May 15, 2006).

[4] Smucker can still contest the appeals board's decision before the patent is officially cancelled.

[5] For earlier journalistic accounts, see Jaffe and Lerner, *op. cit.*, pp. 25-26; David Streitfeld, "This Headline Is Patented," *Los Angeles Times*, Feb. 7, 2003, p. 1A.

[6] See Brian Kahin, "Patent Reform for a Digital Economy," Computer and Communications Industry Association, November 2006 (www.ccianet.org).

[7] Background drawn from Yugi Noguchi, "BlackBerry Patent Dispute Is Settled," *The Washington Post*, March 4, 2006, p. A1; Mike Musgrove, "For NTP, Battle Worth Fighting Ends in Vindication Over Patent," *ibid.*, p. D1.

[8] See Julie Creswell, "So Small a Town, So Many Patent Suits," *The New York Times*, Sept. 24, 2006, sec. 3, p. 1.

[9] See Erica Werner, "Small-time inventors take on Congress, high-tech industry over proposed patent law changes," The Associated Press, Oct. 21, 2005.

[10] Historical background drawn from Donald S. Chisum, *et al.*, *Principles of Patent Law: Cases and Materials* (3d ed.), 2004, pp. 1-23.

[11] The citation is 52 U.S. 248 (1851).

[12] See various entries on http://inventors.about.com.

[13] The cases are *Cuno Engineering Corp. v. Automatic Devices Corp.*, 314 U.S. 84 (1941); *Great Atlantic & Pacific Tea Co. v. Supermarket Equipment Corp.*, 340 U.S. 147 (1950).

[14] The citation is 383 U.S. 1 (1966).

[15] The citation is 447 U.S. 303 (1980).

[16] The citation is 450 U.S. 175 (1981).

[17] See Chisum, *et al.*, p. 23. For data on outcomes of patent-related appeals, see Jaffe and Lerner, *op. cit.*, p. 105.

[18] The ruling is *State Street Bank & Trust Company v. Signature Financial Group, Inc.*, 149 F.3d 1368 (Fed. Cir. 1998). For figures

on business-method patent applications, see Chisum, *op. cit.*, p. 119.

[19] Data on patent applications and patents issued from U.S. Patent and Trademark Office 2005 annual report (www.uspto.gov/web/offices/com/annual/2005). For examiners' salary, workload, see Jaffe and Lerner, *op. cit.*, pp. 131, 135.

[20] See University of Houston Law Center, www.patstats.org (caseload); Jaffe & Lerner, *op. cit.*, p. 123 (jury trials).

[21] *Ibid.*, p. 2.

[22] Federal Trade Commission, "To Promote Innovation: The Proper Balance of Competition and Patent Law and Policy," October 2003.

[23] National Research Council, "A Patent System for the 21st Century," April 2004.

[24] Quoted in Streitfeld, *op. cit.* See also Sabra Chartrand, "The patents commissioner seeks to reinvent a notoriously backlogged office and process," *The New York Times*, Sept. 23, 2002, p. C2.

[25] Quoted in Steve Seidenberg, "Patent Office Receives Criticism for Issuing Patents on Tax Strategies," *Inside Counsel*, December 2006, p. 22.

[26] U.S. Patent and Trademark Office, "Performance and Accountability Report: Fiscal Year 2006," www.uspto.gov/web/offices/com/annual/2006/2006annualreport-2.pdf.

[27] See Government Accountability Office, "Key Processes for Managing Patent Automation Strategy Need Strengthening," June 17, 2005; "USPTO Has Made Progress In Hiring Examiners, But Challenges To Retention Remain," June 15, 2005.

[28] Cecil D. Quillen Jr. and Ogden H. Webster, "Continuing Patent Applications and Performance of the U.S. Patent and Trademark Office — Updated," *Federal Circuit Bar Journal*, Vol. 15, No. 4 (May 2006), pp. 635-677. For a rebuttal to an earlier version, see Robert A. Clarke, "U.S. Continuity Law and Its Impact on the Comparative Patenting Rates of the U.S., Japan and the European Patent Office," *Journal of Patent and Trademark Office Society*, Vol. 85 (April 2003), pp. 335-349.

[29] The decision is *In re Kahn*, 441 F.3d 977 (CAFC 2006).

[30] The case is *MedImmune, Inc. v. Genentech, Inc.*, 05-608.

[31] The case is *Microsoft Corporation v. AT&T Corp.*, 05-1056.

[32] Quoted in Michael T. Burr, "Reinventing the Patent Act," *Corporate Legal Times*, October 2005, p. 38.

FOR MORE INFORMATION

American Intellectual Property Law Association, 2001 Jefferson Davis Highway, #203, Arlington, VA 22202; (703) 415-0780; www.aipla.org. Represents individuals, companies and institutions involved in the practice of patent, trademark, copyright, and unfair-competition law.

Biotechnology Industry Organization (BIO), 1225 I St., N.W., Suite 400, Washington, DC 20005; (202) 962-9200; www.bio.org. Represents biotechnology industry positions to elected officials and regulators.

Coalition for Patent Fairness, 1850 M St., N.W., Suite 550, Washington, DC 20036; www.patentfairness.org. Represents companies and industry groups with an interest in patent reform.

Computer & Communications Industry Association, 666 11th St., N.W., Washington, DC 20001; (202) 783-0070; www.ccianet.org. Promotes open markets, open systems, open networks and open competition.

Federal Circuit Bar Association, 1620 I St., N.W., Suite 900, Washington, DC 20006; (202) 466-3923; www.fedcirbar.org. Represents practitioners before the Court of Appeals for the Federal Circuit.

Generic Pharmaceutical Association (GPhA), 2300 Clarendon Blvd., Suite 400, Arlington, VA 22201; (703) 647-2480; www.gphaonline.org. Represents the manufacturers and distributors of finished generic pharmaceuticals and suppliers of other goods and services to the generics industry.

Pharmaceutical Research and Manufacturers of America (PhRMA), 1100 15th St., N.W., Suite 900, Washington, DC 20005; (202) 835-3400; www.phrma.org. Represents the country's leading pharmaceutical research and biotechnology companies.

Professional Inventors Alliance USA, 1323 West Cook Road, Grand Blanc, MI 48439; (810) 655-8830; www.piausa.org. Represents the interests of independent inventors.

Public Patent Foundation, 1375 Broadway, Suite 600, New York, NY 10018; (212) 796-0570; www.pubpat.org. Represents the public's interests against wrongly issued patents and unsound patent policies.

U.S. Patent and Trademark Office, 401 Dulany St., Alexandria, VA 22314; (571) 272-1000; www.uspto.gov. Department of Commerce agency that handles patent applications and challenges.

About the Author

Associate Editor **Kenneth Jost** graduated from Harvard College and Georgetown University Law Center. He is the author of the *Supreme Court Yearbook* and editor of *The Supreme Court from A to Z* (both *CQ Press*). He was a member of the *CQ Researcher* team that won the 2002 ABA Silver Gavel Award. His recent reports include "Democracy in the Arab World" and "Understanding Islam."

Bibliography

Selected Sources

Books

Chisum, Donald S., Craig Allan Nard, Herbert F. Schwartz, Pauline Newman and F. Scott Kieff, *Principles of Patent Law: Cases and Materials* (3d ed.), Foundation Press, 2004.

The comprehensive legal textbook opens with a compact history of patent law followed by a subject-by-subject treatment of U.S. patent legislation and judicial decisions. Lead author Chisum is a professor at Santa Clara University School of Law.

Jaffe, Adam B., and Josh Lerner, *Innovation and Its Discontents: How Our Broken Patent System Is Endangering Innovation and Progress, and What to Do About It*, Princeton University Press, 2004.

Two economists argue strongly that a series of administrative, legislative and legal changes since the 1980s has created a patent system that encourages the filing and granting of "frivolous" patent applications and costly and disruptive patent litigation. Includes detailed notes. Jaffe is dean of arts and sciences at Brandeis University; Lerner is a professor of investment banking at Harvard Business School.

Articles

Burr, Michael T., "Reinventing the Patent Act," *Corporate Legal Times*, October 2005, p. 38.

The 4,000-word article gives a thorough and balanced account of the proposals for — and obstacles to — patent-reform legislation in Congress.

Davidson, Paul, "Patents Out of Control?" *USA Today*, Jan. 13, 2004, p. 1B.

The reporter examines the effect of purportedly dubious patents and costly litigation on the high-tech industry and other sectors.

Streitfeld, David, "Note: This Headline Is Patented," *Los Angeles Times*, Feb. 7, 2003, p. A1.

The lengthy article uses highly visible examples — such as the controversial patent for a peanut-butter-and-jelly sandwich — to examine the operations of the U.S. patent system at the U.S. Patent and Trademark Office and in the courts. In a second article, the reporter examined the controversial rise of "business-method" patents, especially in e-commerce applications ("E-Commerce Battles 'Me' Commerce," Feb. 8, 2003).

Reports and Studies

Kahin, Brian, "Patent Reform for a Digital Economy: Open Markets, Open Systems, Open Networks," Computer & Communications Industry Association, November 2006.

The 44-page report argues strongly that the U.S. patent system is "in crisis" because of low-quality patents and costly and disruptive litigation. Kahin is a senior fellow with CCIA and an adjunct professor at the University of Michigan School of Information.

Federal Trade Commission, "To Promote Innovation: The Proper Balance of Competition and Patent Law and Policy," October 2003.

The report makes 10 recommendations to overhaul the U.S. patent system, including a new administrative procedure to challenge patents at the U.S. Patent and Trademark Office and an eased standard for invalidating a patent in court.

Maskus, Keith E., "Reforming U.S. Patent Policy: Getting the Incentives Right," Council on Foreign Relations Press, November 2006.

A professor of economics at the University of Colorado argues against what he calls the "misguided" principle that stronger patent protection results in increased innovation.

National Research Council, A Patent System for the 21st Century, National Academies Press, April 2004.

The book-length report urges creation of a mechanism for post-grant challenges to newly issued patents, reinvigoration of the non-obviousness standard to quality for a patent and simplified and less costly litigation.

Schacht, Wendy H., and John R. Thomas, "Patent Reform: Innovation Issues," Congressional Research Service, July 15, 2005.

A CRS specialist in science and technology (Schacht) and Thomas, then a visiting scholar and now a professor at Georgetown University Law Center, examine then-pending bills described as proposing "the most sweeping reforms to the U.S. patent system since the 19th century."

Watson, Jason O., "A History of the United States Patent Office," April 17, 2001 (www.historical-markers.org/uspto-history.cgi).

Historian Watson's compact account of the U.S. patent system includes interesting details on 19th-century inventions. Includes a list of 21 works cited.

On the Web

The U.S. Patent and Trademark Office's Web site (www.uspto.gov) provides well-organized access to official information, including a 27-minute video overview of the PTO's history and current operations. For an unofficial patent-law information service, see the Patently-o blog (www.patentlyo.com), maintained by Dennis Crouch, a visiting assistant professor at Boston University Law School.

The Next Step:

Additional Articles from Current Periodicals

Intellectual Property

Creswell, Julie, "A Wall Street Rush to Patent Profit-Making Methods," ***The New York Times*****, Aug. 11, 2006, p. C7.**

Financial-services firms like Goldman Sachs and Citigroup are stockpiling patents on exotic derivatives and processes like software-based pricing, trading and risk-analysis systems.

Hughlett, Mike, "New Auction on the Block," ***Chicago Tribune*****, Oct. 20, 2006, p. C1.**

Chicago-based Ocean Tomo will put up 250 patents for bid in an "intellectual-property auction."

Litigation

Decker, Susan, "Lawsuit Against Palm Makes Patent-Infringement Claims," ***The Seattle Times*****, Nov. 7, 2006, p. C6.**

Eight months after winning $612.5 million from BlackBerry creator Research in Motion for infringing on its patents, NPT, Inc., is suing Palm, maker of the Treo e-mail phone, for the same reason.

Henderson, Stephen, "High Court Gives Rules For Patent Disputes," ***Charlotte Observer*****, May 16, 2006, p. A6.**

The Supreme Court ruled that online auctioneer eBay shouldn't automatically lose the right to use its "Buy It Now" sales feature because of a patent dispute.

Kesslar, Michelle, "High Court Refuses to Hear BlackBerry-Maker Case," ***USA Today*****, Jan. 24, 2006, p. A1.**

The Supreme Court refused to hear a messy patent lawsuit that could force the maker of the BlackBerry to halt the popular mobile e-mail service in the United States.

Lane, Charles, "A Powerful Voice in Patent Disputes," ***The Washington Post*****, Nov. 6, 2006, p. A19.**

Lane argues that the Office of the Solicitor General is ultimately the real power in patent law these days.

Noguchi, Yuki, "Ipod Patent Dispute Settled," ***The Washington Post*****, Aug. 24, 2006, p. D1.**

Apple Computer Inc. will pay $100 million to Creative Technology Ltd. to settle a patent dispute over competing claims to the software and systems that make their digital music players work.

Slagle, Matt, "Settlement Ends JPEG Lawsuit," ***The Houston Chronicle*****, Nov. 5, 2006, p. 4.**

Texas-based Forgent Networks, which generates most of its revenue from patent licensing and litigation, has reached a settlement over the use of a patent covering the JPEG digital-image format.

Patents

Creswell, Julie, "So Small a Town, So Many Patent Suits," ***The New York Times*****, Sept. 24, 2006, p. 1.**

The Federal District Court in Marshall, Texas, handles the second-highest number of patent-infringement cases because of quick trials and plaintiff-friendly juries.

Gordon, Larry, "Inventiveness Pays at Colleges," ***Los Angeles Times*****, Sept. 12, 2006, p. S8.**

California's state university system has topped the federal government's list of U.S. universities receiving patents for the past 12 years.

Maney, Kevin, "Search for the Most Prolific Inventors is a Patent Struggle," ***USA Today*****, Dec. 7, 2005, p. B3.**

America's most prolific living inventor might be a foreigner, according to Maney's search for the top living U.S. patent holders.

Meller, Paul, "Fresh Opposition to Europe Patent Plan," ***The New York Times*****, June 24, 2006, p. C4.**

Industry groups representing some of the most innovative companies in Europe want the European Commission to abandon its promise to adopt a single patent regime for European Union countries.

Wang, Andrew L., and Matt O'Connor, "Family Saw Anger Build," ***Chicago Tribune*****, Dec. 11, 2006, p. 1.**

The family of Joe Jackson, who shot and killed three people in a Chicago law firm, says he sought revenge against a lawyer he believed stole his idea for a portable toilet.

Zwahlen, Cyndia, "Long Road to a Patent Can Pay Off in Profits," ***Los Angeles Times*****, April 19, 2006, p. C7.**

Getting a patent can take small businesses several years and cost a lot of money, but the potential to profit from an invention while enjoying protection from copycats for up to 20 years is worth it.

Patent Litigation

Davies, Jennifer, "Trade Panel Could Ban Importing Some Chips," ***San Diego Union-Tribune*****, Dec. 12, 2006.**

The U.S. International Trade Commission ruled that Qualcomm is infringing a patent to help cell phones conserve battery power held by Broadcom.

Lane, Charles, "MedImmune Asks For Right to Sue," ***The Washington Post*****, Oct. 5, 2004, p. D4.**

MedImmune asked the Supreme Court for permission to sue Genentech over a patent it holds on an ingredient in MedImmune's drug Synagis.

Patent Reform

Lohr, Steve, "Hoping to Be a Model, I.B.M. Will Put Its Patent Filings Online," *The New York Times*, Sept. 26, 2006, p. C5.

IBM will publish its patents filings on the Web for public review in an effort to help curb patent disputes and litigation.

Patel, Purva, "Bill Would Change U.S. Patent Laws to Conform With Rest of the World," *The Houston Chronicle*, July 27, 2005, p. 2.

Rep. Lamar Smith, R-Texas, introduced a bill in Congress that would overhaul U.S. patent law, creating a process to challenge patents up to nine months after they are awarded and granting patents based on who files first.

Rugaber, Christopher, "High Court Makes Getting a Patent More Difficult," *St. Louis Post-Dispatch*, Nov. 29, 2006, p. B2.

Supreme Court justices signaled a willingness to make patents harder to obtain after hearing arguments in *KSR International v. Teleflex Inc.*

"Swinging Into the Absurd," *St. Louis Post-Dispatch*, Dec. 1, 2006, p. C16.

An editorial highlights a recent trend to seek patents for obvious products or minor adaptations of existing technology.

Patent Trolls

Hughlett, Mike, "Blurry on BlackBerry," *Chicago Tribune*, Feb. 19, 2006, p. C1.

NTP, Inc., holds a patent for an old-fashioned e-mail system and has sued BlackBerry's creator, Research in Motion Ltd., for patent infringement.

Nocera, Joe, "Tired of Trolls, A Feisty Chief Fights Back," *The New York Times*, Sept. 16, 2006, p. C1.

Donald R. Katz, chief executive of Audible.com, felt strongly that patent trolls were hurting small businesses like his and decided to fight Diego, a company that claimed Audible was infringing one of its patents.

Von Bergen, Jane M., "Trials, Traps of Reinventing Patent Law," *Philadelphia Inquirer*, Sept. 28, 2005, p. C1.

Capitol Hill is revisiting patent law after several cases involving "patent trolls," companies that buy rights to dormant patents and sue companies that may be using similar technology.

U.S. Patent and Trademark Office

"Medicines Co. Says U.S. Rejects Patent Extension" www.reuters.com, Dec. 11, 2006.

The Senate adjourned without considering a bill passed by the House that would have allowed the U.S. Patent and Trademark Office to consider patent applications filed unintentionally late.

"U.S. Patent & Trademark Office Rejects Hexagon Patent Claim," www.Yahoo.com, Dec. 12, 2006.

The patent office rejected claims involved in a patent-infringement case filed by Romer-CimCore, a subsidiary of Hexagon, against FARO Technologies, determining that the feature in question was already found in other prior patents.

Decker, Susan, "IBM Tops in U.S. Patents for 13th Straight Year," *The Philadelphia Inquirer*, Jan. 11, 2006, p. C6.

IBM, the world's biggest computer company, received the most U.S. patents for the 13th year in a row.

Harris, Craig, "Starbucks Urged to Sign Pact With Ethiopia Over Coffee Names," *The Seattle Post-Intelligencer*, Nov. 3, 2006, p. E1.

Ethiopia is trying to secure the rights to three Ethiopian coffee names that Starbucks uses.

Maney, Kevin, "Patent Applications So Abundant That Examiners Can't Catch Up," *USA Today*, Sept. 21, 2005, p. B3.

As technology advances, patent applications are getting increasingly complex, making it hard for patent examiners to keep up.

Pollack, Andrew, "Inventor of DNA Sequencing Technique Is Disputed," *The New York Times*, Nov. 16, 2006, p. C2.

The U.S. Patent and Trademark Office will consider whether it awarded a patent to the wrong party for a seminal technique crucial to biotechnology research.

Weiss, Rick, "U.S. Denies Patent for a Too-Human Hybrid," *The Washington Post*, Feb. 13, 2005, p. A3.

The U.S. Patent and Trademark Office rejected a seven-year effort to win a patent on a laboratory-conceived creature that is part human and part animal.

CITING *CQ RESEARCHER*

Sample formats for citing these reports in a bibliography include the ones listed below. Preferred styles and formats vary, so please check with your instructor or professor.

MLA STYLE

Jost, Kenneth. "Rethinking the Death Penalty." CQ Researcher 16 Nov. 2001: 945-68.

APA STYLE

Jost, K. (2001, November 16). Rethinking the death penalty. *CQ Researcher, 11*, 945-968.

CHICAGO STYLE

Jost, Kenneth. "Rethinking the Death Penalty." *CQ Researcher*, November 16, 2001, 945-968.

Published by CQ Press, a division of Congressional Quarterly Inc.

www.cqresearcher.com

Index

January 1991–December 2006

❖ *CQ Researcher* reports are indexed by title under boldface topic headings.

- Titles are followed by the date the report appeared and the first page number of its print version.
- Page numbers followed by an asterisk refer to a sidebar or the "At Issue" (Pro/Con) feature.

❖ This index is updated monthly and available at: http://library.cqpress.com/researcher_index.pdf

❖ *CQ Researcher* can be accessed online at: www.cqresearcher.com

Published by CQ Press, a division of Congressional Quarterly Inc.

 *Indicates sidebar or "At Issue" report section.

 *Indicates sidebar or "At Issue" report section.

 *Indicates sidebar or "At Issue" report section.

 *Indicates sidebar or "At Issue" report section.

 *Indicates sidebar or "At Issue" report section.

 *Indicates sidebar or "At Issue" report section.

 *Indicates sidebar or "At Issue" report section.

 *Indicates sidebar or "At Issue" report section.

 *Indicates sidebar or "At Issue" report section.

 *Indicates sidebar or "At Issue" report section.

 *Indicates sidebar or "At Issue" report section.

 *Indicates sidebar or "At Issue" report section.

 *Indicates sidebar or "At Issue" report section.

 *Indicates sidebar or "At Issue" report section.

 *Indicates sidebar or "At Issue" report section.

 *Indicates sidebar or "At Issue" report section.

 *Indicates sidebar or "At Issue" report section.

 *Indicates sidebar or "At Issue" report section.

 *Indicates sidebar or "At Issue" report section.

 *Indicates sidebar or "At Issue" report section.

 *Indicates sidebar or "At Issue" report section.

 *Indicates sidebar or "At Issue" report section.

 *Indicates sidebar or "At Issue" report section.

 *Indicates sidebar or "At Issue" report section.

 *Indicates sidebar or "At Issue" report section.

 *Indicates sidebar or "At Issue" report section.

 *Indicates sidebar or "At Issue" report section.

 *Indicates sidebar or "At Issue" report section.

 *Indicates sidebar or "At Issue" report section.

 *Indicates sidebar or "At Issue" report section.

 *Indicates sidebar or "At Issue" report section.

 *Indicates sidebar or "At Issue" report section.

 *Indicates sidebar or "At Issue" report section.

 *Indicates sidebar or "At Issue" report section.

 *Indicates sidebar or "At Issue" report section.

 *Indicates sidebar or "At Issue" report section.

 *Indicates sidebar or "At Issue" report section.

 *Indicates sidebar or "At Issue" report section.